WHO'S WHO IN SCOTLAND
1998 (8TH EDITION)

Who's Who
in
Scotland
1998

Carrick Media

Published by Carrick Media
2/1 Galt House, 31 Bank Street, Irvine KA12 0LL
01294 311322

Copyright 1998 Carrick Media

Printed in Great Britain by Bookcraft, Midsomer Norton, Avon

British Library Cataloguing-in-Publication Data
A catalogue record for this book is available from the British Library

ISBN 0 946724 37 7

Preface

In the preface to our last edition, we said that Who's Who in Scotland was a wee burgh of a book: by which we meant that, with a population of around 5,000, it was roughly the size of a typical Scottish town (this being a country of small towns). A recent article in the Spectator magazine, diplomatically entitled "Death to the Scots", claimed that, if the present birth rate continued, there would be very few people left living north of the Border, a prospect that did not seem to trouble the author or the magazine. We are glad to report that Who's Who in Scotland is defying the trend. The population of this particular wee burgh grows steadily year by year: indeed we have had to print 10 more pages of biographical entries in order to accommodate all the people who have qualified to live within its boundaries.

We counted 636 new inhabitants before the book went to bed. Of course, against that, we must set deaths and expulsions. People who come to bide in Who's Who in Scotland are not automatically entitled to residence for life. In the event of their complete withdrawal from public life or, equally dire, emigration to England, they are tactfully asked to leave.

Then again, there are others who, despite impeccable residential qualifications, have to be dragged kicking and screaming into the book. We call these reluctant immigrants "the basics". They are the ones, mercifully few in number, who fail to co-operate with our repeated requests for biographical information and for whom a brief entry must be compiled from whatever sources are available to us.

For example, in all the years we have published the book, the well-known horse-racing tipster, Robin Cook, has not once returned a questionnaire or indeed communicated with us in any way. Every year we write to Mr Cook; every year he ignores us. But we put him in anyway; for our wee burgh would not be quite the same without him.

Within the ranks of the basics, there is a tiny sub-category, the refuseniks, who are so troubled by the possibility of an entry in Who's Who in Scotland that they write to insist that their names never darken our pages. The refuseniks include one of the most prominent ministers in the Church of Scotland and one of our most senior civil servants. Regrettably, we cannot as a matter of course agree to such requests. In the case of the senior civil servant, it is clearly a matter of public interest to know at least the identity of the person holding the office:

his salary is, after all, paid by the taxpayer. Likewise, exclusion of the distinguished clergyman would be perverse. So we include their names and the principal offices they hold, though without embellishment.

These are exceptions. We are more than ever gratified by the help and encouragement of thousands of prominent people from all walks of life, without whose co-operation the book would simply not be possible. Our renewed thanks to all of them.

And finally, may we draw to your attention the enlarged Directory section: these advertisements from prominent Scottish organisations, though in no sense comprehensive, are becoming more useful every year, not only as a supplement to the biographical section but as a valuable source of information in their own right.

February 1998

THE DIRECTORY

1. AGRICULTURE, HORTICULTURE AND BOTANY

MYLNEFIELD RESEARCH SERVICES LTD
INVERGOWRIE, DUNDEE DD2 5DA.
TEL.: 01382 568568. FAX: 01382 568501. e-mail: n.kerby@scri.sari.ac.uk

Contact: Dr. Nigel W. Kerby, Managing Director; Dr. Jonathan B. Snape, Commercial Manager; Professsor John R. Hillman, Deputy Chairman.

Mylnefield Research Services Ltd acts as the gateway to unique skills and services available in biology, agriculture and horticulture at the Scottish Crop Research Institute (SCRI). Considerable emphasis is placed on developing successful partnerships between SCRI's research community and industry. Expertise in plant breeding, plant health, diagnostics, environmental impact analysis, molecular analysis, advisory packages, licensing and technology transfer is available. Core crops include cereals, potatoes, soft-fruit, brassicas, trees and certain tropical crops.

ROWETT RESEARCH INSTITUTE
GREENBURN ROAD, BUCKSBURN, ABERDEEN AB21 9SB.
TEL.: 01224 712751. FAX: 01224 715349. e-mail: enquiries@rri.sari.ac.uk

Contact: Professor W.P.T. James, Director, 01224 716601; Professor I. Bremner, Deputy Director (Science), 01224 716602.

The remit of the Institute is to advance understanding of the biochemical and physiological aspects of mammalian nutrition and growth, and interaction with reproduction, and to investigate aspects of human nutrition. Its mission is to maintain the position of the Institute as the pre-eminent European nutrition centre for integrated research in biological sciences of relevance to health, food and agriculture.

ROYAL BOTANIC GARDEN EDINBURGH
20A INVERLEITH ROW, EDINBURGH EH3 5LR.
TEL.: 0131-552 7171. FAX: 0131-552 0382. e-mail: press@rbge.org.uk

Director: Professor David Ingram, Ext. 288.
Contact: Angela Kilday, Enquiries, Ext. 427; Elaine Carmichael, Development Manager, Ext. 438.

Founded in 1670, as a physic garden, the Royal Botanic Garden Edinburgh is now an executive non-departmental public body and a recognised charity. The Garden's mission is to explore and explain the plant kingdom – past, present and future – and its importance to humanity. Its prime task is to pursue whole plant science, notably through systematic research of the highest quality, on the diversity and relationships of plants, and their significance in the environment.

SCOTTISH CROP RESEARCH INSTITUTE
INVERGOWRIE, DUNDEE DD2 5DA.
TEL.: 01382 562731. FAX: 01382 562426. e-mail: wmacf@scri.sari.ac.uk

Contact: Professor J.R. Hillman, Director; Dr. R.J. Killick, Secretary; Dr. W.H. Macfarlane Smith, Scientific Liaison Officer.

The Institute is financed principally by the Scottish Office Agriculture, Environment and Fisheries Department and external contracts (c. £13m. per annum). It undertakes research to advance knowledge in the biological sciences, to improve the quality of crops, and to control losses due to pests and diseases with due regard to the environment. It is the lead centre in the UK for research on potatoes and soft fruit, and has major inputs into barley, beans and brassicas, and other temperate, tropical and subtropical crops.

2. ANIMALS AND WILDLIFE

ROYAL ZOOLOGICAL SOCIETY OF SCOTLAND
EDINBURGH ZOO, MURRAYFIELD, EDINBURGH EH12 6TS.
TEL.: 0131-334 9171. FAX: 0131-316 4050.

Contact: Professor Roger Wheater, Director; Amanda Alabaster, Marketing Manager.
Exists to promote, through the presentation of our living collections, the conservation of animal species and wild places by captive breeding, environmental education and scientific research. The Royal Zoological Society of Scotland is a charitable, non-profit making organisation devoted to the study and conservation of wildlife. Founded in 1909 to promote a greater knowledge of animal life among the Scottish people, today it is one of the nation's foremost conservation organisations, owning both Edinburgh Zoo and the Highland Wildlife Park.

SCOTTISH WILDLIFE TRUST (SWT)
CRAMOND HOUSE, KIRK CRAMOND, CRAMOND GLEBE ROAD, EDINBURGH EH6 6BT.
TEL.: 0131-312 7765. FAX: 0131-312 8705. e-mail: scotwildtr@aol.com

Contact: Stan Blackley, Press and Information Officer, Ext. 259, e-mail: sblackley@aol.com
Established in 1964, the Scottish Wildlife Trust is the leading voluntary body protecting all forms of Scottish wildlife and Scotland's natural environment. The SWT owns and manages over 120 wildlife reserves, protects over 2,000 wildlife sites, trains 400 individuals in practical conservation work each year and runs high-profile campaigns on a wide variety of cnvironmental issues. As a registered charity, the SWT relies on public support for its funding. The SWT has a network of offices, staff, branches and groups throughout Scotland.

3. ARTISTIC AND CULTURAL

BBC SCOTTISH SYMPHONY ORCHESTRA
Chief Conductor: Osmo Vänskä
BBC BROADCASTING HOUSE, QUEEN MARGARET DRIVE, GLASGOW G12 8DG.
TEL.: 0141-338 2606. FAX: 0141-307 4312. e-mail: bbcsso@bbc.co.uk

Contact: Hugh Macdonald, Director, 0141-338 2489; Alan Davis, Manager, BBC SSO, 0141-338 2606.
Founded in December 1935, the BBC Scottish Orchestra as it was then called, was Scotland's first full-time professional orchestra. Since then it has developed an international reputation with concert tours throughout Europe and to Canada and Hong Kong, and regular appearances at the Edinburgh International Festival and BBC Proms in London. The orchestra is particularly noted for its performances of contemporary music and it has an ambitious commissioning policy, giving special prominence to Scottish composers. In recent years it has recorded extensively, winning *Gramophone* Awards in 1992 and 1993.

BORDERLINE THEATRE COMPANY
NORTH HARBOUR STREET, AYR KA8 8AA.
TEL.: 01292 281010. FAX: 01292 263825.

Contact: Eddie Jackson, Chief Executive; Leslie Finlay, Artistic Director; Sally Stewart, Administrator.
Borderline is one of Scotland's most dynamic and innovative touring theatre companies. Based in Ayr, the company tours throughout the country, playing to in excess of 35,000 people per year. Borderline presents high quality, exuberant theatre that is accessible and seeks to stimulate, enlighten and, above all, entertain. In addition to the touring work the company is unique in having a year-round programme of workshops and projects in schools and communities.

A free reference and lending library for Scotland's poetry in its three languages throughout the centuries and up-to-date, and for British and international poetry. Stock includes books, audio and video tapes, magazines and newscuttings. Specialist lists, indexes and bibliographies may be produced by the computer catalogue, INSPIRE. Lending is free to the public; also by post, and from travelling van and branches. The Library has charitable status: membership £10 (organisations £15) for reading room, newsletter and to support the work.

SCOTTISH SCREEN
74 VICTORIA CRESCENT ROAD, GLASGOW G12 9JN.
TEL.: 0141-334 4445. FAX: 0141-334 8132. e-mail: info@scottishscreen. demon.co.uk
web: http://www.scottishscreen.demon.co.uk
Contact: John Archer, Chief Executive.
The new national body responsible for promoting all aspects of the film and television industry in Scotland. Scottish Screen is the one-stop-shop for support in film development and production, locations, exhibitions, professional training, education, information and festivals. We host the European Union's MEDIA 2 Scottish Antenna, dedicated to developing partnerships abroad and Scottish Screen is the home of the Scottish National Film and Television Archive. Scottish Screen is the major funder of the Edinburgh International Film Festival and of Scotland's regional film theatres.

SOCIETY OF ANTIQUARIES OF SCOTLAND
ROYAL MUSEUM OF SCOTLAND, CHAMBERS STREET, EDINBURGH EH1 1JF.
TEL.: 0131-225 7534.
Contact: Fionna Ashmore, Director.
The Society, founded in 1780, is the second oldest antiquarian society in Britain; an active body, it organises lectures, conferences, seminars and excursions, publishes an annual *Proceedings*, a twice-yearly Newsletter and a Monograph series. It plays an important role in the cultural life and heritage of Scotland, sponsoring all aspects of archaeological and historical research. Drawing on its wide range of available expertise, it provides an impartial and independent voice on heritage matters and is represented on many committees and councils.

4. BUSINESS

BARR HOLDINGS LIMITED
HEATHFIELD, AYR KA8 9SL.
TEL.: 01292 281311. FAX: 01292 618678.
Contact: W.J. Barr, OBE, CEng, FICE, FIMgt, Chairman and Chief Executive; Sir W. Francis, CBE, DSc, LLD, FEng, Director; S.H. Ingall, MA, FCA, Director.
Construction, development, steelwork, quarries, homes, precast concrete, ready mix concrete, ports, joinery, cranes, waste management, facilities management, plant and transport.

CLYDEPORT PLC
16 ROBERTSON STREET, GLASGOW G2 8DS.
TEL.: 0141-221 8733. FAX: 0141-248 3167.
Contact: Tom Allison, Chief Executive; Euan Davidson, Corporate Services Director; Peter McKellar, Corporate Development Director.
Clydeport is Scotland's premier west coast port operator. With comprehensive facilities designed to cater for the needs of both importers and exporters, Clydeport offers unrivalled facilities, speedy turnaround times and above all, excellent service. Our facilities at Glasgow, Greenock, Ardrossan and Hunterston, are each dedicated to specific cargoes such as dry bulks, forest products, containers and cruise liners. The company is also involved in property acquisition and development. At Clydeport, you can always be assured of the best possible service.

5. CHARITABLE AND VOLUNTARY

respite care are heavily dependent upon your generosity. Once you have provided for your family, please see if there is some extra room for us. Communicate your concern by considering a donation, covenant or legacy.

VOLUNTEER DEVELOPMENT SCOTLAND
72 MURRAY PLACE, STIRLING FK8 2BX.
TEL.: 01786 479593. FAX: 01786 449285. e-mail: vds@vds.org.uk
Contact: Liz Burns, OBE, Director.
Volunteer Development Scotland is Scotland's national centre for volunteering. We are committed to extending the range and effectiveness of voluntary work by giving volunteering a voice, promoting good practice and developing new initiatives. We work across all sectors and through national and local networks. Our services include the provision of specialist training, information, advice on policy development, consultancy, publications and development projects with specific groups such as volunteering in the health service, youth and employee volunteering.

6. CONSERVATION

EDINBURGH NEW TOWN CONSERVATION COMMITTEE
13A DUNDAS STREET, EDINBURGH EH3 6QG.
TEL.: 0131-557 5222. FAX: 0131-556 6355.
Contact: Richard Griffith, MA(Cantab), Dip Arch(Cantab), RIAS, Director; Caroline Sibbald, Grant Case Officer.
Established 1970 to halt decay of residential buildings in Georgian New Town. Funded by Scottish Office (Historic Scotland) and City of Edinburgh Council. Remit: to award grants for appropriate external repairs, promote building maintenance, and advise central and local government on major policy issues. Committee representation: City of Edinburgh Council; Historic Buildings Council for Scotland; Scottish Civic Trust; Cockburn Association; Architectural Heritage Society of Scotland; New Town Residents.

EDINBURGH OLD TOWN RENEWAL TRUST
343 HIGH STREET, EDINBURGH EH1 1PW.
TEL.: 0131-225 8818. FAX: 0131-225 8636.
Contact: Kirsteen Thomson, Executive Director.
The Trust's work is to promote and co-ordinate a conservation led economic regeneration strategy for the Old Town of Edinburgh. The aim is to ensure that the Old Town is a place in which people live, work and spend leisure time. The Trust works closely with other agencies to focus resources to achieve development, conservation and town centre management initiatives. In addition, the Trust manages a £500,000 conservation grants programme.

HISTORIC SCOTLAND
LONGMORE HOUSE, SALISBURY PLACE, EDINBURGH EH9 1SH.
TEL.: 0131-668 8600. FAX: 0131-668 8699.
Contact: G.N. Munro, Director and Chief Executive, 0131-668 8696; F.J. Lawrie, Director, Heritage Policy, 0131-668 8727; B. Naylor, Director, Properties in Care, 0131-668 8735; Mrs Paulette M. Hill, Librarian, Room G55, 0131-668 8651, Fax: 0131-668 8749, phill.hs.lh@gtnet.gov.uk
Historic Scotland, an executive agency of The Scottish Office Development Department, protects and promotes public understanding and enjoyment of Scotland's ancient monuments and archaeological sites and landscapes, historic buildings, parks, gardens and designed landscapes. This includes in particular the maintenance and conservation of the Palace of Holyroodhouse, the Scottish Royal Parks and monuments in the care of the Secretary of State for Scotland.

NATIONAL PLAYING FIELDS ASSOCIATION
20 QUEEN STREET, EDINBURGH EH2 1JX.
TEL.: 0131-225 4307. FAX: 0131-225 5763.

Contact: Stephen Barr, Secretary/Treasurer.

Our Royal Charter tasks us with the protection and preservation of playing fields and recreational space and in Scotland we are the guardian trustees of 85 King George V Memorial Playing Fields. The Association's objectives are to provide, maintain, promote and assist in the provision and maintenance of playing fields, recreational grounds, playgrounds, open spaces and other facilities for play and recreation, for the benefit of the community at large and particularly in areas of greatest social need. The Association awards grants and loans to organisations whose aims and objectives are basically in line with our own.

ROYAL COMMISSION ON THE ANCIENT AND HISTORICAL MONUMENTS OF SCOTLAND
JOHN SINCLAIR HOUSE, 16 BERNARD TERRACE, EDINBURGH EH8 9NX.
TEL.: 0131-662 1456. FAX: 0131-662 1477/1499.

Contact: Sir William Fraser, GCB, MA, LLD, FRSE; Mr R.J. Mercer, MA, FSA, FRSE.

The aims of the Royal Commission on the Ancient and Historical Monuments of Scotland are: to survey and record the man-made environment of Scotland; to compile and maintain in the National Monuments Record of Scotland a record of the archaeological and historical environment; and to promote an understanding of this information by all appropriate means.

7. ECONOMIC DEVELOPMENT AND PLANNING

DUNDEE AND TAYSIDE CHAMBER OF COMMERCE AND INDUSTRY
PANMURE STREET, DUNDEE DD1 1ED.
TEL.: 01382 201122. FAX: 01382 229544. e-mail: dundeechamber@sol.co.uk

Contact: Harry Terrell, Chief Executive; Stephanie Brown, Human Resources Manager; Avril Novak, Membership Services Manager.

The Chamber is a non party political voluntary business organisation dedicated to the furtherance of its members' interests by: influencing all relevant bodies in order to create, maintain and improve an environment and infrastructure supportive of the local business community; providing a range of effective and efficient business services that give members a competitive edge; and assisting in the attraction of new industry and commerce to the area.

GLASGOW DEVELOPMENT AGENCY
ATRIUM COURT, 50 WATERLOO STREET, GLASGOW G2 6HQ.
TEL.: 0141-204 1111. FAX: 0141-248 1600.

Contact: Michael Lunn, Chairman; Stuart Gulliver, Chief Executive; Gordon Kennedy, Director, Corporate Development.

Glasgow is the largest city in Scotland in terms of population, jobs, companies and investment. Its sphere of influence affects almost half of the Scottish population. Within the Scottish Enterprise network, Glasgow Development Agency's task of delivering economic development in Glasgow is unique, since it is the only Local Enterprise Company to serve an exclusively inner city area. Glasgow's urban context and scale presents a special set of challenges and problems, as well as genuine advantages and opportunities.

HIGHLAND OPPORTUNITY LIMITED
THE HIGHLAND COUNCIL, GLENURQUHART ROAD, INVERNESS IV3 5NX.
TEL.: 01463 702551. FAX: 01463 710848. e-mail: eic@sprite.co.uk

Contact: Hugh F. Black, Company Manager, Ext. 2551; Isabel Crawford, Company Accountant, Ext. 2558; Caroline Gray-Stephens, European Executive, Ext. 2560.

Highland Opportunity Limited is the Enterprise Trust for the Highlands of Scotland providing financial assistance and business services, particularly to small and medium

THE SCOTTISH CHAMBERS OF COMMERCE
CONFERENCE HOUSE, THE EXCHANGE, 152 MORRISON STREET, EDINBURGH EH3 8EB.
TEL.: 0131-477 8025. FAX: 0131-477 7002.
Contact: Mr Lex Gold, Director.
The Scottish Chambers of Commerce (SCC) is the most extensive business support organisation in Scotland with 21 member Chambers and 8,000 member companies who, in turn, employ more than 50 per cent of the Scottish workforce. SCC co-ordinates member Chamber activities at national and international level. It encourages development of Chamber services such as Export Support and Training and Education. It is the authentic national voice of the business community and plays a major role in influencing Government policy and decisions at all levels.

SCOTTISH ENTERPRISE
120 BOTHWELL STREET, GLASGOW G2 7JP.
TEL.: 0141-248 2700. FAX: 0141-221 3217. e-mail: scotentcsd@scotent.co.uk
Contact: Sir Ian Wood, Chairman; Crawford Beveridge, CBE, Chief Executive.
Helping create jobs and prosperity for Scotland, the Scottish Enterprise Network consists of Scottish Enterprise and 13 Local Enterprise Companies. Scottish Enterprise provides a framework for the operation of the network and carries out Scotland-wide projects and programmes. Through Locate in Scotland, it helps attract jobs to Scotland; through Scottish Trade International it helps Scottish companies compete in world export markets. The Local Enterprise Companies deliver programmes for local needs: company development, business start-up and training programmes.

SCOTTISH ENTERPRISE TAYSIDE
ENTERPRISE HOUSE, 45 NORTH LINDSAY STREET, DUNDEE DD1 1HT.
TEL.: 01382 223100. FAX: 01382 201319. e-mail: set.reception@scotent.co.uk
Contact: Sandra Burke, Communications Manager, 01382 305510, e-mail: sandra.burke@scotent.co.uk; Chris Roberts, PR Executive, 01382 305547, e-mail: chris.roberts@scotent.co.uk
Scottish Enterprise Tayside (SET) is a government-funded enterprise company. It offers a broad range of business services and training programmes to help Tayside businesses and individuals develop their full potential. The company also invests in environmental projects to enhance Tayside's natural character and works with Locate in Scotland to secure jobs through inward investment. SET can help businesses to obtain financial assistance and has specialists dealing with property matters, exporting, environmental matters, European funding and tourism.

8. EDUCATION
(see also Schools)

ABERDEEN COLLEGE
GALLOWGATE CENTRE, GALLOWGATE, ABERDEEN AB25 1BN.
TEL.: 01224 612000. FAX: 01224 612001. e-mail: abcoll-enquiry@abdn.ac.uk
web: http://www.abcol.ac.uk/
Contact: Rae Angus, Principal.
Aberdeen College – Scotland's largest FE college – provides flexible, high quality further and higher education courses, ranging from non-advanced to advanced, professional and post-graduate level. Subject areas comprise: art, design and construction; business studies; communication, language and media studies; engineering technologies; office technology and computing; rural and recreation studies; service industries; social studies. The College's training company, ASET Ltd, offers specialist marine operations courses and hazardous area Ex-Training for offshore industries. Aberdeen College is a member of Scotland's Polytechnic Colleges Group.

CARDONALD COLLEGE
690 MOSSPARK DRIVE, GLASGOW G52 3AY.
TEL.: 0141-883 6151. FAX: 0141-882 0767. e-mail: info_centre@cardonald. ac.uk

Contact: Ros Micklem, Principal, Ext. 201; Ian MacEachern, Depute Principal, Ext. 204; David Baillie, Secretary to Board of Management, Ext. 208.

The College's mission is "to meet the aspirations of each student or client by providing a valuable and enjoyable learning experience". It provides a wide variety of courses at both non-advanced and advanced levels in a range of disciplines, from aromatherapy to water operations. There is increasing emphasis on community outreach and open learning. Most subjects are available on a full-time or part-time basis and a business development unit keeps the College close to market realities.

COMMITTEE OF SCOTTISH HIGHER EDUCATION PRINCIPALS (COSHEP)
ST. ANDREW HOUSE, 141 WEST NILE STREET, GLASGOW G1 2RN.
TEL.: 0141-353 1880. FAX: 0141-353 1881. e-mail: coshep@gcal.ac.uk

Contact: Dr Ronald L. Crawford, Secretary; Ms Rosemary C. Williamson, Deputy Secretary.

"The most effective regional organisation of its kind in the UK" (Commission on Scottish Education). COSHEP is the official "voice" of the Scottish universities and higher education colleges. The present Convener (1996–1998) is Professor Richard Shaw, Principal and Vice-Chancellor of the University of Paisley.

THE UNIVERSITY OF EDINBURGH
OLD COLLEGE, SOUTH BRIDGE, EDINBURGH EH8 9YL.
TEL.: 0131-650 1000. FAX: 0131-650 2147.

Contact: Professor Sir Stewart Sutherland, Principal, 0131-650 2150; Dr Martin Lowe, Secretary, 0131-650 2144, e-mail: Dr.M.J.B.Lowe@ed.ac.uk; Mr Ray Footman, Director of Information and PR Services, 0131-650 2249, e-mail: R.Footman@ed.ac.uk

The University of Edinburgh, with some 17,500 students and over 2,000 academic and research staff, is one of Europe's leading centres of higher education, devoted to excellence in teaching and research across a broad range of disciplines and professions. It especially values its intellectual and economic relationship with the Scottish community that forms its base and provides a wide range of research, educational, commercial and cultural services for its client groups.

EDINBURGH'S TELFORD COLLEGE
CREWE TOLL, EDINBURGH EH4 2NZ.
TEL.: 0131-332 2491. FAX: 0131-343 1218. e-mail: @ed.coll.ac.uk

Contact: Mrs Fiona M. Baikie, Principal and Chief Executive, Ext. 2201, e-mail: fiona@ed.coll.ac.uk; Mrs Kate Arnott, Chair, Board of Management, Ext. 2302; Mr Joe Mooney, Depute Principal, e-mail: joem@ed.coll.ac.uk.

The College mission is "to be accessible, responsive and flexible, and to achieve excellence". It aims to meet the educational and training needs of individuals, industry and the wider community. In pursuit of these goals, it works in partnership with a wide range of local, national and international organisations. The number of students enrolled with the College in 1996-97 exceeded 18,000, many of them studying part-time and by distance learning.

FALKIRK COLLEGE OF FURTHER AND HIGHER EDUCATION
GRANGEMOUTH ROAD, FALKIRK FK2 9AD.
TEL.: 01324 403000. FAX: 01324 403222. e-mail: 101544.3517@ compuserve.com

Contact: Dr Graham Clark, Principal; Mr Allan French, Associate Principal; Mrs Jeanette Johnston, Marketing Manager.

A large comprehensive provider of further and higher education and vocational training in central Scotland. 12,000 students/trainees per year of which half undertake HNC, HND, AD or SVQ level III/IV. Validated by OUVS for BA and BSc vocational degree programmes. A member of Scotland's Polytechnic Colleges Group. Scotvec Approved Centre, accredited under SQMS and an Investor in People.

Motherwell College will develop its role as a key provider of local, national and international learning opportunities, making a full contribution to the economic, social and cultural life of the local community and meeting the needs of individual learners.

NAPIER UNIVERSITY
219 COLINTON ROAD, EDINBURGH EH14 1DJ.
TEL.: 0131-444 2266. FAX: 0131-455 4666. e-mail: info@napier.ac.uk

Contact: Professor John Mavor, FRSE, FEng, Principal, 0131-455 4600, e-mail: j.mavor@napier.ac.uk; Professor Michael Thorne, BSc, PhD, FIMA, FBCS, Vice-Principal, 0131-455 4607, e-mail: m.thorne@napier.ac.uk; Ian Miller, MA, LLB, Secretary and Registrar, 0131-455 4603, e-mail: i.miller@napier.ac.uk
Napier University is the sixth largest HEI in Scotland with 11,500 students following professional, technical and vocational courses. Its five faculties – Arts & Social Science, Engineering, Health Studies, Science, and the Business School – offer degree, honours degree, and postgraduate programmes, diploma and certificate courses, and short courses for industry and commerce. Napier is a vocational university with a strong reputation for applied research and consultancy in biomedicine, building technology, electronics, international law, management, new materials, statistics, tourism and transportation.

QUEEN MARGARET COLLEGE
CLERWOOD TERRACE, EDINBURGH EH12 8TS.
TEL.: 0131-317 3000. FAX: 0131-317 3256.

Contact: Dr Joan Stringer, Principal and Vice Patron; Dr Austin Reid, Assistant Principal (Academic Development); Rosalyn Marshall, Assistant Principal (Strategic Planning and Development).
Queen Margaret College is a university-sector institution with around 2,500 full-time students as well as over 2,000 part-time and short-course students. In 1992 the College was granted Degree Awarding Powers by the Privy Council, in common with all the new universities. The College's courses fall into the categories of Business, Management and Information; Theatre Arts and Health Care which together reflect the vocational and professional emphasis of the College mission. QM is located on three sites, with the majority of teaching taking place at the Corstorphine and Leith campuses. The Department of Drama will soon occupy premises in the Gateway, formerly Edinburgh base for Scottish Television.

SCET (SCOTTISH COUNCIL FOR EDUCATIONAL TECHNOLOGY)
74 VICTORIA CRESCENT ROAD, GLASGOW G12 9JN.
TEL.: 0141-337 5000. FAX: 0141-337 5050. e-mail: scet@scet.org.uk

Contact: Nigel Paine, Chief Executive; Philip Strange, Business Development Manager; Martin Jack, Technology Centre Manager.
SCET aims to enhance the quality of education and training in Scotland, helping people learn effectively through technology. We are actively involved in software development, multi-media production, consultancy, training and providing information and support on all aspects of learning through technology.

SCOTTISH CONSULTATIVE COUNCIL ON THE CURRICULUM
GARDYNE ROAD, BROUGHTY FERRY, DUNDEE DD5 1NY.
TEL.: 01382 455053. FAX: 01382 455046. e-mail: Reception@sccc.ac.uk

Contact: Cameron Harrison, Chief Executive, CHarrison@sccc.ac.uk; Tegwen Wallace, Senior Information Officer, TWallace@sccc.ac.uk; Anne Gerono, Public Relations and Promotions Officer, AGerono@sccc.ac.uk
The Scottish Consultative Council on the Curriculum is the principal advisory body to the Secretary of State on all curriculum matters relating to 3-18 year olds in Scottish schools. It has three main functions: to keep the curriculum under review and inform the government on those areas requiring attention; to consult with local authorities, teachers, parents and other representatives of the community; to provide guidance on curriculum development and practice. The Council publishes support materials for government programmes as well as guidance and discussion documents for teachers on aspects of the curriculum.

SCOTTISH COUNCIL FOR RESEARCH IN EDUCATION
15 ST. JOHN STREET, EDINBURGH EH8 8JR.
TEL.: 0131-557 2944. FAX: 0131-556 9454. e-mail: scre@scre.ac.uk

Contact: Professor Wynne Harlen, OBE, Director, e-mail: wynne.harlen@scre.ac.uk; Mr David Gilhooly, Head of Admin Services, e-mail: david.gilhooly@scre.ac.uk; Ms Rosemary Wake, Head of Information Services, e-mail: r.wake@scre.ac.uk.

SCRE's mission is to conduct research for the benefit of education in Scotland and elsewhere. It supports research through disseminating its own and others' research by conventional and electronic publications and conferences. It supplies information and consultancy to help others conduct and disseminate research and provides training in research methods through workshops and seminars.

SCOTTISH QUALIFICATIONS AUTHORITY
HANOVER HOUSE, 24 DOUGLAS STREET, GLASGOW G2 7NQ.
TEL.: 0141-248 7900. FAX: 0141-242 2244. e-mail: mail@sqa.org.uk

Contact: Ron Tuck, Chief Executive; David Miller, Chairman; Amanda Cornish, Head of Marketing and PR.

The Scottish Qualifications Authority offers a framework for education and training for the whole population of Scotland from school age onwards. It develops and awards most of Scotland's qualifications including Standard and Higher Grades, normally taken at school; Higher National Certificates (HNCs) and Higher National Diplomas (HNDs), usually taken at college; and Scottish Vocational Qualifications (SVQs), the workplace based qualification. The qualifications on offer cover a huge range of skills – both academic and vocational – at all levels.

SCOTTISH SECONDARY TEACHERS' ASSOCIATION
15 DUNDAS STREET, EDINBURGH EH3 6QG.
TEL.: 0131-556 5919. FAX: 0131-556 1419. e-mail: sstateach@aol.com

Contact: David H. Eaglesham, BEd, General Secretary.

The Association was founded to advance education in Scotland and to safeguard and promote the interests of Scottish secondary teachers especially regarding salaries and conditions of service. We represent members within schools, at local authority levels, and nationally through bodies such as the SJNC and GTC. This representation is carried out for individuals as well as the whole membership, and involves shaping the future of education in Scotland as well as offering a comprehensive range of services to members.

SSERC LIMITED (TRADING AS SSERC AND STS SUPPORT SERVICES)
ST. MARY'S BUILDING, 23 HOLYROOD ROAD, EDINBURGH EH8 8AE.
TEL.: 0131-558 8180. FAX: 0131-558 8191. e-mail: sserc@mhie.ac.uk

Contact: John Richardson, Executive Director.

Technical resource support for education. Advisory, information, consultancy, testing and training services on anything connected with the purchase, use (including health and safety), maintenance and repair of equipment and materials for education, health and safety, management training and consultancy.

9. FINANCIAL

ASSOCIATION OF BRITISH INSURERS
51 GRESHAM STREET, LONDON EC2V 7HQ.
TEL.: 0171-600 3333. FAX: 0171-696 8996.

Contact: Vic Rance, Manager, Media, 0171-216 7440; Suzanne Moore, Assistant Manager, Media, 0171-216 7411; Malcolm Tarling, Assistant Manager, Media, 0171-216 7410.

The Association of British Insurers represents around 440 insurance companies, which between them account for over 95 per cent of the business of UK insurance companies. The Association represents insurance companies to the Government and to regulatory and other agencies, and it provides a wide range of services to its members.

CIPFA (The Chartered Institute of Public Finance & Accountancy)
8 North West Circus Place, Edinburgh EH3 6ST.
Tel.: 0131-220 4316. Fax: 0131-220 4305.
Contact: Ian P. Doig, Director (Scotland); Valerie Davidson, Depute Director (Scotland).
CIPFA, the Chartered Institute of Public Finance and Accountancy was founded in 1885 and is the leading accountancy body for public services, whether in the public or private sectors. It is a registered charity and holder of a Royal Charter. CIPFA members are to be found throughout the public services, including local government, central government, healthcare services, higher and further education, housing associations, utility services, charities, as well as in the statutory audit agencies, firms of accountants and management consultants.

The Institute of Chartered Accountants of Scotland
27 Queen Street, Edinburgh EH2 1LA.
Tel.: 0131-225 5673. Fax: 0131-225 3813. e-mail: icas.icas.rog.uk
Contact: Peter W. Johnston, Chief Executive and Secretary; Professor Ian F.Y. Marrian, Deputy Chief Executive and Secretary.
The objective of the Institute of Chartered Accountants of Scotland is to uphold the integrity and standing of the profession of chartered accountancy in the interests of society and the membership, through excellence in education and the development of accountancy, and through service to members and the enforcement of professional standards.

Local Authority (Scotland) Accounts Advisory Committee (LASAAC)
c/o CIPFA Scotland, 8 North West Circus Place, Edinburgh EH3 6ST.
Tel.: 0131-220 4316. Fax: 0131-220 4305.
Contact: Ian P. Doig, Secretary; Valerie Davidson; Bill Dickson, Chair, 01786 442900.
LASAAC, the Local Authority (Scotland) Accounts Advisory Committee is the standard setting body for local authority accounting in Scotland. LASAAC aims to seek continued self-regulation of accounting standards within Scottish local government and achieves this via its involvement in standard setting at a UK level. LASAAC provides guidance to local authority practitioners on accounting matters as well as developing discussion documents on current issues which seek to move the debate forward not only within Scotland but at a UK level.

Scottish Financial Enterprise
91 George Street, Edinburgh EH2 3ES.
Tel.: 0131-225 6990. Fax: 0131-220 1353. e-mail: info@sfe.org.uk
Contact: Professor Grant Baird, Executive Director; Derek Elder, Deputy Director; Bill Brash, Manager, UK Programmes.
SFE was set up in 1986 to promote and represent the Scottish financial community. It is a not-for-profit, private sector organisation with over 200 members, including the major banks, life offices and fund managers together with providers of professional, financial and business services. Its aim is to confirm and enhance Scotland's position as a financial centre of world standing.

10. Health

British Medical Association
3 Hill Place, Edinburgh EH8 9EQ.
Tel.: 0131-662 4820.
Contact: Dr. Brian Potter, Scottish Secretary; Mr Arthur Morris, FRCS, Scottish Council Chairman, 01382 660111, Ext. 6142; Mrs Irene Hamilton, Public Affairs Co-ordinator.
The British Medical Association, founded in 1832, represents doctors from all branches of medicine in the UK. It is a voluntary professional association, independent trade union, scientific and educational body and a publishing house. The BMA and the BMJ Publishing Group, which is one of the most influential medical publishers in the world, produce a wide range of journals, reports and medical books. With a UK membership of 111,000, and nearly 12,000 in Scotland, the BMA is regarded as the voice of the medical profession.

maintenance of high standards of professional competence and conduct. The College shall comprise Honorary Fellows in surgery and Honorary Fellows in dental surgery, ordinary Fellows in surgery and ordinary Fellows in dental surgery.

SCOTTISH ASSOCIATION OF HEALTH COUNCILS
18 ALVA STREET, EDINBURGH EH2 4QG.
TEL.: 0131-220 4101. FAX: 0131-220 4108. e-mail: sahc@sol.co.uk
Contact: Patricia Dawson, Director; Rev. T.W. Tait, Convener; Mr J. Nairn, Vice Convener.
The SAHC seeks to be the national voice of the public in health matters.

11. HOUSING

SCOTTISH COUNCIL FOR SINGLE HOMELESS
WELLGATE HOUSE, 200 COWGATE, EDINBURGH EH1 1NQ.
TEL.: 0131-226 4382. FAX: 0131-225 4382.
Contact: Laurie Naumann, Director; Robert Aldridge, Information Officer; Alison Brown, Training and Development Officer.
Campaigns throughout Scotland, firstly, to highlight the wide-ranging needs of single homeless people for access to secure accommodation according to individual requirements and, secondly, for the prevention of homelessness. SCSH also presses for improvements in the law and in the practices of service providers, publishes a monthly newsletter, undertakes training and research, publishes reports and offers advice and information to individuals and agencies. SCSH works closely with others in the voluntary, statutory and independent sectors and has a particular interest in community care issues.

SCOTTISH FEDERATION OF HOUSING ASSOCIATIONS
38 YORK PLACE, EDINBURGH EH1 3HU.
TEL.: 0131-556 5777. FAX: 0131-557 6028.
Contact: David Orr, Director; Dave Alexander, Policy Manager; Rob Hughes, Member Services Manager.
As the voice of housing associations and co-operatives throughout Scotland, the SFHA promotes, encourages and assists the formation of housing associations and provides services to help them operate. It supports the provision of affordable quality housing for those in need. Negotiating new policy, practice and legislation, it seeks to influence Government and Scottish Homes. As well as conducting national campaigns, the SFHA provides training and advice for all those involved in, or interested in, the Scottish housing association movement.

12. LOCAL GOVERNMENT

ANGUS COUNCIL
THE CROSS, FORFAR DD8 1BX.
TEL.: 01307 461460. FAX: 01307 461874.
Contact: Mr A.B. Watson, Chief Executive, 01307 473023; Councillor Mrs Frances E. Duncan, Provost, 01307 473008; Councillor Ian Hudghton, Leader of Administration, 01307 473006.
Scottish local authority providing full range of services, with the following key themes: to promote the identity of and represent the interests of Angus locally, nationally and internationally; to aim to provide excellent public services, maximising the use of available resources to meet local needs; to improve economic prosperity in Angus; to improve the environment and the quality of life in Angus, with an emphasis on sustainability; to promote equal opportunities/reduce inequalities in Angus; to value staff as the Council's most important asset, and seek to ensure long-term employment prospects for a locally based and directly employed workforce; to develop partnerships.

MIDLOTHIAN COUNCIL
MIDLOTHIAN HOUSE, BUCCLEUCH STREET, DALKEITH, MIDLOTHIAN EH22 1DJ.
TEL.: 0131-663 2881. FAX: 0131-660 7565.
Contact: Trevor Muir, Chief Executive, 0131-663 2881.
Midlothian is situated to the south of Scotland's capital city of Edinburgh. Midlothian Council serves a population of 80,000, covering a geographical area of over 35,515 hectares, incorporating the main towns of Penicuik, Bonnyrigg, Dalkeith, Mayfield and Easthouses, Loanhead and Gorebridge. The Council employs over 4,000 people.

13. MEDIA AND PUBLISHING

GRAMPIAN TELEVISION
QUEEN'S CROSS, ABERDEEN AB15 4XJ.
TEL.: 01224 846846. FAX: 01224 846800. e-mail: gtv@grampiantv.co.uk
Contact: Alistair Gracie, Controller; Hilary Buchan, Head of Public Relations.
Grampian Television serves North Scotland as a producer licensee, with 99 per cent of its wide range of regional programmes made in the area. It produces additional Gaelic programmes funded by the Gaelic Broadcasting Committee, schools programmes for Channel Four, and ITV Network shows which include the highly popular *National TV Awards*. For 36 years, Grampian Television has ensured that its area, larger than Belgium or Denmark, enjoys a service that meets its distinctive regional requirements. The Station has a licence to continue this service until 2002 but it can apply for a 10 year extension before that date.

NORTHSOUND RADIO
45 KINGSGATE, ABERDEEN AB15 4EL.
TEL.: 01224 632234. FAX: 01224 400003. e-mail: webster@srh.co.uk
Contact: Rod Webster, Managing Director; Fiona Stalker, Head of News; Lewis Carnie, Sales Director.
Commercial radio station serving NE Scotland, broadcasting local and national news and weather, local information. Split into two services, Northsound One on FM, and Northsound Two on AM, the station provides entertainment and information as the top-rated broadcaster in national research.

ORDNANCE SURVEY
GRAYFIELD HOUSE, 5 BANKHEAD AVENUE, EDINBURGH EH11 4AE.
TEL.: 0131-442 3985. FAX: 0131-442 4780.
Contact: Graham E. Little, Account Manager (Scotland).
Ordnance Survey is Great Britain's national mapping agency, responsible for the official, definitive topographic mapping of the country. We produce, maintain and market a wide range of maps and computer data products for government, business, administrative, educational and leisure use.

14. POLITICAL

SCOTTISH CONSTITUTIONAL CONVENTION
C/O ROSEBERY HOUSE, 9 HAYMARKET TERRACE, EDINBURGH EH12 5XZ.
TEL.: 0131-474 9200. FAX: 0131-474 9292.
Contact: Douglas Sinclair, Secretary; Canon Kenyon Wright, Chair of Executive Committee.
The membership of the SCC includes political parties, local government, trades unions, churches and a range of civic organisations who are working together to achieve three key objectives: to agree a scheme for a Parliament for Scotland; to mobilise Scottish opinion and ensure the approval of the Scottish people for that scheme; and to assert the right of the Scottish people to secure the implementation of that scheme.

15. PROFESSIONAL AND TRADE ORGANISATIONS

16. RELIGIOUS

17. RURAL, CROFTING, LAND

18. SCHOOLS
(see also Education)

burgesses. Today it is an independent, coeducational day school, deeply rooted in the Scottish tradition. The School which has a unique setting close to the Royal Mile, Edinburgh University and the Castle, has long enjoyed a reputation for educational excellence, pastoral care and sporting achievement. Our aim is to introduce all our pupils to the broadest possible spectrum of academic, cultural and sporting interests and experiences.

HIGH SCHOOL OF DUNDEE
EUCLID CRESCENT, DUNDEE DD1 1IIU.
TEL.: 01382 202921. FAX: 01382 229822.
e-mail: admin@thehighschool. dundeecity.sch.uk
Contact: Mr A. Michael Duncan, MA, BPhil, DipEd, Rector.
A fully co-educational independent school of 1,100 pupils (junior school 400 pupils) offering all through education for pupils from five to 18. Emphasis is placed upon the needs and welfare of the individual. Pupils are prepared for SCE examinations with over 90 per cent of final leavers entering university. There is an extensive range of sporting, cultural and social activities with games, music, drama and debating particularly strong.

KELVINSIDE ACADEMY
33 KIRKLEE ROAD, GLASGOW G12 0SW.
TEL.: 0141-357 3376. FAX: 0141-357 5401.
Contact: J.H. Duff, Rector; Mrs T. Littlefield, Head of Lower School; Mrs J. Macleod, Head of Nursery.
Scotland's leading independent day school for boys caters for ages four and a half to 18. Girls will be admitted up to Primary 5 in 1998, and progressively thereafter. The adjacent nursery department takes boys and girls aged two and a half to five. The aim is to encourage each pupil to achieve his fullest potential in all academic, sporting and cultural fields, in what is a friendly but disciplined environment. Small classes and individual attention are main features. Over 80 per cent of leavers proceed to universities, with others embarking on college or professional courses.

ST. COLUMBA'S SCHOOL, KILMACOLM
DUCHAL ROAD, KILMACOLM, RENFREWSHIRE PA13 4AU.
TEL.: 01505 872238. FAX: 01505 873995.
Contact: Mr A.H. Livingstone, Rector.
Founded in 1897, St. Columba's is one of Scotland's foremost schools with a roll of 600 students. The school is non-denominational and has equal numbers of boys and girls at all stages. It has an excellent academic reputation and, in addition, is strong musically, on the sporting front and in its participation in the Duke of Edinburgh Awards' Scheme.

ST. LEONARDS & ST. KATHERINES SCHOOLS
ST. ANDREWS, FIFE KY16 9QU.
TEL.: 01334 472126. FAX: 01334 479784. e-mail; stleonardssch.fife @campus.bt.com
Contact: Mary James, Headmistress (St. Leonards), 01334 472126; Joan Brittain, Headmistress (St. Katherines), 01334 472446; Fiona Macleod, Business Development Director, 01334 479784.
St Leonards School is a girls' independent boarding and day school. Small class sizes and superb facilities allow this school to offer high quality education on an individual scale for girls from the age of 12. Upper 5th is the year of the GCSEs and in the two 6th form years girls take A level courses and a programme of subsidiary subjects. Examination results at St. Leonards have been consistently excellent and 98 per cent of girls continue on to university or higher education. St Katherines is a small independent school situated on the campus of the senior school, offering nursery and pre-prep education for both boys and girls from age three to seven years and day and boarding education for girls from age seven to 12. Here, every pupil becomes part of a secure, supportive and happy community where confidence and self esteem develop.

19. TRADE UNIONS

20. TRANSPORT

21. YOUTH

Secretary; B.B. UK Headquarters, 01442 231681, e-mail: felden@boys-brigade.org.uk
By the year 2000, The Boys' Brigade will be known for its leading Christian Youth Work
which cares and challenges young people for life. The Boys' Brigade uses and will continue
to use methods of working which are attractive to boys, both those boys from within the
family of the church and those from without. It seeks to provide an atmosphere in which
boys can find enjoyment and fulfilment and in which they will respond to challenges –
physical, intellectual and spiritual. The Boys' Brigade will maintain its position in seeking to
inculcate Christian moral and spiritual values in its membership in an increasingly secular
world.

THE GUIDE ASSOCIATION SCOTLAND
16 COATES CRESCENT, EDINBURGH EH3 7AH.
TEL.: 0131-226 4511. FAX: 0131-220 4828.

Contact: Miss S.J. Pitches, Executive Director; Mrs K.S. McMath, Scottish Chief
Commissioner; Mrs G.R. Patterson, Public Relations Adviser.
The Guide Association is the UK's largest voluntary movement for girls and women. Its
purpose is to enable girls to mature into confident, capable and caring women, determined,
as individuals to realise their potential in their career, home and personal life, and willing, as
citizens, to contribute to their community and the wider world. We believe we can best
develop these qualities in a mutually-supportive, female structure, within an environment of
fun, friendship and adventure, underpinned by spiritual and moral values.

A

Abbott, Mollie Pearson, CBE (1984), DPE, MEd; b. 4.2.28, Peebles. Educ. Edinburgh Ladies' College; Dunfermline College of Physical Education. Assistant Teacher of Physical Education in Edinburgh schools; Temporary Lecturer, Moray House College of Education, Edinburgh, 1952-56; Senior Lecturer, Ripon Training College, 1956-62; Principal Lecturer, Aberdeen College of Education, 1962-63; HM Inspector of Schools, 1964-70; Principal, Dunfermline College of Physical Education, 1970-83. Past Chairman: Association of Higher Academic Staff in Colleges of Education in Scotland, Scottish Central Committee on Physical Education, Scottish Joint Consultative Committee on Physical Education; former Member: General Teaching Council for Scotland, Court of Heriot Watt University, National Committee for the In-Service Training of Teachers, Scottish Arts Council, Scottish Council of Physical Education, Scottish Sports Council. Recreations: gardening; handbell-ringing; swimming. Address: (h.) Janefield House, Kirkcudbright DG6 4UR; T.-01557 330119.

Abercrombie, Ian R., QC, LLB (Hons); b. 7.7.55, Bulawayo. Educ. Milton High School; Edinburgh University. Recreations: travelling; walking. Address: (h.) 7 Lauder Road, Edinburgh EH9 2EW; T.-0131-668 2489.

Aberdeen and Temair, June Marchioness of, CBE, DL, GCStJ, FRCM, FRSE. Musical Director and Conductor, Haddo House Choral and Operatic Society, since 1945. Educ. Southlands School, Harrow; Royal College of Music. Chairman: Scottish Children's League, 1969-84, NE Scotland Music School, since 1975, Advisory Council, Scottish Opera, 1979-90. Address: Haddo House, Aberdeen AB41 0ER; T.-01651 851216.

Abernethy, Hon. Lord, (John Alastair Cameron). Senator, College of Justice, since 1992; b. 1.2.38, Newcastle-upon-Tyne; m., Elspeth Mary Dunlop Miller; 3 s. Educ. St. Mary's School, Melrose; Glenalmond College, Perth; Pembroke College, Oxford. National Service, 2nd Lt., RASC, Aldershot and Malta, 1956-58. Called to the Bar, Inner Temple, 1963; admitted Member, Faculty of Advocates, 1966; Advocate-Depute, 1972-75; Standing Junior Counsel to Department of Energy, 1976-79, Scottish Development Department, 1978-79; QC (Scotland), 1979; Vice-Dean, Faculty of Advocates, 1983-92; President, Pensions Appeal Tribunals for Scotland, 1985-92 (Legal Chairman, 1979-85); Chairman, Faculty Services Ltd., 1983-89 (Director, 1979-89); Hon. Fellow, Pembroke College, Oxford, 1993; Vice-Chairman, Judges' Forum, International Bar Association, 1993-94, Chairman, since 1994; Member, Executive Committee, Society for the Welfare and Teaching of the Blind (Edinburgh and South East Scotland), 1979-92; Trustee, Arthur Smith Memorial Trust, since 1975, Chairman, since 1990; President, Scottish Medico-Legal Society, since 1996. Publications: Medical Negligence: an introduction, 1983; Reproductive Medicine and the Law (Contributor). Recreations: travel; sport; nature conservation; Africana. Address: (b.) Court of Session, Parliament House, Edinbrugh EH1 1RQ; T.-0131-225 2595.

Abram, Henry Charles, LLB, WS. Solicitor, Tods Murray WS, since 1973; b. 11.8.51, Glasgow; m., Leslie Anne Hamilton; 2 s.; 1 d. Educ. Merchiston Castle School; Aberdeen University. Articled Tods Murray WS; qualified, 1976; Partner, 1978; Chairman, Management Board, 1994-97; Chairman, 1998. Member, Council, Law Society of Scotland, 1983-86; Vice-Chairman of Governors, Merchiston Castle School; Member, High Constables and Guard of Honour of Holyrood House. Recreations: shooting; stalking; golf; skiing; running. Address: (b.) 66 Queen Street, Edinburgh EH2 4NE; T.-0131-226 4771.

Adam, Edmund Ian, MBChB, DRCOG. Medical Officer, Company of Merchants of City of Edinburgh, since 1973; b. 26.5.31, Edinburgh; m., Norma Barbara; 2 s. Educ. Daniel Stewart's College, Edinburgh; University of Edinburgh. House Officer (Surgery), General Hospital, Kirkcaldy, 1956-57; House Officer (Medicine), Bangour General Hospital, 1957; Medical Officer (Captain, RAMC), Intelligence Corps Depot, Sussex, 1957-59; House Officer (Obstetrics), Craigtoun Maternity Hospital, St. Andrews, 1959-60; Trainee Assistant, general practice, Dunkeld, 1960-61; Partner, general practice, Edinburgh, 1961-85; School Medical Officer, Daniel Stewart's and Melville College, Edinburgh, 1972-85; Medical Adviser, Lothian Regional Council, 1985-95; Clinical Assistant, Department of Medicine, Western General Hospital, Edinburgh, 1969-97. Moderator, Society of High Constables of Edinburgh, 1987-89; Honorary Physician: Scottish Schools Rugby Union, 1977-94, Scottish Badminton Union, 1977-90. Recreation: golf. Address: (h.) Norian, 60 Hillview Terrace, Edinburgh EH12 8RG; T.-0131-334 3498.

Adam, Ian Clark, CA. Group Finance Director, Christian Salvesen PLC, since 1995; b. 2.9.43, Dundee; m., Betty Anne; 1 s.; 1 d. Educ. Harris Academy, Dundee. Trained as CA, Henderson & Logie, Dundee, 1962-67; Price Waterhouse Peat & Co., Rio de Janeiro, 1967-70; Price Waterhouse, Bristol, 1970-76; Partner, Price Waterhouse, Edinburgh, 1976-86, Senior Partner, Scotland, 1986-95. Governor, Queen Margaret College, Stewarts Erskine Schools. Recreations: golf; reading; walking. Address: (b.) 50 East Fettes Avenue, Edinburgh EH4 1EQ; T.-0131-559 3600.

Adam, Ian Simpson Thomson, OBE, QFSM, GIFireE. Firemaster, Central Scotland Fire Brigade, since 1984; b. 4.5.40, Dunfermline; m., Norma; 1 s. Educ. Beath Secondary, Cowdenbeath. Retained Firefighter, Fife, 1960; wholetime Firefighter, Fife, 1964; Leading Firefighter, Fife, 1968; Sub Officer, Fife, 1969; Station Officer, Fife, 1972; Assistant Divisional Officer, Fife, 1974; Divisional Officer, Fife, 1978; Third Officer, SDO, Fife, 1979; Depute Firemaster, Central, 1982. Recreations: gardening; photography. Address: (b.) Main Street, Maddiston, Falkirk FK2 0LG.

Adams, David Anstey, MA. Principal, Northern College of Education, formerly Aberdeen College of Education, since 1983; b. 2.3.42, Wakefield, Yorkshire; m., Margaret Ishbel; 1 s.; 1 d. Educ. Harris Academy, Dundee; St. Andrews University. Teacher of English and History, High School of Dundee; Principal Teacher of English, Arbroath Academy; Assistant Director of Education: Angus County Council, Tayside Regional Council. Member, Committee of Scottish Higher Education Principals, General Teaching Council for Scotland, Open University Validation Board; Chairman, Independent Television Commission Viewer Consultative Council (Scotland). Recreations: fishing; shooting. Address: (b.) Northern College of Education, (Aberdeen Campus), Hilton Place, Aberdeen AB9 1FA; T.-01224 283500.

Adams, Douglas William, MA, MBA. Business Planning Director Europe, Templeton Global Investors Ltd, since 1988; b. 17.5.53, Perth; m., Jacqueline Mary Ferguson; 1 s.; 1 d. Educ. Perth Academy; Glasgow University; Strathclyde University. Economic Assistant, Scottish Office, Edinburgh, 1975-78; Economist, European Commission, Brussels, 1978-82; Head of Industrial Programmes, Scottish Development Agency, Glasgow, 1982-86; Economist, Scottish Provident, Edinburgh, 1986-88. Recreation: golf.

Address: (b.) Saltire Court, 20 Castle Terrace, Edinburgh EH14 1ER; T.-0131-469 4000.

Adams, Irene, JP. MP (Labour), Paisley North, since 1990; b. 1948. Address: House of Commons, London SW1A 0AA.

Adams, James Gordon Leitch, MA, PhD. Director of Planning and Development, Scottish Tourist Board, since 1988 (formerly Director of Development); b. 17.10.40, Glasgow; m., Rowan Hopwood; 1 s.; 1 d. Educ. Dundee High School; St Andrews University; Queen's University, Canada; McGill University. Economist: Canadian Federal Government, 1966-70, Highlands and Islands Development Board, 1970-75; Lecturer, Glasgow University, 1975-82; Visiting Lecturer in Poland, 1978, and India, 1981. Recreations: mountaineering; golf. Address: (h.) 5 Corrennie Drive, Edinburgh; T.-0131-447 8073.

Adams, Ralph Gange, LLB, CA. Partner in Charge, Scottish and Northern Ireland Offices, Deloitte & Touche, Chartered Accountants, since 1993; b. 30.10.55, Calcutta; m., Kirstine Mary Park; 2 s.; 1 d. Educ. Trinity College, Glenalmond; University of Dundee. Deloitte & Touche: indentured student, 1976-79; qualified as CA, 1979; seconded to Melbourne Office, 1980; seconded to Bank of Scotland, Glasgow and Edinburgh, 1984, Partner, 1986; Partner in Charge, Edinburgh Office, 1990-93, Scottish Offices, since 1993; Member, Board of Partners. Recreations: tennis; golf; music; theatre. Address: (b.) Deloitte & Touche, 39 George Street, Edinburgh EH2 2HZ; T.-0131-225 6834.

Adams, Robert William, OBE, FCMA, FCCA, JDipMA. Director, John Cairney & Co. Ltd., since 1983; Chairman, Hanover Housing Association, since 1995; b. 27.9.22, Glasgow; m., Mary Ann Ritchie; 2 s.; 1 d. Educ. Shawlands Academy, Glasgow. H.C. Stewart & Co., CA, Glasgow; Lieutenant, Parachute Regiment; South of Scotland Electricity Board; James Colledge (Cocoa) Ltd., West Africa; Highland Home Industries Ltd.; Managing Director, A.H. McIntosh & Co. Ltd., until 1982. Member, Glenrothes Development Corporation, 1976-84; former Member: Scottish Sports Council; Council, Institute of Cost and Management Accountants; Scottish Sports Council; former Convenor, Scottish Athletic Coaching Committee; former Scottish Chairman, Writers' Guild. Recreations: tennis; golf. Address: (h.) Achray, Shore Road, Aberdour, Fife; T.-01383 860269.

Adams, Sheenagh, MA (Hons), MCIH. Secretary, Historic Buildings Council for Scotland, since 1995; Head, Grants and Heritage Policy, Historic Scotland, since 1995; b. 31.8.57, Dundee; m., Peter Craig; 2 d. Educ. Harris Academy, Dundee; St. Andrews University. Welfare Rights Officer, Strathclyde Regional Council, 1979-82; Tenant Participation Officer, Clydebank Council and TPAS, 1982-85; Principal Management Officer, Falkirk District Council, 1985-90; Principal, Scottish Office, since 1990. Address: (b.) Longmore House, Salisbury Place, Edinburgh EH9 1SH; T.-0131-668 8799.

Adamson, James G., CBE, FRSA. Vice-Chairman, Financial Services Group (FSG), NCR (Scotland) Ltd.; b. 25.5.41, Rosyth; m., Ann May; 2 s.; 2 d. Educ. Heriot-Watt University. MoD (Navy), Rosyth; Honeywell Computer Systems; ITT; Marconi Space & Defence; NCR, AT&T (now NCR). President, Fife Society for the Blind; Non-Executive Director: Scottish Higher Education Funding Council, Scottish Enterprise, East Board Bank of Scotland; Member: Scottish Economic Council, Advisory Board, SCDI. Recreations: sailing; singing. Address: (b.) St. Davids Drive, Dalgety Bay, Fife; T.-01383 643179.

Adamson, Rev. Sidney, MA, BD. Minister, Church of Scotland; b. 3.8.11, Arbroath; m., Margaret T. Sharpe, JP; 1 s. Educ. Dumbarton Academy; Glasgow University and Trinity College; Royal Scottish Academy of Music and Drama. Ministries: St Ninian's, Sanquhar, 1937-47 (including war service), Trinity Church, Renfrew, 1947-54, High Kirk of Rothesay, 1954-59, St Michael's Inveresk, Musselburgh, 1959-85. Moderator of Presbytery: Dumfries, 1939, Dunoon, 1958, Dalkeith, 1964 and 1965; former Moderator, Synod of Lothian and Tweeddale; Army Chaplain, India, 1944-47; Territorial Army Chaplain, 1952-66; Chaplain, Royal British Legion (Scotland), Paisley, Renfrew, Rothesay, Musselburgh, and Honorary Vice President, Edinburgh & Lothian Area Council, 1973; Industrial Chaplain, Babcock & Wilcox Ltd., Renfrew, 1948-54; Chaplain, British Sailors' Society, 1955-85; Editor, Homeward Bound (Forces magazine, India), 1946-47. Publications: Two Centuries of Service (history of Sanquhar congregation), 1939; St Michael's Kirk at Inveresk (four editions between 1963 and 1984). Recreations: (at suitable periods) ballroom dancing; shooting; swimming; (always) reading; theatre; freelance journalism; ex-service welfare. Address: 48 Hailes Gardens, Colinton, Edinburgh EH13 0JH; T.-0131-441 2471.

Addison, Alexander, MBE, MB, ChB, FRCGP, DObstRCOG. Senior Partner, Addison, Scott, Kane & Ferguson, 1978-95; Chairman, Lanarkshire LMC, 1989-95; Member, Scottish Committee, BMA, since 1984, and Fellow, BMA, since 1993; b. 23.8.30, Kerala; m., Joan Wood; 3 s. Educ. Keith Grammar School; Aberdeen Grammar School; Aberdeen University. House Surgeon and Physician, Woodend General Hospital, Aberdeen, 1954-55; Captain, RAMC; Junior Medical Specialist, Cowglen MH, 1955-58; SHO, Bellshill MH, 1958-59; GP in Douglas and Physician to Lady Home Hospital, 1959-95; Member, West of Scotland Faculty of GP College, 1967-79 and of Scottish Council, 1976-78; Member, Lanarkshire LMC, since 1972, and of AMAC, since 1975; Chairman, Lanarkshire AMAC, 1982-86; Chairman, Scottish Association of General Practitioner Hospitals, 1985-87; Member, Scottish Committee of Medical Commission on Accident Prevention, since 1976; Member, National Medical Consultative Committee, 1977-83; Honorary Surgeon, St. Andrews Ambulance Association, 1959-89. Recreations: curling; golf; reading. Address: (h.) 7 Addison Drive, Douglas, Lanarkshire ML11 0PZ; T.-01555 851302.

Addison, Gordon, LLB, DipLP, NP. Solicitor, since 1989; Partner, Nelsons, Falkirk, since 1996; Secretary, Falkirk District Faculty of Solicitors, since 1995; b. 4.3.67, Lanark; m., Pauline Heather Proudfoot. Educ. Lanark Grammar; Aberdeen University. Traineeship, Drummond & Co. W.S., 1988-90; Associate, More & Co., 1991-92; Partner, Caesar & Howie, 1994-96. Vice President, Corstorphine Curling Club, since 1996. Recreations: curling; golf; the countryside. Address: (b.) Nelsons, 326 Main Street, Camelon, Falkirk; T.-01324 613316.

Agnew of Lochnaw, Sir Crispin Hamlyn. 11th Baronet (created 1629); Chief of the Agnews; Advocate 1982; Queen's Counsel (1995); Unicorn Pursuivant of Arms, 1981-86, Rothesay Herald of Arms, since 1986; Trustee, John Muir Trust; Chairman, Crofting Law Group; b. 13.5.44, Edinburgh; m., Susan Rachel Strang Steel; 1 s.; 3 d. Educ. Uppingham School; Royal Military Academy, Sandhurst. Commissioned Royal Highland Fusiliers, 1964, as 2nd Lieutenant; Major, 1977; Retired, 1981. Member: Royal Navy Expedition to East Greenland, 1966; Joint Services Expedition to Elephant Island, Antarctica, 1970-71; Army Nuptse Himal Expedition, 1975; Army Everest Expedition, 1976; Leader: Army East Greenland Expedition, 1968; Joint Services Expedition to Chilean Patagonia, 1972-73; Army Api Himal Expedition, 1980. Publications: Licensing (Scotland) Act 1976 (4th edition)

(Co-author); Agricultural Law in Scotland, 1996; Connell on the Agricultural Holdings (Scotland) Acts (Co-author) 1996; articles in various newspapers and journals. Recreations: mountaineering; offshore sailing. Address: 6 Palmerston Road, Edinburgh EH9 1TN; T.-0131-668 3792.

Agnew, Ian, MA (Hons) (Cantab). Rector, Perth High School, 1975-92; b. 10.5.32, Newcastle-upon-Tyne; m., Gladys Agnes Heatherill; 1 d. Educ. King's College School, London; Pembroke College, Cambridge. Assistant Teacher of Modern Languages, Melville College, Edinburgh, 1958-63; Assistant Teacher of Modern Languages, then Principal Teacher of Russian, George Heriot's School, Edinburgh, 1964-70; Housemaster, Craigmount Secondary School, Edinburgh, 1970-73; Deputy, Liberton High School, Edinburgh, 1973-75. Non-Executive Director, Perth and Kinross Healthcare NHS Trust; Minute Secretary, Headteachers Association of Scotland, 1979-81; Committee Member, SCCORE; President: Perthshire Musical Festival, 1978-88, Perth Chamber Music Society, 1982-89; Past President, Rotary Club of Perth St. John's; Past Chairman: Barnton and Cramond Conservative Association and West Edinburgh Conservative and Unionist Association; Serving Officer (OStJ), Priory of Scotland of the Most Venerable Order of St. John; Member, Society of High Constables, City of Perth; Governor: Balnacraig School, Perth, since 1981, Kilgraston School, Convent of the Sacred Heart, Bridge of Earn, since 1990; Chairman: Friends of Pskov, Friends of St. John's Kirk, Perth; Secretary, Friends of Perth Festival of the Arts; Member, Advisory Group, Perth College Development Trust. Recreations: music (opera); reading; tennis; gardening. Address: (h.) Northwood, Heughfield Road, Bridge of Earn, Perthshire PH2 9BH; T.-01738 81 2273.

Ailsa, 8th Marquess of (Archibald Angus Charles Kennedy); b. 13.9.56; 2 d. Address: Cassillis House, Maybole KA19 7JN.

Airlie, 13th Earl of (David George Coke Patrick Ogilvy), KT, GCVO, PC, KStJ, JP. Lord Chamberlain of Her Majesty's Household; Ensign, Queen's Body-Guard for Scotland (Royal Company of Archers), since 1975; Chairman, General Accident Fire & Life Assurance Corporation plc, since 1987 (Deputy Chairman, 1975-87); Chancellor, University of Abertay, Dundee, since 1994; Director, Baring Stratton Investment Trust plc, since 1986; Lord Lieutenant, Angus; Chancellor of the Royal Victorian Order; President, National Trust for Scotland, since 1997; Hon. President, Scottish Council, The Scout Association; b. 17.5.26, London; m., Virginia Fortune Ryan; 3 s.; 3 d. Educ. Eton College. Lieutenant, Scots Guards, 1944; serving 2nd Bn., Germany, 1945; Captain, ADC to High Commissioner and C-in-C Austria, 1947-48; Malaya, 1948-49; resigned commission, 1950; Chairman, Ashdown Investment Trust Ltd., 1968-82; Director, J. Henry Schroder Wagg & Co. Ltd., 1961-84 (Chairman, 1973-77); Chairman, Schroders plc, 1977-84; Scottish and Newcastle Breweries plc, until 1983; Director, Royal Bank of Scotland Group, 1983-93; Director, Royal Bank of Scotland plc, 1991-93; Trustee, Royal Collection Trust, 1993; Captain, Queen's Body Guard for Scotland (Royal Company of Archers), 1996. Address: (h.) Cortachy Castle, Kirriemuir, Angus.

Airlie, Countess of (Virginia Fortune Ryan), DCVO. Lady in Waiting to HM The Queen, since 1973; Chairman, National Galleries of Scotland, since 1997 (Trustee since 1995); President, Angus Red Cross, since 1988; b. 9.2.33, London; 3 s.; 3 d. Educ. Brearley School, New York City. Commissioner, Royal Fine Arts Commission; Trustee, Tate Gallery, 1983-95; Trustee, National Gallery, London, 1989-95; Member, Industrial Design Panel, British Rail, 1974-91; Trustee, American Museum in Britain, since 1985; Founder/Governor, Cobham School. Address: (h.) Cortachy Castle, Kirriemuir, Angus; T.-01575 540231.

Aitchison, James Douglas, MA (Hons), MEd (Hons). Head Teacher, Boclair Academy, Bearsden, since 1991 (Head Teacher, Gleniffer High School, Paisley, 1984-91); b. 2.7.47, Glasgow. Educ. High School of Glasgow; Glasgow University; University of Marburg. Teacher, Lycee Faidherbe, Lille; Principal Teacher, Bearsden Academy; Assistant Head Teacher, Gryffe High School, Houston. Recreations: curling; walking; travel. Address: (h.) 44 Keystone Road, Milngavie, Glasgow G62 6QG; T.-0141-956 6693.

Aitchison, Thomas Nisbet, MA, MSc. Chief Executive, City of Edinburgh Council, since 1995; b. 24.2.51, Edinburgh; m., Kathleen Sadler; 1 s.; 2 d. Educ. Glasgow University; Heriot-Watt University. Lothian Regional Council: Policy Planning, 1975-78, PA to Chief Executive, 1978-81, seconded to Chief Executive's Co-ordination Team, 1981-82, Department of Manpower Services, 1982-85, Department of Management and Information Services, 1985-87, Corporate Planning Manager and Depute Director, 1987-91, Depute Chief Executive, 1991-94, Chief Executive, 1994-95. Honorary Secretary, Council, Edinburgh International Festival; Member, Court, Napier University. Recreations: hill-walking; football; music. Address: (b.) City Headquarters, George IV Bridge, Edinburgh EH1 1UQ; T.-0131-200 2000.

Aitken, Professor Adam Jack, MA, DLitt. Editor, A Dictionary of the Older Scottish Tongue, 1956-86; Editorial Consultant and Pronunciation Editor, Concise Scots Dictionary, 1975-85; b. 19.6.21, Edinburgh; m., Norma Ward Manson; 3 s.; 1 d. Educ. Lasswade Secondary School; Edinburgh University. Assistant Lecturer in English Language, Edinburgh University, 1947-48; Research Fellow, Universities of Glasgow, Aberdeen and Edinburgh, 1948-54; Lecturer, Universities of Glasgow and Edinburgh, 1954-64; Edinburgh University: Honorary Senior Lecturer, 1965-71, Senior Lecturer (part-time) in English Language, 1971-75, Reader (part-time) in English Language, 1975-79; Chairman, Language Committee, Association for Scottish Literary Studies, 1971-76; Chairman, Universities' Forum for Research on the Languages of Scotland, 1978-81; Vice-President, Scottish Text Society, since 1985; Hon. President, Forum for Research on the Languages of Scotland and Ulster, 1991-97; Hon. Preses, Scots Language Society, since 1994; Honorary Vice-President: Scottish National Dictionary Association, since 1995, Robert Henryson Society, since 1996; Biennial Sir Israel Gollancz Prize of British Academy, 1981; Honorary Professor, Edinburgh University, since 1984. Publications: Edinburgh Studies in English and Scots, 1971; The Computer and Literary Studies, 1973; Lowland Scots, 1973; Bards and Makars, 1977; Languages of Scotland, 1979. Address: (h.) 5 Bellevue Crescent, Edinburgh EH3 6ND; T.-0131-558 1534.

Aitken, Rev. Ewan, BA (Hons), BD (Hons). Parish Minister, St. Margaret's Church of Scotland, Edinburgh, since 1993; b. 27.4.62, Paisley; m., Hilary Brown. Educ. Woodmill High School, Dunfermline; University of Sussex; University of Edinburgh. Youth Worker, Ruchill Parish Church, 1980-81; Vice President (sabbatical), University of Sussex Union, 1982-83; Regional Secretary, Student Christian Movement, 1985-87; Pastor, West Avenue Presbyterian Church, Buffalo, NY, 1990-91; Assistant Minister, South Leith Parish Church, Edinburgh, 1991-93; Staff Member, St. Andrews Church of Scotland, Tiberias, Israel, 1993-94; Locum Minister, St. Andrews, Gisborne, New Zealand, 1994-95. Branch Secretary, Links/Restalrig Labour Party; Convener, Iona Community Finance and Staffing Committee. Recreations: following Dunfermline Athletic F.C.; vegetarian cookery; laughter; collecting earrings. Address: (b.) 176 Restalrig Road South, Edinburgh EH7 6TD; T.-0131-554 7400.

Aitken, Joan Nicol, JP, MA (Hons), SSC. Solicitor, since 1978, formerly a Partner, Messrs Rollo Davidson and McFarlane, Cupar; Editor, Journal of the Law Society of Scotland; b. 26.2.53, Glasgow; m., Alistair Bruce Dodds; 1 d. Educ. James Gillespie's High School for Girls; Dundee University. Former Member: Scottish Consumer Council and Council, Law Society of Scotland; part-time Chairman, Industrial Tribunals (Scotland), Disability Appeal Tribunal, and Child Support Appeal Tribunal; family law mediator and Convener, CALM; Member, General Dental Council; was first woman member, Society of Solicitors in the Supreme Courts of Scotland. Address: (h.) Shepherd's Lodge, Kiltarlity, Beauly IV4 7HR; T.-01463 741369.

Aitken, Professor Robert Cairns Brown, MB, ChB, DPM, MD, DSc (Hon), FRCPEdin, FRCPsych. Chairman, Royal Infirmary of Edinburgh NHS Trust, since 1994; Professor Emeritus of Rehabilitation Studies, Edinburgh University, 1974-94 (Dean, Faculty of Medicine, 1990-91, Vice-Principal, 1991-94); Honorary Consultant in Rehabilitation Medicine, Lothian Health Board, 1974-94; b. 20.12.33, Dunoon; m., Audrey May Lunn; 1 s.; 1 d. Educ. Dunoon Grammar School; Cargilfield School, Edinburgh; Sedbergh School, Yorkshire; Glasgow University. Institute of Aviation Medicine, RAF, 1959-62; Orpington and Maudsley Hospitals, 1962-66; Senior Lecturer/Consultant Psychiatrist, Royal Infirmary and Royal Edinburgh Hospital, 1967-74. President, International College of Psychosomatic Medicine, 1985-87; Chairman, Napier Polytechnic of Edinburgh Governors, 1983-90; Member, Council for Professions Supplementary to Medicine, 1983-90; Member, General Medical Council, 1991-96; Director, Lothian Health Board, 1991-93; Editor, Journal of Psychosomatic Research, 1979-85; occasional WHO consultant; Foundation Secretary, then President, Society for Research in Rehabilitation, 1981-83; Member, Human Genetics Advisory Commission, since 1996. Publications: papers on measurement of mood; flying phobia; management of disability. Recreations: people, places and pleasures of Edinburgh, Scotland and beyond. Address: (h.) 11 Succoth Place, Edinburgh EH12 6BJ; T.-0131-337 1550.

Aitken, William Duff, MM (FG). Director, William Aitken Highland Exports Ltd., since 1973; Member, Board of Directors, Eden Court Theatre, 1984-88; Member, Inverness District Council, 1984-88; b. 12.3.27, Newton Mearns; m., Eva Alexandra Kjellsson; 2 d. Educ. Terra Nova, Birkdale; Merchant Taylors'; Liverpool Nautical College. Seafaring, 1943-53; tanning industry, 1953-72. Member, SSAT. Recreations: philately; swimming; RNXS; TNAUK. Address: (h) The Thistles, 24 MacLeod Road, Balloch, by Inverness IV1 2JW; T.-01463 791234.

Aitken, William Mackie, JP, DL, ACII. Councillor, City of Glasgow, since 1976; Magistrate, since 1985; Deputy Lord Lieutenant; b. 15.4.47, Glasgow. Educ. Allan Glen's School, Glasgow. Chairman, Scottish Young Conservatives, 1975-77; Convenor, City Licensing Committee and Vice-Convenor, Personnel Committee, 1977-79; Leader of the Opposition, City Council, 1980-84 and 1992-96; Bailie of the City, 1980-84, 1988-92, since 1996. Recreations: football; reading; foreign travel. Address: (h.) 35 Overnewton Square, Glasgow G3 8RW; T.-0141-357 1284.

Aitken, William Russell, MA, PhD, FLA. Bibliographer; b. 7.2.13, Calderbank, Lanarkshire; m., Betsy Mary Murison; 1 d. Educ. Dunfermline High School; Edinburgh University. Assistant Librarian, Scottish Central Library, 1936-40; war service, RAF, 1941-46; County Librarian: Clackmannanshire, 1946-49, Perth and Kinross, 1949-58, Ayr, 1958-62; Lecturer, then Senior Lecturer, latterly Reader, Department of Librarianship, University of Strathclyde, 1962-78. President, Scottish Library Association, 1965; Friends Historical Society, 1989. Editor,

Library Review, 1964-76. Books: A History of the Public Library Movement in Scotland, 1971; William Soutar's Poems in Scots and English (Editor), 1961, 1975; The Complete Poems of Hugh MacDiarmid (Editor, with Michael Grieve), 1978, 1985, 1993; Scottish Literature in English and Scots (a bibliographical guide), 1982; Poems of William Soutar: a new selection (Editor), 1988. Address: (h.) 6 Tannahill Terrace, Dunblane FK15 0AX; T.-Dunblane 823650.

Aitkenhead, John M., MA (Hons), MEd, JP. Principal and Founder, Kilquhanity House International School for Boys and Girls, since 1940; b. 21.5.10, Glasgow; m., Morag MacKinnon; 2 s.; 2 d. Educ. Ardrossan Academy; Glasgow University. Worked in Scottish education system until 1940; conscientious objector during World War II; established school inspired by work and writing of A.S. Neill; ardent Scottish nationalist. Recreations: singing; poetry; Scottish country dancing; Gaelic; gardening. Address: Kilquhanity, Castle Douglas DG7 3DB; T.-01556 650 597.

Aitkin, John, TD, CA. Partner, John J. Welch & Co., Chartered Accountants, since 1961; National Chairman, Royal British Legion Scotland, since 1995; b. 10.9.33, Denholm; m., Elizabeth Charlotte Fraser; 1 s.; 1 d. Educ. Hawick High School. Qualified as a CA, 1956; National Service (commissioned 2nd Lt.), 1956-58; joined John J. Welch & Co., CA, Hawick, 1958; served in TA, 1958-73; Committee of Management, Royal British Legion Housing Association Ltd., 1978-91 (Chairman, 1986-91); Hon. Treasurer, Royal British Legion Scotland, 1985-90; Member, Executive Committee, Earl Haig Fund Scotland, since 1992; Regimental Trustee, King's Own Scottish Borderers, since 1980. Recreations: gardening; reading; walking. Address: (h) Appletreehall House, Hawick TD9 8PW; T.-01450 372424.

Alexander, Professor Alan, MA. Professor of Local and Public Management (Head, Department of Human Resource Management, Strathclyde University, 1993-96, Professor of Local Government, 1987-93); Director, Scottish Local Authorities Management Centre, 1987-93; b. 13.12.43, Glasgow; m., Morag MacInnes (Morag Alexander, qv); 1 s.; 1 d. Educ. Possil Secondary School, Glasgow; Albert Secondary School, Glasgow; Glasgow University. Lecturer/Assistant Professor, Political Science, Lakehead University, Ontario, 1966-71; Lecturer in Politics, Reading University, 1971-87. Member of Board, Housing Corporation, 1977-80; Member, Standing Research Committee on Local and Central Government Relations, Joseph Rowntree Memorial Trust, 1988-92; conducted inquiry into relations between Western Isles Islands Council and BCCI, 1991; Trustee, Quarriers, since 1995. Publications: Local Government in Britain since Reorganisation, 1982; The Politics of Local Government in the UK, 1982; L'amministrazione locale in Gran Bretagna, 1984; Borough Government and Politics: Reading, 1835-1985, 1985; Managing the Fragmented Authority, 1994. Recreations: theatre; cinema; hill-walking; avoiding gardening. Address: (b.) Scottish Local Authorities Management Centre, The Graham Hills Building, 50 Richmond Street, Glasgow G1 1XT; T.-0141-553 4167.

Alexander, Professor David Alan, MA (Hons), CPsychol, FBPS, PhD. Professor of Mental Health, University of Aberdeen, since 1994; Hon. Consultant, Police and Fire Services, since 1989; b. 28.8.43, Ellon. Educ. George Watson's College, Edinburgh; Morgan Academy, Dundee; University of St. Andrews; University of Dundee. MRC Research Scholar; Lecturer then Senior Lecturer in Mental Health; Visiting Lecturer, FBI Academy, Virginia, USA; Visiting Professor to universities in USA, Russia, Croatia, Spain and West Indies. Publications: co-author of three books; numerous professional articles. Recreations: badminton; squash; hill-walking. Address: (b.) Medical School, Foresterhill, Aberdeen AB25 2ZD; T.-01224 681818.

Alexander, Major-General David Crichton, CB. Commandant, Scottish Police College, 1979-87; b. 28.11.26, Aberdour; m., 1, Diana Joyce (Jane) Fisher (deceased); 2, Elizabeth Patricia Fleming; 1 s.; 1 step-s.; 2 d. Educ. Edinburgh Academy; Staff College, Camberley; Royal College of Defence Studies. Royal Marines, 1944-77 (2nd Lieutenant to Major-General, including Equerry and Acting Treasurer to Duke of Edinburgh); Director-General, English Speaking Union, 1977-79. President, Corps of Commissionaires, 1994-97; Member, Civil Service Final Selection Board, 1978-88; Chairman, Edinburgh Academy, 1985-90; Freeman, City of London; Liveryman, Painter Stainers' Company; Member, Transport Users Consultative Committee for Scotland, 1989-93; President, SSAFA Fife, 1990-94. Recreations: fishing; golf; gardening. Address: (h.) Baldinnie, Park Place, Elie KY9 1DH; T.-01333 330882.

Alexander, Rev. Douglas Niven, MA, BD. Minister, Erskine Parish Church, Bishopton, since 1970; b. 8.4.35, Eaglesham; m., Dr. Joyce O. Garven; 1 s.; 2 d. Educ. Hutchesons' Boys' Grammar School, Glasgow; Glasgow University (President, SRC, 1958); Union Theological Seminary, New York. Assistant Minister, St. Ninian's Church, Greenock, 1961-62; Warden, Iona Community House, Glasgow, 1963-70. Secretary, Scottish Union of Students, 1958; Assessor to Lord Rector, Glasgow University, 1969-71; Chaplain to Erskine Hospital, since 1970; Moderator, Paisley Presbytery, 1984; Mair Memorial Lecturer, Glasgow University, 1987; Chairman, British Churches Committee for Channel 4 TV, 1986-88; Convener, Church of Scotland Board of Communication, 1987-91; Member: Scottish Committee, IBA, 1988-90; National Religious Advisory Committee, IBA, 1988-90; Central Religious Advisory Committee, 1988-92; National Religious Advisory Committee, ITC, 1991-92; Scottish Viewers Consultative Committee, ITC, 1991-92; Member, Church of Scotland Board of Social Responsibility, since 1997. Recreation: researching ways of salmon poachers! Address: The Manse, Newton Road, Bishopton, Renfrewshire PA7 5JP; T.-01505 862161.

Alexander, Rev. Eric J., MA, BD. Minister, St. George's-Tron Parish Church, Glasgow, since 1977; b. 9.5.32, Glasgow; m., Margaret D. Connell; 1 s.; 1 d. Educ. Allan Glen's School, Glasgow; Glasgow University. Publications: The Search for God, 1962; Plainly Teaching the Word, 1989. Address: (h.) 12 Dargarvel Avenue, Glasgow G41.

Alexander, Rev. Ian W., BA, BD, STM. Europe, Middle East, North Africa Secretary, Board of World Mission, Church of Scotland, since 1995; b. 28.11.64, Dumfries. Educ. Douglas Ewart High School; Glasgow College; University of Edinburgh; Union Theological Seminary, New York City. Assistant Minister, Palmerston Place Church of Scotland, Edinburgh, 1989-91; Communication and Education Officer (Presbyterian), United Nations Office, New York City, 1992-95. Member, Shared Interest Council; Member, United Nations Association (Edinburgh Committee). Recreations: travel; reading; dancing. Address: (h.) 7 South Oswald Road, Edinburgh EH9 2HQ; T.-0131-667 9054.

Alexander, Professor James, BSc, PhD. Professor, Department of Immunology, Strathclyde University, since 1994; b. 14.11.49, Glasgow; m., Margaret Jean Wendon; 1 s. Educ. St. Mungo's Academy, Glasgow University. Scientific Staff, Division of Leprosy and Mycobacterial Research, National Institute for Medical Research, London, 1975-79; Research Fellow, Department of Biology,

Imperial College of Science and Technology, London, 1979-85; Strathclyde University: Wellcome Trust Lecturer, Immunology, 1985, Senior Lecturer, 1989, Reader, 1990. Recreations: gardening; reading. Address: (b.) Todd Centre, Taylor Street, Strathclyde University, Glasgow G4 0NR; T.-0141-552 4400.

Alexander, John Huston, BLitt, MA, DPhil Oxon. Reader in English, Aberdeen University, since 1996; b. 5.4.41, Coleraine, Northern Ireland; m., Flora Ross; 2 s.; 2 d. Educ. Campbell College, Belfast; St. Edmund Hall, Oxford. Sessional Lecturer in English, University of Saskatchewan, Canada, 1966-67; Lecturer then Senior Lecturer in English, Aberdeen University, 1968-96. Editor, The Scott Newsletter, since 1982; Session Clerk, St. Machar's Cathedral, Aberdeen, since 1975. Publications: Two Studies in Romantic Reviewing, 1976; The Lay of the Last Minstrel: Three Essays, 1978; The Reception of Scott's Poetry By His Correspondents: 1796-1817, 1979; Marmion: Studies in Interpretation and Composition, 1981; Scott and his Influence (Editor, with David Hewitt), 1983; Reading Wordsworth, 1987; The Tavern Sages (Editor), 1992; Walter Scott, Kenilworth: A Romance (Editor), 1993; Scott in Carnival (Editor, with David Hewitt), 1993; Walter Scott, The Bride of Lammermoor (Editor), 1995; Walter Scott, A Legend of the Wars of Montrose (Editor), 1995; Walter Scott, The History of France (Second Series) (Co-Editor), 1996; General Editor, Edinburgh Edition of the Waverley Novels. Recreations: music; walking. Address: (h.) 45A Queen's Road, Aberdeen AB15 4ZN; T.-01224 317424.

Alexander, Keith, BSc (Hons), BArch, RIBA, ARIAS, MBIM. Director, Centre for Facilities Management, Strathclyde University, since 1990; b. 20.9.49, Nottingham; m., Marie-Yvonne; 2 s.; 1 d. Educ. Wellingborough Grammar School; Welsh School of Architecture; University of Wales Institute of Science and Technology. Architect, new town development authorities, 1971-75; Principal, private practice, Northern Ireland and Scotland, 1975-78; Senior Lecturer, Ulster College, Northern Ireland Polytechnic, 1975-78; Consultant, Building Performance Design and Appraisal, 1978-90; Strathclyde University: Lecturer, Department of Architecture and Building Science, 1978-90, Director, Building Performance and Research Unit, 1984-90; Visiting Lecturer, School of Architecture, National University of Singapore, 1982-84; Architect, private practice, Singapore, 1982-84. President, European Facilities Management Network; Editor, International Journal of Facilities Management. Recreations: rugby; golf. Address: (b.) Centre for Facilities Management, Strathclyde Graduate Business School, 199 Cathedral Street, Glasgow G4 0QU. T.-0141-553 4165.

Alexander, Sir Kenneth John Wilson, BSc (Econ), LLD, DUniv, FRSE, CBIM, Hon. Fellow, RIAS; b. 14.3.22, Edinburgh; m., Angela-May; 1 s.; 4 d. Educ. George Heriot's School, Edinburgh; School of Economics, Dundee. Taught at Universities of Leeds, Sheffield and Aberdeen; Professor of Economics, Strathclyde University, 1963-80; Principal and Vice-Chancellor, Stirling University, 1981-86; Chancellor, Aberdeen University, 1986-87. Member, Advisory Committee on University of the Air, 1965; Chairman: Committee on Adult Education in Scotland, 1970-73, Social Science Research Council, 1975-76; President, Section F, British Association, 1974; Chairman, Govan Shipbuilders, 1974-76; Chairman, Highlands and Islands Development Board, 1976-80; Economic Consultant to the Secretary of State for Scotland, 1968-89; Member, Scottish Development Agency, 1975-85; Chairman, Council for Applied Science in Scotland, 1980-85; Governor, Technical Change Centre, 1981-87; Director, Scottish Television Ltd., 1981-92; Member, Council for Tertiary Education in Scotland, 1981-82; Deputy Chairman, Scottish Council (Development and Industry), 1982-91; Honorary President: The Highland Fund, since 1983; Scottish National Dictionary Association Ltd., since 1983;

President, Town and Country Planning (Scottish Section), since 1982; Director, Stakis plc, 1987-93; Chairman, Edinburgh Book Festival, 1987-91; Chairman, Scottish Industrial Trade Exhibitions, since 1990; Trustee, Aegean Archipelago, since 1994. Publications: The Economist in Business, 1967; Fairfields, a study of industrial change (with C.L. Jenkins), 1971; The Political Economy of Change (Editor), 1976. Recreation: Scottish antiquarianism. Address: (h.) 9 West Shore, Pittenweem, Fife KY10 2NV; T.-01333 310593.

Alexander, Professor Michael Joseph, BA, MA (Oxon). Berry Professor of English Literature, St. Andrews University, since 1985; b. 21.5.41, Wigan; m., 1, Eileen Mary McCall (deceased); 2, Mary Cecilia Sheahan; 1 s.; 2 d. Educ. Downside School; Trinity College, Oxford; Perugia University; Princeton University. Editor, William Collins, London, 1963-65; Lecturer, University of California, 1966-67; Editor, Andre Deutsch, London, 1967-68; Lecturer: East Anglia University, 1968-69, Stirling University, 1969; Senior Lecturer, 1977; Reader, 1985. Publications: Earliest English Poems (Translator), 1966; Beowulf (Translator), 1973; Twelve Poems, 1978; The Poetic Achievement of Ezra Pound, 1979; History of Old English Literature, 1983; Macmillan Anthology of English Literature, 1989; Beowulf (Editor), 1995; Sons of Ezra (Editor), 1995; Beowulf and Grendel (Translator), 1995; The Canterbury Tales – The First Fragment (Editor), 1996; The Canterbury Tales : Illustrated Prologue (Editor), 1996. Address: (b.) School of English, St. Andrews University, St. Andrews KY16 9AL; T.-01334 462666.

Alexander, Morag, BA (Hons). Director, Equal Opportunities Commission, Scotland, since 1992; b. 10.10.43, Kilwinning; m., Professor Alan Alexander (qv); 1 s.; 1 d. Educ. Lourdes Secondary School, Glasgow; Glasgow University; Lakehead University, Ontario. Research Assistant, ASTMS, 1971-73; Editor and Researcher, RIPA, 1973-82; freelance journalist and consultant, 1982-90; Founding Editor, Women in Europe, 1985-89, and UK Correspondent, Women of Europe, 1987-92; Founding Director, Training 2000 (Scotland) Ltd., Scottish Alliance for Women's Training, 1990-92; Member, Board, Children in Scotland, Chair, Early Years Forum, since 1995; Member, Scottish Committee, Turning Point, since 1996; Member, Board, Partnership for a Parliament, 1997. Recreations: music; opera; visiting art galleries and museums; hill-walking. Address: (b.) E.O.C., Stock Exchange House, 7 Nelson Mandela Place, Glasgow G2 1QW; T.-0141 248 5834.

Alexander, Samuel, BL. Honorary Sheriff, Dumbarton, since 1983; b. Glasgow; m., Isabella Kerr Ligertwood; 2 s. Educ. Govan High School; Glasgow University. Formerly Consultant and Senior Partner, Keyden Strang & Co., Solicitors, Glasgow. Recreations: golf; reading. Address: (h.) 1 Hillneuk Avenue, Bearsden, Glasgow G61; T.-0141-942 4674.

Alexander, Walter Ronald, CBE. Chairman, Walter Alexander plc, 1979-90 (Managing Director, 1973-79); Company Director; b. 6.4.31; m., 1, Rosemary Anne Sleigh (m. diss.); 2 s.; 2 d.; 2, Mrs Lorna Elwes. Educ. Loretto School; Cambridge University (MA Hons). Chairman and Managing Director, Tayforth Ltd., 1961-71; Chairman, Scottish Automobile Company Ltd., 1971-73; Director: Scotcros plc, 1965-82 (Chairman, 1972-82); Investors Capital Trust plc, since 1967; Clydesdale Bank plc, 1970-96; RIT and Northern plc, 1973-84; Dawson International plc, 1979-96; Chairman, Scottish Appeals Committee, Police Dependants' Trust, 1974-81; President, Public Schools Golfing Society, 1973-79; Chairman: PGA, 1982-85; Royal and Ancient Golf Club of St. Andrews Trust, since 1987; Governor, Loretto School, 1961-89; Comr.,

Queen Victoria School, 1987-92; Scottish Free Enterprise Award, 1977. Recreation: golf. Address: Moonzie Mill, Balmullo, St. Andrews KY16 0AH; T.-01334 870990.

Alexander, Wendy, MA (Hons), MA (Econ), MBA. Special Adviser to Secretary of State for Scotland, since 1997; b. 27.6.63, Glasgow. Educ. Park Mains School, Erskine; Glasgow University; Warwick University; INSEAD, France. Research Officer, Scottish Labour Party, 1988-92; Senior Associate, Booz Allen & Hamilton Int., 1994-97. Address: (b.) Scottish Office, St. Andrew's House, Regent Road, Edinburgh EH1 3DG; T.-0131-244 2437.

Ali, Nasir, MB, BS, DPM, FRCPsych. Consultant Psychiatrist, since 1973; Honorary Senior Lecturer, Aberdeen University, since 1982; b. 21.8.39, Lucknow, India; m., D. Rosemary; 1 s.; 1 d. Address: (h.) Balmachree House, Dalcross, Inverness IV1 2JQ; T.-Inverness 790602.

Allan, Bob. Chief Executive, Clackmannanshire Council. Address: (b.): Greenfield, Alloa FK10 2AD.

Allan, Charles Maitland, MA. Journalist, Economist and Farmer; b. 19.8.39, Stirling; m., Fiona Vine; 2 s.; 2 d. Educ. Dartington Hall; Aberdeen University. Lecturer in Economic History, Glasgow University, 1962-63; Lecturer in Economics, St. Andrews University, 1963-65; Lecturer and Senior Lecturer, Strathclyde University, 1965-74; Editorial Adviser, Leopard Magazine. Publications: Theory of Taxation; Death of a Papermill; Farmer's Diary I, II, III, IV; Neeps and Strae. Recreation: work. Address: (h.) Little Ardo, Methlick, Ellon, Aberdeenshire; T.-01651 806 218.

Allan, D. Stuart, LLB, NP. Solicitor and Notary Public; Head, Law and Administration, Fife Council; b. 11.11.49, Dundee. Educ. Morgan Academy; Dundee University. Chairman, Society of Directors of Administration in Scotland, 1991-92. Address: (b.) Fife House, Glenrothes KY7 5LT; T.-01592 414141.

Allan, Eric, MA (Hons). Head Teacher, St. Michael's Academy, Kilwinning, since 1994; b. 6.9.55, Inverness; m., Elaine; 2 d. Educ. Dingwall Academy; Glasgow University; Jordanhill College. Teacher: St. Andrew's Academy, Saltcoats, St. Brendan's High School, Linwood (Principal Teacher, Geography); Assistant Head Teacher, St. Brendan's, 1987-92; Depute Head Teacher, Trinity High School, Renfrew, 1992-94. Recreations: golf; supporting Kilmarnock FC; reading; music. Address: (h.) 3 Holmes Crescent, Kilmarnock; T.-01563 524199.

Allan, George Alexander, MA (Hons). Headmaster, Robert Gordon's College, Aberdeen, 1978-96; b. 3.2.36, Edinburgh; m., Anne Violet Veevers; 2 s. Educ. Daniel Stewart's College, Edinburgh; Edinburgh University. Teacher of Classics, Glasgow Academy, 1958-60; Daniel Stewart's College: Teacher of Classics, 1960-63, Head of Classics, 1963-73 (appointed Housemaster, 1967); Schoolmaster Fellow Commoner, Corpus Christi College, Cambridge, 1972; Deputy Headmaster, Robert Gordon's College, 1973-77. Former Chairman and former Secretary, Headmasters' Conference (Scottish Division) (Member, National Committee, 1982 and 1983); Governor, Welbeck College, 1980-89; Council Member, Scottish Council of Independent Schools, 1988-96 and since 1997; Director, Edinburgh Academy, since 1997. Recreations: gardening; golf; music. Address: 5 Abbey View, Kelso, Roxburghshire TD5 8HX.

Allan, James Morrison, FRICS, ACIArb, MIPS. Chartered Surveyor; b. 1.10.43, Edinburgh; m., Elizabeth Howie Sneddon Jack; 2 s. Educ. George Watson's College; Heriot Watt College. Joined Phillips Knox & Arthur as Apprentice Quantity Surveyor, 1960; qualified ARICS 1965; FRICS, 1975; RICS: Chairman, National Junior Organisation, 1975-

76; Chairman, Quantity Surveyors Committee in Scotland, 1988-89; Chairman, RICS in Scotland, 1991-92; Member, RICS General Council; Member, RICS Management Board, 1992-95; Chairman, RICS Business Services Ltd. Recreations: family; caravanning and motoring; golf. Address: (h.) 4 Stevenson Way, Longniddry, East Lothian EH32 0PF; T.-01875 852377.

Allan, Sheriff John Douglas, BL, DMS, FBIM. Sheriff of Lanark, since 1988; b. 2.10.41, Edinburgh; m., Helen E.J. Aiton; 1 s.; 1 d. Educ. George Watson's College, Edinburgh; Edinburgh University. Solicitor in private practice, Edinburgh, 1963-67; Procurator Fiscal Depute, Edinburgh, 1967-71; Solicitor, Crown Office, Edinburgh, 1971-76; Assistant Procurator Fiscal, then Senior Assistant Procurator Fiscal, Glasgow, 1976-79; Solicitor, Crown Office, Edinburgh, 1979-83; Procurator Fiscal for Edinburgh and Regional Procurator Fiscal for Lothians and Borders, 1983-88. Part-time Lecturer in Law, Napier College, Edinburgh, 1963-66; Holder, Scout "Medal of Merit". Recreations: Scouts; youth leadership; walking; Church. Address: (b.) Sheriff Court House, Lanark ML11 7NE; T.-01555 661531.

Allan, Richard James Paul, BSc, PhD, FSA (Scot). Chairman, Executive Committee, Royal Zoological Society of Scotland, since 1995; Hon. Vice President: Shetland Sheep Breeders Group, since 1992, Eriskay Pony Society, since 1997; b. 26.5.30, Glasgow; m., Norma Adam Dick; 3 s. Educ. High School of Glasgow; University of Glasgow; Royal Technical College, Glasgow. Technical service with ICI Fibres Division in man-made fibres and development of commercial computing; left industry to develop countryside and wildlife interests and farming; fronted development of rare breeds in Scotland, assisted by Royal Zoological Society of Scotland. Founder Chairman, Border Country Life Association; Member, Scottish Borders Council Heritage Steering Group (preparing series of booklets on Borders history and archaeology). Publications: The Scottish Borderland (Co-Editor, Contributor), 1988; Wool Quality (Co-Author), 1992; many articles on rare breeds. Recreations: photography; gardening; walking; reading; classical music. Address: (h.) Buskinburn House, Coldingham, Eyemouth, Berwickshire TD14 5UA; T.-018907 71215.

Allan, Robert, MBE. Chief Executive, Scottish Fishermen's Federation, since 1982; b. 14.11.33, Peterhead; m., Moira W. Morrison; 2 d. Educ. Aberdeen Grammar School. Audit Assistant, R.C. Kelman & Shirreffs, CA, Aberdeen, 1949-62; Assistant Secretary, latterly Secretary, Aberdeen Fishing Vessel Owners' Association Ltd. and Scottish Trawlers' Federation, 1962-71; Chief Executive, Aberdeen Fishing Vessel Owners' Association Ltd. and Aberdeen Fish Producers' Organisation Ltd., 1971-82. Address: (b.) 14 Regent Quay, Aberdeen AB11 5AE; T.-01224 582583.

Allan, W. Douglas, MA (Oxon). Chairman, Crossroads (Scotland), Caring for Carers, since 1997; Director, J. & P. Coats Ltd., 1984-93; b. 1.11.39, Tongshan, China; m., Joan Blakeborough; 3 s. Educ. Trinity College, Glenalmond; St. John's College, University of Oxford; London Business School. Graduate Trainee, Coats Patons Ltd., 1962; Managing Director, Coats Chile, then Venezuela and Brazil; Chief Executive, Coats South America. Chairman, Cargilfield School, Edinburgh, 1986-88. Recreations: hill-walking; travel; Hispanic affairs; sport. Address: (h.) Fidra, Gryffe Road, Kilmacolm PA13 4BA; T.-01505-872 772.

Allanbridge, Hon. Lord (William Ian Stewart), QC. Senator of the College of Justice in Scotland, 1977-95; b. 8.11.25. Called to the Bar, 1951; Advocate-Depute, 1959-

64; Home Advocate-Depute, 1970-72; Solicitor-General for Scotland, 1972-74; Temporary Sheriff Principal, Dumfries and Galloway, 1974.

Allen, Professor Janet Marjorie, BSc, MD, MRCP (UK). Professor of Molecular Medicine, University of Glasgow, since 1994; b. 22.3.53, Southport. Educ. Haberdashers Askes; Royal Free Hospital School of Medicine; University of London. Pre-registration House Officer: Radcliffe Infirmary, Oxford, Cambridge, 1978-79; Senior House Officer, Hammersmith, National and Guys Hospitals, 1979-80; Registrar, Hammersmith and Ealing Hospitals, 1980-82; Wellcome Trust Fellow: RPMS, London, Harvard University, Boston, 1982-89; Wellcome Trust Senior Clinical Fellow, RPMS, London, 1989-90; Lecturer, University of Cambridge, 1990-94. Address: (b.) Davidson Building, University of Glasgow, Glasgow G12 8QQ; T.-0141-330 5189.

Allen, Professor John Walter, MA, FSAS, FRSE. Professor of Solid State Physics, St. Andrews University, since 1980; b. 7.3.28, Birmingham. Educ. King Edward's High School, Birmingham; Sidney Sussex College, Cambridge. RAF, 1949-51; Staff Scientist, Ericsson Telephones Ltd., 1951-56; Services Electronics Research Laboratory, 1956-68; Visiting Associate Professor, Stanford University, 1964-66; joined Department of Physics, St. Andrews University, 1968. Recreations: archaeology; country dancing. Address: (b.) Department of Physics and Astronomy, St. Andrews University, North Haugh, St. Andrews, Fife KY16 9SS; T.-01334 463331.

Allison, Professor Arthur Compton, BSc, DipNumMath, PhD, FBCS. Vice Principal, Information Services and Professor of Computing Science, Glasgow University, since 1986; b. 24.3.41, Belfast; m., Dr. Joyce Allison; 3 d. Educ. Queen's University, Belfast; Glasgow University. Glasgow University, 1962-67; Smithsonian Institution, Boston, 1967-73; Glasgow University, 1973-83; Northeastern University, Boston, 1983-84; Glasgow University, since 1984. Elder, Church of Scotland. Recreations: running; curling. Address: (b.) Glasgow University, Glasgow G12 8QQ; T.-0141-330 4453.

Allison, Charles William, MBChB, FFARCS. Consultant Anaesthetist, Stracathro Hospital, Brechin, since 1982; Consultant, Dundee teaching hospitals; Honorary Senior Lecturer, Dundee University; b. 1.7.52, Newport on Tay; m., Elspeth Stratton; 2 d. Educ. Madras College, St. Andrews; Dundee University. Training grades in anaesthesia, Dundee, 1976-81; Clinical Research Fellow, Hospital for Sick Children, Toronto, 1982. Publications: papers and book chapter. Recreations: golf; photography. Address: Summerbank House, Brechin, Angus DD9 6HL; T.-01356 623624.

Allsop, Rev. Thomas Douglas, MA, BD. Minister, Beechgrove Church, Aberdeen, since 1977; b. 2.3.34, Kilmaurs; m., Marion Morrison Urie; 2 s.; 1 d. Educ. Kilmarnock Academy; Glasgow University and Trinity College. Assistant Minister, St. Marnock's, Kilmarnock; Minister: Kirriemuir South (after a union called Kirriemuir St. Andrew's), 1959-65; Minister, Knightswood St. Margaret's, Glasgow, 1965-77. Founder Chairman, Kirriemuir Round Table; Moderator, Dumbarton Presbytery, 1975, Aberdeen Presbytery, 1994-95; Burgess, City of Aberdeen. Recreations: photography; golf; musical appreciation. Address: 156 Hamilton Place, Aberdeen AB15 5BB; T.-01224 642615.

Almaini, Professor A.E.A., BSc(Eng), MSc, PhD, CEng, FIEE. Associate Head, Department of Electrical and Electronic Engineering, Napier University, since 1991, Professor, since 1992; b. 1.7.45, Baghdad; m., Shirley May; 2 s.; 1 d. Educ. London University; Salford University;

Loughborough University. Research Scientist, Scientific Research Foundation, 1970-78; Lecturer, then Senior Lecturer, Napier University, 1980-91. Publication: Electronic Logic Systems. Recreation: gardening. Address: (b.) E&EE Department, Craiglockhart Campus, Edinburgh EH14 1DJ; T.-0131-455 4364.

Alstead, Brigadier (Francis) Allan (Littlejohns), CBE, DL, MPhil, FCIT, FIMgt, FIPD, FInstAM, FRSA, FInstD. Chief Executive, Scottish Sports Council, since 1990; b. 19.6.35, Glasgow; m., Joy Veronica Edwards; 2 s. Educ. Glasgow Academy; Royal Military Academy, Sandhurst; Royal Naval Staff College; Joint Services Staff College; Edinburgh University; University of Wales, Aberystwyth. Commissioned into King's Own Scottish Borderers, 1955; commanded 1st Bn., KOSB, 1974-76 (Mention in Despatches); Military Assistant to Quarter-Master-General,, 1976-79; Instructor, Army Staff College, Camberley, 1979-81; Assistant Chief of Staff, BAOR, 1981-84 (Colonel); Commander, 51st Highland Brigade, 1984-87 (Brigadier); NATO Research Fellow, Edinburgh University, 1987-88; NATO Reinforcement Co-ordinator, 1988-90. Member, Royal Company of Archers (Queen's Bodyguard in Scotland); Deputy Lieutenant, City of Edinburgh; Regimental Trustee, KOSB; Trustee, Youth Sport Trust; Deputy Hon. Colonel, City of Edinburgh Universities OTC; Governor: Moray House College, 1991-97, Glasgow Academy; Member, Executive, Scottish Council, Development and Industry; Member, Lowland TAVRA; President, SSAFA, Edinburgh and Midlothian. Recreations: running; swimming; tennis. Address: (b.) South Gyle, Edinburgh EH12 9DQ; T.-0131-317 7200.

Ambler, Professor Richard Penry, MA, PhD, FSAS. Professor of Protein Chemistry, Institute of Cell & Molecular Biology, Edinburgh University; b. 26.5.33, Bexley Heath; m.; 2 d. Educ. Haileybury and ISC; Pembroke College, Cambridge. Research Fellow, Pembroke College, Cambridge, 1959-62; scientific staff, MRC Laboratory of Molecular Biology, Cambridge, 1960-65; joined Department of Molecular Biology, Edinburgh University, 1965. Member, EMBO. Address: (b.) Institute of Cell & Molecular Biology, Darwin Building, University of Edinburgh EH9 3JR; T.-0131-650 5394.

Amin, Professor Sayed-Hassan, LLB, LLM, PhD. Advocate; Mufti International Lawyer; Author; b. 25.11.48, Persia. Educ. University of Tehran; Glasgow University. Publications: 27 books on international, Middle Eastern and Islamic law. Address: (b.) Advocates' Library, Parliament House, Parliament Square, Edinburgh EH1 1RF.

Amyes, Dorothy Mary Gregory, BSc, MSc, MRTPI. Director, Scottish Farm and Countryside Educational Trust, since 1991; b. 17.3.52, Warrington; m., Sebastian Giles Becket Amyes; 1 s.; 1 d. Educ. Warrington High School; Sir John Cass College; University of Strathclyde; University of Edinburgh. Planning Assistant, Lanarkshire, Surrey and Strathclyde, 1973-78; Project Supervisor, Scottish Wildlife Trust, 1985-87; Scottish Executive/Director, Association of Agriculture/British Association of Agriculture, 1988-91. Address: (b.) Royal Highland Centre, Ingliston, Edinburgh EH28 8NF; T.-0131-333 3805.

Amyes, Professor Sebastian Giles Becket, BSc, MSc, PhD, DSc, FRCPath, FIBiol. Professor of Microbial Chemotherapy and Head of Medical Microbiology Department, Edinburgh University; Joint Director, Scottish Antibiotic Reference Laboratory; b. 6.5.49, Stockton Heath; m., Dorothy Mary Gregory; 1 s.; 1 d. Educ. Cranleigh School; University College, London. Edinburgh University, since 1977; Reader, 1988; Professor, 1992. Royal Pharmaceutical Society annual conference award, 1984; C.L. Oakley lectureship, Pathological Society, 1987.

Recreations: fishing; opera; golf; exploring parts of the world that the tour companies have not yet found. Address: (b.) Department of Medical Microbiology, Medical School, Teviot Place, Edinburgh EH8 9AG; T.-0131-650 3163.

Ancram, Earl of (Michael Andrew Foster Jude Kerr), DL. Advocate; MP (Conservative), Devizes, since 1992; Minister of State, Northern Ireland Office, 1994-97; b. 7.7.45; m., 2 d. DL, Roxburgh District.

Andersen, Finn, MA, MSc. Director, Danish Cultural Institute in Britain, since 1985; b. 20.2.44, Denmark; m., Vivien Ann; 1 s.; 1 d. Educ. University of Arhus; Heriot Watt University. Chairman, European Union Cultural Forum in Scotland. Recreations: the arts; travelling. Address: 3 Doune Terrace, Edinburgh EH3 6DY; T.-0131-225 7189.

Anderson, Alastair, CA. Director of Finance, Napier University, since 1989; b. 10.8.49, Glasgow; m., Maureen Wilson; 1 s.; 1 d. Educ. Hutchesons' Boys Grammar School. CA apprentice and audit assistant, 1967-74; Assistant Accountant, 1975; Retail Trade Accountant, 1975-89. Recreations: sailing; squash. Address: (b.) 219 Colinton Road, Edinburgh EH14 1DJ; T.-0131-455 4656.

Anderson, Alex, DipTP, MRTPI. Director of Planning, Transport and Economic Development, Angus Council, since 1995; b. 21.3.47, Dundee; m., Maureen; 2 s. Educ. Grove Academy, Dundee; Duncan of Jordanstone College. Address: (b.) Department of Planning, Transport and Economic Development, St. James House, St. James Road, Forfar DD8 2ZP; T.-01307 473405.

Anderson, Professor Annie S., BSc, PhD, SRD. Research Professor of Food Choice, University of Dundee, since 1996; b. 24.12.57, Torphins; m., Professor Mike Lean; 1 s.; 2 d. Educ. Cults Academy, Aberdeen; RGIT; University of Aberdeen. Dietician, Cambridge Area Health Authority, 1979-81; Research Assistant, Medical School, University of Cambridge, 1982-84; Research Dietician, Grampian Health Board, 1985-86; Postgraduate Research Student, Department of Obstetrics, University of Aberdeen, 1987-91; Research Fellow (Human Nutrition), University of Glasgow, 1991-96. Recreation: genealogy. Address: (b.) School of Management and Consumer Studies, University of Dundee, Dundee; T.-01382 345383.

Anderson, Arthur Andrew, ARAgS. Producer, Landward, BBC Scotland, since 1979; b. 21.11.44, Dumfries; m., Andrea Jane MacKenzie; 2 s.; 2 d. Educ. Barnard Castle School. Copy Boy, The Scotsman, 1961-64; Reporter, Scottish Farmer, 1964-65; Sub-Editor, Glasgow Herald, 1965-66; Agricultural Reporter, The Scotsman, 1967-69; Scottish Correspondent, Farmers Weekly, 1970-73; News/Farming Producer and Reporter, BBC Radio Carlisle, 1973-75; General Programme Producer, BBC Radio Scotland, 1975-77; joined BBC TV, Aberdeen, 1977; former Head of Production, BBC Aberdeen. Winner RICS TV Award, John Deere Journalism Award, Norsk Hydro TV Award, One World Broadcasting Trust Prize, Netherthorpe Award; Member, Aberdeen Children's Panel, 1982-89; Chairman, Guild of Agricultural Journalists, 1997-98; UK Delegate, International Federation of Agricultural Journalists. Recreation: lunching. Address; (h.) Denmill Cottage, Burnett Street, Auchenblae AB30 1XQ; T.-01561 320248.

Anderson, David Rae, MA (Hons), LLB, LLM, WS, NP. Solicitor, since 1961 (Senior Partner, Allan Grant Solicitors); part-time Legal Chairman, Industrial Tribunals, since 1971; Honorary Sheriff, since 1981; accredited solicitor-mediator; b. 27.1.36, Stonehaven; m., Jean Strachan. Educ. Mackie Academy, Stonehaven; Aberdeen University; Edinburgh University; Australian National

University, Canberra. Barrister and Solicitor of Supreme Court of Victoria, Australia, 1962; Legal Officer, Attorney-General's Department, Canberra, 1962-65; part-time research student, Law Faculty, Australian National University, Canberra, and part-time Lecturer in Legal History, 1962-65; returned to Scotland, 1965, in private legal practice, Edinburgh, 1965-67, Alloa and Central Scotland, since 1967; Interim Town Clerk, Burgh of Alva, 1973; former part-time Reporter to Secretary of State for Scotland for public enquiries; former Dean, Society of Solicitors of Clackmannanshire; twice Member, Council, Law Society of Scotland: former Convener, International Relations Committee, 1992 Committee, Committee on the Constitution, and Convener, Specialist Accreditation Committee; Law Society of Scotland Representative, Council, Commonwealth Lawyers Association; former Member, UK Delegation, Council of the Bars and Law Societies of the European Community; Member, Stirling University Conference; Elder, Church of Scotland; Parliamentary candidate, 1970 and 1971; formerly served, RNVR; Past President, Alloa Rotary Club. Recreations: climbing and hill-walking; reading, especially historical biography and English literature; music, especially opera; interested in current affairs, architecture, stately homes and travel. Address: (h.) 3 Smithfield Loan, Alloa FK10 1NJ; T.-01259 213096; (b.) 8 Shillinghill, Alloa FK10 1JT; T.-01259 723201.

Anderson, Dorothy Elizabeth, BSc (Hons), MB, ChB, MRCP(UK), DMRD, FRCR, FRCP(Glas). Consultant Radiologist, Glasgow Royal Infirmary, since 1981; Honorary Clinical Lecturer, then Senior Lecturer, Glasgow University, since 1982; b. 26.9.50, Glasgow; m., David Anderson; 1 s.; 1 d. Educ. Glasgow High School for Girls; Glasgow University. Pre-registration posts, Stobhill Hospital and Glasgow Royal Infirmary; post-registration year, Respiratory Unit, Knightswood Hospital; trained in radiology, Western Infirmary, Glasgow (Registrar, then Senior Registrar). Recreation: choral singing; walking; aerobics. Address: (h.) 18 Milverton Avenue, Bearsden, Glasgow G61 4BE; T.-0141-942 7510.

Anderson, Douglas Kinloch, OBE, MA. Chairman, Kinloch Anderson (Holdings) Ltd., Edinburgh, since 1975; Board Member, Scottish Tourist Board, 1986-92; Deputy Chairman, Edinburgh Marketing Ltd., 1990-92; Director: Lothian and Edinburgh Enterprise Ltd., 1990-95, Scottish Eastern Investment Trust PLC, Fidelity Special Values PLC; b. 19.2.39, Edinburgh; m., Deirdre Anne; 2 s.; 1 d. Educ. George Watson's Boys College; St. Andrews University. Joined Kinloch Anderson Ltd., 1962 (fifth generation in family business); Assistant on Master's Court, Edinburgh Merchant Company, 1976-79; elected Honorary Member, St. Andrew's Society of Washington DC, 1985; Member, Edinburgh Festival Council, 1988-90; President, Edinburgh Royal Warrant Holders Association, 1987-88; former Member, Scottish Committee, Institute of Directors; President, Edinburgh Chamber of Commerce, 1988-90; Master, Edinburgh Merchant Company, 1990-92; President, Royal Warrant Holders Association, 1994; elected Leith High Constable, 1993; Freeman, City of London. Recreations: golf; fishing; watching rugby; travel (non-business). Address: (b.) Commercial Street/Dock Street, Leith, Edinburgh EH6 6EY; T.-0131-555 1355.

Anderson, Gavin Alan, DipArch, MPhil. Head, Community Care Division, Social Work Services Group, Scottish Office, since 1994; b. 5.7.39, Bridge of Allan; m., Margaret Clarke; 1 s.; 1 d. Educ. St. Modan's High School, Stirling; Edinburgh College of Art; Edinburgh University. Architect, Edinburgh University Architecture Research Unit, 1966-73; Architect, then Principal Architect, Scottish Development Department, 1973-85; Assistant Secretary, Scottish Home and Health Department, 1985-90; Deputy Chief Executive, NHS in Scotland, 1990-93. Recreations:

reading; listening to music; art; walking. Address: (b.) James Craig Walk, Edinburgh EH1 3BA; T.-0131-244 5452.

Anderson, Gordon Alexander, CA, FCMA. Chartered Accountant; b. 9.8.31, Glasgow; m., Eirene Cochrane Howie Douglas; 2 s.; 1 d. Educ. High School of Glasgow. Apprentice CA, Moores Carson & Watson, Glasgow, 1949-54; qualified CA, 1955; National Service, Royal Navy, 1955-57 (Sub Lieutenant); Partner, Moores Carson & Watson, 1958 (firm name changed to McClelland Moores, 1958, Arthur Young McClelland Moores, 1968, Arthur Young, 1985, Ernst & Young, 1989), Chairman, Arthur Young, 1987-89; Deputy Senior Partner, Ernst & Young, 1989-90; Director: Lloyds TSB Group plc, since 1993, TSB Bank Scotland plc, since 1991 (Chairman, since 1994), High School of Glasgow Ltd., 1975-81 and since 1990 (Chairman of Governors, since 1992), Merchants House of Glasgow, since 1996; Member, Council on Tribunals and of its Scottish Committee, 1990-96; Chairman, Bitmac Ltd., 1990-96; Director: Douglas Firebrick Co. Ltd., 1960-70; Member, Scottish Milk Marketing Board, 1979-85; Institute of Chartered Accountants of Scotland: Member, Council, 1980-84, Vice President, 1984-86, President, 1986-87. Recreations: golf; gardening; rugby football (as spectator). Address: (h.) Ardwell, 41 Manse Road, Bearsden, Glasgow G61 3PN; T.-0141-942 2803.

Anderson, Rev. Professor Hugh, MA, BD, PhD, DD, FRSE. Professor of New Testament Language, Literature and Theology, Edinburgh University, 1966-85; b. 18.5.20, Galston, Ayrshire; m., Jean Goldie Torbit; 1 s.; 1 s. (deceased); 1 d. Educ. Kilmarnock Academy; Glasgow University. Chaplaincy work, Egypt and Palestine, 1945-46; Lecturer in Old Testament, Glasgow University, 1946-51; Minister, Trinity Church, Pollokshields, Glasgow, 1951-57; Professor of Biblical Criticism, Duke University, North Carolina, 1957-66; special appointments including A.B. Bruce Lecturer in New Testament, Glasgow University, 1954-57; Katharine McBride Visiting Professor, Bryn Mawr College, Pennsylvania, 1972-73; Kenan Distinguished Visiting Professor, Meredith College, North Carolina, 1982-83; Pendergrass Visiting Professor, Florida Southern College, 1985-86, 1987-88. Awarded Schweitzer Medal from North Carolina History and Science Foundation. Publications: Psalms 1-45; Historians of Israel; The New Testament in Historical and Contemporary Perspective (Editor with W. Barclay); Jesus and Christian Origins; Jesus; The Gospel of Mark: Commentary; 3 and 4 Maccabees (Commentary). Recreations: golf; gardening; music. Address: (h.) Morningside Way, 23/13 Maxwell Street, Edinburgh EH10 5HT.

Anderson, Iain Buchanan, MA, DipEd, LGSM. Music Presenter/Sports Commentator, BBC, since 1985; b. 21.6.38, Stirling; m., Marion Elizabeth; 3 s.; 1 d. Educ. Bellahouston Academy, Glasgow; Glasgow University; Guildhall School. Lecturer in Speech and Drama, Jordanhill College, 1967; Arts Editor/Presenter, Radio Clyde, 1974 Former Rugby Correspondent, Scotland on Sunday. Address: (h.) Elmhurst, Station Road, Langbank PA14 6YA; T.-0147 554 0733.

Anderson, James A., MA, MEd, DipEd. Director of Education, Angus Council, since 1995; b. 21.8.49, Aberdeen; m., Linda; 1 s.; 1 d. Educ. Aberdeen Grammar School; Aberdeen University; Edinburgh University; Stirling University. Teacher, Assistant Principal Teacher, Principal Teacher of Mathematics, 1973-84; Tayside Regional Council: Assistant Director of Education, 1984-87, Area Education Officer, 1987-91, Senior Assistant Director of Education, 1991-95, Director of Education, 1995-96. Recreations: golf; bridge. Address: (b.) Angus Council, County Buildings, Market Street, Forfar DD8 3WE; T.-01307 473235.

Anderson, James Frazer Gillan, CBE, JP, DL. Member, Scottish Development Agency, 1986-89; Convener, Central Regional Council, 1974-86; b. 25.3.29, Maddiston, by Falkirk; m., May Harley; 1 s.; 1 d. Educ. Maddiston School; Graeme High School, Falkirk. Convener, Stirling County Council, 1971-75; Member: Health and Safety Commission, 1974-80; Montgomery Committee, 1982-84; Scottish Economic Council, 1983-87; awarded Honorary Degree, Doctor of University (Stirling). Recreations: gardening; walking; reading. Address: California Road, Maddiston, Falkirk.

Anderson, James Killoch, OBE, MB, ChB, FFCM, FCR, JP. Former Unit Medical Officer, Glasgow Royal Infirmary and Royal Maternity Hospital, Glasgow (retired, 1988); b. 3.2.23, Johnstone; m., Irene Webster Wilson; 1 s.; 2 d. Educ. High School of Glasgow; Glasgow University. Deputy Medical Superintendent, Glasgow Royal Infirmary and Associated Hospitals, 1954; appointed Medical Superintendent, 1957; District Medical Officer, Eastern District, Greater Glasgow Health Board, 1974; Unit Medical Officer, Unit East 1, Greater Glasgow Health Board, 1984. Corps Commandant and Council Member, St. Andrew's Ambulance Association, 1957-82; Member of Committee, Scottish Ambulance Service, 1957-74; Director, North Parish, Washing Green Society, Glasgow, since 1957; Member, Scottish Technical Education Council, since 1974; Member, Science Development Team, 16-18s Action Plan, Scottish Education Department. Recreations: gardening; golf. Address: (h.) 15 Kenilworth Avenue, Helensburgh G84 7JR; T.-01436 3739.

Anderson, John Ferguson, LLB (Hons). Chief Executive, Glasgow City Council, since 1995; b. 13.12.47, Kirkcaldy; m., Sandra; 1 s.; 1 d. Educ. Kirkcaldy High School; Queen's Park School, Glasgow; Edinburgh University. Various legal posts, Glasgow Corporation, 1969-75; Strathclyde Regional Council: Principal Solicitor, 1975-78, Assistant Director of Administration, 1978-80, Senior Executive Officer, 1980-86, Principal Executive Officer, 1986-90, Depute Chief Executive, 1990-95. Director, European Urban Institute. Recreations: golf; football; transport; church activities. Address: (b.) City Chambers, Glasgow G2 1DU; T.-0141-287 4739.

Anderson, Professor Kathleen Janette, OBE, FRSE, BSc, PhD, DSc(H), FScotvec, FSQA, CBiol, FIBiol, CChem, FRSC. Depute Principal, Napier Polytechnic of Edinburgh, 1983-92; b. 22.5.27, Glasgow; m., Mark Elliot Muir Anderson; 1 s.; 1 d. Educ. Queens Park School, Glasgow; Glasgow University. Lecturer, West of Scotland Agricultural College, Glasgow, 1948-54; Johnson and Florence Stoney Research Fellow, University of Sydney, Australia, 1952-53; Commonwealth Travelling Research Fellow, Australia and New Zealand, 1953; Sir James Knott Research Fellow, Durham University, 1955-57; King's College, Durham University: Lecturer in Biochemistry, 1958-59, Lecturer in Microbiology, 1962-63, Lecturer (part-time) in Landscape Horticulture, 1963-65, Lecturer (part-time), Extra-Mural Department, 1959-65; Lecturer (part-time), Department of Extra-Mural Studies, Edinburgh University, 1965-68; Napier College, Edinburgh: Senior Lecturer, Department of Biological Sciences, 1968-69, Head of Department, Biological Sciences, 1969-83. Crown Trustee, National Library for Scotland, since 1981; Deacon, Church of Scotland, 1974-78; Elder, since 1978; CNAA Environmental Sciences Board, 1978-84; Chairman, Joint Committee for Biology, SCOTEC, 1979-85; Institute of Biology: Chairman, Scottish Branch, 1977-79, Member of Council, 1977-80, Fellowship Committee, 1980-83, Environment Division, 1982-86; Founder Chairman, Heads of Biology in Tertiary Education, 1975-77; Heads of Biology in Polytechnics, 1974-83; Nurse Education Committee, Royal Edinburgh Hospital, 1974-77; SCOTVEC: Council Member and Chairman, Education Policy Committee, 1984-92, Vice Chairman, 1989-92;

Chairman, Edinburgh Branch, Glasgow Graduates Association, 1985-86; Trustee, Royal Observatory (Edinburgh) Trust, since 1987; Member: Scottish National Committee, English Speaking Union, 1987-92, Radioactive Waste Management Advisory Committee, 1988-92, Agriculture Industries Training Board, 1989-92, Scottish Committee, University Funding Council, 1989-92, Canon Foundation, since 1991, British Council, Scottish Committee, 1991-96, Governing Body, Independent Girls Schools, since 1996, Eastern Board, Scottish Environment Protection Agency, since 1996; Governor, St George's School, since 1989; Governor, George Watson's School, since 1990; founder Chairman, Women of Lothian Lunch, since 1987; Governor, Edinburgh's Telford College, 1992-97. Publications: Discover Lothian Beaches; Holyrood Park Teachers Handbook; Safety in Biological Laboratories. Recreations: grand-children; charity work; gardening; foreign travel. Address: (h.) 40 Barony Terrace, Edinburgh EH12 8RD.

Anderson, Professor Malcolm, MA, DPhil, DLitt (Oxon), FRSE, FRSA. Professor of Politics, Edinburgh University, since 1979, and Director, International Social Sciences Institute; b. 13.5.34, Knutsford; m., Jacqueline Larrieu; 2 s.; 1 d. Educ. University College, Oxford. Lecturer in Government, Manchester University, 1960-63; Research Fellow, Institut National des Sciences Politiques, 1964-65 and 1986-87; Senior Lecturer, then Professor, Warwick University, 1965-79; Visiting Fellow, Institute of Higher Studies, Vienna, 1977-78; Associate Professor, Sorbonne-Pantheon, 1987-88. Chairman, European Community Studies Association. Publications: Government in France, 1970; Conservative Politics in France, 1974; Frontier Regions in Western Europe, 1983; Women, Equality and Europe (Co-editor), 1988; Policing the World, 1989; Policing Across National Boundaries (Co-Editor), 1994; Policing the European Union (with others), 1995; Frontiers, 1996. Recreations:walking; reading; photography. Address: (h.) 72 Dundas Street, Edinburgh EH3 6QZ; T.-0131-556 9300.

Anderson, Professor Michael, MA, PhD, FBA, FRSE. Professor of Economic History, University of Edinburgh, since 1979; b. 21.2.42, Woking; m., Rosemary Elizabeth Kitching; 1 s.; 1 d. Educ. Kingston Grammar School; Queen's College, Cambridge. University of Edinburgh: Assistant Lecturer, 1967-69, Lecturer, 1969-75, Reader, 1975-79, Dean of Faculty of Social Sciences, 1985-89, Vice-Principal, 1989-93, and since 1997, Acting Principal, 1994. Member: Scottish Records Advisory Council, 1984-93, Economic and Social Research Council, 1990-94, Follett Committee on Libraries and Follett Implementation Group, 1993-97, British Library Board, since 1994, Council of British Academy, 1995-98. Publications: Family Structure in Nineteenth Century Lancashire, 1971; Approaches to the History of the Western Family, 1981; Population Change in North-Western Europe 1750-1850; many papers on family sociology and history and historical demography. Recreations: natural history; gardening; study of ancient civilisations. Address: (b.) Department of Economic History, University of Edinburgh, William Robertson Building, George Square, Edinburgh EH8 9JY; T.-0131-650 3844.

Anderson, Moira, OBE. Singer; b. Kirkintilloch; m., Dr. Stuart Macdonald. Educ. Ayr Academy; Royal Scottish Academy of Music, Glasgow. Began with Kirkintilloch Junior Choir, aged six; made first radio broadcast for BBC in Scotland, aged eight; was Teacher of Music in Ayr before becoming professional singer; made first professional broadcast, White Heather Club, 1960; has toured overseas, had her own radio and TV series; has introduced Stars on Sunday, ITV; appeared in summer shows, cabaret, pantomime and numerous other stage shows; several Royal Variety performances.

Anderson, Peter David, MA, PhD, FSA Scot, FRHistS. Deputy Keeper, Scottish Record Office, since 1993; b. 10.3.47, Greenock; m., Jean Johnstone Smith; 1 s.; 1 d. Educ. Hutchesons' Grammar School, Glasgow; St. Andrews University; Edinburgh University. Teacher of History, Cranhill Secondary School, Glasgow, 1972-73; Research Assistant, Scottish Record Office, 1974-80; Registrar, National Register of Archives (Scotland), 1980-83; Secretary, NRA(S), 1984-85; Conservation Officer, 1985-89; Head, Records Liaison Branch, 1989-93. Member: International Council on Archives Committee on Electronic Records, European Commission committee on new archive building; Convener, Society of Archivists Legislation Panel, since 1996; Chair, International Council on Archives Committee on Archive Buildings and Equipment, since 1996; Secretary, Scottish Oral History Group, 1984-88, Deputy Convener, since 1988; Chair, Linlithgow Players, 1994-97. Publications: Robert Stewart, Earl of Orkney, Lord of Shetland, 1533-93, 1982; Black Patie, 1993. Recreations: drawing and painting; drama. Address: (b.) Scottish Record Office, HM General Register House, Edinburgh EH1 3YY; T.-0131-535 1406.

Anderson, Robert Alexander, LLB, DipLP, NP. Solicitor, since 1983; Partner, Lindsay & Kirk, Aberdeen, since 1988; President, Aberdeen Bar Association, since 1996; b. 31.5.60, Nairn; m., Nicola Mary; 1 s.; 1 d. Educ. Nairn Academy; University of Glasgow. Trained at J.A. McGoogan & Co., Coatbridge, 1981-83, Legal Assistant, 1983-85; Legal Assistant, Lindsay & Kirk, Aberdeen, 1985-88. Involved on voluntary basis with Aberdeen Women's Aid; Tutor in Criminal Court Practice, Aberdeen University. Recreation: orienteering. Address: (b.) 39 Huntly Street, Aberdeen AB10 1TJ; T.-01224 641402.

Anderson, Professor Robert David, MA, DPhil. Professor of Modern History, Edinburgh University, since 1994; b. 11.7.42, Cardiff. Educ. Taunton School, Somerset; Queen's and St. Antony's Colleges, Oxford. Assistant Lecturer, Glasgow University, 1967-69; Lecturer, then Senior Lecturer and Reader, Edinburgh University, 1969-94. Publications: Education in France 1848-1870, 1975; France 1870-1914: Politics and Society, 1977; Education and Opportunity in Victorian Scotland, 1983 (winner, Scottish Arts Council Literary Award, 1984); The Student Community at Aberdeen, 1860-1939 (1988); Universities and Elites in Britain since 1800, 1992; Education and the Scottish People 1750-1918, 1995. Address: (b.) Department of History, Edinburgh University, Edinburgh; T.-0131-650 3786.

Anderson, Professor Thomas Alfred, CEng, FICE, FIWEM, FIHT, FIOSH, FIMgt. Member and West Area Chairman, Scottish Water and Sewerage Customers' Council; Independent Adviser to Secretary of State on appointments to executive Non-Departmental Public Bodies; National Council Member and Director, Chartered Institution of Water and Environmental Management; Director: Scottish Greenbelt Foundation, Land Trust Co. Ltd.; Public Sector Management Consultant, Joint Board for Engineering Management; Visiting Professor, Department of Civil, Structural and Environmental Engineering and Department of Biology, Paisley University, since 1992; b. 9.11.34, Glasgow; m., Margaret; 3 d. Educ. Strathbungo Senior Secondary School; Royal Technical College, Glasgow; Paisley College of Technology. City Engineer's Department, Corporation of the City of Glasgow: Senior Civil Engineer, 1964-68, Assistant Chief Civil Engineer, 1968-75; Strathclyde Regional Council: Assistant Director of Sewerage, 1975-81, Depute Director of Sewerage, 1981-91, Director of Sewerage, 1991-94. Institution of Municipal Engineers National Medal and Prize Winner, 1980; Examiner/Reviewer, Institution of Civil Engineers, since 1977; Freeman, City of London – Company of Water Conservators; Member, Industrial Advisory Committee/

Specialist Visiting Lecturer, Glasgow Caledonian University. Publications: technical papers. Recreations: gardening; golf; cricket. Address: (h.) Craigela, Ryefield Avenue, Drumpellier, Coatbridge ML5 1LG; T.-01236 424146.

Anderson, William, CBE. Managing Editor, The Sunday Post (Editor, 1967-90); b. 10.2.34, Motherwell; m., Margaret Cross McClelland; 3 s. Educ. Dalziel High School; Glasgow University. Journalist since first producing school newspapers, with interruptions as cook steward, male nurse, medical student and Army officer. Address: (b.) 2 Albert Square, Dundee DD1 9QG; T.-01382 223131.

Anderson, Professor Sir (William) Ferguson, Kt (1974), OBE, KStJ, MD, FRCP(Lond), (Glas), (Edin), (C), (I), FACP. Professor Emeritus, Geriatric Medicine, Glasgow University; Vice-President, Scottish Retirement Council; Honorary President, Crossroads (Scotland) Care Attendant Scheme; Honorary Vice-President, Age Concern (Scotland); Vice-President, Marie Curie Cancer Care; b. 8.4.14, Glasgow; m., Margaret Gebbie; 1 s.; 2 d. Educ. Glasgow Academy; Glasgow University. Assistant Lecturer, Materia Medica, Glasgow University, 1939-41; Major, RAMC, 1941-46; Senior Lecturer, Materia Medica, Glasgow University, 1946-48; Senior Lecturer, Medicine, Welsh National School of Medicine, 1948-52; Honorary Consultant Physician, Cardiff Royal Infirmary, 1948-52; Consultant Physician in Geriatric Medicine and Advisor in diseases of old age and chronic sickness, Western Regional Board, 1952-65; Professor of Geriatric Medicine, Glasgow University, 1965-79. St. Mungo Prize, City of Glasgow; Ed Henderson Award, American Geriatrics Society; Brookdale Award, Gerontological Society of America. Recreation: golf. Address: (h.) Rodel, Moor Road, Strathblane, Glasgow G63 9EX; T.-Blanefield 770862.

Anderson, Very Rev. Canon William Rutherfoord Turnbull, MA, FTCL. Administrator, St. Mary's R.C. Cathedral, Aberdeen; b. 7.1.31, Glasgow. Educ. George Watson's College, Edinburgh; University of Edinburgh; Sidney Sussex College, Cambridge. Curate, St. David's, Dalkeith, 1960-61; staff, St. Mary's College, Blairs, Aberdeen, 1961-69; Producer, BBC Scotland Religious Department, 1969-77; Spiritual Director, Pontifical Scots College, Rome, 1977-85; staff, St. Mary's College, Blairs, Aberdeen, 1985-86; R.C. Chaplain, University of Aberdeen, 1986-93. Canon, R.C. Diocese of Aberdeen; former Major Scholar, Sidney Sussex College, Cambridge; Poetry Society Gold Medal for verse-speaking, 1980; Preacher of the Year, The Times and College of Preachers, 1996. Recreations: walking; music and poetry; fondness for cats! Address: (b.) 20 Huntly Street, Aberdeen AB10 1SH; T.-01224 640678.

Anderson, Willie. Managing Director, John Smith & Son, since 1994; b. 7.4.48, Glasgow; m., Pat; 2 d. Educ. Sedbergh School. Bookseller for 24 years; President, Booksellers Association of Great Britain and Ireland, 1995-97; Joint Chair, World Book Day Steering Committee, 1997-98; Member, Booker Prize Management Committee, since 1993. Recreations: books; wine; art; keeping my weight down. Address: (h.) Crossburn, Milngavie; T.-0141-221 7472.

Andrew, Hugh, BA (Oxon), FSA Scot. Joint Managing Director, Canongate Books, since 1994; b. 8.4.62. Educ. Glasgow Academy; Magdalen College, Oxford. Set up own sales business, 1990; set up own publishing company, 1992; bought Canongate Books with colleague, 1994. Recreations: reading; music; archaeology; islands. Address: (b.) Unit 8, Canongate Venture, 5 New Street, Edinburgh EH8 8BH; T.-0131-558 1500.

Andrew, John Anthony, MA, FRICS. Chief Estates Officer, Scottish Office, since 1996; b. 10.10.52, Ormskirk; m., Mary MacLeod Mackay; 3 s. Educ. Ormskirk Grammar School; Heanor Grammar School; Downing College, University of Cambridge. Valuation Office, Inland Revenue, Cleveland North, 1976-78; Lecturer in Land Economy, University of Aberdeen, 1978-81; Valuation Office, Inland Revenue, Aberdeen and Dumfries, 1981-89; Principal Estates Surveyor, Scottish Office, 1989-92 and 1994-96; Principal, Scottish Office Agriculture and Fisheries Department, Land Use and Conservation Division, 1992-94. Member: RICS Chairman's Committee, since 1996, Castle Rock Housing Association Ltd. Management Committee, since 1997. Recreations: reading; fishing. Address: (b.) Scottish Office Land and Property Division, 1-H42, Victoria Quay, Edinburgh EH6 6QQ; T.-0131-244 7943.

Andrews, James, IPFA, DPA. Director of Finance, Glasgow City Council, since 1995; Treasurer, Glasgow Humane Society, since 1994; Chairman, Scottish Branch, CIPFA, since 1997; b. 28.11.38, Kilsyth; m., Mary; 1 s.; 2 d. Educ. Kilsyth Academy. Glasgow District Council, since 1976. Recreations: golf; walking; theatre. Address: (b.) City Chambers, Glasgow; T.-0141-287 3837.

Andrews, June, RMN, RGN, MA(Hons). Secretary to Scottish Board, Royal College of Nursing, since 1993; nurse, since 1980; b. Kilwinning. Educ. Ardrossan Academy; Glasgow University; Nottingham University. NHS nursing and management posts, Nottingham and London; adviser on ethics and Aids, RCN; Assistant Director Policy and Research, Royal College of Nursing. Member, Nuffield Council on Bioethics; regular contributor to nursing press. Address: (b.) RCN, 42 South Oswald Road, Edinburgh EH9 2BB; T.-0131-662 1010.

Angus, Rev. James Alexander Keith, LVO, TD, MA. Extra Chaplain to HM The Queen, since 1996; b. 16.4.29, Aberdeen; m., Alison Jane Daly; 1 s.; 1 d. Educ. High School of Dundee; St. Andrews University. Assistant Minister, Glasgow Cathedral, 1955-56; Minister: Hoddam Parish Church, 1956-67, Gourock Old Parish Church, 1967-79; Minister, Braemar and Crathie Parish Churches, 1979-95. TA: Captain, Royal Artillery, 1950-56, Chaplain, 1957-77; Convener, Committee of Chaplains to HM Forces, General Assembly, 1981-85; LVO, 1990; Domestic Chaplain to HM The Queen in Scotland, 1979-96. Recreations: hill-walking; fishing; golf. Address: (h.) Darroch Den, Hawthorn Place, Ballater, Aberdeenshire AB35 5QH; T.-013397 56260.

Angus, Rae, MA (Hons), MLitt, MIMgt, MITD. Principal, Aberdeen College, since 1993; b. 1947, Ellon; m., Alison Hay; 2 d. Educ. Peterhead Academy; Aberdeen University. Further Education Lecturer, 1975; Research Fellow, Aberdeen University, 1978-80; Aberdeen College of Commerce, 1981-90, latterly as Depute Principal; Depute Principal, Aberdeen College of Further Education, 1991-93. Recreations: reading; walking; computing. Address: (b.) Gallowgate, Aberdeen AB25 1BN; T.-01224 612000.

Angus, Col. William Turnbull Calderhead, CEng, MRAeS, FIMgt, FIQA. Honorary Sheriff, North Strathclyde, since 1986; b. 20.7.23, Glasgow; m., Nola Leonie Campbell-Gillies; 2 s.; 2 d. Educ. Govan High School; Glasgow University; Royal Military College of Science. Commissioned Royal Regiment of Artillery, 1944; King's African Rifles and GSO2, DAAG (Major), HQ East Africa Command, 1945-47; Technical Staff Course, Royal Military College of Science, 1949-51; TSO2 (Major), Inspectorate of Armaments, 1951-54; BAOR and Cyprus, 1954-57; GSO2 (Major), G(Tech) HQ BAOR, 1957-60; TSO2 (Major), Ordnance Board, 1960-63; TSO2 (Major), Trials Establishment Guided Weapons, RA, 1963-65;

postgraduate Guided Weapons Course, Royal Military College of Science, 1965-66; TSO1 (Lt. Col.), Royal Armament Research and Development Establishment, 1966-69; Assistant Director, Guided Weapons Trials (Col.), MOD Procurement Executive, 1970-73; Member (Col.), Ordnance Board, 1973-74; retired, 1974; self-employed holiday cottages proprietor, Scottish Manager, Blakes Holidays, 1976-93; Past President, Campbeltown Rotary Club. Recreations: wood-turning and manufacture of spinning wheels; creationism studies. Address: Kilchrist Castle, Campbeltown, Argyll PA28 6PH; T.-01586 553210.

Annand, David Andrew, DA, ARBS, JP. Sculptor; b. 30.1.48, Insch, Aberdeenshire; m., Jean; 1 s.; 1 d. Educ. Perth Academy; Duncan of Jordanstone College of Art, Dundee. Lecturer, Sculpture Department, Duncan of Jordanstone College of Art, Dundee, 1972-74; Art Department, St. Saviour's High School, Dundee, 1975-88; full-time sculptor, since 1988; RSA Latimer Award, 1976; RSA Benno Schotz Award, 1978; RSA Ireland Alloys Award, 1982; Scottish Development Agency Dundee Technology Park Competition, 1986, "Deer Leap", Sir Otto Beit Medal, 1986; Royal Botanic Garden, Edinburgh "Ardea Cinerea", 1987; Winner, Almswall Road Sculpture Competition, Irvine Development Corporation, "The Ring", 1989; Winner, Perth High Street Sculpture Competition, Perth Partnership "Nae Day Sae Dark", 1989; Baxters of Speyside "Royal Stag" cast by Powderhall Bronze, 1993; Tranent Massacre Memorial bronze casting by Powderhall Bronze, 1995; Winner, competition to design sculpture for Lord Street, Wrexham, 1995, "Y Bwa" Civic Society Award, 1995; Winner, competition to design sculpture, Ashworth Roundabout, Blackpool, "Helter-skelter", 1995; Strathcarron Hospice composition, 1996; British High Commission, Hong Kong, "Three Cranes in Flight", 1997. Recreations: music; bird watching; wine and food. Address: Pigscrave Cottage, The Wynd, Kilmany, Cupar, Fife KY15 4PT; T.-01382 330 714.

Annand, Louise Gibson, MBE, MA (Hons), AMA, DU. Artist; b. 27.5.15, Uddingston; m., 1, Alistair Matheson (deceased); 2, Roderick MacFarquhar (deceased). Educ. Hamilton Academy; Glasgow University. Teacher, primary and secondary schools, Glasgow, 1939-49; Assistant, Schools Museum Service, 1949-70; Museums Education Officer, 1970-80. Past Chairman: Scottish Educational Film Association (Glasgow Production Group); Glasgow Lady Artists Club Trust; National Vice-Chairman, Scottish Educational Media Association, 1979-84; President: Society of Scottish Women Artists, 1963-66 and 1980-85; Member, Royal Fine Art Commission for Scotland, 1979-86; Glasgow Society of Women Artists, 1977-79, 1988-91; Visiting Lecturer in Scottish Art, Regina University, 1982; Chairman, J.D. Fergusson Foundation, since 1982 (Trustee, since 1983); Member, Business Committee, General Council, University of Glasgow, 1981-85, 1988-91; Honorary Member, Saltire Society, since 1993; DUniv, Glasgow University, 1994; exhibited widely since 1945; produced numerous 16mm films, including the first on Charles Rennie Mackintosh, 1966. Recreations: mountaineering (Ladies Scottish Climbing Club). Address: (h.) 22 Kingsborough Gardens, Glasgow G12 9NJ; T.-0141-339 8956.

Annandale and Hartfell, 11th Earl of (Patrick Andrew Wentworth Hope Johnstone of Annandale and of That Ilk). Farmer; Chief, Clan Johnstone; Baron of the Barony of the Lands of the Earldom of Annandale and Hartfell, and of the Lordship of Johnstone; Hereditary Steward, Stewartry of Annandale; Hereditary Keeper, Keys of Lochmaben Castle; Deputy Lieutenant, Dumfriesshire, since 1987; b. 19.4.41, Auldgirth, Dumfriesshire; m., Susan Josephine; 1 s.; 1 d. Educ. Stowe School; Royal Agricultural College, Cirencester. Member: Dumfriesshire County Council, 1970-75, Dumfries and Galloway Regional Council, 1975-85, Scottish Valuation Advisory Council, 1982, Solway River

Purification Board, 1973-85; Underwriter, Lloyds, London, 1976. Address: (b.) House of Lords, London SW1.

Anstruther, Sir Ralph (Hugo), of that Ilk, 7th Bt. of Balcaskie and 12th of Anstruther, GCVO, MC, DL, BA. Equerry to the Queen Mother, since 1959, and Treasurer since 1961; b. 13.6.21. Educ. Eton; Magdalene College, Cambridge. Major (ret.), Coldstream Guards. Member, Queen's Bodyguard for Scotland (Royal Company of Archers); DL, Fife, 1960; DL, Caithness-shire, 1965. Address: Balcaskie, Pittenweem, Fife; Watten, Caithness.

Anton, Alexander Elder, CBE, MA, LLB, LLD (Hon), FBA; b. 1922; m., Doris May Lawrence; 1 s. Educ. Aberdeen University. Solicitor, 1949; Lecturer, Aberdeen, 1953-59; Professor of Jurisprudence, Glasgow University, 1959-73; Honorary Professor, 1984, Aberdeen University; Member, Scottish Law Commission, 1966-82; UK Delegate to Hague Conference on Private International Law, 1964-82; Chairman, Scottish Rights of Way Society, 1988-92. Publications: Private International Law, 1967 and 1990; Civil Jurisdiction in Scotland, 1984. Recreation: hillwalking. Address: (h.) 5 Seafield Drive West, Aberdeen AB15 7XA.

Arbuthnot, Peter Geoffrey. Managing Director, Christie's Scotland Limited, since 1989; b. 18.9.50, London; m., Belinda Terry-Engell; 1 s.; 1 d. Educ. Stowe School; Trinity College, Cambridge. Research in Indian Archaeology, 1974-76; Specialist, Ethnographic Art, Christie's Auctioneers, London, 1976-80; Commodity Trader, E.D. and F. Man, 1980-83; Christie's in the City, 1983-88. Governor, Laurel Park School, Glasgow, since 1991. Recreations: squash; skiing; hockey; travel; public speaking. Address (b.) 164-166 Bath Street, Glasgow G2 4TB; T.-0141-332 8134.

Arbuthnott, 16th Viscount of (John Campbell Arbuthnott), KT, CBE, DSC, FRSE, FRSA, BGCOStJ, LLD. Lord Lieutenant, Kincardineshire, since 1977; b. 26.10.24; m.; 1 s.; 1 d. Educ. Fettes College; Gonville and Caius College, Cambridge. Served RNVR (Fleet Air Arm), 1942-46. Member, Countryside Commission for Scotland, 1967-71; Chairman, Red Deer Commission, 1969-75; Member, Aberdeen University Court, 1978-84; President, Scottish Landowners Federation, 1974-79; President, Royal Scottish Geographical Society, 1984-87; Chairman, Scottish Widows' Fund and Life Assurance Society, 1984-87; Lord High Commissioner to the General Assembly of the Church of Scotland, 1986, 1987; President, Royal Zoological Society of Scotland, 1976-96; President, Scottish Agricultural Organisation Society, 1980-83; President, Federation of Agricultural Cooperatives (UK), 1983-87; Deputy Chairman, Nature Conservancy Council, 1980-85, and Chairman, Scottish Committee, NCC; Chairman, Aberdeen and Northern Marts Ltd., 1986-91, Director, 1973-91; Director, Clydesdale Bank PLC, 1985-92 (Northern Area, 1975-85); Director, Britoil, 1988-90; Prior of Scotland, The Order of St. John, 1983-95; Member, Royal Commission on Historical Manuscripts, 1988-95; Member, BP Scottish Advisory Board, 1990-97. Address: (h.) Arbuthnott House, by Laurencekirk, Kincardineshire AB30 1PA.

Arbuthnott, Professor Sir John Peebles, PhD, ScD, FIBiol, HonFTCD, FRSA, FRSE, FIIB, FRCPath, HonFRCPSGlasg. Principal and Vice Chancellor, Strathclyde University, since 1991; Vice-Chairman, Committee of Vice-Chancellors and Principals; b. 8.4.39; m., Elinor Rutherford Smillie; 1 s.; 2 d. Educ. Glasgow University; Trinity College, Dublin. Assistant Lecturer, then Lecturer, Department of Bacteriology, Glasgow University, 1960-67; Fellow of the Royal Society, 1968-72; Senior Lecturer, Department of Microbiology, then Senior Lecturer, Department of Bacteriology, Glasgow University, 1972-75; Professor of Micriobiology, Trinity College,

Dublin, 1976-88; Professor of Microbiology, Nottingham University, 1988-91. Member, Lister Institute; Member, Board, Glasgow Development Agency; Chairman, Higher Education Councils' Joint Information Systems Committee. Recreations: attending soccer matches; golf. Address: (b.) Strathclyde University, Glasgow G1 1XQ; T.-0141-552 4400.

Archer, Gilbert Baird, DL. Chairman,Tods of Orkney Ltd, since 1970; Director (formerly Chairman), John Dickson & Sons Ltd; b. 24.8.42, Edinburgh; m., Irene Conn; 2 d. Educ. Melville College. Vice Convenor, George Watson's College, 1978-80; Governor, Fettes College, 1986-90; Director, Scottish Council of Independent Schools, 1988-91; Council Member, Governing Bodies Association of Independent Schools, 1988-91; Governor, Napier University; Governor, St. Columba's Hospice; Past President, Edinburgh Chamber of Commerce & Manufactures; Past Chairman, Scottish Chambers of Commerce; Deputy President, Association of British Chambers of Commerce; Chairman, Edinburgh Common Purpose, 1991-94; Past Moderator, High Constabulary of the Port of Leith; Liveryman, Worshipful Company of Gunmakers, London; Treasurer, The Company of Merchants of the City of Edinburgh. Recreations: fishing; shooting. Address: (b.) 12 Broughton Place, Edinburgh EH1 3RX; T.-0131-556 4518.

Archer, Professor John Stuart, BSc, PhD, FEng. Principal and Vice-Chancellor, Heriot-Watt University, since 1997; b. 15.6.43, London; m., Lesley; 1 s.; 1 d. Educ. County Grammar School, Chiswick; City University, London; Imperial College of Science, Technology and Medicine. Trainee, ICI (Mond Division); Senior Research Engineer, Imperial Oil (Esso Canada), Calgary; Senior Petroleum Engineer, British Gas Corporation (Exploration Division); Manager Reservoir Studies, D and S Petroleum Consultants, London and Calgary; Director and Co-founder, ERC Energy Resources Consultants Ltd., London; Professor of Petroleum Engineering, Imperial College, London University; Pro Rector (Resources) and Deputy Rector, Imperial College of Science, Technology and Medicine. Director, Centre for Marine and Petroleum Technology; Advisory Editor, Kluwer and Elsevier; Fellow, City and Guilds Institute; Distinguished Faculty Award, Society of Petroleum Engineers; Lubbock-Sambrook Award, Institute of Energy. Recreations: music; art; theatre; golf. Address: (b.) Heriot-Watt University, Riccarton, Edinburgh EH14 4AS; T.-0131-451 3360.

Argyll, 12th Duke of, (Ian Campbell). Chief of Clan Campbell; Hereditary Master of the Royal Household, Scotland; Hereditary High Sheriff of the County of Argyll; Admiral of the Western Coast and Isles; Keeper of the Great Seal of Scotland and of the Castles of Dunstaffnage, Dunoon, and Carrick and Tarbert; b. 28.8.37; m. Iona Mary; 1 s.; 1 d. Address: Inverary Castle, Inverary, Argyll PA32 8XF.

Armour, Professor Sir James, CBE, PhD, Dr hc Utrecht, DVM&S (Edin), FRCVS, FRSE. Vice-Principal (Planning - External Relations), Glasgow University, 1991-95; Dean, Faculty of Veterinary Medicine, 1986-91, and Professor of Veterinary Parasitology (Personal Chair), Glasgow University, since 1976; Chairman, Glasgow Dental Hospital and School NHS Trust, since 1995; b. 17.9.29, Basra, Iraq; m., 1, Irene Morris (deceased); 2, Christine Strickland; 2 s.; 2 d. Educ. Marr College, Troon; Glasgow University. Colonial veterinary service, Nigeria, 1953-60; Research Scientist, Wellcome Ltd., 1960-63; Glasgow University: Research Fellow, 1963-67, Lecturer/Senior Lecturer, 1967-73, Reader, 1973-76. Chairman, Government Committee on Animal Medicines, 1987-95; Chairman, Editorial Board, In Practice (veterinary journal), 1980-90; Chairman, Governing Body, Institute of Animal Health, 1989-97; Member, Governing Body: Moredun Research Institute,

Edinburgh, since 1997, Institute of Aquaculture, Stirling, since 1997. Awards: RCVS John Henry Steel Medal, Royal Agricultural Society Bledisloe Award, BVA Wooldridge Medal, Pfizer WAAVP Award. Publications: joint author of textbook on veterinary parasitology; editor, two books; 150 scientific articles. Recreation: golf. Address: (h.) Mokoia, 11 Crosbie Road, Troon, Ayrshire; T.-01292 314068.

Armour, Mary Nicol Neill, DA, RSA, RSW, RGI, LLD Glasgow (1980). Artist; b. 27.3.02, Blantyre; m., William Armour. Educ. Hamilton Academy; Glasgow School of Art. Elected ARSA, 1941; RSW, 1956; RSA, 1958; RGI, 1977; Honorary President: Glasgow School of Art, 1982; Royal Glasgow Institute of the Fine Arts, 1983; Vice President, Paisley Art Institute, 1983. Guthrie Award, RSA, 1937; Cargill Prize, RGI, 1972; Fellow, Paisley University, since 1989; Hon. Fellowship, Glasgow School of Art, 1993; Awarded Diploma PAI (Paisley Art Institute), 1995. Recreations: gardening; dress-making. Address: Priory Park Private Residential Home, 19 Main Road, Castlehead, Paisley PA2 6AJ; T.-0141-848 1718.

Armour, Robert Malcolm, MBA, LLB (Hons), DipLP, WS, NP. Company Secretary, British Energy plc, since 1995; formerly Director, Performance Development (1993-95) and Company Secretary (1990-95), Scottish Nuclear Limited; Director: IMS Trust, NIRA Limited, Lochside Insurance Limited, Electricity Association Limited, British Energy Trustees Limited, British Energy International Limited, Scottish Nuclear International Ltd.; b. 25.9.59, Edinburgh; m., Anne Ogilvie White. Educ. Daniel Stewart's and Melville College, Edinburgh; Edinburgh University. Solicitor, Haldanes McLaren and Scott, WS, Edinburgh, 1983-86; Partner, Wright, Johnston and MacKenzie, Edinburgh, 1987-90. Recreations: golf; curling. Address: British Energy plc, 10 Lochside Place, Edinburgh EH12 9DF.

Armstrong, Bryan. Editor: Annandale Observer, since 1994, Annandale Herald, since 1994, Moffat News, since 1994; b. 26.6.54, Chester. Educ. Annan Academy. Joined Dumfriesshire Newspaper Group, 1971, as apprentice/compositor; photographer, 1976-79; reporter, 1979-83; Group Assistant Editor, 1983-94. Recreations: cycling; greyhound racing; photography; music; travel. Address: (b.) 96 High Street, Annan DG12 5DW; T.-01461 202417.

Armstrong, Iain Gillies, LLB, DipLP. Clerk of Faculty, Faculty of Advocates, since 1995; b. 26.5.56, Edinburgh; m., Deirdre Elizabeth Mary Mackenzie; 1 s.; 1 d. Educ. Inverness Royal Academy; Glasgow University. Admitted to Faculty of Advocates, 1986. Address: (b.) Advocates Library, Parliament House, Edinburgh EH1 1RF; T.-0131-226 5071.

Armstrong, Richard, CBE. Musical Director, Scottish Opera, since 1993; b. 7.1.43, Leicester. Educ. Wyggeston Grammar School, Leicester; Corpus Christi College, Cambridge. Musical Director, Welsh National Opera, 1973-86; Principal Guest Conductor, Frankfurt Opera, 1987-90. Address: (b.) Scottish Opera, 39 Elmbank Crescent, Glasgow G2.

Arnold, Andy, MA (Hons), DipEd. Founder and Artistic Director, The Arches, Glasgow, since 1991; Theatre Director, since 1980; Community Artist and Cartoonist, since 1974; Teacher, since 1973; b. Southend-on-Sea. Artistic Director, Theatre Workshop, Edinburgh, 1980-85; Director, Bloomsbury Theatre, London, 1986-89; directing credits include: Metropolis: The Theatre Cut, Caligari, The Devils, The Crucible, Sexual Perversity in Chicago, I Licked a Slag's Deodorant; Freelance Director, The Battle of Stirling Bridge, Stirling Castle, 1997. Two Paper Boat awards; Spirit of Mayfest Award. Recreations: holidays;

five-a-side football; Hibernian F.C.; golf. Address: (b.) The Arches, Midland Street, Glasgow G1 4PR; T.-0141-221 9736.

Arnold, James Edward, MBE, MA (Hon), BA, CertEd, FRIAS. Director, New Lanark Conservation Trust, since 1974; b. 16.3.45, Glasgow; m., Rose. Educ. Caludon Castle Comprehensive School; York University; London University. Recreations: New Lanark and life. Address: (b.) Mill Number Three, New Lanark, Lanark; T.-01555 661345.

Arnott, Campbell. Collector, HM Customs and Excise. Address: (b.) 44 York Place, Edinburgh, EH1 3JW.

Arnott, David Cleghorn, FILAM. Administrator, Scottish Association of Local Sports Councils; formerly Director of Leisure Services, Dunfermline District Council; Member: Scottish Sports Council, National Lottery Board – Sport and Sports Match Scotland Panel since 1995; b. 6.2.42, Hamilton; m., Jean McFarlane Lennox; 2 s.; 1 d. Educ. Woodside Secondary, Hamilton. Joined local government with Lanarkshire County Council, 1957. Past Chairman, Scottish Branch, Institute of Leisure and Amenity Management; Hon. Life Member, Scottish Association of Local Sports Councils. Recreations: football; golf; beach-combing. Address: (h.) 37 Donibristle Gardens, Dalgety Bay, Fife KY11 5NQ; T.-01368 820950.

Arnott, James Mackay, TD, BL, WS, SSC. Solicitor; Partner, MacRoberts, Glasgow and Edinburgh, since 1963; b. 22.3.35, Blackford, Perthshire; m., Jean Barbara Allan; 3 s. Educ. Merchiston Castle School, Edinburgh; Edinburgh University. National Service, RAF, 1957-60; TA, 1961-77. Council Member, Law Society of Scotland, 1983-85 (Convenor, Law Reform Committee); Secretary, Scottish Building Contract Committee. Recreation: cricket. Address: (b.) 152 Bath Street, Glasgow G2 4TB; T.-0141-332 9988; 27 Melville Street, Edinburgh EH3 7JF; T.-0131-226 2552.

Arnott, John Michael Stewart, BA. President, Scottish Arctic Club, since 1995; Member, Council, Scottish Wildlife Trust, since 1995; b. 12.6.33; m., Lynne Gladstone-Millar; 1 s.; 1 d. Educ. Peterhouse, Cambridge. Pilot, RAF, 1952-54; Announcer, Producer, Editor Talks and Features, Edinburgh Manager, BBC Scotland, 1960-90; Member, 1982-92, Vice-Chairman, 1986-92, Countryside Commission for Scotland; Chairman, Isle of May Bird Observatory, 1980-85; Chairman, Fair Isle Bird Observatory Trust, 1983-85; Member: Committee for Scotland, Nature Conservancy Council, 1986-91, NCC Advisory Committee on Birds, 1990-91; Chairman, CCS Advisory Panel on Management of Mountain Areas, 1989-90; Member, National Parks of England and Wales Review Panel, 1990; President, Scottish Ornithologists' Club, 1984-87; Member: South East Regional Board, Scottish Natural Heritage, 1992-95, Board, Edinburgh Green Belt Trust, 1992-97. Sony Award for Radio Feature, 1985. Recreations: ornithology; hill-walking. Address: (h.) East Redford House, 133 Redford Road, Edinburgh EH13 0AS; T.-0131-441 3567.

Arnott, Professor Struther, CBE, BSc, PhD, ScD, FKC, FRSE, FRS. Principal and Vice-Chancellor, St. Andrews University, since 1986; b. 25.9.34, Larkhall; m., Greta Edwards; 2 s. Educ. Hamilton Academy; Glasgow University. King's College, London: Scientist, MRC Biophysics Research Unit, 1960-70, Demonstrator, Physics, 1960-67, Director of Postgraduate Studies in Biophysics, 1967-70; Purdue University, Indiana, USA: Professor of Molecular Biology, 1970, Head, Department of Biological Sciences, 1975-80, Vice-President for Research and Dean, Graduate School, 1980-86; Oxford University: Senior Visiting Research Fellow, Jesus College, 1980-81, Nuffield Research Fellow, Green College, 1985-86, Guggenheim

Memorial Foundation Fellow, 1985. Recreations: birdwatching; botanizing. Address: (b.) College Gate, North Street, St. Andrews KY16 9AJ; T.-01334 462551.

Arthur, Adrian, BL. Editor, The Courier, Dundee, since 1993; b. 28.9.37, Kirkcaldy; m., Patricia Mill; 1 s.; 2 d. Educ. Harris Academy, Dundee; St. Andrews University. Joined staff of People's Journal; through the editorial ranks of The Courier (Deputy Editor, 1978-93). Recreations: golf; travel; Rotary. Address: (b.) 80 Kingsway East, Dundee DD4 8SL; T.-01382 223131.

Arthur, Lt. General Sir Norman, KCB (1985); Lord Lieutenant, Stewartry of Kirkcudbright, Dumfries and Galloway Region; b. 6.3.31, London (but brought up in Ayrshire, of Scottish parents); m., Theresa Mary Hopkinson; 1 s.; 1 d.; 1 s. (deceased). Educ. Eton College; Royal Military Academy, Sandhurst. Commissioned Royal Scots Greys, 1951; commanded Royal Scots Dragoon Guards, 1972-74, 7th Armoured Brigade, 1976-77, 3rd Armoured Division, 1980-82; Director, Personal Services (Army), 1983-85; commanded Army in Scotland, and Governor of Edinburgh Castle, 1985-88; retired, 1988; Honorary Colonel, Royal Scots Dragoon Guards, 1984-92; Col. Comdt. Military Provost Staff Corps, 1983-88; Honorary Colonel, 205 (Scottish) General Hospital, Territorial Army, 1988-93; Colonel, The Scottish Yeomanry, since 1992; mentioned in Despatches, 1974. Officer, Royal Company of Archers; President, Scottish Conservation Projects Trust, 1989-93; Vice President, Riding for the Disabled Association, Edinburgh and the Borders, 1988-94; Chairman: Army Benevolent Fund, Scotland, since 1988, Leonard Cheshire Foundation, SW Scotland; Member, Committee, Automobile Association, since 1990; Member, British Olympic equestrian team (three-day event), 1960. Recreations: riding; country sports; country life; reading. Address: (h.) Newbarns, Dalbeattie, Kirkcudbrightshire DG5 4PY; T.-01556 630227.

Ashcroft, Professor Brian Kemp, BA (Hons), MA. Director, Fraser of Allander Institute, Strathclyde University, since 1989; Member, Secretary of State's Panel of Economic Consultants, since 1991; Member, Northern Ireland Economic Council, since 1995; b. 5.3.47, Stockton-on-Tees; m., Janet; 1 s.; 2 d. Educ. Stockton Grammar School; Lancaster University. Rock musician, 1962-65; Construction Industry: labourer, clerk, office manager, 1965-70; Lecturer, Glasgow Polytechnic, 1974-76; Strathclyde University: Lecturer/Senior Lecturer, 1976-89, Research Director, Fraser of Allander Institute, 1989. Publications: over 30 academic papers/books. Recreations: photography; jogging; trying to hide his English origins. Address: (b.) 100 Cathedral Street, Glasgow G4 0LN; T.-0141-552 4400.

Asher, Catherine Archibald, OBE, DUniv, BA, RGN, SCM, RNT. Chairman, National Board for Nursing, Midwifery and Health Visiting for Scotland, 1982-95; b. 6.7.33, Edinburgh. Educ. Woodside School, Glasgow; Edinburgh University; Open University. Ward Sister, Glasgow Royal Infirmary, 1956-61; Nurse Teacher, Senior Tutor, Principal Nursing Officer (Teaching), Glasgow Royal Infirmary School of Nursing, 1963-74; Director of Nurse Education, Glasgow Eastern College of Nursing and Midwifery, 1974-91; Acting Principal, Glasgow College of Nursing and Midwifery, 1991-95; Governor, University of Paisley, since 1996. Recreations: gardening; golf; swimming. Address: (h.) 68 Fifth Avenue, Glasgow G12 0AT; T.-0141-339 5072.

Asher, Professor R. E., BA, PhD, DLitt, FRSE, FRAS. Professor of Linguistics, Edinburgh University, 1977-93, Professor Emeritus and Honorary Fellow, Faculty of Arts, since 1993; b. 23.7.26, Gringley-on-the-Hill, Nottinghamshire. Educ. King Edward VI Grammar School,

Retford; University College, London; University of London; University of Edinburgh. Assistant, Department of French, University College, London, 1951-53; Lecturer in Linguistics, then Lecturer in Tamil, School of Oriental and African Studies, London, 1953-65; joined Department of Linguistics, Edinburgh University, 1965; Dean, Faculty of Arts, 1986-89; Member, University Court, 1989-92; Vice-Principal, 1990-93; Curator of Patronage, 1991-93; Director, Centre for Speech Technology Research, 1994. Visiting appointments: Visiting Professor of Linguistics, University of Illinois, Urbana-Champaign, 1967; Visiting Professor of Tamil and Malayalam, Michigan State University, 1968; Visiting Professor of Linguistics, University of Minnesota, 1969; Chaire des Professeurs Etrangers, Collège de France, 1970; Subrahmaniya Bharati Fellow, Tamil University, Thanjavur, 1984-85; Visiting Professor, International Christian University, Tokyo, 1994-95; first occupant of Vaikom Muhammed Basheer Chair, Mahatma Gandhi University, Kottayam, Kerala, 1995-96. Medal, Collège de France, Paris, 1970; Gold Medal, Kerala Sahitya Akademi, India, 1983. Publications: A Tamil Prose Reader, 1971; Some Landmarks in the History of Tamil Prose, 1973; Me Grandad 'ad an Elephant! (translation), 1980; Towards a History of Phonetics (Co-Editor), 1981; Tamil, 1982; Studies on Malayalam Language and Literature, 1989; National Myths in Renaissance France: Francus, Samothes and the Druids, 1993; Scavenger's Son (translation), 1993; Atlas of the World's Languages (Co-Editor), 1994; Encyclopedia of Language and Linguistics (Editor-in-Chief), 1994; Concise History of the Language Sciences: from the Sumerians to the Cognitivists (Co-Editor), 1995; Malayalam, 1997; The Novels and Stories of Vaikom Muhammed Basheer, 1997. Address: (b.) Department of Linguistics, University of Edinburgh, Adam Ferguson Building, Edinburgh EH8 9LL; T.-0131-650 3484.

Ashmore, Fionna Margaret, BA (Hons), FSA, FSAScot. Director, Society of Antiquaries of Scotland, since 1992; b. 21.5.50, London; m., P.J. Ashmore; 2 s.; 1 d. Educ. Oporto British School, Portugal; Convent of the Sacred Heart, Tunbridge Wells; University College, Cardiff; Glasgow University. Research on Portuguese Iron Age; archaeological indexer; Assistant Editor, Proceedings of the Society of Antiquaries of Scotland, 1978-90; Assistant Secretary, Cockburn Association, 1990-92. Recreations: reading; walking; visiting buildings and archaeological sites. Address: (b.) National Museums of Scotland, Chambers Street, Edinburgh EH1 1JF; T.-0131-225 7534.

Ashworth, Bryan, MA, MD, FRCP(Lond), FRCP(Edin). Honorary Librarian, Royal College of Physicians of Edinburgh, 1982-91; Consultant Neurologist, Royal Infirmary and Western General Hospital, Edinburgh, and Senior Lecturer in Medical Neurology, Edinburgh University, 1971-92; b. 5.5.29, Oundle, Northants. Educ. Laxton School; Oundle School; St. Andrews University. National Service, Captain RAMC, Northern Nigeria, 1953-55; junior hospital posts, Manchester and Bristol; Wellcome-Swedish Travelling Research Fellow, Karolinska Hospital, Stockholm, 1965-66; Lecturer in Clinical Neurology, Manchester University, and Honorary Consultant Physician, Manchester Royal Infirmary, 1967-71; Chairman and Director (non-executive), Robert Bailey and Son, PLC, Stockport, since 1978. Publications: Clinical Neuro-ophthalmology, 2nd edition, 1981; Management of Neurological Disorders, 2nd edition, 1985; The Bramwells of Edinburgh, 1986. Recreations: writing; walking. Address: (h.) 13/5 Eildon Terrace, Edinburgh EH3 5NL; T.-0131-556 0547.

Ashworth, John Brian, OBE, FCA, CBIM. Former Vice Chairman, Seagram Distillers PLC (Managing Director, Chivas Brothers Ltd., 1974-93, and Seagram Distillers PLC, 1984-93); Chairman, Renfrewshire Enterprise Ltd.;

Director, Scotch Whisky Heritage Centre Ltd; b. 2.9.36, Wakefield; m., Valerie; 2 s.; 1 d. Educ. Ackworth School; British College of Accountancy. Articled chartered accountancy, Leeds; Accountant, John Smiths Tadcaster Brewery Co. Ltd.; Commercial Director, Shaw Carpet Co. Ltd.; Founder/Managing Director, Crimpfil Ltd. Governor, Paisley University; Master, Keepers of the Quaich. Recreations: golf; travel. Address: (b.) Woodside, Upper Colquhoun Street, Helensburgh; T.-01436 676050.

Atherton, Brian John, MCommH, FRSA, MMS, AHRIM, MIMgt. General Manager, Shetland Health Board, since 1990; b. 27.1.44, York; m., Margaret; 2 s. Educ. King's School, Pontefract; University of Liverpool. Civil Servant, 1966-71; various NHS posts, including District Planning Officer, Southmead Health Authority, 1983-86, General Administrator, Tayside Health Board, 1986-90. Trustee, Shetland Welfare Trust. Recreations: sailing; photography. Address: (b.) Brevik House, South Road, Lerwick ZE1 0RB; T.-01595 743062.

Atkinson, Professor David, BSc, PhD, FIBiol, CBiol, MIEEM, FRSA, MIPSS. Vice Principal (R. & D.), Scottish Agricultural College; b. 12.9.44, Blyth; m., Elisabeth Ann Cocks; 1 s.; 2 d. Educ. Newlands County Secondary Modern School; Hull University; Newcastle-upon-Tyne University. East Malling Research Station, Maidstone, 1969-85; Macaulay Institute for Soil Research, 1985-87; Macaulay Land Use Research Institute, 1987-88; Professor of Agriculture, Aberdeen University, and Head, Land Resources Department, Scottish Agricultural College, 1988-93; former Deputy Principal (R. &D.) and Dean, Edinburgh Centre, Scottish Agricultural College. Individual Member, BCPC Council, since 1994; Member, IEEM Council, since 1992. Recreations: music; reading thrillers; quotations. Address: (b.) SAC, West Mains Road, Edinburgh EH9 3JG.

Atkinson, Professor Michael David, MA, DPhil. Professor of Computational Science, St. Andrews University, since 1992; b. 4.5.46, Leeds; m., Helen Lawton Smith; 2 s.; 2 d. Educ. Leeds Grammar School; Queen's College, Oxford. Lecturer, University College, Cardiff, 1970-82; Professor, Carleton University, Ottawa, 1982-92. Recreations: bridge; walking; music. Address: 146 North Street, St. Andrews KY16 9AF; T.-01334 478113.

Atkinson, Norman Keir, DipEd, FMA, AMA, FSA(Scot). Vice-Chair, Scottish Museums Council, since 1993; Head of Support Services, Cultural Services, Angus Council, since 1996; b. 8.1.50, Arbroath; m., Noreen; 1 s; 1 d. Educ. Arbroath High; Dundee College of Education; Leicester University. Teacher, Angus County Council, 1972-75; Assistant Keeper, then Acting Keeper, Extension Services, Dundee Museum, 1975-77; District Curator, Angus District Council, 1977-96. Member, Heritage Committee, Society of Antiquaries of Scotland; Past President, Scottish Museums Federation. Recreations: football; archaeology; wildlife. Address: (b.) County Buildings, Forfar DD8 3WF; T.-01307 461460.

Atkinson, Valerie, MA (Hons). Deputy Head, News and Current Affairs, BBC Scotland, since 1997; b. 28.12.44, Glasgow; m., Ian Atkinson; 1 s.; 1 d. Educ. Hillhead High School, Glasgow; University of Glasgow. BBC Scotland: Researcher, Radio Reporter, TV Producer, Deputy Editor, News and Current Affairs, 1988-94, Editor, Current Affairs, 1995-97. Awards: BAFTA Scotland, 1993; ISDD National Television Award, 1993; Industrial Society, 1994. Address: (b.) BBC Current Affairs, Queen Margaret Drive, Glasgow G12 8DG.

Atwell, Brian Harvey. Chair, Marriage Counselling Scotland, since 1994; a Director, Confederation of Scottish Counselling Agencies, since 1995; Vice Convenor, Marriage Counselling Dumfries and Galloway, since 1994;

b. 19.9.39, Glasgow; m., Ann Ramsay; 2 d. Educ. Trinity Academy, Edinburgh. Career civil servant, 1958-94; Industrial Counsellor, Forestry Commission, 1981-89; Marriage Counsellor, since 1977; Trainer, Scottish Association of Counselling, 1979-83; Member, Civil Service Training Advisory Committee, 1982-88; Trustee, Sutherland Trust, since 1997. Recreations: rugby football; jazz music; fly fishing; sailing. Address: (h.) Bartons House, Lockerbie Road, Dumfries DG1 3PG.

Audain, Irene, MA (Hons), DipInfoScience. National Development Officer, Scottish Out of School Care Network, since 1993; b. 10.7.56, Glasgow. Educ. University of Glasgow; University of Strathclyde. Has worked in voluntary sector for 20 years, developing childcare, community development work, campaigning on women's issues, housing rights and children's rights. Tutor in Women's Self-Defence and Adult Literacy; Youth Leader; Board Member: Scottish Childminding Association, Meadowside and Thornwood Housing Association. Recreations: learning British sign language; travel. Address: (b.) Floor 9, Fleming House, 134 Renfrew Street, Glasgow G3 6ST; T.-0141-331 1301.

Austin, Professor Brian, BSc, PhD, DSc, FRSA. Professor, Department of Biological Sciences, Heriot-Watt University; b. 5.8.51, Barnet; m., Dawn Amy; 1 d. Educ. Mount Grace School, Potters Bar; University of Newcastle-upon-Tyne. Research Associate, 1977-78; Senior Scientific Officer, 1978-84; Lecturer, 1984-89; Reader, 1989-92. Recreations: reading; writing; walking. Address: (b.) Heriot-Watt University, Riccarton, Edinburgh EH14 4AS; T. 0131-451 3452.

Austin, Juliet Leathes, BA (Hons). Headmistress, Kilgraston School, since 1993; b. 22.4.44, Reading; m., Anthony James Kirkpatrick Austin; 1 d. Educ. Downe House; Birmingham University. Downe House School, 1972-82, latterly as Head of English; Headmistress, Combe Bank School, 1982-93. Recreations: sailing; walking; painting. Address: (b.) Kilgraston School, Bridge of Earn, Perth PH2 9BQ; T.-01738 812257.

Axford, Nicola Dawn, BA (Hons). General Manager, Royal Lyceum Theatre Company, since 1995; b. 17.10.60, London; m., Prof. Ian Brown. Educ. Bradford University. Director, Big Bird Music Theatre, 1982-86; Administrator, Major Road Theatre Company, 1986-87; Drama Finance Officer, Arts Council of Great Britain, 1987-91; Business Manager, PW Productions Ltd., 1991-92; Administrator, Manchester City of Drama 1994 Ltd., 1993-94. Director: Royal Lyceum Theatre, Major Road Theatre Company; Member, Drama Panel, Scottish Arts Council, since 1997. Address: (h.) 30 Haddington Place, Edinburgh EH7 4AG; T.-0131-556 3987.

B

Bader, Douglas, MA, FRSA, FIL. Rector, Perth Grammar School, since 1985; b. 22.11.41, Stirling; m., May Heather; 3 s. Educ. Larbert High School. Teacher of Modern Languages, High School of Glasgow, 1965-69; Principal Assistant, then Principal Teacher, Alloa Academy, 1969-74; Assistant Rector, Forfar Academy, 1974-79; Depute Rector, Montrose Academy, 1979-85. Member, Headteachers' Association of Scotland. Recreations: singing; basketball; canoeing. Address: (b.) Perth Grammar School, Gowans Terrace, Perth PH1 5AZ; T.-01738 620071.

Bagnall, John Michael, MA (Cantab), DipLib, MIInfSci. University Librarian, Dundee University, since 1987; b. 22.4.45, South Yorkshire. Educ. Mexborough Grammar School; Sidney Sussex College, Cambridge. Diploma in Librarianship, University College, London; Assistant Librarian and Sub-Librarian, Newcastle upon Tyne University. Recreations: music; bird-watching; languages. Address: University Library, Dundee DD1 4HN; T.-01382 344082.

Baikie, Fiona M., BA (Hons), FRSA, MIM. Principal and Chief Executive, Edinburgh's Telford College, since 1996; b. 15.11.44, Leicester; m., Jim (musician). Educ. John Neilson Institute, Paisley; Strathclyde University; Open University. Advertising and publishing assistant, 1965-69; Lecturer, then Senior Lecturer, Telford College, 1969-80; Head, Department of Commerce, Ayr College, 1980-82, Head, Department of Business Studies, 1982-88; Edinburgh's Telford College: Assistant Principal 1988-94, Vice Principal, 1994-96. Member, Board of Directors, Edinburgh Compact; Member, National Art Collections Fund. Recreations: languages and travel; collecting first editions; art. Address: (b.) Crewe Toll, Edinburgh EH4 2NZ; T.-0131-332 2491.

Bailey, Captain Ronald Richard. Master Mariner; Harbour Master, Clydeport, since 1997; b. 22.4.54, Guildford; m., Deborah; 2 s. Educ. London Nautical School. Merchant Navy Officer, Mobil Shipping Company and Maersk Line, 1971-84; Assistant Harbour Master, then Harbour Master, Manchester Ship Canal, 1984-96. Former Director, Walk the Plank Charity. Recreations: golf; skiing; walking; travel. Address: (b.) Clydeport Operations Limited, Estuary Control, Campbell Street, Greenock PA16 8AW; T.-01475 726221.

Baillie, Ian David Hunter, CBE, CQSW. Director of Social Work, Church of Scotland Board of Social Responsibility, since 1990; Director, Social Care Association (Education), since 1987; Auxiliary Minister, United Reformed Church; b. 18.12.40, Dundee; m., Margaret MacCallum McFarlane; 3 d. Educ. Hutchesons Boys Grammar School. Eight years in life assurance; 30 years, to date, in social work; Member, Executive, International Christian Federation for Prevention of Alcoholism and Drug Addiction. Recreations: sport (watching); reading. Address: (b.) Charis House, 47 Milton Road East, Edinburgh EH15 2SR; T.-0131-657 2000.

Baillie, Professor John, MA, CA. Visiting Professor of Accountancy, Heriot-Watt University, Edinburgh, since 1989; Johnstone-Smith Professor of Accountancy, Glasgow University, 1983-88; Partner, Scott-Moncrieff Downie Wilson, since 1993; Partner, KPMG, 1978-92; b. 7.10.44; m., Annette Alexander; 1 s.; 1 d. Educ. Whitehill School. Convenor, Research Committee, Institute of Chartered Accountants of Scotland; member, various technical and professional affairs committees, Institute of Chartered Accountants of Scotland. Recreations: keeping fit; reading;

music; golf. Address: (h.) The Glen, Glencairn Road, Kilmacolm, Renfrewshire; T.-Kilmacolm 3254.

Baillie, William James Laidlaw, PRSA, HRA, PPRSW, RGI, HRHA, HRWA, HFRBS, HBWS, HSSA, DAEdin, DLitt. President, Royal Scottish Academy, since 1990; professional painter, since 1950; b. 19.4.23, Edinburgh; m. Helen Gillon; 1 s.; 2 d. Educ. Dunfermline High School; Edinburgh College of Art. Army Service (mainly Far East) 1942-47; Lecturer/Senior Lecturer in Drawing and Painting, Edinburgh College of Art, 1960-88; President, Royal Scottish Society of Painters in Water Colours, 1974-88; Royal Scottish Academy: Associate, 1968, Academician, 1979, Treasurer, 1980-90; 25 solo exhibitions in UK and abroad. Awards: 1980 EIS Award RSA, Cargill Award RGI, 1989 May Marshall Brown Award RSW, Sir William Gillies Award RSW; DLitt, Heriot Watt University, 1997. Recreations: music; travel. Address: 6A Esslemont Road, Edinburgh EH16 5PX; T.-0131-667 1538.

Bain, Aly. Fiddler; b. 1945, Lerwick. Co-founder, Boys of the Lough, 1972; Soloist; TV and radio anchorman.

Bain, Professor Andrew David, OBE, FRSE. Visiting Professor, Glasgow University, since 1991; Board Member, Scottish Enterprise, since 1991; Economic Consultant, since 1991; b. 21.3.36, Glasgow; m., Eleanor Riches; 3 s. Educ. Glasgow Academy; Cambridge University. Various posts, Cambridge University, 1959-67; Professor of Economics: Stirling University, 1967-77, Strathclyde University, 1977-84; Group Economic Advisor, Midland Bank, 1984-90. Member: Committee to Review the Functioning of Financial Institutions, 1977-80, Monopolies and Mergers Commission, 1980-81; Member, TEC National Council, 1994-97. Publications: The Control of the Money Supply, 1970; The Economics of the Financial System (2nd Edition), 1992. Address: (b.) Department of Economics, Glasgow University, Glasgow G12 8RT; T.-0141-330 6866.

Bain, Iain Andrew, MA. Editor and Proprietor, The Nairnshire Telegraph, since 1987; b. 25.2.49, Nairn; m., Maureen Beattie; 3 d. Educ. Nairn Academy; Aberdeen University. Joined The Geographical Magazine, 1974, Editor, 1981-87. Recreations: reading; writing; photography; golf. Address: (b.) 10 Leopold Street, Nairn IV12 4BG; T.-01667 453258.

Bain, Professor John, MD, FRCGP. Professor of General Practice, University of Dundee, since 1992; b. 18.8.40, Aberdeen. Educ. Inverurie Academy; University of Aberdeen. Principal in General Practice, Livingston; Professor of Primary Medical Care, University of Southampton. Chairman, Association of University Departments of General Practice; Adviser in Primary Care Research, Chief Scientist's Office, Scottish Office. Recreations: golf; hill-walking; photography. Address: (b.) Tayside Centre for General Practice, Kirsty Semple Way, Dundee DD2 4AD; T.-01382 632771.

Baird, Professor David Tennent, BA (Cantab), MB, ChB, DSc, FRCP Edin, FRCOG, FRS(Ed). Medical Research Council Professor of Reproductive Endocrinology, Edinburgh University, since 1985; Consultant Obstetrician and Gynaecologist, Simpson Memorial Maternity Pavilion, Edinburgh Royal Infirmary, since 1970; b. 13.3.35, Glasgow; m., Frances Lichtveld (m. dissolved); 2 s. Educ. Aberdeen Grammar School; Aberdeen University; Trinity College, Cambridge; Edinburgh University. After clinical training in endocrinology as well as obstetrics, spent three years (1965-68) as an MRC travelling Research Fellow at Worcester Foundation for Experimental Biology, Shrewsbury, Mass., USA, conducting research on reproductive endocrinology; Deputy Director, MRC Unit of Reproductive Biology, Edinburgh, 1972-77; Professor of Obstetrics and Gynaecology, Edinburgh University, 1977-

85; served on a number of national and international committees. Publications: four books on reproduction. Recreations: ski mountaineering; music; sport. Address: (b.) Department of Obstetrics and Gynaecology, Edinburgh University, Centre for Reproductive Biology, 37 Chalmers Street, Edinburgh EH3 9EW; T.-0131-229 2575.

Baird, Sheriff John A., LLB (Hons). Floating Sheriff based at Glasgow. Address: (b.): Sheriff Court House, 1 Carlton Place, Glasgow G5 9DA.

Baird, John Alexander, MD, FRCPsych, DCH. Consultant Forensic Psychiatrist, Glasgow, since 1993; b. 28.8.47, Edinburgh; m., Ann Easson; 3 s. Educ. Daniel Stewart's College, Edinburgh; Edinburgh University. Consultant Psychiatrist, State Hospital, Carstairs, 1981-85, Physician Superintendent, 1985-92. Standing Committee on Difficult Prisoners: Member, 1985-88, Chairman, 1988-91; Member, Parole Board for Scotland, 1992-94; Member, Advisory Committee on Prisoner Management, since 1993. Recreations: hill walking; wine; watching rugby. Address: (h.) 50 Munro Road, Jordanhill, Glasgow G13 1SF.

Baird, Robert Grant, FRSE, FCIBS, MA. Executive Director, Scottish Financial Enterprise, since 1994; b. 13.1.43, Arbroath; m., Glynne Anne Ellis; 2 s. Educ. Arbroath High School; St. Andrews University; London School of Economics. Joined Bank of England, 1965; Royal Bank of Scotland, 1970; Chief Economist, Royal Bank of Scotland Group, 1985-91; Chief Executive, Scotland Europa (Brussels), 1991-94. Recreations: writing; opera; military history; European battlefields. Address: (b.) 91 George Street, Edinburgh EH2 3ES; T.-0131-225 6990.

Baird, Susan, CBE, OStJ, JP, DUniv. Lord Provost of Glasgow, 1988-92; Convener, Economic and Industrial Development Committee, Glasgow City Council, since 1995; b. 26.5.40, Glasgow; m., George; 3 s.; 1 d. Educ. St. Mark's Secondary School, Glasgow. Worked in a city centre office; joined Labour Party, 1969; became Councillor for Parkhead, 1974; elected Bailie of the city, 1980; formerly: Convener, Manpower Committee, Vice-Convener, Parks and Recreation Committee. Address: (b.) City Chambers, George Square, Glasgow G2 1DU; T.-0141-287 2000.

Baker, Frances J.T., MBE, MSc, BA, RGN, OHNC, Cert Ed. Occupational Health Adviser, Lothian Occupational Health Research Project, since 1995; President, Federation of Occupational Health Nurses in the EU (FOHNEU); b. 29.4.34, Ayr; m., Alan; 1 s.; 1 d. Educ. Ayr Academy; London University (External); Manchester University. Casualty Staff Nurse, Ayr County Hospital; Sister, NCB, North Staffs; Lecturer, Senior Lecturer, Head of Health and Nursing Studies, Stoke on Trent Cauldon College, 1975-82; Senior Nursing Officer, British Gas Scotland, 1982-95. Member, National Board for Nursing, Midwifery and Health Visiting for Scotland, 1988-93. Publications: Role of Occupational Health Nurse in the Care of the Pregnant Woman at Work; Counselling Role of the Occupational Health Nurse. Recreations: opera and classical music; theatre; swimming; gardening; tapestry; reading. Address: (b.) Lothian Occupational Health Research Project, 26/28 Albany Street, Edinburgh EH1 3QH.

Baker, Professor Michael John, TD, BA, BSc (Econ), DipM, CertITP (Harvard), DBA (Harvard), FCIM, F.SCOTVEC, FCAM, FRSA, FRSE, FAM, FSQA. Professor of Marketing, Strathclyde University, since 1971 (Deputy Principal, 1984-91); b. 5.11.35, Debden; m., Sheila; 1 s.; 2 d. Educ. Worksop College; Bede, Gosforth and Harvey Grammar Schools; Durham University; London University; Harvard University. Royal Artillery, 1956 (2nd Lt.); Richard Thomas & Baldwins (Sales) Ltd., 1958-64; Lecturer: Medway College of Technology, 1964-66, Hull College of Technology, 1966-68; FME Fellow, Harvard Business School, 1968-71; Member, Vice-Chairman and Chairman, SCOTBEC, 1973-85; Member, SSRC Management Committee, 1976-80; Dean, Strathclyde Business School, 1978-84; Marketing Education Group: Chairman, 1974-87, President, since 1987; Chairman, Institute of Marketing, 1987; Member: SHERT, 1983-96, UGC Business and Management Sub-Committee, 1986-89, Chief Scientist's Committee, since 1985, ESRC Research Resources Board, 1994-96; Governor, CAM; Chairman: Westburn Publishers Ltd, Scottish Management Projects Ltd. Publications: Marketing New Industrial Products; Market Development; Marketing Strategy and Management (2nd edition, 1992); Marketing (6th edition, 1996); The Marketing Book (Editor, 3rd edition, 1994); The Role of Design in International Competitiveness; Marketing and Competitive Success; Dictionary of Marketing & Advertising (2nd edition); Research for Marketing; Perspectives on Marketing Management (Editor); Marketing: Theory & Practice (Editor, 3rd edition, 1996); Companion Encyclopedia of Marketing (Editor, 1995). Recreations: sailing; gardening; travel. Address: (b.) Strathclyde University, 173 Cathedral Street, Glasgow G4 ORQ; T.-0141-552 4400.

Baker, Professor Michael John, BSc (Eng), ACGI, DIC, MICE, MIStructE, FSaRS. Professor of Safety Engineering, Aberdeen University, since 1991; b. 20.10.40, Oxford; m., Margaret Eleanor Lucas; 1 s.; 1 d. Educ. Leighton Park School, Reading; Imperial College of Science, Technology and Medicine, London. Civil Engineer, N.C.B., 1962-65; Research Assistant/Fellow, Imperial College, London, 1966-77; Lecturer in Structural Engineering, 1978-86; Reader in Structural Reliability, 1986-91. Vice-Chairman, Commission I, Comite Euro-International du Beton; Member of the Plenum, International Joint Committee on Structural Safety; Member, Research Strategy Board, Offshore Safety Division, Health and Safety Executive. Recreations: mountaineering; gardening. Address: (h.) 2 Thornton Place, Watson Street, Banchory, Kincardineshire AB31 5UB; T.-01330 825495.

Baker, Ray, OBE. Director, GEC Scotland Ltd.; Chairman: Fife Enterprise, Fife Industry Council, Fife European Vocational Training Partnership, Fife Education Industry – The Fife Partnership; Fife Area Board Young Enterprise; b. 15.10.26, Nuneaton. Educ. Lanchester and Dunchurch Colleges. Joined GEC, 1950; former Chairman: Fife Health Board, Fife College of Further and Higher Education, Association of Scottish Colleges, Youth Clubs Fife. Recreations: music; reading; gardening; walking. Address: (b.) Fife Enterprise, Kingdom House, Saltire Centre, Glenrothes, Fife KY6 2AQ; T.-01334 656200.

Baker, Professor Thomas Neville, BMet, PhD, DMet, FIM, FInstP, CEng, CPhys. Professor, Department of Mechanical Engineering – Metallurgy and Engineering Materials Group, Strathclyde University; b. 11.1.34, Southport; m., Eileen May Allison. Educ. King George V School, Southport; Sheffield University. Research Metallurgist, Nelson Research Laboratories, English Electric Co., Stafford, 1958-60; Scientist, Project Leader, Tube Investments Research Laboratories, Hinxton Hall, Cambridge, 1961-64; Department of Metallurgy, Strathclyde University: SRC Research Fellow, 1965, Lecturer, 1966, Senior Lecturer, 1976, Reader, 1983, Professor, 1990, Professor of Metallurgy (1886 Chair), 1992, Vice Dean, School of Chemical and Materials Science, 1979-82, Head, Department of Metallurgy, 1986-87, Head, Division of Metallurgy and Engineering Materials, 1988-90; Committee Member, Institute of Metals, Metal Science Committee, 1980-94, Materials Technology Committee, since 1994, Process Science and Technology Committee since 1996; Chairman, Annual Conference on Metals and Materials, 1982-92. Publications: Yield, Flow and Fracture in Polycrystals (Editor), 1983; Titanium Technology in Microalloyed Steels (Editor),

1997; over 130 learned society publications. Recreations: music; literature; creating a garden. Address: (b.) Department of Mechanical Engineering, Strathclyde University, Glasgow; T.-0141-552 4400.

Baldwin, Professor Norma, BA (Hons), DipSocAdmin, MPhil. Professor of Child Care and Protection, University of Dundee, since 1995; Head, Department of Social Work, since 1996; Member, CCETSW Scottish Committee, since 1996; b. 21.5.39, Hull; 2 s. Educ. Malet Lambert, Hull; University of Manchester; London School of Economics; University of Warwick. Probation Officer, then Senior Probation Officer, Greater Manchester; Principal Officer, Warwickshire Social Services Department; Lecturer, Senior Research Fellow, Senior Lecturer, University of Warwick. Publications: The Power to Care in Children's Homes, 1990; Residents' Rights (Co-Author), 1993; Protecting Children: Promoting their Rights (Editor). Recreations: walking; gardening; theatre; music. Address: (b.) Department of Social Work, University of Dundee, Dundee DD1 4HN; T.-01382 344651.

Bale, Lesley Christine. Managing Director, Aberdeen Airport Ltd., since 1992; Director, Scottish Airports Ltd., since 1990; b. 14.4.59, Glasgow. Educ. Craigholme School, Glasgow; Strathclyde University. Deloitte Haskins & Sells (Glasgow), 1978-81; Coopers & Lybrand (Bermuda), 1981-83; Western International Financial Group (Bermuda): Vice-President, Treasurer and Director, 1983-87; Financial Controller, Prestwick Airport Ltd., 1988-90; Managing Director, Prestwick Airport Ltd., 1990-92. Alumnus of the Year, Strathclyde University, 1994; Scottish Young Business Achievement Award, 1996. Recreations: bridge; golf. Address: Aberdeen Airport Ltd., Dyce, Aberdeen AB21 7DU;T.-01224 725001.

Balekjian, Wahe Hagop, Dr (Law), Dr (pol sc), PhD. Honorary Senior Research Fellow, School of Law, Glasgow University, since 1990 (Reader in European Law, 1976-90, Head of Department, 1976-88); Visiting Titular Professor, University of Salzburg, Austria, since 1981; Titular Professor, European Faculty, Land Use Planning, Strasbourg, since 1982; Honorary Senior Research Fellow, School of Law, Glasgow University, since 1990; b. 2.10.24, Cairo; m., Eva Birgitta. Educ. College of Arts and Sciences, Cairo; Vienna University; Manchester University. Diploma, Hague Academy of International Law. Lecturer, Vienna University, 1957-73; Simon Research Fellow, Manchester University, 1963-65; Head of Department, European Studies, National Institute of Higher Education, Limerick, 1973-76. Publications: Legal Aspects of Foreign Investment in the EEC, 1967 (awarded Prize of European Communities, 1967); The Status of Unrecognised States in International Law (published in German, 1971). Recreations: hill-walking; piano playing; languages. Address: (b.) School of Law, The University, Glasgow G12 8QQ; T.-0141-339 8855, Ext. 5539.

Balfour of Burleigh, Lady (Janet Morgan), MA, DPhil, FRSAS. Writer; Company Director; b. 5.12.45, Montreal; m., Lord Balfour of Burleigh. Educ. Newbury County Girls' Grammar School; Oxford University; Sussex University; Harvard University. Member: Central Policy Review Staff, Cabinet Office, 1978-81; Board, British Council, since 1989; Special Adviser to Director-General, BBC, 1983-86; Chairman, Cable & Wireless Resource Ltd., 1993-97; Non-Executive Director: Cable & Wireless, W.H. Smith, 1989-95, Midlands Electricity, 1990-96, Scottish American Investment Co., Scottish Oriental Smaller Companies Investment Trust, The Scottish Life Assurance Company, Nuclear Generation Decommissioning Fund Ltd, New Medical Technologies plc, since 1997, Scottish Medical Research Fund; Member: Scottish Museums Council Development Resource, 1988-97, Ancient Monuments Board for Scotland, since 1990, Book Trust Scotland, since

1992, Scottish Economic Council, 1993-95; Chairman, Scotland's Book Campaign, 1994-96, Scottish Cultural Resources Access Network, since 1995; Trustee, Carnegie Endowment for the Universities of Scotland, since 1993. Publications: Diaries of a Cabinet Minister 1964-70 by Richard Crossman (4 volumes) (Editor); The Future of Broadcasting, (Co-Editor, 1982); Agatha Christie: a biography, 1984; Edwina Mountbatten: a life of her own, 1991. Recreations: music of Handel; sea bathing; gardens; ice skating out of doors.

Balfour of Burleigh, Lord. Chairman, Capella Nova; Chancellor, Stirling University; b. 6.1.27, London. Educ. Westminster School, London. Graduate Apprentice, English Electric Company, 1951; various positions in manufacturing mangement; started English Electric's manufacturing operations in India as General Manager of new company in Madras, 1957-64; returned to Liverpool as General Manager; appointed General Manager, D. Napier & Son, before leaving the company in 1968; joined Bank of Scotland as a Director, 1968; Deputy Governor, Bank of Scotland, 1977-91. Forestry Commissioner, 1971-74; Chairman: Scottish Arts Council, 1971-80, Scottish Committee, ABSA, 1988-94, United Artists Communications (Scotland) Ltd., until 1996; Director: Scottish Investment Trust plc, 1971-96, William Lawson Distillers Ltd., 1984-96, Television Educational Network, 1990-96, Edinburgh Book Festival, 1981-96 (Chairman, 1981-87); Member, British Railways (Scottish) Board, 1982-92; Treasurer: Royal Society of Edinburgh, 1989-94, Royal Scottish Corporation; President, Friends of Vellore. Recreations: woodwork; hill-climbing; music. Address: House of Lords, London SW1A 0PW.

Balfour, Alastair. Managing Director, The Insider Group, since 1993; b. 15.6.47, Edinburgh; m., Anne Johnstone (second marriage); 2 s.; 3 d. Educ. Royal High School, Edinburgh. Trained as journalist with The Scotsman, 1966-68; became Industrial Reporter in Glasgow, 1974-78; joined Daily Record as Economics Correspondent, 1978-81; Business Editor, Sunday Standard, 1981-83; co-launched Scottish Business Insider, 1984; Editor, 1986-90; Editorial Director, until 1993. Chairman, Newsco Publications Ltd., Manchester; Director, The Entrepreneurial Exchange; Member, Scottish Enterprise Business Birthrate Group. Recreations: family; sailing. Address: (b.) 43 Queensferry Street Lane, Edinburgh EH2 4PF; T.-0131 535 5555; (h.) 32 Glasgow Road, Blanefield, Stirlingshire G63 9BP; T.-01360 770750.

Balfour, 4th Earl of (Gerald Arthur James Balfour), JP; b. 23.12.25; m. Educ. Eton; HMS Conway. Member, East Lothian County Council, 1960-75; farmer. Address: (h.) The Tower, Whittingehame, Haddington.

Balfour, Ian Leslie Shaw, MA, LLB, BD, PhD, SSC, NP. Solicitor (Consultant, Balfour & Manson) since 1995; b. 16.6.32, Edinburgh; m., Joyce Margaret Ross Pryde; 3 s.; 1 d. Educ. Edinburgh Academy; Edinburgh University. Qualified as Solicitor, 1955; commissioned, RASC, 1955-57; 1959-97. Partner, then Senior Partner, Balfour & Manson; Secretary, Oliver & Son Ltd., 1959-89; Fiscal to Law Society of Scotland, since 1981. Baptist Union of Scotland: President, 1976-77, Law Agent, 1964-97, Secretary, Charlotte Baptist Chapel, Edinburgh, since 1980, Secretary, Scottish Baptist College, since 1983; Secretary, Elba Housing Society Ltd., 1969-92; Council, Society for Computers and Law, 1988-92; Director, Edinburgh Medical Missionary Society. Recreations: gardening; home computing; lay preaching. Address: (h.) 38 Murrayfield Road, Edinburgh; T.-0131-337 2880.

Balfour, Peter Edward Gerald, CBE. President, Scottish Council (Development and Industry), 1985-92 (Chairman, 1978-85); Director, Royal Bank of Scotland, 1972-90; Chairman, Charterhouse plc, 1985-91; b. 9.7.21, Woking;

m., 1, Grizelda Ogilvy, 2, Diana Wainman; 3 s.; 2 d. Educ. Eton College. Served Scots Guards, 1940-54; joined William McEwan & Co., brewers, 1954; appointed Director, 1958; Director, Scottish Brewers, 1959; Scottish and Newcastle Breweries, 1961 (Chairman and Managing Director, 1970-83); Director and Vice Chairman, RBS Group, 1978. Recreations: farming; forestry. Address: (h.) Scadlaw House, Humbie, East Lothian; T.-01875 833252.

Balfour, William Harold St. Clair. Solicitor; b. 29.8.34, Edinburgh; m., 1, Patricia Waite (m. dissolved); 1 s.; 2 d.; 2, Alice Ingsay McFarlane; 2 step. d. Educ. Hillfield, Ontario; Edinburgh Academy; Edinburgh University. Partner, Balfour & Manson, since 1962; Clerk to Admission of Notaries Public, 1971-92; Prison Visiting Committee, 1965-70; Chairman, Basic Space Dance Theatre, 1980-86; Friends of Talbot Rice Art Centre, 1982-97, Garvald Trustees, since 1980, Wellspring Management, 1990-97. Recreations: sailing; walking; wine. Address: (b.) 58 Frederick Street, Edinburgh, EH2 1LS; T.-0131 200 1200; (h.) 11 Nelson Street, Edinburgh EH3 6LF; T.-0131-556 7298.

Ball, Derek William, MB, MRCPsych. Composer; Consultant Psychiatrist; b. 30.12.49, Letterkenny, Ireland; m., Marie Knox; 1 d. Educ. Kings Hospital, Dublin; Royal Irish Academy of Music; Trinity College, Dublin. Studied composition with Dr. Archie Potter; writes chamber and orchestral music; numerous performances in Dublin; pieces performed at festivals in Paris and Bordeaux. Founder Member, Association of Young Irish Composers; Secretary/Treasurer, Scottish Society of Composers. Address: (h.) Mazagon, 4 Glen Road, Lennoxtown G65 7JX.

Ball, Geoffrey A., FCA. Chairman, CALA plc (Group Managing Director, since 1974); b. 4.8.43, Bristol; m., Mary Elizabeth; 3 s.; 1 d. Educ. Cotham Grammar School, Bristol. Former Managing Director, Greencoat Properties Ltd.; non-executive Director: Standard Life Assurance Company; Scottish Mortgage & Trust p.l.c. Recreations: golf; music. Address: 26 Hermitage Drive, Edinburgh EH10 5BT; T.-0131-535 5200.

Ball, Graham Edmund, BDS, FDS, RCS (Eng), MHSM. Consultant in Dental Public Health, Fife and Borders Health Boards, since 1995; Honorary Senior Lecturer in Dental Public Health, University of Edinburgh; b. 14.12.53; m., Carolyn Bowyer; 1 s.; 2 d. Educ. King Edward VI School, Southampton; Welsh National School of Medicine. Registrar, Oral and Maxillofacial Surgery, Portsmouth hospitals, 1979-81; Associate Specialist (part-time), Oral Surgery, Wessex Cardiothoracic Unit, 1982-84; general dental practice, 1984-88; Clinical Community Dental Officer, Orkney Health Board, 1988-91; Chief Administrative Dental Officer, Orkney Health Board, 1991-95. Recreations: sailing; walking. Address: (b.) Fife Health Board, Springfield House, Cupar, Fife; T.-01334 656200.

Ballantyne, Professor Colin Kerr, MA, MSc, PhD, FRSE, FRSA. Professor in Physical Geography, St. Andrews University, since 1994; b. 7.6.51, Glasgow; m., Rebecca Trengove. Educ. Hutchesons' Grammar School; Glasgow University; McMaster University; Edinburgh University. Lecturer in Geography, St. Andrews University, 1980-89; Senior Lecturer in Geography and Geology, 1989-94; Gordon Warwick Award, 1987; Presidents' Medal, Royal Scottish Geographical Society, 1991; Newbigin Prize, Royal Scottish Geographical Society, 1992; Scottish Science Award, Saltire Society, 1996. Publications: The Quaternary of the Isle of Skye, 1991; The Periglaciation of Great Britain, 1994. Recreations: music; travel; mountaineering; skiing; writing. Address: (h.) Birchwood, Blebo Craigs, Fife KY15 5UF; T.-01334 850567.

Ballantyne, Fiona Catherine, MA, MCIM. Network Scotland Ltd.: Director since 1991, Chairman since 1997; Member, Board, Queen Margaret College, Edinburgh, since 1995; b. 9.7.50, Bristol; m., A. Neil Ballantyne. Educ. Marr College, Troon; Edinburgh University. Former Market Researcher and Market Research Manager; Research and Planning Manager, Thistle Hotels Ltd., 1975-77; Assistant Marketing Manager, Lloyds & Scottish Finance Group, 1977-79; Scottish Development Agency: Marketing Manager, Small Business Division, 1979-84, Head of Small Business Services, 1984-88, Director, Tayside and Fife, 1988-90; Managing Director, Ballantyne Mackay Consultants, since 1990; Vice-Chair: BBC Broadcasting Council for Scotland, 1991-96, Duncan of Jordanstone College of Art, 1988-94; Director, Edinburgh Healthcare Trust, 1994-96; Member, Board, Scottish Campaign for Learning, since 1997. Recreations: walking; swimming; tapestry; painting. Address: (b.) 2-8 Millar Crescent, Edinburgh EH10 5HW; T.-0131-447 9700.

Ballantyne, Robert, MA (Hons). Assistant Editor, The Scotsman, since 1994; b. 12.4.53, Forfar; m., Aileen; 1 s. Educ. Beath Senior High School, Cowdenbeath; Edinburgh University. Journalist, Evening News, Edinburgh, 1974-79; The Times, 1979-94 (Business Editor, 1993-94). Recreations: theatre; cycling; swimming. Address: (b.) 20 North Bridge, Edinburgh EH1 1YT; T.-0131-243 3384.

Band, Thomas Mollison. Chairman: Perth Theatre Ltd., since 1995 (Director, since 1994), Andersons Enterprises Ltd., since 1994, Edinburgh Europa Ltd., since 1994, Select Line Breaks Ltd., since 1995; Governor: Edinburgh Telford College, since 1990, Queen Margaret College, since 1995; b. 28.3.34, Aberdeen; m., Jean McKenzie Brien; 1 s.; 2 d. Educ. Perth Academy. Principal, Tariff Division, Board of Trade, London, 1969-73; Director (Location of Industry), Department of Industry, Glasgow, 1973-76; Assistant Secretary: (Industrial Policy), Scottish Economic Planning Department, 1976-78, (Housing), Scottish Development Department, 1978-82, (Finance), Scottish Office, 1982-84; Director, Historic Buildings and Monuments, Scottish Development Department, 1984-87; Chief Executive, Scottish Tourist Board, 1987-94; Member, Board of Management, Perth Housing Association, since 1993. Recreations: gardening; skiing; shooting. Address: (h.) Heathfield, Pitcairngreen, Perthshire; T.-01738 583 403.

Banfill, Professor Phillip Frank Gower, BSc, PhD, CChem, FRSC. Professor of Construction Materials, Heriot-Watt University, since 1995; b. 20.3.52, Worthing; m., Patricia; 1 s.; 1 d. Educ. Lancing College; Southampton University; Liverpool University. Former Lecturer, Liverpool University. Publications: three books; 70 papers. Recreations: sailing; choral singing; bee-keeping. Address: (b.) Department of Building Engineering and Surveying, Heriot-Watt University, Riccarton, Edinburgh EH14 4AS; T.-0131-449 5111.

Banks, Iain. Novelist; b. 1954. Educ. schools in North Queensferry, Gourock, Greenock; Stirling University. Hitch-hiked through Europe, Scandinavia, Morocco, 1975, later worked for British Steel and IBM, and as a costings clerk in London. Books: The Wasp Factory, 1984; Walking on Glass, 1985; The Bridge, 1986; Consider Phlebas, 1987; Espedair Street, 1987; The Player of Games, 1988; Canal Dreams, 1989; Use of Weapons, 1990; The State of the Art, 1991; The Crow Road, 1992; Against a Dark Background, 1993; Complicity , 1993 (No. 1 bestseller in paperback); Feersum Endjinn, 1994; Whit, 1995; Excession, 1996; Song of Stone, 1997.

Banks, Professor William McKerrell, BSc, MSc, PhD, CEng, FIMechE, FIM. Professor of Advanced Materials, Strathclyde University, since 1991; Academic Director, Centre for Advanced Structural Materials; Honorary Secretary, Scottish Branch, IMechE; b. 28.3.43, Irvine; m.,

Martha Ruthven Hair; 3 s. Educ. Irvine Royal Academy; Strathclyde University. Senior Research Engineer, G. & J. Weir Ltd., 1966-70; Lecturer, Senior Lecturer, Reader, Professor, Strathclyde University, since 1970. Recreations: family; Bible teaching; gardening. Address: (h.) 19 Dunure Drive, Hamilton ML3 9EY; T.-01698 823730.

Bannister, John Roy, Clerk to the Scottish Traffic Commissioner, since 1987; b. 3.11.46, London; m., Jan; 1 s., 1 d. Educ. Edmonton County Grammar School. Department of Transport; London, 1965-72, 1984-87, Newcastle upon Tyne, 1972-83; Manager, International Road Freight Office, Newcastle upon Tyne, 1983-84. Recreations: home brewing/wine; foreign travel; railways. Address: (h.) 13 Warrender Court, North Berwick, East Lothian; T.-01620 894683.

Barbenel, Professor Joseph Cyril, BDS, BSc, MSc, PhD, LDS RCS(Eng), CBiol, FIBiol, CPhys, FInstP, CEng, FBES, FRSE. Professor, Bioengineering Unit, Strathclyde University, since 1982 (Head, Tissue Mechanics Division, since 1970); Vice-Dean (Research), Faculty of Engineering; b. 2.1.37, London; m., Lesley Mary Hyde Jowett; 2 s.; 1 d. Educ. Hackney Downs Grammar School, London; London Hospital Medical College; Queen's College, Dundee (St. Andrews University); Strathclyde University. Dental House Surgeon, London Hospital, 1960; National Service, RADC, 1960-61 (Lieutenant, 1960, Captain, 1961); general dental practice, London, 1963; student, 1963-67; Lecturer, Department of Dental Prosthetics, Dental School, Dundee, 1967-69; Senior Lecturer, Strathclyde University, 1970-82. Council Member, Institution of Physics and Engineering in Medicine and Biology; Chancellor, International Faculty for Artificial Organs. Recreations: music; theatre. Address: (b.) University of Strathclyde, Bioengineering Unit, 106 Rottenrow, Glasgow G4 ONW; T.-0141-552 4400.

Barbour, Very Rev. Robert Alexander Stewart, KCVO, MC, MA, BD, STM, DD, DipEd. Minister, Church of Scotland, since 1954; Chaplain, then Extra Chaplain to the Queen in Scotland, since 1976; b. 11.5.21, Edinburgh; m., Margaret Pigot; 3 s.; 1 d. Educ. Rugby School; Balliol College, Oxford; St. Mary's College, St. Andrews. Army (Scottish Horse), 1940-45, Territorial Army, 1947-54; Editorial Assistant, Thomas Nelson & Sons, 1948-49; Secretary, Edinburgh Christian Council for Overseas Students, 1953-55; Lecturer and Senior Lecturer in New Testament Language, Literature and Theology, New College, Edinburgh University, 1955-71; Professor of New Testament Exegesis, Aberdeen University, 1971-86; Master, Christ's College, Aberdeen, 1977-82; Prelate, Priory of Scotland, Order of St. John, 1977-93; Moderator, General Assembly of the Church of Scotland, 1979-80; Dean, Chapel Royal in Scotland, 1981-91;Honorary Secretary, Novi Testamenti Societas, 1970-77. Recreations: music; forestry; walking. Address: (h.) Old Fincastle, Pitlochry PH16 5RJ; T.-01796 473209.

Barker, Alan. Music Director, The Scottish Ballet, since 1992; b. Australia. Educ. Melbourne University. Former Musical Director, New Zealand Ballet, and Artistic Director, New Zealand Opera; former Resident Conductor, Australian Ballet, joined American Ballet Theatre, 1978, as Associate Conductor, promoted to Principal Conductor, 1980; Music Director, Pittsburgh Ballet Theatre, 1988-90; has conducted National Ballet of Canada, Royal Danish Ballet, and Birmingham Royal Ballet. Address: (b.) Scottish Ballet, 261 West Princes Street, Glasgow G4 9EE; T.-0141-331 2931.

Barker, Professor John Reginald, BSc, MSc, PhD, FBIS, FRSE. Professor of Electronics, Department of Electronics and Electrical Engineering, University of Glasgow, since 1985; b. 11.11.42, Stockport; m., Elizabeth Carol; 2 s.; 1 d. Educ. New Mills Grammar School; University of Edinburgh; University of Durham; University of Warwick. University of Warwick: SRC Personal Research Fellowship, 1969-70, Lecturer in Physics, 1970-84, Senior Lecturer, 1984-85; Affiliate Professor, Colorado State University, 1979-83; Distinguished Science Lecturer, Yale University, 1992; Irvine Lectures in Chemistry, St. Andrews, 1994; broadcasting: History of the Microchip, 1982; The Magic Micro Mission, 1983. Member, various SERC/DTI committees, 1987-93: Devices Committee, Electronic Materials Committee, National Committee for Superconductivity, Materials Commission, Molecular Electronics Committee (Chairman, 1990-93). Publications: over 160 scientific papers; Physics of Non-Linear Transport in Semi-conductors (Co-Author), 1979; Granular Nanoelectronics (Co-Author), 1991. Recreations: hill-walking; astronomy; reading; cooking. Address: (b.) Nanoelectronics Research Centre, Department of Electronics and Electrical Engineering, University of Glasgow, Glasgow G12 8QQ; T.-0141-330 5221.

Barker, Ralph Fraser, MA (Hons), DipEd. Rector, Alloa Academy, since 1995; b. 10.7.51, Edinburgh; m., Suzanne; 2 s.; 1 d. Educ. Royal High School, Edinburgh; Edinburgh University. Teacher of Mathematics, then Assistant Principal Teacher, Royal High School, 1974-81; Principal Teacher, Knox Academy, 1981-84; Assistant Head Teacher, then Depute Head Teacher, Queensferry High School, 1984-94. Recreation: public transport, especially buses. Address: (b.) Claremont, Alloa FK10 2EQ; T.-01259 214979.

Barlow, Professor (Arthur) John, PhD, DIC, BSc, ACGI, MIEE, CEng. Professor of Electronics, Glasgow University; b. 17.3.34, Nottinghamshire; m., Alma Marshall; 1 s.; 1 d. Educ. Nottingham High School; Imperial College. Turner and Newall Research Fellow, Imperial College, 1958-61; Glasgow University: Lecturer, 1961-66, Senior Lecturer, 1966-68, Reader, 1968-75. Address: (h.) 5 Auchencruive, Milngavie, Glasgow G62 6EE.

Barnet, James Paul, MA, LLB. Partner, Macbeth Currie & Co., Solicitors, since 1965; Honorary Sheriff, Tayside Central and Fife, at Dunfermline; former Dean, Dunfermline District Society of Solicitors; b. 20.7.37, Darlington; m., Margaret Smart; 4 s. Educ. Dunfermline High School; Edinburgh University. Admitted as Solicitor, 1961. Council Member, Law Society of Scotland, 1985-88; Local Secretary, Scottish Garden City Housing Society Ltd.; Captain, Scottish Universities Golfing Society, 1980-81; President, Dunfermline Rotary Club, 1985-86. Recreations: golf; reading; quoting Dr. Johnson. Address: (h.) Bonnyton House, Dunfermline, Fife KY12 9HT; T.-Dunfermline 731011.

Barnett, Robert Hall, FIMI. Managing Director, Barnetts Motor Group Ltd, since 1965; b. 22.1.36, Dundee; m., Alison; 1 s.; 1 d. Educ. Morgan Academy. Dundee and President, Tayside Chamber of Commerce, 1992-93; President, Scottish Motor Trade Association, 1982-84. Recreations: golf; sailing; motorcycling. Address: (b.) Riverside Drive, Dundee; T.-01382 668622.

Barnett, Robert James Charles, LLB (Hons). Director of Administration and Legal Services and Depute Chief Executive, Western Isles Council, since 1986; Returning Officer, Western Isles Area, since 1986; b. 10.5.53, Birmingham; m., Christine Mary; 1 s.; 1 d. Educ. Homelands Technical High School, Torquay; Bristol Polytechnic; Guildford College of Law. Served articles with Torbay Borough Council, 1975-77; qualified as Solicitor, 1978; Assistant Solicitor, then Senior Assistant, then Principal Assistant Solicitor, Plymouth City Council, 1978-86. Recreations: music; reading; walking; family. Address:

(b.) Western Isles Council, Council Offices, Sandwick Road, Stornoway, Isle of Lewis HS1 2BW; T.-01851 703773, Ext. 200.

Barr, Rev. David, MA, BD. Hospital Chaplain, Glasgow Royal Infirmary and Canniesburn Hospital, 1962-84; b. 14.6.14, Airdrie. Educ. Airdrie Academy; Glasgow University and Trinity College. Student Assistant, New Monkland Parish Church, 1935-37; Minister, Kirkintilloch South Church, 1938-42; part-time Hospital Chaplain, Broomhill and Lanfine Hospitals; Minister, St. Mary's, Partick, 1942-62; part-time Hospital Chaplain, Glasgow Western Infirmary, 1960-62. Moderator, Glasgow Presbytery, 1969-70; Chairman, National Association of Whole-Time Hospital Chaplains for England, Scotland and Wales, 1978-82. Recreations: motoring; reading; topography; ecclesiology; medicine. Address: (h.) 17 Victoria Park Gardens South, Broomhill, Glasgow G11 7BX; T.-0141-339 5364.

Barr, David George Dryburgh, MB, ChB, FRCPEd, DCH. Clinical Director, Royal Hospital for Sick Children, Edinburgh; Consultant Paediatrician, Lothian Health Board, since 1971; part-time Senior Lecturer, Department of Child Life and Health, Edinburgh University, since 1977; b. 14.2.36, Edinburgh; m., Anna Blair; 2 s.; 1 d. Educ. Daniel Stewart's College, Edinburgh; Edinburgh University. Senior Registrar, Royal Hospital for Sick Children, Edinburgh, 1965-69; Research Fellow, children's hospital, Zurich, Switzerland, 1969-70; Consultant Paediatrician, Edinburgh Northern and West Fife Hospitals, 1971-77; seconded to Ministry of Health and University of Riyadh, Saudi Arabia, 1980-83. Address: (b.) Royal Hospital for Sick Children, Sciennes Road, Edinburgh.

Barr, Sheriff Kenneth Glen, MA, LLB. Sheriff of South Strathclyde, Dumfries and Galloway, at Dumfries, since 1976; b. 20.1.41, Glasgow. Educ. Royal High School; Edinburgh University. Admitted Faculty of Advocates, 1964. Address: (b.) Sheriff's Chambers, Sheriff Court House, Dumfries DG1 2AN.

Barr, William James, OBE, CEng, FICE, FIMgt. Chairman and Chief Executive, Barr Holdings Limited (which includes Barr Limited, W. & J. Barr and Sons (Scotland) Limited, Alpha Crane Limited, Alpha Services Limited, Alpha Access Limited, Econospace Limited, Barr Quarries Limited, Barmix Concrete, Barr Construction, Solway Engineers, Solway Precast, Solway Crane, Barr Homes, Barr Environmental, Barr Technical Services, Barr Construction Services); Managing Director, Barr Leisure Limited; b. 12.3.39, Ayr; m., Marlean Ramage; 2 s.; 1 d. Educ. Girvan High School; Glasgow University; Paisley University. Chairman, Freeport (Scotland) Ltd; Chairman, Thomas Telford Services Ltd.; Member, Council and Executive, Institution of Civil Engineers; former Chairman, Glasgow and West of Scotland Association, Institution of Civil Engineers; Visiting Professor, Strathclyde University; former Chairman, Craigie College of Education; Chairman, Ayr College Board; Member, Court, Paisley University; Chairman, Ayr Locality Enterprise and Resources Trust; Member, Board, Business Enterprise Scotland; Vice-Chairman, Ayrshire Hospice; Founder Chairman, Laigh Milton Viaduct Conservation Project; former Vice-Chairman, Enterprise Ayrshire; Past President, Ayr Chamber of Commerce; Board Member, Ayrshire Chamber of Commerce and Industry; Past President, Association for Science and Education; Board Member, Ice Hockey Superleague; Member, AME Board. Recreations: the works of Robert Burns and Thomas Telford; walking; reading. Address: (h.) Harkieston, Maybole, Ayrshire, KA19 7LP; T.-01655 883123; (b.) Heathfield, Ayr KA8 9SL; T.-01292 281311.

Barrett, Professor Ann, MB, BS, FRCR, FRCP, MD. Professor of Radiation Oncology, Glasgow University,

since 1986; Consultant, Royal Hospital for Sick Children, since 1986; President, European Society for Therapeutic Radiation Oncology, until 1999; b. 27.2.43, London; m., Adrian Bell; 1 s.; 2 d. Educ. Queen Elizabeth's Grammar School; St. Bartholomew's Hospital. Formerly Consultant in Radiotherapy and Oncology, Royal Marsden Hospital; Director, Beatson Oncology Centre, Glasgow, 1986-91; President, Scottish Radiological Society, 1995-97; Chairman, Scottish Standing Committee, RCR, 1994-97; Associate Editor, Medical and Paediatric Oncology. Former Member: MRC Molecular and Cell Medicine Board, Council, Royal College of Radiologists. Publications: Cancer in Childhood (Co-editor); Practical Radiotherapy Planning (Co-author). Recreations: walking; music; novels. Address: (b.) Beatson Oncology Centre, Western Infirmary, Glasgow; T.-0141-339 8822.

Barrie, Lesley, DPA, MHSM, DipHSM, MBIM. General Manager and Member, Tayside Health Board, since 1993; b. 20.9.44, Glasgow. Educ. Glasgow High School for Girls; Glasgow University. NHS administrative trainee, 1963-66; hospital management, 1966-77; District General Manager: Inverclyde District, 1977-81, Glasgow South East, 1981-83; Director Administrative Services, Glasgow Royal Infirmary, Glasgow Royal Maternity Hospital, Glasgow Dental Hospital, 1983-87; Unit General Manager, Stirling Royal Infirmary, 1987-91; General Manager and Member, Forth Valley Health Board, 1991-93. Hon. Lecturer, Dundee University; Children's Panellist, 1975-79; Chairman, Social Security Appeal Tribunals, 1978-90; Table Tennis Internationalist for Scotland, 1963-70; formerly National and International Secretary, Scottish Table Tennis Association. Recreations: table tennis; badminton; reading. Address: (b.) Gairdrum House, by Balbeggie, Perthshire.

Barron, Professor Laurence David, DPhil, BSc, MInstP, FRSE. Professor of Chemistry, Glasgow University, since 1984; b. 12.2.44, Southampton; m., Sharon Aviva Wolf; 1 s.; 1 d. Educ. King Edward VI Grammar School, Southampton; Northern Polytechnic, London; Lincoln College, Oxford. Post-doctoral research, Cambridge University, 1969-75; Ramsay Memorial Fellow, 1974-75; Glasgow University: Lecturer in Chemistry, 1975-80, Reader, 1980-84. Corday-Morgan Medal, Chemical Society, 1977; G.M.J. Schmidt Memorial Lecturer, Weizmann Institute of Science, 1984; F.L. Conover Memorial Lecturer, Vanderbilt University, 1987; Sir Harold Thompson Award, 1992; EPSRC Senior Fellow, 1995-2000. Publication: Molecular Light Scattering and Optical Activity, 1982. Recreations: water-colour painting; walking; music; radio-controlled model aircraft. Address: (b.) Chemistry Department, The University, Glasgow G12 8QQ; T.-0141-339 8855.

Barrow, Professor Geoffrey Wallis Steuart, MA (Hons), BLitt, DLitt, FBA, FRSE, FSA, FSA Scot, FRHistS, Hon. DLitt (Glasgow and Newcastle upon Tyne). Sir William Fraser Professor of Scottish History and Palaeography, Edinburgh University, 1979-92; b. 28.11.24, Headingley, Leeds; m., Heather Elizabeth Agnes Lownie; 1 s.; 1 d. Educ. St. Edward's School, Oxford; Inverness Royal Academy; St. Andrews University; Pembroke College, Oxford. Royal Navy and RNVR (Sub-Lieutenant), 1943-46; Lecturer in History, University College, London, 1950-61; Professor of Medieval History, Newcastle-upon-Tyne University, 1961-74; Professor of Scottish History, St. Andrews University, 1974-79. Member, Royal Commission on Historical Manuscripts, 1984-90; Royal Historical Society, Council, 1963-74; Joint Literary Director, 1964-74; Vice President, 1982-86; former Chairman: Council, Scottish History Society (President, 1973-77); President: Saltire Society, 1987-90, Scottish Record Society, 1993-97; Vice-President, Commission Internationale de Diplomatique. Publications: Feudal Britain, 1956; Acts of Malcolm IV, 1960; Robert Bruce, 1965 and 1988; Acts of

William I, 1971; The Kingdom of the Scots, 1973; The Scottish Tradition (Editor), 1974; The Anglo-Norman Era in Scottish History, 1980; Kingship and Unity: Scotland 1000-1306, 1981; Scotland and its neighbours, 1992. Recreations: hill-walking; visiting graveyards; travel. Address: (h.) 12A Lauder Road, Edinburgh EH9 2EL; T.-0131-668 2173.

Barry, Stephen. Chief Executive and General Manager, Edinburgh Festival Theatre, since 1997; b. 4.7.45, London; m., Jacqueline; 1 s.; 1 d. Educ. Marlborough College; University of Manchester. Trainee Director, Mermaid Theatre, 1968-69; Assistant Director, Yvonne Arnaud Theatre, 1969-71; Staff Producer, National Theatre, 1971-72; Director and Researcher, Cheltenham Everyman and Granada Television, 1972-74; Artistic Director: Harrogate Theatre, 1974-77, Perth, W. Australia, 1977-82, Redgrave Theatre, Farnham, 1982-86; Theatre Director, Theatre Royal, Bath, 1986-90. Recreations: reading; walking. Address: (b.) 13/29 Nicolson Street, Edinburgh EH8 9FT; T.-0131-662 1112.

Bartholomew, John Christopher, MA, FRSE, FRSGS, FRGS. Editorial Director, John Bartholomew & Son Ltd., 1960-84; b. 15.1.23, Edinburgh; m., Genevieve Achard-James; 5 s. Educ. Edinburgh Academy; Gordonstoun; Edinburgh University. Military Service, Royal Engineers (Survey), Middle East and East Africa, 1943-47; rejoined family firm on graduation, 1950, to share editorial responsibility for The Times Atlas of the World, mid-century edition and all subsequent editions, 1967-82, and other atlases. President, British Cartographic Society, 1970-71; Vice-President, International Cartographic Association, 1972-80; President, Royal Scottish Geographical Society, 1987-93; President, Edinburgh University Graduates' Association, 1980-82; Director, Scottish Rights of Way Society, since 1984. Recreations: nature pursuits; photography. Address: (h.) 26 Braid Farm Road, Edinburgh EH10 6LF; T.-0131-447 2655.

Bartlett, Professor Christopher John, BA, PhD, FRHistS, FRSE. Emeritus Professor of International History, Dundee University (Head of Modern History Department, 1983-88); Member, Scottish Examination Board; b. 12.10.31, Bournemouth; m., Shirley Maureen Briggs; 3 s. Educ. Queen Elizabeth's Grammar School, Wimborne; University College, Exeter; London School of Economics. Assistant Lecturer, Edinburgh University, 1957-59; Lecturer, University of the West Indies, Jamaica, 1959-62; Lecturer, Queen's College, Dundee, 1962-68; Reader, Dundee University, 1968-78. Publications: Great Britain and Sea Power 1815-53; Castlereagh; The Long Retreat; The Rise and Fall of the Pax Americana; A History of Postwar Britain 1945-74; The Global Conflict 1880-1990; British Foreign Policy in the Twentieth Century; The Special Relationship since 1945; Defence and Diplomacy 1815-1914; The Annual Register 1987-97 (UK and Scotland chapters); Peace, War and the European Great Powers, 1814-1914. Address: (b.) Department of History, The University, Dundee.

Bartlett, Professor Robert John, MA, DPhil, FRHS, FBA, FSA. Professor of Mediaeval History, St. Andrews University, since 1992; b. 27.11.50, London; m., Honora Hickey; 1 s.; 1 d. Educ. Battersea Grammar School; Peterhouse, Cambridge; St. John's College, Oxford. Lecturer in History, Edinburgh University, 1980-86; Professor of Medieval History, University of Chicago, 1986-92. Publications: Gerald of Wales 1146-1223, 1982; Trial by Fire and Water: the medieval judicial ordeal, 1986; The Making of Europe, 1993. Recreations: walking; squash. Address: (b.) Department of Mediaeval History, St. Andrews University, St. Andrews KY16 9AL; T.-01334 463308.

Barty, James Webster, OBE (1981), MA, LLB. Retired Solicitor; Honorary President, Scottish Law Agents Society, since 1984; b. 9.3.12, Dunblane; m., Elisabeth Beryl Roebuck; 1 s.; 2 d. Educ. Hurst Grange School, Stirling; Fettes College, Edinburgh; St. Andrews University; Edinburgh University. Qualified as Solicitor, 1935; Partner, Tho. & J.W. Barty, Dunblane, 1937-84; Scottish Law Agents Society: Secretary, 1940-82, President, 1982-84; Honorary Sheriff, since 1970. Clerk, Dunblane Cathedral Kirk Session, 1949-69; Council Member, Friends of Dunblane Cathedral, 1940-84 (Vice-Chairman, 1974-84). Recreations: life-long interest in sport (rugby, tennis, cricket, badminton) and in all arts, including theatre, opera, ballet, literature and painting. Address: (h.) 5 Fir Road, Doune, Perthshire; T.-01786 841 545.

Bastable, Arthur Cyprian, OBE, BSc, CEng, FIEE, FIMgt. General Manager, Ferranti plc, Dundee, 1958-86; Director, Ferranti Astron Ltd., 1983-86; Director, Ferranti Industrial Electronics Ltd., 1984-86; Deputy Chairman, Dundee Port Authority, 1981-92 (Member, since 1967, Convener, Corporate Planning Committee, 1975-92); b. 9.5.23, Kobe, Japan; m., Joan Cardwell; 1 s.; 1 d. Educ. St. Georges School, Harpenden; Manchester University. Joined Ferranti, 1950; President, Dundee & Tayside Chamber of Commerce, 1970-71 (Convener, Overseas Trade and Development, 1973-91); Member, Tayside Development Authority, 1972-75; Vice-Chairman, Board of Governors, Dundee College of Technology, 1975-77; Member, Scottish Council, CBI, 1980; Member, Dundee Project Steering Committee, 1983-91; Director: Edinburgh Instruments Ltd., 1983-85; Taytec Ltd., 1985-88; Dundee and Tayside ITEC Ltd., 1985-88; Chairman, Tayside 1992 Committee, 1988-92. Recreations: sailing; skiing; ornithology. Address: (h.) Hunters Moon, 14 Lorne Street, Monifieth, Dundee DD5 4DU.

Baster, Jeremy, BA, MPhil, MRTPI. Director of Development and Planning, Orkney Islands Council, since 1996; b. 5.2.47, New York; m., Miriam Landor; 2 s.; 1 d. Educ. Leighton Park School, Reading; St. John's College, Oxford; University College, London. Early career in consultancy; Economist, Scottish Council (Development and Industry), 1975-80; Economist, Orkney Islands Council, 1980-85; Director of Economic Development, Orkney Islands Council, 1985-96. Director, Soulisquoy Printmakers Ltd.; Director, Orkney Enterprise. Address: (b.) Council Offices, School Place, Kirkwall KW15 1NY; T.-01856 3535.

Bateman, Malcolm, FCMA. Managing Director, Continental Tyres Ltd., since 1996; Financial Director, since 1986; Chairman, Continental UK Group Holdings, since 1993; Director, Continental Tyre Group, since 1986; Director, Contitech Power Transmission Systems, since 1995; b. 2.3.49, Welwyn Garden City; m., Lynda; 1 s.; 1 d. Educ. Dean Close School, Cheltenham. Recreations: golf; gardening; photography. Address: (b.) Newbridge, Midlothian EH28 8LG; T.-0131-333 2700.

Bateman, Richard Mark, BSc (Geol.), BSc (Biol.), PhD, FLS. Director of Science, Royal Botanic Garden Edinburgh, since 1997; Honorary Research Fellow, University of Edinburgh, since 1997; b. 27.5.58, Bradford; m., Orpah Susan Farrington. Educ. Francis Bacon School, St. Albans; University of Luton; Birkbeck College, University of London. Researcher, Quaternary Paleoenvironmental Unit, Rothamsted Experimental Station, 1977-84; Doctoral Researcher, Birkbeck College, University of London, 1984-88; Lindemann Research Fellow, Smithsonian Institution, 1988-91; Senior Research Fellow, University of Oxford, 1991-94; Principal Scientific Officer, Royal Botanic Garden Edinburgh/Royal Museum of Scotland, 1994-97. Council Member: Systematics Association, UK Systematics Forum; President's Award, Geological Society, 1988; Linnean

Society Bicentenary Medal, 1994. Publications: 45 books and research papers; Editor, Smithsonian Series on Comparative Evolutionary Biology; 120 articles; 75 conference presentations. Recreations: natural history; golf; pontificating while drinking beer. Address: (b.) Royal Botanic Garden, 20a Inverleith Row, Edinburgh EH3 5LR; T.-0131-552 7171.

Bates, Professor David Richard, BA, PhD, FRHistS, FSA. Edwards Professor of Medieval History, University of Glasgow, since 1994; b. 30.4.45, Coventry; m., Helen Mary; 1 s.; 1 d. Educ. King Edward VI Grammar School, Nuneaton; University of Exeter. Research Assistant, Documents Section, Imperial War Museum, 1969-71; Fellow, University College, Cardiff, 1971-73; Lecturer, Senior Lecturer, Reader in History, 1973-94, Head of History and Welsh History, 1988-92, University of Wales, Cardiff. Member, Council, Royal Historical Society. Publications: Normandy Before 1066, 1982; A Bibliography of Domesday Book, 1986; William the Conqueror, 1989; Bishop Remigius of Lincoln 1067-1092, 1992; England and Normandy in the Middle Ages (Co-Editor), 1994; Contributor, The History Today Companion to British History; Conflict and Co-existence: Nationalism and Democracy in Modern Europe: Essays in Honour of Harry Hearder (Co-Editor), 1997; Regesta Regum Anglo-Normannorum: The Acta of William I 1066-1087, 1998; General Editor: The Medieval World series. Recreations: walking; music; reading; watching sport. Address: (b.) Department of History (Medieval History), University of Glasgow, Glasgow G12 8QQ; T.-0141-330 4511.

Bates, Peter James, CertSocAdmin, DipSocWk. Director of Social Work, Dundee City Council, since 1996 (Director of Social Work, Tayside Regional Council, 1987-96); b. 6.5.45, Birmingham; m., Ann Gordon; 1 s.; 3 d. Educ. Birmingham University. Left school at 15 and completed five year apprenticeship; became active in youth work and community action in Handsworth; attended Birmingham University from the age of 23; moved to Scotland, 1969, as a social worker in Greenock; senior social worker, Edinburgh, later Director of a Community Development Project in the Grassmarket; a Social Work Manager with Lothian Regional Council; Principal Child Care Officer, later Deputy Director of Social Work, Strathclyde Regional Council. Recreations: running; climbing; photography. Address: (b.) Social Work Department, Tayside House, 28 Crichton Street, Dundee DD1 3RN; T.-01382 433314.

Bathgate, Gordon, BSc, CEng, FICE, FCIArb. Contracts Adviser, Scott Wilson Kirkpatrick & Co. (Scotland), since 1992; Chairman, Scottish Branch, Chartered Institute of Arbitrators, since 1997; b. 5.10.46, Edinburgh; m., Elizabeth Boddison; 1 s.; 1 d. Educ. Leith Academy; Heriot-Watt University. Graduate Trainee, Robert H. Cuthbertson & Partners, 1968-72; worked in local government, 1972-89; Regional Manager (Scotland), Reinforced Earth Company, 1989-92. Address: 6 Park Circus, Glasgow G3 6AX; T.-0141-332 2258.

Bauckham, Professor Richard John, MA, PhD. Professor of New Testament Studies, St. Andrews University, since 1992; b. 22.9.46, London. Educ. Enfield Grammar School; Clare College, Cambridge. Fellow, St. John's College, Cambridge, 1972-75; Lecturer in Theology, Leeds University, 1976-77; Lecturer in the History of Christian Thought, Manchester University, 1977-87, Reader, 1987-92. Publications: Tudor Apocalypse; Jude, 2 Peter; Moltmann: Messianic Theology in the Making; The Bible in Politics; Jude and the Relatives of Jesus in the Early Church; The Theology of the Book of Revelation; The Climax of Prophecy; The Theology of Jurgen Moltmann. Recreations: walking; novels; poetry; gardening; sleeping.

Address: (b.) St. Mary's College, St. Andrews KY16 9JU; T.-01334 462830.

Baverstock, John Browitt. President, Scottish Dairy Association, since 1997; b. 10.2.42, Blackpool; m., Brenda M. Slidders; 1 s.; 1 d. Educ. Kings School, Rochester; St. Andrews University. Senior buyer, Nestle UK Ltd. Recreations: golf; walking; gardening. Address: (b.) 46 Underwood Road, Paisley PA3 1TL.

Baxby, Keith, BSc, MB, BS, FRCS. Consultant Urological Surgeon, Tayside Health Board, since 1977; Honorary Senior Lecturer, Dundee University, since 1977; Clinical Director, Special Surgical Services, Dundee Royal Infirmary, 1991-95; b. 17.4.44, Sheffield. Educ. King Edward VII School, Sheffield; Durham University. House Officer, Royal Victoria Infirmary, Newcastle-upon-Tyne, 1968-69; Surgical Registrar, Newcastle University Hospitals, 1969-73; Northern Counties Kidney Fund Research Fellow, 1973-74; Senior Urological Registrar, Newcastle General Hospital, 1974-77; Visiting Professor of Urology, Louisiana State University, 1981; WHO Fellow in Clinical Urodynamics, 1984. Recreation: cycling. Address: (b.) Department of Urology, Royal Infirmary, Dundee; T.-01382 660111.

Baxter, Audrey Caroline, BA, DipACC. Managing Director, Baxters of Speyside Ltd.; b. 25.5.61; m., Colin McNiven. Educ. St. Leonard's School; Heriot-Watt University. International banking, Kleinwort Benson Ltd, London, 1983-87; Director, Corporate Planning, Baxters of Speyside, 1988-90. Address: (b.) W.A. Baxter and Sons Ltd, Fochabers, Moray.

Baxter, Brian Newland, BSc, MSc, PhD, CEng, FRINA, FIES. Marine Consultant; Visiting Professor, Department of Ship and Marine Technology, Strathclyde University, since 1980; b. London; m., Nadina McLeod; 2 d. Educ. King's College, Newcastle, Durham University. Scientific Officer, Royal Naval Scientific Service, 1948-50; Lecturer in Naval Architecture, King's College, Newcastle, 1950-57; Chief Representative, Bureau Veritas in the UK, 1957-62; Director, Yarrow & Co., Glasgow, 1962-79; Deputy Managing Director, Yarrow Shipbuilders, Glasgow, 1967-81; Director, British Shipbuilders Training and Education Co., 1981-84. President, Institution of Engineers and Shipbuilders in Scotland, 1979-81; Hon. Secretary, Seagull Trust, since 1984. Recreations: reading; writing; walking; golf. Address: (h.) Dunelm, Kilmacolm, RenfrewshirePA13 4DQ; T.-0150 587 2092.

Baxter, Jim. Footballer; b. 1939, Fife. Glasgow Rangers, 1960-64, later Sunderland and Nottingham Forest. Capped 34 times for Scotland.

Baxter, Mary Ross, MBE, MA, LRAM. Co-Ordinator, The Pushkin Prizes in Scotland; b. 23.9.27, Glasgow. Educ. Park School, Glasgow; Glasgow University. John Smith & Son, Booksellers, Glasgow, 1952-56; British European Airways, Glasgow Office, 1956-60; National Book League (now known as Book Trust), 1960-89; started the Scottish Office in 1961; former President, International PEN Scottish Centre. Honorary Member, Scottish Library Association. Recreations: music; books; home-decorating; cooking; gardening. Address: (b.) 18 Crown Terrace, Glasgow G12 9ES; T.-0141-357 0327.

Baxter, (William) Gordon, OBE, DL, LLD, DBA. President: W.A. Baxter & Sons Ltd., since 1994 (Chairman, 1970-94); b. 8.2.18, Fochabers, Moray; m., Ena E. Robertson; 2 s.; 1 d. Educ. Ashville College, Harrogate; Aberdeen University. ICI Explosives Ltd., 1940-45 (Research and Development Manager, various military projects); joined family business, 1946; Managing Director, 1947-71; Member, British Export Council Committee for

Exports to USA, 1964-72; Member, North American Advisory Group, DTI, 1979-89; former Director, Grampian Regional Board, Bank of Scotland; President, Chartered Institute of Marketing: Northern Branch; Member of Council, Royal Warrant Holders Association, London. Recreations: fishing; tennis. Address: (h.) Speybank House, Fochabers, Moray; T.-01343 821234.

Bayliss, Anthony Paul, MB, ChB, FRCR, DMRD. Consultant Radiologist, Royal Aberdeen Hospitals NHS Trust; b. 7.2.44, Oldham; m., Margaret Anne; 3 s. Educ. Oldham Hulme Grammar School; St. Andrews University. Medical Intern., Mount Sinai Hospital, Minneapolis, 1969-70; House Officer, Ballochmyle Hospital, Ayrshire, 1970-71; Trainee Radiologist, Western Infirmary, Glasgow, 1971-75. Recreation: golf. Address: (h.) Whistlebrae Farmhouse, Banchory Devenick, Aberdeen; Tel:-01224 780596.

Baynham, John William, CBE, Doctor honoris causa (Edinburgh), BSc, PhD, DIC. Chairman, Lothian Health Board, 1990-97; Chairman, Scottish Health Board Chairmen's Group, 1995-97; b. 20.1.29, Blantyre; m., Marie B. Friel; 1 d. Educ. Bathgate Academy; Aberdeen University: Imperial College, London. Scottish Agricultural Industries PLC, 1955-87, latterly as Agribusiness Director. Member, Lothian Health Board, 1987-90; Chairman, Board of Governors, Moray House Institute of Education, Heriot Watt University, 1991-95; Governor, Queen Margaret College, since 1995. Recreations: golf; grandchildren. Address: (h.) 2/18 Succoth Court, Succoth Park, Edinburgh EH12 6BZ; T.-0131-337 2813.

Bealey, Professor Frank William, BSc (Econ), DSc (Econ). Professor of Politics, Aberdeen University, 1964-90; b. 31.8.22, Bilston, Staffordshire; m., Sheila Hurst; 1 s.; 2 d. Educ. King Edward VI Grammar School, Stourbridge; London School of Economics. Seaman, Royal Navy, 1941-46; Extra-Mural Lecturer, Manchester University, 1951-52; Lecturer, Keele University, 1952-64; Temporary Lecturer, Birmingham University, 1958-59. Treasurer and founder Member, Society for the Study of Labour History, 1960-63; Convener, Committee for Social Science, Aberdeen University, 1970-74 and 1986-89; Fellow, Royal Historical Society, 1971; Editorial Board, Political Studies, 1975-83; Visiting Fellow, Yale University, 1980; Organiser, Parliamentary All-Party Group, Social Science and Policy, 1984-89; Trustee, Jan Hus Educational Foundation, since 1981; Co-ordinator: EC Tempus Project (Political Science, Czechoslovakia), 1990-93. Publications: Labour and Politics 1900-1906 (Co-author); Constituency Politics (Co-author); The Social and Political Thought of the British Labour Party; The Post Office Engineering Union; The Politics of Independence (Co-author); Democracy in the Contemporary State. Recreations: reading poetry; darts; eating and drinking; watching football and cricket. Address: (h.) 11 Viewforth Terrace, Edinburgh EH10 4LH.

Beastall, Graham Hedley, BSc, PhD, FRCPath. Top Grade Biochemist (Endocrinology), Glasgow Royal Infirmary, since 1981; Honorary Senior Lecturer, Glasgow University, since 1983; b. 11.12.47, Liverpool; m., Judith; 2 s. Educ. Liverpool Institute High School for Boys; Liverpool University. Lecturer in Biochemistry, Liverpool University, 1971-72; Lecturer in Steroid Biochemistry, Glasgow University, 1972-76; Senior Biochemist (Endocrinology), then Principal Biochemist (Endocrinology), Glasgow Royal Infirmary, 1976-81.Chairman, Association of Clinical Biochemists, since 1994; Chairman, Conference of Clinical Scientists Organisations, since 1996; Area Commissioner, Greater Glasgow Scout Council, 1980-88; Scottish Scout Council Programme and Training Co-ordinator, since 1995. Recreations: Scouting; gardening; sport. Address: (b.) Department of Clinical Biochemistry, Royal Infirmary, Glasgow G4 OSF; T.-0141-211 4632.

Beat, Janet Eveline, BMus, MA. Composer; Lecturer: Royal Scottish Academy of Music and Drama, 1972-96, Glasgow University since 1996; Artistic Director and Founder, Soundstrata (electro-acoustic ensemble); b. 17.12.37, Streetly. Educ. High School for Girls, Sutton Coldfield; Birmingham University. Freelance Orchestral Player, 1960s; Lecturer: Madeley College of Education, 1965-67, Worcester College of Education, 1967-71; founder Member and former Council Member, Scottish Society of Composers; a Director, Scottish Electro-Acoustic Music Association; wrote musical criticism for The Scotsman; G.D. Cunningham Award, 1962; her works have been performed throughout Scotland as well as in Switzerland, Poland, North America, South America, Greece, Australia, and Japan. Recreations: travel; reading; photography. Address: c/o Scottish Music Information Centre, 1 Bowmont Gardens, Glasgow, G12 9LR; T.-0141-334 6393.

Beath, Professor John Arnott, MA, MPhil. Professor of Economics, St. Andrews University, since 1991, and Head, School of Social Sciences; b. 15.6.44, Thurso; m., Dr. Monika Schroder. Educ. Hillhead High School; St. Andrews, London, Pennsylvania and Cambridge Universities. Research Officer, Department of Applied Economics, Cambridge University; Fellow, Downing College, Cambridge; Lecturer, then Senior Lecturer in Economics, Bristol University. Member, Research Priorities Board, Economic and Social Research Council. Publication: The Economic Theory of Product Differentiation. Recreations: gardening; golf; music. Address: (h.) Simonden, Ceres, Cupar KY15 5PP; T.-01334 858920.

Beaton, John David. Editorial Director, Mainstream Publishing, since 1995; b. Edinburgh; m., Jane Belinda Copley; 2 d. Educ. Melville College, Edinburgh; Hove College, Sussex. Commissioning Editor, Caribbean list; Thomas Nelson & Son Ltd., 1975-79; Deputy Publisher, Pelham Books, 1979-90; Managing Editor, Airlife Publishing, 1990-95. Recreations: riding; gardening; walking. Address: (h.) Wester Balchrystie, by Colinsburgh, Fife KY9 1HE.

Beattie, Alistair Duncan, MD (Hons), FRCPGlas, FRCPLond. Consultant Physician, Southern General Hospital, Glasgow, since 1976; Honorary Clinical Lecturer, Glasgow University, since 1977; Chairman, West of Scotland Committee for Postgraduate Medical Education; b. 4.4.42, Laurencekirk; m., Gillian Margaret McCutcheon; 3 s.; 2 d. Educ. Paisley Grammar School; Glasgow University. Junior hospital appointments, Royal Infirmary and Western Infirmary, Glasgow, 1965-69; Department of Materia Medica, Glasgow University: Research Fellow, 1969-73, Lecturer, 1973-74; MRC Research Fellow, Royal Free Hospital, London, 1974-75. Honorary Treasurer, Medical and Dental Defence Union of Scotland. Recreations: golf; music. Address: (h.) 228 Queen Victoria Drive, Glasgow G13 1TN; T.-0141-959 7182.

Beattie, Bryan William, JP, BA. Chairman, Scottish Youth Theatre, since 1993; Chairman, Board of Governors, Eden Court Theatre, since 1996; Chairman, Cultural and Leisure Services Committee, Highland Council, since 1995; b. 3.5.60, Dundee. Educ. High School of Dundee; Stirling University. Director, Stirling Festival, 1984-86; established Stirling Writers Group, Stirling Youth Theatre; Arts Development Officer for Scotland, Scottish Council on Disability, 1986-87; Principal, Creative Services (arts consultancy), since 1992; Councillor, Highland Regional Council, 1994-96, and Highland Council, since 1995; Board Member, Ross and Cromarty Enterprise, since 1996; Member, University of Highlands and Islands Foundation; author of plays for radio and theatre; broadcaster; columnist, Press and Journal; occasional acting. Recreations: music; books; sport; regular breathing; remembering family and friends' names. Address: (h.)

Drumderfit, North Kessock, by Inverness, IV1 1XF; T.- 01463 731596.

Beattie, Johnny. Comedian and entertainer; b. 1926, Glasgow. Established his career as principal comic in Robert Wilson's touring revue. Has appeared frequently in pantomime and in summer seasons at the Gaiety, Ayr.

Beaumont, Professor Phillip Barrington, BEcon (Hons), MEcon, PhD. Professor, Department of Management Studies, Glasgow University, since 1990 (Senior Lecturer, 1984-86, Reader, 1986-90); b. 13.10.49, Melbourne, Australia; m., Patricia Mary Ann McKinlay; 1 s. Educ. Camberwell High School, Melbourne; Monash University, Melbourne; Glasgow University. Research Fellow, then Lecturer, Glasgow University, 1976-84; Visiting Professor: Massachusetts Institute of Technology, Boston, 1982, McMaster University, 1986, Case Western Reserve University, 1988, Cornell University, 1990. Publications: Bargaining in the Public Sector, 1978; Safety at Work and the Trade Unions, 1981; Job Satisfaction in Public Administration, 1983; The Decline of Trade Union Organization, 1987; Change in Industrial Relations, 1990; Public Sector Industrial Relations, 1991; Human Resource Management, 1993; The Future of Employment Management, 1995. Recreations: tennis; badminton; cricket; shooting; fishing. Address: (b.) The University, Glasgow G12 8QQ; T.-0141-339 8855.

Beaumont, Professor Steven Peter, MA, PhD, CEng, MIEE, MIEEE. Professor of Nanoelectronics and Head, Department of Electronics and Electrical Engineering, Glasgow University; b. 20.2.52, Norwich; m., Joanne Mary; 1 s.; 2 d. Educ. Norwich School; Corpus Christi College, Cambridge University. Research Fellow, Glasgow University, 1978-83; Barr and Stroud Lecturer in Electronics, Glasgow University, 1983-86, Senior Lecturer, 1986-89; Director, Intellemetrics Ltd., 1982-90, Scot-Flow Dynamics Ltd. Recreations: walking; crofting. Address: (h.) 13 Kelvinside Terrace South, Glasgow G20 6DW; T.-0141-330 5380.

Bechhofer, Professor Frank, MA. Professor, University of Edinburgh; b. 10.10.35, Nurnberg, Germany; m., Jean Barbara Conochie; 1 s.; 1 d. Educ. Nottingham High School; Queens' College, Cambridge. Junior Research Officer, Department of Applied Economics, Cambridge University, 1962-65; Edinburgh University: Lecturer in Sociology, 1965-71, Reader in Sociology, 1971-87, Director, Research Centre for Social Sciences, 1984-97, Professor of Social Research, 1988-97. Address: (b.) Research Centre for Social Sciences, Old Surgeons' Hall, High School Yards, Edinburgh EH1 1LZ; T.-0131-650 6385.

Beckett, Rev. David Mackay, BA, BD. Minister, Greyfriars Tolbooth and Highland Kirk, Edinburgh, since 1983; b. 22.3.37, Glasgow; m., Rosalie Frances Neal; 2 s. Educ. Glenalmond; Trinity Hall, Cambridge; St. Andrews University. Assistant Minister, Dundee Parish Church (St. Mary's), 1963-66; Minister, Clark Memorial Church, Largs, 1966-83. Convener, Committee on Public Worship and Aids to Devotion, General Assembly, 1978-82; President, Church Service Society, 1986-88; Secretary, General Assembly Panel on Doctrine, 1987-95. Publication: The Lord's Supper, 1984. Address: (h.) 12 Tantallon Place, Edinburgh EH9 1NZ; T.-0131-667 8671.

Bedi, Tarlochan Singh, JP, MB, BS, FRCPsych, DPM. Consultant Psychiatrist and Honorary Clinical Senior Lecturer, Southern General Hospital, Glasgow, since 1980; b. India; m., Dr. T.H. Ratani; 1 s. Educ. Poona University, India. Junior House Officer, Aga Khan Hospital, Nairobi; Senior House Officer, Glenside and Barrow Hospital, Bristol; Registrar, Coneyhill Hospital, Gloucester; Senior Registrar, Gartnavel and Southern General Hospital,

Glasgow; Consultant Psychiatrist, Woodilee Hospital, Lenzie. Past President: Scottish Asian Action Committee, Glasgow; Indian Social and Cultural Association, Glasgow; Indian Graduates Society, Glasgow. Recreations: music; photography; culinary arts. Address: 156 Prestonfield, Milngavie G62 7QA; T.-0141-570 0734.

Beevers, Professor Clifford, BSc, PhD. Professor of Mathematics, Heriot Watt University, since 1993; b. 4.9.44, Castleford; m., Elizabeth Ann; 2 d. Educ. Castleford Grammar School; Manchester University. Senior Lecturer, 1985; Director, CALM, 1985. Chairman, Edinburgh Branch, British Retinitis Pigmentosa Society. Recreations: walking; jogging; music; theatre. Address: (b.) Department of Mathematics, Heriot Watt University, Riccarton, Edinburgh EH14 4AS; T.-0131-451 3233.

Begg, Anne, MA. MP (Labour), Aberdeen South, since 1997; b. 6.12.55, Forfar. Educ. Brechin High School; University of Aberdeen; Aberdeen College of Education. Teacher of English and History, Webster's High, Kirriemuir, 1978-88; Assistant Principal Teacher, then Principal Teacher of English, Arbroath Academy, 1988-97. Recreations: cinema; theatre; reading; public speaking. Address: (b.) House of Commons, London SW1A 0AA; T.- 0171-219 2140.

Begg, David, BA (Hons). Chair of Transport, City of Edinburgh Council (Councillor, since 1986); Professor of Transport, Robert Gordon University; Secretary, Scottish Transport Studies Group; b. 12.6.56, Edinburgh. Educ. Portobello High School; Heriot-Watt University. Economic Researcher, PIEDA, 1979; management employee, BR, 1979-81; Lecturer in Economics, Napier University, 1981-91. Publications: articles on transport economics and local government finance. Recreations: golf; watching Hibernian F.C. Address: (b.) City Chambers, High Street, Edinburgh; T.-0131-529 3262.

Begg, Professor Hugh MacKemmie, MA, MA, PhD, DipTP, FRTPI, FRSA. Consultant Economist and Chartered Planner; part-time Reporter, Scottish Office Inquiry Reporters Unit; External Adjudicator, Scottish Enterprise; b. 25.10.41, Glasgow; m., Jane Elizabeth Harrison; 2 d. Educ. High School of Glasgow; St. Andrews University; University of British Columbia. Lecturer in Political Economy, St. Andrews University; Research Fellow, Tayside Study; Lecturer in Economics, Dundee University; Assistant Director of Planning, Tayside Regional Council; Visiting Professor, Technical University of Nova Scotia; Consultant, UN Regional Development Project, Egypt and Saudi Arabia; Consultant, Scottish Office Industry Department, Scottish Office Agriculture and Forestry Department; Head, School of Town and Regional Planning, Dundee University. Recreations: local history; hill walking; rugby. Address: (h.) 4 Esplanade, Broughty Ferry, Dundee; T.-01382 779642.

Begg, Ian McKerron, DA, FRIAS, FSA Scot. Architect (own practice), since 1983; b. 23.6.25, Kirkcaldy; 3 d. Educ. Kirkcaldy High School; Edinburgh College of Art. Partner, Robert Hurd & Partners, 1951-83; Interim Director, Edinburgh New Town Conservation Committee; Interim Director, Edinburgh Old Town Committee for Conservation and Renewal. Honorary Member, Saltire Society. Recreations: travel, particularly to Paris; supporting Scotland's identity. Address: Ravens'Craig, Plockton, Ross-shire IV52 8UB; T.-01599 544 265.

Begg, Norman Roderick Darroch, MA, LLB. Secretary, Aberdeen University, since 1988; b. 23.12.41, London; m., Fiona Schofield; 3 d. Educ. Aberdeen Grammar School; Aberdeen University. Administrative Assistant, East Anglia University, 1964-66; Aberdeen University, since 1966: Administrative Assistant; Assistant Secretary; Registry

Officer; Clerk to Senatus; Deputy Secretary. Member, Children's Panel, Grampian Region, 1984-87; Past Chairman, Aberdeen Studio Theatre Group; Director, Edinburgh Festival Fringe Society, 1980-83; Hon. Vice-President, Aberdeen Opera Company, since 1988. Recreation: amateur drama. Address: (b.)Aberdeen University, Regent Walk, Aberdeen AB24 3FX.

Begg, Robert William, CBE (1977), DL, DUniv (Glas), MA, CA. Painter; b. 19.2.22; m., Sheena Margaret Boyd; 2 s. Educ. Greenock Academy; Glasgow University. Royal Navy, 1942-46 (Lt., RNVR) (Despatches). Consultant, Moores Rowland, 1987-95 (Partner, Mann Judd Gordon, Glasgow, 1951-86). Honorary Treasurer, Royal Philosophical Society of Glasgow, 1952-62; President, Royal Glasgow Institute of Fine Arts, 1987-90 (Honorary Treasurer, 1975-87); Member, Board of Governors, Glasgow School of Art, 1955-77 (Chairman, 1970-76); Trustee, National Galleries of Scotland, 1974-91 (Chairman, 1980-87); Member: Council, National Trust for Scotland, 1984-90 (Executive, 1985-90), Court, Glasgow University, 1986-90, Museums and Galleries Commission, 1988-91. Address: (h.) 3 Colquhoun Drive, Bearsden, Glasgow G61 4NQ; T.-0141-563 5705.

Begg, William Kirkwood, OBE. Chairman and Managing Director, Begg, Cousland Holdings Ltd.; Chairman, Begg Cousland & Co. Ltd.; b. 5.2.34; m., Thia St Clair; 2 s.; 1 d. Educ. Glenalmond College. Chairman, Scottish Advisory Committee on Telecommunications; Member, CBI SME Council; Privy Council Nominee to General Convocation, Strathclyde University; Director, Weavers' Society of Anderston; Founder Trustee, Dallas Benevolent Fund; Trustee, James Paterson's Trust; Vice Chairman, The Wise Group; Director, Commercially Wise Ltd.; Director, Merchants' House of Glasgow; former Member, Scottish Industrial Development Advisory Board; former Member, CBI Council for Scotland. Recreations: sailing; shooting; DIY. Address: (h.) 3 Mirrlees Drive, Glasgow G12 0SH.

Behan, Professor Peter Oliver, MB ChB, MD, DSc, FACP, FRCP (Glas), FRCP (Lond), FRCP (Ire). Consultant Neurologist, Greater Glasgow Health Board, since 1976; Professor of Neurology, Glasgow University; b. 8.7.35, Co. Kildare; m., Dr. Wilhelmina Behan; 2 s.; 1 d. Educ. Sir John Cass College, London; Leeds University Medical School. Demonstrator in Pathology, Cambridge University, 1965-66; Research Fellow in Psychiatry, Harvard University, 1966-67; Special Research Fellow, Oxford University, 1968-70; Lecturer in Neurology, then Senior Lecturer, then Reader, Glasgow University, from 1971. Patron, Motor Neurone Disease Association of Scotland; awarded Pattison Medal for contributions to neurology; International Dutch prize for study of fatigue states, 1995; Chief Editor, Journal of Neuroimmunology; papers and books on neurology; book on salmon and women (Co-author). Recreations: salmon fishing; Samuel Johnson. Address: (h.) 17 South Erskine Park, Bearsden, Glasgow; T.-0141-942 5713.

Belch, Professor Jill J. F., MB, ChB, FRCP, MD (Hons). Professor of Vascular Medicine, Dundee University, since 1993; Chairman, UK Forum on Angiology, since 1995; b. 22.10.52, Glasgow; m., Tom van der Ham; 1 s.; 3 d. Educ. Morrison's Academy, Crieff; University of Glasgow. University of Glasgow and Royal Infirmary: Research Fellow, 1980, Lecturer, 1984; University of Dundee and Ninewells Hospital: Senior Lecturer, 1987, Reader, 1990. Medical Adviser, Raynaud's and Scleroderma Association. Publications: over 200 peer-reviewed articles in scientific journals. Recreations: family; skiing. Address: (b.) University Department of Medicine, Ninewells Hospital, Dundee DD1 9SY; T.-01382 632457.

Belch, Sir Ross, CBE (1972), LLD Strathclyde (1978), BSc, FRSE, FRINA, CBIM, CEng. Company Director; b. 13.12.20, London; m., 1, Janette Finnie Murdoch (deceased); 4 d.; 2, Dorothy West. Educ. Morrison's Academy, Crieff; Glasgow University. Lithgows Ltd.: Director and General Manager, 1954, Managing Director, 1964; Managing Director, Scott Lithgow Group, 1969-80; Member, Board, British Shipbuilders, 1977-79; President, Shipbuilders and Repairers National Association, 1974-76; Chairman: Irvine Development Corporation, 1985-90, Murray Hotels (Crieff) Ltd., Kelvin Travel Ltd., Altnacraig Shipping plc, Altnamara Shipping plc; Chairman, Trustees, Scottish Maritime Museum. Address: (h.) Altnacraig House, Lyle Road, Greenock PA16 7XT; T.-01475 721124.

Belfall, David J., BA (Hons). Head, Housing and Area Regeneration Group, Scottish Office, since 1995; b. 26.4.47, Colchester; m., Lorna McLaughlan; 1 s.; 1 d. Educ. Colchester Royal Grammar School; St. John's College, Cambridge. Home Office, 1969-88 (Private Secretary to Permanent Under Secretary of State, 1973-74); Scottish Office, since 1988; Under Secretary, Police and Emergency Services, 1988-91; Health Policy and Public Health, 1991-95. Recreations: squash; badminton. Address: (b.) Scottish Office, Victoria Quay, Edinburgh EH6 6QQ.

Bell, Alexander Scott, FFA, FPMI. Group Managing Director, Standard Life Assurance Company, since 1988; b. 4.12.41, Falkirk; m., Veronica Jane Simpson; 2 s.; 1 d. Educ. Daniel Stewart's College, Edinburgh. Joined Standard Life, 1958; Director: Universities Superannuation Scheme Limited, Hammerson plc. Recreations: golf; travel. Address: (b.) 30 Lothian Road, Edinburgh, EH1 2DH; T.-0131-245 6011.

Bell, Sheriff Andrew Montgomery, BL. Sheriff of Lothian and Borders, at Edinburgh, since 1990 (Sheriff of Glasgow and Strathkelvin, at Glasgow, 1984-90); b. 21.2.40, Edinburgh; m., Ann Margaret Robinson; 1 s.; 1 d. Educ. Royal High School, Edinburgh; Edinburgh University. Solicitor, 1961-74; called to Bar, 1975; Sheriff of South Strathclyde, Dumfries and Galloway, at Hamilton, 1979-84. Address: (h.) 5 York Road, Edinburgh EH5 3EJ; T.-0131-552 3859.

Bell, Anne Rutherford, MA, MIPD. Head of Human Resources, Scottish Tourist Board, since 1996; b. 14.4.59, Carlisle. Educ. Annan Academy; Edinburgh University. Personnel Assistant, Hydro-Electric Board, 1984; Personnel Officer, Lothian Regional Council, 1987; Scottish Homes, 1988-96, latterly as Human Resources Development Manager. Recreations: travel; cinema; theatre. Address: (b.) 23 Ravelston Terrace, Edinburgh EH4 3EU.

Bell, Arthur J.A., CBE, BSc, MCIM, FRSA, MIDM. Chairman, Scotland Direct (Holdings) Ltd., and subsidiaries; Marketing Consultant; b. 6.10.46, Brechin; m., G. Susan Bell; 4 c. Educ. Royal High School, Edinburgh; Edinburgh University. Chair, New Lanark Housing Association; former Chair, Scottish Tory Reform Group; Vice Chair, New Lanark Conservation Trust; Director, Small Business Bureau; Editor, Small Business News; Member, Council, Institute of Direct Marketing; three times parliamentary candidate. Publication: Complete Edinburgh Pub Guide/A Flavour of Edinburgh (Co-author). Address: (h.) Culter House, Coulter, Biggar, Lanarkshire; T.-01899 220064.

Bell, Colin John, MA (Hons), HonLLD (Aberdeen). Broadcaster; Journalist; Author; b. 1.4.38, London; m., Caroline Rose Bell; 1 s.; 3 d. Educ. St. Paul's School; King's College, Cambridge. Journalist, The Scotsman, 1960-62 and 1975-78; Journalist/Contributor, London Life, Sunday Times, Sunday Telegraph, Daily Mirror, Sunday Mail, etc.; Lecturer, Morley College, 1965-68; College

Supervisor, King's College, Cambridge, 1968-75; Parliamentary candidate (SNP), West Edinburgh, 1979; European Parliamentary candidate (SNP), North East Scotland, 1979; Vice-Chairman, SNP, 1978-84; Campaign Director, Euro Election, 1984; a Senior Fellow, the 21st Century Trust, 1990; Rector, Aberdeen University, 1991-93. Publications: City Fathers, 1969; Boswell's Johnson, 1971; Scotch Whisky, 1985; Radical Alternative (Contributor), 1978; The Times Reports (Series) (Editor). Recreations: jazz; Scottish history. Address: (h.) Cockburnhill, Balerno, Midlothian.

Bell, Professor Colin Roy, BA, MScEcon, FRSE. Professor of Sociology, Edinburgh University, since 1988; Vice Principal, since 1993; b. 1.3.42, Enfield; m., Dr. Janette Webb; 1 s.; 3 d. Educ. The Judd School, Tonbridge; Keele University; University of Wales. University teaching posts at Essex; Professor of Sociology, Universities of New South Wales and Aston; research posts, Universities of Leicester and Edinburgh. Publications: Middle Class Families; Community Studies; Doing Sociological Research; Property, Paternalism and Power; numerous other academic papers and books. Recreations: jazz and blues; Munros; Penguins; gardening. Address: (b.) Sociology Department, Edinburgh University, 18 Buccleuch Place, Edinburgh EH8; T.-0131-667 1011.

Bell, Professor David Nevin Fraser, MA, MSc, PhD. Professor of Economics, Stirling University, since 1990; b. 16.12.51, Inverness; 1 s.; 1 d. Educ. Dornoch Academy; Aberdeen University; London School of Economics; Strathclyde University. Lecturer, St. Andrews University, 1974-75; Research Fellow: Fraser of Allander Institute, Strathclyde University, 1975-83, Macroeconomic Modelling Bureau, Warwick University, 1983-85; Lecturer, Glasgow University, 1985-90. Address: (b.) Department of Economics, Stirling University, Stirling FK9 4LA.

Bell, Donald Atkinson, BSc, PhD, FIMechE, CEng, MIEE, FBCS. Director, Marchland Consulting Ltd., since 1990 (Director, National Engineering Laboratory, 1983-90); b. 28.5.41, Belfast; m., Joyce Louisa Godber; 2 s. Educ. Royal Belfast Academical Institution; Queen's University, Belfast; Southampton University. National Physical Laboratory, Teddington, 1966-77; Electronics Applications Division, Department of Industry, 1978-82. Address: (b.) Marchland Consulting Ltd., 108 East Kilbride Road, Glasgow G76 8JF; T.-0141-644 2000.

Bell, George Armour, OBE, JP, BSc, MB, ChB. Former Chairman, Monklands and Bellshill Hospitals NHS Trust; Vice President, Tenovus-Scotland; b. 8.7.20, Bellshill; m., Elizabeth Davidson Porteous; 2 s. Educ. Bellshill Academy; Glasgow University. War Service, 609 Squadron – Normandy to Germany, SMO Prestwick, SMO Brize Norton, RAF. Retired General Practitioner, Bellshill; former Member, Lanarkshire Health Board; founder Chairman, Crime Prevention Panel, Bellshill and District; former Red Cross Detachment Medical Officer, Bellshill; founder Chairman, Community Council for Mossend; Honorary Medical Officer, Bellshill Bn., Boys Brigade; President, Bellshill Branch, Arthritis Care; Honorary Member, Rotary; Life Member, BMA; Life Member, RAF Association. Address: (h.) Chudleigh, 449 Main Street, Bellshill, Lanarkshire ML4 1AX; T.-01698 749084.

Bell, G. Susan, ACIS, FSA (Scot), MIDM. Founder Director, Scotland Direct (Holdings) Limited; Bell Lawrie of Biggar (Developments) Ltd.; Board Member, Scottish Centres; Board Member, SALVO; b. 31.8.46; m., Arthur J.A. Bell, CBE; 2 s.; 2 d. Educ. College of Commerce, Glasgow. Investment Analyst, Edinburgh, 1970-74; Conservative Parliamentary candidate: Motherwell, 1970, Caithness & Sutherland, February 1974; Chairman, Conservative Candidates Association, 1971-74; joined Liberal Democrats, 1997; Member, Council, CBI Scotland,

1986-93; Board Member: Scottish Tourist Board, 1983-88, SCOTVEC, 1987-95, Southern General Hospital Trust, 1993-95; Member, Council, National Trust for Scotland, 1983-88; former Chair, Women into Business. Recreations: garden; riding; reading. Address: (h.) Culter House, Coulter, Biggar; T.-01899 220064.

Bell, Robin, MA, MSc. Poet and Broadcaster; b. 4.1.45, Dundee; 2 d. Educ. Morrison's Academy, Crieff; St. Andrews University; Perugia University, Italy; Union College, New York; Columbia University, New York. Formerly: Director of Information, City University of New York, Regional Opportunity Program; Assistant Professor, John Jay College of Criminal Justice, City University of New York; Member, US Office of Education Task Force in Educational Technology; Audio-Visual Editor, Oxford University Press; Editor, Guidebook series to Ancient Monuments of Scotland; Secretary, Poetry Association of Scotland. Scottish Radio and Television Industries Award for Best Radio Feature, 1984; Sony Award, Best British Radio Documentary, 1985. Publications: The Invisible Mirror; Culdee, Culdee; Sawing Logs; Strathinver: A Portrait Album 1945-53; Collected Poems of James Graham, Marquis of Montrose (Editor); Radio Poems; The Best of Scottish Poetry; An Anthology of Living Scottish Poets (Editor); Bittersweet Within My Heart: collected poems of Mary Queen of Scots (Translator/Editor); Scanning the Forth Bridge. Address: (h.) The Orchard, Muirton, Auchterarder PH3 1ND.

Bellany, Dr. John, CBE, RA; b. June, 1942, Port Seton; m., 1, Helen Margaret Percy; 2, Juliet Gray Lister (deceased); 3, for second time, Helen Margaret Bellany; 2 s.; 1 d. Educ. Cockenzie Public School; Preston Lodge, Prestonpans; Edinburgh College of Art; Royal College of Art, London. Lecturer in Fine Art, Winchester School of Art, 1969-73; Head, Faculty of Painting, Croydon College of Art, 1973-78; Visiting Lecturer in Painting, R.C.A., 1975-85; Lecturer in Fine Art, Goldsmiths College, London University, 1978-84; elected Fellow Commoner, Trinity Hall, Cambridge, 1988; one-man exhibitions include: Arts Council touring show; Rosa Esman Gallery, New York; Christine Abrahams Gallery, Melbourne; Ikon Gallery, Birmingham; Walker Art Gallery, Liverpool; Roslyn Oxley Gallery, Sydney; National Portrait Gallery, London; Galerie Krikhar, Amsterdam; Fischer Fine Art, London; retrospective — Scottish National Gallery of Modern Art; Serpentine Gallery, London; Kimsthalle, Hamburg; Museum Ostral, Dortmund; Ruth Siegel Gallery, New York; Raab Gallery, Berlin; Fitzwilliam Museum, Cambridge; Kelvingrove Museum and Art Gallery (50th birthday tribute); Beaux Arts Gallery, Berkeley Square Gallery, London; elected Hon. RSA, 1987; joint 1st prize, Athena International Award, 1985; Awarded Honorary Doctorate, Edinburgh University, 1996. Recreation: motoring around Europe in search of beauty.

Beltrami, Joseph, SSC, BL, NP. Solicitor/Advocate (Beltrami & Co.); b. 15.5.32, Rutherglen; m., Brigid D.; 3 s. Educ. St. Aloysius College, Glasgow; Glasgow University. Intelligence Corps, 1954-56 (Sgt.); qualified as Solicitor, 1956; specialised in criminal law; has instructed in more than 500 murder cases; closely associated with two cases of Royal Pardon; in first batch of Solicitor/Advocates to have rights of audience in High Court and Court of Criminal Appeal. Chairman, soccer testimonials: Jim Johnstone and Bobby Lennox, 1976; Danny McGrain, 1980. Publications: The Defender, 1980; Glasgow - A Celebration (Contributor), 1984; Tales of the Suspected, 1988; A Deadly Innocence, 1989. Recreations: bowls; soccer; snooker; writing; boxing. Address: (h.) 12 Valence Tower, Regents Gate, Bothwell, Lanarkshire; T.-01698 817841.

Benedetti, Giovanni. Chairman: Benedetti International Plc, Pendigo Ltd., Wallace Cameron & Co. Ltd., Wrap Film Systems Ltd., ProPac Ltd., GB Consulting and Management

Services Ltd., KSS Supplies; Director, Prince's Scottish Youth Business Trust; b. 6.3.43, Italy; m., Francesca; 2 d. Arrived in Britain aged 11; worked in uncle's cafe until age of 19; started his own business with two dry-cleaning shops; opened his first factory in Ardrossan, 1970; company bought by BET, 1989. Recreations: skiing; sailing.

Benington, (Charles) Kenneth, BSc, PhD, CEng, FIMechE. Industrial Consultant, since 1996; b. 1.4.31, Belfast; m., Margaret Malcolm; 1 s.; 1 d. Educ. Dalriada Grammar School, Ballymoney; Queen's University, Belfast; Heriot-Watt University. Graduate apprentice and design engineer, Associated Electrical Industries Ltd., 1953-60; Assistant Chief Engineer, Trials, British Ship Research Association, 1960-63; Lecturer, Heriot-Watt University, 1963-72; Senior Engineer, Marine Industries Centre, Newcastle University, 1972-74; Brown Brothers & Co. Ltd.: Systems Manager, 1974-75; Technical Manager, 1975-77; Technical Director, 1977-80; Assistant Managing Director and Technical Director, 1980-81; Managing Director, 1981-86; Technical Director, Vickers Marine Engineering Division, 1986-88; Industrial Adviser to Secretary of State for Scotland, 1988-96; Member, Executive Committee, Scottish Employers' Association, 1984-86; Member, Board of Unilink, Heriot Watt University, 1987-90. Address: (h.) 4 Redfox Crescent, Penicuik, Midlothian EH26 0RQ.

Bennet, Graham Alexander, QPM. Deputy Chief Constable, Fife, since 1991; b. 21.3.43, Insch. Educ. Aberlour High School. Joined Fife Constabulary, 1963; Assistant Chief Constable, 1987. Address: (b.) Detroit Road, Glenrothes, Fife KY6 2RJ.

Bennett, Professor David, BSc (Hons), BVetMed (Hons), PhD, DSAO, MRCVS. Professor and Head, Small Animal Clinical Studies, University of Glasgow, since 1996; Director, Comparative Connective Tissue Research Unit, since 1996; RCVS Specialist in Small Animal Surgery, since 1986; b. 14.3.48, Ipswich; m., Carol Ann; 1 d. Educ. Northgate Grammar, Ipswich; Royal Veterinary College; University of London. Resident House Officer, Royal Veterinary College, 1972-74; Lecturer, Veterinary Surgery, University of Glasgow, 1974-81; Assistant in general practice, 1981-82; Senior Lecturer, 1982-1990, Reader in Comparative Rheumatology, 1990-96, University of Liverpool. Founder Member and Trustee, BVOA. Elanco Literary Award; Veterinary Drug Prize; Central Veterinary Society Centenary Award; BSAVA Simon Award; BEVA Silver Jubilee Prize; Honorary Member, Scottish Rheumatology Club. Publications: over 150 clinical and research publications. Recreations: hockey; gardening; restoring antique furniture and porcelain; bridge. Address :(b.) Department of Veterinary Clinical Studies, University of Glasgow Veterinary School, Bearsden Road, Bearsden, Glasgow G61 1QH; T.-0141-330 6959.

Bennett, David Andrew, MA, LLB, WS, NP. Partner, Bennett & Robertson, Solicitors, Edinburgh and Glasgow, since 1964, b. 27.3.38, Edinburgh; m., Marion Miller Park; 2 d. Educ. Melville College, Edinburgh; Fettes College, Edinburgh; Edinburgh University. Director, Jordan Group Ltd.; Member, Council, Law Society of Scotland, 1984-90. Session Clerk, Liberton Kirk, since 1975; Honorary Secretary, Scottish Hockey Association, 1973-82; Scottish Editor, Palmer's Company Law, since 1970, and Gore-Browne on Companies, since 1975. Recreations: most sports and arts. Address: (b.) 16 Walker Street, Edinburgh EH3 7NN; T.-0131-225 4001.

Bennett, Helen Margaret, PhD, AMA, FSA Scot. Crafts Director, Scottish Arts Council, since 1993; Governor, Edinburgh College of Art, since 1992; b. 25.6.48, Newark; m., Philip Edwin Bennett; 1 d. Educ. Lilley and Stone High School for Girls, Newark; Exeter University; Edinburgh

University. Assistant Curator, Borough of Weston-super-Mare, 1969-71; Curator of Agricultural and Social History, Bristol City Museums, 1971-72; Research Assistant, Costume and Textiles, National Museum of Antiquities of Scotland, 1974-81; freelance arts administrator, 1984-88; Head of Crafts Division, Scottish Development Agency, 1989-91; freelance cultural consultant, 1991-93. Recreations: walking; gardening; textile crafts. Address: (b.) 12 Manor Place, Edinburgh EH3 7DD; T.-0131-226 6051.

Bennie, Norma, DipCOT. Mental Welfare Commissioner, since 1994; Occupational Therapist, since 1968; b. 11.11.46, Beith; m., Ernest H. Bennie; 2 s.; 1 d. Educ. Spier's School, Beith; Glasgow School of Occupational Therapy. Occupational Therapist, Duke Street Hospital, Gartnavel Royal Hospital and Dykebar Hospital, 1968-1993; Service Manager for Mental Health, Dykebar Hospital, 1993-97; Community Care Development and Business Planning Manager, Renfrewshire Healthcare (NHS) Trust, 1997. Recreations: keep-fit; sailing. Address: (b.) Trust HQ, Dykebar Hospital, Paisley PA2 7DE; T.-0141-884 9052.

Bennie, Peter Fraser, MB, ChB, MRCPsych. Consultant Psychiatrist, Parkhead Hospital, Glasgow; b. 7.6.63, New Zealand. Educ. Dollar Academy; Glasgow University. Junior Doctors' Association: Member, UK Committee, since 1990, Deputy Chairman, 1995-97, Chairman, Scottish Committee, 1991-96, Chairman, UK Conference, 1995. Recreations: five a side football; cycling; hill-walking; theatre; cinema; eating and drinking well. Address: (b.) Parkhead Hospital, 83 Salamanca Street, Glasgow G32 5EX; T.-0141-211 8300.

Bennie, Robert William, BSc, CPFA. Director of Finance, Western Isles Council, since 1992; b. 19.8.56, Edinburgh. Educ. Melville College, Edinburgh; Linlithgow Academy; Heriot-Watt University. Trainee Accountant/Accounting Assistant, Falkirk District Council; Chief Technical Assistant, Aberconwy B.C.; Principal Accountant, Vale of White Horse D.C.; District Finance Officer, Hinckley and Bosworth B.C.; Deputy Treasurer, South Northamptonshire D.C. Recreations: mountaineering; rugby; running; music; reading. Address: (b.) Stornoway, Isle of Lewis HS1 2BW; T.-01851 703773, Ext. 230.

Benson, Professor Gordon Mitchell, AADip, SADG, FRIAS, ARIBA. Architect; Partner, Benson and Forsyth; b. 5.10.44, Glasgow; 1 s. 1 d. Educ. Glasgow High School; Glasgow University and Architectural Association. Partner in private practice, since 1978; recent prize work includes Cowgatehead Library, Edinburgh, 1995, New Museum of Scotland (international competition), 1991; Chair of Architecture, Strathclyde University, 1986-90.

Berry, Professor David Richard, MA, MSc, PhD, DSc, CBiol, FIBiol, FIFST. Professor, Department of Bioscience and Biotechnology, Strathclyde University (Head of Department, 1988-95); b. 1.3.41, Huddersfield; m., Elisabeth Ann; 1 s.; 1 d. Educ. Holme Valley Grammar School; St. Peter's College, Oxford. Scientific Officer, Glaxo Ltd., Ulverston, 1962-64; graduate student, 1964-70; Lecturer, then Senior Lecturer, then Reader, Strathclyde University; Former Member, Scottish Examination Board Biology Panel; Chairman, Further and Higher Education Committee, Institute of Biology; Council Member, Institute of Biology, 1996-99. Address: (b.) Department of Bioscience and Biotechnology, Strathclyde University, George Street, Glasgow; T.-0141-552 4400.

Berry, Graham, CA. Director of Finance and Administration, Scottish Arts Council, since 1989; b. 12.1.45, Edinburgh; 1 s.; 1 d. Educ. Royal High School, Edinburgh; CA Apprentice, Edinburgh, 1963-68; CA, Price

Waterhouse, London, 1968-70; Divisional Chief Accountant, Trust House Forte, London, 1970-74; Company Secretary, 1974-86: Scottish Film Council, Scottish Council for Educational Technology, Glasgow Film Theatre, Filmhouse Ltd., Scetlander Ltd.; Finance Officer, Stirling University, 1986-89. Recreations: mountaineering; photography. Address: (b.) Scottish Arts Council, 12 Manor Place, Edinburgh EH3 7DD; T.-0131-226 6051.

Berry, John, CBE (1968), DL (Fife) (1969), BA (Cantab), MA (Cantab), PhD (St. Andrews) Hon. LLD Dundee (1970), HonDSc St. Andrews (1991), FRSE (1936). Adviser and Consultant on environmental and wildlife conservation (retired); b. 5.8.07, Edinburgh; m., Hon. Bride Fremantle; 2 s.; 1 d. Educ. Ardvreck School, Crieff; Eton College; Trinity College, Cambridge. Salmon Research Officer, Fishery Board for Scotland, 1930-31; Biological Research Station, University College, Southampton: Research Officer, 1932-36; Director, 1936-39; Chief Press Censor for Scotland, 1940-44; Biologist and Information Officer, North of Scotland Hydro-Electric Board, 1944-49; Environment Conservation Adviser, 1944-89 (to South of Scotland Electricity Board, 1969-89, to Scottish Landowners Federation, 1984-87); Director of Nature Conservation in Scotland, 1949-67; consultancy work 1968-90. Honorary Life Member, Swiss League for Protection of Nature, 1946; founder Member (1948), International Union for Conservation of Natural Resources and first President, International Union Commission on Ecology; Member, Executive Board, International Waterfowl Research Bureau, 1963-72; Honorary Corresponding Member, Danish Natural History Society, since 1957; Vice-President and Honorary Life Fellow, Royal Zoological Society of Scotland, since 1959; Honorary Life Fellow: Wildfowl Trust, 1983; Glasgow Natural History Society, 1951; Member, Dundee University Court, 1970-78; Director, British Pavilion, Expo 71, Budapest; Member, Scottish Marine Biological Association, 1947-71 (Council, 1947-54 and 1957-66). Recreations: natural history (especially insects, water birds and fish); music. Address: (h.) The Garden House, Tayfield, Newport-on-Tay, Fife DD6 8HA; T.-01382 543118.

Berry, William, MA, LLB, WS, NP. Senior Partner, Murray Beith Murray, WS, Edinburgh; Chairman, Scottish Life Assurance Co.; Director: Scottish American Investment Co. Plc, Fleming Continental European Trust Plc, Alliance Trust plc, Dawnfresh Seafoods Ltd., Inchcape Family Investments Ltd., and other companies; b. 26.9.39, Newport-on-Tay; m., Elizabeth Margery Warner; 2 s. Educ. Ardvreck, Crieff; Eton College; St. Andrews University; Edinburgh University. Interests in farming, forestry, etc. Depute Chairman, Edinburgh Festival Society, 1985-89; Member Council/Board: New Town Concerts Society Ltd., Thistle Foundation. Performer in three records of Scottish country dance music. Recreations: music; shooting; forestry. Address: (b.) 39 Castle Street, Edinburgh EH2 3BH; T.-0131-225 1200.

Bettison, Graeme Hayward, LLB(Hons). Chief Executive, Inverclyde Council, since 1995; b. 29.4.55, Edinburgh; m., Fiona. Educ. Royal High School, Edinburgh; Edinburgh University. West Lothian District Council, 1978-81; Dumfries and Galloway Regional Council, 1981-93; Senior Depute Director of Administration, Grampian Regional Council, 1993-95. President, Junior Chamber, Dumfries, 1984-85. Recreations: golf; reading; gardening. Address: (b.) Municipal Buildings, Greenock PA15 1LY; T.-01475 882701.

Betts, Michael William, CBE, FCIT, FILog. Traffic Commissioner for Scotland, since 1992; Senior Traffic Commissioner, Great Britain, since 1996; b. 3.3.38, Bournemouth; m., Margaret Irene Lussi; 2 d. Educ. Hardye's School, Dorchester; Royal Military Academy, Sandhurst. Commissioned Royal Army Service Corps,

1957; Brigadier Logistics, British Army of the Rhine, 1987-90; Director of Movements (Army), Ministry of Defence, 1991-92; ADC to HM The Queen, 1990-92. Freeman, City of London, 1993; Freeman and Liveryman, Worshipful Company of Carmen, 1993. Recreations: sailing; skiing; bird-watching. Address: (b.) Scottish Traffic Area Office, Floor J, Argyle House, 3 Lady Lawson Street, Edinburgh EH3 9SE; T.-0131-529 8510.

Bevan, John Stuart, BSc (Hons), MBChB (Hons), MD, FRCP (Edin), FRSM. Consultant Physician and Endocrinologist, Aberdeen Royal Infirmary, since 1991; Honorary Senior Clinical Lecturer, Aberdeen University, since 1991; Secretary, Council, Endocrine Section, Royal Society of Medicine; b. 18.9.53, Portsmouth; m., Sheena Mary; 2 s.; 2 d. Educ. Portsmouth Northern Grammar School; Dunfermline High School; Edinburgh University. Registrar in Endocrinology, Radcliffe Infirmary, Oxford, 1981-83; Medical Research Council Training Fellow in Endocrinology, Oxford, 1984-86; Senior Registrar in Medicine and Endocrinology, University Hospital of Wales, Cardiff, 1987-90; Assistant Editor, Clinical Endocrinology, since 1994; Trustee, Pituitary Foundation. Publications: papers on clinical neuroendocrinology, particularly the treatment of human pituitary tumours. Recreations: cricket; guitar; ornithology. Address: (b.) Department of Endocrinology, Aberdeen Royal Infirmary, Ward 25, Foresterhill, Aberdeen AB25 2ZN; T.-01224 681818.

Beveridge, Crawford William, CBE, BSc, MSc. Chief Executive, Scottish Enterprise, since 1991; b. 3.11.45, Edinburgh; m., Marguerite Devoe; 1 s.; 1 d. Educ. Daniel Stewart's College; Edinburgh University; Bradford University Management Centre. Training Officer, Hewlett Packard, 1968; European Personnel Director, Digital, 1977; Vice President: Human Resources, Analog Devices, 1982, Corporate Resources, Sun Microsystems, 1985. Recreations: cooking; music; paperweights. Address: (b.) Scottish Enterprise, 120 Bothwell Street, Glasgow G2 7JP; T.-0141-248 2700.

Bewsher, Colonel Harold Frederick, LVO, OBE. Chairman: The Airborne Initiative (Scotland) Ltd., since 1995, The Atlantic Salmon Trust, since 1995; Brigadier, The Queen's Bodyguard for Scotland, since 1996 (Secretary, 1982-94); b. 13.1.29, Glasgow; m., Susan Elizabeth Cruickshank; 2 s. Educ. Merchiston Castle School; Royal Technical College; Glasgow University; Royal Military Academy, Sandhurst. Regular Army, The Royal Scots, 1949-72; Director-General, Scotch Whisky Association, 1973-94. Chairman: New Club, Edinburgh, 1981-82, Scottish Society for the Employment of Ex-Regular Soldiers, Sailors and Airmen, 1973-83; Freeman, City of London, 1992; Liveryman, Worshipful Company of Distillers, 1993. Recreations: outdoors — salmon fishing, field sports. Address: (b.) 33 Blacket Place, Edinburgh EH9 1RJ; T.-0131-667 4600.

Bicanic, Professor Nenad Josip Nikola, DiplIng, PhD. Regius Professor of Civil Engineering, since 1994, and Head of Department of Civil Engineering, University of Glasgow, since 1997; b. 6.9.45, Zagreb, Croatia; m., Jasna Babic; 1 s.; 1 d. Educ. University of Zagreb; University of Wales, Swansea. Structural Engineer, Zagreb, 1968-69; Consulting Engineer, Arnhem, Netherlands, 1969-72; Lecturer, Docent, Professor, University of Zagreb, 1972-83; Visiting Professor, University of Colorado, 1983-84; Lecturer, Senior Lecturer, Reader, Department of Civil Engineering, University of Wales, Swansea, 1985-94. President, AMAC-UK. Publication: Computational Modelling of Concrete Structures, 1990. Recreations: tennis; skiing; folk dancing. Address: (h.) 20 Ledcameroch Road, Bearsden G61 4AE; T.-0141-942 0711.

Biddulph, 5th Lord (Anthony Nicholas Colin). Interior Designer and Sporting Manager; b. 8.4.59; m., Hon. Sian Gibson-Watt; 1 s. Educ. Cheltenham; RAC, Cirencester. Recreations: shooting; design; fishing. Address: Address: (h.) Makerstoun, Kelso TD5 7PA; T.-01573 460 234.

Biggart, Thomas Norman, CBE (1984), WS, MA, LLB. Partner, Biggart Baillie & Gifford, Solicitors, Glasgow and Edinburgh, 1959-95; b. 24.1.30; m., Eileen Jean Anne Gemmell; 1 s.; 1 d. Educ. Morrison's Academy, Crieff; Glasgow University. Royal Navy, 1954-56 (Sub-Lt., RNVR). Law Society of Scotland: Council Member, 1977-86; Vice-President, 1981-82; President, 1982-83; President, Business Archives Council, Scotland, 1977-86; Member, Executive, Scottish Council (Development and Industry), 1984-94; Member: Scottish Tertiary Education Advisory Council, 1984-87, Scottish Records Advisory Council, 1985-91; Director: Clydesdale Bank, since 1985; Independent Insurance Group, since 1986 (Chairman, 1989-93); Chairman, Beechwood, Glasgow, 1989-97; Trustee, Scottish Civic Trust, since 1989; Member, Council on Tribunals (Chairman, Scottish Committee), since 1990; Honorary Member, American Bar Association, 1982; OStJ, 1968. Recreations: golf; hill-walking. Address: (h.) Gailes, Kilmacolm, Renfrewshire PA13 4LZ; T.-0150 587 2645.

Bills, David James, BSc (For). Director General and Deputy Chairman, Forestry Commission, since 1995; b. 9.2.48, Australia; m., Michele Hartam-Ellis; 1 s.; 2 d. Educ. University of Tasmania; Australian National University. Research Scientist, Forest Research Institute (Australia); Department of Agriculture, Australian Government; various forestry positions, Associated Pulp and Paper Mills, becoming General Manager, North Forest Products (North Ltd.). Past President, National Association of Forest Industries, Australia; former Vice-President, Australian Forest Development Institute. Recreations: sailing; ski-ing; classic cars; music. Address: (h.) 17 Lansdowne Crescent, Edinburgh EH12 5EH; T.-0131-538 4926.

Binnie, Frank Hugh. Chief Executive, The Caledonian Foundation, since 1996; Director, UK Clothing and Textile Initiative, since 1990; b. 1.3.50, Edinburgh; m., Fiona Margaret McLean Nicolson (née Hart); 4 s.; 1 d. Educ. Loughborough Grammar; De Montfort University. Design Management Trainee, Corahs Textiles, Leicester, 1970-73; Manufacturing Manager, Floreal Knitwear, Mauritius, 1973-76; Sales Manager, Kemptons Knitwear, Leicester, 1976-79; General Manager Design, Texport Unilever, 1979-82; Manufacturing Manager, Kilspindie Knitwear, 1982-85; Director and Company Secretary, Midlothian Enterprise, 1985-88; Managing Director, Perkins, Hodgkinson and Gillibrand (Coxmore plc), 1988-90; Chief Executive, Scottish Design (formerly Director, The Design Council Scotland), 1990-96. External Assessor, MBA, University of Westminster; Assessor, Management Course, De Montfort University; Member: Licensing Executive, Coutts Scottish Advisory Committee, Institute of Directors, Scottish Council Development and Industry, Guid Club; Visiting Professor in Engineering Design, Strathclyde University; Fellow, Chartered Society of Designers, Fellow, Royal Society of Arts, Design and Manufacturing; Chairman, Textile Institute Fashion, Product Design and Marketing Group. Recreations: yachting; running. Address: (b.) Caledonian Foundation, 9 Lynedoch Crescent, Glasgow G3 6QE; T.-0141-332 5668; (h.) 18 Fernlea, Bearsden, Glasgow G61 1NB.

Bird, Professor Colin C., MBChB, PhD, FRCPath, FRCPE, FRCSE, FRSE. Dean, Faculty of Medicine, Edinburgh University, since 1995; b. 5.3.38, Kirkintilloch; m., Ailsa M. Ross; 2 s.; 1 d. Educ. Lenzie Academy; Glasgow University. McGhie Cancer Research Scholar, Glasgow Royal Infirmary, 1962-64; Lecturer in Pathology: Glasgow University, 1964-67, Aberdeen University, 1967-72; MRC Goldsmiths Travelling Fellow, Chicago, 1970-71; Senior Lecturer in Pathology, Edinburgh University, 1972-75; Professor and Head, Department of Pathology, Leeds University, 1975-86; Professor of Pathology and Head, Department of Pathology, Edinburgh University, 1986-95. Recreations: golf; hill walking; music. Address: (h.) 45 Ann Street, Edinburgh, EH4 1PL.

Bird, Jackie. Journalist; b. 31.7.62, Bellshill; m., Robert Bird; 1 s.; 1 d. Educ. Earnock High School. Music/Film/Television Editor, Jackie Magazine; Radio News Reporter and Presenter, Radio Clyde; Reporter, Evening Times; Reporter, Sun; Reporter/Presenter, TVS; Presenter, Reporting Scotland. Patron, Glasgow Cat and Dog Home. Recreations: swimming; aerobics; running; music; animal welfare. Address; (b.) BBC, Queen Margaret Drive, Glasgow.

Birley, Tim(othy) Grahame, BSc(Eng), MSc, ACGI, FRTPI, FRICS, FRSA. Independent adviser on sustainable development and public policy, since 1995; b. 13.3.47, Kent; m., Catherine Anne; 1 s.; 2 d. Educ. Sir Roger Manwood's Grammar School; Imperial College, London University; Edinburgh University. Local government, 1965-71; academic appointments, 1973-81; Director, Energy and Environment Research, 1982-85; Scottish Office: Inquiry Reporter, 1985-87, Principal Inquiry Reporter, 1987-88, Deputy Director of Building, 1988-90, Head, Rural Affairs Division, 1990-95. Non-Executive Director, RPT (Scotland), 1989-91; Central Scotland Woodlands, 1991-92; Director, Centre for Human Ecology, Edinburgh University, 1995-96; Chair, Project Selection Panel, Millennium Forest for Scotland Trust; Board Member: Forward Scotland, Landwise. Recreation: family outings. Address: (b.) 6 Malta Terrace, Edinburgh EH4 1HR; T.-0131-332 3499.

Birnie, George David, BSc, PhD. Senior Scientist, Beatson Institute for Cancer Research, since 1969; Honorary Lecturer in Biochemistry, Glasgow University, since 1982; b. 8.8.34, Gourock; m., Jean Gray McCaig; 2 s.; 1 d. Educ. Gourock High School; Greenock High School; Glasgow University. Assistant Lecturer in Biochemistry, Glasgow University, 1959-60; Postdoctoral Fellow, McArdle Memorial Laboratory, University of Wisconsin, 1960-62; Scientist, Imperial Cancer Research Fund Laboratories, London, 1962-69. Kitchener Scholarship, 1952-56; Fulbright Travel Scholarship, 1960-62; US Public Health Service Fellowship, 1960-62; Member: Editorial Advisory Panel, Biochemical Journal, 1981-92, Editorial Board, Biochemical Journal, since 1992. Publications: Editor of five books, author of more than 140 papers. Deacon, Giffnock Congregational Church, 1980-91. Recreation: gardening. Address: (b.) Beatson Institute for Cancer Research, Garscube Estate, Switchback Road, Bearsden, Glasgow G61 1BD; T.-0141-942 9361.

Birss, Rev. Alan David, MA (Hons), BD (Hons). Minister, Paisley Abbey, since 1988; b. 5.6.53, Ellon; m., Carol Margaret Pearson. Educ. Glenrothes High School; St. Andrews University; Edinburgh University. Assistant Minister, Dundee Parish Church (St. Mary's), 1978-80; Minister, Inverkeithing Parish Church of St. Peter, 1982-88. Secretary, Scottish Church Society; Member, Council, Church Service Society. Address: The Manse of Paisley Abbey, 15 Main Road, Castlehead, Paisley PA2 6AJ; T.-0141-889 3587.

Bisset, David W., ALA, AIInfSc, FSA (Scot), DEAB. Secretary, Scottish Esperanto Federation, since 1997; Chairman: Architectural Heritage Society of Scotland (Strathclyde), since 1997, Esperanto Publicity Commission, since 1997; b. 8.8.38, Motherwell; m., Jean; 1 s.; 1 d. Educ. Dalziel High, Motherwell; University of Strathclyde. Librarian, Coatbridge Technical College, 1962-72; Head of Library Services, Bell College of Technology, Hamilton, 1972-95. Various positions within the Esperanto Movement in Scotland and Britain; Hon. Vice-President, Hamilton Civic Society. Recreations: cultural tourism; town walking; architectural history. Address: (h.) 47 Airbles Crescent, Motherwell ML1 3AP; T.-01698 263199.

Bissett-Johnson, Professor Alastair, LLB (Nottingham), LLM (Michigan), Barrister. Professor of Private Law, Dundee University, since 1991; b. Northumberland; m., 1, Dr. Winifred McPherson (deceased); 2, Ann Taylor. Educ. Royal Masonic School, Bushey. Assistant Lecturer, Sheffield University, 1963; Lecturer, Bristol University, 1963-67; Senior Lecturer, Monash University, Melbourne, 1968-71, Leicester University, 1971-76; Associate Professor, McGill University, Montreal, 1976-77; Professor, Dalhousie University, Halifax, Nova Scotia, 1977-90. Publications: Family Law in Australia (Co-author); Cases and Materials on Family Law (Co-author); Matrimonial Property Law in Canada (Co-author); The New Divorce Law (Co-author). Recreations: watercolour painting; music; food and wine. Address: (h.) 7 Shaftesbury Road, Dundee DD2 1HF; T.-01382 645264.

Black, Professor Antony, MA (Cantab), PhD (Cantab). Professor in Political Science, Dundee University, since 1994; Author; b. 23.6.36, Leeds; m., Aileen Pow; 4 s.; 1 d. Educ. Shrewsbury School; King's College, Cambridge. Assistant Lecturer, Department of Political Science, Queen's College, Dundee, 1963-66; Lecturer, Department of Political Science, Dundee University, 1967-80; Visiting Associate Professor, School of Government and Public Administration, The American University, Washington, DC, 1975-76. Publications: Monarchy and Community: political ideas in the later conciliar movement (1430-50); Council and Commune: the Council of Basle and the 15th-century heritage; Guilds and civil society in European political thought from the 12th century to the present; State, Community and Human Desire; Community in Historical Perspective (Editor); Political Thought in Europe, 1250-1450. Address: (b.) Department of Political Science, Dundee University, Dundee; T.-Dundee 344592.

Black, Rev. Archibald Tearlach, BSc. Chairman of Council, The Saltire Society, since 1997; retired Church of Scotland minister; b. 10.6.37, Edinburgh; m., Bridget Mary Baddeley; 2 s.; 1 d. Educ. Merchiston School; St. Andrews University; New College, Edinburgh. St. Andrew's Church, Calcutta, 1964-66; St. Columba's, Pont Street, London, 1966-68 (Assistant); Carstairs with Carstairs Junction, 1969-74; Chaplain, The State Hospital; Ness Bank Church, Inverness, 1974-97. Elected Member of Council, National Trust for Scotland, 1991-96, re-elected, 1997. Recreations: photography; the arts; the conservation and enrichment of all aspects of Scotland's natural and cultural heritage. Address: (h.) 16 Elm Park, Inverness IV2 4QN; T.-01463 230588.

Black, Hugh Finlayson, BSc (Hons), MBA. Head of Business Development, The Highland Council, since 1996; Company Manager, Highland Opportunity Limited, since 1986; Regional Manager, Prince's Scottish Youth Business Trust, since 1988; Director: Business Information Source Ltd., Highland Birchwoods Ltd., North of Scotland European Partnership Ltd.; b. 16.6.46, Johnstone; m., Lydia Mary McRae; 1 s.; 3 d. Educ. Paisley Grammar School; Aberdeen University; Strathclyde University; Glasgow University. Development Officer, West Cumberland Farmers, 1973-75; Regional Manager, Pan Britannica Industries, 1976-79; Principal Officer, Grampian Regional Council, 1980-84; Depute Director Development, Highland Regional Council, 1984-96. Recreations: family; education; farming; history; travel; walking. Address: (b.) Economic Development Service, The Highland Council, Glenurquhart Road, Inverness IV3 5NX; T.-01463 702000, Ext. 2551.

Black, Laurie, FRSA. Chairman, Taste of Scotland, since 1994; Chairman, Taste of Burns Country, since 1995; Joint Partner, Fouters Bistro, Ayr, since 1973; Vice-Chairman, Ayrshire Tourism Industry Forum; b. 10.7.48, West Germany; m., Fran; 1 s.; 1 d. Educ. Horley Secondary School; Bournemouth Technical College. Former policeman; left police, 1973, to open restaurant in Ayr. Member, Scottish Tourist Board working party on natural cooking of Scotland; Director: Taste of Scotland, since 1993, Ayrshire and Arran Tourist Board. Recreations: cooking; travel; walking; music; computing; wine; golf. Address: (b.) 2A Academy Street, Ayr; T.-01292 261391.

Black, Professor Robert, QC, LLB (Hons), LLM, FRSA, FRSE. Professor of Scots Law, Edinburgh University, since 1981; Temporary Sheriff, 1981-94; b. 12.6.47, Lockerbie. Educ. Lockerbie Academy; Dumfries Academy; Edinburgh University; McGill University, Montreal. Advocate, 1972; Lecturer in Scots Law, Edinburgh University, 1972-75; Senior Legal Officer, Scottish Law Commission, 1975-78; practised at Scottish bar, 1978-81; QC, 1987; General Editor, The Laws of Scotland: Stair Memorial Encyclopaedia, 1988-96 (formerly Deputy and Joint General Editor). Publications: An Introduction to Written Pleading, 1982; Civil Jurisdiction: The New Rules, 1983. Recreations: beer and books, not necessarily in that order. Address: (h.) 6/4 Glenogle Road, Edinburgh EH3 5HW; T.-0131-557 3571.

Black, Robert William, MA (Hons, Econ), MSc (Town Planning), MSc (Public Policy). Controller of Audit, Accounts Commission for Scotland, since 1995; b. 6.11.46, Banff; m., Doreen Mary Riach; 3 s.; 1 d. Educ. Robert Gordon's College, Aberdeen; Aberdeen University; Heriot-Watt University; Strathclyde University. Nottinghamshire County Council, 1971-73; City of Glasgow Corporation, 1973-75; Strathclyde Regional Council, 1975-85; Chief Executive: Stirling District Council, 1985-90, Tayside Regional Council, 1990-95. Fellow, Royal Statistical Society. Recreations: the outdoors and the arts. Address: (b.) 18 George Street, Edinburgh EH2 2QU.

Black, W.J. Murray, MBE, BSc, PhD, ARICS, ARAgS, JP. Honorary Senior Lecturer, Edinburgh University, since 1970; Farms Director, Edinburgh School of Agriculture, 1970-97; b. 26.7.35, Reading; m., Ann Warren; 3 d. Educ. Leighton Park School, Reading; Reading University; Durham University; College of Estate Management, Reading. Lecturer in Agriculture, Newcastle University, 1959-64; Principal Scientific Officer, Agricultural Institute, Dublin, 1964-70. Member: Farm Animal Welfare Council, London, since 1988, NCCS (SNH) S.E. Scotland Regional Board, 1991-96; Honorary Secretary/Treasurer, British Society of Animal Science, since 1980; President, BSAS, 1995; Chairman of Governors, St. Margaret's School, Edinburgh, 1990-94. Publications: 45 scientific papers. Recreations: DIY houses and restoration of old cars; holidays in France. Address: Glenburnie, Boghall, Biggar Road, Edinburgh EH10 7OX; T.-0131-445 2247.

Black, William Scott, FCIBS, MBA. Director, Operations, Retail Banking, Royal Bank of Scotland plc, since 1993; b. 8.3.48; m., Margaret Aitken; 1 s.; 1 d. Educ. Kelso High School; Strathclyde University Business School. Joined Royal Bank of Scotland plc, 1964; Treasurer, John Menzies plc, 1981-82; rejoined Royal Bank of Scotland plc, 1982; General Manager (Development), Royal Scottish Assurance, 1990-91; Assistant Director, Network, Royal Bank of Scotland plc, 1991-93. Recreations: golf; gardening; reading; keep fit. Address: (b.) 42 St. Andrew Square, Edinburgh EH2 2YE; T.-0131-523 2844.

Blackadder, Elizabeth, OBE, RA, RSA. Artist; b. 24.9.31, Falkirk. Educ. Falkirk High School; Edinburgh University; Edinburgh College of Art. Lecturer, School of Drawing and Painting, Edinburgh College of Art, 1962-66; first Scottish woman painter elected full member, Royal Academy and Royal Scottish Academy.

Blackford, Ian. Managing Director, Nat West Securities, Scotland, since 1993; b. 14.5.61, Edinburgh; m., Mary; 1 s.; 2 d. Educ. Royal High School, Edinburgh. Assistant Fund Manager, Mercury Asset Managers, London, 1986-88; Analyst, Smith New Court, London, 1988-90; Director, Union Bank of Switzerland, London, 1990-93. SNP candidate, Ayr, General Election, 1997, Paisley South, by-election, 1997; elected Member, National Council, SNP. Recreations: reading; walking; rugby; football. Address: (b.) 74-77 Queen Street, Edinburgh; T.-0131-243 4481.

Blackie, Alan John, BA, DipYCS. Director of Education and Community Services, East Lothian, since 1995; b. 6.6.48, Haddington; 2 d. Educ. Knox Academy, Haddington; Jordanhill College, Glasgow; Open University. Community Education Service, Dunbarton County Council/Strathclyde Regional Council, 1971-79; Community Education Officer, Castlebrae High School, Edinburgh, 1979-87; Education Officer, then Assistant Director of Education, Lothian, 1987-95. Former Chairman, Scottish Youth Work Forum; Chairman, Duke of Edinburgh's Award Advisory Committee (Scotland); Member, Scottish Community Education Council. Recreations: hill-walking; skiing. Address: (h.) Byre Court, East Saltoun, EH34 5ED; T.-01875 340083.

Blackie, Professor John Walter Graham, BA (Cantab), LLB. Professor of Law, Strathclyde University, since 1991 (Senior Lecturer in Scots Law, Edinburgh University, 1988-91, Lecturer, 1975-88); Director, Blackie & Son Ltd., publishers, 1970-93; Advocate, since 1974; b. 2.10.46, Glasgow; m., Jane Ashman. Educ. Uppingham School; Peterhouse, Cambridge; Harvard; Merton College, Oxford; Edinburgh University. Open Exhibitioner, Peterhouse, Cambridge, 1965-68; St. Andrews Society of New York Scholar, Harvard, 1968-69; practised at Scottish bar, 1974-75. Recreations: music; sailing. Address: (h.) 17 Parsonage Square, Glasgow G4 0TA.

Blackshaw, Alan, OBE, VRD. Management Consultant and Author; Associate, Oakwood Environmental Ltd., since 1991; b. 7.4.33; m., 1, Jane Elizabeth Turner (m. dissolved); 1 d.; 2, Dr. Elspeth Paterson Martin; 1 s.; 2 d. Educ. Merchant Taylors' School, Crosby; Wadham College, Oxford (MA). Royal Marines (commissioned), 1954-56, and RM Reserve, 1956-76. Entered Home Civil Service, Ministry of Power, 1956; Principal Private Secretary to Minister of Power, 1967-69; Department of Energy: Under Secretary, 1974, Offshore Supplies Office, 1974-78 (Director-General, 1977-78), Coal Division, 1978-79; Consultant, N.C.B., 1979-86; Consultant Director, Strategy International, 1980-91; Member: Scottish Council Development and Industry, 1974-78, Scottish Sports Council, 1990-95, Scottish Natural Heritage, 1992-97 (Chairman: Task Force on Access, 1992-94, Audit Committee, 1995-97); Member, Adventure Activities Licensing Authority, since 1996; Patron, British Mountaineering Council, since 1979 (President, 1973-76); Chairman, Standing Advisory Committee on Mountain Training Policy, 1980-86 and since 1990, Sports Council's National Mountain Centre, Plas y Brenin, 1986-95, Mountaineering Committee, UIAA, (Berne, Switzerland), since 1990, Access and Conservation Working Group, UIAA, since 1995, UK Mountain Training Board, 1991-94, Scottish National Ski Council, 1991-94, President, since 1994; Honorary Adviser, Mountaineering Council of Scotland, since 1995; Director, Paths for All Partnership, 1996-97; President, Ski Club of Great Britain, since 1997; Freeman, City of London; FRGS; FInstPet. Publication: Mountaineering, 1965. Recreations: mountaineering; skiing. Address: (h.) Coire Mor, East Terrace, Kingussie PH21 1JS; T.-01540 662192.

Blackwood, Rev. Keith Thomas, BD, DipMin. Minister, Bearsden North Parish Church, since 1997; b. 29.5.69, Motherwell; m., Katrina Mary. Educ. Dalziel High School, Motherwell; University of Glasgow. Care Assistant, Church of Scotland Homeless Hostel, 1991-93. Recreations: golf; football. Address: 5 Fintry Gardens, Bearsden, Glasgow G61 4RJ; T.-0141-942 0366.

Blair, (Ann) Kay, MA (Hons). Managing Director, Business Perceptions; Marketing Columnist, The Scotsman, since 1990; Board Member, Scottish Legal Aid Board, since 1994; Non-Executive Director, Edinburgh Sick Children's NHS Trust, since 1994; b. 12.4.53, Edinburgh; m., William; 1 s.; 2 d. Educ. James Gillespie's High School for Girls; St. Andrews University; School of Slavonic and Eastern European Studies, London University. Journalist/ Researcher on Eastern Europe and Manager, Business Information Service, Financial Times, 1977-80; Marketing Information Manager, Scottish Development Agency, 1980-81. Recreations: skiing; cinema; travel. Address: (b.) 8 Winton Terrace, Edinburgh EH10 7AP; T.-0131-477 7477.

Blair, Anna Dempster, DPE. Writer and Lecturer; b. 12.2.27, Glasgow; m., Matthew Blair; 1 s.; 1 d. Educ. Hutchesons' Girls Grammar School, Glasgow; Dunfermline College. Novels: A Tree in the West; The Rowan on the Ridge; Short Stories: Tales of Ayrshire; Scottish Tales; The Goose Girl of Eriska; Seed Corn; social history: Tea at Miss Cranston's; Croft and Creel; More Tea at Miss Cranston's. Recreations: film-making; travel; reading; friendship. Address: (h.) 20 Barrland Drive, Giffnock, Glasgow G46 7QD; T.-0141-638 0676.

Blair, Frank. Director Scotland, Advisory Conciliation and Arbitration Service, since 1995; b. 18.4.48, Wishaw; m., Brenda; 2 s.; 1 d. Various posts, Department of Employment/Employment Service, 1967-82; ACAS Conciliator, 1982-91; Deputy Director Scotland, 1991-95. Recreation: golf. Address: (b.) 123 Bothwell Street, Glasgow; T.-0141-248 1400.

Blair, James Ballantyne, BL, InstAM (Dip). Honorary Sheriff, Grampian, Highland and Islands at Stonehaven, since 1989; b. 16.8.24, Dailly, Ayrshire; m., Margaret M.J. McCafferty (deceased); 2 s.; 2 d. Educ. Peebles High School; Edinburgh University. Post Office, Peebles, 1941-44; Royal Signals, 1944-48 (GHQ (I) Signals, New Delhi, 1945-47); Sheriff Clerk's Offices, Edinburgh, Inverness, Peebles, Dingwall, Glasgow, 1948-73; Sheriff Clerk of Aberdeenshire at Aberdeen, 1973-82. Recreations: opera/operetta; reading (current affairs and law reports). Address: 41 Woodcot Park, Stonehaven AB3 2HG; T.-01569 762067.

Blair, James Eric, BL. Solicitor, since 1948; Honorary Sheriff, since 1980; b. 18.3.23, Airdrie. Educ. Glasgow Academy; Glasgow University. Past Captain, Airdrie Golf Club. Recreation: golf. Address: (h.) Dunedin, Forrest Street, Airdrie.

Blair, John Samuel Greene, OBE (Mil), TD, KStJ, BA, Hon. DLitt (St. Andrews), ChM, FRCSEdin, FICS, D(Obst)RCOG. Senior Lecturer, History of Medicine, St. Andrews University, since 1993; Honorary Senior Lecturer in Surgery, Dundee University, 1967-90; Member, Editorial Board, Vesalius, since 1994; b. 31.12.28, Wormit, Fife; m., Ailsa Jean Bowes; 2 s.; 1 d. Educ. Dundee High School; St. Andrews University (Harkness Scholar, 1946-50). National Service, RAMC, 1952-55; Tutor, Department of Anatomy, St. Salvator's College, St. Andrews, 1955; surgical and research training, Manchester, Dundee, Cambridge, London, 1957-65; Member, Court of Examiners, Royal College of Surgeons of Edinburgh, 1965; Consultant Surgeon, Perth Royal Infirmary, 1965-90; postgraduate Clinical Tutor, Perth, 1966-74; first North American

Travelling Fellow, St. Andrews/Dundee Universities, 1971; Secretary, Tayside Area Medical Advisory Committee, 1974-83; Member, Education Advisory Committee, Association of Surgeons, 1984-88; Secretary, Perth and Kinross Division, British Medical Association, 1982-90; Member, Scottish Council and Chairman's Sub-Committee, BMA, 1985-89; Fellow of the BMA, 1990; Chairman, Armed Forces Committee, BMA, since 1992; President: British Society for the History of Medicine, 1993-95, Scottish Society for the History of Medicine, 1990-93; Honorary Colonel (TA), RAMC; Member, Principal's Council, St Andrews University, since 1989; Elder, Church of Scotland; Hospitaller, Priory of Scotland, Order of St. John of Jerusalem; Mitchiner Lecturer, Army Medical Services, 1994. Publications: books on medical history and anatomy. Recreations: golf; travel; bridge. Address: (h.) 143 Glasgow Road, Perth; T.-Perth 623739.

Blair, Michael, FTS. Marketing Manager, Caledonian MacBrayne, since 1996; b. 5.12.43, Glasgow; m., Margaret; 1 d. Educ. Rothesay Academy. Merchant Navy, 1961-66; Assistant Tourist Officer, Glasgow Corporation, 1966-75; Tourist Officer, Cunninghame District Council, 1975-91; Director, Dunoon and Cowal Tourist Board, 1991-93; Director of Tourism, Bute and Cowal Tourist Board, 1993-96. Recreations: sailing; swimming. Address: (h.) 5 Eaglesham Terrace, Rothesay PA20 9HL; T.-01700 503211.

Blair, Robin Leitch, MB, ChB, FRCSEdin, FRCS(C), FACS. Head, Department of Otolaryngology, Ninewells Hospital and Medical School, Dundee, since 1984; Clinical Director of Otolaryngology, Dundee Teaching Hospitals NHS Trust; b. 28.11.45, Gourock; m., Elizabeth Anne Manson; 2 d. Educ. Greenock Academy; Edinburgh University; University of Toronto. House Surgeon, Royal Infirmary, Edinburgh; Lecturer, Department of Anatomy, Glasgow University; Assistant Professor, Department of Otolaryngology, University of Toronto. Address: (b.) Department of Otolaryngology, Ninewells Hospital and Medical School, Dundee DD1 9SY; T.-01382 660111, Ext. 2162.

Blair, Robin Orr, MA, LLB, WS. Partner, Turcan Connell WS, since 1997, Dundas & Wilson, 1967-97 (Managing Partner, 1976-83 and 1988-91); Chairman, Top Flight Leisure Group; Director, Tullis Russell Group Ltd. Educ. Rugby School; St. Andrews University; Edinburgh University. Purse Bearer to the Lord High Commissioner to General Assembly of Church of Scotland. Address: (b.) Saltire Court, 20 Castle Terrace, Edinburgh, EH1 2EF; T.-0131-228 8111.

Blake, Professor Christopher, CBE, FRSE, MA, PhD. Chairman, Glenrothes Development Corporation, 1987-96; b. 28.4.26; m.; 2 s.; 2 d. Educ. Dollar Academy; St. Andrews University. Royal Navy, 1944-47; teaching posts, 1951-53; Assistant, Edinburgh University, 1953-55; Stewarts & Lloyds Ltd., 1955-60; St. Andrews University, 1960-67: Lecturer, then Senior Lecturer; Dundee University, 1967-88: Senior Lecturer, Professor of Economics, Bonar Professor of Applied Economics; Director, Alliance Trust plc, 1974-94; Director, William Low & Co. plc, 1980-90 (Chairman, 1985-90). Recreation: golf. Address: (h.) Westlea, 14 Wardlaw Gardens, St. Andrews, Fife, KY16 9DW.

Blakey, Rev. Ronald Stanton, MA, BD, MTh. Deputy Secretary, Department of Education, Church of Scotland, since 1981; Secretary, Assembly Council, from 1 Aug., 1988; b. 3.7.38, Glasgow; m., Kathleen Dunbar; 1 s. Educ. Hutchesons' Boys' Grammar School, Glasgow; Glasgow University. Minister: St. Mark's, Kirkconnel, 1963-67; Bellshill West, 1967-72; Jedburgh Old Parish with Edgerston and Ancrum, 1972-81. Member, Roxburgh District Council, 1974-80 (Chairman of Council, 1977-80);

Religious Adviser, Border Television, 1973-81; Member, Borders Region Children's Panel, 1974-80; JP, 1974-80. Publication: The Man in the Manse, 1978. Recreation: collecting antiquarian books on Scotland. Address: (h.) 61 Orchard Brae Avenue, Edinburgh EH4.

Blakey, Wilson, MA (Hons), DipEd. Headteacher, Drumchapel High School, since 1992; b. 28.12.46, Uddingston; m., Ruth; 2 s.; 1 d. Educ. University of Glasgow. Teacher of Modern Studies, St. Augustine's Secondary, 1970-73; Principal Teacher of Modern Studies, Waverley Secondary, 1973-80; Assistant Headteacher, Vale of Leven Academy, 1980-86; Depute Headteacher, Castlehead High School, 1986-90; Headteacher, Crookston Castle Secondary, 1990-92. Past Chair, S.E.B. Panel; setter of Higher Grade Modern Studies. Publication: Contemporary Britain (Co-Author). Recreations: spectator sport (except horses and snow); genealogy; politics. Address: (h.) 150 Prestonfield, Milngavie, Glasgow; T.-0141-956 4822.

Blanchflower, Brian William, BSc (Hons), PGCSE (Distinction). Rector, Lochgelly High School, Fife, since 1996; b. 8.1.56, Belfast; m., Karen Ann Simpson; 1 s.; 1 d. Educ. Dunfermline High School; University of Edinburgh; Moray House College of Education. Teacher of Mathematics and Geography, Inverkeithing High School, 1979-83; Assistant Principal Teacher of Geography, Buckhaven High School, 1983-84; Principal Teacher of Geography, Beath High School, 1984-87; Assistant Rector, 1987-90, Depute Rector, 1990-96, Lochgelly High School. Recreations: rugby; hill-walking. Address: (b.) Lochgelly High School, Station Road, Lochgelly, Fife KY5 8LZ; T.-01592 418000.

Blaxter, Professor John Harry Savage, MA (Oxon), DSc (Oxon), HonDUniv(Stirling), FIBiol, FRSE. Hon. Professor, Stirling University and St. Andrews University; Hon. Research Fellow, Scottish Association for Marine Science; b. 6.1.29, London; m., Valerie Ann McElligott; 1 s.; 1 d. Educ. Berkhamsted School; Brasenose College, Oxford. SO, then SSO, Marine Laboratory, Aberdeen, 1952-64; Lecturer, Zoology Department, Aberdeen University, 1964-69; PSO, 1969, SPSO, 1974, DCSO, 1985-91, Scottish Marine Biological Association, Oban. Recreations: sailing; gardening. Address: (h.) Dems Lodge, Barcaldine, Oban PA37 1SF.

Bleiman, David, MA, MBA, MIPD. Assistant General Secretary (Scotland), Association of University Teachers, since 1982; Member, STUC General Council, since 1990; Member, Industrial Tribunal, since 1992; b. 7.8.53, Cape Town; m., Maureen McGibbon; 1 s.; 1 d. Educ. Haberdashers' Aske's School; Christ's College and King's College, Cambridge. W.E.A. Tutor, 1978; General Secretary, Scottish Further Education Association, 1979-82. Publication: Labour and Scottish Nationalism (Co-author), 1980. Recreations:listening to German language programmes; birdwatching. Address: (b.) 6 Castle Street, Edinburgh EH2 3AT; T.-0131-226 6694.

Bloomer, Keir, BA. Executive Director, Education and Community Services, Clackmannanshire, since 1996; b. 1.7.47, Glasgow; m., Jacquetta Megarry; 1 s.; 1 d. Educ. Greenock Academy; Cambridge University. Teacher, 1969-81; Depute General Secretary, Educational Institute of Scotland, 1981-84; Education Officer, then Depute Director of Education, Strathclyde Regional Council, 1984-95. Address: Lime Tree House, Alloa FK10 1EX; T.-01259 452435.

Bluck, Professor Brian John, BSc, PhD, DSc, FRSE, FGS. Professor of Tectonics and Sedimentation, University of Glasgow, since 1989; b. 29.8.35, Bridgend, S. Wales; m., Barbra Mary; 1 s.; 1 d. Educ. Bridgend County Grammar;

University College, Wales. Visiting Research Scholar, University of Illinois, USA, 1961; NATO Research Fellow, 1962; Assistant Lecturer, 1962, Reader, 1981, University of Glasgow. Awarded Keith Medal, Royal Society of Edinburgh, 1981; Lyell Fund, Geological Society of London, 1981; Saltire/Royal Bank of Scotland Award for contributions to geology in Scotland, 1991. Recreations: hill-walking; music; theatre. Address: (b.) Department of Geology and Applied Geology, University of Glasgow, Glasgow G12 8QQ; T.-0141-330 5447.

Boddy, Francis Andrew, MB, ChB, FRCPEdin, FFPHM, DPH. Director, Public Health Research Unit (formerly Social Paediatric and Obstetric Research Unit), Glasgow University, since 1978; b. 1.3.35, York; m., Adele Wirszubska; 2 d. Educ. Prince Henry's Grammar School, Otley; Edinburgh University. Research Associate, New York City Department of Health; Senior Lecturer, Department of Community Medicine, Glasgow University. Honorary Secretary, Society for Social Medicine, 1982-87, Chairman, 1996; Convener, Scottish Affairs Committee, Faculty of Public Health Medicine, 1991-94. Publications on socio-medical and public health topics. Recreations: fishing; photography. Address: (b.) 1 Lilybank Gardens, Glasgow G12; T.-0141-330 5399.

Bold, Alan. Writer; b. 20.4.43, Edinburgh; m., Alice Howell; 1 d. Educ. Broughton Secondary School; Edinburgh University. Full-time writer and visual artist since 1966; has published numerous books of poetry including: To Find the New; The State of the Nation; a selection in Penguin Modern Poets 15; In This Corner: Selected Poems 1963-83; collaborated on A Celtic Quintet, Haven and Homage to MacDiarmid; Editor, numerous anthologies, including: The Penguin Book of Socialist Verse; The Martial Muse; Cambridge Book of English Verse 1939-75; Making Love; The Bawdy Beautiful; Mounts of Venus; Drink To Me Only; The Poetry of Motion; books of criticism including: Thom Gunn & Ted Hughes; George Mackay Brown; The Ballad; Modern Scottish Literature; MacDiarmid: The Terrible Crystal; Muriel Spark; MacDiarmid: A Critical Biography (McVitie's Prize for Scottish Writer of the Year, 1989); Scotland: A Literary Guide; A Burns Companion; Editor: The Thistle Rises: a MacDiarmid Miscellany; The Letters of Hugh MacDiarmid; Rhymer Rab; author of novel, East Is West; has exhibited illuminated poems and oil paintings in a variety of venues; regular reviewer with Glasgow Herald and contributor to Sunday Times; Royal Philosophical Society of Glasgow annual arts award, 1990; Hon. President, Auchinleck Boswell Society, 1992. Recreations: walking; playing alto saxophone; watching films; gardening. Address: (h.) Balbirnie Burns East Cottage, near Markinch, Glenrothes, Fife KY7 6NE; T.-01592 757216.

Bolland, Alexander, QC (Scot),. BD, LLB; b. 21.11.50, Kilmarnock; m., Agnes Hunter Pate Moffat; 1 s.; 2 d. Educ. Kilmarnock Academy; St. Andrews University; Glasgow University. Admitted Faculty of Advocates, 1978; Captain, Army Legal Services, 1978-80, Standing Junior Counsel to Department of Employment in Scotland, 1988-92; QC (Scot), since 1992; Temporary Sheriff, since 1988; part-time Chairman, Industrial Tribunals, since 1992. Recreations: Hellenistics; walking; reading. Address: (h.) 60 North Street, St. Andrews, Fife; T.-01334 474599.

Bomont, Robert George, DUniv, BSc (Econ), IPFA, JP. University Secretary, Stirling University, 1973-95; General Commissioner of Income Tax, since 1977; b. 6.5.35, Preston; m., Marian; 1 s.; 2 d. Educ. Preston Grammar School; London University. Trainee and qualified accountant, Lancashire County Council, 1951-64; Assistant Finance Officer, Lancaster University, 1964-66; Accountant, then Accountant and Deputy Secretary, Stirling University, 1966-73. Member, Council of Management,

Strathcarron Hospice. Recreations: golf; gardening; DIY. Address: (h.) Wester Ardoch, Feddal Road, Braco, by Dunblane, Perthshire.

Bonallack, Michael Francis, OBE. Secretary, Royal and Ancient Golf Club of St. Andrews, since 1983; b. 31.12.34. Address: (b.) St. Andrews, KY16 9JD.

Bond, Professor Sir Michael R., MD, PhD, FRCSEdin, FRCPsych, FRCPSGlas, DPM, DSc (Leics, Hon). Professor of Psychological Medicine, Glasgow University, since 1973 (former Administrative Dean, Faculty of Medicine); b. 15.4.36, Balderton, Nottinghamshire; m., Jane; 1 s.; 1 d. Educ. Magnus Grammar School, Newark; Sheffield University. Former Vice-Principal, Glasgow University; Chairman, Head Injuries Trust for Scotland; Member, Council, St. Andrews Ambulance Association; Fellow, Royal Society of Arts; Knight Bachelor, 1995. Recreations: reading; music; painting. Address: (b.) Academic Centre, Gartnavel Royal Hospital, 1055 Great Western Road, Glasgow G12 0XH.

Bone, Professor (James) Drummond, MA. Vice-Principal, Glasgow University, since 1995; b. 11.7.47, Ayr; m., Vivian. Educ. Ayr Academy; Glasgow University; Balliol College, Oxford. Lecturer in English and Comparative Literary Studies, Warwick University; Lecturer and Senior Lecturer, English Literature, Glasgow University. Academic Editor and Advisory Editor, The Byron Journal; Editor, Romanticism. Recreations: music; skiing; Maseratis. Address: (h.) The Old Manse, Bow of Fife, Cupar, Fife.

Bone, Professor Thomas R., CBE, MA, MEd, PhD, FCCEA, FRSGS. Professor and Deputy Principal, Strathclyde University, until 1996 (Principal, Jordanhill College, 1972-92); b. 2.1.35, Port Glasgow; m., Elizabeth Stewart; 1 s.; 1 d. Educ. Port Glasgow High School; Greenock High School; Glasgow University; Jordanhill College. Teacher of English, Paisley Grammar School, 1957-62; Lecturer in Education: Jordanhill College, 1962-63, Glasgow University, 1963-67; Head of Education Department, Jordanhill College, 1967-71. Member, Dunning Committee, 1975-77; Chairman, Educational Advisory Council, IBA, 1985-88; Vice-Chairman: Scottish Examination Board, 1977-84; Scottish Tertiary Education Advisory Council, 1984-87; Chairman: Scottish Council for Educational Technology, 1981-87, Standing Conference on Studies in Education, 1982-84, Council for National Academic Awards Board for Organisation and Management, 1983-87, Council for National Academic Awards Committee for Teacher Education, 1987-89, General Teaching Council for Scotland, 1990-91; Member, Complaints Committee, Law Society of Scotland. Publication: School Inspection in Scotland, 1968; articles in journals. Recreation: golf. Address: (h.) 7 Marchbank Gardens, Ralston, Paisley.

Bonnar, Anne Elizabeth, MA. Director, Bonnar Keenlyside; Arts Management Consultant; b. 9.10.55, St. Andrews; m., Fernley Thompson; 2 s.; 2 d. Educ. Dumbarton Academy; Glasgow University; City University, London; Jordanhill College of Education. Theatre Manager, Young Vic Theatre, London, 1980; Director, Circuit, 1982, 1983; Press and Publicity, Mayfest, 1984, 1985; Publicity Officer, Citizens' Theatre, Glasgow, 1981-85; Arts Public Relations Consultant, 1985-86; General Manager, Traverse Theatre, 1986-91. Address: (b.) The Grange, Burntisland, Fife KY3 0AA; T.-01592 874478.

Bonnar, David James. Director (National Lottery), Scottish Arts Council, since 1994; b. 20.10.50, Dunfermline; m., Sally Elizabeth Armour; 2 s. Educ. Dunfermline High School. Royal Bank of Scotland, 1968-73; Theatre Royal, Glasgow, 1975-80; Theatre Royal, Newcastle upon Tyne, 1980-84; General Manager, Perth

Repertory Theatre, 1984-94. Recreations: singing; gardening; opera; architecture. Address: (b.) Scottish Arts Council, 12 Manor Place, Edinburgh; T.-0131-226 6051.

Bonnar, Desmond Michael, PhD, MBA, DipTP. Chief Executive, Lothian and Edinburgh Enterprise Ltd, since 1991; b. 26.7.47, Wishaw; m., Maureen; 1 s.; 1 d. Educ. Reading University; Glasgow University; Glasgow School of Art. Scottish Development Agency: Regional Director, Edinburgh/Lothians, Head, Service Industry Group, Head, Special Projects Division, Project Executive, Glasgow Eastern Area Renewal Project. Recreations: skiing; windsurfing. Address: (b.) Apex House, 99 Haymarket Terrace, Edinburgh EH12 5HD; T.-0131-313 4000.

Bonnington, Alistair James, LLB (Hons). Solicitor, BBC Scotland, since 1992; part-time Lecturer, University of Glasgow, since 1990; b. 28.5.52, Glasgow; m., Alison Margaret; 2 s.; 1 d. Educ. Hillhead High School, Glasgow; University of Glasgow. Apprentice, Biggart, Baillie and Gifford, Solicitors, Glasgow; pursued career in private practice, specialising in court work and media law. Secretary, Scottish Media Lawyers' Society. Publication: Scots Law for Journalists (Co-Author). Recreation: golf. Address: (b.) Broadcasting House, Queen Margaret Drive, Glasgow G12 8DG; T.-0141-338 2352.

Bonomy, Hon. Lord (Iain Bonomy). Senator of the College of Justice, since 1997; b. 15.1.46, Motherwell; m., Jan; 2 d. Educ. Dalziel High School; University of Glasgow. Apprentice Solicitor, East Kilbride Town Council, 1968-70; Solicitor, Ballantyne & Copland, 1970-83; Advocate, 1984-93; Queen's Counsel, 1993-96; Advocate Depute, 1990-96. Address: (b.) Parliament House, Edinburgh; T.-0131-225 2595.

Booker-Milburn, Sheriff Donald, BA, LLB. Sheriff of Grampian Highland and Islands, since 1983. Address: Sheriff Court House, The Castle, Inverness, IV2 3EG.

Borland, Marjorie Kirsteen, DA, RIBA, ARIAS, SpDip, FRTPI. Commissioner, Royal Fine Art Commission for Scotland, 1986-96; b. 13.1.25, Glasgow; m., John Charles Holmes, MC; 1 s.; 1 d. Educ. Westbourne School for Girls; Glasgow School of Architecture; School of Planning, London. Planner, London CC; Partner, Jack Holmes & Partners, Architects; Principal, The Jack Holmes Planning Group; Planning Consultant. Past Convener: RIAS Environment Committee, GIA Environment Committee. Address: (h.) Old Wing, Drumhead, Cardross G82 5EZ; T.-0138 984 1217.

Borley, Lester, CBE, DLitt, FRSGS, FTS, FRSA. Chairman: Icomos (UK), Cultural Tourism Committee; Council Member, Europe Nostra; Adviser, World Monuments Fund; b. 7.4.31, Pontardawe, S. Wales; m., Mary Alison Pearce; 3 d. Educ. Dover County Grammar School; Queen Mary College, University of London. Joined British Travel Association, London, 1955: Assistant to General Manager (USA), New York, 1956-61, Manager, Midwestern States (USA), Chicago, 1961-64, Manager, Australia, 1964-67, Manager, West Germany, Frankfurt, 1967-70; Chief Executive, Scottish Tourist Board, 1970-75; Chief Executive, English Tourist Board, 1975-83; Director, National Trust for Scotland, 1983-93; Secretary General, Europe Nostra, The Hague, 1992-96; Visiting Lecturer, Academia Istropolitana, Slovakia. Vice President, Edinburgh Film House; Trustee: Hopetoun House Trust, Cromarty Arts Trust. Recreations: gardening; visiting museums and galleries; reading social history; music. Address: (h.) 4 Belford Place, Edinburgh EH4 3DH; T.-0131-332 2364.

Borthwick, Alan Charles, LLB, NP. Partner, Brechin Tindal Oatts, Solicitors, Glasgow and Edinburgh, since 1983; b. 25.4.57, Glasgow; m., Sheila; 1 d. Educ. Glasgow Academy; Glasgow University. Brechin Robb, Solicitors, 1977-81; joined Tindal Oatts & Rodger, 1981. Member, Council, Law Society of Scotland, since 1995 (former Vice Convener, Professional Practice and International Relations Committees); Convener, Practice Management Committee and Electronic Services Working Party; Director, Children's Hospice Association Scotland; a Trustee, Parents Oncology Support, Yorkhill. Recreations: golf; skiing; garden; family. Address: (b.) 48 St. Vincent Street, Glasgow G2 5HS; T.-0141-221 8012.

Borthwick of that Ilk, Lord (John Hugh Borthwick). 24th Lord Borthwick; Hereditary Falconer of Scotland to The Queen; b. 14.11.40; m.; 2 d. Educ. Gordonstoun; Edinburgh School of Agriculture. Address: (h.) The Neuk, Heriot, Midlothian EH38 5HS.

Borthwick, Kenneth White, CBE, DL, JP; b. 4.11.15, Edinburgh; m., Irene Margaret; 2 s.; 1 d. Educ. George Heriot's School, Edinburgh. War Service, RAF; Lord Provost and Lord Lieutenant, City of Edinburgh, 1977-80; Chairman, 1986 Commonwealth Games Organizing Committee; Dean of Consular Corps of Edinburgh and Leith, since 1991; Hon. Consul, Republic of Malawi, 1982-94. Recreations: golf; gardening; painting. Address: (h.) 17 York Road, Edinburgh EH5 3EJ; T.-0131-552 2519.

Boswell, Sir Alexander, KCB, CBE, DL. Chairman, Officers' Association Scotland; Chairman, Scottish Veterans' Residences; Member, Executive Committee, Earl Haig Fund (Scotland); Member, Scottish Advisory Committee, Army Benevolent Fund; President, Friends of St. Mary's, Haddington; b. 3.8.28, Malaya (of Scottish parents); m., Jocelyn Pomfret; 5 s. Educ. Merchiston Castle School; RMA, Sandhurst. Enlisted in Army, 1947; commissioned Argyll & Sutherland Highlanders, 1948; regimental appointments, 1949-58; Staff College, Camberley, 1959; Military Assistant (GSO 2) to GOC Berlin, 1960-62; Company Commander, then Second in Command 1 A & SH, Malaya and Borneo, 1963-65; Directing Staff, Staff College, Camberley, 1965-68; Commanding Officer, 1 A & SH, 1968-71; Colonel GS Army Strategic Command, 1971; Brigadier Commanding 39 Infantry Brigade, 1972-74; Chief of Staff, 1st British Corps, 1974-76; National Defence College, Canada, 1976-77; GOC 2nd Armoured Division, 1978-80; Director, Territorial Army and Cadets, 1980-82; GOC Scotland and Governor of Edinburgh Castle, 1982-85; Lieutenant Governor and Commander in Chief, Bailiwick of Guernsey, 1985-90. Address: c/o Bank of Scotland, 52 Shandwick Place, Edinburgh EH2 4SB.

Boswell, Lorne, BA. Scottish Secretary, Equity, since 1990; b. 9.1.59, Bridge of Allan; m., Noreen; 2 s.; 1 d. Freelance theatre worker and stage manager, 1981-89. Address: (b.) 114 Union Street, Glasgow G1 3QQ; T.-0141 248 2472.

Bouchier, Professor Ian Arthur Dennis, CBE, MD, ChB, MD, FRCP, FRCPEdin, FFPHM, Hon. FCP (SAf), FIBiol, FRSE, FRSA. Professor of Medicine, Edinburgh University, 1986-97 (now Emeritus Professor); b. 7.9.32, Cape Town, South Africa; m., Patricia Norma Henshilwood; 2 s. Educ. Rondebosch Boys High School; Cape Town University. Instructor in Medicine, School of Medicine, Boston University, 1964; London University: Senior Lecturer in Medicine, 1965; Reader in Medicine, 1970; Professor of Medicine, Dundee University, 1973-86. Member: Court, Dundee University, Council, Royal Society, Edinburgh, Medical Research Council; former Chief Scientist, Scotland; President, World Organization of Gastroenterology; former Dean, Faculty of Medicine and Dentistry, Dundee University; Past President, British

Society of Gastroenterology. Publications: Clinical Skills (2nd edition), 1982; Gastroenterology (3rd edition), 1982; Gastroenterology: clinical science and practice (2nd edition), 1993. Recreations: music; history of whaling; cooking. Address: (h.) 8A Merchiston Park, Edinburgh EH10 4PN.

Boulton, Professor Geoffrey Stewart, FRS, FRSE, BSc, PhD, DSc, FGS. Regius Professor of Geology and Mineralogy, Edinburgh University, since 1986; Provost and Dean, Faculty of Science and Engineering, since 1994; b. 28.11.40, Stoke-on-Trent; m., Denise Bryers; 2 d. Educ. Longton High School; Birmingham University. Geological Survey of GB, 1962-64; University of Keele, 1964-65; Birmingham University, 1965-67; Water Supply Department, Kenya, 1968; University of East Anglia, 1968-81; Extraordinary Professor, University of Amsterdam, 1981-86. Kirk Bryan Award of the Geological Society of America, 1976; President, Quaternay Research Association, 1991-94; President, British Glaciological Society, 1989-91; President, Geological Society of Edinburgh, 1991-94; Member: Nature Conservancy Council for Scotland Science Board, 1991-92, Natural Environmental Research Council, since 1993 (Chairman, Earth Science and Technology Board), Royal Commission on Environmental Pollution, Scottish Higher Education Funding Council, since 1997, Royal Society Council, since 1997. Recreations: violin; mountaineering. Address: (b.) Department of Geology and Geophysics, University of Edinburgh, Grant Institute, Kings Buildings, West Mains Road, Edinburgh EH9 3JW.

Bovey, Keith S., BL. Solicitor, since 1951; President, Scottish CND; b. 31.7.27, Renfrew; m., Helen Cameron; 1 s.; 1 d. Educ. Paisley Grammar School; Glasgow University. Army, 1944-48. Publication: Misuse of Drugs, A Handbook for Lawyers. Address: (b.) 126 Morningside Road, Edinburgh EH10 4DT; T.-0131-452 8822.

Bowd, Nicholas John, CA. Director of Procurement, Scottish Office, since 1996; b. 3.4.45, Glasgow; m., Marjory; 2 d. Educ. High School of Glasgow; University of Glasgow. Qualified Assistant, Paterson & Steel CA, 1969; IBM UK, 1970-88 and 1991-95; IBM Europe (Paris), 1988-91; Motorola EICD (Swindon), 1996. Recreations: golf; rugby; football; personal investment; cars. Address: (b.) James Craig Walk, Edinburgh EH1 3BA; T.-0131-244 3504.

Bowdler, Timothy John, BSc, MBA. Group Managing Director, Johnston Press plc, since 1994; b. 16.5.47, Wolverhampton; m., Margaretha Eklund; 2 d. Educ. Wrekin College; Birmingham University; London Business School. Recreations: golf; tennis; skiing. Address: (b.) 53 Manor Place, Edinburgh EH3 7EG; T.-0131-225 3361.

Bowen, Edward Farquharson, TD, QC, LLB. Advocate; Sheriff Principal, Glasgow and Strathkelvin, since 1997; b. 1.5.45, Edinburgh; m., Patricia Margaret Brown; 2 s.; 2 d. Educ. Melville College, Edinburgh; Edinburgh University. Admitted Solicitor, 1968; Advocate, 1970; Standing Junior Counsel, Scottish Education Department, 1976; Advocate Depute, 1979-83; Sheriff of Tayside, Central and Fife, at Dundee, 1983-90; Partner, Thorntons WS, 1990-91; resumed practice at Scottish Bar; QC, 1992; Chairman (Part-time) Industrial Tribunals, 1995-97; Member, Criminal Injuries Compensation Board, 1996-97; Governor, Dundee Institute of Technology, 1987-90. Served RAOC TA/TAVR, 1964-80. Recreation: golf. Address: (b.) Sheriff's Chambers, Sheriff Court, 1 Carlton Place, Glasgow G5 9DA.

Bowler, David P., BA, MPhil, FSA (Scot). Director, Scottish Urban Archaeological Trust, since 1993; b. 9.12.55, Southampton. Educ. McGill University, Montreal;

Lincoln College, Oxford. Address: (b.) 55 South Methven Street, Perth PH1 5NX; T.-01738 622393.

Bowlt, Kenneth Stuart, BSc, FRICS. Chartered Surveyor; Member, Royal Institution of Chartered Surveyors Scottish Council, since 1990; b. 7.7.52, Nairn; m., Edith Bowman. Educ. Queen Victoria School, Dunblane; Edinburgh University. Voluntary Service Overseas, Zambia, 1975-80; set up Bowlts (chartered surveyors practice), 1991. Member, Royal Institution of Chartered Surveyors in Scotland Rural Practice Divisional Committee, since 1988, Divisional Council, since 1997; Secretary/Treasurer, West Ross Deer Management Group, since 1991. Recreations: fishing; stalking; five-a-side football; keep fit. Address: (h.) Muirfield, 27 Forteath Avenue, Elgin; T.-01343 552088.

Bowman, (Bernard) Neil, LLB, NP. Senior Partner, Bowman Scottish Lawyers, Solicitors, Dundee and Forfar, since 1984; b. 11.11.43, Dundee; m., Pamela Margaret Munro Wright; 2 d. Educ. High School of Dundee; Edinburgh University; St. Andrews University. Apprenticeship, Sturrock Morrison & Gilruth, Solicitors, Dundee, 1967-69; admitted Solicitor, 1969; Notary Public, 1970; assumed Partner, Gray Robertson & Wilkie (subsequently Bowman Gray Robertson and Wilkie, now Bowman) 1971. Secretary: Dundee Institute of Architects, 1970-96, Dundee Building Trades (Employers) Association, 1970-89, Dundee Construction Industry Group Training Association, 1970-93, Tayside Construction Safety Association, 1975-89; Joint Secretary, Local Joint Council for Building Industry, 1970-89, and Local Joint Apprenticeship Committee for the Building Industry, 1970-89; Clerk, Three United Trades of Dundee and to Mason Trade, Wright Trade and Slater Trade of Dundee, since 1970; Lord Dean of Guild of Guildry Incorporation of Dundee, 1987-90; first Lord President, Court of Deans of Guild of Scotland, 1989; Director, High School of Dundee, 1980-90; Chairman, High School of Dundee Scholarship Fund, 1987-90; Co-opted Member, Law Society of Scotland Committees — Public Relations and Conference, 1982-90, Complaints, 1987-90; Member: Working Party on "Corporate Conveyancing", 1989, School Age Team Sports Enquiry, 1989; Committee Member and National Selector, Scottish Cricket Union, 1974-83; Selector, 1990; President: Scottish Counties Cricket Board, 1981, Scottish Cricket Union, 1989. Recreations: cricketophile; breeding Highland cattle. Address: (b.) 27 Bank Street, Dundee; T.-01382 322267.

Bowman, Sheriff Pamela Margaret Munro, LLB, NP. All Scotland Sheriff; Dean, Society of Procurators and Solicitors of Angus; b. 1.8.44, Larbert; m., (Bernard) Neil Bowman; 2 d. Educ. Beacon School, Bridge of Allan, Stirling High School; Queens College, Dundee, St. Andrews University. Admitted Solicitor and Notary Public, 1967; Member, Scottish Legal Aid Board, 1994-97; Non-Executive Director, Angus NHS Trust, 1994-97. Recreations: theatre; literature; Highland cattle. Address: Newhouse of Balgaries, near Forfar, Angus, DD8 2TH; T.-01307 818258.

Bowman, Professor Emeritus William Cameron, BPharm, PhD, DSc, FIBiol, FRSE, FRSA, FRPharmS, HonFFARCS. Head, Department of Physiology and Pharmacology, Strathclyde University, 1966-87 and 1990-94; b. 26.4.30; m., Anne Wyllie Stafford; 1 s.; 1 d. Educ. London University. RAF (commissioned officer), 1955-57; Lecturer, then Reader in Pharmacology, London University, 1952-66. Dean, School of Pharmaceutical Sciences, Strathclyde University, 1974-77; Vice Principal, Strathclyde University, 1986-90; Visiting Professor: McGill University, Montreal; Cornell University, New York; Ohio Medical College. Member: Nomenclature Committee, BP Commission, 1964-67; Biology Committee, MOD, 1966-75; TCT and SEAR Sub-Committees, CSM, 1972-83; Biomedical Research Committee, SHHD, 1980-85;

Chairman, Committee: British Pharmacological Society, 1981-84 (Foreign Secretary since 1992), Heads of UK Pharmacology Departments, 1990-94; Member: Executive Committee, European Federation of Pharmacologists, 1991-96, Scottish Hospital Endowments Research Trust, since 1996; Secretary General, International Union of Pharmacology, 1994-98. Publications: Textbook of Pharmacology, 1968, 1980; Pharmacology of Neuromuscular Function, 1980, 1990; Dictionary of Pharmacology, 1986; many research articles in scientific journals. Address: Department of Physiology and Pharmacology, Strathclyde University, Glasgow G1 1XW; T.-0141-552 4400.

Bown, Professor Lalage Jean, OBE, MA (Oxon), DrUniv (Open University), DUniv (Paisley), Dr h.c. (Edinburgh), DUniv (Stirling), Hon. FITD, FRSA, FEIS, FRSE. Professor and Director, Department of Adult and Continuing Education, Glasgow University, 1981-92; Hon. Professor, Warwick University, 1992-97; Honorary Professorial Fellow, University of London Institute of Education, 1997-98; b. 1.4.27, Croydon. Educ. Wycombe Abbey School, Buckinghamshire; Cheltenham Ladies' College; Somerville College, Oxford. Resident Tutor: University College of the Gold Coast, 1949-55; Makerere University College, Uganda, 1955-59; successively Tutorial Advisor, Assistant Director, Deputy Director, Extra-Mural Department, Ibadan University, 1960-66 (Associate Professor, 1962-66); Director of Extra-Mural Studies and Professor Ad Personam, University of Zambia, 1966-70; Professor of Adult Education, Ahmadu Bello University, Nigeria, 1971-76; Commonwealth Visiting Professor, Edinburgh University, 1974; successively Professor of Adult Education and Dean of Education, Lagos University, 1977-80; Distinguished Visitor, Curtin University, Perth, Australia, 1995. Chair, Scottish Museums Council, 1993-96; Member: Board of Trustees, National Museums of Scotland, 1987-97, Council, Royal Society of Edinburgh, Commonwealth Standing Committee on Student Mobility and Higher Education Co-operation; former Member: Board, The British Council, Governing Body, Institute of Development Studies, Council, Scottish Poetry Library, Scottish Community Education Council; Past President: British Comparative and International Education Society, Development Studies Association; Vice-President, National Union of Townswomen's Guilds; former Vice-President, WEA; former Trustee, Womankind Worldwide; Vice-Chair, CODE Europe; President, British Association for Literacy in Development; Chair, Ethnological Research Centre, Edinburgh; Co-Chair, Scottish Somali Action. Publications: 10 academic books. Recreation: travel. Address: (h.) 37 Partickhill Road, Glasgow G11 5BP; T.-0141-339 1714.

Bownes, Professor Mary, BSc, DPhil. Personal Chair of Developmental Biology, Edinburgh University, since 1994; b. 14.11.48, Drewsteignton; m., Michael J. Greaves; 1 d. Educ. Maldon Grammar School; Sussex University. Lecturer, Essex University; Lecturer, Senior Lecturer, Reader, Edinburgh University. Publications: 100 research articles and reviews. Address: (b.) Institute of Cell and Molecular Biology, Edinburgh University, Darwin Building, Mayfield Road, Edinburgh EH9 3JR; T.-0131-650 5369.

Bowser of Argaty and the King's Lundies, David Stewart, JP, BA (Agric). Trustee, Scottish Forestry Trust, 1983-89 (Chairman, 1987); Member, Queen's Bodyguard for Scotland (Royal Company of Archers); Chairman, Scottish Council, British Deer Society, 1988-94; b. 11.3.26; m.; 1 s.; 4 d. Educ. Harrow; Trinity College, Cambridge. Captain, Scots Guards, 1944-47; Forestry Commissioner, 1974-82; President, Highland Cattle Society, 1970-72; Member, Perth County Council, 1954-61. Address: Auchlyne, Killin, Perthshire FK21 8RG.

Boxer, Professor David Howell, BSc, PhD. Professor of Biochemistry, Dundee University, since 1991, Head, Biochemistry Department, since 1988, Dean, Science and Engineering Faculty, since 1994; m., Dr. Maureen Boxer; 1 s.; 2 d. Educ. Aberdare Boys' Grammar School; Bristol University. Dundee University: Lecturer in Biochemistry, 1976, Senior Lecturer, 1985. Nuffield Research Fellow, 1983-84; Chairman, Biochemistry Biophysics Sub-Commitee, SERC, 1990-92. Recreations: travelling; skiing. Address: (b.) Department of Biochemistry, Medical Sciences Institute, Dundee University, Dundee DD1 4HN; T.-01382 344834.

Boyd, Rev. Archibald C., MA, BD. Principal, Free Church College. Ordained, 1959. Address: (b.) The Mound, Edinburgh, EH1 2LS.

Boyd, Colin David, QC, BA (Econ), LLB. Solicitor General for Scotland, since 1997; b. 7.6.53, Falkirk; m., Fiona Margaret MacLeod; 2 s.; 1 d. Educ. Wick High School; George Watson's College, Edinburgh; University of Manchester; University of Edinburgh. Solicitor, 1978-82; called to Bar, 1983; Advocate Depute, 1993-95; took Silk, 1995. Legal Associate, Royal Town Planning Institute. Publication: The Legal Aspects of Devolution (Contributor), 1997. Recreations: children; hill-walking; reading. Address: (b.) Crown Office, 25 Chambers Street, Edinburgh EH1 1LA; T.-0131-226 2626.

Boyd, Ian Mair, MSc, CA. Group Finance Director, The Weir Group PLC, since 1981; Director, Glasgow Income Trust plc, since 1990; Director, Inveresk PLC, since 1993; b. 4.9.44, Ayr; m., Theodora; 2 s.; 1 d. Educ. Ayr Academy; London Business School. The Weir Group PLC: Financial Controller International Division, 1975-78, Group Chief Accountant, 1978-81. Council Member, Institute of Chartered Accountants of Scotland, 1987-93; Chairman, Group of Scottish Finance Directors, 1990-91. Recreations: golf; hill-walking; fishing. Address: (b.) The Weir Group PLC, Cathcart, Glasgow G44 4EX; T.-0141-637 7111.

Boyd, Rev. Ian Robert, MA, BD, PhD. Minister, Netherlee Parish Church, since 1997; b. 29.11.61, Ayr; m., Dr. Carolyn Boyd; 2 s.; 1 d. Educ. Prestwick Academy; Glasgow University; Edinburgh University. Probationer Assistant Minister, Knightswood St. Margaret's, 1988-89; Minister, Perceton and Dreghorn, Irvine, 1989-92; postgraduate study, New College, Edinburgh University, 1992-96. Address: 532 Clarkston Road, Netherlee, Glasgow G44 3RT; T.-0141-637 2884.

Boyd, Joe, BSc (Hons), DipEd, MEd. Headteacher, St. David's High, Dalkeith, since 1997; Author, since 1989; b. 10.11.53, Ayr; m., Moira McCabe; 1 s.; 2 d. Educ. St. David's High, Dalkeith; University of St. Andrews; Moray House; University of Edinburgh. President, Students' Union, University of St. Andrews, 1975-76; teaching, various Lothian schools, including Beeslack High School, St. Augustine's High School, St. David's High School, 1977-97. Member, National Joint Working Party (Revised Higher Chemistry), 1987-90; seconded to SOEID, to work with HM Inspectorate, 1996-97; led Inservice workshops for teachers, 1983-97. Publications: co-author of 27 titles, including Understanding Science series, and Scottish Science S-14. Recreations: cycling; hill-walking; football; sailing; skiing; reading. Address: (b.) St. David's High School, Abbey Road, Dalkeith, Midlothian; T.-0131-663 1961.

Boyd, John Morton, CBE, BSc, PhD, DSc, DLitt, FIBiol, CBiol, FRSE, FRSA, HonFRSGS, HonFRZSS. Conservation Consultant to Scottish Hydro-Electric plc, since 1985; Consultant: Forestry Commission, since 1985 (Honorary since 1992), National Trust for Scotland, since

1985; b. 31.1.25, Darvel; m., Winifred Isobel Rome; 4 s. Educ. Darvel School; Kilmarnock Academy; Glasgow University. War service, 1943-47 (Flt. Lt., RAF). Nature Conservancy Council: Regional Officer, 1957-68, Assistant Director, 1969-70, Director (Scotland), 1971-85; Nuffield Travel Fellow, Mid-East and East Africa, 1964-65; Leader, British Jordan Expedition, 1966; Member: Royal Society Aldabra Expedition, 1967, Council, Royal Zoological Society of Scotland, 1963-69, 1980-89, since 1990, BBC Scotland Agricultural Advisory Committee, 1973-76, Council, National Trust for Scotland, 1971-85, Council, Royal Society of Edinburgh, 1978-81, Seals Advisory Committee, NERC, 1973-79, Consultative Panel on Conservation of Phoenix and Line Islands (Central Pacific), 1981-90, Council, Scottish Wildlife Trust, 1985-91, Commission on Ecology, IUCN, 1976-92, CCS Panel on Popular Mountain Areas, 1989, Advisory Committee on Sites of Special Scientific Interest, SNH, 1992-95; Co-Chairman, Area VI Anglo-Soviet Environmental Protection Agreement, 1977-85; Patron: Dynamic Earth, since 1993, Woodland Trust, since 1996; Vice-President: Scottish Conservation Projects Trust, since 1985, Scottish Wildlife Trust, since 1995; General Editor (Island Biology), Edinburgh University Press, 1985-92; Consultant Editor, Discover Scotland, 1989-90; Convenor, Saltire Society Science Award, since 1993; Lecturer, Glasgow University (Honorary), Swan (Hellenic) Ltd., Serenissima Travel Ltd., Noble Caledonia Ltd.; Neill Prize, Royal Society of Edinburgh, 1985; Elder, Colinton Kirk, since 1959; Member, Advisory Committee, Life and Work, since 1993. Publications: St. Kilda Summer (Co-author), 1960; Mosaic of Islands, 1963; Highlands and Islands (Co-author), 1964; Travels in the Middle-East and East Africa, 1966; Island Survivors (Co-editor), 1974; The Natural Environment of the Hebrides (Co-editor), 1979 and 1983; Fraser Darling's Islands, 1986; The Hebrides — a natural history (Co-author), 1990; Fraser Darling in Africa, 1992; The Hebrides – a trilogy (Co-author), 1996. Recreations: hill-walking; travel; painting; photography. Address: (h.) 57 Hailes Gardens, Edinburgh, EH13 0JH; T.-0131-441 3220; Balephuil, Tiree, Argyll; T.-01879 220 521.

Boyes, John, MA (Hons). HM Chief Inspector of Schools; b. 20.5.43, Greenock; m., Margaret Anne Peat; 1 s.; 1 d. Educ. Greenock High School; Glasgow University. Teacher, Alloa Academy and Denny High School, 1967-74. Recreation: mixing metaphors. Address: (b.) Scottish Office Education and Industry Department, Greyfriars House, Gallowgate, Aberdeen; T.-01224 642544.

Boyle, Professor Alan Edward, MA, BCL, Barrister. Professor of International Law, Edinburgh University, since 1994; Barrister, Middle Temple, since 1977; b. 28.3.53, Belfast; m., Caroline Patricia Tuckett. Educ. Royal Belfast Academical Institution; Pembroke College, Oxford University. Lecturer, Senior Lecturer, Reader, Queen Mary and Westfield College, London University, 1978-94; Visiting Professor, College of William and Mary, VA, 1987; Visiting Professor, University of Texas, 1988, 1994; Editor, International and Comparative Law Quarterly, since 1997 Publication: International Law and the Environment (Co-author), 1992. Recreations: gliding; walking; reading. Address: (b.) Faculty of Law, Edinburgh University, Old College, South Bridge, Edinburgh EH8 9YL; T.-0131-650 2019.

Boyle, Rt. Rev. Mgr. Hugh Noonan, PhL, STL, FSA Scot. Canon, Chapter of Metropolitan Cathedral Church of St. Andrew, Glasgow, since 1984; Chapter Secretary, since 1991; Prelate of Honour, since 1987; Archivist, Archdiocese of Glasgow, since 1973; b. 14.1.35, Glasgow. Educ. St. Aloysius' College, Glasgow; Glasgow University; Pontifical Scots College and Pontifical Gregorian University, Rome, 1956-63. National Service, RAF, 1954-56; ordained priest, Rome, 1962; Assistant Priest: St. Philomena's, Glasgow, 1963-66, St. Eunan's, Clydebank,

1966-76; Administrator, Metropolitan Cathedral Church of St. Andrew, Glasgow, 1983-92; Parish Priest, St. Leo's, Dumbreck, 1992-93; Chaplain, Bon Secours Convent Hospital, Glasgow, since 1995; Assistant Catholic Chaplain, Victoria Infirmary, Glasgow, since 1995; Archdiocese of Glasgow: Assistant Archivist, 1967-73; Chancellor, 1976-83. Editor, Catholic Directory for Scotland and Western Catholic Calendar, since issues of 1975; Member: Scottish Catholic Communications Commission, 1979-87; Scottish Catholic Heritage Commission, since 1981; Patron, Hutchesons' Hospital, since 1983. Recreations: music (listening); walking. Address: The Lindens, 36 Mansionhouse Road, Glasgow G41 3DW; T.-0141-649 9226.

Boyle, Iain Thomson, BSc (Hons), MB, ChB, FRCP, FRCP (London and Glasgow), FSA (Scot). Medical Advisor, University of Strathclyde, since 1991; Chairman: National Scientific Advisory Committee, Tenovus-Scotland, since 1997, Organising Committee, Glasgow 2000 National Philatelic Exhibition; Visiting Professor in Physiology/Pharmacology, University of Strathclyde, since 1994; b. 7.10.35, Glasgow; m., Elizabeth Johnston Carmichael; 1 s.; 2 d. Educ. Paisley Grammar School; Glasgow University. Lecturer in Medicine, Glasgow University and Glasgow Royal Infirmary, 1964-70; Hartenstein Research Fellow, Wisconsin University, 1970-72; Senior Lecturer in Medicine, Glasgow University and Glasgow Royal Infirmary, 1973-84; Reader in Medicine, Glasgow University and Glasgow Royal Infirmary, 1984-96. Chairman, Board of Management, Scottish Medical Journal, 1987-96; President, Bone and Tooth Society, 1994-96; Editor, Scottish Medical Journal, 1978-83; Co-Editor, Bone, 1983-93; Council Member, Royal College of Physicians and Surgeons, 1984-88; Secretary: Scottish Society for Experimental Medicine, 1984-88, Scottish Society of Physicians, 1984-88; President: Caledonian Philatelic Society, 1983-84, Association of Scottish Philatelic Societies, 1995-96, Harveian Society of Edinburgh, 1991; Vice President (Medical), Royal College of Physicians and Surgeons of Glasgow, 1992-94, and Hon. Librarian, since 1994. Fletcher Prize, Royal College of Physicians and Surgeons of Glasgow, 1973. Recreations: philately; Scottish social history; France and the French; angling; gardening; golf. Address: (h.) 7 Lochbrae Drive, High Burnside, Rutherglen, Glasgow G73 5QL.

Boyle, John Stirling, MA, DPA, FRSA. Director, Corporate Affairs, ScotRail, since 1994; b. 17.9.39, Paisley; m., Helen Dickson; 2 s.; 1 d. Educ. Camphill School, Paisley; Glasgow University. School Teacher, 1960-61; Reporter, Sunday Post, 1961-62; Technical Writer, Harland Engineering Company, 1962-64; Health Education Officer, Stirling County, 1964-66; Public Relations Officer, Heriot-Watt University, 1966-73; Director, External Relations, Scottish Council (Development and Industry), 1973-83; Director of Public Affairs (Scotland), British Rail, 1983-92; Director, Corporate Affairs (Scotland), British Railways Board, 1992-94. Recreation: motor cycling. Address: (b.) Caledonian Chambers, 87 Union Street, Glasgow G1 3ET; T.-0141-335 4447.

Boyle, Sandy, DGA. Joint Deputy General Secretary, BIFU, since 1992; Member, STUC General Council, since 1992; b. 23.12.45, Falkirk; m., Elizabeth Ross Cockrill; 1 s.; 1 d. Educ. Falkirk High School. Civil Servant, 1964-92. Vice-President, Society of Civil and Public Servants; Deputy President, National Union of Civil and Public Servants (President, NUCPS, 1989-92); STUC: Chair, Home and International Committee, since 1996, Member, Finance and Strategy Committee. Recreations: trade union badge collector; music; reading; bridge; watching Falkirk F.C. Address: (b.) 146 Argyle Street, Glasgow G2 8BL; T.-0141-221 6475.

Bradley, Rev. Dr. Ian Campbell, MA, BD, DPhil. Writer and Broadcaster; Lecturer, Department of Divinity, Aberdeen University; Member: Church of Scotland Panel on Worship, Liturgical Committee, Committee to Revise the Church Hymnary; b. 28.5.50, Berkhamsted; m., Lucy Patricia; 1 s.; 1 d. Educ. Tonbridge School, Kent; New College, Oxford; St. Andrews University. Research Fellow, New College, Oxford, 1971-75; Staff Journalist, The Times, 1976-82; ordained into Church of Scotland, 1990; Head, Religious Broadcasting, BBC Scotland, 1990-91. Publications: The Call to Seriousness, 1974; William Morris and his World, 1975; The Optimists, 1976; The Penguin Annotated Gilbert & Sullivan, 1980; The Strange Rebirth of Liberal Britain, 1982; Enlightened Entrepreneurs, 1986; The Penguin Book of Hymns, 1989; God is Green, 1990; O Love That Wilt Not Let Me Go, 1990; Marching to the Promised Land, 1992; The Celtic Way, 1993; The Power of Sacrifice, 1995; The Complete Annotated Gilbert and Sullivan, 1996; Columba, Pilgrim and Penitent, 1996; Abide with Me – the World of the Victorian Hymn, 1997. Recreations: music; walking; family; spas. Address: (h.) 7 Strathkinness High Road, St. Andrews KY16 9UA; T.-01334 475389.

Bradley, Professor Roy, BSc, MSc, PhD, FIMA, CMath. Head, Department of Mathematics, Glasgow Caledonian University, since 1992; b. 23.9.40, Wolverhampton; m., Ann; 1 s.; 1 d. Educ. Wolverhampton Grammar School; Durham University. Performance Engineer, 1963-65; Lecturer/Senior Lecturer/Principal Lecturer, Department of Mathematics and Statistics, Newcastle upon Tyne Polytechnic, 1965-86; Lecturer/Senior Lecturer, Department of Aerospace Engineering, Glasgow University, 1986-92. Recreation: mountaineering. Address: (b.) Department of Mathematics, Glasgow Caledonian University, Glasgow G4 0BA; T.-0141-331 3610.

Brady, Paul A., BSc (Hons), PhD. Director Finance and Planning, Scottish Enterprise; b. 28.7.49, Glasgow; 2 s.; 1 d. Educ. St. Mungo's Academy, Glasgow; University of Glasgow. Joined Scottish Office, 1974; posts in Industry, Police, and Energy areas, 1974-88; headed team advising on electricity privatisation, 1988-90; led on Higher Education reforms, 1991-92; Director of Policy, Scottish Higher Education Funding Council, 1992-93; Head, Finance Division (industry, transport and agriculture), Scottish Office, 1993-94. Recreations: walking; music; family. Address: (b.) Scottish Enterprise, 120 Bothwell Street, Glasgow G2 7JP; T.-0141 248 2700.

Braid, Peter John, LLB (Hons), WS. Partner, The Morton Fraser Partnership, Solicitors, since 1985; Solicitor Advocate, since 1995; b. 6.3.58, Edinburgh; m., Heather McIntosh; 2 s. Educ. George Watson's College, Edinburgh; University of Edinburgh. Apprentice, 1980-82; has specialised in litigation since 1982, now concentrates on commercial litigation; acted for manufacturer in Lanark Blue Cheese case, 1995. Publications: articles on enforcement of judgements, food safety, YZK. Recreations: golf; bridge; playing the piano badly. Address: (b.) 19 York Place, Edinburgh EH1 3EL; T.-0131-550 1023.

Brailsford, Sidney Neil, QC, BA, LLB. Member, Faculty of Advocates, since 1981; QC (Scotland), since 1994; b. 15.8.54, Edinburgh; m.; 2 s. Educ. Daniel Stewart's College, Edinburgh; Stirling University; Edinburgh University. Recreations: food and wine; travel; horse riding; American history. Address: (h.) 29 Warriston Crescent, Edinburgh, EH3 5LB; T.-0131-556 8320.

Braithwaite, Robert Barclay, BSc, CEng, FICE, MASCE. General Manager, Aberdeen Harbour Board, since 1990 (Assistant, then Deputy General Manager and Harbour Engineer, 1986-89); b. 17.2.48, Glasgow; m., Christine Isobel Ross; 2 s. Educ. Hutchesons' Boys' Grammar School; Strathclyde University. Graduate/Assistant Engineer, Rendel Palmer & Tritton, Consulting Civil Engineers, London, 1969-74; Deputy Harbour Engineer, 1974-75, Harbour Engineer, 1976-86, Aberdeen Harbour Board. Chairman, Aberdeen Maritime Museum Appeal; Council Member, Aberdeen Chamber of Commerce; Council Member, British Ports Association. Recreations: hill running; cycling; reading. Address: (b.) Harbour Office, 16 Regent Quay, Aberdeen AB11 5SS; T.-01224 592571.

Brand, David Allan, LLB (Hons), WS, NP. Solicitor; Senior Lecturer in Law, University of Dundee; Consultant, Thorntons WS, Dundee; b. 4.3.50, Dundee; 1 d. Educ. Grove Academy, Broughty Ferry; Dundee University. Former Member of Council, Law Society of Scotland; former Dean, Faculty of Procurators and Solicitors in Dundee; former Reporter to Scottish Legal Aid Board; former Member, Council, NHBC Scotland; former Chairman: Solicitors Property Centres Group Scotland, Tayside Solicitors Property Centre, Social Security Tribunals. Recreations: all types of music; amateur operatics; theatre. Address: (b.) Department of Law, University of Dundee, Dundee DD1 4HN; T.-01382 223181.

Brand, Janet Mary Valentine, BA (Hons), DipTP, MRTPI. Senior Lecturer, Strathclyde University, since 1973 (Member of Senate, 1984-91 and since 1992; Member of Court, 1989-91; Convener, Programme of Opportunities for Women Committee, 1990-93); b. 19.4.44, Bath; 2 d. Educ. County High School for Girls, Brentwood; Exeter University. Local authority appointments in Departments of Planning, Essex County Council, London Borough of Barking and City of London, 1965-70; Senior Lecturer, South Bank Polytechnic, 1970-73. Specialist Assessor in Town and Country Planning and Landscape, HEFCE, since 1996. Recreations: the environment; gardening; family pursuits; travelling. Address: (b.) Department of Environmental Planning, Strathclyde University, 50 Richmond Street, Glasgow; T.-0141-552 4400, Ext. 3905/6.

Brand, John Arthur. Reader in Government, formerly Politics, Strathclyde University; b. 4.8.34, Aberdeen; 1 d. Educ. Aberdeen Grammar School; Aberdeen University; London School of Economics. Assistant in Politics, Glasgow University, 1959-61; Lecturer in Politics, Reading University, 1961-63; Lecturer in the Politics of Education, London University, 1963-64; joined Strathclyde University as Lecturer in Politics, 1964. Chairman: Campaign for a Scottish Assembly, 1979-83; Glasgow Community Relations Committee, 1968-71. Recreations: skiing; tennis; music. Address: (h.) 17 Kew Terrace, Glasgow, G12 OTE; T.-0141-339 1675.

Brannan, Micheline H., MA. Head, Civil Law Division, Scottish Office Home Department, since 1995; b. 23.10.54, Glasgow; m., Michael N. Brannan; 2 s. Educ. Hutchesons' Grammar School; St. Hilda's College, Oxford. Scottish Office: joined as administrative trainee, 1976, promoted to Principal, 1982, Industry Department for Scotland, 1982-84, Scottish Education Department, 1985-88, Home and Health Department Criminal Justice Group, 1989-95. Recreations: Scottish country dancing; cycling; Jewish cultural activities. Address: (b.) Saughton House, Broomhouse Drive, Edinburgh; T.-0131-244 2258.

Breaks, Michael Lenox, BA, DipLib. University Librarian, Heriot-Watt University, since 1985; b. 12.1.45, Plymouth; m., Barbara Lawson; 1 s.; 1 d. Educ. St. George's College, Weybridge; Leeds University. Assistant Librarian: University College, Swansea, York University; Social Sciences Librarian, University College, Cardiff, 1977-81; Deputy Librarian, University College, Dublin, 1981-85. Chairman, JANET National User Group, 1991-93; Non-Executive Director, UKERNA; Member, SCONUL Executive Board; Editor, New Review of Information

Networking. Recreations: gardening; horse-riding; walking. Address: (h.) 2 Corrennie Gardens, Edinburgh EH10 6DG; T.-0131-447 7193.

Breen, James William, DPE. Deputy Chief Executive, Scottish Sports Council, since 1989; b. 1.7.53, Lennoxtown; m., Fiona; 2 d. Educ. Victoria Drive Secondary School, Glasgow; Jordanhill College, Glasgow. Assistant Director of Leisure Services, Motherwell District Council, 1986-89. Address: (b.) Caledonia House, South Gyle, Edinburgh EH12 9DQ; T.-0131-317 7200.

Breeze, David John, BA, PhD, FSA, PPSA Scot, FRSE, MIFA. Chief Inspector of Ancient Monuments, Scotland, since 1989; Visiting Professor, Department of Archaeology, Durham University, since 1993; Honorary Professor, Edinburgh University, since 1996; b. 25.7.44, Blackpool; m., Pamela Diane Silvester; 2 s. Educ. Blackpool Grammar School; Durham University. Inspector of Ancient Monuments, Scotland, 1969-88; Principal Inspector of Ancient Monuments, Scotland, 1988-89. Member: International Committee of the Congress of Roman Frontier Studies, since 1983, Council, Society of Antiquaries of London, 1984-86; Trustee, Senhouse Roman Museum, since 1985; Chairman: 1989 Hadrian's Wall Pilgrimage, British Archaeological Awards, since 1993; President, Society of Antiquaries of Scotland, 1987-90. Publications: The Building of Hadrian's Wall, The Army of Hadrian's Wall, Hadrian's Wall, and Roman Officers and Frontiers (all Co-author); Roman Scotland: a guide to the visible remains; Roman Scotland: some recent excavations (Editor); The Romans in Scotland (Co-author); The Northern Frontiers of Roman Britain; Roman Forts in Britain; Studies in Scottish Antiquity (Editor); Hadrian's Wall, a souvenir guide; A Queen's Progress, an introduction to the buildings associated with Mary Queen of Scots in Scotland; The Second Augustan Legion in North Britain; Service in the Roman Army (Co-editor); Invaders of Scotland (Co-author); Roman Scotland: Frontier Country; The Stone of Destiny: Symbol of Nationhood (Co-author). Recreations: reading; walking; swimming; travel. Address: (b.) Historic Scotland, Longmore House, Salisbury Place, Edinburgh, EH9 1SH; T.-0131-668 8724.

Bremner, Ian, BSc, PhD, DSc. Deputy Director (Science), Rowett Research Institute, Aberdeen, since 1988; b. 19.2.39, Aberdeen; m., Kathleen Stewart; 3 s. Educ. Robert Gordon's College, Aberdeen; Aberdeen University. Senior Research Biochemist, Fisons Pharmaceuticals Ltd., Cheshire, 1964-65; SSO, Nutritional Biochemistry Department, Rowett Research Institute, 1967, PSO, 1974; Grade 6, Biochemistry Division, 1985. Member, Parent Committee, and Chairman, TEMA International: international symposia on trace elements in man and animals; Underwood Memorial Lecture, 1990. Address: (b.) Rowett Research Institute, Greenburn Road, Bucksburn, Aberdeen, AB21 9SB; T.-01224 716602.

Brett, Timothy Edward William, BSc (Hons), FHSM, DipHSM, GradIPM. Chief Executive, Dundee Teaching Hospitals NHS Trust, since 1993; b. 28.3.49, Gravesend; m., Barbara Jane; 2 s; 1 d. Educ. Gravesend Grammar School for Boys; Bristol University. Unit Administrator, Plymouth General Hospital, 1981-85; Dundee General Hospitals Unit: Unit Administrator, 1985-87, Unit General Manager, 1987-93. Recreations: hill-walking; squash; swimming; theatre; church activities. Address: (h.) Woodend Cottage, Hazelton Walls, Cupar KY15 4QL; T.-01382 632598.

Brett Young, Michael Jonathan, DL. Manager, East Sutherland Village Advisory Service, since 1986; Director: Voluntary Groups, East Sutherland, since 1996, Highland Advice and Information Network Ltd.; Deputy Lieutenant, Sutherland, since 1995; b. 18.10.37, Salisbury; m., Helen Dorothy Anne Barker; 2 s. Educ. Dartmouth. Royal

Australian Navy, 1956-69; Sales and Marketing Manager, 1969-79; Senior Account Manager, 1979-84. Chairman, PR Committee, Retread Manufacturers Association, 1975-79; Executive Member, Community Organisations Group, Scotland, 1990-93; Chairman: East Sutherland Council of Social Service, 1991-94, East Sutherland Local Community Care Forum, since 1993; Executive Member, SSAFA, Sutherland; Chairman, Dornoch Cricket Club, since 1991. Recreations: cricket; naval history; music. Address: (h.) West Shinness Lodge, Lairg, Sutherland; T.-01549 402495.

Brew, David Allan, BA, MSc. Assistant Secretary, Scottish Office, since 1990; b. 19.2.53, Kettering. Educ. Kettering Grammar School; Heriot-Watt University; Strathclyde University; European University Institute, Florence. Administration Trainee and HEO(D), Scottish Office, 1979-81; Administrator, DGV, Commission of the EC, 1981-84; Principal, Scottish Office, Glasgow, 1984-88, Edinburgh, 1988-90; Assistant Secretary, since 1990; Head: Electricity Privatisation Division, 1990-91, European Funds and Co-ordination Division, 1991-95, Sea Fisheries Division, since 1995. Member, Court, Heriot-Watt University, 1985-91. Recreations: languages; music; film; gastronomy. Address (h.) Flat 4, 1 Dundas Street, Edinburgh, EH3 6QG; T.-0131-556 4692.

Bridges, Professor Roy Charles, BA, PhD, FRGS, FRHistS. Emeritus Professor of History, Aberdeen University; b. 26.9.32, Aylesbury; m., Jill Margaret Bridges; 2 s.; 2 d. Educ. Harrow Weald County Grammar School; Keele University; London University. Lecturer in History, Makerere University, Uganda, 1960-64; joined Aberdeen University, 1964; Head, History Department, 1977-82, 1985-88, 1990-94; Secretary, then Chairman, African Studies Group, 1966-94. Chairman, SEB Joint Working Party on Higher and Post-Higher History, 1988-90; Council Member: Royal Historical Society, since 1995, Hakluyt Society, 1991-95; Treasurer, Scottish Institute of Missionary Studies. Publications: Nations and Empires (Co-author), 1969; Africa in Times Atlas of World Exploration; Compassing the Vaste Globe of the Earth (Co-editor), 1996. Recreations: cricket; geology; gardening. Address: (b.) Department of History, King's College, Aberdeen, AB24 3FX; T.-Aberdeen 272452.

Britton, Professor Celia Margaret, MA (Cantab), PhD. Carnegie Professor of French and Director, Centre for Francophone Studies, Aberdeen University, since 1991; b. 20.3.46, Stanmore, Middx. Educ. North London Collegiate School; New Hall, Cambridge. Temporary Lecturer in French, Kings College, London, 1972-74; Lecturer in French Studies, Reading University, 1974-91. Publications: Claude Simon: Writing The Visible, 1987; The Nouveau Roman: fiction, theory and politics, 1992; Claude Simon (Editor), 1993; articles on French literature and cinema, French Caribbean literature. Address: (b.) Department of French, Aberdeen University, Old Aberdeen, AB9 2UB; T.-01224 272163.

Broadie, Professor Alexander, MA, PhD, DLitt, FRSE. Professor of Logic and Rhetoric, Glasgow University. Educ. Royal High School, Edinburgh; Edinburgh University; Balliol College, Oxford. Henry Duncan Prize Lecturer in Scottish Studies, Royal Society of Edinburgh, 1990-93; Gifford Lecturer, Aberdeen University, 1994. Publications: A Samaritan Philosophy, 1981; George Lokert: Late-Scholastic Logician, 1983; The Circle of John Mair, 1985; Introduction to Medieval Logic, 1987; Notion and Object, 1989; The Tradition of Scottish Philosophy, 1990; Paul of Venice: Logica Magna, 1990; Robert Kilwardby O.P.: on time and imagination, 1993; Introduction to Medieval Logic (2nd edition), 1993; The Shadow of Scotus, 1995; The Scottish Enlightenment: an anthology, 1997. Address: (b.) Philosophy Department, The University, Glasgow G12 8QQ; T.-0141-330 5692.

Brock, Professor David John Henry, BA (Oxon), PhD, FRCPath, FRSE, FRCPE. Professor of Human Genetics, Edinburgh University, since 1985; Director, Human Genetics Unit, Edinburgh University, since 1983; Chairman, Department of Medicine, Western General Hospital, since 1994; b. 5.6.36, London; 4 s. Educ. Diocesan College, Cape Town; Cape Town University; Oxford University. Postdoctoral Fellow: Massachussets Institute of Technology, 1962-63; Harvard University, 1963-66; Oxford University, 1966-67; Senior Scientific Officer, ARC Animal Breeding Research Organisation, 1967-68; joined Edinburgh University as Lecturer in Human Genetics, 1968; appointed Reader, 1978. Address: (h.) 14 Silverknowes Avenue, Edinburgh; T.-0131-336 5015.

Brock, Sheila Margaret, MA, PhD. Campaign Director, Museum of Scotland, since 1994; Chair, Visual Arts Committee, Scottish Arts Council, since 1993; Trustee, Paxton House Trust, since 1996; b. Edinburgh; 4 s. Educ. George Watson's Ladies' College; Edinburgh University; St. Hugh's College, Oxford. Various teaching posts, Scotland, England, South Africa; Scholar, Radcliffe Institute, Cambridge; Education Department, Royal Scottish Museum, 1979-83; Head of Public Affairs, National Museums of Scotland, 1983-94. Recreations: reading; music; gardening; travel. Address: (b.) Campaign Office, Royal Museum of Scotland, Chambers Street, Edinburgh EH1 1JF; T.-0131-247 4389.

Brockie, Rev. Colin Glynn Frederick, BSc (Eng), BD. Minister, Kilmarnock: Grange, since 1978; Clerk to Presbytery of Irvine and Kilmarnock, since 1992; Hon. Chaplain, 327 (Kilmarnock) Squadron, Air Training Corps, since 1978; b. 17.7.42, Westcliff on Sea; m., Barbara Katherine Gordon; 2 s.; 1 d. Educ. Musselburgh Grammar School; Aberdeen Grammar School; University of Aberdeen. Probationary year, Aberdeen: Mastrick, 1967-68; Minister, St. Martin's, Edinburgh, 1968-78. Recreations: billiards; photography; computing. Address: Grange Manse, 51 Portland Road, Kilmarnock, Ayrshire KA1 2EQ; T.-01563 525311.

Brocklebank, Ted. TV Producer, Greyfriars Productions; b. 24.9.42, St. Andrews; 2 s. Educ. Madras College, St. Andrews. D.C. Thomson, Dundee, 1960-63; Freelance Journalist, 1963-65; Scottish TV, 1965-70; Grampian Television: Reporter, 1970-76, Head of News and Current Affairs, 1977-85, Head of Documentaries and Features, 1985-95. BAFTA Award for What Price Oil?; Radio Industries Club of Scotland Special Award (Documentary) for Tale of Two Cities; Norwegian Amanda award for eight-part series on world oil business, networked on Channel 4 and throughout USA on PBS; BMA Award for Scotland the Grave. Recreation: Committee Member, Scottish Cancer Research Campaign. Address: (b.) Greyfriars Productions, Greyfriars Garden, St. Andrews KY16 9HG.

Brodie, Robert, CB, MA, LLB. Solicitor to Secretary of State for Scotland, since 1987 (Deputy Solicitor, 1984-87); b. 9.4.38, Dundee; m., Jean Margaret McDonald; 2 s.; 2 d. Educ. Morgan Academy, Dundee; St. Andrews University; Queen's College, Dundee. Scottish Office: Legal Assistant, 1965; Senior Legal Assistant, 1970; Deputy Director, Scottish Courts Administration, 1975; Assistant Solicitor, Scottish Office, 1982. Chairman, Scottish Tourette Syndrome Support Group, since 1993. Recreations: music; hill-walking. Address: (h.) 45 Stirling Road, Edinburgh; T.-0131-552 2028.

Brodie, William, BSc, CBiol, MIBiol. Rector, Wallace High School, Stirling, since 1984; b. 16.9.37, Hamilton; m., Helen Bland; 1 s.; 1 d. Educ. Hamilton Academy; Glasgow University; Paisley College of Technology. Teacher,

Wishaw High School, 1965-67; Principal Teacher of Biology, Hutchesons' Grammar School, Glasgow, 1967-74; Assistant Rector, Graeme High School, Falkirk, 1974-79; Depute Rector, Kirkintilloch High School, 1979-81; Rector, Balfron High School, 1981-84. Recreations: golf; tennis; gardening. Address: (b.) Wallace High School, Dumyat Road, Stirling FK9 5HW; T.-01786 462166.

Brodie of Brodie, (Montagu) Ninian Alexander, DL, JP; b. 12.6.12, Forres; m., Helena Penelope Budgen (deceased); 1 s.; 1 d. Educ. Eton. Trained Webber-Douglas School of Dramatic Art, 1933-35; professional Actor and Director, occasional broadcasts, 1935-40; served with Royal Artillery, including North Africa and Italy, 1940-45; returned to stage, with occasional films and broadcasts, 1945-50; managed estate, market garden, etc., Brodie Castle, from 1950; transferred Brodie Castle and part of estate to National Trust for Scotland, 1979; voluntary work as guide etc., since 1980. Life Member, National Trust for Scotland. Recreations: shooting; hill-walking; collecting paintings. Address: (h.) Brodie Castle, Forres, Moray, IV36 0TE.

Bromage, Professor Niall R., BSc, PhD. Professor of Reproductive Physiology, University of Stirling, since 1994; Assistant Director, Institute of Aquaculture, since 1996; Editor, Aquaculture, since 1991; Technical Adviser, British Trout Association, since 1990; b. 4.7.42, Herts; m., Anne; 1 s.; 1 d. Educ. Welwyn Garden City Grammar School; University of Leicester. Lecturer, University of Aston, 1967-88; Lecturer, then Senior Lecturer, University of Stirling, 1988-94. Publications: author of books on intensive aquaculture, bacterial diseases of fish and broodstock management; over 160 scientific and trade articles. Recreation: squash. Address: (b.) University of Stirling, Stirling FK9 4LA; T.-01786 473171.

Broni, David Alexander Thomas, MIED. Aftercare Executive, Locate in Scotland, since 1995; b. 25.10.57, Glasgow; m., Ann Frances; 1 s.; 1 d. Educ. St. Mungo's Academy. Joined civil service, 1975; Manpower Services Commission, 12 years, Training Agency, 2 years, Scottish Office Industry Department, 2 years; Head of Secretariat, Scottish Enterprise, 4 years. Member, Institute of Economic Development. Recreations: running; cycling; swimming; rugby; opera. Address: (b.) 120 Bothwell Street, Glasgow G2 7JP; T.-0141-228 2854.

Brooke, (Alexander) Keith, FRAgS. Director: Animal Diseases Research Association, now Moredun Foundation for Animal Health and Welfare, 1981-96, Scottish, English & Welsh Wool Growers Ld., 1988-95, Wigtownshire Quality Lamb Ltd., 1991-96; Member, Panel of Agricultural Arbiters appointed by Secretary of State for Scotland; b. 11.2.46, Minnigaff; m., Dilys K. Littlejohn; 1 s.; 3 d. Educ. George Watson's College, Edinburgh. President, Blackface Sheep Breeders Association, 1985-86, Hon. President, 1989-92; Director: Royal Highland and Agricultural Society of Scotland, 1986-93 and since 1994, Wallets Marts PLC, 1989-91; Chairman, Blackface Sheep Breeders' Development Board, since 1996; Member: Council for Awards of Royal Agricultural Societies, since 1997, Council, British Rouge de l'Ouest Sheep Society, since 1986 (Chairman, 1990-92, Treasurer, since 1993). Address: (h.) Carscreugh, Glenluce, Newton Stewart, DG8 0NU; T.-01581 300334.

Brooks, James, BTech (Hons), MPhil, PhD, FRSC, CChem, FGS, FInstPet, AssocBIT. Senior Partner, Brooks Associates Glasgow, since 1986; Visiting Lecturer, Glasgow University, since 1978; Chairman/Director, Petroleum Geology '86 Limited, since 1985; b. 11.10.38, Co. Durham; m., Jan Slack; 1 s.; 1 d. Educ. University of Bradford. Research Scientist, British Petroleum, 1969-75; Senior Research Fellow, Bradford University, 1975-77;

Research Associate/Section Head/Senior Scientist, British National Oil Corporation/Britoil PLC, 1977-86. Geological Society: Vice President, 1984-87, Secretary, 1987-90; Founder and Chairman, The Petroleum Group; AAPG Distinguished Achievement Award for service to petroleum geology and human need, 1993; AAPG Distinguished Lecturer to North America, 1989-90; Chairman, Shawlands Academy School Board, since 1990; Church Secretary, Queen's Park Baptist Church, Glasgow; elected Member, Baptist Union of Scotland Council. Publications: 18 books; 85 research papers. Recreations:travel; reading; writing; sport (English soccer!); Christian work. Address: (h.) 10 Langside Drive, Newlands, Glasgow G43 2EE; T.-0141-632 3068.

Brooks, Patrick William, BSc, MB, ChB, DPM, FRCPsych. Senior Medical Officer, Scottish Office Department of Health, since 1981; b. 17.5.38, Hereford. Educ. Hereford High School; Bishop Vesey's Grammar School, Sutton Coldfield; Edinburgh University. Royal Edinburgh and associated hospitals, including State Hospital, Carstairs, and Western General Hospital, Edinburgh: Senior House Officer, 1964-66; Registrar, 1966-69; Senior Registrar, 1969-74; Medical Officer, Scottish Home and Health Department, 1974-81. A founder Member, Edinburgh Festival Fringe Society, 1959 (Vice-Chairman, 1964-71); Chairman, Edinburgh Playhouse Society, 1975-81; Secretary, Lothian Playhouse Trust, 1981-83; Chairman, The Scottish Society; Joint Vice-Chairman, Royal Lyceum Theatre Club. Recreations: opera; ballet; music; theatre; cinema; modern Scottish art; travel. Address: (h.) 11 Thirlestane Road, Edinburgh EH9 1AL.

Broome, Professor John, BA, MA, PhD. Professor of Philosophy, University of St. Andrews, since 1996; b. 17.5.47, Kuala Lumpur, Malaya; m., Ann; 1 s.; 1 d. Educ. Rugby School; Trinity Hall, Cambridge; Bedford College, London; Massachusetts Institute of Technology. Lecturer in Economics, Birkbeck College, London University, 1972-78; University of Bristol: Reader in Economics, 1979-92, Professor of Economics and Ethics, 1992-95. Publications: The Microeconomics of Capitalism, 1983; Weighing Goods, 1991; Counting the Cost of Global Warming, 1992. Recreation: sailing. Address: (b.) Department of Moral Philosophy, University of St. Andrews, St. Andrews, Fife KY16 9AL; T.-01334 462481.

Broster, Rev. David, BA, DipTh, CPS. Minister, Kilbirnie: St. Columba's, since 1983; Clerk, Ardrossan Presbytery, since 1989; b. 14.3.44, Liverpool; m., Margaret Ann Mercer; 2 d. Educ. Liverpool Institute High School; United Theological College, University of Wales; Open University. Ordained by Presbyterian Church of Wales, 1969; Minister, Park Place, Tredegar, Gwent, 1969-78; Clubmoor Presbyterian Church of Wales, Liverpool, 1978-83; Clerk, Association in East, Presbyterian Church of Wales, 1981-83; Moderator, Synod of Ayr, 1991-92; Secretary, Nan Stevenson Charitable Trust, since 1989. Chairman: Garnock Valley Victim Support, Moorpark School Board; Past Chairman, Garnock Valley Crime Prevention Panel; Treasurer, Garnock Valley Rotary. Recreations: computing; advanced driving; gardening; curling. Address: St. Columba's Manse, Kilbirnie, Ayrshire; T.-01505 683342.

Broun, Janice Anne, BA. Freelance journalist and author; b. 24.3.34, Tipton; m., Canon Claud Broun; 2 s.; 1 d. Educ. Dudley Girls High School; St. Anne's College, Oxford. Publications: Conscience and Captivity: Religion in Eastern Europe, 1988; Prague Winter, 1988; Albania: Religion in a Fortress State, 1989; Bulgaria: Religion Denied, 1989; Romania: Religion in a Hardline State, 1989; six entries in Censorship: An International Dictionary, 1998; frequent contributions to Keston Institute publications. Recreations: swimming; cycling; music; art history; travel. Address:

Martin Lodge, Ardross Place, Alness, Ross-shire, IV17 0PX; T.-01349 882442.

Brown, Alan. Chairman, Scottish Road Safety Campaign, since 1995; Head of Road Safety Branch, Scottish Office, since 1995; b. 9.5.47, Methil; m., Marion Dougal; 1 s.; 1 d. Educ. Buckhaven High School. Joined Scottish Office, 1965: posts in Education, Social Work Services, Transport, Local Government, and Criminal Justice. County Bird Recorder for East Lothian, 1983-89; Member: Lothian Birds Record Committee, 1983-96, Scottish Birds Record Committee, 1984-94 (Secretary, 1984-86), Council, Scottish Ornithologists Club, 1986-90, British Birds Rarities Committee, 1987-95. Recreations: birdwatching in the world's remote places (the ecstasy); supporting Hibernian FC (the agony); rock music. Address: (b.) The Scottish Office, Victoria Quay, Edinburgh EH6 6QQ; T.-0131-244 0836.

Brown, Professor Alan Geoffrey, BSc, MB, ChB, PhD, FRSE, FIBiol. Professor of Veterinary Physiology, Edinburgh University, since 1984; b. 20.4.40, Nottingham; m., Judith Allen; 1 s.; 1 d. Educ. Mundella School, Nottingham; Edinburgh University. Assistant Lecturer, then Lecturer in Veterinary Physiology, Edinburgh University, 1964-68; Beit Memorial Fellow for Medical Research, 1968-71; Research Fellow supported by MRC, 1971-74; Lecturer, then Reader in Veterinary Physiology, Edinburgh University, 1974-84; holder, MRC Research Fellowship for academic staff, 1980-85. Member, Editorial Boards, several scientific journals. Recreations: music; gardening; walking; reading. Address: (b.) Department of Preclinical Veterinary Sciences, Edinburgh University, Edinburgh, EH9 1QH; T.-0131-667 1011.

Brown, Alistair M. Director, Administrative Services, Scottish Office, since 1997; b. 1.3.57, Edinburgh; m., Sarah Thompson; 1 s.; 2 d. Educ. Linlithgow Academy. Scottish Office, since 1974; Personal Assistant to Chief Executive, S.D.A., 1987-89; Scottish Office Industry Department, 1989-93; Grade 5, 1993. Recreations: helping to bring up family; walking. Address: (b.) Scottish Office, Victoria Quay, Edinburgh EH6 6QQ; T.-0131-244 7692.

Brown, Professor Charles Malcolm, BSc, PhD, DSc, FIBiol, FIBrew, FRSE. Professor of Microbiology, Heriot-Watt University, since 1979 (Head, Department of Biological Sciences, 1988-93; Dean of Science, 1993-95, Assistant Principal, 1994-95; Vice Principal, since 1995); b. 21.9.41, Gilsland; m., Diane Mary Bryant; 3 d. Educ. Houghton-le-Spring Grammar School; Birmingham University. Lecturer in Microbiology, Newcastle-upon-Tyne University, 1966-73; Senior Lecturer, Dundee University, 1973-79. Deputy Chairman, C-MIST; Director, Microbiological Research Authority; Editor: Process Biochemistry; Journal of the Institute of Brewing. Recreations: music; walking. Address: (b.) Heriot-Watt University, Riccarton, Edinburgh EH14 4AS; T.-0131-449 5111.

Brown, Professor Ewan, CBE, MA, LLB, CA, FRSA. Merchant Banker; Executive Director: Noble Grossart Ltd., since 1971; Chairman, Dunedin Income Growth Investment Trust Plc; Director, Amicable Smaller Enterprises Trust Plc; John Wood Group Plc; Noble Grossart Investments Ltd.; Scottish Widows Bank plc; Stagecoach Holdings Plc; James Walker (Leith) Ltd.; Scottish Knowledge Plc.; b. 23.3.42, Perth; m., Christine; 1 s.; 1 d. Educ. Perth Academy; St. Andrews University. CA apprentice with Peat Marwick Mitchell, 1964-67. Honorary Professor in Finance, Heriot Watt University; Trustee, Carnegie Trust for the Universities of Scotland; Chairman, University Court, Heriot-Watt University; Master, The Company of Merchants of the City of Edinburgh, 1994-95; Lord Dean of Guild, City of Edinburgh, 1995-97; Council Member:

Institute of Chartered Accountants of Scotland, 1988-91; Scottish Business School, 1974-80; Director: Scottish Transport Group, 1983-88, Scottish Development Finance, 1983-93, Pict Petroleum plc; Governor, Edinburgh College of Art, 1986-89; Session Clerk, Mayfield Church, 1983-88. Recreations: family; golf; skiing; Scottish watercolours; Mah Jongg. Address: (b.) 48 Queen Street, Edinburgh; T.-0131-226 7011.

Brown, Francis Henry, BA (Hons), MHSM, DipHSM. Chief Executive, Perth and Kinross Healthcare NHS Trust, since 1994; b. 17.4.47, Falkirk; m., Marion Muir Crawford; 2 s. Educ. Falkirk High School; Strathclyde University. Joined NHS as graduate trainee, 1975; various management/senior management posts, Borders Health Board, Ayrshire and Arran Health Board, 1977-94. Recreations: music; swimming; cycling; golf. Address: (b.) Perth Royal Infirmary, Taymount Terrace, Perth PH1 1NX; T.-01738 620540.

Brown, Gerard Anthony, LLB, NP. Partner, Livingstone, Brown, Solicitors; Council Member, Law Society of Scotland, since 1995 (Convener: Criminal Law Committee, since 1996, Access to Justice Committee, since 1997); b. 22.6.50, Glasgow; m., Margaret Macleod; 2 s.; 2 d. Educ. Holy Cross High School, Hamilton; Glasgow University. Past President, Glasgow Bar Association; Solicitor-Advocate. Recreations: football; tennis; reading; travel. Address: (b.) 84 Carlton Place, Glasgow G5 9TD; T.-0141-429 8166.

Brown, Gordon Lamont. Scottish Rugby International and British Lion; author and after-dinner speaker; ITV rugby commentator; b. 1.11.47, Troon; m., Linda; 1 s.; 1 d. Educ. Marr College, Troon. Bank clerk, British Linen Bank, 1965-71; Building Society Manager: Leicester Building Society, 1971-76, Bristol & West Building Society, since 1976. Played for Scotland, 30 times; toured with British Isles Rugby Team ("Lions), New Zealand 1971, South Africa 1974, New Zealand 1977; holds world record for number of tries scored by a forward on a tour (eight); former Chairman, now Vice-President, Stars Organisation for Spastics (Scotland). Publications: Broon from Troon (autobiography); Rugby is a Funny Game (rugby anecdotes). Recreation: golf. Address: (h.) 65 Bentinck Drive, Troon, Ayrshire; T.-01292 315125.

Brown, Hamish Macmillan, Hon.D.Litt (St Andrews). Author, Lecturer, Photographer and Mountaineer; b. 13.8.34, Colombo, Sri Lanka. Educ. several schools abroad; Dollar Academy. National Service, RAF, Middle East/East Africa; Assistant, Martyrs' Memorial Church, Paisley; first-ever full-time appointment in outdoor education (Braehead School, Fife; served many years on Scottish Mountain Leadership Board; has led expeditions world-wide for mountaineering, skiing, trekking, canoeing, etc. Publications: Hamish's Mountain Walk, 1979 (SAC award); Hamish's Groats End Walk, 1981 (Smith's Travel Prize shortlist); Time Gentlemen, Some Collected Poems, 1983; Eye to the Hills, 1982; Five Bird Stories, 1984; Poems of the Scottish Hills (Editor), 1982; Speak to the Hills (Co-Editor), 1985; Travels, 1986; The Great Walking Adventure, 1986; Hamish Brown's Scotland, 1988; Climbing the Corbetts, 1988; Great Walks Scotland (Co-author), 1989; Scotland Coast to Coast, 1990; Walking the Summits of Somerset and Avon, 1991; From the Pennines to the Highlands, 1992; The Bothy Brew & Other Stories, 1993; The Fife Coast, The Last Hundred, 1994; 25 Walks - Fife, 1995; Fort William and Glen Coe Walks, 1996; Exploring the Edinburgh to Glasgow Canal, 1997; Compendium: Hamish's Mountain Walks/Climbing the Corbetts, 1997. Recreations: books; music; Morocco. Address: 26 Kirkcaldy Road, Burntisland, Fife, KY3 9HQ; T.-01592 873546.

Brown, Hilary Neilson, DipDomSc, DipEd. Chef/Proprietrix, La Potiniere, since 1975; b. 6.6.52, Glasgow; m., David Richard Brown. Educ. Hutchesons' Girls' Grammar School; Glasgow and West of Scotland College of Domestic Science; Jordanhill College of Education. Teacher, Bellarmine Secondary School, 1973-75. Michelin Star, since 1991; Egon Ronay Star, since 1985; AA Rosettes, since 1977. Publication: La Potiniere and Friends, 1990. Recreations: health and fitness; cinema; France. Address: (b.) La Potiniere, Gullane, East Lothian; T.-01620 843214.

Brown, Ian Forbes, FIB (Scot). Director:Wilson Distributors (Scotland) Ltd.; Credential Holdings Ltd.; Norman Cordiner Ltd., Allied London Scotland Ltd.; Chairman: Anglo Scottish Properties Plc; b. 5.3.29; m., Margaret Catherine; 1 s.; 1 d. Educ. Glasgow High School. Address: (h.) 8 Ardchoille Park, Strathmore Street, Perth PH2 7TL.

Brown, Professor Ian James Morris, MA (Hons), MLitt, PhD, DipEd, FRSA. Playwright, since 1969; Professor of Drama, Queen Margaret College, Edinburgh, since 1995 (Head of Department, since 1996, Reader, 1994-95); b. 28.2.45, Barnet; m., 1, Judith Sidaway; 2, Nicola Axford; 1 s.; 1 d. Educ. Dollar Academy; Edinburgh University; Crewe and Alasager College. Schoolteacher, 1967-69, 1970-71; Lecturer in Drama, Dunfermline College, 1971-76; British Council: Assistant Representative, Scotland, 1976-77, Assistant Regional Director, Istanbul, 1977-78; various posts, Crewe and Alsager College, 1978-86, latterly Leader, BA (Hons) Drama Studies; Programme Director, Alsager Arts Centre, 1980-86; Drama Director, Arts Council of Great Britain, 1986-94. British Theatre Institute: Vice Chairman, 1983-85, Chairman, 1985-87; Member, International Advisory Committee, O'Neill Theatre Center, since 1994; Chair, Scottish Society of Playwrights, 1973-75, 1984-87, since 1997; plays include Mother Earth, The Bacchae, Carnegie, The Knife, The Fork, New Reekie, Mary, Runners, Mary Queen and the Loch Tower, Joker in the Pack, Beatrice, First Strike, The Scotch Play, Bacchai, Wasting Reality. Recreations: theatre; sport; travel; cooking. Address: (b.) Queen Margaret College, Clerwood Terrace, Edinburgh EH12 8TS.

Brown, James Armour, RD, BL, FSA (Scot). Chancellor of the Priory of Scotland, Order of St. John of Jerusalem, since 1992; Partner, Kerr Barrie & Duncan (formerly Kerr, Barrie & Goss), Solicitors, Glasgow, 1957-91 (Consultant, 1991-93); b. 20.7.30, Rutherglen; m., Alexina Mary Robertson McArthur; 1 s. Educ. Rutherglen Academy; Glasgow University. National Service, Royal Navy, 1951-53; commissioned RNVR, 1952; served with Clyde Division, RNVR/RNR, 1953-72; Captain, 1972; Senior Reserve Supply Officer on staff of Admiral Commanding Reserves, 1973-76; Naval ADC to The Queen, 1975-76; Member, Suite of Lord High Commissioner to General Assembly of Church of Scotland, 1961-63; Session Clerk, Stonelaw Parish Church, Rutherglen, 1964-81; Member, Church of Scotland Committee on Chaplains to HM Forces, 1975-82 (Vice-Convener, 1979-82); Clerk, Incorporation of Bakers of Glasgow, 1964-89; Deacon, Society of Deacons and Free Preseses of Glasgow, 1978-80; Member, Glasgow Committee, Order of St. John of Jerusalem, since 1961 (Chairman, 1982-93, Honorary President, since 1995); Member, Chapter of the Priory of Scotland of the Order of St. John, since 1970; KStJ, 1975; Preceptor of Torphichen, Priory of Scotland, 1984-92; Hon. Chairman, Orders and Medals Research Society (Scottish Branch), 1987- 91. Recreations: music; historical research. Address: (h.) 6 Arran Way, Bothwell, Glasgow G71 8TR; T.-01698 854226.

Brown, Rt. Hon. (James) Gordon. MA, PhD, MP. Chancellor of the Exchequer, since 1997; MP (Labour),

Dunfermline East, since 1983; b. 20.2.51. Educ. Kirkcaldy High School; Edinburgh University. Rector, Edinburgh University, 1972-75; Temporary Lecturer, Edinburgh University, 1976; Lecturer, Glasgow College of Technology, 1976-80; Journalist and Current Affairs Editor, Scottish Television, 1980-83. Contested (Labour) South Edinburgh, 1979; Chairman, Labour Party Scottish Council, 1983-84; Opposition Chief Secretary to the Treasury, 1987; Shadow Minister for Trade and Industry, 1989. Publications: The Red Paper on Scotland (Editor), 1975; The Politics of Nationalism and Devolution (Co-Editor), 1980; Scotland: The Real Divide, 1983; Maxton, 1986; Where There is Greed, 1989. Recreations: reading and writing; football; golf; tennis. Address: 21 Ferryhills Road, North Queensferry, Fife.

Brown, J. Craig, BA, DipPE. International Team Manager and Technical Director, Scottish Football Association, since 1993; b. 1.7.40, Glasgow; 2 s.; 1 d. Educ. Hamilton Academy. Professional footballer: Rangers F.C., 1958-60, Dundee F.C., 1960-66, Falkirk F.C., 1966-68; Assistant Manager, Motherwell F.C., 1975-77; Manager, Clyde F.C., 1977-86; Assistant National Coach and Under-21 Coach, 1986-93; Vice President, Union of European Football Trainers; Hon. Lecturer, Paisley University; Sports Photographers' Personality of the Year, 1996; City of Glasgow Sports Personality of the Year, 1997; Bells Manager of the Month, five occasions. Teacher of primary school subjects, Deputy Headteacher, Headteacher and Lecturer in Primary Education, 1963-86. Publication: Activity Methods in the Middle Years, 1975. Recreation: golf. Address: (b.) Scottish Football Association, 6 Park Gardens, Glasgow G3 7YF; T.-0141-353 3522.

Brown, Jenny, MA (Hons). Literature Director, Scottish Arts Council; b. 13.5.58, Manchester; m., Alexander Richardson; 3 s. Educ. George Watson's College; Aberdeen University. Assistant Administrator, Edinburgh Festival Fringe Society, 1980-82; Director, Edinburgh Book Festival, 1983-91; Presenter, Scottish Television book programmes, 1989-94; National Co-ordinator, Readiscovery Campaign, 1994-95. Address: (b.) Scottish Arts Council, 12 Manor Place, Edinburgh EH4.

Brown, Jock, MA (Cantab). General Manager, Football, Celtic F.C., since 1997; b. 7.5.46, Kilmarnock; m., Ishbel; 3 d. Educ. Hamilton Academy; Sidney Sussex College, University of Cambridge. Journalist: Glasgow Herald, 1967, D.C. Thomson & Co. Ltd., 1967-68 and 1970-73; Assistant Secretary, Scottish Football League, 1968-70; Law Apprentice, Ballantyne & Copland, Solicitors, Motherwell, 1973-75, Solicitor, 1975-95; Director, Caledonian Television Ltd., 1993-95; Sports Law Consultant, Harper MacLeod, Solicitors, Glasgow, 1995-97; Sports Commentator: Scottish Television, 1980-90, BSkyB, 1989-95, BBC Scotland, 1990-97. Recreation: golf. Address: (b.) Celtic Park, Glasgow G40 3RE; T.-0141-551 4203.

Brown, Professor John Campbell, BSc, PhD, DSc, FRAS, FRSE, FInstP. Astronomer Royal for Scotland, since 1995; Professor of Astrophysics, Glasgow University, 1984-96; Regius Chair of Astronomy, since 1996; b. 4.2.47, Dumbarton; m., Dr. Margaret I. Brown; 1 s.; 1 d. Educ. Dumbarton Academy; Glasgow University. Glasgow University Astronomy Department: Research Assistant, 1968-70, Lecturer, 1970-78, Senior Lecturer, 1978-80, Reader, 1980-84; Nuffield Fellow, 1983-84; Kelvin Medallist, 1983-86; DAAD Fellow, Tubingen University, 1971-72; ESRO/GROC Fellow, Space Research Laboratory, Utrecht, 1973-74; Visitor: Australian National University, 1975, High Altitude Observatory, Colorado, 1977; NASA Associate Professor, Maryland University, 1980; NSF Fellow, University of California at San Diego, 1984; Brittingham Professor, University of Wisconsin,

1987. SERC Solar System Committee, 1980-83; Council, Royal Astronomical Society, 1984-87, 1990-93 (Vice-President, 1986-87); Member, International Astronomical Union, since 1976. Recreations: cycling; walking; painting; lapidary; conjuring; photography; woodwork. Address: (b.) Department of Physics and Astronomy, Glasgow University, Glasgow G12 8QW; T.-0141-330 5182.

Brown, John Souter, MA (Hons), MIPR. Head of Public Relations and Marketing, Glasgow City Council, since 1996; b. 15.10.48, Glasgow; m., Angela McGinn; 1 s.; 1 d. Educ. Kirkcaldy High School; Edinburgh University. Statistics and Information Officer, Lanark County Council, 1970-72; Senior Officer (Research, Planning Publicity), Manchester City Social Services Department, 1972-75; Press Officer, Strathclyde Regional Council, 1975-80; Journalist and Presenter, Scottish Television, 1980-82; Editor, What's Your Problem?, 1982-84; Ways and Means, 1984-86; Senior Producer (Politics), Scottish Television, 1986-91; North of Scotland TV Franchise Team, 1991; Managing Director, Lomond Television, 1992-93; Head of Public Relations, Strathclyde Regional Council, 1993-96; Chair, Volunteer Centre, Glasgow, since 1992; Director, Scottish Foundation, since 1990. Address: (b.) Public Relations Department, City Chambers, George Square, Glasgow G2 1DU; T.-0141-287 0901.

Brown, Professor Kenneth Alexander, BSc, MSc, PhD, FRSE. Professor of Mathematics and Head of Department, Glasgow University; b. 19.4.51, Ayr; m., Irene M.; 2 s. Educ. Ayr Academy; Glasgow University; Warwick University. Recreations: reading; running. Address: (b.) Mathematics Department, Glasgow University, Glasgow G12 8QW; T.-0141-330 5180.

Brown, Professor Kenneth J., BSc, PhD, FRSE. Professor in Mathematics, Heriot-Watt University, since 1993; b. 20.12.45, Torphins; m., Elizabeth Lobban; 1 s.; 2 d. Educ. Banchory Academy; Robert Gordon's College; Aberdeen University; Dundee University. Lecturer in Mathematics, Heriot Watt University, 1970-81, Senior Lecturer, 1981-91, Reader, 1991-93. Publications: 45 papers. Recreations: coaching athletics; reading. Address: (h.) 3 Highlea Grove, Balerno, Edinburgh EH14 7HQ; T.-0131-449 5314.

Brown, R. Iain F, MBE, MA, MEd, ABPsS, ChPsychol. Senior Lecturer, Department of Psychology, Glasgow University, since 1968; b. 16.1.35, Dundee; m., Catherine G. (qv); 2 d. Educ. Daniel Stewart's College, Edinburgh; St. Andrews University; Edinburgh University; Glasgow University. Education Department, Corporation of Glasgow; Department of Psychological Medicine, Glasgow University. National Training Adviser, Scottish Council on Alcohol, 1979-94; Member, Executive, Scottish Council on Alcohol, 1980-94; Chairman: Society for the Study of Gambling, London, 1987-92, European Association for the Study of Gambling, since 1992, Glasgow Council on Alcohol, since 1985, Confederation of Scottish Counselling Agencies, 1989-93; Member, Lead Body on Advice, Guidance, Counselling and Psychotherapy (UK), since 1992. Various publications, mainly on addictions, in scientific books and journals. Recreations: travel; music. Address: (h.) 13 Kirklee Terrace, Glasgow G12 0TH; T.-0141-339 7095.

Brown, Russell Leslie. MP (Labour), Dumfries, since 1997; b. 17.9.51, Annan; m., Christine Margaret Calvert; 2 d. Educ. Annan Academy. Employed by ICI for 23 years in variety of positions; Local Councillor, since 1986. Recreations: walking; sport, especially football. Address: (h.) 11 Great King Street, Dumfries DG1 1BA; T.-01387 247902.

Brown, Professor Sally, BSc, MA, PhD, FRSE. Professor of Education, Stirling University, since 1990; Deputy

Principal, Stirling University, since 1996; b. 15.12.35, London; m., Professor Charles Brown (deceased); 2 s. Educ. Bromley High School GPDST; University College, London; Smith College, Massachusetts; Stirling University. Lecturer in College of Education, London, and College of Technology, Nigeria; University Lecturer, Nigeria; School Science Teacher, Helensburgh; University Researcher, Stirling; Research Adviser to Scottish Education Department; Director, Scottish Council for Research in Education, 1986-90. Publications: 100 (articles, monographs, books) on educational research and education generally. Recreations: squash; reading; music. Address: (b.) Department of Education, Stirling University, Stirling FK9 4LA.

Brown, Professor Stewart J., BA, MA, PhD, FRHistS. Professor of Ecclesiastical History, Edinburgh University, since 1988; b. 8.7.51, Illinois; m., Teri B. Hopkins-Brown; 1 s.; 1 d. Educ. University of Illinois; University of Chicago. Fulbright Scholar, Edinburgh University, 1976-78; Whiting Fellow in the Humanities, University of Chicago, 1979-80; Assistant to the Dean, College of Arts & Sciences, and Lecturer in History, Northwestern University, 1980-82; Associate Professor and Assistant Head, Department of History, University of Georgia, 1982-88; Visiting Lecturer, Department of Irish History, University College, Cork, 1986; Editor, Scottish Historical Review, since 1993. Publications: Thomas Chalmers and the Godly Commonwealth in Scotland, 1982 (awarded Agnes Mure Mackenzie Prize from Saltire Society); Scotland in the Age of the Disruption (Co-author), 1993; William Robertson and the Expansion of Empire (Editor), 1997; Religion, Politics and Culture in Ireland (Co-editor), 1998. Recreations: swimming; hill-walking. Address: (h.) 160 Craigleith Hill Avenue, Edinburgh EH4 2NB; T.-0131-343 1712.

Browne, Desmond. MP (Labour), Kilmarnock and Loudoun, since 1997; b. 1952. Address: (b.) House of Commons, London SW1A 0AA.

Browning, Rev. Derek, MA, BD, DMin. Minister, Cupar Old Parish Church, since 1987; b. 24.5.62, Edinburgh. Educ. North Berwick High School; Corpus Christi College, University of Oxford; St. Mary's College, University of St. Andrews; Princeton Theological Seminary. Moderator, Presbytery of St. Andrews, 1996-97; Member, General Assembly Panel on Worship, since 1995. Recreations: reading; cooking; travel; croquet. Address: (h.) Eden Manse, Cupar, Fife; T.-01334 653196.

Browning, Professor J. Robin, BA (Hons), FCIBS. Chief Executive, British Linen Bank; General Manager, Bank of Scotland, since 1986 (Divisional General Manager, 1983-86); b. 29.7.39, Kirkcaldy; m., Christine Campbell; 1 s.; 1 d. Educ. Morgan Academy, Dundee; Strathclyde University; Harvard Business School. Bank of Scotland: Assistant Management Accountant, 1971-74, Assistant Manager (Corporate Planning), 1974-77; British Linen Bank Ltd.: Manager, 1977-79, Assistant Director, 1979-81, Director, 1981-82; Assistant General Manager, Bank of Scotland, 1982-83. Former Member of Council, Chartered Institute of Bankers in Scotland, 1994-97; Deputy Chairman, Association for Payment and Clearing Services, 1994-97; Visiting Professor of Banking, University of Stirling. Recreations: curling; gardening; DIY enthusiast. Address: (b.) Bank of Scotland, Head Office, The Mound, Edinburgh EH1 1YZ; T.-0131-243 5541.

Brownlie, Alistair Rutherford, OBE, MA, LLB, SSC; b. 5.4.24, Edinburgh; m., Martha Barron Mounsey. Educ. George Watson's; Edinburgh University. Served as radio operator in 658 Air O.P. Squadron RAF, Europe and India; apprenticed to J. & R.A. Robertson, WS; qualified Solicitor, 1950; in private practice; Member, Committee on Blood Grouping (House of Lords); Solicitor for the poor, 1955-64,

in High Court of Justiciary; Secretary, SSC Society, 1970-95, now Archivist; former Member, Council, Law Society of Scotland; Legal Aid Central Committee; Chairman, Legal Aid Committee, Scottish Legal Aid Board, 1986-90; founder Member, Past President, now Hon. Member, Forensic Science Society; Member, Vice-Chairman, Scottish Council of Law Reporting, 1975-97; Fellow, RSA; Elder, Church of Scotland and Congregational Union of Scotland. Publications: Drink, Drugs and Driving (Co-author); Crime Investigation: art or science (3rd edition, Editor); various papers on forensic science, criminal law and legal aid. Recreations: the pen, the spade, and the saw. Address: (h.) 8 Braid Mount, Edinburgh; T.-0131-447 4255.

Bruce, Alistair James, LLB, NP. Solicitor; Partner, T.P. and J.L. Low, Solicitors, Kirkwall, since 1985; b. 4.12.58, Perth; m., Jane; 2 s. Educ. Perth Academy; University of Dundee. Apprenticeship with A.C. Morrison and Richards, Advocates, Aberdeen, 1980-82; Assistant Solicitor, T.P. and J.L. Low, Kirkwall, 1982-85. Member, Council, Law Society of Scotland, since 1996. Senior Vice President, Rotary Club of Kirkwall; Secretary: Orkney Arts Theatre, J.P. Advisory Committee for Orkney; Past President, Society of the Procurators of Orkney; Past Chairman, Family Mediation, Orkney. Recreations: golf; drama; St. Magnus Cathedral Choir. Address: (b.) 5 Broad Street, Kirkwall, Orkney; T.-01856 873151.

Bruce, Andrew, MA (Hons), MEd. Headteacher, Craigmount High School, Edinburgh, since 1994; b. 26.3.46, Cowdenbeath; m., Jennifer Harkess; 1 s. Educ. Daniel Stewart's College, Edinburgh; Edinburgh University; Aberdeen University. Adviser in English, Dunbarton Division, Strathclyde Region; Assistant Head Teacher, Bankhead Academy, Aberdeen; Resources Development Officer, Grampian Region; Headteacher, Deans Community High School, Livingston; Head, Management Development Unit, Lothian Region. Recreations: squash; reading; motorcycling. Address: (b.) Craigs Road, Edinburgh EH12 8NH; T.-0131-339 6823.

Bruce, David, MA, Chevalier de L'Ordre des Arts et des Lettres. Writer and Consultant; Director, Scottish Film Council, 1986-94; b. 10.6.39, Dundee; m., Barbara; 1 s.; 1 d. Educ. Dundee High School; Aberdeen Grammar School; Edinburgh University. Freelance (film), 1963; Assistant Director, Films of Scotland, 1964-66; Director, Edinburgh International Film Festival, 1965-66; Promotions Manager, Mermaid Theatre, London, 1966-67; Executive Officer, British Universities Film Council, 1967-69; joined Scottish Film Council as Assistant Director, 1969; Depute Director, SFC and Scottish Council for Educational Technology, 1977-86. Chairman, Mental Health Film Council, 1982-84; Chairman, Scottish Society for History of Photography, 1983-86; Chairman, Association of European Film Institutes, 1990-94. Various publications, including Scotland–the movie, 1996. Recreations: movies; music; photo-history. Address: (h.) Rosebank, 150 West Princes Street, Helensburgh G84 8BH.

Bruce, Fraser Finlayson, RD, MA (Hons), LLB, FSA(Scot). Regional Chairman, Industrial Tribunals for Scotland 1993-97 (Permanent Chairman, 1982-93); Solicitor, since 1956; b. 10.10.31, Kirkcaldy; m., Joan Gwendolen Hunter; 2 step-s. Educ. St. Andrews University. National Service, Royal Navy, 1956-58, commissioned Sub-Lieutenant, RNVR; Legal Assistant: Lanark County Council, 1958-60, Inverness County Council, 1960-66; Depute County Clerk: Argyll County Council, 1966-70, Inverness County Council, 1970-72; County Clerk, Inverness County Council, 1972-75; Joint Director of Law and Administration, Highland Regional Council, 1975-82; Temporary Sheriff, 1984-92. Served RNVR, 1956-76, retiring as Lieutenant-Commander RNR. Recreations: hill walking; Gaelic language; reading (in philosophy and naval/military history). Address: (h.) Drumdunan House, by Grantown-on-Spey PH26 3LG;T.-01479 873969.

Bruce, George, OBE (1984), MA, DLitt. Writer/Lecturer; b. 10.3.09, Fraserburgh; m., Elizabeth Duncan; 1 s.; 1 d. Educ. Fraserburgh Academy; Aberdeen University. Teacher, English Department, Dundee High School, 1935-46; BBC Producer, Aberdeen, 1946-56; BBC Talks (Documentary) Producer, Edinburgh, with special responsibility for arts programmes, 1956-70; first Fellow in Creative Writing, Glasgow University, 1971-73; Visiting Professor, Union Theological Seminary, Richmond, Virginia, and Writer in Residence, Prescott College, Arizona, 1974; Visiting Professor of English, College of Wooster, Ohio, 1976-77; Scottish-Australian Writing Fellow, 1982; E. Hervey Evans Distinguished Fellow, St. Andrews Presbyterian College, North Carolina, 1985; Vice-Chairman, Council Member, Saltire Society; Council Member, Advisory Council of the Arts in Scotland; Extra-Mural Lecturer, Glasgow, St. Andrews and Edinburgh Universities; Executive Editor, The Scottish Review, 1975-76; Honorary President, Scottish Poetry Library. Publications: Sea Talk, 1944; Selected Poems, 1947; Landscapes and Figures, 1967; Collected Poems, 1970; The Red Sky, 1985; Perspectives: poems 1970-86, 1987; Scottish Sculpture Today (Co-author), 1947; Anne Redpath, 1974; The City of Edinburgh, 1974; Festival in the North, 1975; Some Practical Good, 1975; A Scottish Postbag (Co-author), 1986; The Scottish Literary Revival, 1962 (Editor); Scottish Poetry Anthologies 1-6 (Co-Editor), 1966-72; The Land Out There, anthology (Editor), 1991. Recreation: visiting friends. Address: 25 Warriston Crescent, Edinburgh EH3 5LB; T.-0131-556 3848.

Bruce, Malcolm Gray, MA, MSc. MP (Liberal Democrat, formerly Liberal), Gordon, since 1983; Liberal Democrat Treasury Spokesman; Member, Treasury Select Committee; b. 17.11.44, Birkenhead; 1 s.; 1 d. Educ. Wrekin College; St. Andrews University; Strathclyde University. Trainee Journalist, Liverpool Daily Post & Echo, 1966-67; Section Buyer, Boots the Chemist, 1968-69; Fashion Retailing Executive, A. Goldberg & Sons, 1969-70; Research and Information Officer, NESDA, 1971-75; Marketing Director, Noroil Publishing, 1975-81; Director, Aberdeen Petroleum Publishing; Editor/Publisher, Aberdeen Petroleum Report, 1981-83; Co-Editor, Scottish Petroleum Annual, 1st and 2nd editions; Called to the Bar (Gray's Inn), 1995. Vice Chairman, Political, Scottish Liberal Party, 1975-84; Rector, Dundee University, 1986-89. Recreations: reading; music; theatre; hill-walking; cycling; travel. Address: (b.) House of Commons, London, SW1A 0AA.

Bruce, Professor Steve, BA, PhD. Professor of Sociology, Aberdeen University, since 1991; b. 1.4.54, Edinburgh; m., Elizabeth S. Duff; 1 s.; 2 d. Educ. Queen Victoria School, Dunblane; Stirling University. Variously Lecturer, Reader and Professor of Sociology, Queen's University of Belfast, 1978-91. Publications: author of numerous books on religion, and on the Northern Ireland conflict. Recreation: farming. Address: (b.) Department of Sociology, Aberdeen University, Aberdeen AB9 2TY; T.-01224 272761.

Bruce, Professor Victoria Geraldine, OBE, BA, MA, PhD, CPsychol, FBPsS, FRSE. Professor of Psychology, Stirling University, since 1992; Deputy Principal (Research), Stirling University, since 1995; b. 4.1.53; m., Professor A.M. Burton. Educ. Newcastle-upon-Tyne Church High School for Girls; Newnham College, Cambridge. Lecturer, then Reader, then Professor of Psychology, Nottingham University, 1978-92. Member, Economic and Social Research Council, 1992-96, and Chair, Research Programmes Board, 1992-96; Member, Executive's Research Advisory Group, Scottish Higher Education Funding Council, since 1993; Editor, British Journal of Psychology, since 1995; Chair, Psychology Panel for 1996 University Funding Councils' Research

Assessment Exercise; Member, Scottish Higher Education Funding Council, since 1995. Publications: numerous papers and several books on visual perception and cognition. Recreations: dogs; walking; games. Address: (h.) The Mill House, Fintry, Stirlingshire G63 0YD; T.-01360 860 342.

Brunt, Professor Peter William, OBE, MD, FRCP(Lond), FRCP(Edin). Consultant Physician, Aberdeen Royal Infirmary, since 1970; Clinical Professor of Medicine, Aberdeen University, since 1996; Physician to The Queen in Scotland, since 1984; non-stipendiary Minister in Episcopal Church of Scotland; b. 18.1.36, Prestatyn; m., Marina Evelyn Anne Lewis; 3 d. Educ. Manchester Grammar School; King George V School; Liverpool University. Recreations: mountaineering; music. Address: (h.) 17 Kingshill Road, Aberdeen AB15 5JY; T.-Aberdeen 314204.

Bryant, Anthony B., FRICS. Regional Director, Highlands, National Trust for Scotland, since 1986; b. 25.1.38; m., Jane E.A.; 1 s.; 1 d. Educ. Bryanston School. Trained as land agent, Chatsworth Estate, 1956-60, returning there 1964-69 after working for the Duchy of Cornwall; joined National Trust for Scotland as Depute Factor, 1969; Factor, 1976; Head Factor, 1984. Recreations: music; painting. Address: (b.) Abertarff House, Church Street, Inverness 1V1 1EU; T.-Inverness 232034.

Bryce, Professor Charles F.A., BSc, PhD, DipEdTech, EurBiol, CBiol, FIBiol, CChem, FRSC. Professor, Dean, Faculty of Science, and Head, Department of Biological Sciences, Napier University, since 1983; b. 5.9.47, Lennoxtown; m., Maureen; 2 s. Educ. Lenzie Academy; Shawlands Academy; Glasgow University; Max Planck Institute, Berlin. Former Executive Editor, Computer Applications in the Biosciences; Member, EFB Task Group on Public Perceptions of Biotechnology; Adviser to the Committee on Science and Technology in Developing Countries (India); former Chairman, UK Deans of Science Committee; Convener, UCAS Biology Panel. Recreations: competitive bridge; collecting wine. Address: (b.) Napier University, 10 Colinton Road, Edinburgh EH10 5DT; T.-0131-455 2525.

Bryce, Colin Maxwell, DA (Edin), CertEd, FCSD, FRSA. Dean, Faculty of Arts and Social Sciences, Napier University, since 1997; b. 14.9.45, Edinburgh; m., Caroline Joy; 2 s. Educ. Royal High School, Edinburgh; Edinburgh College of Art; Moray House College of Education. Art and Design Teacher, Portobello High School, 1968-75; Head of Art and Design, Wester Hailes Education Centre, 1975-85; Education Advisory Officer/Senior Education Officer/Director, The Design Council Scotland, 1985-90; Managing Director, Quorum Graphic Design, 1990-91; Principal, Hunter Maxwell Associates, 1991-92; Head, Department of Design, Napier University, 1992-97. Member, Society of High Constables of Edinburgh. Recreations: looking, listening, and talking. Address: (b.) Napier University, 10 Colinton Road, Edinburgh, EH10 5DT; T.-0131-455 2216.

Bryce, Professor Tom G.K., BSc, MEd, PhD, CPsychol. Professor, Department of Educational Studies, Faculty of Education, Strathclyde University, Jordanhill Campus, since 1993; Vice-Dean (Postgraduate Studies and Research), since 1997; b. 27.1.46, Glasgow; m., Karen Douglas Stewart; 1 s.; 1 d. Educ. King's Park Secondary School, Glasgow; Glasgow University. Teacher of Physics, Jordanhill College School, 1968-71; P.T. of Physics, King's Park Secondary School, 1971-73; part-time Lecturer in Psychology, Glasgow University, 1972-75; Open University Tutor, 1979-84; Lecturer, 1973, Head of Psychology, 1983, Head, Division of Education and Psychology, 1987-94, Jordanhill College of Education. Chairman, Editorial Board, Scottish Educational Review.

Publications include: How to Assess Open-ended Practical Investigations in Biology, Chemistry and Physics, 1991. Recreations: moutaineering; badminton. Address: (b.) Jordanhill Campus, Southbrae Drive, Glasgow, G13 1PP; T.-0141-950 3220.

Bryden, Professor Ian Gordon, BSc, PhD, CEng, CPhys, MIMarE, MInstP. Professor and Head, School of Mechanical and Offshore Engineering, Robert Gordon University, since 1996; b. 12.9.58, Dumfries; m., Fiona Morag; 2 s.; 1 d. Educ. Lockerbie Academy; University of Edinburgh. Research Assistant, Heriot-Watt University; Research Engineer, BMT Ltd.; Lecturer, Heriot-Watt University; Senior Engineer, ICIT/IOE. Recreations: reading; cycling; music. Address: (b.) The Robert Gordon University, Schoolhill, Aberdeen AB10 1FR; T.-01224-262 301.

Brydon, Donald Lithgow, BSc, PhD, CChem, FRSC. Vice Principal, Scottish College of Textiles, since 1988; Dean, Faculty of Textiles, Heriot-Watt University, since 1989; b. 13.12.40, Stirling; m., Sandra Elizabeth Lumsden; 1 s.; 1 d. Educ. Inverurie Academy; University of St. Andrews. Postdoctoral Fellow, Case Western Reserve University, Cleveland, Ohio, 1967-69; Research and Development, Organics and Fibres Divisions, latterly Project Manager, ICI, 1969-80. Publications: range of academic publications. Recreations: tennis; travelling; gardening. Address: (b.) Scottish College of Textiles, Netherdale, Galashiels TD1 3HF; T.-01896 753351.

Bryson, Norval MacKenzie, MSc, DPhil, FFA. Deputy Group Managing Director and Group Finance Director, Scottish Provident; Non-Executive Director, Aberdeen Asset Management PLC; b. 22.1.49, Dundee; m., Pamela Judith Sallie; 1 s.; 2 d. Educ. High School of Dundee; St. Andrews University; Magdalen College, Oxford. Joined Scottish Provident, 1974. Former Member of Council, Faculty of Actuaries. Recreation: walking the dog. Address: (h.) Achmore, 1 Hillview Terrace, Corstorphine, Edinburgh EH12 8RA; T.-0131-334 2614.

Buccleuch, 9th Duke of, and Queensberry, 11th Duke of (Walter Francis John Montagu Douglas Scott), KT (1978), VRD, JP. Hon. Captain, RNR; Captain and President of the Council, Queen's Bodyguard for Scotland (Royal Company of Archers); Lord Lieutenant of Roxburgh, since 1974, and of Ettrick and Lauderdale, since 1975; b. 23.9.23, London; m., Jane McNeill, daughter of John McNeill, QC, Appin, Argyll; 3 s.; 1 d. Educ. Eton; Christ Church, Oxford. Served World War II, RNVR; MP (Conservative), Edinburgh North, 1960-73; PPS to the Scottish Office, 1961-64; Chairman, Royal Association for Disability and Rehabilitation, since 1978, and President, since 1993; President: Royal Highland and Agricultural Society of Scotland, 1969, St. Andrew's Ambulance Association, Royal Scottish Agricultural Benevolent Institution, Scottish National Institution for War Blinded, Royal Blind Asylum and School, Galloway Cattle Society, East of England Agricultural Society, 1976, Commonwealth Forestry Association; President (Scotland), Malcolm Sargent Cancer Fund for Children; President, Royal Scottish Forestry Society, 1994-96; Chairman: Living Landscape Trust, since 1985, Buccleuch Heritage Trust, since 1986; Vice-President: Royal Scottish Society for Prevention of Cruelty to Children, Disablement Income Group Scotland, Disabled Drivers Motor Club, Spinal Injuries Association; Honorary President: Moredun Foundation for Animal Health, Scottish Agricultural Organisation Society; DL: Selkirk, 1955, Midlothian, 1960, Roxburgh, 1962, Dumfries, 1974; Chancellor, Most Ancient & Most Noble Order of the Thistle, since 1992; Chairman, Association of Lord Lieutenants, since 1990. Recreations: travel; country sports; painting; photography; classical music. Address: Bowhill, Selkirk; T.-Selkirk 20732; and Drumlanrig Castle, Thornhill; T.-Thornhill 30248.

Buchan, Alexander Stewart, MB, ChB, FRCA. Consultant in charge of Obstetric Anaesthesia, Simpson Memorial Maternity Pavilion, Edinburgh, since 1988; b. 7.9.42, Aberdeen; m., Henrietta Young Dalrymple; 1 s. Educ. Loretto School; Edinburgh University. Anaesthetic training in Edinburgh, apart from work in Holland, 1972; appointed Consultant in NHS, 1975; Royal Infirmary, Edinburgh, Royal Hospital for Sick Children, and Princess Margaret Rose Orthopaedic Hospital. Publication: Handbook of Obstetric Anaesthesia, 1991. Recreations: sailing; fishing; golf. Address: (h.) 21 Chalmers Crescent, Edinburgh EH9 1TS; T.-0131-667 1127.

Buchan, Alistair. Chief Executive, Orkney Islands Council. Address: (b.) Council Offices, Kirkwall KW15 1NY. T.-01856 873535.

Buchan of Auchmacoy, Captain David William Sinclair, JP, KStJ. Chief of the Name of Buchan; b. 18.9.29; m., The Hon. Susan Blanche Fionodbhar Scott-Ellis; 4 s.; 1 d. Educ. Eton; Royal Military Academy, Sandhurst. Commissioned Gordon Highlanders, 1949; served Berlin, BAOR and Malaya; ADC to GOC-in-C, Singapore, 1951-53; retired 1955. Member, London Stock Exchange; Senior Partner, Messrs Gow and Parsons, 1963-72. Changed name from Trevor through Court of Lord Lyon King of Arms, 1949, succeeding 18th Earl of Caithness as Chief of Buchan Clan. Member: Queen's Body Guard for Scotland (Royal Company of Archers); The Pilgrims; Friends of Malta GC; Alexandra Rose Day Council; Council, St. John's Ambulance, London; Council, Royal School of Needlework; Conservative Millennium Fund; Governor, London Clinic; Vice-President, Bucks CCC; Member, Council for London, Order of St. John; Master, Worshipful Company of Borderers, 1992; President, Ellon Cricket Club. Recreations: cricket; tennis; squash. Address: Auchmacoy House, Ellon, Aberdeenshire AB41 8RB.

Buchanan, James Glen Stewart, MB, ChB, FRCGP, DCH, DRCOG. Chairman, Scottish Council on Alcohol, 1987-95; b. 11.6.24, Annan; m., Elizabeth Urquhart Macgregor; 2 s. Educ. Dumfries Academy; Edinburgh University. General Practitioner, Vale of Leven, 1958-87; Past President, Glasgow Psychosomatic Society. Recreations: hill-walking; fishing; reading. Address: (h.) Landalla Cottage, Glenisla, Blairgowrie, PH11 8PH; T.-01575 582318.

Buchanan, Professor John (Iain) Thomson, BSc, MSc, PhD. Professor of Computer Science, Strathclyde University, since 1988 (and Royal Society Industry Fellow, 1996-98); b. 25.7.46, Glasgow; m., Margaret Moffat. Educ. Allan Glen's School, Glasgow; Glasgow University; Strathclyde University. Lecturer, Manchester University, 1971-75; Lecturer, Strathclyde University, 1976-88. Recreations: yachting; mountains; music; reading; food and wine. Address: (b.) Department of Computer Science, Strathclyde University, Glasgow, G1 1XH, T.-0141-553 3424.

Buchanan, Joyce Mary, BA, Dip SW. Deputy Director, Strategy and Planning, Board of Social Responsibility, Church of Scotland, since 1987; b. 9.4.49, Ayr. Educ. Larkhall Academy; Strathclyde University; Edinburgh University. Social Worker, 1971-74; Training Officer, Board of Social Responsibility, 1974-87; External Assessor to Certificate on Social Service, 1981-86. Secretary of State Appointee, Saughton Prison Visiting Committee; External Verifier for SVQ; Member, Residential Forum, Standards Project Group. Recreations: handcrafts; reading; involvement with local churches in setting up care groups for elderly people. Address: (b.) Church of Scotland, Charis

House, 47 Milton Road East, Edinburgh EH15 2SR; T.-0131-657 2000.

Buchanan, Paul, MA, MSc, MTS. Chief Executive, Ayrshire and Arran Tourist Board; b. 29.2.60, Barnet; m., Elizabeth; 2 s. Educ. Lochaber High School; Edinburgh University; Strathclyde University. Assistant Area Tourist Officer, Kincardine and Deeside Tourist Board; Tourism Manager, City of Dundee Tourist Board. Chairman, Great British Cities Marketing Group. Recreation: photography. Address: (b.) Burns House, Burns Statue Square, Ayr KA7 1UP; T.-01292 262555.

Buchanan, William Menzies, DA. Head of Fine Art, 1977-90, Acting Director, 1990-91, Deputy Director, 1991-92, Glasgow School of Art; b. 7.10.32, Caroni Estate, Trinidad, West Indies. Educ. Glasgow School of Art. Art Teacher, Glasgow, 1956-61; Exhibitions Officer, then Art Director, Scottish Arts Council, 1961-77. Chairman, Stills Gallery, Edinburgh, 1987-92; Member, Fine Art Board, Council for National Academic Awards, 1978-81. Publications: Scottish Art Review, 1965, 1967, 1973; Seven Scottish Painters catalogue, IBM New York, 1965; The Glasgow Boys catalogue, 1968; Joan Eardley, 1976; Mr Henry and Mr Hornel Visit Japan catalogue, 1978; Japonisme in Art (Contributor), 1980; A Companion to Scottish Culture (Contributor), 1981; The Stormy Blast catalogue, Stirling University, 1981; The Golden Age of British Photography (Contributor), 1984; The Photographic Collector (Contributor), 1985; Willie Rodger: A Retrospective (Contributor to catalogue), 1986; Scottish Photography Bulletin (Contributor), 1988; History of Photography (Contributor), 1989; Mackintosh's Masterwork (Editor), 1989; British Photography in the 19th Century (Contributor), 1989; The Art of the Photographer J. Craig Annan, 1992; Photography 1900 (Contributor), 1993; J. Craig Annan: selected texts and bibliography, 1994; Woven Image: Contemporary British Tapestry Catalogue (Contributor), 1996; Studies in Photography (Contributor), 1996; Charles Rennie Mackintosh: Art, Architecture and Design (CD Rom, General Editor), 1997. Recreations: gardening; cooking. Address: (h.) Allan Water School House, by Skelfhill, Hawick TD9 0PH; T.-01450 850311.

Buchanan-Jardine, Sir Andrew Rupert John, MC. Landowner; Deputy Lieutenant; b. 2.2.23, London; 1 s.; 1 d. Educ. Harrow; Royal Agricultural College. Joined Royal Horse Guards, 1941; served NW Europe; retired as Major, 1949. Joint Master, Dumfriesshire Foxhounds, 1950; JP. Recreation: country pursuits. Address: (h.) Dixons, Lockerbie, Dumfriesshire; T.-01576 202508.

Buchanan-Smith, Robin D., BA, ThM; b. 1.2.36, Currie, Midlothian; m., Sheena Mary Edwards; 2 s. Educ. Edinburgh Academy; Glenalmond; Cambridge University; Edinburgh University; Princeton Theological Seminary. Minister, Christ's Church, Dunollie, Oban, 1962-66; Chaplain: St. Andrews University, 1966-73, 8th Argylls, 1962-66, Highland Volunteer, 1967-69; British Council of Churches Preacher to USA, 1968; Commodore, Royal Highland Yacht Club, 1977-81; Member, Board of Directors, Scottish Television, 1982-96 (Chairman, Staff Trust, since 1993); Chancellor's Assessor, St. Andrews University, 1981-85; Chairman: Scotland's Heritage Hotels, 1988-91, Cross Trust, since 1989; Trustee: Carnegie Trust for the Universities of Scotland, since 1986, Scottish Orthopaedic Research Trust into Trauma, since 1992. Recreations: sailing; Scotland. Address: Isle of Eriska, Ledaig, Argyll PA37 1SD; T.-01631 720371.

Buckland, Professor Roger, MA, MPhil. Professor of Accountancy, Aberdeen University, since 1993 (Head, Department of Accountancy, since 1993 and Head, Department of Management Studies, since 1996); b. 22.4.51, Sheffield; m., Dr. Lorna McKee; 2 d. Educ. Aston Woodhouse High School; Selwyn College, Cambridge.

Research Fellow, York University; Lecturer, University of Aston. Publications: The Unlisted Securities Market; Finance for Growing Enterprises. Recreation: hot air balloon pilot; family. Address: (b.) Dunbar Street, Aberdeen AB24 3QY; T.-01224 272206.

Buckland, Professor Stephen T., BSc, MSc, PhD, CStat. Professor of Statistics, St. Andrews University, since 1993 (Head, Statistical Ecology Group, since 1995); b. 28.7.55, Dorchester; m., Patricia A. Peters; 1 d. Educ. Foster's School, Sherborne; Southampton University; Edinburgh University; Aberdeen University. Lecturer in Statistics, Aberdeen University, 1977-85; Senior Scientist, Tuna/Dolphin Program, Inter-American Tropical Tuna Commission, San Diego, 1985-87; Senior Consultant Statistician, Scottish Agricultural Statistics Service, 1988-93, Head, Environmental Modelling Unit, 1991-93. Publications: The Birds of North-East Scotland (Co-editor), 1990; Distance Sampling: estimating abundance of biological populations (Co-author), 1993. Recreations: natural history; walking; reading. Address: (b.) School of Mathematical and Computational Sciences, St. Andrews University, North Haugh, St. Andrews KY16 9SS; T.-01334 463787.

Buckley, Ernest Graham, MD, FRCPE, FRCGP. Director, Scottish Council for Postgraduate Medical and Dental Education, since 1993; b. 16.10.45, Oldham; m., Dr. Felicity Buckley; 2 s.; 1 d. Educ. Manchester Grammar School; Edinburgh University. General Practitioner, Livingston, 1974-93; Editor: British Journal of General Practice, 1982-90, Medical Education. Secretary, Association for the Study of Medical Education. Recreations: gardening; history; upholstery. Address: (b.) 12 Queen Street, Edinburgh EH2 1JE; T.-0131-225 4365.

Budge, Keith Joseph, MA (Hons). Headmaster, Loretto School, since 1995; b. 24.5.57; m., Caroline Ann Gent; 2 s.; 1 d. Educ. Rossall School; University College, Oxford. Assistant Master, Eastbourne College, 1980-84; Marlborough College: Assistant Master, 1984-88 and 1989-91; Housemaster, Cotton House, 1991-95; Instructor in English, Stevenson School, Pebble Beach, CA, 1988-89. Recreations: hill-walking; trout fishing; gadgets; theatre. Address: (b.) Loretto School, Musselburgh, Midlothian EH21 7RE; T.-0131-653 4441.

Bulfield, Professor Grahame, PhD, FIBiol, FRSE. Director and Chief Executive, Roslin Institute (Edinburgh), since 1993; b. 12.6.41. Educ. Kings School, Macclesfield; Leeds University; Edinburgh University. Fullbright Fellow and NIH Postdoctoral Fellow, Department of Genetics, University of California, Berkeley, 1968-70; SRC Resettlement Fellow, 1970-71, and Research Associate, 1971-76, Institute of Animal Genetics, Edinburgh University; Lecturer and Convenor of Medical Genetics, Department of Genetics, Medical School and School of Biological Sciences, Leicester University, 1976-81, Head of Genetics Group, AFRC Poultry Research Centre, Roslin, 1981-86; Head of Gene Expression Group, 1986-88, and Head of Station and Associate Director, 1988-93, Edinburgh Research Station, Institute of Animal Physiology and Genetic Research. Hon. Fellow, 1981-90, and Hon. Professor, since 1990, Division of Biological Sciences, Edinburgh University. Recreations: fell-walking; cricket. Address: (b.) Roslin Institute, Roslin, Midlothian EH25 9PS; T.-0131-527 4457.

Bulloch, Douglas, CQSW, MCC. Director of Social Work, East Ayrshire Council, since 1996; b. 5.2.51, Hamilton; m., Irene Waddell; 1 d. Educ. Hamilton Academy; Jordanhill College; University of Glasgow. Strathclyde Regional Council, 1976-95; Depute Director of Social Work

(Community Care), East Ayrshire Council, 1995-96. Address: (b.) London Road Centre, London Road, Kilmarnock KA3 7BU; T.-01563 576020.

Bunch, Antonia Janette, OBE, MA, FLA, FIInfSc, FSA Scot, FRSA. Freelance writer, editor, researcher; b. 13.2.37, Croydon. Educ. Notting Hill and Ealing High School; Strathclyde University. Assistant Librarian, Scottish Office; Librarian, Scottish Health Service Centre; Lecturer, Strathclyde University; Director, Scottish Science Library. Founding Chairman, Association of Scottish Health Sciences Librarians; Member: Standing Committee on Science and Technology Libraries, IFLA, 1987-91, Advisory Committee, British Library Science Reference and Information Service, 1987-96, Advisory Committee on Telematics for the Scottish Parliament. Publications: Libraries in Hospitals (Co-author), 1969; Hospital and Medical Libraries in Scotland: an Historical and Sociological Study, 1975; Health Care Administration: an Information Sourcebook, 1979. Recreations: breeding and showing Welsh mountain ponies; gardening; music; travelling in Italy. Address: Dove Cottage, Garvald, Haddington, East Lothian EH41 4LL.

Buncle, Tom, BA, MA. Chief Executive, Scottish Tourist Board, since 1994; b. 25.6.53, Arbroath; m., Janet; 2 s. Educ. Trinity College, Glenalmond; Exeter University; Sheffield University. Various overseas posts (North America, Europe, Asia), British Tourist Authority, 1978-91; International Marketing Director, Scottish Tourist Board, 1991-96. Recreations: wind-surfing; scuba diving; cycling; walking, tennis. Address: (b.) Scottish Tourist Board, 23 Ravelston Terrace, Edinburgh EH4 3EU; T.-0131-332 2433.

Bundy, Professor Alan Richard, BSc, PhD, FRSA, FRSE, FAAAI. Professor, Department of Artificial Intelligence, Edinburgh University, since 1990; b. 18.5.47, Isleworth; m., D. Josephine A. Maule; 1 d. Educ. Heston Secondary Modern School; Springgrove Grammar School; Leicester University. Tutorial Assistant, Department of Mathematics, Leicester University, 1970-71; Edinburgh University: Research Fellow, Metamathematics Unit, 1971-74, Lecturer, Department of Artificial Intelligence, 1974-84, Reader, 1984-87, Professorial Fellow, 1987-90. Editorial Board: Artificial Intelligence Journal, Journal of Automated Reasoning, AJ & Society Journal. Publications: Artificial Intelligence: An Introductory Course, 1978; The Computer Modelling of Mathematical Reasoning, 1983; The Catalogue of Artificial Intelligence Tools, 1984. Recreations: wine and beer making; walking; bridge. Address: (b.) Department of Artificial Intelligence, Edinburgh University, 80 South Bridge, Edinburgh EH1 1HN; T.-0131-650 2716.

Burchell, Professor Brian, BSc (Hons), PhD, FRCPath, FRSEdin. Professor of Medical Biochemistry; Honorary Professor, St. Andrews University; b. 1.10.46, Bosworth; m., Ann; 1 s.; 1 d. Educ. King Edward VII Grammar School, Coalville; St. Andrews University. Lecturer in Biochemistry: Loughborough University of Technology, 1974-75, Dundee University, 1976-78; Wellcome Trust Special Research Leave Fellow, 1978-80; Wellcome Trust Senior Lecturer in Biochemistry, Dundee University, 1980-88. Editor and Deputy Chairman, Editorial Board, Biochemical Journal. Publications: over 150 scientific papers and reviews. Recreation: golf. Address: (b.) Department of Molecular and Cellular Pathology, Ninewells Hospital and Medical School, Dundee DD1 9SY.

Burdon, Peter, MA (Cantab), FIA. Chief Executive, Glasgow Chamber of Commerce, since 1997; b. 15.5.47; m., Eileen; 4 s. Educ. Churchill College, University of Cambridge. Friends' Provident Life Office: Actuarial and User Management positions, 1968-79, User Liaison Manager, 1979-82, Manager, Unit Linked Department, 1982-85, Manager, Marketing Department, 1985-86; Deputy Managing Director, FS Assurance (transferred to Britannia Life, 1990), 1986-91; Managing Director, Britannia Life Limited, 1991-96; Marketing and Life Operations Director, Britannia Building Society, 1994-96. Member: UTA External Relations Committee, 1989-93, ABI Smaller Offices Committee, 1989-94, General Purposes Committee of the Associated Scottish Life Offices, 1991-96, Glasgow Discussion Group on Finance & Investment, 1986-96, Glasgow and West of Scotland Regional Committee, IOD, since 1996, Imperial Cancer Research Fund Scottish Advisory Committee, since 1994, Young Enterprise Scotland Business Adviser, since 1996, Scottish Actuaries Club, since 1987. Recreations: golf; squash; music. Address: (b.) Glasgow Chamber of Commerce, 30 George Square, Glasgow G2 1EQ; T.-0141-204 2121.

Burdon, Professor Roy Hunter, BSc, PhD, CBiol, FIBiol, FRSA, FRSE. Professor of Molecular Biology, Strathclyde University; m., Margery Grace Kellock; b. 27.4.38, Glasgow; 2 s. Educ. Glasgow Academy; St. Andrews University. Assistant Lecturer, Glasgow University, 1959; Research Fellow, New York University, 1963; Glasgow University: Lecturer in Biochemistry, 1964, Senior Lecturer, 1967, Reader, 1974, Professor of Biochemistry (Titular), 1977; Guest Professor of Microbiology, Polytechnical University of Denmark, 1977-78; Governor, West of Scotland College of Agriculture; Biochemical Society (UK): Honorary Meeting Secretary, 1981-85, Honorary General Secretary, 1985-89, Chairman, 1989-92; Chairman: British Co-ordinating Committee for Biotechnology, 1991-93, Scientific Advisory Committee, European Federation of Biotechnology, 1991; Auditor, International Union of Biochemistry and Molecular Biology, 1991-94. Recreations: music; painting; golf. Address: (h.) 144 Mugdock Road, Milngavie, Glasgow G62 8NP; T.-0141-956 1689.

Burgess, Charles Douglas, FRICS, IRRV, ACIArb. Partner, David Watson, Property Agents, Surveyors and Valuers, Glasgow, since 1973; Honorary Secretary, Royal Institution of Chartered Surveyors in Scotland, 1993-97; b. 20.12.33, Glasgow; m., Margaret (Rita) Helen Blackwood; 2 d. Educ. High School of Glasgow; Royal Technical College, Glasgow. National Service, 1956-58; Assistant Surveyor, Hendry & Steel, 1958-65; Partner, 1965-73. Chairman, Royal Institution of Chartered Surveyors in Scotland, 1990-91; President, Property Owners and Factors Association, Glasgow, Ltd., 1977-79; President, Property Owners and Factors Association, Scotland Ltd., 1987-88; Past Deacon, Society of Deacons and Free Preseses of Glasgow; Past Preses, Weavers Society of Anderston; Past President, Sandyford Burns Club, Glasgow; Past President, Glasgow and District Burns Association. Recreations: sailing; music. Address: (b.) 926 Govan Road, Glasgow G51 3AE; T.-0141-445 3741.

Burgess, Professor Robert Arthur, LLB, PhD. Professor of Business Law, Strathclyde University, since 1989; b. 24.2.46, Northwich; m., Frances I.L. Burns; 1 s.; 1 d. Educ. Sir John Deane's Grammar School, Northwich; University College, London; Edinburgh University. National Provincial Bank, 1967-69; Lecturer in Law, Southampton University, 1969-72; Lecturer in Taxation and Investment Law, Edinburgh University, 1972-78; Reader in Law, University of East Anglia, 1978-89. Chairman, Glasgow Royal Infirmary University NHS Trust, since 1994. Publications: Perpetuities in Scots Law; Corporate Finance Law; Law of Borrowing. Recreations: food and drink; travel. Address: (b.) Law School, Strathclyde University, 173 Cathedral Street, Glasgow G4 0RQ; T.-0141-552 4400.

Burgon, Robert Douglas, BA, MLitt, APMI. Director and Secretary, Scottish & Northern Ireland Plumbing Employers' Federation, since 1988; Secretary and Pensions Manager, Plumbing Pensions (UK) Ltd., since 1988; b. 3.8.55, Haddington; m., Sheila Georgina Bryson. Educ. North Berwick High School; Heriot Watt University. SNIPEF: Assistant Industrial Relations Officer, 1978, Assistant to the Director, 1979, Secretary, 1983. Recreation: music (church organist). Address: (b.) 2 Walker Street, Edinburgh EH3 7LB; T.-0131-225 2255.

Burley, Elayne Mary, BA (Hons). Director, Department of Partnerships and Enterprise, Napier University, since 1991; b. 17.10.44, Cheshire; 2 s.; 1 d. Educ. Astley Grammar School for Girls; Leeds University. Leeds Polytechnic, 1966-68; Lecturer, Gordon Institute of Technology, Victoria, Australia, 1970-72; Lecturer, Open University in Scotland, 1972-84; Head of Training, Scottish Council for Voluntary Organisations, 1984-91. Convenor, Confederation of Scottish Counselling Agencies; Member, Council, Rotary Club of Edinburgh. Recreations: golf; bridge; performing arts; walking on the beach; collecting blue and white china. Address: (b.) Redwood House, Spylaw Road, Edinburgh; T.-0131-455 5111.

Burley, Lindsay, MB, ChB, FRCPE, FRCGP, MHSM. General Manager, Borders Health Board, since 1995; b. 2.10.50, Blackpool; m., Robin Burley. Educ. Queen Mary School, Lytham; University of Edinburgh. Lothian Health Board: Consultant Physician, Unit General Manager, Director of Planning and Development. Address: (b.) Newstead, Melrose, Roxburghshire TD6 9DB; T.-01896 825515.

Burness, T. J., OBE. Principal, Glenrothes College. Address: (b.) Stenton Road, Glenrothes, KY6 2RA.

Burnet, George Wardlaw, LVO, BA, LLB, WS, KStJ, JP. Lord Lieutenant, Midlothian, since 1992; Chairman, Caledonian Research Foundation, since 1988; b. 26.12.27, Edinburgh; m., Jane Elena Moncrieff; 2 s.; 1 d. Educ. Edinburgh Academy; Lincoln College, Oxford; Edinburgh University. Senior Partner, Murray Beith & Murray, WS, 1983-91; Chairman, Life Association of Scotland Ltd., 1985-93. Brigadier, Queen's Bodyguard for Scotland (Royal Company of Archers); former Midlothian County Councillor; Convenor, Church of Scotland Finance Committee, 1980-83; Hon. Fellow, Royal Incorporation of Architects in Scotland. Address: (h.) Rose Court, Inveresk, Midlothian EH21 7TD.

Burnett, Charles John, KStJ, DA, AMA, FSAScot, FHSS, MLitt. Ross Herald of Arms; Chamberlain, Duff House, Banff, since 1997; Curator of Fine Art, Scottish United Services Museum, Edinburgh Castle, 1985-96; Vice-President, Heraldry Society of Scotland, since 1986; Vice-Patron, Genealogical Society of Queensland, since 1986; b. 6.11.40, Sandhaven, by Fraserburgh; m., Aileen E. McIntyre; 2 s.; 1 d. Educ. Fraserburgh Academy; Gray's School of Art, Aberdeen; Aberdeen College of Education. Advertising Department, House of Fraser, Aberdeen, 1963-64; Exhibitions Division, Central Office of Information, 1964-68 (on team which planned British pavilion for World Fair, Montreal, 1967); Assistant Curator, Letchworth Museum and Art Gallery, 1968-71; Head, Design Department, National Museum of Antiquities of Scotland, 1971-85. Heraldic Adviser, Girl Guide Association in Scotland, since 1978; Librarian, Priory of the Order of St. John in Scotland, since 1987; Vice President, Society of Antiquaries of Scotland, 1992-95; Honorary Citizen of Oklahoma, 1989. Recreations: reading; visiting places of historic interest. Address: (h.) Seaview House, Portsoy, Banffshire, AB45 2RS; T.-01261 843378.

Burnett, James Murray, FRICS, DipTP. Partner, Donaldsons, Chartered Surveyors; Chairman, Royal Institution of Chartered Surveyors in Scotland, 1996-97; Board Member, Cumbernauld Development Corp-oration, since 1990; b. 7.2.44, Edinburgh; m., Elizabeth Anne; 1 s.; 2 d. Educ. Boroughmuir School; Heriot-Watt University; Edinburgh College of Art. Joined Donaldsons in 1970, giving development consultancy advice for large shopping centres; became Partner, 1987. Vice-Chairman, Royal Institution of Chartered Surveyors in Scotland, 1992-93. Recreations: golf; gardening. Address: (h.) 438 Lanark Road, Colinton, Edinburgh; T.-0131-441 2200.

Burnett, Robert Gemmill, LLB, SSC, NP. Solicitor, since 1972; b. 18.1.49, Kilmarnock; m., Patricia Margaret Masson; 1 s.; 2 d. Educ. George Heriot's School, Edinburgh; Edinburgh University. Apprentice, then Assistant, then Partner, Drummond Miller WS; Partner, Burnett Christie. Solicitor to General Teaching Council. Recreations: golf; gardening. Address: (b.) 53 George IV Bridge, Edinburgh; T.-031-225 3456.

Burnett, Rodney Alister, MB, ChB, FRCP, FRIPHH, FRCPath. Consultant Pathologist responsible for diagnostic services, University Department of Pathology, Western Infirmary, Glasgow, since 1985; b. 6.6.47, Congleton; m., Maureen Elizabeth Dunn; 2 d. Educ. Sandbach School; St. Andrews University. Lecturer in Pathology, Glasgow University, 1974-79; Consultant in administrative charge, Department of Pathology, Stobhill Hospital, Glasgow, 1979-85. Member of Council, Royal Institute for Public Health and Hygiene, and Chairman, Board of Education and Examination for Anatomical Pathology Technology. Address: (h.) 134 Brownside Road, Cambuslang, Glasgow G72; T.-0141-641 3036.

Burnett, Rupert Gavin, BCom, CA, FCMA; b. 6.11.39, India; m., Elspeth Maclean; 2 s.; 1 d. Educ. George Watson's College; Edinburgh University; Harvard Business School. Procter & Gamble Ltd., 1963-65; Management Consultant, McLintock, Moores and Murray, 1965-68; Chartered Accountant, Arthur Young (latterly Ernst & Young), 1968-91, Partner, 1970; Honorary Professor, Stirling University, since 1991; Member, Council, Institute of Chartered Accountants of Scotland, 1990-96; Chairman, Glasgow & North Strathclyde Area Committee, 1992-95; CCAB Audit Practices Committee, 1986-91; Chairman, Church of Scotland Investors Trust; General Trustee, Church of Scotland; various non-executive directorships. Recreations: watching rugby; wild brown trout fishing; croft; family. Address: (h.) 7 Ralston Road, Bearsden, Glasgow.

Burnett-Stuart of Crichie, George Slessor. Farmer and Landowner, since 1969; b. 3.1.48, Cobham; m., Patricia De Lavenne; 2 d. Educ. Winchester College; Bordeaux University. Elected Member, Council and Executive, National Trust for Scotland; Council Member, Stewart Society, Scottish Agricultural College; Past Chairman, Grampian Farming Forestry Wildlife Group;Treasurer, Friends of Grampian Stones. Recreations: kite-flying; travelling; tree-planting. Address: Crichie House, Stuartfield, Peterhead AB4 8DY; T.-01771 24202.

Burnie, Joan Bryson. Columnist, Daily Record, since 1987; b. 19.12.41, Glasgow; 1 s.; 1 d. Educ. Hutchesons' Girls' Grammar School. Filed pix, Herald; married; had children; freelanced; Contributing Editor, Cosmopolitan, 1977-81; You (Mail on Sunday), 1984-90; "Just Joan", Daily Record, since 1979; hacks around the air waves for BBC Radio 5 and BBC Scotland. Publications: Scotland The Worst; Post Bus Country. Recreations: lunch; walking dogs; gardening. Address: (b.) 7 Castle Street, Edinburgh EH2; T.-0131-556 0010.

Burns, Frank. Principal, Ayr College. Address: (b.) Dam Park, Ayr, KA8 0EU.

Burns, Dr. Harry J.G. Director of Public Health, Greater Glasgow Health Board. Address: (b.) Dalian House, PO Box 15329, 350 St. Vincent Street, Glasgow G3 8YZ.

Burns, Jessica Martha, BA (Hons), LLB, SSC. Chairman, Independent Tribunal Service with responsibility for Child Support Appeal Tribunals, since 1992; b. 4.10.52, Dumfries; m., Bill Findlay; 2 d. Educ. Carlisle and County High School for Girls; Stirling University; Edinburgh University. Lecturer in Law, Glasgow University, 1983-85; Senior Lecturer, Faculty of Law, Aberdeen University, 1986-92. Member, Parole Board for Scotland, 1990-92; Member, Police Advisory Board for Scotland, 1988-92; Governor, Scottish Police College, 1988-92; Visiting Professor, School of Law, Maryland University, 1988. Recreations: relaxing with family; theatre; music; good company. Address: (b.) ITS, Wellington House, 134 Wellington Street, Glasgow G2 2XL; T.-0141-353 1441.

Burns, Rt. Rev. John Joseph, PhL, STh. Vicar General, Diocese of Motherwell, since 1992; Parish Priest, St. Bride's, Bothwell, since 1992; Vicar General for Pastoral Care and Planning, since 1992; b. 19.2.32, Rutherglen. Educ. Our Lady's High, Motherwell; St. Joseph's College, Dumfries; Gregorian University, Rome; Scots College, Rome. Assistant Priest, Motherwell Cathedral, 1956-65; Full-time Chaplain, Our Lady's High School, Motherwell, 1965-78; Resident at St. Brendan's, Motherwell, 1971-78; Diocesan Master of Ceremonies, 1956-81; Director of Religious Education, Diocese of Motherwell, 1978-85; Resident at Diocesan Centre, Motherwell, 1978-85, Parish Priest, St. Aidan's, Wishaw, 1983-92. Publications: series of Religious Education books for pupils and teachers, S1-S5, 1979-82. Recreations: general reading; walking; football. Address: St. Bride's, Fallside Road, Bothwell, Lanarkshire; T.-01698 852710.

Burnside, David Melville, LLB, NP. Senior Partner, Burnside Kemp Fraser, Solicitors, since 1989; b. 5.3.43, Dumfries; m., Gill; 3 s.; 2 d. Educ. Dumfries Academy; University of Edinburgh. Apprentice Solicitor, Melville & Lindsay W.S., Edinburgh, 1964-67; Assistant Solicitor: National Coal Board Legal Department, 1967-70, Clark & Wallace, Advocates, Aberdeen, 1970-71 (Partner, 1971-89); formed Burnside Advocates (later Burnside Kemp Fraser), 1989; acted for families in Chinook, Brent Spar and Cormorant Alpha helicopter crashes and Piper Alpha explosion (joint lead negotiator for Piper Alpha settlement). Past President: Aberdeen Bar Association, Junior Chamber, Aberdeen; Member, Board of Directors, Legal Defence Union. Recreations: family; music; theatre; tennis; skiing; following the Dons. Address: (b.) 4 Queens Terrace, Aberdeen AB10 1XL; T.-01224 624602.

Burnside, John. Writer; b. 19.3.55, Dunfermline. Scottish Arts Council Book Award, 1988, 1991, 1995; shortlisted for Forward Prize, 1992; Geoffrey Faber Memorial Prize, 1994; shortlisted for T.S. Eliot Prize, 1994; selected for New Generation Poets, 1994. Publications: poetry: The hoop, 1988; Common Knowledge, 1991; Feast Days, 1992; The myth of the twin, 1994; Swimming in the flood, 1995; A Normal Skin, 1997; fiction: The Dumb House, 1997. Address: (b.) c/o Jonathan Cape, Random House, 20 Vauxhall Bridge Road, London SW1V 2SA.

Burt, Gillian Robertson, MA (Hons). Headmistress, Craigholme School, Glasgow, since 1991; b. 7.2.44, Edinburgh; m., Andrew Wallace Burt; 1 s.; 1 d. Educ. Mary Erskine School; Edinburgh University; Moray House College of Education. Teacher of Geography, Tabeetha Church of Scotland School, Jaffa, Israel, 1966-67; Teacher of Geography, Boroughmuir Secondary School, 1967-70; Head of Geography, St. Hilary's School, Edinburgh, 1970-71, 1976-86, Head of Careers, 1986-91 (merged with St. Margaret's School, 1983). Recreations: music; theatre; walking; cooking; foreign travel. Address: (b.) Craigholme School, 72 St Andrews Drive, Glasgow G41 4HS; T.-0141-427 0375.

Burt, John. Principal, Angus College. Address: (b.) Keptie Road, Arbroath, DD11 3EA.

Burt, Peter A. Group Chief Executive, Bank of Scotland. Address: (b.) The Mound, Edinburgh EH1 1YZ.

Burton, Anthony Winston, OBE, BA (Hons). Managing Director, The Planning Exchange; b. 14.10.40, Leicester; 2 s.; 1 d. Educ. Wyggeston; Keele University. Chairman, Strategic Planning Society (Scotland); Deputy Chairman, Consumers' Association; Member, UK Ecolabelling Board. Recreations: cooking; sailing. Address: (b.) 9 Marchmont Terrace, Glasgow G12 9LS; T.-0141-334 7697.

Burton, Lord (Michael Evan Victor Baillie). Landowner and Farmer; b. 27.6.24, Burton-on-Trent; m., 1, Elizabeth Ursula Foster Wise (m. diss., deceased); 2, Coralie Denise Cliffe; 2 s.; 3 d. (1 d. deceased). Educ. Eton; Army. Scots Guards, 1942 (Lt., 1943); Lovat Scouts, 1948; Member, Inverness County Council, 1948-75; JP, 1961-75; Deputy Lieutenant, Inverness, 1963-65; Executive Member, Scottish Landowners Federation, 1963-92; has served on numerous committees. Recreations: shooting, fishing and hunting (not much time); looking after the estate. Address: Dochgarroch Lodge, Inverness IV3 6JX; T.-01463 861252/861218.

Busby, John Philip, NDD, DA (Edin), RSW, ARSA, PPSSA; b. 2.2.28, Bradford; m., Joan; 1 s.; 2 d. Educ. Ilkley Grammar School; Leeds College of Art; Edinburgh College of Art. Lecturer in Drawing and Painting, Edinburgh College of Art, 1956-58; Founder Member, Society of Wildlife Artists; illustrated 30 books on natural history; author and illustrator: Birds in Mallorca, Drawing Birds, John Busby Nature Drawings, The Living Birds of Eric Ennion. Recreations: music; bird-watching; travel. Address: (h.) Easter Haining, Ormiston Hall, East Lothian EH35 5NJ; T.-01875 340512.

Bush, Professor Peter Williams, BA, PhD, FRGS, FRSA. Vice-Principal, Glasgow Caledonian University, since 1989; b. 8.11.45, Liverpool; m., Judy; 1 s.; 1 d. Educ. St. Mary's College, Crosby, Liverpool; University College, London; Leeds University. Lecturer, Senior Lecturer, Principal Lecturer in Geography, Staffordshire University, 1970-81; Head, Department of Humanities, Glasgow College of Technology, 1981-84; Assistant Director, Glasgow Polytechnic, 1985-89. Chair, Scottish Advisory Committee on Credit and Access, 1993-96; Chair, Universities' Association for Continuing Education (Scotland), since 1996; Academic Auditor, Higher Education Quality Council, since 1993; Member: Board of Governors, St. Andrew's College of Education, 1987-95, Northern Ireland Higher Education Council, since 1993, Scottish Qualifications Authority, since 1997. Recreations: sports; music; travel. Address: (b.) Glasgow Caledonian University, Cowcaddens Road, Glasgow G4 0BA; T.-0141-331 3133.

Bushe, Frederick, OBE, RSA (1987), DA, DAE. Sculptor, since 1956; Founder Director, Scottish Sculpture Workshop, 1979-96; b. 1.3.31, Coatbridge; m., Fiona M.S. Marr; 1 d.; 3 s., 1 d. by pr. m. Educ. Our Lady's High School, Motherwell; Glasgow School of Art. Lecturer in Sculpture: Liverpool College of Education, 1962-69, Aberdeen College of Education, 1969-79; full-time Artist since 1979; established Scottish Sculpture Workshop and Scottish Sculpture Open Exhibition; exhibited in numerous one man and group exhibitions, since 1962. Recreations: music; cooking. Address: (h.) Rose Cottage, Lumsden, Huntly, Aberdeenshire AB54 4JJ; T.-01464 861394.

Busuttil, Professor Anthony, MD, FRCPath, FRCP(Glas), FRCPE, DMJ(Path). Regius Professor of Forensic Medicine, Edinburgh University, since 1987; Chairman, European Council for Legal Medicine; Honorary Consultant Pathologist, Royal Infirmary NHS Trust, since 1976; Police Surgeon, Lothian and Borders Police Force, since 1980; b. 30.12.45, Rabat, Malta; m., Angela; 3 s. Educ. St. Aloysius' College, Malta; Royal University of Malta. Junior posts, Western Infirmary, Glasgow; Lecturer in Pathology, Glasgow University. Address: (h.) 78 Hillpark Avenue, Edinburgh EH4 7AL; T.-0131-336 3241.

Bute, 7th Marquess of (John Colum Crichton-Stuart); b. 26.4.58; m.; 1 s.; 2 d. British Formula Three Champion, 1984; Formula One Ferrari Test Driver, 1985; JPS Lotus Grand Prix Driver, 1986; Works Driver for World Champion Sports Prototype Team Silk Cut Jaguar, 1988 (Joint Winner, Le Mans, 1988).

Butler, Vincent Frederick, RSA, RGI. Sculptor. Address: (h.) 17 Deanpark Crescent, Edinburgh EH4 1PH; T.-0131-332 5884.

Butlin, Ron, MA, DipAECD. Poet and Novelist; b. 17.11.49, Edinburgh. Educ. Dumfries Academy; Edinburgh University. Writer in Residence, Lothian Region Education Authority, 1979, Edinburgh University, 1981, 1984-85; Scottish/Canadian Writing Exchange Fellow, University of New Brunswick, 1983-84; Writer in Residence for Midlothian, 1989-90. Publications: poetry: Stretto, 1976; Creatures Tamed by Cruelty, 1979; The Exquisite Instrument, 1982 (Scottish Arts Council Book Award); Ragtime in Unfamiliar Bars, 1985 (SAC Book Award, Poetry Book Society recommendation); prose: The Tilting Room (short stories), 1983 (SAC Book Award); The Sound of My Voice (novel), 1987; Blending In (play), 1989; Histories of Desire (poetry), 1995; Mauritian Voices (Editor), 1996; Night Visits (novel), 1997. Recreations: music; travel. Address: (h.) 7 West Newington Place, Edinburgh EH9 1QT; T.-0131-667 0394.

Butter, Sir David Henry, KCVO, MC. Lord Lieutenant, Perth and Kinross, 1975-95; Landowner and Company Director; b. 18.3.20, London; m., Myra Alice Wernher; 1 s.; 4 d. Educ. Eton College; Oxford University. Served in World War II, 2nd Lt., Scots Guards, 1940; served in Western Desert, North Africa, Sicily and Italy (ADC to GOC 8th Army, 1944); Temporary Major, 1946; retired, 1948; Ensign, Queen's Bodyguard for Scotland (Royal Company of Archers); President, Highland TAVR, 1979-84; Member, Perth County Council, 1955-74; Deputy Lieutenant, Perthshire, 1956; Vice Lieutenant, Perthshire, 1960-71; Lord Lieutenant of County of Perth, 1971-75, of Kinross, 1974-75; Governor, Gordonstoun School, 1954-86. Recreations: golf; skiing; travel; shooting. Address: Cluniemore, Pitlochry, Perthshire; T.-01796 2006.

Butter, Professor Peter Herbert. Regius Professor of English Language and Literature, Glasgow University, 1965-86; b. 7.4.21, Coldstream; m., Bridget Younger; 1 s.; 2 d. Educ. Charterhouse; Balliol College, Oxford. Royal Artillery, 1941-46; Lecturer in English, Edinburgh University, 1948-58; Professor of English, Queen's University, Belfast, 1958-65. Secretary/Treasurer, International Association of University Professors of English, 1965-71. Publications: Shelley's Idols of the Cave, 1954; Francis Thompson, 1961; Edwin Muir, 1962; Edwin Muir: Man and Poet, 1966; Shelley's Alastor, Prometheus Unbound and Other Poems (Editor), 1971; Selected Letters of Edwin Muir (Editor), 1974; William Blake: Selected Poems (Editor), 1982; The Truth of Imagination: Uncollected Prose of Edwin Muir (Editor), 1988; Complete

Poems of Edwin Muir (Editor), 1991. Recreations: gardening; book-collecting. Address: (h.) Ashfield, Prieston Road, Bridge of Weir, Renfrewshire PA11 3AW; T.-01505 613139.

Butterworth, Neil, MA, HonFLCM. Chairman, Scottish Society of Composers, since 1991; Music Critic, Times Educational Supplement, 1983-97; Broadcaster; b. 4.9.34, Streatham, London; m., Anna Mary Barnes; 3 d. Educ. Rutlish School, Surrey; Nottingham University; London University; Guildhall School of Music, London. Lecturer, Kingston College of Technology, 1960-68; Head, Music Department, Napier College, Edinburgh, 1968-87. Conductor: Sutton Symphony Orchestra, 1960-64, Glasgow Orchestral Society, 1975-83 and since 1989; Chairman: Incorporated Society of Musicians, Edinburgh Centre, 1981-86, Inveresk Preservation Society, 1988-95; Churchill Fellowship, 1975. Publications: Haydn, 1976; Dvorak, 1980; Dictionary of American Composers, 1983; Aaron Copland, 1984; Vaughan Williams, 1989; Neglected Music, 1991; Samuel Barber, 1996; The American Symphony, 1998; over 300 compositions. Recreations: autographs; collecting books and records; giant jigsaw puzzles. Address: (h.) 1 Roderick Place, West Linton, Peeblesshire EH46 7ES; T.-01968 661112.

Buxton, Paul Kenneth, MA (Cantab), MB, BChir, FRCP(C), FRCPEdin. Consultant Physician in Dermatology, Fife Health Board and Royal Infirmary, Edinburgh, since 1981; Member, Clinical Teaching Staff, Edinburgh University, since 1981; b. 28.2.36, Harrar, Ethiopia; m., Heather; 1 s.; 1 d. Educ. Trinity College, Cambridge; St. Thomas's Hospital, London. Dermatologist, Royal Jubilee Hospital, Victoria, BC, Canada, 1971-81. President, Fife Branch, BMA, 1986-87; Fellow, Royal Society of Medicine; Member, Ethical Committee, Fife Health Board; Member, Editorial Board, Ethics and Medicine. Publication: ABC of Dermatology. Recreations: seafaring; books; art; country pursuits. Address: (h.) Old Inzievar House, Dunfermline KY12 8HA; T.-01383 852424.

Byers, Eric George, MA, DipTRP, FIMgt, MRTPI. Head, Economic Development Service, Fife Council, since 1995; b. 29.1.51, Aberdeen; m., Nicky. Educ. Aberdeen Grammar School; University of Aberdeen; University of Glasgow. Central Regional Council, 1975-80; Borders Regional Council, 1980-85; Fife Regional Council, 1985-95. Address: (b.) Fife House, North Street, Glenrothes; T.-01592 416294.

Byng, Jamie. Publisher and Joint Managing Director, Canongate Books, since 1994; b. 27.6.69, Winchester; m., Whitney Osborn McVeigh; 1 d. Educ. Winchester College; Edinburgh University. Recreations: tennis; cooking; "deejaying"; reading; drinking. Address: (b.) 14 High Street, Edinburgh EH1 1TE; T.-0131-557 5111.

Byrne, John. Dramatist and stage designer; b. 1940, Paisley. Plays include: The Slab Boys, Cuttin' A Rug, Still Life (trilogy), Normal Service; Cara Coco; television series: Tutti Frutti; Your Cheatin' Heart.

C

Cadell, Patrick Moubray, BA, FSA (Scot). Keeper of the Records of Scotland, since 1991; b. 17.3.41, Linlithgow; m., Sarah King (d. 1996); 2 s.; 1 d. Educ. Merchiston Castle School, Edinburgh; Cambridge University; Toulouse University. Information Officer, British Museum; Assistant Keeper, Department of MSS, British Museum; Keeper of Manuscripts, National Library of Scotland, 1983-90. Bailie, Abbey Court of Holyrood; Past President, West Lothian History and Amenity Society. Recreations: walking; the French language. Address: (b.) Scottish Record Office, HM General Register House, Edinburgh EH1 3YY; T.-0131-535 1312.

Cadell of Grange, William Archibald, DL, MA (Cantab), FRIAS. Architect; Commissioner, Royal Fine Art Commission for Scotland; b. 9.3.33, Aldershot; m., Mary-Jean Carmichael; 3 s. Educ. Merchiston Castle; Trinity College, Cambridge; Regent Street Polytechnic. Robert Matthew, Johnson Marshall and Partners; William A. Cadell Architects, 1968-95; DL, West Lothian, 1982; Member, Buildings and Curatorial Committees, National Trust for Scotland; former Chairman, RIAS Conservation Working Group; former Chairman, West Lothian History and Amenity Society. Recreations: gardening; local history; theatre. Address: Grange, Linlithgow, West Lothian; T.-01506 842946.

Caie, Professor Graham Douglas, MA, PhD. Professor of English Language, Glasgow University, since 1990; b. 3.2.45, Aberdeen; m., Ann Pringle Abbott; 1 s.; 1 d. Educ. Aberdeen Grammar School; Aberdeen University; McMaster University, Canada. Teaching Assistant, McMaster University, 1968-72; Amanuensis and Lektor, Copenhagen University, 1972-90. Chairman, Medieval Centre, Copenhagen University, 1985-90; Visiting Professor: McMaster University, 1985-86, Guelph University, 1989; Associate Fellow, Clare Hall, Cambridge, 1977-78; Chairman, Scottish Language Resource Centre; Member, English Panel: Scottish Examination Board, UCAS; Lead Assessor, SHEFC, TQA in English; Committee, Scottish Texts Society; Erasmus Academic Advisory Group (EU Commission); Board, European Society for the Study of English; Trustee, National Library of Scotland; Member, Council, Dictionary of Older Scottish Tongue. Publications: The Theme of Doomsday in Old English Poetry; Beowulf; Bibliography of Junius XI MS; numerous articles. Address: (h.) 12B Upper Glenburn Road, Bearsden, Glasgow G61 4BW; T.-0141-943 1192.

Cairns, Rev. John Ballantyne, LTh, LLB. Parish Minister, Riverside Church, Dumbarton, since 1985; Chaplain to the Queen, since 1997; b. 15.3.42, London; m., Dr. Elizabeth Emma Bradley; 3 s. Educ. Sutton Valence School, Kent; Bristol University; Edinburgh University. Messrs Macleod, Butler & Co., Solicitors, City of London, 1964-68; Administrative Assistant, East Lothian County Council, 1968-69; Assistant Minister, St. Giles, Elgin, 1973-75; Minister, Langholm, Ewes and Westerkirk Parish Churches, 1975-85, also linked with Canonbie, 1981-85; Clerk, Presbytery of Annandale and Eskdale, 1980-82; Convener, Maintenance of the Ministry Committee and Joint Convener, Board of Ministry and Mission, Church of Scotland, 1984-88; Chairman, Judicial Commission of General Assembly, since 1993; Convener, General Assembly Committee on Chaplains to Her Majesty's Forces, since 1993; Moderator, Presbytery of Dumbarton, 1993-94; Chaplain to Moderator of General Assembly, 1995; Divisional Chaplain, Strathclyde Police. Publications: Keeping Fit for Ministry, 1988; Democracy and Unwritten Constitutions, 1989. Recreations: golf; curling. Address:

(b.) High Street, Dumbarton, G82 1NB; (h.) 5 Kirkton Road, Dumbarton G82 4AS.

Cairns, Robert, MA, DipEd. Member, City of Edinburgh Council, since 1995 (Convener, Planning Committee, since 1995); b. 16.7.47, Dundee; m., Pauline Reidy; 2 s. Educ. Morgan Academy; Edinburgh University; Moray House College of Education. Assistant Editor, Scottish National Dictionary, 1969-74; Parliamentary candidate (Labour), North Edinburgh, 1973, February 1974; Teacher, James Gillespie's High School, 1975-96; Member, City of Edinburgh District Council, 1974-95 (Convener, Planning and Development Committee, 1986-95); Board Member: Old Town Renewal Trust, Old Town Community Development Project; Queen's Hall; Canongate Youth Project; Member, Historic Buildings Council. Recreations: gardening; theatre. Address: (h.) 70 Ratcliffe Terrace, Edinburgh; T.-0131-667 1741.

Cairns, Professor Robert Alan, BSc, PhD, FInstP. Professor, School of Mathematical and Computational Sciences, St. Andrews University, since 1991 (Reader, 1985-91); b. 12.3.45, Glasgow; m., Ann E. Mackay. Educ. Allan Glen's School, Glasgow; Glasgow University. Lecturer in Applied Mathematics, St. Andrews University, 1970-83; Senior Lecturer, 1983-85; Consultant, UKAEA Culham Laboratory, since 1984. Committee Member, Plasma Physics Group, Institute of Physics, 1981-84; Member, SERC Laser Committee, 1990-93; Member, SERC Atomic and Molecular Physics Sub-Committee, 1990-93; Member, Editorial Board, Plasma Physics, 1983-85; Editor, Journal of Plasma Physics, since 1995. Publications: Plasma Physics, 1985; Radiofrequency heating of plasmas, 1991. Recreations: music (listening to and playing recorder and baroque flute); golf; hill-walking. Address: (b.) School of Mathematical and Computational Sciences, St. Andrews University, North Haugh, St. Andrews, Fife KY16 9SS; T.-01334 463707.

Calder, Professor Andrew Alexander, MD, FRCS(Edin), FRCP (Glas and Edin), FRCOG. Professor of Obstetrics and Gynaecology, Edinburgh University, since 1987; Consultant Gynaecologist, Edinburgh Royal Infirmary and Consultant Obstetrician, Simpson Memorial Maternity Pavilion, Edinburgh, since 1987; b. 17.1.45, Aberdeen; m., Valerie Anne Dugard; 1 s.; 2 d. Educ. Glasgow Academy; Glasgow University. Clinical training posts in obstetrics and gynaecology, 1969-72: Queen Mother's Hospital, Western Infirmary, Royal Maternity Hospital and Royal Infirmary, (all Glasgow); Research Fellow, Nuffield Department of Obstetrics and Gynaecology, Oxford University, 1972-75; Lecturer in Obstetrics and Gynaecology, Glasgow University, 1975-78, Senior Lecturer, 1978-86. Secretary, Munro Kerr Society for the Study of Reproductive Biology, 1980-86, Chairman, 1989-96; Blair Bell Memorial Lecturer, RCOG, 1977; WHO Travelling Fellow, 1985; British Exchange Professor, UCLA, 1992. Address: Centre for Reproductive Biology, 37 Chalmers Street, Edinburgh EH3 9EW.

Calder, Angus Lindsay, MA, DPhil. Writer; b. 5.2.42, Sutton, Surrey; m., 1, Jennifer Daiches; 1 s.; 2 d.; 2, Catherine Kyle; 1 s. Educ. Wallington County Grammar School; Kings College, Cambridge. Lecturer in Literature, Nairobi University, 1968-71; Visiting Lecturer, Chancellor College, Malawi University, 1978; Reader and Staff Tutor in Arts, Open University in Scotland, 1979-93; Visiting Professor of English, University of Zimbabwe, 1990; Distinguished Visiting Scholar, University of Waikato, 1995; Member, Board of Directors, Royal Lyceum Theatre Company, 1984-96; Editorial Board, Wasafiri; Member, Panel of Judges, Saltire Society Scottish Book of the Year Award, since 1983; Eric Gregory Award for Poetry, 1967. Publications: The People's War: Britain 1939-1945, 1969 (John Llewellyn Rhys Memorial Prize); Revolutionary Empire, 1981 (Scottish Arts Council Book Award); The

Myth of the Blitz, 1991; Revolving Culture: notes from the Scottish Republic, 1994 (SAC Book Award); Waking in Waikato (poems), 1997. Recreations: curling; cricket. Address: (h.) 15 Spittal Street, Edinburgh EH3 9DY; T.-0131-229 8196.

Calder, Finlay, OBE. Grain Exporter; b. 20.8.57, Haddington; m., Elizabeth; 1 s.; 1 d. Educ. Daniel Stewart's and Melville College. Played rugby for Scotland, 1986-90; captained Scotland, 1989; captained British Isles, 1989. Recreation: work! Address: (b.) Alexander Inglis & Son Ltd., Meadow Stores, Ormiston, Tranent, East Lothian; T.-01875 616161.

Calder, George D., BA (Hons), LLB, MIPM. Senior Civil Servant, Scottish Office, since 1987; b. 20.12.47, Edinburgh; m., Kathleen Bonar; 2 d. Educ. George Watson's College; Pembroke College, Cambridge; Edinburgh University. Department of Employment, 1971-73; European Commission, 1973-76; HM Treasury, 1976-79; Manpower Services Commission Scotland, 1979-83; MSC Director for Northern England, 1983-85; MSC Director for Scotland, 1985-87. Recreations: hill-walking; football; country; writing; book collecting. Address: (b.) 1-577, Victoria Quay, Edinburgh; T.-0131-244 0246.

Calder, Jenni, BA, MPhil. Freelance Writer; Head of Publications, National Museums of Scotland, Edinburgh, since 1987; b. 3.12.41, Chicago, Illinois; 1 s.; 2 d. Educ. Perse School for Girls, Cambridge; Cambridge University; London University. Freelance writer, 1966-78; taught and lectured in Scotland, England, Kenya and USA; Lecturer in English, Nairobi University, 1968-69; Education Officer, Royal Scottish Museum, 1978-87. Publications: Chronicles of Conscience: a study of George Orwell and Arthur Koestler, 1968; Scott (with Angus Calder), 1969; There Must be a Lone Ranger: the Myth and Reality of the American West, 1974; Women and Marriage in Victorian Fiction, 1976; Brave New World and Nineteen Eighty Four, 1976; Heroes: from Byron to Guevara, 1977; The Victorian Home, 1977; The Victorian Home from Old Photographs, 1979; RLS, A Life Study, 1980; The Robert Louis Stevenson Companion (Editor), 1980; Robert Louis Stevenson and Victorian Scotland (Editor), 1981; The Strange Case of Dr Jekyll and Mr Hyde (Editor), 1979; Kidnapped (Editor), 1981; Catriona (Editor), 1981; The Enterprising Scot (Editor), 1986; Island Landfalls (Editor), 1987; Bonny Fighters: The Story of the Scottish Soldier, 1987; Open Guide to Animal Farm and Nineteen Eighty Four, 1987; The Wealth of a Nation (Editor), 1989; St. Ives, a new ending, 1990; Scotland in Trust, 1990; Treasure Islands (Editor), 1994; Mediterranean (poems, as Jenni Daiches), 1995; The Nine Lives of Naomi Mitchison, 1997; Robert Louis Stevenson (Editor), 1997. Recreations: music; films; walking the dog. Address: (h.) 31 Station Road, South Queensferry, West Lothian; T.-0131-331 1287.

Calder, Robert Russell, MA. Critic, Philosophical Writer, Historian of Ideas, Poet, Freelance Journalist, Book Reviewer; b. 22.4.50, Burnbank. Educ. Hamilton Academy; Glasgow University; Edinburgh University. Co Editor, Chapman, 1974-76 and since 1988; Editor, Lines Review, 1976-77; Theatre Critic and Feature Writer, Scot, 1983-86; books: A School of Thinking, 1995; Narcissism, Nihilism, Simplicity (Editor), 1992; poetry: Il Re Giovane, 1976, Ettrick & Annan, 1981; Serapion, 1993. Recreations: music - opera singing; jazz piano. Address: (h.) 23 Glenlee Street, Burnbank, Hamilton ML3 9JB; T.-01698 824244.

Calderwood, Sir Robert, Kt. Chairman, Greater Glasgow Health Board, 1993-97; Chief Executive, Strathclyde Regional Council, 1980-92; b. 1.3.32; m., Meryl Anne; 3 s.; 1 d. Educ. William Hulme's School, Manchester; Manchester University (LLB Hons). Town Clerk: Salford, 1966-69, Bolton, 1969-73, Manchester, 1973-79. Director, Glasgow Garden Festival 1988 Ltd., 1985-88; Chairman,

Strathclyde Buses Ltd., 1989-93; Member: Parole Board for England and Wales, 1971-73, Society of Local Authority Chief Executives, 1974-92 (President, 1989-90), Scottish Consultative Committee, Commission for Racial Equality, 1981-88; Director, European Summer Special Olympic Games 1990 (Strathclyde) Ltd., 1989-90; Member, Council, Industrial Society, 1983-92; Director: GEC (Scotland) Ltd., since 1991, Scottish Opera, 1991-96 (Deputy Chairman, 1991-96); Member: Employers' Panel, Industrial Tribunals in Scotland, since 1992, Local and Central Government Relations Research Committee, Joseph Rowntree Foundation, 1992-97; Director, Quality Scotland Foundation, 1991-92; Honorary Patron, Scottish Overseas Aid, since 1993; Honorary Member, The Incorporation of Coopers, Trades House of Glasgow, since 1994; Member, Court of Governors, Glasgow Caledonian University, 1994-96. Hon. Fellow, IWEM, 1992. Recreations: theatre; watching rugby; interested in United Nations activities. Address:(h.) 6 Mosspark Avenue, Milngavie, Glasgow G62 8NL.

Caldwell, David Cleland, SHNC, MA, BPhil. Secretary, The Robert Gordon University, since 1984; b. 25.2.44, Glasgow; m., Ann Scott Macrae; 1 s.; 1 d. Educ. George Watson's College, Edinburgh; St. Andrews University; Glasgow University. Warwick University: Lecturer in Politics, 1969-76, Administrative Assistant, 1976-77, Assistant Registrar, 1977-80; Registry Officer, Aberdeen University, 1980-84. Member: Warwick District Council, 1979-80, Grampian Regional Council, 1983-84; Parliamentary candidate (Labour), North East Fife, 1983; Member, Aberdeen Grammar School Council, 1983-88 (Chairman, 1985-88); Member, St. Andrews University Court, 1986-94 (Convener, Audit Commitee, 1990-94); Member, Board of Management, and Convener, Finance Committee, Moray College, since 1995; Director, Viscom (Aberdeen) Ltd., 1992-97 (Chairman, 1994-95). Address: (b.) The Robert Gordon University, Schoolhill, Aberdeen AB10 1FR; T.-01224 262010.

Caldwell, David Hepburn, MA, PhD, FSAScot. Curator in Charge of the Scottish Medieval Collections, Royal Museum of Scotland; b. 15.12.51, Kilwinning, Ayrshire; m., Margaret Anne McGovern; 1 s.; 2 d. Educ. Ardrossan Academy; Edinburgh University. Joined staff, National Museum of Antiquities, 1973. Publications: The Scottish Armoury, 1979; Scottish Weapons and Fortifications, 1981. Recreation: travelling. Address: (h.) 3 James Park, Burntisland, Fife KY3 9EW; T.-872175.

Caldwell, Sheila Marion, BA (Hons), ARSGS. Member, Council, Royal Scottish Geographical Society; b. England; m., Major Robert Caldwell, TD. Educ. Tunbridge Wells Grammar School; University College, London. Founder/Principal, Yejide Girls' Grammar School, Ibadan, Nigeria; first Principal, Girls' Secondary (Government) School, Lilongwe, Malawi; Depute Head, Mills Grammar School, Framlingham, Suffolk; Head, St. Columba's School, Kilmacolm, 1976-87; Treasurer, Secondary Heads' Association, Scotland, 1984-87; Public Affairs Liaison, Glasgow Association of Women Graduates. Recreations: travel; art history and architecture; music, opera and ballet; cooking. Address: (h.) 27 Oxford Road, Renfrew PA4 0SJ; T.-0141-886 2296.

Calman, Professor Sir Kenneth Charles, KCB 1996, MD, PhD, FRCP, FRCS, FRSE. Chief Medical Officer, Department of Health, since 1991; Chief Medical Officer, Scottish Home and Health Department, 1989-91; b. 25.12.41, Glasgow; m., Ann; 1 s.; 2 d. Educ. Allan Glen's School, Glasgow; Glasgow University. Lecturer in Surgery, Western Infirmary, Glasgow, 1968-72; MRC Clinical Research Fellow, London, 1972-73; Professor of Oncology, Glasgow University, 1974-84; Dean of Postgraduate Medicine, 1984-89. Recreations: golf; jogging; gardening.

Address: (h.) 585 Anniesland Road, Glasgow; T.-0141-954 9423.

Calvocoressi, Richard. Keeper, Scottish National Gallery of Modern Art, since 1987; b. 5.5.51; m.; 1 s.; 2 d. Educ. Eton; Magdalen College, Oxford.

Cameron, Alasdair, FSA Scot. Farmer and Crofter; b. 12.6.44, Dingwall; m., Jeannette Benzie; 2 d. Educ. Dingwall Academy. Hon. President, Black Isle Farmers Society; Former Vice-Chairman, Crofters Commission; Member: Scottish Farm and Countryside Educational Trust, Highlands and Islands Forum, Scottish Agricultural Arbiters Association, Northern Counties Valuators Association, Scottish Vernacular Buildings Working Group, Historic Farm Buildings UK; Past Chairman: Highland Farming and Forestry Advisory Group, Dingwall Round Table. Recreations: photography; industrial archaeology; local history; the countryside. Address: Wellhouse Farm, Black Isle, Muir of Ord, Ross-shire IV6 7SF; T.-01463 870416.

Cameron, Alexander, BA, CertASS, CQSW. Director of Social Work, South Lanarkshire Council, since 1995; b. 29.4.50, Glasgow; m., Linda Dobbie; 2 s. Educ. Duncanrig Senior Secondary, East Kilbride; Strathclyde University; Aberdeen University. Social Worker, Clackmannan County Council, 1973-75; Central Regional Council: Research/Planning Officer, 1975-79, Principal Officer (Fieldwork), 1979-81, Assistant Director of Social Work, 1981-87; Director of Social Work, Borders Regional Council, 1987-95; former President, Association of Directors of Social Work. Recreations: rugby; Scottish country dancing. Address: (h.) 21 Ballantrac, East Kilbride.

Cameron, Allan John, MBE, DL, JP. Farmer and Landowner, since 1947; b. 25.3.17, Edinburgh; m., Elizabeth Vaughan-Lee; 2 s.; 2 d. Educ. Harrow; Royal Military College. Regular officer, Queen's Own Cameron Highlanders, 1936-47 (ret. Major); Member: Ross and Cromarty County Council, 1955-75 (Chairman, Education Committee, 1962-75), Ross and Cromarty District Council, since 1975 (Convener, since 1991); former Commissioner: Red Deer Commission, Countryside Commission for Scotland; former Member, BBC Council for Scotland; President: Royal Caledonian Curling Club, 1963, International Curling Federation, 1965-69. Recreations: curling; golf; shooting; fishing; gardening. Address: (h.) Allangrange, Munlochy, Ross and Cromarty IV8 8NZ; T.-014638 11249.

Cameron, Rt. Rev. Andrew Bruce. Bishop of Aberdeen and Orkney, Scottish Episcopal Church, since 1992; b. 2.5.41, Glasgow; m., Elaine Cameron; 2 s. Educ. Eastwood Secondary School; Edinburgh Theological College. Curate, Helensburgh and Edinburgh, 1964-70; Chaplain, St. Mary's Cathedral, Edinburgh, 1970-75; Diocesan and Provincial Youth Chaplain, 1969-75; Rector, St. Mary's Church, Dalmahoy, and Anglican Chaplain, Heriot Watt University, 1975-82; Churches Development Officer, Livingston Ecumenical Parish, 1982-88; Rector, St. John's Episcopal Church, Perth, 1988-92; Convener, Mission Board, Scottish Episcopal Church, 1988-92. Recreations: music; theatre; various sports; gardening. Address: (b.) Diocesan Centre, 39 Kings Crescent, Aberdeen AB24 3HP; T.-01224 636653; (h.) Bishop's House, Ashley House, Ashley Gardens, Aberdeen, AB10 6RQ; T.-01224 208142.

Cameron, Colin. Head of Production, BBC Scotland, since 1997; Chair, BAFTA Scotland; b. 30.3.50; m., Christine Main; 2 s. Educ. Glasgow Academy; Duke of York School, Nairobi; Polytechnic of Central London. Journalist, Current Affairs, BBC Scotland, 1973-76; Film Director, That's Life, 1976-77; Producer/Director, Everyman and Heart of the Matter, 1977-85; Editor, Brass Tacks, BBC North, 1985-88; Head of Documentary Features, BBC Television, 1988-91;

Head of Television, BBC Scotland, 1991-96. Board Member, Scottish Film Production Fund; Advisor, Glasgow Common Purpose; RTS International Current Affairs Award, 1984; UN Association Media Peace Prize, 1984. Recreations: dinghy sailing; cycling; hillwalking; cinema; Scottish art. Address: (b.) BBC Scotland, Queen Margaret Drive, Glasgow, G12 8DG; T.-0141-338 2424.

Cameron, David Roderick Simpson, RIBA, ARIAS, MRTPI, FSA Scot. Architect/Planner; Principal, Chambers Design, since 1996; Urban Design Consultant, Broad and Hughes Architects, since 1997; Convener: The Saltire Society Planning and Environment Committee, since 1995, Historic Burghs Association of Scotland (Steering Committee), since 1993, Charles Cameron Conservation Campaign (St. Petersburg), since 1994; Chairman, Sir Patrick Geddes Memorial Trust, since 1991; b. 2.6.41, Inverness; m., Filitsa Boulton; 1 s.; 2 d. Educ. Angusfield and George Watson's College; Edinburgh College of Art; Newcastle University. Architect, Rowand Anderson, Kininmonth and Paul, 1968-71; Conservation Officer, Edinburgh Corporation and Edinburgh District Council, 1971-83; Depute Director of Planning, City of Edinburgh District Council, 1983-96; European Union, ECOS Project Manager (of Edinburgh and Berlin team) for revival of Kazimierz quarter of Krakow, Poland, 1993-95; Chairman, The Saltire Society, 1990-95; Convener: Saltire Performing Arts Committee, 1991-94, Scottish Environment and Amenity Link, 1996-97; Secretary: Saltire Arts and Crafts in Architecture Award Panel, 1987-94, Saltire Housing Award Panel, 1974-83; Hon. Secretary, Edinburgh Architectural Association, 1972-75, and Editor, EAA Review, 1980-84; Member: International Society of City and Regional Planners, since 1987, Executive Committee, Scottish Society of Directors of Planning, 1988-96, Council, Clan Cameron Association, since 1988, and Vice-President, since 1995, Council, National Trust for Scotland, since 1994, Grants Council, The Caledonian Foundation, since 1996, Scottish Homes Advisory Group on Physical Quality, since 1996. Recreations: art; fishing; Scottish and Greek heritage. Address: The Saltire Society, 9 Fountain Close, 22 High Street, Edinburgh EH1 1TF; T.-0131-556 1836.

Cameron, Younger of Lochiel, Donald Angus, MA, FCA, DL. Director, J. Henry Schroder & Co. Limited, since 1984; President, Highland Society of London, 1994-95; b. 2.8.46, London; m., Lady Cecil Kerr; 1 s. 3 d. Educ. Harrow; Christ Church, Oxford. 2nd Lieutenant, Queen's Own Cameron Highlanders (TA), 1966-68; Chartered Accountant, 1971. DL, Lochaber, Inverness, Badenoch and Strathspey. Address: (h.) Achnacarry, Spean Bridge, Inverness-shire.

Cameron of Lochiel, Colonel Sir Donald (Hamish), KT (1973), CVO, TD, JP. 26th Chief of the Clan Cameron; Lord Lieutenant, County of Inverness, 1971-86; Chartered Accountant; b. 12.9.10; m., Margaret Gathorne-Hardy; 2 s.; 2 d. Educ. Harrow; Balliol College, Oxford. Lt.-Col. commanding: Lovat Scouts, 1944-45; 4/5th Bn. (TA), Queen's Own Cameron Highlanders, 1955-57; Colonel, 1957 (TARO); Vice-Chairman, Royal Bank of Scotland, 1969-80; Chairman: Culter Guard Bridge Holdings Ltd., 1970-76, Scottish Widows Life Assurance Society, 1964-67; President: Scottish Landowners Federation, 1979-84, Royal Highland and Agricultural Society of Scotland, 1971, 1979, 1987; Member, Scottish Railways Board (Chairman, 1959-64). Address: (h.) Achnacarry, Spean Bridge, Inverness-shire.

Cameron, Rt. Rev. Douglas M. Bishop of Argyll and the Isles, since 1993; b. 23.3.35, Natal; m., Anne Patricia Purnell; 2 d. Educ. Eastwood Grammar School; Edinburgh Theological College; University of the South, Sewanee, Tennessee. Curate, Christ Church, Falkirk, 1962-65; Priest, Papua New Guinea, 1965-74, Archdeacon, 1972-74; Rector: St. Fillan's and St. Hilda's, Edinburgh, 1974-88, St. Mary's, Dalkeith, and St. Leonard's, Lasswade, 1988-92;

Canon and Synod Clerk, Diocese of Edinburgh, 1990-92; Dean of Edinburgh, 1991-92. Recreations: hill-walking; music; cooking. Address: (b.) The Pines, Ardconnel Road, Oban PA34 5DR; T.-01631 566912.

Cameron, Professor Dugald, DA, FCSD, FRSA. Director, Glasgow School of Art, since 1991; Hon. Professor, Glasgow University, since 1993; Companion, Royal Aeronautical Society, 1996; Director, Squadron Prints, since 1977; Industrial Design Consultant, since 1965; b. 4.10.39, Glasgow; m., Nancy Inglis. Educ. Glasgow High School; Glasgow School of Art. Industrial Designer, Hard Aluminium Surfaces Ltd., 1962-65; Visiting Lecturer, Glasgow School of Art, 1963-70; Head of Product Design, Glasgow School of Art, 1970-82; Head of Design, 1982-91. Member: Engineering Advisory Committee, Scottish Committee, Council of Industrial Design, since 1966, Industrial Design (Engineering) Panel and 3D Design Board, CNAA, since 1978, Scottish Committee of Higher Education, Design Council; commission RAFVR (T), 1974. Publications: Glasgow's Own (a history of 602 City of Glasgow Squadron, Royal Auxiliary Air Force), 1987; Glasgow's Airport, 1990. Recreations: railways; flying (lapsed private pilot). Address: (h.) Achnacraig, Skelmorlie, Ayrshire.

Cameron, Duncan Inglis, OBE, JP, BL, DUniv, CA, FRSGS. Director of Administration and Secretary, Heriot-Watt University, 1965-90; b. 26.8.27, Glasgow; m., Elizabeth Pearl Heron; 2 s.; 1 d. Educ. Glasgow High School; Glasgow University. RAF, 1945-48; CA apprentice, Alfred Tongue & Co., 1948-51; Qualified Assistant, Cooper Brothers & Co., 1951-52; Assistant Accountant, Edinburgh University, 1952-65; Commonwealth Universities Administrative Fellow, 1972. President, Edinburgh Junior Chamber of Commerce, 1962-63; Governor, Keil School, Dumbarton, 1967-85; Chairman of Council, Royal Scottish Geographical Society, 1983-88 (Trustee, since 1973); Governor, Scottish College of Textiles, since 1991; Chairman, Bioscot Ltd., 1983-84; Chairman, Edinburgh Conference Centre Ltd., 1987-90; Director, Heriot-Watt Computer Application Services Ltd., 1987-90; Chairman, SCOT Innovation and Development Ltd., since 1991; Member: Universities Central Council on Admissions, 1967-90, Directing Group, Programme on Institutional Management in Higher Education, OECD, Paris, 1986-90, Executive Committee, Federated Superannuation System for Universities, since 1988, Executive Committee, Scottish Norwegian Business Forum, 1991-96, Board of Management, Petroleum Science and Technology Institute, 1989-93; Chairman, Edinburgh Society of Glasgow University Graduates, 1984-85; Session Clerk, St. Ninian's Church, Corstorphine, 1969-96; Convener, Finance Committee, Action of Churches Together in Scotland, 1993-96; Vice-Convener, Personnel Committee, Church of Scotland, since 1996; Honorary Fellow, Royal Scottish Geographical Society, 1989; Honorary Doctor, Heriot-Watt University, 1991; Officer of the Royal Norwegian Order of St. Olav, 1979. Recreations: travel; photography. Address: (h.) 11 The Hermitage, 1 Kinellan Road, Edinburgh EH12 6FS; T.-0131 316 4454.

Cameron, Professor Iain Thomas, BSc (Hons), MA (Cantab), MD (Edin), MRCOG, MRACOG. Regius Professor, Obstetrics and Gynaecology, Queen Mother's Hospital, Glasgow; b. 21.2.56, Flixton; m., Heidi D. Wade; 1 s.; 1 d.; 2 d by pr. m. Educ. Hutton Grammar School; Edinburgh University. Research Fellow, Department of Obstetrics and Gynaecology, Edinburgh University, 1982-84; Lecturer and Registrar, 1984-86; Clinical Research Fellow, Monash University, 1986-88; Senior Registrar, Royal Women's Hospital, Melbourne, 1988-89; Lecturer, Cambridge University, 1989-92. Recreation: solo piping. Address: (b.) Department of Obstetrics and Gynaecology, The Queen Mother's Hospital, Glasgow G3 8SJ; T.-0141-201 0567.

Cameron, Sheriff Ian Alexander, MA, LLB. Sheriff of Grampian, Highland and Islands, at Wick, Dornoch and Stornoway, since 1993; b. 5.11.38, Elgin; m., Dr. Margaret Anne Innes; 1 s. Educ. Elgin Academy; Edinburgh University; Aberdeen University. Partner, Stewart and McIsaac, Solicitors, Elgin, 1962-86; Sheriff at Edinburgh, 1987-93. Recreation: travel. Address: Braemoray, Elgin, IV30 2NJ; T.-01343 542731; 19/4 Damside, Dean Village, Edinburgh, EH4 3BB; T.-0131-220 1548.

Cameron, Professor Rev. James Kerr, MA, BD, PhD, FRHistS. Professor of Ecclesiastical History, St. Andrews University, 1970 89; b. 5.3.24, Methven; m., Emma Leslie Birse; 1 s. Educ. Oban High School; St. Andrews University; Hartford Theological Seminary, Hartford, Connecticut. Ordained as Assistant Minister, Church of the Holy Rude, Stirling, 1952; appointed Lecturer in Church History, Aberdeen University, 1955; Lecturer, then Senior Lecturer in Ecclesiastical History, St. Andrews University; Dean, Faculty of Divinity, 1978-83. President: Ecclesiastical History Society, 1976-77, British Sub-Commission, Commission Internationale d'Histoire Ecclesiastique Comparee, 1979-92; Vice-President, International Association for Neo-Latin Studies, 1979-81; Co-Editor and Contributor, Theologische Realenzyklopädie (Vol. 17 onwards). Publications: Letters of John Johnston and Robert Howie, 1963; First Book of Discipline, 1972; Contributor to: Acta Conventus Neo-Latini Amstelodamensis, 1973; Advocates of Reform, 1953; The Scottish Tradition, 1974; Renaissance and Renewal in Christian History, 1977; Reform and Reformation: England and the Continent, 1979; Origins and Nature of the Scottish Enlightenment, 1982; A Companion to Scottish Culture; Humanism in Renaissance Scotland, 1990; The Impact of Humanism on Western Europe, 1990. Recreation: gardening. Address: (h.) Priorscroft, 71 Hepburn Gardens, St. Andrews KY16 9LS; T.-01334 473996.

Cameron, J. Gordon, MA, LLB, DipLP, WS, NP. Partner, Stuart & Stuart WS, since 1987; b. 15.11.57, Edinburgh; m., Deborah Jane; 1 s.; 1 d. Educ. George Watson's College; Aberdeen University. Joined Stuart & Stuart WS as assistant, 1985. Hon. Secretary and Treasurer, Royal Celtic Society. Recreations: hill-walking; cycling; keep-fit. Address: (b.) 23 Rutland Street, Edinburgh EH1 2RN; T.-0131-228 6449.

Cameron, John Bell, CBE, FRAgricS, AIAgricE. Chairman, British Railways (Scottish) Board, 1988-93 (Member, 1988-94); Director, South West Trains, since 1995; Chairman, Scottish Beef Council, since 1997; Farmer, since 1961; b. 14.6.39, Edinburgh; m., Margaret Clapperton. Educ. Dollar Academy. Vice President, National Farmers' Union, 1976-79, President, 1979-84; Member, Agricultural Praesidium of EEC, 1979-84; Chairman, EEC Advisory Committee for Sheepmeat, 1982-90; Chairman, World Meats Group, (IFAP), since 1983; Chairman, Board of Governors, Dollar Academy, since 1985; Chairman, United Auctions Ltd., since 1985; Member, Board of Governors, Macaulay Land Use Research Institute, since 1987. Long Service Award, Royal Observer Corps. Recreations: flying; shooting; travelling. Address: (h.) Balbuthie Farm, by Leven, Fife; T.-01333 730210.

Cameron, (John Roderick) Hector, LLB, NP. Solicitor; Director, Telecom Service Centres Ltd.; Director, McColl McGregor Ltd.; b. 11.6.47, Glasgow; m., Rosemary Brownlee; 1 s.; 1 d. Educ. High School of Glasgow; Friends School, Wigton; St. Andrews University. Admitted Solicitor, 1971; Partner, Bishop, Milne Boyd & Co., 1973; Chairman, Glasgow Junior Chamber of Commerce, 1981; Managing Partner, Bishop & Co., 1985; Partner, Dorman Jeffrey & Co., 1990; Director, Merchants House of

Glasgow, 1986; Director, Glasgow Chamber of Commerce, 1987. Recreations: reading; sailing; golf. Address: (h.) 2 Lancaster Crescent, Glasgow G12 0RR.

Cameron, Rev. Dr. John Urquhart, BA, BSc, PhD, BD, ThD. Minister, Parish of Broughty Ferry, since 1974; b. 10.6.43, Dundee; m., Jill Sjoberg; 1 s.; 1 d. Educ. Falkirk High School; St. Andrews University; Edinburgh University; University of Southern California. Marketing Executive, Beechams, London, 1969-73; Assistant Minister, Wellington Church, Glasgow, 1973-74; Chaplain, Royal Naval Reserve, 1976-81; Marketing Consultant, Pergamon Press, Oxford, 1977-81; Religious Education Department, Dundee High School, 1980-87; Sports Journalist and Travel Writer, Hill Publications, Surrey, since 1981; Physics Department, Dundee College of Further Education, 1987-95; Moderator, Presbytery of Dundee, 1993-94; Chaplain, Royal Caledonian Curling Club, 1980-95; Chaplain, Black Watch ACF, since 1994. National and international honours in both summer and winter sports, 1960-85; sports scholarship, University of Southern California, 1962-64. Recreations: golf; skiing; curling. Address: St. Stephen's Manse, 33 Camperdown Street, Broughty Ferry; T.-01382 477403.

Cameron of Lochbroom, Lord (Kenneth John Cameron), Life Baron (1984), PC (1984), MA (Oxon), LLB, QC, FRSE, Hon. FRIAS. Senator of the College of Justice, since 1989; Chairman, Royal Fine Art Commission for Scotland; b. 11.6.31, Edinburgh; m., Jean Pamela Murray; 2 d. Educ. Edinburgh Academy; Corpus Christi College, Oxford; Edinburgh University. Advocate, 1958; Queen's Counsel, 1972; President, Pensions Appeal Tribunal for Scotland, 1976; Chairman, Committee of Investigation Under Agricultural Marketing Act 1958, 1980; Advocate Depute, 1981; Lord Advocate, 1984; Hon. Bencher, Lincoln's Inn; Hon. Fellow, Corpus Christi College, Oxford. Recreations: fishing; sailing. Address: (h.) Stoneyhill House, Musselburgh.

Cameron, Sheriff Lewis, MA, LLB. Solicitor, since 1962; Sheriff of South Strathclyde Dumfries and Galloway at Hamilton, since 1994, at Dumfries, 1988-94; b. 12.8.35, Glasgow; m., Sheila Colette Gallacher; 2 s.; 2 d. Educ. St. Aloysius College; Blairs College; St. Sulpice, Paris; Glasgow University. RAF, 1954-56; admitted Solicitor, 1962. Member, Legal Aid Central Committee, 1970-80; Legal Aid Secretary, Airdrie, 1978-87; Chairman, Social Security Appeal Tribunals, 1983-88; Dean, Airdrie Society of Solicitors, 1984-85; Tutor, Strathclyde University, 1981-88; Treasurer, Monklands Victim Support Scheme, 1983-88; Chairman: Dumfries and Galloway Family Conciliation Service, 1988-92, Dumfries and Galloway, Scottish Association for the Study of Delinquency, 1988-92; Member, Scotland Committee, National Children's Homes; Trustee, Oscar Marzaroli Trust; Chairman, PHEW. Address: (b.) Sheriff Court House, Beckford Street, Hamilton.

Cameron, Roy, QPM. Chief Constable, Lothian and Borders Police. Address: (b.) Fettes Avenue, Edinburgh EH4 1RB. Tel.: 0131-311 3131.

Cameron, Thomas Anthony (Tony). Head of Food and Agriculture, Scottish Office, since 1992; b. 3.2.47; m., Elizabeth Christine Sutherland; 2 s. Educ. Stranraer High School. Department of Agriculture and Fisheries for Scotland, 1966; Private Secretary to Deputy Under Secretary of State, Scottish Office, 1972, to Permanent Under Secretary of State, 1973-74; HEO(D), DAFS, 1974-77; Principal, DAFS, 1977-82; Assistant Secretary, DAFS, 1982-87; Scottish Office Finance Division, 1987-92; Member, Duke of Edinburgh's Sixth Commonwealth Study Conference, Australia. Recreations: reading; mountaineering; cycling. Address: Scottish Office Agriculture and Fisheries Department, Pentland House, 47 Robb's Loan, Edinburgh; T.-0131-244 6032.

Cameron-Jones, Professor Margot, MA, MEd, FRSA. Professor of Teacher Education, Moray House College of Education, Heriot-Watt University, since 1992; b. 11.1.39, Isle of Man; m., Richard John; 1 s. Educ. St. Winifred's School, Llanfairfechan; University of Edinburgh. Schoolteacher, Edinburgh; Research Fellow, University of Dundee; Moray House College of Education, Heriot-Watt University: Lecturer, Head of Department, Director of Teacher Education. Member, Research and Developments Committee, National Board for Scotland. Publications: several papers in the field of teacher education. Recreations: philosophy; hill-walking. Address: (b.) Moray House, Holyrood Road, Edinburgh EH8 8AQ; T.-0131-556 8455.

Campbell, Alan Grant, LLB. Chief Executive, Aberdeenshire Council, since 1995; b. 4.12.46, Aberdeen; m., Susan Black; 1 s.; 2 d. Educ. Aberdeen Grammar School; Aberdeen University. Various legal appointments, Aberdeen County Council, 1968-75; Grampian Regional Council: Assistant Director of Law and Administration, 1975-79, Depute Director, 1979-84, Director of Law and Administration, 1984-91, Chief Executive, 1991-95. Recreations: cycling; gardening. Address: Woodhill House, Westburn Road, Aberdeen AB16 5GB; T.-01224 665400.

Campbell, Alastair James, LLB. Partner, Mitchells Roberton, Solicitors, since 1985; Clerk and Treasurer, Royal Faculty of Procurators in Glasgow, since 1994; b. 29.12.48, Glasgow; m., Pamela Crichton; 3 s. Educ. Merchiston Castle School, Edinburgh; University of Strathclyde. Qualified as Solicitor, 1972; Partner, Mackenzie Roberton & Co. (later Mitchells Roberton), 1975. Secretary, National Burns Homes, Mauchline, Ayrshire, since 1976. Recreations: golf; tennis; curling. Address: (b.) George House, 36 North Hanover Street, Glasgow G1 2AD; T.-0141-552 3422.

Campbell of Airds, Alastair Lorne, OStJ. Chief Executive, Clan Campbell, since 1984; Archivist, Inveraray Castle, since 1984; H.M. Unicorn Pursuivant of Arms, Court of the Lord Lyon, since 1987; b. 11.7.37, London; m., Mary-Ann Campbell-Preston; 3 s.; 1 d. Educ. Eton; R.M.A., Sandhurst. Regular Army, 1955-63 (commissioned Argyll and Sutherland Highlanders); Reid Pye and Campbell, 1963-71 (Managing Director, 1970-71); Waverley Vintners Ltd., 1972-83 (Marketing Director, 1972, Managing Director, 1977). Member: Queen's Bodyguard for Scotland (Royal Company of Archers), Chapter of Scottish Priory, Order of St John; FSA Scot; Patron, Armorial and Heraldry Society of Australasia; Chairman, Advisory Committee on Tartan to the Lord Lyon; Member, Council, National Trust for Scotland; Honorary Research Fellowship, University of Aberdeen, 1996. Publications: Two Hundred Years — The Highland Society of London; The Life and Troubled Times of Sir Donald Campbell of Ardnamurchan. Recreations: painting; fishing; walking. Address: (h.) Inveraw Barn, Taynuilt, Argyll PA35 1HU; T.-0186 62 207.

Campbell, Professor Alexander George Macpherson, MB, ChB, FRCPEdin, DCH. Emeritus Professor of Child Health, Aberdeen University; b. 3.2.31, Glasgow; m., Sheila Mary Macdonald; 1 s.; 2 d. Educ. Dollar Academy; Glasgow University. Paediatric Registrar, Royal Hospital for Sick Children, Edinburgh, 1959-61; Senior House Officer, Hospital for Sick Children, London, 1961-62; Assistant Chief Resident, Children's Hospital of Philadelphia, 1962-63; Fellow in Paediatric Cardiology, Hospital for Sick Children, Toronto, 1963-64; Fellow in Fetal and Neonatal Physiology, Nuffield Institute for Medical Research, Oxford, 1964-66; Lecturer in Child Health, St. Andrews University, 1966-67; Assistant, then Associate Professor of Paediatrics, Yale University School of Medicine, 1967-73; Professor of Child Health, Aberdeen

University, 1973-92. Recreation: golf. Address: (h.) 34 Woodburn Crescent, Aberdeen; T.-01224 319152.

Campbell, Alexandra Speir, MB, ChB, FRCSEd, FRCSGlasg, LLB (Hons), DFM. Secretary, Royal College of Surgeons of Edinburgh, since 1996; b. 9.4.53, Dumfries. Educ. Ayr Academy; Glasgow University; London University. Junior hospital doctor, 1977-85; Consultant in Accident and Emergency, 1985-88; Medical and Dental Defence Union of Scotland, 1988-96, latterly as Senior Medical Adviser. Surgeon Lieutenant Commander, Royal Naval Reserve, 1986-93; private pilot's licence, 1989. Recreations: cookery; gardening; travel; reading. Address: (b.) Royal College of Surgeons of Edinburgh, Nicolson Street, Edinburgh; T.-0131-527 1600.

Campbell, Alistair Bromley, OBE. Farmer; Agricultural Consultant and Valuer; Chairman of Council, Scottish Conservation Projects Trust, 1984-97; b. 23.6.27, Charing, Kent; m., Rosemary Pullar (deceased); 1 s.; 2 d. Educ. Tonbridge School. Training in agriculture, 1944-47; self-employed Farmer, 1948-81; Agricultural Consultant, Arbiter, Valuer, 1968-81; Agricultural Adviser and Valuer, South of Scotland Electricity Board, 1972-81; Vice-Chairman, Countryside Commission for Scotland, 1972-81 (Member from 1969); Member: Secretary of State's Panel of Agricultural Arbiters, 1968-81, Scottish Land Court, 1981-92; Chairman, Executive Committee of Council of Management, Strathcarron Hospice, Denny; former Council Member, British Trust for Conservation Volunteers (Chairman, Scottish Regional Committee, 1975-84); Church Warden, St. Mary's Episcopal Church, Dunblane, since 1960; Honorary Vice-President and a Director, Doune and Dunblane Agricultural Society; former Convener, Legal Committee, NFU of Scotland; General Commissioner of Income Tax, since 1971; Chairman, Scottish Executive Committee, Association of Agriculture, 1980-86; Vice-President and Treasurer, SFACET. Recreations: work; shooting; enjoying countryside; farming. Address: (h.) Grainston Farm, Kilbryde, Dunblane, Perthshire FK15 9NF; T.-01786 823304.

Campbell, Catherine, JP, BSc, BA (Hons), MSc. Educational Psychologist; Member, Scottish Milk Marketing Board, 1981-92; Chairman, Cumbernauld "I" Tech, 1984-88; b. 10.1.40, Glasgow; m., John Campbell; 2 s.; 1 d. Educ. Notre Dame High School; Glasgow University; Open University; Strathclyde University. Teacher of Mathematics, 1962-68; Member: Cumbernauld and Kilsyth District Council, 1969-78, Cumbernauld Development Corporation, 1975-84. Jubilee Medal, 1977; CACDP (stage 3 sign language). Recreations: promotion of equal opportunities for deaf people; cooking; homecrafts. Address: (h.) 10 Westray Road, Cumbernauld G67 1NN; T.-0123 67 24834.

Campbell, Colin Malcolm, QC; b. 1.10.53. Address: (b.) Advocates' Library, Parliament House, Edinburgh, EH1 1RF.

Campbell, Sir Colin Moffat, Bt, MC. Chairman, James Finlay plc, 1975-90; b. 4.8.25; m., Mary Anne Chichester Bain; 2 s.; 1 d. (deceased). Educ. Stowe. Scots Guards, 1943-47 (Captain); joined James Finlay & Co. Ltd., 1947. President, Federation of Kenya Employers, 1962-70; Chairman, Tea Board of Kenya, 1961-71; Chairman, East African Tea Trade Association, 1960-61, 1962-63, 1966-67; Member, Scottish Council, CBI, 1979-85; Member, Council, CBI, 1981-92; Deputy Chairman, Commonwealth Development Corporation, 1983-89, Board, 1981-89.

Campbell, David Ross, CMIM, FInstD. Chairman, Health Education Board for Scotland, since 1995; Deputy Chairman, Enterprise Ayrshire, since 1990; Chairman and Director of a number of private companies; b. 27.9.43, Glasgow; m., Moira. Educ. Whitehill Senior Secondary

School, Glasgow; James Watt Memorial College, Greenock. Officer, Merchant Navy, 1961-68; Sales Executive, 1968-69; various management positions, George Outram & Co. Ltd., 1969-73; Managing Director, Scottish & Universal Newspapers Ltd., 1974-84; Executive Director, Scottish & Universal Investments Ltd.; Chief Executive, Clyde Cablevision Ltd., 1982-84; Chairman and Chief Executive, West Independent Newspapers Ltd., 1984-94; Chairman, Saltire Holdings Ltd., 1991-93. Past President: Scottish Newspaper Proprietors Association, Glasgow Chamber of Commerce; Liveryman and Freeman, City of London; Regional Chairman, PSYBT. Recreations: golf; theatre; reading. Address: (h.) Summerlea, Summerlea Road, Seamill KA23 9HP.

Campbell, Donald. Writer; b. 25.2.40, Wick; m., Jean Fairgrieve; 1 s. Educ. Boroughmuir High School, Edinburgh. Playwright, essayist, lyricist and poet; stage plays include: The Jesuit, 1976; The Widows of Clyth, 1979; Blackfriars Wynd, 1980; Till All The Seas Run Dry, 1981; Howard's Revenge, 1985; Victorian Values, 1986; The Fisher Boy and the Honest Lass, 1990; The Ould Fella, 1993; also active as writer and director in a number of community projects; script co-ordinator, The Dundee Mysteries, Dundee Rep; poetry includes: Rhymes 'n Reasons, 1972; Blether, 1979; Selected Poems: 1970-1990, 1990; other work includes: A Brighter Sunshine (theatre history), 1983, Playing for Scotland (theatre history), 1996, four television plays, 50 radio programmes; Fellow in Creative Writing, Dundee University, 1987-89; William Soutar Fellow, Perth, 1991-93; awards include: three Fringe Firsts; Silver Medal, 1983 New York Radio Festival for A Clydebuilt Man; Radio Industries Club Award for The Miller's Reel, 1987. Address: (h.) 85 Spottiswoode Street, Edinburgh EH9 1BZ; T.-0131-447 2305.

Campbell, Doris Margaret, MD, FRCOG. Senior Lecturer in Obstetrics and Gynaecology and Reproductive Physiology, Aberdeen University, since 1984; part-time secondment to Centre for Educational Development, University of Aberdeen; b. 24.1.42, Aberdeen; m., Alasdair James Campbell; 1 s.; 1 d. Educ. Aberdeen High School for Girls; Aberdeen University. Resident house officer posts, Aberdeen, 1967-69; Research Fellow, Aberdeen University, 1969-73; Registrar in Obstetrics and Gynaecology, Aberdeen Hospitals, 1973-74; Lecturer in Obstetrics and Gynaecology and Physiology, Aberdeen University, 1974-84. Former Member, Scottish Women's Hockey Council. Recreations: bridge; badminton; guiding. Address: (h.) 77 Blenheim Place, Aberdeen; T.-01224 639984.

Campbell, Douglas I., BSc (Psych). Head of PR and Marketing, East Ayrshire Council, since 1995; b. 4.10.64, Kilwinning; m., E.A. McMurrich. Educ. Ardrossan Academy; Stirling University. Assistant Tourism Officer, Stirling District Council, 1986-89; Manager, Ayrshire Valleys Tourist Board, 1989-90; Public Relations Officer, Kilmarnock and Loudoun District Council, 1990-95. Recreation: squash. Address: (b.) Council HQ, London Road, Kilmarnock KA3 7BU; T.-01563 576165.

Campbell, Elizabeth (Libby), OBE, RGN, RM, MSc. Executive Director, Nursing and Quality, West Lothian NHS Trust, since 1993 (Director of Nursing, 1989-93); National Chairman, National Association of Theatre Nurses; b. 9.8.50, Dundee. Educ. Mary Erskine School for Girls, Edinburgh; Edinburgh University. Assistant, then Deputy, Director of Nursing Services, Bangour General Hospital, West Lothian, 1985-89. Former Member, UK Central Council for Nurses, Midwives and Health Visitors. Recreations: singing; travelling; Munro bagging; music. Address: (h.) 8 Fettes Row, Edinburgh EH3 6SE.

Campbell, Wing Commander George, MBE, SBStJ, DL, MIMgt; b. 24.11.22, Renton; m., Marion T.H. Halliday; 1 s.; 1 d. Educ. Vale of Leven Academy. Joined RAF, 1941;

served in UK, India, Burma, Malaya, Singapore; demobilised, 1946, and continued in Royal Air Force Voluntary Reserve (Training Branch), serving with Air Training Corps; formed 2319 (Vale of Leven) Squadron, 1956; appointed to Wing Staff, Glasgow, and Western Wing, 1973; promoted to Wing Commander, 1978; retired, 1983; attended Bisley as competitor, coach, and team captain for 48 years; Vice Chairman, 602 City of Glasgow Squadron, Royal Auxiliary Air Force Squadron Museum; Chairman: 912 Squadron ATC, Duke of Edinburgh Award (County Co-ordinating Committee); Elder, Church of Scotland; County Representative, Royal Air Forces Benevolent Fund; Director, Dumbartonshire Branch, British Red Cross, 1983-92; Past President, Dumbarton Rotary Club; Past Chairman, RNLI, Dumbarton Branch. Address: (h.) Valeview, Comley Bank, Oxhill, Dumbarton; T.-Dumbarton 763700.

Campbell of Croy, Baron (Gordon Thomas Calthrop Campbell), PC (1970), MC (and Bar). Consultant, oil industry, 1975-94; Director, Alliance and Leicester Building Society and Chairman of its Scottish Board, 1975-94; Chairman, Stoic Insurance Services, 1979-93; b. 8.6.21; m.; 2 s.; 1 d. Educ. Wellington. Commissioned, Regular Army, 1939; RA, 1942 (Major); wounded and disabled, 1945; entered HM Foreign Service, 1946 and served in the Foreign Office, at the UN, in the Cabinet Office (Private Secretary to the Secretary of the Cabinet) and in the Embassy in Vienna; MP (Conservative), Moray and Nairn, 1959-74; Government Whip, 1961-62; Lord Commissioner of the Treasury and Scottish Whip, 1962-63; Parliamentary Under-Secretary of State, Scottish Office, 1963-64; Secretary of State for Scotland, 1970-74; Chairman, Scottish Committee, International Year of Disabled, 1981; Partner, Holme Rose Estate and Farms; Trustee, Thomson Foundation, since 1980; Chairman: Advisory Committee on Pollution of the Sea, 1987-89, Scottish Council of Independent Schools, 1976-80; Vice Lord Lieutenant of Nairnshire, since 1988; President, Anglo-Austrian Society, since 1991. Address: (h.) Holme Rose, Cawdor, Nairnshire.

Campbell, Hugh Hall, QC, BA (Hons), MA (Oxon), LLB (Hons), FCIArb. Queen's Counsel, since 1983; b. 18.2.44, Glasgow; m., Eleanor Jane Hare; 3 s. Educ. Glasgow Academy; Trinity College, Glenalmond; Exeter College, Oxford; Edinburgh University. Called to Scottish Bar, 1969; Standing Junior Counsel to Admiralty, 1976. Recreations: carnival, wine, music. Address: (h.) 12 Ainslie Place, Edinburgh EH3 6AS; T.-0131-225 2067.

Campbell, Sir Ian, CBE, OStJ, VRD, JP. Deputy Chairman, Heath (Scotland) Ltd., 1987-95; Chairman, Select Assured Properties PLC, 1989-96; Director, Hermiston Securities, since 1990; b. 3.2.23, Edinburgh; m., Marion Kirkhope Shiel; 1 d. Educ. Daniel Stewart's College, Edinburgh. Royal Navy, 1942-46; Royal Naval Reserve, 1946-64 (retired with rank of Commander); John Line & Sons, 1948-61 (Area Manager, West of England); Managing Director, MacGregor Wallcoverings Ltd., 1965-77; Finance Director, Scottish Conservative Party, 1977-89. Director, Travel System Ltd., 1987-90; Councillor, City of Edinburgh, 1984-88; Member, Transport Users Consultative Committee for Scotland, 1981-87; Freeman, City of Glasgow, 1991. Recreations: golf; vintage cars; water colour painting. Address: (h.) Merleton, 10 Boswall Road, Edinburgh EH5 3RH; T.-0131-552 4825.

Campbell, Sir Ilay Mark, Bt, MA (Oxon). Director, High Craigton Farming Co.; b. 29.5.27, Edinburgh; m., Margaret Minette Rohais Anderson; 2 d. Educ. Eton; Christ Church, Oxford. Christie's: Scottish Agent, 1968, Joint Scottish Agent, 1973-92, Chairman, 1978-96; Honorary Vice-President, Scotland's Garden Scheme; Trustee: Crarae Gardens Charitable Trust, since 1978, Tree Register of the British Isles, since 1988; Chairman, Church Buildings Renewal Trust (Glasgow), since 1993; Past President,

Association for the Protection of Rural Scotland; former Convener, Church of Scotland Committee on Artistic Matters; Member: Historic Buildings Council for Scotland, Gardens Committee, and Argyll, Lochaber and Western Isles Regional Committee, National Trust for Scotland; former Scottish Representative, National Arts Collection Fund. Recreations: heraldry; genealogy; collecting heraldic bookplates. Address: (h.) Crarae Lodge, Inveraray, Argyll PA32 8YA; T.-01546 86274/370.

Campbell, James Hugh, BL. Senior Partner, Bird Semple Fyfe Ireland, WS, 1987-91, Consultant until 1993; b. 13.11.26, Old Kilpatrick; m., Iris Burnside Hercus; 2 s.; 1 d. Educ. Bearsden Academy; Glasgow University. Bird Son & Semple: Partner, 1952-65, then Senior Partner, 1965-73; Senior Partner, Bird Semple Crawford Herron, 1973-87. Member, Council, Law Society of Scotland, 1986-95 (President, 1991-92); President, Glasgow Juridical Society, 1952; Deacon, Incorporation of Wrights in Glasgow, 1980-81; Honorary Member, Royal Faculty of Procurators, Glasgow. Recreations: music; reading; golf. Address: (h.) 24 Woodvale Avenue, Giffnock, Glasgow G46 6RQ; T.-041-638 2630.

Campbell, John Ivor, FCCA. Director of Financial Services, Scottish Borders Council, since 1995; b. 23.8.51, Galashiels; m., Sheila; 2 d. Educ. Kelso High School. Roxburgh County Council, 1970-75; Borders Regional Council, 1975-84; Chief Accountant, Fife Regional Council, 1984-86; Depute Director of Finance, Glenrothes Development Corporation, 1986-88; Director of Finance, Roxburgh District Council, 1988-96. Past President, Scottish Branch, Association of Chartered Certified Accountants. Address: (b.) Council Headquarters, Newtown St. Boswells, Melrose, TD6 0SA; T.-01835 824000.

Campbell, Melfort Andrew. Director, Water Weights Ltd., since 1985; Director, Hiremerit Ltd., since 1990; Member, CBI Scottish Council, since 1989; b. 6.6.56, Exeter; m., Lucy Jane Nickson (Hon. Mrs); 3 d. Educ. Ampleforth College. Joined Water Weights Ltd., 1979; Managing Director, since 1985; founded IMES Ltd., 1993. Member, Queen's Bodyguard for Scotland (Royal Company of Archers). Recreations: rugby; cricket; fishing; shooting. Address: (h.) Mains of Altries, Maryculter, Aberdeen AB12 5GN; T.-01224 734381.

Campbell, Rev. Neil Gregor, BA, BD. Minister, Bargrennan with Penninghame St. John's Church, Newton Stewart, since 1989; Chaplain, Penninghame Prison; b. 5.5.61, Brighton; m., Elizabeth Sharp; 2 s.; 1 d. Educ. George Watson's College; Edinburgh University. Assistant Minister, Palmerston Place Church, Edinburgh, 1987-89. Publications: Penninghame St. John's 1841-1991; Prayers for Today's World (Contributor), 1993. Address: (h.) The Manse, York Road, Newton Stewart DG8 6HH; T.-01671 402259.

Campbell, Neil Martin, MA, BSc, RMN, RGN, DPSN. Board General Manager (Chief Executive), Dumfries and Galloway Health Board, since 1996; b. 9.11.57; m., Debra Ann; 3 s.; 1 d. Educ. St. Dominic's Comprehensive School; De La Salle Grammar School; Liverpool John Moores University; University of Manchester; University of Lancaster. Divisional Manager, Liverpool Priority Services Unit, 1987-89; Director of Operations, North Mersey Community NHS Trust, 1989-91; Co-ordinator for Priority Services, Mersey Regional Health Authority, 1991-93; Director for Service Development and Commissioning, South Cheshire Health Authority, 1993-96. Board Member, Scottish Development Centre for Mental Health Services. Address: (b.) Grierson House, The Crichton, Bankend Road, Dumfries DG1 4ZG; T.-01387 272701.

Campbell, Niall Gordon, BA. Under Secretary, Civil and Criminal Law Group, Scottish Office Home Department:

since 1997 (Social Work Services Group, 1989-97); b. 9.11.41, Peebles; m., Alison M. Rigg; 3 s. Educ. Edinburgh Academy; Merton College, Oxford. Entered Scottish Office 1964; Assistant Secretary, 1978; various posts in Scottish Education Department and Scottish Development Department. Address (h.) 15 Warriston Crescent, Edinburgh.

Campbell, Robert. Provost, South Ayrshire Council, since 1996; b. 22.8.35, Ayr; m., Catherine; 1 s.; 1 d. Educ. Russell Street School, Ayr. Member, Strathclyde Regional Council, 1982-96; Trustee, Burns Cottage; FRSA; Director: Opera West, Ayr College; Director and Vice-Chairman, Ayrshire and Arran Tourist Board; Chairman: Ayrshire Education Business Partnership, Culzean Country Park Joint Committee. Recreations: reading; caravanning; supporting local football team. Address: (b.) County Buildings, Wellington Square, Ayr; T.-01292 612198.

Campbell, Robert Craig, BSc, MCIM. Policy Director, National Farmers' Union of Scotland, since 1996; Chief Economist, Scottish Council (Development and Industry), 1988-96; b. 29.4.47, Glasgow; m., Elizabeth Helen C.; 2 d. Educ. Glasgow Academy; St. Andrews University. Scottish Council: Research Executive, 1970-77, Research Director, 1977-84, Director, Overseas Projects Unit, 1984-86, Policy Research Director, 1986-88. Recreation: angling. Address: (b.) The Rural Centre, West Mains, Ingliston, Newbridge EH28 8LT.

Campbell, (Robert) Mungo (McCready), BA, MPhil. Deputy Director, Hunterian Art Gallery, University of Glasgow, since 1997; b. 8.10.59, Newcastle upon Tyne; m., Teresa Margaret Green. Educ. Royal Grammar School, Newcastle upon Tyne; University of Durham; University of Glasgow. Assistant Keeper, National Gallery of Scotland, Edinburgh, 1987-97. Recreations: walking my dog; cooking good food; eating good food. Address: (b.) Hunterian Art Gallery, 82 Hillhead Street, Glasgow G12 8QQ; T.-0141-330 4735.

Campbell, Rev. Roderick D.M., TD, BD, FSA Scot. Minister, Mearns Parish Church, 1979-97; Vice Chairman, Greater Glasgow Health Board, 1994-96 (Member, 1989-96); Chairman: Greater Glasgow Drug Action Team, 1995-97, Victoria Infirmary NHS Trust, since 1997; Chaplain, 3rd (Volunteer) Battalion The Royal Highland Fusiliers; Staff Chaplain, TA Army HQ, Scotland, since 1997; b. 1.8.43, Glasgow; m., Susan Norman; 2 d. Educ. Daniel Stewart's College, Edinburgh; Arbroath High School; Jordanhill College of Education; New College, Edinburgh University. Teacher, Technical Subjects, Glasgow, Tanzania and London, 1967-70; Associate Minister, St. Andrew's, Nairobi, 1975-78; Chieftain, Caledonian Society of Kenya, 1978; founder Member, Undugu Society of Kenya, 1975; Chairman, Institute of Advanced Motorists (Kenya), 1977-78. Convener, Lodging House Mission, Glasgow Presbytery, 1981-86; Convener, National Church Extension Committee, Church of Scotland, 1987-89; Deacon, Incorporation of Barbers, Trades House, Glasgow, 1992-93. Recreations: swimming; horse-riding; hill-walking. Address: 22 Greenlaw Road, Newton Mearns, Glasgow G77 6ND; T.-0141 639 7328.

Campbell, Professor Thomas, BSc (Hons), PhD, CEng, FIMechE, MSAE, MCIBSE, MInstE. Head, Department of Environment, and Professor, Glasgow Caledonian University, since 1993; Director: Kelvin International, since 1996, Score Environment Limited, since 1996; b. 19.12.51, Glasgow; m., Fiona; 3 s. Educ. Bellahouston Academy; University of Strathclyde. Design Engineer, GEC Reactor Equipment Ltd., 1977-80; Senior Lecturer, 1980-87, Reader, 1987-89, Glasgow Caledonian University; Royal Society Industrial Fellow, Kelvin Diesels, 1989-91. Recreations: athletics; swimming; hill-walking; sailing. Address: (b.) Department of Environment, Glasgow

Caledonian University, 70 Cowcaddens Road, Glasgow G4 0BA; T.-0141-331 3520.

Campbell, (Walter) Menzies, CBE (1987), QC, MA, LLB. MP (Liberal Democrat), North East Fife, since 1987; Advocate, since 1968; Queen's Counsel, since 1982; Member, Select Committee on Defence, since 1992; Member, Parliamentary Assembly of CSCE, until 1997; Member, North Atlantic Assembly, since 1989; Party Spokesman on Defence and Sport, until 1997, Foreign Affairs, Defence and Europe, since 1997; b. 22.5.41, Glasgow; m., Elspeth Mary Urquhart. Educ. Hillhead High School, Glasgow; Glasgow University; Stanford University, California. President, Glasgow University Union, 1964-65; took part in Olympic Games, Tokyo, 1964; AAA 220-yards champion, 1964, 1967; Captain, UK athletics team, 1965-66; 1966 Commonwealth Games, Jamaica; UK 100-metres record holder, 1967-74. Advocate Depute, 1977-80; Standing Junior Counsel to the Army in Scotland, 1980-82. Parliamentary candidate (Liberal): Greenock and Port Glasgow, February, 1974, and October, 1974, East Fife, 1979, North East Fife, 1983; Chairman, Scottish Liberal Party, 1975-77; Member: UK Sports Council, 1965-68; Scottish Sports Council, 1971-81; Chairman, Royal Lyceum Theatre, Edinburgh, 1984-87; Member, Broadcasting Council for Scotland, 1984-87. Recreations: all sports; music; theatre. Address: (b.) House of Commons, London SW1A 0AA; T.-0171-219 4446.

Campbell, William Kilpatrick, MA (Hons). Director, Mainstream Publishing, since 1978; Director, Edinburgh Book Festival, since 1992; b. 1.3.51, Glasgow; m., Marie-France Callie; 2 d. Educ. Kilmarnock Academy; Edinburgh University. Postgraduate research, Universities of Edinburgh and California; world travel, 1975; Publications Manager, Edinburgh University Student Publications, 1976-78. Publications: Alternative Edinburgh (Co-Editor), 1972; Another Edinburgh, 1976. Recreations: soccer; tennis; rugby; wine; books; people. Address: (b.) 7 Albany Street, Edinburgh EH1 3UG; T.-0131-557 2959.

Campbell-Gibson, Lt.Comdr. R.N. (Ret.) Hugh Desmond. Member, Executive and Finance Committees, Scotland's Gardens Scheme; b. 18.8.24; m., Deirdre Wilson; 2 s.; 1 d. Educ. Royal Naval College, Dartmouth. Naval cadet, 1937-41; served Royal Navy, 1941-60; war service convoy duties, Atlantic and Mediterranean; farmed Glenlussa, by Campbeltown, 1960-68; farmed and ran hotel, Dunmor, Seil, Argyll, 1969-83; now manages family woodlands at Melfort. Recreations: gardening; skiing. Address: (h.) Tighnamara, Melfort, Kilmelford, Argyll; T.-Kilmelford 224.

Campion, Nigel Henry, MIFireE. Firemaster, Fife Fire and Rescue Service, since 1996; b. 12.5.45, Leicester; m., Kathryn; 1 s.; 1 d. Formerly with Leicester City Fire Brigade. Recreations: keep fit; walking; reading. Address: (b.) Fire and Rescue Service Headquarters, Strathore Road, Thornton, Kirkcaldy KY1 4DF; T.-01592 774451.

Canavan, Dennis, BSc (Hons), DipEd. MP (Labour), Falkirk West, since 1983; b. 8.8.42, Cowdenbeath. Educ. St. Bride's and St. Columba's Schools, Cowdenbeath; Edinburgh University. Principal Teacher of Mathematics, St. Modan's High School, Stirling, 1970-74; Assistant Head, Holyrood High School, Edinburgh, 1974; Leader, Labour Group, Stirling District Council, 1974; MP, West Stirlingshire, 1974-83; Chair: Scottish Parliamentary Labour Group, 1980-81, PLP Northern Ireland Committee, 1989-97; Member: Foreign Affairs Select Committee, 1982-97, British–Irish Inter-Parliamentary Body, since 1992, International Development Select Committee, since 1997. Founder and Convener, All Party Parliamentary Scottish Sports Group, since 1987; Honorary President, Milton Amateurs Football Club. Recreations: marathon running; hill-climbing; fishing; swimming; football (former

Scottish Universities football internationalist). Address: (b.) Constituency Office, 37 Church Walk, Denny FK6 6DF; T.-01324 825922.

Canavan, Sheriff Vincent Joseph, LLB. Sheriff of South Strathclyde, Dumfries and Galloway at Hamilton, since 1987; b. 13.12.44. Address: (b.) Sheriff Court House, Beckford Street, Hamilton ML3 6AA.

Candlish, Kenneth Henry, BL, JP, DL. Retired Solicitor; Deputy Lieutenant, Berwickshire; b. 22.8.24, Edinburgh; m., Isobel Robertson-Brown; 2 d. Educ. George Watson's; Edinburgh University. Depute County Clerk, West Lothian, 1951-64; County Clerk, Berwickshire, 1964-75. Recreations: photography; wine-making; music. Address: (h.) The Elms, Duns, Berwickshire; T.-Duns 83298.

Canning, Very Rev. Bernard John Canon, FSA Scot. Parish Priest, St. John the Baptist's, Port Glasgow, since 1996; Paisley Diocesan Archivist, since 1983; b. 30.3.32, Derry. Educ. St. Eugene's Boys' School, Derry; St. Columb's College, Derry; St. Kieran's College, Kilkenny. Ordained Priest for the Diocese of Paisley, 1956; Assistant: St. James's, Renfrew, 1956-68, St Fergus', Paisley, 1968-74, St Laurence's, Greenock, 1974-87; Parish Priest: Christ the King, Howwood, and Our Lady of Fatima, Lochwinnoch, 1987-95, St James's, Paisley, 1995-96. Hon. Canon, Paisley Cathedral Chapter, 1989; Member, Editorial Board, The Parish Magazine & Journal, Glasgow, 1962-74; first Press Officer, Paisley Diocese, 1964-88; Member, Board of Governors, National Catholic Press Office, 1968-87. Publications include: Joy and Hope: St. Fergus', Paisley, 1971; A Building from God: St James's, Renfrew 1877-1977, 1977; Padraig H. Pearse and Scotland, 1979; Irish-born Secular Priests in Scotland 1829-1979, 1979; Adventure in Faith: St Ninian's, Gourock 1880-1980, 1980; The Living Stone: St Aloysius', Springburn 1882-1982, 1982; Instruments of His Work : Little Sisters of the Poor, Greenock 1884-1984, 1984; St. Mungo's, Ladyburn, Greenock 1935-1985, 1985; The Charleston Story: St Charles', Paisley, 1986; Bishops of Ireland 1870-1987, 1989; St. Fillan's, Houston 1841-1991, 1991; St. Mary's, Paisley 1891-1991, 1991; The Poor Sisters of Nazareth & Derry 1892-1992, 1992; Bishop Neil Farren, Bishop of Derry 1893-1980, 1993. Recreation: historical research. Address: (b.) St. John's, 23 Shore Street, Port Glasgow PA14 5HD; T.-01475 741139.

Cannon, Steven, MA (Hons). Secretary to the Council, and Director of Finance and Central Services, Scottish Higher Education Funding Council, since 1996; b. 19.12.57, Keighley; m., Joyce. Educ. St. Bedes Grammar School, Bradford; Dundee University. Administrative Assistant, then Admissions Officer, Warwick University, 1983-86; Financial and Administration Manager, Warwick University Science Park, 1986-88; Financial Manager, Ninewells Hospital and Medical School, Dundee, 1988-93; College Secretary, Duncan of Jordanstone College of Art, 1993-94; Deputy Secretary, Dundee University, 1994-96. Recreations: family interests; golf; cricket; music. Address: (b.) Scottish Higher Education Funding Council, Donaldson House, 97 Haymarket Terrace, Edinburgh EH12 5HD.

Cantley, Maurice, OBE, BSc, PhD. Director, Highlands and Islands Enterprise, since 1991; b. 6.6.37, Cambuslang; m., Rosalind Diana Jones; 2 d. Educ. Bedford Modern and Bristol Grammar; Bristol University. Unilever Ltd., 1961-67; McCann Erickson Advertising, London, 1967-76; Director of Recreation and Tourism, Tayside Regional Council, 1976-82; Head of Tourism, HIDB, 1982-85; Marketing Director, Highlands and Islands Development Board, 1985-91. Chairman, Association of Directors of Recreation, Leisure and Tourism, 1980-82; Hon. Education Officer, Society of Cosmetic Chemists of GB, 1963-66. Recreations: driving north of Ullapool; natural history; hill-walking. Address: (h.) Oldshorebeg, Kinlochbervie, Sutherland IV27 4RS; T.-01971 521257.

Caplan, Hon. Lord (Philip Isaac Caplan), MA, LLB, LLD(Hon), QC. Senator of the College of Justice, since 1989; b. 24.2.29, Glasgow; m., Joyce Stone (2nd m.); 2 s.; 2 d. Educ. Eastwood School; Glasgow University. Solicitor, 1952-56; called to Bar, 1957; Standing Junior Counsel to Accountant of Court, 1964-70; Chairman, Plant Varieties and Seeds Tribunal, Scotland, 1977-79; Sheriff of Lothian and Borders, at Edinburgh, 1979-83; Sheriff Principal of North Strathclyde, 1983-88; Member, Sheriff Courts Rules Council, 1984-88; Commissioner, Northern Lighthouse Board, 1983-88; Chairman, Scottish Association for the Study of Delinquency, 1985-89, Hon. Vice President, 1990; Member, Advisory Council on Messengers at Arms and Sheriff Officers, 1987-88; Chairman, Scottish Association of Family Conciliation Services, 1989-94, Honorary President, since 1994; Chairman, James Powell UK Trust. FRPS (1988), AFIAP (1985). Recreations: photography; bridge; music; reading. Address: (b.) Court of Session, Parliament House, Edinburgh.

Capperauld, Ian, MB, ChB, DObst, RCOG, FRCSEdin, FRCSGlas, FRCSEng. Consultant Surgeon, since 1962; Medical Director, Huntly Nursing Home, since 1981; Member, Lothian Health Board, since 1981; b. 23.10.33, New Cumnock; m., Wilma Hyslop Young; 2 s. Educ. Cumnock Academy; Glasgow University; Edinburgh University. Served as Major, RAMC, 1959-69 (Consultant Surgeon); former Executive Director, Research and Development, Ethicon Ltd. Recreations: fishing; shooting. Address: (h.) The Old Mill House, Dalkeith EH22 2AQ; T.-0131-663 2469.

Carbery, Emeritus Professor Thomas Francis, OBE, KSG, MSc, PhD, DPA. Former Professor, Strathclyde Business School, Strathclyde University; Member, Board of Directors, Energy Action Scotland, since 1996; Member, Data Protection Tribunal, since 1985; b. 18.1.25, Glasgow; m., Ellen Donnelly; 1 s.; 2 d. Educ. St. Aloysius' College, Glasgow; Glasgow University; Scottish College of Commerce. Cadet navigator/meteorologist, RAF, 1943-47; civil servant, 1947-61; Lecturer, then Senior Lecturer, Scottish College of Commerce, 1961-64; Strathclyde University: Senior Lecturer in Government-Business Relations, 1964-75, Head, Department of Office Organisation, 1975-79, Professor of Office Organisation, 1979-85, Professor of Business Information, 1985-88; part-time Professor of Marketing, 1988-90. Member: Independent Broadcasting Authority, 1970-79, Broadcasting Complaints Commission, 1981-86, Royal Commission on Gambling, 1975-77, Transport Users Consultative Committee (Chairman, Scottish TUCC), 1975-81, Press Council, 1987-90, Scottish Consumer Council (latterly Vice-Chairman), 1976-84; Chairman, Scottish Transport Research Group, 1983-87; Member, Scottish Legal Aid Board, 1986-92; Chairman, South of Scotland Consumers Committee/Office of Electricity Regulation, 1990-95; Member, Church of Scotland Committee on Higher Education, 1986-87; Chairman, Strathclyde University Inter-denominational Chaplaincy Committee, 1981-87; Joint Editor, Bulletin of Society for Co-operative Studies, 1967-95; Chairman, Scottish Catholic Communications Commission; Member, Scottish Catholic Education Commission, 1980-93. Recreations: conversation; watching television; spectating at association football; very bad golf. Address: (h.) 24 Fairfax Avenue, Glasgow, G44 5AL; T.-0141-637 0514.

Cardownie, Steve. Member, Edinburgh City Council (Convener, Recreation Committee); Director, International Arts Exchange, Street Life Ltd., Scot-Slav Ltd.; b. 1.6.53, Leith; m.; 2 s. Educ. Leith Academy; Telford College. Civil service; National Executive Committee Member, CPSA, five years; Industrial Tribunal Member, 15 years;

Councillor, Edinburgh, eight years; Director: Edinburgh International Festival Council, Edinburgh Festival Theatre, Royal Lyceum Theatre, Traverse Theatre, Edinburgh Science Festival. Recreations: hill-walking; running; Heart of Midlothian FC; theatre; reading; fine wines and ale sampling. Address: (b.) City Chambers, High Street, Edinburgh; T.-0131-529 3266.

Cargill, Kenneth George, MA, LLB. Head of News and Current Affairs, BBC Scotland, since 1994; b. 17.2.47, Arbroath; m., Una Gallacher. Educ. Arbroath High School; Edinburgh University. BBC TV Scotland: Researcher, Current Affairs, 1972; Reporter, Current Account, 1973; Film Director, Public Account, 1978; Producer, Current Account, 1979, Agenda, 1981, People and Power (London), 1983; Editor of the day, Reporting Scotland, 1983; Editor, Scotland 2000, 1986-87; Deputy Editor, News and Current Affairs, Television, 1984-88; Head of TV News, Current Affairs and Sport, 1988-94. Publication: Scotland 2000 (Editor), 1987. Recreations: passive gardening and active consumption of Havana cigars, malt whisky and non-fiction books. Address: (b.) Broadcasting House, Queen Margaret Drive, Glasgow G12 8DG; T.-0141-338 2250.

Carlaw, David Jackson. Deputy Chairman, Scottish Conservative Party, since 1997; Managing Director, Wylies Group, since 1987; Chairman, Scotland, Northern Ireland, Cumbria Ford Dealers, until 1997; b. 12.4.59, Glasgow; m., Wynne Stewart; 2 s. Educ. Glasgow Academy. Wylies Group, since 1977. Vice-Chairman, Scottish Conservative Party, 1992-94, 1995-97; Chairman: Eastwood Conservatives, 1988-92, Scottish Young Conservatives, 1984-86. Recreations: reading; theatre; film; opera; design. Address: (b.) Wylies Ltd., 370 Pollokshaws Road, Glasgow G41 1QR; T.-0141-423 6644.

Carlyle, Robert. Actor and Director. Trained, RSAMD; Duncan Macrae Memorial Prize for Scots verse. Credits include: (film) The Full Monty, Carla's Song, Trainspotting, Riff Raff (lead) (European film of the year); (television) Hamish Macbeth (title role); (theatre) Twelfth Night, Cuttin' A Rug, Othello; as Director of Rain Dog Theatre Company: Wasted, One Flew Over the Cuckoo's Nest (Paper Boat Award), Conquest of the South Pole, Macbeth (Paper Boat Award).

Carmichael of Arthurstone, Major Peter Oliphant, MRAC. Deputy Lieutenant for Perthshire, 1966-96; Justice of the Peace, 1962-96; b. 25.8.21, Broughty Ferry; m., Pamela Muriel Wilson of Ashmore; 3 s.; 1 d. Educ. Stowe School; Cambridge University. Farmer; served in The Scottish Horse, 1941-46, France and Germany; TA, 1951-61. Recreation: country pursuits. Address: (h.) Little Arthurstone, Coupar Angus, Perthshire PH13 9EU; T.-01828 627430.

Carmichael, Peter, CBE, DSc; b. 26.3.33, Dunblane; m., June; 2 s.; 4 d. by pr. m. Educ. McLaren High School, Callander; Glasgow University. Design engineer, Ferranti Ltd., Edinburgh, 1958-65; Hewlett-Packard, South Queensferry: Project Leader, 1965-67, Production Engineering Manager, 1968-73, Engineering Manager, 1973-75, Manufacturing Manager, 1975-76, Division General Manager, 1976-82, Joint Managing Director, 1980-82; Scottish Development Agency: Director, Small Business and Electronics, 1982-88, Group Director East, 1988-89. Former Chairman, Esmee Fairbairn Economic Institute. Address: (h.) 86 Craiglea Drive, Edinburgh; T.-0131-447 6334; Marchbank Cottage, Ballantrae, Ayrshire; T.-0146 5831355.

Carmichael of Carmichael (Richard John). 26th Baron of Carmichael, since 1980; 30th Chief of Name and Arms of Carmichael, since 1981; Chartered Accountant; Farmer; b. 1.12.48, Stamford; m., Patricia Margaret Branson; 1 s.; 2 d. Educ. Hyton Hill Preparatory School; Kimbolton School;

Coventry College of Technology. Audit Senior, Coopers and Lybrand, Tanzania, 1972; Audit Manager, Granger Craig Tunnicliffe, Tauranga, New Zealand, 1974; ACA, 1971; FCA, 1976; Factor/Owner, Carmichael Estate, 1980; Director: Carmichael Heritage Leisure Ltd., World Orienteering Co. Ltd., Scottish Orienteering 6-Day Event Co. Ltd.; claims family titles: Earldom of Hyndford, Viscountcies of Inglisberry and Nemphlar, and Lordship Carmichael of Carmichael. Member, Supreme Council of Scottish Chiefs; Secretary Carmichael Anstruther District Charitable Association; New Zealand Orienteering Champion, 1977; International Controller, International Orienteering Federation, 1994. Recreations: orienteering; skiing; Clan Carmichael Association. Address: Carmichael House, Carmichael, by Biggar, Lanarkshire ML12 6PG; T.-01899 308336.

Carnegie, Leslie Thompson, CBE (1980), BL, JP, Solicitor. Chief Executive, Dumfries and Galloway Regional Council, 1974-85; Honorary Sheriff, since 1960; b. 16.8.20, Aberdeen; m., Isobel Jane McCombie, JP. Educ. Aberdeen Grammar School; Aberdeen University. Legal Department, Aberdeen Corporation, 1939-48; Depute County Clerk, East Lothian, 1948-54; County Clerk, Dumfries County Council, 1954-75. Past President, Society of County Clerks in Scotland; Clerk, Dumfries Lieutenancy, 1954-85. Recreations: gardening; music appreciation; sporting activities. Address: (h.) Marchhill Park, Dumfries.

Carnegy-Arbuthnott, David, TD, DL, LLD, CA. Landowner; b. 17.7.25, London; m., Helen Adamson Lyell; 2 s.; 2 d. Educ. Stowe. Emergency commission, The Black Watch, 1944-47; Chartered Accountant, 1953; in practice, Dundee, 1956-86; TA, 1955-69; Brevet Colonel, 1969; Hon. Colonel, 1st Bn., 51st Highland Volunteers (TA), 1980-89; Deputy Lieutenant, County of City of Dundee, 1973-89, Angus, since 1989; Member, Queen's Bodyguard for Scotland (Royal Company of Archers), since 1959; Governor: Dundee College of Education, 1985-87, Northern College of Education, 1987-91; President, Dundee Chamber of Commerce, 1971-72; Member of Court, Dundee University, 1977-85; Convener, Standing Committee, Scottish Episcopal Church, 1987-92. Recreations: shooting; country pursuits. Address: (h.) Meadowburn, Balnamoon, Brechin, Angus DD9 7RH; T.-01356 660273.

Carnegy of Lour, Baroness (Elizabeth Patricia), DL. Life Peer, since 1982; Member, Council and Finance Committee, Open University, 1984-96; Member, Court, St. Andrews University, 1991-96; b. 28.4.25. Educ. Downham School. Cavendish Laboratory, Cambridge, 1943-46; Girl Guides Association: Training Adviser for Scotland, 1958-62 and for Commonwealth HQ, 1963-65; co-opted Angus County Council Education Committee, 1967-75; Councillor, Tayside Regional Council, 1974-82; Chairman, Education Committee, 1976-82; Chairman, Working Party on Professional Training in Community Education Scotland, 1975-77; Commissioner, Manpower Services Commission, 1979-82, and Chairman, Committee for Scotland, 1980-83; Member, Scottish Economic Council, 1980-92; President for Scotland, Girl Guides Association, 1979-89; Member, Scottish Council for Tertiary Education, 1979-84; Chairman, Scottish Council for Community Education, 1980-88; Honorary Sheriff, 1969-84; Deputy Lieutenant, 1988; Fellow, Royal Society of Arts, 1987; Honorary LLD: Dundee University, 1991, University of St. Andrews, 1997. Address: (h.) Lour, Forfar, Angus DD8 2LR; T.-01307 82 237.

Carr, Isabel Anne, BA. General Secretary (Scotland), YWCA, since 1992; b. 23.6.54, Gifford. Educ. Berwickshire High School; Edinburgh University; Jordanhill College of Education. Rhodesia Ministry of Education, 1976; Lothian Regional Council Community Education, 1978-80; Church of Scotland Board of World Mission and Unity, Pakistan, 1981-85; Area Secretary,

South Scotland, Christian Aid, 1985-92. Address: (b.) 7 Randolph Crescent, Edinburgh EH3 7TH; T.-0131-225 7592.

Carr, John Roger, CBE, JP, FRICS. Chairman, Countryside Commission for Scotland, 1985-92 (Member, since 1979); Member, Macaulay Land Use Research Institute, 1987-97; Director, UK 2000 Scotland, 1990-93; Vice President, FWAG Scotland, since 1993; b. 18.1.27, Ackworth, Yorkshire; m., Cathrine Elise Dickson-Smith; 2 s. Educ. Ackworth & Ayton (Quaker) School. Royal Marines, 1944-47; Gordon Highlanders TA, 1950-55; Factor, Walker Scottish Estates Co., Ballater; Factor, subsequently Director and General Manager, Moray Estates Development Co., Forres; former Convenor, Scottish Recreational Land Association; former Council Member, Scottish Landowners Federation; former District Councillor, Moray. Recreations: most country pursuits. Address: (b.) Goosehill, Invererne Road, Forres, Moray IV360DZ; T.-01309 671320.

Carrie, Professor Allan Stewart, PhD, MSc, BSc (Eng), FIEE, SMIEEE, CEng, FRSA. Professor of Advanced Manufacturing Technology, Department of Design, Manufacture and Engineering Management, University of Strathclyde, since 1987; b. 7.5.42, Glasgow; m., Marie; 2 s. Educ. Fettes College, Edinburgh; Paisley College of Technology; University of London (External Degree); University of Birmingham. Babcock & Wilcox, Renfrew: Student Apprentice, 1960-63, Graduate Engineer, 1963-64, Methods Engineer, 1964-65; Industrial Engineer, Northern Electric, Montreal, 1965-66; University of Strathclyde: Lecturer, 1968-79, Senior Lecturer, 1979-85, Reader, 1985-87. Member, Manufacturing, Production and Business Processes Panel, Foresight 2000. Recreation: Scottish country dancing. Address: (b.) University of Strathclyde, Glasgow G1 1XJ; T.-0141-548 2894.

Carroll, Professor Robert Peter, MA, PhD. Professor of Hebrew Bible and Semitic Studies, Department of Theology and Religious Studies, Glasgow University, since 1991 (Dean, Faculty of Divinity, 1991-94); b. 18.1.41, Dublin; m., Mary Anne Alice Stevens; 2 s.; 1 d. Educ. High School, Dublin; Trinity College, Dublin University; Edinburgh University. After postgraduate degree, worked as swimming pool attendant, barman, brickie's mate, secondary school teacher; Glasgow University: Assistant Lecturer in Semitic Languages, 1968, Lecturer in Old Testament Language and Literature, 1969, Senior Lecturer in Biblical Studies, 1981; Reader, 1986. Publications: When Prophecy Failed, 1979; From Chaos to Covenant, 1981; Jeremiah: A Commentary, 1986; Jeremiah (JSOT Guide), 1989; Wolf in Sheepfold, 1991; The Bible (Co-Editor), 1997. Recreations: cinema; day-dreaming; writing imaginary books in my head. Address: (h.) 5 Marchmont Terrace, Glasgow G12 9LT; T.-0141-339 0440.

Carson, James Grant, MA, DipEd, FSAScot. Chairman, Scottish National Committee, English-Speaking Union in Scotland, since 1996; b. Isle of Fetlar, Shetland; m., Catherine Nisbet; 1 s.; 1 d. Educ. John Watson's; Fettes College, Edinburgh; Trinity College, University of Cambridge. Former Depute Rector, Jordanhill School. Leader, ESU Pupil Exchanges to USA, 1975-94; ESU Debates Convenor; Member, Chorus: Edinburgh Festival, Scottish Opera; Director of plays and operas; Hon. President, Greenock Burns Club, 1986. Recreations: gardening; bridge; reading; travel; food; wine. Address: 23 Atholl Crescent, Edinburgh EH3 8HQ; T.-0131-229 1528.

Carter, Christopher John, BA (Hons), PhD, MRTPI, FRSA. Director, Duncan of Jordanstone College and Deputy Principal, Dundee University, 1994-97; b. 5.2.41, Capel, Surrey; m., Ann Fisher Prince; 1 s.; 1 d. Educ. Ottershaw School, Chertsey, Surrey; Birmingham University; Glasgow University. Town Planning Assistant,

Cumbernauld Development Corporation, 1963-64 and 1967-68; Visiting Lecturer in Geography, Brock University, St. Catharines, Ontario, 1968-69; Lecturer/Senior Lecturer in Planning, Glasgow School of Art, 1969-76; Principal Lecturer in Planning, Coventry (Lanchester) Polytechnic, 1976-78; Senior Lecturer/Head, Department of Town and Regional Planning, Duncan of Jordanstone College of Art, 1978-81; Vice Principal, Duncan of Jordanstone College of Art, 1981-93, Acting Principal, 1993-94. Winner, RTPI Prize, 1970. Member: Board of Governors, Dundee Institute of Technology, 1989-91; Scottish Committee, Universities Funding Council, 1989-92; Scottish Higher Education Funding Council, 1992-93; Member: Board of Governors, Northern College, 1994-95, Board of Management, Elmwood College, since 1997. Publications: Innovations in Planning Thought and Practice at Cumbernauld New Town 1956-62; The Designation of Cumbernauld New Town (case study) (Co-author). Recreations: skiing; running; photography; music. Address: (h.) Etchachan, 12A Deshar Road, Boat of Garten, Inverness-shire PH24 3BN; T.-01479 831732.

Carter, Professor Sir David Craig, MB, ChB, MD, FRCSEdin, FRCSGlas, FRCPEdin, FRCSIre (Hon), FACS (Hon), FRSEd, DSc (Hon), LLD (Hon). Chief Medical Officer (Scotland), since 1997; Surgeon to the Queen in Scotland, since 1993; b. 1.9.40, Penrith; m., Ilske; 2 s. Educ. St. Andrews University. Lecturer in Clinical Surgery, Edinburgh University, 1969-74; 12-month secondment as Lecturer in Surgery, Makerere University, Kampala, Uganda, 1972; Senior Lecturer in Surgery, Edinburgh University, 1974-79;12-month secondment as Associate Professor of Surgery, University of California, 1976; St. Mungo Professor of Surgery, Glasgow University, 1979-88; Honorary Consultant, Glasgow Royal Infirmary, 1979-88; Regius Professor of Surgery, Edinburgh University, 1988-97; Honorary Clinical Consultant, Edinburgh Royal Infirmary, 1988-97. Former Council Member, Royal College of Surgeons of Edinburgh; former Member, Broadcasting Council for Scotland; former Chairman, Scottish Council for Postgraduate Medical and Dental Education; former Co-editor, British Journal of Surgery; Member, Medical Advisory Committee, Higher Education Funding Council, 1994-97; Non-executive Director, Lothian Health Board, 1994-97; President, Surgical Research Society, Association of Surgeons (Great Britain and Ireland), 1996-97. Moynihan Prize, 1973; James IV Association of Surgeons Travelling Fellow, 1975. Recreations: golf; music. Address: (b.) University Department of Surgery, Royal Infirmary, Edinburgh EH3 9YW; T.-0131-536 3812.

Carter, Roger, MBE, BSc, PhD, FTS, MIM. Director, International Tourism Research Group, Napier University, Edinburgh, since 1997; Managing Partner, Tourism Enterprise and Management; b. 8.12.45, Dorking; m., Dee; 3 s. Educ. Dorking County Grammar School; Birmingham University; Strathclyde University. Transport Development Unit, Strathclyde University, 1970; Leader, Research Unit, Greater London and SE Sports Council, 1970-71; Director of Research and Planning, Scottish Tourist Board, 1971-82; Director, Heart of England Tourist Board, 1982-90; former Chief Executive, Edinburgh and Lothians Tourist Board, Edinburgh Tourist Board, 1990-96. Recreation: reading. Address: (b.) ITRG at New Craig, Napier University, Craighouse Campus, Craighouse Road, Edinburgh EH10 5LG; T.-0131-455 6216; (b.) TEAM, 1/1 Liddesdale Place, Edinburgh EH3 5JW; T.-0131-557 5867.

Carty, Matthew John, MB, ChB, FRCSEdin, FRCPSGlas, FRCOG. Consultant Obstetrician and Gynaecologist, Southern General Hospital, Glasgow, since 1977; b. 8.3.42, Hamilton; m., Caroline Martin; 2 s.; 2 d. Educ. St. Aloysius College, Glasgow; Glasgow University. Lecturer in Midwifery, Nairobi University, Kenya, 1970-71; Lecturer in Midwifery, Glasgow University, 1972-77. Recreations:

squash; golf; tennis; jogging. Address: (h.) 31 Monreith Road, Newlands, Glasgow; T.-0141-632 1033.

Casely, (Frederick) Gordon (Polson), OStJ, FSAScot, MIPR. Head of Communications, Aberdeenshire Council, since 1995; Hon. Vice-President, Lonach Highland and Friendly Society, since 1990; b. 29.6.43, Glasgow; m., Valerie Ann Thomas; 1 s. Educ. Hutchesons' Boys Grammar School. Reporter, D.C. Thomson & Co. Ltd., Dundee, Aberdeen and Elgin, 1966-68; Feature Writer, Evening Express, Aberdeen, 1968-73; Public Relations Officer, Greater Glasgow Passenger Transport Executive, 1973-78; public affairs posts in banking, electricity and energy industries, 1978-95 (Assistant Director, CBI Scotland, 1988-91). Founder Member, Heraldry Society of Scotland, 1977; Press Officer, Commonwealth Games Council for Scotland, 1989-93; Member: Scottish Commonwealth Games Team, Auckland, 1990, Guild Burgess of Aberdeen, 1992; President, Aberdeen Welsh Society, 1997-98. Recreations: travelling by bike; promoting heraldry; competing in veteran athletics; remembering 1745. Address: (h.) 45 Beaconsfield Place, Aberdeen AB15 4AB; T.-01224 647927.

Cash, John David, BSc, MB, ChB, PhD, FRCPath, FRCPGlas, FRCPE, FRCSEdin. National Medical and Scientific Director, Scottish National Blood Transfusion Service, since 1979; Honorary Professor, Department of Medicine, Edinburgh University, since 1987; b. 3.4.36, Reading; m., Angela Mary Thomson; 1 s.; 1 d. Educ. Ashville College, Harrogate; Edinburgh University. Edinburgh and South East Scotland Blood Transfusion Service: Deputy Director, 1969, Regional Director, 1974. President, Royal College of Physicians of Edinburgh, 1994; Adviser in Blood Transfusion, WHO. Recreations: fishing; gardening. Address: (b.) Royal College of Physicians of Edinburgh, 9 Queen Street, Edinburgh EH2 1JQ.

Cassidy, Anthony (Tony) F., BSc (Hons). Chief Executive, Renfrewshire Enterprise, since 1991; b. 17.11.44, Kilbarchan; m., Laura Jane; 2 s. Educ. Glasgow University. Lecturer, Mechanical Engineering, Glasgow University, 1969-72; British Council official: India, 1972-76, Japan, 1976-81, France, 1983-84; Director, Japan/Asia, Locate in Scotland, 1984-91. Address: (b.) 27 Causeyside Street, Paisley PA1 1UL; T.-0141-848 0101.

Cassidy, Professor James, MB, ChB, MSc, MD, FRCP (Glasgow, Edinburgh). Professor of Oncology, University of Aberdeen, since 1994; Consultant Oncologist, Aberdeen Royal Hospital NHS Trust, since 1994; b. 28.8.58, Lennoxtown; m., Penelope Jane; 2 s.; 1 d. Educ. St. Mirin's Academy, Paisley; University of Glasgow. General Training, Wales and Scotland MRCP (UK), 1985; Lecturer in Oncology, University of Edinburgh. Member, Board of Governors, ICRF. Recreations: soccer; cycling; music. Address: (b.) Institute of Medical Sciences, Foresterhill, Aberdeen; T.-01224 681818, Ext. 53019.

Cassie, David, ARICS. Managing Director, Coflexip Stena Offshore Ltd., since 1995, Group Vice President, since 1996; b. 18.1.56, Aberdeen; m., Heather Irene; 2 d. Educ. Forrester Academy, Edinburgh; Robert Gordon Institute of Technology. Began career as project quantity surveyor, John Brown Offshore, 1977; joined Stena Offshore, 1987. Recreations: reading; golf; gardening; keep fit; music. Address: (b.) Stena House, Westhill Industrial Estate, Aberdeen AB32 6TQ.

Cater, Isabel McGregor, MCSP. Chairman, North-East Fife District Council, 1992-96; b. 20.5.39, Swansea; m., Dr. John I. Cater; 3 d. Educ. Morrisons Academy, Crieff; School of Physiotherapy, Royal Infirmary, Edinburgh. Chartered Physiotherapist, 1961-83. JP, since 1989; Director, Scottish Rights of Way Society, 1981-85.

Member, Court, St. Andrews University, 1992-97. Recreations: walking; swimming; gardening; reading; cookery. Address: (h.) Woodlands, Gauldry, Newport-on-Tay, DD6 8RW; T.-01382 330 284.

Cates, Professor Michael Elmhirst, MA, PhD. Professor of Natural Philosophy, University of Edinburgh, since 1995; b. 5.5.61, Bristol. Educ. Clifton College; Trinity College, University of Cambridge. Research Fellow, Trinity College, University of Cambridge, 1985-89; Cavendish Laboratory, Cambridge: Royal Society University Research Fellow, 1988-89, University Assistant Lecturer, 1989-92, University Lecturer, 1992-94. Maxwell Medal and Prize, Institute of Physics, 1991; Prix Franco-Britannique de l'Academie des Sciences, Paris, 1994. Publications: 150 publications in scientific journals. Recreations: hill-walking; painting. Address: (b.) Department of Physics and Astronomy, University of Edinburgh, Kings Buildings, Edinburgh EH9 3JZ; T.-0131-650 5296.

Catto, Professor Graeme R.D., MB, ChB (Hons), MD (Hons), DSc, FRCP, FRCPE, FRCPGlas, FRSE. Chief Scientist, NHS in Scotland, since 1997; Vice-Principal, since 1995, Dean, Faculty of Clinical Medicine, since 1992, and Professor in Medicine and Therapeutics, Aberdeen University, since 1988; Honorary Consultant Physician/Nephrologist, since 1977; Vice Chairman, Aberdeen Royal Hospitals NHS Trust, since 1992; Chairman, Robert Gordon's College; b. 24.4.45, Aberdeen; m., Joan Sievewright; 1 s.; 1 d. Educ. Robert Gordon's College; Aberdeen University. Research Fellow/ Lecturer/Senior Lecturer/Reader in Medicine, Aberdeen University, 1970-88; Harkness Fellow of Commonwealth Fund of New York, 1975-77 (Fellow in Medicine, Harvard Medical School and Peter Bent Brigham Hospital, Boston). Recreations: curling; fresh air; France. Address: (b.) Department of Medicine, Aberdeen University, Foresterhill, Aberdeen AB9 2ZB; T.-01224 681818.

Cawdor, 7th Earl of (Colin Robert Vaughan Campbell); b. 30.6.62; m., Lady Isabella Stanhope. Address: Cawdor Castle, Nairn.

Cawthra, David Wilkinson, CBE, BSc, FEng, FICE, CBIM. Principal, Cawthra & Co; b. 5.3.43, Halifax; m., Maureen Mabel Williamson; 1 s.; 1 d. Educ. Heath Grammar School, Halifax; Birmingham University. Mitchell Construction Company Ltd., 1964-73; Tarmac Construction Ltd., 1973-79; Balfour Beatty Ltd., 1979-91; Chief Executive, The Miller Group Limited, 1992-94. Member, NEDO Construction Industry Sector Group, 1990-92; Vice-President, Institution of Civil Engineers, since 1996. Recreations: hill-walking; American history. Address: (b.) 68 Ravelston Dykes, Edinburgh EH12 6HF; T.-0131-337 2155.

Chalmers, David Watson Penn. Director and Deputy Chief Executive, Dunfermline Building Society, since 1995; b. 28.4.46, Dundee; m., Jacky; 1 d. Educ. Harris Academy, Dundee. Joined Dunfermline Building Society, 1968. Director, South Fife Enterprise Trust Ltd.; Member, Committee of Management: Kingdom Housing Association Ltd., Dundee Employment and Aftercare Project; Member, Mortgage Practitioners Panel, Council of Mortgage Lenders; Member, Committee of Management, Dundee Employment and Aftercare Project; Trustee, Scottish Housing Association's Charitable Trust; Director, Business Enterprise Scotland. Recreations: golf; chess; hill-walking; running. Address: (b.) Caledonia House, Carnegie Avenue, Dunfermline KY11 5PJ; T.-01383 627727.

Chalmers, Professor Ian Donald, BSc, PhD, CEng, MInstP, FIEE, SMIEEE. Professor, Department of Electronic and Electrical Engineering, Strathclyde University, since 1988; b. 4.6.40, London; 1 s.; 1 d. Educ. Montrose Academy; Dundee Technical College;

Strathclyde University. CEGB Research Fellow, 1968-73; Lecturer, Department of Electrical Engineering, Strathclyde University, 1973-83, Senior Lecturer, 1983-86, Reader, 1986-88, Professor, 1988. Publications: 70 research papers. Address: (b.) Royal College Building, 204 George Street, Glasgow G1 1XW.

Chalmers, Rev. John Pearson, BD. Depute Secretary, Department of Ministry, Church of Scotland, since 1995; Vice Chairman, Board of Governors, Donaldson's College, since 1991; b. 5.6.52, Bothwell; m., Elizabeth; 2 s.; 1 d. Educ. Marr College; Strathclyde University; Glasgow University. Minister, Renton Trinity, 1979-86;.Clerk, Dumbarton Presbytery, 1982-86; Minister, Palmerston Place, Edinburgh, 1986-95. Recreations: golf; bee-keeping. Address: (b.) 121 George Street, Edinburgh EH2 4YN; T.-0131-225 5722.

Chalmers, Patricia, MA (Hons). Councillor, Glasgow District Council, 1982-96; b. Glasgow; m., Walter Scott Chalmers; 1 s.; 2 d. Educ. Rothesay Academy; Glasgow University. Member, Board, Tron Theatre, since 1992; a Director, Glasgow Cultural Enterprises Ltd., since 1991, Executive Member, Glasgow Building Preservation Trust, since 1991; Chair: West End Festival, St. Vincent Street Church Trust; Trustee, Civic Trust; Hon. Vice-President, Four Acres Charitable Trust. Recreations: conservation; work; the arts. Address: (h.) 92 Southbrae Drive, Glasgow G13 1TZ; T.-0141-959 3131.

Chalmers, Dr. Robert. Principal, Moray College of Further Education. Address: (b.) Hay Street, Elgin, IV30 2NN.

Chamberlain, Rt. Rev. Canon Neville, BA, MA. Episcopal Bishop of Brechin, since 1997; b. 1939. Educ. Nottingham University; Oxford University. Deacon, 1963; ordained Priest, 1964; Curate, St. Paul's, Birmingham, 1963-64; Priest-in-Charge, St. Michael's, Birmingham, 1964-69; Rector, Deer Creek Parish, USA, 1967-68; Vicar, St. Michael's Anglican Methodist Church, 1969-72; Executive Secretary, Lincoln Social Responsibility Commission, 1974-82; Canon and Prebend, Lincoln Cathedral, 1979; Rector, St. John the Evangelist, Edinburgh, 1982-97. Address: (b.) St. Paul's Cathedral, 1 High Street, Dundee DD1 1TD; T.-01382 229230.

Chambers, Ernest George Wilkie, MBA, BSc (Hons). Chief Executive, West of Scotland Water Authority; b. 10.5.47, Dundee; m., Jeanette; 1 s.; 1 d. Educ. Harris Academy, Dundee. Assistant Engineer, East of Scotland Water Board and Lower Clyde Water Board, 1969-75; Strathclyde Regional Council Water Department: Area Engineer (Renfrew), 1975-79, Divisional Operations Engineer, Lower Clyde Division, 1979-84, Assistant Divisional Manager, 1984-86, Assistant Director (Operations & Maintenance), 1986-88; Director, 1988-94; SRC Water Services Department: Director, 1994-95. National President, Institution of Water Officers, 1996-97 (National Senior Vice President, 1995-96); President, Scottish Area, Association of Water Officers, 1991-92. Recreations: DIY; gardening. Address: (b.) 419 Balmore Road, Glasgow G22 6NU; T.-0141-355 5101.

Chapman, Francis Ian, CBE, FRSA, CIMgt, DLitt (Hon). President, Scottish Radio Holdings PLC, since 1996 (Chairman, 1972-96); Deputy Chairman, Guinness Publishing, since 1997 (Chairman, 1991-96); b. 26.10.25, St. Fergus, Aberdeenshire; m., Marjory Stewart Swinton; 1 s.; 1 d. Educ. Shawlands Academy, Glasgow; Ommer School of Music. War Service: RAF air crew cadet, 1943-44; National Service coal mines, 1945-47. William Collins: trainee, 1947, Sales Representative, New York Branch, 1951, General Sales Manager, London, 1955, appointed to main operating Board as Group Sales Director, 1960; appointed to Board, William Collins (Holdings) Ltd. as

Joint Managing Director, 1967; Deputy Chairman, William Collins (Holdings) Ltd., 1976; Chairman, William Collins Publishers Ltd., 1979; Chairman and Chief Executive, William Collins PLC, 1981-89; Chairman, Hatchards Ltd., 1976-89; Pan Books Ltd.: Board Member, 1962-84, Chairman, 1971-73; Chairman, Harvill Press Ltd., 1976-89; Board Member, Book Tokens Ltd., 1981-95; Member, Governing Council, SCOTBIC, since 1983; Board Member, IRN Ltd., 1983-85; President, Publishers Association, 1979-81; Trustee, Book Trade Benevolent Society, since 1982; Board Member, Scottish Opera Theatre Royal Ltd., 1974-79; Director, Stanley Botes Ltd., 1985-89; Non-Executive Director, Guinness PLC, 1986-91; Joint Chairman and Chief Executive, Harper and Row, New York, 1987-89; Director, United Distillers PLC, 1988-93; Chairman and Managing Director, Chapmans Publishers Ltd., 1989-91; Deputy Chairman, Orion Publishing Group, 1993-94. Scottish Free Enterprise Award, 1985; Hon. DLitt, Strathclyde, 1990. Recreations: golf; swimming; music; grandchildren. Address: (b.) Radio Clyde, Clydebank Business Park, Clydebank.

Chapman, Professor John N., MA, PhD, FInstP, FRSE. Professor, Physics and Astronomy, Glasgow University, since 1988; b. 21.11.47, Sheffield; m., Judith M.; 1 d. Educ. King Edward VII School, Sheffield; St. John's College and Fitzwilliam College, Cambridge. Research Fellow, Fitzwilliam College, Cambridge; Lecturer, Glasgow University. Publication: Quantitative Electron Microscopy (Co-Editor). Recreations: photography; walking; squash. Address: (b.) Department of Physics and Astronomy, Glasgow University, Glasgow G12 8QQ; T.-0141-330 4462.

Chapman, Professor Robert, BSc, PhD. Professor of Physics, since 1993, and Head, Department of Electronic Engineering and Physics, since 1996, University of Paisley; b. 10.8.41, Holytown; m., Norma Gilchrist Chapman; 3 d. Educ. Bellshill Academy; University of Glasgow. UKAEA Research Fellow, AWRE, Aldermaston, and AERE, Harwell, 1966-70; University of Manchester: Lecturer, 1970-75, Senior Lecturer, 1975-87, Reader in Physics, 1987-93; Head, Department of Physics, University of Paisley, 1993-96. Recreations: walking; gardening; music. Address: (b.) Department of Electronic Engineering and Physics, University of Paisley, Paisley PA1 2BE; T.-0141-848 3600.

Chapman, Robert Sutherland, MB, ChB (Hons), FRCP(Glas), FRCP(Edin), FRCP(Lond). Consultant Dermatologist, Stobhill NHS Trust and Greater Glasgow Health Board; Clinical Senior Lecturer, Glasgow University, since 1973; b. 4.6.38, Cults, Aberdeenshire; m., Dr. Rosalind S. Slater; 2 s.; 1 d. Educ. Turriff Academy; Aberdeen University. House Officer, Aberdeen Royal Infirmary; Research Fellow, Department of Materia Medica and Therapeutics, Aberdeen University; Registrar and Senior Registrar in Dermatology, Aberdeen Hospitals; Senior Registrar in Dermatology, Middlesex Hospital and St. John's Hospital for Diseases of the Skin, London. Recreations: gardening; hill-walking. Address: (h.) 4 Seafield Avenue, Bearsden, Glasgow G61 3LB; T.-0141-942 8993.

Chapman, Professor Stephen Kenneth, BSc, PhD, CChem, MRSC. Professor of Chemistry, since 1996; b. 12.5.59, Newcastle upon Tyne; m., Karen; 1 s.; 1 d. Educ. Lakes School, Windermere; University of Newcastle. NATO Research Fellow, Massachusetts Institute of Technology, Cambridge, Mass., USA, 1983-85; Department of Chemistry, Edinburgh University: Lecturer, 1986, Senior Lecturer, 1992, Reader, 1995. Publications: 99 scientific publications. Recreations: watching sport; gardening; playing with my children. Address: (b.) Department of Chemistry, University of Edinburgh, West Mains Road, Edinburgh EH9 3JJ; T.-0131-650 4760.

Chatterji, Professor Monojit, BA, MA, PhD. Bonar Professor of Applied Economics, Dundee University, since 1989 (Head, Department of Economic Studies, 1993-97); Associate Dean, Faculty of Arts and Social Sciences, Dundee University, since 1995; b. 15.1.51, Bombay; m., Anjum Rahmatulla; 1 s.; 2 d. Educ. Cathedral School, Bombay; St. Columba's, Delhi; Elphinstone College, Bombay; Christ's College, Cambridge. Recreations: tennis; cinema; history; theology. Address: (b.) Department of Economics, Dundee University, Dundee; T.-01382 23181.

Cheetham, Professor Juliet, OBE, MA. National Co-ordinator, SHEFC Contract Research Staff Initiative, since 1996; Professor and Director, Social Work Research Centre, Stirling University, 1986-95; b. 12.10.39, Jerusalem; m., Christopher Paul Cheetham; 1 s.; 2 d. Educ. St. Andrews University; Oxford University. Probation Officer, Inner London, 1959-65; Lecturer in Applied Social Studies and Fellow of Green College, Oxford University, 1965-86. Member: Committee of Enquiry into Working of the Abortion Act; Northern Ireland Human Rights Commission; Commission of Racial Equality; Social Security Advisory Committee; Council for National Academic Awards; Economic and Social Research Council. Recreation: canal boats. Address: (b.) Department of Applied Social Science, Stirling University, Stirling FK9 4LA.

Chester, Richard Waugh, ARAM, GRSM, ARCM, FRSA. Director, National Youth Orchestra of Scotland, since 1987; b. 19.4.43, Hutton Rudby; m., Sarah Chapman-Mortimer; 1 s.; 2 d. Educ. The Friends' School, Great Ayton; Huddersfield University; Royal Academy of Music. Flautist: BBC Northern Ireland, 1965, Royal Scottish National Orchestra, 1967; Conductor; Teacher; Examiner. Director, Glasgow Festival Strings; Member, Scottish Arts Council (Chairman, Music Committee); Treasurer, European Federation of National Youth Orchestras; Member, Board, World Youth Orchestra Conference; Governor, St. Mary's Music School, Edinburgh. Recreations: tennis; swimming; good food. Address: (h.) Milton of Cardross, Port of Menteith, Stirling FK8 3JY; T.-01877 385634; (b.) National Youth Orchestra of Scotland, 13 Somerset Place, Glasgow G3 7JT; T.-0141-332 8311.

Chesworth, Air Vice Marshal George Arthur, CB, OBE, DFC. Lord-Lieutenant of Morayshire, since 1994.

Cheyne, Rev. Professor Alexander Campbell, MA (Hons), BLitt, BD, HonDLitt (Memorial University, Newfoundland). Professor of Ecclesiastical History, Edinburgh University, 1964-86; Principal, New College, Edinburgh, 1984-86; Moderator, Edinburgh Presbytery, Church of Scotland, 1987-88; b. 1.6.24, Errol, Perthshire. Educ. Kirkcaldy High School; Edinburgh University; Oriel College, Oxford; Basel University, Switzerland. National Service, Black Watch and RAEC (Instructor, Army School of Education), 1946-48; Glasgow University: Assistant Lecturer, 1950-51, Lecturer in History, 1951-53; New College and Basel University 1953-57; Lecturer in Ecclesiastical History, Edinburgh University, 1958-64. Carnegie Scholar, 1948-50; Aitken Fellow, 1956-57; Visiting Professor, Wooster College, Ohio, 1973; Chalmers Lecturer (Trinity College, Glasgow, and Christ's College, Aberdeen), 1976-80; Visiting Fellow, Wolfson College, Cambridge, 1979; Burns Lecturer, Knox College, Dunedin, New Zealand, 1980; Lee Lecturer, 1993; President, Scottish Church History Society, 1986-89. Publications: The Transforming of the Kirk: Victorian Scotland's Religious Revolution, 1983; The Practical and the Pious: Essays on Thomas Chalmers 1780-1847 (Editor), 1985; The Ten Years' Conflict and the Disruption, 1993; contributions to: Reformation and Revolution: Essays presented to Hugh Watt, 1967; introduction to Movements of Religious Thought in Britain during the Nineteenth Century, 1971; The Westminster Confession in the Church Today, 1982;

The Bible in Scottish Life and Literature, 1988; In Divers Manners, 1990; Christ, Church and Society: essays, 1993; William Robertson Smith: Essays in Reassessment, 1995; From Disruption to Diversity: Edinburgh Divinity 1846-1996, 1996. Recreations: classical music; walking; foreign travel. Address: (h.) 12 Crossland Crescent, Peebles EH45 8LF; T.-01721 722288.

Chezeaud, Jacques-Marcel, BA (Hons). Rector, St. Joseph's College, Dumfries, since 1994; b. 16.8.52, Bourges, France; m., Joan I. Campbell; 1 s.; 1 d. Educ. Lycee Alain Fournier, France; Orleans University; Stirling University. Foreign language assistant, Wallace Hall and Sanquhar Academies, 1974-75; manager, wine trade, 1979-80; Teacher, English/French, Biggar High School and St. Mary's Academy, Bathgate, 1980-82; Principal Teacher, Modern Languages, Our Lady's High School, Broxburn, 1982-85; Depute Rector, St. Columba's High School, Perth, 1985-91; Depute Head, St. David's High School, Dalkeith, 1991-94. Member, Executive Committee, Scottish Association for Language Teaching. Recreations: long-distance running; reading; good food and wines. Address: (b.) St. Joseph's College, Craigs Road, Dumfries DG1 4UU; T.-01387 252893.

Chiappelli, Marco Luigi Autimio, CA. Finance Director, Johnston Press plc, since 1980; b. 27.8.44, Glasgow; m., Jane Geddes McLaughlin; 2 d. Educ. Lourdes Senior Secondary School, Glasgow. Indentured Student, Aikman & Glen, CA, Glasgow (later Alexander Sloan), 1963-69; qualified as CA, 1969; Audit Senior, then Audit Manager, Alexander Sloan, 1969-74; joined F. Johnston & Co. Ltd. (later Johnston Press plc), as Company Secretary, 1974. Chairman, Group of Scottish Finance Directors; Board of Governors, St. Margaret's School, Edinburgh, 1995; Finance Director of the Year, 1995. Recreations: golfing; tennis; travel; music. Address: (b.) 53 Manor Place, Edinburgh EH3 7EG; T.-0131-225 3361.

Chick, Jonathan Dale, MA (Cantab), MB, ChB, MPhil, FRCPE, FRCPsych. Consultant Psychiatrist, Royal Edinburgh Hospital, since 1979; part-time Senior Lecturer, Edinburgh University, since 1979; b. 23.4.45, Wallasey; m., Josephine Anna; 2 s. Educ. Queen Elizabeth Grammar School, Darlington; Corpus Christi College, Cambridge; Edinburgh University. Posts in Edinburgh teaching hospitals, 1971-76; scientific staff, MRC Unit for Epidemiological Studies in Psychiatry, 1976-79. Adviser, WHO, Department of Transport; awarded Royal College of Psychiatrists Research Medal and Prize. Publication: Drinking Problems (Co-author). Recreations: wheels, reels, spiels and stichomythia.

Chirnside, Peter Huett, BSc (Hons). National Co-ordinator, Tear Fund, since 1979; Chairman, Scottish Mission Secretaries Fellowship, since 1984; Member, Scottish Lausanne Committee, since 1995; b. 27.12.49, Lancaster; m., Fiona; 1 s.; 1 d. Educ. Silcoates School, Wakefield; University of Dundee. Teacher of Biology, Mackie Academy, 1973-79. Address: (b.) Challenge House, 29 Canal Street, Glasgow G4 0HD.

Chisholm, Duncan Douglas, MB, ChB, FRCPsych, DPM, DPsychother. Consultant Child and Adolescent Psychiatrist, Department of Child and Family Psychiatry, Royal Aberdeen Children's Hospital, since 1975; Clinical Senior Lecturer, Department of Mental Health, Aberdeen University, since 1975; b. 8.10.41, Grantown-on-Spey; m., Rosemary Galloway Doyle; 2 d. Educ. Grantown Grammar School; Aberdeen University. Pre-registration House Officer, Aberdeen, 1965-66; post-registration Senior House Officer/Registrar, Royal Cornhill Hospital and Ross Clinic, Aberdeen, 1966-70; Senior Registrar in Child and Adolescent Psychiatry, 1970-75 (including one-year sabbatical, Clarke Institute of Psychiatry, Toronto, 1973-74). Vice-President, Family Mediation Grampian;

Academic Secretary, Scottish Child and Adolescent Section, Royal College of Psychiatrists. Recreations: reading; chess; crosswords; literature, history and culture of Scotland and Scottish Highlands; bowls. Address: (h.) Figurettes, 6 Crombie Road, Westhill, Aberdeenshire AB32 6PN; T.-01224 620786.

Chisholm, Duncan Fraser, JP. Managing Director, Duncan Chisholm & Sons Ltd., Inverness, since 1979; Chairman, Inverness Town Twinning Committee, since 1992; b. 14.4.41, Inverness; m., Mary Rebecca MacRae; 1 s.; 1 d. Educ. Inverness High School. Member, Inverness District Council, 1984-92; Member, Board of Governors, Eden Court Theatre, Inverness, 1984-88; President, Inverness and Highland Chamber of Commerce, 1983-84 (Vice-President, 1982-83); Member, Highland TAVRA Committee, 1988-92; Vice-Chairman, Inverness, Loch Ness and Nairn Tourist Board, 1988-96; President, Clan Chisholm Society, 1978-89. Recreations: swimming; badminton. Address: (b.) 47-51 Castle Street, Inverness; T.-01463 234599.

Chisholm, Duncan John, FRICS. Assessor and Electoral Registration Officer for Fife (previously for Fife Regional Council), since 1990; b. 22.1.53, Musselburgh; m., Ann Thomson; 1 s.; 1 d. Educ. Trinity Academy, Edinburgh. Apprentice Surveyor, Midlothian County Assessor, 1970-74; Valuer, Midlothian County Assessor, 1974-75; Valuer, Senior Valuer, Divisional Assessor, Lothian Regional Assessor, 1975-89. Recreations: golf; music; eating; real ale. Address (b.) Fife House (03), North Street, Glenrothes, Fife; T.-Glenrothes 414141.

Chisholm, Malcolm. MP (Labour), Edinburgh North and Leith (formerly Edinburgh Leith), since 1992; Parliamentary Under-Secretary of State, Scottish Office (Minister for Local Government and Transport) 1997; b. 7.3.49; m.; 2 s.; 1 d. Former teacher. Address: (b.) House of Commons, SW1A 0AA.

Chisman, Neil, MA, FCCA, MCT. Finance Director, Stakis PLC, since 1989; b. 1.3.47, Southend on Sea; m., Elizabeth Gausden; 1 s.; 1 d. Educ. Preston Manor County Grammar School, Wembley; Fitzwilliam College, University of Cambridge. British Leyland, 1968-70; Mars, 1970-72; BBC, 1972-75; Twinlock, 1975-76; Arabian Construction Co., Abu Dhabi, 1976-77; Abu Dhabi Petroleum Co., 1977-81; Coopers & Lybrand, 1981-85; University of Surrey, 1985-88; Underwoods PLC, 1988-89. Member, Financial Reporting Council. Recreations: work; family; bridge; history. Address: (b.) 3 Atlantic Quay, York Street, Glasgow G2 8JH; T.-0141-304 1038.

Chiswick, Derek, MB, ChB, MPhil, FRCPsych. Honorary Senior Lecturer in Forensic Psychiatry, Edinburgh University; Consultant Forensic Psychiatrist, Edinburgh Healthcare NHS Trust; b. 7.1.45, Hampton, Middlesex; m., Ann Williams; 3 d. Educ. Preston Manor County School, Wembley; Liverpool University. Parole Board for Scotland: Member, 1983-88, Vice-Chairman, 1984-88; Member, Home Office Advisory Board on Restricted Patients. Recreation: relaxing with family. Address: (h.) 6 St. Catherine's Place, Edinburgh EH9 1NU; T.-0131-667 2444.

Christian, Professor Reginald Frank, MA (Hons) (Oxon). Professor of Russian and Head of Department, St. Andrews University, 1966-92, now Honorary Professor; b. 9.8.24, Liverpool; m., Rosalind Iris Napier; 1 s.; 1 d. Educ. Liverpool Institute High School; Queen's College, Oxford. RAF, 1943-46 (aircrew), flying on 231 Sqdn. and 6 Atlantic Ferry Unit (Pilot Officer, 1944); Foreign Office (British Embassy, Moscow), 1949-50; Lecturer and Head of Russian Department, Liverpool University, 1950-55; Senior Lecturer, then Professor of Russian and Head of Department, Birmingham University, 1955-66; Visiting Professor: McGill University, Montreal, 1961-62, Institute

of Foreign Languages, Moscow, 1964-65; Dean, Faculty of Arts, St. Andrews University, 1975-78; Member, University Court, 1971-73, 1981-85. President, British Universities Association of Slavists, 1967-70; Member, International Committee of Slavists, 1970-75; Honorary Vice-President, Association of Teachers of Russian; Member, UGC Arts Sub-Committee on Russian Studies. Publications: Russian Syntax (with F.M. Borras), 1959 and 1971; Korolenko's Siberia, 1954; Tolstoy's War and Peace: A Study, 1962; Russian Prose Composition (with F.M. Borras), 1964 and 1974; Tolstoy: A Critical Introduction, 1969; Tolstoy's Letters, edited, translated and annotated, 1978; Tolstoy's Diaries, edited, translated and annotated, 1985 and 1994. Recreations: violin; fell-walking; formerly association football. Address: (h.) Culgrianach, 48 Lade Braes, St. Andrews, Fife; T.-01334 474407; Scioncroft, Knockard Road, Pitlochry; T.-01796 472993.

Christie, Andrew John McPhedran, BAcc, CA, ATII. Partner, Arthur Andersen (Chartered Accountants), since 1983; b. 17.7.50, Glasgow; m., Barbara Isabel Tait; 2 s. Educ. Hillhead High School, Glasgow; Glasgow University. Joined Arthur Andersen, 1971; appointed Honorary Professor, Heriot-Watt University, 1990. Past Convener, Taxation Committee, ICAS; Member of Council, ICAS; Governor, Edinburgh College of Art. Recreations: golf; skiing. Address: (b.) 18 Charlotte Square, Edinburgh EH2 4DF; T.-031-225 4554.

Christie, Campbell, CBE, DLitt. General Secretary, Scottish Trades Union Congress, since 1986; Visiting Professor, Glasgow Caledonian University; Honorary Professor, Glasgow University; b. 23.8.37, Carsluith, Kirkcud-brightshire; m., Elizabeth Brown Cameron; 2 s. Educ. Albert Senior Secondary School, Glasgow; Woolwich Polytechnic, London. Civil Servant, Department of Health and Social Security, 1954-72; National Officer, then Deputy General Secretary, Society of Civil and Public Servants, 1972-86. Member: EU Economic and Social Committee, Scottish Economic Council, Glasgow Development Agency; Director: Wildcat Theatre Company, Mining (Scotland) Ltd, Scottish Low Pay Unit; Board Member: Falkirk Royal Infirmary Hospital Trust, Edinburgh Festival Theatre; Chairman, Lothian Trade Union and Community Resource Centre. Address: (h.) 31 Dumyat Drive, Falkirk; T.-01324 624555; (b.) 16 Woodlands Terrace, Glasgow G5; T.-0141-332 4649.

Christie, Fergus John Francis, MA, LLB. Solicitor; Partner, Burnett Christie, since 1993; b. 8.5.61, Edinburgh; m., Liesa Spiller; 1 s. Educ. Scotus Academy, Edinburgh; University of St. Andrews; University of Edinburgh. Assistant-Partner, Drummond Miller, 1985-93. Secretary: Edinburgh Bar Association, since 1991, St. Andrews Children's Society. Recreations: golf; antiques. Address: 53 George IV Bridge, Edinburgh; T.-0131-225 3456.

Christie, John, MTheol, DipEd. Director of Education, Scottish Borders Council, since 1995; Non-Executive Director: Scottish Consultative Council on the Curriculum, since 1995; Health Education Board for Scotland, 1991-97; b. 25.12.53, Edinburgh; m., Katherine; 2 d. Educ. Daniel Stewart's College; St. Andrews University; Edinburgh University; Moray House College of Education. Teacher, 1977-83; Principal Assistant, Stockport MBC, 1983-85; Assistant Director of Education, then Depute Director of Education, Tayside Regional Council, 1985-95. Hon. Treasurer, Association of Directors of Education in Scotland. Recreation: house-building. Address: (b.) Council HQ, Newtown St. Boswells TD6 0SA; T.-01835 825095.

Christie, Robert Johnstone Stevenson, BSc (Hons), FRSA. Scottish Secretary, Professional Association of Teachers, since 1989; b. 7.8.46, Edinburgh; m., Anne Elisabeth Fraser Macleod; 3 d. Educ. Grangemouth High School; Paisley College of Technology; Jordanhill College of Education; Glasgow University. Chemist, British Petroleum Chemicals Ltd., 1964-68; Principal Teacher of Physics, Tain Royal Academy, 1976-88. Recreations: family; music; history; sailing. Address: (b.) 4/6 Oak Lane, Edinburgh EH12 6XH; T.-0131-317 8282.

Christie, Terry, BSc (Hons). Headteacher, Musselburgh Grammar School, since 1987; Manager, Stenhousemuir Football Club, since 1992; b. 16.12.42, Edinburgh; m., Susan; 2 s.; 1 d. Educ. Holy Cross Academy, Edinburgh. Headteacher, Ainslie Park, 1982-87. Former professsional footballer; Manager, Meadowbank Thistle, 1980-92; President, Lothian Schools FA. Recreations: reading; golf. Address: (h.) 76 Meadowfield Terrace, Edinburgh EH8 7NU; T.-0131-661 1486.

Chrystie, Kenneth, LLB (Hons), PhD. Partner, McClure Naismith, since 1971; Chairman, Hugh Fraser Foundation, 1988; President, Royal Glasgow Institute of the Fine Arts, since 1997; b. 24.11.46, Glasgow; m., Mary; 1 s.; 2 d. Educ. Duncanrig Senior Secondary; University of Glasgow; University of Virginia. Joined McClure Naismith, 1968. Founder Member and Director, Intellectual Property Lawyers Organisation; Member, DTI Committees, Arbitration Law Reform. Publications: contributor to Encyclopedia of Scots Law, Labour Law Handbook and other legal publications. Recreations: golf; curling; tennis. Address: (b.) 292 St. Vincent Street, Glasgow G2 5TQ; T.-0141-204 2700.

Clapham, David Charles, LLB, SSC. Solicitor (Principal, private practice, since 1984); Secretary, Glasgow, Argyll and Bute and Dunbartonshire Local Valuation Panel, since 1996; part-time Chairman, Social Security Appeal Tribunals, since 1992; Director, Legal Defence Union; b. 16.10.58, Giffnock; m., Debra Harriet Samuels; 1 s.; 2 d. Educ. Hutchesons' Boys' Grammar School, Glasgow; Strathclyde University. Legal apprenticeship, 1979-81; admitted Solicitor, 1981; admitted Notary Public, 1982; founded own legal practice, 1984; Tutor, Strathclyde University, 1984-92; part-time Lecturer, Glasgow University, 1991-94; Secretary, Strathclyde Region Local Valuation Panel, 1988-94; Glasgow Bar Association: Secretary, 1987-91, Vice President, 1991-92, President, 1992-93; Secretary, Scottish Law Agents Society, 1994-97. Recreations: reading and collecting books. Address: (b.) 79 West Regent Street, Glasgow G2 2AW; T.-0141-332 5537.

Clark, Alastair Trevor, CBE (1976), LVO (1974), MA (Oxon), FSA Scot. Barrister (Middle Temple); Member, Race Relations Assessors Panel, Scottish Sheriff Courts, since 1983; b. 10.6.23, Glasgow; m., Hilary Agnes Mackenzie Anderson. Educ. Giffnock Academy; Glasgow Academy; Edinburgh Academy; Magdalen College, Oxford; Inns of Court (Middle Temple); Ashridge Management College. War service, Queen's Own Cameron Highlanders and Royal West African Frontier Force, Nigeria, India and Burma, 1942-46; Administrative Branch, HM Colonial Service (later HMOCS): Nigeria, 1949-59 (Secretary to Cabinet, Northern Region; Senior District Officer), Hong Kong, 1960-72 (Director of Social Welfare; Deputy and Acting Director of Urban Services; Acting Chairman Urban Council; Clerk of Councils; Principal Assistant Colonial Secretary, etc.), Western Pacific, 1972-77 (Chief Secretary Western Pacific High Commission; Deputy and Acting Governor, Solomon Islands); retired, 1977; Vice-President, Hong Kong Scout Association, 1965-72; Joint Founder, HK Outward Bound School; Honorary Secretary, St. John's Cathedral Council, 1963-72; USA State Department Country Leader Fellowship to USA, 1972; Selector, Voluntary Service Overseas, 1978-80; Leverhulme Trust Grant, 1979-81; Chairman, Scottish Museums Council, 1981-84 and 1987-90; Member, Museums Association Council, 1983-86 and 1990-94; Member, Edinburgh International Festival Council, 1980-86 and 1990-94; Vice-Chairman, Committee of Area Museum

Councils, 1983-84; Member, Secretary of State's Museums Advisory Board, 1983-85; Trustee, National Museums of Scotland, 1985-87; a Director, Royal Lyceum Theatre Company, 1982-84; Member: Lothian Health Board, 1981-89, City of Edinburgh District Council, 1980-88, Court of Directors, Edinburgh Academy, 1979-84; a Governor, Edinburgh Filmhouse, 1980-84 and since 1987; Member, National Museums of Scotland Charitable Trust, since 1987; Member, Almond Valley Heritage Trust, since 1990 (Vice Chairman, since 1993); Trustee, Stirling Smith Art Gallery and Museum, since 1993; Volunteer Guide, Royal Museum of Scotland, since 1993. Publication: A Right Honourable Gentleman — Abubakar from the Black Rock, 1991. Recreations: music; books; theatre; netsuke; cartophily. Address: (h.) 11 Ramsay Garden, Edinburgh EH1 2NA; T.-0131-225 8070.

Clark, Alex. Member, Board of Directors, Arran Theatre and Arts Trust; Trustee: James Milne Memorial Trust, Hugh MacDiarmid Memorial Trust, Scottish Working People's History Trust; b. 2.1.22, Larkhall; m., Jessie Beveridge McCulloch; 1 s.; 1 d. Educ. Larkhall Academy. Grain miller, 1936-39; coal miner, 1939-53; political organiser, 1953-69; Scottish and Northern Ireland Secretary, British Actors Equity Association, 1969-84; created the post of STUC Arts Officer, 1985-87; founder Member, Boards, Scottish Youth Theatre, Scottish Theatre Company, Royal Lyceum Theatre Company; Glasgow Jazz Festival, Mayfest (Founder and Honorary President); also served on Boards of Pitlochry Festival Theatre and Cumbernauld Theatre Company, Scottish Ballet, Scottish Opera, Glasgow Film Theatre; Member: Scottish Arts Council's Review Committee on Scottish Theatre Company, 1987, Working Party on a National Theatre for Scotland, 1987, STUC Entertainment and Arts Committee, 1975-94. Lord Provost's Award for services to the city of Glasgow, 1987; Winner, ABSA-Goodman & Reed Elsevier Award for Services to the Arts, 1994. Recreations: reading; music; theatre; walking; gardening. Address: (h.) Ponfeigh, 8 Strathwhillan, Brodick, Isle of Arran.

Clark, Alistair Campbell, MA, LLB, WS. Formerly Senior Partner, Blackadder, Reid, Johnston (formerly Reid, Johnston, Bell & Henderson), Solicitors, Dundee; Honorary Sheriff, Tayside Central & Fife, since 1986; Chairman, Dovetail Enterprises, since 1993; Trustee, Dundee Disabled Children's Association, since 1993; Chairman, Scottish Conveyancing and Executry Services Board, since 1996; b. 4.3.33, Dundee; m., Evelyn M. Clark; 3 s. Educ. Grove Academy, Broughty Ferry; St. Andrews University. Dean, Faculty of Procurators and Solicitors in Dundee, 1979-81, Hon. Life Member, since 1991; President, Law Society of Scotland, 1989-90 (Council Member, since 1982); founder Chairman, Broughty Ferry Round Table; Founder President, Claverhouse Rotary Club, Dundee. Recreations: family; travel; erratic golf. Address: (b.) 34 Reform Street, Dundee; T.-01382 229222.

Clark, Barbara E., MA, DipG. Assistant General Secretary, Scottish Secondary Teachers' Association, since 1997; b. 13.3.46, Stirling; m., John; 1 s.; 1 d. Educ. St. Modan's High School; University of Glasgow; Notre Dame College; Moray House. Alva Academy: Teacher of English, 1968-69 and 1979-85, A.P.T. Guidance, 1969-70 and 1985-90, P.T. Guidance, 1970-73; Guidance Development Officer, Central Region, 1990-93; P.T. Guidance, Bo'ness Academy, 1993-97; Education Liaison Officer, Children's Panel, 1995-96. Member, General Teaching Council, 1992-97; Vice-President then President, S.S.T.A., 1993-97. Recreations: reading; theatre; music; walking; art; travel. Address: (h.) 16 Lothian Crescent, Causewayhead, Stirling FK9 5SB; T.-01786 462968.

Clark, David Findlay, OBE, DL, MA, PhD, CPsychol, FBPsS, ARPS. Deputy Lieutenant, Banffshire, since 1992; Consulting Clinical Psychologist; former Director, Area

Clinical Psychology Services, Grampian Health Board; Clinical Senior Lecturer, Department of Mental Health, Aberdeen University; b. 30.5.30, Aberdeen; m., Janet Ann Stephen; 2 d. Educ. Banff Academy; Aberdeen University. Flying Officer, RAF, 1951-53; Psychologist, Leicester Industrial Rehabilitation Unit, 1953-56; Senior, then Principal Clinical Psychologist, Leicester Area Clinical Psychology Service, and part-time Lecturer, Leicester University and Technical College, 1956-66; WHO short-term Consultant, Sri Lanka, 1977; various lecturing commitments in Canada and USA, since 1968. Honorary Sheriff, Grampian and Highlands; former Governor, Aberdeen College of Education; Member, Grampian Children's Panel, 1970-85; Safeguarder (in terms of Social Work Scotland Act), since 1985; Past Chairman, Clinical Division, British Psychological Society. Publications: Help, Hospitals and the Handicapped, 1984; One Boy's War, 1997; book chapters and technical articles. Recreations: photography; sailing; chess; guitar playing; painting and drawing; golf; hill-walking. Address: (h.) Glendeveron, 8 Deveron Terrace, Banff AB45 1BB; T.-01261 812624.

Clark, Professor Frank, CBE, MHSM, DipHSM. Director, Strathcarron Hospice, since 1996; Honorary Professor, University of Stirling, since 1997; Visiting Professor, Glasgow Caledonian University, since 1993; b. 17.10.46, Aberdeen; m., Linda Margaret; 2 d. Educ. Aberdeen Academy. Greater Glasgow Health Board: Assistant District Administrator, 1977-81, District General Administrator, 1981-83; Lanarkshire Health Board: Director of Administrative Services, 1983-84, Secretary, 1984-85; General Manager, Lanarkshire Health Board, 1985-96; Chairman, Scottish Health Board General Managers Group, 1993-95 (Vice-Chairman, 1995-97). Recreations: reading; music; gardening; driving; swimming; DIY; poetry. Address: (b.) Strathcarron Hospice, Randolph Hill, Denny FK6 5HJ; T.-1324 826222.

Clark, Graham M. BSc, PhD, CChem, FRSC, FIMgt, FRSA. Principal, Falkirk College of Further and Higher Education, since 1992; b. 2.8.41, Dumfries; m., Linda A.; 3 d. Educ. George Watson's College, Edinburgh; Edinburgh University. Research Fellow, Hull University, 1966-67; Lecturer, Huddersfield Polytechnic, 1967-79; Head of Applied Science, North East Surrey College of Technology, 1980-85; Deputy Director, Nene College, Northampton, 1986-89; Principal, Angus College of Further Education, 1990-92. Editor, Thermal Analysis Reviews and Abstracts, 1986-93. Recreations: golf; hill walking; UK philately. Address: (b.) Falkirk College of Further and Higher Education, Grangemouth Road, Falkirk FK2 9AD; T.-01324 403203.

Clark, Guy Wyndham Nial Hamilton, JP, DL. Deputy Lieutenant, Renfrewshire, since 1987; Managing Director (Glasgow), Murray Johnstone Private Investors Ltd., since 1997; b. 28.3.44; m., Brighid Lovell Greene; 2 s.; 1 d. Educ. Eton. Commd. Coldstream Guards, 1962-67; Investment Manager, Murray Johnstone Ltd., Glasgow, 1973-77; Partner, R.C. Greig & Co. (Stockbrokers), Glasgow, 1977-86; Director, Greig, Middleton & Co. Ltd., 1986-97. Member, Executive Committee, Erskine Hospital; Chairman, JP Advisory Committee, since 1991. Recreations: hunting; shooting; fishing; racing. Address: (h.) Braeton, Inverkip PA16 0DU; T.-01475 520 619.

Clark, John Kenneth, BA (Hons), MA. Glasspainter; b. 1.12.57, Dumbarton. Educ. Dumbarton Academy; Glasgow School of Art. Commissions include: Cate Gandolfi, Glasgow (Saltire Award); Paisley Abbey (Saltire Award); Heaton Memorial Window, Ledbury; Lockerbie Memorial Window; Queens Park Synagogue, Glasgow; Beirut Hostages Windows, Broxted; St Petrus Worms — Herrnsheim; St. Konrad, Amberg-Ammersricht; University of Strathclyde Bicentenary Windows; Oakshaw Trinity, Paisley; Pibroch Windows, The Piping Centre, Glasgow.

Address: (h.) 11A Maxwell Drive, Glasgow G41 5DR; T.-0141-429 0987.

Clark, Karen, MA (Hons). Presenter, BBC Radio Scotland, since 1990; b. 11.10.58, Carlisle; m., Dr. Iain Hutchison; 2 s. Educ. Grange Academy, Kilmarnock; University of Edinburgh; University College, Cardiff. News Reporter, Radio Tay, 1981-82; News Reporter, Presenter, Consumer Programme, Radio Forth, 1982-83; News Reporter, LBC, 1984-85; Editor, Capital Radio, 1985-88; Producer, Good Morning Scotland, 1989-90; Presenter: Good Morning Scotland, Newsdrive, 1990-94; The Slice, since 1994, Now You're Talking, since 1997, Radio Scotland. New York Radio Society Award for coverage of London hurricane, 1987. Recreations: fishing; fitness; my family. Address: (b.) BBC Scotland, Beechgrove Terrace, Aberdeen AB15 5ZT; T.-01224 625233.

Clark, M. Lynda, QC. MP (Labour), Edinburgh Pentlands, since 1997. Admitted Advocate, 1977; called to English Bar, 1988; contested Fife North East (Labour), 1992. Address: (b.) House of Commons, London, SW1A 0AA.

Clark, Pamela Ann Dean, LLB (Hons). Executive Director, Highland Community Care Forum, since 1994; b. 18.10.60, Inverness. Educ. Lossiemouth High School; Edinburgh University; Aberdeen College of Education. Welfare Benefits Adviser, Central Regional Council; Legal Services Adviser, Citizens Advice Scotland; Director, Tenant Participation Advisory Service. Member: Scottish Homes Board, Commission on the Future of the Voluntary Sector in Scotland, Scottish New Deal Advisory Task Force; former Member, Scottish Homes Advisory Committee on Housing Information and Advice. Recreations: Irish wolfhound; swimming; cinema. Address: (h.) 8 Burnfarm Cottages, Killen, Avoch, Ross-shire.

Clark, Susan M. BSc, MBA. Director of Corporate Affairs, ScottishPower, since 1995; b. Chesterfield; m., Richard Roberts. Educ. Manchester University; Heriot Watt University. Joined ScottishPower 1992. Recreation: hill-walking. Address: ScottishPower, 1 Atlantic Quay, Glasgow G2; T.-0141-636 4560.

Clarke, (Christopher) Michael, BA (Hons), FRSA. Keeper, National Gallery of Scotland, since 1987; b. 29.8.52, York; m., Deborah Clare Cowling; 2 s.; 1 d. Educ. Felsted School, Essex; Manchester University. Art Assistant, York City Art Gallery, 1973-76; Research Assistant, British Museum, 1976-78; Assistant Keeper in charge of prints, Whitworth Art Gallery, Manchester, 1978-84; Assistant Keeper, National Gallery of Scotland, 1984-87. Visiting Fellow, Yale Center for British Art, 1985. Publications include: The Tempting Prospect; A Social History of English Watercolours; The Arrogant Connoisseur (Co-Editor); Richard Payne Knight; Lighting Up the Landscape – French Impressionism and its Origins; Corot and the Art of Landscape; Eyewitness Art – Watercolours; Corot, Courbet und die Maler von Barbizon (Co-Editor). Recreations: listening to music; tennis; golf. Address: (b.) National Gallery of Scotland, The Mound, Edinburgh EH2 2EL; T.-0131-556 8921.

Clarke, Eric Lionel. MP (Labour), Midlothian, since 1992; b. 9.4.33, Edinburgh; m., June; 2 s.; 1 d. Educ. Holy Cross Academy; W.M. Ramsey Technical College; Esk Valley Technical College. Coal miner, 1949-77; General Secretary, NUM Scottish Area, 1977-89; County Councillor, Midlothian, 1962-74; Regional Councillor, Lothian, 1974-78. Recreations: fly fishing; gardening; carpentry. Address: (h.) 32 Mortonhall Park Crescent, Edinburgh; T.-0131-654 1585.

Clarke, Professor Joseph Andrew, BSc, PhD. Professor, Environmental Engineering, University of Strathclyde, since 1991; Director, Energy Systems Research Unit, since

1987; President, International Building Performance Simulation Association, since 1994; b. 6.3.52, Glasgow; m., Kathryn Ann Clarke; 1 s.; 2 d. Educ. Whitehill Senior Secondary School; University of Strathclyde. SERC (now EPSRC) Research Fellow, 1977-79; SERC Senior Research Fellow, 1979-83; SERC Advanced Research Fellow, 1983-87; Personal Professorship, 1987; Director: Environmental Engineering, 1991, Energy Systems and the Environment MSc, 1988. Royal Society Esso Energy Award, 1989. Publication: Energy Simulation in Building Design, 1985. Recreation: running. Address: (b.) ESRU, Department of Mechanical Engineering, University of Strathclyde, Glasgow G1 1XJ; T.-0141-548 3986.

Clarke, Kevin John, BA. Secretary, University of Stirling, since 1995; b. 8.3.52, Reading; m., Linda Susan Stewart; 2 d. Educ. Presentation College, Reading; University of Stirling. Scientific Officer, British Library Lending Division, 1975-77; Administrative Assistant, Loughborough University, 1977-83; Assistant Registrar, University of Newcastle upon Tyne, 1983-85; Clerk to the Senatus Academicus, 1985-89, Deputy Secretary, 1989-95, University of Aberdeen. Recreations: music; hill-walking; gardening. Address: (b.) University of Stirling, Stirling FK9 4LA; T.-01786 467018.

Clarke, Martin Peter, BA (Hons). Editor, The Scotsman, since 1997; b. 26.8.64. Educ. Gravesend Grammar School; Bristol University. Daily Mail, 1988-94; News Editor, Daily Mirror, 1995; Editor, Scottish Daily Mail, 1995-97. Address: (b.) North Bridge, Edinburgh EH1 1YT.

Clarke, Matthew G., QC. Admitted, Faculty of Advocates, 1978. Address: Advocates' Library, Parliament House, Edinburgh EH1 1RF.

Clarke, Peter, CBE, BSc, PhD, LLD (Hon), CChem, FRSC, DEd(Hon), FInstPet. President, Association for Educational and Training Technology, 1993-95; Chairman, Industrial Training Centre, Aberdeen, 1989-95; b. 18.3.22, Mansfield; m., Ethel; 2 s. Educ. Queen Elizabeth's Grammar School, Mansfield; University College, Nottingham. Principal, Robert Gordon's Institute of Technology, Aberdeen, 1970-85. Chairman: Scottish Vocational Education Council, 1985-91, Aberdeen Enterprise Trust, 1984-92; President, Association of Principals of Colleges, 1980-81; Member, Science and Engineering Research Council, 1978-82; Trustee, Gordon Cook Foundation, since 1988 (Chairman, since 1997). Recreations: walking; gardening. Address: (h.) Dunaber, 12 Woodburn Place, Aberdeen, AB15 8JR; T.-01224 311132.

Clarke, Professor Roger John, ALCM, BA, BTech, MSc, PhD, CEng, MIEE, MIEEE. Professor of Electronic Engineering, Heriot Watt University, since 1989; b. 1.10.40, Ewell, Surrey; m., Yvonne Clarke; 1 s. Educ. Gravesend Grammar School; Loughborough University. Development Engineer, STC Ltd., Woolwich, 1962-64; Research Associate, then Lecturer in Electrical Engineering, Loughborough University, 1964-86; Reader in Electrical Engineering, Heriot Watt University, 1986-89. Recreations: gardening; playing the cello; Shakespeare. Address: (b.) Department of Computing and Electrical Engineering, Heriot Watt University, Riccarton, Edinburgh EH14 4AS; T.-0131-451 3323.

Clarke, Rt. Hon. Thomas, CBE, JP. Minister for Film and Tourism; MP (Labour), Monklands West, since 1983; Shadow Secretary of State for Scotland, 1992-93; b. 10.1.41, Coatbridge. Educ. Columba High School, Coatbridge. Former Assistant Director, Scottish Council for Educational Technology; Provost of Monklands, 1975-82; Past President, Convention of Scottish Local Authorities; MP, Coatbridge and Airdrie, 1982-83; author, Disabled Persons (Services Consultation and Representation) Act, 1986; elected four times to Shadow Cabinet; director,

amateur film, Give Us a Goal. Recreations: films; walking; reading. Address: (h.) 37 Blairhill Street, Coatbridge ML5 1PG; T.-01236 600800.

Clarkson, Euan Neilson Kerr, MA, PhD, DSc, FRSE. Reader in Palaeontology, University of Edinburgh, since 1981; b. 9.5.37; m., Cynthia; 4 s. Educ. Shrewsbury School; Emmanuel College, University of Cambridge. University of Edinburgh: Assistant Lecturer, 1963-65, Lecturer, 1965-78, Senior Lecturer, 1978-81, Director of Studies, 1967-73 and since 1995, Associate Dean, Science Faculty, 1978-81; many university committees. Trustee, Natural History Museum, 1987-92. President: Edinburgh Geological Society, 1983-87, Palaeontological Association, since 1998; Clough Medal, 1993; Keith Medal, 1994. Publications: Invertebrate Palaeontology and Evolution; 80 scientific articles. Recreations: classical music; hillwalking; writing; painting; wine. Address: (b.) Department of Geology and Geophysics, University of Edinburgh, West Mains Road, Edinburgh EH9 3JW.

Clarkson, Graeme Andrew Telford, LLB. Senior Partner, Baird & Company, Solicitors, Kirkcaldy, since 1990; b. 6.9.53, Fraserburgh; m., Moira; 3 s. Educ. High School of Dundee; Aberdeen University. Law Apprentice, Allan MacDougall & Co., Edinburgh; Assistant, Ranken & Reid, Edinburgh; Assistant, then Partner, Baird & Company. Past Chairman, Kirkcaldy Round Table; Council Member, Law Society of Scotland. Address: (b.) 2 Park Place, Kirkcaldy Fife; T.-01592 268608.

Clayson, Christopher William, CBE, OBE, MB, ChB, DPH, MD, FRCPEdin, FRCPLond, Hon.FACP, Hon.FRACP, Hon.FRCP(Glas), Hon.FRCGP, Hon. FRCP Edin. Physician (retired); b. 11.9.03, Ilford. Educ. George Heriot's School, Edinburgh; Edinburgh University. Assistant Physician: Southfield Sanatorium, Edinburgh, 1931-44, City Hospital, Edinburgh, 1939-44; Lecturer, Edinburgh University, 1939-44; Medical Superintendent, Lochmaben Sanatorium, 1944-48; Consultant Physician, Dumfries and Galloway Hospitals, 1948-68; President, RCPEdin, 1966-70; Chairman, Departmental Committee on Scottish Licensing Law, 1971-73; Chairman, Scottish Council on Postgraduate Medical Education, 1970-74; William Cullen Prizeman, RCPEdin, 1978. Address: (h.) Cockieseknowe, Lochmaben, Lockerbie DG11 1RL; T.-01387 810231.

Cleall, Charles, MA(Wales), BMus(Lond), ADCM, FRCO(CHM), GTCL, LRAM, HonTSC. Author and Writer; Tutor in Speech-Training, Scottish Congregational College, and Scottish Churches' Open College, Napier University; b. 1.6.27, Heston, Middlesex; m., Mary Turner; 2 d. Educ. Hampton School, Middlesex; Trinity College of Music; London University; Jordanhill College of Education, Glasgow; University College of North Wales. Organist and Choirmaster, St. Luke's, Chelsea, 1945-46; Command Music Adviser to Royal Navy, Plymouth Command (Instr. Lieut., RN) 1946-48; Professor of Solo Singing and Voice Production, and of ear-training and of choral repertoire, Trinity College of Music, London, 1949-52; Choral Scholar, Westminster Abbey, 1949-52; Organist and Choirmaster, Wesley's Chapel, City Road, London, 1950-52; Conductor, Morley College Orchestra, 1950-52; Conductor, Glasgow Choral Union, 1952-54; BBC Music Assistant, Midland Region, 1954-55; Music Master, Glyn County School, Ewell, 1955-66; Conductor, Aldeburgh Festival Choir, 1957-60; Organist and Choirmaster: St. Paul's, Portman Square, W1, 1957-61, Holy Trinity, Guildford, 1961-65; Lecturer in Music, The Froebel Institute, Roehampton, 1967-68; Adviser in Music, London Borough of Harrow, 1968-72; Northern Divisional music specialist, HM Inspectorate of Schools in Scotland, 1972-87; Editor, Journal, Ernest George White Society, 1983-88; has given many lectures on singing and choir training. Limpus Fellowship Prizeman, Royal College of Organists;

International Composition Prizeman, Cathedral of St. John the Divine, New York. Publications: Voice Production in Choral Technique, 1955/1970; The Selection and Training of Mixed Choirs in Churches, 1960; Sixty Songs from Sankey, 1960 and 1966; John Merbecke's Music for the Congregation at Holy Communion, 1963; Music and Holiness, 1964; Plainsong for Pleasure, 1969; Authentic Chanting, 1969; A Guide to Vanity Fair, 1982; Walking round the Church of St. James the Great, Stonehaven, 1993; scores of articles and book reviews. Recreations: writing; reading; natural history; walking. Address: (h.) 10 Carronhall, Stonehaven, Aberdeen AB39 2QF.

Clements, Professor John Barklie, BSc, PhD, FRSE. Professor of Virology, Glasgow University, since 1995; b. 14.3.46, Belfast. Educ. Belfast Royal Academy; Queen's University, Belfast. Research Fellow, California Institute of Technology, 1971-73; joined Institute of Virology, Glasgow University, 1973; Cancer Research Campaign Travelling Fellow, Department of Biochemistry and Molecular Biology, Harvard University, 1983; Council Member, Society for General Microbiology, 1984-88; Member, MRC Physiological Systems and Disorders Board, 1990-94; Chairman, Grants Committee B, PMIB, 1992-94; Member, Clinical and Biomedical Research Committee, Scottish Home and Health Department, 1990-93. Recreations: walking; golf; music. Address: (b.) Institute of Virology, Glasgow University, Glasgow; T.-0141-330 4027.

Clemson, Gareth, BMus (Auckland), BMus (Edinburgh). Composer; teaches violin and piano at home since retiring in 1994 ; b. 1.10.33, Thames, New Zealand; m., Thora Clyne; 2 s.; 1 d. Educ. St. Peter's School, New Zealand; King's College, New Zealand; Auckland University; Edinburgh University. Music teaching, New Zealand, Edinburgh and West Lothian, 1960-75; String Teacher, West Lothian, 1975-85, Fife Region, since 1985; lessons in composition from Thomas Wilson, 1963-65; chamber works including Nexus I and II, Waters of Separation, The Singing Cat, Invocation; broadcasts, New Zealand and Scotland; recent compositions, Trumpet in the Dust, Blackbird, General Reid's Garb of Old Gaul, two versions (piano and orchestral); Flight of the Kiwi; Pandura (orchestral); Pandura Turning (viola and piano); Rounding the Score (chamber ensemble). Recreations: reading; photography; cats. Address: (h.) Tillywhally Cottage, Milnathort, Kinross-shire KY13 7RN; T.-Kinross 864297.

Clerk of Penicuik, Sir John Dutton, 10th Bt, CBE (1966), VRD, FRSE, JP. Lord Lieutenant of Midlothian, 1972-92; Commodore RNR (Retd); b. 30.1.17; m.; 2 s.; 2 d. Educ. Stowe. Lieutenant, Queen's Bodyguard for Scotland (Royal Company of Archers). Address: (h.) Penicuik House, Penicuik, Midlothian EH26 9LA.

Clifford, Nigel Richard, MA (Cantab), DipInstM, DipCAM, MBA, FIMgmt, FRSA. Chief Executive, Glasgow Royal Infirmary University NHS Trust, since 1994; b. 22.6.59, Emsworth; m., Jeanette; 2 s.; 1 d. Educ. Portsmouth Grammar School; Downing College, Cambridge; Strathclyde University. British Telecom, 1981-92, latterly as Head of Business Strategy, BT Mobile Communications. Founding Trustee, Herald Foundation for Women's Health. Recreations: family life; walking; swimming; running. Address: (b.) 84 Castle Street, Glasgow, G4 0SF; T.-0141-211 4924.

Clifford, Timothy Peter Plint, BA, LLD, AMA, FRSA, FSAScot. Director, National Galleries of Scotland, since 1984; b. 26.1.46; m., Jane Olivia Paterson; 1 d. Educ. Sherborne; Perugia University; Courtauld Institute, London University. Manchester City Art Galleries: Assistant Keeper, Department of Paintings, 1968-72, Acting Keeper, 1972; Assistant Keeper, Department of Ceramics, Victoria and Albert Museum, London, 1972-76; Assistant Keeper, British Art, Department of Prints and Drawings, British Museum, London, 1976-78; Director, Manchester City Art Galleries, 1978-84. Chairman, International Committee for Museums of Fine Art (ICOM), 1980-83; Member, Museums and Galleries Commission, 1983-88; Member, Board, British Council, 1987-92; Member, Executive Committee, Scottish Museums Council; Vice President, Turner Society, 1984-86 and since 1989; Vice-President, Frigate Unicorn Preservation Society, since 1987; Member, Accademia Italiana delle Arti Applicate, since 1988; British Institute of Management's Special Award, 1991; Member, Ateneo Veneto (Italy), since 1997. Cavaliere all'Ordine del Merito della Repubblica Italiana, 1988; Member, Advisory Council, Friends of Courtauld Institute, since 1990; President, NADFAS, since 1996 (Vice-President, 1990-96). HonLLD (St. Andrews University); FRSA; FSA (Scot). Recreations: shooting; bird-watching; entomology. Address: (b.) National Galleries of Scotland, The Mound, Edinburgh, EH2 2EL.

Clinkenbeard, Janette, MB, ChB, FRCGP, DRCOG. Vice-Chairman, Scottish Council, Royal College of General Practitioners, since 1991; General Practitioner, since 1981; b. 11.2.44, Glasgow; m., William Clinkenbeard; 2 s.; 1 d. Educ. Rutherglen Academy; Glasgow University. Member, UK Council, RCGP, 1990-91, 1992-95, Chairman, SES Faculty, 1990-93. Recreations: music; sport; reading. Address: Riccarton Practice, Heriot Watt University, Edinburgh; T.-0131-451 3010.

Clinkenbeard, Rev. William Ward, BSEE, BD, STM. Minister, Carrick Knowe Parish Church, Edinburgh; m., 25.8.37, Nebraska, USA; m., Janette McKay Hunter; 2 s.; 1 d. Educ. Lincoln High School; University of Nebraska; McCormick Theological Seminary; Glasgow University; Yale University. Design Engineer, General Dynamics Corporation; Parish Minister, Wood River Presbyterian Church. Publications: The Contemporary Lesson; Full on the Eye (Co-author). Address: (h.) 40A Harlaw Road, Balerno EH14 7AX; T.-0131-449 6984.

Clive, Eric McCredie, MA, LLB, LLM, SJD. Commissioner, Scottish Law Commission, since 1981; b. 24.7.38, Stranraer; m., Kay McLeman; 1 s.; 2 d. Educ. Stranraer Academy; Stranraer High School; Universities of Edinburgh, Michigan, Virginia. Lecturer, Senior Lecturer, Reader, Professor of Scots Law, Faculty of Law, Edinburgh University, 1962-81. Publications: The Law of Husband and Wife in Scotland (3rd edition), 1982; legal articles. Address: (h.) 14 York Road, Edinburgh EH5 3EH; T.-0131-552 2875.

Clouting, David Wallis, BDS, MSc, LDSRCS (Eng), DDPH. Community Dental Services Manager, Borders Community Health Services NHS Trust, since 1995; b. 29.3.53, London; m., Dr. Margaret M.C. Bacon; 3 s.; 1 d. Educ. Leyton County High School for Boys; University College Hospital Dental School, London; Institute of Dental Surgery, London; Joint Department of Dental Public Health, London Hospital Medical College and University College. Senior Dental Officer for Special Needs, East and North Hertfordshire Health Authorities, 1983-90; Chief Administrative Dental Officer, Borders Health Board, 1990-95. Recreations: amateur radio; DIY; swimming; hill walking; sailing. Address: (b.) Borders Community Health Services NHS Trust, Huntlyburn House, Melrose TD6 9BP; T.-01896 662300.

Clow, Robert George Menzies. Chairman (since 1979) and Managing Director (1969-94), John Smith & Son (Glasgow) Ltd.; b. 27.1.34, Sian, Shensi, North China; m., Katrina M. Watson. Educ. Eltham College, London. Interned by Japanese as a child; National Service, RAF; trained as a bookseller, Bumpus London; worked in Geneva; joined John Smith & Son (Glasgow), 1960. Founded, with others, The New Glasgow Society, 1965 (Chairman 1967, 1968); worked for 12 years in rehabilitating St. Vincent Crescent, Glasgow, as founder member, St. Vincent Crescent Area Association; Secretary, First Glasgow Housing Association, since 1978; Director, St. Vincent Crescent Buildings Preservation Trust; restored Aiket Castle (winner of an Europa Nostra Merit Award, 1989), 1976-79; National Trust for Scotland: elected to Council 1978 and 1991, Executive, 1980-90; Executive Member, Committee, Strathclyde Building Preservation Trust, 1986; appointed to Architectural Heritage Fund Executive, 1989. Recreations: farming; bee keeping; opera; restoring old houses; swimming; skiing; reading on holiday. Address: Aiket Castle, Dunlop, Ayrshire; T.-(b.) 0141-221 7472.

Clyde, The Rt. Hon. The Lord (James John Clyde), PC, Baron (Life Peer), DUniv (Edin), DUniv (Heriot-Watt), DLitt (Napier), BA (Oxon), LLB. Lord of Appeal in Ordinary, since 1996; Senator of the College of Justice, since 1985; b. 29.1.32, Edinburgh; m., Ann Clunie Hoblyn; 2 s. Educ. Edinburgh Academy; Corpus Christi College, Oxford; Edinburgh University. Called to Scottish Bar, 1959; QC, 1971; Advocate Depute, 1973-74; Chancellor to Bishop of Argyll and the Isles, 1972-85; a Judge of the Courts of Appeal of Jersey and Guernsey, 1979-85; Chairman: Medical Appeal Tribunal, 1974-85, Committee of Investigation for Scotland on Agricultural Marketing, 1984-85, Scottish Valuation Advisory Council, 1987-96 (Member, since 1972); Member, UK Delegation to CCBE, 1978-84 (Leader, 1981-84); Chairman of the Inquiry into the removal of children from Orkney, 1991-92. Trustee and Manager, St. Mary's Music School, 1976-93; Trustee, National Library of Scotland, 1978-94; Director, Edinburgh Academy, 1979-88; Vice-President, Royal Blind Asylum and School, since 1987; President, Scottish Young Lawyers' Association, 1988-97; Chairman, St. George's School for Girls, 1989-97; Governor, Napier Polytechnic of Edinburgh, 1989-93; Chancellor's Assessor and Vice Chairman, Court, Edinburgh University, 1993-97; Chairman, Scottish Valuation and Rating Council, since 1996. Recreations: music; gardening. Address: (h.) 12 Dublin Street, Edinburgh, EH1 3PP.

Clyne, Rev. Douglas Roy, BD. Minister, Old Parish Church, Fraserburgh, since 1973; b. 9.11.41, Inverness; m., Annette Taylor; 1 s. Educ. Inverness High School; Aberdeen University. Accountancy, Inverness County Council and Highland Printers Ltd.; studied for ministry; Assistant Minister, Mastrick Parish Church, Aberdeen. Address: (b.) Old Parish Church Manse, 97 Saltoun Place, Fraserburgh AB43 9RY; T.-01346 518536.

Coats, Sir William David, Kt, DL, HonLLD (Strathclyde), 1977. Chairman, Coats Patons PLC, 1981-86; Deputy Chairman, Clydesdale Bank PLC, 1985-93; b. 25.7.24, Glasgow; m., The Hon. Elizabeth L.G. MacAndrew; 2 s.; 1 d. Educ. Eton College. Joined J. & P. Coats Ltd., 1948, as management trainee; held various appointments and became a Director, 1957; appointed Director, Coats Patons PLC, on its formation, 1960; Deputy Chairman, 1979. Recreations: golf; shooting. Address: (h.) The Cottage, Symington, Ayrshire KA1 5QG.

Cobbe, Professor Stuart Malcolm, MA, MD, FRCP. Professor of Medical Cardiology, Glasgow University, since 1985; b. 2.5.48, Watford; m., Patricia Frances; 3 d. Educ. Royal Grammar School, Guildford; Cambridge University. Training in medicine, Cambridge and St. Thomas Hospital, London; qualified, 1972; specialist training in cardiology, National Heart Hospital, London, and John Radcliffe Hospital, Oxford; research work, University of Heidelberg, 1981; Consultant Cardiologist and Senior Lecturer, Oxford, 1982-85. Recreation: walking. Address: (b.) Department of Medical Cardiology, Queen Elizabeth Building, Royal Infirmary, Glasgow G31 2ER; T.-0141-221 4722.

Cochran, Hugh Douglas, BA (Oxon), LLB. Advocate in Aberdeen, since 1958; b. 26.4.32, Aberdeen; m., Sarah Beverly Sissons; 4 s.; 2 d. Educ. Loretto; Trinity College, Oxford; Edinburgh University. Partner: Cochran & Macpherson, 1958-80, Adam, Cochran, 1980-93; Member, Grampian Health Board, 1980-88; Chairman, Castlehill Housing Association, 1974-83. Secretary, Aberdeen Association for the Prevention of Cruelty to Animals, 1972-96; Registrar, Diocese of Aberdeen and Orkney, since 1984. Recreations: cycling; collecting stamps; archaeology. Address: 15 Golden Square, Aberdeen AB10 1WF; T.-Aberdeen 644333.

Cochrane of Cults, 4th Baron (Ralph Henry Vere Cochrane), DL; b. 20.9.26; m.; 2 s. Address: Cults, Cupar, KY15 5RD.

Cockburn, Professor Forrester, CBE, MD, FRCPGlas, FRCPEdin, DCH. Emeritus Professor and Senior Research Fellow, Department of Child Health, Royal Hospital for Sick Children, Yorkhill, Glasgow; formerly Samson Gemmell Professor of Child Health, Glasgow University; b. 13.10.34, Edinburgh; m., Alison Fisher Grieve; 2 s. Educ. Leith Academy; Edinburgh University. Early medical training, Edinburgh Royal Infirmary, Royal Hospital for Sick Children, Edinburgh, and Simpson Memorial Maternity Pavilion, Edinburgh; Research Fellow in Paediatric Metabolic Disease, Boston University; Visiting Professor, San Juan University, Puerto Rico; Nuffield Fellow, Institute for Medical Research, Oxford University; Wellcome Senior Research Fellow, then Senior Lecturer, Department of Child Life and Health, Edinburgh University. Publications: a number of textbooks on paediatric medicine, neonatal medicine, nutrition and metabolic diseases. Recreation: sailing. Address: (b.) University Department of Child Health, Royal Hospital for Sick Children, Yorkhill Glasgow, G3 8SJ; T.-0141-201 0236.

Cockburn, James Masson Thomson, BSc (Hons), CEng, FICE, FIWEM, FIWO, FIMgt. Managing Director, Water Services, North of Scotland Water Authority; b. 22.1.47, Aberdeen; m., Avril; 2 s. Educ. Robert Gordon's College; Dundee University. Assistant Engineer, East of Scotland Water Board, 1969-75; Assistant Divisional Manager (Dundee), Department of Water Services, Tayside Regional Council, 1975-76; Assistant Director, Department of Water and Sewerage, Dumfries and Galloway Regional Council, 1976-79; Depute Director, Department of Water Services, Grampian Regional Council, 1979-88; Director of Water Services, Grampian Regional Council, 1988-95. Past President, Scottish Section, Institution of Water Engineers and Scientists; Member of Council, Institution of Water and Environmental Management, 1987-91; President, Scottish Area Institution of Water Officers, 1994-95; Secretary, Scottish Association of Directors of Water and Sewerage, since 1989; Chairman, Scottish Association of Directors of Water and Sewerage Services, 1995-96. Recreations: hill-walking; sailing; skiing; curling; Rotary. Address: (b.) North of Scotland Water Authority, Cairngorm House, Beechwood Park North, Inverness IV2 3ED; T.-01463 245427.

Cocker, Douglas, DA, ARSA, FRBS. Sculptor; b. 23.3.45, Alyth, Perthshire; m., Elizabeth Filshie; 2 s.; 1 d. Educ. Blairgowrie High School; Duncan of Jordanstone College of Art, Dundee. SED Travelling Scholar, Italy and Greece, 1966; RSA Andrew Carnegie Travelling Scholar, 1967; RSA Benno Schotz Award, 1967; Greenshields Foundation (Montreal) Fellowship, 1968-69 (studies in New York and Greece); RSA Latimer Award, 1970; Arts Council of GB Award, 1977; East Midlands Arts Award, 1979; Scottish Arts Council Major Bursary, 1989; Lecturer in Sculpture, Grays School of Art, Aberdeen, 1982-90; Essex Fine Art Fellowship, 1991-92; Visiting Artist: Newcastle Polytechnic, Duncan of Jordanstone College of Art,

Edinburgh College of Art, Glasgow Art College and Tyler University, Philadelphia. Numerous solo and group exhibitions; various major public commissions. Recreations: reading; travel; sport. Address: (h.) Lundie Mill, Lundie, Angus DD2 5NW.

Coffey, Daniel, JP. Councillor, East Ayrshire; Provost, Kilmarnock and Loudoun District, 1992-96; SNP Group Leader and Leader of the Opposition: Strathclyde Regional Council, 1994-96, East Ayrshire Council, since 1995; b. 19.7.54, Kilmarnock. Educ. St. Joseph's, Kilmarnock. SNP Group Leader: Kilmarnock and Loudoun District, 1988-92, Strathclyde Regional Council, 1986-90; Member, Justices Committee, East Ayrshire; Member, European Committee of the Regions; Bureau Member and Treasurer, European Alliance Group; Convener, Convention of Scottish Local Authorities SNP Group, 1992-96; Member, SNP National Executive, National Council and National Assembly; SNP Depute Spokesperson, Europe and Foreign Affairs; Convener, Association of Nationalist Councillors; Treasurer: Kilmarnock FC Supporters Association, Kilmarnock FC Supporters Travel Club; Hon. President: Burns Federation, Kilmarnock Amateur Operatic Society. Recreations: football supporter; marathon runner; Burns. Address: (h.) 7 Craufurdland Road, Kilmarnock, KA3 2HT; T.-01563 531916; (b.) East Ayrshire Council, London Road Centre, London Road, Kilmarnock KA3 7BU; T.-01563 576055.

Cogdell, Professor Richard John, BSc, PhD, FRSE. Hooker Professor of Botany, Glasgow University, since 1993; b. 4.2.49, Guildford; m., Barbara; 1 s.; 1 d. Educ. Royal Grammar School, Guildford; Bristol University. Post-doctoral research, USA, 1973-75; Botany Department, Glasgow University, 1975-94, now Institute of Biomedical and Life Sciences. Recreations: cricket; aerobics; Scottish dancing; theatre. Address: (b.) Division of Biochemistry and Molecular Biology, Glasgow University, Glasgow G12 8QQ; T.-0141-330 4232.

Coggins, Professor John Richard, MA, PhD, FRSE. Professor of Enzymology and Head, Division of Biochemistry and Molecular Biology, Glasgow University, since 1997; b. 15.1.44, Bristol; m., Dr. Lesley F. Watson; 1 s.; 1 d. Educ. Bristol Grammar School; Queen's College, Oxford; Ottawa University. Post-doctoral Fellow: Biology Department, Brookhaven National Laboratory, New York, 1970-72, Biochemistry Department, Cambridge University, 1972-74; Biochemistry Department, Glasgow University: Lecturer/Senior Lecturer/Professor, 1974-95; Director, Graduate School of Biomedical and Life Sciences, Glasgow University, 1995-97. Chairman: Molecular Enzymology Group, Biochemical Society, 1982-85, Biophysics and Biochemistry Committee, SERC, 1985-88; Managing Director, Biomac Ltd., 1988-94; Member, DTI-Research Councils Biotechnology Joint Advisory Board, 1989-94; Member of Council, AFRC, 1991-94; Biochemistry Adviser to UFC, 1989-92; Member of Council, Hannah Research Institute, since 1994; Governing Member, Caledonian Research Foundation, since 1994; Chairman, HEFC Research Assessment Panel for Biochemistry, 1995-96. Recreations: sailing; travelling. Address: (b.) Division of Biochemistry and Molecular Biology, IBLS, Glasgow University, Glasgow G12 8QQ; T.-0141-330 5267.

Cohen, Professor Anthony Paul, BA, MSc (SocSc), PhD, FRSE. Professor of Social Anthropology, Edinburgh University, since 1989; Provost of Law and Social Sciences, Dean, Social Sciences, Edinburgh University, since 1997; Convener, Scottish Forum for Graduate Education, 1996-98; b. 3.8.46, London; m., Dr. Bronwen J. Cohen; 3 s. Educ. Whittinghame Collge, Brighton; Southampton University. Assistant Professor, Queen's University, Kingston, Ontario, 1970-71; Lecturer/Senior Lecturer in Social Anthropology, Manchester University, 1971-89. Publications: The Management of Myths; The Symbolic Construction of Community; Whalsay: Symbol, Segment and Boundary in a Shetland Island Community; Self Consciousness: an alternative anthropology of identity; Belonging (Editor); Symbolising Boundaries (Editor); Humanising the City? (Co-Editor); Questions of Consciousness (Co-Editor). Recreations: occasional thinking; music; novels. Address: (b.) Adam Ferguson Building, Edinburgh University, George Square, Edinburgh EH8 9LL; T.-0131-650 3934, Ext. 6373.

Cohen, Cyril, OBE, JP, FRCPEdin, FRCPGlas. Honorary Fellow, Dundee University; Past President, Forfarshire Medical Association; retired Consultant Physician, Geriatric Medicine, and Hon. Senior Lecturer, Geriatric Medicine, Dundee University; Chairman, Angus Community Care Forum; b. 2.11.25, Manchester; m., Dr. Sarah E. Nixon; 2 s. Educ. Manchester Central High School; Victoria University, Manchester. Embarked on career in geriatric medicine, 1952. Former Chairman, Advisory Group on Health Education for Elderly People, Health Education Board for Scotland; former Member/Chairman, Angus District and Tayside Area Medical Committees; Secretary/Chairman, Tayside Area Hospital Medical Services Committee; Member, Scottish and UK Central Committee, Hospital Medical Services, and Chairman, Geriatric Medicine Sub-committee; Past Chairman, Scottish Branch, British Geriatric Society (former Council Member); Member, Panel on Nutrition of the Elderly, COMA; Honorary Vice-President, Dundee and District Branch, British Diabetic Association; Life Member, Manchester Medical Society; former Member, Chief Scientist's Committee for Research on Equipment for the Disabled and Health Services Research Committee; Chairman, Angus Access Panel; Honorary Vice-President, Dundee and District Branch, British Diabetic Society; Chairman, Radio North Angus (Hospital Radio); former Member, Brechin and Forfar School Councils, Forfar Academy School Board and Central Committee on Primary Education; Secretary, Aberlemno Community Council; Vice-Chairman, Angus Association of Voluntary Organisations and Member, Brechin Day Care Centre Committee; former Director, Scottish Hospital Advisory Service; Past President, Montrose Burns Club and Brechin Arts Guild; Member, League of Friends, Forfar Hospitals; Past Chairman, Angus Care of the Elderly Group. Publications: many on geriatric medicine and care of the elderly. Recreations: photography; short walks; being at home. Address: (h.) Mansefield, Aberlemno, Forfar DD8 3PD; T.-0130-783 259.

Cohen, George Cormack, MA, LLB. Advocate; b. 16.12.09, Glasgow; m., Elizabeth Wallace; 1 s.; 1 d. Educ. Kelvinside Academy, Glasgow; Glasgow University. Admitted to Faculty of Advocates, 1935; Sheriff of Caithness at Wick, 1944-51; Sheriff of Ayrshire at Kilmarnock, 1951-55; Sheriff of Lothians and Peebles at Edinburgh, 1955-66. Recreations: gardening; travel. Address: (h.) 37B Lauder Road, Edinburgh EH9 1UE; T.-0131-668 1689.

Cohen, Patricia Townsend Wade, BSc, PhD. Head of Molecular Biology and Special Appointments Scientist, Medical Research Council Protein Phosphorylation Unit, Department of Biochemistry, Dundee University; b. 3.5.44, Worsley, Lancashire; m., Professor Philip Cohen (qv); 1 s.; 1 d. Educ. Bolton School; University College, London. Postdoctoral Research Fellow, Department of Medical Genetics, Washington University, Seattle, USA, 1969-71; Department of Biochemistry, Dundee University: Science Research Council Fellowship, 1971-72, Research/Teaching Fellow (part-time), 1972-83, Lecturer (part-time), 1983-90, Senior Lecturer, 1990-91, Reader, 1995. Publications: 100 papers and reviews in scientific journals. Recreations: reading; skiing; golf. Address: (h.) Inverbay II, Invergowrie, Dundee DD2 5DQ; T.-01382 562328.

Cohen, Professor Philip, BSc, PhD, FRS, FRSE, FRSA. Royal Society Research Professor, University of Dundee, since 1984 and Director, Wellcome Trust Building, since 1997; Honorary Director, Medical Research Council Protein Phosphorylation Unit, since 1990; b. 22.7.45, London; m., Patricia Townsend Wade (qv); 1 s.; 1 d. Educ. Hendon County Grammar School; University College, London. Science Research Council/NATO postdoctoral Fellow, Department of Biochemistry, University of Washington, 1969-71; Dundee University: Lecturer in Biochemistry, 1971-78, Reader in Biochemistry, 1978-81, Professor of Enzymology, 1981-84. Publications: 350 papers and reviews, one book. Recreations: bridge; golf; natural history. Address: (h.) Inverbay II, Invergowrie, Dundee; T.-01382 562328.

Coid, Donald Routledge, MSc, BMedSci, BM, BS, FRACMA, FAFPHM, MRCP, FFPHM. Chief Administrative Medical Officer and Director of Public Health, Tayside Health Board, since 1994; b. 13.6.53, Wallingford; m., Susan Kathleen Ramus Crocker; 3 d. Educ. Bromley Grammar School for Boys; Harrow County School for Boys; Nottingham University; London University. Field Medical Officer, Royal Flying Doctor Service of Australia, 1979-80; Medical Officer, Community Health Services, Western Australia, 1981-82; Regional Director of Public Health, Eastern Goldfields, Western Australia, 1982-85; Medical Superintendent, Kalgoorie Regional Hospital, 1984-85; Fife Health Board: Consultant in Public Health, 1985-92; Assistant General Manager, 1992-93. Recreations: golf; singing; cricket; piano. Address: (h.) 90 Hepburn Gardens, St. Andrews KY16 9LN; T.-01334 472710.

Coke, Professor Simon, MA (Oxon). Professor of International Business, Edinburgh University, since 1972; b. 27.6.32, Bicester, Oxfordshire; m., Diana Margaret Evison; 1 s.; 2 d. Educ. Ridley College, Ontario; Pembroke College, Oxford. Marketing Executive, Beecham Overseas, 1958-64; General Manager, Japan, etc., Johnson & Johnson, 1964-68; Head, Department of Business Studies, Edinburgh University, 1984; Dean, Scottish Business School, 1981-83; Director, Edinburgh University Management School, 1991-96; Director: Nippon Asset Trust, Ivory and Sime Optimum Income Trust PLC, Lastolite Ltd. Address: (b.) Department of Business Studies, University of Edinburgh, 50 George Square, Edinburgh EH8 9JY.

Cole-Hamilton, Arthur Richard, CBE, BA, CA, FIB(Scot). Chairman, Stakis plc; Chairman, General Committee, Royal and Ancient Golf Club of St. Andrews; b. 8.5.35, Kilwinning; m., Prudence Ann; 1 s.; 2 d. Educ. Ardrossan Academy; Loretto School; Cambridge University. Partner, Brechin Cole-Hamilton & Co., CA, 1962-67; various appointments, Clydesdale Bank, 1967-82; appointed Chief Executive, 1982, Director, 1984; retired, 1992. Former Council Member, Institute of Chartered Accountants of Scotland (Chairman, Finance and General Purposes Committee, 1981-85); Chairman, Committee of Scottish Clearing Bankers, 1991-92; President, Institute of Bankers in Scotland, 1988-90; former Chairman, Scottish Council (Development and Industry); Director, Glasgow Chamber of Commerce, 1985-91; Trustee: National Galleries of Scotland, 1986-96, Princess Royal Trust for Carers. Recreation: golf. Address: (h.) 26 Lady Margaret Drive, Troon KA10 7AL; T.-01292 311338.

Cole-Hamilton, Professor David John, BSc, PhD, CChem, FRSC, FRSE. Irvine Professor of Chemistry, St. Andrews University, since 1985; b. 22.5.48, Bovey Tracey; m., Elizabeth Ann Brown; 2 s.; 2 d. Educ. Haileybury and ISC; Hertford; Edinburgh University. Research Assistant, Temporary Lecturer, Imperial College, 1974-78; Lecturer, Senior Lecturer, Liverpool University, 1978-85. Sir Edward Frankland Fellow, Royal Society of Chemistry, 1984-85; Corday Morgan Medallist, 1983; President: Chemistry Section, British Association for the Advancement of Science, 1995, Chemistry Sectional Committee, Royal Society of Edinburgh, 1993-95. Address: (b.) Department of Chemistry, The Purdie Building, St. Andrews, Fife KY16 9ST; T.-01334 463805.

Collier, H. Bruce, DCA, MITSA. Director of Community Protection, South Ayrshire Council, since 1995; b. 24.5.46, Dumbarton; m., Margaret; 3 d. Educ. Clydebank High School. Director, Department of Consumer and Trading Standards, Strathclyde Regional Council, 1991-95. Chairman, Association of Petroleum and Explosives Acts Administration, 1973; Chairman, Institute of Trading Standards Scotland, 1986; Director, European Inter-Regional Institute of Consumer Affairs; former Chair, Irvine CAB; Vice-Chairman, Scottish Consumer Council; Council Member, Institute of Trading Standards Administration. Recreations: reading; walking. Address: (b.) South Ayrshire Council, County Buildings, Wellington Square, Ayr KA7 1DR; T.-01292 612429.

Collins, Dennis Ferguson, MA, LLB, WS, FRPSL. Senior Partner, Carlton Gilruth, Solicitors, Dundee (retired); Honorary Sheriff; b. 26.3.30, Dundee; m., Elspeth Margaret Nicoll; 1 s.; 1 d. Educ. High School of Dundee; St. Andrews University. Part-time Lecturer in Scots Law, St. Andrews University, then Dundee University, 1960-79; Agent Consulaire for France in Dundee, 1976-97; Hon. Secretary, Dundee Society for Prevention of Cruelty to Children, 1962-90; Treasurer, Dundee Congregational Church, since 1966; Past President, Dundee and District Philatelic Society; Past President, Association of Scottish Philatelic Societies; Dean, Faculty of Procurators and Solicitors in Dundee, 1987-89. Recreations: Chinese postal history; gardening; Sherlock Holmes pursuits; travelling in France. Address: (h.) Stirling House, Craigiebarn Road, Dundee DD4 7PL; T.-01382 458070.

Collins, Jeffrey Hamilton, DSc, FEng, FRSE, CPhys, FIEE, FIEEE. Specialist Adviser to the Principal and Vice-Chancellor, Napier University, since 1994; b. 22.4.30, Luton; m., Sally; 2 s. Educ. Royal Grammar School, Guildford; University of London. Lecturer, then Senior Lecturer, University of Glasgow, 1957-66; Research Engineer, Stanford University, USA, 1966-68; Director of Physical Sciences, Rockwell International, California, 1968-70; Research Professor, Professor of Industrial Electronics, Professor of Electrical Engineering, University of Edinburgh, 1970-84; Director of Automation and Robotics Research Institute, and Professor of Electrical Engineering, University of Texas at Arlington, 1987-90; Senior Technical Specialist, Lothian Regional Council, Edinburgh, and Chairman, Edinburgh Parallel Computing Centre, 1991-93. Hewlett Packard Europhysics Prize, 1979. Publications: 192 articles in science and engineering journals. Recreations: gardening; music; croquet; tennis. Address: (h.) 28 Muirfield Park, Gullane EH31 2DY; T.-01620 843006.

Collins, Kenneth Darlingston, BSc (Hons), MSc. Member (Labour), European Parliament, since 1979; b. 12.8.39, Hamilton; m., Georgina Frances Pollard; 1 s.; 1 d. Educ. St. John's Grammar School; Hamilton Academy; Glasgow University; Strathclyde University. Steelworks apprentice, 1956-59; University, 1960-65; Planning Officer, 1965-66; WEA Tutor, 1966-67; Lecturer: Glasgow College of Building, 1967-69, Paisley College of Technology, 1969-79; Member: East Kilbride Town and District Council, 1973-79, Lanark County Council, 1973-75, East Kilbride Development Corporation, 1976-79; Chairman, NE Glasgow Children's Panel, 1974-76; European Parliament: Deputy Leader, Labour Group, 1979-84, Chairman, Environment Committee, 1979-84 and since 1989 (Vice-Chairman, 1984-87), Socialist Spokesman on Environment, Public Health and Consumer Protection, 1984-89; Fellow, Royal Scottish Geographical Society; Hon. Fellow,

Chartered Institute of Water and Environment Management; Hon. Senior Research Fellow, Department of Geography, Lancaster University; Member, Advisory Committee, European Public Policy Institute, Warwick University; Director, Institute for European Environmental Policy, London; Fellow, Industry and Parliament Trust. Recreations: music; boxer dogs; cycling. Address: (b.) 11 Stuarton Park, East Kilbride G74 4LA; T.-013552 37282.

Collins, Kenneth E., MPhil, PhD, MRCGP. President, Glasgow Jewish Representative Council, since 1995 (formerly Vice-President); b. 23.12.47, Glasgow; m., Irene Taylor; 1 s.; 3 d. Educ. High School of Glasgow; Glasgow University. General medical practitioner in Glasgow, since 1976; Medical Officer, Newark Lodge, Glasgow, since 1978; Research Associate, Wellcome Unit for the History of Medicine, Glasgow University. Past Chairman, Glasgow Board of Jewish Education. Publications: Aspects of Scottish Jewry, 1987; Go and Learn: International Story of the Jews and Medicine in Scotland, 1988; Second City Jewry, 1990. Address: (h.) 3 Glenburn Road, Giffnock, Glasgow G46 6RE.

Colquhoun of Luss, Captain Sir Ivar (Iain), 8th Bt, JP, DL. Honorary Sheriff; Chief of the Clan; b. 4.1.16.

Coltart, George John Letham, CStJ, TD, MA, MSc, CEng, MICE; b. 2.2.29, Edinburgh; m., Inger Christina Larsson; 1 s.; 1 d. Educ. George Watson's College, Edinburgh; Royal Military Aademy, Sandhurst; King's College, Cambridge; Cornell University, USA. Commissioned, Royal Engineers, 1949; Captain, Adjutant, 23 Engineer Regiment, 1957-58; Staff College, Camberley, 1962; DAA & QMG 5 Bde, 1963-65; OC 51 Field Squadron, 1965-66; transferred to Reserve, 1966; Senior Lecturer in Civil Engineering, Heriot-Watt University, 1966-91 (Deputy Head of Department, 1987-90). Convener, Edinburgh and Heriot-Watt Universities Joint Military Education Committee, 1988-91; Commanding Officer, Edinburgh and Heriot-Watt UOTC, 1971-74; TA Colonel, Lowlands, 1975-80; Chairman, Lowland TAVRA, 1987-90; Priory Secretary, Most Venerable Order of St John of Jerusalem, 1991-96. Recreations: reserve forces; forestry; DIY. Address: Napier House, 8 Colinton Road, Edinburgh EH10 5DS; T.-0131-447 6314.

Coltrane, Robbie, DA. Actor/Director; b. 31.3.50, Glasgow. Educ. Trinity College, Glenalmond; Glasgow School of Art. Film credits: Subway Riders, 1979, Balham Gateway to the South, 1980, Britannia Hospital, 1981, Scrubbers, 1982, Krull, 1983, Ghost Dance, 1983, Chinese Boxes, 1984, The Supergrass, 1984, Defense of the Realm, 1985, Revolution, 1985, Caravaggio, 1985, Absolute Beginners, 1985, Mona Lisa, 1985, Eat the Rich, 1987, The Fruit Machine, 1987, Slipstream, 1988, Bert Rigby, You're a Fool, 1988, Danny Champion of the World, 1988, Let It Ride, 1988, Henry V, 1988, Nuns on the Run, 1989, Perfectly Normal, 1989, Pope Must Die, 1990, Oh What A Night, 1991, Adventures of Huck Finn, 1992, Goldeneye, 1995, Buddy, 1996, Montana, 1997, Frogs for Snakes, 1997; theatre credits: The Bug, 1976, Mr Joyce is Leaving, 1978, The Slab Boys, 1978, The Transfiguration of Benno Blimpie, 1978, The Loveliest Night of the Year, 1979-80, Dick Whittington, 1979, Snobs and Yobs, 1980, Yr Obedient Servant (one-man show), 1987, Mistero Buffo (one-man show), 1990; television credits include: roles in several The Comic Strip Presents productions, lead role in Tutti Frutti (BBC Scotland), Alive and Kicking, 1991, Coltrane in a Cadillac, 1992, Cracker, 1993, 1994, 1995, Ebbtide, 1996. Recreations: vintage cars; sailing; painting; reading; movies. Address: c/o CDA, 19 Sydney Mews, London SW3 6HL.

Colvin, David, CBE. Scottish Secretary, British Association of Social Workers, 1992-96; Scottish Chair, NCH Action for Children, 1992-97; Secretary, Action on Child Exploitation, since 1995; b. 31.1.31, Glasgow; m., Elma; 2 s.; 3 d. Educ. Whitehill School, Glasgow; Glasgow University; Edinburgh University. Probation Officer, Glasgow, 1955-60; Psychiatric Social Worker, Scottish Prison Service, 1960-61; Crichton Royal Hospital, Dumfries, 1961-65; Family Service Unit, Paisley, 1965-66; Adviser in Social Work, then Chief Adviser in Social Work, Scottish Office, 1966-91; Director of Social Work, Shetland, 1991. Former Chair, Dumfries Constituency Labour Party; former Chair, Scottish Marriage Council; Governor, National Institute for Social Work, 1981-91. Recreations: mountaineering; encouragement of fine arts. Address: (h.) The Studio, 53 Windsor Place, Edinburgh EH15 2AF; T.-0131-468 0087.

Comins, David, MA, PGCE. Rector, The Glasgow Academy, since 1994; b. 1.3.48, Scarborough; m., (Christine) Anne Speak; 1 s.; 2 d. Educ. Scarborough Boys' High School; Downing College, Cambridge. Assistant Maths Teacher: Mill Hill School, 1971-75, Strathallan School, 1975-76, Glenalmond College, 1976-80; Head of Maths, then Director of Studies, Glenalmond College, 1980-89; Deputy Head, Queen's College, Taunton, 1989-94. Winston Churchill Fellow, 1981. Recreations: mountaineering; ballet; crosswords; music. Address: (h.) 11 Kirklee Terrace, Glasgow G12 8HE; T.-0141-357 1776.

Comley, David John, BSc, PhD, FIH. Director of Housing, Glasgow City Council, since 1988; b. 25.4.50, Carshalton. Educ. Ashlyns School, Berkhamsted; Birmingham University. Housing Management Trainee, then District Housing Manager, Dudley Metropolitan Borough, 1976-80; District Housing Manager, then Assistant Director, then Depute Director, Glasgow City Council, since 1980. Adviser to COSLA, since 1988; Member, Hamish Allan Trust. Recreations: jazz; classical music; saxophone; hill-walking; literature; cinema; theatre. Address: (b.) Wheatley House, 25 Cochrane Street, Glasgow, G1 1HZ.

Conboy, William Morgan, MA (Oxon), FRSA. Principal, Newbattle Abbey College, since 1993; b. 8.5.31, Edinburgh; m., Irene; 1 s.; 1 d. Educ. Royal High School; Ruskin College and Jesus College, Oxford. Assistant Research Officer, Institute of Economics and Statistics, Oxford University, 1966-69; Staff Tutor, Economics and Industrial Relations, Oxford University, 1969-79; Vice Principal, Ruskin College, Oxford, 1979-94; Acting Principal, Newbattle Abbey College, 1990-93; National President, WEA, 1991-97. Recreations: choral singing; golf. Address: (h.) Principal's Flat, Newbattle Abbey College, Dalkeith EH22 3LL.

Conn, Stewart. Poet and playwright; b. 1936, Glasgow, brought up Kilmarnock. Educ. Glasgow University. Author of numerous stage plays, including The Burning, Herman, The Aquarium, By the Pool, Clay Bull; television work includes The Kite, Bloodhunt; recent poetry includes In the Kibble Palace, The Luncheon of the Boating Party, At the Aviary, In the Blood; his production of Carver (by John Purser) won Gold Medal Award, International Radio Festival, 1991; left BBC, 1992.

Connaghan, John Gerard, BA, DMS, MBA, FBIM. Chief Executive, Western General Hospital, Edinburgh, since 1994; b. 2.9.54, Glasgow; m., Evelyn Joyce; 3 s.; 1 d. Educ. Strathclyde University. General Manager, Charles Letts, Scotland, 1980-87; Chief Executive, Victoria Infirmary, Glasgow, 1987-94. Director, MKJCCT (charity). Recreations: hill-walking; fine wine. Address: (h.) Slieve View, Ruthven PH12 8RG; T.-01575 530242.

Connarty, Michael, BA, DCE. MP (Labour), Falkirk East, since 1992; PPS to Tom Clarke (Minister for Film and Tourism); Member, House of Commons Information Committee; Secretary, PLP Science and Technology Committee; Member, European Directives Committee (on

Agriculture, Environment and Health and Safety); Vice-Chairman, Scottish PLP Group; Vice-Chairman, APG on Chemical Industries; b. 3.9.47, Coatbridge; m., Margaret Mary; 1 s.; 1 d. Educ. Stirling University; Jordanhill College of Education; Glasgow University. Member, Scottish Executive, Labour Party, 1981-92; Chair, Labour Party Scottish Local Government Committee, 1988-90; Member: Convention of Scottish Local Authorities, 1980-90 (Depute Labour Leader, 1988-90), Stirling District Council, 1977-90 (Council Leader, 1980-90); Vice-Chair, Socialist Educational Association, 1983-85; Council Member, Educational Institute of Scotland, 1984-85; Founding Secretary, Labour Coordinating Committee (Scotland); Vice-Chairman, Scottish MAP, since 1988; Scottish Task Force Leader on Skills and Training in Scotland and Youth and Students, 1995-97; Member, Select Committee on the Parliamentary Commissioner for Administration, 1995-97; Chair, Economy, Industry and Energy Committee, Scottish PLP Group, 1993-97; Scottish Co-ordinator, Labour Crime and Drugs Campaign, 1993-97. Recreations: family; hill-walking; reading; music; Falkirk FC; Bo'ness United FC. Address: (b.) 47 Bo'ness Road, Grangemouth FK3 8AP; T.-01324 474832.

Connal, Robert Craig, LLB(Hons). Solicitor, since 1977; Partner, McGrigor Donald, since 1980; Solicitor Advocate, since 1996; b. 7.7.54, Brentwood; m., Mary Ferguson Bowie; 2 d. Educ. Hamilton Academy; University of Glasgow. Apprentice, Brown, Mair, Gemmill & Hislop, 1975-77; Assistant, McGrigor Donald, 1977-1980. Council Member, Royal Faculty of Procurators in Glasgow, since 1995; Member, Thorntonhall Community Council (Chairman, Planning Committee), since 1997. Publications: Contributor, Stair Memorial Encyclopedia; many articles. Recreations: rugby referee; gardens (but not gardening). Address: (b.) Pacific House, 70 Wellington Street, Glasgow G2 6SB; T.-0141-248 6677.

Connell, Anthony Anderson, LLB (Hons). Chief Executive, The Moray Council, since 1995; b. 27.7.53, Aberdeen; m., Sandra; 2 s.; 2 d. Educ. Robert Gordons College, Aberdeen; Aberdeen University. Grampian Regional Council: Principal Solicitor (Litigation), Assistant Director (Law and Administration), Depute Director (Law and Administration), Depute Chief Executive and Director of Administration. Group Leader (Public Administration), Aberdeen University. Recreations: reading; music; collecting; photography; politics as an observer. Address: (b.) Council Headquarters, High Street, Elgin IV30 1BX; T.-01343 543451.

Connell, Douglas Andrew, LLB, NP, WS, FRSA. Joint Senior Partner, Turcan Connell WS; Member: Scottish Arts Council, 1994-97, Edinburgh Festival Council, since 1997; Chairman, Lottery Committee, Scottish Arts Council, 1994-97; b. 18.5.54, Callander; m., Marjorie Elizabeth; 2 s. Educ. McLaren High School; Edinburgh University. Qualified as a solicitor, 1976; admitted as a Writer to the Signet, 1976; President, Scottish Young Lawyers Association, 1975-76; Tutor in Scots Law, Edinburgh University, 1974-76; Partner, Dundas and Wilson, 1979-92. Member, Revenue Committee, Law Society of Scotland, 1979-92; Trustee, Pushkin Prizes in Scotland; Member, Development Resource, Scottish Museums Council; Patron, National Galleries of Scotland; Fellow, Royal Society of Arts; Chairman, Edinburgh Book Festival, 1991-95. Recreations: books; travel; good food. Address: (b.) Saltire Court, 20 Castle Terrace, Edinburgh EH1 2EF; T.-0131-228 8111.

Connelly, David, MA (Oxon), FSAScot. Secretary, Buildings of Scotland Trust, since 1990; b. 23.2.30, Halifax; m., Audrey Grace Salter; 1 s.; 1 d. Educ. Heath Grammar School, Halifax; Queen's College, Oxford. Colonial Administrative Service, Tanganyika, 1954-62; Assistant Secretary, St. Andrews University, 1962-63; Principal, Commonwealth Relations Office, 1963-64; First

Secretary, British High Commission, New Delhi, 1964-66; Principal, Scottish Office, 1966-73; Assistant Secretary, 1973-87; Director, Historic Buildings and Monuments, Scotland, 1987-90; Chairman, Cockburn Conservation Trust, Edinburgh, 1990-96. Recreations: opera; literature; history; architecture; walking the hills; country life. Address: c/o Royal Bank of Scotland plc, 36 St. Andrew Square, Edinburgh EH2 2YB.

Connon, Joyce Blair. Scottish Secretary, Workers Educational Association, since 1992; b. 11.6.47, Edinburgh; m., Neil Connon; 1 s.; 1 d. W.E.A. Tutor Organiser, Lothian, 1988; District Secretary, South-East Scotland, 1989. Recreations: reading; theatre; walking. Address: (b.) W.E.A., Riddle's Court, 322 Lawnmarket, Edinburgh EH1 2PG; T.-0131-226 3456.

Connor, Professor James Michael, MD, DSc, BSc (Hons), MB, ChB (Hons), FRCP. Professor of Medical Genetics and Director, West of Scotland Regional Genetics Service, since 1987 (Wellcome Trust Senior Lecturer and Honorary Consultant in Medical Genetics, Glasgow University, 1984-87); b. 18.6.51, Grappenhall, England; m., Dr. Rachel A.C. Educ. Lymm Grammar School, Cheshire; Liverpool University. House Officer, Liverpool Royal Infirmary; Resident in Internal Medicine, Johns Hopkins Hospital, USA; University Research Fellow, Liverpool University; Instructor in Internal Medicine, Johns Hopkins Hospital, USA; Consultant in Medical Genetics, Duncan Guthrie Institute of Medical Genetics, Yorkhill, Glasgow. Publications: Essential Medical Genetics (Co-author), 1984 (5th edition, 1996); Principles and Practice of Medical Genetics (Co-Editor), (3rd edition, 1996); various articles on aspects of medical genetics. Recreation: windsurfing. Address: (h.) East Collarie Farm, by Fenwick, Ayrshire; T.-Fenwick 600790.

Considine, John, MA, MEd. Rector, Inverness Royal Academy, since 1993; President, Highland Secondary Headteachers Association, since 1997; b. 26.11.50, Glasgow; m., Hellen L. Campbell; 1 s.; 2 d. Educ. St. Aloysius College; Glasgow University. Teacher: St. Margaret Mary's, Glasgow, 1973, Inverness High, 1974, Millburn Academy, Inverness, 1976; Principal Teacher, then Assistant Rector, Charleston Academy, Inverness, 1978-88; Depute Rector, Woodmill High, Dunfermline, 1988-93. Member, Inverness College Board of Management, and Chair, College Personnel Sub-Committee. Recreations: hill-walking; running; squash. Address: (b.) Inverness Royal Academy, Culduthel Road, Inverness; T.-01463 222884.

Constable, Alan W., BSc (Hons), CertEd. Rector, Morgan Academy, Dundee, since 1987; b. 30.8.46, Blairgowrie; m., Irene M.; 2 s. Educ. Blairgowrie High School; Heriot Watt University, Edinburgh; Moray House College, Edinburgh. Design Engineer, 1970-71; Teacher/Principal Teacher/Assistant Headteacher, 1972-83; HMI Technology, Scottish Education Department, 1983-84; Depute Rector, Montrose Academy, 1984-86. Recreations: golf; hockey. Address: (b.) Morgan Academy, Forfar Road, Dundee DD4 7AY; T.-01382 438700.

Conti, Rt. Rev. Mario Joseph, STL, PhL, DD, FRSE. Bishop of Aberdeen, since 1977; Member, Pontifical Council for the Promotion of Christian Unity, Rome, since 1984; Member, International Commission for English in the Liturgy, 1978-87; b. 20.3.34, Elgin. Educ. St. Marie's Convent; Springfield School, Elgin; Blairs College, Aberdeen; Scots College, Pontifical Gregorian University, Rome. Ordained priest, Rome, 1958; Curate, St. Mary's Cathedral, Aberdeen, 1959-62; Parish Priest, St. Joachim's, Wick and St. Anne's, Thurso, 1962. Commendatore, Order of Merit, Italian Republic; President-Treasurer, SCIAF, 1977-85; President, National Liturgy Commission, 1978-86; Chairman, Scottish Catholic Heritage Commission;

President, Commission for Christian Doctrine and Unity, since 1986; first Convener, Central Council, ACTS, 1990; Co-Moderator, Joint Working Group of the World Council of Churches and the Roman Catholic Church, since 1996; Member, Pontifical Commission for the Cultural Heritage of the Church, since 1994; Knight Commander of the Holy Sepulchre, 1989; Conventual Chaplain Ad Honorem, Knights of Malta, 1991, Principal Chaplain to British Association of the Order, since 1995. Recreations: music; art. Address: Bishop's House, 3 Queen's Cross, Aberdeen AB15 4XU; T.-01224 319154.

Convery, Sheriff Daniel. Sheriff of Glasgow and Strathkelvin. Address: (b.) Sheriff Court House, 1 Carlton Place, Glasgow, G5 9DA.

Conway, Rt. Rev. Mgr. Michael Joseph, BA, MSc (Econ). Rector, Scotus College, since 1993; Prelate of Honour, since 1988; b. 5.3.40, Newry. Educ. St. Colman's College, Newry; St. Kieran's College, Kilkenny; University College, Dublin; London School of Economics. St. James's, Coatbridge, 1963-65; St. David's, Plains, Airdrie, 1965-66; St. Theresa's, Newarthill, 1966-69; St. Monica's, Coatbridge, 1975-77; Catholic Chaplain, Glasgow University, 1977-93. Recreations: golf; hill-walking; reading; listening to music. Address: (b.) Scotus College, 2 Chesters Road, Bearsden, Glasgow G61 4AG; T.-0141-942 8384.

Cook, Rev. James Stanley Stephen Ronald Tweedie, BD, DipPSS. Minister, Hamilton West Parish Church, since 1974; b. 18.8.35, Tullibody; m., Jean Douglas Maclachlan; 2 s.; 1 d. Educ. Whitehill Senior Secondary School, Glasgow; St. Andrews University. Apprentice quantity surveyor, Glasgow, 1953-54; regular soldier, REME, 1954-57; Assistant Preventive Officer, Waterguard Department, HM Customs and Excise, 1957-61; Officer, HM Customs and Excise, 1961-69; studied for the ministry, 1969-74. Chairman, Cruse Bereavement Care (Lanarkshire), 1983-93, since 1994; Chairman, Cruse — Scotland, 1992-96; Member, Council, Cruse UK, 1988-94; Member, National Training Group, Cruse, 1987-94; Member, Action Research for Crippled Child Committee, 1977-94; Substitute Provincial Grand Master, Lanarkshire (Middle Ward), 1983-88; Honorary Provincial Grand Chaplain, since 1989; founder Member, Wishaw Victim Support Scheme, 1985; Member, Hamilton Crime Prevention Panel, since 1976, Chairman, 1986-87; President, Hamilton Rotary Club, 1994-95. Recreations: music; photography; DIY; computer work. Address: West Manse, 43 Bothwell Road, Hamilton ML3 0BB; T.-Hamilton 458770.

Cook, Rt. Hon. Robin. MP (Labour), Livingston, since 1983 (Edinburgh Central, 1974-83); Foreign Secretary; b. 28.2.46. Formerly: Opposition Spokesman on Trade and Industry; Opposition Spokesman on Health and Social Security. Address: (b.) House of Commons, London, SW1A 0AA.

Cooke, Professor David John, BSc, MSc, PhD, CPsych, FBPsS. Professor of Forensic Psychology, Glasgow Caledonian University, since 1992; Head of Forensic Clinical Psychology, Greater Glasgow Community and Mental Health Services NHS Trust, since 1984; Glasgow University: Honorary Lecturer, since 1984, Honorary Senior Research Fellow, since 1989, Visiting Professor, since 1997; b. 13.7.52, Glasgow; m., Janet Ruth Salter; 2 d. Educ. Larbert High School; St. Andrews University; Newcastle-upon-Tyne University; Glasgow University. Clinical Psychologist, Gartnavel Royal Hospital, 1976-83; Cropwood Fellow, Institute of Criminology, Cambridge University, 1986. Recreations: sailing; opera; cooking. Address: (b.) Douglas Inch Centre, 2 Woodside Terrace, Glasgow G3 7UY; T.-0141-211 8016.

Cooke, Nicholas Huxley, MA (Oxon), FRSA. Director, The Scottish Conservation Projects Trust, since 1984; b.

6.5.44, Godalming, Surrey; m., Anne Landon; 2 s.; 3 d. Educ. Charterhouse School; Worcester College, Oxford. Retail management, London, 1967; chartered accountancy training, London, 1968-71; British International Paper, London, 1972-78; Director (Scotland), British Trust for Conservation Volunteers, 1978-84. Member: Policy Committee, Scottish Council for Voluntary Organisations; Chair, Youthlink Scotland Chief Officers; Chair, NTO Steering Group, SCVO; Member, Scottish Committee, European Year of the Environment, 1987-88. Recreations: fishing; walking; photography; outdoor conservation work. Address: (b.) Balallan House, 24 Allan Park, Stirling FK8 2QG; T.-01786 79697.

Cooke, Professor Timothy, MD, FRCS, MB, ChB. St. Mungo Professor of Surgery, Glasgow University, since 1989; Honorary Consultant Surgeon, Royal Infirmary, Glasgow; b. 16.9.47, Liverpool; m., Lynn; 1 s.; 1 d. Educ. Birkenhead Institute; Liverpool University. Surgical training, Liverpool University, 1973-79; Lecturer in Surgery, Southampton University, 1980-83; Senior Lecturer and Honorary Consultant Surgeon, Charing Cross & Westminster Medical School, 1983-86; Senior Lecturer and Honorary Consultant Surgeon, Liverpool University and Royal Liverpool and Broadgreen Hospitals, 1986-89. Hunterian Professor, Royal College of Surgeons of England. Publications: numerous scientific articles about cancer research. Recreations: playing wide range of indoor and outdoor sports; lifetime supporter, Liverpool FC. Address: (b.) University Department of Surgery, Royal Infirmary, Glasgow G31 2ER; T.-0141-211 4870.

Coombs, Professor Graham H., BSc, PhD, FRSE. Professor of Biochemical Parasitology, Glasgow University, since 1996; b. 22.9.47, Coventry; m., Isabel; 1 d. Educ. King Henry VIII School, Coventry; University College, London. Research Fellow, University of Kent, 1972-74; Lecturer, Department of Zoology, Glasgow University, 1974-86, Senior Lecturer, 1986-88, Reader, 1988-90, Professor, 1990-96, Head, Department of Zoology, 1991-94. Recreation: golf. Address: (b.) Infection and Immunity, Joseph Black Building, Glasgow University, Glasgow G12 8QQ; T.-0141-330 4777.

Cooper, Rev. David, BA, MPhil. Superintendent Minister, Edinburgh and Forth Circuit, since 1992; Secretary to Synod of Methodist Church in Scotland, since 1995; b. 6.11.49, Seaham; m., Veronica; 3 s.; 1 d. Educ. Bede Grammar School for Boys, Sunderland; University of Manchester; Hartley Victoria Methodist College. Minister: Morpeth Circuit, Newcastle District, 1977, Lerwick, North Roe and North Isles Circuit, Shetland District, 1980, Witney and Faringdon Circuit, Oxford and Leicester District, 1985. World Council of Churches Scholarship, University of Ghana, 1976-77. Recreation: music. Address: (b.) Central Hall, Tollcross, Edinburgh EH3 9BP; T.-0131-229 7937.

Cooper, Sheena M.M., MA. Rector, Aboyne Academy and Deeside Community Centre; b. 7.3.39, Bellshill. Educ. Dalziel High School, Motherwell; Glasgow University. Teacher of History, Dalziel High School, Motherwell, 1962-68; Lecturer in History, Elizabeth Gaskell College of Education, Manchester, 1968-70; Woman Adviser, then Assistant Rector, Montrose Academy, 1970-76; Rector, John Neilson High School, Paisley, 1976-83. Member: Council for Tertiary Education in Scotland, 1979-83, Scottish Examination Board, 1984-92, Scottish Vocational Education Council, 1985-88, Religious Advisory Council, BBC, 1980-91, Broadcasting Council for Scotland, 1991-96, Scottish Higher Education Funding Council, since 1995; President, Education Section, British Association for Advancement of Science, 1978-79. Recreations: walking; skiing. Address: (b.) Aboyne Academy and Deeside Community Centre, Aboyne; T.-01339 86222, Ext. 207.

Copland, Rt. Rev. Mgr. John Forbes. Prelate of Honour to His Holiness the Pope; Vicar General R.C. Diocese of Aberdeen, since 1979; Provost of Cathedral Chapter, since 1996; Parish Priest, St. Thomas', Keith, since 1974; b. 26.12.20, Glenlivet. Educ. Tombae R.C. School; Blairs College Junior Seminary; Gregorian University, Rome; St. Peter's, Glasgow; St Joseph's, London. Ordained Priest, 1946; Curate: St. Peter's, Aberdeen, 1946, St Mary's Cathedral, Aberdeen, 1948; Parish Priest: Church of Annuniciation, Portsoy, 1951, St Andrew's, Braemar, 1964, St Joseph's, Woodside, Aberdeen, 1968. Chairman, Portsoy Improvement Association, 1954-64; Group Scoutmaster, Portsoy, 1952-64; Area Chairman, O.A.P.'s Association, 1958-64, Member, Aberdeenshire Education Committee, 1964-74, Grampian Education Committee, 1974-86; Chairman and Founder Member, Braemar Mountain Rescue Association, 1965-66; Founder Member, Aberdeen Cyrenians, 1970; President, Keith Initiative, since 1990. Recreations: hill-walking; stone polishing; photography. Address: (h.) St. Thomas' Rectory, Chapel Street, Keith, Banffshire AB55 5AL; T.-01542 882352.

Coppock, Emeritus Professor John Terence, CBE, MA, PhD, FBA, FRSE. Secretary and Treasurer, Carnegie Trust for the Universities of Scotland, since 1986; Emeritus Professor of Geography, Edinburgh University; b. 2.6.21, Cardiff; m., Sheila Mary Burnett (deceased); 1 s.; 1 d. Educ. Penarth County School; Queens' College, Cambridge. Civil Servant, 1938-47 (Lord Chancellor's Department, Ministry of Works, Customs and Excise); War Service, Army, 1939-46 (Commissioned, 1941); Departmental Demonstrator, Department of Geography, Cambridge University, 1949-50; University College, London: Assistant Lecturer, 1950-52, Lecturer, 1952-64, Reader, 1964-65; Ogilvie Professor of Geography, Edinburgh University, 1965-86. Institute of British Geographers: Vice-President, 1971-73, President, 1973-74; Vice-President: Royal Scottish Geographical Society, since 1975, British Academy, 1985-87. Recreations: walking; natural history; listening to music. Address: (b.) Carnegie Trust for the Universities of Scotland, Cameron House, Abbey Park Place, Dunfermline KY12 7PZ; T.-01383 622148.

Corcoran, Professor Cornelius David, MA, MLitt(Oxon). Professor of English, University of St. Andrews, since 1996; b. 23.9.48, Cork; m., Gillian Anne Jeffs; 2 s. Educ. Austin Friars, Carlisle; St. Edmund Hall, Oxford; Wolfson College, University of Oxford. Lecturer, then Senior Lecturer in English, University of Sheffield; Professor, University of Wales, Swansea. Publications: Seamus Heaney, 1986; English Poetry since 1940, 1993; After Yeats and Joyce, 1997. Address: University of St. Andrews, St. Andrews KY16 9AJ.

Cormack, John James Callender, MD, FRCPE, FRCGP. General Medical Practitioner; Apothecary to HM Household at the Palace of Holyroodhouse, since 1991; Chairman, Corstorphine Trust, since 1995; b. 21.2.34, Edinburgh; m., Joy Mackenzie Gourlay; 1 s.; 2 d. Educ. Edinburgh Academy; Edinburgh University. House Officer, Grenfell Mission, Canada, 1960-61; Medical Officer, CCAP Mission Hospital, Nyasaland, 1961-62; Principal in general practice, Corstorphine, since 1964; part-time Lecturer, Department of General Practice, Edinburgh University, 1966-76; Member, Panel of Examiners, Royal College of General Practitioners, 1971-82. Elder (former Joint Session Clerk), Corstorphine Old Parish Church; Hon. Librarian and Trustee, Royal Medical Society. Publications: Practice – Clinical Management in General Practice (Co-editor); Teaching General Practice (Co-editor). Recreations: cycling; walking; painting; Scottish history. Address: (b.) Ladywell Medical Centre, Ladywell Road, Edinburgh EH12 7TB; T.-0131-334 3602.

Corner, David John, BA (Oxon), FRHS. Secretary, St. Andrews University, since 1991; Honorary Lecturer, Department of Mediaeval History, St. Andrews University, since 1991; b. 24.10.47, Birmingham; m., Carol Ann; 2 s. Educ. King Edward VI Grammar School, Aston, Birmingham; Worcester College, Oxford. Prize Fellow, Magdalen College, Oxford, 1972-75; Lecturer, Department of Mediaeval History, St. Andrews University, 1975-91. Governor, Newbattle Abbey College, since 1991; President, St. Andrews Association of University Teachers, 1985-88. Recreations: cinema; sport. Address: St. Andrews University, College Gate, North Street, St. Andrews KY16 9AJ; T.-01334 462549.

Cornish, Melvyn David, BSc, PGCE. Deputy Secretary, Edinburgh University, since 1991; b. 29.6.48, Leighton Buzzard; m., Eileen Joyce Easterbrook; 1 s.; 1 d. Educ. Cedars Grammar School, Leighton Buzzard; Leicester University. Chemistry Teacher, Jamaica and Cumbria, 1970-73; Administrator, Leicester Polytechnic, 1973-78; Senior Administrative Officer, Assistant Secretary, Director of Planning, Edinburgh University, 1978-91. Recreations: walking; photography; travel; family. Address: (b.) Old College, South Bridge, Edinburgh; T.-0131-650 2136.

Cornwell, Professor John Francis, PhD, BSc, DIC, ARCS, FRSE. Professor of Theoretical Physics, St. Andrews University, since 1979 (Chairman, Physics Department, 1984-85); b. 28.1.37, London; m., Elizabeth Margaret Burfitt; 2 d. Educ. Ealing Grammar School; Imperial College, London. Lecturer in Applied Mathematics, Leeds University, 1961-67; St. Andrews University: Lecturer in Theoretical Physics, 1967-73, Reader, 1973-79. Publications: Group Theory in Physics, three volumes, 1984, 1989; Group Theory and Electronic Energy Bands in Solids, 1969. Recreations: sailing; hill-walking; tennis; badminton; golf. Address: (b.) Department of Physics and Astronomy, St. Andrews University, North Haugh, St. Andrews, Fife KY16 9SS; T.-01334 476161.

Cornwell, Professor Keith, BSc, PhD, DEng, FIMechE. Professor, Department of Mechanical and Chemical Engineering and Director of Quality, Heriot-Watt University; b. 4.4.42, Abingdon; m., Sheila Joan Mott; 1 s.; 1 d. Educ. City University, London. Research Fellow, then Lecturer, Middlesex Polytechnic; Lecturer, Head of Department, Dean of Engineering, Heriot-Watt University. Secretary, UK Committee on Heat Transfer. Publications: The Flow of Heat; numerous journal papers. Recreations: classic cars; hillwalking. Address: (h.) Strathview, Templar Place, Gullane EH39 2AH.

Corrie, John Alexander. Member (Conservative), European Parliament for Worcestershire and South Warwickshire, since 1994; Chairman, Backbench (1979) Committee of Conservatives in Europe; farms family farm in Galloway; Council Member, Royal Agricultural Society of England, since 1992; b. 1935; m.; 1 s.; 2 d. Educ. Kirkcudbright Academy; George Watson's College, Edinburgh; Lincoln Agricultural College, New Zealand. Nuffield Farming Scholar, 1972; National Chairman, Scottish Young Conservatives, 1964; MP (Conservative): Bute and North Ayrshire, 1974-83, Cunninghame North, 1983-87; PPS to Secretary of State for Scotland, 1979-81; introduced Private Member's Bill to reduce upper limit on abortion, 1979; Member: European Assembly, 1975-76 and 1977-79, Council of Europe, 1983-87, Western European Union (Defence Committee), 1983-87; Senior Instructor, British Wool Board, Agricultural Training Board, 1970-74; elected to Council, Belted Galloway Cattle Society, 1978; Chairman, Scottish Transport Users Consultative Committee, 1988-94; Vice Chairman, Central Transport Consultative Committee, 1988-94; Industrial Fellowship with Conoco and Du Pont, USA, 1987; awarded Wilberforce Plaque for Humane Work, 1981. Publications: Forestry in Europe; Fish Farming in Europe; The Importance of Forestry in the World Today; Towards a

Community Rural Policy (Co-author). Address: (h.) Park of Tongland, Kirkcudbright DG6 4NE.

Corsar, Charles Herbert Kenneth, LVO, OBE, TD, JP, DL, MA. Farmer, since 1953; Secretary for Scotland, Duke of Edinburgh's Award, 1966-87; b. 13.5.26, Edinburgh; m., The Honourable Dame Mary Corsar, DBE, FRSE (qv) ; 2 s.; 2 d. Educ. Merchiston Castle; King's College, Cambridge. Commissioned, The Royal Scots TA, 1948; commanded 8/9 Bn.,The Royal Scots TA, 1964-67; Edinburgh and Heriot-Watt Universities OTC, 1967-72; TA Colonel, 1972-75; Hon. ADC to The Queen, 1977-81; Honorary Colonel, 1/52 Lowland Volunteers, 1975-87; Chairman, Lowland TA and VR Association, 1984-87; Zone Commissioner, Home Defence, East of Scotland; County Councillor, Midlothian, 1958-67; Deputy-Lieutenant, Midlothian; Vice President, Edinburgh Bn., 1970-91 and President, Edinburgh Bn., Boys Brigade, 1969-87 (Hon. President, Edinburgh Bn., since 1987); Chairman, Scottish Standing Conference of Voluntary Youth Organisations, 1973-78; Governor: Merchiston Castle School, Clifton Hall School; Chairman: Wellington List D School, 1978-84, Earl Haig Fund Scotland, 1984-90; Secretary, Royal Jubilee and Princes' Trusts (Lothian and Borders); Member, Scottish Sports Council, 1972-75; Elder, Church of Scotland, since 1956. Recreations: gardening; bee-keeping; shooting. Address: (h.) Burg, Torloisk, Ulva Ferry, Isle of Mull PA74 6NH; T.-01688 500289; 11 Ainslie Place, Edinburgh EH3 6AS; T.-0131-225 6318.

Corsar, Kenneth, MA (Hons), MEd (Hons), FRSA. Director of Education, Glasgow City Council, since 1995; b. 16.7.46, Clackmannan; m., Mary Massie; 2 s. Educ. Alloa Academy; St. Andrews University; Glasgow University. Teacher, Principal Teacher of Classics, 1970-75; Education Officer, Senior Education Officer, Divisional Education Officer, Strathclyde Regional Council, 1975-90; Divisional Education Officer, Depute Director of Education, Strathclyde Regional Council, 1990-95. Vice-President, Association of Directors of Education in Scotland, 1992-93, President, 1993-94. Recreations: golf; calligraphy. Address: (b.) India Street, Glasgow; T.-0141-287 6710; (h.) 9 Eaglesfield Crescent, Strathaven, Lanarkshire; T.-01357 520817.

Corsar, The Hon. Dame Mary Drummond, DBE (1993), FRSE, MA; b. 8.7.27, Edinburgh; m., Colonel Charles H.K. Corsar (qv); 2 s.; 2 d. Educ. Westbourne, Glasgow; St. Denis, Edinburgh; Edinburgh University. Chairman, Women's Royal Voluntary Service, 1988-93; Chairman, Scotland, WRVS, 1981-88; Midlothian Girl Guides: Secretary, 1951-66; County Commissioner, 1966-72; Deputy Chief Commissioner, Girl Guides Scotland, 1972-77; Member: Parole Board for Scotland, 1982-89; Executive Committee, Trefoil Centre, since 1975; Visiting Committee, Glenochil Detention Centre, 1976-94; Management Committee, Church of Scotland Youth Centre, Carberry, 1976-82; Governor, Fettes College; Member of Convocation, Heriot Watt University; Chairman, TSB Foundation for Scotland, 1994-95. Recreation: hill-walking. Address: (h.) Burg, Torloisk, Ulva Ferry, Isle of Mull PA74 6NH; T.-0168 8500289.

Cosgrove, Hon. Lady (Hazel Josephine Aronson), QC, LLB, LLD. Senator of the College of Justice in Scotland, since 1996; b. 12.1.46, Glasgow; m., John A. Cosgrove; 1 s.; 1 d. Educ. Glasgow High School for Girls; Glasgow University. Advocate at Scottish Bar, 1968-79; Sheriff: Glasgow and Strathkelvin at Glasgow, 1979-83, Lothian and Borders at Edinburgh, 1983-96; Temporary Judge, Court of Session and High Court, 1992-96; Past Chairman, Mental Welfare Commission for Scotland. Recreations: swimming; walking; opera; foreign travel. Address: (b.) Parliament House, Edinburgh EH1 1RQ; T.-0131-225 2595.

Costley, William James McCreadie. Owner: Costley and Costley Hoteliers Limited, Airclose Limited; Chairman, Kilmarnock Football Club, since 1997; b. 1.5.52, Dumfries; m., Catherine; 2 s. Educ. Prestwick Public School; Prestwick Academy; Ayr College. Trainee Chef, Turnberry Hotel; Head Chef: Caledonian Hotel, Ayr, Chapeltoun House Hotel, Stewarton; Executive Chef, Hospitality Inn, Irvine; Costley & Costley Hoteliers Limited: bought Highgrove House Hotel, 1988, Lochgreen House, 1990, Cochrane Inn, Gatehead, Brig O'Doon House, Alloway, 1996-97. Recreations: food; eating out; football. Address: Lochgreen Courtyard, Monktonhill Road, Troon KA10 7EN; T.-01292 313343.

Cotter, Elizabeth Faith, LLB. Solicitor; Partner, Stewarts and Murdochs, since 1997; b. 11.9.43, Motherwell; m., James Logan Millar Cotter; 2 s.; 1 d. Educ. Westbourne School; Glasgow University. Stewarts Nicol McCormick, 1966-68; Motherwell and Wishaw District Council, 1968-69; Director, Motherwell Times Ltd., 1966-84; Partner, Bellshill Speaker, 1966-84; Partner, Stewarts Nicol D. & J. Hill, 1984-97. Part-time Commissioner, Mental Welfare Commission for Scotland. Recreations: reading; gardening; fishing; antiques. Address: (b.) 1 Royal Bank Place, Buchanan Street, Glasgow G1 3AA; T.-0141-248 8810.

Coulsfield, Hon. Lord (John Taylor Cameron), QC, BA, LLB. Senator of the College of Justice, since 1987; b. 24.4.34, Dundee; m., Bridget Deirdre Sloan. Educ. Fettes College; Corpus Christi College, Oxford; Edinburgh University. Admitted to Faculty of Advocates, 1960; Queen's Counsel, 1973; Lecturer in Public Law, Edinburgh University, 1960-64; Advocate Depute, 1977-80; Keeper of the Advocates Library, 1977-87; Chairman, Medical Appeal Tribunals, 1985-87; Judge of the Appeal Courts of Jersey and Guernsey, 1986-87; Scottish Judge, Employment Appeal Tribunal, 1992-96.

Coulthard, William George, LLB. Solicitor, since 1971; Honorary Sheriff, since 1988; b. 13.3.48, Whitehaven; m., Fiona Jane McQueen; 1 s.; 2 d. Educ. Glasgow Academy; Glasgow University. Partner in legal firm, since 1974; Dean, Faculty of Procurators, Stewartry of Kirkcudbright, 1986-88; Chairman, Castle Douglas High School Board, 1990-94; President, Castle Douglas Rotary Club, 1995. Recreations: golf; swimming; hill-running. Address: (h.) Netherby, Castle Douglas DG7 1BA; T.-01556 502965.

Courtney, Professor James McNiven, BSc, PhD, Dr sc nat, ARCST, EurChem, CChem, FRSC, FIM. Professor, Bioengineering Unit, Strathclyde University, since 1989 (Reader, 1986-89, Senior Lecturer, 1981-86); Tenured Professor, International Faculty for Artificial Organs, since 1992; Secretary/Treasurer, International Society for Artificial Organs, since 1994; b. 25.3.40, Glasgow; m., Ellen Miller Courtney; 2 s.; 1 d. Educ. Whitehill Senior Secondary School; Royal College of Science and Technology; Strathclyde University. Rubber technologist: MacLellan Rubber Ltd., Glasgow, 1962-65, Uniroyal Ltd., Dumfries, 1965-66; Lecturer, Bioengineering Unit, Strathclyde University, 1969-81. Recreation: football supporter (Glasgow Rangers). Address: (b.) Strathclyde University, Bioengineering Unit, 106 Rottenrow, Glasgow; T.-0141-548 3349.

Cousin, (David) Alastair (Henry), BVMS, MRCVS, DBR, JP. Senior Partner, veterinary practice, Kintyre, since 1972; Honorary Sheriff, Campbeltown Sheriff Court, since 1990; b. 19.4.44, Kincardine on Forth; m., Anne Macleod; 1 s.; 1 d. Educ. Balfron High School; Glasgow University; Liverpool University. Veterinary practice, Campbeltown: Veterinary Assistant, 1966, Junior Partner, 1972, Senior Partner, 1982. Former Commodore, Campbeltown Sailing Club, 1995. Recreations: sailing; shooting; gardening; music. Address: (h.) Southpark, Kilkerran Road, Campbeltown; T.-01586 553108.

Coutts, Rev. Fred, MA, BD. Hospital Chaplain, Aberdeen Royal Hospitals NHS Trust; b. 13.1.47, Forfar; m., Mary Lawson Fraser Gill; 2 s.; 1 d. Educ. Brechin High School; Dollar Academy; St. Andrews University; Edinburgh University. Assistant Minister, Linwood Parish Church, 1972-74; Minister: Buckie North, 1974-84, Mastrick, Aberdeen, 1984-89. Chairman: Buckie Community Council, 1981-83, Moray Firth Community Radio Association, 1982-83. Recreations: music; photography; computing. Address: 9A Millburn Street, Aberdeen, AB11 6SS; T.-01224 583805.

Coutts, Herbert, SBStJ, AMA, FMA, FSAScot. City Curator, Edinburgh City Museums and Art Galleries, since 1973; b. 9.3.44, Dundee; m., Angela E.M. Smith; 1 s.; 3 d. Educ. Morgan Academy, Dundee. Assistant Keeper of Antiquities and Bygones, Dundee City Museums, 1965-68; Keeper, 1968-71; Superintendent, Edinburgh City Museums, 1971-73; Vice-President, Museum Assistants Group, 1969-70; Member: Government Committee on future of Scotland's National Museums and Galleries, 1979-80; Council, Museums Association, 1977-78, 1987-88; Council, Society of Antiquaries of Scotland, 1981-82; Board, Scottish Museums Council, 1985-88; Museums Adviser, COSLA, 1985-90; Member, Paxton House Trust, since 1988; Member, East Lothian Community Development Trust, since 1989; External Examiner, St. Andrews University, since 1994. Member, Board, Museums Training Institute, since 1995; Contested Angus South (Lab), 1970. Publications: Ancient Monuments of Tayside; Tayside Before History; Edinburgh: an illustrated history; Huntly House; Lady Stair's House; The Pharaoh's Gold Mask; Gold of the Pharaohs (Editor); Dinosaurs Alive! (Editor); Sweat of the Sun — Gold of Peru (Editor); Golden Warriors of the Ukrainian Steppes (Editor); StarTrek – the exhibition (Editor); Quest for a Pirate (Editor); Gateway to the Silk Road – Relics from the Han to the Tang Dynasties from Xi'an, China (Editor); Faster, Higher, Stronger – The Story of the Olympic Movement (Editor). Recreations: family; gardening; opera; writing; reading; walking. Address: (h.) Kirkhill House, Queen's Road, Dunbar EH42 1LN; T.-01368 63113.

Coutts, John R.T., BSc, PhD. Reader in Biochemistry, IBLS, Glasgow University, since 1996; b. 10.7.41, Dundee; m., Marjory R.B.; 1 s.; 2 d. Educ. Morgan Academy, Dundee; St. Andrews University. Dundee University: Research Fellow in Obstetrics and Gynaecology, 1966-69, Honorary Lecturer in Obstetrics and Gynaecology, 1969-70; Lecturer, then Senior Lecturer, Glasgow University, 1970-87; Reader, Reproductive Medicine, Glasgow University, 1987-96. Publications: The Functional Morphology of the Human Ovary (Editor); many journal articles. Recreation: bowling. Address: (h.) 7 Spence Street, Glasgow G20 0AW; T.-0141-579 6553.

Coutts, T(homas) Gordon, MA, LLB, QC, FCIArb. Queen's Counsel, since 1973; b. 5.7.33, Aberdeen; m., Winifred K. Scott; 1 s.; 1 d. Educ. Aberdeen Grammar School; Aberdeen University. Advocate, 1959; Chairman, Industrial Tribunals, 1972; Chairman, Medical Appeal Tribunals, 1984; Chairman, VAT Tribunals, 1990; Temporary Judge, Court of Session, 1991; Member, Panel of Arbitrators, CIArb, 1995. Recreations: travel; stamp collecting. Address: (h.) 6 Heriot Row, Edinburgh.

Cowan, Sheriff Annella M., LLB, MSc. Floating Sheriff based at Aberdeen. Address: (b.) Sheriff Court House, Castle Street, Aberdeen AB9 1AP.

Cowan, Brigadier Colin Hunter, CBE, MA, FRSA, CEng, MICE. Chief Executive, Cumbernauld Development Corporation, 1970-85; b. 16.10.20, Edinburgh; m., 1, Elizabeth Williamson (deceased); 1 s.; 1 d.; m., 2, Mrs Janet Burnett. Educ. Wellington College; Trinity College, Cambridge. Commissioned, Royal Engineers, 1940; service in India and Burma, Royal Bombay Sappers and Miners, 1942-46; staff and regimental appointments, UK and Malta, 1951-60; commanded Field Engineer Regiment, Germany, 1960-63; Defence Adviser, UK Mission to UNO, New York, 1964-66; Chief Staff Officer to Engineer-in-Chief (Army), Ministry of Defence, 1966-68; Brigadier, Engineer Plans (Army), Ministry of Defence, 1968-70. Recreations: hill-walking; photography; music. Address: (h.) 12B Greenhill Gardens, Edinburgh, EH10 4BW; T.-0131-447 9768.

Cowan, David Lockhart, MB, ChB, FRCSEdin. Consultant Otolaryngologist, City Hospital, Royal Hospital for Sick Children and Western General Hospital, Edinburgh, since 1974; Honorary Senior Lecturer, Edinburgh University; b. 30.6.41, Edinburgh; m., Eileen M. Masterton; 3 s.; 1 d. Educ. George Watson's College, Edinburgh; Trinity College, Glenalmond; Edinburgh University. Scottish Representative, Council, British Association of Otolaryngologists. Publications: Logan Turner's Diseases of the Ear, Nose and Throat (Co-author); Paediatric Otolaryngology (Co-author). Recreations: golf; all sport. Address: (h.) Kellerstane House, Gogar Station Road, Edinburgh EH12 9BS; T.-0131-339 0293.

Cowan, Professor Edward James, MA. Professor of Scottish History, Glasgow University, since 1993; b. 5.2.44, Edinburgh; widower; 1 s.; 2 d. Educ. Dumfries Academy; Edinburgh University. Lecturer in Scottish History, Edinburgh University, 1967-79; Professor of History and Chair of Scottish Studies, University of Guelph, Ontario, 1979-93. Recreations: hill-walking; Scottish folk music. Address: (b.) 9 University Gardens, Glasgow G12 8QH.

Cowan, Rev. Gordon Leith. Former Moderator, United Free Church of Scotland; Minister, Leith: Ebenezer UF Church of Scotland, since 1987; part-time Chaplain, Eastern General Hospital, Edinburgh, since 1994; b. 2.8.39, Glasgow; m., Agnes Allan Copeland; 2 s.; 2 d. Educ. Whitehill Senior Secondary School, Glasgow; Glasgow University; UF Congregational College, Edinburgh. Former Apprentice CA and book-keeper; Minister: Cumnock St. Andrews UF Church, 1968-76, Glasgow Wynd, 1976-87. Children's Panel Member, 1972-87. Recreations: genealogy; Scotland; watching athletics. Address: (h.) 14 Wardie Crescent, Edinburgh EH5 1AG; T.-0131-552 2349.

Cowan, Lt. Col. John Mervyn, TD, MCIBS. Chairman: Earl Haig Fund (Scotland), since 1993, Royal Artillery Association Scottish Region, since 1991; b. 13.2.30, Oban; m., Marion Neilson Kidd; 1 s.; 2 d. Educ. Oban High School. National Bank of Scotland, National Commercial Bank of Scotland, Royal Bank of Scotland, 1946-90 (retired); TA commission, 1963; commanded 207 (Scottish) Battery RA(V), 1980-82; J.S.L.O., HQ Scotland, 1982-90; Member, RA Council for Scotland. Recreations: travel; charitable works; sport. Address: (h.) 43 Hunter Grove, Bathgate EH48 1NN; T.-01506 655784.

Cowan, Margaret Morton (Lady Cowan), MA, JP. Member, Executive Committee and Council, National Trust for Scotland; Member, Scottish Committee, British Council, since 1991; b. 4.11.33, Newmilns; m., Sir Robert Cowan; 2 d. Educ. St. George's School for Girls, Edinburgh; Edinburgh University. British Petroleum Company, 1955-59; Teacher, West Midlands Education Authority, 1965-76; Consultant and Lecturer in Use of Language, Hong Kong, 1976-81; Convener, The Highland Festival, since 1992; Member, Justice of the Peace Committee, Inverness, since 1985. Address: (h.) The Old Manse, Farr, Inverness-shire IV1 2XA; T.-01808 521209.

Cowe, Alan Wilson, MA, LLB. Secretary and Clerk, Church of Scotland General Trustees, since 1964; b. 9.8.38, Kelso; m., Agnes Cunningham Dick. Educ. Dunfermline High School; Edinburgh University. Law apprentice,

Simpson Kinmont & Maxwell, WS, Edinburgh; Assistant to Secretary, Church of Scotland General Trustees, 1963-64. Recreations: long-distance running; hill-walking. Address: (b.) 121 George Street, Edinburgh EH2 4YR; T.-0131-225 5722.

Cowe, Andrew. Chief Executive, North Lanarkshire Council. Address: (b.) PO Box 14, Civic Centre, Motherwell, ML1 1TW.

Cowie, Professor John McKenzie Grant, BSc, PhD, DSc, CChem, FRSC, FRSE. Professor of Chemistry of Materials, Heriot-Watt University, since 1988; Chairman, British High Polymer Research Group, since 1990; Chairman, Macro Group UK, since 1995; b. 31.5.33, Edinburgh; m., Agnes Neilson Campbell; 1 s.; 1 d. Educ. Royal High School, Edinburgh; Edinburgh University. Assistant Lecturer, Edinburgh University, 1956-58; Research Officer, National Research Council of Canada, Ottawa, 1958-67; Lecturer, Essex University, 1967-69; Senior Lecturer, Stirling University, 1969-73; Professor of Chemistry, Stirling University, 1973-88. Staff Assessor, Bangladesh Agricultural College; Chairman, Scottish Spinal Cord Injury Association, 1991-94; Hon. President, Scottish Council on Disability (Stirling District); Vice Chairman, Scottish Council on Disability, 1989-90; Hon. President, Stirling Association of Voluntary Services. Recreations: reading; painting; listening to music. Address: (h.) Traquair, 50 Back Road, Dollar, Clackmannanshire; T.-Dollar 742031.

Cowie, Julian Martin, BA, CPFA, ACIS, IRRV. Director for Corporate Finance, Dumfries and Galloway Council, since 1995; b. 5.1.52, Castlerea, Eire; m., Anne Marie; 2 s.; 1 d. Educ. St. Joseph's College, Dumfries; Heriot-Watt University. Trainee Accountant, Midlothian CC, 1973-74; Assistant Accountant, Lothian Health Board, 1974-76; Accountant, Lothian RC, 1976-77; Senior Accountant, Fife RC, 1977-79; Chief Accountant, Dumfries and Galloway RC, 1979-85; Depute Director of Finance, Nithsdale District Council, 1985-92; Director of Financial Services, Annandale and Eskdale District Council, 1992-95. Address: (b.) Council Offices, English Street, Dumfries DG1 2DD; T.-01387 260000.

Cowie, Hon. Lord (William Lorn Kerr Cowie), MA (Cantab), LLB (Glas). Senator of the College of Justice in Scotland, 1977-94; Botswana Court of Appeal, 1995-98; b. 1.6.26, Glasgow; m., Camilla Henrietta Grizel Hoyle; 2 s.; 2 d. Educ. Fettes College, Edinburgh; Clare College, Cambridge; Glasgow University. RNVR, 1944-47 (Sub. Lt.); Member, Faculty of Advocates, 1952; QC, 1967. Scottish rugby internationalist, 1953. Recreation: fishing. Address: (h.) 20 Blacket Place, Edinburgh; T.-0131-667 8238.

Cowley of Innerwick, Col. Victor Charles Vereker, TD, JP, DL. Land Owner and Farmer; b. 4.4.18, Glasgow; m., Moyra McClure; 1 s.; 2 d. Educ. St. Mary's, Melrose; Merchiston Castle School. Young master printer, 1937; commissioned, RATA, 1939; served France, North Africa, Sicily, Italy, Burma, Indo China; Col. Depute CRA 51st Highland Division; Chairman, Brownlie Scandrett and Graham Ltd. (retired 1960); Vice Convener, East Lothian County Council, 1973; Regional Councillor, Lothian, 1975; Commissioner of Income Tax, East Lothian, 1965-87. Recreations: shooting; golf. Address: Crowhill, Innerwick, Dunbar EH42 1QT; T.-01368 840279.

Cox, Gilbert Kirkwood, MBE, DL, JP. General Manager Scotland, Associated Perforators & Weavers Ltd., since 1971; Director/Trustee, Airdrie Savings Bank, since 1987 (President, 1996); b. 24.8.35, Chapelhall, Airdrie; m., Marjory Moir Ross Taylor; 2 s.; 1 d. Educ. Airdrie Academy. National Coal Board, 1953-63; David A. McPhail & Sons Ltd., 1963-68; D.A. Monteith Holdings,

1968-71. Deputy Lieutenant, Lanarkshire; founder Member and Past President, Monklands Rotary Club; Member, Scottish Kidney Research Fund. Recreations: golf; gardening; walking. Address: (h.) Bedford House, Commonhead Street, Airdrie ML6 6NS; T.-01236 763331.

Cox, Sheriff Principal Graham Loudon, QC, MA, LLB. Sheriff Principal of South Strathclyde Dumfries and Galloway, since 1993; b. 22.12.33, Newcastle-upon-Tyne; m., Jean Nelson; 3 c. by pr. m. Educ. Hamilton Academy; Grove Academy; Edinburgh University. Army 1956-61 (latterly Major, Directorate of Army Legal Services); called to the Bar, 1962; Advocate-Depute, 1966-68; Sheriff of Tayside Central and Fife, at Dundee, 1968-93; QC, 1993; Secretary, Sheriffs' Association, 1987-91, President, 1991-93; Honorary Vice-President, Scottish Association for the Study of Delinquency, since 1996; Vice-Chairman, Northern Lighthouse Board, since 1997. Recreations: skiing; golf; restoration of decaying property. Address: (h.) Crail House, Crail, Fife; T.-01333 450270.

Cox, Richard Anthony Victor, MA, PhD. Lecturer in Celtic Studies, Aberdeen University, since 1996; Secretary, Scottish Gaelic Texts Society, since 1996; b. 31.5.54, Croydon. Educ. Rugby School; Cambridge Tutors (Croydon); Glasgow University. Editorial Assistant, Historical Dictionary of Scottish Gaelic, Glasgow University, 1985-91; Honorary Lecturer, Department of Gaelic, Glasgow University, 1982-91, 1995-96; Writer/Researcher, 1991-95. Publications: Brigh nam Facal – Faclair Ur don Bhun-sgoil (dictionary); articles in academic journals. Address: (b.) Department of Celtic, Taylor Building, Aberdeen University, Aberdeen AB24 3UB; T.-01224 272544.

Cox, Roy Frederick. Managing Director, A. Richardson & Son Ltd., since 1983; Chairman, Sense Scotland, since 1992; b. 4.11.49, Leicester; m., Elizabeth; 2 s.; 2 d. Educ. New Parks Boys' School; Leicester Polytechnic College. Engineering apprentice; hosiery mechanic; builder. Past President, Rotary Club of Clydebank. Recreations: golf; skiing; football. Address: (b.) 34 Old Mill Road, Duntocher, Clydebank G81 6BX; T.-01389 872436.

Craig, Emeritus Professor Gordon Younger, BSc, PhD, CGeol, FRSE. Emeritus Professor of Geology, Edinburgh University, since 1984; Trustee, Dynamic Earth Charitable Trust, since 1995; b. 17.1.25, Milngavie; m., Mary Thornton; 2 s.; 2 step s.; 1 step d. Educ. Hillhead High School; Bearsden Academy; Glasgow University; Edinburgh University. Joined Edinburgh University as Lecturer, 1947; James Hutton Professor of Geology, 1967-84; Visiting Professor, University of Colorado, 1958-59, UCLA, 1959, 1965; Leverhulme Fellow, ANU, Canberra, 1978; Distinguished Foreign Scholar, Mid-America State Universities, 1980; Green Professor, University of British Columbia, 1977, Texas Christian University, 1994; President: Edinburgh Geological Society, 1967-69, International Commission on the History of the Geological Sciences, 1984-89; Clough Medal, Edinburgh Geological Society, 1987; History of Geology Division Award, Geological Society of America, 1990. Publications: Geology of Scotland (Editor), 1991 (3rd ed.); James Hutton: The Lost Drawings (Co-author), 1977; A Geological Miscellany (Co-author), 1982. Recreations: golf; gardening. Address: (h.) 14 Kevock Road, Lasswade, Edinburgh EH18 1HT; T.-0131-663 8275.

Craig, James Loudon, BA, ALA. Director, Community and Leisure Services, Falkirk Council, since 1995; b. 5.2.46, Hamilton; m., Jennifer Craig; 2 d. Educ. Dalziel High School; Scottish School of Librarianship; Open University. Librarian, Lanarkshire CC, 1966-75; Assistant Chief Librarian, East Kilbride District Council, 1975-80; Depute Director, Libraries and Museums, then Depute Director Leisure Services, Falkirk District Council, 1980-

95. Recreations: reading; cinema; theatre; music; travel. Address: (b.) Kilns House, Kilns Road, Falkirk FK1 5SA; T.-01324 506188.

Craig, Rev. Maxwell Davidson, MA, BD, ThM. General Secretary, Action of Churches Together in Scotland, since 1990 (Minister, St. Columba's Parish Church, Bridge of Don, Aberdeen, 1989-91); Chaplain to the Queen in Scotland, since 1986; b. 25.12.31; m., Janet Margaret Macgregor; 1 s.; 3 d. Educ. Bradford Grammar School; Harrow School; Oriel College, Oxford; Edinburgh University. National Service, 1st Bn., Argyll and Sutherland Highlanders (2nd Lt.), 1954-56. Assistant Principal, Ministry of Labour, 1957-61; Private Secretary to Parliamentary Secretary, 1959-61; left London and civil service to train for ministry of Church of Scotland, 1961; ThM, Princeton, 1965; Minister, Grahamston Parish Church, Falkirk, 1966-73; Minister, Wellington Church, Glasgow, 1973-89; Convener, Church and Nation Committee, Church of Scotland, 1984-88; Chairman: Falkirk Children's Panel, 1970-72, Hillhead Housing Association Ltd., 1975-89; Member, Strathclyde Children's Panel, 1973-86. Recreations: hill-walking; choral singing. Address: (h.) 9 Kilbryde Crescent, Dunblane, Perthshire FK15 9BA; T.-01786 823147.

Craig, Robert, BA, MA, ALA. Director, Scottish Library Association, since 1984; b. 2.7.43, Hamilton; m., Ann Beaton; 1 s.; 1 d. Educ. Dalziel High School; Strathclyde University. Depute County Librarian, Lanark County Council, 1974-75; Principal Education Librarian, Glasgow Division, Strathclyde Regional Council, 1975-79; Lecturer, Strathclyde University, 1979-84. Publications: Scottish Libraries (Editor); Lights in the Darkness (Co-Editor); Scotland 1939 (Co-author). Recreations: reading; gardening; football. Address: (b.) Scottish Centre for Information and Library Services, 1 John Street, Hamilton ML3 7EU; T.-01698 458888.

Craig, Robert Harvey, RD, CA. Chartered Accountant in professional practice 1955-97; Honorary Sheriff, North Strathclyde at Campbeltown, since 1986; b. 18.12.29, Campbeltown; m., Marion Caldwell; 1 s.; 1 d. Educ. Campbeltown Grammar School; Glasgow University. Admitted to Institute of Chartered Accountants of Scotland, 1953; Fleet Air Arm, 1953-55; later commanded a Naval Reserve minesweeper; Director, Loch Fyne Oysters Ltd. and various companies. Recreations: sailing; skiing. Address: (h.) Ferndean, Campbeltown, Argyll, PA28 6EN; T.-01586 552495; (b.) T.-01586 551781.

Craik, Professor Alexander Duncan Davidson, BSc, PhD, FRSE. Professor of Applied Mathematics, St. Andrews University, since 1988 (Reader, 1974-87); b. 25.8.38, Brechin; m., Elizabeth Mary Farmer; 1 s.; 1 d. Educ. Brechin High School; St. Andrews University; Cambridge University. St. Andrews University: Lecturer in Applied Mathematics, 1963-70, Senior Lecturer, 1970-74. Publication: Wave Interactions and Fluid Flows, 1985. Address: (h.) 92 Hepburn Gardens, St. Andrews KY16 9LN.

Craik, Sheriff Roger George, QC (Scot). Sheriff of Lothian and Borders, at Edinburgh, since 1984; b. 22.11.40.

Cramb, Rev. Erik McLeish, LTh. National Co-ordinator, Scottish Churches Industrial Mission; b. 26.12.39, Glasgow; m., Elizabeth McLean; 2 s.; 3 d. Educ. Woodside Secondary School, Glasgow; Glasgow University and Trinity College. Minister: St. Thomas' Gallowgate, Glasgow, 1973-81, St. Paul's United Church, Kingston, Jamaica, 1981-84, Yoker, Glasgow, 1984-89; Organiser for Tayside, Scottish Churches International Mission, 1989-97. Socialist; Member, Iona Community; Chairman, Church Action on Poverty. Recreation: supports Partick Thistle. Address: (h.) 65 Clepington Road, Dundee DD4 7BQ; T.-01382 458764.

Cramond, Ronald Duncan, CBE (1987), MA, FIMgt, FSA (Scot). Chairman, Scottish Greenbelt Foundation (formerly Strathclyde Greenbelt Company), since 1992; Secretary, Intellectual Access Trust, since 1995; b. 22.3.27, Leith; m., Constance MacGregor (deceased); 1 s.; 1 d. Educ. George Heriot's School; Edinburgh University. Commissioned Royal Scots, 1950; entered War Office, 1951; Private Secretary to Parliamentary Under Secretary of State, Scottish Office, 1956; Principal, Department of Health for Scotland, 1957; Mactaggart Fellow, Glasgow University, 1962; Haldane Medallist in Public Administration, 1964; Assistant Secretary, Scottish Development Department, 1966; Under Secretary, 1973; Under Secretary, Department of Agriculture and Fisheries for Scotland, 1977. Deputy Chairman, Highlands and Islands Development Board, 1983-88; Member, Scottish Tourist Board, 1985-88; Trustee: National Museums of Scotland, 1985-96, Cromarty Arts Trust, 1988-91, Bo'ness Heritage Trust, 1989-97, Scottish Civic Trust, 1988-95; Vice President, Architectural Heritage Society of Scotland, 1989-94; Chairman, Scottish Museums Council, 1990-93; Commissioner, Countryside Commission for Scotland, 1988-92. Recreations: golf; hill-walking; testing a plastic hip. Address: (b.) Scottish Greenbelt Foundation, 375 West George Street, Glasgow G2 4NT.

Crampsey, Robert A. McN., MA (Hons), ARCM. Freelance Broadcaster and Writer; b. 8.7.30, Glasgow; m., Dr. Veronica R. Carson; 4 d. Educ. Holyrood School, Glasgow; Glasgow University; London University (External). RAF, 1952-55 (demobilised in rank of Flt. Lt.); Head of History Department, St. Aloysius College, Glasgow, 1967-71; Assistant Head Teacher, Holyrood Secondary School, 1971-74; Rector, St. Ambrose High School, Coatbridge, 1974-86. Winner, Brain of Britain, BBC, 1965; Churchill Fellow, 1970; semi-finalist, Mastermind, 1972-73; BBC Sports Commentator. Publications: History of Queen's Park FC; Puerto Rico; The Manager; The Scottish Footballer; The Edinburgh Pirate (Arts Council Award); The Run Out; Mr Stein (a biography); The Young Civilian; The Glasgow Golf Club 1787-1987; The Empire Exhibition; The Somerset Cricket Quiz Book; The Surrey Cricket Quiz Book; Ranfurly Castle Golf Club — a centenary history; The Official Centenary History of the Scottish Football League; Scottish Railway Connections; The King's Grocer – a Life of Sir Thomas Lipton. Recreations: travel; things Hispanic; listening to and playing music; cricket. Address: (h.) 15 Myrtle Park, Glasgow G42; T.-0141-423 2735.

Cranston, Colin. Firemaster, Lothian and Borders. Address: (b.) Brigade Headquarters, Lauriston Place, Edinburgh, EH3 9DE.

Cranstoun of That Ilk and Corehouse, David Alexander Somerville, TD, MA, MSc, PhD, DL. Cereal Specialist, SAC, since 1982; National List Trials Officer, ESCA, since 1973; Member, Queen's Bodyguard for Scotland (Royal Company of Archers); b. 19.12.43, Washington DC; m., Dr. Iur M M Glättli; 2 s. Educ. Winchester College; Trinity College, Oxford. Director, Scottish Quality Cereals; Hon. Director: Lord Roberts Workshops (Edinburgh), Scottish Union Jack Association. Commissioned Queens Own Lowland Yeomanry (TA), 1964, Lt. Col., 1982; Comd District Specialist Training Team, 1988, TA Col Lowlands, 1990; Recreation: forestry. Address: (h.) Corehouse, Lanark ML11 9TQ.

Crawford, Allan James, MA, LLB, SSC. Solicitor, since 1971; Senior Court Partner, Cochran, Sayers, Cook; Solicitor Advocate, since 1994; Part-time Tutor in Civil Advocacy, University of Strathclyde, since 1990; Temporary Sheriff; b. 9.6.46, Glasgow; m., Patricia; 1 s.; 2 d. Educ. King's Park School, Glasgow; University of Glasgow. Law apprenticeship, Maclay, Murray, Spens, 1969-71; joined Cochran, Sayers, Cook, Solicitors, 1971,

Partner, 1974. Recreations: music; opera; tennis; badminton. Address: (b.) 33a Gordon Street, Glasgow G1 3PQ; T.-0141-248 5961.

Crawford, Barbara Elizabeth, MA (Hons), PhD. Lecturer in Medieval History, St. Andrews University, since 1972; Member, Royal Commission on Ancient and Historical Monuments of Scotland, since 1995; Chair, Treasure Trove Advisory Panel for Scotland, since 1994; b. 5.4.40, Barnsley; m., Robert M.M. Crawford; 1 s. Educ. Queen Margaret's School; St. Andrews University. Carnegie Senior Scholarship, 1968; Temporary Lecturer, Department of History, Aberdeen University, 1969; elected Fellow, Society of Antiquaries London, 1964, Fellow Society of Antiquaries of Scotland, 1974, Member Norwegian Academy of Science and Letters, 1997. Publication: Scandinavian Scotland, 1987. Recreations: exploring areas of Viking settlement in Scotland and North Atlantic. Address: (h.) Kincaple Cottage, St. Andrews KY16 9SH.

Crawford, Ian James, BAcc, ACMA. Director, IBM Greenock Site, since 1996; b. 27.7.54, Peterborough; m., Sheila Crawford. Educ. John Neilson High School, Paisley; Glasgow University. Rolls Royce (1971) Ltd., 1975-78; joined IBM, 1978. Recreations: sub aqua diving; has written and published two books. Address: (b.) IBM UK Ltd., Spango Valley, Greenock; T.-01475 895810.

Crawford, Professor Robert, MA, DPhil. Professor of Modern Scottish Literature, School of English, St. Andrews University, since 1995; Associate Director, St. Andrews Scottish Studies Institute, since 1993; Poetry Editor, Polygon, since 1991; Poet and Critic; b. 23.2.59, Bellshill; m., Alice Wales; 1 s.; 1 d. Educ. Hutchesons' Grammar School, Glasgow; Glasgow University; Balliol College, Oxford. Snell Exhibitioner & Carnegie Scholar, Balliol College, Oxford, 1981-84; Elizabeth Wordsworth Junior Research Fellow, St. Hugh's College, Oxford, 1984-87; British Academy Postdoctoral Fellow, Department of English Literature, Glasgow University, 1987-89; Lecturer in Modern Scottish Literature, School of English, St. Andrews University, 1989-95. Former Co-Editor, Verse Magazine. Publications: The Savage and the City in the Work of T.S. Eliot, 1987; A Scottish Assembly, 1990; Sharawaggi (Co-author), 1990; About Edwin Morgan (Co-Editor), 1990; Other Tongues: young Scottish poets in English, Scots and Gaelic (Editor), 1990; The Arts of Alasdair Gray (Co-Editor), 1991; Devolving English Literature, 1992; Talkies, 1992; Reading Douglas Dunn (Co-Editor), 1992; Identifying Poets, 1993; Liz Lochhead's Voices (Co-Editor), 1993; Twentieth Century Literature of Scotland: a selected bibliography, 1995; Talking Verse (Co-Editor), 1995; Masculinity, 1996; Penguin Modern Poets 9 (Co-Editor), 1996; Robert Burns and Cultural Authority (Editor), 1997; Launch-site for English Studies: Three Centuries of Literary Studies at the University of St. Andrews (Editor), 1997. Recreation: quietness. Address: (b.) School of English, St. Andrews University, St. Andrews, KY16 9AL; T.-01334 476161, Ext. 2666.

Crawford, 29th Earl of, and Balcarres, 12th Earl of (Robert Alexander Lindsay), PC, DL. Premier Earl of Scotland; Head of House of Lindsay; b. 5.3.27; m., Ruth Beatrice Meyer; 2 s.; 2 d. Educ. Eton; Trinity College, Cambridge. Grenadier Guards, 1945-49; MP (Conservative), Hertford, 1955-74, Welwyn and Hatfield, February to September, 1974; Opposition Front Bench Spokesman on Health and Social Security, 1967-70; Minister of State for Defence, 1970-72; Minister of State for Foreign and Commonwealth Affairs, 1972-74; Chairman, Lombard North Central Bank, 1976-80; Director, National Westminster Bank, 1975-88; Director, Scottish American Investment Co., 1978-88; Vice-Chairman, Sun Alliance & London Insurance Group, 1975-91; President, Rural District Councils Association, 1959-65; Chairman, National Association of Mental Health, 1963-70;

Chairman, Historic Buildings Council for Scotland, 1976-83; Chairman, Royal Commission on Ancient and Historical Monuments of Scotland, 1985-95; First Crown Estate Commissioner, 1980-85; Chairman, Joint Committee, RSA and NGS, 1993-96; Deputy Lieutenant, Fife; Chairman, National Library of Scotland, since 1990. Address: (h.) Balcarres, Colinsburgh, Fife KY9 1HL.

Crawford, Robert Caldwell. Composer; b. 18.4.25, Edinburgh; m., Alison Braedine Orr; 1 s.; 1 d. Educ. Melville College, Edinburgh; Keswick Grammar School; Guildhall School of Music, London. Freelance Composer and Critic until 1970; BBC Music Producer, 1970-85; Chairman, Music Advisory Committee for Sir James Caird's Travelling Scholarships Trust, 1978-93. Recreations: carpentry; hill-walking; gardening; beekeeping. Address: (h.) 12 Inverleith Terrace, Edinburgh EH3 5NS; T.-0131-556 3600.

Crawford, Robert Hardie Bruce, JP. Leader, Perth and Kinross Council, since 1995; b. 16.2.55, Perth; m., Jacqueline; 3 s. Educ. Kinross High School; Perth High School. Civil servant, Scottish Office, since 1974; Chairman, Perth and Kinross Recreation Facilities Ltd; Member: Perthshire Tourist Board, Scottish Enterprise Tayside, Perth College. Recreations: watching Dunfermline Athletic; family. Address: (h.) 12 Douglas Crescent, Kinross; T.-01577 863531.

Crawford, Professor Robert MacGregor Martyn, BSc, DocSciNat (Liege), FRSE, FInstBiol. Professor of Plant Ecology, St. Andrews University, since 1977; b. 30.5.34, Glasgow; m., Barbara Elizabeth Hall; 1 s. Educ. Glasgow Academy; Glasgow University; Liege University; Moscow University. Lecturer, then Reader in Botany, St. Andrews University; Past President, Edinburgh Botanical Society; Editor, Flora. Publications: Studies in Plant Survival, 1989; Disturbance and Recovery in Arctic Lands, 1997. Recreations: languages; music; photography. Address: (b.) Sir Harold Mitchell Building, The University, St. Andrews, KY16 9AJ; T.-01334 463370.

Crawford, Ronald Lyndsay, MA, BLitt, Dr h.c., Commander of the Polish Order of Merit, 1989 (Gold Medal, 1982). Secretary, Committee of Scottish Higher Education Principals, since 1993; Secretary, Committee of Scottish University Principals, since 1988; b. 31.1.39, Paisley; m., Evelyn Ewing Knox; 2 s. Educ. Paisley Grammar School; Glasgow University; University of Freiburg. Editor, educational publishing, 1961-63; Strathclyde University: Administrative Assistant, 1963-67, Assistant, then Senior Assistant Registrar, 1967-73, Secretary to Court, 1973-81, Academic Registrar, 1981-93. Honorary Citizen, Lodz, Poland; President, Scottish-Polish Cultural Association, 1985-92. Recreations: fishing; boating; music. Address: (h.) COSHEP, St. Andrew House, 141 West Nile Street, Glasgow G1 2RN; T.-0141-353 1880.

Crawford, Rudy, BSc (Hons), MBChB, FRCS (Glas). Consultant in Accident and Emergency Care, Royal Infirmary, Glasgow, since 1990; Honorary Clinical Senior Lecturer, Glasgow University, since 1991; b. 5.5.49, Glasgow; m., Jane Crawford; 1 s.; 1 d. Educ. Glasgow University. Temporary Lecturer in Anatomy, Glasgow University; general surgery training; specialist training in accident and emergency medicine and surgery, Glasgow and Aberdeen; formerly member of offshore specialist team providing medical support for North Sea oil emergencies; founder Member and Local Project Director, Scottish Trauma Audit Group; Member: Council, St. Andrew's Ambulance Association, Scottish Management Efficiency Group Working Party on Accident and Emergency Services. Recreations: karate; running; photography; travel; Rotary International. Address: (b.) Accident and Emergency Department, Royal Infirmary, Glasgow G4 0SF; T.-0141-211 5166.

Crawford, Thomas, MA. Hon. Reader in English, Aberdeen University, since 1985; b. 6.7.20, Dundee; m., Jean Rennie McBride; 1 s.; 1 d. Educ. Dunfermline High School; Edinburgh University; University of Auckland. University of Auckland: Lecturer in English, 1953-60, Senior Lecturer, 1960-62, Associate Professor, 1963-65; Lecturer in English, Edinburgh University, 1965; Commonwealth Research Fellow, Hamilton, Ontario, 1966; Senior Lecturer in English, then Reader, Aberdeen University, 1967-85; Warnock Fellow, Yale University, various times, since 1978. Past President, Association for Scottish Literary Studies; former Editor, Scottish Literary Journal. Publications: Burns: a study of the poems and songs, 1960; Scott, 1965; Scott, selected poems (Editor), 1972; Love, Labour, and Liberty, 1976; Society and the Lyric, 1980; Boswell, Burns and the French Revolution, 1990; Correspondence of James Boswell and William Johnson Temple 1756-1795 (Editor), 1997; Boswell in Scotland and Beyond (Editor), 1997. Recreations: walking and rambling; music. Address: (h.) 61 Argyll Place, Aberdeen AB25 2HU; T.-01224 635862.

Crawley, David Jonathan, MA (Oxon). Head, Constitution Group – Functions Division, Scottish Office, since 1997; b. 6.5.51, Barnet; m., Anne Anderson; 1 s.; 2 d. Educ. Chichester High School; Christ Church, Oxford. Scottish Office, 1972-81; Department of Energy, 1981-84; Assistant Secretary, Scottish Education Department, 1984-87; Principal Private Secretary to Secretary of State for Scotland, 1987-89; Assistant Secretary, Scottish Home and Health Department, 1989-90; Counsellor, UK Permanent Representation to European Communities, Brussels, 1990-94; Head, Private Finance Unit, Scottish Office, 1995-97. Recreations: family; walking; gardening. Address: (b.) Scottish Office, Victoria Quay, Edinburgh EH6 6QQ; T.-0131-244 7497.

Crean, Gerard Patrick, PhD, FRCPE, FRCPG, FRCPI; President, Scottish Fiddle Orchestra; Former Consultant Physician, Ross Hall Hospital, Glasgow; Consultant Physician and Physician-in-charge, Gastro-Intestinal Centre, Southern General Hospital, Glasgow, 1967-92; b. 1.5.27, Courtown Harbour, County Wexford; m., Janice Dodds Mathieson; 1 s.; 2 d. Educ. Rockwell College, Cashel, County Tipperary; University College, Dublin. House appointments, Mater Misericordiae Hospital, Dublin, Western General Hospital, Edinburgh and Edinburgh Royal Infirmary; Registrar, then Senior Registrar, Western General Hospital, Edinburgh; Member, scientific staff, Medical Research Council Clinical Endocrinology Unit, Edinburgh; Honorary Lecturer, Department of Therapeutics, Edinburgh University; Visiting Professor in Physiology, Pennsylvania University. Clarke Prize, Edinburgh Pathological Club; contributed to several textbooks. Past President, British Society of Gastroenterology. Recreations: fiddle playing; traditional music; history of Antarctic exploration; golf. Address: (h.) St. Ronan's, Duchal Road, Kilmacolm PA13 4AY.

Cresser, Professor Malcolm Stewart, PhD, DIC, BSc, ARCS, FRSC, CChem, CBiol, FIBiol. Professor of Plant & Soil Science, Aberdeen University, since 1989; b. 17.4.46, London; m., Louise Elizabeth Blackburn; 1 s.; 2 d. Educ. St. Ignatius College, Tottenham; Imperial College, London. Lecturer, Senior Lecturer, Reader, Department of Soil Science, Aberdeen University, 1970-89; awarded 11th SAC Silver Medal, 1984. Publications: Solvent Extraction in Flame Spectroscopic Analysis; Flame Spectrometry in Environmental Chemical Analysis; Environmental Chemical Analysis (Co-author); Acidification of Freshwaters (Co-author); Soil Chemistry and its Applications (Co-author). Recreations: painting; drawing; gardening. Address: (b.) Department of Plant and Soil Science, Cruickshank Building, Old Aberdeen AB24 3UU; T.-01224 272259.

Cresswell, Lyell Richard, BMus (Hons), MusM, PhD. Composer; b. 13.10.44, Wellington, New Zealand; m., Catherine Mawson. Educ. Victoria University of Wellington; Toronto University; Aberdeen University. Music Organiser, Chapter Arts Centre, Cardiff; Forman Fellow, Edinburgh University, 1980-82; Canadian Commonwealth scholarship, 1969-70; Dutch Government bursary, 1974-75; Ian Whyte Award, 1978; APRA Silver Scroll, 1979; Cramb Fellow, Glasgow University, 1982-85. Address: (h.) 4 Leslie Place, Edinburgh EH4 1NQ; T.-0131-332 9181.

Crichton, Robin, FRAI. Film Producer and Director, since 1961; b. 14.5.40, Bournemouth; m., Trish Dorrell; 3 d. Educ. Sherborne; Paris; Edinburgh. Built Scotland's first independent film studio, 1968; started film training scheme, now Napier University M.A., 1970; founded first animation studio in Scotland; managed first independent outside broadcast unit in Scotland; Founder Member: Scottish ACTT Committee, Scottish Film Archive; former UK Vice-Chair and Scottish Chair, Independent Programme Producers' Association; former Co-ordinator, Working Party, Scottish Screen; co-initiated Annual Co-production Conference; organised Scottish stand at international TV television markets; Churchill Fellowship, 1990 (to study models for Scottish Screen); Co-production Consultant to various European broadcasters and producers; Project Leader, Eureka Audiovisual Federation; Director, Scottish Screen Locations; Consultant Programme Buyer, Gaelic Television Committee. Publications: Sara; The Curious Case of Santa Claus; Christmas Mouse. Recreations: dancing; gardening; DIY. Address: (b.) Edinburgh Film Productions, by Penicuik, Midlothian EH26 9LT; T.-01968 672131.

Critchlow, Howard Arthur, BDS, FDSRCS(Eng), FDSRCPS(Glas). Consultant Oral Surgeon (Honorary Senior Lecturer), Glasgow Dental Hospital, Stobhill General Hospital and Royal Hospital for Sick Children, Glasgow, since 1976; b. 22.4.43, Littleborough; m., Avril; 1 s.; 1 d. Educ. Nottingham High School for Boys; Sheffield University. General dental practice, Sheffield; oral surgery training post, Sheffield, Southampton, Odstock and Newcastle. Chairman, Greater Glasgow Health Board Dental Ethical Committee. Recreations: gardening; hill-walking; running. Address: (b.) Glasgow Dental Hospital and School, 378 Sauchiehall Street, Glasgow G2 3JZ; T.-0141-211 9600.

Croall, Alastair Menzies, LLB. Chief Executive, Scottish Borders Council, since 1995; b. 18.12.46, Kirkcaldy; m., Pauline; 3 s. Educ. Kirkcaldy High School; Edinburgh University. Worked with Roxburgh County Council, Moray and Nairn Joint County Council, Ross and Cromarty County Council; joined Borders Regional Council, 1975; appointed Depute Chief Executive and Solicitor to the Council, 1986. Recreations: walking; rugby; reading. Address: (b.) Council Headquarters, Newtown St. Boswells, Melrose, TD6 0SA; T.-01835 825055.

Croan, Sheriff Thomas Malcolm, MA, LLB. Sheriff of North Strathclyde at Kilmarnock, since 1983; b. 7.8.32, Edinburgh; m., Joan Kilpatrick Law; 1 s.; 3 d. Educ. St. Joseph's College, Dumfries; Edinburgh University. Admitted to Faculty of Advocates, 1956; Standing Junior Counsel, Scottish Development Department, 1964-65 and (for highways work), 1967-69; Advocate Depute, 1965-66; Sheriff of Grampian, Highland and Islands at Banff and Peterhead, 1969-83. Recreation: sailing. Address: (h.) Overdale, 113 Bentinck Drive, Troon.

Croft, Trevor Anthony, BSc, DipTRP, MRTPI, ARSGS. Director, The National Trust for Scotland, since 1997; b. 9.6.48, Bradford; m., Janet Frances Halley; 2 d. Educ. Belle Vue Boys Grammar School, Bradford; Hull University; Sheffield University. Senior Assistant Planning Officer, N.

Ireland Government, 1971-72; Assistant Planning Officer, Countryside Commission for Scotland, 1972-75; Physical Planning Officer, Office of the President, Malawi Government, 1976-78; Parks Planning Officer, Department of National Parks and Wildlife, Malawi Government, 1978-82; Planning Officer, then Head of Policy Research, then Regional Director, then Deputy Director/Director of Countryside, National Trust for Scotland, 1982-96; Member, Forestry Commission, South Conservancy Regional Advisory Committee, 1987-90. Chairman, Dunfermline Branch, Royal Scottish Geographical Society, 1993-96. Recreations: sailing; travel; photography; equestrian vaulting; hill-walking. Address: (h.) Glenside, Tillyrie, Milnathort, Kinross KY13 7RW; T.-01577 864105.

Crofton, Sir John Wenman, KB, MA, MD, Dr h.c. Bordeaux, FRCP, FRCPE, Hon FRSE; b. 27.3.12, Dublin; m., Eileen Chris Mercer, MBE; 2 s.; 3 d. Educ. Tonbridge; Sidney Sussex College, Cambridge. Professor of Respiratory Diseases, Edinburgh University, 1952-77; Dean, Faculty of Medicine, 1963-66; Vice-Principal, 1969-70; President, Royal College of Physicians of Edinburgh, 1973-76; Vice-Chairman, Scottish Committee, Chest, Heart and Stroke Association, 1976-90; Chairman: Scottish Health Education Co-ordinating Committee, SHHD, 1981-86, Tobacco and Health Committee, International Union Against Tuberculosis and Lung Disease, 1984-88; Edinburgh Medal for Science and Society, 1995. Recreations: history; music; mountains. Address: (h.) 13 Spylaw Bank Road, Edinburgh EH13 0JW; T.-0131-441 3730.

Crofts, Roger Stanley, BA, MLitt, CertEd, FRSA. Chief Executive, Scottish Natural Heritage, since 1991; Visiting Professor in Environmental Management, Royal Holloway, London University; Honorary Professor in Geography, University of Aberdeen; b. 17.1.44, Leicester; m. Lindsay Manson; 1 s.; 1 d. Educ. Hinckley Grammar School; Liverpool University; Leicester University. Research Assistant in Geography: Aberdeen University, 1966-72, University College, London, 1972-74; entered Scottish Office, 1974; Senior Research Officer, 1974-78; Principal Research Officer, 1978-84; Assistant Secretary, Highlands and Tourism Division, Industry Department, 1984-88; Assistant Secretary, Rural Affairs Division, Scottish Development Department, 1988-91. Member, Council: World Commission on Protected Areas (Europe), Royal Scottish Geographical Society, National Trust for Scotland, Scottish Wildlife Trust, Scottish Association of Marine Science. Recreations: gardening; choral singing; hill-walking; wildflower photography. Address: (h.) 6 Old Church Lane, Duddingston Village, Edinburgh EH15 3PX; T.-0131-661 7858.

Cromartie, 5th Earl of (John Ruaridh Grant Mackenzie). Chief of the Clan Mackenzie; b. 12.6.48; m.; 2 s. Explosives Engineer. Publication: Selected Climbs in Skye, 1982. Address: Castle Leod, Strathpeffer, IV14 9AA.

Cromarty, Professor John Alfred, BSc, MSc (Pharmacol), MSc (ClinPharm), CertEd, MRPharmS. Professor of Clinical Pharmacy, The Robert Gordon University, Aberdeen, since 1993; National Specialist in Clinical Pharmacy (Scotland), since 1993; Honorary Consultant Clinical Pharmacist, Dundee Teaching Hospitals NHS Trust; Honorary Clinical Pharmacist, Grampian Health Board, Grampian Healthcare NHS Trust, Aberdeen Royal Hospitals NHS Trust; b. 26.8.51, Kirkwall; m., Evelyn McKenzie; 2 d. Educ. Kirkwall Grammar School; Heriot Watt University; Strathclyde University; Aberdeen College of Education; Aberdeen University. Staff Pharmacist/Lecturer, Oldham AHA/University of Manchester, 1979-80; Principal Pharmacist, North West Thames RHA, 1980-81; Principal Pharmacist/Senior Lecturer, North West Thames RHA/London University, 1981-89; Director, Post Qualification Education for Pharmacists in Scotland/Senior Lecturer, Strathclyde University, 1989-93; Member: National Pharmaceutical Advisory Committee, since 1994, Scottish Intercollegiate Guidelines Network, since 1995, Royal College of Physicians (London) Working Party on Clinical Pharmacology and Therapeutics in a Changing World, 1996, Stonehaven and District Community Council, since 1996. Recreations: wine; natural history; rugby (spectating); poetry. Address: (b.) Clinical Pharmacy Practice Unit, School of Pharmacy, The Robert Gordon University, Schoolhill, Aberdeen AB10 1FR; T.-01224 262540.

Crompton, Professor David William Thomasson, MA, PhD, ScD, FIBiol, FRSE. John Graham Kerr Professor of Zoology, Glasgow University, since 1985; b. 5.12.37, Bolton; m., Effie Mary Marshall; 1 s.; 2 d. Educ. Bolton School; Sidney Sussex College, Cambridge. National Service, commission, King's Own Royal Regiment, 1957; Assistant in Research, Cambridge University, 1963-68; Fellow, Sidney Sussex College, 1964-85; Vice-Master, 1981-83; Lecturer in Parasitology, Cambridge University, 1968-85; Joint Editor, Parasitology, 1972-82; Adjunct Professor, Division of Nutritional Sciences, Cornell University, New York, since 1981; Aquatic Life Sciences Committee, Natural Environment Research Council, 1981-84; Director, Company of Biologists Ltd., since 1985; Member, WHO Expert Committee on Parasitic Diseases, since 1985; Scientific Medal, Zoological Society of London, 1977; Head, WHO Collaborating Centre for soil-transmitted helminthiases, Glasgow University; Chairman, Company of Biologists Ltd. Recreations: mountain walking; fishing; books; bull terriers. Address: (b.) Institute of Biomedical and Life Sciences, Glasgow University, Glasgow, G12 8QQ; T.-0141-330 5395; (h.) Melrose Cottage, Tyndrum, Perthshire FK20 8SA; T.-01838-400 203.

Crompton, Graham Kenneth, MB, ChB, FRCPE, FCCP. Consultant Physician, Lothian Health Board, since 1969; Senior Lecturer in Medicine and Respiratory Medicine, Edinburgh University, since 1969; b. 14.2.35, Salford; m., 1, Dorothy Margaret Graham (deceased); 2 s.; 2, Jane Anne Robertson (née Harrison). Educ. Salford Grammar School; Edinburgh University. Appointed Consultant Physician, 1969; Director of Studies, Faculty of Medicine, 1977-88; Member: Medical Advisory Committee, Asthma Society, 1981-88, Faculty of Medicine Admission Committee, Edinburgh University, since 1994, National Asthma Campaign Therapy Task Force, since 1991; President: British Thoracic Society 1994-95, Scottish Thoracic Society, 1994-96. Publications: Diagnosis and Management of Respiratory Diseases; chapters in 12 medical text books; author or co-author of over 200 scientific publications. Recreation: watching sport. Address: (h.) 14 Midmar Drive, Edinburgh EH10 6BU; T.-0131-447 1022.

Crook, Eunice Campbell, BSc, MBA. Director, The British Council, Scotland, since 1996; b. 24.11.50; m., Philip Crook. Educ. Campbeltown Grammar School; Glasgow University; Jordanhill College of Education. Teacher, Scotland, Seychelles and Botswana, 1972-85; British Council: Finance Division, 1985-90, Director Glasgow/International Arts Officer Scotland, 1990-94; study leave, 1994-96. Recreations: performing arts; travel; bridge. Address: (b.) 3/4 Bruntsfield Crescent, Edinburgh EH10 4HD; T.-0131-447 4716.

Crookall, Simon Philip. Chief Executive, Royal Scottish National Orchestra, since 1997; b. 1.10.60, Macclesfield. Educ. Nantwich and Acton Grammar School; King's College, Cambridge. Academic Assistant/Assistant to Principal/Front of House Manager, Royal Scottish Academy of Music and Drama, Glasgow, 1983-89; General Manager, Queen's Hall, Edinburgh, 1989-95; General Manager, Royal Scottish National Orchestra, 1995-96. Recreations: singing as soloist for Council for Music in

Hospitals; Chorusmaster, Haddo House Choral and Operatic Society, Aberdeen; Member, Order of St. John. Address: (b.) RSNO Centre, 73 Claremont Street, Glasgow G3 7JB; T.-0141-226 3868.

Crosbie, William, BSc(Hons). Headteacher, Castlebrae Community High School, since 1991; b. 14.8.50, Dumbarton; m., Rosemary; 1 s.; 1 d. Educ. Clydebank High School; University of Glasgow; Moray House College of Education. Teacher of Chemistry, Greenfaulds High School, Cumbernauld, 1973-76; Assistant Principal Teacher of Science, Holy Rood R.C. High School, Edinburgh, 1976-78; Castlebrae High School, Edinburgh: Principal Teacher of Chemistry, 1978-87, Assistant Headteacher, 1987-89, Depute Headteacher, 1989-91. Scottish Teacher of the Year, 1993; Scottish Schools Ethos Award, 1997; Chair, Edinburgh Compact Youthstart Steering Group. Recreations: golf; cinema; swimming. Address: (b.) 2a Greendykes Road, Edinburgh EH16 4NY; T.-0131-661 1282.

Crosby, William Scott, CBE (1982), BL. Lawyer; b. 31.7.18, Hawick; m., Margaret Elizabeth Bell; 3 s. Educ. Hawick High School; Edinburgh University. Army Service, 1939-46; Croix de Guerre, 1945; acted as Brigade Major 152 Brigade, 1945; Former Senior Partner, Storie, Cruden & Simpson, Advocates, Aberdeen; Chairman, Grampian Health Board, 1973-82; President, Society of Advocates in Aberdeen, 1984-85. Recreations: golf; swimming; walking; gardening. Address: (h.) 16 Golf Place, Aboyne AB34 5GA; T.-013398 85357.

Crosfield, Rev. Canon George Philip Chorley, OBE, MA (Cantab). Provost, St. Mary's Cathedral, Edinburgh, 1970-90; Hon. Canon, St. Mary's Cathedral, since 1991; b. 9.9.24, London; m., Susan Mary Jullion; 1 s.; 2 d. Educ. George Watson's College, Edinburgh; Selwyn College, Cambridge. Royal Artillery, 1942-46 (Captain); Priest, 1952; Assistant Curate: St. David's, Pilton, Edinburgh, 1951-53, St. Andrew's, St. Andrews, 1953-55; Rector, St. Cuthbert's, Hawick, 1955-60; Chaplain, Gordonstoun School, 1960-68; Canon and Vice-Provost, St. Mary's Cathedral, Edinburgh, 1968-70. Recreations: gardening; walking; carpentry. Address: (h.) 21 Biggar Road, Silverburn, near Penicuik EH26 9LQ; Tel.-01968 676607.

Crowe, David T., LLB, WS, NP. Solicitor, since 1969; Partner, Andrew Haddow & Crowe, W.S., Hawick, since 1971; Temporary Sheriff, since 1984; Chairman, Social Security Appeals Tribunal, since 1991; b. 9.8.45, Kilmarnock; m., Agi Pusztai; 1 s.; 3 d. Educ. Royal Academy, Irvine; University of Edinburgh. Hospital Administrator, Hôpital Protestante, Dabou, Ivory Coast, W. Africa, 1969-71. Dean, Faculty of Procurators for Roxburghshire; Treasurer, Temporary Sheriffs Association. Author: The Shrieval Vade Mecum; The Scottish Courts Companion. Recreations: music; transport; gardening; family. Address: (b.) 3 Oliver Place, Hawick TD9 9BG; T.-01450 372738.

Crowe, Frank Richard, LLB, NP. Regional Procurator Fiscal, South Strathclyde, Dumfries and Galloway, since 1996; Procurator Fiscal, Hamilton, since 1996; Solicitor Advocate; 15.3.52, Kirkcaldy; m., Alison Margaret Purdom; 2 d. Educ. Kirkcaldy High School; Royal High School, Edinburgh; University of Dundee. Law Apprentice, North of Scotland Hydro-Electric Board, 1973-75; Procurator Fiscal Depute: Dundee, 1975-78, Glasgow 1978-81; Senior Legal Assistant, Crown Office, 1981-83; Senior Depute Procurator Fiscal, Edinburgh 1983-87; Senior Depute i/c Crown Office Fraud Unit, 1987-88; Assistant Solicitor i/c High Court Unit, Crown Office, 1988-91; Procurator Fiscal, Kirkcaldy, 1991-96. Member: Management Committee, Lothian Victim Support Scheme, 1983-89, Training Advisory Committee, Victim Support Scotland, since 1994, Council, Law Society of Scotland,

since 1996. Recreations: golf; cycling; racing; music. Address: (b.) Procurator Fiscal's Office, Cameronian House, 315 Almada Street, Hamilton ML3 0HG; T.-01698 284000.

Crowe, William J.J., BSc (Hons). Chief Executive, Scottish Salmon Growers Association, since 1988; b. 2.8.47, Edinburgh; m., Susan A.C. Knott; 1 s.; 1 d. Educ. High School of Glasgow; Aberdeen University. Address: (b.) Drummond House, Scott Street, Perth PH1 5EJ; T.-01738 635420.

Cruickshank, Alastair Harvey, LLB, WS, NP, DL. Solicitor and Partner, Condies, Solicitors, Perth, since 1967; b. 10.8.43, Perth; m., Moira E. Pollock (deceased); 2 s. Educ. Perth Academy; Edinburgh University. Apprentice, then Assistant, Shepherd & Wedderburn, WS, Edinburgh, 1964-67; Assistant, then Partner, Condie Mackenzie & Co. (now Condies), since 1967. Registrar, Diocese of Brechin, since 1974; Member, Perth Society of High Constables. Recreations: hill-walking; sailing; chamber music, opera and classical music generally. Address: (b.) 2 Tay Street, Perth PH1 5LJ; T.-01738 440088.

Cruickshank, Alistair Booth, MA, FRSCS; b. 3.8.31, Dumfries; m., Sheena Carlin Brown; 2 s.; 1 d. Educ. High School of Stirling; Glasgow University; Georgia University. RAF, 1956-58; Glasgow University, 1958-61; Nottingham University, 1961-65; Glasgow University, 1965-86. Director, Royal Scottish Geographical Society, 1986-96; ordained Auxiliary Minister, Church of Scotland, 1991; Deputy Lieutenant, County of Clackmannan, since 1991. Recreations: fly fishing; peoples and places.

Crummy, Helen Murray, MBE, DLitt, DL, JP; b. 10.5.20, Edinburgh; m., Larry Crummy; 3 s. Educ. James Clark's School. Co-Founder Member and Organising Secretary, 23 years, Craigmillar Festival Society; served on Morris Committee (Housing and Social Work); former Member: Scottish Council for Community Education, Scottish Arts Council Development Committee, various Gulbenkian committees, DHSS Appeals Tribunal, Lothian Regional Council Education Advisory Committee. Recreations: writing; historical research; reading; gardening. Address: (h.) 4 Whitehill Street, Newcraighall, Musselburgh EH21 8RA; T.-0131-669 7344.

Cruttenden, Timothy Peter, BEd, DipPhysEd, FILAM. Director of Leisure Services, South Lanarkshire Council, since 1995; b. 6.9.45, Portsmouth; m., Hazel; 2 s. Educ. Warblington School, Havant; Bristol University; St. Paul's, Cheltenham. Taught in Hampshire and Gloucestershire, 1967-72; sports centre management, 1973-77; recreation administration, since 1977; Director of Leisure Services, East Kilbride District Council, 1980-95. Past Chairman, Association of Directors of Recreation, Leisure and Tourism. Recreations: squash; hockey; golf; sailing. Address: (b.) Council Offices, Almada Street, Hamilton ML3 0AA; T.-01698 454028.

Cubie, Andrew, LLB (Hons), NP, WS, FRSA. Senior Partner, Fyfe Ireland WS, since 1994; Chairman, Bird Semple Fyfe Ireland WS, 1991-94; b. 24.8.46, Northallerton; m., Dr. Heather Ann Cubie; 1 s.; 2 d. Educ. Dollar Academy; Edinburgh University. Partner, Fyfe Ireland & Co., WS, 1971; non-executive Director of a number of private companies; Regional Chairman, CBI (former Chairman, Scottish Council); Chairman of Governors, George Watson's College; Chairman, RNLI Scotland; Member, UK and Eire Committee of Management, and Deputy Chairman, Fund-Raising Committee, RNLI; Chairman: Scotland's Health at Work, W.S. Society Education and Training Committee; Member, Napier University Court. Recreation: sailing. Address: (b.) Orchard Brae House, 30 Queensferry Road, Edinburgh EH4 2HG; T.-0131-343 2500.

Cullen, Paul B., QC, LLB. Solicitor-General for Scotland, 1995-97. Address: (b.) Advocates' Library, Parliament House, Edinburgh EH1 1RF.

Cullen, The Rt. Hon. Lord (William Douglas Cullen), PC, LLD, DUniv, FRSE, HonFEng. Lord Justice Clerk, since 1997; Senator of the College of Justice, since 1986; b. 18.11.35, Edinburgh; m., Rosamond Mary Downer; 2 s.; 2 d. Educ. Dundee High School; St. Andrews University (MA); Edinburgh University (LLB). Called to the Scottish Bar, 1960; QC, 1973; Advocate-Depute, 1977-81; Chairman: Inquiry into the Piper Alpha Disaster, 1988-90, Inquiry into the Shootings at Dunblane Primary School, 1996. Member, Royal Commission on the Ancient and Historical Monuments of Scotland, since 1987; Chairman: Cockburn Association, 1984-86, Board of Governors, St. Margaret's School, Edinburgh, since 1994. Recreations: gardening; natural history. Address: (b.) Court of Session, Parliament House, Edinburgh; T.-0131-225 2595.

Culliven, John. Provost, Perth and Kinross Council, since 1996; b. 6.2.37, Glasgow; m., Sheila Elizabeth Grant MacKenzie; 4 s. Regional Councillor, since 1989. Recreations: bagpipes; horse-riding. Address: (h.) Craigmhor, Calvine, Pitlochry; T.-01796 483 250.

Cumming, Lt. Col. Alaistair Michael, OBE. Regimental Secretary to The Highlanders (Seaforth, Gordons and Camerons), since 1995; Commandant, Queen's Own Highlanders Battalion Army Cadet Force; b. 22.12.41, Singapore; m., Hilary Katharine Gray; 2 d. Educ. Bradfield College, Berkshire. Cadet, RMA Sandhurst, 1960-61; commissioned into The Gordon Highlanders, 1962; Major/Company Commander, Northern Ireland, 1976-77; Major/Staff Officer, Edinburgh, 1978-79; Battalion Second in Command, Hong Kong, 1980-81; Major/Staff Officer, Londonderry, 1982-84; Lt. Col.: Commander Ground Liaison Team, Germany, 1985-88; Naval and Military Attache, British Embassy, Poland, 1989-92; Commander Support Weapons Wing, Netheravon, 1992-95. Recreations: cricket; golf; tennis; shooting; skiing. Address: (b.) RHQ, The Highlanders, Cameron Barracks, Inverness IV2 3XD.

Cumming, Alexander James, MA (Hons), CIMA, IPFA. Chief Executive, Aberdeen Royal Hospitals NHS Trust, since 1994; b. 7.3.47, Aberdeen; m., Margaret Callan; 1 s.; 2 d. Educ. Fordyce Academy; Robert Gordon's College; Aberdeen University. VSO, 1968-70; Accountant, Company Secretary, Chief Accountant, 1970-75; joined Grampian Health Board, 1975. Chairman, Langstane Housing Association. Address: (b.) Foresterhill House, Ashgrove Road West, Aberdeen; T.-01224 681818.

Cumming, Eric Alexander, MIMgt, AInstAM, FSA (Scot). Principal, Scottish Court Service HQ, since 1995; b. 9.5.54, Glasgow; m., Isabel Rodger. Educ. Albert Senior Secondary School; Glasgow College of Commerce. Entered Scottish Court Service (Sheriff Clerk's Branch), 1972; posts in Glasgow, Nairn, Ayr, Dumbarton; Depute Clerk of Session and Justiciary, 1983; Sheriff Clerk, Ayr, 1990-92; Deputy Principal Clerk of Justiciary, 1992-95. Recreations: Clyde steamers; reading; naval history. Address: (b.) Hayweight House, 23 Lauriston Street, Edinburgh; T.-0131 221 6822.

Cumming, Ian George, LLB. Director of Legal Services, Glasgow City Council, since 1995. Senior Tutor in Public Administration, Strathclyde University; National Course Leader in Public Administration for Diploma in Legal Practice. Address: (b.) City Chambers, Glasgow G2 1DU; T.-0141-287 5436.

Cumming, Robert Currie, BL, FCIBS, ACIB, FRCSEdin (Hon.), FRSGS; b. 21.5.21, Strathaven; m., Mary Jean McDonald Crombie. Educ. Hutchesons' Grammar School, Glasgow; Glasgow University. Former Executive Director, Royal Bank of Scotland Group PLC and Royal Bank of Scotland PLC; Chairman, English Speaking Union — Scotland, 1984-90; Trustee, Royal Scottish Geographical Society. Recreations: fishing; golf; walking. Address: (h.) 3 Succoth Park, Edinburgh EH12 6BX; T.-0131-337 1910.

Cummings, John Andrew, BA, MA. Headmaster, Keil School, since 1993; b. 15.5.49, Eastbourne; m., Claire; 1 s.; 1 d. Educ. Eastbourne Grammar School; University of Kent; London University. Assistant Master: Glasgow Academy, 1975-80, Tonbridge School, Kent, 1980-89; Melbourne Grammar School, Australia, 1985; Head of English and Drama/Head of Sixth Form, Wycliffe College, 1989-93. Recreations: reading; theatre; hill-walking; tennis. Address: (b.) Keil School, Helenslee Road, Dumbarton G82 4AL; T.-01389 762003.

Cunliffe, Michael James Paton, BSc, MSc, MCIWEM. Director of Corporate Services, East of Scotland Water Authority, since 1995; b. 9.3.47, Sunderland; m., Jocelyn Mary Willoughby; 1 s.; 1 d. Educ. Kendal Grammar School; Edinburgh University. Administration Trainee, Scottish Development Department, 1971-73; Higher Executive Officer, Scottish Economic Planning Department, 1973-75; Principal, Scottish Development and Education Departments, 1975-82; Assistant Secretary, Scottish Development, Industry, and Education Departments, 1982-95. Elder, St. Andrew's and St. George's Church, Edinburgh. Recreations: sailing; country walks; listening to music. Address: (b.) Pentland Gait, 597 Calder Road, Edinburgh EH11 4HJ; T.-0131-453 7526.

Cunningham, David Kenneth, BEd, MEd (Hons), FRSA. Head Teacher, Hillhead High School, Glasgow, since 1993; b. 19.4.48, Saltcoats; m., Marion S. Shedden; 2 d. Educ. Ardrossan Academy; Glasgow University; Jordanhill College of Education. Principal Teacher of English, North Kelvinside Secondary, 1976-80; Assistant Head Teacher, Garthamlock Secondary, 1980-82; Adviser in English, Dunbarton Division, 1982-90, Education Officer (Acting), 1989-90; Member, Board, Glasgow Area, Young Enterprise Scotland; Inspector, Quality Assurance Unit, Strathclyde Regional Council, 1990-93. Executive Member, National Council, Headteachers Association of Scotland. Publications: Reading for 'S' Grade English, 1988. Recreations: various sports; reading; photography; travel; family. Address: (h.) 7 Waterfoot Road, Newton Mearns, Glasgow; T.-0141-639 3367.

Cunningham, Edward, CBE, MA (Cantab), MBA (Harvard), FRSE. Chairman: Scottish Exhibition Centre Ltd., since 1992, The PHQ Agency, since 1990, BUE Marine Ltd., since 1994; Vice-Chair: Scottish Industry Forum, since 1995; b. 15.9.31, Pakistan; m., Sylvia; 2 s. Educ. Trinity Hall, Cambridge; Harvard Business School. World Bank, Washington DC, 1968-77; Scottish Development Agency, 1977-90; Director (Non-Executive), TSB Bank Scotland Plc, 1986-96, Watson & Philip Plc, 1989-95; Business Options Ltd., since 1990. Address: (b.) Business Options Ltd, 8 Wester Coates Avenue, Edinburgh EH12 5LS.

Cunningham, Ian Campbell, MA, BPhil. Keeper of Manuscripts, Maps and Music, National Library of Scotland, since 1991; b. 17.9.38, Falkirk; m., Morvern; 2 d. Educ. Campbeltown Grammar School; Glasgow University; Oxford University. Assistant Keeper, National Library of Scotland, 1963-90. Former Secetary and President, Edinburgh Bibliographical Society. Publications: editions of Herodas and of Auchinleck ms facsimile; Greek Manuscripts in Scotland; David Livingstone: a catalogue of documents. Address: (b.) National Library of Scotland, George IV Bridge, Edinburgh EH1 1EW; T.-0131-226 4531.

Cunningham, Professor Ian M.M., CBE, FRSE, FIBiol, FRAgS, Hon. Assoc. RCVS, Bsc, PhD. Vice-President, Executive Committee and Chairman, Countryside and Nature Conservation Committee, National Trust for Scotland; Chairman, Advisory Committee on Sites of Special Scientific Interest; General Council Assessor, Court, Edinburgh University; Director, Edinburgh Technopole Co. Ltd; b. 30.9.25, Kirknewton; m., Agnes Whitelaw Frew. Educ. Lanark Grammar School; Edinburgh University. Assistant Economist, West of Scotland Agricultural College, 1946-47; Lecturer in Agriculture, Durham School of Agriculture, 1947-50; Lecturer, then Senior Lecturer, Edinburgh University, 1950-68; Director, Hill Farming Research Organisation, 1968-80; Professor of Agriculture, Glasgow University, and Principal, West of Scotland Agricultural College, 1980-87. Member: Farm Animal Welfare Council, Hill Farming Advisory Committee, Scotland; Chairman, Board, Macaulay Land Use Research Institute, 1987-95; George Hedley Memorial Award for services to the sheep industry; Massey Ferguson Award for services to British agriculture; Sir William Young Award for services to livestock production in Scotland; Hon. Assoc., RCVS. Address: (h.) 5 The Bridges, Peebles EH45 8BP.

Cunningham, Very Rev. Monsignor John, JCD. Parish Priest, St. Patrick's Greenock, since 1992; Chairman, Roman Catholic Scottish National Tribunal, 1986-92; Papal Chaplain, since 1994; Vicar General, Diocese of Paisley, since 1997; b. 22.2.38, Paisley. Educ. St. Mary's College, Blairs, Aberdeen; St. Peter's College, Cardross; Scots College and Gregorian University, Rome. Assistant Priest, Our Lady of Lourdes, Bishopton, 1964-69; Professor of Canon Law, St. Peter's College, Cardross and Newlands (Glasgow), 1967-81; Advocate of the Roman Catholic Scottish National Tribunal, 1970-82; Assistant Priest, St. Columba's, Renfrew, 1974-86; Vice-President, RC Scottish National Tribunal, 1982-86. Address: 5 Orangefield Place, Greenock PA15 1YX; T.-01475 720223.

Cunningham, (Robert) Grahame. Divisional Director, Edinburgh Chamber of Commerce and Enterprise, since 1996; Chief Executive, Edinburgh Business Development Ltd., since 1996; Divisional Director, Edinburgh International Trade, since 1997; b. 8.1.44, Edinburgh; m., Elaine Macfie; 3 s.; 1 d. British Transport Hotels, 1963-66 (Trainee Manager); United Biscuits Group of Companies, 1966-87, latterly General Manager (London and Midlands); Assistant Director, EVENT Enterprise Trust, Edinburgh, 1987, which merged with Leith Enterprise Trust, 1992, subsequently Director of Operations in new Capital Enterprise Trust. Director, Edinburgh Community Trust; Director, Craigmillar Opportunities Trust; Director, Edinburgh Business Loan Fund Ltd.; partner in own business, Cunningham & Co. Recreations: golf; renovating classic cars; tennis; motor racing. Address: (h.) 16 Dean Park Crescent, Edinburgh EH4 1PH; T.-0131-315 3302.

Cunningham, Robert Ritchie, MA (Hons). Rector, Inverness High School, since 1991; b. 22.5.53, Stirling; m., Linda; 2 s. Educ. Lenzie Academy; University of Glasgow. Teacher of Geography, Cumbernauld High School, 1977-80; Principal Teacher of Geography, John Neilson High School, Paisley, 1980-84; Field Development Officer, Scottish Examination Board, 1984-86; Adviser in Social Subjects, Highland Region, 1986-91. Publications: author or co-author of over 20 publications, mostly on geography for schools. Recreations: Rotary; writing; playing with my children. Address: (b.) Inverness High School, Montague Row, Inverness IV3 5DZ; T.-01463 233586.

Cunningham, Roseanna, MP. MP (SNP), Perth and Kinross, since 1995; b. 27.7.51, Glasgow. Educ. University of Western Australia. SNP Research Department, 1976-79; law degree, Edinburgh University; Trainee Solicitor, Dumbarton District Council, 1983-86; Glasgow District Council, 1986-89; private practice as a Solicitor, 1989-90; called to the Scottish Bar, 1990. Recreations: martial art; reading; cinema; cats. Address: (b.) House of Commons, Westminster, London, SW1A 0AA.

Cunningham, William Scott, MREHIS. Executive Director, Environmental and Contract Services, Clackmannanshire Council, since 1995; b. 22.8.42, Stirling; m., Jo; 2 d. Educ. Kilsyth Academy. Local government posts, since 1960, with Kilsyth Town Council, Midlothian CC, Clackmannan CC, Clackmannan DC. Recreations: golf; football supporter (Falkirk FC). Address: (h.) 36 Grampian Road, Stirling FK7 9JP; T.-01786 478894.

Cunningham-Jardine, Ronald Charles. Lord Lieutenant, Dumfries, since 1991; Farmer; b. 19.9.31, Edinburgh; m., Constance Mary Teresa Inglis; 1 s.; 1 d. Educ. Ludgrove; Eton; Royal Military Academy, Sandhurst. Royal Scots Greys (retired as Captain), 1950-58. Recreations: all country sports. Address: (h.) Fourmerkland, Lockerbie, Dumfriesshire DG11 1EH; T.-01387 810226.

Curran, Professor Sir Samuel Crowe, Kt, DL, MA, BSc, PhD, DSc, FInstP, FInstE, FRSE, FRS, CEng, DEng, FEng. Visiting Professor of Energy Studies, Glasgow University; Scientific Adviser to various organisations; Fellow of Strathclyde University; b. 23.5.12, Ballymena, Northern Ireland; m.; 3 s.; 1 d. Educ. Wishaw High School; Glasgow University; Cambridge University; California University. Research, Glasgow University, Cambridge University; war research, MAP and Ministry of Supply in radar and atom bomb (Manhattan project); staff, Physics Department, Glasgow University; Chief Scientist, UKAEA at AWRE (also on management board, UKAEA, Harwell); Principal, Royal College of Science and Technology, Glasgow; Principal and Vice-Chancellor, Strathclyde University. Publications: books on nuclear radiation, energy, and issues in science and higher education. Recreations: golf; horology. Address: (h.) 93 Kelvin Court, Glasgow G12 0AH; T.-0141-334 8329.

Currie, Eleanor Jean, MA, DipSecEd. Director of Education, East Renfrewshire Council, since 1995; b. 1.6.50, Ayr; m., Robert L. Currie. Educ. Cumnock Academy; Glasgow University; Jordanhill College. Teacher/Principal Teacher of Modern Studies; seconded to Consultative Committee on the Curriculum; Principal Office (Staffing), then Education Officer (Renfrew Division), then Senior Education Officer (Dumbarton Division), then Divisional Assistant Director of Education (Dumbarton Division), Strathclyde Regional Council. Recreations: keep fit exercising; walking; travel. Address: (b.) Eastwood Park, Rouken Glen Road, Giffnock, G46 6UG; T.-0141-557 3430.

Currie, Rev. Ian Samuel, MBE, BD. Minister, Oakshaw Trinity Church, Paisley, since 1991; b. 14.8.43, Glasgow; m., Jennifer; 1 s.; 1 d. Educ. Bellahouston Academy; Trinity College; University of Glasgow; Minister: Blairhill Dundyvan Church, Coatbridge, 1975-80, St John's Church, Paisley, 1980-91. Chair, Victim Support Scotland, 1993-98; Director, Wynd Centre, Paisley. Recreation: chess. Address: (b.) Oakshaw Trinity Church Office, 6 School Wynd, Paisley PA1 2DB; T.-0141-887 4647.

Currie, Ken. Painter; b. 1960, North Shields. Educ. Paisley College; Glasgow School of Art. Worked on two films about Glasgow and Clyde shipbuilding, 1983-85; specialises in political realism, including a series of murals for the People's Palace Museum, Glasgow, on the socialist history of the city.

Curtis, Professor Adam Sebastian Genevieve, MA, PhD. Professor of Cell Biology, Glasgow University, since 1967; Director, Centre for Cell Engineering, since 1996; b. 3.1.34, London; m., Ann Park; 2 d. Educ. Aldenham School; Kings

College, Cambridge. University College, London: Honorary Research Assistant, 1957-62, Lecturer in Zoology, 1962-67. Director, Company of Biologists Ltd., since 1961; Governor, Westbourne School, 1985-90; Council Member, Royal Society of Edinburgh, 1983-86; President, Society of Experimental Biology, 1991-93; Editor, Scottish Diver magazine, 1978-91, and since 1994; Editor-in-Chief, Experimental Biology Online, since 1996; President, Scottish Sub-Aqua Club, 1972-76. Recreations: sports diving; gardening. Address: (h.) 2 Kirklee Circus, Glasgow G12 0TW; T.-0141-339 2152.

Curtis, Professor David James, BSc, PhD, FZS, CBiol, FIBiol. Professor of Biology, Paisley University, 1990-97 (Visiting Professor, since 1997); Tutor in Biology and Psychology, Open University, since 1973; Ecologist; b. 5.4.45, Liverpool; m., Margaret Angela Lacey; 2 d. Educ. St. Mary's College, Crosby; Liverpool University. Lecturer in Biology, Paisley College of Technology, 1970-81; Senior Lecturer in Biology, Paisley College of Technology, 1981-90; edited five books, written many scientific papers and reports; organised international conferences about environmental conservation; Hon. Secretary, Scottish Environmental Education Council and Director, Scottish Environmental Information Network for Education, 1983-91; Co-Director, Scottish Chough Study Group, 1988-93; Founding Co-Director, European Forum on Birds and Pastoralism, 1988-93; Board Member, Clyde River Purification Board, 1984-92; Member, Species Survival Commission (Steppe and Grassland Birds), IUCN - World Conservation Union, since 1992. Recreations: motor-caravanning; walking; bird-watching; jogging. Address: (b.) Department of Biological Sciences, Paisley University, High Street, Paisley PA1 2BE; T.-0141-848 3119.

Cuschieri, Professor Sir Alfred, MD, ChM, FRCSEd, FRCSEng, FIBiol, MD Liverpool Univ (Hon), FRCSI (Hon), FRCPSGlas (Hon). Professor and Head, Department of Surgery, Dundee University, since 1976; b. 30.9.38, Malta; m., Dr. M.P. Holley; 3 d. Educ. St. Aloysius College; Royal University of Malta; Liverpool University. Lecturer/Senior Lecturer/Reader in Surgery, then Professor of Surgery, Liverpool University. Recreations: fishing; music. Address: (h.) 6 Balnacarron Avenue, St. Andrews KY16 9LT; T.-01382 60111.

Cusine, Professor Douglas James, LLB. Professor, Department of Conveyancing and Professional Practice of Law, Aberdeen University, since 1990; Member: Council, Law Society of Scotland, since 1988, Lord President's Advisory Council on Messengers-at-Arms and Sheriff Officers, since 1989, CCBE, since 1997; Honorary Sheriff, since 1994; b. 2.9.46, Glasgow; m., Marilyn Calvert Ramsay; 1 s.; 1 d. Educ. Hutchesons' Boys' Grammar School; Glasgow University. Solicitor, 1971; Lecturer in Private Law: Glasgow University, 1974-76, Aberdeen University, 1977-82; Senior Lecturer, 1982-90. Publications: Marine Pollution: Law and Practice (Co-Editor), 1980; Cases and Materials in Commercial Law (Co-Editor), 1987; A Scots Conveyancing Miscellany (Editor), 1987; New Reproductive Techniques: a legal perspective, 1988; Law and Practice of Diligence (Co-author), 1989; Reproductive Medicine and the Law (Co-Editor), 1990; Standard Securities, 1990; Missives (Co-Author), 1993; Requirements of Writing (Co-Author), 1995; various articles on medico-legal issues and conveyancing. Recreations: swimming; walking; bird-watching. Address: (b.) Aberdeen University, Taylor Building, Regent Walk, Old Aberdeen AB9 2UB.

Cuthbert, Thomas Paterson, MA (Hons), MEd. Regional Manager (Scotland), ATB — Landbase, since 1993; b. 20.12.57, Dunfermline; m., Margaret; 1 s.; 2 d. Educ. Queen Anne High School, Dunfermline; Edinburgh University. British Universities Soccer Internationalist, 1980. Teacher, Alloa Academy, 1981-87; Research and Development Officer, Scottish Vocational Education Council, 1987-88; Project Development Officer, Fife Education Department, 1989-91; Business Development and Training Manager, Scottish Association of Master Bakers, 1991-93. Recreations: sport, including football, tennis and golf; current affairs; cinema; collecting classic Westerns; reading history. Address: (b.) The Rural Centre, West Mains, Ingliston, Newbridge, Midlothian, EH28 8NZ; T.-0131-472 4131.

Cuthbertson, Iain, MA (Hons), FRSAMD. Actor; b. 4.1.30. Educ. Glasgow Academy; Aberdeen Grammar School; Aberdeen University. General Manager/Director of Productions, Citizens' Theatre, Glasgow, 1962-65; Associate Director, Royal Court Theatre, London, 1965; Director, Perth Theatre, 1967-68; sometime Administrator, Playhouse Theatre, Nottingham; stage performances include title roles in Armstrong's Last Goodnight (Citizens'), The Wallace (Edinburgh Festival), Serjeant Musgrave's Dance (Royal Court), Sutherland's Law (TV series); 1,500 broadcasts; TV work includes Budgie, Charles Endell Esq.; premiere of A Drunk Man Looks at the Thistle, set to music and dance; Hon. LLD, Aberdeen University; former Board Member, Scottish Theatre Company; former Hon. President, SCDA; Visiting Stage Director and Tutor, Royal Scottish Academy of Music and Drama. Recreations: countryside; sailing. Address: (b.) Janet Welch, Personal Management, 32 Hill Street, Richmond, Surrey TW9 1TW.

Cuthbertson, Ian Jardine, LLB, NP, MIPA, MSPI, FInstD. Solicitor, Notary Public and Licensed Insolvency Practitioner; Partner, Dorman, Jeffrey & Co., Solicitors, Glasgow and Edinburgh, since 1979; b. 8.5.51, Glasgow; m., Sally Jane; 1 s.; 2 d. Educ. Jordanhill College School, Glasgow; Glasgow University. Apprenticeship, Messrs Boyds; admitted as Solicitor, 1974; Partner, Messrs Boyds, 1978; jointly founded firm of Dorman Jeffrey & Co., 1979. Recreations: watching football and rugby. Address: (b.) Madeleine Smith House, 6/7 Blythswood Square, Glasgow; T.-0141-221 9880; 20 Ainslie Place, Edinburgh; T.-0131-225 9999.

Cuthbertson, Rev. Malcolm, BA, BD (Hons). Minister, Easterhouse: St. George's and St. Peter's Church of Scotland, since 1984; Non-Executive Director, Glasgow Dental Hospital and School NHS Trust, since 1995; b. 3.4.56, Glasgow; m., Rena Fennel; 1 s.; 2 d. Educ. Grangemouth High School; Stirling University; Aberdeen University. Probationer Assistant, Crown Court Church, London, 1983-84. Recreations: eating out; reading theology. Address: 2 Lochdochart Road, Glasgow G34 0PZ; T.-0141-773 2667.

Cuthell, Rev. Thomas Cuthbertson, MA, BD. Minister, St. Cuthbert's Parish Church, Edinburgh, since 1976; b. 18.2.41, Falkirk. Educ. Bo'ness Academy; University of Edinburgh. Assistant Minister, St. Giles Cathedral, Edinburgh; Minister, North Church, Uphall. Recreations: travel; music; sailing. Address: St. Cuthbert's Parish Church, 5 Lothian Road, Edinburgh EH1 2EP; T.-0131-229 1142.

Cutler, Timothy Robert (Robin), CBE, BSc, DSc. Forestry Consultant; b. 24.7.34, India; m., Ishbel W.M.; 1 s.; 1 d. Educ. Banff Academy; Aberdeen University. Colonial Forest Service, Kenya, 1958-64; New Zealand Government Forestry, 1964-90, latterly Chief Executive, New Zealand Ministry of Forestry; Director General, Forestry Commission, 1990-95. Recreations: tennis; golf; travel. Address: 14 Swanston Road, Edinburgh EH10 7BB; T.-0131-445 5437.

Cywinski, Professor Robert, BSc, PhD, CPhys, MInstP, FRSA. Professor of Physics (Magnetism), School of Physics and Astronomy, University of St. Andrews, since 1995; Director, St. Andrews Centre for Advanced

Materials, since 1996; b. 18.4.52, Huddersfield; 1 d. Educ. Huddersfield New College; University of Manchester; University of Salford. Postdoctoral Research Assistantship, Department of Physics, Imperial College, London, 1976-77; Australian Research Grants Committee Research Fellow, Department of Physics, Monash University, Australia, 1977-80; Senior Scientific Officer, Neutron Division, ISIS, Rutherford Appleton Laboratory, Oxfordshire, 1980-85; Lecturer in Physics, J. J. Thomson Physical Laboratory, University of Reading, 1985-95. UK Delegate and Vice Chairman, European Neutron Scattering Association; Member, Physics College, UK Engineering Physical Sciences Research Council; Member, Neutron Scattering Group Committee, Institute of Physics; Member, Central Laboratories, Research Council's ISIS Muon Instrument Scheduling Panel; Member, European Spallation Source Science Working Group Muon Subcommittee; Chairman, Institut Laue Langevin (Grenoble) Magnetic Structures College, Scientific Council. Publications: Neutron Scattering at a Pulsed Source (Co-Editor); over 130 publications on magnetism, superconductivity, neutron beam science, and muon spin relaxation in international scientific journals. Recreations: photography; music; literature. Address: (b.) School of Physics and Astronomy, University of St. Andrews, St. Andrews, KY16 9SS; T.-01334 463108.

Czerkawska, Catherine Lucy, MA (Hons); MA (postgraduate). Novelist and Dramatist; b. 3.12.50, Leeds; m., Alan Lees; 1 s. Educ. Queen Margaret's Academy, Ayr; St. Michael's Academy, Kilwinning; Edinburgh University; Leeds University. Wrote and published two books of poety (White Boats and a Book of Men); taught EFL in Finland and Poland for three years; returned to Scotland to work as Community Writer in Fife; thereafter, full-time freelance writer working on radio, television and stage plays; author, Shadow of the Stone and The Golden Apple; Pye Radio Award for Best Play of 1980, O Flower of Scotland; Scottish Radio Industries Club Award, 1983, for Bonnie Blue Hen; Wormwood, produced by Traverse Theatre, Edinburgh, 1997. Recreations: travel; films; local history; swimming; genealogy. Address: c/o Peters Fraser and Dunlop, 5th Floor, The Chambers, Chelsea Harbour, Lots Road, London, SW10 0XF; T.-0171-376 7676.

D

Dagg, John Hunter, MD (Hons), FRCPGlas, FRCPEdin. Consultant Physician, Western Infirmary, Glasgow, since 1972; Honorary Lecturer in Medicine, Glasgow University, since 1962; b. 23.3.33, Rutherglen. Educ. High School of Glasgow; Glasgow University. Junior hospital posts, Glasgow and Paisley, 1958-65; Senior US Public Health Service Fellow, University of Washington Medical School, 1965-67; Senior Wellcome Fellow in Clinical Science, University Department of Medicine, Western Infirmary, Glasgow, 1968-72. Member, Board of Examiners, Royal Colleges of Physicians, UK. Recreations: classical music, especially as pianist; hill-walking; gardening. Address: (h.) Ardvulan, Gartmore, By Stirling FK8 3RJ.

Daiches, Professor David, CBE, MA (Edin), DPhil (Oxon), Hon. DLitt (Edinburgh, Glasgow, Sussex, Brown, Guelph), Docteur de l'Universite (Sorbonne), DUniv (Stirling), Dottore in Lettere (Bologna). Writer; b. 2.9.12, Sunderland; m., Isobel J. Mackay (deceased); 1 s.; 2 d. Educ. George Watson's College, Edinburgh; Edinburgh University; Balliol College, Oxford. Professor of English, Cornell University, 1946-51; University Lecturer in English and Fellow of Jesus College, Cambridge, 1951-61; Professor of English, Sussex University, 1961-77; Director, Institute for Advanced Studies in the Humanities, Edinburgh University, 1980-86. President, Saltire Society, 1981-87, now Hon. President; Past President, Association for Scottish Literary Studies. Publications: numerous works of criticism and biography, including A Critical History of English Literature; Robert Burns; Sir Walter Scott and His World; The Paradox of Scottish Culture; God and the Poets (Gifford Lectures, 1983); A Weekly Scotsman and Other Poems. Recreations: music; talking. Address: (h.) 22 Belgrave Crescent, Edinburgh EH4 3AL.

Daiches, Lionel Henry, MA, LLB. Queen's Counsel, since 1956; Fellow, International Academy of Trial Lawyers, since 1976; b. 8.3.11, Sunderland; 2 s. Educ. George Watson's College, Edinburgh; Edinburgh University. Solicitor, Scotland, 1936-39; Army service, 1940-46, including Judge Advocate-General's Branch, Central Mediterranean Forces, North Africa and Italy (including Anzio Beachhead); Advocate, Scots Bar, 1946; QC Scotland, 1956; broadcaster on television and radio. Publication: Russians at Law, 1960.

Dalby, Martin, BMus, ARCM. Composer; freelance music producer; Chairman, Composers' Guild of Great Britain, 1995-98; b. 25.4.42, Aberdeen; m., Hilary. Educ. Aberdeen Grammar School; Royal College of Music. Music Producer, BBC Radio 3, 1965-71; Cramb Research Fellow in Composition, Glasgow University, 1971-72; Head of Music, BBC Scotland, 1972-90; Executive Music Producer, BBC Scotland, 1990-93. Recreations: flying; railways; birdwatching; hill-walking. Address: (h.) 23 Muirpark Way, Drymen, near Glasgow G63 ODX; T.-01360 660427.

Dale, Brian Graeme, LLB, WS, NP. Partner, Brooke & Brown, WS, Dunbar, since 1974; b. 20.11.46, London; m., Judith Gail de Beaufort Franklin; 4 s.; 2 d. Educ. Bristol Grammar School; Aberdeen University. Shepherd & Wedderburn, WS, Edinburgh, 1968-70; Stuart & Stuart WS, Edinburgh, 1970-85; Diocese of Edinburgh, Scottish Episcopal Church: Treasurer, since 1995, Secretary, 1974-90, Registrar, 1974; Honorary Secretary, Abbeyfield Society (Dunbar) Ltd. Recreations: music; armchair sport; singing; family life. Address: (h.) 5 The Doon, Spott, Dunbar, East Lothian; T.-Dunbar 862059.

Dale, Professor John Egerton, BSc, PhD, FRSE, FIBiol. Emeritus Professor of Plant Physiology, Edinburgh University, since 1993; b. 13.2.32, London; m., Jacqueline Joyce Benstock; 1 s.; 2 d. Educ. City of London School; Kings College, London. Plant Physiologist, Empire Cotton Growing Corporation, Uganda, 1956-61; Edinburgh University: Lecturer in Botany, then Reader, 1961-85, Professor of Plant Physiology, 1985-93, Head, Division of Biological Sciences, 1990-93. Secretary, Society for Experimental Biology, 1974-79; Secretary General, Federation of European Societies of Plant Physiology, 1978-84; Trustee, Peter Potter Gallery, since 1994; Convener, Conservation Stategy Committee, Scottish Wildlife Trust (Member, Council, since 1997). Publications: 100 papers on growth of leaves and related topics. Recreations: the arts; travel; gardening. Address: (h.) The Old Bothy, Drem, North Berwick, EH39 5AP; T.-01620 850394.

Dalhousie, Earl of (Simon Ramsay), KT, GCVO, GBE, MC, LLD. Lord Lieutenant, County of Angus, 1967-89; Lord Chamberlain to Queen Elizabeth, the Queen Mother, 1965-92; Chancellor, Dundee University, 1977-92; b. 17.10.14, London; m., Margaret Elizabeth Mary Stirling; 3 s.; 2 d. Educ. Eton; Christ Church, Oxford. Major, 4/5 Black Watch TA; served overseas, 1939-45 (prisoner); MP, Forfar, 1945-50; Conservative Whip, 1946-48; Governor-General, Federation of Rhodesia and Nyasaland, 1957-63. Address: (h.) Brechin Castle, Brechin, Angus; T.-0135-62 2176.

Dalkeith, Earl of (Richard Walter John Montagu Douglas Scott). Deputy Chairman, Independent Television Commission, since 1996; Member, Millennium Commission, since 1994; b. 14.2.54; m., Lady Elizabeth Kerr; 2 s.; 2 d. Son and heir of 9th Duke of Buccleuch (qv). Address: (h.) Dabton, Thornhill, Dumfriesshire.

Dallas, Garry, BA (Hons), DipTP, MSc, MRTPI. Executive Director, Development Services, Clackmannanshire Council, since 1995; b. 15.8.59, Kirkcaldy; m., Ruth. Educ. Glenrothes High School; Strathclyde University; Heriot-Watt University. Planning Officer, Principal Planner, Planning Manager, Property Development Manager, Head of Planning and Property Development, Clackmannan District Council, 1983-95. Founding Director, Alloa Tower Building Preservation Trust. Recreations: motor sports; swimming; golf; heritage site visits. Address: (b.) Clackmannanshire Council, Greenfield, Alloa FK10 2AD; T.-01259 452180.

Dalrymple, Sir Hew (Fleetwood) Hamilton-, 10th Bt (created 1697), KCVO, 1985 (CVO, 1974). Lord Lieutenant, East Lothian, since 1987; Captain General, Queen's Bodyguard for Scotland (Royal Company of Archers); Gold Stick for Scotland, since 1996; b. 9.4.26; m., Lady Anne-Louise Mary Keppel; 4 s. Educ. Ampleforth; Staff College, Camberley, 1957. Commissioned Grenadier Guards, 1944; DAAG HQ 3rd Division, 1958-60; Regimental Adjt., Grenadier Guards, 1960-62; retired, 1962; Vice-Chairman, Scottish & Newcastle Breweries, 1983-86 (Director, 1967-86); Chairman, Scottish American Investment Co., 1985-91 (Director, 1967-94); DL, East Lothian, 1964; JP, 1987. Address: Leuchie, North Berwick, East Lothian; T.-North Berwick 2903.

Dalrymple, John Francis, BA, PhD, MInstP, CPhys, FSS. Director, Scottish Quality Management Centre, Stirling University, since 1990; Governor, BMT Quality Assurance Ltd., since 1990; b. 18.9.49, Rosyth; 1 s.; 3 d. Educ. St. Andrew's High School, Kirkcaldy; Stirling University; Strathclyde University. Research Fellow, then Lecturer, Department of Applied Physics, Strathclyde University, 1974-79; Lecturer, Senior Lecturer, Head, Department of Management Science, Stirling University, 1979-92; Member, Strathclyde Region Children's Panel, since 1977; Chairman, Scottish Association of Children's Panels, 1983-88. Publications: 100 papers and presentations. Recreations:

skiing; walking; reading; swimming. Address: (b.) Management Science, Faculty of Management, Stirling University, Stirling FK9 4LA; T.-01786 467360.

Dalrymple-Hamilton, Christian Margaret, MBE, DL; b. 20.9.19, Devon. Former President: Wigtownshire Girl Guides, Wigtownshire Branch British Red Cross Society. Address: (h.) Cladyhouse, Cairnryan, Stranraer, Wigtownshire.

Dalrymple-Hamilton of Bargany, Captain North Edward Frederick, CVO, MBE, DSC, JP, DL (Ayrshire). Lieutenant, Queen's Bodyguard for Scotland (Royal Company of Archers); b. 17.2.22; m., 1, Hon. Mary Colville (deceased); 2 s.; 2, Antoinette Beech. Educ. Eton. Director of Naval Signals, 1965, Director, Weapons Equipment Surface, 1967, retired, 1970. Address: (h.) Lovestone House, Bargany, Girvan, Ayrshire KA26 9RF; T.-01465 871227.

Dalrymple Hamilton, North John Frederick, OBE, TD, MA (Hons), DL. Farmer and Estate Manager; b. 7.5.50, Edinburgh; m., Sally Anne How; 2 s.; 1 d. Educ. Eton College; Aberdeen University. Scottish and Newcastle Breweries, 1972-82; certificate of farming practice, East of Scotland College of Agriculture, 1982-84; farming of Bargany Estate, since 1984. TA Commission, 1967-95; Member, Queen's Bodyguard for Scotland; Deputy Lieutenant for Ayrshire; President, RBL(S), Maybole Branch. Address: (h.) Houdston, Girvan, Ayrshire KA26 9PH.

Dalyell, Tam. MP (Labour), Linlithgow (formerly West Lothian), since 1962; Weekly Columnist, New Scientist, since 1967; b. 9.8.32, Edinburgh; m., Kathleen Wheatley; 1 s.; 1 d. Educ. Edinburgh Academy; Harecroft; Eton; King's College, Cambridge; Moray House, Edinburgh. National Service, Scots Greys; Teacher, Bo'ness Academy, 1957-61; Deputy Director of Studies, Ship-School Dunera, 1961-62; Member, Public Accounts Committee, 1962-66; PPS to R.H.S. Crossman, 1964-70; Vice-Chairman, Parliamentary Labour Party, 1974-76; Member, European Parliament, 1975-78; Member: National Executive Committee, Labour Party, 1986-87, Advisory Council on Biological Sciences, Edinburgh University; a Vice-President, Research Defence Society; Hon. Doctor of Science, Edinburgh University, 1994. Publications: Case for Ship Schools, 1959; Ship-School Dunera, 1961; Devolution: the end of Britain?, 1978; A Science Policy for Britain, 1983; One Man's Falklands, 1983; Misrule, 1987; Dick Crossman: a portrait, 1989. Address: (h.) The Binns, Linlithgow EH49 7NA; T.-0506-83 4255.

Dalzel-Job, Lt. Cdr. Patrick. Deputy Lieutenant, Lochalsh, since 1979; b. 1.6.13, London; m., Bjorg Bangsund (deceased); 1 s. Educ. Berkhamsted; in Switzerland. Owner/Master, topsail schooner Mary Fortune, mainly Norwegian and Arctic waters, until start of Second World War; as a junior Sub Lt, organised landing of Allied Expeditionary Force, North Norway, 1940, and evacuation of civilians from Narvik before German bombing; thanked by King of Norway; awarded Knight's Cross (1st Class) of St. Olav with swords; Special Service Operations, Norway, France, Germany; Canadian Navy, post-war; retired to West Highlands, 1960; awarded BBC TV Heart of Gold, 1996. Publications: The Settlers, 1957; From Arctic Snow to Dust of Normandy, 1991 (published in English, French and Norwegian). Recreations: skiing; sailing; woodland garden. Address: (h.) Nead-An-Eoin, by Plockton, Rossshire; T.-01599 544 244.

Daniels, Peter. Chief Executive, East Renfrewshire Council. Address: (b.) Eastwood Park, Rouken Glen Road, Giffnock Glasgow G46 6UG.

Dareau, Margaret Grace, MA. Senior Editor, Dictionary of the Older Scottish Tongue, since 1984; b. 11.3.44, Dumfries; m., Michel Dareau; 1 s.; 2 d. Educ. Annan Academy; Edinburgh University. Research Assistant on Middle English Dialects Atlas, 1967; Kennedy Scholarship to study linguistics, MIT, 1967; began work at Dictionary of Older Scottish Tongue, 1968; Editor, Concise Scots Dictionary, 1976-77, 1980-84; Glossary Editor, Edinburgh Encyclopedia of Language and Linguistics. Recreation: horse riding. Address: (h.) The Old Manse, Howgate, Penicuik EH26 8QB; T.-01968 673028.

Dargie, Gordon. Principal, Shetland College of Further Education. Address: (b.) Gremista, Lerwick, Shetland, ZE1 0PX.

Darling, Alistair Maclean, LLB. Chief Secretary to the Treasury, since 1997; MP (Labour), Edinburgh Central, since 1987; Member, Faculty of Advocates, since 1984; b. 28.11.53, London; m., Margaret Vaughan; 1 s.; 1 d. Educ. Loretto School; Aberdeen University. Solicitor, 1978-83; Advocate, since 1984; Member: Lothian Regional Council, 1982-87, Lothian and Borders Police Board, 1982-87; Governor, Napier College, 1985-87. Address: (b.) 78 Buccleuch Street, Edinburgh; T.-0131-662 0123.

Darling, Ian Marshall, FRICS. Chairman, Royal Institution of Chartered Surveyors in Scotland, since 1997; Director, Chesterton Scotland, since 1996; b. 16.4.45, Perth; m., Kate; 1 s.; 1 d. Educ. Perth Academy; London University (College of Estate Management). Qualified as a Chartered Surveyor, 1968; Partner, Bell Ingram, 1974; Managing Partner, 1987. Member, Council, British Trust for Ornithology; Member, Scottish Committee, RSPB; President, Scottish Ornithologists' Club. Recreations: nature conservation; ornithology. Address: (b.) 36 Castle Street, Edinburgh EH2 3HT; T.-0131-226 4791.

Darwent, Rt. Rev. Frederick Charles, LTh (Hon), JP. Bishop of Aberdeen and Orkney, 1978-92; b. 20.4.27, Liverpool; m., 1, Edna Lilian Waugh (deceased); 2 d.; 2, Roma Evelyn Fraser. Educ. Warbreck School, Liverpool; Ormskirk Grammar School; Wells Theological College, Somerset. Followed a banking career, 1943-61; War Service, Far East, 1945-48; ordained Deacon, 1963, Priest, 1964, Diocese of Liverpool; Curate, Pemberton, Wigan, 1963-65; Rector: Strichen, 1965-71, New Pitsligo, 1965-78, Fraserburgh, 1971-78; Canon, St. Andrew's Cathedral, Aberdeen, 1971; Dean of Aberdeen and Orkney, 1973-78. Recreations: amateur stage (acting and production); calligraphy; music. Address: (h.) 107 Osborne Place, Aberdeen AB25 2DD; T.-01224 646497.

Das, Sachinandan, MB, BS, FRCR, DMRT. Consultant in administrative charge, Ninewells Hospital, Dundee, and Head, University Department, Dundee University, since 1987, Clinical Director, since 1991; Chairman, Area Oncology Committee, since 1987; Council Member, Scottish Radiological Society, since 1987; Regional Postgraduate Education Advisor in Radiotherapy and Oncology, since 1987; b. 1.8.44, Cuttack, India; m., Dr. Subhalaxmi; 1 s.; 1 d. Educ. Ravenshaw Collegiate School; SCB Medical College, Cuttack, India; Utkal University. Senior House Officer in Radiotherapy, Plymouth General Hospital, 1969-70; Registrar in Radiotherapy and Oncology, then Senior Registrar, Mersey Regional Centre for Radiotherapy, Liverpool, 1970-77; Member: Standing Scottish Committee, National Medical Consultative Committee, Scottish Paediatric Oncology Group, Joint Radiological Safety Committee, Radiation Hazards Sub-Committee, Unit Medical and Dental Advisory Committee. Recreations: hill-walking; table tennis; reading. Address: (h.) Grapevine, 42 Menzieshill Road, Dundee DD2 1PU; T.-Dundee 642915.

Datta, Dipankar, MB, BS, FRCPGlas. Consultant Physician (with special interest in gastroenterology), since 1975; Honorary Senior Clinical Lecturer and Clinical Sub-Dean, Glasgow University; Chairman, Scottish India Forum; Founder Director, Scottish Overseas Aid; b. 30.1.33, Chittagong, India; m., Dr. J.B. Datta; 1 s.; 1 d. Educ. Calcutta University. Former Vice Chairman, UN Association, Glasgow; former Chairman, Overseas Doctors' Association, Scottish Division; former Chairman, British Medical Association, Lanarkshire; former Member, Central Executive Committee, Scottish Council, United Nations Association; former Member, Lanarkshire Health Board; former Member, Scottish Council, British Medical Association; former Member, Executive Committee, Scottish Council, Royal Commonwealth Society for the Blind; former Member, Senate, Glasgow University; Member, General Medical Council; Chairman, South Asia Voluntary Enterprise. Recreations: reading - history, economics and international politics. Address: (h.) 9 Kirkvale Crescent, Newton Mearns, Glasgow G77 5HB; T.-0141-639 1515.

Davenport, Professor John, BSc, MSc, PhD, DSc, FIBiol, FZS, FRSE. Director, University Marine Biological Station, Millport, since 1991; Professor of Marine Biology, London University; b. 12.2.46; m., Julia Ladner; 2 d. Educ. Bablake School, Coventry; London University; Southampton University; University of Wales. Demonstrator in Marine Biology, University of Wales at Bangor, 1970-72; Researcher, NERC Unit of Marine Invertebrate Biology, 1972-83 (promoted Principal Scientific Officer, 1980); Lecturer, then Senior Lecturer, School of Animal Biology, University of Wales at Bangor, 1983-88; Reader in Marine Biology, School of Ocean Sciences, Marine Sciences Laboratories, Menai Bridge, 1988-91. Publications: Animal Osmoregulation (Co-Author), 1981; Environmental Stress and Behavioural Adaptation, 1985; Animal Life at Low Temperature, 1992. Recreations: skiing; sailboarding; swimming; birding; badminton. Address: (b.) University Marine Biological Station, Isle of Cumbrae KA28 0EG.

Davidson, Alan Ingram, ChM, FRCSEdin, DObstRCOG. Consultant Surgeon, Aberdeen Royal Infirmary, since 1974; Honorary Senior Lecturer in Surgery, Aberdeen University, since 1974; b. 25.3.35, Aberdeen; m., Margaret Elizabeth Mackay; 1 s.; 1 d. Educ. Robert Gordon's College, Aberdeen; Aberdeen University. House Officer, Aberdeen Royal Infirmary, 1959-60; National Service, Royal Army Medical Corps, 1960-62; Lecturer, Department of Pathology, Aberdeen, 1963-64; Registrar and Senior Registrar, Aberdeen Royal Infirmary, 1964-74. Recreations: gardening; watching TV; music. Address: (h.) 20 Hillview Road, Cults, Aberdeen; T.-Aberdeen 867347.

Davidson, Hon. Lord (Charles Kemp Davidson), MA, LLB, FRSE. Chairman, Scottish Law Commission, 1988-96; Senator of the College of Justice, 1983-96; Deputy Chairman, Boundaries Commission for Scotland, 1985-96; b. 13.4.29, Edinburgh; m., Mary Mactaggart; 1 s.; 2 d. Educ. Fettes College, Edinburgh; Oxford University; Edinburgh University. Advocate, 1956; QC (Scot), 1969; Keeper, The Advocates Library, 1972-77; Vice Dean, Faculty of Advocates, 1977-79; Dean, 1979-83; Procurator to the General Assembly of the Church of Scotland, 1972-83; Chairman, National Health Service Tribunal for Scotland, 1970-83. Address: (h.) 22 Dublin Street, Edinburgh EH1 3PP; T.-0131-556 2168.

Davidson, Professor Colin William, BSc, DipER, PhD, CEng, FIEE, FRSA. Consulting Engineer; Vice-President, Institution of Electrical Engineers, since 1995 (and 1990-93); b. 18.9.34, Edinburgh; m., Ranee M.N. Cleland; 2 d. Educ. George Heriot's School; Edinburgh University. Lecturer, Edinburgh University, 1956-61; Electronics Engineer, Nuclear Enterprises (GB) Ltd., 1961-64; Lecturer, Heriot-Watt College/University, 1964-67;

Associate Professor, Chulalongkorn University, Bangkok, 1967-68; Heriot-Watt University: Senior Lecturer, 1968-85, Professor of Electrical Engineering, 1985-88, Dean of Engineering, 1976-79 and 1984-87, Head of Department, 1979-87. Member, Lothian Regional Council, 1990-94; Liveryman, Worshipful Company of Engineers, City of London; Member, Engineering Council Senate and Board for Engineers' Regulation, since 1996. Recreation: sailing (Royal Highland Yacht Club). Address: (h.) 20 East Barnton Avenue, Edinburgh EH4 6AQ; T.-0131-336 5806.

Davidson, Professor Donald Allen, BSc, PhD, FRSE. Professor of Environmental Science, Stirling University, since 1991; b. 27.4.45, Lumphanan; m., Caroline E. Brown; 1 s.; 2 d. Educ. Robert Gordon's College, Aberdeen; Aberdeen University; Sheffield University. Lecturer, St. David's University College, Wales, 1971-76; Lecturer, Senior Lecturer, Reader, Strathclyde University, 1976-86; Reader, Stirling University, 1986-91. Member, Terrestrial Sciences Committee, Natural Environmental Research Council. Publications include: The Evaluation of Land Resources, 1992; many papers. Recreations: exploring the countryside; real ale. Address: (b.) Department of Environmental Science, Stirling University, Stirling FK9 4LA; T.-01786 467840.

Davidson, Duncan Lewis Watt, BSc (Hons), MB, ChB, FRCPEdin. Consultant Neurologist, Tayside Health Board, since 1976; Honorary Senior Lecturer in Medicine, Dundee University, since 1976; b. 16.5.40, Kingston, Jamaica; m., Dr. Anne V.M. Maiden; 4 s.; 1 d. Educ. Knox College, Jamaica; Edinburgh University. House Officer, Senior House Officer, Registrar and Senior Registrar posts in medicine and neurology, Edinburgh, 1966-75; Peel Travelling Fellowship, Montreal, 1973-74; MRC clinical scientific staff, MRC Brain Metabolism Unit, Edinburgh, 1975-76. Recreations: gardening; golf. Address: (h.) Brooksby, Queens Terrace, St. Andrews, Fife; T.-01334 76108.

Davidson, Euan, LLB(Hons). Director, Clydeport plc, since 1994; b. 8.7.58, Bellshill; m., 1, Elspeth Robertson (divorced); 2, Dawn Gaw; 1 s.; 1 d. Educ. Hutchesons' Grammar School, Glasgow; University of Glasgow. Wright, Johnston and Mackenzie, Solicitors, Glasgow: Apprentice, 1979, qualified as Solicitor, 1981, Partner, 1985, Managing Partner, 1991-94; Clydeport plc: Director and Secretary, 1994, Corporate Services Director, 1996. Member of Council, British Ports Association; Session Clerk, Cairngryffe Parish Church. Recreations: hillwalking; gardening. Address: (b.) 16 Roberston Street, Glasgow G2 8DS; T.-0141-221 8733.

Davidson, Ian Graham, MA (Hons). MP (Labour and Co-op), Glasgow Pollok, since 1997 (Glasgow Govan 1992-97); Secretary, Tribune Group; Chair, MSF Group; b. 8.9.50, Jedburgh; m., Morag Mackinnon; 1 s.; 1 d. Educ. Jedburgh Grammar School; Galashiels Academy; Edinburgh University; Jordanhill College of Education. Chairman, Strathclyde Education Committee, 1990-92; Chairman, COSLA Education Committee, 1990-92. Address: (b.) Constituency Office, 1829 Paisley Road West, Glasgow G52 3SS; T.-0141-883 8336.

Davidson, Rev. Ian Murray Pollock, MBE, MA, BD. Minister, Allan Park South Church and Church of the Holy Rude, Stirling, 1985-94; Chairman, General Trustees, Church of Scotland, since 1993; b. 14.3.28, Kirriemuir; m., Isla; 2 s. Educ. Montrose Academy; St. Andrews University. National Service, 1949-51; Minister: Crieff North and West Church (St. Andrew's), 1955-61, Grange Church, Kilmarnock, 1961-67, Cambuslang Old Church, 1967-85; Convener, Maintenance of the Ministry Committee and Board, Church and Ministry Department, 1981-84; General Trustee, since 1975. Publications: At the Sign of the Fish (history of Cambuslang Old Parish

Church), 1975; A Guide to the Church of the Holy Rude. Recreations: travel; photography; reading; writing. Address: (h.) 13/8 Craigend Park, Edinburgh EH16 5XX; T.-0131-664 0074.

Davidson, John F., MB, ChB, FRCPEdin, FRCPath. Consultant Haematologist, Glasgow Royal Infirmary, since 1969; b. 11.1.34, Lumphanan; m., Laura G. Middleton; 1 s.; 1 d. Educ. Robert Gordon's College, Aberdeen; Aberdeen University. Surgeon Lt., RN; Registrar in Medicine, Aberdeen Royal Infirmary; Research Registrar in Medicine, then Senior Registrar in Haematology, Glasgow Royal Infirmary; Honorary Clinical Senior Lecturer, Glasgow University; Honorary Consultant Haematologist, Strathclyde University. Secretary, British Society for Haematalogy, 1983-86; President, British Society for Haematology, 1990-91; Chairman: BCSH Haemostasis and Thrombosis Task Force, 1986-81, Steering Committee NEQAS in blood coagulation, 1986-91; Member, Council, Royal College of Pathologists, two terms; Secretary, Joint Committee on Haematology, Royal College of Pathologists and Royal College of Physicians; Chairman, UK Joint Working Group on Quality Assurance. Editor, Progress in Fibrinolysis, Volumes I to VII; Chairman, International Committee on Fibrinolysis, 1976-84; Co-Editor in Chief, Fibrinolysis, 1986-96. Recreation: gardening. Address: (b.) Department of Haematology, Glasgow Royal Infirmary, Glasgow; T.-0141-211 4669.

Davidson, John Knight, OBE, MD, FRCP (Edin), FRCP (Glas), FRCR, (Hon) FACR, (Hon) FRACR. Consultant Radiologist; expert adviser on bone disease in compressed air and diving medicine; b. 17.8.25, Edinburgh; m., Edith E. McKelvie; 2 s.; 1 d. Educ. George Watson's Boys College, Edinburgh; Edinburgh University. Adviser in Bone Disease in Divers MRC, Aberdeen, US Navy, 1970-92; Non Executive Director, Yorkhill NHS Trust, 1993-95; Member, Council, Medical and Dental Defence Union, 1971-95; Chairman, Health Policy, Council, Scottish Conservative and Unionist Association, 1991-95; Member, BBC Medical Advisory Group, 1988-95; Consultant Radiologist in Administrative Charge, Western Infirmary and Gartnavel General, Glasgow, 1967-90; Royal College of Radiologists: Member, Council, 1984-87, Chairman, Examining Board, 1976-79, Scottish Committee, 1985-89; Member, Council, Royal Glasgow Institute of Fine Arts, 1978-88; Deputy President, Glasgow and Renfrewshire, British Red Cross Society, 1988-93; Honorary Fellow: Royal Australian College of Radiology, 1981, Scottish Radiological Society, 1990, American College of Radiology, 1992, Medical and Dental Defence Union, Scotland, 1995; Honorary Fellow and Medallist, International Skeletal Society, 1995; Rohan Williams Professor, Australasia, 1977; Aggarwal Memorial Oration, India, 1988. Editor, Aseptic Necrosis of Bone and numerous publications. Recreations: golf; painting; bridge; meeting people; skiing. Address: (h.) 15 Beechlands Avenue, Netherlee, Glasgow G44 3YT; T.-0141-637 0290.

Davidson, Julie Wilson. Writer and Broadcaster; Freelance Contributor to radio, television, newspapers and magazines, since 1981; b. Motherwell; m., Harry Reid (qv); 1 d. Educ. Aberdeen High School for Girls. Trainee Journalist, D.C. Thomson Ltd., Dundee, 1961-64; Feature Writer and Sub-Editor, Aberdeen Press & Journal, 1964-67; The Scotsman: Feature Writer, 1967-77, Columnist, 1977-81; Columnist, The Herald, 1995-97; Television Critic, The Herald, 1981-95. Columnist/Critic of the Year, Scottish Press Awards, 1985; Critic of the Year, Scottish Press Awards, 1988-89-92-94-95; Canada Travel Award, 1992. Recreations: reading; walking; travelling; lunching. Address: (h.) 15 Albion Buildings, Ingram Street, Glasgow; T.-0141-552 8403.

Davidson, Neil Forbes, QC, BA, MSc, LLB, LLM; b. 13.9.50. Admitted, Faculty of Advocates, 1979; called to the Bar, Inner Temple, 1990; Commissioner, Scottish Council for International Arbitration, since 1990.

Davidson, Sheriff Richard Alexander, LLB, NP. Sheriff of Tayside Central and Fife at Dundee, since 1994; b. 3.11.47, Lennoxtown; m., Shirley Margaret Thomson; 1 s.; 1 d. Educ. Oban High School; Glasgow University. Apprentice Solicitor, 1969-72; Assistant Solicitor, 1972-76; Partner, Tindal Oatts, 1976-94. Member, Glasgow and North Argyll Legal Aid Committee, 1984-89. Address: (b.) Sheriff Courthouse, West Bell Street, Dundee.

Davidson, Professor Robert, MA, BD, DD, FRSE. Moderator, General Assembly of the Church of Scotland, 1990-91; Professor of Old Testament Language and Literature, Glasgow University, 1972-91; Principal, Trinity College, Glasgow, 1981-91; b. 30.3.27, Markinch, Fife; m., Elizabeth May Robertson; 4 s.; 4 d. Educ. Bell-Baxter School, Cupar; St. Andrews University. Lecturer in Biblical Studies, Aberdeen University, 1953-60; Lecturer in Hebrew and Old Testament Studies, St. Andrews University, 1960-66; Lecturer/Senior Lecturer in Old Testament, Edinburgh University, 1966-72. Publications: The Bible Speaks, 1959; The Old Testament, 1964; Geneses 1 - 11, 1973; Genesis 12 - 50, 1979; The Bible in Religious Education, 1979; The Courage to Doubt, 1983; Jeremiah Volume 1, 1983; Jeremiah Volume 2, Lamentations, 1985; Ecclesiastes, Song of Songs, 1986; Wisdom and Worship, 1990; A Beginner's Guide to the Old Testament, 1992; Go by the Book, 1996. Recreations: music; gardening. Address: (h.) 30 Dumgoyne Drive, Bearsden, Glasgow G61 3AP; T.-0141-942 1810.

Davidson, William Keith, CBE, JP; b. 20.11.26, Glasgow; m., Dr. Mary W.A. Davidson; 1 s.; 1 d. Educ. Coatbridge Secondary School; Glasgow University. Medical Officer, 1st Bn., RSF, 1950; Maj. 2 i/c 14 Field Ambulance, 1950-51; Medical Officer, i/c Holland and Belgium, 1952; General Medical Practitioner, 1953-90; Chairman: Glasgow Local Medical Committee, 1971-75, Scottish General Medical Services Committee, 1972-75; Member, Scottish Council on Crime, 1972-75; Fellow, BMA, 1975; Deputy Chairman, General Medical Services Committee (UK), 1975-79; Member, Scottish Medical Practices Committee, 1968-80; Chairman: Scottish Council, BMA, 1978-81, Scottish Health Services Planning Council, 1984-89; Member, Scottish Health Services Policy Board, 1985-89; Vice President, BMA, since 1983; Hon. President, Glasgow Eastern Medical Society, 1984-85; Member, General Medical Council, 1984-94; Fellow, Royal College of General Practitioners, since 1980; Member, Greater Glasgow Health Board, 1989-91; Chairman: Strathclyde Aids Forum, 1990-93, Greater Glasgow Health Board Aids Forum, 1990-93, Greater Glasgow Health Board Drugs & Alcohol Forum, 1990-93, Chryston High School Board, since 1995; Elder, Church of Scotland, since 1956. Recreation: gardening. Address: (h.) Dunvegan, Hornshill Farm Road, Stepps, Glasgow G33 6DE; T.-0141-779 2103.

Davidson, William Powell, MREHIS, MInstWM, MILAM. Head of Environmental Health, Dumfries and Galloway Council; Chairman, Scottish Food and Drugs Co-ordinating Committee, since 1991; b. 28.8.48, Paisley; m., Elizabeth Ann Davidson; 1 s. Educ. Camphill Senior Secondary School, Paisley; Langside College, Glasgow; Bell College, Hamilton. Trainee, then Assistant Sanitary Inspector, Renfrew County Council, 1966-71; Sanitary Inspector, Paisley Burgh Council, 1971-72; Assistant District Sanitary Inspector, Perth and Kinross Joint County Council, 1972-75; Area Environmental Health Officer, Argyll and Bute District Council, 1975-76; Regional Manager, Ciba Geigy Public Hygiene Project, Saudi Arabia, 1976-77; Senior Environmental Health Officer, Perth and Kinross District Council, 1977-79; Depute Director of Environmental Health, Stewartry District Council, 1979-82; Director of Environmental Health & Leisure Services,

Stewartry District Council, 1982-96. Recreations: golf; gardening; travel; jogging. Address: (b.) Environmental Health Department, Cannonwalls, High Street, Kirkcudbright.

Davie, Ivor Turnbull, MB, ChB, FRCA, FRCPE, HonFCPS(Bd). Consultant Anaesthetist, Western General Hospital, Edinburgh, since 1971; Honorary Senior Lecturer, Edinburgh University, since 1979; Lecturer, Central Midwives Board (Scotland), since 1974; b. 23.2.35, Edinburgh; m., Jane Elizabeth Fleischmann; 1 s.; 1 d. Educ. Royal High School, Edinburgh; Edinburgh University. Member, Board of Examiners, Faculty of Anaesthetists, Royal College of Surgeons of England and Royal College of Anaesthetists, 1978-91; President, Edinburgh and East of Scotland Society of Anaesthetists, 1990-91; Tutor, Faculty of Anaesthetists, 1979-87; Regional Educational Adviser, Royal College of Anaesthetists, 1988-95; Member, Editorial Board, British Journal of Obstetrics and Gynaecology, 1980-84; Visiting Medical Officer, Westmead Centre, Sydney, NSW, 1983. Address: (h.) 26 Kingsburgh Road, Edinburgh EH12 6PZ; T.-0131-337 1117.

Davies, Adrian Hartley Kemp, BA(Econ), CQSW, MPhil, MBA. Director, Glasgow Council on Alcohol, since 1992; b. 7.8.47, Birkenhead; m., Anne; 2 s.; 1 d. Educ. Ellesmere College, Shropshire; University of Manchester; University of Aberdeen; University of Strathclyde. Simon Worker, Simon Community, Liverpool, 1969-71; Trainee Social Worker, Cheshire Social Services Department, 1971-72; Group Leader, St. Mungo Community, London, 1972-74; professional social work training, Aberdeen, 1974-76; Senior Social Worker, Helping Hand Organisation, Manchester, 1976-79; Lecturer, Alcohol Studies Centre, Paisley College of Technology, 1979-83; Hostels Co-ordinator and Depute Housing Manager, Glasgow City Council Housing Department, 1983-92. Recreations: hill-walking; swimming; history. Address: (b.) 9th Floor, Elmbank Chambers, 289 Bath Street, Glasgow G2 4JL; T.-0141-226 3883.

Davies, Alan Graham, LLB(Hons), Dip. Legal Practice. Solicitor in private practice since 1983, Partner, since 1987; Council Member, Law Society of Scotland, since 1996; b. 4.2.59, Perth; m., Fiona; 2 s.; 1 d. Educ. Perth Grammar School; University of Edinburgh. Vice-Chair, People United for Supported Housing; accredited Mediator by Law Society of Scotland. Recreations: squash; golf; football. Address: (b.) 25 South Methven Street, Perth; T.-01738 620451.

Davies, Professor Alun Millward, BSc, MB, ChB, PhD. Professor in Medical Science, St. Andrews University, since 1993; b. 2.8.55, Tredegar. Educ. Pontllanfraith Grammar School; Liverpool University; London University. Lecturer, Middlesex Hospital Medical School, London, 1982-83; Lecturer, then Senior Lecturer, then Reader in Neurobiology, St. George's Hosital Medical School, London, 1983-93. Recreations: playing piano and harpsichord; sailing; scuba diving; building musical instruments. Address: (b.) Bute Medical Building, St. Andrews University, St. Andrews KY16 9TS; T.-01334 63219.

Davies, David Somerville, FTCL, ARCM. Conductor, flautist, composer; Artistic Director, Paragon Ensemble Scotland, since 1980; b. 13.6.54, Dunfermline. Educ. Dunfermline High School; Royal Scottish Academy of Music and Drama; Edinburgh University; Marseille Conservatoire. Assistant Principal Flute, Scottish National Orchestra, 1975-80; Principal Flute, Scottish Opera, 1980-85; Freelance Conductor: Edinburgh International Festival, France, Germany, Iceland, Italy, Luxembourg, Spain, Switzerland, BBC Scottish Symphony Orchestra, Royal Liverpool Philharmonic Orchestra, Royal Scottish National Orchestra, Scottish Chamber Orchestra, Ulster Orchestra;

Director, Scottish Music Information Centre, 1992-94; RSAMD: Head of Woodwind, since 1991, Head of Orchestral Studies, since 1997. Recordings: two volumes of world premiere recordings of Scottish contemporary music, 1991, 1993; one volume of works by MacKenzie with RSNO, 1997. Awards: Clutterbuck Scholarship; Performing Rights Society/Scottish Society of Composers Award for services to contemporary Scottish music with Paragon Ensemble Scotland; Sir James Caird Scholarship; Scottish Arts Council Music Award; Scottish International Education Trust Award; Tovey Memorial Prize. Recreations: computing; gardening; photography; reading. Address: (b.) 20 Renfrew Street, Glasgow G2 3BW; T.-0141-332 9903.

Davies, Professor Sir Graeme John, Kt, BE, MA, PhD, ScD, FEng, FRSE. Principal and Vice-Chancellor, Glasgow University, since 1995; b. 7.4.37, New Zealand; m., Florence; 1 s.; 1 d. Educ. Mt. Albert Grammar School, Auckland; University of Auckland; Cambridge University. Junior Lecturer, University of Auckland, 1960-62; Lecturer, Cambridge University, 1962-77; Professor of Metallurgy, Sheffield University, 1978-86; Vice-Chancellor, Liverpool University, 1986-91; Chief Executive: Universities Funding Council, 1991-93, Higher Education Funding Council for England, 1992-95. Hon. LLD, Liverpool, 1991; Hon. FRSNZ, 1993; Hon. DMet, Sheffield, 1995; Hon. DSc, Nottingham, 1995; Hon. FTCL, 1995; FIMechE; FIM; FRSA; CBIM; DL, Merseyside, 1989-93; Hon. DEng, Manchester Metropolitan University, 1996. Recreations: bird-watching; golf. Address: (b.) Glasgow University, Glasgow G12 8QQ; T.-0141-330 5995.

Davies, Hywel William, MA. Chief Executive, Royal Highland and Agricultural Society of Scotland, since 1991; Director: Scottish Agricultural and Rural Development Centre, since 1991, Scottish Farming and Countryside Educational Trust, since 1991; b. 28.6.45, Wales; b. Patricia Thornhill; 1 s.; 1 d. Educ. Harrow; Magdalene College, Cambridge. Army Officer, commissioned Royal Horse Guards (The Blues), 1965-87; commanded The Blues and Royals, 1984-87; defence and allied industries, 1988-91. Member, Committee, Order of St. John Association (Central Region); Panel Judge, British Driving Society. Recreations: country sports and horses (represented Great Britain at 4-in-hand carriage driving). Address: (h.) Peatland, Gatehead, Ayrshire KA2 9AN; (b.) Ingliston, Edinburgh EH28 8NF; T.-0131-333 2444.

Davies, Ivor, MA, DipEd, PhD. Director of Planning, Scottish Sports Council, since 1975, and Director, Lottery Sports Fund, since 1994; b. Scotland. Educ. Edinburgh University. Founded and developed Department of Geography, Lakehead University, Thunder Bay, Ontario, and became first Chairman of Department. Member, Board, European Association for Sport Management; Member, Grants Council, Caledonian Foundation. Recreations: sport; music. Address: (b.) Caledonia House, South Gyle, Edinburgh EH12 9DQ; T.-0131-317 7200.

Davies, Professor Peter Anthony, BSc, DipEd, PhD, FRSE. Professor of Fluid Dynamics, Dundee University, since 1994; b. 7.11.44, N. Yorks; m., Ann Smith; 1 s. Educ. Grammar School, Yarm-on-Tees; Newcastle upon Tyne University. Royal Society Postdoctoral Fellow, International Meteorological Institute, Stockholm, 1971-73; Senior Research Associate, Department of Physics, Newcastle upon Tyne University, 1973-80; Lecturer, Senior Lecturer, Reader, Professor, Department of Civil Engineering, Dundee University, since 1981. Vice-President, European Geophysical Society, 1981-83; Visiting Professor, Sichuan Union University, Yunnan Polytechnic University, People's Republic of China; Member: College, Engineering and Physical Sciences Research Council, since 1994; Fluid Mechanics Committee, International Association of Hydraulic Research. Publications: two books; 100 scientific publications. Recreations: Newcastle United; sport; reading. Address: (b.) Department of Civil Engineering, The University, Dundee DD1 4HN; T.-01382 344346.

Davies (a.k.a. Glasse-Davies), Professor R. Wayne, MA, PhD, ScD. Robertson Professor of Biotechnology, Glasgow University, since 1989; b. 10.6.44, Cardiff; m., Victoria Glasse; 3 s.; 2 d. Educ. Queen Elizabeth's Hospital, Bristol; St. John's College, Cambridge. Research Fellow, University of Wisconsin, 1968-71; H3 Professor, Universität zu Köln, FRG, 1971-77; Lecturer, University of Essex, 1977-81; Senior Lecturer, UMIST, 1981-83; Vice-President, Scientific and Research Director, Allelix Biopharmaceuticals, Toronto, 1983-89; Neuropa Ltd.: Founding Director, 1996, CEO, 1997. Recreations: poetry and literature; cello; skiing. Address: (b.) Robertson Laboratory of Biotechnology, Institute of Biomedical and Life Sciences, Glasgow University, 54 Dumbarton Road, Glasgow G11 6NU.

Davies, Terry, BSc (Hons), MSc, MInstP, FIPC. Principal, James Watt College of Further and Higher Education, since 1990; b. 14.12.40, Llanelli. Educ. Llanelli Boys' Grammar School; University College of Swansea; Nottingham University. Lecturer (Physics), Middlesex Polytechnic, then Preston Polytechnic, 1964-73; Depute Head, Department of Engineering, Science and Construction, Lewes Technical College, 1973-79; Head, Department of Science, Mathematics and Computing, Telford College of Further Education, Edinburgh, 1979-85; Depute Principal, Telford College of FE, 1985-90. Recreations: rugby; cricket; squash; tennis. Address: (b.) James Watt College, Finnart Street, Greenock, PA16 8HF.

Davies, Trevor John, BA. Independent Television Producer, since 1981; b. 23.1.44, London; lives with Elaine Pidgeon; 1 step-s.; 1 step-d. Educ. University of Leicester. General Secretary, Scottish Union of Students, 1968; Secretary, Open University in Scotland, 1969-74; Assistant Director, Scottish Council of Social Service, 1974-78; Freelance Journalist and Broadcaster, 1978-85; credits include: Producer, The Big Day, Glasgow, 1990; Executive Producer, Hamish MacBeth; Producer, Bombay Blue. Councillor, Edinburgh Town Council, 1971-75; Parliamentary Candidate, 1974; Councillor, Lothian Region Council, 1974-78; Chair: Scottish Volleyball Association, 1979-83, Edinburgh Central Citizens' Advice Bureau, 1980-84; Vice-Chair, Edinburgh Council of Social Service, 1982-84; Director and Vice-Chair, Wester Hailes Community Enterprises, 1983-91; Scottish Convener and UK Council Member, Independent Programme Producers Association, 1988-91; Governor, Scottish Film Council, 1990-95; Chair, Scottish Screen Industry Project, 1991-94. Recreations: jazz; gardening. Address: (b.) 10 Scotland Street, Edinburgh EH3 6PS; T.-0131-557 4580.

Davis, Alan Angus, BSc (Hons). Manager, BBC Scottish Symphony Orchestra, since 1992; b. 7.2.58, Glasgow. Educ. Queen Anne High School, Dunfermline; Aberdeen University. Publicity and Publications Assistant, The Poetry Society, 1981-82; Marketing Officer, Incorporated Society of Musicians, 1982-84; freelance administrator, 1984-92. Council Member, Society for the Promotion of New Music; Director, Chamber Group of Scotland. Recreations: cooking; gardening; American literature. Address: (b.) Broadcasting House, Queen Margaret Drive, Glasgow G12; T.-0141-330 2606.

Davis, Christine A.M., CBE, MA, DipEd. Chairman: Scottish Legal Aid Board, since 1991, Scottish Agricultural Wages Board, since 1995 (Member, since 1990); b. 5.3.44, Salisbury; m., Robin John Davis; 2 d. Educ. Perth Academy; Ayr Academy; St. Andrews University; Aberdeen University; Aberdeen College of Education. Teacher of History and Modern Studies, Cumbernauld High

School and High School of Stirling, 1967-69; joined Dunblane Town Council and Perth and Kinross Joint County Council, 1972; undertook research in Canada on Ontario Hydro and small claims in Ontario courts, 1977-78; Chairman, Electricity Consultative Council for North of Scotland, 1980-90; Member: North of Scotland Hydro Electric Board, 1980-90, Scottish Economic Council, 1987-95, Scottish Committee of the Council on Tribunals, 1989-95; Clerk, Britain Yearly Meeting, Society of Friends (Quakers), 1991-95; a President, Council of Churches for Britain and Ireland, 1990-92; Trustee, Quaker Tapestry at Kendal Ltd, Joseph Rowntree Charitable Trust. Recreations: embroidery; bird-watching; walking. Address: (h.) 24 Newton Crescent, Dunblane, Perthshire FK15 ODZ; T.-Dunblane 823226.

Davis, Gerry. Journalist/Public Relations Consultant, since 1970; TV Producer and Presenter, since 1989; Media Training Provider, since 1991; b. 7.10.35, Glasgow; m., June Imray; 1 s.; 1 d. Educ. Shawlands Academy, Glasgow; Strathclyde University. Trainee analytical chemist, ICI; pharmaceutical chemist; actor; television continuity announcer/programme presenter/reporter, BBC Radio Scotland. Former Radio Reporter of the Year/Presenter of the Year. Recreation: holidaying. Address: (b.) Davis Media, 24 Belvidere Street, Aberdeen AB25 2QS; T.-01224 633024.

Davis, Margaret Thomson. Novelist; b. Bathgate; 2 s. Educ. Albert Secondary School. Worked as children's nurse; Red Cross nurse; short story writer; novelist; author of autobiography, The Making of a Novelist; novels include The Breadmakers, A Baby Might Be Crying, A Sort of Peace, The Prisoner, The Prince and the Tobacco Lords, Roots of Bondage, Scorpion in the Fire, The Dark Side of Pleasure, A Very Civilised Man, Light and Dark, Rag Woman Rich Woman, Daughters and Mothers, Wounds of War, A Woman of Property, A Sense of Belonging, Hold Me Forever, Kiss Me No More,A Kind of Immortality, Burning Ambition. Committee Member: International PEN (Scottish Branch); Society of Authors; Lecturer in Creative Writing; Honorary President, Strathkelvin Writers Club. Recreations: reading; travelling; being with friends. Address: c/o Heather Jeeves Literary Agency, Kingsfield Crescent, Witney, Oxon OX8 6JB.

Davis, Robert Clive, CEng, MIMarE. Marine Engineer Superintendent, Scottish Fisheries Protection Agency, since 1991; b. 29.8.38, Brighton; m., Elizabeth Mary Warren; 2 s. Educ. Marist Brothers, Durban, South Africa; Glasgow College of Nautical Studies. Apprenticeship, James Brown, Durban, South Africa; joined Merchant Navy, 1959; served with Safmarine, Bank Line, Jardine Matheson; Boiler Inspector, 1970-72; joined Scottish Office, 1972; promoted Chief Engineer, 1979. Recreations: golf; gardening; DIY. Address: (h.) 19 Duddingston Park South, Edinburgh EH15 3NY; T.-0131-669 5320.

Davison, Timothy Paul, BA (Hons), MHSM, DipHSM, MBA. Chief Executive, Greater Glasgow Community and Mental Health Services NHS Trust, since 1994; b. 4.6.61, Newcastle upon Tyne; m., Hilary Williamson; 1 s. Educ. Kenton School, Newcastle upon Tyne; Stirling University; Glasgow University. Appointments in Stirling Royal Infirmary, Royal Edinburgh Hospital, Glasgow Royal Infirmary, 1984-90; Sector General Manager, Gartnavel Royal Hospital, 1990-91; Unit General Manager, Mental Health Unit, Glasgow, 1991-92, Community and Mental Health Unit, Glasgow, 1992-94. Member, Council, Glasgow and West of Scotland Institute of Public Administration. Recreations: tennis; military and political history. Address: (b.) Gartnavel Royal Hospital, 1055 Great Western Road, Glasgow G12 0XH; T.-0141-211 3782.

Dawson, James Ronald, FRICS, MIPS. Honorary Secretary, Royal Institution of Chartered Surveyors in

Scotland, since 1997; Director, Institution of Planning Supervisors, since 1996; b. 28.5.41, Glasgow; m., Marion; 1 s.; 1 d. Educ. High School of Glasgow; Stow College of Building, Glasgow. Apprentice Quantity Surveyor, 1958-63; Partner, Robert H. Soper & Co., 1965-72; Founding Partner, Robertson and Dawson, Edinburgh and Galashiels, since 1972; Chairman, RICS in Scotland, 1992-93. President, Edinburgh Junior Chamber of Commerce, 1974-75; Captain, Ward XXIII, Society of High Constables of Edinburgh, 1992. Recreations: hill-walking; golf; opera. Address: (b.) 6 Manor Place, Edinburgh; T.-0131-225 2219.

Dawson, Professor John Alan, BSc, MPhil, PhD, MIPDM. Professor of Marketing, Edinburgh University, since 1990; Visiting Professor, Escuela Superior de Administración y Dirección de Empresas (ESADE), Barcelona; b. 19.8.44, Hyde; m., Jocelyn Barker; 1 s.; 1 d. Educ. Lady Manners School, Bakewell; University College, London; Nottingham University. Lecturer, Nottingham University; Lecturer, Senior Lecturer, Reader, St. David's University College, Wales; Fraser of Allander Professor of Distributive Studies, Stirling University; Visiting Lecturer, University of Western Australia; Visiting Research Fellow, Australian National University; Visiting Professor: Florida State University, Chuo University. Chairman, National Museums of Scotland Retailing Ltd. Publications: Evaluating the Human Environment, 1973; Man and His World, 1975; Computing for Geographers, 1976; Small-Scale Retailing in the UK, 1979; Marketing Environment, 1979; Retail Geography, 1980; Commercial Distribution in Europe, 1982; Teach Yourself Geography, 1983; Shopping Centre Development, 1983; Computer Methods for Geographers, 1985; Retailing in Scoland 2005, 1988; Evolution of European Retailing, 1988; Retailing Environments in Developing Countries, 1990; Competition and Markets, 1992. Recreations: sport; writing. Address:(b.) Edinburgh University, 50 George Square, Edinburgh; T.-0131-650 3828.

Dawson, Patricia, MBA, DipLSc/Nursing, RGN, RNMD. Director, Scottish Association of Health Councils, since 1994; b. 14.7.56, Edinburgh; m., David; 1 d. Educ. James Gillespie's High School; Queen Margaret College, Edinburgh; Napier University, Edinburgh. Various nursing posts, 1974-94; Co-founder and former Chairperson, Scottish Society of Anaesthetic and Recovery Nurses; Chairperson, Balgreen Out of School Care Club. Recreations: gardening; swimming; reading; holidays in Greece. Address: (b.) Scottish Association of Health Councils, 18 Alva Street, Edinburgh EH2 4QG; T.-0131-220 4101.

Dawson, Hon. Lord (Thomas Cordner Dawson), QC (Scot), LLB. Senator of the College of Justice in Scotland, since 1995; b. 14.11.48; m., 2 s. Educ. Royal High School of Edinburgh; Edinburgh University. Advocate, 1973; QC, 1986; Lecturer, Dundee University, 1971-74; Advocate Depute, 1983-87; Solicitor-General for Scotland, 1992-95. Address: Court of Session, Parliament House, Parliament Square, Edinburgh, EH1 1RQ.

Dawson Scott, Robert, MA, MLitt. Arts Editor, The Scotsman, since 1997; b. 24.7.56, London; 3 d. Educ. Oxford University; Strathclyde University. Recreations: skiing; hill-walking. Address: (b.) 20 North Bridge, Edinburgh EH1 1YT; T.-0131-225 2468.

Deakins, Professor David Arthur, BSc(Econ.), BA(Bus. Studs.), MA(Bus. Econ.), FRSA. Renfrewshire Enterprise Professor of Enterprise Development, University of Paisley, since 1994; b. 5.1.50, Cheshire; m., June Patricia Eglen; 1 s.; 2 d. Educ. Sutton Secondary Modern Boys' School; University of London (External Degree); University of Essex. Lecturer: Rotherham College of Technology, 1975-81, Chelmsford College of Further Education, 1981-88, University of Central England, Birmingham, 1988-94.

Vice-President, Institute for Small Business Affairs. Publications: Enterpreneurship and Small Firms, 1996; Entrepreneurship in the Nineties, 1997. Recreations: cycling; walking; mountain biking. Address: (b.) Paisley Enterprise Research Centre, University of Paisley, Paisley PA1 2BE; T.-0141-848 3433.

Deane, Robert Fletcher, MB, ChB, MSc, FRCSEdin, FRCSGlas. Consultant Urological Surgeon, since 1971; b. 25.3.38, Glasgow; m., Sylvia Alison Yuill; 3 s. Educ. Hillhead High School, Glasgow; Glasgow University. Consultant Urologist, Western Infirmary, Glasgow, since 1971; Senior Consultant Surgeon to Family Planning Association, Glasgow; Member, Specialist Advisory Committee (Urology); Founder, Board of Intercollegiate Specialty Board in Urology. Publication: Urology Illustrated. Recreations: golf; music. Address: (b.) 27 Bellshaugh Lane, Glasgow G12 0PE; T.-0141-334 8102.

Deans, Rev. Graham Douglas Sutherland, MA, BD(Hons). Parish Minister, St. Mary's Parish Church, Dumfries, since 1987; b. 15.8.53, Aberdeen; m., Marina Punler. Educ. Mackie Academy, Stonehaven; University of Aberdeen; Westminster College, University of Oxford. Assistant Minister, Craigsbank Parish Church, Corstorphine, 1977-78; Parish Minister, Denbeath with Methilhill, 1978-87. Depute Clerk and Treasurer, Presbytery of Kirkcaldy, 1981-87; Chaplain, Randolph Wemyss Memorial Hospital, 1980-87; Moderator, Presbytery of Dumfries and Kirkcudbright, 1994-95; Convener: Committee on Glebes, 1991-92, Committee on Music and Worship, 1993-96, Committee on the Maintenance of the Ministry, since 1997 (Member, since 1991, Vice-Convener, 1991-96); Conductor, Dumfries and Kirkcudbright Presbytery Choir, 1994-96; Member, Assembly Committee on Probationers, 1991-97, Maintenance of the Ministry Committee, since 1991. Publications: A History of Denbeath Church, 1980; Children's Addresses in the Expository Times, 1983. Recreation: music. Address: (h.) 47 Moffat Road, Dumfries DG1 1NN; T.-01387 254873.

Deans, Joyce Blair, MBE, DUniv, BArch, PPRIAS, RIBA, ACIArb, FRSA. Architect; President, Royal Incorporation of Architects in Scotland, 1991-93 (first woman President); b. 29.1.27, Glasgow; m., John Albert Gibson Deans; 2 s.; 2 d. Educ. Laurel Bank School for Girls; University of Strathclyde. Re-entered profession as Assistant, private practice, 1968; appointed Associate, 1972; established own practice, 1981; elected Member, Council: Glasgow Institute of Architects, 1975-90 (first female President, 1986-88), Royal Incorporation of Architects, 1979-95; first female Vice President, Royal Incorporation of Architects in Scotland, 1986-88; Member, Building Standards Advisory Committee, 1987-96; Chairman: BSAC (Research), 1988-96, Scottish Construction Industry Group, 1995-96 (Member, since 1991); Director: Cairn Housing Association, since 1988, Glasgow West Conservation Trust, since 1987; Governor: Laurel Bank (now Laurel Park) School for Girls since 1981, Glasgow School of Art, since 1989 (Vice-Chairman, since 1992); Member, Court, Strathclyde University, since 1992 Deputy Chairman of Court (Estates), since 1993; elected Vice President, Royal Institute of British Architects, 1993-95; Member: RIBA Council, since 1993, Patrick Geddes Award Panel, since 1993; Industrial Assessor (Architecture), SHEFC, 1994-95; External Examiner, Part 3, since 1994; Hon. DUniv (University of Strathclyde), 1996. Recreations: gardening; golf; walking; reading; theatre. Address: 11 South Erskine Park, Bearsden, Glasgow G61 4NA; T.-0141-942 6795.

Deans, Leslie George, LLB, NP. Chairman, Heart of Midlothian PLC, since 1996; Senior Partner, Leslie Deans & Co., Solicitors, since 1986; b. 10.8.51, Edinburgh. Educ. George Watson's, Edinburgh; Edinburgh University. Professional life as practising solicitor; with C.P. Robinson acquired controlling interest in Heart of Midlothian, 1994. Recreations: cycling; bridge; travel; fine wines. Address: (b.) Tynecastle Stadium, Gorgie Road, Edinburgh; T.-0131-200 7200.

Deans, Mungo Effingham, BSc(Econ), LLB. Regional Adjudicator, Immigration Appellate Authority, since 1996; b. 25.5.56, Lytham St. Annes; m., Kathryn Atkinson; 3 s. Educ. Fettes College, Edinburgh; London School of Economics; University of Edinburgh. Admitted as Solicitor, 1981; Lecturer, Department of Law: Napier University, 1981-82, Dundee University, 1983-96; Chairman: Social Security Appeal Tribunals, 1989, Disability Appeal Tribunals, 1992; Immigration Adjudicator, 1994. Publication: Scots Public Law, 1995. Recreations: Scottish history; fine art. Address: (b.) Immigration Appellate Authority, 5th Floor, Portcullis House, 21 India Street, Glasgow G2 4PZ; T.-0141-221 3489.

Deary, Professor Ian John, BSc, PhD, MBChB, FRCPE, AFBPSS, CPsychol, MRCPsych. Professor of Differential Psychology, University of Edinburgh, since 1995; b. 17.5.54, Carluke; m., Ann Marie Barclay; 1 s.; 2 d. Educ. Hamilton Academy; University of Edinburgh. House Officer, Royal Informary of Edinburgh, 1983-84; Senior House Officer in Psychiatry, Maudsley Hospital, London, 1984-85; Department of Psychology, University of Edinburgh: Lecturer, 1985-90, Senior Lecturer, 1990-92, Reader, 1992-95. Member, Board, and President-Elect, Directors of the International Society for the Study of Individual Differences; Executive Committee Member, European Association of Personality Psychology; Distinguished International Affiliate, Laboratory for the Cross-Cultural Study of Individual Differences, University of Haifa, Israel. Publications: Personality Traits (Co-author); editor of two books on personality; over 100 refereed scientific papers, principally on human cognitive ability and personality. Recreations: saxophone; lyric-writing; late Victorian novels; English Romantic composers; Motherwell F.C. Address: (b.) Department of Psychology, University of Edinburgh, 7 George Square, Edinburgh EH8 9JZ; T.-0131-650 3452.

DeFelice, Hilda, BA (Hons). Headteacher, St. Luke's High School, Barrhead, since 1993; b. 16.2.49, Glasgow; m. Gordon Herriot; 1 s.; 1 d. Educ. Holyrood Secondary School, Glasgow; Strathclyde University. Teacher, 1973-76; Assistant Principal Teacher, 1976-79; Principal Teacher, 1979-86; Assistant Head Teacher, St. Ninian's High School, Giffnock, 1986-90; Depute Head Teacher, St. Bride's High School, East Kilbride, 1990-93. Recreations: reading; guitar; music. Address: (b.) St. Luke's High School, Springfield Road, Barrhead, G78 2SG; T.-0141-577 2400.

Della Sala, Professor Sergio F., MD, PhD. Chair of Psychology, Aberdeen; b. 23.9.55, Milan. Senior Neurologist, Milan teaching hospital; Head, Neuropsychology Unit, Veruno, Italy. Address: (b.) King's College, Aberdeen University, Aberdeen.

Demarco, Professor Richard, OBE, RSW, SSA, Hon. FRIAS, FRSA, DA, Hon. DFA, ACA, Hon. LLD (Dundee). Artist and Writer; Director, Richard Demarco Gallery, since 1966; b. 9.7.30, Edinburgh; m., Anne Muckle. Educ. Holy Cross Academy, Edinburgh; Edinburgh College of Art. National Service, KOSB, 1954-56; Art Master, Duns Scotus Academy, Edinburgh, 1957-67; Vice-Chairman, Board, Traverse Theatre Club, 1963-67; Director, Sean Connery's Scottish International Education Trust, 1972-73; Member: Board of Governors, Carlisle School of Art, 1970-74, Edinburgh Festival Society, 1971-86; Contributing Editor, Studio International, 1982-84; External Assessor, Stourbridge College of Art, 1988-90; Artistic Director, European Youth Parliament, since 1993; Professor of European Cultural Studies, Kingston University, since

1993; Director, Demarco European Art Foundation, since 1993; Trustee, Kingston-Demarco European Cultural Foundation, since 1993; Honorary Member, Scottish Arts Club; Elected Member, L'Association International des Critiques D'Art (AICA), 1994. Awards: Gold Order of Merit, Polish People's Republic; Chevalier de L'Ordre Des Arts Et Des Lettres; Order of Cavaliere Della Republica d'Italia; Scottish Arts Council Award for services to Scotland's visual arts, 1975; Medal, International Theatre Institutes of Great Britain and Poland, 1992; Honorary Doctorate, Atlanta College of Art, 1993; Arts Medal, Royal Philosophical Society of Glasgow, 1995; appointed Commander, Military and Hospitaller Order of St. Lazarus of Jerusalem, 1996. Publications: The Road to Meikle Seggie; The Artist as Explorer; A Life in Pictures; Kunst=Kapital: The Adam Smith Lecture, 1995; Honouring Colmcille, 1997. Recreation: walking "The Road to Meikle Seggie". Address: (h.) 23(a) Lennox Street, Edinburgh EH4 1PY; T.-0131-343 2124.

Dempsey, John, JP, CEng, MICE, MIBC. Chartered Civil Engineer, since 1963; Provost, East Dunbartonshire Council, since 1995; b. 24.11.35, Lennoxtown; 1 d. Educ. St. Machans, Lennoxtown; St. Ninian's High School, Kirkintilloch. District Councillor, Strathkelvin DC, 1980-95. Address: (b.) Tom Johnston House, Kirkintilloch, Glasgow G66; T.-0141-776 9000.

Dempster, Alastair Cox, FCIBS. Chief Executive, TSB Bank Scotland plc, since 1992; b. 22.6.40, Glasgow; m., Kathryn; 2 s. Educ. Paisley Grammar School. Royal Bank of Scotland, 1955-62; various managerial appointments, Scotland, Hong Kong, New York, 1962-81; AGM, International Division, Royal Bank of Scotland, 1981-86; Director of Commercial Banking and International/Executive Director, TSB Scotland plc, 1986-91; TSB Bank Channel Islands Ltd.: Chief Executive, 1991-92; Deputy Chairman, 1992-96. Chairman, Committee of Scottish Clearing Bankers, 1993-95; President, Chartered Institute of Bankers in Scotland, 1995-97; Member, Scottish Council Development and Industry and Executive Committee; Convener, Heriot Watt Audit Committee; Member, Heriot Watt University Court; Director, Scottish Homes; Director: Office of the Banking Ombudsman, Scottish Financial Enterprise; Direct Aberforth Split Level Trust plc; Member, Board of Governors, Edinburgh College of Art. Recreations: golf; tennis; bridge. Address: (b.) TSB Bank Scotland plc, Henry Duncan House, 120 George Street, Edinburgh EH2 4TS; T.-0131-225 4555.

Denholm, James Allan, CBE, CA. Director, William Grant & Sons Ltd., 1975-96; Director, Scottish Mutual Assurance Society, since 1987 (Deputy Chairman, since 1992); Director, Scottish Cremation Society Limited, since 1980; Director, Abbey National plc, 1992-97; b. 27.9.36, Glasgow; m., Elizabeth Avril McLachlan, CA; 1 s.; 1 d. Educ. Hutchesons Boys Grammar School, Glasgow; Institute of Chartered Accountants of Scotland. Apprenticed, McFarlane Hutton & Patrick, CA, Glasgow (Sir William McLintock prizeman); Chief Accountant, A. & W. Smith & Co. Ltd., Glasgow, 1960-66; Secretary, William Grant & Sons Ltd., 1968-96; Chairman, East Kilbride Development Corporation, 1983-94 (Member, since 1979). Council Member, Institute of Chartered Accountants of Scotland, 1978-83, 1989-93 (President, 1992-93); Director and Treasurer, Glasgow YMCA, 1966-79; Chairman, Glasgow Junior Chamber of Commerce, 1972-73; Elder, New Kilpatrick Parish Church, since 1971; Visitor of the Incorporation of Maltmen in Glasgow, 1980-81; President, The Deacons' Association of Glasgow, 1994-95; Preses, The Weavers' Society of Anderston, 1994-95; Collector, Society of Deacons and Free Preseses of Glasgow, 1997-98; President, 49 Wine and Spirit Club of Scotland, 1983-84; Trustee, Scottish Cot Death Trust; Fellow, Society of Antiquaries of Scotland, since 1987; Collector, The Trades House of Glasgow, 1996-97; Fellow,

Royal Society for the Encouragement of Arts, Manufactures and Commerce, 1993. Recreations: shooting; golf. Address: (h.) Greencroft, 19 Colquhoun Drive, Bearsden, Glasgow G61 4NQ; T.-0141-942 1773.

Denholm, John Clark, MA (Hons), MIPA. Chairman, Leith Advertising Agency Ltd., since 1995; Chairman, One to One Direct Communications Ltd., since 1990; b. 10.9.50, Chesterfield; m., Julia; 1 s.; 1 d. Educ. Buckhaven High School; St. Andrews University. Product Manager, The Boots Company, Nottingham, 1972-76; Brand Manager, Scottish & Newcastle Breweries, 1976-80; Account Director, Hall Advertising, Edinburgh, 1980-84. Recreation: golf. Address: (b.) The Canon Mill, Canon Street, Edinburgh; T.-0131-557 5840.

Denholm, Sir John Ferguson (Sir Ian), Kt, DL. Chairman, J. & J. Denholm Ltd. Address: (b.) Inter City House, 80 Oswald Street, Glasgow G1 4PX.

Dennis, Richard Benson, PhD, BSc. Managing Director, Edinburgh Instruments Ltd.; Director, Edinburgh Sensors Ltd.; Founder, Mütek GmbH, West Germany; b. 15.7.45, Weymouth; m., Beate Stamm; 2 d. Educ. Weymouth Grammar School; Reading University. SRC Postdoctoral Fellow, Reading; Guest Fellow, Freiburg University, 1968-70; Lecturer/Senior Lecturer, Heriot-Watt University, 1970-91; Alexander von Humboldt Fellow, Munich University, 1976-78; Treasurer, UK Laser and Electro-Optic Trade Association; Council Member, Scottish Consultative Committee on the Curriculum, 1991-94; Chairman, Balerno High School Board, 1990-94; Joint Winner, Department of Industry EPIC Award (Education in Partnership with Industry and Commerce), 1982. Recreations: bridge; sport. Address: (b.) Edinburgh Instruments Ltd., Riccarton, Currie, Edinburgh; T.-0131-449 5844.

Dennis, Roy, MBE. Wildlife Consultant/Ornithologist; Specialist, species recovery projects, UK and overseas; crofter, since 1985; b. 4.5.40; m., Marina MacDonell; 2 s.; 1 d. Educ. Price's School. Migration Research Assistant, UK Bird Observatories, 1958-59; Warden, Lochgarten Osprey Reserve, 1960-63; Warden, Fair Isle Bird Observatory, 1963-70; Highland Officer, RSPB, 1971-87, Regional Officer (North Scotland), 1987-91; Main Board Member, Scottish Natural Heritage, 1992-97; Director, Cairngorms Partnership, 1995-97. Publications: Ospreys and Speyside Wildlife; Birds of Badenoch and Strathspey; Puffins; Ospreys; Peregrine Falcons; Divers; The Loch; Golden Eagles. Recreations: travel; photography; cross-country skiing; bird-watching. Address: Inchdryne, Nethybridge, Invernessshire PH25 3EF; T.-01479 831 384.

Denniston, Rev. David William, BD, DipMin. Minister, North Church, Perth, since 1996; b. 23.4.56, Glasgow; m., Jane Ross; 2 s.; 1 d. Educ. Hutchesons' Boys Grammar School, Glasgow; University of Glasgow. Minister: Ruchazie Parish Church, Glasgow, 1981-86, Kennoway, Fife, 1986-96. Recreations: hill-walking; fishing; music. Address: (h.) 127 Glasgow Road, Perth PH2 0LU; T.-01738 625728.

Denny, Margaret Bertha Alice, OBE, DL, BA (Hons), PhD. Member, Council and Executive Committee, National Trust for Scotland, since 1974 (Vice President, 1981-91); b. 30.9.07, Chatham; m., Edward Leslie Denny. Educ. Dover County School; Bedford College for Women, London University. Entered Civil Service as Principal, Ministry of Shipping, 1940; Assistant Secretary, 1946; Under Secretary, 1957; Governor, Bedford College; Member: Scottish Advisory Council for Civil Aviation, 1958-67, Western Regional Hospital Board, 1960-74, Scottish Committee, Council of Industrial Design, 1961-71, General Advisory Council, BBC, 1962-66, General Nursing Council, Scotland, 1963-78, Board of Management, State Hospital, Carstairs, 1966-76; Vice-Chairman, Argyll and Clyde

Health Board, 1974-77; County Commissioner, Girl Guides, Dunbartonshire, 1958-68; DL, Dunbartonshire, since 1973; Officer, Order of Orange Nassau, 1947. Recreations: gardening; needlework; music. Address: (h.) Dalnair House, Croftamie, Glasgow G63 0EZ; T.-01360 660106.

Denyer, Professor Peter Brian, BSc, PhD. Managing Director, Vision Group plc, since 1990, and Professor of Integrated Electronics, Edinburgh University, since 1986; b. 27.4.53, Littlehampton; m., Fiona Margaret Lindsay; 2 d. Educ. Worthing Technical High School; Loughborough University. Wolfson Microelectronics Institute, 1976-80; Lecturer, then Reader, Edinburgh University, 1981-86. Chairman, SERC/DTI Microelectronics Design Sub-Committee, 1989-91. Publications: Introduction to MOSLSI Design, 1983; VLSI Signal Processing: A Bit-Serial Approach, 1985. Recreations: family; walking; renovation.

Deregowski, Professor Jan Bronislaw, BSc, BA, PhD, DSc, FBPsS, FRSE. Professor of Psychology, Aberdeen University, since 1986 (Reader, 1981-86); b. 1.3.33, Pinsk, Poland; m., Eva Loft Nielsen; 2 s.; 1 d. Educ. London University. Lecturer, then Senior Lecturer, Aberdeen University, 1969-81. Publications: Illusions, Patterns and Pictures: a cross-cultural perspective; Distortion in Art; Perception and Artistic Style (Co-author). Address: (b.) Department of Psychology, King's College, Old Aberdeen AB9 2UB; T.-Aberdeen 272247.

Dervaird, Hon. Lord (John Murray), MA (Oxon), LLB (Edin), FCIArb. Dickson Minto Professor of Company Law, Edinburgh University, since 1990, Dean, Faculty of Law, 1994-96; b. 8.7.35, Stranraer; m., Bridget Jane Godfrey; 3 s. Educ. Stranraer schools; Edinburgh Academy; Corpus Christi College, Oxford; Edinburgh University. Advocate, 1962; QC, 1974; Law Commissioner (part-time), 1979-88; Senator of the College of Justice, 1988-89; Chairman, Scottish Council for International Arbitration, since 1989; Council Member, London Court of International Arbitration, since 1990; Trustee, David Hume Institute, since 1992; Member, ICC Committee on Business Law, Paris, since 1992; Chairman, BT Scottish Ensemble, since 1988; Member: City Disputes Panel, since 1994, Panel of Arbitrators, International Centre for Settlement of Investment Disputes; Hon. President, Advocates' Business Law Group, since 1988; Chairman, Edinburgh Wigtownshire Association, since 1997. Publications: Stair Encyclopaedia of Scots Law (Contributor); articles on legal and ornithological subjects. Recreations: farming; gardening; bird-watching; music; curling. Address: (b.) Faculty of Law, Old College, South Bridge, Edinburgh.

Devereux, Alan Robert, CBE, DL, CEng, MIEE, CBIM. Chairman, Scottish Ambulance Service NHS Trust, 1995-97; Founder, Quality Scotland Foundation; International Director, Gleneagles PLC, since 1990; Director, Scottish Mutual Assurance Society, since 1976; b. 18.4.33, Frinton-on-Sea; m., 1, Gloria Alma Hair (deceased); 1 s.; 2, Elizabeth Tormey Docherty. Educ. Colchester School; Clacton County High School; Mid Essex Technical College. Marconi's Wireless Telegraph Company: apprentice, 1950-55, Standards Engineer, 1955-56; Technical Production Manager, Halex Division, British Xylonite Company, 1956-58; Technical Sales Manager, SPA Division, Sanitas Trust, 1958-65; General Manager, Dobar Engineering, 1965-67; various managerial posts, Norcros Ltd., 1967-69; Group Managing Director, Scotcros Ltd., 1969-78; Deputy Chairman, Scotcros Ltd., 1978-80. CBI: Chairman, Scotland, 1977-79 (Deputy Chairman, 1975-77), Council Member, 1972-84, Member, President's Advisory Committee, 1979; UK Regional Chairman, 1979; Chairman, Small Industries Council for Rural Areas of Scotland, 1975-77; Member, Scottish Development Agency, 1977-83; Chairman: Scottish Tourist Board, 1980-90, Glasgow City Mission; Director, Children's Hospice

Association for Scotland; Scottish Free Enterprise Award, 1978; Deputy Lieutenant, Renfrewshire, since 1985. Recreations: work; amateur radio; reading. Address: (h.) South Fell, 24 Kirkhouse Road, Blanefield, Glasgow G63 9BX; T.-0360 770464.

Devine, Bernard. Chief Executive, North Ayrshire Council. Address: (b.) Cunninghame House, Irvine, KA12 8EE.

Devine, John, FRICS, IRRV. Member, Lands Tribunal for Scotland, since 1991; b. 23.10.29, Glasgow; m., Agnes Susan McLaughlin; 2 s.; 1 d. Educ. St. Mary's College, Blairs, Aberdeen; Glasgow College of Technology; College of Estate Management. Apprentice and qualified assistant, Thomas Binnie & Hendry, Chartered Valuation Surveyors, 1947-57; Senior Valuer, Fife County Council's Assessor's Department, 1957-62; Partner, then Senior Partner, Graham & Sibbald, Chartered Surveyors, 1962-91. Member: Board of Management, Fife College of Further and Higher Education, since 1992, Scottish Valuation and Rating Council, since 1996. Recreation: golf. Address: (h.) 80 Milton Road, Kirkcaldy KY1 1TP; T.-01592 264806.

Devine, Rt. Rev. Joseph, PhD. Bishop of Motherwell, since 1983; b. 7.8.37, Glasgow. Educ. St. Mary's College, Blairs, Aberdeen; St. Peter's College, Cardross; Pontifical Scots College, Rome. Ordained Priest, Glasgow, 1960; Private Secretary to Archbishop of Glasgow, 1964-65; Assistant Priest, St. Robert Bellarmine, Glasgow, 1965-67; St. Joseph's, Helensburgh, 1967-72; on staff, St. Peter's College, Cardross, 1967-74; Assistant Chaplain, Catholic Chaplaincy, Glasgow University, 1974-77; nominated Titular Bishop of Voli, and Auxiliary Bishop to Archbishop of Glasgow, 1977. Vice-Convener, Central Council, ACTS; President, Catholic Communications Commission. Recreations: reading; watching sport. Address: (b.) Diocesan Centre, Coursington Road, Motherwell ML1 1PW; T.-01698 269114.

Devine, Professor Thomas Martin, BA, PhD, DLitt, FRHistS, FRSE, FBA. Professor of Scottish History, Strathclyde University, since 1988, Director of the Research Centre in Scottish History and Deputy Principal of the University; b. 30.10.46, Motherwell; m., Catherine Mary Lynas; 2 s.; 3 d. Educ. Our Lady's RC High School, Motherwell; Strathclyde University. Lecturer, then Senior Lecturer and Reader, Department of History, Strathclyde University, 1969-88 (Head of Department, 1990-92); Dean, Faculty of Arts and Social Sciences, Strathclyde University, 1993-94; Visiting Professor, University of Guelph, Canada, 1983 and 1988 (Adjunct Professor in History, since 1988); Adjunct Professor in History, University of North Carolina; Governor, St. Andrews College of Education, 1990-94. Joint Founding Editor, Scottish Economic and Social History, 1980-84. British Academy/Leverhulme Trust Senior Research Fellow, 1992-93; Trustee, National Museums of Scotland, since 1995; Winner: Senior Hume Brown Prize, 1977, Agnes Mure MacKenzie Prize, Saltire Society, 1992, Henry Duncan Prize, Royal Society of Edinburgh, 1995. Publications: The Tobacco Lords, 1975; Lairds and Improvement in Enlightenment Scotland, 1979; Ireland and Scotland 1600-1850 (Co-Editor), 1983; Farm Servants and Labour in Lowland Scotland 1770-1914, 1984; A Scottish Firm in Virginia 1767-77, 1984; People and Society in Scotland 1760-1830 (Co-Editor), 1988; The Great Highland Famine, 1988; Improvement and Enlightenment (Editor), 1989; Conflict and Stability in Scottish Sociey (Editor), 1990; Irish Immigrants and Scottish Society in the Eighteenth and Nineteenth Centuries (Editor), 1991; Scottish Emigration and Scottish Society, 1992; Scottish Elites, 1993; The Transformation of Rural Scotland, 1994; Clanship to Crofters' War, 1994; Industry, Business and Society in Scotland since 1700 (Co-Editor), 1994; Glasgow: I, Beginnings to 1830, 1995; St. Mary's, Hamilton: a social history; Exploring the Scottish Past,

1995; Scotland in the Twentieth Century (Co-Editor), 1996. Recreations: walking and exploring the Hebrides; watching skilful football; travelling in Italy. Address: (b.) Research Centre in Scottish History, McCance Building, 16 Richmond Street, Glasgow G1 1XQ; T.-0141-548 4531.

de Vink, Peter Henry John, BComm. Managing Director, Edinburgh Financial and General Holdings Ltd., since 1978; b. 9.10.40, Amsterdam; m., Julia Christine (Krista) Quarles van Ufford; 1 s.; 1 d. Educ. Edinburgh University. National Service, Dutch Army, 1961-63; Edinburgh University, 1963-66; Ivory and Sime Investment Managers, 1966-78, latterly as Director. Address: (h.) 7 Howe Street, Edinburgh EH3 6TE; T.-0131-225 6661; (h.) Huntly Cot, Temple, Midlothian EH23 4TS; T.-01875 830345.

Dewar, The Rt Hon. Donald Campbell, PC, MA, LLB. Secretary of State for Scotland, since 1997; MP (Labour), Glasgow Anniesland, since 1997 (MP, Garscadden, 1978-96; Labour Chief Whip); b. 21.8.37, Glasgow; 1 s.; 1 d. Educ. Glasgow Academy; Glasgow University. Practised as Solicitor in Glasgow; MP, Aberdeen South, 1966-70; PPS to Tony Crosland, 1967; Chairman, Select Committee on Scottish Affairs, 1980-81; Member, Scottish front bench team, 1981-83; elected to Shadow Cabinet, 1984; Opposition Spokesman on Scottish Affairs, 1983-92, Social Security, 1992-95; Privy Councillor, 1996. Address: (h.) 23 Cleveden Road, Glasgow G12; T.-0141-334 2374.

Dewar, Douglas, MA (Hons), CA. Finance Director, Scottish Airports Ltd., since 1992; b. 18.6.47, Glasgow; m., Nancy; 1 s.; 1 d. Educ. High School of Glasgow; Glasgow University. Arthur Young McClelland Moores; Scottish Co-ordinated Investments Ltd.; Scottish Express Ltd. (Finance Director); Stansted Airport Ltd. (Finance Director). Address: (b.) Scottish Airports Ltd., St. Andrews Drive, Glasgow Airport, Glasgow PA3 2SW; T.-0141-848 4298.

Dewar, Ian McGregor, CA. Partner in Charge, Price Waterhouse, East of Scotland, since 1995; b. 21.8.46, Helensburgh; m., Avril; 2 s. Educ. Hutchesons' Grammar School, Glasgow. Qualified as CA, 1969; joined Price Waterhouse, Glasgow, 1969, Partner, 1979. Past President, Junior Chamber, Scotland. Recreations: golf; shooting. Address: (b.) 58 Albany Street, Edinburgh EH1 3QR; T.-0131-559 9900.

Dewar, Lawrence, MBE. Chief Executive, Scottish Grocers' Federation, since 1980; b. 12.1.36, Blackford; m., Nancy Kelly; 2 s.; 2 d. Educ. Dunfermline High School. Grocer of the Year, 1967; President, Scottish Grocers' Federation, 1975; Member, Board, SCOTBEC, 1981-85; Member, Sector Sector Board 5, SCOTVEC, 1986-97; Recreations: golf; reading; TV. Address: (h.) 222/224 Queensferry Road, Edinburgh EH4 2BN.

Dewar-Durie, Andrew Maule. Chairman, Allied Distillers Ltd., since 1997; Chairman, CBI Scotland, since 1997; b. 13.11.39, Bath; m., Marguerite Kottulinsky; 2 s.; 1 d. Educ. Wellington College. Regular soldier, Argyll and Sutherland Highlanders, 1958-68, retiring with rank of Captain; Export Representative to Senior Export Director, White Horse Distillers, 1968-83; International Sales Director, Long John International, 1983-87; James Burrough Distillers: International Sales Director, 1987-89, Managing Director, 1990; Chief Executive Officer, James Burrough Ltd., 1990-91, Managing Director, 1991-92; Managing Director, Allied Distillers Ltd., 1992-97. Deputy Lieutenant, Dunbartonshire, since 1996; CBI Scotland: Council Member, 1993, Vice Chairman, 1996; Non-Executive Director, Dumyat Investment Trust PLC, since 1995; Director, Scotch Whisky Association, since 1992; Keeper of the Quaich, since 1989, Master, since 1992; Liveryman, Worshipful Company of Distillers, since 1986; Council Member, Gin and Vodka Association of GB, since 1997; Member, Scottish Economic Council, since 1997.

Recreations: tennis; rough shooting; sailing; theatre; cinema. Address: (b.) 2 Glasgow Road, Dumbarton G82 1ND; T.-01389 765111.

Dewing, Irene Isabel Joan, DL; b. 21.9.36, Inverness; m., William Beresford Dewing; 2 d. Educ. Heatherley, Inverness. Deputy Lieutenant. Address: (h.) The Hollies, Kildary, Rossshire; T.-01862 842204.

Dick, David, OBE, DIC, CEng, FIEE. H.M. Lay Inspector of Fire Services for Scotland, since 1994; b. 20.3.29, Edinburgh; m., Muriel Elsie Margaret Buchanan; 5 d. Educ. Boroughmuir School, Edinburgh; Heriot-Watt College, Edinburgh; Imperial College, London. Electrical Engineer, North of Scotland Hydro-Electric Board, 1951-54; Lecturer, Dundee College of Technology, 1954-60; Head, Department of Electrical Engineering, Coatbridge Technical College, 1960-64; Depute Principal, Napier College of Science and Technology, Edinburgh, 1964-69; Principal, Stevenson College of Further Education, Edinburgh, 1969-87. Manpower Services Commission: Chairman, Lothian District Manpower Committee, 1981-82, Member, Lothian and Borders Area Manpower Board, 1982-85; Member and Chairman, various committees: Scottish Technical Education Council, Scottish Business Education Council, 1969-87; Chairman, Fire Services Examination Board (Scotland), 1968-86; Member, Construction Industry Training Board, 1976-85; Member: Electrical Engineering Services Committee, CITB, 1976-88, General Convocation, Heriot-Watt University, Edinburgh, 1970-73; Past Chairman, Scottish Committee, Institution of Electronic and Radio Engineers; former Honorary President, Edinburgh and District Spastics Association. Publications: Capital Walks in Edinburgh – The New Town, 1994; Street Biographies of the Royal Burgh of Haddington, 1997. Recreations: music (flute); gardening; writing historical biographies. Address: (h.) West Lodge, Clerkington, near Haddington, East Lothian.

Dick, James, OBE, BA, DMS. Director of Social Work, The Highland Council, since 1996; b. 19.5.39, Kirkcaldy; m., Isabel; 1 d. Educ. Buckhaven High School; Schumacher High School, Ontario; Jordanhill College; Open University; RGIT. Probation Officer, Edinburgh, 1967; Child Care Officer, Moray and Nairn, 1969; Area Team Leader, Perth and Kinross, 1971; Principal Social Work Officer, Selkirk County Council, 1973; Divisional Officer, Child Care, Borders Regional Council, 1975; Divisional Officer, Grampian Regional Council, 1975; Highland Regional Council: Senior Depute Director of Social Work, 1985, Director of Social Work, 1985-96. Past President, Association of Directors of Social Work. Recreations: golf; gardening; reading; bowls. Address: (b.) Kinmylies Building, Leachkin Road, Inverness IV3 6NN; T.-01463 703444.

Dick, Jill (Gillian Avril). Director: Scottish Cultural Press, since 1992, Scottish Children's Press, since 1995; b. 9.4.49, Croydon; 3 s. Educ. Croham Hurst School, South Croydon. Variety of positions with Aberdeen University Press for 10 years, until its collapse at the death of Robert Maxwell. Recreations: crosswords; reading; walking; good food and drink. Address: (b.) Unit 14, Leith Walk Business Centre, 130 Leith Walk, Edinburgh EH6 5DT; T.-0131-555 5950.

Dick, Rev. John Hunter Addison, MA, MSc, BD. Parish Minister, Aberdeen: Ferryhill, since 1982; Vice-Convener, Church of Scotland Board of Parish Education, since 1997; b. 27.12.45, Dunfermline; m., Gillian A. Ogle-Skan; 3 s. Educ. Dunfermline High School; Edinburgh University. Research Assistant, Department of Geography, Edinburgh University, 1967-70; Senior Tutor, Department of Geography, Queensland University, 1970-78; student of divinity, 1978-81; Assistant Minister, Edinburgh: Fairmilehead, 1981-82. Governor, Robert Gordon's College, since 1994. Recreations: music; bowls. Address: Ferryhill

Manse, 54 Polmuir Road, Aberdeen AB11 7RT; T.-01224 586933.

Dickie, Bobbie, MSc, CQSW, DipOT, DipComCare, LRCCO. Executive Director Housing and Social Services, Clackmannanshire Council, since 1995; b. 18.11.43, Glasgow; m., Greig Stobo; 1 d. Educ. The Academy, Hamilton; Stirling University; Glasgow University; Suffolk College. Team Leader, Child Protection, NSPCC, London, 1973-78; Children and Family work, St. Albans Social Services, 1978-81; Central Region: Team Manager, Learning Disabilities, 1981-89; Principal Professional Officer, Disabilities, 1989-93; Head of Service, Adult Care, 1993-95. Recreations: travel; motoring; gardening; DIY. Address: (b.) Limetree House, Castle Street, Alloa FK10 1EX; T.-01259 452416.

Dickie, Jim, MA, DipSW, MCC. Director of Social Work: East Ayrshire Council, 1995-96, North Lanarkshire Council, since 1996; b. 23.3.47, New Lanark; m., Jean; 2 d. Educ. Lanark Grammar School; Glasgow University; Jordanhill College. Assistant Governor, HM Prison Service; Project Administrator, New Careers Project, Bristol; Senior Social Worker, Greenock; Social Education Adviser, Assistant District Manager, Strathclyde Region. Recreations: sailing; mycology; walking. Address: (b.) Scott House, Merry Street, Motherwell ML1 1JE; T.-01698 332027.

Dickie, Thomas, JP. Chairman: Commercial Services Committee, North Ayrshire Council, since 1996, Scottish ADLO Vehicle Maintenance and Transportation Working Group, since 1993, Scottish ADLO Building Division, since 1996, National ADLO Vehicle Maintenance and Transportation Advisory Group, since 1992, National ADLO, 1997-98; Member: National ADLO Committee on Competitive Tendering, since 1994, National ADLO Council, since 1994; b. 5.12.30, Beith; m., Janette Coulter Brown. Educ. Beith Academy; Speirs Secondary School; Glasgow and West of Scotland Commercial College. From office boy to Personnel Manager, Redpath Engineering Ltd., 1946-80; Member, Cunninghame District Council, 1975-96, serving as Convener, 1980-84, Chairman, Licensing Board, 1980-92, Chairman, Housing Committee, 1992-96. Member, Board, Irvine Development Corporation, 1981-84; Chairman, Garnock Valley Development Executive, 1984-88; Secretary: Cunninghame North Constituency Labour Party, 1990-92, Garnock Labour Social Club, since 1972. Recreations: reading; music; walking. Address: (h.) 45 Loadingbank Court, Kilbirnie, Ayrshire KA25 6JX; T.-01505 682205.

Dickinson, Professor Harry Thomas, BA, DipEd, MA, PhD, DLitt, FRHistS. Professor of British History, Edinburgh University, since 1980; Professor of British History, Nanjing University, since 1987; b. 9.3.39, Gateshead; m., Jennifer Elizabeth Galtry; 1 s.; 1 d. Educ. Gateshead Grammar School; Durham University; Newcastle University. Teacher of History, Washington Grammar School, 1961-64; Earl Grey Fellow, Newcastle University, 1964-66; History Department, Edinburgh University: Assistant Lecturer, 1966-68, Lecturer, 1968-73, Reader, 1973-80; Associate Dean (Postgraduate), 1992-96; Visiting Professor, Nanjing University, China, 1980-83-87-94; Fulbright Scholar, 1973; Huntington Library Fellowship, 1973; Folger Shakespeare Library Fellowship, 1973; Winston Churchill Fellow, 1980; Leverhulme Award, 1986-87; Ahmanson Fellowship, UCLA, 1987; Anstey Lecturer, University of Kent, 1989; Douglas Southall Freeman Professor, University of Richmond, Virginia, 1987; Chairman, Publications Committee, Historical Association, 1991-94; Vice-President: Royal Historical Society, 1991-95, Historical Association, 1995-97 (Deputy President, since 1997); Member, Humanities Committee, CNAA, 1991-93; National Auditor, Higher Education Quality Council, 1993-95; Team Assessor, History, TQA,

SHEFC, 1995-96; Member, Marshall Aid Commonwealth Commission, since 1987; Editor, History. Publications: Bolingbroke; Walpole and the Whig Supremacy; Liberty and Property; British Radicals and the French Revolution; The Correspondence of Sir James Clavering; Politics and Literature in the 18th Century; The Political Works of Thomas Spence; Caricatures and the Constitution 1760-1832; Britain and the French Revolution; The Politics of the People in Eighteenth-century Britain; many pamphlets, essays and reviews. Recreations: reading; films. Address: (h.) 44 Viewforth Terrace, Edinburgh EH10 4LJ; T.-0131-229 1379.

Dickinson, Professor Keith William, BSc, MEng, PhD, CEng, MICE, FIHT. Assistant Principal, Academic Development, Napier University, since 1997; b. 17.9.48, Liverpool; m., Dorothy Mills; 1 s. Educ. Ormskirk Secondary School; Sheffield Polytechnic; University of Sheffield. A.M. Voorhees & Associates, 1975-76; South Yorkshire County Council, 1973-79; Department of Civil and Structural Engineering, University of Sheffield, 1980-85; Senior Lecturer and Director, Transport Engineering Research Unit, Napier Polytechnic, 1986-90; Napier University: Head, Civil & Transportation Engineering, 1990-94, Dean, Faculty of Engineering, 1994-97. Recreations: walking; travelling; fishing; drawing. Address :(b.) Napier University, 10 Colinton Road, Edinburgh EH10 5DT; T,-0131-455 2401.

Dickson, Alastair Ronald. Senior Partner, Dickson Minto WS, since 1985; b. 16.1.51, Glasgow; m., Josephine; 2 s.; 1 d. Educ. Glenalmond College; Edinburgh University. Trained, Dundas & Wilson, 1971-73; Maclay, Murray & Spens, 1973-76; Dundas & Wilson, 1976-85 (Partner, from 1985); Founding Partner, Dickson Minto WS, 1985. Recreations: golf; squash; hill-walking. Address: (b.) 11 Walker Street, Edinburgh EH3 7NE; T.-0131-225 4455.

Dickson, Captain Alexander Forrest, OBE, RD, FRIN. Commissioner of Northern Lighthouses, since 1979; b. 23.6.20, Edinburgh; m., Norma Houston; 3 s.; 2 d. Educ. George Watson's; Leith Nautical College. Apprentice, P. Henderson and Co., 1936-39; Royal Navy service in destroyers, 1939-45; Lecturer, Leith Nautical College, 1945-49; Shell International Marine Co. Ltd., 1949-79 (Director Operations, 1968-79). Honorary Sheriff, Perth. Recreations: fishing; gardening; golf. Address: (h.) Birchburn, Kenmore, Perthshire; T.-018873 283.

Dickson, Campbell S., MA, DipEd. Rector, Nairn Academy, since 1987; b. 25.11.44, Edinburgh; 2 s. Educ. Boroughmuir High School, Edinburgh; Edinburgh University. Teacher of Modern Languages, Dunfermline High School, 1968-71; Principal Teacher of Modern Languages, Golspie High School, 1971-79; Assistant Rector, Banff Academy, 1979-82; Depute Rector, Lochaber High School, 1982-87. Member, Scottish Central Committee on Modern Languages, 1977-80. Address: (b.) Nairn Academy, Duncan Drive, Nairn IV12 4RD; T.-01667 453700.

Dickson, James Holms, BSc, MA, PhD, FLS, FRSE. Reader in Botany, University of Glasgow, since 1993; b. 29.4.37, Glasgow; m. Camilla A. Lambert, 1 s.; 1 d. Educ. Bellahouston Academy; University of Glasgow; University of Cambridge. Fellow, Clare College, University of Cambridge, 1963-70; Lecturer then Senior Lecturer in Botany, University of Glasgow, 1970-93. Leader, Trades House of Glasgow Expedition to Papua, New Guinea, 1987; Consultant, Britoil, Glasgow Garden Festival, 1988; currently working on plant remains found with 5,300 year old Tyrolean Iceman. Neill Medallist, Royal Society of Edinburgh, 1996; twice Past President, Glasgow Natural History Society; Past President, Botanical Society of Scotland. Publications: three books, including Wild Plants of Glasgow; many papers on Scottish flora, Ice Age plants,

archaeo-botany. Address: (b.) Graham Kerr Building, Glasgow University; T.-0141-330 4364.

Dickson, Leonard Elliot, CBE, MC, TD, DL, BA (Cantab), LLB. Retired Solicitor; b. 17.3.15, Edinburgh; m., Mary Elisabeth Cuthbertson; 1 s.; 1 d. Educ. Uppingham; Magdalene College, Cambridge; Glasgow University. 1st Bn., Glasgow Highlanders HLI, 1939-46; former Senior Partner, Dickson, Haddow & Co., Solicitors, Glasgow (retired, 1985); Clerk, Clyde Lighthouses Trust, 1953-65; Secretary, Glasgow Society of Sons of Clergy, 1953-83; serving Officer, TA, 1939-55 (Lt. Col. commanding 1st Bn., Glasgow Highlanders, 1952-55), Chairman, Lowland TAVR, 1968-70; Member, Glasgow Executive Council, NHS, 1956-74 (Vice Chairman, 1970-74). Recreations: travel; gardening. Address: (h.) Bridge End, Gartmore, Stirling FK8 3RR; T.-01877 382 220.

Dickson, Sheriff Robert Hamish, LLB, WS. Sheriff of South Strathclyde, Dumfries & Galloway at Airdrie, since 1988; b. 19.10.45, Glasgow; m., Janet Laird Campbell; 1 s. Educ. Glasgow Academy; Drumtochty Castle; Glenalmond; Glasgow University. Solicitor, Edinburgh, 1969-71, and Glasgow, 1971-86; Partner, Brown Mair Gemmill & Hislop, Solicitors, Glasgow, 1973-86; appointed floating Sheriff of South Strathclyde, Dumfries & Galloway at Hamilton, 1986. Publication: Medical and Dental Negligence, 1997. Recreations: golf; music; reading. Address: (b.) Airdrie Sheriff Court, Airdrie; T.-Airdrie 751121.

Dillon, J. Shaun H., DRSAM (Comp), FSA Scot. Professional Musician; Composer, Oboist and Teacher of Woodwind; b. 30.12.44, Sutton Coldfield. Educ. Berwickshire High School; Fettes College; Royal Scottish Academy of Music; Guildhall School of Music. Studied composition with Frank Spedding and Edmund Rubbra; awarded prize for composition for Leicestershire Schools Orchestra, 1965; commissions from various bodies, including Scottish Amateur Music Association; Instructor of Woodwind: Edinburgh Corporation, 1967-72, Aberdeen Corporation (latterly Grampian Region), 1972-81; Freelance Musician, since 1981; sometime Director of Music, St. Mary's Cathedral, Aberdeen; two suites of Airs and Graces for strings published; Secretary, Association of Instrumental and Vocal Specialists, 1975-78. Recreations: reading, especially history, literature; crosswords; playing flute (badly) in ceilidh bands. Address: (b.) 34 Richmond Street, Aberdeen AB2 4TR; T.-Aberdeen 630954.

Dilworth, Rt. Rev. Gerard Mark, OSB, MA, PhD, FRHistS, FSA Scot. Abbot, Fort Augustus Abbey, since 1991; b. 18.4.24. Educ. St. Andrew's School, Edinburgh; Fort Augustus Abbey School, Invernessshire; Oxford University; Edinburgh University. Fort Augustus Abbey School: Senior Modern Languages Master, 1956-59, Headmaster, 1959-72; Parish Priest, Fort Augustus, 1974-79; Editor, The Innes Review, 1979-84; Keeper, Scottish Catholic Archives, 1979-91. Publications: The Scots in Franconia; George Douglas: priest and martyr; Scottish Monasteries in the Late Middle Ages, 1995. Address: (b.) The Abbey, Fort Augustus, Inverness PH32 4DB; T.-01320 366232.

Divers, Tom. General Manager, Lanarkshire Health Board. Address: (b.) 14 Beckford Street, Hamilton ML3 0TA.

Dixon, Brian Ringrose, ACIB. Scotland Director, Barclays Bank PLC, since 1983; Non-Executive Director, EJ Stiell Group Limited; Member, Court, Strathclyde University; b. 4.1.38, Market Weighton; m., Annette Robertson; 2 s. Educ. Pocklington School, York. Member, Executive Council, Scottish Council Development and Industry. Recreations: rugby; gardening; golf; walking. Address: (b.) 90 St. Vincent Street, Glasgow G2 5UQ; T.-0141-221 9585.

Dixon, Professor Geoffrey Richard, BSc, PhD, FIHort, FIBiol, CBiol. Professor of Horticulture, University of Strathclyde; independent international Consultant, specialising in biotechnology, horticulture, landscape, education; Director, Green Gene Ltd.; Head, Vice-Dean, Department of Horticulture, Director, Scottish Horticultural Advisory Service, SAC, 1987-97; b. 13.6.42, London; m., Kathleen Hilda Edwards; 1 s.; 1 d. Educ. Pewley County School, Guildford; Wye College, University of London. Plant Pathologist, National Institute of Agricultural Botany, Cambridge, 1968-78; Head, Horticulture Division and Chairman, Crop Production and Protection Group, and Senior University Lecturer, Aberdeen School of Agriculture, 1978-87; Chairman, International Clubroot Working Group; Visiting Professor, Mansourah University, Egypt; Honorary Professor, Von Humboldt University, Berlin; Senior Research Scholar, University of Wisconsin; Visiting Lecturer, University of Horticulture, Budapest; Vice-Chairman, Education and Training Committee; former Chairman, Scottish Branch, Institute of Horticulture; Member, Examinations Board, Royal Horticultural Society; created Freeman Citizen of Glasgow and Member, Incorporation of Gardeners of Glasgow; Member of the Master Court; Liveryman, Worshipful Company of Fruiterers of the City of London; Member, Agricultural Sciences Committee, Institute of Biology. Wain Fellowship, BBSRC; Nuffield Foundation Fellowship, European Community Erasmus Programme Co-ordinator. Publications: Vegetable Crop Diseases; Plant Pathogens and their control in Horticulture; 200 scientific papers. Recreations: gardening; photography; travel; hill-walking. Address: (h.) Helenton Mote, Symington, by Ayr KA1 5PP; T.-01563 830251.

Dixon-Carter, Clare, OBE. Vice-Chairman, British Red Cross Society; Chairman, Scottish Central Council Branch, British Red Cross Society; b. 18.9.38, London. Educ. Moira House School, Eastbourne. Technical staff, EMI; hotel management, 1959-65; Assistant Regional Organiser for Scotland, World Worldlife Fund, 1969-77; joined Invernessshire Branch, British Red Cross Society, 1965; Branch Director, 1979-86; awarded Voluntary Medical Service Medal, 1983; BRCS Badge of Honour for distinguished service and life membership of society, 1986; Vice-Chairman, Scottish Central Council Branch, 1986-90. Recreations: photography; travel; music. Address: (h.) Easter Balnabaan, Drumnadrochit, Invernessshire IV3 6UX; T.-01456 450310.

Dobie, Margaret G.C., OBE, MA, DipSocStud. Hon. Vice President, Scottish Association for the Study of Delinquency; Chair, Dumfries & Galloway Valuation Appeal Panel, since 1987; Chairman, National Children's Homes Action for Children, Dumfries and Galloway Family Mediation Service; b. Galloway; m., James T.J. Dobie; 3 s. Educ. Benedictine Convent, Dumfries; Dumfries Academy; Edinburgh University. Medical Social Worker; Chair, Dumfries and Galloway Regional Children's Panel, 1971-77; Social Worker, Child Guidance Service, Dumfries; National Secretary, Scottish Association for the Study of Delinquency, 1982-87; Member, Broadcasting Council for Scotland, 1987-91; Chair, Dumfries and Galloway Children's Panel Advisory Committee, 1982-89; Chair, Children's Panel Advisory Group, 1985-88. Recreations:travel; tennis; reading. Address: (h.) 8 New Abbey Road, Dumfries DG2 7ND; T.-01387-254 595.

Dobie, Rev. Rachel Jean Wayland, LTh. Minister, Broughton, Glenholm, Kilbucho linked with Skirling, linked with Stobo, Drumelzier linked with Tweedsmuir; Contributor, BBC religious broadcasting; b. 17.8.42, Forres; m., Kirkpatrick H. Dobie; 1 s.; 1 d. Educ. Dumfries Academy; Jordanhill College; Edinburgh University. Primary schoolteacher, 1963-80; Auxiliary Minister, Dalbeattie with Urr, 1990-93; Church of Scotland Sunday School Adviser, 1976-86; Reader, 1982-90; Chair, Marriage Guidance, Dumfries, 1984-86; Member, General Assembly Youth Education Committee, 1985-93; Vice-Convener, General Assembly Board of Parish Education 1993-97. Publication: Time Together, 1981. Recreations: music; fine arts. Address: (h.) The Manse, Broughton, Biggar ML12 6HQ; T.-01899 830331.

Docherty, Michael. Depute Chief Executive (Corporate Strategy), South Lanarkshire Council; b. 12.1.52, Glasgow; m., Linda; 2 s.; 1 d. Educ. St. Mungo's Academy, Glasgow. Trainee Accountant, Electricity Board, 1971-74; Accountancy Assistant, Coatbridge Town Council, 1974-75; Accountant, Monklands District Council, 1975-77; Stirling District Council, 1977-79; Senior Accountant, Monklands District Council, 1979-82; Principal Accountant, Renfrew District Council, 1982-84; Depute Director of Finance, Motherwell District Council, 1984-91; Director of Finance, Hamilton District Council, 1991-92; Chief Executive, Hamilton District Council, 1992-96. Recreations: running; reading; hill-walking. Address: (b.) Council Offices, Almada Street, Hamilton ML3 0AA.

Dodd, Raymond Henry, PhD, MA, BMus, ARAM. Cellist and Composer; b. 31.3.29; m., Doreen Joyce; 1 s.; 1 d. Educ. Bryanston School; Royal Academy of Music; Worcester College, Oxford. Music Master, Sedbergh School, 1951-55; Aberdeen University: Lecturer in Music, 1956, Senior Lecturer in Music, 1971-91, Head of Department, 1981-88; Visiting Professor of Music, Wilson College, USA, 1972-73. Various orchestral, vocal and chamber music compositions; awarded Szymanowski Medal, Polish Ministry of Art and Culture, 1982. Address: (h.) 14 Giffordgate, Haddington, East Lothian EH41 4AS; T.-01620 824618.

Doig, Ian, CPFA, FCCA. Scottish Director, Chartered Institute of Public Finance and Accountancy (CIPFA); Secretary, Local Authority (Scotland) Accounts Advisory Committee, since 1986; Director, FSF LTD.; b. 25.11.45, Glasgow; m., Barbara; 1 d. Educ. Alva and Alloa Academies; Strathclyde University. Address: (b.) CIPFA Scotland, 8 North West Circus Place, Edinburgh EH3 6ST; T.-0131-220 4316.

Doig, John Scott. Regional Sheriff Clerk, Tayside Central and Fife; b. 24.11.38, Dundee; m., Margaret; 1 s.; 1 d. Educ. Harris Academy, Dundee. Sheriff Clerk Service since 1956 in Glasgow, Perth, Campbeltown, Linlithgow, Dumbarton, Inverness, Dundee; Secretary, Sheriff Court Rules Council, 1973-79. Recreations: bowls; curling. Address: (b.) Sheriff Courthouse, 6 West Bell Street, Dundee; T.-01382 229961.

Doig, P. Michael R., MA (Hons), FRSA. Head Teacher, Cumbernauld High School, since 1992; b. 2.5.48, Glasgow; m., Catherine; 2 s. Educ. High School of Glasgow; Glasgow University. Teacher/Assistant Principal Teacher/Principal Teacher of Modern Languages, 1972-81; Assistant Head Teacher, Hermitage Academy, Helensburgh, 1981-85; Depute Head Teacher, Kirkintilloch High School, 1985-92. Member, National Council, Headteachers' Association of Scotland; Editor, Scottish Headlines. Recreations: music; golf; current affairs. Address: (b.) Cumbernauld High School, Ring Road, S. Carbrain, Glasgow G67 2UF; T.-01236 725511.

Donachie, Professor William David, BSc, PhD, MAcadEurop. Professor of Bacterial Genetics, Edinburgh University, since 1993; b. 27.4.35, Edinburgh; m.,Millicent Masters, BS, MS, PhD; 1 s. Educ. Dunfermline High School; Edinburgh University. Assistant Lecturer in Genetics, Edinburgh University, 1958-62; Research Associate in Biochemical Sciences, Princeton University, 1962-63; Lecturer in Genetics, Edinburgh University, 1963-65; Scientific Staff, MRC Molecular Genetics Unit, London and Edinburgh, 1965-74; Senior Lecturer/Reader in Molecular Biology, Edinburgh University, 1974-93.

Publications: 70 research papers. Recreations: drawing; natural history; T'ai Chi. Address: (b.) Institute of Cell and Molecular Biology, Edinburgh University, Darwin Building, King's Buildings, Mayfield Road, Edinburgh EH9 3JR; T.-0131-650 5354.

Donald, Colin Dunlop, BA (Cantab), LLB, DUniv, FRSA, DL. b. 24.7.34, Strathaven; m., Theresa Ann Gilliland; 2 s.; 1 d. Educ. Cargilfield; Rugby; Gonville and Caius College, Cambridge; Glasgow University. National Service, 1953-55, 2nd Lt., The Cameronians (Scottish Rifles); Partner and latterly Consultant, McGrigor Donald, Solicitors, Glasgow, 1966-94. President and Chairman, Council, The Thistle Foundation, Edinburgh and Renfrew; Vice-President, National Trust for Scotland; Deputy Chairman, Universities Superannuation Scheme Ltd.; Trustee: Lloyds, TSB Foundation for Scotland; a Deputy Lieutenant of Stirling and Falkirk. Recreations: golf and other outdoor sports. Address: (h.) 33 Park Terrace, Stirling FK8 2JS; T.-01786 473565.

Donald, George Malcolm, RSA, RSW, DA, ATC, MEd. Lecturer, Edinburgh College of Art; Director, Centre for Continuing Studies, ECA; b. 12.9.43, Ootacamund, South India; 1 s.; 1 d. Educ. Robert Gordon's College; Aberdeen Academy; Edinburgh College of Art; Hornsey College of Art; Edinburgh University. Joined Edinburgh College of Art as Lecturer, 1969; Visiting Lecturer, five Faculties of Art in India, 1979; Visiting Professor: University of Central Florida (Art, 1981, Drawing and Anatomy, 1985), Strasbourg, 1986, Belgrade, 1987, Sechuan Fine Art Institute, China, 1989, Chinese Academy of Fine Art, 1994; Latimer Award, RSA, 1970; Guthrie Award, RSA, 1973; Scottish Arts Council Bursary, 1973; RSA Gillies Bequest Travel Award to India, 1978; RSA Gillies Prize, 1982; RSW Mary Marshall Brown Award, 1983; RGI Cargill Award, 1987; former Council Member, Printmakers Workshop (Edinburgh); one man shows: Florida, 1985, Helsinki, 1985, Edinburgh Festival, 1985, Belgrade, 1987, Florida, 1987, Edinburgh, 1988, 1990, London, 1992-94, Edinburgh 1993-94-95. Address: (h.) Bankhead, by Duns, Berwickshire TD11 3QJ; T.-01361 883014.

Donald, Rev. Peter Harry, MA, PhD, BD. Minister, Leith St. Serf's Parish Church, since 1991; b. 3.2.62, Edinburgh; m., Brigid Mary McNeill; 1 s.; 1 d. Educ. George Watson's College; Gonville and Caius College, University of Cambridge; University of Edinburgh. Scouloudi Research Fellow, Institute of Historical Research, University of London, 1986-87; Probationer Assistant, St. Michael's Church, Edinburgh, 1990-91. Hon. Secretary, Scottish Church History Society; Board Member, Faith and Order Commission. Publication: An Uncounselled King: Charles I and the Scottish Troubles 1637-1641, 1990. Recreations: golf; swimming; racquet sports; piano; singing; walking; family. Address: 1 Denham Green Terrace, Edinburgh EH5 3PG; T.-0131-552 4059.

Donaldson, Rev. David, MA, BD (Hons), DipEd. Minister, Duddingston Kirk, Edinburgh, since 1990; b. 6.7.43, Glasgow; m., Jean Lacey; 1 s.; 3 d. Educ. Glasgow Academy; Glasgow University. Missionary, Church of Scotland, Taiwan, 1969-75; Minister: St. David's Bathgate, 1975-83, Whitfield, Dundee, 1983-90. Convener, Diaconate Committee, Church of Scotland, 1990-95. Recreations: tennis; badminton. Address: (h.) Duddingston Manse, 5 Old Church Lane, Edinburgh EH15 3PX; T.-0131-661 4240.

Donaldson, Professor Gordon Bryce, MA, PhD, FInstP, FRSE. Professor of Applied Physics and Head of Department, Strathclyde University, since 1993; b. 10.8.41, Edinburgh; m., Christina Martin; 1 s.; 1 d. Educ. Glasgow Academy; Christ's College, Cambridge. Cavendish Laboratory, Cambridge, 1962-65; Lecturer in Physics, Lancaster University, 1966-75; Strathclyde University:

Lecturer, 1976, Senior Lecturer, 1978; Visiting Scientist and Fulbright Scholar, University of California, 1975; Visiting Professor, University of Virginia, 1981; Chairman, Institute of Physics Low Temperature Group, 1990-93; DTI/SERC Coordinator for National Superconductivity Programme, 1990-93. Address: (b.) Department of Physics and Applied Physics, Strathclyde University, Glasgow G4 0NG.

Donaldson, Professor Iain Malcolm Lane, BSc, MB, ChB, MA, FRCPE, MRCP. Professor of Neurophysiology, Edinburgh University, since 1987; b. 22.10.37; m.; 1 s. Educ. Edinburgh University. House Physician and Surgeon, Research Fellow, Honorary Lecturer, Honorary Senior Registrar, Departments of Medicine and Surgical Neurology, Edinburgh University, 1962-69; Anglo-French Research Scholarship, University of Paris, 1969-70; Research Officer, University Laboratory of Physiology, Oxford, 1970-79; Fellow and Tutor in Medicine, St. Edmund Hall, Oxford, 1973-79; Professor of Zoology, Hull University, 1979-87; Emeritus Fellow, St. Edmund Hall, Oxford, since 1979. Recreation: studying the past. Address: (b.) Centre for Neuroscience, Edinburgh University, Appleton Tower, Crichton Street, Edinburgh EH8 9LE.

Donaldson, James Andrew, BDS, BA, DFM. Principal in general dental practice; b. 28.2.57, Glasgow; m., Patricia H. Winter; 1 s.; 3 d. Educ. Coatbridge High School; Dundee University; Open University; Glasgow University. Dental Adviser, British Antarctic Survey, 1986-97; Member: National Council, General Dental Practitioners Association, since 1989, Scottish General Dental Services Committee, 1991-93, Aberdeen District Council, 1984-86, Grampian Regional Council, 1986-88; Director, "Open Wide" Dental Courses. Recreations: skiing; squash; scuba diving. Address: (h.) Ellon Castle, Ellon, AB41 9QN; T.-01358 721865.

Donaldson, Marion. Fashion Designer; b. 1944, Glasgow. Trained as primary school-teacher; with husband, founded fashion company, mid-1960s.

Donaldson, William, MA, PhD. Writer, Researcher, Traditional Musician; b. 19.7.44, Fraserburgh. Educ. Fraserburgh Academy; Aberdeen University. Publications: Popular Literature in Victorian Scotland, 1986; The Jacobite Song, 1988; The Language of the People, 1989. Recreation: piobaireachd. Address: (b.) 13 Mile End Avenue, Aberdeen.

Donegan, Kate. Governor, HM Prison and Institution, Cornton Vale, since 1996; b. 21.4.53, Newport on Tay; m., Chris Donegan; 2 s. Educ. Kirkcaldy High School. Assistant Governor: Cornton Vale, 1977-84, Barlinnie Prison, 1984-87; Deputy Governor: Reading Prison, 1987-89, Perth Prison, 1989-91; Head, Operational Manpower, Planning Unit, 1991-93; seconded to Staffing Structure Review Team, 1993-94; Deputy Governor, Barlinnie Prison, 1994-95; Deputy Chief Inspector of Prisons, 1995-96. Recreations: gardening; reading; computing. Address: (b.) HM Prison and YOI, Cornton Vale, Cornton Road, Stirling FK9 5NU; T.-01786 832591.

Donnachie, Ian, MA, MLitt, PhD, FRHistS, FSA (Scot). Senior Lecturer in History, since 1985, Staff Tutor, since 1970, Director, Centre for Scottish Studies, Open University in Scotland; b. 18.6.44, Lanark. Educ. Lanark Grammar School; Glasgow University; Strathclyde University. Research Assistant, Galloway Project, Strathclyde University, 1967-68; Lecturer in Social Studies: Napier Polytechnic, 1968-70, Deakin University, Victoria, 1982; Visiting Fellow: Deakin University, Victoria and Sydney University, NSW, 1985; Vice-Chairman, Scottish Brewing Archive; Consultant: National Library of Scotland, Scottish Tourist Board, Scottish Office Education Department, Scottish Consultative Committee on the

Curriculum, SHEFC, HEFCE; Member: Universities Association for Continuing Education (Scotland), International Council for Distance Education; Conference Secretary, Economic and Social History Society of Scotland. Publications include: A History of the Brewing Industry in Scotland; Industrial Archaeology in the British Isles (jointly); Scottish History 1560-1980 (jointly); That Land of Exiles: Scots in Australia (jointly); Forward! Labour Politics in Scotland 1888-1988 (Co-Editor); A Companion to Scottish History from the Reformation to the Present (jointly); The Manufacture of Scottish History (Co-editor); Historic New Lanark: the Dale and Owen Industrial Community since 1785 (Co-author); Studying Scottish History, Literature and Culture. Recreations: walking; curling; eating; drinking. Address: (b.) 10 Drumsheugh Gardens, Edinburgh EH3 7QJ; T.-0131-226 3851.

Donnelly, Dougie. Radio and Television Broadcaster, since 1976; b. 7.6.53, Glasgow; m., Linda; 3 d. Educ. Hamilton Academy; Strathclyde University. Studied law at University; Presenter, BBC Sports: Grandstand, Sportscene, World Championship snooker and bowls, golf; Radio Clyde mid-morning show, 1979-91. Scottish Radio Personality of Year, 1979, 1982 and 1985; Scottish TV Personality of Year, 1982; Member: Stars Organisation for Spastics, Lords Taverners. Recreations: golf; reading; socialising; work. Address: (b.) c/o David John Associates, 90 Barrington Drive, Glasgow G4 9ET; T.-0141-357 0532.

Donnison, Professor David. Honorary Research Fellow, Glasgow University; Visiting Professor, Warwick University; b. 19.1.26. Lecturer: Manchester University, 1950-53, Toronto University, 1953-55; London School of Economics and Political Science: Reader, 1956-61, Professor, 1961-69; Director, Centre for Environmental Studies, London, 1969-75; Chairman, Supplementary Benefits Commission, 1975-80; Professor of Town and Regional Planning, Glasgow University, 1980-90. Address: (b.) Glasgow University, Glasgow G12 8RT.

Donohoe, Brian H. MP (Labour), Cunninghame South, since 1992; b. 10.9.48, Kilmarnock; m., Christine; 2 s. Educ. Irvine Royal Academy; Kilmarnock Technical College. Secretary, Irvine and District Trades Council, 1973-81; Chair: North Ayrshire and Arran LHC, 1977-79, Cunninghame Industrial Development Committee, 1975-79; former full-time trade union official (NALGO). Recreation: gardening. Address: (h.) 5 Greenfield Drive, Irvine, Ayrshire; T.-01294 274419.

Donovan, Professor Robert John, BSc, PhD, CChem, FRSC, FRSE. Professor of Chemistry, Edinburgh University, since 1979; b. 13.7.41, Nantwich; m., Marion Colclough; 1 d. Educ. Sandbach School; University College of Wales, Aberystwyth; Cambridge University. Research Fellow, Gonville and Caius College, 1966-70; Edinburgh University: Lecturer in Physical Chemistry, 1970-74, Reader in Chemistry, 1974-79. Member: Physical Chemistry Panel, Science & Engineering Research Council, 1977-80, Management Committee, SERC Synchrotron Radiation Source, Daresbury, 1977 80, SERC Synchroton Radiation Facility Committee, 1979-84; Chairman, SERC Laser Facility Committee, 1989-92; Member, SERC Science Board, 1989-92; Chairman, Faculties Commission, SERC, 1993-94; awarded Corday-Morgan Medal and Prize, Royal Society of Chemistry, 1975; Member: Faraday Council, Royal Society of Chemistry, 1981-83, 1991-93, Royal Society of Edinburgh Council, since 1996; Tilden Prize, Royal Society of Chemistry, 1995. Recreations: hill-walking; skiing; sail-boarding; cross-country riding. Address: (b.) Department of Chemistry, Edinburgh University, West Mains Road, Edinburgh EH9 3JJ; T.-0131-650 4722.

Doran, Frank, LLB(Hons). MP (Labour), Aberdeen Central, since 1997; b. 13.4.49; 2 s. Educ. Leith Academy;

University of Dundee. Solicitor, 1977-87; MP (Labour), Aberdeen South, 1987-92; Co-ordinator, National Trade Union Political Fund Ballot Campaign, 1993-96. Address: (b.) House of Commons, London SW1A 0AA; T.-0171-219 3000.

Dorman, Arthur Brian, LLB, FIMgt. Solicitor; Founding and Senior Partner, Dorman, Jeffrey & Co., Glasgow and Edinburgh; b. 21.6.45, Glasgow; 1 s.; 1 d. Educ. Hillhead High School; Glasgow University. Recreation: occasional golf. Address: (b.) Madeleine Smith House, 6/7 Blythswood Square, Glasgow G2 4AD; T.-0141-221 9880.

Dorrian, Leeona J., QC, LLB. Admitted Faculty of Advocates, 1981. Address: Advocates' Library, Parliament House, Edinburgh, EH1 1RF.

Dorward, David Campbell, MA, GRSM, LRAM. Composer, since 1944; Music Producer, BBC, 1962-91; b. 7.8.33, Dundee; m., Janet Offord; 1 s.; 2 d. Educ. Morgan Academy, Dundee; St. Andrews University; Royal Academy of Music. Teaching, 1960-61; Freelance, 1961-62. Arts Adviser, Lamp of Lothian Collegiate Trust, since 1967; Member, Scottish Arts Council, 1972-78; Consultant Director, Performing Right Society, 1985-90; Patron's Fund Award, 1958; Royal Philharmonic Prizewinner, 1958; compositions include four string quartets, two symphonies, four concertos, Tonight Mrs Morrison (one-act opera), A Christmas Carol (musical), and incidental music for TV, radio, film and stage. Recreations: photography; computers; walking in the country. Address: (h.) 10 Dean Park Crescent, Edinburgh EH4 1PH; T.-0131-332 3002.

Dorward, David Keay, CPFA. Director of Finance, Dundee City Council, since 1995; Depute Director of Finance, Tayside Regional Council, since 1993; Chief Financial Policy Officer, Tayside Regional Council, since 1986; b. 24.5.54, Dunfermline; m., Gail; 3 d. Educ. Kinross High School; Perth High School; Perth College of Further Education; Dundee College of Commerce; Glasgow College of Technology. Director: Dundee Energy Recycling Limited, Dundee Small Business Finance. Recreations: supporting Dundee United; golf; bowls; listening to music. Address: (h.) 4 Norrie Street, Broughty Ferry, Dundee; T.-01382 793006; (b.) T.-01382 433359.

Dorward, David Philip, MA (Hons), LLB; b. 10.4.31, Dundee; m., Joy Stewart; 2 s. Educ. Dundee High School; St. Andrews University. Joined St. Andrews University as Administrative Assistant, 1959; successively Assistant Secretary, Deputy Secretary, Secretary; retired; Honorary Sheriff, Tayside, Central and Fife at Cupar, since 1995. Publications: Scottish Surnames; Scotland's Place-Names. Recreations: music; golf; gardening; walking; European travel. Address: (h.) 7 Drumcarrow Crescent, Strathkinness, Fife KY16 9XT; T.-0133 485630.

Douglas, Alan. Journalist and Broadcaster; b. 16.10.51, Dundee; m., Viv Lumsden (qv); 2 d. Educ. Forfar Academy. Local newspapers, 1970-74; BBC Local Radio Reporter and Producer, 1974-78; Reporter/Presenter, BBC TV Scotland, 1978-89; freelance broadcaster and journalist, BBC TV and Radio, corporate and Scottish TV (co-presenting The Home Show with his wife); Partner, The Broadcasting Business (media consultancy); Motoring Columnist, Glasgow Evening Times; Member: Guild of Motoring Writers, Association of Scottish Motoring Writers. Recreations: cars; walking; eating; drinking. Address: 9 Lethington Road, Glasgow G46 6TA.

Douglas, Rev. Andrew Morrison, MA. Clerk to the Presbytery of Aberdeen, since 1995; b. 23.2.30; b. Orange, Australia; m., Margaret Rennie; 2 s.; 2 d. Educ. Robert Gordons College, Aberdeen; University of Aberdeen. Minister: Lochcraig, Fife, 1957-62, Bon Accord St Paul's, Aberdeen, 1963-72, Southesk, Brechin, 1972-77, High

Church Hilton, Aberdeen, 1977-95. Recreations: golf; gardening; choral singing. Address: (b.) Aberdeen Presbytery Office, c/o Mastrick Parish Church, Greenfern Road, Aberdeen AB16 6TR; T.-01224 690494.

Douglas, Rev. Colin Rutherford, MA, BD, STM. Minister, Livingston Ecumenical Parish, since 1987; b. 10.4.42, Leven; Educ. Loretto College; University of St. Andrews; University of Edinburgh. Scottish Schoolboys Half-mile Champion, 1960. Address: 27 Heatherbank, Ladywell, Livingston EH54 6EE; T.-01506 432326.

Douglas, David Pringle, DipTP, MRTPI. Chief Executive, Scottish Borders Enterprise, since 1990; b. 13.5.39, Edinburgh; m., Diane; 1 s.; 1 d. Local government, 1957-86; Material International, USA, 1986-87; Roger Tym & Partners, Glasgow, 1987-90. Recreations: golf; walking. Address: (b.) Bridge Street, Galashiels TD1 1SW; T.-01896 758991.

Douglas, Gavin Stuart, RD, QC, MA, LLB; b. 12.6.32. Educ. South Morningside School; George Heriot's School; Edinburgh University. Qualified as Solicitor, 1955; National Service, Royal Navy; admitted to Faculty of Advocates, 1958; Sub-editor (part-time), The Scotsman, 1957-61; Member, Lord Advocate's Department in London, (as Parliamentary Draftsman) 1961-64; returned to practice at Scots Bar, 1964; Counsel to Scottish Law Commission, 1965-96; Hon. Sheriff, 1965-71; a Chairman of Industrial Tribunals, 1966-78; Counsel to Secretary of State for Scotland under Private Legislation Procedure (Scotland) Act 1936, 1969-1975, Senior Counsel under that Act since 1975; Member, Lothian Health Board, 1981-85; Editor, Session Cases, seven volumes, 1976-82; Temporary Sheriff, since 1990. Recreations: golf; skiing. Address: (b.) Parliament House, Parliament Square, Edinburgh EH1 1RF.

Douglas, Sheriff Neil. Sheriff of North Strathclyde at Paisley. Address: (b.) Sheriff Court House, 106 Renfrew Road, Paisley, PA3 4DD.

Douglas, Professor Neil James, MD, FRCP. Professor of Respiratory and Sleep Medicine, Edinburgh University; Director, Scottish National Sleep Laboratory; Dean, Royal College of Physicians of Edinburgh; Consultant Physician, since 1983; b. 28.5.49, Edinburgh; m., Dr. Sue Galloway; 1 s.; 1 d. Educ. Dundee High School; Trinity College, Glenalmond; St. Andrews University; Edinburgh University. Lecturer in Medicine, Edinburgh University, 1974-83; MRC Travelling Fellow, University of Colorado, 1980-81. Recreations: fishing; gardening; eating. Address: (b.) Respiratory Medicine Unit, Department of Medicine, Royal Infirmary, Lauriston Place, Edinburgh EH3 9YW; T.-0131 536 3252.

Douglas, Patricia, MBE. Director, Charles Rennie Mackintosh Society; m., Thomas H. Douglas; 2 s. Recreations: tennis; bridge. Address: (b.) Queen's Cross, 870 Garscube Road, Glasgow G20 7EL; T.-0141-946 6600.

Douglas, Sadie Naomi, MBE. Administrative Director, Scottish Civic Trust, 1983-93; b. Huddersfield; m., Alexander Douglas (deceased); 1 s. Educ. Longley Hall, Huddersfield; Huddersfield Technical College. Worked with Oxfam, 1966-70; Organising Secretary, Facelift Glasgow, 1970-73; Trust Secretary, Scottish Civic Trust, 1973-83. Member: Countrywide Holiday Association (Past President, Glasgow CHA Club), Scottish Countryside Activities Council; Chairman, West Kilbride Amenity Society. Recreation: hill-walking. Address: (h.) Hillhouse, Ardneil Avenue, West Kilbride, Ayrshire KA23; T.-01294 822465.

Douglas-Home, Lady (Lavinia) Caroline, DL, FSA Scot. Estate Factor, Douglas and Angus Estates, 1960-95; Trustee, National Museum of Antiquities of Scotland, 1982-

85; Deputy Lieutenant, Berwickshire, since 1983; b. 11.10.37 (daughter of Baron Home of the Hirsel, KT, PC). Educ. privately. Woman of the Bedchamber (Temporary) to Queen Elizabeth the Queen Mother, 1963-65; Lady-In-Waiting (Temporary) to HRH Duchess of Kent, 1966-67. Recreations: fishing; reading; antiquities. Address: (h.) Heaton Mill House, Cornhill-on-Tweed, Northumberland; T.-01890 882303.

Dover, Sir Kenneth James, BA, MA, DLitt, Hon.LLD (St. Andrews, Birmingham), Hon.LittD (St. Andrews, Bristol, London, Liverpool, Durham), Hon.DHL (Oglethorpe), FRSE, FBA. Chancellor, St. Andrews University, since 1981; b. 11.3.20, Croydon; m., Audrey Ruth Latimer; 1 s., 1 d. Educ. St. Paul's School, London; Balliol College, Oxford; Merton College, Oxford. Fellow and Tutor, Balliol College, Oxford, 1948-55; Professor of Greek, St. Andrews, 1955-76; President, Corpus Christi College, Oxford, 1976-86. Served in Royal Artillery, 1940-45; President, Hellenic Society, 1971-74; President, Classical Association, 1975; President, British Academy, 1978-81; Foreign Honorary Member, American Academy of Arts and Sciences, since 1979; Foreign Member, Royal Netherlands Academy, since 1979; Honorary Fellow, Balliol, Corpus Christi and Merton Colleges, Oxford. Recreations: lonely country; historical linguistics. Address: (h.) 49 Hepburn Gardens, St. Andrews, Fife KY16 9LS; T.-01334 473589.

Dow, Professor Alexander Carmichael, MA, PhD. Professor and Head, Department of Economics, Glasgow Caledonian University, since 1989; b. 28.8.46; m., Sheila Christine; 2 d. Educ. Perth Academy; St. Andrews University; Simon Fraser University; University of Manitoba. Research Officer, Commonwealth Secretariat; Lecturer and Assistant Professor, University of Toronto; Lecturer, Stirling University. Recreations: curling; travel. Address: (b.) Department of Economics, Glasgow Caledonian University, Cowcaddens Road, Glasgow G4 0BA; T.-0141-331 3310.

Dow, Alister, CA, FCMA. Chief Executive, Scottish Motor Trade Association, since 1992; Managing Director, Scottish Motor Show Ltd., since 1995; Managing Director, Scotsure Insurance Company, since 1993; Director, Ivory and Sime Optimum Trust PLC, since 1989; b. Cupar; m., Jacqueline; 2 d. Educ. Bell Baxter High School; Edinburgh University. Cost and Management Accountant, Ethicon Ltd., Edinburgh; Financial Director, Operations Director, Managing Director, Devro Ltd., Glasgow; Chairman, Forth Investments PLC, Edinburgh, and Hibernian Football Club, Edinburgh. Recreations: golf; hill-walking; Rotary; amateur operatics; gardening. Address: (h.) 23 Victoria Place, Stirling FK8 2QT; T.-01786 475995.

Dow, Rear-Admiral Douglas Morrison, CB, DL. Director, The National Trust for Scotland, 1992-97; b. 1.7.35; m., Felicity Margaret Mona Napier; 2 s.; Educ. George Heriot's School; BRNC Dartmouth. Joined RN, 1952; served Staff of C-in-C Plymouth, 1959-61; HMS Plymouth, 1961-63; RN Supply Sch., 1963-65; Staff of Comdr FEF, 1965-67; HMS Endurance, 1968-70; BRNC Dartmouth, 1970-72; Cdr 1972; Assistant Director, Officer Appointments (S), 1972-74; Sec to Comdr British Navy Staff, Washington, 1974-76; HMS Tiger, 1977-78; NDC Latimer, 1978-79; Captain 1979; CSO(A) to Flag Officer Portsmouth, 1979; Sec to Controller of Navy, 1981; Captain, HMS Cochrane, 1983; Commodore, HMS Centurion, 1985; RCDS, 1988; Rear Admiral, 1989; Director General, Naval Personal Services, 1989-92. Vice-Chairman, George Heriot's Trust, since 1996. Recreations: rugby union; fly fishing; shooting; golf; gardening. Address: (h.) Tor Lodge, 1 Eskbank Terrace, Dalkeith, Midlothian EH22 3DE.

Dow, Professor Sheila Christine, MA (Hons), PhD. Professor in Economics, Stirling University, since 1996;

Director, MSc in Banking and Finance; b. 16.4.49, Dumfries; m., Professor Alexander Dow; 2 d. Educ. Hawick High School; St. Andrews University; University of Manitoba; McMaster University; Glasgow University. Overseas Office, Bank of England, 1970-72; Economist, then Senior Economist, Department of Finance, Government of Manitoba, 1973-77; Lecturer, then Reader, Department of Economics, Stirling University, 1979-96. Publications: Macroeconomic Thought, 1985; Financial Markets and Regional Economic Development, 1990; Money Matters (Co-author), 1982; Money and the Economic Process, 1993; The Methodology of Macroeconomic Thought, 1996. Recreations: travel; various sports. Address: (b.) Department of Economics, Stirling University, Stirling FK9 4LA; T.-01786 467474.

Downes, Robert, DipTP, BPhil. Director, Scottish Business, Scottish Enterprise, since 1997 (Director, Industry and Skills, 1994-97); b. 10.8.51, Belfast; m., Pauline; 2 s. Educ. Portora Royal School, Enniskillen; Dundee University; Duncan of Jordanstone College of Art, Dundee. Local government, 1976-82; Dundee Project, 1982-84; SDA, 1984-87; Director: North East, SDA, 1987-90, Conran Roche Planning, London, 1990-92; independent consultant, 1992-93; Chief Executive, Dumfries and Galloway Enterprise, 1993-94; Director, Scottish and International Operations, Scottish Enterprise, 1994; Advisor, Ulster Community Conference and Flax Trust, Belfast, since 1994; part-time Lecturer, Strathclyde University, since 1994; Director: Wise Group, Glasgow, since 1997, Emerging Business Trust, Belfast, since 1996, Ulster Community Investment Trust, Belfast, since 1995; Member, Board, National Council for Urban Economic Development, Washington D.C., since 1996. Recreations: running; cycling; live music; travelling; films; pub crack; Jim Thompson novels; journalists' biographies; Kelvin walkway. Address: (h.) 18 Cleveden Gardens, Kelvinside, Glasgow G12 0PT; T.-0141-357 1651.

Downie, Rev. Alan Frew Munro, MA, BD. Parish Minister, St. Mungo's, Alloa, since 1996; b. 17.11.46, Uddingston; m., Margaret Elizabeth Moore; 2 s.; 2 d. Educ. Hamilton Academy; Langside College; University of Glasgow. Trainee Underwriter, 1964-68; Probationer Assistant Minister: Largs St. Columba's, 1976-77; Minister, Dun l/w Hillside, 1977-96. Area Chaplain, Clackmannanshire Scouts. Recreations: hillwalking; curling; music. Address: (h.) 37a Claremont, Alloa FK10 2DG; T.-01259 213872.

Downie, Professor Robert S., MA, BPhil, FRSE. Professor of Moral Philosophy, Glasgow University, since 1969 (Stevenson Lecturer in Medical Ethics, 1984-88); b. 19.4.33, Glasgow; m., Eileen Dorothea Flynn; 3 d. Educ. High School of Glasgow; Glasgow University; Queen's College, Oxford. Tutor, Worcester College, Oxford, 1958-59; Glasgow University: Lecturer in Moral Philosophy, 1959-68, Senior Lecturer, 1968-69; Visiting Professor: Syracuse University, New York, 1963-64, Dalhousie University, Nova Scotia, 1976. Publications: Government Action and Morality, 1964; Respect for Persons, 1969; Roles and Values, 1971; Education and Personal Relationships, 1974; Caring and Curing, 1980; Healthy Respect, 1987; Health Promotion: models and values, 1990; The Making of a Doctor, 1992; Francis Hutcheson, 1994; The Healing Arts: an Oxford illustrated anthology, 1994; Palliative Care Ethics, 1996; Medical Ethics, 1996. Recreation: music. Address: (b.) Department of Philosophy, Glasgow University G12 8QQ; T.-0141-339 8855.

Doyle, Professor Christopher John, BA, MSc. Head: Management Division, since 1997, Applied Economics and Agricultural Systems Department, since 1989, Scottish Agricultural College, Auchincruive; Adjunct Professor of Agricultural Economics, Glasgow University, since 1989; Vice Dean (Education), 1991-94, and Professor of Agricultural Economics, since 1994, Scottish Agricultural College, Auchincruive; b. 21.8.48, Sale, Cheshire; m., Alice; 1. d. Educ. St. Ambrose College, Cheshire; Keele University; Newcastle upon Tyne University. Departmental Demonstrator in Agricultural Economics, Oxford University, 1972-76; Research Officer, Centre for Agricultural Strategy, Reading University, 1976-79; Principal Scientific Officer, Institute for Grassland and Animal Production, 1979-86; Senior Economist, Ruakura Research Centre, MAF, New Zealand, 1987; Principal Scientific Officer, Institute for Grassland and Animal Production, 1988-89. Publications: 100 scientific papers and publications. Recreations: languages; foreign travel; modern history; theatre. Address: (b.) Scottish Agricultural College, Auchincruive, Ayr KA6 5HW; T.-01292 525053.

Doyle, Rev. David Wallace, MA(Hons), BD(Hons). Minister, St. Mary's Parish Church, Motherwell, since 1987; b. 12.4.48, Glasgow; m., Alison W. Britton; 1 s.; 1 d. Educ. High School of Glasgow; University of Glasgow; Corpus Christi, University of Cambridge. Assistant Minister, East Kilbride Old Parish Church, 1973-74; Minister, Tulliallan and Kincardine Parish Church, Fife, 1977-87. Recreations: music, gardening. Address: (h.) Manse of St. Mary's, 19 Orchard Street, Motherwell ML1 3JE; T.-01698 263472.

Doyle, Rev. Ian Bruce, MA, BD, PhD. Pastoral Assistant, Palmerston Place Church, Edinburgh, 1991; General Secretary, Department of National Mission, 1989-91; b. 11.9.21, Methil, Fife; m., Anne Watt Wallace; 2 s. Educ. Buckhaven High School; St. Andrews University; New College, Edinburgh. Served with Church of Scotland Huts, Germany, 1945-46; Assistant to Rev. D.P. Thomson, Evangelist, 1946; Minister: St. Mary's, Motherwell, 1946-60, Eastwood, Glasgow, 1960-77; Convener: Home Mission Committee, 1970-74, Home Board, 1974-77; Secretary, Department of Home Mission, 1977-84; Joint Secretary, Department of Ministry and Mission, 1984-89; General Secretary, Board of National Mission, 1989-91; Secretary, Prison Chaplaincies Board, 1977-91. Publications: This Jesus; Reformation and Revolution (Contributor); The Word for All Seasons (Contributor); Local Church Evangelism (Contributor); D.P.: a memoir of Dr. D.P. Thomson. Recreation: reading. Address: (h.) 21 Lygon Road, Edinburgh; T.-0131-667 2697.

Doyle, Roberta, BA. Director of Marketing and Press, Scottish Opera, since 1992; b. 5.1.60, Glasgow; m., Mahmut Cemal Öztürk. Educ. Notre Dame High School, Glasgow; University of Strathclyde. Marketing Manager, Citizens' Theatre, 1986; Director of Marketing and Press, Scottish Ballet, 1990. Chair, Clyde Unity Theatre Co.; Board Director, Anatomy Performance Co; Member, Theatrical Management Association Marketing Committee. Recreations: theatre; film; travel; riding. Address: (b.) Scottish Opera, 39 Elmbank Crescent, Glasgow G2 4PT; T.-0141-248 4567.

Draper, Professor Paul Richard, BA, MA, PhD. Walter Scott and Partners Professor of Finance, University of Edinburgh, since 1997; b. 28.12.46, Hayes; m., Janet Margaret; 1 s.; 1 d. Educ. Exeter, Reading and Stirling Universities. Lecturer: St. Andrews and Edinburgh Universities; Professor of Finance, Strathclyde University, 1986-97 (Head, Department of Accounting and Finance, 1990-95, Vice Dean, Strathclyde Business School, 1993-97). Publication: Scottish Financial Sector (Co-author), 1988; Investment Trust Industry in the UK, 1989. Recreations: renovating country cottages; home computing. Address: (h.) 19 Upper Gray Street, Newington, Edinburgh; T.-0131-667 4087.

Drewry, James Michael, FITSA, DCA. Director of Environmental and Consumer Services, City of Edinburgh Council, since 1996; b. Hexham. Trained, Northumberland County Council; Inspector of Weights and Measures,

Cheshire County Council; Senior Assistant Chief Trading Standards Officer, Humberside County Council, 1976-79; County Consumer Protection Officer, Durham County Council, 1980-89; Director of Trading Standards, Lothian Regional Council, 1989-96. Past Chairman, Institute of Trading Standards Administration; Chairman, Prosafe (Product Safety Enforcement Forum of Europe); President, European Consumer Product Safety Association; Adviser, Convention of Scottish Local Authorities. Recreations: squash; golf; travel. Address: (b.) Chesser House, 500 Gorgie Road, Edinburgh EH11 3YJ; T.-0131-469 5454.

Drummond, Humphrey, MC. Writer and Farmer; Proprietor and Managing Director, The Historical Press; b. 18.9.22, Old Buckenham, Norfolk; m., Cherry Drummond, 16th Baroness Strange; 3 s.; 3 d. Educ. Eton; Trinity College, Cambridge. Captain, 1st Mountain Regiment; former General Secretary, Council for Preservation of Rural Wales; Welsh Representative, National Trust; Chairman, Society of Authors (Scotland), 1976-82. Publications: Our Man in Scotland; The Queen's Man; The King's Enemy; Falconry For You; Falconry; Balkan Assault; Nazi Gold. Recreations: mechanical musical instruments; pre-Raphaelitism. Address: Megginch Castle, Errol, Perthshire; T.-01821 642 222.

Drummond, Rev. John Whiteford, MA, BD. Minister, Rutherglen West Parish Church, since 1986; b. 27.6.46, Glasgow; m., Barbara S. Grant; 1 s.; 3 d. Educ. Bearsden Academy; University of Glasgow. Probationer Assistant, St. Francis-in-the-East Church, Bridgeton, 1970-71; Ordained Assistant, King's Park Parish Church, Glasgow, 1971-73; Minister, Linwood Parish Church, 1973-86. Recreations: reading; television; family. Address: (h.) 12 Albert Drive, Rutherglen G73 3RT; T.-0141-569 8547.

Drummond, Rev. Norman Walker, MA, BD. BBC National Governor and Chairman, Broadcasting Council for Scotland, since 1994; Minister, Kilmuir and Stenscholl, Isle of Skye, since 1996; Headmaster, Loretto School, 1984-95; b. 1.4.52, Greenock; m., Lady Elizabeth Kennedy; 3 s.; 2 d. Educ. Merchiston Castle School; Fitzwilliam College, Cambridge; New College, Edinburgh. Chaplain to the Forces, 1976-82; Depot, The Parachute Regiment and Airborne Forces, 1977-78; 1st Bn., The Black Watch (Royal Highland Regiment), 1978-82; Chaplain, Fettes College, 1982-84; Chaplain to Her Majesty the Queen in Scotland; Member, Queen's Bodyguard for Scotland (Royal Company of Archers); President: Victoria League for Overseas Students in Scotland, since 1995, Edinburgh Bn., Boys' Brigade; Governor: Gordonstoun School, Aiglon College, Switzerland; Member, Scottish Committee for Imperial Cancer Research; Trustee, Foundation for Skin Research; former Member, Scottish Committee, Duke of Edinburgh's Award Scheme; former Member, Court, Heriot-Watt University; former Chairman, Musselburgh and District Council of Social Services. Publications: The First Twenty Five Years (the official history of the Black Watch Kirk Session); Mother's Hands. Recreations: rugby football; cricket; golf; curling; traditional jazz. Address: BBC Scotland, Broadcasting House, Queen Margaret Drive, Glasgow G12 8DG; T.-0141 338 2835.

Dry, Philip John Seaton, LLB. Partner, Biggart Baillie, Solicitors, since 1971; b. 21.4.45, Lincolnshire; m., Joyce Christine Hall; 1 s.; 1 d. Educ George Watson's College; Greenock Academy; Glasgow University. Apprenticeship with Biggart Lumsden & Co., 1966-68; Assistant Solicitor, 1968-70; Director: Westscot Homes PLC and Westscot Homes II PLC, Fyfe Chambers (Glasgow) Ltd.; Council Member, Law Society of Scotland; Vice President, Law Society of Scotland, 1997-98; Member, Post Office Users' Council for Scotland, since 1995; Director, Glasgow Renfrewshire Society. Recreations: sailing; the garden; opera; swimming; travel. Address: (b.) Dalmore House, 310 St. Vincent Street, Glasgow G2 5QR; T.-0141-228 8000.

Dryden, Professor Myles Muir, BSc (Econ), MBA, PhD. Professor of Management Studies, Glasgow University, since 1972; b. 21.9.31, Dundee; m., Margaret Mary Cargill; 1 s.; 1 d. Educ. Kirkcaldy High School; London School of Economics; Cornell University. National Service, 1st Bn., Black Watch, BAOR, 1950-52; Assistant Professor of Finance, Sloan School of Industrial Management, Massachusetts Institute of Technology, 1960; Lecturer, then Reader in Economics, Edinburgh University, 1963-72; appointed to first Chair of Management Studies, Glasgow University, 1972 (Head of Department, until 1980); Member, Scottish Business School Council, 1975-79; has published in a number of professional journals; research on capital budgeting, share price behaviour and portfolio management. Recreations: pottering about in the garden or with computers. Address: (b.) Department of Management Studies, 55 Southpark Avenue, Glasgow G12 8LF; T.-0141-330 4664.

Drysdale, Thomas Henry, LLB, WS. Solicitor; Deputy Keeper of Her Majesty's Signet, since 1991; Partner, Shepherd & Wedderburn, WS, Edinburgh, since 1967 (Managing Partner, 1988-94); b. 23.11.42, Buchlyvie; m., Caroline Shaw; 1 s.; 2 d. Educ. Cargilfield; Glenalmond; Edinburgh University. Chairman, Edinburgh Solicitors Property Centre, 1981-88; Chairman John Watson's Trust; Chairman, Legal Education Advisory Committee, Clark Foundation for Legal Education; Vice-Chairman, Scottish Council of Law Reporting. Recreations: skiing; walking; reading. Address: (b.) Saltire Court, 20 Castle Terrace, Edinburgh EH1 2ET; T.-0131-228 9900.

Dudgeon, Alexander (Sandy) Stewart, MA, CA. Managing Director, Martin Currie Unit Trusts Ltd.; b. 16.10.57, Edinburgh; m., Jennifer J.K. Waddell; 2 s.; 1 d. Educ. Trinity College, Glenalmond; Aberdeen University. Recreations: racing; farming; squash; golf; bridge. Address: (h.) 8 Cluny Drive, Edinburgh EH10 6DW; T.-0131-229 5252.

Dudley Edwards, Owen, BA, FRHistS. Reader in History, Edinburgh University; b. 27.3.38, Dublin; m., Barbara Balbirnie Lee; 1 s.; 2 d. Educ. Belvedere College, Dublin; University College, Dublin; Johns Hopkins University, Baltimore. Visiting Lecturer in History, University of Oragon, 1963-65; Assistant Lecturer in History, Aberdeen University, 1966-68; Lecturer in History, Edinburgh University, 1968-79; Visiting Lecturer, California State University of San Francisco, 1972-73; Visiting Associate Professor, University of South Carolina, 1973; Sir David Owen Evans Lecturer, University College of Wales, Aberystwyth, 1987; Journalist and Broadcaster, notably for Irish Times, since 1959, and BBC, since 1969; contributor to various journals, especially The Scotsman. Life Member: American Historical Association, Organisation of American Historians, Royal Medical Society (Edinburgh University), Royal Lyceum Theatre Club; External Examiner: Queen's University, Belfast, Bradford University, Manchester University, Sorbonne, University College Cardiff. Publications. Celtic Nationalism (with Gwynfor Evans, Ioan Rhys and Hugh MacDiarmid), 1968; The Sins of Our Fathers - Roots of Conflict in Northern Ireland, 1970; The Mind of an Activist - James Connolly, 1971; P.G. Wodehouse - a Critical and Historical Essay, 1977; Burke and Hare, 1980; The Quest for Sherlock Holmes: a Biographical Study of Arthur Conan Doyle, 1982; Eamon de Valera, 1987; Macaulay (Historians on Historians), 1988; The Edinburgh Festival, 1990; City of 1000 Worlds — Edinburgh in Festival, 1991; as Editor/Contributor: 1916 - The Easter Rising (with Fergus Pyle), 1968; Conor Cruise O'Brien Introduces Ireland, 1969; James Connolly: Selected Political Writings (with Bernard C. Ransom), 1973; Scotland, Europe and the American Revolution (with George Shepperson), 1976; Christmas Observed (with Graham Richardson), 1981; Edinburgh (with Graham Richardson), 1983; A Claim of Right for Scotland, 1989;

The Fireworks of Oscar Wilde, 1989; A. Conan Doyle: The Exploits of Brigadier Gerard, 1991; The Oxford Sherlock Holmes (General Editor), 1993. Address: (b.) Department of History, Edinburgh University, 50 George Square, Edinburgh, EH8 9JY.

Duff, John Hume, MA (Cantab), MA (Edin), DipEd (Oxon). Rector, Kelvinside Academy, since 1980; Chairman, HMC (Scottish Division), 1996; b. 24.4.40, Edinburgh. Educ. St. Mary's School, Melrose; Edinburgh Academy; Corpus Christi College, Cambridge; Edinburgh University; Brasenose College, Oxford. Housemaster and Head of History Department, Kelly College, Tavistock, Devon, 1967-80. Major, TA; Governor, Wellbeck College, since 1996. Recreations: squash rackets; skiing; hill-walking; foreign travel. Address: (b.) Kelvinside Academy, 33 Kirklee Road, Glasgow G12 OSW; T.-0141-357 3376.

Duffty, Paul, MB, ChB, FRCP, FRCPE, LMCC. Consultant Paediatrician, since 1982; Senior Lecturer in Child Health, Aberdeen University, since 1982; b. 1.9.46, Leeds; m., Lesley Marjory Macdonald; 2 d. Educ. Leeds Central High School; Aberdeen University. Lecturer in Child Health, Aberdeen University, 1972-75; Trainee in General Practice, Aberdeen, 1975-76; Lecturer in Child Health, Aberdeen University, 1976-78; Fellow in Neonatology, Toronto University, 1978-80; Staff Paediatrician, Hospital for Sick Children, Toronto, and Assistant Professor, Toronto University, 1980-82. Recreations: hill-walking; cross-country skiing; philately. Address: (h.) 13 Louisville Avenue, Aberdeen; T.-01224 317072.

Duffus, Professor Carol Margaret, BSc, MS, PhD, DIC, DSc, FRSE. Vice-Dean, Scottish Agricultural College, since 1991; Head, Crop Science and Technology Department, since 1991; Professor, since 1997; b. Belfast; m., John Henderson Duffus; 2 d. Educ. Victoria College, Belfast; Queens's University, Belfast; University of Michigan, Ann Arbor, USA; Imperial College, London; University of Edinburgh. Lecturer in Biochemistry, School of Molecular Sciences, University of Warwick, 1966; Lecturer, University of Edinburgh and East of Scotland College of Agriculture, 1968; Scottish Agricultural College: Head, Agricultural Biochemistry Department, 1987, Head, Crop Sciences Division, 1990, Chairman, School of Plant and Environmental Sciences, 1991. Hon. Senior Lecturer, Institute of Ecology and Resource Management, University of Edinburgh; Member: Scottish Natural Heritage, South East Regional Board, Scientific Advisory Committee, 1990-97, Law Society of Scotland Complaints Committee, 1993-95; Vice-President, Association of Applied Biologists, 1997-98 (President, 1999-2000). Publications: Carbohydrate Metabolism in Plants (Co-Author), 1984; Toxic Substances in Crop Plants (Co-Author), 1991. Recreations: gardening; chamber music; golf. Address: (b.) Scottish Agricultural College, King's Buildings, West Mains Road, Edinburgh EH9 3JG; T.-0131-535 4060.

Duffus, George McKay, FREHIS. Director of Environmental and Consumer Protection, Aberdeen City Council, since 1995; b. 10.7.45, Aberdeen; m., Patricia; 2 s. Educ. Aberdeen Grammar School. Corporation of City of Aberdeen, 1964-79; City of Aberdeen District Council, 1979-96. Recreations: walking; reading; listening to music. Address: (b.) Environmental and Consumer Protection Department, St. Nicholas House, Broad Street, Aberdeen; T.-01224 522210.

Duffus, John Henderson, BSc, PhD, DSc, CBiol, MIBiol, CChem, FRSC. Director, Edinburgh Centre for Toxicology (EdinTox). Educ. Arbroath High School; Edinburgh University; Heriot-Watt University. Research Fellow: Warwick University, 1965-67, Edinburgh University, 1967-70; Lecturer, Heriot-Watt University, 1970-80; Senior Lecturer in Environmental Toxicology, Heriot-Watt University, 1980-97; WHO Consultant, Toxicology and Chemical Safety, since 1981; Member, UK Department of the Environment Advisory Committee on Hazardous Substances, since 1991; Titular Member, IUPAC Commission on Toxicology, since 1991; Member, RSC Committee on Environment, Health and Safety. Publications: Environmental Toxicology, 1980; Environmental Toxicology and Ecotoxicology, 1986; Magnesium in Mitosis and the Cell Cycle (Co-author), 1987; Yeast: A Practical Approach (Co-Editor), 1988; The Toxicology of Chemicals, Series 1, Carcinogenicity, Vol III, Vol IV (Co-Editor/Author), 1991-93; Toxic Substances in Crop Plants (Co-Editor/Author), 1991; Cancer and Workplace Chemicals, 1995; Carcinogenicity of Inorganic Substances (Chief Editor/Author), 1997. Address: (b.) Edinburgh Centre for Toxicology, 43 Mansionhouse Road, Edinburgh EH9 2JD.

Duffy, Mgr. Francis. Former Vicar General to RC Bishop of Galloway; Resident Chaplain, Nazareth House, Kilmarnock, since 1992; b. 15.10.14, Edinburgh. Educ. Holy Cross Academy, Edinburgh; Blairs College, Aberdeen; Pontifical Scots College, Rome; Gregorian University, Rome. Ordained Priest (Rome), 1938; Curate, Ayr, 1939-41; Professor, Blairs College, Aberdeen, 1941-55; parish work in various towns, since 1955; Monsignor, since 1972. RC Religious Adviser, Scottish Television, 1958-78; Member, Dumfries Education Committee, 1963-72; Composer of congregational Church music and hymns. Address: Nazareth House, 23 Hill Street, Kilmarnock KA3 1HG.

Duffy, Graham Woodburn. Partner, Graphic Partners Design Consultants, since 1971; Director: Edinburgh Chamber of Commerce, since 1992, Scottish Design, since 1994; Fellow, Royal Society of Arts; b. 19.6.42, Edinburgh; m., Rosemary Jean; 1 s.; 1 d. Educ. Royal High School, Edinburgh; Heriot Watt College/Edinburgh College of Art. Andrew Grant Scholar, Edinburgh College of Art, 1961-63; Graphic Designer, Pillans and Wilson, 1963-67; Graphic Designer/ Typographer, Forth Studios, 1967-68; self-employed Design Consultant, 1969-71. Recreations: masters rowing; skiing; English literature; music; theatre; film. Address: (b.) 179 Canongate, Edinburgh; T.-0131-557 3558.

Duffy, Professor John Alastair, BSc, PhD, DSc, CChem, FRSC. Professor of Chemistry, Aberdeen University, since 1996; Quality Assessor for Scottish Higher Education Funding Council, 1993-94; b. 24.9.32, Birmingham; m., Muriel F.L. Ramsay; 1 s.; 1 d. Educ. Solihull School, Warwickshire; Sheffield University. Research Chemist, Albright & Wilson, Oldbury, 1958-59; Lecturer in Inorganic Chemistry, Wolverhampton Polytechnic, 1959-61; Senior Lecturer in Inorganic Chemistry, NE Wales Institute, 1961-65; Lecturer, Senior Lecturer, Reader in Chemistry, Aberdeen University, 1966-96; Assessor in Inorganic Chemistry for Ordinary and Higher National Certificates and Diplomas in Scotland, 1971-82; Consultant to Schott Glaswerke, Mainz, West Germany, 1984-86; Past Chairman, NE Scotland Section, Royal Society of Chemistry. Publications: General Inorganic Chemistry, 1966; Bonding Energy Levels and Bands in Inorganic Solids, 1990. Recreations: 20th-century opera; music. Address: (h.) 35 Beechgrove Terrace, Aberdeen AB15 5DR; T.-01224 641752.

Duffy, John Charles, BSc, MSc, CStat. Research Manager, Chief Scientist Office, Scottish Office Department of Health, since 1996; b. 6.3.49, Glasgow; m., Rosemary Clare Arthur; 2 s.; 1 d. Educ. St. Andrew's High School, Kirkcaldy; Edinburgh University; Reading University. Lecturer, Department of Statistics, Edinburgh University, and Non-Clinical Scientist, Medical Research Council, 1970-89; Senior Lecturer, Department of Statistics, Edinburgh University, 1990-96; Director, Statistics and

Information, Alcohol Research Group, Edinburgh University, 1990-96. Hon. Secretary, Association of University Teachers (Scotland), 1992-96; President, Association of University Teachers (Scotland), 1988-90. Recreations: reading; music; computers; puzzles; conversation. Address: (b.) Scottish Office Department of Health, St. Andrew's House, Edinburgh EH1 3DG; T.- 0131-244 2254.

Duffy, Sheila Sinclair, MA. Women's Editor, Radio Clyde, since 1973; Freelance Journalist, since 1967; b. 6.8.46, Silloth, Cumberland; m., Paul Young; 2 d. Educ. St. Joseph's, Nicosia; Boroughmuir School, Edinburgh; Edinburgh University. Auxiliary nurse, Edinburgh Royal Infirmary, 1965-66; croupier, Edinburgh night club, 1966-67; graduate trainee, Scottish Television, 1967-68; Reporter, Scottish Television, 1968-73; Presenter, Dateline Early/Edinburgh Film Festival programmes/Moneywise; Member, Visiting Committee, Glenochil Young Offenders Institution, since 1995. Glenfiddich Food Writer Award, 1986. Recreations: children; husband; genealogy; cooking; reading; cake decorating; walking; sampler embroidery. Address: c/o Young Casting Agency, 7 Beaumont Gate, Glasgow; T.-0141-339 5180.

Dukes, Professor Paul, BA (Cantab), MA, PhD. Professor of History, Aberdeen University, since 1988; b. 5.4.34, Wallington; m., Rosemary Mackay; 1 s.; 1 d. Educ. Wallington County Grammar School; Cambridge University. Advisory Editor, History Today. Publications: several books on aspects of Russian, American, European and world history. Recreations: hill-walking; travel. Address: (b.) History Department, Aberdeen University, Aberdeen; T.-01224 272465.

Dun, Thomas Dixon Connochie. Farmer; Hon. Secretary, Royal Highland Agricultural Society, since 1995; Hon. President, North Country Cheviot Sheep Society, since 1970; b. 16.8.30, Selkirk; m., Jacqueline Joan Bruce; 3 s.; 1 d. Educ. Dollar Academy; Edinburgh Agriculture College. Farming, since 1953. Chairman, Royal Highland Agricultural Society, 1992-93, Director, 1972-94; President, North Country Cheviot Sheep Society, 1967-68; Council Member, National Sheep Association, since 1960; winner, George Hedley Memorial Award, 1991. Recreations: horse-racing; rugby. Address: Nether Brotherstone, Heriot, Midlothian EH38 5YS; T.-01875 835225.

Dunbar, Sir Archibald Ranulph, MA, DipAgric (Cantab), DTA (Trin). Retired; b. 8.8.27, London; m., Amelia M.S. Davidson; 1 s.; 2 d. Educ. Wellington College; Pembroke College, Cambridge. Military Service, Cameron Highlanders (attached Gordon Highlanders), 1945-48; Imperial College of Tropical Agriculture, Trinidad, 1952-53; Agricultural Officer, Colonial Service, Uganda (later Overseas Civil Service, Uganda) 1953-70; Landowner, Duffus Estate, Elgin, since 1970. Honorary Sheriff, Sheriff Court District of Moray, since 1989; Knight of Honour and Devotion, Sovereign Military Order of Malta, 1989. Recreations: swimming; railways; model railways; military models. Address: (h.) The Old Manse, Duffus, Elgin, Moray; T.-01343 830270.

Dunbar, Ian Duncan, LLB. Partner, Miller Hendry, Solicitors, since 1990; b. 31.10.48, Dundee; m., Susan Young. Educ. Lawside Academy, Dundee; Queens College, Dundee/St. Andrews University. Law apprentice, Soutar Reid & Mill, Dundee, 1969-71; Assistant Solicitor, Sneddon Campbell & Munro, Perth, 1971-72, Partner, 1972-85; merged to form Miller Sneddon, 1985, Partner, 1985-90; merged to form Miller Hendry, 1990. President, Law Society of Scotland, 1993-94. Recreations: golf; rugby; cooking; wine. Address: (h.) Craigrownie, Forgandenny Road, Bridge of Earn, Perth PH2 9HA; T.- 01738 812255.

Dunbar, John Greenwell, MA, FSA, FSA Scot, HonFRIAS. Secretary, Royal Commission on the Ancient and Historical Monuments of Scotland, 1978-90; b. 1.3.30, London; m., Elizabeth Mill Blyth. Educ. University College School, London; Balliol College, Oxford. joined staff, Royal Commission on the Ancient and Historical Monuments of Scotland, 1953; Member, Ancient Monuments Board for Scotland, 1978-90. Publications: The Historic Architecture of Scotland, 1966; Accounts of the Masters of Works, Volume 2 (1616-1649), (Joint Editor), 1982. Address: (h.) Paties Mill, Carlops, by Penicuik, Midlothian EH26 9NF; T.-01968 660250.

Dunbar, Lennox Robert, DA, ARSA. Head of Printmaking, Grays School of Art, since 1987; Painter and Printmaker; b. 17.5.52, Aberdeen; m., Jan Storie; 2 s.; 1 d. Educ. Aberdeen Grammar School; Grays School of Art. Part-time Lecturer, 1975-82; Etching Technician, Peacock Printmakers, 1978-82; Education Officer, Peacock Printmakers, 1982-86; appointed Lecturer in Painting and Printmaking, Grays School of Art, 1986; Visiting Lecturer, Duncan of Jordanstone College of Art, Dundee, and Newcastle University; Visiting Artist/Tutor, Louisiana State University; participated in many group and one-man exhibitions; numerous awards including Latimer Award, 1978, Guthrie Award, 1984, Shell Expro Premier Award, 1991 and 1993; work in many private and public collections.

Dunbar, Morrison Alexander Rankin, FCIOB, FFB, FBIM, FRSAMD, FRSA. Chairman: Royal Scottish Academy of Music and Drama Trust, since 1992, Scottish Philharmonic Trust; b. 27.4.29, Glasgow; m., Sally Joan Sutherland; 2 s.; 1 d. Educ. Belmont House; Gresham House. Managing Director, Morrison Dunbar Ltd. Builders, 1957-81. President: Scottish Building Contractors Association, 1968, Scottish Building Employers Federation, 1975, Building Employers Confederation, 1980, Builders Benevolent Institution, 1987; Lord Dean of Guild, Merchants House of Glasgow, 1991-93; Chairman: Epilepsy Association of Scotland, 1990-93, Royal Scottish Academy of Music and Drama, 1987-91, Royal Scottish National Orchestra, 1993-97; Trustee, University of Strathclyde Foundation; Member, Trades House of Glasgow. Recreations: music; art galleries; golf. Address: (h.) 18 Devonshire Terrace Lane, Glasgow G12 9XT; T.- 0141-357 1289.

Dunbar-Nasmith, Professor Emeritus Sir James Duncan, CBE, BA, DA, RIBA, PPRIAS, FRSA, FRSE. Chairman, Scottish Civic Trust; Partner, Law and Dunbar-Nasmith, Architects, Edinburgh, Forres, and Wiesbaden, since 1957; b. 15.3.27, Dartmouth. Educ. Lockers Park; Winchester College; Trinity College, Cambridge; Edinburgh College of Art. Lt., Scots Guards, 1945-48; ARIBA, 1954; President: Edinburgh Architectural Association, 1967-69, Royal Incorporation of Architects in Scotland, 1971-73; Member, RIBA Council, 1967-73 (Vice-President and Chairman, Board of Architectural Education, 1972-73), Council, ARCUK, 1976-84, Board of Education, 1976-88 (Vice Chairman, 1977); Professor and Head, Department of Architecture, Heriot-Watt University and Edinburgh College of Art, 1978-88; Member: Royal Commission on Ancient and Historical Monuments of Scotland, 1972-96, Ancient Monuments Board for Scotland, 1969-82 (interim Chairman, 1972-73), Historic Buildings Council for Scotland, 1966-93; Trustee, Architectural Heritage Fund, Theatres Trust, 1983-95; Trustee, Holyrood Brewery Foundation; Member: Edinburgh New Town Conservation Committee, Council of Europa Nostra; Deputy Chairman, Edinburgh Festival Society, 1981-85. Recreations: music; theatre; skiing; sailing. Address: (b.) 16 Dublin Street, Edinburgh EH1 3RE; T.-0131-556 8631.

Duncan, A. Craig, MA, FRSA. Depute General Secretary, Scottish Secondary Teachers' Association, since 1993; b.

15.11.39, Ayr; m., Jane Warnock Rutherford; 2 s. Educ. Ayr Academy; University of Glasgow; Jordanhill College of Education. Teacher of Classics, Kilmarnock Academy, 1963-70; Principal Teacher of Classics, Auchenharvie Academy, Stevenston, 1970-80; Assistant General Secretary, Scottish Secondary Teachers' Association, 1980-93. Elder, Davidson's Mains Church of Scotland, Edinburgh; Member, Presbytery of Edinburgh; General Committee Member, Royal Scots Club. Recreation: choral singing. Address: (b.) 15 Dundas Street, Edinburgh EH3 6QG; T.-0131-556 5919/0605.

Duncan, Sheriff Agnes Lawrie Addie, LLB. Sheriff of Glasgow and Strathkelvin, since 1982; b. 17.6.47. Admitted Solicitor, 1969; called to the Scottish Bar, 1976.

Duncan, Professor Archibald Alexander McBeth, MA, FBA, FRSE, FRHistS. Emeritus Professor of Scottish History, Glasgow University, 1962-93, currently Honorary Research Fellow; b. 17.10.26, Pitlochry; m., Ann Hayes Sawyer; 2 s.; 1 d. Educ. George Heriot's School, Edinburgh; Edinburgh University; Balliol College, Oxford. Lecturer: Balliol College, 1950-51, Queen's University, Belfast, 1951-53, Edinburgh University, 1953-61; Leverhulme Fellow, 1961-62; Clerk of Senate, Glasgow University, 1978-83. Publications: Scotland, The Making of the Kingdom; revised 3rd edition of W.C. Dickinson's Scotland from Earliest Times to 1603; Regesta Regum Scottorum, v., The Acts of Robert I 1306-29, 1988; edition of John Barbour's The Bruce, 1997. Recreation: swimming. Address: (h.) 17 Campbell Drive, Bearsden, Glasgow G61 4NF: T.-0141-942 5023.

Duncan, Geoffrey Cheyne Calderhead, BL. Lord Dean of Guild, Merchants House of Glasgow, 1993-95; b. 6.10.29, Whitecraigs, Glasgow; m., Lorna Dowling (deceased); 1 s.; 1 d. Educ. Belmont House School; Glasgow Academy; Glasgow University. Partner, Aitken, Hamilton & Duncan, 1951-70; Partner, Kerr, Barrie & Duncan, 1970-91; Chairman, Glasgow Junior Chamber of Commerce, 1963-64; Director, The Girls' School Company Ltd., 1964-90 (Chairman, 1977-90); Chairman, St. Columba's School, 1972-83; Director, The West of Scotland School Company Ltd., 1972-92 (Chairman, 1989-92); Member: Board of Management, Glasgow South Western Hospitals, 1964-69, Clyde River Purification Board, 1969-75; Director, Glasgow Chamber of Commerce, 1972-92; Chairman, Glasgow Post Office Advisory Committee, 1974-84; Member, Post Office Users' National Council, 1974-87; Chairman: Post Office Users' Council for Scotland, 1984-87, Advisory Committee on Telecommunications for Scotland, 1984-87; Director, The Merchants' House of Glasgow, since 1982; Trustee, Ferguson Bequest Fund, 1987-97; Member: Executive Committee, Abbeyfield Quarrier's Society (now Abbeyfield Strathgryffe Society), 1981-97 (Chairman, 1988-96), Council of Management, Quarrier's Homes, 1985-93; Director, The Scottish Cremation Society Ltd. (Chairman, since 1993); Member, Iona Cathedral Management Board, 1990-93; Director, Iona Abbey Ltd., 1993-96; Chairman, Renfrewshire Valuation Appeal Panel, since 1993; General Commissioner for Income Tax, since 1994; Patron and Member, Executive Committee, Royal Incorporation of Hutcheson's Hospital, since 1995; Patron, Unity Enterprise, 1997. Recreations: golf; gardening; photography. Address: (h.) Mid Clevans, Bridge of Weir, Renfrewshire PA11 3HP; T.-01505 612566.

Duncan, Professor James Lindsay, BVMS, PhD, MRCVS. Professor in Veterinary Parasitology, Glasgow University, since 1987; b. 26.2.41, Law, Carluke; m., Helen M.; 1 s.; 1 d. Educ. Wishaw High School; Glasgow University. Veterinary Practice, UK, and clinical teaching posts, Kenya, 1964-70; Glasgow University: Research Fellow, Department of Veterinary Parasitology, 1970-76, Lecturer, 1976-79, Senior Lecturer, 1979-82, Reader, 1982-

87; Vice-Dean, Faculty of Veterinary Medicine, 1994-96; Consultant, international animal health agencies and multinational pharmaceutical companies; Co-author of several textbooks. Recreations: farming; gardening; music. Address: (h.) Eastfield of Wiston, Biggar, Lanarkshire; T.-Lamington 270.

Duncan, James Wann, MBE, JP, MIMFT. Rector's Assessor, University of Dundee; former Vice-Chairman, Tayside Health Board (Convener, General Purposes Committee); Convener, Personnel and Accommodation Sub-Committee, Management Committee, Common Services Agency for the Scottish Health Service; retired Senior Chief Maxillofacial Technician, Dundee Royal Infirmary; b. 14.7.25, Dundee; m., Hilda Mackenzie Gray; 3 d. Educ. Stobswell Secondary School; Dundee College of Technology. Former Convener, Property Equipment Supplies Committee, General Board of Management, Dundee General Hospitals; former Vice-Convener, General Purposes Committee, General Board of Management, Dundee Northern Hospitals; former Member, Dundee Town Council (Senior Magistrate); former Convener: Dundee Art Galleries and Museums Committee, Further Education Committee, Dundee Police Committee; former Member, Board of Governors, Scottish Police College; Member, Dundee District Council, 1974-77 (Convener, Planning and Development Committee); Chairman, Dundee City Labour Party, 1960-62; former Member, Scottish Council, SDP; former Scottish Representative, National Committee for Dental Technicians, USDAW; former Member, STUC Health and Social Services Committee; former Member, University of Dundee Court. Recreations: golf; gardening; DIY. Address: (h.) 13 Clive Road, Downfield, Dundee DD3 8LP; T.-01382 825488.

Duncan, Leslie James, CA. Managing Partner, Scottish Region, Grant Thornton, since 1989; b. 17.11.44, Glasgow; m., Liz; 2 s. Educ. George Heriot's, Edinburgh; Robert Gordon's, Aberdeen; Aberdeen University. Grant Thornton: Partner, Glasgow Office, 1975, Managing Partner, Glasgow Office, 1988. Recreation: Treasurer, Riley RM Club. Address: (b.) 112 West George Street, Glasgow G2 1QF; T.-0141-332 7484.

Duncan, Peter W. Principal, Central College of Commerce. Address: (b.) 300 Cathedral Street, Glasgow, G1 2TA.

Duncan, William, BSc (Hons), GradIPM, PhD. Executive Secretary, Royal Society of Edinburgh, since 1985; Executive Secretary, RSE Scotland Foundation, since 1996; Secretary to Trustees, Scottish Science Trust, since 1997; b. 6.12.50, Edinburgh. Educ. Linlithgow Academy; Edinburgh University. Greater London Council, 1975-78; Lothian Regional Council, 1978-85. Recreations: contemporary music; opera. Address: (b.) 22/24 George Street, Edinburgh EH2 2PQ; T.-0131-225 6057.

Duncan Millar, Ian Alastair, CBE, MC, MA, MICE, CEng, FIFM, DL. Vice President, Scottish Landowners Federation, 1986-90; Member, Queen's Bodyguard for Scotland (Royal Company of Archers); b. 22.11.14, Alloa; m., Louise Reid McCosh; 2 s.; 2 d. Educ. Greshams School, Holt; Trinity College, Cambridge. Civil Engineer, Sir Alexander Gibb & Partners, 1937-51 (except War years); War Service, Corps of Royal Engineers, Western Desert, Europe (with Highland Division); wounded; twice mentioned in Despatches; retired as Major; Resident Engineer i/c Pitlochry Dam and Power Station, 1946-51; Member: Perth and Kinross County Council, 1946-74 (Convener, 1970-74), Tayside Regional Council, 1974-78 (Convener, 1974-78), North of Scotland Hydro Electric Board, 1956-70 (Depute Chairman, 1970-72); Director: Macdonald Fraser & Co., Perth, 1961-84, United Auctions (Scotland) Ltd., 1963-74 (Chairman, 1967-74); fought Parliamentary elections as Liberal, Banff, 1945, Kinross and West Perth, 1949 and 1963. Director, Hill Farming Research Organisation, 1966-78; Chairman: Scottish Branch, Institute of Fisheries Management, 1980-83, Consultative Committee on Freshwater Fisheries, 1981-86; Vice President, Royal Highland and Agricultural Society of Scotland, 1972. Publications: A Countryman's Cog, 1990; A Bit of Breadalbane, 1995. Recreations: care of the countryside; fishing; knowing about salmon. Address: (h.) Reynock, Remony, Aberfeldy, Perthshire; T.-Kenmore 400.

Dundas, Ronald Edgar, MA (Hons). Chief Financial Editor, The Herald, since 1993; b. 11.7.42, Glasgow; m., Elizabeth; 1 s.; 1 d. Educ. Hutchesons' Grammar School, Glasgow; St. Salvators College, St. Andrews University. Glasgow Herald: Sub-Editor, 1964, Leader Writer, 1965, Chief Leader Writer, 1967, Business Editor, 1973. Conservative candidate: Greenock, 1966, Glasgow Kelvingrove, 1970; Chairman, East Renfrewshire Conservative Association, 1971-73. Address: (b.) The Herald, 195 Albion Street, Glasgow; T.-0141-552 6255.

Dundas-Bekker, Althea Enid Philippa, DL. Deputy Lieutenant, Midlothian, since 1991; b. 4.11.39, Gorebridge; m., Aedrian Ruprecht Bekker (deceased); 2 d. Secretarial work abroad, in London, and with the National Trust for Scotland; inherited Arniston House, 1970, and restoring ever since. National Trust for Scotland: Member, Council, Curatorial Committee, Regional Committee; Commissioner, Royal Commission on Historical Manuscripts; Trustee: Arniston Village Improvement Trust, Scottish Businessman's Achievement Award Trust; Member, Historic Buildings Council for Scotland. Recreation: Scottish history; Scottish songs; walking dogs. Address: (h.) Arniston House, Gorebridge, Midlothian EH23 4RY; T.-01875 830238.

Dundee, 12th Earl of (Alexander Henry Scrymgeour). Hereditary Royal Standard-Bearer for Scotland; b. 5.6.49; m.; 1 s.; 3 d. Address: Farm Office, Birkhill, Cupar, Fife.

Dundonald, 15th Earl of (Iain Alexander Douglas Blair); b. 17.2.61; m., Marie Beatrice Louise Russo; 2 s.; 1 d. Educ. Wellington College; Royal Agricultural College, Cirencester. Company Director; Hon. Chilean Consul to Scotland. Recreations: marine and rural environment; rural housing; Scottish affairs. Address: Lochnell Castle, Ledaig, Argyll.

Dunion, Kevin Harry, MA (Hons), MSc, FRSA. Director, Friends of the Earth Scotland, since 1991; b. 20.12.55, Bridge of Allan; 2 s. Educ. St. Andrew's High School, Kirkcaldy; St. Andrews University; Edinburgh University. HM Inspector of Taxes, 1978-80; Administrator, Edinburgh University Students Association, 1980-84; Scottish Campaigns Manager, Oxfam, 1984-91. Editor, Radical Scotland, 1982-85; Chair: Scottish Education and Action for Development, 1990-92, Friends of the Earth International, since 1996 (Treasurer, 1993-96), Scottish Environmental Forum; Member: Secretary of State's Advisory Group on Sustainable Development, Lord Provost's Commission on Sustainable Development for Edinburgh. Publication: Living in the Real World: An International Role for Scotland's Parliament. Address: (b.) Bonnington Mill, 72 Newhaven Road, Edinburgh EH6 5QG; T.-0131-554 9977.

Dunion, Linda M., BSc (Soc Sci). Director, Scottish Down's Syndrome Association; b. 15.9.56, Perth. Educ. Morrisons Academy Girls' School, Crieff; Edinburgh University. Administrator, Scottish War on Want; Councillor, Edinburgh District Council; formerly Director, SEAD (Scottish Education and Action for Development). Council Member, Scottish Civic Assembly. Address: (b.) 158-160 Balgreen Road, Edinburgh EH11 3AU; T.-0131 313 4225.

Dunlop, Alastair Barr, OBE, FRICS. Deputy Chairman, Lothians Ethics of Medical Research Committee; General Commissioner for Income Tax, since 1991; b. 27.12.33, Calcutta; m., Catriona C.L.H. MacLaurin; 1 s.; 1 d. Educ. Radley. Member, British Schools Exploring Society Expedition, Arctic Norway, 1950. National Service, 1952-54 (active service, Malaya: 2nd Lt., 1st Bn., RWK); commerce, City of London, 1954-58; agricultural student, 1959-61; Land Agent, Inverness, 1962-71 (Partner, Bingham Hughes & Macpherson); Joint Founding Director, Martin Paterson Associates Ltd., 1971; ecology studies, Edinburgh University, 1973-74. Member, Lothian Health Board, 1983-91 (Vice-Chairman, 1989-91); Chairman: Edinburgh and Borders Branch, RICS, 1977, Paintings in Hospitals Scotland; Life Member, Institute of Directors; Past President, Edinburgh South Conservative Association; Chairman: South Edinburgh Conservative Association, 1980-84 and 1992-98, Central and South, Scottish Conservative and Unionist Association, 1985-88, Edinburgh Branch, World Wildlife Fund, 1982-96; elected Member, Council, National Trust for Scotland, 1992-97. Recreations: golf; skiing; fine arts. Address: 46 Dick Place, Edinburgh EH9 2JB; T.-0131-667 5343.

Dunlop, Eileen. Children's Writer; b. 13.10.38, Alloa; m., Antony Kamm (qv). Educ. Alloa Academy; Moray House College. Publications: Robinsheugh, 1975; A Flute in Mayferry Street, 1976; Fox Farm, 1978; The Maze Stone, 1982 (SAC Book Award); Clementina, 1985 (SAC Book Award); The House on the Hill, 1987 (commended, Carnegie Medal); The Valley of Deer, 1989; Finn's Island, 1991; Tales of St. Columba, 1992; Green Willow's Secret, 1993; Finn's Roman Fort, 1994; Tales of St. Patrick, 1995; Castle Gryffe, 1995; Waters of Life, 1996; The Ghost by the Sea, 1997; Co-author, with Anthony Kamm: Scottish Verse to 1800, 1985; A Book of Old Edinburgh, 1983. Recreations: reading; gardening; theatre. Address: (h.) 46 Tarmangie Drive, Dollar FK14 7BP; T.-01259 742007.

Dunlop, Sheriff William, LLB. Sheriff of North Strathclyde, since 1995; b. 7.3.44, Glasgow; m., Janina Marthe; 1 s.; 2 d. Educ. High School of Glasgow; Glasgow University. Solicitor, 1968-84; called to Scottish Bar, 1985. Address: (b.) Sheriff Court, Castlehill, Campbeltown, PA28 6AN; T.-01586 552503.

Dunn, Bill, BA. Chief Executive, Ayr Locality Enterprise Resource Trust (ALERT), since 1988; b. 26.2.48, Ayr; m., Sheila; 2 s.; 2 d. Educ. Ayr Academy; Strathclyde University. Transport Manager, National Freight Corporation/British (later Scottish) Road Services, 1970-73; Administrator, Ayrshire Joint Police Committee, 1973; Internal Audit Department, British Steel Corporation, Glasgow, 1973-81; Garnock Valley Task Force: Project Co-ordinator, 1981-83, Business Development Consultant, 1983-84; Managing Director, Development Executive, 1984-88. Recreations: family; golf; football; music; DIY; model railways. Address: (b.) 16 Smith Street, Ayr KA7 1TD; T.-01292 264181.

Dunn, Professor Douglas Eaglesham, BA, FRSL, Hon.LLD (Dundee, 1987), Hon.DLitt (Hull, 1995). Professor and Head, School of English, St. Andrews University, since 1991, and Director, St. Andrews Scottish Studies Institute, since 1993; b. 23.10.42, Inchinnan. Educ. Renfrew High School; Camphill Senior Secondary School, Paisley; Hull University. Books of poems: Terry Street, 1969; The Happier Life, 1972; Love or Nothing, 1974; Barbarians, 1979; St. Kilda's Parliament, 1981; Elegies, 1985; Selected Poems, 1986; Northlight, 1988; Dante's Drum-Kit, 1993; Secret Villages (short stories), 1985; Boyfriends and Girlfriends (short stories), 1995; Andromache (translation), 1990; Poll Tax: The Fiscal Fake, 1990; Editor: Choice of Lord Byron's Verse, 1974, The Poetry of Scotland, 1979, A Rumoured City: New Poets from Hull, 1982; Two Decades of Irish Writing: a Critical

Survey, 1975; The Essential Browning, 1990; Scotland: an anthology, 1991; Faber Book of Twentieth Century Scottish Poetry, 1992; Oxford Book of Scottish Short Stories, 1995; author of plays, and TV films using commentaries in verse. Gregory Award, 1968; Somerset Maugham Award, 1972; Geoffrey Faber Memorial Prize, 1975; Hawthornden Prize, 1982; Whitbread Award for Poetry and Whitbread Book of the Year Award, 1985; Cholmondeley Award, 1989. Honorary Visiting Professor, Dundee University, 1987; Fellow in Creative Writing, St. Andrews University, 1989-91; Honorary Fellow, Humberside College, 1987. Address (b.) School of English, St. Andrews University, St. Andrews KY16 9AL.

Dunn, Ian Campbell, DipTP. Convenor, Outright Scotland (founded as S.M.G.), 1969-74 and since 1995; Vice Chairman, Mansfield Traquair Trust, since 1993; Community Councillor, Edinburgh, since 1990; b. 1.5.43, Glasgow. Educ. Hillhead High School; Edinburgh College of Art. Meteorological Office, 1961-69; Edinburgh College of Art/Heriot-Watt University, 1969-74; City of Edinburgh Planning Department, 1974-96; Elan Planning Consultancy, since 1996. Founded, with four friends, Gay Movement in Scotland, 9 May 1969; author and editor of many publications on homosexuality in Scotland. Recreations: gardening; reading. Address: 30A Gayfield Square, Edinburgh EH1 3PA; T.-0131-557 1662.

Dunne, John Joseph, MA (Hons), MPhil, PhD, AFBPsS, CPsychol. Consultant Clinical Psychologist and Head, Community Clinical Psychology Service, Central Scotland Healthcare NHS Trust; Honorary Senior Lecturer in Psychology, Stirling University, since 1994; Honorary Clinical Senior Lecturer, Department of Nursing Studies, University of Glasgow, since 1996; Honorary Fellow, Edinburgh University, since 1984; b. 31.8.42, Kirkcaldy; m., Marie Anne Cecile. Educ. Blairs College, Aberdeen; Gregorian University, Rome; St. Andrews University; Edinburgh University. Clinical Psychologist, Royal Edinburgh Hospital, 1977-81; Senior Clinical Psychologist (Primary Care), Dedridge and Craigshill Health Centres, Livingston, 1981-85; Honorary Lecturer in Psychology, Stirling University, 1986-94 (Director, Macmillan Nursing Research Project, 1987-91). Member: Scottish Office Home & Health Department's National Panel for the Care of the Dying and Bereaved in Scotland, 1992-96, steering group for establishment of BACUP (Scotland), since 1995, working group to develop guidelines in palliative and cancer care, 1993, Advisory Group to "Partnership in Cancer Care"; Consultant in Clinical Psychology, Cancer Relief Macmillan Fund, since 1993. Address: (b.) Community Clinical Psychology Service, Department of Psychology, Stirling University, Stirling; T.-01786 467680.

Dunnett, Sir Alastair (MacTavish), HonLLD (Strathclyde). Director, Thomson Scottish Petroleum Ltd., 1979-87; b. 26.12.08, Kilmacolm; m., Dorothy Halliday (see Dorothy Dunnett); 2 s. Educ. Overnewton School; Hillhead High School, Glasgow. Entered Commercial Bank of Scotland Ltd., 1925; Co-Founder, The Claymore Press, 1933-34; Glasgow Weekly Herald, 1935-36; The Bulletin, 1936-37; Daily Record, 1937-40; Chief Press Officer, Secretary of State for Scotland, 1940-46; Editor: Daily Record, 1946-55, The Scotsman, 1956-72; Managing Director, Scotsman Publications Ltd., 1962-70 (Chairman, 1970-74); Chairman, Thomson Scottish Petroleum Ltd., Edinburgh, 1971-79; Member, Executive Board, Thomson Organisation Ltd., 1973-78; Director, Scottish Television, 1975-79; a Governor, Pitlochry Festival Theatre, 1958-84; Member: Press Council, 1959-62, Scottish Tourist Board, 1962-70, Council, National Trust for Scotland, 1962-70, Scottish International Education Trust, Scottish Theatre Ballet Committee, Scottish Opera Committee. Publications: Treasure at Sonnach, 1935; Heard Tell, 1946; Quest by Canoe, 1950 (new edition published as The Canoe Boys, 1995); Highlands and Islands of Scotland, 1951; The

Donaldson Line, 1952; The Land of Scotch, 1953; The Duke's Day, No Thanks to the Duke, 1978; Among Friends (autobiography), 1984; The Scottish Highlands (Co-author), 1988; End of Term, 1989; author of plays: The Original John Mackay, 1956; Fit to Print, 1962 (Duke of York's, London). Recreations: sailing; riding; walking. Address: (h.) 87 Colinton Road, Edinburgh EH10 5DF; T.-0131-337 2107.

Dunnett, Dorothy, OBE. Writer, since 1960; Portrait Painter, since 1950; b. 25.8.23, Dunfermline; m., Sir Alastair M. Dunnett (qv); 2 s. Civil Service: Assistant Press Officer, Scottish Government Departments, Edinburgh, 1940-46, Executive Officer, Board of Trade, Glasgow, 1946-55; Trustee for the Secretary of State for Scotland, Scottish National War Memorial, 1962-96; Non-Executive Director, Scottish Television p.l.c., 1979-92; Fellow, Royal Society of Arts, since 1986; Trustee, National Library of Scotland, since 1986; Director, Edinburgh Book Festival, 1990-95. Publications (novels): Game of Kings, 1961; Queens' Play, 1964; The Disorderly Knights, 1966; Dolly and the Singing Bird, 1968; Pawn in Frankincense, 1969; Dolly and the Cookie Bird, 1970; The Ringed Castle, 1971; Dolly and the Doctor Bird, 1971; Dolly and the Starry Bird, 1973; Checkmate, 1975; Dolly and the Nanny Bird, 1976; King Hereafter, 1982; Dolly and the Bird of Paradise, 1983; Niccolo Rising, 1986; The Spring of the Ram, 1987; The Scottish Highlands (Co-author), 1988; Race of Scorpions, 1989; Moroccan Traffic, 1991; Scales of Gold, 1991; The Unicorn Hunt, 1993; To Lie with Lions, 1995; Caprice and Rondo, 1997; Contributor, Scottish Short Stories, anthology, 1973. Recreations: travel; medieval history; opera; orchestral music; ballet. Address (h.) 87 Colinton Road, Edinburgh EH10 5DF; T.-0131-337 2107.

Dunnett, Major G.T., TD. Lord-Lieutenant of Caithness.

Dunning, Norman Moore, BA (Oxon), CQSW. Director, Enable, since 1991; b. 15.4.50, Crewe; m., Diana Mary; 2 s. Educ. Sandbach School; Jesus College, Oxford; Manchester University. Probation Officer, City of Manchester and Salford, 1973-75; Social Worker, NSPCC, 1975-77; Leader, RSSPCC Overnewton Centre, Glasgow, 1978-87; Divisional Manager (East and North Scotland), RSSPCC, 1987-91. Recreations: running; cycling; swimming. Address: (h.) 7 The Ness, Dollar, Clackmannanshire; T.-01259 43354.

Dunphy, Elaine Margaret, MA, ALA. Director of Information, The Robert Gordon University, Aberdeen, since 1997; b. 19.9.50; m., Jimmy. Educ. Paisley Grammar School; University of Aberdeen. Dundee University Library, St. Andrews University Library, 1972-74; Robert Gordon Institute of Technology/Robert Gordon University: Librarian, 1975-79; Lecturer A, School of Librarianship and Information Studies, 1980-83; Chief Librarian, 1983-88; Institute Secretary (Acting), 1988-90; Library and Special Projects Director, 1990; Chief Librarian, 1990-97. Address: (b.) The Robert Gordon University, St. Andrew Street, Aberdeen AB25 1HG; T.-01224 262620.

Dunrossil Viscount (John William Morrison), CMG, JP, MA, KStJ. Lord Lieutenant, Western Isles, since 1993; Consultant, Bank of Bermuda, since 1989; Director, International Registries Inc., since 1993; b. 22.5.26, London; m., Diana; 3 s.; 3 d. Educ. Fettes College; Oriel College, Oxford. RAF (Pilot), 1945-48 and 1951; HM Diplomatic Service, 1951-88; served in Australia, East Pakistan, South Africa; International Maritime Consultative Organization, 1968-70; Counsellor and Head of Chancery, Ottawa, 1970-74; Counsellor, Brussels, 1975-78; High Commissioner: Fiji and Tuvalu, 1978-82, Barbados, 1982-83; Governor, Bermuda, 1983-88. Recreation: music. Address: (h.) Dunrossil House, Clachan Sands, Lochmaddy, Isle of North Uist HS6 5AY; T.-01876 500 213.

Dunsire, Thomas, MA, LLB, WS. Partner, then Consultant, J. & J. Milligan, WS, Edinburgh (now Morton, Fraser & Milligan, WS), 1951-90; b. 16.11.26, Rangoon, Burma; m., Jean Mary. Educ. Morrison's Academy, Crieff; Edinburgh University. Royal Navy; Solicitor and WS, 1950. Chairman, Governors, Morrison's Academy, 1984-96. Recreations: formerly rugby, football, golf and cricket. Address: (h.) 40 Liberton Brae, Edinburgh.

Durham, Jane Mary Stow, MBE. Council Member, Society of Antiquaries for Scotland, since 1995; Vice President, Architectural Heritage Society of Scotland, since 1985; President, Tain and Easter Ross Civic Trust, since 1990; Trustee: Scottish Redundant Churches Trust, since 1996, Scottish Historic Buildings Trust; b. 26.5.24, Invergordon; m., P.E. Durham, RN (retd.); 3 s. FSA Scot; Commissioner, Royal Commission for Ancient and Historical Monuments of Scotland, 1983-95; former Chairman, Scottish Vernacular Buildings Group. Recreations: trying to save church buildings within medieval parish boundaries; identifying settlement patterns from the past; driving a gig. Address: (h.) Scotsburn, Kildary, Rossshire IV18 0PE; T.-0186 284 2241.

Durie, Roy Ross, FRICS, FSVA, MIMgt. A Senior Partner, Ryden, Edinburgh, since 1979; Chairman, Ryden Plant & Machinery Ltd., since 1989; b. 11.5.48, Edinburgh; m., Dorothy; 1 s.; 3 d. Educ. Edinburgh Academy; Britannia Royal Naval College, Dartmouth. Royal Navy Officer (Lt. R.N.), 1966-72; Trainee Surveyor, Richard Ellis, Glasgow, 1972-74; Surveyor, Ryden, Edinburgh, 1974-79. Governor: Stewarts Melville School, Mary Erskine School; Elder, St. Giles, Edinburgh; Past Chairman, ISVA, Scotland. Recreations: walking; swimming; sailing; skiing; golf; rugby. Address: (b.) Ryden, 46 Castle Street, Edinburgh EH2 3BN; T.-0131-225 6612.

Durrani, Professor Tariq Salim, BSc (Hons), MSc, PhD, FIEE, FEng, FIEEE, FRSE. Professor, Department of Electronic and Electrical Engineering, Strathclyde University, since 1986; b. 27.10.43, Amraoti, India; m., Clare Elizabeth; 1 s.; 2 d. Educ. Marie Colaco High School, Karachi; Engineering University, Dacca; Southampton University. Research Fellow, Southampton University, 1970-76; joined academic staff, Strathclyde University, 1976, Chairman, Department of Electronic and Electrical Engineering, 1986-90, Deputy Principal, 1990-91; Special Advisor, IT, 1991-94; Director/ Chairman, Scottish Electronics Technology Group; President, IEEE Signal Processing Society, 1993-94; Chair: IEEE Periodicals Council, since 1996, Management Committee, IT Associate Companies Scheme (ITACS). Publications: six books; over 250 technical research papers. Recreation: playing occasional golf badly. Address: (b.) Department of Electronic and Electrical Engineering, Strathclyde University, Glasgow; T.-0141-548 2883.

Durward, William Farquharson, MB, ChB, FRCP(Edin), FRCP(Glas). Consultant Neurologist, Greater Glasgow and Lanarkshire Health Boards, since 1977; Honorary Clinical Senior Lecturer in Neurology, Glasgow University, since 1978; Director, Cloburn Quarry Co. Ltd.; b. 16.9.44, Kilmarnock; m., Ann Roy Paterson; 1 s.; 1 d. Educ. Kilmarnock Academy; Glasgow University; Boston University. Employed by NHS, since 1968; specialist training grades, 1969-77. Recreations: walking; reading; railway conservation. Address: (h.) Overdale, 20 South Erskine Park, Bearsden, Glasgow G61 4NA; T.-0141-942 3143.

Duthie, Sir Robert (Robin) Grieve, CBE (1978), CA, LLD, CBIM, FRSA, FRIAS, DTech (Napier). Chairman, Neill Clerk Group plc, since 1993; Director: Carclo Engineering Group PLC, since 1986, Royal Bank of Scotland plc, since 1978, British Assets Trust plc, since 1977, Devol Engineering Ltd., since 1993; Member, Board of Governors, Beatson Institute for Cancer Research, since 1989; Vice Chairman, BP Advisory Board Scotland, since 1990; b. 2.10.28, Greenock; m., Violetta Noel Maclean; 2 s.; 1 d. Educ. Greenock Academy. Apprentice Chartered Accountant, Thomson Jackson Gourlay and Taylor, CA, 1946-51; joined Blacks of Greenock, 1952; appointed Managing Director, 1962; Chairman, Black & Edgington, 1972-83. Chairman, Inverkip Society, 1966; Director, Greenock Chamber of Commerce, 1966; Member, Clyde Port Authority, 1971-83 (Chairman, 1977-80); Chairman, Scottish Development Agency, 1979-88; Chairman, Britoil PLC, 1988-90; Director, Greenock Provident Bank, 1969-75 (Chairman, 1975); Member, Scottish Telecommunications Board, 1972-77; Council Member, Institute of Chartered Accountants of Scotland, 1973-78; Member: East Kilbride Development Corporation, 1976-78, Strathclyde Region Local Valuation Appeal Panel, 1976-83; CBI Tax Liaison Officer for Scotland, 1976-79; Chairman, Made Up Textile Association of Great Britain, 1972; Member: British Institute of Management Scottish Committee, 1976, Glasgow and West of Scotland Committee, Scottish Council (Development and Industry), 1975-79; Chairman, Greenock Club, 1972; Captain, Greenock Cricket Club, 1960-61; Commissioner, Queen Victoria School, Dunblane, 1972-89; Commissioner, Scottish Congregational Ministers Pension Fund, since 1973; Member, Scottish Economic Council, 1980-96; Member of Council, Royal Caledonian Curling Club, 1984-88; Treasurer, Nelson Street EU Congregational Church, Greenock, since 1970. Awarded Honorary Degree of Doctor of Laws, Strathclyde University, 1984. Recreations: curling; golf. Address: (h.) Fairhaven, 181 Finnart Street, Greenock, PA16 8JA; T.-01475 722642.

Du Vivier, Paul Eastwood, FIMgt. Chief Executive, Scottish Fisheries Protection Agency, since 1995; b. 24.5.45, Bath; m., Diana Rochsoles Robertson; 1 s.; 2 d. Educ. Malvern College; Britannia Royal Naval College, Dartmouth. Service at sea, 1965-88; in command, HMS Maxton, 1974-76, HMS Achilles, 1980-81; service in MoD Naval Secretary's Department, 1977-79, Naval Plans, 1981-84; BRNC Dartmouth, 1984-86; HMS Dryad, 1989-91; Board President, Admiralty Interview Board, 1991; Director, Joint Maritime Operational Training Staff, 1991-94; Chief of Staff to Flag Officer Scotland, Northern England and Northern Ireland, 1994-95; Member, Institute of Directors; selected Naval Member, Lowland TAVRA. Recreation: sport (golf). Address: (b.) Pentland House, 47 Robb's Loan, Edinburgh EH14 1TY; T.-0131-244 6059.

Duxbury, Professor Geoffrey, BSc, PhD, CPhys, FInstP, FRSE. Professor, Chemical Physics, Strathclyde University; b. 6.11.42, Blackburn; m., Mary R.; 1 s.; 1 d. Educ. Cheadle Hulme School; Sheffield University. Junior Research Fellow, National Physical Laboratory, 1967-69; Research Assistant, Research Associate, Lecturer in Chemical Physics, Bristol University, 1970-80; Senior Lecturer/Reader, Strathclyde University, 1981-86. Marlow Medal, Faraday Division, Royal Society of Chemistry, 1975. Address: (b.) Department of Physics and Applied Physics, Strathclyde University, Glasgow, G4 0NG; T.-0141-548 3271.

Dyer, James A.T., MB, ChB (Hons), FRCPsych. Medical Commissioner, Mental Welfare Commission for Scotland, since 1991, and Director, since 1993; b. 31.12.46, Arbroath; m., Suzanne Whitaker; 2 s.; 1 d.; 1 step-s.; 2 step d. Educ. Bo'ness Academy; Robert Gordon's College, Aberdeen; Aberdeen University. Trainee General Practitioner, Skene, Aberdeenshire, 1971-72; junior clinical appointments, then Senior Registrar in Psychiatry, Royal Edinburgh Hospital, 1972-77; Scientific Officer, MRC Unit for Epidemiological Studies in Psychiatry, Edinburgh, 1977-80; Consultant Psychiatrist, Royal Edinburgh Hospital, 1981-91; Executive Member, Scottish Division, Royal College of Psychiatrists; Member, Medical Action for Global Security. Recreations:

walking; reading; photography. Address: (b.) 37 Lauder Road, Edinburgh EH9 1UE; T.-0131-667 2479.

Dyer, Robert Lynch, MSAE, EngTech, AMIPD, DIP Scottish Law. Heating and Ventilating Contractors Association: Scottish Secretary and Regional Officer, since 1992, Scottish and Northern Ireland Secretary, since 1996; Secretary, Scottish Joint Consultative Committee for Codes of Practice, since 1994; b. 28.2.49, Edinburgh. Educ. Gracemount Secondary School; Napier College of Further Education. Member: Scottish Qualification Authority Sector Committee, since 1996, Society of Association Executives, 1997, Institute of Personnel and Development, 1994; Adviser, Construction Industry Training Board, 1984; Scottish Representative, Northern Ireland Joint Consultative Committee and Confederation of Associations of Specialist Engineering Contractors, 1997; Member, Scottish CASEL, 1994, Scottish Contractual Law Joint Committee, 1997. Recreations: reading; swimming; travelling. Address: (b.) Bush House, Bush Estate, Midlothian EH26 0SB; T.-0131-445 5580.

E

Eagles, John Mortimer, MBChB, MPhil, FRCPsych. Consultant Psychiatrist, Royal Cornhill Hospital, Aberdeen, since 1985; Honorary Senior Lecturer in Mental Health, Aberdeen University, since 1985; b. 21.10.52, Newport-on-Tay; m., Janette Isobel Rorke; 2 d. Educ. Bell-Baxter High School, Cupar; Aberdeen University. Resident House Officer posts, Aberdeen, 1977-78; Senior House Officer/Registrar in Psychiatry, Royal Edinburgh Hospital, 1978-82; Lecturer, Department of Mental Health, Aberdeen University, 1982-85; Psychiatric Tutor for trainee psychiatrists, Aberdeen, 1987-92. Chairman, North-East Regional Postgraduate Medical Education Committee, 1990-95. Recreations: cricket; golf; travel; reading. Address: (h.) 41 Binghill Park, Milltimber, Aberdeenshire AB13 0EE; T.-01224 732434.

Eassie, Lord (Ronald Mackay). Senator of the College of Justice, since 1997; b. 1945. Address: Parliament House, Parliament Square, Edinburgh EH1 1RQ.

Eastmond, Clifford John, BSc, MD, FRCP, FRCPE. Clinical Director of Medicine, since 1995, and Consultant Rheumatologist, since 1979, Aberdeen Royal Hospitals NHS Trust; Clinical Senior Lecturer, Aberdeen University, since 1979; b. 19.1.45, Ashton-under-Lyne; m., Margaret Wadsworth; 2 s.; 1 d. Educ. Audenshaw Grammar School; Edinburgh University. House Officer posts, Edinburgh, one year; moved to Liverpool for further training, subsequently to Rheumatism Unit, Leeds. Elder, Church of Scotland. Recreations: skiing; hill-walking; music. Address: (h.) The Rowans, Skene, Aberdeenshire AD32 6YP; T.-01224 790370.

Easton, Rev. David John Courtney, MA, BD. Minister, Burnside Parish Church, Glasgow, since 1977; Moderator, Glasgow Presbytery, 1989-90; 7.10.40, Bogota, Colombia; m., Edith Stevenson; 2 s.; 1 d. Educ. Arbroath High School; Aberdeen University. Minister, Hamilton-Bardrainney Parish Church, Port Glasgow, 1967-77. Member, Rutherford House Council. Recreation: music. Address: 59 Blairbeth Road, Burnside, Rutherglen, Glasgow G73 4JD; T.-0141-634 1233.

Easton, Lorna, MA, MSc. Director of UK Marketing, Scottish Tourist Board; b. 8.8.60, Hawick. Educ. Hawick High School; Edinburgh University; Strathclyde University. Economic Development, Central Regional Council, 1984-87; Lothian Regional Council, 1987-90; joined Scottish Tourist Board, 1990. Governor, Eden Court Theatre. Address: (b.) Scottish Tourist Board, Thistle House, Beechwood Park North, Inverness IV2 3ED; T.-01463 716996.

Easton, Sir Robert William Simpson, CBE (1980), DUniv, CEng, FIMechE, FIMarE, FRINA. Director: Caledonian MacBrayne Ltd., since 1997, West of Scotland Water Authority, since 1995; Chairman, GEC Scotland, since 1990; Chancellor, University of Paisley, since 1993; b. 30.10.22, Glasgow; m., Jean Fraser; 1 s.; 1 d. Educ. Govan High School, Glasgow; Royal Technical College, Glasgow. Apprentice, Marine Engineer, 1939-51; Manager, Yarrow & Co. Ltd., 1951-65; Yarrow Shipbuilders Ltd.: Director, 1965-70, Deputy Managing Director, 1970-77, Managing Director, 1977-91; Main Board Director, Yarrow & Co. Ltd., 1971-77; Chairman: Yarrow Shipbuilders Ltd., 1979-94, GEC Naval Systems, 1991-94; Chairman, Clyde Port Authority, 1983-93; Director: Supermarine Consortium Ltd., 1986-94, Glasgow Development Agency, 1990-94. Vice-President, Clyde Shipbuilders Association, 1972-79; Freeman, City of London, 1982; Council Member, RINA, 1983; Trustee, Seagull Trust, 1984; Director, Merchant House of Glasgow, 1994; Member, Incorporation of Hammermen, 1989; Past President, Institute of Welding; President, Institute of Engineers and Shipbuilders, Scotland, since 1997. Recreations: sailing; golf; walking; family. Address: (h.) Springfield, Stuckenduff Road, Shandon, Argyllshire G84 8NW; T.-01436 820 677.

Easton, Robin Gardner, OBE, MA, DipEd. Rector, High School of Glasgow, since 1983; b. 6.10.43, Glasgow; m., Eleanor Mary McIlroy; 1 s.; 1 d. Educ. Kelvinside Academy; Sedbergh School; Christ's College, Cambridge; Wadham College, Oxford. Teacher of French and German, Melville College, Edinburgh, 1966-72; Housemaster and Deputy Head, French Department, Daniel Stewart's and Melville College, 1972-78; Head, Modern Languages, George Watson's College, 1979-83. Elder, Church of Scotland. Recreations: watching rugby; tennis; hill-walking; visiting ancient monuments. Address: (h.) 21 Stirling Drive, Bearsden, Glasgow G61 4NU; T.-0141-943 0368.

Eastwood, Martin Anthony, MB, MSc, FRCPE. Honorary Librarian, Royal College of Physicians of Edinburgh; retired Gastroenterologist; b. 7.8.35, Hull; m., Jenny; 3 s.; 1 d. Educ. Minster Grammar School, Southwell; Edinburgh University. Publications: papers on physiology of the colon and nutrition; History of Western General Hospital Edinburgh (Co-Author), 1995; Principles of Human Nutrition, 1996. Address: (h.) Hill House, North Queensferry KY11 1JJ.

Eccles, Alexander Charles William Anderson, RD—, BA, LLB, WS. Temporary Sheriff, since 1984; part-time Chairman, Social Security Appeals Tribunals, since 1985, and Rent Assessment Committee, since 1975; part-time Chairman, Industrial Tribunals, since 1991; b. 8.1.33, Newcastle upon Tyne; m., Judith Margaret Hardy; 2 s.; 2 d. Educ. Loretto; Gonville and Caius College, Cambridge; Edinburgh University. National Service, 1951-53 (commissioned HLI); TA, Royal Scots, 1953-59; qualified Solicitor and WS, 1960; Assistant with various firms and local authorities, 1960-68; Partner, J.L. Anderson & Co., Solicitors, Cupar, Kinross, Glenrothes and Cowdenbeath, 1968-84. Lt. Cdr., RNR, 1966-85; Rugby Blue, Edinburgh University (played for Scottish Universities and Durham County). Recreations: rugby; squash; reading military history. Address: (h.) Ringwood House, 33A High Street, Auchtermuchty, Fife.

Eckford, James Millar, OBE, FCIS, FHSM, FIM, FRSA. Health Management Consultant; Chairman: Ayrshire Careers Partnership Ltd., Dalmellington and District Conservation Trust; Member, Board, Ayr College; District Secretary, Rotary District 1230; b. 8.7.36, Leith; m., Joan Miller. Educ. George Heriot's School, Edinburgh. District Administrator, East Fife District, Fife Health Board, 1974-79; Board Secretary, Forth Valley Health Board, 1979-85; Board General Manager, Ayrshire and Arran Health Board, 1985-95. Recreations: Rotary; bowling; fishing; curling; Ayr United. Address: (h.) 22 Abbots Way, Doonfoot, Ayr KA7 4EY, T.-01292 42323.

Eddie, Rev. Duncan Campbell, MA (Hons), BD (Hons). Minister, Old Cumnock: Crichton West linked with St. Ninian's, since 1992; b. 17.2.63, Fraserburgh; m., Dr. Carol Buchanan; 1 s. Educ. Mackie Academy, Stonehaven; Aberdeen University; Edinburgh University. Assistant Minister, Edinburgh, 1990-91. Recreations: music; reading. Address: 46 Ayr Road, Cumnock KA18 1DW; T.-01290 420119.

Edge, David Owen, BA, MA, PhD, FRSE, FRAS, FRSA. Reader Emeritus in Science Studies, since 1992, Edinburgh University; b. 4.9.32, High Wycombe; m., Barbara Corsie; 2 s.; 1 d. Educ. Aberdeen Grammar School; Leys School, Cambridge; Gonville and Caius College, Cambridge. Assistant Physics Master, Perse School, Cambridge;

Producer, Science Unit, Talks Department, BBC Radio, London, 1959-66; Senior Fellow, Society for the Humanities, and Senior Research Associate, Science, Technology and Society Program, Cornell University, 1973; Reader in Science Studies, Edinburgh University, 1979-92. Scottish HQ Adviser for Students, Scout Association, 1966-85; President (Past Chairman), Scout & Guide Graduate Association; Circuit Steward, Methodist Church, Edinburgh and Forth Circuit, 1983-86; Editor, Social Studies of Science, since 1971; Member: various CNAA panels and committees, since 1972, Edinburgh University Court, 1983-86, DQA Auditing Team, HEQC, 1991-93, ABRC Working Party on Peer Review, 1990-91; Chair, Board of Science Policy Support Group, 1989-93; President, Society for Social Studies of Science (4S), 1985-87. John Desmond Bernal Prize, 1993; Fellow, American Association for the Advancement of Science, 1989; Fellow, Royal Society of Edinburgh, 1992. Publications: Astronomy Transformed (Co-author), 1976; Science in Context (Co-Editor), 1982. Recreations: hill-walking; music; watching sport - especially soccer and baseball. Address: (h.) 25 Gilmour Road, Edinburgh EH16 5NS; T.-0131-667 3497.

Edgeler, Ian George, MIMgt. Garden Secretary (Head of Administration, Finance and Personnel), Royal Botanic Garden Edinburgh, since 1993; b. 2.12.49, Gravesend; m., Jane; 4 s. Educ. Springhead School; Britannia Royal Naval College, Dartmouth. Joined Royal Navy as Cadet Seaman Officer, 1968; specialised as aircrew (Observer), 1976; flying and specialist operations posts; promoted to Commander, 1988; retired from Royal Navy, 1993. Recreations: amateur gardener and exhibitor; travel; family pursuits. Address: (b.) Royal Botanic Garden Edinburgh, 20a Inverkeith Row, Edinburgh EH3 5LR; T.-0131-552 7171.

Edward, Judge David Alexander Ogilvy, CMG, QC, MA, LLD, FRSE. Judge of the Court of Justice of the European Communities, since 1992 (Judge of the Court of First Instance, 1989-92); Advocate, since 1962; b. 14.11.34, Perth; m., Elizabeth Young McSherry; 2 s.; 2 d. Educ. Sedbergh School; University College, Oxford (Hon. Fellow, 1995); Edinburgh University. National Service, RNVR, 1956-57 (Sub-Lt.); Clerk, Faculty of Advocates, 1967-70, Treasurer, 1970-77; President, Consultative Committee, Bars and Law Societies of the European Community, 1978-80; Salvesen Professor of European Institutions, Edinburgh University, 1985-89 (Hon. Professor, since 1990); Member: Law Advisory Committee, British Council, 1974-88, Panel of Arbitrators, International Centre for Settlement of Investment Disputes, 1981-89; Chairman, Continental Assets Trust plc, 1986-89; Director, Adam & Company plc, 1984-89; Director, Harris Tweed Association Ltd., 1985-89; Specialist Adviser to House of Lords Select Committee on the European Communities, 1985-88; Trustee: National Library of Scotland, 1966-95, Industry and Parliament Trust, since 1995, Carnegie Trust for the Universities of Scotland, since 1995, Hopetoun Foundation (Chairman, Hopetoun House Preservation Trust, 1988-92); President, Franco-Scottish Society, since 1996; Hon. President, Scottish Council for International Arbitration; President, Johnson Society, 1995-96. Hon. Bencher, Gray's Inn, 1992; Hon. LLD: Edinburgh University,1993, Aberdeen University, 1997. Address: (h.) 32 Heriot Row, Edinburgh EH3 6ES; (b.) EC Court of Justice, L-2925 Luxembourg; T.-00-352-43032203.

Edward, Ian, MA, LLB. Consultant, Ledingham Chalmers, Solicitors, Aberdeen, since 1997; part-time Chairman of Industrial Tribunals, since 1997; b. 3.9.35, Aberdeen; m., Marguerite Anne Leiper (deceased); 2 s.; 1 d. Educ. Robert Gordon's College, Aberdeen; University of Aberdeen; Fitzwilliam College, University of Cambridge. HM Colonial Service (District Officer, Northern Rhodesia), 1959-63; C. & P. H. Chalmers, Solicitors, Aberdeen (now Ledingham Chalmers): Legal Assistant, Partner, Senior

Partner, 1963-97. Chairman, Scottish Motor Neurone Disease Association; Trustee, Grampian Hospitals Art Trust; Archivist, Royal Aberdeen Golf Club. Recreations: golf; gardening. Address: (b.) 17 Golden Square, Aberdeen; T.-01224 408428.

Edwards, Frederick Edward, LVO, RD, DUniv, MUniv, FIMgt. President, Volunteer Development Scotland, since 1993; b. 9.4.31, Liverpool; 2 s.; 1 d. Educ. St. Edward's College, Liverpool; Glasgow University. Midshipman to Second Officer, Alfred Holt & Co., 1948-57; awarded Perm. Commn. RNR, 1953; Lt.-Cmdr., 1963; Reserve Decoration, 1972; Clasp, 1982; Management Trainee, Morgan Crucible Group, 1957-60; Probation Service, Liverpool, 1960-69; Director of Social Work: Joint County Council of Moray and Nairn, 1969-75, Grampian Region, 1975-76, Strathclyde Regional Council, 1976-93; Visiting Professor of Social Administration and Social Work, Glasgow University, 1988-93; Trustee, New Lanark Conservation Trust, since 1993; President, Disability Scotland, since 1995; Member: Board, East Region SEPA, 1996, Council, Scottish Wildlife Trust, 1994; Chairman, Capability Scotland, 1997. Awarded Hon. Doctorate, Paisley University, 1993. Recreations: hill-walking; natural history; Scottish country dancing. Address: (h.) Gardenfield, Ninemileburn, by Penicuik EH26 9LT; T.-01968 674566.

Edwards, George Lowden, CEng, MIMechE, MIEE, FIM, FInstPet, FRSA. Chairman, GPC Market Access Scotland; Associate, Smythe Dorward Lambert; Director: Network Scotland Limited, European Editions PLC; Trustee, Scottish Civic Trust; b. 6.2.39, Kirriemuir; m., Sylvia Izatt; 1 d. Educ. Webster's Seminary, Kirriemuir; Dundee Institute of Technology. Production Engineer, Burroughs Machines Ltd., Cumbernauld, 1961-64; Development Division, Scottish Council (Development and Industry), Edinburgh, 1964-67; General Manager, GR Designs Ltd., Perth, 1967-68; London Director, Scottish Council (Development and Industry), 1968-78; Manager, Public Affairs Scotland, Conoco (UK) Ltd., Aberdeen, 1978-83; Manager, Public Affairs, Conoco (UK) Ltd., London, 1983-85; Head of Corporate Affairs, Clydesdale Bank PLC, 1988-96. Recreations: music; travel; food and wine. Address: (h.) 1 Back Dean, Ravelston Terrace, Edinburgh EH4 3UA.

Edwards, Gordon, MA, CPFA. Director of Finance, Aberdeen City Council, since 1996; b. 1.4.56, Aberdeen; m., Diane; 2 d. Educ. Aberdeen Grammar School. Assistant Director of Finance, Grampian Regional Council, 1991-96. Address: (b.) Town House, Broad Street, Aberdeen AB10 1AH.

Edwards, Neil, DMS, DCA, MITSA. Head of Trading Standards, Fife Council, since 1996; b. 6.10.45, Wrexham, N. Wales. Educ. Yale High School, Wrexham; Liverpool Polytechnic. Inspector of Weights and Measures, Denbighshire CC, 1967-74; Area Officer, Standards of Trading Standards, Clywd CC, 1974-78; retail management, Italy, 1978-81; Trading Standards Officer, Durham CC, 1981-83; Principal Trading Standards Officer, West Midlands CC, 1983-86; Depute Director of Trading Standards, Dumfries and Galloway RC, 1986-88; Director of Trading Standards and Consumer Protection, Fife Regional Council, 1988-96. Recreation: sport. Address: (b.) Fife House (03), North Street, Glenrothes, Fife KY7 5LT; T.-01592 416353.

Edwards, Rob (Robert Philip), MA. Consultant, New Scientist, since 1994; Freelance Journalist, since 1980; Television Producer, since 1990; b. 13.10.53, Liverpool; m., Fiona Grant Riddoch; 2 d. Educ. Watford Boys Grammar School; Jesus College, University of Cambridge. Organiser, Scottish Campaign to Resist the Atomic Menace, 1977-78; Campaigns Organiser, Shelter (Scotland), 1978-80; Research Assistant to Robin Cook M.P., 1980-83; Freelance

Journalist, writing for Social Work Today, The Scotsman, New Statesman, 1980-89; Environment Editor, Scotland on Sunday, 1989-94; Correspondent, The Guardian and Columnist, Edinburgh Evening News, 1989-94; Freelance Journalist, writing for New Scientist, Scotland on Sunday, The Scotsman, The Observer etc., since 1994; Member, Scottish Advisory Council, World Wildlife Fund; various media awards. Publications: Co-author of four books, including Still Fighting for Gemma, 1995. Recreations: music; opera; mountains. Address: 53 Nile Grove, Edinburgh EH10 4RE; T.-0131-447 2796.

Edwards, Susan Spencer, MA (Oxon), DipHistArt, ACIS. Administrator, National Galleries of Scotland, since 1990; b. 25.8.46, London. Educ. Paddington & Maida Vale High School for Girls; Lady Margaret Hall, Oxford. Early career teaching; Tutor-Counsellor, Open University, 1977-80; joined North of Scotland College of Agriculture; Secretary and Treasurer, 1982-90. Publication: Biographical Dictionary of Scottish Painters. Recreations: clarinet; calligraphy; riding; cooking; theatre. Address: (b.) 13 Heriot Row, Edinburgh EH3 6HP; T.-0131-556 8921.

Eilbeck, Professor John Christopher, BA, PhD, FIMA, FRSE. Professor, Department of Mathematics, Heriot-Watt University, since 1986 (Head of Department, 1984-89); b. 8.4.45, Whitehaven; 3 s. Educ. Whitehaven Grammar School; Queen's College, Oxford; Lancaster University. Royal Society European Fellow, ICTP, Trieste, 1969-70; Research Assistant, Department of Mathematics, UMIST, Manchester, 1970-73; Heriot-Watt University: Lecturer, Department of Mathematics, 1973-80, Senior Lecturer, 1980-85, Reader, 1985-86; Long-term Visiting Fellow, Center for Nonlinear Studies, Los Alamos National Laboratory, New Mexico, 1983-84. Publications: Rock Climbing in the Lake District (Co-author), 1975; Solitons and Nonlinear Wave Equations (Co-author), 1982. Recreation: mountaineering. Address: (b.) Department of Mathematics, Heriot-Watt University, Riccarton, Edinburgh EH14 4AS; T.-0131-451 3220.

Elder, Dorothy-Grace. Columnist, Scotland on Sunday, Scottish Daily Express, and Daily Express; Television Scriptwriter and Producer; m., George Welsh; 1 s.; 2 d. D.C. Thomson newspapers; Glasgow Herald as reporter, news feature writer, leader writer; TV and radio news, BBC Scotland; feature writer and columnist, Scottish Daily News Co-operative; freelance feature writer and columnist, Sunday Mail; productions for Scotland and the network, BBC and Scottish TV. Trustee, Yorkhill Children's Fund, Royal Hospital for Sick Children; Member, ACHE UK Committee (opposing child pornography); Oliver Award winning columnist, 1995-96; British Reporter of the Year, UK Press Awards, 1996-97. Address: Scotland on Sunday, 20 North Bridge, Edinburgh EH1 1YT.

Elders, Rev. (Iain) Alasdair, MA, BD. Minister, Broughton St. Mary's Parish Church, Edinburgh, since 1992; b. 17.4.39, Sunderland; m., Hazel Stewart Steven; 1 s.; 1 d. Educ. Daniel Stewart's College, Edinburgh; Edinburgh University. Assistant Minister: Edinburgh: St. Andrew's, 1961-63, Edinburgh: High (St. Giles Cathedral), 1963-65; Minister, Cumbernauld: Abronhill (church extension charge), 1965-73; Minister, Edinburgh: Broughton McDonald, 1973-92; Secretary, Cumbernauld Council of Churches, 1967-72; Chairman: Council of East End Churches of Edinburgh, 1978-82, New Town Community Council, 1986-89 and since 1992; Scout Commissioner, 1966-90; Secretary, East End Churches Together, since 1989; Vice-Chairman, Edinburgh and East of Scotland Society for the Deaf, 1978-97; Moderator, Edinburgh Presbytery, 1994. Address: Broughton St. Mary's Manse, 103 East Claremont Street, Edinburgh EH7 4JA; T.-0131-556 7313.

Elgin, 11th Earl of, and Kincardine, 15th Earl of, (Andrew Douglas Alexander Thomas Bruce), KT (1981), DL, JP; 37th Chief of the Name of Bruce; Lord Lieutenant of Fife, since 1987; Lieutenant, Queen's Bodyguard for Scotland (Royal Company of Archers); President, Royal Scottish Automobile Club; b. 17.2.24; m., Victoria Usher; 3 s.; 2 d. Educ. Eton; Balliol College, Oxford. President, Scottish Amicable Life Assurance Society, 1975-94; Chairman, National Savings Committee for Scotland, 1972-78; Member, Scottish Postal Board, 1980-96; Lord High Commissioner, General Assembly, Church of Scotland, 1980-81; Grand Master Mason of Scotland, 1961-65; President, Royal Caledonian Curling Club, 1968-69; Hon. LLD, Dundee, 1977, Glasgow, 1983. Address: (h.) Broomhall, Dunfermline KY11 3DU.

Eliott of Redheugh, Margaret Frances Boswell. Chief of Clan Elliot; Chairman, Elliot Clan Society and Sir Arthur Eliott Memorial Trust; b. 13.11.48; m., 1, Anthony Vaughan-Arbuckle (deceased); 1 s.; 1 d.; 2, Christopher Powell Wilkins. Educ. Hatherop Castle School. Address: Redheugh, Newcastleton, Roxburghshire.

Ellington, Marc Floyd, DL. Baron of Towie Barclay (Feudal Barony); Laird of Gardenstown and Crovie; Deputy Lieutenant, Aberdeenshire, since 1984; b. 16.12.45; m., Karen Leigh; 2 d. Member: National Committee, Architectural Heritage Society of Scotland, British Heritage Commission (representing Scottish Tourist Board), Historic Buildings Council for Scotland, since 1980; Vice-President, Buchan Heritage Society; Trustee, Scottish Historic Building Trust; Chairman: Grampian Regional Council Tourism Task Force, Heritage Press (Scotland); Director: Grampian Enterprise Ltd., Aberdeen University Research Ltd., Gardenstown Estates Ltd., Soundcraft Audio; Partner, Heritage Sound Recordings; Producer, documentary films and television programmes. Saltire Award, 1973; Civic Trust Award, 1975; European Architectural Heritage Award, 1975; SBStJ; FSA. Recreations: sailing; historic architecture; art collecting; music. Address: Towie Barclay Castle, Auchterless, Turriff, Aberdeenshire AB53 8EP; T.-01888 511347.

Elliot, Alison Janet, MA, MSc, PhD. Convener, Church and Nation Committee, Church of Scotland, since 1996; Vice-Convener, ACTS Commission on Justice, Peace, Social and Moral Issues, since 1995; Member, Central Committee, Conference of European Churches, since 1997; b. 27.11.48, Edinburgh; m., John Christian Elliot; 1 s.; 1 d. Educ. Bathgate Academy; Edinburgh University; Sussex University. Research Associate, Department of Linguistics, Edinburgh University, 1973-74; Lecturer in Psychology, Lancaster University, 1974-76, Edinburgh University, 1977-85; Member, Church of Scotland's Committee on Church and Nation, since 1988; Elder, Greyfriars Kirk, Edinburgh. Publication: Child Language, 1981. Recreations: music; cookery. Address: (b.) Church of Scotland Offices, 121 George Street, Edinburgh EH2 4YN; T.-0131-225 5722.

Elliot, Frances Mary, MB, ChB, DRCOG, DCH. Principal in general practice; Member, Scottish General Medical Services Committee, BMA, since 1994; Non-executive Member, Board, HEBS, since 1996; b. 13.4.60, Edinburgh; m., John Gordon Elliot. Educ. St. Columba's High School, Dunfermline; Glasgow University. Hon. Secretary, Fife Local Medical Committee, 1990-97; Member, BMA Scottish Council, 1994-97. Recreations: hill-walking; cycling; swimming; photography. Address: (h.) 10 Durie Vale, Windygates, Leven KY8 5EF; T.-01333 351509.

Elliot, Sir Gerald Henry; b. 24.12.23, Edinburgh; m., Margaret Ruth Whale; 2 s.; 1 d. Educ. Marlborough College; New College, Oxford. Chairman: Christian Salvesen PLC, 1981-88, Scottish Provident Institution, 1983-89, Scottish Arts Council, 1980-86, Prince's Scottish

Youth Business Trust, 1987-94; Vice Chairman, Scottish Business in the Community, 1987-89; Trustee, National Museums of Scotland, 1987-91; Member of Court, Edinburgh University, 1984-93; Chairman: Scottish Unit Managers Ltd., 1984-88, Martin Currie Unit Trusts, 1988-90; Chairman, Scottish Opera, 1987-92; Chairman of Trustees, David Hume Institute, 1985-95; Chairman, Institute of Directors, Scottish Division, 1989-92; Trustee and Director, Edinburgh Festival Theatre, 1995-97; Member, Court of Regents, Royal College of Surgeons, since 1990; President, UN50 Scotland, 1994-95; Fellow, Royal Society of Edinburgh, since 1977; Honorary Consul for Finland in Edinburgh and Leith, 1957-89; Hon. d.h.c., Edinburgh University, 1989; Hon. LLD, Aberdeen University, 1991. Address: (b.) 8 Howe Street, Edinburgh EH3 6TD; T.-0131-220 3739.

Elliot, John. Farmer; Vice Chairman, British Wool Marketing Board and Member for Southern Scotland; b. 29.5.47, Duns, Berwickshire; m., Joan Kathleen Wight; 1 s.; 1 d. Educ. St. Mary School, Melrose; Edinburgh Academy. Nuffield Scholar, US and Canada, 1982. Recreations: spectator sports; reading; writing; agriculture. Address: Roxburgh Mains, Kelso TD5 8NJ.

Elliot, Robert John, LLB, WS. Solicitor; b. 18.1.47, Edinburgh; m., Christine; 1 s.; 1 d. Educ. Loretto School; Edinburgh University. Partner, Lindsays WS, since 1973; President, Law Society of Scotland, 1996-97. Recreations: golf; Scottish country dancing; detective novels; argument. Address: (b.) 11 Atholl Crescent, Edinburgh EH3 8HE; T.-0131-229 1212.

Elliot, Thomas, MBE, JP. Farmer; a Director, Animal Diseases Research Association; Member, Hill Farming Advisory Committee for Scotland; b. 6.4.26, Galashiels; m., Patrena Jennifer Mundell; 1 s.; 2 d. Educ. St. Mary's School; Loretto. President: South Country Cheviot Society, 1971-73, Border Area, NFU of Scotland, 1974-76; Chairman, Selkirk Branch, 1968; Member, Southern Regional Committee, British Wool Board. Played rugby, Gala RFC, 1945-58; 14 caps for Scotland, 1955-58; Barbarians, 1956; British Lions, South African tour, 1955. "Border Man of the Year", Tweeddale Press, 1979; Elder and Session Clerk, Caddonfoot Church. Recreations: watching rugby; reading books; farming. Address: Newhall, Clovenfords, Galashiels; T.-01896-850 260.

Elliott, Professor Alex, BA, PhD, DSc, CPhys, FInstP, FIPEM. Director, West of Scotland Health Boards' Department of Clinical Physics and Bioengineering, since 1990 (Clinical Director, Laboratory Medicine and Clinical Physics, since 1996); Professor of Clinical Physics, Glasgow University, since 1991; b. 1.2.49, Edinburgh; m., Barbara; 2 d. Educ. Trinity Academy, Edinburgh; Stirling University; Glasgow University. Temporary Lecturer, Nuclear Medicine Unit, Strathclyde University, 1974-75; Lecturer in Nuclear Medicine, Middlesex Hospital Medical School, 1975-77; Principal Physicist, Department of Nuclear Medicine, St. Bartholomew's Hospital, London, 1977-81; Chief Physicist, Western Infirmary/Gartnavel General Hospital, Glasgow, 1981-90. Publications: 200 papers and presentations. Recreations: cycling; orienteering; squash. Address: (b.) 22 Western Court, 100 University Place, Glasgow G12 8SQ; T.-0141-211 2948.

Elliott, Rev. Gavin John, MA, BD. Minister, Biggar Kirk, since 1995; Convenor, Sub-Saharan Africa Committee, Board of World Mission, Church of Scotland, since 1995; b. 12.6.50, Perth; m., Rachel Ann Jones; 2 s.; 2 d. Educ. Perth Academy; Aberdeen University. Minister, Carntyne Old, 1976-82; Missionary, United Church of Zambia, 1982-89; Minister, South Uist, 1989-95. WCC Delegate to WCC Assembly, 1998. Recreations: hill-walking; music. Address: 61 High Street, Biggar ML12 6DA; T.-01899 220227.

Elliott, Professor Robert F., BA (Oxon), MA. Professor of Economics, Aberdeen University, since 1990; b. 15.6.47, Thurlow, Suffolk; m., Susan Elliott Gutteridge; 1 s. Educ. Haverhill Secondary Modern School, Suffolk; Ruskin College and Balliol College, Oxford; Leeds University. Joined Aberdeen University, 1973, as Research Fellow, then Lecturer; Chair, Review of Area Cost Adjustment commissioned by Department of the Environment; acted as Consultant to numerous public and private sector organisations, including Megaw Committee of Inquiry into Civil Service Pay, the EEC Commission, HM Treasury OECD, Highlands and Islands Development Board, on issues of pay and employment. Publications: books on Pay in the Public Sector, 1981; Incomes Policies, Inflation and Relative Pay, 1981; Incomes Policy, 1981; Unemployment and Labour Market Efficiency, 1989; Labour Market Analysis, 1990. Recreations: music; reading; golf. Address: (h.) 11 Richmondhill Place, Aberdeen AB15 5EN; T.-01224 314901.

Elliott, Hon. Lord (Walter Archibald Elliott), QC, MC, BL. President, Lands Tribunal for Scotland, 1971-92; Chairman, Scottish Land Court, 1978-92; Ensign, Queen's Bodyguard for Scotland (Royal Company of Archers); b. 6.9.22, London; m., Susan Isobel MacKenzie Ross; 2 s. Educ. Eton College; Edinburgh University. 2nd Bn., Scots Guards, 1943-45 (Staff Captain, 1947); Advocate and at the Inner Temple, Barrister-at-Law, 1950; QC (Scotland), 1963; conducted Edinburgh ring road inquiry, 1967. Publications: Us and Them: a study of group consciousness, 1986; Esprit de Corps, 1995. Recreations: gardening; shooting. Address: (h.) Morton House, 19 Winton Loan, Edinburgh EH10 7AW; T.-0131-445 2548.

Ellis, Charles William, OBE, BA (Hons), LLD. Chairman, Grampian Health Board, 1982-89; Member, Whitley Council for Professions Allied to Medicine, 1987-89; b. 15.11.21, Horsham, Sussex; m., Maureen Patricia Radley; 1 s.; 3 d. Educ. Oxted County School; University College London. Indian Army and Royal Artillery, 1941-64; completed degree in modern history, 1964-66 (begun in 1940-41); Junior Lecturer to Head, School of Social Studies, Robert Gordon's Institute of Technology, Aberdeen, 1966-85. Councillor, City of Aberdeen, 1971-75 (Convener, Education Committee, 1974-75); Councillor, Grampian Regional Council, 1974-78 (Leader, Labour Group). Recreations: International affairs; family; genealogy. Address: (h.) 78 Kirk Brae, Cults, Aberdeen AB1 9QQ; T.-Aberdeen 861581.

Ellis, Richard Tunstall, OBE, DL, MA, LLB, LLD (Hon); b. 6.9.18, Liverpool; m., Jean Bruce Maitland Porter (deceased); 2 s.; 2 d. Educ. Merchant Taylors School, Crosby; Silcoates School, Wakefield; Aberdeen University. Captain, Royal Signals, 1939-45 (POW, Germany); Partner, Paull & Williamsons, Advocates, Aberdeen, 1949-83; Senior Partner, 1970-83; Chairman: Trustee Savings Bank Scotland, 1983-86, TSB Scotland p.l.c., 1986-89; Director, TSB Group p.l.c., 1986-89; Chairman, Board of Governors, Dunfermline College of Physical Education, 1964-67; Governor, Aberdeen College of Education, 1969-75; Member: Scottish Board, Norwich Union Insurance Society, 1973-80, Aberdeen Board, Bank of Scotland, 1972-82, Aberdeen University Court, 1984-93, Council, National Trust for Scotland, 1984-89; Chairman, Scottish Division, Institute of Directors, 1988-89. Recreations: golf; hill-walking; skiing. Address: (h.) 18 Rubislaw Den North, Aberdeen AB15 4AN; T.-01224 316680.

Elvidge, John William, BA (Oxon). Head of Economic Infrastructure Group, Scottish Office Development Department; b. 9.2.51, Edmonton, Middlesex. Educ. Sir George Monoux School, Walthamstow; St. Catherine's College, Oxford. Recreations: appreciating other people's creativity; observing other people's politics. Address: (b.) Victoria Quay, Edinburgh EH6; T.-0131-244 0629.

Embrey, John Derek, FCA, MCT. Director, Nimrod House Ltd., since 1994; b. 14.7.45, Shrewsbury; m., Carol Anne. Educ. Bishop Vesey's School. Finance Director, Dawson International PLC, 1983-94; Member, Investment Committee, Carnegie Trust for the Universities in Scotland; Non-Executive Adviser, Company Growth Team, Scottish Enterprise. Recreations: equestrian activities; theatre. Address: (b.) Nimrod House, Muckhart, Dollar, Clackmannanshire FK14 7JN.

Emmanuel, Professor Clive Robert, BSc (Econ), MA, PhD, ACIS. Professor of Accounting and Director of CIFA; Adjunct Professor, Deakin University, Australia, since 1997; b. 23.5.47; m.; 1 s.; 2 d. Educ. UWIST; Lancaster University; UCW, Aberystwyth. Steel Company of Wales, Port Talbot, 1964-68; Lecturer, Lancaster University, 1974-78; Senior Lecturer, then Reader, UCW, Aberystwyth, 1978-87; Associate Professor, University of Kansas, 1980-82. Address: (b.) Department of Accounting and Finance, Glasgow University, Glasgow.

Emslie, Rt. Hon. Lord (George Carlyle), MBE, PC, LLD, FRSE. Lord Justice General of Scotland, 1972-89; Lord President of the Court of Session, 1972-89; b. 6.12.19, Glasgow; m., Lilias Ann Mailer Hannington; 3 s. Educ. High School of Glasgow; Glasgow University. Commissioned A. & S.H., 1940; served War of 1939-45 (Despatches), North Africa, Italy, Greece, Austria, 1942-46; p.s.c. Haifa, Chief Instructor, Brigade Major (Infantry), 1944-46; Advocate, 1948; Advocate-Depute (Sheriff Courts), 1955; QC (Scotland), 1957; Sheriff of Perth and Angus, 1963-66; Dean, Faculty of Advocates, 1965-70; Senator of the College of Justice, 1970-72; Chairman, Scottish Agricultural Wages Board, 1969-73; Member, Council on Tribunals (Scottish Committee), 1962-70; Hon. Bencher, Inner Temple, 1974, and Inn of Court of N. Ireland, 1981; PC, 1972; Baron (Life Peer), created 1980. Recreation: golf. Address: (h.) 47 Heriot Row, Edinburgh EH3 6EX; T.-0131-225 3657.

Emslie, Hon. (George) Nigel (Hannington), QC; b. 17.4.47. Admitted to Faculty of Advocates, 1972; part-time Chairman, Medical Appeal Tribunals, since 1988.

Emslie-Smith, Donald, OStJ, MD (Hons), FRCP, FRCPEdin, FSA Scot. Honorary Fellow, Dundee University (Reader in Medicine, 1971-87; Head, Department of Medicine, 1986-87); Honorary Consultant Physician (Cardiologist), Tayside Health Board, 1961-87; b. 12.4.22, Aberdeen; m., Ann Elizabeth Milne; 1 s.; 1 d. Educ. Trinity College, Glenalmond; Aberdeen University. House Physician, Aberdeen Royal Infirmary; RAFVR (Medical Branch), UK and Middle East; Registrar in Cardiology, Dundee Royal Infirmary; Edward Wilson Memorial Research Fellow, Baker Institute, Melbourne; Tutor and Senior Registrar in Medicine, Royal Postgraduate Medical School and Hammersmith Hospital, London; Senior Lecturer in Medicine, St. Andrews University. Member for Scotland, Executive Committee, Association of Physicians of Great Britain and Ireland, 1977-80; Chairman, British Cardiac Society, 1987; President, Harveian Society of Edinburgh, 1986-87; Harveian Orator, 1987. Publications: Textbook of Physiology (Co-author and Editor) (8th to 11th editions); Accidental Hypothermia, 1977. Recreations: fly-fishing; dinghy-sailing; music; painting. Address: (b.) University Department of Medicine, Ninewells Hospital and Medical School, Dundee DD1 9SY; T.-01382 660111.

Engeset, Jetmund, FRCSE, FRCSG. Consultant Surgeon, Grampian Health Board, since 1987; Surgeon to the Queen in Scotland, since 1985; b. 22.7.38.

Entwistle, Professor Noel James, BSc, PGCE, PhD, FilD (h.c.), FBPsS. Bell Professor of Education, Edinburgh University, since 1978; Director, Godfrey Thomson Unit for Educational Research and Centre for Research on Learning and Instruction, since 1978; b. 26.12.36, Bolton; m., Dorothy Bocking; 1 d. Educ. King's School, Ely; Sheffield University; Aberdeen University. Teacher, Rossall School, Fleetwood, 1961-64; Research Fellow, Aberdeen University, 1964-68; Department of Educational Research, Lancaster University: Lecturer, 1968, Senior Lecturer, 1971, Professor, 1972. Editor: British Journal of Educational Psychology, 1975-79, Higher Education, since 1993. Recreations: reading; walking; golf. Address: (b.) 10 Buccleuch Place, Edinburgh EH8 9JT; T.-0131-650 4333.

Entwistle, Raymond Marvin, FCIB. Managing Director, Adam & Company Group Plc, since 1993; b. 12.6.44, Croydon; m., Barbara Joan Hennessy; 2 s.; 1 d. Educ. John Ruskin Grammar School. Several managerial appointments with Lloyds Bank. Governor, Edinburgh College of Art; Chairman, Fruit Market Gallery, Edinburgh; Non-executive Director: John Davidson (Holdings) Ltd, 1992-96, JW International Plc., 1995-96. Recreations: golf; shooting; fishing; antiques. Address: (b.) 22 Charlotte Square, Edinburgh EH2 4DF; T.-0131-225 8484.

Erdal, David Edward, MA, MBA. Director, Tullis Russell & Co. Ltd. (Chairman, 1985-96); Chairman: Job Ownership Ltd., Baxi Partnership Ltd.; Trustee, FI Group Shareholders' Trust; Director, China Heartland Fund; b. 29.3.48, Umtali, Zimbabwe; 1 s.; 1 d. Educ. Glenalmond; Brasenose College, Oxford; Harvard Business School. English Language Teacher, London, 1972-74; Foreign Language Institute, People's Republic of China, 1974-76; joined Tullis Russell, 1977. Trustee, Baxi Partnership; Fellow, Royal Society of Arts. Recreations: sailing; skiing; reading. Address: (b.) Tullis Russell & Co. Ltd., Markinch, Glenrothes KY7 6PB; T.-01592 753311.

Erickson, Professor John, MA, FRSE, FBA, FRSA. Honorary Fellow, Centre for Defence Studies, Edinburgh University; b. 17.4.29, South Shields; m., Ljubica; 1 s.; 1 d. Educ. South Shields High School; St. John's College, Cambridge. Research Fellow, St. Antony's College, Oxford; Lecturer, Department of History, St. Andrews University; Lecturer/Reader, Department of Government, Manchester University; Reader/Professor, Defence Studies, Edinburgh University. President, Association of Civil Defence and Emergency Planning Officers, until 1984; Visiting Professor, Yale University, 1987; Hon. Fellow, Aerospace Academy of Ukraine, 1995. Publications: The Soviet High Command, 1962; The Road to Stalingrad, 1975; The Road to Berlin, 1984; Soviet Ground Forces, An Operational Assessment, 1986; Barbarossa, The Axis and the Allies (Editor and Contributor), 1994; The Soviet Armed Forces, 1918–1992: Research Guide to Soviet Forces (jointly), 1996; The Russian General Staff 1700-1994, forthcoming. Recreation: model-making. Address: (b.) 13 Ravelston House Road, Edinburgh EH4 3LP; T.-0131-650 4263.

Eriksen, Gunn; b. 28.12.56, Grimstad, Norway; m., Fred Brown. Educ. Grimstad, Norway; tutored in ceramics by Rolf Tiemroth. Worked as ceramicist in Norway and Scotland; exhibited ceramics and weaving in Norway; since 1980 has run Altnaharrie Inn with Fred Brown; various awards, including maximum ratings in Good Food Guide, AA Restaurant Guide, Egon Ronay etc. Recreations: reading; sailing; skiing; design. Address: (b.) Altnaharrie Inn, Ullapool IV26 2SS; T.-01854 633230.

Ermarth, Professor Elizabeth Deeds, BA, MA, PhD. Saintsbury Professor of English Literature, Edinburgh University, since 1994; b. 30.11.39, Denver, Colorado; m., Professor Thomas Vargish; 1 s. Educ. Carleton College, Minn.; University of California at Berkeley; University of Chicago. Taught at Northwestern University, Illinois, 1969-71; Dartmouth College, New Hampshire, 1972-74; Reed College, Oregon, 1974-78; University of Maryland, Baltimore, 1979-94 (Presidential Research Professor, 1991-

95); Fullbright Senior Fellow and Overseas Fellow, Churchill College, Cambridge, 1992-93. Publications: numerous works of cultural history and theory, including: The English Novel in History, 1840-1895; Sequel to History: Postmodernism and the Crisis of Representational Time; George Elliot; Realism and Consensus in the English Novel. Recreations: music; hiking; travel. Address: (b.) English Department, Edinburgh University, David Hume Tower, George Square, Edinburgh, EH8 9JX; T.-0131-650 3612/3618; (h.) T.-0131-447 0617.

Erskine, Donald Seymour, DL, FRICS. Factor and Director of Estates, National Trust for Scotland, 1961-89; b. 28.5.25, London; m., Catharine Annandale McLelland; 1 s. 4 d. Educ. Wellington College. RA (Airborne), 1943-47 (Captain); Pupil, Drumlanrig Estate, 1947-49; Factor, Country Gentlemen's Association, Edinburgh, 1950-55; Factor to Mr A.L.P.F. Wallace, 1955-61. Member, Queen's Bodyguard for Scotland (Royal Company of Archers); Deputy Lieutenant, Perth and Kinross; Elder and General Trustee, Church of Scotland. Recreations: golf; shooting; singing. Address: (h.) Cleish House, Cleish, Kinrossshire KY13 7LR; T.-01577 850232.

Eva, David, BCom, CPFA. Director of Finance, Shetland Health Board, since 1974; b. 2.12.42, Romford; m., Marina; 2 s. Educ. Merchant Taylors; University of Liverpool. Auditor, Halifax Borough Council; Zetland County Council: Assistant County Treasurer, Depute County Treasurer. Past President, Shetland Rotary Club; Treasurer, Lerwick Methodist Church. Recreations: bird-watching; record collecting; foreign travel. Address: (b.) Brevik House, South Road, Lerwick, Shetland ZE1 0RB; T.-01595 696767.

Evans Charles, CEng, MIMechE, MIRTE. Chief Executive and Managing Director, Lothian Region Transport plc, since 1986; b. 30.8.37, Chadderton, Lancashire; m., Cherie; 3 s.; 1 d. Educ. North Chadderton Secondary Modern School; Oldham Technical College. Apprentice Engineer/Engineer, Oldham Corporation Passenger Transport, 1952-63; Assistant Engineer, Manchester Corporation, 1963-65; Edinburgh Corporation: Assistant Chief Engineer, 1965-71, Chief Engineer, 1971-75; Depute Director, Lothian Regional Council, 1975-78; Director of Public Transport, Lothian Regional Council, 1978-86. President, Bus and Coach Council, 1986-87 (Chairman, Scotland, 1987-88); Director, Edinburgh Chamber of Commerce, 1990-93. Recreations: golf; caravanning. Address: (b.) 1-4 Shrub Place, Leith Walk, Edinburgh EH7 4PA; T.-0131-554 4494.

Evans, David Pugh, ARCA, RSA, RSW; paints in Edinburgh; b. 20.11.42, Gwent. Educ. Newbridge Grammar School; Newport College of Art; Royal College of Art. Lecturer, Edinburgh College of Art, 1965-68; Fine Art Fellow, York University, 1968-69; Lecturer, Edinburgh College of Art, since 1969; travelled and painted throughout USA, 1975; solo exhibitions: Marjorie Parr Gallery, London; Mercury Gallery, London; York University; Fruitmarket Gallery, Edinburgh; Open Eye Gallery, Edinburgh. Address: (h.) 17 Inverleith Gardens, Edinburgh EH3 5PS; T.-0131-552 2329.

Evans, Sheriff George James, MA, LLB. Sheriff of Glasgow and Strathkelvin, at Glasgow, since 1983; b. 16.7.44. Address: (b.) Sheriff Court House, 1 Carlton Place, Glasgow, G5 9DA.

Evans, James, MBE, RD, DL, BSc, CEng, FRINA, MIMechE. Managing Director: Thomas Evans (Berwick) Ltd.; Consultant Naval Architect, since 1990; b. 9.5.33, South Shields; m., Patricia Alexena Kerr; 1 s.; 2 d. Educ. Merchiston Castle School; Kings College, Durham. Apprenticeship, 1950-56; Royal Navy, 1956-58; YARD, 1958-63; UKAEA, 1963-68; RNR, 1956-80 (retired as

Captain (E) RNR); Member, Eyemouth Burgh Council, 1972-75; Berwickshire County Council; Vice-Chairman and Finance Chairman, Berwickshire District Council, 1974-80; Managing Director, Eyemouth Boat Building Co. Ltd., 1988-90; Deputy Lieutenant, Berwickshire, since 1978; Chairman: Berwick Freemen's Guild, since 1975, Fishing Boat Builders Association, 1979-90, Berwickshire District Council, 1980-96; Lord President, Court of Deans of Guild Scotland, 1994-95. Awarded Silver Medal, Nuclear Engineering Society, 1962; Hon ADC, The Queen, 1979-80. Address: (h.) Makore, Northburn View, Eyemouth, Berwickshire; T.-Eyemouth 50231.

Eveling, Stanley, BA, BPhil. Fellow, Edinburgh University; Playwright; b. 4.8.25, Newcastle upon Tyne; m., Kate Howell; 2 s.; 2 d. Educ. King's College, Durham University; Lincoln College, Oxford. Recreations: golf; tennis; going abroad. Address: (b.) 30 Comely Bank, Edinburgh EH4 1AJ.

Everett, John William, BSc, CEng, MICE. Chairman: J. & J. E. (Contractors), Ltd., Edinburgh, since 1970; Chairman, Scottish Cricket Union, since 1996; b. 22.11.29, London; m., Jean Fishwick; 1 s.; 2 d. Educ. George Watson's College, Edinburgh; University of Edinburgh. RAF Commission, Airfield Construction Branch, 1952-56; Civil Engineer, J. White (Contractors) Ltd., Edinburgh, 1956-69 (Director, 1965-69). Chairman, East of Scotland Lighthouse Club. Recreations: golf; cricket; squash (Scottish Internationalist, 1948-53). Address: (h.) 11 Old Farm Avenue, Edinburgh; T.-0131-441 1273.

Everett, Peter, BSc (Hons), SPMB. Director: Scottish Hydro-Electric, since 1989, Forth Ports Authority, since 1989, Edinburgh Java Trust plc, since 1995, Ramco Energy Ltd., since 1993; b. 24.9.31, London; m., Annette Patricia Hyde; 3 s.; 1 d. Educ. George Watson's College; Edinburgh University. Royal Engineers, 1953-55 (2nd Lt.); joined Shell International Petroleum Company, 1955; Managing Director: Brunei Shell Petroleum Co. Ltd., 1979-84, Shell UK Exploration and Production, 1985-89; retired, 1989. Honorary Professor, Heriot Watt University, 1989. Recreation: golf. Address: (h.) Cluain, Castleton Road, Auchterarder, Perthshire PH3 1JW.

Ewart, Michael. Chief Executive, Scottish Court Service. Address: (b.) Hayweight House, 23 Lauriston Street, Edinburgh EH3 9DQ.

Ewing, David John, MA, MD, FRCP(Ed). Senior Medical Officer, Scottish Office Home and Health Department; b. 27.8.40, London; m., E. Anne Bellamy; 2 d. Educ. Dulwich College; Jesus College, Cambridge; Guy's Hospital, London. Lecturer in Medicine, Edinburgh University, 1970-80; Wellcome Trust Senior Lecturer in Medicine, Edinburgh University, and Hon. Consultant Physician, Lothian Health Board, 1980-91. Castelli-Pedroli Prize, 1987, European Association for the Study of Diabetes. Recreations: walking; reading; cathedral and church architecture. Address: (b.) Scottish Office Department of Health, St. Andrew's House, Edinburgh EH1 3DE.

Ewing of Kirkford, Lord (Harry Ewing), DL. Deputy Lord Lieutenant, Fife, since 1995; Joint Chair, Scottish Constitutional Convention, 1987-96; b. 20.1.31; m., Margaret; 1 s.; 1 d. MP (Labour), Stirling and Falkirk Burghs, 1971-74, Stirling, Falkirk and Grangemouth, 1974-83, Falkirk East, 1983-92; Under Secretary of State for Scotland, 1974-79; Opposition Spokesman on Scottish Affairs, 1979-83, UK Trade and Industry, 1983-84, Scottish Affairs, 1984-87; Chairman, Ewing Inquiry into availability of housing for wheelchair disabled, since 1993; Chairman, Scottish Disability Foundation, since 1994; Member, Council of Europe, 1987-92; Opposition Spokesman on Transport and Scottish Affairs, House of Lords, since 1992.

Address: (h.) Gowanbank, 45 Glenlyon Road, Leven KY8 4AA.

Ewing, Margaret Anne, MA, BA (Hons). MP (Moray), since 1987; Parliamentary Leader, SNP, since 1987; b. 1.9.45, Lanark; m., Fergus Stewart Ewing. Educ. Biggar High School; Glasgow University; Strathclyde University; Jordanhill College. Schoolteacher, 1968-74 (Principal Teacher of Remedial Education, St. Modan's, Stirling, 1972-74); SNP MP (East Dunbartonshire), 1974-79; Freelance Journalist, 1979-81; Co-ordinator, West of Scotland CSS Scheme, 1981-87. Recreations: gardening; reading; arts in general. Address: (h.) Burns Cottage, Tulloch's Lane, Tulloch's Brae, Lossiemouth, Moray IV31 6QY; T.-0134381 3218/2222.

Ewing, Winifred Margaret, MA, LLB, NP. Member (SNP), European Parliament, since 1975; President, Scottish National Party; b. 10.7.29, Glasgow; m., Stewart Martin Ewing; 2 s.; 1 d. Educ. Queen's Park School; Glasgow University. Solicitor, since 1952; former Secretary and President, Glasgow Bar Association; President, Soroptimist Club (Glasgow), 1966; MP (SNP), Hamilton, 1967-70, Moray and Nairn, 1974-79; Doctor, Open University; Doctor of Laws, Glasgow University. Recreations: walking; reading; painting; swimming. Address: (h.) Goodwill, Miltonduff, Elgin IV30 3TL.

F

Fair, James Stuart, CBE, MA, LLB, WS, LLD. Solicitor; formerly Senior Partner, Thorntons, WS, Dundee; Honorary Sheriff and Temporary Sheriff; Director of private investment trust companies; b. 30.9.30, Perth; m., Anne Lesley Cameron; 2 s.; 1 d. Educ. Perth Academy; St. Andrews University; Edinburgh University. Past Chairman: University Court, Dundee, Review Committee, Perth Prison, Dundee Port Authority, Dundee Teaching Hospitals NHS Trust; Past President: Dundee and Tayside Chamber of Commerce & Industry, Dundee Choral Union; former Member, Scottish Solicitors' Discipline Tribunal; former Member, Committee on Medical Ethics, Ninewells Hospital and Medical School, Dundee; former Clerk, Commissioners of Inland Revenue (Dundee District); Trustee, Sir James Caird's Travelling Scholarship Trust; Chairman, Dundee Incubator Company; Hon. Doctor of Laws, Dundee University. Address: (h.) Beechgrove House, 474 Perth Road, Dundee DD2 1LL.

Fairbairn, Alasdair. Chief Executive, Sea Fish Industry Authority. Address: (b.) 18 Logie Mill, Logie Green Road, Edinburgh EH7 4HG.

Fairbairn, The Hon. Mrs Elizabeth, BA. Chairman: Edinburgh New Town Conservation Committee, Lothian Housing Association, Live Music Now! Scotland; Trustee, Scottish National War Memorial; Council Member, The Cockburn Association; President, Clan Mackay Society; b. 21.6.38; 3 d. Address: 38 Moray Place, Edinburgh EH3 6BT; T.-0131-225 2724.

Fairgrieve, Brian David, OBE, DL, MB, ChB, FRCSEd. Deputy Lieutenant, Falkirk and Stirling Districts; General Surgeon, Falkirk Royal Infirmary, 1960-87; b. 21.2.27, Glasgow. Educ. Glasgow Academy; Glasgow University. RMO, 2/6th Gurkha Rifles, 1952-54; initial medical training, Western Infirmary, Glasgow, Stobhill General Hospital, Killearn Hospital; Area Scout Commissioner, 21 years; President, Forth Valley Area Scout Council; Past President, Rotary Club of Falkirk; Lecturer and Examiner, Scotish Police College; Member, Council, St. Andrew's Ambulance Association; former Director, Incorporated Glasgow Stirlingshire & Sons of the Rock Society; Hon. Vice President, Grangemouth Rugby Club; awarded Silver Wolf, 1983, and OBE, 1986, for services to International Scouting. Recreations: photography; travel. Address: (h.) 19 Lyall Crescent, Polmont, Falkirk FK2 0PL; T.-01324 715449.

Fairgrieve, James Hanratty, DA, ARSA, RSW. Painter; Senior Lecturer in Drawing and Painting, Edinburgh College of Art, since 1968; b. 17.6.44, Prestonpans; m., Margaret D. Ross; 2 s.; 1 d. Educ. Preston Lodge Senior Secondary School; Edinburgh College of Art. Postgraduate study, 1966-67; Travelling Scholarship, Italy, 1968; President, SSA, 1978-82; exhibited in Britain and Europe, since 1966. Recreation: angling. Address: (h.) Burnbrae, Gordon, Berwickshire; T.-Gordon 357.

Fairgrieve, Sir (Thomas) Russell, CBE, TD, JP. Former Chairman, Bain Hogg Scotland; former Chairman, Quality Guaranteed PLC; b. 3.5.24, Galashiels; m., Millie Mitchell; 1 s.; 3 d. Educ. St. Mary's School, Melrose; Sedbergh School, Yorkshire. Commissioned, 8th Gurkha Rifles (Indian Army), 1943; Company Commander, 1/8th Gurkha Rifles, 1944-46 (Burma, Malaya and Java); TA, 4th KOSB, 1947-63 (Major). Director, Laidlaw & Fairgrieve Ltd., 1953-68 (Managing Director, 1958-68); Director, Dawson International PLC, 1961-73 (Group Yarn Sales Director, 1965-68); Chairman, Scottish Young Conservatives, 1950-51; President, Scottish Conservative Association, 1965-66; MP, Aberdeenshire West, 1974-83; Chairman, Scottish Conservative Group for Europe, 1974-78; Scottish Conservative Whip, 1975; Chairman, Scottish Conservative Party, 1975-80; Under-Secretary of State for Scotland, 1979-81; Member, Consultative Assembly, Council of Europe and WEU, 1982-83.

Fairhead, Nigel Derek, FCA. Director of Finance, National Trust for Scotland, since 1991; b. 17.10.52, Malaya; m., Morag McGregor; 1 s.; 1 d. Educ. Brighton College; Hendon College. Trained with Spain Brothers & Co., Kent; qualified as a chartered accountant, 1976; Price Waterhouse, Paris, 1978-79; Marcus Hazelwood, Cheltenham, 1979-81; joined National Trust for Scotland, 1981. Address: (b.) 5 Charlotte Square, Edinburgh EH2 4DU; T.-0131-226 5922.

Fairley, Janet Christine, PhD, MPhil, BA (Hons). Director, Edinburgh Book Festival, 1995-97; Hon. Fellow, Institute of Latin American Studies, since 1996; b. 16.3.49, Birkenhead; 1 s.; 2 d. Taught, Catholic University, Temuco, Chile, 1971-73; Leverhulme Research Fellow, 1992; British Council-Andes Foundation Visiting Professor in Musicology, University of Chile, 1994; Editorial Board, Popular Music Journal, Cambridge University Press, since 1988; freelance journalist since late 1980s; freelance broadcaster, since 1989, producing arts programmes (Presenter, Earthbeat, 1989-93); music critic, Folk Roots; numerous academic publications; contributor, Rough Guide to World Music; UK Chair, International Vice-Chair, International Association for the Study of Popular Music, 1985-92. Recreations: yoga; Latin and flamenco dancing; tennis; swimming; reading; singing; music; theatre; film. Address: (h.) 7A Cluny Gardens, Edinburgh EH10 6BE.

Fairlie, Andrew Patrick. Executive Chef, One Devonshire Gardens, Glasgow; b. 21.11.63, Perth; m., Gillian Laird Ashley; 2 d. Educ. Perth Academy; Westminster Hotel School, London. Began apprenticeship aged 15 at Station Hotel, Perth; Chef de Partie, Boodles, London; studied with Michael Guererd, Eugene-les-Bains, S.W. France; worked in establishments in Paris (Hotel de Crillion), French Alps, Sydney and East Africa, and aboard Royal Scotsman train; Senior Sous Chef, Ritz, London; worked in Adare Manor, S. Ireland; Head Chef, Disneyland Hotel, Euro Disney, Paris. Winner, first Michael Roux Scholarship, 1985; Scottish Chef of the Year 1996; Member, Academie Culinaire de France; awarded Michelin Star, 1996, 1997. Recreation: hill-walking. Address: (b.) One Devonshire Gardens, Glasgow G12 0UX; T.-0141-339 2001.

Fairlie of Myres, David Ogilvy, MBE. Landowner; b. 1.10.23, Edinburgh; m., Jane Bingham-Newland. Educ. Ampleforth College, York; Oriel College, Oxford. Officer, Royal Signals, Europe, Ceylon, Singapore, Java, Malaya, Korea, SHAPE Paris; retired, 1959; Fife Area Scouts: President, former County Commissioner; former Cupar District Commissioner for Scouts; awarded Silver Acorn and Silver Wolf; DL, Fife; JP; Member, Queen's Bodyguard for Scotland; Knight Commander with Star of the Equestrian Order of the Holy Sepulchre of Jerusalem, Lieutenant of Scotland. Publication: Fairlie of that Ilk. Recreations: genealogy; photography; bee-keeping. Address: Myres Castle, Auchtermuchty, Cupar, Fife KY14 7EW.

Fairlie, Peter James Morrison. Director, The Macallan Distillers Ltd., since 1996; Member, Scottish Tourist Board, since 1995; b. 18.12.57, Bridge of Allan; m., Anne (Louise) Moon; 1 s.; 1 d. Educ. Strathallan School. Glenturret Distillery Ltd., 1977-96 (Managing Director, 1989-96).Vice Chairman, Association of Scottish Visitor Attractions, 1988-94; Member, Scottish Sports Council, 1990-93; Member, Scottish Tourist Board Seasonality Working Group, 1994-97; Member, Board of Governors, Strathallan School, since 1994. Recreations: squash (Internationalist,

1980-87); golf; skiing; angling. Address: (b.) The Macallan Distillers Ltd., West Kinfauns, Perth PH2 7XZ; T.-01738 443777.

Fairweather, Andrew Burton, OBE, TD, BA, MIMgt. General Secretary, Abbeyfield Society for Scotland, since 1991; b. 26.2.31, Edinburgh; m., Elizabeth Brown; 3 s. Educ. Royal High School, Edinburgh; Edinburgh University; Open University. Clerical Officer, HM Customs and Excise, 1949; Executive Officer: Accountant of Court for Scotland, 1949, Department of Health for Scotland, 1951 (Secretary, Scottish Medical Practices Committee, 1954-58); Higher Executive Officer, Department of Health for Scotland and Scottish Development Department, 1958; Senior Executive Officer, Scottish Development Department, 1965 (Secretary, Rent Assessment Panel for Scotland, 1965-67); Principal: Chief Administrative Officer, Civil Service College, Edinburgh, 1970, Scottish Economic Planning Department, 1972, Scottish Development Department, 1974 (Secretary, Local Government Staff and Property Commissions, 1974-77), Scottish Office Central Services, 1981; Senior Principal, Scottish Office Central Services, 1982. Rifle Brigade, RAEC; Royal Scots (TA) and Royal Corps of Transport (TA); Commanding Officer, 495 Liaison Unit (BAOR), Royal Corps of Transport (TA), 1977-81; Colonel, Regular Army Reserve of Officers, 1982. Address: (h.) 127 Silverknowes Gardens, Edinburgh.

Fairweather, Ann Beatrice, MBA. Director of Marketing and Communications, Scottish Sports Council, since 1992; b. 19.11.55, London; m., Clive Bruce Fairweather; 1 s.; 1 d. Educ. Dundalk Grammar School; College of Business Studies, Belfast; Open University. Various PR and press related jobs, 1975-82; freelance journalist, 1982-89; Business Development Manager, Reiach and Hall, Architects, 1989-94. Recreations: discovering the countryside on a bicycle. Address: (b.) Scottish Sports Council, South Gyle, Edinburgh EH12 9DQ; T.-0131-317 7200.

Fairweather, Clive Bruce, OBE. HM Chief Inspector of Prisons for Scotland, since 1994; b. 21.5.44, Edinburgh; m., Ann; 1 s.; 1 d. Commanding Officer: Scottish Division Depot, 1984-87, 1st Bn., King's Own Scottish Borderers, 1987-89; Divisional Colonel, The Scottish Division, 1991-94. Address: (b.) Scottish Office, St. Andrews House, Edinburgh; T.-0131-244 8481.

Fairweather, Henry, MA. Group Personnel and Services Director, Scottish and Newcastle plc, since 1986; Independent Director, Havelock Europa plc, since 1991; Non-executive Director, Western General Hospitals NHS Trust, since 1994; b. 16.7.46, Edinburgh; m., Lesley; 2 s. Educ. Edinburgh Academy; St. Andrews University. Scottish and Newcastle, since 1969. Director, Edinburgh Academy; FIPD. Recreations: squash; golf. Address: (b.) 111 Holyrood Road, Edinburgh EH8 8YS; T.-0131-556 2591.

Fairweather, Rev. Ian C.M., MA (Hons), BD. Associate Minister, Glasgow Cathedral, 1985-90; b. 7.3.20, Glasgow; m., Joan Margaret Dickinson. Educ. Hutchesons' Boys' Grammar School, Glasgow; Glasgow University. Professor of Philosophy, Scottish Church College, Calcutta, and Murray College, Sialkot, 1945-47; Minister, Perceton & Dreghorn Parish Church, 1948-63; Lecturer in Religious Studies and Religious Education, Jordanhill College of Education, 1964-82. Church of Scotland Representative, General Teaching Council for Scotland, 1983-91; Hon. Fellow, New College, Edinburgh, 1984-85. Publications: The Quest for Christian Ethics: an inquiry into ethics and Christian ethics (Co-author); Religious Education (Co-author). Recreation: gardening. Address: (h.) Seaforth, 10 Hillside Road, Cardross G82 5LX; T.-01389 841551.

Falconer, Alexander. Member (Labour), Mid Scotland and Fife, European Parliament, since 1984; b. 1.4.40, Dundee; m., Margaret Cavell Aldridge; 1 s.; 1 d. Educ. St. John's Junior Secondary School, Dundee. Former foundry worker; Royal Navy stoker, 1959-68; Rosyth Dockyard, 1969-84; Shop Steward, TGWU, 1970-84; Chair, Fife Federation of Trades Councils. Address: (b.) 25 Church Street, Inverkeithing, Fife KY11 1LH; T.-01383 419330.

Falconer, Professor Kenneth John, MA, PhD (Cantab). Professor in Pure Mathematics, St. Andrews University, since 1993; b. 25.1.52, Middlesex; m., Isobel Jessie Nye; 1 s.; 1 d. Educ. Kingston Grammar School; Corpus Christi College, Cambridge. Research Fellow, Corpus Christi College, Cambridge, 1977-80; Lecturer, then Reader, Bristol University, 1980-93; Visiting Professor, Oregon State University, 1985-86. Publications: The Geometry of Fractal Sets; Fractal Geometry — Mathematical Foundations and Applications; Techniques in Fractal Geometry; Unsolved Problems in Geometry (Co-author); 70 papers. Recreations: hill-walking and long distance walking (National Committee Member, Long Distance Walkers Association, 1987-92, and Editor of its magazine Strider). Address: (h.) Lumbo Farmhouse, St. Andrews, Fife; T.-01334 478507.

Falconer, Lake. Solicitor (retired); b. 21.10.27, Oban; m., Winifred Margaret Payne; 2 s. Educ. Oban High School; Glasgow University. RAF, 1946-48; qualified Solicitor, 1951; Partner, then Senior Partner, D.M. MacKinnon & Co., WS, Oban, 1953-89; Council Member, Law Society of Scotland, 1980-90; Vice President, 1985-86; Dean, Oban Faculty of Solicitors, 1983-86; Honorary Sheriff of North Strathclyde at Oban, since 1988; Chairman, Oban Social Security Appeal Tribunal; Commodore, Royal Highland Yacht Club, 1974-77; Chairman and Depute Launching Authority, Oban Lifeboat, since 1972; Chairman, North Argyll District Scout Council, since 1982; Session Clerk, Kilmore and Oban Church of Scotland, 1974-93; President, Oban Burns Club. Recreation: enjoying his grandchildren. Address: (h.) Birkhill, Glenmore, Oban PA34 4PG; T.-01631 562940. .

Falkland, 15th Viscount (Lucius Edward William Plantagenet Cary). Premier Viscount of Scotland on the Roll; b. 8.5.35, London; 2 s.; 3 d. (1 deceased). Educ. Wellington College; Alliance Francaise, Paris. Formerly journalist, theatrical agent, chief executive of international trading company; entered Parliament, 1984 (SDP), 1987 (Liberal Democrats); Deputy Chief Whip, House of Lords, for Liberal Democrats, since 1987; Culture, Sport and Media Spokesman, since 1994. Recreations: golf; motor-cycling; cinema. Address: (b.) House of Lords, London SW1.

Fallick, Professor Anthony Edward, BSc, PhD, FRSE, FRSA. Professor of Isotope Geosciences, University of Glasgow, since 1996; Head of Isotope Geosciences Unit, Scottish Universities Research and Reactor Centre, East Kilbride, since 1986; b. 21.4.50, Chatham; Educ. St. Columba's High School, Greenock; University of Glasgow. Research Fellow: McMaster University, Canada, 1975-78; University of Cambridge, 1978-80; Research Fellow, Lecturer, Reader, Professor, Scottish Universities Research and Reactor Centre, East Kilbride, since 1980. Address: (b.) S.U.R.R.C., Rankine Avenue, East Kilbride, Glasgow G75 0QF; T.-0141-339 8564.

Fallon, Edward Brian. Member, City of Edinburgh Council, since 1995; Deputy Chairman, Labour Group; Convener: General Purposes and Consumer Services Committee, Lothian Valuation Joint Board, since 1996; b. 10.11.47, Edinburgh; m., Jennifer Mary; 1 s.; 1 d. Educ. St. Anthony's School, Edinburgh; Napier College; Edinburgh School of Building. Elected, Lothian Regional Council, 1982, Deputy Leader, 1990-96, and Chair, General

Purposes Committee, 1986-96; Convener, Protective Services Committee, COSLA, 1990-96; Vice-President, ECOSA; Hon. Vice-President, ITSA; Deputy Chair, LACOTS. Recreations: golf; football; rugby; reading; swimming. Address: (b.) City Chambers, High Street, Edinburgh, EH1 1YJ; T.-0131-529 3271.

Fannin, A. Lorraine, BA (Hons), DipEd. Director, Scottish Publishers Association, since 1987; b. Belfast; m., Nigel Fannin; 2 s.; 1 d. Educ. Victoria College, Belfast; Queen's University, Belfast; Reading University. Teacher of Modern Languages, Henley-on-Thames and Edinburgh; opened children's bookshop, 1979. Recreations: theatre; gardening; antique-hunting; reading. Address: (b.) 137 Dundee Street, Edinburgh EH11 1BG; T.-0131-228 6866.

Farley-Sutton, Captain Colin David, RN, CEng, FIMechE, DL. Independent Consulting Engineer; Deputy Lieutenant, Caithness, since 1986; b. 20.12.31, Rugby; m., Sheila Wilson Baldwin; 2 s.; 2 d. Educ. Rugby College of Technology and Arts; RN Engineering College, Plymouth; RN College, Greenwich. Royal Navy, 1950-82 (Captain Superintendent, HMS Vulcan, Dounreay, 1980-82). President, Caithness Branch, Red Cross, since 1991; Member, Scottish Council of Red Cross, since 1993. Address: (h.) Shepherd's Cottage, Lynegar, Watten, Caithness KW1 5YJ; T.-01955 621697.

Farmer, Sir Tom, CBE, KCSG. Chairman and Chief Executive, Kwik-Fit Holdings PLC, since 1984; b. 10.7.40, Edinburgh; m., Anne Drury Scott; 1 s.; 1 d. Educ. Holy Cross Academy. Address: (b.) 17 Corstorphine Road, Edinburgh; T.-0131-337 9200.

Farquhar, Charles Don Petrie, JP, DL. Member, Dundee City Council (Chairman, Leisure Services Committee); b. 4.8.37, Dundee; 2 d. Educ. Stobswell Secondary School; Dundee Trades College; NCLC. Time-served engineer; elected Dundee Corporation, 1965; former Magistrate and Chairman of various Committees; served Royal Engineers (TRG NCO); Supervisory Staff, Plant Engineering Division, NCR; elected Dundee District Council, 1974; Lord Provost and Lord Lieutenant, City of Dundee District, 1975-77; Past Chairman, Tayside and Fife Committee for Employment of Disabled People. Recreations: fresh-water angling; numismatics; DIY; pool; golf; bowls. Address: (h.) 2 Killin Avenue, Dundee DD3 6EB.

Farquhar, Margaret, LLD, JP. Lord Provost of Aberdeen; Lord Lieutenant of Aberdeen; b. 14.3.30, Aberdeen; m., Councillor W. Farquhar (deceased); 1 s.; 1 d. Educ. Ruthrieston Secondary School, Aberdeen; Webster's College, Aberdeen. Elected as a Councillor, 1971; held various Convenerships; Vice Chairman, St Machar Housing Co-operative; Hon. President, Grampian Girls' Brigade, since 1988; former Board Member, Grampian Enterprise Ltd. Hon. LLD, University of Aberdeen, 1996. Recreations: bowling; television; driving; working with elderly and young. Address: (b.) Town House, Aberdeen AB10 1LP; T.-01224 522514.

Farquhar, William John, MA, DSA, FHSM. Secretary, Clinical Resource and Audit Group, NHS in Scotland, since 1989; b. 29.5.35, Maud, Aberdeenshire; m., Isabel Henderson Rusk; 4 s. Educ. Peterhead Academy; Aberdeen University; Manchester University. National Administrative Trainee, Scottish Health Service; Hospital Secretary, Whitehaven Hospital, Cumberland; Deputy Secretary and Treasurer, West Cumberland Hospital Management Committee; Regional Staff Officer, South-Eastern Regional Hospital Board; Deputy Secretary, Eastern Regional Hospital Board; Lothian Health Board: District Administrator, South Lothian District, then Administrator, Operational Services. Secretary, Scottish Health Service Planning Council, 1985-89; Director, Planning Unit, Scottish Home and Health Department, 1987-90; Secretary,

Scottish Health Service Advisory Council, 1989-93; Council of Europe Medical Fellowship, 1988; Elder, Colinton Parish Church; Vice-Convener, Church of Scotland Board for National Mission, 1991-94; Convener, Health Care Advisory Group, Board of World Mission, since 1991; Member, Executive Committee, Crossroads, Edinburgh. Recreations: gardening; walking. Address: (h.) Craigengar, 7 Harelaw Road, Colinton, Edinburgh EH13 0DR; T.-0131-441 2169.

Farquharson, Angus Durie Miller, OBE, DL, MA, FRICS. Vice Lord Lieutenant, Aberdeenshire, since 1988 (DL, 1984); b. 27.3.35, Haydon Bridge; m., Alison Mary Farquharson of Finzean; 2 s.; 1 d. Educ. Trinity College, Glenalmond; Downing College, Cambridge. Chartered Surveyor, Estate Factor, Farmer and Forester; Council Member, Scottish Landowners Federation, 1980-88; Member: Regional Advisory Committee, Forestry Commission, 1980-94; Red Deer Commission, 1986-92; Nature Conservancy Committee for Scotland, 1986-91; NE Committee, SNH, 1991-94; Hon. President, Kincardine/Deeside Scouts; Director, Lathallan School; Elder and General Trustee, Church of Scotland. Recreations: shooting; fishing; gardening; nature conservation. Address: (h.) Finzean House, Finzean, Banchory, Aberdeenshire, AB31 6NZ; T.-01330850 229.

Farquharson, Captain Colin Andrew, JP, DL, FRICS. Lord Lieutenant of Aberdeenshire, since 1987; Chartered Surveyor and Land Agent, since 1953; b. 9.8.23; m., 1, Jean Sybil Mary Hamilton (deceased, 1985); 2 d.; 1 d. deceased; 2, Clodagh, JP, DL, widow of Major Ian Houldsworth of Dallas, Morayshire; 3 step s.; 2 step d. Educ. Rugby. Grenadier Guards, 1942-48; ADC to Field Marshal Sir Harald Alexander (Earl Alexander of Tunis), 1945; Member, Board of Management, Royal Cornhill Hospitals, 1962-74; Director, MacRobert Farms (Douneside), 1971-87; Chairman, Gordon Local Health Council, 1975-81; Member, Grampian Health Board, 1981-89; DL, Aberdeenshire, 1966; Vice Lord Lieutenant, Aberdeenshire, 1983-87; Member, Queen's Bodyguard for Scotland (Royal Company of Archers), since 1964. Recreations: shooting; fishing; farming. Address: Whitehouse, Alford, Aberdeenshire AB33 8DP.

Farquharson, Sir James Robbie, KBE, BSc, CEng, FICE. Upland farmer, since 1965; b. 1.11.03, Kirriemuir; m., Agnes Binny Graham; 2 s. Educ. Websters High School, Kirriemuir; Royal Technical College, Glasgow; Glasgow University. Trainee Civil Engineer, LMS Railway, 1923-25; Civil Engineer, Kenya and Uganda Railway, 1925-37; Tanganyika Railway: Assistant to General Manager, 1937-41, Chief Engineer, 1941-45, General Manager, 1945-48; Deputy General Manager and Chief Engineer, East African Railways and Harbours, 1948-52; General Manager: Sudan Railways, 1952-57, East African Railways and Harbours, 1957-61; Assistant Crown Agent and Engineer-in-Chief, Crown Agents, 1961-65. Fellow, Scottish Council Development and Industry; Former Member, Executive Committee, Scottish Council Development and Industry; undertook missions to Nigeria, Malawi, Jordan and Philippines for Overseas Development Administration; advised African Development Bank on transport matters. Publication: Tanganyika Transport, 1945. Recreation: farming in retirement. Address: (h.) Kinclune, Kirriemuir, Angus DD8 5HX; T.-01575 574710.

Farrell, Sheriff James Aloysius, MA, LLB. Sheriff of Lothian and Borders, since 1986; b. 14.5.43, Glasgow; m., 1, Jacqueline Allen (divorced); 2, Patricia McLaren; 2 d. Educ. St. Aloysius College; Glasgow University; Dundee University. Admitted to Faculty of Advocates, 1974; Advocate-Depute, 1979-83; Sheriff: Glasgow and Strathkelvin, 1984-85, South Strathclyde, Dumfries and Galloway, 1985-86. Recreations: sailing; cycling; hill-walking. Address: (b.) Sheriff's Chambers, Edinburgh; T.-0131-226 7181.

Farrell, William John. Secretary, Board of Stewardship and Finance, Church of Scotland, since 1993; b. 10.5.35, Glasgow; m., Mary Elizabeth Kelly. Educ. Whitehill School; Glasgow Technical College. Church of Scotland Elder and Reader. Recreations: walking; swimming; reading; joking. Address: (b.) 121 George Street, Edinburgh; T.-0131-225 5722.

Farrington, Dennis Joseph, BSc, DPhil, LLM, FRSA. Deputy Secretary and Clerk to the Court, Stirling University, since 1995; b. 13.8.47, Ellesmere Port; m., Julia Baverstock; 1 s.; 1 d. Educ. Ellesmere Port County Grammar School; University of Kent; University of Ulster. Civil Service, 1972-81: Customs and Excise, 1972-73, Northern Ireland Office, 1973-78, HM Stationery Office, 1978-81; Personnel Officer, Hull University, 1981, Administrative Secretary, 1986; Deputy Secretary and Registrar, Stirling University, 1986-95. Secretary, Conference of University Administrators, 1982-88; Chairman, Cancer Research Campaign, Stirling, 1987-91. Publications: Universities and the Law (Co-author), 1990; The Law of Higher Education, 1994; Going to University, 1996. Recreations: DIY; home computing. Address: (b.) Stirling University, Stirling FK9 4LA; T.-01786 467017.

Farry, James. Chief Executive, The Scottish Football Association Ltd., since 1990 (Secretary, The Scottish Football League, 1979-89); 1.7.54, Glasgow; m., Elaine Margaret; 1 s.; 1 d. Educ. Queens Park Secondary School; Hunter High School; Claremont High School. Recreations: occasional fishing; regular spectating football matches. Address: (b.) 6 Park Gardens, Glasgow G3 7YF; T.-0141-332 6372.

Fass, Rev. Michael J., MA. Director, Partners in Economic Development Ltd., since 1992; b. 22.6.44, Sonning, Berks; m., Iola Mary Ashton; 1 s.; 2 d. Educ. Eton College; Trinity College, Cambridge; IMD, Lausanne. Served C Squadron (Berkshire Yeomanry) Berkshire and Westminster Dragoons (TA), 1963-68; worked in industry at Hays Wharf, Miles Druce-GKN, and DTI's Small Firms Service; Director, West Lothian Enterprise Ltd., 1983-92. Director, Prince's Scottish Youth Business Trust, 1989-97; Priest in Charge, Collegiate Church of St. Matthew, Rosslyn Chapel, Roslin (Scottish Episcopal Church). Publication: The Vital Economy, Integrating Training and Enterprise (Co-Author). Address: 60 Braid Road, Edinburgh EH10 6AL.

Faulkner, Professor Douglas, WhSch, PhD, DSc, RCNC, FEng, FRINA, FIStructE, FRSA, FSNAME. President, Institution of Engineers and Shipbuilders in Scotland, since 1995; Head, Department of Naval Architecture and Ocean Engineering, Glasgow University, 1973-95; b. 29.12.29, Gibraltar; m., Isobel Parker Campbell; 3 d. Educ. Sutton High School, Plymouth; HM Dockyard Technical College, Devonport; Royal Naval College, Greenwich. Aircraft carrier design, 1955-57; production engineering, 1957-59; structural research, NCRE Dunfermline, 1959-63; Assistant Professor of Naval Construction, RNC, Greenwich, 1963-66; Structural Adviser to Ship Department, Bath, 1966-68; Naval Construction Officer attached to British Embassy, Washington DC, 1968-70; Member, Ship Research Committee, National Academy of Sciences, 1968-71; Research Associate and Defence Fellow, MIT, 1970-71; Structural Adviser, Ship Department, Bath, and Merrison Box Girder Bridge Committee, 1971-73; UK Representative, Standing Committee, International Ship Structures Congress, 1973-85; Member, Marine Technology Board, Defence Scientific Advisory Council; Expert Assessor: Lord Donaldson's Assessment (Derbyshire), 1995, Department of Transport (re. Derbyshire survey), 1996. Awarded: David W. Taylor Medal; William Froude Medal; Peter the Great Medal.

Recreations: hill-walking; music; croquet; GO. Address: (h.) 4 Murdoch Drive, Milngavie, Glasgow G62 6QZ; T.-0141-956 5071.

Fearon, Brian Joseph, BSSc, MA, DipASocStud. Director of Social Services, East Dunbartonshire Council, since 1995; b. 8.11.48, Belfast; m., Roseanne; 2 d. Educ. St. Mary's CBS Grammar School, Belfast; Queens University, Belfast; Sheffield University; Middlesex University. Social Worker, LB of Waltham Forest, 1973-75; Senior/Assistant Principal Social Worker, Eastern Health and Social Services Board, N. Ireland, 1975-79; Principal Social Worker (Field Work), Northern Health and Social Services Board, 1979-80; Central Regional Council, 1980-95, latterly as Head of Child Care. Member, Northern Ireland Supplementary Benefits Commission, 1978-80. Publications: Cost of Caring; In Defence of the Welfare State; Social Work and Citizenship. Recreation: golf. Address: (b.) 2-4 West High Street, Kirkintilloch G66 1AD; T.-0141-775 9000.

Fedak, Professor Michael A., BA, MA, PhD. Professor, School of Environmental and Evolutionary Biology, University of St. Andrews, since 1996; b. 22.4.43, New Jersey; m., Wendy Brown; 1 s.; 1 d. Educ. Rutgers University; Duke University. Research Associate, Duke University; Lecturer, Harvard University; Biologist (Principal Scientific Officer), Natural Environment Research Council, 1979-96. Address: (b.) Sea Mammal Research Unit, Gatty Marine Laboratory, University of St. Andrews, St. Andrews, Fife KY16 8LB; T.-01334 462630.

Fee, Kenneth, MA, FRCS. Editor, Scots Independent, since 1985; b. 14.7.31, Glasgow; m., Margery Anne Dougan; 3 s.; 1 d. Educ. Gourock High School; Hamilton Academy; Glasgow University. President, Glasgow University SRC and Scottish Union of Students; Editor, Gum, Ygorra and GU Guardian; sometime in military intelligence; Sub-Editor, Glasgow Herald; Strathclyde Publishing Group; itinerant teaching; Member, Scottish Executive, NASUWT, since 1983; various SNP branch, constituency and national offices, since 1973. Publication: How to Grow Fat and Free. Recreations: chess; gastronomy; campaigning. Address: (h.) 157 Urrdale Road, Dumbreck G41 5DG; T.-0141-427 0117.

Fenton, Professor Emeritus Alexander, CBE, MA, BA, DLitt, HonDLitt (Aberdeen), FRSE, FSA, FRSGS, HRSA, FSA Scot. Director, European Ethnological Research Centre, since 1989; Honorary Professor of Antiquities to Royal Scottish Academy, since 1996; b. 26.6.29, Shotts; m., Evelyn Elizabeth Hunter; 2 d. Educ. Turriff Academy; Aberdeen University; Cambridge University. Senior Assistant Editor, Scottish National Dictionary, 1955-59; part-time Lecturer, English as a Foreign Language, Edinburgh University, 1958-60; National Museum of Antiquities of Scotland: Assistant Keeper, 1959-75, Deputy Keeper, 1975-78, Director, 1978-85; part-time Lecturer, Department of Scottish History, Edinburgh University, 1974-80; Research Director, National Museums of Scotland, 1985-89; Chair of Scottish Ethnology and Director, School of Scottish Studies, Edinburgh University, 1990-94; Honorary Fellow, School of Scottish Studies, since 1969; Foreign Member: Royal Gustav Adolf Academy, Sweden, since 1978, Royal Danish Academy of Sciences and Letters, since 1979; Honorary Member: Volkskundliche Kommission fur Westfalen, since 1980, Hungarian Ethnographical Society, since 1983; Jury Member, Europa Prize for Folk Art, 1975-95; President, Permanent International Committee, International Secretariat for Research on the History of Agricultural Implements; President, Scottish Vernacular Buildings Working Group; President, Scottish Country Life Museums Trust; Secretary and Trustee, Friends of the Dictionary of the Older Scottish Tongue; Secretary and Trustee, Scotland Inheritance Fund; Co-Editor: Tools and Tillage, since 1968, The Review of Scottish Culture, since 1984. Publications: The Various Names of Shetland, 1973, 1977; Scottish

Country Life, 1976 (Scottish Arts Council Book Award); The Diary of a Parish Clerk (translation from Danish), 1976; The Island Blackhouse, A Guide to the Blackhouse at 42 Arnol, Lewis, 1978 (re-issued, 1989); A Farming Township, A Guide to Auchindrain, the Museum of Argyll Farming Life, 1978; The Northern Isles, Orkney and Shetland, 1978 (Dag Stromback Award); The Rural Architecture of Scotland (Co-author), 1981; The Shape of the Past 1, 1985; If All The World Were a Blackbird (translation from Hungarian), 1985; The Shape of the Past II, 1986; 'Wirds an' Wark 'e Seasons Roon on an Aberdeenshire Farm, 1987; Country Life in Scotland, Our Rural Past, 1987; Scottish Country Life, 1989; The Turra Coo, 1989; Cruiters...or Twenty Buchan Tales, 1995. Recreation: languages. Address: (b.) European Ethnological Research Centre, National Museums of Scotland, Chambers Street, Edinburgh, EH1 1JF; T.-0131-225 7534.

Fenton, Professor George Wallace, MB, FRCPEdin, FRCPLond, FRCPsych, MRCP, DPM. Emeritus Professor of Psychiatry, Dundee University, since 1996 (Professor, 1983-96); Consultant, Neuropsychiatry, Kathleen May Albrecht Trust; m.; 1 s. Educ. Ballymena Academy; Queen's University, Belfast. Lecturer, Academic Department of Psychiatry, Middlesex Hospital, 1962-66; Maudsley Hospital, London: Consultant Psychiatrist, 1967-75, Consultant in Charge, Epilepsy Unit, 1969-75, Consultant Neurophysiologist, 1968-75; Senior Lecturer, Institute of Psychiatry, London University, 1967-75; Professor of Mental Health, Queen's University, Belfast, 1976-83. Chairman, Scottish Division, Royal College of Psychiatrists, 1988-93. Publications: Event Related Potentials in Personality and Psychopathology (Co-author), 1982; numerous papers on clinical neurophysiology and neuropsychiatry. Recreations: sailing; history; literature. Address: (b.) University Department of Psychiatry, Ninewells Hospital and Medical School, Dundee, DD1 9SY; T.-01382 660111, Ext. 3111; (h.) Invergowrie House, Dundee DD2 1UA; T.- 01382 668224.

Fenwick, Hubert Walter Wandesford. Architectural Historian and Lecturer; Chairman, Royal Martyr Church Union; b. 17.7.16, Glasgow. Educ. Huntley School, New Zealand; Royal Grammar School, Newcastle-upon-Tyne. Architectural student; qualified, 1950; office of Ian G. Lindsay, then Lorimer & Matthew, Edinburgh; gave up architectural career, 1958; RIBA Examiner for Scotland in History of Architecture, until post abolished; Assistant Secretary and PRO, Scottish Georgian Society, 1960-65; Council Member, Cockburn Association, 1966; Scottish Editor, Church Illustrated, 1959-64; Editor and Manager, Edinburgh Tatler and Glasgow Illustrated, 1966-67; regular contributor to Scots Magazine, 25 years, and other journals. Publications: Architect Royal; Auld Alliance; Scotland's Historic Buildings; Scotland's Castles; Chateaux of France; Scotland's Abbeys and Cathedrals; View of the Lowlands; Scottish Baronial Houses. Recreations: foreign travel; architectural history; sketching and photography (for own books and articles); gardening. Address: The Priory, Pittenweem, Fife KY10 2LJ; T.-013333 311 453.

Ferguson, Professor Allister Ian, BSc, MA, PhD, FInstP, CPhys. Professor of Photonics, Strathclyde University, since 1989; Technical Director, Institute of Photonics, University of Strathclyde, since 1996; Managing Director, Microlase Optical Systems Ltd.; b. 10.12.51, Aberdeen; m., Kathleen Ann Challenger. Educ. Aberdeen Academy; St. Andrews University. Lindemann Fellow, Stanford University, 1977-79; SERC Research Fellow, St. Andrews, 1979-81; SERC Advanced Fellow, Oxford, 1981-83; Junior Research Fellow, Merton College, Oxford, 1981-83; Lecturer, then Senior Lecturer, Southampton University, 1983-89. Fellow: Royal Society of Edinburgh, since 1993, Institute of Physics, Optical Society of America. Address: (b.) Department of Physics and Applied Physics,

Strathclyde University, Glasgow, G4 0NG; T.-0141-548 3359.

Ferguson, Charles, LLB(Hons), NP. Solicitor; Senior Partner, Charles Ferguson & Co.; Solicitor Advocate; writer and broadcaster of legal programmes, Scot FM; b. 19.7.63, Glasgow; 4 s.; 2 d. Educ. University of Dundee. Chairman, Hamilton South Conservative and Unionist Party; Election Agent, Conservative and Unionist Party. Address: (b.) 43 Quarry Street, Hamilton ML3 7AH; T.-01698 285885.

Ferguson, Duncan John, MA, MEd, FSA Scot. Rector, Plockton High School, since 1992; Director, Skye and Lochalsh Local Enterprise Company, since 1993; Vice-Chair, Highland Secondary Headteachers' Association, since 1997; b. 26.2.53; m., Catriona; 1 s.; 1 d. Educ. Keil School; University of Glasgow. Teacher of Classics, Albert Secondary School, Glasgow, 1976-79; Head of Classics, Lochgilphead High School, Argyll, 1979-86; Depute Headteacher, Tobermory High School, Mull, 1986-92. Schoolteacher Fellow, British School at Rome, 1992; part-time Lecturer in Scottish History, Continuing Education Departments, Glasgow and Aberdeen Universities; Evening Class Tutor in Gaelic; Vice-Chair, Gaelic Learners' Association; Member, Board, Leirsinn (Centre for Research in Gaelic Affairs); Trustee, Catherine MacKichan Trust; ceilidh compere; five times Winner, National Mod traditional storytelling trophy; Chair, BBC Gaelic Advisory Committee, 1992-95; Vice-Chair, Comunn na Gaidhlig, 1992-93; Church Elder. Recreations: family archaeological rambles and picnics; family holidays in Auvergne; supporting children's musical and sporting pursuits; Hebridean islandhopping; walking on Hadrian's Wall; collecting books, reading; Irish literature and drama; arts generally; passionate and eclectic interest in Scottish culture; French wine; Italian food; Islay's west coast beaches; politics; Gaelic/Celtic issues; research (life of John Stuart Blackie; Lordship of the Isles). Address: (b.) Plockton High School, Plockton IV52 8TU; T.-01599 544372.

Ferguson, James, BSc, PhD, DSc, CChem, FRSC. Professor, Chemistry Department, University of Strathclyde, since 1991; Scientific Consultant, since 1963; b. 30.3.35, Paisley; m., Jean Leslie; 2 s.; 2 d. Educ. Camphill Secondary, Paisley; University of Glasgow. Research Chemist, Shell Research, Manchester, 1960-63; University of Strathclyde: Lecturer in Fibre Chemistry, 1963, Senior Lecturer, 1975, Reader and Head of Fibre and Textile Research Unit, 1982; Consultant: MoD, several international companies. Member, Council, European Society of Rheology; Treasurer, Association of Deacons, Trades House (President, 1999-2000); Board Member, Eastwood High School; Royal Society of Medicine Rheology Award, 1986; Polish Minister of Education's Award, 1991. Publication: Applied Fluid Rheology. Recreations: golf; walking; DIY. Address: (b.) Department of Pure and Applied Chemistry, University of Strathclyde, Glasgow G1 1XL; T.-0141-548 2161.

Ferguson, James Murray, BSc (Econ), MPhil, DipEd, FCIS, FIPM, FBIM, FSA Scot; b. 21.4.28, Almondbank, Perthshire; m., Moira McDougall, BA; 2 d. Educ. Perth Academy; London University; Edinburgh University; Dundee University; Moray House College of Education. Military Service, 1946-79: full-time, Army Emergency Reserve, Territorials, T&AVR, Regular Army Reserve of Officers (final rank of Major); variety of business appointments, mainly in insurance, investment and finance, 1952-64; lectureships in range of management subjects, various higher educational establishments, 1965-76; Principal, Elmwood College, Fife, 1976-82; Principal, Aberdeen College of Commerce, 1982-90; Principal and Chief Executive, Aberdeen College, 1990-93. Governor: Further Education Staff College, Coombe Lodge, Bristol, 1982-87, Aberdeen College of Education, 1983-87.

Recreations: sporting: badminton, tennis, hill-walking; non-sporting: reading, writing, public speaking, local history studies. Address: (h.) Crosslands, Meethill Road, Alyth PH11 8DE; T.-Alyth 2701.

Ferguson, Joan P.S., MA, ALA, FRCPEdin. Hon. Secretary, Scottish Genealogy Society, since 1960; b. 15.9.29, Edinburgh. Educ. George Watson's Ladies College; Edinburgh University. Scottish Central Library, 1952-66; Librarian, Royal College of Physicians of Edinburgh, 1966-94. Member, Scottish Records Advisory Council, 1987-93; Compiler: Scottish Newspapers, Scottish Family Histories; Contributor, Companion and New Companion to Scottish Culture. Recreations: genealogy; gardening; reading. Address: (h.) 21 Howard Place, Edinburgh EH3 5JY; T.-0131-556 3844.

Ferguson, Rev. John, Lth, BD. Minister, Portree, Isle of Skye, since 1980; b. 30.3.37, North Uist; m., Effie MacPhail; 2 s.; 1 d. Educ. Paible Junior Secondary School; Faith Mission Bible College; Glasgow University. Minister, Ness, Isle of Lewis, 1973-80. DD, Canada Christian College. Publications: children's version of Pilgrim's Progress (Gaelic); Slainte Mhath (booklet for Skye and Lochalsh Council on Alcoholism). Recreations: hill-walking; art; gardening. Address: The Manse, Portree, Isle of Skye; T.-01478 612019.

Ferguson, Professor Michael Anthony John, BSc (Hons), PhD. Professor of Molecular Parasitology, Department of Biochemistry, Dundee University, since 1994; b. 6.2.57, Bishop Auckland; m., Dr. Maria Lucia Sampaio Guther; 1 s. Educ. St. Peters School, York; UMIST; London University. Research Associate, Rockefeller University, New York, 1982-85; Research Assistant, Oxford University, 1985-88; Lecturer, then Reader, Dundee University, 1988-94. FRSE; Colworth Medal, 1991; Howard Hughes International Research Scholar. Address: (b.) Department of Biochemistry, Dundee University, Dundee DD1 4HN; T.-01382 229595.

Ferguson, Moira, MBE, BA (Hons). President, Scottish Childminding Association; b. 28.5.35, Glasgow; m., Douglas Ferguson; 3 d. Educ. Glasgow High School for Girls; Open University. J. & P. Coats; Glasgow Education Department; Greater Glasgow Health Board. Chairman, SPPA, 1982-84; Chairman, Scope in Scotland, 1984-85; National Executive Officer, Scottish Pre-school Play Association, 1988-95. Recreations: reading; walking. Address: (b.) 29 Elmwood Avenue, Glasgow G11 7ED; T.-0141 339 0390.

Ferguson, Rev. Ronald, MA, BD, ThM. Minister, St. Magnus Cathedral, Orkney, since 1990 (Leader, Iona Community, 1981-88); Columnist, The Herald, since 1997; b. 27.10.39, Dunfermline; m., Cristine Jane Walker; 2 s.; 1 d. Educ. Beath High School, Cowdenbeath; St. Andrews University; Edinburgh University; Duke University. Journalist, Fife and Edinburgh, 1956-63; University, 1963-71; ordained Minister, Church of Scotland, 1972; Minister, Easterhouse, Glasgow, 1971-79; exchange year with United Church of Canada, 1979-80; Deputy Warden, Iona Abbey, 1980-81. Publications: Geoff: A Life of Geoffrey M. Shaw, 1979; Grace and Dysentery, 1986; Chasing the Wild Goose, 1988; The Whole Earth Shall Cry Glory (Co-Editor), 1985; George MacLeod, 1990; Daily Readings by George MacLeod (Editor), 1991; Black Diamonds and the Blue Brazil, 1993; plays: Every Blessed Thing, 1993, Orkneyinga, 1997; poetry: Pushing the Boat Oot (Contributor), 1997. Recreation: supporting Cowdenbeath Football Club. Address: (h.) Cathedral Manse, Berstane Road, Kirkwall, Orkney KW15 1NA; T.-01856 3312.

Ferguson, R. Scott, BA. Controller, Scottish Television, since 1997; b. 10.11.58, Glasgow; m., Teri Lally; 2 d. Educ. Cumbernauld High School; Strathclyde University.

Journalist, D.C. Thomson, 1980-82; Researcher, BBC Network Current Affairs, London, 1982-84; Assistant Producer, BBC Scotland News and Current Affairs, 1984-86; Scottish Television: Producer/Director, 1986-90, Senior Producer, 1990-93; Editor, News, Sport and Current Affairs, Scottish Television, 1993-96; Channel Head, Sky Scottish Television, 1996-97. Gold Medallist, New York Television Festival. Recreations: television; cinema; football; cooking. Address: (b.) Scottish Television, Cowcaddens, Glasgow G2 3PR; T.-0141-300 3000.

Ferguson, William James, OBE, FRAgS. Farmer, since 1954; Chairman, Aberdeen Milk Company; former Vice Chairman, Scottish Agricultural College; Director, Hannah Research Institute, since 1995; Deputy Lieutenant, Aberdeenshire; b. 3.4.33, Aberdeen; m., Carroll Isobella Milne; 1 s.; 3 d. Educ. Turriff Academy; North of Scotland College of Agriculture. National Service, 1st Bn., Gordon Highlanders, 1952-54, serving in Malaya during the emergency. Former Director, Rowett Research Institute, Aberdeen; former Member, Scottish Country Life Museums Trust Ltd. Recreations: golf; field sports. Address: Rothiebrisbane, Fyvie, Turriff, Aberdeenshire AB53 8LE; T.-01651 891 213.

Fergusson of Kilkerran, Sir Charles, 9th Bt; b. 10.5.31; m., Hon. Amanda Mary Noel-Paton; 2 s.

Fergusson, Professor David Alexander Syme. MA, BD, DPhil. Professor of Systematic Theology, Aberdeen University, since 1990; b. 3.8.56, Glasgow; m., Margot McIndoe; 2 s. Educ. Kelvinside Academy; Glasgow University; Edinburgh University; Oxford University. Assistant Minister, St. Nicholas Church, Lanark, 1983-84; Associate Minister, St. Mungo's Church, Cumbernauld, 1984-86; Lecturer, Edinburgh University, 1986-90. Chaplain to Moderator of the General Assembly, 1989-90. Publications: Bultmann, 1992; Christ, Church and Society, 1993. Recreations: football; golf; jogging. Address: 44 Ashley Road, Aberdeen AB10 6RJ; T.-01224 583817.

Ferrier, Professor Robert Patton, MA (Cantab), BSc, PhD, FInstP, FRSE. Professor of Natural Philosophy, Glasgow University, since 1973; b. 4.1.34, Dundee; m., Valerie Jane Duncan; 2 s.; 1 d. Educ. Morgan Academy, Dundee; Queen's College, Dundee, St. Andrews University. Scientific Officer, AERE Harwell, 1959-61; Research Associate, Massachusetts Institute of Technology, 1961-62; Senior Research Assistant, Cavendish Laboratory, Cambridge, 1962-65; Fellow, Fitzwilliam College, Cambridge, 1964-73; Assistant Director of Research, Cavendish Laboratory, Cambridge, 1965-71; Lecturer in Physics, Cambridge University, 1971-73; Guest Scientist, IBM Research Division, California, 1972-73. Member, Physics Committee, SERC, 1979-82 (Chairman, Semiconductor and Surface Physics Sub-Committee, 1979-82). Recreations: tennis; reading crime novels; garden and house maintenance. Address: Department of Physics and Astronomy, The University, Glasgow G12 8QQ; T.-0141-330 5388.

Fewson, Professor Charles Arthur, BSc, PhD, FRSE, FIBiol. Professor and Director, Institute of Biomedical and Life Sciences, Glasgow University, since 1994; b. 8.9.37, Selby, Yorkshire; m., Margaret C.R. Moir; 2 d. Educ. Hymers College, Hull; Nottingham University; Bristol University. Research Fellow, Cornell University, New York, 1961-63; Department of Biochemistry, Glasgow University: Assistant Lecturer, 1963-64, Lecturer, 1964-68, Senior Lecturer, 1968-79, Reader, 1979-82; Titular Professor, 1982-94. Address: (h.) 39 Falkland Street, Glasgow G12 9QZ; T.-0141-339 1304.

Field, Christopher David Steadman, MA, DPhil, ARCM. Hon. Fellow, Faculty of Music, Edinburgh University; b. 27.4.38, Frimley; m., Elizabeth Ann. Educ. Winchester

College Choir School; Radley College; New College, Oxford. Lecturer in Music, St. Andrews University, 1974-76, Senior Lecturer, 1976-87; Senior Lecturer in Music, Edinburgh University, 1987-95, Dean, Faculty of Music, 1993-95; Associate Director, Scottish Early Music Consort, since 1979; Member, Governing Board, RSAMD, 1973-82. Recreation: gardening. Address: (h.) 2 Maynard Road, St. Andrews KY16 8RX.

Fife, 3rd Duke of (James George Alexander Bannerman Carnegie); b. 23.9.29; m., Hon. Caroline Cecily Dewar (m. diss.); 1 s.; 1 d. Educ. Gordonstoun. National Service, Scots Guards, Malaya, 1948-50; Royal Agricultural College; Clothworkers' Company and Freeman, City of London; President, ABA, 1959-73; Vice Patron, ABA, 1973-94; Ships President, HMS Fife, 1964-87; a Vice-Patron, Braemar Royal Highland Society; a Vice-President, British Olympic Association. Address: Elsick House, Stonehaven, Kincardineshire AB39 3NT.

Findlay, A.F. (Sandy). Chairman and Chief Executive, Hewden Stuart Plc; b. 19.5.36, Mintlaw; m., Marty; 2 d. Educ. Peterhead Academy; Robert Gordon's Technical College. Engineer/draughtsman; design/development engineer; engineer/area manager, Atlas Copco, 1963-69; joined Hewden Stuart Plc, 1969, and worked through the ranks to main board; main board, since 1982. Recreations: golf; gardening; grand-children. Address: (h.) Pitfour, 1 Leewood Park, Dunblane FK15 0NX.

Findlay, Alastair Donald Fraser, MA. Chief Executive, North of Scotland Water Authority, since 1995; b. 3.2.44, Perth; m., Morag Cumming Peden; 1 s.; 3 d. Educ. Pitlochry High School; Kelso High School; Edinburgh University. Assistant Principal, DAFS, 1966-70; Private Secretary to Joint Parliamentary Under Secretary, Scottish Office, 1970-71; Principal, 1971-74; on loan to Diplomatic Service as First Secretary (Agriculture and Food), The Hague, 1975-78; Assistant Secretary, Higher Education, SED, 1979-82; Fisheries Division, 1982-85, Livestock Products Division, 1985-88, DAFS; Under Secretary, Scottish Office Industry Department, 1988-93; Fisheries Secretary, Scottish Office Agriculture and Fisheries Department, 1993-95. Recreations: golf; walking; watching rugby and football. Address: (b.) North of Scotland Water Authority, Cairngorm House, Beechwood Park North, Inverness IV2 3ED; T.-01463 245424.

Findlay, Donald Russell, QC, LLB (Hons), MPhil, FRSA. Advocate, since 1975; Vice-Chairman, Glasgow Rangers FC; Lord Rector, St. Andrews University; Newspaper Columnist; Writer; Broadcaster; b. 17.3.51, Cowdenbeath; m., Jennifer E. Borrowman. Educ. Harris Academy, Dundee; Dundee University; Glasgow University. Sometime Lecturer in Commercial Law, Heriot-Watt University. Recreations: Glasgow Rangers FC; Egyptology; archaeology; wine; ethics; travelling first class. Address: (b.) Advocates Library, Parliament House, Parliament Square, Edinburgh EH1 1RF; T.-0131-226 2881.

Findlay, Richard Martin, LLB, NP. Entertainment Lawyer and Partner, Tods Murray WS, Edinburgh, since 1990; b. 18.12.51, Aberdeen. Educ. Gordon Schools, Huntly; Aberdeen University. Trained, Wilsone & Duffus, Advocates, Aberdeen; Legal Assistant, Commercial Department, Maclay Murray & Spens, Glasgow and Edinburgh, 1975-78; Partner, Ranken & Reid SSC, Edinburgh, 1979-90. Member: International Association of Entertainment Lawyers, International Entertainment and Multimedia Law and Business Network, International Bar Association, BAFTA, The Writers' Guild, New Producers Alliance, Scottish Media Lawyers Society, Business in the Arts Placement Scheme; Associate and Scottish Legal Adviser, Theatrical Management Association; Director, Gallus Theatre Company, Dance Base Ltd.; Trustee, Peter Darrell Trust; Managing Editor, i2i (The Business Journal

of the International Film Industry); Company Secretary: Edinburgh Capital Group Limited, Edinburgh Arts and Entertainment Limited, Scottish Arts Lobby, French Film Festival Ltd., Edinburgh International Jazz Festival, Italian Film Festival, Arts Research and Development Scotland, Great Distribution Ltd, Moonstone International Ltd.. Recreations: music; theatre; opera; cinema. Address: (b.) 66 Queen Street, Edinburgh EH2 4NE; T.-0131-226 4771.

Fink, Professor George, MB, BS, MD, MA, DPhil, FRSE. Director, MRC Brain Metabolism Unit, since 1980; Honorary Professor, Edinburgh University, since 1984; b. 13.11.36, Vienna; m., Ann Elizabeth; 1 s.; 1 d. Educ. Melbourne High School; Melbourne University; Hertford College, Oxford. House Officer appointments, Royal Melbourne and Alfred Hospitals, 1961-62; Demonstrator and Lecturer, Department of Anatomy, Monash University, 1963-64; Nuffield Dominions Demonstrator, Oxford, 1965-67; Senior Lecturer, Monash University, 1968-71; University Lecturer, Oxford, 1971-80; Official Fellow and Tutor in Physiology and Medicine, Brasenose College, Oxford, 1974-80. Member of Council, European Neuroscience Association, 1980-82, since 1994; President, European Neuroendocrine Association 1991-95; Chairman, EU Biomed Assessment Panel, 1991-96. Publications: Neuropeptides: Basic and Clinical Aspects (Co-Editor), 1982; Neuroendocrine Molecular Biology (Co-Editor), 1986; Neuropeptides: a Methodology (Co-Editor); 320 papers. Recreations: skiing and squash. Address: (b.) MRC Brain Metabolism Unit, Department of Pharmacology, Edinburgh University, 1 George Square, Edinburgh EH8 9JZ; T.-0131-650 3548.

Finlay, Ian Gardner, BSc, MB, ChB, FRCS (Glas), FRCS (Edin.), FCPSP (Hon.). Consultant Colorectal Surgeon, Royal Infirmary, Glasgow, since 1987; b. 24.5.52, Leven; m., Patricia Mary Whiston; 1 s.; 1 d. Educ. St. Andrews University; Manchester University. House Surgeon; Casualty Officer; Demonstrator in Anatomy; Registrar in Surgery; Senior Registrar in Surgery: Royal Infirmary, Glasgow; St. Mark's Hospital, London; University of Minnesota. Hon. Treasurer, Royal College of Physicians and Surgeons of Glasgow. Publications: more than 100 relating to disorders of the large bowel. Recreations: sailing; skiing; ornithology; antique furniture. Address: (b.) Department of Coloproctology, Ward 61, Royal Infirmary, Glasgow; T.-0141-211 4084.

Finlay, Robert Derek, BA, MA, FInstD, MIMC, MCIM. Chairman, Dawson International PLC, since 1995; b. 16.5.32, London; m., Una Ann Grant; 2 s.; 1 d. Educ. Kingston Grammar School; Emmanuel College, Cambridge. Ltd., Gordon Highlanders, 1950-52; Mobil Oil Co. UK, 1953-61; Associate, Principal, Director, McKinsey & Co., 1961-79; Managing Director, H.J. Heinz Co. Ltd., 1979-81; Senior Vice-President, World HQ, H.J. Heinz Co., 1981-93. Recreations: tennis; rowing; music; theatre. Address: (h.) Grantully Castle, by Aberfeldy, PH15 2EG.

Finlayson, Robert William, LLB, BCom, CA, ATII. Managing Partner, Edinburgh, Ernst & Young, since 1991; Director, Ernst &Young Financial Management Ltd., since 1989; b. 16.12.49, Glasgow; m., Jennifer Catherine; 2 s.; 1 d. Educ. Glasgow Academy; Edinburgh University. Touche Ross, Glasgow, 1972-75; Arthur Young: Glasgow, 1976-77, Edinburgh, 1977-79, Birmingham, 1979-82 (Tax Manager/Tax Partner), Edinburgh, since 1982 (Head of Tax, Office Managing Partner). Member, Scottish Committee, Wooden Spoon Society; Chairman, Wooden Spoon Society "BT Pay to Play" Scheme. Recreations: golf; sailing; skiing; hill-walking. Address: (b.) Ernst & Young, Ten George Street, Edinburgh EH2 2DZ; T.-0131-226 6400.

Finn, Anthony, MA (Hons), FEIS (1997). Rector, St. Andrew's High School, Kirkcaldy, since 1988; Teachers'

Representative, National Committee for the Staff Development of Teachers; Governor, Moray House College of Education; b. 4.6.51, Irvine; m., Margaret Caldwell. Educ. St. Joseph's Academy, Kilmarnock; Glasgow University. Teacher, Principal Teacher, Assistant Head Teacher, Depute Head Teacher, Acting Head Teacher, St. Andrew's Academy, Saltcoats, 1975-88. Member: General Teaching Council (Convener, Education Committee); Member, Catholic Education Commission for Scotland; Assessor, Teacher Education, Scottish Higher Education Funding Council, 1994-95; Chair, Fife Secondary Head Teachers Association, until 1997. Recreations: sport; travel; literature; current affairs. Address: (h.) 1 Blair Place, Kirkcaldy KY2 5SQ; T.-01592 640109.

Finnie, James Ross, CA. Member, Inverclyde Council, since 1995 (Member, Inverclyde District Council, 1977-96); Ross Finnie & Co., Chartered Accountants; Chairman, Systems Reliability Scotland Ltd., Finance Director, Buko Holdings Ltd.; Director, Mico Ltd; b. 11.2.47, Greenock; m., Phyllis Sinclair; 1 s.; 1 d. Educ. Greenock Academy. Member, Executive Committee, Scottish Council (Development and Industry), 1976-87; Chairman: Scottish Liberal Party, 1982-86, Scottish Liberal Democrats General Election Campaign, 1997. Address: (h.) 91 Octavia Terrace, Greenock PA16 7PY; T.-01475 631495.

Firth, Professor William James, BSc, PhD, CPhys, FInstP, FRSE. Professor of Physics, Strathclyde University (Head, Department of Physics and Applied Physics, 1990-93); b. 23.2.45, Holm, Orkney; m., Mary MacDonald Anderson; 2 s. Educ. Perth Academy; Edinburgh University; Heriot-Watt University. Lecturer to Reader, Physics, Heriot-Watt University, 1967-85. Fellow, Optical Society of America. Recreation: sports (Edinburgh University Hockey Blue, 1967-68). Address: (b.) John Anderson Building, 107 Rottenrow, Glasgow G4 0NG.

Fisher, Archie. Folk singer, guitarist, composer, broadcaster; b. 1939, Glasgow. First solo album, 1966; presenter, Travelling Folk, BBC Radio; Artistic Director, Edinburgh International Folk Festival, 1988-92.

Fisher, Gregor. Actor (television, theatre, film). Credits include (BBC TV): Rab C. Nesbitt series (leading role), Naked Video series, Scotch and Wry, Para Handy. Best Actor award, Toronto Festival, for One, Two, Three.

Fisher, Kenneth Holmes, BA, ACIS, AInstM, DipABCC. Depute Principal, North Glasgow College, since 1987; b. 19.3.41, Glasgow. Educ. Hillhead High School, Glasgow. Administrative appointments, Colvilles Ltd., 1957-67; Lecturer and Senior Lecturer, Anniesland College, Glasgow, 1967-75; Head: Department of Business Studies, Cumbernauld College, 1975-80, Department of Commerce, Anniesland College, Glasgow, 1980-86. Address: (b.) 110 Flemington Street, Glasgow G21 4BX; T.-0141-558 9001.

Fitzgerald, Professor Alexander Grant, BSc, PhD, DSc, CPhys, FInstP. Head, Department of Applied Physics and Electronic and Mechanical Engineering and Professor of Analytical Electron Microscopy, Dundee University, since 1992; b. 12.10.39, Dundee; m., June; 1 s.; 2 d. Educ. Perth Academy; Harris Academy; St. Andrews University; Cambridge University. Research Fellow, Lawrence Berkeley Laboratory, University of California; Lecturer, Senior Lecturer, Reader, Professor, Dundee University. Publications: 130 conference and journal papers; book: Quantitative Microbeam Analysis (Co-editor). Recreations: swimming; golf. Address: (b.) Department of Applied Physics and Electronic and Mechanical Engineering, Dundee University, Dundee, DD1 4HN; T.-01382 344553.

Fitzgerald, Maren L., LLB, MICFM. National Organiser, Scotland, RNLI; b. 20.4.47, Glasgow; 2 s. Educ. Glasgow High School for Girls; Glasgow University. Appeal

Director, Strathcarron Hospice, 1989-92; Director of Fundraising, Scottish Medical Research Fund, 1992-94; Administrator, Scottish Hospital Endowments Research Trust, 1993-94; Depute Campaign Director, Children 1st, 1994-96. Member, Business Committee, General Council, Glasgow University, 1982-92, and Convenor, Social Affairs Committee of the Business Committee, 1988-92; Trustee, University of Glasgow Trust, 1989-97. Recreation: golf. Address: (b.) Bellevue House, Hopetoun Street, Edinburgh EH7 4ND; T.-0131-557 9171.

Fitzsimons, Sheriff J.T. Sheriff of North Strathclyde. Address: (b.) Dumbarton Sheriff Court, Sheriff Court House, Church Street, Dumbarton, G82 1QR.

Flanagan, Andrew, BAcc, CA. Chief Executive, Scottish Media Group, since 1997; b. 15.3.56, Glasgow; m., Ginni; 1 s. Educ. Hillhead High School; Glasgow University. Trainee Accountant, Touche Ross, 1976-79; Senior Auditor, Price Waterhouse, Brussels, 1979-81; Manager of Financial Control, ITT Inc., Brussels, 1981-86; Finance Director, PA Consulting, London, 1987-91; Group Finance Director, BIS Group, London, 1991-93; Group Finance Director, then Managing Director, Scottish Television, 1993-97. Recreations: golf; skiing. Address: (b.) Cowcaddens, Glasgow G2 3PR; T.-0141-300 3066.

Fleetwood, Gordon, LLB, NP, WS. Partner, Fleetwood & Robb, Solicitors, since 1986; Solicitor-Advocate, since 1994; b. 3.10.51, Elgin; m., Jean Arthur; 2 d. Educ. Elgin Academy; University of Edinburgh. Recreations: fishing; curling. Address: (b.) 11 Queensgate, Inverness IV1 1DF; T.-01463 226232.

Fleming, Alistair, BSc. Chairman, Scottish Council for Educational Technology, since 1994; Chief Executive, Forth Ports PLC, since 1996; b. 31.3.44, Glasgow; m., Sandra; 1 s.; 2 d. Educ. Shawlands Academy; Strathclyde University. Corpus Christi Petrochemicals/ICI America, 1975-80; Britoil, 1980-87; General Manager of Projects, BP Exploration, 1987-89; Managing Director, Eurotunnel, 1990; Director, The Weir Group, 1991-96. Address: (b.) Forth Ports PLC, Tower Place, Leith, Edinburgh EH6 7DB; T.-0131-554 6473.

Fleming, Archibald Macdonald, MA, BCom, PhD, FRSA. Director of Continuing Education, Strathclyde University, since 1987 (Director, Management Development Programmes, Strathclyde Business School, 1984-87); Lecturer, Department of Information Science, Strathclyde University, since 1968; Consultant on Management Training and Development, since 1970; b. 19.6.36, Glasgow; m., Joan Moore; 1 s.; 1 d. Educ. Langholm Academy; Dumfries Academy; Edinburgh University. W. & T. Avery, 1961-63; IBM (UK) Ltd., 1963-64; Sumlock Comptometer Ltd., 1964-68; Consultancies: Scottish Co-operative Wholesale Society, 1969, Hotel and Catering Industry Training Board, 1971, Scottish Engineering Employers Association, 1973. Member: Strathclyde Children's Panel, Committee on Food Processing Opportunities in Scotland, Scottish Council (Development and Industry), Council, Royal Philosophical Society of Glasgow, since 1995, International Vocational Education and Training Association, Church of Scotland Education Committee, American Association of Adult and Continuing Education; Vice-Chairman, Universities Council for Adult and Continuing Education (Scotland), since 1990. Publication: Collins Business Dictionary (with B. McKenna). Recreation: reading, observing and talking on Scotland and the Scots. Address: (b.) 40 George Street, Glasgow G1 1QE.

Fleming, Professor George, BSc, PhD, FEng, FRSE, FICE, MIWEM. Professor of Civil Engineering, Strathclyde University, since 1985, and Managing Director of Envirocentre, since 1995; Vice President, Institution of

Civil Engineers; b. 16.8.44, Glasgow; m., Irene Fleming; 2 s.; 1 d. Educ. Knightswood Secondary School, Glasgow; Strathclyde University; Stanford University, California. Research Assistant, Strathclyde University, 1966-69, Stanford University, 1967; Senior Research Hydrologist, Hydrocomp International, California, 1969-70; Research Associate, Stanford University, 1969-70; Director and Vice President, Hydrocomp International, Palo Alto and Glasgow, 1970-79; Lecturer, then Senior Lecturer, then Reader in Civil Engineering, Strathclyde University, 1971-85; Visiting Professor, University of Padova, Italy, since 1980; Vice Dean, Engineering Faculty, Strathclyde University, 1984-87. Member, Scottish Exports Forum. Publications: Computer Simulation in Hydrology, 1975; The Sediment Problem, 1977; Deterministic Models in Hydrology, 1979. Recreations: farming; fishing; food. Address: (b.) John Anderson Building, 107 Rottenrow, Glasgow G4 0NG; T.-0141-553 4169.

Fleming, Sheriff Grahame R, QC. Sheriff of Lothian and Borders, since 1993; b. 13.2.49. Address: (b.) Linlithgow Sheriff Court, Sheriff Court House, High Street, Linlithgow, EH49 7EQ.

Fleming, Maurice. Editor, The Scots Magazine, 1974-91; b. Blairgowrie; m., Nanette Dalgleish; 2 s.; 1 d. Educ. Blairgowrie High School. Trained in hotel management before entering journalism; worked on various magazines; has had five full-length plays performed professionally, as well as one-act plays by amateurs; founder Member: Traditional Music and Song Association of Scotland, Scottish Poetry Library; Chairman, Blairgowrie, Rattray and District Civic Trust; Past Chairman, Blair in Bloom. Publications: The Scots Magazine — A Celebration of 250 Years (Co-Editor); The Ghost O' Mause and Other Tales and Traditions of East Perthshire; Old Blairgowrie and Rattray; The Real Macbeth and Other Stories from Scottish History. Recreations: theatre; reading; bird-watching; enjoying the countryside; folksong and folklore. Address: (h.) Craigard, Perth Road, Blairgowrie; T.-Blairgowrie 873633.

Fleming, Tom, OBE. Actor and Director; b. 29.6.27, Edinburgh. Professional theatre debut, 1945, in company led by Edith Evans; Co-Founder, Edinburgh Gateway Company, 1953; joined Royal Shakespeare Company at Stratford upon Avon, 1962, and played several classical roles, including Prospero, Brutus, Cymbeline, Buckingham and Kent; toured with RSC in USSR, USA and Europe, 1964; appointed Director, new Royal Lyceum Theatre Company, 1965; there played title role in Galileo; Director, Scottish Theatre Company, 1982-87; awarded Roman Szlydowski Prize for his production of The Thrie Estaites, Warsaw, 1986; TV work includes portrayals of Robert Burns, William Wallace, Jesus of Nazareth, Henry IV, Weir of Hermiston, and Sir John Reith; Television commentator on royal and state occasions, including silver jubilee celebrations, two royal weddings, 10 state funerals, Queen's birthday parade and annual Cenotaph service (30 years), D-Day remembrance service and VE Day 50th anniversary celebrations; commentator, Edinburgh Military Tattoo, since 1966; Hon. doctorate, Heriot-Watt University; FRSAMD.

Fletcher, Sheriff Michael John, LLB. Sheriff of South Strathclyde Dumfries & Galloway at Dumfries, since 1994; b. 5.12.45, Dundee; m., Kathryn Mary; 2 s. Educ. High School of Dundee; St. Andrews University. Solicitor, 1968-94. Recreations: golf; gardening.

Fletcher, Professor Roger, MA, PhD, FIMA, FRSE. Professor of Optimization, Department of Mathematics and Computer Science, Dundee University, since 1984; b. 29.1.39, Huddersfield; m., Mary Marjorie Taylor; 2 d. Educ. Huddersfield College; Cambridge University; Leeds University. Lecturer, Leeds University, 1963-69; Principal

Research Fellow, then Principal Scientific Officer, AERE Harwell, 1969-73; Senior Research Fellow, then Senior Lecturer, then Reader, Dundee University, 1973-84. Publications: Practical Methods of Optimization, 2nd edition, 1987. numerous others. Recreations: hill-walking; music; bridge. Address: (h.) 43 Errol Road, Invergowrie, Dundee DD2 5BX; T.-01382 562452.

Flett, Ian Stark, CBE (1984), MA, MEd, ABPS; b. 26.1.20, Aberdeen; m., Moyra. Educ. Aberdeen Grammar School; Aberdeen University; Aberdeen College of Education. RAF, Signals and Intelligence Branch, 1940-46; Teacher, Aberdeen, 1947-49; Adviser, Durham, 1949-54; Assistant Education Officer, Lancashire, 1954-59; Deputy, 1959-63; Deputy Education Officer, City of Hull, 1963-66; Member, Dalegacy Institute of Education, Hull University, 1963-66; Director of Education, Fife, 1966-85; General Secretary, Association of Directors of Education in Scotland, 1975-85; President, 1979-80; Adviser to Association of County Councils, 1970-74; Principal Adviser, Convention of Scottish Local Authorities, 1975-84; Member: Consultative Committee on the Curriculum, 1977-87, General Teaching Council, 1976-84; Governor, Craiglockhart College of Education, 1977-83; Chairman: Scottish Association of Educational Management and Administration, 1981-84, Scottish Centre for Tuition of the Disabled, 1980-89, National Association for Gifted Children Scotland, 1985-93. Publication: The Years of Growth 1945-75, 1989. Recreations: music; gardening. Address: (h.) 5 Townsend Place, Kirkcaldy, Fife KY1 1HB; T.-01592 260279.

Flett, James. JP. Honorary Sheriff, Lothians and Borders; Past Chairman, City of Edinburgh Valuation Appeal Committee; b. 26.1.17, Findochty; m., Jean Walker Ross; 1 s. Educ. Findochty Public School; Heriot-Watt University; Royal Military College, Sandhurst. Commissioned Seaforth Highlanders; Chief Official, Royal Burgh of Linlithgow (retired). Governor, West Lothian Educational Trust; former Member, JP Advisory Committee; former Member, Scottish Home Department Interviewing Committee at Edinburgh Prisons; former Member, West Lothian Licensing Board. Recreations: gardening; travel; walking. Address: (h.) Craigenroan, Linlithgow, West Lothian; T.-Linlithgow 842344.

Flint, Professor David, TD, MA, BL, CA. Professor of Accountancy, Glasgow University, 1964-85 (Vice-Principal, 1981-85); b. 24.2.19, Glasgow; m., Dorothy Mary Maclachlan Jardine; 2 s.; 1 d. Educ. High School of Glasgow; Glasgow University. Royal Signals, 1939-46 (Major; mentioned in Despatches); Partner, Mann Judd Gordon & Company, Chartered Accountants, Glasgow, 1951-71; Lecturer (part-time), Glasgow University, 1950-60; Dean, Faculty of Law, 1971-73. Council Member, Scottish Business School, 1971-77; Institute of Chartered Accountants of Scotland: President, 1975-76, Vice-President, 1973-75, Convener, Research Advisory Committee, 1974-75 and 1977-84, Convener, Working Party on Future Policy, 1976-79, Convener, Public Sector Committee, 1987-89, Convener, Taxation Review and Research Sub-Committee, 1960-64; Trustee, Scottish Chartered Accountants Trust for Education, 1981-87; Member: Management Training and Development Committee, Central Training Council, 1966-70, Management and Industrial Relations Committee, Social Science Research Council, 1970-72 and 1978-80, Social Sciences Panel, Scottish Universities Council on Entrance, 1968-72; Chairman, Association of University Teachers of Accounting, 1969; Member, Company Law Committee, Law Society of Scotland, 1976-85; Scottish Economic Society: Treasurer, 1954-62, Vice-President, 1977-88, Hon. Vice-President, since 1988; Member, Commission for Local Authority Accounts in Scotland, 1978-80; President, European Accounting Association, 1983-84. Publication: Philosophy and Principles of Auditing, 1988. Recreation:

golf. Address: (h.) 16 Grampian Avenue, Auchterarder, Perthshire PH3 1NY; T.-01764 663978.

Flockhart, (David) Ross, OBE, BA, BD; b. 20.3.27, Newcastle, NSW, Australia; m., Pamela Ellison Macartney; 3 s.; 1 d.; 1 d. (deceased). Educ. Knox Grammar School, Sydney; Sydney University; Edinburgh University. Royal Australian Engineers, 1945-46; Chaplain to Overseas Students, Edinburgh, 1955-58; Parish Minister (Church of Scotland), Northfield, Aberdeen, 1958-63; Warden, Carberry Tower, Musselburgh, 1963-66; Lecturer and Senior Lecturer, School of Community Studies, Moray House College of Education, 1966-72; Director, Scottish Council for Voluntary Organisations, 1972-91. Member: Scottish Arts Council, 1976-82, Court, Stirling University, since 1989, Council, National Trust for Scotland; former Trustee and Vice-Chairman, Community Development Foundation. Recreations: bee-keeping; sailing. Address: (h.) Longwood, Humbie, East Lothian EH36 5PN; T.-01875 833208.

Florey, Professor Charles du Ve, MD, MPH, FFCM, FRCPE. Professor of Epidemiology and Public Health, Dundee University, since 1983. Instructor, Assistant Professor, Yale University, 1963-69; Member, Scientific Staff, MRC, 1969-71; Senior Lecturer, then Reader, then Professor, St. Thomas's Hospital Medical School, 1971-83; Member, Committee on Data Protection, 1976-78; Chairman, Commissioning Group, Health Technology Assessment. Publications: Introduction to Community Medicine; Methods for Cohort Studies of Chronic Airflow Limitation. Address: (b.) Department of Epidemiology and Public Health, Ninewells Hospital and Medical School, Dundee DD1 9SY; T.-01382 632124.

Flowerdew, Stuart Alan, LLB(Hons), DipLP, NP. Solicitor; Associate, John MacRitchie & Co., SSC, Peterhead, since 1997; Secretary and Treasurer, Faculty of Solicitors in Peterhead and Fraserburgh, since 1993; b. 5.2.67, Kings Lynn; m., Natalie Anne Lamb. Educ. Forres Academy; University of Dundee. Trainee/Assistant, Miller Hendry, Perth, 1989-92; Assistant: Stewart and Watson, Peterhead, 1992-94, Masson & Glennie, Peterhead, 1994-96. Recreation: cricket. Address: (b.) The Townhouse, Broad Street, Peterhead; T.-01779 478877.

Foot, Professor Hugh Corrie, BA, PhD, FBPsS. Professor of Psychology, Strathclyde University, since 1992; b. 7.6.41, Northwood, Middx; m., Daryl M.; 1 s.; 1 d. Educ. Durham University; Queen's College, Dundee. Research Fellow, Dundee University, 1965-68; University of Wales Institute of Science and Technology: Lecturer, 1968-77, Senior Lecturer, 1977-88; Reader, University of Wales College of Cardiff, 1989-91. Recreations: tennis; hill walking. Address: Department of Psychology, Strathclyde University, 40 George Street, Glasgow, G1 1QE; T.-0141-552 4400, Ext. 2580.

Forbes, Professor Charles Douglas, DSc, MD, MB, ChB, FRCP, FRCPGlas, FRCPEdin, FRSA, FRSE. Professor of Medicine, Dundee University, and Honorary Consultant Physician, Tayside Health Board, since 1987; b. 9.10.38, Glasgow; m., Janette MacDonald Robertson; 2 s. Educ. High School of Glasgow; Glasgow University. Assistant Lecturer in Materia Medica, Glasgow University; Lecturer in Medicine, Makerere, Uganda; Registrar in Medicine, Glasgow Royal Infirmary; Reader in Medicine, Glasgow University; Fellow, American Heart Association; Fullbright Fellow; Director, Regional Haemophilia Centre, Glasgow. Recreation: gardening. Address: (h.) East Chattan, 108 Hepburn Gardens, St. Andrews KY16 9LT; T.-01334 472428.

Forbes, David Fraser, LLB (Hons). Regional Officer, Scottish Health Visitors' Association/UNISON; b. 11.4.56, Glasgow; m., Isabel Hamilton; 3 d. Educ. Greenock

Academy; Edinburgh University. Porter, Royal Edinburgh Hospital, and Senior Shop Steward, NUPE, 1978-87; Diploma in Accountancy, Stirling University, 1987-88. Address: (b.) Douglas House, 60 Belford Road, Edinburgh, EH4 3UQ.

Forbes, Very Rev. Graham J.T., MA, BD. Provost, St. Mary's Cathedral, Edinburgh, since 1990; b. 10.6.51, Edinburgh; m., Jane Miller; 3 s. Educ. George Heriot's School, Edinburgh; Aberdeen University; Edinburgh University. Curate, Old St. Paul's, Edinburgh, 1976-82; Provost, St. Ninian's Cathedral, Perth, 1982-90. Chairman: Canongate Youth Project, 1977-83, Lothian Association of Youth Clubs, 1981-88, Scottish Intermediate Treatment Resource Centre, 1982-89, Youth Affairs Group, Scottish Community Education Council, 1982-88; Member: Edinburgh Area Board, Manpower Services Commission, 1980-83, Scottish Community Education Council, 1982-88, Parole Board for Scotland, 1991-95, Scottish Consumer Council, since 1996, General Medical Council, since 1996; Non-Executive Director, Radio Tay, 1987-90; HM (Lay) Inspector of Constabulary, since 1995. Address: 8 Lansdowne Crescent, Edinburgh EH12 5EQ.

Forbes, Sheriff John Stuart, MA, LLB. Sheriff of Tayside, Central and Fife, at Dunfermline, since 1980; b. 31.1.36.

Forbes, 22nd Lord (Nigel Ivan Forbes), KBE (1960), JP, DL. Premier Lord of Scotland; Chairman, Rolawn Ltd., since 1975; b. 19.2.18; m., Hon. Rosemary Katharine Hamilton-Russell; 2 s.; 1 d. Educ. Harrow; Sandhurst. Retired Major, Grenadier Guards; Representative Peer of Scotland, 1955-63; Minister of State, Scottish Office, 1958-59. Member: Scottish Committee, Nature Conservancy, 1961-67, Aberdeen and District Milk Marketing Board, 1962-72, Sports Council for Scotland, 1966-71; Chairman, River Don District Board, 1962-73; President: Royal Highland and Agricultural Society of Scotland, 1958-59, Scottish Scout Association, 1970-88; Chairman, Scottish Branch, National Playing Fields Association, 1965-80; Deputy Chairman, Tennant Caledonian Breweries Ltd., 1964-74. Address: (h.) Balforbes, Alford, Aberdeenshire AB33 8DR; T.-019755 62516.

Ford, Gordon J.W., BA, DipEd. Headmaster, Broughton High School, since 1993;' b. 1.5.52, Inverkeithing; m., Audrey; 1 s.; 2 d. Educ. Kirkcaldy High School; Knox Academy; Stirling University. Teacher of History, Modern Studies, 1974-87; Assistant Headteacher, Greenhall High School, 1987-89; Depute Headteacher: Ainslie Park High School, 1989-91, Armadale Academy, 1991-93. Publication: Timetabling Explained. Recreations: coaching rugby; tennis; music; tai chi. Address: (b.) Broughton High School, Carrington Road, Edinburgh EH4 1EG; T.-0131-332 7805.

Ford, Professor Ian, BSc, PhD. Professor of Statistics and Director, Robertson Centre for Biostatistics, Glasgow University, since 1991; b. 4.2.51, Glasgow; m., Carole Louise Ford; 1 s. Educ. Hamilton Academy; Glasgow University. Visiting Lecturer, University of Wisconsin, Madison, 1976-77; Lecturer, then Senior Lecturer, Reader and Personal Professor, Glasgow University, since 1977. Publications: 60 papers. Recreations: gardening; travel. Address: (b.) Robertson Centre for Biostatistics, Boyd Orr Building, Glasgow University, Glasgow; T.-0141-330 4744.

Ford, James Allan, CB, MC. Author; b. 10.6.20, Auchtermuchty; m., Isobel Dunnett; 1 s.; 1 d. Educ. Royal High School, Edinburgh; Edinburgh University. Employment Clerk, Ministry of Labour, 1938-39; Executive Officer, Inland Revenue, 1939-40; Captain, The Royal Scots, 1940-46 (POW, Far East, 1941-45); Executive Officer, Inland Revenue, 1946-47; Department of Agriculture for Scotland, 1947-66 (Assistant Secretary,

1958); Registrar General for Scotland, 1966-69; Under Secretary, Scottish Office, 1969-79. Trustee, National Library of Scotland, 1981-91. Publications (novels): The Brave White Flag, 1961; Season of Escape, 1963; A Statue for a Public Place, 1965; A Judge of Men, 1968; The Mouth of Truth, 1972. Recreation: gardening. Address: (h.) 6 Hillpark Court, Edinburgh EH4 7BE; T.-0131 336 5398.

Ford, James Angus, OBE, MB, ChB, FRCPEdin, FRCPGlas, FRCP (Lond), FRCPCH, DCH. Consultant Paediatrician, since 1975; Chairman: Scottish Joint Consultants Committee, National Medical Advisory Committee; b. 5.11.43, Arbroath; m., Dr. Veronica T. Reid. Educ. Kelvinside Academy; Glasgow University. House appointments: Glasgow Royal, Southern General, Stobhill, Belvidere; Registrar/Senior Registrar, Stobhill; Consultant appointments: Rutherglen Maternity Hospital, Royal Hospital for Sick Children, Glasgow; Territorial Army: six years, 6/7th Bn., Cameronians (Scottish Rifles), Captain; BMA: former Chairman, Scottish Council, Chairman, Hospital Junior Staff Committee (Scotland), Deputy Chairman, HJSC (UK), Member of Council (Scottish and UK), Member, Joint Consultants Committee (Scottish and UK). Recreation: gardening. Address: (h.) 20 Ralston Road, Bearsden, Glasgow; T.-0141-942 4273.

Ford, John Noel Patrick, CStJ, FInstD. Director of Administration and Finance, Scottish Civic Trust, since 1993; Regional Chairman, Glasgow, Princes Scottish Youth Business Trust, since 1993; Chairman, Glasgow Committee, Order of St. John, since 1993; Trustee, New Lanark Conservation Trust, since 1994; b. 18.12.35, Surbiton; m., Roslyn Madeleine Penfold; 2 s.; 2 d. Educ. Tiffin School, Kingston on Thames. Retired, 1992, as Chairman, Scotland and Northern Ireland, and Marketing Director, OCS Group Ltd. Deacon, Incorporation of Masons of Glasgow, 1985-86; Deacon Convener, Trades House of Glasgow, 1991-92; Governor, Hutchesons' Educational Trust, since 1986; General Commissioner of Inland Revenue, Glasgow North. Recreations: golf and sport in general; gardening. Address: (b.) 42 Miller Street, Glasgow G1 1DT; T.-0141 221 1466.

Ford, Margaret. Chairman, Lothian Health Board. Address: (b.) 148 The Pleasance, Edinburgh EH8 9RS.

Forrest, Professor Sir (Andrew) Patrick (McEwen), Kt (1986), BSc, MD, ChM, FRCS, FRCSEdin, FRCSGlas, DSc (Hon), LLD (Hon), FACS (Hon), FRACS (Hon), FRCSCan (Hon), FRCR (Hon), FIBiol, FRSE. Professor Emeritus, Edinburgh University; b. 25.3.23, Mount Vernon, Lanarkshire; m., 1. Margaret Beryl Hall (deceased); 1s.; 1d.; 2. Margaret Anne Steward; 1 d. Educ. Dundee High School; St. Andrews University. House Surgeon, Dundee Royal Infirmary; Surgeon Lieutenant, RNVR; Mayo Foundation Fellow; Lecturer and Senior Lecturer, Glasgow University; Professor of Surgery, Welsh National School of Medicine; Regius Professor of Clinical Surgery, Edinburgh University; Visiting Scientist, National Cancer Institute, USA; Associate Dean of Clinical Studies, International Medical College, Malaysia; Chief Scientist (part-time), Scottish Home and Health Department, 1981-87; Chairman, Working Group, Breast Cancer Screening, 1985-86; President: Surgical Research Society, 1974-76, Association of Surgeons of Great Britain and Ireland, 1988-89; Lister Medal, Royal College of Surgeons of England, 1987; Member, Kirk Session, St. Giles Cathedral. Publications: Prognostic Factors in Breast Cancer (Co-author), 1968; Principles and Practice of Surgery (Co-author), 1985; Breast Cancer: the decision to screen, 1990. Recreations: sailing; golf. Address: (h.) 19 St. Thomas Road, Edinburgh EH9 2LR; T.-0131-667 3203.

Forrest, Peter, ATI. Managing Director, Dawson International PLC, since 1995, Main Board Director, since 1994; Managing Director, Todd & Duncan Ltd., Kinross,

since 1991; b. 2.5.38, Dewsbury; m., Evelyn Margaret; 3 s. Educ. Batley Grammar School; Huddersfield College of Textiles. Yorkshire textile industry, 1959-70; founded and become Managing Director, Dundee Fabrics Ltd., 1971-76; Dundee Fabrics taken over, 1976, continuing as MD until 1980, also joining board of Courtaulds Northern Weaving Division; Operations Director, Legler Industria Tessile, Italy, 1980-91. Recreations: sailing; walking; classical music. Address: (h.) Whinfield House, Kinross KY13 7AU.

Forrest, Robert Jack, OBE, FRAgS, DL. Director: Royal Highland & Agricultural Society of Scotland, since 1979 (Hon. Treasurer, 1985-88, Chairman, 1989-90, Hon. Secretary since 1991), Scottish Agricultural College, since 1996; b. 4.1.39, Duns; m., Jennifer McCreath; 2 s.; 1 d. Educ. Loretto School; East of Scotland College of Agriculture. Director, Robert Forrest Ltd. (Farmers), since 1960, Chairman since 1986; President, British Simmental Cattle Society, 1983-84; President, Scottish Agricultural Arbiters Association, 1993-94; Vice Chairman, Scottish Agricultural Benevolent Institution, 1991; Council Member, Royal Agricultural Society of the Commonwealth; Director, Scottish Borders Enterprise, since 1994; Elder, Bonkyl Church. Address: (h.) Preston, Duns, Berwickshire TD11 3TQ; T.-01361 882826.

Forrester, Rev. Professor Duncan Baillie, MA (Hons), BD, DPhil. Dean, Faculty of Divinity, New College, Edinburgh, since 1996 (Principal, 1986-96) and Professor of Christian Ethics and Practical Theology, since 1978; Church of Scotland Minister; b. 10.11.33, Edinburgh; m., Rev. Margaret McDonald; 1 s.; 1 d. Educ. Madras College, St. Andrews; St. Andrews University; Chicago University; Edinburgh University. Part-time Assistant in Politics, Edinburgh University, 1957-58; Assistant Minister, Hillside Church, Edinburgh, and Leader of St. James Mission, 1960-61; as Church of Scotland Missionary, Lecturer and then Professor of Politics, Madras Christian College, Tambaram, South India, 1962-70; ordained Presbyter, Church of South India, 1962; part-time Lecturer in Politics, Edinburgh University, 1966-67; Chaplain and Lecturer in Politics, Sussex University. Member, WCC Faith and Order Commission, 1983-96; President: Society for Study of Theology, 1991-93, Society for Study of Christian Ethics, 1991-94. Publications: Caste & Christianity, 1980; Encounter with God (Co-author), 1983; Studies in the History of Worship in Scotland (Co-Editor), 1984; Christianity and the Future of Welfare, 1985; Theology and Politics, 1988; Just Sharing (Co-author), 1988; Beliefs, Values and Policies, 1989; Worship Now Book II (Co-editor), 1989; Theology and Practice (Editor), 1990; The True Church and Morality, 1997; Christian Justice and Public Policy, 1997. Recreations: hill-walking; reading; listening to music. Address: (h.) 25 Kingsburgh Road, Edinburgh, EH12 6DZ; T.-0131-337 5646.

Forrester, Frederick Lindsay, MA (Hons), DipEd, FEIS. Depute General Secretary, Educational Institute of Scotland, since 1992; b. 10.2.35, Glasgow; 1 s.; 1 d. Educ. Victoria Drive Senior Secondary School, Glasgow; Glasgow University; Jordanhill College of Education. Teacher of English, Glasgow secondary schools, 1962-64; Teacher of English and General Studies, Coatbridge Technical College, 1964-67; Assistant Secretary, Educational Institute of Scotland, 1967-75, Organising Secretary, 1975-92. Recreations:walking; cycling; swimming; foreign travel. Address: (h.) 2/6 East Farm of Gilmerton, Edinburgh EH17 8TQ; T.-0131 672 1638.

Forrester, Ian Stewart, QC, MA, LLB, MCL. Honorary Visiting Professor in European Law, Glasgow University, since 1991; Member, European Advisory Board, Tulane University Law School, since 1992; b. 13.1.45, Glasgow; m., Sandra Anne Therese Keegan; 2 s. Educ. Kelvinside Academy, Glasgow; Glasgow University; Tulane University of Louisiana. Admitted to Faculty of Advocates,

1972; admitted to Bar of State of NY, 1977; called to Bar, Middle Temple, 1996. Maclay, Murray & Spens, 1968-69; Davis Polk & Wardwell, 1969-72; Cleary Gottlieb Steen & Hamilton, 1972-81; established independent chambers, Brussels, 1981; Co-Founder, Forrester & Norall, 1981 (Forrester Norrall & Sutton, 1989), practising before European Commission and Courts. Chairman: British Conservative Association, Belgium, 1982-86, European Trade Law Association, since 1989 ; Member, European Committee of British Invisibles; Elder, St. Andrew's Church of Scotland, Brussels. Recreations: politics; wine; cooking; restoring old houses. Address: Advocates' Library, Parliament House, Edinburgh EH1 1RF.

Forrester, Professor John V., MD (Hons), FRCS(Ed), FRCOphth, FRCS(G). Cockburn Professor of Ophthalmology, since 1984; Editor, British Journal of Ophthalmology, since 1992; b. 11.9.46, Glasgow; m., Anne Gray; 2 s.; 2 d. Educ. St. Aloysius College, Glasgow; Glasgow University. Various hospital appointments, Glasgow, 1971-78; MRC Travelling Fellow, Columbia University, New York, 1976-77; Consultant Ophthalmologist, Southern General Hospital, 1979-83; Spinoza Professor, University of Amsterdam, 1997. Recreation: family. Address: (b.) Department of Ophthalmology, Aberdeen University, Aberdeen AB9 2ZD; T.-01224 681818.

Forrester, Rev. Margaret Rae, MA, BD. Minister, St. Michael's, Edinburgh, since 1980; b. 23.11.37, Edinburgh; m., Duncan B. Forrester; 1 s.; 1 d. Educ. George Watson's Ladies' College; Edinburgh University and New College. Assistant Pastor, Madras; Minister, Telscombe Cliffs URC, Sussex; Assistant Minister, St. George's West, Edinburgh; Chaplain, Napier College, Edinburgh. Convener, Board of World Mission and Unity, Church of Scotland, 1992-96. Recreation: gardening. Address: 25 Kingsburgh Road, Edinburgh EH12 6DZ; T.-0131-337 5646.

Forsyth of That Ilk, Alistair Charles William, JP, KHS, FSCA, FSA Scot, FInstPet, CStJ. Baron of Ethie; Chief of the Name and Clan of Forsyth; b. 7.12.29; m., Ann Hughes; 4 s. Educ. St. Paul's School; Queen Mary College, London. Company Director; CStJ, 1982; KHS, 1992; Freeman of the City of London; Liveryman of the Scriveners Company. Recreations: Scottish antiquities. Address: (h.) Ethie Castle, by Arbroath, Angus DD11 5SP.

Forsyth, Bill. Film Director and Script Writer; b. 1947, Glasgow. Films include: Gregory's Girl, 1981, Local Hero, 1983, Comfort and Joy, 1984, Housekeeping, 1988, Breaking In, 1990, Being Human, 1993. BAFTA Awards: Best Screenplay, 1982, Best Director, 1983.

Forsyth, Janice, MA (Hons). Broadcaster; b. Glasgow. Educ. Glasgow High School for Girls; Glasgow University. Presenter, Janice Forsyth Show, The Usual Suspects, The Learning Curve (Radio Scotland); Live at the Fringe (Radio 5); TV includes: Filmnight (C4), Don't Look Down, NB and Festival Cinema (all Scottish); Columnist, Scotsman/Scotland on Sunday. Board Member, Giant Productions. Recreations: cinema; travel; theatre.

Forsyth, Kathleen, MA. National Convener, Church of Scotland Guild, since 1997; b. 19.12.38, Edinburgh. Educ. Mary Erskine School for Girls; Edinburgh University; Moray House College of Education (Diploma in Religious Education). Teacher of Primary and Religious Education, St. Denis School, 1960-71; Deputy Head, Letham Primary, Livingstone, 1971-74; Head Teacher: Hillwood Primary, Ratho Station, 1974-78, Broughton Primary, Edinburgh, 1978-93. Past Chairman: Association of Christian Teachers, Edinburgh District Council of Scripture Union. Recreations: music; tapestry; reading. Address: (h.) 10 Meggetland Terrace, Edinburgh EH14 1AR; T.-0131-443 2083.

Forsyth, Rt. Hon. Sir Michael (Bruce), PC, Kt, MA. MP (Conservative), Stirling, 1983-97; Secretary of State for Scotland, 1995-97; Director, Robert Fleming & Co. Ltd.; b. 16.10.54, Montrose; m., Susan Jane; 1 s.; 2 d. Educ. Arbroath High School; St. Andrews University. National Chairman, Federation of Conservative Students, 1976; Member, Westminster City Council, 1978-83; Member, Select Committee on Scottish Affairs; Parliamentary Private Secretary to the Foreign Secretary, 1986-87; Chairman, Scottish Conservative Party, 1989-90; Parliamentary Under Secretary of State and Minister of State, Scottish Office, 1987-92; Minister of State, Department of Employment, 1992-94; Minister of State, Home Office, 1994-95. Recreations: mountaineering; astronomy; gardening. Address: (h.) Na Laban, Aberfoyle, Stirling FK8 3TJ.

Forsyth, Roderick Hugh (Roddy). Journalist; b. 22.9.53, Lennoxtown; m., Marian Charlotte Reilly; 2 d. Educ. Allan Glen's School, Glasgow. Journalist, D.C. Thomson & Co., 1972-74; Scottish Daily News, 1975; Editor, Carnoustie Times, 1976-77; Editor, What's On in Glasgow, 1978-79; Editor, Clyde Guide, 1979-80; Journalist, Glasgow Herald, 1980-81; Sunday Standard, 1982-83; freelance, since 1983; Scottish Football Correspondent: The Times, 1988-93, Daily and Sunday Telegraph, since 1993, BBC Radio Sport, since 1983, RTE Ireland, since 1988, Ireland on Sunday, since 1996. Publications: The Only Game, 1990; Fields of Green, 1996; Blue and True, 1996.

Forteviot, 4th Baron (John James Evelyn Dewar). Director, John Dewar & Sons Ltd., since 1965; Member, Queen's Bodyguard for Scotland (Royal Company of Archers); b. 5.4.38. Educ. Eton. Black Watch (RHR), 1956-58. Address: (h.) Aberdalgie House, Perth.

Forty, Professor Arthur John, CBE, BSc, PhD, DSc, LLD, DUniv, FRSE. Principal and Vice-Chancellor, Stirling University, 1986-94; b. 4.11.28, Shrivenham; m., Alicia Blanche Hart Gough; 1 s. Educ. Headlands School, Swindon; Bristol University. RAF, 1953-56; Senior Scientist, Tube Investments Ltd., 1956-58; Lecturer, Bristol University, 1958-64; founding Professor of Physics, Warwick University, 1964-86; Pro-Vice-Chancellor, Warwick Univ., 1970-86; Member, Physics and Materials Science Committees, SERC, 1970-74; Member: UGC, 1982-86 (Vice-Chairman, 1985-86), Computer Board, Universities and Research Councils, 1982-85 (Chairman, 1988-91); Chairman, Committee of Scottish University Principals, 1990-92; Member, British Library Board, 1987-94; Chairman, Information Systems Committee, UFC, 1991-92; Hon. Fellow and Chairman, EPCC, Edinburgh University, 1994-97; Member, Board of Trustees, National Library of Scotland, since 1995; author of "Forty Report" on future facilities for advanced research computing. Recreations: dinghy sailing; gardening. Address: (h.) Port Mor, St. Fillans, Perthshire PH6 2NF.

Foster, Alan, MA, MEd, MBA, PhD, MICFM, FRSA. Chief Executive, Scottish Council on Alcohol, since 1997; b. 2.4.50, St. Andrews; m., Elizabeth Jessie Margaret Denham; 3 d. Educ. Kirkcaldy High School; Lancaster Royal Grammar School; Edinburgh, Dundee and Glasgow Universities. Lothian Regional Council Department of Education, 1979-83; Save the Children Fund, 1983-89; Chief Executive, Glasgow and West of Scotland Society for the Blind, 1989-97. Recreations: sailing; hill-walking; cricket; opera; running (slowly). Address: (b.) 166 Buchanan Street, Glasgow G1 2NH.

Foster, Ann, MA. Director, Scottish Consumer Council, since 1991; Non-executive Director, Scottish Ambulance Service NHS Trust; b. 28.9.49, St. Andrews. Educ. Hutchesons' Girls' Grammar School, Glasgow; St. Andrews University; Reading University. Lecturer, ILEA, 1972-78; Consultant, National Consumer Council, 1978-91; Member: National Disability Council, Committee on

Medical Aspects of Food Policy, Scottish Diet Action Group, Advisory Group on Sustainable Development, Council of Rail Regulator. Recreations: skiing; theatre; opera. Address: (b.) Royal Exchange House, 100 Queen Street, Glasgow G1 3DN; T.-0141-226 5261.

Foster, Elizabeth. BA, MSc, MBA. Director, Family Mediation Scotland, since 1997; b. Glasgow; 1 d. Educ. Albert Secondary School, Glasgow; Strathclyde University; Glasgow University. Research Officer, National Children's Bureau, 1979-83; Projects Manager, Aberlour Child Care Trust, 1983-86; Assistant Divisional Director, Save the Children, 1986-96. Recreations: walking; skiing; sailing; reading; music; films. Address: (b.) 127 Rose Street South Lane, Edinburgh EH2 4BB; T.-0131-220 1610.

Foster, James Richard Charles, pce, jsdc, RN (Retd). General Manager, WS Society, since 1993; b. 7.11.48, Arbroath; m., Kathryn Taylor; 1 s.; 2 d. Educ. George Heriot's School; Hampton School; Britannia Royal Naval College. Former naval officer, submariner and sometime commander of a Polaris submarine. Recreations: hill-walking (Munros); sailing. Address: (b.) The Signet Library, Parliament Square, Edinburgh EH1 1RF; T.-0131-225 4923.

Foster, John, CBE, FRICS, FRTPI, RIBA, ARIAS, FRSA. President, Ramblers Association (Scotland); b. 13.8.20, Glasgow; m., Daphne Househam. Educ. Whitehill School, Glasgow; Royal Technical College, Glasgow. Surveyor with private firm in Glasgow, 1937; Air Ministry during War; Assistant Planning Officer: Kirkcudbright County Council, 1945-47, Holland Joint Planning Committee, Lincolnshire, 1947-48; Deputy County Planning Officer, Holland County Council, 1948-52; Deputy Planning Officer, Peak Park Planning Board, 1952-54; Director: Peak District National Park Board, 1954-68, Countryside Commission for Scotland, 1968-85. Honorary Vice-President, Countrywide Holidays Association; Honorary Fellow, Royal Scottish Geographical Society; Member, Executive Committee, Scottish Council for National Parks; Honorary Member and Past Vice Chairman, Commission on National Parks and Protected Areas, World Conservation Union; Hon. Member, European Federation of Nature and National Parks; Vice-Chairman, Heritage Unit Advisory Board, Robert Gordon University, Aberdeen; Life Member, National Trust for Scotland; George Waterston Memorial Award, 1991. Recreations: walking; swimming; photography; philately; reading; travel. Address: (h.) Birchover, Ferntower Road, Crieff PH7 3DH; T.-01764 652336.

Foster, Professor John Odell, MA, PhD. Professor of Applied Social Studies, Paisley University, since 1981; b. 21.10.40, Hertford; m., Renee Prendergast; 1 d. Educ. Guildford Grammar School; St. Catherine's College, Cambridge. Postdoctoral Research Fellow, St. Catherine's College, Cambridge, 1965-68; Lecturer in Politics, Strathclyde University, 1966-81. Secretary, Scottish Committee, Communist Party of Britain, since 1988. Publications: Class Struggle and the Industrial Revolution, 1974; Politics of the UCS Work-In, 1986; Track Record: the Caterpillar Occupation, 1988; Paying for the Piper (Co-author), 1996. Recreation: hill-walking. Address: (h.) 845 Govan Road, Glasgow G51.

Foulds, Emeritus Professor Wallace Stewart, CBE, MD, ChM, FRCS, FRCSGlas, DO, Hon. FRCOphth, Hon. DSc (Strathclyde), Hon. FRACO, Hon. FCMSA. Emeritus Professor of Ophthalmology, Glasgow University; Visiting Professor, National University of Singapore and Singapore National Eye Centre; b. 26.4.24, London; m., Margaret Holmes Walls; 1 s.; 2 d. Educ. George Watson's Boys College, Edinburgh; Paisley Grammar School; Glasgow University. RAF Medical Branch, 1946-49; training posts, Moorfields Eye Hospital, London, 1952-54; Research

Fellow, Institute of Ophthalmology, London University, and Senior Registrar, University College Hospital, London, 1954-58; Consultant Ophthalmologist, Addenbrookes Hospital, Cambridge, 1958-64; Tennent Professor, Glasgow University, 1964-89; Honorary Lecturer, Cambridge University and Research Fellow, London University, 1958-64; Past President: Ophthalmological Society of UK, Faculty of Ophthalmologists; Past Chairman, Association for Eye Research; Past President, Royal College of Ophthalmologists. Recreations: sailing; diving; DIY; natural history. Address: Kinnoul Place, 68 Downanside Road, Glasgow G12 9DL; T.-0141-334 2463.

Foulis, Alan Keith, BSc, MD, MRCPath, FRCP(Ed). Consultant Pathologist, Royal Infirmary, Glasgow, since 1983; b. 25.5.50, Glasgow; m., Anne Don Martin; 1 s.; 1 d. Educ. Glasgow Academy; Glasgow University. Trained in pathology, Western Infirmary, Glasgow, following brief flirtation with surgery at Aberdeen Royal Infirmary; C.L. Oakley Lecturer, Pathological Society, Oxford, 1987; Bellahouston Medal, Glasgow University, 1987; R.D. Lawrence Lecturer, British Diabetic Association, Manchester, 1989. Publications: research papers on diseases of the pancreas. Recreations: choral and Leider singing; walking; cycling; arctophilia; natural history. Address: (h.) 32 Tannoch Drive, Milngavie, Glasgow; T.-0141-956 3092.

Foulkes, George, JP, BSc. Parliamentary Under-Secretary of State, Department for International Development; MP (Labour and Co-operative), Carrick, Cumnock and Doon Valley, since 1979; b. 21.1.42, Oswestry; m., Elizabeth Anna; 2 s.; 1 d. Educ. Keith Grammar School; Haberdashers' Aske's School; Edinburgh University. Opposition Spokesman on Foreign Affairs, 1984-92, Defence, 1992-93, Overseas Development, 1994-97. President, Scottish Union of Students, 1964-66; Director: European League for Economic Co-operation, 1967-68, Enterprise Youth, 1968-73, Age Concern Scotland, 1973-79; Chairman: Lothian Region Education Committee, 1974-79, Education Committee, COSLA, 1975-79; Rector's Assessor, Edinburgh University, 1968-71; Treasurer, Parliamentarians for Global Action. Recreations: boating; watching football (Heart of Midlothian and Ayr United). Address: (h.) 18A Ewenfield Road, Ayr KA7 2QB; T.-01292 265776.

Foulner, Joan, BA(Hons), Dip. Teaching, Dip. SLD (RSA). English/History/Remedial Teacher, Dunedin School Co-operative Ltd., since 1997; b. 15.7.41, Edinburgh; m., Norman; 2 s.; 1 d. Educ. Boroughmuir Senior Secondary; Open University; Callendar Park College. Clerk, Inland Revenue, 1957-62; Teacher, Edinburgh City and Lothian Region, 1966-77. Advisor, Duke of Edinburgh's Award for City of Edinburgh Guides; Judge, Scottish Gymnastics. Recreations: yoga; coaching gymnastics. Address: (b.) Dunedin School Co-operative Ltd., Miller Hall, 5 Gilmerton Road, Edinburgh EH16 5TY; T.-0131-664 1328.

Fourman, Professor Michael Paul, BSc, MSc, DPhil. Professor of Computer Systems, Edinburgh University, since 1988; b. 12.9.50, Oxford; m., Jennifer Robin Head; 2 s.; 1 d. Educ. Allerton Grange, Leeds; Bristol University; Oxford University. Junior Research Fellow, Wolfson College, Oxford, 1974-78; J.F. Ritt Assistant Professor of Mathematics, Columbia University NY, 1976-82; Department of Electrical & Electronic Engineering, Brunel University: Research Fellow, 1983-86, Hirst Reader in Integrated Circuit Design, 1986, Professor of Formal Systems, 1986-88. Recreations: cooking; sailing. Address: (b.) Computer Science Department, JCMB, King's Buildings, Edinburgh EH9 3JZ; T.-0131-650 5197.

Fowkes, Professor Francis Gerald Reid, MB, ChB, PhD, FRCPE, FFPHM. Professor of Epidemiology, Edinburgh University, since 1994; Director, Wolfson Unit for Prevention of Peripheral Vascular Diseases, since 1989;

Hon. Consultant Public Health Medicine, since 1985; b. 9.5.46, Falkirk; 1 s.; 1 d. Educ. George Watson's College, Edinburgh; Edinburgh University. Senior Lecturer, University of Wales, 1980-85; Reader/Professor, Edinburgh University, since 1985. Address: (b.) Department of Public Health Sciences, Edinburgh University, Teviot Place, Edinburgh EH8 9AG; T.-0131-650 3220.

Fowler, Agnes Isobel, BSc, FRSAMD. Director of Finance and Administration, Royal Scottish Academy of Music and Drama; b. 13.2.42, Glasgow; m., William M. Fowler; 2 s.; 1 d. Educ. Jordanhill College School; Glasgow University. Governor, Associated Board, Royal Schools of Music. Recreations: hill-walking; swimming; gardening; Church. Address: (h.) Hillside, 7 Main Street, Drymen, Glasgow; T.-01360 660009.

Fowlie, Hector Chalmers, OBE, MB, ChB, FRCPEdin, FRCPsych, DPM. Retired Consultant Psychiatrist; Member of Court, Abertay University, Dundee; b. 21.6.29, Dundee; m., Christina N.M. Walker; 2 s.; 1 d. Educ. Harris Academy, Dundee; St. Andrews University. House Officer, Maryfield Hospital, Dundee, and Perth Royal Infirmary; Registrar, Dundee Royal Mental Hospital; Lecturer, Department of Psychiatry, Medical School, Dundee University; Consultant Psychiatrist and Deputy Physician Superintendent, Gartnavel Royal Hospital, Glasgow; Physician Superintendent, Royal Dundee Liff and Strathmartine Hospitals; Consultant Psychiatrist, Tayside Health Board. Vice-Chairman, Mental Welfare Commission for Scotland, 1984-89; sometime Vice-Chairman, Parole Board for Scotland; Member, Tayside Health Board; Council of Europe Scholar; Consultant, WHO; Past Chairman: Dundee Association for Mental Health, Dundee Healthcare NHS Trust. Recreations: reading; walking. Address: (h.) 21 Clepington Road, Dundee; T.-01382 456926.

Fox, Andrew John Arthur, MA. General Manager, H. M. Frigate Unicorn, since 1994; b. 1.5.53, Bristol; m., Lyubov Mikhailovna Yampolskaya; 1 s. Educ. Dundee High School; University of Aberdeen. Assistant Collector of Taxes, Dundee and London, 1977-78; Teacher of English, Invergordon Academy, 1979-80; Information Worker, Dundee Association for Social Services, 1985-86; H.M. Frigate Unicorn: Curator, 1987-90, Project Supervisor, 1992-94. Publications: three books of poetry. Recreations: writing; reading; swimming. Address: (b.) H. M. Frigate Unicorn, Victoria Dock, Dundee DD1 3JA; T.-01382 200900.

Fox, Christopher Howard Christian, MRAC, ARICS. Chartered Surveyor and Director (Estates), Scottish Greenbelt Company, since 1996; b. 13.1.41, Whitehaven; m., Caroline Jane Porter; 1 s.; 1 d. Educ. Fettes College, Edinburgh; Royal Agricultural College, Cirencester. Assistant Land Agent: W.H. Cooke & Arkwright, Chartered Surveyors, Hereford, 1963-69, Nature Conservancy Council, Edinburgh, 1969-73; Area Land Agent, North Scotland, Nature Conservancy Council, 1973-79; Senior Land Agent (Scotland), Nature Conservancy Council, 1983-91; Regional Director: South West Scotland, Nature Conservancy Council for Scotland, 1991-92, South West Region, Scottish Natural Heritage, 1992-96. Director, Scottish Agricultural College, Auchincruive, 1991-94; Member, Advisory Committee, Scottish Agricultural College. Recreations: country sports; contemporary Scottish painters; music. Address: (h.) 3 Brandon Terrace, Edinburgh EH3 5EA; T.-0131-557 4481.

Fox, Professor Keith Alexander Arthur, BSc (Hons), MB, ChB, FRCP. Duke of Edinburgh Professor of Cardiology, Edinburgh University, since 1989; Honorary Consultant Cardiologist, Royal Infirmary of Edinburgh; b. 27.8.49, Salisbury, Rhodesia; m., Aileen E.M.; 1 s.; 1 d. Educ. Falcon College; Edinburgh University. Assistant

Professor of Medicine, Washington University School of Medicine, 1980-85; Senior Lecturer in Cardiology and Consultant Cardiologist, University Hospital of Wales College of Medicine, 1985-89. Address: (b.) Department of Cardiology, Royal Infirmary of Edinburgh, Lauriston Place, Edinburgh EH3 9YW; T.-0131 536 2743.

Fraile, Emeritus Professor Medardo, PhD. Writer; Emeritus Professor in Spanish, Strathclyde University, since 1985; b. 21.3.25, Madrid; m., Janet H. Gallagher; 1 d. Educ. Madrid University. Teacher of Spanish language and literature, Ramiro de Maeztu Secondary School, Madrid, 1956-64; Assistant in Spanish, Southampton University, 1964-67; Strathclyde University: Assistant Lecturer in Spanish, 1967-68, Lecturer, 1968-79, Reader, 1979-83, Personal Professor, 1983-85. Travelling Scholarship for authors, 1954; Premio Sesamo for short story writing, 1956; literary grant, Juan March Foundation, 1960; Book of the Year award, 1965; La Estafeta Literaria Prize for short stories, 1970; Hucha de Oro Prize for short stories, 1971; research grant, Carnegie Trust, 1975; Ibanez Fantoni Prize for journalism, 1988. Publications: El Weir de Hermiston by R.L. Stevenson (Translator), 1995; short stories translated into eight languages (Complete Short Stories, Madrid, 1991); five books for children; a novel; books of essays and literary criticism; contributor to periodicals in many countries. Recreations: swimming; walking. Address: (h.) 24 Etive Crescent, Bishopbriggs, Glasgow G64 1ES; T.-0141-772 4421.

Frame, John Neil Munro, LLB. Director, Stocktrade; Director, The Caledonian Foundation; Trustee, The Sportsman's Charity; b. 8.10.46, Edinburgh; m., Susan Macmillan; 2 s.; 2 d. Educ. Edinburgh University. Recreations: jogging slowly downhill; golfing erratically; reading profusely; hill-walking with friends who have a compass. Address: 30 Murrayfield Road, Edinburgh EH12 6ER; T.-0131-346 0077.

Frame, Roger Campbell Crosbie, CA. Secretary, Royal Scottish Society of Painters in Water Colours, since 1986; Secretary, Glasgow Eastern Merchants and Tradesmen's Society, since 1983; Treasurer, Glasgow Group of Artists, 1983-88; b. 7.6.49, Glasgow; m., Angela M. Evaristi; 2 s.; 1 d. Educ. Glasgow Academy. Qualified CA, 1973; formed Frame & Co., CA, 1976. Deacon, Incorporation of Coopers of Glasgow, 1985-86. Recreations: clay pigeon shooting; art. Address: (b.) 29 Waterloo Street, Glasgow G2 6BZ; T.-0141-226 3838.

France, Anthony James, MA, MB, BChir, FRCP. Consultant Physician, Dundee Teaching Hospitals, since 1989; Honorary Senior Lecturer, Dundee University, since 1989; b. 5.4.54, London; m., Rosemary; 1 s.; 2 d. Educ. Perse School, Cambridge; Magdalene College, Cambridge; St. Thomas' Hospital, London. Qualified 1978; specialises in management of HIV infection, communicable diseases and respiratory medicine. Recreations: photography; gardening; decorating an old house. Address: (b.) King's Cross Hospital, Clepington Road, Dundee DD3 8EA; T.-01382 660111.

France, Professor Peter, MA, PhD, FBA. Professor of French, Edinburgh University, 1980-90, Endowment Fellow, since 1990; b. 19.10.35, Londonderry; m., Sian Reynolds; 3 d. Educ. Bradford Grammar School; Magdalen College, Oxford. Fellow, Magdalen College, Oxford, 1960-63; Lecturer, then Reader in French, Sussex University, 1963-80; French Editor, Modern Language Review, 1979-85; President: British Comparative Literature Association, since 1992, International Society for the History of Rhetoric, 1993-95. Publications: Racine's Rhetoric, 1965; Rhetoric and Truth in France, 1972; Poets of Modern Russia, 1982; Diderot, 1982; Rousseau: Confessions, 1987; Politeness and its Discontents, 1992; New Oxford Companion to Literature in French, 1995; Translator: An

Anthology of Chuvash Poetry, 1991, Gennady Aygi: Selected Poems, 1997. Address: (b.) 60 George Square, Edinburgh EH8 9JU; T.-0131-650 8417.

Francis, Professor Arthur, BSc, ACGI, FRSA. Professor of Corporate Strategy, Glasgow University, since 1992; b. 16.12.44, Leamington Spa; m., Janice Mary; 1 s.; 2 d. Educ. Warwick School; Imperial College, London. Research Officer, Imperial College, 1967-73; Nuffield College, Oxford, 1973-76; Lecturer/Senior Lecturer, Imperial College, 1976-92, Head, Business Policy Group, 1986-92. Member, Council, British Academy of Management; Fellow, Royal Society of Arts. Publications: six books; numerous journal articles. Recreations: music; literature. Address: (b.) 59 Southpark Avenue, Glasgow G12 8LF; T.-0141-330 4130.

Francis, David, MA. Artistic Director, Edinburgh Folk Festival, since 1996; Traditional Music Co-ordinator, Scottish Arts Council, since 1997; Folk Musician, since 1983; Dance Teacher; b. 14.9.54, Dumfries; m., Mairi Campbell. Educ. Dumfries Academy; University of Aberdeen. Former Librarian, Printer, Publisher, Radio Researcher and Presenter; albums, with The Cast: The Winnowing, 1993; Colours of Lichen, 1996; Founder Member, Scottish Traditions of Dance Trust. Recreations: food; conversation; listening to anything except folk music. Address: 34 Prince Regent Street, Edinburgh EH6 4AT; T.-0131-554 3092.

Francis, John Michael, BSc, ARCS, PhD, DIC, FRSGS, FRSE, FRZSS. Senior Policy Adviser, Home Department, Scottish Office, since 1995; b. 1.5.39, London; m., Eileen; 2 d. Educ. Gowerton Grammar School, near Swansea; Imperial College of Science and Technology, London University. CEGB Berkeley Nuclear Laboratories, 1963-70; Director, Society, Religion and Technology Project, Church of Scotland, 1970-74; Senior Research Fellow, Heriot-Watt University, 1974-76; Principal, Scottish Development Department, 1976-81; Assistant Secretary, Scottish Office, 1981-84, and 1992-95; Director – Scotland, Nature Conservancy Council, 1984-91, then Chief Executive, Nature Conservancy Council for Scotland. Consultant, World Council of Churches, 1971-83; Chairman, SRT Project, Church of Scotland, 1979-94; Member: Oil Development Council for Scotland, 1973-76, Advisory Committee for Scotland, Nature Conservancy Council, 1973-76, Council, National Trust for Scotland, 1984-92; Chairman, Edinburgh Forum, 1986-92; Professional Member, World Future Society, Washington DC, since 1992; Member: John Muir Trust, since 1994, British Association for the Advancement of Science; UK Representative, Millennium Project, United Nations University. Publications: Scotland in Turmoil, 1972; Changing Directions, 1973; Facing Up to Nuclear Power, 1976; The Future as an Academic Discipline, 1975; The Future of Scotland, 1977; North Sea Oil and the Environment (Jointly), 1992; contributions to scientific journals. Recreations: theatre; hill-walking; ecumenical travels. Address: (h.) 49 Gilmour Road, Newington, Edinburgh EH16 5NU; T.-0131-667 3996.

Franklin, Ian Maxwell, BSc, MB, ChB, FRCP (Lond, Glasg, Edin), FRCPath, PhD. Professor of Transfusion Medicine, Glasgow University, since 1996; National Medical and Scientific Director, Scottish National Blood Transfusion Service, since 1997; Honorary Consultant, Bone Marrow Transplant Unit, Glasgow Royal Infirmary; b. 6.9.49, London; m., Dr. Anne Christine Bush; 1 s.; 1 d. Educ. Owen's Boys School, Islington; Leeds University; University College London Medical School. MRC Research Training Fellow, University College London Medical School, 1977-80; Consultant Haematologist, Queen Elizabeth Hospital, Birmingham, 1982-92; Director of Haematology, Central Birmingham Health Authority, 1989-91; Director, Glasgow and West of Scotland Blood

Transfusion Service, 1996-97; Consultant-in-Administrative Charge, Bone Marrow Transplant Unit, Glasgow Royal Infirmary, 1992-97; Co-Editor, Blood Reviews. Scientific Secretary, British Society for Haematology, since 1995; Chairman, Working Party on Relationship Between Blood Banks and Bone Marrow Transplant Units, Council of Europe, 1995-96; author of various papers. Recreations: sailing; cycling; eating and drinking; music. Address: (b.) Department of Medicine, Glasgow University, Royal Infirmary, 10 Alexandra Parade, Glasgow; T.-0141-211 1202.

Fransman, Professor Martin, BA, MA, PhD. Professor of Economics, University of Edinburgh, since 1996; Director, Institute for Japanese-European Technology Studies, since 1988; b. 17.4.48, Johannesburg; m., Tamar Ludwin; 1 s.; 2 d. Educ. University of the Witwatersrand; University of Sussex. Lecturer: University of Swaziland, 1971-77, University of London, 1977-78; University of Edinburgh: Lecturer, 1978-86, Reader, 1987-96. Publications: The Market and Beyond, 1990 (Masayoshi Ohira Prize, 1991); Japan's Computer and Communications Industry, 1995. Recreations: hill-walking; foreign travel; music; cinema. Address: (b.) Institute for Japanese-European Technology Studies, University of Edinburgh, 25 Buccleuch Place, Edinburgh EH8 9LN; T.-0131-650 4060.

Fraser, Alan Alexander, BSc (Hons), MBChB, MRCPsych. Consultant Psychiatrist, Southern General Hospital, Glasgow, since 1987; Honorary Clinical Senior Lecturer in Psychiatry, Glasgow University, since 1988; Visiting Consultant: Langside Priory Hospital, Glasgow Nuffield Hospital, Bon Secours Hospital, Glasgow; b. 17.10.55, Kilbirnie. Educ. Spier's School, Beith; Glasgow University. Address: (h.) 65 Dowanside Road, Glasgow G12 9DL; T.-0141-357 2283.

Fraser, Alan William, BSc, PhD. Rector, Arbroath High School, since 1995; b. 12.3.47, Forres; m., Edith; 1 s.; 2 d. Educ. Forres Academy; Aberdeen University. Teacher, Buckhaven High, Kirkcaldy High; Assistant Rector, Montrose Academy, 1985-88; Depute Rector, Webster's High School, Kirriemuir, 1988-95; served on a number of national science committees and projects. Publication: Starting Science. Recreations: hill-walking; sports; music; church work. Address: (h.) High Croft, Usan Road, Ferryden, Montrose; T.-01674 671879.

Fraser, Alan William, MA (Hons). Head, Enterprise and Tourism Division, Scottish Office Education and Industry Department, since 1993; b. 17.12.51, Lennoxtown; m., Joan; 2 s.; 1 d. Educ. Daniel Stewart's College; Banff Academy; Aberdeen University. Entered Scottish Office, 1973; Assistant Secretary to Inquiry into UK Prison Services, 1978-79; Private Secretary to Minister of State, 1979-81; secondment to Aberdeen District Council, 1981-82; Head, New Towns Branch, IDS, 1982-85; Manager, Scottish Office Efficiency Unit, 1985-88; Head, Industrial Policy and Technology Division, SOID, 1988-91; Principal Private Secretary to Secretary of State for Scotland, 1991-93. Recreations: hill-walking; skiing; wind-surfing. Address; (b.) Scottish Office Education and Industry Department, Victoria Quay, Edinburgh EH6 6QQ; T.-0131-244 7588.

Fraser, Callum George, BSc, PhD, FAACB. Clinical Director of Biochemical Medicine, Ninewells Hospital and Medical School, since 1983; Honorary Senior Lecturer, Dundee University, since 1983; Honorary Senior Lecturer, St. Andrews University, since 1988; b. 3.1.45, Dundee; m., Stella Sim; 2 d. Educ. Dunfermline High School; Perth Academy; Aberdeen University. Postdoctoral Fellow, National Research Council of Canada, 1969-70; Lecturer in Chemical Pathology, Aberdeen University, and Honorary Biochemist, Grampian Health Board, 1970-75; Chief Clinical Biochemist, Flinders Medical Centre, South

Australia, 1975-83; Honorary Senior Lecturer, then Honorary Associate Professor, Flinders University of South Australia, 1975-83. Former Chairman, Education Division, International Federation of Clinical Chemistry; former Member, Commission on Teaching of Clinical Chemistry, International Union of Pure and Applied Chemistry; Member, Editorial Board, Advances in Clinical Chemistry. Recreations: sailing; gardening; reading; travel. Address: (b.) Department of Biochemical Medicine, Ninewells Hospital, Dundee DD1 9SY; T.-01382 660111.

Fraser, Sir Campbell, FRSE, DCom, DUniv, DL, LLD, CBIM. Chairman, Tandem Computers Ltd., since 1987; Non-Executive Director, Bridgewater Paper Ltd., since 1985; Chairman, Riversoft Ltd., since 1997; b. 2.5.23, Dunblane; m., Myar McLaren (deceased); 2 d. Educ. McLaren High School, Callander; Dundee School of Economics; University of Glasgow; McMaster University. Economist, Raw Cotton Company; Staff, Economist Intelligence Unit; many positions with Dunlop Holdings (Chairman, 1978-83); Non-Executive Director, Morgan Crucible; Chairman, Scottish Television, 1975-91; Non-Executive Director, 3 i's; Non-Executive Director, B.A.T. Industries Ltd.; Non-Executive Director, British Petroleum PLC and associated companies; Past President, Confederation of British Industry; Chairman: Wells Fargo's International Advisory Council, Barkers (Scotland) Ltd., Tandem Inc. (International Advisory Council (Director, Tandem Inc.); Trustee: The Economist, Institute of Hepatology; Governor, N.I.E.S.R.; Visiting Professor: University of Stirling, University of Strathclyde; Chairman, Business School, Strathclyde University. Recreations: watching Dundee F.C.; reading history; writing. Address: (h.) Pine Lodge, 23 Doune Road, Dunblane FK15 9AT; T.-0181-660 1703.

Fraser, Sir Charles Annand, KCVO, WS, DL. Partner, W. & J. Burness, 1956-92 (retired); Chairman, Adam and Company PLC; Director: British Assets Trust PLC, Scottish Television PLC, Scottish Business in the Community, Stakis PLC; b. 16.10.28, Humbie, East Lothian; m., Ann Scott-Kerr; 4 s. Educ. Hamilton Academy; Edinburgh University. Purse Bearer to Lord High Commissioner to General Assembly of Church of Scotland, 1969-88; served on Court, Heriot-Watt University, 1972-78; Council Member, Law Society of Scotland, 1966-72; Chairman, Lothian & Edinburgh Enterprise, 1991-94. Recreations: gardening; skiing; piping. Address: (h.) Shepherd House, Inveresk, Midlothian; T.-0131-665 2570.

Fraser, David James, MA, MHSM, MIPD. Chief Executive, North Ayrshire and Arran NHS Trust, since 1993; b. 1.7.52, Fraserburgh; m., Anne; 1 s. Educ. Peterhead Academy; Aberdeen University. Peat Marwick Mitchell & Co., City of London, 1974-75; Scottish Health Service Management Training Scheme, 1975-77; Lothian Health Board, 1977-93. Recreations: gardens; photography; opera. Address: (b.) Crosshouse Hospital, Kilmarnock KA2 0BE; T.-01563 572230.

Fraser, Eugenie, Writer, since 1980, b. 10.12.05, Archangel, Russia; m., Ronald Fraser; 2 s. Educ. Archangel; Bruce's Business College, Dundee. Housewife since marriage in 1935; spent 26 years travelling to and from India; four years to and from Thailand. Scottish Arts Council Award-winner. Recreations: swimming; sewing; embroidery; travel. Address: (h.) 5 Braid Crescent, Edinburgh EH10 6AX; T.-0131-447 3855.

Fraser, Hugh Donald George, MBE, QPM, DipSM, OStJ, FBIM, MIPM, MIIRSM. Councillor, City of Edinburgh Council, since 1996; Honorary Secretary, Scottish Chamber of Safety, since 1979; former Senior Assistant Secretary, Heriot-Watt University; b. Edinburgh; m., Margaret Jane Stothard; 1 s.; 2 d. War Service, RAF Aircrew, 1939-45 (Pilot); Edinburgh City Police, 1941-71; Chief

Superintendent, Research and Planning Branch, Home Office, London, 1966-68; Deputy Commandant, Scottish Police College, 1968-71. Honorary Secretary, Edinburgh and District Spastic Association, 14 years; Member: Edinburgh Accident Prevention Council, Lothian Retirement Committee; Member, Lothian Regional Council, 1982-96. Recreations: Burns' enthusiast; work with senior citizens; jogging; the theatre. Address: (h.) 181 Braid Road, Edinburgh EH10 6JA; T.-0131-447 1270.

Fraser, James Edward, CB, MA (Aberdeen), BA (Cantab), FSA (Scot). Assistant Local Government Boundary Commissioner for Scotland, since 1997; Secretary of Commissions for Scotland, 1992-94; b. 16.12.31, Aberdeen; m., Patricia Louise Stewart; 2 s. Educ. Aberdeen Grammar School; Aberdeen University; Christ's College, Cambridge. Royal Artillery, 1953-55 (Staff Captain, "Q", Tel-El-Kebir, 1954-55); Assistant Principal, Scottish Home Department, 1957-60; Private Secretary to Permanent Under-Secretary of State, Scottish Office, 1960-62; Private Secretary to Parliamentary Under-Secretary of State, Scottish Office, 1962; Principal, 1962-69: SHHD, 1962-64, Cabinet Office, 1964-66, HM Treasury, 1966-68, SHHD, 1968-69; Assistant Secretary: SHHD, 1970-76, Scottish Office Finance Division, 1976; Under Secretary, Local Government Finance Group, Scottish Office, 1976-81, Scottish Home and Health Department, 1981-91. President: Scottish Hellenic Society, Edinburgh and Eastern Scotland, 1987-93, Aberdeen Grammar School Former Pupils' Club, 1997-98. Recreations: reading; music; walking; Greece, ancient and modern; DIY. Address: (h.) 59 Murrayfield Gardens, Edinburgh EH12 6DH; T.-0131-337 2274.

Fraser, Sheriff James Owen Arthur, MA, LLB. Sheriff of Grampian, Highland and Islands, since 1984; b. 9.5.37. Solicitor, 1967-84. Address: (b.) Sheriff Court House, Ferry Road, Dingwall, IV15 9QX.

Fraser, Jeremy William, LLB (Hons), DipLP, NP. Solicitor; Legal Adviser and Company Secretary, TSB Bank Scotland plc, since 1990; b. 2.5.62, Inverness; m., Claudia Bölling; 2 s.; 1 d. Educ. Alloa Academy; Edinburgh University. Lindsay Duncan & Black WS; Lloyds Bowmaker Ltd. Recreations: hockey; squash; golf; hill-walking. Address: (b.) 120 George Street, Edinburgh; T.-0131-225 4555.

Fraser, John, MA (Hons), FRSA. Rector, Mackie Academy, Stonehaven, since 1975; b. 8.8.36, Inverness; m., 1, Judith Helen Procter; 2 d.; 2, Ella Scott. Educ. Inverness Royal Academy; Aberdeen University; Aberdeen College of Education. Teacher, Harris Academy, 1960-66; Principal Teacher of History, Buckie High School, 1966-72; Assistant Head Teacher and Depute Rector, Peterhead Academy, 1972-75; Governor, Aberdeen College of Education, 1984-88; Member: GTC, 1979-83, 1990-91, and since 1994; Grampian Region Education Committee, 1975-78; Regional Convener, SSTA, 1976-86. Conductor: Buckie Choral Union, 1968-72, Peterhead Choral Society, 1972-75; Organist in various churches; President, Stonehaven Rotary Club, 1988-89. Recreations: music; DIY. Address: (b.) Slug Road, Stonehaven; T.-01569 762071.

Fraser, John A., DipEd, DipPhysEd. Rector, Mearns Academy, since 1993; b. 3.6.52, Inverness; m., Moira; 2 s.; 1 d. Educ. Kingussie High School; Jordanhill College of Education. P.E. Teacher, Northfield Academy; Principal Teacher of Guidance, Northfield Academy; Assistant Head Teacher, Hazlehead Academy; Depute Rector, Mearns Academy. Recreation: sport. Address: (b.) Mearns Academy, Laurencekirk AB30 1AJ; T.-01561 378817.

Fraser, John A.W., MA, FEIS, JP, DL. Deputy Lieutenant for Shetland, since 1985; b. 9.11.28, Lerwick; m., Jane Ann Jamieson; 2 s. Educ. Anderson Educational Institute;

Edinburgh University; Moray House College of Education. Education Officer, RAF, 1950-52; Teacher, Baltasound Junior Secondary School, 1952-54; Head Teacher: Haroldswick Primary School, 1954-59, Aith Junior High School, 1959-66, Scalloway Junior High School, 1966-88. Former Member, National Council, EIS; Chairman, Scalloway Development Association; Member, Shetland Valuation Appeals Committee; Director, Scalloway Waterfront Trust; General Commissioner of Income Tax. Recreations: genealogy; travel; gardening. Address: (h.) Broadwinds, Castle Street, Scalloway, Shetland; T.-01595 880644.

Fraser, Lindsey M., BA (Hons), PGCE. Executive Director, Book Trust Scotland, since 1991; b. 15.8.61, Edinburgh. Educ. George Watson's College; York University; Froebel Institute, London. Manager, Heffers Children's Bookshop, Cambridge, 1986-91. Recreations: reading; music. Address: (b.) Book Trust Scotland, Scottish Book Centre, 137 Dundee Street, Edinburgh EH11 1BG; T.-0131-229 3663.

Fraser, Lady Marion Anne, LT, MA, LRAM, ARCM, LLD. Chairman, Scottish International Piano Competition, since 1995; Chair, Scottish Association of Mental Health, since 1995; b. 17.10.32, Glasgow; m., Sir William Kerr Fraser; 3 s.; 1 d. Educ. Hutchesons' Girls' Grammar School; University of Glasgow; RSAMD. Lord High Commissioner to General Assembly of the Church of Scotland, 1994; Her Majesty's High Commissioner to the General Assembly of the Church of Scotland, 1995. Formerly Director: RGI, Scottish Opera, Laurel Bank School; Founder Chairman, Friends of the RSA; Director, St. Mary's Music School; Chair: Board, Christian Aid, 1990-97; Trustee, Scottish Churches Architectural Heritage Trust; President, Scotland's Churches' Scheme, 1997; Member, Sponsoring Group, Churches' Enquiry into Unemployment and the Future of Work, 1995-97. Recreations: family and friends; people and places. Address: (h.) Broadwood, Edinburgh Road, Gifford, East Lothian EH41 4JE; T.-01620 810 319.

Fraser of Carmyllie, Lord (Peter Fraser), PC, QC. Minister of State, Department of Trade and Industry, 1995-97; b. 29.5.45; m., 1 s.; 2 d. MP (Conservative), Angus South, 1979-83, Angus East, 1983-87; Solicitor-General for Scotland, 1982-89; Lord Advocate, 1989-92; Minister of State, Scottish Office, 1992-95.

Fraser, Robert Dunbar, MA (Hons), MIMgt. Rector, Kirkcaldy High School, since 1989; b. 30.11.45, Dingwall; m., Annice; 2 s.; 2 d. Educ. Dingwall Academy; Aberdeen University. Depute Rector, Culloden Academy, 1979-84; Rector, Keith Grammar School, 1984-89. Recreations: sports; golf; DIY; being with family. Address: (h.) Elphinstone Lodge, 77 Hepburn Gardens, St. Andrews, Fife.

Fraser, Sheriff Simon William Hetherington, LLB, NP. Sheriff of North Strathclyde at Dumbarton, since 1989; b. 2.4.51, Carlisle; m., Sheena Janet; 1 d. Educ. Glasgow Academy; Glasgow University. Solicitor, 1973; Partner, Flowers & Co., Solicitors, Glasgow, 1976-89; Temporary Sheriff, 1987-89. Glasgow Bar Association: Secretary, 1977-79, President, 1981-82. Recreation: cricket. Address: (b.) Sheriff Court, Church Street, Dumbarton; T.-01389 63266.

Fraser, William Alexander Elrick, OStJ, JP. Provost, Inverness District Council, 1992-96; Councillor, since 1962; b. 19.8.27, Inverness; m., Margaret Elizabeth; 2 s.; 2 d. Educ. Inverness Royal Academy. Past President: Inverness Round Table, Inverness Rotary, Inverness Master Butchers, Inverness Amateur Swimming Club, Highland District Swimming Association; former Chairman: Inverness Harbour Trust, Governors of Eden Court Theatre; Director: Highland Hospice Ltd., Highland Prospect Ltd.,

Highland Opportunity Ltd., Inverness and Loch Ness Horizons Ltd.; Patron, Inverness Sea Cadets; Hon. President, Inverness Opera Company, Inverness Festival Association, Inverness Tattoo Committee; Past President, Scottish Accident Prevention Council; Chairman, Princes Scottish Youth Business Trust, Highland Area; Chairman, Seagull Trust. Address: (h.) Balwearie, Drummond Road, Inverness IV2 4NA; T.-01463 233345.

Fraser, Professor William Douglas, BSc, MSc, PhD, FRICS. Professor and Head, Department of Land Economics, Paisley University, since 1986; b. 3.1.40, Edinburgh. Educ. Edinburgh Academy; London University; Strathclyde University. Partner, Bingham, Hughes and Macpherson, Chartered Surveyors, Inverness, 1970-72; Lecturer: Department of Land Economics, Paisley College, 1972-83, Centre for Property Valuation and Management, City University, London, 1983-86. Publication: Principles of Property Investment and Pricing, 1984. Recreations: climbing; gardening. Address: (b.) Department of Land Economics, Paisley University, High Street, Paisley PA1 2BE; T.-0141-848 3450.

Fraser, Professor William Hamish, MA, DPhil, FRHistS. Professor of History, Strathclyde University (Dean, Faculty of Arts and Social Studies, 1987-93); b. 30.6.41, Keith; m., Helen Tuach; 1 d. Educ. Keith Grammar School; Aberdeen University; Sussex University. Lecturer in History, Strathclyde University, 1966-77. Publications: Trade Unions and Society 1850-1880, 1973; Workers and Employers, 1981; The Coming of the Mass Market, 1982; Conflict and Class: Scottish Workers 1700-1838, 1988; People and Society in Scotland 1830-1914, 1990; Glasgow 1830-1914 (Co-author), 1996; Alexander Campbell and the Search for Socialism, 1996. Recreations: hill-walking; skiing. Address: (h.) 112 High Station Road, Falkirk FK1 5LN; T.-01324 622868.

Fraser, Sir William Kerr, GCB (1984), LLD, FRSE. Chancellor, Glasgow University, since 1996; Chairman, Royal Commission on the Ancient and Historical Monuments of Scotland, since 1995; b. 18.3.29; m., Lady Marion Fraser, LT (qv); 3 s.; 1 d. Educ. Eastwood Secondary School; Glasgow University. RAF, 1952-55; various posts in Scottish Office, 1955-88, including Permanent Under Secretary of State, Scottish Office, 1978-88; Principal and Vice Chancellor, Glasgow University, 1988-95. Director, Scottish Mutual Assurance plc; Chairman, Scottish Inheritance Fund; Governor, Caledonian Research Foundation. Address: (h.) Broadwood, Edinburgh Road, Gifford, East Lothian EH41 4JE; T.-01620 810 319.

Frazer, Rev. Richard Ernest, BA, BD, SBStJ. Minister, St. Machar's Cathedral, Old Aberdeen, since 1993; b. 20.11.57, Stirling; m., Katherine Tullis Sinclair; 2 s.; 1 d. Educ. Doncaster Grammar School; University of Newcastle upon Tyne; University of Edinburgh. Assistant Minister, St. Giles Cathedral, Edinburgh, 1985-87; Minister, Schoharie, Breakabeen, N. Bleheim, New York, USA, 1987-88; Minister, Cargill-Burrelton with Collace, 1988-93. Publication: A Collace Miscellany: a History of the Parish of Collace (Co-Editor and Contributor), 1992. Recreations: walking; squash; rummaging in the attic. Address: (b.) St. Machar's Cathedral, The Chanonry, Old Aberdeen AB24 1RQ; T.-01224 485988.

Freeman, James Martin, BSc, MSc, DipEduc. Rector, Lawside R.C. Academy, Dundee, since 1986; b. 7.11.34; m., Mary Agnes; 2 s.; 1 d. Educ. St. Anthony's, Edinburgh; University of Edinburgh; University of East Anglia. Chemistry Teacher, Broughton Secondary School, Edinburgh, 1963-65; Chemistry Teacher/Depute Head, Makerere College School, Kampala, 1966-69; Lecturer in Education, Makerere University, Kampala, 1969-73; Principal Teacher, Gracemount High School, 1974-76; Assistant Headteacher, Liberton High School, Edinburgh,

1976-82; Depute Headteacher, Holy Rood High School, Edinburgh, 1982-86. Recreations: walking; theatre; sport. Address: (b.) West School Road, Dundee DD3 8RT; T.-01382 436100.

Freemantle, Andrew, MBE, FIMgt. Chief Executive, Scottish Ambulance Service, since 1991; b. 26.9.44, Bournemouth; m., Patricia Mary; 4 d. Educ. Framlingham College; Royal Military College of Science. Commissioned, Royal Hampshire Regiment (Germany, Malaya, Borneo), 1965-69; Australian SAS Regiment (Australia, South Vietnam), 1969-72; Royal Hampshire Regiment, (Hong Kong, UK, Northern Ireland), 1972-76; Staff College, Camberley, 1978; Directing Staff, Staff College, 1983-84; Commanding Officer, Royal Hampshire Regiment (mention in Dispatches, 1987), 1985-87; Commander, 19 Infantry Brigade (Brigadier), 1987-89; Member, Royal College of Defence Studies, 1990. Recreations: running; cooking; field sports. Address: (b.) National Headquarters, Scottish Ambulance Service NHS Trust, Tipperlinn Road, Edinburgh EH10 5UU; T.-0131-447 7711.

Freer, Professor John Henry, BSc, MSc, PhD. Personal Professor in Microbiology, Glasgow University, since 1986; Deputy Director, Institute of Biomedical and Life Sciences; b. 17.11.36, Kasauli, India; m., Jocelyn Avril Williams; 4 d. Educ. Durham University; Nottingham University; Birmingham University. Lecturer in Microbiology, New South Wales University, Australia, 1962-65; New York University Medical Centre: Associate Research Scientist, then Assistant Professor, Microbiology, 1965-68; Senior Lecturer, Microbiology Department, Glasgow University, 1968-82; Reader in Microbiology, 1982-86; Editor-in-Chief, Journal of General Microbiology, 1990-95. Publications: Bacterial Protein Toxins (Joint Editor), 1988; Sourcebook of Bacterial Protein Toxins, 1991; 100 scientific articles. Address: (b.) Joseph Black Building, Glasgow University, Glasgow, G12 8QQ.

French, William Allan, DL, BSc, MSc, CEng, FIM, FIEE, FIBF. Associate Principal, Falkirk College of Further and Higher Education, since 1986; Depute Lieutenant, Stirling and Falkirk Districts, since 1994; Director, Careers Central Ltd., since 1995; b. 30.12.41, Falkirk; m., Joyce; 2 d. Educ. George Watson's College, Edinburgh; Strathclyde University. Scientific Officer, UKAEA, Dounreay; Production Manager, British Aluminium Co. Ltd., Falkirk; Lecturer, Napier College, Edinburgh; Head, Department of Industrial Engineering, Falkirk College of Technology. Secretary, Forth Valley Area Scout Association; District Scout Commissioner; founder Area Chairman, Central Scotland Round Table; Past President, Larbert Rotary Club. Recreations: golf; bridge; bowling; scouting; rotary; music. Address: (b.) Falkirk College of Further and Higher Education, Falkirk FK2 9AD; T.-01324 403210.

Frew, Rev. Michael William, BSc, BD. Parish Minister, Carluke: St. John's, since 1991; b. 16.5.51, Edinburgh; m., Margaret; 3 s.; 1 d. Educ. Broughton Senior Secondary; University of Edinburgh. Parish Minister: Alloa West; Organiser for Evangelism, Church of Scotland Department of National Mission. Recreations: cycling, walking; football. Address: 18 Old Bridgend, Carluke, Lanarkshire ML8 4HN; T.-01855 772259.

Friel, Professor Edward J. Chief Executive, Greater Glasgow and Clyde Valley Tourist Board, since 1997; Broadcaster and Writer; b. 20.9.41, Londonderry; m., Eleanor; 3 s. Educ. Northern Ireland; London; Strathclyde. Northern Ireland Tourist Board: Director, North America, Chief Executive, 1991; Director, Marketing and Public Relations, Scottish Opera; Proprietor, Eddie Friel Associates, since 1992; Chief Executive, Greater Glasgow Tourist Board and Convention Bureau, 1993-97. Former Chairman: Theatre Royal, Glasgow 1990 Marketing; former Member, Board of Directors, Scottish Opera; a Director,

Glasgow Chamber of Commerce, Scottish National Youth Orchestra; Visiting Professor, Scottish Hotel school, Strathclyde University. Recreations: golf; music; theatre; opera. Address: (b.) 11 George Square, Glasgow G2 1DY; T.-0141-566 4001.

Friend, James, MA, MB, ChB, FRCPEdin. Consultant in Thoracic Medicine, Grampian Health Board, since 1973; Clinical Reader in Medicine and Therapeutics, Aberdeen University, since 1996; b. 2.6.38, Edinburgh; m., Elizabeth; 1 s.; 2 d. Educ. Edinburgh Academy; Gonville and Caius College, Cambridge; Edinburgh University. Hospital posts in Edinburgh and Oxford; Dorothy Temple Cross Fellowship, Seattle, 1971-72; British Thoracic Society: Council Member, 1983-91, Treasurer, 1984-91, Vice President, 1997; Chairman, Grampian Action on Smoking and Health, 1989-97. Recreation: the Scottish hills. Address: (b.) Aberdeen Royal Infirmary, Aberdeen AB25 2ZN.

Frier, Brian Murray, BSc (Hons), MD, FRCP (Edin), FRCP (Glas). Consultant Physician, Royal Infirmary, Edinburgh, since 1987; part-time Reader in Medicine, Edinburgh University, since 1995; b. 28.7.47, Edinburgh; m., Dr. Isobel M. Wilson; 1 d. Educ. George Heriot's School, Edinburgh; Edinburgh University. Medical Registrar, Ninewells Hospital, Dundee, 1974-76; Research Fellow in Diabetes and Metabolism, Cornell University Medical Centre, The New York Hospital, 1976-77; Senior Medical Registrar, Royal Infirmary, Edinburgh, 1978-82; Consultant Physician, Western Infirmary and Gartnavel General Hospital, Glasgow, 1982-87. R.D. Lawrence Lecturer, British Diabetic Association, 1986; Governor, George Heriot's Trust, Edinburgh, 1988-94. Recreations: appreciation of the arts; ancient and modern history. Address: (h.) 100 Morningside Drive, Edinburgh EH10 5NT; T.-0131-447 1653.

Frith, Professor Simon, BA, MA, PhD, FRSA. Director, John Logie Baird Centre, since 1987, and Professor of English Studies, since 1988, University of Strathclyde; Director, ESRC Media Economics and Media Culture Programme, since 1995; b. 25.6.49, England. Educ. Leys School, Cambridge; Balliol College, University of Oxford; University of California, Berkeley. Lecturer, then Senior Lecturer in Sociology, University of Warwick, 1972-87; Rock Critic, Sunday Times, 1982-86; Pop Critic, Observer, 1987-91; Chair of Judges, Mercury Music Prize. Publications: Sound Effects, 1981; Art into Pop, 1987; Music for Pleasure, 1988; Performing Rites, 1996. Recreations: music; reading; walking. Address: (b.) John Logie Baird Centre, University of Strathclyde, Glasgow G1 1XH; T.-0141-553 4150.

Frizzell, Edward W. MA (Hons). Chief Executive, Scottish Prison Service, since 1991; Board Member, Quality Scotland Foundation, since 1991; b. 4.5.46, Paisley; m., Moira Calderwood; 2 s.; 1 d. Educ. Paisley Grammar School; Glasgow University. Scottish Milk Marketing Board, 1968-73; Scottish Council (Development and Industry), 1973 76; DAFS, Scottish Office, 1976-78; First Secretary, Fisheries, Office of the UK Permanent Representative to European Communities, Brussels (Foreign and Commonwealth Office), 1978-82; Assistant Secretary (Grade 5), Scottish Education Department, Higher Education Division, 1982-86; Scottish Office Finance Division, 1986-89; Director, Locate in Scotland, Scottish Office Industry Department (Grade 4), 1989-91. Address: (b.) Calton House, 5 Redheughs Rigg, Edinburgh, EH12 9HW; T.-0131-244 8522.

Frizzell, Rev. Robert Stewart, BD. Minister, Wick Old Parish Church, since 1998; Chaplain, Army Cadet Force, Queen's Own Highlanders Battalion, since 1993; Chaplain, Caithness General Hospital, Wick, since 1991; b. 24.6.34, Motherwell; m., Elizabeth Brown; 2 d. Educ. Bellshill

Academy; University of Glasgow. Ordained 1961; Minister: Vale of Leven; Kirkintilloch; Partick Anderson Church, Glasgow; Balshagray Parish Church, Broomhill, Glasgow. Recreations: touring with car; grandchildren; foreign holidays. Address: (h.) Old Parish Manse, Miller Avenue, Wick, Caithness; T.-01955 604252.

Frost, Patricia. General Manager, Fife Health Board. Address: Springfield House, Cupar, Fife, KY15 5UP.

Frutin, Bernard Derek, MBE, FRSA, MInstPkg. Inventor; Chairman and Managing Director: Rocep Lusol Holdings Ltd., since 1973, Rocep Pressure Packs Ltd., since 1987; b. 7.2.44, Glasgow; 3 d. Educ. Kelvinside Academy, Glasgow. Winner of nine international innovator awards since 1989, including John Logie Baird and British Institute of Packaging Environmental Awards; Innovator of the Year, 1989 (Institute of Packaging); Finalist, 1992 Prince of Wales Award. Recreations: sailing; skiing; fine food; listening to music. Address: (b.) Rocep Lusol Holdings Ltd., Rocep Business Park, Kings Inch Road, Deanpark, Renfrew PA4 8XY; T.-0141-885 2222.

Fry, Professor Stephen C., BSc, PhD, FRSE. Professor of Plant Biochemistry, Edinburgh University, since 1995; b. 26.11.53, Sheffield; m., Verena Ryffel; 3 d. Educ. Thornbridge School, Sheffield; Leicester University. Postdoctoral Research Fellow, Cambridge University, 1978-79; Royal Society Rosenheim Research Fellow, Cambridge University, 1979-82; Senior Research Associate, University of Colorado, 1982-83; Lecturer in Botany, then Reader in Plant Biochemistry, Edinburgh University, 1983-95. President's Medal, Society for Experimental Biology, 1988. Publication: The Growing Plant Cell Wall: Chemical and Metabolic Analysis, 1988. Recreations: hill-walking; paper chromatography. Address: (b.) Division of Biological Sciences, Edinburgh University, King's Buildings, Mayfield Road, Edinburgh EH9 3JH; T.-0131-650 5320.

Fullarton, John Hamilton, ARIAS, DipTP. Consultant Architect and Town Planner; b. 21.2.31, Dalry, Ayrshire; m., Elvera Peebles; 1 s. Educ. Dalry High School; Glasgow School of Art; Royal Technical College, Glasgow; Edinburgh College of Art. Architect with local authorities before joining Scottish Office, 1964; Superintending Architect, Scottish Development Department, 1970-78; Head of New Towns, Construction Industry Division, Scottish Economic Planning Department, 1978-79; Director of Technical Services, Scottish Special Housing Association, 1979-89. Research Fellowship, Urban Planning, Edinburgh College of Art, 1966-67. Publication:Waverley Park Conservation Study, 1977. Address: (h.) 7 Queens Crescent, Edinburgh EH9 2AZ; T.-0131-667 5809.

Fulton, Rev. John Oswald, BSc, BD. General Secretary, United Free Church of Scotland, since 1994; b. 9.7.53, Glasgow; m., Margaret P.; 1 d. Educ. Clydebank High School; Glasgow University. Ordained as minister, 1977; Minister, Croftfoot U.F. Church, Glasgow, 1977-94. Recreations: reading; gardening; photography. Address: (b.) 11 Newton Place, Glasgow G3 7PR; T.-0141-332 3435.

Fulton, Rikki, OBE, DLitt, DArts. Actor; b. 15.4.24, Glasgow; m., Kate Matheson. Educ. Whitehill Secondary School. Invalided out of RNVR as Sub-Lt., 1945; began professional career broadcasting with BBC in Glasgow; Presenter, BBC Showband, London, 1951-55; appeared in numerous pantomimes and revues with Howard & Wyndham from 1955, including Five Past Eight shows; television work including Scotch & Wry (creator, Rev. I.M. Jolly) and starring roles in The Miser and A Winter's Tale; films including The Dollar Bottom, Gorky Park, Local Hero, Comfort and Joy and The Girl in the Picture. Scottish TV Personality of the Year, 1963 and 1979; Best Light

Entertainment Performance of the Year, 1969 and 1983; President's Award, Television and Radio Industries Club, 1988; Lifetime Achievement Award, BAFTA Scotland, 1993. Recreations: bridge; chess; reading; music (listening and piano); writing; painting.

Fulton, William Francis Monteith, BSc, MD (Hons), MB, ChB, FRCP, FRCPGlas, FRCPEdin. Reader, Department of Materia Medica, Glasgow University, 1977-84; Consultant Physician, Stobhill General Hospital, Glasgow, 1958-84; b. 12.12.19, Aberdeen; m., Dr. Frances I. Melrose; 1 s.; 1 d. Educ. Bryanston School, Dorset; Glasgow University. Resident Physician and Surgeon, Western Infirmary, Glasgow, 1945-46; National Service, Merchant Navy, 1946-48 (Ship's Surgeon); joined National Health Service, 1950; Research Assistant, Cardiology, Edinburgh University, 1952-53; Senior Lecturer, Department of Materia Medica, Glasgow University, 1958-77; Senior Fellow, Cardiology, Johns Hopkins Hospital, Baltimore, 1963-64; Foundation Professor of Medicine, Nairobi University, 1967-72. Publications: The Coronary Arteries, 1965; Modern Trends in Pharmacology and Therapeutics, 1967. Address: (h.) Woodhill, Braemar AB35 5XX; T.-0133 97 41239.

Fulton, Sheriff William J. Sheriff of Grampian, Highland and Islands at Inverness. Address: (b.) The Castle, Inverness, IV2 3EG.

Furnell, Professor James R.G., MA (Hons), DCP, PhD, LLB, FBPsS, DipLP. Consultant Clinical Psychologist (Child Health), Forth Valley Health Board, since 1990; Advocate (called to Scottish Bar, 1993); Honorary Fellow, Edinburgh University, since 1987; b. 20.2.46, London; m., Lesley Anne Ross; 1 s.; 1 d. Educ. Leighton Park Society of Friends School, Reading; Aberdeen University; Glasgow University; Stirling University; Dundee University. Clinical Psychologist, Royal Hospital for Sick Children, Glasgow, 1970-72; Senior Clinical Psychologist, Forth Valley Health Board, 1972-80. Member: National Consultative Committee of Scientists in Professions Allied to Medicine, 1984-87 (Secretary, Clinical Psychology Sub-Committee), Forth Valley Health Board, 1984-87; Chairman, Division of Clinical Psychology, British Psychological Society, 1988-89; Visiting Professor, Caledonian University, since 1996. Recreations: flying; cross-country skiing. Address: (h.) Glensherup House, Glendevon, by Dollar, Perthshire FK14 7JY; T.-01259 781234.

Furness, Professor Raymond Stephen, BA, MA, PhD. Professor of German, St. Andrews University, since 1984; b. 25.10.33, Builth Wells; m., Janice Fairey; 1 s.; 2 d. Educ. Welwyn Garden City Grammar School; University College, Swansea. Modern Languages Department, University of Manchester Institute of Science and Technology; Department of German, Manchester University. Publications: Expressionism; Literary History of Germany 1890-1945; Wagner and Literature; A Companion to Twentieth Century German Literature; An Introduction to German Literature 1871-1989; The Dedalus Book of German Decadence. Recreation: sleeping. Address: (h.) Dirdale, Boarhills, St. Andrews KY16 8PP; T.-01334 88469.

Furness, Col. Simon John, DL. Landowner; Vice Lord Lieutenant, Berwickshire, since 1990; b. 18.3.36, Ayton. Educ. Charterhouse; RMA, Sandhurst. Commissioned Durham Light Infantry, 1956, 2nd Lt.; served Far East, UK, Germany; active service, Borneo, Northern Ireland; retired, 1978; Deputy Colonel (Durham) The Light Infantry, 1989-93. Member, Executive, National Trust for Scotland, 1986-96; Chairman: Berwickshire Civic Society, since 1996, Eyemouth Museum Trust, since 1981. Recreations: field sports; gardening. Address: The Garden House, Netherbyres, Eyemouth, Berwickshire TD14 5SE; T.-01890 750337.

Furness, William Arthur, BA, MSc. National Manager for Scotland, BT; b. 6.9.45, London. Educ. St. Benedict's Abbey School, Ealing; Exeter University; London University. Various posts within BT. Board Member: Edinburgh Chamber of Commerce, Edinburgh Science Festival, Quality Foundation Scotland; Executive Committee Member: Scottish Council Development and Industry, Scottish Business in the Community. Recreations: travel; dogs; reading; art. Address: (b.) Telephone House, 357 Gorgie Road, Edinburgh EH11 2RP; T.-0131-345 1380.

Fyfe, Andrew, MA (Hons). Managing Director, Glasgow and North Clyde, Scottish Homes, since 1997; b. 26.6.54, Glasgow; m., Louise Drummond; 2 d. Educ. Hutchesons', Glasgow; Glasgow University. Research Assistant, Strathclyde University, 1975-78; Senior Development Officer, Govanhill Housing Association, 1978-81; Director: Shettleston Housing Association, Glasgow, 1982-89, Strategic Development, Scottish Homes, 1989-92, Operations, Scottish Homes, 1992-97. Member, Executive Council, Scottish Business in the Community; Chairman, Scottish Federation of Housing Associations, 1987-89. Address: (b.) Highlander House, 58 Waterloo Street, Glasgow G2 7DA; T.-0141-305 4151.

Fyfe, Maria, BA (Hons). MP, Glasgow Maryhill, since 1987; Chair, Labour Backbench Committee on International Development, since 1997; Member, Council of Europe, since 1997; b. 25.11.38, Glasgow; 2 s. Educ. Notre Dame High School, Glasgow; Strathclyde University. Glasgow District Councillor, 1980-87; Senior Lecturer, Central College of Commerce, 1977-87; Member, Scottish Executive Committee, Labour Party, 1981-87; Opposition Spokesperson on Women, 1988-91; Scottish Affairs Spokesperson, 1992-95. Address: (b.) House of Commons, London, SW1A 0AA; T.-0171-219 4430; 0141-945 1495.

G

Gage, Simon Martin, BSc, MSc, PhD. Research Physicist, University of Edinburgh, since 1985; Events Manager, since 1990, and Director, since 1994, Edinburgh International Science Festival; b. 18.5.62, London; m., Sarah Price; 1 d. Educ. Ivybridge Comprehensive School; University of Bristol; University of Dundee; University of Edinburgh. Publications: author of science books for children, including Light and Illusion Activity Pack. Recreations: cycle touring; classical music; walking on hot coals and other demonstrations of unusual scientific principles. Address: (b.) Edinburgh International Science Festival, 149 Rose Street, Edinburgh EH2 4LS; T.-0131-220 3977.

Galbraith, Professor Roderick Allister McDonald, BSc, PhD (Cantab), CEng, MRAeS. Head of Aerospace Engineering, Glasgow University, since 1989; b. 4.8.47, Lowmoor, England; m., Lynn Margaret Fraser. Educ. Greenock High School; James Watt Memorial College; Paisley College of Technology; Cambridge University. Apprentice Draughtsman/Engineer, Scott's Shipbuilding & Engineering Co. Ltd., 1964-72; Department of Aerospace Engineering, Glasgow University: joined 1975; Reader, 1989, Professor, 1992. Publications: over 100 reports and publications on aerodynamics. Recreations: sailing; walking. Address: (b.) Department of Aerospace Engineering, Glasgow University, Glasgow G12 8QQ; T.-0141-330 5295.

Galbraith, Samuel Laird, BSc, MBChB, MD, FRCSGlas. MP (Labour), Strathkelvin and Bearsden, since 1987; Parliamentary Under-Secretary of State, Scottish Office (Minister for Health, the Arts and Children); Neurosurgeon; b. 18.10.45. Address: (b.) House of Commons, London, SW1A 0AA.

Galbraith, William C., QC, BA, LLB; b. 25.2.35. Parliamentary Counsel, Scottish Law Commission, 1975-95.

Gale, William Stuart, QC, LLB (Hons); b. 10.6.55. Advocate, 1980. Address: Advocates' Library, Parliament House, Edinburgh EH1 1RF.

Gallacher, Tom. Writer; b. 16.2.34, Alexandria. Stage plays: Our Kindness to 5 Persons, 1969; Mr Joyce is Leaving Paris, 1971; Revival, 1972; Three to Play, 1972; Schellenbrack, 1973; Bright Scene Fading, 1973; The Only Street, 1973; Personal Effects, 1974; A Laughing Matter, 1975; Hallowe'en, 1975; The Sea Change, 1976; A Presbyterian Wooing (adapted from Pitcairne's The Assembly), 1976; The Evidence of Tiny Tim, 1977; Wha's Like Us - Fortunately!, 1978; Stage Door Canteen, 1978; Deacon Brodie (adapted from Stevenson and Henley), 1978; Jenny, 1979; Natural Causes, 1980; The Parole of Don Juan, 1981; The Treasure Ship (adapted from Brandane), 1982; Renée Houston Rehearses her Life, 1995; Of Time and Loss, 1997. Publications: (fiction): Hunting Shadows, 1981; Apprentice, 1983; Journeyman, 1984; Survivor, 1985; The Jewel Maker, 1986; The Wind on the Heath, 1987; The Stalking Horse, 1989; Gainful Perjury, 1990; The Last of Zenda, 1996; Remembering Clare and Herald Stories, 1997. Address: (b.) 25 Linn Walk, Garelochhead, Dunbartonshire G84 0DS.

Gallagher, Jim, BSc, MSc. Head, Local Government (1) Division, Scottish Office, since 1996; b. 23.9.54, Clydebank; m., Una Green; 1 s.; 2 d. Educ. St. Aloysius College, Glasgow; Glasgow University; Edinburgh University. Administration Trainee, Scottish Office, 1976; Private Secretary to Minister for Home Affairs and Environment, 1980-82; Principal, Criminal Justice Division, 1982-86; Secretary, Scottish Office Management Group, 1986-88; Head, Urban Policy Division, 1988-89; Private Secretary to successive Secretaries of State for Scotland, 1989-91; Director (Human Resources), Scottish Prison Service, 1991-96. Address: (b.) Scottish Office, Victoria Quay, Edinburgh; T.-0131-244 7018.

Gallagher, Sister Maire T., CBE, MA (Hons), MEd, FScotVec, DCE, FSQA. Retired Headteacher; Sister of Notre Dame Religious Congregation, since 1959; b. 27.5.33, Glasgow. Educ. Notre Dame High School, Glasgow; Glasgow University; Notre Dame College of Education. Principal Teacher of History, Notre Dame High School, Glasgow; Lecturer in Secondary Education, Notre Dame College of Education; Headteacher, Notre Dame High School, Dumbarton, 1974-87; Chairman, Scottish Consultative Council on the Curriculum, 1987-91 (Member, Consultative Committee on the Curriculum, since 1976). Member, Executive, Secondary Heads Association (Scottish Branch), 1976-83; Coordinator, Christian Life Movement Groups, West of Scotland; Fellow, Scottish Qualifications Authority, 1997. Recreations: reading; dress-making; bird-watching. Address: (h.) Sisters of Notre Dame, 67 Moorpark Avenue, Penilee, Glasgow G52 4ET; T.-0141 810 4214.

Gallie, Philip Roy, TEng, MIPlantE. Vice-Chairman, Scottish Conservative and Unionist Party, since 1995; MP (Conservative), Ayr, 1992-97; business advisor; b. 3.6.39, Portsmouth; m., Marion Wands. Educ. Dunfermline High School; Kirkcaldy Technical College. Apprenticeship, H.M. Dockyard, Rosyth, 1955-60; Merchant Navy, 1960-64; electricity industry, 1964-92. Recreations: sports; politics. Address: (b.) 35 Auchentrae Crescent, Ayr; T.-01292 619350.

Galloway, George. MP (Glasgow Hillhead), since 1987; Vice-Chair, Parliamentary Foreign Affairs Committee; b. 16.8.54, Dundee; 1 d. Educ. Harris Academy, Dundee. Production Worker, Michelin Tyres, 1974; Dundee Labour Party Organiser, 1977; General Secretary, War on Want, 1983. Chairman, Scottish Labour Party, 1981-82; Member, Scottish Labour Party Executive Committee, 1974-84; Founder and first General Secretary, Trade Union Friends of Palestine, 1979. Recreations: football; music; films. Address: (b.) House of Commons, Westminster, London; T.-0171-219 4084.

Galloway, Janice. Writer; b. 2.12.56, Kilwinning. Educ. Ardrossan Academy; Glasgow University. Variety of paid and unpaid work, including 10 years' teaching English in Ayrshire; music criticism for Glasgow Herald, The Observer, Scotland on Sunday; fiction writing, including two collections of short stories and two novels; Co-Editor, New Writing Scotland, 1990-92. Publications: The Trick Is To Keep Breathing, 1990; Blood, 1991; Foreign Parts, 1994; Where You Find It, 1996; Staged work: The Trick is to Keep Breathing; Fall. Song cycle: Clara (Co-Writer); Monster, for orchestra and voices (Co-Writer).

Galloway, 13th Earl of (Randolph Keith Reginald Stewart); b. 14.10.28; m. Address: Senwick House, Brighouse Bay, Borgue, Kirkcudbrightshire, DG6 4TP.

Galt, Sheriff Eric. Sheriff of Glasgow and Strathkelvin. Address: (b.) Sheriff Court House, 1 Carlton Place, Glasgow, G5 9DA.

Gamble, Alan James, LLB(Hons), LLM, Advocate. Full-time Chairman, Independent Tribunal Service, Glasgow, since 1993; Deputy Social Security and Child Support Commissioner, Edinburgh, since 1994; b. 29.4.51, Glasgow; m., Elizabeth Waugh; 2 s.; 1 d. Educ. High School of Glasgow; University of Glasgow; Harvard Law School, USA. Law Apprentice, 1973-76; admitted to

Faculty of Advocates, 1978; Lecturer, then Senior Lecturer in Law, University of Glasgow, 1976-93. Bible Teacher, Christian Brethren Assemblies; Trustee, Interlink, and other charitable trusts; Dr J. McCormick Prize, 1972; Harkness Fellow, 1972-74. Publications: Contributor, Stair Memorial Encyclopedia; articles in legal journals. Recreations: reading; hill-walking. Address: (b.) Wellington House, 134-136 Wellington Street, Glasgow G2 2XL; T.-0141-353 1441.

Gamble, Kevin George Alfred, BEng. Executive Director, Weir Group PLC, since 1995; b. 1.9.47, Liverpool; m., Marie-Luise Paganetty; 2 s.; 1 d. Educ. Liverpool College; University of Liverpool. Stewarts & Lloyds, Bilston, Staffs, 1965-1970; Stone Manganese Marine Ltd., 1970-82; G.E.C. Turbine Generators Ltd., Rugby, 1982-88; Managing Director, Express Lift Co. Ltd., Northampton, 1988-92; Executive Director, Senior Engineering Group plc, 1992-95. Director, Northamptonshire Training and Enterprise Council, 1989-94. Recreations: tennis; family; garden. Address: (b.) Weir Group plc, 149 Newlands Road, Cathcart, Glasgow G44 4EX; T.-0141-308 2006.

Gammell, James Gilbert Sydney, MBE, CA; b. 4.3.20, Camberley; m., Susan Patricia Bowring; 5 s.; 1 d. Educ. Winchester College. Major, Grenadier Guards, Second World War; Partner, Ivory & Sime, 1949, Chairman, 1974-85; former Director, Bank of Scotland, Standard Life. Recreation: farming. Address: (h.) Foxhall, Kirkliston, West Lothian EH29 9ER; T.-0131-333 3275.

Gani, Professor David, BSc, DPhil, CChem, FRSC, FRSE. Purdie Professor of Chemistry and Professor of Organic Chemistry, St. Andrews University, since 1990; b. 29.9.57, Beckenham; m., Julie Margaret; 4 d. Educ. Rawlins Grammar School, Quorn; Sussex University; Croydon Technical College. Royal Society University Fellow, Southampton University, 1983-88; Lecturer in Bioorganic Chemistry, then Senior Lecturer, Southampton University, 1988-90, Research Co-ordinator and Financial Controller, Institute of Biomolecular Sciences, 1987-90. ICI Research Award, 1990; Corday Morgan Medal and Prize, 1991; Hickinbottom Prize Fellowship, 1992-93; Pfizer Prize, 1997. Publications: 115 papers; one book. Recreations: chess; guitar; music; swimming. Address: (b.) School of Chemistry, Purdie Building, St. Andrews University, St. Andrews; T.-01334 63860.

Garbutt, David Charles Gemmell, QPM, GradIPD. HM Assistant Inspector of Constabulary for Scotland, Edinburgh, since 1997; b. 16.8.45, Harthill; m., Moira Murdoch; 1 s.; 1 d. Educ. College of Commerce, Hull; Napier, Edinburgh. Joined Edinburgh City Police, 1964; transferred to Kingston upon Hull, 1967; returned to Edinburgh, 1970; promoted Chief Superintendent, 1987, as Divisional Commander, West Lothian; promoted Assistant Chief Constable, Lothian and Borders Police, 1991; appointed Deputy Chief Constable, Grampian Police, 1992. Recreations: hill-walking; cycling; curling. Address: (b.) HM Inspectorate of Constabulary, 2 Greenside Lane, Edinburgh EH1 3AII, T.-0131-244 5614.

Garden, Neville Abbot. Broadcaster; Writer and Lecturer on musical and media matters; b. 13.2.36, Edinburgh; m., Jane Fowler; 1 s., 1 d.; 3 d. by pr. m. Educ. George Watson's College, Edinburgh. Reporter, Sub-Editor, Feature Writer, Evening Dispatch, 1953-63; Daily Columnist and Music Critic, Edinburgh Evening News, 1963-64; Senior Feature Writer, Scottish Daily Express, 1964-78; Presenter, Good Morning Scotland, BBC Radio Scotland, 1978-90, Queen Street Garden, 1990-93; Music Critic and Columnist, Sunday Standard, 1981-83; Music Writer, Scotland on Sunday, since 1988; Conductor: Edinburgh Grand Opera, seven years; Edinburgh Ballet Theatre, nine years. Publication: Bloomsbury Good Music Guide.

Gardiner, Iain Derek, FRICS. Chartered Surveyor, since 1957; Consultant, Souter & Jaffrey, Chartered Surveyors (Senior Partner, 1986-95); b. 22.12.33, Glasgow; m., Kathleen Elizabeth Johnson; 2 s.; 1 d. Educ. Hutcheson's Grammar School, Glasgow; Royal Technical College, Glasgow. Trainee and Assistant Quantity Surveyor, John H. Allan & Sons, Glasgow, 1950-57; National Service, Royal Engineers, 1957-59; Souter & Jaffrey, Inverness: Quantity Surveyor, 1959-63, Partner, 1963-86. Past Chairman, Royal Institution of Chartered Surveyors in Scotland; Chairman: Inverness Area, RICS in Scotland, 1969-70, Quantity Surveyors Committee, RICS in Scotland, 1989-90, Friends of Eden Court Theatre, 1981-82, Inverness Area Scout Council. Recreations: swimming; travel; cookery. Address: (h.) 77 Stratherrick Road, Inverness IV2 4LL; T.-01463 235607.

Gardiner, John Ronald, BL, WS, NP. Senior Partner, Brodies W.S, Solicitors, since 1992 (Partner, since 1964); b. 25.10.38, Rangoon; m., Aileen Mary Montgomery; 1 s.; 1 s. (deceased); 1 d. Educ. Fettes College; University of Edinburgh. Admitted Solicitor, 1963; admitted Writer to the Signet, 1964; Partner, Brodie Cuthbertson & Watson W.S. (now Brodies W.S.), 1964; Notary Public, 1966. Governor, Fettes Trust, 1986-96; Member, Rent Assessment Panel for Scotland, 1973-97; Hon. Secretary: Standing Council of Scottish Chiefs, 1970-72, Salmon and Trout Association (Scottish Branch), 1971-84. Recreations: fishing; shooting; golf; gardening. Address: (b.) 15 Atholl Crescent, Edinburgh EH3 8HA; T.-0131-228 3777.

Gardner, Angela Joy, BSc (Hons). Independent Public Affairs Consultant, AJ Enterprises, since 1994; b. 16.9.62, Wolverhampton; m., Andrew Ronald Gardner; 1 d. Educ. Codsall High School; UMIST. BP Chemicals Ltd., South Wales and Grangemouth, 1984-90; BP Schools Link Officer, 1985-90; Senior Public Affairs Officer, BP, 1990-94. Member, General Teaching Council for Scotland, since 1990. Address: (h.) 72 Craigcrook Road, Edinburgh EH4 3PN; T.-0131-336 5164.

Gardner, Dianne Alicia, BA (Hons). Headmistress, Wellington School, Ayr, since 1988; b. 15.9.47, Wolverhampton; m., John W. Gardner. Educ. Ounsdale School; Liverpool University. Museum Assistant, 1969-71; Teacher of History, 1971-72; Head of History, then Senior Mistress, Wellington School, 1972-88. Recreations: painting; gardening. Address: (b.) Carleton Turrets, Ayr KA7 2XH; T.-01292 269321.

Gardner, James, BSc. Rector, Dunblane High School, since 1989; b. 3.2.41, Glasgow; m., Margaret Catherine; 1 s.; 1 d. Educ. Allan Glen's School, Glasgow; Glasgow University; Strathclyde University. Teacher of Mathematics, Allan Glen's School, 1968-76; Principal Teacher of Mathematics, Cranhill Secondary, Glasgow, 1976-80; Assistant Head Teacher, Dunoon Grammar School, 1980-84; Depute Rector, Wallace High School, Stirling, 1984-89. Member, British Antarctic Survey, 1963-66. Recreations: climbing; skiing; orienteering; chess; golf. Address: (b.) Dunblane High School, Highfields, Dunblane; T.-01786 823823.

Garland, Harry Mitchell, MBE, CQSW, FBIM. Chairman, Secretary of State's Advisory Committee on Scotland's Travelling People, since 1987; b. 7.7.28, Aberdeen; m., Phyllis Sandison; 1 s.; 1 d. Educ. Rockwell Academy, Dundee; Robert Gordon's College, Aberdeen; Moray House College, Edinburgh; Edinburgh University. Probation Officer/Senior Probation Officer/Principal Probation Officer, 1958-69; Depute Director of Social Work, Aberdeen and Kincardine Counties, 1969-73; Director of Social Work: Paisley Burgh, 1973-74, Western Isles, 1974-78, Central Region, 1978-86. Chairman, National Association of Probation Officers in Scotland, 1968-69; President, Association of Directors of Social

Work, 1983; Member, Forth Valley Health Board, 1986-90. Recreations: voluntary work; church; golf; walking. Address: (h.) 7 Cromarty View, Nairn IV12 4HX; T.-01667 453684.

Garner, John Angus McVicar, MB, ChB, DRCOG, DCH, FRCGP. Principal in general practice, since 1980; Past Chairman, Scottish General Medical Services Committee; British Medical Association: Vice Chairman, Scottish Council, Member, Council; Director, Medical and Dental Defence Union of Scotland; Treasurer, General Medical Services Defence Fund Ltd.; b. 4.9.50, London; m., Catherine Lizbeth; 1 s.; 1 d. Educ. Eltham College; Edinburgh University. Lothian Local Medical Committee: Secretary, 1986-89, Chairman, 1991-92; Member: General Medical Services Committee, since 1989, National Medical Advisory Committee, 1989-95. Recreations: amphibians and photographing fungi. Address: (h.) 25 Murrayfield Avenue, Edinburgh EH12 6AU; T.-0131-337 6120.

Garrett, Graeme Frederick, LLB, SSC. Solicitor; Partner, Digby Brown Solicitors, Edinburgh, since 1997; b. 23.1.53, Milan; m., Kathleen McGowan; 2 d. Educ. Royal High School, Edinburgh; Edinburgh University. Partner: Allan McDougall & Co., SSC, 1979-91, Thompsons Solicitors, Edinburgh, 1991-97. Council Member, Law Society of Scotland, 1993-96. Recreations: rugby; fishing; whisky. Address: (b.) 7 Albyn Place, Edinburgh EH2 4NG; T.-0131-220 7198.

Garrick, Sir Ronald, FEng, FRSE. Managing Director and Chief Executive, The Weir Group Plc, since 1982; b. 21.8.40; m.; 2 s.; 1 d. Non-Executive Director, Scottish Power, Shell UK; Member, Scottish Economic Council. Address: (b.) Weir Group PLC, 149 Newlands Road, Glasgow, G44 4EX.

Garrity, Rev. Thomas Alan Whiteway, BSc, BD, MTh. Ministe, Auld Kirk of Ayr, since 1982; b. 13.7.43, Glasgow; m., Elizabeth Caroline Whiteford; 2 d. Educ. Allan Glen's School; University of Glasgow; University of Edinburgh. Minister, Fraserburgh South, 1971-82. Recreations: golf; photography; woodwork. Address: 58 Monument Road, Ayr; T.-01292 262580.

Garrod, Professor Neil, BSc (Hons), PhD, ACIS. Professor of Financial Analysis and Head, Department of Accounting and Finance, Glasgow University, since 1993; b. 7.6.54; m., Sonja Gortnar; 1 s.; 1 d. Educ. Guthlaxton Upper School, Wigston; Manchester Institute of Science and Technology. Lecturer in Business Finance, University College of Wales, Aberystwyth, 1979-87; Associate Professor, Graduate Management Institute, Union College, New York, 1987-89; Senior Lecturer in Accounting and Finance, University of Wales, Bangor, 1989-90, Royal Insurance Professor of Finance and Accounting, 1990-93. Recreation: running. Address: (b.) Department of Accounting and Finance, Glasgow University, Glasgow G12 8LE; T.-0141-339 8855, Ext. 5426.

Gartside, Peter, BEd (Hons). UNICEF Educational Representative; Freelance education and training consultant; b. 31.10.32, Oldham; m., Kathleen; 1 s. Educ. East Oldham High School; Chester Diocesan Training College; Charlotte Mason College of Education. National Service, Royal Scots Greys, 1951-53; Teacher, Hollinwood County Secondary School, Oldham, 1955-57; Teacher, The Blue Coat School, Oldham, 1957-68; Head of House, Hattersley County Comprehensive School, 1968-70; Warden, Workington Teachers' Centre, Cumbria, 1970-76; Education Department, Independent Broadcasting Authority, 1977-78; Warden, West Cumbria Teachers' Centre, 1978-79; Adviser, Scottish Council for Educational Technology, 1980-86; Research Officer, Scottish Council for Research in Education, 1987-88; Secretary: Scottish Committee on Open Learning, 1983-86, National Committee of Teachers' Audio/Visual Aids Groups; former Member, BBC Radio Carlisle Education Education Advisory Panel. Recreations: walking; travel; music. Address (h.) 73 Argyle Way, Dunblane FK15 9DY.

Gaskin, Professor Maxwell, DFC (and bar), MA. Jaffrey Professor of Political Economy, Aberdeen University, 1965-85; b. 18.11.21, Liverpool; m., Brenda Stewart; 1 s.; 3 d. Educ. Quarry Bank School, Liverpool; Liverpool University. War Service, RAF, 1941-46; Lecturer and Senior Lecturer in Economics, Glasgow University, 1951-65; Head, Department of Political Economy, Aberdeen University, 1965-81; Economic Consultant to Secretary of State for Scotland, 1965-87; Member, Scottish Agricultural Wages Board, 1972-90; Chairman: Foresterhill and Associated Hospitals Board, 1972-74, Flax and Hemp and Retail Bespoke Tailoring Wages Councils, 1978-93; Member, Civil Engineering EDC, 1978-84; Chairman, Section F, British Association, 1978-79; President, Scottish Economic Society, 1981-84; Fellow, Royal Economic Society. Publications: The Scottish Banks: A Modern Survey, 1965; North East Scotland: A Survey of its Development Potential (Co-author), 1969; Economic Impact of North Sea Oil on Scotland (Co-author), 1978; Employment in Insurance, Banking and Finance in Scotland, 1980; The Political Economy of Tolerable Survival (Editor), 1981. Recreations: music; gardening. Address: (h.) Westfield, Ancrum, Roxburghshire TD8 6XA; T.-018353 830237.

Gaston, Rev. Arthur Raymond Charles, MA, BD. Secretary for Staffing, Board of World Mission, Church of Scotland, since 1993; Secretary, Presbytery of Europe, since 1997; b. 25.5.36, Atherstone; m., Evelyn Wilson Mather; 1 s.; 2 d. Educ. The Gordon Schools, Huntly; Aberdeen University. Teacher of Mathematics, 1961-62; Principal of theological college in Madagascar, 1962-67; Missionary with London Missionary Society, 1967-69; Minister, Sauchie Parish Church, 1969-75, Dollar with Muckhart with Glendevon, 1975-89, Scottish Church, Knox's Chapel, Geneva, 1989-93. Recreations: water colour painting; walking; choral singing; wildlife. Address: (h.) 137 Newhaven Road, Edinburgh EH6 4NP; T.-0131-554 6579.

Gautam, Prasanna Chandra, MBBS (Hon), MRCP (UK), FRCPEdin; FRCPGlas, MFCH. Consultant Physician, since 1989; Clinical Senior Lecturer in Medicine, Medical School, Aberdeen, since 1989; b. 3.4.45, Nepal; m., Leela Mani; 1 s.; 1 d. Educ. Padmodaya High School, Kathmandu; Bangalore Medical College, India. HMG of Nepal: Medical Officer, 1970-76, Senior Medical Officer, 1977-78; Senior House Officer in General Medicine, UK, 1977-81; Registrar in Cardiology, Liverpool, 1981-84; Registrar in Geriatric Medicine, Liverpool, 1984-86; Senior Registrar in General Medicine and Geriatrics, 1986-89. Former Chairman, Nepalese Doctors Association (UK); former Executive Member, Scottish Branch, BGS. Publications: several books in Nepali; publications on hypothermia and cardiac problems in the elderly. Recreations: chess; travelling; gardening; walking. Address: (b.) Department of Medicine for the Elderly, Woodend Hospital, Aberdeen; T.-01224 663131, Ext. 56319.

Gavin, Anthony John, BSc, DipEd. Head Teacher, St. Margaret's Academy, Livingston, since 1993; Member, Strategy Group, Higher Still Development Programme Scotland; b. 11.10.41, Perth; m., Charlotte Duffy; 2 d. Educ. Perth Academy; St. Andrews University. Teacher, St. Andrew's High School, Kirkcaldy, 1964-71; Principal Teacher/Assistant Headteacher, St. David's High School, Dalkeith, 1971-77; Depute Headteacher, St. Augustine's High School, Edinburgh, 1977-79; Headteacher, St. Saviour's High School, Dundee, 1979-93; TVEI Adviser Scotland, 1986-90. Member, Scottish Community Education Council, since 1993; Chair, Catholic Headteachers' Association of Scotland, 1994-96.

Recreations: music; golf. Address: (h.) 5 Colinton Court, Glenrothes KY6 3PE; T.-01592 743462.

Gavin, Derek, FRICS, IRRV. Chartered Surveyor, since 1971; Executive Director, Stirling Enterprise Park and Stirling Enterprise, since 1984; Board Director: Stirling Business Links Ltd., Business Enterprise Scotland Ltd.; b. 12.12.46, Perth; m., Terry; 1 s. Educ. Perth Academy; College of Estate Management. Trainee Surveyor, Bell Ingram, Perth, 1964-69; Management Surveyor, Scottish Industrial Estates Corporation, Glasgow, 1969-72; Valuation Surveyor, Bell Ingram, Perth, 1972-77; Estates Property Manager, Central Regional Council, 1977-84. Recreations: curling; golf. Address: (b.) John Player Building, Players Road, Stirling; T.-01786 463416.

Gavin, Kevin George, MA (Hons), DipEd. Director of Education, The Moray Council, since 1995; b. 4.7.48, Aberdeen; m., Jessie M.C. Connell; 1 d. Educ. Aberdeen Academy; Aberdeen University; Aberdeen College of Education. Assistant Head Teacher, Silverwood Primary School, Kilmarnock, 1974-77; Head Teacher, Monkton Primary School, 1977-80; Adviser in Primary Education: Grampian, 1980-83, Strathclyde, 1983-85; HM Inspector of Schools, 1985-90; Chief Adviser, Strathclyde Regional Council Education Department, 1990-95. Recreations: walking; gardening; food and drink; motor-cycling. Address: (h.) Monymusk, Benslie Village, by Kilwinning, KA13 7QY.

Gawthrop, Professor Peter John, MA, DPhil, MIEE, MInstMC, CEng, EurIng. Wylie Professor of Mechanical Engineering, Glasgow University, since 1987; b. 10.3.52, Seascale; 2 d. Educ. Whitehaven Grammar School; Queen's College, Oxford. W.W. Spooner Research Fellow, New College, Oxford; Lecturer, then Reader, Sussex University. Recreation: hill-walking. Address: (b.) Department of Mechanical Engineering, James Watt Building, Glasgow University, Glasgow G12 8QQ; T.-0141-339 8855.

Gemmell, Curtis Glen, BSc, PhD, MIBiol, FRCPath. Reader and Head of Academic Department of Bacteriology, Glasgow University; Honorary Bacteriologist, Greater Glasgow Health Board, since 1976; Director, Scottish MRSA Reference Laboratory; b. 26.8.41, Beith, Ayrshire; m., Anne Margaret; 2 d. Educ. Spier's School, Beith; Glasgow University. Glasgow University: Assistant Lecturer, 1966-68, Lecturer, 1968-69; Paisley College of Technology: Lecturer, 1969-71, Senior Lecturer, 1971-76; Glasgow University: Senior Lecturer, 1976-90, Reader, 1990-94; Visiting Assistant Professor, University of Minnesota, Minneapolis, 1979-80. Recreations: gardening; golf. Address: (h.) Sunninghill, 19 Lawmarnock Crescent, Bridge of Weir PA11 3AS; T.-Bridge of Weir 613350.

Gemmell, Gavin John Norman, CA. Senior Partner, Baillie, Gifford & Co., since 1989 (Partner, since 1967); Chairman, Toyo Trust Baillie Gifford Ltd., since 1989; Deputy Chairman, Scottish Widows Fund & Life Assurance Society, since 1995; Director: Guardian Baillie Gifford Ltd., since 1990, TSB Bank Scotland PLC, since 1991; b. 7.9.41, Edinburgh; m., Kathleen Fiona Drysdale; 1 s.; 2 d. Educ. George Watson's College. Qualified CA, 1964; joined Baillie, Gifford & Co., 1964; Chairman, Standing Committee, Scottish Episcopal Church, since 1997; Member, Court, Heriot Watt University, since 1993. Recreations: golf; foreign travel. Address: (b.) 1 Rutland Court, Edinburgh EH3 8EY; T.-0131-222 4000.

Gemmell, William Ruthven, LLB, WS. Partner, Murray Beith Murray WS, since 1987; Director, Inchcape Family Investments Ltd., Lawshare Ltd., and other companies; b. 4.4.57; m., Fiona Elizabeth Watson; 1 s.; 1 d. Educ. Loretto; Edinburgh University; Aberdeen University. Apprentice at Law, Brodies WS, 1979-82; Trainee Accountant, Arthur Young CA, 1983-85; Solicitor, Murray Beith Murray WS,

1985-87. Law Society of Scotland: Chairman, Investor Protection Committee, since 1992, Council Member, since 1993; Member, Financial Services Tribunal, since 1993; Director, Association of Solicitor Investment Managers. Address: (b.) 39 Castle Street, Edinburgh EH2 3BH; T.-0131-225 1200.

Gemmill, Robert, MA, FIMC. Member, Business Committee, General Council, Glasgow University, since 1987 and Assessor of the General Council on the Court, since 1990; b. 20.2.30; m., 1, Anne MacMurchy Gow (deceased); 2, Elisabeth Mary MacLennan; 2 s.; 1 d. Educ. High School of Glasgow; Glasgow University. Manufacturing management, Procter & Gamble Ltd., 1953-56; Management Consultant, PA Management Consultants Ltd., 1956-85. Played rugby football for Glasgow High School FP, Northumberland, Cheshire, Barbarians and Scotland, 1950-51. Recreations: golf; travel; music. Address: (h.) 123 Fotheringay Road, Glasgow G41 4LG; T.-0141-423 1860.

Gennard, Professor John, BA (Econ), MA (Econ), FIPM. Professor of Human Resource Management, Strathclyde University, since 1981; b. 26.4.44, Manchester; m., Florence Anne Russell; 1 s.; 1 d. Educ. Hulme Grammar School for Boys; Sheffield University; Manchester University. Research Officer, Industrial Relations Department, then Lecturer in Industrial Relations, London School of Economics, 1968-81. Publications: The Reluctant Militants (Co-author), 1972; Financing Strikers, 1978; Industrial Relations and Job Security, 1979; The Closed Shop in British Industry, 1984; A History of the National Graphical Association, 1990; A History of the Society of Graphical and Allied Trades, 1995; Employee Relations, 1997. Recreations: football; swimming; politics; trade unions; food and drink. Address: (h.) 4 South Avenue, Carluke, Lanarkshire; T.-01555 51361.

George, John Charles Grossmith, FSAScot, FHS. Kintyre Pursuivant of Arms, since 1986; b. 15.12.30, London; m., Margaret Mary Maria Mercedes Weld. Educ. Ampleforth. Lt., Hertfordshire Yeomanry, 1951-54; films and television advertising, 1952-62; College of Arms, 1962-72; Earl Marshal's Liaison Officer with the Churchill family, 1965; Green Staff Officer, Prince of Wales's Investiture, 1969; Garioch Pursuivant, 1976. Chairman, Philbeach Light Opera Society, 1961-63; Vice President, BBC "Mastermind" Club, 1979-81; Knight of Obedience, Sov. Mil. Ord. of Malta; Commander, Ord. Pro Merito Melitensi; Knight Constantinian Order of St. George. Publications: The Puffin Book of Flags, 1975; The French Heralds (paper), 1985; numerous historical articles. Recreations: English light opera and musical comedies; hagiographies; sports. Address: (h.) 115 Henderson Row, Edinburgh EH3 5BB; T.-0131-557 1605.

George, Judith Wordsworth, MA (Oxon), PhD. Deputy Scottish Director, The Open University, since 1984; b. 26.8.40, Bradford; 2 d. Educ. Heath Grammar School, Halifax; Somerville College, Oxford. Tutor in Philosophy, St. Andrews University; Lecturer in History of Fine Art, Manchester University; Tutor in Classics, Open University; Senior Counsellor, Open University in Scotland. Recreations: gardening; classical music; hill-walking. Address: (b.) 10 Drumsheugh Gardens, Edinburgh EH3 7QJ; T.-0131-260 7130.

George, Professor William David, MB, BS, FRCS, MS. Professor of Surgery, Glasgow University, since 1981; b. 22.3.43, Reading; 1 s.; 3 d. Educ. Henley Grammar School; London University. Lecturer in Surgery, Manchester University, 1973-77; Senior Lecturer in Surgery, Liverpool University, 1977-81. Member, National Committees, British Association of Surgical Oncology and Surgical

Research Society. Recreations: veteran rowing; golf. Address: (b.) University Department of Surgery, Western Infirmary, Glasgow G11 6NT; T.-0141-339 8822.

Gerber, Pat, MA (Hons). Writer, since 1982; Lecturer (part-time), Glasgow University, since 1985; b. 17.3.34, Glasgow; m., Cyril Gerber; 3 s.; 2 d. Educ. St. Leonard's School; Glasgow University. Committee Member: Scottish Book Marketing Group, Society of Authors in Scotland. Publications: The Stone of Destiny; Maiden Voyage; several plays. Recreations: reading; travel; swimming; tennis; hill-walking; sailing; cars; sewing; music. Address: (h.) 6 Golf Road, Clarkston, Glasgow G76 7LZ; T.-0141-638 2269.

Gerrard, John Henry Atkinson, MBE, FRIAS, DA (Edin), MA (Cantab), FRSA, FSA(Scot). Technical Director, Scottish Civic Trust, since 1984; b. 15.9.34, Leicester; m., Dr. Margaret Mackay. Educ. Abbotsholme; Corpus Christi College, Cambridge; Edinburgh College of Art. Assistant Architect: Sheffield Corporation, 1961-63, Planning Department, Oxford City Council, 1965-68; Assistant Director, Scottish Civic Trust, 1968-84. Recreation: travelling hopefully. Address: (b.) The Tobacco Merchant's House, 42 Miller Street, Glasgow G1 1DT; T.-0141-221 1466.

Gerrie, Ian. Controller, Inland Revenue Scotland. Address: (b.) Clarendon House, 114-116 George Street, Edinburgh EH2 4LH.

Gerson, Jack Barton. Dramatist and Novelist; b. 31.7.28, Glasgow; 1 d. Educ. Hillhead High School, Glasgow. RAF, two years; worked in advertising and cinema distribution, 1949-59; writing full-time since 1959; won BBC Television Play Competition, 1959, for Three Ring Circus; has written more than 100 hours of television drama; created two series, The Regiment and The Omega Factor; 14 radio plays; novels include Whitehall Sanction, Assassination Run, Treachery Game, The Back of the Tiger, Deaths Head Berlin, The Evil Thereof, The Fetch. Recreations: cinema; reading; swimming; Caribbean Islands; sleeping in front of television set. Address: (b.) c/o Harvey Unna & Stephen Durbridge, 24 Pottery Lane, Holland Park, London W11 4LZ.

Gerstenberg, Frank Eric, MA (Cantab), PGCE, FRSA. Principal, George Watson's College, Edinburgh, since 1985; b. 23.2.41, Balfron; m., Valerie MacLellan; 1 s.; 2 d. Educ. Trinity College, Glenalmond; Clare College, Cambridge; London University. Assistant Master, Kelly College, Tavistock, 1963-67; Housemaster and Head of History, Millfield School, 1967-74; Headmaster, Oswestry School, 1974-85. Recreations: skiing; sailing; travelling; music. Address: (h.) 27 Merchiston Gardens, Edinburgh EH10 5DD; T.-0131-337 6880.

Gerver, Professor Elisabeth, BA (Hons), MA, PhD. Professor and Director of Continuing Education, University of Dundee, 1990-97; b. 15.4.41, Winnipeg; m., Dr. David Gerver (deceased); 1 s.; 1 d. Educ. Wolfville High School, Nova Scotia; Dalhousie University, Canada; Toronto University; King's College, London. Lecturer in Communications, Newcastle upon Tyne Polytechnic, 1968-69; part-time staff, Open University, 1971-84; Lecturer in Communication, Queen Margaret College, Edinburgh, 1974-83; Director: Scottish Community Education Microelectronics Project, Glasgow, 1981-82, Scottish Institute of Adult and Continuing Education, 1983-90. Member, Council: Scottish Community Education Council, 1979-83, BBC Continuing Education Advisory Council, 1983-86; Vice-President, European Bureau of Adult Education, 1986-90; Executive Member, Universities Association for Continuing Education, 1992-97; Governor, Queen Margaret College, 1985-88; Member: Board, Tayside Education Business Partnership, 1992-96, IBA

Educational Advisory Council, 1988-90, Education Panel, Research Assessment Exercise, 1992 and 1996, Post-Qualification Education Board for Pharmacists (Scotland), 1996-98. Publications: Computers and Adult Learning, 1984; Humanising Technology, 1985; Strategic Women: how do they manage in Scotland? (Co-author), 1991. Recreations: travel; the performing arts; hill-walking; sailing. Address: (h.) 65 Magdalen Yard Road, Dundee DD2 1AL; T.-01382 566794.

Gibb, Alexander Russell. Director and General Manager, Royal Mail Scotland and Northern Ireland, since 1996; b. 19.9.46, Motherwell; m., Elizabeth Ann Watney. Educ. Wishaw High School. Management Trainee, Post Office, 1965; Assistant Controller, Royal Mail, 1968; Assistant Head Postmaster, Oxford, 1976; Head Postmaster, Aberdeen, 1984; Operations Controller, Scotland, Royal Mail, 1986; Operations Director, Scotland, Royal Mail, 1992. Director, Quality Scotland Foundation; Chairman, Head Postmaster Fellowship, Scotland; President, Post Office Sports Association (Scotland and Northern Ireland). Recreations: sport; walking; family; travel. Address: (b.) 102 West Port, Edinburgh EH3 9HS; T.-0131-228 7400.

Gibb, Andrew Thomas Fotheringham, LLB (Hons), SSC, NP. Solicitor, since 1972; Chairman and Head, Family Law Team, Balfour & Manson, Edinburgh, since 1995; b. 17.8.47, Perth; m., Patricia Anne Eggo; 2 s. Educ. Perth Academy; University of Edinburgh. Qualified 1971; joined Balfour & Manson, 1972: Partner, 1975. Solicitor, Educational Institute of Scotland, since 1983; President, Law Society of Scotland, 1990-91 (Member, Council, 1981-93); Joint Editor, Family Law Bulletin. Recreations: music; golf. Address: (b.) 58 Frederick Street, Edinburgh EH2 1LS.

Gibb, Francis. General Manager, Common Services Agency. Address: (b.) Trinity Park House, South Trinity Road, Edinburgh, EH5 3SE.

Gibbons, John Ernest, PhD, DipArch, DipTP, ARIBA, ARIAS, FSA(Scot), FRSA. Director of Building and Chief Architect, Scottish Office, since 1984; b. 20.4.40, Halesowen; m., Patricia Mitchell; 1 s.; 2 d. Educ. Oldbury Grammar School; Birmingham School of Architecture, Aston University; Edinburgh University. Lecturer, Birmingham School of Architecture and Aston University, 1962-65; Research Fellow, Architecture Research Unit, then Lecturer in Architecture, Edinburgh University, 1966-72; Principal, Architect's Division, Scottish Development Department, 1972-78; Visiting Research Scientist, CSIRO, Melbourne, 1975; Assistant Director, Building Directorate, SDD, 1978; Deputy Director, Scottish Office Building Directorate, 1982-84. Member, Council: EAA and RIAS, 1977-80, ARCUK, since 1984; Assessor, Design Council, 1984-88. Address: (h.) Crichton House, Pathhead, Midlothian EH37 5UX; T.-01875 320085.

Gibbs, Lavinia. Trustee, National Galleries of Scotland, since 1986; Member: Brodick Country Park Committee, since 1980, Ayrshire and Arran Health Council, since 1994; b. 7.6.39, London; m., Stephen Gibbs; 2 s.; 1 d. Educ. Heathfield, Ascot; Ipswich Civic College. Librarian, Courtauld Institute of Art, London, 1960-66; Child Care Officer/Social Worker, Royal Borough of Kensington and Chelsea, 1968-73; Representative for Norfolk, National Art Collections Fund, 1968-73; Member, Council, National Trust for Scotland, 1975-80, and Curatorial Committee, 1982-92. Recreation: gardening. Address: (h.) Dougarie Lodge, Isle of Arran KA27 8EB; T.-0177 084 0229.

Gibbs, Ronald Percy, OBE. President, Phab Scotland, since 1992 (Chairman, 1984-92); a Director, Handicabs (Lothian), since 1985; Convener, History Section, The Cramond Association, since 1983; b. 1.6.21, London; m., Margaret Eleanor Dean; 3 s.; 1 d. Educ. Owen's School,

Islington. Ministry (later Department) of Transport, 1938-81; set up the Ports Office for Scotland in Edinburgh, 1973, and remained Head of that Office until retiral in 1981. Recreations: transport and communications; music; Scottish and industrial history; photography. Address: (h.) 13 Inveralmond Drive, Edinburgh EH4 6JX; T.-0131-312 6034.

Gibbs, Stephen Cokayne, Director, Vaux Group PLC, since 1970; b. 18.7.29, Hertingfordbury, England; m., Lavinia Bacon; 2 s.; 1 d. Educ. Eton College. Served with KRRC (60th Rifles), 1947-49; TA, service with QVR (TA), 1951-63: Lt., 1951, Captain, 1956, Major, 1958; Port Line Ltd., 1949-62: Assistant Manager, 1957, London Manager, 1959; Charles Barker PLC, 1962-87: Director, 1962, Deputy Chairman, 1982-87. National Trust for Scotland: Member, Executive, since 1987 and Council, 1991-96; Member: TUCC for Scotland, since 1992, Red Deer Commission, since 1993; Chairman: Association of Deer Management Groups, since 1994, Isle of Arran District Salmon Fishery Board, since 1990. Recreations: shooting; fishing. Address: The Estate Office, Dougarie, Isle of Arran KA27 8EB; T.-01770 840259.

Gibson, Edgar Matheson, MBE, TD, DL, DA. Deputy Lieutenant, Orkney, since 1976; Honorary Sheriff, Grampian, Highlands and Islands, since 1992; full-time professional artist since 1990; b. 1.11.34, Kirkwall; m., Jean McCarrick; 2 s.; 2 d. Educ. Kirkwall Grammar School; Gray's College of Art, Aberdeen. National Service, 1958-60; TA and TAVR service to 1985 with Lovat Scouts, reaching Lt. Col.; Battalion Second in Command, 2/51 Highland Volunteers, 1973-76; Joint Services Liaison Officer for Orkney, 1980-85; Cadet Commandant, Orkney Lovat Scouts ACF, 1979-86, Honorary Colonel, since 1986; Member, Orkney Health Board, since 1991; Vice Chairman, Italian Chapel Preservation Committee, since 1994; Hon. President: Society of Friends of St. Magnus Cathedral, since 1994, Orkney Craftsmen's Guild, since 1997 (Chairman, 1962-82); President, Orkney Branch, SSFA and FHS, since 1997 (Chairman, 1990-97); Chairman: St. Magnus Cathedral Fair Committee, since 1982, Northern Area, Highland TA&VR Association, 1987-93. Recreation: whisky tasting. Address: (h.) Transcona, New Scapa Road, Kirkwall, Orkney; T.-0856 2849.

Gibson, Rev. Henry Montgomerie, MA, BD, PhD. Minister, The High Kirk, Dundee, since 1979; b. 11.6.36, Wishaw; m., Dr. Anne Margaret Thomson; 1 s. Educ. Wishaw Academy; Hamilton Academy; Glasgow University. Assistant Minister, Glasgow Cathedral, 1960; Minister: Carmunnock Parish Church, Glasgow, 1961-71, Aberfeldy, 1971-79; Convener, Church of Scotland Working Party on Alcohol and Drugs, 1975-81; Moderator, Dundee Presbytery, 1996-97. Recreations: reading; table tennis (occasionally). Address: High Kirk Manse, 6 Adelaide Place, Dundee DD3 6LF; T.-Dundee 322955.

Gibson, Ian Ford, BSc, BA(Hons). Headteacher, Woodfarm High School, Thornliebank, since 1995; b. 16.4.49, Girvan; m., Marion. Educ. Hamilton Academy; University of Glasgow; Open University. Teacher of Mathematics: Hamilton Grammar, 1972-74, Earnock High, Hamilton, 1974-80; Barrhead High: Teacher of Mathematics, 1980-85, Assistant Head Teacher, 1985-91, Depute Head Teacher, 1991-95. Recreations: bowling; gardening. Address: (b.) Woodfarm High School, Rosslee Road, Thornliebank, Glasgow G46 7HG; T.-0141-577 2600.

Gibson, Ian Robert Lusk, MA, DipHSM. Regional Director, Scotland and Northern Ireland, Macmillan Cancer Relief, since 1996; b. 15.5.53, Kilmarnock; m., Rosemary Margaret Copland. Educ. Dollar Academy; Edinburgh University. Commissioning Administrator, Crosshouse Hospital, Ayrshire, 1978-79; Assistant Administrator,

Stobhill Hospital, Glasgow, 1979-83; Administrator, Western General Hospital, Edinburgh, 1983-86; Assistant General Manager, Royal Infirmary of Edinburgh, 1986-89; Civil Servant, 1989-90; Operations Director, Mediguard Services, 1990-92; Regional Director, Scottish Ambulance Service, 1992-96. Trustee, Edinburgh Cyrenians, since 1993. Recreations: golf; tennis; skiing; hill-walking; gardening; foreign languages. Address: (b.) 9 Castle Terrace, Edinburgh; T.-0131-229 3276.

Gibson, John Alan, MB, ChB, MD, FRCGP, FRSMed, DObstRCOG, CBiol, FIBiol, FLS, FZS, FRGS, FRMS, FGS, FSA (Scot). Senior Honorary Secretary, British Medical Association, since 1979; Chairman, Scottish Natural History Library, since 1974; Editor, the Scottish Naturalist, since 1972; b. 15.5.26, Kilbarchan; m., Dr. Mary M. Baxter; 1 d. Educ. Lindisfarne School; Paisley Grammar School; Glasgow University. Family doctor, village of Kilbarchan; Hon. Secretary, Renfrewshire Division, BMA, 1957-95; last Secretary, Renfrewshire Local Medical Committee; first Secretary, Argyll and Clyde Area Medical Committee; Member, Central Council, Central Ethical Committee, Scottish Council and Scottish GMS Committee, BMA; Past President, West of Scotland Branch, BMA; Hon. President, Renfrewshire Division, BMA; Fellow, Royal Society of Medicine; Life Fellow, Royal College of General Practitioners; Scottish Representative and Vice-President, Society for the Bibliography of Natural History; Scientific Meetings Secretary, Vice-President and Hon. Member, Society for the History of Natural History; Chairman: Friends of Glasgow University Library, Scottish Natural History Trust, Clyde Area Branch, Scottish Wildlife Trust; President, Renfrewshire Natural History Society; Secretary and Honorary Life Member, Scottish Society for the Protection of Birds; Life Fellow: RSPB, Royal Zoological Society of Scotland; Chairman, Clyde Bird Club; Honorary President, Kintyre Bird Club; Secretary, Royal Physical Society of Edinburgh; Gold Medal, Scottish Society for the Protection of Birds, 1967; Queen's Silver Jubilee Medal, 1977; Fellowship, BMA, 1982. Publications: Mammals of West of Scotland; Birds of Clyde Area; Atlas of Clyde Vertebrates; Regional Bibliography of West of Scotland Vertebrates; Bibliography of Scottish Vertebrate Zoology; 300 scientific papers, books and reports on Scottish natural history, 1939-97. Recreations: natural history; golf (Royal Troon). Address: (h.) Foremount House, Kilbarchan PA10 2EZ; T.-01505 702410.

Gibson, John Sibbald. Author (Scottish history); b. 1.5.23, Barrhead; m., Moira Helen Gibson; 1 s.; 1 d. Educ. Paisley Grammar School; Glasgow University. Army Service, 1941-46 (Lieut., 1 Commando); returned to Glasgow University; joined administrative grade, Civil Service, 1947 and served in Scottish Office until 1985, retiring as Under Secretary. Vice Chairman, Saltire Society, since 1995. Publications: Ships of the '45; Deacon Brodie; The Thistle and the Crown; Playing the Scottish Card; The Jacobite Threat; Summer Hunting A Prince; Lochiel of the '45; Edinburgh in the '45. Recreation: writing on historical themes. Address: (h.) 28 Cramond Gardens, Edinburgh EH4 6PH; T.-0131 336 2931.

Gibson, Robert Irvine, MA(Hons). Rector, Eastwood High School, since 1995; b. 14.8.47, Ayr; m., Elizabeth; 1 s.; 2 d. Educ. John Neilson Institution, Paisley; University of Glasgow. Teacher, Paisley Grammar School; Principal Teacher, then Assistant Headteacher, Woodfarm High School; T.R.I.S.T. Co-ordinator, Renfrew Division, Strathclyde Council; Depute Headteacher, Greenock High School. Member, Mearns Parish Kirk Trust. Address: (b.) Eastwood High School, Capelrig Road, Newton Mearns G77 6NQ; T.-0141-577 2200.

Gibson, Sheriff William Erle, BA, LLB. Sheriff, since 1989; b. 30.8.34, Glasgow; m., Anne; 1 s.; 2 d. Educ. Dollar Academy; Trinity Hall, Cambridge; Glasgow University.

Solicitor in Glasgow, 1961-89; Clerk to General Commissioners of Taxes, City of Glasgow, 1968-89; Clerk to General Council, Glasgow University, 1976-86. Member, European Ethical Review Committee, since 1976. Recreations: golf; fishing; piping; hill-walking; the family. Address: (h.) 7A Briarwell Road, Milngavie, Glasgow; T.-0141-956 2770.

Gilchrist, Allan C., BSc, DipEd, FRSA. Director of Education, Highland Council, since 1994; b. 12.9.38, Paisley; m., Margaret Porteous; 2 s. Educ. John Neilson Institution; Glasgow University. Teacher, 1962-69; Head Teacher, 1969-74; Education Officer, 1974-85; Depute Director of Education, 1985-94. Recreations: walking; golf; travel; reading. Address: (b.) Highland Council, Glenurquhart Road, Inverness IV3 5NX; T.-01463 702801.

Gilchrist, Archibald, OBE, MA. Director, RMJM Ltd., since 1988; Vice-Chairman, Scottish Friendly Assurance Society Ltd. (Director, since 1988); b. 17.11.29, Glasgow; m., Elizabeth Jean; 2 s.; 1 d. Educ. Loretto School; Pembroke College, Cambridge. Barclay Curle & Co. Ltd., 1954-64; Brown Bros. & Co. Ltd., 1964-72; Govan Shipbuilders Ltd., 1972-79; Vosper Pte Ltd., Singapore, 1980-86; Director, Caledonian MacBrayne Ltd., 1990-97. Recreations: shooting; fishing; golf. Address: (h.) 35 Barnton Avenue, Edinburgh EH4 6JJ; T.-0131-336 4288.

Gilchrist, Bernard, MBE, MA (Hons) (Oxon); b. 20.5.19, Manchester; m., Jean W. Gregory; 2 s.; 1 d. Educ. Manchester Grammar School; Queen's College, Oxford. Tanganyika: Forest Officer, HM Colonial/Overseas Civil Service, 1942-62 (Conservator of Forests, 1960), Conservator of Forests, Tanganyika/Tanzania Government Service, 1962-65; Chief Executive, Scottish Wildlife Trust, 1965-85. Recreations: countryside; natural history; hill-walking; photography. Address: (h.) 9 Murrayfield Gardens, Edinburgh EH12 6DG; T.-0131-337 3869.

Gilchrist, Thomas, BSc, PhD, CChem, FRSC. Managing Director, Giltech Ltd., since 1984; b. 18.6.36, Ayr; m., Fiona Christina Brown; 2 d. Educ. Ayr Academy; Glasgow University. Assistant Lecturer in Chemistry, Glasgow University, 1961-62; Research Chemist: Canadian Industries Ltd., Quebec, 1962-64, ICI Ltd., Stevenston, Ayrshire, 1964-69; Strathclyde University: Lecturer in Bioengineering, 1969, Head, Division of Artificial Organs, Bioengineering Unit, 1972, Senior Lecturer in Bioengineering, 1975-84. Recreations: golf; curling. Address: (h.) The Lodge, 67 Midton Road, Ayr KA7 2TW; T.-Ayr 266088.

Giles, Cecilia Elspeth, CBE, MA. Member, Rail Users Consultative Committee for Scotland, since 1989; b. Dumfries. Educ. Queen Margaret's School, Yorkshire; Edinburgh University. Administrative staff, Khartoum University, 1956-57; joined Administrative staff, Edinburgh University, 1957; Assistant Secretary, Edinburgh University, 1972-87; Committee of Vice-Chancellors and Principals' Administrative Training Officer (seconded part-time), 1983-85. President, Edinburgh University Graduates' Association, 1889-91; Member, Business Committee, General Council, Edinburgh University, 1988-93, Convener, Constitutional Sub-Committee, 1991-93; Member, Church of Scotland Board of Stewardship and Finance, 1986-93, Vice Convener 1990-93; Member, Church of Scotland Assembly Council, 1993-96. Publication: Scotland for the Tourist (Co-author). Recreations: entertaining friends, family and godchildren; theatre. Address: (b.) Graduates' Association, 5 Buccleuch Place, Edinburgh EH8 9LW.

Gilhooly, Professor Mary Lynn Martin, BSc, MEd, MPhil, PhD, CPsychol, AFBPsyS. Professor of Health Studies and Director, Centre of Gerontology and Health Studies, University of Paisley, since 1994; b. 22.1.47,

Tacoma, Washington; m., Kenneth; 1 s. Educ. Hood River High School, Oregon; David Douglas High School, Oregon; University of Oregon; University of Aberdeen; University of Glasgow. Scientific Officer, MRC Medical Sociology Unit, Aberdeen, 1979-83; Fellow, Andras Gerontology Centre, University of Southern California, 1983-84; Senior Scientific Officer, Grampian Health Board, 1984-85; Lecturer, Behavourial Sciences, Faculty of Medicine, University of Glasgow, 1984-94; Editor, Generations Review. Member, Rights and Legal Protection Sub-committee, Alzheimer's Scotland-Action on Dementia; Member, National Board for Nursing, Midwifery and Health Visiting for Scotland Research and Development Committee; Member, Ayrshire and Arran Community Healthcare NHS Research Ethics Committee. Address: (b.) Centre for Gerontology and Health Studies, University of Paisley PA1 2BE; T.-0141-848 3771.

Gill, Hon. Lord (Brian Gill), MA, LLB, PhD. Senator of the College of Justice in Scotland, since 1994; Chairman, Scottish Law Commission; b. 25.2.42; m.; 5 s.; 1 d. Educ. St. Aloysius College; Glasgow University; Edinburgh University. Advocate, 1967; Advocate-Depute, 1977-79; Standing Junior Counsel: Foreign and Commonwealth Office (Scotland), 1974-77, Home Office (Scotland), 1979-81, Scottish Education Department, 1979-81; QC, 1981; called to the Bar, Lincoln's Inn, 1991; Keeper, Advocates' Library, 1987-94. Address: (b.) Court of Session, Parliament House, Parliament Square, Edinburgh, EH1 1RQ.

Gill, Professor Roger William Thomas, BA (Hons), BPhil, MA, PhD, AFBPsS, FIPD, FIMgt, FRSA, CPsychol. Director, Research Centre for Leadership Studies, The Leadership Trust, and Visiting Professor of Business Administration (Human Resource Management), Strathclyde University Graduate Business School, since 1992; b. 3.10.45, Cumbria; 1 s.; 1 d. Educ. Merchant Taylors' School, Crosby; St. Peter's College, Oxford; Liverpool University; Bradford University. English Electric, 1967-68; Inbucon/AIC Management Consultants, 1969-71; Personnel Manager, De La Rue, 1971-72; Manpower Manager, Associated Weavers, 1972-74; Lecturer, Bradford University Management Centre, 1974-78; Assistant Professor, State University of New York at Binghamton, 1979-82; Managing Director, Roger Gill & Associates, Singapore, 1982-90; Regional Manager (Asia), PA Consulting Group, Singapore, 1990-91. Publications: numerous articles and research reports. Recreations: music; theatre; food and wine; reading; doing nothing. Address: (b.) 199 Cathedral Street, Glasgow, G4 0QU; T.-0141-553 6141.

Gillespie, Professor Thomas Alastair, BA, PhD, FRSE. Professor of Mathematical Analysis, University of Edinburgh, since 1997; b. 15.2.45, Torrance; m., Judith Anne Nelmes; 2 s.; 1 d. Educ. Glasgow Academy; University of Cambridge; University of Edinburgh. Lecturer, 1968-87, Senior Lecturer, 1987-92, Reader in Mathematics, 1992-97, University of Edinburgh; Visiting Professor, Indiana University, 1973-74, 1983-84. Recreations: gardening; making music; jogging. Address: (b.) Department of Mathematics and Statistics, James Clerk Maxwell Building, Edinburgh EH9 3JZ; T.-0131-650 5081.

Gillespie, Professor William John, TD, BSc, MB, ChB, ChM, FRCSEd, FRACS. Professor of Orthopaedic Surgery, Edinburgh University, since 1993; b. 16.6.40, Stirling; m., Lesley Diane Wood; 2 s. Educ. George Watson's College; Edinburgh University. Professor of Orthopaedic Surgery: Christchurch School of Medicine, University of Otago, 1981-89, University of Newcastle, New South Wales, 1989-93. Address: (b.) Princess Margaret Rose Orthopaedic Hospital, Fairmilehead, Edinburgh EH10 7ED; T.-0131-536 4667.

Gillies (nee McCall-Smith), Anne Bethea, MA, LLB. Advocate; Honorary Sheriff of South Strathclyde, Dumfries and Galloway, at Lanark, since 1960; b. 12.4.22, Lochgilphead, Argyll; m., Sheriff Principal M.G. Gillies, T.D., Q.C. (d. 1997). Educ. Sherborne School for Girls, Dorset; Edinburgh University. Served in WAAF, until 1946; called to Scottish Bar, 1951; married, 1954. Member, Valuation Appeal Panel, Strathclyde, 1974-88. Recreations: gardening; cats. Address: (h.) The Coach House, Broadgait, Gullane, East Lothian EH31 2DH; T.-01620 842857.

Gillies, Anne Lorne, MA, PhD, PGCE, LRAM, Drhc. Singer and Writer, since 1962; Lecturer in Gaelic, University of Strathclyde, since 1995; Member, National Executive, Scottish National Party, since 1996; b. 21.10.44, Stirling; 1 s.; 2 d. Educ. Oban High School; Edinburgh University; London University; Jordanhill College of Education; Glasgow University. Singer: TV, radio, concert, recital, theatre, recording; writer: scripts, children's books, novels, articles, autobiography, songs; education/ community development: teacher, resource development; National Education Officer, Comunn na Gaidhlig, 1988-90, Arts Development Officer, Govan Initiative Ltd., 1991-93; Producer and Writer, Scottish Television 1993-95. Recreation: married bliss. Address: (h.) 54 Terregles Avenue, Glasgow G41 4LX.

Gillies, Norman Neil Nicolson, BA, MIMgt, FRSA. Director, Sabhal Mor Ostaig, since 1988; b. 1.3.47, Flodigarry, Isle of Skye; m., Jean Brown Nixon; 1 s.; 2 d. Educ. Portree High School; Strathclyde University; Open University. College Secretary, Sabhal Mor Ostaig, 1983-88; Director: Skye and Lochalsh Enterprise Ltd., Sabhal Mor Ostaig (Developments) Ltd., Canan Ltd, UHI Ltd.; Member: Barail (Centre for Highlands and Islands Policy Studies); Leirsinn Research Centre; University of the Highlands and Islands Academic Council; Gaelic Broadcasting Committee; Gaelic Television Training Trust. Recreations: reading; broadcasting; family. Address: (h.) Innis Ard, Ardvasar, Isle of Skye IV45 8RU; T.-01471 844 281.

Gillies, Rev. Dr. Robert Arthur, BD, PhD. Rector, St. Andrew's Episcopal Church, St. Andrews, since 1991; b. 21.10.51, Cleethorpes; m., Elizabeth; 3 s. Educ. Barton-upon-Humber Grammar School; Edinburgh University; St. Andrews University. Medical Laboratory Technician, 1968-72; Curate: Christ Church, Falkirk, 1977-80, Christ Church Morningside, and Chaplain, Napier College, 1980-84; Chaplain, Dundee University, 1984-90. Hon. Lecturer, Department of Philosophy, Dundee University, 1985-95. Publications: A Way for Healing, 1995; Informing Faith, 1996; Healing: Broader and Deeper, 1998. Recreations: family; garden; Scotland's mountains. Address: St. Andrew's Rectory, Queen's Terrace, St. Andrews, Fife KY16 9QF; T.-01334 473344.

Gillies, Valerie, MA, MLitt, FSAScot. Poet; Writer in Residence, Edinburgh University, since 1995; b. 4.6.48, Edmonton, Canada; m., William Gillies; 1 s.; 2 d. Educ. Edinburgh University; University of Mysore, S. India. Writer to the School, Boroughmuir High School and Edinburgh Academy; Radio and Television Scriptwriter; Poet to Borders Festival; Writer in Residence, Duncan of Jordanstone College of Art and Dundee District Libraries; Writer in Residence, East Lothian and Midlothian District Libraries; Senior Arts Worker (Hospital Arts), Artlink. Publications: Each Bright Eye; Bed of Stone; Tweed Journey; The Chanter's Tune; The Ringing Rock; St. Kilda Song. Recreations: whippet-racing; field-walking; Taichi; swimming. Address: (h.) 67 Braid Avenue, Edinburgh EH10 6ED; T.-0131-447 2876.

Gillies, Professor William, MA (Edin), MA (Oxon). Professor of Celtic, Edinburgh University, since 1979; b. 15.9.42, Stirling; m., Valerie; 1 s.; 2 d. Educ. Oban High School; Edinburgh University; Corpus Christi College, Oxford; Dublin University. Dublin Institute for Advanced Studies, 1969-70; Lecturer, Edinburgh University, 1970-79; Fellow, Royal Society of Edinburgh, 1990. Director, SNDA Ltd. Recreations: walking; gardening; music. Address: (h.) 67 Braid Avenue, Edinburgh EH10 6ED.

Gillis, Charles Raphael, MD, FRCP(Glas), FFCM. Director: West of Scotland Cancer Surveillance Unit, since 1973, WHO Collaborating Centre; Honorary Clinical Senior Lecturer, Glasgow University, since 1973; Honorary Professor, Glasgow University, since 1997; b. 23.10.37, Glasgow; m., Judith Ann Naftalin; 1 s.; 1 d. Educ. High School of Glasgow; Glasgow University. Lecturer in Epidemiology and Preventive Medicine, then Senior Lecturer and Honorary Consultant Epidemiologist, Glasgow University, 1965-73. Past Chairman: Cancer Education Co-ordinating Group of the UK and Republic of Ireland, West of Scotland Oncological Organisation. Address: (b.) West of Scotland Cancer Surveillance Unit, Ruchill Hospital, Bilsland Drive, Ruchill, Glasgow G20 9NB; T.-0141-946 7120.

Gillon, Hamish William, FFA, FPMI. Group Actuary, Scottish Provident Institution, since 1988; b. 22.1.40, Edinburgh; m., Sandra; 1 s.; 1 d. Educ. Royal High School, Edinburgh. Various appointments, Scottish Provident Institution, since 1965. Vice President, Faculty of Actuaries, 1993-96; Hon. Treasurer (Scotland), The Scout Association. Address: (b.) 7-11 Melville Street, Edinburgh EH3 7YZ; T.-0131-527 1100.

Gilmour, Colonel Sir Allan Macdonald, KCVO, OBE, MC (and Bar), DSC (USA). Lord Lieutenant of Sutherland, 1972-96; b. 23.11.16, Edinburgh; m., Jean Wood; 3 s.; 1 d. Educ. Cargilfield, Edinburgh; Winchester College; Trinity College, Oxford. Commissioned Seaforth Highlanders, 1939; served War in Middle East, Sicily and NW Europe; Regimental and Staff appointments, 1945-69, including Instructor, Staff College, Quetta, and Chief of Staff, Ghana Armed Forces; Member, Sutherland County Council, 1970; Member, Highland Health Board, 1974 (Chairman, 1982-84); DL, Sutherland, 1969; Member, Highlands and Islands Development Consultative Council, 1980-88; Chairman: Sutherland District Council, 1974-78, East Sutherland Council of Social Service, 1972-76; Member: Board, Scottish National Orchestra Society, 1976-86, Highland Regional Council, 1976-96; President, Highland Territorial & Auxiliary Reserve Association, 1988-91; Chairman, Highland River Purification Board, 1994-96. Recreation: fishing. Address: (h.) Invernauld, Rosehall, Lairg, Sutherland; T.-0154 984 204.

Gilmour, Andrew Parr, BSc (Hons). Rector, Rothesay Academy, since 1983; b. 26.4.46, Glasgow; m., Elizabeth Morrison MacPherson; 1 s.; 2 d. Educ. Allan Glen's School, Glasgow; Glasgow University. Teacher of Chemistry, Allan Glen's School, 1969; Dunoon Grammar School: Principal Teacher of Chemistry, 1972, Assistant Rector, 1975; Depute Head Teacher, Mearns Castle High School, 1981. Recreations: golf; badminton; rugby (spectating nowadays); swimming, cycling; windsurfing; gardening. Address: (h.) Millford, 34 Mount Stuart Road, Rothesay, Isle of Bute; T.-Rothesay 503336.

Gilmour, Douglas Graham, BSc (Hons), MB, ChB, MD, FRCS. Consultant Vascular Surgeon, Glasgow Royal Infirmary, since 1983; b. 15.4.47, Glasgow; m., Evelyn Jean; 2 s.; 2 d. Educ. Kelvinside Academy, Glasgow; Glasgow University. House Surgeon/Physician, then Senior House Officer/Registrar in Surgery, Western Infirmary, Glasgow, 1971-77; Glasgow Royal Infirmary: Senior Registrar in Surgery, 1977-80, Senior Lecturer (Honorary Consultant) in Surgery, 1980-83. Recreations: family; golf; skiing; sailing. Address: (b.) Vascular Surgery Department, Royal Infirmary, Glasgow; T.-0141-211 4772.

Gilmour, John, DL, MFH. Farmer; b. 15.7.44, Edinburgh; m., Valerie Jardine Russell; 2 s.; 2 d. Educ. Eton; Aberdeen College. Captain, FFY/SH (TA); Member, Queen's Bodyguard for Scotland (Royal Company of Archers); Trustee, ADRA (Moredun Foundation). Recreations: fishing; reading. Address: Balcormo Mains, Leven, Fife; T.-01333 360229.

Gilmour, John Andrew George, MA, LLB, NP. Solicitor; Marketing Consultant; Honorary Sheriff at Dumbarton, since 1991; b. 17.11.37, Balloch; m., Roma Aileen; 3 d. Educ. Morrison's Academy, Crieff; Edinburgh University. Partner, McArthur Brown Robertson; Partner, McArthur Stanton; President, Strathclyde Junior Chamber of Commerce, 1973; Director, Dumbarton Enterprise Trust, since 1985; Dean, Faculty of Dunbartonshire Solicitors, 1988-90; Law Society accredited Liquor Licensing Specialist, 1993. Recreations: sport; music; gastronomy. Address: (h.) Cramond Cottage, 19 East Lennox Drive, Helensburgh; T.-01436 675057.

Gilmour, Col. Sir John Edward, 3rd Bt, DSO, TD, JP, BA. Lord Lieutenant of Fife, 1980-87; b. 24.10.12, Edinburgh; m., Ursula Mabyn Wills; 2 s. Educ. Eton College; Trinity Hall, Cambridge; Dundee School of Economics. Served with Fife and Forfar Yeomanry, 1939-45; served on Fife County Council, 1951-61; MP (Conservative), East Fife, 1961-79; Chairman, Conservative Party in Scotland, 1965-67; Lord High Commissioner, General Assembly, Church of Scotland, 1982, 1983. Recreation: gardening. Address: (h.) Montrave, Leven, Fife, KY8 5NY; T.-Leven 426159.

Gilmour, William McIntosh, OStJ, BL. Honorary Sheriff, Dumbarton; Lawyer; b. 9.3.23, Newcastle-upon-Tyne; m., Elinor Adams. Educ. Hillhead High School; Cally House, Gatehouse of Fleet; Glasgow University. Early experience with legal firms in Glasgow; became Partner, latterly Senior Partner, in firm in Dunbartonshire; now retired; former Dean, Faculty of Solicitors in Dunbartonshire; founder Member and Past President, Clydebank Rotary Club; Past Deacon, Society of Deacons and Free Presces; former Chairman for Dunbartonshire, Order of St. John; Member, Incorporation of Gardeners (Glasgow Trades House). Recreations: dog-walking (formerly, motor sport). Address: (h.) 65 Killermont Road, Bearsden, Glasgow; T.-0141-942 0498.

Gimblett, Sheriff Margaret, MA. Sheriff, Glasgow and Strathkelvin, since 1995; b. 24.9.39, Perth; m., Iain; 1 s.; 1 d. Educ. St. Leonards, St. Andrews; University of Edinburgh; University of Glasgow. Retail Management, John Lewis Partnership, London, until 1970; Partner, Russel and Aitken, Solicitors, 1972-95; Temporary Sheriff, 1994-95; Churchill Fellow. Recreations: gardening; tourism. Address: (b.) Glasgow Sheriff Court, Carlton Place, Glasgow G5 9DA; T.-0141-429 8888.

Gingham, Alison Caroline, BSc(Hons), CIBiol, PGCE. Director, Kindrogan Field Centre, since 1994; b. 14.2.54, Aberdeen; m., Timothy Avery. Educ. St. Margaret's School for Girls, Aberdeen; University of Edinburgh. Biology Teacher, 1978-84; Head of Ecology, Cranedale Field Studies Centre, 1984-94. British Ecological Society: Council Member 1991-95; Member, Education and Careers Committee. Address: (b.) Kindrogan Field Centre, Enochdhu, Blairgowrie, Perthshire PH10 7PG; T.-01250 881 286.

Gimingham, Professor Charles Henry, OBE, BA, PhD, ScD, FRSE, FIBiol. Regius Professor of Botany, Aberdeen University, 1981-88; b. 28.4.23, Leamington; m., Elizabeth Caroline Baird; 3 d. Educ. Gresham's School, Holt, Norfolk; Emmanuel College, Cambridge. Research Assistant, Imperial College, London, 1944-45; Department of Botany, Aberdeen University: Assistant, 1946-48,

Lecturer, 1948-61, Senior Lecturer, 1961-64, Reader, 1964-69, Professor, since 1969, Head of Department, 1981-88; Member: Scottish Committee of Nature Conservancy, 1966-69, Scottish Advisory Committee, Nature Conservancy Council, 1970-80, Countryside Commission for Scotland, 1980-92; President, Botanical Society of Edinburgh, 1982-84; Vice-Chairman, NE Regional Board, Nature Conservancy Council for Scotland, 1991-92; Member: NE Regional Board, SNH, 1992-96, Board of Management, Hill Farming Research Organisation, 1981-87, Governing Body, Aberdeen College of Education, 1981-87, Council of Management, Macaulay Institute for Soil Research, 1983-87, Board of Management, Macaulay Land Use Research Institute, 1987- 90; British Ecological Society: Joint Secretary, 1956-61, Vice-President, 1962-64, Joint Editor, Journal of Ecology, 1975-78, President, 1986-87. Publications: Ecology of Heathlands, 1972; Introduction to Heathland Ecology, 1975; Lowland Heathland Management Handbook, 1992. Recreations: hill-walking; photography; history and culture of Japan. Address: (h.) 4 Gowanbrae Road, Bieldside, Aberdeen.

Gimson, George Stanley, QC (Scot); b. 1915. Educ. High School of Glasgow; Glasgow University. Advocate, 1949; QC, 1961; Sheriff Principal: Aberdeen, Kincardine and Banff, 1972-74; Grampian, Highland and Islands, 1975-82; Member, Edinburgh Central Hospitals Board, 1960-70 (Chairman, 1964-70); Director, SNO Society Ltd., 1962-80; Trustee, National Library of Scotland, 1963-76; Chairman, Pensions Appeals Tribunals, Scotland, 1971-95, RSSPCC, Edinburgh, 1972-76, Scottish Far-East P.O.W. Association, since 1996; Hon. LLD, Aberdeen, 1981. Address: (h.) 16 Royal Circus, Edinburgh EH3 6SS.

Girdwood, Professor Ronald Haxton, CBE, MB, ChB (Hons), MD, PhD, FRCPEd, FRCP, FRCPI, FRCPath, Hon. FACP, Hon. FRACP, FRSE. President, Royal College of Physicians of Edinburgh, 1982-85; Chairman, Scottish National Blood Transfusion Association, 1980-95; b. 19.3.17, Arbroath; m., Mary Elizabeth Williams; 1 s.; 1 d. Educ. Daniel Stewart's College, Edinburgh; Edinburgh University; Michigan University. Army service, RAMC, UK and India, 1942-46, successively as Lt., Captain, Major and Lt.-Col. (when posted to Burma); Lecturer, then Senior Lecturer, Reader in Medicine, Edinburgh University, 1946-62; Research Fellow, Michigan University, 1948-49; Consultant Physician, Edinburgh Royal Infirmary, 1950-82; Professor of Therapeutics and Clinical Pharmacology, Edinburgh University, 1962-82 (Dean, Faculty of Medicine, 1975-79); Chairman, Scottish Group, Nutrition Society, 1961-62; President, British Society for Haematology, 1963-64; Chairman, Executive Committee, Edinburgh and SE Scotland Blood Transfusion Association, 1970-95; Member, UK Committee on Safety of Medicines, 1972-83; Chairman, Medico-Pharmaceutical Forum, 1985-87; President, University of Edinburgh Graduates' Association, 1991-92; Member, Board of Governors, St. Columba's Hospice, 1985-97; Suniti Panja Gold Medal, Calcutta School of Tropical Medicine, 1980; given the Freedom of Sirajgunj, Bangladesh, 1984; Oliver Memorial Award for services to blood transfusion, 1991. Publications: Travels with a Stethoscope, 1991; editor of four medical books and more than 300 medical papers. Recreations: writing; photography. Address: (h.) 2 Hermitage Drive, Edinburgh EH10 6DD; T.-0131-447 5137.

Glasby, Michael Arthur, BM, BCh, MA, MSc (Oxon), MA (Cantab), CBiol, MIBiol, FICS, FRCS (Edin), FRCS (Eng). Reader in Anatomy, Edinburgh University, since 1992; b. 29.10.48, Nottingham; m., Celia M.E. Robinson. Educ. High Pavement Grammar School, Nottingham; Christ Church, Oxford; Oxford Medical School. Senior Scholar and Assistant Tutor in Physiology, Christ Church, Oxford, 1971-76; Surgeon, Harefield Hospital Transplant Trust, 1981-83; Fellow and Lecturer in Anatomy, New Hall, Cambridge, 1983-87; Lecturer in Anatomy, Royal College of Surgeons of England, 1984-87; joined Edinburgh University as Lecturer, 1987. Editor, anatomy textbook for surgeons and physiology textbook for surgeons; numerous articles. Recreations: golf; Latin and Greek literature; music; beekeeping; wine. Address: (b.) Department of Anatomy, Edinburgh University, Edinburgh EH8 9AG; T.- 0131-650 3112.

Glasgow, 10th Earl of (Patrick Robin Archibald Boyle). Television Director/Producer; b. 30.7.39; m., Isabel Mary James; 1 s.; 1 d. Educ. Eton; Paris University. Sub.-Lt., RNR, 1959-60; Producer/Director, Yorkshire TV, 1968-70; freelance Film Producer, since 1971; created Kelburn Country Centre (leisure park), and now manages this and Kelburn Estate. Address (b.) Kelburn Castle, Fairlie, Ayrshire KA29 0BE; T.-01475 568685.

Glasier, Anna, MB, ChB, BSc, FRCOG, MD. Director, Lothian Health Board Family Planning and Well Woman Services, since 1990; Senior Lecturer, Department of Obstetrics and Gynaecology, Edinburgh University, since 1990; Consultant Gynaecologist, Lothian Health Board, since 1989; b. 16.4.50, Salisbury. Educ. Lord Digby's School, Sherborne. Clinical Research Scientist, Medical Research Council Centre for Reproductive Biology, Edinburgh, 1989-90. Recreations: ski mountaineering; sailing. Address: (b.) 18 Dean Terrace, Edinburgh EH4 1NL; T.-0131-332 7941.

Glass, Alexander, OBE, MA, DipEd. Rector, Dingwall Academy, 1977-97; b. 1.6.32, Dunbar; m., Edith Margaret Duncan Baxter; 3 d. Educ. Dunbar Grammar School; Edinburgh University; Heidelberg University; University of Aix-en-Provence. Teacher of Modern Languages, Montrose Academy, 1958-60; Special Assistant Teacher of Modern Languages, Oban High School, 1960-62; Principal Teacher of Modern Languages, Nairn Academy, 1962-65; Principal Teacher of French and Assistant Rector, Perth Academy, 1965-72; Rector, Milne's High School, Fochabers, 1972-77. Chairman, COSPEN; former President, Highland Secondary Headteachers' Association; former Chairman: Highland Region Working Party for Modern Languages, Children's Panel Chairmen's Group; Chairman, Highland Children's Panel; Reader, Church of Scotland; Licentiate, Auxiliary Ministry, Church of Scotland; Scottish Community Drama Association; Chairman, Inverness District, Divisional Secretary/Festival Organiser, Highland Division, Member, General Council; Chairman and Secretary, Scottish Secondary Schools' Travel Trust; Member, Highland Health Council; Churchill Fellow, 1991. Recreations: amateur drama; foreign travel; Rotary. Address: (h.) Craigton, Tulloch Avenue, Dingwall IV15 9LH; T.-01349 863258.

Glass, Douglas James Allan, MB, ChB. General Practitioner, Ballater, since 1987; Apothecary to HM Household, Balmoral, since 1988; Partner in farm (D.L. Glass), since 1982; b. 8.10.53, Dinnet, Aboyne; m., Suzanne; 1 s.; 2 d. Educ. Aboyne Academy; Banchory Academy; Aberdeen University. Junior House Officer, 1977-78; Senior House Officer, 1978-79; General Practitioner Trainee, 1979-80; General Practice, Australia and New Zealand, 1980-81; General Practice Principal, Peterhead, 1981-87. Church Elder. Recreations: dry stane dyking; golf; snooker; football. Address: (h.) Deecastle, Dinnet, Aboyne, Aberdeenshire; T.-013397 55686.

Glasser, Lesley Scott Dent, MBE, BA (Cantab), PhD, DSc, CChem, FInstP, CPhys, FRSE. Director, SATRO North Scotland, since 1986; Managing Director, Satrosphere, since 1989; b. 19.5.32, Grimsby; m., Professor Fredrick Paul Glasser; 1 s.; 2 d. Educ. Wintringham Grammar School; Newnham College, Cambridge; Aberdeen University. Research Fellow, Lecturer, Senior Lecturer, Reader, Aberdeen University Department of Chemistry, 1958-85. President, ASE Scotland, 1996;

Secretary, UK Crystallographic Council; 1978-82; Trustee, National Museums of Scotland; Member, Council: Royal Society of Edinburgh, British Association for the Advancement of Science; Chairman, Scottish Branch, Institute of Physics, 1995-97. Recreation: gardening. Address: (b.) SATRO North Scotland, Marischal College, Aberdeen; T.-01224 273161.

Glen, Alexander Iain Munro, MB, ChB, FRCPsych, FRCP (Glas), DPM. Hon. Consultant Psychiatrist, Highland Health Board; Hon. Senior Lecturer, Aberdeen University, since 1986; Research Director, Highland Psychiatric Research Group, since 1981; Member (SNP), Highland Regional Council, since 1990; Member, SNP National Council; SNP Shadow Health Spokesperson; b. 25.5.30, Glasgow; m., Dr. Evelyne Glen; 2 s.; 2 d. Educ. Albert Road Academy, Glasgow; Glasgow Academy; Glasgow University. National Service as Surgeon Lt., RNVR, 3rd Frigate Squadron, Far East, 1955-57; Research Fellow, Psychiatry, Glasgow University, 1964-68; Medical Research Council: Clinical Psychiatry Unit, 1968-72, Brain Metabolism Unit, Research Fellow, Pharmacology, Edinburgh University, 1972-81. Recreations: politics; poetry; Scotland. Address: (h.) Dalnavert Community Co-operative, Dalnavert, by Kincraig PH21 1NG; T.-0154 04 347.

Glen, Duncan Munro. Writer and Lecturer; Sole Owner, Akros Publications, since 1960; b. 11.1.33, Cambuslang; m., Margaret Eadie; 1 s.; 1 d. Educ. West Coats, Cambuslang; Edinburgh College of Art. Book Designer, London; Lecturer in Typography; Editor, Robert Gibson & Co. Ltd.; Lecturer, then Senior Lecturer, then Head of Graphic Design, Lancashire Polytechnic; Professor and Head, Department of Visual Communication, Nottingham Trent University (Emeritus Professor); Member, Council for Academic Awards, 1979-89; Editor: Akros, poetry magazine, 1-51, ZED 2 0, 1-10, Scottish Poetry Library Newsletter. Author and editor of many books including Hugh MacDiarmid and The Scottish Renaissance, Selected Essays of Hugh MacDiarmid, In Appearances: Poems, The Autobiography of a Poet, Makars' Walk, The Poetry of the Scots, Selected Poems 1965-1990, Hugh MacDiarmid: Out of Langholm and Into the World; A Nation in a Parish; Four Scottish Poets; Splendid Lanarkshire; New Selected Poems, 1987-96. Recreation: walking. Address: (h.) 33 Lady Nairn Avenue, Kirkcaldy, Fife KY1 2AW; T.-01592 651522.

Glen, Eric Stanger, MB, ChB, FRCSGlas, FRCSEdin. Consultant Urological Surgeon, Walton Urological Teaching and Research Centre, Southern General Hospital, Glasgow; Honorary Clinical Senior Lecturer, Glasgow University; Member, Surgical Examination Panel, Royal College of Physicians and Surgeons of Glasgow; b. 20.10.34, Glasgow; m., Dr. Patricia. Educ. Glasgow University. Pre-Consultant posts, Western and Victoria Infirmaries, Glasgow; Ship Surgeon, Royal Fleet Auxiliary. Chairman, Greater Glasgow Health Board Incontinence Resource Group; Past Chairman, Area Medical Committee; Founder and former Secretary, International Continence Society; Founder, Urological Computing Society. Publications: chapters in books; papers on urodynamics, urology and computing. Recreations: travel; writing; computer applications. Address: (h.) 9 St. John's Road, Pollokshields, Glasgow G41 5RJ; T.-0141-423 0759.

Glen, Norman MacLeod, CBE, TD, MA, JP. Former Member, Dumbarton District Council, 1975-96; b. 22.12.11, Glasgow; m., Dr. Janet M.S. Glen (deceased); 2 s.; 2 d. Educ. Glasgow Academy; Glasgow University. Retail trade as Buyer, Director and Managing Director, John Glen & Co. Ltd., Glasgow, 1932-74; War Service, six years; TA (mostly 474 HAA Regt RA), 1938-56 (Lt. Colonel, 1954-56); Parliamentary candidate (Liberal), 1945, (Conservative), 1951, 1955, 1959, 1964, 1966 and By-Election, Woodside, 1962; elected, Helensburgh Town

Council, 1966 (last Provost of Helensburgh, 1970-75); Member, Dunbartonshire County Council, 1966-75; Elder, West Kirk of Helensburgh. Recreation: walking. Address: (h.) Flat 11, Queen's Court, Helensburgh G84 7AH; T.-01436 673497.

Glen, Robbie, BA, FIMgt. After Dinner Speaker and Event Management Consultant, since 1996 (Partner, Glen Enterprises and Kintra Consultants); Governor, H.M. Institution, Cornton Vale, 1994-96; b. 31.5.46, Hamilton; m., Elspeth Reyburn; 2 d. Educ. Hamilton Academy; Strathclyde University. Assistant Governor: Polmont Borstal, 1969, Longriggend Remand Institution, 1972; Deputy Governor, Edinburgh Prison, 1976; seconded to Prison HQ Admin Branch, 1979; Governor: Castle Huntly Borstal, 1981, Dungavel Prison, 1984; seconded to Prisons Inspectorate, 1986; returned to Dunvagel, 1987, transferred to Prisons HQ Operations Branch; Deputy Governor/Acting Governor, Barlinnie Prison, 1991. Barker, Variety Club of Great Britain; Member: Stars Organisation for Spastics Scotland, Lord's Taverners. Recreations: golf; reading; writing; speaking; holidaying on Arran. Address: (b.) 22 Lochaber Road, Strathaven, Lanarkshire ML10 6HZ; T.- 01357 522531.

Glen, William Hamish. Artistic Director, Dundee Rep, since 1992; b. 20.12.57, Edinburgh; m., Denise Maria Winford. Educ. Edinburgh Academy. ASM, Traverse Theatre, 1979-81; Trainee Director, Tron Theatre, 1986-87, Associate Director, 1988-89; Artistic Director, Winged Horse, 1990-92; worked as freelance director in Lithuania and Finland. Address: (b.) Tay Square, Dundee; T.-01382 227684.

Glenarthur, 4th Baron (Simon Mark Arthur), Bt, DL, MCIT, FRAeS. DL, Aberdeenshire, since 1987; Consultant: British Aerospace PLC, since 1989, Hanson PLC, since 1989, Imperial Tobacco Ltd., since 1996; Deputy Chairman, Hanson Pacific Ltd., since 1994; Director: Millennium Chemicals Inc., since 1996, Whirly Bird Services Ltd., since 1995; b. 7.10.44; m.; 1 s.; 1 d. Educ. Eton. Retired Major, 10th Royal Hussars (PWO); Helicopter Captain, British Airways, 1976-82; a Lord in Waiting, 1982-83; Parliamentary Under Secretary of State: Department of Health and Social Security, 1983-85, Home Office, 1985-86; Minister of State: Scottish Office, 1986- 87, Foreign and Commonwealth Office, 1987-89. Chairman, St. Mary's Hospital, Paddington, NHS Trust, since 1991, British Helicopter Advisory Board, since 1992, European Helicopter Association, since 1996; President, National Council for Civil Protection, since 1991; Member (Brigadier), Queen's Bodyguard for Scotland (Royal Company of Archers); Scottish Patron, The Butler Trust, since 1994. Address: (b.) House of Lords, London SW1A 0PW.

Glennie, John Ellis, FCCA, CIPFA. Chief Executive, Borders General Hospital NHS Trust, since 1995; b. 28.9.48, Keith; 2 s; 1 d. Educ. Keith Grammar School. Joined NHS as a trainee accountant, Aberdeen, 1966, and progressed through a number of posts to become Director of Finance, Darlington Health Authority, 1982; Director of Finance, Information and Computing, Central Manchester Health Authority, 1985-91; Director of Finance, then Deputy Chief Executive/Director of Operations, Central Manchester Healthcare NHS Trust, 1992-95. National Treasurer, Healthcare Financial Management Association. Address: (b.) Borders General Hospital NHS Trust, Melrose TD6 9BS; T.-01896 754333.

Gloag, Ann. Executive Director, Stagecoach Holdings plc; b. 10.12.42. Educ. Perth High School. Nursing, 1960-80; Founding Partner, Stagecoach, 1980. Address: (b.) Charlotte House, 20 Charlotte Street, Perth PH1 5LL.

Gloag, Matthew Irving. Director, Matthew Gloag & Son Ltd., since 1971; b. 1.12.47, Perth; m., Dilly Moon; 2 d. Chairman, Scottish Licensed Trade Association, 1984-85 and 1995-96. Address: (b.) West Kinfauns, Perth PH2 7EF; T.-01738 440000.

Glover, Professor David Moore, BA, PhD, FRSE. Professor of Molecular Genetics, Dundee University, since 1989; Director, Cancer Research Campaign Cell Cycle Group, since 1989; b. 28.3.48, Chapeltown. Educ. Broadway Grammar School, Barnsley; Fitzwilliam College, Cambridge. Postdoctoral Fellow, Stanford University, California, 1972-75; Imperial College, London, 1975-89, latterly as Head, Biochemistry Department. Publications: 120 scientific papers; two books; Editor, 18 books. Address: (b.) CRC Laboratories, Medical Sciences Institute, Dundee DD1 4HN; T.-01382 344793.

Glover, Rev. Robert Lindsay, BMus, BD, ARCO. Minister, Chalmers Memorial, Cockenzie and Port Seton, since 1997; b. 21.7.45, Watford; m., Elizabeth Mary Brown; 2 s.; 2 d. Educ. Langholm Academy; Dumfries Academy; Glasgow University. Minister: Newton Parish, near Dalkeith, 1971-76, St. Vigeans Parish, Arbroath, 1976-85, Knox's, Arbroath, 1982-85, St. George's West, Edinburgh, 1985-97. Recreations: music (organ, piano, accordion); caravanning; following Heart of Midlothian FC; reading. Address: Braemar Villa, 2 Links Road, Port Seton, Prestonpans, East Lothian EH32 0HA.

Glover, Sue, MA. Writer; b. 1.3.43, Edinburgh; m., John Glover; 2 s. Educ. St. George's School, Edinburgh; Montpellier University; Edinburgh University. Original drama and other scriptwriting for radio, television and theatre; theatre productions include: The Seal Wife, Edinburgh Festival, 1980; An Island in Largo, Byre Theatre, 1981; The Bubble Boy, Glasgow Tron, 1981; The Straw Chair, Traverse Theatre, 1988; Bondagers, Traverse Theatre, 1991 (winner, 1990 LWT Plays on Stage Award); Sacred Hearts, 1994; Artist Unknown, 1996; television work includes: The Spaver Connection; Mme Montand and Mrs Miller; Dear Life; televised version of The Bubble Boy won a silver medal, New York Film and Television Festival, and a merit, Chicago International Film Festival, 1983. Publications: The Bubble Boy, 1991; Bondagers (Made in Scotland), 1995; Bondagers and The Straw Chair, 1997. Recreations: house and garden. Address: Castlefield Cottage, Castlebank Road, Cupar, Fife; T.-Cupar 653664.

Godden, Anthony John, BSc (Hons), FRSH, AIHE. Principal, West Lothian College, since 1987; b. 26.3.46, Swansea; m., Kelly; 1 s.; 1 d. Educ. Dynevor Grammar School; North East London Polytechnic; Open University. Lecturer, Bridgnorth College of Further Education, 1970- 73; Social Tutor, Airedale and Wharfedale College of Further Education, 1973-75; Warden, Mildmay Hall, and Head, Section of General Studies and Information Sciences, Essex Institute of Higher Education, 1975-78; Assistant Inspector, Kent County Council Education Department, 1978-82; Principal, Gainsborough College of Further Education, 1982-86.Knight of the Holy Sepulchre of Jerusalem; Chairman, Almond Housing Association, Livingston. Recreations: armchair sport; theatre; guitar; travel. Address: (b.) West Lothian College, Marjoribanks Street, Bathgate EH48 1QJ; T.-01506 634300.

Godden, Tony Richard Hillier, CB, BSc (Econ). Secretary, Friends of the Royal Scottish Academy, since 1988; b. 13.11.27, Barnstaple; m., Marjorie Florence Snell; 1 s.; 2 d. Educ. Barnstaple Grammar School; London School of Economics. Commissioned, RAF Education Branch, 1950; entered Civil Service, 1951; first appointed to Colonial Office; Private Secretary to Parliamentary Under Secretary of State, 1954-55; seconded to Cabinet Office, 1957-59; joined Scottish Home Department, 1961; Assistant Secretary, Scottish Development Department,

1964; Under Secretary, 1969; Secretary, Scottish Economic Planning Development, 1973-80; Secretary, Scottish Development Department, 1980-87. Member: The Council on Tribunals and its Scottish Committee, 1988-94, Advisory Board on Ancient Monuments, 1990-95. Address: 9 Ross Road, Edinburgh EH16 5QN.

Godfray, Martin Francis, BSc, CChem, FRSC, MChemA. Consultant Scientist and Microscopist; Public Analyst, Official Agricultural Analyst and Scientific Adviser, Lothian, Borders and Highland Regional Councils and Orkney and Shetland Islands Councils, 1980-96; b. 10.5.45, Barry, Glamorgan; m., Heather Jean; 1 s.; 2 d. Educ. Barry Boys Grammar Technical School; Birmingham University. Deputy Public Analyst and Deputy Agricultural Analyst, London Boroughs of Southwark, Greenwich, Islington and Tower Hamlets, 1973-80. Address: (b.) 27 Burnbrae, Edinburgh, EH12 8UB; T.-0131-339 1212.

Godfrey, Professor Alan Dearn, BA (Hons), FCCA. Professor of Accounting and Head, Department of Finance and Accounting, Glasgow Caledonian University; b. 12.5.46, Falkirk; 1 s.; 1 d. Educ. Falkirk High School; Strathclyde University. Financial Consultant, Engineering Services Ltd., 1972-76; Lecturer, then Senior Lecturer, Glasgow College, 1976-88; Depute Head of Department, then Acting Head of Department, Glasgow Polytechnic, 1988-93. Recreations: music; golf. Address: (b.) Department of Finance and Accounting, Glasgow Caledonian University, Glasgow G4 0BA; T.-0141-331 3361.

Godman, Norman. MP (Labour), Greenock and Inverclyde (formerly Greenock and Port Glasgow) since 1983; b. 1938. Address: (b.) House of Commons, London, SW1A 0AA.

Gold, Lex. Director, Scottish Chambers of Commerce; Chairman, Hibernian Football Club; b. 14.12.40, Rigside; m., Eleanor; 1 s.; 1 d. Educ. Lanark Grammar School. Sub-Editor, Daily Record; professional footballer; joined Civil Service, Glasgow, 1960; Inland Revenue, two years, Civil Service Department, four years, Home Office, 21 years, Training Agency, three years; former Managing Director, Scottish Enterprise; former Director, CBI Scotland. Address: (b.) 152 Morrison Street, Edinburgh EH3 8EB.

Goldberg, Professor Sir Abraham, KB, MD, DSc, FRCP, FRCPEdin, FRCPGlas, FRSE. Regius Professor of the Practice of Medicine, Glasgow University, 1978-89; Founder President, Faculty of Pharmaceutical Medicine of Royal Colleges of Physicians of UK, 1989; b. 7.12.23, Edinburgh; m., Clarice Cussin; 2 s.; 1 d. Educ. Sciennes School, Edinburgh; George Heriot's School, Edinburgh; Edinburgh University. House Physician, Royal Hospital for Sick Children, Edinburgh, 1946-47; RAMC, 1947-49 (granted rank of honorary Major on discharge); Nuffield Research Fellow, UCH Medical School, London, 1952-54; Eli Lilly Travelling Fellow in Medicine (MRC), Department of Medicine, Utah University, 1954-56; Glasgow University; Lecturer in Medicine, 1956-59, Titular Professor of Medicine, 1967-70, Regius Professor of Materia Medica, 1970-78. Chairman, Grants Committee 1, Clinical Research Board, MRC, 1973-77; Member, Chief Scientist's Committee, SHHD, 1977-83; Chairman, Biomedical Research Committee, SHHD, 1977-83; Editor, Scottish Medical Journal, 1962-63; Chairman, Committee on Safety of Medicines, 1980-86; Fitzpatrick Lecturer, Royal College of Physicians, London, 1988; Goodall Memorial Lecturer, Royal College of Physicians and Surgeons of Glasgow, 1989; City of Glasgow Lord Provost's Award, 1988. Publications: Disorders of Porphyrin Metabolism (Co-Author), 1987; Recent Advances in Haematology (Joint Editor), 1971; Clinics in Haematology "The Porphyrias" (Co-Author), 1980. Recreations: medical history; literature; writing; walking;

swimming. Address: (h.) 16 Birnam Crescent, Bearsden, Glasgow G61 2AU.

Goldie, Annabel MacNicoll, DL, LLB, NP. Deputy Lord Lieutenant, Renfrewshire, since 1993; Deputy Chairman, Scottish Conservative Party, since 1995 (Chairman, March–July 1997); Director, Prince's Scottish Youth Business Trust, since 1994; b. 27.2.50, Glasgow. Educ. Greenock Academy; Strathclyde University. Solicitor in private practice, since 1978. Elder, Church of Scotland; Member, West of Scotland Advisory Board, Salvation Army; Member, Strathclyde University Court. Recreations: weeding; walking; dogs; swimming Address: (h.) Levernholm, Gledstane Road, Bishopton PA7 5AU; T.-0141-248 3020.

Good, John Russell. Secretary, Royal Highland and Agricultural Society of Scotland, since 1981; b. 9.8.41, Kirkcudbright; m., Muriel Law Bathgate; 2 s.; 1 d. Educ. Kirkcudbright Academy. Trainee and junior bank officer, 1958-64; Group Secretary in North Lanarkshire, NFU of Scotland, 1964--66; Procedures Analyst, Caterpillar Tractor Co., Uddingston, 1966-67; joined RHASS, 1967. Address: (b.) Royal Highland Centre, Ingliston, Edinburgh EH28 8NF.

Goodall, Alexander, OBE, MA (Hons). Principal, Wester Hailes Education Centre, since 1982; b. 25.8.38, Dolphinton, Peebles-shire; 1 s.; 1 d. Educ. Portobello High School; Edinburgh University; Moray House College of Education. Teacher of History, Niddrie Marischal Secondary School, 1961-64; Education Officer, Teso College, Uganda, 1964-69; Preston Lodge High School: Principal Teacher of History, 1969-74, Assistant Head Teacher, 1974-78; Depute Principal, Wester Hailes Education Centre, 1978-82. Editor, Scottish History Teaching Review. Publication: Economics and Development (Co-author). Recreations: trout angling; rubber bridge. Address: (b.) 5 Murrayburn Drive, Edinburgh; T.-0131-442 2201.

Gooday, Professor Graham W., BSc, PhD, FRSE, FIBiol. Professor of Microbiology, Aberdeen University, since 1984; b. 19.2.42, Colchester; m., Margaret A. Mealing; 1 s.; 2 d. Educ. Hove Grammar School for Boys; Bristol University. VSO, Sierra Leone, 1964; Research Fellowships: Leeds University, 1967, Glasgow and Oxford Universities, 1969; Lecturer, Senior Lecturer, Reader, Aberdeen University, 1972-84; Honorary Professorial Fellow, Rowett Research Institute, 1992; Member: Aquatic Life Sciences Committee, NERC, 1984-87, Council, Society for General Microbiology, 1976-80; British Mycological Society: Member, Council, 1974-77, President, 1993, Centenary Fellow, 1996; awarded first Fleming Lectureship, Society for General Microbiology, 1976. Recreation: open countryside. Address: (b.) Department of Molecular and Cell Biology, Institute of Medical Sciences, University of Aberdeen, Aberdeen AB25 2ZD; T.-01224 273147.

Goodman, Professor Anthony Eric, MA (Oxon), BLitt (Oxon), FRHistS. Professor of Medieval and Renaissance History, Edinburgh University, since 1993; b. 21.7.36, London; m., Jacqueline; 1 d. Educ. Selhurst Grammar School, Croydon; Magdalen College, Oxford. Joined staff, Edinburgh University, 1961. Secretary, Edinburgh Branch, Historical Association, since 1975. Publications: The Loyal Conspiracy, 1971; A History of England from Edward II to James I, 1977; The Wars of the Roses, 1981; A Traveller's Guide to Medieval Britain (Co-author), 1986; The New Monarchy, 1471-1534, 1988; John of Gaunt, 1992. Address: (h.) 23 Kirkhill Gardens, Edinburgh EH16 5DF; T.-0131-667 5988.

Goodman, Professor Timothy Nicholas Trewin, BA, MSc, DPhil. Professor of Applied Analysis, Dundee

University, since 1994; b. 29.4.47, London; m., Choo-Tin; 3 d. Educ. Judd School; St. John's College, Cambridge; Warwick University; Sussex University. Teacher, VSO, 1973; Teacher, Singapore, 1974-75; Lecturer, Universiti Sains Malaysia, 1975-79; Lecturer, Dundee University, 1979-90; Professor Texas A&M University, 1990-91; Reader, Dundee University, 1992-94. Recreations: walking; Scottish country dancing; music. Address: (b.) Department of Mathematics, Dundee University, Dundee; T.-01382 344488.

Goodsman, James Melville, CBE. Chairman, Michael Fraser & Co. Ltd; Director Scotland, ICP Ltd.; Consultant, Democracy International Ltd.; b. 6.2.47, St. Andrews; m., Victoria Smitherman. Educ. Elgin Academy. Conservative Party Agent, 1968-80; Deputy Central Office Agent, North West Area, 1980-84; Assistant Director (Community Affairs), CCO, 1984-89; Head, Community and Legal Department, CCO, 1989-90; Director, Conservative Party in Scotland, 1990-93; Chairman, Edinburgh Morayshire Club, 1996-97. Recreations: golf; Church music; gardening. Address: (b.) The Old Schoolhouse, Collessie, Fife KY15 7UU; T.-01337 810745.

Goodwin, Frederick Anderson, LLB, CA, FCIBS. Chief Executive Officer and Director, Clydesdale Bank PLC and Yorkshire Bank PLC, since 1997; b. 17.8.58, Paisley; m., Joyce; 1 s. Educ. Paisley Grammar School; Glasgow University. Partner, Touche Ross, 1988-95; Executive Director, Short Brothers plc, 1989-92; Chief Operating Officer, BCCI Liquidation, 1992-95; Clydesdale Bank PLC: Deputy C.E.O., 1995-96, Chief Executive Officer, 1996-97. Recreations: cars; golf. Address: (b.) 30 St. Vincent Place, Glasgow G1 2HL; T.-0141-223 2011.

Goodwin, Sir Matthew Dean, CA. Former Chairman, Hewden Stuart PLC; b. 12.6.29, Dalserf; m., Margaret Eileen Colvil; 2 d. Educ. Glasgow Academy.

Goodwin, Michael David, OBE, FIMgt. Managing Director, Electrical Contractors' Association of Scotland, since 1991; Director: Scottish Electrical Contractors' Insurance, since 1991, Scottish Joint Industry Board, since 1993; Trustee, Scottish Electrical Charitable Training Trust, since 1991; b. 18.1.40, Colombo; m., Anne Dundas, nee Finlay; 2 s.; 2 d. Educ. Stowe School; Britannia Royal Naval College, Dartmouth. Graduated as full career commission officer, Royal Navy, 1960; retired as Commander, 1978; NATO appointments, 1980-86; retired, 1988; Assistant Director, Administration, Information and Settlement Division, International Stock Exchange, 1988-91. Recreations: tennis; theatre; music; reading; clay shooting; swimming. Address: (b.) Bush House, Bush Estate, Midlothian EH26 0SB; T.-0131-445 5577.

Gordon, Alexander. Principal, Banff and Buchan College of Further Education. Address: (b.) Henderson Road, Fraserburgh, AB43 5GA.

Gordon, Donald Neil, MA, LLB, WS, NP, MSI, TEP. Partner, Carltons, Solicitors, since 1979; Senior Tutor, Diploma in Legal Practice, University of Dundee, since 1994; Vice Dean, Faculty of Procurators and Solicitors in Dundee, since 1997; b. 30.3.51, Aberdeen; m., Alison Mary Whyte; 1 s.; 1 d. Educ. Robert Gordon's College, Aberdeen; University of Aberdeen; University of Edinburgh. Law Apprenticeship, Edinburgh, 1973-75; Assistant Solicitor, Carlton & Reid, Dundee, 1975-79. WS, 1975; Notary Public, 1975; Chairman, Dundee Citizens Advice Bureau, 1996; France Consular Agent, Dundee, 1996; Secretary, Abertay Rotary Club, 1995; Treasurer, Dundee Orchestral Society, since 1978; Past Chairman, High School of Dundee Parents Association. Recreations: music; gardening. Address: (b.) 30 Whitehall Street, Dundee DD1 AAL; T.-01382 200111.

Gordon, Professor George, MA (Hons), PhD. Director of Academic Practice, Strathclyde University, since 1987; b. 14.11.39, Edinburgh; m., Jane Taylor Collins; 2 d. Educ. George Heriot's School; Edinburgh University. Edinburgh University: Vans Dunlop Scholar, 1962-64, Demonstrator, 1964-65; Strathclyde University: Assistant Lecturer, 1965-66, Lecturer, 1966-80, Dean, Faculty of Arts and Social Studies, 1984-87; served on SUCE and SCE Geography Panels, SCOVACT, and General Teaching Council for Scotland; Convener, Publications Committee, Royal Scottish Geographical Society; Vice President, British Association for the Advancement of Science; former Member, General Assembly of Open University; Member, Senate, Strathclyde University; Governor, Jordanhill College of Education, 1982-93 (Chairman, 1987-93). Publications: Regional Cities of the UK 1890-1980 (Editor), 1986; Perspectives of the Scottish City (Editor), 1985; Scottish Urban History, 1983; The Making of Scottish Geography (Co-Author), 1984; Settlement Geography, 1983; Urban Geography (Co-Author), 1981; Scottish Urban History (Co-Editor), 1983; Settlement Geography (Co-Author), 1983. Recreations: theatre-going; watching sport. Address: (b.) Centre for Academic Practice, Strathclyde University, 50 George Street, Glasgow; T.-0141-548 2637.

Gordon, George, MB, ChB, FRCSE, FRCOG. Consultant Obstetrician and Gynaecologist, Dumfries and Galloway, since 1969; b. 4.9.36, Markinch, Fife; m., Rosemary Gould Hutchison; 1 s.; 1 d. Educ. Bell Baxter School; Edinburgh University. Senior Registrar, Western General Hospital, Edinburgh, 1966-69; Chairman, Scottish Confidential Enquiry into Maternal Mortality; Member, Central Midwives Board for Scotland, 1978-84; Examiner, FRCS Edinburgh, MRCOG and DRCOG London; Clinical Director, Local Acute and Maternity Hospitals Trust; Honorary Secretary, Dumfries and Stewartry Division, BMA, 1975-87; Fellow of BMA. Recreations: music; Scottish literature; golf; gardening. Address: (b.) Dumfries and Galloway Royal Infirmary, Bankend Road, Dumfries DG1 4AP.

Gordon, Sheriff Gerald Henry, CBE, QC, MA, LLB, PhD, LLD. Sheriff of Glasgow and Strathkelvin, since 1978; Temporary Judge, Court of Session and High Court of Justiciary, since 1992; b. 17.6.29, Glasgow; m., Marjorie Joseph; 1 s.; 2 d. Educ. Queen's Park Senior Secondary School; Glasgow University. Advocate, 1953; Procurator Fiscal Depute, Edinburgh, 1960-65; Edinburgh University: Head, Department of Criminal Law and Criminology, 1965-72, Personal Professor of Criminal Law, 1969-72, Dean, Faculty of Law, 1970-73, Professor of Scots Law, 1972-76; Sheriff of South Strathclyde, Dumfries and Galloway, at Hamilton, 1976-77; Member: Interdepartmental Committee on Scottish Criminal Procedure, 1970-77, Committee on Criminal Appeals and Miscarriages of Justice, 1995-96. Publications: Criminal Law of Scotland, 1967, 1978; Renton & Brown's Criminal Procedure (Editor), 1972, 1983, 1996. Recreations: Jewish studies; coffee conversation; swimming. Address: (b.) Sheriff Court, Glasgow; T.-0141-429 8888.

Gordon, Giles Alexander Esme, FRSL. Director, Curtis Brown Ltd., Literary Agents, since 1995; b. 23.5.40, Edinburgh; m., 1, Margaret Anna Eastoe (divorced); 1 s.; 1 s. (deceased); 1 d.; 2, Maggie McKernan; 2 d. Educ. Edinburgh Academy; Edinburgh College of Art. Trainee Publisher, Oliver & Boyd, Edinburgh, 1959-63; Advertising Manager, Secker & Warburg, 1963-64; Editor, Hutchinson, 1964-66; Plays Editor, Penguin Books, 1966-67; Editorial Director, Victor Gollancz, 1967-73; Literary Agent, Anthony Sheil Associates, later Sheil Land Associates, 1973-95. C. Day Lewis Fellow in Writing, KCL, 1974-75; Secretary and Chairman, Society of Young Publishers; Member: Literature Panel, Arts Council, 1968-72; Committee of Management, Society of Authors; Committee, Association of Authors' Agents; Council, RSL,

1992-94; Committee, Authors Club, since 1992; Lecturer: Tufts University in London, 1970-74, Hollins College, London, 1983-86; Theatre Critic: Spectator, London Daily News, Drama; Books Columnist, The Times, 1993-95; Editor, Drama; Editor, Bloomsbury Classics Short Stories, since 1995, Clarion Tales, since 1996. Publications: Pictures from an Exhibition, 1970; The Umbrella Man, 1971; About a Marriage, 1972; Girl with Red Hair, 1974; Factions (Co-Editor), 1974; Walter and the Balloon (Co-Author), 1974; Beyond the Words (Editor), 1975; Farewell, Fond Dreams, 1975; Prevailing Spirits (Editor), 1976; 100 Scenes from Married Life, 1976; Members of the Jury (Co-Editor), 1976; You Always Remember the First Time (Co-Editor), 1976; A Book of Contemporary Nightmares (Editor), 1977; Enemies, 1977; The Illusionist, 1978; Modern Scottish Short Stories (Co-Editor), 1978; Ambrose's Vision, 1980; Shakespeare Stories (Editor), 1982; English Short Stories 1940-80 (Editor), 1982; Best Short Stories (Co-Editor, annually), 1986-95; English Short Stories: 1900 to the present (Editor), 1988; The Twentieth Century Short Story in English: a bibliography (Editor), 1989; Aren't We Due a Royalty Statement?, 1993; The Best of Best Short Stories 1986-95 (Co-Editor), 1995; Scotland from the Air, 1996. Recreations: theatre; opera; walking; travelling; eating; drinking; book collecting. Address: 6 Ann Street, Edinburgh EH4 1PJ; T.-0131-332 1993.

Gordon, Rev. Canon Hugh. Chaplain, St. Joseph's House, Edinburgh; b. 18.11.10, Inverness. Educ. Stonyhurst College, Lancashire; Heriot-Watt College, Edinburgh; Oscott College, Birmingham. Ordained, 1937; Curate, Inverness, 1937; Army Chaplain, 1940 (Egypt and El Alamein, 51st Highland Division); Osnabruck, 1946, developing civilian parish church and first Catholic school in Germany after the fall of Hitler; Priest: Stirling, Selkirk, St. Andrews, Edinburgh St. Margaret's and St. John the Evangelist, Linlithgow St. Michael's; founded Linlithgow Scripture Centre for Christian Unity; former Executive Member, Scottish Catholic Lay Apostolate Council; Member: Commission for Christian Doctrine and Unity; Order of Christian Unity; Fellowship of St. Andrew. Recreations: anything to help restoration of Christian unity; stopped tennis, golf, fishing. Address: 45 Gilmore Place, Edinburgh EH3 9NG; T.-0131-228 9084.

Gordon of Strathblane, Lord (James Stuart Gordon), CBE, DLitt., MA (Hons). Chairman, Scottish Radio Holdings, since 1996; Director: Clydeport plc, since 1992, Johnston Press plc, since 1996, The AIM Trust plc, since 1996; Member: Board, Scottish Tourist Board, since 1997, BP Scottish Advisory Board, since 1991, Glasgow University Court, since 1984; b. 17.5.36, Glasgow; m., Anne Stevenson; 2 s.; 1 d. Educ. St. Aloysius College, Glasgow; Glasgow University (President of the Union, 1958-59). Political Editor, STV, 1965-73; Managing Director, Radio Clyde, 1973-96; Chief Executive, Scottish Radio Holdings, 1991-96. Winner, Observer Mace Debating Tournament, 1957; Sony Special Award for Services to Radio, 1984. Chairman, Scottish Exhibition Centre, 1983-89; Member, Scottish Development Agency, 1981-90. Recreations: his children; genealogy, golf. Address: (b.) Scottish Radio Holdings, Clydebank Business Park, Clydebank; T.-0141-565 2202.

Gordon, Canon Kenneth Davidson, MA. Rector, St. Devenick's Episcopal Church, Bieldside, Aberdeen, since 1971; Synod Clerk, Diocese of Aberdeen and Orkney, since 1996; Warden of Lay Readers, Diocese of Aberdeen and Orkney, since 1978; b. 27.12.35, Edinburgh; m., Edith Jessica Newing; 2 s. Educ. George Heriot's School, Edinburgh; Edinburgh University; Tyndale Hall, Bristol. Curate, St. Helens Parish Church, Lancashire, 1960-66 (with charge of St. Andrew's Mission Church, 1962-66); Vicar, St. George the Martyr's Parish Church, Bolton, 1966-71; Examining Chaplain to Bishop of Aberdeen and Orkney, 1978-86; Canon, St. Andrew's Cathedral,

Aberdeen, since 1981. Member, ACTS Commission on Mission, Education and Evangelism; Representative, Scottish Episcopal Church, Church Pastoral Aid Society. Address: The Rectory, Bieldside, Aberdeen AB15 9AP; T.-01224 861552.

Gordon, Robert, QFSM, GIFireE. Firemaster, Highland and Islands Fire Brigade, since 1995; b. 21.11.42, Nairn; m., Pamela; 1 s.; 1 d. Educ. Nairn Academy; Inverness Technical College. Joined Northern Fire Brigade, 1964; Highland and Islands Fire Brigade, since 1983. Queen's Fire Service Medal, 1995; Chairman, Appliances, Equipment and Uniform Committee, Chief and Assistant Chief Fire Officers Association District No. 7 (Scotland); Member, National AEU Committee. Recreations: sailing; golf; painting and sketching; vegetable gardening; running. Address: (b.) 16 Harbour Road, Inverness IV1 1TB; T.-01463 227000.

Gordon, Robert Smith Benzie, MA. Head, Constitution Group, Scottish Office, since 1997; b. 7.11.50, Aberdeen; m., Joyce Cordiner; 2 s.; 2 d. Educ. Gordon Schools, Huntly; Aberdeen University. Joined Scottish Office, 1973; Principal, Scottish Development Department, 1979-85; Principal Private Secretary to Secretary of State for Scotland, 1985-87; Assistant Secretary: Department of Agriculture and Fisheries, 1988-90, Management, Organisation and Industrial Relations Division, Scottish Office, 1990-91; Director, Administrative Services, 1991-97. Address: (b.) Victoria Quay, Edinburgh EH6 6QQ; T.-0131-556 8400.

Gordon, Professor William Morrison, MA, LLB, PhD, FRSE. Douglas Professor of Civil Law, Glasgow University, since 1969; Solicitor (non-practising), since 1956; b. 3.3.33, Inverurie; m., Isabella Evelyn Melitta Robertson; 2 s.; 2 d. Educ. Inverurie Academy; Robert Gordon's College, Aberdeen; Aberdeen University. National Service, Royal Navy, 1955-57; Assistant in Jurisprudence, Aberdeen University, 1957-60; Glasgow University: Lecturer in Civil Law, 1960-65, Senior Lecturer in Law, 1965-69 (and Sub-Dean of Faculty); Dean of Faculty, 1974-76. Elder and Session Clerk, Jordanhill Parish Church; Literary Director, The Stair Society. Publications: Studies in Transfer of Property by Traditio, 1970; Scottish Land Law, 1989; Stair Society Miscellany III, 1992; European Legal History (2nd Ed.), (with others), 1994. Recreation: golf. Address: (b.) School of Law, Stair Building, University, Glasgow G12 8QQ; T.-0141-339 8855, Ext. 5387.

Gordon-Duff-Pennington, Patrick Thomas, OBE, DL. Chairman, Deer Commission for Scotland, since 1993; b. 12.1.30, London; m., Phyllida Rosemary; 4 d. Educ. Eton; Trinity College, Oxford. Farmed in Dumfriesshire, 1959-82; Hon. President, Scottish NFU, 1981-83; Convenor, Scottish Landowners Federation, 1988-91; DL, Cumbria; Vice-President, Field Studies Council. Address: (b.) 82 Fairfield Road, Inverness IV3 5LH; T.-01463 231751.

Goring, Rev. Iain McCormick, BSc, BD. Minister, Callander Kirk, since 1985; b. 22.7.50, Edinburgh; m., Janet Page; 2 s.; 1 d. Educ. Dunfermline High School; University of Edinburgh. Minister, Lochwood Parish Church, Easterhouse, Glasgow, 1977-85. Address: (h.) The Manse, Aveland Park Road, Callander, Perthshire FK17 8EN; T.-01877 330097.

Gorman, Professor Daniel Geelan, BSc, PhD, DSc, CEng, FIMechE. Professor of Mechanical Engineering, University of Aberdeen, since 1995; b. 9.8.47, Bellshill; m., Dr. June Neilson; 1 s.; 1 d. Educ. Holy Cross High School, Hamilton; Strathclyde University. Honeywell Ltd., 1968-69; E. Scragg & Sons Ltd., 1969-74; PhD student, 1974-77; Trinity College, Dublin, 1977-80; University of Limerick, 1980-81; Queen Mary and Westfield College, London,

1981-89; Robert Gordon University, 1989-95; Editor-in-Chief, Machine Vibration, 1991-95. Recreations: golf; motor cars. Address: (h.) The Linns, Catterline, Stonehaven, Kincardineshire AB39 2UL; T.-01569 750273.

Gorrie, Donald Cameron Easterbrook, OBE, MA, JP. MP (Liberal Democrat), Edinburgh West, since 1997; Leader, Liberal Democrat Group: City of Edinburgh Council, 1995-97, City of Edinburgh District Council, 1980-96, Lothian Regional Council, 1974-96; b. 2.4.33, India; m., Astrid Salvesen; 2 s. Educ. Hurst Grange, Stirling; Oundle School; Corpus Christi College, Oxford. Schoolmaster: Gordonstoun School, 1957-60, Marlborough College, 1960-66; Scottish Liberal Party: Director of Research, 1969-71, Director of Administration, 1971-75; Edinburgh Town Councillor, 1971-75. Director, 'Edinburgh Translations'; Member, Board: Royal Lyceum Theatre Company, Queens Hall, Lothian Association of Youth Clubs, Edinburgh Youth Cafe, Diverse Attractions, Castle Rock and Lothian Housing Associations; former Member, Board: Edinburgh Festival, Scottish Chamber Orchestra; former Scottish native record holder, 880 yards. Address: (h.) 9 Garscube Terrace, Edinburgh EH12 6BW; T.-0131-337 2077.

Gossip, Michael A.J., OBE, JP, BL, FBIM. Honorary Sheriff, Dunoon, since 1989, and Campbeltown, since 1997; Clerk, Presbytery of South Argyll, since 1996; b. 27.4.33, Edinburgh; m., Margaret; 1 s.; 2 d. Educ. George Watson's Boys' College, Edinburgh; Edinburgh University. Legal Assistant, Midlothian County Council, 1955-57; Dumfries County Council: Senior Legal Assistant, 1957-60, Depute County Clerk, 1960-71; Argyll County Council: Depute County Clerk, 1971-72, County Clerk, 1972-75; Chief Executive, Argyll and Bute District Council, 1974-96. Recreations: bowls; gardening. Address: (h.) Tigh-na-Coille, Ardrishaig, Argyll PA30 8EP; T.-01546 603454.

Gotts, Iain McEwan, DipLE, DipTP, FRICS, MRTPI. Chief Executive, PIEDA plc, Planning, Economic and Development Consultants, since 1976; b. 26.2.47, Glasgow; m., Pamela; 1 s.; 2 d. Educ. Jordanhill College School, Glasgow; Paisley College of Technology; Heriot-Watt University/Edinburgh College of Art. Trainee Surveyor, British Rail Property Department, Glasgow, 1965-68; further education, 1968-72; Surveyor/Land Economist, Wright & Partners, Edinburgh, 1972-76. Governor, Stewart's Melville College and Mary Erskine School, since 1992. Recreations: music; golf; rugby. Address: (b.) 10 Chester Street, Edinburgh EH3 7RA; T.-0131-225 5737.

Gould, Robert. Leader, Glasgow City Council, since 1995 (previously Leader, Strathclyde Regional Council); b. 8.2.35; m., Helen; 2 s.; 2 d. Elected to Glasgow Corporation, 1970; JP and magistrate, 1971; elected to Strathclyde Regional Council, 1974; Chair: National Joint Council Manual Workers, 1980-92, National Joint Council Fire Brigades, 1980-88; elected Depute Leader, SRC, 1986; Chairman, National Joint Council (Employer), APT&C and Manual Workers, 1986; Director: SECC, Glasgow Cultural Enterprises Ltd., Royal Concert Hall Board. Recreations: golf; hill-walking; sports; theatre. Address: (b.) Glasgow City Council, City Chambers, Glasgow; T.-0141-287 5432.

Gow, Alistair Martin, MBA, BSc, FICE, FIHT. Director of Roads and Transportation, Argyll and Bute Council, since 1995; b. 17.4.47, Glasgow; m., Rosalind; 2 d. Educ. Hyndland Secondary School, Glasgow; Glasgow University. Argyll County Council, 1969-74; City of Glasgow, 1974-75; Strathclyde Regional Council, 1975-95. Elder, Church of Scotland. Recreations: sailing; hill-walking; reading. Address: (h.) Oakbank, Churchill Wood, Inverneill, Ardrishaig, Argyll PA30 8ES; T.-01546 606222.

Gow, Sir (James) Michael, GCB, DL (Edinburgh), FSAScot. President, Royal British Legion Scotland, 1986-96; President, Earl Haig Fund (Scotland), 1986-96, Vice-President, since 1996; Vice-President, Officers' Association Scotland, since 1986 (President, 1985-86); Vice-President, Scottish Institution for the War Blinded, since 1986; b. 3.6.24; m., Jane Emily Scott; 1 s.; 4 d. Educ. Winchester College. Enlisted, Scots Guards, 1942; commissioned, 1943; served NW Europe 1944-45, Malayan Emergency, 1949; Equerry to the late HRH Duke of Gloucester, 1952-53; Brigade Major, 1955-57; Regimental Adjutant, Scots Guards, 1957-60; Instructor, Army Staff College, 1962-64; Command, 2nd Bn Scots Guards, Kenya and England, 1964-66; GSO1, HQ London District, 1966-67; Command, 4th Guards Brigade, 1968-69; Imperial Defence College, 1970; Brigadier General Staff (Int.) HQ, BAOR and Assistant Chief of Staff, G2 HQ, Northag, 1971-73; GOC 4th Div., BAOR, 1973-75; Director of Army Training, 1975-78; General Officer Commanding, Scotland, Governor of Edinburgh Castle, 1979-80; Commander-in-Chief, BAOR and Commander, Northern Army Group, 1980-83 (awarded die Plakette des deutschen Heeres); ADC Gen. to the Queen, 1981-84; Commandant, Royal College of Defence Studies, 1984-86. Colonel Commandant: Intelligence Corps, 1973-86, Scottish Division, 1979-80; Ensign, Queen's Body Guard for Scotland, (Royal Company of Archers); UK Member, Eurogroup US Tour, 1983; UK Kermit Roosevelt Lecturer, USA, 1984; Vice President: Queen Victoria School, Dunblane, 1979-80, Royal Caledonian Schools, Bushey, since 1980; County Commissioner, British Scouts, W. Europe, 1980-83 (Silver Acorn); Elder, Church of Scotland, since 1988; President, National Association of Sheltered Employment, since 1993; Freeman: City of London, 1980, State of Kansas, USA, 1984; Freeman and Liveryman, Painters' and Stainers' Company, 1980. Publications: Trooping the Colour: A History of the Sovereign's Birthday Parade by the Household Troops, 1989; Jottings in a General's Notebook, 1989; General Reflections, 1991. Recreations: sailing; music; travel; reading. Address: (h.) 18 Ann Street, Edinburgh EH4 1PJ; T.-0131-332 4752.

Gow, Sheriff Neil, QC (Scot). Sheriff of South Strathclyde, at Ayr, since 1976; b. 24.4.32. Address: Sheriff Court House, Wellington Square, Ayr, KA7 1DR.

Grace, Professor John, BSc, PhD, FIBiol, FRSE. Professor of Environmental Biology, Edinburgh University, since 1992; b. 19.9.45, Northampton; m., Elizabeth Ashworth; 2 s.; 1 d. Educ. Bletchley Grammar School; Sheffield University. Lecturer, then Reader in Ecology, Edinburgh Univrsity, 1970-92. Co-Editor, Functional Ecology, since 1986; Technical Editor, International Society for Biometeorology, since 1983; Member, Terrestrial Life Sciences Committee, Natural Environment Research Council, 1986-89; Council Member, British Ecological Society, since 1983. Publications: Plant Response to Wind, 1977; Plants and their Atmospheric Environment (Co-Editor), 1981; Plant-atmosphere Relationships, 1983. Recreations: hill-walking; cycling; fishing; bridge. Address: (h.) 25 Craiglea Drive, Edinburgh EH10 5PB; T.-0131-447 3030.

Grace, Paul Henry, BSc, FFA. Managing Director and Actuary, Scottish Equitable Policyholders Trust Ltd., since 1994; b. 25.9.38, Bletchley; m., Aileen Anderson; 1 d. Educ. Bedford Modern School; St. Andrews University. Joined Scottish Equitable as Actuarial Trainee, 1960; joined Zurich Life Assurance Co. as Actuary and Life Manager, 1965; rejoined Scottish Equitable, 1980. President, Faculty of Actuaries, 1996-97. Publication: Introduction to Life Assurance, 1988. Recreations: golf; gardening. Address: Edinburgh Park, Edinburgh EH12; T.-0131-549 3013.

Gracie, Alistair. Head of News and Current Affairs, Grampian Television, since 1986; b. 25.2.48, Aberdeen; m., Wendy; 1 s.; 2 d. Educ. Aberdeen Grammar School. Joined Aberdeen Journals as Trainee Journalist, 1966; worked on

Press and Journal as Reporter and Evening Express as Sub-Editor; moved into television as Researcher/Reporter, 1972; Grampian Television: News Editor, 1974, Programme Editor, 1978. Recreations: mountaineering; squash; running; photography; reading; painting. Address: (b.) Grampian TV, Queen's Cross, Aberdeen AB9 2XJ.

Graham, Rev. A. David M., BA, BD. Minister, Rosemount Parish Church, Aberdeen, since 1990; b. 17.7.40, Tralee; m., Mary A. Taylor; 2 s.; 1 d. Educ. Wesley College, Dublin; Methodist College, Belfast; Queen's University, Belfast; Glasgow University. Assistant, South Leith Parish; Secretary for Christian Education, Scottish National Council of YMCAs, Minister, Anderston Parish, Glasgow; Warden, Iona Abbey; Minister, Rutherford Parish, Aberdeen. Recreations: jogging; climbing. Address: 22 Osborne Place, Aberdeen AB2 4DA; T.-01224 648041.

Graham. Rev. Alasdair Giffen, BD, Dip. Ministry. Minister, Arbroath West Kirk, since 1990; Part-time Chaplain, Arbroath Infirmary; b. 20.4.54, Lanark; m., Joan Janet Forsyth; 1 d. Educ. Gordon Schools, Huntly; Kirkcaldy High School; University of Glasgow. Probationary Assistant, Mastrick Church, Aberdeen, 1980-81; Minister, Redgorton and Stanley Churches, Perthshire, 1981-86; Chaplain, HM Prison, Perth; Minister, St Margaret's Church, Arbroath, 1986-90. District Scout Chaplain; Chaplain, Angus Training Group. Recreations: time with family; badminton; swimming. Address: (h.) 1 Charles Avenue, Arbroath DD11 2EY; T.-01241 872244.

Graham, Professor David I., MB, ChB, PhD, FRCPath, FRCPS, FRSE. Professor of Neuropathology, Glasgow University, since 1983; b. 20.7.39, Glasgow; m., Joyce; 1 s.; 1 d. Educ. Penarth County Grammar School; Welsh National School of Medicine, Cardiff. Registrar, Western Infirmary, Glasgow, 1965-68; Lecturer, Department of Neuropathology, Glasgow, 1968-72; Fogarty Fellow, Laboratory of Neuropathology, Philadelphia, 1972-74; Senior Lecturer, Glasgow, 1974-83. Publications: several books; 300 papers. Recreations: hill-walking; music. Address: (b.) Department of Neuropathology, Institute of Neurological Sciences, Southern General Hospital, Govan Road, Glasgow G51 4TF; T.-0141-201 2113.

Graham, Lord Donald, BSc, MBA. Director of Information Technology, Adam & Company plc, since 1991; Director: Fruit Market Gallery, since 1992, KDCL Ltd., Property Developers, since 1992, Children's Music Foundation, since 1995; b. 28.10.56, Salisbury, Southern Rhodesia; m., Bridie; 3 d. Educ. St. Andrews College, South Africa; St. Andrews University; INSEAD. Recreations: piping; music. Address: (b.) Adam & Company plc, 22 Charlotte Square, Edinburgh EH2 4DF; T.-0131-225 8484.

Graham, Elspeth Forbes, MA, PhD. Senior Lecturer in Geography, St. Andrews University, since 1997; Member, Local Government Boundary Commission for Scotland, since 1994; b. 7.2.50, Edinburgh; 1 s.; 1 d. Educ. George Watson's Ladies College, Edinburgh; St. Andrews University; Durham University. Visiting Lecturer, University of Minnesota, 1979-80. Publications: Postmodernism and the Social Sciences (Co-editor), 1992; research papers on population policies and issues. Recreations: horse-riding; Celtic music. Address: (b.) Department of Geography, St. Andrews University, St. Andrews KY16 9ST; T.-01334 463908.

Graham, Ian, BSc(Econ) (Hons), DipEdTech (CNAA). Principal, John Wheatley College, Glasgow, since 1992; b. 26.6.51, Devizes. Educ. Queen Victoria School, Dunblane; London Universty (External). Lecturer/Senior Lecturer, Reid Kerr College, Paisley, 1975-86; Head of Department, Clydebank College, 1986-88; Further Education Officer, Strathclyde Regional Council, 1988-89; HM Inspector of Schools, 1989-90; Assistant Director of Education (FE), Strathclyde Region, 1990-92. Fellow, Royal Society of Arts; Fellow, Institute of Personnel and Development; Member, Board: Scottish Community Education Council, Association of Scottish Colleges; Chair: Strathclyde European Partnership Board, West of Scotland Colleges' European Partnership. Recreations; reading; cinema; foreign travel; admiring Burmese cats. Address: (b.) 1346 Shettleston Road, Glasgow G32 9AT; T.-0141-778 2426.

Graham, John James, OBE, MA, MUniv (Aberdeen) FEIS. Joint Editor, The New Shetlander, since 1956; b. 12.7.21, Lerwick; m., Beryl Smith; 3 s.; 2 d. Educ. Lerwick Central Secondary School; Edinburgh University. RAF Training Command, 1941-44, Bomber Command, 1944-46; Principal Teacher of English, Anderson Educational Institute, Lerwick, 1950-66; Headmaster: Lerwick Central Secondary School, 1966-70, Anderson High School, Lerwick, 1970-82; Member: Consultative Committee on the Curriculum, 1976-80, Broadcasting Council for Scotland, 1981-84; President, Shetland Folk Society. Publications: A Grammar and Usage of the Shetland Dialect (Co-author); Northern Lights (Joint Editor); The Shetland Dictionary; Shadowed Valley (novel); Strife in the Valley (novel). Recreations: local history; golf. Address: (h.) 10 Reform Lane, Lerwick, Shetland; T.-Lerwick 3425.

Graham, John Michael Denning, LLB (Hons), NP, FRSA. Solicitor and Notary Public, since 1970; Senior Partner, Paterson Roberson & Graham, since 1971; Senior Tutor in Law, Glasgow University; Director, John Smith & Son (Glasgow) Ltd.; Non Executive Director, West Glasgow Hospitals University NHS Trust; b. 7.9.44, Kirkintilloch; m., Christina Jeanne Sinclair; 2 s. Educ. Royal Belfast Academical Institution; Queen's University, Belfast. Chairman: Rent Assessment Committee, Glasgow, since 1983, Child Support Appeal Tribunal, since 1993, Social Security Appeal Tribunal, since 1995; Governor, Glasgow Caledonian University. Recreations: tennis; golf; hang-gliding. Address: (b.) 12 Royal Crescent, Glasgow G3 7SL; T.-0141-353 0550.

Graham, John Strathie, BA. Principal Finance Officer, Scottish Office, since 1996; b. 27.5.50, Edinburgh; m., Anne Graham; 2 s.; 1 d. Educ. Edinburgh Academy; Corpus Christi College, Oxford. Joined Scottish Office, 1972; Principal, Scottish Economic Planning Department, 1976; Assistant Secretary, Industry Department for Scotland, 1982; Private Secretary to Secretary of State, 1983; Assistant Secretary: Planning Division, Scottish Development Department, 1985, Finance Division 1, 1990; Under Secretary, Local Government Group, 1991. Recreations: exploring Scotland; listening to music. Address: (b.) Victoria Quay, Edinburgh EH6 6QQ.

Graham, Keith H.R., LLB, WS. Principal Clerk, Scottish Land Court, since 1982; b. 29.5.47, Edinburgh; m., Patricia; 2 d. Educ. George Watson's College; Edinburgh University. Apprenticeship, Davidson & Syme, WS, 1968-70; private practice, 1970-72; Legal Assessor, Scottish Land Court, 1972-82. Publication: The Scottish Land Court: Practice and Procedure. Address: (b.) 1 Grosvenor Crescent, Edinburgh EH12 5ER; T.-0131-225 3595.

Graham, Professor Neil Bonnette, BSc, PhD, CChem, FRSC, FIM, FRSE. Professor in Chemical Technology, Strathclyde University, since 1973; b. 23.5.33, Liverpool; 1 s.; 3 d. Educ. Alsop High School, Liverpool; Liverpool University. Research Chemist, Research Scientist, Canadian Industries Ltd., MacMasterville PQ, Canada, 1956-67; Assistant Group Head, then Group Head, Polymer Chemistry, ICI, Runcorn, Cheshire. Member: Advisory Committee on Dental and Surgical Materials, 1980-86; Expert Advisor to the Secretary of State on Active Medical Implants, since 1993; sometime member of various committees, Society of Chemical Industry, Royal Society of

Chemistry and Plastics and Rubber Institute; Member, International Editorial Boards, Biomedical Polymers; Founder and Technical Director, Polysystems Ltd., 1980-90; Governor and Trustee, Keil School; Trustee, James Clerk Maxwell Trust. Recreations: music; walking. Address: (b.) Strathclyde University, Department of Pure and Applied Chemistry, Thomas Graham Building, 295 Cathedral Street, Glasgow G1 1XL; T.-0141-552 4400, Ext. 2133.

Graham, Nigel John O. Member, Highland Council (previously Member, Highland Regional Council); b. 28.7.27, Worcestershire; m., Margaret; 2 s.; 2 d. Educ. Marlborough College. Highland Light Infantry, 1945-53; TA, Queen's Own Cameron Highlanders, 1953-61; farmer, 1953-83; Member, Nairn County Council, 1966-72; Member, N.E. Board, Scottish Natural Heritage. Recreation: bird-watching; photography. Address: (h.) Househill, Nairn; T.-Nairn 453241.

Graham, Sir Norman William, Kt (1971), CB (1961), MA, DLitt (Heriot-Watt), DUniv (Stirling), FRSE; b. 11.10.13, Dundee; m., Catherine Mary Strathie; 2 s.; 1 d. Educ. High School of Glasgow; Glasgow University. Assistant Principal, Department of Health for Scotland, 1936; Principal, Ministry of Aircraft Production, 1941; Principal Private Secretary to Minister, 1944; Assistant Secretary, Department of Health for Scotland, 1945; Under Secretary, 1956; Secretary, Scottish Education Department, 1964-73.

Graham, Lieutenant General Sir Peter, KCB, CBE, DLitt. Chairman, Regimental Trust Fund, The Gordon Highlanders, since 1986; Chairman, The Gordon Highlanders Museum Management Committee, since 1994; b. 14.3.37; m., Dr Alison Mary Morren; 3 s. Educ. Fyvie Village School, Aberdeenshire; Hall School, Hampstead; St. Paul's School, London; RMA Sandhurst. Commissioned The Gordon Highlanders, 1956; regimental appointments, Dover, Germany, Scotland, Kenya, 1957-62; HQ Highland Brigade, 1962-63; Adjutant 1 Gordons, Kenya, Edinburgh, Borneo (Despatches), 1963-66; Staff Captain, HQ 1 Br Corps, 1966-67; Australian Staff College, 1968; Company Commander, 1 Gordons, Germany, 1969-70; Brigade Maj., HQ 39 Brigade, Northern Ireland, 1970-72; 2nd i/c, 1 Gordons, Ulster, Singapore, 1972-74; Military Assistant to Adjutant General MoD, 1974-75; CO, 1 Gordons, Scotland, Ulster, 1976-78; COS, HQ 3 Armoured Division, Germany, 1978-82; Comd UDR, Ulster (Despatches), 1982-84; Canadian National Defence College, Ontario, 1984-85; Deputy Military Secretary, MoD, 1985-87; GOC Eastern District, 1987-89; Commandant RMA, Sandhurst, 1989-91; GOC Army in Scotland and Governor, Edinburgh Castle, 1991-93. Colonel, The Gordon Highlanders, 1986-96; Member, Royal Company of Archers, since 1985. Publications: The Gordon Highlanders Pipe Music Collection (Co-author), 1983 and 1985; DLitt, Robert Gordon University, 1996. Recreations: stalking; hill-walking; shooting; reading; pipe music; gardening under my wife's directions. Address: (b.) The Gordon Highlanders Museum, Viewfield Road, Aberdeen AB1 7XH; T.-01224 311200.

Graham, Riddell, BSc, MTS. Chief Executive, Scottish Borders Tourist Board, since 1996, Director, 1990-96; b. 13.2.54, Galashiels; m., Sandra; 1 s. Educ. Galashiels Academy; Edinburgh University. Borders Regional Council, 1976-83, latterly as Assistant Tourist Officer; joined Scottish Borders Tourist Board, 1983, as Assistant Director of Tourism. Recreations: mountain biking; watching rugby. Address: (b.) Shepherds Mill, Whinfield Road, Selkirk; T.-01750 20555.

Graham, Ronald Cairns, CBE, MB, ChB, DipSocMed, FRCP, FFCM. Honorary Senior Lecturer, Dundee University, since 1969; b. 8.10.31, Airdrie; m., Christine Fraser Osborne; 2 s.; 1 d. Educ. Airdrie Academy; Glasgow University. Deputy Medical Superintendent, Edinburgh Royal Infirmary; Assistant Senior Administrative Medical Officer, South-Eastern Regional Hospital Board; Eastern Regional Hospital Board: Deputy Senior Administrative Medical Officer, Senior Administrative Medical Officer; Tayside Health Board: Chief Administrative Medical Officer, 1973-85, General Manager, 1985-93. Recreation: fishing. Address: (h.) 34 Dalgleish Road, Dundee; T.-Dundee 455426.

Graham, Thomas. MP (Labour), Renfrew West, since 1987; b. 1944. Address: (b.) House of Commons, London, SW1A 0AA.

Graham, Rev. William Peter, MA, BD. Clerk, Edinburgh Presbytery, since 1993; b. 24.11.43, Edinburgh; m., Isabel Arnot Brown; 2 s. Educ. George Watson's College, Edinburgh; Edinburgh University. Assistant Minister, Dundee (St. Mary's) Parish Church, 1966-68; Minister, Chirnside Parish Church, 1968-93, Bonkyl & Preston, 1973-93, Edrom-Allanton, 1978-93; Clerk, Duns Presbytery, 1982-93; Convener, General Assembly's Nomination Committee, 1990-93; Vice-Convener, Committee on Education for Ministry, since 1996. Recreations: golf; theatre; reading. Address: (b.) 10 Palmerston Place, Edinburgh EH12 5AA; T.-0131-225 9137.

Graham-Bryce, Ian James, DPhil, BA, MA, BSc, FRSC, CChem, FRSE, FRSA. Principal and Vice-Chancellor, Dundee University, since 1994; b. 20.3.37; m., Anne Elisabeth Metcalf; 1 s.; 3 d. Educ. William Hulme's Grammar School, Manchester; University College, Oxford. Lecturer, UCNW, Bangor, 1961-64; Senior Scientific Officer, Rothamsted Experimental Station, 1964-70; Senior Research Officer, ICI Plant Protection Division, Berks, 1970-72; Imperial College of Science and Technology: Special Lecturer in Pesticide Chemistry, Department of Zoology and Applied Entomology, 1970-72, Visiting Professor, 1976-79, Governor, since 1985; Rothamsted Experimental Station: Head, Department of Insecticides and Fungicides, 1972-79, Deputy Director, 1975-79; Director, East Malling Research Station, 1979-86; Cons. Director, Commonwealth Bureau of Horticulture and Plantation Crops, 1979-86; Head, Environmental Affairs Division, Shell Internationale Petroleum Maatschappij BV, 1986-94. Society of Chemical Industry, London: President, 1982-84, Member, Council, 1969-72, 1974-89, Hon. Secretary, Home Affairs, 1977-80; President: Association of Applied Biologists, 1988; British Crop Protection Council, since 1996; Member, NERC, 1989-96 (Chairman, Polar Sciences Committee, 1995-96); Member, Board of Directors: Educational Counselling Service, British Council; Member, Board of Directors, Quality Assurance Agency for Higher Education (Chairman, Scottish Advisory Committee). Publications: Physical Principles of Pesticide Behaviour, 1980; papers on soil science, plant nutrition, crop protection and environmental matters. Recreations: music (especially opera); sport. Address: (b.) Dundee University, Dundee DD1 4HN.

Grahame, David Currie, MA (Hons). Executive Director, LINC Scotland, since 1993; b. 10.12.53, Hawick. Educ. Langholm Academy; Lockerbie Academy; St. Andrews University. Hotelier and company director, 1980-87; Small Business Consultant, 1987-90; Area Manager, Princes Scottish Youth Business Trust, 1990-91; Head of Business Development, Glasgow Opportunities Enterprise Trust, 1991-93; Founding Director, LINC Scotland (National Business Angels Network). Member, Bank of England Small Firms Advisory Group for Scotland. Recreations: music; classic cinema; food and wine. Address: (b.) 30 George Square, Glasgow G2 1BB; T.-0141-221 3321.

Grainger, John McGregor Leighton, MBE, FTS. Chief Executive, Perthshire Tourist Board, since 1982; b. 3.9.43, Aberdeen; m., Kathleen; 1 s. (deceased); 2 d. Assistant Tourist Officer, Aberdeen Town Council, 1959-67; Tourism Manager: Dunbar Town Council, 1967-69, Perth Tourist Association, 1969-74; Senior Tourist Officer, Tayside Regional Council, 1974-82. Recreations: fishing; hill-walking. Address: (b.) Lower City Mills, West Mill Street, Perth PH1 5QP; T.-01738 627958.

Grains, Florence Barbara, OBE, JP. Member, Shetland Islands Council, since 1986; Director, Shetland Careers Service; former Chairman, Shetland Health Board; b. 2.11.32, Shetland; m., Alistair M. Grains; 4 s. Educ. Whiteness School, Shetland; Lerwick FE Centre. Retired Sub-postmaster, Whiteness, Shetland. Chairman, Alting Debating Society; Trustee, Shetland Amenity Trust; Chairman, Shetland Branch, Post Office Users Council for Scotland; Member, Shetland Area Licensing Board; Trustee, Walls and District Agricultural Society; Supervisor, Whiteness and Weisdale Playgroup; GCSL, 1st Whiteness/Weisdale; Chairman, Foula Electricity Trust. Address: (h.) Hoove, Whiteness, Shetland; T.-01595 84 243.

Grant, Donald Blane, CBE, TD, LLD, CA; b. 8.10.21, Dundee; m., Lavinia Margaret Ruth Ritchie; 3 d. Educ. Dundee High School. Royal Artillery, 1939-46 (retired as Major); Partner, Thomson, McLintock & Co., 1950-86. Chairman, Tayside Health Board, 1984-91; Chairman: Scottish Legal Aid Board, 1986-91, Mathew Trust, Caird Travelling Scholarships Trust. Recreations: golf; fishing; shooting; gardening. Address: (h.) 24 Albany Road, Broughty Ferry, Dundee DD5 1NT.

Grant, Dr. Douglas, TD, FRSE, FSA Scot; b. 6.1.18; m., Enid Whitsey; 3 s. Educ. George Watson's College; University of St. Andrews. Lt.-Col., RA (served W. Africa and staff), 1939-46; Scottish Widows Fund, 1936-39; Director: Oliver and Boyd Ltd., 1947-67, Edinburgh C. of C., 1952-56, New Education Ltd., 1962-66, Bracken House Publications Ltd., 1963-67, Sprint Productions Ltd., 1963-80, E. & S. Livingston Ltd., 1963-67, Darien Press Ltd., 1963-68, R. & R. Clark Ltd., 1963-80, Port Seton Offset Printers Ltd., 1965-75, T. & A. Constable Ltd., 1965-75, British Journal of Educational Psychology, 1970-91, Pindar (Scot) Ltd., 1986-89, Macdonald Lindsay (Printers) Ltd., 1988-89; Chairman: Scottish Journal of Theology Ltd., 1948-91, Robert Cunningham & Sons Ltd., 1952-76, Hunter and Foulis Ltd., 1963-75, Port Seton Offset Printers Ltd., 1965-75, Multi Media (AU) Services Ltd., 1967-75, Church of Scotland Publications Committee, 1971-76, Scottish Academic Press Ltd., 1969-91, Scottish International Review Ltd., 1970-75, Handsel Press Ltd., 1975-91, Scottish Academic Press (Journals) Ltd., 1976-91, Clark Constable Printers Ltd., 1978-89; Consultant Editor, Scottish Academic Press, since 1991. Trustee, The Lodge Trust (Natural History), 1949-85, Darling (Ogilby) Investment Trust, 1955-78, Kilwarlin Trust, since 1964, Esdaile Trust, since 1975, Society for the Benefit of Sons and Daughters of the Clergy of the Church of Scotland, since 1990; Committee Member: Scottish Council of Law Reporting, 1950-93 (Consultant, since 1993), Police Dependents' Trust (Lothian and Borders Police), since 1956, NEDO, 1968-75, New College University of Edinburgh Board, since 1970, University of Edinburgh Court, 1972-84, Scottish Arts Council, 1975-79; President: Edinburgh Master Printers' Association, 1962-64, Edinburgh Bookseller Society, 1977-80, Edinburgh Amateur Angling Club, 1978-80; Honorary Fellow, Edinburgh Geological Society, 1992; Hon. DLitt, University of St. Andrews, 1986. Address: Flat G, The Lodge, 2 East Road, North Berwick, East Lothian EH39 4HN; T.-01620 894972.

Grant, (Helen) Rae. Administrator, Scottish Liberal Democrats, since 1989; b. 17.12.40, Edinburgh; m., James Sturrock Grant; 2 d. Educ. Boroughmuir High School; Torphichen Commercial College. Party Secretary, 1974-89. Recreations: reading; swimming; walking. Address: (b.) 4 Clifton Terrace, Edinburgh EH12 5DR; T.-0131-337 2314.

Grant, Ian David, CBE, FRAgS. Chairman, Scottish Tourist Board, since 1990; Crown Estate Commissioner; b. 28.7.43, Dundee; m., Eileen May Louisa Yule; 3 d. Educ. Strathallan School; East of Scotland College of Agriculture. Chairman, EEC Cereals Working Party, 1982-88 and International Federation of Agricultural Producers, Grains Committee, 1984-90; President, NFU of Scotland, 1984-90; Director: Scottish Hydro Electric, East of Scotland Farmers Ltd., NFU Mutual Insurance Society Ltd., Clydesdale Bank PLC, 1989-97; Member: Scottish Council, CBI, 1984-96, Board, British Tourist Authority, since 1990, Scottish Economic Council, 1993-97; Vice President, Royal Smithfield Club. Recreations: shooting; swimming; music. Address: (h.) Leal House, Alyth PH11 8JQ. Tel.: 01828 632695.

Grant, Ian Faulconer Heathcoat, JP, DL. Managing Director, Glenmoriston Estates Limited; Chairman, Pacific Assets Trust PLC; Director: Royal Bank of Scotland PLC, Royal Bank of Scotland Group plc, Redruth Brewery (1972) Ltd., Worldwide Value Fund Inc. (USA), Banco Santander S.A., Holland Pacific Fund N.V., Grandom International Limited, Dransfield Holdings Limited; b. 3.6.39, Singapore; m., Sally; 1 s.; 3 d. Educ. Cargilfield; Sedbergh; Liverpool College of Commerce. ICI Ltd., 1957-62; various positions, Jardine Matheson & Co. Ltd., Hong Kong, 1962-73, culminating in directorship on Main Board. Address: (b.) Glenmoriston Estates Ltd., Glenmoriston, near Inverness; T.-01320 351202.

Grant, Major James MacAlpine Gregor, TD, NDA, MRAC. Landowner and Farmer, since 1961; b. 18.2.38, Nakuru, Kenya; m., Sara Marjory, DL; 3 d. Educ. Eton; Royal Agricultural College, Cirencester. National Service, Queen's Own Cameron Highlanders, 1957-58; TA with 4/5th Queen's Own Cameron Highlanders; Volunteers with 51st Highland Volunteers. Address: Roskill House, Munlochy, Rossshire IV8 8PA; T.-01463 811207.

Grant, James Shaw, CBE, LLD, FRSE, FRAgS, MA. Author; b. 22.5.10, Stornoway; m., Catherine Mary Stewart. Educ. Nicolson Institute, Stornoway; Glasgow University. Editor, Stornoway Gazette, 1932-63; Governor, Pitlochry Festival Theatre, 1954-84 (Chairman, 1971-83); Member, Crofters Commission, 1955-78 (Chairman, 1963-78); Director, Grampian TV, 1969-80; Member: Highlands and Islands Development Board, 1970-82, Scottish Advisory Committee, British Council, 1972-94; Chairman, Harris Tweed Association Ltd., 1972-84; Member, Council, National Trust for Scotland, 1979-84; Governor, Eden Court Theatre, 1980-96 (Vice Chairman, 1987-96); author of plays: Tarravore, The Magic Rowan, Legend is Born, Comrade the King. Publications: Highland Villages, 1977, Their Children Will See, 1979; The Hub of My Universe, 1982; Surprise Island, 1983; The Gaelic Vikings, 1984; Stornoway and the Lews, 1985; Discovering Lewis and Harris, 1987; Enchanted Island, 1989; A Shilling for Your Scowl, 1992. Address: (h.) Ardgranach, Inshes, Inverness; T.-Inverness 231476.

Grant, Professor John Paxton, LLB, LLM. Professor, School of Law, Glasgow University, since 1988 (Dean, Faculty of Law and Financial Studies, 1985-89 and 1992-96); b. 22.2.44, Edinburgh; m., Elaine E. Sutherland. Educ. George Heriot's School, Edinburgh; Edinburgh University; Pennsylvania University. Lecturer, Faculty of Law: Aberdeen University, 1967-71, Dundee University, 1971-74; Senior Lecturer, Department of Public International Law, Glasgow University, 1974-88; Visiting Professor:

Saint Louis University School of Law, 1981, Northwestern School of Law, Lewis and Clark College, 1984, 1986, 1998. Editor, The Juridical Review, since 1988. Publications: Independence and Devolution (Editor), 1976; The Impact of Marine Pollution: Law and Practice (Joint Editor), 1980; The Encyclopaedic Dictionary of International Law (Joint General Editor), 1985; Legal Education 2000 (Joint Editor), 1988; English–Estonian Law Glossary (Joint Editor), 1993; English for Lawyers (Joint Editor), 1995. Recreations: walking; travelling. Address: (h.) 87 Warrender Park Road, Edinburgh EH9 1EW; T.-0131-229 7705.

Grant, Lesley Dunbar, MBE, MA. Member, Scottish Sports Council; b. Banchory. Educ. Banchory Academy; Aberdeen University; Aberdeen College of Education. Former teacher/head teacher; Past Chairman, Northern Area, Scottish Conservative and Unionist Association; former Councillor, Dean of Guild and Hon. Treasurer, Banchory Town Council; former Handicap Adviser and Selector, Scottish Ladies Golf Association; Elder, Banchory-Ternan East Church. Recreations: current affairs; travel; caring; some holes of golf. Address: (h.) Ordeans, Arbeadie Terrace, Banchory AB31 5TN; T.-01330 822782.

Grant, Very Rev. Malcolm Etheridge, BSc (Hons), BD (Hons). Provost and Rector, Cathedral Church of S. Andrew, Inverness, Rector, S. Paul's, Strathnairn and Priest-in-charge, S. Mary's-in-the-Fields, Culloden, since 1991; b. 6.8.44, Maidstone; m., Katrina Russell Nuttall; 1 s.; 1 d. Educ. Dunfermline High School; Edinburgh University; Edinburgh Theological College. Assistant Curate: S. Mary's Cathedral, Glasgow, 1969-72, Grantham Parish Church, in charge of Church of the Epiphany, Earlesfield, 1972; Team Vicar, Earlesfield, Grantham Team Ministry, 1972-78; Priest-in-charge, S. Ninian's, Invergordon, 1978-81; Provost and Rector, Cathedral Church of S. Mary the Virgin, Glasgow, 1981-91; Examining Chaplain to Bishop of Moray, Ross and Caithness, 1979-81; Member, Highland Region Education Committee, 1979-81. Address: 15 Ardross Street, Inverness IV3 5NS; T.-01463 233535.

Grant, Sir (Matthew) Alistair, DL, FRSE. Chairman, Scottish and Newcastle plc, since 1997; b. 6.3.37, Haddington; m., Judith Mary Grant; 2 s. ; 1 d. Educ. Woodhouse Grove School, Yorkshire. Unilever, 1958-63; J. Lyons, 1963-65; Connell May & Steavenson, 1965-68; Marketing Director, Fine Fare Ltd., 1968-72; Managing Director, Oriel Foods Ltd., 1973-77; Managing Director of companies which formed Argyll Group, 1977-86; Deputy Chairman, Chief Executive, Chairman, Argyll Group, 1986-97. Chairman, Biotechnology and Biological Sciences Research Council; Ordinary Director, Bank of Scotland; Non-Executive Director, Scottish & Newcastle PLC; Visiting Professor, Strathclyde University; Trustee: National Museums of Scotland, National Heritage Memorial Fund; Regent, Royal College of Surgeons, Edinburgh. Recreations: hunting; fishing; reading; music.

Grant, Professor Nigel Duncan Cameron, MA, MEd, PhD, FRSE. Professor of Education, Glasgow University, 1978-95; b. 8.6.32, Glasgow; m., Valerie Keeling Evans; 1 s.; 1 d. Educ. Inverness Royal Academy; Glasgow University. Teacher of English, Glasgow secondary schools, 1957-60; Lecturer in Education, Jordanhill College of Education, 1960-65; Lecturer in Educational Studies, then Reader, Edinburgh University, 1965-78. Past Chairman and President, British Comparative and International Education Society; former Executive Member, Comparative Education Society in Europe; Past Chairman: Scottish Educational Research Association, Scottish Universities Council for Studies in Education; Educational Consultant, Comann Sgoiltean Da-Chananach Ghlaschu; Member: Executive Committee, Advisory Council for the Arts in Scotland, Editorial Board, Comparative Education; Trustee, Urras Foghlam na Gaidhlig; Member, Scottish

Constitutional Steering Committee; Hon. President, Glasgow Educational Colloquium. Publications: Soviet Education, 1964; Society, Schools and Progress in Eastern Europe, 1969; Education and Nation-Building in the Third World (Editor and Co-Author), 1971; A Mythology of British Education (Co-Author), 1974; Scottish Universities: The Case for Devolution (Co-Author), 1976; Patterns of Education in the British Isles (Co-Author), 1977; The Crisis of Scottish Education, 1982. Recreations: theatre; music; poetry; natural history; languages; art; travel; calligraphy.

Grant, Peter James, CBE. Chairman, Sun Life Corporation PLC, 1983-95; Chairman, Sun Life Assurance Society PLC, 1983-95; b. 5.12.29, London; m., Paula Eugster; 2 s.; 3 d. Educ. Winchester; Magdalen College, Oxford. Lieutenant, Queen's Own Cameron Highlanders. Vice-Chairman, 1983-85, Deputy Chairman, 1985-88, Lazard Bros & Co.; Director: Scottish Hydro, 1990-95, London Merchant Securities PLC, BNP UK Holdings Ltd.; Chairman, Highlands & Islands Airports Ltd.; Member: Council, Institute of Directors, Cromarty Firth Port Authority, since 1994; awarded CBE, 1997. Recreations: fishing; shooting; golf. Address: (h.) Mountgerald, near Dingwall, Rossshire IV15 9TT; T.-01349 62244.

Grant, Professor Peter Mitchell, PhD, CEng, FIEE, FIEEE, FRSE, FEng. Professor of Electronic Signal Processing, Edinburgh University, since 1987; b. 20.6.44, St. Andrews; m., Marjory Renz; 2 d. Educ. Strathallan School; Heriot-Watt University; Edinburgh University. Publications: Digital Communications (Co-Author), 1997; Signal Processing and Coding (Co-Author), 1988. Address: (b.) Department of Electrical Engineering, Edinburgh University, Edinburgh EH9 3JL; T.-0131-650 5569.

Grant, Richard Anthony, BSocSc, MSc. Head of Division, Land Use and Crofting, Scottish Office Agriculture and Fisheries Department, since 1991; b. 12.6.48, Leicester; m., Jacqueline Claire; 1 s.; 1 d. Educ. Loughborough College School; Birmingham University; Strathclyde University. Research Officer/Senior Research Officer, Scottish Education Department and Scottish Development Department, 1969-75; Principal Research Officer, Housing Research Unit, Scottish Development Department, 1975-77; Principal, Sports Policy Branch, Scottish Education Department, 1977-79; Principal Research Officer, Housing and Urban Renewal Research Unit, Scottish Development Department, 1979-85; Principal: Land Use and Conservation Branch, Department of Agriculture and Fisheries, 1986-89, NHS Management Executive, 1989-91. Recreations: cycling; hill-walking; cross-country skiing. Address: (b.) Room 102, Pentland House, Robbs Loan, Edinburgh; T.-0131-224 6190.

Grant of Dalvey, Sir Patrick Alexander Benedict, 14th Bt, FSA Scot, LLB. Chieftain of Clan Donnachy; Company Director; b. 5.2.53.

Grant, Sara Marjory. Deputy Lieutenant, Ross and Cromarty, since 1996; b. 7.12.45, Urray; m., James Grant; 3 d. Educ. St. James's, West Malvern. Team Leader, Day Hospice Volunteers, Highland Hospice. Recreations: walking; swimming; sewing; cooking; flower arranging. Address: (h.) Roskill House, Munlochy, Ross-shire IV8 8PA; T.-01463 811207.

Grant of Rothiemurchus, John Peter, DL. Landowner; b. 22.10.46, Rothiemurchus; m., Philippa; 1 s.; 2 d. Educ. Gordonstoun. Chairman and Director, Scot Trout Limited, 1989-95; Past Chairman, Highland Region, Forestry, Farming and Wildlife Advisory Group; Patron, Highland Hospice; Vice-President, Scottish Landowners' Federation, since 1991; Deputy Lieutenant, Districts of Lochaber, Inverness, Badenoch and Strathspey, since 1986; Member: Council, National Trust for Scotland, 1990-95, Native Woodlands Advisory Panel to the Forestry Commission, since 1993, National Access Forum, since 1993, Cairngorm Partnership, since 1995; Chairman, Tourism and Enivronment Task Force, since 1995; President, Royal Zoological Society of Scotland, since 1996. Recreations: skiing; shooting. Address: (b.) Doune of Rothiemurchus, by Aviemore; T.-01479 810647.

Grant Peterkin, Brigadier Anthony Peter, OBE, BA. Army Officer, since 1967; Army Director of Manning and Career Management, since 1996; Landowner; b. 6.7.47, London; m., Joanna Young; 1 s.; 1 d. Educ. Ampleforth College; University of Durham; University of Madras. Commissioned into Queen's Own Highlanders, 1967: service in Middle East, Germany, Northern Ireland, Belize, Hong Kong and India; ADC to CGS; Command of 1st Bn. Queen's Own Highlanders, Belize and Germany, 1987-89; Higher Command and Staff Course, Camberley, 1991; Military Adviser to UN Mission, Iraq and Kuwait, 1991; Commander, 24 Airmobile Brigade, 1993-94; Royal College of Defence Studies, 1995. Recreation: travelling off the beaten track in Indochina. Address: (h.) Grange Hall, Forres, Morayshire; T.-0171-727 5399.

Grassie, Professor Norman, BSc, PhD, DSc, CChem, FRSC, FRSE. Emeritus Professor of Chemistry, since 1973; b. 28.5.24, Aberdeen; m., Catherine Beaton; 1 s.; 2 d. Educ. Nicolson Institute, Stornoway; University of Aberdeen. DSIR Senior Research Fellow, University of Birmingham, 1948-50; University of Glasgow: ICI Research Fellow, 1950-55, Lecturer, 1955, Senior Lecturer, 1963, Reader, 1967, Titular Professor, 1971; Editor, Polymer Degradation and Stability: an international journal, 1977-95. Publications: numerous books and articles on topics related to polymer degradation and stability. Recreations: hill-walking; bridge; grandchildren; church activities. Address: (h.) The Stables, West Balgrochan Farm, West Balgrochan Road, Torrance, Glasgow G44 4DQ; T.-01360-620 433.

Gravestock, Martin John. Crown Estate Receiver for Scotland, since 1985; b. 31.8.52, Carshalton, Surrey; m., Olwyn Claire; 3 s. Educ. Sutton County Grammar School. Crown Estate Office, since 1969: Legal, Foreshore and Seabed, General, and London Branches; Head, Personnel Branch, 1984; Head, Foreshore and Seabed Branch, 1984-85. Recreations: cars; gardening. Address: (b.) 10 Charlotte Square, Edinburgh; T.-0131-226 7241.

Gray, Adam, OBE, NDA, NDD, FRAgS. Farmer; b. 6.8.29, Borgue, Kirkcudbright; m., Elaine West Russell; 3 s. Educ. George Watson's Boys College; West of Scotland Agricultural College. Nuffield Scholar, 1955; Past President, Stewartry NFU; Member, NFU Council; Director: Royal Highland & Agricultural Society (Honorary Vice-President, 1994-95), Scottish Milk Marketing Board, 1981-94; former Council Member, British Simmental Cattle Society; former Chairman: SW Scotland Grassland Society, Kirkcudbright District Council, UK Milk Publicity Council; Past President, Scottish Agricultural Arbiters Association; former Director, Scottish Pride Ltd.; Honorary President, Stewartry Agricultural Society; Secretary, Kirkcudbright Burns Club; Past President, Kirkcudbright Rotary Club. Awarded OBE, 1994, FRAgS, 1997. Publications: Borgue Academy; White Gold?; A Scots Agricultural Glossary. Recreations: rugby; local history. Address: (h.) Ingleneuk, Borgue, Kirkcudbright; T.-0155 870 208.

Gray, Alasdair. Artist and Writer; b. 28.12.34, Glasgow; m., Morag McAlpine; 1 s. Educ. Whitehill Senior Secondary School; Glasgow Art School. Part-time Art Teacher, 1958-62; Scene Painter, 1963-64; has since lived by drawing, painting, writing; Glasgow People's Palace has a collection of his portraits and cityscapes; extant murals: Palacerigg nature reserve, Cumbernauld; Abbots House local history museum, Dunfermline. Publications: novels: Lanark; 1982 Janine; The Fall of Kelvin Walker; Something Leather; McGrotty and Ludmilla; A History Maker; Poor

Things; Mavis Befrage; short story collections: Unlikely Stories, Mostly; Lean Tales (this last also containing work by Jim Kelman and Agnes Owens); Ten Tales Tall and True; Five Glasgow Artists (an exhibition catalogue); Saltire Self-Portrait No. 4; Why Scots Should Rule Scotland (1992 and 1997), Working Legs, a play for people without them. Scottish National Library has a collection of his unpublished plays and other material. Recreations: reading; talking to friends; drinking; walking.

Gray, Alexander, OBE, MA, LLB, DUniv, FSA Scot. Honorary Sheriff, Dumbarton; b. 6.5.12, Glasgow; m., Margaret; 2 s. Educ. Hillhead High School; Glasgow University; Edinburgh University. Town Clerk, Cove and Kilcreggan, 1948-67; Queen's Coronation Medal, 1953; Dean, Faculty of Procurators, Dumbarton, 1972; Clerk of Peace, Dunbartonshire, 1974. Fundraiser, Glasgow University Centre for Rheumatic Diseases. Recreations: archaeology; Gaelic; arthritis charity. Address: (h.) (h.) Borraichill, 116 Frederick Crescent, Port Ellen, Isle of Islay PA42 7BQ.

Gray, 22nd Lord (Angus Diarmid Ian Campbell-Gray); b. 3.7.31; m.; 1 s.; 3 d. by pr. m. Address: Airds Bay House, Taynuilt, Argyll, PA35 1JR.

Gray, Charles Ireland, CBE, FRSA, JP. Chair, Education, North Lanark Council; b. 25.1.29, Gartcosh; m., Catherine; 3 s.; 2 d. Educ. Coatbridge High School. Local government, since 1958; Leader, Strathclyde Regional Council, 1986-92 (Deputy Leader, 1978-86); former Director, Scottish Exhibition and Conference Centre; former Member: Scottish Enterprise Board, East Kilbride Development Corporation, Scottish Development Agency, Clyde Port Authority; former Vice-Chairman, Planning Exchange; UK Vice-President, European Committee of Regions. Recreations: music; reading; local government. Address: (b.) Civic Centre, Motherwell ML1 1TW.

Gray, David, DipArch (Aberdeen), RIBA, FRIAS, DipTP (Strath). Director of Architectural and Related Services, Strathclyde Regional Council, 1991-95; b. 2.10.37, Aberdeen; m., Margaret Ross Allen Gordon; 1 s.; 2 d. Educ. Robert Gordon's College; Scott Sutherland School of Architecture; Strathclyde University. Apprentice architect/archict, Aberdeen, 1956-62; architect, Lanark County Council, 1962-66; architect/planner, East Kilbride Development Corporation, 1966-67; Group Leader/ Assistant County Architect, then Depute County Architect, Renfrew County Council, 1967-75; Strathclyde Regional Council: Area Architect (Renfrew Division), 1975-76, Depute Director (Renfrew/Dumbarton/Argyll), 1976-78, Depute Director (Glasgow Division), 1978-87, Senior Depute Director, 1987-91. Past President, Association of Chief Architects of Scottish Local Authorities; Vice-Chair, Investigations Committee, Royal Incorporation of Architects in Scotland. Recreations: sport; theatre; gardening. Address: (h.) 73A Broomfield Avenue, Newton Mearns, Glasgow G77 5JR; T.-0141-639 4366.

Gray, Ethel Marian, CBE, JP, MA, LLD, DUniv, FEIS. Patron, LEAD (Scotland), since 1997 (Board Member, and Chairman, Advisory Committee, 1987-95); Patron and Board Member, LEAD Telematics, since 1995; b. 19.4.23, Glasgow; m., George Deans Gray (deceased). Educ. Hutchesons' Girls Grammar School; Paisley Grammar School; Glasgow University. Teacher of English, 1946-52; Lecturer in English and Drama, Jordanhill College, 1952-63; Founding Principal, Craigie College of Education, Ayr, 1963-75; Director, Scottish Adult Literacy Agency, 1976-79; Chairman, National Book League Scotland, 1977-81; Convener, Adult Access to Education, Scottish Institute of Adult and Continuing Education, 1988-89 (President of Institute, 1984-87); Vice-Chairman, Board of Governors, The Queen's College, Glasgow, 1980-88; Chairman, Education Project for Older People, Age Concern Scotland,

1982-85; Member of Court, Chairman of Staffing Committee and Joint Faculty Staff Review Board, Heriot-Watt University, 1979-84; Adviser in Adult Education, IBA, 1983-88; Member: Scottish Tertiary Education Advisory Council, 1984-87, Scottish Advisory Committee, British Council, 1968-89, STV Education Advisory Committee, 1981-92, Scottish Community Education Council, 1979-85 (Chairman, Communications and Technology Group and Chairman, Management Committee, Micro-Electronics Project), Crawford Commission on Radio and Television Coverage, 1973-75, Committee of Enquiry on the Police, 1977-79, Consultative Committee on the Curriculum, 1965-71. Recreations: reading; travelling; theatre. Address: (h.) 7 Greenbank Crescent, Edinburgh EH10 5TE; T.-0131-447 5403.

Gray, George Bovill Rennie, OBE, DL. Farmer; Chairman, G.B.R. Gray Ltd., since 1952; Trustee, Scottish Society for Crop Research, Invergowrie; a Director, Cruden Foundation, ; b. 5.3.20, Edinburgh; m., Anne Constance Dale; 4 s.; 2 d. Educ. Clayesmore, Dorset; Edinburgh and East of Scotland College of Agriculture. Past Chairman, East Lothian Area, National Farmers Union of Scotland; former Convenor, Cereals Committee, NFU of Scotland; Member, Seed Production Committee, National Institute of Agricultural Botany, Cambridge; a Director, West Cumberland Farmers Ltd., 1955-85; Director, Moredun Foundation, 1958-97; Member, Pig Industry Development Authority, 1958-68; Chairman, Oxford Farming Conference, 1972; Member: Agricultural and Veterinary Sub-Committee, UGC, 1972-82, Lothian Regional Council, 1974-82. Recreations: gardening; arboriculture. Address: Smeaton-Hepburn, East Linton, EH40 3DT; T.-01620 860275.

Gray of Contin, Lord (Hamish Gray), PC, DL. Business and Parliamentary Consultant, since 1986; b. 28.6.27, Inverness; m., Judith W. Brydon; 2 s.; 1 d. Educ. Inverness Royal Academy. Queen's Own Cameron Highlanders, 1945-48; Director, family and other private companies, 1949-70; MP, Ross and Cromarty, 1970-83; Government Whip, 1971-74; Opposition Spokesman on Energy, 1975-79; Minister of State for Energy, 1979-83; Minister of State for Scotland, 1983-86; Spokesman for Government in Lords for Scotland, Employment and Energy, 1983-86. Non-Executive Director, Dove Energy Ltd.; Non-Executive Chairman, Union Advertising Agency Ltd.; Vice President, Neighbourhood Energy Action (President, Energy Action Scotland), Scottish Association of Youth Clubs; Lord Lieutenant, Invernessshire, since 1996. Recreations: golf; cricket; hill-walking; rugby. Address: (h.) Achneim House, Flichity, Invernessshire IV1 2XE.

Gray, James Allan, MB, ChB, FRCPEdin. Principal Medical Officer, Scottish Widows' Fund, Edinburgh, 1990-97; President, British Society for the Study of Infection, 1989-91; b. 24.3.35, Bristol; m., Jennifer Margaret Newton Hunter; 1 s.; 2 d. Educ. St. Paul's School, London; Edinburgh University. House Surgeon and Physician posts, Edinburgh and Middlesbrough; Short Service Commission, RAF Medical Branch, 1960-63; Senior House Officer, Research Fellow and Registrar posts, Edinburgh, 1965 67; Registrar, Bristol Royal Infirmary, 1967-68; Senior Registrar, Royal Free Hospital (Department of Infectious Diseases), London, 1968-69; Consultant in Communicable Diseases, City Hospital, Edinburgh, 1969-95; Assistant Director of Studies (Medicine), Edinburgh Post-Graduate Board, 1976-84; Honorary Senior Lecturer, Department of Medicine, Edinburgh University, 1992-95; Fellow, Royal Medical Society (Senior President, 1958-59); Founder Editor, Res Medica, 1957-58; Assistant Editor, Journal of Infection, 1979-86. Publications: Antibacterial Drugs Today (Co-author), 1983; Infectious Diseases (Co-author), 1984, 1992. Recreations: hill-walking; pottery collecting; photography. Address: (h.) St. Andrews Cottage, 15 Lauder Road, Edinburgh EH9 2EN; T.-0131-667 4124.

Gray, Professor James Robertson, OBE, BSc, FRSGS, DipActMaths, FFA, FIMA, CMath, FSS. Professor and Head, Department of Actuarial Mathematics and Statistics, Heriot-Watt University, 1971-89 (now Emeritus); b. 21.2.26, Dundee; m., Catherine McAulay Towner. Educ. High School of Dundee; Edinburgh University. Actuarial Trainee, Scottish Life Assurance Company, 1947-49; St. Andrews University: Lecturer in Mathematics, 1949-50, Lecturer in Statistics, 1950-62, Senior Lecturer in Statistics (also Head of Department), 1962-71; Heriot-Watt University: established first Department of Actuarial Science in UK; Dean, Faculty of Science, 1978-81; Council Member, Faculty of Actuaries, 1969-87 (Vice President, 1983-87); Vice-Chairman, Scottish Examination Board, 1984-90 (Convener of Examinations Committee, 1982-90); former Member, Council, Royal Scottish Geographical Society and former Convener, Lecture Committee; former Vice-Chairman, Scottish Universities Council on Entrance; Past Chairman: Scottish Branch, Institute of Mathematics and Its Applications, Edinburgh Branch, Royal Statistical Society. Recreations: golf; hill-walking; bridge; music; Probus. Address: (h.) Green Gables, 9 Cammo Gardens, Edinburgh EH4 8EJ; T.-0131-339 3330.

Gray, John Bullard, CA. Finance Director, Scottish Hydro-Electric plc, since 1989; b. 4.7.41, Prestwick; m., Isobel Margaret Craig; 2 s. Educ. Strathallan School. Glenfield and Kennedy Ltd.; McLintock Moores and Murray Ltd.,; Marathon Shipbuilding (UK) Ltd.; David Brown-Vosper (Offshore) Ltd.; Cammell Laird Shipbuilders Ltd.; Vosper Thornycroft UK Ltd.; VSEL Consortium PLC; North of Scotland Hydro Electric Board. Recreations: golf; hill-walking; music. Address: (b.) 10 Dunkeld Road, Perth PH8 0BA.

Gray, John William Reid, MA, LLB, Advocate; b. 24.12.26, Aberdeen. Educ. Aberdeen Grammar School; Aberdeen University. Resident Magistrate, Uganda, 1954-62; Temporary Procurator-Fiscal Depute, Glasgow, 1962-63; Lecturer in Private Law, Queen's College, Dundee, then Dundee University, 1964-84; Warden, Airlie Hall, 1966-75; Member of Senate, 1971-75. Fellow, Saltzburg Seminar, 1964. Publications: articles in legal journals; The Administration of Justice Act, 1982. Address: (h.) Rhynuie, 41 Golf Road, Ballater, Aberdeenshire AB35 5RS. T.-013397 55656.

Gray, Michael Maxwell, OBE, DL. Chairman and Chief Executive, McQueen Ltd., since 1982; b. 5.5.47, Galashiels; m., Trish; 2 s. Educ. Galashiels Academy. Joined McQueen as management trainee, 1964; management buy-out, 1976. Board Member, Scottish Enterprise; Member, IR Committee, Scottish Print Employers Federation. Recreations: rugby; cricket; golf; reading. Address: (b.) McQueen Ltd., Nether Road, Galashiels TD1 3HE; T.-01896 754866.

Gray, Muriel, BA (Hons). Broadcaster; Joint Managing Director, Ideal World Productions; b. Glasgow. Educ. Glasgow School of Art. Worked as an illustrator; then as a designer with National Museum of Antiquities; was member of rock band, The Family Von Trapp; had own show with Radio Forth; was frequent presenter on Radio 1; co-presented The Tube, Channel 4; had own arts programme, The Works, Tyne Tees; own music programme, Studio 1, Border TV; presented Casebook Scotland, BBC Scotland; Frocks on the Box, Thames TV; Acropolis Now, ITV; presented The Media Show, Channel 4; Co-Producer and Presenter, Walkie Talkie, Channel 4; first woman Rector, Edinburgh University; Producer/Presenter/Director, The Munro Show, Scottish TV; Producer/Presenter, Art is Dead...Long Live TV!, Channel Four; The Golden Cagoule, BBC; Ride On. Publications: The First Fifty; The Trickster (novel); Furnace (novel). Recreation: being in the Scottish Highlands — gets grumpy and miserable if can't be up a mountain every few weeks.

Address: (b.) St. Georges Studios, 93-97 St. Georges Road, Glasgow G3 6JA.

Gray, Professor Peter Michael David, MA, DPhil, FBCS. Professor, Department of Computing Science, Aberdeen University, since 1989; b. 11.2.40, Abingdon; m., Doreen F. Ross; 1 s.; 1 d. Educ. Abingdon School; Queens' College, Cambridge; Jesus College, Oxford. Systems Analyst, Plessey Co., Poole, 1966-68; Research Fellow, Computer Research Group, Aberdeen University, 1968-72; Lecturer in Computing Science, Aberdeen University, 1972-84; Visiting Associate Professor, University of Western Ontario, 1985; Senior Lecturer, 1985-89. Reader, Church of Scotland. Publication: Logic, Algebra and Databases. Recreation: croquet. Address: (b.) Department of Computing Science, King's College, Aberdeen, AB24 3UE; T.-01224 272292.

Gray, Professor Robert Hugh, BSc (Econ), MA (Econ), FCA, FCCA, FRSA. Mathew Professor of Accounting and Information Systems, Dundee University, since 1990; b. 1.4.52, Manchester; 2 s. Educ. De La Salle College, Salford; Hull University; Manchester University. Qualified as accountant with KPMG Peat Marwick, 1976; Lecturer, Lancashire Polytechnic, UCNW Bangor, University of East Anglia; Editor, Social and Environmental Accounting; Director, Centre for Social and Environmental Accounting Research. Publications: over 100 articles; various books including Accounting for the Environment; The Greening of Accountancy; Accounting and Accountability. Recreations: golf; sailing; rock music. Address: (b.) Department of Accountancy and Business Finance, Dundee University, Dundee DD1 4HN; T.-01382 344789.

Gray, Sir William (Stevenson), Kt (1974), JP, BL, DL, HonLLD (Strathclyde), HonLLD (Glasgow), FRSA. Solicitor and Notary Public, since 1958; b. 3.5.28, Glasgow; m., Mary Rodger; 1 s.; 1 d. Educ. Hillhead High School, Glasgow; Glasgow University. Chairman: Scottish Special Housing Association, 1966-72, Clyde Tourist Association, 1972-75, Scotland West Industrial Promotion Group, 1972-75, WPHT Scotland Ltd. (formerly World of Property Housing Trust Scottish Housing Association Ltd.), since 1974, Irvine New Town Development Corporation, 1974-76, Scottish Development Agency, 1975-79, The Oil Club, since 1975, Research Trust for Institute of Neurological Sciences, 1978-94, Glasgow Independent Hospital Ltd., 1982-89, Webtec Industrial Technology Ltd., 1984-91, Barrell Selection Ltd., since 1987, Norcity Homes PLC, 1988-95, Gap Housing Association Ltd., since 1988, Gap Housing Association (Ownership) Ltd., since 1988, Clan Homes plc, since 1988, Manchester Village Homes plc, 1989-97, Norhomes plc, 1989-97, Norcity II Plc, 1989-96, Paragon Group, since 1990, Home Partners Plus Plc, 1991-95, Paragon Protected Growth, since 1993, Norcity III and IV plc, since 1993, Clan FM Ltd., since 1997. Member: Lower Clyde Water Board, 1971-72, National Trust for Scotland, 1971-72, Scottish Opera Board, 1971-72, Executive, Scottish Council (Development and Industry), 1971-75, Convention of Royal Burghs, 1971-75, Clyde Port Authority, 1972-75, Scottish National Orchestra Society, 1972-75, Advisory Council for Energy Conservation, 1974-84, Scottish Economic Council, 1975-83, Central Advisory Committee on JPs, since 1975, Glasgow Advisory Committee on JPs, since 1975, Third Eye Centre, 1984-91 (Chairman, 1975-84), Hodgson Martin Ltd. Advisory Board, 1988-94, Dermalase Ltd., 1989-91; Vice President: Charles Rennie Mackintosh Society, since 1974, Glasgow Citizens' Theatre, since 1975 (Member, Board of Directors, 1970-75), Strathclyde Theatre Group, 1975-86, Scottish Association for Care and Resettlement of Offenders, 1982-86 (Chairman, 1975-82); Governor, Glasgow School of Art, 1961-75; Patron: Scottish Youth Theatre, 1978-86, Scottish Pakistani Society, since 1984; Member: Court, Glasgow University, 1972-75, Council, Strathclyde University Business School, 1978-88, Glasgow Corporation, 1958-75

(Chairman, Property Management Committee, 1964-67); Treasurer, City of Glasgow, 1971-72; Lord Provost and Lord Lieutenant of the City of Glasgow, 1972-75. Recreations: sailing; theatre. Address: (b.) 13 Royal Terrace, Glasgow G3 7NY; T.-0141-332 8877.

Green, Geoffrey, MA, PhD. Proprietor and Managing Director, T. & T. Clark Ltd., Professional and Academic Publishers, since 1991; b. 22.8.47, Bradford; m., Ellen Hughes; 1 s.; 1 d. Educ. Bootham School, York; University of Edinburgh. Director, T. & T. Clark Ltd., 1975 (Managing Director, 1990). Address: (b.) 59 George Street, Edinburgh EH2 2LQ; T.-0131-225 4703.

Green, Malcolm. Chief Executive, Shetland Islands Council. Address: (b.) Town Hall, Lerwick, ZE1 0HB.

Green, Malcolm Robert, MA, DPhil. Member, City of Glasgow Council (Convener, Education Committee; Member: Arts and Culture Committee, Policy and Resources Committee, Roads and Transportation Committee); Lecturer in Roman History, Glasgow University, since 1967; b. 4.1.43, Leicester; m., Mary Margaret Pratley; 1 s.; 2 d. Educ. Wyggeston Grammar School, Leicester; Magdalen College, Oxford. Formerly Member, Strathclyde Regional Council: Chairman, Environment Committee; Chairman, Education Committee, 1982-90; Chairman, Education Committee, Convention of Scottish Local Authorities, 1978-90. Address: (b.) City Chambers, George Square, Glasgow G2 1DU.

Green, Professor Roger Philip Hywel, MA, BLitt. Professor of Humanity (Latin), since 1995, and Head, Department of Classics, since 1997, University of Glasgow; b. 14.6.43, High Wycombe; m., Anne Mary Perry; 1 s.; 1 d. Educ. Royal Grammar School, High Wycombe; Balliol College, University of Oxford. University of St. Andrews: Assistant Lecturer, 1967-70, Lecturer, 1970-92, Senior Lecturer, 1992-94, Reader, 1994-95. Former Secretary, International Association of Neo-Latin Studies. Publications include: The Works of Ausonius, 1991; Augustine on Christian Teaching, 1997. Recreations: walking; cycling; rail travel; birdwatching; gardening; music; architecture. Address: (b.) Department of Classics, University of Glasgow, Glasgow G12 8QQ; T.-0141-330 4276.

Greenberg, Rabbi Philip T., BA, MPhil. Rabbi, Giffnock and Newlands Hebrew Congregation, Glasgow, since 1981; b. 28.6.37, Liverpool; m., Hannah Barber-Kestenberg; 1 s.; 1 d. Educ. Quarry Bank Grammar, Liverpool; Jews College, London University. Minister, Chingford Hebrew Congregation, 1959-68; Rabbi, Nottingham Hebrew Congregation, 1968-72; Head, Mishna Stream, Hasmonean Boys Grammar School, London, 1972-81. Member, Executive, Glasgow Council of Christians and Jews; Rabbi, Glasgow Shechita Board and Glasgow Kashrut Authority; Chairman, Glasgow Rabbinical Committee (Va'ad Harabbonim). Recreations: music; reading; photography. Address: (h.) 20 Ayr Road, Giffnock, Glasgow G46 6RY; T.-0141-638 0309.

Greene, John Gerald, MA, PhD, FBPsS. Registrar, Board of Examiners in Clinical Psychology, British Psychological Society; Clinical Lecturer, Glasgow University; b. 10.3.38, Glasgow; m., Dr. Elisabeth Rose Hamil; 2 s.; 2 d. Educ. St. Aloysius College, Glasgow; Glasgow University. Clinical Tutor, Glasgow University Master of Applied Science degree in Clinical Psychology, 1976-95; Chairman, National (Scotland) Scientific Consultative Committee on Clinical Psychological Services, 1985-87; Secretary and Treasurer, Scottish Branch Committee, Division of Clinical Psychology, 1977-81. Publications: The Social and Psychological Origins of the Climacteric Syndrome, 1984; Clinical Psychology in the Scottish Health Service (Co-author), 1984. Recreations: music; tennis; skiing. Address: (b.) Psychology Department, Gartnavel Royal Hospital, Glasgow G12 0XH.

Greene, John Henderson, MA, LLB. Former Partner, MacRoberts, Solicitors, Glasgow, Edinburgh and London; b. 2.6.32, Kilmarnock; m., Catriona McGillivray Scott; 1 s. Educ. Merchiston Castle School, Edinburgh; Edinburgh University. Assistant: Joseph Kirkland & Son, Solicitors, Saltcoats, 1958-60, MacRoberts, Solicitors, 1960 (appointed Partner, 1961); Law Society of Scotland: former Vice-Convener, Company Law Committee, former Member, Bankruptcy and Liquidation Committee; former Council Member, Royal Faculty of Procurators, Glasgow; founder Chairman, Troon Round Table, 1964; Captain, Royal Troon Golf Club, 1989-90; Elder, Portland Church, Troon; President, Glasgow Ayrshire Society, 1985-86 and 1993-94; Vice-Chairman, Ayrshire and Arran Health Board. Publication: Law and Practice of Receivership in Scotland (Co-Author). Recreations: golf; gardening. Address: (h.) Silvertrees, 7 Lady Margaret Drive, Troon KA10 7AL; T.-Troon 312482.

Greenhill, Patricia Anne, OBE, JP. Board Member, Scottish Homes, since 1996; J.P. Advisory Committee for Stirling, since 1992; Trustee, Dunblane Fund; Chairman of Trustees, Dunblane Help Fund, since 1996; b. 20.12.46, Aberdeen; m., Donald; 2 s. Educ. Perth Academy. Clydesdale Bank Ltd., 1963-72; Councillor, Dunblane, Doune and Deanston, 1984-96; Provost, Stirling District, 1992-96; Member of Court, University of Stirling, 1991-96. Trustee, Friends of Logie Kirk; Hon. MA (Stirling). Address: (b.) Scottish Homes, Thistle House, 91 Haymarket Terrace, Haymarket, Edinburgh; T.-0131-479 5220.

Greenman, Professor Jonathan Vaughan, BA, MA, PhD. Professor of Mathematics and Its Applications, Stirling University, since 1990; b. 3.3.39, Cardiff; m., Barbara Phyllis; 2 s. Educ. Kingston Grammar School; Cambridge University. Harkness Scholar, University of California, Berkeley; Department of Physics, MIT; Stanford Research Institute, California; Department of Mathematics, Essex University; Tutor, Open University; Senior Analyst, Corporate Planning, British Petroleum plc; Industry Analyst, Centre for Global Energy Studies. Recreations: cinema; walking; travel. Address: (b.) Department of Mathematics, Stirling University, Stirling, FK9 4LA; T.-01786 467460.

Greenock, William, MA. Principal, Clydebank College, since 1984; b. 3.2.37, Glasgow; 2 d. Educ. Allan Glen's School; Glasgow University. Teacher, secondary schools, 1959-65; David Dale College, 1965-68; Langside College, 1968-70; Reid Kerr College, 1970-75; Anniesland College, 1975-82; Ayr College, 1982-84. Session Clerk, Langside Parish Church, Glasgow. Recreation: golf. Address: (b.) Clydebank College, Kilbowie Road, Clydebank, G81 2AA; T.-0141-952 7771.

Greenshields, David, MA, DipEd. Headteacher, Uddingston Grammar School, since 1997; b. 24.7.49, Bellshill; 2 d. Educ. Biggar High School; University of Edinburgh; Moray House College. History Teacher, Lanark Grammar, 1971; Assistant Principal Teacher, Social Subjects, Auchmuty High, Fife, 1973; Assistant Principal Teacher, Guidance, Lanark Grammar, 1974; various posts, Uddingston Grammar School, since 1978. Recreation: supporter of Heart of Midlothian F.C. Address: (b.) Uddingston Grammar School, Station Road, Uddingston G71 7BS; T.-01698 327400.

Greensted, Professor Christopher Stanford, BSc, MSc. Director, Strathclyde Graduate Business School, since 1986; b. 10.9.41, Leeds; m., Candace Helen; 1 s.; 1 d.; 1 s. by pr. m. Educ. Cranbrook School, Kent; Sir John Cass College, London; Strathclyde University. Chemist in

pharmaceuticals, 1960-65; operational research/consultancy in food industry, 1966-68; appointed Lecturer in OR, Strathclyde, 1969, then in Accounting and Finance, 1974; was part-time Director of yacht chandlery company, eight years. RNR officer, eight years. Publications: three books; several articles on business statistics and management development. Recreations: sailing; golf; theatre and concerts. Address: (h.) 18 Carrick Drive, Glasgow, G32 0RW; T.-0141-778 9120.

Greer, Professor Ian Andrew, MB, ChB, MD (Glas), MRCP(UK), FRCP(Glas), MFFP, MRCOG, MAE. Muirhead Professor and Head, Department of Obstetrics and Gynaecology, Glasgow University, since 1991; Honorary Consultant Obstetrician and Gynaecologist, Glasgow Royal Infirmary and Glasgow Royal Maternity Hospital, since 1991; b. 16.4.58, Glasgow. Educ. Allan Glen's School, Glasgow; Glasgow University. Registrar in General Medicine, Glasgow Royal Infirmary; Registrar in Obstetrics and Gynaecology, Glasgow Royal Maternity Hospital and Glasgow Royal Infirmary; Lecturer in Obstetrics and Gynaecology, Edinburgh University; Clinical Research Scientist/Consultant Obstetrician and Gynaecologist, MRC Reproductive Biology Unit, Edinburgh. MRCOG Gold Medal; Blair-Bell Lectureship, Royal College of Obstetricians and Gynaecologists 1989; Travelling Fellowship, RCOG, 1989; Watson Prize Lecture, Royal College of Physicians and Surgeons of Glasgow, 1990. Address: (b.) Department of Obstetrics and Gynaecology, Glasgow University, Glasgow Royal Infirmary, Glasgow G31 2ER; T.-0141-552 8316.

Gregson, William Derek Hadfield, CBE, DL, DFH, CEng, FIEE, CBIM, FRSA. Former Commissioner of Northern Lighthouses; former Director: Anderson Strathclyde, Brammer plc, East of Scotland Industrial Investments PLC; former Consultant, ICI; b. 27.1.20; m., Rosalind Helen Reeves; 3 s.; 1 d. Educ. UK and Switzerland. Director, Ferranti Holdings, 1983-85; Deputy Chairman, British Airports Authority, 1975-85; Director, British Telecom (Scotland), 1977-85; Past President: EEA, BEAMA. Recreations: woodwork; books; automation in the home. Address: (h.) Murrayfield House, 66 Murrayfield Avenue, Edinburgh EH12 6AY. T.-0131-337 3858.

Greig, Rev. Alan, BSc, BD. Minister, Kintore Parish Church, since 1992; b. 19.11.51, Helensburgh; m., Ruth D. Evans; 2 s. Educ. Coatbridge High School; University of Strathclyde; University of Edinburgh. Probationer Minister, Northfield Parish, Aberdeen, 1976-77; Minister, Hurlford Reid Memorial Church, Ayrshire, 1977-83; Church of Scotland Missionary working with United Church of Zambia, 1983-92. Recreations: swimming; cycling; walking. Address: 6 Forest Road, Kintore, Inverurie AB51 0XG; T.-01467 632219.

Greig, Christopher George, BSc, PhD. Non-Executive Chairman: William Grant & Sons Ltd., PPL Therapeutics plc; Non-Executive Director, Robert Wiseman Dairies plc; m., Anne; 1 s.; 2 d. Educ. Harris Academy; St. Andrews University; London University. Invergordon Distillers Group PLC, 1966-94 (Managing Director, 1983-94); Director (Non-Executive): Simpsons Malt Ltd., Belhaven Brewery Group plc, Edinburgh Green Belt Trust, Scottish Quality Cereals, Heriot Watt Trading, Canongate Technology Ltd., The Airborne Initiative (Scotland) Ltd.; Director: Scotch Whisky Association, C.G. (Farms) Ltd., Mosszone Ltd; Trustee, Scottish Civic Trust. Address: (h.) North Mains, Ormiston, East Lothian EH35 5NG; T.-01875 613721.

Greig, G. Andrew, MA. Author; b. 23.9.51, Bannockburn. Educ. Waid Academy, Anstruther; Edinburgh University. Full-time writer, since 1979; Writer-in-Residence, Glasgow University, 1979-81; Scottish-Canadian Exchange Fellow, 1981-82; Writer-in-Residence, Edinburgh University, 1993-

94; climbed on Himalayan expeditions. Publications: six volumes of poetry including Men on Ice, Surviving Passages, The Order of the Day, Western Swing; two mountaineering books; novels: Electric Brae, Return of John Macnab. Recreations: climbing; fishing; music. Address: Stirling's Dairy, 2 Brewery Close, South Queensferry; T.-0131-331 2535.

Grier, Arnold Macfarlane, MB, ChB, FRCSEdin. Consultant Ear, Nose and Throat Surgeon, Highland Health Board, since 1962; National Vice-President, Scottish Association for the Deaf; b. 5.9.21, Musselburgh; m., Elisabeth J. Kluten; 2 s.; 1 d. Educ. Musselburgh Grammar School, Edinburgh University. Recreations: gardening; aviculture; painting. Address: (h.) Elmbank, 68 Culduthel Road, Inverness; T.-Inverness 234682.

Grier, Scott, OBE, MA, CA, MCIT. Chairman: Loganair Limited, Scottish Tanning Industries Limited; b. 7.3.41, Kilmacolm; m., Frieda Gardiner; 2 s. Educ. Greenock High School; Glasgow University. Apprenticed, Grahams Rintoul & Co., 1962-66; Accountant, Ardrossan Harbour Company Ltd./Clydeport, from 1967; various posts, Loganair, since 1976; Director: Glasgow Chamber of Commerce, since 1990, Caledonian MacBrayne Limited, since 1996; Chairman: Bridge of Weir Leather Co. Ltd., Andrew Muirhead & Son Ltd., W. J. & W. Lang Ltd., NCT Leather Ltd., since 1997; Governor, Scottish Sports Aid Foundation, since 1993. Recreations: golf; philately. Address: (h.) Lagavulin, 15 Corsehill Drive, West Kilbride, KA23 9HU; T.-01294 823138.

Grieve, Professor Andrew Robert, DDS, BDS, FDS RCSEd. Professor of Conservative Dentistry, since 1980, Dean of Dentistry, 1993-97, Dundee University; Consultant in Restorative Dentistry, since 1980; b. 23.5.39, Stirling; m., Frances M. Ritchie; 2 d. Educ. Perth Academy; St. Andrews University. Junior hospital appointments and general dental practice, 1961-63; Lecturer in Operative Dental Surgery and Dental Therapeutics, St. Andrews University, 1963-65; Lecturer in Conservative Dentistry, Birmingham University, 1965; appointed Senior Lecturer and Consultant in Restorative Dentistry, Birmingham Area Health Authority (Teaching), 1975. Member, Dental Council, Royal College of Surgeons of Edinburgh, 1983-88; President: British Society for Restorative Dentistry, 1986-87, Royal Odonto-Chirurgical Society of Scotland, 1994-95 (Council Member, 1985-88); Chairman: Tayside Area Dental Advisory Committee, 1987-90, Legislation Committee, General Dental Council, since 1994 (Member, since 1989). Recreations: hill-walking; travel in France and study of French language and culture. Address: (b.) The Dental School, The University, Dundee DD1 4HN; T.-01382 26041.

Grieve, John. Actor; b. 14.6.24, Glasgow. Trained, Royal Scottish Academy of Music and Drama (James Bridie Gold Medallist), followed by five full seasons, Citizens' Theatre, Glasgow; also appeared in Guthrie's production of The Anatomist, Citizens', 1968; numerous other performances on the Scottish stage, including leading roles in The Bevellers, The Flouers o' Edinburgh, The Good Soldier Schweik, Twelfth Night; television work includes The Vital Spark, Oh Brother, Doctor at Sea, New Year shows; numerous appearances in pantomime; appeared with Scottish Theatre Company in Waiting for Godot and The Thrie Estaites.

Grieve, Professor Robert, MA, PhD, CPsych, FBPsS. Professor of Psychology, Edinburgh University, since 1987; b. 2.8.44, Bathgate; m., Anne; 1 s.; 2 d. Educ. Edinburgh University. Lecturer in Psychology, St. Andrews University; Senior Lecturer in Psychology, then Associate Professor of Psychology, University of Western Australia. Address: (b.) Department of Psychology, Edinburgh

University, 7 George Square, Edinburgh EH8 9JZ; T.-0131-650 3441.

Grieve, Hon. Lord (William Robertson Grieve), VRD (1958), QC (Scot), MA, LLB. Senator of the College of Justice in Scotland, 1972-88; Chairman, Board of Governors, St. Columba's Hospice, since 1983; b. 21.10.17, Glasgow; m., Lorna St. John Benn (deceased); 1 s.; 1 d. Educ. Glasgow Academy; Sedbergh School; Glasgow University. Served with Royal Navy as an RNVR officer, 1939-45; Advocate, Scots Bar, 1947; QC, 1957; Sheriff Principal, Renfrew and Argyll, 1964-72; Judge of Appeal, Jersey and Guernsey, 1971-72; Procurator, Church of Scotland, 1968-72; Chairman, Governors, Fettes Trust, 1978-86. President, Glasgow University Union, 1938. Recreations: golf; painting. Address: (h.) 20 Belgrave Crescent, Edinburgh EH4 3AJ; T.-0131-332 7500.

Griffith, Richard Jeremy, MA (Cantab), DipArch (Cantab), RIAS. Director, Edinburgh New Town Conservation Committee, since 1994; b. 18.3.47, London. Educ. Malvern Boys College; St. John's College, Cambridge. Choral Scholar, 1966-69; RIBA, 1974; International Centre for Conservation and Restoration of Monuments, 1977; Listed Buildings Case Officer, Greater London Council's Historic Buildings Division, 1979-86; Senior Statutory Officer, English Heritage, London Region, 1986-94. Member, Council, Cockburn Association. Recreations: travel; music; skiing. Address: (b.) 13a Dundas Street, Edinburgh EH3 6QG; T.-0131-557 5222.

Griffiths, Nigel. Minister for Competition and Consumer Affairs, since 1997; MP (Labour), Edinburgh South, since 1987; Opposition Spokesman on Consumer Affairs, 1989-97; Vice President, Institute of Trading Standards Administration, since 1994; b. 20.5.55; m., Sally McLaughlin. Educ. Hawick High School; Edinburgh University; Moray House College of Education. Secretary, Lothian Devolution Campaign, 1978; Rights Adviser, Mental Handicap Pressure Group, 1979-87; City of Edinburgh District Councillor, 1980-87 (Chairperson, Housing Committee); Member: Edinburgh Festival Council, 1984-87, Edinburgh Health Council, 1982-87; Executive Member, Edinburgh Council of Social Service, 1984-87; Member, Wester Hailes School Council, 1981; Executive Member, Scottish Constitutional Convention (Chair, Finance Committee). Recreations: travel; live entertainment; badminton; hill-walking; rock-climbing; architecture; reading; politics. Address: (h.) 30 McLaren Road, Edinburgh EH9 2BN; T.-0131-667 1947.

Griffiths, Professor Peter Denham, CBE, BSc, MD, LRCP, MRCS, FRCPath, FIMgt, FRSA. Emeritus Professor of Biochemical Medicine, Dundee University (Vice-Principal, 1979-85, Dean of Medicine and Dentistry, 1985-89); Director and Trustee, Scottish Hospitals Endowment Research Trust, since 1994; b. 16.6.27, Southampton; m., Joy Burgess; 3 s.; 1 d. Educ. King Edward VI School, Southampton; Guy's Hospital, London University. House appointments, Guy's Hospital, 1956-57; Junior Lecturer in Physiology, Guy's Hospital, 1957-58; Registrar and Senior Registrar, Guy's and Lewisham Hospitals, 1958-64; Consultant Pathologist, Harlow Hospitals Group, 1964-66; Senior Lecturer in Clinical Chemistry/Honorary Consultant, St. Andrews University, then Dundee University, 1966-68. Member, General Medical Council, 1986-93; President, 1987-89, and sometime Chairman of Council, Association of Clinical Biochemists; Consultant, Tayside Health Board, 1986-89; former Director, Dundee Repertory Theatre. Recreations: music; domestic activities. Address: (h.) 52 Albany Road, West Ferry, Dundee DD5 1NW; T.-01382 776772.

Grimble, Professor Michael John, BSc, MSc, PhD, DSc, BA, CEng, FIEE, FInstMC, FIMA, FIEEE. Professor of Industrial Control, University of Strathclyde, since 1981;

Technical Director, ISC, since 1988; b. 30.10.43, Grimsby; m., Wendy; 1 s.; 1 d. Educ. Armstrong Street School, Grimsby; University of Birmingham. Design Engineer, GEC Electrical Projects, and seconded, Imperial College of Science and Technology, 1971-74; Senior Design Engineer, GEC Electrical Projects Limited, 1974-75; Senior Lecturer then Reader in Control Systems, Sheffield City Polytechnic, 1975-81. Awarded IEE Heaviside Premium, 1978, Coopers Hill War Memorial Prize Medal, 1979, Honeywell International Medal, 1991. Recreations: theatre; reading; family; travel and sightseeing; eating out. Address: (b.) University of Strathclyde, ICC, Graham Hills Building, 50 George Street, Glasgow G1 1QE; T.-0141-548 2378.

Grimmond, Iain William, BAcc (Hons), CA. Director of Finance, Erskine Hospital for Disabled Ex-Servicemen, since 1981; b. 8.8.55, Girvan; m., Marjory Anne Gordon Chisholm; 1 s.; 2 d. Educ. Hutchesons' Boys Grammar School; Glasgow University. Trainee CA, Ernst & Whinney, Glasgow, 1976-79; Assistant Treasurer, Erskine Hospital, 1979-81. Elder, Giffnock South Parish Church. Recreations: golf; football; reading. Address: (h.) 9 Wemyss Avenue, Crookfur, Newton Mearns, Glasgow G77 6AR; T.-0141-639 4894.

Grimson, Dermot, FRSA. Director, Rural Forum, since 1987; Secretary, Trans European Rural Network; Chairman, UK Rural Development Network; Member: National Rural Partnership, BBC Rural Advisory Committee, SCVO Policy Committee, Equal Opportunities Commission for Scotland Advisory Committee, Scottish Episcopal Church Rural Commission, Board of Enterprise Music Scotland; b. 22.5.52, Glasgow. Educ. Kelvinside Academy; Glasgow School of Art. Planner, Renfrew District Council; Planner, Banff and Buchan District Council. Former Member of Banff and Buchan Health Council; Past Chairman, Buchan Countryside Group; former Secretary, Banff and Buchan Constituency Labour Party; Past Chairman, Perth Civic Trust. Address: (h.) 10 St. John's Place, Perth; T.-01738 630014.

Grinyer, Professor John Raymond, MSc, FCA. Professor of Accountancy and Business Finance, Dundee University, since 1976 and Deputy Principal, since 1997 (Head, Department of Accountancy and Business Finance, 1976-90, Dean, Faculty of Law, 1984-85 1991-1993); b. 3.3.35, London; m., Shirley Florence Marshall; 1 s.; 2 d. Educ. Central Park Secondary Modern School, London; London School of Economics. London Electricity Board, 1950-53; National Service, RAMC, 1953-55; Halifax Building Society, 1955-56; Martin Redhead & Co., Accountants, 1956-60; Hope Agar & Co., Chartered Accountants, 1960-62; Kemp Chatteris & Co., Chartered Accountants, 1962-63; Lecturer, Harlow Technical College, 1963-66; City of London Polytechnic, 1966-71; Cranfield School of Management, 1971-76; Chairman, British Accounting Association, 1980-81 and 1990, and Scottish Representative, 1984-93. Recreations: golf; dinghy sailing; Member, Royal Tay Yacht Club. Address: (b.) The University, Dundee DD1 4HN; T.-Dundee 344192.

Grinyer, Professor Peter Hugh, MA (Oxon), PhD. Emeritus Professor, since 1997, and Professorial Fellow, St. Andrews University; b. 3.3.35, London; m., Sylvia Joyce Boraston; 2 s. Educ. Balliol College, Oxford; London School of Economics. Senior Managerial Trainee, Unilever Ltd., 1957-59; Personal Assistant to Managing Director, E.R. Holloway Ltd., 1959-61; Lecturer and Senior Lecturer, Hendon College of Technology, 1961-64; Lecturer, The City University, London, 1965-69; The City University Business School: Senior Lecturer and Co-ordinator of Research, 1969-72, Reader, 1972-74, Professor of Business Strategy, 1974-79; Esmee Fairbairn Professor of Economics (Finance and Investment), St. Andrews University, 1979-93; Chairman, Department of Economics, 1979-85; Vice-Principal, 1985-87 (Acting Principal, 1986); Chairman,

Department of Management, 1987-89; Chairman: St. Andrews Management Institute, 1989-96, St. Andrews Strategic Management Ltd.; Member, Sub-Committee on Management and Business Studies, University Grants Committee, 1979-85; Consultant to NEDO on Sharpbenders Project, 1984-86; Visiting Professor, New York University; Non-Executive Director: Glenrothes Enterprise Trust, 1983-86, John Brown plc, 1984-86, Don Bros. Buist plc (now Don and Low (Holdings) Ltd.) 1985-91, Ellis and Goldstein plc, 1987-88; Chairman (non-executive), McIlroy Coates, 1991-95; Member, Scottish Legal Aid Board, since 1992 (Convener, Business Committee, since 1995); Erskine Fellow, University of Canterbury, New Zealand, 1994. Recreations: mountain walking; golf; listening to music. Address: (b.) University of St. Andrews, Department of Management, Kinnessburn, Kennedy Gardens, St. Andrews KY16 9UL; T.-01334 462871.

Groat, John Malcolm Freswick, MBE, JP, DL. Company Director: J.M.F. Groat & Sons Ltd., Orkney Seaport Supplies Ltd.; Postmaster, Longhope, Orkney, since 1964; b. 9.9.23, Longhope, Orkney; m., Edna Mary Yule. War service: joined RAFVR as Air Crew Cadet, 1943; operational service with No. 576 and No. 150 Lancaster Squadrons No. 1 Group, Bomber Command, RAF, until 1945, then in India and as Officer i/c transport, Air Command South East Asia, Changi, Singapore, until 1947; Clerk, Hoy and Walls District Council, 1953-74; Clerk, School Management Committee, Walls and Flotta, 1953-74; Registrar of Births etc., Hoy and Walls, 1953-74; Secretary, Longhope Lifeboat, 1962-95; Provincial Grand Master, Orkney and Zetland, 1979-84; Member, Orkney Health Board, 1979-91; Agent, Shipwrecked Mariners Society; Secretary, Longhope British Legion, 1948-53; Secretary, Longhope Sailing Club, 1950-60; former Member, Orkney Pilotage Committee; Director, Orkney Islands Shipping Co., 1974-87; Member, Coastguard Lifesaving Company, Longhope, 1947-61; Founder Member, Orkney Flying Club, 1949; Secretary/Treasurer, Walls and Hoy Agricultural Society, 1950-60; R.W. Master, Lodge St. Colm No. 1022, 1964-69. Address: (h.) Moasound, Longhope, Orkney.

Grossart, Sir Angus McFarlane McLeod, CBE, LLD, DL, MA, CA. Advocate; Merchant Banker; Vice Chairman, Royal Bank of Scotland, since 1996; Chairman, Scottish Daily Record and Sunday Mail, since 1998; Chairman of the Trustees, National Galleries of Scotland, 1988-97; Director: Hewden Stuart plc, since 1988, American Trust PLC, since 1973, Edinburgh Fund Managers PLC, since 1983 (Deputy Chairman), Noble Grossart Limited, since 1969, The Scottish Investment Trust PLC, since 1973 (Chairman); b. 6.4.37, Glasgow; m., Gay Kerr Dodd; 1 d. Educ. Glasgow Academy; Glasgow University. CA, 1962; Advocate, Scottish Bar, 1963-69; Managing Director, Noble Grossart Ltd., since 1969. Former Scottish Editor, British Tax Encyclopaedia and British Tax Review. Recreations: golf; decorative arts. Address: (b.) 48 Queen Street, Edinburgh EH2 3NR; T.-0131-226 7011.

Grosset, Alan George, MA, LLB, WS, NP. Partner, Alex. Morison & Co., WS; b. 18.1.42, Edinburgh; 1 s.; 1 d. Educ. Royal High School, Edinburgh; Edinburgh University. Law Society of Scotland "Troubleshooter" from inception of scheme, until 1987; President, Scottish Lawn Tennis Association, 1983-84; Council Member, Lawn Tennis Association, 1980-89; first Chairman, Scottish Sports Association, 1984-90; Vice-Chairman, Scottish Sports Council, since 1994 (Member since 1984); Captain, Duddingston Golf Club, 1992-94; Founder Member, Scottish Branch, Society for Computers and Law; first Secretary, British Sports Forum, 1991-95 (Member, since 1991). Recreations: golf; tennis; squash. Address: (b.) 68 Queen Street, Edinburgh; T.-0131-226 6541.

Grosz, David Peter, BA (Hons). Vice-Chairman, Ramblers' Association, since 1995; b. 2.4.39, London. Educ. Wyggeston Boys' Grammar School, Leicester; Nottingham University; School of Education, Leicester University. School Teacher, Leicester, 1962-78, West Lothian, 1978-84. Member: RA National Executive Committee, since 1983, Board of Directors, Scottish Rights of Way Society, 1984-92, Council, National Trust for Scotland, 1989-94; Chairman: Friends of New Lanark, 1985-89, Ramblers' Association Scottish Council, 1985-96; Founding Member and Committee Member, Scottish Council for National Parks, 1991-95. Recreations: walking; reading; campaigning with passion for public access and countryside conservation. Address: (h.) 57 Harburn Avenue, Deans, Livingston EH54 8NH; T.-01506 410493.

Groves, C. Arthur, JP. Chairman: Borders Region Valuation Panel, 1991-94, Justices Committee, Ettrick and Lauderdale, 1984-94, General Inland Revenue Commissioners, since 1983; b. 28.11.24, London. Educ. Raine's Foundation, London. Selkirk Town Council, 1961-75 (Hon. Treasurer); former Selkirk County Councillor (Chairman, Finance Committee). Recreation: equestrian activities. Address: (h.) 24 Hillview Crescent, Selkirk TD7 4AZ; T.-01750 21126.

Guest, Andrew, MA, Director, Scottish Sculpture Trust, since 1990; b. 8.11.51, Edinburgh; m., Elizabeth Cuthbert; 1 s.; 1 d. Educ. Charterhouse School; University of St. Andrews; University of Edinburgh. Museum Assistant, Geffrye Museum, 1975-77; Interpretive Projects Officer, Montgomery Canal, 1980-83; Exhibitions Officer, Smith Art Gallery and Museum, Stirling, 1983-90. Publications: Platform for Partnership (Editor), 1990; The City is a Work of Art - Glasgow, 1994; The City is a Work of Art - Edinburgh, 1996. Address: (h.) Shirgarton House, Kippen, Stirling FK8 3EA; T.-01786 870604.

Guest, Peter David. Chairman: Lineplan Ltd., Perth, since 1992, Powerplan (Scotland), Ltd., since 1994, Epilepsy Association of Scotland, since 1996; b. 25.10.39, Solihull; m., Kathleen Althea Ward; 1 s.; 3 d. Educ. King Edward's School, Birmingham; College of Advanced Technology, Birmingham. Sales Director, Bonar Long Ltd., Dundee, 1982; Vice-President, National Industri, Norway, 1985; Managing Director, E.B. Power Projects Ltd., 1985; Deputy Managing Director, Nitran, Dundee, 1989. Member, Court of Governors, Abertay University Dundee. Recreations: fishing; shooting. Address: (h.) The Well, Kirkinch, by Meigle, Blairgowrie, Perthshire PH12 8SL; T.-01828 640790.

Guild, Ivor Reginald, CBE, FRSE, MA, LLB, WS; b. 2.4.24, Dundee. Educ. Cargilfield; Rugby; New College, Oxford; Edinburgh University. Director: Fulcrum Investment Trust, Scottish Oriental Smaller Companies Trust PLC; former Partner, Shepherd & Wedderburn, WS; former Procurator Fiscal to the Lyon Court. Recreations: golf; genealogy. Address: (b.) Saltire Court, 20 Castle Terrace, Edinburgh, EH1 2ET; T.-0131-225 8585.

Guild, Stuart Alexander, TD, BL, WS, NP. Writer to the Signet, since 1950; Senior Partner, Guild and Guild WS, 1958-89; b. 25.1.24, Edinburgh; m., Fiona Catherine MacCulloch; 1 s.; 2 d. Educ. Edinburgh Academy; George Watson's College, Edinburgh; Queen's University, Belfast; Edinburgh University. Royal Artillery, 1942-47; Territorial Army (RA), 1947-65; County Cadet Commandant, Lothian Bn., ACF, 1967-69 (Hon. Lt-Col.); Honorary Treasurer, 1976-91, Shooting Convener, 1969-94, and Vice Chairman, since 1995, Army Cadet Force Association (Scotland); 1969-94; Member: Council, Army Cadet Force Association, 1976-91, Royal Artillery Council of Scotland, 1982-84 and

1985-93; President, Lothian & Peebles Home Guard Rifle Association, 1980-91; Vice-President, Lothian Smallbore Shooting Association, 1985-92; Governor, Melville College Trust, 1976-91 (now Hon. Governor); Chairman, Sandilands Memorial Trust, 1980-94; Assistant, The Company of Merchants of the City of Edinburgh, 1972-75; Vice-Convener, Mary Erskine School for Girls, 1973-75. Recreations: golf; target shooting; photography. Address: (h.) 7 Lockharton Gardens, Edinburgh EH14 1AU.

Gulliver, Stuart, BSc (Econ). Chief Executive, Glasgow Development Agency, since 1991; b. 10.1.42, Sheffield; m., Barbara McKewan; 3 s.; 1 d. Educ. Firth Park Grammar School; London School of Economics. Research Fellow in Economics, Leeds University; Senior Lecturer, Leeds Polytechnic; commercial development, Warrington New Town Development Corporation; Regional Director, Scottish Development Agency. Visiting Professor in Economic and Social Research, Glasgow University. Recreations: cricket; tennis; watching football; music, especially modern jazz; theatre. Address: (b.) Atrium Court, 50 Waterloo Street, Glasgow G2 6HQ; T.-0141-204 1111.

Gunn, Alexander MacLean, MA, BD. Minister, Aberfeldy with Amulree and Strathbraan with Dull and Weem, since 1986; b. 26.2.43, Inverness; m., Ruth T.S.; 1 s.; 1 d. Educ. Edinburgh Academy; Beauly; Dingwall Academy; Edinburgh University and New College. Parish Minister: Wick St. Andrews and Thrumster, 1967-73; Member, Caithness Education Committee, 1968-73; Parish Minister, Glasgow St. David's Knightswood, 1973-86; Convener: Church of Scotland Rural Working Group, 1988-90, General Assembly's Presbytery Development Committee, 1990-92, General Assembly's Mission and Evangelism Resource Committee, 1992-95; Interim Convener, Board of National Mission, 1996. Chairman, Breadalbane Academy School Board, 1989-92. Address: The Manse, Taybridge Terrace, Aberfeldy PH15 2BS; T.-01887 820656.

Guy, Professor John Alexander, MA, PhD, FRHistS. Professor of Modern History, since 1991, and Head, School of History and International Relations, 1992-94, St. Andrews University; Provost, 1994-97, and Vice-Principal, 1996-97, St. Leonard's College; b. 16.1.49, Australia; m., Rachel Hooper; 1 s.; 1 d. Educ. King Edward VII School, Lytham; Clare College, Cambridge. Research Fellow, Selwyn College, Cambridge, 1970-73; Assistant Keeper of Public Records, Public Record Office, London, 1973-78; Visiting Lecturer in British History, University of California, Berkeley, 1977; History Department, Bristol University, 1978-90; British Academy Marc Fitch Research Reader, 1987-89; John Hinkley (Visiting) Professor, Johns Hopkins University, Baltimore, 1990; Richard L. Turner Professor of Humanities, and Professor of History, University of Rochester, 1990-91. Publications: The Cardinal's Court; The Public Career of Sir Thomas More; Law and Social Change in British History (Co-Editor); The Court of Star Chamber and its Records to the Reign of Elizabeth I; Christopher St. German on Chancery and Statute; Reassessing the Henrician Age (Co-Author); The Complete Works of Thomas More, Vol. X (Co-Editor); Tudor England; The Tudors and Stuarts (Co-Author); The Reign of Elizabeth I. Address: School of History, St. Andrews University, College Gate, St. Andrews KY16 9AJ.

Guy, Roger Robert, MSc, PhD, CEng, MICE. Director for Environment and Infrastructure, Dumfries and Galloway Council, since 1995; b. 8.8.47. Educ. Westminster City School; Imperial College, London University; Manchester University. Research Fellow, Edinburgh University, 1972; South West of Scotland Water Board, 1973; Dumfries County Council, 1974; Dumfries and Galloway Regional Council, 1975: Assistant Director (Transportation), 1987,

Director Roads and Transportation, 1991. Henrici Medal, 1967; Unwin Medal, 1968. Recreation: outdoor pursuits. Address: (b.) Militia House, Council Offices, Dumfries DG1 2DD; T.-01387 260100.

Gwilt, George David, MA, FFA, FBCS. Director: European Assets Trust NV, since 1979, Scottish Mortgage & Trust plc, since 1983, Hodgson Martin Ltd., since 1989, Edinburgh Festival Society Ltd., 1989-95; b. 11.11.27, Edinburgh; m., Ann Sylvester; 3 s. Educ. Sedbergh; St. John's College, Cambridge. Standard Life, 1949-88, latterly as Managing Director; President, Faculty of Actuaries, 1981-83; Trustee, South of Scotland TSB, 1966-83; Member: Younger Committee on Privacy, 1970-72, Monopolies and Mergers Commission, 1983-87; Convener, Scottish Poetry Library, since 1988. Recreations: flute playing; squash. Address: (h.) 39 Oxgangs Road, Edinburgh EH10 7BE; T.-0131-445 1266.

H

**Haddington, 13th Earl of (John George Baillie-Hamilton); b. 21.12.41; m.; 1 s.; 2 d. Address: Mellerstain, Gordon, Berwickshire, TD3 6LG.

Hadley, Geoffrey, BSc (Hons), PhD. Honorary Senior Lecturer, Aberdeen University, since 1985; Consultant Microbiologist, since 1985; b. 7.2.32, Stoke-on-Trent; m., Margaret Murison; 3 d. by pr. m. Educ. Longton High School; Birmingham University. Research Fellow, Nottingham University, 1956-58; Lecturer, Glasgow University, 1958-60; Lecturer, then Senior Lecturer, Aberdeen University, 1960-85; seconded to University of Malaya, 1967-68; Member, Aberdeen County Council, 1973-75, Grampian Regional Council, 1974-94; Convener, Grampian Regional Council, 1986-90; Vice-President, British Mycological Society, 1987; Editor, Mycologist; Chairman, Aberdeen Civic Society; Chairman, Grampian Heart Campaign, 1991-96; Member, Management Committee, Hanover (Scotland) Housing Association. Recreations: classical music; home brewing and wine-making; cricket; cycling; DIY. Address: (h.) 74 Don Street, Old Aberdeen, Aberdeen AB24 1UU; T.-01224 494472.

Hadley, Ruth, MCGB. Chef; b., 18.4.49, Liverpool; m., Anthony; 1 s.; 1 d. Educ. Holly Lodge High School for Girls, Liverpool. Taste of Scotland Restaurant of the Year, 1989; Macallan Scottish Restaurant of the Year, 1993. Address: The Cross, Kingussie; T.-01540 661166.

Hafren, Paul Anthony, BA(Hons), MA, MBA. Depute Principal, Inverness College, since 1996; b. 22.9.55, London; m., Jane; 1 s. Educ. Chatham House Grammar School, Ramsgate; University of Bristol; University of East Anglia; South Bank University. Secondary Teacher: Gloucester, 1979-80, East Devon College, 1980-84, Norfolk College, 1984-89, Stafford College, 1989-96. Executive Officer, National Association of Student Services. Recreations: mountaineering; kayaking; skiing; windsurfing. Address: (b.) 3 Longman Road, Longman South, Inverness IV1 1SA; T.-01463 256039.

Hagart-Alexander of Ballochmyle, Sir Claud, Bt, DL, JP, BA, CEng, MInstMC. Vice Lord-Lieutenant, Ayrshire and Arran, since 1983; b. 6.1.27, Peking; m., Hilda Etain Acheson; 2 s.; 2 d. Educ. Sherborne; Corpus Christi College, Cambridge. Address: (h.) Kingencleugh House, Mauchline, Ayrshire KA5 5JL; T.-01290 550217.

Haggart, David Ballantine, JP, MA. Writer and Broadcaster; b. 15.3.34, Dundee; m., Gwendolen Hall; 3 s. Educ. Aberdeen Grammar School; Aberdeen University. National Service, Band of Royal Corps of Signals, 1956-58; Teacher, Perth and Kinross County Council, 1958-59; Youth Employment Officer, City of Aberdeen, 1959-63; Head of Careers Service, Aberdeen University, 1963-92; Member, Justices' Committee, Aberdeen, since 1976, Justice of the Peace Advisory Committee, since 1991; Chairman: Ferryhill Community Council, 1976-82, Castlehill Housing Association, 1991-94, Aberdeen and NE Scotland Music Festival, 1982-84; Writer and Producer, educational television programmes, including The Interview (Royal Television Society award); Editor, Current Vacancies, 1986-93; Columnist, Prospects Today, Evening Express; regular radio broadcasts, mainly on religious programmes; Presenter, Sunday Best, Northsound Radio, since 1981, Producer, since 1988. Recreations: music; motoring; local history. Address: (h.) 24 Polmuir Road, Aberdeen AB11 7SY; T.-01224 584176.

Haggart, Mary Elizabeth, OBE; b. 8.4.24, Leicester; m., Rt. Rev. A.I.M. Haggart. Educ. Wyggeston Grammar School for Girls, Leicester; Leicester Royal Infirmary and Children's Hospital. Leicester Royal Infirmary: Staff Nurse, 1947-48, Night Sister, 1948-50, Ward Sister, 1950-56, Night Superintendent, 1956-58, Assistant Matron, 1958-61; Assistant Matron, Brook General Hospital, London, 1962-64; Matron, Dundee Royal Infirmary and Matron Designate, Ninewells Hospital, Dundee, 1964-68; Chief Nursing Officer, Board of Managements, Dundee General Hospitals and Ninewells Hospital, 1968-73; Chief Area Nursing Officer, Tayside Health Board, 1974-82; President, Scottish Association of Nurse Administrators, 1972-77; Member: Scottish Board, Royal College of Nursing, 1965-70, General Nursing Council for Scotland, 1965-70 and 1978-82; Chairman, Scottish Board of Nursing Midwifery and Health Visiting, 1980-83; Member: Standing Nursing and Midwifery Committee, 1971-74 (Vice Chairman, 1973-74), Action on Smoking and Health Scotland, 1978-82 (Chairman, Working Party, Smoking and Nurses); Governor, Dundee College of Technology, 1978-82; Honorary Lecturer, Department of Community Medicine, Dundee University and Medical School, 1980-82; Member: Management Committee, Carstairs State Hospital, 1982-92, United Kingdom Central Council for Nursing Midwifery and Health Visiting, 1980-82, Scottish Hospital Endowments Research Trust, 1986-96. Recreations: walking; music; travel. Address: (h.) 14/2 St. Margaret's Place, Edinburgh EH9 1AY.

Haggarty, William McLaughlan, TD, BL. Solicitor, since 1950; Senior Partner, Mathie-Morton Black & Buchanan, Ayr; Honorary Sheriff, South Strathclyde, Dumfries and Galloway; b. 22.2.26, Glasgow; m., Olive Dorothy Mary Speirs; 1 s.; 1 d. Educ. High School of Glasgow; Glasgow University. War Service, Merchant Navy, 1943-47; Chairman, National Insurance Tribunal, North and South Ayrshire, 1963-88; Lt. Col. Commanding 264 (Scottish) Regiment, Royal Corps of Transport (TA), 1966; Dean, Ayr Faculty of Solicitors, 1982; Governor, Craigie College of Education, Ayr, 1983-91. Recreations: golf; travel; gardening. Address: (b.) 4 Alloway Place, Ayr; T.-01292 263549.

Haig, Andrew James Newton, BSc, PhD, CBiol, FIBiol, FCIWEM. Regional Scientist, Scottish Environment Protection Agency (West Region), since 1996; b. 2.4.47, London; m., Barbara Mary Jackson; 1 s.; 1 d. Educ. King's School, Bruton; London University; Leeds University. Research Assistant, Leeds University Wellcome Marine Laboratory, 1968-71; Clyde River Purification Board: Marine Biologist, 1971-74, Assistant Marine Survey Officer, 1974-75, Marine Survey Officer, 1975-89, Assistant Director, 1989-92, Depute Director (Chief Scientist), 1992-96. Member, Scottish Council, Institute of Biology, 1978-81; Consultant/Adviser, World Health Organisation, Copenhagen 1978, Lisbon 1978, Athens 1979; NATO Invited Specialist, Lisbon 1977; Member, Fish Farming Advisory Committee, since 1994. Recreations: natural history; gardening; music. Address: (b.) SEPA West, 5 Redwood Crescent, Peel Park, East Kilbride, Glasgow G74 5PP; T.-01355 574200.

Haig of Bemersyde, The Earl (George Alexander Eugene Douglas), OBE, DL, MA, ARSA, KStJ. Painter; b. 15.3.18, London; 1 s.; 2 d. Educ. Cargilfield; Stowe School; Christ Church, Oxford. 2nd Lt., Royal Scots Greys, 1938; retired on account of disability (rank of Captain); attended Camberwell School of Arts and Crafts; paintings in many public and private collections; served Second World War; taken prisoner, 1942; Member, Royal Fine Art Commission for Scotland, 1958-61; Chairman, SE South East Scotland Disablement Advisory Committee, 1960-73; Trustee, Scottish National War Memorial, 1961-96; Trustee, National Galleries of Scotland, 1962-72; Member, Scottish Arts Council, 1968-74; Past Chairman, Royal British Legion Scotland; President: Earl Haig Fund Scotland/Royal British Legion Scotland, 1980-86, Scottish

Branch, Officers Association, 1978-95, Scottish Craft Centre, 1952-73; Vice President, Scottish National Institution for War Blinded and of Royal Blind Asylum, since 1960. Recreations: fishing; shooting. Address: (h.) Bemersyde, Melrose TD6 9DP; T.-018352 2762.

Haines, Gerald, MA. Rector, Keith Grammar School, since 1989; b. 28.7.38, Glamorgan; m., Avril Esther Shearer; 1 s.; 1 d. Educ. Eastwood Senior Secondary, Glasgow; Glasgow University. Teacher of English, Cumbernauld High School, 1964-69; Principal Teacher of English, then Assistant Head Teacher, Lossiemouth High School, 1969-78; Depute Rector, Keith Grammar School, 1978-89. Recreations: bridge; gardening; golf. Address: (b.) School Road, Keith AB55 5ES; T.-01542 882461.

Hajducki, Andrew Michael, QC, MA. Advocate, since 1979; QC (Scot), since 1994; Temporary Sheriff, since 1987; b. 12.11.52, London; 2 s.; 1 d. Educ. Dulwich College; Cambridge University (Downing). Called to English Bar (Gray's Inn), 1976; Reporter, Session Cases, 1980; Tutor, Edinburgh University, 1979-81; Safeguarder: Lothian Children's Panel, 1987-97. Fellow, Royal Society of Antiquaries of Scotland. Publications: three books on the railways of East Lothian and Berwickshire; Scottish Civic Government Licensing Law (Co-author); Civil Jury Trials. Recreations: travel by train, tram, and Land Rover; reading fiction, topography, and history. Address: (b.) Advocates Library, Parliament House, Edinburgh.

Halcro-Johnston, Hugh. Convener, Orkney Islands Council. Address: (b.) Council Offices, Kirkwall KW15 1NY.

Halcrow, James George, MA, BMus (Hons), DipEd. Director of Education and Community Services, Shetland Islands Council, since 1996; b. 28.2.45, Lerwick; m., Anne; 2 d. Educ. Anderson Educational Institute, Lerwick; Edinburgh University. Teacher of Music, Royal High School, Edinburgh, 1970-71; Principal Teacher of Music, Anderson High School, Lerwick, and part-time County Music Organiser, 1971-74; Shetland Islands Council: Adviser in Music, 1974-89, Home/School Adviser, 1989-92. Chairman, Association of Music Advisers in Scotland, 1988-90; Convenor, Music Panel, Scottish Examination Board, 1991. Recreations: performing music; DIY. Address: (b.) Education Office, Schlumberger Base, Gremista Industrial Estate, Lerwick ZE1 0PX; T.-01595 744303.

Haldane of Gleneagles, James Martin, MA, CA, FRSA. 26th Laird of Gleneagles; Partner, Chiene & Tait, CA, since 1989; Director: Scottish Life Assurance Co., since 1990, Investors Capital Trust PLC, since 1995, Stace Barr Angerstein PLC, Shires Investment plc, since 1996; Chairman, Queen's Hall (Edinburgh) Ltd., since 1987; b. 18.9.41, Edinburgh; m., Petronella Victoria Scarlett; 1 s.; 2 d. Educ. Winchester College; Magdalen College, Oxford. Partner, Arthur Young, 1970-89. Chairman, Scottish Chamber Orchestra, 1978-85; Chairman, Craighead Investments PLC, 1982-90; Trustee, D'Oyly Carte Opera Trust, 1985-92; Treasurer, Queen's Bodyguard for Scotland (Royal Company of Archers), since 1992; Member: Council, Edinburgh Festival Society, 1985-89, Northern and Scottish Board, Legal and General Assurance Co., 1984-87, Council, National Trust for Scotland, 1992-97, Court, Stirling University, since 1997. Recreations: music; golf. Address: (h.) Gleneagles, Auchterarder PH3 1PJ; T.-01764 682 388.

Haldane, Professor John Joseph, BA, PGCE, BA, PhD, Hon LLD, FRSA, FRSE. Professor of Philosophy, St. Andrews University, since 1994; Director, Centre for Philosophy and Public Affairs, St. Andrews University, since 1988; b. 19.2.54, London; m., Hilda Marie Budas; 2 s.; 2 d. Educ. St. Aloysius College, Glasgow; Wimbledon

School of Art; London University. Art Master, St. Joseph's Grammar School, Abbey Wood, 1976-79; Lecturer in Moral Philosophy, St. Andrews University, 1983-90, Reader, 1990-94; Member, Editorial Board: The Philosophical Quarterly, since 1984, Journal of Medical Ethics, Journal of Philosophy of Education, American Journal of Jurisprudence, Cambridge Studies in Philosophy, Innes Review. Fellow: Royal Society of Arts, Royal Society of Edinburgh. Recreations: reading; photography; gardening; art. Address: (b.) Department of Moral Philosophy, St. Andrews University, St. Andrews KY16 9AL; T.-01334 462488.

Hale, Professor Bob, BA, BPhil. Professor of Metaphysical Philosophy, University of Glasgow, since 1995; British Academy Research Reader, since 1997; b. 4.5.45, Aldershot; m., Maggie; 2 s.; 1 d. Educ. Woking County Grammar School for Boys; University of Bristol; University of Oxford. Part-time Lecturer in Philosophy, University of Nottingham; Lecturer in Philosophy, University of Lancaster; Lecturer then Reader in Logic and Metaphysics, University of St. Andrews. Publications: Abstract Objects, 1987; Reading Putnam, 1994; Blackwell Companion to Philosophy of Language (Co-Author), 1997. Recreations: film; theatre; music; reading; hill-walking. Address: (b.) Department of Philosophy, University of Glasgow, Glasgow G12 8QQ; T.-0141-330 5173.

Halford-MacLeod, Col. (ACF), Retired Lt. Col. Aubrey Philip Lydiat, MA (Hons), late Black Watch (RHR); retired Army Officer; Schools Liaison Officer (Scotland), Army HQ Scotland; Director: Living History in Scotland, Round Tower Ltd., since 1993; b. 28.4.42, Bagdad; m., Alison Fiona Brown; 2 s.; 1 d. Educ. Winchester College; RMA Sandhurst; Magdalen College, Oxford. Commissioned into Black Watch, 1962; Lt., 1964; Capt., 1968; Maj., 1975; Lt. Col., 1985; appointed Commanding Officer, Glasgow and Strathclyde Universities OTC, 1985; Chief of Staff, The Scottish Division, 1988; UK Liaison Officer (as Colonel), US European Command Stuttgart, 1991; SO1 G1 Action and Support Team (Demob Cell), Army HQ Scotland, 1992; Commandant, The Black Watch ACF Battalion, 1993. Recreations: walking the dogs; shooting; fishing; opera; model soldiers; curling; country dancing. Address: (b.) Craigiehall, Edinburgh EH30 9TN; T.-0131-310 2190; (h.) The Old Manse, 28 Skene Street, Strathmiglo KY14 7QL; T.-01337 860715/868930.

Halford-MacLeod, Aubrey Seymour, CMG, CVO, MA (Oxon); b. 15.12.14, Birmingham; m., Giovanna M. Durst; 3 s.; 1 d. Educ. King Edward's School, Birmingham, and abroad; Magdalen College, Oxford. HM Diplomatic Service, Third Secretary, Foreign Office, 1937; Bagdad, 1939; Office of Minister of State, Algiers, 1943; reopened Embassy, Rome, 1944; Secretary, Advisory Council Italy, and Political Adviser to Allied Control Commission, 1943-46; PPS to Permanent Under Secretary, Foreign Office, 1946-49; Deputy Secretary-General, Council of Europe, 1949-52; Tokyo, 1953-55; Libya, 1955-57; Kuwait, 1957-59; Munich, 1959-65; Ambassador to Iceland, 1966-70. Director, Scottish Opera, 1972-77; President, Scottish Society for Northern Studies, 1972-75; Vice-President, Clan MacLeod Society of Scotland, 1973-77; Adviser, Scottish Council (Development and Industry), 1970-77. Recreations: fishing; ornithology. Address: (h.) Mulag House, North Harris, Western Isles HS3 3AB; T.-Harris 2054.

Hall, Diana M., MA(Hons), DipEdTech. Vice Principal, Central College of Commerce, since 1996; b. 22.5.49, Glasgow; m., J.C. Russell Hall; 1 s.; 2 step-d. Educ. Glasgow High School for Girls; University of Glasgow; Jordanhill College of Education; Dundee College of Education. English Teacher: Eastwood High School, 1971, St. George's School, Switzerland, 1974, King's Park Secondary, 1975; Lecturer then Senior Lecturer in English and General Studies, Cardonald College, 1976; joined

Central College of Commerce, 1987: Staff Development and Equality Officer, Head of Staff Services, Vice Principal, Staff Development Officer (on secondment), Scottish Wider Access Programme, West of Scotland, 1989-91. Recreations: reading; walking. Address: (b.) 300 Cathedral Street, Glasgow G1 2TA; T.-0141-552 3941.

Hall, Professor Graham Stanley, BSc, PhD, FRSE. Professor of Mathematics, University of Aberdeen, since 1996; b. 5.9.46, Warrington; 1 s.; 1 d. Educ. Boteler Grammar School, Warrington; University of Newcastle upon Tyne. Lecturer in Mathematics, University of Aberdeen, since 1973 (Senior Lecturer, 1982, Reader, 1990, Head of Department, 1992-95). Publication: General Relativity (Co-Editor), 1996. Recreation: music (playing piano); sport. Address: (b.) Department of Mathematical Sciences, University of Aberdeen, Aberdeen AB24 3QY; T.-01224 272748.

Hall, Hugh, MBA, CPFA(Hons). Director of Finance and Regulation, Scottish Homes, since 1997; b. 30.5.58, Glasgow; m., Jan; 2 d. Educ. St. Ambrose High School; University of Edinburgh. Scottish Office (Health/Education), 1978-91; Scottish Higher Education Funding Council, 1991-95; Finance Director, Occupational Health and Safety Agency, 1995-97. Member, CIPFA Examination Board; Quality Assessor, Advanced Diploma for Finance (CIPFA). Recreations: family; walking; reading. Address: (b.) Thistle House, 91 Haymarket Terrace, Edinburgh EH12 5YA; T.-0131-479 5210.

Hall, Jacqueline, MA (Hons), DMS, DipM. Executive Director, Gordon Enterprise Trust, since 1990; b. 17.1.65, Aberdeen. Educ. Bankhead Academy, Aberdeen; Aberdeen University; Robert Gordon's University. Executive Officer, Civil Service, 1986-87; Assistant Director, Moray Enterprise Trust, 1987-90. Scottish Young Career Woman of the Year, 1991; Member: Board, Grampian Young Enterprise Scotland, Assessment Panel, Investors in People Scotland; Advisor, Young Enterprise Scotland. Recreations: scuba diving; running; swimming; aerobics; reading; salmon fishing. Address: (b.) Thainstone Business Centre, Inverurie, Aberdeenshire AB51 5TB; T.-01467 621166.

Hall, James Firth, Comendator OM (Portugal), Medhalha de Vasco da Gama (Portugal), OStJ, FRCIS. Honorary Consul of Portugal (Scotland), since 1973; retired Chartered Surveyor; b. 1.12.27, Edinburgh; m., Helen Davidson Smith. Educ. George Watson's Boys College. Senior Partner, D.M. Hall & Son, 1966-88; former Member, Valuation Appeal Committee. Recreations: golf; sailing; shooting. Address: 25 Bernard Street, Edinburgh EH6 6SH.

Hall, Major General Jonathan Michael Francis Cooper, OBE (1987). General Officer Commanding Scotland and Governor of Edinburgh Castle, 1995-97; b. 10.8.44, Wilmslow; m., Sarah Linda Hudson; 2 d. Educ. Taunton School; RMA Sandhurst. Commnd 3rd Carabiniers, 1965; Staff College, Camberley, 1977; Comd Offr, Royal Scots Dragoon Guards, 1984-86; Higher Comd and Staff Course, 1988; Comd 12th Armoured Bde, 1989-90; Member, Royal College of Defence Studies, 1991; Dep Mil Sec (A), Ministry of Defence, 1992-94; Director, Royal Armoured Corps, 1994-95. Committee Member, Cavalry and Guards' Club, since 1981; Col Comdt, The Scottish Division, 1995-97; Col Comdt, The Royal Army Veterinary Corps, since 1995; Col, The Royal Scots Dragoon Guards from July 1998. Recreations: country pursuits; tennis; skiing; travel. Address: (b.) c/o Home Headquarters, The Royal Scots Dragoon Guards, The Castle, Edinburgh EH1 2YT; T.-0131-310 5100.

Hall, Rev. Keith Ferrier, BD(Hons). Minister, Dundee Parish Church (St. Mary's), since 1994; Chaplain, Dundee High School, since 1994; b. 20.10.55, Arbroath; m., Amilia Elaine Donaldson; 2 s.; 1 d. Educ. Arbroath High School;

University of St. Andrews. Minister: Blairgowrie, St. Mary's South, 1981-87, Alloa Parish, St. Mungo's, 1987-94. Recreations: family; gardening; golf; theatre. Address: (b.) Dundee Parish Church (St. Mary's), Nethergate, Dundee DD1 4DG; T.-01382 226271.

Hall, Professor Peter Anthony, BSc, PhD, MD, MRCPath. Professor of Cellular Pathology, Dundee University, since 1993; b. 2.2.58, Italy. Educ. Tunbridge Wells Technical School; London University. Lecturer in Pathology, London University; Research Fellow, Imperial Cancer Research Fund; Senior Lecturer, Royal Postgraduate Medical School; Professor of Histopathology, London University. Recreation: walking.

Hall, William, CBE, DFC, FRICS. Honorary Sheriff, Paisley, since 1974; b. 25.7.19, Paisley; m., Margaret Semple Gibson; 1 s.; 3 d. Educ. Paisley Grammar School. Pilot, RAFVR, 1939-45 (Despatches); Senior Partner, R. & W. Hall, Chartered Surveyors, Paisley, 1949-79; Chairman, Royal Institution of Chartered Surveyors in Scotland, 1971; Member: Valuation Advisory Council, 1970-80, Lands Tribunal for Scotland, 1971-91, Lands Tribunal for England and Wales, 1979-91; Executive Member, Erskine Hospital, since 1976. Recreation: golf. Address: (h.) Windyridge, Brediland Road, Paisley PA2 9HF.

Hall, William Andrew McDonald, MA (Hons). Head Teacher, Dalry Secondary School, Kirkcudbrightshire, since 1973; b. 12.2.37, Airdrie; m., Catherine R.; 1 s.; 2 d. Educ. Airdrie Academy; Glasgow University. Teacher of History, Hamilton Academy, 1962-66; Principal Teacher of History, Mackie Academy, Stonehaven, 1966-73. Recreations: reading; golf; Airdrieonians Football Club; cinema. Address: (b.) Dalry Secondary School, St. John's Town of Dalry, Kirkcudbrightshire DG7 3UU; T.-01644 430259.

Hall, (William) Douglas, OBE (1985), BA, FMA; b. 9.10.26, London; m., 1, Helen Elizabeth Ellis (m. diss.); 1 s.; 1 d.; 2, Matilda Mary Mitchell. Educ. University College School, Hampstead; University College and Courtauld Institute of Art, London University, 1948-52. Intelligence Corps, 1945-48 (Middle East); Manchester City Art Galleries: Keeper, Rutherston Collection, 1953-58, Keeper, City Art Gallery, 1958-59, Deputy Director, 1959-61; Keeper, Scottish National Gallery of Modern Art, 1961-86. Recreations: music; travel; gardening; wall-building. Address: (h.) Wellgate, Morebattle, Roxburghshire TD5 8QN; T.-01573 440687.

Halliburton, Ian Scott. Director, Bell Lawrie Investment Management; b. 30.1.43, Huddersfield; m., Anne Whitaker; 1 s.; 1 d. Educ. Royal High School, Edinburgh; Royal Scottish Academy of Music and Drama. General banking training, Royal Bank of Scotland, 1961-63; RSAMD, 1963-66; professional actor, 1967-70; sales consultant, 1970-71; insurance broker, 1971-78. Director, Enterprise Music Scotland. Recreations: hill-walking; listening to music; supporting the arts. Address: (h.) 259 Garrioch Road, Glasgow G20 8QZ; T.-0141-946 5426.

Halliday, James, MA, MLitt, JP. Chairman, Scots Independent Newspapers; b. 27.2.27, Wemyss Bay; m., Olive Campbell; 2 s. Educ. Greenock High School; Glasgow University. Teacher: Ardeer FE Centre, 1953, Kildonan Secondary School, Coatbridge, 1954-56, Uddingston Grammar School, 1956-58, Dunfermline High School, 1958-67; Lecturer in History, Dundee College of Education, 1967-79; Principal Lecturer in History, 1979-87. Chairman, Scottish National Party, 1956-60; Parliamentary candidate: Stirling and Falkirk Burghs, 1955 and 1959, West Fife, 1970. Publications: World in Transformation — America; Scotland The Separate; A Concise History of Scotland; 1820: The Radical War; Story of Scotland (Co-author). Recreations: reading; folk music; football spectating. Address: (h.) 72 Fintry Place, Broughty Ferry, Dundee DD5 3BH.

Halliday, Rt. Rev. Robert Taylor, MA, BD. Bishop of Brechin, 1990-96; b. 7.5.32, Glasgow; m., Dr. Gena M. Chadwin; 1 d. Educ. High School of Glasgow; Glasgow University, Trinity College, Glasgow; Episcopal Theological College, Edinburgh. Deacon, 1957; Priest, 1958; Assistant Curate, St. Andrew's, St. Andrews, 1957-60, St. Margaret's, Newlands, Glasgow, 1960-63; Rector, Holy Cross, Davidson's Mains, Edinburgh, 1963-83; External Lecturer in New Testament, Episcopal Theological College, Edinburgh, 1963-74; Canon, St. Mary's Cathedral, Edinburgh, 1973-83; Rector, St. Andrew's, St. Andrews, 1983-90; Tutor in Biblical Studies, St. Andrews University, 1984-90. Recreations: walking; reading; gardening. Address: 28 Forbes Road, Edinburgh EH10 4ED; T.-0131-221 1490.

Halling, Professor Peter James, BA, PhD, FRSE. Robertson Professor of Bioprocess Technology, Strathclyde University, since 1996; b. 30.3.51, London. Educ. Calday Grammar School; Churchill College, Cambridge; Bristol University. Postdoctoral Fellow, University College, London, 1975-78; Research Scientist, Unilever Research, Bedford, 1978-83; Professor of Biocatalyst Science, Strathclyde University, 1990-96. Recreation: orienteering. Address: (h.) 34 Montague Street, Glasgow G4 9HX; T.-0141-552 4400.

Halliwell, Professor Francis Stephen, MA, DPhil(Oxon). Professor of Greek, University of St. Andrews, since 1995; b. 18.10.53, Wigan; m., Helen Ruth Gainford; 2 s. Educ. St. Francis Xavier's, Liverpool; Worcester College, University of Oxford. Lecturer in Classics and Drama, Westfield College, London, 1980-82; Fellow in Classics, Corpus Christi College, University of Cambridge, 1982-84; Lecturer, Senior Lecturer, Reader in Classics, University of Birmingham, 1984-95; Visiting Professor in Classics, University of Chicago, 1990; Visiting Faculty Fellow, University of California at Riverside, 1993; Visiting Professor, University of Rome, 1998. Publications: various books on Greek literature and philosophy. Recreations: music; golf. Address: (b.) Department of Greek, Swallowgate, University of St. Andrews, St. Andrews KY16 9AL; T.-01334 462617.

Halls, Michael, FREHIS, FRSH, MInstWM. President, International Federation of Environmental Health, 1996-98; b. 6.12.39, Galashiels; m., Sheila; 1 s.; 1 d. Educ. Galashiels Academy; Heriot-Watt. Trainee Burgh Surveyor, Galashiels Town Council, 1959-63; Additional Public Health Inspector, Thame Urban District Council, 1963-64; Galashiels Town Council: Assistant Burgh Surveyor and Sanitary Inspector, 1964-68, Depute Burgh Surveyor, 1968-71, Burgh Surveyor, 1971-75; Director of Environmental Services, Ettrick and Lauderdale District Council, 1975-96. Last Honorary Secretary, Scottish Institute of Environmental Health, 1978-83; President, Royal Environmental Health Institute of Scotland, 1984-85. Recreation: golf; philately; wine-making/drinking; music; eating; photography. Address: (h.) Eastfield, 16 Abbotsford Road, Galashiels TD1 3DS; T.-01896 752624.

Hamblen, Professor David Lawrence, MB, BS, PhD, FRCS, FRCSEdin, FRCSGlas. Professor of Orthopaedic Surgery, Glasgow University, since 1972; Chairman, Greater Glasgow Health Board, since 1997; Honorary Consultant in Orthopaedic Surgery, Greater Glasgow Health Board, since 1972; Visiting Professor to National Centre for Training and Education in Prosthetics and Orthotics, Strathclyde University, since 1981; Hon. Consultant Orthopaedic Surgeon to Army in Scotland; b. 31.8.34, London; m., Gillian; 1 s.; 2 d. Educ. Roan School, Greenwich; London University. The London Hospital,

1963-66; Teaching Fellow in Orthopaedics, Harvard Medical School/Massachusetts General Hospital, 1966-67; Lecturer in Orthopaedics, Nuffield Orthopaedic Centre, Oxford, 1967-68; Senior Lecturer in Orthopaedics/ Honorary Consultant, Edinburgh University/South East Regional Hospital Board, 1968-72. Member, Chief Scientist Committee and Chairman, Committee for Research on Equipment for Disabled, 1983-90; Chairman, Journal of Bone and Joint Surgery, since 1995 (Member, Editorial Board, 1978-82 and 1985-89); Secretary and Treasurer, JBJS Council of Management, 1992-95; Member, Physiological Systems Board, Medical Research Council, 1983-88; President, British Orthopaedic Association, 1990-91 (Chairman, Education Sub-Committee, 1986-89); Non-Executive Director, West Glasgow Hospitals University NHS Trust, 1994-97. Recreation: golf. Address: (b.) University Department of Orthopaedic Surgery, Western Infirmary, Glasgow G11 6NT; T.-0141-211 2678/2264.

Hamer-Hodges, David William, MS, FRCS, FRCSE. Consultant Surgeon, Western General Hospital, Edinburgh, since 1979; Honorary Senior Lecturer, Edinburgh University, since 1979; b. 17.10.43, Portsmouth; m., Gillian Landale Kelman; 3 s.; 1 d. Educ. Portsmouth Grammar School; University College London. Senior Registrar, Aberdeen Teaching Hospitals; Research Fellow, Harvard Medical School; Resident Surgical Officer, St. Mark's Hospital, London. Address: (b.) 38 India Street, Edinburgh; T.-0131-226 5720.

Hamill, J. Secretary, Scottish Office Home Department. Address: (b.) Saughton House, Broomhouse Drive, Edinburgh, EH11 3XD.

Hamill, Sir Patrick, Kt (1984), QPM, OStJ, BA. Chief Constable of Strathclyde, 1977-85; b. 29.4.30, Clydebank; m., Nellie Gillespie; 4 s.; 1 d. Educ. St. Patrick's High School, Dumbarton. Joined Dunbartonshire Constabulary, 1950, and rose through the ranks until promoted Chief Superintendent, 1970; transferred to City of Glasgow Police, 1972; appointed Assistant Chief Constable, 1974; joined Strathclyde Police, 1975, and attended the Royal College of Defence Studies, 1976; President, Association of Chief Police Officers (Scotland), 1982-83, Honorary Secretary and Treasurer, 1983-85; Member, Board of Governors: St. Aloysius College, Glasgow, 1983-90, St. Andrew's College of Education, Bearsden, 1987-88.

Hamilton, Alex. Writer of fiction; b. 14.4.49, Glasgow. Publications: Three Glasgow Writers, 1976; Gallus, Did You Say?, 1982; Abdul the Tobacco Curer, forthcoming; The Formulae, forthcoming; many articles, songs, stories, reviews, broadcasts, audio and videotapes. Recreations: language; literature; music; theatre. Address: (h.) 12 Woodlands Drive, Glasgow G4 9EH; T.-0141-339 2258.

Hamilton, Alexander Macdonald, CBE, JP, MA, LLB. Former Vice Chairman: Royal Bank of Scotland Group plc, Royal Bank of Scotland plc; b. 11.5.25, Motherwell; m., Catherine; 2 s.; 1 d. Educ. Hamilton Academy; Glasgow University. Former Senior Partner, subsequently Consultant, McGrigor Donald, Solicitors, Glasgow; former Member, Council, Law Society of Scotland, now Convener, Insolvency and Diligence Sub Committees; President of the Society, 1977-78; former Member, Court House Committee, Royal Faculty of Procurators of Glasgow; Past President, Glasgow Juridical Society; former Chairman, Scottish Committee, The Scout Association; Secretary, Cambuslang Old Parish Church; former Vice-Chairman and Legal Adviser, Cambuslang Community Council. Recreations: sailing; golf. Address: (h.) 30 Wellshot Drive, Cambuslang; T.-0141-641 1445.

Hamilton, 15th Duke of, (Angus Alan Douglas Douglas-Hamilton), MA, CEng, MIMechE, FBIS. Premier Peer of Scotland; Hereditary Keeper of Palace of Holyroodhouse; b.

13.9.38; m., Sarah Scott (deceased); 2 s.; 2 d. Educ. Eton; Balliol College, Oxford. Joined RAF, 1956; Flt.-Lt., 1963; flying instructor, 1965; Instrument Rating Examiner, 1966; invalided, 1967; Senior Commercial Pilot, 1968; Test Pilot, Scottish Aviation, 1971-72; Knight of St. John, 1974, Prior for Scotland, 1975-82; Patron, British Airways Pipe Band, 1977; Member: European Community Sub-Committee on Energy and Transport, 1975-77, Queen's Bodyguard for Scotland (Royal Company of Archers), since 1976, Royal Scottish Pipers Society, 1977, Piobaireachd Society, 1979, Council, Cancer Research Campaign, 1978; Honorary Air Commodore, No. 2 (City of Edinburgh) Maritime Headquarters Unit, R.Aux.AF, 1982-93. Publication: MARIA R, 1991. Address: (b.) Lennoxlove, Haddington, East Lothian, EH41 4NZ; T.-0162 082 3720; (h.) Archerfield, by Dirleton, East Lothian EH39 5HQ; T.-0162 085 0298.

Hamilton, Hon. Lord (Arthur Campbell Hamilton), QC, BA (Oxon), LLB (Edin). Senator of the College of Justice, since 1995; b. 10.6.42, Glasgow; m., Christine Ann; 1 d. Educ. High School of Glasgow; Glasgow University; Worcester College, Oxford; Edinburgh University. Advocate, 1968; Standing Junior Counsel to Scottish Development Department, 1975-78, Inland Revenue (Scotland), 1978-82; Queen's Counsel, 1982; Advocate Depute, 1982-85; Judge of the Courts of Appeal of Jersey and of Guernsey, 1988-95; President, Pensions Appeal Tribunals for Scotland, 1992-95. Recreations: hill-walking; fishing; music; history. Address: (b.) Parliament House, Edinburgh EH1 1RQ; T.-0131-225 2595.

Hamilton, Christine M., MA. Depute Director, Performing Arts and Venues, Glasgow City Council, since 1997; b. 9.8.54, Hamilton. Educ. Kirkcaldy High School; Harris Academy, Dundee; Glasgow University; City University, London (Diploma, Arts Administration). House Manager, Citizens' Theatre, Glasgow; Administrator: 7:84 Theatre Company, Tag Theatre Company; Arts Officer, Scottish Trades Union Congress; Depute Director and Director, Planning and Development, Scottish Arts Council, 1991-97. Recreations: arts; hill-walking; swimming. Address: (b.) Exchange House, 229 George Street, Glasgow G1 1QU; T.-0141 287 5464.

Hamilton, Gordon MacMillan, MB, ChB, DFM, MPhil, CLEM. Medical Director, Glasgow University Health Service, since 1989; Hon. Senior Lecturer, Glasgow University, since 1989; Branch Medical Officer, Glasgow and Renfrewshire Branch, British Red Cross, since 1992; b. 6.2.54, Motherwell. Educ. Glasgow University. Various hospital appointments, 1977-89. Past Chairman, Friends of the S.N.O.; Member, Glasgow Art Club. Recreations: tennis; squash; keep-fit; art; antiques; music. Address: (h.) Gorrisholm, 2 Holm Road, Crossford ML8 5RG; T.-01555 860 877.

Hamilton, Ian Robertson, QC (Scot), BL, LLD (Hon); b. 13.9.25, Paisley; m., Jeannette Patricia Mari Stewart; 1 s.; 1 s., 2 d. by pr. m. Educ. John Neilson School, Paisley; Allan Glen's School, Glasgow, Glasgow University; Edinburgh University. RAFVR, 1944-48; called to Scottish Bar, 1954, and to Albertan Bar, 1982; Founder, Castle Wynd Printers, Edinburgh, 1955; Advocate Depute, 1962; Director of Civil Litigation, Republic of Zambia, 1964-66; Hon. Sheriff of Lanarkshire, 1967; retired from practice to work for National Trust for Scotland and later to farm in Argyll, 1969; returned to practice, 1974; Sheriff of Glasgow and Strathkelvin, May-December, 1984; returned to practice. Chief Pilot, Scottish Parachute Club, 1979-90; Student President, Heriot-Watt University, 1990-96; Rector, Aberdeen University, 1994-96. University of Aberdeen, 1997: LLD (Hon), Hon Research Fellow. Publications: No Stone Unturned, 1952; The Tinkers of the World, 1957 (Foyle award-winning play); A Touch of Treason, 1990; The Taking of the Stone of Destiny, 1991; A Touch More

Treason, 1993. Recreation: motor-biking. Address: (b.) Advocates' Library, Parliament House, Edinburgh EH1 1RF.

Hamilton, Rev. Ian William Finlay, BD, LTH, ALCM, AVCM. Minister, Nairn Old Parish Church, since 1986; b. 29.11.46, Glasgow; m., Margaret McLaren Moss; 1 s.; 2 d. Educ. Victoria Drive Senior Secondary School, Glasgow; University of Glasgow and Trinity College. Employed in banking, then music publishing; ordained, Alloa North Parish Church, 1978. Moderator, Presbytery of Inverness, 1990-91; Member: General Assembly Parish Re-appraisal Committee, 1994-97, General Assembly Maintenance of the Ministry Committee, since 1995; has participated in five pulpit exchanges, Reformed Church, New Jersey, USA; Presenter, Reflections (Grampian TV), Crossfire (Moray Firth Radio). Publications: Reflections from the Manse Window; Second Thoughts; They're Playing My Song; A Century of Christian Witness; several children's talks published in The Expository Times; regular contributor to Manse Window page in People's Friend. Recreations: music (piano and organ); writing; broadcasting on radio and television. Address: (h.) Nairn Old Parish Manse, 3 Manse Road, Nairn IV12 4RN; T.-01667 452203.

Hamilton, James Watt, JP, DL; b. 24.2.31, East Kilbride; m., Mabel; 1 s.; 1 d. Educ. Hutchesons' Grammar School. Founder, Hamilton's Dairies Ltd. Trustee: Turnberry Trust, Malin Court; Non-Executive Director, Hairmyres and Stonehouse Hospital Trust. Recreation: building a nine-hole golf course for use by charities. Address: (h.) Mains Farm, East Kilbride; T.-01355 276670.

Hamilton, John Patterson, QPM, BA (Hons), MBA, BSc. Chief Constable, Fife Constabulary, since 1996; b. 27.1.44, Belfast; m., Patricia; 1 s.; 1 d. Educ. Templemore Avenue School, Belfast; Open University. RUC (latterly as Chief Superintendent 1963-90); Assistant Chief Constable, Greater Manchester Police, 1990-96; seconded to National Criminal Intelligence Service, Home Office (Deputy Director General), 1994-96. Address: (b.) Police HQ, Detroit Road, Glenrothes, Fife; T.-01592 418888.

Hamilton, Loudon Pearson, CB (1987), MA (Hons). Chairman: Scottish Food Quality Certification Company since 1995, Scottish Agricultural and Rural Development Centre, since 1992; b. 12.1.32, Glasgow; m., 1, Anna Mackinnon Young (deceased); 2, Rosemary Hutton; 2 s. Educ. Hutchesons Grammar School, Glasgow; Glasgow University. National Service, RA, 1953-55 (2nd Lt.); Inspector of Taxes, Inland Revenue, 1956-60; Assistant Principal, Department of Agriculture and Fisheries for Scotland, 1960; Private Secretary to Parliamentary Under Secretary of State for Scotland, 1963-64; First Secretary, Agriculture, British Embassy, Copenhagen and The Hague, 1966-70; Assistant Secretary, Department of Agriculture and Fisheries for Scotland, 1973-79; Principal Establishment Officer, Scottish Office, 1979-84; Secretary, Scottish Office Agriculture and Fisheries Department, 1984-92. Chairman, Corstorphine Trust, 1990-95. Address: (h.) 8a Dick Place, Edinburgh EH9 2JL; T.-0131-667 5908.

Hamilton, Thomas Banks, BAcc, CA. Chairman and Chief Executive, Ashbourne PLC, since 1988; Managing Director, Elders PLC, since 1988; European President, Sun Healthcare Group Inc., since 1990; b. 22.11.55, Glasgow; 3 s.; 1 d. Educ. Glasgow Academy; Glasgow University. Director, West Highland Way PLC; Chairman, Bon Secours Health Systems Ltd. Recreations: hill-climbing; golf; painting; drawing. Address: (b.) Sun House, 58 West Regent Street, Glasgow G2 2QZ; T.-0141-331 2222.

Hamilton, William, MB, ChB, MD, FRCPGlas, FRCPEdin, DPH, DCH. Paediatric Endocrinologist, in private practice; b. 22.12.22, Holytown, Lanarkshire; m., Elizabeth Janet Beveridge; 2 s. Educ. Holytown Public

School; Dalziel High School, Motherwell; Glasgow University. House Physician/House Surgeon posts, Glasgow, 1952-54; general practice, 1954-56; Registrar medical post, Inverness, 1957-61; Senior Registrar in Paediatrics, 1961-62; Paediatrician and Paediatric Endocrinologist, Department of Child Health, Royal Hospital for Sick Children, Glasgow, 1961-89; University Senior Lecturer, 1962-89. Hon. Member, Österreichische Geschelschaft für Kinder und Jugend Heilkunde, 1996. Publications: Clinical Paediatric Endocrinology, 1972; Surgical Treatment of Endocrine Disease; chapters in Diseases of the Fetus and Newborn, 1994. Recreations: gardening; vintage car enthusiast. Address: (h.) 81 Woodend Drive, Glasgow G13 1QF; T.-0141-954 9961.

Hamilton-Grierson, Philip John, OBE, MA. Chairman, Raigmore NHS Trust; Director: Cromarty Firth Port Authority, Investors in People Scotland Ltd., A1 Welders Ltd., Made in Scotland Ltd.; b. 10.10.32, Inveresk; m., Pleasaunce Jill Cardew; 1 s.; 2 d. Educ. Rugby School; Corpus Christi College, Oxford. Contracts Manager, Bristol Aircraft Ltd.; Economic Adviser, Joseph Lucas Industries Ltd.; Secretary to Liberal Parliamentary Party; Director, Gallaher Ltd. Fellow, Royal Society of Arts. Recreations: hill-walking; tennis; music. Address: Pitlundie, North Kessock, Rossshire IV1 1XG; T.-01463 731392.

Hammerton, Professor Desmond, OBE, BSc, CBiol, FIBiol, FIWEM, FIMgt, FRSE. Visiting Professor, Department of Biology, Paisley University; b. 17.11.29, Wakefield, Yorkshire; m., Jean Taylor; 2 s.; 2 d. Educ. Harrow Weald County School; Birkbeck College, London University. Assistant Biologist, Metropolitan Water Board, 1953-55; Research Biologist, Bristol Waterworks, 1955-58; Principal Assistant, Lothians River Purification Board, 1958-62; Director, Hydrobiological Research Unit, Khartoum University, 1962-71; Deputy Director, Clyde River Purification Board, 1971-74, Director, 1975-94; Consultant, World Health Organisation, 1977-90; Member: Aquatic Life Sciences Grants Committee, Natural Environment Research Council, 1975-79, Marine Pollution Monitoring Management Group and its Steering Committee, 1974- 91, Steering Committee for the Development of Environmental Quality Objectives and Standards, Department of Environment, 1981-94, Scottish Council, Institute of Biology, 1973-76; elected to Committee of Environment Division, Institute of Biology, 1977 (Chairman, Environment Division, 1980-82), Terrestrial and Freshwater Sciences Committee, Natural Environment Research Council, 1985-89, Court, University of Paisley, Advisory Committee on Sites of Special Scientific Interest, since 1995, Board, Institute of Offshore Engineering, Heriot-Watt University, since 1995, West Regional Board, Scottish Environmental Protection Agency, since 1996; Chairman, Scottish Council, Institute of Biology, 1995-97. Recreations: chess; tennis; hill-walking. Address: (h.) Mansefield Lodge, Ancaster Square, Callander, Stirling FK17 8BL; T.-01877 330105.

Hampson, Stephen F., MA, BPhil. Under Secretary, Scottish Office, since 1993; b. 27.10.45, Grimsby; m., Gunilla Brunk; 1 s.; 1 d. Educ. The Leys School, Cambridge; University College, Oxford. Lecturer, Department of Political Economy, Aberdeen University, 1969-71; Economist, National Economic Development Office, 1971-75; Economic Adviser, Scottish Office, 1975-78 and 1982-84; First Secretary, British High Commission, New Delhi, 1978-81; Assistant Secretary, Scottish Office, 1984-93. Recreations: hill-walking; theatre. Address: (h.) Glenelg, Park Road, Kilmacolm, Renfrewshire; T.-Kilmacolm 872615.

Hampton, Robert. Principal Dancer, Scottish Ballet, since 1986; b. London. Trained, Legat Russian Ballet School; joined Scottish Ballet, 1979, making his principal debut as James in La Sylphide, 1983; has danced all the danseur

noble roles in the company's repertoire: La Sylphide, Giselle, Swan Lake, The Nutcracker, Coppelia, and Cinderella; Patron, Russian Ballet Society, since 1992. Address: (b.) Scottish Ballet, 261 West Princes Street, Glasgow G4 9EE.

Hankey, Maurice S., BSc, PhD. Director, Scottish Landowners Federation, since 1996; b. 3.7.54, Newcastle upon Tyne; m., Catherine; 1 s.; 1 d. Educ. Royal Grammar School, Newcastle upon Tyne; Wye College, London; Newcastle upon Tyne University. Specialist Adviser, East of Scotland College of Agriculture, 1978-80; Lecturer, Newcastle upon Tyne University, 1980-83; farming, 1983-90; Land Use Specialist, Scottish Landowners Federation, 1992-96. Member, Scottish Agricultural Wages Board. Recreations: landscape gardening; computing; rural interests. Address: (b.) Scottish Landowners Federation, 25 Maritime Street, Edinburgh EH6 5PW; T.-0131-555 1031.

Hanley, Clifford. Writer and Performer; b. 28.10.22, Glasgow; m., Anna Clark (deceased); 1 s.; 2 d. Educ. Eastbank Academy, Glasgow. Journalist, since 1940; Novelist, since 1957; Songwriter; Broadcaster; Member: Scottish Arts Council, 1965-72, Inland Waterways Advisory Council, 1970-73; Writer in Residence, York University, Toronto, 1979-80. Publications: Dancing in the Streets; Love from Everybody; The Taste of Too Much; Nothing but the Best; The System; The Redhaired Bitch; It's Different Abroad; The Italian Gadget; The Chosen Instrument; The Scots; Another Street, Another Dance; History of Scotland. Recreations: music; talk.

Hannay of Kirkdale and That Ilk, Ramsay William Rainsford. Retired Landowner, Farmer, Caravan Park Operator; Barrister-at-Law, Inner Temple; b. 15.6.11, India; m., Margaret Wiseman; 1 s.; 1 d. Educ. Winchester College; Trinity College, Cambridge (Hons. degree in Law). Called to the Bar and practised in the Bankruptcy Court; called up for service in the Forces, 1939; commissioned, HLI; served throughout the War in Europe, with a short spell in USA and Canada; demobilised with rank of Major; Legal Assistant, then Assistant Solicitor, Board of Trade, 1946-64; Honorary Sheriff, Stewartry of Kirkcudbright; Member, Queen's Bodyguard for Scotland (Royal Company of Archers); President, Dumfries and Galloway Boy Scouts Association; Chief of the Clan Hannay; former President, Drystane Walling Association of Great Britain. Recreations: sailing; shooting; fishing. Address: (h.) Cardoness, Gatehouse-of-Fleet, Kirkcudbrightshire; T.-01557 840286.

Hanson, William Stewart, BA, PhD, FSA, FSA Scot. Vice-President, Council for British Archaeology, since 1995; Senior Lecturer in Archaeology, Glasgow University, since 1990; b. 22.1.50, Doncaster; m., Lesley Macinnes; 1 d. Educ. Gravesend Grammar School; Manchester University. Lecturer in Archaeology, Glasgow University, 1975; Chairman: Scottish Field School of Archaeology, 1982-89, Scottish Archaeological Link, 1990-96; Member, Executive Committee, Council for British Archaeology, since 1989; President, Council for Scottish Archaeology, 1989-96; Director, large-scale archaeological excavations at several sites in Scotland and northern England, including complete excavation of the Roman Fort at Elginhaugh, Dalkeith; recipient, Glenfiddich Living Scotland Award, 1987. Publications include: Agricola and the conquest of the north; Rome's north-west frontier: the Antonine Wall (Co-Author); Scottish archaeology: new perceptions (Co-Editor); papers and articles. Recreations: tennis; film. Address: (h.) 4 Victoria Road, Stirling FK8 2RH; T.-01786 465506.

Happs, John Henderson, MA (Hons). Head Teacher, Mainholm Academy, Ayr, since 1994; b. 1.9.47, Irvine; m., Jean; 4 s.; 1 d. Educ. Irvine Royal Academy; Glasgow University; Jordanhill College. Teacher of English/Principal Teacher of English, Ravenspark Academy, 1970-80;

Assistant Head Teacher/Depute Head Teacher/Acting Head Teacher, Kilwinning Academy, 1980-94. Recreations: caravanning; music; reading; computing; playing with grand-daughter. Address: (b.) Mainholm Academy, Mainholm Road, Ayr KA8 0QQ; T.-01292 267300.

Hardie of Blackford, Rt. Hon Lord (Andrew Rutherford Hardie), QC (Scot). Lord Advocate, since 1997; b. 8.1.46, Alloa; m., Catherine Storrar Elgin; 2 s.; 1 d. Educ. St. Modan's High School, Stirling; Edinburgh University. Enrolled Solicitor, 1971; Member, Faculty of Advocates, 1973; Advocate Depute, 1979-83; Dean, Faculty of Advocates, 1994-97. Address: (b.) Crown Office, 25 Chambers Street, Edinburgh EH1 1LA.

Hardie, Donald Graeme, KStJ, TD, JP, FIM. Director, Hardie Polymers Ltd., since 1976; Director, Ronaash Ltd., since 1988; Chairman, Scottish Suppliers Forum, since 1996; b. 23.1.36, Glasgow; m., Rosalind Allan Ker (separated); 2 s. Educ. Blairmore and Merchiston Castle. Commissioned 41st Field Regiment RA, 1955; Battery Commander 277 (Argyll & Sutherland Highlanders) Regiment RA (TA), 1966; Commanding Officer GSVOTC, 1973; TA Col. Lowlands, 1976; TA Col. DES, 1980; TA Col. Scotland, 1985; ACF Brigadier Scotland, 1987. UTR Management Trainee, 1956-59; F.W. Allan & Ker, Shipbrokers, 1960-61; J. & G. Hardie & Co. Ltd., 1961-81; Director, Gilbert Plastics Ltd., 1973-76. Lord Lieutenant, Dunbartonshire, since 1990; Hon. Col. 105, Air Defence Regiment RA (V); Hon. Col. Glasgow & Lanarkshire ACF; Chairman, Scottish Gunner Council; Vice President, ACFA Scotland; Keeper, Dumbarton Castle, since 1996. Recreations: skiing; sailing; shooting; fishing. Address: (h.) Dun Ruadh, Gartocharn, Dunbartonshire G83 8SB.

Hardie, Sir Douglas Fleming, CBE, LLD. Chairman, Edward Parker & Co. Ltd., since 1960; Non-Executive Chairman, Drug Development (Scotland), Ltd. (Contract Clinical Research), since 1997; b. 26.5.23, Dundee; m., Dorothy Alice Warner; 2 s.; 1 d. Educ. Trinity College, Glenalmond. Trooper, 58 Training Regt., RAC, 1941; commissioned RMA Sandhurst, 1942, 1 Fife & Forfar Yeomanry Flamethrowing Tank Regt., NW Europe, 1942-46 (Despatches), Major. Director, Dayco Rubber (UK) Ltd., 1956-86; Chairman, CBI Scotland, 1976-78; Director: Clydesdale Bank plc, 1981-92, The Alliance Trust plc, 1982-93, The Second Alliance Trust plc, 1982-93, Alliance Trust (Finance) Ltd., 1982-93, SECDEE Leasing, 1982-93, Alliance Trust (Nominees) Ltd., 1982-93; Chairman, A.G. Scott Textiles, 1985-87; Deputy Chairman, Scottish Development Agency, 1978-91; Chairman, Grampian Television PLC, 1989-93; Member: CBI Grand Council, London, 1976-85, Scottish Economic Council, 1977-91; Councillor, Winston Churchill Memorial Trust, since 1985; Vice Chairman, Prince's Scottish Youth Business Trust, 1987; Past President, Dundee Rotary Club; Vice-President, Fife & Forfar Yeomanry Regimental Association; Deacon Convener, Nine Incorporated Trades of Dundee, 1951-54; Elder, Dundee Parish Church (St. Mary's). Recreations: golf; fishing. Address: (h.) 6 Norwood Terrace, West Park, Dundee DD2 1PB.

Hardie, William Dunbar, MBE, MA, BA, MUniv. Writer and Entertainer; b. 4.1.31, Aberdeen; m., Margaret Elizabeth Simpson; 1 s.; 1 d. Educ. Robert Gordon's College, Aberdeen; Aberdeen University; Sidney Sussex College, Cambridge. Administrative Assistant, then Assistant Secretary, NE Regional Hospital Board; District Administrator, North District, Grampian Health Board; Secretary, Grampian Health Board, 1976-83. Co-Writer and performer, Scotland The What? (comedy revue); Writer, Dod'N'Bunty column, Aberdeen Evening Express. Recreations: reading; TV-watching; film and theatre-going; sport; avid and totally biased follower of Aberdeen's

football team, Scotland's rugby team, and England's cricket team. Address: (h.) 50 Gray Street, Aberdeen AB1 6JE; T.-01224 310591.

Harding, Professor Dennis William, MA, DPhil, FRSE. Abercromby Professor of Archaeology, University of Edinburgh, since 1977; b. 11.4.40. Educ. Keble College, University of Oxford. Assistant Keeper, Department of Antiquities, Ashmolean Museum, University of Oxford, 1965; Lecturer in Celtic Archaeology, University of Durham, 1966 (Senior Lecturer, 1975); Dean, Faculty of Arts, 1983-86, Vice-Principal, 1988-91, University of Edinburgh. Member, S.A.A.S. Studentships Committee, since 1982 (Chairman, since 1997); Trustee, Urras Nan Jursachan, since 1985. Address: (h.) Department of Archaeology, The Old High School, Infirmary Street, Edinburgh EH1 1LT; T.-0131-650 2364.

Hardy, Herbert Charles. Deputy Chairman and Chief Executive, The Scotsman Publications Ltd., since 1996; Chief Executive, The European, since 1995. Managing Director, News International, 1976, Chief Executive, 1977; Chief Executive, Associated Newspapers Ltd., 1989-94; Chairman, Evening Standard Co. Ltd., 1989-94; Director Teletext Holdings, 1995-96; Director, Channel One Television, 1994-95. Recreations: golf; horse racing. Address: (b.) The Scotsman Publications Ltd., 20 North Bridge, Edinburgh, EH1 1YT; T.-0131-225 2468.

Hare, Professor Paul Gregory, BA, BPhil, DPhil. Professor of Economics since 1985, and Head, School of Management, Heriot-Watt University, since 1997; b. 19.3.46, Hull; m., Susan Jennifer Robertson; 1 s.; 2 d. Educ. Malet Lambert High School, Hull; St. John's College, Cambridge; Nuffield College, Oxford. Technical Officer, ICI, 1967-68; Lecturer, Birmingham University, 1971-72; Lecturer, Senior Lecturer, Reader, Stirling University, 1972-85. Member, Lothian Region Children's Panel, 1981-89. Recreations: hill-walking; reading; listening to choral music. Address: (h.) 34 Saughtonhall Drive, Edinburgh EH12 5TN; T.-0131-337 7329.

Hare Duke, Rt. Rev. Michael Geoffrey, BA, MA, DD. Bishop of St. Andrews, Dunkeld and Dunblane, 1969-94 (retired); Chairman, Age Concern Scotland, since 1994; b. 28.11.25, Calcutta; m., Grace Judy Frances Dodd; 1 s.; 3 d. Educ. Bradfield College; Trinity College, Oxford; Westcott House, Cambridge. Sub-Lt., RNVR, 1944-46; Deacon, 1952; Priest, 1953; Curate, 1952-56; Vicar, Bury, 1956-62; Pastoral Director, Clinical Theology Association, 1962-64; Vicar, St. Paul's Daybrook and Officiating Chaplain, E. Midlands District HQ, 1964-69. Chairman, Scottish Association for Mental Health; Member, Anglican Communion Peace and Justice Network, Convener, 1992-94. Publications: The Caring Church (Co-author); First Aid in Counselling (Co-author); Understanding the Adolescent; The Break of Glory; Freud; Good News; Stories Signs and Sacraments of the Emerging Church; Praying for Peace, reflections on the Gulf crisis; Hearing the Stranger. Recreations: walking; writing; broadcasting. Address: (h.) 2 Balhousie Avenue, Perth PH1 5HN; T.-01738 622642.

Hargreave, Timothy Bruce, MB, MS, FRCSEdin, FRCS, FEB (Urol). Consultant Urological Surgeon, Western General Hospital, Edinburgh, since 1978; b. 23.3.44, Lytham; m., Molly; 2 d. Educ. Harrow; University College Hospital, London University. Senior Registrar: Western Infirmary, Glasgow, University College Hospital, London; Medical Officer, Paray Mission Hospital, Lesotho. Publications: Diagnosis and Management of Renal and Urinary Disease; Male Infertility (Editor); Practical Urological Endoscopy; The Management of Male Infertility. Recreation: skiing. Address: (h.) 20 Cumin Place, Edinburgh.

Harkess, Ronald Dobson, OBE, BSc, MS, PhD, NDA, CBiol, MIBiol, FRAgS, FRSA. Agricultural Scientist and Consultant; b. 11.7.33, Edinburgh; m., Jean Cuthbert Drennan; 2 d. Educ. Royal High School, Edinburgh; Edinburgh University; Cornell University. Senior Fison Research Fellow, Nottingham University, 1959-62; Assistant Grassland Adviser, West of Scotland Agricultural College, Ayr, 1962-72; Senior Agronomist, 1972-86; Technical Secretary, Council, Scottish Agricultural Colleges, 1986-90, Company Secretary, 1987-90; Company Secretary, Scottish Agricultural College, 1990-91; Assistant Principal, Scottish Agricultural College, 1991-93. Member, Earn Community Council, since 1997; Chairman, Friends of Perth Festival of the Arts, since 1997; President, Perth Philatelic Society, since 1997. Recreations: amateur radio; philately; gardening. Address: (h.) Friarton Bank, Rhynd Road, Perth PH2 8PT; T.-01738 643435.

Harkness, Very Rev. James, CB, OBE, MA, FRSA, OStJ. Dean of the Chapel Royal in Scotland, since 1996; Moderator, General Assembly of the Church of Scotland, 1995-96; Chaplain to The Queen; b. 20.10.35, Thornhill; m., Elizabeth Anne; 1 s.; 1 d. Educ. Dumfries Academy; Edinburgh University. Assistant Minister, North Morningside Parish Church, 1959-61; Chaplain: KOSB, 1961-65, Queen's Own Highlanders, 1965-69; Singapore, 1969-70; Deputy Warden, RAChD, 1970-74; Senior Chaplain, Northern Ireland, 1974-75; 4th Division, 1975-78; Staff Chaplain, HQ BAOR, 1978-80; Assistant Chaplain, Scotland, 1980-81; Senior Chaplain, 1st British Corps, 1981-82; BAOR, 1982-84; Deputy Chaplain General, 1985-86; Chaplain General to the Forces, 1987-95. QHC, 1982-95; General Trustee, Church of Scotland, since 1996; Member, Committee on Chaplains to HM Forces, since 1997; Member, Board of World Mission, since 1997; President, Army Cadet Force Association Scotland; Hon. Chaplain to BLESMA, Royal British Legion Scotland; Patron, St. Mary's Music School, Edinburgh, Napier University. Recreations: walking; reading; watching sport. Address: (h.) 13 Saxe-Coburg Place, Edinburgh EH3 5BR; T.-0131-343 1297.

Harlen, Professor Wynne, OBE, MA (Oxon), MA (Bristol), PhD, FRSA. Director, Scottish Council for Research in Education, since 1990; Visiting Professor, Liverpool University, since 1990; b. 12.1.37, Swindon; 1 s.; 1 d. Educ. Pate's Grammar School for Girls, Cheltenham; St. Hilda's College, Oxford; Bristol University. Teacher/Lecturer, 1958-66; Research Associate, Bristol University School of Education, 1966-73; Research Fellow, Project Director, Reading University, 1973-77; Research Fellow, Centre for Science Education, King's College, London, 1977-84; Sidney Jones Professor of Science Education, Liverpool University, 1985-90. Chair, Children in Scotland Early Years Forum, 1991-95; Member, Secretary of State's Working Party on the Development of the National Curriculum in Science, 1987-88; President, British Educational Research Association, 1993-94. Publications: 23 books, and contributions to 35 others; 136 papers. Recreations: concerts; opera; hill-walking. Address: (h.) 26 Torphin Road, Colinton, Edinburgh EH13 0HW; T.-0131-441 6130.

Harper, Professor Alexander Murray, MB, ChB, MD (Hons). Emeritus Professor of Surgical Research, and Honorary Senior Research Fellow, Glasgow University, since 1996; Honorary Consultant Clinical Physiologist, Greater Glasgow Health Board, since 1970; b. 31.5.33, Glasgow; m., Charlotte Maria Fossleitner; 2 s., 1 d. Educ. Hutchesons' Grammar School; Glasgow University. House Physician and Surgeon, Southern General Hospital and Glasgow Royal Infirmary, 1957-58; McIntyre Research Scholar in Clinical Surgery, Glasgow Royal Infirmary, 1958-60; Scientific Assistant, Medical Research Council, 1960-63; Wellcome Senior Research Fellow in Clinical Science and Honorary Lecturer in Surgery, Glasgow University, 1963-68; Glasgow University: Senior Lecturer in Surgery and Surgical Physiology, 1968-69, Reader, 1969-81; Professor of Surgical Research, 1981-96. Editor in Chief, Journal of Cerebral Blood Flow and Metabolism, 1981-89; Editor, Cerebrovascular and Brain Metabolism Reviews, 1989-96; David Patey Prize, Surgical Research Society, 1966; H.G. Wolff Award, American Association for Study of Headache, 1968; Gold Medal, British Migraine Association, 1976; Honorary Fellow, American Heart Association (Stroke Council), 1980. Recreations: fishing; contract bridge; gardening. Address: (b.) Wellcome Surgical Institute, Glasgow University, Garscube Estate, Bearsden Road, Glasgow G61 1QH; T.-0141-330 5826.

Harper, Rev. Anne J. McInroy, BD, STM, MTh. Chaplain, Glasgow Royal Infirmary University NHS Trust, since 1990; b. 31.10.49, Glasgow. Educ. Camphill Senior Secondary School, Paisley; Glasgow University; Union Theological Seminary, New York. Graduate Fellow, Union Theological Seminary, and Assistant Minister, 2nd Presbyterian Church, New York City, 1974-75; research, Church history and liturgics, Glasgow University, 1975-78; Assistant Minister, Abronhill Church, Cumbernauld, 1978-79; Christian Education Field Officer, Church of Scotland Department of Education, 1979-84; Minister, Linthouse St. Kenneth's Parish Church, 1984-90. Holder (first woman), The Scots Fellowship awarded by Union Theological Seminary, New York, 1974. Address: The Chaplain's Office, Glasgow Royal Infirmary, Glasgow G4 0SF; T.-0141-211 4000.

Harper, Professor Anthony John, BA, MA, PhD, CertEd. Professor of German Studies, Strathclyde University, since 1979; b. 26.5.38, Bristol; m., Sandra; 1 s.; 2 d. Educ. Clifton College, Bristol; Bristol University; Exeter University. Lecturer, Department of German, Edinburgh University, 1962-79. Publications: German Today (Co-author), 1967; David Schirmer - A Poet of the German Baroque, 1977; Time and Change, Essays on German and European Literature, 1982; Schriften zur Lyrik Leipzigs 1620-1670, 1985; The Song-Books of Gottfried Finckelthaus, 1988 ; Studien zum deutschen weltlichen Lied (Co-author), 1992; The European Emblem (Co-author), 1992; edition of Chr. Brehme; Lustige Gediehte, 1994. Address: (b.) Department of Modern Languages, Strathclyde University, 26 Richmond Street, Glasgow G1 1XQ; T.-0141-552 4400.

Harper, Professor David John, BSc(Hons), PhD, CEng, FBCS. Head, School of Computer and Mathematical Sciences, Robert Gordon University, Aberdeen, since 1993; b. 28.2.52, Melbourne; m., Morna G. Stewart; 1 s. Educ. Blackburn South High School, Victoria, Australia; Monash University; Jesus College, University of Cambridge. Analyst/Programmer, Lincoln Agricultural College, New Zealand; Research Scientist, Commonwealth Scientific and Industrial Research Organisation, Melbourne; Lecturer, Department of Computer Science, University College, Dublin; Lecturer, Department of Computing Science, University of Glasgow. Recreations: shooting; fishing; skiing; sailing; hill-walking. Address: (b.) Robert Gordon University, S.C.M.S., St. Andrew Street, Aberdeen AB25 1HG; T.-01224 262701.

Harper, Rev. David Little, BSc, BD (Hons). Minister, St. Meddan's Church, Troon, since 1979; b. 31.10.47, Moffat; m., Janis Mary Clark; 2 s. Educ. Morton Academy, Thornhill; Dumfries Academy; Edinburgh University. Assistant Minister, Cumbernauld St. Mungo's, 1971-72; first Minister, New Erskine Parish Church, 1972-79. Moderator, Presbytery of Ayr, 1991-92; Member, Scottish Advisory Committee, Independent Broadcasting Authority, 1974-79; Scottish Member, Religious Advisory Panel, IBA, 1978-79. Recreations: golf; hill-walking; swimming. Address: St. Meddan's Manse, 27 Bentinck Drive, Troon, Ayrshire; T.-01292 311784.

Harper, Douglas Ross, BSc, MD, FRCSEdin, FRCSEng, FRCSGlas. Consultant Surgeon, since 1976, Medical Director, since 1994, Falkirk and District Royal Infirmary NHS Trust; Examiner: Royal College of Surgeons of Edinburgh, since 1979, Royal College of Surgeons of Glasgow, since 1987; Honorary Senior Lecturer, Department of Clinical Surgery, Edinburgh University, since 1976; b. 16.2.40, Aberdeen; m., Dorothy Constance Wisely; 1 s.; 3 d. Educ. Aberdeen Grammar School; Aberdeen University. House Officer, Registrar and Fellow in Vascular Surgery, Aberdeen Royal Infirmary, 1967-73; Senior Registrar, Edinburgh Royal Infirmary, 1973-76. Elder, Bridge of Allan Chalmers Church of Scotland. Recreations: hill-walking; geology; woodwork. Address: (h.) Glenallan, 16 Upper Glen Road, Bridge of Allan, Stirlingshire FK9 4PX; T.-01786 832242.

Harper, Edward James, MA, BMus, ARCM, LRAM. Composer, since 1957; Reader in Music, Edinburgh University, since 1990; Director, New Music Group of Scotland, 1973-91; b. 17.3.41, Taunton; m., Dorothy Caroline Shanks. Educ. King Edward VI School, Guildford; Royal College of Music, London; Christ Church, Oxford. Main works as a Composer: Piano Concerto, 1971; Bartok Games, 1972; Ricercari in Memoriam Luigi Dallapiccola, 1975; Fanny Robin (chamber opera), Chester Mass, 1979; Clarinet Concerto, 1981; Hedda Gabler (opera, commissioned for Scottish Opera), 1985; Fantasia V (for chamber orchestra), 1985; The Mellstock Quire (chamber opera), 1987; Homage to Thomas Hardy (baritone and orchestra), 1990; The Fiddler of the Reels (str. orch.), 1993; And Winds Austere and Pure (choir and piano duet), 1993; Psalm 150 (unacc. choir), 1996; Trio (cl., cello, piano), 1997. Address: (h.) 7 Morningside Park, Edinburgh EH10 5HD; T.-0131-447 5366.

Harper, George, MA, DipTP, MRTPI. Director of Planning, Economic Development and Tourism, Argyll and Bute Council, since 1976; b. 21.3.51, Perth; m., Katherine; 1 s.; 1 d. Educ. Perth Academy; Aberdeen University; Heriot-Watt University (Diploma, Town and Country Planning). Planner, Dundee Corporation, 1972-75; Planner/Senior Planner, Tayside Regional Council, 1975-88; Depute Director of Planning, Argyll and Bute District Council, 1988-90; Director of Planning, Development and Tourism, Argyll and Bute District Council, 1990-96. Director, Strathclyde Building Preservation Trust. Recreations: hill-walking; football; golf; gardening; family. Address: (b.) Kilmory Castle, Lochgilphead, Argyll; T.-01546 604225.

Harper, John Ross, CBE, MA, LLB. Senior Partner, Ross Harper & Murphy and Harper Macleod, Solicitors, since 1962; b. 20.3.35, Glasgow; m., Ursula; 2 s.; 1 d. Educ. Hutchesons' Boys' Grammar School; Glasgow University. Parliamentary Commissioner; Professor of Law, Strathclyde University; Past President: Law Society of Scotland, Scottish Conservative & Unionist Association, International Bar Association; former Chairman, Society of Scottish Conservative Lawyers; former Parliamentary candidate (Conservative), Hamilton and West Renfrewshire; Deputy Chairman: Mining (Scotland) Ltd., Scottish Coal Company; Member, Board of Trustees, National Galleries of Scotland; Trustee, Strathclyde Foundation Board. Publications: Glasgow Rape Case; My Client My Lord; A Practitioner's Guide to the Criminal Courts; Fingertip Criminal Law; Rates Revaluation; Devolution; New Unionism; Scotland '97; Referendums are Dangerous. Recreations: angling; bridge. Address: (b.) The Ca'd'oro, 45 Gordon Street, Glasgow, G1 3PE; T.-0141-221 8888; (h.) 23 Clabon Mews, Cadogan Square, London SW1X 0EG.

Harris, Rev. John William Forsyth, MA. Minister, Bearsden South Church, since 1987; b. 10.3.42, Hampshire; m., Ellen Lesley Kirkpatrick Lamont; 1 s.; 2 d. Educ. Merchant Taylors' School, London; St. Andrews University; New College, Edinburgh. Ordained Assistant, St. Mary's Church, Haddington, 1967-70; Minister: St. Andrew's Church, Irvine, 1970-77, St. Mary's Church, Motherwell, 1977-87. Convener: Scottish Churches' Christian Aid Committee, 1986-90, Scottish Christian Aid Committee, since 1990, Scottish Television's Religious Advisory Committee, since 1990; Member: Board, Christian Aid, since 1990, Executive, Church and Nation Committee, 1985-91, Executive, Scottish Churches' Council, 1986-90; Vice-Convener, Board of World Mission, since 1996; Moderator, Dumbarton Presbytery, 1994-95. Fencing Blue, St. Andrews and Edinburgh; Scottish Fencing Team, 1963-66. Recreations: holiday home in Kintyre; Cruban walking. Address: 61 Drymen Road, Bearsden, Glasgow G61 2SU; T.-0141-942 0507.

Harris, Marshall James, DPA. Director, Scottish Educational Trust for United Nations and International Affairs, since 1986; b. 14.3.28, Edinburgh; m., Matilda Currie Main; 2 s.; 1 d. Educ. Armadale Secondary; Glasgow University. Accountancy, pre-1958; Scottish National Officer, UN Association, 1958-86; Secretary, Scottish Standing Committee for Voluntary International Aid. Former Liberal and Alliance candidate. Recreations: reading; member of Rotary, Liberal International and Royal Institute of International Affairs. Address: (h.) Hopetoun, Charlotte Street, Brightons, Falkirk; T.-01324 715203.

Harris, Paul Anthony, MA(Hons). Writer, since 1967; b. 22.7.48, Dartford. Educ. Bradford Grammar School; Elgin Academy; University of Aberdeen. Pirate Radio, 1966-71; Publisher, 1967-85; Publishing Consultant, 1985-97; Journalist (Foreign Correspondent), 1990-97. Lecturer, Cunard World University Programme; British Press Award (Bosnia), 1992. Publications: 28 books including: When Pirates Ruled the Waves, 1968, The Garvie Trial, 1969, Dictionary of Scottish Painters, 1990, Somebody Else's War, 1992, Cry Bosnia, 1995. Recreations: photography; travel. Address: (h.) Whittingehame House, Haddington EH41 4QA; T.-01368 850369.

Harrison, Albert, MA, BA, ALA, MIInfSc. Librarian, Strathclyde University, since 1982; b. 19.7.34, Lancaster; m., Margaret. Educ. Storey's Institute, Lancaster; University of Cape Town. Librarian: University of Zimbabwe, 1967-78; St. Patrick's College, Maynooth, 1980-82. Recreations: tennis; sailing. Address: (b.) University Library, Strathclyde University, Glasgow G4 0NS; T.-0141-552 3701.

Harrison, Professor Bryan Desmond, CBE, BSc, PhD, FRS, FRSE, Hon. DAgric. Emeritus Professor of Plant Virology, Dundee University, since 1997 (Professor of Plant Virology, 1991-96); b. 16.6.31, Purley, Surrey; m., Elizabeth Ann Latham-Warde; 2 s.; 1 d. Educ. Whitgift School, Croydon; Reading University. Agricultural Research Council Postgraduate Research Student, 1952-54; Scientific Officer, Scottish Horticultural Research Institute, 1954-57; Senior and Principal Scientific Officer, Rothamsted Experimental Station, 1957-66; Scottish Horticultural Research Institute/Scottish Crop Research Institute: Principal Scientific Officer, 1966, Senior Principal Scientific Officer (Individual Merit), 1969, Deputy Chief Scientific Officer (Individual Merit), 1981; Head, Virology Department, 1966-91; Honorary Professor, Department of Biochemistry and Microbiology, St. Andrews University, 1987; Honorary Visiting Professor, Dundee University, 1987-91; Past President, Association of Applied Biologists. Recreation: gardening. Address: (b.) Scottish Crop Research Institute, Invergowrie, Dundee DD2 5DA.

Harrison, Cameron, BSc (Hons), MEd. Chief Executive, Scottish Consultative Council on the Curriculum, since 1991; b. 27.8.45, Mauchline, Ayrshire; m., Pearl; 1 s.; 1 d. Educ. Cumnock Academy; Strathclyde University; Glasgow University; Stirling University. Teacher, Greenock

Academy, 1968-71; Principal Teacher of Physics, Graeme High School, Falkirk, 1971-79; Depute Rector, Kirkcudbright Academy, 1979-82; Rector, The Gordon Schools, Huntly, 1982-91; Member: SEB, several research advisory committees; CCC Sub-Committees (Member, JWP on Higher Physics, 1976-79); General Secretary, CIDREE. Recreations: lay preacher; used to play rugby (still pretends to!); music. Address: (b.) Gardyne Road, Broughty Ferry, Dundee DD5 1NY.

Harrison, Professor Robert Graham, BSc (Hons), PhD, FRSE. Professor of Physics, Heriot-Watt University, since 1987; b. 26.2.44 Oxford; m., Rowena Indrania; 1 s.; 1 d. Educ. Wanstead High School; London University. Postgraduate and postdoctoral research, Royal Holloway College, London, and Culham Laboratories, UKAEA, 1966-72; Lecturer, Bath University; joined Physics Department, Heriot-Watt University. Publications: 200 scientific publications, including editorship of five books. Address: (b.) Physics Department, Heriot-Watt University, Riccarton, Currie, Edinburgh EH14 4AS; T.-0131-449 5111.

Harrison, Sydney, OBE. Proprietor, Paisley and Renfrewshire Gazette Group, 1963-87; Chairman, James Paton Ltd., Printers, 1970-87; Editor, Scot, 1981-87; b. 13.4.13, Glasgow; m., Joan Morris. Educ. Whitehill School, Glasgow. Journalist, various newspapers, 1927-37; Sub-Editor, Glasgow Herald, 1938-39; Army, 1939-46 (Lt.-Col., 1944); Editor, Scottish Field, 1946-63; Director, Scottish Counties Newspapers, 1950-63; Councillor, 4th District, Renfrewshire, 1956-67; Member, Council of Industrial Design, Board of Trade, 1955-65; Honorary Member, Scottish PEN; Past President: Paisley Burns Club, Rotary Club of Paisley. Recreations: curling; motoring; caravanning; travel. Address: (h.) 17 Stanley Drive, Brookfield, Renfrewshire PA5 8UG; T.-01505 320634.

Hart, Maidie (Jenny Marianne), MA (Hons); b. 15.12.16, Brookfield, Renfrewshire; m., William Douglas Hart; 2 d. Educ. St. Columba's School for Girls, Kilmacolm; St. Andrews University. Church of Scotland: Vice Convener, Home Board, 1967-70, National Vice-President, Woman's Guild, 1967-70, National President, Woman's Guild, 1972-75, Elder, since 1974; Executive Member, Women's National Commission, 1974-76; Member, Coordinating Committee, UK International Woman's Year, 1974-76 (Chairwoman, Scottish Steering Committee); first Chairwoman, Scottish Convention of Women, 1977; Vice President, British Council of Churches, 1978-81; Church of Scotland Delegate to World Council of Churches, 5th Assembly, 1975, WCC European Conference, 1978, WCC Human Rights and Mission Women's Conference, 1980, WCC Sheffield International Conference, 1981. Recreations: travel; walking; family; reading; garden; cooking. Address: (h.) Westerlea, Chapelhill, Dirleton, East Lothian, EH39 5HG; T.-01620 850278.

Hart, Morag Mary, JP, DL, RGN, RSCN. Deputy Lieutenant, Dunbartonshire, since 1989; Director, Scotsell Ltd., since 1982; b. 19.4.39, Glasgow; m., Tom Hart; 1 s.; 1 d. Educ. Westbourne School for Girls, Glasgow. Sick Children's Hospital, Glasgow, 1956-59; Western General Hospital, Edinburgh, 1960-62. County Commissioner, Dunbartonshire Girl Guides, 1982-90; Chairman, Dunbartonshire Area Scouts, since 1994; Member, The Guide Association Council for Scotland, since 1996. Recreations: reading; gardening; walking. Address: (h.) 18 Campbell Drive, Bearsden, Glasgow G61 4NE; T.-0141-942 1216.

Hart, Professor Robert Albert, BA (Hons), MA. Professor of Economics, Stirling University, since 1986; b. 7.1.46, Hartlepool; m., Shirley; 3 d. Educ. Hartlepool Grammar School; Liverpool University. Economics Lecturer, Aberdeen University, 1969-73, Leeds University,

1974-75; Senior Lecturer, Strathclyde University, 1976-80; Senior Research Fellow, Science Centre, Berlin, 1980-86; Head, School of Management, Stirling University, 1991-94. Recreations: walking; reading; drinking beer. Address: (b.) Department of Economics, Stirling University, Stirling FK9 4LA; T.-01786 467471.

Hart, Professor Susan Jane Ritchie, BA (Hons), PhD, DipMRS. Professor of Marketing, University of Stirling, Edinburgh, since 1995; b. 18.7.60, Edinburgh. Educ. Bearsden Academy; Strathclyde University. Universite de Technologie de Compiegne, 1982-83; Procter and Gamble PLC, 1983-84; Research Assistant/Lecturer/Senior Lecturer, Department of Marketing, Strathclyde University, 1984-93; Professor of Marketing, Heriot-Watt University, 1993-95. Publications: Marketing and Competitive Success (Co-Author); New Product Development, 1996; papers. Recreations: hill-walking; skiing. Address: (b.) Department of Marketing, University of Stirling, Stirling FK9 4LA; T.-01786 467387.

Hart, Thomas, MA, LLB. Chairman, Scottish Transport Studies Group, since 1994; Vice President, Scottish Association for Public Transport, since 1976; Lecturer, Department of Economic and Social History, Glasgow University, since 1965; b. 15.11.39, Kilmarnock; m., Ellen Elizabeth Jones; 2 s. Educ. Spiers School, Beith; Glasgow University. Consultant on transport and environmental issues, since 1990; Founder Member and Secretary, Scottish Transport Studies Group; Founder Member, Scottish Railway Preservation Association (Secretary, 1962-67, Vice Chairman, 1967-72); Chairman, Scottish Association for Public Transport, 1972-76; Member, Board, TRANSform Scotland, since 1997. Recreations: walking; travel; gardening. Address: (h.) Birchfield, Kings Road, Beith, Ayrshire KA15 2BN; T.-01505 502164.

Harte, Professor Ben, BA, MA, PhD(Cantab), FRSE. Professor of Metamorphism, Edinburgh University, since 1991; b. 30.5.41, Blackpool; m., Angela Elizabeth; 1 s.; 2 d. Educ. Salford Grammar School; Trinity College, Cambridge University. Lecturer/Reader, Edinburgh University, 1965-91; Guest Research Investigator, Carnegie Institution of Washington, 1974-75; Visiting Associate Professor, Yale University, 1982; Visiting Research Fellow, University of Cape Town, 1990. Address: (b.) Department of Geology and Geophysics, King's Buildings, Edinburgh EH9 3JW; T.-0131-650 8528.

Hartley, Clive, BA, DipTP, MRTPI. Chief Executive, Dumfries and Galloway Tourist Board, since 1996; b. 20.4.47; m, Joyce Walker. Educ. Nelson Secondary Technical School; Hull University; Central London Polytechnic. Assistant Research Officer, Countryside Commission for England and Wales; Research Officer, Department of the Environment; Principal Planning Officer, Dumfries and Galloway Regional Council; Depute Director of Economic Development, Dumfries and Galloway Regional Council; Director of Tourism, Dumfries and Galloway Tourist Board. Past President: Galloway Mountaineering Club, Dumfries and Galloway Architectural and Engineering Society. Recreations: hill-walking; gardening; natural history; photography. Address: (b.) Campbell House, Bankend Road, Dumfries DG1 4TH; T.-01387 250434.

Hartley, Graeme Edward, BA. Deputy Director, Royal Institution of Chartered Surveyors in Scotland, since 1990; Secretary, Scottish Construction Industry Group, since 1996; b. 9.4.61, Edinburgh; m., Lee Adams Rankine; 1 s. Educ. Perth High School; Napier University. Dundee Chamber of Commerce, 1983-85; Electrical Contractors' Association of Scotland, 1985-90. Member, Scottish Building Contract Committee, since 1986. Recreations: golf; running; X-C skiing. Address: (b.) 9 Manor Place, Edinburgh EH3 7DN; T.-0131-225 7078.

Hartley, Keith Scott, BA, MA. Assistant Keeper, Scottish National Gallery of Modern Art, since 1979; b. 27.1.49, Evesham. Educ. Prince Henry's Grammar School, Evesham; St. Catherine's College, University of Oxford; Courtauld Institute; University of London; Freie Universität, Berlin. Curator of numerous exhibitions, and author of corresponding catalogues, including: Scottish Art Since 1900, 1989, Otto Dix, Tate Gallery, 1992, The Romantic Spirit in German Art 1790-1990, 1994. A Director, Art in Partnership (Scotland). Recreations: travel; reading. Address: (b.) Scottish National Gallery of Modern Art, Belford Road, Edinburgh EH4 3DR; T.-0131-624 6328.

Hartnett, Frank Ernest Lawrence, OBE, BSc (Econ), CertEd, DipEdTech. General Manager, Grampian Health Board, since 1991; b. 3.9.40, Alton; m., 1, Catherine Mary Adams (deceased); 2, Louisa MacAllan; 1 s.; 1 d. Educ. Lord Wandsworth College; London University; Southampton University; Sussex University. Head, Economics Department, Cheshunt Grammar School; commissioned RAF, 1965; lead role in achieving organisational change in RAF training, 1972-75; involved in fast jet operations, RAF Germany, 1975-78; introduction of Tornado into RAF, 1978-81; OFFR and aircrew selection, 1982; OC Trg WG, RAF Hereford, 1982-85; OC Admin WG, RAF Cosford, 1985-87; Grampian Health Board: General Manager, Maternity and Child Health, 1987-89, General Manager, Mental Health, 1989-91. Recreations: hill-walking; shooting; badminton. Address: (b.) Summerfield House, 2 Eday Road, Aberdeen AB15 6RE; T.-01224 404000.

Hartnoll, Mary C., CBE, Hon. LLD, BA (Hons). Director of Social Work, Glasgow City Council, since 1996; b. 31.5.39, Bristol. Educ. Colston's Girls School, Bristol; Bedford College, London University; Liverpool University. Child Care Officer, Dorset County Council, 1961-63; various posts, Reading County Borough, 1963-74; Berkshire County Council: Assistant Director, 1974-75, Divisional Director, 1975-77; Director of Social Work, Grampian Regional Council, 1978-93; Director of Social Work, Strathclyde Regional Council, 1993-96. Recreations: natural history; walking. Address: (b.) Strathclyde House, 20 India Street, Glasgow G2 4PF.

Harvey, Professor Alan L., BSc, PhD, MBA, CBiol, FIBiol. Director, Strathclyde Institute for Drug Research, since 1988; Professor in Physiology and Pharmacology, Strathclyde University, since 1986; b. 23.6.50, Glasgow. Educ. Hutchesons', Glasgow; Strathclyde University. Lecturer in Physiology and Pharmacology, Strathclyde University, 1974-83; Senior Lecturer, 1983-86. British Pharmacological Society Sandoz Prize, 1983; British Pharmaceutical Conference Science Award, 1983. Publications: Toxicon (Editor); Snake Toxins, 1991. Address: (b.) Department of Physiology and Pharmacology, Strathclyde University, Glasgow, G1 1XW; T.-0141-553 4155.

Harvey, Alexander, BSc(Hons), DipEd. Headteacher, All Saints Secondary School, Glasgow, since 1982; b. 19.5.41, Glasgow; m., Phyllis; 3 s.; 1 d. Educ. St. Augustine's Secondary, Glasgow; University of Glasgow; Jordanhill College. St. Augustine's Secondary School, Glasgow: Teacher of Science, 1963-65, Principal Teacher of Physics, 1965-73; Assistant Headteacher, St. Andrews, Glasgow, 1973-79; Depute Headteacher, Turnbull High School, Bishopbriggs, 1979-82. Address: (b.) All Saints Secondary School, 21 Scotsburn Road, Glasgow G21 3HX; T.-0141-558 1241.

Harvey, Jake, DA, RSA. Sculptor and Lecturer; Acting Head of Sculpture, Edinburgh College of Art; b. 3.6.48, Kelso; m., Anne Penelope; 1 s.; 2 d. Educ. Kelso High School; Edinburgh College of Art. Latimer Award, RSA, 1975; Benno Schotz Sculpture Prize, RSA, 1976; Macaulay Prize, RSA, 1996; ARSA, 1977; Hugh MacDiarmid Memorial Sculpture, 1982-85; William Gillies Bursary, 1989; RSA, 1989; has shown in many solo and group exhibitions; major retrospective exhibition, Talbot Rice Gallery, 1993; commissions include: Hugh MacDiarmid Memorial Sculpture, 1982, Charles Mackintosh Sculpture, Glasgow, 1985, Newcraighall Mining Sculpture, 1987, Poacher's Tree, 1991, Motherwell Heritage Centre Sculpture, 1996, Sculpture for Hunterian Museum, Glasgow, 1996. Recreations: fishing; walking. Address: (h.) Maxton Cross, Maxton, St. Boswells, Roxburghshire; T.-01835 822650.

Harvey, Rev. William John, BA (Hons), BD (Hons). Staff Member, Craighead Institute, Glasgow; Minister, Church of Scotland, since 1964; Leader, The Iona Community, 1988-95; b. 17.5.37, Glasgow; m., Isabel Mary Douglas; 2 s.; 2 d. Educ. Fettes College, Edinburgh; Oxford University; Glasgow University. National Service, Argyll & Sutherland Highlanders, 1956-58; Ordained Assistant, Govan Old Parish Church, 1964-66; Member, Gorbals Group Ministry, 1963-71; Minister, Laurieston-Renwick Parish Church, Glasgow, 1968-71; Warden, Iona Abbey, 1971-76; Minister: Raploch Parish Church, Stirling, 1976-81, Govan Old Parish Church, 1981-88. Member, Church of Scotland Committee on Church and Nation, 1978-86; Kerr Lecturer, Glasgow University, 1987. Recreations: reading; history; bread and wine-making; sea-bird watching. Address: (h.) 501 Shields Road, Glasgow G41 2RF; T.-0141-429 3774.

Harvey-Jamieson, Lt.-Col. Harvey Morro, OBE, TD, DL, WS; b. 9.12.08, Edinburgh; m., Frances Ridout; 3 s. Educ. Edinburgh Academy; RMC, Sandhurst; Edinburgh University (BL). 2nd Lt., 1st Bn., King's Own Scottish Borderers, 1928; Captain, 1938; Major, RA TA, 1939; Lt. Col., 1943; CO 3rd Edinburgh Home Guard Bn. Royal Scots, 1954-57; Member, Royal Company of Archers (Queen's Bodyguard for Scotland), since 1934; served Belgium, Holland and Germany, 1944-45; Secretary and Legal Adviser, The Company of Merchants of City of Edinburgh, 1946-71; Member, Committee on Conveyancing Legislation, 1964-66; Chairman, Scottish Committee HMC Association of Governing Bodies of Boys and Girls Public Schools, 1956-70; Member, Council, Cockburn Association, 1957-78; Deputy Lieutenant, Edinburgh, since 1968. Recreation: travel. Address: (h.) 20 Dean Terrace, Edinburgh; T.-0131-332 4589.

Haslett, Professor Christopher, BSc (Hons), MBChB (Hons), FRCP Edin, FRCP Lond. Professor of Respiratory Medicine, Edinburgh University, and Director, The Rayne Laboratories, since 1990; Honorary Consultant Physician, Lothian Health Board, since 1990; Chairman, Department of Medicine, Royal Infirmary, since 1995; Visiting Professor, Department of Medicine, Royal Postgraduate Medical School, since 1990; b. 2.4.53, Chester; m., Jean Margaret; 1 s.; 1 d. Educ. Wirral Grammar School; Edinburgh University Medical School. House Physician, Department of Medicine, Royal Infirmary, Edinburgh, 1977-87; Rotating Medical Registrar, Ealing Hospital and Hammersmith Hospital, London, 1980-82; MRC Travelling Fellow, National Jewish Hospital, Denver, Colorado, 1982-85; MRC Senior Clinical Fellow and Senior Lecturer, Department of Medicine, Royal Postgraduate Medical School, Hammersmith Hospital, London, 1986-90. Vice-Chairman, National Asthma Campaign Research Committee; Member, MRC Molecular and Cellular Medicine Board; Member and Vice Chairman, MRC Systems "A" Grants Committee; Secretary, Lung Injury Section, European Respiratory Society. Recreation: rugby union. Address: (b.) Respiratory Medicine Unit, Department of Medicine, Royal Infirmary, Edinburgh EH3 9YW; T.-0131-229 2477.

Hastings, Gavin, OBE, DUniv (Paisley). Former rugby player; b. 1962, Edinburgh. Educ. George Watson's

College, Edinburgh; Paisley University; Cambridge University. 61 Scotland Caps, 1986-95 (20 as Captain); 3 World Cups, 1987, 1991, 1995; 2 British Lions Tours: 1989, Australia, 3 Tests, 1993, New Zealand (Captain), 3 Tests; Marketing Consultant, Hastings International.

Hastings, Professor Gerard Bernard, BSc, PhD. Director, Centre for Social Marketing, Department of Marketing, Strathclyde University, since 1987; Head, Department of Marketing; Member, Board, SACRO; b. 5.10.54, Ilkley; 3 s. Educ. St. Michael's College, Leeds; Newcastle upon Tyne Polytechnic; Strathclyde University. Recreations: hill-walking; travel; books. Address: (b.) Department of Marketing, Strathclyde University, 173 Cathedral Street, Glasgow G4 0RQ; T.-0141-552 4400.

Hathorn, (Alexander) Michael, CA, CPFA. Managing Partner, Scott-Moncrieff Downie Wilson, since 1990; Chairman, Moore Stephens (UK), Ltd., since 1991; b. 5.6.48, Peterborough; m., Deborah Christian; 2 s.; 1 d. Educ. Stranraer High School; Sedbergh. Joined Scott-Moncrieff Thomson-Shiells, CA (later Scott-Moncrieff Downie Wilson), 1967: qualified 1972, Partner, 1974. Financial Advisor, Edinburgh International Festival; Trustee and Treasurer, Age Concern Scotland. Recreations: art; music. Address: (b.) 17 Melville Street, Edinburgh EH3 7PH; T.-0131-473 3500.

Hatton, Wai-yin. General Manager, Ayrshire and Arran Health Board. Address: Boswell House, 10 Arthur Street, Ayr KA7 1QJ.

Hatwell, Anthony, DFA(Lond). Sculptor; Head, School of Sculpture, Edinburgh College of Art, 1969-90; b. 21.6.31, London; m., Elizabeth; 2 d. Educ. Dartford Grammar School; Slade School of Fine Art; Borough Polytechnic; Bromley College of Art. Some exhibitions: Scottish Arts Council Edinburgh Festival Exhibition, 1978; British Sculpture in the 20th Century, Whitechapel Gallery, 1981; Built in Scotland exhibition in Edinburgh, Glasgow, and London, 1983; Slade Postgraduate Scholarship, 1956; Boise Travelling Scholarship, 1957; Assistant to Henry Moore, 1958; Member, London Group, 1959-69 (Vice-President, 1961-63); works in collections of Scottish National Gallery of Modern Art, Arts Council of GB, Scottish Arts Council and private collections. Address: (h.) 4 North Street, Belhaven, Dunbar, East Lothian.

Haughan, Barbara, LLB. Director of Support Services, East Ayrshire Council, since 1995; b. 27.8.51, Glasgow; m., Alistair. Educ. Hamilton Academy; University of Glasgow. Legal Apprentice, Sutherland County Council, 1972-74; Legal Apprentice and Legal Assistant, Ayr Burgh, 1974-75; Kyle and Carrick District Council: Legal Assistant and Senior Legal Assistant, 1975-79, Assistant Director of Administration, 1979-90, Assistant Chief Executive, 1990-95. Address: (b.) East Ayrshire Council, Council Headquarters, London Road, Kilmarnock KA3 7BU; T.-01563 576061.

Havenga, Frances. Chairman, Tayside Health Board. Address: (b.) Gateway House, Luna Place, Technology Park, Dundee DD2 1TP.

Havergal, Giles Pollock, OBE, MA, DLitt (Glasgow, Strathclyde), FRSE, FRSAMD. Director, Citizens Theatre, Glasgow, since 1969; b. 9.6.38, Edinburgh. Educ. Harrow; University of Oxford. Director, Palace Theatre, Watford, 1964-69. Awarded St. Mungo Prize, Glasgow, 1995. Address: (b.) Citizens Theatre, Gorbals, Glasgow G5 9DS; T.-0141-429 5561.

Hawkins, Anthony Donald, BSc, PhD, FSA Scot, FRSE. Director of Fisheries Research for Scotland, since 1987; Honorary Professor, Aberdeen University; b. 25.3.42, Dorset; m., Susan Mary; 1 s. Educ. Poole Grammar School;

Bristol University. Entered Scottish Office as Scientific Officer, Marine Laboratory, Aberdeen, 1965; Senior Scientific Officer, 1969, Principal Scientific Officer, 1972, Senior Principal Scientific Officer, 1978, Deputy Chief Scientific Officer, 1983; Deputy Director of Fisheries Research for Scotland, 1983; conducts research into behaviour and physiology of fish; awarded A.B. Wood Medal, Institute of Acoustics, 1978; Chairman, The Green Wedge. Publications: books on fish physiology and aquarium systems. Recreations: reading; angling; soccer; breeding whippets. Address: (b.) Marine Laboratory, PO Box 101, Victoria Road, Torry, Aberdeen; T.-01224 876544.

Hay, Francis (Frank) Walker Christie, OBE, DL, MA (Hons). Deputy Lieutenant, Banffshire, since 1988; Honorary Sheriff, Banff, since 1992; Member, Committee of Management, Cairn Housing Association Ltd.; Vice-President, Aberdeen, Banff and Kincardine Area, Royal British Legion Scotland; b. 20.3.23, Aberdeen; m., Margaret Anne Castel; 2 s.; 1 d. Educ. Robert Gordon's College, Aberdeen; Aberdeen University. Commissioned into Reconnaissance Corps, 1943; gazetted Captain, 1947; Teacher of History, 1950-58; Special Assistant, Turriff Academy, 1958-63; Principal Teacher of History, Breadalbane Academy, Banff Academy, 1963-74; Assistant Rector, Banff Academy, 1974-88; Member, Banffshire Education Committee, 1961-75. Recreations: furniture making; Banff Choral Society. Address: (h.) 11 Fife Street, Banff AB45 1JB; T.-01261 812285.

Hay, Ian, FCIBS, FRSA, FSAE. Chief Executive, Scottish Association of Master Bakers, since 1989; b. 31.8.39, Aberdeen; m., Amelia Robertson; 3 s.; 1 d. Educ. Ellon Academy. Thirty years with Clydesdale Bank PLC, including senior positions as General Manager London and Regional Director with responsibilities for East of Scotland; appointed Chief Executive, Craft Bakery Training Organisation, 1993; Chairman, Scottish Council of National Training Organisations; Member: Board of Management, Scottish Qualifications Authority, Board, NTO National Council, Industrial Tribunal Panel. Recreations: golf; football; reading; complementary medicine. Address: (b.) 4 Torphichen Street, Edinburgh EH3 8JQ; T.-0131-229 1401.

Hay, J. Iain, FRICS, IRRV. J. Iain Hay, Chartered Surveyors, since 1992; Director, KDCL Ltd., since 1992; b. 17.7.44, Ayr; m., Elizabeth; 2 d. Educ. Kelvinside Academy. Thomas Binnie & Hendry, Chartered Surveyors, 1962-66; Dunbarton County Assessors Office, 1966-69; Bovis Homes, 1969-70; Senior Surveyor, Millar Macrae and Stewart, 1970-72, Partner, 1972-86; Partner, Knight Frank & Rutley, 1986-91 (Consultant, 1991-93); Director, Montrose Estates (1982) Ltd., 1986-93; Chairman, Royal Institution of Chartered Surveyors in Scotland, 1993-94; Past President, Property Agents International. Recreations: golf; gardening. Address: (h.) Castle House, Drymen, Glasgow; T.-01360 660550.

Hay, James Taylor Cantlay, MBE, BSc (Hons), DTech, FInstPet, AAPG. Oil and Gas Consultant; Chairman: Scottish Sub-sea Technology Group, since 1991, Grampian Enterprise Training Services, since 1992; b. 13.6.35, Huntly; m., Mary Gordon Davidson; 1 s.; 2 d. Educ. Banchory Academy; Aberdeen University. Geologist, Iraq Petroleum Co. Ltd., Iraq, 1958-66; Head of Geology, Abu Dhabi Petroleum Co. Ltd., Abu Dhabi, 1967-71; Lecturer in Geology, Aberdeen University, 1971-74; Senior Production Geologist, Burmah Oil, London, 1974-76; various management roles, BNOC, Aberdeen and Glasgow, 1977-80; General Manager: BNOC/Britoil, Aberdeen, 1980-87, BP Exploration, Aberdeen, 1988-91. Recreations: golf; shooting. Address: (h.) 67 Fountainhall Road, Aberdeen; T.-01224 645955.

Hay, John McWhirter. Sheriff Clerk, Kirkcaldy, since 1993; b. 27.4.43, Glasgow; m., Mary Wilkie Munro; 3 d. Educ. Clydebank High School. Clerical Officer: Glasgow Sheriff Court, 1960-63, Dumbarton Sheriff Court, 1963-65; Second Class Depute, Glasgow Sheriff Court, 1965-71; First Class Depute, Ayr Sheriff Court, 1971-80; Sheriff Clerk, Dunfermline, 1980-88; Project Sponsor, Scottish Courts Administration, 1988-93. Captain: Troon St. Meddans Golf Club, 1975, Dunfermline Golf Club, 1989-91. Recreations: versatile sportsman, first love golf (single figure handicap, since 1972). Address: (b.) Sheriff Clerk's Office, Whytescauseway, Kirkcaldy; T.-01592 260171.

Hay, Michael James, BSc (Hons), DipEd. Head Teacher, Tynecastle High School, since 1987; b. 8.3.47, Newport Pagnell; m., Rosalind Margaret Gibling; 1 s.; 1 d. Educ. Perth Academy; Edinburgh University. Teacher of Mathematics, Royal High School, 1968-71; Principal Teacher of Mathematics: John Watson's School, 1971-73, Leith Academy, 1973-79; Assistant Head Teacher, Penicuik High School, 1979-83; Depute Head Teacher, Tynecastle High School, 1983-87. Recreations: music (organist and choirmaster); hill-walking; recreational computing. Address: (b.) Tynecastle High School, McLeod Street, Edinburgh EH11 2NJ; T.-0131-337 3488.

Hay, Sheriff Principal Robert Colquhoun, CBE, MA, LLB, WS. Sheriff Principal of North Strathclyde, since 1989; b. 22.9.33, Glasgow; m., Olive Black; 2 s.; 2 d. Educ. Edinburgh University. Legal practice, 1956-63, 1968-76; Depute Procurator Fiscal, 1963-68; Chairman, Industrial Tribunals (Scotland), 1976-81, President, 1981-89; Commissioner of Northern Lights, since 1989, Chairman, 1992-93; Member, Sheriff Court Rules Council, 1990-95, Chairman, 1993-95; Commissioner for Clan Hay, since 1995. Address: (b.) Sheriff Principal's Chambers, Sheriff Court House, St. James Street, Paisley PA3 2HW; T.-0141-887 5291.

Hay, Robert King Miller, BSc, MSc, PhD, FIBiol. Director, Scottish Agricultural Science Agency, since 1990; b. 19.8.46, Edinburgh; m., Dorothea Harden Vinycomb; 2 s.; 1 d. Educ. Forres Academy, Moray; Aberdeen University; University of East Anglia. AFRC Research Fellow, Edinburgh University, 1971-74; Lecturer in Crop Production: University of Malawi, 1974-76, Edinburgh University, 1976-77; Lecturer in Environmental Sciences, Lancaster University, 1977-82; Leverhulme European Fellow, Agricultural University of Norway, 1981; Head of Plant Sciences, Scottish Agricultural College, Ayr, 1982-90; British Council Research Fellow, University of Western Australia, 1989; Visiting Scientist, McGill University, Montreal, 1997. Publications: Environmental Physiology of Plants; Chemistry for Agriculture and Ecology; Introduction to the Physiology of Crop Yield; Volatile Oil Crops (Editor); Science Policies in Europe: Unity and Diversity (Editor); Annals of Botany (Editor); 60 scientific papers. Recreations: walking; skiing; mending walls; music; Scotland. Address: (h.) 16 Polton Road, Lasswade EH18 1AA.

Hay, Professor Robert Walker, BSc, PhD, CChem, FRSC, FRSE. Professor of Chemistry, St. Andrews University, since 1988; b. 17.9.34, Stirling; m., Alison Laird; 1 s.; 3 d. Educ. Stirling High School; Glasgow University. Assistant Lecturer, Glasgow University, 1959; subsequently worked at Esso Research; Lecturer, Senior Lecturer and Reader, Victoria University, Wellington, New Zealand, 1961; Reader, Stirling University, 1971; Professor, Stirling University, 1984; Pro Dean of Science (Graduate Studies), 1993-96; Governor, Morrisons Academy, Crieff. Publications: Bioinorganic Chemistry, 1984; numerous scientific papers. Recreations: walking; travel; gardening; reading. Address: (b.) School of Chemistry, St. Andrews University, St. Andrews KY16 9ST; T.-01334 463827.

Hayes, Sir John Osler Chattock, KCB, OBE; b. 9.5.13; m., Hon. Rosalind Mary Finlay; 2 s.; 1 d. Educ. Royal Naval College, Dartmouth. War service, 1939-45, Atlantic/HMS Repulse/Singapore/Russian Convoys/Malta; Real Admiral, Naval Secretary to First Lord of Admiralty, 1962-64; Vice Admiral/Rear Admiral, Flag Officer 2nd in command Western Fleet, 1964-66; Vice Admiral, Flag Officer Scotland and Northern Ireland, 1966-68; President, King George's Fund for Sailors, Scotland, 1968-79; Vice Patron, Royal National Mission for Deep Sea Fishermen, 1968-94; Deputy Chairman, Gordonstoun School, 1977-86; Lord Lieutenant of Ross and Cromarty, Skye and Lochalsh, 1977-88. Publication: Face the Music: a sailor's story, 1991. Recreations: music; writing; walking. Address: (h.) Wemyss House, Nigg, Tain, Ross and Cromarty IV19 1QW; T.-Nigg 212.

Hayes, Michael George, BA, MCD, MRTPI. Director of Planning and Development, Glasgow City Council; Visiting Professor, University of Strathclyde; b. 20.2.47, Liverpool; m., Elizabeth; 1 s.; 2 d. Educ. Bootle Grammar School; Leeds University; Liverpool University. Assistant Planner, Bootle CB, 1971; Principal Planning Officer, Sefton MD, 1974; Assistant Divisional Planning Officer, Liverpool, 1979; City Planning Officer, Liverpool, 1985; Director of Planning, City of Glasgow District Council, 1993. Member: Historic Areas and Buildings Advisory Committee, English Heritage, Executive Committee, Scottish Society of Directors of Planning. Recreations: Reader in Anglican church; cycling; hill-walking; music; theatre. Address: (b.) 231 George Street, Glasgow G1 1RX; T.-0141-287 5903.

Haythornthwaite, Professor Josephine Angela, BA, PhD, FLA, FInstInfSc. Chief Librarian, Glasgow Caledonian University, since 1989; Visiting Profesor in Information Management, Leicester De Montfort University, since 1993; b. 24.6.38, Leamington Spa. Educ. St. Margaret's School, Ludlow, Strathclyde University. Began career as librarian, 1962; Depute Librarian, Glasgow College of Technology, 1971-78; Lecturer: Strathclyde University, 1978-82, Loughborough University, 1983-89. Publications: Distance Education in Library and Information Studies (Co-author); Business Information Maze; Scotland in the Nineteenth Century. Recreations: theatre; music; cooking; entertaining; travel. Address: (b.) Glasgow Caledonian University, Cowcaddens Road, Glasgow G4 0BA; T.-0141-331 3860.

Hazel, George McLean, BSc, MSc, PhD, CEng, MICE, MCIT, MIHT. Director of City Development, City of Edinburgh Council, since 1996; b. 27.1.49, Dunfermline; m., Fiona Isabella Gault; 1 s.; 2 d. Educ. Dunfermline High School; Heriot-Watt University; Cranfield Institute of Technology. Transportation Engineer: City of Edinburgh Corporation, five years, Lothian Regional Council, four years; Lecturer, Senior Lecturer, Head of Department and Professor, Napier College/Polytechnic/University, 11 years; Director, Oscar Faber TPA, three years; Director of Transportation, Lothian Regional Council, two years; Royal Academy of Engineers Visiting Professor, Heriot-Watt University; Visiting Professor, Napier University. Member, Secretary of State for Scotland's Advisory Group on Sustainable Development; Chairman: Edinburgh and East of Scotland Association, Institution of Civil Engineers, Institution of Highways and Transportation (Central and Southern Scotland Branch). Recreations: golf; gardening; music; vintage cars. Address: (h.) 7 Glenlockhart Valley, Edinburgh EH14 1DE.

Heading, Robert Campbell, BSc, MD, FRCPE, FRCP. Consultant Physician, Edinburgh Royal Infirmary, since 1975; Reader in Medicine, Edinburgh University, since 1992; b. 3.7.41, Stepps, Lanarkshire; m., Patricia Mary Goldie; 2 s.; 1 d. Educ. Birkenhead School; King Edward's

School, Birmingham; Edinburgh University. Address: (h.) 20 Frogston Road West, Edinburgh EH10 7AR; T.-0131-445 1552.

Heald, Professor David Albert, BA, ACMA. Professor of Accountancy, Aberdeen University, since 1990; Specialist Adviser: Treasury and Civil Service Committee, House of Commons, since 1989, Scottish Affairs Committee, House of Commons, 1980-81, 1983, 1993-96; b. 25.9.47, York; m., Yvonne Duncan. Educ. Nunthorpe Grammar School, York; Leicester University; Jordanhill College. Accountant, Raleigh Industries, 1969-70, British Steel Corporation, 1971-72; Lecturer in Economics, Glasgow College of Technology, 1972-78; Lecturer in Economics, later in Management Studies, Glasgow University, 1978-90. Labour Parliamentary candidate, Roxburgh, Selkirk and Peebles, 1979. Publications: several books, including: Making Devolution Work; Financing Devolution within the UK: a study of the lessons from failure; Public Expenditure: its defence and reform; Financing a Scottish Parliament: options for debate; and numerous articles on topics such as public expenditure, government accounting, privatisation and the Private Finance Initiative. Recreations: theatre; cinema; everything French; squash; boating on the Moray Firth. Address: (b.) Department of Accountancy, Aberdeen University, Edward Wright Building, Aberdeen, AB24 3QY; T.-01224 272213.

Heaney, (Alison) Jane, BEd. Teacher of Physical Education, since 1975; General Commissioner of Taxes, since 1994; Member, Scottish Sports Council, since 1996; b. 25.3.53, Inverness; m., Robert J. Heaney, JP, FRICS; 1 s.; 1 d. Educ. St. Leonards School for Girls, St. Andrews; Dunfermline College of Physical Education. Teacher of Physical Education, 1975-78; Partner in catering business, 1978-81; Director of property development company, 1985-90; Partner in farming business, since 1980; Teacher of Physical Education, since 1993. Secretary, Dalkeith and District Pony Club, 1995-96; President, Scottish Lacrosse Association, 1994-96. Recreations: golf; tennis; sailing; skiing; interior design; cooking; gardening. Address: (h.) Pogbie House, Humbie, East Lothian EH36 5PN; T.-01875 833 332.

Heaney, Henry Joseph, OBE, MA, FLA, FRSA, FRSE. University Librarian and Keeper of the Hunterian Books and MSS, Glasgow University, since 1978; b. 2.1.35, Newry, Northern Ireland; m., Mary Elizabeth Moloney. Educ. Abbey Grammar School, Newry; Queen's University, Belfast. Assistant Librarian, Queen's University, Belfast, 1959-62; Librarian, Magee University College, Londonderry, 1962-69; Deputy Librarian, New University of Ulster, 1967-69; Assistant Secretary, Standing Conference of National and University Libraries, 1969-72; Librarian: Queen's University, Belfast, 1972-74, University College, Dublin, 1975-78. Member, Advisory Committee on Public Library Service, Northern Ireland, 1965; Chairman, NI Branch, Library Association, 1966, 1973; Trustee, National Library of Scotland, 1980-91; Chairman, British Library Ad Hoc Working Party on Union Catalogues, 1982; Member: British Library Board, 1989-95, British Library Reference Division Advisory Committee, 1982-89, British Library Lending Division Advisory Committee, 1983-86, British Eighteenth Century Short Title Catalogue Committee, since 1983, Standing Committee, University Libraries Section, IFLA, 1986-91; Trustee, National Manuscripts Conservation Trust, 1989-95; Chairman, Consortium of University Research Libraries, 1995-97; Editor, World List of Abbreviations of Organisations; President, Scottish Library Association, 1990. Address: (b.) Glasgow University Library, Hillhead Street, Glasgow G12 8QE; T.-0141-330 5633.

Hearne, John Michael, BMus, MMus. Publisher (Longship Music); Freelance Composer and Professional Singer; b. 19.9.37, Reading; m., Margaret Gillespie Jarvie.

Educ. Torquay Grammar School; St. Luke's College, Exeter; University College of Wales, Aberystwyth. Teaching, Rugeley, Staffordshire, 1959-60; Warehouseman/ Driver, Torquay, 1961-64; Teaching: Tonlistarskoli Borgarfjardar, Iceland, 1968-69, UCW Aberystwyth, 1969-70; Lecturer, Aberdeen College of Education, 1970-87. Composer, vocal, instrumental and incidental music: BBC commission for BBCSSO, 1990 (trumpet concerto); McEwen Commission, Glasgow University, 1979; A Legend of Margaret, commissioned to celebrate 150th anniversary of St. Margaret's School, Aberdeen, 1996; Member, John Currie Singers; Awarded Radio Forth Trophy, 1985, for most outstanding work on Edinburgh Festival Fringe; joint winner, Gregynog Composers' Award for Wales, 1992. Chorus Manager, Aberdeen International Youth Festival, since 1978; Chairman: Scottish Music Advisory Committee, BBC, 1986-90, Gordon Forum for the Arts, 1991-94; Conductor, Stonehaven and District Choral Society; Past Chairman, Scottish Society of Composers; District Councillor, Incorporated Society of Musicians; Member: Executive Committee, Composers' Guild GB, Board, National Youth Choir of Scotland. Recreations: motoring and travel (1954 Daimler Roadster). Address: (h.) Smidskot, Fawells, Keith-Hall, Inverurie AB51 OLN; T.-01651 882 274.

Heatly, Sir Peter, CBE, DL, BSc, CEng, FICE. Chairman, Peter Heatly & Co. Ltd., since 1958; b. 9.6.24, Edinburgh; m., Mae Calder Cochrane. Educ. Leith Academy; Edinburgh University. Structural Designer, Redpath Brown & Co. Ltd., 1946; Lecturer in Civil Engineering, Edinburgh University, 1948. Chairman: Scottish Sports Council, 1975-87, Commonwealth Games Federation, 1982-90, International Diving Committee, 1984-88; Master, Edinburgh Merchant Company, 1988-90; awarded Honorary Doctorate, Edinburgh University, 1992, Queen Margaret College, 1994. Recreations: swimming; gardening; travel. Address: (h.) Lanrig, Balerno, Edinburgh EH14 7AJ; T.-0131-449 3998.

Hector, Alistair. Headmaster, George Heriot's School, since 1998. Address: (b.) Lauriston Place, Edinburgh EH3 9EQ.

Hector, Gordon Matthews, CMG, CBE (OBE, 1955), MA (Oxon). Honorary Vice President, The St. Andrew Society; b. 9.6.18, Aberdeen; m., Dr. Mary Forrest Gray; 1 s.; 2 d. Educ. St. Mary's School, Melrose; Edinburgh Academy; Lincoln College, Oxford. HM Colonial Administrative Service and Overseas Civil Service, 1946-66: District Commissioner, Kenya, Secretary, Kenya Road Authority, Secretary to Government of Seychelles, 1952-55, Acting Governor, 1953, Deputy Resident Commissioner and Government Secretary, Basutoland (now Lesotho), 1956-64, Deputy British Government Representative, Lesotho, 1965-66; Aberdeen University: Clerk to University Court, 1967, Deputy Secretary, 1976-80; Secretary to Assembly Council, General Assembly of Church of Scotland, 1980-85. Fellow, Commonwealth Fund, 1939; Burgess of Guild, Aberdeen; Chairman, West End Community Council, Edinburgh, 1986-89; Court of Directors, Edinburgh Academy, 1967-75; Chairman: Great North of Scotland Railway Association, 1990-92, Scottish Council, Victoria League, 1983-88; Member, sometime Chairman, Board of Managers, Oakbank List D School, 1969-90. Recreations: town and country walking; railways ancient and modern; grandchildren. Address: (h.) 4 Montgomery Court, 110 Hepburn Gardens, St. Andrews KY16 9LT; T.-01334 473784.

Hedderwick, Alexander Mark. Managing Director, Adam & Company Investment Management, since 1989; Director, Adam & Company Group PLC, since 1992; b. 13.12.48. Hedderwick Borthwick, Stockbrokers, 1969-73; Langton Underwriting Agents, Lloyds, 1973-84. Recreations:

family; gardening; bee-keeping. Address: (b.) 22 Charlotte Square, Edinburgh EH2 4DF; T.-0131-225 8484.

Hedderwick, Mairi Crawford, DA (Edin). Illustrator, Writer and Public Speaker; b. 2.5.39, Gourock; 1 s.; 1 d. Educ. St. Columba's School, Kilmacolm; Edinburgh College of Art; Jordanhill College of Education. Art Teacher, mid-Argyll primary schools, 1962; Hebridean "dropping out", crofting, child rearing, 1964-73; part-time art teaching 1979-86; community co-operative worker, Highlands and Islands, 1986-88. Publications: for children: Katie Morag series, Peedie Peebles series, Carpenter MacPheigh; for adults: An Eye on the Hebrides, Highland Journey. Recreations: a day outside ending round a table with friends, food and wine.

Heggie, Professor Douglas Cameron, MA, PhD, FRAS, FRSE. Professor of Mathematical Astronomy, Edinburgh University, since 1994; b. 7.2.47, Edinburgh; m., Linda Jane Tennent; 2 d. Educ. George Heriot's School, Edinburgh; Trinity College, Cambridge. Research Fellow, Trinity College, Cambridge, 1972-76; Lecturer in Mathematics, Edinburgh University, 1975-85, Reader, 1985-94; Council Member, Royal Astronomical Society, 1982-85; President, Commission 37, International Astronomical Union, 1985-88. Publications: Megalithic Science; scientific papers on dynamical astronomy. Recreations: family life; walking; music. Address: (b.) Edinburgh University, Department of Mathematics and Statistics, King's Buildings, Edinburgh EH9 3JZ; T.-0131-650 5035.

Heilig, James Leedom, BSc. Chief Executive, Low & Bonar PLC, since 1995; b. 9.10.35, United States; m., Susie; 2 s.; 1 d. Educ. Oregon State University. Background in sales and marketing; former Vice-President – Operations, Flexible Packaging Group, James River Corporation, Cincinnati, Ohio; joined Low & Bonar Group, 1992; became C.E.O. and President of Group's North American operations and member of Group Board. Recreations: golf; travel; reading. Address: (b.) Bonar House, Faraday Street, Dundee DD1 9JA; T.-01382 818171.

Heller, Martin Fuller Vernon, FRSAMD. Actor, since 1947; b. 20.2.27, Manchester; m., Joyce Allan; 2 s.; 4 d. Educ. Rondebosch Boys High School, Cape Town; Central School of Speech Training and Dramatic Art, London. Compass Players, 1948-52; repertory seasons and/or individual productions at following Scottish theatres: St. Andrews Byre, Edinburgh Gateway, Glasgow Citizens' (eight seasons), Edinburgh Royal Lyceum, Edinburgh Traverse, Dundee Repertory, Perth Repertory, Pitlochry Festival; Founder/Artistic Director, Prime Productions; extensive television and radio work; Member: Scottish Arts Council, 1975-82 (latterly Chairman, Drama Committee), Board, Pitlochry Festival Theatre; Governor, Royal Scottish Academy of Music and Drama, 1982-94. Recreations: politics; history; listening to music. Address: (h.) 54 Hermiston, Currie, Midlothian EH14 4AQ; T.-0131-449 4055.

Helms, Professor Peter Joseph, MB, BS, PhD, FRCP. Professor of Child Health, Aberdeen University, since 1991; Consultant Paediatrician, since 1982; b. 26.6.47, Melbourne; m., Kathleen Mary; 1 s.; 3 d. Educ. Wimbledon College; Royal Free Hospital School of Medicine; London University. SHO, Hospital for Sick Children, Great Ormond Street, 1976; Lecturer in Paediatrics, Charing Cross Hospital Medical School, 1977-78; Research Fellow, Institute of Child Health, London, 1978-81, National Heart and Lung Institute, London, 1981-82; Senior Lecturer, Institute of Child Health, 1982-91; Honorary Consultant Paediatrician, Hospital for Sick Children, Great Ormond Street, 1982-91. Recreations: music; hill-walking; European history. Address: (b.) Department of Child Health, Foresterhill, Aberdeen, AB25 2ZD; T.-01224 681818.

Henderson, Andrew Kerr, MB, ChB, FRCP. Consultant Physician and Clinical Director, Lorn and the Islands District General Hospital, Oban; Honorary Clinical Senior Lecturer, Glasgow University; b. 1.3.46, Hawick; m., Doreen Innes Wilkinson; 1 s.; 2 d. Educ. Glasgow Academy; Glasgow University. Medical Registrar, Western Infirmary, Glasgow; Medical Registrar/Senior Registrar, Glasgow Royal Infirmary. Chairman, Counties Branch, Scottish Schoolboys' Club. Recreations: gardening; hill-walking. Address: (h.) Birkmoss, North Connel, Argyll; T.-01631 710379.

Henderson, Douglas Mackay, CBE, BSc, FLS, FRSE, VMH, Queen's Botanist in Scotland, since 1987; b. 30.8.27, Blairgowrie; m., Julia Margaret Brown; 1 s.; 2 d. Educ. Blairgowrie High School; Edinburgh University. Scientific Officer, Department of Agriculture, Scotland, 1948-50; Research Botanist, Royal Botanic Garden, Edinburgh, 1950-70; Curator, Royal Society of Edinburgh, 1978-87; Secretary, International Association of Botanical Gardens, 1969-81; Regius Keeper, Royal Botanic Garden, Edinburgh, 1970-87; Honorary Professor, Edinburgh University, since 1982; Administrator, Inverewe Garden, National Trust for Scotland, 1987-92; Council Member, National Trust for Scotland, since 1993; Secretary, Help the Aged Highland Committee. Recreations: natural history; painting; sailing; cooking. Address: (h.) Larachan, 54 Lonemore, Gairloch, Ross-shire IV21 2DB; T.-01445 2391.

Henderson, Elizabeth Kidd, MA (Hons), MEd (Hons). Governor, Glasgow Academy; Headmistress, Westbourne School, 1970-88; b. 25.5.28, Dunfermline. Educ. Dunfermline High School; Edinburgh University; St. Andrews University. Mathematics Teacher, Morrison's Academy, Crieff; Second Master, Mathematics, Dundee High School; Principal Teacher of Mathematics, Aberdeen High School; former Secretary, Mathematics Panel, Scottish Examination Board; President, Scottish Area, Secondary Heads Association; former Member, Church of Scotland Education Committee; President, Glasgow Mathematical Association; Chairman, Community Council. Publication: Modern Mathematics for Schools (Co-author). Recreations: walking; golf. Address: (h.) 16 George Reith Avenue, Glasgow G12 0AN; T.-0141-334 8545.

Henderson, Hamish Scott, MA, Hon.LLD, Hon.DUniv, Dr.h.c. Lecturer/Research Fellow, School of Scottish Studies, Edinburgh University, since 1952 (Honorary Fellow, since 1988); b. 11.11.19, Blairgowrie; m., Felicity Schmidt; 2 d. Educ. Blairgowrie High School; Dulwich College; Downing College, Cambridge University. Wartime: Intelligence Officer, 51st Highland Division and other Infantry Divisions, Egypt, Libya, Tunisia, Sicily, Italy; mentioned in Dispatches, 1945; District Secretary, WEA, 1947-49; Assistant to Alan Lomax in folklore collection and editing, 1950-51; first translator of Gramsci into English. Publications: Elegies for the Dead in Cyrenaica, 1948 (Somerset Maugham Award, 1949); Ballads of World War II (published by Lili Marlene Club of Glasgow), 1947; Alias MacAlias (anthology of essays), 1992; The Armstrong Nose: selected letters, 1996; Gramsci's Prison Letters, 1996. Recreations: writing; singing; song-writing. Address: (h.) 20 Melville Terrace, Edinburgh; T.-0131-667 5143.

Henderson, James. Registrar of Companies for Scotland, since 1992; b. 22.11.48, Kilmarnock; m., Patricia Mazs; 2 d. Educ. Kilmarnock Academy. Joined the Queen's and Lord Treasurer's Remembrancer, 1967; Department of Trade and Industry, 1981; became Companies House DTI's first agency, 1988. Recreations: bowls; rugby (spectating); reading; gardening. Address: (b.) 37 Castle Terrace, Edinburgh EH1 2EB; T.-0131-535 5855.

Henderson, James Gunn, MBE. Editor, Northern Times, 1975-96; b. 10.7.31, Wick; m., 1, Catherine Maclean (deceased); 2 d.; 2, Christine Mackay; 4 s. Educ. Wick High School. Reporter, John O'Groat Journal, 1948-53; Scottish Daily Express: Reporter, 1953-60, Deputy Chief, Edinburgh, 1960-65, Deputy News Editor, Glasgow, 1965-69, News Features Editor, Glasgow, 1969-75.Trustee, Moray Firth Radio Charity, Highland Community Foundation. Recreation: reading newspapers. Address: (h.) Littleferry, Golspie, KW10 6TD; T.-01408 633548.

Henderson, John Gunn, BA, FRSA. Head of Private Finance Unit and Assistant Director of Finance, Scottish Office, since 1997; b. 29.5.53, Edinburgh; m., Caroline; 1 s.; 2 d. Educ. Broughton Secondary, Edinburgh; Open University. Scottish Development Department, 1970-78; Department of Agriculture and Fisheries for Scotland, 1978-85; Scottish Development Department, Trunk Roads Division, 1985-88; Scottish Office Education and Industry Department, 1988-97 (Head, Further Education Funding Unit, 1992-97). Recreations: reading; gardening; beachcombing. Address: (b.) Scottish Office, Victoria Quay, Edinburgh EH6 6QQ; T.-0131-244 7497.

Henderson, Major Richard Yates, TD, JP, BA (Oxon), LLB. Lord Lieutenant, Ayrshire and Arran, since 1991; b. 7.7.31, Nitshill; m., Frances Elizabeth Chrystal; 3 s. (inc. 1 s. dec.); 1 d. Educ. Rugby; Hertford College, Oxford; Glasgow University. Royal Scots Greys, 1950-52; TA Ayrshire (ECO) Yeomanry, 1953-69 (Major); Deputy Lieutenant, Ayrshire and Arran, 1970-90; Partner, Mitchells Roberton, Solicitors, 1958-90, Consultant, 1991-92. Brigadier, Queen's Bodyguard for Scotland (Royal Company of Archers); President, Lowland TAVRA, since 1996; Hon. Colonel, Ayrshire Yeomanry Sqn., Scottish Yeomanry, 1992-97; Honorary Sheriff, South Strathclyde Dumfries and Galloway at Ayr, since 1997. Recreations: shooting; tennis; golf. Address: (h.) Blairston, by Ayr; T.-01292 441601.

Henderson, Robert Ewart, QC, BL; b. 29.3.37. Admitted to Faculty of Advocates, 1963. Address: (b.) Advocates' Library, Parliament House, Edinburgh, EH1 1RF.

Henderson, Simon, LLB(Hons), DLP. Solicitor, Digby Brown Solicitors, since 1997; b. 11.4.72, Bellshill. Educ. Belmont Academy, Ayr; University of Aberdeen. Completed legal training with Jeffrey Aitken Solicitors. Vice-President, Glasgow Juridical Society. Recreations: travel; music; motorsport; hockey umpiring. Address: (b.) Savoy Tower, 77 Renfrew Street, Glasgow G2 3BZ; T.-0141-566 9494.

Henderson, Stewart Alexander, RIBA, FRIAS. Director of Property Services, City of Edinburgh Council; b. 18.1.47, Glasgow; 1 s.; 1 d. Educ. Falkirk High School; Glasgow School of Art. Private practice, Glasgow; Principal Architect, Stewartry District; Depute Director of Architectural Services, Stornoway; Chief Architect, Clydesdale District; Chief Architect, Scottish & Newcastle; Executive Director of Property Services, Edinburgh District Council. Recreations: shooting; stalking; fishing. Address: (b.) 329 High Street, Edinburgh; T.-0131-529 4916.

Henderson, Thomas Wilson. Director, John Turnbull & Sons Ltd., Hawick, since 1983; Member, Scottish Borders Council, since 1995 (formerly Member, Ettrick and Lauderdale District Council, and Provost of Selkirk); b. 28.9.41, Selkirk; m., Catherine Helen Herbert; 2 s. Educ. Selkirk Public School; Selkirk High School; Scottish College of Textiles; Paisley College of Technology. Served apprenticeship as dyer with George Roberts & Co. Ltd., Selkirk, 1957-61; Dyer, Grays Carpets, Ayr, 1961-70; Assistant Manager, John Turnbull & Sons Ltd., Hawick, 1978-83; involved in management buy-out, 1983; Member, Selkirk Town Council, 1973-75; Corporate Member, Society of Dyers and Colourists; holder of various offices, Transport and General Workers Union, since 1970;

Organiser, Scottish National Party, Ayr Constituency, 1967-70. Recreations: hill-walking; horse-riding; reading; folk music; jazz; football; cricket. Address: (h.) Triglav, 29 Shawpark Crescent, Selkirk; T.-01750 20821.

Henderson-Howat, David Barclay, BSc, MA, MBA. Chief Conservator, Forestry Authority, Scotland, since 1996; b. 23.1.54, Trinidad; m., Jean Buchanan-Smith; 1 s.; 3 d. Educ. Abingdon School; University of Edinburgh; Magdalene College, University of Cambridge; University of Strathclyde. Scottish Office, 1976-79; Personal Assistant to Chief Executive, Scottish Development Agency, 1979-80; Harvesting and Marketing Manager, Thetford Forest, 1980-84; Forest Manager, Shiselweni Forest, Swaziland, 1984-86; Forest District Manager, Aberfoyle, Perthshire, 1986-90; Forestry Commission Headquarters, 1990-96. Member, Lamancha, Newlands and Kirkurd Community Council, 1992-95. Recreations: walking; sailing. Address: (b.) Forestry Commission, 231 Corstorphine Road, Edinburgh EH12 7AR; T.-0131-314 6162.

Hendrie, Eric. Chairman/Director, Grampian Careers; b. 11.9.25, Glasgow; m., Isabel; 1 s.; 1 d. Educ. Lambhill School, Glasgow; Royal Technical College, Glasgow. Councillor: Aberdeen Corporation, 1970-75, Grampian Regional Council, 1975-94 (Convener of Education, 1990-94). Address: (h.) 37 New Park Road, Aberdeen, AB16 6UT; T.-01224 691723.

Hendron, Frances, MA (Cantab). Director, Celtic Film and Television Association, since 1994. Educ. St. Michael's High School, Lurgan; Newnham College, Cambridge. Address: (b.) 1 Bowmont Gardens, Glasgow G12 9LR; T.-0141-342 4947.

Hendry, Alan. Editor: John O'Groat Journal, since 1988, Caithness Courier, since 1988; b. 26.3.62, Wick; m., Yvonne; 2 s. Educ. Wick High School; Aberdeen College of Commerce. Address: (b.) 42 Union Street, Wick, Caithness KW1 5ED; T.-01955 604242.

Hendry, Professor Alan, BSc (Hons), PhD, CEng, FIM, MInstP, FRSA. Dean, Faculty of Engineering, Strathclyde University; b. 29.1.47, Ochiltree; m., Jean Carey Kerr; 1 s.; 1 d. Educ. Cumnock Academy; Strathclyde University. Postdoctoral Research Associate, Newcastle University, 1971-75; Research Officer, Midlands Region, CEGB, 1975-76; Lecturer in Metallurgy and Assistant Director, Wolfson Research Group for High Strength Materials, Newcastle University, 1976-85; Strathclyde University: Reader in Ceramics, 1985-88, Professor of Metallurgy and Engineering Materials, since 1988, Head of Department of Metallurgy and Engineering Materials, 1990-96. President, Scottish Association for Metals, 1990-92; Member, Materials Commission, SERC, 1989-92, Materials College, EPSRC, since 1994; Member, International Academy of Ceramics; Allan B. Dove Medal, Wire Assoc. Int., 1993. Address: (h.) Ardleven, 23 Campbell Drive, Bearsden, Glasgow G61 4NF; T.-0141-942 3169.

Hendry, Douglas, LLB, DipLP. Director of Legal Services, Argyll and Bute Council, since 1995; b. 24.7.60, Dunoon. Educ. Dunoon Grammar School; Aberdeen University. Argyll and Bute District Council: Trainee Solicitor, 1982, Solicitor, 1984, Principal Officer, 1985, Depute Director of Administration, 1988. Recreations: exotic motor cars; Persian cats; football. Address: (b.) Kilmory Castle, Lochgilphead PA31 8RT; T.-01546 604119.

Hendry, Joy McLaggan, MA (Hons), DipEd. Editor, Chapman Magazine, since 1972; Writer; Writer-in-Residence, Stirling District Council, 1991-93; b. 3.2.53, Perth; m., Ian Montgomery. Educ. Perth Academy; Edinburgh University. Former teacher; Co-Editor, Chapman, 1972-76, Sole Editor, since 1976; Deputy Convener, Scottish Poetry Library Association, 1983-88;

Convener, Committee for the Advancement of Scottish Literature in Schools; Member AdCas; Scottish National Theatre Steering Committee; Campaign for a Scottish Assembly; Member, Drama Committee, Scottish Arts Council; writes poetry; gives lectures and talks and performances of poetry and song; radio critic, The Scotsman, 1988-97; theatre reviewer. Publications: Scots: The Way Forward; Poems and Pictures by Wendy Wood (Editor); The Land for the People (Co-Editor); Critical Essays on Sorley MacLean (Co-Editor); Critical Essays on Norman MacCaig (Co-Editor); Gang Doun wi a Sang (play); radio: The Wa' at the World's End, Radio 3 (play); A Many-Faceted Thing (Memory), Radio 4 (major 4-part series). Recreations: going to theatre; cinema; reading. Address: 4 Broughton Place, Edinburgh EH1 3RX; T.-0131-557 2207.

Hendry, Professor Leo Brough, MSc, MEd, PhD, DLitt, FBPS, FECSS. Professor of Education, Aberdeen University, since 1989, and Visiting Professor in Health Psychology, Norwegian University of Science and Technology, Trondheim; b. 12.11.35, Glasgow; m., Philomena Walsh; 2 d. Educ. Hermitage Academy, Helensburgh; Jordanhill College of Education, Glasgow; Bradford University; Leicester University; Aberdeen University. School Teacher in Scottish and English schools, including two posts as Head of Department, 1957-64; Lecturer in Education and Physical Education, College of St. Mark and St. John's, Chelsea, London University Institute, 1964-66; Head of Human Movement Studies, Trinity and All Saints' Colleges, Leeds University Institute, 1966-71; Lecturer in Education, then Senior Lecturer, Aberdeen University, 1971-88; Head, Education Department, 1988-94; Member, Scottish Council for Research in Education, 1983-86. Publications: School, Sport, Leisure: three dimensions of adolescence, 1978; Adolescents and Leisure, 1981; Growing Up and Going Out, 1983; Personality and Performance in Physical Education and Sport (Co-Author), 1974; Physical Education in England (Co-Author), 1976; Towards Community Education (Co-Author), 1980; The Nature of Adolescence (Co-Author), 1990; Young People's Leisure and Lifestyles (Co-Author), 1993; Educating for Health (Co-Author), 1995; New Perspectives on Youth Disaffection (Co-Author), 1997; book chapters; research articles. Recreations: golf; writing; broadcasting; presenting papers at international conferences. Address: (b.) Centre for Educational Research, Department of Sociology, Aberdeen University, Aberdeen AB9 2UB; T.-01224 272731.

Hendry, Stephen, MBE. Professional snooker player; b. 13.1.69; m., Mandy. Youngest-ever Scottish Amateur Champion (aged 15); has won 64 major titles worldwide; youngest player to attain No. 1 ranking; youngest player to win World Championship, 1990; World Champion six times; UK Champion, five times; Masters Champion, six times. Address: (b.) Cuemasters Ltd., Kerse Road, Stirling, FK7 7SG; T.-01786 462634.

Henley, Professor John Sebastian, BSc(Eng), PhD. Professor of International Management, Department of Business Studies, University of Edinburgh, since 1996; b. 5.4.43, Malvern; m., Sarah J. Sieley; 2 d. Educ. King Edward's School, Birmingham; University College, London; London School of Economics. Personnel Officer, Glaxo Laboratories, 1966-68; Lecturer, Industrial Relations Department, London School of Economics, 1968-72; Lecturer, Faculty of Commerce, University of Nairobi, 1972-75; joined Department of Business Studies, University of Edinburgh, 1975. Publications: co-author of three books; editor of two books; author of over 50 academic papers. Recreations: gardening; theatre; opera; sailing. Address: (b.) Department of Business Studies, University of Edinburgh, 50 George Square, Edinburgh EH8 9JT; T.-0131-650 3814.

Henley, Rt. Rev. Michael Harry George, CB. Bishop of St. Andrews, Dunkeld and Dunblane, since 1995; b. 16.1.38; m.; 2 d.

Henrie, Hugh. Leader, Renfrewshire Council. Address: (b.) Municipal Buildings, Cotton Street, Paisley, PA1 1BU.

Henry, Sheriff A.C., MA, LLB. Sheriff of Glasgow and Strathkelvin, at Glasgow. Admitted, Faculty of Advocates, 1969. Address: (b.) Sheriff Court House, 1 Carlton Place, Glasgow, G5 9DA.

Henry, Captain Michael Charles, DL, RN (Rtd.) Deputy Lieutenant, Dunbartonshire, since 1989; Director, Merchants House of Glasgow, 1990-96; b. 4.6.28, London; m., Nancie Elma Nicol; 2 s.; 3 d. Educ. Royal Naval College, Dartmouth. Naval career, Cadet to Captain, 1942-78; submarine specialist; commanded HM Submarines Seraph, Trump and Resolution, Britain's first Polaris submarine; fired first British missile, Cape Canaveral, and conducted first deterrent patrol, 1968; commanded 10th (Polaris) Submarine Squadron, Faslane, and Queen's Harbour Master, Clyde, 1972-74; commanded HMS Hampshire, 1975-76; Director of Naval Operations and Trade, 1976-78; Marine Manager, British National Oil Corporation, Aberdeen, 1978-80; Naval Regional Officer Scotland and Northern Ireland, Glasgow, 1980-90. Recreation: sailing. Address: (h.) Aldavhu, Garelochhead, Dunbartonshire G84 0EL; T.-01436 810533.

Henshelwood, James, JP, FISMM, MCIM, MInstM, AMNI. Director, Glasgow Building Preservation Trust, since 1982; Member, St. John Association of Scotland; Member, Central Advisory Committee on Justices of the Peace; b. 18.2.22, Glasgow; m., Mavis Irene Watson (deceased); 3 s.; 2 d. Educ. Allan Glen's School; Whitehill Senior Secondary School; Royal Technical College, Glasgow. Joined Merchant Navy as cadet, 1938, and "swallowed the anchor" in 1953 as Master Mariner; Special Services, RNR; Independent Councillor, Johnstone, 1966-69 (Burgh Treasurer); President, Chartered Institute of Marketing, West of Scotland Branch; Immediate Past Chairman, Nautical Institute, West of Scotland; Governor, RNLI; Vice-Chairman, Scottish Pre-Retirement Council; Past President, Glasgow Bute Benevolent Society; former Director, Glasgow Chamber of Commerce; Captain, Bute Golf Club. Recreations: golf; sailing; walking. Address: (h.) 72 Globe Court, Calderwood, East Kilbride, Glasgow G74 3QZ; T.-013552 38851.

Herald, Sheriff John Pearson, LLB, NP, SSC. Sheriff of North Strathclyde at Greenock and Rothesay, since 1992; b. 12.7.46, Glasgow; m., Catriona; 1 d. Educ. Hillhead High School, Glasgow; Glasgow University. Partner, Carlton Gilruth, Solicitors, Dundee, 1970-91; Depute Town Clerk, Newport-on-Tay, 1970-75; Member, Angus Legal Aid Committee, 1970-79, Secretary, 1979-87; Member, Legal Aid Central Committee, 1981-87; Temporary Sheriff, 1984-91; part-time Chairman, Industrial Tribunals, 1984-91. Chairman, Dundee Citizens Advice Bureau, 1972-79 and 1982-91; President, Rotary Club of North Fife, 1989. Recreations: football; golf; reading. Address: (b.) Sheriff Court House, Nelson Street, Greenock; T.-01475 787073.

Herbert, Professor Rodney Andrew, BSc, PHD, CBiol, FIBiol. Professor of Microbiology, Dundee University, since 1992; b. 27.6.44, York; m., Helen Joyce Macpherson Millard; 2 s. Educ. Archbishop Holgate's Grammar School, York; Bradford University; Aberdeen University. Research Fellow, Edinburgh University, 1970-71; Lecturer/Reader in Microbiology, Dundee University, 1971-92. General Secretary, Society for General Microbiology, 1989-94; President, Society for Applied Microbiology, 1997-99; Senior Visiting Scientist: British Antarctic Survey, 1976-77, Ross Sea, Antarctica, 1982-83. Recreations: music;

walking; gardening. Address: (b.) Department of Biological Sciences, Dundee University, Dundee DD1 4HN; T.-Dundee 23181, Ext. 4262.

Herd, James Peter, MBE, WS, NP. Consultant, Beveridge, Herd & Sandilands, WS, Kirkcaldy (Partner, 1951-97); Honorary Sheriff, Kirkcaldy, since 1987; b. 18.5.20, Kirkcaldy; m., Marjory Phimister Mitchell; 3 s.; 2 d. Educ. Edinburgh Academy; St. Andrews University; Edinburgh University. Army Service as Major, Black Watch, UK and South East Asia, 1939-46; Local Director, Royal Insurance Group, since 1951; Trustee, Kirkcaldy and District Trustee Savings Bank, 1952-83; Director: Kirkcaldy Ice Rink Limited, 1982-88, Kirkcaldy Abbeyfield Society, 1970-92. Recreations: curling; gardening. Address: (b.) 1 East Fergus Place, Kirkcaldy, Fife KY1 1XT; T.-01592 261616.

Herd, John Downie, BL, NP, FRSA. Managing Director, Scottish Prudential Investment Association Ltd., since 1984; Director, Vice Chairman, Dunfermline Building Society; Chairman, Accord Hospice; b. 23.3.34, Paisley; m., Morag; 1 s.; 1 d. Educ. Paisley Grammar School; Glasgow University. Partner, McFadyen-Semple, Solicitor, Paisley, 1960; resigned partnership to become Consultant (position still held), 1984; Director, Paisley Building Society, 1981 – became Edinburgh & Paisley, latterly Dunfermline Building Society; various other non-executive directorships. Chairman, Blythswood Housing Association; Regional Chairman, Princes Scottish Youth Business Trust. Recreations: reading; Rotary; travel; gardening. Address: (h.) Rydale, South Avenue, Paisley PA2 7SP; T.-0141-884 7744.

Herdman, John Macmillan, MA (Hons), PhD (Cantab), DipTh. Writer, since 1963; b. 20.7.41, Edinburgh. Educ. Merchiston Castle School, Edinburgh; Magdalene College, Cambridge. Creative Writing Fellow, Edinburgh University, 1977-79; Scottish Arts Council bursaries, 1976 and 1982; Scottish Arts Council Book Awards, 1978 and 1993; Hawthornden Writer's Fellowship, 1989 and 1995; William Soutar Fellowship, 1990-91. Publications: Descent, 1968; A Truth Lover, 1973; Memoirs of My Aunt Minnie/Clapperton, 1974; Pagan's Pilgrimage, 1978; Stories Short and Tall, 1979; Voice Without Restraint: Bob Dylan's Lyrics and Their Background, 1982; Three Novellas, 1987; The Double in Nineteenth Century Fiction, 1990; Imelda and Other Stories, 1993; Ghostwriting, 1996; Cruising (play), 1997. Recreations: reading; walking; listening to music. Address: (h.) Roselea, Bridge of Tilt, Blair Atholl, Perthshire; T.-01796 481437.

Heron, Garth McAllen Drennan, BA, FIPM, FRSA. Managing Partner, Garth Heron Search and Consultancy, since 1995; b. 21.5.49, Belfast; m., Louise Dick; 1 s.; 1 d. Educ. Friend's School, Lisburn; Queen's University, Belfast; Strathclyde University. Personnel Officer, United Dominions Trust Ltd., 1971-73; Personnel Manager: Alcan Aluminium Ltd., 1973-76, Bourns Ltd., Fife, 1976-78; Personnel Director, Honeywell Ltd., Bracknell, 1978-87; General Manager, Personnel Division, Clydesdale Bank, 1987-93; Personnel Director, United Distillers, 1993-95. Elder, Cramond Kirk. Recreations: family; church; sports; cinema. Address: (b.) 4 Wemyss Place, Edinburgh EH3 6DH.

Herron, Very. Rev. Andrew, ATCL, MA, BD, LLB, DD, LLD. Moderator, General Assembly of Church of Scotland, 1971; b. 29.9.09, Glasgow; m., Joanna Fraser Neill; 4 d. Educ. Strathbungo H.G. School; Albert Road Academy; Glasgow University and Trinity College. Minister: Linwood, 1936-40, Houston and Killellan, 1940-59; Clerk, Glasgow Presbytery, 1959-81. Baird Lecturer, 1985; William Barclay Lecturer, 1989. Publications: Record Apart, 1974; Guide to the General Assembly, 1976; Guide to Congregational Affairs, 1979; Guide to the Presbytery, 1982; Kirk by Divine Right, 1985; Guide to the Ministry,

1987; Guide to Ministerial Income, 1987; The Law and Practice of the Kirk; Minority Report, 1990; Inter Alia, 1995. Address: (h.) 36 Darnley Road, Glasgow G41 4NE; T.-0141-423 6422.

Hetherington, Professor Emeritus (Hector) Alastair, Dhc (Lille), MA, Hon. Fellow RIAS. Emeritus Professor in Media Studies, Stirling University, since 1987; b. 31.10.19, Llanishen, Glamorgan; m., 1, Miranda; 2 s.; 2 d.; 2, Sheila; 1 step s.; 2 step d. Educ. Corpus Christi College, Oxford. Army, 1940-46; Glasgow Herald, 1946-50; The Guardian, 1950-75 (Foreign Editor, 1953-56, Editor, 1956-75); BBC Scotland, 1976-79; Director, Scotquest (film company), 1982-89; Chairman, The Scott Trust (owners, The Guardian and Manchester Evening News), 1984-89; various films for Channel Four. Publications: Guardian Years, 1981; News, Newspapers and Television, 1985; Perthshire in Trust, 1988; News in the Regions, 1989; Highlands and Islands, a generation of progress, 1990; Cameras in the Commons, 1990; Inside BBC Scotland 1975-1980, 1992; A Walker's Guide to Arran, 1995. Recreation: hill-walking. Address: (h.) 38 Chalton Road, Bridge of Allan FK9 4EF; T.-01786 833316.

Hewitt, Professor David S., MA, PhD, FRSE. Professor in Scottish Literature, Aberdeen University, since 1994 (Reader, 1991-94); b. 22.4.42, Hawick; m., Angela Catherine Williams; 1 s.; 1 d. Educ. Melrose Grammar School; George Watson's College, Edinburgh; Edinburgh University; Aberdeen University. Aberdeen University: Assistant Lecturer in English, 1964, Lecturer, 1968, Senior Lecturer, 1982; Treasurer, Association for Scottish Literary Studies, 1973-96; Editor-in-Chief, Edinburgh Edition of the Waverley Novels, 1984; President, Edinburgh Sir Walter Scott Club, 1988-89; Fellow, Royal Society of Edinburgh, 1990; Elder, Cathedral Church of St. Machar, Old Aberdeen; Managing Editor, New Writing Scotland, 1983-86. Publications: Scott on Himself (Editor), 1982; Literature of the North, 1983; Scott and His Influence, 1984; Longer Scottish Poems, Vol. 2 1650-1830, 1987; Scottish in Carnival, 1993; The Antiquary, 1995; Northern Visions, 1996; The Edinburgh Edition of the Waverley Novels: A Guide for Editors, 1996; Redgauntlet, 1997. Address: (b.) Department of English, Aberdeen University, Aberdeen AB24 3UB; T.-01224 273777.

Heys, Steven Darryll, BMedBiol, MB, ChB, MD, PhD, FRCS(Glas). Director, Surgical Nutrition and Metabolism Unit, Aberdeen University, since 1995; Reader in Surgery, Aberdeen University, since 1996; Consultant Surgeon, Aberdeen Royal Infirmary, since 1992; b. 5.7.56, Accrington; m., Margaret Susan Proctor; 2 s.; 1 d. Educ. St. Mary's College, Blackburn; Aberdeen University Medical School. House Officer/SHO, Surgery, Aberdeen Royal Infirmary, 1981-84; Registrar, Grampian Health Board, 1984-87; Wellcome Research Training Fellow, Rowett Research Institute, 1987-89; Lecturer in Surgery, Aberdeen University, 1989-92; Senior Lecturer, 1992-96. Examiner in Surgery, Royal College of Surgeons of Glasgow. Publications: numerous scientific papers on aspects of breast cancer, oncology, nutrition and metabolism; book chapters. Recreations: karate; hill-walking; golf. Address: (b.) University Medical Buildings, Foresterhill, Aberdeen AB9 2ZD.

Heywood, Barry Keith, MA, LLB. Regional Procurator Fiscal, Dundee, since 1991; b. 24.7.46, Oldham; m., Mary A.; 1 s.; 1 d. Educ. Kirkcaldy High School; Edinburgh University. Procurator Fiscal Depute, Ayr, 1971-77, Glasgow, 1977-78; Procurator Fiscal, Wick, 1978-83; Assistant Procurator Fiscal, Glasgow, 1983-86; Procurator Fiscal, Inverness, 1986-91. Recreations: walking; Roman and Byzantine history; "railway buff". Address: (b.) 15 West Bell Street, Dundee DD1 1HB; T.-01382 27535.

Hickman, Richard Michael, BA (Hons), MA, DipTP, MRTPI. Chief Inquiry Reporter, since 1997; b. 30.4.42, Beckenham; m., Sandie Randall; 3 s; 1 d. Educ. Kingswood School, Bath; London School of Economics; University of British Columbia. Work in town and country planning for London County Council, Greater London Council, Lower Mainland Regional Planning Board (British Columbia), Scottish Development Department; Scottish Office Inquiry Reporters Unit, since 1979. Hon. Visiting Fellow, Department of Planning and Housing, Edinburgh College of Art. Recreations: walking; cycling; sailing; skiing. Address: (b.) 2 Greenside Lane, Edinburgh EH1 3AG; T.-0131-244 5644.

Higgins, Sheriff Colin Kirk, LLB. Sheriff of North Strathclyde at Paisley, since 1990; b. 9.11.45, Slough; m., Anne Marie McMahon; 1 s.; 2 d. Educ. St. Patrick's High School, Coatbridge; Glasgow University. Law Apprentice, Coatbridge, 1967-69; Legal Assistant, Coatbridge, 1969-70; Legal Assistant, James Bell & Sons, 1970-73; Partner, Bell, Russell & Co., 1973-90. Dean, Airdrie Society of Solicitors, 1989-90. Recreations: reading; travel; walking; theatre. Address (b.) Court House, St. James' Street, Paisley; T.-041-887 5291.

Higgs, Professor Peter Ware, BSc, MSc, PhD, FRS, FRSE, DSc (Hon). Professor of Theoretical Physics, Edinburgh University, 1980-96; b. 29.5.29, Newcastle-upon-Tyne; m., Jo Ann Williamson; 2 s. Educ. Cotham Grammar School, Bristol; King's College, London. Postdoctoral Fellow, Edinburgh University, 1954-56, and London University, 1956-58; Lecturer in Mathematics, University College, London, 1958-60; Lecturer in Mathematical Physics, then Reader, Edinburgh University, 1960-80. Hughes Medal, Royal Society, 1981; Rutherford Medal, Institute of Physics, 1984; James Scott Prize, Royal Society of Edinburgh, 1993; Paul Dirac Medal and Prize, Institute of Physics, 1997; High Energy and Particle Physics Prize, European Physical Society, 1997. Recreations: music; walking; swimming. Address: (h.) 2 Darnaway Street, Edinburgh EH3 6BG; T.-0131-225 7060.

Hill, Richard Inglis, OBE, BSc (Hons), CEng, FICE, FIHT. Director of Technical Services, Scottish Borders Council, since 1996; b. 8.5.33, Callander; m., Margaret; 2 s. Educ. McLaren High School, Callander; Royal College of Science and Technology, Glasgow. Perth and Kinross Joint County Council: student assistant, 1951-53, graduate assistant, 1954-56, Assistant Engineer, 1958-59, Senior Engineer, 1959-61, Senior Supervisory Engineer, 1961-65, Assistant County Surveyor, 1965-72; County Surveyor and Engineer, Selkirk County Council, 1972-75; Director of Roads and Transportation, Borders Regional Council, 1974-96. Past Secretary and Chairman, Scottish Branch, County Surveyors' Society; former Secretary and Chairman, Institution of Highways and Transportation, Central and Southern Scotland Branch; Adviser on Roads and Transportation to COSLA; Past Chairman, Edinburgh and East of Scotland Division, Association of Municipal Engineers. Recreations: walking; music. Address: (b.) Council HQ, Newtown St. Boswells, Melrose TD6 QSA; T.-St Boswells 23301.

Hill, Professor William George, BSc, MS, PhD, DSc, FRSE, FRS. Professor of Animal Genetics, Edinburgh University, since 1983; Head, Division of Biological Sciences, since 1993; b. 7.8.40, Hemel Hempstead; m., C. Rosemary Austin; 1 s.; 2 d. Educ. St. Albans School; London University; University of California; Iowa State University; Edinburgh University. Edinburgh University: Assistant Lecturer, 1965-67, Lecturer, 1967-74, Reader, 1974-83, Head, Department of Genetics, 1989-90, and Institute of Cell, Animal and Population Biology, 1990-93; Visiting Research Associate, Iowa State University, 1967-68-69-72; Visiting Professor: University of Minnesota, 1966, Iowa State University, 1978, North Carolina State

University, 1979, since 1985; Consultant Geneticist: Cotswold Pig Development Co., since 1965, Holstein Friesian Society, since 1978; Editor, Genetical Research, since 1996; Member: AFRC Animals Research Grant Board, 1986-92, Director's Advisory Group, AFRC Animal Breeding Research Organisation, 1982-86, AFRC Institute of Animal Physiology and Genetics Research, 1986-93, Governing Council, Roslin Institute, since 1994, Council, Royal Society, 1993-94. Recreations: farming; bridge. Address: (h.) 4 Gordon Terrace, Edinburgh EH16 5QH; T.-0131-667 3680.

Hillhouse, Sir (Robert) Russell, KCB, FRSE. Permanent Under-Secretary of State, Scottish Office, since 1988; b. 23.4.38, Glasgow; m., Alison Fraser; 2 d. Educ. Hutchesons' Grammar School, Glasgow; Glasgow University. Entered Home Civil Service as Assistant Principal, Scottish Education Department, 1962; Principal, 1966; HM Treasury, 1971; Assistant Secretary, Scottish Office, 1974; Scottish Home and Health Department, 1977; Principal Finance Officer, Scottish Office, 1980; Under-Secretary, Scottish Education Department, 1985; Secretary, 1987. Recreation: making music. Address: (b.) St. Andrew's House, Regent Road, Edinburgh EH1 3DG; T.-0131-556 8400.

Hillier, Professor Stephen Gilbert, BSc, MSc, PhD, DSc, FRCPath. Professor, Department of Obstetrics and Gynaecology, Edinburgh University, since 1994, Director, Reproductive Medicine Laboratory, since 1985 and Director, Graduate School of Life Sciences, since 1997; b. 16.1.49, Hillingdon; m., Haideh; 2 d. Educ. Hayes County Grammar School; Leeds University; Welsh National School of Medicine. Postdoctoral Research Fellow, National Institutes of Health, USA, 1976-78; Research Scientist, University of Leiden, 1978-82; Senior Lecturer: Reproductive Biochemistry, RPMS, London University, 1982-85, Department of Obstetrics and Gynaecology, Edinburgh University, 1985-94. Member: Interim Licensing Authority for Human Fertilisation and Embryology, 1987-91, Human Fertilisation and Embryology Authority, 1990-96; 1991 Society for Endocrinology Medal. Publications: Ovarian Endocrinology, 1991; Scientific Essentials of Reproductive Medicine, 1996. Recreations: fly-fishing; walking. Address: (b.) Edinburgh University Centre for Reproductive Biology, 37 Chalmers Street, Edinburgh EH3 9EW; T.-0131-229 2575.

Hillman, John Richard, BSc, PhD, HonDSc, CBiol, FIBiol, FLS, FIM, FRSE. Director, Scottish Crop Research Institute, since 1986; Visiting Professor, Dundee University, Edinburgh University and Glasgow University; Deputy Chairman, Mylnefield Research Services Ltd.; Chairman, UK Technology Foresight Programme; b. 21.7.44, Farnborough, Kent; m., Sandra Kathleen Palmer; 2 s. Educ. Chislehurst and Sidcup Grammar School; University of Wales. Assistant Lecturer, 1968, and Lecturer, 1969, Physiology and Environmental Studies, Nottingham University; Lecturer, 1971, Senior Lecturer, 1977, Reader, 1980, Professor of Botany, 1982, Glasgow University; Chairman, Agriculture, Natural Resources and Environment Sector Panel, 1994-95, Agriculture, Horticulture and Forestry Sector Panel, 1995-97. Recreations: landscaping; building renovations; horology; reading. Address: (b.) Scottish Crop Research Institute, Invergowrie, Dundee DD2 5DA; T.-01382 562731.

Hills, Professor Sir Graham (John), PhD, DSc, FRSE, Hon DSc (Lodz, Southampton, Lisbon), Hon. LLD (Glasgow, Waterloo and Strathclyde), DUniv (Paisley). National Governor for Scotland, BBC, 1989-94; Principal and Vice-Chancellor, Strathclyde University, 1980-91; b. 9.4.26, Leigh-on-Sea; m., 1, Brenda Stubbington; 2, Mary Jane McNaughton; 1 s.; 3 d. Educ. Westcliff High School for Boys; Birkbeck College and Imperial College, London University. Lecturer in Physical Chemistry, Imperial

College, 1949-62; Professor of Physical Chemistry, Southampton University, 1962-80; Visiting Professor, University of Western Ontario, 1968; Visiting Professor and National Science Foundation Fellow, Case-Western Reserve University, Ohio, 1968-69; Visiting Professor, Buenos Aires University, 1976; Member, Advisory Council on Science and Technology, 1987-93; (Non-Executive) Member, Scottish Post Office Board, since 1986; Non-Executive Director, Scottish Enterprise, 1988-94; Fellow, Birkbeck College; Fellow, Royal Scottish Academy of Music and Drama; Honorary Fellow, Chartered Society of Designers, 1996; Fellow, University of East London; Director, Glasgow Chamber of Commerce, since 1981; President: Friends of Glasgow Cathedral, 1987-95, Society of Chemical Industry, 1991-93; Chairman, Quarriers Homes, since 1992; Commander Insignia: Order of Merit of Polish People's Republic, Royal Norwegian Order of Merit. Publications: Reference Electrodes, 1961; Polarography, 1964. Recreations: music; crofting; European politics. Address: (b.) Sunnyside of Threepwood, Laigh Threepwood, Beith, Ayrshire KA15 2JW.

Hind, Archie. Novelist and Playwright; b. 1928. Author of The Dear Green Place, 1966.

Hine, Professor Harry Morrison, MA, DPhil (Oxon). Scotstarvit Professor of Humanity, St. Andrews University, since 1985; b. 19.6.48, Portsmouth; m., Rosalind Mary Ford; 1 s.; 1 d. Educ. King Edward's School, Birmingham; Corpus Christi College, Oxford. P.S. Allen Junior Research Fellow, Corpus Christi College, 1972-75; Lecturer in Humanity, Edinburgh University, 1975-85. Editor (Joint), The Classical Review, 1987-93. Publications: An Edition with Commentary of Seneca, Natural Questions, Book Two, 1981; Studies in the Text of Seneca's Naturales Quaestiones, 1996; L. Annaei Senecae Naturales Quaestiones (Editor), 1996. Recreations: walking; reading. Address: (h.) 33 Drumcarrow Road, St. Andrews, Fife KY16 8SE; T.-01334 474459.

Hird, David Forbes, CA. General Manager, Forth Valley Health Board, since 1993; b. 11.5.43, Aberdeen; m., Irene; 1 s.; 2 d. Educ. Robert Gordon's College, Aberdeen; Aberdeen University. Range of finance posts in NHS, since 1966; District Finance Officer, East Fife District, 1974, North Lothian District, 1979; Director of Finance, Forth Valley Health Board, 1984. Recreation: curling. Address: (b.) 33 Spittal Street, Stirling FK8 1DX; T.-01786 457248.

Hirst, Sir Michael William, LLB, CA, FRSA. Chairman, Scottish Conservative and Unionist Party, 1993-97; b. 2.1.46, Glasgow; m., Naomi Ferguson Wilson; 1 s.; 2 d. Educ. Glasgow Academy; Glasgow University. Partner, Peat Marwick Mitchell & Co., Chartered Accountants, until 1983; Director of and Consultant to various companies; contested: Central Dunbartonshire, February and October, 1974, East Dunbartonshire, 1979; MP (Conservative), Strathkelvin and Bearsden, 1983-87; Member, Select Committee on Scottish Affairs, 1983-87; Parliamentary Private Secretary, Department of Energy, 1985-87; Vice-Chairman, Scottish Conservative Party, 1987-89; President, Scottish Conservative and Unionist Association; Chairman, Scottish Conservative Candidates Association, 1978-81; Hon. Secretary, British Diabetic Association; Chairman, The Park School Educational Trust; Member, Court, Glasgow Caledonian University; Director, Children's Hospice Association Scotland; Member, Executive Committee, Princess Louise Scottish Hospital, Erskine; Elder, Kelvinside Hillhead Parish Church. Recreations: golf; hill-walking; skiing. Address: (h.) Glentirran, Kippen, Stirlingshire FK8 3JA.

Hitchman, Professor Michael L., BSc, DPhil, CChem, FRSC, FRSA, FRSE. Young Professor of Chemistry, Strathclyde University, since 1984; b. 17.8.41, Woburn, Bedfordshire; m., Pauline J. Thompson; 1 s.; 2 d. Educ.

Stratton Grammar School, Biggleswade; Queen Mary College and King's College, London University; University College, Oxford. Assistant Lecturer in Chemistry, Leicester Regional College of Technology, 1963-65; Junior Research Fellow, Wolfson College, Oxford, 1968-70; ICI Postdoctoral Research Fellow, Physical Chemistry Laboratory, Oxford University, 1968-70; Chief Scientist, Orbisphere Corporation, Geneva, 1970-73; Staff Scientist, Laboratories RCA Ltd., Zurich, 1973-79; Lecturer, then Senior Lecturer, Salford University, 1979-84; Strathclyde University: Chairman, Department of Pure and Applied Chemistry, 1986-89, Vice-Dean, Faculty of Science, 1989-92; Honorary Professor, Taiyuan University of Technology, China, since 1994; Editor, Advanced Materials CVD, since 1995. Royal Society of Chemistry: Chairman, Electro-analytical Group, 1985-88, Treasurer, Electrochemistry Group, 1984-90; Member, Chemistry and Semiconductor Committees, Science and Engineering Research Council; Member, since 1985, Chairman, 1989-92, International Advisory Board, EUROCVD; Medal and Prize, British Vacuum Council, 1993. Publications: Ring-disk Electrodes (Co-Author), 1971; Measurement of Dissolved Oxygen, 1978; Chemical Vapor Deposition (Co-Editor), 1993. Recreations: humour; cooking; eating; rambling; losing weight. Address: (b.) Department of Pure and Applied Chemistry, Strathclyde University, 295 Cathedral Street, Glasgow G1 1XL; T.-0141-552 4400.

Hobsbaum, Professsor Philip Dennis, MA, PhD, DLitt, LRAM, LGSM. Poet and Critic; Professor of English Literature, Glasgow University, 1985-97, and Honorary Professorial Research Fellow, since 1997; b. 29.6.32, London; m., Rosemary Phillips. Educ. Belle Vue Grammar School, Bradford; Downing College, Cambridge; Sheffield University. Lecturer in English, Queen's University, Belfast, 1962-66; Lecturer, Senior Lecturer, Reader in English Literature, Glasgow University, 1966-85; Chairman of writers' groups in London, 1955-59, Belfast, 1962-66, Glasgow, 1966-75. Publications: A Group Anthology (Co-Editor), 1963; The Place's Fault, 1964; In Retreat, 1966; Coming Out Fighting, 1969; Ten Elizabethan Poets (Editor), 1969; A Theory of Communication, 1970; A Reader's Guide to Charles Dickens, 1972; Women and Animals, 1972; Tradition and Experiment in English Poetry, 1979; A Reader's Guide to D.H. Lawrence, 1981; Essentials of Literary Criticism, 1983; A Reader's Guide to Robert Lowell, 1988; Wordsworth: Selected Poetry and Prose (Editor), 1989; Channels of Communication (Co-editor), 1992; Metre, Rhythm and Verse Form, 1996; over 100 articles in learned journals; over 1,000 book reviews. Recreations: walking the dog; playing the piano. Address (h.) 10 Oban Drive, Glasgow G20 6AF; T.-0141 946 6653.

Hodge, Robin Mackenzie, BA (Hons). Publisher, The List magazine, since 1985; b. Edinburgh. Educ. Edinburgh Academy; Clifton College, Bristol; Durham University. Certificat Europeen en Administration de Projects Culturels (Bruelles). Director, Canongate Publishing Ltd., 1981-84; restoration of 16th-century buildings around Tweeddale Court, Edinburgh Old Town, 1981-88; founded The List, 1985. Address: (b.) 14 High Street, Edinburgh EH1 1TE; T.-0131-558 1191.

Hogg, Lt. Col. Colin Grant Ogilvie, DL. King's Own Scottish Borderers (KOSB), since 1962; Regimental Secretary, since 1991; b. 6.12.43, Glasgow; m., Cynthia Rose Mackenzie; 2 d. Educ. St. Mary's Preparatory School; Merchiston Castle School. Commissioned into KOSB, 1965; service with 1st Battalion in Aden, Hong Kong, Borneo, BAOR, Berlin, Northern Ireland; Deputy Assistant Adjutant General, HQ of 1st Armoured Division, Germany, 1981-83; on directing staff, Royal Military Academy, Sandhurst, 1983-84; Commanding Officer, 2nd Battalion, 52 Lowland Volunteers, 1985-88; SOI, Foot Guards and Infantry Manning and Records Office, 1988-91; retired from active list, 1991; Honorary Colonel of the Lothian and

Border Army Cadet Force, since 1997. Member: Queen's Bodyguard for Scotland, since 1986, Ancient Order of Mosstroopers; Chairman, Borders Branch, SSAFA, since 1993; Member, Board, South of Scotland Youth Awards Scheme, since 1994; Chairman, Roxburgh and Berwickshire Conservative and Unionist Association, since 1995; Governor: Oxenfoord Castle School, 1986-93, St. Mary's School, Melrose, 1994-98; Vice President, Jedburgh Branch, Royal British Legion Scotland, since 1994; Deputy Lieutenant, Roxburgh, Ettrick and Lauderdale, since 1995. Recreations: foxhunting; shooting; all equestrian events. Address: (h.) Mounthooly, Jedburgh TD8 6TJ; T.-01835 863368.

Hogg, Ian Alisdair Lawrence, MA, CA. Secretary, Scottish Rugby Union, since 1983; b. 13.6.40, Edinburgh; m., Louise; 1 s.; 1 d. Educ. George Watson's College; Edinburgh University. Chartered Accountant, 1961-78; Treasurer, Scottish Rugby Union, 1978-83. Recreations: rugby; cricket. Address: (b.) Scottish Rugby Union, Murrayfield, Edinburgh EH12 5PJ; T.-0131-346 5000.

Hogg of Cumbernauld, Lord (Norman), MP, Cumbernauld and Kilsyth, 1983-97 (MP, East Dunbartonshire, 1979-83); Non-executive Director, Kelvin Central Buses Ltd., since 1991; b. 12.3.38, Aberdeen; m., Elizabeth M. Christie. Educ. Ruthrieston Secondary School, Aberdeen. Local Government Officer, Aberdeen Town Council, 1953-67; District Officer, NALGO, 1967-79; Member: Transport Users Consultative Committee for Scotland, 1977-79, Select Committee on Scottish Affairs, 1979-82; Scottish Labour Whip, 1982-83; Chairman, Scottish Parliamentary Labour Group, 1981-82; Deputy Chief Opposition Whip, 1983-87; Scottish Affairs Spokesman, 1987-88; Member, Chairman's Panel, since 1988; Member, Public Accounts Committee, 1991-92. Recreation: music. Address: House of Lords, Westminster, London SW1A 0PW; T.-0171-219 3000.

Hogwood, Professor Brian Walter, BA, PhD. Professor of Politics, Department of Government, Strathclyde University, since 1991; b. 29.6.50, Glasgow; m., Patricia Brearey. Educ. Hamilton Academy; Glenrothes High School; Keele University. Economics Sub-Editor, Cambridge University Press, 1974-75; appointed Lecturer in Politics, Strathclyde University, 1975; Senior Lecturer, 1985; Reader, 1988. Recreations: cooking; computing; cross-country running. Address: (b.) Department of Government, Strathclyde University, McCance Building, 16 Richmond Street, Glasgow; T.-0141-552 4400, Ext. 2919.

Holland, Professor John, BSc, MBA, PhD. Professor of International Finance and Banking, since 1996, Head, Department of Accounting and Finance, since 1997, and Director of Postgraduate Studies, since 1990, University of Glasgow; b. 16.6.47; m., Janet Laurie; 1 s.; 1 d. Educ. Ullathorne Grammar School, Coventry; Aston University; University of Liverpool. Research Fellow, London Guildhall University, 1972-75; Lecturer, University of Bath, 1975-79; Lecturer, 1979-85, Senior Lecturer, 1986-95, University of Glasgow. Publications: many publications on international financial management, banking, corporate communication. Recreations: walking; theatre; eating out. Address: (b.) Department of Accounting and Finance, University of Glasgow, 65-71 Southpark Avenue, Glasgow G12 8LE; T.-0141-330 4136.

Holloway, Most Rev. Richard Frederick, BD, STM, DUniv (Strathclyde), DD (Aberdeen), FRSE. Gresham Professor of Divinity, since 1997; Bishop of Edinburgh, since 1986; Primus of the Scottish Episcopal Church, since 1992; b. 26.11.33; m., Jean Elizabeth Kennedy; 1 s.; 2 d. Educ. Kelham Theological College; Edinburgh Theological College; Union Theological Seminary, New York. Curate, St. Ninian's, Glasgow, 1959-63; Priest-in-charge, St. Margaret and St. Mungo's, Glasgow, 1963-68; Rector, Old

St. Paul's, Edinburgh, 1968-80; Rector, Church of the Advent, Boston, Mass, 1980-84; Vicar, St. Mary Magdalen's, Oxford, 1984-86. Recreations: running; long-distance walking; reading; going to the cinema; listening to music. Address: (h.) 3 Eglinton Crescent, Edinburgh EH12 5DH.

Holmes, George Dennis, CB (1979), FRSE, FICfor. Forestry Consultant, since 1987; b. 9.11.26, Conwy; m., Sheila Rosemary; 3 d. Educ. John Bright's School, Llandudno; University of Wales, Bangor. Forestry Commission, 1948-86 (Director General, 1976-86). Recreations: fishing; golf. Address: (h.) 7 Cammo Road, Barnton, Edinburgh EH4 8EF; T.-0131-339 7474.

Home Robertson, John David. MP (Labour), East Lothian, since 1983 (Berwick & East Lothian, 1978-83); b. 5.12.48, Edinburgh; m., Catherine Brewster; 2 s. Educ. Ampleforth College; West of Scotland Agricultural College. Farmer; Member: Berwickshire District Council, 1974-78, Borders Health Board, 1975-78; Chairman, Eastern Borders Citizens' Advice Bureau, 1976-78; Member, Select Committee on Scottish Affairs, 1979-83; Chairman, Scottish Group of Labour MPs, 1983; Scottish Labour Whip, 1983-84; Opposition Front Bench Spokesman on Agriculture, 1984-87, on Scotland, 1987-88, on Agriculture, 1988-90; Member, Select Committee on Defence, 1990-97. Address: (b.) House of Commons, Westminster, London, SW1A OAA.

Homfray, John L., MBE, TD, FCA. Director, Iona Abbey Ltd., since 1993; b. 5.8.16, Darjeeling, India; m., Elizabeth M. Shand; 2 s.; 1 d. Educ. Sherborne. Captain, RA 80 Field Regiment, 1940-45 (mentioned in Despatches); Director, Clyde Shipping Co. Ltd., Glasgow, 1948-81; Deputy Lieutenant, Dunbartonshire, 1975-90; Chairman, Iona Cathedral Trust Management Board, 1982-92; Lt. Col., City of Glasgow Artillery, RATA, 1953-57; Director, Glasgow Aged Seamen Relief Fund; Director, Sailors Orphan Society of Scotland. Recreation: travelling. Address: (h.) Ardballachan, Bracklinn Road, Callander, Perthshire; T.-01877 330256.

Hood, James. MP (Labour), Clydesdale, since 1987; b. 16.5.48, Lesmahagow; m., Marion; 1 s.; 1 d. Educ. Lesmahagow High School; Nottingham University. Local councillor, 1973-87; official of NUM, 1973-87; Leader, Nottingham striking miners, 1984-85; Chairman, Miners' Parliamentary Group, 1991-92; former Chairman, All-Party Group on ME; Chairman, European Legislation Select Committee; Convenor, Scottish Labour Group of MPs Home Affairs Committee; sponsor of three Private Members' Bills on under-age drinking and a Bill on ME. Address: (b.) House of Commons, London SW1A 0AA; T.-0171-219 4585.

Hood, Professor Neil, FRSE, MA, MLitt. Professor of Business Policy, Department of Marketing, Strathclyde University, since 1979; Director, Strathclyde International Business Unit, since 1992; b. 10.8.43, Wishaw; m., Anna Watson Clark; 1 s.; 1 d. Educ. Wishaw High School; Glasgow University. Research Fellow, Scottish College of Textiles, 1966-68; Lecturer/Senior Lecturer, Paisley College of Technology, 1968-78; Economic Adviser, Scottish Economic Planning Department, 1979; Director: Locate in Scotland, 1987-89, Employment and Special Initiatives, SDA, 1989-90; Visiting Professor: International Business, University of Texas, Dallas, 1981, Institute of International Business, Stockholm School of Economics, since 1982; Director, Euroscot Meat Exports Ltd., 1981-85; Economic Consultant to Secretary of State for Scotland, 1980-87; Director, Scottish Development Finance Ltd., 1984-90 and 1993-96; Deputy Chairman, Scottish Equity Partnership, since 1997; Investment Adviser, Castleforth Fund Managers, 1984-87; Director, LIFE Ltd., 1984-86; Board Member, Irvine Development Corporation, 1985-87;

Director: Prestwick Holdings PLC, 1986-87, Lamberton (Holdings) Ltd., 1989-92, GA (Holdings) Ltd., 1990-92, Shanks and McEwan PLC, 1990-94, I & S UK Smaller Companies Trust plc, since 1993, I & S Trustlink Ltd., since 1994, Kwik-Fit plc, since 1991, Grampian Holdings plc, since 1993; Corporate Adviser, Scottish Power, since 1989; Chairman, John Dickie Group Ltd., since 1995; Director, FI Group plc, since 1997; President, European International Business Association, 1985-86. Publications: Industrial Marketing — A Study of Textiles (Co-Author), 1970; Chrysler UK: A Corporation in Transition (Co-Author), 1977; The Economics of Multinational Enterprise (Co-Author), 1979; European Development Strategies of US Multinationals Located in Scotland (Co-Author), 1980; Multinationals in Retreat: The Scottish Experience (Co-Author), 1982; Multinational Investment Strategies in the British Isles (Co-Author), 1983; Industry, Policy and the Scottish Economy (Co-Editor), 1984; Transnational Corporations in the Textile Industry (Co-Author), 1984; Foreign Multinationals and the British Economy (Co-Author), 1987; Strategies in Global Competition (Co-Editor), 1987; Scottish Financial Sector (Co-Author), 1988; Marketing in Evolution (Co-Editor), 1996; Transition in Baltic States: Microlevel Studies (Co-Editor), 1997; Multinational Corporate Evolution and Subsidiary Development (Co-Editor), 1998. Recreations: swimming; reading; gardening. Address: (h.) 95 Mote Hill, Hamilton ML3 6EA; T.-01698 424870.

Hook, Professor Andrew Dunnet, MA, PhD. Bradley Professor of English Literature, Glasgow University, since 1979; b. 21.12.32, Wick; m., Judith Ann (deceased); 2 s.; 1 d. (deceased). Educ. Wick High School; Daniel Stewart's College, Edinburgh; Edinburgh University; Manchester University; Princeton University. Edinburgh University: Assistant Lecturer in English Literature, 1961-63, Lecturer in American Literature, 1963-70; Senior Lecturer in English, Aberdeen University, 1970-79; Chairman, Committee for Humanities and Member, Committee for Academic Affairs, CNAA, 1987-92; Chairman: Scottish Universities Council on Entrance English Panel, 1986-92, Universities and Colleges Admissions Service English Panel, since 1995; Member: Scottish Examination Board, 1984-92, Scottish Qualifications Authority English Panel, since 1996; President, Eighteenth-Century Scottish Studies Society, 1990-92. Publications: Scotland and America 1750-1835, 1975; American Literature in Context 1865-1900, 1983; Scott's Waverley (Editor), 1971; Charlotte Brontë's Shirley (Editor, with Judith Hook), 1974; Dos Passos: A Collection of Critical Essays (Editor), 1974; The History of Scottish Literature II, 1660-1800 (Editor), 1987; Scott Fitzgerald, 1992; The Glasgow Enlightenment (Co-Editor), 1995. Recreations: theatre; opera; catching up on reading. Address: (b.) Department of English Literature, Glasgow University, Glasgow G12 8QQ; T.-0141-339 8855, Ext. 4226.

Hooper, Ian Ross, BA. Depute Director (Resources), National Museums of Scotland, since 1989; Director, Museum of Scotland Project, since 1990; b. 26.5.49, Edinburgh; m., Julie Ellen Vaughan; 1 s.; 1 d. Educ. Hornchurch Grammar School; University of East Anglia. Administrator, Department of the Environment, 1973-89; seconded to English Heritage, 1984-85, responsible for historic buildings policy. Recreations: historic buildings; hill-walking; golf. Address: (b.) Royal Museum of Scotland, Edinburgh EH1 1JF; T.-0131-225 7534.

Hooper, Professor Martin Leslie, MA, PhD, FRSE. Professor of Molecular Pathology, University of Edinburgh, since 1996; b. 1.3.47, Walsall. Educ. Queen Mary's School, Walsall; University of Cambridge. MRC Research Scholar, MRC Laboratory of Molecular Biology, University of Cambridge, 1968-71; EMBO Research Fellow, Centre de Génétique Moléculaire, Gif-sur-Yvette, 1972-73; Research Fellow, Institute of Genetics, Glasgow, 1973-80; University of Edinburgh: Senior Lecturer in Experimental Pathology, 1980-90, Reader, Department of Pathology, 1990-96. Co-recipient, Margaret MacLellan Award, Tenovus Scotland, 1996. Recreations: walking; watching cricket; opera. Address: (b.) Sir Alastair Currie CRC Laboratories, Molecular Medicine Centre, Western General Hospital, Edinburgh EH4 2XU; T.-0131-651 1071.

Hope, Colin John Filshill, OStJ, BA, FCII, FCIS, FCIT, FBIM, MCIM, DipM. Director, Merchants House of Glasgow, 1981-87, 1988-94, 1995; Governor, Glasgow Educational and Marshall Trust, since 1986; b. 24.6.24, Dullatur; m., Jean Calder Douglas; 1 s.; 2 d. Educ. Glasgow High School; Glasgow Academy; Open University. RAF, 1942-47; joined Stenhouse & Partners, 1947; appointed Director, 1949; served in many capacities, including Managing Director, Stenhouse International; joined Norman Frizzell Scotland Ltd. as Managing Director, 1974; additionally Director, Norman Frizzell UK Ltd., 1976-81; Director, G.T. Senior, 1981-83 (Consultant, 1983-85); a Director, Glasgow Chamber of Commerce, 1979-88. Member: Scottish Consumer Council, 1979-85, Electricity Consultative Council for Scotland, 1979-87, General Convocation, Strathclyde University, 1980-90, Council, Insurance Ombudsman Bureau, 1981-94, Glasgow Airport Consultative Committee, since 1984; Governor, Keil School, 1986-91; former Chairman, Scottish Transport Users Consultative Committee; Member: Air Transport Committee, Association of British Chambers of Commerce, 1986-90, South of Scotland Electricity Consultative Committee, 1990-91; Director, Glasgow Native Benevolent Association, 1988-91 and since 1992; Member, Dumbartonshire Committee, Order of St. John, 1987-93. Address: (h.) Omaha, 4 Munro Drive East, Helensburgh G84 9BS; T.-01436 673091.

Hope of Craighead, Rt. Hon. Lord (James Arthur David Hope), PC. A Lord of Appeal in Ordinary, since 1996; b. 27.6.38, Edinburgh; m., Katharine Mary Kerr; 2 (twin) s.; 1 d. Educ. Edinburgh Academy; Rugby School; St. John's College, Cambridge (BA); Edinburgh University (LLB); Hon. LLD, Aberdeen (1991), Strathclyde (1993), Edinburgh (1995). National Service, Seaforth Highlanders, 1957-59; admitted Faculty of Advocates, 1965; Standing Junior Counsel to Inland Revenue, 1974-78; QC, 1978; Advocate Depute, 1978-82; Chairman, Medical Appeal Tribunal, 1985-86; Legal Chairman, Pensions Appeal Tribunal, 1985-86; Dean, Faculty of Advocates, 1986-89; A Senator of the College of Justice, Lord Justice General of Scotland, and Lord President of the Court of Session, 1989-96. President, The Stair Society, 1993; Hon. Professor of Law, Aberdeen, 1994; Baron (Life Peer), 1995. Publications: Gloag and Henderson's Introduction to Scots Law (Joint Editor, 7th edition, Assistant Editor, 8th and 9th editions); Armour on Valuation for Rating (Joint Editor, 4th and 5th editions); (Contributor) Stair Memorial Encyclopaedia of Scots Law. Address: (h.) 34 India Street, Edinburgh EH3 6HB; T.-0131-225 8245.

Hope, William, MA. Rector, Elgin High School, since 1978; b. 26.9.43, Scotland; m., Patricia Miller. Educ. Dalbeattie High School; Kirkcudbright Academy; Edinburgh University; Jordanhill College of Education. Alloa Academy: Assistant Teacher, Principal Teacher of Guidance; Assistant Rector, Lochaber High School. Chairman, Moray Branch, UNICEF; Vice Chairman, Elgin and District Branch, Cancer Relief; President: Forres St. Lawrence Cricket Club, North of Scotland Cricket Association. Recreations: umpiring hockey and cricket; fishing; public speaking. Address: (b.) Elgin High School, High School Drive, Elgin, Moray; T.-01343 545181.

Hopwood, Sylvia Elaine, MB, ChB, DPM. Psychiatrist, Tayside Region, and Honorary Lecturer, Dundee University, since 1962; b. 25.2.38, Salford; 2 d. Educ. Leeds University. Medical and neurological training, Leeds,

1960-62; psychiatric training, Dundee, 1962. Chairman, Gowrie Housing Association; Member, National Schizophrenia Fellowship and Manic Depressive Fellowship. Publications: many articles on alcoholism, depression and schizophrenia. Recreations: lace-making; embroidery; gardening. Address: (h.) 6 Strips of Craigie Road, Dundee DD4 7PZ; T.-01382 462265.

Horden, Professor John Robert Backhouse, MA, MLitt, DHL, FSA, FSA Scot, FRSL. Professor Emeritus of Bibliographical Studies, Stirling University; b. Warwickshire; m., Aileen Mary Douglas (deceased); 1 s. Educ. Oxford University; Cambridge University; Heidelberg University; Sorbonne; Lincoln's Inn. Former Director: Centre for Bibliographical Studies, Stirling University, Institute of Bibliography and Textual Criticism, Leeds University; former Tutor and Lecturer in English Literature, Christ Church, Oxford; Visiting Professorial appointments, Universities of Pennsylvania State, Saskatchewan, Erlangen-Nurnberg, Texas at Austin, Munster; Editor, Dictionary of Scottish Biography, since 1982; Cecil Oldman Memorial Lecturer, 1971; Marc Fitch Prize for Bibliography, 1979. Publications: Francis Quarles: A Bibliography of his Work to 1800, 1953; Francis Quarles' Hosanna and Threnodes (Editor), 1960; Annual Bibliography of English Language and Literature (Editor), 1967-75; English and Continental Emblem Books (22 vols.) (Editor), 1968-74; Art of the Drama, 1969; Dictionary of Concealed Authorship, Vol. 1 (Editor), 1980; initiator and first editor, Index of English Literary Manuscripts, twelve volumes, 1980-93; Everyday Life in Seventeenth-Century England, 1974; Techniques of Bibliography, 1977; John Freeth: Political Ballad Writer and Inn Keeper, 1985; Bibliographia (Editor), 1992. Recreations: golf (represented England, Warwickshire, Oxford, Cambridge); music; painting. Address: (b.) Department of English Studies, Stirling University, Stirling FK9 4LA.

Horn, David Bowes, BSc, PhD, CChem, FRSC, FRCPath, CBiol, FIBiol, FRSE; b. 18.8.28, Edinburgh; m., Shirley Kay Riddell; 2 d. Educ. Daniel Stewart's College, Edinburgh; Heriot-Watt University, Edinburgh; Edinburgh University. Senior Grade Biochemist: Vale of Leven Hospital, Alexandria, 1956, Queen Elizabeth Hospital, Birmingham, 1959; Biochemist, Royal Victoria Infirmary, Newcastle-upon-Tyne, and Honorary Lecturer, Department of Clinical Biochemistry, Newcastle-upon-Tyne University, 1959; Head, Department of Clinical Chemistry, Western General Hospital, Edinburgh, 1966-87; Honorary Senior Lecturer in Clinical Chemistry, Edinburgh University, 1966-87. Past Chairman: Scottish Region, Association of Clinical Biochemists (former Member, ACB National Council), Scientific Services Advisory Group Clinical Chemistry Sub-Committee; Royal Society of Chemistry Representative, Mastership in Clinical Biochemistry Examination Board, 1973-88. Recreations: computation; gardening; walking. Address: (h.) 2 Barnton Park, Edinburgh EH4 6JF; T.-0131-336 3444.

Horne, Allan Maxwell, BL, Solicitor (retired); Honorary Sheriff, Elgin, since 1981; b. 24.2.17, Brora; m., Margaret Ross; 1 d. Educ. Elgin Academy; Edinburgh University. Royal Artillery, 1940-46: commissioned 128th Field Regiment, 51st (H) Division, served as Air Observation Pilot, 1945-46, demobilised with rank of Captain; Legal Assistant, Inverness, 1946-49; Partner, Grigor & Young, Solicitors, Elgin, 1949-83, retiring as Senior Partner; Burgh Prosecutor, Elgin, 1950-75. Recreation: golf. Address: (h.) Melford, 11 Fleurs Place, Elgin; T.-Elgin 542833.

Horne, Rev. Archibald Sinclair. Minister, Reformed Presbyterian Church of Scotland, since 1955; Secretary and Lecturer, Scottish Reformation Society, since 1964; b. 9.3.27, Port Seton; m., Margaret Robertson Paterson; 2 s.; 1 d. Educ. Preston Lodge Secondary; London Bible College (External Student); New College, University of Edinburgh.

Publications: Torchbearers of the Truth, 1966; In the Steps of the Covenanters, 1974. Recreations: golf; gardening; photography; producing video films. Address: (b.) Magdalene Chapel, 41 Cowgate, Edinburgh EH1 1EE; T.-0131-220 1450.

Horner, Professor Robert Malcolm Wigglesworth, CEng, BSc, PhD, MICE, MIM. Professor of Engineering Management, since 1986 and Chair, School of Engineering and Physical Sciences, since 1997, Dundee University; Atlantic Power and Gas Ltd.: Non-executive Director, since 1991, Director, Research and Development, 1993-97; Chairman, Winton Caledonian Ltd., 1995-97, b. 27.7.42, Bury; m., Beverley Anne Wesley; 1 s.; 1 d. Educ. The Bolton School; University College, London. Civil Engineer, Taylor Woodrow Construction Ltd., 1966-77; Lecturer, Senior Lecturer, Head, Department of Civil Engineering, Dundee University, 1977-91; Managing Director, International Maintenance Management, 1996-97. Founder Chairman, Dundee Branch, Opening Windows on Engineering; Winner, CIOB Ian Murray Leslie Award, 1980 and 1984; Director, Dundee Rep., since 1991; Member, Council, National Conference of University Professors, 1989-93; Director, Scottish International Resource Project, 1994-95; Member: Technology Foresight Construction Sector Panel, since 1994, British Council Advisory Committee on Science and Engineering, since 1994; Chairman, Friends of St. Paul's Cathedral, 1993-95. Recreations: squash; gardening. Address: (h.) Westfield Cottage, 11 Westfield Place, Dundee DD1 4JU; T.-01382 225933.

Hornibrook, John Nevill, OBE, VRD, FEng, FIChemE. A Director, Renfrewshire Healthcare NHS Trust; Chairman, Awarding Body for Vocational Qualifications for the Chemical and Pharmaceutical Industries; Member, Court, and Chairman, Waste Management Centre, University of Paisley; b. 25.10.28, Gerrards Cross, Buckinghamshire; m., Dr. (Norma) Gillian Newbury; 2 d. Educ. Wellington College; Birmingham University. Various industrial appointments at home and overseas; Roche Products, Dalry, 1972-93, Divisional Director, 1981-93. Former Chairman, Enterprise Ayrshire. Recreations: sailing; gardening. Address: (h.) Cruachan, West Glen Road, Kilmacolm PA13 4PN; T.-01505 873265.

Horobin, John Charles, BSc, PhD. Head of Conference and Group Services, St. Andrews University, since 1989; Member: Kingdom of Fife Tourist Board, Council, British Universities Accommodation Consortium Ltd.; b. 13.2.45, Long Eaton; 1 s.; 1 d. Educ. Long Eaton Grammar School; King's College, London University; Durham University. Tutor-Organiser, WEA, Plymouth and West Devon, 1971-74; Assistant Director of Adult Education, St. Andrews University, 1974-89. Address: (b.) Residence and Business Services, St. Andrews University, 79 North Street, St. Andrews KY16 9AJ; T.-01334 462520.

Horsburgh, Sheriff John Millar Stewart, QC. Sheriff of Lothian and Borders, at Edinburgh, since 1990; b. 15.5.38. Admitted to Scots Bar, 1965. Address: (b.) Sheriff Court House, 27 Chambers Street, Edinburgh, EH1 1LB.

Horsfall, Sheriff A.C., MA, LLB. Member, Lands Tribunal for Scotland. Admitted Faculty of Advocates, 1953.

Houlihan, Professor Dominic Francis Joseph, BSc, PhD. Professor in Zoology, since 1992, and Head, Department of Zoology, since 1993, University of Aberdeen; b. 2.8.45, London; m., Margaret Swanston Catto; 2 s.; 1 d. Educ. St. Bonaventure's Grammar School, London; University of Bristol. Lecturer, 1970-84, Senior Lecturer, 1984-87, Reader, 1987, Personal Chair in Zoology, 1992, University of Aberdeen; Ciba-Geigy Senior Research Fellow, CNRS, Laboratory, Strasbourg, 1983-84; Visiting Professor, University of Naples, 1987; Member, SERC, AFRC,

BBSRC. Grant Awarding Committees; Senate Assessor to University Court, since 1996; External Examiner, undergraduate degree programmes, PhD, DSc. Publications: over 100 publications in scientific journals on animal physiology; seven reviews on protein metabolism in animals. Address: (b.) Department of Zoology, University of Aberdeen, Tillydrone Avenue, Aberdeen AB24 2TZ; T.-01224 272393.

Housden, Stuart David, BSc (Zoology). Director Scotland, RSPB, since 1993; b. 24.6.53, Croydon; m., Catherine Juliet Wilkin; 3 d. Educ. Selhurst Grammar School; Royal Holloway College, London University. Freshwater biologist, Thames Water, 1976; RSPB: Species Investigation Officer, 1977-79, Parliamentary Officer, 1979-82, Manager — Government Unit, 1982-85, Head, Conservation Planning Department, 1985-90, Head, Conservation Planning, 1990-93. Member, Cairngorms Partnership Board, since 1995; Churchill Fellow, 1992. Publications: Important Bird Areas in the UK (Co-Editor); numerous articles. Recreations: ornithology; travel; rugby football; politics; work. Address: (b.) 17 Regent Terrace, Edinburgh EH7 5BN; T.-0131-557 3136.

Houslay, Professor Miles Douglas, BSc, PhD, FRSE, FRSA, FIBiol, CBiol. Gardiner Professor of Biochemistry, Glasgow University, since 1984; b. 25.6.50, Wolverhampton; m., Rhian Mair; 2 s.; 1 d. Educ. Grammar School, Brewood, Stafford; University College, Cardiff; King's College, Cambridge; Cambridge University. ICI Research Fellow and Fellow, Queens' College, Cambridge, 1974-76; Lecturer, then Reader in Biochemistry, UMIST, 1976-82; Selby Fellow, Australian Academy of Science, 1984; Colworth Medal, Biochemical Society of Great Britain, 1984; Honorary Research Fellow, California Metabolic Research Foundation, since 1981; Editor in Chief, Cellular Signalling; Deputy Chairman, Biochemical Journal, 1984-89; Editorial Board, Biochimica Biophysica Acta; Member: Committee, Biochemical Society, 1982-85, Research Committee, British Diabetic Association, 1986-91; Chairman, Grant Committee A, Cell and Disorders Board, Medical Research Council, 1989-92; Member: Scientific and Medical Grant Committee, Scottish Home and Health Department, 1991-94, Advisory Board for External Appointments, London University, 1990-92, HEFC RAE Basic Medical and Dental Sciences Panel, since 1996, Wellcome Trust BMB Grant Panel, since 1996; Chairman, British Heart Foundation Project Grant Panel; Member, British Heart Foundation Chairs and Programme Grant Panel, since 1997; Trustee, British Heart Foundation, since 1997. Publication: Dynamics of Biological Membranes; over 300 scientific papers. Address: (b.) Department of Biochemistry, Glasgow University, G12 8QQ; T.-0141-330 5903.

Housley, Edward, MB, ChB, FRCPEdin, FRCP. Consultant Physician, Edinburgh Royal Infirmary, since 1970; Honorary Senior Lecturer, Department of Medicine, Edinburgh University, since 1970; Medical Specialist, Armed Forces Scotland, since 1975; b. 10.1.34, Chester, USA; 1 d. Educ. Mundella Grammar School, Nottingham; Birmingham University. Postgraduate training, Department of Medicine, Birmingham University and McGill University, Montreal. Recreation: crossword puzzles. Address: (h.) 6 Kew Terrace, Edinburgh, EH12 5JE.

Houston, Major General David, CBE. Lord Lieutenant of Sutherland, since 1991; b. 24.2.29.

Houston, Rev. Dr. Graham Richard, BSc (Hons), BD (Hons), MTh, PhD. Chaplain, Heriot-Watt University, since 1990; b. 3.5.50, Glasgow; m., Irene Elizabeth Robertson; 1 s.; 2 d. Educ. Hutchesons' Boys' Grammar School, Glasgow; Strathclyde University; Aberdeen University. Assistant, project, Govan, 1972-73; Assistant Minister, Palmerston Place Church, Edinburgh, 1976-77; Minister:

Kildonan and Loth Church, Sutherland, 1978-82, Letham St. Mark's Church, Perth, 1982-90. Publications: Prophecy Now, 1989; Virtual Morality, 1998. Recreations: squash; golf; cricket. Address: (h.) 3 Ramsay Place, Penicuik, Midlothian EH26 9JS; T.-01968 672752.

Houstoun, Andrew Beatty, OBE, MC, JP, DL. Vice President, Scottish Landowners Federation, since 1984; b. 15.10.22, Cranleigh; m., Mary Elizabeth Spencer-Nairn; 4 s. Educ. Harrow. Regular Army, 1941-56; retired as Major, 1st The Royal Dragoons; farming, Angus and Perthshire, since 1956; commanded Fife and Forfar Yeomanry/Scottish Horse (TA), 1962-65; retired Brevet Col. and Lt. Col, 1965; Angus County Councillor, 1966-75 (Vice Chairman, Education Committee); Convener, Scottish Landowners Federation, 1979-82; Chancellor's Assessor, Dundee University Court, 1981-92; Vice Lord Lieutenant, Angus, since 1986. Address: Kirkhill, Lintrathen, Kirriemuir, Angus DD8 5JH; T.-01575 560228.

Howard, Professor Ian, MA (Hons), ARSA. Professor of Fine Art, Duncan of Jordanstone College of Art, Dundee, since 1986; b. 5.11.52, Aberdeen; m., Ruth D'Arcy; 2 d. Educ. Aberdeen Grammar School; Edinburgh College of Art; Edinburgh University. Travelling scholarship to Italy, 1976; part-time Lecturer in Painting, Gray's School of Art, Aberdeen, 1977 (appointed full-time, 1980); Scottish Arts Council Award, 1979, Bursary, 1985-86; numerous one-man and group exhibitions; appointed to Faculty of Fine Art, British School at Rome. Recreations: reading; music; cooking. Address: (b.) School of Fine Art, Duncan of Jordanstone College of Art, University of Dundee, Dundee; T.-01382 345227.

Howard, Philip, MA (Hons) (Cantab), MLitt. Artistic Director, Traverse Theatre, Edinburgh, since 1996; b. 27.5.63, York. Educ. Ampleforth College, York; Girton College, Cambridge; St. Andrews University. Assistant Director, Royal Court Theatre, London, 1988-90; Director, National Gaelic Youth Theatre, Isle of Benbecula, 1989-92. Director, TOSG Gaelic Theatre Company, since 1996. Address: (b.) Traverse Theatre, Cambridge Street, Edinburgh, EH1 2ED; T.-0131-228 3223.

Howe, Professor James Alexander Macgregor, MA, PhD, FAAAI. Head, Department of Artificial Intelligence, Edinburgh University, 1978-96 (Professor of Artificial Intelligence, 1985-97); b. 7.7.37, Glasgow; m., Nan Harvie Bell; 1 s.; 2 d. Educ. Kelvinside Academy, Glasgow; St. Andrews University; Cambridge University. Senior Assistant in Research, Laboratory of Experimental Psychology, Cambridge University, 1964-66; Research Fellow, Lecturer, Senior Lecturer, Reader, Department of Artificial Intelligence, Edinburgh University, 1967-85; Founder Director, Conversational Software Ltd., 1969-73; Founder and Chairman, Artificial Intelligence Applications Institute, Edinburgh University, since 1984; Governor, Scottish Council for Educational Technology, 1981-84; Chairman, Society for the Study of Artificial Intelligence and the Simulation of Behaviour, 1982-85; Chairman, Alvey Directorate's IKBS Advisory Group, 1983-88; Chairman, SERC/DTI Systems Engineering – Committee A, 1988-91; Member, Ordnance Survey Science and Technology Advisory Committee, 1987-92; Member, Court, Edinburgh University, 1994-97. Publications: contributor to 60 books and journals. Recreations: skiing; curling; gardening; golf. Address: (h.) 26 Essex Road, Edinburgh, EH4 6LJ; T.-0131-339 5390.

Howie, Andrew Law, CBE, FRAgrS. Chairman: Robert Howie & Sons, since 1982, Scottish Milk Ltd., 1994-95; b. 14.4.24, Dunlop; m., Joan Duncan; 2 s.; 2 d. Educ. Glasgow Academy. Joined Robert Howie & Sons, 1941; War Service, RN; became Director, 1965; President, Scottish Compound Feed Manufacturers, 1968-70 and 1983-85; President, Compound Animal Feed Manufacturers National

Association, 1971-72; Director, Scottish Corn Trade, 1976-78; Vice-President/Feed, UK Agricultural Supply Trade Association, 1980-81; Chairman, Scottish Council, UKASTA, 1985-87; Director, Scottish Milk Marketing Board, 1980-94 (Chairman, 1982-94); Member, CBI Scottish Council, 1989-95. Recreations: golf; gardening. Address: (h.) Newmill House, Dunlop, Kilmarnock KA3 4BQ; T.-01560 484936.

Howie, Professor John Garvie Robertson, CBE, MD, PhD, FRCPE, FRCGP. Professor of General Practice, Edinburgh University, since 1980; b. 23.1.37, Glasgow; m., Elizabeth Margaret Donald; 2 s.; 1 d. Educ. High School of Glasgow; Glasgow University. Registrar, Laboratory Medicine, Western Infirmary, Glasgow, 1962-66; General Practitioner, Glasgow, 1966-70; Lecturer/Senior Lecturer in General Practice, Aberdeen University, 1970-80; Member: Biomedical Research Committee, SHHD, 1977-81, Health Services Research Committee, SHHD, 1982-86, Chief Scientist Committeee, SHHD, 1987-97, Committee on the Review of Medicines, 1986-91; Chairman, Heads of Departments of General Practice Group. Publication: Research in General Practice. Recreations: golf; gardening; music. Address: (h.) 4 Ravelrig Park, Balerno, Midlothian EH14 7DL; T.-0131-449 6305.

Howie, Professor John Mackintosh, CBE, MA, DPhil, DSc, FRSE. Regius Professor of Mathematics, St. Andrews University, 1970-97; b. 23.5.36, Chryston, Lanarkshire; m., Dorothy Joyce Miller; 2 d. Educ. Robert Gordon's College, Aberdeen; Aberdeen University. Assistant in Mathematics, Aberdeen University, 1958-59; Assistant, then Lecturer in Mathematics, Glasgow University, 1961-67; Senior Lecturer in Mathematics, Stirling University, 1967-70; visiting appointments:Tulane University, 1964-65, State University of New York at Buffalo, 1969-70, University of Western Australia, 1968, Monash University, 1979, Northern Illinois University, 1988, University of Lisbon, 1996; Dean of Science, St. Andrews University, 1976-79. President, Edinburgh Mathematical Society, 1972-73; Vice-President, London Mathematical Society, 1984-86 and since 1990; Convener, SCEEB Mathematics Panel, 1970-73; Chairman, Scottish Central Committee on Mathematics, 1975-81; Member, Committee to Review Examinations (Dunning Committee), 1975-77; Chairman, Governors, Dundee College of Education, 1983-87; Keith Prize, Royal Society of Edinburgh, 1979-81; Chairman, Committee to review Fifth and Sixth Years (Howie Committee), 1990-92. Publications: An Introduction to Semigroup Theory, 1976; Automata and Languages, 1991; Fundamentals of Semigroup Theory, 1995; papers in mathematical journals. Recreations: music; gardening. Address: (b.) Mathematical Institute, St. Andrews University, North Haugh, St. Andrews, KY16 9SS; T.-01334 463746.

Howie, Professor Peter William, MD, FRCOG, FRSE, FRCP (Glas). Professor of Obstetrics and Gynaecology, Dundee University, since 1981 (Deputy Principal, Dundee University, since 1996, Dean, Medicine and Dentistry, 1990-93); b. 21.11.39, Aberdeen; m., Anne Jardine Quigg; 1 s.; 1 d. Educ. High School of Glasgow; Glasgow University. Astor Foundation Research Fellow, Royal College of Pathologists, 1970-71; Lecturer, then Senior Lecturer, Department of Obstetrics and Gynaecology, Glasgow University, 1971-78; Clinical Consultant, Medical Research Council Reproductive Biology Unit, Edinburgh, 1978-81. Recreations: golf; music. Address: (h.) 8 Travebank Gardens, Monifieth, Angus DD5 4ET; T.-01382 534802.

Howie, William Forbes, DL, JP, BSc, CEng, MIEE, BA. Justice of the Peace, since 1974; Deputy Lieutenant, Stirling and Falkirk District, since 1981; General Commissioner of Income Tax, since 1983; b. 13.8.20, Falkirk; m., Janet M. Campbell; 2 s.; 1 d. Educ. Falkirk High School; Glasgow University; Open University. RAF, during Second World War (demobbed as Flight Lieutenant); Managing Director, Thomas Laurie & Co. Ltd., 1956-81; appointed Chairman, Children's Panel Advisory Committee, Falkirk, 1970; Chairman, Supplementary Benefit Appeal Tribunal, Stirling and Falkirk, 1973-88; Past Chairman, Forth Valley Scouts; former Session Clerk St. Andrews Church, Falkirk; set up Stirling and District Amateur Football Association, 1951 (its first Secretary); set up Falkirk Section, Scottish Wildlife Trust, 1984. Recreations: golf; bowls; colour photography; gardening; wildlife. Address: 12 Gartcows Crescent, Falkirk FK1 5QH; T.-Falkirk 24128.

Howison, John Andrew, BSc, MSc, CEng, MICE, ACIArb. Deputy Chief Engineer, Roads Directorate, Scottish Office Industry Department, since 1992; b. 12.8.46, Ruislip; m., Teresa Maria; 2 s.; 2 d. Educ. Surbiton Grammar School; Edinburgh University; Heriot Watt University. Edinburgh Corporation, 1968-70; Livingston Development Corporation, 1970-73; Department of Environment/Department of Transport/Scottish Office, since 1973. Address: (b.) Victoria Quay, Edinburgh; T.-0131-244 7204.

Howson, Peter. Painter; b. 1958, London. Studied, Glasgow School of Art, 1975-77. Official artist, Gulf War.

Hoy, William. Director of Communications, Scottish Homes, since 1992; b. 23.4.50, Dalkeith; m., Sheena; 2 s.; 1 d. Educ. Dalkeith High School; Esk Valley College. Scottish Office: Information Officer, 1978-82, Senior Information Officer, 1982-90, Principal Information Officer, 1990-92. Recreations: golf; gardening; art; reading. Address: (h.) 5 New Meadowspott, Eskbank, Midlothian; T.-0131-663 5986.

Ho-Yen, Darrel Orlando, BMSc (Hons), MBChB, MD, FRCPath. Consultant Microbiologist, Raigmore Hospital, Inverness, since 1987; Director, Scottish Toxoplasma Reference Laboratory, since 1987; Honorary Clinical Senior Lecturer, Aberdeen University, since 1987; b. 1.5.48; m., Jennifer Nicholls; 2 s. Educ. Dundee University. Ninewells Hospital and Medical School, Dundee, 1974-83; Regional Virus Laboratory, Ruchill Hospital, Glasgow, 1983-87. Publications: Better Recovery from Viral Illnesses; Diseases of Infection (Co-Author); Unwind; Human Toxoplasmosis (Co-Author); Climbing Out. Address: (b.) Microbiology Department, Raigmore Hospital, Inverness IV2 3UJ; T.-01463 704206.

Hubbuck, Professor John Reginald, BA (Cantab), MA, DPhil (Oxon), FRSE, FRSA, CMath, FIMA. Professor of Mathematics, Aberdeen University, since 1978; b. 3.5.41, Girvan; m., Anne Neilson; 1 s.; 1 d. Educ. Manchester Grammar School; Queens' College, Cambridge; Pembroke College, Oxford. Fellow: Gonville and Caius College, Cambridge, 1970-72, Magdalen College, Oxford, 1972-78; President, Edinburgh Mathematical Society, 1985-86. Recreation: hill-walking. Address: (h.) 8 Fonthill Terrace, Aberdeen AB1 2UR; T.-01224 588738.

Hudson, Christopher Sydney, DSO (and Bar), FInstM, CIPD; b. 1.8.16, Tunbridge Wells; m., Ruth Julia Risse; 1 d. Educ. privately, in Switzerland. Army Service, Royal Fusiliers and SOE, 1940-45 (Lt.-Col.); Control Commission for Germany (British and US Sectors), 1946-53; Personnel Manager in overseas companies, Shell International Petroleum Co., Israel, Trinidad, Congo, Algeria; seconded to International Labour Organisation, Geneva, 1966; Executive in charge of Personnel, Training and Industrial Relations, Bank of Scotland, 1968-80. Croix de Guerre with Palme. Recreations: golf; swimming. Address: (h.) Invereil House, North Berwick, East Lothian EH39 5DH; T.-01620 893646.

Hudson, Rev. Eric Vallance, LTh. Minister, Westerton Fairlie Memorial Church, since 1990; b. 22.2.42, Glasgow;

m., Lorna Mary Miller; 1 s.; 1 d. Educ. Paisley Grammar School; Wollongong High School, NSW; Christ's College, Aberdeen and Aberdeen University. Sub-Editor, D.C. Thomson & Co. Ltd., Dundee, 1961-66; Student Assistant, West Kirk of St. Nicholas, Aberdeen, 1966-69; Senior Assistant Minister, New Kilpatrick Parish Church, Bearsden, 1971-73; Minister, Kintore Parish Church, 1973-78; Religious Programmes Officer, Scottish Television, 1978-89; Convener, Association of Bearsden Churches, since 1997; Member: Religious Advisory Committee, Radio Clyde, Church of Scotland Board of Social Responsibility, since 1997. Address: 3 Canniesburn Road, Bearsden, Glasgow G61 1PW.

Huggins, Martin, MA, FRSA. Co-Founder and Principal, Edinburgh School of English, since 1969; b. 14.4.39, Edinburgh; m., 1, Astrid Chalmers Watson (m. diss.); 2 d.; 2, Margot Learmond. Educ. George Watson's College; Edinburgh University. Chairman, Scottish Craftsmanship Association, 1977-84; Governor, Edinburgh College of Art, 1980-92; Director, Edinburgh Chamber of Commerce, 1982-86; Chairman, ARELS, 1984-86; Member, British Council Recognition Advisory Committee, 1984-86; Chairman, Board of Governors, Edinburgh College of Art, 1990-92; President, Scottish Arts Club, 1990-92; Assistant, Masters Court, Edinburgh Merchant Company, 1992-95; Trustee, Hospitalfield Trust, since 1994. Recreations: music; travel; lunching at the Arts Club. Address: (h.) 13 Ainslie Place, Edinburgh EH3 6AS; T.-0131-226 1246.

Hughes, Rev. Clifford Eryl, MA, BD, CertEd. Minister, St. Mary's Parish Church, Haddington, since 1993; b. 16.12.36, Newport, S. Wales; m., Kathleen Mackenzie Craig; 1 s.; 1 d. Educ. Dulwich College, London; King's College, University of Cambridge; New College, University of Edinburgh. Teacher, Hurst Grange School, Stirling; Headmaster, Beaconhurst School, Bridge of Allan; Headmaster, Loretto Junior School. Professional singer (opera, concert hall, radio and television performances). President, Haddington Club, 1998. Recreations: listening to and reviewing music. Address: St. Mary's Manse, 21 Sidegate, Haddington EH41 4BZ; T.-01620 823109.

Hughes, Professor John, BSc, CEng, FIMechE, FISPO. Professor and Director, National Centre for Prosthetics and Orthotics, Strathclyde University, since 1972; b. 20.4.34, Renfrew; m., Margaret Scoular Crichton; 2 d. Educ. Camphill School; Strathclyde University. Worked in shipbuilding and engineering, 1950-63; Strathclyde University: Lecturer in Mechanical Engineering Design, 1963-67, Senior Lecturer, Bioengineering Unit, 1967-72; Past President, International Society for Prosthetics and Orthotics. Recreations: golf; gardening. Address: (b.) Strathclyde University, Curran Building, 131 St. James' Road, Glasgow G4 OLS; T.-0141-552 4049.

Hughes of Woodside, Lord (Robert Hughes). MP (Labour), Aberdeen North, 1970-97; b. 3.1.32; m.; 2 s.; 3 d. Educ. Powis Secondary School, Aberdeen; Robert Gordon's College, Aberdeen; Benoni High School, Transvaal; Pietermaritzburg Technical College, Natal. Engineering apprenticeship, South African Rubber Company, Natal, 1949-54; draughtsman, C.F. Wilson & Co., Aberdeen, 1954-70; Member, Aberdeen City Council, 1962-71; Chairman, Aberdeen City Labour Party, 1961-69; Member, Select Committee on Scottish Affairs, 1971; Opposition Junior Spokesman on Scottish Affairs, 1972-74; Parliamentary Under Secretary of State, Scottish Office, 1974-75; Chairman, Select Committee on Scottish Affairs, 1981; Opposition Junior Spokesman on Transport, 1981-83; Opposition Principal Spokesman on Agriculture, 1984-85, on Transport, 1985-87; Member, General Medical Council, 1976-79; Chairman: Anti Apartheid Movement, 1976-94, Action for Southern Africa (ACTSA), since 1994; Vice-Convenor, Scottish Group, Labour MPs, 1989; Convenor, Scottish Group of Labour MPs, 1990-91; Member, Select Committee on Scottish Affairs, 1992-97. Address: (b.) House of Lords, London.

Hughes, Rt. Hon. Lord (William Hughes), PC (1970), CBE (1956), DL, LLD. Company Director; b. 22.1.11, Dundee; m., Christian Clancher Gordon (deceased); 2 d. Educ. Balfour Street School; Dundee Technical College. ARP Controller, Dundee, 1939-43; Armed Forces, 1943-46 (commissioned 1944, demobilised as Captain, 1946, served India, Labuan and Burma); Member, Dundee Town Council, 1933-36 and 1937-61; City Treasurer, 1946-47; Lord Provost, 1954-60; Chairman, Eastern Regional Hospital Board, 1948-60; Member: Court, St. Andrews University, 1954-63, Council, Queen's College, Dundee, 1954-63, Committee on Civil Juries, 1958-59, Committee to Inquire into Registration of Title to Land, 1960-62, North of Scotland Hydro Electric Board, 1957-64, Scottish Transport Council, 1960-64; Chairman: Glenrothes Development Corporation, 1960-64, East Kilbride Development Corporation, 1975-82, Royal Commission on Legal Services in Scotland, 1976-80; Joint Parliamentary Under Secretary of State for Scotland, 1964-69; Minister of State for Scotland, 1969-70 and 1974-75; President, Scottish Federation of Housing Associations, 1975-93; Member, Council of Europe and Western European Union, 1976-87; Hon. Member, Council of Europe, since 1987. Recreation: gardening. Address: (h.) The Stables, Ross, Comrie, Perthshire; T.-01764 670557.

Hughes, William Young, CBE. Chairman and Chief Executive, Grampian Holdings plc, since 1985 (Chief Executive, 1976-85); Chairman, Aberforth Smaller Companies Trust PLC, since 1990; Treasurer, Scottish Conservative Party, since 1993 (Deputy Chairman, 1989-92); Director, Central Scotland Healthcare NHS Trust, since 1994; b. 12.4.40, Milnrow, Lancaster; m., Anne Macdonald Richardson; 2 s.; 1 d. Educ. Firth Park Grammar School, Sheffield; Glasgow University; Strathclyde University; Heriot-Watt University. Partner, R. Gordon Drummond, 1966-70; Managing Director, MSJ Securities Ltd., 1970-76. Chairman, CBI Scotland, 1987-89; Member, Governing Council, Scottish Business in the Community. Recreations: Member, Glenbervie Golf Club. Address: (b.) Stag House, Castlebank Street, Glasgow G11 6DY; T.-0141-357 2000.

Hughes Hallett, Professor Andrew Jonathan, BA (Hons), MSc (Econ), DPhil, FRSA. Professor of Economics, Strathclyde University, since 1989; Research Fellow, Centre for Economic Policy Research, since 1985; Consultant to World Bank, UN, EEC, etc., since 1986; Professor and Fulbright Fellow, Princeton University, 1992-94; Jean Monet Professor, since 1996; b. 1.11.47, London; m., Claudia; 2 s.; 1 d. Educ. Radley College; Warwick University; LSE; Oxford University. Lecturer in Economics, Bristol University, 1973-77; Associate Professor, Erasmus University, Rotterdam, 1977-85; David Dale Professor, Newcastle University, 1985-89. Publications: four books; 145 papers. Address: (b.) 100 Cathedral Street, Glasgow G4 0LN; T.-0141-552 4400.

Hughes Hallett, David John, FRICS. Director, Scottish Wildlife Trust, since 1989; Main Board Member, Scottish Environment Protection Agency, since 1995; Chairman, Balerno High School Board, since 1995; b. 19.6.47, Dunfermline; m., Anne Mary Wright; 2 s.; 1 d. Educ. Fettes College; Reading University. Chartered Surveyor, rural practice, 1966-76; Land Use Adviser, then Director, Scottish Landowners' Federation, 1976-89. Convener, Association of Chief Officers of Scottish Voluntary Organisations; Member, Policy Committee, Scottish Council for Voluntary Organisations. Recreations: sailing; cycling; singing. Address: (h.) 8 Crosswood Crescent, Balerno, Edinburgh EH14 7HS; T.-0131-449 2244.

Hughson, A.V. Mark, MD, MB, ChB, FRCPsych, DPM. Consultant Psychiatrist, Leverndale Hospital, Glasgow, since 1990; Honorary Clinical Senior Lecturer, Glasgow University, since 1991; b. 12.3.47, Edinburgh; m., Joan Scally; 2 s. Educ. George Watson's College, Edinburgh; Glasgow University. Recreations: playing the organ (not too badly); skiing (badly). Address: (h.) 1 Cleveden Gardens, Glasgow G12 0PU; T.-0141-334 2473.

Hull, John Hewett, FRSE, BSc (Hons), MSc, CGeol, FGS. Assistant Director, British Geological Survey, 1982-94; Senior Officer in Scotland and Head, Geological Survey of Scotland, N. Ireland and Northern England, 1982-94; Head, Petroleum Geology, Geophysics and Offshore Surveys, 1985-94; b. 18.6.34, Manchester; m., Peggy Dunning. Educ. Manchester Central Grammar School; Birmingham University. H.M. Geological Survey of Great Britain, 1958-65; Natural Environment Research Council, 1966-94; Hon. Research Fellow, Edinburgh University; Vice-President, Edinburgh Geological Society, 1993-97. Publications: numerous books, professional papers and maps. Recreations: sport; visual arts; music. Address: (h.) 14 Laverockdale Park, Colinton, Edinburgh EH13 0QE; T.-0131-441 7563.

Hume, Sir Alan (Blyth), Kt, CB, MA; b. 5.1.13, Broxburn; m., Marion Morton Garrett; 1 s.; 1 d. Educ. George Heriot's School, Edinburgh; Edinburgh University. Scottish Office: entered, 1936, Under Secretary, Scottish Home Department, 1957-59, Assistant Under Secretary of State, 1959-62, Under Secretary, Ministry of Public Building and Works, 1963-64, Secretary, Scottish Development Department, 1965-73. Chairman: Ancient Monuments Board for Scotland, 1973-81, Edinburgh New Town Conservation Committee, 1975-90. Recreations: golf; fishing. Address:(h.) 12 Oswald Road, Edinburgh EH9 2HJ; T.-0131-667 2440.

Hume, James Douglas Howden, CBE, BSc, CEng, FIMechE, Hon. LLD (Strathclyde). Chairman and Managing Director, Drimard Limited, since 1988; Non-Executive Director, Magnum Power PLC Ltd.; b. 4.5.28, Melbourne, Australia; m., June Katharine Spriggs; 1 s.; 2 d. Educ. Loretto; Strathclyde University; Glasgow University. Royal Artillery, 1944-46 (2nd Lt.); engineering training: James Howden & Company Limited, 1948-54, Production Engineering Limited, 1954-55; James Howden & Company Limited: Production Manager, 1955-56, appointed Director, 1957, Joint Managing Director 1960, Managing Director, 1963; Howden Group PLC: Managing Director, 1968, Deputy Chairman and Managing Director, 1973, appointed Chairman, 1987 (resigned, November 1987). Member, Court, Strathclyde 1989-92. Address: (b.) Drimard Limited, 22 East Lennox Drive, Helensburgh, Dunbartonshire G84 9JD; T.-01436 75132.

Hume, John Robert, BSc, ARCST, FSA, FSA Scot, Hon FRIAS. Chief Inspector of Historic Buildings, Historic Scotland; Member, Inland Waterways Amenity Advisory Council, since 1974; Member, Industrial Archaeology Sub-Committee, English Heritage, since 1985; Honorary Life President, Seagull Trust, since 1994 (Chairman, 1978-93); Trustee, Scottish Maritime Museum, since 1983; Honorary Vice-President, Association for Industrial Archaeology; b. 26.2.39, Glasgow; m., Catherine Hope Macnab; 4 s. Educ. Hutchesons' Boys' Grammar School; Glasgow University; Royal College of Science and Technology. Assistant Lecturer, Lecturer, Senior Lecturer in Economic History, Strathclyde University, 1964-91. Member, Ancient Monuments Board for Scotland, 1981-84; Director, Scottish Industrial Archaeology Survey, 1978-84. Publications: The Industrial Archaeology of Glasgow; The Industrial Archaeology of Scotland; as Co-Author: Workshop of the British Empire: Engineering and Shipbuilding in the West of Scotland; Beardmore: the History of a Scottish Industrial Giant; The Making of Scotch Whisky; A Bed of Nails: a History of P. MacCallum & Sons Ltd.; Shipbuilders to the World: a History of Harland and Wolff; Steam

Entertainment; Historic Industrial Scenes: Scotland; Industrial History in Pictures: Scotland; Glasgow's Railway Stations. Recreations: photography; reading. Address: (h.) 28 Partickhill Road, Glasgow G11 5BP.

Hume, Krystyna D., BSc. Head Teacher, St. Serf's School, Edinburgh, since 1992; b. 2.10.43, Edinburgh; m., Bill Hume; 2 s. Educ. James Gillespie's High School for Girls; Edinburgh University. Teacher of Mathematics: Portobello Secondary School, 1966-74 (Housemistress, 1970-74), St. Serf's School, 1981-92. Recreations: reading; going to the theatre and concerts; listening to music. Address: (b.) St. Serf's School, 5 Wester Coates Gardens, Edinburgh EH12 5LT; T.-0131-337 1015.

Hume, Robert, BSc, MBChB, PhD, FRCP(Edin), FRCPCH. Reader in Developmental Medicine, Dundee University; Consultant Paediatrician and Honorary Consultant in Biochemical Medicine, Dundee Teaching Hospitals NHS Trust; b. 5.4.47, Edinburgh; m., Shaena Finlayson Blair; 2 d. Educ. Dalkeith High School; Edinburgh University. MRC Fellow, Department of Biochemistry, Edinburgh University, 1975-78; Lecturer, Department of Child Life and Health, Edinburgh University, 1978-80; Senior Lecturer, Department of Child Life and Health, Edinburgh University, 1980-92. Medical and Dental Defence Union of Scotland Specialist Advisor. Address: (b.) Centre for Research into Human Development, Departments of Child Health, Obstetrics and Gynaecology, Ninewells Hospital and Medical School, Dundee DD1 9SY; T.-01382 660111.

Humfrey, Professor Peter Brian, BA, MA, PhD. Professor of Art History, University of St. Andrews, since 1995; b. 9.4.47, Cyprus; m., Margaret Zarina; 2 s. Educ. Cranleigh School, Surrey; Trinity College, Dublin. Lecturer in Art History, University of St. Andrews, 1977; Senior Visiting Fellow, Center for Advanced Studies in the Visual Arts, National Gallery of Art, Washington D.C., 1986; Fellow, Harvard Center for Italian Renaissance Studies, Villa I Tatti, Florence, 1987, 1991; Member, Institute for Advanced Study, Princeton, 1988. Publications: Cima da Conegliano, 1983; The Altarpiece in Renaissance Venice, 1993; Painting in Renaissance Venice, 1995; Lorenzo Lotto, 1997. Address: (b.) School of Art History, University of St. Andrews, St. Andrews KY16 9AL; T.-01334 462400.

Humphrey, James Malcolm Marcus, CBE, DL, OStJ, MA, FRICS. Member, Aberdeenshire Council, since 1995 (Member, Grampian Regional Council, 1974-94); Deputy Lieutenant, Aberdeenshire, since 1989; Alternate Member, European Committee of the Regions; Non-Executive Director, Grampian Healthcare NHS Trust; b. 1.5.38, Montreal, Canada; m., Sabrina Margaret Pooley; 2 s.; 2 d. Educ. Eton College; Oxford University. Conservative Parliamentary candidate, North Aberdeen, 1966, Kincardine and Deeside, 1991; Council Member, National Farmers Union of Scotland, 1968-73; Member, Aberdeen County Council, 1970-75 (Chairman of Finance, 1973-75); Grampian Regional Council, 1974-78: Leader of the Council, Chairman of Finance, Leader, Conservative Group; Grand Master Mason of Scotland, 1983-88; former Chairman, Clinterty Agricultural College Council; Member, Queen's Bodyguard for Scotland (Royal Company of Archers); Chairman, North of Scotland Board, Eagle Star Group, 1973-91. Recreations: shooting; fishing; photography. Address: (h.) Dinnet, Aboyne, Aberdeenshire.

Hunt, Major John Henry. Salvation Army Officer, since 1964; Divisional Commander, East Scotland, since 1994; b. 2.3.40, Romford; m., Sheila; 2 s.; 1 d. Educ. Wallington County Grammar. Corps Officer, Salvation Army, 1964-88; Divisional Officer (Finance and Administration), 1988-94. Recreations: classical music; reading; following cricket and golf. Address: (b.) 5 East Adam Street, Edinburgh EH8 9TF; T.-0131-662 3300.

Hunter, A. Colin J., BA. Head Teacher, Tiree High School, since 1985; b. 26.9.47, Falkirk; m., June Sinclair Stark; 2 s.; 1 d. Educ. Falkirk High School; Stirling University. Entered teaching, 1972; Teacher, Falkirk High School and Forres Academy; Principal Teacher of Biology, Whitfield High School, Dundee; Depute Head Teacher, Auchtercairn Secondary School, Gairloch. Recreations: gardening; golf; walking. Address: (h.) Cornaigmore Schoolhouse, Isle of Tiree, Argyll PA77 6XA; T.-01879 220556.

Hunter, Allison Carnegie. Director of Organisation, Scottish National Party, since 1990; b. 8.1.42, Glasgow; m., Ian James Hunter; 1 s.; 2 d. Educ. Pollokshields Senior Secondary School; Jordanhill College of Education. Schoolteacher, 1961-65 and 1971-90. Recreations: cooking; reading; music. Address: (h.) 4 Tantallon Road, Shawlands, Glasgow G41 3BX; T.-0141-649 1093.

Hunter, Archibald Sinclair, DL, CA. Senior Partner, Scotland, KPMG; b. 20.8.43, Glasgow; m., Pat; 2 s.; 1 d. Educ. Queen's Park School, Glasgow. Trained with Mackie & Clark, CA, Glasgow; qualified as CA, 1966; joined Thomson McLintock, 1966; Partner, 1974. President, Institute of Chartered Accountants of Scotland; Member, Council, Scotbic. Recreations: golf; swimming; walking. Address: (b.) 24 Blythswood Square, Glasgow G2 4QS; T.-0141-226 5511.

Hunter, Christopher G.W., MA, FNI, MRIN. Principal, Glasgow College of Nautical Studies, since 1991; b. 8.10.42, Bristol; m., Irene Mary; 3 d. Educ. Pangbourne College. Seafaring career, Deck Officer to Master, 1960-77; Fleet Training Manager/Deputy Personnel Manager, Cunard Shipping Services Ltd., 1978-84; Principal, National Sea Training College, Kent, 1984-91. Vice-Chairman, Merchant Navy Training Board; Chairman, Thistle Education and Consultancy Ltd.; Chairman: Adelphi Management Company Ltd., International Association of Maritime Institutions; Vice Chairman, West of Scotland Ports Welfare Committee; Director, The Gorbals Initiative. Recreation: family. Address: (b.) 21 Thistle Street, Glasgow G5 9XB; T.-0141-565 2550.

Hunter, Colin M., MB, ChB, DRCOG, FRCGP. Chairman, Scottish Council, Royal College of General Practitioners, since 1996; Hon. Secretary, N.E. Scotland Faculty, RCGP, 1989-96; Hon. Fellow, Association of Managers in General Practice, since 1996; b. 28.4.58, Stirling. Educ. High School of Stirling; Aberdeen University. Principal in general practice, Skene Medical Group, 1986; Teaching Fellow, Aberdeen University, 1988; first member, RCGP in Scotland, to attain Fellowship of Royal College by Assessment, 1993; Sally Irvine Lecture, Glasgow, 1996. Recreations: hill-walking; singing. Address: The Langdales, 1 Craigston Gardens, Westhill, Aberdeen AB32 6NL; T.-01224 742594.

Hunter, Professor Geoffrey, BSc, PhD, CChem, FRSC. Professor of Chemistry, Dundee University, since 1993, and Head, Department of Chemistry, since 1990; b. 28.6.43, Co. Durham; m., Jacqueline; 1 d. Educ. Stanley Grammar School; Sheffield University. Research Fellow, Simon Fraser University, Vancouver, 1967; Scientific Officer, Atomic Energy Research Establishment, Harwell, 1968; Lecturer, Dundee University, 1969, Senior Lecturer, 1988; Visiting Fellow, Princeton University, 1980, 1982; Visiting Professor, University of Victoria, 1986; Gast Professor, University of Vienna, 1994. Publications: author/co-author of more than 90 publications. Recreation: sailing. Address: (b.) Chemistry Department, Dundee University, Dundee DD1 4HN.

Hunter, George Alexander, OBE (1980), CStJ. Secretary, Commonwealth Games Council for Scotland, since 1978; Founder Governor, Scottish Sports Aid Foundation, since 1980; Member, Edinburgh City Council, since 1992; b. 24.2.26, Edinburgh; m., Eileen Elizabeth. Educ. George Watson's College, Edinburgh. Served with Cameronians, seconded to 17th Dogara Regiment, Indian Army, 1944-47 (Captain); Lawson Donaldson Seeds Ltd., 1942-82 (Director, 15 years); Secretary, Scottish Amateur Rowing Association, 1948-78 (President, 1978-84); Adviser, Sports Aid Foundation, since 1979; Treasurer, Commonwealth Games Council for Scotland, 1962-78; Member, Scottish Sports Council, 1976-84 (Chairman, Games and Sports Committee, 1976-84); Chairman, Scottish Standing Conference for Sport, 1977-84. Address: (h.) 1 Craiglockhart Crescent, Edinburgh EH14 1DZ; T.-0131-443 2533.

Hunter, James, MA (Hons), PhD. Writer, Historian, Journalist and Broadcaster; Chairman, Skye and Lochalsh Enterprise; Member, Scottish Tourist Board; Member, Northern Areas Board, Scottish Natural Heritage; b. 22.5.48, Duror, Argyll; m., Evelyn; 1 s.; 1 d. Educ. Oban High School; Aberdeen University; Edinburgh University. Former Director, Scottish Crofters Union. Publications: The Making of the Crofting Community, 1976; Skye: The Island, 1986; The Claim of Crofting, 1991; Scottish Highlanders: A People and their Place, 1992; A Dance Called America: The Scottish Highlands, the United States and Canada, 1994; On the Other Side of Sorrow: Nature and People in the Scottish Highlands, 1995; Glencoe and the Indians, 1996. Address: (b.) 22 Borve, Portree, Isle of Skye IV51 9PE; T.-01470 532421.

Hunter, Professor John Angus Alexander, OBE, BA, MD, FRCPEdin. Grant Professor of Dermatology, Edinburgh University, since 1981; b. 16.6.39, Edinburgh; m., Ruth Mary Farrow; 1 s.; 2 d. Educ. Loretto School; Pembroke College, Cambridge; Edinburgh University. Research Fellow, Institute of Dermatology, London, 1967; Registrar, Department of Dermatology, Edinburgh Royal Infirmary, 1968-70; Exchange Research Fellow, Department of Dermatology, Minnesota University, 1968; Lecturer, Department of Dermatology, Edinburgh University, 1970-74; Consultant Dermatologist, Lothian Health Board, 1974-80; Member: Executive Committee of Investigative Group, British Association of Dermatologists, 1974-76; Executive Committee, British Association of Dermatologists, 1977-79; SEC, Scottish Dermatological Society, 1980-82; Specialist Advisory Committee, (Dermatology), Joint Committee on Higher Medical Training, 1980-87 (Chairman, 1986-90); Medical Appeal Tribunal, since 1982; Scottish Committee for Hospital Medical Services, 1983-85; President: Section of Dermatology, Royal Society of Medicine, 1993-94, Scottish Dermatological Society, 1994-97. Publications: Common Diseases of the Skin (Co-author); Clinical Dermatology (Co-author); Skin Signs in Clinical Medicine (Co-author). Recreations: music; gardening; tropical fish; golf. Address: (h.) Leewood, Rosslyn Castle, Roslin, Midlothian EH25 9PZ; T.-0131-440 2181.

Hunter, Hon. Lord (John Oswald Mair Hunter), VRD. Senator of the College of Justice in Scotland, 1961-86; b. 21.2.13. Chairman, Scottish Law Commission, 1971-81.

Hunter, Kirk John, MA (Hons). Secretary, Scottish Dairy Association, since 1989; b. 1.12.54, Glasgow; m., June Wilson. Educ. George Heriots School; Dundee University. Graduate Trainee, SSEB, 1977-79; Trade Association Executive, Thomson McLintock, Glasgow, 1980-83; Commercial Officer, Metal Trades Confederation, London and Glasgow, 1983-86; Peat Marwick McLintock, Glasgow, 1986-89. Recreations: golf; gardening; cycling. Address: (h.) 18 Ravelston Road, Bearsden, Glasgow G61 1AW; T.-0141-942 3799.

Hunter, Sir Laurence Colvin, Kt, MA, DPhil, FRSE. Professor of Applied Economics, Glasgow University, since 1970; b. 8.8.34, Glasgow; m., Evelyn Margaret Green; 3 s.; 1 d. Educ. Hillhead High School, Glasgow; Glasgow University; University College, Oxford. Assistant Lecturer, Manchester University, 1958-59; 2nd Lt., RAEC, 1959-61; Walgreen Postdoctoral Fellow, University of Chicago, 1961-62; joined Glasgow University as Lecturer, 1962; Vice-Principal, 1982-86; Director: External Relations, 1987-90, Business School since 1996. Council Member, ACAS, 1974-86; Chairman, Police Negotiating Board, since 1986; Council Member, Economic and Social Research Council, 1989-92; Editor, Scottish Journal of Political Economy, 1966-97; President, Scottish Economic Society, 1993-96. Recreations: golf; painting; curling. Address: (h.) 23 Boclair Road, Bearsden, Glasgow G61 2AF; T.-0141-563 7135.

Hunter, Mark S. Managing Director, Chesterton Scotland Ltd., Edinburgh, since 1993; Director, Northern Retail Property Fund, since 1994; b. 2.11.51, Newcastle upon Tyne; m., Rosalind (deceased); 1 s.; 2 d. Educ. Rugby School; Royal Agricultural College, Circencester. Weatherall, Green and Smith, London; Chestertons, London; Associate Director, Conrad Ritblat, Glasgow; Associate Director, Leavers, Edinburgh; Joint Founder/Chairman, Conroy Hunter, Edinburgh. Trustee, Young Musicians Trust. Recreations: music; opera; fishing; shooting; wine; Scottish art; family. Address: (b.) 36 Castle Street, Edinburgh EH2 3HT; T.-0131-226 4791.

Hunter, Mollie. Writer; b. 30.6.22, Longniddry; m., Thomas McIlwraith; 2 s. Educ. Preston Lodge School. Freelance Journalist, until 1960; Past Chairman, Society of Authors in Scotland; writer of various types of fiction (fantasy, historical novels, "realism") for children of varying age groups; 30 titles published, including Talent Is Not Enough, on the craft of writing for children; travelled extensively (Australia, New Zealand, Canada, USA); Lecturer on writing for children; Writer-in-Residence, Dalhousie University, Halifax, Canada, on two occasions; awarded Arbuthnot Lectureship, 1975, and Carnegie Medal, 1975. Recreations: reading; gardening; music. Address: Rose Cottage, 7 Mary Ann Court, Inverness IV3 5BZ; T.-01463 713914.

Hunter, Robert Daniel, JP, FCCA. Director of Financial Services, North Ayrshire Council, since 1995; b. 25.1.41, Paisley; m., Ishbel; 3 d. Educ. John Neilson School, Paisley; Mellow Lane Comprehensive, Hayes; Glasgow Central College. Accountant, Rutherglen Burgh Council, 1965-70, Port Glasgow Town Council, 1970-72; Accountant/Auditor, Irvine Town Council, 1972-75; Assistant Director of Finance, then Depute, then Director of Finance, Cunninghame District Council, 1975-95. Recreations: hill-walking; caravanning; curling. Address: (b.) Cunninghame House, Irvine KA12 8EE; T.-01294 324511.

Hunter, Russell. Actor; b. 18.2.25, Glasgow. Former shipyard worker; began acting as an amateur; made professional debut with Glasgow Unity Theatre, 1947; appeared in repertory with Edinburgh Gateway, Edinburgh Traverse and Glasgow Citizens'; acted with the RSC, Bristol Old Vic and at the Old Vic, London; played title role in The Servant o' Twa Maisters, 1965, opening production of Edinburgh Civic Theatre Company; played The Pope in Galileo, also at Royal Lyceum; played The Gravedigger in Hamlet, Assembly Hall, Edinburgh Festival; took title role in Cocky, one-man play, 1969; played Jock, solo play, 1972.

Hunter, Thomas Blane, BA. Chief Executive Officer, Sports Division, since 1984; b. 6.5.61, Irvine. Educ. Cumnock Academy; University of Strathclyde. Address: (b.) Olympic Business Park, Drybridge Road, Dundonald KA2 9BE.

Hunter, William, MA. Columnist, The Herald, retired 1996; b. 16.8.31, Paisley; m., Mo (deceased); 1 s.; 1 d. Educ. Paisley Grammar School; Glasgow University. Publications: The Saints; Bell the Cage!; Dear Happy Ghosts. Recreation: weeding. Address: (h.) 233 Fenwick Road, Glasgow; T.-0141-638 1323.

Hunter, William Hill, CBE, CA, JP, DL. Partner, McLay, McAlister & McGibbon, CA, 1946-91, Consultant, since 1991; Director, J. & G. Grant, Glenfarclas Distillery, 1966-92; b. 5.11.16, Cumnock; m., Kathleen Cole; 2 s. Educ. Cumnock Academy. Enlisted as private, RASC, 1940; commissioned Royal Artillery, 1941; Staff Captain, Middle East, 1944-46; Director: Abbey National Building Society (Scottish Advisory Board), 1966-86, City of Glasgow Friendly Society, 1966-88 (President, 1980-88); Member: CBI Scottish Council, 1978-84, Institute of Directors West of Scotland Committee, 1980-91; President, Renfrew West and Inverclyde Conservative and Unionist Association, since 1972, Scottish Young Unionist Association, 1958-60, Scottish Unionist Association, 1964-65; contested (Unionist), South Ayrshire, 1959 and 1964; Hon. Treasurer, Quarrier's Homes, 1972-94 (Chairman, 1991-94); Hon. Financial Advisor, Erskine Hospital, since 1981; Session Clerk, Kilmacolm Old Kirk, 1972-77; Chairman: Salvation Army Advisory Board in Strathclyde, 1982-93, Salvation Army Housing Association Scotland Ltd., 1986-91; admitted to Distinguished Order of Auxiliary Service of Salvation Army, 1981; Deacon Convener, Trades House of Glasgow, 1986-87; Honorary Vice President, Royal Scottish Agricultural Benevolent Institution, since 1994; Honorary President, Friends of Glasgow Botanic Gardens, since 1994. Recreations: gardening; golf; swimming; music. Address: (h.) Armitage, Kilmacolm PA13 4PH; T.-0150587 2444.

Hunter Blair, Francis, JP. Hill Farmer; Vice-President and Past Chairman, Galloway Cattle Society of Great Britain and Ireland; b. 29.10.30, Lincoln; m., Joyce Adeline Mary Graham; 4 s.; 1 d. Educ. Royal Naval College, Dartmouth; West of Scotland Agricultural College. President, Stewartry Branch, National Farmers' Union of Scotland, 1968-69; Council Member, NFU of Scotland, 1969-70; Vice President, Royal Highland and Agricultural Society of Scotland, 1987; several periods of office as Secretary and President, local agricultural shows; Past Chairman, Carsphairn Community Council; Elder and Session Clerk, Carsphairn Kirk. Recreations: country pursuits; reading. Address: Marbrack, Carsphairn, Castle Douglas, Stewartry of Kirkcudbright; T.-Carsphairn 207.

Hunter Blair, James, DL. Landowner and Forester; b. 18.3.26, Ayr. Educ. Eton; Oxford. Scots Guards, 1944-48; University, 1948-50; merchant bank, London, 1951-53; managed family estate, since 1953. Past President, Royal Scottish Forestry Society; former Vice-President, Royal Highland Society; Past Chairman, Historic Houses Association for Scotland; Trustee, National Galleries of Scotland; Member, Historic Buildings Council for Scotland. Recreations: shooting; fishing; going to the opera. Address: Blairquhan, Maybole, Ayrshire; T.-Straiton 239.

Hunter Gordon, Nigel, MA, FCA, ATII. Managing Partner, Ernst & Young, Highlands and Islands, since 1993; b. 2.9.47, Camberley; m., Linda; 2 s. Educ. Ampleforth College; St. Andrews University. Secretary, Highlands and Islands Area Group, CBI; Member, Scottish Council, Institute of Directors. Recreations: skiing; gardening. Address: (b.) Moray House, 16 Bank Street, Inverness IV1 1QY; T.-01463 237581.

Huntly, 13th Marquess of (Granville Charles Gomer Gordon). Premier Marquess of Scotland; Chief, House of Gordon; b. 4.2.44; m.; 1 d.; 1 s., 2 d. by pr. m. Address: Aboyne Castle, Aberdeenshire, AB34 5JP.

Huq, Mohammed Mozammel, BA(Hons), MA, MLitt, PhD. Senior Lecturer in Economics, since 1990, and Associate Director, Developing Countries Research Unit, since 1991, University of Strathclyde; President, North Bengal College, Kakina, Lalmonirhat, Bangladesh, since 1994; b. 29.11.40, Kakina, Bangladesh; m., Kumkum; 1 s.; 1 d. Educ. Kakina M.R.M. High School; Carmichael College, Rangpur; University of Rajshahi, Bangladesh; University of Glasgow. Lecturer in Economics, then Associate Professor, University of Rajshahi, Bangladesh; postgraduate research, University of Glasgow; returned to Bangladesh, 1974, as Researcher; Researcher, David Livingstone Institute of Overseas Development Studies, University of Strathclyde, 1976-87; Senior Research Fellow (on secondment), Centre for Development Studies, University of Ghana, 1982-84; Lecturer in Economics, University of Strathclyde, 1987. President, North Bengal College, Bangladesh; Chairman, Third World Science, Technology and Development Forum UK; President, Scottish Asian Action Committee. Publications: author of several books and co-editor of two books. Recreations: tennis; bridge. Address: (b.) Department of Economics, University of Strathclyde, Glasgow G4 0LN; T.-0141-548 3863.

Hurford, Professor James Raymond, BA, PhD. Professor of General Linguistics, Edinburgh University, since 1979; b. 16.7.41, Reading; m., Sue Ann Davis; 2 d. Educ. Exeter School; St. John's College, Cambridge; University College, London. Assistant Professor, Department of English, University of California, Davis, 1968-71; Lecturer, then Senior Lecturer, Department of Linguistics, Lancaster University, 1972-79. Publications: Language and Number: the emergence of a cognitive system; Semantics: a coursebook (Co-author); The Linguistic Theory of Numerals; Grammar: a student's guide. Address: (b.) Edinburgh University, Edinburgh EH8 9YL.

Hurman, David Charles, MBChB, DTM&H, DMRT, FRCR, HonMD (Manitoba). Consultant in Clinical Oncology, Aberdeen Royal Hospitals NHS Trust (Head of Department, since 1991); Visiting Consultant, Shetland Health Board, since 1988; Clinical Senior Lecturer, Aberdeen University, since 1988; b. 9.2.52, London; m., Dr. Dorothy Elizabeth McMurray; 1 s.; 1 d. Educ. Ashford County Grammar School; Liverpool University. Pre-registration and junior medical posts, Southport General Infirmary and Christiana Hartley Maternity Hospital, 1975-77; Medical Officer, Trans-Borneo Expedition, 1978; Mersey Regional Centre for Radiotherapy and Oncology, Clatterbridge Hospital, Bebington, 1979-86; Clinical Research Fellow, Cross Cancer Institute and University of Alberta, 1986-87; Senior Medical Officer, International Scientific Support Trust Expedition to Java and Kalimantan, 1994. Recreations: foreign travel; football; cricket; hills and mountains; rock music. Address: (h.) 85 Cairnfield Place, Aberdeen AB15 5LX; T.-01224 638411.

Hurst, Professor Andrew, CGeol, FGS. Professor of Production Geoscience, Aberdeen University, since 1992; b. 5.9.53, Stoke-on-Trent; m., Liv Christiansen; 1 s.; 1 d. Educ. Cheadle Grammar School; Aberdeen University; Reading University. Geologist, Norway, 1981-82; Senior Geologist, Norway, 1982-90; Senior Geologist, Unocal UK, 1990-91; Advising Geologist, Unocal UK, 1991-92. Executive Editor, Sedimentary Geology; William Smith Fund Award, Geological Society of London, 1993; Chief Editor, Petroleum Geoscience; editor of five books. Recreations: squash; music; natural history. Address: (b.) Department of Geology and Petroleum Geology, King's College, Aberdeen AB9 2UE; T.-01224 273713.

Hurtado, Professor Larry Weir, BA, MA, PhD. Professor of New Testament Language, Literature and Theology, Faculty of Divinity, Edinburgh University, since 1996; b. 29.12.43, Kansas City; m., Shannon Hunter; 1 s.; 2 d. Educ.

Case Western Reserve University. Pastor, North Shore Assembly of God, Illinois, 1971-75; Assistant Professor of New Testament, Regent College, Vancouver BC, 1975-78; Professor of Religion, University of Manitoba, Winnipeg, 1978-96. Associate Editor, Critical Review of Books in Religion. Address: (b.) New College, Mound Place, Edinburgh EH1 2LX; T.-0131-650 8920.

Hutcheon, Rev. Douglas John. Superintendent, Baptist Union of Scotland, since 1993; b. 27.7.38, Buckie; m., Helen Smith; 2 s.; 2 d. Educ. Buckie High School; Milnes High School, Fochabers; Bible Training Institute. Bank of Scotland, 1953-57; Minister of the Baptist Church, since 1962. Recreations: reading; hill-walking; watching football; music. Address: (b.) 14 Aytoun Road, Glasgow G41 5RT; T.-0141-423 6169.

Hutcheson, John Mitchell. Executive Officer, Royal Scottish Pipe Band Association, since 1990; b. 25.5.31, Glasgow. Educ. Allan Glen's School, Glasgow. Director, Hugh Baird & Sons Ltd., 1976-85; Chairman, Institute of Brewing (Scotland), 1986-88. Recreations: golf; cricket; reading; philately. Address: (h.) 29 Victoria Park Drive North, Glasgow G14 9NL; T.-0141-959 3501.

Hutcheson, Rev. Norman McKenzie, MA, BD. Minister, Dalbeattie and Urr Parish Churches; b. 11.10.48, Leven; m., Elizabeth; 2 d. Educ. Hillhead High School, Glasgow; Glasgow University; Edinburgh University. Minister, St. Andrews, Kirkcaldy, 1973-88. Recreations: photography; travel; reading. Address: (h.) 36 Mill Street, Dalbeattiew DG5 4HE; T.-01556 610029.

Hutchins, Michael John Patrick, FCIB. Director UK Retail Banking, Royal Bank of Scotland Plc, since 1995; b. 19.4.44, Sale; m., Rosemary Isabelle; 1 s.; 2 d. Educ. Burnage Grammar School, Manchester. Career banker with William Deacon's Bank, Williams & Glyns Bank and Royal Bank of Scotland; Manager of a group of bank branches in Sheffield and Nottingham; a senior manager, International Division, running North of England and Midlands area; a branch area manager covering Cheshire and Derbyshire; Local Director, Yorkshire and North East of England; ran all branch banking operations in North of England and Midlands from Manchester, as Director; moved to Edinburgh in 1995. Director: Royal Scottish Assurance, Royal Bank of Scotland Unit Trust Management, Royal Exchange Theatre (Manchester). Recreations: all sports; theatre. Address: (b.) Royal Bank of Scotland, PO Box 31, 42 St. Andrew Square, Edinburgh; T.-0131-556 8555.

Hutchinson, Peter, PhD, FIFM. Assistant Secretary, North Atlantic Salmon Conservation Organization, since 1986; b. 26.5.56, Glasgow; m., Jane MacKellaig; 1 s.; 1 d. Educ. Queen Elizabeth's Grammar School, Blackburn; Edinburgh University. Project Co-ordinator, Surface Water Acidification; Research Biologist: Institute of Terrestrial Ecology, Edinburgh University; Member, Consular Corps in Edinburgh and Leith, since 1991. Recreations: golf; squash; rugby union; angling. Address: (h.) 3 St. Ronan's Terrace, Morningside, Edinburgh.

Hutchison, David, MA, MLitt. Senior Lecturer in Communication Studies, Glasgow Caledonian University, since 1975; b. 24.9.44, West Kilbride; m., Pauleen Frew; 2 d. Educ. Ardrossan Academy; Glasgow University. Tutor/Organiser, WEA (West of Scotland), 1966-69; Teacher, Reid Kerr College, Paisley, 1969-71; Lecturer in Communication Studies, Glasgow College of Technology, 1971-75; Member, West Kilbride District Council, 1970-75 (Chairman, 1972-75); Governor, Scottish Film Council, 1987-95; Member, General Advisory Council, BBC, 1988-96; author of play, Deadline, Pitlochry Festival Theatre, 1980. Publications: The Modern Scottish Theatre, 1977; Headlines: the Media in Scotland (Editor), 1978; various articles/chapters. Recreations: walking; swimming; the arts.

Address: (b.) Department of Language and Media, Caledonian University, Cowcaddens Road, Glasgow G4 OBA; T.-0141-331 3255.

Hutchison, Ian Somerville, OBE, JP. Member, East Renfrewshire Council; Member: Historic Buildings Council for Scotland, since 1983, Renfrewshire Valuation Appeals Committee, Management Committee, Renfrewshire Enterprise, Scottish Council Development and Industry Executive; Delegate to COSLA, since 1975 (Vice-President, 1979-82); Managing Director, Timbertection Ltd., since 1973; Director, The Planning Exchange; Vice Chairman, Scottish Housing Planning Council; b. 10.4.28, Glasgow; m., Aileen Wallace; 2 s.; 2 d. Educ. Hutchesons' Boys' Grammar School. Former Member: Eastwood District Council, Renfrew County Council, First (Eastwood) District Council, Scottish Valuation Advisory Council. Recreations: gardening; fishing. Address: (h.) 39 Hazelwood Avenue, Newton Mearns, Glasgow G77 5QT; T.-0141-639 2186.

Hutchison, James Carswell, BA (Hons), DipEd. Rector, Woodlands High School, Falkirk, since 1996; b. 16.9.47, Kilsyth; m., Eileen Hamilton Todd; 1 s. Educ. Kilsyth Academy; Strathclyde University; Glasgow University; Jordanhill College. Airdrie Academy, 1969-86, latterly as Principal Teacher of History; Assistant Head Teacher, Calderhead High School, 1986-91; Depute Rector, Denny High School, 1991-96; Member, Stirling University and General Teaching Council of Scotland groups reviewing management of teacher training; Lay preacher. Publications: Weavers, Miners and the Open Book; Sierra Leone Challenge. Recreations: swimming; badminton; walking; running; foreign travel; local history; local radio broadcasting. Address: (h.) 3 Castle Grove, Kilsyth, Glasgow G65 9HD; T.-Kilsyth 823726.

Hutchison, Sir Peter Craft, Bt, CBE, FRSE. Chairman, Forestry Commission, since 1994; formerly Chairman, Hutchison & Craft Ltd., Insurance Brokers; b. 5.6.35, London; m., Virginia Colville; 1 s. Educ. Eton; Magdalene College, Cambridge. National Service, Royal Scots Greys (2nd Lt.); Northern Assurance Co. (London); Director of various companies; Past Chairman, Ailsa Shipbuilding Co. Ltd.; Director, Stakis plc, 1979-91; Board Member, Scottish Tourist Board, 1981-87; Vice Chairman, British Waterways Board, since 1988; Chairman: Board of Trustees, Royal Botanic Garden, Edinburgh, 1985-94, Loch Lomond and Trossachs Working Party, 1991-93; Deacon, Incorporation of Hammermen of Glasgow, 1984-85. Recreations: plant hunting; gardening; calligraphy. Address: (h.) Broich, Kippen, Stirlingshire FK8 3EN; T.-01786 870317.

Hutton, Alasdair Henry, OBE, TD. Chairman, Calchou Electronics; Writer and Broadcaster; Writer and Narrator, Edinburgh Military Tattoo and other public events; Member, Social Security Advisory Committee; Scottish Trustee, Community Service Volunteers; Senior Consultant, Coutts Career Consultants, Scotland; Chairman, Disease Prevention Organisation; Member, Kelso and Jedburgh Advisory Committee, Scottish Borders Enterprise; Member, International Relations Committee, Law Society of Scotland; b. 19.5.40, London; m., Deirdre Mary Cassels (see Deirdre Mary Hutton); 2 s. Educ. Dollar Academy; Brisbane State High School. Journalist, The Age, Melbourne, 1959-61, Aberdeen Journals, 1962-64; Broadcaster, BBC, 1964-79; Member, European Parliament, 1979-89. Member, Queen's Bodyguard for Scotland (Royal Company of Archers); Former 2ic, 15th (Scottish Volunteer) Bn., The Parachute Regiment; Vice-President, Kelso Branch, Royal British Legion; Elder, Kelso North Church of Scotland; Patron ROKPA; Vice-Chairman and Life Member, John Buchan Society; Life Member, Edinburgh Sir Walter Scott Club; Fellow, Industry and Parliament Trust; Honorary President, Scottish Association of CB Clubs; Patron, Kelso Laddies' Association; Member, Ancient Order of Mosstroopers; Honorary Chairman, Hawick Conservative Club. Address: (b.) Rosebank, Shedden Park Road, Kelso, TD5 7PX; T.-01573 224369.

Hutton, Deirdre Mary. Vice-Chairman, National Consumer Council, since 1997; Chairman: Scottish Consumer Council, since 1991, Rural Forum, since 1992, Personal Investment Authority Ombudsman Council, since 1997 (Member, Personal Investment Authority Consumer Panel, since 1994); b. 15.3.49, Haddington; m., Alasdair Hutton (qv); 2 s. Educ. Sherborne School for Girls; secretarial college. Research Assistant, Glasgow Chamber of Commerce, 1976-81; seconded to Scotland is British Campaign and Scotland Says No Campaign during devolution referendum, 1979; Founder Chairman, Enterprise Music Scotland Ltd. Recreations: music; reading. Address: (h.) Rosebank, Shedden Park Road, Kelso TD5 7PX; T.-01573 224368.

Hutton, V. Rosemary S., MA, PhD, FRAS, FRSE. Honorary Fellow, Department of Geology and Geophysics, University of Edinburgh, since 1990; b. 22.10.25, Dundee. Educ. Harris Academy, Dundee; University of St. Andrews; University of London. Research Physicist, British Jute Trade Research Association, Dundee, 1949-53; Lecturer in Physics, University of Ghana, Accra, 1954-62; Senior Lecturer/Reader in Physics, Ahmadu Bello University, Zaria, Nigeria, 1963-67; Associate Professor of Physics, University of Ibadan, Nigeria, 1968-69; University of Edinburgh: Lecturer in Geophysics, 1969-73, Senior Lecturer, 1973-82, Reader, 1982-90. Former Member of several international scientific committees; guest lectureships at universities and research institutes in Russia, Australia, Italy and India. Publications: over 60 articles in international scientific journals. Recreations: video photography; painting; gardening. Address: (h.) Kerfield Grange, Innerleithen Road, Peebles EH45 8BG; T.-01721 720376.

Hyslop, John Michael, OBE, FInstD, FInstPet, FIM. Chairman, Brown and Root AOC (part of the Halliburton Group); b. 31.8.37, Pontypridd; m., Marjorie Lorraine Rowe; 1 s. Educ. Pontypridd Grammar School; Glamorgan Technical College. Former Managing Director and Chairman, AOC International; Director, Fairhaven International plc, 1988-93; former Managing Director, OGC International plc; Grampian Industrialist of the Year, 1991; elected FRSA, 1993. Recreations: game shooting; rugby; golf; country pursuits. Address: (b.) Alba Gate, Stoneywood Park, Dyce, Aberdeen AB21 7HW; T.-01224 770033.

I

Ibbett, Professor Roland Norman, BSc, MSc, PhD, FRSE, CEng, FBCS, FRSA. Professor of Computer Science, Edinburgh University, since 1985, Vice-Principal, since 1994; b. 21.6.41, Burton upon Trent; m., Janet; 3 s.; 3 d. Educ. Burton upon Trent Grammar School. Lecturer in Computer Science, Manchester University, 1967-75, Senior Lecturer, 1975-82, Reader, 1982-85. Chairman, Conference of Professors and Heads of Computing, 1993-95. Publications: two books; 40 papers. Recreations: gardening; DIY; listening to music. Address: (b.) Department of Computer Science, Edinburgh University, King's Buildings, Edinburgh EH9 3JZ; T.-0131-650 5119.

Idiens, Dale, BA, DipEd. Depute Director (Collections) and Keeper, Department of History and Applied Art, National Museums of Scotland; b. 13.5.42, Prestatyn. Educ. Wycombe High School, High Wycombe; Leicester University. Royal Scottish Museum, Department of Art and Archaeology: Assistant Keeper in Charge of Ethnography, 1964, Deputy Keeper, 1979, Keeper, 1983. Address: (b.) Royal Museum of Scotland, Chambers Street, Edinburgh; T.-0131-225 7534.

Ingle, Professor Stephen James, BA, MA (Econ), DipEd, PhD. Professor of Politics (and Head, Politics Department), Stirling University; b. 6.11.40, Ripon; m., Margaret Anne; 2 s.; 1 d. Educ. The Roan School, London; Sheffield University; Wellington University, NZ. Lecturer in Politics, Hull University, 1967-80; Senior Lecturer, 1980-91; Head of Department, 1985-90. Secretary, Political Studies Association, 1988-89; Member, East Yorkshire Health Authority, 1985-90. Publications: Socialist Thought in Imaginative Literature, 1979; Parliament and Health Policy, 1981; British Party System, 1987, 1989; George Orwell: a political life, 1993. Recreations: reading; music; hill-walking. Address: (b.) Department of Politics, Stirling University, Stirling FK9 4LA; T.-01786 467593.

Inglis, George Finlay, CA. Director of Finance and Administration, Scottish Tourist Board, since 1988; b. 2.1.46, Edinburgh; m., Catherine; 1 s.; 1 d. Educ. Royal High School, Edinburgh. Recreations: sport; literature; good wine; good food. Address: (h.) 67 Hillpark Avenue, Edinburgh EH4 7AL; T.-0131-336 2338.

Inglis, Professor Emeritus James Alistair Macfarlane, CBE (1984), MA, LLB. Emeritus Professor, Glasgow University; Professor of Conveyancing, Glasgow University, 1979-93; Professor of Professional Legal Practice, Glasgow University, 1984-93; Partner, McClure, Naismith, Anderson & Gardiner, Solicitors, Glasgow, 1956-93; Honorary Member, Court of Patrons, Royal College of Physicians and Surgeons of Glasgow, since 1995; b. 24.12.28, Kilmarnock; m., Mary Elizabeth Howie; 2 s.; 3 d. Educ. Kilmarnock Academy; Fettes College; Glasgow University; Glasgow University. Qualified as Solicitor, 1952; Member: Board of Management, Victoria and Leverndale Hospitals, 1964-74, Greater Glasgow Health Board, 1975-83; President, Rent Assessment Panel for Scotland, 1976-87; Chairman, Glasgow Hospitals Auxiliary Association, since 1985; Dean, Royal Faculty of Procurators in Glasgow, 1989-92; Convener, Ad Hoc Committee, Church of Scotland, into Legal Services of Church, 1978-79; Session Clerk, Caldwell Parish Church, since 1963; General Trustee, Church of Scotland, since 1994. Address: (h.) Crioch, Uplawmoor, Glasgow; T.-01505 850315.

Inglis, John, RSW, FSA(Scot), DA. Painter and Lecturer; b. 27.7.53, Glasgow; m., Heather; 2 s.; 2 d. Educ. Hillhead High School; Gray's School of Art. Travelling scholarships to Italy, 1976; Member, Dundee Group, 1979-84; one-man exhibitions: Aberdeen, 1976 and 1977; Glasgow, 1980; Skipton, 1981; Aberdeen Hospitals, 1989; Alloa Museum, 1989; Smith Art Gallery, Stirling, 1993; Illinois, USA, 1997. Scottish Arts Council Award, 1981; RSA Keith Prize, 1975; SAC Bursary, 1982; RSA Meyer Oppenheim Prize, 1982; RSW EIS Award, 1987; SAC Grant, 1988; May Marshall Brown Award, 1994. Address: (h.) 21 Hillview Road, Larbert, Stirlingshire; T.-01324 558891.

Ingram, Adam. Minister of State for Northern Ireland, since 1997; MP (Labour), East Kilbride, since 1987; b. 1.2.47, Glasgow; m., Maureen McMahon. Educ. Cranhill Senior Secondary School. Programmer/analyst, 1965-1970; systems analyst, 1970-77; full-time union official, 1977-87; Councillor, East Kilbride District Council, 1980-87 (Leader of the Council, 1984-87); PPS to Neil Kinnock, Leader of the Opposition, 1988-92; Labour Opposition Spokesperson on Social Security, 1993-95, Science and Technology, 1995-97; JP. Recreations: fishing; cooking; reading. Address: (b.) House of Commons, London SW1A 0AA; T.-0171-219 4093.

Ingram, Professor David Stanley, BSc, PhD, MA, ScD, FLS, FIBiol, FIHort, FRSE. Regius Keeper (Director), Royal Botanic Garden, Edinburgh, since 1990; Visiting Professor, Glasgow University, since 1991; Hon. Professor, Edinburgh University, since 1991; Honorary Professor of Horticulture, Royal Horticultural Society, since 1995; President: British Society for Plant Pathology, International Congress of Plant Pathology; b. 10.10.41, Birmingham; m., Alison W.; 2 s. Educ. Yardley Grammar School, Birmingham; Hull University; Cambridge University. Research Fellow, Glasgow University, 1966-68, Cambridge University, 1968-69; Senior Scientific Officer, Unit of Developmental Botany, Cambridge, 1969-74; Lecturer, then Reader in Plant Pathology, Botany Department, Cambridge University, 1974-90; Fellow (also Tutor, Dean and Director of Studies in Biology), Downing College, Cambridge, 1974-90; author of several books and many papers in learned journals. Recreations: gardening; literature; film; theatre; music; travel. Address: (b.) Royal Botanic Garden, Edinburgh EH3 5LR; T.-0131-552 7171.

Ingram, Greig Webster, MA. Rector, High School of Stirling, since 1994; b. 20.11.47, Burnhervie; m., Patricia Annette Miller. Educ. Mackie Academy, Stonehaven; Aberdeen University; Aberdeen College of Education. Teacher of Modern Studies and History, 1970-74; Principal Teacher of Modern Studies, St. Margaret Mary's Secondary, Glasgow, 1974-84; Assistant Head Teacher, Eastbank Academy, Glasgow, 1984-89, Depute Head Teacher, 1989-94. Recreations: reading; music; travel; running; soccer. Address: (b.) Ogilvie Road, Stirling FK8 2PA; T.-01786 472451.

Ingram, Hugh Albert Pugh, BA (Cantab), PhD (Dunelm). Chairman, Council, Scottish Wildlife Trust, since 1996 (Vice-Chairman, Conservation and Science, 1982-87); b. 29.4.37, Rugby; m., Dr. Ruth Hunter; 1 s.; 1 d. Educ. Lawrence Sheriff School, Rugby; Rugby School; Emmanuel College, Cambridge; Hatfield College, Durham. Demonstrator in Botany, University College of North Wales, Bangor, 1963-64; Staff Tutor in Natural Science, Department of Extra-Mural Studies, Bristol University, 1964-65; Lecturer, then Senior Lecturer in Botany (Ecology), Dundee University, 1966-97; Editor, Journal of Applied Ecology, 1991-97; Member: Executive Committee, Scottish Field Studies Association, since 1989, Museums and Galleries Commission Working Party on the non-national museums of Scotland, 1984-86; Trustee, National Museums of Scotland, 1987-94. Publications: numerous scientific research papers on hydrological aspects of the ecology of peat bogs and other mires. Recreations: music (clarinet, piano); literature; rural history; hill-walking. Address: Johnstonfield, Dunbog, Cupar, Fife KY14 6JG.

Ingram, Professor Malcolm David, BSc, PhD, DSc, CChem, FRSC. Professor of Chemistry, Aberdeen University, since 1993; b. 18.1.39, Wallasey; m., Lorna Hardman; 1 s.; 1 d. Educ. Oldershaw Grammar School; Liverpool University. Aberdeen University: Lecturer in Physical Chemistry, 1965-78, Senior Lecturer in Chemistry, 1978-90, Reader, 1990-93. Chairman, Aberdeen and North of Scotland Section, Royal Society of Chemistry, 1990-93. Publications: 150 in scientific journals. Recreations: gardening; foreign travel. Address: (b.) Department of Chemistry, Aberdeen University, Aberdeen AB9 2UE; T.-01224 272905.

Innes, James, BSc, CEng, FICE, FIHT. Director of Roads and Chief Road Engineer, Scottish Office Development Department, since 1995; Visiting Professor of Civil Engineering, Strathclyde University, since 1992; Chairman, Scottish Construction Clients' Forum, since 1995; b. 7.8.44, Helmsdale; m., June Pearson; 1 s.; 1 d. Educ. Woodside Secondary School, Glasgow; Strathclyde University. Lanark County Council, 1966-67; Inverness County Council, 1967-73; Scottish Development Department, 1973-84; Department of Transport (Superintending Engineer), 1984-85; Assistant Chief Road Engineer, Scottish Office Industry Department, 1985-88; Deputy Chief Road Engineer, Scottish Office Industry Department, 1988-95. Recreations: golf; foreign travel. Address: (b.) 3-H 42 Victoria Quay, Edinburgh EH6 6QQ; T.-0131-244 0626.

Innes, Professor John, BCom, PhD, CA, FCMA. Professor of Accountancy, Dundee University, since 1991; b. 11.7.50, Edinburgh; m., Ina. Educ. George Watson's College; Edinburgh University. Student accountant and staff auditor, KPMG, 1972-75; International Operational Auditor, Uniroyal Inc., 1975-78; Lecturer and Senior Lecturer in Accounting, Edinburgh University, 1978-91. Canon Foundation Visiting Research Fellow, 1992-93; SHEFC Lead Assessor in Accounting, 1995-96. Recreations: golf; squash; tennis. Address: (b.) Department of Accountancy & Business Finance, Dundee University, Dundee DD1 4HN; T.-01382 344197.

Innes, Norman Lindsay, OBE, BSc, PhD, DSc, FIBiol, FRSE. Agricultural Research Consultant; b. 3.5.34, Kirriemuir; m., Marjory Niven Farquhar; 1 s.; 1 d. Educ. Websters High School, Kirriemuir; Aberdeen University; Cambridge University. Senior Cotton Breeder: Sudan, 1958-66, Uganda, 1966-71; Head, Cotton Research Unit, Uganda, 1972; National Vegetable Research Station, Wellesbourne: Head, Plant Breeding Section, 1973-84, Deputy Director, 1977-84; Scottish Crop Research Institute: Deputy Director, 1986-94, Head, Plant Breeding Division, 1984-89; Honorary Lecturer, then Honorary Professor, Birmingham University, 1973-84; Governing Board Member, International Crops Research Institute for Semi-Arid Tropics, India, 1982-88; Honorary Professor, Dundee University, 1988-95; Governing Board Member, International Potato Centre, Peru, 1988-95, Chairman, 1991-95; Vice-President, Association of Applied Biologists, 1990-92, President, 1993-94; Governing Council Member, since 1996, Chairman, since 1997, International Centre of Insect Physiology and Ecology, Kenya, British Association of Plant Breeders, 1982-84; Member, Oxfam Council of Trustees, 1982-85. Recreations: golf; photography; travel. Address: (b.) Scottish Crop Research Institute, Invergowrie, Dundee DD2 5DA; T.-01382 562731.

Innes of Edingight, Sir Malcolm Rognvald, KCVO, MA, LLB, WS, KStJ. Lord Lyon King of Arms, since 1981; Secretary to Order of the Thistle, since 1981; b. 25.5.38, Edinburgh; m., Joan Hay; 3 s. Educ. Edinburgh Academy; Edinburgh University. Carrick Pursuivant, 1958; Marchmont Herald, 1971; Lyon Clerk and Keeper of the Record, 1966; Member, Queen's Bodyguard for Scotland (Royal Company of Archers); President, Scottish Heraldry Society. Recreation: shooting. Address: (b.) Court of the Lord Lyon, HM New Register House, Edinburgh; T.-0131-556 7255.

Inverarity, James Alexander (Sandy), CBE, FRSA, FRAgS, CA. Farmer and Landowner; Chairman: Scottish Agricultural College, since 1990, Scottish Agricultural Securities Corporation, plc, since 1987; President, Scottish Farm and Countryside Educational Trust, since 1990; b. 17.9.35; m., Jean; 1 s.; 2 d. Educ. Loretto School. President, National Farmers Union of Scotland, 1970-71; Member: Eggs Authority, 1971-74, Farm Animal Welfare Council, 1978-88, Panel of Agricultural Arbiters, since 1983, Governing Body, Scottish Crop Research Institute, 1984-97, Dairy Produce Quota Tribunal for Scotland, 1984-85; Director, United Oilseed Producers Ltd., 1985-97 (Chairman, 1987-97). Recreations: shooting; curling. Address: Cransley, Fowlis, Dundee DD2 5NP; T.-01382 580327.

Ireland, Dr. Kenneth, OBE, DUniv, BL, FRSA, FTS. Consultant, Hanover Fine Arts (Edinburgh); b. 17.6.20, Edinburgh; m., Moira Lamb; 2 s. Educ. Edinburgh Academy; Edinburgh University. Law Apprentice, Steedman Ramage & Co., WS, Edinburgh, 1938-41; War service: Royal Artillery, L. Bdr., 1941-42, Intelligence Corps, WO II, 1942-46; Lt. (TA), 1948-52; General Manager: Park Theatre, Glasgow, 1946-49, Pitlochry Festival Theatre, 1951-52; Pitlochry Festival Society Ltd.: General Manager and Secretary, 1953-57, Festival Director and Secretary, 1957-83 (retired, 1984); Board Member, Scottish Tourist Board, 1966-69; Chairman, Tourist Association of Scotland, 1967-69; Deputy Chairman, Scottish Tourist Consultative Council, 1977-83; ESU Scotland Thyne Scholarship, 1970; Bill Heron Trophy, 1981 (first recipient for services to tourism). Recreations: foreign travel; drama; music; art; literature. Address: (h.) 10 Ravelston Rise, Edinburgh EH4 3LH; T.-0131-346 2292.

Ireland, Kenny. Artistic Director, Royal Lyceum Theatre Company. Address: (b.) Grindlay Street, Edinburgh, EH3 9AX.

Ireland, Sheriff Ronald David, QC, HonLLD. Sheriff Principal, Grampian, Highland and Islands, 1988-93; b. 13.3.25, Edinburgh. Educ. George Watson's College, Edinburgh; Balliol College, Oxford (Scholar); Edinburgh University. Advocate, 1952; Clerk, Faculty of Advocates, 1957-58; Professor of Scots Law, Aberdeen University, 1958-71; QC, 1964; Dean, Faculty of Law, Aberdeen University, 1964-67; Chairman, Board of Management, Aberdeen General Hospitals, 1964-71; Sheriff, Lothian and Borders at Edinburgh, 1972-88; Director, Scottish Courts Administration, 1975-78. Address: (h.) 6A Greenhill Gardens, Edinburgh EH10 4BW.

Irons, James Fraser, BSc, CEng, FICE, FIHT. Director of Roads and Transport, Perth and Kinross Council, since 1995; b. 25.6.47, Dundee; m., Frances Heron; 1 s.; 1 d. Educ. Morgan Academy, Dundee; Dundee University. Graduate Engineer, Perth and Kinross County Council, 1969-74; Senior Engineer, Dundee Corporation, 1974-76; Project Engineer, Government of Bahrain, 1976-78; Senior Engineer, Principal Engineer, Assistant Director Roads and Transport, Depute Director Roads and Transport, Tayside Regional Council, 1978-95. Recreations: golf; rugby; squash; caravanning; theatre. Address: (b.) 5 Whitefriars Crescent, Perth PH2 0ZA; T.-01738 476501.

Irons, Norman MacFarlane, CBE, DL, DLitt, DUniv, Hon. FRCSE, CEng, MIMechE, MCIBSE, JP. Lord Provost and Lord Lieutenant of the City of Edinburgh, 1992-96; Partner, Building Services Consulting Engineers, since 1993; b. 4.1.41, Glasgow; m., Anne Buckley; 1 s.; 1 d. Held various posts as Consulting Engineer; founded own practice, 1983. SNP Member, City of Edinburgh District Council, 1976-96. Recreation: rugby football. Address: (h.)

141 Saughtonhall Drive, Edinburgh EH12 5TS; T.-0131-337 6154.

Ironside, Leonard, JP. Member, Aberdeen City Council, since 1995 (Convener, Social Work Committee); Chairman, Aberdeen International Youth Festival), since 1996; Director: Foxlane Special Needs Garden Centre, Crown St. Day Centre, Voluntary Service, Aberdeen; Patron, Grampian Special Olympics for Handicapped; Commonwealth Professional Wrestling Champion, since 1981; Athletics Coach, Bon Accord (Special Needs); appointed Justice of the Peace, 1997; b. Aberdeen; m., Wendy; 1 d. Educ. Hilton Academy, Aberdeen. Member, Grampian Regional Council, 1982-96; Inspector, contributions agency, DHSS, since 1990; former Chairman, Grampian Initiative; won Commonwealth Professional Wrestling Championship at Middleweight, 1979; lost Championship, 1981; regained title, 1981; gained European Lightweight title, 1985, relinquished title, 1989; Grampian Ambassador, 1996. Former Director: Grampian Enterprise Ltd., Scottish Sub-Sea Technology Group; Member: Grampian Racial Equality Commission, Aberdeen Sports Council. Recreations: yoga teacher; also plays tennis, squash, badminton; cycling. Address: (h.) 42 Hillside Terrace, Portlethen, Kincardineshire; T.-Aberdeen 780929.

Irvine, Andrew Robertson, MBE (1979), BSc, FRICS. Rugby Player; b. 16.9.51, Edinburgh; m., Audrey; 1 s.; 3 d. Educ. George Heriot's School, Edinburgh; Edinburgh University. Captained George Heriot's School, Scottish Schools, Heriots FP, Edinburgh, Scotland; holds record for most tries scored by a full back (10); made international debut against All Blacks, 1972; 51 Scottish caps.

Irvine, Joseph Andrew, BSc. Head Teacher, Brae High School, since 1988; b. 18.6.44, Lerwick; m., Ishbel; 2 s. Educ. Anderson Educational Institute, Lerwick; Aberdeen University. Teacher of Maths/Science, Lerwick Central School, 1967-68; Teacher of Maths, Assistant Principal Teacher, Principal Teacher, Anderson High School, 1968-84; Field Officer, Shetland Islands Council, 1984-88. Chairman: Northern Sports Development Trust, Shetland Recreational Trust. Recreations: sailing; photography. Address: (b.) Brae High School, Brae, Shetland ZE2 9QG; T.-01806 522 370.

Irvine-Fortescue, James William, MA (Hons), CA, JP, DL, KLJ, FSA Scot; b. 7.6.17, Wilmslow; m., Margaret Guise Yates; 3 s.; 1 d. Educ. Aberdeen Grammar School; Edinburgh Academy; Aberdeen University. War Service: Royal Army Pay Corps, 1940-46, service in India and Ceylon, 1942-46 (Major and Staff Paymaster); JP and Magistrate, Kincardineshire, 1957; Member, Kincardine County Council, 1952-73; Commissioner of Income Tax, County of Kincardine, 1957-92; Chairman: Lower Deeside District Council, 1964-73; Grampian Region Valuation Appeal Committee, 1975-90. President, Deeside Field Club, 1981-86; a Vice President, Royal Society for Asian Affairs, 1983-86; Past President, Auchinleck Boswell Society; Past Chairman, Aberdeen Music Festival. Recreations: family history research; foreign travel. Address: (h.) Kingcausie, Maryculter, Kincardineshire AB12 5FR; T.-01224 732224.

Irving, George Livingston, MSc, CSW, MIM. Director of Social Work, North Ayrshire Council, since 1996; Convener, Association of Directors of Social Work, Criminal Justice Standing Committee, since 1996; Board Member, Scottish Association for the Care and Resettlement of Offenders, since 1997; Honorary Lecturer, Caledonian University, since 1990; b. 11.11.41, Glasgow; m., Dorothy; 1 s.; 1 d. Educ. Whitehill Secondary School, Glasgow; University of Strathclyde. Residential Social Worker, Approved School Service, 1964-68; Social Worker, Paisley Town Council, 1968-70; Senior Social Worker/Area Officer, Ferguslie Park, Paisley, 1970-72; Director, Community Development Project, Paisley, 1972-

75; Divisional Organiser (Ayr Division), Strathclyde Region, 1975-86; District Social Work Manager: Glasgow North West, 1986-90, North Ayrshire, 1990-96. Representative, European Children's Trust (Romanian Orphanage Trust); six years voluntary child care work in Romania. Recreations: bowling; hill-walking; art; grandchildren. Address: (b.) Elliott House, Redburn Estate, Kilwinning Road, Irvine KA12 8TB; T.-01294 317723/5.

Irving, Gordon, MA (Hons). Writer, Journalist and Broadcaster; b. 4.12.18, Annan; m., Elizabeth Dickie (deceased); 1 s. Educ. Dumfries Academy; Edinburgh University. Staff Journalist, Daily Record, Edinburgh and Glasgow; Reuters' News Agency, London; TV Guide, Scotland; The Viewer, Scotland; Freelance Writer/Journalist, since 1964; Travel Correspondent, UK and overseas media; Scotland Correspondent, Variety, New York. Publications: Great Scot! (biography of Sir Harry Lauder); The Good Auld Days; The Solway Smugglers; The Wit of the Scots; The Wit of Robert Burns; The Devil on Wheels; Brush Up Your Scotland; Annie Laurie; Take No Notice and Take No More Notice! (World's Funniest Signs); The First 200 Years (Story of Dumfries and Galloway Royal Infirmary); 90 Glorious Years (Story of the King's Theatre, Glasgow). Recreations: making video films of personal travels; collecting trivia; researching Scottish music-hall history; fighting bumbling bureaucrats; reading all the Sunday broadsheets; surfing the World Wide Web on Internet. Address: (h.) 36 Whittingehame Court, Glasgow G12 OBG; T.-0141-357 2265.

Irving, Margaret Anne, MB, ChB, MFCH, FRCPCH. Consultant Paediatrician, Child and Family Health, Dumfries and Galloway Community HS Trust; b. 28.4.43, Glasgow; m., Dr. John Bruce Irving (qv); 2 s.; 1 d. Educ. Bathgate Academy; Glasgow University. Registrar in Bacteriology, Western Infirmary, Glasgow; Principal in general practice, Ayrshire; CMO in Child Health, Salford Health Authority; Senior Clinical Medical Officer in Child Health, Dumfries & Galloway Health Board; Medical Adviser to Regional Adoption and Fostering Panel; Chairman, Scottish Medical Group, British Agencies for Adoption and Fostering, 1990-93. Recreations: gardening; opera. Address: (h.) Bonshaw Tower, Kirtlebridge, Lockerbie, Dumfriesshire DG11 3LY; T.-01461 500256.

Irwin, Professor David George, MA, PhD, FSA, FRSA. Professor Emeritus, History of Art, Aberdeen University (Professor and Head of Department, 1970-96); b. 24.6.33, London; m., Francina Sorabji; 1 s.; 1 d. Educ. Holgate Grammar School, Barnsley; Queen's College, Oxford (Exhibitioner); Courtauld Institute of Art, London University. Lecturer in History of Fine Art, Glasgow University, 1959-70; Past President, British Society for 18th Century Studies; former Council Member, Walpole Society; former Member, Art Panel, Scottish Arts Council; Member, Editorial Board, British Journal of 18th Century Studies; Committee Member: Aberdeen Art Gallery, Architectural Heritage Society of Scotland; elected Member, International Association of Art Critics; won Laurence Binyon Prize, Oxford, 1956. Publications: English Neoclassical Art; Paul Klee; Visual Arts, Taste and Criticism; Designs and Ornaments of Empire Style; Winckelmann, Writings on Art; John Flaxman, Sculptor, Illustrator, Designer; Neoclassicism; Scottish Painters, At Home and Abroad, 1700 to 1900 (with Francina Irwin). Recreations: travel; painting. Address: (b.) Department of History of Art, King's College, Old Aberdeen, Aberdeen AB24 3UG; T.-01224 272458.

Ivory, Brian Gammell, MA (Cantab), CA, FRSA. Group Chief Executive, The Highland Distilleries Company plc, since 1994; b. 10.4.49, Edinburgh; m., Oona Mairi MacPhie Bell-Macdonald (see Oona Mairi MacPhie Ivory); 1 s.; 1 d. Educ. Eton College; Magdalene College, Cambridge. CA apprentice, Thomson McLintock, 1971-75; joined Highland

Distilleries, 1976, became Director, 1978, Managing Director, 1988; Director, Matthew Gloag and Son Ltd., 1987, Chairman, since 1994; Director, Orpar SA, since 1990; Director, Remy Cointreau SA, since 1991; Member, Scottish Arts Council, 1983-92 (Vice-Chairman, 1988-92); Member, Arts Council of GB, 1988-92; Chairman, The Piping Centre, since 1996. Recreations: the arts; farming; hill-walking. Address: (h.) Brewlands, Glenisla, by Blairgowrie, Perthshire, PH11 8PL; 12 Ann Street, Edinburgh, EH4 1PJ; (b.) 106 West Nile Street, Glasgow G1 2QY; T.-0141-332 7511.

Ivory, Oona Mairi MacPhie, MA (Cantab), ARCM, FRSA. Professional Musician; former Chairman, Scottish Ballet; Governor, Royal Scottish Academy of Music and Drama; Trustee, The Piping Trust; Founder Director, The Piping Centre; b. 21.7.54, Ayr; m., Brian Gammell Ivory (qv); 1 s.; 1 d. Educ. King's College, Cambridge; Royal Scottish Academy of Music and Drama; Royal Academy of Music. Recreations: visual arts; sailing. Address: (h.) Brewlands, Glenisla, by Blairgowrie, Perthshire PH11 8PL; 12 Ann Street, Edinburgh EH4 1PJ.

Izat, Alexander John Rennie, MA. Chairman: United Auctions (Scotland) Ltd., since 1992, Moredun Research Institute, since 1995, Shires Income Trust, since 1996; Partner, John Izat & Partners (Farmers), since 1975; Director: Glasgow Investment Managers, since 1990, Moredun Foundation, 1992-97, Shires Smaller Companies Trust, since 1997, Pentlands Science Park Ltd.; b. 14.7.32, London; m., Frederica Ann McNiel; 1 s.; 2 d. Educ. Glenalmond; Oriel College, Oxford. Partner, Williams de Broe & Co., Stockbrokers, 1955-75; farming at Balliliesk and Naemoor, 1975-87; farming at High Cocklaw, since 1987; former Member, Council, Scottish NFU; Director, Moredun Scientific Ltd., 1992-97; Past President, Fife and Kinross NFU and Kinross Agricultural Association; Director, Royal Highland Agricultural Society, 1985-97 (Hon. Treasurer, 1992-96); Member, Council, Glenalmond College, 1975-95 (Chairman, Committee of Council, 1989-95); President, Northern Area, Suffolk Sheep Society, 1989-91. Address: (b.) High Cocklaw, Berwick-upon-Tweed TD15 1UZ; T.-01289 86591.

Izod, (Kenneth) John, BA (Hons), PhD. Senior Lecturer, Department of Film and Media Studies, Stirling University, since 1978 (Dean, Faculty of Arts, since 1995); b. 4.3.40, Shepperton; m., Irene Chew Geok Keng (divorced 1994); 1 s.; 1 d. Educ. Prince Edward School, Harare City, Zimbabwe; Leeds University. Clerk articled to Chartered Accountant, 1958-63; Projectionist, mobile cinema unit, 1963; Lecturer in English, New University of Ulster, 1969-78; former Governor, Scottish Film Council; Chairman, Stirling Film Theatre, 1982-89 and 1991-92; Member, National Film and Video Forum, since 1994. Publications: Reading the Screen, 1984; Hollywood and the Box Office 1895-1986, 1988; The Films of Nicolas Roeg, 1991; Introduction to Television Documentary (Co-Author). Address: (b.) Film and Media Studies, University, Stirling FK9 4LA; T.-01786 473171.

J

Jack, David, BSc (Agric), DipAgric (Cantab), ARAgS. Honorary President, National Farmers Union of Scotland, 1996-97; Chairman, Scottish Quality Cereals Ltd., since 1994; Vice-Chairman, H-GCA, Cereals R. & D. Committee, since 1992; b. 9.8.32, Peterhead; m., Isabell Cowie; 2 s.; 2 d. Educ. Aberdeen Grammar School; Aberdeen University; Cambridge University. Farmer in Aberdeenshire; Member, Council, NFU of Scotland, 1988-97; Convener, Cereals Committee, 1990-96, EU Commission Cereals Advisory Committee, 1990-96. Recreations: golf; music. Address: Jackstown, Rothienorman, Inverurie, Aberdeenshire AB51 8UR; T.-01467 671205.

Jack, Professor Robert Barr, CBE, MA, LLB. Senior Partner, McGrigor Donald, Solicitors, Glasgow, Edinburgh and London, 1990-93 (Partner, 1957-93); Professor of Mercantile Law, Glasgow University, 1978-93; b. 18.3.28; m., Anna Thorburn Thomson; 2 s. Educ. Kilsyth Academy; High School of Glasgow; Glasgow University. Admitted a Solicitor in Scotland, 1951; Member, Scottish Law Commission, 1974-77; Scottish Observer, Department of Trade's Insolvency Law Review Committee, 1977-82; Member, Council for the Securities Industry, 1983-85; Lay Member, Council of the Stock Exchange, 1984-86; Independent Member, Board, Securities and Futures Authority (formerly Securities Association), 1986-94; Board Member, Securities and Investments Board, 1994-97; Chairman, Review Committee on Banking Services Law, 1987-89; Member: Panel on Takeovers and Mergers, since 1992, Financial Law Panel, since 1993; Chairman: Brownlee plc, Timber Merchants, Glasgow, 1984-86 (Director, 1974-86); Joseph Dunn (Bottlers) Ltd., Soft Drink Manufacturers, Glasgow, since 1983; Director: Bank of Scotland, 1985-96, Scottish Metropolitan Property plc, since 1980 (Deputy Chairman, since 1991), Scottish Mutual Assurance plc, since 1987 (Chairman, since 1992), Clyde Football Club Ltd., 1980-96, Gartmore Scotland Investment Trust PLC, since 1991, Glasgow Development Agency, 1992-97; President, Scottish National Council of YMCAs, since 1983 (Chairman, 1966-73); Governor, Hutchesons' Educational Trust, Glasgow, 1978-87 (Chairman, 1980-87); Chairman, The Turnberry Trust, since 1983; Member, Scottish Higher Education Funding Council, 1992-96; Governor, Beatson Institute for Cancer Research, since 1989. Publications: lectures and articles on various aspects of company law, the statutory regulation and self-regulation of the City, and banking and insolvency law. Recreations: golf; music; hopeful supporter of one of Scotland's less fashionable football teams; a dedicated lover of the Isle of Arran. Address: (h.) 50 Lanton Road, Lanton Park, Newlands, Glasgow G43 2SR; T.-0141-637 7302.

Jack, Professor Ronald Dyce Sadler, MA, PhD. Professor of Scottish and Medieval Literature, Edinburgh University, since 1987; b. 3.4.41, Ayr; m., Kirsty; 2 d. Educ. Ayr Academy; Glasgow University; Edinburgh University. Department of English Literature: Assistant Lecturer, 1965, Lecturer, 1968, Reader, 1978, Associate Dean, Faculty of Arts, 1971-73; Visiting Professor, Virginia University, 1973-74; Director, Universities Central Council on Admissions, 1988-94 (Member, 1973-76); Pierpont Morgan Scholar, British Academy, 1976; Advising Editor: Scotia, 1980-96, Scottish Literary Journal, since 1996; Member, Scottish Universities Council on Entrance, since 1981; Governor, Newbattle Abbey College, 1984-89; Beinecke Fellow, Yale, 1992; Visiting Professor, Strathclyde University, 1993; Lynn Woods Neag Distinguished Visiting Professor of British Literature, University of Connecticut, 1998. Publications: Robert MacLellan's Jamie the Saxt (Co-Editor), 1970; Scottish Prose 1550-1700, 1972; The Italian Influence on Scottish Literature, 1972; A Choice of Scottish Verse 1560-1660, 1978; The Art of Robert Burns (Co-Author), 1982; Sir Thomas Urquhart, The Jewel (Co-Author), 1984; Alexander Montgomerie, 1985; Scottish Literature's Debt to Italy, 1986; The History of Scottish Literature, Volume 1, 1988; Patterns of Divine Comedy, 1989; The Road to the Never Land, 1991; Of Lion and of Unicorn, 1993; The Poems of William Dunbar, 1997; The Mercat Anthology of Early Scottish Literature (Co-Editor). Address: (b.) Department of English Literature, Edinburgh University, David Hume Tower, George Square, Edinburgh EH8 9JX.

Jackson, Anthony Arthur, MA, MSc, FICDDip, MIED, AIEMgt. Senior Lecturer and Course Director in Environmental Management, School of Town and Regional Planning, Dundee University, since 1991; Founding Partner, St. Andrews Economic Services, 1986; b. 18.6.46, London; m., Alicia; 3 d. Educ. Westminster City School; Gonville and Caius College, Cambridge; Reading University. Agricultural Economist, Malawi Government, 1968-71; St. Andrews University: Stanley Smith Senior Fellow, 1971-73, Lecturer in Economics, 1973-91; FAO/FFHC Food and Nutrition Consultant, Malawi Government, 1973-76; Warning Officer, 1975-81, and Sector Scientific Adviser, UKWMO, 1981-91; Editor, Journal of Institute of Civil Defence, 1982-89; Group Leader, Conservative Group, Fife Regional Council, 1982-86; Director: Claverhouse Group, since 1992, Byre Theatre, 1980-89; Home Office Civil Defence Medal, 1990. Recreations: theatre; cricket; philately. Address: (h.) Creinch, Peat Inn, by Cupar, Fife KY15 5LH; T.-01334-840275.

Jackson, Eileen. Author; b. 18.4.26, Bristol; m., John Tunnard Jackson; 3 d. Short story/article writer, 1935-74; novels, since 1974; first novel, published USA, 1976, UK, 1978; 21 novels in over 65 editions and 10 languages; pseudonyms: Helen May, Linda Comer, Elizabeth Warne; also publishes as Eileen Jackson; President, Strathclyde Writers, since 1985; Lecturer. Recreations: reading; book collecting; swimming; golf; travel. Address: (h.) Girvan Lodge, Blairquhan, Maybole, Ayrshire KA19 7QP; T.-01655 770639.

Jackson, Jack, BSc (Hons), PhD, FIBiol, CIBiol. HM Staff Inspector of Schools with responsibility for science subjects; b. 31.5.44, Ayr; m., Sheilah Margaret Fulton; 1 s.; 3 d. Educ. Ayr Academy; Glasgow University; Jordanhill College of Education. Demonstrator, Zoology Department, Glasgow University, 1966-69; Lecturer in Zoology, West of Scotland Agricultural College, 1969-72; Assistant Teacher of Biology, Cathkin High School, 1972-73; Principal Teacher of Biology, Ayr Academy, 1973-83. Senior Examiner and Setter, Scottish Examination Board, 1978-83; Director, Board, Scottish Youth Theatre, 1979-82; Member: Scottish Council, Institute of Biology, 1980-83, School Board, Balerno High School, since 1989. Recreations: family life; gardening; hill-walking; conservation. Address: (b.) HM Inspector of Schools' Office, Saughton House, Broomhouse Drive, Edinburgh EH11 3XD; T.-0131-244 8324.

Jackson, Jim, OBE, BA. Executive Director, Alzheimer Scotland – Action on Dementia, since 1994; b. 10.2.47, Bradford; m., Jennifer; 1 s.; 1 d. Educ. Stand Grammar School; West Ham College of Technology; Open University. Playleader, 1969-72; Community Development Worker, 1972-77; Principal Assistant, Community Services and Development, Wirral, 1977-81; Consultant, Home Office Voluntary Services Unit, 1981-84; Assistant Director, Scottish Council for Voluntary Organisations, 1984-93; Director, Alzheimer's Scotland, 1993-94. Recreations: hill-walking; modern jazz. Address: (b.) 22 Drumsheugh Gardens, Edinburgh, EH3 7RN; T.-0131-243 1453.

Jackson, Professor Michael Herbert, BA, PhD, CBiol, MIBiol, FRSH, FRSA, MREHIS, MIEH. Professor and Head, Division of Environmental Health, Strathclyde University; b. 17.7.40, Hornchurch; m., Diana Evans; 2 d. Educ. Nantwich and Acton Grammar School; Open University; Strathclyde University. Lecturer in Environmental Health, Strathclyde University, 1977-86; previously public health inspector and environmental health officer; Editor-in-Chief, International Journal of Environmental Health Research. Recreations: gardening; reading; holidaying. Address: (b.) Department of Civil Engineering, Strathclyde University, John Anderson Building, Glasgow G4 0NG; T.-0141-548 3437.

Jackson, Professor Michael Peart, BA, MA, GradIPM. Senior Deputy Principal, Stirling University, since 1991; b. 1.7.47, Oldham; m., Sylvia; 1 s.; 1 d. Educ. Hulme Grammar School, Oldham; Hull University. Lecturer and Senior Lecturer in Sociology, Professor of Human Resource Management, Stirling University. JP; author of 12 books on industrial relations and employment policy. Address: (b.) Deputy Principal's Office, Stirling University, Stirling; T.-01786 467013.

Jackson, Philip, LLB. Reporter Manager for West Scotland, since 1996; b. 3.12.50, Glasgow; m., Miriam E. Levy; 1 s.; 1 d. Educ. Allan Glen's School, Glasgow; University of Glasgow. Assistant Reporter, Glasgow Corporation, 1974; Area Reporter: Strathclyde Region (Hamilton), 1976, Glasgow South West, 1988; Divisional Reporter, Strathclyde South, 1994. Recreations: cinema; calligraphy; history. Address: (b.) Merchant Exchange, 20 Bell Street, Glasgow; T.-0141-567 7957.

Jackson, Richard Dodds, MA, DipEd. Assistant Secretary (Post-Sixteen Qualifications), Scottish Office Education Department, since 1990; b. 13.9.37, Galashiels; m., Brenda Routledge Faurcus; 1 s.; 1 d. Educ. St. Mary's School, Melrose; Royal High School, Edinburgh; St. Andrews University; Moray House College of Education. Teacher of English, Broughton Secondary School, Edinburgh, and Daniel Stewart's College, Edinburgh, 1961-70; HM Inspector of Schools and FE Colleges, 1970-75; Scottish Education Department: Temporary Principal, Arts Branch, 1975-78, Assistant Secretary, Social Work Services Group, 1978-82; Deputy Director (Personnel and Supplies), Scottish Prison Service, 1982-86; Assistant Secretary (Primary Health Care), Scottish Home and Health Department, 1986-90. Recreations: theatre and opera work. Address: (b.) First Floor West, Victoria Quay, Edinburgh; T.-0131-244 0278.

Jackson, Robert Penman, MIBM. Director, Dundee Contract Services, Dundee City Council, since 1996; b. 2.4.47, Dunfermline; m., Helen Paxton; 1 s.; 1 d. Educ. Beath Senior High School, Cowdenbeath; Napier College of Science and Technology, Edinburgh. RSAS Diploma. Burgh Surveyor and Sanitary Inspector, Lochgelly Town Council, 1971-75; Assistant Director of Technical Services, Dunfermline District Council, 1975-84; Director of Public Works, City of Dundee District Council, 1984-96. Honorary Secretary, Lochgelly Old Folks' Reunion Committee. Recreation:golf. Address: (b.) 353 Clepington Road, Dundee; T.-Dundee 434729.

Jackson, Ronald William, LLB. Director of Law and Administration, Perth and Kinross Council, since 1995; Member, Policy Committee, Society of Directors of Administration, since 1979; Member, Competition Joint Committee, CIPFA, since 1990; b. 31.7.49, Dundee; m., Morag; 2 d. Educ. Dundee High School; Dundee University. Banff and Buchan District Council: Depute Director of Administration and Legal Services, 1975-79; Director of Administration and Legal Services and Joint Chief Officer, 1979-89; Depute Director of Corporate Services, Fife Regional Council, 1989-95. Recreations:

golf; skiing. Address: (b.) PO Box 77, 2 High Street, Perth PH1 5PH; T.-01738 475101.

Jackson, William Gordon, QC, LLB. Queen's Counsel; b. 5.8.48, Saltcoats; m., Anne; 1 s.; 2 d. Educ. Ardrossan Academy; St. Andrews University. Advocate Depute, 1987-90. Address: (b.) Advocates Library, Parliament House, Edinburgh; T.-0131-226 2881.

Jamal, Goran A., MB, ChB (Hons), MD, PhD, MRCP, FRCP. Consultant, Department of Neurology, Southern General Hospital, Glasgow, since 1988; Senior Clinical Lecturer, Glasgow University, since 1989; Senior Lecturer in Neuroscience, Strathclyde Region, since 1989; b. 19.7.53, Iraqi Kurdistan; m., Dr. Vian M.S. Anber; 1 s.; 1 d. Educ. Central Secondary School, Baghdad; Glasgow University. Research Fellow, Glasgow University Department of Neurology, 1981-86; Senior Registrar, Department of Neuroscience, St. Bartholomew's Hospital and London University, 1986-88. Publications: several chapters in books and more than 100 papers. Address: (b.) Department of Neurology, I.N.S., Southern General Hospital, Glasgow G51 4TF; T.-0141-201 2462.

James, David Sheard, MB, ChB, DipEd, DCH, DPM, FRCPsych, FRCP (Glas). Consultant Child Psychiatrist, Royal Hospital for Sick Children, Glasgow, since 1971; Honorary Clinical Senior Lecturer, Child and Adolescent Psychiatry, Glasgow University, since 1991; b. 19.2.39, Harrogate; m., Hilary; 1 s.; 2 d. Educ. Warwick School; Sheffield University. Paediatrics, Sheffield Children's Hospital; Registrar in Psychiatry, Mapperley Hospital, Nottingham; Research Registrar, United Sheffield Hospitals; Senior Registrar, Child Psychiatry, Birmingham Children's Hospital and Charles Burns Clinic. Publication: Families Without Hope (Co-Author), 1975. Recreations: motor vehicles; model railway. Address: (h.) Waterside, Lochlibo Road, Uplawmoor, Glasgow G78 4AA; T.-01505 850269.

James, Professor Keith, BSc, PhD, DSc, FIBiol, FRCPath, FRSE. Professor in Immunology, Edinburgh University, since 1991; b. 15.3.38, Cumbria; m., Valerie Spencer Jubb; 3 s. Educ. Whitehaven Grammar School; Birmingham University. Research Fellow, Birmingham University, 1962-64; Research Assistant, University of California, 1964-65; Senior Lecturer, Edinburgh University, 1965-77, Reader, 1977-91; Past Chairman, Treasurer, Education Secretary and Trustee, British Society for Immunology; Secretary General, International Union of Immunological Societies; serves on the editorial board of a number of journals. Publications: Introducing Immunology (Co-Author); numerous scientific papers. Recreations: hillwalking; photography. Address: (h.) 23 Crosswood Crescent, Balerno, Edinburgh EH14 7LX; T.-0131-449 5583.

James, Mary Charlotte, BA (Hons). Headmistress, St. Leonards School, St. Andrews, since 1988; b. 2.4.44, Bilston, Staffs; m., Lawrence Edwin James; 2 s. Educ. St. Leonards School; York University; St. Anne's College, Oxford. Head of History, Casterton School, Kirkby Lonsdale, 1979-84; Headmistress, Queen Ethelburga's School, Harrogate, 1984-88. Chairman, Demarco European Cultural Initiative, since 1997; Member, Scottish Council, ISCO, since 1988; SCIS: Member, Governing Board, Member, Working Party on Marketing and PR, since 1996. Recreations: reading; cooking; walking; sleeping. Address: St. Leonards House, St. Andrews, Fife; T.-01334 472126.

James, Stuart, BA, FLA, MIInfSc, FRSA. Librarian, Paisley University, since 1989; b. 17.3.44, Borehamwood; m., Gillian Margaret Buckman; 1 s.; 1 d. Educ. Bushey Grammar School; Birmingham University. Leeds City Libraries, 1965-69; Northampton Development Corporation, 1970-71; Irvine Development Corporation

(Librarian/ Information Specialist), 1971-78; Depute Librarian, Paisley College, 1978-89. Editor, Library Review; Editor, Reference Reviews; Convenor, Scottish Academic Libraries Co-operative Training Group, 1987-92; Member, Council of Polytechnic Librarians Executive Committee, 1991-93; Honorary Secretary, Library Association Cataloguing and Indexing Group, 1992-97; Chairman, Cataloguing and Indexing Group in Scotland; Member, British Library National Bibliographic Service Advisory Board, 1995-97; Chairman, Open Learning Foundation Library and Learning Support Group, since 1997. Recreations: history of aviation; reading; book collecting. Address: (b.) Library, Paisley University, High Street, Paisley PA1 2BE; T.-0141-848 3750.

James, Professor (William) Philip (Trehearne), CBE, MA, MD, DSc, FRCP, FRCPEdin, FRSE, MFPHM. Director, Rowett Research Institute, Aberdeen, since 1982; Research Professor, Aberdeen University, since 1983; b. 27.6.38, Liverpool; m., Jean Hamilton Moorhouse; 1 s.; 1 d. Educ. Bala School, North Wales; Ackworth School, Yorkshire; University College, London. Senior House Physician, Whittington Hospital, London, 1963-65; Clinical Research Scientist, Medical Research Council Tropical Metabolism Research Unit, Kingston, Jamaica, 1965-68; Harvard Research Fellow, Massachusetts General Hospital, 1968-69; Wellcome Trust Research Fellow, MRC Gastroenterology Unit, London, 1969-70; Senior Lecturer, Department of Human Nutrition, London School of Hygiene and Tropical Medicine, and Honorary Consultant, UCH, 1970-74; Assistant Director, MRC Dunn Nutrition Unit, and Honorary Consultant Physician, Addenbrooke's Hospital, Cambridge, 1974-82. Sir David Cuthbertson Lecturer; Van den Berghs & Jurgens Reporting Award; Amos Memorial Lecturer; Sir Thomas Middleton Memorial Lecturer; Sir Stanley Davidson Memorial Lecturer; Minshull Lecture; Member, COMA and its Sub-Committees; Chairman, Panel on Novel Foods; Member: Nutrition Task Force; Advisory Committee on Novel Foods and Processes; Chief Executive's Research Advisory Group, Scottish Higher Education Funding Council; President, National Food Alliance; WHO Committee on Nutrition Policy, 1989; FAO Commission on National Energy Needs, 1987-88; Department of Health Task Force on Obesity, 1994; Royal College of Physicians of Edinburgh Working Party on Management of Obesity in the NHS, 1994-96; Association of Professors of Human Nutrition, since 1994; International Task Force on Obesity Management, since 1995; Planning Group, European Young Nutrition Leadership Courses, since 1994; European Panel for European Heart Foundations' Analysis of Cardiovascular Risk, since 1994; Member: EC Scientific Committee for Food, 1992-95, World Cancer Research Fund International Panel on Diet and Cancer, since 1994, EC Scientific Steering Committee, since 1997; Adviser, European Directors of Agricultural Research on Diet and Health, since 1995; Chairman, UN Commission on Global Nutrition for the 21st Century, since 1997; author: WHO report on nutrition and European health, FAO book on human energy requirements; editor, textbook on human nutrition and dietetics, 1992. Address: (b.) Rowett Research Institute, Greenburn Road, Bucksburn, Aberdeen AB2 9SB; T.-01224 712751.

Jameson, John, QFSM, CIMgt, AIFireE. Firemaster, Strathclyde Fire Brigade, since 1991; b. 12.4.46, Chapelhall; m., Helen Mulvey; 1 s.; 1 d. Educ. St. Aloysius and St. Patrick's High School, Coatbridge. Lanarkshire Fire Brigade, 1965-70; Glasgow Fire Service, 1970-75; Strathclyde Fire Brigade: joined 1975, Assistant Firemaster, 1987-88, Deputy Firemaster, 1988-91. Fire Brigade Long Service and Good Conduct Medal, 1985; Strathclyde Regional Council Medal for Bravery, 1987; Churchill Fellowship, 1983. Recreations: historic buildings; golf. Address: (b.) Fire Headquarters, Bothwell Road, Hamilton ML3 0EA.

Jameson, John Valentine McCulloch, OBE, JP, DL, BSc, FRICS. Chairman, West of Scotland Water; Partner, G.M. Thomson & Co., Chartered Surveyors, since 1970; b. 5.10.33, Twynholm, Stewartry of Kirkcudbright; m., Mary Irene Butters; 1 s.; 2 d. Educ. Rugby School; College of Estate Management (External). Commissioned 4/7 Royal Dragoon Guards, 1952-54; Shell Petroleum Co., London, 1954-57; Richard Costain (Canada) Ltd., Toronto, 1958-64. Member and Bailie, Gatehouse-of-Fleet Town Council, 1970-75; Member, Dumfries and Galloway Regional Council, 1974-94: Chairman, Finance Committee, 1974-83, Convener, 1983-90; Chairman: Dumfries and Galloway Tourist Association, 1978-82, Royal Institution of Chartered Surveyors in Scotland, 1981-82; Council Member, National Trust for Scotland, 1980-84; Chairman, Dumfries & Galloway Enterprise Co. Ltd., 1993-94; Treasurer, Anwoth and Girthon Kirk Session. Recreations: golf; shooting; squash; hill-walking. Address: (h.) Laghead, Gatehouse-of-Fleet; T.-01557 814389.

Jameson, Brigadier Melville Stewart, CBE. Producer, Edinburgh Military Tattoo, since 1995; b. 17.7.44, Clunie; m., Sarah Amy Walker Munro; 2 s. Educ. Glenalmond; RMA, Sandhurst. Commissioned into Royal Scots Greys, 1965; served with regiment in Germany, Northern Ireland, Cyprus, Middle East and Edinburgh (where, in 1971, regiment amalgamated with 3rd Carbiniers to form Royal Scots Dragoon Guards); following tour as Chief of Staff 52 Lowland Brigade, commanded Royal Scots Dragoon Guards, 1986-88, at Tidworth; posted as Instructor to Joint Service Defence College Greenwich; Colonel PB17 on Military Secretary's staff, Ministry of Defence; Command, 51 Highland Brigade, 1994-96 based in Perth. Member, Royal Company of Archers; Honorary Colonel: Aberdeen University OTC, The Scottish Yeomanry. Recreations: shooting; gardening; polo; music (Highland bagpipes). Address: (b.) Tattoo Office, 32 Market Street, Edinburgh EH1 1QB; T.-0131-225 4783.

Jamie, Kathleen, MA. Writer; b. 13.5.62, Johnstone. Educ. Currie High School; Edinburgh University. Publications: The Way We Live; The Autonomous Region; The Queen of Sheba; The Golden Peak.

Jamieson, Rev. Gordon David, MA, BD. Minister, Barnhill St. Margaret's Parish Church, Dundee, since 1986; b. 1.3.49, Glasgow; m., Annette; 1 s.; 1 d. Educ. Hamilton Academy; Edinburgh University. Assistant Minister, Tron Moredun, Edinburgh, 1973-74; Minister: Schaw Kirk, Drongan, 1974-79, Elie Parish Church, linked with Kilconquhar or Colinsburgh Parish Church, 1979-86; Vice-Convener, Committee on the Maintenance of the Ministry, 1993-95; Interim Convener, Church of Scotland Board of Ministry, 1995-96. Address: The Manse, Invermark Terrace, Broughty Ferry, Dundee DD5 2QU; T.-01382 779278.

Janes, Derek Charles, MA, AMA. Assistant Head of Museums and Galleries, Edinburgh City Museums, since 1985; b. 24.3.48, Bristol; m., Diane; 1 s.; 1 d. Educ. Bristol Grammar School; George Watson's College; Edinburgh University. Lancaster City Museum, 1969-71; Assistant Curator, Bury County Borough Museum and Art Gallery, 1972-74; Keeper of Social History, Bury Metropolitan Borough Museum, 1974-76; Senior Keeper, Social History, Coventry City Council Herbert Art Gallery, 1976-84. Publication: Lancaster. Recreations: garden; house; music; towns; reading. Address: (b.) City Art Centre, 2 Market Street, Edinburgh EH1 1DE. T.-0131-529 3951.

Jardine, Sir (Andrew) Rupert (John) Buchanan-, 4th Bt, MC, DL. Landowner; b. 2.2.23; m., Jane Fiona Edmonstone (m. diss.); 1 s.; 1 d. Educ. Harrow; Royal Agricultural College. Retired Major, Royal Horse Guards; Joint Master, Dumfriesshire Foxhounds, 1950; Deputy Lieutenant,

Dumfriesshire, 1978. Address: (h.) Dixons, Lockerbie, Dumfriesshire.

Jardine, Ian William, BSc, PhD. Director of Strategy and Operations (East), Scottish Natural Heritage; b. 22.5.59, Edinburgh; m., Anne Daniel; 2 s. Educ. Royal High School, Edinburgh; Durham University; Leeds University. Joined Scottish Office, 1984; worked in various departments, including Scottish Development and Industry Departments; Private Secretary to Ian Lang MP; involved in setting-up of urban partnership initiatives and management of Castlemilk Partnership; joined Scottish Natural Heritage, 1992. Recreations: acting; gardening; natural history. Address: (b.) Battleby, Redgorton, Perth PH1 3EW; T.-01738 444177.

Jardine, Leslie Thomas, LLB. Director for Community Resources, Dumfries and Galloway Council, since 1995; b. 4.6.49, Dumfries; m., Angela; 1 s. Educ. Dumfries Academy; Glasgow University. Law apprentice, then Legal Assistant, Dumfries County Council, 1972-75; Policy Planning Assistant, then Regional Public Relations Officer, then Director of Economic Development, Dumfries and Galloway Regional Council, 1985-96. Solicitor. Recreation: riding. Address: (b.) 118 English Street, Dumfries; T.-01387 61234.

Jarvie, Sheriff Elizabeth, QC. Sheriff of Lothian and Borders at Edinburgh. Address: Sheriff Court House, 27 Chambers Street, Edinburgh EH1 1LB.

Jarvie, Norman Dobson, MB, ChB, FRCGP, FRCP(G), DObstRCOG. General Practitioner, Crieff; b. 31.3.36, Glasgow; m., Dr. Anne Jarvie; 2 s.; 1 d. Educ. Rutherglen Academy; Glasgow University. Medical Officer to Crieff Hospital, Ardvreck School, Morrison's Academy and Crieff Hydro; Chairman, Local Medical Committee, Perth and Kinross Division, 1978-80; President, Perth and Kinross Division, BMA, 1980; Chairman, Scottish Association of General Practitioner Community Hospitals, 1981-85; General Practitioner Tutor, Dundee University; Chairman, Scottish Council, Royal College of General Practitioners, 1987-90; Provost, East Scotland Faculty, RCGP, 1987-90; Chairman, National Medical Advisory Committee, 1990-95; Chairman, Area Drug and Therapeutics Committee, Tayside Health Board, 1994-97. Recreations: skiing; sailing; golf. Address: (b.) Health Centre, Crieff PH7 3SA; T.-01764 652456.

Jarvis, Geoffrey, FRIBA, FRIAS. Architect; b. 9.1.28, London; m., Rosalind Bailey; 2 s.; 2 d. Educ. Kelvinside Academy; Glasgow Academy; Glasgow School of Architecture. Worked for two years in Philadelphia and New York (Marcel Breuer); returned to Glasgow, setting up in private practice; Consultant to National Trust for Scotland, 1972-87; principal works include Culzean Country Park Centre; Clan Donald Centre, Skye; Chatelherault, Hamilton; Edinburgh Castle Visitor Reception Feasibility Study; Past Chairman, Glasgow Tree Lovers' Society; Founder, former Honorary Secretary and Chairman, New Glasgow Society; Co-Founder and Vice-Chairman, Clyde Fair International, 1972-73; Co-founder, Clydebuilt, 1991; RIBA national award, Regenerating Scotland Award, three Europa Nostra Diplomas of Merit; two Civic Trust Awards; Founder and Vice Chair, Clyde Heritage Trust; Founder Director, Clyde Festival Gardens 1999 Ltd. Recreations: travel and sight-seeing; local and Scottish history; Glasgow; family. Address: (b./h.) Manse Brae, Baldernock, Milngavie G62 6HA; T.-0141-956 3899.

Jarvis, Professor Paul Gordon, PhD, Fil dr, FRS (London), FRSE, FRS (Uppsala), FIBiol, FIChFor. Professor of Forestry and Natural Resources, Edinburgh University, since 1975; b. 23.5.35, Tunbridge Wells; m., Margaret Susan Gostelow; 1 s.; 2 d. Educ. Sir Anthony Brown's School, Brentwood; Oriel College, Oxford. PhD study, Sheffield University, 1957-60; Postdoctoral Fellow, NATO, Institute of Plant Physiology, Uppsala University, 1960-62; Fil dr, Uppsala University, 1963; Senior Lecturer in Plant Physiology, Royal College of Agriculture, Uppsala; Aberdeen University: Lecturer in Botany, 1966-72, Senior Lecturer, 1972-75. Council Member, Society for Experimental Biology, 1977-80, President, 1993-95; Commissioner, Countryside Commission for Scotland, 1976-78; Council Member, National Trust for Scotland, since 1987; Trustee, John Muir Trust, since 1989; Member, Governing Body, Scottish Crops Research Institute, 1977-86; Co-Founder and Sectional Editor, Plant, Cell and Environment; present interests: environmental change, biodiversity, forest ecology; serves on various editorial and review boards. Recreations: hill-walking; gardening; growing trees. Address: (h.) Belmont, 47 Eskbank Road, Dalkeith, Midlothian EH22 3BH; T.-0131-663 8676.

Jauncey of Tullichettle, Lord (Charles Eliot Jauncey), PC. Lord of Appeal in Ordinary, since 1988; Senator of the College of Justice in Scotland, 1979-88; b. 8.5.25; m., Sarah Camilla Cathcart; 2 s.; 2 d. Educ. Radley; Christ Church, Oxford; Glasgow University. Advocate, 1949; Kintyre Pursuivant of Arms, 1955; QC, 1963; Sheriff Principal of Fife and Kinross, 1971. Member, Historic Buildings Council for Scotland, 1971-92. Recreations: fishing; shooting; bicycling; genealogy. Address: (h.) Tullichettle, Comrie, Perthshire PH6 2HU; T.-01764 670349.

Jeeves, Professor Malcolm Alexander, CBE, MA, PhD (Cantab), Hon. DSc (Edin), FBPsS, FRSE. President, Royal Society of Edinburgh, since 1996 (Vice-President, 1990-93); Professor of Psychology, St. Andrews University, since 1969; b. 16.11.26, Stamford, England; m., Ruth Elisabeth Hartridge; 2 d. Educ. Stamford School; St. John's College, Cambridge University. Lt., 1st Bn., Sherwood Foresters, BAOR, 1945-48; Exhibitioner, St. John's College, Cambridge, 1948-52; research and teaching, Cambridge and Harvard Universities, 1952-56; Lecturer, Leeds University, 1956-59; Professor and Head, Department of Psychology, Adelaide University, 1959-69 (Dean, Faculty of Arts, 1963-64); Member: Council, SERC, 1985-89, Neuroscience and Mental Health Board, MRC, 1985-89, Council, Royal Society of Edinburgh, 1985-88 (Vice President, 1990-93); Director, Medical Research Council Cognitive Neuroscience Research Group, 1983-88; Vice-Principal, St. Andrews University, 1981-85; Chairman, Executive Committee, International Neuropsychological Symposium, 1986-91; Editor-in-Chief, Neuropsychologia, 1990-93; Cairns Memorial Lecturer, Australia, 1986; New College Lecturer, University of NSW, 1987. Honorary Sheriff, Fife, since 1986. Publications: Analysis of Structural Learning (Co-Author); Psychology Survey No. 3 (Editor); Experimental Psychology: An introduction for biologists; The Effects of Structural Relations upon Transfer (Co-Author); Thinking in Structures (Co-Author); Behavioural Science and Christianity (Editor); Free to be Different (Co-Author); Psychology and Christianity: The View Both Ways; The Scientific Enterprise and Christian Faith; Psychology: Through the eyes of faith (Co Author); Mind Fields; Human Nature at the Millennium. Recreations: walking; music; fishing. Address: (b.) Department of Psychology, St. Andrews University, St. Andrews KY16 9JU; T.-01334 76161.

Jeffares, Professor Alexander Norman, AM, MA, PhD, DPhil, Ddel'U, DLitt, FAHA, FRSE, FRSL, FRSA. Professor of English Studies, Stirling University, 1974-86; Honorary Professor, since 1987; Managing Director, Academic Advisory Services Ltd.; Director, Colin Smythe Ltd.; b. 11.8.20, Dublin; m., Jeanne Agnes Calembert; 1 d. Educ. The High School, Dublin; Trinity College, Dublin; Oriel College, Oxford. Lecturer in Classics, Trinity College, Dublin, 1943-45; Lector in English, Groningen University, 1946-48; Lecturer in English Literature, Edinburgh University, 1949-51; Professor of English Language and

Literature, Adelaide, 1951-56; Professor of English Literature, Leeds, 1957-74. Secretary, Australian Humanities Research Council, 1954-57; Honorary Fellow, Australian Academy of Humanities; Founding Chairman, Association for Commonwealth Literary and Language Studies, 1966-68 (Honorary Life Fellow); Founding Chairman, International Association for Study of Anglo-Irish Literature, 1968-70 (Honorary Life President, since 1973); Member, Scottish Arts Council (Chairman, Literature Committee, 1977-83, Vice Chairman, 1980-84); Member, Arts Council of GB, 1980-84; Chairman, National Book League Scotland, 1985-87, Book Trust Scotland, 1987-89; Board Member, Book Trust, 1987-89; President, International PEN, Scottish Centre, 1986-89; Vice-President, Royal Society of Edinburgh, 1988-89; Vice-Chairman, Muckhart Community Council, 1979-86; Chairman of Judges, McVitie Prize, 1988-91. Publications: Yeats: Man and Poet; Seven Centuries of Poetry; The Scientific Background (Co-Author); A Commentary on the Poems of Yeats; A Commentary on the Plays of Yeats (Co-Author); History of Anglo-Irish Literature; Restoration Drama; New Commentary on Poems of Yeats; Brought up in Dublin (poems); Brought up to Leave (poems); An Irish Childhood (Co-Editor); A Jewish Childhood (Co-Editor); Yeats: a new biography; Yeats's Poems; Yeats's Vision; Yeats: the love poems; Always Your Friend (Co-Editor); Swift, the selected poems; Joycechoyce (Co-Editor); Ireland's Women (Co-Editor); Collins Dictionary of Quotations (Co-Editor); Images of Imagination (essays); Victorian Love Poems; Irish Love Poems. Recreations: drawing; painting; restoring old houses. Address: (h.) Craighead Cottage, Fife Ness, Crail, Fife; T.-01333 450898.

Jeffcoat, Marilyn Annette, BCom, FCCA. Chairman, D.M. Vaughan & Co. Ltd., Accountants; Member of Court, Napier University, since 1990; Commissioner, Mental Welfare Commission, since 1992; b. 7.4.47, Birmingham; 5 s.; 1 d. Educ. Erdington Grammar School, Birmingham; Edinburgh University. Worked in investment management, tax accountancy and audit with Baillie Gifford, Ivory & Sime, and Coopers & Lybrand until 1978, qualifying as a certified accountant in 1976; public practice since 1979. Convener, One Parent Families, Scotland; Director, St. Mary's Cathedral Workshop Ltd.; Treasurer: Society of Scottish Artists, St. Mary's Episcopal Cathedral, Edinburgh, Royal Scottish Country Dance Society; Administrator, Mendelssohn on Mull Festival; Trustee, Scottish Hospital Trust. Recreations: theology; mathematics; dance. Address: (b.) 10 Gloucester Place, Edinburgh; T.-0131-225 8282.

Jeffery, Professor Jonathan, MA, BSc, DPhil, DSc, CChem, FRSC, CBiol, FIBiol, FRSA, FRSE. Professor of Biochemistry, Aberdeen University, since 1983; b. 29.7.35, Liverpool; m., Christa Torriano-Williams; 2 d. Educ. Liverpool Institute High School; Jesus College, Oxford University. Research Biochemist, ICI, 1962-66; Aberdeen University: Lecturer in Chemical Pathology, 1966-72, Lecturer in Biochemistry, 1972-74, Senior Lecturer in Biochemistry, 1974-83. Recreations: country walks; some interest in theatre, visual arts and music. Address: (b.) Department of Molecular and Cell Biology, Aberdeen University, Marischal College, Aberdeen, AB10 1YS; T.-01224 272000.

Jeffrey, Dr. Robin Campbell, FEng. Chief Executive, Scottish Nuclear Ltd., since 1992; Chairman, Scottish Nuclear, since 1995; Deputy Chairman, British Energy plc, since 1995; Non-Executive Director, London Regional Transport; b. 19.2.39, Kirkintilloch; m., Barbara; 2 s.; 1 d. Educ. Lenzie Academy; Kelvinside Academy; Royal College of Science and Technology, Glasgow; Glasgow University; Cambridge University. Babcock and Wilcox, Renfew, 1956-60 and 1964-79; joined SEEB (later ScottishPower), 1979: Technical Services Manager, 1979-80, Torness Project Manager, 1980-88, Chief Engineer, 1988-89, Managing Director, Engineering Resources Business, 1989-92. Visiting Professor, University of Strathclyde. Recreations: squash; tennis; real tennis; skiing. Address: (h.) 71D Partickhill Road, Glasgow; T.-0141-357 3079.

Jeffreys-Jones, Professor Rhodri, BA (Wales), PhD (Cantab), FRHistS. Professor of American History, Edinburgh University, since 1997; b. 28.7.42, Carmarthen; m., Mary Fenton; 2 d. by pr. m. Educ. Ysgol Ardudwy; University of Wales; Cambridge University; Michigan University; Harvard University. Tutor: Harvard, 1965-66, Fitzwilliam College, Cambridge, 1966-67; Assistant Lecturer, Lecturer, Senior Lecturer, Reader, Edinburgh University, 1967-97; Fellow, Charles Warren Center for the Study of American History, Harvard, 1971-72; Canadian Commonwealth Visiting Fellow and Visiting Professor, University of Toronto, 1993. Publications: Violence and Reform in American History; American Espionage: From Secret Service to CIA; Eagle Against Empire: American Opposition to European Imperialism 1914-82 (Editor); The Growth of Federal Power in American History (Joint Editor); The CIA and American Democracy; North American Spies (Joint Editor); Changing Differences: Women and the Shaping of American Foreign Policy, 1917-1994; Eternal Vigilance? – 50 years of the CIA (Joint Editor). Recreations: snooker; vegetable gardening. Address: (b.) Department of History, Edinburgh University, William Robertson Building, George Square, Edinburgh EH8 9JY; T.-0131-650 3773/3780.

Jenkins, Blair, MA (Hons). Director of Broadcasting, Scottish Television, since 1994; b. 8.1.57, Elgin; 3 d. Educ. Elgin Academy; Edinburgh University. Joined Evening Express, Aberdeen, from school, 1974; Young Journalist of the Year, Scottish Press Awards, 1977; university, 1976-80; joined BBC in London, becoming chief sub-editor, Television News, 1982; Producer, Nine O'Clock News, 1983; returned to Scotland, 1984, to produce Reporting Scotland, BBC; joined Scottish TV, 1986, to re-launch Scotland Today; Editor, News and Current Affairs, 1990-93; Head of Regional Broadcasting, 1993-94. Recreations: his daughters; good books; Aberdeen Football Club. Address: (b.) Scottish Television plc, Cowcaddens, Glasgow G2 3PR; T.-0141-300 3780.

Jenkins, David, BMus, PhD, MBA. Academic Registrar, Moray House Institute of Education, since 1984; b. 30.5.44, Dundee; m., Dr. Janet Jenkins; 2 s.; 1 d. Educ. Perth Academy; Edinburgh University. Assistant Teacher, Tynecastle Secondary School, Edinburgh, 1968-70; Lecturer, then Vice-Principal, Callendar Park College of Education, Falkirk, 1970-82; Lecturer and Clerk to Board of Studies, Moray House College of Education, 1982-84. Recreations: music; gardening. Address: (h.) 18 Blacket Place, Edinburgh EH9 1RL; T.-0131-667 2885.

Jenkins, Robin, MA. Novelist; b. 11.9.12. Author of: So Gaily Sings the Lark, Happy for the Child, The Thistle and the Grail, The Cone-Gatherers, Guests of War, The Missionaries, The Changeling, Some Kind of Grace, Dust on the Paw, The Tiger of Gold, A Love of Innocence, The Sardana Dancers, A Very Scotch Affair, The Holy Tree, The Expatriates, A Toast to the Lord, A Far Cry from Bowmore, A Figure of Fun, A Would-be Saint, Fergus Lamont, The Awakening of George Darroch, Just Duffy, Poverty Castle, Willie Hogg, Leila, Lunderston Tales. Address: (h.) Fairhaven, Toward, Dunoon PA23 7UE.

Jennett, Professor Bryan, MD, FRCS. Professor of Neurosurgery, Glasgow University, 1968-91 (Dean, Faculty of Medicine, 1981-86); Member, Court, Glasgow University, 1987-91; b. 1.3.26, Twickenham, Middlesex; m., Professor Sheila Jennett; 3 s.; 1 d. Educ. King's College, Wimbledon; King George V School, Southport; Liverpool University. Lecturer in Neurosurgery, Manchester University; Rockefeller Travelling Fellow,

University of California; Hunterian Professor, Royal College of Surgeons of England. Member: Medical Research Council, 1979-83, Chief Scientist Committee, Scotland; Rock Carling Fellow. Publications: Epilepsy After Non-Missile Head Injuries; Introduction to Neurosurgery; High Technology Medicine - Benefits and Burdens. Recreations: writing; cruising under sail. Address: (h.) 83 Hughenden Lane, Glasgow G12 9XN.

Jennings, James, JP. Member, North Ayrshire Council, since 1996 (Chair, Social Work Committee); Former Convener, Strathclyde Regional Council; Honorary Sheriff, Kilmarnock, since 1991; Chairman, Police Negotiating Board, since 1990; b. 18.2.25; m., 1, Margaret Cook Barclay (deceased); 3 s.; 2 d.; 2, Margaret Mary Hughes, JP; 2 d. Educ. St. Palladius School, Dalry; St. Michael's College, Irvine. Steel industry, 1946-79. Member: Ayr County Council, 1958, Strathclyde Regional Council, 1974 (Vice-Convener, 1982-86); Chairman: Ayr CC Police and Law Committee, 1964-70, Ayrshire Joint Police Committee, 1970-75, North Ayrshire Crime Prevention Panel, 1970-82, Police and Fire Committee, Strathclyde Regional Council, 1978-82; contested Perth and East Perthshire, 1966; Vice-President, St. Andrew's Ambulance Association; Patron, Association of Youth Clubs in Strathclyde; Honorary President: Scottish Retirement Council, Princess Louise Scottish Hospital (Erskine Hospital); Honorary Vice-President: SNO Chorus, Royal British Legion Scotland (Dalry and District Branch); JP, Cunninghame, 1969 (Chairman, Cunninghame Justices Committee, since 1974); Vice-Chairman, Official Side, Police Negotiating Board, 1984-86, Chairman, 1986-88; Chairman, Garnock Valley Development Executive, since 1988. Recreation: local community involvement. Address: (h.) 4 Place View, Kilbirnie KA25 6BG; T.-Kilbirnie 3339.

Jennings, Kevin, MB, FRCP. Consultant Cardiologist, Aberdeen Royal Infirmary, since 1983; b. 9.3.47, Charleville, Eire; m., Heather; 2 s.; 1 d. Educ. Downside; St. Bartholomew's Hospital, London. Registrar: King's College Hospital, London, London Chest Hospital; Senior Registrar, Freeman Hospital, Newcastle-upon-Tyne. Recreations: theatre; ballet; golf; windsurfing. Publication: Acute Cardiac Care. Address: 58 Rubislaw Den South, Aberdeen AB15 4AY; T.-Aberdeen 311466.

Jensen-Butler, Professor Christopher Nigel, BA, PhD. Professor, Department of Economics, University of St. Andrews, since 1996; b. 5.6.45, Derby. Educ. Bemrose School, Derby; University College, University of Durham. University of Aarhus, Denmark: Assistant Professor, 1969-72, Associate Professor, 1972-87, Department of Geography, Associate Professor, Department of Mathematics, 1987-91, Associate Professor, Department of Political Science, 1991-95; Professor of Urban and Regional Planning, Department of Geography, University of St. Andrews, 1995-96; Guest Professor, University of Lisbon, 1987. Member, National Committee for Geography. Publication: European Cities in Competition (Co-Editor), 1997. Recreations: sailing; hill-walking; classical music. Address: (b.) Department of Economics, University of St. Andrews, Castlecliffe, The Scores, St. Andrews, Fife KY16 9AL; T.-01334 478074.

Jessamine, Rev. Alistair Lindsay, MA, BD. Minister of Dunfermline Abbey, since 1991; b. 17.6.49, Hill of Beath; m., Eleanor Moore. Educ. Beath High School, Cowdenbeath; University of Edinburgh. Assistant Minister, Newlands South Parish Church, Glasgow, 1978-79; Minister, Rankin Parish Church, Strathaven linked with Chapelton, 1979-91; Chaplain: HM Prison, Dungavel, 1979-91, RAF Pitreavie Castle, 1991-95; Moderator, Presbytery of Dunfermline, 1993-94. Recreations: travel; cooking; golf. Address: Abbey Manse, 12 Garvock Hill, Dunfermline, Fife KY12 7UU; T.-01383 721022.

Jessop, Sheriff Alexander Smethurst, MA, LLB. Sheriff at Aberdeen, since 1990; b. 17.5.43, Montrose; m., Joyce Isobel Duncan; 2 s.; 1 d. Educ. Montrose Academy; Fettes College; Aberdeen University. Partner, Campbell, Middleton, Burness and Dickson, Montrose; Procurator Fiscal Depute, Perth, 1976-78; Assistant Solicitor, Crown Office, 1978-80; Senior Assistant Procurator Fiscal, Glasgow, 1980-84; Regional Procurator Fiscal, Aberdeen, 1984-87, Glasgow, 1987-90. Member, Scottish Legal Aid Board; Chairman, Aberdeen Victim Support. Recreation: golf (Vice-Captain, Royal Montrose Golf Club). Address: (b.) Sheriff Court House, Aberdeen AB9 1AP; T.-01224 648316.

Johnson, David (Charles), MA, BA, PhD. Composer; Musical Historian; Cellist, McGibbon Ensemble, since 1979; 27.10.42, Edinburgh; 1 s. Educ. Aberdeen University; St. John's College, Cambridge. Research Fellow in Scottish Music, Napier University, 1995; Tutor, Edinburgh University Music Faculty, 1988-94; awarded Scottish Arts Council composer's bursary, 1992-93; compositions include four operas, an orchestral suite, chamber music, songs, a piano concerto, church music. Publications: Music and Society in Lowland Scotland, 1972; Scottish Fiddle Music in the 18th Century, 1984; contributions to the New Grove Dictionary of Music, 1981; The Scots Cello Book, 1990; Stepping Northward, 1991; 12 Preludes and Fugues, 1995. Address: (h.) 8 Shandon Crescent, Edinburgh EH11 1QE. T.-0131-337 4621.

Johnson, Ian M., BA, FLA, MIInfSc, MIMgt. Head, School of Information and Media, Robert Gordon University, Aberdeen, since 1989; Chairman: Heads of Schools and Departments Committee, British Association for Information and Library Education and Research, 1997-2000; b. 17.3.45, Sheffield; m., Jean Trevena. Educ. King Edward VII School, Sheffield; Liverpool College of Commerce; Leeds Polytechnic. Sheffield City Libraries, 1962-74; Department of Education and Science (Office of Arts and Libraries), 1970-72 (on secondment); Rotherham M.B. Council, 1974-78; College of Librarianship Wales, 1978-89. Chairman, Professional Board, International Federation of Library Associations and Institutions, 1993-95; Chairman, Library Association Personnel Training and Education Group, 1994-95; Member, Library Association Council, since 1996. Recreations: theatre; cinema; travel. Address: (b.) 352 King Street, Aberdeen AB9 2TQ; T.-Aberdeen 262951.

Johnson, Professor Keith Jack, BSc, PhD, MRCPath. Professor of Genetics, University of Glasgow, since 1995; b. 17.5.55, Dorset; m., Margot Ross; 1 s.; 1 d. Educ. Brockenhurst Grammar School, Hants; University of Dundee. Charing Cross and Westminster Medical School: Lecturer, 1989-93, Senior Lecturer, 1993-95. Recreations: golf; crosswords. Address: (b.) Division of Molecular Genetics, Anderson College, 56 Dumbarton Road, Glasgow; T.-0141-330 5101.

Johnston, Hon. Lord (Alan Charles Macpherson), BA (Hons) (Cantab), LLB. Senator of the College of Justice, since 1994; Queen's Counsel (1980); b. 13.1.42, Stirling; m., Anthea Jean Blackburn; 3 s. Educ. Edinburgh Academy; Loretto School; Jesus College, Cambridge; Edinburgh University. Advocate, 1967; Standing Junior Counsel, Scottish Home and Health Department, 1972; Advocate Depute, 1978-82; Chairman: Industrial Tribunal, 1982-85, Medical Appeal Tribunal, 1985-89; Treasurer, Faculty of Advocates, 1977-89, Dean, Faculty of Advocates, 1989-93. Publication: Introduction to Law of Scotland 7th Edition (Joint Editor). Address: (h.) 3 Circus Gardens, Edinburgh; T.-0131-225 1862.

Johnston, Sheriff Alexander Graham, LLB, BA. Sheriff of Glasgow and Strathkelvin, at Glasgow, since 1985 (Grampian, Highland and Islands, 1982-85); b. 16.7.44.

Johnston, Alistair, BSc (Hons). Rector, Kelso High School, since 1975; b. 2.5.39, Stirling; m., Elizabeth; 2 s.; 1 d. Educ. High School of Stirling; Glasgow University. Teacher, George Heriot's School, 1962-65; Principal Teacher of Physics, Galashiels Academy, 1965-71; Depute Rector, Banff Academy, 1971-75. Past President, Headteachers' Association of Scotland. Recreations: gardening; walking; sailing; skiing; golf. Address: (b.) Kelso High School, Bowmont Street, Kelso TD5 7EG; T.-01573 224444.

Johnston, Frederick Patrick Mair, CBE, FRSA, MA. Chairman, Johnston Press plc (formerly F. Johnston & Co. Ltd.), since 1973; Director, TSB Bank Scotland plc, since 1996; b. 15.9.35, Edinburgh; m., Elizabeth Ann Jones; 2 s. Educ. Morrison's Academy, Crieff; Lancing College, Sussex; New College, Oxford. Editorial Department, Liverpool Daily Post and Echo, 1959; Assistant Secretary, The Times Publishing Co. Ltd., 1960; Company Secretary, F. Johnston & Co. Ltd., 1969. Chairman, Central Scotland Manpower Committee, 1976-83; Member, Press Council, 1974-88; President, Scottish Newspaper Proprietors' Association, 1976-78; Treasurer, Society of Master Printers of Scotland, 1981-86; President, The Newspaper Society, 1989-90; Director, Scottish Mortgage & Trust plc, since 1991; Chairman, Edinburgh Book Festival, since 1996. Recreations: reading; travelling. Address: (b.) 53 Manor Place, Edinburgh EH3 7EG; T.-0131-225 3361.

Johnston, Geoffrey Edward Forshaw, LLB, CA, FCIT. Managing Director, Cambria Investments Ltd. (Arbuckle, Smith Group), since 1972; Director: Scottish Friendly Assurance Society Ltd., since 1995, Central College of Commerce, since 1995; President, Glasgow Chamber of Commerce, 1994-95 (Director since 1981); b. 20.6.40, Burton, Wirral; m., Elizabeth Anne Lockhart; 2 d. Educ. Loretto School; St. Andrews University. Wilson, Stirling & Co., 1959-65; joined Arbuckle, Smith Holdings Ltd., 1965; Director, 1968; Managing Director, 1972; management buy-out, 1984; National Chairman, British International Freight Association, 1990-91; Belgian Consul (Scotland West and North), 1989-95; Chairman, Scottish Chambers of Commerce, 1996; Member, Scottish Valuation Advisory Council; Governor, Lomond School Ltd. Recreations: sailing; skiing; hill-walking; golf; DIY. Address: (b.) Ferry Road, Yorkhill, Glasgow G3 8QU; T.-0141-337 8000.

Johnston, George Hermiston, Dip., Youth and Community Work. Chief Executive, Scottish Standing Conference of Voluntary Youth Organisations, since 1992; Chairman, Scottish Youth Work Partnership, since 1995; b. 22.11.36. Director, Clermiston Centre and Youth Secretary, Edinburgh YMCA, 1964-70; General Secretary, Belfast YMCA, 1970-74; Training Officer, Northern Ireland Association of Youth Clubs, 1974-76, Director, 1976-92. Past President, European Confederation of Youth Clubs. Recreations: photography; music; walking; art. Address: (b.) YouthLink Scotland, Central Hall, West Tollcross, Edinburgh EH3 9BP; T.-0131-229 0339.

Johnston, Grenville Shaw, OBE, TD, KCSG, DL, CA. Chartered Accountant, since 1968; Vice Lord Lieutenant of Moray, since 1996; Territorial Army Officer, 1964-89 (Lt. Col.); b. 28.1.45, Nairn; m., Marylyn Jean Picken; 2 d. Educ. Blairmore School; Fettes College. Qualified in Edinburgh with Scott Moncrieff Thomson & Sheills; Thomson McLintock & Co., Glasgow, 1968-70; joined family firm, W.D. Johnston & Carmichael, Elgin, 1970; Senior Partner, 1975. Commanding Officer, 2nd 51st Highland Volunteers, 1983-86; Hon. Col., 3rd Highland Volunteers, 1997; Knight Commander, Order of St. Gregory, 1982, for work for Pluscarden Abbey; OBE for services to Territorial Army; Chairman, Grampian Committee, Royal Jubilee Trusts, 1982-91; Member, Cairngorm Recreation Trust Ltd.; Vice Chairman, Gordonstoun School; Council Member, Institute of

Chartered Accountants of Scotland (Highland Area); Trustee and Council Member: Queens Own Highlanders, The Highlanders; Member, Grampian Committee, Princes Scottish Youth Business Trust. Recreations: shooting; fishing; hockey; golf; skiing; singing (tenor). Address: (h.) Spynie Kirk House, Spynie, By Elgin, Moray IV30 3XJ.

Johnston, Professor Ian Alistair, BSc, PhD, FRSE. Chandos Professor of Physiology, Director, Gatty Marine Laboratory and Head, School of Environmental and Evolutionary Biology, St. Andrews University, since 1985; b. 13.4.49, Barking, Essex. Educ. Addey and Stanhope Grammar School, London; Hull University. NERC Postdoctoral Research Fellow, Bristol University, 1973-75; Lecturer in Physiology, St. Andrews University, 1976-84; Reader, 1984-85; Visiting Senior Lecturer, Department of Veterinary Physiology, Nairobi University, 1981; Visiting Scientist, British Antarctic Survey base, Signy Island, South Orkneys, 1983-84; Council Member: NERC, Scottish Association for Marine Science; Chairman, NERC Marine Science and Technology Board; Director, Company of Biologists; awarded Scientific Medal, Zoological Society of London. Recreations: photography; walking; reading. Address: (b.) School of Environmental and Evolutionary Biology, St. Andrews University, St. Andrews KY16 8LB; T.-01334 463440.

Johnston, John Robert, BSc, PhD, FIBiol. Reader, Department of Bioscience and Biotechnology, Strathclyde University, since 1983; b. 6.10.34, Leven, Fife; m., Janet Bonthrone Reekie (deceased); 3 s. Educ. Buckhaven High School; St. Andrews University. Teaching Associate, University of California, Berkeley; Research Scientist, Brewing Research Foundation, Nutfield, Surrey; Royal Society Latin America Exchange Fellow, 1970-71, Mexico City; Lecturer, then Senior Lecturer, Strathclyde University, 1964-83; Visiting Research Professor, University of California, Berkeley, 1987-98; Vice-President, Royal Philosophical Society of Glasgow, 1987-90. Recreations: outdoor activities; theatre and music; community affairs. Address: (h.) 83 Castlehill Road, Bearsden, Glasgow G61 4DX; T.-0141-942 1461.

Johnston, Joyce Sara Ramsay, BA, MEd. Principal, Fife College of Further and Higher Education, Kirkcaldy, since 1996; b. Brisbane, Australia. Educ. Knightswood School, Glasgow; University of Strathclyde; University of Edinburgh. Tourism Research, Australia, 1970-80; Education Administration, Dundee College, 1980-83; Depute Principal, Glenrothes College, 1983-89; Principal, Anniesland College, Glasgow, 1989-92; H.M.I., Scottish Office Education and Industry Department, 1992-96. Recreations: reading; gardening; cinema. Address: (b.) St. Brycedale Avenue, Kirkaldy KY1 1EX; T.-01592 268591.

Johnston, Professor Marie, BSc, PhD, DipClinPsych, FBPsS, CPsychol. Professor in Psychology, St. Andrews University, since 1992; b. 6.7.44, Aberdeen; m., Derek Johnston. Educ. High School for Girls, Aberdeen; Aberdeen University; Hull University. Research Officer, Oxford University, 1971-77; Lecturer, Senior Lecturer, Reader, Royal Free Hospital School of Medicine, 1977-90; Reader, Professor of Psychology, St. Andrews University, since 1990; Honorary Clinical Psychologist, Tayside and Fife Health Boards, since 1991; first Chair, Section of Health Psychology, British Psychological Society; Past President, European Health Psychology Society. Recreation: gardening. Address: (b.) School of Psychology, St. Andrews University, St. Andrews KY16 9JU; T.-01334 62060.

Johnston, Peter William, MA, LLB, FRSA. Chief Executive and Secretary, Institute of Chartered Accountants of Scotland, since 1989; b. 8.2.43, Peebles; m., Patricia Sandra; 1 s.; 1 d. Educ. Larbert High School; Glasgow University. Partner, MacArthur & Co., Solicitors, Inverness,

1971-76; Procurator Fiscal Service, 1976-89. Recreations: music; languages; sailing. Address: (b.) 27 Queen Street, Edinburgh, EH2 1LA; T.-0131-225 5673.

Johnston, Robin Alexander, BSc, MB, BCh, BAO, MD, FRCS (Edin). Consultant Neurosurgeon, since 1985 (of Queen Elizabeth National Spinal Injury Unit, since 1992); Honorary Clinical Senior Lecturer, Glasgow University, since 1990; b. 30.3.49, Belfast; m., Ann. Educ. Belfast Royal Academy; Queens University, Belfast. Various surgical posts, UK, 1974-77; neurosurgical training, Belfast, Dallas, Glasgow, 1977-85. Address: (b.) Institute of Neurological Sciences, Southern General Hospital, Glasgow; T.-0141-201 2021.

Johnston, Thomas Lothian, MA, PhD, DL, FRSA, FRSE, CIMgt, FIPD, DrHC, DEd, LLD, DUniv, DLitt, FEIS. President, Royal Society of Edinburgh, 1993-96; Chairman, Scottish Committee, Royal Society of Arts, 1991-95; b. 9.3.27, Whitburn; m., Joan Fahmy; 2 s.; 3 d. Educ. Hawick High School; Edinburgh University; Stockholm University. Served RNVR (Sub. Lieut.), 1944-47; Lecturer in Political Economy, Edinburgh University, 1953-65; Professor of Economics, Heriot-Watt University, 1966-76; Vice-Chancellor, Heriot-Watt University, 1981-88; industrial relations arbitrator and mediator; Chairman, Manpower Services Committee for Scotland, 1977-80; Member, Scottish Economic Council, 1977-91; Chairman, Enquiry into Staff Representation, London Clearing Banks, 1978-92; Member, Review Committee, New Zealand Universities, 1987; Scottish Chairman, Industry Year, 1986, and Industry Matters, 1987-89; Trustee, National Galleries of Scotland, 1989-95; academic appointments in other countries: Illinois University, 1957, 1962-63, Queen's University, Canada, 1965, Western Australian Institute of Technology, 1979, Visiting Professor, International Institute for Labour Studies, Geneva, 1973. Publications: Collective Bargaining in Sweden, 1962; Economic Expansion and Structural Change, 1963; The Structure and Growth of the Scottish Economy (Co-Author), 1971; Introduction to Industrial Relations, 1981; translations from Swedish. Recreations: gardening; walking. Address: (h.) 14 Mansionhouse Road, Edinburgh EH9 1TZ; T.-031-667 1439.

Johnston, Very Rev. William Bryce, MA, BD, DD, DLitt. Minister, Colinton Parish Church, 1964-91; Chaplain to The Queen in Scotland, 1981-91, Extra Chaplain, since 1991; b. 16.9.21, Edinburgh; m., Ruth Margaret Cowley; 1 s.; 2 d. Educ. George Watson's College, Edinburgh; Edinburgh University. Chaplain to the Forces, 1945-49; Minister: St. Andrew's Church, Bo'ness, 1949-55, St. George's Church, Greenock, 1955-64; Chaplain, HM Prison, Greenock, 1959-64; Convener, General Assembly Committees: Adult Christian Education, 1970-72, Church and Nation, 1972-76, Inter-Church Relations, 1979-81; Moderator of the General Assembly, 1980; Cunningham Lecturer, New College, 1968-71; Visiting Lecturer in Social Ethics, Heriot-Watt University, 1966- 88; Member, Broadcasting Council for Scotland, 1983-87. Publications: translations of Karl Barth and John Calvin; Ethics and Defence (Contributor). Recreations: organ music; bowls. Address: (h.) 15 Elliot Road, Edinburgh EH14 1DU; T.-0131-441 3387.

Johnston, William John, BSc (Hons), DipEd(Tech). Rector, Aberdeen Grammar School, since 1987; b. 17.8.47, Kilmarnock; m., Katie Mary Maclean; 3 d. Educ. Spier's School, Beith; Glasgow University. Marketing Assistant, ICI Silicones, 1969-70; Teacher: Cranhill Secondary, 1971-73, Perth High School, 1973-75; Assistant Principal Teacher, Glenrothes High School, 1975-78; Principal Teacher, Millburn Academy, 1978-81; Assistant Rector, Kingussie High School, 1981-84; Depute Rector, Culloden Academy, 1984-87. Address: (b.) Aberdeen Grammar School, Skene Street, Aberdeen; T.-01224 642299.

Johnstone, Professor Alexander Henry, BSc, PhD, DipREd, CChem, FRSC. Professor in Science Education, Glasgow University, since 1990 (Head, Science Education Research Group, since 1972); Director: Centre for Science Education, Glasgow University, since 1989, Teaching and Learning Service, Glasgow University, until 1997; b. 17.10.30, Edinburgh; m., Martha Y. Cuthbertson; 2 s. Educ. Leith Academy; Edinburgh University; Glasgow University; Moray House College of Education. Commissioned, Royal Corps of Signals; Assistant Teacher of Chemistry, George Watson's College, Edinburgh; Head, Chemistry Department, High School of Stirling; Lecturer, then Senior Lecturer in Chemistry, then Reader in Chemical Education, Glasgow University. Vice-President, Royal Society of Chemistry (President, Education Division). Recreations: hill-walking; photography; archaeology; lay preaching. Address: (b.) Centre for Science Education, Kelvin Building, Glasgow University, Glasgow G12 8QQ; T.-0141-330 5172.

Johnstone, Sir Raymond, CBE, BA, CA. Director, RJ KILN & Co. Ltd., since 1995; Director, Lomond Underwriting plc (Chairman, since 1993); Chairman: Historic Buildings Council for Scotland, since 1995, The Nuclear Generation Decommissioning Fund Limited, since 1996, The Nuclear Trust, since 1996, Patrons of the National Galleries of Scotland, since 1995; b. 27.10.29, London; m., Susan Sara; 5 step s.; 2 step d. Educ. Eton; Trinity College, Cambridge. Investment Analyst, Robert Fleming & Co. Ltd., London, 1955-60; Partner (CA), Brown, Fleming & Murray (later Whinney Murray & Co.), 1960-68; Director: Dominion Insurance Co. Ltd., 1973-95 (Chairman, 1978-95); Scottish Financial Enterprise, 1986-91 (Chairman, 1989-91); Summit Group PLC (Chairman, since 1989); Murray Income PLC, since 1989; Murray International PLC, since 1989; Murray Smaller Markets PLC, since 1989; Murray Ventures PLC, since 1984; Murray Enterprise PLC, since 1989; Chairman, Murray Johnstone Ltd., 1984-91 (Managing Director, 1968-88); Chairman, Forestry Commission, 1989-94; Chairman, Murray Split Capital Trust PLC, since 1991; Director, Scottish Amicable Life Assurance Society, 1971-97 (Chairman, 1983-85); Hon. President, Scottish Opera. Recreations: fishing; shooting; opera; farming. Address: (h.) Wards, Gartocharn, Dunbartonshire G83 85B.

Johnstone, Professor William, MA (Hons), BD. Professor of Hebrew and Semitic Languages, Aberdeen University, since 1980; Minister, Church of Scotland, since 1963; b. 6.5.36, Glasgow; m., Elizabeth M. Ward; 1 s.; 1 d. Educ. Hamilton Academy; Glasgow University; Marburg University. Lecturer in Hebrew and Semitic Languages, Aberdeen University, 1962-72, Senior Lecturer, 1972-80, Dean, Faculty of Divinity, 1983-87; President, Society for Old Testament Study, 1990. Recreation: alternative work. Address: (h.) 37 Rubislaw Den South, Aberdeen AB15 4BD; T.-Aberdeen 316022.

Jolliffe, Professor Ian, BSc, DPhil. Professor of Statistics, Aberdeen University, since 1992; b. 22.12.45, Isle of Wight; m., Jean Peddar; 1 s.; 1 d. Educ. Sandown Grammar School; Sussex University. Lecturer, then Senior Lecturer, Kent University; visiting positions, Dalhousie University, University of Guelph. Recreations: running; dinghy sailing; folk music. Address: (b.) Department of Mathematical Sciences, Aberdeen University, King's College, Aberdeen, AB25 3UE; T.-01224 272611.

Jonathan, Professor Ruth Madeline, BA(Hons), PGCE, MA, PhD. Professor of Educational Theory and Policy (Personal Chair), University of Edinburgh, since 1993; b. 25.6.41; 1 s.; 2 d. Educ. Arnold High School, Blackpool; Liverpool; Sorbonne; Leicester. Seven years teaching English and Modern Languages, in Finland, E. Africa and England; five years as Teacher Trainer and Educational Researcher; Teacher and Researcher in Educational Theory and Philosophy, University of Edinburgh, for 17 years; Member, GTC; former Member, SCCC; Past Chair: SUSCE, Philosophy of Education Society GB (Life Vice-President). Publications: Illusory Freedoms, Liberalism, Education and the Market, 1997; many other publications over the past 20 years. Recreations: family; friends; baroque music; gardening; travel. Address: (b.) University of Edinburgh, South Bridge, Edinburgh; T.-0131-650 4326.

Jones, Professor Charles, MA, BLitt, FRSE. Forbes Professor of English Language, Edinburgh University, since 1990; b. 24.12.39, Glasgow; m., Isla Shennan. Educ. St. Aloysius College, Glasgow; Glasgow University. Lecturer in Linguistics, Hull University, 1964-67; Lecturer, Department of English Language, Edinburgh University, 1967-78; Professor of English Language, Durham University, 1978-90. Convenor, Scots Language Resource Centre Association, 1993-95; former Council Member, Saltire Society (Convenor, Education Committee); Member, Edinburgh University Court, 1993-96. Publications: An Introduction to Middle English; Phonological Structure and the History of English; Grammatical Gender in English; A History of English Phonology; A Treatise on the Provincial Dialect of Scotland (Editor); Historical Linguistics (Editor); A Language Suppressed; The Edinburgh History of the Scots Language (Editor). Recreation: breeding Soay sheep. Address: (h.) Laggan Cottage, Faladam, Midlothian, EH37 5SU; T.-01875 833 652.

Jones, Professor Huw, BA, MA. Professor of Geography and Dean, Faculty of Arts and Social Sciences, Dundee University; b. Llanidloes; 2 s. Educ. Newtown Boys Grammar School, Powys; University College of Wales, Aberystwyth. Editor, International Journal of Population Geography. Address: (b.) Department of Geography, Dundee University, Dundee DD1 4HN; T.-01382-344 427.

Jones, Keith Greig, LLB. Head of Law and Administration (North Division), Aberdeenshire Council, since 1996; b. 10.9.48, Edinburgh; m., Margaret. Educ. Aberdeen Grammar School; Aberdeen University. Various appointments in private legal practice, 1969-75; joined Law and Administration Department, Kincardine and Deeside District Council, 1975: Director of Legal Services and Depute Chief Executive, 1985-97. Trustee: Grampian Transport Museum Trust, Kinneff Old Church Preservation Trust, 1979-97. Address: (b.) St. Leonard's, Sandyhills Road, Banff.

Jones, Mark Ellis Powell, MA, FSA, FSA Scot. Director, National Museums of Scotland, since 1992; b. 5.2.51, Bogota; m., Dr. A.C. Toulmin; 2 s.; 2 d. Educ. Eton College; Oxford University; London University. Assistant Keeper of Coins and Medals, British Museum, 1974-90; Keeper of Coins and Medals, 1990-92. Founding Director, Scottish Cultural Resources Access Network (SCRAN); President, Fédération Internationale de la Médaille; Member, Royal Mint Advisory Committee. Address: (h.) 39 Regent Street, Portobello, Edinburgh EH15 2AY; T.-0131-657 3335.

Jones, Professor Peter (Howard), MA, FRSE, FRSA, FSA Scot. Professor of Philosophy, University of Edinburgh, since 1984; Director, Institute for Advanced Studies in the Humanities, since 1986; b. 18.12.35, London; m., Elizabeth Jean Roberton; 2 d. Educ. Highgate School; Queens' College, Cambridge. Regional Officer, The British Council, London, 1960-61; Research Scholar, University of Cambridge, 1961-63; Assistant Lecturer in Philosophy, Nottingham University, 1963-64; University of Edinburgh: Lecturer in Philosophy, 1964-77, Reader, 1977-84; Visiting Professor of Philosophy: University of Rochester, New York, 1969-70, Dartmouth College, New Hampshire, 1973, 1983, Carleton College, Minnesota, 1974, Oklahoma University, 1978, Baylor University, 1978, University of Malta, 1993; Distinguished Foreign Scholar, Mid-America

State Universities, 1978; Visiting Fellow, Humanities Research Centre, Australian National University, 1984; Calgary Institute for the Humanities, 1992; Lothian Lecturer, 1993; Gifford Lecturer, University of Aberdeen, 1994-95; Loemker Lecturer, Emory University, 1996; Trustee: National Museums of Scotland, since 1987, University of Edinburgh Development Trust, Morrison's Academy, Crieff, Fettes College; Founder Member, The Hume Society, 1974. Publications: Philosophy and the Novel, 1975; Hume's Sentiments, 1982; A Hotbed of Genius, 1986; Philosophy and Science in the Scottish Enlightenment, 1988; The Science of Man in the Scottish Enlightenment, 1989; Adam Smith Reviewed, 1992. Recreations: opera; chamber music; the arts; architecture. Address: (b.) Institute for Advanced Studies in the Humanities, Hope Park Square, Edinburgh EH8 9NW; T.-0131-650 4671.

Jones, Trevor, IPFA, FCCA, ACIS, MIMgt. General Manager, Lothian Health Board, since 1995; b. 23.12.50, Penshaw, Co. Durham; m., Hazel Oliver. Entered NHS, 1978; Northern Regional Health Authority; South Manchester Health Authority; Waltham Forest Health Authority; Chief Executive, Forest Healthcare NHS Trust, 1991-95. Recreations: golf; squash; Durham CCC; Sunderland AFC. Address: (b.) Lothian Health Board, 148 Pleasance, Edinburgh EH8 9RS; T.-0131-536 9001.

Jones, Rev. William Gerald, MA, BD, ThM. Minister, Kirkmichael with Straiton St. Cuthbert's, since 1985; Moderator, Presbytery of Ayr, 1997-98; b. 2.11.56, Irvine; m., Janet Blackstock. Educ. Dalry High School; Garnock Academy, Kilbirnie; Glasgow University; St. Andrews University; Princeton Theological Seminary, Princeton, New Jersey. Assistant Minister, Glasgow Cathedral, 1983-85. Freeman Citizen of Glasgow, 1984; Member, Incorporation of Gardeners of Glasgow, 1984; Convener, Administration Committee, Presbytery of Ayr, 1988-91; Member: General Assembly Panel on Worship, 1987-91, Council, Church Service Society, since 1986, Committee to Nominate the Moderator of the General Assembly, 1988-92, Societas Liturgica, since 1989; AssChLJ (Assistant Chaplain, Order of St. Lazarus of Jerusalem), 1995; Member, Society for Liturgical Study, since 1995. Publications: Prayers for the Chapel Royal in Scotland, 1989; Worshipping Together (Contributor), 1991; Common Order (Contributor), 1994. Recreations: music; liturgies; reading; writing. Address: The Manse, Kirkmichael, Maybole, Ayrshire KA19 7PJ; T.-01655 750286.

Jordan, Professor Grant, MA, PhD. Professor of Politics, Aberdeen University, since 1990; b. 12.10.48, Forfar; m., Susan Allardice; 1 s.; 2 d. Educ. Forfar Academy; Aberdeen University. Entered market research, 1971; moved to Keele University, 1973, Aberdeen University, 1974. Recreations: books; skiing; Montrose FC. Address: (b.) Department of Politics and International Relations, Aberdeen University, Aberdeen AB9 2TY; T.-01224 272722.

Jordan, Brigadier Howard Alfred John, MBE, FCIT. Chief Executive, Scottish Engineering, since 1980; Vice Chairman, Lowland TAVRA, since 1994; b. 26.3.36, Edinburgh; m., Patricia Ann Tomlin; 1 s.; 1 d. Army, 1954-80; Lt. Col., Royal Corps of Transport; commanded 154 (Lowland) Transport Regiment RCT(V). Chairman: Carmunnock Community Council, since 1980, Strathclyde Group, National Council for Conservation of Plants and Gardens, since 1983; Honorary President, Carmunnock British Legion, since 1980; Member, Lowland TA Council, since 1981; Commandant, ACF Scotland, Chairman, ACFA Scotland, 1994-97; Member, Court, Glasgow Caledonian University, since 1995. Address: (b.) 105 West George Street, Glasgow G2 1QL; T.-0141-221 3181.

Joseph, Professor John E., BA, MA, PhD, FRSA. Professor of Applied Linguistics and Head, Department of

Applied Linguistics, University of Edinburgh, since 1997; b. 30.10.56, Monroe, Michigan, USA; m., Jeannette; 1 s. Educ. Monroe High School, Michigan; University of Michigan, Ann Arbor. Lecturer in Linguistics, Université Paul Valéry, Montpellier, France, 1980-81; Assistant then Associate Professor of French and Italian, Oklahoma State University, 1981-85; Visiting Associate Professor of French, University of Maine, 1986; Assistant, then Associate Professor of French and English Linguistics, University of Maryland at College Park, 1986-93; University Fellow, National Endowment for the Humanities, 1993; Camargo Foundation Fellow, Cassis, France, 1993; Professor of English Language and Linguistics and Head, Department of of English, University of Hong Kong, 1993-96. Publications: Eloquence and Power, 1987; Ideologies of Language (Co-Author), 1990; Linguistic Theory and Grammatical Description (Co-Author), 1991. Recreations: playing piano; reading literature and philosophy; theatre; concerts; swimming. Address: (b.) Department of Applied Linguistics, University of Edinburgh, Edinburgh EH8 9LN; T.-0131-650 3497.

Jowitt, Professor Paul William, PhD, DIC, BSc(Eng), ACGI, CEng, FICE. Professor of Civil Engineering Systems, Heriot-Watt University, since 1987 (Head, Civil Engineering Department, 1989-91; Head, Civil and Offshore Engineering, since 1991); Editor, Civil Engineering Systems, since 1985; b. 3.8.50, Doncaster; m., Jane Catriona Urquhart; 1 s.; 1 d. Educ. Maltby Grammar School; Imperial College. Lecturer in Civil Engineering, Imperial College 1974-86 (Warden, Falmouth Hall, 1980-86); Director, Tynemarch Systems Engineering Ltd., 1984-91 (Chairman, 1984-86). Recreations: painting; Morgan 3-wheelers; restoring old houses. Address: (h.) 22 Fountainhall Road, The Grange, Edinburgh EH9 2LW; T.-0131-667 5696.

Jung, Roland Tadeusz, BA, MA, MB, BChir, MD, MRCS, LRCP, MRCP, FRCPEdin, FRCPLond. Consultant Physician (Specialist in Endocrinology and Diabetes), since 1982; Honorary Reader, Dundee University; Director, Research and Development for Tayside NHS Consortium, since 1997; b. 8.2.48, Glasgow; m., Felicity King; 1 d. Educ. St. Anselm's College, Wirral; Pembroke College, Cambridge; St. Thomas Hospital and Medical School, London. MRC Clinical Scientific Officer, Dunn Nutrition Unit, Cambridge, and Honorary Senior Registrar, Addenbrooke's Hospital, Cambridge, 1977-79; Senior Registrar in Endocrinology and Diabetes, Royal Postgraduate Medical School, Hammersmith Hospital, London, 1980-82; Clinical Director of General Medicine, Dundee Teaching Hospitals Trust, 1991-94. Publication: Endocrine Problems in Oncology (Co-Editor), 1984; Colour Atlas of Obesity, 1990. Recreation: gardening. Address: (b.) Diabetes Centre, Ninewells Hospital and Medical School, Dundee; T.-Dundee 660111.

K

Kamm, Antony, MA. Author; b. 2.3.31, London; m., Eileen Dunlop (qv). Educ. Charterhouse; Worcester College, Oxford. Editorial Director, Brockhampton Press, 1960-72; Senior Education Officer, Commonwealth Secretariat, 1972-74; Managing Editor (Children's Books), Oxford University Press, 1977-79; Consultant to UNESCO and other international organisations, 1963-76; part-time Lecturer in Publishing Studies, Stirling University, 1988-95; Chairman, Children's Book Group, The Publishers Association, 1963-67, and of Children's Book Circle, 1963-64; played cricket for Middlesex, 1952. Publications include: Collins Biographical Dictionary of English Literature, 1993; The Jacobites, 1995; The Romans: an Introduction, 1995; Wallace, Bruce, and the Wars of Independence, 1996; (with Eileen Dunlop): The Story of Glasgow, 1983; Kings and Queens of Scotland, 1984, and other information books for children on Scottish themes; several anthologies. Recreations: work; watching sport on TV. Address: (h.) 46 Tarmangie Drive, Dollar FK14 7BP; T.-01259 742007.

Kane, Jack, OBE, JP, DL, Dr hc (Edin). Honorary Vice-President, Age Concern Scotland, since 1986; Honorary President: Workers Educational Association (SE Scotland), Craigmillar Festival Society, Jack Kane Centre; b. 1.4.11, Addiewell, Midlothian; m., Anne Murphy; 1 s.; 2 d. Educ. Bathgate Academy. Librarian, 1937-55; War Service, Royal Artillery, 1940-46; District Secretary, Workers Educational Association (SE Scotland), 1955-76; Chairman, South of Scotland Electricity Consultative Council, 1977-80; Chairman, Board of Trustees, National Galleries of Scotland, 1975-80; Councillor, Edinburgh, 1938-75 (Bailie, 1947-51, Lord Provost, 1972-75). Recreations: reading; walking.

Kane, Liam James, ACMA. Managing Director, Scottish Daily Record and Sunday Mail Ltd, 1997-98; b. 11.1.50, Glasgow; m., Gillian Willie; 2 s.; 3 d. Educ. Holyrood Senior Secondary School; Central College, Glasgow. Commercial apprentice, G. & J. Weir, 1967-70; Accountant to Deputy Managing Director, Scottish Daily Record and Sunday Mail Ltd., 1970-84; M.D., Grant Forrest Advertising Ltd., 1985; Deputy General Manager, News Group Newspapers, 1985; General Manager, News (Scotland) Ltd., 1986; General Manager, Today newspaper, 1987-89; General Manager, Sky Television PLC, 1989-91; Chief Executive, Caledonian Publishing Ltd., 1991-97.

Kane, Patrick Mark, MA (Hons). Lead Singer, Hue and Cry (pop group); former Rector, Glasgow University; Writer and Broadcaster; b. 10.3.64, Glasgow; m., Joan McAlpine; 1 d. Educ. St. Ambrose RC Secondary, Coatbridge; Glasgow University. Worked in London as a freelance writer; returned to Scotland to start professional music career with brother Gregory; achieved Top 10 and Top 20 singles and albums successes, 1987-89; Columnist, The Herald; TV arts presenter. Recreations: being with family; listening to music; reading abstruse social theory.

Kavanagh, Rev. Joseph Anthony, BD(Hons), DipPTh. Minister, Girvan North, Church of Scotland, since 1992; b. 27.1.57, Glasgow; m., Mary; 2 s.; 2 d. Educ. St. Mirin's Academy, Paisley; University of St. Andrews. Recreations: golf; football; reading. Address: (h.) 38 The Avenue, Girvan; T.-01465 713203.

Kay, Stefan George, BSc, CEng, FIMechE, CIMgmt, FRSA. Group Managing Director, Inveresk PLC, since 1989; Non-Executive Director, Dunedin Enterprise Investment Trust PLC, since 1995; b. 25.7.44, Peebles; m., Helen Eugenia; 2 d. Educ. Holy Cross Academy; Heriot-Watt University. Graduate Trainee, Production Superintendent, Chief Chemist, Thames Board Ltd., 1967-73; Production Manager, Dexter Ltd., Berwickshire, 1973-78; Mill MD, St. Regis Paper Co. Ltd., Berwickshire and Devon, 1979-88. Past President, Paper Federation of Great Britain; awarded paper industry Gold Medal, 1996; Vice Chairman, Environment Committee, Confederation of European Paper Industries; Honorary President, Students' Association and Member, Court, Heriot-Watt University. Recreations: railway history; classical music. Address: (b.) Inveresk PLC, 3 Pitreavie Court, Dunfermline KY11 5PU; T.-01383 622333.

Kay, William, MA. Freelance Broadcaster/Writer/Producer; b. 24.9.51, Galston, Ayrshire; m., Maria Joao de Almeida da Cruz Dinis; 1 s.; 2 d. Educ. Galston High School; Kilmarnock Academy; Edinburgh University. Producer, Odyssey series, Radio Scotland; produced about 40 documentaries on diverse aspects of working-class oral history; Writer/Presenter, TV documentaries, including Miners, BBC Scotland; Presenter, Kay's Originals, Scottish TV. Commandeur d'Honneur, Commanderie du Bontemps de Medoc et des Graves; won Australasian Academy of Broadcast Arts and Sciences Pater award, 1987, 1988; Medallist, International Radio Festival of New York, 1990-92; Sloan Prize for writing in Scots, 1992; Wine Guild of UK 1994 Houghton Award, for Fresche Fragrant Clairettis; Winner: Heritage Society Award, 1995, Wines of France Award, 1996. Publications: Odyssey: Voices from Scotland's Recent Past (Editor); Odyssey: The Second Collection (Editor); Knee Deep in Claret: A Celebration of Wine and Scotland (Co-author); Made in Scotland (poetry); Jute (play for radio); Scots — The Mither Tongue; They Fairly Mak Ye Work (for Dundee Repertory Theatre); Lucky's Strike (play for radio); The Dundee Book. Recreations: the weans; languages; films; Dundee United. Address: (h.) 72 Tay Street, Newport on Tay, Fife DD6 8AP.

Kaye, Professor Stanley Bernard, BSc, MD, FRCP (Glas, Edin, Lond). CRC Professor of Medical Oncology, University of Glasgow, since 1986; b. 5.9.48, Leeds; m., Anna; 2 s.; 1 d. Educ. Roundhay School, Leeds; Charing Cross Hospital Medical School; University of London. Junior hospital posts, London, 1972-80; Staff Specialist, Sydney, Australia, 1980; Senior Lecturer, Department of Medical Oncology, Glasgow, 1981-85. Chairman of scientific/clinical committees, Cancer Research Campaign, European Organisation for Research and Treatment of Cancer. Publications: 280 peer-reviewed papers relating to cancer therapy. Recreations: various sports, including tennis, golf and football. Address: (b.) Department of Medical Oncology, Garscube Estate, Glasgow G61 1BD; T.-0141-330 4884.

Kayne, Steven Barry, PhD, MBA, LLM, BSc, MRPharmS, MCPP, DAgVetPharm, LFHom(Pharm), MPS(NZ), ACNZP, MIPharmM, MBIM. Consultant Homoeopathic and Veterinary Pharmacist; medical journalist; b. 8.6.44, Cheltenham Spa; m., Sorelle; 2 s. Educ. Westcliff High School; Aston University; Strathclyde University; Glasgow University; University of Wales. Lecturer; Visiting Lecturer, University of Strathclyde School of Pharmacy; Pharmacy Tutor to UK Faculty of Homoeopathy; Research Co-ordinator, Glasgow Homoeopathic Hospital; Member: UK Faculty of Homoeopathy Council and Education Committee; Faculty of Homoeopathy (Scotland) Council and Education Committee; Council, British Homoeopathic Association; Natural Medicine Advisory and Research Committee; Pharmacy Practice Adjudication Panel, British Pharmaceutical Conference; Government Advisory Board on Homoeopathic Registration; Homoeopathic Research Committee; Chairman, British Homoeopathic Research Group; Member, Board of Directors, Epilepsy Association,

Scotland. Publication: Homoeopathic Pharmacy, 1997. Recreations: walking in Spey Valley; watching rugby; photography. Address: (h.) 79 Milverton Road, Whitecraigs, Giffnock, Glasgow; T.-0141-638 3216.

Keane, Sheriff Francis Joseph, PhL, LLB. Sheriff of Lothians and Borders, since 1993; b. 5.1.36, Broxburn; m., Lucia Corio Morrison; 2 s.; 1 d. Educ. Blairs College, Aberdeen; Gregorian University, Rome; Edinburgh University. Partner, McCluskey, Keane & Co., 1959; Procurator Fiscal Depute, Perth, 1961, Edinburgh, 1963; Senior PF Depute, Edinburgh, 1971; Senior Legal Assistant, Crown Office, Edinburgh, 1972; Procurator Fiscal, Airdrie, 1976; Regional Procurator Fiscal, South Strathclyde, Dumfries and Galloway, 1980; Sheriff of Glasgow and Strathkelvin, 1984-93. President, Procurators Fiscal Society, 1982-84. Recreations: music; tennis; walking; painting. Address: (b.) 27 Chambers Street, Edinburgh EH1 1LB; T.-0131-225 2525.

Keane, Professor Simon Michael, MA, LLB, PhD, CA. Professor of Accountancy, Glasgow University, since 1983; b. 8.4.35, Glasgow; m., Mary; 1 d. Educ. St. Aloysius College; Glasgow University. Investigating Accountant, Admiralty, 1965-67; Lecturer, Glasgow College of Commerce, 1967-69; Glasgow University: Lecturer, 1969-81, Reader, 1981-83. Publications: Efficient Market Hypothesis, 1980; Stock Market Efficiency, 1983. Recreations: golf; painting. Address: (b.) 67 Southpark Avenue, Glasgow G12; T.-0141-339 8855.

Kearney, Sheriff Brian, MA, LLB. Sheriff of Glasgow and Strathkelvin, since 1977; b. 25.8.35.

Kearns, Mary Elizabeth, LLB(Hons), DipLP, DipTA. Consultant, Brodies W.S., Solicitors, since 1997 (Partner, 1995-97); Accredited Employment Law Specialist, since 1995; Solicitor Advocate, since 1995; b. 25.4.61, London; m., Dr. Patrick Kearns; 2 s.; 2 d. Educ. St. Georges School, Harpenden, Hertfordshire; University of Edinburgh. Trainee Solicitor, W. & J. Burness W.S., Edinburgh, 1986-88; Brodies W.S., Edinburgh: Assistant Solicitor, 1988-93, Associate, 1993-95. Nominated by Secretary of State for Scotland to General Teaching Council for Scotland, 1995; Scottish Representative, Employment Lawyers' Association, 1996; Member, Scottish Council on Bioethics. Recreation: hill-walking. Address: (b.) 15 Atholl Crescent, Edinburgh EH3 8HA; T.-0131-228 3777.

Kee, Professor A. Alistair, MA, BD, STM, PhD, DLitt. Professor of Religious Studies, Edinburgh University; b. 17.4.37, Alexandria; m., Anne Paterson; 1 s.; 1 d. Educ. Clydebank High School; Glasgow University; Union Theological Seminary, New York. Lecturer: University College of Rhodesia, 1964-67, Hull University, 1967-76; Glasgow University: Senior Lecturer, then Reader (Head, Department of Religious Studies, 1976-88); Visiting Professor: Augusta College, Georgia, 1982-83, Dartmouth College, New Hampshire, 1990,1995; Director, SCM Press Ltd.; delivered Jaspers Lectures, Ripon Hall, Oxford, 1975; Ferguson Lectures, Manchester University, 1986. Publications: The Way of Transcendence; A Reader in Political Theology; Constantine Versus Christ; Being and Truth; Domination or Liberation; The Roots of Christian Freedom; Marx and the Failure of Liberation Theology; From Bad Faith to Good News. Address: (b.) Department of Theology and Religious Studies, Edinburgh University, New College, Mound Place, Edinburgh EH1 2LX; T.-0131-650 8953.

Keeble, Professor Neil Howard, BA, DPhil, DLitt, FRHistS. Professor of English, Stirling University, since 1995; b. 7.8.44, London; m., Jenny Bowers; 2 s.; 1 d. Educ. Bancroft's School, Woodford Green; St. David's College, Lampeter; Pembroke College, Oxford. Foreign Lektor,

Department of English, University of Aarhus, Denmark, 1969-72; Lecturer in English, Aarhus, 1972-74; Lecturer in English, Stirling University, 1974-88; Reader in English, Stirling University, 1988-95. Publications: Richard Baxter: Puritan Man of Letters; The Literary Culture of Nonconformity in later seventeenth-century England; The Autobiography of Richard Baxter (Editor); The Pilgrim's Progress (Editor); John Bunyan: Conventicle and Parnassus (Editor); A Handbook of English and Celtic Studies in the United Kingdom and the Republic of Ireland (Editor); The Cultural Identity of Seventeenth-Century Woman (Editor); Lucy Hutchinson, Memoirs of the Life of Colonel Hutchinson (Editor); Calendar of the Correspondence of Richard Baxter (Co-Compiler). Recreations: books and book-collecting; films; the Midi; gardening. Address: Duncraggan House, Airthrey Road, Stirling FK9 5JS; T.-01786 473758.

Keen, Richard Sanderson, LLB (Hons). Queen's Counsel; b. 29.3.54, Rustington; m., Jane Carolyn Anderson; 1 s.; 1 d. Educ. King's School, Rochester; Dollar Academy; Edinburgh University. Admitted to Faculty of Advocates, 1980; Standing Junior Counsel in Scotland to DTI, 1986-93; QC, 1993. Recreations: golf; skiing; shooting; opera. Address: (b.) Parliament House, Parliament Square, Edinburgh; T.-0131-226 5071.

Keighley, Brian Douglas, MB, ChB, FRCGP. General Practitioner Principal, Balfron, since 1975; Chairman, Scottish General Medical Services Committee (BMA), since 1995; Chairman, Joint Committee on Postgraduate Training for General Practice; b. 21.5.48, Glasgow; m., Ruth Patricia Maguire; 2 s. Educ. Glasgow Academy; Glasgow University. House Officer, Law Hospital, Stobhill Hospital, 1972-73; SHO, Robroyston Hospital, 1973; SHO, Falkirk Royal Infirmary, 1974; Trainee GP, Balfron, 1974. Member: GMSC (UK) since 1992, General Medical Council, since 1994, Scottish Council for Postgraduate Medical and Dental Education (Chairman, Audit Committee), BMA Scottish Council, National Medical Advisory Committee. Publication: Guide to Postgraduate Medical Education, 1996. Recreations: reading; politics; angling; jogging; squash. Address: (h.) Hector Cottage, Banker's Brae, Balfron G63 0PY; T.-01360 440520.

Keir, Professor Hamish Macdonald, BSc, PhD, DSc, CBiol, FIBiol, CChem, FRSC, FRSE. Professor of Biochemistry, Aberdeen University, 1968-96 (Vice-Principal, 1982-84); Vice-Chairman, Governors, Macaulay Land Use Research Institute, since 1987; b. 5.9.31, Moffat; m., 1, Eleanor Campbell; 1 s.; 2 d.; 2, Linda Gerrie; 2 d.; 3, Evelyn Cook. Educ. Ayr Academy; Glasgow University; Yale University. Hon. Secretary, The Biochemical Society, 1970-77, Chairman, 1986-89; Member, Cell Board, Medical Research Council, 1970-74; Scottish Home and Health Department, BRC, 1974-78; Ethical and Research Committees, Grampian Health Board; Science and Engineering Research Council (Biology), 1980-84; University Grants Committee (Biology), 1984-90; Royal Society — British National Committee for Biochemistry, 1986-90; Board of Governors: North of Scotland College of Agriculture, 1976-91, Longridge Towers School, since 1988; Tenovus — Scotland, Grampian Region, 1980-86; Committees of the International Union of Biochemistry, 1974-82; Chairman: Natural Environment Research Council, Institute of Marine Biochemistry, 1969-84, Universities of Scotland Purchasing Consortium, 1988-96, Board of Governors, Rowett Research Institute, 1989-93; President, European Union of Societies for Experimental Biology, 1989-96; European Science Foundation, since 1989; President, Council, Federation of European Biochemical Societies, 1980-83; Member, Executive, Ross, Skye and Inverness West Conservative and Unionist Association, since 1996. Recreations: piano; politics; travel. Address: (b.) Institute of Medical Sciences, University of Aberdeen, Aberdeen AB25 2ZD; T.-01224 273121; (h.)

Dundalachie, The Black Isle, Ross and Cromarty IV10 8TB; T.-01381 621239.

Kelbie, Sheriff David, LLB (Hons); Sheriff of Grampian, Highland and Islands, at Aberdeen and Stonehaven, since 1986 (North Strathclyde, at Dumbarton, 1979-86); b. 28.2.45, Inverurie; m., Helen Mary Smith; 1 s.; 1 d. Educ. Inverurie Academy; Aberdeen University. Passed Advocate, 1968; Associate Lecturer, Heriot-Watt University, 1971-76; Secretary, Scottish Congregational College, 1974-82; Member, UK/Ireland Committee of Christian Aid, 1986-90; Member, Scottish Christian Aid Committee, 1986-95; Editor, Scottish Civil Law Reports, since 1996. Recreations: sailing; reading; music. Address: (h.) 38 Earlspark Drive, Bieldside, Aberdeen.

Kellas, Professor James Grant, MA, PhD, FRHistS. Professor in Politics, Glasgow University, since 1984; b. 16.5.36, Aberdeen; m., Norma Rennie Craig; 2 s.; 1 d. Educ. Aberdeen Grammar School; Aberdeen University; London University. Tutorial Fellow in History, Bedford College, London University, 1961-62; Assistant in History, Aberdeen University, 1962-64; Glasgow University: Lecturer in Politics, 1964-73; Senior Lecturer, 1973-77, Reader, 1977-84. Member, Study of Parliament Group. Publications: Modern Scotland, 1968, 1980; The Scottish Political System, 1973, 1975, 1984, 1989; The Politics of Nationalism and Ethnicity, 1991. Recreations: mountaineering; music. Address: (b.) Department of Politics, Glasgow University, Glasgow G12 8RT; T.-0141-339 8855.

Kelly, Alexander Joseph, MA, MEd. Rector, Auchmuty High School, Glenrothes, since 1990; b. 18.6.46, Dunoon; m., Ann Smith; 3 s.; 1 d. Educ. Dunoon Grammar School; Glasgow University. Teacher, Assistant Principal Teacher, Principal Teacher, St. Mary's, Glasgow, 1969-75; Principal Teacher, St. Mungo's Academy, 1975-79; Assistant Head Teacher, St. Columba's, Dunfermline, 1979-84; Deputy Head Teacher, St. Andrew's High, Kirkcaldy, 1984-90. Recreations: Rotary; golf; photography; walking. Address: (h.) Blythswood, 101 Main Street, Aberdour, Fife; T.-01383 860369.

Kelly, Barbara Mary, CBE, DL, LLD, DipEd. President, Rural Forum Scotland; Member, Scottish Economic Council; Member, Broadcasting Council for Scotland; Member, Board, Scottish Natural Heritage (Chair, South West Region); Member, Scottish Advisory Board: BT, BP plc; Chairman, Architects' Registration Board; Chair, Training 2000; Director, Clydesdale Bank plc; Convener, Millennium Forest for Scotland Trust; Trustee, Caledonian Foundation; Partner in dairy farming enterprise; b. 27.2.40, Dalbeattie; m., Kenneth A. Kelly; 1 s.; 2 d. Educ. Dalbeattie High School; Kirkcudbright Academy; Moray House College. Past Chairman, Scottish Consumer Council; former Member: National Consumer Council, Scottish Enterprise Board, Scottish Tourist Board, Priorities Board, MAFF; former Vice-Chairman, SWRI; Duke of Edinburgh's Award: former Chairman, Scottish Advisory Committee and former Member, UK Advisory Panel; former EOC Commissioner for Scotland; Past Chairman, Dumfries and Galloway Area Manpower Board, Manpower Services Commission; former Member: Scottish Enterprise Board, Scottish Tourist Board. Recreations: painting; music. Address: (h.) Barncleugh, Irongray, Dumfries DG2 9SE; T.-01387 730210.

Kelly, John Lewis, MBE, BSc(Hons). Regimental Secretary, Royal Highland Fusiliers, since 1997; b. 9.7.50, Glasgow; m., Alison; 1 s.; 1 d. Educ. Allan Glen's School, Glasgow; Glasgow University. Regular Army Officer, Royal Highland Fusiliers, 1974-97. Deputy Commandant, Glasgow and Lanark Battalion ACF; City and Guilds Insignia Award. Recreation: keeping the house up and the garden down. Address: (b.) 518 Sauchiehall Street, Glasgow G2 3LW; T.-0141-332 5639.

Kelly, Michael, CBE (1983), OStJ, JP, BSc(Econ), PhD, LLD, DL, FCIM. Public Relations Consultant, since 1984; Honorary Vice-President, Children 1st, since 1996 (Chairman, Royal Scottish Society for the Prevention of Cruelty to Children, 1987-96); Secretary, Scottish Industry Forum, since 1995; Member, National Arts Collection Fund, since 1990; Columnist, The Scotsman; b. 1.11.40, Glasgow; m., Zita Harkins; 1 s.; 2 d. Educ. St. Joseph's College, Dumfries. Assistant Lecturer in Economics, Aberdeen University, 1965-67; Lecturer in Economics, Strathclyde University, 1967-80; Lord Provost of Glasgow, 1980-84; Rector, Glasgow University, 1984-87; Director, Drumkinnon Development Company; British Tourist Authority Medal for services to tourism, 1984; Robert Burns Award from University of Old Dominion, Virginia, for services to Scottish culture, 1984; Scot of the Year, 1983; Radio Scotland News Quiz Champion, 1986, 1987; Radio Scotland Christmas Quiz Champion, 1987; Honorary Mayor of Tombstone, Arizona; Kentucky Colonel, 1983. Publications: Paradise Lost: the struggle for Celtic's soul, 1994; London Lines: the capital by underground, 1996. Recreations: philately; golf. Address: (b.) 50 Aytoun Road, Pollokshields, Glasgow G41 5HE.

Kelly, Patrick Joseph, BSc, CEng, MICE. Scottish Officer, Public Services, Tax and Commerce Union, since 1986; President, STUC General Council; Director, Lothian and Edinburgh Enterprise, since 1992; b. 26.10.50, Glasgow; m., Rhona; 1 s.; 3 d. Educ. St. Mungo's Academy, Glasgow; Glasgow University. Civil Engineer, Central Regional Council, 1973-86; full-time trade union official, since 1986. Member, Executive, European Federation of Agricultural Workers; Member, Management Committee, War on Want. Recreations: golf; sailing; football. Address: (b.) 6 Hillside Crescent, Edinburgh EH7 5DZ; T.-0131-556 0407.

Kelly, Tom. Chief Officer, Association of Scottish Colleges, since 1996; b. 4.5.49, Loughborough. Educ. Hinckley Grammar School; Clare College, Cambridge. Home Civil Service, 1970-96; Head, Higher Education Division, Scottish Office, 1992-96. Address: (b.) Argyll Court, Castle Business Park, Stirling FK9 4TY; T.-01786 892100.

Kelly, Rev. William Wilson, BSc, BD. Minister, Troqueer Parish Church, Dumfries, since 1994; b. 25.11.49, Beith; m., Joy; 1 s.; 1 d. Educ. Speir's School, Beith, Ayrshire; University of Glasgow. Part-time Prison Chaplain. Recreations: reading; computers; music. Address: The Manse, Troqueer Road, Dumfries; T.-01387 253043.

Kelman, James. Novelist; b. 1946, Glasgow. Works include: The Busconductor Hines; A Chancer; Greyhound for Breakfast; A Disaffection; How Late It Was How Late (Booker Prize, 1994).

Kelnar, Christopher J.H., MA, MD, FRCP, FRCPCH, DCH. Consultant Paediatric Endocrinologist, Royal Hospital for Sick Children, Edinburgh, since 1983; Senior Lecturer, Department of Child Life and Health, Edinburgh University, since 1983; b. 22.12.47, London; m., Alison; 1 s.; 2 d. Educ. Highgate School, London; Trinity College, Cambridge; St. Bartholomew's Hospital, London. Research Fellow, Paediatric Endocrinology, Middlesex Hospital, London, 1979-81; Senior Registrar, Hospital for Sick Children, Great Ormond Street, London, and Tutor, Institute of Child Health, London, 1981-83. Publications: The Sick Newborn Baby, 1981 (3rd edition, 1995); Childhood and Adolescent Diabetes, 1995; chapters and papers on paediatric endocrinology. Recreations: music;

gardening. Address: (b.) Royal Hospital for Sick Children, Sciennes Road, Edinburgh EH9 1LF; T.-0131-536 0000.

Kelso, David Elliot, BSc, MEd. HM Chief Inspector, Scottish Office Education and Industry Department; b. 25.3.45, Glasgow; m., Dorothy Louise Christie; 1 s.; 2 d. Educ. St. Joseph's College, Dumfries; Edinburgh University; Glasgow University; Dundee University. Personnel Officer, Singer (UK) Ltd., Clydebank, 1968-69; Personnel Manager, Rank Organisation, Kirkcaldy, 1969-71; Lecturer in Management, Glasgow College, 1971-73; Senior Lecturer, Dundee College of Commerce, 1973-76; Head, Department of Commerce and Business Studies, Falkirk College, 1976-83; Assistant Principal, 1983-85; HMI, 1985. Recreations: running; esperanto; hill-walking. Address: (h.) Lomond, St. Mary's Drive, Dunblane, Perthshire; T.-01786 822605.

Kemball, Professor Emeritus Charles, CBE, MA, ScD, HonDSc, CChem, FRSC, MRIA, FRSE, FRS. Emeritus Professor of Chemistry, Edinburgh University, since 1983; b. 27.3.23, Edinburgh; m., Kathleen Purvis Lynd; 1 s.; 2 d. Educ. Edinburgh Academy; Trinity College, Cambridge. Fellow, Trinity College, 1946-54 (Junior Bursar, 1949-51, Assistant Lecturer, 1951-54); Demonstrator in Physical Chemistry, Cambridge University, 1951-54; Professor of Physical Chemistry, Queen's University, Belfast, 1954-66 (Dean, Faculty of Science, 1957-60, Vice-President, 1962-65); Professor of Chemistry, Edinburgh University, 1966-83 (Dean, Faculty of Science, 1975-78). President, Royal Institute of Chemistry, 1974-76; President, Royal Society of Edinburgh, 1988-91; Meldola Medal, RIC, 1951; Corday-Morgan Medal, 1958; Tilden Lecturer, 1960; Surface and Colloid Chemistry Award, Chemical Society, 1972; Ipatieff Prize, American Chemical Society, 1962; Gunning-Victoria Jubilee Prize, Royal Society of Edinburgh, 1976-80. Recreations: hill-walking; card games; wine-making. Address: (h.) 24 Main Street, Tyninghame, Dunbar, East Lothian EH42 1XL; T.-01620 860710.

Kemp, Professor Alexander George, MA (Hons). Professor of Economics, Aberdeen University, since 1983; Member, Energy Advisory Panel to UK Minister of Energy, since 1993; b. Blackhall, Drumoak, Aberdeenshire. Educ. Robert Gordon's College, Aberdeen; Aberdeen University. Economist, Shell International Petroleum, London, 1962-64; Lecturer in Economics, Strathclyde University, 1964-65; Lecturer, then Senior Lecturer, then Reader, Aberdeen University, 1966-83. Specialist Adviser to House of Commons Select Committee on Energy, 1980-92. Publications: 150 books and papers on petroleum economics. Address: (b.) Department of Economics, King's College, Aberdeen AB24 3QY.

Kemp, Arnold, MA. Editor, The Herald, 1981-94; b. 15.2.39; 2 d. Educ. Edinburgh Academy; Edinburgh University. Sub-Editor: The Scotsman, 1959-62, The Guardian, 1962-65; The Scotsman: Production Editor, 1965-70, London Editor, 1970-72, Deputy Editor, 1972-81, Publication: The Hollow Drum, 1993. Recreations: music; reading; theatre.

Kemp, Professor Peter Anthony, BSc(Hons), MPhil, DPhil. Professor of Housing and Urban Studies, University of Glasgow, since 1996; Director, ESRC Centre for Housing Research, since 1996; b. 25.12.55, Romford; 2 d. Educ. University of Southampton; University of Glasgow; University of Sussex. Researcher, SHAC (London Housing Aid Centre), 1983-85; Research Fellow, ESRC Centre for Housing Research, University of Glasgow, 1985-87; Lecturer in Housing Studies, University of Salford, 1987-90; Joseph Rowntree Professor of Housing Policy and Director, Centre for Housing Policy, University of York, 1990-95. Publications include: The Private Provision of Rented Housing, 1988; Tax Incentives and the Revival of

Private Renting, 1991; Housing and Social Policy, 1990; Single Homeless People, 1993; Managing Social Housing, 1993; Housing Benefit: an appraisal, 1992; A Comparative Study of Housing Allowances, 1997. Recreation: cycling. Address: (b.) Department of Urban Studies, University of Glasgow, 25 Bute Gardens, Glasgow G12 8RS; T.-0141-330 3665.

Kempton, Rodney Alistair, MA, BPhil, CStat. Director, Biomathematics and Statistics Scotland (formerly Scottish Agricultural Statistics Service), since 1986; b. 2.7.46, London; m., Annelise; 2 s.; 1 d. Educ. Chislehurst and Sidcup Grammar School; Wadham College, Oxford. Rothamsted Experimental Station, Harpenden, 1970-76; Head, Statistics Department, Plant Breeding Institute, Cambridge, 1976-86. President, British Region, International Biometric Society, 1994-96. Recreations: hill-walking; cycling. Address: (b.) BioSS, The King's Buildings, Edinburgh University, Edinburgh EH9 3JZ; T.-0131-650 4902.

Kendell, Robert Evan, CBE, MD, FRCP, FRCPsych. President, Royal College of Psychiatrists; Chief Medical Officer, Scottish Office Home and Health Department, 1991-96; b. 28.3.35, Rotherham; m., Ann Whitfield; 2 s.; 2 d. Educ. Mill Hill School; Cambridge University; King's College Hospital Medical School. Visiting Professor, University of Vermont College of Medicine, 1969-70; Reader in Psychiatry, Institute of Psychiatry, London University, 1970-74; Professor of Psychiatry, Edinburgh University, 1974-91, and Dean, Faculty of Medicine, 1986-90. Gaskell Medal, Royal College of Psychiatrists, 1967; Paul Hoch Medal, American Psychopathological Association, 1988; Marcé Society Medal, 1994; Fellow, Royal Society of Edinburgh, 1993; Honorary Fellow: Royal College of Surgeons of Edinburgh, since 1995, Royal College of Physicians and Surgeons of Glasgow, since 1995. Publications: The Classification of Depressive Illnesses, 1968; The Role of Diagnosis in Psychiatry, 1975; Companion to Psychiatric Studies (Editor), 1983, 1988, 1993. Recreations: walking up hills; overeating. Address: (h.) 3 West Castle Road, Edinburgh EH10 5AT.

Kendle, Professor Keith Emery, BPharm (Hons), PHD, MRPharmS. Professor of Clinical Pharmacy, Robert Gordon University, since 1992; b. 24.8.41, Hetton-Le-Hole. Educ. Houghton Le Spring Grammar School; School of Pharmacy, London University. Endocrinologist,. then Deputy Head of Endocrinology, BDH Research Ltd.; Senior Lecturer, Robert Gordon's Institute of Technology. Recreations: hill-walking; music. Address: (b.) School of Pharmacy, Robert Gordon University, Schoolhill, Aberdeen; T.-01224 262537.

Kennedy, Alison Louise, BA (Hons). Writer; b. 22.10.65, Dundee. Educ. High School of Dundee; Warwick University. Community Arts Worker, 1988-89; Writer in Residence, Project Ability, 1989-94; Writer in Residence, Hamilton/East Kilbride Social Work Department, 1990 92; fiction critic for Scotsman, etc.; Booker Prize Judge, 1996; four S.A.C. book awards; Saltire Best First Book Award; Saltire Best Book Award; John Llewellyn Rees/Mail on Sunday Prize; listed, Sunday Times Best of Young British Novelists; Encore Award; Festival Fringe First; Social Work Today Award. Publications: Night Geometry; Garscadden Trains; Looking for the Possible Dance; Now That You're Back; So I Am Glad; Original Bliss; The Life and Death of Colonel Blimp (essay); The Audition (play); Stella Does Tricks (film); Delicate (performance piece). Recreations: cinema; clarinet; fencing.

Kennedy, (Alistair James) Spencer, MA, LLB, SSC, NP. Partner, Balfour & Manson, since 1991; b. 3.5.45, Dumfries; m., Joan Margaret Whitelaw. Educ. Royal High School of Edinburgh; Edinburgh University. Estate Duty

Office, 1965-68; Connell & Connell, 1968-70; Nightingale & Bell, SSC, 1970-90; Past President, Society of Solicitors in the Supreme Courts of Scotland. Recreations: hill-walking; horticulture. Address: (b.) 58 Frederick Street, Edinburgh EH1 1LS; T.-0131-225 8291.

Kennedy, Professor Angus Johnston, MA, PhD, Officier dans l'Ordre des Palmes Academiques. Professor of French Language and Literature, Glasgow University; b. 9.8.40, Port Charlotte; m., Marjory McCulloch Shearer; 2 d. Educ. Bearsden Academy; Glasgow University. Glasgow University: Assistant Lecturer in French, 1965, then Lecturer, Senior Lecturer, Reader; former Secretary, British Branch, International Arthurian Society. Publications: books on Christine de Pizan. Address: (b.) French Department, Glasgow University, Glasgow; T.-0141-339 8855.

Kennedy, Professor Arthur Colville, CBE, MD, FRCP(Lond), FRCPE, FRCP(Glas), FRCPI, FRSE, FACP(Hon.), FRACP (Hon.). Consultant Physician, Royal Infirmary, Glasgow, 1959-88; Muirhead Professor of Medicine, Glasgow University, 1978-88; President, Royal College of Physicians and Surgeons of Glasgow, 1986-88; b. 22.10.22, Edinburgh; m., Agnes White Taylor; 1 s. (deceased); 2 d. Educ. Whitehill School, Glasgow; Glasgow University. Medical Officer, RAFVR, 1946-48; junior NHS posts, 1948-57; Lecturer in Medicine, Glasgow University, 1957; Senior Lecturer, 1961; Reader, 1966; Titular Professor, 1969; responsible for establishment of Kidney Unit, Glasgow Royal Infirmary, 1959; Chairman, MRC Working Party in Glomerulonephritis, 1976-88; Member, Executive Committee, National Kidney Research Fund, 1976-83; Expert Adviser to WHO on Renal Disease; Adviser to EEC on Nephrology in Developing Countries; Chairman, Professional and Linguistic Assessments Board (PLAB), GMC, 1987-89; President: Royal Medico-Chirurgical Society of Glasgow, 1971-72, European Dialysis and Transplant Association, 1972-75, Scottish Society of Physicians, 1983-84, Harveian Society of Edinburgh, 1985; Member: Greater Glasgow Health Board, 1985-89, General Medical Council, 1989-92; President, British Medical Association, 1991-92. Recreations: gardening; walking; reading; photography. Address: (h.) 16 Boclair Crescent, Bearsden, Glasgow G61 2AG; T.-0141-942 5326.

Kennedy, Charles Peter, MA (Hons). MP (SLD, formerly SDP), Ross, Cromarty and Skye, since 1983, Ross, Skye and Inverness West, since 1997; Liberal Democrat Spokesman on Agriculture and Rural Affairs, since 1997; b. 25.11.59, Inverness. Educ. Lochaber High School, Fort William; Glasgow University; Indiana University. President, Glasgow University Union, 1980-81; Winner, British Observer Mace for Student Debating, 1982; Journalist, BBC Highland, Inverness, 1982; Fulbright Scholar, Indiana University (Bloomington Campus), 1982-83. Chairman, SDP Council for Scotland, 1986-88; SDP Spokesman on Health and Social Services, and Scotland, 1983-87; Alliance Election Spokesman, Social Security, Jan.-June, 1987; Member, Select Committee on Social Services, 1985-87; SLD Interim Joint Spokesman, Social Security, 1988; SLD Spokesman, Trade and Industry, 1988-89; President, Liberal Democrats, 1989-94; Liberal Democrat Spokesman: Health, 1989-92, Europe, 1992-97; Member: Select Committee on House of Commons Televising, 1988, Standards and Privileges Committee, since 1997. Recreations: reading; writing. Address: (b.) House of Commons, London SW1A 0AA; T.-0171-219 5090.

Kennedy, Garfield. Chief Executive, Gosh That's Big Entertainment and Gosh Films (formerly Garfield Kennedy Company), since 1984; b. 21.8.51, Belfast; m., Carrie Rolls; 2 d. Educ. Coleraine Academical Institution; Edinburgh University. Reporter, Radio Forth, 1975; Television Researcher, Granada TV, 1975-78; Associate Producer, Anglia TV, 1978-81; Television Producer/Director, TVS, responsible for four series of science series, The Real World, 1981-84; Producer and Director, The Garfield Kennedy Company, 1984-97. Science Writer of the Year, 1988. Recreations: cycling; skiing; hill-walking. Address: (b.) 420 Sauchiehall Street, Glasgow G2 3JD; T.-0141-353 0456.

Kennedy, Professor Gavin, BA, MSc, PhD, FCIM. Professor, Edinburgh Business School, Heriot-Watt University; Managing Director, Negotiate Ltd., Edinburgh; b. 20.2.40, Collingham, Yorkshire; m., Patricia Anne; 1 s.; 2 d. Educ. London Nautical School; Strathclyde University. Lecturer: Danbury Management Centre, NE London Polytechnic, 1969-71, Brunel University, 1971-73. Lecturer, National Defence College, Latimer, 1972-74; Senior Lecturer in Economics, Strathclyde University, 1973-83; Professor, Defence Finance, Heriot-Watt University, 1983-86. Publications: Military in the Third World, 1974; Economics of Defence, 1975; Bligh, 1978 (Yorkshire Post Book of the Year, 1979); Death of Captain Cook, 1978; Burden Sharing in NATO, 1979; Mathematics for Innumerate Economists, 1982; Defence Economics, 1983; Invitation to Statistics, 1983; Everything is Negotiable, 1984; Negotiate Anywhere, 1985; Macro Economics, 1985; Superdeal, 1985; The Economist Pocket Negotiator, 1987; Captain Bligh: the man and his mutinies, 1988; Do We Have A Deal?, 1991; Simulations for Training Negotiators, 1993; The Perfect Negotiation, 1993; Negotiation, 1994; Local Pay Bargaining, 1995; The Negotiate Trainer's Manual, 1996; Practical Negotiation Works, 1996; Kennedy on Negotiation, 1997. Recreation: reading. Address: (h.) 22 Braid Avenue, Edinburgh; T.-0131-447 3000.

Kennedy, Rev. Gordon, BSc, BD. Church of Scotland Minister, New Cumnock Parish Church, Ayrshire, since 1993; b. 15.9.63, England. Educ. Crookston Castle Secondary; University of Strathclyde; University of Glasgow. Graduate Civil Engineer, Strathclyde Regional Council, 1985-89; Probationer Assistant, Bearsden North Parish Church, 1992-93. Address: 37 Castle, New Cumnock, Ayrshire KA18 4AG; T.-01290 338296.

Kennedy, Professor Peter Graham Edward, MB, BS, MPhil, MLitt, PhD, MD, DSc, FRCPath, FRCPLond, FRCPGlas, FRSE. Burton Professor of Neurology and Head of Department, Glasgow University, since 1987; Consultant Neurologist, Institute of Neurological Sciences, Southern General Hospital, Glasgow, since 1986; b. 28.3.51, London; m., Catherine Ann; 1 s.; 1 d. Educ. University College School, London; University College, London; University College Medical School. Medical Registrar, University College Hospital, 1977-78; Hon. Research Assistant, MRC Neuroimmunology Project, University College, London, 1978-80; Research Fellow, Institute of Virology, Glasgow University, 1981; Registrar and Senior Registrar, National Hospital for Nervous Diseases, London, 1981-84; Assistant Professor of Neurology, Johns Hopkins University School of Medicine, 1985; "New Blood" Senior Lecturer in Neurology and Virology, Glasgow University, 1986-87. BUPA Medical Foundation "Doctor of the Year" Research Award, 1990; Linacre Medal and Lectureship, Royal College of Physicians of London, 1991; T.S. Srinivasan Endowment Lecturer and Gold Medal, 1993; Fogarty International Scholar, NIH, USA, 1993-94; Associate Editor, Journal of Neurovirology; Member: Medical Research Advisory Committee, Multiple Sclerosis Society, Association of Physicians Great Britain and Ireland, Association of British Neurologists. Publications: Infections of the Nervous System (Co-Author); numerous papers on neurology, neurovirology and neurobiology. Recreations: reading and writing; music; astronomy; tennis; walking in the country; philosophy. Address: (b.) Institute of Neurological Sciences, Southern General Hospital, Glasgow G51; T.-0141-201 2474.

Kennedy, Peter Norman Bingham, TD, CA, DL. Investment Director, since 1979; Landowner; b. 11.10.42, Kings Lynn; 4 d. Educ. Rugby. Qualified as CA, 1967; worked for R.C. Greig & Co., Alex. Lawrie Factors Ltd. and Duncan Lawrie Ltd.; Managing Director, Gartmore Scotland Limited, 1988-96. Served with Ayrshire Yeomanry/ Queen's Own Yeomanry (TA), 13 years; Chairman, River Doon Fishery Board, since 1980; Deputy Lieutenant, Ayrshire and Arran. Address: (h.) Doonholm, Ayr.

Kennedy, Professor Robert Alan, BA, PhD, FBPsS, FRSE. Professor of Psychology, University of Dundee, since 1972; b. 1.10.39, Stourbridge; m., Elizabeth Wanda; 1 s. Educ. King Edward VI Grammar School, Stourbridge. Senior Tutor then Lecturer in Psychology, University of Melbourne, 1963-65; Lecturer in Psychology: Queen's College, University of St. Andrews, University of Dundee, 1965-72; Senior Lecturer in Psychology, University of Dundee, 1972. Member, Psychology Committee, Social Science Research Council (UK), 1980-82; Committee Member, Experimental Psychology Society, 1984-88; Member, Scientific Affairs Board, British Psychological Society, 1986-88; Member, MRC Neuropsychology Sub-committee, 1982-89; Editorial Board: Acta Psychologica, 1980-88, Psychological Research, 1978-88; Founder Member, European Conference on Eye Movements, since 1980; Convener, Scottish Group of Professors of Psychology, 1985-91; Governor, Dundee College of Education, 1974-78; Member of Court, University of Dundee, 1976-80 and since 1990; Convener, University Research Committee, 1994-97. Publications: Studies in Long-Term Memory (Co-author); The Psychology of Reading. Recreations: hill-walking; playing the piano. Address: (b.) Psychology Department, University of Dundee, Dundee DD1 4HN; T.-01382 344622.

Kent, Roger Williamson, CBE, CQSW, DipAppSocStud. Co-opted Member, East Lothian Education Committee; b. 27.12.31, Portsmouth; m., Angela Mary; 1 d. Educ. Royal Naval College, Dartmouth; London University; Newcastle University. Royal Navy, 1945-61; approved schools, 1962-64; social worker, 1964-73; Director: Social Services, Doncaster, 1973-79, Social Work, Lothian Region, 1979-89, Waverley Care Trust, 1989-95; Convener, Scottish Council for Voluntary Organisations, 1990-96. Commissioner for Scotland, CRE, 1989-93. Recreations: watching cricket; walking dog. Address: (h.) Strawfields, Foulden, Berwickshire TD15 1UH.

Kerby, Nigel Wells, BSc, PhD, CBiol, FBiol. Managing Director, Mylnefield Research Services Ltd., since 1993; b. 5.4.53, Anglesey; m., Marigold; 1 s. Educ. Sedbergh School; United World College of the Atlantic; Leeds University. SERC Fellowship, Leeds University, 1979-82; AFRC Fellowship, Dundee University, 1982-90; Lecturer in Microbiology, Dundee University, 1990-93; Hon. Lecturer, Dundee University. Member, Institute of Directors, Institute of Advanced Motorists. Recreations: gardening; flying kites; wine; golf. Address: (b.) Mylnefield Research Services Ltd., Invergowrie, Dundee, DD2 5DA; T.-01382 568568.

Kermack, Sheriff Stuart Ogilvy, BA (Oxon), LLB. Sheriff of Tayside, Central and Fife, at Forfar, Perth, Arbroath, and Dundee, 1971-93; b. 9.7.34, Edinburgh; m., Barbara Mackenzie; 3 s.; 1 d. Educ. Glasgow Academy; Jesus College, Oxford; Glasgow University. Called to Scottish Bar, 1958. Address: (h.) 23 South Learmonth Gardens, Edinburgh; T.-0131-332 1898; 1 Linshader, Isle of Lewis; T.-01851 621201.

Kernohan, Robert Deans, OBE, MA. Journalist, Writer and occasional Broadcaster; b. 9.1.31, Mount Vernon, Lanarkshire; m., Margaret Buchanan Bannerman; 4 s. Educ. Whitehill School, Glasgow; Glasgow University; Balliol College, Oxford. RAF, 1955-57; Editorial Staff, Glasgow Herald, 1957-67 (Assistant Editor, 1965-66, London Editor, 1966-67); Director-General, Scottish Conservative Central Office, 1967-71; Freelance Journalist and Broadcaster, 1972; Editor, Life and Work, The Record of the Church of Scotland, 1972-90. Chairman, Federation of Conservative Students, 1954-55; Conservative Parliamentary candidate, 1955, 1959, 1964; Member: Newspaper Panel, Monopolies and Mergers Commission, 1987-97, Ancient Monuments Board for Scotland, 1990-97, Broadcasting Standards Council, 1994-97, Broadcasting Standards Commission, since 1997; Chairman, Scottish Christian Conservative Forum, 1991; HM Inspector of Constabulary for Scotland (Lay Inspector), 1992-95; Director, Handsel Press Ltd; Trustee, Carberry Tower; Elder, Cramond Kirk, Edinburgh. Publications: Scotland's Life and Work, 1979; William Barclay, The Plain Uncommon Man, 1980; Thoughts through the Year, 1985; Our Church, 1985; The Protestant Future, 1991; The Road to Zion, 1995. Recreations: rugby-watching; travel; pontification. Address: (h.) 5/1 Rocheid Park, Edinburgh EH4 1RP; T.-0131-332 7851.

Kerr, Sheriff B.A., QC, BA, LLB. Sheriff of Glasgow and Strathkelvin at Glasgow. Admitted to Faculty of Advocates, 1973. Address: (b.) Sheriff Court House, 1 Carlton Place, Glasgow, G5 9DA.

Kerr, David Alexander, MC, TD, JP, DL; b. 30.9.16, Inverkip; m., Elizabeth Phoebe Coxwell Cresswell; 1 s.; 1 d. Educ. Canford School. Joined Westburn Sugar Refineries Ltd., Greenock, 1936; joined 5/6 Bn., Argyll & Sutherland Highlanders, 1936; mobilised, 1939, serving in France, Belgium, North Africa, Italy, Palestine and Syria; MC, 1945; mentioned in Despatches; Territorial Decoration, 1948; returned to Westburn, 1946; Technical Director, 1949; Refinery Director, 1955; Joint Managing Director, 1960; Managing Director, 1967; Chairman, 1972; Director, The Sankey Sugar Company Ltd., 1965; Managing Director, Maubre Sugars Ltd., 1972; Director, Tate & Lyle Refineries Ltd., 1976-79; retired, 1979. County Commissioner, County of Renfrew Scout Association, 1964-70, County Chairman, 1971-73; Area President, 1976-93; Chief Commissioner for Scotland, 1977-81; Honorary Vice President, since 1981; a County Vice President, Renfrewshire Guide Association. Recreations: garden; philately; photography. Address: (h.) Whitefarland, 88 Octavia Terrace, Greenock PA16 7PY; T.-01475 631980.

Kerr, Douglas J., JP. Convenor, Edinburgh City Council Licensing Board, since 1996, and of City Licensing Committee, 1995-97; b. 9.1.57, Perth. Educ. Perth High School. Vice-Chair, Edinburgh District Council Planning Committee, 1990-96. Recreations: cricket; golf; football; skiing. Address: (b.) City Chambers, High Street, Edinburgh EH1 1YJ, T.-0131-529 3279.

Kerr, Rev. Fergus Gordon Thomson, OP, STM, MA, DD. Prior, since 1992; Honorary Senior Lecturer in Theology, University of Edinburgh, since 1995; Editor, New Blackfriars, since 1995; b. 16.7.31, Banff. Educ. Banff Academy; University of Aberdeen. Flying Officer, Royal Air Force, 1953-55; entered Order of Preachers, 1956; ordained Priest, 1962; Prior, Blackfriars, Oxford, 1969-78; Member, Theology Faculty, University of Oxford, 1978-86; President, Catholic Theological Association of Great Britain, 1990-92; Stanton Lecturer, University of Cambridge, 1995. Publications: Theology after Wittgenstein, 1986; Immortal Longings, 1997. Recreation: reading. Address: (h.) Blackfriars, 25 George Square, Edinburgh EH8 9LD; T.-0131-650 0901.

Kerr, Finlay, MB, ChB, DObsRCOG, FRCPEdin, FRCPGlas. Consultant Physician, Raigmore Hospital, Inverness, since 1976; Honorary Senior Lecturer, Aberdeen University, since 1976; Board Director, Highland Hospice, 1985-90 (Chairman, Board of Directors, 1985-87); Chairman, Area Medical Committee, 1993-96; b. 8.8.41, Edinburgh; m., Margaret Ann Carnegie Allan; 1 s.; 2 d. Educ. Keil School; Glasgow University. House Physician and Surgeon, Western Infirmary, Glasgow; House Physician, Ruchill Hospital, Glasgow; House Surgeon, Queen Mother's Hospital, Glasgow; Senior House Officer, Western Infirmary, Glasgow; Fellow, University of Southern California; Lecturer in Medicine, then Senior Registrar in Medicine, Edinburgh Royal Infirmary. Recreations: sailing; windsurfing; skiing; golf. Address: (h.) The Birks, 2 Drummond Place, Inverness.

Kerr, Rev. Philip John, PhB, STL. Parish Priest, Our Lady and St. Ninian, Bannockburn, and Sacred Heart, Cowie; R.C. Chaplain, Stirling University; Lecturer in Systematic Theology, Scotus College, Bearsden, 1993-96; b. 23.4.56, Edinburgh. Educ. Holy Cross Academy; St. Augustine's High School, Edinburgh; Scots College and Gregorian University, Rome. Assistant Priest, St. Francis Xavier's, Falkirk, 1980-82; Lecturer in Systematic Theology, St. Andrew's College, Drygrange, 1982-86; Vice-Rector and Lecturer in Systematic Theology, Gillis College, Edinburgh, 1986-93. Recreations: squash; walking. Address: Catholic Presbytery, Quakerfield, Bannockburn FK7 8HJ; T.-01786 812249.

Kerr, Robert James, MA (Hons), PhD. Rector, Peebles High School, since 1986; b. 14.6.47, Jedburgh; m., Isobel Grace Atkinson; 2 s.; 1 d. Educ. Kelso High School; Edinburgh University. Assistant Teacher, Lochaber High School, 1973-75; Assistant Principal Teacher of Geography, Forrester High School, 1976-77; Principal Teacher of Geography, Douglas Ewart High School, 1977-82; Assistant Rector, Elgin High School, 1982-85; Depute Rector, Forres Academy, 1985-86. Chairman, "Higher Still" Specialist Group in PSE, 1994-97. Recreations: fishing; rugby supporter; hill-walking/mountaineering; mountain biking; ornithology; skiing; travel. Address: (h.) Enniskerry, Eshiels, Peebles EH45 8NA; T.-01721 722131.

Kerr, Professor William John Stanton, BDS, FDS, RCSEdin, MDS, FFD, RCSIrel, DOrthRCS, FDS RCPS Glas, DDS. Professor of Orthodontics, Glasgow Dental Hospital and School, since 1993; Honorary Consultant in Orthodontics, since 1978; b. 12.7.41, Belfast; m., Marie-Francoise; 1 d. Educ. Campbell College, Belfast; Queen's University, Belfast. Address: (b.) Glasgow Dental Hospital and School, 378 Sauchiehall Street, Glasgow G2 3JZ; T.-0141-211 9665.

Kerrigan, Herbert Aird, QC, MA, LLB (Hons); b. 2.8.45, Glasgow; 1 s. Educ. Whitehill School, Glasgow; Aberdeen University; Keele University; Hague Academy. Admitted to Faculty of Advocates, 1970; Lecturer in Criminal Law and Criminology, Edinburgh University, 1969-73; Lecturer in Scots Law, Edinburgh University, 1973-74; Member, Longford Commission, 1972; Church of Scotland: Elder, 1967 (now at Greyfriars Tolbooth and Highland Kirk), Reader, 1969, elected Member, Assembly Council, 1981-85; called to the English Bar (Middle Temple), 1990; joined Chambers of Edmund Lawson, QC, 1991; appointed QC in Scotland, 1992. Publications: An Introduction to Criminal Procedure in Scotland, 1970; Ministers for the 1980s (Contributor), 1979; The Law of Contempt (Contributing Editor), 1982; The Law of Sport (2nd edition) (Contributor), 1995. Recreation: travel. Address: (h.) 20 Edinburgh Road, Dalkeith, Midlothian EH22 1JY; T.-0131-660 3007.

Kidd, Professor Cecil, BSc, PhD, FIBiol, FRSA. Regius Professor of Physiology, Aberdeen University, since 1984;

b. 28.4.33, Shotley Bridge, Co. Durham; m., Margaret Winifred; 3 s. Educ. Queen Elizabeth Grammar School, Darlington; King's College, Newcastle-upon-Tyne; Durham University. Demonstrator in Physiology, King's College, Newcastle-upon-Tyne; Lecturer/Senior Lecturer/Reader in Physiology, Senior Research Associate in Cardiovascular Studies, Leeds University; Head, Department of Biomedical Sciences. Recreations: squash; gardening. Address: (b.) Department of Biomedical Sciences, Medical School, Aberdeen University, Aberdeen AB25 2ZD; T.-01224 273005.

Kidd, David Hamilton, LLB, LLM, WS, NP. Partner, Biggart Baillie, since 1978; Solicitor Advocate, since 1994; Member, Council, W.S. Society, since 1995; b. 21.9.49, Edinburgh; m., Geraldine Stephen; 2 s.; 1 d. Educ. Edinburgh Academy; Edinburgh University. Recreations: cycling; skiing; sailing. Address: (b.) 7 Castle Street, Edinburgh EH2 3AP; T.-0131-226 5541.

Kidd, Mary Helen (May), JP, MA. National Chairman, Scottish Women's Rural Institutes, 1993-96; Member: Scottish Consumer Council, 1991-96, Advisory Board and Council, Scottish Agricultural College, since 1991, Women's National Commission, since 1993; m., Neil M.L. Kidd; 2 s. Educ. Brechin High School; Edinburgh University. Partner in family farming business; former Member, WNC International Committee; Member: MAFF Consumer Panel, Committee, Associated Countrywomen of the World. Recreations: playing piano and organ; creative writing. Address: (h.) Holemill of Kirkbuddo, Forfar, Angus DD8 2NQ; T.-01307 820 318.

Kiddie, Charles, BSc (Hons). Rector, Perth High School, since 1993; b. 3.4.49, Dundee; m., Esther Linda Power; 2 s. Educ. Harris Academy, Dundee; Aberdeen University; University of Kansas; Dundee College of Education. Teacher, Forfar Academy; Principal Teacher, Breadalbane Academy, Aberfeldy; Assistant Head Teacher, Whitfield High School, Dundee; Adviser in Social Subjects, Tayside Regional Council; Rector, Auchterarder High School. Recreations: family; ice hockey. (b.) Perth High School, Oakbank Road, Perth; T.-01738 628271/2.

Killick, Roger John, BSc, MBA, MA, PhD, CBiol, MIBiol. Secretary, Scottish Crop Research Institute, since 1988; b. 27.5.45, London; m., E. Marion Smith; 1 s.; 1 d. Educ. Purley County Grammar School for Boys; London University; Birmingham University; Dundee University; Leicester University. Research Geneticist, Scottish Plant Breeding Station, 1969-82; Assistant to Director, Scottish Crop Research Institute, 1982-88. Recreations: hill-walking; watching ballet. Address: (h.) Hilltops, 19 Sidlaw Terrace, Birkhill, Dundee DD2 5PY; T.-01382 580396.

Kilpatrick, Lord (Robert Kilpatrick), MD, FRCP(Edin), FRCP, FRCPS(Glas), HonFRCS, HonFRCP(Dub), HonFRCS(Edin). Chairman, Scottish Hospital Endowment Research Trust, since 1996; b. 29.7.26, Wemyss; m., Elizabeth Forbes; 2 s.; 1 d. Educ. Buckhaven High School; Edinburgh University. House Officer, Senior House Officer, Registrar, Edinburgh, 1949-54; Lecturer and Senior Lecturer, Sheffield University, 1955-66; Professor of Clinical Pharmacology, Sheffield University, 1966-75; Professor of Clinical Pharmacology and Medicine, Leicester University, 1975-89; President, General Medical Council, 1989-95. Hon. Degrees: DrHc (Edin), LLD (Dundee), DSc (Hull), DSc (Leics), LLD (Sheff). Recreation: golf. Address: (h.) 12 Wester Coates Gardens, Edinburgh EH12 5LT; T.-0131-337 7304.

Kilshaw, David Andrew George. Solicitor, since 1979; Chairman, Borders Health Board, since 1993; b. 18.3.53, Glencoe; 3 s. Educ. Keil School, Dumbarton. Traineeship, Brunton Miller, Solicitors, Glasgow, 1975-80; Solicitor, Borders Regional Council, 1980-83; Partner, Cullen

Kilshaw Solicitors, Galashiels and Melrose, since 1983. Safeguarder, Borders Region Children's Panel, since 1987; Director of Rugby, Peebles Rugby Football Club. Recreations: golf; fishing; walking; self-improvement. Address: (b.) 27 Market Street, Galashiels; T.-01896 758311.

Kimbell, Professor David Rodney Bertram, MA, DPhil, LRAM, FRSA. Professor of Music, Edinburgh University, since 1987 (Professor of Music, St. Andrews University, 1979-87); b. 26.6.39, Gillingham, Kent; m., Ingrid Else Emilie Lübbe; 1 s.; 2 d. Educ. Dartford Grammar School; Kent College, Canterbury; Worcester College, Oxford. Lecturer in Music, Edinburgh University, 1965-78. Publication: Verdi in the Age of Italian Romanticism, 1981; Italian Opera, 1991. Address: (h.) 3 Bellevue Crescent, Edinburgh EH3 6ND; T.-0131-556 5480.

Kincraig, Hon. Lord (Robert Smith Johnston), QC (Scot), BA (Hons), LLB. Senator of the College of Justice in Scotland, 1972-88; Chairman, Parole Review Body for Scotland; b. 10.10.18, Glasgow; m., Margaret Joan Graham (deceased); 1 s.; 1 d. Educ. Strathallan; St. John's College, Cambridge; Glasgow University. Member, Faculty of Advocates, 1942; Advocate-Depute, 1953-55; QC (Scot), 1955; contested (Unionist), Stirling and Falkirk Burghs, General Election, 1959; Home Advocate Depute, 1959-62; Sheriff of Roxburgh, Berwick and Selkirk, 1964-70; Dean, Faculty of Advocates, 1970-72. Recreations: gardening; golf. Address: (h.) Westwood Cottage, Southfield Farm, Longniddry EH32 0PL; T.-01875 853583.

King, Professor Bernard, MSc, PhD, FIWSc, CBiol, FIBiol. Principal and Vice-Chancellor, University of Abertay, Dundee, since 1992; b. 4.5.46, Dublin; m., Maura Antoinette Collinge; 2 d. Educ. Synge St. Christian Brothers School, Dublin; College of Technology, Dublin; University of Aston in Birmingham. Research Fellow, University of Aston, 1972-76; Dundee Institute of Technology, 1976-91: Lecturer, Senior Lecturer, Head, Department of Molecular and Life Sciences, Dean, Faculty of Science; Assistant Principal, Robert Gordon Institute of Technology/Robert Gordon University, 1991-92. Director, Dundee Healthcare Trust; Governor, Unicorn Preservation Society; Vice-Chairman, Committee of Principals of Scottish Centrally-Funded Colleges. Recreations: reading; music; sailing. Address: (h.) 11 Dalhousie Place, Arbroath, DD11 2BT; T.-01382 308012.

King, Elspeth Russell, MA, FMA.Director, Smith Art Gallery and Museum, Stirling, since 1994; b. 29.3.49, Lochore, Fife. Educ. Beath High School; St. Andrews University; Leicester University. Curator, People's Palace, Glasgow, 1974-91, with responsibility for building up the social history collections for the city of Glasgow; Director, Dunfermline Heritage Trust, 1991-94; responsible for restoration of, and new displays in, Abbot House. Address: (b.) Smith Art Gallery and Museum, Dumbarton Road, Stirling FK8 2RQ; T.-01786 471917

King, Geoffrey Harry, BA (Oxon), DPhil. Director of Projects, Scottish Environment Protection Agency, since 1995; b. 25.8.46, Swindon; m., Deborah Anne King; 2 d. Educ. Commonweal Grammar School, Swindon; Balliol College, Oxford; Sussex University. Research Manager, Unilever, 1972-74; Lecturer in Analytical Chemistry, Dorset Institute of Higher Education, 1974-77; Programme Manager, Renewable Energy Research and Development, Energy Technology Support Unit, 1977-83; Manager, Energy Efficiency Demonstration Scheme, 1983-87; Business Planning Manager, Thames Water Authority, 1987-89; Business Services and Market Testing Manager, NRA, 1989-95. Recreations: railways; walking; listening to music; sailing. Address: (h.) 43 Grange View, Linlithgow EH49 7HY; T.-01506 846108.

King, Robert Lees Lumsden. Secretary: Post Office Users' Council for Scotland, since 1988, Scottish Advisory Committee on Telecommunications, since 1988; b. 23.3.49, Peebles; m., Yvonne Mary Black. Educ. Leith Academy. Department of Agriculture and Fisheries for Scotland, 1966-70; Department of Environment, 1970-72; Forestry Commission, 1972-79; Nature Conservancy Council, 1979-88. Recreations: country life; shooting; reading; travel. Address: (b.) 2 Greenside Lane, Edinburgh EH1 3AH; T.-0131-244 5576.

King, Thomas Robertson, BL. Director, Corporate Affairs, Standard Life Assurance Company, since 1996; b. 29.6.41, Edinburgh; m., Sheila; 2 d. Educ. Lasswade Senior Secondary; University of Edinburgh. Joined Standard Life, 1967: Sales Manager, South of England, 1973, General Manager (Marketing), 1985, Director, 1992. Recreation: golf. Address: (b.) Standard Life House, 30 Lothian Road, Edinburgh EH1 2DH; T.-0131-245 0324.

Kingarth, Lord (Hon. Derek Emslie). Senator of the College of Justice, since 1997; b. 21.6.49. Educ. Cambridge University; Edinburgh University. Advocate, 1974; Advocate Depute 1985-1988. Address: Parliament Square, Edinburgh EH1 1RQ.

Kinnaird, Alison, MBE, MA, FGE. Glass Engraver and Artist; Clarsach Player; b. 30.4.49, Edinburgh; m., Robin Morton; 1 s.; 1 d. Educ. George Watson's Ladies College; Edinburgh University. Freelance glass artist, since 1971; exhibitions in Edinburgh, 1978, 1981, 1985, in London, 1988, 1995; work in many public and private collections; professional musician, since 1970; has produced three LPs as well as film and TV music; served on Council, Scottish Craft Centre, 1974-76; Council, SSWA, 1975-76; Member: BBC Scottish Music Advisory Committee, 1981-84, BBC Broadcasting Council for Scotland, 1984-88, SAC Crafts Committee, 1993-96; awarded: SDA/CCC Craft Fellowship, 1980, Glass-Sellers of London Award, 1987, MBE, for services to music and art, 1997. Recreations: children; cooking; garden. Address: (h.) Shillinghill, Temple, Midlothian EH23 4SH; T.-01875 830328.

Kinnis, William Kay Brewster, PhD, FRSA. Solicitor and Notary Public; Consultant Lawyer with Cannon, Orpin & Murdochs, Solicitors, Glasgow, since 1995; Director, East Neuk Properties Ltd., Kilrymont Properties Ltd., Culdee Properties Ltd., Madras Properties Ltd., Swilcan Properties Ltd., Rock & Spindle Properties Ltd., Christian Action Glasgow Housing Trust Ltd.; b. 5.1.33, St. Andrews; m., Agnes Inglis Erskine, MA; 2 d. Educ. Hamilton Academy; Glasgow University; London University (External). Partner: MacArthur Stewart & Orr, Solicitors, Oban and Lochgilphead, 1959-62; Town Clerk and Burgh Chamberlain, Lochgilphead, 1960-62; Partner, Murdoch Jackson, Solicitors, Glasgow, 1963-92; Senior Partner: Miller Jackson, Solicitors, Lenzie, 1982-92, Cannon, Orpin & Murdochs, 1992-95; Council Member, Member, Royal Faculty of Procurators, 1980-83; Governor, Baillie's Institution, 1983-94. Choral Scholar, Glasgow University, 1954-58; Choirmaster, Lochgilphead Parish Church, 1959-62; Reader, Church of Scotland, since 1960; Member, Church of Scotland Board of Practice and Procedure and Law Committee, since 1990. Recreations: choral singing; swimming; reading; travel. Address: (b.) 78 Queen Street, Glasgow G1 3DW; T.-0141-204 1155.

Kinross, Lord (Christopher Patrick Balfour), LLB, WS. Solicitor, since 1975; b. 1.10.49, Edinburgh; m., Susan Jane Pitman; 2 s. Educ. Eton College; Edinburgh University. Member, Royal Company of Archers, Queen's Bodyguard for Scotland; James IV Association of Surgeons. Recreations: off-road motorsport; shooting. Address: (b.) Taylor Kinross Legal Partnership, 27 Stafford Street, Edinburgh; T.-0131-623 1997.

Kinsey, Rev. Louis, BD, DipMin. Parish Minister, St. Columba's Church of Scotland, Bridge of Don, Aberdeen, since 1991; b. 11.12.59, Wingate, Co. Durham; m., Sally Anne Stewart; 2 s. Educ. Milton School, Bulawayo, Zimbabwe; New College, University of Edinburgh. British Army, 1976-83; Assistant Minister, St. Giles and St. Columba's, Elgin, 1990-91. Recreations: playing with my children; amateur trumpet-playing; surfing the Internet. Address: (h.) 151 Jesmond Avenue, Bridge of Don, Aberdeen AB22 8UG; T.-01224 705337.

Kintore, 13th Earl of (Michael Canning William John Keith); b. 22.2.39; m.; 1 s.; 1 d. Address: The Stables, Keith Hall, Inverurie, AB51 0LD.

Kirk, David, MA, BM, BCh, DM, FRCS (Eng), FRCS-RCPS (Glas), FRCS Edin). Consultant Urological Surgeon, Greater Glasgow Health Board, since 1982; Honorary Professor, Glasgow University, since 1995; b. 26.5.43, Bradford; m., Gillian Mary Wroot; 1 s.; 2 d. Educ. King Edwards School, Birmingham; Balliol College, Oxford; Oxford University Clinical Medical School. Resident House Physician and House Surgeon, Radcliffe Infirmary, Oxford; University Demonstrator, Oxford; clinical surgical posts, Oxford and Bristol; Arris and Gale Lecturer, Royal College of Surgeons (England), 1980-81; rotating surgical Registrar appointment, Sheffield; academic surgical research, Sheffield University; Senior Registrar in General Surgery, then in Urology, Bristol; Honorary Clinical Lecturer, Glasgow University, 1984-95. Secretary/Treasurer, 1983-85, Chairman, 1985-88, Scottish Urological Oncology Group; Council Member: Urology Section, Royal Society of Medicine, 1984-87, British Association of Urological Surgeons, 1988-91; Chairman: Prostate Forum, 1991-94, Intercollegiate Board in Urology, 1994-97; Specialist Adviser in Urology, National Medical Advisory Committee (Scottish Office). Recreations: skiing; hill-walking; classical music. Address: (h.) Woodend, Prospect Road, Dullatur, Glasgow G68 0AN; T.-01236 720778.

Kirk, Professor Gordon, MA, MEd, FRSA. Principal, Moray House Institute of Education, since 1981; Vice-Convener, General Teaching Council, since 1992; b. 8.5.38, Dunfermline; m., Jane D. Murdoch; 1 s.; 1 d. Educ. Camphill Secondary School, Paisley; Glasgow University. Lecturer in Education, Aberdeen University, 1965-74; Head, Education Department, Jordanhill College of Education, 1974-81; Member, Munn Committee on the Curriculum of the Secondary School, 1974-77; Chairman: Educational Broadcasting Council, Scotland, 1985-91, Scottish Council for Research in Education, 1984-92; Member: General Teaching Council for Scotland, since 1984, Consultative Committee on the Curriculum, 1984-91, Council for National Academic Awards, 1979-93; Vice-Convener, Committee of Scottish Higher Principals, 1993-94. Publications: Scottish Education Looks Ahead (Assistant Editor), 1969; Curriculum and Assessment in the Scottish Secondary School, 1982; Moray House and Professional Education (Editor), 1985; The Core Curriculum, 1986; Teacher Education and Professional Development, 1988; Handbook of Educational Ideas and Practices (Associate Editor), 1990; Scottish Education and the European Community (Editor), 1992; 5-14: Scotland's National Curriculum (Editor), 1994; Moray House and Change in Higher Education (Editor), 1995; Professional Issues in Education series (Co-Editor). Recreations: walking; golf; bridge. Address: (h.) Craigroyston, Broadgait, Gullane, East Lothian; T.-01620 843299.

Kirk, James, MA, PhD, DLitt, FRHistS, FRSE. Reader in Scottish History, Glasgow University, since 1990; b. 18.10.44, Falkirk. Educ. Stirling High School; Edinburgh University. Lecturer in Scottish History, Glasgow University, 1972-89; Senior Lecturer, 1989-90; David Berry Prize, Royal Historical Society, 1973; Wolfson Award,

1977; British Academy Major Research Awards, 1989-96; ESRC Research Award, 1993-95. President, Scottish Church History Society, 1989-92; Hon. Secretary: Scottish Record Society, since 1973, Scottish Society for Reformation History, 1980-90; Member, Council, Scottish History Society, 1989-93; Scottish Section Editor, Royal Historical Society, Annual Bibliography of British and Irish History. Publications: The University of Glasgow 1451-1577, 1977; Records of the Synod of Lothian and Tweeddale, 1977; The Second Book of Discipline, 1980; Stirling Presbytery Records, 1981; Visitation of the Diocese of Dunblane, 1984; Patterns of Reform, 1989; Humanism and Reform (Editor), 1991; The Books of Assumption of the Thirds of Benefices: Scottish Ecclesiastical Rentals at the Reformation, 1995; Scotland's History (Editor), 1995; The Medieval Church in Scotland (Editor), 1995; Her Majesty's Historiographer, 1996; Calendar of Scottish Supplications to Rome 1447-1471, vol. 5 (Editor), 1997; Contributor to: Encyclopedia of the Reformed Faith, 1992, Dictionary of Scottish Church History and Theology, 1993, The Oxford Encyclopedia of the Reformation, 1996. Recreations: living in Wester Ross; viticulture. Address: (h.) Woodlea, Dunmore, Stirlingshire FK2 8LY; T.-01324 831240.

Kirk, William, CPFA. Director of Finance, South Lanarkshire Council, since 1995; Treasurer, Strathclyde Fire Board, since 1995; Treasurer, Lanarkshire Joint Valuation Board, since 1995; b. 21.8.50, Holytown; m., Eleanor; 2 d. Educ. Hamilton Academy. Lanarkshire County Council, 1968-75; Hamilton District Council, 1975-96. Recreations: sport; reading. Address: (b.) Council Offices, Almada Street, Hamilton; T.-01698 454530.

Kirkhill, Lord (John Farquharson Smith); b. 7.5.30; m.; 1 step d. Lord Provost of Aberdeen, 1971-75; Minister of State, Scottish Office, 1975-78; Chairman, North of Scotland Hydro-Electric Board, 1979-82; Delegate, Parliamentary Assembly, Council of Europe, since 1987. Address: (h.) 3 Rubislaw Den North, Aberdeen, AB2 4AL; T.-01224 314167.

Kirkness, Professor Colin Mainland, BMedBiol, MBChB, FRCS(Edin), FRCS (Glas), FRCOphth. Tennent Professor of Ophthalmology, Glasgow University, since 1991; President-Elect, European Board of Ophthalmology; Secretary, EUPO; Vice-President, Royal College of Ophthalmologists; b. 4.5.49, Kirkwall. Educ. Fraserburgh Academy; Aberdeen University. Resident Surgical Officer and Senior Resident, Moorfields Eye Hospital, London, 1980; Lecturer, 1983, Senior Lecturer and Director, 1989, Pocklington Eye Transplant Unit, Institute of Ophthalmology, London; Honorary Consultant, Moorfields Eye Hospital, 1987. Publications: books on ophthalmology; papers. Address: (b.) Tennent Institute, 38 Church Street, Glasgow G11 6NT; T.-0141-211 2000, Ext. 2640.

Kirkpatrick, William, BSc. Rector, Blairgowrie High School, since 1995; b. 5.8.46, Kirkcaldy; m., Jenifer; 1 s. Educ. Kirkcaldy High; University of Edinburgh. Teacher of Physics, Kirkcaldy High School; Principal Teacher of Physics: Kirkland High School, Kirkcaldy High School; Assistant Head Teacher, Auchmuty High; TVEI Co-ordinator then Senior Adviser, Fife Region; Depute Rector, Auchmuty High. Address: (b.) Beeches Road, Blairgowrie PH10 6PW; T.-01250 873445.

Kirkwood, Archy, BSc. MP (Liberal Democrat), Roxburgh and Berwickshire, since 1983; Chairman, Social Security Select Committee, since 1997; Commissioner, House of Commons; b. 22.4.46, Glasgow; m., Rosemary Chester; 1 s.; 1 d. Educ. Cranhill School; Heriot-Watt University. Solicitor, Notary Public; Aide to Sir David Steel, 1971-75, 1977-78; Liberal Spokesman on Health and Social Services, and on Social Security, 1985-87; Alliance Spokesman on

Overseas Development, 1987; Liberal Spokesman on Scotland, 1987-88; Social and Liberal Democrat Convener on Welfare, Health and Education, 1988-89; Liberal Democrat Deputy Chief Whip, and Spokesman on Welfare and Social Security, 1989-92, Community Care, 1994-97. Trustee, Joseph Rowntree Reform Trust, since 1985. Recreations: music; photography. Address: (b.) House of Commons, London SW1A 0AA.

Kirkwood, Professor Daniel, BSc (Hons), PhD, EurIng, CEng, FIM, FICorr, FIES. Professor and Head, Department of Engineering, Glasgow Caledonian University, since 1994; b. 14.2.48, Kilmarnock. Educ. Kilmarnock Academy; University of Strathclyde. Robert Gordon's Institute of Technology: Lecturer, School of Mechanical Engineering, 1975-78, Senior Lecturer, 1978-85, Deputy Head, 1985-88, Acting Head, 1988-89, School of Mechanical and Offshore Engineering; Technical Director, Welltrain International Ltd., Aberdeen, 1989-91; Professor and Senior Lecturer, School of Mechanical and Offshore Engineering, Robert Gordon University, Aberdeen; Chair, Glasgow Panel, REMAP Scotland (technical help for disabled people). Recreations: cycling, DIY. Address: (b.) Glasgow Caledonian University, Cowcaddens, Glasgow G4 0BA; T.-0141-331 3529.

Kirkwood, Hon. Lord (Ian Candlish Kirkwood). Senator of the College of Justice, since 1987; b. 8.6.32. Advocate, 1957; QC, 1970. Address: (b.) Court of Session, Parliament House, Edinburgh, EH1 1RQ.

Kirkwood, Professor (James) Michael, MA, DipSovStud, MA. Professor in Slavonic Languages and Literatures, Glasgow University, since 1993; b. 6.3.41, Glasgow; m., Melanie Claire McMath; 1 s.; 1 d. Educ. Hillhead High School, Glasgow; Glasgow University. Assistant Lecturer, Lecturer, Senior Lecturer in Russian, Lancaster University, 1966-82; Senior Lecturer in Russian, School of Slavonic and East European Studies, London University, 1982-92; Reader in Russian Studies, SSEES, 1992-93. Recreations: skiing; windsurfing; hill-walking; bird-watching; squash; golf. Address: (b.) Department of Slavonic Languages and Literatures, Hetherington Building, Glasgow University, Glasgow G12 8QQ; T.-0141-330 4731.

Kirkwood, Ralph C., BSc, PhD, FRSE, FIBiol. Reader in Biology, Strathclyde University, since 1981; b. 6.7.33, Glasgow; m., Mair Enid; 3 s. Educ. Jordanhill College School, Glasgow; Glasgow University; University of Wales, Aberystwyth. Lecturer, Botany Department, West of Scotland Agricultural College, 1959-64; Strathclyde University: Lecturer, Biology Department, 1964-72, Senior Lecturer, 1972-81; Member, Advisory Committee, Scottish Agricultural College; Member, West Areas Board and Scientific Advisory Committee, S.N.H. Publications: Target sites for herbicide action (Editor); Clean Technology and the Environment (Co-Editor). Recreations: sailing; photography; natural history; walking. Address: (b.) Department of Bioscience and Biotechnology, Todd Centre, Strathclyde University, Glasgow, G1 1XW; T.-0141-548 3624.

Kirwan, Frank, BA, MA. Director Privilege Insurance, since 1997; Chairman, Crystal Media Group, since 1997; Visiting Professor, University of Strathclyde, since 1997; Member, Accounts Commission, since 1995; b. 16.7.52, Dublin; m., Moira; 1 s.; 1 d. Educ. Colaiste Mhuire, Dublin; Trinity College, University College, Dublin. Economic and Social Research Institute, 1974-76; Strathclyde University, 1976-81; Lund University, 1981-82; Fraser of Allander Institute, 1983-84; Scottish Development Agency, 1984-88; Royal Bank of Scotland, 1988-97. Recreation: gardening. Address: (h.) Gateside House, Hill Road, Gullane EH31 2BE.

Kitchen, John Philip, MA, BMus, PhD (Cantab), FRCO, LRAM. Senior Lecturer in Music, Edinburgh University, since 1987; Harpsichord Consultant, Royal Scottish Academy of Music and Drama; Concert Organist, Harpsichordist, Pianist; b. 27.10.50, Airdrie. Educ. Coatbridge High School; Glasgow University; Cambridge University. Lecturer in Music, St. Andrews University, 1976-87; Harpsichordist/Organist, Scottish Early Music Consort, Stanesby Recorder Trio, St. Andrews Baroque Trio; BBC and commercial recordings; music reviewer; Organist, Old St. Paul's Episcopal Church, Edinburgh. Recreations: more music; entertaining. Address: (b.) Faculty of Music, Alison House, 12 Nicolson Square, Edinburgh EH8 9DF; T.-0131-650 2432.

Klein, Bernat, CBE, FCSD, Hon. FRIAS; b. 6.11.22, Senta, Yugoslavia; m., Margaret Soper; 1 s.; 2 d. Educ. Senta, Yugoslavia; Bezalel School of Arts and Crafts, Jerusalem; Leeds University. Designer: Tootal, Broadhurst, Lee, 1948-49, Munrospun, Edinburgh, 1949-51; Chairman and Managing Director, Colourcraft, 1952-62; Managing Director, Bernat Klein Ltd., 1962-66; Chairman and Managing Director: Bernat Klein Design Ltd., 1966-81, Bernat Klein Ltd., 1982-92. Member: Design Council, 1962-68, Royal Fine Art Commission for Scotland, 1981-87. Publications: Eye for Colour, 1965; Design Matters, 1975. Recreations: tennis; reading. Address: High Sunderland, Galashiels; T.-01750 20730.

Kleinpoppen, Professor Hans, DiplPhysicist, Chart Phys, Dr re nat & habil, FInstPhys, FRAS, FRSA, FRSE, Fellow, American Physical Society. Professor of Experimental Physics, Stirling University, 1968-96, Professor Emeritus, since 1996; b. 30.9.28, Duisburg, Germany. Educ. Giessen University; Heidelberg University; Tuebingen University. Visiting Fellow, Colorado University, 1967; Visiting Associate Professor, Columbia University, New York, 1968; Stirling University: Head, Physics Department, 1970-72, Director, Institute of Atomic Physics, 1975-81, Head, Unit of Atomic and Molecular Physics, School of Natural Sciences, since 1989. Visiting Professor, Bielefeld University, since 1979; Visiting Fellow, Fritz Haber Institut, Max Planck Gessellschaft, since 1991. Co-Director, three International Summer Schools; Chairman, several national and international Conferences on Atomic Physics. Publications: editor of 13 books; research papers; articles in many journals; monograph series on physics of atoms and molecules (Co-Editor). Address: (b.) Unit of Atomic and Molecular Physics, Stirling University, Stirling.

Knight, Alanna, FSA Scot. Novelist; b. Co. Durham; m., Alistair Knight; 2 s. Educ. Jesmond High School. Writing career began, 1965; novels: Legend of the Loch, 1969 (RNA First Novel Award), The October Witch, 1971, This Outward Angel, 1971, Castle Clodha, 1972, Lament for Lost Lovers, 1972, The White Rose, 1974, A Stranger Came By, 1974, The Wicked Wynsleys, 1977; historical novels: The Passionate Kindness, 1974, A Drink for the Bridge, 1976, The Black Duchess, 1980, Castle of Foxes, 1981, Colla's Children, 1982, The Clan, 1985; Estella, 1986; detective novels: Enter Second Murderer, 1988, Blood Line, 1989, Deadly Beloved, 1989, Killing Cousins, 1990, A Quiet Death, 1991, To Kill A Queen, 1992; The Evil that Men Do, 1993, The Missing Duchess, 1994, Inspector Faro and the Edinburgh Mysteries, 1994, The Bull Slayers, 1995; Murder by Appointment, 1996; Inspector Faro's Second Casebook, 1996; crime novels: the Sweet Cheat Gone, 1992, This Outward Angel, 1994; Angel Eyes, 1997; plays: The Private Life of R.L.S., 1973, Girl on an Empty Swing, 1977; non-fiction: The Robert Louis Stevenson Treasury, 1985; RLS in the South Seas, 1986, Bright Ring of Words (Co-Author), 1994; radio short stories, plays and documentaries. Recreations: walking; reading; painting. Address: (h.) 24 March Hall Crescent, Edinburgh EH16 5HL; T.-0131-667 5230.

Knill-Jones, Jennifer Gillian, MB, BS, LRCP, MRCS, MRCPsych. Consultant Psychiatrist, since 1986; b. 15.8.36, Stockton-on-Tees; 3 d. Educ. Sutton High School; St. Bartholomew's Hospital Medical School. House Officer posts, Luton and Dunstaple Hospital, Elizabeth Garrett Anderson Hospital, London, St. Bartholomew's Hospital, London; Clinical Assistant, Gartnavel Royal Hospital, Glasgow; Senior Registrar in Psychiatry, Greater Glasgow Health Board. Recreations: walking; Scottish country dancing. Address: (b.) Parkhead Hospital, Salamanca Street, Glasgow G32; T.-0141-211 8300.

Knops, Professor Robin John, BSc, PhD, FRSE. Professor of Mathematics, Heriot-Watt University, Edinburgh, since 1971 (Vice Principal, 1988-95; Special Adviser to the Principal, 1995-97); b. 30.12.32, London; m., Margaret; 4 s.; 2 d. Educ. Nottingham University. Nottingham University: Assistant Lecturer in Mathematics, 1956-59, Lecturer in Mathematics, 1959-62; Newcastle-upon-Tyne University: Lecturer in Applied Mathematics, 1962-68, Reader in Continuum Mechanics, 1968-71; Head, Department of Mathematics, Heriot-Watt University, 1971-83; Visiting Professor: Cornell University, 1967 and 1968; University of California, Berkeley, 1968; Pisa University, 1974; Ecole Polytechnique Federale Lausanne, Switzerland, 1980; Royal Society of Edinburgh: Council Member, 1982-92, Executive Committee Member, 1982-92, Meetings Secretary, 1982-87, Chief Executive Editor, Proceedings A, 1982-87, Curator, 1987-92; President: Edinburgh Mathematical Society, 1974-75, International Society for the Interaction of Mechanics and Mathematics, 1991-95 (Vice-President, since 1995). Publications: Uniqueness Theories in Linear Elasticity (Co-author), 1971; Theory of Elastic Stability (Co-author), 1973. Recreations: walking; reading. Address: (b.) Lord Balerno Building, Heriot-Watt University, Edinburgh EH14 4AS; T.-0131-449 5111.

Knowler, Professor John T., PhD, CBiol, FIBiol. Head, Department of Biological Sciences, Glasgow Caledonian University, since 1990; b. 19.10.42, Whitstable; m., Susan Penelope; 2 d. Educ. Canterbury Technical School; Glasgow University. Insecticide and pharmaceutical industries, 1962-69; pre-doctoral research, 1969-72; post-doctoral research, 1972-73; Lecturer then Senior Lecturer, Biochemistry, Glasgow University, 1973-90. Publications: 75 papers, 11 chapters in academic books, two authored books. Recreations: bird-watching and other aspects of natural history; gardening. Address: (b.) Department of Biological Sciences, Glasgow Caledonian University, Cowcaddens Road, Glasgow G4 0BA; T.-0141-331 3210.

Knox, Col. Sir Bryce Muir, KCVO, MC (and Bar), CStJ, TD, BA (Cantab); b. 4.4.16, Edinburgh; m., Patricia Mary Dunsmuir; 1 s.; 1 d. Educ. Stowe; Trinity College, Cambridge. County of Ayr: Deputy Lieutenant, 1953, Vice Lieutenant, 1970-74, Ayrshire and Arran Lord Lieutenant, 1974-91; Chairman, W. & J. Knox Ltd., Kilbirnie, 1970-78; Vice-Chairman, Lindustries Ltd., 1979 (Director, 1953-79); served with Ayrshire (ECO) Yeomanry, 1939-45, North Africa and Italy (CO, 1953-56, Hon. Col., 1960-71); Honorary Colonel, Ayrshire Yeomanry Squadron, Queen's Own Yeomanry, 1971-77; Member, Queen's Bodyguard for Scotland (Royal Company of Archers), since 1974; President, Royal Highland Agricultural Society of Scotland, 1990-91. Publications: brief historical notes of the Ayrshire Yeomanry; History of the Eglinton Hunt. Recreation: country sports. Address: (h.) Martnaham Lodge, by Ayr KA6 6ES; T.-01292 560204.

Knox, John, BA, BD. General Secretary, Scottish National Council of YMCAs, since 1992; b. 28.1.35, Larne, Co. Antrim; m., Patricia Ringland; 1 s.; 1 d. Educ. Larne Grammar School; Queen's University, Belfast; Edgehill College; London University. Methodist Minister, Dublin, Donegal and Belfast, 1959-69; General Secretary, Methodist Youth Department, Ireland, 1969-78; Associate Secretary, Irish Council of Churches, 1978-82; Chief Officer, Scottish Standing Conference of Voluntary Youth Organisations, 1982-92. Recreations: gardening; mountain walking; music. Address: (b.) 11 Rutland Street, Edinburgh EH1 2AE; T.-0131-228 1464.

Knox, William. Author and Journalist; b. 20.2.28, Glasgow; m., Myra Ann McKill; 1 s.; 2 d. Educ. Eastwood School. Deputy News Editor, Evening News, Glasgow, 1957; Scottish Editor, Kemsley Newspapers, Glasgow, 1957-60; News Editor, Scottish Television, 1960-62; Freelance Author and Broadcaster, since 1962; author of more than 60 books, including novels of crime, sea and adventure: most recent novel, Blood Proof, 1997; awarded Police Review Award for best novel of British police procedures, 1987 (The Crossfire Killings); Presenter Crime Desk, STV, 1977-88; William Knox Collection established Boston University, USA; Past President and Honorary Member, Association of Scottish Motoring Writers; former Member, Scottish Committee, Society of Authors; Past President, Eastwood Rotary Club; Honorary Editor, Scottish Lifeboat, RNLI; Fellow, Paul Harris Foundation, Rotary International, 1989. Recreations: motoring; photography; dogs. Address: (h.) 55 Newtonlea Avenue, Newton Mearns, Glasgow G77 5QF.

Knox, William James. Member, Council, ACAS, since 1992; President, Rotary Club of Greenock, 1995-96; Member, Executive, Scottish Council Development and Industry, since 1995; Member, Council, Scottish Bowling Association, since 1995; UK Employment Spokesman, Federation of Small Businesses: b. 4.8.44, Glasgow; m., Ann May; 1 d. Educ. Greenock High School; Reid Kerr College, Paisley. Partner, A.F. McPherson & Co., Builders and Merchants, since 1962; Board Member, Scottish National Federation of Building Trade Employers, 1970-79; Member, Social Security Tribunal, 1978-84; Director, Morton Football and Athletic Club, 1986-89; Chairman, Morton Development Club, 1986-89; Member: Board of Directors, Greenock Arts Guild, since 1993, Executive, Scottish Constitutional Convention, 1989-90; Chairman: UK Federation of Small Businesses, 1989-92, Inverclyde Megawatt Festival, 1994-95. Recreations: football; bowling; photography; canals. Address: (h.) 3 Moorfield Road, Gourock PA19 1DD; T.-01475 633327.

Kuenssberg, Nicholas Christopher, BA (Hons) (Oxon), FCIS, FIoD, CIMgt. Chairman: David A. Hall Ltd., since 1996, GAP Group Ltd., since 1996, Institute of Directors, Scotland, since 1997, Association for Management Training and Education in Scotland, since 1996; Non-executive Director: Scottish Power Plc, since 1984, Standard Life Assurance Company, since 1988, Baxi Partnership, since 1996, Stoddard Sekers International PLC; Member: Scottish Advisory Group on Sustainable Development, since 1996, Scottish Legal Aid Board, since 1996; b. 28.10.42, Edinburgh; m., Sally Robertson; 1 s.; 2 d. Educ. Edinburgh Academy; Wadham College, Oxford. Director, J. & P. Coats Ltd., 1978-91; Chairman, Dynacast International Ltd, 1978-91; Director, Coats Patons Plc, 1985-91; Director, Coats Viyella PLC, 1986-91; Dawson International plc: Director, 1991, Managing Director, 1994-95; Non-executive Director, Bank of Scotland West of Scotland Board, 1984-88; Visiting Professor, Strathclyde Business School, 1988-91. Recreations: languages; opera; travel; sport. Address: (b.) 6 Cleveden Drive, Glasgow, G12 0SE.

Kuenssberg, Sally, BA, DipAdEd. Chairman, Scottish Children's Reporter Administration, since 1995; Non-Executive Director, Yorkhill NHS Trust, since 1993; b. 30.7.43, Edinburgh; m., Nicholas; 1 s.; 2 d. Educ. St Leonard's School; University of Oxford. Language Teaching, Europe and South America, 1966-78; Partner, Heatherbank Press, Milngavie, 1981-90; Children's Panel Training Organiser, Department of Adult and Continuing

Education, University of Glasgow, 1990-95. Adult Literacy Tutor, 1979-83; Member, Children's Panel, Glasgow, 1984-90. Address: (b.) SCRA, Ochil House, Springkerse Business Park, Stirling FK7 7XE.

Kyle, James, CBE, DSc, MCh, FRCS. Chairman, Raigmore Hospital NHS Trust, Inverness; b. 26.3.25, Ballymena, Northern Ireland; m., Dorothy Elizabeth Galbraith; 2 d. Educ. Ballymena Academy; Queen's University, Belfast. Scholarship to Mayo Clinic, USA, 1950; Tutor in Surgery, Royal Victoria Hospital, Belfast, 1952; Lecturer in Surgery, Liverpool University, 1957; Senior Lecturer in Surgery, Aberdeen University, 1959-60, and Surgeon, Aberdeen Royal Infirmary, 1959-89. Member, Grampian Health Board, 1973-77, Chairman, 1989-93; Chairman, Scottish Committee for Hospital Medical Services, 1976-79; elected Member, General Medical Council, since 1979; Chairman: Scottish Joint Consultants Committee, 1984-89, Representative Body, British Medical Association, 1984-87; President, Aberdeen Medico-Chirurgical Society, 1989-90; Examiner: Belfast, Dublin, Dundee, Edinburgh, Sydney, University of West Indies; Burgess of Aberdeen. Publications: Peptic Ulcer; Pye's Surgical Handicraft; Crohn's Disease; Scientific Foundations of Surgery. Recreations: Fellow, Royal Philatelic Society, London; licensed radio amateur, GM4 CHX. Address: (h.) 7 Fasaich, Gairloch IV21 2BD; T.-01445 712398.

Kyle, Peter McLeod, MBChB, FRCS(Edin), FRCS(Glas), FRCOphth. Consultant Ophthalmologist, Southern General Hospital NHS Trust, since 1982 (Clinical Director of Ophthalmology, since 1995); Honorary Clinical Senior Lecturer, Glasgow University, since 1985; Member, Medical Appeal Tribunals, Scotland, since 1986; b. 19.8.51, Rutherglen; m., Valerie Anne Steele; 1 s.; 2 d. Educ. High School of Glasgow; Glasgow University. Lecturer in Ophthalmology, Glasgow University, 1980-84. Convener, Ophthalmology Sub-committee, Royal College of Physicians and Surgeons of Glasgow; Member, Opthalmology Specialist Advisory Board, Royal College of Surgeons of Edinburgh. Recreations: walking; skiing. Address: (h.) 36 Sutherland Avenue, Glasgow; T.-0141-427 4400; The Stables, Earlsferry, Fife; T.-01333 330647.

Kynoch, George Alexander Bryson, BSc. Non-Executive Chairman, Silvertech International plc, since 1997; MP (Conservative), Kincardine and Deeside, 1992-97; Parliamentary Under Secretary of State for Scotland – Minister for Industry and Local Government, 1995-97; b. 7.10.46, Keith; m., Dr. Rosslyn Margaret McDevitt; 1 s.; 1 d. Educ. Cargilfield School, Edinburgh; Glenalmond College, Perth; Bristol University. Plant Engineer, ICI Ltd., Nobel Division, 1968-71; G. and G. Kynoch PLC, 1971-92, latterly as Group Executive Director; Non-Executive Director: Kynoch Group PLC, Aardvark Clear Mine Ltd., 1992-95; Member, Aberdeen and District Milk Marketing Board, 1988-92; Director, Moray Badenoch and Strathspey Local Enterprise Co. Ltd., 1991-92; Chairman, Scottish Woollen Publicity Council, 1983-90; President, Scottish Woollen Industry, 1990-91; Vice Chairman, Northern Area, Scottish Conservative and Unionist Association, 1991-92. Recreations: golf; skiing; travel. Address: (h.) Newton of Drumduan, Dess, Aboyne, Aberdeenshire AB34 5BD.

L

Lacey, Professor Andrew Alfred, BA, MSc, DPhil, MA, FRSE. Professor of Mathematics, Heriot-Watt University, since 1996; b. 1.12.53, Newcastle upon Tyne. Educ. Royal Grammar School, Newcastle upon Tyne; New College, University of Oxford. Royal Commission for the Exhibition of 1851 Research Fellow, University of Oxford, 1979-80, 1982; Postdoctoral Research Fellow, Victoria University of Wellington, New Zealand, 1980-82; Lecturer in Mathematics, 1982-87, Reader, 1987-96, Heriot-Watt University. Joint Winner, Sir Edmund Whittaker Memorial Prize, 1989. Publications: Non-Classical Continuum Mechanics (Co-Editor), 1987; Reaction-Diffusion Equations (Co-Editor), 1990. Recreations: photography; walking. Address: (b.) Department of Mathematics, Heriot-Watt University, Riccarton, Edinburgh EH14 4AS; T.-0131-451 3228.

Lacy, Rev. David William, BA, BD. Minister, Henderson Parish Church, Kilmarnock, since 1989; Vice Convener, General Assembly Business Committee, since 1996; Member, Judicial Commission of General Assembly; b. 26.4.52, Inverness; m., Joan Stewart Roberston; 1 s.; 1 d. Educ. Aberdeen Grammar School; High School of Glasgow; University of Strathclyde; University of Glasgow and Trinity College. Assistant Minister, St. George's West, Edinburgh, 1975-77; Minister, Knightswood: St. Margaret's, Glasgow, 1977-89. Chaplain, "U" Division, Strathclyde Police; Chaplain, Kilmarnock College. Recreations: sailing; snooker; choral singing. Address: 52 London Road, Kilmarnock, Ayrshire KA3 7AJ; T.-01563 523113.

Laidlaw, Bruce, ACIS. Administrative Secretary, Royal Scottish Academy, since 1995; b. 11.7.45, Edinburgh; m., Sandra; 1 s.; 1 d. Educ. Royal High School; Napier College, Edinburgh. Assistant Secretary, Cranston London Hotels Co. Ltd., 1963-65; public service, Edinburgh City, 1966-74; Elections Officer, Lothian Regional Council, 1975-79; public service, Lothian Regional Council, 1980-95. Recreations: fishing; skiing. Address: (b.) Royal Scottish Academy, The Mound, Edinburgh EH2 2EL; T.-0131-225 6671.

Laidlaw, Professor Emeritus James Cameron, MA, PhD. Emeritus Professor of French, Aberdeen University (Professor of French, 1975-92); Honorary Fellow, Arts Faculty, Edinburgh University; b. 3.3.37, Ecclefechan; m., Elizabeth Fernie Bosomworth; 1 s.; 2 d. Educ. George Watson's College, Edinburgh; Edinburgh University; Trinity Hall, Cambridge. Research Fellow, Trinity Hall, Cambridge, 1961-63; Lecturer in Medieval French, Queen's University, Belfast, 1963-65; University Assistant Lecturer (from 1969 University Lecturer) in French, and Fellow, Trinity Hall, Cambridge, 1965-74; Visiting Fellow, Gonville and Caius College, Cambridge, 1986-87; Visiting Professor, Victoria University of Wellington, New Zealand, 1990-91; Vice-Principal, Aberdeen University, 1984-86. Member Arts Sub-Committee, University Grants Committee, 1980-89; Adviser in Modern Languages, Universities Funding Council, 1989-91; Honorary Secretary, Modern Humanities Research Association, 1961-67; Chevalier des palmes académiques. Publications: The Future of the Modern Humanities (Editor), 1969; The Poetical Works of Alain Chartier, 1974; Alain Chartier: poemes, 1988. Recreations: walking; cycling. Address: (h.) Orchard Walls, Traquair, Innerleithen EH44 6PU; T.-01896 831227.

Laing, David Kemlo, LLB. Managing Partner, Ledingham Chalmers, since 1996; b. 17.6.53, Aberdeen; m., Marina Maclean; 2 d. Educ. Robert Gordon's College, Aberdeen; University of Edinburgh. Clark and Wallace, Aberdeen, 1974-76; C. and P. H. Chalmers, Aberdeen, 1976-78, Partner, 1978-90; Partner, Ledingham Chalmers, 1991. Recreations: music; outdoors. Address: (b.) 1 Golden Square, Aberdeen AB10 1HA; T.-01224 408510.

Laing, The Hon. Mark Hector, MA. Managing Director, Simmers of Edinburgh, since 1996; Chairman, Capital Enterprise Trust; Member, Executive Council, Scottish Business in the Community; b. 22.2.51, London; m., Susanna Crawford; 1 s.; 2 d. Educ. Eton College; Cambridge University. United Biscuits p.l.c., 1972-96: Factory Director, Glasgow, 1985; Production Director, McVities, 1988; Managing Director, Simmers Biscuits, 1990. Recreations: walking; gardening; fishing; shooting. Address: (b.) Simmers of Edinburgh Ltd., 90 Peffermill Road, Edinburgh EH16 5UU; T.-0131-661 3384.

Lally, Patrick James, JP, HRGI, FRSA. Rt. Hon. Lord Provost of the City of Glasgow and Lord Lieutenant, City of Glasgow; Commandeur, Ordre National du Merite (France); Chairman, Greater Glasgow and Clyde Valley Tourist Board, since 1996; Director, Glasgow Cultural Enterprises, since 1988; b. Glasgow; m., Margaret Beckett McGuire; 2 s. Elected, Corporation of Glasgow, 1966-75 (Deputy Leader, 1972-75); elected City of Glasgow Council, 1975-77, and 1980-96; City Treasurer, 1984-86; Leader, City of Glasgow District Council, 1986-92 and 1994-96; Chairman, Greater Glasgow Tourist Board, 1989-96; Director: Scottish Exhibition Centre Ltd., Glasgow International Jazz Festival; Hon. Director, Chinese Peoples Association for Friendship with Foreign Countries; Hon. Member, Royal Glasgow Institute of Fine Arts; Hon. Citizen, Dalian, China. Recreations: enjoying the arts; reading; watching TV; football. Address: (b.) City Chambers, George Square, Glasgow; T.-0141-287 4201.

Lamb, Rev. A. Douglas, MA, FSA (Scot). Parish Minister, Dalry: St. Margaret's, since 1973; Convener, Mission and Evangelism Resource Committee, Board of National Mission, Church of Scotland, since 1995; b. 9.11.36, Glasgow; m., Jean A. Beattie; 3 s.; 1 d. Educ. Hermitage School, Helensburgh; Glasgow University; Princeton Seminary. Assistant Minister: First Presbyterian, Philadelphia, Airdrie West; Parish Minister, Unst (Shetland). Recreations: hill-walking; history; continental travel. Address: St. Margaret's Manse, Dalry KA24 4DA; T.-01294 832234.

Lamb, Alan Francis, MSc, BSc. Chairman, Scottish Gymnastics, since 1995; b. 17.1.52, Ashby-de-la-Zouch; m., Carol Ann; 1 s.; 1 d. Educ. Ashby-de-la-Zouch Boys' Grammar School; Heriot-Watt University. British National Gymnastics judge; Past President, Dunfermline Gymnastic Club; Past Chairman, Dunfermline Federation of Gym Clubs. Recreations: walking; gardening. Address: (h.) 34 Inchcolm Drive, North Queensferry, Fife.

Lamb, Professor Joseph Fairweather, MB, ChB, BSc, PhD, FRCPEdin, FRSE, FRSA. Honorary Professor; Chandos Professor of Physiology, St. Andrews University, 1969-93; Chairman, Save British Science Society, 1986-97; b. 18.7.28, Brechin; m., 1, Olivia Jane Horne; 3 s.; 1 d.; 2, Bridget Cecilia Cook; 2 s. Educ. Brechin High School; Edinburgh University. National Service, 1947-49; House Surgeon, Dumfries Royal Infirmary, 1955-56; House Physician, Eastern General Hospital, Edinburgh, 1956; Research Scholar, then Lecturer, Edinburgh University, 1957-61; Lecturer, then Senior Lecturer, Glasgow University, 1961-69; Editor, Journal of Physiology, 1968-74; Senior Secretary, Physiological Society, 1982-85; Chairman, Gas Greed campaign, 1994-95. Publication: Essentials of Physiology, 1980. Recreations: boat-building; sailing; amateur radio. Address: (h.) Kenbrae, 23 Millbank, Cupar KY15 5DP.

Lamb, Colonel Tom Bell Maxwell, OBE, CStJ, MA, FSA (Scot), DL. Retired Colonel, HM Forces; Deputy Lord Lieutenant, Argyll & Bute, since 1987; b. 23.11.18, Lanark; m., Sheina Barclay Dempster; 2 s.; 1 d. Educ. Lanark Secondary School; Heriot-Watt College. Commercial Bank of Scotland, 1935-38; Chartered Bank of India, 1938-39; Regular Officer, Queen's Own Cameron Highlanders, 1940-70; staff, Stirling University, 1970-75; Controller, The Burn, Edzell, 1975-84. Croix de Guerre, 1945; Meritorious Service Decoration (Singapore), 1964; mentioned in Despatches, 1945; Commander of St. John, 1982. Recreation: golf (Member, R. & A.). Address: (h.) Seafield, Kilchattan Bay, Isle of Bute; T.-Kilchattan Bay 682.

Lambie, David, BSc (Hons), DipEd, FEIS. Chairman, Development Committee and Member, Management Committee, Cunninghame Housing Association, since 1992; Chairman, Saltcoats Labour Party, 1992-96; MP (Labour), Cunninghame South, 1970-92; b. 13.7.25, Saltcoats; m., Netta Merrie; 1 s.; 4 d. Educ. Ardrossan Academy; Glasgow University; Geneva University. Teacher, Glagow Corporation, 1950-70. Secretary, All Party Committee for Energy Studies, 1980-92; chaired Select Committee on Scottish Affairs, 1981-87; UK Member, Council of Europe and Western European Union, 1987-92; Chairman, PLP Aviation Committee, 1988-92. Recreation: watching junior football. Address: (h.) 11 Ivanhoe Drive, Saltcoats, Ayrshire KA21 6LS; T.-01294 464843.

Lammie, Neil Robertson, FCCA. Director of Finance and Executive Board Member, Ayrshire and Arran Health Board, since 1992; b. 4.11.41, Ayr; m., Winnie; 2 s.; 1 d. Educ. Marr College, Troon. Treasurer, Fife Health Board, 1979-85; Treasurer, Ayrshire and Arran Health Board, 1985-91. Recreations: sport in general, rugby union and golf in particular. Address: (b.) Seafield House, Doonfoot Road, Ayr KA7 4DW; T.-01292 611040.

Lamont, Colin C., MA, PhD. Headteacher, Ross High School, Tranent, since 1989; b. 6.10.44, Glasgow; m.; 2 s. Educ. Robert Gordon's College, Aberdeen; Aberdeen University; Edinburgh University. Teacher, Merchiston Castle School, Edinburgh; Principal Teacher, Robert Gordon's College, Aberdeen; Adviser in English, Renfrew Division, Strathclyde; Headteacher, Gracemount High School, Edinburgh. Address: (b.) Ross High School, Well Wynd, Tranent, East Lothian EH33 2EQ; T.-01875 610433.

Lamont, Rev. Stewart Jackson, BSc, BD. Minister, Church of Scotland, since 1972; Freelance Journalist and Broadcaster (Religious Affairs Correspondent, Glasgow Herald), since 1980; Parish Minister, Kinning Park, Glasgow, since 1991; b. 8.1.47, Broughty Ferry; m., Larisa V. Gaidakova. Educ. Grove Academy, Broughty Ferry; St. Andrews University. General Council Assessor, St. Andrews University Court, 1970-82; Producer, BBC Religious Department, 1972-80; Freelance Radio and Television Presenter and Producer, 1980-91; part-time Minister, Abernyte, 1980-82. Publications: The Third Angle, 1978; Is Anybody There?, 1980; Religion and the Supernatural (Co-Author), 1985; Religion Inc. (Scientology), 1986; Scotland 2000 (BBC TV, 1987; Church and State, 1989; In Good Faith, 1989; The Swordbearer: John Knox, 1991; Glasgow Herald Book of Glasgow (Contributor); St. Andrews Rock, 1993; Life of St. Andrew, 1997. Winner, Scottish Schools Debating Competition, 1965; President of the Union, St. Andrews, 1969. Recreations: cooking; music; foreign travel. Address: Apartment 9, 10 Mavisbank Gardens, Glasgow G51 1HG; T.-0141-427 2191.

Lamont, William David Dawson, CA, IRRV. Head of Revenues, Finance Service, The Highland Council, since 1996; b. 14.11.49, Irvine; m., Eleanor; 1 s.; 1 d. Educ. Irvine Royal Academy; Institute of Chartered Accountants of Scotland (Glasgow University). Alexander Sloan & Company, Glasgow, 1966-73; Depute Burgh Chamberlain, Royal Burgh of Irvine, 1973-75; Depute Director of Finance, Argyll & Bute District Council, 1975-90; Director of Finance, Argyll & Bute District Council, 1990-96. Recreations: family; travel; music; Rotary. Address: (b.) The Highland Council, Glenurquhart Road, Inverness IV3 5NX; T.-01463 702404.

Lamont-Brown, Raymond, MA, AMIET, MJS, FSA (Scot). Author and Broadcaster; Lecturer, Centre for External Services, St. Andrews University, since 1978, Centre for Continuing Education, Dundee University, since 1988; Founder, Japan Research Projects, since 1965; b. 20.9.39, Horsforth, Leeds; m., Dr. Elizabeth Moira McGregor. Educ. Wheelwright Grammar School, Dewsbury; Bradford Technical College; SOAS; Nihon Daigaku, Japan. Honorary Secretary/Treasurer, Society of Authors in Scotland, 1982-89; Past President, St. Andrews Rotary Club; Vice-Chairman, St. Andrews Community Council, 1988-91; Chairman, Arthritis Care Liaison Committee (Central, Fife and Tayside), since 1991; Member, Council, Arthritis Care, since 1991. Publications: 50 published books, including Discovering Fife; Phantoms of the Sea; The Life and Times of Berwick-upon-Tweed; The Life and Times of St. Andrews; Royal Murder Mysteries; Scottish Epitaphs; Scottish Superstitions; Scottish Traditions and Festivals; Famous Scots; Scottish Witchcraft; Around St. Andrews; Scottish Folklore; Kamikaze: Japan's Suicide Samurai; Scotland of 100 Years Ago; Kempeitai: Japan's Dreaded Military Police. Address: (h.) 11 Seabourne Gardens, Broughty Ferry, Dundee DD5 2RT; T.-01382 732032.

Lamprell-Jarrett, Peter Neville, KCSG, KCHS, PPIAAS, FIAS, FFB, FSA(Scot), FRSA. Partner, Archard & Partners, Architects and Surveyors, since 1954; b. 23.6.19, Margate; m., Kathleen Furner; 1 s.; 1 d. Educ. Vernon House Preparatory School; Cliftonville College. Architectural Assistant, LCC (later GLC) Housing Department, 1947-49; Deputy Controller of Works, Land Settlement Association, 1950-54; President, Incorporated Association of Architects and Surveyors, 1967-68; Kt. Commander: Equestrian Order Holy Sepulchre of Jerusalem, 1974, Pontifical Order of St. Gregory the Great, 1975; responsible for design of many Catholic schools and churches; Freeman, City of London; Life Vice President, London Caledonian Catholic Association; Past Chairman, Archdiocese of Westminster Catholic Parents and Electors Association; Liveryman, Worshipful Company of Wheelwrights, since 1978. Recreations: painting; walking; fishing; classical music. Address: (h.) Carrick House, Carrick Castle, by Lochgoil, Argyll PA24 8AF; T.-Lochgoilhead 703394.

Landale, Sir David William Neil, KCVO, DL. Chairman, Malcolm Sargent Fund in Scotland, since 1996; b. 27.5.34, London; m., (Norah) Melanie; 3 s. Educ. Eton School; Balliol College, Oxford (MA). Black Watch, Royal Highland Regiment, 1952-54; Jardine Matheson & Co. Ltd., 1958-75, served in Hong Kong, Thailand, Taiwan and Japan (Director, 1967-75); Director, Matheson & Co. Ltd., 1975; Secretary and Keeper of the Records, Duchy of Cornwall, 1987-93; Member, Royal Company of Archers, Queen's Bodyguard for Scotland, since 1966. Recreations: all countryside pursuits; theatre; reading (history). Address: (h.) Dalswinton, Dumfries; T.-01387 740 208/279.

Lander, Ronald, BSc, Comp. IEE, FScotvec, FSQA. Chairman and Managing Director: Scotlander plc, since 1985, Scetlander Ltd., since 1986; b. 5.8.42, Glasgow; m., Elizabeth Stirling; 2 s. Educ. Allan Glen's School; Glasgow University. Chairman and Managing Director, Lander Grayburn & Co. Limited, 1970-83; Deputy Managing Director, Lander Alarm Company (Scotland) Limited, 1975-79; Managing Director, Lander Alarms Limited and

Lander Alarms (Scotland) Limited, 1979-85; Chairman, Lander & Jess Limited, 1983-87; Director, Centre for Entrepreneurial Development, Glasgow University, 1985-88. Member, CBI Scottish Council, 1977-83, 1984-90 and since 1992; (founding) Chairman, CBI Scotland's Smaller Firms' Working Group, 1977-80; founding Chairman, Entrepreneurial Exchange, 1995-96; founder Member, CBI Industrial Policy Committee, London, 1978-86; Chairman, CBI Scotland Smaller Firms' Committee, 1993-95; Chairman, Scottish Fire Prevention Council, 1979-80; Member, Glasgow University Appointments Committee, since 1979; CBI Representative, Home Office/CBI/TUC Joint Committee on Prison Industries, 1980-87; Industrial Member, Understanding British Industry, Scotland, 1981-89; Member, Council, Scottish Business School, 1982-87; Director, British Security Industry Association Council, 1984-85; Governor, Scottish Sports Aid Foundation, 1985-88; Vice-Chairman, CBI Scotland Education and Training Committee, 1986-87; Member: Kincraig Committee (review of parole system and related matters), 1987-89, Manpower Services Committee for Scotland (later the Training Agency), 1987-88; founder Chairman, Local Employer Network (LENS) Scottish Co-ordinating Committee, 1987; Chairman, CBI Scotland Education and Training Committee, 1987-89; Director, SCOTVEC, 1987-93; Member, CBI Business/Education Task Force (the Cadbury Report), 1988; Member, Scottish Consultative Council on the Curriculum, 1988-91; Vice-Convener, Scottish Education/Industry Committee, 1988-91; founder Member, Glasgow Action, 1985; Member, Secretary of State for Scotland's Crime Prevention Committee, 1984-87; Companion IEE, 1986; Board Member, Glasgow Development Agency, since 1991; Visiting/Honorary Professor, Glasgow University, since 1991; National Judge, National Training Awards, 1989-92. Address: (b.) Lander Software, Glasgow Software Centre, 1 Atlantic Quay, Broomielaw, Glasgow, G2 8JE; T.-0141 226 5611.

Lane, Professor David Philip, BSc, PhD, FRSE, FRS, FRCPath. Professor of Molecular Oncology, Department of Biochemistry, Dundee University, since 1990; Director, Cancer Research Campaign Cell Transformation Group, since 1990; Gibb Fellow, Cancer Research Campaign, since 1990; b. 1.7.52, London; m., Professor Ellen Birgitte Lane (qv); 1 s.; 1 d. Educ. John Fisher School, Purley; University College, London. Lecturer in Zoology, then Lecturer in Biochemistry, Imperial College, London; Principal Scientist, Imperial Cancer Research Fund, South Mimms. Publications: (book) Antibodies, a laboratory manual; 200 articles. Recreations: walking; tennis; motor bikes. Address: (b.) CRC Laboratories, Dundee University, Dundee DD1 4HN; T.-01382 344982.

Lane, Professor Ellen Birgitte, BSc, PhD. Cox Professor of Anatomy and Cell Biology, Dundee University, since 1991; Director, Cancer Research Campaign Cell Structure Research Group, since 1990; b. 24.12.50, Welwyn Garden City; m., David Philip Lane (qv); 1 s.; 1 d. Educ. Withington Girls' School, Manchester; University College, London. Research Assistant, Imperial College of Science and Technology, 1975-77, University College, 1977-78, Cold Spring Harbour Laboratories, New York, 1978-80; Imperial Cancer Research Fund, 1980-90; ICRF Clare Hall Laboratories, 1985-90. Publications: scientific papers in cell biology and cancer research. Address: (b.) CRC Laboratories, Department of Anatomy and Physiology, Medical Sciences Institute, Dundee University, Dundee DD1 4HN; T.-01382 344921.

Lang, Lt.-Gen. Sir Derek, KCB (1967), DSO (1944), MC (1941), DL; b. 7.10.13, Guildford; 1 s.; 1 d. Educ. Wellington College; RMC, Sandhurst. Director of Army Training, 1964-66; GOC-in-C, Scottish Command, and Governor of Edinburgh Castle, 1966-69. President, Army Cadet Force Association (Scotland), 1974-86. Recreations:

golf; fishing; shooting; music. Address: (h.) Templeland, Kirknewton, Midlothian EH27 8DJ; T.01506 883211.

Lang of Monkton, Baron (Ian Bruce Lang), PC, OStJ, BA. President of the Board of Trade, 1995-97; Life Peer; b. 27.6.40, Glasgow; m., Sandra Caroline Montgomerie; 2 d. Educ. Lathallan School; Rugby School; Sidney Sussex College, Cambridge. MP (Conservative) Galloway and Upper Nithsdale, 1983-97 (Galloway, 1979-83); Member, Select Committee on Scottish Affairs, 1979-81; Honorary President, Scottish Young Conservatives, 1982-84; Trustee, Glasgow Savings Bank and West of Scotland TSB, 1969-82; Lord Commissioner of HM Treasury, 1983-86; Scottish Whip, 1981-83; Vice-Chairman, Scottish Conservative Party, 1983-87; Parliamentary Under Secretary of State, Scottish Office, 1986-87, and at Department of Employment, 1986; Minister of State, Scottish Office, 1987-90; Secretary of State for Scotland, 1990-95. Member, Queen's Bodyguard for Scotland (Royal Company of Archers), since 1974; Insurance Broker and Company Director, 1962-81. Address (b.) House of Lords, Westminster, London SW1A OPW.

Langford, Professor David Anthony, FCIOB, MSc, MPhil, MIMgt, FRSA. Barr Professor of Construction, Strathclyde University, since 1991; b. 6.5.50, Nottingham; m., Victoria; 1 d. Educ. Barstable School, Basildon; Bristol Polytechnic; Aston University; Cranfield School of Management. MSc Course Director, Department of Building Technology, Brunel University, 1975; Director of Postgraduate Studies, Bath University, 1987. Address: (b.) Department of Civil Engineering, Strathclyde University, Glasgow G4 0NG; T.-0141-552 4400.

Langley, Crawford James, LLB (Hons), DPA, ACIS, NP. Director of Legal and Corporate Services, Aberdeen City Council, since 1995; Advocate in Aberdeen; b. 21.11.51, Glasgow; m., Janette Law Hamilton. Educ. Bellahouston Academy, Glasgow; Glasgow University. Legal apprentice, Corporation of Glasgow, 1973-75; various legal posts, Strathclyde Regional Council, 1975-89, Principal Solicitor, 1984-89; Depute Director of Law and Administration, Tayside Regional Council, 1989-91; Director of Law and Administration, Tayside Regional Council, 1991-95. Part-time Tutor in Public Administration, Dundee University; Assistant Area Commissioner, Scout Association. Recreations: travel; gardening. Address: (h.) Canouan, Eassie, Angus DD8 1SG; T.-Glamis 518.

Lansdowne, 8th Marquess of (George John Charles Mercer Nairne Petty-Fitzmaurice); b. 27.11.12; 2 s.; 1 d. Minister of State for Colonial Affairs, 1962-64, for Commonwealth Relations, 1963-64. Address: Meikleour House, Perthshire, PH2 6EA.

Larg, Fiona Margaret, BA (Hons), CA. Chief Executive, Inverness and Nairn Enterprise, since 1991; b. 6.3.58, Inverness. Educ. Inverness Royal Academy; Stirling University. Trainee Chartered Accountant, 1980-84; Investment Manager, Senior Investment Manager, Highlands and Islands Development Board, 1984-89; Member, LEC Unit, Scottish Office, 1989-90 (seconded to establish local enterprise company network in Highlands and Islands); Project Manager, Inverness and Nairn Enterprise, 1990-91. President, Soroptimist International of Inverness, 1996-98. Recreations: reading; walking; theatre. Address: (b.) Castle Wynd, Inverness IV2 3DW; T.-01463 713504.

Larg, Ian, FCCA, MInstMgt. Chief Executive, North of Scotland Milk Co-operative Society Ltd., since 1996; Director, Claymore Dairies Ltd., since 1996; b. 12.8.56, Dundee; m., Elaine Elizabeth; 2 s.; 1 d. Educ. Morgan Academy, Dundee; Dundee College of Technology. Scott Oswald & Co., CA, Inverness; Group Chief Accountant, A. Tulloch & Sons (Holdings) Ltd., 1983-86; Financial

Controller, Elbar PLC, 1986; Financial Director, North of Scotland Milk Marketing Board, 1987-94; Financial Director, North of Scotland Milk Co-operative Society, 1995-96. Recreation: hill-walking. Address: (h.) The Rowan, Loch Flemington, Gollanfield, Inverness; T.-01667 462469.

Larkin, Professor Maurice John Milner, MA, PhD. Professor of Modern European History, Edinburgh University, since 1976; b. 12.8.32, Harrow on the Hill; m., Enid Thelma Lowe; 1 s.; 1 d. Educ. St. Philip's Grammar School, Birmingham; Trinity College, Cambridge. Assistant Lecturer, then Lecturer, Glasgow University, 1958-65; Lecturer, then Senior Lecturer, then Reader, Kent University, 1965-76. Publications: Gathering Pace: Continental Europe 1870-1945, 1969; Church and State after the Dreyfus Affair, 1974; Man and Society in Nineteenth-Century Realism, 1977; France since the Popular Front, 1988; Religion, politics and preferment in France since 1890, 1995. Recreations: bird-watching; music; films. Address: (b.) History Department, Edinburgh University, Edinburgh EH8 9JY; T.-0131-650 3754.

Last, Professor Frederick Thomas, DSc, ARCS, FRSE, SHM. Applied Biologist; Honorary Professor, Institute of Ecology and Resource Management, Edinburgh University, since 1972; b. 5.2.28, Wembley; m., Pauline Mary Cope; 2 s. Educ. Haberdashers' Aske's Hampstead School; Imperial College of Science and Technology, London. Rothamsted Experimental Station, Herts, 1950-61; Chief Plant Pathologist to Government of Sudan, 1956-58; Head, Mycology and Bacteriology, Glasshouse Crops Research Institute, Sussex, 1961-69; Visiting Professor, Pennsylvania State University, 1969-70; Member of Directorate, Institute of Terrestrial Ecology, Midlothian, 1970-86; Commissioner, Red Deer Commission, 1981-86; Visiting Professor, Agriculture and Environmental Science, Newcastle upon Tyne University, 1986-94; Chairman, Advisory Committee on Sites of Special Scientific Interest, 1992-96; Chairman, Tree Advice Trust, since 1993; Advisor, Chongqing Institute of Environmental Science, since 1993; Board Member, Scottish Natural Heritage, since 1996; Member, Joint Nature Conservation Committee, since 1996. Publications: Tree Physiology and Yield Improvement (Joint Editor), 1976; Land and its Uses, Actual and Potential: An Environmental Appraisal (Joint Editor), 1986; Acidic Deposition, Its Nature and Impacts (Joint Editor). Recreations: gardening; philately; travelling. Address: (h.) Furuly, Seton Mains, Longniddry, East Lothian EH32 0PG; T.-01875 852102.

Lathe, Professor Richard Frank, BSc, Dr. ès Sci. Professorial Fellow, Edinburgh University, since 1989; b. 23.4.52, London; m., Margaret. Educ. Edinburgh University; Universite Libre de Bruxelles. Assistant Scientific Director, Transgene SA, Strasbourg; Principal Scientific Officer, ABRO, Edinburgh; Professor of Genetics/Genetic Engineering, University of Strasbourg; Director/Scientific Director, Ecole Superieure de Biotechnologie de Strasbourg. Publications: more than 100 scientific papers. Recreations: guitar; squash. Address: (b.) King's Buildings, West Mains Road, Edinburgh EH9 3JQ; T.-0131-650 5890.

Lauderdale, Earl of (Patrick Francis Maitland), BA (Hons) (Oxon). Company Director; b. 17.3.11, Walsall; m., Stanka Lozanitch; 2 s.; 2 d. Educ. Lancing College; Brasenose College, Oxford. Journalist, Fleet Street, 1934-39; War Correspondent, Poland, 1939; Balkans/Danubian Correspondent, The Times, 1939-41; War Correspondent, the Pacific, News Chronicle, 1941-43; Foreign Office, 1943-45; Editor, The Fleet Street Letter Service, 1945-51; MP (Conservative), Lanark, 1951-59; Peer, since 1968; Chairman, Lords Energy Committee, 1974-79; Founder/Deputy Chairman, Parliamentary Group for Energy Studies, since 1983; Guardian, Shrine of Our Lady

of Walsingham, since 1955 (now Emeritus); Chairman, Parliamentary 'Church in Danger' Group, 1988-95; Hereditary Bearer of the National Flag of Scotland. Recreations: reading; travel; pilgrimages to St. Mary's, Haddington.

Laurenson, Arthur Bruce, OBE, FRSA. Consultant; Chairman, Shetland Catch Ltd., since 1992; b. 22.7.31, Lerwick; m., Janet S. Mullay; 2 d. Educ. Anderson High School. Assistant Clerk and Collector, Lerwick Harbour Trust, 1947-64; Assistant Clerk and Treasurer, 1964-1968; General Manager and Clerk, 1972; Consultant, since 1991. Honorary Sheriff; Member, Lerwick Lifeboat Committee. Recreations: crofting; breeding Shetland ponies; gardening. Address: (h.) Vatnagarth, 2 Lovers Loan, Lerwick, Shetland ZE1 0BA; T.-01595 692799.

Laurenson, James Tait, FCA. Chairman, Erskine Stewart's Melville Governing Council; Non-Executive Director: I & S UK Smaller Companies Trust plc, since 1983, Hiscox Harrison Ltd., since 1992, Frizzell Bank, Ltd., since 1996, Fidelity Special Values plc, since 1994, Contra-Cyclical Investment Trust plc, since 1996; Chairman, Nippon Assets Investments SA, since 1983; b. 15.3.41, Farnborough; m., Hilary Josephine; 1 s.; 3 d. Educ. Eton College; Magdalene College, Cambridge. Ivory & Sime PLC: joined 1968; Partner, 1970; Director, 1975; left 1983; Managing Director, Tayburn Design Group Limited, 1983-84 (Chairman, 1984-88); Managing Director, Adam & Company Group plc, 1984-93. Recreations: spending time with the family; gardening. Address: (h.) Hill House, Kirknewton, Midlothian EH27 8DR; T.-01506 881990.

Laurie, Thomas, OBE, FRICS. Senior Partner, Keillor Laurie Martin Partnership, since 1991; b. 11.11.38, Wishaw; m., Jennifer Rose Dunthorne; 1 s.; 2 d. Educ. Hamilton Academy; Glasgow Technical College. Partner, Robert H. Soper & Co., Cumbernauld, 1964-77; Sole Principal, Thomas Laurie Associates, Cumbernauld and Glasgow, 1977-90. Founder Member, Cumbernauld Theatre Group, 1961; Board Member: Cottage Theatre, Cumbernauld, 1964-72, Traverse Theatre, 1972-76 (Chairman), WASPS; Member: Drama Panel, Scottish Arts Council, 1973-82, SAC, 1976-82. Recreations: traditional singing; all forms of art appreciation; hill-walking. Address: (h.) 21 Dunglass Avenue, Glasgow G14 9ED; T.-0141-959 4025.

Laver, Professor John David Michael Henry, MA (Hons), DipPh, PhD, DLitt, FBA, FRSE, FRSA, FIoA. Chairman, Humanities Research Board of the British Academy; Professor of Phonetics, Edinburgh University, since 1985; b. 20.1.38, Nowshera, Pakistan; m., Sandy Hutcheson; 3 s.; 1 d. Educ. Churcher's College, Petersfield; Edinburgh University. Assistant Lecturer, then Lecturer in Phonetics, Ibadan University, 1963-66 (Exchange Lecturer, Edinburgh University, 1964-65); Edinburgh University: Lecturer, then Senior Lecturer in Phonetics, 1966-80, Reader in Phonetics, 1980-84, Director, Centre for Speech Technology Research, 1984-89, Vice Principal, 1994-97; Visiting Assistant Professor, Department of Linguistics, University of California, 1971; Visiting Research Fellow, Macquarie University, Sydney, 1982; Information Technology Fellowship, Edinburgh, 1983-84; President, International Phonetic Association, 1991-95; Vice-President, Royal Society of Edinburgh, 1996-99. Publications: Communication in Face to Face Interaction (Joint Editor), 1972; Phonetics in Linguistics (Joint Editor), 1973; Voice Quality, 1979; The Phonetic Description of Voice Quality, 1980; The Cognitive Representation of Speech (Joint Editor), 1981; The Prospect of Future Speech Technology (Co-Author), 1987; Proceedings of the European Conference on Speech Technology (Co-Editor), 1987; Aspects of Speech Technology (Co-Editor), 1988; The Gift of Speech, 1991; Principles of Phonetics, 1994; Menschen und ihre Stimmen (Co-Author), 1994; The

Handbook of Phonetic Sciences (Co-Editor). Address: (b.) Humanities Research Board of the British Academy, Edinburgh University, Playfair Library, Old College, Edinburgh; T.-0131-650 2088.

Laverock, Edward, MA, LLB. Retired Solicitor; b. 21.10.19, Dunlop; m., Helen Moffat Harriet Mackison; 1 s.; 1 d. Educ. Hutchesons' Grammar School, Glasgow; Glasgow University. Partner, J. & W. Buchan, Peebles, 1945-86 (Senior Partner, 1954-86); Town Clerk, Peebles, 1948-75; Procurator Fiscal, Peeblesshire, 1949-76. Honorary Sheriff, since 1983. Address: (h.) Craigmount, Bonnington Road, Peebles; T.-01721 720314.

Law, Professor Robin C. C., BA, PhD, FRHS. Professor of African History, University of Stirling, since 1993; b. 7.8.44, Chester. Educ. Southend-on-Sea High School; Balliol College, University of Oxford; Centre of West African Studies, Birmingham. Research Assistant in African History, University of Lagos, Nigeria, 1966-69; Research Fellow in West African History, University of Birmingham, 1970-72; University of Stirling: Lecturer in History, 1972-78, Senior Lecturer, 1978-83, Reader, 1983-93. Editor, Journal of African History, 1974-82, 1991-95. Publications: The Oyo Empire c.1600-c.1836, 1977; The Horse in West African History, 1980; The Slave Coast of West Africa, 1550-1750, 1991. Address: (b.) Department of History, University of Stirling, Stirling FK9 4LA; T.-01786 833772.

Lawrence, Professor Andrew, BSc, PhD, FRAS. Regius Professor of Astronomy, Edinburgh University, since 1994; b. 23.4.54, Margate; partner, Debbie Ann Capel; 2 s.; 1 d. Educ. Chatham House Grammar School, Ramsgate; Edinburgh University; Leicester University. Exchange Scientist, Massachusetts Institute of Technology, 1980-81; Senior Research Fellow, Royal Greenwich Observatory, 1981-84; Research Assistant, then SERC Advanced Fellow, School of Mathematical Sciences, Queen Mary College, London, 1984-89; Lecturer, Physics Department, Queen Mary and Westfield College, London, 1989-94. Publications: over 60 in learned journals. Recreations: painting electrons and teasing publishers; acting. Address: (b.) Institute for Astronomy, Edinburgh University, Royal Observatory, Blackford Hill, Edinburgh.

Lawrie, Frank James. Director of Heritage Policy, Historic Scotland, since 1991; Member, Board of Management, Buildings of Scotland Trust; Trustee, Rainbow Sports Trust; Assessor, Railway Heritage Trust; Assessor, Edinburgh Old Town Renewal Trust; b. 30.10.45, Edinburgh; m., Ann Macamon Kerr; 2 s.; 1 d. Educ. Royal High School, Edinburgh. Executive Officer, Department of Agriculture and Fisheries for Scotland, 1964-70; Higher Executive Officer, Scottish Office Finance Division, 1970-78; Senior Executive Officer, 1978-81; Principal, Department of Agriculture and Fisheries for Scotland, 1981-88; Deputy Director, Historic Buildings and Monuments, Scotland, 1988-91. Recreations: railway archaeology; cricket; golf. Address: (b.) Longmore House, Salisbury Place, Edinburgh EH9 1SH; T.-0131 668 8727.

Lawrie, Nigel Gilbert, BSc, PhD. Head Teacher, Port Glasgow High School, since 1985; Member, Board of Management, Scottish Qualifications Authority, since 1997; b. 2.6.47, Edinburgh; m., Janet Clark Warnock; 1 d. Educ. Bearsden Academy; Strathclyde University. Chemistry Teacher, Hermitage Academy, Helensburgh, 1972-75; Principal Teacher of Chemistry, Dunoon Grammar School, 1975-81; Assistant Head Teacher, Garnock Academy, 1981-84; Depute Head Teacher, Castlehead High School, Paisley, 1984-85. President, Scottish Association for Teachers of Social and Vocational Skills, 1984-88; Member, National Council, Headteachers' Association of Scotland, since 1991; Member: Scottish Examination Board, 1994-97, Board, SCOTVEC, 1995-97. Recreations:

reading; gardening; football. Address: (b.) Port Glasgow High School, Marloch Avenue, Port Glasgow; T.-01475 705921.

Lawson, Alexander Adamson Hutt, MD, FRCPEdin. Consultant Physician, Fife Health Board, 1969-95; Honorary Senior Lecturer, Edinburgh University, 1979-95; Medical Member and Chairman, War Pensions Appeal Tribunal, Scotland, since 1979; b. 30.7.37, Dunfermline; m., Barbara Helen Donnet; 3 s.; 1 d. Educ. Dunfermline High School; Edinburgh University. Consultant Member, Clinical Teaching Staff, Faculty of Medicine, Edinburgh University, 1971-95; Postgraduate Tutor in Medicine, West Fife, 1973-81; Medical Assessor, General Medical Council, since 1982; Member, Fife Health Board, 1981-91 (Vice-Chairman, 1989-91); President: Scottish Society of Physicians, 1989-90, West Fife Medical Society, 1982-83; Life Trustee: Carnegie Dunfermline Trust and Carnegie United Kingdom Hero Fund, since 1980 (Vice Chairman, 1995-98, Chairman, since 1998), Carnegie United Kingdom Trust, since 1983; Member: Committee of Safety, Efficacy and Adverse Reactions of Drugs (Committee, Safety of Medicines, DHSS, London), 1982-84, Specialist Advisory Committee (UK) HCMT - General (Internal) Medicine, 1984-88; UK Representative to European Union of Medical Specialties, Monospecialty Committee for General Medicine, 1986-95. Publications: Common Acute Poisonings; Acute Poisoning in Principles and Practice of Medicine; Toxicology and Drug Monitoring in Chemical Diagnosis of Disease; scientific papers. Address: (h.) 16 Green Wood, Kinross, Tayside KY13 7FG; T.- Kinross 865193.

Lawson, John Philip, BSc, FEIS. Chairman, Scottish Youth Hostels Association, since 1980; Headteacher, St. Joseph's School, Linlithgow, 1974-94; b. 19.8.37, Bathgate; m., Diana Mary Neal. Educ. St. Mary's Academy, Bathgate; Edinburgh University; Moray House College of Education. Teacher, West Lothian, 1962-94; held various offices in the Educational Institute of Scotland, including President, West Lothian Local Association and Chairman, Lothian Regional Executive; Member, West Lothian Children's Panel, 1972-81; Member, SYHA National Executive, since 1966; Vice-Chairman, SYHA, 1975-80; awarded: Richard Schirrmann Medal by German Youth Hostels Association, 1988, Gezel van de Rugzak, Flemish Youth Hostels Association, 1993; a Director, Scottish Rights of Way Society Ltd., since 1979; a Director, Gatliff Hebridean Hostels Trust, since 1988; President, West Lothian Headteachers Association, 1986-88; President, Federation of Youth Hostels Associations in the European Community, since 1990; First Vice-President, International Youth Hostel Federation, since 1994. Recreations: hill-walking; music; reading. Address: (h.) Ledmore, Carnbee, Anstruther KY10 2RU; T.-01333 720312.

Lawson, Rev. Kenneth Charles, MA. Tutor-Organiser, Department of Parish Education, Church of Scotland, since 1984; Director, Ecumenical Spirituality Programme, Scottish Churches Open College, since 1991; b. 24.12.34, Agadir, Morocco; m., Mary Elizabeth Anderson; 3 s. Educ. Royal High School, Edinburgh; Preston Lodge School; Stranraer High School; Edinburgh University. Assistant Minister, Brechin Cathedral; Sub-Warden, St. Ninian's Training Centre, Crieff; Minister: Paisley South, Cumbernauld St. Mungo. Recreations: walking; reading; painting. Address: (b.) St. Colm's Education Centre and College, 18-23 Inverleith Terrace, Edinburgh EH3 5NS; T.- 0131-332 0343.

Lawson, Lilian Keddie, BSc (Hons), MBA. Service Director, Scotland, Royal National Institute for Deaf People, since 1993; b. 23.2.49, Pittenweem; m., John McDonald Young, OBE; 2 d. Educ. Donaldson's School, Edinburgh; Mary Hare Grammar School, Newbury; Edinburgh University; Strathclyde University.

Administrative Assistant, progressing to Head of Administration, British Deaf Association, 1981-92; Manager, Sign Language Interpreting Services, Strathclyde Regional Council, 1992-93. Publication: Words in Hand (Co-Author), 1984. Recreations: gardening; her children. Address: (b.) 9 Clairmont Gardens, Glasgow G3 7LW; T.-0141-332 0343.

Lawson, Rev. Ronald George, MA, BD. Minister, Wellpark Mid Kirk, Greenock, since 1988; b. 9.9.33, Glasgow; m., Beryl Read; 2 s.; 1 d. Educ. Allan Glen's School, Glasgow; University of Glasgow. Probationer, St. Martin's, Port Glasgow, 1961-63; Minister: Perceton and Dreghorn, Irvine, 1964-76, St. Andrew's, Dumbarton, 1976-88. Chaplain to various schools, and in industry, hospital, police. Recreations: walking; reading. Address: 101 Brisbane Street, Greenock PA16 8PA; T.-01475 721741.

Laybourn, Professor Peter John Robert, MA (Cantab), PhD, FIEE, FRSE. Professor of Electronic Engineering, Glasgow University, since 1985; b. 30.7.42, London; m., Ann Elizabeth Chandler; 2 d. Educ. William Hulme's Grammar School; Bristol Grammar School; Clare College, Cambridge. Research Assistant, Leeds University, 1963-66; Research Fellow, Southampton University, 1966-71; Lecturer, then Senior Lecturer, then Reader, Glasgow University, 1971-85; Honorary Editor, IEE Proceedings: Optoelectronics. Recreations: sailing; boat-building; plant collecting. Address: (h.) Ashgrove, Waterfoot Row, Thorntonhall, Glasgow; T.-0141-644 3992.

Lazarowicz, Mark, MA, LLB, DipLP. Advocate; b. 8.8.53. Educ. St. Andrews University; Edinburgh University. Member, Edinburgh District Council, 1980-96: Leader of the Council, 1986-93, Chairperson, Labour Group, 1993-94; Deputy Leader, COSLA Labour Group, 1990-93; Vice-Chairperson: Labour Party in Scotland, 1988-89, 1989-90, Edinburgh International Conference Centre Ltd., 1992-93; Chairperson, Edinburgh Tourist Board, 1993-94. Address: (h.) 17 Bellevue Place, Edinburgh; T.-0131-556 4438.

Leach, Professor Donald, CBE, BSc, CMath, FIMA, CPhys, MInstP, CEng, MBCS, FRSA. President, Edinburgh Chamber of Commerce, 1996-98; Principal, Queen Margaret College, Edinburgh, 1985-96; b. 24.6.31, Croydon; m., June Valentine Reid; 2 s.; 1 d. Educ. John Ruskin Grammar School, Croydon; London University (External). Pilot Officer, Navigator, RAF, 1951-53; Physicist, British Jute Trade Research Association, Dundee, 1955-65; Technical Director, A.R. Bolton & Co. Ltd., Edinburgh, 1965-66; Napier College: Lecturer and Senior Lecturer in Mathematics, 1966-68, Head, Department of Mathematics and Computing, 1968-74, Assistant Principal/Dean, Faculty of Science, 1974-85. Member, South-Eastern Regional Hospital Board, 1969-74, and Lothian Health Board, 1977-81; Member: Scottish Health Service Information Processing and Computer Systems Advisory Group, 1979-86, Computer Steering Committee (Chairman), 1981-86; Institute of Mathematics: Council Member, 1978-81, Chairman, Scottish Branch, 1980-83, Member, Joint IMA-Royal Society of London Mathematical Education Committee, 1981-84; Council for National Academic Awards: Member, various boards, 1975-79, Science Technology and Society Board, 1979-82 (Chairman, 1981-82), Committee for Scotland, 1987-92; Chairman: Science Technology and Society Association, 1982-85, Mathematics and Computing Course Committees, SCOTEC/SCOTBEC, 1981-85; Hon. Secretary, Committee of Principals and Directors of Scottish Central Institutions (COPADOCI), 1985-88, Chairman, 1988-92; Member: Council for Professions Supplementary to Medicine, since 1985, Executive, Scottish Council (Development and Industry), since 1987, Board of Directors, Edinburgh Chamber of Commerce, since 1991, Council, World Association for Cooperative Education, 1991-97, Board of

Directors, Higher Education Quality Council, 1992-96, Board of Directors, Capital Enterprise Trust, since 1993; President, Leith Chamber of Commerce, 1994-96; Honorary Fellow, Society of Chiropodists and Podiatrists, 1991; Liberal candidate, West Edinburgh, 1959, East Fife, 1961; Labour candidate, West Perthshire, 1970. Recreations: badminton; walking; skiing; cooking. Address: (h.) 8 Ravelston House Park, Edinburgh EH4 3LU; T.-0131-332 3826.

Leake, Professor Bernard Elgey, BSc (Hons), PhD, DSc (Bristol), DSc (Glas). Professor of Geology and Keeper of the Geological Collections in the Hunterian Museum, Glasgow University, 1974-97 (Professor Emeritus, since 1997); b. 29.7.32, Grimsby; m., Gillian Dorothy Dobinson; 5 s. Educ. Wirral Grammar School; Liverpool University. Leverhulme Postdoctorate Research Fellow, Liverpool University, 1955-57; Lecturer in Geology, then Reader, Bristol University, 1957-74. Lyell Medal, Geological Society, 1977; FRSE; President: Geological Society, 1986-88, (Treasurer, 1981-85 and 1989-96), Mineralogical Society, 1998-2000; Treasurer, Geologists' Association, since 1997. Address: (b.) Department of Geology, Glasgow University; T.-0141-330 5435.

Lean, Professor Michael E. J., MA, MD, FRCP (Edin), FRCPS (Glas). Professor of Human Nutrition, University of Glasgow, since 1992; Honorary Consultant Physician, Greater Glasgow Health Board, since 1990; b. 16.3.52, Chester; m., Annie S. Anderson; 3 s.; 2 d. Educ. Glenalmond; Downing College, Cambridge; St. Bartholomews Medical School. RHO, 1976-77; Registrar, Aberdeen Royal Infirmary, 1977-80; MRC Clinical Scientist, Dunn Nutrition Laboratory, Cambridge, 1980-84; Senior Registrar in General Medicine, Diabetes and Endocrinology, Aberdeen Royal Infirmary, 1984-89; Senior Lecturer, Department of Human Nutrition, University of Glasgow. Member, Health Education Board for Scotland, since 1995. Author of books and papers on diabetes, obesity and nutrition. Recreations: Scottish fiddling; violin making; hill running; mountains. Address: (h.) Hatton Castle, Newtyle, Blairgowrie PH12 8UN; T.-01828 650404.

Lederer, Peter J, OBE. Managing Director, Gleneagles Hotels plc, since 1987; General Manager, The Gleneagles Hotel, since 1983; Director, Guinness Enterprises, since 1987; Board Member, Scottish Tourist Board; b. 30.11.50; m., Marilyn Ruth MacPhail. Four Seasons Hotels, Canada, 1972-79; Vice President, Wood Wilkings Ltd., Toronto, 1979-81; General Manager, Plaza Group of Hotels, Toronto, 1981-83. Governor, Ardvreck School, Crieff; Chairman, Tourism Training Scotland; Chairman, Hospitality Industry Trust Scotland; Freeman, City of London; Member, Advisory Scottish Council for Education and Training Targets; FHCIMA; Master Innholder. Recreations: Matthew and Mark; TVR. Address: (b.) The Gleneagles Hotel, Auchterarder, Perthshire PH3 1NF; T.-01764 662231.

Ledger, Philip Stevens, CBE, FRSE, HonLLD (Strathclyde), MA, MusB, FRCM, HonRAM, FRNCM, HonGSM, FRCO. Principal, Royal Scottish Academy of Music and Drama, since 1982; b. 12.12.37, Bexhill-on-Sea; 1 s.; 1 d. Educ. Bexhill Grammar School; King's College, Cambridge. Master of the Music, Chelmsford Cathedral, 1962-65; East Anglia University: Director of Music, 1965-73, Dean, School of Fine Arts and Music, 1968-71; Conductor, Cambridge University Musical Society, 1973-82; Director of Music and Organist, King's College, Cambridge, 1974-82; President: Royal College of Organists, 1992-94, Incorporated Society of Musicians, 1994-95; Chairman, Committee of Principals of Conservatoires, 1994-98; Editor, Anthems for Choirs 2 and 3; Composer/Editor, Six Carols with Descants. Publication: The Oxford Book of English Madrigals (Editor). Recreations: swimming; theatre. Address: (b.) Royal

Scottish Academy of Music and Drama, 100 Renfrew Street, Glasgow G2 3DB; T.-0141-332 4101.

Ledingham, Professor Iain McAllan, MD(Hons), FRCS(Ed), FRCP(Ed, Glas), FInstBiol, FCCM, FRSE. Professor of Medical Education, Faculty of Medicine, Dentistry and Nursing, University of Dundee, since 1995; Honorary Consultant Physician, Dundee Teaching Hospitals NHS Trust, since 1995; b. 26.2.35, Glasgow; m., Eileen; 3 s. Educ. King's Park Senior Secondary, Glasgow; Central School, Aberdeen; University of Glasgow. Early training in surgery/trauma/intensive care; MRC Senior Research Fellow in hyperbaric medicine; first UK Professor of Intensive Care Medicine, University of Glasgow, 1980; Chair, Intensive Therapy Unit, Western Infirmary, Glasgow, 1985; Foundation Chair, Department of Emergency and Critical Care Medicine, Faculty of Medicine and Health Sciences, United Arab Emirates University, 1988 (Dean, FMHS, 1989). First Chair, Intensive Care Society, UK; President: European Shock Society, European Society of Intensive Care Medicine; Bellahouston Medal, University of Glasgow; La Médaille de la Ville de Paris. Recreations: jogging; hill-walking; gardening; music; reading; woodworking; occasional bad golf. Address: (b.) Clinical Skills Centre, Ninewells Hospital and Medical School, Dundee DD1 9SY; T.-01382 632615.

Lee, Professor Clive Howard, MA, MLitt (Cantab). Professor of Historical Economics, Aberdeen University, since 1991; Convener of Council, since 1994; b. 21.4.42, Leeds; m., Christine Ann. Educ. West Leeds High School; Fitzwilliam College, Cambridge. Assistant Lecturer to Professor, Aberdeen University, since 1966; Editor, Scottish Economic and Social History, 1989-93. Publications include: The British Economy since 1700: A Macroeconomic Perspective, 1986; British Regional Employment Statistics 1841-1971, 1979; Scotland and the United Kingdom: The Economy and the Union in the Twentieth Century, 1995. Recreations: watching and playing football; gardening; going to pub. Address: (b.) Department of Economics, Aberdeen University, Regent Walk, Aberdeen; T.: 01224 272198.

Lee, Professor Michael Radcliffe, MA, DM, DPhil (Oxon), FRCP, FRCPE, FRSE. Emeritus Professor of Clinical Pharmacology, Edinburgh University; b. 21.11.34, Manchester; m., Judith Ann Horrocks; 1 s.; 1 d. Educ. Manchester Grammar School; Brasenose College, Oxford. Beit Memorial Fellow for Medical Research; Lecturer in Medicine, Oxford University; Lecturer in Medicine, St. Thomas's Hospital Medical School; Medical Director, then Managing Director, Weddel Pharmaceuticals Ltd.; Senior Lecturer in Clinical Pharmacology, Leeds University. Publications: books on medicine and hypertension. Recreations: gardening; walking; old trains; old books. Address: (h.) 112 Polwarth Terrace, Edinburgh EH11 1NN; T.-0131-337 7386.

Leech, Michael J. Principal, Stevenson College. Address: (b.) Bankhead Avenue, Edinburgh, EH11 4DE.

Lees, James George Grahame, MA, LLB, NP. Partner, McLean & Stewart, Solicitors, Dunblane, since 1974; Vice Chairman, Judicial Commission, Church of Scotland; b. 22.6.46, Perth; m., Hazel Margaret Raffan; 1 s.; 2 d. Educ. Dundee High School; St. Andrews University; Edinburgh University. Solicitor, J. & F. Anderson, WS, Edinburgh, 1969-72; Solicitor, McLean & Stewart, Solicitors, Dunblane, since 1972. Elder, Dunblane Cathedral Church of Scotland. Recreations: walking; photography; fishing. Address: (h.) Northbank, St. Margaret's Drive, Dunblane, FK15 ODP; T.-Dunblane 822928.

Lees, Robert Ferguson, LLB. Regional Procurator Fiscal, Lothian and Borders, since 1991; b. 15.9.38, Bellshill; m.,

Elizabeth. Educ. Bellshill Academy; Strathclyde University. Entered Procurator Fiscal Service, 1972; Legal Assistant, Paisley, 1972-75; Legal Assistant/Senior Legal Assistant/Senior Depute Procurator Fiscal, Glasgow, 1975-81; Assistant Procurator Fiscal, Dundee, 1982-88; Regional Procurator Fiscal, North Strathclyde, 1989-91. Recreations: music; travel; foreign languages. Address: (b.) Procurator Fiscal's Office, Sheriff Court House, 29 Chambers Street, Edinburgh EH1 1LD.

Lefevre, Frank Hartley, MA, LLB, NP. Solicitor and Advocate in Aberdeen, since 1959; Senior Partner, Frank Lefevre Practice, since 1988; Chairman, Quantum Claims Compensation Specialists Ltd., since 1988; b. 4.12.34, Aberdeen; m., Hazel Gray; 1 s.; 2 d. Educ. Robert Gordon's College, Aberdeen; Aberdeen University. Commenced legal practice, 1959; set up, 1988, Britain's first no-win no-fee professional compensation company. Treasurer, Aberdeen Society of Advocates, 1994, President 1995; Past President, Grampian Squash Racquets Association (now Honorary President); accredited by the Law Society of Scotland as specialist in employment law, 1993, and as solicitor/ mediator, 1995; part-time Chairman, Industrial Tribunals (Scotland), 1996; Member, Council, Royal Aberdeen Golf Club, 1993-95. Recreations: squash; golf; music. Address: (h.) Braco Lodge, 11 Rubislaw Den North, Aberdeen; T.-01224 317170.

Leggat, James, BA, DipEd. Rector, Annan Academy, since 1994; b. 8.5.53, Glasgow; m., Susan Renshaw. Educ. Glasgow Academy; Stirling University. Teacher of English, Renfrewshire and Glasgow; Principal Teacher of English, Eastbank Academy, Glasgow; Assistant Rector, Carluke High School, Glasgow; Depute Rector, Hunter High School, East Kilbride. Address: (b.) Annan Academy, St. John's Road, Annan DG12 6AP.

Leggat, (John) Brian, WS. Partner, since 1973, and Head of Education Group, since 1996, Dundas and Wilson CS; b. 29.7.48; m., Iona Aitken; 1 s.; 1 d. Educ. Edinburgh Academy; University of Edinburgh. Trainee, Lindsay, Duncan and Black, 1969-71; Assistant Solicitor, Dundas and Wilson, 1971-73; Head of Commercial Property Group, 1983-93; Chairman of Partnership, 1993-96. Member, IPF Scottish Education Committee. Recreations: rugby; golf; curling; sailing; horse-riding, music. Address: (b.) Saltire Court, 20 Castle Terrace, Edinburgh; T.-0131-228 8000.

Leggate, Peter James Arthur, JP, FRICS. Chartered Surveyor, since 1967; Chairman, Lowland Insurance Brokers Ltd.; Director: Isla Mines Ltd., James Gammell & Son Ltd., Ptarmigan International Capital Trust Plc, Cheviot Investments Ltd.; b. 17.10.43; m., Jennifer Susan Gammell; 1 s.; 1 d. Educ. Wrekin College. Qualified as Chartered Surveyor, 1967; Kenneth Ryden & Partners, 1967-70; P.G. Matineau, Jedburgh, 1970-72; Founder, P.J. Leggate & Co., Edinburgh, 1973 (Sole Principal, since 1979). Recreations: horses; sailing; skiing. Address: (h.) Greenlawdean House, Greenlaw, Berwickshire, TD10 6XP.

Leiper, Joseph, MA, DipEd, ACII. Rector, Oldmachar Academy, since 1983; elected Vice Convener, Business Committee, General Council, Aberdeen University, 1997; b. 13.8.41, Aberdeen; m., Moira Taylor; 2 d. Educ. Aberdeen Grammar School; Aberdeen University. Inspector, Commercial Union Assurance, until 1967; Aberdeen University, 1967-72; Aberdeen College of Education, 1971-72; Teacher of English, since 1972. Recreation: sailing. Address: (b.) Oldmachar Academy, Jesmond Drive, Bridge of Don, Aberdeen AB2 8ZJ; T.-01224 820887.

Leishman, Brian Archibald Scott. Consultant, Edinburgh Military Tattoo (Business Manager, 1978-97); b. 16.9.36; 1 s.; 1 d. Educ. Fettes College, Edinburgh. Retired Regular Army Officer; commissioned The Cameronians (Scottish Rifles); re-badged King's Own Scottish Borderers; service in the Arabian Gulf, East Africa and Europe; Italian Staff College, 1971-73; Assistant Defence Attache, British Embassy, Rome, 1974-76; Ticketing Consultant, XIII Commonwealth Games in Edinburgh, 1986; Board Member, Edinburgh Military Tattoo Ltd. and Edinburgh Military Tattoo (Charities) Ltd.; Chairman, Edinburgh International Jazz and Blues Festival; Founder Member, Edinburgh Capital Group (Edinburgh Entertains). Recreations: sailing; music; photography. Address: (b.) Tattoo Office, 32 Market Street, Edinburgh EH1 1QB; T.-0131-225 4783.

Leishman, Marista Muriel, MA, FRSA. Senior Partner, The Insite Consultancy for Management and Training; b. 10.4.32, Beaconsfield; m., Murray Leishman; 1 s.; 3 d. Educ. St. George's School, Ascot; St. Andrews University. First Head of Education, National Trust for Scotland, 1979-86; two National Training Awards recognising Insite's innovatory programmes supporting disabled access. Recreations: music; painting; writing; hill-walking. Address: 9/23 St. Leonard's Crag, Edinburgh EH8 9SP; T.-0131-667 1246.

Leishman, Mark Murray. Secretary and Head of Corporate Affairs, BBC Scotland; b. 4.3.62, Perth. Educ. Firrhill High School, Edinburgh; Napier College, Edinburgh. Press and PR, National Trust for Scotland, 1979-81; Reporter, United News Service, 1982-84; Reporter, Fife Free Press, Kirkcaldy, 1986-87; Chief Reporter, Radio Forth/Tay, 1987-88; Reporter, Radio Clyde, 1988-90; Reporter, Political Correspondent, Sunday Times, 1990-93; Presenter, Good Morning Scotland, BBC Scotland, 1993-95. Recreations: fishing; running; golf; gym work; reading; cinema; music. Address: (h.) 34 Polwarth Street, Glasgow G12 9TX.

Leitch, Donald H., DMS, MHCIMA, MCFA. Depute Principal, Glasgow College of Food Technology, since 1991; b. 2.4.48, Glasgow; m., Mary B.; 2 s. Educ. Hyndland Senior Secondary School; Langside College, Glasgow; Glasgow College of Technology. Catering management, Health Service, 1967-70; Depute Catering Officer, Glasgow University, 1970-74; Lecturer then Senior Lecturer, Glasgow College of Food Technology, 1974-85; Head of Department, Cambuslang College, Glasgow, 1985-91. Past Chairman, Scottish Division, Cookery and Food Association. Recreations: hill-walking; gardening. Address: (b.) 230 Cathedral Street, Glasgow G1 2TG; T.-0141-552 3751.

Lenman, Professor Bruce Philip, MA (Aberdeen), MLitt, LittD (Cantab), FRHistSoc. Professor of Modern History, St. Andrews University, since 1992 (formerly Reader in Modern History); b. 9.4.38, Aberdeen. Educ. Aberdeen Grammar School; Aberdeen University; St. John's College, Cambridge. Assistant Professor, Victoria University, Canada, 1963; Lecturer in Imperial and Commonwealth History, Queen's College, Dundee (St. Andrews University), 1963-67; Lecturer, Dundee University, 1967-72; United College, St. Andrews; Lecturer, Department of Modern History, 1972-78, Senior Lecturer, 1978-83; British Academy Fellow, Newberry Library, Chicago, 1982; John Carter Brown Library Fellow, Brown University, Providence, RI, 1984; Harrison Professor, College of William & Mary, VA, 1988-89; Bird Fellow, Emory University, Atlanta, GA, 1998. Publications: Esk to Tweed, 1975; An Economic History of Modern Scotland 1660-1976, 1977 (Scottish Arts Council Award); The Jacobite Risings in Britain 1689-1746, 1980 (Scottish Arts Council Award); Scotland 1746-1832, 1981; The Jacobite Clans of the Great Glen 1650-1784, 1984; The Jacobite Cause, 1986; The Jacobite Threat (Co-Author), 1990; The Eclipse of Parliament, 1992; Editor, Chambers Dictionary of World History, 1993. Recreations: golf; tennis; swimming. Address: (b.) Department of Modern History, St. Andrews University, St. Andrews KY16 9AL; T.-01334 476161.

Leonard, Professor Thomas, BSc, ARCS, MSc, PhD. Chair of Statistics, Professor of Mathematics and Statistics, University of Edinburgh, since 1995; Director, University of Edinburgh Statistical Laboratory, since 1996; statistical expert witness in legal cases, since 1985; b. 24.3.48, Plympton; 2 d. Educ. Sutton High School, Plymouth; Imperial College, London; University College, London. Predoctoral Research Fellow, American College Tertiary Program, Iowa City, 1971, 1972; Co-Founder and Lecturer, Department of Statistics, University of Warwick, 1972-80 (Co-Founder, MORSE degree, 1975); Senior Medical Statistician, Queen's University, Kingston, Ontario, 1978; Associate Professor, Mathematics Research Center, University of Wisconsin-Madison, 1979-86; Associate, then full Professor, Department of Statistics, University of Wisconsin-Madison, 1979-96. Publications: Statistical Inference, Data Analysis and Robustness (Co-Author), 1983; Bayesian Methods (Co-Author), 1998; 60 papers in scientific journals. Recreations: chess (Edinburgh Premier League Team Champion, 1996); football supporter (Green Bay Packers, Newcastle United). Address: (b.) Department of Mathematics and Statistics, University of Edinburgh, The King's Buildings, Mayfield Road, Edinburgh EH9 3JZ; T.-0131-650 8569.

Leonard, Wilfred. Member, Island Policy Committee, Scottish Accident Prevention Council; Honorary President, Harris Local Supporters Network (promoting jobs in Harris); b. 9.5.12, Humberton, Brafferton, Yorkshire; m., Margaret Ross (deceased); 1 s.; 2 d. Educ. Brafferton Church of England School. Staffordshire County Police, 1935-67 (retired in rank of Inspector); Member, Inverness County Council, 1973-74; Past Chairman: Harris District Council, South Harris Agricultural Society, Harris Council of Social Service; former Member: Highlands and Islands Consultative Council; Highlands and Islands Manpower Board, MSC; Member, Western Isles Islands Council, 1974-86 (Chairman, Planning and Development, 1980-86). Recreation: gardening. Address: (h.) Cnoc-Na-Ba, Finsbay, Isle of Harris, T.-01859 530 232.

Leslie, Professor Frank Matthews, JP, BSc, PhD, DSc, FIMA, FInstP, FRSE, FRS. Professor of Mathematics, Strathclyde University, since 1982; Chairman, British Liquid Crystal Society, 1987-91; b. 8.3.35, Dundee; m., Ellen Leitch Reoch; 1 s.; 1 d. Educ. Harris Academy; Queen's College, Dundee; Manchester University. Assistant Lecturer, Manchester University, 1959-61; Research Associate, MIT, USA, 1961-62; Lecturer, Newcastle University, 1962-68; Visiting Assistant Professor, Johns Hopkins University, USA, 1966-67; Strathclyde University: Senior Lecturer, 1968-71, Reader, 1971-79, Personal Professor, 1979-82; Consultant, DRA Malvern; Annual Award, British Society of Rheology, 1982; Sykes Gold Medal, St. Andrews University, 1996; G.W. Gray Medal, British Liquid Crystal Society, 1997. Recreations: golf; hill-walking. Address: (b.) Department of Mathematics, Strathclyde University, Livingstone Tower, 26 Richmond Street, Glasgow G1 1XH; T.-0141-548 3655.

Leslie, John, MRPharmS. Chairman, Orkney Health Board, since 1991; b. 1.1.35, Kirkwall; m., Evelyn MacGillivray; 1 s. Educ. Kirkwall Grammar School; Robert Gordon's Institute of Technology, Aberdeen. Member, NHS Executive Council for Orkney, 1968-74; Chairman, Kirkwall Chamber of Commerce, 1973-74; Member, Orkney Health Board, 1979-85 and since 1987. Past President, Kirkwall Rotary Club. Recreations: participating in amateur music and drama groups; simple electronics/computing. Address: (h.) Failte, Bignold Park Road, Kirkwall, Orkney; T.-01856 874002.

Lessels, Norman, CBE, CA. Senior Partner, Chiene & Tait, CA; Chairman: Standard Life Assurance Company, Cairn Energy PLC, Havelock Europa PLC; Director: Scottish Eastern Investment Trust PLC, Robert Wiseman Diaries

PLC; b. 2.9.38, Edinburgh; m., Christine Stevenson; 1 s. Educ. Edinburgh Academy. Partner, Ernst & Whinney, until 1980; President, Institute of Chartered Accountants of Scotland, 1987-88. Recreations: golf; music; bridge. Address: (b.) 3 Albyn Place, Edinburgh; T.-0131-225 7515.

Lester, Andrew, BArch, RIBA, ARIAS. Partner, Aitken and Turnbull Architects, since 1986; Chairman, Scottish Society for Autistic Children, since 1993; b. 15.6.49, Glasgow; m., Kate; 1 s.; 2 d. Educ. High School of Dundee; Heriot-Watt University. Architect, Sir Basil Spence, Glover and Ferguson, Edinburgh; Architect, Forgan and Stewart, Edinburgh; Architect, Aitken and Turnbull, Duns. Member, Executive Committee, Scottish Society for Autistic Children, since 1982. Recreations: football supporter; amateur dramatics; opera. Address: (h.) Wellfield Cottage, Preston Road, Duns, Berwickshire TD11 3DZ; T.-01361 883445.

Levein, Charles Peter Alexander, MA, PhD, FRSGS. Chief Research Officer, Scottish Office, since 1988; b. 16.5.40, Devonport; 1 s.; 2 d. Educ. Dunfermline High School; Edinburgh University. Demonstrator, Geography Department, Edinburgh University; Research Officer, Central Planning Research Unit, Scottish Development Department; Senior Research Officer, WC Scotland Planning Team; Principal Research Officer, Scottish Office Urban Deprivation Unit; Senior Principal Research Officer, Scottish Office. Recreations: golf; bowls; theatre. Address: (h.) 45 The Wynd, Dalgety Bay, Fife; T.-01383 822952.

Leven and Melville, Earl of (Alexander Robert Melville). Lord Lieutenant of Nairn, since 1969; Honorary President, Scottish National Ski Council; b. 13.5.24, London; m., Susan Steuart-Menzies; 2 s.; 1 d. Educ. Eton. Coldstream Guards, 1942-52 (retired as Captain); ADC to Governor General of New Zealand, 1951-52; Convener, Nairn County Council, 1970-74. Chairman of Governors, Gordonstoun School, 1971-89; President, British Ski Federation, 1981-85. Address: (h.) Glenferness House, Nairn IV12 5UP; T.-01309 651202.

Levinthal, Terrence Scott, BES, DipUD, FSAScot. Secretary, The Cockburn Association (Edinburgh Civic Trust), since 1992; Advisory Board Member: Transport Research Institute, Lothian and Edinburgh Action Research Network; b. 9.12.61, Winnipeg. Educ. University of Waterloo; Heriot-Watt/Edinburgh College of Art. Investigator, Royal Fine Art Commission for Scotland, 1988-92. Recreations: hill-walking, skiing, cycling and other outdoor pursuits; the arts; woodworking. Address: (b.) Trunk's Close, 55 High Street, Edinburgh EH1 1SR; T.-0131-557 8686.

Levison, Professor David Annan, MD, FRCPath. Dean of Faculty of Medicine, Dentistry and Nursing and Professor of Pathology, University of Dundee, since 1995; b. 4.1.44, Perth; m., Rosemary Ann; 4 s.; 2 d. Educ. George Watson's Boys College; Kirkcaldy High School; St. Andrews University. Lecturer in Pathology, Dundee University, 1969-77; Senior Lecturer (Hon. Consultant) in Histopathology, St. Bartholomew's Hospital, London, 1978-88; Professor of Clinical Histopathology, UMDS, Guy's Hospital, London, 1988-94. Treasurer, Pathological Society of Great Britain and Ireland; Pathology Editor, Surgery; author of 100 scientific papers. Recreations: sailing; hill-walking; family. Address: (h.) Huntly, 8 Glamis Drive, Dundee, DD2 1QL; T.-01382 668150.

Levison, Rev. Mary Irene, BA, BD, DD. Minister of the Church of Scotland (retired); (Extra) Chaplain to the Queen in Scotland, since 1991; Vice-President, St. Leonard's School, since 1996; b. 8.1.23, Oxford; m., Rev. Frederick Levison. Educ. St. Leonard's School, St. Andrews; Oxford University; Edinburgh University. Administrative Assistant, Scottish Home Department, 1943-46; Deaconess, Church of

Scotland, Musselburgh, 1954-58; Tutor, St. Colm's College, 1958-61; Assistant Chaplain, Edinburgh University, 1961-64; Assistant Minister, St. Andrew's and St. George's Church and Chaplain to the retail trade, Edinburgh, 1978-83; Moderator, Edinburgh Presbytery, 1988. Publication: Wrestling with the Church, 1992. Recreations: gardening; music; travel. Address: (h.) 2 Gillsland Road, Edinburgh EH10 5BW; T.-0131-228 3118.

Levy, Professor Roger P., BA (Hons), MPhil, PhD. Acting Dean, Faculty of Management, since 1997, and Head, School of Public Administration and Law, Robert Gordon University, since 1991; b. 14.12.50, London. Educ. Southgate Technical College; Leicester University; Glasgow University; McGill University. Tutor in Government, Glasgow University, 1974-75; Lecturer in Public Administration, Bell College, 1975-79; worked in Canada, 1979-83; Education Development Officer, Scottish Civil Liberty Trust, Glasgow, 1983; Lecturer/Senior Lecturer in Public Administration, Glasgow Polytechnic, 1983-91. Publications (books): A Guide to Civil Liberties in Scotland (Co-Author), 1980; Young People and the Law (Co-Author), 1985; Scottish Nationalism at the Crossroads, 1990; numerous book chapters and articles. Address: (b.) Robert Gordon University, School of Public Administration and Law, 352 King Street, Aberdeen AB24 5BN; T.-01224 262900.

Lewis, Andrew Douglas Fyfe, MBA, FInstD. Director, The Goldcrest Company (UK) Ltd., since 1982; b. 11.2.43, Aberdeen; m., Cathrine Diana; 1 s.; 1 d. Educ. Fettes College, Edinburgh; University of Aberdeen; Robert Gordon University. Trainee, Ernst & Young, 1963; Trawler Manager, Associated Fisheries PLC, 1964-68; Director, Trawling Division, John Lewis & Sons Limited, 1969-72; Director, Trawling Scotland, Associated Fisheries PLC, 1972-82. Honorary Consul, Federal Republic of Germany, since 1976; Chairman, Northsound Local Commercial Radio, Aberdeen, since 1979; President, Aberdeen Chamber of Commerce; Board of Governors, Robert Gordon University, since 1993; Chairman, National Art Collections Fund, Grampian Area, since 1994; Board, North of Scotland Water Authority, since 1995. Cross of the Order of Merit of Federal Republic of Germany. Recreations: Scottish art; tennis; running; reading biographies; work; listening to music. Address: The Glebe House, Kirkton of Durris, Kincardineshire AB31 6BQ; T.-01330 844 414.

Lewis, John Ivor, MSc, CEng, FIEE. Managing Director, Operations, United Distillers, since 1992; b. 24.2.45, Shrewsbury; m., Karolyn Richards; 1 s.; 1 d. Educ. Adams Grammar School, Shropshire; Birmingham University; INSEAD. With Rolls Royce for 10 years; Management Consultancy, 1972-81; J. C. Bamford Excavators, 1981-85; Rover Cars, 1985-91; Director, Gleneagles Hotels. Member, Council, CBI Scotland; Member, Council, and Treasurer, Scotch Whisky Association; Member, Board, Scottish Natural Heritage; Member, Management Committee, Keepers of the Quaich. Recreations: shooting; riding; photography; reading. Address: (h.) 21 Rothesay Terrace, Edinburgh; T.-0131-519 2306.

Lewis, Penelope Frances, BSc(Hons). Head of Fundraising and Sponsorship, Scottish Opera, since 1992; b. 7.7.58; m., Roy Lewis; 1 s.; 1 d. Educ. Kendal High School; University of Edinburgh. Worked in tourism in Italy, 1980-86; Scottish Development Agency (Locate in Scotland and Tourism Departments), 1986-89; Commercial Manager, Scottish Chamber Orchestra, 1989-92. Founder Committee Member, West of Scotland Businesswomen's Club. Recreations: spending time with the family; hill-walking; gardening; going to the theatre. Address: (b.) Scottish Opera, 39 Elmbank Crescent, Glasgow G2 4PT; T.-0141-248 4567.

Liddell, Colin. Partner, Liddell Thomson, Management Consultants; b. 28.8.47, Falkirk; m., Sheena Wood Mackay.

Educ. Denny High School. Journalist, Johnston Newspaper Group, 1964-69; Editor, Linlithgow Journal & Gazette, 1968-69; Journalist, Scotsman Publications, 1969-77; Senior Press Officer, Scottish Development Agency, 1977-82; PR Director, then Chief Executive, Charles Barker Scotland, 1982-86; Public Affairs Director, United Distillers, 1986-93; Corporate Communications Director, Scottish Power plc, 1993-95. Non-Executive Director: Royal Scottish National Orchestra, Scotland the Brand; Advisory Director, Barclays Bank Scotland; Member, Board, Roger Billcliffe Fine Art. Recreations: golf; gardening. Address: (b.) 225 West George Street, Glasgow G2 2ND.

Liddell, David, BSc (Hons), DipSW. Director, Scottish Drugs Forum, since 1993 (Co-ordinator, since 1986); b. 1957, Kingston. Educ. Riddlesdown School; Sheffield University; Edinburgh University. Project Worker, Bristol Cyrenians and Dublin Simon Community; Researcher, Queen Charlotte's Hospital, London; Biochemist, Children's Hospital, Dublin; Youth Worker, Dublin Committee for Travelling People; Field Worker, Standing Conference on Drug Abuse. Publications: Drug Problems in Edinburgh District, 1987 (Co-author); Drugfax (Co-author), 1991. Recreations: travel; cycling; working on allotment. Address: (b.) Shaftsbury House, 5 Waterloo Street, Glasgow, G2 6AY.

Liddell, Faith Ann, MA(Hons), DEML. Director, Edinburgh Book Festival, since 1997; b. 9.4.65, Lanark. Educ. Dalkeith High School; University of Aberdeen; Napier University. Box-Office Manager, Traverse Theatre, 1989-90; Press and Publicity Officer, Royal Lyceum Theatre, 1990-91; Marketing and Press Manager, Edinburgh Festival Fringe, 1992-94; Press Officer, Edinburgh Book Festival, 1995; Freelance Arts and Events Manager, since 1995. Recreations: literature; theatre; film; travel. Address: (b.) The Book Centre, 137 Dundee Street, Edinburgh EH11 1BG; T.-0131-228 5444.

Liddell, Helen Lawrie, BA. Economic Secretary to the Treasury, since 1997; MP (Labour), Airdrie and Shotts (formerly Monklands East), since 1994; b. 6.12.50, Coatbridge; m., Dr. Alistair H. Liddell; 1 s.; 1 d. Educ. St. Patrick's High School, Coatbridge; Strathclyde University. Head, Economic Department, STUC, 1971-76; Economics Correspondent, BBC, 1976-77; Scottish Secretary, Labour Party, 1977-88; Scottish Daily Record and Sunday Mail Ltd.: Director of Personnel and Public Affairs, 1988-91, Director of Corporate and Public Affairs, 1991-92; Chief Executive, Business Venture Programme, 1993-94; Labour Candidate, East Fife, 1974. Publication: Elite, 1990. Address: (b.) House of Commons, London SW1A 0AA; T.-0171-219 3000.

Liddle, Robert Christie, CA. Consultant (former Partner), Robb Ferguson CA; Secretary: Royal Glasgow Institute of the Fine Arts, since 1986, Scottish Artists Benevolent Association, since 1993; b. 2.8.33, Hamilton: m., Elizabeth Jean Smith; 2 s.; 1 d. Educ. Hamilton Academy. Partner, Russ Ferguson & Maclennan, CA, 1958. Recreations: travel; bowling. Address: (b.) 5 Oswald Street, Glasgow G1 4QR; T.-0141-248 7411.

Lidgate, Professor David, BEng, PhD, CEng, FIEE, FInstE. Professor and Head, Department of Electrical and Electronic Engineering, Napier University, since 1994; b. 11.7.46, Gosforth; m., Janet; 2 d. Educ. Royal Grammar School, Newcastle upon Tyne; Liverpool University. Research Engineer, A. Reyrolle & Co. Ltd., 1965-75; Lecturer, UMIST, 1975-88; Head, School of Engineering, Greenwich University, 1988-94. Member, Electricity Consumers Committee for Southern Scotland. Recreations: genealogy; model railways. Address: (b.) 219 Colinton Road, Edinburgh EH14 1DJ; T.-0131-455 4361.

Light, John V. Rector, The Edinburgh Academy. Address: (b.) 42 Henderson Row, Edinburgh, EH3 5BL.

Lilley, Professor David Malcolm James, FRSE. Professor of Molecular Biology, Dundee University, since 1989; b. 28.5.48, Colchester; m., Patricia Mary; 2 d. Educ. Gilberd School, Colchester; Durham University. Joined Biochemistry Department, Dundee University, 1981; awarded: Colworth Medal by Biochemical Society, 1982, Gold Medal of G. Mendel, Czech Academy of Sciences, 1994, Gold Medal of V. Prelog in Stereochemistry, ETH, Zurich. Publications: over 180 scientific papers. Recreation: foreign languages. Address: (b.) Department of Biochemistry, Dundee University, Dundee DD1 4HN; T.-01382 344243.

Lillico, William Allan, MREHIS, MInstWM. Director of Protective Services, Scottish Borders Council, since 1996; b. 8.3.45, Galashiels; m., Doreen Ann; 2 d. Educ. Galashiels Academy; Napier College, Edinburgh. Burgh of Galashiels: Trainee Burgh Surveyor/Sanitary Inspector, 1964-68, Junior Assistant Burgh Surveyor/Sanitary Inspector, 1968-71, Assistant Burgh Surveyor/Sanitary Inspector, 1971-72, Depute Burgh Surveyor/Sanitary Inspector, 1972-75; Ettrick and Lauderdale District Council: Area Inspector, Technical Services Department, 1975-76, Depute Director of Environmental Services, 1976-96. Member, Ettrick and Lauderdale Crime Prevention Panel. Recreation: golf. Address: (b.) Protective Services Department, Scott House, Sprouston Road, Newton St. Boswells TD6 0QD; T.-01835 825111.

Lindsay, Frederic, MA (Hons). Writer; b. 12.8.33, Glasgow; m., Shirley; 1 s.; 3 d. Educ. North Kelvinside Senior Secondary School; Glasgow University; Jordanhill College; Edinburgh University. Worked as library assistant, teacher, lecturer; since becoming full-time writer in 1979, has published four novels: Brond, 1984, Jill Rips, 1987, A Charm Against Drowning, 1988, After the Stranger Came, 1992, Kissing Judas, 1997; has written plays for Scottish Youth Theatre; radio plays for children; adapted Brond as serial for Channel 4. Former Chair, Society of Authors in Scotland; former Vice-President, PEN Scotland; former Member, Scottish Arts Council, Literature Committee. Recreations: cinema; theatre; television; reading; walking in the Pentlands. Address: (b.) 2a Hopelands Road, Silverburn, Penicuik EH26 9LH; T.-01968 678498.

Lindsay, James Kerr, MA. Manager, Scottish Fisheries Museum Trust Ltd., since 1989; b. 13.7.34, Dundee; m., Dorothy Pattullo; 1 s.; 1 d. Educ. Morgan Academy, Dundee; St. Andrews University. Production Controller/Finishing Manager, Alex. Pirie & Sons, 1958-66; Head of Fisheries Division, Highlands and Islands Development Board, 1966-89. Governor, Unicorn Preservation Society, Dundee; Council Member, Scottish Museums Council, Edinburgh. Recreations: ornithology; chess. Address: (h.) 5 St. Ayles Crescent, Anstruther, Fife; T.-01333 310028.

Lindsay, 16th Earl of (James Randolph Lindesay-Bethune). Parliamentary Under Secretary of State, Scottish Office, 1995-97; b. 19.11.55; m., Diana Mary Chamberlayne-Macdonald. Educ. Eton; Edinburgh University; University of California, Davis. President, International Tree Foundation, since 1995; Member, Advisory Panel, Railway Heritage Trust, since 1990; Director, Tay Forth Marketing Group Ltd., since 1990; Chairman, Landscape Foundation, 1992-95; Member: Advisory Council, World Resource Foundation, since 1994, Select Committee, Sustainable Development, 1994-95; Lord in Waiting (Government Whip), 1995; Green Ribbon political award, 1995. Address: (h.) Lahill, Upper Largo, Fife KY8 9JE.

Lindsay, John. Chief Executive, East Lothian Council. Address: Council Buildings, Court Street, Haddington, EH41 3HA.

Lindsay, Professor John Gordon, BSc, PhD. Professor of Medical Biochemistry, Glasgow University, since 1992; b. 9.8.45, Birkenhead; m., Joan Cameron Barr; 2 s. Educ. Bellshill Academy; Glasgow University. Lecturer in Biochemistry, then Senior Lecturer, then Reader, Glasgow University, 1973-92. Fulbright Scholar, 1979-80; Editorial Adviser, Biochemical Journal; 110 publications in learned journals. Recreations: playing and coaching cricket; golf; classical music. Address: (b.) Division of Biochemistry and Molecular Biology, Institute of Biomedical and Life Sciences, Glasgow University, Glasgow G12 8QQ; T.-0141-330 4720.

Lindsay, John Maurice, CBE, TD, DLitt, HonFRIAS. Consultant, Scottish Civic Trust (Director, 1967-83); b. 21.7.18; m., Aileen Joyce Gordon; 1 s.; 3 d. Educ. Glasgow Academy; Scottish National Academy of Music. Drama Critic, Scottish Daily Mail, 1946-47; Music Critic, The Bulletin, 1946-60; Border Television: Programme Controller, 1961-62, Production Controller, 1962-64, Features Executive and Chief Interviewer, 1964-67. Atlantic-Rockefeller Award, 1946; Editor: Scots Review, 1949-50, The Scottish Review, 1975-85; Member, Historic Buildings Council for Scotland, 1976-87; Secretary-General, Europa Nostra, 1983-91; Council Member, Association of Scottish Literary Studies, 1983-94, President, 1988-90; Trustee: New Lanark Conservation Trust, 1983-94, National Heritage Memorial Fund, 1980-84; HonDLitt, Glasgow, 1982. Publications: poetry: The Advancing Day, 1940; Perhaps To-morrow, 1941; Predicament, 1942; No Crown for Laughter: Poems, 1943; The Enemies of Love: Poems 1941-45, 1946; Selected Poems, 1947; Hurlygush: Poems in Scots, 1948; At the Wood's Edge, 1950; Ode for St. Andrew's Night and Other Poems, 1951; The Exiled Heart: Poems 1941-56, 1957; Snow Warning and Other Poems, 1962; One Later Day and Other Poems, 1964; This Business of Living, 1969; Comings and Goings: Poems, 1971; Selected Poems 1942-72, 1973; The Run from Life, 1975; Walking Without an Overcoat, Poems 1972-76, 1977; Collected Poems, 1979; A Net to Catch the Winds and Other Poems, 1981; The French Mosquitoes' Woman and other diversions and poems; Requiem for a Sexual Athlete; Collected Poems 1940-90; On the Face Of It: Collected Poems, Vol. 2; News of the World: Last Poems; Speaking Likenesses: A Postscript; prose: Pocket Guide to Scottish Culture; The Scottish Renaissance; The Lowlands of Scotland: Glasgow and the North; Robert Burns: The Man, His Work, The Legend; Dunoon: The Gem of the Clyde Coast; The Lowlands of Scotland: Edinburgh and the South; Clyde Waters: Variations and Diversions on a Theme of Pleasure; The Burns Encyclopedia; Killochan Castle; By Yon Bonnie Banks: A Gallimaufry; Environment: A Basic Human Right; Portrait of Glasgow; Robin Philipson; History of Scottish Literature; Lowland Scottish Villages; Francis George Scott and the Scottish Renaissance; The Buildings of Edinburgh (Co-Author); Thank You For Having Me: A Personal Memoir; Unknown Scotland (Co-Author); Castles of Scotland: A Constable Guide; Count All Men Mortal: The Story of the Scottish Provident Institution; Victorian and Edwardian Glasgow; An Illustrated Guide to Glasgow; The Comic Poems of William Tennant (Co-Editor); Edinburgh Past and Present (Co-Author); The Youth and Manhood of Cyril Thornton (Editor); The Scottish Dog (Co-Author); A Pleasure of Gardens (Co-Author); The Scottish Quotation Book (Co-Author); The Music Quotation Book (Co-Author); The Theatre and Opera Lover's Quotation Book (Co-Author); The Burns Quotation Book (Co-Author); The Chambers Guide to Good Scottish Gardens (Co-Author). Recreations: music; walking. Address: (h.) 7 Milton Hill, Milton, Dumbarton G82 2TS; T.-Dumbarton 762655.

Lindsay, Ranald Bruce, LLB(Hons), DipLP, NP. Solicitor-Advocate, since 1993; Solicitor, since 1986; b. 18.3.62, Bellshill; m., Jennifer Vesey; 1 s.; 1 d. Educ. Wishaw High; University of Glasgow. Trained with Bishop & Co., Glasgow, 1984-86; qualified as first Solicitor Advocate in both civil and criminal law, 1993; established own practice, 1994. Recreations: reading; films; history; computing; getting away from it all. Address: (b.) Lindsay Solicitors, 33 Buccleuch Street, Dumfries DG1 2AB; T.-01387 259236.

Lindsay, Stephen James. Regimental Secretary, The Black Watch (RHR), since 1997; b. 2.3.40, London; m., Ann Powell; 3 s.; 1 d. Educ. Eton College; Royal Military Academy, Sandhurst. Commissioned into The Black Watch, 1959; commanded Royal Guard, Balmoral, 1978; Commanding Officer, 1st Bn., 51st Highland Volunteers, 1984-86; retired in rank of Lt. Col., 1995. Recreations: piping; painting. Address: (b.) Balhousie Castle, Perth PH1 5HR; T.-01738 441784.

Lingard, Joan Amelia. Author; b. Edinburgh; 3 d. Educ. Bloomfield Collegiate School, Belfast; Moray House College of Education, Edinburgh. Member, Scottish Arts Council, 1980-85; Chair, Society of Authors in Scotland, 1980-84; a Director, Edinburgh Book Festival, since 1994; first novel published, 1963; has also written plays for TV, including 18-part series, Maggie, adapted from quartet of teenage books; novels: Liam's Daughter, 1963; The Prevailing Wind, 1964; The Tide Comes In, 1966; The Headmaster, 1967; A Sort of Freedom, 1968; The Lord on our Side, 1970; The Second Flowering of Emily Mountjoy, 1979; Greenyards, 1981; Sisters By Rite, 1984; Reasonable Doubts, 1986; The Women's House, 1989; After Colette, 1993; Dreams of Love and Modest Glory, 1995; 30 children's books. Recreations: reading; walking; travelling. Address: (b.) David Higham Associates, 5-8 Lower John Street, Golden Square, London W1R 4HA.

Lingard, Robin Anthony, MA, FTS. Independent Consultant; Project Director, University of the Highlands and Islands Project, 1993-97; b. 19.7.41, Enfield; m., Margaret; 2 d. Educ. Felsted School; Emmanuel College, Cambridge. Joined Ministry of Aviation, 1963; Private Secretary to Joint Parliamentary Secretary, Ministry of Technology, 1966-68; appointments, Department of Industry, DTI, etc., to 1984; Head, Enterprise Unit, Cabinet Office, 1984-85; Head, Small Firms and Tourism Division, Department of Employment, 1985-87; full-time Board Member, Highlands and Islands Development Board, 1988-91; Director of Training and Social Development, Highlands and Islands Enterprise, 1991-93. Member, Scottish Tourist Board, 1988-92; Chairman, Prince's Trust Committee for Highlands, Western Isles and Orkney; Member, Management Board, Prince's Trust and Royal Jubilee Trusts, 1989-95. Recreations: watching birds; walking; reading; aviation history; dinghy sailing. Address: (h.) Kinnairdie House, Dingwall IV15 9LL; T.-01349 61044.

Linklater, Professor Karl Alexander, BVM&S, PhD, CBiol, FIBiol, FRAgS, FRCVS. Vice Principal and Professor, Scottish Agricultural College, since 1997; (Member, Veterinary Products Committee, since 1990); a Director, The Moredun Foundation, since 1991; Director, Vet CPD, since 1991; b. 1.9.39, Stromness, Orkney; m., Margaret Carr Gibb; 1 s.; 1 d. Educ. Robert Gordon's College, Aberdeen; Edinburgh University. General veterinary practice, Tarland, Aberdeenshire, 1962-66; North of Scotland College of Agriculture, Aberdeen, 1966-67; Royal (Dick) School of Veterinary Studies, Edinburgh University, 1967-73; East of Scotland College of Agriculture, St. Boswells, 1973-86; Director, SAC Veterinary Services, 1986-97. President: Sheep Veterinary Society, 1983-85, British Veterinary Association, 1996-97, Association of Veterinary Teachers and Research Workers

(Scotland), 1988-90, Scottish Branch, British Veterinary Association, 1992-94, Scottish Metropolitan Division, BVA, 1979-80; Alan Baldry Award, 1982. Recreations: sport; gardening; sheep breeding. Address: (h.) Bridge Park, Old Bridge Road, Selkirk TD7 4LG; T.-01750 20571.

Linklater, Magnus Duncan. Writer and Broadcaster; Chairman, Scottish Arts Council, since 1996; b. 21.2.42, Harray, Orkney; m., Veronica Lyle; 2 s.; 1 d. Educ. Eton College; Cambridge University. Reporter, Daily Express, Manchester, 1965-66; London Evening Standard: Diary Reporter, 1966-67, Editor, Londoner's Diary, 1967-69; Sunday Times: Editor, Spectrum, 1969-72, Editor, Colour Magazine, 1972-75, News Editor/Features Editor, 1975-83; Managing Editor, The Observer, 1983-86; Editor, London Daily News, 1986-87; Editor, The Scotsman, 1988-94; Chairman, Edinburgh Book Festival, 1994-96. Publications: Hoax: the Howard Hughes-Clifford Irving Affair (Co-Author); Jeremy Thorpe: A Secret Life (Co-Author); The Falklands War (with Sunday Times Insight team); Massacre — the story of Glencoe; The Fourth Reich — Klaus Barbie and the Neo-Fascist Connection (Co-Author); Not With Honour — the inside story of the Westland Affair (Co-Author); For King and Conscience — John Graham of Claverhouse, Viscount Dundee (Co-Author); Anatomy of Scotland (Co-Editor); Highland Wilderness; People in a Landscape. Honorary Doctor of Arts, Napier University; Honorary Doctor of Law, Aberdeen University. Recreations: book-collecting; fishing. Address: (h.) 5 Drummond Place, Edinburgh EH3 6PH; T.-0131-557 5705.

Linklater of Butterstone, Baroness (Veronica Linklater). Founder and Executive Chairman, The New School, Butterstone, since 1991; President, Society of Friends of Dunkeld Cathedral, since 1989; Trustee, Esmée Fairbairn Charitable Trust, since 1991; b. 15.4.43, Meikleour, Perthshire; m., Magnus Duncan Linklater (qv); 2 s.; 1 d. Educ. Cranborne Chase; Sorbonne; University of Sussex; University of London. Child Care Officer, London Borough of Tower Hamlets, 1967-68; Co-Founder, Visitors Centre, Pentonville Prison, 1971-77; Governor, three Islington schools, 1970-85; Prison Reform Trust Winchester Prison Project, 1981-82; Founder, Administrator, Consultant, Butler Trust, 1983-87 (Trustee, since 1987); JP, Inner London, 1985-88; Co-ordinator, Trustee, Vice Chairman, Pushkin Prizes (Scotland), since 1989; Member, Children's Panel, Edinburgh South, 1989-97; Committee Member, Gulliver Award for the Performing Arts in Scotland, 1990-96; Patron, Sutherland Trust, since 1993; Trustee, Young Musicians Trust, 1993-97; Candidate (Liberal Democrat), Perth & Kinross By-Election, 1995; Director, Maggie Keswick Jencks Caring Centres Trust, since 1997; Life Peer, since 1997. Recreations: music; theatre; gardening. Address: (h.) 5 Drummond Place, Edinburgh EH3 6PH; T.-0131-557 5705.

Linkston, Alexander Millar, IPFA. Chief Executive Officer, West Lothian Council, since 1996; b. 13.12.49, Bathgate; m., Margaret Cuddihy; 2 d. Educ. Lindsay High School, Bathgate; Glasgow College of Commerce. Joined West Lothian County Council as trainee accountant, 1965. Recreations: horse riding; swimming; Rotary. Address: (b.) West Lothian Council, West Lothian House, Livingston EH54 6QG; T.-01506 777100.

Linlithgow, 4th Marquess of (Adrian John Charles Hope). b. 1.7.46; m.; 1 s.; 1 d.; 2 s. by pr. m. Address: Hopetoun House, South Queensferry, West Lothian, EH30 9SL.

Lisgo, John, BSc (Econ) (Hons), DipEd (Hons). Principal, Jewel and Esk Valley College, Edinburgh, since 1986 (Lauder Technical College, Dunfermline, 1983-86); b. 8.7.40, Seaham, Durham; m., Norma Ranson Peel; 1 s. Educ. Ryhope School, Sunderland; London School of Economics and Political Science; Durham University.

Assistant Teacher of History and Mathematics, Boldon Secondary School, 1962-63; Assistant Lecturer in Economics, then Liaison Officer for Adult Education, Monkwearmouth College of Further Education, 1963-72; Stevenson College of Further Education: Senior Lecturer in Social Studies, 1972-75, Head, Department of Language and Social Studies, 1975-80, Assistant Principal, 1980-83. Board Member: JEVCEL, Craigmillar Opportunities Trust, Midlothian Enterprise. Recreation: swimming. Address: (b.) 24 Milton Road East, Edinburgh EH15 2PP; T.-0131-660 1010.

Lishman, Professor Joyce, MA (Oxon), PhD, DipSW. Head, School of Applied Social Studies, Robert Gordon University, since 1993; m., Dr. J.R. Lishman; 1 s.; 1 d. Educ. Normanton Girls High School; St. Hilda's College, Oxford University; Edinburgh University; Aberdeen University. Social Worker/Senior Social Worker, Departments of Child and Family Psychiatry, Edinburgh; Research Assistant/Research Fellow, Aberdeen University; Editor, Research Highlights Series; Malcolm Sargent Social Worker, Royal Aberdeen Children's Hospital; Lecturer/Senior Lecturer, RGIT; Lead Assessor, Quality Assessment of Social Work, 1995-96. Publications: Handbook of Theory for Practice; Teachers in Social Work (Editor); Communication in Social Work; Research Highlights in Social Work series (General Editor). Recreations: family and friends; music; theatre; reading; cycling; swimming. Address: (b.) School of Applied Social Studies, The Robert Gordon University, Kepplestone Annexe, Queen's Road, Aberdeen AB9 2PG; T.-01224 263201.

Lister-Kaye, Sir John, 8th Bt. of Grange, DUniv. Naturalist, Author, Lecturer; Member, International Committee, World Wilderness Foundation, since 1984; Chairman, Scottish Committee, RSPB, 1985-92; Member, Committee for Scotland, NCC, 1989-90; NW Regional Chairman, NCC, 1991; NW Regional Chairman, Scottish Natural Heritage, 1992-96; b. 8.5.46; m., 1, Lady Sorrel Deirdre Bentinck; 1 s.; 2 d.; 2, Lucinda Anne Law. Educ. Allhallows School. Founded Field Studies Centre, Highlands, 1970; founder Director, Aigas Trust, 1979; Director, AigasQuest Ltd., 1997. Honorary Doctorate, University of Stirling, 1995. Publications: The White Island, 1972; Seal Cull, 1979; The Seeing Eye, 1980; One for Sorrow, 1994; Ill Fares the Land, 1995. Address: (h.) House of Aigas, Beauly, Inverness-shire IV4 7AD.

Lithgow, Sir William (James), 2nd Bt. of Ormsary, DL, LLD, CEng, FRINA, CBIM. Industrialist; Farmer; Chairman, Lithgows Limited, since 1959 (Director, since 1956); b. 10.5.34; m., 1, Valerie Helen Scott (deceased); 2, Mary Claire Hill; 2 s.; 1 d. Educ. Winchester College. Chairman, Hunterston Development Company Limited, 1987 (Director, since 1971); Director: Lithgows Limited, Lithgows Pty Limited; Chairman, Scott Lithgow Drydocks Ltd., 1967-78; Vice-Chairman, Scott Lithgow Ltd., 1968-78; Chairman, Western Ferries (Argyll) Ltd., 1972-85; Director, Bank of Scotland, 1962-86. Member: British Committee, Det Norske Veritas, 1966-92, Greenock District Hospital Board, 1961-66, General Board (Royal Society Nominee), Nat. Physical Lab., 1963-66; Honorary President, Students Association, and Member, Court, Strathclyde University, 1964-69; Member: Executive Committee, Scottish Council Development and Industry, 1969-85, Scottish Regional Council, CBI, 1969-76, Clyde Port Authority, 1969-71, West Central Scotland Plan Steering Committee, 1970-74, Board, National Ports Council, 1971-78, Scottish Milk Marketing Board, 1979-83; Chairman, Iona Cathedral Trustees Management Board, 1979-83; Council Member, Winston Churchill Memorial Trust, 1979-83; Member, Queen's Body Guard for Scotland (Royal Company of Archers), 1964; Fellow, Scottish Council Development and Industry; Honorary President: West Renfrewshire Battalion Boys' Brigade, Mid-Argyll

Agricultural Society. Recreations: rural life; invention; photography. Address: (b.) PO Box 7, Lochgilphead, Argyll PA31 8JH; T.-01880 770244.

Little, Professor John Anthony, BSc, MSc, MBA, PhD, CEng, MICE, CGeol, FGS. Assistant Principal, since 1997, and Professor and Head, Department of Civil, Structural and Environmental Engineering, Paisley University, since 1992; Associate Dean, Faculty of Engineering, since 1993; b. 24.11.48, Catterick; m., Gail; 1 s.; 2 d. Educ. Chatham House Grammar School, Ramsgate; University of Wales; Durham University; City University; Edinburgh University. Research engineer, construction industry, 1972-76; Senior Lecturer, Hatfield Polytechnic, 1976-86; Lecturer/Senior Lecturer, Heriot-Watt University, 1986-92. Chairman, Scottish Geotechnical Group, since 1992; Co-ordinator, Scotland Science Engineering and Technology, 1996; Member, Women into Science and Engineering Scotland Committee, since 1996. Address: (b.) Paisley University, High Street, Paisley PA1 2BE; T.-0141-848 3250.

Little, Keith, MB, ChB, MD, FRCP, FRCSEdin, FFAEM. Consultant in Accident and Emergency Medicine, Edinburgh Royal Infirmary; b. 26.4.43, Yeadon, Yorkshire; 2 s.; 2 d. Educ. Dalbeattie High School; Dumfries Academy; Edinburgh Medical School. First posts in Edinburgh; moved to Derby as a Registrar in Accident and Emergency Medicine; Consultant, Chester Royal Infirmary, 1974-78. Past President, British Association for Accident and Emergency Medicine; President, Faculty of Accident and Emergency Medicine. Publication: Accident and Emergency Resuscitation (Co-Author). Recreations: golf; tennis. Address: (b.) Accident and Emergency Department, Royal Infirmary, Edinburgh; T.-0131-536 4007.

Littlejohn, Professor David, BSc, PhD, CChem, FRSC. Professor of Analytical Chemistry, Strathclyde University, since 1988; b. 1.5.53, Glasgow; m., Lesley Shaw MacDonald. Educ. Duncanrig Secondary School, East Kilbride; Strathclyde University. Technical Officer, ICI Petrochemicals Division, Wilton, Middlesborough, 1978-80; Lecturer/Senior Lecturer in Chemistry, Strathclyde University, 1981-88. Awarded 15th SAC Silver Medal by Royal Society of Chemistry, 1987; joint Editor in Chief, Talanta, International Journal of Pure and Applied Analytical Chemistry, 1989-91. Publications: 140 research papers, 10 reviews, one book. Address: (b.) Department of Pure and Applied Chemistry, Strathclyde University, 295 Cathedral Street, Glasgow G1 1XL; T.-0141-548 2067.

Littlejohn, Doris, JP, BL, DUniv. President, Industrial Tribunals (Scotland), since 1991; b. 19.3.35, Glasgow; m., Robert; 3 d. Educ. Queen's Park School, Glasgow; University of Glasgow. Solicitor in private practice in Stirling until 1977; Chairman, Industrial Tribunals, until 1988, Regional Chairman, until 1991. Member of Court, University of Stirling; Non-Executive Director, Stirling Royal Infirmary; Member, Human Genetics Advisory Commission; former Member: Broadcasting Council for Scotland, General Advisory Committee, BBC. Address: (b.) Central Office of the Industrial Tribunals, Eagle Building, 215 Bothwell Street, Glasgow G2 7TS; T.-0141-204 0730.

Littlejohn, Robert King, MA (Aberdeen), MA (Sussex), MIPD. Registrar, Royal College of Physicians and Surgeons of Glasgow, since 1996; b. 17.3.46, Aberdeen; m., Anna; 1 s.; 2 d. Educ. Morrison's Academy, Crieff; Aberdeen University; Moray House College; Sussex University. Administrative (Education) Officer, RAF, 1969-96 including: Directorate of Air Staff Briefing and Co-ordination, 1987-90; Officer Commanding Administration Wing, RAF Leeming, 1990-93; Head of RAF Resettlement Service, 1993-96; retired in rank of Wing Commander. Recreations: golf; hill-walking; opera; Aberdeen FC. Address: (b.) 232-242 St. Vincent Street, Glasgow G2 5RJ; T.-0141-221 6072.

Littlejohn, William Hunter, RSA, RSW, RGI; b. 16.4.29, Arbroath. Educ. Arbroath High School; Dundee College of Art. Art teaching in Angus schools, 1953-56; Art teaching, Arbroath High School, 1956-66; Gray's School of Art, Aberdeen: Lecturer, 1966-72, Head of Painting, then Head of Fine Art, 1972-86; retired from teaching, 1986. Address: (h.) 16 Colvill Place, Arbroath DD11 1RB; T.-01241 874402.

Livesay, Admiral Sir Michael Howard, KCB, CIMgt. President, Royal British Legion Scotland, since 1996; President, Earl Haig Fund Scotland, since 1996; Non-Executive Director: Scottish Nuclear, since 1993, Interexec Scotland Ltd., since 1994; Commissioner, Northern Lighthouse Board, since 1994 (Chairman, 1997); b. 5.4.36, Middlesbrough; m., Sally House; 2 d. Educ. Acklam Hall Grammar School; Britannia Royal Naval College. Joined Royal Navy, 1952; Commissioned 1957; Aircraft Direction Specialist, 1959; served HM Ships: Loch Alvie, Hermes, Aisne, Victorious; in command, HMS Hubberston, 1966; promoted Commander, 1970 and in command HMS Plymouth; promoted Captain, 1975; Captain, Fishery Protection and Mine Counter Measures at South Queensferry; first Commanding Officer, HMS Invincible, 1980; Director, Naval Warfare, 1982; promoted Rear Admiral, 1984; Flag Officer, Sea Training, 1984-86; Assistant Chief of Naval Staff, 1986-89; promoted Vice Admiral, 1989; Flag Officer, Scotland and Northern Ireland, 1989-91; promoted Admiral, 1991; Second Sea Lord and Chief of Naval Personnel, 1991-93; retired from RN 1993. Governor, Ardvreck School; Member, Council, Thistle Foundation. Recreations: fishing; golf; gardening; reading; outdoor sports. Address: c/o Naval Secretary, Victory Building, HM Naval Base, Portsmouth PO1 3LS.

Livingstone of Bachuil, Alastair, MA, LLB, FSA Scot. Baron of Bachuil; b. 1.9.14, Blantyre, Nyasaland; m., Valerie Collins; 2 s.; 3 d. Educ. Loretto School; Edinburgh University; Cambridge University. Sudan Political Service, 1938-40; 1940-43: commissioned into West Yorkshire Regiment in Khartoum, later Brigade Intelligence Officer, 9th Indian Infantry Brigade, active service in Eritrea and Western Desert; seconded to Palestine Government as Assistant District Commissioner, 1943-47; Executive, Iraq Petroleum Company Ltd., 1948-73. Chairman, Lismore Community Council, 1977-80; Member, Convention of the Baronage of Scotland; Hereditary Keeper of the Pastoral Staff of Saint Moluag; Past Chairman, 1745 Association; Co-Editor, Muster Roll of Prince Charles Edward Stuart's Army, 1746. Recreations: genealogy; Scottish history; country pursuits. Address: (h.) Bachuil, Isle of Lismore, Argyll; T.-01631 760 256.

Livingstone, Bill (William). Editorial Director, Dunfermline Press Group, since 1997; Chairman, Guild of Editors (Scotland), 1994-96; Life Trustee, Carnegie Dunfermline and Hero Fund Trusts, since 1991; b. 23.7.44, Dunfermline; m., Margaret Stark; 2 s.; 2 d. Educ. Dunfermline High School. Entire career with Dunfermline Press Group: Editor, Dunfermline Press, 1984-96. Elder, St. Paul's Parish Church, Dunfermline; Hon. Vice-President, Dunfermline and District Bn., Boys' Brigade. Address: (b.) Pitreavie Business Park, Dunfermline, Fife KY11 5QS; T.-01383 728201.

Livingstone, Ian Lang, OBE, BL, NP. Chairman: Lanarkshire Health Board, since 1993, Lanarkshire Development Agency, since 1991, Board, Motherwell College, 1989-97; Consultant Solicitor, since 1989; b. 23.2.38, Hamilton; m., Diane; 2 s. Educ. Hamilton Academy; Glasgow University. Qualified as Solicitor, 1960; Partner, Senior Partner, Ballantyne & Copland, Solicitors, Motherwell, 1962-86; Chairman and Director, family property investment and development company, since 1987. Former Chairman, Motherwell Football Club; Member, Dalziel High School Board; Hon. President,

Motherwell Conservative Association; Governor, David Livingstone Memorial Trust; Elder, St. Mary's Parish Church, Motherwell. Recreations: walking; football; music. Address: (h.) 223 Manse Road, Motherwell ML1 2PY; T.- 01698 253750.

Lloyd, Douglas Mathon Gent, BSc, DSc(Bristol), DSc(St. Andrews), CChem, FRSC, FRSE. Honorary Reader in Chemistry, University of St. Andrews, since 1985; b. 19.7.20, Bristol; m., Lydia Morris. Educ. Colston's School, Bristol; University of Bristol. University of Sheffield, 1942-45; University of Bristol, 1945-46; Lecturer, Senior Lecturer, Reader, 1947-85, University of St. Andrews; Provost, St. Leonard's College, University of St. Andrews, 1973-78. Member, Council: Chemical Society, 1974-77, Royal Society of Chemistry, 1985-88; Member, Perkin Division Council, Royal Society of Chemistry, 1983-86; Chairman, Tayside Section, Royal Society of Chemistry, 1971-73. Recreations: organist; travel (especially by sea); interest in wine and theatre. Address: (b.) Department of Chemistry, Purdie Building, University of St. Andrews, St. Andrews KY16 9ST; T.-01334 463845.

Lloyd, Ivor Graham, BA, DipLib, MLib, ALA. Head of Information Services, University of Abertay Dundee, since 1996; b. 28.10.50, Edinburgh; m., Rosemary; 1 s.; 1 d. Educ. Ainslie Park Secondary School, Edinburgh; University of Strathclyde; University of Wales. Assistant Librarian, Kirkcaldy Technical College, 1975-76; Subject Librarian, Duncan of Jordanstone College of Art, 1976-84; Depute Chief Librarian, Dundee College of Technology, 1984-89; Chief Librarian, University of Abertay Dundee, 1989-96. Recreations: golf; gardening. Address: (b.) University of Abertay Dundee, Bell Street, Dundee; T.- 01382 308866.

Lloyd-Jones, Glyn Robin, MA, BA. Author and Novelist; Vice President, Scottish PEN International, since 1993; Co-ordinator, Scottish Forum for Development Education in Schools (SFDES), since 1996; b. 5.10.34, London; m., Sallie Hollocombe; 1 s.; 2 d. Educ. Blundell's School, Tiverton; Selwyn College, Cambridge University; Jordanhill College of Education. Teaching in Scottish secondary schools; Director, Curriculum Development Centre, Clydebank; English-Speaking Union Thyne Travel Scholarship to America, 1974; President, Scottish Association of Writers, 1981-86; Adviser, Education Department, Dunbartonshire, 1972-89; radio drama: Ice in Wonderland, 1992 (winner, Radio Times new drama script award); Rainmaker, 1995. Publications: children's: Where the Forest and the Garden Meet, 1980; novels: Lord of the Dance (Winner, BBC/Arrow First Novel Competition, 1983); The Dreamhouse, 1985; Fallen Angels, 1992; education books: Assessment: From Principles to Action, 1985; How to Produce Better Worksheets, 1985; non-fiction: Argonauts of the Western Isles, 1989. Recreations: mountaineering; sea-kayaking; photography; chess. Address: (h.) 26 East Clyde Street, Helensburgh G84 7PG; T.-01436 672010.

Lo, Professor Kwok Lun, MSc, PhD, CEng, FIEE. Professor of Power Systems, Strathclyde University, since 1989; Visiting and Consultant Professor to several overseas universities, since 1987; power systems consultant, since 1970; b. 23.6.43; m., Dr. K.K.N. Lo; 2 s. Educ. St. Joseph's College, Hong Kong; UMIST. Began career with South Wales Switchgear Ltd., Central Electricity Generating Board, South Wales Electricity Board; joined Department of Electrical Engineering, Paisley College of Technology, 1971; joined Strathclyde University, 1977, as Lecturer, then Senior Lecturer, then Reader; author/co-author of more than 200 technical publications. Recreations: swimming; walking. Address: (b.) Department of EEE, Royal College, 204 George Street, Strathclyde University, Glasgow; T.- 0141-552 4400, Ext. 2169.

Lobban, Alexander James, MIFireE. Firemaster, Grampian Fire Brigade, since 1993; b. 16.2.47, Aberdeen; m., Caroline; 2 d. Educ. Inverurie Academy. Joined Fire Service, 1966; Course Director — Command Studies, Fire Service College, Moreton-in-Marsh, 1984; joined Grampian as Deputy Firemaster, 1989. Recreations: sailing; skiing. Address: (b.) 19 North Anderson Drive, Aberdeen AB15 6DW; T.-01224 696666.

Lochhead, Liz. Poet and Playwright; b. 1947, Motherwell. Educ. Glasgow School of Art. Combined teaching art and writing for eight years; became full-time writer after selection as first holder, Scottish/Canadian Writers' Exchange Fellowship, 1978; former Writer in Residence, Tattenhall Centre, Chester. Publications include: Memo for Spring, Islands, Grimm Sisters, Dreaming of Frankenstein, True Confessions; plays include: Blood and Ice, Dracula, Same Difference, Sweet Nothings, Now and Then, True Confessions, Mary Queen of Scots Got Her Head Chopped Off, The Big Picture.

Lockett, Patrick Gordon, CA. Director, James Finlay PLC; Director, Scottish National Trust PLC, since 1996; b. 3.5.46, Glasgow; m., Erica; 1 s.; 1 d. Educ. Wellington College, Berkshire; Harvard Business School. Partner, Whinney Murray & Co., 1979; Partner, Ernst & Young, 1979-95. Director, Cumbernauld Development Corporation, 1989-97. Recreations: field sports; tennis; travel. Address: (h.) Swindridgemuir, Dalry, Ayrshire; T.-01294 832079.

Lockhart, Sheriff Brian Alexander, BL. Sheriff, Glasgow and Strathkelvin, since 1981; b. 1.10.42, Ayr; m., Christine Ross Clark; 2 s.; 2 d. Educ. Glasgow Academy; Glasgow University. Partner, Robertson Chalmers and Auld, Solicitors, 1967-79; Sheriff, North Strathclyde, at Paisley, 1979-81; Member, Parole Board for Scotland; Secretary, Sheriffs' Association. Recreations: fishing; golf; squash; family. Address: (h.) 18 Hamilton Avenue, Glasgow G41; T.-0141-427 1921.

Lockhart, Brian Robert Watson. MA (Hons), DipEd. Headmaster, Robert Gordon's College, Aberdeen, since 1996; b. 19.7.44, Edinburgh; m., Fiona Anne Sheddon; 1 s.; 2 d. Educ. George Heriot's School, Edinburgh; Aberdeen University. Teacher of History and Economic History, George Heriot's School, 1968-72; Principal Teacher of History, 1972-81; Deputy Rector, High School of Glasgow, 1981-96. Headteachers' Association of Scotland: Member, Council, 1988-97, Member, Executive, 1989-94; Member, Universities and Colleges Admissions Service Scottish Standing Committee; Member, Higher Still Implementation Group. Recreations: reading biographies; sport; films; politics. Address: (h.) 80 Gray Street, Aberdeen AB10 6JE; T.-01224 315776.

Lockhart of the Lee, Angus Hew; b. 17.8.46, Dunsyre; m., Susan Elizabeth Normand; 1 s.; 1 d. Educ. Rannoch School, Perthshire; North of Scotland College of Agriculture. Recognised as Chief of the Name Lockhart, 1957; Owner and Manager, Lee and Carnwath Estates; Member, Standing Council of Scottish Chiefs. Recreations: shooting; skiing. Address: (h.) Newholm, Dunsyre, Lanark ML11 8NQ; T.- 01968 682254.

Lockhead, Moir, OBE, IEng, MCIT, MIRTE. Deputy Chairman and Chief Executive, FirstBus plc; b. 25.4.45, Sedgefield; m., Audrey; 3 s.; 1 d. Educ. West Cornforth Secondary School; Darlington Technical College; Middlesborough Polytechnic. Former Head of Engineering, Strathclyde Passenger Transport Executive; joined Grampian Regional Transport as General Manager, 1985; Executive Chairman, GRT Bus Group PLC, 1989. Address: (b.) 395 King Street, Aberdeen AB24 5RP; T.-01224 650102.

Lockley, Stephen Randolph, BSc, CEng, MICE, FICT, MIHT, DipTE. Transport Consultant, since 1997; b. 19.6.43, Manchester; m., Angela; 2 d. Educ. Morecambe Grammar School; Manchester University. Highway and Planning Engineer, Lancashire County Council, 1964-72; Transportation and Planning Engineer, Lanarkshire County Council, 1972-75; Strathclyde Regional Council: Principal Engineer (Transportation), 1975-77, Depute Director of Policy Planning, 1977-80, Principal Executive Officer, 1980-86; Director General, Strathclyde Passenger Transport Executive, 1986-97. Address: 64 Townhead Street, Strathaven, Lanarkshire ML10 6DJ; T.-01357 529395.

Lodge, Professor Raymond Anthony, BA, PhD. Professor of French Language and Linguistics, University of St. Andrews, since 1995; b. 12.7.42, Leeds; m., Janet Mary Martin; 2 s.; 1 d. Educ. Pudsey Grammar School; University of Manchester. Lecturer then Senior Lecturer in French, University of Aberdeen, 1967-84; Professor of French, University of Newcastle upon Tyne, 1984-95. Publication: French: From Dialect to Standard, 1993. Recreation: singing. Address: (b.) French Department, University of St. Andrews, St. Andrews KY16 9AJ; T.-01334 463636.

Logan, Alec, MB, ChB, FRCGP. Editor, Hoolet (Scottish magazine, Royal College of General Practitioners), since 1994; Deputy Editor, British Journal of General Practice, since 1997; b. 18.11.59, Bellshill; m., Janice Crofts; 2 s. Educ. Hutchesons' Grammar School; Glasgow University. Medical Officer, Royal Navy, 1980-88; GP, Wishaw, since 1988. Recreations: sailing; reading; music. Address: (h.) 47 Orchard Street, Motherwell ML1 3JE; T.-01698 258201.

Logan, Andrew, SDA, NDA, FIHort. Farmer; Director, Scottish Nuclear Stock Association, since 1983; Chairman, Dorward Gray Ltd.; b. 24.3.40, Cupar; m., M.L. Fleming; 3 s.; 1 d. Educ. Strathallan School; Edinburgh School of Agriculture. Director: Fifegro, 1973-79, Elba, 1979-84, Central Farmers, 1974-83; Chairman, Soft Fruit and Field Vegetable Committee, Scottish NFU, 1979-83; Member, Scottish Agricultural Development Council, 1983-86; Governor: Scottish Crop Research Institute, 1986-87, National Vegetable Research Station, 1977-87, Strathallan School, since 1986; Director, East of Scotland Growers, 1987-89; Member, Horticultural Development Council, 1986-92; Member, Home Grown Cereals Authority Research and Development Committee, 1987-89; Director, Scotfresh, 1984-89; Governor, Institute of Horticultural Research, 1987-89; Member, Scottish Agricultural Research and Development Advisory Council, 1987-90; Director, Futursky, since 1988; Director, Top Hat Holdings, since 1989; Council Member, Scottish Agricultural Organisation Society, 1991-97. Recreations: skiing; golf. Address: (h.) Tarvit Home Farm, Cupar, Fife; T.-Cupar 652808.

Logan, Jimmy. Actor/Manager; Comedian; b. 4.4.28, Glasgow. One of five children who appeared on stage as The Logan Family; toured as an accordionist, juvenile lead and comedian's feed; for many years starred in Five Past Eight (summer revue) and numerous pantomimes; wrote and produced Lauder (one-man show); nine appearances at Royal performances.

Logan, Rev. Robert James Victor, MA, BD. Minister, Crown Church, Inverness, since 1970; b. 8.6.38, Kilmarnock; m., Catherine Steel Young. Educ. Dundee High School; St. Andrews University; Edinburgh University. Assistant Minister, Auld Kirk of Ayr, 1962-64; Minister, Newton Parish Church, Dalkeith, 1964-70; Member, Church Boundaries' Commission, 1974-75; Clerk: Synod of Moray, 1972-75, Synod of the Southern Highlands, 1976-92, Inverness Presbytery, 1980-96; Convener, Nomination Committee, General Assembly,

1979-82; Chairman, successful group applying for franchise to operate Moray Firth Radio, 1979-81. Publication: The Lion, The Pit and the Snowy Day. Recreations: classical music; opera; bridge; reading history. Address: (h.) 39 Southside Road, Inverness IV2 4XA; T.-01463 231140.

Logan, Rt. Rev. Vincent, DipRE. Roman Catholic Bishop of Dunkeld, since 1981; b. 30.6.41, Bathgate. Educ. Blairs College, Aberdeen; St. Andrew's College, Drygrange. Ordained Priest, 1964; Assistant Priest, St. Margaret's, Edinburgh, 1964-66; Corpus Christi College, London, 1966-67; Chaplain, St. Joseph's Hospital, Rosewell, Midlothian, 1966-67; Adviser in Religious Education, Archdiocese of St. Andrews and Edinburgh, 1967; Parish Priest, St. Mary's, Ratho, 1977-81; Vicar Episcopal for Education, Edinburgh, 1978. Address: Bishop's House, 29 Roseangle, Dundee DD1 4LS; T.-01382 224327.

Logan, (William) Bruce, BA (Cantab), LLB, NP, WS. Partner, W. & J. Burness, WS, Solicitors, since 1969; b. 7.9.41, Forfar; m., Jennifer Mary; 3 d. Educ. Fettes College, Edinburgh; Cambridge University; Edinburgh University. Director: Art in Partnership Scotland Ltd, Scottish Rights of Way Society Ltd. Recreations: music; contemporary art; cycling; walking. Address: (b.) 16 Hope Street, Edinburgh; T.-0131-226 2561.

Logie, John Robert Cunningham, MB, ChB, PhD, FRCS(Eng), FRCS(Edin), FRCS(Glas). Consultant General Surgeon, Inverness Hospitals, since 1981; Member, Council, Royal College of Surgeons of Edinburgh, since 1991; b. 9.9.46, Aberdeen; m., Sheila C. Will. Educ. Robert Gordon's College, Aberdeen; Trinity College, Glenalmond; Aberdeen University. House Officer, then Senior House Officer, then Lecturer, Department of Surgery, then Senior Registrar, Aberdeen Royal Infirmary. Recreations: rugby refereeing; garden; railways; ornamental waterfowl. Address: (h.) The Darroch, Little Cantray, Culloden Moor, Inverness IV1 2EG; T.-01463 792090.

Logue, James, CEng, FIMechE, MIMgt. Personnel Director, ScotRail Train Operating Company; since 1994; Board Member: Institution of Mechanical Engineers, since 1990, Strathkelvin Enterprise Trust, since 1987; b. 13.5.39, Glasgow; m., Pamela; 1 s.; 2 d. Educ. St. Mungo's, Glasgow; Stow College, Glasgow. ScotRail: Area Engineer, 1978-89, Quality Programmes Manager, 1989-92, Retail Manager, 1992-94; Chairman, IMechE Railway Division, Scottish Branch. Recreations: golf; DIY; car maintenance; socialising. Address: (h.) 1 Linnhe Avenue, Bishopbriggs, Glasgow G64 1HG; T.-0141-563 6598.

Lonie, James William Laing, MA. Head of Arts and Cultural Heritage Division, Scottish Office Education and Industry Department; b. 24.6.41, Falkirk; m., Nuala Clare Ward. Educ. Falkirk High School; Edinburgh University; Gonville and Caius College, Cambridge. HM Treasury, 1967-76; joined Scottish Office, 1976. Recreations: music; walking; languages. Address: (b.) 1-A21, Education and Industry Department, Victoria Quay, Edinburgh, EH6 6QQ; T.-0131-244 0246.

Lord, Geoffrey, OBE, MA, AIB, FRSA. Founder Trustee, The ADAPT Trust, since 1992; b. 24.2.28, Rochdale; m., Jean; 1 s.; 1 d. Educ. Rochdale Grammar School; Bradford University. Midland Bank Ltd., 1946-58; Greater Manchester Probation and After-Care Service, 1958-76 (Deputy Chief Probation Officer, 1974-76); Secretary and Treasurer, Carnegie UK Trust, 1977-93; Vice-President, Selcare Trust; Chairman, Pollock Memorial Missionary Trust; Honorary Fellow, Manchester Metropolitan University, 1987; Trustee, HomeStart UK; Chairman, The Unemployed Voluntary Action Fund, 1990-95; Past President, Centre for Environmental Interpretation.

Publications: The Arts and Disabilities, 1981; Interpretation of the Environment, 1984. Recreations: the arts; philately; walking; enjoying life. Address: (h.) 9 Craigleith View, Edinburgh.

Lord, John, BA, FRSA. Director, EDAW, economic development and planning consultants, since 1996; b. 15.4.52, Bristol; m., Wendy; 2 s.; 1 d. Educ. Australia; Woking County Grammar School; Kingston College of Further Education; Warwick University. Freelance journalist and writer; Administrative Trainee, Department of Employment; Area Manager, Training Agency, 1989-90; Chief Executive, Enterprise Ayrshire, 1990-93; Director Strategy, Scottish Enterprise, 1993-96. Publication: The Floating Harbour – A Landscape History of Bristol City Docks. Recreations: architectural history; football; the arts. Address: (b.) EDAW, 219 St. Vincent Street, Glasgow G2 5QY.

Lord, Jonathan Christopher, MA. Secretary, Royal Scottish Automobile Club, since 1991; b. 29.4.53, Alverstoke; m., Angela Phillips; 1 s. Educ. Dollar Academy; St. Andrews University. Ministry of Defence (Naval), 1975-76; Royal Scottish Automobile Club, since 1976; Member, RAC British Motor Sports Council, since 1991; RAC Rallies Committee, since 1982; FIA Observer for International Rallies; RACMSA Steward; Clerk of the Course, RSAC International Scottish Rally, since 1982; Standing Joint Committee of RAC, AA and RSAC: Joint Secretary, 1986, Member, since 1991; Secretary, RSAC (Motor Sport) Limited, since 1982; Secretary to the Vestry, St. Bride's Episcopal Church, Glasgow, since 1991. Recreations: music (especially choral singing); cricket; motor sport; following Dunfermline Athletic FC. Address: (h.) 11 Melrose Gardens, Glasgow G20 6RB; T.-0141-946 5045.

Lorimer, A. Ross, MD, FRCP, FRCPGlas, FRCPEdin. Honorary Professor, Glasgow University; Consultant Physician and Cardiologist, Glasgow Royal Infirmary, since 1970; b. 5.5.37, Bellshill; m., Fiona Marshall; 3 s. Educ. Uddingston Grammar School; High School of Glasgow; Glasgow University. Recreations: reading; walking. Address: (b.) Department of Cardiology, Royal Infirmary, Glasgow.

Lothian, Sheriff Andrew, MA, LLB. Sheriff of Lothian and Borders at Edinburgh. Advocate, 1968. Address: (b.) Sheriff Court House, 27 Chambers Street, Edinburgh, EH1 1LB.

Lothian, Professor Niall, BA, CA, FRSA. Professor, Graduate School of Business, Heriot-Watt University, since 1996; b. 27.2.48, Edinburgh; m., Carol Miller; 1 s.; 1 d. Educ. Daniel Stewart's College, Edinburgh; Heriot-Watt University. Lecturer, Senior Lecturer, Professor and Head, Department of Accountancy and Finance, Heriot-Watt University, 1973-96; Visiting Professor: IMEDE, Lausanne, 1979-80, INSEAD, Fontainebleau, since 1984; Consultant, United Nations Industrial Development Organisation, Vienna, since 1980; President, Institute of Chartered Accountants of Scotland, 1995-96. Publications: Accounting for Inflation: Issues and Managerial Practices, 1978; Audit Quality and Value for Money, 1983; How Companies Manage R. & D., 1984; Corporate Performance Indicators, 1987. Address: (b.) Graduate School of Business, Heriot-Watt University, PO Box 807, Riccarton, Edinburgh EH14 4AT; T.-0131-451 3090.

Lothian, 12th Marquess of (Peter Francis Walter Kerr), KCVO, DL; b. 8.9.22, Melbourne, near Derby; m., Antonella Newland; 2 s.; 4 d. Educ. Ampleforth College, York; Christ Church, Oxford. Parliamentary Under Secretary, Ministry of Health, 1964; Parliamentary Under Secretary, Foreign and Commonwealth Office, 1970-72; Lord in Waiting, 1972-73; Lord Warden of the Stannaries, 1977-83. Knight of Malta; Lieutenant, Queen's Bodyguard for Scotland; Chairman of Council, Scottish Branch, British Red Cross, 1973-83. Recreation: music. Address: Ferniehirst Castle, Jedburgh, Roxburghshire; T.-01835 864021/0835 862872.

Loudon, Alasdair John, LLB, NP, WS. Senior Partner, Loudons WS, Edinburgh, since 1992; President, Edinburgh Bar Association, since 1996; b. 7.4.56, Edinburgh; m., Mary V.; 2 s.; 1 d. Educ. Edinburgh Academy; Dundee University. Apprentice, Tods, Murray and Jamieson, WS, 1978-80; Qualified Assistant, Warner & Co., 1980-82, Partner, 1982-92; founded Loudons WS, 1992; accredited as specialist in family law. Recreations: golf (Bruntsfield Links and Luffness New); football (Heart of Midlothian supporter). Address: (b.) 29 St. Patrick Square, Edinburgh; T.-0131-662 4193.

Loudon, John Alexander, LLB, NP, SSC. Partner, MacRoberts, Edinburgh; specialist in Liquor Licensing Law; b. 5.12.49, Edinburgh; m., Alison Jane Bruce Laird; 2 s. Educ. Edinburgh Academy; Dundee University. Apprenticeship, Tindal, Oatts and Roger, Solicitors, Glasgow. Former Member, Council, Law Society of Scotland; Secretary, Scottish Division, British Hospitality Association; Legal Adviser, Scottish Decorators Federation and Edinburgh and Lothians Decorators' Association; High Constable, City of Edinburgh Ward XV. Recreations: children; shooting; stalking; skiing; occasional use of a mountain bike and even more occasional golf. Address: (h.) 27 Melville Street, Edinburgh EH3 7JF; T.-0131-226 2552.

Loudon, John Bruce, MB, ChB, FRCPsych, DPM. Consultant Psychiatrist, Royal Edinburgh Hospital, since 1978; Principal Medical Officer (part-time, on secondment), Department of Health, Scottish Office, since 1997; Honorary Senior Lecturer, Department of Psychiatry, Edinburgh University; b. 12.8.43, Edinburgh; m., Susan Mary Lay; 3 s. Educ. Edinburgh Academy; Edinburgh University. Clinical Director, General Psychiatry, Royal Edinburgh Hospital, 1991-94; Head, Mental Health Service, Edinburgh Healthcare NHS Trust, 1994-96. Address: (b.) Andrew Duncan Clinic, Morningside, Edinburgh EH10 5HF; T.-0131-537 6452.

Love, Frances Mary. Director, Marriage Counselling Scotland, since 1987; Tutor and Lecturer, Scottish Human Relations and Counselling Course, since 1986; Organisational Consultant, SIHR, since 1986; b. 2.7.38, Edinburgh; m., James Love; 1 d. Educ. Broughton Secondary School. Edinburgh Public Library Service; voluntary playleader, Edinburgh Toddlers Playcentres; Pre-School Playgroup Association: playgroup supervisor, fieldworker, Scottish Adviser; General Secretary, Pre-School Playgroups Association; Executive Officer/Company Secretary, Scottish Council for Opportunities in Play Experience (SCOPE). Member, Management Board, Scottish Council of Voluntary Organisations; Member, Executive Committees, Scottish Child & Family Alliance and Scottish Council for Single Parents; Member, Council, Stepfamily Scotland. Recreations: gardening; reading; theatre; dress-making. Address: (b.) 105 Hanover Street, Edinburgh EH2 1DJ; T.-0131-225 5006.

Love, Robert Malcolm, MA (Hons), FRSAMD. Controller of Drama, Scottish Television, since 1979; b. 9.1.37, Paisley. Educ. Paisley Grammar School; Glasgow University; Washington University, St. Louis. Actor and Director, various repertory companies, including Nottingham Playhouse, 1962-65; Producer, Thames TV, 1966-75, including Public Eye, Van Der Valk; freelance Producer, 1976-79, including Thames TV, LWT, Seacastle

Film Productions, Scottish TV. Awards including: Commonwealth Festival, New York TV and Film Festival, Chicago Film Festival, BAFTA Scotland, nominated for International Emmy, New York, 1982; productions for Scottish include Taggart, High Road, Doctor Finlay, McCallum. Governor, RSAMD, since 1994; Member, Scottish Arts Council, since 1994. Recreations: literature; music; theatre; travel. Address: (b.) Scottish Television, Cowcaddens, Glasgow.

Lovelace, 5th Earl of (Peter Axel William Locke King); b. 26.11.51; m. Address: Torridon House, Torridon, IV22 2HA.

Low, Alistair James, BSc, FFA. Director, William M. Mercer Ltd., Actuaries and Employee Benefit Consultants, since 1986; Non-Executive Director, Scottish Widows Fund, since 1984; b. 2.8.42, Dundee; m., Shona Wallace; 2 s.; 1 d. Educ. Dundee High School; St. Andrews University. Recreations: golf; skiing; bridge. Address: (h.) Thornfield, Erskine Loan, Gullane, East Lothian.

Low, Bet, ARSA, RSW, RGI. Freelance Artist; b. 27.12.24, Gourock. Educ. Greenock Academy; Glasgow School of Art; Hospitalfield College of Art. Joined Unity Theatre Company, set designing etc., 1946; exhibited in international exhibition, Warsaw, 1954; co-founder and exhibitor, first open-air exhibition on railings at Botanic Gardens, Glasgow; worked part-time as art therapist, early 60s; Co-Founder and Co-Director, New Charing Cross Gallery, Glasgow, 1963-68; major retrospective exhibition, Third Eye Centre, 1985; exhibited widely in Britain and Europe and recently in Hong Kong. Recreations: reading; opera; Glasgow Art Club; beach-combing; just pottering. Address: 53 Kelvinside Gardens, Glasgow G20 6BQ; T.-0141-946 1377.

Low, Eur Ing. Sir James (Richard) Morrison-, 3rd Bt, DL, DFH, CEng, MIEE. Director, Osborne & Hunter Ltd., Glasgow, 1956-89; b. 3.8.25; m., Ann Rawson Gordon; 1 s.; 3 d. Educ. Ardvreck; Harrow; Merchiston; Faraday House, London. Royal Corps of Signals, 1943-47 (Captain). President, Electrical Contractors Association of Scotland, 1982-84; Director, National Inspection Council of Electrical Installation Contractors, 1982-88 (Chairman, Scottish Committee, 1982-88); Chairman, Electrical Industry Liaison Committee, 1986-88; Chairman, Fife Area Scout Council, 1966-84; Chairman, Cupar Branch, East Fife Conservative Association, 1965-78; Trustee, TSB, 1960-80; President, Elecrical Contractors Association of Scotland, 1982-84; DL, Fife, 1978.

Low, William, CBE, LLD, JP. Chairman, Dundee Heritage Trust, 1986-96; b. 12.9.21, Dundee; m., Elizabeth Ann Stewart Sime; 2 s. Educ. Merchiston Castle School, Edinburgh. Chairman: Don & Low (Holdings) Ltd., 1975-89, UBI Scotland, 1984-89, European Association for Textile Polyolefins, 1982-85, British Polyolefin Association, 1971-73 and 1978-79; President, Dundee & Tayside Chamber of Commerce & Industry, 1973-74; Chairman, Scottish Enterprise Tayside, 1991-94. Past President, Scottish Lawn Tennis Association; Provost, Burgh of Kirriemuir, 1973-75; appointed Fellow, Scottish Council (Development & Industry), 1989. Recreations: shooting; fishing; golf; gardening. Address: (h.) Herdhill Court, Kirriemuir, Angus DD8 5LG; T.-01575 572215.

Lowden, Professor Gordon Stuart, MA, LLB, CA. Director, Dundee and London Investment Trust PLC, since 1981; b. 22.5.27, Bangkok; m., Kathleen; 2 s.; 1 d. Educ. Dundee High School; Strathallan School; St. John's College, Cambridge; St. Andrews University. Trained with Moody Stuart & Robertson, CA, Dundee; became Partner, 1959; part-time Lecturer/Senior Lecturer, Dundee University, 1955-83; Honorary Professor, Department of Accountancy and Business Finance, Dundee University, since 1987; Member, Board of Governors, Strathallan School; Honorary Sheriff, since 1991; former Chairman, Dundee Port Authority; Past President, Institute of Chartered Accountants of Scotland. Recreations: golf; watching rugby; bridge. Address: (h.) 169 Hamilton Street, Barnhill, Dundee DD5 2RE; T.-01382 778360.

Lowe, Professor Gordon Douglas Ogilvie, MB, ChB, MD, FRCPEdin, FRCPGlas, FRCPLond. Professor of Vascular Medicine, Glasgow University, since 1993; Consultant Physician, Glasgow Royal Infirmary, since 1985; Co-Director, West of Scotland Haemophilia Centre, since 1987; b. 2.1.49, London; m., Ann Harvie; 1 s.; 1 d. Educ. Dundee High School; St. Andrews University. House Officer, Royal Infirmary and Maryfield Hospital, Dundee, 1972-73; Senior House Officer, City Hospital, Nottingham, 1973-74; Registrar, Royal Infirmary, Glasgow, 1974-77; Lecturer, Glasgow University, 1978-85, Senior Lecturer, 1985-92, Reader, 1992-93. Past President, British Society for Haemostasis and Thrombosis. Publications: editor of books and author of publications on thrombosis and bleeding disorders. Recreations: travel; railways; gardening. Address: (b.) Department of Medicine, Royal Infirmary, Glasgow G31 2ER; T.-0141-211 5412.

Lowe, Janet, BA (Hons), MBA, MIPD. Principal, Lauder College, Dunfermline, since 1996; b. 27.9.50, South Normanton; m., Donald Thomas Stewart. Educ. Swanwick Hall Grammar School; Hull University; Dundee University. Immigration Officer, Home Office, 1973-76; Administrative Assistant, Hull University, 1976-80; Administrator, Lothian Region Social Work Department, 1980-82; Napier University: Examinations Assistant, Personnel Officer, Assistant Academic Registrar, 1982-88; Secretary and Registrar, Duncan of Jordanstone College of Art, 1988-93; Depute Principal, Lauder College, 1993-96. Member: Scottish Consultative Council on the Curriculum, since 1995, Board of Management, Scottish Further Education Unit, since 1993. Recreations: travel; literature; outdoor pursuits. Address: (b.) Lauder College, Halbeath, Dunfermline KY11 5DY; T.-01383 845002.

Lowe, Sheriff John Duncan, CB, MA, LLB. Sheriff of Glasgow and Strathkelvin, since 1997; Crown Agent, 1991-96; b. 18.5.48, Alloa; m., Jacqueline M.; 2 s. Educ. Hamilton Academy; Glasgow University. Procurator Fiscal Depute, Kilmarnock, 1974-77; Legal Assistant, Crown Office, 1977-79; Senior Procurator Fiscal Depute, Glasgow, 1979-80; Assistant Procurator Fiscal, Glasgow, 1980-83; Assistant Solicitor, Crown Office, 1983-84; Deputy Crown Agent, 1984-88; Regional Procurator Fiscal, Lothian and Borders, 1988-91. Address: (b.) Sheriffs' Chambers, Glasgow Sheriff Court, 1 Carlton Place, Glasgow G5 9DA; T.-0141-429 8888.

Lowe, Martin John Brodie, BSc, PhD. Secretary to Edinburgh University, since 1990; b. 10.4.40, Dorking; m., Janet MacNaughtan; 3 s.; 1 d. Educ. Dunfermline High School; St. Andrews University. British Council Officer, with service in Tanzania and South India, 1965-69; Strathclyde University: Administrative Assistant, 1969-71, Assistant Registrar, 1971-73, Secretary to Senate, 1973-81; Secretary and Registrar, St. Andrews University, 1981-89. National Council, Voluntary Service Overseas, 1976-83; Honorary Secretary, then Chairman, Glasgow and West of Scotland VSO Committee, 1973-81; Hon. Secretary, Royal Scottish Pipers' Society, since 1997. Recreations: piping; hill-walking; family interests. Address: (b.) Old College, South Bridge, Edinburgh EH8 9YL; T.-0131-650 2143.

Ludlam, Christopher A., BSc (Hons), MB, ChB, PhD, FRCP, FRCPath. Consultant Haematologist, Edinburgh Royal Infirmary, since 1980; Director, Edinburgh Haemophilia Reference Centre, since 1980; part-time Reader in Medicine, Edinburgh University, since 1997; b.

6.6.46, Edinburgh. Educ. Edinburgh University. MRC Research Fellow, 1972-75; Senior Registrar in Haematalogy, University Hospital of Wales, Cardiff, 1975-78; Lecturer in Haematology, University of Wales, 1979. Address: (b.) Department of Haematology, Royal Infirmary, Edinburgh; T.-0131-536 2122.

Lumsden, Iain C., MA, FFA. Group Finance Director and Appointed Actuary, Standard Life Assurance Company, since 1990; b. 6.6.46, Perth; m., Rosemary; 1 s.; 1 d. Educ. Exeter College, Oxford University. Standard Life, since 1967. Address: (b.) 30 Lothian Road, Edinburgh EH1 2DH; T.-0131 225 2552.

Lumsden, James Alexander, MBE, TD, MA, LLB, DL. Director, Bank of Scotland, 1958-85; Director, Scottish Provident Institution, 1968-85; b. 24.1.15, Arden, Dunbartonshire; m., Sheila Cross; 3 s. Educ. Cargilfield School, Edinburgh; Rugby School; Corpus Christi College, Cambridge; Glasgow University. Territorial Army, 193746; Partner, Maclay Murray & Spens, Solicitors, Glasgow and Edinburgh, 1947-82; Director of certain Investment Trust companies managed by Murray Johnstone Ltd., 1967-85; Director, Burmah Oil, 1957-76; Member, Queen's Body Guard for Scotland (Royal Company of Archers), 1963; Commissioner of Income Tax, County of Dumbarton, 1964-90; Member, Committee on Company Law, 1960-62; Fellow, Law Society of Scotland. Recreations: shooting; fishing; other country pursuits. Address: (h.) Bannachra, by Helensburgh, Dunbartonshire G84 9EF; T.-01389 850653.

Lumsden, Professor Keith Grant, MA, PhD, FRSE. Professor and Director, Edinburgh Business School, Heriot-Watt University; b. 7.1.35, Bathgate; m., Jean Baillie MacDonald; 1 s. Educ. Bathgate Academy; Edinburgh University; Stanford University, California. Instructor, Department of Economics, then Assistant Professor, Graduate School of Business, Stanford University, 1960-67; Research Associate, Stanford Research Institute, 1965-71; Director, Stanford University Conference: NDTE, 1966, RREE, 1968; Associate Professor, Graduate School of Business, Stanford University, 1968-75; Visiting Professor of Economics, Heriot-Watt University, 1969-70; Director: Economics Education Project, 1969-74, Behavioral Research Laboratories, 1970-72, Capital Preservation Fund Inc., 1971-75, Nielsen Engineering Research Inc., 1972-75; Member, American Economic Association Committee on Economic Education, 1978-81; Academic Director, Sea Transport Executive Programme (STEP), since 1979; Professor of Economics, Advanced Management College, Stanford University, since 1971; Affiliate Professor of Economics, INSEAD, France; Member: Economics Education 14-16 Project, Manchester University, Advisory Council, David Hume Institute, since 1984, Board of Directors, Hewlett Packard Ltd., 1982-92; Henry Villard Award, Economics America, 1994. Publications: The Free Enterprise System, 1963; The Gross National Product, 1964; International Trade, 1965; Microeconomics: A Programmed Book, 1966; Macroeconomics: A Programmed Book, 1966; New Developments in the Teaching of Economics (Editor), 1967; Excess Demand and Excess Supply In World Tramp Shipping Markets, 1968; Recent Research in Economics Education (Editor), 1970; Basic Economics: Theory and Cases, 1973; Efficiency in Universities: The La Paz Papers (Editor), 1974; Economics Education in the United Kingdom, 1980; Economics: a distance learning study programme, 1991. Recreations: tennis; deep sea sports fishing. Address: (h.) 40 Lauder Road, Edinburgh EH9 1UE.

Lumsden, Vivien Dale Victoria, DSD, CDS. Presenter, Scottish Television, since 1989; b. 22.11.52, Edinburgh; m., Alan Douglas (qv); 1 s.; 1 d. Educ. James Gillespie's High School for Girls, Edinburgh; RSAMD. Full-time member, 1975-82; AA Traffic News Reporter, 1982-84; BBC Scotland: Breakfast Newsreader, 1984-85, Reporting Scotland Presenter, 1985-89, Garden Party, 1988; joined Scottish TV as Presenter, Scotland Today, 1989; also presented chat show, Telethon, BAFTA Awards, Business Game, Home Show. Trustee, Parents Oncology Support Yorkhill. Address: (b.) Scottish Television, Cowcaddens, Glasgow.

Lumsden, William Hepburn Russell, DSc, MD, DTM, DTH, FIBiol, FRCPEdin, FRSE. Scientific and Medical Writer; b. 27.3.14, Forfar; m., Pamela Kathleen Bartram; 2 s.; 1 d. (deceased). Educ. Queen Elizabeth's Grammar School, Darlington; Glasgow University; Liverpool University. MRC Fellow in Tropical Medicine, 1938-41; active service, Malaria Field Laboratories, RAMC, 1941-46; Yellow Fever (subsequently East African Virus) Research Institute, Entebbe, 1947-57; Director, East African Trypanosomiasis Research Organisation, Tororo, 1957-63; Lecturer, Department of Bacteriology, Edinburgh University Medical School, 1963-64; Senior Lecturer, Department of Animal Health, Royal (Dick) School of Veterinary Studies, Edinburgh University, 1964-68; Visiting Professor, Toronto University, 1968; Professor of Medical Protozoology, London School of Hygiene and Tropical Medicine, London University, 1968-79; Senior Editor, Advances in Parasitology, 1978-82; Member: Council, Royal Society of Tropical Medicine and Hygiene, 1969-73, 1974-77, Council, Royal Zoological Society of Scotland, 1967-68, Expert Advisory Panel on Parasitic Diseases (Trypanosomiasis), WHO, 1962-84, Trypanosomiasis Panel, Ministry of Overseas Development, 1973-79, International Malaria Review Teams, Bangladesh, 1978, Nepal, 1979, Sri Lanka, 1980; Editing Secretary, Berwickshire Naturalists' Club, 1988-91. Publications: Techniques with Trypanosomes, 1973; Biology of the Kinetoplastida (Editor), 1976 and 1979. Recreation: hill-walking. Address: (h.) 16A Merchiston Crescent, Edinburgh EH10 5AX; T.-0131-229 2702.

Lunan, Charles Burnett, MD, FRCOG, FRCS. Consultant Obstetrician, Royal Maternity Hospital, Glasgow, since 1977; Consultant Gynaecologist, Royal Infirmary, Glasgow, since 1977; b. London; m., Helen Russell Ferrie; 2 s.; 1 d. Educ. High School of Glasgow; Glasgow University. Lecturer, Obstetrics and Gynaecology, Aberdeen University, 1973-75; Senior Lecturer, University of Nairobi, 1975-77; WHO Consultant, Family Planning Programme, Bangladesh, 1984-85. Treasurer, 1982-90, Vice-President, 1990-91, President, Royal Medico-Chirurgical Society of Glasgow, 1991-92; Secretary, Glasgow Obstetrical and Gynaecological Society, 1978-82. Recreations: gardening; photography; hill-walking. Address: (h.) 1 Moncrieff Avenue, Lenzie, Glasgow G66 4NL; T.-0141-776 3227.

Lunan, Duncan Alasdair, MA (Hons), FBIS, DipEd. Author; b. 24.10.45; m., Linda Joyce Donnelly (m. diss.). Educ. Marr College, Troon; Glasgow University. Management Trainee, Christian Salvesen (Managers) Ltd., 1969-70; self-employed (Author), 1970-78 and since 1980; Manager, Astronomy Project, Glasgow Parks Department, 1978-79; SF Critic, Glasgow Herald, 1971-82, and SF competition organiser, 1986-91; Photo-Archivist, Glasgow 1990 Press Centre, 1990-91; regular astronomy column in various papers and magazines; Council Member, Association in Scotland to Research into Astronautics (ASTRA), since 1963 (President, 1966-72, 1978-85, and 1991-97); Treasurer, 1965-66, 1977-78, and since 1997; Secretary, 1985-89). Publications: Man and the Stars, 1974; New Worlds for Old, 1979; Man and the Planets, 1983; Starfield (Editor), 1989. Recreation: folk music. Address: Flat 65, Dalriada House, 56 Blythswood Court, Anderston, Glasgow G2 7PE; T.-0141-221 7658.

Lunney, James Thomas, LLB, NP. Full-time Chairman, Independent Tribunal Service, since 1995; Director, Paisley Hammermen Society, since 1990; b. 24.7.54, Glasgow; m.,

Patricia Anne Lunney, BDS; 2 d. Educ. St. Mirin's Academy, Paisley; Strathclyde University. Apprentice to Pattison & Sim, Solicitors, Paisley, 1979-81; Assistant, 1981-83; Partner, 1983-95; part-time Chairman, Independent Tribunal Service, 1992-95. Recreations: golf; rugby; reading; architecture. Address: (b.) Wellington House, 134-136 Wellington Street, Glasgow G2 2XL.

Lunny, Sheriff William Francis, MA, LLB. Sheriff of South Strathclyde, Dumfries and Galloway, since 1984; b. 10.12.38. Advocate, 1977. Address: (b.) Sheriff Court House, Beckford Street, Hamilton, ML3 6AA.

Lusby, John David, MEd, BA. Rector, Buckhaven High School, since 1997; b. 23.10.50, Wales; m., Hazel Ann; 2 s.; 1 d. Educ. Kirkton High School; Jordanhill College; Dundee University. Teacher, 1971-74; Youth Tutor, 1975-76; Principal Teacher of Guidance, 1976-82; Assistant Head Teacher, 1982-84; TVEI Co-ordinator, 1986-89; Rector, Arbroath Academy, 1989-97. Board, Angus College, 1990-97. Recreations: cycling; music; reading. Address: (h.) 11 Lawside Road, Dundee DD3 6BP; T.-01382 229496.

Luscombe, Rt. Rev. Lawrence Edward, ChStJ, MA, MPhil, PhD, LLD, DLitt, CA, FRSA, FSA Scot. Primus of the Scottish Episcopal Church, 1985-90, and Bishop of Brechin, 1975-90; b. 10.11.24; m., Dr. Doris Morgan (deceased); 1 d. Educ. Kelham College; King's College, London; Dundee University. Indian Army, 1942-47; Major; Chartered Accountant, 1952; Partner, Galbraith Dunlop & Co. (later Watson and Galbraith), CA, 1953-63; Curate, St. Margaret's, Glasgow, 1963-66; Rector, St. Barnabas', Paisley, 1966-71; Provost, St. Paul's Cathedral, Dundee, 1971-75. Honorary Canon, Trinity Cathedral, Davenport, Iowa, since 1983; Member, Education Committee, Renfrew County Council, 1967-71; Chairman, Governing Body: Glenalmond College, Edinburgh Theological College, 1985-90; Governor: Lathallan School, Dundee College of Education; Chairman, Inter-Anglican Finance Committee, 1989-93; Member, Tayside Health Board, 1989-93; Honorary Research Fellow, Dundee University, since 1993; Member, Court, Corporation of Sons of the Clergy. Address: (h.) Woodville, Kirkton of Tealing, by Dundee DD4 0RD; T.-01382 380331.

Lyall, Fiona Jane, MBE, DL, MB, ChB, DPH. Family Doctor, Laurencekirk, since 1959; Director, Grampian Television PLC, since 1980; Non-Executive Director: Aberdeen Royal Hospitals NHS Trust, since 1992, Templehill Community Council, since 1990; Deputy Lieutenant, Kincardineshire, since 1985; b. 13.4.31, Inverness; m., Dr. Alan Richards Lyall; 1 s.; 1 d. Educ. Inverness Royal Academy; Aberdeen University. Former Member, Laurencekirk Burgh Council; former Kincardine County and Grampian Regional Councillor; Member: Grampian Health Board, 1974, and Kincardine & Deeside Health Council, 1974, Children's Panel Advisory Committee, 1974, Grampian Valuation Appeals Committee, Prince's and Royal Jubilee Trust for Grampian; Treasurer, Action Research for Crippled Child; Trustee, Kincardineshire Silver Jubilee Trust, since 1985. Recreations: skiing; riding; golf. Address: Melrose Bank, Laurencekirk AB30 1AL; T.-01561 377220.

Lyall, Ian Alastair, DSC, VRD, DL, FICS; b. 16.3.17, Bangor, Co. Down; m., Eileen Patricia Bennet; 1 d. Educ. Hillhead High School, Glasgow; College of Nautical Studies, Glasgow. Chairman and Managing Director, Roxburgh Henderson & Co. Ltd., 1967-80; Director: British & Burmese Steam Navigation Co. Ltd., 1971-80, Henderson Line Ltd., 1971-80; President, Glasgow Chamber of Commerce, 1978-79; retired Lt. Commander, RNR, 1963. Recreations: sailing; fishing; shooting. Address: (h.) 21 Chapelacre, Helensburgh G84 7SH; T.-01436 673976.

Lyall, Michael Hodge, MB, ChB, ChM, FRCSEdin. Consultant Surgeon, Tayside Health Board, since 1975; Honorary Senior Lecturer, Dundee University, since 1975; b. 5.12.41, Methilhill, Fife; m., Catherine B. Jarvie; 3 s. Educ. Buckhaven High School; St. Andrews University. President, Tayside Division, Ileostomy Association of Great Britain; Past President, North Fife Rotary Club. Recreation: computing. Address: (h.) 26 Linden Avenue, Newport on Tay, Fife DD6 8DU.

Lyddon, William Derek Collier, CB, DLitt, BA, RIBA, DipTP, FRTPI, FRSGS. Vice Chairman, Edinburgh Old Town Renewal Trust; Chief Planner, Scottish Development Department, 1967-85; Honorary Professor, Heriot-Watt University; Governor, Edinburgh College of Art; b. 17.11.25, Loughton, Essex; m., Marian Louise Kaye Charlesworth; 2 d. Educ. Wrekin College; University College, London. Depute Chief Architect Planner, Cumbernauld Development Corporation; Chief Architect Planner, Skelmersdale Development Corporation. President, International Society of City and Regional Planners, 1981-84; Chairman, The Planning Exchange, 1992-95. Address: (h.) 31 Blackford Road, Edinburgh EH9 2DT; T.-0131-667 2266.

Lyell, 3rd Baron (Charles Lyell), Bt. Parliamentary Under-Secretary of State, Northern Ireland Office, 1984-89; b. 27.3.39. Educ. Eton; Christ Church, Oxford. Scots Guards, 1957-59; CA; Opposition Whip, 1974-79; Government Whip, 1979-84; Member, Queen's Bodyguard for Scotland (Royal Company of Archers); DL, Angus, 1988. Address: (h.) Kinnordy House, Kirriemuir, Angus.

Lyle, David Angus, MA, LLB, NP, SSC, FCIS, FIMgt, FInstD, FIAM, FRSA. Consultant, Solicitor, and Chartered Company Secretary, in private practice, since 1993; b. 7.9.40; m., Dorothy Ann Clark; 1 s.; 3 d. Educ. George Watson's College, Edinburgh; Edinburgh University. Account Executive, Advertising Agencies, London; Indentured, Edinburgh Corporation; Solicitor, Lloyds and Scottish Finance Ltd., Edinburgh; Depute County Clerk, East Lothian County Council; Director of Administration and Law, Dumfries and Galloway Regional Council; Agency Secretary, Scottish Development Agency; Director/Company Secretary, Scottish Enterprise. Recreations: shooting; golf; bridge. Address: (b.) The Caledonian Suite, St Andrew House, 141 West Nile Street, Glasgow G1 2RN; T.-0141-333 1119.

Lynch, Alexander McKay, ACMA, MCIT. Deputy Managing Director/Finance Director, ScotRail, since 1994; b. 6.10.49, Greenock; m., Christina Keenan; 2 d. Educ. St. Columba's High School, Greenock; Central College of Commerce and Distribution, Glasgow. BR management posts, since 1976. Hon. President, Railway Staff Association, Scotland. Recreations: youth football; TV; music. Address: (b.) Caledonian Chambers, 87 Union Street, Glasgow G1 3TA; T.-0141-335 4180.

Lyon, George. NSc, ARAgS. Vice-President, National Farmers' Union of Scotland, since 1996; Director, Scotch Quality Beef and Lamb Association; Farmer; b. 16.7.56, Rothesay; m., Patricia; 3 d. Educ. Rothesay Academy. Left school to work on family farm, 1972; took over running of farms, 1980; family partnership split 1992; took on two more farms, 1994; now farms 1350 acres. National Farmers' Union of Scotland: Convener, Livestock Committee, since 1996; Past Director, Ayr Country Lamb Group; Nuffield Scholar, 1987. Recreations: soccer; skiing; politics. Address: Kildavannan Farm, Rothesay, Isle of Bute; T.-01700 504237.

Lyon, Robert Alexander, MA, CA, CMA. Dean, Faculty of Law and Accountancy, Dundee University, since 1994; Member, Council, Institute of Chartered Accountants of Scotland, since 1994; Non-Executive Director, Dundee

Teaching Hospitals NHS Trust, since 1993; b. 18.2.48, Dundee. Educ. Morgan Academy, Dundee; Dundee University. CA student, Dundee, 1969-73; Senior Accountant, Peat, Marwick, Mitchell & Co., USA, Germany, Scotland, 1973-76; Lecturer, then Senior Lecturer, Dundee University, since 1976. Address: (b.) Faculty of Law and Accountancy, Dundee University, Dundee DD1 4HN; T.-01382 344195.

Mac/Mc

McAllion, John, MA (Hons). MP (Lab), Dundee East, since 1987; b. 13.2.48, Glasgow; m., Susan Jean; 2 s. Educ. St. Augustine's Secondary, Glasgow; St. Andrews University. Teacher, History and Modern Studies, St. Saviour's Secondary, Dundee, 1973-78, Social Studies, Balgowan List D School, Dundee, 1978-82; Research Assistant to Bob McTaggart, MP, 1982-86; Regional Councillor, 1984-87; Convener, Tayside Regional Council, 1986-87. Member, Scottish Executive, Labour Party, 1986-88; Senior Vice Chairperson, Dundee Labour Party, 1986, 1987. Recreations: football; reading; music. Address: (h.) 3 Haldane Street, Dundee DD3 0HP; T.-01382 200329.

McAlpine, Joan, MA (Hons). Columnist and Feature Writer, Sunday Times, since 1996; b. 28.1.64, Gourock; m., Pat Kane (qv); 2 d. Educ. St. Columba's RC Comprehensive, Greenock; Glasgow University; City University, London. Reporter, Greenock Telegraph, The Scotsman; Feature Writer, Columnist, The Scotsman, 1992-95; joined Daily Record as Feature Writer and Columnist, 1995. Publications: A Time to Rage (Co-author), 1994; The Best of The Scotsman (Contributor), 1995. Recreations: spending time with my children; reading. Address: (b.) Sunday Times, 124 Portman Street, Kinning Park, Glasgow G41 1EJ; T.-0141-420 1000.

McAlpine, Thomas, BSc, CEng, MIEE. Business Consultant; b. 23.9.29, Motherwell; m., Isobel Lindsay; 2 s.; 1 d. Educ. Dalziel High School, Motherwell; Strathclyde University. National Service, REME, 1952-54 (2nd Lt.); Chief Engineer, Belmos Co. Ltd., Bellshill, 1954-58; Chief Development Engineer, Mine Safety Appliances, Glasgow, 1958-62; Managing Director: Rowen Engineering Co. Ltd., Glasgow, 1962-71, Chieftain Industries PLC, Livingston, 1971-85. Former Executive Vice Chairman Administration, Scottish National Party (former Vice President, SNP); Parliamentary candidate, Clydesdale (Lanark), 1974, 1979, 1983, Dumfries, 1987; District Councillor, Clydesdale, 1988-96, now South Lanarkshire Councillor. Recreations: when young, played rugby, swimming and tennis. Address: (h.) 9 Knocklea Place, Biggar, Lanarkshire ML12 6DZ; T.-01899 220423.

McAndrew, Nicolas, CA. Chairman, Murray Johnstone Ltd., since 1992; Deputy Chairman, Burn Stewart Distillers PLC, since 1991; Board Member: Highlands and Islands Enterprise, since 1994, North of Scotland Water Authority, since 1995; b. 9.12.34, London; 2 s.; 1 d. Educ. Winchester College. National Service (The Black Watch) commission, 1953-55; articled clerk, Peat Marwick Mitchell, 1955-61; qualified CA, 1961; S.G. Warburg & Co. Ltd., Merchant Bankers, 1962-78; became Chairman, Warburg Investment Management Ltd., and Director, Mercury Securities Ltd.; Managing Director, N.M. Rothschild & Sons Ltd., Merchant Bankers, 1979-88. Master, Worshipful Company of Grocers, 1978-79. Recreations: fishing; shooting; golf. Address: (h.) Kilcoy Castle, Killearnan, Muir of Ord, Ross-shire IV6 7RX; T.-01463 871 393.

McArdle, Professor Colin S., MD, FRCS, FRCSEdin, FRCSGlas. Professor of Surgery, University of Edinburgh, Western General Hospital, Edinburgh, since 1996; b. 10.10.39, Glasgow; m., June M.C. Merchant; 2 s.; 1 d. Educ. Jordanhill College School; Glasgow University. Senior Registrar in General Surgery, Western Infirmary, Glasgow, 1972-75; Consultant Surgeon: Victoria Infirmary, Glasgow, 1975-78, Glasgow Royal Infirmary, 1978-80; University Department of Surgery, Glasgow Royal Infirmary, 1981-96. Address: (h.) 6 Collylinn Road, Bearsden, Glasgow.

McArthur, Alasdair, LLB. Chairman of Industrial Tribunals, since 1993; b. 29.5.43, Balfron; m., Edith Mary Patricia; 1 s.; 2 d. Educ. Hutchesons' Grammar School, Glasgow; Glasgow University. Solicitor, John Wilson & Co., Glasgow, 1968-93; former Member, Glasgow and North Argyll Legal Aid Committee; Member, Council, Law Society of Scotland, 1981-87 (Convener, Judicial Procedure and Law Reform Committees). Recreations: outdoor pursuits; gardening; reading; music. Address: (b.) Eagle Building, 215 Bothwell Street, Glasgow G2 7TS.

MacArthur, Rev. Allan Ian, BD, JP. Minister, Lochcarron Parish, since 1973; District Councillor, 1984-96; b. 22.5.28, Marvig, Isle of Lewis; m., Effie Macleod; 1 s.; 6 d. Educ. Nicolson Institute, Stornoway; Glasgow University and Trinity College. Meteorologist, Air Ministry and Falkland Islands Dependencies Survey, Antarctica; teaching; Minister of Religion and Presbytery Clerk. Member, Crofters Commission, 1984-90. Address: Church of Scotland Manse, Lochcarron, Ross-shire IV54 8YD; T.-01520 722278.

McArthur, Archibald Roderick, CPFA. Director of Finance, Perth and Kinross Council, since 1995; b. 1.3.51, Greenock; m., Marilyn; 2 d. Educ. Greenock Academy. Trainee Accountant, Greenock Town Council, 1969; Accountant, Tayside Regional Council, 1975; Perth and Kinross District Council: Management Accountant, 1978, Depute Director of Finance, 1981, Director of Finance, 1992. Recreations: member of Blairgowrie Golf Club; supporter, St. Johnstone F.C. Address: (b.) Council Building, 2 High Street, Perth PH1 5PH; T.-01738 475501.

McArthur, Douglas B., BSc (Hons). Managing Director, Radio Advertising Bureau, since 1992; Director, RAJAR Ltd.; Chairman, Strategic Marketing Scotland Ltd; b. 17.3.51, Dundee; m., Elizabeth M.A.; 3 d. Educ. Kirkton High School, Dundee; Glasgow University. Marketing management roles, Proctor and Gamble, Scottish & Newcastle, Campbell's Soups Ltd., Radio Clyde; marketing and advertising consultancy roles with Hall Advertising and Baillie Marshall Advertising. Director, Drumchapel Opportunities Ltd.; Member, Scottish Arts Council (Chairman, Drama Committee, 1989-94); Director, Balgray Communications Group Ltd. and subsidiaries, 1984-92; Fellow: Radio Academy, CAM Foundation. Recreations: swimming; music; visual arts; drama. Address: (h.) 33 Victoria Crescent Road, Glasgow G12 9DD.

Macarthur, Edith. Actress; b. Ardrossan, Ayrshire. Educ. Ardrossan Academy. Began career, 1948, with Wilson Barrett Company, then Perth Repertory, Gateway Theatre Company, Citizens' Theatre, Glasgow, Bristol Old Vic, Royal Shakespeare Company, Ochtertyre Theatre, Royal Lyceum Theatre Company, West End; television work includes The Borderers, Sunset Song, Weir of Hermiston, Sutherland's Law, Take the High Road, Dr. Finlay, Hamish Macbeth; Taggart; Golden Wedding; nominated for Scottish BAFTA award in The Long Roads, 1993; recent stage appearances: solo-performance play, Marie of Scotland, Jamie the Saxt and The Thrie Estates for the Scottish Theatre Company at Edinburgh Festivals and Warsaw International Festival, 1986, Judith Bliss in Hay Fever, Royal Lyceum Theatre, 1987, Charley's Aunt, Death of a Salesman, Royal Lyceum, 1988, Daphne Laureola, Pygmalion, Pride and Prejudice, Pitlochry Festival Theatre, 1988; The Cherry Orchard, Royal Lyceum, 1989; The Cherry Orchard, The Circle, Arsenic and Old Lace, Pitlochry, 1990; Driving Miss Daisy, Perth, 1991; Cinderella, Glasgow and Edinburgh, 1990, 1991; Good, Glasgow and Edinburgh, 1992; Long Day's Journey into Night, Dundee, 1994 (TMA/Martini Best Actress nomination); The Prime of Miss Jean Brodie, London, 1994-95; The Flou'ers o' Edinburgh; On Golden Pond; Long Day's Journey into Night, Pitlochry Festival Theatre, and tour, 1996; Widows, Traverse Theatre, and tour, 1997.

Recreations: music; books. Address: c/o Larry Dalzell Associates Ltd., Suite 12, 17 Broad Court, London WC2B 5QN.

McArthur, George, OBE. Chairman, Scottish Churches Housing Agency, since 1993; Convener: Edinburgh Peace and Justice Resource Centre, since 1992; b. 22.7.30, Edinburgh; m., Margaret Moffat Wilson; 1 s.; 1 d. Educ. Leith Academy. Missionary (youth worker), Church of Scotland, South Africa, 1956-71; Official Correspondent for Church of Scotland's List D schools, 1972-77; involved in formation of Kirk Care Housing Association Ltd., 1973, becoming its first Director, 1978, retired, 1992. Chairman, Council, Scottish Federation of Housing Associations, 1984-86; a Vice-President, Churches National Housing Coalition, 1995. Recreations: golf; supporting Hibernian F.C.; walking; reading. Address: (h.) 3 Craigcrook Road, Edinburgh EH4 3NQ; T.-0131-477 0312.

McArthur, John Duncan, BSc (Hons), MB, ChB (Hons), DM, FRCPGlas, MRCP, FRCPEdin. Consultant Physician and Cardiologist, Western Infirmary and Gartnavel General Hospital, Glasgow, since 1978; Honorary Clinical Senior Lecturer, Glasgow University, since 1978; b. 7.1.38, Hamilton; m., Elizabeth A. Bowie; 2 s.; 1 d. Educ. Hamilton Academy; Glasgow University. Junior doctor, Royal Infirmary, Glasgow, and in Ayrshire, 1963-67; St. Colm's College, Edinburgh, 1967-68; Missionary, Church of Scotland, working as Cardiologist at Christian Medical College Hospital, Vellore, India, 1968-73; Senior Registrar, Glasgow Teaching Hospitals, 1974-78. Elder, Killermont Parish Church; Council Member, Interserve, Scotland. Recreations: DIY; gardening. Address: (h.) 8 Durness Avenue, Bearsden, Glasgow, G61 2AQ; T.-0141-563 9068.

Macartney, W.J. Allan, MA, BLitt, PhD. Member of the European Parliament for North East Scotland, since 1994; Staff Tutor, Social Sciences, The Open University in Scotland, 1975-94; Honorary Fellow, Edinburgh University, since 1981; Member, National Executive Committee, Scottish National Party, since 1984, Vice President, 1990-92, Senior Vice-Convener and Foreign Affairs Spokesperson, since 1992; b. 1941, Accra, Ghana; m., J.D. Anne Forsyth; 2 s.; 1 d. Educ. Elgin Academy; Tuebingen University; Marburg University; Edinburgh University; Glasgow University. Teacher, Eastern Nigeria, 1963-64; Lecturer, University of Botswana, Lesotho and Swaziland, 1966-74; Executive Member, Unit for the Study of Government in Scotland, Scottish Self-Government College, Saint Andrew Society; Church of Scotland Elder, since 1979; Member, Church and Nation Committee, 1989-96; Chairman, National Flag Trust, since 1991; Parliamentary candidate (SNP), 1970, 1979, 1983, 1987, 1992; Euro candidate, 1989; President, UN Association (Edinburgh), since 1991. Publications: Readings in Boleswa Government, 1971; The Referendum Experience, 1981; Islands of Europe, 1984; Self-Determination in the Commonwealth, 1987; Towards 1992, 1989; Asking the People, 1992. Recreations: music; languages; walking; vexillology. Address: (b.) 70 Rosemount Place, Aberdeen AB25 2XJ; T.-01224 623150.

McAteer, Charles, MA, BA (Hons). Rector, Dumfries Academy, since 1995; Chairman, Dumfries and Galloway Secondary Headteachers, since 1995; Minutes Secretary, Headteachers' Association of Scotland; b. 5.5.50, Glasgow; m., Anne Neil; 1 s.; 3 d. Educ. Our Lady's High School, Motherwell; Edinburgh University; Jordanhill College; Strathclyde University. Teacher of English, St. Augustine's High School, Edinburgh, 1972-74; Principal Teacher of English, St. Kentigern's Academy, W. Lothian, 1974-83; Depute Rector, Moffat Academy, 1983-88; Rector, Dalbeattie High School, 1988-95. Recreations: squash; indoor football; reading; walking; film; family. Address: (b.) Dumfries Academy, Academy Street, Dumfries, DG1 1DD; T.-01387 252846.

Macaulay, Rev. Donald, OBE, JP. Former Minister, Park, Isle of Lewis; former Convener, Western Isles Council; b. 25.2.26, Great Bernera; m., Catherine Macleod; 3 s.; 3 d. Educ. Great Bernera School; Aberdeen University. Several years a fisherman; Member: Ross and Cromarty County Council, 1969-75, Lewis District Council, 1969-75, COSLA Policy Committee, 1975-82; Director, Western Isles Enterprise. Recreations: fishing; travel; local history; silviculture. Address: Garymilis, Great Bernera, Isle of Lewis; T.-01851 612341.

MacAulay, Professor Emeritus Donald, MA, BA, DipGenLing. Professor of Celtic, Glasgow University, 1991-96; b. 21.5.30, Isle of Lewis; m., Ella Murray Sangster; 1 s.; 1 d. Educ. Nicolson Institute, Stornoway; Aberdeen University; Cambridge University. Lecturer in English Language, Edinburgh University, 1957-60; Lecturer in Irish and Scottish Gaelic, Trinity College, Dublin, 1960-63; Lecturer in Applied Linguistics, Edinburgh University, 1963-67; Senior Lecturer in Celtic, then Reader in Celtic, Aberdeen University, 1967-91. Publications: Seobhrach as a' Chlaich; Nua-bhardachd Ghaidhlig; The Celtic Languages. Recreations: poetry; surviving. Address: (b.) 7 Ledcameroch Park, Bearsden Glasgow G61 4AT; T.-0141-942 9801.

Macaulay of Bragar, Rt. Hon. Lord (Donald Macaulay), QC. Advocate, 1963; QC (Scot), 1975; Life Peer, since 1989. Address: (b.) Advocates' Library, Parliament House, Edinburgh, EH1 1RF.

McAveety, Frank (Francis), BA (Hons). Councillor, Glasgow City Council, since 1995 (Convenor, Arts and Culture Committee); Councillor, Glasgow District Council, 1988-96; Teacher of English, St. Brendan's High School, Linwood, since 1994; b. 27.7.62, Glasgow; m., Anita Mitchell; 1 s. Educ. All Saints Secondary School, Glasgow; Strathclyde University; St. Andrew's College, Bearsden. Teacher of English: Holyrood Secondary School, Glasgow, 1984-86, St. Gregory's Secondary School, Glasgow, 1986-89, Garthamlock Secondary School, Glasgow, 1989-94. Director: Citizens' Theatre, Glasgow, Glasgow Jazz Festival Board; Chairperson, Glasgow North Co-operative Party. Recreations: labour history; record collecting; football. Address: (h.) 156 Glenbuck Avenue, Robroyston, Glasgow G33 1LW; T.-0141-558 1341.

McAvoy, Thomas McLaughlin. Government Whip, Comptroller of Her Majesty's Household, since 1997; MP (Labour and Co-operative), Glasgow Rutherglen, since 1987; b. 14.12.43, Rutherglen; m., Eleanor Kerr; 4 s. Member, Strathclyde Regional Council, 1982-87; Opposition Whip, 1990-93. Address: (b.) House of Commons, London SW1A 0AA.

McBryde, Professor William Wilson, LLB, PhD, LLD, FRSE. Professor of Scots Law, Dundee University, since 1987, Deputy and Vice Principal, 1991-94; Solicitor, since 1969; b. 6.7.45, Perth; m., Joyce Margaret Gossip; 1 s.; 2 d. Educ. Perth Academy; Edinburgh University. Apprentice and Assistant, Morton, Smart, Macdonald & Milligan, WS, Edinburgh, 1967-70; Court Procurator, Biggart, Lumsden & Co., Glasgow, 1970-72; Lecturer in Private Law, Glasgow University, 1972-76; Member, Scottish Law Commission Working Party on Contract Law, since 1975; Senior Lecturer in Private Law, Aberdeen University, 1976-87; Specialist Parliamentary Adviser to House of Lords Select Committee on the European Communities, 1980-83; Member: Scottish Consumer Council, 1984-87, Scottish Advisory Committee on Arbitration, since 1986; Director, Scottish Universities' Law Institute, 1989-95; Honorary Sheriff, Tayside, Central and Fife, at Dundee, since 1991; Member, DTI Working Party on Rights in Security over Moveables, since 1994. Recreations: walking; photography. Address: (b.) Faculty of Law, Dundee University, Dundee DD1 4HN; T.-01382 23181.

McBurnie, Gavin John, MB, ChB, MBA, DRCOG, MHSM. Director, Primary Care, Fife Health Board, since 1994; b. 9.9.59, Edinburgh; m., Doreen Elizabeth; 3 s. Educ. Royal High School, Edinburgh; Glasgow University; Edinburgh University. Junior doctor, 1982-86; general medical practitioner, 1986-91; Assistant Director, Strategic Planning and Contracts, 1993-94. Recreations: rugby union; r. and b. Address: (h.) 25 Ferryfield, Cupar, Fife; T.-01334 656572.

McCabe, Primrose Smith, CA. Senior Partner, The McCabe Partnership, since 1987; b. 21.9.40, Gorebridge; m., Ernest McCabe. Educ. Ayr Academy. Trained with Stewart Gilmour, Ayr; qualified as CA 1963; joined Romanes & Munro, Edinburgh, 1964; progressed through manager ranks to Partner, Deloitte Haskins & Sells, 1981-87; set up own practice, Linlithgow, 1987; moved practice to Edinburgh, 1997. Member, Accounts Commission, 1988-92; Non-Executive Director: Dunfermline Building Society, 1990, Northern Venture Trust plc, 1995; Institute of Chartered Accountants of Scotland: Member, Council, since 1988, first Convener, GP Committee, 1990, Vice President, 1992-94, President, 1994-95; Honorary Treasurer, Hospitality Industry Trust Scotland, 1994; Fellow, SCOTVEC, 1994. Recreation: walking her three dogs. Address: (b.) The McCabe Partnership, 56 Palmerston Place, Edinburgh EH12 5AY; T.-0131-225 6366.

McCabe, Thomas. Leader, South Lanarkshire Council, since 1995; Vice-Convener, Strathclyde Joint Police Board; Leader, Hamilton District Council, 1992-96; Member: Lanarkshire Development Agency Board, Labour Party Scottish Executive; b. 28.4.54, Hamilton. Educ. St. Martin's Secondary; Bell College of Technology. Senior shop steward, Hoover Ltd., 1974-93; welfare rights officer, since 1993. Recreations: walking; reading; gardening; cinema. Address: (b.) South Lanarkshire Council, Council Offices, Almada Street, Hamilton ML3 0AA; T.-01698 454192.

McCafferty, Rev. Allan, BSc, BD (Hons). Minister, Kirkwall East Church, since 1993; b. 19.1.67, Motherwell. Educ. Garrion Academy, Wishaw; Glasgow University; Edinburgh University. Probationer Minister, Holy Trinity Church, Bridge of Allan, 1991-93. Recreations: choral singing; hill-walking. Address: East Church Manse, Thoms Street, Kirkwall KW15 1PF; T.-01856 875469.

McCaffrey, Rev. Kenneth, BEd, DTheol, DAREd. Parish Priest, St. Mungo's, Alloa, since 1995; Convenor, Joint Prison Chaplaincies Board, since 1997; b. 27.5.47, Glasgow. Educ. St. Thomas Aquinas Secondary School, Glasgow; Manchester University; St. Patrick's College, Thurles, Eire. Ordained priest, 1982; Assistant Priest, St. Ninian's, Dundee, 1982-86; Parish Priest, St. John's, Alva, 1986-95. Chaplain, Glenochil Prison. Recreations: soccer; reading. Address: 25 Mar Street, Alloa FK10 1HR; T.-01259 212486.

McCall, Frances, MBE. Board Member, Scottish Homes, since 1988; Member, Management Committee, Calvay Housing Co-operative, since 1984; b. 2.7.37, Glasgow; m., Thomas McCall; 2 s.; 1 d. Educ. St. Columba of Iona School; Notre Dame College. Recreations: grand-children; voluntary work. Address: (h.) 45 Calvay Road, Barlanark, Glasgow G33 4RQ; T.-0141-771 4294.

McCall, Professor James, BSc, MEd, PhD, CPsychol, AFBPsS, FRSA. Professor, Department of Educational Studies, Strathclyde University, since 1993; b. 14.7.41, Kilmarnock; m., Mary Elizabeth Stuart Maclean; 3 s. Educ. Kilmarnock Academy; Glasgow University; Aberdeen University; Jordanhill College of Education. Teacher of Science, Hillhead High School, Glasgow; Principal Teacher of Physics, Queen's Park Secondary School, Glasgow; Lecturer in Educational Psychology, Aberdeen College of Education; Jordanhill College of Education: Head,

Psychology Department, Vice Principal, 1983-92, Acting Principal, 1992-93, Dean, Faculty of Education, 1993-97; Member: Board of Governors, Glasgow School of Art, since 1986, CNAA Committee on Teacher Education, 1989-92, General Teaching Council for Scotland, 1992-97. Publications: Techniques for the Assessment of Practical Skills in Foundation Science, 1983; Techniques for Assessing Process Skills in Practical Science, 1988; Teacher Education in Europe, 1990; How to assess open-ended practical investigations in Biology, Chemistry and Physics, 1991. Recreations: bridge; golf. Address: (b.) Jordanhill Campus, Strathclyde University, Southbrae Drive, Glasgow G13 1PP; T.-0141-950 3200.

McCall, Kathleen Mary, DL, LRAM. Deputy Lieutenant for Borders Region, District of Tweeddale, since 1988; Patron, Tweeddale Branch, British Red Cross Society, since 1993; b. 20.2.33, Karachi; m., J.A.G. McCall, CMG. Educ. Calder Girls' School, Seascale; Royal Scottish Academy of Music and Drama. Held various teaching posts; voluntary offices with Red Cross in Nigeria. Recreations: music; walking; the arts. Address: (h.) Burnside, West Linton EH46 7EW; T.-01968 660488.

McCall Smith, Professor Alexander, LLB, PhD. Professor, Faculty of Law, Edinburgh University; Author; b. 24.8.48, Zimbabwe; m., Dr. Elizabeth Parry; 2 d. Publications: (non-fiction): Law and Medical Ethics (Co-Author); Butterworth's Medico-Legal Encyclopaedia (Co-Author); Scots Criminal Law (Co-Author); The Duty to Rescue (Co-Author); The Criminal Law of Botswana; Forensic Aspects of Sleep (Co-Author); fiction: Children of Wax; Heavenly Date; numerous books for children. Recreation: wind instruments. Address: (h.) 16A Napier Road, Edinburgh EH10 5AY; T.-0131-229 6083.

MacCallum, Alasdair Norman, BSc (Hons). Chief Executive, Don & Low Holdings, since 1986; Director, Hamish Morison Ltd., Vico Properties PLC; b. 27.1.36, Connel, Argyll; m., Helga Diana; 1 s.; 1 d. Educ. Keil School; Glasgow University. National Service Commission, Royal Artillery; Unilever, six years; Culter Guard Bridge Paper Co. Ltd., seven years; Devro Ltd. (Production Director, Managing Director), 14 years; Baxters of Fochabers (Managing Director), one year. Chairman: Montrose Harbour Trust, CBI Scotland, 1991-93, New South Mills Ltd.; Member, Board, North of Scotland Water Authority; Chairman, Scottish Crop Research Institute. Recreations: angling; shooting; gardening; theatre; music; reading. Address: (h.) Inverossie, Rossie Braes, Montrose DD10 9TJ; T.-01674 673013.

McCallum, Sir Donald Murdo, CBE, DL, BSc, DSc, LLD, DUniv, FEng, FIEE, FRAeS, CBIM, FRSE, FScotVec, FRSGS; b. 6.8.22, Edinburgh; m., 1, Barbara Black (deceased); 1 d.; 2, Margaret Illingworth (nee Broadbent). Educ. George Watson's Boys' College; Edinburgh University. Admiralty Signal Establishment, 1942-46; Standard Telecommunication Laboratories, 1946; joined Ferranti, 1947; General Manager, Ferranti Scottish Group, 1968-85; Director, Ferranti plc, 1970-87; Chairman, Scottish Tertiary Education Advisory Council, 1984-87; Chairman, Scottish Council Development and Industry, 1985-91, President, 1991-93; Chairman, Scottish Committee, Universities Funding Council, 1989-91; Chairman, Laser Ecosse Ltd., 1990-95; former Trustee, National Library of Scotland; former Member, Court, Napier University; Governor, Edinburgh College of Art, 1987-93; Member, Scottish Economic Council, 1983-91. Recreations: fishing; photography. Address: (h.) 46 Heriot Row, Edinburgh EH3 6EX; T.-0131-225 9331.

MacCallum, Professor James Richard, BSc, PhD, DSc, CChem, FRSC, FRSE. Professor of Polymer Chemistry, St. Andrews University (Vice-Principal, 1992-96); b. 3.5.36, Kilmartin; m., Eleanor Margaret Thomson; 2 s.; 1 d. Educ.

Dumfries Academy; Glasgow University. Technical Officer, ICI Fibres Division, 1961-62; ICI Research Fellow, Aberdeen University, 1962-63; Lecturer, St. Andrews University, 1964; Master, United College, 1988-92. Elder, St. Leonards Church, St. Andrews. Recreation: golf. Address: (h.) 9 Cairnsden Gardens, St. Andrews, Fife; T.-01334 473152.

MacCallum, Kenneth. Principal, Bell College of Technology. Address: (b.) Almada Street, Hamilton ML3 0JB.

MacCallum, Neil Robb, Poet, Critic and Editor; Editor, Lallans, since 1996; Convener, Edinburgh Branch, Scots Language Society, since 1995 (Preses of the Society, 1993-95); Committee Member, Poetry Association of Scotland, since 1995; b. 15.5.54, Edinburgh. Educ. Firrhill High School; Napier College, Edinburgh. Lothian Health Board, 1973-87; Edinburgh City Councllor, 1977-80; Assistant National Secretary, SNP, 1980-81, National Secretary, 1981-86; Arts Columnist, Scots Independent; Editor, Scots Glasnost, 1991-95; Committee Member, Scottish Poetry Library, 1989-95; Vice-Convener, Scots Language Resource Centre, 1993-95. Publications: Report of the SNP Commission of Inquiry (Editor), 1984; Portrait of a Calvinist, 1991; Mak It New (Co-Editor), 1995; Sing Frae the Hert, (Editor), 1996, A Stern's Light, 1997. Recreations: reading; theatre; fitness and weight-training; running. Address: (h.) 18 Redford Avenue, Edinburgh EH13 0BU; T.-0131-441 3724.

Maccallum, Professor Norman Ronald Low, BSc, PhD, CEng, FIMechE. Emeritus Professor, Honorary Research Fellow, Department of Mechanical Engineering, Glasgow University; b. 18.2.31, Walston, Lanarkshire; m., Mary Bentley Alexander; 1 s.; 2 d. Educ. Allan Glen's School, Glasgow; Glasgow University. Assistant in Mechanical Engineering, Glasgow University, 1952-55; National Service, Royal Navy, 1955-57 (final rank: Sub-Lt.); Lecturer in Mechanical Engineering, Glasgow University, 1957-61; Performance Engineer, Rolls-Royce Ltd. (Scottish Group), 1961-62; Lecturer in Mechanical Engineering/ Senior Lecturer/Reader/Professor, Glasgow University. Chairman, Glasgow Panel, IMechE. Joint Session Clerk, Trinity St. Paul's Church, Cambuslang. Recreation: singing. Address: (h.) 43 Stewarton Drive, Cambuslang, Glasgow G72 8DQ.

McCalman, Ian Alister, MA (Hons). President, Educational Institute of Scotland, 1997-98; Member, STUC Education Committee, 1997-98; b. 26.4.42, Elgin; m., Gilllian; 1 s.; 1 d. Educ. Elgin Academy; Aberdeen University; Jordanhill College. Research in history, Balliol College, Oxford, 1964-67; Lecturer in History, Aberdeen University, 1967-70; Teacher in Glasgow, 1970-97; Teacher of History and Modern Studies, 1970-86, of Learning Support, 1986-97. Recreations: reading; cinema. Address: (h.) 18 Mossgiel Road, Glasgow G43 2DF.

McCann, Fergus John, MBA, CA, Chairman and Managing Director, Celtic plc; b. Stirling; moved to Canada 1963 to work for Touche Ross & Co.; financial executive posts: Cott Beverages (Canada) Ltd., Distillers Corporation Seagrams Limited, Pretty Polly Canada Ltd.; founded International Golf Inc., Montreal, 1973; President, World Golf Management Ltd., Bermuda, 1982-87; joined Board, Celtic Football Club, 1994. Address: (b.) Celtic Plc, Celtic Park, Glasgow G40 3RE.

McCann, James Aloysius, MA, LLB. Solicitor and Notary Public; a founding Director, Legal Defence Union in Scotland, 1987, Chairman, since 1990; b. 14.8.39, Glasgow; m., Jane Marlow; 3 s.; 1 d. Educ. St. Mungo's Academy, Glasgow; Glasgow University. Former Member, Legal Aid Central Committee; Dean, Faculty of Dunbartonshire Solicitors, 1986-88; Convenor for Law Society PQLE

Advocacy Training Courses, 1983-91; Senior Tutor (Professional Legal Practice), Glasgow University, 1981-91; Member, Law Society of Scotland Legal Aid Committee, 1987-97; Reporter, Scottish Legal Aid Board (Co-opted Member, Criminal Applications Committee, 1987-93); appointed Honorary Sheriff at Dumbarton, 1990; commission as Temporary Sheriff, 1991. Recreations: sailing/windsurfing; chess; music. Address: (b.) 499 Kilbowie Road, Clydebank G81 2AX.

McCann, Peter Toland McAree, CBE (1977), OStJ, DL, JP, BL. Solicitor and Notary Public, since 1947; b. 2.8.24, Glasgow; m., Maura Eleanor Ferris, 1 s. Educ. St. Mungo's Academy, Glasgow; Glasgow University. Councillor, Corporation of Glasgow, 1961-75; River Bailie, 1962; Magistrate, 1963-66; Police Judge, 1967-74; JP, since 1967; Lord Lieutenant, 1975-77; Lord Provost, City of Glasgow District, 1975-77; Depute Lieutenant, since 1977; Chairman, St. Thomas More Society for Lawyers, 1960; Chairman, McCann Committee for Provision of Secondary Education for Physically Disabled Children, 1968; awarded two Golden Swords from HRH Prince Fawaz of Saudi Arabia, 1977-78; awarded Silver and Golden Swords from City of Jeddah, 1975-78; awarded Medal of King Faisal of Saudi Arabia, 1976. Recreations: music; history; model railways; collecting model cars and model soldiers. Address: (h.) Craig En Ross, 31 Queen Mary Avenue, Crosshill, Glasgow G42 8DS.

McCarthy, James, BSc, FRZSS (Hon). Lecturer/Conservation Consultant; b. 6.5.36, Dundee; m.; 2 s.; 1 d. Educ. Harris Academy, Dundee; Aberdeen University; University of East Africa, Kampala. Military Service, 1954-56 (Royal Marines, commissioned Black Watch, seconded King's African Rifles); Leverhulme Scholar, Makerere College, Kampala, 1959-61; Assistant Conservator of Forests, Tanzania, and Lecturer in Forest Ecology, Forest Training School, 1961-63; Deputy Regional Officer (North England), Nature Conservancy, 1963-69; Deputy Director (Scotland), Nature Conservancy Council, 1975-91; Member, Board, Scottish Natural Heritage. Churchill Fellow, USA, 1976; Nuffield/ Leverhulme Fellow, 1988. Recreation: cross-country skiing. Address: (h.) 6a Ettrick Road, Edinburgh; T.-0131-229 1916.

McClellan, John Forrest, MA, Hon. FDIT. Director, Scottish International Education Trust, since 1986; Member, Management Committee, Hanover (Scotland) Housing Association, since 1986; b. 15.8.32, Glasgow; m., Eva Maria Pressel; 3 s.; 1 d. Educ. Aberdeen Grammar School; Aberdeen University. 2nd Lt., Gordon Highlanders and Nigeria Regiment, Royal West African Frontier Force, 1954-56; entered Civil Service, 1956; Assistant Principal, Scottish Office, 1956-59; Private Secretary to Permanent Under Secretary of State, Scottish Office, 1959-60; Principal, Scottish Office, 1960-68; Civil Service Fellow, Glasgow University, 1968-69; Assistant Secretary, Scottish Office, 1969-77; Under Secretary, Scottish Office, 1977-85. Publication: Then A Soldier (novel), 1991. Recreations: gardening; walking. Address: (h.) 7 Cumin Place, Edinburgh EH9 2JX; T.-0131 667 8446.

McClelland, Professor John Ferguson, CBE, CIMgt, FRSA, FRSE. Vice-President, Worldwide Manufacturing, Digital Corporation, since 1995; Visiting Professor and Fellow, Paisley University, since 1993; Main Board Member, Digital UK Ltd., since 1995; b. 27.3.45, Glasgow; m., Alice; 1 d. Educ. North Kelvinside School; Glasgow College. South of Scotland Electricity Board, 1963-68; IBM Corporation, 1968-95: Controller, Greenock Manufacturing, 1977, European Director of Operations, 1980, European Manufacturing Controller, 1983, Director of Manufacturing, Greenock, 1987, Director of UK Manufacturing, 1992, Vice President, Worldwide Manufacturing, 1994. Chairman: Judging Panel, Quality Scotland Excellence Award, Higher

Education Funding Council's Quality Assessment Committee, CBI UK Technology and Innovation Committee. Recreations: golf; football; gardening. Address: (b.) Digital Ltd., Crompton Way, Irvine KA11 4DY; T.-01294 203162.

McClements, Rev. Duncan Elliott, MA (Hons), BD (Hons), MTh. Parish Minister, Falkirk Grahamston United, since 1976; Clerk, Falkirk Presbytery, since 1989; Convener, Committee on Ecumenical Affairs, Church of Scotland, since 1994; b. 28.8.40, Glasgow; m., Dorothy Jean Easton; 1 s.; 1 d. Educ. Daniel Stewart's College; Edinburgh University. Assistant Minister, Carrick Knowe Parish, Edinburgh, 1965-66; Parish Minister, Hurlford Reid Memorial, 1966-76. Sometime Chairman, Kirk Care Housing Association. Recreations: gardening; reading; watching sport; Rotary. Address: 30 Russel Street, Falkirk FK2 7HS; T.-01324 624461.

McClure, Judith, MA (Oxon), DPhil, FRSA, FSAScot. Head, St. George's School, Edinburgh, since 1994; Chairman, Scottish Region and Member, Council, Girls' Schools Association; b. 22.12.45, Stockton; m., Dr. Roger Collins. Educ. Newlands Grammar School, Middlesbrough; Somerville College, Oxford. Sir Maurice Powicke Research Fellow, Lady Margaret Hall, Oxford, 1976-77; Lecturer in Medieval Latin and Medieval History, Liverpool University, 1977-79; Lecturer in History, Oxford University (Jesus, Somerville and Worcester Colleges), 1979-81; Teacher and Head of Department in History and Politics, School of St. Helen & St. Katherine, Abingdon, 1981-84; Deputy Head, Kingswood School, Bath, 1984-87; Head, Royal School, Bath, 1987-93. Member: Court, University of Bath, 1989-92, General Convocation, Heriot Watt University, since 1994, Board of Governors, Clifton Hall School, since 1995, Governing Body, Scottish Council of Independent Schools, since 1995. Publication: Bede: The Ecclesiastical History (Co-author), 1994. Recreations: reading; using a computer; travelling. Address: (b.) St. George's School for Girls, Garscube Terrace, Edinburgh EH12 6BG; T.-031-332 4575.

McCluskey, Baron (John Herbert McCluskey), LLD (Dundee). Senator of the College of Justice in Scotland, since 1984; Life Peer, since 1976; b. 12.6.29, Glasgow; m., Ruth Friedland; 2 s.; 1 d. Educ. St. Bede's Grammar School, Manchester; Holy Cross Academy, Edinburgh; Edinburgh University; MA, LLB. Admitted Faculty of Advocates, 1955; Standing Junior Counsel to Ministry of Power (Scotland), 1963; Advocate-Depute, 1964-71; QC (Scot), 1967; Chairman, Medical Appeal Tribunals for Scotland, 1972-74; Sheriff Principal of Dumfries and Galloway, 1973-74; Solicitor General for Scotland, 1974-79. Chairman, Scottish Association for Mental Health, 1985-94; Independent Chairman: Scottish Football League Compensation Tribunal, SFA Appeals Tribunal; Reith Lecturer, BBC, 1986; Editor, Butterworth's Scottish Criminal Law and Practice series. Publications: Law, Justice and Democracy, 1987; Criminal Appeals, 1992. Recreations: tennis; pianoforte. Address: (b.) Court of Session, Parliament House, Edinburgh EH1 1RF; T.-0131-225 2595.

McCluskey, Mary, DCE. Artistic Director, Scottish Youth Theatre, since 1992; freelance Theatre Director/Drama Tutor, since 1985; b. 16.9.54, Glasgow. Educ. West Senior High School, Garden City, Michigan, USA; Hamilton College of Education; Royal Scottish Academy of Music and Drama. President, Hamilton College of Education SRC, 1975-76; Teacher, Glenlee Primary, Hamilton, 1976-79; Assistant Stage Manager, Dundee Repertory Theatre, 1980-81; YOP Supervisor, Community Projects Agency (East End), 1981-83; YTS Training Officer, Community Projects Agency (South East), 1983-85; Associate Director, Scottish Youth Theatre, 1989-91; Education Officer, Royal Shakespeare Company, 1991-92. Adapted: Wee

MacGreegor, Wee MacGreegor Enlists, Medea. Recreations: theatre; films; books; visiting historic sites. Address: (b.) Scottish Youth Theatre, The Old Athenaeum, 179 Buchanan Street, Glasgow; T.-0141-332 5127.

McCoist, Alistair (Ally) Murdoch, MBE. Footballer, Glasgow Rangers; b. 24.9.62, Bellshill; m., Allison; 1 s. Educ. Hunter High School. Debut for St. Johnstone aged 16; signed for Sunderland, 1981; joined Rangers, 1983; became club's leading goal-scorer, August 1997 (421 goals); 57 caps for Scotland, since 1986; Member, Scotland squad, 1990 World Cup Finals, 1992 European Championships; regular contributor to Question of Sport, BBC TV; chat-show host, McCoist and MacAulay, BBC Scotland. Scottish Sports Personality of the Year, 1992; Scottish Sports Writers' Player of the Year, 1992. Recreations: reading autobiographies; listening to music; playing pranks on his team-mates. Address: (b.) Carnegie Sports International Ltd., 4 Redheughs Rigg, South Gyle, Edinburgh EH12 9DQ; T.-0131-317 7773.

McColgan, Elizabeth. Athlete; b. 24.5.64, Dundee; m., Peter Conor McColgan. Educ. University of Alabama. Commonwealth Games Gold medallist (10,000 metres), 1986; Silver medallist, World Cross-Country Championships, 1987; Olympic Games Silver medallist (10,000 metres), 1988; Silver medallist, World Indoor Championships, 1989; Gold medallist (10,000 metres) and Bronze medallist (3,000 metres), Commonwealth Games, 1990; Winner, 1996 London Marathon.

McColl, James Hamilton, MBE, NDH, SDH, SHM. Freelance Horticulturalist; b. 19.9.35, Kilmarnock; m., Billie; 1 s.; 1 d. Educ. Kilmarnock Academy; West of Scotland Agricultural College. Staff Member, WSAC, Auchincruive, Ayr, 1956-59; Assistant Head Gardener, Reading University Botanic Garden, 1959-61; Horticultural Adviser/Lecturer, Shropshire Education Authority, 1961-67; Horticultural Adviser: MAFF, Leicestershire, Northants and Rutland, 1967-73, North of Scotland College of Agriculture, 1973-78; former PRO, Morrison Bowmore Distillers Ltd.; Co-Presenter, The Beechgrove Garden, BBC TV Scotland, 1978-89, since 1994. Recreations: golf; music; rugby. Address: (h.) Ayrshire House, Oldmeldrum, Aberdeenshire; T.-01651 873955.

McConachie, Neil Alexander, BSc, MSc, MRPharmS. General Manager, Argyll and Clyde Health Board, since 1995; b. 23.5.50, Aberdeen; m., Judy McLennan; 1 s.; 1 d. Educ. Fettes College; Robert Gordon's University; Strathclyde University. Pharmacist, NHS, 1974-75; Wellcome Foundation, 1976-78; Pharmacist, North West Thames, 1978-82; various positions in Britain and overseas, DuPont, 1982-95. Recreations: golf; travel. Address: (h.) 19 Lochend Road, Bearsden, Glasgow G61 1DX. T.-0141-942 6862.

McConnell, Charles Stephen, BA (Hons), MPhil. Chief Executive, Scottish Community Education Council, since 1993; Board Member, International Association for Community Development, since 1990; b. 20.6.51, Harrogate. Educ. Huyton Hill School, Ambleside; Granby Park School, Harrogate; City of Birmingham Polytechnic; Paisley College of Technology. Community Educator; Lecturer in Community Studies, Clydebank Technical College; Action Researcher, Community Education, Scottish Local Government Unit; Lecturer in Community Education, Dundee College of Education; Senior Policy Development Officer, National Consumer Council; Development Director, Action Resource Centre; Public and European Affairs Director, Community Development Foundation. Publications: Community Worker as Politiciser of the Deprived; Deprivation, Participation and Community Action; Community Education and Community Development; Post 16 — Developments in Continuing Education in Scotland; Classroom Commercials — business sponsorship of education; Consumer Action and Community Development; Community Development — the European dimension; A Citizen's Europe; Promoting Community Development in Europe; Community Development and Urban Regeneration; Community Education: The Making of an Empowering Profession. Recreations: fell-walking; reading political biography. Address: (b.) Rosebery House, 9 Haymarket Terrace, Edinburgh EH12 5EZ; T.-0131-313 2488.

McConnell, Jack Wilson, BSc, DipEd. General Secretary, Scottish Labour Party, since 1992; b. 30.6.60, Irvine; m., Bridget, 1 s., 1 d. Educ. Arran High School; Stirling University. Mathematics Teacher, Lornshill Academy, 1983-92; Member, Stirling District Council, 1984-92, Council Leader, 1990-92, Treasurer, 1988-92, Chair, Leisure and Recreation Committee, 1986-88, Equal Opportunities Committee, 1986-90; President, 1980-82, Hon. President, 1991-93, Stirling University Students Association; Chair, Board of Directors, Stirling Windows Ltd., 1988-92; Member, Labour Party Scottish Executive Committee, 1989-92; Parliamentary candidate, Perth and Kinross, 1987. Publication: Proposals for Scottish Democracy, 1989. Address: (h.) 10a Argyll Avenue, Stirling FK8 1UL; T.-01786 479470.

McConnell, Rodger Raymond, FRICS, MBA. Director of Property Services, Glasgow City Council, since 1995; Chairman, General Practice Division, Royal Institution of Chartered Surveyors in Scotland, 1996; b. 13.5.47, Bellshill; m., Rosalind; 3 s.; 1 d. Educ. Our Lady's High School, Motherwell; College of Estate Management; Glasgow University. Trainee Valuer, District Valuer's Office, Glasgow, 1966-71; Senior Assistant, Richard Ellis, 1971-75; Strathclyde Regional Council: Assistant Head of Estates, 1975-78, Depute Director of Estates, 1978-91; City Estates Surveyor, Glasgow District Council, 1992-95. Member, Association of Chief Estates Surveyors and Property Managers in Local Government. Recreations: family activities; following sport; theatre. Address: (b.) Tontine Building, 20 Trongate, Glasgow G1 5EY; T.-0141-287 8400.

McConnell, Walter Scott, OBE, FRPharmS, PhC. Community Pharmacist, since 1962; Vice Chairman, Ayrshire and Arran Community Health Care Trust; Chairman, Advisory Committee on Prisoner Management, Scottish Prison Service; b. 7.4.36, Kilmarnock; m.; 1 s.; 3 d. Educ. Kilmarnock Academy; Royal Technical College, Glasgow. Former Chairman, Pharmaceutical General Council (Scotland). Recreations: curling; golf. Address: (h.) 27 Mauchline Road, Hurlford, Kilmarnock KA1 5AB; T.-01563 525393.

McCool, Thomas Joseph, CBE, BSc (Hons), HonDEd, FRSA. Chief Executive, Scottish Vocational Education Council, 1986-97; b. 1.3.39, Bellshill; m., Anne McGurk; 2 d. Educ. Our Lady's High School, Motherwell; Glasgow University; Jordanhill College of Education. Various teaching appointments, 1961-71; Assistant Director of Education, then Depute Director, Renfrewshire, 1971-76; Divisional Education Officer, Renfrew Division, Strathclyde, 1976-86.

McCormack, Ian Andrew. Editor, West Highland Free Press, since 1976; b. 5.2.48, Kilmarnock; 2 d. Educ. Kilmarnock Academy. Trainee Journalist, Evening Times, Glasgow, 1965, Kilmarnock Standard, 1966-67; Reporter, Glasgow Herald, 1968-69; joined West Highland Free Press, 1975. Address: (b.) Broadford, Isle of Skye; T.-01471 822464.

McCormack, Jean Elizabeth Wallace, DL. Provost, Perth and Kinross District Council, 1992-96; b. 13.6.38, Duundee; m., Peter McCormack; 1 s.; 1 d. Educ. Harris

Academy, Dundee; Dundee College of Education. Address: Grangeside, Grange Road, Errol, Perth PH2 7SR

MacCormick, Professor (Donald) Neil, MA, LLD, Hon. LLD (Uppsala), Hon.LLD (Saarland), Hon.LLD (Queen's University, Ontario), FRSE, FBA. Vice-Principal, 1997-2000, and Regius Professor of Public Law, Edinburgh University, since 1972; b. 27.5.41, Glasgow; m., 1, Karen (Caroline) Rona Barr (m. diss.); 3 d.; 2, Flora Margaret Britain. Educ. High School of Glasgow; Glasgow University; Balliol College, Oxford. Lecturer in Jurisprudence, Queen's College, Dundee, 1965-67; Fellow, Balliol College, Oxford, 1967-72; Oxford University: CUF Lecturer, 1968-72, Pro-Proctor, 1970-71; Dean, Faculty of Law, Edinburgh University, 1973-76 and 1985-88; Senate Assessor, University Court, 1982-85; Provost, Faculty Group of Law and Social Sciences, 1993-97; Member, Broadcasting Council for Scotland, 1985-89; Vice President: International Association for Legal and Social Philosophy, 1991-95, Royal Society of Edinburgh, 1991-94; Member, Economic and Social Research Council, since 1995; Member, Scottish Examination Board, 1994-97. President, Oxford Union, 1965; Executive Member, Scottish National Party, 1978-81, Council Member, 1978-84 and 1989-97; Foreign Member, Finnish Academy of Science. Publications: as author or editor, books on philosophy of law, political philosophy, etc. Address: (h.) 19 Pentland Terrace, Edinburgh EH10 6AA; T.-0131-447 7945.

McCormick, John, MA, MEd. Controller, BBC Scotland, since 1992; b. 24.6.44; m., Jean Frances Gibbons; 1 s.; 1 d. Educ. St. Michael's Academy, Irvine; Glasgow University. Former schoolteacher; joined BBC as Education Officer, 1970; Senior Education Officer, Scotland, 1975-82; Secretary and Head of Information, BBC Scotland, 1982-87; Secretary of BBC Scotland, 1987-92. Member, Glasgow Children's Panel, 1972-77; Visiting Committee, Glenochil Young Offenders' Institution, 1979-85; Vice-Chairman, Youth-At-Risk (Scotland); Chairman, Edinburgh International Film Festival, since 1996; Hon. Joint Chairman, BAFTA Scotland, since 1992; Lay Member, Court, University of Strathclyde, since 1996. Recreations: theatre; cinema; biography; newspapers. Address: (b.) Broadcasting House, Queen Margaret Drive, Glasgow, G12 0TT; T.-0141-339 8844.

McCormick, John William Penfold, BSc, PhD. Chairman, Scottish Association for Public Transport, since 1988; Information Technology Manager, Weir Group Management Systems, since 1979; b. 9.6.46, Renfrew; m., Linda M.L.; 1 d. Educ. Paisley Grammar School; Glasgow University. Research Fellow, Glasgow University, 1971-74; computer management, since 1975. Recreations: hill-walking; transport; music. Address: (b.) 5 St. Vincent Place, Glasgow G1 2HT; T.-0141-639 3697.

McCormick, Julie Elizabeth, LLB (Hons), DipLP, NP. Solicitor; Membership Secretary, Scottish Young Lawyers Association; Member, Admissions Committee, Law Society of Scotland; b. 10.12.71, Farnborough, Kent. Educ. John Paul Academy, Glasgow; Strathclyde University. Joined Allan McDougall & Co, SSC, as trainee Solicitor, 1994; Qualified Solicitor, since 1996. Recreations: cinema; theatre; Celtic music; food and drink. Address: (b.) 3 Coates Crescent, Edinburgh EH3 7AL; T.-0131-225 2121.

McCormick, Patrick. Scottish Divisional Officer, USDAW, since 1985; Member, Industrial Tribunals, since 1986; Chairperson, General Council, Scottish TUC, 1995-96; b. 21.5.33, Greenock; m., May; 1 d. Educ. St. Columba's High School, Greenock. Recreations: photography; walking; music; DIY. Address: (b.) USDAW, 342 Albert Drive, Glasgow G41 5PG; T.-0141-427 6561.

McCosh, Professor Andrew Macdonald, BSc, DBA, HonMBA, CA. Professor of Finance Emeritus and University Fellow, Edinburgh University, since 1995; b. 16.9.40, Glasgow; m., Anne; 3 d. Educ. Edinburgh Academy; Edinburgh University; Harvard University. Associate Professor of Accounting, University of Michigan, 1964-71; Research Assistant, Visiting Professor of Business Administration, Harvard Business School, 1964-75; Professor of Management Accounting, Manchester Business School, 1971-85; Professor of the Organisation of Industry and Commerce, Edinburgh University, 1986-95; Director, The Lexington Mutual Funds, New York, USA, since 1996. Recreations: mountaineering; fishing; golf. Address: (b.) Department of Business Studies, William Robertson Building, 50 George Square, Edinburgh EH8 9JY; T.-0131-650 3801.

McCourt, Arthur David, BSc (Hons). Chief Executive, Highland Council, since 1995; b. 11.7.47, Newburgh, Fife; m., Jan; 1 d. Educ. Bell-Baxter High School, Cupar; Edinburgh College of Art; Heriot-Watt University. Various posts with Northumberland County Council, Central Regional Council, Stirling District Council; Assistant Chief Executive, Tayside Regional Council, 1990-93. Recreation: mountaineering. Address: (b.) Glenurquhart Road, Inverness IV3 5NX; T.-01463 702838.

McCreadie, Robert Anderson, LLB, PhD, Advocate; b. 17.8.48, St. Andrews. Educ. Madras College, St. Andrews; Edinburgh University; Christ's College, Cambridge. Lecturer, Dundee University, 1974-78, Edinburgh University, 1978-93; called to Scottish Bar, 1992; Standing Junior Counsel, Department of Transport, 1994-95, Scottish Home and Health Department, 1995; Member: Scottish Consumer Council, 1977-82, Social Security Appeal Tribunals, 1987-92; Labour Parliamentary Candidate, Edinburgh South, 1983; joined Scottish Liberal Party, 1985; Parliamentary Candidate: Livingston, 1987, Glasgow Central, 1989, Edinburgh South, 1992; Vice Chairman, Scottish Liberal Democrats, 1988-92; Executive Committee, Scottish Constitutional Convention, 1989-92; Chairman, Scottish Legal Action Group, 1980-82; Fellow, British-American Project, 1985. Publication: You and Your Rights: An A to Z Guide to the Law in Scotland, 1984 (Joint Editor). Recreations: music; Scottish history; walking. Address: (h.) 40 Marchmont Crescent, Edinburgh EH9 1HG; T.-0131-667 1383.

McCreadie, Robin G., DSc, MD, FRCPsych. Director of Clinical Research, Crichton Royal Hospital, Dumfries, since 1982; Medical Commissioner, Mental Welfare Commission, Edinburgh, since 1994; b. 21.2.42, Troon; 2 d. Educ. Ayr Academy; Glasgow University. Lecturer in Psychological Medicine, Glasgow University; Consultant Psychiatrist, Gartnavel Royal Hospital, Glasgow. Recreations: hill-walking; all things Italian. Address: (b.) Crichton Royal Hospital, Dumfries; T.-01387 255301.

McCrone, Alasdair Iain, DDA. Artistic Director, Mull Theatre, since 1995; b. 21.10.59, Glasgow; m., Alicia Hendrick. Educ. Dalziel High School, Motherwell; Glasgow University; Royal Scottish Academy of Music and Drama. Freelance actor, 1984-90; twice toured Highlands with one-man plays; directed The Vanek Plays (Havel) as part of Glasgow's 1990 celebrations; Drama Director, Banff and Buchan Council, 1991-92 and 1993; Director, Mull Little Theatre, 1992-93; resigned, 1994, to resume freelance work; appeared as Stan Laurel, Laurel and Hardy; re-appointed to Mull Theatre, 1995; directing credits include: The Road to Mecca, The Bend, Not About Heroes, Speed-The-Plow, Whisky Galore, Death and the Maiden, all for Mull Theatre; Columcille, Stray Theatre; Highland Voices, Traverse Theatre. Recreations: golf; cycling; rail travel; Gaelic choir; reading; walking. Address: (h.) Thornliebank, Argyll Terrace, Tobermory, Isle of Mull; T.-01688 302602.

McCrone, Iain Alistair, CBE (1987), SDA. Farmer and Company Director; b. 29.3.34, Glasgow; m., Yvonne Findlay; 4 d. Educ. Glasgow Academy; Trinity College, Glenalmond; West of Scotland Agricultural College. Farming on own account, since 1956; Managing Director, McCrone Farmers Ltd., since 1958; began fish farming, 1968; Director: Highland Trout Co. (now Marine Harvest McConnell), Otter Ferry Salmon Ltd., since 1974; Member: Fife Regional Council, 1978-82; Parliamentary candidate (Conservative), Central Fife, 1979, Council, National Farmers Union of Scotland, 1977-82, Board, Glenrothes Development Corporation, 1980-96, Fife Health Board, 1983-91; Nuffield Farming Scholar, 1966; President, Scottish Conservative and Unionist Association, 1985-87. Recreations: golf; rugby (spectator). Address: (h.) Cardsknolls, Markinch, Fife KY7 6LP; T.-01337 830267.

McCrone, Professor Robert Gavin Loudon, CB, MA, MSc, PhD, Hon.LLD, FRSE. Visiting Professor, Department of Business Studies, since 1994, and Hon. Fellow of the Europa Institute, since 1992, Edinburgh University; Deputy Chairman, Royal Infirmary of Edinburgh NHS Trust, since 1994; Board Member, Scottish Opera, since 1992; b. 2.2.33, Ayr; m., Alexandra Bruce Waddell; 2 s.; 1 d. Educ. St. Catharine's College, Cambridge; University of Wales; Glasgow University. Fisons Ltd., 1959-60; Lecturer in Economics, Glasgow University, 1960-65; Fellow, Brasenose College, Oxford, 1965-70; Consultant, UNESCO, 1964; Member, NEDC Working Party on Agricultural Policy, 1967-68; Adviser, House of Commons Select Committee on Scottish Affairs, 1969-70; Senior Economic Adviser, Scottish Office, 1970-72; Under Secretary, 1972-80; Secretary, Industry Department for Scotland, 1980-87; Secretary, Scottish Office Environment Department, 1987-92; Chief Economic Adviser, Scottish Office, 1972-92. Member, Economic and Social Research Council, 1986-89, Council, Royal Economic Society, 1977-82, Council, Scottish Economic Society, 1982-91, Advisory Committee, Inquiry into Implementation of Constitutional Reform, 1995-97. Publications: The Economics of Subsidising Agriculture, 1962; Scotland's Economic Progress 1951-60, 1963; Regional Policy in Britain, 1969; Scotland's Future, 1969; Housing Policy in Britain and Europe (Co-Author), 1995; European Monetary Union and Regional Development, 1997. Recreation: walking. Address: (b.) Department of Business Studies, Edinburgh University, 50 George Square, Edinburgh EH8 9JY; T.-0131 650 4603.

McCrorie, Ian, BSc. Chorusmaster, Scottish Festival Singers, since 1991; Assistant Rector, Greenock Academy, since 1975; b. 6.5.41, Greenock; m., Olive Simpson Bolton; 2 s. Educ. Greenock Academy; Glasgow University. Founded Toad Choir, Greenock, which appeared in numerous BBC Songs of Praise programmes and won 1975 National Choral Competition, Royal Albert Hall, London); this choir became the nucleus of the Scottish Philharmonic Singers (1976-91); Organist and Choirmaster, Mid Kirk of Greenock, 1964-93; conducted at Festivals in France and Poland, and took SPS to Israel and the London Proms; Member, Greenock Presbytery, and Panel on Worship, General Assembly; Past President and Convener of Cruising, now Review Editor, Clyde River Steamer Club; author of numerous books and articles on Clyde and West Highland steamers. Recreations: as above! Address: (h.) 72 Newton Street, Greenock; T.-01475 726689.

McCrossan, Margaret B.P., MA, CPFA. Director of Finance, Inverclyde Council, since 1995; b. 12.1.61, Helensburgh; m., Bill; 1 s. Educ. Braidfield High School; University of Glasgow. Joined Strathclyde Regional Council as Trainee Accountant, 1981; various accountancy, audit and systems development posts since qualifying in 1986. Recreations: golf; travel. Address: (b.) Department of Finance, Municipal Buildings, Greenock PA15 1LX; T.-01475 882201.

McCue, William, OBE (1982), LRAM, ARAM. Bass Singer; b. 17.8.34, Allanton, Shotts; m., Patricia Carrick; 1 d. Educ. Calderhead High School; Royal Scottish Academy of Music; Royal Academy of Music. Began professional singing career in 1960; his work has included opera, oratorio, recital, concert, cabaret, pantomime and stage musical, radio and TV; has travelled throughout the world, making numerous visits to USA, Canada, USSR, Iceland, Europe and Israel; has made various recordings of Scots songs and Negro spirituals; Director, Scottish Singers Company; Honorary Life Member, Saltire Society; former Member, Scottish Arts Council. Recreations: watching all sport; listening to all kinds of music; gardening; escaping to the Scottish countryside. Address: (h.) Sweethope House, Bothwell, Glasgow G71 8BT; T.-01698 853241.

McCulloch, Andrew Grant, LLB, BSc(Soc Sci). Partner, Drummond Miller WS, since 1979; b. 10.2.52, Edinburgh; m.; 1 s.; 1 d. Educ. Glasgow Academy; Edinburgh University. Trained, then Assistant, Drummond & Co., 1974-79; Partner, since 1979; Member, Council, Law Society of Scotland, since 1987, President of Society, 1996-97; Solicitor Advocate, since 1992; Temporary Sheriff, since 1991. President, Grange Sports Club, 1990-92. Recreations: golf; cricket; wine. Address: (b.) 31/2 Moray Place, Edinburgh; T.-0131-226 5151.

McCulloch, Ian, DA, ARSA. Painter and Printmaker; b. 4.3.35, Glasgow; m., Margery Palmer; 2 s. Educ. Eastbank Academy; Glasgow School of Art. Elected Member, Society of Scottish Artists, 1964; elected Associate, Royal Scottish Academy, 1989; paintings in many private and public collections; numerous one-man and group exhibitions; 1st prize, Stirling Smith Biennial, 1985; winner, Glasgow International Concert Hall Mural Competition, 1989-90; Fine Art Fellow, Strathclyde University, since 1994. Address: (h.) 51 Victoria Road, Lenzie, Glasgow G66 5AP; T.-0141-776 1053.

McCulloch, Professor James, BSc, PhD. Professor of Neuroscience, Glasgow University, since 1988; b. 7.4.51, Irvine; m., Mailis Christina; 2 s. Educ. Spiers School, Beith; Glasgow University. Lecturer, 1978-86, Reader, 1986-88, Glasgow University; Secretary, International Society for Cerebral Blood Flow and Metabolism, since 1989. Publications: four books; 190 scientific papers. Recreations: squash; golf; skiing. Address: (b.) Glasgow University, Bearsden Road, Glasgow, G61 1QH; T.-0141-330 5828.

McCulloch, John David, CA, DL. Deputy Lieutenant, Midlothian, since 1992; Clerk to Church of Scotland Presbytery of Lothian, since 1994; Chartered Accountant, since 1963; b. 5.4.37, Edinburgh; m., Cicely Blackett; 2 s.; 1 d. Educ. Belhaven Hill, Dunbar; Marlborough College. Address: (h.) Auchindinny House, Penicuik EH26 8PE; T.-Penicuik 672943.

McCulloch, Margery Palmer, BA, MLitt, PhD, LRAM. University teacher and writer; m., Ian McCulloch; 2 s. Educ. Hamilton Academy; London University, Glasgow University. Convener, Glasgow Branch, Saltire Society. Publications: The Novels of Neil M. Gunn: a critical study, 1987; The Man Who Came Back: short stories and essays by Neil M. Gunn, 1991; Edwin Muir: poet, critic and novelist, 1993. Recreation: music. Address: (h.) 51 Victoria Road, Lenzie, Glasgow G66 5AP; T.-0141-776 1053.

McCulloch, Tony, BSc, MEd, MA, FRSA. Rector, Charleston Academy, Inverness, since 1991; b. 12.12.50, Glasgow; m., Anne C.; 1 s.; 1 d. Educ. St. Pius Secondary, Glasgow; University of Ulster; Edinburgh University; Open University. Taught in Glasgow, Cumbernauld, Edinburgh, and Armadale (formerly Depute Rector, Armadale Academy, West Lothian). Recreations: traditional music; mandolin. Address: (b.) Charleston Academy, Kinmylies, Inverness; T.-01463 234324.

McCunn, Archibald Eddington, OBE, BSc (Hons), CEng, MIMechE, FIMgt. Board Member, Scottish Greenbelt Foundation; b. 27.5.27, Motherwell; m., Olive Isobel Johnston; 1 s.; 1 d. Educ. Dalziel High School; Strathclyde University. Engineering Management, Colvilles Ltd. BSC, 1952-64; Senior Consultant, Inbucon/AIC, 1964-67; Divisional Chairman, Stenhouse Industries, 1967-71; Divisional Chairman/Consultant, Grampian Holdings plc, 1971-89; Board Member, Highlands and Islands Development Board, 1985-89; Director: A.E. McCunn Consultants Ltd., 1985-95; Chairman, Craftpoint Ltd., 1986-91; Director, McConnell Salmon Ltd., 1990-94; Vice Chairman and Trustee, Argyll and Bute Countryside Trust, 1990-95; Hon. Vice-President, Scottish Salmon Growers Association, 1990-95; Board Member: State Hospital, 1992-96, Scottish Natural Heritage (South West), 1992-97. Recreations: painting; music; writing; cycling; gardening. Address: (h.) 2 McIntosh Way, Motherwell ML1 3BB; T.-01698 253500.

McDaid, Professor Seamus, CA, MBA. Vice Principal, University of Paisley, since 1997; b. 23.7.52, Glasgow; m., Alice; 2 d. Educ. St. Mungo's Academy; Glasgow University; Strathclyde University. Qualified as CA, 1974; trained with Wylie & Bisset, CA; worked for Coopers & Lybrand; joined Glasgow College as Lecturer, 1976; Senior Lecturer, 1980, Head, Department of Finance and Accounting, 1987; Dean, Faculty of Business, Glasgow Caledonian University, 1992. Recreations: football; badminton. Address: (b.) University of Paisley, Paisley PA1 2BE; T.-0141 848 3000.

McDevitt, Professor Denis Gordon, DSc, MD, FRCP, FRCPI, FRCPEd, FFPM, FRSE. Professor of Clinical Pharmacology, Dundee University Medical School, since 1984, and Dean, Faculty of Medicine, Dentistry and Nursing, 1994-97; Honorary Consultant Physician, Tayside Health Board, since 1984; Civil Consultant in Clinical Pharmacology, RAF, since 1987; Member, General Medical Council, since 1996; b. 17.11.37, Belfast; m., Anne McKee; 2 s.; 1 d. Educ. Campbell College, Belfast; Queen's University, Belfast. Assistant Professor of Medicine and Consultant Physician, Christian Medical College, Ludhiana, North India, 1968-71; Senior Lecturer in Clinical Pharmacology and Consultant Physician, Queen's University Medical School, 1971-76; Merck International Fellow in Clinical Pharmacology, Vanderbilt University, Nashville, Tennessee, 1974-75; Reader in Clinical Pharmacology, Queen's University Medical School, 1976-78; Professor of Clinical Pharmacology, Queen's University of Belfast and Consultant Physician, Belfast Teaching Hospitals, 1978-83. Chairman, Clinical Section, British Pharmacological Society, 1985-88 (Secretary, 1978-82); Member, Medicines Commission, 1986-95; President, Association of Physicians of Great Britain and Ireland, 1987-88. Recreations: golf; classical music. Address: (h.) 1 Godfrey Street, Barnhill, Dundee DD5 2QZ.

McDonald, Rt. Rev. Alexander, BA, CMIWS. Moderator of the General Assembly, Church of Scotland; General Secretary, Department of Ministry, Church of Scotland, since 1988; b. 5.11.37, Bishopbriggs; m., Essdale Helen McLeod; 2 s.; 1 d. Educ. Bishopbriggs Higher Grade School; Whitehill Senior Secondary School, Glasgow; Glasgow University and Trinity College. RAF, 1954-56; Management in timber trade: 1952-54, 1956-58; motor trade, 1958-62; student, 1962-68; Minister: St. David's Bathgate, 1968-74, St. Mark's, Old Hall, Paisley, 1974-88. Trustee, Scottish Television Staff Trust; wide range of involvement with Boys' Brigade in Scotland, Scottish Spastics, mentally handicapped children, ACCORD, Christian Aid and many others; regular broadcaster. Recreations: reading; walking; fishing. Address: Church of Scotland, 121 George Street, Edinburgh EH2 4YN; T.-0131-225 5722.

McDonald, Alexander John. Breed Secretary, Galloway Cattle Society, since 1990; b. 12.6.39, Fochabers. Educ. Milnes High School. RAF, 1958-90. Editor and Publsher, The Galloway Journal. Recreations: country pursuits; photography. Address: (b.) 15 New Market Street, Castle Douglas DG7 1HY; T.-01556 502753.

MacDonald, Sheriff Alistair Archibald, MA, LLB, DL, KHS. Sheriff of Grampian, Highland and Islands, at Kirkwall and Lerwick, 1968-91; b. 8.5.27, Edinburgh; m., Jill Russell; 1 s.; 1 d. Educ. Broughton School; Edinburgh University. Army Service, Intelligence Corps, 1945-48; called to Scottish Bar, 1954; Sheriff Substitute of Caithness, Sutherland, Orkney and Shetland, at Lerwick, 1961-68; Deputy Lieutenant of Shetland, since 1986; Knight of the Equestrian Order of the Holy Sepulchre of Jerusalem, 1987. Address: (h.) Westhall, Shetland Isles; T.-Lerwick 2711.

Macdonald, Alister Gordon, BSc, PhD, DSc. Reader in Physiology, Aberdeen University, since 1984; b. 25.1.40, London; m., Jennifer; 1 s.; 2 d. Educ. Boys' High School, Trowbridge, Wiltshire; Bristol University. University of East Anglia, 1963-69; joined Aberdeen University as Lecturer in Physiology, 1969. Publications: Physiological Aspects of Deep Sea Biology, 1975; Effects of High Pressure on Biological Systems, 1993. Recreations: hillwalking; badminton; music; Scottish country dancing. Address: (b.) Department of Biomedical Sciences, c/o Zoology Building, Tillydrone Avenue, Aberdeen AB24 2TZ; T.- Aberdeen 272399.

MacDonald, Allan, MA. Managing Director: MNE Television, since 1989, Corrodale Ltd., since 1988; (first) Chairman, CRANN Ltd; (first) Chairman, Federation of TAC, REALT, CRANN and Breton TV (independent sector for film/TV/radio in Celtic countries); b. 11.6.53, Eriskay; m., Marion Margaret; 1 d. Educ. St. Vincent's College, Langbank; Blairs College, Aberdeen; Glasgow University. Senior Producer, BBC Highland, Inverness; Senior Producer/Manager, BBC Radio Nan Eilean, Stornoway; Manager, BBC Highland, Inverness; Television Producer, BBC Scotland, Glasgow; Head of Gaelic Television, Grampian TV, 1992-94. Member, Board of Management, Lews Castle College, 1992-95. Address: (h.) 39 Hughenden Gardens, Hyndland, Glasgow G12 9YH.

Macdonald, Angus David, MA (Hons) (Cantab), DipEd. Headmaster, Lomond School, Helensburgh, since 1986; b. 9.10.50, Edinburgh; m., Isabelle Marjory Ross; 2 d. Educ. Portsmouth Grammar School; Cambridge University; Edinburgh University. Assistant Teacher, Alloa Academy, 1972-73; Assistant Teacher, Edinburgh Academy, 1973-82 (Exchange Teacher, King's School, Parramatta, NSW, 1978-79); George Watson's College, Edinburgh: Principal Teacher of Geography, 1982, Deputy Principal, 1982-86. Recreations: outdoor recreation; sport; piping; gardening. Address: 8 Millig Street, Helensburgh, Argyll; T.-01436 679204.

MacDonald, Very Rev. Canon Bernard Gordon. Parish Priest, St. Mary's, Fochabers, since 1997; b. 25.12.24, Dufftown. Educ. Blairs College, Aberdeen; St. Edmund's, Herts. Curate, St. Mary's, Aberdeen, 1948-54; Parish Priest: Holy Family, Mastrick, 1954-61, St. Lawrence's, Dingwall, and St. Joseph's, Invergordon, 1961-79, St. Ninian's, Inverness, 1979-89, St. Anne's, Thurso, and St. Joachim's, Wick, 1989-97. Recreations: English literature; bowling; golf; art. Address: St Mary's, 22 South Street, Fochabers IV32 7ED; T.-01343 820 285.

MacDonald, Calum Alasdair, PhD. MP (Labour), Western Isles, since 1987; Parliamentary Under-Secretary of State, Scottish Office, since 1997; b. 7.5.56, Stornoway. Address: (b.) House of Commons, London, SW1; T.-071-219 4609.

MacDonald, Professor Caroline Mary, BSc, PhD, CBiol, FIBiol. Assistant Principal, since 1997, and Professor and Head, Department of Biological Sciences, Paisley University, since 1992; b. 4.9.51, Edinburgh; m., Alastair MacDonald; 2 d. Educ. Glasgow High School for Girls; Glasgow University. Lecturer/Senior Lecturer, Strathclyde University, 1983-92; Chairman, European Society for Animal Cell Technology, since 1994 (Secretary and Treasurer, 1991-94); Chief Editor, Genetic Engineer and Biotechnologist; Member, Executive Committee, and Secretary, Heads of University Biological Sciences. Recreations: family; gardening; travel. Address: (b.) Department of Biological Sciences, Paisley University, High Street, Paisley PA1 2BE; T.-0141-848 3101.

MacDonald, Colin Cameron, BA. Under Secretary, Principal Establishment Officer, Scottish Office; b. 13.7.43, Glasgow; m., Kathryn Campbell; 1 s.; 1 d. Educ. Allan Glen's School; Strathclyde University. Scottish Development Department: Research Officer, Research Services, 1967-70, Senior Research Officer, Research Services, 1970-71, Principal Research Officer, Central Planning Research Unit, 1971-75; Senior Principal Research Officer, Scottish Office Central Research Unit, 1975-81; Chief Research Officer, 1981-88; Assistant Secretary, Housing, 1988-91. Non-Executive Director, TSB Bank Scotland PLC, since 1994. Recreations: tennis; fishing; music. Address: (b.) 16 Waterloo Place, Edinburgh EH1 3DN; T.-0131-244 3938.

Macdonald, David Robert, BSc (Hons), MBA. Chief Executive, Enterprise Ayrshire, since 1993; b. 10.4.51, Edinburgh; m., Mary-Anne Turner; 2 d. Educ. Daniel Stewart's College, Edinburgh; University of Stirling; University of Strathclyde. Research Assistant, University of Dundee, 1974; Economic Analyst, West Midlands County Council, 1975-77; Head of Industrial Projects, Government of Papua New Guinea, 1978-81; Senior Economist, West Midlands County Council, 1982; Industrial Economist, Project Executive and Head of Service Industries, Scottish Development Agency, 1983-85; Director, Glasgow Action, 1985-91; Director, Glasgow Development Agency, 1991-93. Recreations: cycling; skiing; MGs; youth church; family. Address: Enterprise Ayrshire, 17-19 Hill Street, Kilmarnock KA3 1HA; T.-01563 526623.

MacDonald, Professor Donald Gordon, RD**, BDS, PhD, FRCPath, FDSRCPS(G). Professor of Oral Pathology, Glasgow University, since 1991; Consultant Oral Pathologist, Glasgow Dental Hospital, since 1974; b. 5.7.42, Glasgow; m., Emma Lindsay Cordiner; 2 s. Educ. Kelvinside Academy, Glasgow; Glasgow University. Assistant, then Lecturer, Glasgow University, 1964-69; Visiting Associate Professor in Oral Pathology, University of Illinois, 1969-70; Lecturer, Senior Lecturer, Reader in Oral Medicine and Pathology, Glasgow University, 1970-91; Editor, Glasgow Dental Journal, 1969-75; Honorary Consultant Forensic Odontologist, Strathclyde Police, since 1976; Vice President, Association of Head and Neck Oncologists of Great Britain, 1987-90; President, British Society for Oral Pathology, 1988-91; Commodore, Royal Naval Reserves, 1995-97. Recreations: golf; curling. Address: (h.) 2 Dougalston Gardens South, Milngavie, Glasgow; T.-0141-956 2075.

MacDonald, Donald John, BSc. Rector, Nicolson Institute, Stornoway, since 1989; b. 25.5.39, Glasgow; 1 s.; 2 d. Educ. Hill's Trust School, Glasgow; Lionel School, Lewis; Govan High School, Glasgow; Glasgow University; Jordanhill College of Education. Teacher of Science, Govan High School; Principal Teacher of Physics: Kirkwall Grammar School, Govan High School; Assistant Head, Linwood High School; Depute Rector, Dingwall Academy; Assistant Divisional Education Officer, Highland Region; Rector, Thurso High School, 1980-89. Address: (b.) Springfield Road, Stornoway PA87 2PZ.

MacDonald, Professor Donald Murray, MB, ChB, FRCS(Edin), Dip.Theol. Moderator, Free Church of Scotland, since 1997; Professor of Apologetics and Pastoral Theology, Free Church College, since 1997; b. 16.1.44, Kildonan, Sutherland; m., Joan; 1 s.; 3 d. Educ. Golspie Senior Secondary School; Edinburgh University. Medical and surgical training posts, Edinburgh area, 1967-73; Medical Superintendent, Lakhnadon Christia Hospital, Seoni District, India, 1973-88; divinity training, Free Church College, 1988-90; Minister Bishopbriggs Free Church of Scotland, 1990-97. Address: (b.) Free Church College, The Mound, Edinburgh EH1 2LS; T.-0131-226 5286.

Macdonald, Rev. Fergus, MA, BD. General Secretary, National Bible Society of Scotland, since 1981; President, Campaigners youth movement, since 1993; Executive Chair, Lausanne Committee for World Evangelization, since 1994; b. 2.3.36, Evanton; m., Dolina M. Mackay; 1 s.; 4 d. Educ. Edinburgh University. Assistant Minister, Hope Street Free Church, Glasgow, 1960-62; Minister, St. Andrew's Evangelical Presbyterian Church, Lima, Peru, 1962-67; Minister, Cumbernauld Free Church of Scotland, 1968-81. Address: (b.) 7 Hampton Terrace, Edinburgh EH12 5XU; T.-0131-337 9701.

Macdonald, Rev. Finlay Angus John, MA, BD, PhD. Principal Clerk, General Assembly of the Church of Scotland; b. 1.7.45, Watford; m., Elizabeth Mary Stuart; 2 s. Educ. Dundee High School; St. Andrews University. Assistant Minister, Bo'ness Old Kirk, 1970-71; Minister, Menstrie Parish Church, 1971-77; Junior Clerk and Treasurer, Stirling and Dunblane Presbytery, 1973-77; Minister, Jordanhill Parish Church, Glasgow, 1977-96; Convener, General Assembly Board of Practice and Procedure, 1988-92; Convener, General Assembly Business Committee, 1989-92; Depute Clerk, General Assembly, 1993-96. Recreations: music; hill-walking; reading; gardening. Address: (b.) 121 George Street, Edinburgh EH2 4YN; T.-0131-225 5722.

Macdonald, Fiona Margaret Taylor, LLB, NP. Solicitor, since 1981; Member, Western Isles Health Board, since 1993; b. 14.4.56, Glasgow; m., Norman Lewis Macdonald; 1 s. Educ. Hillpark Secondary School; Dundee University. Solicitor, Inverclyde District Council, 1981-83; Solicitor, Bird Semple & Crawford Heron, Stornoway, 1983-89; Solicitor, Western Isles Islands Council, since 1989. Member, Council, Law Society of Scotland, 1992-96; Local Secretary, Cancer Research Campaign (Scotland). Recreation: founder member, Goathill Ceilidh Band. Address: (h.) Valasay, Goathill Crescent, Stornoway HS1 2TA; T.-01851 70 6364.

McDonald, Gerard, MA, BA (Hons). Head Teacher, Our Lady and St. Patrick's High School, Dumbarton, since 1989; b. 26.11.39, Motherwell; m., Eileen Mary; 2 s. Educ. St. Aloysius' College, Glasgow; Glasgow University; Strathclyde University. Principal Teacher, then Assistant Head Teacher, St. Roch's Secondary, 1971-80; Depute Head Teacher, St. Ninian's High School, 1980-83; Head Teacher, St. Leonard's Secondary, 1983-89. Past President, Glasgow Schools' Rugby Association. Recreations: rugby; golf. Address: (b.) Hawthornhill Road, Dumbarton; T.-01389 762101.

Macdonald, Gibson Torbett. Conservative Group Leader, South Ayrshire Council; b. 21.1.33; m., Muirkirk; m., Mary Hastings Logan Lambie; 1 s.; 1 d. Educ. Kilmarnock Academy. National President, Junior Chamber Scotland; Executive Vice President, Junior Chamber International; Chairman, Ayr Branch, Ayr Conservative Association; Chairman, Ayr Conservative Constituency; Town Councillor, Royal Burgh of Ayr; District Councillor, Kyle and Carrick District (Provost, 1984-88 and 1992-96; held Convenership of Planning, Employment and Policy and

Resources Committees); Chairman, Culzean Country Park Joint Committee; Member, COSLA Planning and Town Twinning Committees. Treasurer, Ayrshire Decorative and Fine Arts Society; Past President, Ayr Town Twinning Association; Secretary, Franco Scottish Society (Ayrshire); President, Ayr Chamber of Commerce, 1990-92; Dean of Guildry, 1991-92; Vice-President, Ayrshire Chamber of Commerce and Industry, since 1993. Recreations: bowling; bridge; computing; philately. Address: (h.) 14 Belmont Avenue, Ayr KA7 2JN.

Macdonald, 8th Baron, (Godfrey James Macdonald of Macdonald). Chief of the Name and Arms of Macdonald; b. 28.11.47; m., Claire Catlow; 1 s.; 3 d. Address: (h.) Kinloch Lodge, Isle of Skye.

Macdonald, Gus, CBE. Chairman, Scottish Television, now Scottish Media Group plc; Television Journalist; b. 20.8.40, Larkhall; m., Teen; 2 d. Educ. Allan Glen's School, Glasgow. Marine engineer, Stephens, Linthouse, 1955-62; Circulation and Publicity Manager, Tribune, 1963-65; Investigative Journalist, The Scotsman, 1965-66; Editor, Financial Scotsman, 1966-67; Investigative Bureau, World in Action, Granada, 1967-69; Editor/Executive Producer, World in Action, 1969-75; successively Head of Current Affairs, Head of Regional Programmes, Head of Features, Granada, 1975-82; Writer/Presenter, Camera: Early Photography, 1979-80, MacDiarmid: Hammer and Thistle; Presenter, variously, World in Action, What the Papers Say, Devil's Advocate, Union World; Election and Party Conference coverage; C4 Viewers Ombudsman, Right to Reply, 1982-88; BAFTA Award, Best Factual Series, 1973; National Viewers and Listeners' Association Award, 1984; Scottish Business Elite Award, Services Sector, 1993; founder Chairman, Edinburgh International Television Festival, 1976; Visiting Professor, Film and Media Studies, Stirling University, since 1985; Chairman, Edinburgh International Film Festival, 1993-96; Governor, National Film and Television School, 1986-97; Vice President, Royal Television Society, since 1994; Board, GMTV, since 1991; Chairman, ITV Broadcast Board, 1992-94; Member, Board, Scottish Screen, since 1997, Board, Glasgow 1999 Festival Company Limited, since 1996, Board, Bail'ur Ostaig (Gaelic College, Skye), since 1996; President, Paths For All Initiative, Scottish Natural Heritage. Publications: Grierson: Television and Documentary, 1977; Camera: Victorian Eyewitness, 1979. Recreations: words; music; pictures; sports; hills. Address: (b.) Scottish Media Group, Cowcaddens, Glasgow G2 3PR.

Macdonald, Ian Hamish, OBE, FCIBS, CIMight. Chairman, Clan Donald Lands Trust; Director, AIB Group Northern Ireland PLC, 1992-96; b. 30.12.26, Inverness; m., Patricia Lace; 1 d. Educ. Inverness Royal Academy; Inverness Technical High School. RAFVR, 1944; Queen's Own Cameron Highlanders, 1945 (Hon. Captain, 1948); Mercantile Bank, 1948-59; The Hongkong and Shanghai Banking Corporation: Manager, 1959-72, General Manager, India, 1972-73, General Manager International, 1973-80, Executive Director, 1980-83; Chairman, Hongkong Bank of Canada, 1981-83; Chief General Manager, TSB Scotland, 1983-86, and TSB Scotland PLC, 1986-87; Director, TSB Group PLC, 1986-87; Director, Scottish Power PLC, 1987-92; Chairman, Clairmont PLC, 1987-91, First Edinburgh Homes PLC, 1988-92, EFM Dragon Trust, 1987-92, Scottish Council Foundation, 1983-92; Director, Macdonald Orr, 1987-93, TSB Northern Ireland PLC, 1987-92, Morgan Grenfell Scotland Ltd., 1987-91; Member, Court, Edinburgh University, 1989-92. Recreations: fishing; golf; bridge. Address: (h.) Minewood Cottage, 11 Abercromby Drive, Bridge of Allan, FK9 4EA.

Macdonald, Professor Ian Robert, MA, PhD. Senior Vice-Principal, and Professor in Spanish, Aberdeen University, since 1991; b. 4.5.39, The Hague; m., Frances Mary; 3 s. Educ. Whitgift School; St. Andrews University.

United Steel Cos. Ltd., 1961-64; research student, 1964-65; Lecturer, then Senior Lecturer, Aberdeen University, 1965-90. Recreations: walking; digging; carpentry. Address: (h.) 47 North Deeside Road, Peterculter, Aberdeenshire; T.-01224 732284.

McDonald, Rev. James Ian Hamilton, MA, BD, MTh, PhD, FEIS. Reader in Christian Ethics and New Testament Studies, Edinburgh University, since 1992; b. 7.2.33, Stonehouse; m., Jenny Paterson Fleming. Educ. Rutherglen Academy; Glasgow University; Edinburgh University. Parish Minister, Johnstone West; Baird Research Fellow in Christian Education; Lecturer in Religious Education, Moray House, Edinburgh; Lecturer in Christian Ethics and Practical Theology, then Senior Lecturer in Christian Ethics and New Testament, Edinburgh University; Associate Dean, Faculty of Divinity, 1991-94; Head, Department of Christian Ethics, since 1995; Convener, Church of Scotland Education Committee, 1985-89; Honorary President, Scottish Church Theology Society, 1997. Recreations: walking; reading; painting. Address: (b.) New College, Mound Place, Edinburgh EH1 2LX; T.-0131-650 8923.

McDonald, Professor Janet B.I., MA, FRSE, FRSAMD, FRSA. Professor of Drama, Glasgow University, since 1979; b. 28.7.41, Netherlee, Renfrewshire; m., Ian James McDonald; 1 d. Educ. Hutchesons' Girls' Grammar School; Glasgow University. Member: Governing Body, Royal Scottish Academy of Music and Drama, 1979-94, Academic Council, since 1994, Board, Citizens' Theatre, 1979-82 and since 1989 (Chair, since 1991); Member, Glasgow University Court, 1991-94; Council Member, Royal Society of Edinburgh, since 1994; Chairman: Drama and Theatre Board, Council for National Academic Awards, 1981-85, Standing Committee of University Departments of Drama, 1982-85, Drama Committee, Scottish Arts Council, 1985-88; Chair, Creative and Performing Arts Committee, CNAA, 1989-91. Address: (b.) Gilmorehill Centre for Theatre, Film and Television, University of Glasgow; T.-0141-330 5162.

MacDonald, John. Editor, Inverness Courier, since 1991; b. 6.4.45, Haddington; m., Jean Nimmo; 1 d. Educ. Dunbar Grammar School. Reporter, Haddingtonshire Courier, 1960-65; Assistant Editor, Barrow News series, 1965-68; Editor, Linlithgow Journal & Gazette, 1968-73; Editor, Lincolnshire Chronicle, 1973-75; Chief Sub-Editor, Farmers Weekly, 1975-77; Senior Editor, Reader's Digest, 1977-82; Executive Editor, Telegraph Sunday Magazine, 1982-86; Sub-Editor, The Times, 1986-89; Editor, Northern Scot, 1989-91. Publications: Great Battlefields of the World; Great Battles of World War II; Great Battles of the American Civil War. Recreations: military history; photography; travel. Address: (b.) 12-14 Seafield Road, Inverness IV1 1SG; T.-01463 233059.

Macdonald, Father John Angus, STB, MA, MLitt. Parish Priest, Fort William, and R.E. Adviser, Diocese of Argyll and the Isles, since 1991; Member: Scottish Catholic Education Commission, since 1993, Rural Forum Action Network for Scotland, since 1997; Commissioner for South Argyll, Argyll Islands and Southern Isles, Crofters Commission, since 1997; Treasurer, Burns–Gaelic Trust, since 1997; b. 6.12.45, Askernish, South Uist. Educ. Daliburgh J.S. School; St. Mary's College, Blairs; Royal Scots College, Spain (Comillas University); Aberdeen University. Ordained, 1970; Curate, 1970-72; Staff, St. Mary's College, Blairs, 1972-83, Depute Rector, 1978-83; Administrator, St. Mary's, Arisaig, 1983-85; Parish Priest: St. Mary's, Bornish, 1985-87, St. Peter's, Daliburgh, 1987-91. School Board Member, Fort William R.C. School, since 1991; Editor, Cnamh, Aberdeen University Celtic Society magazine, 1974-78; Spanish language translator for Concilium, 1981-90; Member: Western Isles Islands Council Education Committee, 1985-91, Gaelic Advisory Committee, BBC, 1986-90, Western Isles Health Board,

1989-92. Recreations: music; reading; local and church history; hill-walking; languages; DIY. Address: (h.) St. Mary's, Belford Road, Fort William PH33 6BT; T.-01397 702174.

MacDonald, Major-General John Donald, CB, CBE, DL. Joint Secretary, Royal British Legion Scotland, and The Earl Haig Fund Scotland; b. 5.4.38; m., Mary Warrack; 1 s.; 2 d. Educ. George Watson's College, Edinburgh; RMA, Sandhurst; RMCS, Shrivenham; DSSC, India; National Defence College, Latimer. Commissioned King's Own Scottish Borderers, 1958, RASC, 1963, Royal Corps of Transport, 1976-78; Commander, Armd. Division Transport Regiment, BAOR, 1978-80 (Lt.-Col.); Exchange Instructor, Australian Army Cmd. and Staff College, 1980-82; Head of Personnel and Logistics, Armd. Division, BAOR, 1983-86 (Col.); Head of Personnel and Officer for Human Resources, MoD, London, 1987-88; Distribution and Transport Director, 1 Br Corps, BAOR, 1988-91 (Brigadier); Director General, Transport and Movement (Distribution), Army, 1991-93 (Major-General). FCIT; FILDM. Recreations: travel; music; art; rugby (internationalist); athletics (internationalist); golf; skiing. Address: (b.) New Haig House, Logie Green Road, Edinburgh EH7 4HR.

MacDonald, Margo. Freelance journalist and broadcaster; b. Hamilton; m., Jim Sillars; 1 step s.; 2 d.; 1 step-d. Educ. Hamilton Academy; Dunfermline College. Teacher, 1963-65; barmaid and mother, 1965-73; Member of Parliament, 1973-74; Broadcaster/Writer, 1974-78; Director, Shelter, Scotland, 1978-81; Radio Forth: Broadcaster, 1981-83, Editor, Topical Programmes, 1983-85; political and current affairs broadcasting as reporter/presenter, 1985-91; former Chief Executive, Network Scotland.

Macdonald, Rev. Professor Murdo Ewen, MA, BD, DD (St. Andrews), DD (McGill University). Emeritus Professor, Trinity College, Glasgow University; b. 28.8.14, Isle of Harris; 2 s. Educ. Sir Edward Scott School, Harris; Kingussie Secondary School; St. Andrews University. Minister, Portree, Isle of Skye, 1939-40; Chaplain to 4th Camerons, 1940-42; Chaplain to 2nd Paras, 1942; wounded and taken prisoner, North Africa, and spent rest of War in Germany (acted as Chaplain to American Air Force); awarded Bronze Star; Pollock Lecturer in Preaching, Canada; Syme Lecturer in Theology and Preaching, Lutheran Colleges, USA; Ferrie Lecturer in Preaching and Theology, Australia. Publications: Vitality of Faith; Need to Believe; Call to Obey; Crisis of Belief; Call to Communicate; Lost Provinces of Religion. Address: (h.) 68 Lauderdale Gardens, Glasgow, G12 9QW; T.-041-334 2087.

Macdonald, Rev. Neil, MA. Free Church Minister, Fearn, Ross-shire; Moderator, General Assembly, Free Church of Scotland, 1996; b. 1932, Skye; m.; 1 s.; 2 d. Educ. Portree High School; Edinburgh University; Moray House College; Free Church College. Ordained and inducted, 1959; first charge, Lochalsh; Minister, Fearn, 26 years.

MacDonald, Norman Hamilton, FRSA, FSAScot. Chairman, The 1745 Association, since 1991; President, Clan Donald Society of Edinburgh, since 1993; President, Edinburgh Gaelic Choir, since 1995; b. 4.3.33, Edinburgh; m., Morag Young McKenzie. Educ. Royal High School, Edinburgh. RAF, 1953-55; accountancy, 1955-63; S.E. Regional Hospital Board, 1963-67; Edinburgh Corporation, later Edinburgh District Council, 1967-91 (retired). Editor, Clan Donald Magazine. Publications: histories of MacDonalds of Glengarry and Keppoch; two cassette recordings of Gaelic and Scots songs. Address: (h.) Ceapach, 8 Ethel Terrace, Edinburgh EH10 5NB: T.-0131-447 3970.

Macdonald, Norman Malcolm. Writer and Dramatist; b. 24.7.27, Thunder Bay, Canada; m., Mairi F. Educ. Nicolson Institute; Newbattle Abbey College. New Zealand Air Force, 1949-57; journalism and administration at various periods; Administrator and Writer, Fir Chlis (Gaelic theatre company), 1978-80; Secretary and Writer in Residence, Sabhal Mor Ostaig Gaelic College, 1982-83. Publications: Calum Tod (novel); An Sgaineadh (novel); Fad (poetry); Bathach Chaluim, Anna Chaimbeul, The Catechist, The Brahan Seer, Sublime Savage, Aimhreit Aignis, The Teuchtar's Tale, Or an Amadain, Ordugh na Saorsa (plays); Call Na h'Iolaire, Clann-Nighean a Sgadain (historical); The Shutter Falls (television); Portrona Community Play, 1996. Recreation: walking. Address: 14 Tong, Isle of Lewis.

Macdonald, Peter Cameron, DL, SDA. Vice-President, Scottish Landowners' Federation, since 1990 (Convener, 1985-88); Farmer, 1961-96; Director, J. Dickson & Son, Gunmakers, since 1968, Chairman, since 1997; b. 14.12.37, Edinburgh; m., Barbara Helen Drimmie Ballantyne; 2 steps. Educ. Loretto; East of Scotland College of Agriculture. Council Member: Scottish Landowners Federation, since 1976, Blackface Sheepbreeders Association, 1970-74; Member, Forth River Purification Board, 1979-87; Director, Royal Highland and Agricultural Society of Scotland, 1985; Deputy Lieutenant, West Lothian, since 1987. Recreations: fishing; shooting; golf. Address: Waterheads, Eddleston, Peeblesshire EH45 8QX; T.-01721 730229.

Macdonald, Rhoda Mairi, MA. Head of Gaelic, Scottish Television, since 1991; b. 18.10.58, Stornoway. Educ. Nicolson Institute, Stornoway; Glasgow University; Jordanhill College. Freelance Television Presenter, 1979-88; Scottish Television: Researcher, 1988, Programme Executive, Gaelic, 1989. Director, Scottish Television Enterprises. Recreations: reading; cinema; cooking. Address: (b.) Scottish Television, Cowcaddens, Glasgow G2 3PR; T.-0141-332 9999.

McDonald, Hon. Lord (Robert Howat McDonald), MC (1944), MA, LLB. Senator of the College of Justice in Scotland, 1973-89; b. 15.5.16, Paisley; m., Barbara Mackenzie. Educ. John Neilson Institution, Paisley; Glasgow University. Admitted Solicitor, 1938; KOSB, 1939-46 (mentioned in Despatches); admitted, Faculty of Advocates, 1946; QC (Scot), 1957; Sheriff of Ayr and Bute, 1966-71; Member, Criminal Injuries Compensation Board, 1964-71; Chairman: Mental Welfare Commission for Scotland, 1964-83, General Nursing Council for Scotland, 1970-73. Address: (h.) 5 Doune Terrace, Edinburgh EH3 6EA.

Macdonald, Roderick, BSc(Agri), MSc. Member, Scottish Land Court, since 1986; b. 6.2.27, Benbecula; m., Elizabeth MacLeod; 3 d. Educ. Portree High School; Aberdeen University; Michigan State University, USA. Bayer Agriculture, 1952-54; Lands Division, Department of Agriculture and Fisheries for Scotland, 1954-67 and 1972-86, latterly as Assistant Chief; Head, Land Development Division, Highlands and Islands Development Board, 1967-72; appointed Gaelic Speaking Member, Scottish Land Court, 1986; Trustee and Surveyor, Glebes Committee, Church of Scotland, since 1994; Secretary, Highland Fund, since 1993. Recreations: golf; fiddle playing; fishing. Address: 19 Cherrytree Loan, Balerno, Edinburgh; T.-0131-449 3600.

Macdonald, Rt. Rev. Mgr. Roderick, STL. Parish Priest, Glencoe/Kinlochleven, since 1990; Delegate to Diocesan Administrator, since 1996; b. 4.11.25, Mallaig. Educ. Blairs College, Aberdeen; Gregorian University, Rome. Assistant, St. Columba's Cathedral, Oban, 1950-56, St. Peter's, Daliburgh, South Uist, 1956-58; Parish Priest: St. Mun's, Glencoe, 1958-62, St. Kieran's, Campbeltown, 1962-69, St.

Mun's, Dunoon, 1969-90. Address: (b.) St. Mun's, Ballachulish, Argyll PA39 4JG; T.-01855 811203.

Macdonald, Vice-Admiral Sir Roderick (Douglas), KBE (1978). Painter; b. 25.2.21, Java; m., 1, Joan Willis (m. diss.); 2 s.; 1 s. deceased; 2, Mrs Pamela Bartosik. Educ. Fettes (Captain, Scottish Schoolboys' rugby, 1937-38). Entered Royal Navy, 1939; served at sea throughout War, 1939-45: Norway, Battle of Atlantic, Malta convoys, Indian Ocean, Normandy and East Coast convoys; Comd. six HM ships, one minesweeper and two frigate squadrons; Cyprus (Despatches, 1957); Commander, Naval Forces Borneo, 1965 (CBE); Captain of the Fleet, 1970; COS to C-in-C, Naval Home Command, 1973-76; ADC to The Queen, 1975; COS to Comdr., Allied Naval Forces Southern Europe, 1976-79. Chieftain, Skye Highland Games; President, Skye Piping Society; Fellow, Nautical Institute (Vice-President, 1976-85); Trustee and Executive, Clan Donald Lands Trust; President, Inverness Sea Cadets Unit; own exhibitions, Naples, Edinburgh (2), London (5). Publication: The Figurehead, 1993. Recreations: sailing; Highland bagpipe, gardening. Address: (h.) Ollach, Braes, Skye IV51 9LJ.

Macdonald, Roderick Francis, QC; b. 1.2.51. Advocate, 1975. Address: (b.) Advocates' Library, Parliament House, Edinburgh, EH1 1RF.

McDonald, Professor Ronald, BA, MA, PhD. Professor of International Finance, Strathclyde University, since 1993; b. 23.4.55, Glasgow. Educ. Falkirk High School; Heriot Watt University; Manchester University. Midland Bank Fellow in Monetary Economics, Loughborough University, 1982-84; Lecturer in Economics, Aberdeen University, 1984-88; Senior Lecturer, 1988-89; Robert Fleming Professor of Finance and Investment, Dundee University, 1989-93; Visiting Professor, Queen's University, Canada, 1988, University of New South Wales, Australia, 1989; Visiting Scholar, International Monetary Fund, Washington DC, since 1991; Consultant to the European Commission. Publications: Floating Exchange Rates; International Money: theory evidence and institutions (Co-Author); five co-edited books; over 100 journal articles. Recreations: music; photography; hill-walking. Address: (b.) Department of Economics, Strathclyde University, Glasgow, G4 0LN; T.-0141-552 4400.

McDonald, Sheena Elizabeth, MA. Television and Radio Broadcaster/Producer. Educ. George Watson's Ladies' College; Edinburgh University; Bristol University. BBC Radio Scotland, 1978-81; Scottish Television, 1981-87; Radio Presenter: The World At One, The World This Weekend, Beyond the Millennium, Mediumwave, BBC Radio; Television Presenter: Channel 4 News, House to House, McLibel, Midnight Special, Power and the People, Right to Reply, Channel 4 Television. Address: (b.) Curtis Brown, 28/9 Haymarket, London SW1Y 4SP.

MacDonald, Professor Simon Gavin George, MA, PhD, FInstP, FRSE; b. 5.9.23, Beauly, Inverness-shire; m., Eva Leonie Austerlitz; 1 s.; 1 d. Educ. George Heriot's, Edinburgh; Edinburgh University. Junior Scientific Officer, Royal Aircraft Establishment, Farnborough, 1943-46; Lecturer in Physics, St. Andrews University, 1948-57; Senior Lecturer in Physics: University College of the West Indies, 1957-62, St. Andrews University, 1962-67; Dundee University: Senior Lecturer in Physics, 1967-73, Professor of Physics, 1973-88, Dean of Science, 1970-73, Vice-Principal, 1974-79, Head, Department of Physics, 1979-85; Chairman, Statistics Committee, Universities Central Council on Admissions, 1989-93; Member, Scottish Universities Council on Entrance, 1969-82 (Vice-Convener, 1973-77, Convener, 1977-82); Chairman, Technical Committee, UCCA, 1979-83; Deputy Chairman, UCCA, 1983-89; Chairman, Board of Directors, Dundee Repertory

Theatre, 1975-89. Publications: Problems and Solutions in General Physics; Physics for Biology and Premedical Students; Physics for the Life and Health Sciences. Recreations: bridge; golf; fiction writing. Address: (b.) 10 Westerton Avenue, Dundee DD5 3NJ; T.-01382 778692.

McDonald, William, JP, CA. Bursar, The Carnegie Trust for the Universities of Scotland, since 1990; b. 9.11.29, Perth; m., Anne Kidd Laird McDonald; 1 s.; 1 d. Educ. Perth Academy. RAF, 1952-54; Secretary, South Mills and Grampian Investment, Dundee, 1957-62; The Company of Merchants of the City of Edinburgh: Chamberlain, 1962-90, Secretary, 1971-90; Clerk and Treasurer, Incorporation of Guildry in Edinburgh, 1975-90; Joint Secretary, Scottish Council of Independent Schools, 1978-90. Scout Association: Deputy Chief Commissioner of Scotland, 1977-79, Hon. Treasurer, Scotland, 1989-93, Chairman, UK Finance Sub-Committee, since 1993; Hon. Treasurer, European Scout Region (Brussels), 1995; Member, High Constables of Edinburgh, since 1982; Chairman: Scottish Environmental and Outdoor Education Centres, 1987-92, Lothian Valuation Appeal Committee, since 1995. Recreations: Scout Association; bridge. Address (h.) 1/3 Wyvern Park, The Grange, Edinburgh EH9 2JY; T.-0131-662 4145.

McDonald, Very Rev. William James Gilmour, MA, BD, Hon. DD (Edinburgh); b. 3.6.24, Edinburgh; m., Patricia Watson; 1 s.; 2 d. Educ. Daniel Stewart's College; Edinburgh University; Gottingen University. Royal Artillery and Indian Artillery, 1943-46; Parish Minister, Limekilns, 1953-59; Minister, Mayfield Parish Church, Edinburgh, 1959-92; Convener: Committee on Education for the Ministry, 1974-78, Assembly Council, 1984-87; Moderator, General Assembly of Church of Scotland, 1989-90. Chaplain, Edinburgh Merchant Company; Chaplain, National Trust for Scotland; Hon. Chaplain, Loretto School; Warrack Lecturer, 1993-95; Turnbull Trust Preacher, Melbourne, 1993-94. Recreations: music; cinema. Address: (h.) 7 Blacket Place, Edinburgh EH9 1RN; T.-0131-667 2100.

MacDonell of Glengarry, Air Cdre. Aeneas Ranald Donald, CB, DFC. 22nd Chief of Glengarry; Member, Standing Council of Scottish Chiefs; Trustee, Clan Donald Lands Trust; Trustee, Finlaggan Trust; b. 15.11.13, Baku, Russia; m., 1, Diana Dorothy Keane; 2 s.; 1 d.; 2, Lois Eirene Frances Streatfeild; 1 s.; 1 d. Educ. Hurtspierpoint College; Royal Air Force College, Cranwell. RAF Officer, 1931-64; seconded to Fleet Air Arm, 1935-37; Flying Instructor, 1938-39; Air Ministry; Officer Commanding Spitfire Squadron during Battle of Britain; POW, Germany, 1941-45; Chief Flying Instructor, RAF College, Cranwell; Air Attache, Moscow, 1956-58; Director of Management and Work Study, Ministry of Defence, 1960-64; retired from RAF; Construction Industry Training Board, 1967-72; Head, Commercial Department, Industrial Society, 1972-76; Partner, John Courtis & Partners, Management Selection Consultants; finally retired and moved to Scotland, 1981. Honorary President, Ross and Cromarty Branch, Soldiers', Sailors' and Airmen's Families Association, 1983-86. Recreation: bird watching. Address: (h.) Elonbank, 23 Castle Street, Fortrose, Ross-shire IV10 8TH; T.-01381 620121.

McDonnell, Michael Anthony, BD, DipCE, FIRSO. Road Safety Manager (Scotland), ROSPA, since 1990; Secretary, Scottish Accident Prevention Council, since 1990; b. 13.5.55, Bellshill; m., Rosemary Boyle; 1 s. Educ. St. Patrick's High School, Coatbridge; Hamilton College of Education; Chesters College, Glasgow. Strathclyde Regional Council, 1976-81, 1982-83, 1988-90, latterly as Assistant Road Safety Training Officer. Recreations: football; golf; cinema. Address: (b.) Slateford House, 53 Lanark Road, Edinburgh EH14 1TL; T.-0131-455 7457.

McDougall, Professor Bonnie S., BA, MA, PhD. Professor of Chinese, Edinburgh University, since 1990; b. 12.3.41, Sydney; m., A. Hansson; 1 s. Educ. University of Sydney. Lecturer in Chinese, University of Sydney; Nuffield Fellow, London University; Visiting Lecturer, Harvard University; editor, translator and teacher, Peking; Professor of Modern Chinese, University of Oslo. President, British Association of Chinese Studies. Recreations: reading; travelling. Address: (b.) Department of East Asian Studies, Edinburgh University, 8 Buccleuch Place, Edinburgh EH8 9LW; T.-0131-650 4227.

McDougall, Douglas Christopher Patrick, MA. Investment Manager; Senior Partner, Baillie Gifford & Co., since 1989; Chairman, Investment Management Regulatory Organisation, since 1997; b. 18.3.44, Edinburgh; m., Hon. Carolyn Griffiths; 2 d. Educ. Edinburgh Academy; Christ Church, Oxford. Baillie Gifford & Co.: joined, 1965; Partner, 1969; Chairman: Association of Investment Trust Companies, 1995-97, Institutional Fund Managers Association, 1993-95; Director: Baillie Gifford Japan Trust, since 1989, Pacific Horizon Trust, since 1993, Provincial Insurance, 1989-94; Member, Investments Committee, Cambridge University. Address: (b.) 1 Rutland Court, Edinburgh EH3 8EY; T.-0131-222 4000.

MacDougall, John William, JP, FIIM. Convener, Fife Council, since 1996; Leader of Administration, Fife Regional Council, 1987-96; Trustee, St. Andrews Links Trust; Member, Court, St. Andrews University; b. 8.12.47, Dunfermline; m., Catherine; 1 s.; 1 d. Educ. Templehall Secondary Modern; Rosyth Dockyard College; Fife College; Glenrothes College. Vice-President/Treasurer, Association of European Regions; Member, COSLA International Affairs Committee; former Board Member: Glenrothes Development Corporation, Fife Enterprise Company; Founder Member and Chairman, East of Scotland European Consortium. Recreations: DIY; sport. Address: (b.) Fife House, North Street, Glenrothes, Fife; T.-01592 414141, Ext. 6209.

McDougall, Peter. Screenwriter; b. 1947, Greenock. Television and film work includes: Just Another Saturday, 1974 (Prix Italia); Elephant's Graveyard, 1976; Just A Boy's Game, 1979; Shoot for the Sun, 1985; Down Where The Buffalo Go, 1988; Down Among The Big Boys, 1993.

MacDougall, Robert Hugh, MB, ChB, DMRT, FRCS, FRCR, FRCPEdin. Clinical Director, Department of Clinical Oncology, Western General Hospitals, Edinburgh, and Honorary Senior Lecturer in Clinical Oncology, Edinburgh University, since 1986; Honorary Senior Lecturer, St. Andrews University; b. 9.8.49, Dundee; m., Moira Jean Gray; 1 s.; 2 d. Educ. High School of Dundee; St. Andrews University; Edinburgh University. Demonstrator in Anatomy, St. Andrews University; Registrar in Surgery, Aberdeen Royal Infirmary; Lecturer in Clinical Oncology, Edinburgh University; Consultant Radiotherapist and Oncologist, Tayside Health Board. Recreation: reading. Address: (b.) Department of Clinical Oncology, Western General Hospital, Edinburgh.

McDowall, Linda, MA. Chief Executive, East Kilbride Business Centre, since 1993; Member: Lanarkshire Health Board, since 1995, New Lanarkshire Ltd., since 1996; Director, EICBC, since 1997; b. 29.1.55, Glasgow; m., Colin McDowall. Educ. Glenwood Secondary School; Glasgow University. Entered civil service, 1977; joined Motherwell Enterprise Development Co., 1989. Panel Member, Investors in People (Scotland) Ltd. Recreations: swimming; keep-fit; sailing; skiing. Address: (b.) PO Box 1, James Watt Building, Scottish Enterprise Technology Park, East Kilbride G75 0NS; T.-01355 238456; Platthorn Road, East Kilbride G74 1NW; T.-01355 245096.

McDowall, Stuart, CBE, MA. Local Government Boundary Commissioner for Scotland, since 1982; b. 19.4.26, Liverpool; m., Margaret B.W. Gyle; 3 s. Educ. Liverpool Institute; St. Andrews University. Royal Air Force, 1944-47; Lecturer then Senior Lecturer in Economics, St. Andrews University, 1961-91; Deputy Chairman, Central Arbitration Committee, 1976-96; Master, United College of St. Salvator and St. Leonard, St. Andrews University, 1976-80; Member: Monopolies and Mergers Commission, 1985-90, Restrictive Practices Court, 1993-96; Chairman, Fife Healthcare NHS Trust, 1994-96; Secretary, Scottish Economic Society, 1970-76. Recreations: golf; gardening; music. Address: (h.) 10 Woodburn Terrace, St. Andrews, Fife KY16 8BA; T.-01334 473247.

MacDowell, Professor Douglas Maurice, MA, DLitt, FRSE, FBA. Professor of Greek, Glasgow University, since 1971; b. 8.3.31, London. Educ. Highgate School; Balliol College, Oxford. Schoolmaster, 1954-58; Manchester University: Assistant Lecturer, 1958-61, Lecturer, 1961-68, Senior Lecturer, 1968-70, Reader, 1970-71; Visiting Fellow, Merton College, Oxford, 1969; President, Glasgow Centre, Classical Association of Scotland, 1973-75, 1977-79, 1982-84, 1988-90; Chairman, 1973-76, and Vice President, since 1976, Scottish Hellenic Society; Chairman, Council, Classical Association of Scotland, 1976-82. Publications: Andokides: On the Mysteries, 1962; Athenian Homicide Law, 1963; Aristophanes: Wasps, 1971; The Law in Classical Athens, 1978; Spartan Law, 1986; Demosthenes: Against Meidias, 1990; Aristophanes and Athens, 1995. Address: (b.) Department of Classics, Glasgow University, Glasgow G12 8QQ.

McEachran, Colin Neil, QC, MA, LLB, JD. QC, since 1981; b. 14.1.40, Glasgow; m., Kathrine Charlotte; 2 d. Educ. Glenalmond College; Merton College, Oxford; Glasgow University; University of Chicago. Advocate, since 1968; Advocate Depute, 1974-77; QC, 1981; Member, Scottish Legal Aid Board, since 1990; President, Pension Appeal Tribunal Scotland; Chairman, Commonwealth Games Council for Scotland. Recreations: target shooting; hill-walking. Address: 13 Saxe Coburg Place, Edinburgh; T.-0131-332 6820.

McElroy, Professor(Arthur) Rennie, MA, MBA, DipLib, FLA. University Librarian, Napier University, since 1985; b. 21.10.45, Falkirk; 1 d. Educ. George Heriot's School; Edinburgh, Strathclyde and Glasgow Universities. Napier College: Assistant Librarian, 1968-70, Tutor Librarian, 1970-79, Depute Librarian, 1980-84. President, Scottish Library Association, 1989; Member: Council, Library Association, 1989-92, Scottish Library and Information Council; author/editor of several books, reports, articles. Recreations: sport; travel; walking; reading. Address: (b.) Napier University, Sighthill, Edinburgh EH11 4BN; T.-0131-455 3301.

McEwan, Sheriff Robin Gilmour, QC, LLB, PhD. Sheriff of Ayr, since 1988 (of Lanark, 1982-88); Temporary Judge, Court of Session and High Court of Justiciary, since 1991; b. 12.12.43, Glasgow; m., Sheena McIntyre; 2 d. Educ. Paisley Grammar School; Glasgow University. Faulds Fellow in Law, Glasgow University, 1965-68; admitted to Faculty of Advocates, 1967; Standing Junior Counsel, Department of Energy, 1974-77; Advocate Depute, 1976-79; Chairman, Industrial Tribunals, 1981; Member, Scottish Legal Aid Board, 1989-96. Publications: Pleading in Court, 1980; A Casebook on Damages (Co-author), 1983; Contributor to Stair Memorial Encyclopaedia of the Laws of Scotland, 1986. Recreations: formerly: football, boxing; skating; now: golf, tennis. Address: (b.) Sheriff Court, Ayr KA7 1DR; T.-Ayr 268474.

McEwan, Roy James, BSc (Econ), DAARL, FRSA. Managing Director, Scottish Chamber Orchestra, since 1993; Member, Board: Association of British Orchestras, since 1993, Scottish Music Information Centre, since 1994; b. 12.5.51, Dumfries. Educ. Dumfries High School; Carlisle Grammar School; London School of Economics; Polytechnic of Central London. House Manager, St. George's Theatre, London, 1977-78; Manager, Whitechapel Art Gallery, 1978-79; Administrator, then Director, MacRobert Arts Centre, Stirling, 1979-91; Director of Arts Development, North West Arts Board, Manchester, 1991-93. Chairman, Federation of Scottish Theatres, 1988-91; Member, Drama Committee, Scottish Arts Council, 1991. Address: (b.) 4 Royal Terrace, Edinburgh EH7 5AB.

McEwen, Professor James, MB, ChB, FRCP (Glasgow), FFPHM, FFOM, DIH. Henry Mechan Professor of Public Health, Glasgow University, since 1989; Consultant in Public Health Medicine, Greater Glasgow Health Board; b. 6.2.40, Stirling; m., Elizabeth May Archibald; 1 s.; 1 d. Educ. Dollar Academy; St. Andrews University. Lecturer in Industrial Medicine, Dundee University; Senior Lecturer in Community Medicine, Nottingham University; Chief Medical Officer, The Health Education Council; Professor of Community Medicine, King's College, University of London. Recreations: church; gardening. Address: (b.) 2 Lilybank Gardens, Glasgow G12 8RZ. T.-0141-330 5013.

McEwen, John, MB, ChB, PhD, FRCPE, FFPM. Medical Director, Drug Development (Scotland) Ltd., since 1983; Honorary Professor, Dundee University, since 1995; Honorary Consultant, Tayside Health Board, since 1984; b. 11.4.43, Uddingston; m., Veronica Rosemary Iverson; 1 s.; 1 d. Educ. Ecclesfield Grammar School; St. Andrews University. Resident Physician/Surgeon, Dundee Hospitals, 1966-67; Lecturer in Therapeutics, Dundee University, 1969-75; Visiting Fellow in Clinical Pharmacology, Vanderbilt University, Tennessee, 1972-74; Head of Clinical Pharmacology, Hoechst, UK, 1975-82. Recreations: keyboard instruments; hill-walking; choral singing. Address: (h.) 1 Osborne Place, Dundee DD2 1BE; T.-Dundee 641060.

MacEwen, Robert Rule (Robin), BL. Solicitor; Honorary Sheriff, Inverness, since 1984; b. 31.1.07, Inverness; m., 1, Elsie Ellis; 2, Marion Pringle or Jack; 1 s. Educ. Inverness Royal Academy; St. Peter's School, York; Edinburgh University. Partner, Stewart, Rule & Co., 1930-67, Rule MacEwen & Co., 1967-77; Consultant, MacLeod & MacCallum, 1977-81; War Service: RAOC, France and Germany, 1944-45 (mentioned in Despatches); Member, Inverness Town Council, 1950-56 (Magistrate and Chairman, Planning Committee); Member, Northern Regional Hospital Board, 1953-56; Dean, Faculty of Solicitors of the Highlands, 1976-79; Chairman: Federation of Scottish Film Societies, 1955, Inverness Civic Trust, 1967-72, Highlands and Islands Film Guild, 1974-77, The Balnbin Trust, 1974-87, Hon. President, since 1987; Member, National Trust Advisory Committee on Culloden; Chairman, Inverness Liberal Association, 1980-81. Address: (h.) Brangan Cottage, 7 Crown Circus, Inverness IV2 3NH; T. 01463 225385.

McFadden, Jean Alexandra, CBE, JP, DL, MA, LLB. Member, Glasgow City Council; (Convener, 1995-96, Convener, Labour Group, since 1995, Convener, Social Strategy Committee, since 1996); Lecturer in Law, Strathclyde University; b. 26.11.41, Glasgow; m., John (deceased). Educ. Hyndland Secondary School; Glasgow University; Strathclyde University. Principal Teacher of Classics, Strathclyde schools, 1967-86; entered local government as Member, Cowcaddens Ward, Glasgow Corporation, 1971; Glasgow District Council: Member, Scotstoun Ward, 1984, Chairman, Manpower Committee, 1974-77, Leader, Labour Group, 1977-86, and 1992-94, Council, 1980-86, and 1992-94, Treasurer, 1986-92; Vice Lord Lieutenant, City of Glasgow, 1980-92; President, COSLA, 1990-92; Convener, Scottish Local Government

Information Unit, since 1984; Member, Board, Scottish Development Agency, 1989-91, GDA, since 1992; Chairman, Mayfest, 1983-97; Member, Secretary of State's Health Appointments Advisory Committee, since 1994. Recreations: cycling; theatre; walking; golf; West Highland terriers. Address: (h.) 16 Lansdowne Crescent, Glasgow G20 6NG; T.-0141-334 3522.

Macfadyen, Hon. Lord (Donald James Dobbie Macfadyen), LLB, FCIArb. Senator of the College of Justice; b. 8.9.45, Glasgow; m., Christine Balfour Gourlay Hunter; 1 s.; 1 d. Educ. Hutchesons' Grammar School, Glasgow; Glasgow University. Advocate, 1969; Standing Junior Counsel, Department of Agriculture and Fisheries for Scotland, 1977-79, Scottish Home and Health Department, 1982-83; Advocate-Depute, 1979-82; QC, 1983; part-time Chairman, Medical Appeal Tribunals, 1989-95; Vice-Dean, Faculty of Advocates, 1992-95; Temporary Judge, Court of Session, 1994-95. Address: (h.) 66 Northumberland Street, Edinburgh EH3 6JE; T.-0131-556 6043.

McFadyen, Thomas, MB, ChB. Director of Medical Services, Erskine Hospital, since 1978; b. 30.11.39, Glasgow. Educ. Allan Glen's School; Glasgow University. Appointments, Glasgow Royal Infirmary, Law Hospital, Carluke and Royal Alexandra Infirmary, Paisley. Recreation: golf. Address: (h.) Tigh-Na-Coille, Erskine Hospital, Bishopton PA7 5PU; T.-0141-812 7555.

McFall, John, BSc (Hons), BA, MBA. Lord Commissioner of the Treasury, since 1997; MP (Labour), Dumbarton, since 1987. Serves on: Information Committee, Parliamentary and Scientific Committee, Executive Committee – Parliamentary Group for Energy Studies; Treasurer, British/Hong Kong Group; Vice Chairman, British/Italian Group; Joint Secretary, British/Peru Group; Secretary, Retail Industry Group; Member, Roads Study Group; Treasurer, Scotch Whisky Group; Hon. Secretary, Parliamentary and Scientific Committee; formerly Opposition Whip with responsibility for Foreign Affairs, Defence and Trade and Industry (resigned post at time of Gulf War); formerly Deputy Shadow Secretary of State for Scotland. Recreations: jogging; reading; golf. Address: (b.) House of Commons, Westminster, London.

MacFarlane, Professor Alistair George James, CBE, PhD, DSc, MA, ScD, FIEE, FEng, FRS, FRSE. Principal and Vice Chancellor, Heriot-Watt University, 1989-96; Chairman, Scottish Council for Research in Education, since 1993; Chairman, Scottish Library and Information Council, since 1994; b. 1931, Edinburgh; m., Nora; 1 s. Educ. Hamilton Academy; Glasgow University. Metropolitan-Vickers Electrical Company Ltd.: Electronic Engineer, Radar and Servo Division, Group Leader, Moving Target Indication and Receiver Laboratories; Lecturer, Electrical Engineering, Queen Mary College, London University, 1959 (Reader, 1965); UMIST: Reader in Control Engineering, 1966, Professor, 1969; Cambridge University: Chair, Engineering, 1974, Head, Information Engineering Division, Fellow, Selwyn College, 1974 (Vice-Master, 1980-88); Non-Executive Director, BNFL plc, since 1994; Member, BT Advisory Forum in Scotland, since 1996; Consultant Editor, International Journal of Control. Past Member: SERC Computer Board, Joint Policy Committee for National Facilities for Advanced Research Computing, Advisory Committee on Safety of Nuclear Installations. American Society of Mechanical Engineers Centennial Medal, 1980; Sir Harold Hartley Medal, Institute of Measurement and Control,1982; IEE Achievement Medal, 1992; IEE Faraday Medal, 1993.

Macfarlane, Rev. Alwyn James Cecil, BA, MA; b. 14.6.22, Edinburgh; m., Joan Cowell Harris; 1 s.; 1 d. Educ. Cargilfield School, Edinburgh; Rugby School; New College, Oxford; New College, Edinburgh. Captain, 6th Black Watch, North Africa, Italy and Greece, 1940-45;

entered Ministry, Church of Scotland, 1951; Minister: Fodderty and Strathpeffer, 1952-59, St. Cuthbert's Church, Edinburgh (Associate), 1959-63, Portobello Old, Edinburgh, 1963-68, Newlands (South), Glasgow, 1968-85; Associate Minister, The Scots' Church, Melbourne, 1985-88. Chaplain to The Queen in Scotland; Member, The Queen's Household in Scotland. Recreations: photography; travel. Address: 4/9 Belhaven Place, Edinburgh.

McFarlane, Sheriff C., QC, LLB. Sheriff of Glasgow and Strathkelvin at Glasgow. Address: (b.) Sheriff Court House, 1 Carlton Place, Glasgow, G5 9DA.

MacFarlane, Professor Colin John, BSc, CEng, FRINA, MIMarE, FRSA. Lloyd's Register Professor of Subsea Engineering, Strathclyde University, since 1986; Governor, Centre for Advanced Maritime Studies, since 1988; b. 4.3.50, Inverkip; m., Sheila Gardner; 1 s.; 1 d. Educ. Uddingston Grammar School; Strathclyde University. P&O Steam Navigation Company and Three Quays Marine Services, 1973-80; BP Engineering (specialist naval architect), 1981-86. Recreations: family; reading; gardening. Address: (b.) Strathclyde University, Department of Ship and Marine Technology, 100 Montrose Street, Glasgow; T.-0141-552 4400.

Macfarlane of Bearsden, Lord, (Norman (Somerville) Macfarlane), KT, DL, FRSE, HRSA, HRGI, Hon.FRIAS, Hon.FScotvec, Hon.FRCPSGlas, Hon. LLD (Strathclyde, 1986; Glasgow, 1988; Glasgow Caledonian, 1993; Aberdeen, 1995), DUniv (Stirling, 1992); Dr. h.c. (Edinburgh, 1992). Chairman, Macfarlane Group (Clansman) PLC, since 1973 (Managing Director, 1973-90); Honorary Life President, United Distillers (Chairman, 1987-96); b. 5.3.26; m., Marguerite Mary Campbell; 1 s.; 4 d. Educ. High School of Glasgow. Commissioned, Royal Artillery, 1945, served Palestine, 1945-47; founded N.S. Macfarlane & Co. Ltd., 1949 (became Macfarlane Group (Clansman) PLC, 1973); Underwriting Member of Lloyd's, since 1978; Chairman: The Fine Art Society PLC, since 1976, American Trust PLC, since 1984 (Director, since 1980), Guinness PLC, 1987-89 (Joint Deputy Chairman, 1989-92); Deputy Chairman, Clydesdale Bank PLC, 1993-96 (Director, 1980-96); Director: General Accident Fire and Life Assurance Corporation plc, 1984-96, Edinburgh Fund Managers plc, since 1980, Glasgow Chamber of Commerce, 1976-79; Member: Council, CBI Scotland, 1975-81, Board, Scottish Development Agency, 1979-87; Chairman, Glasgow Development Agency, 1985-92; Vice-Chairman, Scottish Ballet, 1983-87 (Director, since 1975); Director, Scottish National Orchestra, 1977-82; Lord High Commissioner, General Assembly of Church of Scotland, 1992-93); President, Royal Glasgow Institute of the Fine Arts, 1976-87; Member, Royal Fine Art Commission for Scotland, 1980-82; Scottish Patron, National Art Collection Fund, since 1978; Governor, Glasgow School of Art, 1976-87; Trustee: National Heritage Memorial Fund, 1984-97, National Galleries of Scotland, since 1986; Director, Third Eye Centre, 1978-81; Chairman, Governors, High School of Glasgow, 1979-92; Member, Court, Glasgow University, 1979-87; President: Stationers' Association of GB and Ireland, 1965, Company of Stationers of Glasgow, 1968-70, Glasgow High School Club, 1970-72; Honorary President, Charles Rennie Mackintosh Society, since 1988; Hon. Fellow, Glasgow School of Art, since 1993; knighted, 1982; created a Life Peer, 1991; created Knight of the Thistle, 1996. Recreations: golf; cricket; theatre; art. Address: (b.) Macfarlane Group (Clansman) PLC, Sutcliffe Road, Glasgow, G13 1AH; (h.) 50 Manse Road, Bearsden, Glasgow G61 3PN.

Macfarlane, Professor Peter Wilson, BSc, PhD, FBCS, FESC, FRSE. Professor of Electrocardiology, Glasgow University, since 1995; b. 8.11.42, Glasgow; m., Irene Grace Muir; 2 s. Educ. Hyndland Senior Secondary School, Glasgow; Glasgow University. Glasgow University:

Assistant Lecturer in Medical Cardiology, 1967, Lecturer, 1970, Senior Lecturer, 1974, Reader, 1980, Professor, 1991; President, 5th International Congress on Electrocardiology, Glasgow, 1978; Chairman, 15th and 18th Annual Conferences, International Society of Computerized Electrocardiology, 1990, 1993; Author/Editor, 13 books. Recreations: watching football; running half-marathons; playing violin. Address: (h.) 12 Barrcraig Road, Bridge of Weir PA11 3HG; T.-01505 614443.

Macfarlane, Ray, MA, LLB, MBA, NP, FRSA. Managing Director, Scottish Enterprise Operations, since 1996; m., John Macfarlane; 1 d. Educ. Spier's School, Beith; University of Glasgow. Solicitor, McGrigor Donald; Principal Solicitor and Project Manager, Scottish Development Agency; Director: Corporate Affairs and Property, Scottish Borders Enterprise, Network Services, Scottish Enterprise. Director: Quality Scotland, Scottish Development Finance, Scottish Screen. Address: (b.) 120 Bothwell Street, Glasgow G2 7UP; T.-0141-248 2700.

MacFarlane, Professor Thomas Wallace, DDS, DSc, FRSE, FRCPath, FDSRCPSGlas. Professor of Oral Microbiology, Glasgow University, since 1991; Honorary Consultant in Oral Microbiology; Dean of the Dental School, since 1995; b. 12.12.42, Glasgow; m., Nancy McEwan; 1 s. Educ. Hyndland Senior Secondary School; Glasgow University. Assistant Lecturer, Dental Histology and Pathology, 1966-69; trained in Medical Microbiology and Histopathology, Glasgow Royal Infirmary; Lecturer in Oral Medicine and Pathology, 1969-77; organised and ran the diagnostic service in Oral Microbiology, Glasgow Dental Hospital and School; Senior Lecturer in Oral Medicine and Pathology and Consultant in Oral Microbiology, 1977; Reader in Oral Medicine and Pathology, 1984-91; Head, Department of Oral Sciences, 1992-95. Recreations: music; reading; painting; walking. Address: (b.) Glasgow Dental Hospital and School, 378 Sauchiehall Street, Glasgow G2 3JZ; T.-0141-211 9701.

McFarlane, William Stewart, CA; b. 26.3.33, Glasgow; m., Sandra; 1 d. Educ. High School of Glasgow. Trained as Chartered Accountant, Wilson Stirling (now Touche, Ross & Co.), Glasgow; Parlane McFarlane CA, 1957-58; National Service (Second Lieutenant, Royal Corps of Signals), 1959-60; Partner, McFarlane, Son & Co., CA, 1961-62 (merged with Dickson, McFarlane & Robinson, CA, 1963-84, merged with Wylie & Bisset, CA, since 1985). Member, Council, Institute of Chartered Accountants of Scotland, 1971-76, Institute's representative, directorate of Glasgow Chamber of Commerce, 1970-88; President, Glasgow Chamber of Commerce, 1990-92; Past Finance Convener, Scottish Golf Union; Past Treasurer, Scottish Squash Rackets Association; Captain, Association of Golf Club Secretaries, 1980; Director, The Laurel Park School Co. Ltd.; Past Deacon, Incorporation of Masons of Glasgow; Past President, Rotary Club of Charing Cross. Recreations: golf; curling; swimming; squash. Address: (b.) 135 Wellington Street, Glasgow G2 2XE; T.-0141-248 3904.

McGeoch, Duncan J., BSc, PhD, FRSE. Director, Medical Research Council Virology Unit, Glasgow, since 1995; Honorary Professor, Glasgow University, since 1996. Educ. Hutchesons' Grammar School; Glasgow University. Jane Coffin Childs Memorial Fund Fellow, Department of Microbiology and Molecular Genetics, Harvard Medical School, 1971-73; Researcher, Division of Virology, Department of Pathology, University of Cambridge, 1973-76; Staff Member, MRC Virology Unit, Glasgow, since 1976. Fleming Award, Society for General Microbiology, 1980; Editor, Journal of General Virology, 1984-87, Editor-in-Chief, 1988-92. Address: (b.) MRC Virology Unit, Church Street, Glasgow G11 5JR.

McGeough, Professor Joseph Anthony, FRSE, BSc, PhD, DSc, CEng, FIMechE, FIEE. Regius Professor of Engineering, Edinburgh University, since 1983; Honorary Professor, Nanjing Aeronautical and Astronautical University, China, since 1991; Visiting Professor: University Federico II of Naples, 1994, Glasgow Caledonian University, 1997-2000; b. 29.5.40, Kilwinning; m., Brenda Nicholson; 2 s.; 1 d. Educ. St. Michael's College; Glasgow University; Aberdeen University. Research Demonstrator, Leicester University, 1966; Senior Research Fellow, Queensland University, Australia, 1967; Research Metallurgist, International Research and Development Co. Ltd., Newcastle upon-Tyne, 1968-69; Senior Research Fellow, Strathclyde University, 1969-72; Lecturer in Engineering, Aberdeen University, 1972-77 (Senior Lecturer, 1977-80, Reader, 1980-83). Chairman, Dyce Academy College Council, 1980-83; Honorary Vice-President, Aberdeen University Athletic Association, since 1981; Chairman: Edinburgh and S.E. Scotland Panel, IMechE, 1988-92, Scottish Branch, IMechE, 1993-95; Hon. President, Lichfield Science and Engineering Society, 1987-88; Member, Engineering Research Board, AFRC, 1992-94; Editor, Journal of Processing of Advanced Materials, 1991-94; CIRP Editor, Journal of Materials Processing Technology, since 1991. Publications: Principles of Electrochemical Machining, 1974; Advanced Methods of Machining, 1988. Recreations: gardening; golf; athletics. Address: (h.) 39 Dreghorn Loan, Colinton, Edinburgh EH13 0DF; T.-0131-441 1302.

McGettrick, Professor Andrew David, BSc, PhD, FRSE, FIEE, FBCS, CEng. Head, Computer Science Department, since 1996, Professor of Computer Science, Strathclyde University, since 1984; b. 15.5.44, Glasgow; m., Sheila Margaret Girot; 5 s.; 1 d. Educ. St. Aloysius College, Glasgow; Glasgow University; Cambridge University. Lecturer, then Reader, then Professor, Strathclyde University, since 1969; Editor, Addison Wesley's International Computer Science series; Chairman, IEE Safety Critical Systems Committee; Chairman, UK Computer Science Professors Conference, 1991-93. Publications: four books as author, three books edited. Recreations: running; golf; squash. Address: (b.) Strathclyde University, Glasgow G1 1XH; T.-0141-548 3589.

McGettrick, Professor Bartholomew John, OBE, FRSAMD, KCHS, DHLitt, FRSA, BSc (Hons), MEd (Hons), Silver Palm of Jerusalem (1996). Honorary Professor, Glasgow University; Principal, St. Andrew's College of Education, since 1985; Member: Scottish Consultative Council on the Curriculum, since 1988 (Deputy Chairman, since 1991), General Teaching Council for Scotland, since 1986, various CNAA committees; Chairman, Committee on Assessment 5-14; b. 16.8.45, Glasgow; m., Elizabeth Maria McLaughlin; 2 s.; 2 d. Educ. St. Aloysius' College, Glasgow; Glasgow University. Teacher and Head, Department of Geography, St. Aloysius' College, Glasgow, 1968-72; Educational Psychologist, Scottish Centre for Social Subjects, 1972-75; Assistant Principal, then Vice-Principal, Notre Dame College of Education (latterly St. Andrew's College of Education), 1975-85. Chairman, Catholic Education Commission for Scotland, 1981-87; Chair, "Higher Still" Task Group – Staff Development; Member: Council for Educational Technology, 1982-86, SCOTVAC, 1984-88; Chairman, Committee of Principals of Colleges of Education, 1990-92; President, Association Catholique Internationale des Institutions de Sciences de L'Education, 1995-97; Chairman, Board of Governors, St. Aloysius' College, Glasgow; Governor: Kilgraston School, Craighalbert Centre; Chairman, Governors, Craighead Institute; Member, International Committee for the Education of Teachers; Vice Chair: Educational Broadcasting Council for Scotland, Advisory Group on Sustainable Development; Chairman, Education for Sustainable Development Group; Chairman,

Scottish Council for Independent Schools, since 1997; Chairman, Committee of Scottish Higher Education Principals in Scotland (COSHEP) Staff Development Committee, since 1997. Recreations: sports (golf, rugby). Address: (h.) 174 Carmunnock Road, Glasgow G44 5AJ; T.-0141-637 8112.

McGhee, Professor Charles N.J., MB, BSc (Hons), FRCS(G), FRCOphth, FRSA. Professor of Ophthalmology, Dundee University, since 1996; Honorary Consultant Ophthalmic Surgeon, Ninewells Hospital and Medical School, Dundee, since 1996; b. 26.1.59, Motherwell; m., J. Jane Oliver-McGhee. Educ. Our Lady's High School, Motherwell; Glasgow University. Junior medical posts, Glasgow and Eidnburgh before ophthalmology training in Southern General Hospital and Tennant Institute of Ophthalmology, Glasgow, 1986-93; sub-specialty training in corneal diseases, Lions Eye Institute, Perth, Australia, 1991-92; Consultant Ophthalmologist and Honorary Professor of Ocular Therapeutics, Sunderland Eye Infirmary, 1993-96. President, British Excimer and Keratorefractive Laser Society, 1994-97; Privy Council appointment to General Optical Council, since 1996. Publications: Excimer Lasers in Ophthalmology (textbook); many scientific articles. Recreations: art; photography; travel; architectural restoration; guitar. Address: (b.) Department of Ophthalmology, Ninewells Hospital and Medical School, Dundee DD1 9SY; T.-01382 632714.

McGhie, Hon. Lord (James Marshall), QC, LLB (Hons). Queen's Counsel, since 1983; Chairman, Scottish Land Court; President, Lands Tribunal for Scotland, since 1996; b. 15.10.44, Perth; m., Ann M. Cockburn; 1 s.; 1 d. Educ. Perth Academy; Edinburgh University. Advocate-Depute, 1983-86; part-time Chairman, Medical Appeal Tribunals, 1987-92; Member, Criminal Injuries Compensation Board, 1992-96. Address: (b.) 1 Grosvenor Crescent, Edinburgh; T.-0131-225 3595.

McGibbon, David Campbell, FCMA, DipMS, FBIM. Finance Director, Grampian Holdings plc, since 1984; Director (Non-Executive), Pittencrieff Resources plc, since 1994; Member, Stock Exchange Regional Advisory Group, since 1995; b. 3.12.47, Airdrie; m., Anne Ferguson; 2 d. Educ. Coatbridge High School; Glasgow College of Technology. Accountancy posts, 1967-78; joined Grampian Holdings plc as Group Accountant, 1978; Group Financial Controller, 1983-84. Past Chairman, Group of Scottish Finance Directors; Director, Atholl Preparatory School, Milngavie. Recreation: golf. Address: (b.) Stag House, Castlebank Street, Glasgow G11 6DY; T.-0141-357 2000.

McGill, Rt. Rev. Stephen, PSS, STL. Bishop of Paisley, 1968-88; b. 4.1.12, Glasgow. Educ. St. Aloysius College, Glasgow; Blairs College, Aberdeen; Institut Catholique, Paris. Staff, Le Grand Seminaire, Bordeaux, 1939, Le Grand Seminaire, Aix-en-Province, 1940; Spiritual Director, then Rector, Blairs College, Aberdeen, 1940-60; Bishop of Argyll and the Isles, 1960-68. Recreations: calligraphy; golf. Address: 13 Newark Street, Greenock PA16 7UH.

McGillivray, Rev. (Alexander) Gordon, MA, BD, STM; b. 22.9.23, Edinburgh; m., Winifred Jean Porter; 2 s.; 2 d. Educ. George Watson's Boys' College, Edinburgh; Edinburgh University; Union Theological Seminary, New York. Royal Artillery, 1942-45; Assistant Minister, St. Cuthbert's Parish Church, Edinburgh; Minister: Waterbeck Church, 1951-58, Nairn High Church, 1958-73; Clerk, Presbytery of Edinburgh, 1973-93; Clerk, General Assembly of Church of Scotland, 1971-94, retired. Recreations: golf; theatre. Address: 7 Greenfield Crescent, Balerno, Midlothian EH14 7HD; T.-0131-449 4747.

McGillivray, Elizabeth Norma, LLB (Hons), NP. Solicitor; part-time University Lecturer; b. 16.1.48, Perth;

m., Robert Gordon McGillivray. Educ. Grove Academy, Broughty Ferry; Dundee University. Partner, Bowmans Solicitors, Dundee, since 1985; part-time Tutor, Dundee University, 1984-92, part-time Lecturer, since 1989. Member: Council, Law Society of Scotland, Board of Management, Angus College; Founder Chairman, Tayside Cancer Support Group. Recreations: music; walking; reading. Address: (h.) Lochtyknowe, Carnoustie, Angus; T.-01241 854887.

McGinlay, Alan Douglas, BSc. Head Teacher, Hillpark Secondary School, since 1994; b. 14.4.50, Glasgow; m., Lynn; 1 s.; 1 d. Educ. Queen's Park Secondary School; Glasgow University. Assistant Head Teacher, then Depute Head and Acting Head, James Hamilton Academy, 1984-91; Head Teacher, Govan High School, 1991-94. Address: (b.) 36 Cairngorm Road, Glasgow G43 2XA; T.-0141-637 1071.

McGirr, Professor Emeritus Edward McCombie, CBE, BSc, MD, DSc (Hon.), FRCP, FRCPEdin, FRCPGlas, FFCM, FACP (Hon.), FRSE; b. 15.6.16, Hamilton; m., Diane Curzon Woods (deceased); 1 s.; 3 d. Educ. Hamilton Academy; Glasgow University. RAMC, 1941-47, including posts as graded physician and specialist in medicine ; appointments in University Department of Medicine, Glasgow Royal Infirmary, 1947-78, latterly Muirhead Chair of Medicine, Glasgow University, and Physician in charge of wards, Glasgow Royal Infirmary; Dean, Faculty of Medicine, Glasgow University, 1974-81; Administrative Dean and Professor of Administrative Medicine, Glasgow University, 1978-81; Emeritus Professor, Glasgow University, since 1981 (Dean of Faculties, 1992-94); President, Royal College of Physicians and Surgeons of Glasgow, 1970-72; Chairman, Scottish Health Service Planning Council, 1978-84; Honorary Physician to the Army in Scotland, 1975-81; Chairman, Scottish Council for Postgraduate Medical Education, 1979-85; sometime Member: Greater Glasgow Health Board, National Radiological Protection Board, General Nursing Council for Scotland, National Board for Nursing, Midwifery and Health Visiting; Past President, Royal Medico-Chirurgical Society of Glasgow; Chairman, Scottish Council for Opportunities for Play Experience (SCOPE), 1985-87; Chairman, Clyde Estuary Amenity Council, 1986-90. Recreations: reading; curling. Address: (h.) Anchorage House, Bothwell, by Glasgow G71 8NF; T.-01698 852194.

McGlynn, Archie Smith, BA (Hons), MPhil, DipComm. HM Chief Inspector of Schools, since 1987; Director, HMI Audit Unit, since 1992; b. Tarbert, Argyll; m., Leah Sutherland Ross; 1 s.; 1 d. Educ. Tarbert Secondary School; Campbeltown Grammar School; Strathclyde University; Glasgow University. Industry and commerce, 1962-64 and 1966-67; Teacher in schools and further/higher education colleges, 1964-69; Depute Principal, Glenrothes College, 1969-75; HM Inspector of Schools, 1976-87. Recreations: hedgehog preservation; following Fife Flyers. Address: (b.) Room 2C-91, Victoria Quay, Edinburgh EH6 6QQ; T.-0131-244 0748.

McGlynn, Rt. Rev. Lord Abbot (James Aloysius) Donald, OCSO, STL, SLJ. Monk, Order of Cistercians of Strict Observance, since 1952; Abbot of Nunraw, since 1969; b. 13.8.34, Glasgow. Educ. Holyrood School, Glasgow; St. Bernardine's School, Buckinghamshire; Gregorian University, Rome. President: Scottish Council of Major Religious Superiors, 1974-77, British Isles Regional Council of Cistercian Abbeys, 1980-84; Chairman, Union of Monastic Superiors, 1985-89; Official Roman Catholic Visitor to the General Assembly, Church of Scotland, 1976 and 1985; Commandeur Ecclesiastique, Military & Hospitaller Order of St. Lazarus of Jerusalem, 1985; Patron, Friends of the Beatitudes, Madras; Patron, Haddington Pilgrimage of St. Mary & the Three Kings. Recreations: iconography; farm work; computer printing. Address:

Sancta Maria Abbey, Nunraw, Garvald, Haddington EH41 4LW; T.-0162 083 0223.

McGougan, Donald, CPFA. Director of Finance, City of Edinburgh Council, since 1995; Director, Edinburgh Military Tattoo, since 1995; b. 26.12.50; Glasgow; m., Mandy; 1 s.; 1 d. Educ. Hermitage Academy, Helensburgh. Trainee Accountant, Midlothian County Council, 1971; Professional Assistant, City of Edinburgh District Council, 1975; Falkirk District Council: Principal Assistant, 1979, Depute Director of Finance, 1981; Depute Director of Finance, City of Edinburgh District Council, 1987. Recreations: family; golf; football. Address: (b.) Council Headquarters, George IV Bridge, Edinburgh EH1 1UQ; T.-0131-469 3005.

McGowan, Professor David Alexander, MDS, PhD, FDSRCS, FFDRCSI, FDSRCPSG. Professor of Oral Surgery, Glasgow University, since 1977 (Dean of Dental Education, 1990-95); Consultant Oral Surgeon, Greater Glasgow Health Board, since 1977; b. 18.6.39, Portadown, Co. Armagh; m., Margaret Vera Macaulay; 1 s.; 2 d. Educ. Portadown College; Queen's University, Belfast. Oral surgery training, Belfast and Aberdeen, 1961-67; Lecturer in Dental Surgery, Queen's University, Belfast, 1968; Lecturer, then Senior Lecturer and Deputy Head, Oral and Maxillofacial Surgery, London Hospital Medical College, 1968-77. Postgraduate Adviser in Dentistry, Glasgow University, 1977-90; Chairman, Dental Committee, Scottish Council for Postgraduate Medical Education, 1980-90; Dean, Dental Faculty, and Member of College Council, Royal College of Physicians and Surgeons of Glasgow, 1989-92; Member and Vice-Chairman of Executive, General Dental Council; Member, Court, Glasgow University, 1995-99; Chairman, National Dental Advisory Committee; Member, EC Advisory Committee on training of dental practitioners; former Council Member, British Association of Oral and Maxillofacial Surgeons. Recreations: sailing; music. Address: (b.) Department of Oral Surgery, Glasgow Dental Hospital and School, 378 Sauchiehall Street, Glasgow G2 3JZ; T.-0141-211 9700.

McGowan, Ian David, MA, PhD. Director, Centre for Publishing Studies, Stirling University, since 1988, and Senior Lecturer in English Studies, since 1992; Member, Scottish Arts Council, and Chairman, Literature Committee, 1993-97; b. Glasgow. Educ. Pembroke College, Oxford. Joined Stirling University as Lecturer in English Studies, 1973. Member and Chairman, Grants to Publishers Panel, since 1985, Chairman, Grants to Magazines Panel, since 1992, Scottish Arts Council; Member, Executive Committee, Book Trust Scotland, 1986-93; Trustee, Arts Trust of Scotland. Publications: The Restoration and the Eighteenth Century; Charles Dickens: Little Dorrit; Journey to the Hebrides; articles and chapters. Address: (b.) Centre for Publishing Studies, Stirling University, Stirling FK9 4LA; T.-01786 473171.

McGowan, Ian Duncan, BA. Librarian, National Library of Scotland, since 1990; b. 19.9.45, Liverpool; m., Elizabeth Ann Weir; 2 d. Educ. Liverpool Institute; Exeter College, Oxford. Assistant Keeper, National Library of Scotland, 1971-78; Keeper (Catalogues and Automation), 1978-88; Secretary of the Library, 1988-90. Address: (b.) National Library of Scotland, George IV Bridge, Edinburgh EH1 1EW; T.-0131-226 4531.

McGowan, Sheriff John, LLB. Sheriff in Glasgow, since 1993; b. 15.1.44, Kilmarnock; m., Elise Smith; 2 s. Educ. St. Joseph's Academy, Kilmarnock; Glasgow University. Admitted Solicitor, 1967; Temporary Sheriff, 1986-93; Council Member, Law Society of Scotland, 1982-85. Recreations: golf; tennis; curling; cricket; listening to music. Address: (h.) 19 Auchentrae Crescent, Ayr.

McGowan, Kenneth John, LLB (Hons), SSC, CIMgt. Managing Partner, Balfour & Manson, since 1996; b. 27.4.58, Irvine; m., Nancy McFadzean; 3 s. Educ. Prestwick Academy; University of Edinburgh; Napier University. Recreations: travel; wine; family. Address: (b.) 54-66 Frederick Street, Edinburgh EH2 1LS; T.-0131-200 1200.

McGowan, Neal L., DipTechEd. Head Teacher, Gracemount High School, Edinburgh, since 1997; b. 12.5.63, Edinburgh. Educ. Musselburgh Grammar School; Moray House College of Education. Teacher, Assistant Principal Teacher, Principal Teacher, all of CDT; Depute Head Teacher, Selkirk High School. Publications: three books on technological studies. Recreation: golf. Address: (b.) Gracemount High School, Lasswade Road, Edinburgh EH16 6TZ; T.-0131-664 7440.

McGown, Archibald M, OStJ. Director, Scottish Pre-Retirement Council, since 1987; b. 15.11.33, Paisley; m., Janet Robertson; 1 s.; 2 d. Educ. Rutherglen Academy. Managing Director, Elvestead Canned Meat Co. Ltd., 1976-86. Chairman, Royal Scottish Automobile Club, 1992-94. Recreations: curling; bowling. Address: (b.) Alexandra House, 204 Bath Street, Glasgow G2 4HL; T.-0141-332 9427.

McGrail, Frank Robert, MA (Hons), DipEd. Head Teacher, Drummond Community High School, Edinburgh, since 1995; b. 7.2.52, Edinburgh; 2 d. Educ. St. Augustine's High School, Edinburgh; Edinburgh University. Teacher of History, then Principal Teacher of History; Assistant Head, Tynecastle High, Edinburgh; Depute Head, Craigmount High, Edinburgh. Recreations: swimming; walking; adventure sports; theatre; cinema. Address: (b.) 41 Bellevue Place, Edinburgh EH7 4BS; T.-0131-556 2651.

McGrath, John. Playwright; Theatre, Film and TV Director; Artistic Director, 7:84 Theatre Company (Scotland), 1973-88; Producer/Director, Freeway Films, since 1982; Director, Moonstone International, since 1997; b. 1.6.35, Birkenhead; m., Elizabeth MacLennan; 2 s.; 1 d. Educ. Alun Grammar School, Mold, Clwyd; St. John's College, Oxford. Playwright (more than 40 plays produced professionally in UK and abroad); Writer of film screenplays for feature films and TV plays; Director in theatre and TV; Poet and Songwriter; plays for theatre including Events While Guarding the Bofors Gun, The Cheviot, The Stag and the Black, Black Oil, Blood Red Roses, Border Warfare, John Brown's Body, Watching for Dolphins, The Wicked Old Man, The Last of the MacEachans, The Four Estaites. Visiting Judith E. Wilson Fellow, Cambridge, 1979 and 1989; recent film and television productions: Border Warfare, John Brown's Body, The Dressmaker, Mairi Mhor, Carrington, Half the Picture. Publications: A Good Night Out (lectures); The Bone Won't Break; many plays, including 6-Pack, Six Plays for Scotland (1996). Address: (b.) Freeway Films, 67 George Street, Edinburgh EH2 2JG; T.-0131-225 3200.

McGrath, Professor John Christie (Ian), BSc, PhD. Regius Professor of Physiology, Glasgow University, since 1991; Co-Director, Clinical Research Initiative in Heart Failure, since 1994; Head of Division, Department of Neuroscience and Biomedical Systems, Institute of Biomedical and Life Sciences; b. 8.3.49, Johnstone; m., Wilma Nicol; 1 s.; 1 d. Educ. John Neilson Institution, Paisley; Glasgow University. Glasgow University: Research Fellow in Pharmacology and Anaesthesia, 1973-75, Lecturer, 1975-83, Senior Lecturer, 1983-88, Reader, 1988-89, Titular Professor, 1987-91. Sandoz Prizewinner, British Pharmacological Society, 1980; Pfizer Award for Biology, 1983. Recreations: running; politics; travel. Address: (b.) Institute of Physiology, Glasgow University, Glasgow; T.-041-330 4483.

McGrath, Tom. Playwright and Poet; b. 1940, Rutherglen. Educ. Glasgow University. Founder Editor, International Times, 1966-67; Musical Director, Great Northern Welly Boot Show; Director, Third Eye Centre, Glasgow, 1974-77; plays include: Laurel and Hardy, 1976, The Hardman, 1977.

McGregor, Rev. Alistair Gerald Crichton, QC, BD, BA, LLB, WS. Minister, North Leith Parish Church, Edinburgh, since 1987; Temporary Sheriff, 1984-87; b. 15.10.37, Sevenoaks, Kent; m., Margaret Dick Lees or McGregor; 2 s.; 1 d. Educ. Charterhouse; Pembroke College, Oxford; Edinburgh University. Solicitor; Advocate; QC; former Standing Junior Counsel to Queen's and Lord Treasurer's Remembrancer, to Scottish Home and Health Department and to Scottish Development Department; Past Chairman, Discipline Committee, Potato Marketing Board; former Clerk, Rules Council, Court of Session; former Tutor in Scots Law, Edinburgh University; former Chairman, Family Care; Director, Apex (Scotland) Ltd; Executive Committee, Kirk Care Housing Association Ltd. Publication: Obscenity (Co-Author). Recreations: squash; tennis; swimming; travel; cinema. Address: (h.) 22 Primrose Bank Road, Edinburgh EH5; T.-0131-551 2802.

McGregor, Bill, MA, MEd. Rector, James Hamilton Academy, Kilmarnock, since 1989; b. 14.2.44, Kilmarnock; m., Elspeth Barbara Greene; 1 s.; 1 d. Educ. Kilmarnock Academy; Glasgow University. Teacher, Assistant Rector, Depute Rector, Mainholm Academy, Ayr, 1968-89. Publications: bus histories. Recreations: photography (transport); writing. Address: (h.) 25 Blackburn Drive, Ayr KA7 2XN; T.-01292 282043.

MacGregor, Professor Bryan Duncan, BSc, MSc, PhD, DipSurv, MRTPI, ARICS. MacRobert Professor of Land Economy, Aberdeen University, since 1990; b. 16.10.53, Inverness; m., Nicola; 2 d. Educ. Inverness Royal Academy; Edinburgh University; Heriot Watt University; Cambridge University; College of Estate Management. Lecturer, Department of Land Management, Reading University, 1981-84; Lecturer, Department of Town and Regional Planning, Glasgow University, 1984-87; Deputy, then Property Research Manager, Prudential Portfolio Managers, 1987-90. Recreations: hill-walking; football; literature; music; thinking. Address: (b.) Department of Land Economy, St. Mary's, King's College, Aberdeen University, Aberdeen AB24 3UF; T.-01224 272356.

McGregor, Very Rev. Canon Charles Cameron, BA. Parish Priest, Banchory, since 1982; b. 6.9.26, Buckie. Educ. Our Lady's High School, Motherwell; Blairs College, Aberdeen; Allen Hall, St. Edmund's College, Ware. Army Service, 1945-48; ordained Priest, St. Bridget's, Baillieston, 1954; Parish Priest, Inverurie, 1956-62, Kincorth, 1962-72; Cathedral Administrator, Aberdeen, 1972-82; Dean, St. Mary's, since 1979; Dean, St. Columba's, since 1982; appointed to Cathedral Chapter, 1994; Broadcaster, BBC, 1958-84; Religious Adviser, Grampian TV, 1965-85; Army Chaplain, TAVR, 1965-72, 1st Bn., Lowland Volunteers; Chairman, Scottish Catholic International Aid Fund, 1988-92. Recreations: reading; theatre; historical buildings; Doric prose and verse. Address: (h.) Corsee Cottage, High Street, Banchory AB31 5RP; T.-01330 822835.

Macgregor, Rt. Rev. Gregor, MA, BD (Hons). Bishop of Moray, Ross and Caithness, since 1994; b. 17.11.33, Glasgow; m., Elizabeth Jean; 1 s.; 3 d. Educ. Hutchesons' Boys Grammar School, Glasgow; St. Andrews University. Deaconed and priested, 1977; St. Michael's, Elie, 1978-81; St. Luke's, Glenrothes, 1981-86; St. James', Dollar, 1986-90; St. Luke's, Wester Hailes, 1991-93. Recreations: hill-walking; rugby. Address: (b.) 11 Kenneth Street, Inverness IV3 5NR; T.-01463 226255.

MacGregor of MacGregor, Brigadier Sir Gregor, 6th Bt. 23rd Chief of Clan Gregor; b. 22.12.25; m., Fanny Butler; 2 s. Educ. Eton. Commissioned, Scots Guards, 1944; commanding 1st Bn., Scots Guards, 1966-69; Col. Recruiting, HQ Scotland, 1971; Lt.-Col. commanding Scots Guards, 1971-74; Defence and Military Attache, British Embassy, Athens, 1975-78; Comdr., Lowlands, 1978-80; Grand Master Mason of Scotland, 1988-93; Member, Queen's Bodyguard for Scotland (Royal Company of Archers). Address: (h.) Bannatyne, Newtyle, Blairgowrie, Perthshire.

McGregor, Iain. Honorary Secretary, SABRE (Scotland Against Being Ruled By Europe); b. 19.3.37, Stirling. Educ. Selkirk High School; Kelso High School. Army Service, REME; International Trade Exhibitions Publicist, London; Editor, BIPS International Photo-Feature Agency; Journalist, Fleet Street and provinces; Writer and Lecturer in Journalism, Asia, Europe, North America; Founding Director, Institute for Christian Media (Canada); Editor, The Patriot for Scotland; Editor and Publisher, Social Credit International; Scotland Representative, European Anti-Maastricht Alliance; Council Member, Heritage Society of Scotland; Lecturer and Board Member, British–Israel World Federation. Recreations: local history; travel; music; theatre; film; books. Address: (h.) 8 Baileyfield Road, Edinburgh EH15 1DL.

Macgregor, Janet Elizabeth, OBE, BSc, MB, ChB, MD, FRCPath, FRCOG. Former Director, Harris Birthright Research Centre, Aberdeen University; b. 12.1.20, Glasgow; m., Professor A.G. Macgregor (deceased); 3 s.; 1 d. Educ. Bearsden Academy; Glasgow University. Captain, RAMC, 1943-45; Medical Officer, Maternity and Child Welfare, Glasgow, Sheffield and Edinburgh, 1946-59; Research Fellow, Department of Obstetrics and Gynaecology, Aberdeen University, 1960-66; Medical Assistant, Grampian Health Board, 1966-73; appointed Senior Lecturer, Aberdeen University, 1973. Member, Cytology Sub-Committee, Royal College of Pathologists, 1980-82; Chairman and President, British Society for Clinical Cytology, 1977-83; former Member, Medical Advisory Committee, Women's National Cancer Control Campaign; Member, IARC (WHO) Study Group on Cervical Cancer, 1978-84; Fellow, International Academy of Cytology, since 1963. Address: (h.) Ardruighe, Clachan, Isle of Seil, Argyll; 22 Ovington Square, London, SW3 1LR.

Macgregor, Jimmie, MBE, DA. Radio and Television Presenter; Author; Lecturer. Educ. Springburn Academy; Glasgow School of Art. Forefront of British folk revival for more than 20 years; countless radio and TV appearances, tours in Britain and abroad; more than 20 albums recorded; own daily radio programme, Macgregor's Gathering, for more than 10 years; regular TV series on long-distance walks; various books on folk song and the outdoors; has written theme music for TV and radio, illustrated books; gives regular lectures and slide shows; Life Member, RSPB, Scottish Wildlife Trust, Friends of Loch Lomond; President, Friends of River Kelvin; Vice-President, Scottish Conservation Projects and Scottish Youth Hostels Association; twice Scot of the Year; Hon. Fellow, Royal Zoological Society of Scotland. Recreations: collecting paintings, pottery, glass, furniture; the outdoors; wildlife; hill-walking; theatre; art; music; antiques; old cars; anything and everything Scottish.

McGrenary, Thomas Joseph, BSc (Hons). Principal, Cumbernauld College, since 1985; b. 12.2.39, Hamilton; m., Marlyn; 4 s. Educ. Our Lady's High School, Motherwell; University of Strathclyde. Research Scientist: Ministry of Aviation, General Electric Company; Lecturer, Aberdeen Technical College; Senior Lecturer, Glasgow College of Food Technology; Further Education Officer, Strathclyde Regional Council; Depute Principal, Ayr

College. Recreations: sport; reading (non-fiction). Address: (h.) 42 Buchanan Drive, Rutherglen G73 3PE; T.-(b.) 01236 731811.

McGrigor, Captain Sir Charles Edward, 5th Bt. Life Vice-President, RNLI; Member, Queen's Bodyguard for Scotland (Royal Company of Archers); a Deputy Lieutenant, Argyll and Bute; b. 5.10.22; m., Mary Bettine (eldest daughter of the late Sir Archibald Edmonstone, 6th Bt. of Duntreath); 2 s.; 2 d. Educ. Eton. Joined Army, 1941; Rifle Brigade, North Africa, Italy, Austria (mentioned in Despatches); ADC to Duke of Gloucester, 1945-47.

McGuire, Anne, MP, MA (Hons). MP (Labour), Stirling, since 1997; b. 26.5.49, Glasgow; m., Len McGuire, JP, CA; 1 s.; 1 d. Educ. Our Lady and St. Francis School, Glasgow; University of Glasgow. Development Officer, Community Service Volunteers, 1984-88; National Officer, CSU, 1988-93; Depute Director, Scottish Council for Voluntary Organisations, 1993-97. Address: (b.) 38 Forth Crescent, Stirling FK8 1LG; T.-01786 446515.

McGuire, Edward, ARCM, ARAM. Composer; b. 15.2.48, Glasgow. Educ. Junior Department, RSAMD; Royal Academy of Music, London; State Academy of Music, Stockholm. Won National Young Composers Competition, 1969; Rant selected as test piece for 1978 Carl Flesch International Violin Competition; Proms debut, 1982, when Source performed by BBC SSO; String Quartet chosen for 40th Anniversary Concert, SPNM, Barbican, 1983; featured composer, Park Lane Group series, Purcell Room, 1993, Bath International Guitar Festival, 1996, Proms, 1997; frequent commissions and broadcasts including Euphoria (EIF/Fires of London), Songs of New Beginnings (Paragon Ensemble), Quintet II (Lontano), Peter Pan (Scottish Ballet), A Glasgow Symphony (NYOS), The Loving of Etain (Paragon Opera), Trombone Concerto (Aix-en-Provence Festival), plays flute with and writes for Whistlebinkies folk group. Address: c/o Scottish Music Information Centre, 1 Bowmont Gardens, Glasgow G12 9LR; T.-0141-334 6393.

McGurk, John C. Editor, Scotland on Sunday, since 1997; b. 12.12.52, Edinburgh; m., Karen Ramsay; 1 s.; 1 d. Educ. Tynecastle Secondary School, Edinburgh. Deputy Editor, Sunday Mail, 1987-89; Editor, Sunday Sun, Newcastle-upon-Tyne, 1989-91; Deputy Editor, Daily Record, 1991-94; Editor, Evening News, 1994-97. Runner Up, UK Regional Editor of the Year, 1991. Recreation: paying for children. Address: (b.) 20 North Bridge, Edinburgh EH1 1YT; T.-0131-225 2468.

McHaffie, Rev. Robin Dunlop, BD (Hons). Minister, Linton, Morebattle and Hownam, Yetholm, since 1991; b. 12.7.48, Glasgow; m., Hazel Wallace Lyons; 3 d. Educ. Bishopbriggs High School; Whitehill Secondary School; Glasgow University. Insurance Trainee, Management Trainee, Templeton Carpets; Publicity Manager, Philips Welding; Minister; Calton Mission, Kinning Park Church. Past Chair, Churches Together Through Garden Festival and Year of Culture. Address: (b.) The Manse, Kirk Yetholm, Kelso TD5 8PF; T.-01573 420308.

McHardy, Stuart Andrew, MA (Hons), FSAScot. Director, Scots Language Resource Centre, Perth, since 1993; Chairman, Pictish Arts Society; Lecturer on Scottish History and Folklore; b. 19.4.47, Dundee; m., Sandra Davidson; 1 s. Educ. Morgan Academy, Dundee; Edinburgh University. Formerly worked in advertising and marketing and as professional musician, writer, broadcaster, journalist and poet. Publications: Strange Secrets of Ancient Scotland; Tales of Whisky and Smuggling; The Wild Haggis an the Greetin-Faced Nyaff. Recreations: music; hill-walking. Address: (b.) S.L.R.C., A.K. Bell Library, 2-8 York Place, Perth PH2 8EP.

McIldowie, James Robert, MA, LLB, NP. Solicitor, since 1962; Honorary Sheriff, since 1986; b. 24.9.37, Crieff; m., Isabella Junor (June) Anderson; 2 d. Educ. Morrison's Academy, Crieff; Edinburgh University. Apprentice and Assistant in Edinburgh; joined McLean & Stewart, Dunblane and Callander, 1962; became a Partner, 1963; now Senior Partner. Accredited Expert in Agricultural Law; former Secretary and Treasurer, Highland Pony Society. Recreations: golf; music; theatre; all sports. Address: (b.) 51-53 High Street, Dunblane, Perthshire; T.-01786 823217.

McIlvanney, William. Novelist and Poet; b. 1936, Kilmarnock. Educ. Kilmarnock Academy; Glasgow University. Teacher (Assistant Rector (Curriculum), Greenwood Academy, Irvine, until 1975); Creative Writing Fellow, Strathclyde University, 1972-73; author of Remedy is None, 1966 (joint winner, Geoffrey Faber Memorial Award, 1967), A Gift from Nessus, 1968 (Scottish Arts Council Publication Award, 1969), Docherty, 1975 (Whitbread Award for Fiction, 1975), Laidlaw, 1977, The Papers of Tony Veitch, 1983, The Big Man, 1985, Strange Loyalties, 1990; three books of poetry: The Longships in Harbour, 1970, Weddings and After, 1983, In Through the Head, 1985; Surviving the Shipwreck (essays and collected journalism), 1991.

McIlwain, Alexander Edward, CBE, MA, LLB, SSC, WS. Retired Solicitor, formerly Senior Partner, Leonards, Solicitors, Hamilton; Honorary Sheriff, South Strathclyde, Dumfries and Galloway, at Hamilton, since 1981; b. 4.7.33, Aberdeen; m., Moira Margaret Kinnaird; 3 d. Educ. Aberdeen Grammar School; Aberdeen University. Commissioned, Royal Corps of Signals, 1957-59; Burgh Prosecutor then District Prosecutor, Hamilton, 1966-76; Dean, Society of Solicitors of Hamilton, 1981-83; Chairman, Legal Aid Central Committee, 1985-87; President, Law Society of Scotland, 1983-84; Member: Central Advisory Committee for Scotland on Justices of the Peace, 1986-96; Lanarkshire Health Board; The Scout Council (UK); Honorary Member, American Bar Association; Chairman, Lanarkshire Scout Area, 1981-91; Chairman, Hamilton Sheriff Court Project, 1990-94; Temporary Sheriff, since 1984; President, Temporary Sheriffs Association, since 1994; Member: Criminal Injuries Compensation Panel, Judicial Studies Committee. Publications: Time Costing and Time Recording (in collaboration); Supporting Victims in the Criminal Justice System. Recreations: work; gardening. Address: (h.) 7 Bothwell Road, Uddingston, Glasgow; T.-01698 813368.

MacInnes, Hamish, OBE, BEM, DUniv. Writer and Designer; b. 7.7.30, Gatehouse of Fleet. Educ. Gatehouse of Fleet. Mountaineer with numerous expeditions to Himalayas, Amazon and other parts of the world; Deputy Leader, 1975 Everest SW Face Expedition; film Producer/Advisor/safety expert, with Zinnemann, Connery, Eastwood, Putnam, etc.; Advisor, BBC TV live outside broadcasts on climbing; author of 20 books on travel and adventure, including two autobiographies and fiction; designed the first all-metal ice axe, Terodactyl ice climbing tools, the MacInnes stretchers; Founder, Search and Rescue Dog Association; Honorary Member, Scottish Mountaineering Club; former President, Alpine Climbing Group; world authority on mountain rescue; Doctor of Laws (Hons), Glasgow University; Hon. DSc: Heriot Watt University, Aberdeen University; Doctor of the University, University of Stirling, 1997; President, Guide Dogs Adventure Group; past Leader, Glencoe Mountain Rescue Team. Recreations: as above. Address: (h.) Glencoe, Argyll; T.-0855 811258.

McInnes, Sheriff John Colin, QC, BA (Hons) (Oxon), LLB (Edin), HonLLD (St. Andrews), DL. Advocate; Sheriff, Tayside, Central and Fife, since 1974; Deputy Lieutenant for Fife, since 1997; b. 21.11.38, Cupar, Fife; m., Elisabeth Mabel Neilson; 1 s.; 1 d. Educ. New Park

School, St. Andrews; Cargilfield School, Edinburgh; Merchiston Castle School, Edinburgh; Brasenose College, Oxford; Edinburgh University. 2nd Lt., 8th Royal Tank Regiment, 1956-58; Lt., Fife and Forfar Yeomanry, Scottish Horse, TA, 1958-64; Advocate, 1963; Director, R. Mackness & Co. Ltd., 1963-70; Chairman, Fios Group Ltd., 1970-72; Parliamentary candidate (Conservative), Aberdeen North, 1964; Tutor, Law Faculty, Edinburgh University, 1965-72; in practice, Scottish Bar, 1963-73; Sheriff of Lothian and Peebles, 1973-74. Member, St. Andrews University Court, 1983-91; Chairman, Fife Family Conciliation Service, 1988-90; Member and Vice-President: Security Service Tribunal, since 1989, Intelligence Services Tribunal, since 1994; President, The Sheriffs' Association, 1995-97; Member: Scottish Criminal Justice Forum, since 1996, Judicial Studies Committee, since 1996. Publication: Divorce Law and Practice in Scotland, 1990. Recreations: fishing; shooting; hill-walking; skiing; photography. Address: (h.) Sheriff Court, Tay Street, Perth PH2 8NL.

McInnes, Professor William McKenzie, MSc, PhD, CA, FRSA. Professor of Accounting, since 1994, and Head, Department of Accountancy and Finance, since 1995, Stirling University; Vice-Dean, Faculty of Management, Stirling University, since 1996; b. 24.5.42, Hawick; m., Christine Mary; 1 s.; 1 d. Educ. George Watsons College, Edinburgh; Durham University; Glasgow University. Management Accountant, IBM (UK) Ltd., 1966-68; Lecturer, Kirkcaldy Technical College, 1968-70; Audit Senior, Coopers and Lybrand, Bermuda, 1970-72; Senior Lecturer, Newcastle upon Tyne Polytechnic, 1974-76; Lecturer, then Senior Lecturer, Strathclyde University, 1976-91; Director of Research, Institute of Chartered Accountants of Scotland, 1992-93; SHEFC Team Leader for Quality Assessment of Finance and Accounting, 1995-96; Elder, Cadder Parish Church. Recreations: golf; tennis; music. Address: (b.) Department of Accountancy and Finance, Stirling University, Stirling FK9 4LA; T.-01786 467280.

McIntosh, Rev. Colin George, MA, BD (Hons). Minister, Dunblane Cathedral, since 1988; b. 5.4.51, Glasgow; m., Linda Mary Henderson; 2 d. Educ. Govan High School; Glasgow University. Assistant Minister, Corstorphine, Edinburgh, 1975-76; Minister, St. John's-Renfield Church, Glasgow, 1976-88. Chairman, Leighton Library Trustees; Trustee, Dunblane Cathedral Museum; Director, Church of Scotland Selection Schools, since 1992. Recreations: gardening; music; reading. Address: (h.) Cathedral Manse, The Cross, Dunblane FK15 0AQ.

McIntosh, David Bainbridge, MA, MHSM, FIPD. Founder and Director, Bainbridge McIntosh International Management Consultants; b. 28.10.46, Oxford; m., Judith Mary Mitchell; 4 d. Educ. Edinburgh Academy; Christ Church, Oxford; London School of Economics. Industrial Relations Adviser, Coats Patons (UK) Ltd., 1972-73; Personnel Manager: J. & P. Coats (UK) Ltd., 1974-79, J. & P. Coats Ltd., 1979-81; Mill Manager: Comphanhia De Linha Coats & Clark LDA Portugal, 1981-84, Hilos Cadena SA Colombia, 1984-87; Director, Scottish Health Service Management Development Group, 1987-90; General Manager, Scottish National Blood Transfusion Service, 1990-96; former Chairman, Scotland, The Association for Quality in Health Care; former Member, Broadcasting Council for Scotland. Recreations: golf; sailing; skiing; squash; fishing. Address: 6 Oswald Court, Oswald Road, Edinburgh EH9 2HY.

Macintosh, Farquhar, CBE, MA, DipEd, DLitt, Dr. hc (Edinburgh), FEIS, FScotvec, FSQA. Chairman: Sabhal Mor Ostaig, since 1991, Highlands and Islands Education Trust, since 1988, Gaelic Education Action Group, since 1994, Argyromont Movement (Scotland), since 1996; b. 27.10.23, Isle of Skye; m., Margaret M. Inglis; 2 s.; 2 d. Educ. Portree High School; Edinburgh University; Glasgow

University; Jordanhill College of Education. Taught, Greenfield Junior Secondary School, Hamilton, Glasgow Academy and Inverness Royal Academy; Headmaster: Portree High School, Oban High School; Rector, Royal High School, Edinburgh, 1972-89; Member, Highlands and Islands Development Consultative Council and Convener, Education Sub-Committee, 1965-82; Chairman: Jordanhill Board of Governors, 1970-72, BBC Secondary Programme Committee, 1972-80, Scottish Examination Board, 1977-90, School Broadcasting Council for Scotland, 1981-85; Vice-Chairman, School Broadcasting Council for UK, 1984-86; Chairman, Scottish Association for Educational Management and Administration, 1979-82; Member, Court, Edinburgh University, 1976-91; Governor, St. Margaret's School, since 1989 (and Vice-Chairman of Governors, since 1996), Royal Blind School, Edinburgh, since 1990; Gaelic Correspondent, Weekly Scotsman, 1953-57. Recreations: hill-walking; travel; Gaelic. Address: 12 Rothesay Place, Edinburgh EH3 7SQ; T.-0131-225 4404.

McIntosh, Professor Francis George, BSc, MSc, CEng, MIEE, FRSA. Professor of Electronic and Electrical Engineering, Robert Gordon University, since 1984 (Assistant Principal and Dean of Science and Technology, since 1988); b. 19.3.42; 1 d. Previously Head, School of Electronic and Electrical Engineering, RGIT. Register of advisors, IEE accreditation; Member, COSHEP Research Advisory Group, Scottish Higher Education Funding Council Executive Research Advisory Group. Address: (b.) Robert Gordon University, Schoolhill, Aberdeen AB10 1FR; T.-01224 262020.

McIntosh, Gordon, BSc, CAS. Director of Economic Development, Aberdeen City Council, since 1996; Director, Aberdeen Exhibition and Conference Centre, since 1997; b. 10.8.56; m., Lesley; 2 s.; 1 d. Educ. Keith Grammar School; Glasgow University; Aberdeen University. KPMG (Thomson McLintock), Chartered Accountants, 1979-84; Grampian Regional Council, 1984-96. Chairman, Scottish Local Authorities Economic Development Officers; Member, Scottish Export Forum; Past Chairman, Aberdeen and St. John Mountain Rescue Association; President, Junior Chamber. Recreations: mountaineering; angling; golf. Address: (b.) Economic Development Department, Aberdeen City Council, 74-76 Spring Garden, Aberdeen AB25 1GN; T.-01224 522020.

McIntosh, Iain Redford. Sculptor; b. 4.1.45, Peterhead; m., Freida; 2 d. Educ. Peterhead Academy; Gray's School of Art. Recreation: sculpture. Address: (h.) 53 Kilrymont Road, St. Andrews, Fife.

McIntosh, Professor Jean Barbara, PhD, BSc, SRN, CMB. Professor of Community Nursing Research, Glasgow Caledonian University, since 1993; Non-Executive Director, Greater Glasgow Community and Mental Health Services NHS Trust, since 1994; b. 16.8.44, Fulmer; m., Dr. James R.B. McIntosh; 2 s. Educ. Watford Girls' Grammar School; LSE; University College Hospital, London. Former student nurse and staff nurse; Research Fellow, Aberdeen University, 1972-76; Senior Nurse Research, Greater Glasgow Health Board, 1981-88; Reader, then Professor, Glasgow Caledonian University, since 1989. Publications: one book; numerous papers. Recreations: hill-walking; gardening; classical music. Address: (b.) Department of Nursing and Community Health, Glasgow Caledonian University, 70 Cowcaddens Road, Glasgow G4 0BA; T.-0141-331 3461.

Macintosh, Joan, CBE (1978), MA (Oxon), LLD (Hon., Dundee and Strathclyde), DUniv. (Stirling); b. 23.11.19. Chairman, Scottish Consumer Council, 1975-80; Vice-Chairman, National Consumer Council, 1976-84; Lay Observer for Scotland, 1982-89; Chairman, Scottish Child Law Centre, 1989-92; Member: Council, Victim Support Scotland, 1992-96, Commission, Scottish Constitutional

Convention, 1993-95; Hon. President, Scottish Legal Action Group; Member, Auchterarder District Community Council. Address: (h.) Wynd End, Auchterarder, Perthshire PH3 1AD.

McIntosh, Neil William David, CBE, ACIS, FIPM, FRSA. Convener, Scottish Council for Voluntary Organisations; Chairman, National Companies Implementation Group; Head, COSLA Consultancies; b. 30.1.40, Glasgow; m., Marie Elizabeth Lindsay. Educ. King's Park Senior Secondary School, Glasgow. O. and M. Trainee, Honeywell Controls Ltd., Lanarkshire, 1959-62; O. and M. Assistant, Berkshire, Oxford and Reading Joint Management Services Unit, 1962-64; O. and M. Officer, Stewarts and Lloyds Ltd., Lanarkshire, 1964-66; Senior O. and M. Officer, Lanark County Council, 1966-69; Establishment/O. and M. Officer, Inverness County Council, 1969-75; Personnel Officer, Highland Regional Council, 1975-81; Director of Manpower Services, Highland Regional Council, 1981-85; Clerk, Dumfries Lieutenancy, 1985; Chief Executive, Dumfries and Galloway Regional Council, 1985-92; Chief Executive, Strathclyde Regional Council, 1992-96.

McIntosh, Peter William, BA, FIMgt. Assistant Principal, Robert Gordon University, since 1988, and Dean, Faculty of Management, since 1988; b. 9.4.51, Dunfermline; m., Christine; 1 s.; 1 d. Educ. Dunfermline High School; Strathclyde University. Lecturer in Economics, Strathclyde University, 1974-75; Lecturer in Business Studies, Bell College, Hamilton, 1975-78; Lecturer, Senior Lecturer, Head of Department and Dean, Faculty of Professional Studies, Napier Polytechnic, 1978-88. Recreations: sport; music; travel. Address: (b.) Faculty of Management, Robert Gordon University, Kepplestone Annexe, Queen's Road, Aberdeen; T.-01224 263352.

McIntosh, Robert, BSc, PhD, FICF. Chief Executive, Forest Enterprise, since 1997; b. 6.10.51, Edinburgh; m., Elizabeth Ann. Educ. Linlithgow Academy; Edinburgh University. Joined Forestry Commission, 1973: District Manager, Research Scientist, Operations Director. Recreations: shooting; farming; fishing. Address: (b.) 231 Corstorphine Road, Edinburgh EH12 7AT; T.-0131-314 6456.

Macintosh, Robert Macfarlan, MA, LLB. Solicitor; Chairman, Rent Assessment Committee, Glasgow, since 1966; Honorary Sheriff Substitute, Dumbarton, since 1975; b. 16.6.17, Dumbarton; m., Ann McLean Kelso; 1 s. Educ. Dumbarton Academy; George Watson's College, Edinburgh; Glasgow University. Qualified as Solicitor, 1949; Local Secretary, Dumbarton Legal Aid Committee, 1950-84; Dean, Faculty of Procurators, Dumbarton, 1973; Chairman: Dunbartonshire Rent Tribunal, 1960, Glasgow Rent Tribunal, 1974; Clerk to Commissioners of Income Tax, East and West Dunbartonshire, since 1973; President, Dumbarton Burns Club; President, Cardross Golf Club. Recreation: golf. Address: (h.) Ardmoy, Peel Street, Cardross, Dunbartonshire.

McIntosh, Stewart, BA (Hons). Journalist; b. 7.5.48, Glasgow; m., Marion; 2 d. Educ. Rutherglen Academy; Strathclyde University. Assistant Secretary, STUC, 1976-79; Education Officer, GMB, 1979-83; Freelance Researcher/Reporter, BBC Scotland, 1983-87; Freelance Journalist and Writer, since 1987. UK Property Writer of the Year, 1997. Recreations: athletics; mountain biking; Rioja; Tennent's Bar; Spain. Address: (b.) 29 Cleveden Road, Glasgow G12 0PQ; T.-0141-334 8475.

McIntosh, Alasdair Duncan, CBE, BSc, DSc, FRSE, FIBiol, FRSA. Chairman: Marine Forum for Environmental Issues, since 1990, Atlantic Frontier Environmental Forum, since 1996, Buckland Foundation, since 1994; President, Sir Alister Hardy Foundation for Ocean Science, since 1992; Emeritus Professor of Fisheries and Oceanography,

Aberdeen University, since 1986; b. 17.11.26, Helensburgh; m., Catherine Helen; 1 d. Educ. Hermitage School, Helensburgh; Glasgow University. Senior Principal Scientific Officer in charge of environmental team, Marine Laboratory, Aberdeen, 1973-79; Deputy Director, Department of Agriculture and Fisheries for Scotland, Marine Laboratory, Aberdeen, 1979-83; Director of Fisheries Research for Scotland, 1983-86; Co-ordinator, UK Fisheries Research and Development, 1986; President, Estuarine and Coastal Sciences Association, 1992-95; Member, Research Board, Scottish Natural Heritage, 1992-96; Editor, Fisheries Research. Hon. doctorate, Stirling University, 1997. Recreations: reading; food and wine; walking. Address: (h.) 63 Hamilton Place, Aberdeen AB15 5BW; T.-01224 645633.

McIntyre, Archibald Dewar, CBE, MB, ChB, DPH, FFCM, FRCPE, DIH, DTM&H; b. 18.2.28, Dunipace; m., Euphemia Hope Houston; 2 s.; 2 d. Educ. Falkirk High School; Edinburgh University. Senior Medical Officer, Overseas Civil Service, Sierra Leone; Depute Medical Officer of Health, Stirling County Council; Depute Secretary, Scottish Council for Postgraduate Medical Education; Senior Medical Officer, Scottish Home and Health Department; Principal Medical Officer, Scottish Home and Health Department, 1977-93. Recreations: gardening; photography. Address: (h.) Birchlea, 43 Falkirk Road, Linlithgow EH49 7PH; T.-01506 842063.

Macintyre, Iain Melfort Campbell, MB, ChB, MD, FRCSE, FRCPE. Consultant Surgeon, Edinburgh, since 1979; Director of Education, Royal College of Surgeons, Edinburgh, since 1997; Chairman, Edinburgh Postgraduate Board for Medicine, since 1995; b. 23.6.44, Glasgow; m., Tessa Lorna Mary Millar; 3 d. Educ. Daniel Stewart's College, Edinburgh; Edinburgh University. Lecturer in Surgery, Edinburgh University, 1974-78; Visiting Professor, University of Natal, 1978-79; Council of Europe Travelling Fellow, 1986; Member: Council, Royal College of Surgeons of Edinburgh, since 1991, National Medical Advisory Committee, 1992-95. Recreations: historical postcards; photography; flying light aircraft; skiing. Address: (b.) Department of Surgery, Western General Hospital, Edinburgh; T.-0131-537 1549.

McIntyre, Rev. Mgr. John, MA (Hons), STL, PhL, DipEd. Parish Priest, St. Bridget's, Baillieston, since 1995; Member, Scottish Catholic Heritage Commission, since 1981; b. 12.11.37, Airdrie. Educ. St. Aloysius College, Glasgow; Gregorian University, Rome; Glasgow University; Jordanhill College of Education. Ordained to priesthood, Rome, 1961; Assistant, St. Monica's, Coatbridge, 1962-63; student, 1963-68; staff, St. Vincent's College, Langbank, 1968-69, St. Mary's College, Blairs, Aberdeen, 1969-86 (Rector, 1985-86); Parish Priest, St. Bride's, East Kilbride, 1986-89; Rector, Scots College, Rome, 1989-95. Bradley Medal, Glasgow University, 1967. Publication: Scotland and the Holy See, 1982. Recreations: English literature; bird-watching; history. Address: 15 Swinton Road, Baillieston, Glasgow G69 6DT; T.-0141-771 1058.

McIntyre, Very Rev. Professor John, CVO, MA, BD, DLitt, DD, DHL, Dr hc, FRSE. Professor of Divinity, Edinburgh University, 1956-86; Honorary Chaplain to The Queen in Scotland, 1974-86 (Extraordinary Chaplain, since 1986); Dean of the Order of the Thistle, 1974-89; b. 20.5.16, Glasgow; m., Jessie Brown Buick; 2 s.; 1 d. Educ. Bathgate Academy; Edinburgh University. Ordained, 1941; Locum Tenens, Parish of Glenorchy and Inishail, 1941-43; Minister, Fenwick, Ayrshire, 1943-45; Hunter Baillie Professor of Theology, St. Andrew's College, Sydney University, 1946-56; Principal, St. Andrew's College, 1950-56, Hon. Fellow, since 1991; Principal Warden, Pollock Halls of Residence, Edinburgh University, 1960-71; Acting Principal and Vice-Chancellor, Edinburgh University,

1973-74, 1979; Principal, New College, and Dean, Faculty of Divinity, 1968-74; Moderator, General Assembly of the Church of Scotland, 1982; Convener, Board of Education, Church of Scotland, 1983-87; former Council Member (1980-86) and Vice President (1983-86), Royal Society of Edinburgh. Publications: St. Anselm and his Critics, 1954; The Christian Doctrine of History, 1957; On the Love of God, 1962; The Shape of Christology, 1966; Faith, Theology and Imagination, 1987; The Shape of Soteriology, 1992; Theology after the Storm, 1997; The Shape of Pneumatology, 1997. Recreation: travel. Address: (h.) 22/4 Minto Street, Edinburgh EH9 1RQ; T.-0131-667 1203.

Macintyre, Lorn, BA (Hons), PhD. Freelance Writer; b. 7.9.42, Taynuilt, Argyll; m., Mary. Educ. Stirling University; Glasgow University. Novelist and Short Story Writer; publications include Cruel in the Shadow and The Blind Bend in Chronicles of Invernevis Series. Recreations: Scottish country dancing; nightjars; the paranormal. Address: (h.) Priormuir, by St. Andrews, Fife; T.-01334 476428.

Macintyre, Professor Sally, BA, MSc, PhD. Director, Medical Research Council Medical Sociology Unit, since 1983; Honorary Professor, Glasgow University, since 1991; b. 27.2.49, Edinburgh; m., Dr. Guy Muhlemann. Educ. Durham, London and Aberdeen Universities. Research Fellow, Aberdeen University, 1971-75; Researcher, MRC Medical Sociology Unit, Aberdeen, 1975-83. Fellow, Royal Society of Medicine; Hon. Member, Faculty of Public Health Medicine. Recreations: skiing; hill-walking; climbing. Address: (b.) MRC Medical Sociology Unit, 6 Lilybank Gardens, Glasgow G12 8QQ; T.-0141-357 3949.

MacIver, Alistair. President, Scottish Crofters Union, 1995-97; Chairman, Caithness and Sutherland Constituency Labour Party, 1985-97; Branch Secretary, General, Municipal and Boilermakers' Union, since 1971; b. 13.5.30, Brora. Educ. Lairg Senior School. Member: Rogart Community Council, since 1982, Sutherland Council on Alcohol, since 1990. Recreations: reading; indoor bowling. Address: (h.) Elcama, Inchcape, Rogart IV28 3UD; T.-01408 641373.

MacIver, Donald John Morrison, MA (Hons). Education Adviser, Western Isles Council, since 1989; b. 12.11.42, Stornoway; m., Alice Macleod; 1 s. Educ. Nicolson Institute; Aberdeen University. Teacher of Gaelic, 1968-73; Principal Teacher of Gaelic, Nicolson Institute, 1973-89. President, An Comunn Gaidhealach, 1985-90; former Director, National Gaelic Arts Project; former Member, Gaelic Books Council; Director, Acair Publishing Co.; former Editor, Sruth (newspaper of An Comunn Gaidhealach). Publications: Gaelic Oral Composition; Gaelic Language Practice; Gaelic O-Grade Interpretation; Sgriobh Seo; Feuch Seo; Feuch Freagairt; Faic Is Freagair; Camhanaich; Eadar Peann Is Paipear; Coinneach Odhar; Grian is Uisge; Co Rinn E?; A'Chlach; Bonaidean is Breacain. Recreations: writing (prose and poetry); computing; reading poetry; gardening; Coronation Street. Address: (h.) 32 Goathill Road, Stornoway, Isle of Lewis PA87 2NL; T.-01851 702582.

MacIver, Ian, BSc, DipEd, MSc, PhD. Principal, Coatbridge College, since 1989; b. 25.11.38, Stornoway; m., Anne Maureen Ramsay; 3 s.; 2 d. Educ. Nicolson Institute, Stornoway; Portree High School; Glasgow University. Secondary school teacher, 1962-64; studied and taught, University of Alberta, University of Chicago, and York University, Toronto, 1964-73; returned to Scotland and held posts, Langside College, 1973-74, Jordanhill College, 1975-76, James Watt College, 1977-82, Anniesland College, 1982-89. Elder, Free Church of Scotland. Recreations: distance running; reading; loafing. Address: (b.) Coatbridge College, Kildonan Street, Coatbridge ML5 3LS; T.-01236 422316.

Maciver, Sheriff K. M. Sheriff of Glasgow and Strathkelvin. Address: Sheriff Court House, 1 Carlton Place, Glasgow, G5 9DA.

MacIver, Matthew M., MA, MEd, FRSA. Rector, Royal High School, Edinburgh, since 1989; b. 5.7.46, Isle of Lewis; m., Katrina; 1 s.; 1 d. Educ. Nicolson Institute, Stornoway; Edinburgh University; Moray House College. History Teacher, 1969-72; Principal Teacher of History, Craigmount High School, 1972-80; Assistant Rector, Royal High School, 1980-83; Depute Head Teacher, Balerno High School, 1983-86; Rector, Fortrose Academy, 1986-89. Chairman: Gaelic Broadcasting Committee, Highlands and Islands Educational Trust, Higher Still Specialist Group on Classical Studies. Recreation: Gaelic culture. Address: (h.) 21 Durham Road, Edinburgh EH15 1NY; T.-0131-669 5029.

McKay, Alexander, BSc (Hons), CertEd. Head of Education, Fife Council, since 1995; b.11.9.49, Buckie; m., Jennifer; 1 s. Educ. Fordyce Academy; Banff Academy; Aberdeen University; Aberdeen College of Education. Teacher, Perth Academy, 1972-76; Assistant Principal Teacher, Ellon Academy, 1976-78; Principal Teacher, Elgin High School, 1978-81; secondment to Scottish Curriculum Development Service as Munn-Dunning Development Officer (Mathematics) for Northern Division, 1981-83; General Adviser, Fife Regional Council, 1983-90; Chief Adviser, Fife Regional Council, 1990-93; Assistant Director of Education, Fife Regional Council, 1993-95. Recreations: cricket; walking; reading; jogging and trying to keep fit; holidays with family. Address: (b.) Fife House, North Street, Glenrothes KY7 5LT; T.-01592 414141.

Mackay, Angus Victor Peck, OBE, MA, BSc (Pharm), PhD (Cantab), MB, ChB, FRCPsych, FRCP (Ed). Physician Superintendent and Clinical Director, Argyll and Bute Hospital, and MacKintosh Lecturer in Psychological Medicine, Glasgow University, since 1980; Hon. Senior Lecturer, Department of Psychology, St. Andrews University; Medical Director, Argyll & Bute NHS Trust; Chairman, National Working Group on Mental Illness, since 1993; Psychiatric Representative, Committee on Safety of Medicines, DHSS, since 1983; b. 4.3.43, Edinburgh; m., Elspeth M.W. Norris; 2 s.; 2 d. Educ. George Heriot's School, Edinburgh; Edinburgh University; Churchill and Trinity Colleges, Cambridge. MRC Research Fellow, Cambridge; Member, senior clinical staff, MRC Neurochemical Pharmacology Unit, Cambridge, with appointment as Lector in Pharmacology, Trinity College (latterly, Deputy Director of Unit). Deputy Chairman, Health Services Research Committee of the Chief Scientist for Scotland; Chairman: Argyll and Clyde Area Psychiatric Sub-Committee, Research and Clinical Section, Royal College of Psychiatrists (Scotland); Member: Research Committee, Mental Health Foundation, Scottish Executive, Royal College of Psychiatrists. Recreations: rowing; sailing; rhododendrons. Address: (h.) Tigh an Rudha, Ardrishaig, Argyll; T.-01546 603272.

McKay, Bob, BA (Hons), DipEd. Director of Education, Perth and Kinross Council, since 1995; President, Association of Directors of Education, 1995-96; b. 2.11.43, Glasgow; m., Norma; 1 s.; 1 d. Educ. St. Mungo's Academy, Glasgow; Strathclyde University. Teacher, Principal Teacher, Assistant Headteacher, 1969-85 (mainly at St. Augustine's Secondary, Glasgow, first Strathclyde Community School); seconded to regional headquarters to promote community school concept, 1985-86; Education Officer, Dunbarton Division, 1986-88; Assistant Director of Education, Strathclyde Regional Council, 1988-91; Senior Depute Director, Tayside Regional Council, 1991-95. Publication: Contemporary Britain (textbook). Recreations: theatre; music; art; reading; Spain and things Spanish; sport. Address: (b.) Education Offices, Blackfriars, Perth; T.-01738 476201.

McKay, Sheriff Colin Graham, MA, LLB. Sheriff of North Strathclyde at Oban, since 1990; b. 20.1.42. Solicitor, 1966; private practice, 1966-90.

MacKay, Colin Hinshelwood, MA (Hons), FSA Scot. Partner, Colin MacKay Associates; Broadcaster and Writer; b. 27.8.44, Glasgow; m., Olive E.B. Brownlie; 2 s. Educ. Kelvinside Academy, Glasgow; Glasgow University; Jordanhill College of Education. Reporter/Presenter: Border Television Ltd., 1967-70, Grampian Television Ltd., 1970-73; Political Editor, Scottish Television PLC, 1973-92 (Presenter, Ways and Means, 1973-86), Parliamentary Lobby Correspondent, 1985-95; recent programmes include: People and Power (BBC Radio Scotland); Talk-In Sunday (Radio Clyde); Westminster File (Border TV); Eikon (Scottish TV); General Assembly (BBC TV/Radio); contributions to BBC World Service, Radio 4; ITV Commentator: Papal Visit to Scotland, 1982, CBI Conference, Glasgow, 1983. Winner, Observer Mace, 1967 (British Universities Debating Championship); Member, two-man British Universities Canadian Debating Tour, 1967; Commonwealth Relations Trust Bursary to Canada, 1981; Member, Scottish Arts Council, 1988-94. Publications: Kelvinside Academy: 1878-1978, 1978; The Scottish Dimension in Central and Eastern Canada, 1981. Recreations: music (especially opera); reading; writing.

McKay, Colin Ian, LLB (Hons). Legal and Policy Adviser, Enable (Scottish Society for the Mentally Handicapped), since 1989; Member, Mental Welfare Commission for Scotland, since 1996; b. 21.8.59, Dundee; m., Allison Brisbane; 1 s.; 1 d. Educ. North Berwick High School; Edinburgh University. Legal Trainee/Legal Assistant, 1982-86; Assistant Solicitor, Lothian Regional Council, 1986-88. Norman McEwan Award. Publications: The Care Maze (Co-author); Sex, Laws and Red Tape; Invisible Citizens (Editor). Address: (b.) 6th Floor, 7 Buchanan Street, Glasgow G1 3HL; T.-0141-226 4541.

McKay, David Sutherland. Director and General Manager, JVC Manufacturing UK Ltd., since 1988; Director, SETG Ltd., since 1984; Chairman, Lanarkshire Quality Forum; b. 28.8.38, Wick; m., Catherine Margaret; 2 d. Educ. Wick High School; Robert Gordon's College. Apprenticeship in control engineering; Design Engineer, British Oxygen Co.; joined Honeywell Control Systems as Design Engineer; appointed Technical Director, 1983. Member, Bell College Management Board; Member, Scottish Electronic Forum; Visiting Professor, Strathclyde University. Recreation: gardening; DIY. Address: (h.) Green Garth, Nethan Glen, Crossford ML8 5QU; T.-Crossford 309.

Mackay, Professor David William, CBiol, FIBiol, FIWEM, FBIM, MIFM. Regional Director (North), Scottish Environment Protection Agency, since 1996; Visiting Professor, Institute of Aquaculture, Stirling University, since 1992; Board Member, Scottish Marine Biological Association, since 1991; b. 6.4.36, Stirling; m., Maureen. Educ. High School of Stirling; Strathclyde University; Paisley College. Experimental Officer, Freshwater Fisheries Laboratory, Pitlochry; Freshwater Biologist, then Marine Survey Officer, Clyde River Purification Board; Principal Environmental Protection Officer, Government of Hong Kong; Depute Director, Clyde River Purification Board; Head of Environmental Services, Ove Arup and Partners, Hong Kong; General Manager and Clerk, North East River Purification Board, Aberdeen; Chief Officer, North East River Purification Board. Vice President and Secretary, Scottish Anglers National Association, 1970-89. Recreations: farming; fishing. Address: (b.) SEPA, North Region Headquarters, Graesser House, Fodderty Way, Dingwall, IV15 9XB; T.-01349 862021.

Mackay, Donald George, MA PhD. Honorary Research Fellow, Aberdeen University, since 1990; b. 25.11.29; m.,

Elizabeth Ailsa Barr; 2 s.; 1 d. Educ. Morgan Academy, Dundee; St. Andrews University; Aberdeen University. Assistant Principal, Scottish Home Department, 1953; Assistant Private Secretary to Secretary of State for Scotland, 1959-60; Assistant Secretary, Royal Commission on the Police, 1960-62; Secretary, Royal Commission on Local Government in Scotland, 1966-69; Assistant Secretary, Scottish Development Department, 1969-79; Assistant Secretary, 1980-83, Under Secretary, 1983-85, Department of Agriculture and Fisheries for Scotland; Under Secretary, Scottish Development Department, 1985-88. Member, Scottish Agricultural Wages Board, since 1991. Publication: Scotland's Rural Land Use Agencies, 1995. Recreation: hill walking; photography; music. Address: (h.) 38 Cluny Drive, Edinburgh EH10 6DX; T.-0131-447 1851.

MacKay, Professor Sir Donald Iain, MA, FRSE, FRSGS. Chairman, Pieda Consulting, since 1976; Honorary Professor, Heriot-Watt University, since 1982; b. 27.2.37, Kobe, Japan; m., Diana Marjory Raffan; 1 s.; 2 d. Educ. Dollar Academy; Aberdeen University. Professor of Political Economy, Aberdeen University, 1971-76; Professor of Economics, Heriot-Watt University, 1976-82; Chairman, Scottish Enterprise, 1993-97; Director: Grampian Holdings, Highland Distilleries; Vice President, Scottish Association of Public Transport; Member, Scottish Economic Council; Economic Consultant to Secretary of State for Scotland; Governor, National Institute of Economic and Social Research; Chairman, Edinburgh Business School Ltd. Recreations: tennis; bridge. Address: (h.) Newfield, 14 Gamekeepers Road, Edinburgh; T.-0131-336 1936.

Mackay, Donald John, MA, FRSA, FIMgt. Chairman, Highland Communities NHS Trust, 1994-96; Chief Executive, Harris Tweed Association, 1982-93; b. 8.6.30, North Uist; m., Rhona MacLeod; 3 d. Educ. Portree High School; Aberdeen University; London University. District Commissioner and Private Secretary/Aide de Camp to Governor, Sierra Leone, 1954-58; Scottish Agricultural Organisation Society, 1958-61; AEA, Dounreay, 1961-63; British Aluminium, 1964-65; Director, An Comunn Gaidhealach, 1965-70; Primary Division, British Aluminium, 1970-82. Member, Red Deer Commission, 1966-74; Member, Highland Disablement Committee, 1970-91, Chairman, 1991-94; Member: Highland Area Group, Scottish Council, 1971-93, North of Scotland Electricity Council, 1981-84; Secretary, CBI Highland Area Group, 1978-87, Chairman, 1988-91; Member: HIDB Consultative Council, 1978-81, 1988-91, Nature Conservancy Council Scottish Advisory Committee, 1979-86; MSC Chairman, Highlands & Islands, 1981-88; Member, Executive Committee, Scottish Council, 1982-93; Chairman: CNAG, 1984-86, Albyn Housing Society, 1979-83; Director, Fearann Eilean Iarmain, 1972-91; Member, Industrial Tribunal Panel, since 1986; Deputy Chairman, Sabhal Mor Ostaig, 1981-85; Member: Highland River Purification Board, 1981-83, Highland Health Board, 1991-93. Recreations: sailing; shooting; fishing; Gaelic. Address: (h.) Kildonan, Teandalloch, Beauly, by Inverness.

Mackay, Donald M. Convener, Western Isles Council. Address: (b.) Council Offices, Sandwick Road, Stornoway, PA87 2BW.

Mackay of Drumadoon, Rt. Hon. Lord (Donald Sage Mackay), QC, LLB, LLM. Former Lord Advocate; b. 30.1.46; m., 1 s.; 2 d. Educ. George Watson's; University of Edinburgh; University of Virginia. Called to Scottish Bar, 1976.

MacKay, Donald Stewart, BA, DipPE, AUPE. Director of Education, Midlothian, since 1996; b. 18.4.50, Edinburgh; 2 s. Educ. Firrhill Secondary, Boroughmuir Secondary, Edinburgh; Moray House College of Education; Open

University. Teacher/Assistant Head Teacher/Headteacher, Fife; Curriculum Development Officer, Fife; Advisor in Primary Education, Lothian; Assistant Director of Education, Lothian. Recreations: skiing; football. Address: (b.) Midlothian House, Buccleuch Street, Dalkeith EH22 1DJ; T.-0131-660 7738.

Mackay, Rev. Canon Douglas Brysson. Rector, Church of the Holy Rood, Carnoustie, since 1972; Synod Clerk, Diocese of Brechin, since 1981; Canon, St. Paul's Cathedral, Dundee, since 1981; Tutor, Primary Care, Tayside Centre for General Practice; b. 20.3.27, Glasgow; m., Catherine Elizabeth; 2 d. Educ. Possil Senior Secondary School; Edinburgh Theological College. Precentor, St. Andrew's Cathedral, Inverness, 1958; Rector, Gordon Chapel, Fochabers, 1961 (also Priest-in-Charge, St. Margaret's Church, Aberlour, 1964); Canon, St. Andrew's Cathedral, Inverness, 1965; Synod Clerk, Diocese of Moray, Ross, Caithness, 1965; Honorary Canon, St. Andrew's Cathedral, Inverness, 1972; Convenor of Youth, Moray Diocese, 1965; Brechin Diocese: Convenor, Social Service Board, 1974, Convenor, Joint Board, 1974, Convenor, Administration Board, 1982; Chairman, Truth and Unity Movement, 1980-87. President: British Red Cross, Carnoustie, 1974-82, British Legion, Carnoustie, 1981; Vice-Chairman, Carnoustie Community Care, 1981; Chairman, Carnoustie Community Council, 1979-81; President, Carnoustie Rotary Club, 1976; Joint Founder and Vice Chairman, Carnoustie Community Care. Recreations: golf; snooker; reading; music. Address: Holy Rood Rectory, Carnoustie DD7 6AB; T.-01241 852202.

Mackay, Douglas Ian, QC, LLB; b. 10.8.48. Advocate, 1980. Address: (b.) Advocates' Library, Parliament House, Edinburgh, EH1 1RF.

Mackay of Talmine, Rev. Hugh, GCLJ, MA, FSAScot, CF3(rtd). Minister, Duns Parish Church, since 1967; b. 5.1.30, Edinburgh. Educ. Daniel Stewart's College, Edinburgh; Edinburgh University and New College. Student Assistant, Canongate Kirk, Edinburgh, 1955-57; Senior Assistant, St. Machar's Cathedral, Old Aberdeen, 1957-58; Minister, St. Bride's Parish Church, Glasgow, 1958-67. Chaplain to Moderator of General Assembly, 1972-73; Founder Chairman, Duns Community Council, 1977-78; Clerk, Synod of the Borders, 1982-92; Principal Chaplain, ACF Scotland, 1987-97; Chancellor of Grand Bailiwick of Scotland, Order of St. Lazarus of Jerusalem, 1988-91; Depute Grand Master of Grand Lodge of Scotland, 1988-91; Third Grand Principal, SG Royal Arch Chapter; Grand Prior, Great Priory of the Temple & Malta. Recreations: singing; drawing; Heraldry; too many other things. Address: Manse of Duns, Berwickshire TD11 3DP; T.-Duns 883755.

MacKay, Lt. Col. Hugh David Ruthven. Secretary to the Trustees, Scottish National War Memorial, since 1997; b. 29.12.28, Blackheath, Kent; m., Suzanne Dimoline; 3 d. Educ. Epsom College; Royal Military Academy, Sandhurst. Served in the Highland Light Infantry and Royal Highland Fusiliers, 1949-68; Adjutant, 1st Bn., HLI, Cyprus and Germany, 1956-58; Nigerian Military Forces, 1958-60; Instructor, Royal Canadian School of Infantry, 1962-64; Commander, Edinburgh/Heriot Watt Universities OTC, 1974-77; Abbey Life Assurance Co., Broker Division, 1972-80; Skandia Life Assurance Co. Ltd., 1982-93, latterly as Regional Director Scotland. Chairman, Perth and Kinross Conservative Association, 1990-93; Hon. Treasurer, Scottish Conservative and Unionist Association, 1994-96; Chairman, Supervisory Board, BLESMA Home, Crieff, 1993-96. Recreations: current affairs; history; antiques; shooting; walking. Address: (b.) Scottish National War Memorial, The Castle, Edinburgh EH1 2YT; T.-0131-310 5130.

Mackay, Ian Munro, BCom, CA. Principal, Mackay & Co., Chartered Accountants, Golspie and Dornoch, since 1979; Honorary Sheriff, Dornoch Sheriff Court, since 1985; b. 14.9.47, Brora; m., Maureen; 2 s.; 2 d. (1 d. deceased). Educ. Golspie High School; Edinburgh University. Trained as CA in Edinburgh, qualifying in 1973; has worked in the profession since, spending three years in United Arab Emirates, returning to UK in 1979 to set up own practice. Auditor, Treasurer, Secretary of several local charities and sporting organisations; Secretary, Dornoch Curling Club; President, Sutherland Curling Province, 1991-93; Treasurer, Brora Ice Rink Club. Recreations: curling; local history; garden; following most sports. Address: (h.) 4 Sutherland Road, Dornoch, Sutherland; T.-01862 810333.

Mackay, James Alexander, MA, DLitt. Author and Journalist; Numismatic and Philatelic Correspondent, Financial Times, since 1972; b. 21.11.36, Inverness; m., Renate Finlay-Freundlich. Educ. Hillhead High School, Glasgow; Glasgow University. Lt., RA Guided Weapons Range, Hebrides, 1959-61; Assistant Keeper, Department of Printed Books, British Museum, in charge of philatelic collections, 1961-71; returned to Scotland as a full-time Writer, 1972; Editor-in-Chief, IPC Stamp Encyclopedia, 1968-72; Columnist on antiques, Financial Times, 1967-72, philately and numismatics, 1972-85; Editor: the Burns Chronicle, 1978-91, The Burnsian, 1986-89; Consultant Editor: Coin News, since 1992, Stamp and Coin Mart, since 1995, International Stamp and Exhibition News, since 1996; Trustee, James Currie Memorial Trust, since 1987, Burns-Gaelic Trust, since 1992; Secretary, West of Scotland Numismatic Society, since 1993; Publisher of books on philately and postal history; author of 170 books on aspects of the applied and decorative arts, numismatics, philately, postal history; Scottish books include Robert Bruce, King of Scots, 1974; Rural Crafts in Scotland, 1976; Scottish Postmarks, 1978; The Burns Federation 1885-1985, 1985; The Complete Works of Robert Burns, 1986; The Complete Letters of Robert Burns, 1987; Burnsiana, 1988; Burns-Lore of Dumfries and Galloway, 1988; Burns at Ellisland, 1989; Scottish Post Offices, 1989; Burns A-Z, 1990; Kilmarnock, 1992; Burns, a biography, 1992; Vagabond of Verse, 1995; William Wallace Brave Heart, 1995; Land o' Burns, 1996; Allan Pinkerton, The Eye Who Never Slept, 1996; Michael Collins, 1996; Sounds out of Silence, a life of Alexander Graham Bell, 1996; Under the Gum, 1997; Little Boss: a life of Andrew Carnegie, 1997; The Man who Invented Himself: a life of Sir Thomas Lipton, 1997. Recreations: travel; languages; music (piano-playing); photographing post offices. Address: (h.) 67 Braidpark Drive, Glasgow G46 6LY; T.-0141-633 5422.

Mackay of Clashfern, Lord (James Peter Hymers), Baron (1979), PC (1979), FRSE, Hon. FRICE, FRCOG. Lord High Chancellor of Great Britain, 1987-97; Chancellor, Heriot Watt University, since 1991; b. 2.7.27, Edinburgh; m., Elizabeth Gunn Hymers; 1 s.; 2 d. Educ. George Heriot's School, Edinburgh; Edinburgh University. Lecturer in Mathematics, St. Andrews University, 1948-50; Major Scholar, Trinity College, Cambridge, in Mathematics, 1947, taken up, 1950; Senior Scholar, 1951; BA (Cantab), 1952; LLB Edinburgh (with distinction), 1955; admitted, Faculty of Advocates, 1955; QC (Scot), 1965; Standing Junior Counsel to: Queen's and Lord Treasurer's Remembrancer, Scottish Home and Health Department, Commissioners of Inland Revenue in Scotland; Sheriff Principal, Renfrew and Argyll, 1972-74; Vice-Dean, Faculty of Advocates, 1973-76; Dean, 1976-79; Lord Advocate of Scotland, 1979-84; a Senator of the College of Justice in Scotland, 1984-85; a Lord of Appeal in Ordinary, 1985-87. Part-time Member, Scottish Law Commission, 1976-79; Hon. Master of the Bench, Inner Temple, 1979; Fellow, International Academy of Trial Lawyers, 1979; Fellow, Institute of Taxation, 1981; Director, Stenhouse Holdings Ltd., 1976-77; Member, Insurance Brokers' Registration Council, 1977-79; a Commissioner of Northern

Lighthouses, 1975-84; Hon. LLD: Edinburgh, 1983, Dundee, 1983, Strathclyde, 1985, Aberdeen, 1987, Cambridge, 1989, Birmingham, 1990, Leicester University, 1996; Hon. DCL, Newcastle, 1990; Hon. Doctor of Laws, College of William and Mary, 1989; Hon. Fellow, Institution of Civil Engineers, 1988; Hon. Fellow, Trinity College, Cambridge, 1989; Hon. Fellow, Royal College of Surgeons, Edinburgh, 1989; Hon. Fellow, Royal College of Physicians of Edinburgh, 1990; Hon. Fellow, Royal College of Obstetricians and Gynaecologists, 1996; Fellow, American College of Trial Lawyers, 1990. Recreation: walking. Address: House of Lords, London, SW1A 0PW.

MacKay, John, OBE, MB, ChB, FRCGP. Retired General Medical Practitioner; Member, General Medical Council; Member, Scottish National Board for Nursing, Midwifery and Health Visiting; b. 24.7.26, Glasgow; m., Matilda MacLennan Bain; 2 s.; 2 d. Educ. Govan High School; Glasgow University. Junior House Doctor, Victoria Infirmary and Southern General Hospital, Glasgow, 1949; Ship's Surgeon, 1950; Assistant in General Practice, Govan, 1951-52 (Principal, since 1953); Member, Board of Management, Glasgow South West Hospitals, prior to 1973; Tutor, University Department of General Practice, Glasgow; part-time Medical Referee, Scottish Home and Health Department; Honorary Life Manager, Govan Weavers Society; Member, Scottish General Medical Services Committee. Recreations: angling; golf; gardening. Address: (h.) Moorholm, Barr's Brae, Kilmacolm, Renfrewshire PA13 4DE; T.-Kilmacolm 3234.

MacKay, John Angus, MA. Director, Gaelic Broadcasting Fund, since 1991; Board Member, Highlands and Islands Enterprise; Director, Comunn Na Gaidhlig, since 1985; Chairman, Gaelic Television Training Trust; Board Member, National Gaelic Arts Ltd; b. 24.6.48, Shader, Stornoway; m., Maria F.; 4 s. Educ. Nicolson Institute; Aberdeen University; Jordanhill College. Aberdeen Circulation Rep., D.C. Thomson, 1970-71; Jordanhill College, 1971-72; Teacher, 1972-77; Field Officer, then Development Officer, then Senior Administrative Officer, HIDB, 1977-85. Chairman: Gaelic Youth Radio Trust, Sabhal Mor Ostaig, 1987-91; Director, Acair. Recreations: reading; skiing; swimming; running. Address: (h.) Druimard, Arnol, Isle of Lewis; T.-01851 71479.

McKay, John Henderson, CBE (1987), DL, JP, BA (Hons), PhD, Dr h.c. (Edinburgh). Chairman: Scottish Working Peoples' History Trust, since 1992, Edinburgh Quartet Trust, since 1996; Hon. Vice-President, St. Andrew Society, since 1989; Hon. President, Scottish Craftsmanship Association, since 1987; Patron, Scotland Yard Adventure Centre, since 1988; b. 12.5.29, Kirknewton; m., Catherine Watson Taylor; 1 s.; 1 d. Educ. West Calder High School; Open University. Labourer and Clerk, Pumpherston Oil Co. Ltd., 1948-50; National Service, Royal Artillery, 1950-52; Customs and Excise, 1952-85; Lord Provost of Edinburgh, 1984-88. Vice President, Royal Caledonian Horticultural Society, 1984-88 and 1993-96, Secretary and Treasurer, 1988-93; Convener, Business Committee, General Council, Edinburgh University, 1992-96; General Council Assessor, Edinburgh University Court, since 1996. Recreations: gardening; reading; listening to music. Address: (h.) 2 Buckstone Way, Edinburgh EH10 6PN; T.-0131-445 2865.

MacKay of Ardbrecknish, Rt. Hon Lord (John Jackson MacKay), PC, DL, BSc, DipEd, JP. Life Peer, since 1991; Opposition Spokesman on Constitutional Affairs, the Treasury and Social Security, since 1997; b. 15.11.38, Lochgilphead; m., Sheena Wagner; 2 s.; 1 d. Educ. Dunoon Grammar School; Campbeltown Grammar School; Glasgow University; Jordanhill College of Education. Member: Oban Town Council, 1969-74, Argyll Water Board, 1969-74; Principal Teacher of Mathematics, Oban High School, 1969-79; MP for Argyll, 1979-83, for Argyll & Bute, 1983-87; Parliamentary Private Secretary to

Secretary of State for Scotland, 1982; Parliamentary Under Secretary of State, Scottish Office, 1982-87; Chief Executive, Scottish Conservative Party, 1987-90; Chairman, Sea Fish Industry Authority, 1990-93; Member, Select Committee on the European Communities, 1992-93; Under Lord in Waiting (Government Whip in the House of Lords), 1993-94; Secretary of State, Department of Transport, January-July, 1994; Minister of State, Social Security, 1994-97. Recreations: fishing; sailing. Address: (h.) Innishail, 51 Springkell Drive, Pollokshields, Glasgow G41 4EZ.

Mackay, Rev. Professor John L., MA, MLitt, BD. Principal Clerk of Assembly, Free Church of Scotland. Address: (b.) 15 North Bank Street, The Mound, Edinburgh, EH1 2LS.

McKay, Rev. Johnston Reid, MA (Glasgow), BA (Cantab). Senior Producer, Religious Programmes, BBC, since 1987; b. 2.5.42, Glasgow. Educ. High School of Glasgow; Glasgow University; Cambridge University. Assistant Minister, St. Giles' Cathedral, 1967-71; Church Correspondent, Glasgow Herald, 1968-70; Minister, Bellahouston Steven Parish Church, 1971-78; frequent Broadcaster; Governor, Paisley College; Minister, Paisley Abbey, 1978-87; Editor, The Bush (newspaper of Glasgow Presbytery), 1975-78; Chairman, Scottish Religious Advisory Committee, BBC, 1981-86; Stanley Mair Lecturer on Preaching, Glasgow University, 1995. Publications: From Sleep and From Damnation (with James Miller), 1970; Essays in Honour of William Barclay (Joint Editor), 1976; Through Wood and Nails, 1982; This Small Pool, 1996. Recreations: good music and bad golf. Address: (b.) 41 Stakehill, Largs KA30 9NH; T.-01475 672960.

MacKay, Professor Norman, CBE, MD, FRCP(Glas), FRCP(Edin), FRCS(Edin), FRCGP, FCPSP, FACP(Hon), FRACP(Hon), FAMS, FAMM, FRCS(Eng), FRCS(I), FRCP(I), FCPSBangl., FCCP(Hon). Dean of Postgraduate Medicine and Professor of Postgraduate Medical Education, Glasgow University, since 1989; Consultant Physician, Victoria Infirmary, Glasgow, since 1974; President, Royal College of Physicians and Surgeons of Glasgow, 1994-97; b. 15.9.36, Glasgow; m., Grace Violet McCaffer; 2 s.; 2 d. Educ. Govan High School; Glasgow University. Honorary Secretary: Royal College of Physicians and Surgeons of Glasgow, 1973-83, Standing Joint Committee, Scottish Royal Colleges, 1978-82, Conference of Royal Colleges and Faculties in Scotland, 1982-91; Speciality Adviser in Medicine, West of Scotland Committee of Postgraduate Medical Education, 1982-89; President, Royal Medico-Chirurgical Society of Glasgow, 1982-83; Member, Area Medical Committee, Greater Glasgow Health Board, 1987-89; President, Southern Medical Society, 1989-90. Address: (b.) Department of Postgraduate Medical Education, 124 Observatory Road, Glasgow G12 8UZ; T.-0141-330 5273.

Mackay, Peter, CB. Director, British Linen Bank; Member, Board, Scottish Agricultural College; Member, Board, Scottish Natural Heritage, since 1997; Member, Court, Napier University; Board Member, Scottish Ballet; Member, Monopolies and Mergers Commission, since 1996; Trustee, Scottish Maritime Museum; Visiting Professor, Strathclyde Graduate Business School; b. 6.7.40, Arbroath; m., Sarah Holdich; 1 s.; 2 d. Educ. Glasgow High School; St. Andrews University. Teacher, New South Wales, Australia, 1962-63; Private Secretary to Secretaries of State for Scotland, 1973-75; Director for Scotland, Manpower Services Commission, 1983-85; on secondment from Scottish Office to Department of Employment, London, 1985; Under Secretary, Scottish Education Department (Further and Higher Education, Arts and Sport), 1987-89; Secretary and Chief Executive, Scottish Office Industry Department, 1990-95; Executive Director, Advanced Management Programme in Scotland, 1995-97. Recreations: Scotland; high altitudes and latitudes; dinghy sailing; sea canoeing; tennis. Address: (h.) 6 Henderland Road, Edinburgh EH12 6BB; T.-0131-337 2830.

McKean, Professor Charles Alexander, BA, FRSA, FSA Scot, HonFRIBA, Hon FRIAS. Professor of Architecture, Duncan of Jordanstone College, Dundee University; Secretary, Royal Incorporation of Architects in Scotland, 1979-94; b. 16.7.46, Glasgow; m., Margaret Yeo; 2 s. Educ. Fettes College; Bristol University. RIBA: Secretary, London Region, 1968-76, Secretary, Eastern Region, 1972-79, Secretary, Community Architecture, 1976-79; Architectural Correspondent, The Times, 1977-83; Trustee, Thirlestane Castle; author of architectural guides to Edinburgh, Dundee, Stirling, London, Cambridge, Moray, Central Glasgow, Banff and Buchan; General Editor, RIAS/Landmark Trust Guides to Scotland. Publications: The Scottish Thirties; Edinburgh: Portrait of a City. Recreations: books; glasses; gardens; stately homes. Address: (b.) Duncan of Jordandstone College, Perth Road, Dundee DD1 4HT; T.-01382 345231.

McKechin, Ann, LLB, DipLP. Solicitor, since 1983; Secretary, Strathkelvin Association of Solicitors, since 1992; b. 22.4.61, Johnstone. Educ. Paisley Grammar School; Strathclyde University. Partner, Pacitti Jones, Solicitors, since 1991 (Associate, 1987-91). Secretary, Glasgow Kelvin Labour Party; Chair, Glasgow World Development Movement. Recreations: art history; Scottish country dancing; music. Address: (b.) Pacitti Jones, 64 Townhead, Kirkintilloch, Glasgow G66 1NZ; T.-0141-777 8899.

McKechnie, George. Editor, The Herald, 1994-97; b. 28.7.46, Edinburgh; m., Janequin Claire Seymour Morris; 2 s. Educ. Portobello High School, Edinburgh. Reporter: Paisley & Renfrewshire Gazette, 1964-66, Edinburgh Evening News, 1966, Scottish Daily Mail, 1966-68, Daily Record, 1968-74; Deputy News Editor/News Editor, Sunday Mail, 1974-76; Assistant Editor, Evening Times, 1976-80; Editor, Glasgow Evening Times, 1981-94. Recreation: reading.

McKee, Graham Hamilton, BSc, BPhil. Chief Executive, Scottish Enterprise Tayside, since 1994; b. 11.9.51; m., Pilar; 1 s.; 2 d. Educ. Hutchesons' Grammar School, Glasgow; Glasgow University; Newcastle-upon-Tyne University. Assistant Planner, Burnley Borough Council, 1975-77; Scottish Development Agency, 1977-91, latterly as Regional Manager; Director Economic Development, Scottish Enterprise Tayside, 1991-93. Recreation: family. Address: (b.) Scottish Enterprise Tayside, Enterprise House, 45 North Lindsay Street, Dundee DD1 1HT; T.-01382 223100.

McKee, Professor (James Clark St. Clair) Sean, BSc, MA, PhD, DSc, FIMA, CMath, FRSE. Professor of Mathematics, Strathclyde University, since 1988; b. 1.7.45, Belfast. Educ. George Watson's College, Edinburgh; St. Andrews University; Dundee University; Oxford University. NCR Research Fellow, 1970-72; Lecturer in Numerical Analysis, Southampton University, 1972-75; Fellow, Hertford College, Oxford, 1975-86; Professor of Industrial Mathematics, Strathclyde University, and Consultant Mathematician, Unilever Research, 1986-88. Member, Council: IMA, ECMI; President, Scottish Branch, Institute of Mathematics and Its Applications; Member, IMA Programmes Committee. Publications: 100 papers; Industrial Numerical Analysis (Co-Editor), 1986; Vector and Parallel Computing (Co-Editor), 1989; Artificial Intelligence in Mathematics (Co-Editor), 1994. Recreations: climbing Munros; golf; theatre; running conferences. Address: (b.) Department of Mathematics, Strathclyde University, Glasgow G1 1XH; T.-0141-552 4400.

McKellar, Kenneth, BSc. Singer, Composer, Writer; b. 23.6.27, Paisley. Gave first concert in local hall, aged 13;

continued singing while at school, university and during his first two years working in forestry; has made numerous records of classical and popular music; numerous tours, especially in Australia and New Zealand; has appeared a number of times at the London Palladium.

McKellar, Peter Archibald, LLB (Hons). Corporate Development Director, Clydeport plc, since 1995; b. 28.5.65, Glasgow; m., Kathleen Scarlett; 1 s. Educ. Daniel Stewart's and Melville College, Edinburgh; Edinburgh University. J.P. Morgan, Investment Bank, New York and London, 1986-88; EFT Group PLC, Corporate Finance Division, 1988-89; London and Edinburgh Trust plc, 1989-90; Co-Founder, Barry McKellar Ltd., 1990-95. Recreations: golf; shooting; swimming. Address: (b.) 16 Robertson Street, Glasgow G2 8DS; T.-0141-221 8733.

McKenna, Rosemary, CBE, DCE, JP. MP (Labour), Cumbernauld and Kilsyth; Chair: Standing Committee of UK Women Elected Members, CEMR Standing Committee of European Women Elected Members; Member, Committee of the Regions of European Union; Member, Executive Committee, Scottish Council Development and Industry; b. 8.5.41, Kilmacolm; m., James Stephen McKenna; 3 s.; 1 d. Educ. St. Augustine's Secondary School, Glasgow; St. Andrew's College, Bearsden. Taught in various primary schools, 1974-93; Leader of Council, Cumbernauld and Kilsyth, 1984-88, Provost 1988-92, Leader of Council, 1992-94; former Member, North Lanarkshire Council; former Policy Board Member: Local Government Management Board, Local Government International Bureau; former Member, Board, Scottish Enterprise; Member, Executive, Scottish Constitutional Convention; Immediate Past President, Convention of Scottish Local Authorities. Recreations: reading; cooking. Address: (h.) 9 Westray Road, Cumbernauld G67 1NN.

MacKenzie, Angus Alexander, CA. Chartered Accountant, since 1955; b. 1.3.31, Nairn; m., Catherine; 1 d. Educ. Inverness Royal Academy; Edinburgh University. National Service, RAF, 1955-57; in private practice as CA Assistant in Edinburgh, 1957-59, Inverness, 1959-61; commenced in practice on own account, 1961; Chairman, Highland Group, Riding for the Disabled Association. Recreations: shooting; stalking; hill-walking; gardening. Address: (h.) Tigh an Allt, Tomatin, Inverness-shire; T.-01808 511270.

Mackenzie, Anne, MA (Hons). Broadcaster; b. Stornoway, Isle of Lewis; m., Neil McConaghy. Educ. Nicolson Institute, Stornoway; Glasgow University. Reporter, News Presenter, Political/Current Affairs Presenter, Grampian TV, 1981-95 (Presenter, North Tonight, Crossfire, We The Jury, etc.); Presenter, BBC Scotland, Glasgow, 1995-97 (Good Morning Scotland, Reporting Scotland, Campaign Scotland, election/devolution specials); Reporter/Presenter, Here and Now, BBC London, 1996; Presenter, Westminster Live, BBC London, since 1998. Recreations: gardening; antiques; history; old movies.

Mackenzie, Professor Ann Logan, MA. Ivy McClelland Research Professor of Spanish, Glasgow University, since 1995; General Editor, Bulletin of Hispanic Studies, since 1992; b. Greenock. Educ. Greenock Academy; Glasgow University. Lecturer, Senior Lecturer, Reader, Department of Hispanic Studies, Liverpool University, 1968-95. Publications: numerous articles and books on golden-age drama in Spain; books on the history of higher education. Recreations: walking; theatre-going; animals. Address: (b.) Department of Hispanic Studies, Hetherington Building, Glasgow University, Glasgow G12 8RS; T.-0141-330 5665.

MacKenzie, Archibald MacIntosh, DL. Vice Lord Lieutenant, Dunbartonshire, since 1990; b. 3.6.33, Inveraray; m., Margaret Young Ritchie; 1 s.; 1 d. Educ. Hermitage School, Helensburgh. Assistant Chief Constable,

British Transport Police, 1982-92; Vice-President and Member, Executive Committee, Royal National Lifeboat Institution (Chairman, Dumbarton Branch); Convenor, Scottish Lifeboat Council; Chairman, Scottish Lifeboat Executive Committee, 1990-96; Member, Committee of Management, Royal National Lifeboat Institution; Director, Dunbartonshire Branch, British Red Cross, 1992-95; Member, Loch Lomond Rescue Committee; Non-Executive Director, Lomond Health Trust; Chairman, 2319 Sqd. ATC Committee; Governor, Keil School; Elder, Church of Scotland. Recreations: sailing; golf; reading; classical music. Address: (h.) Millerston, 10 Boghead Road, Dumbarton; T.-Dumbarton 763654.

Mackenzie, Major Colin Dalzell, MBE, MC, DL. Vice Lieutenant, Inverness-shire, 1986-95; b. 23.3.19, Fawley; m., Lady Anne Fitz Roy; 1 s.; 3 d. Educ. Eton; RMC, Sandhurst. Page of Honour to King George V, 1932-36; joined Seaforth Highlanders, 1939; ADC to Viceroy of India, 1945-46; Deputy Military Secretary to Viceroy of India, 1946-47; retired, 1949; TA, 1950-56; Inverness County Council, 1949-52; Director, various companies. Recreation: fishing. Address: (h.) Farr House, Inverness, IV1 2XB.

Mackenzie, Sheriff Colin Scott, DL, BL, NP. Sheriff of Grampian Highland and Islands, at Lerwick and Kirkwall, since 1992; b. 7.7.38, Stornoway; m., Christeen E.D. MacLauchlan. Educ. Nicolson Institute; Fettes College; Edinburgh University. Procurator Fiscal, Stornoway, 1969-92; Burgh Prosecutor, Stornoway, 1971-75; JP Fiscal, 1971-75; Deputy Lieutenant and Clerk to Lieutenancy of the Western Isles, 1975-92; Vice Lord Lieutenant of Islands Area, Western Isles, 1984-92; Founder President, Stornoway Flying Club, 1970; Founding Dean, Western Isles Faculty of Solicitors; elected Council Member, Law Society of Scotland, 1985-92; Convener, Criminal Law Committee, 1991-92; Elder, Church of Scotland, since 1985; Member, Board of Social Responsibility, Church of Scotland, 1990-96; Convener, Assembly Study Group on Young People and the Media, 1991-93; author of article on Lieutenancy, Stair Memorial Encyclopaedia of Law of Scotland, 1987; President, Stornoway Rotary Club, 1977; President, Lewis Pipe Band. Recreation: fishing. Address: (h.) Park House, Matheson Road, Stornoway, Lewis; Middlebank, Bells Road, Lerwick, Shetland.

MacKenzie, Hugh D., MA (Hons), FEIS, JP, FRSA. Headteacher, Craigroyston Community High School, 1972-93; Director, Craigroyston Curriculum Project, since 1980; b. 29.5.33, Edinburgh; m., Helen Joyce; 1 s.; 1 d. Educ. Royal High School; Edinburgh University; Moray House College of Education, Edinburgh. Education Officer, RAF, 1956-58; Assistant Teacher, Niddrie Marischal Junior Secondary School and Falkirk High School, 1958-62; Principal Teacher: Broxburn Academy, 1962-64, Liberton High School, 1964-70; Deputy Headteacher, Craigmount High School, 1970-72; Scottish Representative, Northern Regional Examination Board, 1973-88; Vice-Chairman, Lothian Regional Consultative Committee, 1984-87; a Director, Royal Lyceum Theatre, Edinburgh, since 1985, Scottish Community Education Council, 1985-88; President, Royal High School Rugby Club; President and Founder Member, Edinburgh Golden Oldies Rugby Club. Publication: Craigroyston Days, 1995. Recreations: rugby; squash; golf; ornithology; philately; jazz. Address: (h.) 3 Beechwood Mains, Edinburgh.

MacKenzie, Ian Kenneth, OBE, JP. Member, Council and Executive Committee, National Trust for Scotland; Chairman, Red Deer Commission, 1984-92; Chairman, Highlands and Islands Development Consultative Council, 1988-91; Landowner; b. 1.3.31, Nairn; m., Margaret Vera Matheson; 2 s.; 2 d. Educ. Inverness Royal Academy. Member: Scottish Agricultural Consultative Panel, Secretary of State's Panel of Arbiters; Director, Royal

Highland and Agricultural Society of Scotland, 1980-84. Recreation: field sports. Address: Leanach House, Culloden Moor, Inverness IV1 2EJ.

Mackenzie, Rev. Ian Murdo. Church of Scotland Minister; Writer, Broadcaster, Organist; b. b. 3.8.31, Fraserburgh; m., Elizabeth Alice Whitley; 1 s.; 1 d. Educ. Strichen School; Fettes College; Edinburgh University. Assistant Organist, St. Giles Cathedral, 1952-58; Editor, The Student, Sooth and Breakthrough; Founder Member, Telephone Samaritans Scotland, 1960; Columnist, Edinburgh Evening Dispatch; Conductor, Calton Singers; Music Organiser, Iona Abbey; Assistant Minister, St. Giles, 1960-62; Founder, Edinburgh University CND, 1962; Scottish Secretary, Student Christian Movement, 1962-63; Assistant General Secretary, Student Christian Movement, 1963-64; Secretary, University Teachers Group, 1963-65; Religious Adviser and Executive Producer, Religious Programmes, ABC TV, 1964-68; LWT, 1968-69; conceived and produced From Inner Space, Looking for an Answer, Don't Just Sit There, Question '68, Roundhouse; Religious Columnist, The Times, 1966-68; Minister, Peterhead Old Parish Church, 1969-73; Presenter, For Christ's Sake and What The Religious Papers Say, Grampian TV; Chairman, Scottish Religious Panel, IBA, 1970-72; Head of Religious Programmes, BBC Scotland, 1973-89; conceived Eighth Day, Voyager, Angles, Gates to Space, The Quest; Writer/Presenter, He Turned Up, Channel Four, 1990; Baird Lectures on Church Music, 1990; Presenter/Improviser on hymns and other programmes, Radio Scotland. Publications: Tunes of Glory; Vision and Belief; various papers, articles and essays. Recreations: attending concerts, cathedrals, and newsagents; driving with majestic care and attention; writing novels; wondering about God; preaching about wondering. Address: (h.) 1 Glenan Gardens, Helensburgh, Dunbartonshire, G84 8XT; T.-01436 673429.

MacKenzie, Kenneth, MB, ChB, FRCA, DRCOG. Chairman, Scottish Committee for Hospital Medical Services, since 1995; Clinical Director, Anaesthesia, Ayr Hospital, since 1993; b. 13.1.48, Paisley; m., Anne Scott; 1 s.; 1 d. Educ. Paisley Grammar School; Glasgow University. Consultant Anaesthetist, Ayrshire and Arran Health Board; Honorary Medical Officer, Western Meeting Club. Recreation: golf; reading. Address: (h.) Arden, Maidens Road, Turnberry KA26 9LS; T.-01655 331239.

MacKenzie, Robert, BA (Hons), DipM, MRTPI. Chief Executive, Fife Enterprise Company, since 1991; b. 1.5.56, Edinburgh. Educ. Daniel Stewart's College, Edinburgh; Glasgow School of Art; Strathclyde University. Offshore contracts, North Sea and North America, 1977-80; Development Officer, GDHA Limited, 1980-82; Regional Manager, Property Development, Scottish Development Agency, 1982-87; Mid-West Office, Chicago, USA, Locate in Scotland, 1987-91. Recreations: running; sailing; motorcycling; reading; films, travel. Address: (b.) Kingdom House, Saltire Centre, Glenrothes, Fife KY6 2AQ.

Mackenzie, Rory Donald, BEd, MEd. Headteacher, Balerno High School, since 1995; b.10.10.48, Edinburgh; m., Agnes; 1 d. Educ. Edinburgh Rudolf Steiner School; Telford College; Stevenson College; Edinburgh University. Teacher of English, James Gillespie's High School; APT, Guidance, Craigroyston High School; PT, Guidance, Deans Community High School; Assistant Headteacher, Blackburn Academy; Depute Headteacher, Broxburn Academy. Recreations: apart from my young daughter: golf; holidays; gardening; football. Address: (b.) 5 Bridge Road, Balerno EH14 7AQ; T.-0131-477 7788.

Mackenzie, Ruth, OBE. General Director, Scottish Opera, since 1997; b. 1957. Educ. London, Paris and Cambridge. Editor's Assistant, Time Out, 1980-81; Fellow in Theatre, Bradford University, 1982-84; Artistic Director, Bradford

Multicultural Festival, 1983; Drama Officer, Arts Council of GB, 1984-86; Head of Strategic Planning, South Bank Centre, 1986-90; Executive Director, Nottingham Playhouse, 1990-97. Board Member, London International Festival of Theatre; Member, Lottery Panel and Touring Panel, Arts Council of England; Director, New Millennium Experience Company Ltd. Address: (b.) Scottish Opera, 39 Elmbank Crescent, Glasgow G2 4PT; T.-0141-248 7646.

McKenzie Smith, Ian, OBE, RSA, PRSW, LLD, FSA (Scot), FMA; b. 3.8.35; m., Mary Rodger Fotheringham; 2 s.; 1 d. Educ. Robert Gordon's College, Aberdeen; Gray's School of Art, Aberdeen; Hospitalfield College of Art, Arbroath. Teacher of Art, 1960-63; Education Officer, Council of Industrial Design, Scottish Committee, 1963-68; Director, Aberdeen Art Gallery and Museums, 1968-89; City Arts and Recreation Officer, City of Aberdeen, 1989-96. Work in permanent collections: Scottish National Gallery of Modern Art, Scottish Arts Council, Arts Council of Northern Ireland, Contemporary Art Society, Aberdeen Art Gallery and Museums, Glasgow Art Gallery and Museums, Abbot Hall Art Gallery, Kendal, Hunterian Museum, Glasgow, Nuffield Foundation, Carnegie Trust, Strathclyde Education Authority, Lothian Education Authority, Royal Scottish Academy, Department of the Environment, City Art Centre, Edinburgh, Perth Art Gallery, IBM, Robert Fleming Holdings; Member, Scottish Arts Council, 1970-77; Member, Scottish Museums Council, 1980-87; President, RSW, since 1988; Deputy President, RSA, 1990-91, Treasurer, 1990, Secretary, since 1991; Governor: Edinburgh College of Art, 1976-88, The Robert Gordon University, 1989-95; Member: National Heritage Scottish Group, since 1977, National Trust for Scotland Curatorial Committee, since 1991, National Trust for Scotland Council, since 1995; FSS; FRSA. Address: (h.) 70 Hamilton Place, Aberdeen AB15 5BA; T.-01224 644531.

Mackenzie-Stuart, Lord (Alexander John Mackenzie-Stuart); b. 18.11.24; m., Anne Burtholme Millar; 4 d. Educ. Fettes College; Sidney Sussex College, Cambridge; Edinburgh University (LLB). Admitted Faculty of Advocates (Scottish Bar), 1951; Honorary Keeper, Advocates' Library, 1969; Sheriff-Principal of Aberdeen, Kincardine and Banff, 1971; Senator of the College of Justice, 1972; Judge of the Court of Justice of the European Communities, 1973; elected President of the Court, 1984; retired from Court of Justice, 1988; since retirement, Woodrow Wilson Center for International Scholars, Washington; lectures on Community Law and other matters in UK and Europe; international arbitration; Honorary Doctorates: Stirling, Exeter, Edinburgh, Glasgow, Aberdeen, Cambridge, Birmingham; Prix Bech for services to Europe, 1989; Honorary Bencher, Middle Temple, King's Inn, Dublin; created Life Baron, 1988, as Lord Mackenzie-Stuart of Dean; FRSE; President: British Academy of Experts, 1989-92, European Movement (Scotland). Publication: A French King at Holyrood, 1995. Address: (h.) 7 Randolph Cliff, Edinburgh EH3 7TZ; T.-0131-225 1089.

McKeown, James Patrick, LLB, DipLP, NP. Solicitor; b. 17.3.59, Coatbridge; m., Pamela Mary; 2 s.; 1 d. Educ. Aberdeen University. Assistant, Esslemont & Cameron, Aberdeen, 1983-85; Company Secretary, Sysdrill Ltd., 1985-86; Assistant, C. & D. Mactaggart, 1986, appointed Partner, 1987; Chairman, Social Security Appeal Tribunal. Vice-Chairman, Scottish Liberal Democrats, Argyll and Bute, 1990-97. Recreation: politics. Address: (b.) Castlehill, Campbeltown, Argyll PA28 6AR; T.-01586 552317.

McKerrell of Hillhouse, Charles James Mure. Baron of Dromin; Hereditary Keeper of Cashel; Hereditary Niadh Nask (ancient Gaelic Irish Knightly Order); OSt.J; Knight Order of St. Michael of the Wing; Knight Commander, Order of Polonia Restituta; Knight Grand Cross of Justice Order of St. Lazarus of Jerusalem; Honorary Captain, Canadian Bush Pilots' Squadron; recognised as McKerrell of Hillhouse and Head of the Name by Lord Lyon, 1973, and as 15th Head of the Name by Chief Herald of Ireland 1974; b. 2.1.41; m., May Weston Cochrane, Niadh Nask, DLJ, FSA (Scot). Educ. Cranleigh. Chancellor to The Mac Carthy Mor, Prince of Desmond, Head of the Royal House of Munster; Chancellor of the Niadh Nask. FSA (Scot); Vice-Chairman, International Commission for Orders of Chivalry; Member: Royal Celtic Society, Royal Stuart Society, Heraldry Society of Scotland, Corona Legitima, Monarchist League (Scotland); Founder Member, Heraldry Society of Ireland. Address: (h.) Magdalene House, Lochmaben, Dumfries DG11 1PD; T.-01387 810439.

McKerrell, Douglas Gordon, LLB. Partner: Kidstons & Co., Solicitors, Glasgow, since 1992, Maclay Murray and Spens, 1976-92; b. 18.8.44, Edinburgh; m., Elizabeth Anne (Lizanne) Brown; 3 s.; 1 d. Educ. Royal High School, Edinburgh; High School of Glasgow; Glasgow University. After training and qualifying, spent several years in private practice in London and Glasgow; Tutor/Senior Tutor, Finance and Investment, Diploma in Legal Practice, Glasgow University, 1980-89; Chairman, Rent Assessment Panel for Scotland, 1980-89; Scottish Representative, UK Committee, UNICEF, 1985-88; Chairman: Scottish Music Information Centre, 1990-93, Scottish SPCA, 1988-93; Trustee, Scottish International Piano Competition; Secretary, Children's Music Foundation in Scotland; Trustee, Scottish Musicians' Benevolent Fund; Board Member, Edinburgh International Film Festival. Publication: The Rent Acts: A Practitioner's Guide, 1985. Recreations: music; theatre; cinema; collecting records. Address: (b.) 1 Royal Bank Place, Buchanan Street, Glasgow; T.-0141-221 6551.

MacKessack-Leitch, Hilda Jane Marshall. Deputy Lieutenant, Moray, since 1993; Elgin Local Organiser, WRVS, since 1976; b. 4.9.40, Rothes; m., 1, Dr. Ernest V. C. Dawson (deceased); 2, David C. MacKessack-Leitch; 2 s. Educ. Elgin Academy. Past County Commissioner, The Guide Association, Moray; Past Chairman, Cancer Research Campaign Committee, Elgin and District. Recreations: cooking; walking; reading; music. Address: (h.) Inchstelly House, Alves, Elgin, Moray IV30 3UY. T.-01343 850203.

Mackey, Professor James Patrick, PhD, LPh, BD, STL, DD, BA. Thomas Chalmers Professor of Theology, Edinburgh University, since 1979; b. 9.2.34; m., Hanorah Noelle Quinlan; 1 s.; 1 d. Educ. Mount St. Joseph College, Roscrea; National University of Ireland; Pontifical University, Maynooth; Queen's University, Belfast; Oxford University; London University; Strasbourg University. Lecturer in Philosophy, Queen's University, Belfast, 1960-66; Lecturer in Theology, St. John's College, Waterford, 1966-69; Associate Professor and Professor of Systematic and Philosophical Theology, San Francisco University, 1969-79; Visiting Professor: University of California, Berkeley, 1974, Dartmouth College, New Hampshire, 1989; Member, Centre for Hermeneutical Studies, Berkeley, 1974-79; Dean, Faculty of Divinity, Edinburgh University, 1984-88, Associate Dean and Director of Graduate School, since 1995; Editor, Studies in World Christianity (international journal), since 1995. Publications: The Modern Theology of Tradition, 1962; Life and Grace, 1966; Tradition and Change in the Church, 1968; Contemporary Philosophy of Religion, 1968; Morals, Law and Authority (Editor), 1969; The Church: Its Credibility Today, 1970; The Problems of Religious Faith, 1972; Jesus: The Man and the Myth, 1979; The Christian Experience of God as Trinity, 1983; Religious Imagination (Editor), 1986; Modern Theology: A Sense of Direction, 1987; New Testament Theology in Dialogue, (Co-Author), 1987; Introduction to Celtic Christianity, 1989; The Cultures of Europe: the Irish contribution, 1993; Power and Christian

Ethics, 1994. Recreations: yachting; rediscovery of original Celtic culture of these islands. Address: (h.) 10 Randolph Crescent, Edinburgh EH3 7TT; T.-0131-225 9408.

McKichan, Duncan James, OBE, BL. Solicitor (former Senior Partner, Maclay Murray & Spens); Honorary Consul for Canada, 1986-92; Dean, Royal Faculty of Procurators in Glasgow, 1983-86; b. 28.7.24, Wallington, Surrey; m, Leila Campbell Fraser; 2 d. Educ. George Watson's College, Edinburgh; Solihull School; Downing College, Cambridge; Glasgow University. Royal Navy, 1943-46; qualified as Solicitor, 1950. Recreations: gardening; walking; sailing; skiing. Address: (h.) Invermay, Queen Street, Helensburgh; T.-01436 674778.

Mackie, Michael James, BMedBiol, MBChB, MD, FRCP, FRCPath. Consultant Haematologist, since 1981; Area Director, Haematology Services, 1991-93; b. 17.11.48, Aberdeen; 1 s.; 1 d. Educ. Robert Gordon's College, Aberdeen; Aberdeen University. Junior appointments in Aberdeen and Canada; Consultant and Senior Lecturer, Liverpool University, 1981-86; Consultant Haematologist, Western General Hospital, Edinburgh, since 1986. Recreation: tennis. Address: (b.) Department of Haematology, Western General Hospital, Crewe Road, Edinburgh; T.-0131-537 1902.

MacKie, Professor Rona McLeod, MD, DSc, FRCP, FRCPGlas, FRCPLond, FRCPath, FRSE, FInstBiol. Professor of Dermatology, Glasgow University, since 1978; Honorary Consultant Dermatologist, Greater Glasgow Health Board, since 1978; b. 22.5.40, Dundee; m., Sir James Black; 1 s.; 1 d. Educ. Laurelbank School, Glasgow; Glasgow University. Registrar, Department of Dermatology, Western Infirmary, Glasgow, 1970-71; Lecturer in Dermatology, Glasgow University, 1971-72; Consultant Dermatologist, Greater Glasgow Health Board, 1972-78. Publications: textbooks and papers on skin cancer. Recreations: opera; gardening; skiing. Address: Department of Dermatology, Glasgow University, Glasgow G11 6NU; T.-0141-339 8855, Ext. 4006.

McKiernan, Professor Peter, BA, MA, PhD, MIM, FRSA. Professor of Strategic Management, St. Andrews University, since 1992; b. 28.12.53, Accrington; m., Morna; 1 s.; 1 d. Educ. Preston Catholic College; Lancaster University; Surrey University. Former M.D. of mechanical engineering company; Lecturer in Management, St. Andrews University; Senior Lecturer in Strategic Management, Warwick University. Publications: Sharpbenders; Strategies of Growth; Inside Fortress Europe; Historical Evolution of Strategic Management. Recreations: cricket; poetry. Address: (b.) Department of Management, St. Andrews University KY16 9AL; T.-01334 462795.

McKillop, Professor James Hugh, BSc, MB, ChB, PhD, FRCP, FRCR. Muirhead Professor of Medicine, Glasgow University, since 1989; Honorary Consultant Physician, Glasgow Royal Infirmary, since 1982; b. 20.6.48, Glasgow; m., Caroline A. Oakley; 2 d. Educ. St. Aloysius' College, Glasgow, Glasgow University. Hall Fellow in Medicine, then Lecturer in Medicine, Glasgow University, 1974-82; Postdoctoral Fellow, Stanford University Medical Center, California, 1979 and 1980; Senior Lecturer in Medicine, Glasgow University, 1982-89. Watson Prize Lectureship, Royal College of Physicians and Surgeons of Glasgow, 1979; Harkness Fellowship, Commonwealth Fund of New York, 1979-80; Robert Reid Newall Award, Stanford University, 1980; Honorary Treasurer, Scottish Society of Experimental Medicine, 1982-87; Honorary Secretary, British Nuclear Cardiology Group, 1982-87; Symposium Editor, Scottish Medical Journal, 1984-93; Council Member, British Nuclear Medicine Society, 1985-94 (Hon. Secretary, 1988-90, President, 1990-92); Editor, Nuclear Medicine Communications, since 1990; Congress President, European Association of Nuclear Medicine, 1997, Member,

Executive Committee, 1995-98; Chairman, Administration of Radioactive Substances Advisory Committee, Department of Health, since 1996 (Vice Chairman, 1989-95); Member, National Medical Advisory Committee, since 1995. Recreations: music (especially opera); history; football. Address: (b.) University Department of Medicine, Royal Infirmary, Glasgow G31 2ER; T.-0141-211 4675.

McKinlay, Peter, MA (Hons). Chief Executive, Scottish Homes, since 1991; Chairman, Bute Beyond 2000 (formerly Bute Partnership), since 1996; Member, Board, The Wise Group, since 1996; Director, St. Mary's Cathedral Workshop, since 1994; b. 29.12.39, Campbeltown; m., Anne Thomson; 2 s.; 1 d. Educ. Campbeltown Grammar School; Glasgow University. Assistant Postal Controller, GPO HQ, Edinburgh; Assistant Principal, PS to Secretary, Scottish Development Department; Principal, Housing, SDD; Principal Private Secretary to Rt. Hon. Bruce Millan, Minister of State; Principal, Local Government Finance; Assistant Secretary, Finance; Assistant Secretary, Industry Department for Scotland; Director, Scottish Prison Service, 1988-91. Non-Executive Director, D.S. Crawford; Badminton Blue, Glasgow University; Member, National Executive, First Division Association, 1977-80. Recreations: reading; gardening; family; friends. Address: (b.) Thistle House, 91 Haymarket Terrace, Edinburgh EH12 5HE; T.-0131-313 0044.

McKinney, Alan. National Director, Scottish Decorators' Federation; Director of Organisation and Headquarters, Scottish National Party, 1977-90; b. 16.10.41, Glasgow; m., Elma; 1 s.; 1 d. Educ. Brechin High School. Time-served refrigeration engineer before entering politics full-time as National Organiser, SNP, 1977; former Election Agent, Dundee East; former elected Member, NEC. Played football for Brechin City. Recreation: golf. Address: (b.) 222 Queensferry Road, Edinburgh EH4 2BN; T.-0131-343 3300.

McKinnon, David Douglas, BSc, FFA, CMath, FIMA. Director, General Manager and Actuary, Scottish Mutual Assurance Society, 1982-90, Director, 1981-91, Director, Scottish Mutual Assurance plc, 1992-96; b. 18.7.26, Larbert; m., Edith June Kyles; 1 s.; 2 d. Educ. High School of Stirling; Glasgow University. Faculty of Actuaries: Fellow, since 1951, President, 1979-81; Member of Council, International Actuarial Association, 1972-89 and Secretary for the UK, 1975-89; Member, Investment Advisory Committee, Glasgow University Court, since 1982; Chairman, Associated Scottish Life Offices, 1988-90; Member, Board of Association of British Insurers, 1988-90; Session Clerk, Larbert West Church, 1968-87; Vice-Chairman, Church of Scotland Trust, 1984-89, Chairman, 1991-96; Member, Church of Scotland Assembly Council, 1987-96; Director: Church of Scotland Insurance Company Ltd., since 1992, Scotsure Insurance Company Ltd., 1992-97; Member, Trinity College (Glasgow) Financial Board, 1977-97; President, Falkirk and District Battalion, The Boys' Brigade, 1972-77. Recreations: music; gardening. Address: (h.) 4 Carronvale Road, Larbert, Stirlingshire FK5 3LZ; T.-01324 562373.

Mackinnon, Donald McDougall, CEng, MIW, LCG. Chairman, Scottish Inland Waterways Association, since 1981; President, Forth and Clyde Canal Society, since 1986; b. 14.11.29, Glasgow; m., Regine; 1 s.; 2 d. Educ. Hillhead High School; Stow College, Glasgow; London University. Lecturer in Welding Technology and Metallurgy, 1955-78; Senior Lecturer in Welding and Heavy Fabrication, 1978-81; Depute Head, Department of Fabrication, 1981-82; Head, Department of Fabrication and Heating, Ventilation and Refrigeration, 1982-91. Vice-President, Scottish Maritime Heritage Association; Member: Forth and Clyde Canal Local Plan Working Group, Forth and Clyde Canal

Local Plan Advisory Committee, Marine Safety Agency Inland Waterway Committee. Address: (h.) 8 Kelvin Way, Kirkintilloch, Glasgow G66 1BX; T.-0141-776 3812.

MacKinnon, Major John Farquhar, MC, DL, JP; b. 27.1.18, Melbourne; m., Sheila Pearce (deceased); 1 s.; 1 d. (deceased); 2, Mrs Anne Swann. Educ. Geelong, Australia; Corpus Christi College, Cambridge (MA). Army, Queen's Own Cameron Highlanders, 1939-46 (Major); twice wounded; Middle East, 1940-41; ADC, Governor General, Union of South Africa, 1942; Staff, UK, 1943-46 (left service due to wounds); Staff TA, 1949-54; ICI Ltd., 1949-73, Regional Manager; Secretary, British Field Sports Society, Berwickshire, 1974-80; Elder, Kirk of Lammermuir; JP, 1966; Deputy Lieutenant, Berwickshire, since 1987. Recreation: fishing. Address: (h.) Craigie Lodge, Longformacus, by Duns, Berwickshire; T.-Longformacus 890251.

McLachlan, Alastair Stevenson, MA (Hons). Rector, Lornshill Academy, Alloa, since 1988; b. 7.8.40, Glasgow; m., Anne Rutherford; 1 s.; 1 d. Educ. High School of Glasgow; Glasgow University. Recreations: family; golf; after-dinner speaking; singing. Address: (b.) Lornshill Academy, Tullibody Road, Alloa FK10 2ES; T.-01259 214331.

Maclachlan, Alistair Andrew Duncan, BA (Hons), FRSA. Rector, Forres Academy, since 1982; b. 14.3.46, Perth; m., Alison M.S. Love; 2 s. Educ. Perth Academy; Strathclyde University. Teacher in various schools, 1969-71; Principal Teacher of Economics and Business Studies, 1971-74; Assistant Rector, Keith Grammar School, 1974-78; Depute Rector, Elgin High School, 1978-82; Member, SCCC. Secretary and Treasurer, Keith Agricultural Show, 1972-82; Past Chairman, Elgin Squash Club; Chairman, Moray Swing Band. Recreations: keeping fit; squash; reading; music. Address: (h.) 82 Duncan Drive, Elgin, Moray IV30 2NH; T.-Elgin 542193.

Maclagan, Ian, LLB, FSAScot. Partner, Macbeth and Maclagan, Solicitors, Rothesay, since 1970; b. 21.5.43, Rothesay; m., Marjorie; 1 s. Educ. Rothesay Academy; George Watson's College; Edinburgh University. Solicitor in private practice, since 1967; Hon. Sheriff of North Strathclyde at Rothesay; Dean, Faculty of Solicitors in Bute. Trustee, Bute Museum; Past President, Buteshire Natural History Society. Recreations: walking; local history; archaeology; reading. Address: (b.) 34 Castle Street, Rothesay, Bute; T.-01700 503157.

MacLaren, Archie, CBE, FRICS. Chief Valuer (Scotland), Valuation Office Agency, since 1992; b. 28.1.40, Kilsyth; m., Dolina Archina MacIsaac; 1 s.; 1 d. Educ. Kilsyth Academy; College of Estate Management, London. Partner, W.R. Patterson & Houston, 1964-67; Estates Surveyor, Glenrothes Development Corporation, 1968-70; Principal Valuer, Valuation Office Inland Revenue, 1971-74, First Class Valuer, 1975-77; District Valuer, Dumbarton & Argyll, 1977-91. Recreations: photography; gardening. Address: (b.) Meldrum House, 15 Drumsheugh Gardens, Edinburgh, EH3 7UN; T.-0131-225 4938.

McLaren, Bill. Rugby Union Commentator, BBC; b. 16.10.23. Played wing forward for Hawick; had trial for Scotland but forced to withdraw because of illness; became reporter on local newspaper; first live radio broadcast, Glasgow v. Edinburgh, 1953; former teacher of physical education.

MacLaren, Iain Ferguson, MB, ChB, FRCSEdin, FRCS, FRCP Edin. Consultant Surgeon, Royal Infirmary, Edinburgh, 1974-92; b. 28.9.27, Edinburgh; m., Dr. Fiona Barbara Heptonstall; 1 s.; 1 d. Educ. Edinburgh Academy; Fettes College; Edinburgh University. Captain, RAMC, Egypt, 1950-52; Surgical Registrar, Royal Hospital for Sick

Children, Edinburgh, 1956-58; Senior Surgical Registrar, Royal Infirmary, 1959-63 and 1964-67; Fellow in Surgical Research, Hahnemann Medical College and Hospital, Philadelphia, 1963-64; Consultant Surgeon, Deaconess Hospital, Edinburgh, 1967-85; Vice-President, Royal College of Surgeons of Edinburgh, 1983-86 (Council Member, 1977-83 and 1987-94); Fellow, Royal Medical Society (Honorary Treasurer, 1979-85); Chairman, Royal Medical Society Trust, since 1985; Honorary Pipe-Major, Royal Scottish Pipers' Society, 1959-62; Honorary Secretary: Harveian Society of Edinburgh, 1968-87, Aesculapian Club, since 1978; Hon. Secretary, Royal College of Surgeons of Edinburgh, 1972-77; Secretary, Edinburgh University General Council, 1993-97; Chairman: Professional and Linguistic Assessments Board, General Medical Council, since 1996, Clan MacLaren Society, 1968-91; Chieftain, Clan Lathran, 1991. Recreations: music; the study of military history; all aspects of Scottish culture. Address: (h.) 3 Minto Street, Edinburgh EH9 1RG; T.-0131-667 3487.

McLatchie, Cameron, CBE, LLB. Chairman and Chief Executive, British Polythene Industries, formerly Scott & Robertson PLC, since 1988; Non-executive Chairman, Hiscox Select PLC; Member, Board, Scottish Environmental Protection Agency; b. 18.2.47, Paisley; m., Helen Leslie Mackie; 2 s.; 1 d. Educ. Boroughmuir School, Edinburgh; Largs High School; Ardrossan Academy; Glasgow University. Whinney Murray & Co., Glasgow, 1968-70; Thomas Boag & Co. Ltd., Greenock, 1970-75; Chairman and Managing Director, Anaplast Ltd., Irvine, 1975-83; this company purchased by Scott & Robertson. Recreations: bridge; golf. Address: (b.) 96 Port Glasgow Road, Greenock; T.-01475 501000.

McLaughlin, Mary, MA. Head Teacher, Notre Dame High School, Glasgow, since 1990; b. 18.8.48, Glenboig; m., William J. McLaughlin; 1 d. Educ. St. Patrick's High School, Coatbridge; Glasgow University; Notre Dame College of Education. Principal Teacher of Modern Languages, St. Margaret's High, Airdrie; Assistant Head Teacher, Taylor High School, New Stevenston. Recreations: reading; music; cycling; walking. Address: (b.) 160 Observatory Road, Glasgow G12 9LN; T.-0141-339 3015.

Maclay, Baron (Joseph Paton Maclay), 3rd Baron; Bt. Deputy Lieutenant, Renfrewshire, since 1986; Director, Altnamara Shipping Plc, since 1994; Group Marketing Executive, Acomant Group, since 1993; Commissioner, Northern Lighthouse Board, since 1996; b. 11.4.42; m., Elizabeth Anne Buchanan; 2 s.; 1 d. Educ. Winchester; Sorbonne. Managing Director: Denholm Maclay Co. Ltd., 1970-83, Denholm Maclay (Offshore) Ltd., Triport Ferries (Management) Ltd., 1975-83; Deputy Managing Director, Denholm Ship Management Ltd., 1982-83; Director: Milton Shipping Co. Ltd., 1970-83, Marine Shipping Mutual Insurance Company, 1982-83; President, Hanover Shipping Inc., 1982-83; Director: British Steamship Short Trades Association, 1978-83, North of England Protection and Indemnity Association, 1976-83; Chairman, Scottish Branch, British Sailors Society, 1979-81; Vice-President, Glasgow Shipowners & Shipbrokers Benevolent Association, 1982-83; Director, Denholm Ship Management (Holdings) Ltd., 1991-93. Address: (h.) Duchal, Kilmacolm, Renfrewshire.

McLay, Louisa Mary, MA. Headmistress, Fernhill School, Rutherglen, since 1992; b. 14.8.45, Glasgow; m., Dr. Arthur McLay. Educ. Notre Dame High School; Glasgow University. Primary Teacher, 1966-73; Fernhill School: Teacher of English, French, History, 1973-76, Principal Teacher of English, 1976-94, Deputy Headmistress, 1978-92. Recreations: music; gardening. Address: (b.) Fernhill School, Fernbrae Avenue, Burnside, Rutherglen, Glasgow; T.-0141-634 2674.

MacLean, Rev. Andrew Thomas, BA, BD. Parish Minister, St. Andrew's, Port Glasgow, since 1993; b. 1.2.50, Abadan, Iran; m., Alison Douglas Blair; 1 s.; 1 d. Educ. Bearsden Academy; Clydebank Technical College; Stirling University; Edinburgh University. Co-operative Insurance Society, 1967-70; Partner, Janus Enterprises, 1970-72; Probationer, Loanhead, 1979-80; Minister, Aberdeen Stockethill, 1980-85; Chaplain, Strathclyde University, 1985-93. Member: Woman's Guild Central Committee, since 1995, Church of Scotland Board of Practice and Procedure, since 1995; Convener, Church of Scotland Board of Social Responsibility, 1989-93; Moderator, Greenock Presbytery, 1997 98. Recreations: sound recording; photography; parachuting; desk top publishing. Address: St. Andrew's Manse, Barr's Brae, Port Glasgow PA14 5QA; T.-01475 741486.

McLean, Angus, BL, SSC. Solicitor; Honorary Sheriff, Argyll (Dunoon); b. 26.10.12, Kilmartin, Argyll; m., Celia Jane Oliver; 1 s.; 1 d. Educ. Dunoon Grammar School; Glasgow University. Solicitor (Corrigall Ritchie & McLean, Dunoon), 1935; Royal Artillery, 1940-46; seconded Indian Army, 1942, Major (DAAG), 1945. Member, Council, Law Society of Scotland, 1950-74 (Vice President, 1964); Past President, Dunoon Business Club and Dunoon Rotary Club. Publications: History of Dunoon; Place Names of Cowal. Recreations: local history; travel; gardening. Address: (h.) 21 Ravelston Dykes, Edinburgh EH4 3JE; T.-0131-332 4774.

Maclean of Dunconnel, Sir Charles (Edward), Bt; b. 31.10.46; m.; 3 d. Educ. Eton; New College, Oxford. Publications: The Wolf Children; The Watcher; Island on the Edge of the World (Co-author); Scottish Country; Romantic Scotland; The Silence. Address: (h.) Inverglen, Strachur, Cairndow, Argyll PA27 8DG.

MacLean, Charles Hector, BL, AE, DL. Former Senior Partner, Montgomerie & Co., Solicitors, Glasgow; Chairman, Association for Relief of Incurables in Glasgow and West of Scotland, 1964-94; Deputy Lieutenant, County of Renfrew, since 1987; b. 9.12.13, Glasgow; m., Rachael Malcolm Hutchesson; 2 s.; 2 d. Educ. Canford School; Glasgow University. Pilot Officer, 602 Squadron Auxiliary Air Force, 1936; mobilised, 1939; severely wounded, 1940, as Flt. Commander in Battle of Britain; released in rank of Wing Commander, 1945; re-commissioned as wing Commander, RAuxAF to raise and command 3602 Fighter Control Unit. Member, Committee, Earl Haig Fund Scotland, 1965-94; Vice President, Officers Association, Scottish Branch, 1983-97; Address: (h.) 71 Lochwinnoch Road, Kilmacolm, Renfrewshire.

Maclean, Christian. Manager, Floris Books, since 1976; b. 14.2.50, Edinburgh; m., Astrid; 2 s.; 1 d. Educ. Rudolf Steiner School. Treasurer, Scottish Publishers Association; Director, Scottish Book Source. Address: (b.) 15 Harrison Gardens, Edinburgh; T.-0131-337 2372.

MacLean, Colin R., BSc (Hons), DipEd, MSc. Chief Statistician, Scottish Office Education and Industry Department, since 1996; Chief Professional Officer (Statistics), Scottish Office, since 1997; b. 22.5.51, Dundee; m., Ilse; 2 s.; 1 d. Educ. Forfar Academy; Edinburgh University. Teacher of Mathematics, Edinburgh, 1973-79; Education Adviser (Microelectronics/Computing), Lothian Regional Council, 1980-85; HM Inspector of Schools, 1985-96. Recreations: gardening; swimming; travel; trying not to be humiliated when playing computer games with my children. Address: (b.) 1-A75, Victoria Quay, Edinburgh; T.-0131-244 0302.

Maclean, Sir Donald, FCOptom. Ophthalmic Optician, since 1952; Chairman, Ayrshire Medical Support Ltd.; Chairman, Bell Hollingworth Ltd; b. Annan; widower; 1 s.; 1 d. Educ. Morrison's Academy, Crieff; Heriot-Watt,

Edinburgh. Ophthalmic Optician in Edinburgh, Newcastle, Perth and now Ayr; Chairman, Ayrshire Local Optical Committee, 1986-88; former Member, Transport Users Local Consultative Committee; Chairman, Ayr Constituency Conservative Association, 1971-75; Chairman, West of Scotland Area Council, Scottish Conservative Association, 1977-78-79; President, Scottish Conservative and Unionist Association, 1983-85; Scottish Conservative Party: Deputy Chairman, 1985-89, Vice Chairman, 1989-91; Dean of Guildry, Ayr Guildry, 1993-95; Elder, Church of Scotland; Past President, West Highland Steamer Club; Liveryman of the Worshipful Copany of Spectacle Makers, Freeman, City of London. Recreations: photography; reading. Address: (b.) 59 Newmarket Street, Ayr KA7 1LL.

MacLean, Sheriff Hector Ronald. Sheriff of Lothian and Borders, at Linlithgow, since 1988; b. 6.12.31. Advocate, 1959. Address: (b.) Sheriff Court House, Court Square, Linlithgow, EH49 7EQ.

MacLean, Ian Hamish, MBChB, FFPHM. Chief Administrative Medical Officer and Director of Public Health, Dumfries and Galloway Health Board, since 1989; Honorary Clinical Senior Lecturer, Glasgow University, since 1989; b. 9.10.47, Bishop's Stortford, Herts; m., Anne; 1 s.; 1 d. Educ. Felsted School; Dundee University. Consultant in Public Health Medicine, Borders Health Board, 1980-89. Recreations: music; sailing; flying; house restoration; photography. Address: (b.) Dumfries and Galloway Health Board, Nithbank, Dumfries DG1 2SD; T.-01387 246246.

MacLean, Ian Teasdale, MA, LLB. Solicitor; Senior Partner, Mackie & Dewar, 1982-97 (Partner, since 1968); Honorary Treasurer, Aberdeen YMCA, since 1970; b. 3.6.40, Stornoway; m., Lavinia May Symonds; 1 s.; 1 d. Educ. Nicolson Institute, Stornoway; Aberdeen University. Qualified as Solicitor, 1964, after three years' indenture with Morice & Wilson, Advocates in Aberdeen; salaried Solicitor, J.D. Mackie & Dewar, Advocates in Aberdeen, 1965-68. Address: (b.) 18 Bon-Accord Square, Aberdeen; T.-01224 596341.

McLean, Jack, DA, MSIAD. Journalist and Broadcaster; b. Irvine, Ayrshire. Educ. Allan Glen's School, Glasgow; Edinburgh College of Art. Apprentice Welder, 1962-65; various jobs until 1968; Studio Artist, uncertificated Art Teacher, 1968-70; Edinburgh Art College; Jordanhill College of Education; Teacher of Art in Glasgow schools, until 1988; began writing with Times Educational Supplement with regular column; Columnist, The Scotsman, 1967-81; Columnist, Glasgow Herald, 1981-97; Columnist, The Scotsman, since 1997; Scottish Vice-Chairman and National Executive Member, National Union of Students, 1970-74; Member, Scottish Council, Educational Institute of Scotland, 1981-82; Member, Strathclyde Regional Council Education Committee, 1986-88. Commendation, Scottish Press Awards, 1985, 1986; Runner up, Columnist of the Year, British Press Awards, 1985; Scottish Feature Writer of the Year, 1989; commended Columnist of the Year, 1989. Publications: The Bedside Urban Voltaire; More Bedside Urban Voltaire; The Sporting Urban Voltaire; City of Glasgow. Recreations: drinking in public houses; flashy dressing; talking. Address: The Scotsman, 20 North Bridge, Edinburgh EH1 1YT.

McLean, James Angus, BA, LLB, WS. Partner, W. & J. Burness, since 1974; b. 25.4.47, Gosforth; m., Carol Inglis; 1 s.; 2 d. Educ. Dunoon Grammar School; Fettes College; Sidney Sussex College, Cambridge; Edinburgh University. Solicitor, 1972. Member, High Constables of Edinburgh; Member, Scottish Lawyers European Group; Member, various committees, Law Society of Scotland. Recreations: swimming; cycling; theatre. Address: (b.) 16 Hope Street, Charlotte Square, Edinburgh EH2 4DD.

McLean, John David Ruari, CBE, DSC, Croix de Guerre. Typographer and Author; b. 10.6.17, Minnigaff; m., Antonia Maxwell Carlisle (deceased); 2 s.; 1 d. Educ. Dragon School, Oxford; Eastbourne College. Royal Navy, 1940-45; Tutor in Typography, Royal College of Art, 1948-51; Typographic Adviser, Hulton Press, 1953-60; The Observer, 1960-62; Art Editor, The Connoisseur, 1962-73; Founder-Partner, Rainbird, McLean Ltd., 1951-58; Founder Editor, Motif, 1958-67; Honorary Typographic Adviser to HM Stationery Office, 1966-80; Senior Partner, Ruari McLean Associates Ltd., 1960-81; Trustee, National Library of Scotland, 1981. Publications include: Modern Book Design, 1958; Victorian Book Design and Colour Printing, 1963; Magazine Design, 1969; Jan Tschichold, Typographer, 1975; The Thames & Hudson Manual of Typography, 1980; Benjamin Fawcett, Engraver and Colour Printer, 1988; Edward Bawden, war artist, and his letters home 1940-45 (Editor), 1989; Nicolas Bentley drew the pictures, 1990; Typographers on Type (Editor), 1995; Jan Tschichold: a life in typography, 1997. Recreations: sailing; acquiring books. Address: (h.) Pier Cottage, Carsaig, Mull PA70 6HD; T.-01681 704 216.

Maclean, John Robert, DL; b. 24.5.51, Lossiemouth; m., Veronica Mary Lacy Hulbert-Powell; 1 s.; 2 d. Educ. Milton Abbey School. Commissioned into Queen's Own Highlanders, 1971; left Army, 1978, and returned home to farm via Royal Agricultural College, Cirencester; Deputy Lieutenant, County of Moray, since 1987; Member, Royal Company of Archers (Queen's Bodyguard for Scotland), since 1987; Chairman, Elgin Branch, Earl Haig Fund. Recreations: shooting; field sports. Address: (h.) Westfield House, near Elgin, Moray.

Maclean of Duart, Major The Hon. Sir Lachlan, DL. Major, Scots Guards retired; 28th Chief of Clan Maclean; b. 25.8.42.

MacLean, Rev. Marjory Anne, LLB, BD, DipLP. Minister, Stromness Parish Church, since 1992; Depute Clerk, General Assembly, Church of Scotland, since 1996; b. 11.6.62, Forfar. Educ. Forfar Academy; Edinburgh University. Trainee to Qualified Solicitor, T.P. & J.L. Low, Kirkwall, 1985-87; Probationer to Assistant Minister, Fairmilehead Parish Church, Edinburgh, 1990-92. Company Member, St. Magnus Festival, Orkney. Recreations: chamber singing; indifferent golf. Address: 5 Manse Lane, Stromness, Orkney KW16 3AP; T.-01856 850203.

Maclean, Hon. Lord (Ranald Norman Munro Maclean), BA, LLB, LLM. Senator of the College of Justice, since 1990; Queen's Counsel, since 1977; b. 18.12.38, Aberdeen; m., Pamela Ross (m. dissolved); 2 s.; 1 d. Educ. Inverness Royal Academy; Fettes College, Edinburgh; Cambridge University; Edinburgh University; Yale University. Advocate, 1964; Advocate Depute, 1972-75; Advocate Depute (Home), 1979-82; Chairman of Governors, Fettes College, since 1996. Recreations: hill-walking; bird watching. Address: (h.) 38 Royal Terrace, Edinburgh EH7 5AH.

Maclean, Sir Robert (Alexander), KBE (1973), Kt (1955), LLD. Honorary Life President, A.F. Stoddard & Co. Ltd.; Deputy Lieutenant, Renfrewshire; b. 11.4.08, Cambuslang; m., Vivienne Neville Bourke; 2 s.; 2 d. Educ. High School of Glasgow. Partner, later a Senior Partner, James Templeton & Co., Glasgow, 1937-45; Chairman, A.F. Stoddard & Co. Ltd., 1946-83. Chairman, Glasgow Junior Chamber of Commerce, 1940; President, Glasgow Chamber of Commerce, 1956-58; Chairman, Scottish Council of Chambers of Commerce, 1960-62; President, Association of British Chambers of Commerce, 1966-68; Regional Controller (Scotland), Board of Trade, 1944-46; Regional Controller, Factory and Storage Control, 1941-44; Chairman: Scottish Industries Exhibitions, 1949, 1954, 1959, Scottish Exports Committee, 1966-70; Scottish Industrial Estates Corporation, 1955-72; President, British Industrial Exhibition, Moscow, 1966; Member: BNEC, 1966-70, Scottish Aerodromes Board, 1950-61, Export Council for Europe, 1960-64; Vice-Chairman, Scottish Board for Industry, 1952-60; a Vice-President, Scottish Council (Development and Industry), 1955-82. Recreations: golf; fishing. Address: (h.) South Branchal Farm, Bridge of Weir, Renfrewshire PA11 3SJ; T.-Kilmacolm 2162.

McLean, Professor Sheila Ann Manson, LLB, MLitt, PhD, FRSE, FRCP(Edin), FRSA. International Bar Association Professor of Law and Ethics in Medicine, University of Glasgow, since 1990; Director, Institute of Law and Ethics in Medicine, since 1985; b. 20.6.51, Glasgow; m., Alan McLean (divorced). Educ. Glasgow High School for Girls; University of Glasgow. Area Reporter to Children's Panel, 1972-75; School of Law, University of Glasgow: Lecturer, 1975-85, Senior Lecturer, 1985-90. Previously: Chair, committee reviewing Professions Supplementary to Medicine Act, Member, Scottish Office Working Group on the Confidentiality of Personal Health Information at the Interface between Medical and Social Services, Member, BMJ Working Party on Rationing and Health Care, Member, External Advisory Group of Review on the Ethics of Clinical Trials, Member, West Ethics Committee, Member, Broadcasting Council for Scotland; currently: appointed by Department of Health to review consent provisions of the Human Fertilisation and Embryology Act, Member, Scottish Higher Education Funding Council, Member, UK Xenotransplantation Interim Regulatory Authority, Vice-Chair, Multi-Centre Research Ethics Committee for Scotland, Member, Advisory Group to Data Protection Registrar, Member, Audit Committee, International Association of Medical Law, Secretary of State Appointee to United Kingdom Central Council for Nursing, Midwifery and Health Visiting, Trustee, Scottish Civil Liberties Trust, Trustee, Joyce Watson Memorial Fund, Member, College Patient Liaison Committee, Royal College of Physicians of Edinburgh, Member, Sectional Committee, Philosophy, Theology and Law, Royal Society of Edinburgh, Member, Editorial Board, International Journal of Medical Practice and the Law, Member, Editorial Board, Medical Law International, Member, Editorial Board, Bulletin of Medical Ethics, Academic Reviewer, European Journal of Public Health, Member, Research Board of Advisers, American Biographical Association, Review Editor, Medical Law International. Publications: monographs: Medicine, Morals and the Law, 1983; A Patient's Right to Know: Information Disclosure, the Doctor and the Law, 1989; The Case for Physician Assisted Suicide, 1997; Old Law, New Medicine, 1998; edited books: Legal Issues in Medicine, 1981; Human Rights: From Rhetoric to Reality, (Co-Editor), 1986; The Legal Relevance of Gender (Joint Editor), 1988; Legal Issues in Human Reproduction, 1989; Law Reform and Human Reproduction, 1992; Compensation for Personal Injury: An International Perspective, 1993; Law Reform and Medical Injury Litigation, 1995; Law and Ethics in Intensive Care, 1996; Death, Dying and the Law, 1996; Contemporary Issues in Law, Medicine and Ethics, 1996. Recreations: music; reading; playing guitar; singing. Address: School of Law, University of Glasgow, Glasgow G12 8QQ; T.-0141-330 5577.

McLean, Una. Actress; b. 1930, Strathaven. Trained, Royal Scottish Academy of Music and Drama; professional debut, Byre, St. Andrews, 1955; pantomime debut, Mother Goose, 1958; joined Citizens' Theatre, Glasgow, 1959; appeared in Five Past Eight revue, 1960s; many television appearances.

Maclean, Professor William James, DA, RSA, RGI, FSA Scot. Professor of Fine Art, Duncan of Jordanstone College, University of Dundee; b. 12.10.41, Inverness; m., Marian Forbes Leven; 2 s.; 1 d. Educ. Inverness Royal Academy; HMS Conway; Grays School of Art, Aberdeen.

Postgraduate and Travel Scholarship, Scottish Education Trust Award, Visual Arts Bursary, Scottish Arts Council; Benno Schotz Prize; one-man exhibitions in Rome, Glasgow, Edinburgh and London; group exhibitions in Britain, Europe and North America; represented in private and public collections including Arts Council, British Museum, Scottish National Gallery of Modern Art, Fitzwilliam Museum, Cambridge, and several Scottish galleries. Address: (h.) Bellevue, 18 Dougall Street, Tayport, Fife.

MacLeary, Alistair Ronald, MSc, DipTP, FRICS, FRTPI, FBIM, FRSA. Honorary Fellow, Commonwealth Association of Surveying and Land Economy; Member, Lands Tribunal for Scotland; MacRobert Professor of Land Economy, Aberdeen University, 1976-89 (Dean, Faculty of Law, 1982-85); b. 12.1.40, Glasgow; m., Claire Leonard; 1 s.; 1 d. Educ. Inverness Royal Academy; College of Estate Management; Heriot-Watt University; Strathclyde University. Assistant Surveyor, Gerald Eve & Co., Chartered Surveyors, 1962-65; Assistant to Director, Murrayfield Real Estate Co. Ltd., 1965-67; Assistant Surveyor and Town Planner/Partner, Wright & Partners, 1967-76; seconded to Department of the Environment, London, 1971-73; Member: Committee of Inquiry into the Acquisition and Occupancy of Agricultural Land, 1977-79, Home Grown Timber Advisory Committee, Forestry Commission, 1981-87; Chairman, Board of Education, Commonwealth Association of Surveying and Land Economy, 1981-90; President, Planning and Development Division, Royal Institution of Chartered Surveyors, 1984-85; Editor, Land Development Studies, 1986-90; Member, Natural Environment Research Council, 1988-91. Recreations: shooting; golf. Address: (h.) St. Helen's, St. Andrew's Road, Ceres, Fife KY15 5NQ; T.-01334 828862.

McLeary, Bernard, MA. Director of Education Services, Inverclyde Council, since 1995; b. 29.10.51, Greenock; m., Anne Marie; 2 d. Educ. St. Columba's High School; University of Glasgow; Notre Dame College of Education. Teacher, Principal Teacher, Assistant Head Teacher, St. Stephen's High School, 1973-84; Education Adviser, Dunbarton Division, 1984-88; Education Officer: Dunbarton Division, 1988-90, Argyll and Bute, 1990-93, Glasgow Division, 1993-95. Chairman, Working Groups on Curriculum and Special Needs; consultant to national organisations on educational matters. Recreations: collecting books on Russia; keeping fit; theatre and arts. Address: (b.) Department of Education Services, 105 Dalrymple Street, Greenock PA15 1HT; T.-01475 882824.

MacLeay, Very Rev. John Henry James, MA. Dean of Argyll, since 1987; Rector, St. Andrew's, Fort William, since 1978; Canon, St. John's Cathedral, Oban, since 1980; b. 7.12.31, Inverness; m., Jane Speirs Cuthbert; 1 s.; 1 d. Educ. St. Edmund Hall, Oxford. Ordained Deacon, 1957; Priest, 1958; Curate: St. John's, East Dulwich, 1957-60, St. Michael's, Inverness, 1960-62; Rector, St. Michael's, Inverness, 1962-70; Priest-in-Charge, St. Columba's, Grantown-on-Spey and St. John's, Rothiemurchus, 1970-78. Recreations: fishing; reading; visiting churches and cathedrals. Address: St. Andrew's Rectory, Parade Road, Fort William PH33 6BA; T.-01397 702979.

MacLehose of Beoch, Baron (Crawford Murray MacLehose), KT (1983), GBE (1976), KCMG (1971), KCVO (1975), DL, Hon. LLD (York, 1983, Strathclyde, 1984). Chairman, School of Oriental and African Studies, 1983-91; Chairman, Scottish Trust for the Physically Disabled and Margaret Blackwood Housing Association, 1983-91; Life Peer; 16.10.17; m.; 2 d. Educ. Rugby; Balliol College, Oxford. Served Second World War (Lt., RNVR); joined Foreign Service, 1947; Governor and C-in-C, Hong Kong, 1971-82. Address: (h.) Beoch, Maybole, Ayrshire.

McLeish, Henry Baird. MP (Labour), Fife Central, since 1987; Minister of State, Scottish Office (Minister for Home Affairs and Devolution), since 1997; b. 15.6.48; 1 s.; 1 d. Educ. Buckhaven High School, Methil; Heriot-Watt University. Former Research Officer and Planning Officer in local government; former Member, Kirkcaldy District Council and Fife Regional Council (Leader, 1982-87); Scottish Front Bench Spokesman for Education and Employment, 1988-89, for Employment and Training, 1989-92; Shadow Scottish Minister of State, 1992-94; Shadow Minister of Transport, 1994-95; Shadow Minister for Health, 1995-97. Recreations: reading; history; life and work of Robert Burns, malt whisky, Highlands and Islands. Address: House of Commons, London SW1A 0AA.

McLellan, Rev. Andrew Rankin Cowie, MA, BD, STM. Minister, St. Andrew's and St. George's, Edinburgh, since 1986; b. 16.6.44, Glasgow; m., Irene L. Meek; 2 s. Educ. Kilmarnock Academy; Madras College, St. Andrews; St. Andrews University; Glasgow University; Union Theological Seminary, New York. Assistant Minister, St. George's West, Edinburgh, 1969-71; Minister: Cartsburn Augustine, Greenock, 1971-80, Viewfield, Stirling, 1980-86; Member, Inverclyde District Council, 1977-80; Tutor, Glasgow University, 1978-82; Chaplain, HM Prison, Stirling, 1982-85; Convener, Church and Nation Committee, General Assembly, 1992-96. Publication: Preaching for these People, 1997. Recreations: golf; family; theatre; travel; books. Address: 25 Comely Bank, Edinburgh EH4 1AJ; T.-031-332 5324.

McLellan, Douglas Richard, MD, FRCPath, DipFM. Consultant Pathologist, Victoria Infirmary, Glasgow, since 1989; Honorary Senior Lecturer, Glasgow University, since 1989; b. 13.6.55, Glasgow; m., Caitriona; 3 s. Educ. High School of Glasgow; Glasgow University. Registrar in Pathology, Southern General Hospital, Glasgow, 1978-81; Honorary Senior Registrar in Neuropathology (MRC Head Injury Project), Institute of Neurological Sciences, Glasgow, 1981-84; Senior Registrar in Pathology, Western Infirmary, Glasgow, 1984-89. Recreations: bibliomania; Celtology. Address: (h.) 8 Calderwood Road, Newlands, Glasgow G43 2RP.

McLellan, James Alexander, LLB. Chief Executive, Argyll and Bute Council, since 1995 (Director of Administration, Argyll and Bute District Council, 1978-95); b. 23.12.50, Lochgilphead; m., Alexis; 2 s.; 1 d. Educ. Keil School; Glasgow University. Recreations: fishing; gardening. Address: (b.) Kilmory, Lochgilphead, Argyll PA31 8RT; T.-01546 602127.

Maclennan, Professor Alexander Hope, BSc, PhD, PGCE, CChem, FRSC. Director of Corporate Communications, University of Paisley, since 1996; b. 17.3.53, Glasgow; m., Alison. Educ. Bellahouston Academy; Paisley College of Technology. Research and Development Chemist, CIBA Geigy, 1979; Development Chemist, Glaxo, 1983; Paisley College: Lecturer in Organic Chemistry, 1985, CATS Co-ordinator, Credit Accumulation and Transfer Scheme, 1990, Director, CATS Unit, 1991; Director of CATS and Continuing Education, University of Paisley, 1993; Head, Department of Continuing Education, 1995. Recreations: golf; curling; wine. Address: (b.) University of Paisley, Paisley PA1 2BE; T.-0141-848 3730.

MacLennan, David Peter Hugh, LLB (Hons), WS, NP. Vice-President, Scottish Law Agents Society, since 1995; Secretary, Edinburgh Legal Dispensary, since 1988; Member, Advisory Council on Messengers-at-Arms and Sheriff Officers, since 1993; b. 6.9.47, Edinburgh; m., Joan Isobel; 2 s.; 1 d. Educ. Edinburgh Academy; Edinburgh University. Apprentice Solicitor/Assistant Solicitor, 1969-73; admitted as a Solicitor, 1971; Assistant Solicitor/Partner, Balfour & Manson, Edinburgh, since 1973; Solicitor to the Society of Messengers-at-Arms and Sheriff

Officers; Elder, Gorgie Parish Church, and Member, Edinburgh Presbytery; Director, Edinburgh City Mission; Member, Westray Buildings Preservation Trust; Honorary Member, Clan Gregor Society. Recreations: hill-walking; swimming; cycling; genealogy; enjoying the county of Sutherland. Address: (b.) 54-66 Frederick Street, Edinburgh EH2 1LS; T.-0131-200 1215.

Maclennan, Professor Duncan, CBE, MA, MPhil. Mactaggart Professor of Land Economics and Finance, Glasgow University; Director, ESRC Cities Programme; Member, Board, Scottish Homes; b. 12.3.49, Glasgow; 1 s.; 1 d. Educ. Allan Glen's Secondary School; Glasgow University. Lecturer in Applied Economics, Glasgow University, 1974-76; Lecturer in Political Economy, Aberdeen University, 1976-78; Lecturer in Applied Economics, Glasgow University, 1979-82. Address: (b.) Department of Urban Studies, 25 Bute Gardens, Glasgow; T.-0141-330 4615.

Maclennan, Rt. Hon. Robert Adam Ross, PC. MP (Lib. Dem.), Caithness, Sutherland and Easter Ross; Lib. Dem. President and Spokesman on Constitutional Affairs, National Heritage and Broadcasting; Barrister-at-Law; b. 26.6.36, Glasgow; m., Helen Cutter Noyes; 2 s.; 1 d. Educ. Glasgow Academy; Balliol College, Oxford; Trinity College, Cambridge; Columbia University, New York. Parliamentary Private Secretary to Secretary of State for Commonwealth Affairs, 1967; Opposition Spokesman on Scottish Affairs and Defence, 1970; Parliamentary Under-Secretary of State, Department of Prices and Consumer Protection, 1974-79; Opposition Spokesman on Foreign Affairs, 1979; Member, Public Accounts Committee, since 1979; Founder Member, SDP, 1981; Parliamentary Spokesman on Agriculture, 1981, Home Affairs, 1983, Economic Affairs, 1987; elected Leader, SDP, 1987; Recreations: music; theatre; visual arts. Address: (b.) House of Commons, London SW1A 0AA; T.-0171-219 6553.

MacLennan, Professor William Jardine, MD, FRCP, FRCPEdin, FRCPGlas. Professor of Geriatric Medicine, Edinburgh University, 1986-96; Honorary Consultant Physician in Geriatric Medicine, Lothian Health Board, 1986-96; b. 11.2.41, Glasgow; m., Fiona Hannah Campbell; 2 s. Educ. Hutchesons' Boys' Grammar School; Glasgow University. House Physician, Stobhill Hospital, Glasgow, 1964; Hansen Research Scholar, then Assistant Lecturer, then Lecturer, Department of Materia Medica, Glasgow University, 1965-69; Senior Registrar in Geriatric Medicine, Stobhill General Hospital and Glasgow Western Infirmary, 1969-71; Senior Lecturer in Geriatric Medicine, Southampton University, 1971-80; Senior Lecturer, then Reader in Geriatric Medicine, Dundee University, 1980-86; Member of Trustees, Dementia Services Development Centre. Publications: books on clinical care of the elderly, drugs in the elderly and bone disease in the elderly, metabolic and endocrine disorders in the elderly, infections in elderly patients. Recreations: hill-walking; ship-modelling; playing classical guitar badly. Address: (h.) 26 Caiystane Avenue, Fairmilehead, Edinburgh; T.-0131-445 1755.

MacLeod, Ally; b. 1931, Glasgow. Played for Third Lanark, St. Mirren, Blackburn, Hibernian, Ayr United; Manager, Ayr United, Aberdeen, Motherwell, Airdrie, Queen of the South; led Scotland to World Cup, Argentina, 1978.

MacLeod, Andrew Kenneth, BA. Head, Skills and Lifelong Learning Division, Scottish Office Education and Industry Department; b. 28.3.50, Elgin; m., Sheila Janet; 2 d. Educ. Fettes College, Edinburgh; St. John's College, Oxford. Nuffield College, Oxford, 1971-74; National Economic Development Office, 1974-78; Economic Adviser, Manpower Services Commission, Office for Scotland, 1978-83; Economic Adviser/Principal, Scottish

Office, 1983-90; Head, Fisheries Division III, 1990-91; Chief Executive, Scottish Fisheries Protection Agency, 1991-95. Address: (b.) Victoria Quay, Leith, Edinburgh EH6 6QQ; T.-0131-244 0812.

MacLeod, Archibald, OBE, NDA, NDD. Member: Scottish Advisory Committee, RSPB, since 1993, Red Deer Commission, 1989-95; b. 23.3.28, Kames, Argyll; m., Sheena Fleming Ferguson; 2 s.; 1 s deceased. Educ. Greenock High School; West of Scotland Agricultural College. Research Assistant, West of Scotland Agricultural College, 1949-53; Officer-in-Charge, Lephinmore Research Farm, Hill Farming Research Organisation, 1953-56; Senior Adviser (North Argyll), West of Scotland Agricultural College, 1956-66; Head of Advisory Services, Argyll Area, 1966-86. Chairman, Crofters Commission, 1986-89; Past President: Oban Rotary Club, Oban Speakers Club; founder Chairman, West Cowal YFC; Honorary Vice-President, Lorn Agricultural Society. Recreations: curling; gardening; reading. Address: (h.) Glendale, 24 Brinckman Terrace, Westhill, Inverness IV1 2BL.

MacLeod, Calum Alexander, CBE, MA, LLB, LLD. Chairman: Grampian Television, since 1993, Grampian Health Board, since 1993, Britannia Building Society, since 1994, Abtrust Scotland Investment Company PLC, since 1986, Albyn of Stonehaven Ltd., since 1973; Deputy Chairman: Scottish Eastern Investment Trust plc, since 1988, Scottish Media Group plc, since 1997; Director: Bradstock Group PLC, since 1994, Macdonald Hotels plc, since 1995, Scotia Holdings PLC, since 1997; Aberdeen Board Member, Bank of Scotland, since 1980; b. 25.7.35, Stornoway; m., Elizabeth M. Davidson; 2 s.; 1 d. Educ. Nicolson Institute; Glenurquhart High School; Aberdeen University. Partner, Paull & Williamsons, Advocates, Aberdeen, 1964-80; Member, White Fish Authority, 1973-80; Member: North of Scotland Hydro-Electric Board, 1976-84, Highlands and Islands Development Board, 1984-91; Chancellor's Assessor, Aberdeen University, 1979-90; Chairman of Governors, Robert Gordon's College, 1981-94; Chairman, Scottish Council of Independent Schools, 1991-97. Recreations: golf; motoring; hill-walking; reading; music. Address: (b.) Grampian Television, Queen's Cross, Aberdeen AB15 4XJ; T.-01224 846600.

Macleod, Rev. Professor Donald, MA. Professor of Systematic Theology, Free Church College, since 1978; Editor, The Monthly Record, 1977-90; Vagrant Preacher, since 1978; b. 24.11.40, Ness, Isle of Lewis; m., Mary Maclean; 3 s. Educ. Nicolson Institute, Stornoway; Glasgow University; Free Church College. Ordained Guy Fawkes Day, 1964; Minister: Kilmallie Free Church, 1964-70, Partick Highland Free Church, Glasgow, 1970-78. Recreations: dreaming about cricket, fishing and gardening; Gaelic music.

Macleod, Donald Angus David, MB, ChB, FRCS Edin, FRCPEdin, DipSpMed, FISM. Consultant General Surgeon, since 1976; b. 4.3.41, Selkirk; m., Lucile Janette Kirkpatrick; 1 s.; 2 d. Educ. Gordonstoun; Edinburgh University. Chairman, Lothian Health Board Basic Surgical Training Committee, 1986-91; Director of Studies (Surgery), Edinburgh Postgraduate Board for Medicine, 1976-86; Chairman: Scottish Committee, Medical Commission for Accident Prevention, 1980-85, West Lothian Medical Staff Committee, 1986-89; Member, West Lothian Unit Management Team, 1987-89; Hon. Medical Adviser, Scottish Rugby Union, since 1969; Member, International Rugby Football Board Medical Advisory Committee, since 1978; Vice-Chairman, Medical Advisory Committee, 13th Commonwealth Games, Scotland, 1984-86; Chairman, Sports Medicine and Sports Science Consultative Group, Scottish Sports Council, 1990-93; Associate Post Graduate Dean, Lister Post Graduate Institute, since 1993; Councillor, Royal College of Surgeons of Edinburgh, since 1992; Chairman,

Intercollegiate Board for General Surgery, UK and Ireland, 1995-98, Intercollegiate Basic Surgical Training and Examinations Committee, UK and Ireland, 1996-99; Member, Intercollegiate Academic Board for Sport and Exercise Medicine, UK, since 1996; awarded Robert Atkins Award for services to sports medicine, 1992. Recreation: orienteering. Address: (h.) The Haining, Woodlands Park, Livingston, West Lothian EH54 8AT.

MacLeod, Donald Ian Kerr, RD—, MA, LLB, WS. Partner, Shepherd & Wedderburn, WS, since 1964; b. 19.4.37, Edinburgh; m., Mary St. Clair Bridge; 1 s.; 2 d. Educ. Aberdeen Grammar School; Aberdeen University, Edinburgh University. Apprentice, MacPherson & Mackay, WS, 1957-60; Assistant, Shepherd & Wedderburn, 1960-64; Solicitor in Scotland to HM Customs and Excise and Department for Education and Employment, since 1970, and Health and Safety Executive, since 1974. Lt.-Cdr. RNR (Retd.); Member, Court of Session Rules Council; Governor, Rannoch School; Church Elder. Recreations: hockey; golf; walking. Address: (b.) Saltire Court, Castle Terrace, Edinburgh EH1 2ET; T.-0131-228 9900.

MacLeod, Duncan James, CBE. Director, Scottish Provident Institution, since 1976; Chairman, Scottish Industrial Development Advisory Board, since 1989 (Director, since 1980); b. 1.11.34, Edinburgh; m., Joanna Bibby; 2 s.; 1 d. Educ. Eton College. Partner, Brown, Fleming and Murray, Glasgow (now Ernst and Young), 1960; Managing Partner, Ernst and Whinney, Glasgow, 1985-89; Director: Harry Ramsden Plc, since 1989, Motherwell Bridge Holdings Ltd., since 1990, Hunterston Development Co. Ltd., since 1983, Macleod Hotels Ltd., since 1960, de Jersey Co. Ltd., since 1991. Recreations: golf; shooting; fishing. Address: Monkredding House, Kilwinning; T.-01294 552336.

McLeod, Iain Alasdair. Assistant Director of Finance, Scottish Office, since 1995; b. 28.9.44, Glasgow. Educ. Allan Glen's School. Ministry of Social Security, 1968-70; Department of Trade and Industry, 1970-75; Scottish Office, SEPD, Glasgow, 1975-78; Glasgow District Council (on secondment), 1978-80; Scottish Development Department, 1980-85; Scottish Office Finance Group, since 1985. Address: (b.) Victoria Quay, Edinburgh EH6 6QQ.

MacLeod, Professor Iain Alasdair, BSc, PhD, CEng, FICE, FIStructE. Professor of Structural Engineering, Strathclyde University, since 1981; b. 4.5.39, Glasgow; m., Barbara Jean Booth; 1 s.; 1 d. Educ. Lenzie Academy; Glasgow University. Design Engineer, Crouch and Hogg, Glasgow, 1960-62; Assistant Lecturer in Civil Engineering, Glasgow University, 1962-66; Design Engineer, H.A. Simons Ltd., Vancouver, 1966-67; Structural Engineer, Portland Cement Association, Illinois, 1968-69; Lecturer in Civil Engineering, Glasgow University, 1969-73; Professor and Head, Department of Civil Engineering, Paisley College of Technology, 1973-81; Chairman, Scottish Branch, Institution of Structural Engineers, 1985-86; Vice-President, Institution of Structural Engineers, 1989-90; Member, Standing Committee on Structural Safety, 1989-97. Recreations: climbing; sailing. Address: (b.) Department of Civil Engineering, Strathclyde University, 107 Rottenrow, Glasgow; T.-0141-548 3275.

Macleod, Ian Buchanan, BSc, MB, ChB, FRCSEdin. Honorary Secretary, Royal College of Surgeons of Edinburgh, 1993-96; Consultant Surgeon, Royal Infirmary, Edinburgh, 1969-93; Honorary Senior Lecturer, Department of Clinical Surgery, Edinburgh University, 1969-93; Surgeon to the Queen in Scotland, 1987-93; b. 20.5.33, Wigan; m., Kathleen Gillean Large; 1 s.; 1 d. Educ. Wigan Grammar School; Edinburgh University. House Surgeon and House Physician, Royal Infirmary, Edinburgh, 1957-59; National Service, RAMC, Malaya, Singapore, Nepal, 1959-61; appointments, Department of Clinical Surgery,

Edinburgh University and Royal Infirmary, Edinburgh, since 1961. Editor, Journal, Royal College of Surgeons of Edinburgh, 1982-87. Publications: Principles and Practice of Surgery (Co-author), 1985, 1989, 1995; Farquharson's Text Book of Operative Surgery (Contributor), 1986; Companion to Medical Studies (Contributor), 1981, 1985. Recreations: golf; photography. Address: (h.) Derwent House, 32 Cramond Road North, Edinburgh EH4 6JE; T.-0131-336 1541.

Macleod, Iseabail Campbell, MA. Editorial Director, Scottish National Dictionary Association Ltd., since 1986; b. 27.5.36, Glasgow. Educ. Clydebank High School; Lenzic Academy; Glasgow University. Teacher, 1958-64; Editorial Assistant, Europa Publications, 1965-66; Editor of bilingual dictionaries, Collins, Glasgow, 1966-74; Dictionaries Editor, Editorial Director, W. & R. Chambers, Edinburgh, 1974-77. Publications: Pocket Guide to Scottish Words, 1986; Pocket Scots Dictionary (Co-Editor), 1988; Scots Thesaurus (Co-Editor), 1990; Concise English-Scots Dictionary (Co-Editor), 1993; Scots School Dictionary (Co-Editor), 1996; Edinburgh Pocket Guide, 1996. Recreations: hill-walking; cooking; languages; music. Address: (h.) 11 Scotland Street, Edinburgh EH3 6PU; T.-0131-556 5683.

Macleod, Professor James Summers, LLM, CA, FTII. Partner, Ernst & Young, Edinburgh, since 1973; Professor, Department of Accountancy, Edinburgh University, since 1986; Member, Scottish Industrial Development Advisory Board, since 1996; b. 3.8.41, Dumfries; m., Sheila Stromier; 2 s.; 1 d. Educ. Dumfries Academy; Glasgow University. Lecturer, Edinburgh University, 1965-68; Lecturer, Heriot Watt University, 1968-71; joined Arthur Young (now Ernst & Young), 1971. Publications: Taxation of Insurance Business (Co-author), 3rd edition, 1992; 200 papers. Recreations: bridge; music; reading. Address: (h.) 2 Bonaly Road, Edinburgh; T.-0131-441 4144.

MacLeod of MacLeod, John. 29th Chief of Clan MacLeod; b. 10.8.35; m.; 1 s.; 1 d. Educ. Eton. Address: Dunvegan Castle, Isle of Skye.

Macleod, John Alasdair Johnston, DL, FRCGP, DCH, DObsRCOG. General Practitioner, North Uist, since 1973; Secretary, Western Isles Local Medical Committee (GP), 1977-91; Deputy Lieutenant, Western Isles, since 1979; b. 20.1.35, Stornoway; m., Lorna Jean Ferguson; 2 s.; 1 d. Educ. Nicolson Institute; Keil School; Glasgow University. National Service, Royal Navy, 1957-59; hospital posts, Glasgow and London, 1963-73; Non-Executive Director, Olscot Ltd., 1969-93; trainer in general practice, 1975-95; Visiting Professor, Department of Family Medicine, University of North Carolina, 1985; Member, World Organisation of National Colleges Academique of Family Practice, since 1989 (Member, WONCA World Group "Recruitment for Rural Practice", since 1992); Member, General Practitioner Writers Association, since 1986. Member, Committee of North Uist Highland Gathering; Fellow, Royal Society of Medicine; Admiralty Surgeon and Agent, 1974-91; author of papers and articles, singly and jointly, on aspects of isolated practice. Recreations: boating; horticulture; photography; time-sharing. Address: (h.) Tigh-Na-Hearradh, Lochmaddy, Isle of North Uist HS6 5AE; T.-01876 500224.

Macleod, John Francis Matheson, MA, LLB, NP. Solicitor in Inverness, 1959-94; b. 24.1.32, Inverness; m., Alexandra Catherine; 1 s. Educ. Inverness Royal Academy; George Watson's College; Edinburgh University. Solicitor, Fife County Council, 1957-59; in private practice, 1959-94; Parliamentary candidate (Liberal): Moray and Nairn, 1964, Western Isles, 1966; Chairman, Highland Region, Scottish Liberal Party, until 1978; former Vice-Chairman, Broadcasting Council for Scotland; Dean, Faculty of Solicitors of the Highlands, 1988-91; Chairman, Crofters Commission, 1978-86; Member, Council, Law Society of

Scotland, 1988-92; Chairman of Council, Gaelic Society of Inverness, 1996-97. Address: (h.) Bona Lodge, Aldourie, Inverness; T.-01463 751327.

Macleod, John Murray, MA. Freelance Journalist and Broadcaster; b. 15.4.66, Kilmallie, Inverness-shire. Educ. Jordanhill College School, Glasgow; James Gillespie's High School, Edinburgh; Edinburgh University. Columnist, The Herald and The Scotsman, 1989-92; Columnist/Writer-at-large, The Herald, since 1992; also writer of interviews/profiles. Scottish Journalist of the Year, 1991; Young Scottish Journalist of the Year, 1991-92; Commended, Columnist of the Year, 1992; Commended, Feature Writer of the Year, 1996; Columnist of the Year, UK Press Gazette Regional Newspaper Awards, 1996. Recreations: beach-combing; corresponding; photography; poaching; applied Free Presbyterianism. Address: (h.) Twin Peaks, Scott Road, Harris, Western Isles HS3 3DL; T.-01859 50 2187.

MacLeod, Lorne Buchanan, BA, CA. Chief Executive, Skye and Lochalsh Enterprise, since 1992; b. 13.4.63, Oban. Educ. Oban High School; University of Strathclyde. Trainee Chartered Accountant, Ernst and Whinney, Inverness, 1983-87; Highlands and Islands Development Board, 1987-92. Member: An Comunn Gaidhealach, Scottish Crofters Union, Talisker Quality Awards Trust. Recreations: hillwalking; sailing; Gaelic music and culture. Address: (b.) King's House, The Green, Portree, Isle of Skye; T.-01478 612841.

MacLeod, Professor Emeritus Malcolm, MD (Hons), FRCPEdin. Professor Emeritus in Renal Medicine, Aberdeen University; b. 9.12.16, Glasgow; m., Elizabeth Shaw Ritchie; 1 s. Educ. Nicolson Institute, Stornoway; Aberdeen University. Military Service, Africa, India, SE Asia, 1940-46 (Medical Specialist, RAMC); Lecturer, Senior Lecturer, Reader in Medicine, 1947-80; Personal Professor in Renal Medicine, Aberdeen University, 1981; Honorary Consultant Physician, Aberdeen Royal Infirmary, 1955-82 and Honorary Consultant in charge, Medical Renal Unit, 1966-82; President, Scottish Society of Physicians, 1980. Recreation: natural history. Address: (h.) 76 Hamilton Place, Aberdeen AB15 5BA; T.-01224 635537.

McLeod, Professor Malcolm Donald, MA, BLitt (Oxon), FRSE. Director, Hunterian Museum and Art Gallery, Glasgow University, since 1990; Chairman, Scottish Museums Council, since 1996; b. 19.5.41, Edinburgh; m., I.V. Barry; 2 s.; 1 d. Educ. Birkenhead School; Hertford and Exeter Colleges, Oxford. Research Assistant, Institute of Social Anthropology, Oxford, 1964-65; Lecturer, Sociology Department, University of Ghana, 1967-69; Assistant Curator, Museum of Archaeology and Ethnology, Cambridge, 1969-74; College Lecturer and Director of Studies, Magdalene and Girton Colleges, Cambridge, 1969-74; Fellow, Magdalene College, 1972-74; Keeper of Ethnography, British Museum, 1974-90; Honorary Lecturer, Department of Anthropology, UCL, 1976-81; Honorary Lecturer, Department of Archaeology, University of Glasgow, since 1992. Publications: The Asante, 1981; Treasures of African Art, 1981; Ethnic Sculpture (Co-author), 1985; Jacob Epstein Collector (Co-author), 1989. Address: (h.) Mossfennan, Bowden, Melrose, TD6 0ST; 13 Kirklee Terrace, Glasgow G12 8QQ.

Macleod, Murdoch, MBE, JP. Honorary Sheriff; b. 11.8.32, Shawbost, Isle of Lewis; m., Crisybil; 1 s.; 1 d. Educ. Nicolson Institute, Stornoway. Ross and Cromarty Council: Highways Department, 1955-57, Education Department, 1957-65; Stornoway Town Council: Town Clerk's Department, 1965-68, Town Clerk, 1968-75; General Manager, Secretary and Treasurer, Stornoway Pier and Harbour Commission, 1975-96. Former Deputy Chairman, Transport Users Consultative Committee for Scotland; Past Chairman, District Courts Association;

Chairman, Western Isles Justices Committee; former Member, Council, British Ports Asssociation; former Chairman, Scottish Port Members, British Ports Association; Director, Western Isles Development Fund Ltd.; Honorary President, Lewis Pipe Band; former Member, British Airways Consumer Council for Highlands and Islands; Chairman, League of Friends, Stornoway Hospitals and Homes. Recreation: reading. Address: (h.) 46 Barony Square, Stornoway, Isle of Lewis; T.-01851 703024.

MacLeod, Sheriff Principal Norman Donald, QC, MA, LLB. Sheriff Principal of Glasgow and Strathkelvin, since 1986; Commissioner of Northern Lighthouses, since 1986; b. 6.3.32, Perth; m., Ursula Jane Bromley; 2 s.; 2 d. Educ. Mill Hill School; George Watson's Boys College; Edinburgh University; Hertford College, Oxford. Called to the Bar, 1956; District Officer and Crown Counsel, Colonial Service, East Africa, 1957-63; at the Bar, 1963-67; Sheriff at Glasgow, 1967-86. Recreation: rustic pursuits. Address: (b.) 1 Carlton Place, Glasgow G5 9DA; T.-0141-429 8888.

McLeod, Norman Duff, FCCA. Group Finance Director, Low & Bonar PLC, since 1990; b. 2.8.51, Dundee; m., Alison; 1 s.; 1 d. Educ. Grove Academy, Dundee. Henderson & Loggie, CAs, Dundee, 1968-77; Bonar Long Ltd., 1977-84, latterly as Finance Director and Company Secretary; Low & Bonar PLC, since 1984. Recreation: golf. Address: (b.) Bonar House, Faraday Street, Dundee, DD1 9JA; T.-01382 818171.

MacLeod, Peter, MCIBS. Retired Banker; yachting journalist; Honorary Sheriff, Oban, since 1988; b. 9.6.33, Ruaig, Isle of Tiree; m., Jean MacDonald Buchanan; 2 s. Educ. Oban High School. Served as Captain, Royal Signals, AER; joined Royal Bank of Scotland, 1949; Bank Manager: Tobermory, Kinlochleven, Wick, Oban. Past Commodore, Royal Highland Yacht Club. Publication: History of Royal Highland Yacht Club, 1881-1986. Recreations: sailing; island wandering; impromptu ceilidhs; beachcombing. Address: (h.) The Wheelhouse, Ganavan, Oban, Argyll; T.-01631 563577.

MacLeod, Rev. Roderick, MA (Hons), BD, PhD (Edin), PhD (Open). Minister, Cumlodden, Lochfyneside and Lochgair, Argyll, since 1985; b. 24.6.41, Lochmaddy. Educ. Paible Secondary School; Portree High School; Edinburgh University. Minister, Berneray, North Uist, 1966-85; Member: Western Isles Islands Council, 1974-82, Western Isles Health Board, 1975-79; Clerk, Uist Presbytery, 1981-85; Mackinnon Memorial Lecturer, Cape Breton College, 1979; Visiting Scholar, Harvard Divinity School, 1981; Editor, Gaelic Supplement, Life and Work, since 1980; Depute Clerk, Presbytery of South Argyll, since 1995; President, Scottish Gaelic Texts Society, since 1996; Founder, Cruisgean (Gaelic newspaper); author of several Gaelic books; writes and broadcasts on Highland affairs in Gaelic and English. Recreations: walking; shinty. Address: Furnace, Inveraray, Argyll, PA32 8XU.

MacLeod, Roderick John, LLB (Hons). Advocate; Member, Broadcasting Council for Scotland, since 1992; b. 7.12.52, Skye; m., Lorna Jane Robertson. Educ. Portree High School; Edinburgh University. Research Assistant, BBC Scotland, 1976-78; Solicitor, 1979-93. Director, Highland Fund Ltd.; former Chairman, Club Gniomhachas nan Gaidheal; Founder Director, Comunn na Gaidhlig. Recreations: Gaelic literature; reading; cycling; football. Address: (h.) 19 South Oswald Road, Edinburgh EH9 2HQ; T.-0131-667 2829.

McLernan, Sheriff Kieran Anthony, KHS, MA, LLB. Sheriff of Grampian Highlands and Islands at Banff and Peterhead, since 1991; b. 29.4.41, Wemyss Bay; m., Joan Doherty; 1 s.; 3 d. Educ. St. Aloysius College, Glasgow;

Glasgow University. Solicitor, 1965-91; Temporary Sheriff, 1986-91; Tutor, Glasgow University, 1987-91. Recreations: golf; hockey; skiing. Address: (h.) Peockstone Farm, Lochwinnoch, Renfrewshire; T.-01505 842128.

McLetchie, David William, LLB (Hons), WS. Solicitor, since 1976; Vice Chairman, Scottish Conservative and Unionist Party, since 1997; b. 6.8.52, Edinburgh; m., Barbara Gemmell Baillie (deceased); 1 s. Educ. George Heriot's School; Edinburgh University. Solicitor, Tods Murray WS, 1976-80; Partner, Tods Murray WS, since 1980. President, Scottish Conservative and Unionist Association, 1994-97. Recreations: golf; football (Heart of Midlothian); rock and pop music. Address: (h.) 13 Keith Crescent, Edinburgh EH4 3NH; T.-0131-332 4691.

McLuskie, Norman Cardie, CA. Managing Director, Operations Division, Royal Bank of Scotland, since 1990; Group Executive Director, Royal Bank of Scotland, since 1992; b. 23.8.44, Uddingston; m., Anne Gibb; 1 s.; 2 d. Educ. Kings Park School, Glasgow. Qualified with Touche Ross & Co., 1969; various senior executive positions; joined Royal Bank of Scotland plc as Management Accountant, 1982; appointed: Assistant General Manager, Group Management and Cost Accounting, 1985, Group Controller, Management Accounting, 1986, Assistant Director, Finance, 1988. Director, IBOS Limited, Tesco Personal Finance Ltd., RBS Cards Ltd.; Chairman: BACS Ltd, RoyScot Financial Services Limited, RBS Advanta; Deputy Chairman, APACS. Recreations: golf; travel. Address: (b.) 42 St. Andrew Square, Edinburgh EH2 2YE; T.-0131-523 2415.

McMahon, Hugh Robertson, MA (Hons). Member (Labour), European Parliament, Strathclyde West, since 1984; b. 17.6.38, Saltcoats; m., Helen Paterson Grant; 1 s.; 1 d. Educ. Stevenston High School; Ardrossan Academy; Glasgow University. Schoolteacher in Ayrshire (Largs High, Stevenston High, Irvine Royal Academy, Mainholm Academy); Assistant Head, Ravenspark Academy, 1971-84. Vice-Chair, EP Social Affairs, Employment and Working Environment Committee, 1992-94; Member, Social Affairs, Fisheries and Transport Committees; Chair, EP Delegation with Norway, 1989-92; currently Member, Delegation with Hungary. Recreation: golf. Address: (b.) Euro Office, 9 Low Road, Paisley PA2 6AQ.

MacMahon, Rev. Janet P.H., BD, MSc, LCST, LLCM. Chaplaincy Co-ordinator, Southern General Hospital, Glasgow, since 1992; b. 31.5.44, Glasgow; m..., Professor M.K.C. MacMahon (qv); 1 s.; 1 d. Educ. Glasgow High School for Girls; Glasgow University; Glasgow School of Speech Therapy. Senior Speech Therapist, 1965-80; Chief Speech Therapist, 1980-82; Senior Speech Therapist, Scottish Council for Spastics, 1983-85; Assistant Minister, Cairns Church, Milngavie, and Govan Old Church, 1989-90; Research and Development Officer in special educational needs, Department of Education, Church of Scotland, 1990-92. Publications include: Walk in God's Ways, 1993. Recreations: reading crime novels; watching TV soaps. Address: (h.) 6 Jubilee Gardens, Bearsden, Glasgow G61 2RT; T.-0141-942 3671.

MacMahon, Professor Michael Kenneth Cowan, BA, PhD, DipLing. Professor of Phonetics, Glasgow University, since 1977; b. 7.8.43, Winchester; m., Rev. Janet P.H. MacMahon (qv); 1 s.; 1 d. Educ. Hymers College, Hull; Durham University; Gottingen University; Glasgow University; Reading University. Lecturer in Phonetics and Linguistics, Jordanhill College, Glasgow, 1966-72; Lecturer in Linguistics and Phonetics, 1972-83, Lecturer in English Language, 1983-87, Senior Lecturer in English Language, 1987-97, Glasgow University. Member, Council, Phonetic Association; Member, Executive Committee, Henry Sweet Society; Archivist and Secretary, British Association of Academic Phoneticians. Publications include: Basic

Phonetics. Recreations: singing; playing the flute. Address: (h.) 6 Jubilee Gardens, Bearsden, Glasgow G61 2RT; T.-0141-942 3671.

MacMahon, Peter, BSc (Hons). Scottish Political Editor, The Scotsman, since 1995; b. 31.7.59, Dublin; m., Seonag MacKinnon; 2 s.; 1 d. Educ. St. Augustine's High School, Edinburgh; St. Andrews University. Reporter, Cambrian News Agency, Cardiff; Reporter, Northampton Chronicle and Echo; Political Correspondent, Central Press Features, Westminster; Political Correspondent, Daily Star; Westminster Editor, Scotland on Sunday; Political Editor, Sunday Mirror. Recreations: music; sport. Address: (b.) 20 North Bridge, Edinburgh EH1 1YT; T.-0131-225 2468.

McManus, James. Commissioner, Scottish Prisons Complaints Commission. Address: (b.) Government Buildings, Broomhouse Drive, Edinburgh EH11 3XD. T.-0131-244 8423.

McManus, Professor John, DSc, PhD, ARCS, DIC, FRSE, CGeol, MIEnvSci. Professor of Geology, St. Andrews University, since 1993 (Reader, 1988-93); Honorary Director, Tay Estuary Research Centre, 1979-92; b. 5.6.38, Harwich; m., J. Barbara Beveridge; 2 s.; 1 d. Educ. Harwich County High School; Imperial College, London University. Assistant, then Lecturer, St. Andrews University, 1964-67; Lecturer, Senior Lecturer, Reader, Dundee University, 1967-88; UNESCO Representative, International Commission on Continental Erosion, 1980-84 and 1986; Member: Scottish Natural Heritage East Areas Board and Scientific Advisory Committee, Secretary of State's Committee on Waste Discharges into the Marine Environment; President, Estuarine and Brackish Water Sciences Association, 1995-98; Member, Eden Estuary Nature Reserve Management Committee; former Treasurer, British Sedimentological Research Group; Consultant on Coastal Erosion and Protection to four Regional Councils; Executive Editor, Transactions of the Royal Society of Edinburgh, Earth Sciences, 1988-95; Associate Editor, Continental Shelf Research. President: Cupar Choral Association, 1968-78, Cupar Amateur Opera, 1979-91. Recreations: music; bird-watching; swimming; stamp collecting. Address: (b.) School of Geography and Geology, Purdie Building, St. Andrews University, St. Andrews, Fife KY16 9ST.

McManus, Rev. Matthew Francis. Parish Priest, Kilwinning; b. 22.9.40, Rutherglen. Educ. Sacred Heart High School, Girvan; St. Andrew's College, Drygrange. Ordained, 1965, Assistant Priest, St. Margaret's, Ayr; Parish Priest, New Cumnock, Kirkconnel and Sanquhar, 1976-81, Kirkcudbright, 1981-88; Chairman: Dumfries and Galloway Local Health Council, 1985-87, Castle Douglas District CAB, 1984-87, Stewartry Council of Voluntary Service, 1985-88, Stewartry School Council, 1985-87; Member, Scottish Consumer Council, 1983-90; Convenor, Association of Scottish Local Health Councils, 1983-92; Complaints Reporter, Law Society of Scotland, 1985-97; Secretary, Association of Vocations Directors of Scotland, 1987-96; Member, Ayrshire and Arran Health Council, 1988-97; Non-Executive Director, Ayshire and Arran Health Board, since 1996; Member, North Ayrshire Education Committee, since 1996; Acting Chair, Minerva Housing Association, since 1996. Address: St. Winin's, St. Winning's Lane, Kilwinning KA13 6EP; T.-Kilwinning 552276.

McMaster, Brian John, CBE. Director and Chief Executive, Edinburgh International Festival, since 1991; b. 9.5.43. General Administrator, subsequently Managing Director, W.N.O., 1976-91. Address: (b.) 21 Market Street, Edinburgh, EH1 1BW.

McMath, Katherine Sally, MCSP. Scottish Chief Commissioner, The Guide Association, since 1997; b.

29.10.53, Edinburgh; m., Robert Patrick John McMath; 1 s.; 1 d. Educ. Lansdowne House School, Edinburgh; School of Physiotherapy, Royal Infirmary, Edinburgh. Chartered Physiotherapist. County Commissioner, West Lothian Guide Association, 1990-96; Scottish Guide Public Relations Adviser, 1987-90. Recreations: choral singing; music; badminton; tennis. Address: (b.) Scottish Guide HQ, 16 Coates Crescent, Edinburgh EH3 7AH; T.-0131-226 4511.

McMicking, Major David John, LVO, MSc. Consultant, Human Resources/Sporting, since 1986; b. 29.4.39, Jerusalem; m., Janetta; 1 s.; 1 d. Educ. Eton; RMA, Sandhurst; Strathclyde University. Career soldier, Black Watch, rising to rank of Major; left Army, 1973; executive positions, John Menzies Holdings Ltd., 1973-86; family farming interests, since 1996. Extra Equerry, Queen Elizabeth The Queen Mother; Chairman, Officers Association Scotland; Earl Haig Fund: Chairman, North, South and East Scotland, for 15 years an Executive Member and Chairman, Investment Committee; Secretary, Friends of St. Andrew's, Jerusalem. Recreation: field sports. Address: (b.) 10 Albert Terrace, Edinburgh EH10 5EA; T.-0131-447 6192.

MacMillan, Emeritus Professor Andrew, OBE, RSA, MA, FRIAS, RIBA. Emeritus Professor, University of Glasgow, since 1994; Professor of Architecture and Head, Mackintosh School of Architecture, Glasgow University, 1973-94; b. 11.12.28, Glasgow; m., Angela Lillian McDowell; 1 s.; 3 d. Educ. North Kelvinside Secondary School; Glasgow School of Architecture. Glasgow Corporation, 1945-52; East Kilbride Development Corporation, 1952-54; joined Gillespie Kidd & Coia, 1954 (Partner, 1966); has served as a Member of: CNAA Architecture Board, ARCUK Board of Architectural Education, Scottish Arts Council WASPS Board, GIA Education Committee; Vice President for Education, RIBA; Vice President, Prince and Princess of Wales Hospice, 1981; RIBA Bronze Medal, 1965; RIBA Award for Architecture, four times; RSA Gold Medal, 1975; Concrete Society Award, 1978; Carpenter Award, 1982, 1983; various Saltire Society and Civic Trust awards; Member, Forum, Scottish Churches Architectural Heritage Trust; Patron, Arts Education Trust, since 1988. Recreations: travel; sailing; water colour. Address: (b.) Mackintosh School of Architecture, Glasgow University and Glasgow School of Art, 177 Renfrew Street, Glasgow G3 6RQ.

Macmillan, Angus. Chief Executive, Western Isles Tourist Board; b. 3.12.55, Ness, Isle of Lewis; m., Isabel; 2 d. Educ. Govan High School, Glasgow. Address: (b.) 26 Cromwell Street, Stornoway HS1 2DD; T.-01851 703088.

MacMillan of MacMillan and Knop, George Gordon, MA (Cantab). Chief of Clan MacMillan; Deputy Lieutenant, Renfrewshire; b. 20.6.30, London; m., (Cecilia) Jane Spurgin; 2 s. Educ. Aysgarth School; Eton; Trinity College, Cambridge. Schoolmaster, Wellington College, 1953-63; Lecturer, Trinity College, Toronto, 1963-64; Lecturer, Bede College, Durham, 1965-74. Owner, small historic house with gardens and woods open to the public. Address: (h.) Finlaystone, Langbank, Renfrewshire PA14 6TJ; T.-01475 540285.

Macmillan, Very Rev. Gilleasbuig Iain, MA, BD. Minister, St. Giles', The High Kirk of Edinburgh, since 1973.

MacMillan, Hector. Playwright; b. 1929, Glasgow. Plays include: The Rising, 1970; The Sash, 1973.

Macmillan, Iain Alexander, CBE, LLD, BL. Sheriff of South Strathclyde, Dumfries and Galloway, at Hamilton, 1981-92; b. 14.11.23, Oban; m., Edith Janet McAulay; 2 s.; 1 d. Educ. Oban High School; Glasgow University; Scottish Commercial College. RAF (France, Germany, India), 1944-47; Solicitor (Sturrock & Co., Kilmarnock), 1952-81; Council Member, Law Society of Scotland, 1964-79 (President, 1976-77); Chairman: Lanarkshire Branch, Scottish Association for the Study of Delinquency, 1986-92, Kilmarnock Victim Support Scheme; President: Temporary Sheriffs Association, 1993-94, Glasgow Ayrshire Society. Recreations: golf; music. Address: (h.) 2 Castle Drive, Kilmarnock, Ayrshire; T.-01563 525864.

McMillan, Iain Macleod, FCIB, FCIBS, FFA, FIMgt, FRSA. Director, CBI Scotland, since 1995; Member, Board, Scottish Qualifications Authority; Chairman, Higher Still Employment and Training Group; b. 25.4.51, Glasgow; m., Guiseppina; 3 s. Educ. Bearsden Academy. Trainee Banker, 1970-76; TSB Group plc: Manager, 1976-89, Senior Manager, 1989-93; Assistant Director, CBI Scotland, 1993-95. Publications: Manufacturing Matters (Co-Author), 1994; The Challenge for Government in Scotland (principal author), 1996, Scottish Manufacturing: a shared vision (Co-author), 1997. Recreations: squash; walking. Address: (b.) Beresford House, 5 Claremont Terrace, Glasgow G3 7XT; T.-0141-332 8661.

MacMillan, James Loy, BMus, PhD. Composer and Conductor; Affiliate Composer, Scottish Chamber Orchestra, since 1990; b. 16.7.59, Kilwinning; m., Lynne; 1 s.; 2 d. Educ. Cumnock Academy; Edinburgh University; Durham University. Principal compositions: The Confession of Isobel Gowdie, London Proms, 1990; Busqueda, Edinburgh International Festival, with Diana Rigg, 1990; featured composer, Musica Nova, 1990, Huddersfield Contemporary Music Festival, 1991; Veni, Veni, Emmanuel, percussion concerto for Evelyn Glennie, London Proms, 1992; Visitatio Sepulchri, one act opera, Mayfest, 1993; Ines de Castro, for Scottish Opera, Edinburgh International Festival, 1996; Triduum, series of three orchestral works for London Symphony Orchestra, 1996-1997; featured composer, Edinburgh International Festival, 1993; recording of Tryst and The Confession of Isobel Gowdie by BBC SSO won Gramophone Award, contemporary music category, 1993; Seven Last Words, BBC TV, 1994; nominated for Mercury Music Prize, 1995. DUniv, (Paisley); DLitt (University of Strathclyde); FRASMD; HonFRIAS.

McMillan, John Boyd, BSc. Rector, Invergordon Academy, since 1986; b. 16.12.41, Irvine; m., Kathleen Miller (deceased); 2 s. Educ. Irvine Royal Academy; Glasgow University; Jordanhill College of Education. Mathematics Teacher: Irvine Royal Academy, 1964-67, Gloucester School, Hohne, 1967-72, Invergordon Academy, 1972-74; Principal Teacher of Mathematics, Thurso High School, 1974-82; Assistant Rector, Alness Academy, 1982-86; In-Service Training Co-ordinator, HRC, Inverness, 1986; Chairman, Highland Education Industry Liaison Committee, 1990-91; President: Highland Secondary Heads Association, 1988-90, Invergordon Highland Gathering, Highland Family History Society. Football Blue. Recreations: gardening; public speaking; genealogy; sailing; photography. Address: (b.) Invergordon Academy, Academy Road, Invergordon IV18 0LD; T.-0349 852362.

Macmillan, Professor (John) Duncan, MA, PhD, FRSA, HRSA. Professor of the History of Scottish Art, Edinburgh University; Curator, Talbot Rice Gallery and University Collections, Edinburgh University, since 1979; Hon. Keeper of Portraits, Royal College of Surgeons, Edinburgh; Art Critic, The Scotsman; b. 7.3.39, Beaconsfield; m., Vivien Rosemary Hinkley; 2 d. Educ. Gordonstoun School; St. Andrews University; London University; Edinburgh University. Lecturer, then Senior Lecturer, then Reader, Department of Fine Art, Edinburgh University. Chairman, Edinburgh Galleries Association. Recreation: walking. Address: (h.) 20 Nelson Street, Edinburgh; T.-0131-556 7100.

McMillan, Joyce Margaret, MA (Hons), DipEd. Journalist and Arts Critic; Arts/Political Columnist, The Herald, since 1997; b. 29.8.52, Paisley. Educ. Paisley Grammar School; St. Andrews University; Edinburgh University. Theatre Reviewer, BBC Radio Scotland and The Scotsman, 1979-81; Theatre Critic, Sunday Standard, 1981-83; Radio Critic, The Herald, 1983-95; Scottish Theatre Critic, The Guardian, 1984-93; Scotland on Sunday: Social/Political Columnist, 1989-97, Theatre Critic, 1993-97. Chair, NUJ Freelance Branch, Edinburgh; Member, National Executive Committee, NUJ, London; Chair, Scottish Constitutional Commission, 1994; Executive Member, Helsinki Citizens' Assembly, Prague. Publications: The Traverse Story, 1963-88, 1988; Charter for the Arts in Scotland, 1992. Recreations: food; drink; films; music; talking politics. Address: 8 East London Street, Edinburgh, EH7 4BH; T.-0131-557 1726.

McMillan, Michael Dale, BSc, LLB, NP. Managing Partner, Burnett & Reid, Solicitors, Aberdeen; Partner, Macdonalds Sergeants, Solicitors, East Kilbride and Glasgow, 1971-92; b. 15.2.44, Edinburgh; m., Isobel Ross Mackie; 2 s.; 1 d. Educ. Edinburgh Academy; Edinburgh University. Secretary: East Kilbride Chamber of Commerce, 1971-86, East Kilbride Chamber of Trade, 1971-92; Member, East Kilbride Development Corporation, 1979-84; Secretary, Pilgrim Legal Users' Group, 1985-92; Captain, East Kilbride Golf Club, 1979; Chairman, Strathaven Academy School Board, 1991-92; President, East Kilbride Burns Club, 1989-91; Captain, Inchmarlo Golf Club (Banchory), 1997-99. Recreations: golf; sailing; skiing. Address: (h.) Belnies, Strachan, Banchory, Aberdeenshire AB31 6LU; T.-01330 850249.

McMillan, William Alister, BL. Solicitor, since 1955; b. 19.1.34, Ayr; m., Elizabeth Anne; 3 d. Educ. Strathallan; Glasgow University. Clerk of the Peace, County of Ayr, 1974-75; Honorary Sheriff, Ayr; Governor, Strathallan School. Recreations:sailing; golf; philately. Address: (h.) Afton Lodge, Mossblown, by Ayr; T.-01292 520 710.

Macmillan, Very Rev. William Boyd Robertson, MA, BD, HonLLD (Dundee), Hon. DD (Aberdeen). Minister, Dundee Parish Church (St. Mary's), 1978-93; Extra Chaplain to The Queen in Scotland, since 1997 (Chaplain in Ordinary to The Queen, 1988-97); President, Scottish Church Society, 1993-97; b. 3.7.27, Keith; m., Mary Adams Bisset Murray. Educ. Royal High School, Edinburgh; Aberdeen University. Royal Navy, 1946-48; Aberdeen University, 1948-54 (President, SRC, 1953-54); Minister: St. Andrew's Church, Bo'ness, 1955-60, Fyvie Parish Church, 1960-67, Bearsden South Church, 1967-78. Convener, Board of Practice and Procedure, 1984-88, and of Business Committee, 1985-88, General Assembly, Church of Scotland; Moderator, General Assembly, 1991-92; Chaplain, City of Dundee District Council, 1978-93; Freeman of Dundee, 1991; Prelate, Order of St. John of Jerusalem (Scotland), 1993-96; Chairman of Directors, High School of Dundee, 1993-96; Chairman, The Murray Home for Scottish Veterans, 1994-96; Trustee, Scottish National War Memorial, since 1994; Committee Member, Royal Society for the Relief of Indigent Gentlewomen of Scotland, since 1994. Recreations: golf; reading. Address: (h.) 3/5 Craigend Park, Edinburgh EH16 5XY.

Macnab of Macnab, Hon. Mrs, DL. Honorary Vice President, Scotland's Gardens Scheme, since 1991 (Chairman, 1983-91); Chairman, East Fife Members' Centre, National Trust for Scotland; President, Central and North Fife Preservation Society; Deputy Lieutenant, Fife, since 1992; b. 6.6.36, Edinburgh; m., J.C. Macnab of Macnab (qv); 2 s.; 2 d. Address: (h.) Leuchars Castle Farmhouse, Leuchars, St. Andrews KY16 0EY; T.-01334 838777.

Macnab of Macnab, James Charles — The Macnab. Senior Consultant, Hill Samuel Investment Services Ltd., 1982-92, now retired; 23rd Chief, Clan Macnab; b. 14.4.26, London; m., Hon. Diana Mary Anstruther-Gray (see Hon. Mrs. Macnab of Macnab); 2 s.; 2 d. Educ. Radley College; Ashbury College, Ottawa. Served, RAF and Scots Guards, 1944-45; Lt., Seaforth Highlanders, 1945-48; Assistant Superintendent and Deputy Superintendent, Federation of Malaya Police Force, 1948-57; Captain, Seaforth Highlanders (TA), 1960-64; managed family estate and farms, 1957-82; County Councillor, Perth and Kinross Joint County Council, 1964-75; District Councillor, Perth, 1961-64; JP, 1968-86; Member: Central Regional Council, 1978-82, Queen's Bodyguard for Scotland (Royal Company of Archers). Address: (h.) Leuchars Castle Farmhouse, Leuchars, St. Andrews KY16 0EY; T.-01334 838777.

McNair, James Burt Oliver, BSc (Hons), DipEd. Secretary, Headteachers' Association of Scotland; b. 20.7.33, Bargeddie, Lanarkshire; m., Muriel Eadie; 1 s.; 2 d. Educ. Woodside Secondary School, Glasgow; Glasgow University. Taught, Gambia High School; Principal Teacher of Physics and Assistant Head, North Kelvinside Secondary School; Depute Head, John Street Secondary School; Head, Waverley Secondary School, 1976-92. Chairman, SED Joint Working Party on Social and Vocational Skills; Member, Scottish Examination Board; Chairman: Drumchapel Citizens' Advice Bureau, 1981-84, Scripture Union — Scotland. Publication: Basic Knowledge Physics. Address: (b.) Strathclyde University, Jordanhill Campus, Southbrae Drive, Glasgow G13 1PP.

Macnair, Terence Crawford, LLB, NP. Solicitor, since 1967; Director, Argyll and the Islands Enterprise Company, since 1996; Honorary Sheriff, North Strathclyde, since 1988; b. 16.12.42, Kingston, Jamaica; m., Ishbel Ross Hunter; 1 s. Educ. High School of Glasgow; Glasgow University. Town Clerk, Lochgilphead, 1970-75; Partner, MacArthur Stewart & Orr, 1970-81; Senior Partner, MacArthur Stewart, since 1981; Assistant Clerk, Tarbert Harbour Authority, since 1970; Clerk, Awe District Salmon Fishery Board, since 1979; President, Oban Rotary Club, 1988-89; Past Chairman, Oban Tennis and Squash Club; Secretary/Treasurer, Oban and District Licensed Trade Association, since 1977; Chairman, North Argyll Development Agency, since 1994. Recreations: tennis; squash; golf; curling; bridge; music. Address: (b.) Boswell House, Oban; T.-01631 562215.

McNally, Rt. Rev. Anthony Joseph. Rector, Gillis College, Edinburgh, since 1987; Vicar General, Archdiocese of St. Andrews and Edinburgh, since 1985; b. 27.5.32, Edinburgh. Educ. Blairs College, Aberdeen; Seminaire St. Sulpice, Paris. Ordained Priest, 1955; Assistant Priest, Methil, Fife, 1955-63; Missioner, Calabar and Bauchi Province, Nigeria, 1963-67; Assistant Priest, Bonnybridge, 1967-72; Parish Priest, Burntisland, 1972-80, St. Peter's, Morningside, 1980-85; Parish Priest, Musselburgh, and Vicar General, Archdiocese, 1985; Parish Priest, St. Columba's, Edinburgh, since 1993. Recreations: reading; walking. Address: (b.) St. Columba's, 9 Upper Gray Street, Edinburgh EH9 1SN.

McNaught, Peter Cairn, MA, MLitt, DUniv, FRSA. Principal, Craigie College of Education, Ayr, 1976-87; b. 29.5.25, Glasgow; m., Else Kristine Sandvad; 1 s.; 1 d. Educ. Hutchesons' Boys' Grammar School, Glasgow; Glasgow University. Teacher, Queen's Park and Hutchesons' Boys' Grammar Schools, Glasgow, 1952-58; Lecturer in English, Moray House College of Education, Edinburgh, 1958-60; Principal Lecturer in English, Aberdeen College of Education, 1960-61; Moray House College of Education: Senior Assistant Principal, 1961-70, Vice-Principal, 1970-75. Vice-Chairman, Scottish Council for the Validation of Courses for Teachers; Member, General Teaching Council for Scotland; Vice-Chairman,

West Sound; Chairman, STV Education Committee; Member, STV Staff Trust; Visiting Professor in English Studies, Strathclyde University, 1988; Director, Wider Access Programme, 1988-1992. Address: (h.) 1a Victoria Drive, Troon KA10 6EN; T.-01292 312200.

McNaughton, John Ewen, OBE, JP, FRAgS. Chairman, Scotch Quality Beef & Lamb Association, 1981-97; Vice President, Royal Highland and Agricultural Society of Scotland, 1997-98; Member: British Wool Marketing Board, since 1975, Panel of Agricultural Arbiters, since 1973, Red Deer Commission, 1975-92; b. 28.5.33, Edinburgh; m., Jananne Ogilvie Honeyman; 2 s.; 2 d. Educ. Cargilfield; Loretto. Born and bred a hill sheep farmer; after a short spell in America, began farming at Inverlochlarig with father; served on Council, NFU of Scotland; Elder, Church of Scotland. Recreations: yachting; stalking. Address: Inverlochlarig, Balquhidder, Lochearnhead, Perthshire FK19 8PH; T.-01877 384 232.

Macnaughton, Professor Sir Malcolm Campbell, MD, LLD, FRCPGlas, FRCOG, FFFP, FRSE, FSLCOG (Hon.), FACOG (Hon.), FRCA (Hon.), FRACOG (Hon.). Vice President, Royal College of Midwives; Professor of Obstetrics and Gynaecology, Glasgow University, 1970-90; b. 4.4.25, Glasgow; m., Margaret-Ann Galt; 2 s.; 3 d. Educ. Glasgow Academy; Glasgow University. RAMC, 1949-51; Lecturer in Obstetrics and Gynaecology, Aberdeen University, 1957-61; Senior Lecturer, St. Andrews University, 1961-66; Consultant, Eastern Regional, 1966-70. Member: Chief Scientist Committee, SHHD, Biomedical Research Committee and Health Service Research Committee, SHHD, MRC Grant Committee and Cell Systems Board, MRC, Scientific Committee, Hospital Recognition Committee, RCOG; President: RCOG, 1984-87, British Fertility Society, 1993-95; Chairman: Scottish Perinatal Mortality Advisory Group, SCOTMEG Working Party on Accident and Emergency Services in Scotland. Recreations: walking; fishing; curling. Address: (h.) 15 Boclair Road, Bearsden, Glasgow G61 2AF; T.-0141-942 1909.

McNay, W. Gordon, OBE, DL, JP, BL; b. 11.12.25, Wishaw; m., Margaret C. MacKay. Educ. Wishaw High School; Glasgow University. Depute Town Clerk, Burgh of Airdrie, 1952-53; Senior Depute Town Clerk, Burgh of Motherwell and Wishaw, 1953-63; Town Clerk, Burgh of East Kilbride, 1963-75; Chief Executive, East Kilbride District Council, 1975-88. Deputy Lieutenant, County of Lanark; Honorary Freeman, East Kilbride District. Recreations: golf; photography; philately. Address: (h.) Solbakken, 17 Kibblestane Place, Strathaven ML10 6EL; T.-01357 520889.

MacNeacail, Aonghas. Writer (poetry, journalism, scriptwriting for TV, film and radio, librettoes); b. 7.6.42, Uig, Isle of Skye; m., Gerda Stevenson (qv); 1 s. Educ. Portree High School; Glasgow University. Writing fellowships: Sabhal Mor Ostaig, 1977-79, An Comunn Gaidhealach, 1979-81, Ross and Cromarty District Council, 1988-90, Glasgow and Strathclyde Universities, 1993-95, Sabhal Mor Ostaig, 1995-98; tours to Ireland, Germany, North America, Japan, Israel, etc.; opera librettoes for Alasdair Nicolson and William Sweeney; songs for Capercaillie, Phil Cunningham; art with Simon Fraser and Kenny Munro; short-listed, Paul Hamlyn Foundation Award for Poets, 1977; winner, Stakis Scottish Writer of the Year Award. Publications: books: An Seachnadh, 1986; Rock-Water, 1990; Oideachadh Ceart, 1996; poems widely anthologised. Recreations: newsprint; red wine; thinking about walking. Address: (h.) The Rock, Carlops, Peeblesshire EH26 9NF; T.-01968 661058.

McNee, Sir David Blackstock, Kt, QPM, FBIM, FRSA, KStJ. President, National Bible Society of Scotland, 1983-96; Non-Executive Director and Adviser to a number of public limited companies; b. 23.3.25; m., Isabella Clayton Hopkins; 1 d. Educ. Woodside Senior Secondary School, Glasgow. Joined City of Glasgow Police, 1946; Deputy Chief Constable, Dunbartonshire Constabulary, 1968; Chief Constable: City of Glasgow Police, 1971-75, Strathclyde Police, 1975-77; Commissioner, Metropolitan Police, 1977-82. Honorary Vice-President, Boys' Brigade, since 1980; Vice-President, London Federation of Boys Clubs, since 1982; Patron, Scottish Motor Neurone Association, 1982-97; Freeman, City of London, 1977; President, Glasgow City Committee, Cancer Relief, 1987-92. Recreations: fishing; golf; music.

McNee, Ian. Member, Parole Board for Scotland, since 1989 (Chairman, since 1995); b. 22.4.32, Edinburgh; m., Betty; 1 s.; 1 d. Educ. Boroughmuir School. Former Managing Director, now Chairman, MacDonald Lindsay Pindar PLC. Member, Lothian Region Children's Panel, 1972-88, Chairman, 1985-88; Past President, Edinburgh Master Printers; Past Captain, Kingsknowe Golf Club. Recreation: golf. Address: (h.) 16 Camptoun, Drem, East Lothian, EH39 5BA; T.-01620 880 631.

MacNee, Professor William, MB, ChB, MD(Hons), FRCP(Glas), FRCP(Edin). Professor of Respiratory and Environmental Medicine, Edinburgh University; Visiting Professor, Department of Biological Sciences, Napier University; Honorary Consultant Physician, Lothian Health Board, since 1987; Clinical Director, Respiratory Medicine Unit; b. 18.12.50, Glasgow; m., Edna Marina Kingsley; 1 s.; 1 d. Educ. Coatbridge High School; Glasgow University. House Physician/House Surgeon, Glasgow and Paisley, 1975-76; SHO/Registrar in Medicine, Western Infirmary/Gartnavel Hospitals, Glasgow, 1976-79; Registrar in Respiratory Medicine, City Hospital, Edinburgh, 1979-80; MRC Research Fellow/Honorary Registrar, Department of Respiratory Medicine, Royal Infirmary, Edinburgh, 1980-82; Lecturer, Department of Respiratory Medicine, City Hospital, Edinburgh, 1982-83; Senior Registrar, Respiratory Medicine/Medicine, Lothian Health Board, 1983-87; MRC Research Fellow, University of British Columbia, Vancouver, 1985-86; Senior Lecturer in Respiratory Medicine, 1987-93; Reader in Medicine, Edinburgh University, 1993-97. Council Member, Scottish Thoracic Society, 1990-93; Hon. Secretary, British Lung Foundation (Scotland); Chairman, British Lung Foundation Grants Committee. Recreations: music; theatre; sport. Address: (b.) Department of Medicine, Royal Infirmary, Lauriston Place, Edinburgh EH3 9XW; T.-0131-536 3254.

Macneil of Barra, Ian Roderick, BA, LLB, FSA Scot. Wigmore Professor of Law, Northwestern University, Chicago, since 1980; b. 20.6.29, New York City; m., Nancy C. Wilson; 2 s.; 1 d. Educ. Scarborough School; University of Vermont; Harvard University. Lt., AUS, 1951-53; Commissioned Officer, USAR, 1950-67; practised law, 1956-59; Member, Cornell Law School Faculty, 1959-72, 1974-80; Visiting Professor, University College, Dar es Salaam, 1965-67; Duke Law School, 1971-72; Professor of Law and Member, Centre for Advanced Studies, Virginia University, 1972-74; Visiting Fellow, Centre for Socio-Legal Studies, Wolfson College, Oxford, 1979, and Edinburgh University Faculty of Law, 1979, 1987; Visiting Professor, Harvard University, 1988-89; Guggenheim Fellow, 1978-79. Member, Standing Council of Scottish Chiefs; author of numerous books and articles. Recreations: walking; reading; historical studies. Address: (h.) Kisimul Castle, Isle of Barra HS9; T.-Castlebay 300; 95/6 Grange Loan, Edinburgh EH9 2ED; T.-0131-667 6068.

McNeil, Neil, MB, ChB, DPH, DPA, FFCM, FFPHM, MREHIS. Consultant in Public Health Medicine/Director of Community Medicine/Unit Medical Officer/District Medical Officer, Lanarkshire Health Board, 1976-92; Honorary Senior Clinical Lecturer/Honorary Clinical Lecturer, Department of Public Health, Glasgow

University, 1976-92; b. 4.6.31, Glasgow; m., Florence Ward Butterworth; 2 s.; 1 d. Educ. Govan High School; Glasgow University. SHO, Senior Resident, House Physician and House Surgeon, Western Infirmary, Glasgow, 1956-58; Hall Fellow, Glasgow University, 1958-60; Registrar, Western Infirmary, Glasgow, 1960-61; Divisional Medical Officer of Health, City of Glasgow, 1962-65; Principal Lecturer in Health Education and Medical Officer, Jordanhill College, Glasgow, 1965-68; Medical Officer of Health, North-East Hampshire, and Honorary Consultant, Aldershot, 1968-69; Medical Officer, Scottish Home and Health Department, 1969-73; Honorary Lecturer, Departments of Materia Medica and Community Medicine, Glasgow University, 1973-74; Consultant Epidemiologist, Communicable Diseases (Scotland) Unit, Ruchill Hospital, 1973-74; Senior Medical Officer, Scottish Home and Health Department, 1974-76. Dr. MacKinlay Prize in Public Health and Preventive Medicine, Glasgow University, 1962. Publications on community medicine, environmental medicine, public health, immunisation and infectious disease control. Recreations: tennis; photography; natural history; Gaelic language and culture; Scottish history and archaeology. Address: (h.) Claddach, 25 Waterfoot Road, Newton Mearns, Glasgow G77 5RU.

MacNeill, Deirdre, M., QC, LLB. Admitted, Faculty of Advocates, 1981. Address: Advocates' Library, Parliament House, Edinburgh, EH1 1RF.

McNeill, James Walker, QC. Advocate, since 1978; b. 16.2.52, Dunoon; m., Katherine Lawrence McDowall; 2 s.; 1 d. Educ. Dunoon Grammar School; Sidney Sussex College, Cambridge; Edinburgh University. QC, 1991; Standing Junior Counsel, Department of Transport in Scotland, 1984-88, Inland Revenue, 1988-91. Member of Council, Scottish Universities Law Institute. Recreations: music; hill-walking; golf; sailing; travel. Address: (b.) Advocates' Library, Parliament House, Edinburgh EH1 1RF; T.-0131-226 5071.

McNeill, Robert John, BA (Hons), MSc, MPhil, FInstD, FIMgt. Deputy Director, Regime Development, Scottish Prison Service, since 1996; Chief Executive, SACRO, 1991-96; b. 7.7.45, Belfast; m., Margaret Alison McCartney; 1 s.; 2 d. Educ. Annadale Grammar School, Belfast; Queen's University, Belfast; Open University; Edinburgh University. Probation Officer, Northern Ireland Probation Service, 1972-73; Governor, N.I. Prison Service, 1973-80, Scottish Prison Service, 1980-85; Depute Director, SACRO, 1985-91. Hon. Treasurer, International Federation of Settlements; Cropwood Fellow, Institute of Criminology, Cambridge University, 1985; Associate, Centre for Criminology and the Social and Philosophical Study of Law, Edinburgh University. Recreations: fly fishing; golf. Address: (b.) Calton House, 5 Redheughs Rigg, Edinburgh EH12 9HW.

McNeill, Sheriff Peter Grant Brass, PhD, MA (Hons), LLB, QC. Formerly Sheriff of Lothian and Borders at Edinburgh; b. 3.3.29, Glasgow; m., Matilda Farquhar Rose; 1 s.; 3 d. Educ. Hillhead High School, Glasgow; Morrison's Academy, Crieff; Glasgow University. Law apprentice, Biggart Lumsden & Co., Glasgow, 1952-55; Carnegie Fellowship, 1955; Faulds Fellowship, 1956-59; Scottish Bar, 1956; Honorary Sheriff Substitute of Lanarkshire, and of Stirling, Clackmannan and Dumbarton, 1962; Standing Junior Counsel to Scottish Development Department (Highways), 1964; Advocate Depute, 1964; Sheriff of Lanarkshire, subsequently of Glasgow and Strathkelvin, at Glasgow, 1965-82; Temporary Sheriff, 1996; President, Sheriffs' Association, 1982-85; Chairman: Council, Stair Society, 1990, Scottish Legal History Group, 1990. Publications: Balfour's Practicks (Editor), 1962-63; An Historical Atlas of Scotland c. 400 - c. 1600 (Co-Editor), 1975; Adoption of Children in Scotland, 1982, 2nd ed., 1986; Atlas of Scottish History to 1707 (Co-Editor), 1996.

Recreations: legal history; gardening; book-binding. Address: (h.) 31 Queensferry Road, Edinburgh EH4 3HB.

McNeill, William Alistair, BA. Deputy Director, Scottish Office Information Directorate, since 1993; b. 11.8.43, Edinburgh; m., Norma; 1 s.; 1 d. Educ. Ross High School, East Lothian; Open University. Journalist: Scotsman Publications, Scottish County Press, West Midland News Association, Glasgow Herald, 1961-67; joined Government Information Service as Press Officer, 1967; seconded Press and Publicity Officer, Scottish Health Education Unit, 1971-75; Principal Information Officer, 1987-92 (including five years heading press office at Scottish Office, Whitehall). Recreations: walking; golf; the Scots fiddle; theatre. Address: (b.) St. Andrew's House, Edinburgh EH1 1DG; T.-0131-244 2705.

McNeilly, Professor Alan S., BSc, PhD, DSc, FRSE. Acting Director, MRC Reproductive Biology Unit, Edinburgh, since 1996; b. 10.2.47, Birmingham; m., Judy; 1 s.; 3 d. Educ. Handsworth Grammar School, Birmingham; Nottingham University; Reading University; Edinburgh University. Research Lecturer, Department of Reproductive Medicine, St. Bartholomew's Hospital, London, 1971-75; Visiting Professor, University of Manitoba, Canada, 1975-76; Research Scientist, MRC Reproductive Biology Unit, Edinburgh, since 1976, Deputy Director, since 1986. Recreations: walking; golf; orienteering; bee-keeping; gardening. Address: (b.) 37 Chalmers Street, Edinburgh EH3 9EW; T.-0131-229 2575.

McNicoll, Professor Iain Hugh, BA, PhD, FRSA. Professor of Applied Economics, Strathclyde University, since 1987; Senior Research Advisor, Fraser of Allander Institute, since 1991; b. 24.6.51, Glasgow; m. Educ. St. Mungo's Academy, Glasgow; Stirling University. Leverhulme Research Fellow, Industrial Science, Stirling University, 1974-76; Lecturer, Business Studies, Edinburgh University, 1976-79; Fellow/Senior Fellow, Director of Research, Acting Director/Director, Fraser of Allander Institute, 1979-89. Publications: two books; 15 monographs; 60 academic journal and book articles. Recreations: hi-fi; golf; astronomy. Address: (b.) Department of Economics, Strathclyde University, 100 Cathedral Street, Glasgow G4 0LN; T.-0141-552 4400.

MacNish, Alastair J.H., FCCA, MIPD. Chief Executive, South Lanarkshire Council, since 1995; b. 4.2.47, Greenock; m., Jean Ferguson Bell; 1 s.; 2 d. Educ. Gourock High School. Chief Auditor, Renfrew County Council, 1973-75; Principal Accountant, then Assistant Director of Education, then Depute Director of Social Work, Strathclyde Regional Council, 1975-95. Recreations: golf; curling; bridge. Address: (b.) South Lanarkshire Council, Regional Offices, Almada Street, Hamilton ML3 0AA; T.-01698 454208.

McNiven, David Martin. Songwriter, Music Director and Producer, Composer, Actor; b. 4.11.45, Glasgow; m., Angela Rew; 1 s.; 2 d. Educ. High School of Glasgow; Royal Scottish Academy of Music and Drama. Traverse Theatre Company, 1970-73; Young Lyceum, 1974-76; Mickery Theatre, 1976; Oxford and Cambridge Shakespeare Company, 1977-78; Wildcat, 1978-83; Royal Lyceum, 1987-88; various TV comedy series for ITV and BBC, since 1983, including Naked Video, Rab C. Nesbitt, The Baldy Man, etc.; Board Member, Wildcat Stage Productions and Hullaballoo Children's Theatre; three albums for Decca Records; Edinburgh Festival Fringe First Award for Hot Burlesque, 1981. Recreations: walking; photography.

Macniven, Duncan, TD, MA, MLitt. Head of Police, Fire and Emergencies Group, Scottish Office, since 1997; b. 1.12.50, Edinburgh; m., Valerie Clark (see Valerie Macniven); 2 d. Educ. Melville College, Edinburgh;

Aberdeen University. Graduate trainee, Scottish Office, 1973-78, Principal, 1978-86, Assistant Secretary, 1986-90; Deputy Director, Historic Scotland, 1990-95; Head of Police Division, Scottish Office, 1995-97. Recreations: walking; Scottish dancing; swimming; cycling; exploring; Scottish history. Address: (b.) St. Andrew's House, Edinburgh; T.-0131-244 2154.

Macniven, Valerie Margaret, MA (Hons). Head of Division, Scottish Office Home Department, since 1996; b. 14.1.51, Perth; m., Duncan Macniven (qv); 2 d. Educ. Aberdeen High School for Girls; Edinburgh University. Scottish Office, 1973-82 and since 1987. Elder, Church of Scotland. Recreations: Scottish country dancing; tennis; travel. Address: (b.) James Craig Walk, Edinburgh EH1 3BA; T.-0131-244 5434.

McNulty, Des, BA. Member, Glasgow City Council, since 1995 (Chair, Policy Formulation and Monitoring Committee, since 1995); Chair, Glasgow 1999 Festival Company Limited, since 1996; b. 28.7.52, Stockport. Educ. St. Bede's College Manchester; University of York. Senior Lecturer in Sociology, Glasgow Caledonian University; Member, Strathclyde Regional Council, 1990-96 (responsibility for dealing with issues associated with local government reorganisation and for organising the 1994 Strathclyde Water Referendum); Vice Chair, Policy and Resources Committee, Glasgow City Council. Member of Court, University of Glasgow; Board Member: The Wise Group, Scottish Opera; Member, Kemp Commission on the Voluntary Sector. Address: (b.) City Chambers, George Square, Glasgow G2 1DU; T.-0141-287 4007.

McOwan, Rennie, DUniv, FSA Scot. Writer and Broadcaster; b. Stirling; m., Agnes Mooney; 3 s.; 1 d. Educ. Alva Academy. Reporter, Stirling Journal; Sub-Editor, Kemsley Newspapers, Daily Record; Public Relations, Roman Catholic Church; Sub-Editor, Features Writer, Scotsman Publications; Assistant Publicity Secretary, National Trust for Scotland; now: Scottish Arts Council Lecturer under Writers in Schools and Writers in Public schemes; Guest Lecturer, Film and Media Studies, Stirling University; Contributor to newspapers and magazines in Britain and overseas; radio and TV scripts and research. Publications: Light on Dumyat; The White Stag Adventure; The Day the Mountain Moved; Robert Burns for Beginners; St. Andrew for Beginners; Magic Mountains; Walks in the Trossachs and the Rob Roy Country; The Green Hills; Kilchurn Castle: a history; contributed to: Walking in Scotland; Poetry of the Scottish Hills; Speak to the Hills; Wild Walks; The Story of Scotland; Discover Scotland; Great Walks, Scotland; Classic Coastal Walks of Britain; On Foot Through History. Recreations: mountaineering; Scottish history and literature. Address: 7 Williamfield Avenue, Stirling FK7 9AH; T.-01786 461316.

McPartlin, Sheriff Noel, MA, LLB. Sheriff of Grampian, Highland and Islands, at Elgin, since 1985; b. 25.12.39.

McPhail, Angus William, MA (Oxon). Headmaster, Strathallan School, since 1993; b. 25.5.56, Ipswich; m., Elizabeth Hirsch; 2 s.; 1 d. Educ. Abingdon School; University College, Oxford. Overseas Department, Bank of England, 1978-82; Assistant Master, Glenalmond College, 1982-85; Head of Economics and Housemaster, Sedbergh School, 1985-93. Recreations: cricket; golf; walking; music; theatre. Address: (h.) Strathallan School, Forgandenny, Perth PH2 9EG; T.-01738 812546.

Macphail, Sheriff Iain Duncan, QC, MA (Hons), LLB. Sheriff of Lothian and Borders at Edinburgh, since 1995; b. 24.1.38; m., Rosslyn Graham Lillias Hewitt; 1 s.; 1 d. Educ. George Watson's College; Edinburgh University; Glasgow University. Admitted Faculty of Advocates, 1963; practice, Scottish Bar, 1963-73; Faulds Fellow in Law, Glasgow University 1963-65; Lecturer in Evidence and Procedure,

Strathclyde University, 1968-69, Edinburgh University, 1969-72; Standing Junior Counsel to Scottish Home and Health Department and Department of Health and Social Security, 1971-73; Extra Advocate-Depute, 1973; Sheriff of Glasgow and Strathkelvin (formerly Lanarkshire), 1973-81; Sheriff of Tayside, Central and Fife at Dunfermline and Alloa, 1981-82; Sheriff of Lothian and Borders at Linlithgow, 1982-88, at Edinburgh, 1988-89. Member, Scottish Law Commission, 1990-94; Chairman, Scottish Association for the Study of Delinquency, 1978-81; Hon. LLD, Edinburgh, 1992. Publications: Evidence, 1987; Sheriff Court Practice, 1988. Address: (b.) Sheriff Court House, 27 Chambers Street, Edinburgh EH1 1LB; T.-0131-225 2525.

Macphail, Madeline, BSc, DipEd. Board Member, Scottish Tourist Board, since 1997; Board Member, Thurso College, since 1994; Chair, Assynt Care Ltd., since 1990; b. 23.5.39, Dundee; m., Pat Macphail; 1 s.; 1 d. Educ. Morgan Academy, Dundee; Queen's College, Dundee, St. Andrews University. Teacher of Mathematics, Glasgow and Lanark; Tourism operator. Recreations: reading; walking. Address: (h.) 216 Clashmore, Stoer, by Lairg IV27 4JQ; T.-01571 855295.

McPhee, George, MBE, BMus, FRCO, DipMusEd, RSAM, Hon. FRSCM. Visiting Professor of Organ, St. Andrews University; Chairman, Paisley International Organ Festival; Organist and Master of the Choristers, Paisley Abbey, since 1963; b. 10.11.37, Glasgow; m., Margaret Ann Scotland; 1 s.; 2 d. Educ. Woodside Senior Secondary School, Glasgow; Royal Scottish Academy of Music and Drama; Edinburgh University. Studied organ with Herrick Bunney and Fernando Germany; Assistant Organist, St. Giles' Cathedral, 1959-63; joined staff, RSAMD, 1963; Conductor, Scottish Chamber Choir, 1971-75; Conductor, Kilmarnock and District Choral Union, 1975-84; since 1971, has completed 12 recital tours of the United States and Canada; has been both Soloist and Conductor with Scottish National Orchestra; numerous recordings and broadcasts; has taken part in numerous music festivals as Soloist; Adjudicator; Examiner, Associated Board, Royal Schools of Music; Special Commissioner, Royal School of Church Music; Silver Medal, Worshipful Company of Musicians; Honorary Doctorate, University of Paisley. Recreations: golf; walking. Address: (h.) 17 Main Road, Castlehead, Paisley PA2 6AJ; T.-0141-889 3528.

Macpherson, Sheriff Alexander Calderwood, MA, LLB. Sheriff of South Strathclyde, Dumfries and Galloway, at Hamilton, since 1978; b. 14.6.39.

Macpherson, Archie. Sports broadcaster and journalist; b. 1935, Glasgow. Former headmaster; football commentator, BBC Scotland, until 1990; reported Olympic Games, 1984 and 1988, for BBC network; author of Action Replays, 1991.

McPherson, Duncan James, CBE, MA, SDA. Farmer; Member, Highland Council; formerly Convener, Highland Regional Council; b. 29.10.30, Santos, Brazil; m., Vivian Margaret; 1 s.; 1 d. Educ. Robert Gordon's College, Aberdeen; Aberdeen University. Member, Cromarty Town Council, 1964-75, Ross and Cromarty County Council, 1972-75; Fellow, Scottish Council (Development and Industry), since 1990; former Member, Board, Scottish Natural Heritage; President, Rosemarkie Golf Club. Recreations: golf; curling; formerly rugby (Scottish trialist, 1951-56). Address: Cromarty Mains, Cromarty, Ross-shire; T.-01381 600 232.

Macpherson, Rev. Duncan James, BSc(Eng), BD. Minister, Annan Old Parish Church, since 1997; b. 26.4.67, Hardgate; m., Jillian Margaret. Educ. Glasgow Academy; Glasgow University. Associate and Youth Minister, Christ Church, Bermuda; part-time Ordained Assistant, Canonbie with Langholm and Westerkirk. Recreations: volleyball; squash; diving; kite flying; singing; drumming. Address: 12 Plumdon Park, Annan DG12 6EY; T.-01461 201405.

McPherson, James Alexander Strachan, CBE, MA, BL, LLB, FSA Scot, JP. Lord Lieutenant, Grampian Region (Banffshire), since 1987; Consultant, formerly Senior Partner, Alexander George & Co., Solicitors, Macduff; Honorary Sheriff, Grampian, Highland and Islands at Banff, since 1972; b. 20.11.27, Wormit, Fife; m., Helen Marjorie Perks, MA; 1 s.; 1 d. Educ. Banff Academy; Aberdeen University. Member, Macduff Town Council and Banff County Council, 1958-75; Provost of Macduff, 1972-75; Convener, Banff County Council, 1970-75; Member: Grampian Health Board, 1974-82, Post Office Users National Council for Scotland, 1976-80, Police Advisory Board for Scotland, 1974-86, Grampian Regional Council, 1974-90; Chairman, Public Protection Committee, 1974-86; Governor, Scottish Police College, 1974-86; Chairman, Banff and Buchan JP Advisory Committee, since 1987; Member, Scottish Solicitors Discipline Tribunal, 1990-94; Vice President, Highland Territorial and Reserve Forces Association; Member, Aberdeen University Court, since 1993. Recreations: reading; sailing; swimming. Address: (h.) Dun Alastair, 126 Gellymill Street, Macduff; T.-Macduff 832377.

Macpherson of Drumochter, Lord (James) Gordon Macpherson), 2nd Baron, JP, FRES, FRSA, FZS. Chairman and Managing Director, Macpherson, Train & Co. Ltd., since 1964; Chairman, A.J. Macpherson & Co. Ltd., since 1973; b. 22.1.24; m., 1, Dorothy Ruth Coulter (deceased); 2 d.; 1 s. deceased; 2, Catherine MacCarthy; 1 s.; 2 d. Educ. Loretto; Wells House, Malvern. RAF, 1939-45; Member, Council, London Chamber of Commerce, 1952-73; Chief, Scottish Clans Association of London, 1972-74; Chairman, Macpherson Clan Association, 1963-64; Life Managing Governor, Royal Scottish Corporation; Freeman, City of London. Address: (h.) Kyllachy, Tomatin, Inverness-shire.

Macpherson, John Hannah Forbes, CBE, OStJ, CA, DUniv. Lord Dean of Guild, Glasgow; Chairman of Court, University of Glasgow; b. 23.5.26, Glasgow; m., Margaret Graham Roxburgh; 1 s. Educ. Glasgow Academy; Merchiston Castle School, Edinburgh. Royal Naval Volunteer Reserve, 1943; Apprentice CA, Wilson Stirling & Co., 1947 (qualified, 1949); Partner, Wilson Stirling & Co. (subsequently Touche Ross & Co.), 1956-86; Chairman: Glasgow Junior Chamber of Commerce, 1965, Scottish Mutual Assurance Society, 1971, Scottish Industrial Estates Corporation, 1972, Irvine Development Corporation, 1976, TSB Scotland plc, 1984, Glasgow Development Agency, 1990; President, Glasgow Chamber of Commerce, 1980; Director: Scottish Metropolitan Property plc, 1986, TSB Group plc, 1985; Deputy Chairman, Hill Samuel Bank Ltd., 1991; Director, PCT Group plc, 1992; Governor, Merchiston Castle School, 1988; Member, Charity Appeals Committee for Prince and Princess of Wales Hospice; Director, Glasgow Native Benevolent Society. Recreations: travel; gardening; reading. Address: (h.) 16 Collylinn Road, Bearsden, Glasgow; T.-0141-942 0042.

McPherson, Malcolm Henry, LLB. Solicitor (Henderson Boyd Jackson); b. 22.5.54, Edinburgh; m., Fiona Sutherland Hogg; 1 s.; 3 d. Educ. George Watson's College, Edinburgh; Edinburgh University. Apprentice, Henderson & Jackson, WS, 1975-77; Partner, 1978; Managing Partner, 1982; development of commercial practice, 1982-86; merged with Wilson Pyle & Co., WS, Allan Dawson Simpson & Hampton, WS, Boyd Jameson, WS. Lay Member, ICAS Investigation Committee. Recreations: shooting; sailing; golfing. Address: (b.) 19 Ainslie Place, Edinburgh EH3 6AU; T.-0131-226 6881.

Macpherson, Peter, FRCP, FRCR, DTCD, FLS. Emeritus Consultant Neuroradiologist, Institute of Neurological Sciences; President: British Society of Neuroradiologists, 1990-92, Botanical Society of the British Isles, 1991-93; b. 10.10.25, Inveraray; m., Agnes Cochrane Davidson; 4 d. Educ. Inveraray Grammar School; Keil School, Dumbarton; Anderson College, Glasgow. House Surgeon, Royal Infirmary, Stirling; Junior Hospital Medical Officer, Robroyston Hospital, Glasgow; Chest Physician, Argyll; Registrar/Senior Registrar, Western Infirmary, Glasgow. Commodore, Oban Sailing Club, 1958-60; President, Glasgow Natural History Society, 1979-81 and 1983-86; Honorary Secretary, Botanical Society of the British Isles, Committee for Scotland, 1977-95, Chairman, since 1995; Plant Recorder for Lanarkshire, since 1978; Elder, Church of Scotland, since 1957. Recreations: natural history; sailing. Address: (h.) Ben Alder, 15 Lubnaig Road, Glasgow; T.-0141-632 0723.

Macpherson of Cluny (and Blairgowrie), The Honourable Sir William, KB (1983), TD, MA. 27th Hereditary Chief of the Clan Macpherson (Cluny-Macpherson); b. 1.4.26; m., Sheila McDonald Brodie; 2 s.; 1 d. Educ. Summer Fields, Oxford; Wellington College; Trinity College, Oxford. Scots Guards, 1944-47 (Captain); 21st Special Air Service Regiment (TA), 1951-65 (Lt.-Col. Commanding, 1962-65); Honorary Colonel, 21st SAS, 1983-91. Called to the Bar, Inner Temple, 1952; Queen's Counsel, 1971-83; Recorder of the Crown Court, 1972-83; Member, Senate and Bar Council, 1979-83; Bencher, Inner Temple, 1978; Judge of the High Court of Justice (of England and Wales), Queen's Bench Division, 1983-96; Honorary Member, Northern Circuit, since 1987. Member, Queen's Bodyguard for Scotland (Royal Company of Archers), since 1976, Brigadier, 1989; Vice President, Royal Scottish Corporation; President, Highland Society of London, 1991-94. Recreations: golf; fishing; rugby football. Address: (h.) Newton Castle, Blairgowrie, Perthshire.

Macquaker, Donald Francis, MA (Oxon), LLB. Partner, T.C. Young & Son, Writers, Glasgow, 1957-93; Director, Lithgows Limited, since 1987; b. 21.9.32, Stair; m., Susan Elizabeth Finlayson; 1 s.; 1 d. Educ. Winchester College; Trinity College, Oxford; Glasgow University. Greater Glasgow Health Board: Chairman, Finance and General Purposes Committee, 1974-83, Chairman, 1983-87; Chairman, Scottish Health Service Common Services Agency, 1987-91; former Member, Board of Management, Glasgow Royal Maternity Hospital and Associated Women's Hospitals (latterly Vice-Chairman); Director, Prince and Princess of Wales Hospice, Glasgow, 1991-94; Chairman, Western Meeting Club (Ayr Racecourse), since 1996. Recreations: shooting; fishing; gardening. Address: (h.) Blackbyres, by Ayr; T.-0292 441088.

MacQueen, Professor Hector Lewis, LLB (Hons), PhD, FRSE. Professor of Private Law, Edinburgh University, since 1994; Director, David Hume Institute, Edinburgh, since 1991; b. 13.6.56, Ely; m., Frances Mary Young; 2 s.; 1 d. Educ. George Heriot's School, Edinburgh; Edinburgh University. Lecturer, Senior Lecturer, Reader, all in Law, Edinburgh University, 1979-94; Visiting Professor, Cornell University, 1991; Secretary, Scottish Historical Review, since 1986; Editor, Hume Papers on Public Policy, since 1993; Editor, Edinburgh Law Review, since 1996; Scottish Representative, European Contract Commission, since 1995. Publications: Common Law and Feudal Society in Medieval Scotland; Studying Scots Law; Copyright, Competition and Industrial Design. Recreations: Scotland; cricket; walking; reading. Address: (b.) Faculty of Law, Edinburgh University, Edinburgh EH8 9YL; T.-0131-650 2060.

MacQueen, Professor Emeritus Jack (John), MA (Glasgow), MA (Cantab), Hon DLitt, FRSE. Professor Emeritus, Edinburgh University, since 1988, and Hon.

Fellow, Faculty of Arts, since 1993; b. 13.2.29, Springboig; m., Winifred W. MacWalter; 3 s. Educ. Hutchesons' Boys Grammar School; Glasgow University; Christ's College, Cambridge. RAF, 1954-56 (Pilot Officer, Flying Officer); Assistant Professor of English, Washington University, St. Louis, Missouri, 1956-59; Edinburgh University: Lecturer in Medieval English and Scottish Literature, 1959-63, Masson Professor of Medieval and Renaissance Literature, 1963-72; Director, School of Scottish Studies, 1969-88; Professor of Scottish Literature and Oral Tradition, 1972-88; Endowment Fellow, 1988-92. Publications: St. Nynia, 1961, 1990; Robert Henryson, 1967; Ballattis of Luve, 1970; Allegory, 1970; Progress and Poetry, 1982; Numerology, 1985; Rise of the Historical Novel, 1989; Scotichronicon III and IV (with W. MacQueen), 1989; Scotichronicon I and II (with W. MacQueen), 1993; Scotichronicon V and VI (with W. MacQueen and D.E.R. Watt), 1995; Oxford Book of Scottish Verse (with T. Scott), 1966; A Choice of Scottish Verse 1470-1570 (with W. MacQueen), 1972; Humanism in Renaissance Scotland (Co-Author), 1990. Recreations: walking; occasional archaeology; music; astronomy. Address: (h.) Slewdonan, Damnaglaur, Drummore, Stranraer DG9 9QN.

McQueen, James Donaldson Wright, MA, PhD, ARSGS. Dairy Industry Consultant; Honorary Research Fellow, Department of Geography and Topographic Science, University of Glasgow; Director, Scottish Dairy Conference; Council Member, Royal Scottish Geographical Society; b. 14.2.37, Dumfries; m., Jean Evelyn Brown; 2 s.; 1 d. Educ. King's Park School, Glasgow; Glasgow University. Assistant Lecturer, Department of Geography, Glasgow University, 1960-61; Junior Manager, Milk Marketing Board (England and Wales), 1961-62; Scottish Milk Marketing Board, 1963-89 (Deputy Managing Director, 1985-89); Chief Executive, Scottish Dairy Trade Federation (latterly Scottish Dairy Association), 1989-95. Member: CBI Scottish Council, 1987-89, CBI National Council, 1991-94. Recreations: golf; gardening; photography. Address: (h.) Ormlie, 53 Kingston Road, Bishopton, Renfrewshire PA7 5BA; T.-Bishopton 862380.

McQueen, William Robert James, BSc, MA, MBA. Head, Transport Division, Scottish Office, since 1995; b. 19.4.51, Widnes; m., Maureen Frances Hall; 2 d. Educ. Kirkham Grammar School; London University; University of California; Strathclyde University. Social Science Research Council, 1973-74; joined Scottish Office, 1974. Recreations: tennis; skiing; music. Address: (b.) Victoria Quay, Edinburgh EH6 6QQ; T.-0131-244 0862.

McQuillin, Robert, BSc, MSc, MInstPet, FGS, FRSE. Managing Director, Hydrocarbon Management International Ltd., since 1991; Senior Consultant, R. McQuillin & Associates, since 1990; b. 28.5.35, Cumbria; m., Angela; 2 s. Educ. White House School, Brampton; Durham University; London University. British Geological Survey: Staff Geophysicist, 1957-66; set up offshore geophysical exploration of UK shelf, 1966-73; Head, Marine Geophysics Unit, 1973-85, Deputy Director, Marine Surveys, Hydrocarbons and Geothermal Energy Division, 1983-85; Britoil: Chief Geophysicist, 1985-88, Chief Scientist and Deputy Exploration Manager, 1986-88; Scientific Adviser, BP NW Europe, Exploration and Production, 1988-89; Oil Industry Consultant, 1990-91. Former Vice-President, Geological Society of London and of Geological Society of Edinburgh. Publication: An Introduction to Seismic Interpretation (principal author), 1986. Recreations: wine and food; good hotels; golf; history of art of china. Address:(b.) HMI Ltd., 94 Liberton Drive, Edinburgh EH16 6NR; T.-0131-664 2193.

Macrae, John Grant, CA, CPFA, FRSA. Partner in charge Public Sector Practice, KPMG; b. 9.11.50, Glasgow; m., Inez; 1 s.; 2 d. Educ. Melville College. Former Convener, ICAS Public Sector Committee; Member, ICAS

Accounting Standards Committee; former Chairman, Scottish Branch, CIPFA. Recreations: skiing; golf; walking. Address: (b.) Saltire Court, 20 Castle Terrace, Edinburgh EH1 2EG; T.-0131-222 2000.

MacRae, Kenneth. Chief Executive, Student Awards Agency for Scotland, since 1994; b. 4.11.39, Kirkintilloch; m., Elizabeth Marjorie. Joined Board of Trade, 1960; transferred to Scottish Office, 1973; various posts, Industry Department for Scotland, 1973-84; Principal, Scottish Development Department Housing Division, 1984-86; Assistant Secretary, Scottish Education Department, 1986-94. Recreations: motor racing (voluntary senior official); gardening. Address: (b.) Gyleview House, 3 Redheughs Rigg, Edinburgh EH12 9HH; T.-0131-244 5867.

Macrae, Col. Sir Robert Andrew Alexander Scarth, KCVO, MBE (1953). Lord Lieutenant of Orkney, 1972-90; Farmer; b. 14.4.15; m., Violet Maud MacLellan (d., 1997); 2 s. Educ. Lancing; RMC, Sandhurst. Commissioned Seaforth Highlanders, 1935; active service, BEF 1940 (PoW, 1940-45), NW Europe, 1945 (Despatches, 1945), Korea, 1952-53, East Africa, 1953-54; retired from Army, 1968; farming in Orkney, since 1967; Councillor, Orkney CC, 1970-74; Orkney Islands Council, 1974-78; Vice-Chairman, Orkney Hospital Board, 1971-74; Orkney Health Board, 1974-79; Honorary Sheriff, Grampian Highlands and Islands, 1974; JP, 1975; Freedom of Orkney, 1990. Recreations: sailing; gardening (watching the cabbages being blown out to sea). Address: (h.) Grindelay, Orphir, Orkney KW17 2RD.

McSwan, Malcolm, OBE, CA. Managing Director, Racal-MESL Ltd., since 1983; Chairman, Adaptive Engineering Group Ltd., since 1995; Proprietor, Knapp Tree Farm; b. 31.8.39, Glasgow; m., Juliet Cowper-Jackson; 2 s. Educ. Royal High School, Edinburgh. Recreations: renovation; trees. Address: (b.) Lochend Industrial Estate, Newbridge, Midlothian; T.-0131-333 2000.

MacSween, Iain MacLean, BA (Econ), MPhil. Chief Executive, Scottish Fishermen's Organisation, since 1982; b. 20.9.49, Glasgow; m., Jean Gemmill Martin; 3 s.; 1 d. Educ. Knightswood Secondary School; Strathclyde University; Glasgow University. Fisheries Economics Research Unit, 1973-75; Department of Agriculture and Fisheries for Scotland, 1975-77; Scottish Fishermen's Organisation, since 1977; President, European Federation of Fishermen's Organisations. Address: (b.) 601 Queensferry Road, Edinburgh EH2 6EA; T.-0131-339 7972.

MacSween, Professor Roderick Norman McIver, BSc, MD, FRCPGlas, FRCPEdin, PRCPath, FRSE, FIBiol. Professor of Pathology, Glasgow University, since 1984; Honorary Consultant Pathologist, Western Infirmary, Glasgow, since 1970; President, Royal College of Pathologists, since 1996; b. 2.2.35, Kinloch, Lewis; m., Marjory Pentland Brown; 1 s.; 1 d. Educ. Inverness Royal Academy; Glasgow University. Honorary Fellow, South African Society of Pathologists, 1982; Otago Savings Bank Visiting Professor, Otago University, 1983; Hans Popper Lecturer in Liver Pathology, Columbia University College of Physicians and Surgeons, New York, 1988; Henry Moon Lecturer, University of California, San Francisco, 1993; Basil Morson Lecturer, British Society of Gastroenterology, 1995; President, Royal Medico-Chirurgical Society of Glasgow, 1978-79; President, International Academy of Pathology, British Division, 1988-90; Editor, Histopathology (Journal), 1985-96. Publications: Muir's Textbook of Pathology, 13th edition (Co-Editor); Pathology of the Liver, 3nd edition (Co-Editor); Recent Advances in Histopathology, Nos. 11-17; Recent Advances in Hepatology, No. 1. Former Captain, Dunaverty and Machrihanish Golf Clubs. Recreations: golf; gardening; opera; hill-walking; more golf! Address: (b.) University

Department of Pathology, Western Infirmary, Glasgow G11 6NT; T.-0141-211 2233.

MacTaggart, Kenneth Dugald, BA, PhD. Directory of Strategy, Highlands and Islands Enterprise, since 1995; b. 15.4.53, Glasgow; m., Caroline McNicholas; 2 d. Educ. Allan Glen's School, Glasgow; Glasgow University; Paisley College; Aston University. Economic research, Aston University, 1976-80; Editor, Export Times, London, 1980-84; Editor, Property International, London and Bahrain, 1984-87; Director, Inc Publications, London, 1987-88; Senior Economist, HIDB, 1988-91. Recreations: hill-walking; piano; photography. Address: (h.) The Sutors, 28 Broadstone Park, Inverness IV2 3LA; T.-01463 233717.

MacVicar, Angus, MA, DUniv. Author; b. 28.10.08, Argyll; m., Jean Smith McKerral (deceased); 1 s. Educ. Campbeltown Grammar School; Glasgow University. Reporter, Campbeltown Courier, 1931-33; Freelance Author; Army Service, 1940-45 (Captain, RSF); Freelance Author, Journalist, Radio and TV Scriptwriter; published 78 books, including adult novels, children's novels, adult and children's non-fiction, plays; Honorary Sheriff-Substitute, Argyll, 1965; Doctorate, Stirling University, 1985. Recreations: golf; gardening; amateur drama. Address: (h.) Achnamara, Southend, Campbeltown, Argyll PA28 6RW; T.-01586 830228.

McVicar, George Christie, DipMusEd, RSAM; Hon.FTSC. Chairman, Scottish Amateur Music Association, 1982-95; b. 17.3.19, Dumbarton. Educ. Dumbarton Academy; Royal Scottish Academy of Music and Drama. Teacher of Music, Dunbartonshire Schools, 1946-54; Lecturer in Music, Moray House College of Education, 1954-56; Adviser in Music to Stirlingshire and subsequently Central Region, 1956-79. Adjudicator Member, British Federation of Music Festivals; Examiner, Trinity College of Music, 1979-91; Hon. Vice President, Scottish Amateur Music Association, since 1995. Publications: The Saltire Scottish Song Book (formerly Oxford Scottish Song Book); Saltire Two-Part Scottish Song Book; The New Scottish Song Book. Address: (h.) 22 Queen Street, Stirling FK8 1HN; T.-01786 72074.

McVie, John, BL, WS, NP. Retired Solicitor; Honorary Sheriff-Substitute, Lothian and Borders; b. 7.12.19, Edinburgh; m., Lindsaye Woodburn Mair; 1 s.; 1 d. Educ. Royal High School; Edinburgh University. Captain, 7/9th Bn., The Royal Scots, 1940-46 (Signal Officer, North West Europe); mentioned in Despatches; Town Clerk, Royal Burgh of Haddington, 1951-75. Address: (h.) Ivybank, Haddington, East Lothian; T.-0162-082 3727.

MacWalter, Ronald Siller, BMSc (Hons), MB, ChB (Hons), MRCP(UK); FRCP(Edin); FRCP (Glas). Consultant Physician in General Medicine, Ninewells Hospital, Dundee, since 1997; Consultant Physician in Medicine for the Elderly, Royal Victoria Hospital, Dundee, 1986-97; Honorary Senior Lecturer in Medicine, Dundee University, Ninewells Hospital, Dundee, since 1986; b. 14.12.53, Broughty Ferry; m., Sheila Margaret Nicoll; 2 s. Educ. Harris Academy, Dundee; Dundee University. Registrar in Medicine and Haematology, Department of Clinical Pharmacology, Ninewells Hospital, Dundee; Senior Registrar in General Medicine and Geriatric Medicine, Nuffield Department of Medicine, John Radcliffe Hospital, Oxford. Publication: Aids to Clinical Examination.

McWilliam, James, OBE, MA (Hons), DipEd. Rector, Lochaber High School, 1970-88; Chairman, Highland Health Board, 1983-91; b. 4.10.27, Portsoy, Banffshire; m., Helen C. Brodie; 3 d. Educ. Fordyce Academy, Banffshire; Glasgow University. Teacher of English, Calderhead School, Shotts, 1951; National Service (Royal Army Education Corps), 1951-53; Teacher, Coatbridge High School, 1953; Special Assistant, Beath High School,

Cowdenbeath, 1958; Principal Teacher of English, Campbeltown Grammar School, 1961-70. Member, Highland Health Board, since 1978 (Chairman, Practitioners' Committee, 1981); Honorary Sheriff, Grampian, Highlands and Islands, since 1978; Past President: Lochaber Rotary Club, Lochaber EIS, Highland Secondary Headteachers Association. Recreations: music; TV; golf (occasionally). Address: (h.) 19 Seafield Street, Portsoy, Banff; T.-01261 843148.

McWilliam, Rev. Thomas Mathieson, MA, BD. Minister, Contin Parish, Ross-shire, since 1997; b. 12.11.39, Glasgow; m., Patricia Jane Godfrey; 1 s.; 1 d. Educ. Eastwood Secondary School; Glasgow University; New College, Edinburgh. Assistant Minister, Auld Kirk of Ayr, 1964-66; Minister: Dundee St. David's North, 1966-72, East Kilbride Greenhills, 1972-80, Lylesland Parish Church, Paisley, 1980-97; Convener, Youth Education Committee, General Assembly, 1980-84; Moderator, Paisley Presbytery, 1985-86; Convener, Board of Practice and Procedure, General Assembly, 1992-96. Recreations: walking; reading; gardening; bowling. Address: (h.) Contin Manse, Contin, Strathpeffer IV14 9ES; T.-01997 421380.

M

Maan, Bashir Ahmed, JP, MSc, DL, FRSA; b. 22.10.26, Maan, Pakistan; 1 s.; 3 d. Educ. D.B. High School, Quila Didar Singh; Punjab University. Involved in the struggle for creation of Pakistan as a student, 1943-47; organised rehabilitation of refugees from India in Maan and surrounding areas, 1947-48; emigrated to UK and settled in Glasgow, 1953; Founder Secretary, Glasgow Pakistan Social and Cultural Society, 1955-65 (President, 1966-69); Member, Executive Committee, Glasgow City Labour Party, 1969-70; Vice-Chairman, Glasgow Community Relations Council, 1970-75; Member, Glasgow Corporation, 1970-75 (Magistrate, City of Glasgow, 1971-74; Vice-Chairman, then Chairman, Police Committee, 1971-75); Member, National Road Safety Committee, 1971-74 and Scottish Accident Prevention Committee, 1971-75; Member, BBC Immigrant Programmes Advisory Committee, 1972-80; Convenor, Pakistan Bill Action Committee, 1973; contested East Fife Parliamentary seat, February 1974; President, Standing Conference of Pakistani Organisations in UK and Eire, 1974-77; Police Judge, City of Glasgow, 1974-75; Member: City of Glasgow District Council, 1975-84, Glasgow City Council, since 1995 (Bailie, since 1996); Deputy Chairman, Commission for Racial Equality, 1977-80; Member, Scottish Gas Consumers Council, 1978-81; Bailie, City of Glasgow, 1980-84; Member, Greater Glasgow Health Board, 1981-92; Deputy Lieutenant, Glasgow, since 1982; Hon. Research Fellow, Glasgow University, 1988-91; Founder Chairman, Scottish Pakistani Association, 1984-91, and since 1994; Judge, City of Glasgow District Courts; Chairman, Strathclyde Community Relations Council, 1986-93 and since 1994; Member, BBC General Advisory Council, 1992-95; a Governor, Jordanhill College of Further Education, 1987-91; Chairman, Mosque Committee, Islamic Centre, Glasgow, 1986-91. Publication: The New Scots. Recreations: golf; reading. Address: (h.) 8 Riverview Gardens, Glasgow G51 8EL; T.-0141-429 7689.

Macara, (John David) Murray, LLB, SSC, NP. Solicitor, since 1973; Solicitor Advocate, since 1993; b. 22.7.49, Glasgow; m., Elaine; 1 d. Educ. Loretto School; Glasgow University. Apprentice and Assistant, McGrigor Donald & Co., 1970-73; Beltrami & Co., Solicitors, since 1973, Partner, since 1975. Recreations: golf; hockey; travel. Address: (b.) 93 West Nile Street, Glasgow G1 2FH; T.-0141-221 0981.

Machin, Professor George Ian Thom, MA, DPhil, FRHistS. Professor of British History, Dundee University, since 1989, Head, Department of Modern History, 1992-95; b. 3.7.37, Liverpool; m., Dr. Jane Margaret Pallot; 2 s. Educ. Silcoates School, near Wakefield; Jesus College, Oxford. Research Student and Tutor, Oxford University, 1958-61; Assistant Lecturer, then Lecturer in History, Singapore University, 1961-64; Lecturer in Modern History, St. Andrews University, 1964-67; Lecturer, then Senior Lecturer, then Reader, Dundee University, 1967-89; Course Tutor, Open University in Scotland, 1971-82. Member, History Panel, Scottish Universities Council on Entrance, 1990-94; Observer, Scottish Examination Board, 1991-94; Universities' Member, History Panel, Scottish Qualifications Authority, since 1997 (Scottish Examination Board, 1996-97); sometime External Examiner, Universities of Cambridge, St. Andrews, Aberdeen, Hull, Leicester, Sussex, Stirling; Treasurer: Abertay Historical Society, 1966-73; Treasurer, Dundee Branch, Historical Association, 1981-92, President, 1992-95; Elder, Church of Scotland, since 1981. Publications: The Catholic Question in English Politics 1820 to 1830, 1964; Politics and the Churches in Great Britain 1832 to 1868, 1977; Politics and the Churches in Great Britain 1869 to 1921, 1987; The Liberal

Governments 1905-15, 1991; Disraeli, 1995. Recreations: the arts; hill-walking; photographing historic sign-posts. Address: (h.) 50 West Road, Newport-on-Tay, Fife DD6 8HP; T.-01382 543371.

Mack, Douglas Stuart, MA, PhD, FRSE. Reader, Stirling University, since 1994; General Editor, Association for Scottish Literary Studies, 1980-90; General Editor, Stirling/South Carolina Edition of James Hogg, since 1990; President, The James Hogg Society, since 1982; b. 30.1.43, Bellshill; m., Wilma Stewart Grant; 2 s. Educ. Uddingston Grammar School; Glasgow University; Stirling University. Research Assistant, National Library of Scotland, 1965-66; Assistant Librarian: St. Andrews University, 1966-70, Stirling University, 1970-86; Lecturer, Stirling University, 1986-94. Editor of various books by James Hogg and Sir Walter Scott. Recreations: watching Hamilton Accies; sailing on paddle steamers. Address: (h.) 2 Law Hill Road, Dollar FK14 7BG; T.-Dollar 742452.

Mack, Jimmy, MBE. Broadcaster and Journalist; Presenter, The Jimmy Mack Show, Radio Clyde 2, since 1990; b. 26.6.34, Greenock; m., Barbara; 1 s.; 1 d. Educ. Lenzie Academy; Bathgate Academy. Insurance Inspector, Guardian Royal Exchange Assurance Co., 1956-70; Producer and Presenter, various programmes, BBC Radio Medway, Kent, 1970-79; Presenter, Radio 1 Club, BBC Radio 1, 1967-70; Presenter, The Early Show, Night Ride, Junior Choice, BBC Radio 2, 1971-76; Producer, You and Yours, Woman's Hour, In Britain Now, BBC Radio 4, 1977-78; Presenter: The Jimmy Mack Show and Jimmy Mack's Old Gold, BBC Radio Scotland, 1979-89; Top Club and Best Years of Their Lives, Grampian TV, 1980-84; Scotland Today, Scottish TV, 1984-85; I Believe You Believe, BBC TV, 1986. Television and Radio Industries Club of Scotland Award for best live radio programme, 1986; MBE, for services to charity in Scotland, 1996. Patron, Scottish Motor Neurone Disease Association. Publication: Jimmy Mack Show Book, 1984. Recreation: photography. Address: (b.) Radio Clyde, Clydebank Business Park, Glasgow G81 2RX; T.- 0141-306 2200.

Mack, Thomas Angus, MBE, DL, MRPharmS. Proprietor Pharmacist, since 1963; b. 20.9.30, Menstrie; m., Lynne; 2 d. Educ. Alva Academy; Heriot-Watt University. After five years in retail pharmacy management opened own retail pharmacy in Tillicoultry. Scout Leader, Menstrie Scout Group, 1953-95 (District Commissioner 1964-85); Scout Awards: Medal of Merit, 1963, Silver Acorn, 1980, Silver Wolf, 1990. Recreations: mountaineering; skiing; canoeing; gardening; photography. Address: (h.) 36 Middleton, Menstrie, Clackmannanshire FK11 7HD; T.-01259 761465.

Mackie, Dugald Mabon, MA, FRSA. Secretary to University Court, University of Glasgow, since 1996; b. 26.12.52, Ayr. Educ. Ayr Academy; University of Edinburgh. Administrative Assistant: Didsbury College of Education, 1974-76, University of Aston, 1976-80; University of Strathclyde: Faculty Officer, 1980-89, Deputy Registrar, 1989-92; Secretary, Scottish Higher Education Funding Council, 1992-96. Recreations: mountaineering; gardening; railways. Address: (b.) University of Glasgow, Glasgow G12 8QQ; T.-0141-330 4246.

Mackie of Benshie, Baron (George Yull Mackie), CBE, DSO, DFC, LLD. Farmer; Liberal Democrat Spokesman, House of Lords, on Devolution, Agriculture, Scotland, Industry; Member, Council of Europe and Western European Union, 1986-96; b. 10.7.19, Aberdeen; m., 1, Lindsay Lyall Sharp; 1 s. (deceased); 3 d.; 2, Mrs Jacqueline Lane. Educ. Aberdeen Grammar School; Aberdeen University. Bomber Command and Air Staff, 1944. Contested South Angus, 1959; Vice-Chairman (Organisation), Scottish Liberal Party, 1959-64; MP (Liberal), Caithness and Sutherland, 1964-66; Chairman, Scottish Liberal Party, 1965-70; contested Caithness and

Sutherland, 1970; contested NE Scotland, European Parliamentary Election, 1979; Member, EEC Scrutiny Committee (D), House of Lords; Executive, Inter-Parliamentary Union; Chairman: Industrial Appeal Committee, Pitlochry Festival Theatre, 1979, Angus Committee, Salvation Army, 1976-84; Rector, Dundee University, 1980-83; Director, Scottish Ballet, 1986-88. Address: (h.) Benshie Cottage, Oathlaw, by Forfar, Angus.

Mackie, Joyce Grant, BA (Hons), DipCE, DL. Vice-President, National Trust for Scotland, since 1988; Partner, farming business, since 1963; b. 7.5.40, Forfar; m., Bruce Stephen Mackie; 2 s.; 2 d. Educ. St. Margaret's School for Girls, Aberdeen; Moray House College of Education. Teacher, Dalmilling School, Ayr, 1961-63. National Trust for Scotland: Member, Council, 1974-79, 1985-90, Member, Executive Committee, 1976-86; former Member, Aberdeen Committee, Scottish Children's League (RSSPCC), Trustee, David Gordon Memorial Trust, since 1977; Director, Lathallan Preparatory School, Montrose, since 1979, Chairman, since 1990; Member, Council, Glenalmond College, since 1991; Member, Church of Scotland Nomination Committee, 1985-88; former Member, Executive Committee, Aberdeen University Quincentenary Campaign. Recreations: gardening; art; Scotland. Address: (h.) Balquhindachy, Methlick, Ellon, Aberdeenshire AB41 7BY; T.-01651 806373.

Mackie, Maitland, CBE, BSc, MA, LI.D. Farmer; Owner, Mackie's; Chairman: Farmdata, Grampian Enterprise Ltd; Vice Chairman, Scottish Agricultural College; Director, Rowett Research Institute and Rowett Research Services; Member, Priorities Board for Agricultural Research; b. 21.9.37, Aberdeen; m., Dr. Halldis Mackie; 1 s.; 2 d. Educ. Aberdeen Grammar School; Aberdeen University. Former Chairman, Food and Animal Committees, Agricultural and Food Research Council; former Chairman, Farm Assured Scotch Livestock; former Chairman, Scottish Pig Industry Initiative; former Vice-President, National Farmers Union of Scotland; Recreations: skiing; sailing; Norway. Address: Westertown, Rothienorman, Aberdeenshire; T.-01467 671466.

Mackie, Marie Watson-Watt, MA (Hons), EdB (Dip). National Chairman, Scottish Women's Rural Institutes, 1987-93; Chairman, Borders Arts Network; Non-Executive Director, Borders Community Health NHS Trust; b. Kilmarnock; m., Alex. O. Mackie, MA (Hons), FSA Scot. Educ. Kilmarnock Academy; Glasgow University. County Federation Chairman, SWRI, Roxburghshire, 1975-81; National Vice-Chairman, SWRI, 1981-87; Member, Women's National Commission, 1987-89; former Executive Member, Scottish Institute of Adult Education; Producer, Lecturer and Adjudicator, amateur drama; Chairman, Roxburghshire Drama Association; Britain in Bloom Judge, 1975-84; SWRI Delegate to ACWW Hague conference, 1992; Member: Borders Enterprise Focus on Community Sustainability Steering Group, 1993, Council, Scottish Association of Young Farmers Clubs, 1987-94, Council, Rural Forum (Scotland), 1987-90, House Management Committee and Clinical Services Sub Committee, Sue Ryder Home (Borders), Community Sub-Group, Borders Environmental Education Forum. Recreations: interior design; 19th-century pottery; Samoyed dogs; enjoying the countryside of Scotland; art and architecture. Address: (h.) Linton Downs, Kelso, Roxburghshire.

Maddox, Professor Christopher Edward Ralph, BSc, PhD, CBiol, MIBiol, DipManEd. Principal, Scottish College of Textiles, Galashiels, since 1988 (Vice Principal, Queen Margaret College, Edinburgh, 1983-88); Professor, Heriot-Watt University, since 1991; b. 21.11.40; m., Janet; 2 s. Educ. Priory School, Shrewsbury; Birmingham University. MRC Research Fellow, Warwick University, 1965-66; Senior Lecturer, Luton University, 1966-67; Senior Lecturer, then Principal Lecturer, then Assistant Dean of Studies, Manchester Metropolitan University, 1967-77; Head, Department of Molecular and Life Sciences, University of Abertay, 1977-83. Member: SCOTEC Committees for Biology and Medical Laboratory Sciences, 1978-83, Council, Scottish Branch, Institute of Biology, 1979-82, CNAA Combined Studies Board, 1983-87, CNAA Health Studies Committee, 1987-89, Health Visiting Joint Committee, UK Central Council for Nursing, Midwifery and Health Visiting, 1983-88; Director: Scottish Borders Enterprise Company, since 1990, SCOT Innovation & Development, since 1992, Higher Education Statistics Agency, since 1993; Member, Scottish Examination Board, 1992-97. Recreations: reading; watching sports. Address: (b.) Scottish College of Textiles, Galashiels TD1 3HF; T.-01896 753351.

Madsen, Johan, BA, MBA, DipM, MIMgt, MCIM, FIBA. Managing Director, Business Enterprise for North Ayrshire; Director, Ayrshire Marketing Ltd., since 1991; b. 15.4.40, Aarhus, Denmark; m., Dr. Sheila Madsen; 2 d. Educ. Open University; Strathclyde University; Chartered Institute of Marketing. Manager, subsidiary of Danish company, 1969-72; Sales Manager for Scotland, Stimorol (UK) Ltd., 1972-86. Recreations: music; photography. Address: (b.) APL Centre, Stevenston Industrial Estate, Stevenston, Ayrshire.

Magee, William F., LLB. Secretary, Accounts Commission for Scotland, since 1995; b. 25.1.50, Glasgow; m., Helen McCann; 2 s. Educ. St. Aloysius College, Glasgow; Glasgow University. Legal work with various Scottish local authorities; Depute Director of Administration, Edinburgh District, 1984-88; Director of Administration and Legal Services, Central Region, 1988-95. Past Chairman, Society of Directors of Administration in Scotland. Recreations: music; golf. Address: (b.) 18 George Street, Edinburgh; T.-0131-477 1234.

Maginnis, Elizabeth, BA. Convener, Education Committee, City of Edinburgh Council, since 1996; b. 14.12.53, Edinburgh; m., Michael; 2 s.; 1 d. Educ. Trinity Academy; Edinburgh University. Recreations: reading; writing; watching football; gardening. Address: (h.) 2 Grierson Avenue, Edinburgh EH5 2AP; T.-0131-552 3674.

Maguire, Francis Thomas, PHB, LLB. Solicitor Advocate; Thompsons, Glasgow, since 1987 (Thompsons, Edinburgh, 1981-87); b. 4.10.55, Glasgow; m., Fiona Macdonald; 3 s. Educ. St. Vincent's College, Langbank; Gregorian University, Rome; St. Mary's College, Blairs; Aberdeen University. Apprentice, McLauchlan & McKenzie, Edinburgh, Robin Thompson & Partners, Edinburgh; Assistant Solicitor, Robin Thompson & Partners; Salaried Partner, Thompsons; Equity Partner, Thompsons. Member, Law Society Panel for Solicitor Advocates. Recreations: sailing; windsurfing; mountain biking; jogging; insurance companies. Address: (b.) Berkeley House, 285 Bath Street, Glasgow G2 4HQ; T.-0141-221 8840.

Maguire, Sheriff John, PhD, LLB, QC. Sheriff Principal, Tayside, Central and Fife, since 1990; b. 30.11.34, Kirkintilloch; m., Eva O'Hara; 2 s.; 2 d. Educ. St. Ninian's High School, Kirkintilloch; St. Mary's College, Blairs; Pontifical Gregorian University, Rome; Edinburgh University. Standing Junior Counsel, Ministry of Public Buildings and Works, 1962-68; Sheriff at Airdrie, 1968-73; Sheriff at Glasgow, 1973-90; Secretary, Sheriffs Association, 1982-87, President, 1988-90. Co-Founder and Chairman, PHEW, 1985-90; Chairman, Northern Lighthouse Board, 1995-97. Recreations: reading; thinking about doing the garden. Address: (b.) Sheriff Principal's Chambers, Perth Sheriff Court, Tay Street, Perth; T.-01738 620546.

Magnusson, Magnus, KBE (Hon.), MA (Oxon), FRSE, FRSA, FSA Scot. Writer and Broadcaster; Chairman, Scottish Natural Heritage, since 1992; b. 12.10.29, Reykjavik, Iceland; m., Mamie Baird; 1 s.; 3 d. Educ. Edinburgh Academy; Jesus College, Oxford. Reporter, Scottish Daily Express; Features Writer, The Scotsman; Co-Presenter, Tonight, BBC TV, 1964-65; Presenter: Chronicle, Cause for Concern, Checkpoint, All Things Considered, Mainly Magnus, BC - The Archaeology of the Bible Lands, Living Legends, Vikings!, Mastermind; Rector, Edinburgh University, 1975-78.

Mahmood, Tahir Ahmed, MB, BSc, DObstRCP, MD, MRCOG, FRCP(Ireland); MFFP. Consultant Obstetrician and Gynaecologist, Forth Park Hospital, Kirkcaldy, since 1990; Clinical Senior Lecturer, Obstetrics and Gynaecology, Aberdeen University, since 1990; Senior Lecturer, School of Biological and Medical Sciences, St. Andrews University, since 1995; Clinical Senior Lecturer, University of Edinburgh, since 1996; b. 7.10.53, Pakistan; m., Aasia Bashir; 2 s. Educ. King Edward Medical College, Lahore, Punjab University. Member, Scottish Hospital Staffing Review Committee, sub-speciality of obstetrics and gynaecology, 1986-88; Member, Minimal Invasive Surgery Subgroup and Clinical Resource Management — Procurement Group for Acute Unit, Fife, 1991-92; Ethicon RCOG Travelling Fellowship, 1991; Member, Senate, Aberdeen University, since 1992; Hon. Secretary, Northern Obstetrical and Gynaecological Society, since 1993; Member, Area Medical Committee, Fife, since 1993, Chairman, since 1995; Member, Council, Royal College of Obstetricians and Gynaecologists, since 1994, and of Scottish Executive Council, since 1994. Recreations: squash; jogging; reading; history; walking. Address: (b.) Forth Park Hospital, 30 Bennochy Road, Kirkcaldy, Fife; T.-01592 261155.

Main, Professor Alan, TD, MA, BD, STM, PhD. Professor of Practical Theology, Christ's College, Aberdeen, since 1980; Moderator, General Assembly, Church of Scotland, 1998-99; b. 31.3.36, Aberdeen; m., Anne Louise Swanson; 2 d. Educ. Robert Gordon's College, Aberdeen; University of Aberdeen; Union Theological Seminary, New York. Minister, Chapel of Garioch Parish, Aberdeenshire, 1963-70; Chaplain, University of Aberdeen, 1970-80; Chaplain, 153(H) Artillery Support Regiment, RCT(V), 1970-92; Provost, Faculty of Divinity, Aberdeen University, 1990-93; Master, Christ's College, Aberdeen, since 1992. Moderator: Garioch Presbytery, 1969-70, Aberdeen Presbytery, 1984-85; Adviser in Religious Broadcasting, Grampian Television, 1976-86; Chairman: Grampian Marriage Guidance, 1977-80, Cruse, 1981-84. Recreations: music, golf; beekeeping. Address: (h.) Kirkfield, Barthol Chapel, Inverurie AB51 8TD; T.-01651 806602.

Main, Professor Brian G.M., BSc, MBA, MA, PhD. Professor of Economics, Edinburgh University, since 1991 b. 24.8.47, St. Andrews; m., June Lambert; 2 s.; 1 d. Educ. Buckhaven High School; St. Andrews University; University of California, Berkeley. Lecturer, then Reader in Economics, Edinburgh University, 1976-87; Professor of Economics and Chairman, Department of Economics, St. Andrews University, 1987-91. Recreation: fishing. Address: (b.) Department of Economics, Edinburgh University, George Square, Edinburgh EH8 9JY; T.-0131-650 8361.

Main, Carol B.L.D., BA. Director, National Association of Youth Orchestras, since 1979; Scottish Director, Live Music Now, since 1984; Classical Music Editor, The List, since 1985; b. 21.12.58, Kirkcaldy; 1 d. Educ. Kirkcaldy High School; Edinburgh University. Freelance music critic, mainly with Scotsman. Board Director: Edinburgh Festival Fringe Society, Enterprise Music Scotland. Address: (b.) 14 Lennox Street, Edinburgh EH4 1QA; T.-0131 332 2110.

Main, Kirkland, ARSA, RSW, DA, FEIS. Head, School of Drawing and Painting, Edinburgh College of Art (Deputy Principal, 1991-97); b. 1.7.42, Edinburgh; m., Geraldine Francis; 1 d. Educ. Daniel Stewart's College; Edinburgh College of Art. Assistant to Vice Principal, Edinburgh College of Art, 1980-83 (Governor, 1979-85); Member, Central Institutions Staffs Salaries Committee, 1977-81; Member, Scottish Joint Negotiating Committee, Further Education, 1982-87; Chairman, Association of Lecturers in Scottish Central Institutions, 1982-86.

Main, Sir Peter (Tester), ERD, MD, LLD (Hon.), FRCPE, CIMgt; b. 21.3.25, Aberdeen; m., 1, Margaret Tweddle (deceased); 2 s.; 1 d.; 2, May Heatherington McMillan. Educ. Robert Gordon's College; Aberdeen University. House Surgeon, Aberdeen Royal Infirmary, 1948-49; Captain, RAMC, 1949-51; Medical Officer with Field Ambulance (Suez), 1956; Lt. Col., RAMC (AER), retired 1964; general practice, 1953-57; The Boots Co. PLC: joined Research Department, 1957; Director of Research, 1968; Managing Director, Industrial Division, 1979; Director, 1973-85, Vice Chairman, 1980-81, Chairman, The Boots Co. PLC, 1982-85; Director: Scottish Development Agency, 1986-91, W.A. Baxter & Sons Ltd., 1985-91. Member, National Economic Development Council, 1984-85; Chairman, Committee of Inquiry into Teachers' Pay and Conditions, Scotland, 1986; Governor, Henley Management College, 1983-86. Recreations: fishing; Scottish music. Address: Ninewells House, Chirnside, Duns, Berwickshire TD11 3XF; T.-01890 818191.

Main, Lt. Col. William. Divisional Commander, West Scotland, Salvation Army; b. 15.7.35, Edinburgh; m., Sylvia Ann; 3 s.; 1 d. Educ. David Kilpatrick School, Leith. Entered Salvation Army Training College, London, 1960; served for 20 years on Corps work before serving on Youth Work and Finance; appointed Leader, Salvation Army in Ireland, 1987; moved to East Midlands; returned to Glasgow, 1995. Recreations: reading; golf. Address: (b.) 4 Buchanan Court, Cumbernauld Road, Stepps, Glasgow G33 6HZ; T.-0141-779 5000.

Mair, Alexander, MBE (1967). Governor, Robert Gordon's College, Aberdeen, since 1988; b. 5.11.22, Echt; m., Margaret Isobel. Educ. Skene Central School; School of Accountancy, Glasgow. Company Secretary, Grampian TV, 1961-70; appointed Director, 1967; Director and Chief Executive, 1970-87. President, Aberdeen Chamber of Commerce, 1989-91; Chairman: Aberdeen International Football Festival, 1988-91, Oil Industry Community Fund, since 1993, RGIT Limited, since 1989. Recreations: golf; skiing; gardening. Address: (h.) Ravenswood, 66 Rubislaw Den South, Aberdeen AB15 4AY; T.-01224 317619.

Mair, Alistair S.F., MBE, DL, BSc, FIMgt. Chairman, since 1991, Managing Director, since 1977, Caithness Glass Ltd.; Chairman, CBI Scotland, 1989-91, and Member, CBI Council, since 1985; President, British Glass Manufacturers Confederation; b. 20.7.35, Drumblade; m., 1, Anne Garrow (deceased); 2, Mary Bolton; 4 s.; 1 d. Educ. Robert Gordon's College, Aberdeen; Aberdeen University. Rolls Royce, Glasgow, 1957-71: graduate apprentice, PA to General Manager, Production Control Manager, Product Centre Manager; RAF, 1960-62 (short-service commission, Technical Branch); Managing Director, Caithness Glass Ltd., 1971-75; Marketing Director, Worcester Royal Porcelain Co., 1975-76. Non-Executive Director: Grampian Television, since 1986, Crieff Hydro Ltd., since 1994 (Chairman, since 1996); Governor, Morrison's Academy, Crieff, since 1985 (Chairman, since 1996); Commissioner, Queen Victoria School, Dunblane, 1992-97; Member, Aberdeen University Court, since 1993; Chairman, Crieff Auxiliary Association (Richmond House); Patron, Perth and Kinross Association of Voluntary Services, since 1994. Recreations: reading; history; gardening; walking; current affairs. Address: (h.) Dungora, Heathcote Road, Crieff, Perthshire PH7 4AG; T.-01764 652191.

Mair, Professor Douglas, FRSA. Professor, Department of Economics, Heriot-Watt University, Edinburgh, since 1993; b. 3.6.39, Arbroath; m., Ishbel Fraser; 2 s.; 1 d. Educ. Arbroath High School; St. Andrews University. Ford Motor Company, 1960-63; Scottish Council (Development and Industry), 1963-67; joined Heriot-Watt University, 1967. Recreation: golf. Address: (b.) Department of Economics, Heriot-Watt University, Riccarton, Edinburgh EH14 4AS; T.-0131-451 3491.

Mair, Henry. Poet; b. 4.3.45, Kilmarnock; m., Etta; 1 s.; 1 d. Educ. St. Joseph's High School, Kilmarnock. Originator, 1972, and Secretary, Scottish National Open Poetry Competition; guest, USSR Writers' Union, 1980. Publications: I Rebel, 1970; Alone I Rebel, 1974; Flowers in the Forest, 1978; The Prizewinners, 1987. Address: (h.) 42 Tollerton Drive, Irvine, Ayrshire; T.-Irvine 76381.

Mair, William Wallace, MA, MBA, FRSA. Secretary, Faculty of Actuaries in Scotland, since 1974; b. 19.6.49, Bellshill; m., Sandra Cunningham; 1 s.; 1 d. Educ. Uddingston Grammar School; Glasgow University; Edinburgh University. Assistant Secretary, Royal Institution of Chartered Surveyors, 1969-72; Secretary, Scottish National Federation of Building Trades Employers, 1972-73. Recreations: badminton; cricket; hill-walking; lay preaching; photography. Address: (h.) 17 Thistle Street, Edinburgh EH2 1DF; T.-0131-220 4555.

Maitland, Peter Salisbury, BSc, PhD, FRSE. Independent Consultant in Freshwater Ecology, since 1986; Secretary, Scottish Freshwater Group, since 1968; Member, SEPA South East Regional Board, since 1996; b. 8.12.37, Glasgow; m., Kathleen Ramsay; 1 s.; 2 d. Educ. Bearsden Academy; Glasgow University. Lecturer in Zoology, Glasgow University, 1959-67; Senior Scientific Officer, Nature Conservancy, 1967-70; Principal Scientific Officer, Institute of Terrestrial Ecology, 1970-86; Senior Lecturer in Ecology, St. Andrews University, 1978-82. Royal Society of Edinburgh Fellowship, 1980; Neill Medal, 1993; Freshwater Biological Association Fellowship, 1996. Publications: eight books; 200 scientific papers. Recreations: wildlife conservation; fish-keeping; gardening; walking; music. Address: (h.) Nether Sunnyside, Gladshot, Haddington EH41 4NR; T.-01620 823691.

Maitland-Carew, The Hon. Gerald Edward Ian, DL; b. 28.12.41, Dublin; m., Rosalind Averil Speke; 2 s.; 1 d. Educ. Harrow School. Army Officer, 15/19 The Kings Royal Hussars, 1960-72; looked after family estates, since 1972; Member, Royal Company of Archers; Chairman, Lauderdale Hunt; Chairman, Lauderdale and Galawater Branch, Royal British Legion Scotland; Deputy Lieutenant, Ettrick and Lauderdale and Roxburgh, 1989; elected Member, Jockey Club, 1989; Chairman, Musselburgh Racecourse, 1993; Member: Border Area, TA Committee, Council, International League for the Protection of Horses, 1993; President, Border Rifle League, 1994; Chairman, Gurkha Welfare Trust of Scotland, 1996; Racecourse Steward at Ayr, Kelso, Newcastle, Cheltenham and Newmarket. Recreations: racing; hunting; shooting. Address: (h.) Thirlestane Castle, Lauder, Berwickshire; T.-01578 722 254.

Maizels, Professor Rick, BSc, PhD. Professor of Zoology, Edinburgh University, since 1995; Head, Institute of Cell, Animal and Population Biology, since 1997; b. 14.5.53, London. Educ. University College London. MRC Scientific Staff, NIMR, Mill Hill, 1979-83; Lecturer, Reader and Professor, Department of Biology, Imperial College, London, 1983-95. Address: (b.) Ashworth Laboratories, Edinburgh University EH9 3JT; T.-0131-650 5511.

Makin, Keith, BSc, MSc, DipSocAdmin, CQSW, MInstM, FRSA. Director of Social Services, Dumfries and Galloway Council, since 1995; b. 22.4.53, Luton; m., Margaret Louise; 1 s.; 2 d. Educ. Kingsbury Grammar School, Dunstable; Cardiff University; Manchester University; Birmingham University. Social Worker, Cheshire County Council, 1975-80; Senior Social Worker, Oxfordshire, 1980-83; Team Manager/Operations Manager, Warwickshire, 1983-89; Divisional Director, Northumberland, 1990-93; Depute Director, then Director of Social Work, Dumfries and Galloway Regional Council, 1994-95. Executive Committee Member, Association of Directors of Social Work. Recreations: fishing; driving; music; cookery; sailing. Address: (b.) Grierson House, The Crichton, Bankend Road, Dumfries DG1 4ZH.

Malcolmson, Peter, OBE, JP, CQSW. Councillor, Shetland Islands Council (Vice Chairman, Education Committee); former Director of Social Work, Shetland Islands Council; b. 27.7.39, Lerwick; m., Grace Eleanor Robson; 2 s.; 2 d. Educ. Anderson High School, Lerwick; Moray House College, Edinburgh. Social Worker, 1963-90. Recreations: voluntary social work; guizing and sailing Viking Longship. Address: (h.) Skersund, Upper Sound, Lerwick, Shetland Isles ZE1 0SU.

Malik, Hanzala Shaheed, BSc. Member, Glasgow City Council, since 1995; Chair, West of Scotland Community Relations Council, since 1995; Chair, Ethnic Minority Respite Care Project, since 1995; Chair, North West Advisory Council, since 1995; Chair, Woodlands Education Development Group, since 1996; b. 26.11.56, Glasgow; m., Haleema Sadia; 1 s.; 1 d. Educ. North Kelvinside Secondary School; Clydebank College; Paisley University. Strathclyde Police Special Constable, 1975-76; Strathclyde Police Traffic Warden, 1976-82; Manager, Dhool Farms Ltd, 1982-87; Financial Consultant, Allied Dunbar Plc, 1987-88; Director, Azad Video Link Ltd, 1988-92. Glasgow City Council: Member, Policy and Resources (Budget and Financial Monitoring) Sub-committee; Member, Equality Committee (and Gay and Lesbian Issues Working Group and Race Working Group); Finance Committee; Housing Committee; Licensing Committee; Social Strategy Committee (and Community Councils Sub Committee); Social Work Committee (and Care Planning Sub Committee); Committee Member: Queens Cross Housing Association, Charing Cross Housing Association; Director, Queens Cross Workspace; Member, North West Action Group; Member, Scottish Pakistani Friends Society. Recreations: badminton; charity work; cooking; football; gardening; overseas travel; philately; swimming. Address: (b.) Glasgow City Chambers, George Square, Glasgow G2 1DU; T.-0973 633 120.

Mallinson, Edward John Harold, MPharm, FRPharmS, FIMgt, FRSH. Chief Administrative Pharmaceutical Officer, Lanarkshire Health Board, since 1984; b. 15.3.50, Bingley; m., Diana Gray; 2 d. Educ. Bradford Grammar School; Bradford University. Staff Pharmacist (Ward Pharmacy Services), Bradford Royal Infirmary, 1973-78; District Pharmaceutical Officer, Perth and Kinross District, 1978-83. Chairman, Scottish Chief Administrative Pharmaceutical Officers' Group, 1990-92, and since 1997; Royal Pharmaceutical Society of Great Britain: Hon. Secretary, Bradford & District Branch, 1978, Hon. Secretary, Dundee & Eastern Scottish Branch, 1979-83, Hon. Secretary and Treasurer, Lanarkshire Branch, since 1984; Member of Council, Royal Society of Health, 1992-96, Honorary Treasurer, 1996; Vice Chairman and Secretary, Pharmaceutical Group, Royal Society of Health, 1986-89; Chairman, Strathclyde Police/Lanarkshire Health Board Drug Liaison Committee, 1985-91; Member, General Synod, Scottish Episcopal Church, 1986-95; Honorary Treasurer, Comunn Gaidhlig na h-Eaglais Easbaigich; Honorary Treasurer, Affirming Apostolic Order; Secretary, Lanarkshire Branch, British Institute of Management, 1989-

91, Chairman, 1991-94. Recreations: genealogy; Gaelic language and culture; walking and cooking. Address: (h.) Malden, North Dean Park Avenue, Bothwell, Glasgow G71 8HH; T.-01698 852973.

Mallon, Con. Chief Executive, East Dunbartonshire Council. Address: (b.) Tom Johnston House, Civic Way, Kirkintilloch, G66 4TJ.

Malone, Wilson, CA, MPhil. Head, Industrial Assistance Division, Scottish Office Education and Industry Department, since 1994; b. 20.6.55, Glasgow; m., Anna Tunn; 1 s. Educ. Hillhead High school; Glasgow Technical College; Glasgow University. CA trainee, 1975-79; Accountant, John G. Kincaid & Co., 1980-82; Civil Servant, since 1983; Deputy Director, Locate in Scotland, 1988-94. Recreations: sailing; music. Address: (b.) Meridian Court, 5 Cadogan Street, Glasgow G2 6AT; T.-0141-242 5801.

Mann, Professor David George, BSc, PhD. Senior Principal Research Scientist, Royal Botanic Garden, Edinburgh, since 1996; Hon. Professor, Glasgow University, since 1996; b. 25.2.53, Romford, Essex; m., Lynn Barbara; 1 s.; 1 d. Educ. Brentwood School; Bristol University. Edinburgh University: Demonstrator, 1978-81, Lecturer, 1981-90, Director of Studies, 1989-90; Deputy Regius Keeper (Deputy Director), Royal Botanic Garden, Edinburgh, 1990-96. Member, Council, International Society for Diatom Research; G.W. Prescott Award, 1991. Publications: editor/author of 65 papers and books. Recreations: classical piano; watercolour painting. Address: (b.) Royal Botanic Garden, Inverleith Row, Edinburgh EH3 5LR; T.-0131-552 7171.

Mann, Gordon Laurence, DipTP, MRTPI, MInstPet. Managing Director, The Crichton Trust; b. 28.4.48, Dundee. Director of Planning, Shetland Islands Council, 1980-87; Director of Physical Planning, Dumfries and Galloway Regional Council, 1987-96; Chief Planning Officer, Dumfries and Galloway Council, 1996-97. Address: (b.) Grierson House, The Crichton, Dumfries DG1 4ZE; T.-01387 247544.

Manning, Professor Aubrey William George, BSc, DPhil, FInstBiol, Dr (h c) (Toulouse), FRSE. Professor of Natural History, Division of Biological Sciences, Edinburgh University, 1973-97, Professor Emeritus, since 1997; b. 24.4.30, London; m.; 3 s., inc. 2 by pr. m. Educ. Strode's School, Egham; University College, London; Merton College, Oxford. Research, 1951-54; National Service, Royal Artillery, 1954-56; Lecturer, then Reader in Zoology, Edinburgh University, 1956-73; Secretary-General, International Ethological Committee, 1971-79; President: Association for the Study of Animal Behaviour, 1981-84, Biology Section, British Association for the Advancement of Science, 1993; Member: Scottish Advisory Committee, Nature Conservancy Council, 1982-89, Advisory Committee on Science, NCC, 1985-89; Chairman of Council, Scottish Wildlife Trust, 1990-96; Trustee, National Museums of Scotland, since 1997. Association for the Study of Animal Behaviour Medal, 1997; Dobzhansky Memorial Award, Behavioural Genetics Association, 1996. Publication: An Introduction to Animal Behaviour, 5th edition, 1998; research papers in biological journals. Recreations: woodland conservation; walking; architecture. Address: (h.) The Old Hall, Ormiston, East Lothian; T.-Pencaitland 340536.

Mansfield and Mansfield, 8th Earl of (William David Mungo James Murray), JP, DL; b. 7.7.30; m., Pamela Joan Foster; 2 s.; 1 d. Educ. Eton; Christ Church, Oxford. National Service, Malayan Campaign; called to Bar, Inner Temple, 1958; Barrister, 1958-71; Member, British Delegation to European Parliament, 1973-75; Minister of State, Scottish Office, 1979-83; Minister of State, Northern Ireland Office, 1983-84; Director: General Accident Fire and Life Assurance Corporation Ltd., 1972-79, and since 1985; The American Trust Ltd., since 1985; Pinneys of Scotland Ltd., 1985-89; Ross Breeders Ltd., 1989-90; Hon. President, St. Andrews Society of Glasgow, 1972-92; President, Royal Scottish Country Dance Society, since 1977; Hon. Member, RICS; First Crown Estate Commissioner, 1985-95. Address: (h.) Scone Palace, Perthshire PH2 6BE.

Manson, Alexander Reid, CBE, SDA, FRAgS. Farmer; Member, Meat and Livestock Commission, 1986-95; General Commissioner of Income Tax, since 1991; Director, National Animal Data Centre, 1992-95; b. 2.9.31, Oldmeldrum; m., Ethel Mary Philip; 1 s.; 2 d. Educ. Robert Gordon's College; North of Scotland College of Agriculture. Member, Oldmeldrum Town Council, 1960-65; founder Chairman, Aberdeen Beef and Calf Ltd., 1962; Past President, Scottish Agricultural Organisation Society Ltd.; Chairman, Buchan Meat Producers Ltd., 1982-92; Past President, Federation of Agricultural Cooperatives; Member, Williams Committee of Enquiry, 1989; Member, EU Beef Advisory Committee, 1986-96. Recreations: golf; bird-watching. Address: (h.) Kilblean, Oldmeldrum, Inverurie AB51 0DN; T.-01651 872226.

Manson, Frank, MA, MIOSH, MIIRSM. Managing Director, Registers of Scotland, since 1996; b. 18.3.50, Lerwick; m., Mary. Educ. Anderson Educational Institute, Lerwick; Edinburgh University. HM Inspector of Factories, Health and Safety Executive, 1976-80; Technical Executive, BP Detergents International, 1980-84; Production Controller, William Moir Ltd., 1984-85; Business Development Manager, Unisys Corporation, 1985-89; Management Consultant, 1989-92; Assistant Director of Property, Tayside Region, 1992-96; Head of Central Services, Angus Council, 1995-96. Recreations: reading; walking; rugby. Address: (b.) Meadowbank House, 153 London Road, Edinburgh; T.-0131-479 3615.

Manson, Richard U., MCIH. General Manager, State Hospital, Carstairs, since 1990; b. 2.5.51, Glasgow; m., Barbara; 2 s.; 1 d. Educ. Shawlands Academy; Glasgow College of Commerce; Glasgow College of Building. District Housing Manager, then Management Auditor, Glasgow District Council, 1979-87; Operations Director, Quality Street Ltd., 1987-89; Managing Director, Homesense Ltd., 1989-90. Address: (b.) State Hospital, Carstairs, Lanark ML11 8RP; T.-01555 840293.

Mappin, Rev. Michael Graeme, BA (Cantab). Clerk, Presbytery of Caithness, since 1974; b. 16.3.32, Shenfield; m., Catherine Rendall; 4 s.; 2 d. Educ. Radley College; Pembroke College, Cambridge. Assistant Curate, St. Paul's and St. George's, Edinburgh, 1960-62, St. Mungo's Episcopal Church, Balerno, 1962-64; Rector, St. Mungo's, 1964-69; Assistant Minister, Corstorphine Old Parish Church, 1969-70; Minister, Bower with Watten, 1970-98. Recreations: gardening; joiner work. Address: The Manse, Watten, by Wick KW1 5YN; T.-01955 621220.

Mar and Kellie, Earl of (James Thorne Erskine). Estate Worker; Scottish Liberal Democrat Peer; b. 10.3.49, Edinburgh; m., Mary Irene; 1 step s.; 4 step d. Educ. Eton; Moray House College of Education; Inverness College. Community Service Volunteer, York, 1967-68; Youth and Community Worker, Craigmillar, 1971-73; Social Worker, Sheffield, 1973-76, Grampian Region, 1976-78; Social Worker, Prison Social Worker, Community Service Supervisor, Highland Region, 1979-87; Builder, Kincardine, 1990-92; Project Worker, SACRO, Falkirk, 1992-93; Royal Auxiliary Air Force Regiment, 1979-85; Royal Naval Auxiliary Service, 1985-88; Chairman, Strathclyde Tram Inquiry, 1996. Recreations: canoeing; hill-walking; boat building; Alloa Tower. Address: House of Lords, London, SW1A 0PW; Erskine House, Clackmannan FK10 4JF.

Maran, Professor Arnold George Dominic, MB, ChB, MD, FRCS, FACS, FRCP, FRCS (Eng), FDS (Hon). Professor of Otolaryngology, Edinburgh University, since 1988; President, Royal College of Surgeons; Consultant Surgeon, Royal Infirmary and City Hospital, Edinburgh, since 1974; b. 16.6.36, Edinburgh; m., Anna; 1 s.; 1 d. Educ. Daniel Stewart's College; Edinburgh University; University of Iowa. Trained in Otolaryngology in Edinburgh and America; former Consultant Otolaryngologist, Tayside Health Board, and Professor of Otolaryngology, West Virginia University. Fifteen Visiting Professorships to foreign universities; Honorary Fellowship, Royal College of Surgeons of South Africa, and Royal College of Surgeons of Hong Kong. Publications: six books and 150 scientific papers. Recreations: golf; music; travel. Address: (h.) 27 Learmonth Terrace, Edinburgh EH4 1NZ; T.-0131-332 0055.

Marjoribanks, Gerald Brian, BA, LRAM, ALAM. Officer for Scotland, Independent Television Commission, previously Independent Broadcasting Authority, since 1983; b. 22.7.42, Falkirk; m., Kathleen; 2 s.; 2 d. Educ. Falkirk High School; Edinburgh College of Speech and Drama; Open University. Sports Presenter, Sportsreel, Sportscene, Sportsound, BBC Scotland, 1966-83; Lecturer in Drama, Notre Dame College of Education, 1967-79; Co-ordinator of Learning Resources, Dunfermline College of Physical Education, 1979-80; Head of Public Relations, Cumbernauld Development Corporation, 1980-83. Recreations: drama adjudication; badminton; photography. Address: (h.) 11 Majors Place, Falkirk FK1 5QS.

Marjoribanks, Sir James Alexander Milne, KCMG (1965), MA. HM Diplomatic Service, 1934-71; b. 29.5.11, Edinburgh; m., Sonya Patricia Stanley de Brandon (deceased); 1 d. Educ. Edinburgh Academy; Edinburgh University; Strasbourg University. Served in Peking, Hankow, Marseilles, Jacksonville, New York, Bucharest, Canberra, Luxembourg, Bonn, Brussels, London; Assistant Under-Secretary of State, Foreign Office, 1962-65; Ambassador to European Communities, 1965-71. Director, Distillers PLC, 1971-76; Member, Edinburgh University Court, 1976-80; Governing Member, Caledonian Research Foundation; Chairman, Scotland in Europe, 1979-91; Member, Committee for European Community Cultural Co-operation. Recreation: hill-walking. Address: (h.) 13 Regent Terrace, Edinburgh EH7 5BN; T.-0131-556 3872.

Markland, John A., MA, PhD, ACIS. Chief Executive, Fife Council, since 1995; b. 17.5.48, Bolton; m., Muriel Harris; 4 d. Educ. Bolton School; Dundee University. Demographer, Somerset County Council, 1974-76; Senior Professional Assistant, Tayside Regional Council; Personal Assistant to Chief Executive, then Assistant Chief Executive, then Chief Executive, Fife Regional Council, 1979-95; Chairman, Forward Scotland Ltd.; Director, Fife Enterprise; Clerk to Lord Lieutenant of Fife. Recreations: climbing Scotland's Munros; cycling. Address: (b.) Fife House, North Street, Glenrothes, Fife; T.-01592 414141.

Marks, Frederick Charles, OBE, MA, LLB, FIMgt. Commissioner for Local Administration in Scotland (Local Government Ombudsman); Local Government Adjudicator; Vice Chairman, Queen Margaret Hospital, Dunfermline, NHS Trust; b. 3.12.34, Bellshill; m., Agnes M. Bruce; 3 s.; 1 d. Educ. Wishaw High School; Glasgow University. Depute Town Clerk, Dunfermline, 1963-68; Town Clerk, Hamilton, 1968-75; Chief Executive, Motherwell, 1974-83; General Manager, Scottish Special Housing Association, 1983-89; Deputy Chairman, Local Government Boundary Commission for Scotland, 1989-94. Address: (b.) 23 Walker Street, Edinburgh EH3 7HX; T.-0131-225 5300.

Marnoch, Hon. Lord (Michael Stewart Rae Bruce), QC (Scot), MA, LLB. Senator of the College of Justice, since 1990; b. 26.7.38; m., Alison M. Stewart; 2 d. Educ.; Loretto; Aberdeen University. Advocate, 1963; QC, 1975; Standing Counsel to Department of Agriculture and Fisheries for Scotland, 1973; to Highlands and Islands Development Board, 1973; Advocate-Depute, 1983-86; Member, Criminal Injuries Compensation Board, 1986-89. Chairman for Scotland, Salmon and Trout Association, 1989-94. Recreations: golf; fishing. Address: (b.) Parliament House, Edinburgh; T.-0131-225 2595.

Marnoch, Derek George, MBE, BSc, ACMA. Chief Executive, Aberdeen Chamber of Commerce, since 1983; b. 30.10.35, Aberdeen; m., Kathleen Howard (deceased); 3 s. Educ. Aberdeen Grammar School; Aberdeen University. Recreation: golf. Address: (h.) Fairways, The Drive, Edzell, Brechin, Angus DD9 7XX.

Marquis, Alistair Forbes, BA, MEd, DipCE, FCollP. Chairman, Scottish Committee of The Boys' Brigade, since 1991; elected Representative, UK Brigade Executive for East Lowland District, since 1989; Scottish Member, UK Management Committee, since 1991; Hon. Vice President: The Scout Association, The Scottish Council, since 1996; b. 13.1.50, Glasgow; m., Margaret Jarvie Greenlees; 1 d. Educ Queen's Park Secondary School; Jordanhill College, Glasgow; Open University; Edinburgh University. Teacher/Assistant Head Teacher/Head Teacher; HM Inspector of Schools, 1989. Member, Scottish Committee on Special Educational Needs, 1985-88; Chairman, Lanthorn Community Complex Management Committee, 1979-82; SFA Football Referee, 1972; Church of Scotland Elder; Member, Rotary International. Recreations: gardening; reading; walking. Address: (h.) 39 Bankton Drive, Murieston, Livingston EH54 9EJ; T.-01506 414406.

Marr, Derek Shepherd, QFSM, FIFireE. Firemaster, Tayside Fire Brigade, since 1990; Secretary, Scottish Chief & Assistant Chief Fire Officers Association, since 1991; b. 6.7.48, Arbroath; m., Edna; 1 s.; 1 d. Educ. Arbroath High School. Joined fire service, 1967. Chairman, Tayside Fire Liaison Panel; COSLA Adviser to Protective Services Committee; Council Member, Chief & Assistant Chief Fire Officers Association. Recreations: reading; golf. Address: (b.) Fire Brigade Headquarters, Blackness Road Dundee.

Marr, Norman G., CStJ, DipArch, ARIBA, FRIAS. Consultant Architect/Planner; Director of Planning and Development, Kincardine and Deeside District Council, 1975-92; b. 19.5.37, Aberdeen. Educ. Aberdeen Grammar School; Scott Sutherland School of Architecture, Aberdeen. Architectural Assistant, Aberdeen County Council, 1961-66; Senior Research Assistant, Corporation of the City of Aberdeen, Town Planning Department, 1967-69 (Principal Development Assistant, 1970-75). Organist and Choirmaster, Denburn Parish Church, Aberdeen, since 1956; Secretary, Scottish Federation of Organists, 1970-92 (President, 1993-94); Cross Bearer, Priory of the Order of St. John in Scotland, and Member, Aberdeen Committee of the Order; Member, Church of Scotland Property Commission; Vice-Chairman, Friends of St. Machar's Cathedral, Aberdeen, and Friends of the Kirk of St. Nicholas, Aberdeen. Recreations: organ playing/building; swimming; long-distance running; hill-walking; books; entertaining. Address: (h.) 63 Devonshire Road, Aberdeen, AB10 6XP; T.-01224 322937.

Marrian, Ian Frederic Young, MA, CA. Chief Executive and Deputy Secretary, Institute of Chartered Accountants of Scotland, since 1994 (Director of Education, since 1981); b. 15.11.43, Kilwinning; m., Moira Selina McSwan; 1 s.; 2 d. Educ. Royal Belfast Academical Institution; Queens University, Belfast; Edinburgh University. Qualified as CA, 1969; Deloitte Haskins & Sells: audit practice, Rome, 1969-72, London, 1972-73, Audit Partner, Edinburgh, 1973-78,

Technical Partner, London, 1978-81. Recreations: gardening in the grand scale; wines. Address: (h.) Bowerhouse, Dunbar EH42 1RE; T.-0131-247 4815.

Marshall, David. MP (Labour), Glasgow Shettleston, since 1979; b. 1941. Address: (b.) House of Commons, London, SW1A 0AA.

Marshall, Enid Ann, MA, LLB, PhD, Assoc. RICS, ACIArb, FRSA. Solicitor; Reader, Scots Law Research Unit, Stirling University, since 1994; Editor, Scottish Law Gazette, since 1983; Chairman, Social Security Appeal Tribunal, Stirling and Falkirk, since 1984; b. 10.7.32, Boyndie, Banffshire. Educ. Banff Academy; Bell-Baxter School, Cupar; St. Andrews University. Apprentice Solicitor, 1956-59; Lecturer in Law, Dundee College of Technology, 1959-72; Lecturer, then Senior Lecturer, then Reader in Business Law, Stirling University, 1972-94. Departmental Editor, Arbitration Section, Journal of Business Law, since 1976. Publications: General Principles of Scots Law; Scottish Cases on Contract; Scottish Cases on Agency; Scottish Cases on Partnerships and Companies; Scots Mercantile Law; Gill on Arbitration; Charlesworth and Morse Company Law (Scottish Editor); Notes on the Law of Property in Scotland (Editor, 3rd edition); M.C. Oliver's Company Law (10th, 11th, 12th editions). Recreations: veganism; animal welfare. Address: (h.) 24 Easter Cornton Road, Stirling FK9 5ES; T.-Stirling 478865/467285.

Marshall, Professor Ian Howard, MA, BD, PhD (Aberdeen), BA (Cantab), DD (Asbury). Professor of New Testament Exegesis, Aberdeen University, since 1979; b. 12.1.34, Carlisle; m., Joyce Elizabeth; 1 s.; 3 d. Educ. Aberdeen Grammar School; Aberdeen University; Cambridge University; Göttingen University. Assistant Tutor, Didsbury College, Bristol; Methodist Minister, Darlington; Lecturer, then Senior Lecturer and Reader in New Testament Exegesis, Aberdeen University. Publications: Kept by the Power of God; Luke: Historian and Theologian; The Origins of New Testament Christology; New Testament Interpretation (Editor); The Gospel of Luke; I Believe in the Historical Jesus; The Epistles of John; Acts; Last Supper and Lord's Supper; Biblical Inspiration; 1 and 2 Thessalonians; Jesus the Saviour; 1 Peter; Philippians; The Acts of the Apostles. Address: (b.) Department of Divinity with Religious Studies, King's College, Aberdeen AB24 3UB; T.-01224 272388.

Marshall, Janet Ann, ALA. Chairman, Scottish Society for the Prevention of Cruelty to Animals, since 1993; b. 3.7.47, Inchinnan; m., Allan W. Marshall; 2 s. Educ. John Neilson Institution, Paisley; Strathclyde University. Glasgow Public Libraries, 1965-67; Children's Librarian, 1969-73; School Librarian, 1973-75; Senior Education Resources Librarian, 1975-79; Farmer, 1979-92. Member, East Ayrshire Children's Panel. Recreation: gardening. Address: (h.) Silverhill Farm, Dunlop, Kilmarnock KA3 4BN; T.-01560 484807.

Marshall, Professor Mary Tara, MA, DSA, DASS. Director, Dementia Services Development Centre, Stirling University; b. 13.6.45, Darjeeling, India. Educ. Mary Erskine School for Girls; Edinburgh University; London School of Economics; Liverpool University. Child Care Officer, London Borough of Lambeth, 1967-69; Social Worker, Personal Service Society, Liverpool, 1970-74; Research Organiser, Age Concern, Liverpool, 1974-75; Lecturer in Social Studies, Liverpool University, 1975-83; Director, Age Concern Scotland, 1983-89. Depute Chair, Edinvar Housing Association Board; Governor, Centre for Policy on Ageing; Vice Chair, Comic Relief, UK Grants Committee; Member: Journal of Dementia Care Advisory Board, Health and Social Care in the Community Editorial Advisory Board, Royal Commission on Long-term Care of

the Elderly. Publications: I Can't Place This Place At All: Working with people with dementia and their carers, 1996; The State of Art in Dementia Care, 1997. Recreations: photography; bird-watching. Address: (b.) Dementia Services Development Centre, Stirling University, Stirling FK9 4LA; T.-01786 467740.

Marshall, Maud Evelyn, MA (Hons), MSc, MRTPI. Chairperson, Building Standards Advisory Committee; Chairperson, Lottery Capital Committee, Scottish Arts Council; Member, Scottish Arts Council; b. 24.1.50, Glasgow. Educ. Park School, Glasgow; Edinburgh University; Swiss Federal Institute of Technology; Strathclyde University. Managing Director, South and West, Scottish Homes. Recreations: skiing; music; travel. Address: (b.) St. James House, 25 St. James Street, Paisley PA3 2HQ; T.-0141-842 3209.

Marshall, Thomas Graham, LLB, WS, FCIArb. Solicitor; Partner, Bishop and Robertson Chalmers, Edinburgh, since 1988; Solicitor Advocate, since 1995; b. 2.4.57, Kilmacolm; m., Anne Gibson; 3 s.; 1 d. Educ. Loretto School; Dundee University. Collector of Taxes, 1980-81; Law Apprentice, then Assistant Solicitor, Bishop & Co., Glasgow, 1982-86; Senior Assistant, Bishop and Robertson Chalmers, Glasgow, 1986-88. Secretary, Eurocopy Complainers Advisory Group, 1991-95; Fellow, Chartered Institute of Arbitrators, since 1993; Chair, Dunfermline East Constituency Labour Party, since 1992. Publications: The Scots Dimension to Cross Border Litigation (Contributor), 1996. Recreations: family; Fife Opera; cricket (Largo C.C.). Address: (b.) 22 Ainslie Place, Edinburgh EH3 6AJ; T.-0131-220 3355.

Martin, Daniel, MA, BSc, PhD, FRSE, CMath, FIMA. Honorary Lecturer in Mathematics, Glasgow University, since 1980; b. 16.4.15, Carluke. Educ. High School of Glasgow; Glasgow University. Lecturer in Mathematics, Royal Technical College, Glasgow, 1938-47; Scientific Officer, Air Navigation Section, Royal Aircraft Establishment, Farnborough, 1941-45; Lecturer/Senior Lecturer in Mathematics, Glasgow University, 1947-80; Snell Visitor to Balliol College, Oxford, 1975-76. President: Glasgow Mathematical Association, 1958-59, Edinburgh Mathematical Society, 1960-61; former Assessor, Church of Scotland's selection schools for candidates for the Ministry. Publications: Solving Problems in Complex Numbers, 1968; An Introduction to Vector Analysis (Reviser), 1970; Manifold Theory: an introduction for mathematical physicists, 1991. Recreations: theology; local history; Gaelic. Address: (b.) Department of Mathematics, Glasgow University, Glasgow G12 8QW; T.-0141-339 8855, Ext. 6537.

Martin, David McLeod, DA, RSW, RGI. Painter; b. 30.12.22, Glasgow; m., Isobel Agnes Fowlie Smith; 4 s. Educ. Govan High School; Glasgow School of Art; Jordanhill College of Education. RAF, 1942-46. Principal Teacher, Hamilton Grammar School, 1973-83; retired early to paint full-time; exhibits regularly in Scotland; exhibited RA, 1984; numerous group shows; one man shows, Glasgow, Edinburgh, Perth, Greenock, Newcastle, Stenton, London; former Vice President, RSW. Address: (h.) The Old Schoolhouse, 53 Gilmour Street, Eaglesham, Glasgow G76 0LG.

Martin, David Weir, BA (Econ), MA. Member (Labour), European Parliament, for Lothians, since 1984; Vice-President, European Parliament, since 1989; b. 26.8.54, Edinburgh; m., Margaret Mary Cook; 1 s.; 1 d. Educ. Liberton High School; Heriot-Watt University; Leicester University. Worked as stockbroker's assistant and animal rights campaigner; became Lothian Regional Councillor, 1982; Vice-President, Mobile Projects; Director, St. Andrew Animal Fund; Rapporteur, Intergovernmental Conferences. Publications: Bringing Common Sense to the

Common Market — A Left Agenda for Europe; European Union and the Democratic Deficit; Europe — An Ever Closer Union; Towards a Wider, Deeper, Federal Europe; Maastricht in a Minute; 1996 and all that; A Partnership Democracy for Europe. Recreations: soccer; reading. Address: (b.) 4 Lothian Street, Dalkeith EH22 1DS.

Martin, Donald, MA. Editor, Evening Express, Aberdeen, since 1997; b. 23.4.64, Glasgow. Educ. Bishopbriggs High School; Glasgow University. Assistant Editor/Deputy Editor, Thames Valley Newspapers; Launch Editor, Edinburgh and Lothians Post; Group Editor, Thames Valley Newspapers; Production Editor/Chief Sub, Evening Post; Deputy Editor, Cambridge Evening News; Editor, North West Evening Mail. Recreations: golf; football; sailing. Address: (b.) Aberdeen Journals Ltd., Lang Stracht, Mastrick, Aberdeen AB15 6DP; T.-01224 690222.

Martin, Professor Ged, BA, MA, PhD, FRHistS. Professor and Director, Centre of Canadian Studies, Edinburgh University, since 1983; Past President, British Association for Canadian Studies; b. 22.5.45, Hornchurch; m., Ann Barry. Educ. Royal Liberty School, Romford; Magdalene College, Cambridge. Research Fellow, Magdalene College, Cambridge, 1970-72, Australian National University, 1972-77; Lecturer, then Statutory Lecturer, University College, Cork, 1977-83. Canadian High Commissioner's Award for Service to British-Canadian Relations, 1989. Publications: ten books, including Canada's Heritage in Scotland (Co-author), 1989. Recreations: reading and writing history; music; talking to cats. Address: (b.) 21 George Square, Edinburgh EH8 9LD; T.-0131-667 1011, Ext. 6801.

Martin, Graham Dunstan, MA, BLitt, GradCertEd. Writer; Senior Lecturer, Edinburgh University, since 1982; b. 21.10.32, Leeds; m., 1, Ryllis Daniel; 2 s.; 1 d.; 2, Anne Crombie; 2 s. Educ. Leeds Grammar School; Oriel College and Linacre College, Oxford. Schoolteacher, 1956-65; Assistant Lecturer, then Lecturer, in French, Edinburgh University, 1965-82. Publications: (philosophy) Language, Truth and Poetry, 1975; The Architecture of Experience 1981, Shadows in the Cave, 1990; (novels) Giftwish, 1980; Catchfire, 1981; The Soul Master, 1984; Time-Slip, 1986; The Dream Wall, 1987; Half a Glass of Moonshine, 1988; poems and poetry translations. Recreations: music; jazz; walking; good food; the Celtic past. Address: (b.) French Department, Edinburgh University, 60 George Square, Edinburgh EH8 9JU; T.-0131-650 8409.

Martin, Rev. James, MA, BD, DD. Minister, High Carntyne, Glasgow, 1954-87; b. 21.1.21, Motherwell; m., Marion Gordon Greig; 2 d. Educ. Dalziel High School, Motherwell; Glasgow University. Minister, Newmilns West Church, 1946-54; Convener, Publications Committee, General Assembly, 1978-83 and Board of Communications, 1983-87. Publications: Did Jesus Rise from the Dead?; The Reliability of the Gospels; Letters of Caiaphas to Annas; Suffering Man, Loving God; The Road to the Aisle; People in the Jesus Story; A Plain Man in the Holy Land; Listening to the Bible; William Barclay: A Personal Memoir; My Friend Bobby; It's You, Minister; It's My Belief; Travels in the Holy Land; God-Collared; William Barclay in a Nutshell; You Can't Be Serious; A Parish Minister's Hats; More About Bobby. Recreations: football; tennis; conversation. Address: 9 Magnolia Street, Wishaw; T.-01698 385825.

Martin, John Sharp Buchanan, BSc. Under Secretary, School Education and Sport, Scottish Office, since 1992; b. 7.7.46, West Kilbride; m., Catriona Meldrum; 1 s.; 1 d. Educ. Bell-Baxter High School, Cupar; St. Andrews University. Assistant Principal, 1968-73; Private Secretary to Parliamentary Under Secretary of State, 1971-73; Principal, 1973-79; Rayner Scrutinies, 1979-80; Assistant Secretary, Highlands and Tourism Division, 1980-84; Housing Division 1, 1984-89; Transport and Local Roads

Division, 1989-92. Recreations: tennis; cricket; golf; philately. Address: (b.) Victoria Quay, Leith, Edinburgh; T.-0131-244 7108.

Martin, Michael John. Deputy Speaker of the House of Commons, since 1997; MP (Labour), Glasgow Springburn, since 1979; Chairman, Scottish Grand Committee, since 1987; b. 3.7.45, Glasgow; m., Mary McLay; 1 s.; 1 d. Educ. St. Patrick's Boys' School, Glasgow. Member, Glasgow Corporation, 1973-74, and of Glasgow District Council, 1974-79. Member, Speaker's Panel of Chairmen, since 1987; Fellow, Parliament and Industry Trust; Secretary, British-Italian Parliamentary Group; Member, College of Piping. Recreations: hill-walking; studying history of Forth and Clyde Canal; listening to pipe band music. Address: (h.) 144 Broomfield Road, Glasgow G21 3UE; T.-0141-558 2975.

Martin, Robert (Roy) Logan, QC, LLB. Advocate, since 1976; Barrister, since 1990; b. 31.7.50, Glasgow; m., Fiona Frances Neil; 1 s.; 2 d. Educ. Paisley Grammar School; Glasgow University. Solicitor, 1973-76; Member, Sheriff Courts Rules Council, 1981-84; Standing Junior Counsel, Department of Employment (Scotland), 1983-84; Advocate-Depute, 1984-87; admitted to Bar of New South Wales, 1987; Queen's Counsel, 1988; called to the Bar, Lincoln's Inn, 1990; Chairman (part-time), Industrial Tribunals, 1990-96; Chairman, Scottish Planning, Local Government and Environmental Bar Group, 1991-96. Affiliate, Royal Incorporation of Architects in Scotland, 1995; Honorary Secretary, The Wagering Club, 1982-91. Recreations: shooting; skiing; modern architecture; vintage motor cars. Address: (h.) Hardengreen House, Dalkeith EH22 3LF; T.-0131-660 5997.

Martin, Professor Roderick, MA, DPhil, DLitt. Professor of Organizational Behaviour, Glasgow University, since 1992 (Director, Glasgow University Business School, 1992-96); b. 18.10.40, Lancaster; 1 s.; 2 d. Educ. Royal Grammar School, Lancaster; Balliol College, Oxford; University of Pennsylvania; Nuffield College, Oxford. Lecturer, York University, 1964-66; Lecturer in Sociology, Oxford University, 1966-69; Fellow and Tutor in Politics and Sociology, Trinity College, Oxford, 1969-84; Professor of Industrial Sociology, Imperial College, London, 1984-88; Fellow, Templeton College, Oxford, 1988-91. Member, ESRC Research Grants Board, 1987-91. Publications: eight books, including Bargaining Power, 1992. Recreations: reading; listening to music. Address: (b.) 55-59 South Park Avenue, Glasgow G12 8LF; T.-0141-330 5410.

Martin, Professor Ursula Hilda Mary, MA, PhD, CEng, FRSA. Professor, School of Mathematical and Computational Sciences, University of St Andrews, since 1992; b. 3.8.53, London. Educ. Cambridge University. Lecturer, London University, 1978-81; Visiting Professor, University of Illinois, 1981-83; Lecturer, Manchester University, 1983-87; Reader, then Professor, London University, 1987-92. Address: (b.) School of Mathematical and Computational Sciences, Computer Science Division, University of St Andrews, North Haugh, St. Andrews KY16 9SS; T.-01334 463252.

Martin-Bates, Robert Stuart, BL. Honorary Sheriff, Perth, since 1989; b. 8.5.21, Perth; m., Ursula Louise Sarena Peter; 2 s. Educ. Glenalmond College; Edinburgh University. Served in Royal Navy, 1941-46; private practice as solicitor in Perth and Pitlochry, 1948-90; Burgh Prosecutor, Crieff, 1960-74; Depute Burgh Prosecutor, Perth, 1963-74. Member and Past Moderator, Perth Society of High Constables, since 1957; Past President, Society of Solicitors of the City and County of Perth; Member: Committee, Perth Model Lodging House Association, 1950-85 (Chairman, 1968-85), Committee, Perthshire & Kinrosshire Society for the Blind, 1979-89, including three years as Chairman, now Hon. Vice-President. Recreations:

golf; gardening; reading. Address: (h.) Immeriach, Glencarse, Perth PH2 7NF; T.-01738 860284.

Marwick, George Robert, SDA, JP. Lord Lieutenant for Orkney, 1997 (Vice Lieutenant, 1995, Deputy Lieutenant, 1976); Chairman, Swannay Farms Ltd., since 1972; Chairman, Campbeltown Creamery (Holdings) Ltd., 1974-90; b. 27.2.32, Edinburgh; m., 1, Hanne Jensen; 3 d.; 2, Norma Gerrard. Educ. Port Regis; Bryanston; Edinburgh School of Agriculture. Councillor, local government, 1968-78; Vice-Convener, Orkney County Council, 1970-74, Convener, Orkney Islands Council, 1974-78; Chairman, North of Scotland Water Board, 1970-73; Member, Scottish Agricultural Consultative Panel, since 1972 (formerly Winter Keep Panel, 1964-72); Director: North Eastern Farmers Ltd., since 1968, Orkney Islands Shipping Co., 1972-87; Member: Countryside Commission for Scotland, 1978-86, Council, National Trust for Scotland, 1979-84. Recreations: shooting; tennis; motor sport. Address: (h.) Swannay House, by Evie, Orkney; T.-01856 721365.

Mason, Christopher Michael, MA, PhD. Chairman, Clyde Maritime Trust Ltd., since 1991; Member, City of Glasgow Council, since 1995; b. 8.3.41, Hexham; m., Stephanie Maycock; 2 d. Educ. Marlborough College; Magdalene College, Cambridge. Lecturer in Politics, Glasgow University, 1966-93; Alliance candidate, Glasgow, European Elections, 1984; Liberal Democrat candidate in General Elections, Glasgow Hillhead, 1992, Eastwood, 1997; Chairman, Scottish Liberal Party, 1987-88; Member, Strathclyde Regional Council, 1982-96; Leader, Strathclyde Liberal Democrat Group, 1986-96; Member, Scottish Constitutional Convention, 1989-97. Publication: Effective Management of Resources: The International Politics of the North Sea, 1979. Recreation: sailing. Address: (b.) City Chambers, Glasgow G2 1DU; T.-0141 287 4448.

Mason, Professor Sir David Kean, KB, CBE, BDS, MD, FRCS, FDS, FRCPath, Hon. DSc, Hon. DChD, Hon. LLD, Hon. FFD, Hon. FDS, Hon. FRCS. President, General Dental Council, 1989-94; Honorary Consultant Dental Surgeon, since 1965; b. 5.11.28, Paisley; m., Judith Armstrong; 2 s.; 1 d. Educ. Paisley Grammar School; Glasgow Academy; St. Andrews University; Glasgow University. RAF Dental Branch, 1952-54; Registrar in Oral Surgery, Dundee, 1954-56; Senior Lecturer in Dental Surgery and Pathology, Glasgow University, 1964-67; Professor of Oral Medicine, Glasgow University, 1967-92 (Dean of Dental Education, 1980-90); Chairman, National Dental Consultative Committee, 1976-80; Member: Medicines Commission, 1976-80, Dental Committee, MRC, 1973-83, Physiological Systems Board, MRC, 1976-80, GDC, 1976-93, Dental Strategy Review Group, 1980-81, Dental Review Working Party, UGC, 1986-87, WHO Expert Committee on Oral Health, since 1991; Convener, Dental Council, RCPSGlas, 1977-80; John Tomes Prize, RCS England, 1979; Colyer Prize RCS England, 1993; Honorary Member, British Dental Association, 1993; Honorary Member, American Dental Association, 1994. Publications: Salivary Glands in Health and Disease (Co-Author); Introduction to Oral Medicine (Co-Author); Self Assessment: Manuals I and II (Co-Editor); Oral Manifestations of Systemic Disease. Recreations: golf; tennis; gardening; enjoying the pleasure of the countryside. Address: (h.) Greystones, Houston Road, Kilmacolm, Renfrewshire; T.-Kilmacolm 2001.

Mason, Derek Stevens, CBE (1986), JP, FRICS, FFB. Partner, John Baxter, Dunn and Gray, Chartered Quantity Surveyors, since 1970; Chairman, Hutchesons' Educational Trust (Governor, since 1972); Chairman, West Glasgow Hospitals University NHS Trust, since 1996; b. 21.5.34, Glasgow; m., Jeanette M. Mason, OBE, JP; 2 s.; 1 d. Educ. Allan Glen's School, Glasgow; Royal Technical College (part-time). RICS: Chairman, West of Scotland Junior Sub-Branch, 1965-66, Chairman, Scottish Junior Branch, 1966-

67, Chairman, Scottish Branch, Faculty of Building, since 1994; Councillor, Glasgow Corporation, 1970 and 1972-75, Glasgow District Council, 1974-84 (Deputy Leader, Conservative Group, 1977-80, Bailie, 1977-80); Chairman, Glasgow Sports Promotion Council, 1977-80 (Hon. Vice-President, since 1980); Preceptor, Hutchesons' Hospital, 1978-80; JP, since 1977; Past Deacon, Incorporation of Masons of Glasgow; Chairman, Scottish Special Housing Association, 1981-89; Member: Merchants House of Glasgow, SCOTVEC Council, 1993-97, Glasgow Eastern Merchants Association, Incorporation of Tailors of Rutherglen, Incorporation of Wrights in Glasgow; Elder, Newlands South Church of Scotland. Recreations: reading; current affairs; watching football. Address: (h.) Carinya, 77 Newlands Road, Glasgow G43 2JP; T.-0141-649 2665.

Mason, Douglas C., BSc. Member, Glenrothes Development Corporation, 1985-96; Parliamentary Research Assistant, 1979-97; Freelance Journalist, since 1977; b. 30.9.41, Dunfermline. Educ. Bradford Grammar School; St. Andrews University. Conservative Party Organising Secretary, 1969-77; Member: Fife County Council, 1967-70, Kirkcaldy District Council, 1974-88, Scottish Housing Advisory Committee, 1978-80; contested Central Fife, General Election, 1983; Convener, General Council Business Committee, St. Andrews University. Domestic Policy Adviser, Adam Smith Institute, since 1984. Publications: Allocation and Transfer of Council Houses (Co-Author), 1980; The Qualgo Complex, 1984; Revising the Rating System, 1985; Room for Improvement, 1985; University Challenge, 1986; Time to Call Time, 1986; Ex Libris, 1986; Expounding the Arts, 1987; Licensed to Live, 1988; Pining for Profit, 1988; A Home for Enterprise, 1989; Privatizing the Posts, 1989; Wiser Councils and Shedding a Tier, 1989; Wood for the Trees, 1991; City in the Mist (Co-Editor), 1995. Recreations: books; music. Address: (h.) 84 Barnton Place, Glenrothes, Fife; T.-01592 758766.

Mason, John Kenneth, BA (Oxon), MPhil. Head of Industrial Policy, The Scottish Office, since 1996; b. 26.6.56, Chichester; m., Alison Margaret Cruickshanks; 1 s.; 2 d. Educ. Chichester High School; Hertford College, Oxford; University College, London. Kent County Council, 1980-85; Department of Environment, 1985-90; Scottish Office, 1990-94; Registers of Scotland, 1994-96. Recreations: photography; gardening. Address: (b.) Meridian Court, 5 Cadogan Street, Glasgow G2 6AT; T.-0141-242 5537.

Mason, Professor Emeritus John Kenyon French, CBE, MD, LLD, FRCPath, DMJ, FRSE. Regius Professor of Forensic Medicine, Edinburgh University, 1973-85; b. 19.12.19, Lahore; m., Elizabeth Latham (deceased); 2 s. Educ. Downside School; Cambridge University; St. Bartholomew's Hospital. Regular Officer, Medical Branch, RAF, following War Service; Consultant in charge, RAF Department of Aviation and Forensic Pathology, 1957-73. President, British Association in Forensic Medicine, 1981-83; Swiney Prize in Jurisprudence, 1978. Publication: Forensic Medicine for Lawyers, 3rd Edition; Law and Medical Ethics, 4th Edition (Co-Author); Medico-legal Aspects of Reproduction and Parenthood, 2nd Edition; Human Life and Medical Practice. Address: (h.) 66 Craiglea Drive, Edinburgh EH10 5PF; T.-0131-447 2301.

Massie, Allan Johnstone, BA, FRSL. Author and Journalist; b. 16.10.38, Singapore; m., Alison Langlands; 2 s.; 1 d. Educ. Drumtochty Castle; Trinity College, Glenalmond; Trinity College, Cambridge. Schoolmaster, Drumtochty Castle, 1960-71; taught EFL, 1972-75; Creative Writing Fellow, Edinburgh University, 1982-84, Glasgow and Strathclyde Universities, 1985-86; Editor, New Edinburgh Review, 1982-84; Fiction Reviewer, The Scotsman, since 1975; Television Critic, Sunday Standard, 1981-83 (Fraser of Allander Award, Critic of the Year,

1982); Sports Columnist, Glasgow Herald, 1985-88; Columnist: Daily Telegraph, Daily Mail. Publications: (novels): Change and Decay in all around I see; The Last Peacock; The Death of Men (Scottish Arts Council Book Award); One Night in Winter; Augustus; A Question of Loyalties; The Sins of the Father; Tiberius; The Hanging Tree; Caesar; These Enchanted Woods; The Ragged Lion; King David; (non-fiction): Muriel Spark; Ill Met by Gaslight; The Caesars; Portrait of Scottish Rugby; Colette; 101 Great Scots; Byron's Travels; Glasgow; Edinburgh; (as Editor): Edinburgh and the Borders in Verse; (radio play): Quintet in October; (plays): The Minstrel and the Shirra; First-Class Passengers. Recreations: reading; watching rugby, cricket, racing; walking the dogs. Address: (h.) Thirladean House, Selkirk, TD7 5LU; T.-Selkirk 20393.

Masson, Alastair H.B., BA, MB, ChB, FRCSEdin, FRCA; b. 30.1.25, Bathgate; m., Marjorie Nan Paisley-Whyte; 3 s.; 1 d. Educ. Bathgate Academy; Edinburgh University. Consultant Anaesthetist, Edinburgh Royal Infirmary (retired); Visiting Professor of Anesthesiology, South Western Medical School, Dallas, Texas, 1962-63. President: Scottish Society of Anaesthetists, 1978-79, British Society of the History of Medicine, 1989-91; Honorary Archivist, Royal College of Surgeons, Edinburgh; President, Scottish Society of the History of Medicine, 1984-87. Publication: Portraits, Paintings and Busts in the Royal College of Surgeons of Edinburgh, 1995. Recreations: golf; hillwalking; music; travel. Address: (h.) 28 Beechmount Park, Edinburgh.

Masterman, Eileen Mary, MA (Hons), ACIArb. Director, Royal Institution of Chartered Surveyors in Scotland, since 1992; Member, Committee of Investigation for Great Britain, since 1995; Member, Extra Parliamentary Panel, since 1996; b. Spennymoor, Co. Durham; m., Norman A. Fiddes; 2 d. Educ. St. Anthony's School for Girls, Sunderland; Dundee University. Research Assistant, Dundee University, 1976-80; Investigator and Complaints Examiner, Commissioner for Local Administration in Scotland, 1980-90; Advocates' Clerk/Business Manager, Faculty of Advocates, 1990-92. Member, Building Standards Advisory Committee, 1994-97; Director, Edinburgh Chamber of Commerce, 1994-97. Recreations: walking; reading. Address: (b.) 9 Manor Place, Edinburgh EH3 7DN; T.-0131-225 7078.

Masters, Christopher, BSc (Hons), PhD, AKC. Chief Executive, Christian Salvesen PLC, since 1989; Executive Chairman Designate, Aggreho plc, since 1997; b. 2.5.47, Northallerton; m., Gillian Mary Hodson; 2 d. Educ. Richmond School; King's College, London; Leeds University. Shell Research BV/Shell Chemicals UK Ltd., 1971-77; joined Christian Salvesen as Business Development Manager, 1979; transferred to Christian Salvesen Inc., USA, 1982, as Director of Planning; Managing Director, Christian Salvesen Seafoods, 1983; Managing Director, Industrial Services Division, 1985; appointed a Director, Christian Salvesen PLC, 1987. Member, Scottish Board of Young Enterprise, since 1994; Chairman, Quality Assessment Committee of Higher Education Funding Council, 1991-95; Member, Scottish Higher Education Funding Council, since 1995; Non-Executive Director: British Assets Trust, since 1989, Scottish Widows, since 1991, Scottish Chamber Orchestra Trust, since 1993; Vice Chairman, Scottish Opera, since 1996. Recreations: wines; music. Address: (b.) Aggreho plc, 121 West Regent Street, Glasgow G2 2SD; T.-0141-225 5900.

Masterton, Gavin George, FIB (Scot). Treasurer and Chief General Manager, Bank of Scotland, since 1996; b. 19.11.41, Dunfermline; m., Sheila; 3 d. Educ. Dunfermline High School; Harvard University (AMP). Began banking career with British Linen Bank, 1957; branch banking for several years, then to various Head Office functions;

initiated bank's move into structured finance and management buy-out market. Address: (b.) Bank of Scotland, The Mound, Edinburgh.

Mather, John, CBE, FSCA, FCIS, FCIT. Former Executive Chairman, Clydeport Ltd.; b. 17.12.36, Glasgow. Former President, International Association of Ports and Harbors of the World.

Matheson, Alexander (Sandy), OBE, FRPharmS, MRSH, DL, JP. Chairman, Western Isles Health Board (Member, since 1973; Vice-Chairman, 1991-93); b. 16.11.41, Stornoway; m., Irene Mary Davidson, BSc, MSc; 2 s.; 2 d. Educ. Nicolson Institute, Stornoway; Robert Gordon's Institute of Technology, Aberdeen. Chairman, Stornoway Pier and Harbour Commission, since 1991 (Member, since 1968); Member, Stornoway Trust Estate, since 1967 (Chairman, 1971-81); Chairman: Stornoway Branch, RNLI, Western Isles Development Fund, since 1972; Member, Stornoway Town Council, 1967-75; Provost of Stornoway, 1971-75; Member: Ross and Cromarty County Council, 1967-75, Western Isles Islands Council, 1974-94 (Chairman, Development Services, 1974-80, Vice-Convener, 1980-82, Convener, 1982-90); President, Islands Commission of the Conference of Peripheral Maritime Regions of Europe, 1987-91 and 1993-94; Honorary Sheriff, since 1972; Vice Lieutenant, Western Isles Islands Area; Director, Harris Tweed Authority; Director, Callanish Ltd.; Chairman and Superintendent Pharmacist, Roderick Smith Ltd., Stornoway. Address: (h.) 33 Newton Street, Stornoway, Isle of Lewis; T.-01851 702082.

Matheson, Allen Short, CBE, FRIBA, PPRIAS, MRTPI. Retired Partner, Matheson Gleave Partnership; b. 28.2.26, Egypt; m., Catherine Anne; 2 s. Educ. George Watson's College; Edinburgh College of Art. Past President, Royal Incorporation of Architects in Scotland; Past Chairman, Scottish Construction Industry Group; former Vice-Chairman, Board of Governors, Glasgow School of Art; former Director, Glasgow Chamber of Commerce; former Member, Royal Fine Art Commission for Scotland; Past Chairman, Joint Standing Committee of Architects, Surveyors and Building Contractors. Address: (h.) 11 Spence Street, Glasgow G20 0AW; T.-0141-946 5670.

Matheson, Lindsay S.G., MA, MLitt. Rector, Madras College, St. Andrews, since 1997; b. 2.10.44, Edinburgh; m., Katherine R.; 2 d. Educ. Otago Boys' High School, Dunedin; George Watson's, Edinburgh; St. Andrews University; Oxford University. History Teacher, Banff Academy, 1970-72; Principal Teacher of History, Lochaber High School, 1972-80; Assistant Rector, Inverurie Academy, 1980-85; Headmaster, Milne's High School, Fochabers, 1985-97. Recreations: cycling; golf; bridge. Address: (h.) 52 Largo Road, St. Andrews, Fife; T.-01334 472744.

Matheson, Susan Margaret Graham, BSc (Soc Sci). Chief Executive, Sacro, since 1996; b. 6.6.49, Tarbert, Harris; 1 d. Educ. St. George's School for Girls, Edinburgh; Edinburgh University. Antique dealer, 1971-73; Research Officer, then Senior Research Officer, Scottish Office Central Research Unit, 1973-88; Director, Family Mediation Scotland, 1988-96. Publications: several Government research reports and other publications. Recreation: skiing. Address: (b.) 31 Palmerston Place, Edinburgh EH12 5AP; T.-0131-226 4222.

Mathews, Very Rev. Canon Eugene Joseph, JCL. Parish Priest of Girvan, since 1982; b. 2.9.21, Dumfries. Educ. St. Joseph's College, Dumfries; Blairs College, Aberdeen; Scots College, Rome; St. Peter's College, Bearsden; Gregorian University, Rome. Ordained Priest, St. Andrew's Cathedral, Glasgow, 1946; Curate, St. Mary's, Saltcoats, 1949-56; Parish Priest: Kirkconnel, 1956-63, Maybole, 1963-67, Kilbirnie, 1967-73, St. Michael's, Kilmarnock,

1973-82. Publications: Counting My Blessings; Counting My Joys. Recreation: reading. Address: 17 Harbour Street, Girvan KA26 9AJ; T.-01465 713331.

Mathewson, David Carr, BSc, CA. Merchant Banker; Director, Noble Grossart Limited, since 1989; b. 26.7.47, Broughty Ferry; m., Jan McIntyre; 1 s.; 1 d. Educ. Daniel Stewart's College, Edinburgh; St. Andrews University. Deloitte Haskins & Sells, Edinburgh, 1968-72; Williams Glyn & Co., London, 1972-75; Nedbank Group, South Africa, 1976-86; Noble Grossart Limited, since 1986; Director, Quicks Group plc, since 1991, Rodime plc, since 1992. Recreations: family interests; golf; skiing; athletics. Address: (b.) 48 Queen Street, Edinburgh EH2 3NR; T.-0131-226 7011.

Mathewson, George Ross, CBE, BSc, PHD, MBA, LLD, FRSE, CEng, MIEE, CBIM, FCIBS. Group Chief Executive, Royal Bank of Scotland Group plc, Royal Bank of Scotland plc, since 1992; Director, Strategic Planning and Development, Royal Bank of Scotland Group plc, Royal Bank of Scotland plc, since 1987; Director: Scottish Investment Trust Ltd., since 1981, Citizens Financial Group, since 1999, Direct Line Insurance plc, since 1990; b. 14.5.40, Dunfermline; m., Sheila Alexandra Graham Bennett; 2 s. Educ. Perth Academy; St. Andrews University; Canisius College, Buffalo, New York. Assistant Lecturer, St. Andrews University, 1964-67; Systems Engineer (various positions), Bell Aerospace, Buffalo, New York, 1967-72; ICFC: Executive in Edinburgh Area Office, 1972-81, Area Manager, 1974-79, Director and Assistant General Manager, 1979-81; Chief Executive, Scottish Development Agency, 1981-87. Recreations: tennis; skiing; geriatric rugby; golf; business. Address: (h.) 29 Saxe Coburg Place, Edinburgh EH3 5BP.

Mathieson, John George, CBE, TD, DL, BL, WS. Solicitor; Chairman, Thorntons, WS, Tayside, 1990-97; b. 15.6.32, Argyll; m., Shirley Bidder; 1 s.; 1 d. Educ. George Watson's College, Edinburgh; Glasgow University. Territorial Army, 1951-86: Commanding Officer The Highland Regiment RA, TA Colonel for Highlands, Honorary Colonel 105 Regiment RA(TA), Chairman, Highlands TA Association; ADC TA, the Queen, 1975-80. Commenced practice as Solicitor, Glasgow, 1955; Partner, Clark Oliver, Arbroath, 1959; Scottish Director, Woolwich Building Society, 1975; Chairman: Independent Tribunal Service, 1992, Arbroath Branch, Royal British Legion and Earl Haig Fund; Deputy Lieutenant, Angus, 1977; Chairman: Scottish Solicitors Discipline Tribunal, 1986-92, Royal Artillery Council for Scotland; Honorary President, Angus Bn., Boys' Brigade; Elder, Colliston Parish Church. Recreations: shooting; golf; gardening. Address: (h.) Willanyards, Colliston, Arbroath, Angus; T.-01241 890286.

Matthews, Baird, BL. Solicitor in private practice, since 1950; Honorary Sheriff, Kirkcudbright and Stranraer; b. 19.1.25, Newton Stewart; m., Mary Thomson Hope; 2 s.; 1 d. Educ. Douglas Ewart High School; Edinburgh University. Commissioned, Royal Scots Fusiliers, 1944; demobilised as Captain, 1st Bn., 1947; Partner, A. B. & A. Matthews, Solicitors, Newton Stewart, since 1950; Clerk to General Commissioners of Income Tax, Stranraer and Newton Stewart Districts, from 1952; Burgh Prosecutor, Newton Stewart, from 1968; Depute Procurator Fiscal for Wigtownshire, 1970; Chairman, Board of Local Directors, General Accident Fire and Life Assurance Corporation, 1988; Director, Newcastle Building Society (Scottish Board), 1991; Dean of Faculty of Stewartry of Kirkcudbright Solicitors, 1979; Dean of Faculty of Solicitors of the District of Wigtown, 1983; Chairman, Appeals Tribunal, 1984; President, Newton Stewart Golf Club 1996 (Centenary Year). Recreations: golf; curling. Address: (b.) Bank of Scotland Buildings, Newton Stewart, Wigtownshire; T.-01671 404100.

Matthews, Herbert Eric, MA (Oxon), BPhil (Oxon). Professor of Philosophy, Aberdeen University, since 1995 (Head, Department of Philosophy, 1989-96); b. 24.10.36, Liverpool; m., Hellen Kilpatrick Matthews; 2 s. Educ. Liverpool Institute High School for Boys; St. John's College, Oxford. Lecturer, Department of Logic, Aberdeen University, 1963; Reader in Philosophy, 1993. Publications: numerous articles in learned journals; translations of works of German philosophy; The Philosophy of Thomas Reid (Editor); Philosophy and Health Care (Editor); Twentieth Century French Philosophy. Recreations: cinema; reading; walking; cycling. Address: (b.) Department of Philosophy, Aberdeen University, Aberdeen AB24 3UB; T.-01224 272367.

Matthews, Hugh, QC, LLB. Sheriff of Glasgow and Strathkelvin at Glasgow. Admitted, Faculty of Advocates, 1979. Address: (b.) Sheriff Court House, 1 Carlton Place, Glasgow, G5 9DA.

Matthews, Professor John Burr Lumley, MA, DPhil, FRSE. Secretary, Scottish Association for Marine Science; Honorary Professor, Stirling University, since 1984; b. 23.4.35, Isleworth; m., Jane Rosemary; 1 s.; 2 d. Educ. Warwick School; Oxford University. Research Scientist (Zooplankton), Oceanographic Laboratory, Edinburgh, 1961-67; Senior Lecturer, Department of Marine Biology, then Professor of Marine Biology, University of Bergen, 1967-84; Visiting Professor, University of British Columbia, 1977-78; Director, NERC Dunstaffnage Marine Laboratory, 1988-94; Deputy Chairman, South West Regional Board, Scottish Natural Heritage, 1994-97. Recreations: cross country skiing; gardening; wine-making. Address: (h.) Grianaig, Rockfield Road, Oban PA34 5DH; T.-01631 562734.

Matthews, Peter A.H., LLB, WS, NP. Solicitor, since 1977; Senior Partner, A.B. & A. Matthews, since 1997; b. 30.12.54, Dumfries; m., Mary Josephine; 2 d. Educ. Edinburgh Academy; Edinburgh University. Tods Murray & Jamieson, WS, Edinburgh, 1975; Shepherd & Wedderburn, WS, Edinburgh, 1977; A.B. & A. Matthews, since 1979. Dean, Wigtown District Faculty of Solicitors. Address: (b.) Bank of Scotland Buildings, Newton Stewart DG8 6EG.

Maver, Professor Thomas Watt, BSc (Hons), PhD, FInstE, FRSA, HonFRIAS. Professor of Computer Aided Design, Department of Architecture and Building Science, and Director of the Graduate School, Strathclyde University, since 1982 (Head of Department, 1983-85, 1988-91, Vice-Dean, Faculty of Engineering, 1993-96); b. 10.3.38, Glasgow; m., Avril Elizabeth Cuthbertson; 2 d. Educ. Eastwood Secondary School; Glasgow University. Special Research Fellow, Engineering Faculty, Glasgow University, 1961-67; Strathclyde University: Research Fellow, School of Architecture, 1967-70, Director, Architecture and Building Aids Computer Unit, Strathclyde, since 1970; Visiting Professor: Technical University Eindhoven, Universiti Sains Malaysia, University of Rome (La Sapienza); Past Chairman, Design Research Society; Royal Society Esso Gold Medal, 1989; Founder, CAAD Futures and ECAADE. Recreation: experiencing Europe. Address: (h.) 8 Kew Terrace, Glasgow G12 0TD; T.-0141-339 7185.

Mavor, Professor John, BSc, PhD, DSc(Eng), FRSE, FEng, FIEEE, CEng, FIEE, CPhys, FInstP. Principal and Vice-Chancellor, Napier University, since 1994; b. 18.7.42, Kilwinning; m., Susan Christina; 2 d. Educ. Bromley Technical High School; City University; London University. AEI Research Laboratories, London, 1964-65; Texas Instruments Ltd., Bedford, 1968-70; Emihus Microcomponents Ltd., Glenrothes, 1970-71; Edinburgh University: joined 1971, first holder, Lothian Chair of Microelectronics, 1980-86, Head, Department of Electrical

Engineering, 1984-89, Chairman, School of Engineering, 1987-89, Dean, Faculty of Science & Engineering, 1989-94, Chair of Electrical Enginering, 1986-94. Recreations: steam railways; hill-walking. Address: (b.) Napier University, Craiglockhart Campus, 219 Colinton Road, Edinburgh EH14 1DJ; T.-0131-455 4600.

Mavor, Ronald Henry Moray, CBE, MB, ChB, FRCP(Glas); b. 13.5.25, Glasgow; m., Sigrid Bruhn (m. diss.); 1 s.; 1 d.; 1 d. deceased. Educ. Glasgow University. In medical practice, 1948-57; Drama Critic, The Scotsman, 1957-65; Director, Scottish Arts Council, 1965-71; Professor and Head, Department of Drama, University of Saskatchewan, 1977-90; Deputy Chairman, Edinburgh Festival, 1975-81. Author of plays: The Keys of Paradise, Aurelie, War of Huntershill, The Partridge Dance, A Private Matter, The Quartet, A House on Temperance, The Grand Inquisitor; also Dr Mavor and Mr Bridie (biography). Address: (h.) 19 Falkland Street, Glasgow G12 9PY; T.-0141-339 3149.

Maxton, John Alston. BA (Oxon), DipEd (Oxon). MP (Labour), Glasgow Cathcart, since 1979; b. 5.5.36, Oxford; m., Christine Elspeth; 3 s. Educ. Lord Williams Grammar School, Thame; University College, Oxford. Lecturer in Social Studies, Hamilton College of Education, before entering Parliament; Chairman, Association of Lecturers in Colleges of Education in Scotland, 1974-78; Member, Scottish Select Committee, 1980-83, Public Accounts Committee, 1983-84; Opposition Treasury and Scottish Whip, 1984-85; Opposition Scottish Front Bench Spokesperson on Health, Local Government and Transport, 1985-87, on Industry and Local Government Finance, 1987-92; Member: National Heritage Select Committee, Speaker's Panel of Chairmen. Recreations: listening to jazz (Director, Glasgow International Jazz Festival); running. Address: (h.) 37 Larch Grove, Hamilton ML3 8NF; T.-01698 458473.

Maxwell, Donald, MA. Professional Singer; b. 12.12.48, Perth; m., Alison Jayne Norman; 1 d. Educ. Perth Academy; Edinburgh University. Former Teacher of Geography; since 1976, professional Singer with British opera companies and orchestras; Principal Baritone, Scottish Opera, 1978-82; Principal Baritone, Welsh National Opera, 1982-85; guest appearances, BBC Proms, Edinburgh Festival, Royal Opera House, London, Vienna, Paris, Milan, Tokyo, New York, Buenos Aires – notably as Falstaff; comedy – The Music Box with Linda Ormiston. Recreation: railways. Address: (b.) c/o 6 Murray Crescent, Perth.

Maxwell, Gordon Stirling, MA, FSA, FSA Scot. Archaeologist and Author; b. 21.3.38, Edinburgh; m., Kathleen Mary King; 2 d. Educ. Daniel Stewart's College, Edinburgh; St. Andrews University. Investigator (Archaeological), Royal Commission on the Ancient and Historical Monuments of Scotland, 1964-86; Head of Field Survey, RCAHMS, 1986-91, Head of Archaeology, 1991-95; President, Society of Antiquaries of Scotland, 1993-96; Hon. Professor, School of History, University of St. Andrews, since 1997. Publications: Rome's North-West Frontier: The Antonine Wall (Co-author), 1983; The Impact of Aerial Reconnaissance on Archaeology (Editor), 1983; The Romans in Scotland, 1989; A Battle Lost: Romans and Caledonians at Mons Graupius, 1990. Recreations: archaeology; gardening; aviation; Scottish literature. Address: (h.) Micklegarth, 72A High Street, Aberdour, Fife KY3 0SW; T.-01383 860796.

Maxwell, Ingval, DA, RIBA, FRIAS, FSA Scot. Director, Technical Conservation Research and Education, Historic Scotland, since 1993; b. 28.5.44, Penpont; m., Susan Isabel Maclean; 1 s.; 1 d. Educ. Dumfries Academy; Duncan of Jordanstone College of Art, Dundee. Joined Ministry of Public Buildings and Works as Architect, 1969; Area Architect, then Principal Architect, Ancient Monuments Branch, 1972-85; Assistant Director of Works, Historic Scotland, 1985-93; RIBA Research Award, 1970-71; RIAS Thomas Ross Award, 1988; Chairman, Scottish Vernacular Buildings Working Group, 1990-94; Chairman: Scottish Conservation Forum in Training and Education, since 1994, Scottish Stone Liaison Group, since 1997; Member, RIAS Conservation Working Group; Member, European Commission Cost Action C5, since 1996. Publications: Historic Scotland International Lime Conference Proceedings (Co-Editor), 1995; Building Materials of the Scottish Farmstead, 1996; Historic Scotland Traditional Building Materials Conference Proceedings (Co-Editor), 1997. Recreations: photography; astronomy; aircraft; buildings. Address: (h.) 135 Mayfield Road, Edinburgh EH9 3AN.

Maxwell, (Thomas) Fordyce, MBE. Diary Editor, Columnist, Agricultural Editor, The Scotsman, since 1989; b. 21.8.45, Northumberland; m., Liz (Elizabeth Duncan); 1 s.; 1 d. Educ. Berwick Grammar School; Harper Adams Agricultural College. Farming News, 1967-69; The Scotsman: Assistant Agricultural Editor, 1969-75, Agricultural Editor, 1975-77; farming/freelance, 1977-89; rejoined The Scotsman, 1989. Seaton Award, 1992; author of three books. Recreations: family; gardening; reading. Address: (b.) 20 North Bridge, Edinburgh; T.-0131-243 3323.

Maxwell, Professor Thomas Jefferson, BSc, PhD, CBiol, FIBiol, FRSE, FRSGS. Director, Macaulay Land Use Research Institute, since 1987 and Chief Executive, Macaulay Research and Consultancy Services, since 1994; Honorary Research Professor, Aberdeen University; b. 7.10.40, Aspatria, Cumbria; m., Christine Patrick Speedie; 1 s.; 1 d. Educ. Silcoates School, Wakefield; Edinburgh University. Specialist Animal Production Adviser, East of Scotland College of Agriculture, 1967-70; Research Scientist, then Head, Animal Production Department, Hill Farming Research Organisation, 1970-87. Recreations: reading; hill-walking; gardening. Address: (b.) Macaulay Land Use Research Institute, Craigiebuckler, Aberdeen.

Maxwell-Irving, Alastair Michael Tivey, BSc, CEng, MIEE, MIMgt, FSAScot. Antiquarian and Archaeologist; b. 1.10.35, Witham, Essex; m., Esther Mary Hamilton, MA, LLB. Educ. Lancing College; London University; Stirling University. General Electric Company, 1957; English Electric Company, 1960; Assistant Factor, Annandale Estates, 1966; Weir Pumps Ltd., 1970-91; founder Member and Secretary, 1975-78, Central Scotland Branch, British Institute of Management. Publications: Genealogy of the Irvings of Dumfries, 1965; The Irvings of Bonshaw, 1968; The Irvings of Dumfries, 1968; Lochwood Castle, 1968; Early Firearms and their Influence on the Military and Domestic Architecture of the Borders, 1974; Cramalt Tower: Historical Survey and Excavations, 1977-79, 1982; Borthwick Castle: Excavations 1979, 1982; Andrew Dunlop (Clockmakers' Company 1701-32), 1984; Hoddom Castle: A Reappraisal of its Architecture and Place in History, 1989; Lochwood Castle, 1990; The Castles of Buittle, 1991; Lockerbie Tower, 1992; Torthorwald Castle, 1993; Scottish Yetts and Window Grilles, 1994. Recreations: architecture and history of the Border towers of Scotland; archaeology; family history and genealogy; Florence and the art and architecture of Tuscany; horology; heraldry; photography; gardening. Address: (h.) Telford House, Blairlogie, Stirling FK9 5PX.

Maxwell-Scott, Dame Jean (Mary Monica), DCVO (1984). Lady in Waiting to Princess Alice, Duchess of Gloucester, since 1959; b. 8.6.23. VAD Red Cross Nurse, 1941-46; great-great-great grand-daughter of Sir Walter Scott. Address: (h.) Abbotsford, Melrose, Roxburghshire TD6 9BQ.

Maxwell-Scott, Patricia Mary, OBE. Honorary Sheriff of Selkirk, since 1971; b. 11.3.21, Curragh, Dublin; m., Harold Hugh Christian Boulton. Educ. Convent des Oiseaux, Westgate on Sea, Kent. ATP, 1942-45. Great-great-great grand-daughter of Sir Walter Scott. Recreations: travelling; reading. Address: (h.) Abbotsford, Melrose TD6 9BQ; T.-01896 752043.

May, David Jeans, MA (Hons). Rector, Craigie High School, Dundee, since 1990; b. 28.12.45, Aberdeen; m., Anne Elizabeth Raeside Eastop; 1 s.; 1 d. Educ. Robert Gordon's College, Aberdeen; Aberdeen University; Jordanhill College of Education. Teacher, St. Columba's, Gourock, 1973-74; Assistant Principal Teacher of Social Subjects, Castlehead High, Paisley, 1974-78; Principal Teacher of Modern Studies/Economics, Grange Secondary, Glasgow, 1978-84; Assistant Head Teacher, Dunoon Grammar School, 1984-87; Deputy Rector, Montrose Academy, 1987-90. Convener, SEB Modern Studies Panel; Member: Secretary of State for Scotland's Working Group on Environmental Education, Steering Committee, Scottish Office Education and Industry Department Improving School Effectiveness Project. Recreations: hill-walking; golf; gardening. Address: (h.) Evanston, Lamondfauld Lane, Hillside, Montrose DD10 9HY; T.-0167 4830673.

May, Douglas James, LLB. Queen's Counsel, since 1989; b. 7.5.46, Edinburgh. Educ. George Heriot's; Edinburgh University. Advocate, 1971; Temporary Sheriff, since 1984; Social Security Commissioner, Child Support Commissioner, since 1993; Parliamentary candidate (Conservative), Edinburgh East, 1974, Glasgow Cathcart, 1983. Recreations: golf (Captain: Scotland Universities Golfing Society, 1990-91, Merchants of Edinburgh Golf Club, 1997); photography (ARPS, 1997, President, Edinburgh Photographic Society); travel. Address: 23 Melville Street, Edinburgh; T.-0131-225 2201.

May, Malcolm Stuart, BA, BD, STM, CQSW. Chief Officer, Dundee Voluntary Action, since 1979; b. 9.9.40, Isle of Shapinsay, Orkney; m., Alison Wood; 1 s.; 1 d. Educ. Kilmarnock Academy; The Gordon Schools, Huntly; Hamilton Academy; Queen's University, Belfast; Glasgow University; Union Theological Seminary, New York. Assistant Minister, The Old Kirk, West Pilton, Edinburgh, 1966-68; staff, Iona Community, Glasgow, 1968-72; social work training, 1972-73; Training Officer, Scottish Council for Voluntary Organisations, 1973-78. Member, Board of Management, Dundee College; Non-Executive Director, Tayside Health Board. Recreations: reading; choral singing; hill-walking. Address: (b.) Kandahar House, 71 Meadowside, Dundee DD1 1EN.

Mayfield, Hon. Lord (Ian MacDonald), MC (1945), QC (Scot). Former Senator of the College of Justice in Scotland; b. 26.5.21. Sheriff Principal of Dumfries and Galloway, 1973; President, Industrial Tribunals for Scotland, 1973-81; Scottish Chairman, Employment Appeal Tribunal, 1986-92.

Meek, Brian Alexander, OBE, JP. Columnist, The Herald; Chairman, Conservative Group, City of Edinburgh Council, since 1995; b. 8.2.39, Edinburgh; m., Frances C. Horsburgh; 1 s.; 1 d. Educ. Royal High School, Edinburgh; Edinburgh Secretarial College. Joined Scotsman Publications as trainee, then Sub-Editor, Features Writer; transferred to Express Newspapers as Feature Writer, Leader Writer and Rugby Correspondent; elected, Edinburgh Corporation, 1969; Leader, Conservative Group, 1970-72; elected as Bailie, 1972; Convener, Lothian Regional Council, 1982-86; Member, Edinburgh District Council, 1992-96; Vice-President, Scottish Conservative and Unionist Association, 1989-92. Address: (b.) City of Edinburgh Council, City Chambers, High Street, Edinburgh EH1 1YJ; T.-0131-529 4953.

Meek, David, MA, MEd. Rector, Queen Anne High School, Dunfermline, since 1997; b. 20.7.54, Bonnybridge; m., Sheena Flora Meek; 2 s. Educ. Falkirk High School; Glasgow University. Teacher, Renfrew High School; Assistant Principal Teacher, Vale of Leven Academy; Principal Teacher of English, then Assistant Head Teacher, Boclair Academy; Inspector, Quality Assurance Unit, Strathclyde; Rector, Portree High School. Address: (b.) Broomhead, Dunfermline, Fife KY12 0PQ.

Meek, Professor Donald Eachann MacDonald, MA (Cantab), MA, PhD (Glas), FRHistS. Professor of Celtic, Aberdeen University, since 1993; b. 16.5.49, Glasgow, brought up in Tiree; m., Rachel Jane Rogers; 2 d. Educ. Oban High School; Glasgow University; Emmanuel College, Cambridge. Lecturer, Senior Lecturer and Reader in Celtic, Edinburgh University, 1979-92. Assistant Editor, Historical Dictionary of Scottish Gaelic, Glasgow University, 1973-79; Honorary Secretary, Gaelic Society of Glasgow, 1974-79; Member, Gaelic Advisory Committee to Broadcasting Council for Scotland, 1976-78 and of Gaelic Panel, National Bible Society of Scotland, since 1978; President, Edinburgh and Lothians Baptist Association, 1992-93; Clerk and Treasurer, Board of Celtic Studies (Scotland), since 1994; Editor, 1992 edition, Gaelic Bible; a General Editor, Dictionary of Scottish Church History and Theology, 1993; Baptist lay preacher. Publications: books include Mairi Mhor nan Oran, 1977; The Campbell Collection of Gaelic Proverbs and Proverbial Sayings, 1978; Island Harvest: A History of Tiree Baptist Church, 1988; Sunshine and Shadow: the story of the Baptists of Mull, 1991; A Mind for Mission: essays (Editor), 1992; Tuath is Tighearna: Poetry of the Clearances and the Land Agitation (Editor), 1995. Recreations: family activities; getting to know the Highlands. Address: (h.) 50 Dunecht Road, Westhill, Aberdeenshire AB32 6RH; T.-01224 742668.

Meldrum, Angus Alexander, BSc, DIA. Managing Director, Tennent Caledonian Breweries Ltd., since 1992; Director, Bass Ireland Ltd., since 1981; Director, Maclay's Brewery & Co. Ltd., since 1992; b. 7.11.45, Stornoway; m., Anne-Marie; 1 s. Educ. Kingussie School; Edinburgh University; Bath University Management School. Joined Bass plc, London, 1971; Tennent Caledonian Breweries Ltd., 1978; Brands Marketing Director, Bass Brewers Ltd., Burton-on-Trent, 1990-92. President, Brewers Association of Scotland, 1992-94. Recreations: fishing; shooting; sport. Address: (b.) 110 Bath Street, Glasgow G2 2ET; T.-0141-552 6552.

Meldrum, James, MA. Registrar General for Scotland, since 1994; b. 9.8.52, Kirkintilloch. Educ. Lenzie Academy; Glasgow University. Administration Trainee/HEO (Admin), Scottish Office, 1973-79; Principal grade posts, Scottish Economic Planning Department, Scottish Development Department, Scottish Office Personnel Division, 1979-86; Deputy Director, Scottish Courts Administration, 1986-91; Head, Investment Assistance Division, Scottish Office Industry Department, 1991-94. Address: (b.) New Register House, Edinburgh EH1 3YT; T.-0131-334 0380.

Mellows, Susan Mary, BSc, PhD, DIC. Academic Registrar, Strathclyde University, since 1993; b. 20.1.44, Brackley, Northants. Educ. Brackley High School; Edinburgh University; Imperial College, London. Kodak Ltd., 1966-67; Science and Engineering Research Council, London, 1970-85; YARD Ltd., Glasgow, 1985-90 (Manager, System Dynamics and Underwater Engineering Group); joined Strathclyde University, 1990, as Deputy Registrar. Recreations: hill-walking; other outdoor activities; books; music. Address: (b.) John Anderson Campus, Strathclyde University, Glasgow G1 1XG; T.-0141-552 4400, Ext. 2002.

Melville, Ian Dunlop, MB, ChB, FRCPGlas, FRCPLond. Consultant Neurologist, Institute of Neurological Sciences, Glasgow, 1965-88; Honorary Clinical Lecturer, Glasgow University, 1968-88; b. 9.11.27, Glasgow; m., Eliza Duffus; 1 s.; 3 d. Educ. Shawlands Academy; Glasgow University. RAF Medical Branch; Medical Registrar, Glasgow Royal Infirmary; Academic Registrar, National Hospital for Nervous Diseases, London; Clinical Research Fellow, Medical Research Council, London; Senior Medical Registrar, Glasgow. Artist Member, Committee, Paisley Art Institute; Editor, Bulletin of Royal College of Physicians and Surgeons, Glasgow. Recreations: golf; photography; watercolour painting. Address: (h.) 9 Mirrlees Drive, Glasgow G12 OSH; T.-0141-339 7085.

Mennie, Alastair Douglas, LLB, PhD, FSA Scot. Academic and practising lawyer; b. 2.10.57, Aberdeen. Educ. Aberdeen University; Edinburgh University. Advocate, since 1982; Part-time Lecturer in Law, 1987-92; Professor of Law, ESADE Business School, Barcelona, 1992-94; Visiting Professor, University of Toulouse, 1994-95; Professor of Law, Abat Oliba University Centre, Barcelona, since 1995; Visiting Professor: Aarhus University, 1996-97; Belgrano University, Buenos Aires, 1997; Guest Lecturer, Universities of Paris II and Bologna; Visiting Scholar, Cornell Law School, 1997; Director of Studies, Hague Academy of International Law, 1997. Publications: Domicile Flowcharts, 1991; numerous articles in British and foreign law journals. Recreations: visiting prehistoric sites; viewing modern art exhibitions. Address: (h.) 25 Panmure Place, Edinburgh EH3 9HP; T.-0131-229 5604.

Mennie, William Patrick, BL, NP, IAC. Partner, Grigor & Young, Solicitors, Elgin and Buckie, since 1964 (Senior Partner, since 1984); b. 11.10.37, Elgin; m., Patricia Leslie Bogie; 2 s.; 1 d. Educ. Elgin Academy; Edinburgh University. Solicitor, 1960; Honorary Sheriff at Elgin, since 1993; accredited by Law Society of Scotland as a specialist in agricultural law; Secretary, Malt Distillers Association of Scotland. Recreation: game shooting. Address: (h.) Innesmill, Urquhart, Elgin; T.-01343 842643.

Menzies, Duncan A.Y., QC, MA (Oxon), LLB. Queen's Counsel, since 1991; b. 28.8.53, Edinburgh; m., Hilary Weston; 2 s. Educ. Edinburgh Academy; Cargilfield; Glenalmond; Wadham College, Oxford; Edinburgh University. Advocate, 1978; Standing Junior Counsel to The Admiralty, 1984-91; accredited mediator, 1992; Temporary Sheriff, 1996; Chairman, Scottish Planning, Local Government and Environmental Bar Group, 1997. Parliamentary Candidate, Midlothian, 1983, Edinburgh Leith, 1987; founder, Scottish Wine Society, 1976. Recreations: shooting; golf; wines. Address: (h.) Leaston House, Humbie, East Lothian; T.-01875 833219.

Menzies, George Macbeth, BA, LLB. Partner, W. & J. Burness, Solicitors, since 1974; b. 18.4.43, Edinburgh; m., Patricia Mary; 1 s.; 2 d. Educ. Edinburgh Academy; Corpus Christi College, Oxford; Edinburgh University. Past Chairman, North British Steel Group (Holdings) PLC; Non-Executive Director, Cairn Petroleum Oil & Gas Ltd., 1986-88; Chairman, Fruitmarket Gallery, 1984-88; President, Edinburgh Academical Football Club, 1990-92; Chairman, Endeavour Training (Scotland) Ltd., 1983-97; Director, Scottish Council (Development and Industry), since 1990; Director, Greencastle Farming Plc, since 1995. Recreations: walking; contemporary arts; rugby. Address: (b.) 16 Hope Street, Edinburgh; T.-0131-226 2561.

Menzies, Gordon, MA (Hons), DipEd. Independent Producer (retired Head of Educational Broadcasting, BBC Scotland); b. 30.7.27, Logierait, Perthshire; m., Charlotte; 2 s.; 1 d. Educ. Breadalbane Academy, Aberfeldy; Edinburgh University. Producer/Director, Who Are the Scots?, 1971, The Chiel Amang Us, 1974, Ballad Folk, 1975, History Is

My Witness, 1976, Play Golf with Peter Alliss, 1977, Scotch and Wry, 1978-79, Two Views of Burns, 1979, Barbara Dickson in Concert, 1981-84-86, The World of Golf, 1982, The Celts, 1987, Play Better Golf with Peter Alliss, 1989, Scotch and Wry Hogmanay, 1980-91; Editor, The Afternoon Show, 1981-85; Play Snooker with Dennis Taylor, 1990; Play Bridge with Zia, 1991. Publications: Who Are the Scots?, 1971; The Scottish Nation, 1972; History Is My Witness, 1976; Play Golf, 1977; The World of Golf, 1982; Scotch and Wry, 1986; Double Scotch and Wry, 1988; Play Better Golf, 1989. Recreations: golf; snooker; curling; theatre. Address: (h.) 8 Ingleside, Lenzie, Glasgow G66 4HN.

Menzies, John Maxwell. Life President, John Menzies PLC (Chairman, 1952-97); b. 13.10.26; m., Patricia Eleanor Dawson; 4 d. Educ. Eton. Lt., Grenadier Guards; Member, Berwickshire County Council, 1954-57; Director: Scottish American Mortgage Co., 1959-63, Standard Life Assurance Co., 1960-63, Vidal Sassoon Inc., 1969-80, Gordon & Gotch plc, 1970-85, Atlantic Assets Trust, 1973-88, Ivory and Sime Enterprise Capital PLC (formerly Independent Investment Co. plc), 1973-96 (Chairman, 1983-96), Fairhaven International, 1980-88, Rocky Mountains Oil & Gas, 1980-85, Ivory & Sime plc, 1980-83, Personal Assets PLC, 1981-92, Bank of Scotland, 1984-94, Guardian Royal Exchange, 1985-96, Malcolm Innes & Partners Ltd., since 1989. Life Vice President, Newstr Aid Benevolent Institution (Trustee, 1974-95, President, 1968-74, Newsvendors' Benevolent Institution); Member: Royal Company of Archers, Queen's Bodyguard for Scotland, Board of Trustees, National Library of Scotland, since 1991. Recreations: farming; shooting; reading; travel. Address: (b.) 108 Princes Street, Edinburgh EH2 3AA; T.-0131-225 8555.

Menzies, Neil Graham Finlay, BSc, FRSA. Corporate Adviser; Scottish Adviser to Chemical Industries Association; b. 14.10.41, Meiklour; m., Lorna; 2 d. Educ. Lower School of John Lyon, Harrow; St. Andrews University. Voluntary Service Overseas, Nigeria, 1964-66; ICI, 1966-93, lately Scottish Affairs Adviser; Deputy Chairman, Scottish Water and Sewerage Customers Council; Member, Executive, Scottish Council Development and Industry; Director, Royal Lyceum Theatre Company; Member, Investors in People Recognition Panel for Scotland; Lay Member, Scottish Office, Education Department, HM Inspectorate; Non-Executive Director, Scottish Ambulance Service. Address: (h.) 13 Northumberland Street, Edinburgh EH3 6LL; T.-0131-557 4321.

Mercer, John, MA, DipEd. Headmaster, Belmont House School, since 1972; b. 11.8.40, Glasgow; m., Eileen Margaret; 2 s.; 1 d. Educ. Eastwood Senior Secondary School; Glasgow University; Jordanhill College of Education. Teacher of English/History, Mossvale Secondary School, Paisley, 1962-66; Head Teacher of English, Belmont House School, 1966-72. Elder and Session Clerk, Mearns Parish Kirk, President, Eastwood Rotary Club, 1986-87. Recreations: golf; skiing; walking; reading; palaeontology. Address: (b.) Belmont House School, Newton Mearns, Glasgow G77 5DU; T.-0141-639 2922.

Mercer, Roger James, MA, FSA, FRSE, FSA Scot, MIFA. Secretary, Royal Commission for the Ancient and Historical Monuments (Scotland); b. 12.9.44, Hertfordshire; m., Susan; 1 s.; 1 d. Educ. Harrow County Grammar School; Edinburgh University. Inspector of Ancient Monuments, AM Division, Department of the Environment, London, 1969-74; Lecturer and Reader, Department of Archaeology, Edinburgh University, 1974-89. Treasurer, Society of Antiquaries of Scotland, 1977-87; Vice President: Society of Antiquaries of Scotland, 1988-91, Prehistoric Society, 1987-91; Council for British Archaeology, 1991-94.

Recreations: music; reading; learning. Address: (b.) RCAHMS, John Sinclair House, 16 Bernard Terrace, Edinburgh EH8 9NX.

Merchant, Bruce Alastair, OBE, LLB. Solicitor; Partner, South, Forrest, Mackintosh & Merchant, Inverness, since 1971; Member, Accounts Commission for Scotland; b. 17.5.45, Edinburgh; m., Joan Isobel Sinclair Hamilton; 1 s.; 2 d. Educ. Inverness Royal Academy; Aberdeen University. Council Member, Law Society of Scotland, 1982-88 (Convener, Guarantee Fund Committee, 1984-87, Convener, Finance Committee, 1987-88); Member: Highland Health Board, 1981-91, Board of Management for Inverness Hospitals, 1971-74, Inverness Local Health Council, 1975-81; Dean, Faculty of Solicitors of the Highlands, 1994-96. Address: (h.) 3 Crown Circus, Inverness; T.-01463 239980.

Meston, Professor Michael Charles, MA, LLB, JD. Professor of Scots Law, Aberdeen University, 1971-96; b. 13.12.32, Aberdeen; m., Dorothea Munro; 2 s. Educ. Robert Gordon's College, Aberdeen; Aberdeen University; Chicago University. Lecturer in Private Law, Glasgow University, 1959-64; Aberdeen University: Senior Lecturer in Comparative Law, 1964-68, Professor of Jurisprudence, 1968-71; Dean, Faculty of Law, 1970-73 and 1988-91; Honorary Sheriff, Grampian Highland and Islands, since 1972; Temporary Sheriff, since 1993; Vice Principal, Aberdeen University, 1979-82; Trustee, National Museum of Antiquities of Scotland, 1982-85; Governor, Robert Gordon's College, Aberdeen; Member, Grampian Health Board, 1985-91; Non-Executive Director, Aberdeen Royal Hospitals NHS Trust, since 1992. Publications: The Succession (Scotland) Act 1964; The Matrimonial Homes (Family Protection) (Scotland) Act 1981; The Scottish Legal Tradition, 1991. Recreations: golf; photography. Address: (h.) 4 Hamilton Place, Aberdeen AB15 4BH; T.-Aberdeen 641554.

Michels, David Michael Charles, FHCIMA. Chief Executive, Stakis plc, since 1991; b. 8.12.46, London; m., Michele; 1 s.; 1 d. Educ. Hendon College. Sales and Marketing Manager: Grand Metropolitan Hotels, Ladbroke Leisure; Managing Director: Ladbroke Leisure, Ladbroke Hotels; Executive Vice President, Hilton International; Non Executive Director: Aberforth, Split Level Trust PLC. DLitt, Caledonian. Address: (b.) 3 Atlantic Quay, York Street, Glasgow G2 8JH; T.-0141-204 4321.

Michie, Professor David Alan Redpath, OBE, RSA, RGI, RWA, DA, FRSA. Professor, Heriot Watt University, 1988-90; Head, School of Drawing and Painting, Edinburgh College of Art, 1982-90; b. 30.11.28, St. Raphael, France; m., Eileen Anderson Michie; 2 d. Educ. Hawick High School; Edinburgh College of Art. Travelling Scholarship, Italy, 1954-55; Lecturer, Grays School of Art, Aberdeen, 1957-61; Lecturer, Edinburgh College of Art, 1961 (Vice Principal, 1974-77). President, Society of Scottish Artists, 1961-63; Member: General Teaching Council for Scotland, 1975-80, Court, Heriot-Watt University, 1979-82, Council, British School at Rome, 1980-85, Museums and Galleries Commission, 1991-96; Guthrie Award, RSA, 1964; David Cargill Prize, RGI, 1977; Lothian Region Award, 1977; Sir William Gillies Award, 1980; RGI Prize, 1990; Cornelissen Prize, RWA, 1992; one-man exhibitions, Mercury Gallery, London, eight times, 1966-96, Lothian Region Chambers, 1977, The Scottish Gallery, 1980, 1994, Loomshop Gallery, Lower Largo, 1981, 1987, Mercury Gallery, Edinburgh, 1986; Baarn and Amsterdam, 1991; Visiting Professor, Faculty of Art Studio Department, UCLA, Santa Barbara, 1992. Address: (h.) 17 Gilmour Road, Edinburgh EH16 5NS.

Michie, Donald, MA (Oxon), DPhil (Oxon), DSc (Oxon), Hon. DSc (NCAA), Hon. DSc (Salford), Hon. DUniv (Stirling). Scientific Worker, since 1949; Treasurer,

Human-Computer Learning Foundation, since 1995; b. 11.11.23, Rangoon; m., Jean Hayes; 2 s.; 2 d. Educ. Rugby School; Oxford University. War Service, F.O., Bletchley Park, 1942-45; Research Associate, London University, 1952-58; Edinburgh University: Senior Lecturer, Reader, in Surgical Science, 1958-65, Director, Experimental Programming Unit, 1965-67, Professor of Machine Intelligence, 1967-84; Turing Institute, Glasgow: Chairman, 1984-86, Chief Scientist, 1986-92. Pioneer Award, International Embryo Transfer Society (jointly), 1988. Publications: The Creative Computer (Co-author), 1984; Machine Intelligence and Related Topics (Co-author), 1982; On Machine Intelligence, 1986. Recreation: travel. Address: (h.) 6 Inveralmond Grove, Edinburgh EH4 6RA; T.-0131-336 3826.

Michie, (Janet) Ray. MP (Lib. Dem.), Argyll and Bute, since 1987; b. 4.2.34; m.; 3 d. Educ. Aberdeen High School for Girls; Lansdowne House School, Edinburgh; Edinburgh School of Speech Therapy. Former Area Speech Therapist, Argyll and Clyde Health Board. Address: (b.) House of Commons SW1A 0AA.

Micklem, Professor Henry Spedding, MA, DPhil (Oxon). Freelance Musician and Lecturer; Professor of Immunobiology, Edinburgh University, 1980-92, Emeritus, since 1992; b. 11.10.33, Oxford; m., 1, Lisel Ruth Thomas (deceased); 2, Damaris Manson; 3 s. 1 d. Educ. Rugby School; Oriel College, Oxford. Scientific Staff, Medical Research Council; Research Fellow, Institut Pasteur, Paris; Academic Staff, Department of Zoology, Edinburgh University; Visiting Professor, Department of Genetics, Stanford University; Visiting Fellow, Department of Pathology, New York University Medical School. Address: (h.) 1 Dryden Place, Edinburgh, EH9 1RP; T.-0131-667 5618.

Micklem, Rosalind, BA (Hons), PGCE, MPhil. Principal, Cardonald College, since 1997; b. 7.6.56, Surrey. Educ. St. Paul's Girls' School, London; Oxford University; Leicester University; London University. Lecturer, North Oxfordshire Technical College, 1979-84; Education Officer, Northants and Hounslow, 1985-89; Vice Principal, Enfield College, 1989-95; Deputy Principal, Wirral Metropolitan College, 1995-97. Address: (b.) Cardonald College, 690 Mosspark Drive, Glasgow G52 3AY; T.-0141-883 6151.

Middleton, Robert, JP, Hon. DLitt, HonLLD. Member, Aberdeen City Council, since 1995 (Vice Convener, Economic Development); b. 28.7.32, Aberdeen; m., Audrey Ewen; 2 s. Educ. Aberdeen Grammar School. Started apprenticeship with Post Office Telephones, 1948; Aberdeen Town Council: elected, 1961, appointed Magistrate, 1963, Chairman of Magistrates, 1965-66, Chairman, Education Committee, 1966-69; Chairman, Labour Party in Scotland, 1986-87; contested Banffshire as Labour candidate, 1966; contested Aberdeen South, 1974 (twice) and 1983; elected, Grampian Regional Council, 1975 (Convener, 1990-95); President, North Sea Commission of the Conference of Peripheral Maritime Regions, 1992-95. Publications: North Sea Brose; Grampian Homeland. Recreations: golf; reading; writing not very good poetry; travel; bridge; bowls. Address: (h.) 9 Stronsay Avenue, Aberdeen AB2 6HX; T.-01224 313366.

Midgley, Professor John Morton, BSc, MSc, PhD, CChem, FRSC, FRPharmS. Professor of Pharmaceutical and Medicinal Chemistry, Strathclyde University, since 1984 (Chairman and Head of Department, 1985-90); b. 14.7.37, York; m., Jean Mary Tillyer; 2 s. Educ. Nunthorpe Grammar School, York; Manchester University; London University. Demonstrator, Manchester University, 1959-61; Assistant Lecturer, School of Pharmacy, London University, 1962-65; Research Associate, Massachusetts Institute of Technology, 1965-66; Lecturer, then Senior Lecturer, School of Pharmacy, London University, 1965-

83; Member: Committee on the Review of Medicines, 1984-92, British Pharmacopoeia Commission, since 1985, Committee on the Safety of Medicines, since 1990, Council of Royal Pharmaceutical Society of GB, 1991-92, Science and Engineering Research Council Pharmacy Panel, since 1985. Recreations: fly fishing; fisheries management; training labradors; gardening; music. Address: (b.) Strathclyde University, Department of Pharmaceutical Sciences, Royal College, 204 George Street, Glasgow G1 1XW; T.-0141-552 4400, Ext. 2125.

Milburn, Professor George Henry William, PhD, CChem, FRSC, FBIM, Dr (h.c.), FRSA. Head, Department of Applied Chemical and Physical Sciences, Napier University, since 1973; b. 25.11.34, Wallasey; m., Jean Muriel; 1 s.; 1 d. Educ. Wallasey Grammar School; Leeds University. Short service commission, Royal Corps of Signals, 1959-63; Staff Demonstrator, Leeds University, 1963-66; Research Fellow, Sydney University, 1967-68; Senior Scientific Officer, Agricultural Research Council, 1968-69; Lecturer, Plymouth Polytechnic, 1969-70; Senior Lecturer, Sheffield Polytechnic, 1970-73. Convener, Committee of Scottish University Heads of Chemistry Departments, 1994-97; Honorary Doctorate, Technical University, Budapest, 1988; Silver Star Laureate, Poland, 1996. Publications: more than 50 scientific publications including a textbook on crystal structure analysis. Recreations: golf; bridge; photography. Address: (h.) 9 Orchard Court, Longniddry, East Lothian; T.-01875 853228.

Mill, Douglas Russell, LLB, BA, MBA, WS, NP. Secretary, Law Society of Scotland, since 1997; b. 3.1.57, Paisley; m., Christine; 2 s.; 1 d. Educ. Paisley Grammar School; Glasgow University. Former Depute Director, Centre for Professional Legal Studies, Strathclyde University; former Partner, MacFarlane Young & Co., Solicitors, Paisley; former Member, Council, Law Society of Scotland. Publication: Successful Practice Management, 1992. Recreations: golf; rugby. Address: (h.) Foxburn, South Avenue, Paisley PA2 7SP; T.-0141-884 6164.

Millan, Rt. Hon. Bruce, PC, CA. European Commissioner, 1989-95; b. 5.10.27, Dundee; m., Gwendoline May Fairey; 1 s.; 1 d. Educ. Harris Academy, Dundee. MP, Glasgow Craigton, 1959-83, Glasgow Govan, 1983-88; Parliamentary Secretary for the RAF, 1964-66; Parliamentary Secretary, Scottish Office, 1966-70; Minister of State, Scottish Office, 1974-76; Secretary of State for Scotland, 1976-79; Opposition Spokesman on Scottish Affairs, 1979-83. Address: (h.) 1 Torridon Avenue, Glasgow G41 5LA; T.-0141-427 6483.

Millan, Professor Charles Gordon, MA, PhD, FRSA. Professor of French, Strathclyde University, since 1991; Chairman, Department of Modern Languages, since 1994; Vice-Dean, Faculty of Arts and Social Sciences, since 1995; b. 25.9.46, Kirkcaldy; m., Margaret Anne Robbie; 1 s.; 1 d. Educ. Kirkcaldy High; Merrywood Grammar, Bristol; Edinburgh University. Temporary Lecturer, Edinburgh University, 1970-71; Teacher, Broughton High School, 1972-76; Strathclyde University, since 1976; Director, Languages for Business Unit, since 1990 (Languages for Export Award, 1994). Publications include: Pierre Louÿs ou le Culte de l'Amitié, 1979, Stéphane Mallarmé, Poésies (jointly), 1985; A Throw of the Dice: The Life of Stéphane Mallarmé, 1994. Recreations: cinema; reading. Address: (b.) Livingstone Tower, Richmond Street, Glasgow G1 1XH; T.-0141-552 4400.

Millan, William Robert, LLB, NP. Director of Central Services, Scottish Borders Council, since 1995; Clerk to the JP Advisory Committee, since 1993; Clerk of the Peace (Scottish Borders Commission Area), since 1996; Clerk to the Licensing Board and District Court, since 1996; b. 17.8.52, Glasgow; m., Margaret Hamilton McCulloch; 1 s.;

1 d. Educ. Hillhead High School; Glasgow University. Bannatyne, Kirkwood, France & Co., Writers, Glasgow, 1973-75; Senior Legal Assistant, Cumnock and Doon Valley District Council, 1975-79; Roxburgh District Council: Depute Director of Administrative and Legal Services, 1979-86, Director of Administrative and Legal Services, 1986-96, Chief Executive, 1993-96. Recreations: reading; DIY; gardening; skiing; badminton; golf; photography. Address: (b.) Council Headquarters, Newtown St. Boswells, Melrose TD6 0SA.

Millar, Professor Alan, MA, PhD. Professor of Philosophy, Stirling University, since 1994; b. 14.12.47, Edinburgh; m., Rose-Mary Marchand; 1 s. Educ. Edinburgh University; Cambridge University. Stirling University: Lecturer in Philosophy, 1971, Senior Lecturer, 1991, Head, Department of Philosophy, 1988-94. Member, Postgraduate Studentship Selection Committee, Student Awards Agency for Scotland; former Convener, Religious Studies Panel, Scottish Universities Council on Entrance; awarded Mind Association Research Fellowship, 1996-97; Visiting Fellow, Clare College, Cambridge, 1997. Publications: Reasons and Experience, 1991; articles in the philosophy of mind, epistemology, philosophy of religion, history of ethics. Recreations: reading; walking; films; cooking. Address: (b.) Stirling University, Stirling FK9 4LA; T.-01786 467555.

Millar, Bob, MA, CA. Director of Finance, Miller Homes, since 1997; b. 30.3.50, Edinburgh; m., Sandra; 1 s.; 1 d. Educ. George Heriot's School; Edinburgh University. Chartered Accountant, Touche Ross; Financial Accountant, Bredero UK Ltd., Castle Rock Housing Association; Head of Registration, Housing Corporation; Director of Strategy, Scottish Homes. Address: (b.) Miller House, 18 South Groathill Avenue, Edinburgh EH4 2LW.

Millar, Douglas Andrew Terris. Deputy Director, Scottish Chambers of Commerce, since 1997; b. 18.6.55, Dunfermline. Educ. Queen Anne High School, Dunfermline; Aberdeen College of Commerce. Civil Servant, Scottish Office, 1972-97, latterly Head of Film, Broadcasting and Gaelic Policy Branch, Education and Industry Department. Elder, Dunfermline Abbey. Recreations: youth work; football. Address: (b.) Conference House, The Exchange, 152 Morrison Street, Edinburgh EH3 8EB; T.-0131-477 8025.

Millar, Helen Jean, MA, FRSA. Chairman, Rail Users Consultative Committee for Scotland; Member, Air Transport Users Council, since 1991; Member, Advisory Committee on Novel Foods and Processes, since 1991; Member, Glasgow Local Health Council; Member, Executive Committee, Scottish Association of Health Councils; Member, Multi Centre Research Ethics Committee for Scotland; Vice Chairman, Consumer Congress; b. 10.10.31, Glasgow; 3 s.; 2 d. Educ. Craigholme School, Glasgow; Glasgow University. Chairman, Consumers in European Community Group, 1988-91; Chairman, Consumer's Committee for Scotland, 1980-89; Member and Vice Chairman, Scottish Consumer Council, 1979-87; Chairman, Strathclyde Children's Panel, 1979-81; Vice-Chairman, New Glasgow Society, 1980-87; former Lecturer in charge, Children's Panel Training, Glasgow University; Founder Member, Board, Tron Theatre Club, Glasgow. Recreations: theatre; arts in general; Glasgow; arguing. Address: (h.) 33 Aytoun Road, Glasgow G41; T.-0141-423 4152.

Millar, Henry Rankin, MB, ChB, BMedBiol (Hons), FRCPsych. Consultant Psychiatrist, Royal Cornhill Hospital, Aberdeen, since 1991; b. 23.4.47, Aberdeen; m., Frances Morgan; 3 d. Educ. Aberdeen Grammar School; Aberdeen University. House Officer, Aberdeen Royal Infirmary, 1972-73; Junior Fellow in Community Medicine and Honorary Senior House Officer in Medicine, Aberdeen

University and Aberdeen Royal Infirmary, 1973-74; Senior House Officer/Registrar in Psychiatry, Royal Edinburgh Hospital, 1975-77; Senior Registrar and Lecturer, Dundee Psychiatric Services and Dundee University, 1977-80; Consultant Psychiatrist, Southern General Hospital, Glasgow, 1980-91. Recreation: walking. Address: (h.) Failte, Quarryhill, Mid Auguston, Peterculter, Aberdeen AB14 OPP.

Millar, Professor Keith, BA, PhD, CPsychol, FBPsS. Professor of Behavioural Science, Medical Faculty, Glasgow University, since 1988; b. 27.6.50, Dundee; m., Dr. Margaret Elspeth Reid; 1 step s. Educ. Dundee High School; Stirling University; Dundee University. Research Scientist, MRC Applied Psychology Unit, Cambridge, 1976-79; Lecturer, Department of Psychiatry, University Hospital and Medical School, Nottingham, 1979-84; Senior Lecturer, Behavioural Sciences Group, Medical Faculty, Glasgow University, 1984-88. Publications: papers and edited book on topics relating psychology to medicine. Recreations: reading; travelling; hill-walking; procrastination. Address: (h.) 33 West Chapelton Crescent, Bearsden, Glasgow G61 2DE; T.-0141-942 4978.

Millar, Mary Armour, MB, ChB, FRCPGlas, FRCR. Consultant Radiologist, Victoria Infirmary, Glasgow, since 1972; b. 10.8.39, Glasgow. Educ. Queen's Park Senior Secondary School; Glasgow University. Resident House Officer: Stobhill Hospital, Glasgow Royal Infirmary; Victoria Infirmary: Registrar in Medicine, Registrar in Radiology, Senior Registrar. Medical Advisor, Overseas Missionary Fellowship in Scotland; Member, Congregational Board, Sandyford Henderson Memorial Church. Recreations: reading; gardening; hill-walking. Address: (h.) 1 Rosslea Drive, Giffnock, Glasgow G46 6JW; T.-0141-638 3036.

Millar, Peter Carmichael, OBE, MA, LLB, WS. Chairman, Medical Appeal Tribunals, since 1991, and of Pension Appeal Tribunals, since 1992; b. 19.2.27, Glasgow; m., Kirsteen Lindsay Carnegie; 2 s.; 2 d. Educ. Aberdeen Grammar School; Glasgow University; St. Andrews University; Edinburgh University. Royal Navy, 1944-47; Partner, W. & T.P. Manuel, WS, 1954-62; Partner, Aitken Kinnear & Co., WS, 1963-87; Partner, Aitken, Nairn WS, 1987-92; Clerk, Society of Writers to HM Signet, 1964-83; Deputy Keeper of Her Majesty's Signet, 1983-91; Chairman: Church of Scotland General Trustees, 1973-85, Mental Welfare Commission for Scotland, 1983-91. Recreations: golf; hill-walking; music. Address: (h.) 25 Cramond Road North, Edinburgh EH4 6LY.

Millar, Rev. Peter William, MA, BD, MTh. Minister, Church of Scotland, since 1970; Warden, Iona Abbey, since 1995; b. 24.5.43, Edinburgh; m., Dr. Dorothy Millar; 2 s.; 1 d. Educ. George Heriot's School, Edinburgh; Edinburgh University; Princeton University; Chicago University. Parish Minister, 1970-76; Priest, Church of South India, 1976-88; Director, Ecumenical Retreat Centre, 1989-94. Publications: Letters from Madras, 1988; Words from the Cross, 1989; Set Free, 1989; Prayers from a Columban House, 1990; Notes for a Pilgrim, 1991; Pilgrim Guide to Iona, 1997; Prayers from Iona, 1998. Recreations: walking; writing; travelling. Address: (b.) Iona Abbey, Argyll PA76 6SN; T.-01681 700404.

Millar, William Mungall. Editor, Scottish Business Insider, since 1996; b. 13.12.50, Falkirk; 2 s.; 1 d. Address: (b.) 43 Queensferry Street Lane, Edinburgh EH2 4PF; T.-0131-535 5512.

Miller, Professor Alan, LLB (Hons), NP. Visiting Professor of Law, specialising in human rights, Strathclyde University, since 1996; Director, Scottish Human Rights Centre; Convener, Standing Conference on Justice; practising Solicitor; b. 9.4.52, Irvine; m., Brenda; 2 s.; 2 d.

Educ. Ardrossan Academy; Edinburgh University. Admitted as practising Solicitor, 1984; published draft Bill of Rights for Scotland, 1992. Executive Committee Member, Glasgow Bar Association; Secretary, Common Cause. Recreation: time with family. Address: (b.) Scottish Council for Civil Liberties, 146 Holland Street, Glasgow G2 4NG; T.-0141-332 5960.

Miller, Professor Alan, BSc, PhD, CPhys, FInstP, FRSE. Professor of Semiconductor Physics and Head, School of Physics and Astronomy, St. Andrews University, since 1993; Professor of Physics and Electrical Engineering, University of Central Florida, since 1989; b. 5.6.49, Dunfermline; m., Susan Linklater; 3 d. Educ. Gibraltar Grammar School; Edinburgh University; Bath University. Research Fellow, Heriot-Watt University, 1974-79; Visiting Assistant Professor, North Texas University, 1979-81; Senior Principal Scientific Officer, Royal Signals and Radar Establishment, Malvern, 1981-89. Editor, Optical and Quantum Electronics, and of Cambridge Studies in Modern Optics (series of monographs); Chairman, Committee of Scottish Professors of Physics; Vice-Chairman, Scottish Branch, Lasers and Electro-Optics Society. Publications: Nonlinear Optics in Signal Processing (Editor); Nonlinear Optical Materials and Devices for Applications in Information Technology (Editor); Laser Sources and Applications (Editor); 150 research papers. Address: (b.) Department of Physics and Astronomy, North Haugh, St. Andrews KY16 9SS; T.-01334 463122.

Miller, (Alan) Cameron, MA, LLB, FCIT. Advocate; Past Chairman (Scotland), Institute of Transport; b. 10.1.13, Killin, Perthshire; m., Audrey Main; 1 s. (deceased); 1 d. Educ. Fettes College; Edinburgh University. Member, Faculty of Advocates, since 1938; Royal Navy, 1940-45; Sheriff, Fort William, 1946-52; Legal Adviser (Scotland) to: British Transport Commission, 1952-62, British Railways Board, 1962-72. Voluntary Tutor, Fettes College, 1974-93. Recreations: golf; music. Address: (h.) 12A Quality Street, North Berwick; T.-01620 5035.

Miller, Alan Douglas, LLB (Hons), DipLP. Principal Reporter, Scottish Children's Reporter Administration, since 1995; b. 30.11.59, Edinburgh; m., Alison; 1 s.; 2 d. Educ. Stewart's/Melville College, Edinburgh; Edinburgh University. Assistant/Area Reporter, Strathclyde, 1985-90; Regional Reporter, Dumfries and Galloway, 1990-95; Secretary, Association of Children's Reporters, 1990-93. Associate Member, Iona Community; Elder, Church of Scotland. Address (b.): Ochil House, Springkerse Business Park, Stirling FK7 7XE; T.-01786 459500.

Miller, Alastair Robert John Dunlop, BSc, MAg, NDA, FRAgS. Farmer; Chairman, Scotfresh (1997) Ltd.; b. 5.3.37, Tranent; m., Margaret Eileen Lees-Brown; 3 d. Educ. Edinburgh Academy; Rugby; Edinburgh University; Purdue University, USA. Scottish Horticulture Medal; Fellow, Royal Agricultural Societies. Recreations: golf; travel. Address: (h.) Ferrygate, North Berwick, East Lothian.

Miller, Professor Andrew, MA, BSc, PhD, FRSE, FIBiol. Principal and Vice-Chancellor, University of Stirling, since 1994; b. 15.2.36, Kelty, Fife; m., Rosemary S.H. Fyvie; 1 s.; 1 d. Educ. Beath High School; Edinburgh University. Assistant Lecturer in Chemistry, Edinburgh University, 1960-62; Postdoctoral Fellow, CSIRO, Melbourne, and Tutor in Chemistry, Ormond College, Melbourne University, 1962-65; Staff Scientist, MRC Laboratory of Molecular Biology, Cambridge, 1965-66; Lecturer in Molecular Biophysics, Oxford University and (from 1967) Fellow, Wolfson College, 1966-83 (Honorary Fellow, since 1994); on secondment as first Director, European Molecular Biology Laboratory, Grenoble Antenne, France, 1975-80. Committee Member: British Biophysical Society, 1972-74, SERC Synchrotron Radiation Facility Committee, 1979-82,

Biological Sciences Committee, 1982-85, Neutron Beam Research Committee, 1982-85; Council Member, Institut Laue-Langevin, 1981-85; Member: MRC Joint Dental Committee, 1984-86, UGC Biological Sciences Committee, 1985-89; (part-time) Director of Research, European Synchrotron Radiation Facility, Grenoble, 1986-91; Member: Advisory Board, AFRC Food Research Institute, 1985, UFC Advisory Groups on Biological Sciences and Pre-clinical Medicine, 1989, Scientific Council, Grenoble University, 1989; Vice-Dean of Medicine, Edinburgh University, 1991-93; Professor of Biochemistry, Edinburgh University, 1984-94; Vice-Principal, Edinburgh University, 1993-94. Address: (b.) University of Stirling, Stirling FK9 4LA.

Miller, Andrew, MA, FLA. Director of Libraries and Archives, Glasgow City Council, since 1981; b. 25.12.36, Hamilton; m., Jean Main Freeland; 2 d. Educ. St. John's Grammar School; Hamilton Academy; Glasgow and West of Scotland Commercial College. Assistant, Hamilton Public Libraries and Glasgow District Libraries; Depute Burgh Librarian, Motherwell and Wishaw, 1963-74; Depute Director of Libraries, Glasgow District Council, 1974-81. Chairman of Council and Past President, Scottish Library Association; Past President: Strathclyde Librarians' Club, Motherwell Speakers' Forum. Recreations: reading; travelling; public speaking; planning. Address: (b.) Mitchell Library, North Street, Glasgow G3 7DN; T.-0141-287 2801.

Miller, Bill, BSc, DipTP. Member, European Parliament, Glasgow, since 1994; b. 22.7.54, Gartocharn; 1 s.; 1 d. Educ. Paisley Technical College; Kingston Polytechnic. Strathclyde Regional Councillor, 1986-94. Recreations: ties; records; Kilmarnock F.C. Address: 9 Chisholm Street, Glasgow G1 5HA; T.-0141-552 2234.

Miller, Brian, BSc (Hons). Rector, Dalziel High School, Motherwell, since 1990; b. 4.1.51, Glasgow; m., Margaret; 1 s.; 1 d. Educ. High School of Glasgow; Strathclyde University. Teacher of Mathematics, 1974-77; Assistant Principal Teacher, 1977-80; Principal Teacher, 1980-84; Assistant Head Teacher, Cranhill Secondary School, Glasgow, 1984-86; Depute Head Teacher, Stonelaw High School, Glasgow, 1986-90. Recreation: bowls. Address: (b.) Crawford Street, Motherwell ML1 3AG.

Miller, Rev. Charles W., MA. Chaplain, Royal Dundee Liff Hospital, since 1980; b. 4.2.26, Kinross; m., Isabella Russell Stewart, MA; 3 s. Educ. St. Mary's School, Dunblane; McLaren High School, Callander; Aberdeen University; St. Andrews University. Assistant Minister, Auld Kirk of Ayr, 1953-54; Minister: Torthorwald, Dumfries, 1953-59, Munro Church, Rutherglen, 1959-65, Cruden, Aberdeenshire, 1965-72, Anstruther Parish Church, 1972-80, Fowlis Easter and Liff Parish Church, 1980-94; former Convener: Overseas Committee, Dumfries Presbytery; Church and Nation and Social Responsibility Committees, Aberdeen Presbytery; Social Responsibility Committee, St. Andrews Presbytery; Church of Scotland Pulpit Supply Agent (Dundee and Tayside); Member, Scottish Churches Consultative Committee on Road Safety; Institute of Advanced Motorists: Member, Governing Council, 1962-95, elected Fellow, since 1996, Founder Member and President, Institute's Groups Association in Scotland. Recreations: caravanning; swimming; landscape painting; hospital radio broadcasting. Address: Palm Springs, Parkside, Auchterhouse, Dundee DD3 0RF; T.-01382 320407.

Miller, Sheriff Colin Brown, LLB, SSC. Sheriff of South Strathclyde, Dumfries and Galloway, since 1991; b. 4.10.46, Paisley; m., Joan Elizabeth Blyth; 3 s. Educ. Paisley Grammar School; Glasgow University. Partner, McFadyen & Semple, Solicitors, Paisley, 1971-91; Council Member, Law Society of Scotland, 1983-91 (Convener, Conveyancing Committee, 1986-89; Convener, Judicial Procedure Committee, 1989-91; Chairman, Working Party on Rights of Audience in Supreme Courts, 1990-91); Dean, Faculty of Procurators in Paisley, 1991. Recreations: Clyde steamers; railways; photography; travel. Address: (b.) Ayr Sheriff Court, Wellington Square, Ayr; T.-01292 268474.

Miller, Sir Donald John, DSc, DUniv, BSc, FEng, FIMechE, FIEE, FRSE; b. 9.2.27, London; m., Fay G. Herriot; 1 s.; 2 d. Educ. Banchory Academy; Aberdeen University. Metropolitan-Vickers, 1947-53; British Electricity Authority, 1953-55; Preece Cardew & Rider (Consulting Engineers), 1955-66; Chief Engineer, North of Scotland Hydro-Electric Board, 1966-74; SEEB: Director of Engineering, 1974, appointed Deputy Chairman, 1979; Chairman, Scottish Power, 1982-92. Chairman, Power Division, IEE, 1977. Recreations: gardening; walking; sailing. Address: (h.) Puldohran, Gryffe Road, Kilmacolm, Renfrewshire; T.-Kilmacolm 3652.

Miller, George Richardson, OBE. Managing Director, L.S. Starrett Co. Ltd., Jedburgh, since 1995; b. 31.3.32, Jedburgh; m., Margaret; 1 d. Educ. Jedburgh Grammar School; Galashiels Technical College. Past National Chairman, Royal British Legion Scotland. Recreations: curling; fishing; rugby football. Address: (h.) 3 Howden Drive, Jedburgh; T.-01835 862202.

Miller, Hugh Craig, BSc, MB, ChB, FRCPEdin. Consultant Cardiologist, Edinburgh Royal Infirmary, since 1975; b. 7.4.42, Edinburgh; m., Isobel Margaret; 1 s.; 1 d. Educ. George Watson's College; Edinburgh University. Registrar, Edinburgh Royal Infirmary, 1969-72; Senior Registrar, Brompton Hospital, London, 1972-75; Research Fellow, Duke University, North Carolina, 1973-74; Fulbright Scholar. Recreations: skiing; sailing. Address: (h.) 12 Dick Place, Edinburgh; T.-0131-667 4235.

Miller, Professor Hugh Graham, OBE, BSc, PhD, DSc, FICFor, FIBiol, FRSE, FRSA. Professor and Head, Department of Forestry, Aberdeen University, since 1984; b. 22.11.39, Ndola, Zambia; 1 s.; 1 d. Educ. Kaptagat School, Kenya; Strathallan School; Sutton High School; Aberdeen University. Joined Department of Peat and Forest Soils, Macaulay Institute for Soil Research, 1986. Awarded Institute of Foresters Silvicultural Prize, 1974; selected for International Union of Forest Research Organization's Scientific Achievement Award, 1981; President, Institute of Chartered Foresters, 1994-96; OBE, 1996. Recreation: curling. Address: (b.) Department of Forestry, Aberdeen University, St. Machar Drive, Aberdeen AB9 2UD; T.-01224 272666.

Miller, Ian George Tweedie, BSc, AFIMA, MBCS, CEng, FRSA. Principal, North Glasgow College, since 1990; Chairman, Skill (Scotland), since 1992; b. 5.8.42, Hamilton; m., Una; 1 s.; 1 d. Educ. George Heriot's, Edinburgh; Heriot Watt University. Research Assistant, Hatfield Polytechnic; Lecturer, Computer Science, Strathclyde University; Director, Computer Centre, Paisley College; Depute Principal, Stevenson College. Recreations: golf; bowling. Address: (b.) 110 Flemington Street, Glasgow G21 4BX; T.-0141-558 9001.

Miller, Rev. Ian Hunter, BA, BD. Minister, Bonhill, since 1975; b. 30.5.44, Johnstone; m., Joan Elizabeth Parr; 2 s. Educ. Johnstone High School; Glasgow University; Open University. Travel agent, latterly Branch Manager, A.T. Mays, 1962-69; Assistant Minister, Renfrew Old Kirk, 1974-75. Moderator, Dumbarton Presbytery, 1985-87 (Convener, Presbytery Planning and Re-adjustment); Non-executive Director, Lomond Healthcare NHS Trust. Recreations: golf; badminton; music; drama. Address: Bonhill Manse, 1 Glebe Gardens, Bonhill, Alexandria G83 9HR; T.-Alexandria 53039.

Miller, Ian James, MA, LLB. Secretary and Academic Registrar, Napier University, Edinburgh, since 1987; Director, Edinburgh Healthcare NHS Trust, since 1995; b. 21.10.38, Fraserburgh; m., Sheila Mary Hourston; 1 s.; 2 d. Educ. Fraserburgh Academy; Aberdeen University; Edinburgh University. Private legal practice, 1963-68; Senior Legal Assistant, Inverness County Council, 1968-70; Depute County Clerk, then County Clerk, Ross and Cromarty County Council, 1970-75; Chief Executive, Inverness District Council, 1975-77; Director of Law and Administration, Grampian Regional Council, 1977-84; Director, Kildonnan Investments Ltd., Aberdeen, 1984-87. Recreations: golf; curling. Address: (b.) 219 Colinton Road, Edinburgh EH14 1DJ; T.-0131-455 4603.

Miller, Dr. Jack Elius, OBE, JP, OStJ, FRCGP. Director, The Medical Insurance Agency Ltd., since 1978; b. 7.3.18, Glasgow; m., Ida Warrens; 1 s. Educ. Hillhead High School; Glasgow University. General Medical Practitioner in Glasgow (retired); Captain, Royal Army Medical Corps, 1944-46; Chairman (founder Member), Glasgow Marriage Guidance Council, 1956-61 (Hon. Vice-President, since 1961); Hon. Vice-President, Scottish Marriage Guidance Council, since 1967; Chairman: Scottish General Services Committee, 1969-72, Association of Jewish Ex-Servicemen and Women of Scotland, 1952-61 and 1964-68; President, Glasgow Jewish Representative Council, 1969-72; Member, Council, BMA, 1964-81 (National Treasurer, 1972-81; Gold Medallist, 1982); Freeman, City of London; Member, Board of Deputies of British Jews, 1979-88; Vice-President, Prince and Princess of Wales Hospice, since 1981; Co-Chairman, Scottish Jewish Archives Committee, since 1986; Chairman, Scottish Health Authorities Review of Priorities for the Eighties, 1985-87. Publications: Glasgow Doctors' Handbook (three editions); Sharpen report. Recreations: travel; reading; communal affairs. Address: (h.) 38 Fruin Court, Fruin Avenue, Newton Mearns, Glasgow G77 6HJ; T.-0141-639 7869.

Miller, James, CBE (1986), MA, FCIOB, FCIArb, CBIM. Chairman, since 1970, Managing Director, 1970-91, The Miller Group Ltd. (formerly James Miller & Partners); Director, British Linen Bank Ltd., since 1983 (Chairman, British Linen Bank Group Limited, since 1997); Member, Advisory Board, British Petroleum, since 1990; Chairman, Court, Heriot-Watt University, 1990-96; Director: Bank of Scotland, since 1993, Royal Scottish National Orchestra, since 1996; b. 1.9.34, Edinburgh; m., 1, Kathleen Dewar (deceased); 2, Iris Lloyd-Webb; 1 s.; 3 d. Educ. Edinburgh Academy; Harrow School; Balliol College, Oxford. National Service, Royal Engineers. James Miller & Partners Ltd.: joined, 1958, appointed Director, 1960; Scottish Representative, Advisory Committee to the Meteorological Services, 1980-92; Chairman, Federation of Civil Engineering Contractors, 1985-86, President, 1990-93; Deacon Convener, Incorporated Trades of Edinburgh, 1974-77; President, Edinburgh Chamber of Commerce, 1981-83; Assistant, 1982-85, Treasurer, 1990-92, Master, 1992-94, Merchant Company of Edinburgh. Recreation: shooting. Address: (b.) The Miller Group Ltd., Miller House, 18 South Groathill Avenue, Edinburgh EH4 2LW; T.-0131-315 6000.

Miller, James David Frederick, CBE, DUniv(Stirling, Paisley), MA (Cantab), CIMgt, FIPD, FRSA. Chairman: SQA (Scottish Qualifications Authority), since 1996, SCOTVEC, since 1992, Scottish Examination Board, since 1995, University of Stirling Court, since 1992, Wolverhampton and Dudley Breweries PLC, since 1992; Vice-Chairman, Forth Valley Enterprise, since 1996; Director: J. and J. Denholm Ltd., Edinburgh Military Tattoo Ltd., since 1990, Scottish Life Assurance Company, since 1995; Member, Scottish Advisory Council for Education and Training Targets, since 1993; b. 5.1.35, Wolverhampton; m., Saffrey Blackett Oxley; 2 s. (1 deceased); 1 d. Educ. Emmanuel College, Cambridge;

London School of Economics. National Service, Argyll and Sutherland Highlanders (commissioned South Staffords); Council Member, Outward Bound Limited; Member, Court, Stirling University, 1978-84; Vice-Chairman, Royal National Orchestra; Director, Edinburgh Academy, 1985; Member, CBI Employee Involvement Panel; Governor, Scottish College of Textiles, 1989. Recreations: gardening; golf; walking. Address: (h.) Blairuskin Lodge, Kinlochard, Aberfoyle, by Stirling FK8 3TP; T.-01877 387 249.

Miller, Rev. John Stewart Abercromby Smith, MA, BD, STM. Minister, Morningside United Church, Edinburgh, since 1980; b. 3.5.28, Gibraltar; m., Lorna Vivien Fraser; 1 s.; 1 d. Educ. Lanark Grammar School; Edinburgh University; Union Theological Seminary, New York. Assistant Minister, St. Giles' Cathedral, Edinburgh, 1953-54; Minister: St. Andrew's, Hawick, 1954-59, Sandyhills, Glasgow, 1959-67, Mortlach and Cabrach, Banffshire, 1967-75, North Morningside, Edinburgh, and Morningside Congregational Church, 1975-80; Visiting Instructor, Columbia Theological Seminary, Georgia, 1986; Honorary Associate Minister, Peachtree Presbyterian Church, Atlanta, 1986; Chaplain, Sea Cadet Corps; Moderator, Edinburgh Presbytery, 1996-97. Recreations: reading; listening to music; exploring Britain. Address: (h.) 54 Hayfield, East Craigs, Edinburgh EH12 8UH; T.-0131 339 0537.

Miller, Josephine L., BA, BMus, MLitt. Course Leader, BA (Scottish Music), Royal Scottish Academy of Music and Drama, since 1996; Lecturer in Scottish Music and Ethnomusicology, since 1989; freelance musician and teacher; b. 1.10.62, Carluke; m., Steven Sutcliffe; 1 s. Educ. Kirkcudbright Academy; RSAMD; Glasgow University; Edinburgh University. Provision of teaching materials and teacher support for Scottish music in schools; freelance singer and fiddler, solo and with bands; Lecturer in Traditional Arts, Glasgow Arts Centre, 1990-92. Publications: music transcriptions for Come Gie's A Sang, 1995; The Music of Scotland (teacher support package). Recreations: gardening; walking; reading. Address: (b.) RSAMD, 100 Renfrew Street, Glasgow G2 3DB.

Miller, Keith Manson, BSc (Hons), DipMS. Chief Executive, Miller Group, since 1994; b. 19.3.49, Edinburgh. Educ. Loretto; Heriot-Watt University; Glasgow University. Managing Director: Miller Mining, 1976-90, Miller Developments, 1990-94. Director, Aberforth Smaller Companies Trust PLC. Recreations: sailing; skiing. Address: (b.) Miller Group Ltd., 18 South Groathill Avenue, Edinburgh EH4 2LW; T.-0131-315 6000.

Miller, Professor Kenneth, LLB, LLM, PhD. Professor of Law, Strathclyde University, since 1992; Vice-Dean (Academic), Strathclyde Business School; b. 11.12.51, Paisley; m., Margaret Macleod. Educ. Paisley Grammar School; Strathclyde University; Queen's University, Canada. Lecturer in Law, then Senior Lecturer, Strathclyde University, 1975-91; Deputy General Editor, Stair Memorial Encyclopaedia of the Laws of Scotland, 1990-96; Member, Employment Law Committee, Law Society of Scotland. Publications: Employment Law in Scotland (Co-Author); Property Law (Co-Author); Law of Health and Safety at Work in Scotland. Recreations: reading; golf; theatre. Address: (b.) Law School, Strathclyde University, 173 Cathedral Street, Glasgow; T.-0141-552 4400.

Miller, Sir Ronald Andrew Baird, CBE (1985), CA, DSc. former Chairman, Dawson International PLC; b. 13.5.37, Edinburgh. Non-Executive Director: Christian Salvesen PLC, Scottish Amicable Life Assurance Society, Securities Trust of Scotland PLC; Member, Court, Napier University. Address: (b.) 7 Doune Terrace, Edinburgh EH3 6DY.

Miller, Professor Timothy John Eastham, PhD, BSc, FIEE, CEng, FIEEE, FRSE. Lucas Professor in Power Electronics, Glasgow University, since 1986; b. 25.9.47,

Wigan; m., Janet Ann; 3 d. Educ. Atlantic College; Glasgow University; Leeds University. Research Fellow, Department of Electrical and Electronic Engineering, Leeds University, 1973-77; joined Corporate Research and Development Center, General Electric, NY, 1979, Manager, Power Electronics Control Program, 1983-86; appointed GEC Titular Professor in Power Electronics, Glasgow University, 1986. Publications: five textbooks and reference book; 100 papers. Ten patents. Recreation: racing cyclist. Address: (b.) Department of Electronics and EE, Glasgow University, Glasgow G12 8LT; T.-0141-330 4922.

Miller, Professor William L., MA, PhD, FBA, FRSA. Edward Caird Professor of Politics, Glasgow University, since 1985; b. 12.8.43, Glasgow; m., Fiona Thomson; 2 s.; 1 d. Educ. Aberdeen Grammar School; Royal High School, Edinburgh; Edinburgh University; Newcastle University. Formerly Lecturer, Senior Lecturer and Professor, Strathclyde University; Visiting Professor, Virginia Tech., Blacksburg, Virginia, 1983-84; also taught at Universities of Essex and Cologne; frequent Contributor to Press and TV; Member, Editorial Boards: Electoral Studies, Political Studies. Publications: Electoral Dynamics, 1977; The End of British Politics?, 1981; The Survey Method in the Social and Political Sciences, 1983; Elections and Voters, 1987; The Quality of Local Democracy, 1988; How Voters Change, 1990; Media and Voters, 1991; Alternatives to Freedom, 1995; Political Culture in Contemporary Britain, 1996; Values and Political Change in Postcommunist Europe, 1997. Address: (b.) Department of Politics, Glasgow University G12 8RT; T.-0141-339 8855.

Millham, Richard H. G. Principal, Motherwell College. Address: (b.) Dalzell Drive, Motherwell, ML1 2DD.

Milligan, Eric. Lord Provost and Lord Lieutenant, City of Edinburgh; since 1996; b. 27.1.51, Edinburgh; m., Janis. Educ. Tynecastle High School; Napier College of Commerce and Technology. Edinburgh District Councillor, 1974-78; Lothian Regional Councillor, 1978-96; Chairman, Finance Committee, 1980-82, 1986-90; President, COSLA, 1988-90; Convener, Lothian Regional Council, 1990-96; City of Edinburgh Councillor, since 1995. Address: (b.) City Chambers, High Street, Edinburgh EH1 1YJ.

Milligan, Hon. Lord (James George Milligan). Senator of the College of Justice, since 1988; b. 10.5.34. Advocate, 1959; QC, 1972; Advocate Depute, 1971-78; Chairman, Medical Appeal Tribunal (Scotland), 1979-88. Address: (b.) Court of Session, Parliament House, Edinburgh EH1 1RQ.

Mills, Professor Colin Frederick, OBE, MSc, PhD, CChem, FRSC, FRSE. Professorial Research Fellow and Director, Postgraduate Studies, Rowett Research Institute, since 1986 (Head, Biochemistry Division, 1966-86); Co-ordinator, Nutrition Monitoring Unit for Relief Programmes; b. 8.7.26, Swinton, Lancashire; m., D. Beryl; 1 d. Educ. Altrincham Grammar School; Reading University; London University. ARC Unit for Micronutrient Research, Long Ashton Research Station, Bristol University, 1946-47; Assistant Lecturer in Biochemistry, Wye College, London University, 1947-51; joined Rowett Research Institute, 1951. Member, WHO/FAO Experts Committee on Trace Elements in Human Nutrition; Chairman, International Committee for Symposia on Trace Elements in Man and Animals; Royal Society for Chemistry John Jeye Gold Medallist (Environmental Studies); Visiting Professor, Nutritional Biochemistry, University of Newcastle-upon-Tyne. Recreations: music; sailing. Address: (b.) Rowett Research Institute, Bucksburn, Aberdeen AB21 9SB; T.-01224 712751.

Mills, Harold Hernshaw, CB, BSc, PhD. Secretary and Head of Department, Scottish Office Development Department, since 1992; b. 2.3.38, Greenock; m., Marion Elizabeth Beattie. Educ. Greenock High School; Glasgow University. Cancer Research Scientist, Roswell Park Memorial Institute, Buffalo, New York, 1962-64; Lecturer, Chemistry Department, Glasgow University, 1964-69; Principal, Scottish Home and Health Department, 1970-76; Assistant Secretary: Scottish Office, 1976-81, Privy Council Office, 1981-83, Scottish Development Department, 1983-84; Under Secretary, Scottish Development Department, 1984-88; Principal Finance Officer, Scottish Office, 1988-92; Secretary, Scottish Office Environment Department, 1992-95. Address (b.) Scottish Office Development Department, Victoria Quay, Edinburgh EH6 6QQ; T.-0131-244 0759.

Mills, Ian Thomas, BSc, MPhil, MIMgt. Director of Education and Leisure Services, East Dunbartonshire Council, since 1995; b. 20.5.48, Hamilton; m., Margaret; 2 d. Educ. Dalziel High School, Motherwell; Glasgow University; Strathclyde University. Chemistry Teacher, Dalziel High School, Motherwell, 1970-75; Senior Housemaster, Lanark Grammar School, 1975-78; Assistant Head Teacher, then Depute Head Teacher, Carluke High School, 1978-85; Area Education Officer, Perth and Kinross, 1985-91; Assistant Director of Education, Tayside Regional Council, 1991-95. Adviser to Scottish Arts Council; Church of Scotland Elder; Past President, Rotary Club of Perth St. Johns. Recreations: music; family-based activities; various sports (curling, walking). Address: (b.) Department of Education, Boclair House, 100 Milngavie Road, Bearsden G61 2TQ; T.-0141-942 9000.

Mills, Thomas, BEd, CBiol, MIBiol, MIM. Head Teacher, St. Patrick's High School, Coatbridge, since 1996; b. 17.2.47, Lennoxtown; m., Janice Alexis; 1 s.; 1 d. Educ. St. Mungo's Academy; St. Andrew's College; Paisley University. Teacher of Biology, John Bosco Secondary School, 1974-77; A.P.T., Biology, Lourdes Secondary School, 1977-83; Principal Teacher of Biology, Our Lady and St. Francis Secondary School, 1983-87; Assistant Head Teacher, Our Lady's High School, Motherwell, 1987-92; Depute Headteacher, John Ogilvie High School, Hamilton, 1992-96. Recreations: keep-fit; DIY; music; caravanning. Address: (b.) St. Patrick's High School, Muiryhall Street, Coatbridge ML5 3NN; T.-01236 426191.

Milne, Alastair David, OBE, FRSE, PhD, MSc, BSc, CEng, FIEE, SMIEEE. Managing Director, Wolfson Microelectronics Ltd., since 1984; b. 8.11.42, Edinburgh; m., Rosemary C.; 1 s.; 2 d. Educ. George Watson's College; Heriot-Watt University; Bristol University. Research Fellow, Bristol University, Edinburgh University; Director, Wolfson Microelectronics Institute. Vice-President, Royal Society of Edinburgh. Recreations: climbing; sailing; skiing. Address: (h.) 17 Napier Road, Edinburgh; T.-0131-229 2161.

Milne, Brian, MB, ChB, FRCOG. Consultant Gynaecologist and Obstetrician, Raigmore Hospital NHS Trust, Inverness, since 1978; Clinical Senior Lecturer, Aberdeen University, since 1978; h. 9.1.42, Elgin; m., Mary I.B.; 2 s. Educ. Keith Grammar School; Aberdeen University. House Officer and Senior House Officer appointments, Aberdeen Royal Infirmary; Registrar appointments, Raigmore Hospital, Inverness and Southern General Hospital, Glasgow; Senior Registrar, Obstetrics and Gynaecology, Leicester Royal Infirmary, 1974-78. Recreations: golf; curling. Address: (h.) Muirfield House, 28 Muirfield Road, Inverness; T.-01463 222134.

Milne, Colin McLeod, LLB. Regional Chairman of Employment Tribunals, since 1994; b. 14.3.47, Glasgow; m., Margaret; 1 s.; 1 d. Educ. Kilmarnock Academy; Glasgow University. Partner, Wright Johnston & Mackenzie, Solicitors, Glasgow, until 1991; appointed Chairman of Industrial Tribunals, 1991, Regional Chairman, 1994. Address: (b.) Central Office of

Employment Tribunals, Eagle Building, 215 Bothwell Street, Glasgow G2 7TS; T.-0141-204 0730.

Milne, George, BSc (Hons), MEd. Headteacher, Peterhead Academy since 1991; b. 4.6.49, Aberdeen; m., Elizabeth Kerr; 2 s.; 1 d. Educ. Aberdeen Grammar School; Aberdeen University. Maths Teacher, 1972-81; Principal Teacher of Maths, Peterhead Academy, 1981-84; Assistant Head Teacher, then Depute Head, Mintlaw Academy, 1984-91. Recreations: Rotary activities; golf; reading. Address: (b.) Peterhead Academy, Prince Street, Peterhead AB42 1SY; T.-01779 472231.

Milne, John Alexander, BA, BSc (Hons), PhD. Deputy Director and Head, Ecology and Animal Science Group, Macaulay Land Use Research Institute; b. 22.11.43, Edinburgh; m., Janet Erskine; 1 s. Educ. Edinburgh Academy; Edinburgh University; London University; Open University. Deputy Editor, Grass and Forage Science; Address: (b.) Craigiebuckler, Aberdeen AB9 2QJ.

Milne, Professor John Sim, BSc (Hons), CEng, FIMechE, FRSA. Professor Emeritus, University of Abertay, Dundee, since 1996 (Professor of Mechatronics, 1993-96); b. 22.6.36, Arbroath; m., Isabella Paton; 2 s. Educ. Arbroath High School; Strathclyde University. Lecturer, then Senior Lecturer in Mechanical Engineering, Dundee Institute of Technology, 1958-93. Member, Higher Still Specialist Group on Design, Engineering and Technology; Consultant on Mechatronics for the Scottish Qualifications Authority; co-author of two textbooks and invited contributor to two engineering reference books. Recreations: cycling; hill-walking. Address: (h.) 45 Monymusk Road, Arbroath DD11 2BZ; T.-01241 873988.

Milne, Robert Hughes, MBE, JP. Managing Director, Aberdeen Fish Curers and Merchants Association Ltd., since 1987 (Chief Executive/Secretary, 1983-87); b. 4.6.39, Pittenweem; m., Helen Wilma Masson; 1 s. Educ. Waid Academy, Anstruther. Assistant Chief Fisheries Advisor, then Regional Officer, Herring Industry Board, 1962-73; Development Officer/Secretary, then Secretary General, Scottish Federation of Fishermen's Co-operatives Ltd., Fishing Co-operative Trading (Scotland) Ltd. and Fishing Co-operatives (Manufacturing) Ltd., 1973-83. Served, European Community Social Problems Fisheries Committee, European Community Advisory Committee on Fisheries and Association of European Agricultural and Fisheries Co-operatives, 1973-83; Member: Isle of Man Government's Commission of Inquiry, 1982-83, Sea Fish Industry Authority Research and Development Committee and Sea Fish Training Council, since 1983; Secretary, Scottish Fish Merchants Federation Ltd., since 1984. Burgess of Guild, City of Aberdeen; Council Member, Aberdeen Chamber of Commerce. Recreations: gardening; church activities. Address: (b.) South Esplanade West, Aberdeen AB9 2FJ; T.-01224 897744.

Milner, Professor A.D., MA, DipPsych, PhD, FRSE. Professor of Neuropsychology, St. Andrews University, since 1990 (Dean, Faculty of Science, 1992-94, Head, School of Psychology, 1994-97); b. 16.7.43, Leeds. Educ. Bradford Grammar School; Lincoln College, Oxford. Research Worker, Institute of Psychiatry, London, 1966-70; Lecturer, then Senior Lecturer, St. Andrews University, 1970-85, Reader, 1985-90. Publications: The Neuropsychology of Consciousness (Editor); The Visual Brain in Action, 1995. Address (b.) Psychological Laboratory, St. Andrews University, St. Andrews KY16 9JU; T.-01334 462065.

Milton, Ian Murray, MCIM. Chairman, Milton Hotels Ltd.; Director, Nevis Range Development Company PLC; b. 25.7.45, Glasgow; m., Ann; 1 s.; 3 d. Educ. Lochaber High School; Scottish Hotel School, Glasgow. Began Milton Hotels with brother, 1965. Recreations: golf; skiing.

computing. Address: (b.) Milton Hotels Ltd., North Road, Fort William PH33 6TG; T.-01397 703139.

Minto, 6th Earl of (Gilbert Edward George Lariston Elliot-Murray-Kynynmound), OBE (1986), JP. Brigadier, Queen's Bodyguard for Scotland (Royal Company of Archers); President, Scottish Council on Alcohol, since 1988; Vice Lord-Lieutenant, Roxburgh, Ettrick and Lauderdale, since 1992; former Convenor, Borders Regional Council; b. 19.6.28; m., 1, Lady Caroline Child-Villiers (m. diss.); 1 s.; 2, Mary Elizabeth Ballantine (deceased); 3, Mrs Caroline Larlham. Educ. Eton; Sandhurst. Former Captain, Scots Guards. Address: (h.) Minto, Hawick.

Miquel, Raymond Clive, CBE (1981), CIM. Chairman, Lees of Scotland Ltd., since 1993; b. 28.5.31. Managing Director, Arthur Bell & Sons Ltd., 1973-85; Chairman, Scottish Sports Council, 1987-91.

Mirodan, Vladimir, MA, FRSA. Director of Drama, Royal Scottish Academy of Music and Drama, since 1996; Vice-Chair, Directors' Guild of Great Britain, since 1992; b. 29.7.51, Bucharest; m., Barbara Berkery; 1 s. Educ. St. Sava, Bucharest; Drama Centre, London; Royal Holloway College, London University. Artistic Director, Attitude Theatre Company, 1978-85; Director, New End Theatre, London, 1981-83; Director, School of Performance, Rose Bruford College, 1989-94. Publication: The Balkan Cook Book. Recreation: horse-riding. Address: (b.) RSAMD, 100 Renfrew Street, Glasgow G2 3DB; T.-0141-332 4101.

Misra, Prem Chandra, BSc, MBBS, DPM (RCP&S, Edin and Glas), FAGS. Consultant Psychiatrist, Parkhead Hospital; Clinical Senior Lecturer, Glasgow University, since 1976; b. 24.7.41, Lucknow, India; m., Sandhya; 1 s.; 2 d. Educ. KK Degree College and King George's Medical College, Lucknow, India; Lucknow University. Rotating Intern, King George's Medical College Hospital, Lucknow, 1967; Demonstrator, Department of Human Physiology, Lucknow University, 1967; Resident Senior House Officer, General Medicine and Geriatrics, Wigan and Leigh Group of Hospitals, 1968-69; Resident House Surgeon, General Surgery, Wigan Royal Infirmary, 1968-69; Resident House Physician, General Medicine, Whelley Hospital, Wigan, 1969-70; Resident Senior House Officer in Psychiatry, then Resident Registrar in Psychiatry, Bolton District General Hospital, 1970-73; Senior Psychiatric Registrar (Midland Area Consultant Training Scheme), Hollymoor Hospital, Birmingham, 1973-76; Consultant Psychiatrist, Solihull Area Health Authority, 1976; appointed Consultant Psychiatrist, Glasgow Royal Infirmary and Duke Street Hospital, 1976; Consultant in Charge, Acorn Street Day Hospital, 1979; Deputy Physician Superintendent, Gartloch and Parkhead Hospitals, Glasow, 1984-92. President, Indian Association of Strathclyde, since 1981; Member, Executive Committee: Strathclyde Community Relations Council, 1981-85, Scottish Council for Racial Equality, 1982; Member: Social and Welfare Committee, CRC, for Ethnic Groups and Vietnam Refugees, 1982, Board of Directors, Scottish Refugee Council, since 1995; Secretary, Division of Psychiatry, Eastern District of Glasgow, 1980-94; President, British Society of Medical and Dental Hypnosis (Scotland), 1987-89; Member: Executive Committee, British Society of Research on Sex Education, International Scientific Committee on Sexuality and Handicap, International Advisory Board of Israel Society of Clinical and Experimental Hypnosis, International Committee of Sexologists, Society for the Advancement of Sexual Health; Executive Committee Member, European Society of Hypnosis; Justice of the Peace; awarded Ludwika Bierkoskigo Medal by Polish Medical Association for "outstanding contributions in the prevention and treatment of disabilities". Publications: Modern Trends in Hypnosis; research papers. Address: (b.) Parkhead Hospital, 81 Salamanca Street, Glasgow G31 5BA; T.-0141-211 8300.

Mitcalfe, Kirsteen, BA. Deputy Lieutenant of Moray, since 1991; Member, Gordonstoun School Board of Governors, 1982-94; b. 23.7.36, Edinburgh; m., Hugh Mitcalfe; 4 d. Educ. Oxenfoord Castle School; Open University. Recreations: skiing; tennis; reading. Address: (h.) Milton Brodie, Forres, Moray IV36 0UA; T.-01343 850281.

Mitchell, Rev. Alexander Bell, DipTechEd, BD. Minister, St. Leonard's Church, Dunfermline, since 1981; b. 28.6.49, Baillieston; m., Elizabeth Brodie; 1 s.; 2 d. Educ. Uddingston Grammar School; New College, Edinburgh. Assistant Minister, Dunblane Cathedral, 1979-81. Recreations: golf; hill-walking. Address: 12 Torvean Place, Dunfermline KY11 4VY; T.-01383 721054.

Mitchell, Anne Clouston, MA (Hons). Principal, St. Margaret's School, Edinburgh, since 1994; b. 24.2.46, Aberdeen. Educ. Lossiemouth High School; Elgin Academy; Aberdeen University. Assistant Teacher of English, Kirkcaldy and Lossiemouth; Teacher of English as a Foreign Language, Germany; Teacher of English/Assistant Housemistress, St. Leonards School; Principal Teacher of English, North Berwick High School and Balerno High School; Assistant Headteacher, then Depute Head, Dunbar Grammar School; seconded as Lothian Region Arts Co-ordinator. Co-author, Heinemann Core English Series. Recreations: theatre; reading; gardening. Address: (h.) 22 Cedar Drive, Port Seton EH32 0SN; T.-01875 815187.

Mitchell, Colin Malcolm, BSc, CBiol, MIBiol, MIMgt. Headteacher, Dumfries High School, since 1990; b. 11.6.50, Paisley; m., Pamela Margaret; 2 s. Educ. Forrester Secondary School, Edinburgh; Heriot Watt University. Teacher of Science/Biology, then Principal Teacher of Biology, Craigroyston High School, Edinburgh; Assistant Headteacher, then Depute Headteacher, Maxwelltown High School, Dumfries. Deputy team leader, Moffat Mountain Rescue Team; Chairman: Dumfries Group, Scottish Wildlife Trust, Dunscore Community Council. Recreations: mountaineering; bird-watching. Address: (b.) Dumfries High School, Marchmont, Dumfries DG1 1PX.

Mitchell, Rev. Duncan Ross, BA (Hons), BD (Hons). Minister, St. Andrews Church, West Kilbride, since 1980; b. 5.5.42, Boddam, Aberdeenshire; m., Sandra Brown; 2 s.; 1 d. Educ. Hyndland Senior Secondary School, Glasgow; Strathclyde University; Glasgow University. Worked in insurance industry, four years; Minister, Craigmailen UF Church, Bo'ness, 1972-80; Convener, Assembly Youth Committee, UF Church, 1974-79; Member: Scottish Joint Committee on Religious Education, 1974-79, Multilateral Conversation in Scotland, 1976-79, Board of Social Responsibility, Church of Scotland, 1983-86; Ardrossan Presbytery: Convener, World Mission and Unity, 1984-88, Convener, Stewardship and Finance, 1988-91; Convener, General Assembly Board of World Mission and Unity, Local Involvements Committee, and Executive Member of the Board, 1987-92; Church of Scotland Delegate to Council of Churches for Britain and Ireland Assembly; Moderator, Ardrossan Presbytery, 1992-93. Recreations: cycling; supporting Partick Thistle; writing poetry and short stories. Address: St. Andrew's Manse, 7 Overton Drive, West Kilbride; T.-01294 823142.

Mitchell, Professor Falconer, BCom, CA. Professor of Management Accounting, Edinburgh University; b. 24.11.50, Stirling; m., Maureen Wilson; 2 s. Educ. High School of Stirling; Edinburgh University. Audit apprenticeship, KPMG Edinburgh; Lecturer in Accounting, Heriot Watt University; Lecturer, Senior Lecturer, Edinburgh University. Canon Foundation in Europe Visiting Fellow, 1990-91. Recreations: bowling; gardening; reading; travel. Address: (b.) Department of Accounting, Edinburgh University, George Square, Edinburgh EH8 9JY; T.-0131-650 8340.

Mitchell, George Edward, FCIBS. General Manager, Bank of Scotland, since 1994; b. 7.4.50, Edinburgh; m., Agnes; 3 d. Educ. Forrester High School, Edinburgh. Bank of Scotland, since 1966. Recreations: football; tennis; family. Address: (b.) Bank of Scotland, Teviot House, 41 South Gyle Crescent, Edinburgh EH12 9DR; T.-0131-317 5700.

Mitchell, George Watson, MA. Director of Programmes, Grampian TV, 1989-97; b. 24.3.49, Edinburgh. Educ. Royal High School, Edinburgh; Edinburgh University. Thomson Regional Newspapers, 1971-73; BBC, 1974-80; ATV, Birmingham, 1980-81; Central Television, 1982-88 (Editor, Current Affairs, East Midlands TV Centre); Programme Controller, Grampian TV, 1988-89.

Mitchell, Iain Grant, QC, LLB (Hons), FSA Scot, FRSA. Queen's Counsel, since 1992; Temporary Sheriff, since 1992; Honorary Secretary, Scottish Conservative and Unionist Association, since 1993; b. 15.11.51, Edinburgh. Educ. Perth Academy; Edinburgh University. Called to Scottish Bar, 1976; Past President, Diagnostic Society of Edinburgh; former Vice-President, Edinburgh University Conservative Association; Conservative candidate, Falkirk West, General Election, 1983, Kirkcaldy, General Election, 1987, Cumbernauld and Kilsyth, General Election, 1992, Dunfermline East, General Election, 1997; Chairman, Trust for an International Opera Theatre of Scotland; Vice-Chairman, Scottish Baroque Ensemble Ltd.; Member: Scottish Committee, Royal Institute of International Affairs, Executive Committee of European Movement (Scottish Council), Executive Committee, Scottish Lawyers' European Group, Conservative Group for Europe, Scottish Committee, Society for Computers and Law. Recreations: music and the arts; photography; cinema; walking; history; travel; writing; finding enough hours in the day. Address: (b.) Advocates Library, Parliament House, High Street, Edinburgh; T.-0131-226 5071.

Mitchell, Sheriff J.K., LLB. Sheriff of Glasgow and Strathkelvin at Glasgow. Advocate, 1979. Address: (b.) Sheriff Court House, 1 Carlton Place, Glasgow, G5 9DA.

Mitchell, John, BSc. Head Teacher, Kilsyth Academy, since 1985; President, Headteachers' Association of Scotland, 1995-96; b. 4.1.45, Kirkintilloch; m., Irene; 1 s.; 1 d. Educ. Lenzie Academy; Glasgow University. Taught in Glasgow; Principal Teacher of Physics, Balfron High School and Bishopbriggs High School; Assistant Head Teacher, Kilsyth Academy; Deputy Head Teacher, Knightswood Secondary School. Address: (h.) Kilsyth Academy, Balmalloch, Kilsyth G65 9NF; T.-01236 822244.

Mitchell, (John) Angus (Macbeth), CB, CVO, MC, LLD(Hon), (Dundee), DUniv (Stirling). b. 25.8.24, Ootacamund, India; m., Ann Williamson; 2 s.; 2 d. Educ. Marlborough College; Brasenose College, Oxford. Royal Armoured Corps (Captain), 1943-46; Scottish Office, 1949-84; Principal Private Secretary to Secretary of State for Scotland, 1958-59; Under Secretary, Social Work Services Group, 1969-74; Secretary, Scottish Education Department, 1976-84. Order of Orange-Nassau, 1946; Chairman, Scottish Marriage Guidance Council, 1965-69; Vice-Convener, Scottish Council of Voluntary Organisations, 1986-91; Member, Commission for Local Authority Accounts in Scotland, 1985-89; Chairman of Court, Stirling University, 1984-92; Chairman, Scottish Action on Dementia, 1986-94; Member, Historic Buildings Council for Scotland, 1988-94; Co-ordinator, Recording Scottish Graveyards Project, since 1992; Secretary, Greyfriars Kirkyard Trust. Publications: Scottish Office Ministers 1885-1985; Procedures for the Reorganisation of Schools in England, 1986. Recreations: old Penguins; gravestones; family history. Address: (h.) 20 Regent Terrace, Edinburgh EH7 5BS; T.-0131-556 7671.

Mitchell, John Gall, QC, MA, LLB. Social Security (formerly National Insurance) Commissioner, since 1979, and Child Support Commissioner, since 1992; b. 5.5.31, Edinburgh; m., 1, Anne Bertram Jardine (deceased); 3 s.; 1 d.; 2, Margaret Galbraith. Educ. Royal High School, Edinburgh; Edinburgh University. Advocate, 1957; Standing Junior Counsel, Customs and Excise, Scotland, 1964-70; a Chairman, Industrial Tribunals, Scotland, 1966-80; Honorary Sheriff of Lanarkshire, 1970-74; Chairman, Supreme Court Legal Aid Committee, 1974-79; a Chairman, Pensions Appeal Tribunals, Scotland, 1974-80. Address: (b.) 23 Melville Street, Edinburgh; T.-0131-225 2201.

Mitchell, John Logan, QC, LLB (Hons). Queen's Counsel, since 1987; Advocate Depute, 1981-85; b. 23.6.47, Dumfries; m., Christine Brownlee Thomson; 1 s.; 1 d. Educ. Royal High School, Edinburgh; Edinburgh University. Called to Bar, 1974; Standing Junior Counsel to Forestry Commission; Standing Junior Counsel, Department of Agriculture and Fisheries. Past President, Royal High School F.P. Club. Recreations: running; golf. Address: (h.) 17 Braid Farm Road, Edinburgh; T.-031-447 8099.

Mitchell, Jonathan James, BA, LLB, QC. Deputy Social Security Commissioner, since 1995; Advocate, 1979; Queen's Counsel, since 1992; Temporary Sheriff, 1988-95; b. 4.8.51, Edinburgh; m., Melinda McGarry; 1 s.; 1 d. QC, 1992. Publication: Eviction and Rent Arrears, 1995. Address: (h.) 30 Warriston Crescent, Edinburgh; T.-0131-557 0854.

Mitchell, Louise C., MA. Director, Glasgow Royal Concert Hall, since 1996; b. 12.8.56, London. Educ. Lady Margaret School, London; St. Andrews University; City University, London. Assistant Manager, Scottish Baroque Ensemble, 1979-81; Concerts Manager, London Sinfonietta, 1982-87; Assistant Director, Edinburgh International Festival, 1989-91; Music Programme Manager, Barbican Centre, 1992-94; Concerts Director, London Philharmonic Orchestra, 1994-96. Committee Member, International Society for Contemporary Music; Trustee, Microtonal Arts Trust. Recreations: travel; food and wine. Address: (b.) 2 Sauchiehall Street, Glasgow G2 3NY; T.-0141-332 6633.

Mitchell, Lyn, BSc (SocSci), MMedSci, RGN, SCM, RSCN, RNT. Chief Executive, National Board for Nursing, Midwifery and Health Visiting for Scotland, since 1986; b. 26.4.40, Elgin; m., David Mitchell; 1 step s.; 1 step d. Educ. Elgin Academy; Edinburgh University; Nottingham University. Ward Sister: Sheffield Children's Hospital, Aberdeen Royal Infirmary; Nurse Teacher, Foresterhill College, Aberdeen; Senior Health Education Officer, Grampian Health Board; Lecturer, Department of Nursing Studies, Edinburgh University; Nursing Adviser, Scottish Health Education Group. Address: (b.) 22 Queen Street, Edinburgh EH2 1NT; T.-0131-226 7371.

Mitchell, Professor Emeritus Ross Galbraith, MD, FRCPEdin, FRCPCH, DCH. Professor of Child Health, Dundee University, 1973-85, now Emeritus; b. 18.11.20; m., June Phylis Butcher; 1 s.; 3 d. Educ. Kelvinside Academy, Glasgow; Edinburgh University. Surgeon Lt., Royal Naval Volunteer Reserve, 1944-47; junior medical posts, Edinburgh, Liverpool and London, 1947-52; Rockefeller Research Fellow in Physiology, Mayo Clinic, USA, 1952-53; Lecturer in Child Health, St. Andrews University, 1952-55; Consultant Paediatrician, Dundee Teaching Hospitals, 1955-63; Professor of Child Health, Aberdeen University, 1963-72. Chairman: Editorial Board, Mac Keith Press, 1980-95, Scottish Advisory Council on Child Care, 1966-68; Dean, Faculty of Medicine and Dentistry, Dundee University, 1978-81; Chairman, Aberdeen Association of Social Service, 1971-72; President: Scottish Paediatric Society, 1982-84, Harveian Society of Edinburgh, 1982-83; Member, General Medical Council, 1983-85; Vice-Chairman, Scottish Child and Family Alliance, 1985-92. Recreations: fishing; gardening; languages. Address: (h.) Craigard, Abertay Gardens, Broughty Ferry, Dundee DD5 2RR; T.-01382 776983.

Mitchell, Rev. Sheila Margaret, BD, MTh. Minister, Lesmahagow Old Parish Church, since 1995; b. 24.7.70, Edinburgh. Educ. Arran High School; New College, Edinburgh University. Assistant Minister, St. Giles' Cathedral, Edinburgh. Address: (h.) 103 New Trows Road, Lesmahagow ML11 0ER; T.-01555 892425.

Mitchison, Professor John Murdoch, ScD, FRS, FRSE. Professor Emeritus and Honorary Fellow, Edinburgh University (Professor of Zoology, 1963-88); b. 11.6.22; m., Rosalind Mary Wrong; 1 s.; 3 d. Educ. Winchester College; Trinity College, Cambridge. Army Operational Research, 1941-46; Research Scholar, then Fellow, Trinity College, Cambridge, 1946-54; Lecturer, then Reader in Zoology, Edinburgh University, 1953-62; Member, Edinburgh University Court, 1971-74, 1985-88; Dean, Faculty of Science, 1984-85; Member: Academia Europaea, Scottish Marine Biological Association, 1961-67; Executive Committee Member, International Society for Cell Biology, 1964-72; Member: Biological Committee, SRC, 1972-75, Royal Commission on Environmental Pollution, 1974-79, Science Board, SRC, 1976-79, Working Group on Biological Manpower, DES, 1968-71, Advisory Committee on Safety of Nuclear Installations, Health and Safety Executive, 1981-84; President, British Society for Cell Biology, 1974-77. Publication: The Biology of the Cell Cycle. Address: (h.) Great Yew, Ormiston, East Lothian EH35 5NJ; T.-Pencaitland 340530.

Mitchison, Naomi, CBE. Writer; b. 1.11.97, Edinburgh; m., Dick Mitchison; 3 s.; 2 d. Educ. Dragon School, Oxford; St. Anne's College, Oxford. Member: Argyll County Council, 1945-65, Highland Panel, 1945-65, Highland and Island Advisory Council, 1965-75; contested Scottish Universities Parliamentary constituency for Labour; author of about 80 books, including: The Corn King and the Spring Queen; Blood of the Martyrs; The Bull Calves; The Big House; Lobsters on the Agenda; Five Men and a Swan; Cleopatra's People; volumes of autobiography; The Cleansing of the Knife; Images of Africa; Memoirs of a Space Woman; Travel Light; Early in Orcadia; A Girl Must Live. Address: (h.) Carradale House, Carradale, Campbeltown, Argyll.

Mitchison, Professor Rosalind Mary, Hon DLitt, HonDUniv, FRSE, FRHistS, MA. Professor of Social History, Edinburgh University, 1981-86; b. 11.4.19, Manchester; m., J.M. Mitchison (qv); 1 s.; 3 d. Educ. Channing School, Highgate; Lady Margaret Hall, Oxford. Assistant Lecturer, Manchester University, 1943-46; Tutor, Lady Margaret Hall, Oxford, 1946-47; Assistant: Edinburgh University, 1954-57, Glasgow University, 1962-63; Lecturer, Glasgow University, 1966-67; Lecturer, then Reader, Edinburgh University, 1967-81. President, Scottish History Society, 1981-84. Publications: Agricultural Sir John, 1962; A History of Scotland, 1970; British Population Change since 1860, 1977; Life in Scotland, 1978; Lordship to Patronage: Scotland 1603-1745, 1983; Sexuality and Social Control: Scotland 1660-1780 (Co-Author), 1989; Coping with destitution: poverty and relief in Western Europe, 1991. Recreation: walking. Address: (h.) Great Yew, Ormiston, East Lothian EH35 5NJ; T.-Pencaitland 340530.

Mithen, Dallas Alfred, CB, BSc, FICFor. President, Institute of Chartered Foresters, 1984-86; Chairman, Forestry Training Council, 1984-92; b. 5.11.23; m., 1, Peggy Clarke (deceased); 2, Avril Teresa Dodd; 1 s.; 1 d. Educ. Maidstone Grammar School; University College of North Wales, Bangor. Fleet Air Arm, 1942-46; joined Forestry Commission as District Officer, 1950; Deputy

Surveyor, New Forest, and Conservator, SE (England), 1968-71; Senior Officer, Scotland, 1971-75; Head, Forest Management Division, Edinburgh, 1975-76; Commissioner for Harvesting and Marketing, Forestry Commission, 1977-83. Trustee, Central Scotland Countryside Trust, 1985-97; President, Forestry Section, BAAS, 1985. Recreations: swimming; walking; gardening. Address: (h.) 12 Stanehead Park, Biggar, South Lanarkshire ML12 6PU; T.-01899 221 308.

Mochrie, Ronald George. Deputy Chief Executive/Support Services Director, Scottish SPCA, since 1988; b. 10.8.36, Bonnybridge; m., Helen Joan Farquhar; 1 s.; 1 d. Educ. Denny High School; Falkirk Technical College. Company Secretary/Accountant, Gilbert Plastics Ltd., 1974-77; Secretary and Treasurer, Glasgow and West of Scotland SPCA, 1977-87. Leader Trainer, The Scout Association. Recreations: gardening; walking; photography. Address: (b.) Braehead Mains, 603 Queensferry Road, Edinburgh EH4 6EA.

Moffat, Alistair Murray, MA (Hons), MPhil. Chief Executive, Scottish Television Enterprises, since 1993 (Director of Programmes, 1990-93); b. 16.6.50, Kelso; m., Lindsay Thomas; 1 s.; 2 d. Educ. Kelso High School; St. Andrews University; Edinburgh University; London University. Ran Edinburgh Festival Fringe, 1976-81; Arts Correspondent/Producer/Controller of Features, Scottish Television. Publications: The Edinburgh Fringe, 1978; Kelsae — A History of Kelso from Earliest Times, 1985; Remembering Charles Rennie Mackintosh, 1989. Recreations: sleeping; supporting Kelso RFC. Address: (b.) Scottish Television, Cowcaddens, Glasgow G2 3PR.

Moir, Dorothy Carnegie, MB, ChB, MD, FFPHM, FRCP, DipMgt. Chief Administrative Medical Officer/Director of Public Health, Lanarkshire Health Board, since 1994; Community Medicine Specialist, since 1979; Honorary Senior Clinical Lecturer in Public Health, Aberdeen University; Honorary Senior Clinical Lecturer, Department of Public Health, Glasgow University; b. 27.3.42, Aberdeen; m., Alexander D. Moir; 3 s. Educ. Albyn School for Girls, Aberdeen; Aberdeen University. Research Fellow in Therapeutics and Pharmacology, 1966-69; Lecturer in Community Medicine, 1970-79; Chief Administrative Medical Officer/Director of Public Health, Forth Valley Health Board, 1988-94. Address: (b.) 14 Beckford Street, Hamilton ML3 0TA.

Moir, Rev. Ian Andrew, MA, BD. Church of Scotland Adviser for Urban Priority Areas, since 1991; Minister, Old Kirk of Edinburgh, 1983-91; b. 9.4.35, Aberdeen; m., Elizabeth; 3 s. Educ. Aberdeen Grammar School; Aberdeen University. Sub-Warden, St. Ninian's Training Centre, Crieff, 1959-61; Superintendent, Pholela High School, Natal, 1962-73; Assistant Secretary, Church of Scotland Overseas Council, 1974-83. Recreations: walking; golf. Address: (h.) 47 Millersneuk Drive, Lenzie G66 5JE.

Molana, Professor Hassan, BA, MA, PhD. Professor of Economics, Dundee University, since 1993; b. 16.5.53, Tehran. Educ. Southampton University; Essex University. Research Assistant, Essex University; Research Officer, Southampton University; Lecturer, then Senior Lecturer, Glasgow University; Senior Lecturer, Dundee University. Recreation: classical music. Address: (b.) Department of Economics, Dundee University DD1 4HN; T.-01382 344375.

Mole, George Alexander (Sandy). President, National Farmers Union of Scotland, 1996-97; Vice-Chairman, Coastal Grains Ltd., since 1994; Vice-Chairman, Scottish Agricultural and Rural Centre Ltd., since 1992; b. 7.6.43, Duns; m., Jean Mitchell; 1 s.; 2 d. Educ. St. Mary's, Melrose; Merchiston Castle. NFU of Scotland: President, Mid and East Berwick; Chairman, AFRC Cereal Consultative; Convener, Cereals Committee; Member: EEC Commission Cereals Advisory Committee, Home Grown Cereals Authority R. & D. Committee, Institute of Brewing Cereal Publicity. Recreations: golf; shooting. Address: Greenburn, Reston, Eyemouth TD14 5LP.

Mollison, Professor Denis, ScD. Professor of Applied Probability, Heriot-Watt University, since 1986; Trustee, John Muir Trust, since 1986 (Co-Founder,1983); b. 28.6.45, Carshalton; m., Jennifer Hutton; 1 s.; 3 d. Educ. Westminster School; Trinity College, Cambridge. Research Fellow, King's College, Cambridge, 1969; Lecturer in Statistics, Heriot-Watt University, 1973. Elected Member of Council, National Trust for Scotland, 1979-84; Trustee, Mountain Bothies Association, 1978-94. Address: (h.) The Laigh House, Inveresk, Musselburgh EH21 7TD; T.-0131-665 2055.

Molloy, Daniel Frances. Provost, Midlothian Council, since 1996; Member, Edinburgh and Lothians Tourist Board, since 1996; b. 16.10.52, County Donegal; m., Mara; 1 s.; 1 d. Educ. St. Connells School, Co. Donegal. Member, Lothian Health Board, 1979-87; Convener, Midlothian District Council, 1992-96; Chairman, Midlothian Tourism Association, 1988-96. Recreations: reading; walking in the countryside. Address: (h.) 57 Woodburn Bank, Dalkeith EH22 2HP; T.-0131-663 2120.

Moncreiff, 5th Baron (Harry Robert Wellwood Moncreiff), Bt; b. 4.2.15; m., Enid Marion Watson Locke (deceased); 1 s. Educ. Fettes College, Edinburgh. Lt.-Col. (Hon.), RASC (retired). Address: (h.) Tulliebole Castle, Fossoway, Kinross-shire.

Moncur, Charles C., MA (Hons), MIPR. Chairman, Commission on Scottish Education, since 1994; b. 22.3.41, Aberdeen; m., Sheila; 2 d. Educ. Culter School; Aberdeen University. Economic Analyst, ICI, Harrogate, 1969-72; Economic Adviser, Scottish Office Industry Department, 1972-85; Senior Planning Officer, BP Exploration, Aberdeen, 1985-88; Manager Community Affairs, BP Exploration, Glasgow, 1988-92; Manager Public Affairs Scotland, British Petroleum Co. plc, 1992-95. Formerly: Member, Executive Council, Scottish Business in the Community, Member, Executive Council, Scottish Council Development and Industry, Board of Management, Marine Biological Research Station, Millport, Advisory Committee, UBI Scotland. Recreations: golf; football. Address: (h.) 60 Cammo Gardens, Barnton, Edinburgh EH4 8HF; T.-0131-339 5219.

Mone, Rt. Rev. John Aloysius. Bishop of Paisley, formerly Titular Bishop of Abercorn and Auxiliary Bishop of Glasgow; b. 22.6.29, Glasgow. Educ. Holyrood Secondary School; Seminaire St. Sulpice and Institut Catholique, Paris. Ordained Priest, 1952; Assistant: St. Ninian's, Knightswood, Glasgow, 1952-75, Our Lady and St. George, Glasgow, 1975-79; Parish Priest, St. Joseph's, Tollcross, Glasgow, 1979-84. Scottish President, Scottish Catholic Marriage Care; Chairman, Scottish Catholic International Aid Fund, 1975-77; President, National Justice and Peace Commission, 1987-96; President, National Social Care Commission since 1996; President/Treasurer, Scottish Catholic International Aid Fund, since 1985. Address: (b.) Cathedral House, 8 East Buchanan Street, Paisley PA1 1HS.

Monelle, Raymond, MA, BMus, PhD, ARCM. Writer on music; Reader in Music, Edinburgh University; b. 19.8.37, Bristol; 2 d. Educ. Bristol Grammar School; Pembroke College, Oxford; Royal College of Music. Publication: Linguistics and Semiotics in Music, 1992. Address: (h.) 80 Marchmont Road, Edinburgh EH9 1HR.

Monro of Langholm, Rt. Hon The Lord (Hector), PC, AE, DL, JP, FRAgS, MP (Conservative), Dumfries, 1964-

97; Under Secretary of State, Scottish Office, 1992-95; Privy Councillor, since 1995; Farmer; b. 4.10.22, Edinburgh; m., 1, Lady (Anne) Monro (deceased); 2 s.; 2, Lady (Doris) Monro. Educ. Canford School; Cambridge University; Dundee School of Economics. RAF, 1941-46; Royal Auxiliary Air Force, 1946-53, Honorary Air Commodore, since 1981, Inspector General since 1990; Member, Dumfries County Council, 1952-67 (Chairman, Planning Committee and Joint Police Committee); Scottish Conservative Whip, 1967-70; Lord Commissioner, HM Treasury, 1970-71; Minister of Health and Education, Scottish Office, 1971-74; Opposition Spokesman on Scottish Affairs, 1974-75, Sport, 1974-79; Minister of Sport and Rural Affairs, 1979-81; Member: Nature Conservancy Council, 1982-91, Area Executive, NFU, 1964-97, Council, National Trust for Scotland, 1983-92; Vice-President, Scottish Rugby Union, 1975, President, 1976-77; Member, Queen's Bodyguard for Scotland (Royal Company of Archers); President: NSRA, 1987-92, ACU, 1983-90. Recreations: rugby; golf; flying; vintage cars; country sports. Address: (h.) Williamwood, Kirtlebridge, Lockerbie, Dumfriesshire; T.-01461 500213.

Montagu-Smith, Group Captain Arthur, DL, RAF (Retd); b. 17.7.15; m., Elizabeth Hood Alexander; 1 s.; 1 d. Educ. Whitgift School; RAF Staff College. Commissioned RAF, 1935; Adjutant 99 Squadron, 1938-39; served Second World War, European Theatre, North Africa and Mediterranean; Flt. Cdr., 264 Squadron, 1940, and 221 Squadron, 1941; OC 248 Squadron, 1942-43; Battle of Britain Gold Rosette, 1940; mentioned in Despatches, 1942; Deputy Director, RAF Training, USA (Washington), 1944; OC 104 Wing, France, 1945; Hon. ADC, Governor, N.I., 1948-49; Air Adviser, New Delhi, 1949-50; RAF Representative, Chiefs of Staff Committee, UN, New York, 1951-53; HM Air Attache, Budapest, 1958-60; retired at own request, 1961; Regional Executive, Small Industries Council and Scottish Development Agency, 1962-80; Member, Elgin District Council, 1967-75; Member, Moray TAFA, 1961-68; Director, Elgin and Lossiemouth Harbour Company, 1966-90; Deputy Lieutenant, Morayshire, 1970-91; Hon. County Representative, Moray and Nairn, RAF Benevolent Fund, since 1964; Chairman, Elgin and Lossiemouth Scottish SPCA, 1971-82; Past President, Victoria League, Moray and Nairn; Past Chairman, Moray Association of Youth Clubs. Recreations: outdoor interests; travel; animal welfare. Address: (h.) Woodpark, by Elgin, Moray IV30 3LF; T.-0134 384 2220.

Montgomery, Sir (Basil Henry) David, 9th Bt, JP, DL. Lord Lieutenant, Perth and Kinross, since 1995; Chairman, Forestry Commission, 1979-89; b. 20.3.31.

Montgomery, David Andrew, MA, CertEd. Chief Executive, East Ayrshire Council, since 1995; b. 22.10.46, Irvine; 2 s.; 1 d. Educ. Irvine Royal Academy; Glasgow University; Jordanhill College of Education. Teacher, Principal Teacher, Assistant Head Teacher, 1969-81; Strathclyde Regional Council: Principal Officer (Teacher Staffing), 1982-84; Education Officer, 1984-86; Assistant Director of Education, then Depute Director of Education, then Senior Depute, 1986-95. Recreations: photography; aviation. Address: (b.) Council Headquarters, London Road, Kilmarnock KA3 7BU; T.-01563 576002.

Montrose, 8th Duke of (James Graham), OStJ. Brigadier, Queen's Bodyguard for Scotland (Royal Company of Archers), since 1986 (Member, since 1965); b. 6.4.35; m., Catherine Elizabeth MacDonell; 2 s.; 1 d. Educ. Loretto. Council Member, National Farmers' Union of Scotland, 1982-84, 1987-90. Address: (h.) Buchanan, Drymen, Glasgow.

Moonie, Lewis George, MB, ChB, DPM, MRCPsych, MSc, MFCM. MP (Labour), Kirkcaldy, since 1987;b. 25.2.47, Dundee; m., Sheila Burt; 2 s. Educ. Nicolson Institute, Stornoway; Grove Academy, Dundee; St. Andrews University. A variety of junior and senior medical posts, 1970-87, latterly Consultant in Public Health Medicine, Fife Health Board. Member: Fife Regional Council, 1982-86, Social Services Select Committee, 1987-88, Treasury Select Committee, 1989-90; Opposition Front-Bench Spokesman on Technology, 1990-92, Science and Technology, 1992-94, Industry, since 1994, National Heritage Spokesman on Broadcasting, 1995-97. Address: (b.) 25 High Street, Kirkcaldy, Fife; T.-01592 201873.

Moore, Andrew F., BL. Director, SCIENTIA (Scottish Commercial & Industrial Education & Training International Association), since 1995; b. 5.12.39, Leven; m., Anne MacGregor; 2 s.; 1 d. Educ. Buckhaven High School; Edinburgh University. Examiner, Estate Duty Office, Edinburgh, 1958-63; Assistant, then Depute Secretary, Scottish Council for Commercial Education, 1963-73; Depute Chief Officer, Scottish Business Education Council, 1973-80; Chief Officer, SCOTBEC, 1980-86; seconded to Stirling University, 1987-89; Director: Scottish Chambers of Commerce, 1989-95, Chinese Enterprise Management Development Programmes, 1989-94. Governor, Scottish Council for Educational Technology, 1976-84; Director, Filmhouse, Edinburgh, 1980-85; British Association for Commercial and Industrial Education: Honorary Treasurer, 1979-81, Honorary Secretary, 1966-80; President: International Society for Business Education, 1993-97, Pedagogical Committee, International Society for Business Education and Member, ISBE/SIEC Executive, since 1980; Member, Scottish Council for Research in Education, 1984-87; Hon. Secretary, Scottish Students' Song Book Committee Ltd., 1980-93; Session Clerk, Scoonie Kirk, Leven, 1982-92; President, Leven YMCA 1972-95; Member: Council, Association of British Chambers of Commerce; Executive Committee, Scottish Business in the Community; Executive Committee, Scottish Council (Development & Industry); Forces Resettlement Committee for Scotland, 1989-95; RNIB Alwyn House Advisory Committee, 1994; Director: Fife Enterprise, 1994, North of Scotland European Partnership, 1994, Fife Careers Ltd., 1996; Chairman, Economic Affairs, Fife Chamber of Commerce, 1995; Chairman, Finance Committee, Glenrothes College; Chairman, Steering Group on Health Promotion in SMEs, 1995; Director: Centre for Europe, 1995, QTAC, since 1997; Member, Board of Management, Fife College of Further and Higher Education, since 1997. Recreations: golf; foreign travel. Address: (h.) Annandale, Linksfield Street, Leven, Fife; T.-01333 422644.

Moore, David Arthur, MB, BS, DPH, DIH, DTM&H, FFOM. Chairman, Scottish Council on Alcohol, since 1995; b. 5.2.40, South Shields; m., Susan Thomley; 1 s.; 2 d. Educ. Jarrow Grammar School; Durham University. Consultant Occupational Physician, Hon. Clinical Teacher, Edinburgh University. Recreations: yachting; books; music. Address: (h.) 94 Murrayfield Gardens, Edinburgh EH12 6DJ; T.-0131-346 0861.

Moore, George, LLB (Hons). Solicitor and Solicitor Advocate; Joint Senior Partner, Hamilton Burns Moore, since 1973; b. 7.11.47, Kilmarnock; m., Ann Beattie; 2 s.; 1 d. Educ. High School of Glasgow; Glasgow University. Member, Glasgow and North Argyll Legal Aid Committee, 1979; Reporter to Scottish Legal Aid Board, 1986; part-time Chairman, Industrial Tribunals in Scotland, 1986; Member, Sheriff Court Rules Committee, 1987. Recreations: tennis; golf; windsurfing. Address: (b.) 13 Bath Street, Glasgow G2 1HY; T.-0141-353 2121.

Moore, Malcolm Robert, LLB. Director of Legal Services, South Lanarkshire Council, since 1995; b. 15.11.48, Lennoxtown; m., Betty; 1 s.; 1 d. Educ. Broxburn Academy; Edinburgh University. Law Apprentice, Leonards, Solicitors, 1970-73; Legal Assistant, Burgh of

Hamilton, 1973-75; Legal Manager, then District Solicitor, then Director of Corporate Services, Hamilton District Council, 1974-96. Recreations: photography; walking; reading; cinema. Address: (b.) Council Offices, Almada Street, Hamilton; T.-01698 454829.

Moore, Michael, MA, CA. MP (Liberal Democrat), Tweeddale, Ettrick and Lauderdale, since 1997; b. 3.6.65. Educ. Strathallan School; Jedburgh Grammar School; Edinburgh University. Manager, Corporate Finance practice, Coopers and Lybrand. Recreations: jazz; films; walking; golf. Address: (b.) House of Commons, London SW1A 0AA.

Moore, Rev. William Haisley, MA, Secretary for Scotland, Boys Brigade, 1990-96; b. 9.7.35, Donaghadee; m., Geraldine Ann Moorhead; 1 s.; 2 d. Educ. Bangor Grammar School; Magee University College, Londonderry; Dublin University; Presbyterian College, Belfast. Chaplain to the Forces, attached Royal Highland Fusiliers, 1966-70; Minister, Church of Scotland, 1970-90. Convener, Church of Scotland Youth Education Committee. Recreations: golf; gardening. Address: (h.) Stedfast, 62 Foxknowe Place, Eliburn, Livingston EH54 6TX; T.-01506 462390.

Moorhouse, John Edwin, DL (Edinburgh). Director, Scottish Business in the Community, since 1990; b. 7.10.41, Stone, Staffs; m., Susan; 2 s.; 2 d. Educ. Bridlington School. With Royal Dutch/Shell Group of companies, 1963-94; Director: CTF Training, The Scottish Ballet, Young Enterprise Scotland, and various other charitable organisations. Recreations: music; swimming; theatre. Address: (b.) 43 Station Road, Corstorphine, Edinburgh EH12 7AF; T.-0131-334 9876.

Moorhouse, Professor Robert Gordon, MA, PhD, FRSE, FRAS, ChP, FInstP. Honorary Senior Research Fellow, Glasgow University, since 1994; Theoretical Physicist; b. 14.3.26, Huddersfield; m., Peggy Gee; 1 s. Educ. Huddersfield College; Cambridge University; Birmingham University. Glasgow University, 1950-61; Rutherford-Appleton Laboratory, 1961-67; Glasgow University, 1967-94 (Emeritus Professor, since 1994). Publication: The Pion-Nucleon System, 1973. Recreation: history. Address: (b.) Department of Physics and Astronomy, Glasgow University, Glasgow G12 8QQ; T.-0141-330 5160.

Moos, Khursheed Francis, OBE, MB, BS, BDS, FRCSEdin, FDS RCS (Eng, Edin), FDS RCPS (Glas). Consultant Oral and Maxillofacial Surgeon; Honorary Professor, Glasgow University; Chairman, Intercollegiate Board in Oral and Maxillofacial Surgery; b. 1.11.34, London; m., Katharine Addison; 2 s.; 1 d. Educ. Dulwich College; Guy's Hospital, London; Westminster Hospital. National Service, RADC, Lt., 1959, Capt., 1960; Registrar in Oral Surgery, Mount Vernon Hospital, Middlesex, 1966-67; Senior Registrar, Oral Surgery, University of Wales, Cardiff, 1967-69; Consultant Oral Surgeon, S. Warwicks and Coventry Hospitals, 1969-74; Consultant Oral and Maxillofacial Surgeon, Canniesburn Hospital, Glasgow, since 1974; Dean, Dental Faculty, Royal College of Physicians and Surgeons of Glasgow, 1992-95; Civilian Consultant to Royal Navy, since 1976; President: Craniofacial Society of Great Britain, 1994-95, British Association of Oral and Maxillofacial Surgeons, 1991-92; Down Surgical Prize, 1988; Colyer Medal, Royal College of Surgeons of England, 1997. Publications include contributions to books and various papers. Recreations: music; natural history; philately; Eastern philosophy; gardening. Address: (h.) 43 Colquhoun Street, Helensburgh, Dunbartonshire G84 9JW; T.-01436 673232.

Moray, Earl of (Douglas John Moray Stuart), BA, FRICS. Chairman, Moray Estates Development Co., since 1974; b. 13.2.28, Johannesburg; m., Malvina Dorothea Murray; 1 s.; 1 d. Educ. Hilton College, Natal; Trinity College, Cambridge. Address: (h.) Doune Park, Doune, Perthshire.

Morbey, Gillian, OBE, BA (Hons), RGN. Director, Sense Scotland, since 1989; Trustee, Family Fund, since 1996; b. 11.6.53, Glasgow; m., Jeremy Morbey; 1 s.; 1 d. Educ. Williamwood High School; Strathclyde University. Nursing career within NHS; first Development Officer, Sense Scotland, 1985. Past Chairperson, West of Scotland Branch, Scottish Association for the Deaf; Chairperson, Glasgow Council of Voluntary Services, 1994-97. Recreations: supporter of Worldwide Fund for Nature; reading; music; walking. Address: (b.) 8 Elliot Place, Clydeway Centre, Glasgow G3 8EP; T.-0141-221 7577.

Morgan, Alasdair, MP, MA, BA. MP (SNP), Galloway and Upper Nithsdale, since 1997; Vice President, Scottish National Party; Member, Select Committee for Trade and Industry; b. 21.4.45, Aberfeldy; m., Anne Gilfillan; 2 d. Educ. Breadalbane Academy, Aberfeldy; Glasgow University. SNP: National Treasurer, 1983-90, Senior Vice-Convener, 1990-91, National Secretary, 1992-97. Recreation: hill-walking. Address: (h.) Nether Cottage, Crocketford, Dumfries.

Morgan, David Ivor, MA (Hons), LLB, NP. Regional Chairman of Industrial Tribunals (Scotland), since 1997; Member, Panel of Chairmen, Reserve Forces Appeal Tribunal, since 1997; b. 7.12.36, Giffnock; m., Diane Scott; 1 s.; 1 d. Educ. Hutchesons Grammar School; Aberdeen Grammar School; Aberdeen University. Assistant Solicitor, 1961-64; Partner, Davidson and Garden, Advocates in Aberdeen, 1964-89; full-time Chairman of Industrial Tribunals (Scotland), 1989-97. Burgess, City of Aberdeen. Recreations: hill-walking; fishing. Address: (b.) Inverlair House, 84 West North Street, Aberdeen; T.-01224 643307.

Morgan, Edwin (George), OBE, MA, Hon. DLitt (Loughborough, Glasgow, Edinburgh), Hon.DUniv (Stirling, Waikato); Hon. MUniv (Open). Freelance Writer (Poet, Critic, Translator), since 1980; Emeritus Professor of English, Glasgow University, since 1980; Honorary Professor, University College of Wales, Aberystwyth, since 1990; b. 27.4.20, Glasgow. Educ. Rutherglen Academy; High School of Glasgow; Glasgow University. War Service, Royal Army Medical Corps, 1940-46; Glasgow University: Assistant Lecturer in English, 1947, Lecturer, 1950, Senior Lecturer, 1965, Reader, 1971, Titular Professor, 1975; Visiting Professor of English, Strathclyde University, 1987-90; received Cholmondeley Award for Poets, 1968; Hungarian PEN Memorial Medal, 1972; Scottish Arts Council Book Awards, 1968, 1973, 1977, 1978, 1983, 1985, 1988, 1991, 1992; Saltire Society and Royal Bank Scottish Literary Award, 1983; Soros Translation Award (New York), 1985. Publications: (poetry): The Vision of Cathkin Braes, 1952, Beowulf, 1952, The Cape of Good Hope, 1955, Poems from Eugenio Montale, 1959, Sovpoems, 1961, Collins Albatross Book of Longer Poems (Editor), 1963, Starryveldt, 1965, Emergent Poems, 1967, Gnomes, 1968, The Second Life, 1968, Proverbfolder, 1969, Twelve Songs, 1970, The Horseman's Word, 1970, Scottish Poetry 1-6 (Co-Editor), 1966-72; Glasgow Sonnets, 1972, Wi the Haill Voice, 1972, The Whittrick, 1973, From Glasgow to Saturn, 1973, Fifty Renascence Love-Poems, 1975, Rites of Passage, 1976, The New Divan, 1977, Colour Poems, 1978, Platen: Selected Poems, 1978, Star Gate, 1979, Scottish Satirical Verse (Editor), 1980, Poems of Thirty Years, 1982, Grafts/Takes, 1983, Sonnets from Scotland, 1984, Selected Poems, 1985, From the Video Box, 1986, Themes on a Variation, 1988; Tales from Limerick Zoo, 1988; Collected Poems, 1990; Hold Hands Among the Atoms, 1991; Sweeping Out the Dark, 1994; Collected Translations, 1996; prose: Essays, 1974, East European Poets, 1976, Hugh MacDiarmid, 1976, Twentieth Century Scottish Classics, 1987; Nothing Not Giving Messages, 1990; Crossing the Border, 1990;

Evening Will Come They Will Sew The Blue Sail, 1991; plays: The Apple-Tree, 1982; Master Peter Pathelin, 1983; Cyrano de Bergerac, 1992. Address: (h.) 19 Whittingehame Court, Glasgow G12 OBG; T.-0141-339 6260.

Morgan, Jean R., MA. Secretary, Scottish Motor Neurone Disease Association, since 1996; President, Bearsden Orchestral Society, since 1976; m., Trefor Morgan (deceased); 2 s.; 2 d. Educ. Glasgow High School for Girls; Glasgow University. Working life spent mainly in employment rehabilitation centres as social worker; Church of Scotland Elder. Recreations: music; theatre; reading. Address: (h.) 65 Russell Drive, Bearsden, Glasgow G61 3BB; T.-0141-942 2868.

Morgan, Leslie, DMS, DPE, FILAM, MIM. Managing Director, Slainte Mhath; b. 7.8.53, Perth; m., Jill; 1 s.; 1 d. Educ. Perth Academy; Jordanhill College; Glasgow College of Technology. Sports Officer, Magnum Leisure Centre, Irvine; Deputy Manager, Bishopbriggs Sports Centre; Manager, Spectrum Leisure Centre, Co. Durham; Chief Leisure Officer, Wear Valley District Council; Director of Leisure and Economic Development, Wear Valley D.C.; Chief Executive, Moray District Council; General Manager, Hoskyns Forres BPD (first Business Process Management Centre in Europe). British Leisure Personality of the Year, 1990. Recreations: basketball; skiing; squash. Address: (h.) The Orchard Dyke, near Forres, Moray IV36 0TF; T.-01309 641364.

Morgan, Tom, CBE, DL, NDD, CDD; b. 24.2.14, Aberdeenshire; m., Mary Montgomery McLauchlan (deceased); 2 s. Educ. Longside School; North and West of Scotland Colleges of Agriculture. Unigate PLC, 38 years (Regional Director, Scotland); Councillor, City of Edinburgh Corporation, 1954-71, City of Edinburgh District Council, 1977-84; City Treasurer, 1968-71; Lord Provost and Lord Lieutenant, 1980-84; Chairman, Edinburgh Military Tattoo and Edinburgh International Festival, 1980-84. Recreations: golf; gardening. Address: (h.) 400 Lanark Road, Edinburgh EH13 0LX; T.-0131-441 3245.

Morison, Hon. Lord (Alastair Malcolm Morison), QC, MA, LLB. Senator of the College of Justice, 1985-97; b. 12.2.31, Edinburgh; m., Birgitte Hendil; 1 s., 1 d. by pr. m. Educ. Winchester College; Edinburgh University. Advocate, 1956; QC, 1965. Recreations: golf; fishing.

Morison, Hugh, MA, DipEd. Director General, Scotch Whisky Association, since 1994; b. 22.11.43, Bognor Regis; m.; 2 d. Educ. Chichester High School for Boys; St. Catherine's College, Oxford. Assistant Principal, Scottish Home and Health Department, 1966-69; Private Secretary to Minister of State, Scottish Office, 1969-70; Principal: Scottish Education Department, 1971-73; Scottish Economic Planning Department, 1973-79 (seconded to Offshore Supplies Office, Department of Energy, 1974-75); Assistant Secretary, Scottish Economic Planning Department, 1979-82; Gwilym Gibbon Research Fellow, Nuffield College, Oxford, 1982-83; Assistant Secretary, Scottish Development Department, 1983-84; Under Secretary, Scottish Home and Health Department, 1984-88, Scottish Office Industry Department, 1988-93; Non-Executive Director, Weir Group PLC, 1988-93; Member, Executive Committee, Barony Housing Association, since 1996. Publications: The Regeneration of Local Economics, 1987; Dauphine (Co-Author), 1991. Recreations: hill-walking; archaeology; literature. Address: (b.) Scotch Whisky Association, 20 Atholl Crescent, Edinburgh, EH3 8HF; T.-0131-222 9201.

Morkis, Jerzy Tomasz, BSc. Editor, Fife Free Press, since 1993; b. 29.9.56, Leven; m., Judith Anne Spencer; 1 s.; 1 d. Educ. Buckhaven High School; Stirling University. Joined Fife Free Press Group, 1978; Chief Reporter, East Fife Mail, 1982; Editor, East Fife Mail, 1990. Trustee, T.S.

Murray Award; Member, Media and Communication Programme Committee, Fife College. Recreations: tennis; reading; travel. Address: (b.) 23 Kirk Wynd, Kirkcaldy KY1 1EP; T.-01592 261451.

Morrice, Graeme. Leader, West Lothian Council; b. 23.2.59, Edinburgh. Educ. Broxburn Academy; Napier University. Recreations: playing guitar; reading; listening to music. Address: (h.) 39 Burnside Road, Uphall, Broxburn EH52 5DE; T.-01506 853266.

Morrice, Ken, MD, DPM, FRCPsych. Poet and Writer, since 1965; Psychiatrist, since 1956; b. 14.7.24, Aberdeen; m., Norah Thompson; 1 s.; 2 d. Educ. Robert Gordon's College; Aberdeen University. Hon. Fellow, Aberdeen University Mental Health Department. Publications: Crisis Intervention; Studies in Community Care; seven volumes of poetry; numerous papers; short stories. Recreations: golf; walking; TV. Address: (h.) 30 Carnegie Crescent, Aberdeen; T.-Aberdeen 310136.

Morris, Alistair Lindsay, LLB, DipLP. Solicitor; Director, Sinclair Osborne Financial Services Ltd., since 1987; Partner, Pagan Osborne & Grace Services Ltd.; b. 30.7.58, Dunfermline; m., Sandra Willins; 2 s. Educ. Queen Anne High School, Dunfermline; Aberdeen University. Council Member, Law Society of Scotland, since 1992, and Convenor, Professional Practice Committee, since 1996. Recreations: motor sport; football; rugby. Address: (b.) 83 Market Street, St. Andrews, KY16 9NX; T.-01334 475001.

Morris, Arthur MacGregor, MA, MB, BChir, FRCSEdin, FRCSEng, LRCP. Consultant Plastic Surgeon, Dundee Teaching Hospitals, since 1975; Honorary Senior Lecturer in Surgery, Dundee University, since 1975; b. 6.5.41, Heswall; m., Victoria Margaret Whitaker; 1 s.; 1 d. Educ. Dulwich College; Cambridge University; Guy's Hospital. House Officer, 1965-66; Anatomy Demonstrator, Newcastle, 1966-67; Rotating Surgical Trainee in Surgery, Bristol, 1967-69; Research Registrar, then Casualty Registrar, Guy's Hospital, 1969-71; Plastic Surgery Registrar, Canniesburn Hospital, Glasgow, 1972; Plastic Surgery Senior Registrar, Bangour General Hospital and Royal Hospital for Sick Children, Edinburgh, 1972-75. Chairman, Scottish Council, BMA; Deputy Chairman, Scottish Joint Consultants Committee. Publications: Complications of Plastic Surgery (book); papers. Recreations: golf; curling; photography; bee-keeping; gardening; fishing. Address: (b.) Plastic Surgery Unit, Dundee Royal Infirmary, Barrack Road, Dundee; T.-01382 660111.

Morris, Professor Arthur Stephen, BA, MA, PhD. Professor, Department of Geography, Glasgow University; b. 26.12.36, Broadway, Worcestershire; m., Estela C.; 1 s.; 1 d. Educ. Chipping Campden; Exeter College, Oxford University; University of Maryland; University of Wisconsin. Instructor/Assistant Professor, Western Michigan University, 1964-67; Lecturer, Senior Lecturer, Reader, Glasgow University; Visiting Professor: Central University of Venezuela 1976-77, CEPEIGE, Quito, 1980, Colegio Mexiquense, Mexico, 1987. Publications: South America; Latin America. Recreations: gardening; music; sailing. Address: (h.) The Old Manse, Shandon, near Helensburgh; T.-0141-339 8855.

Morris, Professor Christopher David, BA, DipEd, MIFA, FSA, FSA Scot, FRHistS, FRSE. Professor of Archaeology, Glasgow University, since 1990; b. 14.4.46, Preston; m., Dr. Colleen E. Batey. Educ. Queen Elizabeth's Grammar School, Blackburn; Durham University; Oxford University. Assistant Lecturer, Hockerill College of Education, Bishops Stortford, 1968-72; Lecturer, then Senior Lecturer in Archaeology, 1972-88, Reader in Viking Archaeology, 1989-90, Durham University. Member: Ancient Monuments Board for Scotland, since 1990, Court,

University of Glasgow. Recreations: classical music; opera; theatre; walking; skiing. Address: (b.) Department of Archaeology, Gregory Building, Lilybank Gardens, Glasgow University, Glasgow G12 8QQ; T.-0141-339 8855, Ext. 5690/4422.

Morris, James, CBE, BSc. Chief Executive, Scottish Society for the Prevention of Cruelty to Animals, since 1991; President, Scottish Area, Royal Air Forces Association, since 1991; Chairman, ATC Council for Scotland and NI, since 1995; President, Scottish Union Jack Association, since 1995; b. 8.7.36, Kirkcaldy; m., Anna W. Provan; 3 s. Educ. Kirkcaldy High School; Edinburgh University. Entered RAF, 1957; commanded No. 201 Squadron, 1975-77; commanded RAF Kinloss, 1981-84; Director Operational Requirements (Air), 1986-89; Air Officer, Scotland and Northern Ireland, 1989-91 (Air Vice Marshal); HM Commissioner, Queen Victoria School, since 1995. Recreations: sailing; curling. Address: (b.) Braehead Mains, 603 Queensferry Road, Edinburgh EH4 6EA; T.-0131-339 0222.

Morris, James Shepherd, RSA, RIBA, FRIAS, ALI. Principal, Morris and Steedman, Architects and Landscape Architects, since 1956; Hon. Treasurer, Royal Scottish Academy, since 1992; b. 22.8.31, St. Andrews; m., Eleanor Kenner Smith; 2 s.; 1 d. Educ. Daniel Stewart's College, Edinburgh; Edinburgh School of Architecture; University of Pennsylvania. Lt., Royal Engineers, 1957-59. Member, Council: RIAS and Edinburgh Architectural Association, 1969-71, Cockburn Association, Edinburgh; Convenor, Fellowship Committee, RIAS, 1985-87; Trustee, Museum of Antiquities, 1980-86; Member, Arts Council of GB, 1973-80; Vice Chairman, Scottish Arts Council, 1976-80; Member, Management Committee, Traverse Theatre; ARSA, 1975; RSA, 1989; two RIBA awards for Scotland; British Steel Award; 10 Civic Trust awards. Recreations: painting; golf; skiing; tennis. Address: (b.) 38 Young Street, Edinburgh EH2 4JD; T.-0131-226 6563.

Morris, Jean Daveena Ogilvy, CBE, MA, MEd, LLD (Dundee and St. Andrews), OStJ. Member, Court, University of St. Andrews, since 1994; Chairman, Parole Board for Scotland, 1980-92; b. 28.1.29, Kilmarnock; m., Rev. William J. Morris (qv); 1 s. Educ. Kilmarnock Academy; St. Andrews University. Clinical Psychologist: Royal Hospital for Sick Children, Edinburgh, St. David's Hospital, Cardiff, and Church Village, Pontypridd; Member, Bailie and Convener of Housing, Peterhead Town Council; Member, Aberdeen County Council; Columnist, Aberdeen Press and Journal; Chairman, Christian Action Housing Association; Member, Scottish Federation of Housing Associations; Chairman: Government Committee on Links Between Housing and Social Work (Morris Committee), Local Review Committee, Barlinnie Prison, Glasgow Abbeyfield Society; Vice Chairman, TSB Foundation; Director, Scottish Advisory Board, Abbey National; Chairman, Scotia House Development Company. Badminton Blue, St. Andrews University. Recreations: swimming; holidays in France. Address: (h.) 1 Whitehill Grove, Newton Mearns, Glasgow G77 5DH; T.-0141-639 6327.

Morris, Philip T., BSc, FCA. Finance Director, Adam & Company Group PLC, since 1993; b. 23.10.52, Malaysia. Educ. Morrisons Academy, Crieff; St. Andrews University. Arthur Young, Chartered Accountants, London, Stavanger, Norway and Dundee Offices, 1974-87; Royal Bank of Scotland Group (Corporate Finance), 1987-93. Recreations: travel; circuit training; crosswords. Address: (b.) 22 Charlotte Square, Edinburgh EH2 4DF; T.-0131-225 8484.

Morris, Professor Richard Graham Michael, MA, DPhil, FRSE, FRS. Director, Centre for Neuroscience, Edinburgh University, (Professor, since 1993, Reader, 1989-93); b. 27.6.48, Worthing; m., Hilary Ann; 2 d. Educ. St. Albans,

Washington DC; Marlborough College; Cambridge University; Sussex University. Addison Wheeler Fellow, Durham University, 1973-75; SSO, British Museum (Natural History), 1975-77; Researcher, BBC Television, 1977; Lecturer, St. Andrews University, 1977-86; MRC University Research Fellow, 1983-86. Member, MRC Neurosciences Grants Committee, 1981-85, MRC Neurosciences Board, since 1993; Hon. Secretary, Experimental Psychological Society, 1985-89; Chairman: Brain Research Association, 1990-94, Sectional Committee for Medicine and Biomedical Sciences, Royal Society of Edinburgh, 1995-97; Member, Council, European Neuroscience Association. Publications: academic papers and books; Learning and Memory (Co-Editor). Recreation: sailing. Address: (b.) Centre for Neuroscience, Edinburgh University, Crichton Street, Edinburgh EH8 9LE; T.-0131-650 3518/4562.

Morris, Professor Robert John, BA, DPhil. Professor of Economic and Social History, Edinburgh University, since 1993; b. 12.10.43, Sheffield; m., Barbara; 1 s.; 1 d. Educ. Acklam Hall, Middlesbrough; Keble and Nuffield Colleges, Oxford. Lecturer and Senior Lecturer in Economic and Social History, Edinburgh University, since 1968. Founding Editor, History and Computing. Recreation: watching vegetables grow. Address: (b.) 55 George Square, Edinburgh EH8 9JU.

Morris, Professor Robert Lyle, BSc, PhD. Professor of Parapsychology, Edinburgh University, since 1985; b. 9.7.42, Canonsburg, Pennsylvania; m., Joanna Du Barry; 2 d. Educ. Crafton High School; University of Pittsburgh; Duke University. Research Fellow, Duke University, 1969-71; Research Co-ordinator, then Research Associate, Psychical Research Foundation, 1971-74; Lecturer in Parapsychology, University of California, Santa Barbara, 1974-78; Lecturer, School of Social Sciences, University of California, Irvine, 1978-80; Research Coordinator, Communication Studies Laboratory, and Senior Research Scientist, School of Computer and Information Sciences, Syracuse University, 1980-85. Member: Council, Parapsychological Association, Council, British Society for Psychical Research; President, Psychology Section, British Association for the Advancement of Science, 1995-96. Publication: Foundations of Parapsychology: Exploring the Boundaries of Human Capability (Co-Author), 1986; Guidelines for Testing Psychic Claimants (Co-Author), 1996. Address: (b.) Psychology Department, University of Edinburgh, 7 George Square, Edinburgh EH8 9JZ; T.-0131-650 3343.

Morris, William, BA (Hons), FIOP, FScotvec, FSQA; b. 15.5.24, Aberdare, Wales; m., Pauline; 1 s.; 2 d. Educ. Aberdare Boys' Secondary School; Cardiff School of Art; Garnet College, London; London School of Printing and Graphic Arts; Open University. Compositor/Typographer; Royal Artillery, 1942-45; Lecturer in Typography, LSP&GA, 1951-58; Head, Department of Typography and Related Subjects; Deputy Principal, Glasgow College of Building and Printing, 1959-81; Principal, Anniesland College, 1981-89; Assistant General Secretary, Association of Principals of Colleges, 1991-96. Board Member, Printing and Publishing Industry Training Board, 1968-82; Member, City and Guilds of London Institute; Board Member and Director, Scottish Vocational Education Council, 1987-91; Past Chairman, Association of Principals of Colleges (Scottish Branch); Past Chairman, Association of College Management (Scottish Branch); Secretary, Employers' Association for Scottish Further Education Colleges, 1992-93; Secretary to the Vestry, St. Cyprian's Church, Lenzie, 1981-94; Vice-President, Glasgow Welsh Society, since 1992; President: Probus Club of Kirkintilloch, 1996, Rotary Club of Kelvin, 1997-98. Recreations: golf; gardening; painting. Address: (h.) 26 Laurel Avenue, Lenzie, Kirkintilloch, Glasgow G66 4RU; T.-0141-776 2716.

Morris, Rev. William James, KCVO, ChStJ, JP, BA, BD, PhD, LLD, DD, Hon. FRCP&SGlas. Minister, Glasgow Cathedral, since 1967; Chaplain in Ordinary to The Queen in Scotland, since 1969; Chairman, Iona Cathedral Trust, since 1979; Dean, Chapel Royal in Scotland, 1991-96; Chaplain to The Queen's Body Guard in Scotland (Royal Company of Archers), since 1994; b. 22.8.25, Cardiff; m., Jean Daveena Ogilvy Howie (see Jean Daveena Ogilvy Morris); 1 s. Educ. Cardiff High School; University of Wales (Cardiff and Aberystwyth); Edinburgh University. Ordained, 1951; Assistant, Canongate Kirk, Edinburgh, 1949-51; Minister: Barry Island and Cadoxton Presbyterian Church of Wales, 1951-53, St. David's, Buckhaven, 1953-57, Peterhead Old Parish Church, 1957-67; Chaplain, Peterhead Prison, 1963-67; Chaplain to Lord High Commissioner, 1975-76; Moderator, Deer Presbytery, 1965-66; Chaplain: Strathclyde Police, Glasgow Academy, High School of Glasgow, Glasgow District Council, Trades House of Glasgow, West of Scotland Engineers Association, Royal Scottish Automobile Club; Member, Independent Broadcasting Authority, 1979-84 (Chairman, Scottish Advisory Committee); Member, Convocation, Strathclyde University; Honorary President, Glasgow Society of Social Service. Publication: A Walk Through Glasgow Cathedral, 1986. Recreation: being good, careful, and happy (not always simultaneously). Address: (h.) 1 Whitehill Grove, Newton Mearns, Glasgow G77 5DA; T.- 0141 639 6327.

Morrison, Alexander Fraser, CBE, FRSA, BSc, CEng, FICE, MIHT, FScotvec, FCIOB. Chairman, Highlands and Islands Enterprise; Executive Chairman, Morrison Construction plc, since 1996; Director, Clydesdale Bank PLC; Member, Scottish Economic Council; Vice President, Royal Highland and Agricultural Society of Scotland, 1995-96; b. 20.3.48, Dingwall; m., Patricia Janice Murphy; 1 s.; 2 d. Educ. Tain Royal Academy; Edinburgh University. Morrison Construction Group, since 1970; Managing Director, 1976-84. National Federation of Civil Engineering Contractors: Chairman, 1993-94, Vice President, 1994-96; Director, Aberforth Split Level Trust plc; winner, 1991 Scottish Business Achievement Award; Hon. Doctor of Technology: Napier University, 1995, Glasgow Caledonian University, 1997. Recreations: rugby; golf; skiing; opera; theatre; art. Address: (b.) Morrison House, 12 Atholl Crescent, Edinburgh EH3 8HA; T.-0131-228 4188.

Morrison, Rev. Alistair Hogarth, BTh, DipYCS. Minister, St. Mark's-Oldhall, Paisley, since 1989; b. 12.9.43, Glasgow; 1 s.; 1 d. Educ. Jordanhill College School; Aberdeen University; Jordanhill College of Education. City of Glasgow/Strathclyde Police, 1962-81 (resigned with rank of Inspector to train for Ministry); Minister, Elgin High Church, 1985-89. Strathclyde Medal for Bravery, 1976. Recreations: hill-walking; general fitness. Address: 36 Newtyle Road, Paisley PA1 3JX; T.-0141-889 4279.

Morrison, Andrew Neil, CBE. Chief Inspector of Fire Services for Scotland, since 1993; b. 8.9.37, Arbroath; m., Kathleen; 1 s. Educ. Arbroath High School; Dundee College of Technology. Angus Fire Brigade, 1962-75; Tayside Fire Brigade, 1976-80; Deputy Firemaster, then Firemaster, Grampian Fire Brigade, 1980-93. Queen's Fire Service Medal; Hon. Doctor of Technology. Recreations: curling; golf. Address: (b.) Scottish Office, Saughton House, Edinburgh EH11 3XD; T.-0131-244 2342.

Morrison, Rev. Angus, MA, BD. Minister, Associated Presbyterian Churches, Viewforth Congregation, Edinburgh, since 1989; b. 30.8.53, Oban; m., Marion Jane Matheson; 2 s.; 1 d. Educ. Oban High School; Glasgow University; London University; Edinburgh University. Minister, Free Presbyterian Church of Scotland Oban Congregation, 1979-86, Edinburgh Congregation, 1986-89; Moderator, Southern Presbytery, Free Presbyterian Church, 1987-88; Moderator, APC Scottish Presbytery, 1993-94.

Member, Council, Rutherford House, Edinburgh; Contributor, Dictionary of Scottish Church History and Theology, 1993; Member, Gaelic Panel, National Bible Society of Scotland. Recreations: reading; swimming. Address: (h.) 6 Frogston Grove, Edinburgh EH10 7AG; T.- 0131-445 3673.

Morrison, Rev. Angus Wilson, MA, BD. Minister, Kildalton and Oa Parish, Islay, since 1989 (Minister, Braid Parish Church, Edinburgh, 1977-89); b. 14.2.34, Glasgow; m., Isobel M.S. Taylor; 1 s.; 2 d. Educ. Epsom College, Surrey; Trinity College, Oxford; New College, Edinburgh. Minister: Whithorn, 1961-67, Cults West, Aberdeen, 1967-77; various periods of service on General Assembly Committees, including Overseas Council, Inter-Church Relations, Board of Education and Selection Schools; Observer for World Alliance of Reformed Churches, Vatican Council II, 1963. Recreations: travel; family. Address: The Manse, Port Ellen, Isle of Islay PA42 7DB; T.-01496 302447.

Morrison, Colin Andrew, BA, MEd, DipM, MCIM, CertEd. Director of Education, Chartered Institute of Bankers in Scotland, since 1991; b. 14.10.61, Ellon; m., Stella Ross Ingram. Educ. Peterhead Academy; Robert Gordon's Institute of Technology; Aberdeen College of Education; Edinburgh University. Former Outdoor Pursuits Instructor and F.E. Lecturer/Senior Lecturer; Head of Business Studies, Stevenson College, 1990-91. Recreations: dinghy sailing; skiing. Address: (b.) 19 Rutland Square, Edinburgh EH1 2DE; T.-0131-229 9869.

Morrison, David Ralston. Writer; b. 4.8.41, Glasgow; m., Edna May Wade; 1 s.; 1 d. Educ. Glasgow High School for Boys; Hamilton Academy; Strathclyde University. Librarian: Lanark County, Edinburgh College of Art, Caithness. Founded and ran Scotia Review, Wick Folk Club, Wick Festival of Poetry, Folk and Jazz; author of numerous books of poetry; edited Essays on Neil M. Gunn, Essays on Fionn MacColla. Recreations: walking; drystanedyking; reading; music. Address: (h.) 18 MacArthur Street, Wick KW1 5AX; T.-01955 603703.

Morrison, James, RSA, RSW, DA, DUniv (Stirling). Painter in oil and watercolour; b. 11.4.32, Glasgow; m., Dorothy McCormack; 1 s.; 1 d. Educ. Hillhead High School; Glasgow School of Art. Taught part-time, 1955-58; won Torrance Memorial Prize, RGI, 1958; Visiting Artist, Hospitalfield, 1962-63; Council Member, SSA, 1964-67; staff, Duncan of Jordanstone College of Art, 1965-87; won Arts Council Travelling Scholarship to Greece, 1968; painting in various regions of France, 1976-82; numerous one-man exhibitions since 1956, in Scotland, London, Italy, West Germany, Canada; four works in private collection of Duke of Edinburgh and numerous other works in public and private collections; several group exhibitions since 1980 in UK and Europe; regular series of expeditions to paint in Canadian and Greenland High Arctic, since 1990. Publication: Aff the Squerr. Recreation: playing in a chamber music group. Address: (h.) Craigview House, Usan, Montrose, Angus; T.-Montrose 672639.

Morrison, Jean Turner, DipHE. National President, The Girls' Brigade in Scotland, since 1993; b. 14.5.41, Hamilton. Educ. Eastbank Academy, Glasgow; Glasgow and West of Scotland College of Domestic Science. Formerly Principal Teacher, Garthamlock Secondary School, Glasgow. Elder, Shettleston Old Parish Church, Glasgow. Recreations: walking; gardening; reading; travelling. Address: (b.) B.B. House, 168 Bath Street, Glasgow G2 4TQ; T.-0141-332 1765.

Morrison, Neil, MA (Hons), DipEd. Rector, Eyemouth High School, since 1990; b. 5.10.47, Aberdeen; m., Lorna; 2 d. Educ. Robert Gordon's College, Aberdeen; Aberdeen University. Teacher, Principal Teacher, 1971-81; Assistant

Rector, Mintlaw Academy, 1981-87; Depute Rector, Culloden Academy, 1987-90. Recreation: gardening. Address: (b.) Eyemouth High School, Eyemouth TD14 5BY.

Morrison, Sheriff Nigel Murray Paton, QC. Sheriff of Lothian and Borders at Edinburgh, since 1996; b. 18.3.48, Paisley. Educ. Rannoch School. Called to the Bar of England and Wales, Inner Temple, 1972; admitted to Scottish Bar, 1975; Assistant Editor, Session Cases, 1976-82; Assistant Clerk, Rules Council, 1978-84; Clerk of Faculty, Faculty of Advocates, 1979-86; Standing Junior Counsel to Scottish Development Department (Planning), 1982-86; Temporary Sheriff, 1982-96; Chairman, Social Security Appeal Tribunals, 1982-91; Second (formerly Junior) Counsel to the Lord President of the Court of Session, 1984-89; First Counsel to the Lord President, 1989-96; Counsel to Secretary of State under Private Legislation Procedure (Scotland) Act 1936, 1986-96; QC, 1988; Chairman, Medical Appeal Tribunals, 1991-96; Trustee, National Library of Scotland, since 1989. Publications: Green's Annotated Rules of the Court of Session; Green's Civil Practice Bulletin; Stair Memorial Encyclopaedia of the Laws of Scotland (Contributor); . Recreations: music; riding; Scottish country dancing; being taken by his black labrador for walks. Address: 9 India Street, Edinburgh EH3 6HA; T.-0131-225 2807.

Morrison, Peter, MA, LLB. Singer and Solicitor; b. 14.8.40, Greenock; m., Irene; 1 s.; 1 d. Educ. Greenock Academy; Glasgow University. Private legal practice, since 1968; own legal practice, 1977-96; currently Consultant, Paton Farrell Solicitors, Glasgow; began professional singing engagements at University; first television series, Castles in the Air, 1971; Songs of Scotland, 1973-79; television, theatre and concert appearances throughout UK, USA, Europe, Australia and Far East. Recreations: golf; non-participating cricket and rugby supporter. Address: (b.) 180 Hope Street, Glasgow; T.-0141-331 1798.

Morrison, Rev. Roderick, MA, BD. Minister, Partick Gardner Street Church, Glasgow, since 1994; b. 3.7.43, Lochmaddy; m., Christina Ann MacDonald; 1 s.; 1 d. Educ. Lochportan Public School; Glasgow University and Trinity College. Assistant Minister, Drumchapel Old Parish Church, Glasgow, 1973-74; Minister: Carinish Parish Church, North Uist, 1974-81, High Church, Stornoway, Lewis, 1981-94. Recreations: sailing; fishing; shooting. Address: 148 Beechwood Drive, Broomhill, Glasgow G11 7DX; T.-0141-563 2638.

Morrison, Valerie Louise, MA, PhD. Research Psychologist, since 1984; Lecturer in Health Psychology, Queen Margaret College, Edinburgh, since 1995; Chair, Scottish Drugs Forum, since 1995; b. 9.10.61, Dundee; m., David Robinson; 1 d. Educ. St. Brides School, Helensburgh; St. Andrews University; Edinburgh University. Project Leader, Cambridge Cyrenians and City Council Bus Project, 1984-85; Research Assistant, Addiction Research Unit, Strathclyde University, 1986-87; Research Associate, Alcohol Research Group, Edinburgh University, 1987-91; School of Psychology, St. Andrews University, 1991-95. Governing Council Member, Institute for Study of Drug Dependence, 1990-96. Recreations: visiting friends; good food; reading. Address: (b.) Scottish Drugs Forum, Shaftesbury House, 5 Waterloo Street, Glasgow G2 6AY; T.-0141-221 1175.

Morrison, William Garth, CBE, BA, CEng, MIEE, DL. Farmer; Chief Scout, 1988-96; Member, World Scout Committee, since 1992; Chief Commissioner of Scotland, The Scout Association, 1981-88; b. 8.4.43, Edinburgh; m., Gillian Cheetham; 2 s.; 1 d. Educ. Pangbourne College; Pembroke College, Cambridge. Service, Royal Navy, 1961-73, retiring with rank of Lt.; farming, since 1973; Member, Lothian Region Children's Panel, 1976-83 (Chairman,

Midlothian/East Lothian Area Panel, 1978-81); Lamp of Lothian Trustee, 1978; Member: Lothian, Borders and Fife Committee, Prince's Trust, 1979, Lothian and Borders Committee, Prince's and Royal Jubilee Trusts, 1983-88, Society of High Constables of Holyroodhouse, 1979; Deputy Lieutenant, East Lothian, 1984; Member, Scottish Community Education Council, 1988-95; Chairman, East and Midlothian NHS Trust, since 1993; SCEC Honorary Fellowship, 1995; Member, National Lottery Charities Board, since 1995; S.E. Regional Chairman, Scottish Landowners Federation, since 1996; Vice President, Commonwealth Youth Exchange Council, since 1997. Recreations: golf, sailing; Scouting. Address: West Fenton, North Berwick, East Lothian; T.-01620 842154.

Morrocco, Alberto, OBE, RSA, RSW, RP, RGI, LLD, DUniv. Painter, since 1938; b. 14.12.17, Aberdeen; 2 s.; 1 d. Educ. Sunnybank School, Aberdeen; Gray's School of Art, Aberdeen. Former Member, Grants Committee, Scottish Arts Council; former Member, Royal Fine Art Commission for Scotland. Carnegie Award, Royal Scottish Academy: Guthrie Award, San Vito Romano Prize; elected to Royal Society of Edinburgh, 1995; elected to Royal Institute of Architects in Scotland, 1995. Address: Binrock, 456 Perth Road, Dundee; T.-01382 69319.

Morrow, John, MB, ChB, FRCP(Glas), FRCP(Lond). Chairman, Ayrshire and Arran Health Board, since 1997; b. 19.3.32, Glasgow; m., Clare Patricia; 2 s.; 1 d. Educ. St. Mungo's Academy, Glasgow; University of Glasgow. National Service (RAMC), 1957-59; training posts, Stobhill Hospital and Western Infirmary, Glasgow; Consultant Physician: Ballochmyle Hospital, 1969, Kilmarnock Infirmary, 1981, Crosshouse Hospital, 1983; Clinical Director (Medicine), Crosshouse Hospital, 1992-97; retired 1997. Member, Ayrshire and Arran Health Board, 1981-89; President, Scottish Society of Physicians, 1993. Recreations: reading (biographies and poetry); walking. Address: (h.) 12 Glenpark Place, Ayr KA7 4SQ; T.-01292 441995; (b.) Boswell House, Arthur Street, Ayr; T.-01292 885885.

Morton, Rev. Alasdair J., MA, BD, DipEd, DipRE, FEIS. Minister, Bowden linked with Newtown St. Boswells, since 1991; b. 8.6.34, Inverness; m., Gillian M. Richards; 2 s.; 2 d. Educ. Bell-Baxter School, Cupar; St. Andrews University; Hartford Theological Seminary. District Missionary/Minister, Zambia (Northern Rhodesia), 1960-65; Chaplain and Religious Education Lecturer, Malcolm Moffat Teachers' College, Serenje, Zambia, 1966-67; Principal, David Livingstone Teachers' College, Livingstone, Zambia, 1968-72; Minister, Greyfriars Parish Church, Dumfries, 1973-77; General Secretary, Department of Education, Church of Scotland, 1977-91. Recreations: choral singing; gardening. Address: The Manse, Newtown St. Boswells TD6 0SG; T.-01835 822106.

Morton, Rev. Andrew Reyburn, MA, BD, DD. Associate Director, Centre for Theology and Public Issues, University of Edinburgh, since 1994; b. 24.5.28, Kilmarnock; m., Marion Armstrong Chadwin; 2 s.; 2 d. Educ. Kilmarnock Academy; Glasgow University; Edinburgh University; Bonn University. Scottish Secretary, Student Christian Movement, 1953-56; Minister, Moncreiff Parish, East Kilbride, 1956-64; Chaplain, Edinburgh University, 1964-70; Warden, Wolfson Hall and Co-ordinating Warden, Halls of Residence, Glasgow University, 1970-74; Social Responsibility Secretary and, latterly, Secretary, Division of Community Affairs and Assistant General Secretary, British Council of Churches, 1974-81; Secretary, Inter-Church Relations Committee and Assistant Secretary, Overseas Council, subsequently Assistant Secretary, Board of World Mission and Unity, Church of Scotland, 1982-88; Deputy General Secretary, Board of World Mission and Unity, Church of Scotland, 1988-93. Recreation: walking.

Address: (h.) 11 Oxford Terrace, Edinburgh, EH4 1PX; T.-0131-332 6592.

Morton, Archibald Campbell, MA, BA (Hons). Director of Education, Argyll and Bute Council, since 1995; b. 15.2.42, Kilmarnock; m., Shirley; 2 s.; 1 d. Educ. Dumfries Academy; Edinburgh University; Moray House College of Education. Teaching, 1964-83, latterly Depute Head Teacher, Cowdenknowes High School, Greenock; Education Officer, Renfrew Division, 1983-89; Senior Education Officer, Glasgow Division, 1990-93; Assistant Director of Education, Strathclyde Regional Council, 1993-95. Recreations: curling; sailing. Address: (b.) Argyll House, Alexandra Parade, Dunoon PA23 8AJ; T.-01369 704000.

Morton, Elizabeth Stewart, NP, LicIPD, FIMgt. Director of Law and Administration, Falkirk Council, since 1995; Solicitor; b. 21.8.56, Glasgow. Educ. Dalmellington High School; Ayr Academy; Glasgow University. Entered local government, 1974, as a legal apprentice; worked for Ayr County, Cunninghame District, Cumnock and Doon Valley District, Kyle and Carrick District; moved to Hamilton District as Chief Administrative Officer, 1990; returned to Ayrshire as Director of Administration and Legal Services, 1993. Address: (b.) Municipal Buildings, Falkirk FK1 5RS; T.-01324 506075.

Morton, 22nd Earl of (John Charles Sholto Douglas), DL; b. 19.3.27. Lord-Lieutenant, West Lothian, since 1985.

Morton, William John Keirs, DipTP, MRTPI. Chief Executive, Forth Valley Enterprise, since 1990, and Director, Senior Staff Development, Scottish Enterprise, since 1997; b. 14.6.49, Glasgow; m., Jan; 2 s.; 1 d. Educ. Bearsden Academy; Glasgow College of Art. Planning Assistant, Royal Burgh of Inverness, 1973-75; Project Officer, East Kilbride Development Corporation, 1975-76; SDA, 1976-87, latterly as Project Manager (Coatbridge Project); Chief Executive, Aberdeen Beyond 2000, 1987-89; Head of Urban Regeneration, SDA, 1989-90. Recreations: family; travel; cycling; reading. Address: (b.) Laurel House, Laurelhill Business Park, Stirling FK7 9JQ; T.-01786 451919.

Moss, Professor Michael Stanley, MA. Professor of Archival Studies, since 1997, and Archivist, Glasgow University, since 1974; b. 11.4.47, Harrogate; m.; 2 d. Educ. King Edward's School, Bath; Worcester College, Oxford. Registrar, Western Survey, National Register of Archives (Scotland). Publications include: The Workshop of the British Empire (Co-Author); The Making of Scotch Whisky (Co-Author); Shipbuilders to the World (Co-Author); An Invaluable Treasurer (Co-Author); The Royal (Co-Author). Recreations: swimming; climbing; gardening; stable management. Address: (b.) The Archives, Glasgow University, Glasgow G12 8QQ; T.-0141-330 5516.

Moule, Rev. Gerald Christopher, BA, BD. Parish Minister, Moffat linked with Wamphray, since 1975; b. 31.8.45, Guildford; m., Patricia Rosemary Parker; 1 s.; 2 d. Educ. Edinburgh Academy; Kelvinside Academy, Glasgow; St. Andrews University; Newcastle upon Tyne University; Edinburgh University (New College). Chartered accountancy articles; Assistant Minister, West Church of St. Nicholas, Aberdeen, 1973-75; Moderator, Presbytery of Annandale and Eskdale, 1980-81 and 1988-89; Secretary and Treasurer, Scottish Journal of Theology; World Council of Churches Consultant for Disaster Preparedness, Central and Eastern Europe, since 1995; Representative, UK Faith Communities in Civil Emergency Planning, Home Office, since 1990. Recreations: cricket; travel; swimming; gardening. Address: St. Andrew's Manse, Moffat DG10 9EJ; T.-01683 220128.

Mounfield, J. Hilary, MA (Hons), MICFM. Chief Executive, Epilepsy Association of Scotland, since 1995; Secretary, Joint Epilepsy Council; b. 19.7.41, Edinburgh; 2 s.; 1 d. Educ. Boroughmuir School; Edinburgh University. Research, Scottish Development Department and Ministry of Housing, 1963-66; teaching, London, 1973-84; fundraising for charities, 1984-91; Appeals Director, Penumbra, 1991-95. Chair: ICFM, Scotland, 1993-95, Bighearted Scotland, 1993-96; Council Member, Edinburgh Common Purpose. Recreations: gardening; reading; walking. Address: (b.) 48 Govan Road, Glasgow G51 1JL; T.-0141-427 4911.

Mowat, Ian Robert, MA, BPhil, FLA, FRSA. Librarian, Edinburgh University, since 1997; b. 20.4.46, Dingwall; m., Margaret Louise; 1 s.; 1 d. Educ. Robert Gordon's College, Aberdeen; Aberdeen University; Sheffield University; St. Andrews University. Assistant Librarian, St. Andrews University, 1970-72, Heriot-Watt University, 1972-75; Assistant Keeper, National Library of Scotland, 1975-78; Sub-Librarian/Associate Librarian, Glasgow University, 1978-86; Librarian, Hull University, 1986-92, Newcastle University, 1992-97. Recreations: music; architectural history; walking. Address: (b.) Edinburgh University Library, George Square, Edinburgh EH8 9LJ; T.-0131-650 3378.

Mowat, Sheriff Principal John Stuart, MA, LLB, QC. Sheriff Principal of South Strathclyde, Dumfries and Galloway, 1988-93; b. 30.1.23, Manchester; m., Anne Cameron Renfrew; 2 s.; 2 d. Educ. High School of Glasgow; Merchiston Castle School; Glasgow University. Served RAF Transport Command, 1942-46 (Flt.-Lt.); Journalist, 1947-52; Advocate, 1952-60; Sheriff of Fife and Kinross, at Dunfermline, 1960-72, at Cupar and Kinross, 1972-74, of Glasgow and Strathkelvin, 1974-88; Chairman, Sheriff Court Rules Council, 1989-92; Office-Bearer, Scottish Liberal Party, 1954-58; Parliamentary candidate, Caithness and Sutherland, 1955; Secretary, Sheriffs Association, 1968-75 (President, 1988); Trustee: Carnegie Dunfermline Trust, 1967-74, Carnegie United Kingdom Trust, 1970-74. Recreations: golf; curling; watching football. Address: (h.) Old Mill of Camserney, Aberfeldy, Perthshire PH15 2JF.

Mowat, Norman Ashley George, MB, ChB, MRCP (UK), FRCP, FRCP (Edin). Consultant Physician and Gastroenterologist, Aberdeen Teaching Hospitals, since 1975; Clinical Senior Lecturer in Medicine, Aberdeen University, since 1975; b. 11.4.43, Cullen; m., Kathleen Mary Cowie; 1 s.; 2 d. Educ. Fordyce Academy; Aberdeen University. House Officer, then Senior House Officer, then Registrar, Aberdeen Teaching Hospitals, 1966-72; Lecturer in Medicine, Aberdeen University, 1972-73; Lecturer in Gastroenterology and Research Associate, Medical College of St. Bartholomew's, London, 1973-75. Formerly Visiting Physician to Shetland Islands; publications include Integrated Clinical Sciences: Gastroenterology (Co-Editor), 1985. Recreations: sailing; golf; soccer; reading; photography. Address: (h.) Bucholie, 13 Kings Cross Road, Aberdeen AB2 4BF; T.-01224 319223.

Mowat, William George, MBE, JP. Honorary Sheriff, Caithness; Chairman, Caberfeidh Court, Royal British Legion Housing Association Ltd., 1978-93; Chairman, Caithness Voluntary Group, since 1991; Chairman, Caithness Justices, 1992-94; b. 12.5.28, Lybster; m., Aline Cameron Johnston; 3 d. Educ. Robert Gordon's College, Aberdeen. Provost of Wick, 1967-75; Chairman, Royal Burgh of Wick Community Council, 1977-91; Member, Caithness County Council, 1957-75. Hon. President, 1285 Squadron ATC Caithness; Chairman, Friends of Hempriggs Residential Home, Wick; Elder, Church of Scotland. Recreations: golf; bowls; flying; used to fish a little. Address: (h.) Buchollie, Coronation Street, Wick KW1 5LS; T.-01955 4794.

Muckart, Rev. Graeme Watson MacKinnon, MSc, MTheol, FSA Scot. Minister, North Church of St. Andrew, Aberdeen, since 1997; b. 11.12.43, Dunfermline; m., 1, Mary Elspeth Small; 1 s.; 1 d.; 2, Elizabeth M. Miller, PhD; 1 d. Educ. Royal Naval Schools, Malta; Willesden County Grammar School; Portsmouth Southern Grammar School; Highbury Technical College, Portsmouth; Leeds College of Art; Open University; St. Andrews University; Stirling University. Barclays Bank, 1962-64; Trainee Architect, 1964-69; architectural appointments, 1969-76; resident staff, Iona Abbey, 1976-78; divinity studies, 1978-82; Assistant Minister, Carrick Knowe, Edinburgh, 1982-83; Minister, Erskine Parish Church, Falkirk, 1983-90; Locum Minister, Carriden Parish Church, Bo'ness, 1990-92; Minister, St. Andrew's Church, Colombo, 1992-96. Chair, Falkirk Council of Churches, 1987-89. Recreations: painting; calligraphy; heraldry; reading; walking. Address: The Manse, 51 Osborne Place, Aberdeen AB25 2BX; T.-01224 646429.

Muir, Alastair James, BA (Hons). Chief Executive, Clydebank Economic Development Company, since 1989; b. 21.10.57, Paisley; m., Dr. Sarah Louise Davidson; 2 d. Educ. John Neilson, Paisley; Paisley College. Centre for Study of Public Policy, Strathclyde University, 1984-86; Depute Chief Executive, ASSET, 1986-89. Recreations: skiing; sailing; hill-walking. Address: (b.) Phoenix House, 7 South Avenue, Clydebank G81 2LG; T.-0141-951 1131.

Muir, Richard. Chairman and Chief Executive, James Finlay PLC. Address: (b.) 10 West Nile Street, Glasgow, G1.

Muir, Trevor. Chief Executive, Midlothian Council, since 1995; b. 10.7.49, Glasgow; m., Christine Ann; 1 s.; 1 d. Educ. High School of Glasgow; Langside College; Strathclyde University. Scottish Special Housing Association, 1973-77; City of Glasgow District Council, 1977-81; Director of Housing, City of Aberdeen District Council, 1981-87; Chief Executive, Midlothian District Council, 1987-96. Recreations: squash; family life. Address: (b.) Midlothian House, Buccleuch Street, Dalkeith, Midlothian EH22 1DJ.

Mulholland, Francis, LLB (Hons), MBA, DipLP, SSC, NP. Solicitor Advocate; Advocate Depute, since 1997; b. 18.4.59, Coatbridge; m., Marie Elizabeth. Educ. Columba High School, Coatbridge; Aberdeen University; Edinburgh University. Trainee, Bird Semple & Crawford Herron, Solicitors, Glasgow, 1982-84; Procurator Fiscal Depute: Greenock, 1984-87, Glasgow, 1987-91; Solicitor, Crown Office, Edinburgh, 1991-96; Procurator Fiscal Depute, Edinburgh, 1996. First Solicitor Advocate and Member of Procurator Fiscal Service to be appointed to office of Advocate Depute; Member, Council, SSC Society; Member, Council, Society of Solicitor Advocates. Recreations: football; squash; military history. Address: (b.) Crown Office, 25 Chambers Street, Edinburgh; T.-0131-226 2626.

Mulholland, Henry, JP. Leader, Inverclyde Council, since 1996; b. 10.5.30, Greenock; m., Mary Ann McNeil Scullion; 1 s.; 3 d. Educ. St. Columba's, Greenock. Councillor, Greenock, since 1970; Director, Renfrewshire Enterprise Company. Address: (h.) 119 Mallard Crescent, Greenock PA16 7BE; T.-01475 723665.

Mullen, Frank, BSc, MPhil, MCP. Director, Scottish Convention Bureau, since 1994; b. 12.5.58, Kilmarnock. Educ. James Hamilton Academy, Kilmarnock; Glasgow University; University of Pennsylvania. Policy Researcher, Strathclyde Regional Council, 1980-85; Area Manager, Scottish Tourist Board, 1985-87; Marketing Director, Greater Glasgow Tourist Board and Convention Bureau, 1987-94. Recreations: keep-fit; theatre. Address: (b.) 23

Ravelston Terrace, Edinburgh EH4 3EU; T.-0131-332 2433.

Mullen, Ian M., BSc, MRPharmS. Freelance consultant on healthcare and pharmaceutical issues; b. 11.5.46, Stirling; m., Veronica Drummond; 2 s.; 1 d. Educ. St. Modan's High School, Stirling; Heriot-Watt University. Registered MPS, 1970; self-employed community pharmacist, 1971-97; elected to Pharmaceutical General Council, 1974; Vice-Chairman, 1983; Chairman, Pharmaceutical General Council (Scotland), 1986-88; Vice-Chairman, National Pharmaceutical Consultative Committee, 1987-89; Member, UK Advisory Committee on Borderline Substances, 1986-89; Vice-Chairman, Forth Valley Health Board, 1989-91; Director, Common Services Agency of the NHS in Scotland, 1991-94, Vice-Chairman, 1993; Director, Scottish Aids Research Foundation; contributor to All-Party Parliamentary Group on Aids; Director, Central Scotland Chamber of Commerce, 1990-93; Chairman: St. Andrew's School Board, 1990-94, Falkirk and District Royal Infirmary NHS Trust; Member: Scottish Dental Practice Review Board, 1991-92, Shields Committee for the NHS in Scotland, 1995-96. Recreations: walking; golf; swimming. Address: (h.) Ardenlea, 11 Arnothill, Falkirk FK1 5RZ; T.-01324 621806.

Mullen, Veronica C., BA, DipEd, FRSA. Chairman, Scottish Marriage Care, since 1995; Chairman, Scottish Marriage Care, Falkirk and Stirling Centres, since 1991; b. 20.6.46, Stirling; m., Ian M. Mullen; 2 s.; 1 d. Educ. St. Modan's High School, Stirling; Craiglockhart College of Education; Heriot-Watt University. Primary school teaching, 1966-71; partner in retail pharmacy business, 1984-96; partner in healthcare consultancy, since 1990. Recreations: tennis; travel; golf. Address: Ardenlea, 11 Arnothill, Falkirk, FK1 5RZ; T.-01324 621806.

Mundell, John Weir. Director of Connect Services, East Dunbartonshire Council; b. Edinburgh; m., Karen; 3 s. Educ. Currie High School; Heriot-Watt University. Entered local government, 1974; Head of Central Contracts, Central Regional Council, 1994-95. Recreations: swimming; karate; gymnastics (coach); farming. Address: (b.) East Dunbartonshire Council, Broomhill Industrial Estate, Kilsyth Road, Kirkintilloch; T.-0141-777 5501.

Munn, Charles William, BA, PhD, FCIBS, FRSA. Chief Executive, Chartered Institute of Bankers in Scotland; Vice President, European Bank Training Network; b. 26.5.48, Glasgow; m., Andrea Cuthbertson; 1 s.; 1 d. Educ. Queen's Park Secondary School, Glasgow; Langside College; Strathclyde University; Glasgow University; Jordanhill College. British Linen Bank, 1964-67; Glasgow College of Technology, Department of Finance and Accounting, 1975-78; Lecturer in Economic History, Glasgow University, 1978-86, Senior Lecturer, 1986-88. Editor, The Scottish Banker; Member: Church of Scotland Church and Nation Committee, 1990-94, Board, Scottish Qualifications Authority, since 1997. Publications: Clydesdale Bank: the First 150 Years, 1988; The Scottish Provincial Banking Companies 1747-1864, 1981. Recreation: golf. Address: (b.) 19 Rutland Square, Edinburgh EH1 2DE; T.-0131-229 9869.

Munn, Sir James, OBE, MA, DEd, LLD, DUniv; b. 27.7.20, Bridge of Allan; m., Muriel Jean Millar Moles; 1 d. (deceased). Educ. Stirling High School; Glasgow University. Indian Civil Service, 1941-48; various teaching appointments, Glasgow, 1949-57; Principal Teacher of Modern Languages, Falkirk High School, 1957-66 (Depute Rector, 1962-66); Principal Examiner in Modern Languages, Scottish Examination Board, 1965-66; Rector: Rutherglen Academy, 1966-70, Cathkin High School, 1970-83; Member, University Grants Committee, 1973-82; Member, Consultative Committee on the Curriculum, 1968-80, Chairman, 1980-87; Chairman, Committee to review the

Structure of the Curriculum at S3 and S4, 1975-77; Member of Court, Strathclyde University, 1983-91; Manpower Services Commission/Training Commission Chairman for Scotland, 1984-88, Chairman, GB, 1987-88; University Commissioner, 1988-95. (h.) 4 Kincath Avenue, Rutherglen, Glasgow G73 4RP; T.-0141-634 4654.

Munn, Professor Pamela, MA, MLitt, CertEd. Professor of Curriculum Research, Moray House Institute of Education, since 1994; b. 31.3.49, Glasgow; m., Graham Hamilton Munn. Educ. Hermitage School, Helensburgh; Aberdeen University. Teacher of History, 1972-78; Research Fellow, Stirling University, 1974-84; Lecturer in Applied Research in Education, York University, 1984-86; Senior Research Officer, then Depute Director, Scottish Council for Research in Education, 1986-94. Member, Scottish Consultative Council on the Curriculum; Fellowship, CIDREE, 1996; SCRE Silver Medal, 1984. Publications: The Changing Face of Education 14-16; Education in Scotland: policy and practice from pre-school to secondary, 1997; Parents and Schools: customers, managers or partners?, 1993. Recreations: hill-walking; gardening; reading, especially crime fiction. Address: (b.) Moray House Institute of Education, Holyrood Road, Edinburgh EH8 8AQ; T.-0131-558 6175.

Munro, Alexander, MB, ChB, ChM, FRCS. Consultant General Surgeon, Raigmore Hospital, Inverness, since 1978; Clinical Senior Lecturer in Surgery, Aberdeen University, since 1978; b. 5.6.43, Ross and Cromarty; m., Maureen E. McCreath; 2 s.; 1 d. Educ. Fortrose Academy; Aberdeen University. Training in General Surgery at Registrar and Senior Registrar level, Aberdeen Hospitals, 1971-78; specialist training, St. Mark's Hospital, 1977. Recreation: gardening. Address: (h.) 23 Eriskay Road, Inverness; T.-Inverness 223804.

Munro, Angus Cunningham, BSc, PhD. Director, Scottish Antibody Production Unit, since 1984; b. 12.1.44, Dundee; m., Christine Renwick; 2 s.; 1 d. Educ. Harris Academy, Dundee; Edinburgh University. Senior Scientist and Project Manager, Beecham Pharmaceuticals, 1969-74; Principal Scientist, Glasgow and West of Scotland Blood Transfusion Service, 1974-84. Recreations: music; astronomy; collecting. Address: (b.) Scottish Antibody Production Unit, Law Hospital, Carluke, Lanarkshire ML8 5ES; T.-01698 351161.

Munro, Professor Colin Roy, BA, LLB. Professor of Constitutional Law, Edinburgh University, since 1990, Dean, Faculty of Law, 1992-94; Chief Examiner, London University LLB (External) Degree, since 1991; b. 17.5.49, Aberdeen; m., Ruth Elizabeth Pratt; 1 s.; 1 d. Educ. Aberdeen Grammar School; Aberdeen University. Lecturer in Law, Birmingham University, 1971-72, Durham University, 1972-80; Senior Lecturer in Law, then Reader in Law, Essex University, 1980-85; Professor of Law, Manchester University, 1985-90. Publications: Television, Censorship and the Law; Studies in Constitutional Law. Recreations: sport; cinema and theatre; real ale. Address: (b.) Faculty of Law, Old College, South Bridge, Edinburgh EH8 9YL; T.-0131-650 2056.

Munro, David Mackenzie, BSc, PhD, FRGS, FSAScot. Director and Secretary, Royal Scottish Geographical Society, since 1996; Member, Council, National Trust for Scotland; Member, Advisory Board, Graduate School of Environmental Studies, Strathclyde University; Member, Permanent Committee on Geographical Names for British Official Use; b. 28.5.50, Glasgow. Educ. Daniel Stewart's College; Edinburgh Academy; Edinburgh University. Research Associate, then Research Fellow, Edinburgh University, 1979-96; Leader/Co Leader, Edinburgh University expeditions to Central America, 1981, 1986, 1988, 1991. Chairman, Kinross-shire Civic Trust; Chairman, Michael Bruce Trust. Publications: Chambers

World Gazetteer (Editor); Oxford Dictionary of the World (Editor); Gazetteer of the Baltic States; A World Record of Major Conflict Areas; Loch Leven and the River Leven – a Landscape Transformed; numerous articles and reports on land use in Central America. Recreations: walking; travel; exploring landscapes. Address: (b.) 40 George Street, Glasgow G1 1QE; T.-0141-552 3330.

Munro, Rev. David Peacock, MA, BD, STM. Minister, Bearsden North Church, 1967-96; Clerk, Presbytery of Dumbarton, since 1986; b. 7.9.29, Paisley; m., Jessie Scott McPherson; 3 d. Educ. Paisley Grammar School; Glasgow University; Union Theological Seminary, New York. Minister, Aberluthnott Parish Church, 1953-56, Castlehill Church, Ayr, 1956-67. Vice-Convener, General Assembly Council, 1988-90, Convener, 1990-95; Chairman, General Assembly Board of Education, 1974-79; Convener, General Assembly Education Committee, 1981-85. Recreations: golf; gardening. Address: (h.) 14 Birch Road, Killearn, Glasgow G63 9SDQ; T.-01360 550098.

Munro, Donnie, DA. Former Guitarist and Lead Singer, Runrig; b. Skye; m.; 3 children. Former Art Teacher, Inverness and Edinburgh; Rector, Edinburgh University, 1991-94; contested (Labour) Ross, Skye and Inverness West, 1997. Dr. HC, Edinburgh, 1994.

Munro, Graeme Neil, MA. Director and Chief Executive, Historic Scotland, since 1991; b. 28.8.44, Edinburgh; m., Nicola Susan Wells (qv); 1 d. Educ. Daniel Stewart's College, Edinburgh; St. Andrews University. Assistant Principal, Scottish Development Department, 1968-72; Principal, Scottish Development Department and Scottish Home and Health Department, 1972-79; Assistant Secretary, Department of Agriculture and Fisheries for Scotland, SHHD, and Central Services, 1979-90; Director, Historic Buildings and Monuments, Scottish Office Environment Department, 1990-91. Recreations: walking; reading; local history; gardening; swimming. Address: (b.) Longmore House, Salisbury Place, Edinburgh EH9 1SH; T.-0131-668 8696.

Munro of Foulis, Hector William, ARICS. 31st Chief of Clan Munro; b. 20.2.50; m., Sarah Duckworth; 1 s.; 2 d. Educ. Oratory School; Agricultural College, Cirencester. Farmer and Landowner. Address: (h.) Foulis Castle, Evanton, Ross-shire.

Munro, Hugh Murray, BA, MEng, CA. Office Managing Partner, Ernst & Young, Aberdeen, since 1989; b. 30.12.46, Kirkcaldy; m., Valerie Ingram; 1 s.; 1 d. Educ. Aberdeen Grammar School; Strathclyde University; Glasgow University. Arthur Andersen & Co., Glasgow, 1968-73 (Partner, 1981-87); Arthur Young, Aberdeen, 1987-89 (Office Managing Partner). Recreations: skiing; curling; gardening. Address: (b.) Ernst & Young, 50 Huntly Street, Aberdeen AB10 1ZN; T.-01224 653262.

Munro, Jack, DPE. Chief Executive, Edinburgh and Lothians Tourist Board, since 1997; b. 18.9.49, Cromarty; m., Lynn Prentice Roberts. Educ. Fortrose Academy; Jordanhill College of Education. Assistant Director of Tourism and Recreation, North East Fife District Council, 1975-82; Conference Manager, Inverness District Council, 1984-86; Director, Greater Glasgow Convention Bureau, 1986-90; Director, Edinburgh Convention Bureau, 1990-93. Chief Executive, Greater Glasgow Tourist Board, 1993-96; Chief Executive, Greater Glasgow and Clyde Valley Tourist Board, 1996-97. Chairman, British Association of Conference Towns, 1992-93; Co-Chair, International Task Force, IACUB; Member, Ministerial Advisory Group, Business Tourism. Recreations: rugby; golf; Scottish history; gardening. Address: (b.) 4 Rothesay Terrace, Edinburgh EH3 7RY; T.-0131-226 6800.

Munro, Jean Mary, BA (Hons), PhD. Chairman, Council, Scottish History Society, 1989-93; b. 2.12.23; m., Robert William Munro. Educ. London University; Edinburgh University. WRNS, 1944-47; freelance historical researcher; Member, Council, National Trust for Scotland, 1964-69 and 1987-92 (Executive, 1968-80); Chairman, Council, Scottish Genealogy Society, 1983-86 (Vice-President, since 1987); Chairman, Council, Scottish Local History Forum, 1984-88. Publications (as Jean Dunlop): the British Fisheries Society; the Clan Chisholm; the Clan Mackenzie; the Clan Gordon; the Scotts; the Clan Mackintosh; (with R.W. Munro): Tain through the Centuries; The Scrimgeours; The Acts of the Lords of the Isles. Recreations: reading; walking. Address: (h.) 15a Mansionhouse Road, Edinburgh EH9 1TZ; T.-0131-667 4601.

Munro, Professor J. Forbes, MA, PhD. Associate Director, Centre for Business History, Glasgow University; b. 15.3.40, Grantown-on-Spey. Educ. Dingwall Academy; Edinburgh University; Wisconsin University. Lecturer in Economic History, Senior Lecturer, Reader, Professor, Glasgow University, 1965-96. Editor, Journal of African History, 1982-87; Dean of Social Sciences, 1987-89, Clerk of Senate, 1991-96, Glasgow University. Publications: Colonial Rule and the Kamba, 1975; Africa and the International Economy, 1976; Britain in Tropical Africa, 1984. Recreation: curling. Address: (b.) 4 University Gardens, Glasgow University, Glasgow G12 8QQ.

Munro, John Forbes, OBE, FRCPEdin, FRCPGlas, FRCPLond. Honorary Fellow, Edinburgh University, since 1992; b. 25.6.33, Edinburgh; m., Elizabeth Jean Durell Caird; 3 d. Educ. Edinburgh Academy; Chigwell School, Essex; Edinburgh University. Former Consultant Physician, Eastern General and Edenhall Hospitals and part-time Senior Lecturer, Edinburgh University; Registrar, Royal College of Physicians, Edinburgh, 1993-97. Recreations: art; gardening. Address: (h.) Backhill, Carberry, near Musselburgh, East Lothian; T.-0131-663 4935.

Munro, Rev. John P.L., MA, BD, PhD. Faithshare Secretary, Church of Scotland Department of World Mission, since 1990; b. 11.5.47, Edinburgh; m., Pat Lawson; 1 s.; 1 d. Educ. Edinburgh Academy; Christ's College, Cambridge; Edinburgh University. Church of Scotland Chaplain, Stirling University, 1977-82; Lecturer, St. Paul's Theological College, Kenya, 1982-85; Minister, St. Vigeans and Knox's Church, Arbroath, 1986-90. Recreations: music; hill-walking; motor-cycle touring. Address: (b.) 121 George Street, Edinburgh EH2 4YN; T.-0131-225 5722.

Munro, Kenneth Alexander, MA, FRSA. Head of Representation in Scotland, European Commission, since 1988; b. 17.12.36, Glasgow; m., Elizabeth Coats Forrest McCreanor; 2 d. Educ. Hutchesons' Boys' Grammar School; Glasgow University. Economic research, Scottish American Investment Company, 1963-66; Senior Research Officer, ETU, 1966-67; Secretary, Economic Development Committee, NEDO, 1967-69; Industrial Relations Manager, Ford Motor Co., 1969-74; joined European Commission, 1974. Recreations: walking; swimming; cinema; theatre. Address: (b.) 9 Alva Street, Edinburgh EH2 4PH; T.-0131-225 2058.

Munro, Nicola Susan, BA (Hons). Under Secretary, Scottish Office Public Health Policy, since 1995; b. 11.1.48, Hitchin; m., Graeme Neil Munro (qv); 1 s.; 1 d. Educ. Harrogate Grammar School; Warwick University. Joined Scottish Office, 1970. Recreations: travel; reading; gardening. Address: (b.) St. Andrews House, Edinburgh EH1 3DG; T.-0131-244 2133.

Munro, Robert William. Author and Journalist; b. 3.2.14, Kiltearn, Ross-shire; m., Jean Mary Dunlop. Educ.

Edinburgh Academy. War Service, Seaforth Highlanders and Inter-Services Public Relations Directorate (India), 1940-46; Editorial Staff, The Scotsman, 1933-59 and 1963-69; Editor-in-Chief, Highland News Group, 1959-63; Chairman, Edinburgh Press Club, 1955-57 (President, 1969-71); Honorary Editor, Clan Munro Association, 1939-71 (Vice-President, since 1963); former Council Member: Society of Antiquaries of Scotland, Scottish History Society, Scottish Genealogy Society; Trustee, National Museum of Antiquities of Scotland, 1982-85. Publications: Lachlan MacQuarrie of Ulva, 1944; Donald Monro's Western Isles of Scotland and Genealogies of the Clans 1549 (Editor), 1961; Tain Through the Centuries (Co-Author, with wife), 1966; The Glorious Privilege: The History of The Scotsman (Co-Author), 1967; Kinsmen and Clansmen, 1971; The Northern Lighthouses, 1976; Highland Clans and Tartans, 1977; Edinburgh and the Borders, 1977; The Munro Tree 1734, 1978; Scottish Lighthouses, 1979; Taming the Rough Bounds, Knoydart 1745-1784, 1984; Acts of the Lords of the Isles 1336-1493 (Co-Author, with wife), 1986; Clan MacQuarrie: A History, 1996. Recreations: historical research and writing; walking; visiting islands. Address: (h.) 15A Mansionhouse Road, Edinburgh EH9 1TZ; T.-0131-667 4601.

Murby, David Frigast, LLB (Hons). Partner, Shepherd & Wedderburn, WS, since 1974; Procurator Fiscal to Lyon Court; b. 7.3.47, Nigeria; m., Morag; 2 s. Educ. Edinburgh Academy; Edinburgh University. Shepherd & Wedderburn: Trainee Solicitor, 1969-71, Solicitor, 1971-74. Recreations: sport; reading; music. Address: (b.) Saltire Court, 20 Castle Terrace, Edinburgh; T.-0131-228 9900.

Murchison, Lilian Elizabeth, MB, ChB, PhD, FRCPE, FRCP(Lond). Consultant Physician and Honorary Clinical Senior Lecturer in Medicine, Aberdeen University, since 1976; b. 29.4.36, Aultbea. Educ. Invergordon Academy; Edinburgh University; Glasgow University. Member, Scientific Staff, Atheroma Research Unit, Western Infirmary, Glasgow, 1963-68; Senior Tutor/Senior Registrar, Department of Medicine, Queen's University, Belfast, 1969-71; Lecturer, Department of Therapeutics and Clinical Pharmacology, Aberdeen University, 1971-76. Recreations: overseas travel; hill-walking. Address: (h.) 9 Highgate Gardens, Aberdeen, AB11 7TZ; T.-01224 588532.

Murchison, Maurine, OBE, MA (Hons); b. 25.11.35, London; m., Dr. Murdoch Murchison (qv); 3 s.; 2 d. Educ. James Allen's Girls School, Dulwich; Edinburgh University. Secondary school teaching, 1958-59; homemaker and mother, since 1960; Member, Inverness County Children's Panel, 1971-75 (Chairman, 1972-75); Chairman, Highland Region Children's Panel, 1975-80; Member, Inverness Prison Visiting Committee, 1984-85; Member, Panel for Appeals Tribunal, set up under Social Work Scotland Act 1968, since 1983; Assessor under Race Relations Act, since 1982; Church Representative, Grampian Education Committee, 1990-94; Chairman, Children's Panel Advisory Committee, Highland Region, 1980-85; Member: Consultative Committee on the Curriculum, 1980-87, Highlands and Islands Development Consultative Council, 1978-86, Police Advisory Board for Scotland, 1985-93; Lay Member, Schools Inspectorate, 1994; Mediator and Counsellor, A.C.C.; Member, Rape/Abuse Line. Publication: Not Without Cost, 1996. Recreations: embroidery; group Bible study; reading (ethics and theology). Address: (h.) Ord House, Strathpeffer, Ross-shire IV14 9AX; T.-01997 421117.

Murdoch, Professor Brian Oliver, BA, PhD, LittD, AMusTCL. Professor of German, Stirling University, since 1991; b. 26.6.44, London; m., Ursula Irene Riffer; 1 s.; 1 d. Educ. Sir George Monoux Grammar School; London; Exeter University; Jesus College, Cambridge. Lecturer in German, Glasgow University; Assistant/Associate Professor of German, University of Illinois; Lecturer/Senior Lecturer in German, Stirling University; Visiting Fellow, Trinity Hall, Cambridge, 1989; Visiting Fellow and Waynflete Lecturer, Magdalen College, Oxford, 1994; Hulsean Lecturer in Divinity, University of Cambridge, 1997-98; author of a number of books and articles on medieval German and Celtic literature, also on literature of the World Wars. Recreations: jazz; numismatics; books. Address: (b.) German Department, Stirling University, Stirling FK9 4LA; T.-01786 467546.

Murdoch, Professor George, MBChB, FRCS (Edin), DSc. Professor Emeritus of Orthopaedic Surgery, since 1966; Visiting Professor, Strathclyde University; b. 30.11.20, Denny; m., Elizabeth Ann Rennie; 2 s.; 3 d. Educ. Falkirk High School; St. Andrews University. Squadron Leader, RAF; Consultant Orthopaedic Surgeon; Professor of Orthopaedic Surgery, Dundee University. Travelling Fellow, World Health Association; Honorary Fellow and Past President, International Society for Prosthetics and Orthotics. Publications: papers on surgery, prosthetics, orthotics; Editor of five books on prosthetics, orthotics. Recreations: reading; writing. Address: (h.) Middle Church, Flat C, 6 Tay Street, Perth PH1 5LQ; T.-01738 445772.

Murdoch, Jane, BA, MMus(Hons). Leader, Edinburgh Quartet, since 1996; b. 19.4.68, Glasgow. Educ. RSAMD, Glasgow; Glasgow University. Leader, London City Ballet Orchestra; Member, Academy of St. Martin in the Fields. Address: (b.) 119 Craigleith Road, Edinburgh EH14 2EH; T.-0131-332 8691.

Mure, Kenneth Nisbet, QC. Advocate, Scotland, since 1975; Barrister, Grays Inn, since 1990; Fellow, Institute of Taxation, since 1981; b. 11.4.47, Glasgow. Educ. Glasgow High School; Glasgow University. Address: (b.) Advocates' Library, Edinburgh.

Murning, Lt. Col. Ian Henry, TD, LLB (Hons), DPA, FRICS, MIMgt. Partner, Ian H. Murning Associates, Chartered Surveyors, since 1994; Lecturer, Napier University; b. 24.12.43, Chapelhall; m., Seona Jean Meiklejon; 1 s.; 2 d. Educ. Dalziel High School; Glasgow University; London University; College of Estate Management. Valuer, Stirling Valuation Office, Highlands and Islands; Office of Chief Valuer (Scotland); District Valuer, Dumfries and Galloway, 1988-94. Chairman, Royal Institution of Chartered Surveyors in Scotland, 1995-96; Member, General Council, Royal Institution of Chartered Surveyors, 1994-96; Commander, Royal Engineers (Home Defence), Army HQ Scotland, 1991-95; Commander, District Specialist Training Team, Army HQ Scotland, 1996-97; served with 52(L) Div/Dist Engrs (TA), 1963-67, Royal Monmouthshire Royal Engineers (Militia), 1967-68, 71 (Scottish) Engineer Regt (V), 1968-74; Member: Society of High Constables of Edinburgh, 1993, Merchant Company of Edinburgh, 1995, Territorial Auxiliary and Volunteer Reserve Association for the Lowlands, 1997. Address: (b.) 86 Craiglockhart Drive South, Otterburn Park, Edinburgh EH14 1JY; T.-0131-443 8839.

Murphy, Sheriff Andrew John, MA, LLB. Sheriff of Tayside, Central and Fife at Falkirk, since 1991; b. 16.1.46. Called to Scottish Bar, 1970; called to Bar, Middle Temple, 1990. Address: (b.) Sheriff Court House, Camelon, Falkirk FK1 4AR.

Murphy, Hugh Joseph, MA, LLB. Chairman of Industrial Tribunals, since 1992; b. 24.4.42, Kilmarnock; m., Ashley C.; 1 s.; 3 d. Educ. St. Joseph's, Kilmarnock; Glasgow University. Assistant Solicitor, private practice, 1968-75; Partner, R. Maguire Cook & Co., 1975-92. Recreations: music; books; watching football; keep-fit. Address: (b.) 215 Bothwell Street, Glasgow G2 7TS; T.-0141-204 0730.

Murphy, James Barrie, MB, ChB, DPM, FRCPsych. Medical Director, Greater Glasgow Community Mental Health Services NHS Trust; Honorary Clinical Senior Lecturer; b. 27.7.42, Glasgow; m., Jean Wynn Kirkwood; 1 s.; 1 d. Educ. High School of Glasgow; Glasgow University. Consultant Psychiatrist, Dykebar Hospital, Paisley, 1973-80; Medical Executive, Community and Mental Health Unit, Gartnavel Royal Hospital, Glasgow. Address: (b.) Gartnavel Royal Hospital, 1055 Great Western Road, Glasgow G12 0XH; T.-0141-211 3824.

Murphy, Sheriff James Patrick, BL. Sheriff of Glasgow and Strathkelvin, since 1989; (Sheriff of North Strathclyde, 1976-89); b. 24.1.32.

Murphy, Jim. MP (Labour), Eastwood, since 1997; b. 23.8.67, Glasgow; m., Claire Cook. Educ. Milnerton High School, Cape Town; Strathclyde University. President, NUS (Scotland), 1992-94; President, NUS (UK), 1994-96. Recreations: football; jazz; popular cinema. Address: (h.) 28 Field Road, Busby, East Renfrewshire G76 8SE; T.-0141-644 3250.

Murphy, Vernon Leslie, MA (Cantab), FCIT, FRSA. Chairman and Managing Director, Scottish Airports Ltd., since 1988; Deputy Chairman, Renfrewshire Enterprise, since 1993; b. 28.7.44, Shrewsbury; m., Joan Bridget Mary; 2 d. Educ. Westminster; Gonville and Caius College, Cambridge. Joined B.A.A., 1966; former General Manager, Aberdeen Airport, and Deputy Managing Director, Gatwick Airport Ltd. Recreations: steam engines; photography; music; cricket. Address: (b.) St. Andrews Drive, Glasgow Airport, Paisley PA3 2SW; T.-0141-848 4583.

Murray, Professor Alan Fraser, BSc, PhD, CEng, FIEE, SMIEEE. Professor of Neural Electronics, Edinburgh University, since 1994; b. 26.2.53, Edinburgh; m., Glynis Ruth; 1 s.; 1 d. Educ. Currie High School; Edinburgh University. NATO Fellow, Atomic Energy of Canada, 1978-80; Research Fellow, Edinburgh University, 1980-81; Wolfson Microelectronics Institute, 1981-84; Lecturer, then Reader, Department of Electrical Engineering, Edinburgh University, 1984-94. Publications: 133. Recreations: singer, guitarist, songwriter, and follower of Rupert Bear. Address: (b.) Department of Electrical Engineering, Edinburgh University, Mayfield Road, Edinburgh EH9 3JL; T.-0131-650 5589.

Murray, Alexander George, KStG, KLJ, BSc, FBSC(Lond), FSA Scot. Former National Director, Crossroads (Scotland) Care Attendant Schemes; m., Margaret Elizabeth; 1 d. Educ. Whitehill School, Glasgow; Glasgow University. Former Scottish Manager, British subsidiary of Chase Manhatten Bank of America; formed several companies in investment/credit field. Led first Scottish delegation to UNESCO, 1955-56; established Scottish Worldfriends Society and became its first National Director; active in Highland societies; Scot of the Year, 1986; Founder and Convener, Caledonian Country Dancing Clubs; former Secretary, West of Scotland Refugee Committee; Past President, East Kilbride Sea Cadet Corps; Member, Organising Committee, East Kilbride National Mod, 1974-75; Provincial Grand Master Mason. Publications: A History of Scottish Contra Dancing; 40 Popular Scottish Dances. Recreations: bowling; swimming; walking. Address: (h.) Failte, 51 Eaglesham Road, Clarkston, Glasgow G76 7TR.

Murray, Athol Laverick, PhD, MA, LLB, FRHistS, FSA Scot. Vice-President, Society of Antiquaries of Scotland, 1989-92; Keeper of the Records of Scotland, 1985-90; b. 8.11.30, Tynemouth; m., Irene Joyce Cairns; 1 s.; 1 d. Educ. Lancaster Royal Grammar School; Jesus College, Cambridge; Edinburgh University. Research Assistant, Foreign Office, 1953; Scottish Record Office: Assistant Keeper, 1953-83, Deputy Keeper, 1983-84. Recreations:

historical research; bowling. Address: (h.) 33 Inverleith Gardens, Edinburgh EH5 5PR; T.-0131-552 4465.

Murray, David Edward. Chairman, Murray International Holdings; Chairman, The Rangers Football Club plc; Founder, David Murray Foundation, 1997; b. 14.10.51, Ayr; m., Louise (deceased); 2 s. Educ. Fettes College; Broughton High School. Young Scottish Business Man of the Year, 1984; Hon. Doctorate, Heriot-Watt University, 1986; Chairman, UK 2000 (Scotland), 1987; Governor, Clifton Hall School, 1987. Recreations: sports sponsorship; collecting wine. Address: (b.) South Gyle, Edinburgh; T.-0131-317 7000.

Murray, Donald, MA. Head Teacher, Sir Edward Scott School, Tarbert, Isle of Harris, since 1981; b. Port of Ness, Isle of Lewis; 2 d. Educ. Nicolson Institute, Stornoway; Glasgow University. Teacher, Calder Street Secondary School, Glasgow; Teacher, Achnamara Residential School, Argyll; Principal Teacher of Guidance, Victoria Drive Secondary School, Glasgow; Assistant Head Teacher (Curriculum), Kingsridge Secondary School, Glasgow. Recreations: angling; gardening; reading. Address: (h.) Balranald, West Tarbert, Isle of Harris; T.-01859 502339.

Murray, Rev. Douglas Millar, MA, BD, PhD. Principal of Trinity College, since 1997, and Lecturer in Ecclesiastical History, Glasgow University, since 1989; b. 1946, Edinburgh; m., Dr. Freya M. Smith. Educ. George Watson's College, Edinburgh; Edinburgh University; New College, Edinburgh; Fitzwilliam and Westminster Colleges, Cambridge. Minister: St. Bride's Church, Callander, 1976-80, John Ker Memorial Church in deferred union with Candlish Church, Edinburgh, 1980-81, and Polwarth Church, 1981-89. Editor, Liturgical Review, 1979-81; Associate Editor, Scottish Journal of Theology, 1981-87; Convener, Panel on Doctrine, General Assembly, Church of Scotland, 1986-90; Chalmers Lecturer, 1991. Publication: Studies in the History of Worship in Scotland (Co-Editor); Freedom to Reform, 1993. Recreations: golf; Scottish country dancing; hill-walking. Address: 28 Sherbrooke Drive, Glasgow G41 5AA; T.-0141-427 9524.

Murray, Frank McDonald, EurEng, BSc (Hons), CEng, FIMinE. Secretary-General, Federation of European Explosives Manufacturers; Director, Ayrshire Chamber of Commerce; Chairman, Comitee Europeen de Normalisation, TC 321 Harmonisation of Explosives Standards, Europe; Secretary General, Sofex International; b. 7.9.36, Dunfermline; m., Nancy McDermott; 1 s.; 1 d. Educ. Kirkcaldy High School; Edinburgh University. Coal mining/gold mining, 1957-62; joined ICI as explosives engineer, 1962; Managing Director, ICI Nobel's Explosives Co., 1988-93. Recreation: golf. Address: (b.) McGowan House, Lundholm Road, Stevenston KA20 3LJ; T.-01294 487287.

Murray, George Malcolm, CBE, FFA. Chief General Manager, Scottish Life Assurance Company, since 1987; President, Faculty of Actuaries in Scotland, 1994-96; Chairman, Baillie Gifford Japan Trust PLC, since 1981; Director, Trinity International Holdings PLC; b. 25.12.37, Hawick; m., Muriel; 2 s.; 1 d. Educ. Hawick High School. Joined Scottish Life, 1955; Assistant Actuary, 1962; held various appointments, including Investment Manager. Member, Scottish Sports Council; Trustee, Edinburgh University Trust Funds. Recreations: almost all sports and cultural activities, especially rugby, golf, jogging, and theatre. Address: (b.) 19 St. Andrew Square, Edinburgh EH2 1YE; T.-0131-456 7777.

Murray, Gordon Lindsay Kevan. Partner, W.J. Burness WS, since 1982; Secretary, Scottish National Orchestra Society Ltd., 1985-90; Director, 1990-93, Secretary and Treasurer, since 1985, Royal Scottish National Orchestra Endowment Trust; b. 23.5.53, Glasgow; m., Susan Patricia;

1 s.; 3 d. Educ. Lenzie Academy; Edinburgh University. President, Scottish Young Lawyers Association, 1977-78. Address: (b.) 16 Hope Street, Charlotte Square, Edinburgh EH2 4DD; T.-0131-226 2561.

Murray, Gregor Cumming, MA, MBA. Executive Director, Midlothian Enterprise Trust, since 1992; b. 16.4.57, Edinburgh; 2 d. Educ. George Watson's College, Edinburgh; Trinity College, Oxford; Edinburgh University Management School. Bank of Scotland; Investors in Industry; Leith Enterprise Trust. Board Member: Jewel and Esk Valley College, Lothian Investment Fund for Enterprise. Recreations: fly fishing; golf; music; tennis; hill-walking. Address: (b.) 29A Eskbank Road, Dalkeith EH22 1HJ; T.-0131-654 1234.

Murray, Isobel (Mary), MA, PhD. Writer and Critic; Reader in English, Aberdeen University, since 1974; b. 14.2.39, Alloa; m., Bob Tait. Educ. Dollar Academy; Edinburgh University. Assistant Lecturer, Lecturer, Senior Lecturer, Department of English, Aberdeen University; books include several editions of Oscar Wilde, introductions to new editions of J. MacDougall Hay's Gillespie, Ian MacPherson's Shepherds' Calendar and Robin Jenkins' Guests of War; edited, Beyond This Limit: Selected Shorter Fiction of Naomi Mitchison; A Girl Must Live: stories and poems by Naomi Mitchison; Ten Modern Scottish Novels (with Bob Tait), 1984; Scottish Writers Talking, 1996. Address: (b.) Department of English, King's College, Old Aberdeen, Aberdeen AB24 2UB; T.-Aberdeen 272644.

Murray, Professor James, BSc, ARTC, CEng, FIMechE, FIEE, FIM. Vice Principal, Napier University, 1992-95, now Emeritus Professor; b. 25.7.30, Glasgow; m., Emily Lamb Beveridge; 1 s.; 1 d. Educ. Allan Glen's School, Glasgow; Glasgow University. Development Engineer, Ferranti Ltd., Edinburgh, 1952-62; Lecturer, Department of Mechanical Engineering, Heriot-Watt University, 1962-67; Head, Department of Production Engineering, Napier College, 1967-72; Head, Department of Industrial Studies, 1972-74; Assistant Principal and Dean, Faculty of Professional Studies, 1974-82; Assistant Principal/Dean, Faculty of Technology, 1982-92. Former Member, Council: SCOTEC, EITB, IProdE; Past Chairman, IProdE, Edinburgh Section and Scotland Region; Past Chairman: CEI Scotland, CNAA Engineering Board and Research Committee; former Member, Transport Tribunal, Scotland; Governor, Moray House College of Education; Member of Convocation, Heriot-Watt University; Trustee, National Museums of Scotland, since 1997. Recreations: watching rugby; golf; gardening; studying light rail transport systems; opera. Address: (h.) 40 Elliot Road, Edinburgh EH14 1DZ.

Murray, Professor Sir Kenneth, BSc, PhD, FRS, FRSE, FRCPath. Professor of Molecular Biology, Edinburgh University, since 1976; b. 30.12.30, East Ardsley; m., Noreen E. Parker (see Noreen Elizabeth Murray). Educ. Henry Mellish Grammar School; Birmingham University. Postdoctoral work, Stanford University, California, 1959-64; MRC Scientific Staff, Cambridge, 1964-67; joined Edinburgh University, 1967; leave of absence at European Molecular Biology Laboratory, Heidelberg, 1979-82. Recreations: musical appreciation; reading. Address: (b.) Institute of Cell and Molecular Biology, Edinburgh University, Mayfield Road, Edinburgh EH9 3JR; T.-0131-650 5387.

Murray, Leonard G., JP, KHS, BL, SSC. Solicitor; former Senior Partner, now Consultant to, Levy & McRae, Solicitors; b. 16.8.33, Glasgow; m., Elizabeth Wilson; 3 s. Educ. St. Mungo's Academy, Glasgow; Glasgow University. Chairman, Murray Inns Ltd. After-dinner speaker; Associate, Institute of Linguists; part-time

Chairman, Industrial Tribunals. Recreations: golf; gardening. Address: (h.) 23 Courthill, Bearsden, Glasgow G61 3SN.

Murray, Professor Maxwell, BVMS, DVM, FRCPath, FRSE, PhD. Professor of Veterinary Medicine, Glasgow University, since 1985; Head, Department of Veterinary Clinical Studies; b. 3.5.39, Glasgow; m., Christine Madelaine; 1 s.; 2 d. Educ. Shawlands Senior Secondary School; Glasgow University. Animal Health Trust Research Scholarship, 1962-63; Lecturer in Veterinary Pathology, University of Nairobi, 1963-65; Lecturer in Veterinary Pathology, then Senior Lecturer, Glasgow University, 1965-75; Senior Scientist, International Laboratory for Research on Animal Diseases, Nairobi, 1975-85. Address: (b.) Glasgow University Veterinary School, Bearsden Road, Bearsden, Glasgow G61 1QH.

Murray, Professor Noreen Elizabeth, FRS, PhD, FRSE. Professor, Institute of Cell and Molecular Biology, Edinburgh University; b. 26.2.35, Burnley; m., Kenneth Murray (qv). Educ. Lancaster Girls' Grammar School; King's College, London; Birmingham University. Research Associate, Department of Biological Sciences, Stanford University, 1960-64; Research Fellow, Botany School, Cambridge, 1964-67; Edinburgh University: Member, MRC Molecular Genetics Unit, Department of Molecular Biology, 1968-74, Lecturer, then Senior Lecturer, Department of Molecular Biology, 1974-80; Group Leader, European Molecular Biology Laboratory, Heidelberg, 1980-82; rejoined Edinburgh University as Reader, 1982. Recreation: gardening. Address: (b.) Institute of Cell and Molecular Biology, Edinburgh University, Mayfield Road, Edinburgh EH9 3JR; T.-0131-650 5374.

Murray, Norman Loch, BA, CA, FRSA. Chief Executive, Morgan Grenfell Development Capital Limited, since 1996 (Deputy Chief Executive, 1989-96); Executive Director, Deutsche Morgan Grenfell; Non-Executive Director: Morgan Grenfell Development Capital France SA, Deutsche Morgan Grenfell Development Capital Italy SA, Deutsche Morgan Grenfell Private Equity Asia Fund Limited; b. 17.3.48, Kilmarnock; m., Pamela Anne Low; 2 s. Educ. George Watson's College; Heriot-Watt University; Harvard University Graduate School of Business Administration. Scottish & Newcastle Breweries PLC, 1971-73; Arthur Young, 1973-76; Peat Marwick Mitchell & Co. (Hong Kong), 1977-80; Royal Bank of Scotland PLC, 1980-85; Director, Charterhouse Development Capital Ltd., 1985-89. Former directorships (non-executive): Bristow Helicopter Group Limited, Eurodollar (Holdings) Ltd., Taunton Cider plc, Burn Stewart Group Ltd.; Institute of Chartered Accountants of Scotland: Member of Council, Convener, Finance and General Purposes Committee; Member, Research Committee, 1986-91; Chairman, Lothian Borders and Central Area Committee, 1992-95; Chairman, Legal and Technical Committee, British Venture Capital Association, 1992-96; Member, Governing Council and Finance Committee, George Watson's College. Publication: Making Corporate Reports Valuable (Co-Author), 1988. Recreations: squash; golf; climbing; travel. Address: (b.) 5 St. Andrew Square, Edinburgh EH2 2AD; T.-0131-557 8600.

Murray, Raymond. Principal, Thurso College. Address: (b.) Ormlie Road, Thurso, Caithness, KW14 7EE.

Murray, Robert John, MSc, MCIBS, JP. Deputy Leader, Angus Council, and Convenor, Personnel and Property Committee, since 1995; Vice Convenor: Tayside Valuation Joint Board, since 1995, Tayside Contracts Joint Committee, since 1995; b. 3.2.51, Montrose; m., Linda; 1 s.; 1 d. Educ. Montrose Academy; University of Abertay, Dundee. Recreations: cycling; golf. Address: (h.) 26 Adderley Terrace, Monifieth, DD5 4DR; T.-01382 534908.

Murray, Rt. Hon. Lord (Ronald King Murray), PC (1974), MA, LLB, Dr.h.c.(Edin). Senator of the College of Justice in Scotland, 1979-95; b. 15.6.22; m., Sheila Winifred Gamlin. Educ. George Watson's College; Edinburgh University; Jesus College, Oxford. Advocate, 1953; QC, 1967; MP (Leith), 1970-79; Lord Advocate, 1974-79. Assessor, Edinburgh University Court, 1981-93 (Vice-Chairman, 1990-93). Recreations: sailing; astronomy. Address: (h.) 1 Inverleith Grove, Edinburgh EH3 5PB; T.-0131-551 5330.

Murray, Professor Thomas Stuart, MD, PhD, FRCGP, FRCPGlas, FRCPEdin, DRCOG. West of Scotland Director of Postgraduate General Practice Education, since 1985; Professor of General Practice, Glasgow University, since 1992; b. 22.7.43, Muirkirk; m., Anne Smith; 1 s.; 2 d. Educ. Cumnock Academy. Trained in medicine and cardiology, then general practice; principal in general practice, 1971; Senior Lecturer in General Practice, Glasgow University, 1977. Member, Joint Committee for Postgraduate Training in General Practice. Recreations: sport; travel; reading. Address: (b.) Department of Postgraduate Medicine, 1 Horselethill Road, Glasgow G12 9LX; T.-0141-330 5276.

Murray-Smith, Professor David James, MSc, PhD, CEng, FIEE, MInstMC. Dean, Faculty of Engineering and Professor of Engineering Systems and Control, Glasgow University; b. 20.10.41, Aberdeen; m., Effie Smith; 2 s. Educ. Aberdeen Grammar School; Aberdeen University; Glasgow University. Engineer, Inertial Systems Department, Ferranti Ltd., Edinburgh, 1964-65; Glasgow University: Assistant, Department of Electrical Engineering, 1965-67, Lecturer, 1967-77, Senior Lecturer, 1977-83, Reader, 1983-85. Past Chairman, United Kingdom Simulation Council. Recreations: hill-walking; photography; strong interest in railways. Address: (b.) Department of Electronics and Electrical Engineering, Glasgow University, Glasgow G12 8QQ; T.-0141-330 5222.

Muscatelli, Professor Vito Antonio, MA (Hons), PhD, FRSA. Daniel Jack Professor of Political Economy, Department of Economics, Glasgow University, since 1994; b. 1.1.62, Bari, Italy; m., Elaine Flood; 1 d. Educ. High School of Glasgow; Glasgow University. Lecturer, Senior Lecturer, Glasgow University, 1984-94; Visiting Professor: University of Parma (Italy), 1989, Catholic University, Milan, 1991, University of Bari (Italy), since 1995; Editor, Scottish Journal of Political Economy, since 1989; Member, Council, Scottish Economic Society, since 1989; Member, Editorial Advisory Board, International Review of Economics and Business, since 1995. Hon. Fellow, Societa Italiana Degli Economisti, 1996. Publications: Macroeconomic Theory and Stabilisation Policy (Co-author), 1988; Economic and Political Institutions in Economic Policy (Editor of volume), 1996; articles in journals. Recreations: music; literature; football; strategic games. Address: (b.) Department of Economics, Adam Smith Building, Glasgow University, Glasgow G12 8RT; T.-0141-330 5062.

Musgrave, Ralph Gilbert, BSc, PhD. Director of Corporate Services, City of Edinburgh Council, since 1995; b. 10.4.39, Edinburgh; m., Patricia E. Smith; 2 s. Educ. Broughton High School, Edinburgh; Edinburgh University. ICI Ltd., 1965; Lecturer, Falkirk College of Technology, 1966-71; Depute Director of Education, East Lothian County Council, 1971-75; Assistant Director of Education, Lothian Regional Council, 1975-86; Director of Management and Information Services, Lothian Regional Council, 1986-96. Recreations: curling; golf. Address: (b.) Council Headquarters, George IV Bridge, Edinburgh EH1 1UQ; T.-0131-469 3003.

Musson, John Nicholas Whitaker, MA (Oxon). Director and Trustee, Scottish European Aid and Mercy Corps

Europe, since 1996; Governor, Clifton College, Bristol, since 1989; b. 2.10.27; m., Ann Priest; 1 s.; 3 d. Educ. Clifton College; Brasenose College, Oxford. Served as Guardsman and Lt., Lancashire Fusiliers, 1945-48; HM Colonial Administrative Service, 1951-59 (District Officer, N. Nigeria and Lecturer, Institute of Administration, Nigeria); British Petroleum Co., London, 1959-61; Assistant Master and Housemaster, Canford School, Dorset, 1961-72; Warden, Glenalmond College, 1972-87; Scottish Division Chairman, Headmasters' Conference, 1981-83; Scottish Director, Independent Schools Careers Organisation, 1987-93; Governor, George Watson's College, Edinburgh, 1989-98. Recreations: hill-walking; fishing; Egyptology. Address: (h.) 47 Spylaw Road, Edinburgh EH10 5BP; T.-0131-337 0089.

Mutch, Alexander Fyvie, CBE, JP. Member, Grampian Regional Council, 1974-90 (first Convener, 1974-82); b. 23.3.24, Aberdeen; m., Freda Mutch; 1 d. Educ. Aberdeen Central School. Convener, Aberdeen Corporation Cleansing Committee, 1963; Vice-Chairman, North-East Water Board, 1968-70; Magistrate, Aberdeen, 1967; Senior Magistrate, 1968; Chairman, Aberdeen Licensing Court, 1968; Member, Aberdeen University Court, 1974-82; Chairman, South Aberdeen Conservative Association, 1964-68 (President, 1968-72); Senior Vice-President, Conservative Party in Scotland, 1972-73 (President, 1973-74); Leader, Conservative Group, Aberdeen Town Council, 1974-75; Governor, Robert Gordon's College, Aberdeen, 1968-70 and since 1974; Honorary President, Grampian-Houston Association; Honorary Citizen, Houston, Texas. Address: (h.) 28 Salisbury Terrace, Aberdeen; T.-Aberdeen 591520.

Mutch, William Edward Scott, OBE, BSc, PhD, FRSE, FICFor. Forestry and Land Use Consultant; b. 14.8.25, Salford; m., Margaret Isobel McKay; 1 d. Educ. Royal High School, Edinburgh; Edinburgh University. HM Colonial Service (Forest Department, Nigeria, as Assistant Conservator of Forests and Silviculturist), 1946; Research Assistant, Oxford University, 1952; Lecturer in Forestry, Edinburgh University, 1953. Head, Department of Forestry and Natural Resources, Edinburgh University, 1981-87; President, Institute of Chartered Foresters, 1982-84 (Institute Medal, 1986); Member: Countryside Commission for Scotland, 1988-92; National Forestry Research Advisory Committee; Nature Conservancy Council, 1988-91; NCC for Scotland, 1991-92; Scottish Natural Heritage, Chairman S.E. Scotland, 1992-94; Director, Central Scotland Woodlands Ltd., 1989-93, and Central Scotland Countryside Trust, 1992-97. Publications: Farm Woodland Management; Tall Trees and Small Woods. Recreations: cabinet making; travel; painting. Address: (h.) 19 Barnton Grove, Edinburgh EH4 6EQ; T.-0131-339 1400.

Myles, Andrew Bruce, LLB, MA (Hons). Chief Executive, Scottish Liberal Democrats, since 1992; b. 25.10.57, Edinburgh. Educ. Holt School; Merchiston Castle School; Dundee University. Former General Services Manager (Mental Illness), Tayside Mental Health Unit. Designer/Director, E.I.F. Fringe Productions, 1976-79. Recreations: gardening; films; books; cats; holidays. Address: (b.) 4 Clifton Terrace, Edinburgh EH13 5DR; T.-0131-337 2314.

Myles, David Fairlie, CBE. Hill Farmer; Member, Angus District Council, 1984-96; Chairman, Dairy Produce Quota Tribunal for Scotland, since 1984; Member, Potato Marketing Board, 1988-97; b. 30.5.25, Cortachy, Kirriemuir; m., Janet I. Gall; 2 s.; 2 d. Educ. Brechin High School. Auctioneer's clerk, 1941-43; Royal Marines, 1943-46; Tenant Hill Farmer, since 1946; Director of auction company, 1963-81; Member, Transport Users Consultative Committee for Scotland, 1973-79; Council Member, NFU of Scotland, 1970-79 (Convener, Organisation and Publicity Committee, 1976-79); Member, Meat Promotion Executive, MLC, 1975-79; Chairman, North Angus and Mearns Constituency Conservative Party, 1971-74; MP (Conservative), Banff, 1979-83; Joint Secretary, Backbench Conservative Committee, 1979-83; Secretary, Backbench Conservative European Committee, 1980-83; Member: Select Committee on Agriculture and Select Committee on European Legislation, 1979-83, North of Scotland Hydro-Electric Board, 1985-89, Angus Tourist Board, 1984-92; Dean, Guildry of Brechin, 1993-94; Lord President, Court of Deans of Scotland, 1995-96; Session Clerk, Edzell-Lethnot Parish Church, since 1996; Elder, Edzell-Lethnot Parish Church. Recreations: curling; traditional Scottish fiddle music; works of Robert Burns. Address: (h.) The Gorse, Dunlappie Road, Edzell, Brechin DD9 7UB; T.-0135 64 207.

Myles, William Mackay Stanley, TD (with bar). Senior Partner, Myles Brothers, Wholesale Ironmongers, Edinburgh, since 1954; Member, Executive Committee, National Trust for Scotland, since 1988; b. 6.3.27, Edinburgh; m., Margaret Shiela Grace Bruce; 3 s. Educ. Sciennes and James Clark's, Edinburgh; Bell-Baxter, Cupar. Royal Scots, 1945-66; India & Pakistan 1st Bn., 1946-47, 7/9 and 8/9 TA Bns., 1948-66, as Rifle Company Commander, 1951-66; Member, Regimental Council, since 1977; Mountaineering Council of Scotland: Training Officer, 1974-90, Hon. Secretary, 1977-83, Vice-President, 1984-88; Chairman: The Royal Scots Club, Edinburgh, since 1977, Edinburgh West End Community Council, 1989-95; Director, Lord Roberts Workshops for Disabled Ex-Servicemen; Council Member, Earl Haig Fund; Elder, Church of Scotland, since 1950; Director, Drumsheugh Baths Club Ltd., Edinburgh, since 1972; President, Rotary Club of Edinburgh, 1983-84. Recreations: hill-walking; swimming; painting in oils; gardening. Address: (h.) 1 Chartwell, 4b Church Hill, Edinburgh EH10 4BQ; T.-0131-452 8331.

N

Nairn, Nicholas Cameron Abell. Chef/Director, Nairns Restaurant, Glasgow, since 1997; Chef/Director, Braeval Restaurant, Aberfoyle, since 1986; Hon. President, Drambuie Scottish Chefs National Cookery Centre, since 1997; b. 12.1.59, Stirling; m., Fiona. Educ. McLaren High School, Callander. Merchant Navy, 1976-83. Presenter: Wild Harvest, BBC2, 1996, Ready Steady Cook, BBC2, since 1996, Who'll Do the Pudding, BBC1, 1996-97, Wild Harvest Two, BBC2, 1997, Island Harvest, BBC2, 1998; Chef/Consultant, Tesco; Winner, Scottish Field/Charles Heidsieck Scottish Restaurant of the Year, 1990; Good Food Guide County Restaurant of the Year, 1991; Macallan/Decanter Scottish Restaurant of the Year, 1992; Scottish Field/Bowmore Restaurant of the Year, 1992; Member, Advisory Board, Scottish Chefs Association; Member, Masterchefs of GB. Recreations: cycling; windsurfing; wine; eating out; travel; Scottish art; theatre; fly fishing; diving. Address: (b.) 13 Woodside Crescent, Glasgow G3 7UP; T.-0141-353 0707.

Nairn, Tom. Sociologist; b. 1932, Freuchie, Fife. Educ. Edinburgh University; Oxford University. Taught social philosophy, Birmingham University, and sociology, Hornsey College of Art; Editor, Bulletin of Scottish Politics, 1981-82; Columnist, The Scotsman. Publications: The Left Against Europe; The Break-Up of Britain?; The Enchanted Glass: Britain and its Monarchy.

Nairne, Andrew, MA (Hons). Director, Dundee Contemporary Arts, since 1997; b. 10.2.60, Guildford; m., Nicola Dandridge; 1 s. Educ. Radley College; St. Andrews University. Assistant Curator, Kettle's Yard, Cambridge University, 1984-85; Deputy Director, Ikon Gallery, Birmingham, 1985-86; Exhibitions Director, Centre for Contemporary Arts, Glasgow, 1986-93; Visual Arts Director, Scottish Arts Council, 1993-97. Recreations: modern history; jazz. Address: (h.) 46 Randolph Road, Glasgow G11 7LG; T.-0141-337 2199.

Nandy, Kashinath, BSc, MSc (Calcutta), MSc (Edinburgh), PhD, FRAS, FRSE. Deputy Chief Scientific Officer, Royal Observatory, Edinburgh, 1977-86; Visiting Professor, Rome University, 1987; Honorary Professor, School of Mathematics, University of Wales, Cardiff, since 1994; b. 1.12.27, Santipur, West Bengal, India; m., Smritilekha; 1 d. Educ. Calcutta University; Edinburgh University. Observatory Assistant, Presidency College Observatory, Calcutta, 1952-59; received International Astronomical Union Grant for Studies Abroad, 1959-60; held Robert Cormack Bequest Fellowship (Royal Society of Edinburgh), 1960-63; Royal Observatory, Edinburgh: Research Fellow, 1963-68, Principal Scientific Officer, 1968-72, Senior Principal Scientific Officer, 1972-77. Fellow, Royal Astronomical Society; Member, International Astronomical Union; Founder Member, European Astronomical Society; Honorary Fellow, Edinburgh University, 1973-87; Honorary Research Fellow, University College, London, 1979-86, re-elected, 1989; elected Fellow, Royal Society of Edinburgh, 1973; Fellow, Royal Society of Liege, 1980. Recreations: reading; travel; photography; surfing. Address: (h.) 36 West Mains Road, Edinburgh EH9 3BG; T.-0131-667 6131.

Nanjiani, Shereen, MA (Hons). Journalist, Scottish Television, since 1983; b. 4.10.61, Elderslie. Educ. John Neilson High School, Paisley; Glasgow University. Joined STV as a trainee journalist, 1983; moved to reporting two years later; became presenter of Scotland Today, 1985; also presented Eikon (religious magazine); chaired debate programmes on youth issues. Address: (b.) Scottish Television, Cowcaddens, Glasgow, G2 3PR.

Napier, 14th Lord, and Ettrick, 5th Baron (Francis Nigel Napier), KCVO, DL. Private Secretary, Comptroller and Equerry to Princess Margaret, Countess of Snowdon, since 1973; b. 5.12.30; m.; 2 s.; 2 d. Address: Thirlestane, Ettrick, Selkirkshire.

Nash, Professor Andrew Samuel, BVMS, PhD, CBiol, FIBiol, DipECVIM, MRCVS. Professor of Small Animal Medicine, Division of Small Animal Clinical Studies, Department of Veterinary Clinical Studies, Glasgow University Veterinary School, since 1992, and Director of the Veterinary Hospital, 1993-96; Royal College of Veterinary Surgeons Recognised Specialist in Small Animal Medicine, since 1994; Vice-Dean for Student Affairs, since 1995; b. 1.8.44, Birmingham; m., Rosemary Truscott Hamilton; 1 s.; 1 d. Educ. Judd School, Tonbridge; Glasgow University. General veterinary practice, Ilfracombe, 1967-72; House Physician, Glasgow University Veterinary School, 1973-75, then Lecturer/Senior Lecturer, 1975-92. Silver Medal in Veterinary Clinical Medicine, 1967; RSPCA Humane Award, 1970; Member, Board of Directors, Glasgow Dog and Cat Home, 1981-95; Hon. President, Scottish Cat Club, since 1990; Member, Glasgow Presbytery, 1991-94; President, European Society of Veterinary Nephrology and Urology, 1992-94; Member, Board of Directors, Scottish Society for the Prevention of Cruelty to Animals, since 1995; author of more than 100 papers, articles, book chapters. Recreations: music; gardening; DIY; church work (church organist). Address: (b.) University of Glasgow Veterinary School, Bearsden Road, Glasgow G61 1QH; T.-0141-330 5700.

Nash, Victoria Jane, BSc, PhD. Director, Scottish Water and Sewerage Customers Council, since 1996; b. 17.6.57, Northampton; m., Robin Campbell; 2 step d. Educ. Cheadle Hulme School; Oxford Polytechnic; Stirling University. Senior Research Officer, Scottish Office Education Department, 1982-83; Project Co-ordinator, Scottish Council for Educational Technology, 1983-85; Policy Analyst, then Assistant Chief Executive, then Chief Executive, Fife Regional Council, 1985-96. Recreations: singing; swimming; cats. Address: (b.) Ochil House, Springkerse Business Park, Stirling FK7 7XE; T.-01786 430200.

Naumann, Laurie M. Director, Scottish Council for Single Homeless; b. 1943, Saffron Walden; m., Barbara; 2 s.; 3 d. Educ. Edinburgh, Gloucester and Nuremberg Rudolf Steiner; Leicester University. Furniture maker, Gloucestershire; Probation and After Care Officer, Leeds; Social Worker, Edinburgh; Council of Europe Social Fellowship to Finland to study services for the drunken offender, 1976; jointly won Rosemary Delbridge Memorial Trophy for influencing Parliament to legislate, 1983; on secondment to Scottish Office Social Work Services Inspectorate, 1992-95; Secretary, Hamish Allan Trust; Board Member, Kingdom and Old Town Housing Associations and Garvald Centre, Edinburgh; Panel Member, Scottish Health Advisory Service. Recreations: travel; reading; walking; woodwork. Address: (h.) St. Ann's, Alexander III Street, Kinghorn, Fife KY3 9SD; T.-01592 890346.

Naylor, Brian, BSc, MPhil. Director (Properties in Care), Historic Scotland, since 1995; b. 10.2.49, Altrincham; m., 1, Mary Halley (deceased), 2 s.; 2, Moira Hillen; 2 step s. Educ. Lymm Grammar School; Leicester University; Edinburgh University. Scottish Office: graduate trainee, 1976-82; Principal, 1982-89; Assistant Secretary, 1989-95. Partner, Naylor's Delicatessen, Gullane. Recreations: fishing; theatre; swimming; walking. Address: (b.) Longmore House, Salisbury Place, Edinburgh EH9 1SH; T.-0131-668 8735.

Neal, Andrew, BSc. Consumer Marketing Director, United Distillers UK, since 1993; b. 6.12.58, London; m., Janet; 1 s.; 2 d. Educ. Eastwood High School; Strathclyde University. Recreation: sport. Address: (b.) United Distillers UK, Cherrybank, Perth PH2 0NG; T.-01738 621111.

Neil, Alex., MA (Hons). Policy Vice-Convener, Scottish National Party, since 1994; Economic Consultant; b. 22.8.51, Irvine; m., Isabella Kerr; 1 s. Educ. Dalmellington High School; Ayr Academy; Dundee University. Scottish Research Officer, Labour Party, 1975; General Secretary, Scottish Labour Party (SLP), 1976; Marketing Manager, 1979-83; Director: Cumnock and Doon Enterprise Trust, 1983-87, Prince's Scottish Youth Business Trust, 1987-89; Chairman, Network Scotland Ltd., 1987-93. Recreations: family; golf; gardening; travel. Address: (h.) 26 Overmills Road, Ayr KA7 3LQ; T.-01292 286675.

Neil, Andrew, MA (Hons). Editor-in-Chief, The Scotsman, since 1996; b. 21.5.49. Educ. Paisley Grammar School; Glasgow University. Conservative Research Department, 1971-72; joined The Economist, 1973; Reporter, Ulster, 1973-74; Lobby Correspondent, 1974-75; Labour Correspondent, 1975-78; American Correspondent, 1979-82; UK Editor, London, 1982-83; Editor, Sunday Times, 1983-94; Chairman, Sky TV, 1988-90; author of Full Disclosure (autobiography). Address: (b.) North Bridge, Edinburgh EH1 1YT.

Neil, Rev. James Duncan, BD. Moderator, United Free Church of Scotland, since 1997; Minister, Cathcart United Free Church, since 1979; b. 25.8.45, Glasgow; m., Janette Wilson; 3 s. Educ. Whitehill Secondary School; Glasgow University and Trinity College. Apprentice, Electricity Board, 1963-68; ordained to charge of Moncrieff U.F. Church, Alloa, 1974-79. Former local Branch Chairman, National Bible Society of Scotland. Recreations: golf; swimming; hill-walking. Address: (h.) 72 Berridale Avenue, Glasgow G44 3AE; T.-0141-637 3944.

Neil, James W. M. Principal, Dumfries and Galloway College of Technology. Address: (b.) Heathhall, Dumfries, DG1 3QZ.

Neill, Gordon Webster McCash, DSO, SSC, NP, FInstD. Solicitor and Notary Public; Honorary Sheriff; b. Arbroath; m., Margaret Mary Lamb; 1 s.; 1 d. Educ. Edinburgh Academy. Legal apprenticeship, 1937-39; Pilot, RAF, 1939-46 (DSO, French Croix de Guerres with silver gilt star and silver star); Partner, Neill & Gibb, SSC, 1947; Chairman, Dundee Area Board, British Law Insurance Co. Ltd., 1954; Principal, Neill & Mackintosh, SSC, 1967; Consultant, Thorntons WS, 1989-96; Past Chairman, Scottish Gliding Association and Angus Gliding Club Ltd.; Past President, Chamber of Commerce, Arbroath Rotary Club and Society of Solicitors and Procurators in Angus. Recreations: gliding; shooting; fishing. Address: (h.) 29 Duncan Avenue, Arbroath, Angus DD11 2DA; T.-01241 872221.

Neill, William Wilson, MA (Hons). Poet; b. 22.2.22, Prestwick; m., Doris Marie; 2 d. (by pr. m.). Educ. Ayr Academy; Edinburgh University. Served, RAF; won Sloane Verse Prize and Grierson Verse Prize while at Edinburgh University; Teacher; crowned Bard, Aviemore Mod, 1969; former Editor, Catalyst; former Editor, Lallans (Scots Language magazine); SAC Book Award, 1985; broadcasts, essays in Scotland's three tongues. Publications: Scotland's Castle, 1969; Poems, 1970; Four Points of a Saltire (Co-author), 1970; Despatches Home, 1972; Buile Shuibhne, 1974; Galloway Landscape: Poems, 1981; Cnu a Mogaill: Poems, 1983; Wild Places: Poems, 1985; Blossom, Berry, Fall: Poems 1986; Making Tracks: Poems, 1988; Straight Lines, 1992; Tales frae the Odyssey, 1992; Selected Poems,

1994. Address: (h.) Burnside, Crossmichael, Castle Douglas DG7 3AP; T.-055-667 265.

Neilson, Sheriff Hugh S. Floating Sheriff of South Strathclyde Dumfries and Galloway based at Hamilton. Address: (b.) Sheriff Court House, Beckford Street, Hamilton ML3 6AA.

Neilson, Margaret Marion, MA (Hons), LLB, DipLP, SSC, NP. Litigation Partner, Balfour & Manson, since 1987; b. Falkirk; m., Raymond A. McMenamin. Educ. Mary Erskine School, Edinburgh; Edinburgh University. Balfour & Manson: Trainee, 1983, Assistant, 1985. Secretary, Industrial Law Group, Fiscal Society of Solicitors in Supreme Courts of Scotland; Member, Joint Committee of Legal Societies of Edinburgh and Midlothian. Recreations: skiing; hill-walking; scuba diving; travel. Address: (b.) 54-64 Frederick Street, Edinburgh EH2 1LS; T.-0131-200 1200.

Nelson, (Peter) Frederick, BSc, CEng, MIEE. Chairman, Scottish Sports Association, 1990-96; Member, Scottish Sports Council, since 1990; b. 2.9.52, Glasgow; m., (Caroline) Ann; 3 s. Educ. John Neilson; Strathclyde University. President, Scottish Canoe Association, 1980-90; Member, Commonwealth Games Council for Scotland, since 1982; Elder, Davidson's Mains Parish Church. Recreations: canoeing; cycling; DIY. Address: (h.) 11 Barnton Park Place, Edinburgh EH4 6ET; T.-0131-336 4779.

Ness, James Iain, LLB, NP. Solicitor; Member, Council, Law Society of Scotland, since 1990; Senior Partner, Austins, since 1995; b. 5.7.57, Johannesburg; m., Elaine; 1 s.; 1 d. Educ. Robert Gordon's, Aberdeen; Edinburgh University. Apprenticed, Connel & Connel, Edinburgh; Assistant, then Partner, then Senior Partner, Austins. Chairman, Competence Committee, Law Society of Scotland; Past President, Rotary Club of Dalbeattie; Secretary, Cancer Relief Macmillan Fund, Dalbeattie and District; Dean, Faculty of Procurators for the Stewartry of Kirkcudbright. Recreation: skiing. Address: (b.) 52 High Street, Dalbeattie, DG5 4AB; T.-01556 610259.

Neumann, Jan, CBE, BSc, FEng, FIMechE, FIMarE, FIES. Director, Scottish Nuclear Ltd.; b. 26.6.24, Prague; m., 1, Barbara Joyce Gove (deceased); 2 s.; 2, Irene McCusker. Educ. Friends' School, Great Ayton; London University. Flight Engineer, RAF; Design Engineer, English Electric Co., Rugby; various engineering design and management positions in Yarrow Admiralty Research Department; Director: YARD Ltd., 1969-88 (Managing Director, 1978-87), Yarrow PLC, 1978-86; Board Member: SSEB, 1986-88, Scottish Nuclear, 1989-93; President, Institution of Engineers and Shipbuilders in Scotland, 1993-95; received Denny Gold Medal, IMarE, and Thomas Lowe Gray Prize, IMechE. Recreations: swimming; bowls. Address: (h.) 38 Norwood Park, Bearsden, Glasgow G61 2RZ.

Newall, John, LLB, WS, NP. Solicitor, since 1966; Member, Council, Law Society of Scotland, since 1993; b. 6.8.42, Dumfries; m., Gaye Tuddenham; 1 s.; 2 d. Educ. Dumfries Academy; Edinburgh University. Solicitor, 1966; WS, 1970; Partner, Skene, Edwards and Garson, 1970-78; Partner, McGrigor, Donald, since 1978. Recreations: flying; golf; music. Address: (b.) McGrigor Donald, Erskine House, 68-73 Queen Street, Edinburgh; T.-0131-226 7777.

Newall, Stephen Park, DL, Hon. LLD (Strathclyde). Deputy Chairman, Court, University of Strathclyde, since 1993 (Chairman, Court, 1988-93); Deputy Lieutenant, Dunbartonshire, since 1985; b. 12.4.31, Bearsden, Dunbartonshire; m., Gay Sommerville Craig; 4 s.; 1 d. Educ. Loretto. Commissioned and served with Parachute Regiment, National Service, 1949-51; Sales Manager, A.P.

Newall & Co., 1951-57; Managing Director, Bulten-Kanthal Stephen Newall Co. Ltd., 1957-80. Chairman: Epilepsy Association of Scotland, 1982-86, Finance Committee, University of Strathclyde, 1985-88; Council Member: Quarrier's Homes, 1983-88, Scottish Business School, 1983-85; Secretary of State for Scotland's Nominee on Court of Cranfield, 1985-92; Deacon Convener, Trades of Glasgow, 1983-84. Recreations: farming; hill-walking; sailing; music. Address: (h.) Rowaleyn, Rhu, Dunbartonshire; T.-01436 820 521.

Newell, Professor Alan F., BSc, PhD, FIEE, CEng, FBCS, FRSE, HonFCSLT. NCR Professor of Electronics and Microcomputer Systems, Dundee University, since 1980; Director, Dundee University Microcomputer Centre, since 1980; Head, Department of Applied Computing, since 1997 (Head, Applied Computer Studies Division, 1994-97; Deputy Principal, 1993-95); b. 1.3.41, Birmingham; m., Margaret; 1 s.; 2 d. Educ. St. Philip's Grammar School; Birmingham University. Research Engineer, Standard Telecommunication Laboratories; Lecturer, Department of Electronics, Southampton University. Recreations: family life; skiing; sailing. Address: (b.) Department of Applied Computing, Dundee University, Dundee, DD1 4HN; T.-01382 344144 .

Newis, Kenneth, CB, CVO, MA, FRSAMD. President, Queen's Hall (Edinburgh) Ltd.; Trustee, RSAMD Trust; Director, Scottish Churches Housing Agency; b. 9.11.16, Crewe; m., Kathleen Barrow; 2 d. Educ. Manchester Grammar School; St. John's College, Cambridge. HM Office of Works, London, 1938-70; Under Secretary, Scottish Development Department, 1970-73; Secretary, 1973-76. Recreation: music. Address: (h.) 10/9 St. Margaret's Place, Edinburgh EH9 1AY; T.-0131-447 4138.

Newlands, Rev. Professor George McLeod, MA, BD, PhD. Professor of Divinity, Glasgow University, since 1986 (Dean, Faculty of Divinity, 1988-90); Convener, Panel on Doctrine, Church of Scotland, since 1995; Principal, Trinity College, 1991-97; 12.7.41, Perth; m., Mary Elizabeth Wallace; 3 s. Educ. Perth Academy; Edinburgh University; Heidelberg University; Churchill College, Cambridge. Assistant Minister, Muirhouse, Edinburgh, 1969; Lecturer in Divinity, Glasgow University, 1969; University Lecturer in Divinity, Cambridge, 1973; Dean, Trinity Hall, Cambridge, 1982. Publications: Hilary of Poitiers; Theology of the Love of God; The Church of God; Making Christian Decisions; God in Christian Perspective; Generosity and the Christian Future. Recreations: walking; music. Address: (b.) Faculty of Divinity, 4 The Square, Glasgow University, Glasgow G12 8QQ.

Newlands, William Jeffrey, MB, ChB, FRCSEdin. Consultant Ear, Nose and Throat Surgeon, Grampian Health Board and Orkney and Shetland Health Boards, since 1981; Clinical Senior Lecturer in Otolaryngology, Aberdeen University, since 1981; b. 9.9.29, Edinburgh; m., Patricia Kathleen St. Quintin Gee; 2 s.; 2 d. Educ. Daniel Stewart's College, Edinburgh; Edinburgh University. House Physician and House Surgeon, Western General Hospital, Edinburgh, 1952-53; Captain, RAMC, 1953-55; specialist training, 1958-65, Royal Infirmary, Edinburgh, Western Infirmary, Glasgow, Royal National Throat, Nose and Ear Hospital, London; Otolaryngologist, Brown Clinic, Calgary, 1966; Consultant ENT Surgeon: Grampian Health Board, 1967-77, County Hospital, Uddevalla, Sweden, 1977-78, Lothian Health Board, 1978-79; Professor of Otolaryngology, King Faisal University College of Medicine, Saudi Arabia, 1979-81. Examiner in Otolaryngology, Part 2 Examination, FRCSEdin, 1975-90; Visiting Surgeon, Mount Elizabeth Hospital, Singapore; Visiting Professor, Faculty of Medicine, National University of Malaysia, Kuala Lumpur. Recreations: travel; music. Address: (h.) 43 Westholme Avenue, Aberdeen AB15 6AB; T.-01224 312987.

Newsome, Eric Leslie, LLB, Solicitor of the Supreme Court of England and Wales. Full-time Chairman of Social Security, Disability, Medical and Child Support Appeal Tribunals, since 1993; full-time Chairman of Vaccine Damage Tribunals, since 1996; Deputy Social Security Commissioner, since 1997; b. 2.4.44, Bradford; m., Vivienne Susan; 1 s. Educ. Carlton Grammar School, Bradford; Sheffield University. Local Government Legal Officer, 1966-69; Lecturer in Local Government Law, Norwich College, 1970-72; Lecturer, Senior Lecturer, Principal Lecturer in Law, Manchester Polytechnic/Manchester Metropolitan University, 1973-93; Consultant in trading standards law, specialising in motor vehicle law, 1975-93; part-time Chairman, Social Security Appeal Tribunals, 1985-93; Consultant in statute law revision, Law Commission of England and Wales, 1988-92; part-time Immigration Adjudicator, 1990-94; Training Consultant, Safeway PLC, 1991-93; Visiting Lecturer in Law, University of Hong Kong, 1991-93; part-time Chairman, Disability Appeal Tribunals, 1991-93. Publications: The Trades Descriptions Acts and the Motor Vehicle, 1977; articles and papers. Recreations: boxing; history of the theatre; snooker; old movies; wining and dining. Address: (b.) Independent Tribunal Service, Wellington House, 134-136 Wellington Street, Glasgow G2 2BR.

Nicholls, Brian, BSc (Econ). Senior Business Consultant, Scottish Enterprise, since 1991; Vice President, Scottish Council Development and Industry, since 1991; Director, Scottish Opera, since 1993; b. 21.9.28, London; m., Mary Elizabeth Harley; 1 s.; 2 d. Educ. Haberdashers' Aske's School; London University; Harvard Business School. George Wimpey Ltd., 1951-55; Constructors John Brown Ltd., 1955-75; Director, CJB Projects Ltd., 1972-75; Director, CJB Pipelines Ltd., 1974-75; Deputy Chairman, CJB Mohandessi Iran Ltd., 1974-75; Industrial Adviser to Secretary of State for Trade, 1975-78; Director: John Brown Engineering Ltd., 1978-91, John Brown Engineering Gas Turbines Ltd., 1978-91, Rugby Power Company Ltd., 1990-91; Vice President, John Brown Power Ltd., 1987-90; Member: Council, British Railway Export Group, 1976-78, British Overseas Trade Board, 1978. Recreations: music; reading; walking. Address: (h.) Croy, Shandon, by Helensburgh G84 8NN; T.-01436 820388.

Nicholson, Sheriff Principal (Charles) Gordon (Brown), QC, MA, LLB. Sheriff Principal of Lothian and Borders, since 1990; Commissioner, Scottish Law Commission, 1982-89; b. 11.9.35, Edinburgh; m., Hazel Mary Nixon; 2 s. Educ. George Watson's College, Edinburgh; Edinburgh University. Admitted to Faculty of Advocates, 1961; Advocate Depute, 1968-70; Sheriff of Dumfries and Galloway, at Dumfries, 1970-76; Sheriff of Lothian and Borders, at Edinburgh, 1976-82; Honorary President: Scottish Association for the Study of Delinquency, Victim Support Scotland; Commissioner, Northern Lighthouse Board, since 1990 (Chairman, 1994-95). Publication: The Law and Practice of Sentencing in Scotland, 1981 (2nd edition, 1992). Recreation: music. Address: (h.) Back O'Redfern, 24C Colinton Road, Edinburgh EH10 5EQ; T.-0131-447 4300.

Nicholson, Liz, MA. Director, Shelter Scotland, since 1995; b. 27.9.46, Birmingham; m., Colin Nicholson; 2 s.; 1 d. Educ. Our Lady of Mercy Grammar School, Wolverhampton; Edinburgh University. Research Associate, Edinburgh University, 1988-89; Housing Campaign Worker, Shelter, 1989-92; Depute Chief Executive, Citizens Advice Scotland, 1989-92. Address: (b.) Shelter, Scotiabank House, 6 South Charlotte Street, Edinburgh EH2 4AW.

Nicholson, Peter Alexander, LLB (Hons). Managing Editor, W. Green, The Scottish Law Publisher, since 1989; General Editor, Scots Law Times, since 1985; Scottish Editor, Current Law, 1985-96; General Editor, Greens

Weekly Digest, since 1986; b. 22.5.58, Stirling; m., Morag Ann Fraser; 1 s.; 2 d. Educ. St. David's RC High School, Dalkeith; Edinburgh University. Admitted as Solicitor, 1981. Lay Minister of the Eucharist. Recreations: choral singing; gardening; keeping fit. Address: (h.) 91 Greenbank Road, Edinburgh EH10 5RT; T.-0131-447 1842.

Nickson of Renagour, Lord (David Wigley Nickson), KBE (1987), CBE (1981), DL, CBIM, FRSE. Life Peer; Chairman, Clydesdale Bank, since 1991 (Director, since 1981); Deputy Chairman, General Accident plc; Director, National Australian Group (UK) Ltd., since 1993; Chancellor, Glasgow Caledonian University, since 1993; Vice Lieutenant, Stirling and Falkirk, since 1997 (Deputy Lieutenant, 1982-97);b. 27.11.29, Eton; m., Helen Louise Cockcraft; 3 d. Educ. Eton College; Royal Military Academy, Sandhurst. Commissioned, Coldstream Guards, 1949-54; William Collins: joined, 1954, Director, 1961-85, Joint Managing Director, 1967, Vice-Chairman, 1976-83, Group Managing Director, 1979-82; Director: Scottish United Investors plc, 1970-83, Scottish & Newcastle Breweries plc, 1981-95 (Chairman, 1983-89), Radio Clyde Ltd., 1982-85, National Australia Bank Ltd., 1991-96; Chairman, Pan Books, 1982-83; Chairman, Scottish Enterprise, 1990-93 (SDA, 1988-90); President, CBI, 1986-88; Chairman, CBI in Scotland, 1979-81; Chairman, Countryside Commission for Scotland, 1983-86; Member: Scottish Industrial Development Advisory Board, 1975-80, Scottish Committee, Design Council, 1978-81, Scottish Economic Council, 1980-95, National Economic Development Council, 1985-88; Chairman, Atlantic Salmon Trust, 1988-95; Chairman, Senior Salaries Review Body, 1989-95; President, Association of District Salmon Fisheries Board, since 1996; Chairman, Secretary of State for Scotland's Scottish Salmon Strategy Task Force, 1995-97; Chairman, Scottish Advisory Committee, Imperial Cancer Research Fund, since 1994; Trustee: Princes Youth Business Trust, 1987-90, Princess Royal's Trust for Carers, 1990-94; Brigadier, Queen's Bodyguard for Scotland (Royal Company of Archers); D.Univ, Stirling, 1986; Hon. DBA Napier Polytechnic, 1990; Honorary Fellow, Paisley College, 1992. Recreations: fishing; bird-watching; the countryside. Address: (h.) Renagour House, Aberfoyle, Stirling FK8 3TF; T.-01877 382275.

Nicol, Alexander David, CA. Director and Deputy Chief Executive, British Linen Bank Ltd.; Managing Director, British Linen Leasing Ltd.; Managing Director, British Linen Properties plc; b. 11.7.38, Kirkcaldy; m., Sheila Giffen; 1 s.; 2 d. Educ. Buckhaven High School; Harvard AMP. Managing Director, NEI Peebles, 1976-83. Member, Edinburgh University Advisory Committee on Business Studies. Address: (b.) 4 Melville Street, Edinburgh EH3 7NZ; T.-0131-243 8304.

Nicol, Rev. Douglas Alexander Oag, MA, BD (Hons). General Secretary, Church of Scotland Department of National Mission; b. 5.4.48, Dunfermline; m., Anne Wilson Gillespie; 2 s.; 1 d. Educ. Kirkcaldy High School; Edinburgh University; Glasgow University. Assistant Warden, St. Ninian's Centre, Crieff, 1972-76; Minister, Lochside, Dumfries, 1976-82; Minister, St. Columba, Kilmacolm, 1982-91. Chairman, Board of Directors, National Bible Society of Scotland, 1984-87; Convener, Board of National Mission, Church of Scotland, 1990-91. Recreations: family life and family history; hill-walking; running. Address: (h.) 24 Corbiehill Avenue, Blackhall, Edinburgh EH4 5DR; T.-0131-336 1965.

Nicol, Rev. James Gerard, PhB, STB, JCL. President, Roman Catholic Scottish National Tribunal, since 1992; Priest, Motherwell Diocese, since 1978; Judicial Vicar of all Scottish R.C. Dioceses, since 1992; b. 8.10.54, Coatbridge. Educ. St. Patrick's High School, Coatbridge; Blairs College, Aberdeen; Pontifical Gregorian University, Rome; Scots College, Rome. Parochial appointments, since 1979;

Tribunal: Judge Instructor, 1979-81, Co-ordinator, Motherwell Diocese, 1981-84; Defender of the Bond, 1984-86; Instructor/Defender, 1986-89; Vice-President, 1989-92; Assistant Youth Co-ordinator, Motherwell Diocese, 1979-85. Recreations: cooking; travel; reading; collecting ducks; listening to music. Address: R.C. Scottish National Tribunal, 22 Woodrow Road, Glasgow G41 5PN; T.-0141-427 3036.

Nicol, Rev. John Chalmers, MA, BD, MHSM, DipHSM. Minister, Holy Trinity Church, Bridge of Allan, since 1985; b. 6.4.39, Greenock; m., Anne Morrison MacDonald; 1 s.; 1 d. Educ. Greenock Academy; Glasgow University; Princeton Theological Seminary. Assistant Minister, Westwood Parish Church, East Kilbride, 1964-65; Minister: St. Andrew's Church, Buenos Aires, 1965-69, Bonnyrigg Parish Church, 1970-75; Secretary, Edinburgh Local Health Council, 1975-78; Principal Administrative Assistant, Argyll and Clyde Health Board, 1978-85. Recreations: fishing; Charles Rennie Mackintosh. Address: (h.) 29 Keir Street, Bridge of Allan FK9 4QJ; T.-01786 832093.

Nicol, Rev. Thomas James Trail, LVO, MBE, MC, MA, DD. Minister, Church of Scotland; Extra Chaplain to The Queen, since 1979; b. 24.1.17, Skelmorlie, Ayrshire; m., Mary Barnfather Taylor; 2 d. Educ. Edinburgh Academy; Dundee High School; Glasgow Academy; Aberdeen Grammar School; Aberdeen University. OCTU and Commission, Black Watch, 1939-42; ordained as Chaplain to the Forces, 1942; RAChD, 1942-46, attached 51 (H) Division; Minister, St. Luke's, Broughty Ferry, 1946-49; regular commission, RAChD, 1949-72; Assistant Chaplain-General, HQ Scotland, 1967-72; Minister, Crathie, 1972-77; Domestic Chaplain in Scotland to the Queen, 1972-79. Recreations: hill-walking; gardening; golf. Address: (h.) Beech Cottage, Dalginross, Comrie, Perthshire PH6 2HB; T.-01764 670430.

Nicoll, Eric Hamilton, CBE, FSA Scot, BSc (Hons), FICE, FCIWEM (Dip). Deputy Chief Engineer, Scottish Development Department, 1976-85; b. 15.5.25, Edinburgh; m., Helen Elizabeth Barnes; 1 s.; 1 d. Educ. George Heriot's School, Edinburgh; Edinburgh University. Engineering Assistant: Midlothian County Council Roads Department, 1945-46, Edinburgh Corporation Water Department, 1946-51; Chief Assistant County Engineer, Midlothian County Council, 1951-62; Scottish Development Department: Engineering Inspector, 1962-68, Senior Engineering Inspector, 1968-72, Assistant Chief Engineer, 1972-75. US Water Pollution Control Federation Arthur Sidney Bedell Award, 1985; Chairman: Edinburgh Recorded Music Society, 1993-95, Pictish Arts Society and Archivist, 1992-95; elected Professional Member of Society, Scottish Artists and Artist Craftsmen, 1995. Publications: Small Water Pollution Control Works: Design and Practice, 1988; A Pictish Panorama (Editor), 1995. Recreations: wood sculpture; music; antiquities. Address: (h.) 35 Wardie Road, Edinburgh EH5 3LJ.

Nicolson, David M., CA. Partner, KPMG Edinburgh, since 1988; b. 22.4.42, Edinburgh; m., Elizabeth Finlay Smith; 1 s.; 1 d. Educ. Royal High School, Edinburgh. Qualified as CA with Robertson & Maxtone Graham, Edinburgh, 1964; Peat Marwick Mitchell & Co., London, 1964-67; returned to Robertson & Maxtone Graham, 1967 (now KPMG). President: Edinburgh Junior Chamber of Commerce, 1975-76, Edinburgh Chamber of Commerce and Enterprise, 1994-96; former Member of Council, Institute of Chartered Accountants of Scotland. Recreations: golf; tennis; skiing; gardening. Address: (b.) Saltire Court, 20 Castle Terrace, Edinburgh EH1 2EG; T.-0131-222 2000.

Nicolson, John Alick (Jan). Board Member, Highlands and Islands Enterprise; founder Chairman, Skye and Lochalsh Enterprise; Trustee, Urras Clann Mhicneacil Lands Trust; Scottish Commissioner, Clan Nicolson of Scorrybreac; b.

26.9.45, Inverness; m., Effie; 1 s. Educ. Portree High School. Partner, Jansvans Home and Garden Store, Portree, Jansvans Gas Services Ltd., Jansport, Almond Bank Guest House. Fund-Raising Chairman, HIE-Screen Ltd.; Founder Member and Past Chairman, Isle of Skye Round Table. Recreations: collecting vintage vehicles; community affairs. Address: (h.) Almondbank, Viewfield Road, Portree, Isle of Skye IV51 9E4; T.-01478 612696.

Nicolson, Roy Macdonald, FFA, FPMI. Managing Director, Scottish Amicable, since 1990; b. 12.6.44, Glasgow; m., Jennifer; 1 s.; 1 d. Educ. Paisley Grammar School. Joined Scottish Amicable, 1960. Recreations: golf; bridge. Address: (b.) Scottish Amicable, Craigforth, Stirling FK9 4UE; T.-01786 448844.

Nimmo, Mae Morrison, DL. President, South Lanarkshire Girl Guides, since 1977; Member, Lanarkshire Health Board, since 1990; Company Director; b. 6.11.34, near Lanrk; m., W. Nimmo, CBE; 3 s.; 1 d. Educ. Lanark Grammar School; Glasgow and West of Scotland College of Domestic Science. Recreations: painting; hill-walking; enjoying the company of grand-children; gardening. Address: (h.) Auchenglen House, Auchenglen Road, Braidwood, Carluke ML8 5PH; T.-01555 772021.

Nimmo, Professor Myra A., BSc, PhD. Professor of Exercise Physiology, Faculty of Education, Strathclyde University; b. 5.1.54, Edinburgh; m., Dr. J.A. Macaskill; 2 s. Educ. Westbourne School for Girls; Glasgow University. Temporary Lecturer, Glasgow University, 1978-80; Wellcome Research Fellow, 1980-82; Lecturer in Physiology, Queen's College, Glasgow, 1982-84, Senior Lecturer in Physiotherapy and research, 1984-87, Acting Head, Department of Physiotherapy, 1987-88; Assistant Director, Scottish Vocational Education Department, 1988-91; Member, Scottish Sport Council, Scottish Sport World Class Advisory Group (Member, Scottish Sports Council, 1990-94); Olympic athlete. Recreation: general fitness. Address: (b.) Strathclyde University, Jordanhill Campus, Southbrae Drive, Glasgow G13 1PP; T.-0141-950 3722.

Nimmo, William, CBE, BArch, RIBA, FRIAS, FRSA. Senior Partner, William Nimmo & Partners, since 1956; b. 1.4.29; m., Mae Morrison; 3 s.; 1 d. Educ. Wishaw High School; Mackintosh School of Architecture. Commissioned, Corps of Royal Engineers, 1954-55. Recreations: farming; hill-walking; touring in UK and Europe. Address: (h.) Auchenglen House, Braidwood, Carluke ML8 5PH; T.-01555 772021.

Nimmo Smith, Hon. Lord (William Austin Nimmo Smith), QC, BA, LLB. Senator of the College of Justice, since 1996; b. 6.11.42, Edinburgh; m., Dr. Jennifer Nimmo Smith; 1 s.; 1 d. Educ. Eton; Balliol College, Oxford; Edinburgh University. Advocate, 1969; Standing Junior Counsel, Department of Employment, 1977-82; QC, 1982; Advocate Depute, 1983-86; Chairman, Medical Appeal Tribunals and Vaccine Damage Tribunals, 1986-91; part-time Member, Scottish Law Commission, 1988-96; Temporary Judge, Court of Session, 1995-96. Recreations: mountaineering; music. Address: (b.) Parliament House, Edinburgh EH1 1RQ.

Nisbet, James Barry Consitt, LLB, NP, JP. Stipendiary Magistrate, Glasgow, since 1984; b. 26.7.42, Forfar; m., Elizabeth McKenzie; 2 d. Educ. Forfar Academy; Edinburgh University. Legal Assistant, Warden Bruce & Co., WS, Edinburgh, 1967-68; Legal Assistant, then Junior Depute Town Clerk, then Depute Town Clerk, Perth City Council, 1968-75; Senior Depute Director of Administration, Perth and Kinross District Council, 1975-84. Lay Elector and Head Server, St. Ninian's Episcopal Cathedral, Perth; Secretary-General, Scottish Guild of Servers. Recreations: transport, especially railways and tramways; archaeology; music; foreign travel; genealogy.

Address: (b.) District Court Chambers, 21 St. Andrews Street, Glasgow G1 5PW; T.-0141-227 5424.

Niven, Catharine, BSc, AMA, FSA(Scot) Curator, Inverness Museum and Art Gallery, since 1984; b. 23.9.52, Denbigh; m., Roger Niven. Educ. Loughton High School; Leicester University. Freelance archaeologist, working in Britain and Scandinavia; Keeper of Antiquities, Rotherham Museum, 1979-81; Assistant Curator (Archaeology), Inverness Museum and Art Gallery, 1981-84. Recreation: music. Address: (b.) Castle Wynd, Inverness IV2 3ED; T.-01463 237114.

Niven, Professor Catherine Ann, RGN, BSc (Psychology), PhD. Professor of Nursing and Midwifery Studies and Head, Department of Nursing and Midwifery, Stirling University, since 1996; b. 26.8.45; m., Eric Brodie; 1 s.; 1 d. Educ. Notre Dame High School, Glasgow; Dowanhill Nurse Training School; Victoria Infirmary, Glasgow; Stirling University. Staff nurse; Sister, Victoria Infirmary, Glasgow, and Gartnavel General, Glasgow; Lecturer/Reader, Glasgow Caledonian University. Publications: Psychological Care for Families: before, during and after birth; The Health Psychology of Women (Co-editor); The Psychology of Reproduction (Co-editor). Recreations: Eric; eating; drinking; gardening. Address: (b.) Department of Nursing and Midwifery, Stirling University, Stirling FK9 4LA; T.-01786 466340.

Niven, Stuart Matthew, BSc, DipEd, FIMgt. President Emeritus, International Vocational Education and Training Association; Chairman, Board of Management, Clydebank College; b. 1.3.36, Clydebank; m., Jean K. McPhee; 1 s.; 1 d. Educ. Clydebank High School; Glasgow University. Teacher of Mathematics and Physics: Clydebank High School, 1959, Stow College of Engineering, 1961; Head, Department of Mathematics and Physics, Kilmarnock College, 1964; Jordanhill College of Education: Lecturer in Mathematics, 1967, Senior Lecturer in Further Education, 1968, Principal Lecturer, 1970; Director, Scottish School of Further Education, Strathclyde University, 1983-97. Member, CNAA Further Education Board, 1978-84; Chairman, Editorial Board, Journal for Further and Higher Education in Scotland, 1976-83; Chairman, National Liaison Committee on Training of Teachers of Nursing, Midwifery and Health Visiting, 1983-88; Member, National Board for Scotland for Nursing, Midwifery and Health Visiting, 1989-93; Member, UK Central Council for Nursing, Midwifery and Health Visiting, since 1989; President, International Vocational Education and Training Association, 1994-96 (Vice President, Europe, 1990-92, President (Elect), 1992-94); President, International Section, American Vocational Association; Member, Royal Philosophical Society of Glasgow. Publications: Vocational Further Education in Scotland, 1982; Professional Development of Further Education Lecturers in Scotland: Towards Comprehensive Provision, 1987. Publication: The First Twenty-Five Years. Recreation: golf. Address: 5 Netherblane, Blanefield, Glasgow G63 9SW; T.-01360 770060.

Nixon, Christopher William, NDA, CertEd, ARAgs. Principal, Oatridge Agricultural College, since 1985; b. 7.11.45, Grappenhall; m., Susan Doreen Presley; 1 s.; 2 d. Educ. Normain College, Chester; Harper Adams Agricultural College. Lecturer in Agriculture/Extra Mural Lecturer, Newton Rigg, Penrith; Lecturer in Sheep Production/Senior Lecturer, Extra Mural, Bishop Burton; Depute Principal, Oatridge Agricultural College. Address: (h.) Woodbank Farm, Bathgate, West Lothian EH48 3BE; T.-01501 733217.

Nixon, Mary MacKenzie, OBE, MA (Hons), DipEd. Archivist, Scottish Girl Guides Association, 1979-90; b. Port Arthur, Canada. Educ. High School of Stirling; St. Andrews University. Assistant English Teacher, Riverside

School, Stirling; Responsible Assistant, History, High School of Stirling, Falkirk High School; Responsible Assistant, English, Falkirk High School; Head, English Department, Grangemouth High School. Girl Guides Association: County Camp Adviser and Chairman, Training Committee, Stirlingshire; Scotland: Ranger Adviser, Training Adviser, Deputy Scottish Chief Commissioner; Co-ordinator, Silver Jubilee Scheme for Unemployed; Chairman, Netherurd Committee, Scottish Girl Guides Association Training Centre, 1981-85. Recreations: genealogy; archaeology; poetry. Address: (h.) Gartlea, 19 Station Road, Bannockburn FK7 8LE.

Noad, Elaine, BA, MSc, DPA, DASS, CQSW. Director of Community Services, South Ayrshire Council, since 1995; b. 7.7.56, London; m., Peter Noad; 2 s.; 1 d. Educ. Chorley College; Newcastle Polytechnic; Aberdeen University. Social Worker: Lothian, 1980-85, Grampian, 1985-87; Development Worker, Scottish Council on Disability, 1987-89; Principal Officer (Corporate Services), City of Edinburgh District Council, 1989-90; Social Work Manager, Tayside Regional Council, 1990-94; Assistant Director of Social Work, Grampian Regional Council, 1994-95. Recreations: swimming; hill-walking; travel; sports. Address: (b.) South Ayrshire Council, County Buildings, Wellington Square, Ayr KA7 1DR; T.-01292 612419.

Noble, Rev. Alexander Buchan, MA, BD (Hons), ThM. Minister, Dunbar Parish Church, since 1993; b. 23.5.55, Fraserburgh; m., Patricia Anne. Educ. Fraserburgh Academy; Dalziel High School, Motherwell; Glasgow University; Aberdeen University; Princeton Theological Seminary. Minister, St. Mark's Parish Church, Stirling, 1982-93. Recreations: football; swimming; reading; writing; travel. Address: Bayswell Road, Dunbar EH42 1AB; T.-01368 863749.

Noble, Sheriff Alistair William, LLB. Sheriff of North Strathclyde at Dunoon, since 1992; b. 10.1.54. Advocate, 1978. Address: (b.) Sheriff Court House, George Street, Dunoon, PA23 8BQ.

Noble, David Hillhouse, LLB, DipMan. Chief Executive, Highlands of Scotland Tourist Board, since 1997; b. 27.4.48, Paisley; m., Hilary; 1 s.; 2 d. Educ. Greenock Academy; Glasgow University. Solicitor in private practice, Glasgow, 1970-72; Legal and Administrative Officer, Argyll County Council, 1972-73; Senior Legal and Administrative Officer, Inverness County Council, 1973-75; Chief Executive, Skye and Lochalsh District Council, 1975-96; Director, Skye and Lochalsh Enterprise, 1992-95; Area Manager, Skye and Lochalsh, The Highland Council, 1996-97. Recreations: music; running. Address: (b.) Peffery House, Strathpeffer, Ross-shire IV14 9HA; T.-01997 421160.

Noble (or Nobail), Sir Iain, Bt. of Ardkinglas and Eilean Iarmain, OBE, MA. Chairman, Noble Group Ltd.; entrepreneur and businessman; b. 8.9.35, Berlin. Educ. in China, Argentina and England; University College, Oxford. Scottish Council (Development and Industry), 1964-69; Co-founder and Joint Managing Director, Noble Grossart Ltd., Edinburgh, 1969-72. Chairman, Seaforth Maritime PLC, 1972-77; Director: Adam and Company plc, 1983-94, Independent Insurance Group PLC, since 1986, Premium Trust PLC, since 1993; and other companies; Chairman: Skye Bridge Ltd., 1994-96, Pràban na Linne Ltd ("The Gaelic Whiskies"); Proprietor, Fearann Eilean Iarmain (rural estate in Isle of Skye), since 1972; Member, Edinburgh University Court, 1970-73; Co-founder, first Chairman and Trustee, College of Sabhal Mòr Ostaig, 1975-85; Trustee: National Museums of Scotland, 1986-90, NMS Charitable Trust, since 1990; Scotsman of the Year Award, 1982 (Knights Templar); President, Saltire Society, 1993-96; Editor, Sources of Finance, 1967-69; other

interests: conservation; land management; heritage architecture; community development. Recreations: deasbad, comhradh, orain is ceol le deagh chompanaich. Address: An Oifig, Eilean Iarmain, An t-Eilean Sgitheanach, IV43 8QR; T.-01471 833 266; 76 George Street; T.-0131-225 9677.

Noble, Lillias Mary, BEd. Director, LEAD-Scotland (Linking Education and Disability), since 1988; part-time Commissioner, Mental Welfare Commission, since 1992, Vice Chairman, since 1995; b. 11.9.54, Vancouver. Educ. Larkhall Academy; Hamilton College of Education; Strathclyde University. Teacher of English and Assistant Principal Teacher, Thurso High School, 1975-80; Assistant Principal Teacher, Wester Hailes Education Centre, 1980-85; Save the Children Fund (Scotland), 1985-88. Recreation: climbing mountains. Address: (b.) LEAD-Scotland, Queen Margaret College, Clerwood Terrace, Edinburgh EH12 8TS; T.-0131-317 3439.

Noble, Simon John. Owner, Ardkinglas Estate, Argyll, since 1972; Chairman, Loch Fyne Oysters Ltd., since 1977; Director, Noble Group Ltd., since 1977; b. 31.10.36, London. Educ. Eton; Magdalen College, Oxford. S.G. Warburg & Co., 1959-64; wine trade – French and Foreign Wines Ltd. (Founder), 1964-81; Director (non-Executive), Edinburgh Tapestry Co. Ltd., since 1972; Chairman (non-Executive), Wine Importers Edinburgh Ltd., since 1975. Recreation: country life. Address: (b.) Loch Fyne Oysters Ltd., Cairndow, Argyll PA26 8BH; T.-014996 264.

Noble, Sir (Thomas Alexander) Fraser, Kt (1971), MBE (1947), MA, LLD, FRSE; b. 29.4.18, Cromdale; m., Barbara A.M. Sinclair; 1 s.; 1 d. Educ. Nairn Academy; Aberdeen University. Indian Civil Service, 1940-47; Lecturer in Political Economy, Aberdeen University, 1948-57; Secretary, Carnegie Trust for Scottish Universities, 1957-62; Vice-Chancellor, Leicester University, 1962-76; Principal, Aberdeen University, 1976-81; Past Chairman of numerous public service committees, including Scottish Standing Conference of Youth Service Organisations, Home Office Advisory Committee for Probation and After Care, Television Research Committee; Chairman, UK Committee of Vice Chancellors, 1970-72; former Member of Council, Association of Commonwealth Universities. Recreations: golf; listening to music. Address: (h.) Hedgerley, Victoria Street, Nairn; T.-Nairn 453151.

Noble, Timothy Peter, MA, MBA. Chief Executive, Noble Group Ltd.; Director: Waverley Mining Finance plc, Hardy Underwriting Group, British Ski and Snowboard Federation Ltd.; Chairman, Royal Scottish National Orchestra Endowment Trust; b. 21.12.43; m., Elizabeth Mary Aitken; 2 s.; 1 d. Educ. University College, Oxford; Gray's Inn, London; INSEAD, Fontainebleau. Recreations: skiing; tennis; bridge; wine; astronomy; poetry. Address: (h.) Ardnahane, Barnton Avenue, Edinburgh; T.-0131-336 3565.

Noel-Paton, (Frederick) Ranald, BA. Deputy Chairman, John Menzies plc, since 1997 (Group Managing Director, 1986-97); b. 7.11.38, Bombay; m., Patricia Anne Stirling; 4 d. Educ. Rugby School; McGill University. Investment Analyst, Greenshields Inc., 1962-63; Management Trainee, United Biscuits, 1964; various posts, British United Airways Ltd., 1965-70; various senior executive posts, British Caledonian Airways, 1970-86 (General Manager, West Africa, 1975-79, General Manager, Far East, 1980-86, Director, Caledonian Far East Airways, 1984-86); Director: Pacific Assets Trust plc, since 1986, General Accident plc, since 1987. Recreations: fishing; walking; bird-watching; the arts. Address: (b.) 108 Princes Street, Edinburgh EH2 3AA; T.-0131-225 8555.

Normand, Andrew Christie, MA, LLB, LLM. Crown Agent for Scotland, since 1996; b. 7.2.48, Edinburgh; m.,

Barbara Jean Smith; 2 d. Educ. George Watson's College, Edinburgh; Edinburgh University; Queen's University, Kingston, Ontario. Address: (b.) Crown Office, 25 Chambers Street, Edinburgh EH1 1LA; T.-0131-226 2626.

Norrie, Rev. Graham, MA, BD. Minister, Forfar: East and Old Parish Church, since 1978; b. 14.5.41, Dundee; m., Irene Seward Pearce; 2 s.; 2 d. Educ. Morgan Academy, Dundee; St. Andrews University; Edinburgh University. Assistant Minister, St. Ninian's Church, Corstorphine, 1965-67; Minister, Alloa: West Church, 1967-78. Recreations: hill-walking; football spectating. Address: (h.) The Manse, Lour Road, Forfar DD8 2BB; T.-01307 464303.

North, Michael James, MA, PhD. Reader in Biochemistry, Stirling University, 1989-97; b. 20.1.48, London; m., Barbara Lockwood (deceased); 1 d., Sophie (deceased, victim at Dunblane Primary School). Educ. East Barnet Grammar School; Hertford College, Oxford; Newcastle upon Tyne University. SRC Postdoctoral Fellow, Leicester University and Essex University, 1973-75; Lecturer in Biochemistry, Stirling University, 1975-85; Senior Lecturer, 1985-89. Convener, Scottish Branch, Society for General Microbiology, 1988-93; Editor, Microbiology (formerly Journal of General Microbiology), 1988-94. Founder Member, Gun Control Network. Publication: Biochemical Protozoology (Joint Editor). Recreations: gardening; music; supporting Tottenham Hotspur FC. Address: (h.) Lawers, Aberfeldy, Perthshire PH15 2PA.

Norwell, Peter Smith, OBE, TD, JP. Honorary Sheriff, Perth; b. 14.4.12, Perth; m., Elisabeth May Edwards; 3 d. Educ. Dollar Academy. Lt.-Col., RASC, 1944; Secretary, Perthshire Territorial Army Association, 1960-62; Assistant Secretary, Angus, Perthshire and Fife Territorial Army Association, 1962-67; Managing Director, Norwells Perth Footwear Ltd., 1935-60; Town Councillor, Perth, 1946-52; Chairman, Perth Theatre Company, 1968-72. Address: (h.) Dura Den, Pitcullen Terrace, Perth PH2 7EQ; T.-Perth 626789.

O

O'Brien, Sir Frederick William Fitzgerald, QC, MA, LLB. Sheriff Principal, Lothian and Borders, 1978-89; Convener of Sheriffs Principal, 1972-89; b. 19.7.17, Edinburgh; m., Audrey Muriel Owen; 2 s.; 1 d. Educ. Royal High School, Edinburgh; Edinburgh University. Called to Scottish Bar, 1947; QC, 1960; Commissioner, Mental Welfare Commission, 1962-65; Senior Advocate Depute, Crown Office, 1964-65; Sheriff Principal, Caithness, Sutherland, Orkney and Shetland, 1965-75; Interim Sheriff Principal, Aberdeen, Kincardine and Banff, 1969-71; Sheriff Principal, North Strathclyde, 1975-78; Interim Sheriff Principal, South Strathclyde, 1981; Member: Scottish Medical Practices Committee, 1973-76, Scottish Records Advisory Council, 1974-83; Chairman, Sheriff Court Rules Council, 1975-81; Convener, General Council Business Committee, Edinburgh University, 1980-84; Past President, Royal High School FP Club (Honorary President, 1982-91); Chairman, Edinburgh Sir Walter Scott Club, 1989-92; Commissioner, Northern Lighthouse Board, 1965-89. Recreations: music; golf. Address: (h.) 22 Arboretum Road, Edinburgh EH3 5PN; T.-0131-552 1923.

O'Brien, James Paul, MA (Hons), MEd, DipEdTech. Vice-Principal, Moray House Institute of Education, Heriot-Watt University, since 1993; b. 23.4.50, Stirling; m., Elaine Margaret Kathleen Smith; 1 d. Educ. St. Mirin's Academy, Paisley; Glasgow University. Teacher, 1973-85; Lecturer, St. Andrew's College of Education, 1985-88, Director, 1988-93, Assistant Principal, 1992-93. Recreations: golf; music; reading. Address: (b.) Holyrood Campus, Holyrood Road, Edinburgh EH8 8AQ; T.-0131-558 6164.

O'Brien, Most Rev. Keith Michael Patrick, BSc, DipEd. Archbishop of St. Andrews and Edinburgh, since 1985; b. 17.3.38, Ballycastle, Northern Ireland. Educ. Saint Patrick's, Dumbarton; Holy Cross Academy, Edinburgh; Edinburgh University; St. Andrew's College, Drygrange; Moray House College of Education. Teacher, St. Columba's High School, Fife; Assistant Priest, Kilsyth, then Bathgate; Spiritual Director, St. Andrew's College, Drygrange; Rector, Blairs College, Aberdeen; ordained Archbishop by Cardinal Gray, 1985. Recreations: music; walking. Address: Saint Bennet's, 42 Greenhill Gardens, Edinburgh EH10 4BJ.

O'Farrell, Professor Patrick Neil, BA, PhD, MIPI. Professor of Economics, Heriot-Watt University, since 1986 (Assistant Principal, since 1995, Dean, Faculty of Economic and Social Studies, 1992-95); b. 18.4.41; m.; 3 d. Educ. Trinity College, Dublin. Assistant in Geography, Trinity College, Dublin, 1963-65; Assistant Lecturer and Lecturer in Geography, Queen's University, Belfast, 1965-70; Lecturer in Geography, New University of Ulster, 1971-73; Lecturer, Senior Lecturer and Reader in Planning, UWIST, 1973-86. Recreations: golf; talking; music. Address: (b.) Heriot-Watt University, Riccarton, Edinburgh EH14 4AS.

Ogilvie, Lorna Margaret, BSc, MSc, FRMetS. Headmistress, St. Margaret's School for Girls, Aberdeen, since 1989; b. 22.3.47, Edinburgh. Educ. Mary Erskine School for Girls; Edinburgh University; University of Calgary; Moray House College of Education. Geography Teacher, Inverness High School, 1972-73; Head of Geology and Teacher of Geography, Royal Russell School, Croydon, 1973-82; Assistant Rector, Morrison's Academy, Crieff, 1982-88. Recreations: Scottish country dancing; skiing; golf; theatre; travel; reading. Address: (b.) 17 Albyn Place, Aberdeen AB10 1RU; T.-01224 584466.

Ogilvie, Margaret Elizabeth. Owner/Gardener, Pitmuies Gardens, since 1966; b. 21.12.29, Co. Down; m., Douglas Farquhar Ogilvie (deceased); 1 s.; 2 d. Educ. Central School of Art and Crafts, London. Prior to marriage, advertising manager and book designer/typographer; National Trust for Scotland: Member, Council (three times), Member, Executive Committee (twice); Historic Houses Association: Member, Executive Council, Scottish Representative; Gardens Committee; Association for Protection of Rural Scotland: Member, Representative Committee, Member, judging panel for Annual Award; Member, Scottish Council for National Parks; Member, Committee, Scottish Museums of Year Award; Fellow RSA. Recreations: riding; skiing; music; travelling. Address: (h.) House of Pitmuies, by Forfar, Angus; T.-01241 828245.

Ogilvie-Laing of Kinkell, Gerald, NDD, FRBS. Sculptor; b. 11.2.36; 4 s.; 1 d. Educ. Berkhamsted School; RMA, Sandhurst. Commissioned Fifth Fusiliers, 1955-60; resigned commission and attended St. Martin's School of Art, 1960-64; lived in New York, 1964-69; Artist in Residence, Aspen Institute for Humanistic Studies, Colorado, 1966; moved to north of Scotland, 1969, and restored ruins of Kinkell Castle; Civic Trust Award, 1971; established a tapestry workshop in north of Scotland; Visiting Professor, University of New Mexico, 1976-77; set up bronze foundry, Kinkell Castle, to produce own work; Member, Art Committee, Scottish Arts Council, 1978-80; Professor of Sculpture, Columbia University, New York, 1986-87; Commissioner, Royal Fine Art Commission for Scotland, 1987-95; divides time between north of Scotland and New York; public sculpture includes Callanish, 1971; Frieze of the Wise and Foolish Virgins, 1980; Fountain of Sabrina, 1982; Conan Doyle Memorial, 1991; Axis Mundi, 1991; Bank Underground Station Dragons, London, 1995; St. George and Dragon Series, Harrow, 1996; Four Rugby Players, Twickenham, 1996; portrait bust, John Paul Getty III, National Gallery, London, 1997. Address: (h.) Kinkell Castle, Dingwall IV7 8AT; T.-01349 861485.

Ogilvy, Sir Francis (Gilbert Arthur), 14th Bt, ARICS. Chartered Surveyor; b. 22.4.69; m., Dorothy Margaret Stein. Educ. Edinburgh Academy; Glenalmond College; Royal Agricultural College, Cirencester; BSc (Hons) (Reading). Address: (h.) Winton House, Pencaitland, East Lothian EH34 5AT.

O'Grady, Richard John Peard, MA (Hons). Director/Secretary, Zoological Society of Glasgow and West of Scotland, since 1972; b. 6.7.49, Cambridge; m., Maria Ann; 2 s. Educ. King's School, Bruton; Dundee University. Address: (b.) Glasgow Zoo, Calderpark, Uddingston, Glasgow, G71 7RZ; T.-0141-771 1185.

Ogston, Rev. David Dinnes, MA, BD. Minister, St. John's Kirk of Perth, since 1980; b. 25.3.45, Ellon, Aberdeenshire; m., Margaret Macleod; 2 d. Educ. Inverurie Academy; King's College and Christ's College, Aberdeen. Assistant Minister: St. Giles' Cathedral, Edinburgh, 1969-73, Balerno, 1973-80. Publication: White Stone Country; Dry Stone Days. Recreations: late-night films on TV; Greek and Russian Ikons. Address: 15 Comely Bank Perth; T.-Perth 621755

Ogston, Professor Derek, CBE, MA, MD, PhD, DSc, FRCPEdin, FRCP, FIBiol, FRSE, FRSA. Professor of Medicine, Aberdeen University, 1983-97 (Dean, Faculty of Medicine, 1984-87; Vice-Principal, 1987-97); b. 31.5.32, Aberdeen; m., Cecilia Marie; 1 s.; 2 d. Educ. King's College School, Wimbledon; Aberdeen University. Aberdeen University: Lecturer in Medicine, 1962-69, Senior Lecturer in Medicine, 1969-75, MRC Travelling Fellow, 1967-68, Reader in Medicine, 1975-76, Regius Professor of Physiology, 1977-83. Member, Grampian Health Board, 1991-97 (Vice-Chairman, 1993-97); Member, General Medical Council, 1985-94. Publications: Haemostasis: Biochemistry, Physiology and Pathology (Joint Editor), 1977; The Physiology of Hemostasis, 1983;

Antifibrinolytic Drugs: Chemistry, Pharmacology and Clinical Usage, 1984; Venous Thrombosis: Causation and Prediction, 1987. Recreation: gardening. Address: (h.) 64 Rubislaw Den South, Aberdeen AB15 4AY; T.-Aberdeen 316587.

Ohara, Noriko. Principal Ballerina, Scottish Ballet; b. Japan. London Ballet, 1974; London Festival Ballet (as principal dancer), 1975; joined Scottish Ballet, 1976; has danced all the major roles in the company's repertoire; regular jury member, Prix de Lausanne; Associate Director, Asami Maki Ballet Company, Tokyo. Address: (b.) 261 West Princes Street, Glasgow, G4 9EE.

Oliver, Ian Thomas, QPM, LLB, MPhil, PhD, FRSA. Chief Constable, Grampian Police; b. 24.1.40, London; m., Elsie; 2 s.; 1 d. Educ. Grammar School, Hampton, Middlesex; Nottingham University; Strathclyde University. RAF, 1959-61; Constable to Superintendent, Metropolitan Police, 1961-77; Northumbria Police: Chief Superintendent, 1977, Assistant Chief Constable (Management Services), 1978; Chief Constable, Central Scotland, 1979. President, Association of Chief Police Officers in Scotland, 1983 and 1993; Churchill Fellow, 1986. Publication: Police, Government and Accountability, 1987. Address: (b.) Police Headquarters, Queen Street, Aberdeen, AB10 1ZA; T.-Aberdeen 639111.

Oliver, James Kenneth Murray, OBE. Farmer; b. 1.2.14, Hawick; m., Rhona Mary Purdom Wilkinson; 1 s.; 1 d. Educ. Merchiston Castle, Edinburgh. Army, 1939-46; as racehorse trainer, trained 1,000 winners under National Hunt Rules; rode winner, Scottish Grand National, 1950; trained five winners, Scottish Grand National; four times runner-up, Grand National; trained winners for the Queen Mother; Director and Vice President, Doncaster Bloodstock Sales Ltd. Address: (h.) Hassendean Bank, Hawick.

Olver, Professor Richard Edmund, BSc, MB, FRCP, FRCPE. James Mackenzie Professor of Child Health, Dundee; b. 26.10.41, Ayr; m.; 2 s.; 2 d. Educ. London University. House Officer and Senior House Officer posts, St. Thomas's, Addenbrookes and Brompton Hospitals, 1966-69; Lecturer, Senior Lecturer, Reader, Department of Paediatrics, University College, London, 1969-85; MRC Travelling Fellow, Cardiovascular Research Institute, San Francisco, 1973-74; Consultant Paediatrician, University College Hospital, London, 1975-85. Address: (b.) Dundee University, Dundee.

O'Neil, Brian. Director of Personnel, Historic Scotland, since 1997; b. 14.5.50, Edinburgh; m., Irene; 2 d. Educ. Gracemount Secondary School, Edinburgh. Joined Scottish Office, 1966; Head of Branch, Local Government Division, 1990-95. Recreations: golf; reading; gardening. Address: (b.) Historic Scotland, Longmore House, Salisbury Place, Edinburgh EH9 1SH; T.-0131-668 8667.

O'Neill, Rev. Professor John Cochrane, BA, BD, PhD. Professor of New Testament Language, Literature and Theology, Edinburgh University, 1985-96; b. 8.12.30, Melbourne; m., Judith Beatrice Lyall (see Judith Beatrice O'Neill); 3 d. Educ. Melbourne Church of England Grammar School; Melbourne University; Ormond College Theological Hall; University of Göttingen; Clare College, Cambridge. Senior Tutor in History, Melbourne University, 1953-55; Lecturer in New Testament Studies, Ormond College Theological Hall, Melbourne, 1960-64; Dunn Professor of New Testament Language, Literature and Theology, Westminster College, Cambridge, 1964-85. Publications: Paul's Letter to the Romans, 1975; The Bible's Authority: a portrait gallery of thinkers from Lessing to Bultmann, 1991; Who Did Jesus Think He Was?, 1995. Recreations: swimming; camping. Address: (h.) 9 Lonsdale Terrace, Edinburgh EH3 9HN; T.-0131-229 6070.

O'Neill, Judith Beatrice, MA, PGCE. Author of fiction for older children; b. 30.6.30, Melbourne; m., John Cochrane O'Neill (qv); 3 d. Educ. University of Melbourne; University of London. University Tutor, 1954-56, Melbourne, 1970-72, UK; School Teacher, Cambridge, 1974-82, and part-time author; full-time author, since 1982. Publications: Jess and the River Kids; Stringybark Summer; Deepwater; The Message; So Far from Skye; Hearing Voices, 1996; Spindle River, 1998. Recreations: reading; walking; music; camping; theatre. Address: (h.) 9 Lonsdale Terrace, Edinburgh EH3 9HN; T.-0131-229 6070.

O'Neill, Martin (John), BA (Econ). MP (Labour), Ochil, since 1997 (Clackmannan, 1983-97, East Stirlingshire and Clackmannan, 1979-83); b. 6.1.45; m., Elaine Samuel; 2 s. Educ. Trinity Academy, Edinburgh; trades union and evening classes; Heriot-Watt University; Moray House College of Education. President, Scottish Union of Students, 1970-71; school teacher, 1974-79; Tutor, Open University, 1976-79. Member, Select Committee, Scottish Affairs, 1979-80; Opposition Spokesman, Scottish Affairs, 1980-84; Opposition Spokesman on Defence, 1984-88; Shadow Defence Secretary, 1988-92; Shadow Spokesman on Energy, 1992-95; Chair, Trade and Industry Select Committee, since 1996. Recreations: watching football; reading; listening to jazz; cinema. Address: (b.) 19 Mar Street, Alloa FK10 1HR; T.-01259 721536.

O'Neill, Maureen Patricia, BA (Hons), DMS. Director, Age Concern Scotland, since 1993; b. 11.5.48, Uganda; m., Jonathan Clogstoun-Willmott; 1 s.; 1 d. Educ. St. Margaret's School, Hastings; Charlton Park School, Cheltenham; Birkbeck College, London University. General Secretary, Edinburgh YWCA, 1982-87; Principal Officer, Policy, Research and Development, Scottish Association for Mental Health, 1987-93; Chairperson, Edinburgh Voluntary Organisations Council. Recreations: reading; theatre; sport. Address: (b.) 113 Rose Street, Edinburgh EH2 3DT; T.-0131-220 3345.

O'Neill, Michael, MA (Hons). Director of Education, North Lanarkshire Council, since 1995; b. 13.3.49, Govan; m., Mary; 1 d. Educ. Bellarmine Secondary School, Glasgow; Glasgow University; Jordanhill College, Glasgow. Town Planner, 1971-73; teaching, 1974-84; Assistant Head, Lourdes Secondary School, 1985-89; Adviser in Social Subjects, Dunbarton Division, Strathclyde Regional Council, 1989-90; Senior Adviser, 1990-91; Education Officer, Lanark and Dunbarton, 1991-95. Recreations: golf; running; football; music. Address: (b.) Municipal Buildings, Kildonan Street, Coatbridge ML5 3BT; T.-01236 812336.

O'Neill, Patrick. Provost, West Dunbartonshire Council, since 1996; Magistrate and Justice of the Peace, since 1970; b. 3.5.28, Dumbarton; m., Mary Jane Connolly; 1 s.; 1 d. Educ. St. Patrick's High School, Dumbarton. AEU Branch Secretary, Dumbarton No. 2, 1967-92; AEU Award of Merit, 1992, for 39 years service; Chairman, West Dumbarton Constituency Labour Party, 12 years; Burgh and District Councillor intermittently since 1962. Hon. Life Member, Dumbarton Burns Club, since 1996. Recreations: chess; photography; opera; former amateur boxer (boxed for Queen's Own Cameron Highlanders). Address: (h.) 26 Bellsmyre Avenue, Dumbarton G82 3AR.

O'Neill, Thomas (Tam), CA. Managing Director, Pilkington Optronics (formerly Barr and Stroud Ltd., Glasgow); b. 30.8.43, Methlick. Educ. St. Mungo's Academy, Glasgow; Glasgow University. PA to Chairman, Reed International Ltd., London; Finance Director, Scott Lester Ltd., London; Finance Director, Southern Construction Ltd., Portsmouth; Divisional Finance Director, Norcros Ltd., Reading; Divisional Finance Director, N.E.I. Ltd., Newcastle; Finance Director, Barr & Stroud, Glasgow,

1988-90. Address: (b.) 1 Linthouse Road, Glasgow G51 4BZ.

O'Reilly, Denis St. John, MSc, MD, FRCPath. Consultant Clinical Biochemist, Royal Infirmary, Glasgow, since 1984; b. 30.3.51, Cork; m., Margaret M.P. Lucey; 2 s.; 1 d. Educ. Presentation Brothers College, Cork; University College, Cork; Birmingham University. Registrar, Queen Elizabeth Medical Centre, Birmingham, 1976-78; Senior Registrar, Bristol Royal Infirmary, 1978-84; Ainsworth Scholar-Research Fellow, Norsk Hydro Institute for Cancer Research, Oslo, 1982. Recreation: hill-walking. Address: (h.) 47 Strathblane Road, Milngavie G62 8HA.

Ormiston, Linda, MA, DRSAMD. Singer — Mezzo Soprano; b. 15.1.48, Motherwell. Educ. Dalziel High School, Motherwell; Glasgow University; Royal Scottish Academy of Music and Drama; London Opera Centre. Has sung all over Britain, France, Belgium, Italy, Germany, Austria, Holland and Yugoslavia; has sung regularly at Scottish Opera, Opera North, and Glyndebourne; also well-known in lighter vein and as a member of The Music Box; recordings include Noyes Fludde, HMS Pinafore and Ruddigore with New Sadlers Wells Opera and Tell Me Pretty Maiden; has appeared at New York, Vancouver, Monte Carlo, Brussels and Tokyo; debut, Frankfurt Opera, 1993; debut, Salzburg Festival, 1994; debut, English National Opera, 1995; Presenter, BBC Radio 3 and Radio Scotland. Recreations: playing the piano; skating; golf.

O'Rourke, Daniel (Donny), MA. Poet, journalist, film-maker, broadcaster, and teacher; Fellow in Creative Writing, Universities of Glasgow and Strathclyde, since 1995; b. 5.7.59, Port Glasgow. Educ. St. Mirin's Academy, Paisley; Glasgow University. Chairman, Scottish Youth Council, 1982-84; Producer, BBC TV and Radio Scotland, 1984-86; Reporter, Scottish Television, 1986-87, Producer, 1987-92, Head of Arts, 1992-93, Head of Arts and Documentaries, 1993-94; Executive Producer, BBC Scotland, 1994-95. Member, Manpower Services Commission Youth Training Board, 1982-84; Member, Scottish Community Education Council, 1981-84. Publications: Second City, 1991; Rooming Houses of America, 1993; Dream State, the new Scottish poets, 1994; chapter in Burns Now, 1994; Eftirs/Afters, 1996; poems in various anthologies and textbooks. Recreations: playing guitar; Irish literature; Americana. Address: (h.) 63 Barrington Drive, Glasgow, G4 9ES.

Orr, David Campbell, MA. Director, Scottish Federation of Housing Associations, since 1990; b. 27.3.55, Kirkconnel; m., Carol; 1 s.; 2 d. Educ. Dundee University. Deputy Warden, Iona Community, Community House, 1976-77; Team Leader, then Co-ordinator, Centrepoint, Soho, 1977-86; Director, Newlon Housing Trust, 1986-90. Former Chair, Young Homelessness Group, Homeless Network, Threshold H.A. Recreations: watching sport — playing badly; cinema. Address: (b.) 38 York Place, Edinburgh EH1 3HU; T.-0131-556 5777.

Orr, John, OBE, OStJ, QPM, BA, CIMgt. Chief Constable, Strathclyde, since 1996; Hon. President, Association of Chief Police Officers in Scotland, 1997-98; Member, Secretary of State's Crime Prevention Council; b. 3.9.45, Kilmarnock; m., Joan; 2 s.; 1 d. Educ. James Hamilton Academy, Kilmarnock; Open University; Glasgow University. Entered police as cadet, Renfrew and Bute, 1961; progressed through ranks to rank of Detective Chief Superintendent and Joint Head of Strathclyde CID; Deputy Chief Constable, Dumfries and Galloway, 1990-96; seconded 1994 to HM Inspectorate of Constabulary as Assistant Inspector of Constabulary for Scotland. Recreations: Rotary; reading; gardening; angling. Address: (b.) Police Headquarters, 173 Pitt Street, Glasgow G2 4JS.

Orr, Nigel Wilson, MA, LLB, DipEd. Solicitor, since 1982; Solicitor Advocate, since 1994; b. 11.9.54, Edinburgh. Educ. Jordanhill College School, Glasgow; Glasgow University; Edinburgh University; Besancon University; Freiburg University. Procurator Fiscal Depute: Lanark, 1984, Airdrie, 1988; Senior Legal Assistant, Crown Office, 1990; Principal Procurator Fiscal Depute, Dundee, 1997; currently Manager of Regional Precognition/Fraud Unit, Tayside, Central and Fife. Recreations: sailing; hill-walking. Address: (b.) Caledonian House, Greenmarket, Dundee; T.-01382 227535.

Orr Ewing, Major Edward Stuart, DL, JP. Lord Lieutenant, Wigtown District, since 1989; b. 28.9.31, London; m., 1, F.A.B. Farquhar (m. dissolved); 2, Diana Mary Waters; 1 s.; 2 d. Educ. Sherborne; RMCS, Shrivenham. Black Watch RHR, 1950-69 (Major); Farmer and Landowner, since 1964. Recreations: country sports; skiing; sailing; painting. Address: (h.) Dunskey, Portpatrick, Stranraer; T.-01776 810211.

Orskov, Egil Robert, OBE, BSc, PhD, DSc, FRSE. Director, International Feed Resource Unit, Rowett Research Institute, since 1990; International Consultant, United Nations Organization, since 1980; b. 24.5.34, Denmark; m., Joan P.; 2 s.; 1 d. Post-doctoral work, USDA, Washington, 1966-67; Rowett Research Institute: Head, Sheep Section, 1967-75, Dairy Cattle Section, 1975-85, Head, Ruminant Nutrition, 1985-90. Publications: four books; 510 papers. Recreations: music; travel; antique collector. Address: (b.) Rowett Research Institute, Bucksburn, Aberdeen; T.-01224 716614.

Osborne, Avril, MA, MSc, PhD. Director, Community Social Services, Orkney, since 1993; b. 9.4.47, Johnstone. Educ. Gourock High School; St. Andrews University; Nottingham University; Lancaster University; Aberdeen University. Child Care Officer, 1969-72; Senior Social Worker, 1972-76; Senior Lecturer, 1976-79; Consultant, 1979-82; Leverhulme Fellow, 1982-84; Assistant Director, Social Work, Highland, 1984-93; seconded to Scottish Office, 1991-93. Recreation: walking. Address: (b.) Orkney Islands Council, School Place, Kirkwall, Orkney; T.-01856 873535.

Osborne, Hon. Lord (Kenneth Hilton Osborne), QC (Scot). Senator of the College of Justice, since 1990; b. 9.7.37. Advocate, 1962; QC, 1976; Chairman, Local Government Boundary Commission, since 1990.

Osborne, Michael, BSc, MICFor. Director, Royal Scottish Forestry Society, since 1992; b. 11.8.52, Solihull. Educ. Prices Grammar School, Fareham; University College of North Wales, Bangor. Recreation: bird-watching. Address: (b.) The Stables, Dalkeith Country Park, Dalkeith EH22 2NA; T.-0131-660 9480.

Osborne, Sandra. MP (Labour), Ayr, since 1997; b. 1956. Address: (b.) House of Commons, London SW1A 0AA.

Osler, Douglas Alexander, MA (Hons). HM Senior Chief Inspector of Schools, Scottish Office Education and Industry Department; b. 11.10.42, Edinburgh; m., Wendy I. Cochrane; 1 s.; 1 d. Educ. Royal High School, Edinburgh; Edinburgh University; Moray House College of Education. Assistant Teacher of History/Careers Master, Liberton Secondary School, Edinburgh, 1965-68; Principal Teacher of History, Dunfermline High School, 1968-74. English Speaking Union Fellowship to USA, 1966; International Visitor Program to USA, 1989. Publications: Queen Margaret of Scotland; Sources for Modern Studies, Volumes 1 and 2. Address: (b.) 3-B01 Victoria Quay, Edinburgh EH6 6QQ.

O'Sullivan, Very Rev. Canon Basil, JCL. Parish Priest, Holy Family Church, Dunblane, since 1988; b. 1932,

Fishguard. Educ. St. Finbarr's College, Cork; All Hallow's College, Dublin; Pontifical University of St. Gregory, Rome. Assistant Priest: St. Joseph's, Dundee, 1959-63, St. Andrew's Cathedral, Dundee, 1963-70; R.C. Chaplain, Dundee University, 1964-70; Parish Priest: St. John Vianney's, Alva, 1970-74, St. Columba's, Dundee, 1974-88. Canon of Dunkeld Chapter, since 1992. Recreations: reading; gardening; walking. Address: (h.) St. Clare's, Claredon Place, Dunblane FK15 9HB; T.-01786 822146.

Oswald, Rev. John, BSc, BD, PhD. Minister, Lorne and Lowland Parish Church, since 1997; b. 10.10.47, Glasgow; m., Barbara R.; 1 s. Educ. Kelvinside Academy; Edinburgh University. Management posts, Nickerson Seed Specialists; Managing Director, David Bell Ltd., Penicuik; candidate for ministry; Assistant Minister, Eddleston linked with Peebles Old. Recreations: tennis; gardening; reading. Address: Lorne and Lowland Manse, Castlehill, Campbeltown PA28 6AN; T.-01586 552468.

Ovens, Iain Stanley, BA, MA, DMS, MIPD. Principal, Dundee College, since 1996; b. 9.10.47, Glasgow; m., June Sangster. Educ. Duncanrig Senior Secondary School, East Kilbride; Strathclyde University. Lecturer, Barmulloch College of F.E.; Senior Lecturer, Head of Department, Head of Centre for Industrial Studies, Assistant Principal, Depute Principal, Glenrothes College of F.E.; Principal, Angus College. Address: (b.) Dundee College, Old Glamis Road, Dundee DD3 8LE; T.-01382 834834.

Overing, Professor Joanna Adrienne, BA (Hons), MA, PhD. Professor and Chair, Social Anthropology, St. Andrews University, since 1995; Director, Centre for Indigenous American Studies, St. Andrews University, since 1997; b. 12.8.38, Washington, DC; m., Napier Russell. Educ. University of Connecticut; Brandeis University. Instructor, then Assistant Professor, Anthropology, Vanderbilt University, 1971-74; Lecturer, then Senior Lecturer, Social Anthropology of Latin America, London School of Economics and Institute of Latin American Studies, 1974-92; Senior Lecturer, LSE, 1992-95. Visiting Professor: University of Sao Paulo, 1992, Eotvos University, Budapest, 1993, University of Goteborg, 1994, UNICAMP, Brazil, 1994. Publications: The Piaroa, a People of the Orinoco Basin, 1975; Social Time and Social Space in Lowland South American Societies, 1977; Reason and Morality, 1985. Address: (b.) Department of Social Anthropology, St. Andrews University, St. Andrews KY16 9AL; T.-01334 462979.

Owen, Professor David Gareth, MA, BD (Hons), PhD, FICE, CEng, FRSA. Professor of Offshore Engineering, Heriot-Watt University, since 1986, and Dean of Engineering, since 1996; b. 6.11.40, Brecon, Wales; m., Ann Valerie Wright; 2 d. Educ. Christ College, Brecon; Downing College, Cambridge. Graduate Engineer, John Laing & Son, London; Aerospace Engineer, Marconi Space and Defence Systems, Portsmouth; Lecturer in Civil Engineering, Heriot-Watt University; Visiting Professor, University of New Hampshire; Senior Lecturer, Department of Offshore Engineering, Heriot-Watt University. Recreations: music; travelling. Address: (h.) 7 Oak Lane, Edinburgh EH12 6XH; T.-0131-339 1740.

Owen, Professor Douglas David Roy, MA, PhD. Professor of French, St. Andrews, 1972-88; b. 17.11.22, Norton, Suffolk; m., Berit Mariann; 2 s. Educ. Cambridge and County High School; Nottingham High Pavement School; Nottingham University; St. Catharine's College, Cambridge. St. Andrews University: Lecturer, 1951-64, Senior Lecturer, 1964-71, Reader, 1971-72; General Editor, Forum for Modern Language Studies. Publications: Fabliaux (Joint Editor), 1957; The Evolution of the Grail Legend, 1968; The Vision of Hell, 1970; Arthurian Romance: Seven Essays (Editor), 1970; Two Old French Gauvain Romances (Joint Editor), 1972; The Song of

Roland (Translator), 1972 (new edition, 1990); The Legend of Roland, 1973; Noble Lovers, 1975; Chrétien de Troyes, Arthurian Romances (Translator), 1987; A Chat Round the Old Course, 1990; Guillaume le Clerc, Fergus of Galloway (Translator), 1991; Eleanor of Aquitaine: Queen and Legend, 1993; The Romance of Reynard the Fox (Translator), 1994; William the Lion 1143-1214: Kingship and Culture, 1997. Recreation: golf. Address: (h.) 7 West Acres, St. Andrews, KY16 9UD; T.-01334 473329.

Owens, Agnes. Author; b. 24.5.26, Milngavie; m., Patrick Owens; 2 s.; 4 d. Educ. Bearsden Academy. Worked in shops, factories and offices; came to writing by accident; author of Gentlemen of the West (Autumn Book Award, 1984), Like Birds in the Wilderness, A Working Mother, People Like That; short stories in Lean Tales, The Seven Deadly Sins and The Seven Cardinal Virtues; wrote a play with Liz Lochhead which toured Scotland for three months. Recreations: walking; reading. Address: (h.) 21 Roy Young Avenue, Balloch, Dunbartonshire; T.-Alexandria 50921.

P

Pacione, Professor Michael, MA, PhD. Professor of Geography, Strathclyde University, since 1990; b. 14.10.47, Dundee; m., Christine Hopper; 1 s.; 1 d. Educ. Lawside Academy, Dundee; Dundee University. Lecturer in Geography, Queens University, Belfast, 1973-75; Lecturer, Senior Lecturer, Reader, Strathclyde University, Glasgow, 1975-89; Visiting Professor, University of Guelph, 1984, and University of Vienna, 1995. Publications: author of three books; editor of 17 books; 90 research papers. Recreations: sport; travel, photography. Address: (b.) Department of Geography, Strathclyde University, 50 Richmond Street, Glasgow G1 1XH; T.-0141-548 3793.

Pack, Professor Donald Cecil, CBE, MA, DSc, FIMA, FEIS, FRSE. Emeritus Professor, Strathclyde University, since 1986; b. 14.4.20, Higham Ferrers; m., Constance Mary Gillam; 2 s.; 1 d. Educ. Wellingborough School; New College, Oxford. Ordnance Board, Cambridge, 1941-43; Armament Research Department, Ministry of Supply, Fort Halstead, 1943-46; Lecturer in Mathematics, St. Andrews University, 1947-52; Visiting Research Associate, Maryland University, 1951-52; Lecturer in Mathematics, Manchester University, 1952-53; Professor of Mathematics, Strathclyde University, 1953-82 (Vice-Principal, 1968-72); Honorary Professor, 1982-86; Member, various Government scientific boards and committees, 1952-84; Member, Defence Scientific Advisory Council, 1975-80; First Hon. Member, European Consortium for Mathematics in Industry, 1988; Chairman, Scottish Certificate of Education Examination Board, 1969-77; Chairman, Committee of Inquiry into Truancy and Indiscipline in Scottish Schools, 1974-77 ("Pack Report" published by HMSO, 1977); Hon. President, National Youth Orchestra of Scotland (Chairman from foundation, 1978-88); Member, Scottish Arts Council, 1980-85; Member, UK Committee for European Music Year 1985 and Chairman, Scotland Advisory Committee, 1983-86; Member: General Teaching Council for Scotland, 1966-73, Dunbartonshire Education Committee, 1960-66; Governor, Hamilton College of Education, 1976-81; Council Member, Royal Society of Edinburgh, 1960-63; Honorary Treasurer and Council Member, Institute of Mathematics and its Applications, 1964-72; Member: International Advisory Committee on Rarefied Gas Dynamics Symposia, 1976-88, British National Committee for Theoretical Mechanics, 1973-78, Council, Gesellschaft fuer angewandte Mathematik und Mechanik, 1977-83; Guest Professor: Technische Universitaet, Berlin, 1967, Bologna University and Politechnico Milan, 1980, Technische Hochschule, Darmstadt, 1981; other visiting appointments, Warsaw University, 1977, Kaiserslautern University, 1980 and 1984. Past President: Edinburgh Mathematical Society, Glasgow Mathematical Association; Honorary President, Milngavie Music Club (President, 1983-93). Recreations: music; gardening; golf. Address: (h.) 18 Buchanan Drive, Bearsden, Glasgow G61 2EW; T.-0141-942 5764.

Pagan, Graeme Henry, BL, WS. Solicitor, Hosack & Sutherland, Oban, since 1960; Chairman, Oban Housing Association, since 1971; Honorary Sheriff of North Strathclyde at Oban, since 1988; b. 20.3.36, Cupar; m., Heather; 1 s.; 2 d. Educ. New Park, St. Andrews; Bedford School; Edinburgh University. Part-time Procurator Fiscal, Oban, 1970-79; Regional Organiser, Shelter Campaign for the Homeless, 1968-75; Founder Member, Oban Abbeyfield Society; Organiser, Scottish Solicitors Will Aid; Chairman, Argyll and Bute Liberal Democrats. Recreations: family; jazz; malt whisky; politics; wandering in the Highlands on foot and bike. Address: (h.) Neaveton, Oban, Argyll; T.-01631 563737.

Page, Professor Alan Chisholm, LLB, PhD. Professor of Public Law, Dundee University, since 1985; b. 7.4.52, Broughty Ferry; m., Sheila Duffus; 1 s.; 1 d. Educ. Grove Academy; Edinburgh University. Lecturer in Law, University College, Cardiff, 1975-80; Senior Lecturer in Law, Dundee University, 1980-85; Head, Department of Law, 1980-95; Dean, Faculty of Law, 1986-89; SHEFC Lead Assessor in Law, 1995-96; Member, Tax Law Review Committee, since 1994. Publications: Legislation; Investor Protection. Recreation: mountaineering. Address: (h.) Westlands, Westfield Road, Cupar, Fife KY15 5DR.

Paine, Nigel, Chief Executive, Scottish Council for Educational Technology, since 1990; b. 25.4.52. Educ. Haberdasher's Aske's Hatcham Boys' School; Reading University; East Anglia University. Visiting Professor, Napier University; English Speaking Union Thyne Scholar, 1984; Trustee, National Extension College, since 1987; Vice-Chair, Anniesland College, since 1993. Board Member, Network Scotland; Chairman, LEAD, LEAD Telematics; Fellow, Institute of Training and Development; Fellow, Royal Society of Arts. Recreations: running; reading. Address: 74 Victoria Crescent Road, Glasgow G12 9JN; T.-0141-337 5000.

Paisley of Westerlea (Duncan Wilson), FRSA, FSA (Scot). Landowner; Company Director; 16th Head of the Name; 5th Laird of the Barony of Westerlea; Captain, Balgonie Castle; Ambassador (Overseas), Capability Scotland; Patron, Westerlea School, Edinburgh; b. 30.8.48, Woodcote; m., Valerie R. Alcantra; 3 d. Educ. Cannock House School; Westwood. Regular Army, 1966-90 (Gordon Highlanders, RAOC) General List; King's Own Scottish Borderers, 1990-95; Regional Liaison Officer, Scottish Landowners' Federation, 1992-93; since 1993: Chief Assessor (Scotland), Guild of Master Craftsmen; Director, Delta One Security; Chairman, Westerlea Trust; President, Scottish Tartan Society; Director, Register of all Publicly Known Tartans; Freeman of Glasgow. Recreations: hill-walking; Scottish domestic architecture; family history. Address: (h.) Glen Annan House, Moffat, Dumfriesshire DG10 9RS; T.-01683 220014.

Palmer, Sheriff Charles William, LLB. Sheriff of Tayside, Central and Fife at Dunfermline, since 1992; b. 17.12.45. Sheriff of North Strathclyde at Dunoon and Dumbarton, 1986-92. Address: (b.) Dunfermline Sheriff Court, 1/6 Carnegie Drive, Dunfermline, KY12 7HJ.

Panton, John, MBE. Professional Golfer; b. 9.10.16, Pitlochry. Won PGA Match-Play Championship, 1956 (Runner-up, 1968); PGA British Seniors', 1967-69; World Seniors', 1967 (defeated Sam Snead for title); Silver King, 1950; Daks, 1951; North British-Harrogate, 1952; Goodwin Foursomes, 1952; Yorkshire Evening News, 1954; Gleneagles-Saxone Am.-Pro. Foursomes, 1956; Woodlawn Invitation Open (West Germany), 1958-59-60; leading British player, Open Championship, 1956; Leader, PGA Order of Merit (Vardon Trophy), 1951, won Scottish Professional Championship, seven times (and joint Champion, once); Ryder Cup player, 1951-53-61; awarded Golf Writers' Trophy, 1967; Hon. Professional, Royal and Ancient Golf Club, St. Andrews.

Paolozzi, Professor Sir Eduardo Luigi. Her Majesty's Sculptor in Ordinary for Scotland, since 1986; b. Leith, 7.3.24; 3 d. Full-time study, Edinburgh College of Art, Slade School of Fine Art, 1943-47; first exhibition, 1947; Instructor, Central School of Art and Design, 1949-55; Lecturer, St. Martin's School of Art, 1955-58; Tutor in Ceramics, Royal College of Art, London, 1968-89; Professor of Ceramics, Cologne, 1977-81; Professor of Sculpture, Munich, 1981-91; numerous awards, commissions, one-man and group exhibitions. Lives in London.

Park, Ian Michael Scott, CBE, MA, LLB. Partner, Paull & Williamsons, Advocates, Aberdeen, 1961-91, Consultant, since 1991; Member: Criminal Injuries Compensation Board, since 1983, Criminal Injuries Compensation Appeals Panel, since 1996; b. 7.4.38, Aberdeen; m., Elizabeth M.L. Struthers; 2 s. Educ. Aberdeen Grammar School; Aberdeen University. Assistant to, subsequently Partner in, Paull & Williamsons; Member, Society of Advocates in Aberdeen, since 1962, Treasurer, 1991-92, President, 1992-93; sometime part-time Assistant, Department of Public Law, Aberdeen University; President, Law Society of Scotland, 1980-81 (Council Member, 1974-85); Chairman, Aberdeen Citizens Advice Bureau, until 1988; Secretary, Aberdeen Granite Association, 1962-84; Temporary Sheriff, 1976-84; Honorary Sheriff at Aberdeen, since 1996; part-time Chairman, Medical Appeals Tribunals, until 1996; frequent broadcaster on legal topics. Recreations: golf; gardening. Address: (h.) 46 Rubislaw Den South, Aberdeen.

Park, Neil Ferguson, BSc, MBA. Administrator, Scottish Athletics Federation, since 1993; b. 26.9.62, Gosport; m., Judith Frances; 1 s.; 1 d. Educ. Daniel Stewart's and Melville College, Edinburgh; Aberdeen University; Edinburgh University. Former Assistant Secretary, Royal Highland and Agricultural Society; Executive Member: British Institute of Sports Administrators, Scottish Sports Association. Recreations: rugby; golf; road-running. Address: (b.) Caledonia House, South Gyle, Edinburgh EH12 9DQ.

Parker, Cameron Holdsworth, OBE, DL, BSc. Managing Director, Lithgows Limited, 1984-92, Vice-Chairman, 1992-97; b. 14.4.32, Dundee; m., Marlyne Honeyman; 3 s. Educ. Morrison's Academy, Crieff; Glasgow University. Managing Director, latterly also Chairman, John G. Kincaid & Co. Ltd., Greenock, 1967-80; Chairman and Chief Executive, Scott Lithgow Ltd., Port Glasgow, 1980-83; Board Member, British Shipbuilders, 1977-80, 1981-83; Chief Executive, Prosper Enginering Ltd., Irvine, 1983-84. Liveryman, Worshipful Company of Shipwrights; Member, Council, CBI Scotland, 1986-92; Member, Argyll and Clyde Health Board, 1991-95; Board Member, Scottish Homes, 1992-96; Director, Clyde Shaw Ltd., 1992-94. Recreation: golf. Address: (b.) Netherton, Langbank, Renfrewshire PA14 6YG; T.-01475 540692.

Parker, Professor Denis Michael, BA, PhD, CPsychol, FBPsS. Professor of Psychology, Glasgow Caledonian University, since 1996; Head, Department of Psychology, since 1996; b. 26. 6.43, Cork; m., Mannell Ruth; 3 s. Educ. St. Ignatius College, London; Durham University. Addison Wheeler Research Fellow, Durham University, 1969-71; Lecturer/Senior Lecturer/Reader in Psychology, Aberdeen University, 1972-95; Visiting Professor, University of Konstanz, 1995. Recreations: hill-walking; reading; cogitating. Address: (b.) Department of Psychology, Glasgow Caledonian University, Cowcaddens Road, Glasgow G4 0BA; T.-0141-331 3120.

Parker, Nicholas Sherren, MA (Cantab), FCA. Chartered Accountant; Partner, Coopers & Lybrand, since 1978 (Partner in charge, Corporate Finance Scotland); b. 11.6.46, Edinburgh; m., Julia Caroline Hamilton Dunlop; 1 s.; 2 d. Educ. Edinburgh Academy; St. Catharine's College, Cambridge. Recreations: shooting; golf; squash; fishing. Address: (b.) Erskine House, 68/73 Queen Street, Edinburgh EH2 4NH; T.-0131-226 4488.

Parker, Timothy Robert Walter, LLB. Depute Secretary to Church of Scotland General Trustees, since 1982; b. 7.10.44, Aberdeen; m., Janet Helen Nicol; 3 d. Educ. Trinity College, Glenalmond; Aberdeen University. Private practice as Solicitor, 1969-82. Chairman, Lothian Primary Schools Chess League; Past Chairman, Trinity Academy P.T.A.; Secretary, Lothian Federation of P.T.A.s; Committee Member, Viewpoint Housing Association.

Recreations: bowling; walking; watching other sports; listening to music. Address: (h.) 35 Dudley Avenue, Edinburgh EH6 4PL; T.-0131-554 2076.

Parkins, Professor James J., BSc (Hons), PhD, CBiol, FIBiol. Professor of Animal Health, Glasgow Veterinary School (Director, Cochno Farm and Research Centre); b. 27.7.45, Tynemouth; m., Elma; 1 s.; 1 d. Educ. Wolverhampton Grammar School; Glasgow University. Lecturer in Veterinary Animal Husbandry, 1970; Senior Lecturer, 1983, Reader, 1990, Glasgow University Veterinary School. Publications: over 100 papers. Recreations: the country; golf; music. Address: (b.) Glasgow University Veterinary School, Bearsden Road, Glasgow G61 1QH; T.-0141-330 5700.

Parnell, Brian K., BSc, ACGI, DipTP, FRTPI. Planning Consultant; Vice-Chairman and Hon. Secretary, Scottish Council for National Parks, since 1991; Visiting Professor, Centre for Planning, Strathclyde University, since 1991; b. 18.12.22, Brighton; 2 s.; 1 d. Educ. Varndean School, Brighton; London University; Edinburgh College of Art. Captain, EME, 1943-47; Department of Planning, Midlothian County Council, 1949-57; Depute Planning Officer, Stirling County Council, 1957-64; joined Glasgow School of Art, 1964, Head, Department of Planning, 1976-87; Commissioner, Countryside Commission for Scotland, 1968-80; part-time Planning Inquiry Reporter, Scottish Office, 1982-93. Chairman, Scottish Branch, Royal Town Planning Institute, 1972-73; Executive Committee Member, National Trust for Scotland, 1973-83; Trustee, Scottish Civic Trust, since 1985; Convener, Stirling Civic Trust, since 1994. Recreations: sailing; swimming; hill-walking; travel. Address: (h.) 15 Park Terrace, Stirling FK8 2JT; T.-01786 465714.

Parr, Professor John Brian, BSc (Econ), MA, PhD. Professor of Regional and Urban Economics, Glasgow University, since 1989; Chairman, British-Irish Section, Regional Science Association, 1981-85; b. 18.3.41, Epsom; m., Pamela Jean Harkins; 2 d. Educ. Henry Thornton School; London University; University of Washington. Instructor, University of Washington, 1966; Assistant Professor/Associate Professor, University of Pennsylvania, 1967-75; joined Glasgow University as Lecturer, 1975. Editor, Papers of the Regional Science Association, 1968-75; Associate Editor, Journal of Regional Science, since 1979; Co-Editor, European Research in Regional Science, since 1990; Member, Board of Management, Urban Studies, since 1981; Associate Editor, Annals of Regional Science, 1993-96; Member, Editorial Board, International Regional Science Review, since 1995; Member, Editorial Board, Review of Urban and Regional Development Studies, since 1995. Publications: numerous journal articles on urban and regional analysis; Christaller Central Place Structures (Co-Author); Regional Policy: Past Experience and New Directions (Co-Editor); Analysis of Regional Structure: Essays in Honour of August Lösch (Co-Editor); Market Centers and Retail Location (Co-Author). Address: (b.) Department of Urban Studies, Glasgow University, Glasgow G12 8RS; T.-0141-339 8855, Ext. 4724/5048.

Parratt, Professor James Roy, BPharm, MSc, PhD, DSc, MD (h.c.), FRCPath, DipRelStudies (Cantab), FRPharmS, FESC, FIBiol, FRSE. Professor of Cardiovascular Pharmacology, Strathclyde University, since 1983 (Head, Department of Physiology and Pharmacology, 1986-90); b. 19.8.33, London; m., Pamela Joan Lyndon Marels; 2 s.; 1 d. Educ. St. Clement Danes Holborn Estate Grammar School; London University. Spent nine years in Nigeria as Head of Pharmacology, Nigerian School of Pharmacy, then in Physiology, University Medical School, Ibadan; joined Strathclyde University, 1967; appointed Reader, 1970; Personal Professor, Department of Physiology and Pharmacology, 1975-83. Chairman, Cardiac Muscle Research Group, 1980-83; Vice President, European Shock

Society, since 1995; Gold Medal, Szeged University, 1975; Honorary Member, Hungarian Pharmacological Society, 1983; Honorary Doctorate, Albert Szent-Gyorgi Medical University, Hungary, 1989; Gold J.E. Purkyne Honorary Medal, Academy of Sciences of Czech Republic, 1995; Sodalem honoris causa, Slovak Medical and Cardiological Societies, 1997; Chairman, Universities and Colleges Christian Fellowship, 1984-90; former Vice-Chairman, Scripture Union; Past Chairman, SUM Fellowship; Lay Preacher, Baptist Unions of Scotland and Great Britain; Honorary President, Baptist Lay Preachers Association of Scotland, 1985-90. Recreation: music. Address: (h.) 16 Russell Drive, Bearsden, Glasgow G61 3BD; T.-0141-942 7164.

Parsons, Professor Ian, BSc, PhD, FRSE. Professor of Mineralogy, Edinburgh University, since 1988, Head, Department of Geology and Geophysics, 1993-96; b. 5.9.39, Manchester; m., Brenda Mary Reah; 3 s. Educ. Beckenham and Penge Grammar School; Durham University. DSIR Research Fellow, Manchester University, 1963-64; Aberdeen University: Assistant Lecturer, 1964-65, Lecturer, 1965-77, Senior Lecturer, 1977-83, Professor, 1983-88. Member, NERC Earth Sciences Research Grants and Training Awards Committee; President, Mineralogical Society, 1994-95; Member, NCC Committee for Scotland, 1985-90. Recreations: skiing; hill-walking; music. Address: (b.) Department of Geology and Geophysics, Edinburgh University, West Mains Road, Edinburgh, EH9 3JW; T.-0131-650 8512.

Parvin, Gilmour W., MA, AIIMR. Investment Consultant; Chair, Scottish Tory Reform Group. Educ. Glasgow University. Address: (h.) 26 Cramond Avenue, Edinburgh EH4 6NE; T.-0131-312 7803.

Paternoster, Rev. Canon Michael Cosgrove, MA. Rector, St. James' Episcopal Church, Aberdeen, since 1990; Honorary Canon, St. Paul's Cathedral, Dundee, since 1981; b. 13.5.35, East Molesey, Surrey; m., Careth Osborne. Educ. Kingston Grammar School; Pembroke College, Cambridge; Cuddesdon Theological College. Deacon, 1961; Priest, 1962; Curate, St. Andrew's, Surbiton, 1961-63; Chaplain to Anglican students in Dundee, 1964-68; Secretary, Fellowship of St. Alban and St. Sergius, 1968-71; Rector, St. James', Dollar, 1971-75; Rector, St. James's, Stonehaven, 1975-90; Secretary, Inter-Church Relations Committee, Scottish Episcopal Church, 1975-82; Member, Doctrine Committee, Scottish Episcopal Church, 1980-91; Aberdeen and N.E. Wing Chaplain, Air Training Corps, 1985-92; Director of Ordinands, Diocese of Aberdeen and Orkney, since 1995. Publications: Thou art There Also, 1967; Stronger Than Death, 1972. Recreations: reading; sketching; bird-watching; listening to music. Address: 31 Gladstone Place, Aberdeen AB10 6UX; T.-01224 322631.

Paterson, Professor Alan Alexander, LLB (Hons), DPhil (Oxon), FRSA, FRSE. Professor of Law, Strathclyde University, since 1984; b. 5.6.47, Edinburgh; m., Alison Jane Ross Lowdon; 2 s.; 1 d. Educ. Edinburgh Academy; Edinburgh University; Pembroke College, Oxford. Research Associate, Oxford Centre for Socio-Legal Studies, 1972-73; Lecturer, Law Faculty, Edinburgh University, 1973-84; Visiting Professor, University of New Mexico Law School, 1982, 1986. Former Chairman, Scottish Legal Action Group and British and Irish Legal Education and Technology Association; Chairman, Legal Services Group, Citizens Advice Scotland. Publications: The Law Lords, 1982; The Legal System of Scotland (Co-author), 1993. Address: (b.) Strathclyde University Law School, 173 Cathedral Street, Glasgow G4 ORQ; T.-0141-552 4400, Ext. 3341.

Paterson, Brenda, MA (Hons). News and Current Affairs Presenter, BBC Scotland, since 1991; b. 1.6.59, Aberdeen.

Educ. Inverness Royal Academy; Edinburgh University. Reporter, Radio Clyde, 1984-86; BBC Network Radio, 1986-89 (Producer, Today, Radio 4, Newsbeat, Radio 1, and From Our Own Correspondent, Radio 4); Reporter/Presenter, Scottish Television, 1989-91. Recreations: yoga (qualified teacher); theatre; massive amount of reading. Address: (b.) BBC Scotland, Queen Margaret Drive, Glasgow G12 8DG.

Paterson, Douglas McCallum, MA, MEd, DMS, DipM, MIM. Chief Executive, Aberdeen City Council, since 1995; b. 20.11.49, Macduff; m., Isobel Beaton; 2 d. Educ. Banff Academy; Aberdeen University; Robert Gordon University. John Wood Group, 1971-75; Grampian Regional Council: Teacher, 1976-81, Head Teacher, 1981-86, Advisor, 1986-90, Depute Director of Education, 1990-92, Senior Depute Director, 1992-94, Director of Education, 1994-95. Recreations: local history; fishing industry; music; walking; theatre. Address: (b.) Town House, Aberdeen; T.-01224 522500.

Paterson, Lt. Col. Howard Cecil, TD, FSA Scot. International Tourism Consultant and Artist; b. 16.3.20, Edinburgh; m., Isabelle Mary; 1 s. Educ. Daniel Stewart's College, Edinburgh; Edinburgh College of Art. Army, 1939-49; combat duties during War; personnel selection afterwards; Territorial Army, 1949-70; serves on East Scotland TAVR Committee; Founder, Gunner Heritage Appeal; Member, City of Edinburgh Artillery Officers' Association; Member, 52nd Lowland Division Officers' Club; Assistant Personnel Manager, Jute Industries Ltd., Dundee, 1949-51; Organising Secretary, Scottish Country Industries Development Trust, 1951-66; Senior Director, Scottish Tourist Board, 1966-81. Chairman, Taste of Scotland Ltd., 1984-86; Vice-Chairman, John Buchan Society, 1990-95; Member, Scottish Committee, British Horse Society; Chairman, Trekking and Riding Society of Scotland. Publications: Tourism in Scotland; Flavour of Edinburgh (with Catherine Brown). Recreations: fishing; shooting; riding; writing; drawing and painting; natural history; history. Address: (h.) Dovewood, West Linton, Peeblesshire, EH46 7DS; T.-01968 60346.

Paterson, Sheriff James Veitch, MA (Oxon), LLB (Edin). Sheriff of Lothian and Borders at Jedburgh, Selkirk and Duns, since 1963; b. 16.4.28; m., Ailie Campbell Clark Hutchison; 1 s.; 1 d. Educ. Edinburgh Academy; Lincoln College, Oxford; Edinburgh University. Admitted Faculty of Advocates, 1953.

Paterson, Rev. John Love, MA, BD, STM, FSA Scot. Minister, St. Michael's Parish Church, Linlithgow, since 1977; Chaplain to The Queen, since 1996; b. 6.5.38, Ayr; m., Lorna Begg (see Lorna Marion Paterson). Educ. Ayr Academy; Glasgow University; Edinburgh University; Union Theological Seminary, New York. Minister: Presbyterian Church of East Africa, 1964-72, St. Andrew's, Nairobi, 1968-72; Chaplain, Stirling University, 1973-77. Moderator, West Lothian Presbytery, 1985. Recreation: gardening. Address: St. Michael's Manse, Linlithgow, West Lothian; T.-01506 842195.

Paterson, John Moore, JP. Provost, Stirling Council, since 1996; b. 25.7.44, Stirling; m., Isabel; 1 s.; 3 d. Educ. Riverside Secondary School. Former Stirling District Councillor; Convener, Stirling Shadow Council, 1995-96. Recreations: walking; listening to music; oil painting. Address: (h.) 26 Craighall Street, Stirling.

Paterson, Very Rev. John Munn Kirk, ACII, MA, BD, DD. Minister Emeritus, St. Paul's Church, Milngavie; b. 8.10.22, Leeds; m., Geraldine Lilian Parker; 2 s.; 1 d. Educ. Hillhead High School; Edinburgh University. Pilot, RAF, 1940-46; Insurance official, 1946-58; ordained Minister, Church of Scotland, 1964; Minister, St. John's Church,

Bathgate, 1964-70; Minister, St. Paul's Church, Milngavie, 1970-87. Moderator, General Assembly, Church of Scotland, 1984-85; Life Member, Chartered Insurance Institute; Hon. Doctorate, Aberdeen University, 1986. Recreations: fishing; gardening. Address: (h.) 58 Orchard Drive, Edinburgh EH4 2DZ; T.-0131-332 5876.

Paterson, Lorna Marion, MA, Dip.Rel.Ed. General Secretary, Church of Scotland Guild, since 1985; b. 26.1.38, Unst; m., Rev. John L. Paterson (qv). Educ. Inverurie Academy; Aberden University; Aberdeen College of Education. Teacher of English, History, Geography and Religious Education, 1960-62; Teacher of English, 1962-66; Administrative Assistant, Strathclyde University, 1966-68; Deputy Academic Registrar, then Education Administrator, Stirling University, 1968-79. Guider (Division Commissioner, West Lothian, 1982-85); Vice Chairman, Linlithgow Arts Guild, since 1996; Elder, St. Michael's Parish Church, Linlithgow, since 1995. Recreations: singing; homemaking; church activities; the arts; people. Address: (h.) St. Michael's Manse, Kirkgate, Linlithgow EH49 7AL; T.-0131-225 5722.

Paterson, Mary Sylvia. Secretary, Edinburgh Consumer Group, since 1977; Chairman, Morningside Community Council, since 1995; b. 28.7.37, Hampstead Heath, London; m., Richard Cruickshanks Paterson (deceased); 2 s. Educ. Hornsey High School, London. Westminster Bank Ltd., 1954-55; GPO Continental Telephone Exchange, 1955-56; Scottish Widows Fund, 1957-61; freelance market research. Member, Edinburgh CAB Executive Committee, several years; Member, Post Officers Users' Council for Scotland, 1976-82; Member, Scottish Committee, Meat and Livestock Commission, 1990-95; Member, Executive, National Federation of Consumer Groups, 1993-97.Recreations: music; walking; crosswords. Address: (h.) 9 Comiston Terrace, Edinburgh EH10 6AJ; T.-0131-447 4148.

Paterson, Stuart Andrew. Dumfries and Galloway Arts Association/Scottish Arts Council Writing Fellow, 1996-98; poet; b. 31.1.66, Truro. Educ. James Hamilton Academy, Kilmarnock; Stirling University. Writing Fellow, Morven Day Care Centre, Kilmarnock, 1995-96; Founder/Editor, Spectrum (poetry/prose review), 1991-97; Writers' Workshop Leader, Harbour Arts Centre, Irvine, 1996; poems anthologised in UK and America; Eric Gregory Award, 1992; SAC Writer's Bursary, 1993. Publications: Mulaney of Larne and Other Poems, 1991; Saving Graces, 1997. Recreations: travel; music; football; malts. Address: (b.) Gracefield Arts Centre, 28 Edinburgh Road, Dumfries DG1 1JQ; T.-01387 260445.

Paterson, (Thomas) Michael, DA. Artist; Educational Television Producer and Consultant; b. 14.4.38, Kirkcaldy; m., Joan; 1 s.; 2 d. Educ. George Watson's Boys' College; Edinburgh College of Art; Moray House College of Education. Teacher of Art, Waid Academy, Anstruther, 1960-64; Special Assistant, George Heriot's, Edinburgh, 1964-67; Head of Art, Marr College, Troon, 1967-69; Lecturer and Programme Director, College Television Service, Craigie College of Education, 1969-80, Governor, 1979-80; Assistant Head of Educational Programmes, Scottish Television, 1981-89, Head of Education, 1989-91. ETMA: Chairman (Scotland), 1979-80, 1993-95, National Executive, since 1978, National Deputy Chairman, 1993-94, Chairman, 1994-96; RTS Awards Convener, 1981-86, Chairman, RTS Scottish Centre, and Member of Council, 1986-88; Member, Publicity Committee, General Assembly, Church of Scotland, 1983-86, Board of Communication, 1986-90, 1994-95, Convener, A/V Production Committee, 1986-88; Chairman, Editorial Board, Journal of Educational Media, 1994-96; Member, Educational Services Committee, South Ayrshire Council, since 1996. Publication: A Primary Art Course (Co-author). Recreations: golf at Turnberry; travel; gardening; reading. Address: (h.) 1 Laurelbank Road, Maybole KA19 8BE.

Paterson, William, BSc (Eng), CEng, FIEE, MRAeS. Director of Engineering, Northern Lighthouse Board, since 1987; b. 24.7.40, Neilston; m., Margaret Quirie Forrest Gerrard; 2 s.; 2 d. Educ. Paisley Grammar School; Strathclyde University. Radio Officer, Merchant Navy; Technician, then Engineer, Civil Aviation Authority; Head, Radio Department, Northern Lighthouse Board. Recreation: gardening; golf. Address: (b.) 84 George Street, Edinburgh EH2 3DA; T.-0131-226 7051.

Paterson, (William) Guthrie (Wilson), BSc, MSc, CertEd. Vice-Principal, Scottish Agricultural College, since 1989; b. 5.6.40, Blantyre; m., Mary Isabel; 1 s.; 1 d. Educ. Hamilton Academy; Glasgow University; Jordanhill College of Education; Aberdeen University. Lecturer in Crop Husbandry, North of Scotland College of Agriculture, 1965-73; Senior Agronomy Specialist, West of Scotland Agricultural College, 1973-83; Head, Crop Production Department, North of Scotland College of Agriculture, 1983-93. Recreations: golf; gardening; music; reading. Address: (b.) The Scottish Agricultural College, Ferguson Building, Craibstone Estate, Bucksburn, Aberdeen AB21 9YA; T.-01224 711000.

Paterson, Wilma, DRSAM. Freelance Composer/ Writer/Journalist; b. 23.4.44, Dundee; 1 s.; 1 d. Educ. Harris Academy; Royal Scottish Academy of Music. Composition study with Luigi Dallapiccola in Florence; writes all types of music (chamber, orchestral, incidental); music reviews for Glasgow Herald and The Independent; broadcasts and writes on food, plants, travel. Publications: A Country Cup; Was Byron Anorexic?; Shoestring Gourmet; Flowers and Herbs of the Bible; Lord Byron's Relish; Salmon & Women, The Feminine Angle; Songs of Scotland (with Alasdair Gray). Address: Greystones, 30 Kelvinside Gardens, Glasgow G20 6BB; T.-0141-946 2236.

Paterson-Brown, June, CBE, MBChB. Commonwealth Chief Commissioner, Girl Guides Association, 1985-90; Vice-Chairman, Princes Trust, 1982-92; Non-Executive Director, Border Television plc, since 1980; b. 8.2.32, Edinburgh; m., Peter Neville Paterson-Brown (qv); 3 s.; 1 d. Educ. Esdaile School; Edinburgh University. Medical Officer, Family Planning and Well Woman's Clinics, 1959-85; Past Chairman: County of Roxburghshire Youth Committee, Roxburgh Duke of Edinburgh Award Committee; Scottish Chief Commissioner, Girl Guides Association, 1977-82; Chairman, Borders Region Children's Panel Advisory Committee, 1982-85; Chairman, Scottish Standing Conference of Voluntary Youth Organisations, 1983-85; Trustee, MacRobert Trusts, since 1987; Trustee, Prince's Trust, 1982-94; Paul Harris Fellow, 1990; Deputy Lieutenant, Roxburgh, Ettrick and Lauderdale, since 1990. Address: (h.) Norwood, Hawick, Roxburghshire TD9 7HP; T.-01450 372352.

Paterson-Brown, Peter Neville, MBChB, DObst RCOG. Medical Practitioner, since 1957; b. 23.3.51, Hawick; m., June Garden (see June Paterson-Brown); 3 s.; 1 d. Educ. Merchiston Castle School; Edinburgh University. Medical Adviser, Red Cross Scotland, 1981-94; Member, Scottish Committee, Medical Commission on Accident Prevention, since 1978; Director, Children's Hospice Association Scotland, since 1993; Vice President, React, since 1991. Red Cross Badge of Honour, 1995. Publication: A Matter of Life or Death. Recreations: skiing; shooting; golf; fishing. Address: (h.) Norwood, Hawick, Roxburghshire; T.-01450 372352.

Paton, Alasdair Chalmers, BSc, CEng, FICE, FCIWEM. Chief Executive, Scottish Environment Protection Agency, since 1995; Director and Chief Engineer, Engineering, Water and Waste Directorate, Scottish Office Environment Department, 1991-95; b. 28.11.44, Paisley; m., Zona G. Gill; 1 s.; 1 d. Educ. John Neilson Institution, Paisley; Glasgow University. Assistant Engineer, Clyde Port

Authority, 1967-71; Assistant Engineer, DAFS, 1971-72; Senior Engineer, SDD, 1972-77; Engineer, Public Works Department, Hong Kong Government, 1977-80; Senior Engineer, then Principal Engineer, SDD, 1980-87; Deputy Chief Engineer, 1987-91. Recreations: Rotary; sailing; golf. Address: (b.) Erskine Court, Castle Business Park, Stirling FK9 4TR; T.-01786 457701.

Paton, Ann, QC, MA, LLB. Admitted to Scottish Bar, 1977. Address: (b.) Advocates' Library, Parliament House, Edinburgh.

Paton, David Romer, OBE, FRICS, IRRV, FSA Scot. Chartered Surveyor; b. 5.3.35, Aberdeen; m., Juliette Burney; 2 s. Educ. Gordonstoun School; Keble College, Oxford. Chartered Surveyor in own practice; Past President, Aberdeen Chamber of Commerce; Past Chairman: Gordon Conservative and Unionist Association, Royal Northern & University Club, Scottish Chambers of Commerce, Aberdeen Beyond 2000, Grampian-Houston Association; former Member: North East River Purification Board, Salmon Advisory Committee; Secretary of State Appointee, Scottish Office Scottish Salmon Strategy Task Force; Chairman: Aberdeen Harbour Board, North East Scotland Preservation Trust, Don District Salmon Fishery Board, NE Committee and Vice President, Scottish Council (Development and Industry); Member, Aberdeen Committee, Order of St. John, and of Aberdeen Committee, St. John Association; Member, Aberdeen Macmillan Cancer Relief; President: Aberdeen Civic Society, Friends of Grampian Stones; Member: North of Scotland Water Authority, Architectural Heritage Society of Scotland, Association of Scottish District Salmon Fishery Boards; Trustee, Scottish Civic Trust; Grampian Initiative Ambassador. Address: Grandhome, Aberdeen AB22 8AR; T.-01224 722202.

Paton, George, MA, MEd, FEIS, FITD. Director, Scottish Council for Educational Technology, 1986-90; b. 5.12.31, Rutherglen; m., 1, Barbara Thomson (deceased); 2 s.; 2, J. Honor Smith. Educ. Rutherglen Academy; Glasgow University. National Service, RAEC, 1953-55; Schoolteacher, 1955-61; Lecturer in English, Jordanhill College of Education, 1961-63; Principal Lecturer in English, then Assistant Principal, Dundee College of Education, 1963-69; Principal, Hamilton College of Education, 1970-81; Depute Director, Scottish Council for Educational Technology, 1982-86. President, International Council for Educational Media, 1989-91; Member, Library Information Service Committee (Scotland), 1984-91; Executive Committee Member, Commonwealth Institute Scotland, 1985-96; Governor, David Livingstone Memorial Trust, since 1971 (Chairman, since 1994); former Convener, Education Committee, General Teaching Council for Scotland; Chairman, Strathclyde Committee, Tenovus–Scotland (for medical research in Scotland), since 1991; Elder, Church of Scotland. Recreations: singing; drama; gardening. Address: (h.) 16 Old Bothwell Road, Bothwell, Glasgow G71 8AW.

Paton, William, BSc (Hons). Chief Executive, National Engineering Assessment Group; Director, National Engineering Laboratory; b. 29.11.41, Kilwinning; m., Elizabeth Anne; 2 s. Educ. Douglas Ewart School, Newton Stewart; Glasgow University. Consulting Geophysicist, Seismograph Services Ltd., 1963; Management Trainee, Colvilles Ltd., Ravenscraig, 1964; Research Scientist in Materials, NEL, 1965-76; Offshore Supplies Office, 1976-77; Divisional Manager, Materials Engineering Division, then Controller, Design, Materials and Systems Department, NEL, 1977-87. Recreation: golf. Address: (b.) National Engineering Laboratory, East Kilbride, Glasgow; T.-East Kilbride 20222.

Patrick, James McIntosh, OBE (1997), RSA, LLD, ROI, ARE. Artist and Landscape Painter; b. 4.2.07, Dundee; m.,

Janet Watterston (deceased); 1 s.; 1 d. Educ. Morgan Academy, Dundee; Glasgow School of Art. Guthrie Award, RSA, 1935; paintings in numerous national and municipal collections; Hon. LLD, Dundee, 1973; Fellowship: Duncan of Jordanstone College of Art, Glasgow School of Art; D.Arts, Abertay University, Dundee, 1995. Address: (h.) The Shrubbery, Magdalen Yard Road, Dundee.

Patrick, Sheriff (Lilian) Gail, MA, LLB. Sheriff of Tayside, Central and Fife at Kirkcaldy, since 1991; b. 24.12.41. Enrolled as Solicitor, 1966; former Lecturer and Tutor, Glasgow University and Edinburgh University; admitted to Faculty of Advocates, 1981; called to the Bar, Lincoln's Inn, 1990.

Patterson, Professor Henry Desmond, BSc, MSc, DSc, CMath, FRSE. Honorary Professor, Mathematics and Statistics Department, Edinburgh University, since 1985; b. 17.7.24, Whitby; m., Janet Mary Roffe; 1 s. Educ. Northallerton Grammar School; Pickering Grammar School; Ripon Grammar School; Leeds University. Department of Scientific and Industrial Research, 1946-47; Rothamsted Experimental Station, 1947-67; Agricultural Research Council Unit of Statistics, Edinburgh University, 1967-85. Recreations: music; mathematical and statistical programming. Address: (h.) 15 Kings Grove, Longniddry EH32 0QW; T.-01875 853012.

Patterson, Rev. John Wallace, BA, BD. Clerk, Presbytery of St. Andrews, since 1974; b. 7.1.23, Coleraine; m., Catherine Mackay Cape; 4 d. Educ. Coleraine Academical Institution; Trinity College, Dublin; St. Andrews University. Minister: Church of the Holy Rude, Stirling, 1948-50; Prestwick North Church, 1950-58; St. Andrews Martyrs Church, 1958-89. Address: 34 Claybraes, St. Andrews KY16 8RS; T.-01334 473606.

Patterson, Lindy Ann, LLB (Hons), ACIArb. Lawyer; Partner, MacRoberts; b. 12.9.58, Berwick-upon-Tweed. Educ. Eyemouth High School; Edinburgh University. UK National Vice-President, Association Internationale de Jeunes Avocats, 1991-94; Member, Commercial Court Consultative Committee; Member, Law Commission Contract Law Advisory Group; Scotland's first female Solicitor Advocate (May, 1993); Member, Judicial Procedure Committee and Rights of Audience Working Party, Law Society of Scotland. Recreations: skiing; hill-walking. Address: (b.) 27 Melville Street, Edinburgh.

Patterson, Walter Moffat, MSc, BSc. HM Staff Inspector (Computing Studies); b. 14.6.45, Airdrie; m., Colleen McCrone (Toronto); 1 s.; 1 d. Educ. Coatbridge High School; Strathclyde University. Lecturer in Statistics, Paisley College; Development Officer, Glacier Metal Co., Kilmarnock, 1973-74; Lecturer in Statistics, Paisley College, 1974-83; Senior Lecturer in Information Technology, MEDC, Paisley College, 1983-86. Recreations: gardening; computing; golf. Address: (b.) EID:PS, Floor 1 West, Victoria Quay, Edinburgh, EH6 6QQ; T.-0131-244 0902.

Pattison, David Arnold, BSc, PhD. Director of Leisure and Tourism Consulting, Scott Wilson Resource Consultants; Hon. President, Scottish Youth Hostels Association; Hon. Professor, Queen Margaret College, Edinburgh; b. 9.2.41, Kilmarnock; m., Anne Ross Wilson; 2 s.; 1 d. Educ. Kilmarnock Academy; Glasgow University. Planning Assistant, Ayr County Council, 1963-64; PhD studies, Glasgow University, 1964-66; Planning Assistant, Dunbarton County Council, 1966-67; Lecturer, Strathclyde University, 1967-70; Head of Tourism, Highlands and Islands Development Board, 1970-81; Chief Executive, Scottish Tourist Board, 1981-85; Director Leisure & Tourism Consulting, Ernst & Young, 1985-89. External Examiner for postgraduate tourism courses, Strathclyde University, 1981-84. Recreations: reading; watching soccer and rugby; golf; gardening. Address: (h.) 7 Cramond Glebe Gardens, Cramond, Edinburgh EH4 6NZ.

Pattison, Rev. Kenneth John, MA, BD, STM. Minister, Kilmuir and Logie Easter, Ross-shire, since 1996; b. 22.4.41, Glasgow; m., Susan Jennifer Brierley Jenkins; 1 s.; 2 d. Educ. Lenzie Academy; Glasgow University; Union Theological Seminary, New York. Minister, Church of Central Africa Presbyterian, Malawi, 1967-77; Minister, Park Parish Church, Ardrossan, 1977-84; Chaplain, Glasgow Royal Infirmary, 1984-90; Associate Minister, St. Andrew's and St. George's, Edinburgh, 1990-96. Convener, Chaplaincies Committee, Church of Scotland, 1993-96. Recreations: hill-walking; swimming; gardening; family history. Address: (h.) The Manse, Delny, Invergordon, IV18 0NW; T.-01862 842 280.

Pattullo, Sir (David) Bruce, Kt, CBE, BA, LLD (Hon), DUniv, FRSE, FCIB (Scot). Governor: Bank of Scotland, since 1991; Director (Non-Executive): British Linen Bank, since 1977, Bank of Wales PLC, since 1986, NWS Bank, since 1986; b. 2.1.38, Edinburgh; m., Fiona Jane Nicholson; 3 s.; 1 d. Educ. Belhaven Hill School; Rugby; Hertford College, Oxford. National Service commission, Royal Scots (seconded to West Africa); joined Bank of Scotland, 1961; winner, first prize, Institute of Bankers in Scotland, 1964; Manager, Investment Services Department, 1967-71; Deputy Manager, Bank of Scotland Finance Co. Ltd., 1971-73; Chief Executive, Group Merchant Banking Activities, 1973-78; Deputy Treasurer, 1978; Treasurer and General Manager, 1979-88; Group Chief Executive and a Deputy Governor, Bank of Scotland, 1988-91. Chairman, Committee of Scottish Clearing Bankers, 1987-89. Recreations: tennis; hill-walking. Address: (b.) Bank of Scotland, Head Office, The Mound, Edinburgh EH1 1YZ; T.-0131-243 5555.

Paul, Eur Ing Professor John P., BSc, PhD, ARCST, FEng, FIMechE, FISPO, cFBOA, FRSA, FRSE, FIPEMB. Professor, Bioengineering Unit, Strathclyde University, since 1972; Visiting Professor, Queen Margaret College, Edinburgh, since 1992; b. 26.6.27, Sunderland; m., Elizabeth R. Graham; 1 s.; 2 d. Educ. Aberdeen Grammar School; Allan Glen's School, Glasgow; Royal College of Science and Technology, Glasgow; Glasgow University. Successively Research Assistant, Lecturer and Senior Lecturer in Mechanics of Materials, Royal College of Science and Technology, subsequently Strathclyde University, 1949-69; Visiting Professor, West Virginia University, 1969-70; Reader, then Professor, Bioengineering Unit, Strathclyde University, since 1970. President, International Society of Biomechanics, 1987-89; Chairman, British Standard, European Standard and International Standard Committees on Joint Replacements, 1992. Publications: Computing in Medicine (Senior Editor), 1981; Biomaterials in Artificial Organs (Senior Editor), 1984; Disability (Co-Editor), 1979; Total Knee Joint Replacement (Co-Editor), 1988. Recreations: formerly rugby; gardening; home maintenance; light reading. Address: (h.) 25 James Watt Road, Milngavie, Glasgow G62 7JX; T.-0141-956 3221.

Pawley, Professor G. Stuart, MA, PhD, FRSE, FRS. Professor of Computational Physics, Edinburgh University, since 1985; b. 22.6.37, Ilford; m., Anthea Jean Miller; 2 s.; 1 d. Educ. Bolton School; Corpus Christi College, Cambridge. Lecturer, Edinburgh University, 1964; Reader, 1970; Personal Chair, 1985; Guest Professor, Aarhus University, Denmark, 1969-70. Recreations: choral singing; mountain walking. Address: (b.) Physics Department, Kings Buildings, Edinburgh University EH9 3JZ; T.-0131-650 5300.

Paxton, Professor Roland Arthur, MBE, MSc, CEng, FICE, FRSE, AMCST. Chairman, Institution of Civil Engineers Panel for Historical Engineering Works, since

1990; Commissioner, Royal Commission on the Ancient and Historic Monuments of Scotland, since 1993; Hon. Professor, Civil and Offshore Engineering, Heriot Watt University, since 1994; b. 29.6.32, Altrincham; m., Ann; 2 d. Educ. Altrincham Grammar School; Manchester College of Science and Technology; Heriot Watt University. Cartographic surveyor, Ordnance Survey, 1953-55; Civil Engineer, Corporations of Manchester, Leicester, Edinburgh, and Lothian Regional Council, retiring as Senior Principal Engineer, 1959-90; Hon. Senior Research Fellow, Heriot Watt University, 1990-94. Chairman, Forth Bridges Visitor Centre Trust; Secretary and Director, Laigh Milton Viaduct Conservation Project; President, Edinburgh Bibliographical Society, 1992-95; author of books and papers on technical innovation and historical engineering. Address: (b.) Civil and Offshore Engineering, Heriot Watt University, Edinburgh EH14 4AS; T.-0131-449 5111.

Payne, Professor Peter Lester, BA, PhD, FRHistS, FRSE. Emeritus Professor, Aberdeen University; Professor of Economic History, Aberdeen University, 1969-95; b. 31.12.29, London; m., Enid Christine Rowntree; 1 s.; 1 d. Educ. Brockley County School, London; Nottingham University. Visiting Lecturer in American Economic History, Johns Hopkins University, 1957-58; Lecturer in Economic and Social History, Nottingham University, 1958-59; Colquhoun Lecturer in Business History, Glasgow University, 1959-69; Senior Lecturer in Economic History, Glasgow University, 1964-69; Sherman Fairchild Distinguished Scholar, California Institute of Technology, Pasadena, 1977-78. Vice-President, Business Archives Council; Member, Business Archives Council of Scotland; President, Aberdeen and North of Scotland Philatelic Society, 1995-97. Publications include: Rubber and Railways in the Nineteenth Century; British Entrepreneurship in the Nineteenth Century; Colvilles and the Scottish Steel Industry; The Early Scottish Limited Companies; The Hydro; Growth and Contraction: Scottish Industry c. 1860-1990; Northern Scotland (Editor). Recreations: philately; woodwork. Address: (h.) 7 Kirkton Road, Westhill, Skene, Aberdeenshire, AB32 6LF; T.-01224 744703.

Peacock, Professor Sir Alan Turner, Kt (1987), DSC (1945), MA, HonDUniv (Stirling), Hon. DEcon (Zurich), Hon. DScEcon (Buckingham), HonDUniv (Brunel), HonDUniv (York), HonLLD (St. Andrews), HonLLD (Dundee), HonDSc (Edinburgh), Hon. Fellow (LSE), Lib Doc (Catania), FBA, FRSE. Research Professor in Public Finance, Edinburgh Business School, Heriot-Watt University, since 1985; b. 26.6.22, Ryton-on-Tyne; m., Margaret Martha Astell-Burt; 2 s.; 1 d. Educ. Grove Academy; Dundee High School; St. Andrews University. Royal Navy, 1942-45; Lecturer in Economics, St. Andrews, 1947-48; Lecturer, then Reader in Economics, London School of Economics, 1948-56; Professor of Economic Science, Edinburgh University, 1956-62; Professor of Economics, York University, 1962-78 (Deputy Vice Chancellor, 1963-69); Professor of Economics, University College, Buckingham, 1978-80; Principal, then Vice Chancellor, Buckingham University, 1980-84; Chief Economic Adviser, Department of Trade and Industry (on secondment), 1973-76. Member, Royal Commission on the Constitution, 1970-73; Member, Inquiry into Retirement Provision, 1983-85; SSRC Council, 1972-73; President, International Institute of Public Finance, 1966-69; Chairman, Committee on Financing the BBC, 1985-86; Chairman, Rowntree Inquiry on Takeovers, 1989-91; Executive Director, David Hume Institute, Edinburgh, 1985-91; Chairman, Scottish Arts Council, 1986-92; Chairman, Academic Advisory Council, Institute of Economic Affairs, 1991-93; Head, UN Advisory Mission to Russia on Social Protection, 1992; Non-Executive Director, Caledonian Bank, 1991-96; Chairman, Hebrides Ensemble, since 1994; Scottish Free Enterprise Award, 1987; Keynes Lecturer, British Academy, 1994; Fellow, Accademie

Nazionale dei Lincei, Rome. Publications: 25 books, over 200 articles on economic questions. Recreations: attempting to write music; hill-walking. Address: (h.) Clinton Grange, 146/4 Whitehouse Loan, Edinburgh EH9 2AN; T.-0131-447 5917.

Peacock, Peter James. Convener, Highland Council; Member, Highland Regional Council, 1982-96 (held positions of Vice-Convener, Finance Chairman, Chairman, Policy and Resources Committee); Vice-President, Convention of Scottish Local Authorities; Member, Scottish Economic Council; Training, Organisation and Policy Consultant; Board Member, Centre for Highlands and Islands Policy Studies; Board Member, Scottish Natural Heritage; b. 27.2.52, Edinburgh; 2 s. Educ. Hawick High School; Jordanhill College of Education, Glasgow. Community Worker, Orkney Islands, 1973-75; former Area Officer, Highlands, Islands, Grampian, Scottish Association of Citizens Advice Bureaux. Co-author, Vice-Chairman, subsequently Chairman of successful applicant group for Independent Local Radio franchise, Moray Firth; Member, Highland Area Committee, SCDI; former Chairman, Scottish Library and Information Council; Appointed Member, European Committee of the Regions, 1993. Recreations: ornithology; golf; watching rugby union. Address: (h.) 68 Braeside Park, Balloch, Inverness; T.-01463 790371.

Peaker, Professor Malcolm, FRS, DSc, PhD, FZS, FLS, FIBiol, FRSE. Director, Hannah Research Institute, Ayr, since 1981; Hannah Professor, Glasgow University, since 1981; b. 21.8.43, Stapleford, Nottingham; m., Stephanie Jane Large; 3 s. Educ. Henry Mellish Grammar School, Nottingham; Sheffield University, BSc Zoology; DSc; University of Hong Kong, SRC NATO Scholar; PhD. ARC Institute of Animal Physiology, 1968-78; Head, Department of Physiology, Hannah Research Institute, 1978-81. Member, Editorial Board: Journal of Dairy Science, 1975-78, International Zoo Yearbook, 1978-82, Journal of Endocrinology, 1981-91; Editor, British Journal of Herpetology, 1977-81. Publications: Salt Glands in Birds and Reptiles, 1975; Avian Physiology (Editor), 1975; Comparative Aspects of Lactation (Editor), 1977; Physiological Strategies in Lactation (Co-Editor), 1984; Intercellular Signalling in the Mammary Gland (Editor), 1995; Biological Signalling and the Mammary Gland (Editor), 1997; papers. Recreations: vertebrate zoology; natural history; golf; grumbling about bureaucrats. Address: (h.) Hannah Research Institute, Ayr KA6 5HL.

Pears, John Charles, BSc (Hons). Rector, Paisley Grammar School, since 1995; b. 13.10.50, Castle Douglas; m., Margaret Blackwood; 2 s. Educ. Kirkcudbright Academy; Strathclyde University; Jordanhill College. Teacher, Kirkcudbright Academy; Principal Teacher: Braidhurst High School, Lenzie Academy; Assistant Rector, Kilmarnock Academy; Depute Rector, Johnstone High School. Elder, Church of Scotland. Recreations: sport; music; gardening. Address: (b.) Paisley Grammar School, Glasgow Road, Paisley; T.-0141-889 3484.

Pearson, Francis Salmond Gillespie, MA (Oxon). Painter in oils, since 1984; b. 31.7.35, Edinburgh. Educ. Fettes College, Edinburgh; University College, Oxford; Edinburgh University. National Service, Cameron Highlanders; Assistant Master, Harrow School, 1960-61 and 1967-73; Member, Faculty of Advocates, since 1964; Headmaster, Truro Cathedral School, 1974-79; Head of Arts and Languages, Welbeck College, 1979-83. Trustee, Hopetoun House Preservation Trust. Address: (h.) 28 Douglas Crescent, Edinburgh EH12 5BA; T.-0131-225 4736.

Pearson of Rannoch, Lord (Malcolm Everard MacLaren Pearson). Life Peer; b. 20.7.42; m.; 2 d.; 1 d. by pr. m. Chairman, PWS Holdings plc; founded Rannoch Trust, 1984.

Peart, Geoff, BA, MA, MIED, MRTPI. Director of Strategic Services, Falkirk Council; former Director of Development and Planning, Central Regional Council; Director: Stirling University Innovation Park, Falkirk Enterprise Action Trust; b. 25.10.46, Jarrow; m., Kathryn; 1 s.; 1 d. Educ. Dame Allan's Boys Grammar School, Newcastle upon Tyne; Southampton University; Nottingham University. Member, Scottish Office/COSLA Scottish Statistical Liaison Committee, 1975-91; Technical Adviser to Scottish Office/COSLA Local Government Finance Distribution Committee, 1985-91; Member, COSLA European Policy Advisory Group, 1989-91; Member, Royal Town Planning Institute Retail Working Party, 1986-87. Recreations: hill-walking; squash; cricket; reading. Address: (b.) Abbotsford House, David's Loan, Bainsford, Falkirk; T.-Falkirk 504948.

Peat, George Waddell, CA. Hon. Treasurer, Scottish Football Association, since 1997; Chairman, Airdrieonians Football Club, 1990-97; b. 29.10.40, Coatbridge; m., Evelyn; 1 s.; 1 d. Educ. Coatbridge High School; Glasgow University. CA: General Motors, Transport Development Group, Plessey PLC, J.W. Galloway Ltd.; private practice as CA, first on own account, then in partnership as Peat & McConnachie; Secretary, Airdrieonians FC, since 1978, Director, since 1985. Recreations: sport; music. Address: (b.) Scottish Football Association, 6 Park Gardens, Glasgow G3 7YF.

Peat, Jeremy Alastair, BA, MSc, FRSA. Chief Economist, Royal Bank of Scotland, since 1993; Honorary Professor, Heriot-Watt University; b. 20.3.45, Haywards Heath; m., Philippa Ann; 2 d. Educ. St. Paul's School, London; Bristol University; University College London. Economic Assistant/Economic Adviser, Ministry of Overseas Development, 1969-77; Economic Adviser, Manpower Services Commission, 1978-80; Head, Employment Policy Unit, Ministry of Finance and Development Planning, Government of Botswana, 1980-84; Economic Adviser, HM Treasury, 1984-85; Senior Economic Adviser, Scottish Office, 1985-93. Recreations: walking; reading; tennis; listening to music. Address: (b.) 42 St. Andrew Square, Edinburgh EH2 2YE; T.-0131-523 2277.

Peat, William Wood Watson, CBE, OStJ, JP, FRAgS. Farmer; National Governor for Scotland, BBC, and Chairman, Broadcasting Council for Scotland, 1984-89; b. 14.12.22, Denny; m., Jean McHarrie; 2 s.; 1 d. Educ. Denny Public School. Lt., Royal Signals, NW Europe and India, 1940-46; Broadcaster; National Chairman, subsequently President, Scottish Association of Young Farmers Clubs; Member, Stirling County Council, 1959-75 (Vice Convener, 1967-70); Council Member, NFU of Scotland, 1959-78 (President, 1966-67); Member, Scottish River Purification Advisory Committee, 1960-79; Board of Management, RSNH, 1960-72; General Commissioner of Income Tax, since 1962; Chairman, Scottish Advisory Committee, Association of Agriculture, 1974-79 (Vice-President, since 1979); Council, Hannah Research Institute, 1963-82; Council Member, Scottish Agricultural Organisation Society Ltd., since 1963 (President, 1974-77); Member, British Agricultural Council, 1974-84; Member, Board of Management, Oatridge Agricultural College, 1967-75; Governor, West of Scotland Agricultural College (Chairman, 1983-88); Chairman, Scottish Agricultural Colleges Ltd., 1987-90; Director, FMC plc, 1974-83; Member, Central Council for Agricultural and Horticultural Co-operation, 1967-83; Member, Co-operative Development Board, 1983-89; Member, Board of Management, British Farm Produce Council, 1964-83, BFP Committee, Food from Britain, 1984-87; Chairman, BBC Scottish Agricultural Advisory Committee, 1971-76. Recreations: amateur radio; flying. Address: (h.) 61 Stirling Road, Larbert FK5 4SG.

Peckham, Professor Gordon E., MA, PhD. Professor, Department of Physics, Heriot Watt University, since 1992; b. 29.10.36, Bristol; 1 s.; 1 d. Educ. Bristol Grammar School; Trinity College, Cambridge. Lecturer: Reading University, 1966, Heriot Watt University, 1971; Reader, Heriot Watt, 1972. Address: (b.) Physics Department, Heriot Watt University, Riccarton, Edinburgh EH14 4AS; T.-0131-451 3028.

Peddie, Richard L., MA, MEd, AFBPsS. Retired; Hon. Lecturer, Strathclyde University; formerly Vice Principal, Craigie College of Education; b. 11.6.28, Grangemouth; m., Nan K. Bell; 1 s.; 2 d. Educ. Grangemouth High School; Glasgow University. Royal Signals Officer, Allied Supreme HQ (SHAPE), 1951-53; Teacher, Stirlingshire, 1953-56; Educational Psychologist, Ayrshire, 1956-59; Lecturer, Jordanhill College, 1959-64; Head, Psychology Department, Assistant Principal, Vice-Principal, Craigie College of Education, 1964-88; Member, General Teaching Council for Scotland, 1970-78; External Examiner in Education, London University Institute, 1971-76; External Examiner, Hamilton College of Education, 1977-80; Member, Scottish Examination Board, 1980-84; Member, Education Committee, British Psychological Society, 1964-68; Chairman, Glasgow University Educational Colloquium, 1966-67; Chairman, Association of Lecturers in Colleges of Education in Scotland (ALCES), 1967-69; Member, Scottish Council for Research in Education, 1962-78; Member, Executive Committee, Scottish Division of Educational and Child Psychology, 1979-84; Chairman, Association of Higher Academic Staff in Colleges of Education, 1984-87; Captain, 51 (H) Infantry Division Signals Regiment (TA), 1953-60; Vice-Chairman, Ayr Children's Panel, 1970-74; Paul Harris Fellow, Rotary Award, 1986; Church of Scotland Elder; Dean of Guild, Burgh of Ayr, 1992-93. Recreations: reading; Rotary; driving; golf. Address: (h.) 14 Glenpark Place, Alloway, Ayr KA7 4SQ; T.-01292 441996.

Peden, Professor George Cameron, MA, DPhil. Professor of History, Stirling University, since 1990; b. 16.2.43, Dundee; m., Alison Mary White; 3 s. Educ. Grove Academy, Broughty Ferry; Dundee University; Brasenose College, Oxford. Sub-Editor, Dundee Evening Telegraph, 1960-68; mature student, 1968-75; Tutorial Assistant, Department of Modern History, Dundee University, 1975-76; Temporary Lecturer, School of History, Leeds University, 1976-77; Lecturer in Economic and Social History, then Reader in Economic History, Bristol University, 1977-90; Visiting Fellow, All Souls College, Oxford, 1988-89. Publications: British Rearmament and the Treasury 1932-39, 1979; British Economic and Social Policy: Lloyd George to Margaret Thatcher, 1985; Keynes, The Treasury and British Economic Policy, 1988. Recreation: hill-walking. Address: (h.) Ardvurich, Leny Feus, Callander FK17 8AS; T.-01877 30488.

Peden, Professor James McKenzie, BSc, MEng, PhD, CEng. Shell UK Research Professor, Heriot-Watt University, since 1987; Managing Director, Pitac Ltd., since 1985, Awa Ltd., since 1996; b. 27.9.47, Edinburgh; m., Jacqui; 1 s.; 1 d. Educ. Darwen Grammar School; Heriot-Watt University. Shell UK Ltd., 1970-73; Henry Balfour & Co., 1973-74; Distillers Co. Ltd., 1974-75; Shell International Petroleum Co., 1976-78; joined Heriot-Watt University, Department of Petroleum Engineering, 1978 (Head of Department, 1986-91); Director and Founder, Horizontal Well Technology Unit, 1991-97. Recreations: walking; music. Address: (h.) Meadowcroft, Middleton, Milnathort KY13 7SD; T.-01577 862708.

Peebles, Gillian Margaret, LLB, WS. Advocate, since 1995; Board Member, Scottish Legal Aid Board, 1992-96; b. 31.1.55, Glasgow; m., Sheriff Iain A.S. Peebles. Educ. Laurel Bank School; Glasgow University. Solicitor, 1977-94; WS, 1988. First woman president, Glasgow University

Conservative Club, 1975. Recreations: travel; the arts. Address: (h.) 70 Dublin Street, Edinburgh EH3 6NP; T.-0131-556 1150.

Peebles, Sheriff I. A. S., QC, LLB. Sheriff of Glasgow and Strathkelvin at Glasgow. Admitted, Faculty of Advocates, 1979. Address: (b.) Sheriff Court House, 1 Carlton Place, Glasgow, G5 9DA.

Peggie, Robert Galloway Emslie, CBE, FCCA. Chairman, Local Government Staff Commission for Scotland, 1994-97; b. 5.1.29, Bo'ness; 1 s.; 1 d. Educ. Lasswade High School. Trainee Accountant, 1946-52; Accountant in industry, 1952-57; Edinburgh Corporation, 1957-72: O. and M. Officer, Assistant City Chamberlain, Deputy City Chamberlain, Reorganisation Steering Committee; Chief Executive, Lothian Regional Council, 1974-86; Commissioner (Ombudsman) for Local Administration in Scotland, 1986-94. Member, Court, Heriot-Watt University (Convener, Finance Committee); Governor, Edinburgh College of Art; Trustee, Lloyds TSB Foundation. Recreation: golf. Address: 9A Napier Road, Edinburgh EH10 5AZ; T.-0131-229 6775.

Pelham Burn, Angus Maitland, LLD, JP, DL. Director, Bank of Scotland, since 1977, Chairman, Aberdeen Local Board; Chairman, Scottish Provident, since 1995; Chairman, Aberdeen Asset Management PLC (formerly, Aberdeen Trust PLC); Chairman, Aberdeen Airport Consultative Committee, since 1986; Director, Abtrust Scotland Investment Company, 1989-96; b. 13.12.31, London; m., Anne; 4 d. Educ. Harrow; North of Scotland College of Agriculture. Hudson's Bay Company, 1951-58; Farmer and Company Director, since 1958; Member, Kincardine County Council, 1967-75 (Vice Convener, 1973-75); Member, Grampian Regional Council, 1974-94; Member, Accounts Commission for Scotland, 1980-94 (Deputy Chairman, 1987-94); Chairman, Aberdeen Airport Consultative Committee, since 1986; Director, Aberdeen Association for Prevention of Cruelty to Animals, 1975-95; Chairman, Order of St. John (Aberdeen) Ltd.; Council Member, Winston Churchill Memorial Trust, 1984-94; Member, Queen's Bodyguard for Scotland (Royal Company of Archers), since 1968; Vice Lord Lieutenant, Kincardineshire, since 1978; Honorary Degree of Doctor in Business Administration (Robert Gordon University), 1996. Recreations: gardening; wildlife photography. Address: (b.) 68 Station Road, Banchory AB31 6JS; T.-01330 823343.

Pelly, Frances, RSA. Sculptor; b. 21.7.47, Edinburgh. Educ. Morrison's Academy, Crieff; Duncan of Jordanstone College of Art, Dundee. Part-time lecturing, Dundee, 1974-78; full-time lecturing, Grays School of Art, Aberdeen, 1979-83. Recreations: riding; wildlife; gardening. Address: Costa Schoolhouse, Evie, Orkney; T.-0185 675 1326.

Peltenburg, Professor Edgar, BA, PhD, FSA (Scot). Professor of Archaeology, Edinburgh University, since 1993; b. 28.5.42, Montreal; m., Marie Wright; 3 s.; 1 d. Educ. Montreal; Birmingham University. Assistant Lecturer, Classics, McGill University, Montreal, 1963-66; Research Fellow in Archaeology, Birmingham University, 1966-69; Lecturer in Archaeology, Glasgow University, 1969-78; Lecturer in Near Eastern Archaeology, then Reader, Edinburgh University, 1978-93; director of excavations, Syria and Cyprus. Publications: six books; many scientific papers. Recreations: jazz; skiing. Address: (b.) Department of Archaeology, Old High School, Infirmary Street, Edinburgh; T.-0131-650 2379.

Pender, Sheriff David James, LLB (Hons). Sheriff of North Strathclyde, since 1995; b. 7.9.49, Glasgow; m., Elizabeth; 2 s.; 2 d. Educ. Queen's Park Senior Secondary School, Glasgow; Edinburgh University. Partner, MacArthur Stewart, Solicitors, Oban, 1977. Recreations:

reading; travel; bridge. Address: (b.) Sheriff Courthouse, St. James Street, Paisley; T.-0141-887 5291.

Penman, David Roland, DA (Edin), DipTP (Edin), FRTPI, ARIAS, FSAScot. Reporter, Scottish Office Inquiry Reporters' Unit, since 1994; b. 6.6.36, Manchester; m., Tamara Scott; 2 s.; 1 d. Educ. George Watson's Boys' College, Edinburgh; Edinburgh College of Art. Assistant Architect, private practices, 1960-67; Partner, Bamber Hall & Partners, Edinburgh, 1967-71; Depute County Planning Officer, Argyll County Council, 1971-73; County Planning Officer, Perth & Kinross Joint County Council, 1973-75; Director of Planning, Perth and Kinross District Council, 1975-94. Chairman, RTPI Scotland, 1984, Member of Council, 1978-85; President, Dundee Institute of Architects, 1988, Member of Council, 1980-90; Chairman, Scottish Urban Archaeological Trust, since 1990; former Chairman, Duncan of Jordanstone College of Art; former Vice-Chairman, Scottish Conservation Projects Trust; Director, Action Environment Ltd.; former Council Member, National Trust for Scotland. Recreations: hill-walking; art galleries; theatre; DIY; Scots history; travel. Address: (h.) 17 Gannochy Road, Perth, PH2 7EF; T.-01738 627775.

Pennington, Christopher Royston, BSc (Hons), MB, ChB, MRCP, MD, FRCP, FRCPEdin. Consultant Physician (General Medicine and Gastroenterology), since 1979; Clinical Director, General Medicine, since 1995; Honorary Senior Lecturer in Medicine, Dundee University, since 1979; Examiner, MRCP (UK), since 1986; b. 22.2.46, Chard; m., Marcia Jane Barclay; 1 d. Educ. Shebbear College; Manchester University. House Officer, Manchester Royal Infirmary, 1970-71; Registrar in Medicine, Aberdeen Royal Infirmary, 1971-74; Lecturer in Medicine, Dundee University, 1974-79. External Examiner in Medicine, Aberdeen University, 1983-86; Examiner, Edinburgh College of Physicians; Specialty Adviser, Medical Defence Union of Scotland. Publications: Therapeutic Nutrition: A Practical Guide, 1988; book chapters and papers. Address: (h.) Balnagowan, Braehead, Invergowrie, Dundee.

Penrose, Hon. Lord (George William Penrose), QC (Scot). Senator of the College of Justice, since 1990; b. 2.6.38. Advocate, 1964; QC, 1978; Procurator to General Assembly of Church of Scotland, 1984-90.

Pentland, Brian, BSc, MB, ChB, FRCPE. Consultant Neurologist in Rehabilitation Medicine, since 1982; Senior Lecturer in Rehabilitation Studies, Edinburgh University, since 1983; b. 24.6.49, Glasgow; m., Gillian Mary Duggua; 4 s. Educ. Liberton High School, Edinburgh; Edinburgh University. Junior hospital appointments in Edinburgh, Cumbria and Dundee; formerly Lecturer in Neurology in Edinburgh. Recreation: hill-walking. Address: (b.) Astley Ainslie Hospital, Grange Loan, Edinburgh EH9 2HL; T.-0131-537 9039.

Peoples, J. A., QC, LLB. Admitted Faculty of Advocates, 1979. Address: Advocates' Library, Parliament House, Edinburgh EH1 1RF.

Peppé, William Lawrence Tosco, OBE, JP, DL, FIMgt; b. 25.11.37, India; m., Deirdre Eva Preston Wakefield; 3 s. Educ. Wellington College; King's College, Cambridge. Naval Officer, 1955-91 – Commander. Recreation: country. Address: (h.) Glendrynoch Lodge, Carbost, Isle of Skye IV47 8SX; T.-01478 640218.

Percy, Professor John Pitkeathly (Ian), CBE, CA, FRSA. Former Senior Partner, Grant Thornton, Scotland; Chairman: The Accounts Commission, MacDonald Orr Ltd.; Deputy Chairman, Scottish Provident Institution; Non-Executive Director: Morgan Grenfell (Scotland) Ltd., Beale Dobie (Scot) Ltd., William Wilson (Holdings) Ltd., The Weir Group PLC, The Edinburgh Academy (Chairman, Court of Directors); Vice Chairman, UK Auditing Practices Board; Member, International Auditing Practices Committee; Chairman, International Task Force on Corporate Governance; b. 16.1.42, Southport; m., Sheila; 2 d. Educ. Edinburgh Academy; Edinburgh University. Managing Partner, Grant Thornton, London, 1981-88; Honorary Professor of Accounting, Aberdeen University, 1988. Freeman, City of London; Member, British Academy of Experts; Elder, St. Cuthbert's Church of Scotland; President, Institute of Chartered Accountants of Scotland, 1990-91. Recreations: golf; fishing. Address: (b.) 1 St. Colme Street, Edinburgh EH3 6AA; T.-0131-220 8214; (h.) 30 Midmar Drive, Edinburgh; T.-0131-447 3645.

Perfect, Hugh Epton, BSc. Senior Assistant Principal, Moray House Institute of Education, Heriot-Watt University; b. 9.4.41, London; m., Susan; 2 d. Educ. Haberdasher's Askes' School, Hampstead; Imperial College, London. Teacher, Windsor Grammar School; Lecturer, Bulmershe College of Education, Reading; Lecturer/Senior Lecturer, Biology Department, Moray House College of Education. Recreations: badminton; gardening; micro-computers. Address: (b.) Moray House Institute of Education, Holyrood Road, Edinburgh EH8 8AQ; T.-0131-558 6168.

Perry, Professor Clive Graham, MA (Cantab), Hon. MA (Leicester). Festival Director, Pitlochry Festival Theatre, since 1987; Professor of Theatre, Queen Margaret College, Edinburgh, since 1997; (Professor and Head, Department of Drama, Queen Margaret College, Edinburgh, 1990-96); b. 17.3.36, Harrow. Educ. Wolverhampton Grammar School; Harrow County Grammar School; Cambridge University. Awarded Thames TV Scholarship to regional theatre, 1960-61; Assistant Director, Derby Playhouse; Associate Director, Castle Theatre, Farnham; Director of Productions, Phoenix Theatre, Leicester; Director, Royal Lyceum Theatre, Edinburgh, 1966-76 (Director of Theatres in Edinburgh, 1971-76); Director, Birmingham Repertory Theatre, 1976-87. Recreation: theatre. Address: (b.) Pitlochry Festival Theatre, Port-Na-Craig, Pitlochry PH16 5DR; T.-01796 473054.

Perry, John Scott (Jack), BSc, CA, CPA. Office Managing Partner, Ernst and Young, Glasgow, since 1995; b. 23.11.54, Glasgow; m., Lydia Margaret Cox; 1 s.; 2 d. Educ. Glasgow Academy; Glasgow University; Strathclyde University. Joined Ernst and Young, 1976; transferred to Ernst and Young, Dallas, Texas, 1981-83; seconded to Scottish Development Finance, 1987-88; appointed Partner, Ernst and Young, Glasgow, 1988; Head of Audit, 1994-95. Member, CBI Scotland Council, since 1995; Director, Pollok School Company. Recreations: golf; skiing. Address: (b.) George House, 50 George Square, Glasgow G2 1RR; T.-0141-552 3456.

Perry of Walton, Rt. Hon. Lord (Walter Laing Macdonald Perry), Kt, OBE, MB, ChB, MD, DSc, FRCP, FRCPE, FRSE, FRS. President, Videotel Marine International; Life Peer, since 1979; b. 16.6.21, Dundee; m., 1, Anne Grant (m. dissolved); 3 s.; 2, Catherine Crawley; 2 s.; 1 d. Educ. Morgan Academy; Ayr Academy; Dundee High School; University College Dundee, St. Andrews University. Medical Officer, Colonial Service, 1944-46; RAF, 1946-47; Medical Research Council: member of staff, 1947-52, Director, Department of Biological Standards, 1952-58; Professor of Pharmacology, Edinburgh University, 1958-68; Vice-Chancellor, The Open University, 1968-81. Member, Editorial Board, Encyclopaedia Britannica, since 1971; Member of Kuratorium, Fernuniversitat, Hagen, W. Germany, since 1976; Hon. Director, International Centre for Distance Learning, since 1983; Member, Academic Advisory Committee, University of E. Asia, Macau, since 1984; Member, Board, University of the World, since 1987; Member, Select Committee of Science and Technology, House of Lords, since 1997. Recreations: golf; music;

reading. Address: (h.) 2 Cramond Road South, Edinburgh EH4 6AD.

Perth, 17th Earl of (John David Drummond), PC (1957); b. 13.5.07; m., Nancy Seymour Fincke; 2 s. Educ. Downside; Cambridge University. Lt., Intelligence Corps, 1940; War Cabinet Offices, 1942-43; Ministry of Production, 1944-45; Minister of State for Colonial Affairs, 1957-62; First Crown Estate Commissioner, 1962-77; Member, Court, St. Andrews University, 1967-86; Trustee, National Library of Scotland, 1968-95. Hon. LLD; Hon. FRIBA; Hon. FRIAS. Address: (h.) Stobhall, by Perth PH2 6DR; T.-01821 640 332.

Petch, Professor Alison Jean, BA, MA, PhD, DipSW. Nuffield Professor of Community Care Studies, Glasgow University, since 1993; b. 5.4.50, Leeds; m., David Jarman; 2 s. Educ. Central Newcastle High School; Cambridge University. Research Planner, Livingston Development Corporation, 1973-75; Research Fellow, Edinburgh University, 1983-86; Research Fellow, then Senior Research Fellow, Social Work Research Centre, Stirling University, 1986-93. Member, Management Committee, Scottish Association for Mental Health; Council Member, Alzheimer Scotland. Address: (b.) Nuffield Centre for Community Care Studies, 7 Lilybank Gardens, Glasgow G12 8RZ; T.-0141-330 5600.

Peterken, Laurence Edwin, CBE, MA. Consultant; Member, Criminal Injuries Compensation Appeal Panel, since 1997; Director, Special Projects, NHS in Scotland, 1993-96; Visiting Professor Elect, Glasgow Caledonian University; b. 2.10.31, London; m., 1, Hanne Birgithe Von Der Recke (deceased); 1 s.; 1 d.; 2, Margaret Raynal Blair; 1 s.; 1 d. Educ. Harrow School (Scholar); Peterhouse, Cambridge (Scholar). Pilot Officer, RAF Regt., Adjt. No. 20 LAA Sqdn., 1950-52; Service Divisional Manager, Hotpoint Ltd., 1961-63; Commercial Director, then Managing Director, British Domestic Appliances Ltd., 1963-68; Director, British Printing Corporation Ltd., 1969-73; Managing Director, Fashion Multiple Division, Debenhams Ltd., 1974-76; Management Auditor, 1976-77; Controller, Operational Services, GLC, 1977-85; President, GLC Chief Officers' Guild, 1983-85; Acting Director, Royal Festival Hall, 1983-85; General Manager, Greater Glasgow Health Board, 1986-93; Chairman, Glasgow and West of Scotland Institute of Public Administration, since 1993; Member, Scottish Committee, Council for Music in Hospitals, since 1996. Recreations: opera; swimming. Address: (h.) Langdales, Houston House, Houston, Renfrewshire PA6 7AR.

Peters, Kenneth Jamieson, CBE, JP, DL, FRSA, FSA Scot, Assoc. MCIT. Deputy Lieutenant, City of Aberdeen, since 1978; Vice-Chairman, Peterhead Bay Authority, 1989-96; b. 17.1.23, London; m., Arunda Merle Jane Jones. Educ. Aberdeen Grammar School; Aberdeen University. Served Second World War; commissioned Queen's Own Cameron Highlanders; also King's Own Scottish Borderers; editorial staff, Scottish Daily Record and Evening News Ltd., 1947-51; Assistant Editor, Aberdeen Evening Express, 1951-52; Assistant Editor, Manchester Evening Chronicle, 1952-53; Editor, Aberdeen Evening Express, 1953-56; Editor, Press and Journal, Aberdeen, 1956-60; Managing Director, Aberdeen Journals Ltd., 1960-80, Chairman, 1980-81; Director: Thomson North Sea, 1981-88, Thomson Scottish Petroleum, 1981-86, Thomson Forestry Holdings, 1982-88, Highland Printers Ltd., 1968-83; President, Scottish Daily Newspaper Society, 1964-66 and 1974-76; Member, Press Council, 1974-77; Director, Thomson Regional Newspapers, 1974-81; Director, Aberdeen Association of Social Service, 1973-78; Member, British Railways (Scottish) Board, 1982-92; Member, Girobank, Scotland Board, 1984-90; Member, Executive, Scottish Council (Development and Industry), 1982-88 (Chairman, Aberdeen and North-East Committee, 1982-88); Fellow,

SCDI, 1989; Member, Scottish Advisory Committee, British Council, 1967-84; National Committee Member, Films of Scotland, 1970-82; Burgess of Guild, City of Aberdeen, 1963. Publications: The Northern Lights, 1978; Burgess of Guild, 1982; Great North Memories, Vol. 1 and Vol. 2 (Editor). Recreations: walking; cricket; rugby football. Address: 47 Abergeldie Road, Aberdeen AB10 6ED; T.-01224 587647.

Peterson, George Sholto, NP. Solicitor and Notary Public, since 1956; Honorary Sheriff, since 1982; b. 18.9.27, Lerwick; m., Dorothy Hilda Spence; 2 s.; 4 d. Educ. Lerwick Central Public School; Edinburgh University. Secretary, The Shetland Trust; Factor for the Marquess of Zetland; Senior Partner, Tait & Peterson, Solicitors and Estate Agents, Lerwick; Dean, Faculty of Solicitors in Shetland; Honorary Pastor, Ebenezer Church, Lerwick. Recreations: studying theology; reading; fishing. Address: (b.) Bank of Scotland Buildings, Lerwick, Shetland; T.-01595 693010.

Pethrick, Professor Richard Arthur, BSc, PhD, DSc, FRSC, FRSE. Professor in Chemistry, Strathclyde University, since 1983 (Head of Department, since 1992); b. 26.10.42; m., Joan Knowles Hume; 1 s. Educ. North Gloucestershire College, Cheltenham; London University; Salford University. Editor: British Polymer Journal, Polymer Yearbook, Polymer International, International Journal of Polymer Materials; Member, Polymer Committee, European Science Foundation; Member, Committee, MACRO Group, 1979-84; Member, SERC Polymer Materials Committee, since 1994; Elder, Merrylea Church of Scotland. Address: (b.) Department of Pure and Applied Chemistry, University of Strathclyde, Thomas Graham Building, Cathedral Street, Glasgow G1 1XL.

Petrie, Professor James Colquhoun, CBE, FRCPEdin, FRCP, FFPM, FRCP Ireland. Professor of Clinical Pharmacology, since 1985, Head, Department of Medicine and Therapeutics, Aberdeen University, since 1994; Honorary Consultant Physician, Aberdeen Teaching Hospitals, since 1971; b. 18.9.41, Aberdeen; m., Dr. M. Xanthe P.; 2 s.; 2 d. Educ. Anieres, Geneva; Robert Gordon's College, Aberdeen; Aberdeen University. Senior Lecturer, 1971-81, Reader, 1981-85, Aberdeen University. Chairman, Lecht Ski Company, since 1976. Recreations: ski; golf; fishing. Address: (b.) Department of Medicine and Therapeutics, Aberdeen Royal Infirmary, Foresterhill, Aberdeen AB9 2ZB; T.-01224 681818.

Peyton Jones, Professor Simon Loftus, MA (Cantab), DipCompSci, MBCS, CEng. Professor of Computing Science, Glasgow University, since 1989; b. 18.1.58, Cape Town, South Africa; m., Dorothy Helen. Educ. Marlborough College; Trinity College, Cambridge. Systems Engineer, Beale Electronic Systems Ltd, 1980-82; University College London: Lecturer in Computer Science, 1982-86, Senior Lecturer in Computer Science, 1986-89. Publication: The Implementation of Functional Programming Languages, 1987. Recreations: cycling; reading; singing. Address: (b.) Department of Computing Science, University of Glasgow Glasgow G12 8QQ; T.- 0141-330 4500.

Phelps, Professor Alan David Reginald, MA, DPhil, CPhys, FInstP, FRSE. Professor, Physics and Applied Physics, Strathclyde University, since 1993, Deputy Head of Department, since 1993; Chairman, Plasma Physics Group, Institute of Physics, since 1995; b. 2.6.44, Basingstoke; m., Susan Helen Marshall; 1 d. Educ. Haverfordwest Grammar School; King's College, Cambridge; University College, Oxford. Research Associate, National Academy of Sciences (USA), 1972-73; Research Officer, Oxford University, 1973-78; Lecturer, then Senior Lecturer, then Reader in Physics, Strathclyde University, 1978-93. Publications: 200 research papers and reports. Recreations: hill-walking; country pursuits. Address: (b.) Department of Physics and Applied Physics, John Anderson Building, Strathclyde University, Glasgow G4 0NG; T.-0141-548 3166.

Philip, Hon. Lord (Alexander Morrison). Senator of the College of Justice, since 1996; b. 3.8.42, Aberdeen; m., Shona Mary MacRae; 3 s. Educ. Glasgow High School; St. Andrews University; Glasgow University. Solicitor, 1967-72; Advocate, 1973; Advocate Depute, 1982-85; QC, 1984; Chairman, Medical Appeal Tribunals, 1988-92; Chairman, Scottish Land Court, 1993-96; President, Lands Tribunal for Scotland, 1993-96. Recreations: piping; golf. Address: (b.) Parliament House, Edinburgh EH1 1RQ; T.-0131-225 2595.

Philips, Douglas John, MHSM, DipHSM. Director of Priority Services and Joint Planning, Argyll and Clyde Health Board, since 1997 (Director of Community Care Development, 1992-97); b. 30.4.53, Edinburgh; m., Morag S. Hall. Educ. Dalkeith High School. Formerly General Manager, Northern Unit, Highland Health Board. Winston Churchill Memorial Trust Fellow, 1996. Recreations: walking the Dalmatians; hill-walking; rambling; cycling; gardening; reading fiction; music; Coronation Street. Address: (h.) Windsong, Blairuskinmore, Kinlochard, Stirling FK8 3TP; T.-01877 387236.

Phillips, Professor John Clifford, BSc, CMath, FIMA, FRSA, MIMgt. Vice-Principal, Glasgow Caledonian University, since 1993; Chief Executive, Glasgow Caledonian University Company, since 1995; Chairman, Glasgow Caledonian University Nominee Company Ltd., since 1996; b. 29.1.43, Dyfed; m., Margaret; 1 s.; 1 d. Educ. Llandeilo Grammar School; University of Wales, Aberystwyth. Lecturer, Lancashire Polytechnic, 1967-69, Leeds Polytechnic, 1969-71; Leeds Polytechnic: Senior Lecturer, 1971-77, Principal Lecturer, 1977-86, Head, School of Mathematics and Computing, 1986-87, Dean, Faculty of Engineering and Computing, 1987-88, Senior Executive, External Development, 1988-90; Principal, The Queen's College, Glasgow, 1991-93. Former Member, North Yorkshire County Council. Recreations: reading; walking; architectural conservation. Address: (b.) Glasgow Caledonian University, Cowcaddens Road, Glasgow G4 0BA.

Phillips, Professor John H., MA, PhD. Professor of Biology Teaching and Vice-Provost of Medicine and Veterinary Medicine, Edinburgh University, since 1996; b. 19.2.41, York; m., Kerstin B. Halling; 2 d. Educ. Leighton Park School, Reading; Christ's College, Cambridge. Lecturer in Biochemistry, Makerere University, Uganda, 1967-69; scientific staff, MRC Laboratory of Molecular Biology, Cambridge, 1969-74; Department of Biochemistry, Edinburgh University, 1974-88, Director of Biology Teaching, 1988-93, Head, Department of Biochemistry, 1993-96. Recreations: natural history; Scottish mountains; visits to Sweden. Address: (h.) 46 Granby Road, Edinburgh EH16 5NW; T.-0131-667 5322.

Phillipson, Peter W. Managing Director, United Distillers UK, since 1996; b. 6.3.54, Newcastle-upon-Tyne; m., Julie; 1 s.; 2 d. Educ. St. Mary's School, Newcastle-upon-Tyne; Newcastle-upon-Tyne Polytechnic/Insead. Gillette Company, 1983-90; United Distillers UK, 1990-92; United Distillers plc, 1992-94; First Choice Holidays and Flights Ltd., 1994-96. Recreations: golf; football; cars. Address: (b.) Cherrybank, Perth PH2 0NG; T.-01738 621111.

Pia, Paul Dominic, LLB (Hons), WS. Senior Partner, Burness (formerly W. & J. Burness WS), since 1974; Chairman, Japan Society of Scotland, since 1996; b. 29.3.47, Edinburgh; m., Anne Christine Argent; 3 d. Educ. Holy Cross Academy, Edinburgh; Edinburgh University;

University of Perugia. Law apprentice, Lindsays WS, 1968-70; admitted as Solicitor and member of Society of Writers to HM Signet, 1971; Solicitor, W. & J. Burness WS, 1971-74. Publication: Care Diligence and Skill (handbook for directors). Recreations: hill-walking; travel; foreign languages. Address: (b.) 50 Lothian Road, Edinburgh; T.-0131-473 6000.

Pickard, Willis Ritchie, MA (Hons), Hon. LLD (Aberdeen), FSQA. Editor, Times Educational Supplement Scotland, since 1977; Rector, Aberdeen University, 1988-90; b. 21.5.41, Dunfermline; m., Ann; 2 d. Educ. Daniel Stewart's College; St. Andrews University. The Scotsman: Leader Writer, 1967-72, Features Editor, 1972-77. Former Member, Scottish Arts Council; Chairman, Book Trust Scotland, 1991-95; Liberal candidate, East Fife, 1970 and February, 1974. Address: (b.) 37 George Street, Edinburgh EH2 2HN; T.-0131-220 1100.

Pickett, James, BSc (Econ), MLit. Professor Emeritus, Strathclyde University, since 1995; b. 7.6.29, Greenock; m., Janet Clelland; 1 s.; 3 d. Educ. Greenock Academy; School of Economics, Dundee; Edinburgh University; Glasgow University; University of Paris. Statistician, Dominion Bureau of Statistics, Canada; Lecturer, Senior Lecturer, Professor and Director, Livingstone Institute of Overseas Development, Strathclyde University, 1961-95; Special Economic Adviser, UN Economic Commision for Africa; Visiting Professor, University of Saskatchewan; Economic Adviser, African Development Bank; UN Chief Economic Adviser to Ethiopian Government, 1992-95; Consultant to British, Canadian and Ghanian Governments, UN, OECD; author and editor, seven books and numerous papers; FRSA; sometime President, Scottish Union of Students. Recreations: hill-walking; listening to music; photography; computing; long-suffering supporter of Greenock Morton F.C. Address: (h.) 1 Divert Road, Gourock PA19 1DR; T.-01475 631046.

Pidgeon, Professor Carl R., BSc, PhD, FRSE. Professor of Semiconductor Physics and Head, Physics Department, Heriot Watt University; b. 27.11.37, London; 1 s.; 1 d. Educ. Reading University. Staff Member, National Magnet Laboratory, MIT, 1964-71; Reader in Physics, Heriot Watt University, 1971-83. Recreations: golf; skiing. Address: (b.) Physics Department, Heriot Watt University, Edinburgh.

Pike, (Kathryn) Lorna, MA (Hons). Editor, Dictionary of the Older Scottish Tongue, since 1986; b. 8.8.56, Fort William. Educ. Lochaber High School, Fort William; Edinburgh University. Editor, Concise Scots Dictionary, 1979-83; Assistant Editor, Dictionary of the Older Scottish Tongue, 1984-86. Secretary, Scottish Text Society. Recreations: riding; photography; handicrafts. Address: (b.) 27 George Square, Edinburgh, EH8 9LD; T.-0131-650 4147.

Pilcher, Rosamunde. Author; b. 22.9.24, Lelant, Cornwall. Began publishing short stories in Woman and Home, 1945; since then has published hundreds of short stories. Novels include Sleeping Tiger, Under Gemini, Wild Mountain Thyme, The Carousel, Voices in Summer, The Shell Seekers, September, The Blue Bedroom, Flowers in the Rain, Coming Home; play: The Dashing White Sergeant. Address: (h.) Penrowan, Longforgan, Perthshire; T.-Dundee 360393.

Piper, Professor Ronald Allen, BA, BD, PhD. Principal, St. Mary's College, St. Andrews University, since 1992, Head, School of Divinity, since 1992, Professor of Christian Origins, since 1997; b. 27.3.48, U.S.A.; m., Faith Elizabeth Woodhouse; 1 d. Educ. Pomona College, Claremont, California; London University. Lecturer in New Testament Studies, Aberdeen University, 1979-80; Lecturer in New Testament Language and Literature, St. Andrews

University, 1980-92, Reader in New Testament, 1992-97. Secretary, British New Testament Society. Publications: Wisdom in the Q-Tradition, 1989; The Gospel Behind the Gospels, 1995; numerous journal articles. Address: (b.) St. Mary's College, St. Andrews KY16 9JU; T.-01334 462850.

Pippard, Professor Martin John, BSc, MB, ChB, FRCPath, FRCP. Professor of Haematology, Dundee University, since 1989; Honorary Consultant Haematologist, Dundee Teaching Hospitals Trust, since 1989; b. 16.1.48, London; m., Grace Elizabeth; 2 s.; 1 d. Educ. Buckhurst Hill County High School; Birmingham University. House Physician and House Surgeon, 1972-73; Senior Medical House Officer, 1973-75; Research Fellow, Nuffield Department of Clinical Medicine, Oxford, 1975-78; MRC Travelling Research Fellow, University of Washington, Seattle, 1978-80; Wellcome Trust Research Fellow and Clinical Lecturer, Nuffield Department of Clinical Medicine, 1980-83; Consultant Haematologist, MRC Clinical Research Centre and Northwick Park Hospital, 1983-88. Recreations: gardening; fell-walking. Address: (b.) Department of Molecular and Cellular Pathology, Ninewells Hospital and Medical School, Dundee DD1 9SY; T.-01382 660111.

Pirie, Professor Hugh Munro, BVMS, PhD, MRCVS, FRCPath, DipECVP. Professor of Systematic Veterinary Pathology, Department of Veterinary Pathology, Glasgow University; b. 10.4.36, Glasgow; m., Myrtle Elizabeth Stewart Levack; 1 d. Educ. Coatbridge High School; Glasgow University. Scientific Editor, Research in Veterinary Science, 1981-88; British Council Specialist, Argentina, 1982, Ethiopia, 1986-88. President, Association of Veterinary Teachers and Research Workers, 1984; Secretary, European Association of Establishments for Veterinary Education, 1988-92; Chairman, Veterinary Panel, Royal College of Pathologists, 1988-93; Member, Council, Royal College of Veterinary Surgeons, 1993-98; Diplomate, European College of Veterinary Pathologists, 1995; Member, Board, European Society of Veterinary Pathology, 1994-98; Member, Editorial Board, European Journal of Veterinary Pathology, since 1994; Charter Diplomate, European College of Veterinary Pathologists, 1995. Recreations: travel; gardening; hill-walking; swimming; gastronomy. Address: (h.) North East Corner, Buchanan Castle Estate, Drymen G63 0HX; T.-01361 660781.

Pirie, Sheriff Iain Gordon, MA, LLB. Sheriff of Glasgow and Strathkelvin, since 1982; b. 15.1.33, Dundee; m., Dr Sheila B. Pirie; 2 s.; 1 d. Educ. Harris Academy, Dundee; St. Andrews University. Procurator Fiscal, Dumfries, 1971-76, Ayr, 1976-79; Sheriff of South Strathclyde, Dumfries and Galloway, 1979-82. Address: (b.) Sheriff Court, 1 Carlton Place, Glasgow G5 9DA; T.-0141-429 8888.

Pitches, Sally Jane, LLB, NP. Executive Director, The Guide Association, since 1997; b. 5.6.57, Edinburgh. Educ. Currie High School; Strathclyde University. Solicitor, private practice, Edinburgh. Founding President, Edinburgh Breakfast Rotary Club; Senator, Junior Chamber International. Recreations: cookery; bridge; travel. Address: (b.) 16 Coates Crescent, Edinburgh; T.-0131-226 4545.

Pitt, Professor Douglas Charles, BA, MA, PhD, FBIM. Professor of Organisational Analysis, Strathclyde University, since 1989; Dean, Strathclyde Business School; b. 13.7.43, Greenock; m., Jean Hamilton Spowart. Educ. Varndean Grammar School, Brighton; Exeter University; Manchester University. Executive Officer, Civil Service, 1961-64; Lecturer, then Senior Lecturer and Reader, Strathclyde University, 1973-89. Current research interest: telecommunications deregulation in Britain and the USA. Publications: The Post Office Telecommunications Function, 1980; Public Administration: An Introduction, 1980; Government Departments: An Organisational Analysis, 1981; The Computer Revolution in Public Administration, 1984. Recreations: German; riding; swimming; fishing; skiing; sailing; traditional jazz; bluegrass; opera. Address: (h.) 19 Waterfoot Road, Newton Mearns, Glasgow G77 5RU; T.-0141-639 5359.

Pitt, Stuart. Director, Royal Observatory. Address: (b.) Blackford Hill, Edinburgh EH9 3HJ.

Pittock, Professor Murray G.H., MA, DPhil, FRHistS, FSAScot. Professor in Literature, Strathclyde University, since 1996; Editor, Scottish Literary Journal, since 1995; b. 5.1.62; m., Anne Grace Thornton Martin; 2 d. Educ. Aberdeen Grammar School; Glasgow University; Balliol College, Oxford (Snell Exhibitioner). Lecturer, Pembroke College, Oxford, 1987; British Academy Postdoctoral Fellow, Aberdeen University, 1988; Lecturer, Edinburgh University, 1989, Reader, 1994 (from 1995 Co-ordinator, University in Scotland Initiative). Royal Society of Edinburgh BP Humanities Research Prize, 1992-94. Publications: The Invention of Scotland, 1991; Spectrum of Decadence, 1993; Poetry and Jacobite Politics in Eighteenth-Century Britain and Ireland, 1994; The Myth of the Jacobite Clans, 1995; Inventing and Resisting Britain, 1997. Address: (b.) English Studies, Strathclyde University, Richmond Street, Glasgow, G1 1XH; T.-0141-548 4490.

Pittock-Wesson, Joan Hornby, BA, MA, PhD. Honorary Research Fellow in English, Aberdeen University, since 1995; Director of Research, Thomas Reid Institute for Interdisciplinary Research in the Humanities, Sciences and Medicine, Aberdeen University, 1994-95; b. 1.5.30, Featherstone; 1 s. Educ. Normanton High School for Girls; Victoria University of Manchester. Extra-Mural and Adult Education Lecturer, 1955-64; Lecturer in English, Senior Lecturer, Aberdeen University, 1966-95; founder Director, Cultural History Centre, Aberdeen University, 1985-94; founder Director, Institute for Cultural Studies (Thomas Reid Institute), 1990-94. Editor, British Journal for Eighteenth Century Studies, 1978-80; President, British Society for Eighteenth Century Studies, 1980-82. Publications: Ascendancy of Taste, 1973; Aberdeen and the Enlightenment (Co-Editor), 1987; Interpretation and Cultural History (Co-Editor), 1991; Poetry and The Redemption of History, 1998. Recreation: walking. Address: (b.) Department of English, Aberdeen University, Aberdeen; T.-01224 272629.

Pitts, Professor Nigel Berry, BDS (Hons), PhD, FDS, RCSEng, FDS, RCSEdin. Director, Dental Health Services Research Unit, since 1985; Head, Department of Dental Health, Dundee University, 1990-97, and Professor of Dental Health, since 1991; Dean of Dentistry, since 1997; b. 1954, London; m., Elizabeth Ann; 3 s. Educ. Royal Liberty School; London Hospital Medical College Dental School, London University. House Officer/Senior House Officer, The London Hospital; Lecturer, Department of Conservative Dentistry, London Hospital Medical College Dental School; Lecturer, then Senior Lecturer, Department of Conservative Dentistry, University of Hong Kong; Director, Chief Scientist's Office Dental Health Services Research Unit. Past President, British Association for the Study of Community Dentistry; President, Diagnostic Systems Group, International Association for Dental Research. Recreations: family; photography. Address: (b.) Dental School, Park Place, Dundee DD1 4HR; T.-01382 635959.

Platt, Joseph, LLB. Founding Partner, Philpott Platt and Niblett, Solicitors, Dumbarton; part-time Tutor, Glasgow University; Member, Council, Law Society of Scotland; b. 22.5.51, Dumbarton; m., Christina Susan; 2 s. Educ. Dumbarton Academy; Glasgow University. Qualified as Solicitor, 1974; Partner, J.W. Dunn & Co., 1976. Recreations: hill-walking; photography; reading. Address: 105 Glasgow Road, Dumbarton; T.-01389 733777.

Plotkin, Professor Gordon David, BSc, PhD, FRS, FRSE. Professor in Computer Science, Edinburgh University; Director, Laboratory for the Foundation of Computer Science; b. 9.9.46, Glasgow; m.; 1 s. Educ. Glasgow High School for Boys; Glasgow University; Edinburgh University. Lecturer, then Reader, Edinburgh University; Director, Laboratory for the Foundation of Computer Science; Member, Academia Europaea; Editor: Information and Computation, Mathematical Structures in Computer Science, Theoretical Computer Science. Recreations: chess; hill-walking. Address: (b.) Department of Computer Science, King's Buildings, Edinburgh University, Edinburgh; T.-0131-650 5158.

Pollacchi, Derek Albert Paterson. Chief Executive, Central Scotland Healthcare NHS Trust, since 1994; b. 23.7.51, Dumbarton; m., Jean Lindsay Mullan; 2 d. Educ. St. Mungo's Academy, Glasgow. Various junior/middle management positions, 1972-79; Senior Administrator, Mearnskirk General Hospital, Glasgow, 1979-83; Leverndale Hospital, Glasgow, 1983-84; Director of Administrative Services, Lennox Castle Hospital/Stobill General Hospital and associated community health services, 1984-87; General Manager, Mental Handicap Services, Forth Valley Health Board, 1987-92; Chief Executive, Royal Scottish National Hospital and Community NHS Trust, 1993-94. Recreations: swimming; badminton; hill-walking; reading. Address: (b.) Old Denny Road, Larbert FK5 4SD; T.-01324 570700.

Pollen, Roger Alan, ARCM. Managing Director, BT Scottish Ensemble, since 1988, Deputy Chairman, since 1997; Director, Theatre Cryptic, since 1997; b. 5.8.62. Educ. Royal Belfast Academical Institution; City of Belfast School of Music; RSAMD. Freelance cellist, since 1984; Musical Director, T. Flynn Productions Ltd., 1985; Co-ordinator, Scottish Piano Competition, 1985-86; Orchestra Manager, Scottish Chamber Orchestra, 1986-88. Member, Management Committee, Scottish International Piano Competition. Recreations: collecting and restoring vintage and classic cars; sailing; skiing; para-gliding; athletics; tree-planting. Address: (b.) 2 Anchor Lane, Glasgow G1 2HW; T.-0141-221 2222.

Pollock, Sheriff Alexander, MA (Oxon), LLB. Sheriff of Grampian, Highland and Islands, at Aberdeen and Stonehaven, since 1993; b. 21.7.44, Glasgow; m., Verena Francesca Gertraud Alice Ursula Critchley; 1 s.; 1 d. Educ. Rutherglen Academy; Glasgow Academy; Brasenose College, Oxford; Edinburgh University; Perugia University. Partner, Bonar Mackenzie & Kermack, WS, 1971-73; called to Scottish Bar, 1973; Conservative candidate: West Lothian, General Election, February 1974, Moray and Nairn, General Election, October 1974; MP, Moray and Nairn, 1979-83, Moray, 1983-87; Parliamentary Private Secretary to Secretary of State for Scotland, 1982-86; PPS to Secretary of State for Defence, 1986-87; Advocate Depute, 1990-91; Sheriff (Floating) of Tayside, Central and Fife, at Stirling, 1991-93. Member, Queen's Bodyguard for Scotland (Royal Company of Archers), since 1984. Recreations: walking; music. Address: (h.) Drumdarrach, Forres, Moray.

Polson, Alison. Secretary, Scottish Conservative and Unionist Association, since 1995; b. 11.6.39; m., Alick Polson (deceased). Educ. Chadderton Grammar School; Whitelands College, London. Head of Geography, then Senior Mistress, Hollin High School, Middleton, Manchester; Agent, Tweeddale Ettrick and Lauderdale, from 1989; Senior Agent for the Borders, 1993-95; Chairman, Scottish Conservative Agents, 1994-95. Recreations: music; travel; gardening; old films with happy endings. Address: (h.) Rosemount, Innerleithen Road, Peebles EH45 8BE.

Ponsonby, Bernard Joseph. Reporter/Presenter, Scottish Television, since 1990; b. Glasgow. Educ. Trinity High School, Rutherglen; Strathclyde University. Researcher to Rt. Hon. Dr. Dickson Mabon, 1987; Press Officer, Scottish Liberal Democrats, 1988-89; party's first Parliamentary candidate, Glasgow Govan, 1988; PR and Media Consultant, freelance Reporter for BBC Radio Scotland, 1989-90; Principal Presenter of political, election, and by-election programmes, Scottish Television; presented Platform, since 1996, Scottish Voices, Scottish Questions, Trial by Night. Recreations: golf; Celtic Football Club. Address: (b.) Scottish Television, Cowcaddens, Glasgow G2 3PR; T.-0141-300 3000.

Ponton, Professor John Wylie, BSc, PhD, FIChemE, FEng. Professor of Chemical Engineering, Edinburgh University, since 1989; b. 2.5.43, Edinburgh; m., Katherine Jane Victoria Eachus. Educ. Melville College, Edinburgh; Edinburgh University. Recreations: engineering; amateur radio; music. Address: (b.) Department of Chemical Engineering, Edinburgh University, EH9 3JL; T.-0131-650 4860.

Poole, Sheriff Isobel Anne, LLB. Sheriff of Lothian and Borders; b. 9.12.41, Oxford. Educ. Oxford High School for Girls (GPDST); Edinburgh University. Advocate. Recreations: country; arts; gardens; friends. Address: (b.) Sheriffs' Chambers, Sheriff Court, Edinburgh.

Porteous, Brian William, BSc (Hons), MILAM, DipRM. Depute Director, Parks and Recreation, Glasgow City Council, since 1994; b. 6.2.51, Falkirk; m., Shena; 3 s. Educ. Falkirk High School; St. Andrews University; Moray House College of Education; Loughborough University of Technology. Joined Scottish Sports Council as Development Officer, 1979, appointed Director of Operations, 1989. Honorary Secretary, British Orienteering Federation, 1974-76; former Member, Board, National Coaching Foundation; President, Scottish Orienteering Association, since 1996. Publication: Orienteering, 1979. Recreations: golf; orienteering; amateur opera/musicals; caravanning. Address: (h.) Croft House, 2 Spoker's Loan, Balfron, Glasgow G63 0PA; T.(b.)-0141-287 5520.

Porter, Adrian, MA, BD. Head Master, St. Aloysius' College, Glasgow, since 1995; b. 17.11.59, Bristol. Educ. St. Brendan's, Bristol; Campion Hall, Oxford; Heythrop, London. Member, Society of Jesus (Jesuits), since 1978. Recreation: theatre. Address: (b.) St. Aloysius' College, 45 Hill Street, Glasgow G3 6RJ; T.-0141-332 3190.

Porter, Professor Richard William, MB, ChB, FRCSE. Director of Education and Training, Royal College of Surgeons of Edinburgh, since 1995; b. 16.2.35, Doncaster; m., Christine; 4 s. Educ. Oundle School; Edinburgh University. Consultant Orthopaedic Surgeon, Doncaster Royal Infirmary, 1978-91; Sir Harry Platt Chair of Orthopaedic Surgery, Aberdeen University, 1991-95. Chairman, Educational Committee, British Orthopaedic Association. Publication: Management of Back Pain, 1993. Address: (b.) Royal College of Surgeons of Edinburgh, Nicolson Street, Edinburgh EH8 9DW.

Potter, Brian Thomas, BSc, MB, ChB, MRCGP. Scottish Secretary, British Medical Association, since 1995; b. 25.8.52, Edinburgh; 1 s.; 2 d. Educ. Scotus Academy, Edinburgh; Edinburgh University Medical School. Registrar posts, Accident and Emergency Medicine, Renal Medicine, Royal Infirmary, Edinburgh, and Geriatric Medicine, City Hospital, Edinburgh; Principal in General Practice, Edinburgh; Medical Officer, Marks and Spencer, Edinburgh; Medical Practitioner, Glencorse Army Depot; Occupational Physician, City Hospital; Senior Medical Officer, Scottish Office Home and Health Department, 1992-95. Former Secretary, Lothian Division, BMA; Secretary, Lothian Area Medical Committee; former

Member, Scottish Council, BMA. Recreations: swimming; keep-fit; singing. Address: (b.) BMA, Scottish Office, 3 Hill Place, Edinburgh EH8 9EQ; T.-0131-662 4820.

Pottinger, Graham, LLB, CA, ACMA. Chief Executive, Scottish Mutual Assurance plc, since 1997; Managing Director, Abbey National Financial and Investment Services plc, since 1997; Director, Abbey National Life plc, since 1992; b. 14.6.49, Glasgow; m., Dorothy; 1 s.; 1 d. Educ. Jordanhill College School, Glasgow; Glasgow University. Peat Marwick Mitchell & Co., 1966-72; Partner, Deloitte Haskins & Sells, 1972-79; Controller, UK and Africa, Cargill Plc, 1980-92; Finance Director, Scottish Mutual Assurance plc, 1992-96. Member, Council, Institute of Chartered Accountants of Scotland. Recreations: swimming; gardening. Address: (b.) Abbey National House, 301 St. Vincent Street, Glasgow G2 5HN; T.-0141-275 8654.

Pounder, Professor Derrick John, MB, ChB, FRCPA, FFPathRCPI, FCAP, MRCPath, FHKCPath. Professor of Forensic Medicine, Dundee University, since 1987; b. 25.2.49, Pontypridd; m., Georgina Kelly; 1 s.; 2 d. Educ. Pontypridd Boys' Grammar; Birmingham University. Senior Lecturer (Forensic Pathology), University of Adelaide; Deputy Chief Medical Examiner, Edmonton, Alberta, and Associate Professor, Universities of Alberta and Calgary, 1985-87. Freeman of Llantrisant. Recreations: photography; medieval architecture; almost lost causes. Address: (b.) Department of Forensic Medicine, Royal Infirmary, Dundee DD1 9ND; T.-01382 200794.

Power, Professor David Martin, BCom, MSc(Econ), PhD. Professor of Business Finance, Dundee University, since 1996; b. 20.7.64, Waterford, Ireland. Educ. De La Salle College, Waterford; University College, Cork; London School of Economics. Lecturer/Senior Lecturer, Dundee University, 1987-96. Fellow, Royal Society of Arts. Recreations: golf; tennis. Address: (b.) Department of Accountancy and Business Finance, Dundee University, Dundee DD1 4HN; T.-01382 344854.

Power, Graham, QPM, MA (Oxon). Deputy Chief Constable, Lothian and Borders Police, since 1994; b. 2.6.47, Middlesbrough; m.; 2 s.; 1 d. Educ. Stainsby Boys School, Middlesbrough; Queen's College, Oxford. Constable to Superintendent, Cleveland, 1966-88; Chief Superintendent, North Yorks, Harrogate, 1988-91; Assistant Chief Constable, Lothian and Borders, 1991-94. Recreation: trout fishing. Address: (b.) Police HQ, Fettes Avenue, Edinburgh EH4 1RB; T.-0131-311 3100.

Prag, Thomas Gregory Andrew, MA, FIMgt. Managing Director, Moray Firth Radio; b. 2.1.47, London; m., Angela; 3 s. Educ. Westminster School; Brasenose College, Oxford. Joined BBC, 1968, as Studio Manager; Producer, BBC Radio Oxford; Programme Organiser, BBC Radio Highland; first Chief Executive, Moray Firth Radio, 1981. Trustee, Highland Community Foundation; Director, Commercial Radio Companies Association; President, Inverness and District Chamber of Commerce. Recreations: good intentions towards restoration of 1950 Daimler; keeping clock collection wound; family; growing vegetables; chasing deer off vegetables. Address: (b.) Moray Firth Radio, PO Box 271, Inverness IV3 6SF.

Pratt, Roger Allan, CBE. Director, The Conservative Party in Scotland, since 1993; b. 28.12.50, Birmingham; m., Lynn. Educ. King Edwards Five Ways Grammar School. YC Organiser and Youth Officer, 1971-74; Conservative Party Agent, 1975-76; National YC Organiser, 1976-79; Agent, 1980-84; Deputy Central Office Agent, N.W. Area, 1984-89; Central Office Agent, then Regional Director, North West Area, 1989-93. Address: (b.) Suite 1/1, 14 Links Place, Leith, Edinburgh, EH6 7EZ; T.-0131-555 2900.

Prescott, Paul G., PhD. Director, Railtrack Scotland Zone, since 1993; b. 12.1.51, Oldbury; m.; 1 s.; 1 d. Educ. King Edward's School, Birmingham; Gonville and Caius College, Cambridge; Imperial College, London. Water Resources Board, 1973-76; Marketing Manager, BR Provincial Sector, 1985-90; Planning and Marketing Manager, ScotRail, 1990-93. Recreations: hill-walking; genealogy; linguistics; travel. Address: (b.) Buchanan House, 58 Port Dundas Road, Glasgow G4 0LQ; T.-0141-335 2424.

Press, Professor Jeffrey Ian, BA (Hons) (Spanish), BA (Hons) (Russian), PhD. Established Professor in Russian (Comparative Linguistics), St. Andrews University, since 1995; b. 23.3.47, Oldham; m., Marie-Christine; 1 s.; 1 d. Educ. Hulme Grammar School, Oldham; London University. Lecturer in Russian, Queen Mary College, London University, 1970-79, SSEES and Queen Mary College, 1979-87, Senior Lecturer, 1987-89; Professor of Slavonic and Comparative Linguistics, London University, 1990-95. Publications: books on Breton, Slavonic languages, Ukranian and Lithuanian linguistics. Recreations: astronomy; photography; walking; learning languages. Address: (b.) St. Andrews University, St. Andrews KY16 9AL; T.-01334 463631.

Presslie, Sheriff George. Sheriff of Lothian and Borders at Haddington. Address: (b.) Sheriff Court, Court Street, Haddington, EH41 3HN.

Preston, David Michael, LLB, NP. Solicitor, since 1976; b. 26.8.52, Glasgow; m., Sheila Elizabeth; 2 s. Educ. Hillhead High School; Dundee University. Part-time Depute Procurator Fiscal, 1976-79; Clerk to General Commissioners of Income Tax, since 1976; Registrar, Episcopal Diocese of Argyll and the Isles, since 1977; Partner, Hosack and Sutherland, since 1978; Member, Council, Law Society of Scotland, since 1990 (Convenor: Update Committee, 1992-96, Remuneration Committee, since 1996). Past Chairman and first Hon. President, Oban Round Table; Chairman, Oban Youth and Community Association, since 1980; Commodore, Oban Sailing Club, 1992-93; Secretary, Atlantis Leisure, since 1991. Recreations: sailing; skiing; rugby spectating; logistical supporter (travel and finance) of two sons. Address: (h.) Westbank, Duncraggan Road, Oban; T.-01631 563228.

Preston, George Dawson Chrystal, MA. Secretary and Treasurer, Queen's Nursing Institute Scotland, since 1992; b. 20.4.31, Hampton; m., Elizabeth Anne Rennie; 1 d. Educ. Fettes College; Gonville and Caius College, Cambridge. Science Staff, Fettes College, 1955-91, Housemaster, 1959-64, and 1969-81, Senior Master, 1981-91. Keeper of Records, Fettes College. Recreations: gardening; computing; social court games. Address: (b.) 31 Castle Terrace, Edinburgh, EH1 2EL; T.-0131-229 2333.

Preston, Ian Mathieson Hamilton, CBE, BSc, PhD, FEng, MInstP, FIEE. Chartered Engineer; Chairman, East of Scotland Water; Chairman, Scottish Council Development and Industry, since 1993; Chief Executive, Scottish Power, 1990-95; Non-Executive Director: Scottish Coal Co., Motherwell Bridge Holdings, Clydeport plc, Morgan Grenfell (Scotland) Ltd., Hub Power Co. (Pakistan); b. 18.7.32, Bournemouth; m., Sheila Hope Pringle; 2 s. Educ. Kilmarnock Academy; Glasgow University. University Assistant Lecturer, 1957-59; joined SSEB as Assistant Reactor Physicist, 1959; various appointments until Chief Engineer, Generation Design and Construction Division, 1972; Director General, Central Electricity Generating Board, Generation Development and Construction Division, 1977-83; Deputy Chairman, South of Scotland Electricity Board, 1983-90. Address: East of Scotland Water, Pentland Gait, 597 Calder Road, Edinburgh EH11 4HJ.

Preston, Robert John, ACIS. Group Commercial Director, Marshall Food Group Ltd., since 1996 (previously Finance

Director/Company Secretary); b. 23.2.44, Watlington; m., Sandra Lena; 1 s. Educ. Grove Academy, Dundee; Dundee Institute of Art and Technology. Joined Marshall Food Group, 1989. Member, Council, CBI Scotland. Recreations: golf; reading; sports spectating. Address: (b.) Marshall Food Group Ltd., Newbridge, Midlothian; T.-0131-333 3341.

Price, Professor Allan, PhD, MB, BCh, FRCP(Edin), FRCR. Professor of Radiation Oncology, Edinburgh University, since 1996; b. 3.6.58, Cardiff; m., Lesley; 2 s. Educ. Yeovil School; Welsh National School of Medicine. General medical training, Swansea, Middlesborough; oncology training, Edinburgh, Hammersmith and Royal Marsden Hospitals; ICRF Clinical Research Fellow, 1988-92; Consultant Clinical Oncologist, Addenbrooke's and Papworth Hospitals, Cambridge, 1995-96. Scientific Adviser, Melville Trust; Consultant, Lilly Oncology. Recreations: squash; skiing. Address: (b.) Department of Clinical Oncology, Western General Hospital, Edinburgh EH4 2XU; T.-0131-537 2205.

Price, Barclay. Depute Director (Planning and Development), Scottish Arts Council, since 1997; b. 26.7.45, Glasgow; m., Fiona Dick. Educ. Hillhead High School. Head of Development, Crafts Council; Administrator, Hoxton Hall Community Theatre; Visual Arts Subsidy Officer, Arts Council of GB; Officer, Clydesdale Bank. Address: (b.) Scottish Arts Council, 12 Manor Place, Edinburgh EH3 7DD; T.-0131-225 9833.

Price, Janet Elisabeth, BA, PGCE, DipAppLing. Principal, Inverness College, since 1995; Member, North West Regional Board, Scottish Natural Heritage, since 1996; b. 24.2.40, Rugby. Educ. London University; Edinburgh University. Lecturer in Languages, London, 1967-70, Oxford, 1970-75 (both in FE sector); Lecturer, Newcastle University, 1975-82; Head of Voluntary Sector, Adult Education Institute, Brighton, 1982-86; Assistant Principal, Stevenson College, Edinburgh, 1986-91; Vice-Principal, York College of Further and Higher Education, 1991-95. Recreations: creative writing; hill-walking; languages. Address: (h.) 3 Broadstone Park, Inverness, IV2 3JZ.

Price, Professor Nicholas Charles, MA, DPhil. Professor of Biochemistry, Stirling University, since 1994; b. 12.8.46, Stafford; m., Margaret Hazel Millen; 1 s.; 2 d. Educ. King Edward VI School, Stafford; Merton College, Oxford. Fereday Fellow, St. John's College, Oxford, 1969-74; Harkness Fellow, University of Pennsylvania, 1971-72; Demonstrator, Department of Biochemistry, Oxford University, 1973-74; Lecturer/Senior Lecturer/Reader in Biochemistry, Stirling University, 1974-94. Publications: three books; over 100 journal articles. Recreations: church activities; fund-raising. Address: (b.) Department of Biological and Molecular Sciences, Stirling University, Stirling FK9 4LA; T.-01786 467765.

Price, Rev. Peter Owen, CBE, QHC, BA, FPhS. Minister, Blantyre Old Parish Church, Glasgow, 1985-96; b. 18.4.30, Swansea; m., 1, Margaret Winifred Trevan (deceased); 2, Mary Hamill Robertson; 3 d. Educ. Wyggeston School, Leicester; Didsbury Theological College, Bristol; Open University. Chaplain, Royal Navy, 1960-84, latterly Principal Chaplain, Church of Scotland and Free Churches (Naval), Ministry of Defence, 1981-84; appointed Honorary Chaplain to the Queen, 1981. Recreations: clay pigeon shooting; rugby; warm water sailing; golf. Address: Duncraigan, 20A Old Bothwell Road, Bothwell, Glasgow G71 8AW; T.-01698 854032.

Prickett, Professor (Alexander Thomas) Stephen, MA, PhD, DipEd, FAHA. Regius Professor of English Language and Literature, Glasgow University, since 1990; b. 4.6.39, Freetown, Sierra Leone; m., Maria Angelica; 2 d. Educ.

Kent College, Canterbury; Trinity Hall, Cambridge; University College, Oxford. English Teacher, Methodist College, Uzauakoli, E. Nigeria, 1962-64; Lecturer/Reader, Sussex University, 1967-82; Professor of English, Australian National University, Canberra, 1983-89. Publications: Do It Yourself Doom, 1962; Coleridge and Wordsworth: the Poetry of Growth, 1970; Romanticism and Religion, 1976; Victorian Fantasy, 1979; Words and the Word: language poetics and Biblical interpretation, 1986; England and the French Revolution, 1988; Reading the Text: Biblical criticism and literary theory, 1991; Origins of Narrative: The Romantic Appropriation of the Bible, 1996; World's Classics Bible (Editor), 1997. Recreations: walking; skiing; tennis; drama. Address: (b.) Department of English Literature, Glasgow University, Glasgow; T.-0141-339 8855.

Pride, Professor Stephen James, BSc, PhD, FRSE. Professor of Mathematics, Glasgow University, since 1992 (Reader in Mathematics, 1987-92); b. 8.1.49, Melbourne. Educ. Hampton High School, Melbourne; Monash University, Melbourne; Australian National University, Canberra. Research Fellow, Open University, 1974-78; Temporary Lecturer in Mathematics, King's College, London University, 1978-79; Lecturer in Mathematics, Glasgow University, 1979-87. Member, Editorial Board, London Mathematical Society; Member, Mathematics College, Engineering and Physical Sciences Research Council. Publications: more than 60 articles on algebra (mainly group theory). Recreations: cycling; travelling; cinema; gardening. Address: (h.) 54 Airlie Street, Glasgow G12 9SN; T.-0141-339 7395.

Priest, Professor Eric Ronald, BSc, MSc, PhD, FRSE. Professor of Theoretical Solar Physics, St. Andrews University, since 1983; b. 7.11.43, Birmingham; m., Clare Wilson; 3 s.; 1 d. Educ. King Edward VI School, Birmingham; Nottingham University; Leeds University. St. Andrews University: Lecturer in Applied Mathematics, 1968, Reader, 1977; SERC Senior Fellow, 1992-97. Elected Member, Norwegian Academy of Sciences and Letters, 1994; Chairman, RSE Mathematics Committee; Member, HEFC Research Assessment Exercise Committee. Recreations: bridge; walking; swimming; swingnastics; children. Address: (b.) Mathematical and Computational Sciences Department, St. Andrews University, St. Andrews KY16 9SS; T.-01334 463709.

Pringle, Kevin James, MA (Hons). Director of Communications and Research, Scottish National Party, since 1995; b. 30.12.67, Dundee. Educ. Perth High School; Aberdeen University. Research Officer, SNP, 1989-95. Recreations: cinema; reading. Address: (b.) 6 North Charlotte Street, Edinburgh EH2 4JH.

Pritchard, Kenneth William, OBE, BL, WS. Secretary, Law Society of Scotland, 1976-97; Temporary Sheriff, since 1995; b. 14.11.33, London; Honorary Sheriff, Dundee; m., Gretta Murray; 2 s.; 1 d. Educ. Dundee High School; Fettes College; St. Andrews University. National Service, Argyll and Sutherland Highlanders, 1955-57; 2nd Lt., 1956; TA, 1957-62 (Captain); joined J. & J. Scrimgeour, Solicitors, Dundee, 1957; Senior Partner, 1970-76; Member, Sheriff Court Rules Council, 1973-76, Lord Dunpark's Committee considering Reparation upon Criminal Conviction, 1973-77; Hon. Visiting Professor, Law School, Strathclyde University; Hon. Member, Law Institute of Victoria, 1985; Hon. Member, Law Society of New Zealand, 1987; Hon. Member, Faculty of Procurators and Solicitors in Dundee; Member, University Court of Dundee, 1989-93; President, Dundee High School Old Boys Club, 1975-76. Recreation: golf. Address: (h.) 22/4 Kinellan Road, Edinburgh EH12 6ES; T.-0131-337 4294.

Procter, Rev. Robert Hendy, MA. Secretary, Scottish Council, The Scout Association, 1982-96; b. 22.1.31, Alloa; m., Elizabeth Rosemary; 1 s.; 2 d. Educ. Fettes College; Trinity Hall, Cambridge. Commissioned, Royal Corps of Signals, 1950; Patons & Baldwins Ltd., 1954-79 (General Manager, from 1969); Director, John Gladstone & Co. Ltd., Galashiels, 1980-82. General Commissioner of Income Tax, Clackmannan Division, 1976-80; Honorary Sheriff, Tayside Central and Fife, at Alloa, 1975-97; Edinburgh Diocese training for ministry, 1988-91; Team Priest, Christ Church Morningside, 1994; Member, Lothian Valuation Appeal Panel, 1994; Chairman, Garleton Singers, 1996. Recreations: hill-walking; choral singing. Address: (h.) 2 Braid Avenue, Morningside, Edinburgh EH10 6DR; T.-0131-447 1140.

Proctor, Alan. Editor, Evening Telegraph and Sporting Post, Dundee, since 1995; b. 4.9.40, Forfar; m., Sheila Morrison Kerr; 2 d. Educ. Brechin High School. D.C. Thomson, since 1959. Recreations: walking; reading. Address: (b.) D.C. Thomson & Co. Ltd., 80 Kingsway East, Dundee DD4 8SL; T.-01382 223131.

Prosser, Professor James Anthony William (Tony), LLB. John Millar Professor of Law, Glasgow University, since 1992; b. 3.5.54, Ludlow. Educ. Ludlow Grammar School; Liverpool University. Research Assistant in Law, Southampton University, 1974-76; Lecturer in Law, Hull University, 1976-79; Lecturer, Senior Lecturer, Sheffield University, 1980-92; Jean Monnet Fellow, European University Institute, Florence, 1987-88. Publications: Test Cases for the Poor; Nationalised Industries and Public Control; Law and the Regulators; Privatizing Public Enterprises (Co-author); Waiving the Rules (Co-editor). Recreations: walking; cinema; jazz. Address: (b.) School of Law, Glasgow University, Glasgow G12 8QQ; T.-0141-339 8855, Ext. 4180.

Prosser, (Leslie) Charles, DFA, DAEd. Secretary, Royal Fine Art Commission for Scotland, since 1976; b. 27.10.39, Harrogate; m., Coral; 1 s.; 2 d. Educ. Bath Academy of Art at Corsham Court; Slade School of Fine Art, London University. Assistant Lecturer in Fine Art, Blackpool School of Art, 1962-64; Fine Art research, Royal Academy, Stockholm, 1964-65; Lecturer in Fine Art, Leeds/Jacob Kramer College of Art, 1965-76; research in Art Education, Leeds University, 1974-75. Leverhulme European Arts Research Award, 1964. Recreations: Scottish dancing and hill-walking. Address: (h.) 28 Mayfield Terrace, Edinburgh EH9 1RZ; T.-0131-668 1141.

Prosser, Hon. Lord QC, MA (Oxon), LLB, HonFRIAS. Senator of the College of Justice in Scotland and Lord of Session, since 1986; b. 23.11.34, Edinburgh; m., Vanessa Lindsay; 2 s.; 2 d. Educ. Edinburgh Academy; Corpus Christi College, Oxford; Edinburgh University. Advocate, 1962; Queen's Counsel, 1974; Vice-Dean, Faculty of Advocates, 1979-83, Dean of Faculty, 1983-86. Chairman, Royal Lyceum Theatre Company, 1987-92; Chairman, Royal Fine Art Commission for Scotland, 1990-95; Chairman, Scottish Architectural Education Trust; Chairman, Scottish Historic Buildings Trust; Chairman, Chamber Group of Scotland; Member, Franco-British Council. Address: 7 Randolph Crescent, Edinburgh EH3 7TH; T.-0131-225 2709.

Proudfoot, Edwina Valmai Windram, MA, DipEd, FSA, FSA Scot, MIFA. Archaeologist; Director, St. Andrews Heritage Services, since 1988; Honorary Research Fellow, St. Andrews University, since 1985; b. 9.3.35, Dover; m., Professor V. Bruce Proudfoot (qv); 2 s. Educ. Invergordon Academy; Inverness Royal Academy; Edinburgh University. Lecturer (including Adult Education) in Archaeology, since 1959; director of excavations, numerous projects; Editor, Discovery and Excavation in Scotland, 1977-90; President, Council for Scottish Archaeology,

1983-89; Founder, first Chairman, Tayside and Fife Archaeological Committee, 1975-82; Member, Ancient Monuments Board for Scotland, since 1986; Chairman, St. Andrews Preservation Trust, 1988-93; Council Member, National Trust for Scotland, 1984-89 and since 1993; Member, Executive Committee, NTS, since 1994. Recreations: gardening; music; walking. Address: 12 Wardlaw Gardens, St. Andrews, KY16 9DW; T.-01334 473293.

Proudfoot, Professor V. Bruce, OBE, BA, PhD, FSA, FRSE, FRSGS, FSA Scot. Chair of Council, Royal Scottish Geographical Society; Emeritus Professor of Geography, St. Andrews University; b. 24.9.30, Belfast; m., Edwina Valmai Windram Field; 2 s. Educ. Royal Belfast Academical Institution; Queen's University, Belfast. Research Officer, Nuffield Quaternary Research Unit, Queen's University, Belfast, 1954-58; Lecturer in Geography: Queen's University, Belfast, 1958-59, Durham University, 1959-67; Hatfield College, Durham: Tutor, 1960-63, Librarian, 1963-65; Visiting Fellow, University of Auckland and Commonwealth Visiting Fellow, Australia, 1966; Alberta University, Edmonton: Associate Professor, 1967-70, Professor, 1970-74; Co-ordinator, Socio-Economic Opportunity Studies and Staff Consultant, Alberta Human Resources Research Council, 1971-72; Professor of Geography, St. Andrews University, 1974-93. Royal Society of Edinburgh: Convener, Earth Sciences Committee, 1983-85, Vice-President, 1985-88, Convener, Grants Committee, 1988-91, General Secretary, 1991-96; Chairman, Society for Landscape Studies, 1979-83; Vice-President, Society of Antiquaries of Scotland, 1982-85; President, Section H, BAAS, 1985; Chairman, Rural Geography Study Group, Institute of British Geographers, 1980-84; Vice-President and Chairman of Council, since 1993, Chairman of Dundee Centre, since 1993, Royal Scottish Geographical Society; Hon. President, Scottish Association of Geography Teachers, 1982-84; Trustee, National Museum of Antiquities of Scotland, 1982-85. Recreation: gardening. Address: (h.) Westgate, Wardlaw Gardens, St. Andrews KY16 9DW; T.-01334 473293.

Provan, James Lyal Clark. Member, European Parliament, South Downs West, since 1994 (Chief Whip Conservative Group), Member: Fisheries Committee, Agricultural Committee, Transport and Tourism Committee; Chairman, EP Tourism Group; Chairman, Rowett Research Institute, Aberdeen (Board Member, since 1990); Non-Executive Director, New Holland N.V. and New Holland (Holdings), N.V. Farmer; b. 19.12.36, Glenfarg, Perthshire; m., Roweena Adele Lewis; 2 s.; 1 d. Educ. Ardvreck School, Crieff; Oundle School, Northants; Royal Agricultural College, Cirencester. National Farmers Union of Scotland: Area President, Kinross, 1965, Fife and Kinross, 1971; Tayside Regional Councillor, 1978-81; Member, Tay River Purification Board, 1978-81; Member (Conservative), European Parliament, NE Scotland, 1979-89; European Democratic (Conservative) Spokesman on Agriculture and Fisheries, 1981-87; Questor of European Parliament, 1987-89; former Executive Director, Scottish Financial Enterprise; Chairman, McIntosh of Dyce Ltd., McIntosh Donald Ltd., 1989-94; Member, Agriculture and Food Research Council, 1990-94. Recreations: country pursuits; sailing; flying; politics; agriculture. Address: Summerfield, Glenfarg, Perthshire PH2 9QD; Middle Lodge, Barns Green, Horsham, West Sussex RH13 7NL.

Pugh, Professor John Richard, BSc, PhD, CPhys, CEng, FInstMC, MInstP, MIEE. Head, Department of Physical Sciences and Professor of Physics, Glasgow Caledonian University, since 1992; Member, Board of Directors, Centre for Industrial Bulk Solids Handling, since 1993; b. 16.4.52, Shrewsbury; m., Christine Haldane; 3 s. Educ. Cumbernauld High School; Whitley Bay Grammar School; Glasgow University. Research Fellow, Glasgow University, 1976-80; Physicist, Barr and Stroud Ltd.,

Glasgow, 1980-91; Lecturer, then Senior Lecturer, Glasgow College, 1981-90; Professor of Physics and Depute Head, Glasgow Polytechnic, 1990-92. Tuba player, Bellshill Brass Band. Recreations: music; house restoration; gardening. Address: (b.) Department of Physical Sciences, Glasgow Caledonian University, Cowcaddens Road, Glasgow G4 0BA; T.-0141-331 3670.

Punter, Professor David Godfrey, BA, MA, PhD. Professor of English Studies, Stirling University, since 1988; b. 19.11.49, London; m., Caroline Mary Case-Punter; 1 s.; 2 d. Educ. John Lyon School, Harrow; Fitzwilliam College, Cambridge. Lecturer, University of East Anglia, 1973-84, Professor, Fudan University, Shanghai, 1983; Senior Lecturer, University of East Anglia, 1984-86; Director, Development of University English Teaching Project, 1985-86; Professor, Chinese University of Hong Kong, 1986-88. Publications: three books; 31 articles; 26 chapters contributed; 11 books edited. Recreations: child-minding; dog-minding; walking; squash. Address: (b.) Stirling University, Stirling, FK9 4LA; T.-01786 467495.

Purser, John Whitley, MA, PhD. Composer and Lecturer; Poet, Playwright, Musicologist, and Broadcaster; b. 10.2.42, Glasgow; 1 s.; 1 d. Educ. Fettes College; Glasgow University; Royal Scottish Academy of Music and Drama. Part-time Lecturer in English Literature, Glasgow University, 1981-85; Manager, Scottish Music Information Centre, 1985-87; compositions include two operas, numerous orchestral and chamber works; three books of poetry, The Counting Stick, A Share of the Wind and Amoretti; six radio plays and two radio series, A Change of Tune and Scotland's Music; music history: Is the Red Light On?, Scotland's Music; literary criticism: The Literary Works of Jack B. Yeats; awards: McVitie Scottish Writer of the Year, 1992; Glenfiddich Living Scotland Award, 1991; Giles Cooper Award, 1992; New York International Radio Festival Gold Medal, 1992; Sony Gold Medal, 1993; Oliver Brown Award, 1993; Scottish Heritage Award, 1993; Hon. Life Member, Saltire Society, 1993. Recreations: numerous. Address: (b.) 3 Drinan, Elgol, Isle of Skye IV49 9BG; T.-01471 866262.

Purves, David, BSc, PhD. Editor, Lallans Magazine, 1987-95; Playwright; b. 9.4.24, Selkirk; m., Lilian Rosemary; 3 s. Educ. Galashiels Academy; Edinburgh University. Head, Trace Element Department, Edinburgh School of Agriculture, 1956-82; Supervisor, Central Analytical Department, 1982-87; author of Trace Element Contamination of the Environment, 1985; poetry collections: Thrawart Threipins, 1976, Herts Bluid, 1995; many poems in Scots published; Fringe First play, The Puddok an the Princess and rendering in Scots of Macbeth published, 1992; Joint Editor, Mak It New, anthology of 21 years of writing in Lallans, 1995; Past Preses, Scots Language Society. Address: (h.) 8 Strathalmond Road, Edinburgh EH4 8AD; T.-0131-339 7929.

Purves, Rev. John Peter Sandison, BSc, PhD. Parish Minister, Dollar, Glendevon, Muckhart, since 1990; Chaplain, Dollar Academy, since 1990; b. 6.8.48, Edinburgh; m., Patricia Kennedy; 1 s.; 1 d. Educ. Bathgate Academy; Edinburgh University; Aberdeen University. VSO Teacher, Malawi, 1970-72; Adventure Playground Leader, Gorbals, Glasgow, 1972-74; Assistant Minister, Stonelaw Church, Rutherglen, 1977-78; Assistant Chaplain, Aberdeen University, 1978-82; Missionary, Mount Olivet, Jamaica, 1983-89. Kentucky Colonel, 1997. Recreation: gardening. Address: (h.) 2 Manse Road, Dollar FK14 7AJ; T.-01259 743432.

Purves, Rev. John S., LLB, BD. Minister, Drumchapel St. Andrew's, since 1984; b. 8.1.58, Edinburgh. Educ. Stewart's Melville College, Edinburgh; Edinburgh University. Assistant, King's Park Parish Church, 1982-84; Minister, Drumchapel Old Parish Church, 1984-95. Publication: King

David. Recreations: football; fanatical Hearts supporter; sports cars. Address: (h.) 6 Firdon Crescent, Glasgow G15 6QQ; T.-0141-944 4566.

Purves-Hume, Ian Campbell, FIMgt. Director, Royal Scottish Agricultural Benevolent Institution, since 1990; b. 22.7.38, London; m., Jill Cairns Fairbairn; 2 d. Educ. Ottershaw; Royal Military Academy, Sandhurst. Army Officer, Argyll and Sutherland Highlanders, 1958-90, to rank of Brigadier. Recreations: walking; bird-watching. Address: (b.) RSABI, Ingliston, Edinburgh EH28 8NB; T.-0131-333 1023/1027.

Purvis, John Robert, CBE, MA (Hons). International Business Consultant (Managing Partner, Purvis & Co.), since 1973; Director: James River UK Holdings Ltd., 1984-95, Johnson Fry European Utilities Trust PLC, since 1994, Jamont NV, 1994-95, Curtis Fine Papers Ltd., since 1995, Crown Vantage Ltd., since 1995, Kingdom Radio Ltd., since 1997; b. 6.7.38, St. Andrews; m., Louise Spears Durham; 1 s.; 2 d. Educ. Glenalmond; St. Andrews University. 2nd Lt., Scots Guards, 1956-58; First National City Bank (Citibank NA), London, New York City, Milan, 1962-69; Treasurer, Noble Grossart Ltd., Edinburgh, 1969-73; Director and Secretary, Brigton Farms Ltd., 1969-86; Managing Director, Founder, Owner, Gilmerton Management Services Ltd., 1973-92; Member, European Parliament, Mid Scotland and Fife, 1979-84 (Deputy Chief Whip, Group Spokesman on Monetary Affairs, Energy, Research and Technology) Vice Chairman, European Parliament Delegation to the Gulf States; Chairman, IBA Scottish Advisory Committee, 1985-89; Member for Scotland, IBA, 1985-89; Member of Council, St. Leonards School, St. Andrews, 1981-89; Chairman, Economic Affairs Committee, Scottish Conservative and Unionist Association, 1986-97, Vice-President of Association, 1987-89; Member, Scottish Advisory Committee on Telecommunications, 1990-97. Recreations: Italy and Scotland. Address: Gilmerton House, Dunino, St. Andrews KY16 8NB; T.-01334 75830.

Pyper, Mark Christopher Spring-Rice, BA. Headmaster, Gordonstoun School, since 1990; b. 13.8.47, Seaford; m., Jennifer L.; 1 s.; 2 d. Educ. Winchester College; Oxford University; London University. Assistant Master, Stoke Brunswick School, East Grinstead, 1966-68; Assistant Master, then Joint Headmaster, St. Wilfrid's School, Seaford, 1969-79; Registrar, Housemaster, then Deputy Headmaster, Sevenoaks School, 1979-90; Director, Sevenoaks Summer Festival, 1979-90. Address: (h.) Headmaster's House, Gordonstoun School, Elgin IV30 2RF; T.-01343 830445.

Q

Quinault, Francis Charles, BSc, PhD. Hebdomadar, St. Andrews University, since 1994; former Assistant Principal for External Affairs and Senior Lecturer in Psychology, St. Andrews University; b. 8.5.43, London; m., Wendy Ann Horton; 1 s.; 2 d. Educ. Dulwich College; St. Catharine's College, Cambridge; Bristol University. Ford Foundation Scholar, Oslo University, 1969-70. Member, National Committee for the Training of University Teachers, 1981-87. Recreations: acting; singing; hill-walking. Address: (b.) University of St. Andrews, 71 North Street, St. Andrews KY16 9AJ; T.-01334 462240.

Quinn, Terence James. Editor, Daily Record, since 1994; b. 17.11.51; m., Patricia Anna-Maria Gillespie; 1 s.; 1 d. Educ. St. Aloysius College, Glasgow. Editor: Telegraph & Argus, Bradford, 1984-89, Evening News, Edinburgh, 1989-92; Deputy Editorial Director, 1992-94, Editorial Director, 1994, Thomson Regional Newspapers. Recreations: tennis; reading; newspapers. Address: (b.) Daily Record, Anderston Quay, Glasgow G3 8DA; T.-0141-248 7000.

Qureshi, Robina Zia. Director, Positive Action on Housing Ltd., since 1995; Columnist, East Newspaper, since 1997; b. Glasgow; 1 s. Educ. Bellahouston Academy; Bearsden Academy. Advice Worker, Glasgow West Advisory Service, 1986-87; Welfare Adviser, Woodlands Advice Centre, 1987-90; Project Leader, Race and Housing Project, 1990-92; Race and Housing Officer, Housing Equality Action Unit, 1992-95; Editor, Race and Housing News, 1993-96. Ujima Pookar Award for outstanding contribution to black community. Recreations: horse-riding; arguing with friends at my favourite Italian restaurant on Queen Street. Address: (b.) 98 West George Street, Glasgow G2 1PJ; T.-0141-353 2220.

R

Racey, Professor Paul Adrian, MA, PhD, DSc, FIBiol, FRSE. Regius Professor of Natural History, Aberdeen University, since 1993 (Professor of Zoology, 1985-93); b. 7.5.44, Wisbech, Cambridgeshire; m., Anna Priscilla Notcutt; 3 s. Educ. Ratcliffe College, Leicester; Downing College, Cambridge. Rothamsted Experimental Station, Harpenden, 1965-66; Zoological Society of London, 1966-70; Unit of Reproductive Biology, Liverpool University, 1970-73; joined Department of Zoology, Aberdeen University, 1973. Recreations: riding; sailing; skiing. Address: (b.) Department of Zoology, Aberdeen University, Aberdeen AB24 2TZ; T.-01224 272858.

Radford, Andrew. Chef/Managing Director, Atrium Restaurant, Edinburgh, since 1993; Managing Director, blue bar cafe, since 1997; Founder Member, Scottish Chefs Association, since 1994; b. 9.2.58, Cheltenham; m., Lisa; 2 s.; 1 d. Educ. Maidstone Grammar School; Stafford College of Further Education. Assistant Manager, Cromlix House Hotel, Dunblane, 1984-85; Head Chef, Royal Scotsman Touring Train, 1985-86; Head Chef, Hansel's Restaurant, Edinburgh, 1986-88; Assistant to Sir Bernard Ashley, Ashley Inns, America, 1989; Head Chef, Queen of Scots Touring Train, 1990; Head Chef, Waterloo Place Restaurant, Edinburgh, 1991-92. Winner, Scottish Field Newcomer, 1993; Good Food Guide Newcomer, 1994; Caterer Newcomer, 1994; three AA Rosettes, 1995-98; Michelin Red M, 1996-97; Egon Ronay Star, 1997; Taste of Scotland Personality of Year, 1995; Chef of the Year. Recreations: design; travel; family. Address: (b.) Atrium, 10 Cambridge Street, Edinburgh EH1 2ED; T.-0131-228 8882.

Rae, David, DipTP, MRTPI. Head of Planning, Fife Council, since 1996; b. 10.9.45; m., Ella; 2 s.; 1 d. Educ. Buckhaven High School; Edinburgh College of Art. Various planning posts, Fife, Perth, Dunbarton, 1962-75; Depute Director of Planning/Director of Planning, Kirkcaldy District Council, 1975-90; Divisional Manager, Property and Development Services, Kirkcaldy District Council, 1990-96. Past Chair, Scottish Society of Directors of Planning. Recreations: music; dogs; following East Fife F.C. Address: (b.) Fife Council, Fife House, North Street, Glenrothes KY7 5LT; T.-01592 416200.

Rae, Hugh Crauford. Novelist; b. 22.11.35, Glasgow; m., Elizabeth Dunn; 1 d. Educ. Knightswood School. Prolific popular novelist; author of more than 50 tiles, under a variety of pseudonyms, including Stuart Stern, James Albany and Jessica Stirling; books include (as Hugh C. Rae) Skinner, The Marksman, The Shooting Gallery, Harkfast and Privileged Strangers and (as Jessica Stirling) The Spoiled Earth, The Hiring Fair, The Dark Pasture, Treasures on Earth, Creature Comforts, Hearts of Gold, The Good Provider, The Asking Price, The Wise Child, The Welcome Light, Lantern for the Dark, The Penny Wedding, The Workhouse Girl. Recreation: golf. Address: (h.) Drumore Farm Cottage, Balfron Station, Glasgow G63 0NJ.

Rae, Sheriff Rita Emilia Anna, QC, LLB (Hons). Sheriff of Glasgow and Strathkelvin, since 1997. Educ. St. Patrick's High School, Coatbridge; Edinburgh University. Apprentice, Biggart, Lumsden & Co., Glasgow, 1972-74; Assistant Solicitor: Balfour & Manson, Edinburgh, 1974, Biggart, Baillie & Gifford, Glasgow, 1974-76; Solicitor and Partner, Ross Harper & Murphy, Glasgow, 1976-81; Advocate, 1982; Queen's Counsel, 1992. Member, Scottish Joint Medico-Legal Committee on Bioethics; Member, Sacro; Life Member, Scottish Association for the Study of Delinquency. Recreations: theatre; driving; walking; opera; music; Italy; cycling.

Rae, Scott Alexander, LLB (Hons), WS, NP, TEP. Partner, Morton Fraser Milligan WS, Edinburgh, since 1970; b. 17.12.44, Edinburgh; m., Annabel Riach; 3 s. Educ. Daniel Stewarts College, Edinburgh; Edinburgh University. Sometime Tutor and Course Leader, Edinburgh University; Law Society of Scotland Examiner in Taxation and Chairman, Board of Examiners. Member, VAT Tribunal (Scotland); Clerk, Incorporated Trades of Edinburgh; Secretary, International Academy of Estate and Trust Law; Collector, Society of Writers to the Signet; Convener, Law Society of Scotland Tax Law Committee. Recreations: fishing; farming; travel. Address: (b.) 15-19 York Place, Edinburgh; T -0131-556 8444.

Rae, Shelagh, BSc. Director of Education, Renfrewshire Council, since 1995; b. Hamilton; m., Ian A. Rae. Educ. St. Joseph's Convent, Hartlepool; St. Andrew's High School, Kirkcaldy; Edinburgh University. Teacher of Mathematics, 1972-74; Assistant Principal Teacher, then Principal Teacher, 1974-85; Curriculum Officer, Lothian Regional Council, 1985-87; Adviser in Mathematics, then Assistant Director of Education, then Head of School Development Services, Central Regional Council, 1987-95. Recreations: reading; walking; swimming; golf. Address: (b.) Renfrewshire Council, Cotton Street, Paisley PA1 1LE; T.-0141-842 5601.

Rae, William, QPM. Chief Constable, Dumfries and Galloway Constabulary. Address: Cornwall Mount, Dumfries DG1 1PZ.

Raeburn, James B., FCIS. Director, Scottish Print Employers' Federation and Scottish Newspaper Publishers' Association, since 1984; Director, Scottish Daily Newspaper Society, since 1996; b. 18.3.47, Jedburgh; m., Rosemary Bisset; 2 d. Educ. Hawick High School. Edinburgh Corporation, 1964-69; Roxburgh County Council, 1969-71; Electrical Contractors' Association of Scotland, 1972-83 (Secretary, 1975-83). Consultative Member, The Press Council, 1984-90; Director, Press Standards Board of Finance Ltd., since 1990; Director, Advertising Standards Board of Finance Ltd., since 1988; Director, National Council for the Training of Journalists, since 1993. Recreation: golf. Address: (b.) 48 Palmerston Place, Edinburgh EH12 5DE; T.-0131-220 4353.

Raeburn, Emeritus Professor John Ross, CBE, FRSE, FIBiol, BSc, MA, PhD. Consultant; b. 20.11.12, Kirkcaldy; m., Mary Roberts; 1 s.; 3 d. Educ. Manchester Grammar School; Edinburgh University; Cornell University. Professor, Agricultural Economics, Nanking University, 1936-37; Research Officer, Oxford University, 1938-39; Statistician, then Head of Agricultural Plans Branch, Ministry of Food, 1939-46; Senior Research Officer, Oxford University, 1946-49; Reader in Agricultural Economics, London University, 1949-59; Professor and Head, Department of Agriculture, Aberdeen University, 1959-78; Principal, North of Scotland College of Agriculture, 1963-78; Consultant to World Bank, 1979-88; Vice-President, International Association of Agricultural Economists, 1964-70; President, Agricultural Economics Society, 1964-65. Publications: Agriculture: Foundations, Principles and Development; The History of the International Association of Agricultural Economists (Co-author). Recreations: travel; gardening; photography. Address: (h.) 30 Morningfield Road, Aberdeen, AB15 4AQ; T.-01224 314010.

Raeburn, Sheriff Susan Adiel Ogilvie, LLB, QC. Sheriff of Glasgow and Strathkelvin, since 1993; b. 23.4.54, Ellon. Educ. St. Margaret's School for Girls, Aberdeen; Edinburgh University. Admitted, Faculty of Advocates, 1977; took silk, 1991; part-time Chairman, Social Security Appeal Tribunals, 1986-91; Temporary Sheriff, 1988-92; part-time Chairman, Medical Appeal Tribunals, 1992-93; Reporter to Scottish Legal Aid Board, 1990-93. Recreations: salmon fishing; the arts; travel. Address: (b.) Sheriff Court, P.O. Box 23, 1 Carlton Place, Glasgow G5 9DA; T.-0141-429 8888.

Raffe, Professor David James, BA, BPhil. Professor of Sociology of Education, Edinburgh University, since 1992 (Director, Centre for Educational Sociology, since 1994; Co-Director, Institute for the Study of Education and Society, since 1996); b. 5.5.51, Felixstowe; m., Shirley Paine; 1 s.; 1 d. Educ. The Leys School; New College, Oxford; Nuffield College, Oxford. Edinburgh University: Research Fellow, Centre for Educational Sociology, 1975-79, Lecturer in Education, 1979-85; Reader in Education, 1985-92; Deputy Director, Centre for Educational Sociology, 1979-87, Co-Director, 1987-94. Publications: Reconstructions of Secondary Education, 1983; Fourteen to Eighteen, 1984; Education and the Youth Labour Market, 1988. Recreations: squash; hill-walking. Address: (b.) 7 Buccleuch Place Edinburgh EH8 9LW; T.-0131-650 4191.

Rainey, John Bruce, BSc, MB, ChB, ChM, FRCSEdin. Consultant Surgeon, St. John's Hospital, Howden, Livingston, since 1988; Honorary Senior Lecturer in Surgery, Edinburgh University, since 1988; b. 18.5.52, Belfast; m., Dr. Linda Margaret King; 2 s.; 1 d. Educ. Royal Belfast Academical Institution; Edinburgh University. Trained in general surgery; Examiner in surgery and accident and emergency medicine for Royal College of Surgeons of Edinburgh. Aris and Gale Lecturer, Royal College of Surgeons of England, 1985. Recreations: family; sport; history and military history. Address: (h.) 23 Hatton Place, Edinburgh EH9 1UB, T.-0131-667 6216.

Raistrick, Evlyn, MA. Chairman, Scottish Hockey Union, 1992-96; Tournament Director, Atlanta Olympics, from 1996; Member, Rules Board, Competitions Committee, International Federation, since 1990; Member, Scottish Sports Council, since 1993; Vice-Chairman, Executive, Scottish Sports Association, since 1993; b. 13.8.42, Edinburgh; m., David William; 3 s. Educ. Boroughmuir School; Edinburgh University. Maths Teacher, Liberton High, 1964-72. Recreations: hockey; squash; golf. Address: (h.) St. Michaels, Inveresk, Musselburgh EH21 7UA; T.-0131-665 3055.

Ramage, Alan W. Keeper of the Registers of Scotland, since 1994; b. 4.12.43, Edinburgh; m., Fiona Lesslie. Educ. Boroughmuir School, Edinburgh. Recreations: running; reading; working. Address: (b.) Meadowbank House, 153 London Road, Edinburgh EH8 7AU; T.-0131-659 6111.

Ramsay, Major General Charles Alexander, CB, OBE. Landowner and Company Director; b. 12.10.36, North Berwick; m., Hon. Mary Margaret Hastings MacAndrew; 2 s.; 2 d. Educ. Eton; Sandhurst. Commissioned Royal Scots Greys, 1956; Staff College, Canada, 1967-68; Commanded Royal Scots Dragoon Guards, 1977-79; Commander 12th Armoured Brigade, 1980-82; Dep DMO MOD, 1983-84; GOC Eastern District, 1984-87; Director, General Army Organisation and Territorial Army, 1987-89; Chairman, The Wine Company (Scotland) Ltd., 1992-93, Cockburns of Leith PLC, 1993; Director, John Menzies Plc, Grey Horse Properties Ltd., Edinburgh Military Tattoo Ltd., Potomac Holdings Inc (USA), Morningside Developments Ltd. (USA), Caledonian Eagle. Colonel, The Royal Scots Dragoon Guards, 1992; Member, Royal Company of Archers (Queen's Bodyguard for Scotland). Recreations: field sports; equitation; travel; motor-yachting; motoring. Address: (h.) Bughtrig, Coldstream, Berwickshire TD12 4JP; T.-01890 840678.

Ramsay, Lord (James Hubert Ramsay), DL. Company Director; Brigadier, Queen's Bodyguard for Scotland (Royal Company of Archers); Deputy Lieutenant, Angus; b. 17.1.48; m.; 1 s.; 2 d. Educ. Ampleforth. Address: (h.) Dalhousie Lodge, Edzell, Angus DD9 7TU.

Randall, Rev. David James, MA, BD, ThM. Minister, Church of Scotland, Macduff, since 1971; b. 5.6.45, Edinburgh; m., Nan Wardlaw; 3 s.; 1 d. Educ. George Heriot's School; Edinburgh University; Princeton Theological Seminary. Recreations: jogging; reading. Address: The Manse, Macduff AB45 3QL; T.-01261 832316.

Randall, John Norman, BA, MPhil. Assistant Secretary, Rural Affairs and Natural Heritage Unit, Scottish Office Agriculture, Environment and Fisheries Department, since 1995; b. 1.8.45, Bromley, Kent; 1 s.; 1 d. Educ. Bromley Grammar School; Bristol University; Glasgow University. Department of Economic Affairs; Scottish Office. Recreation: hill-walking. Address: (b.) Pentland House, Edinburgh; T.-0131-244 6416.

Ranicki, Professor Andrew Alexander, MA (Cantab), PhD, FRSE. Professor of Algebraic Surgery, Edinburgh University, since 1995; b. 30.12.48, London; m., Dr. I. Thompson; 1 d. Educ. King's School, Canterbury; Trinity College, Cambridge. Research Fellow, Trinity College, Cambridge, 1972-77; Princeton University, 1977-82. Junior Whitehead Prize, 1983, Senior Berwick Prize, 1994, London Mathematical Society; author of books on algebraic theory. Address: (b.) Department of Mathematics and Statistics, Edinburgh University, Edinburgh; T.-0131-650 5073.

Rankeillour, Rt. Hon. The Lord. Peer (Conservative); Member, House of Lords, since 1968; descendant of King Robert the Bruce; Rear Commodore, House of Lords Yacht Club; Farmer and Landowner; b. 29.5.35. Educ. Ampleforth. Recreations: agricultural and horticultural equipment/machinery inventor; hunting; grandscale landscaping. Address: (h.) The Achaderry Estate, Roy Bridge, Western Inverness-shire; T.-Spean Bridge 206.

Rankin, Sir Alick Michael, CBE (1986). Chairman, Scottish & Newcastle plc, since 1989; Director: Christian Salvesen PLC, since 1986 (Chairman, since 1992), Bank of Scotland, since 1987, Sears plc, since 1991, Scottish Financial Enterprise, since 1991, Securities Trust of Scotland plc, since 1991, James Finlay PLC, since 1994, General Accident PLC, since 1995 (Deputy Chairman); b. 23.1.35, London; m., Suzetta Nelson; 1 s.; 3 d. Educ. Eton College; Oxford University. Scots Guards, 1953-55; investment banking, Toronto, 1956-59; Scottish & Newcastle Breweries plc, since 1960. Past President, The Brewers' Society. Recreations: fishing; shooting; golf; tennis. Address: (b.) General Accident plc, Perth, Scotland.

Rankin, Professor David W.H., MA, PhD, FRSC, CChem, FRSE. Professor of Structural Chemistry, Edinburgh University, since 1989; b. 8.6.45, Birkenhead; m., Stella M. Thomas; 3 s.; 1 d. Educ. Birkenhead School; King's College, Cambridge. Edinburgh University: ICI Research Fellow, 1969, Demonstrator, 1971, Lecturer, 1973, Reader, 1980, Professor, 1989. Publication: Structural Methods in Inorganic Chemistry. Address: (b.) Department of Chemistry, Edinburgh University, West Mains Road, Edinburgh EH9 3JJ; T.-0131-650 4728.

Rankin, Emeritus Professor Robert Alexander, MA, PhD, ScD, FRSAMD, FRSE. Emeritus Professor of Mathematics, Glasgow University, since 1982; b. 27.10.15, Garlieston, Wigtownshire; m., Mary Ferrier Llewellyn; 1 s.; 3 d. Educ. Whithorn School; Fettes College; Clare College, Cambridge. Fellow, Clare College, 1939-51; War work on rockets, 1940-45; Lecturer, Cambridge University, 1945-51; Assistant Tutor, Clare College, 1947-51; Mason Professor of Pure Mathematics, Birmingham University, 1951-54; Professor of Mathematics, Glasgow University, 1954-82 (Clerk of Senate, 1971-78, Dean of Faculties, 1985-88). Vice-President, Royal Society of Edinburgh, 1960-63; Keith Prize, RSE, 1961-63; Member, Secretary of State's

Advisory Council on Education, 1959-61; Honorary President, Gaelic Society of Glasgow, since 1969; Vice-President, London Mathematical Society, 1966-68; LMS Senior Whitehead Prize, 1987; President, Edinburgh Mathematical Society, 1957-58 and 1978-79, Honorary member, since 1990. Recreations: music; hill-walking; Gaelic studies. Address: (h.) 98 Kelvin Court, Glasgow G12 OAH; T.-0141-339 2641.

Rankin, Thomas John, MA, MA(Ed), AdvDipEd, FCollP. Head Teacher, Sgoil Dhalabroig, South Uist, since 1981; b. 29.3.47, Glasgow; m., Jean Helen; 2 d. Educ. Strathbungo Secondary School, Glasgow; Glasgow University; Open University. Teacher, Bernard Street Secondary School, Glasgow; taught in Zambia; i/c Cambridge School Certificate and Overseas Examinations, Ministry of Education, Lusaka, Zambia; Head Teacher, Libala Secondary School, Lusaka; Teacher, West Derby Comprehensive School, Liverpool, Chryston High School, Lanarkshire. Recreation: gardening. Address: (b.) Daliburgh School, Isle of South Uist H58 5SS; T.-01878 700276.

Ransford, Tessa, MA, RSA. Director, Scottish Poetry Library; Poet; Editor, Lines Review; b. 8.7.38, Bombay; 1 s.; 3 d. Educ. St. Leonard's School, St. Andrews; Edinburgh University; Craiglockhart College of Education. Publicity Department, Oxford University Press, 1958; in Pakistan as wife of missionary, 1960-68; Assistant to the Director, Scottish Institute of Adult Education, 1982-83; books of poetry: Poetry of Persons, 1975, While It Is Yet Day, 1976, Light of the Mind, 1980, Fools and Angels, 1984; Shadows from the Greater Hill, 1987; A Dancing Innocence, 1988; Seven Valleys, 1991; Medusa Dozen and other poems, 1994; When It Works It Feels Like Play, 1998; first prize, Jubilee poetry competition, Scottish Association for the Speaking of Verse, 1974; Scottish Arts Council Book Award, 1980; Howard Sergeant Award for services to poetry, 1989; Honorary Member, The Saltire Society, 1993; Heritage Society of Scotland Annual Award, 1996; Member, Scottish International PEN; Founder and Organiser, School of Poets (open learning workshop for practising poets). Recreation: grandchildren. Address: (b.) Scottish Poetry Library, Tweeddale Court, 14 High Street, Edinburgh EH1 1TE; T.-0131-557 2876.

Rapport, Professor Nigel Julian, BA, MA, PhD. Professor of Anthropological and Philosophical Studies, St. Andrews University, since 1996; b. 8.11.56, Cardiff; m., Elizabeth J.A. Munro; 1 s. Educ. Clifton College, Bristol; Cambridge University; Manchester University. Research Fellow and Associate, Institute of Social and Economic Research, Memorial University of Newfoundland, 1983-87; Lecturer, Blaustein Institute for Desert Research, Ben-Gurion University of the Negev, Israel, 1988; Lecturer, Department of Social Anthropology, Manchester University, 1989; joined St. Andrews University as Lecturer, 1993. Hon. Secretary, Association of Social Anthropologists of the UK and Commonwealth, since 1994; 1996 Royal Society of Edinburgh prize lectureship in the humanities, 1996; Royal Anthropological Institute, Curl Essay Prize, 1996. Publications: Talking Violence: an anthropological interpretation of conversation in the city, 1987; Diverse World-Views in an English Village, 1993; The Prose and the Passion: anthropology, literature and the writing of E.M. Forster, 1994; Transcendent Individual, towards a literary and liberal anthropology, 1997; Questions of Consciousness (Co-editor), 1995. Recreations: travel; sport; literature. Address: (b.) Department of Social Anthropology, St. Andrews University, St. Andrews KY16 9AL; T.-01334 462977.

Raven, Professor John Albert, MA, PhD, FRS, FRSE, Hon.PhD. Boyd Baxter Professor of Biology, Dundee University, since 1995; b. 25.6.41, Essex; m., Dr. Linda Lea Handley. Educ. Friend's School, Saffron Walden; Cambridge University (St. John's College). Research Fellow, St. John's College,Cambridge, 1966-69; University Demonstrator in Botany, Cambridge, 1968-71; Official Fellow, St. John's College, Cambridge, 1970-71; Lecturer, 1971-76, Reader, 1976-80, Personal Chair, 1980-95, Department of Biological Sciences, Dundee University. Publications: Energetics and Transport in Aquatic Plants, 1984; Aquatic Photosynthesis (Co-author), 1997; numerous papers. Recreations: aviation; jogging; literature. Address: (b.) Department of Biological Sciences, Dundee University, Dundee DD1 4HN; T.-01382 344281.

Rea, John Malcolm, OBE, BA, MSc, CQSW. Director of Fundraising, Children's Hospice Association Scotland, since 1993; Scottish Member, Anglican Consultative Council, Joint ACC/Primates Standing Committee; Anglican Observer to UN Advisory Group, since 1997; b. 28.2.44, Bradford; m., Della; 1 s.; 1 d. Educ. Bradford and Circencester Grammar Schools; Durham, Newcastle and Stirling Universities. Principal Adviser for Children, Newcastle Social Services, 1973-76; Scottish Director (Child Care), Barnardos, 1976-91; Director-General, Quarriers, 1991-93; founding Chairman, Edinburgh Stopover, 1981-85; founding Vice-Chair, Scottish Child and Family Alliance (now Children in Scotland), 1982-87; Consultant to Lambeth Conference, 1988; Management Group, Anglican International Family Network, since 1988; Scottish Consultant, Charities Aid Foundation Consultants, since 1991; Member, Anglican International Refugees Network, since 1991. Recreations: voluntary work; tennis; sailing; skiing; walking; travel; church social and political action. Address: (h.) Beaconhill, Kirknewton, Midlothian EH27 8AA; T.-01506 880637.

Read, Edward Reginald, MIMgt. Consultant, Ayrshire Marketing Executive, since 1989; General Secretary, Tenovus Scotland, since 1986; b. 6.12.29, Sydenham; 1 s.; 3 d. Educ. Ilkley Grammar School; Marr College, Troon. National Service, 1948-50; J. & P. Coats Ltd., 1950-85. Town Councillor, Troon, 1964-71; Past Chairman, Royal Scottish Automobile Club. Recreations: travel; cars; golf. Address: (h.) 3 Windyhaugh, 119 South Beach, Troon KA10 6EH; T.-01292 311276.

Read, Professor Paul, BSc, MSc, PhD, CBiol, FIBiol, MIWEM. Associate Head, Department of Biological Sciences, Napier University, since 1990; b. 1.1.48, Saffron Walden; m., Jane. Educ. Palmers Grammar School, Grays; Hull University; Aston University. Research Technician, Essex Water Authority, 1969-70; Research Assistant, University of Aston, 1971-72; Research Fellow, then Lecturer, Napier College, 1972-82; Senior Lecturer, Napier Polytechnic, 1982-90. Fifty publications. Recreations: offshore sailing/cruising; gardening; hill-walking. Address: (b.) Department of Biological Sciences, Napier University, Colinton Road, Edinburgh EH10 5DT; T.-0131-455 2625.

Reed, Gavin Barras, BA. Chairman, John Menzies plc; b. 13.11.34, Newcastle upon Tyne; m. Muriel Joyce; 1 s.; 3 d. Educ. Eton; Trinity College, Cambridge. National Service, Fleet Air Arm; joined The Newcastle Breweries, 1958; Vice-Chairman, Scottish & Newcastle plc, 1991-94. Director: Wainholmes plc (Chairman), Ivory & Sime Enterprise Capital plc (Chairman), Ivory & Sime Trustlink Ltd (Chairman), Burtonwood Brewery plc, CNC Properties plc. Recreations: shooting; tennis. Address (h.) Whitehill, Aberdour, Burntisland, Fife KY3 0RW; Broadgate, West Woodburn, Northumberland NE48 2RN.

Reed, Malcolm Christopher, MA, DPhil, FCIT. Director General, Strathclyde Passenger Transport Executive, since 1997; b. 24.11.44, Cardigan, Wales; 2 d. Educ. Royal Grammar School, Newcastle upon Tyne; St. Catherine's College and Nuffield College, Oxford. Assistant, Bodleian Library, Oxford; Lecturer, Glasgow University; Researcher/Associate Director, Planning Exchange, Glasgow; Planner/Chief Public Transport Co-ordinator,

Greater Glasgow P.T.E.; Chief Policy Planner/Senior Executive Officer, Strathclyde Regional Council, latterly Assistant Chief Executive. Member, Scottish Section Committee, Chartered Institute of Transport; Deputy Chairman, Railway Heritage Committee. Recreations: hill-walking; listening to music; travel. Address: (b.) Consort House, 12 West George Street, Glasgow G2 1HN; T.-0141-333 3100.

Reed, Professor Peter, BA, RIBA, FRIAS, FRSA. Professor of Architecture, Strathclyde University; b. 31.1.33, Hayes, Middlesex; m., Keow Chim Lim; 2 d. Educ. Southall Grammar School; Manchester University (State Scholar); Open University. Commissioned Officer, RAF, 1960-61; Assistant Lecturer, University of Hong Kong, 1961-64; Architect in practice, Malaysia, 1964-70; joined Strathclyde University as Lecturer, 1970; Professor, 1986; Dean, Faculty of Engineering, 1988-90; Vice-Principal Elect, 1990-92; Vice-Principal, 1992-94. Secretary, Kilsyth Civic Trust, 1975-80; Chairman, Kilsyth Community Council, 1975-78; GIA Council, 1982-84; ARCUK Board of Education, 1985-95; Governor, Glasgow School of Art, 1982-94; Director, Glasgow West Conservation Trust, since 1990, Convener, since 1996; Chairman, Council, Charles Rennie Mackintosh Society, 1991-94. Publications include Glasgow: The Forming of the City (Editor). Recreations: opera; wine; cricket. Address: (b.) Department of Architecture and Building Science, Strathclyde University, 131 Rottenrow, Glasgow G4 0NG; T.-0141-552 4400.

Reed, Robert John, QC, LLB, DPhil. Advocate, since 1983; b. 7.9.56, Edinburgh; m., Jane Elizabeth Mylne; 2 d. Educ. George Watson's College, Edinburgh; Edinburgh University; Balliol College, Oxford. Standing Junior Counsel: Scottish Education Department, 1988-89, Scottish Office Home and Health Department, 1989-95; called to English Bar, 1991; QC, 1995; Advocate Depute, since 1996. Recreations: music; visual arts. Address: (b.) Parliament House, Edinburgh EH1 1RF.

Reekie, Iain Robert, BA. Artistic Director, 7:84 Theatre Company Scotland; b. 14.2.67, Edinburgh; 1 s. Educ. Firhill High School, Edinburgh; RSAMD. Freelance director, 1989-90; Publicity Officer, Mayfest, 1990; Assistant Director, 7:84 Theatre Company Scotland, 1990-91; Assistant Director, Nottingham Playhouse, 1991. Address: (b.) 2 Port Dundas Place, Glasgow G2 3LB.

Reekie, Tony. Director, Scottish International Children's Festival, since 1995; b. 20.12.64, Edinburgh; m., Gillian Robertson. Educ. Firrhill High School, Edinburgh. Freelance arts administrator, 1986-92; Development Officer, Tag Theatre Co., 1992-93; General Manager, Visible Fictions, 1993-95. Recreations: watching Hibernian F.C.; eating good food to get over watching Hibernian F.C. Address: (b.) 22 Laurie Street, Edinburgh EH6 7AB; T.-0131-554 6297.

Reeks, David Robin, TD, DL, BSc(Eng). Consulting Engineer, Axiom Consulting Engineers Ltd., since 1996; Principal Associate, Avondale Associates, since 1996; b. 15.6.35, Parkstone; m., Kathleen Veronica Stephens; 1 s.; 1 d. Educ. Canford School; London University. Rig Engineer, UKAEA Dounreay, 1962-67; Senior Engineer, SSEB, 1967-90; Reactor Thermal Performance Engineer, Scottish Nuclear Ltd., 1990-94. Committee Member and Volunteer Convoy Leader, Edinburgh Direct Aid to Bosnia; Deputy Lieutenant of Lanarkshire; TA Royal Engineers/Royal Corps of Transport, 1962-90. Recreations: hill-walking; Scottish country dancing. Address: 3 Cedar Place, Strathaven, Lanarkshire ML10 6DW; T.-01357 521695.

Rees, Alan Tait, MBE, MA (Cantab), CQSW; b. 4.8.31, Shanghai, China; m., Alison Margaret; 2 s.; 2 d. Educ. Kingswood School, Bath; Gonville and Caius College, Cambridge; London School of Economics; University College, Swansea. Community Development Officer, Tanzania; Lecturer in Youth and Community Studies, Moray House College; Organising Secretary, Board for Information in Youth and Community Service, Scotland; Senior Community Development Officer, Council of Social Service for Wales; Assistant Director, Edinburgh Voluntary Organisations' Council, retired 1993; Chair, Scotland Yard Adventure Centre, Edinburgh; Member, Scotland Committee, British Association of Social Workers and Editor, Rostrum; Trustee, Seagull Trust; Vice Chair, Handicabs; Scottish National Representative, International Association for the Child's Right to Play; Member: Board, Lothian Centre for Integrated Living; Policy Committee, Scottish Council for Voluntary Organisations. Recreations: gardening; painting. Address: (h.) 20 Seaforth Drive, Edinburgh EH4 2BZ; T.-0131-332 7317.

Rees, Professor Elmer Gethin, BA (Cantab), PhD (Warwick), MA (Oxon), FRSE. Professor, Department of Mathematics and Statistics, Edinburgh University, since 1979; Chairman, Executive Committee, International Centre for Mathematical Sciences, since 1993; b. 19.11.41, Llandybie, Wales; m., Mary Elene; 2 s. Educ. Llandeilo Grammar School; St. Catharine's College, Cambridge; Warwick University. Lecturer, Department of Pure Mathematics, Hull University, 1967-69; Member, Institute for Advanced Study, Princeton, 1969-70; Lecturer, Department of Pure Mathematics, University College of Swansea, 1970-71; Tutorial Fellow, St. Catherine's College, Oxford and Lecturer in Mathematics, Oxford University, 1971-79. Vice President, London Mathematical Society, 1994-96. Publications: Notes on Geometry; Homotopy Theory. Address: (h.) 23 Blacket Place, Edinburgh EH9 1RJ; T.-0131-667 2747.

Rees, Jennifer Linda, BSc, FRSS, MIMgt. Assistant Principal (Academic), Bell College of Technology, since 1995; b. 2.7.51, Edinburgh; m., Richard; 1 s.; 1 d. Educ. George Watson's Ladies College, Edinburgh; Edinburgh University. Operational Research Analyst, then Statistical Quality Control Manager, Scottish & Newcastle Breweries Ltd.; Lecturer, Department of Business Studies, Edinburgh University; Head, Department of Management Studies, Scottish College of Textiles. Recreations: swimming; skiing; playing piano badly. Address: (b.) Bell College of Technology, Almada Street, Hamilton ML3 0JB.

Reeves, Philip Thomas Langford, RSA, RSW, RE, RGI, ARCA. Artist; b. 7.7.31, Cheltenham; m., Christine MacLaren (deceased); 1 d. Educ. Naunton Park School, Cheltenham; Cheltenham School of Art; Royal College of Art, London. Lecturer in Graphic Design, Glasgow School of Art, 1954-70, Head of Printmaking, 1970-91. Address: (h.) 13 Hamilton Drive, Glasgow G12 8DN; T.-0141-339 0720.

Reid, Alexander N., WS, NP, LLB. Senior Partner, Steedman Ramage WS, since 1993; b. 15.9.54, Aberdeen; m., Maria; 2 s. Educ. Robert Gordon's College, Aberdeen; Aberdeen University. Steedman Ramage WS: apprentice lawyer, 1975-77, Assistant, 1977-80, Partner, 1980-93. Recreations: family; sport; music. Address: (b.) 6 Alva Street, Edinburgh; T.-0131-226 3781.

Reid, Alison Hamilton, MA, DMS, MCIM, FRSA. Chief Executive, Scottish Further Education Unit, since 1995; Depute Principal, Perth College. Educ. Montrose Academy; Edinburgh University; Strathclyde University. Marketing and business development in commercial sector, 1973-81; Lecturer and Manager in Further Education, 1981-95. Address: (b.) Argyll Court, Castle Business Park, Stirling; T.-01786 892000.

Reid, Professor Colin Turriff, MA, LLB. Professor of Environmental Law, Dundee University, since 1995; b. 10.6.58, Aberdeen; m., M. Anne Palin; 2 d. Educ. Robert

Gordon's College, Aberdeen; University College, Oxford; Gonville and Caius College, Cambridge. Lecturer in Public Law, Aberdeen University, 1980-90; Senior Lecturer in Law, Dundee University, 1991-95. Publications: Nature Conservation Law; Environmental Law in Scotland (Editor). Recreations: cricket; hockey. Address: (b.) Department of Law, Dundee University, Dundee DD1 4HN; T.-01382 344461.

Reid, David C., MA, MEd. Rector, Kinross High School, since 1985; b. 4.9.43, Motherwell; m., Alison W. Ewing; 1 s.; 1 d. Educ. Wishaw High School; Glasgow University; Jordanhill College; Edinburgh University. Teacher of English, Kirkcaldy High School, 1966-71; Principal Teacher of English, Currie High School, 1971-80; Assistant Rector, Inverkeithing High School, 1980-85. Member/Chairman, English Panel, Scottish Examination Board, 1976-82; Member, IBA Educational Advisory Council (Schools Panels), 1975-86; Chairman, Channel 4 Scottish Schools Committee. Recreations: hill-walking; angling; conversation; reading; Scottish traditional architecture. Address: (b.) Kinross High School, Kinross, Kinross-shire KY13 7AW; T.-01577 862430.

Reid, David Ronald, MA(Hons), LLB. Partner, W. & J. Burness WS, since 1965; b. 23.6.37, Larbert; m., Ruth Edith; 1 d. Educ. Daniel Stewart's College, Edinburgh; Edinburgh University. Apprenticeship with W. & J. Burness, 1959-62, Assistant, 1962-65. Former Council Member, WS Society. Recreations: golf; hill-walking; music; reading. Address: (b.) 16 Hope Street, Edinburgh EH2 4DD; T.-0131-226 2561.

Reid, Derek Donald, MA. Deputy Chairman, Sea Fish Industry Authority, since 1996; Deputy Chairman, Scotland The Brand, since 1997; various directorships of small companies; b. 30.11.44, Aberdeen; m., Janice Anne Reid; 1 s.; 1 d. Educ. Inverurie Academy; Aberdeen University; Robert Gordon University. Cadbury-Schweppes, 1968-85 (latterly Divisional Director); founding Director/Owner, Premier Brands, 1985-90; Chief Executive, Scottish Tourist Board, 1994-96. Honorary Doctorate, Business Administration, Robert Gordon University; Fellow, George Thomas Society. Recreations: golf; fishing; modern art; fine food/wine. Address: Bonhard House, Scone, Perth PH2 7PQ; T.-01738 553911.

Reid, Rev. Donald, LLB, MPhil, BD. Anglican Chaplain, Universities in Glasgow, since 1995; Team Priest, St. Mary's Cathedral, Glasgow, since 1995; Chair, Jubilee 2000 Scottish Coalition, since 1997; b. 25.2.58, Bellshill. Educ. High School of Glasgow. Curate, St. John's, Greenock, 1985-88; Rector, St. John's, Ballieston, St. Serf's, Shettleston, 1988-95; Convener, Overseas Committee, Scottish Episcopal Church, since 1994; Trustee, Scottish Churches' World Exchange, since 1994; Convener, Scottish Churches' World Action. Recreations: cinema; photography. Address: (h.) 1/2 212 Wilton Street, Glasgow G20 6BL; T. 0141 946 1145.

Reid, Professor Gavin Clydesdale, MA, MSc, PhD. Professor in Economics, St. Andrews University, since 1991; Director, Centre for Research into Industry, Enterprise, Finance and the Firm (CRIEFF), since 1991; b. 25.8.46, Glasgow; m., 1, Margaret Morrice or McGregor (m. diss.); 1 s.; 1 step-s.; 2, Maureen Johnson or Bagnall; 1 s.; 2 d.; 1 step.-s. Educ. Lyndhurst School; Frimley and Camberley Grammar School; Aberdeen University; Southampton University; Edinburgh University. Lecturer, Senior Lecturer, Reader in Economics, Edinburgh University, 1971-91; Visiting Associate Professor: Queen's University, Ontario, 1981-82, Denver University, Colorado, 1984; Visiting Scholar, Darwin College, Cambridge, 1987-88; Visiting Professor, University of Nice, 1998; Leverhulme Trust Research Fellowship, 1989; Nuffield

Foundation Social Science Research Fellowship, 1997-98. Editorial Board: Scottish Journal of Political Economy, since 1986, Small Business Economics, since 1997; Member, Council, Scottish Economic Society, since 1990. Publications: The Kinked Demand Curve Analysis of Oligopoly, 1981; Theories of Industrial Organization, 1987; The Small Entrepreneurial Firm (Co-author), 1988; Classical Economic Growth, 1989; Small Business Enterprise, 1993; Profiles in Small Business (Co-author), 1993. Recreations:music; reading; running; badminton. Address: (h.) 23 South Street, St. Andrews KY16 9QS; T.-01334 472932.

Reid, Graham D.M., BL. Solicitor, since 1960; Secretary and Treasurer, Glasgow Society of Sons of Ministers of Church of Scotland, since 1983; b. 12.6.36, Greenock; m., Maureen; 1 s.; 1 d. Educ. Glasgow Academy; Fettes College; Glasgow University. Partner, Brechin Tindal Oatts (formerly Tindal Oatts & Rodger), since 1965. General Trustee, Church of Scotland; Chairman, Mugdock Children's Trust; Session Clerk, Kelvinside Hillhead Parish Church. Recreations: curling; walking; planting trees. Address: (b.) 48 St. Vincent Street, Glasgow; T.-0141-221 8012.

Reid, Harry William, BA (Hons), FRSA. Editor, The Herald, since 1997; b. 23.9.47, Glasgow; m., Julie Davidson (qv); 1 d. Educ. Aberdeen Grammar School; Fettes College; Oxford University. The Scotsman: Education Correspondent, 1973-77, Features Editor, 1977-81; Sports Editor, Sunday Standard, 1981-82; Executive Editor, Glasgow Herald, 1982-83, Deputy Editor, 1983-97. Publication: Dear Country: a quest for England, 1992. Recreations: reading; walking; supporting Aberdeen Football Club. Address: (h.) 15 Albion Buildings, Ingram Street, Glasgow; T.-0141-552 8403.

Reid, Heather M.M., BSc(Hons), MSc, CPhys, MInstP, FRMS. Weather Forecaster, Met Office, since 1993; BBC Scotland Weather Forecaster, since 1994; b. 6.7.69, Paisley. Educ. Camphill High School, Paisley; Edinburgh University. Joined Met Office to work in satellite image research; became forecaster because of "TV potential" (Met Office idea); now known as "Heather the Weather" to viewers. Vice-Chair, Institute of Physics (Scottish Branch), since 1997; active involvement in Edinburgh Science Festival, Techfest, and promoting the public understanding of science. Recreations: apart from lecturing and giving talks in spare time – watch cricket; holidays abroad. Address: (b.) Glasgow Weather Centre, 220 St. Vincent Street, Glasgow G2 5QD; T.-0141-248 3451.

Reid, Professor Ian Cameron, MB, ChB, BMedBiol, PhD, MRCPsych. Professor of Psychiatry, Dundee University, since 1995; b. 13.10.60, Dunfermline; m., Isla; 1 d. Educ. Dollar Academy; Aberdeen University; Edinburgh University. Lecturer in Mental Health, Aberdeen University; Research Fellow, Department of Pharmacology, then Lecturer in Psychiatry, Edinburgh University; Senior Lecturer in Mental Health, Aberdeen University. Recreation: curry. Address: (b.) Department of Psychiatry, Ninewells Hospital and Medical School, Dundee DD1 9SY; T.-01382 632853.

Reid, James Gordon, LLB (Hons), FCIArb. Queen's Counsel (Scotland), since 1993; Barrister, Gray's Inn, London, since 1995; b. 24.7.52, Edinburgh; m., Hannah Hogg Hopkins; 3 s.; 1 d. Educ. Melville College, Edinburgh; Edinburgh University. Solicitor, 1976-80; Advocate, 1980-93; Standing Junior Counsel, Scottish Office Environment Department, 1986-93; admitted as Barrister, Inner Temple, 1991. Recreations: general fitness; computers and music. Address: (h.) Blebo House, by St. Andrews, Fife KY15 5TZ; T.-01334 653274.

Reid, Jimmy. Journalist and Broadcaster; b. 1932. Former Engineer; prominent in campaign to save Upper Clyde Shipbuilders; former Convener of Shop Stewards, AUEW; former (Communist) Member, Clydebank Town Council; joined Labour Party and contested Dundee East, General Election, 1979; Rector, Glasgow University, 1971-74; Founder, Seven Days magazine; Columnist, The Herald, Glasgow.

Reid, John, PhD. MP (Labour), Motherwell North, since 1987; b. 8.5.47, Bellshill; m., Catherine McGowan (deceased); 2 s. Educ. St. Patrick's Senior Secondary School, Coatbridge; Stirling University. Scottish Research Officer, Labour Party, 1979-83; Political Adviser to Rt. Hon. Neil Kinnock, 1983-85; Scottish Organiser, Trade Unionists for Labour, 1986-87. Recreations: crosswords; football; reading. Address: (b.) House of Commons, Westminster, London; Parliamentary Office, Montrose House, 154 Montrose Crescent, Hamilton ML3 6LL; T.-01698 454672.

Reid, Rev. John Kelman Sutherland, CBE, TD, MA, DD. Member, Editorial Board, Scottish Journal of Theology, since 1948; b. 31.3.10, Leith; m., Margaret Winifrid Brookes (deceased). Educ. George Watson's College, Edinburgh; Edinburgh University; Heidelberg University; Basel University; Marburg University; Strasburg University. Professor of Philosophy, Calcutta University, 1935-37; Minister, Craigmillar Park Parish Church, Edinburgh, 1939-52; Chaplain to the Forces with Parachute Regiment, 1942-46; Professor of Theology, Leeds University, 1952-61; Chaplain, Territorial Army, 1948-62; Professor of Systematic Theology, Aberdeen University, 1961-76. Publications: Calvin's Theological Treatises (Editor and Translator), 1954; The Biblical Doctrine of the Ministry, 1955; The Authority of Scripture, 1957; Calvin's Concerning the Eternal Predestination of God (Editor and Translator), 1961; Our Life in Christ, 1963; Presbyterians and Unity, 1966; Christian Apologetics, 1969. Recreation: golf. Address: (h.) 8 Abbotsford Court, 18 Colinton Road, Edinburgh EH10 5EH; T.-0131-447 6855.

Reid, Professor John Low, MA, DM, FRCP, FRSE. Regius Professor of Medicine and Therapeutics, Glasgow University, since 1989; Consultant Physician, Western Infirmary; b. 1.10.43, Glasgow; m., Randa Pharaon; 1 s.; 1 d. Educ. Fettes College; Oxford University. MRC Research Fellow, Royal Post Graduate Medical School, London, 1970-73; Travelling Fellow, US National Institutes of Health, Washington, USA, 1973-75; Senior Wellcome Fellow in Clinical Science and Reader in Clinical Pharmacology, Royal Post Graduate Medical School, London, 1975-78; Regius Professor of Materia Medica, Glasgow University, 1978-89; Editor, Journal of Hypertension. Publications: Lecture Notes in Clinical Pharmacology (Co-author); Clinical Science, 1982-84 (Editor); Handbook of Hypertension (Editor). Recreations: outdoors; gardening. Address: (b.) Gardiner Institute, Western Infirmary, Glasgow; T.-0141-211 2886.

Reid, Professor John William, MEd, FCII, FIRM, MIOSH. Professor, Department of Risk and Financial Services, Glasgow Caledonian University, since 1993; b. 7.12.39, Liverpool; m., Mary McKenna; 3 s. Educ. De La Salle Grammar School, Liverpool; Edinburgh University. Joined Glasgow Polytechnic as Lecturer, 1977. Recreation: hill-walking. Address: (b.) Department of Risk and Financial Services, Caledonian University, Cowcaddens Road, Glasgow, G4 0BA; T.-0141-331 3152.

Reid, Professor J.S. Grant, BSc, PhD. Professor of Plant Biochemistry, Stirling University, since 1994; b. 27.3.42, Huntly; m., Mary E. Edwards; 1 s.; 2 d. Educ. Gordon Schools, Huntly; Aberdeen University. Lecturer, University of Fribourg, Switzerland, 1970-73; Lecturer in Biochemistry, Stirling University, 1974-78; Visiting Associate Professor, University of Calgary, 1977-78; Senior Lecturer, then Reader, Stirling University, 1978-94; Visiting Professor, Unilever Research Laboratories, Netherlands, 1988. Address: (b.) Department of Biological and Molecular Sciences, Stirling University, Stirling FK9 4LA; T.-01786 467762.

Reid, Professor Kenneth Gilbert Cameron, MA, LLB. Professor of Property Law, Edinburgh University, since 1994; Law Commissioner for Scotland, since 1995; b. 25.3.54, Glasgow; m., Elspeth Christie; 2 s.; 1 d. Educ. Loretto; St. John's College, Cambridge; Edinburgh University. Admitted as a Solicitor, 1980; Lecturer in Law, Edinburgh University, 1980. Author of numerous books and papers on the law of property. Recreation: classical music. Address: (b.) Department of Private Law, Old College, South Bridge, Edinburgh EH8 9YL; T.-0131-650 2015.

Reid, Robert Russell, JP. Chairman, Argyll and Bute NHS Trust, formerly Chairman, Argyll and Clyde Health Board; Member, West of Scotland Water Authority; Honorary Sheriff; Farmer; b. 26.12.32, Campbeltown; m., Rebecca Simpson Hunter; 3 s.; 1 d. Educ. Campbeltown Grammar School; Thorpe House; Rothesay Academy. Address: (h.) Eriskay, 13 Ardmory Road, Rothesay, Bute PA20 0PG; T.-01700 50 3238.

Reid, Seona Elizabeth, BA,DArt, FRSA. Director, Scottish Arts Council, since 1990; b. 21.1.50, Paisley. Educ. Park School, Glasgow; Strathclyde University; Liverpool University. Business Manager, Theatre Royal, Lincoln, 1972-73; Press Officer, Northern Dance Theatre, Manchester, 1973-76; PRO, Ballet Rambert, London, 1976-79; freelance arts consultant, 1979-81; Director, Shape, London, 1981-87; Assistant Director, Greater London Arts, 1987-90. Recreations: walking; travel; the arts. Address: (b.) 12 Manor Place, Edinburgh EH3 7DD; T.-0131-226 6051.

Reid, William James, ACII, FBIBA. Chairman, Reid Enterprise Ltd., City Business Venue (Scotland) Ltd., Nickleby & Co. (Scotland) Ltd.; Hon. Vice-President, Children 1st; b. 18.9.32, Edinburgh; m., Patricia; 2 s. Educ. George Heriot's School. Director, Collins Halden & Co. Ltd., 1960-68, Joint Managing Director, 1968-72, Chairman and Chief Executive, 1972-78; Director, Halden McQuaker & Co. Ltd., Glasgow, 1964-73; Director, Collins Halden & Burnett Ltd., Aberdeen, 1962-74; Director, Hogg Robinson Ltd., London, 1978-84; Chief Executive, Hogg Robinson (Scotland) Ltd., 1978-84; Chairman and Chief Executive: Collins Halden (Scotland) Ltd., 1984-90, Heath Collins Halden (Scotland) Ltd., 1990-92, C.E. Heath (Scotland) Ltd., 1990-92; President, Insurance Society of Edinburgh, 1978-79; Chairman, Corporation of Insurance Brokers Scotland, 1969-70; Member, National Council, Corporation of Insurance Brokers, 1968-71; Freeman of the City of London. Address: (h.) Ravensworth, 38 Pentland Avenue, Edinburgh EH13 0HY; T.-0131-441 3942.

Reid, Sir William Kennedy, KCB, MA, LLD, FRCPEd. Chairman, Mental Welfare Commission for Scotland; Chairman, Advisory Committee on Distinction Awards; Chairman of Council, St. George's School for Girls; b. 15.2.31, Aberdeen; m., Ann Campbell; 2 s.; 1 d. Educ. Robert Gordon's College; George Watson's College; Edinburgh University; Trinity College, Cambridge. Civil Servant, 1956-89, Department of Education and Science, Cabinet Office, Scottish Office; Member, Council on Tribunals and Its Scottish Committee, 1990-96; Member, Commission for Local Administration in England, 1990-96; Member, Commission for Local Administration in Wales, 1990-96. A Director, International Ombudsman Institute, 1992-96; Parliamentary Commissioner for Administration, 1990-97; Health Service Commissioner for England, Scotland, Wales, 1990-97. Recreations: verse; hill-walking. Address: (h.) 11 Inverleith Terrace, Edinburgh.

Reid, Sheriff William Macpherson, MA, LLB. Sheriff of Tayside, Central and Fife, since 1983; b. 6.4.38. Advocate, 1963; Sheriff of Lothian and Borders, 1978, Glasgow and Strathkelvin, 1978-83. Address: (b.) Sheriff Court House, County Buildings, Mar Street, Alloa, FK10 1HR.

Reid, (William) Russell. Editor, The Sunday Post, since 1989; b. 27.1.36, Dundee; m., Patricia Rutherford (deceased); 2 d. Educ. Harris Academy, Dundee; Arbroath High School. Joined D.C. Thomson & Co. Ltd. as Reporter on Courier and Evening Telegraph, 1953; joined Sunday Post as Reporter and Feature Writer, 1957; Deputy Editor, 1983. Member, Code Committee, Press Complaints Commission, since 1994. Recreations: music; walking; reading; talking. Address: (b.) Albert Square, Dundee DD1 9QJ; T.-01382 223131.

Reith, David Stewart, LLB, NP, WS. Partner, Lindsays WS, Solicitors, Edinburgh, since 1976; b. 15.4.51, Edinburgh; m., Elizabeth Julia Hawkins; 1 s.; 1 d. Educ. Edinburgh Academy; Fettes College; Aberdeen University. Director: Scottish Historic Buildings Trust, Cockburn Conservation Trust, Scottish Lime Centre Trust, Scottish Sculpture Trust, Boilerhouse Theatre Company Ltd.; Secretary: Ponton House Trust, Cockburn Conservation Trust; Clerk, Incorporation of Cordiners; Honorary Solicitor, Architectural Heritage Society of Scotland and Fet-Lor Youth Centre. Recreations: gardening; photography; wine. Address: (h.) Pilmuir House, Haddington, East Lothian EH41 4HS; T.-01875 340008.

Remp, Stephen Edward, BA, MA HonDTech. Chairman and Chief Executive, Ramco Energy plc, since 1977; b. 5.5.47, California, USA; m., Janine Beverley; 2 s.; 1 d. Educ. American International School; Claremont Men's College; John Hopkins University. Saltire Award, 1977, and Civic Trust Award, 1977 (Harthill Castle); Scottish Business Achievement Award, 1984; Grampian Industrialist of the Year Award, 1996; Burgess of Guild of City of Aberdeen. Recreations: skiing; tennis; shooting; swimming; music. Address: (b.) 4 Rubislaw Place, Aberdeen AB10 1XN; T.-01224 626224.

Rennie, Rev. Adrian James Tait, BA, BD. Minister, Drylaw Parish Church, Edinburgh, since 1996; b. 8.4.63, Aberdeen; m., Jean Gibson; 1 s. Educ. Paisley Grammar School; Strathclyde University; Trinity College, Glasgow University. Minister, Calton, Glasgow, 1988-94; Warden, MacLeod Centre, Isle of Iona, and Warden, Adventure Centre, Isle of Mull, for Iona Community, 1994-95. Chairperson, Scottish CND, 1993-94. Recreations: fly fishing; swimming; parenting. Address: (h.) 23 Hillview, Blackhall, Edinburgh EH4 2AF; T.-0131-343 1643.

Rennie, Alan Craig. Editor, Stirling Observer, since 1983; b. 28.3.51, Stirling; m., Mary. Educ. High School of Stirling. Joined George Outram & Co. as trainee journalist, 1969; junior reporter, Stirling Journal, 1970; reporter, Perthshire Advertiser, 1971-79; Chief Reporter, Stirling Observer, 1979-83. Scottish Chairman, Guild of Editors, 1992-94; UK Delegate to International Society of Weekly Newspaper Editors, USA, 1992. Publication: edited book on history of Stirling, 1986. Recreations: Member, Stirling County R.F.C., Stirling Golf Club, Carse of Stirling Rotary Club. Address: (b.) 40 Craigs, Stirling FK8 2DW; T.-01786 451110.

Rennie, Alistair Gillies, LLB. Hon. Assoc. RICS. Deputy Keeper, Registers of Scotland, Executive Agency; b. 1.2.44, Edinburgh; m., Eleanor Sutherland; 2 d. Educ. Trinity Academy, Edinburgh; Edinburgh University. Joined Department of Registers of Scotland, 1962; Principal Establishment Officer, 1988; Director, Land Register, 1990; Senior Director, Production, 1992; Deputy Keeper, 1994. Director, East of Scotland Society for Welfare and Teaching of the Blind; Member, Deacon's Court, Royal and Ancient Burgh of Linlithgow. Recreations: reading; walking; swimming. Address: (b.) Meadowbank House, 153 London Road, Edinburgh; T.-0131-659 6111.

Rennie, Archibald Louden, CB, LLD, FDS, RCS(Eng); b. 4.6.24, Guardbridge, Fife; m., Kathleen Harkess; 4 s. Educ. Madras College, St. Andrews; St. Andrews University. Experimental Officer, Minesweeping Research Division, 1944-47; joined Department of Health for Scotland, 1947; Private Secretary to Secretary of State for Scotland, 1962-63; Assistant Secretary, Scottish Home and Health Department, 1963-69; Registrar General for Scotland, 1969-73; Under Secretary, Scottish Economic Planning Department, 1973-77; Secretary, Scottish Home and Health Department, 1977-84. Vice-Chairman, Advisory Committee on Distinction Awards, 1985-94; Chancellor's Assessor, St. Andrews University, 1985-89; Member, Scottish Records Advisory Council, 1985-93; Member, Council on Tribunals, and its Scottish Committee, 1987-88; Trustee, Lockerbie Air Disaster Appeal, 1988-91; Chairman, Disciplined Services Pay Review Committee, Hong Kong, 1988; Chairman, Blacket Association, 1971-73; Commodore, Elie and Earlsferry S.C., 1992-94; Chairman, Elie Harbour Trust, since 1993. Recreations: sailing; sea-fishing; walking; reading. Address: (h.) Well Wynd House, South Street, Elie, Fife KY9 1DN; T.-01333 330741.

Rennie, Professor Michael John, BSc, MSc, PhD, FRSE. Symers Professor of Physiology, Dundee University, since 1983; b. 28.7.46, Wallsend on Tyne; m., Anne Macgregor; 1 s.; 2 d. Educ. Newcastle Royal Grammar School; Hull University; Manchester University; Glasgow University. MRC Travelling Fellow, Washington University Medical School, St. Louis, 1974-76; Lecturer and Wellcome Senior Lecturer, Department of Medicine, University College London, 1976-83. Editor, British Journal of Intensive Care. Publications: 200 scientific papers. Recreations: walking; cycling; reading; eating. Address: (b.) Department of Anatomy and Physiology, Dundee University, Dundee DD1 4HN; T.-01382 344572.

Rennie, Professor Robert, LLB, PhD, FRSA. Partner, Ballantyne & Copland, Solicitors, Motherwell, since 1972; Professor of Conveyancing, Glasgow University, since 1993; b. 30.6.47, Glasgow; m., Catherine Mary McGregor; 1 s.; 3 d. Educ. Lenzie Academy; Glasgow University. Apprentice then Legal Assistant, Bishop Milne Boyd & Co., Solicitors, Glasgow; joined Ballantyne & Copland as Legal Assistant, 1971; Past Convener, Law Society of Scotland Conveyancing Committee; Board Member, Capability Scotland; Member, Local Interview Committee, Prince's Scottish Youth Business Trust; Director, Taggarts (Motor Holdings) Limited. Recreation: classical music. Address: (b.) Torrance House, Knowetop, Motherwell ML1 2AF; T.-01698 66200.

Rennilson, John Douglas, MA, MSc, MRTPI, ARICS, MIMgt. Director of Planning, The Highland Council, since 1996; b. 12.2.47, Edinburgh; m., Susan M.; 1 s.; 1. Educ. George Watson's College, Edinburgh; Edinburgh University; University of Wales. Lanarkshire County Council, 1970-74, latterly as Senior Planning Officer; Suffolk County Council, 1974-84, latterly as Assistant County Planning Officer (Environment); County Planning Officer, North Yorkshire County Council, 1984-96. Member, Executive, County Planning Officers Society (Chairman, Committee 3, 1989-91, and from 1995). Recreations: walking; golf; Scottish country dancing; branch line railways. Address: (b.) Glenurquhart Road, Inverness IV3 5NX; T.-01463 772251.

Renshaw, Professor Eric, BSc, ARCS, DipStats, MPhil, PhD, CStat, FRSE. Professor of Statistics, Strathclyde University, since 1991; b. 25.7.45, Preston; m., Anne Renshaw. Educ. Arnold School, Blackpool; Imperial College, London; Manchester University; Sussex

University; Edinburgh University. Lecturer, then Senior Lecturer in Statistics, Edinburgh University, 1969-91. Publication: Modelling Biological Populations in Space and Time. Recreations: skiing; golf; hill-walking; photography. Address: (b.) Department of Statistics and Modelling Science, Livingstone Tower, Strathclyde University, 26 Richmond Street, Glasgow G1 1XH; T.-0141-552 4400.

Renton, Rev. Ian Paterson, OStJ, FSA Scot, JP. Minister, St. Colm's Parish Kirk, Dalry, Edinburgh, 1966-91; b. 22.3.26, Kirkcaldy; m., Ann Gordon Mutter Macpherson; 2 s.; 1 d. Educ. Sinclairtown and Viewforth Schools, Kirkcaldy; Newbattle Abbey College; Glasgow University; St. Mary's College, St. Andrews. Shipping Clerk, Robert Wemyss & Co., Kirkcaldy, 1941-44; Sergeant, 3rd Bn., Scots Guards, 1944-47; Ministry of Labour, Kirkcaldy, 1947-48; Newbattle Abbey College, 1948-50; Youth Clubs Organiser, Roxburghshire, 1950-53; divinity studies, 1953-58; Assistant Minister, North Kirk, Aberdeen, 1958-60; Minister, St. Mark's Church, Greenwich, London, 1960-66. Member, Edinburgh City Education Committee, 1970-76; Governor: Moray House College, 1971-79, Donaldson's School, Edinburgh, 1972-75, Newbattle Abbey College, 1973-76; Member, General Assembly Committee on Education, 1973-79; Joint Chairman, Scottish Joint Committee on Religious Education, 1974-79; Member, Lothian Region Education Committee, 1977-78; Member, Edinburgh Children's Panel, 1971-74; Executive Member, Broadcasting Council, Radio Forth, 1976-79; Member, DHSS Social Security Tribunal, 1978-84; Member, Church of Scotland Board of Education, 1983-85; Member, Lothian Health Board Committee on Medical Ethics, 1984-96; regular Contributor, BBC, STV, Radio Forth, since 1973; Moderator, Edinburgh Presbytery, 1989-90; Chaplain to Astley Ainslie Hospital, Edinburgh. Recreations: gardening; drystane diking; tai chi. Address: Roseneath, Newbattle Terrace, Edinburgh EH10 4SF.

Renton, Janice Helen, LLB. Deputy Commissioner for Local Administration in Scotland, since 1991; Deputy Local Government Adjudicator for Scotland, since 1990; b. 20.4.47, Falkirk. Educ. Bo'ness Academy; Edinburgh University. Legal Assistant, Clackmannan County Council, 1969; Depute Reporter, Children's Panel, Glasgow Corporation, 1971; Senior Legal Assistant, Aberdeen County Council, 1972; Depute Director of Law and Administration, Grampian Regional Council, 1974; Senior Depute Director of Administration, City of Edinburgh, 1976-84; joined Commissioner's Office, 1989. Secretary, Edinburgh International Festival Society, 1982-84. Recreations: eating; talking. Address: 23 Walker Street, Edinburgh EH3 7HX.

Renton, Stuart, MBE, RSA, DA. Architect; Chairman, Board of Governors, Edinburgh College of Art, 1992-98; Visiting Professor, Department of Architecture, Strathclyde University, 1992-98; b. 15.9.29, Edinburgh; m., Ethnie Sloan; 1 s.; 1 d. Educ. Royal High School, Edinburgh; Edinburgh College of Art (Andrew Grant Scholar, 1949-52; Civic Medalist, 1952). Military Service, RAF and RAFVR; Partner, Alan Reiach and Partners, Architects, Edinburgh, 1959; Partner, Reiach and Hall, 1965, Senior Partner, 1982-91, with particular responsibility for design direction, gaining three RIBA awards, three Civic Trust awards and commendations among successes in other national award schemes. External Examiner, several universities; Assessor for architectural awards schemes; Member, Visiting Board Panel, RIBA Education Board, 1984-95; Governor, Edinburgh College of Art, since 1985. Recreations: skiing; game fishing; Italian hill villages. Address: Grianan, Killichonan, Rannoch, Perthshire PH17 2QW; T.-01882 633247.

Renwick, Professor John Peter, MA, PhD, DLitt, FRHistS, Officier des Palmes Academiques. John Orr Professor of French, Edinburgh University, since 1980; b.

25.5.39, Gillingham; m., Claudette Gorse; 1 s.; 1 d. Educ. Gillingham Grammar School; St. Bartholomew's Grammar School, Newbury; St. Catherine's College, Oxford; Sorbonne; British Institute in Paris (Leverhulme Research Scholar). Assistant Lecturer, then Lecturer, Glasgow University, 1964-66; Fellow, Churchill College, Cambridge, 1966-72; Maitre de Conferences Associe, Departement de Francais, Universite de Clermont-Ferrand, 1970-71, 1972-74; Professor of French, New University of Ulster, 1974-80 (Pro-Vice-Chancellor, 1978-80). Publications: La destinee posthume de Jean-Francois Marmontel, 1972; Marmontel, Memoires, 1972; Marmontel, Voltaire and the Belisaire affair, 1974; Marmontel, Correspondence, 1974; Catalogue de la bibliotheque de Jean-Baptiste Massillon, 1977; Voltaire et Morangies, ou les Lumieres l'ont echappe belle, 1982; Chamfort devant La Posterite, 1986; Catalogue de la Bibliotheque du Comte D'Espinchal, 1988; Language and Rhetoric of the French Revolution, 1990; Voltaire, La Guerre Civile de Genève, 1990; Catalogue de la Bibliotheque du College de L'Oratoire de Riom 1619-1792, 1997. Address: (b.) 60 George Square, Edinburgh EH8 9JU.

Rettie, James Philip, CBE, TD. Farmer; Partner, Rettie Farming Co.; Director, Rettie & Co.; Director, Edinburgh and Glasgow Investment Co.; Trustee, Scottish Civic Trust, since 1982; b. 7.12.26, Dundee; m., 1, Helen Grant; 2, Diana Harvey; 2 s.; 1 d. Educ. Trinity College, Glenalmond. Royal Engineers, 1945-48. Chairman, Sea Fish Industry Authority, 1981-87; Chairman, William Low & Co. PLC, 1980-85. Hon. Colonel, 117 and 277 FDSQNS RE (V), 1983-89. Recreations: shooting; gardening; walking. Address: (h.) Hill House, Ballindean, Inchture, Perthshire PH14 9QS; T.-01828 686337.

Reynolds, Professor Siân, BA, MA, PhD. Professor of French, Stirling University, since 1990; Translator; b. 28.7.40, Cardiff; m., Peter France; 3 d. Educ. Howell's School, Llandaff; St. Anne's College, Oxford. Lecturer and Senior Lecturer, Sussex University, 1974-89; Lecturer, Edinburgh University, 1989-90. Publications: Women, State and Revolution (Editor); Britannica's Typesetters; France Between the Wars, gender and politics; translations. Address: (b.) Stirling University, Stirling FK9 4LA; T.-01786 467530.

Rhodes, Joseph, MA (Hons). Rector, Dunoon Grammar School, since 1981; b. 9.12.45, Irvine; m., Ann Robertson; 3 s.; 3 d. Educ. Ayr Academy; Glasgow University. Teacher of History, Kilmarnock Academy, 1969-71; Principal Teacher, Auchenharvie Academy, 1971-74; Assistant Rector, Garnock Academy, 1974-77; Depute Rector, Oban High School, 1977-81. Recreations: gardening; cricket. Address: (b.) Dunoon Grammar School, Kirn, Dunoon; T.-01369 705010.

Rice, Professor C. Duncan, MA, PhD. Principal and Vice-Chancellor, Aberdeen University, since 1996; b. 20.10.42, Aberdeen; m., Susan Ilene; 2 s.; 1 d. Educ. Aberdeen University; Edinburgh University. Lecturer, Aberdeen University, 1966-69; Assistant Professor of History, then Associate Professor of History, Yale University, New Haven, 1970-79; Professor of History, Hamilton College, Clinton, New York, 1979-85; Professor of History, Dean of Faculty of Arts and Sciences, New York University, 1985-94 (Vice-Chancellor, 1991-96). Member, Board, James Inglis Rice Trust for Conservation in Hebrides; Trustee, The Peddie School; Director, Beneficial Bank plc. Publications: The Rise and Fall of Black Slavery; The Scots Abolitionists 1831-1961; various articles and reviews. Recreations: hill-waking; cycling. Address: (b.) Aberdeen University, Regent Walk, Aberdeen; T.-01224 272134.

Richards, Professor Bryan Edward, BSc (Eng), DIC, PhD, CEng, FRAeSoc, AFAIAA. Mechan Professor of Aerospace Engineering, Glasgow University, since 1980; b.

30.6.38, Hornchurch; m., Margaret Owen; 2 s.; 2 d. Educ. Palmer's School, Grays; Queen Mary College, London University. Aerodynamicist, Bristol Aeroplane Company, Filton, 1960-62; Research Assistant, Imperial College, London University, 1962-66; Assistant Professor, Associate Professor, Professor, Von Karman Institute, Belgium, 1967-79; Head, Department of Aerospace Engineering, Glasgow University, 1980-90; Dean of Engineering, 1984-87. Publications: 110 articles. Recreations: sailing; hill-walking. Address: (h.) Ravenswood, 32 Suffolk Street, Helensburgh G84 9PA; T.-01436 672112.

Richards, John Deacon, CBE, AADip, DUniv, RSA, RIBA, PPRIAS. Architect; Principal, John Richards Associates, Architects, since 1986; b. 7.5.31, Shanghai; m., Margaret Brown; 1 s.; 3 d. Educ. Cranleigh School, Surrey; Architectural Association School of Architecture, London. Partner, Robert Matthew, Johnson-Marshall & Partners, 1964-86 (Chairman, 1983-86); Member, Royal Fine Art Commission for Scotland, 1975-89; Agrement Board, 1980-83; Member, Williams Committee on National Museums and Galleries, 1981; Gold Medallist, RSA, 1972; Past President, Royal Incorporation of Architects in Scotland, 1983-85; Trustee, National Galleries of Scotland, 1986-90; Chairman, Scottish Committee, Housing Corporation, 1983-89; Board Member, Scottish Homes, 1988-93, Deputy Chairman, 1989-93; Housing Association Ombudsman for Scotland, since 1993. Recreations: gardening; fishing. Address: (h.) Lady's Field, Whitekirk, East Lothian; T.-01620 870206.

Richards, Professor Robert Michael Edward, OBE, BPharm, PhD, DSc, DPharmSc, FRPharmS, PhC (Thai & Zimb). Professor and Head, School of Pharmacy, Robert Gordon University, Aberdeen, since 1986; b. 5.12.32, Morton, England; m., Joan Mallett Maybrey; 2 s.; 3 d. Educ. Clay Cross Tupton Hall Grammar School; School of Pharmacy, London University. University College Hospital, London, 1954-55; 23rd Parachute Field Ambulance, 1955-57; Medical Missionary and University Lecturer in Thailand with Overseas Missionary Fellowship, 1958-70; Lecturer, Heriot-Watt University, 1970-73; Inaugural Professor of Pharmacy, University of Rhodesia, 1973-78; Senior Lecturer, Strathclyde University, 1978-83; OMF Home Staff and British Council Consultant, Khon Kaen, Thailand and Nanjing, 1983-86. Director of project to establish Faculty of Pharmacy, Mahasarakham University, Thailand, since 1996; Director, WHO Collaborating Centre, School of Pharmacy, Robert Gordon University, since 1995; Chairman, Scottish Council, University and Colleges Christian Fellowship, 1989-95; UK Academic Representative on EC Committee for Training of Pharmacists in Europe; Chairman, Scottish Examiners, Pharmacist's Registration Examination. Publications: Clinical Pharmacy and Hospital Drug Management, 1983; Pharmaceutical Practice, 1998; 100 scientific papers. Recreations: travel; languages; classical music; photography; spectator sports. Address: (b.) School of Pharmacy, Robert Gordon University, Schoolhill, Aberdeen AB10 1FR; T.-01224 262500.

Richardson, Professor John Stuart, MA, DPhil, FRSE. Professor of Classics, Edinburgh University, since 1987, Dean, Faculty of Arts, and Provost, Faculty Group of Arts, Divinity and Music, 1992-97; b. 4.2.46, Ilkley; m., Patricia Helen Robotham; 2 s. Educ. Berkhamsted School; Trinity College, Oxford. Lecturer in Ancient History, Exeter College, Oxford, 1969-72, St. Andrews University, 1972-87; Priest, Scottish Episcopal Church, since 1980; Anglican Chaplain, St. Andrews University, 1980-87; Team Priest, St. Columba's, Edinburgh, since 1987. Publications: Roman Provincial Administration, 1976; Hispaniae, 1986; The Romans in Spain, 1996; papers on ancient history. Recreation: choral singing. Address: (h.) 29 Merchiston Avenue, Edinburgh EH10 4PH; T.-0131-228 3094.

Riches, Christopher Gabriel, BSc. Editorial Director, Reference, Harper Collins Publishers, since 1994; b. 25.3.52, Oxford; m., Catherine Mary Gaunt; 3 s. Educ. Marlborough College; Manchester University. Copy Editor, Penguin Books, 1973-74; Oxford University Press: Science Education Editor, 1974-76, Publishing Manager, Hong Kong, 1976-81, Reference Editor, 1981-88; Publishing Manager, Collins Reference, Glasgow, 1989-94. Council Member, Scottish Publishers' Association, since 1995; Hon. Secretary, St. Mary's Episcopal Church, Aberfoyle, since 1994; Chair, School Boad, Killearn Primary School, since 1997. Recreations: book collecting; gardening; walking. Address: (h.) Achadhu House, Main Street, Killearn G63 9RJ; T.-01360 550544.

Riches, Professor John Kenneth, MA. Professor of Divinity and Biblical Criticism, Glasgow University; b. 30.4.39, London; m., Renate Emmy Therman; 2 s.; 1 d. Educ. Cranleigh School; Corpus Christi College, Cambridge. Assistant Curate, St. Edmund's, Norfolk, 1965-68; Chaplain, Fellow and Director of Studies in Theology, Sidney Sussex College, Cambridge, 1968-72; Lecturer, Department of New Testament Language and Literature, Glasgow University, 1973-86; Senior Lecturer, Department of Biblical Studies, Glasgow University, 1986-91; Chairman, Balmore Trust, since 1980; Convener, Doctrine Committee, Scottish Episcopal Church, 1991-96. Publications: Jesus and the Transformation of Judaism; The World of Jesus; A Century of New Testament Study. Recreations: hill-walking; third world trading. Address: (h.) Viewfield, Balmore, Torrance, Glasgow G64 4AE; T.-01360 620254.

Richmond, Professor John, CBE, MD, FRCPE, FRCP, FRSE. President, Royal College of Physicians of Edinburgh, 1988-91; Emeritus Professor of Medicine, Sheffield University, since 1989; b. 30.5.26, Doncaster; m., Jenny Nicol; 2 s.; 1 d. Educ. Doncaster Grammar School; Edinburgh University. RAMC, Africa, 1949-50; rural general practice, Galloway, 1950-52; Lecturer, Senior Lecturer, Reader in Medicine, Edinburgh University, 1954-73; Research Fellow, Memorial Sloan Kettering Cancer Center, New York, 1958-59; Professor of Medicine, Sheffield University, 1973-89 (Dean of Medicine, 1985-88). Senior Censor and Senior Vice-President, Royal College of Physicians of London, 1984-85; Chairman, MRCP (UK) Examining Board, 1984-88; Member, Board of Advisors in Medicine, London University, 1984-93; External Advisor, Chinese University of Hong Kong, since 1982; Member, Department of Health Clinical Standards Advisory Group, 1991-94; Member, Scottish Advisory Board, British Council, 1991-97; Member, Scottish Committee, Marie Curie Memorial Foundation, since 1992; FRCPSG, FRCPI, FACP(Hon), FFPM(Hon), FRCSE, FFPHM(Hon), FCP(SA)(Hon), FRACP(Hon). Address: (h.) 15 Church Hill, Edinburgh, EH10 4BG.

Richmond, John Kennedy, JP, DL. Chairman, Glasgow Airport Consultative Committee, since 1979; b. 23.4.37, Glasgow; m., Elizabeth Margaret; 1 s.; 1 d. Educ. King's Park Secondary School. Conservative Member, Glasgow Corporation, 1963-75; Member, Glasgow District Council, 1975-84; Deputy Lord Provost, 1977-80; Conservative Group Leader, 1975-77. Recreations: tennis; music; travel. Address: (h.) 84 Merrylee Road, Newlands, Glasgow G43 2QZ; T.-0141-637 7705.

Rickets, Brigadier Reginald Anthony Scott. Managing Director, Irvine Development Corporation, 1981-95; Trustee, Scottish Maritime Museum (Irvine); Director, Enterprise Ayrshire, since 1990; Chairman, Scottish Committee, German/British Chamber of Industry and Commerce; Director, Kelvin Travel; Depute Chairman, Irvine Housing Association, since 1996; Director, Nobel Exhibition Trust, since 1997; b. 13.12.29; m., Elizabeth Ann Serjeant; 1 s.; 1 d. Educ. St. George's College,

Weybridge; Royal Military Academy, Sandhurst. 2nd Lt., RE, 1949; served with Airborne, Armoured and field Engineers, UK, Cyrenaica, Egypt, Malaya, Borneo, Hong Kong and BAOR; special employment military forces, Malaya, 1955-59; Staff College, Camberley, 1962; Brigade Major, BAOR, 1963-66; Gurkha Independent Field Squadron, 1966-68; Directing Staff, Army Staff College, 1968-70; Commandant, Gurkha Engineers, and Commander, Royal Engineers Far East, 1970-73; Chief of Staff, Berlin, 1973-77; Brigadier Chief Engineer, UK Land Forces, 1978-81; President, Ayrshire Chamber of Industries, 1986; Vice President, Ayrshire Chamber of Industry and Commerce, 1991. Recreation: sailing (DTI Ocean Skipper, RYA Coach/Examiner, Commodore REYC, 1979). Address: 10 Waterside Street, Largs KA30 9LN; T.-01475 672838.

Rickman, David Edwin, BCom (Hons). Rules Secretary, Royal and Ancient Golf Club of St. Andrews, since 1996; b. 9.10.64, St. Andrews; m., Jennifer Mary Cameron; 1 d. Educ. Madras College, St. Andrews; Edinburgh University. Joined R. & A. staff, 1987; appointed Assistant Secretary (Rules), 1990. Recreations: sport, especially golf. Address: (b.) c/o Royal and Ancient Golf Club, St. Andrews, Fife KY16 9JD; T.-01334 472112.

Rickman, Professor Geoffrey Edwin, MA, DPhil (Oxon), FBA, FSA. Professor of Roman History, St. Andrews University, 1981-97; Master of the United College of St. Salvator and St. Leonard, 1992-96; Pro Vice Chancellor, 1996-97; b. 9.10.32, Cherat, India; m., Ann Rosemary Wilson; 1 s.; 1 d. Educ. Peter Symonds' School, Winchester; Brasenose College, Oxford. Junior Research Fellow, Queen's College, Oxford; St. Andrews University: Lecturer in Ancient History, Senior Lecturer, Professor; Visiting Fellow, Brasenose College, Oxford. Council Member, Society for Promotion of Roman Studies; British School at Rome: Member, Faculty of Archaeology, History and Letters, (Chairman, 1984-87), Chairman, Council, since 1997. Publications: Roman Granaries and Storebuildings, 1971; The Corn Supply of Ancient Rome, 1980. Recreations: opera; swimming. Address: (h.) 56 Hepburn Gardens, St. Andrews, Fife; T.-St. Andrews 472063.

Riddle, Gordon Stewart, MA. Principal and Chief Ranger, Culzean Country Park, since 1976 (Deputy Administrator, Culzean Castle and Country Park, since 1982); b. 2.10.47, Kelso; m., Rosemary Robb; 1 s.; 1 d. Educ. Kelso High School; Edinburgh University; Moray House College of Education. Biology and History Teacher, Lasswade High School, 1970-71; National Ranger Training Course, 1971-72; Ranger and Depute Principal, Culzean Country Park, 1972-75; National Park Service (USA) Training Course, 1978; Winston Churchill Travelling Fellowship, USA, 1981. Member, Royal Society for the Protection of Birds, Scottish Committee, since 1995; Chairman, South Strathclyde Raptor Study Group, since 1994. Publications: The Kestrel; Seasons with the Kestrel. Recreations: sport; gardening; birds of prey; photography; hill-walking; music; writing. Address: (h.) Swinston, Culzean Country Park, by Maybole, Ayrshire; T.-01655 760 662.

Riddoch, Lesley, BA (Hons). Associate Editor, The Scotsman, 1996-97, Assistant Editor, 1994-96; Presenter, Midnight Hour, BBC2, since 1996; Presenter, You and Yours, BBC Radio 4, since 1996; Speaker, The People's Parliament, Channel 4, since 1994; b. 21.2.60, Wolverhampton; m., George Gunn (separated). Educ. High School of Glasgow; Wadham College, Oxford; University College, Cardiff. Sabbatical President, Oxford University Students Union, 1980; Reporter, BBC Radio Scotland, 1985-88; Co-Presenter, Head On, 1988-90; Presenter, Speaking Out, 1990-94; Founder and Director, Harpies and Quines (feminist magazine). Member, Isle of Eigg Trust, since 1993. Norman McEwen Award, 1992; Cosmopolitan Woman of the Year (Communications), 1992; Plain English

Award, 1993. Recreations: drinking; playing pool; walking. Address: (h.) Crannach Ha', Fowlis Wester, Crieff PH7 3NL.

Ridley, Nicholas John, OBE. Director, Florence Nightingale Fund, since 1994; b. 25.3.41, India; m., Isabel Susan Spencer-Nairn; 1 s.; 1 d. Educ. Edinburgh Academy; Shrewsbury School; R.M.A., Sandhurst. Enlisted Queen's Own Cameron Highlanders, 1959; commissioned, Queen's Own Highlanders, 1962; Lt. Col., 1980, and commanded 1st Bn., 1982; Col., 1984, and Military Director of Studies, Royal Military College of Science, Shrivenham, 1984-87; Brigadier and Commander, 54 Infantry Brigade, 1988-91; Deputy Commandant, RMCS, Shrivenham, 1991-93; Chief Executive, Faculty of Advocates, 1993-94; Managing Director, MA Associates, 1995-97. Recreations: field sports; music; golf; cabinet-making. Address: (h.) 5 Grant Avenue, Edinburgh EH13 ODS; T.-0131-441 7674.

Ridley, Professor Tom, BSc (Eng), BArch, DIC, FRSE, Hon.FRIAS, RIBA, FICE, FIStructE, MConsE. Chartered Architect and Engineer, in private practice; Visiting Professor, Strathclyde University; Member, Royal Fine Art Commission for Scotland, since 1992; Consultant to Royal Scottish Academy; b. 15.8.27, Gateshead-on-Tyne; m., Carolyn Anne; 3 d. Educ. Imperial College, London University; Strathclyde University. Yorkshire Hennibique Contracting Co., 1948-54; Ove Arup & Partners, 1954-91; opened Scottish Office for Arups, 1960, and responsible for all work in Scotland; won Leverhulme Scholarship. Recreations: fishing; golf. Address: (h.) Marlyn, West Linton EH46 7HW; T.-01968 660604.

Riemersma, Rudolph Arend, BSc, MSc, PhD, FRCPE. Assistant Director, Cardiovascular Research Unit, Edinburgh University, since 1975 (British Heart Foundation Senior Lecturer in Cardiac Biochemistry, since 1979); Professor in Medical Physiology, University of Tromso, Norway, since 1994; b. 9.5.43, Hengelo, Netherlands; m., Eva J. Nieuwenhuis; 1 s.; 1 d. Educ. Charlois Lyceum, Rotterdam; Leyden University; Edinburgh University. Biochemist, Department of Cardiology, Academic Hospital, Utrecht; postgraduate research, Royal Postgraduate Medical School, Hammersmith Hospital, London; Research Fellow, Edinburgh University, 1973. Former Vice-President, European Society of Clinical Investigation. Recreations: orienteering; skiing; hill-walking; botany. Address: (b.) Cardiovascular Research Unit, Hugh Robson Building, George Square, Edinburgh; T.-0131-650 3699.

Rifkind, Rt. Hon Sir Malcolm Leslie, KCMG, QC, LLB, MSc. Secretary of State for Foreign and Commonwealth Affairs, 1995-97; Secretary of State for Defence, 1992-95; Secretary of State for Transport, 1990-92; MP (Conservative), Edinburgh Pentlands, 1974-97; b. 21.6.46, Edinburgh; m., Edith Amalia Steinberg; 1 s.; 1 d. Educ. George Watson's College, Edinburgh; Edinburgh University. Lecturer, University of Rhodesia, 1967-68; called to Scottish Bar, 1970; Opposition Front-Bench Spokesman on Scottish Affairs, 1975-76; Member, Select Committee on European Secondary Legislation, 1975-76; Chairman, Scottish Conservatives' Devolution Committee, 1976; Joint Secretary, Conservative Parliamentary Foreign and Commonwealth Affairs Committee, 1977-79; Member, Select Committee on Overseas Development, 1978-79; Parliamentary Under-Secretary of State, Scottish Office, 1979-82; Parliamentary Under-Secretary of State, Foreign and Commonwealth Office, 1982-83; Minister of State, Foreign and Commonwealth Office, 1983-86; Secretary of State for Scotland, 1986-90; Member, Queen's Bodyguard for Scotland (Royal Company of Archers); Hon. Col., 162 Movement Control Regiment, Royal Logistic Corps. Address: (h.) Duddingston Village, Edinburgh.

Rigg, David, MA (Hons). University Registrar and Depute Secretary, Paisley University, since 1987; b. 15.3.48, Insch;

m., Margaret Taylor Mechie; 1 s.; 1 d. Educ. Daniel Stewart's College, Edinburgh; West Calder High School; Dundee University. British Gas, 1971-73; Administrative Assistant, Strathclyde University, 1973-79; Assistant Secretary, Paisley College, 1979-87. Recreations: cutting grass; reading; theatre; supporting Hibernian Football Club. Address: (b.) Paisley University, High Street, Paisley PA1 2BE; T.-0141-848 3677.

Rigg, John Alexander, BA, MA, PhD. Senior Economic Adviser, Scottish Office Education and Industry Department, since 1995; b. 16.11.54, Leeds; m., Angela Mary English; 1 s.; 1 d. Educ. Roundhay School, Leeds; Trinity College, Cambridge. Research Assistant, Queen Mary College, London University, 1981-82; Senior Economic Analyst, Henley Centre for Forecasting, London, 1982-85; Director, Henley Centre, 1986-92; Economic Adviser, Scottish Office, 1992-95. Recreations: cinema; cricket; family history; rugby league. Address: (b.) Scottish Office Education and Industry Department, Meridian Court, 5 Cadogan Street, Glasgow G2 6AT; T.-0141-242 5565.

Rimer, Jennifer, BMusHon, LRAM, DipEd. Headteacher, St. Mary's Music School, Edinburgh, since 1996; SQA Examiner, Setter and Marker, since 1978; b. 16.10.47, Kirkcaldy; m., David Rimer; 3 d. Educ. Buckhaven High School; Edinburgh University. Music Teacher, Newcastle, 1970-72; Principal Music Teacher, Lothian Region, 1972-77; St. Mary's Music School: Piano Teacher/Academic Music Teacher, 1982-93; Head of Guidance, Careers and Academic Music, 1993-95. Governor, George Heriot's School; Director, Edinburgh Youth Orchestra. Recreations: family; reading; yoga; walking; accompanying. Address: (b.) St. Mary's Music School, Coates Hall, 25 Grosvenor Crescent, Edinburgh; T.-0131-538 7766.

Rinning, Andy. Director, Red Deer Commission, since 1990; b. 15.9.49, Balerno; m., Jeanette Legg; 1 s.; 1 d. Educ. Currie Senior Secondary School. Department of Agriculture and Fisheries for Scotland, 1969-75; Scottish Office Finance Division, 1975-78; Scottish Development Department, 1978-82; Scottish Office Finance Division, 1982-85; Assistant Private Secretary to Secretaries of State for Scotland, 1985-88; Scottish Office Finance Division, 1988-90. Recreations: curling; gardening; golf. Address: (b.) Knowsley, 82 Fairfield Road, Inverness IV3 5LH; T.-01463 231751.

Risk, Sheriff Douglas James, QC, MA, LLB. Sheriff Principal of Grampian, Highland and Islands, since 1993; Honorary Professor, Faculty of Law, Aberdeen University, since 1993; b. 23.1.41; m., Jennifer Hood Davidson; 3 s.; 1 d. Educ. Glasgow Academy; Gonville and Caius College, Cambridge; Glasgow University. Admitted Advocate, 1966; Standing Junior Counsel to Scottish Education Department, 1975; Sheriff of Lothian and Borders at Edinburgh, 1977-79; Sheriff of Grampian, Highland and Islands, at Aberdeen and Stonehaven, 1979-93; Temporary Judge, Court of Session and High Court, 1992-93; QC, 1992; Honorary Lecturer, Faculty of Law, Aberdeen University, 1981-93. Address: (b.) Sheriff Court House, Castle Street, Aberdeen AB10 1WP; T.-01224 648316.

Risk, Sir Thomas Neilson, BL, LLD (Glasgow), Dr. h.c. (Edin), FRSE; b. 13.9.22, Glasgow; m., Suzanne Eiloart; 4 s. (1 dec.) Educ. Kelvinside Academy, Glasgow; Glasgow University. Flt. Lt., RAF, 1941-46; RAFVR, 1946-53; Partner, Maclay, Murray & Spens, Solicitors, 1950-81; Bank of Scotland: Director, 1971-77, Deputy Governor, 1977-81, Governor, 1981-91; Chairman, Standard Life Assurance Company, 1969-77; Director, Shell UK Ltd., 1983-92; Director, MSA (Britain) Ltd., since 1958; Director, The Merchants Trust plc, 1973-94; Director, British Linen Bank Limited, 1977-91 (Governor, 1977-86); Director, Bank of Wales, 1986-91; Director, Howden Group, 1971-87; Chairman, Scottish Financial Enterprise,

1986-89; Director, Barclays Bank, 1983-85; Member, Scottish Economic Planning Council, 1983-91; Member, National Economic Development Council, 1987-91; Member, Scottish Industrial Development Board, 1972-75; Chairman: Edinburgh International Festival Endowment Fund, 1989-97, University of Glasgow Trust; Trustee: Royal Air Force Museum, Hamilton Bequest. Address: (h.) 10 Belford Place, Edinburgh EH4 3DH.

Ritchie, Alastair Newton Bethune; b. 30.4.21, London; m., Isobel Sinclair; 1 s.; 1 d. Educ. Harrow School; Corpus Christi College, Cambridge; Stirling University. Scots Guards, 1940-58; campaign North-West Europe, 1944-45; wounded; mentioned in Despatches; active service, Malaya and Far East, 1947-49; Canadian Army Staff College, 1951; Assistant Military Attache, Canada, 1952-53; active service, Canal Zone, Egypt, 1954; retired as Major, 1958; Argyll and Sutherland Highlanders TA, 1966-68; Partner, Drunkie Farms, Callander, 1967-81; Partner, Sheppards and Chase, Stock and Money Brokers and Member, Stock Exchange, 1960-85; Member, Stirling District Council, 1977-90; Member, Queen's Bodyguard for Scotland (Royal Company of Archers), since 1966; Deputy Lieutenant, Stirling and Falkirk, 1979-96. Recreations: gardening; fishing; music. Address: (h.) The Steading at East Mains, Callander, Perthshire FK17 8AZ; T.-01877 330078.

Ritchie, Alexander John, BSc, DipEd. General Manager, Scottish Cricket Union, since 1991; b. 2.4.35, Alloa; m., Margaret; 1 s.; 1 d. Educ. Dollar Academy; St. Andrews University. Teacher, Larbert High School, 1958-63; Principal Teacher, Grangemouth High School, 1963-69; Assistant Director of Education, Dumfries-shire, 1969-75, Dumfries and Galloway, 1975-82; Senior Education Officer, Strathclyde (Argyll and Bute Division), 1982-91. Address: (h.) 22 South Street, Cambuskenneth, Stirling FK9 5NL; T.-01786 448743.

Ritchie, Andrew, BD, DipMin. Minister, Craiglockhart Parish Church, Edinburgh, since 1991; Assistant Chaplain, Royal Hospital for Sick Children, since 1996; b. 17.4.52, Dunfermline; m., Sheila; 3 s. Educ. Queen Anne School, Dunfermline; Edinburgh University and New College. Assistant Minister, Dundee Parish Church, 1983-84; Minister, Clarkston Parish Church, Airdrie, 1984-91; Convener, Parish Assistance Committee, 1988-90; Vice-Convener, Parish Reappraisal Committee, 1990-93; Convener, Field-Staff Committee, 1993-96. Recreations: music; reading; walking. Address: (h.) 202 Colinton Road, Edinburgh EH14 1BP; T.-0131-443 2020.

Ritchie, Anna, OBE, BA, PhD, FSA, FSA Scot. Freelance archaeologist; Member, Ancient Monuments Board for Scotland, since 1990; Trustee, National Museums of Scotland, since 1993; b. 28.9.43, London; m., Graham Ritchie; 1 s.; 1 d. Educ. Woking Grammar School for Girls; University of Wales; Edinburgh University. Excavations on Neolithic, Pictish and Viking sites in Orkney; public and university lectures; archaeological research and writing; Editor, Proceedings of the Society of Antiquaries of Scotland, 1972-79; Secretary, Society of Antiquaries of Scotland, 1986-88; Vice-President, Society of Antiquaries of London, 1988-92; President, Society of Antiquaries of Scotland, 1990-93. Publications: The Kingdom of the Picts, 1977; Orkney and Shetland, 1985; Scotland BC, 1988; Picts, 1989; Viking Scotland, 1993; Prehistoric Orkney, 1995; Iona, 1997; co-author with Graham Ritchie of several works including Scotland: Archaeology and Early History, 1981. Recreations: walking; early music. Address: (h.) 50/1 Spylaw Road, Edinburgh EH10 5BL; T.-0131-228 5962.

Ritchie, Anne Clarke, MA (Hons), DipEd, DCG. Scottish Director, Independent Schools' Careers Organisation, since 1993; b. 5.12.44, Glasgow. Educ. Hutchesons' Girls' Grammar School, Glasgow; Glasgow University. Assistant Teacher of Modern Languages, Allan Glen's School; Head of Modern Languages, St. Columba's School, Kilmacolm; Principal Teacher of Modern Languages, Jordanhill College School; Senior Mistress, Giggleswick School; Headmistress: Sutherland House School, Norfolk, Runton and Sutherland School, Norfolk. Director, Craigholme School, Glasgow; Governor, Kilgraston School; Member, Governing Board, Scottish Council of Independent Schools. Recreations: music; painting; theatre; reading; travel; hill-walking. Address: 18 Castlemains Road, Milngavie, Glasgow G62 7QQ; T.-0141-956 5027.

Ritchie, Anthony Elliot, CBE, MA, DSc, MD, FCSP, FRCPEd, FRSE, LLD. Secretary and Treasurer, Carnegie Trust for the Universities of Scotland, 1969-86; b. 30.3.15, Edinburgh; m.; Elizabeth Lambie Knox; 1 s.; 3 d. Educ. Edinburgh Academy; Aberdeen University; Edinburgh University. Carnegie Scholar, Lecturer and Senior Lecturer in Physiology, Edinburgh University, 1941-48; Professor of Physiology, St. Andrews University, 1948-69; Honorary Consultant, Eastern Regional Hospital Board, 1950-69; Chairman, Scottish Committee on Science Education, 1970-78; Chairman, Scottish University Entrance Board, 1963-69; Member, British Library Board, 1973-80; Member, Houghton Committee on Teachers' Pay; Trustee, National Library of Scotland, Carnegie Trust; Royal Society of Edinburgh: Fellow, 1951, General Secretary, 1966-76, Bicentenary Gold Medal, 1983; Hon. DSc (St. Andrews); Hon. LLD (Strathclyde). Recreations: reading; hill-walking; mechanics; electronics. Address: (h.) 12 Ravelston Park, Edinburgh EH4 3DX; T.-0131-332 6560.

Ritchie, Astrid Ilfra, JP, MA, FRSA, DipSocAdmin. Chair, Learning Initiatives in Scottish Adult Education; Member: Adult Education Guidance Initiative Scotland, Scottish Qualifications Authority; Patron, RSA Scottish Campaign for Learning; m., 1, Martin Huggins (m. dissolved); 2 d.; 2, Professor David Scarth Ritchie. Educ. Harrogate College; Edinburgh University. Former Member: European Year of Lifelong Learning Scottish Steering Group, Scottish Skills Forum, Scottish Community Education Council; former Chairman, Scottish Adult Education Forum. Address: (h.) 11 Ann Street, Edinburgh EH4 1PL; T.-0131-332 1455.

Ritchie, Cameron, LLB. Procurator Fiscal, Stirling, since 1996; Solicitor Advocate; b. 25.9.52, Paisley; m., Hazel; 2 s. Educ. John Neilson Institution, Paisley; Glasgow University. Apprentice Solicitor, Wright and Crawford, Paisley, 1972-74; Procurator Fiscal Depute, Ayr, 1974-75, Glasgow, 1975-88; Senior Procurator Fiscal Depute, Hamilton, 1988-93; Assistant Procurator Fiscal, Dundee, 1993-96. Recreations: golf; rugby coaching; watching cricket; military history. Address: (b.) Sheriff Court, Stirling; T.-01786 462021.

Ritchie, Professor David Scarth, MA (Cantab), FRSE. Governor, Paisley University, 1984-95; Trustee and Director, James Clerk Maxwell Foundation; m., 1 Heather McLennan (deceased); 2 s.; 2 d.; 2, Astrid Ilfra Chalmers Watson. Educ. Edinburgh Academy; Cambridge University; Royal Naval College, Greenwich. Lt., Royal Navy, 1944-47; Technical Director, Barr & Stroud Ltd., 1969-85; Chairman, Scottish Education Department survey on industrial liasion in Central Institutions, 1985-88. Visiting Professor in Management of Technological Innovation, Strathclyde University, 1986-94. Address: (h.) Southwood, Newbyth, East Linton EH40 3DU; T.-01620-860-211.

Ritchie, James S., BA. Secretary, Scottish Casec, since 1995 (Secretary, Confederation of Associations of Specialist Engineering Contractors, Scottish Branch, 1991-94); Secretary, Scottish Joint Consultative Committee for Building, 1991-94; b. 20.12.36, Dunfermline; m., Patricia; 2 s.; 1 d. Joined Electrical Contractors' Association of Scotland (ECAS), 1990, following an eclectic career in contracting. Member, Scottish Building Contracts

Committee; Member, Committee, Scottish Construction Industry Group. Recreations: reading; contemplating exercise; drafting letters to the editor. Address: (b.) Bush House, Bush Estate, Midlothian EH26 0SB; T.-0131-445 5577.

Ritchie, John Douglas, CA. Partner, Pannell Kerr Forster, since 1985 (Chairman, Edinburgh office, 1993-97); b. 9.10.52, Edinburgh; m., Joan Moira. Educ. George Watson's College. Barstow & Millar, CA, 1971-85 (Partner, 1978-85); Member, National Board for Nursing, Midwifery and Health Visiting for Scotland, 1988-93, Hon. Consultant, since 1993; Member, Management Committee, Viewpoint Housing Association, since 1991; Trustee, Viewpoint Trust, since 1991; President, Rotary Club of Braids, 1991-92; Member, Morningside Christian Council, 1985-92; Member, Church of Scotland Board of Parish Education, since 1994; Treasurer, Scottish Churches Open College, since 1995; Member, Merchant Company of the City of Edinburgh, since 1985; Trustee, Bequest Fund for Ministers in Outlying Districts of the Church of Scotland, since 1994. Address: (b.) 17 Rothesay Place, Edinburgh EH3 7SQ; T.-0131-225 3688.

Ritchie, Murray. Scottish Political Editor, The Herald, since 1997; b. 5.9.41, Dumfries; m.; 1 s.; 2 d. Educ. High School of Glasgow. Scottish Farmer, 1958-60; Dumfries and Galloway Standard, 1960-65; Scottish Daily Record, 1965-67; East African Standard, 1967-71; joined Glasgow Herald, 1971. Journalist of the Year, Fraser Press Awards, 1980. Address: (b.) The Herald, 195 Albion Street, Glasgow G1 1QP.

Ritson, Bruce, MD, FRCPsych, FRCP(Ed), DipPsych. Clinical Director and Consultant Psychiatrist, Royal Edinburgh Hospital, since 1972; Senior Lecturer in Psychiatry, Edinburgh University, since 1972; Consultant, Royal Edinburgh Hospital, since 1972; b. 20.3.37, Elgin; m., Eileen Carey; 1 s.; 1 d. Educ. Edinburgh Academy; Edinburgh University; Harvard University. Trained in medicine, Edinburgh; postgraduate training in psychiatry, Edinburgh, Harvard and California; Director, Sheffield Region Addiction Unit, 1968-71; at present Consultant with special responsibility for alcohol-related problems; World Health Organisation consultant; Chairman, Howard League in Scotland; Chairman, Medical Council on Alcoholism; Chairman, Substance Misuse Faculty, Royal College of Psychiatrists; Member, Advisory Group on Substance Misuse, WHO; Chairman, Advisory Panel on Alcohol, DVLA. Recreations: friends; squash; theatre. Address: (b.) Andrew Duncan Clinic, Royal Edinburgh Hospital, Morningside Park, Edinburgh; T.-0131-537 6297.

Roach, Professor Gary Francis, BSc, MSc, PhD, DSc, ScD. Professor of Mathematics, Strathclyde University, since 1979 (Dean, Faculty of Science, since 1982); b. 8.10.33, Penpedairheol, South Wales; m., Isabella Grace Willins Nicol. Educ. University College, South Wales and Monmouthshire; London University; Manchester University. RAF (Education Branch), Flying Officer, 1955-58; Research Mathematician, British Petroleum Co. Ltd., 1958-61; Lecturer, Manchester University Institute of Science and Technology, 1961-66; Visiting Professor, University of British Columbia, 1966-67; Strathclyde University: Lecturer, 1967-70, Senior Lecturer, 1970-71, Reader, 1971-79. Fellow, Royal Astronomical Society; Fellow, Institute of Mathematics and its Applications; Fellow, Royal Society of Arts; Fellow, Royal Society of Edinburgh; Past President, Edinburgh Mathematical Society. Recreations: mountaineering; photography; philately; gardening; music. Address: (b.) Department of Mathematics, Strathclyde University, Livingstone Tower, 26 Richmond Street, Glasgow G1 1XH; T.-0141-552 4400, Ext. 3800.

Roads, Elizabeth Ann, MVO, FSA (Scot). Lyon Clerk and Keeper of the Records, since 1986; Carrick Pursuivant of Arms, since 1992; b. 5.7.51; m., Christopher George William Roads; 2 s.; 1 d. Educ. Lansdowne House School, Edinburgh; Cambridge College of Technology; Study Centre for Fine Art, London. Christie's, Art Auctioneers, 1971-74; Court of the Lord Lyon, since 1975; temporarily Linlithgow Pursuivant Extraordinary, 1987. Recreations: history; reading; countryside activities. Address: (b.) Court of the Lord Lyon, HM New Register House, Edinburgh.

Robb, Professor Alan, DA, MA, RCA. Head, School of Fine Art, Duncan of Jordanstone College of Art, Dundee, since 1983; b. 24.2.46, Glasgow; m., Cynthia J. Neilson; 1 s.; 1 d. Educ. Robert Gordon's College, Aberdeen; Grays School of Art; Royal College of Art. Assistant Art Master, Oundle School, 1972-75; Crawford School of Art: Lecturer in Painting, 1975-78, Head of Painting, 1978-80, Head of Fine Art, 1980-83. Member, Fine Art Panel, CNAA, 1986-87; Specialist Advisor, CNAA, since 1987; Director, Art in Partnership, 1987-92; Director, British Health Care Arts Centre, 1988-93; Member, SHEFC Research Advisory Group, since 1993; Lead Assessor for Fine Art, SHEFC Quality Assessment; first one-man exhibition, New 57 Gallery, 1973; Arts Council touring two-man exhibition, 1978-79; regularly exhibits in Scotland; solo exhibitions: In the Mind's Eye, 1996, True Knowledge, East West Gallery, London, 1997. Publication: Irish Contemporary Art, 1980. Address: (b.) Duncan of Jordanstone College, University of Dundee, Perth Road, Dundee DD1 4HT.

Robb, John Weddell. Chairman, British Energy plc, since 1995; Chairman, Logitron Holdings plc; Non-Executive Director, Unigate plc; Deputy Chairman, Horse Race Betting Levy Board; Non-Executive Director, Allied-Domecq plc; b. 27.4.36, Edinburgh; m., Janet Teanby; 2 s.; 1 d. Educ. Stewart's College, Edinburgh. Non-Executive Director, NFC plc, 1983-95 (Deputy Chairman, 1991-95); Group Managing Director, Beecham Group plc, 1985-88; Non-Executive Director, STC plc, 1985-89; Wellcome plc, 1989-95 (Chief Executive, 1990-93; Chairman and Chief Executive, 1993-95). Recreations: golf; horse-racing; gardening. Address: (b.) 10 Lochside Place, Edinburgh EH12 9DF; T.-0131-527 2000.

Robb, Kenneth Richard, LLB (Hons), NP. Solicitor; Partner, Marshall, Wilson, Falkirk; b. 3.9.54, Larbert; m., Susan Margaret Ringrose; 1 d. Educ. Falkirk High School; Edinburgh University. Private legal practice, since 1976; Member, Council, Law Society of Scotland, 1987-97; Member, Board, Scottish Child Law Centre; part-time Chairman, Child Support Appeal Tribunals. Recreations: history; hill-walking; gardening. Address: (h.) 9 Bryanston Drive, Dollar, Clackmannanshire; T.-01259 743430.

Robbins, Oliver Charles Gordon, BA (Hons), MIMgt. Principal, Cambuslang College of Further Education, since 1992; b. 28.4.36, Edinburgh; m., Andrewena Henderson Briggs; 4 s.; 1 d. Educ. Bellevue Secondary School; Open University; Napier College. Apprentice engineer, 1952-57; draughtsman, 1957-60; design draughtsman, Rolls Royce/Ferranti Ltd., 1960-69; Lecturer, Senior Lecturer, Head of Department, Moray College of FE. Recreations: caravanning; martial arts. Address: (h.) 11 Strathaven Road, Lesmahagow, Lanarkshire; T.-Lesmahagow 894617.

Roberton, Esther A., BA. Director, Scotland Forward; Coordinator, Scottish Constitutional Covention, 1995-97; Member, Executive, Scottish Council Development and Industry, since 1991; Member, Tayside and Fife Committee, SCDI, since 1994; b. 24.6.56, Kirkcaldy; m., William J. Roberton; 1 s. Educ. Buckhaven High School; Edinburgh University. Education and Training Executive, Scottish Development Agency, 1985-88; Project Manager, Scottish Council Development and Industry, 1988-90; Executive Director, Scottish Community Education

Council, 1990-93. Member, Executive, Campaign for a Scottish Parliament. Recreations: juggling; piano-playing; singing; yoga; walking; travel. Address: (h.) 23 High Street, Aberdour KY3 0SH; T.-01383 860909.

Roberts, Professor Bernard, BSc, PhD, FRAS, FRSE. Professor of Solar Magnetohydrodynamics, since 1994; Chairman, UK Solar Physics Community, since 1992; b. 19.2.46, Cork; m., Margaret Patricia Cartlidge; 4 s. Educ. Bletchley Secondary Modern and Bletchley Grammar Schools; Hull University; Sheffield University. Lecturer in Applied Mathematics, St. Andrews University, 1971-87, Reader, 1987-94. Recreations: hill walking; squash. Address: (b.) Mathematical Sciences, St. Andrews University, St. Andrews KY16 9SS; T.-01334 463722.

Roberts, James Graeme, MA, PhD, FRSA. Vice Principal and Dean, Faculty of Arts and Divinity, Aberdeen University, since 1996; b. 7.11.42, Glasgow; m., Elizabeth Watson Milo Tucker; 2 s.; 2 d. Educ. Hutchesons' Boys' Grammar School, Glasgow; St. Andrews University; Aberdeen University. Aberdeen University: Assistant Lecturer in English, 1964, Lecturer in English, 1968, Senior Lecturer, 1985, Head, Department of English, 1993; elected Member, University Court, 1981-89, since 1995. Trustee, Aberdeen International Football Festival; Elder, Ferryhill Parish Church, Aberdeen. Recreations: walking; swimming; music. Address: (b.) Aberdeen University, Regent Walk, Aberdeen AB24 3FDX; T.-01224 272640.

Roberts, Professor Peter Ward, BA, MA, CertEd, MRTPI, FRSA. Professor of European Strategic Planning, Dundee University, since 1995; Member, Scientific Committee on the Regions of Europe, since 1992; Chairman, British Urban Regeneration Association – Best Practice Committee, since 1994; b. 17.7.47, Birkenhead; m., Josephine Blythe; 1 s. Educ. Rock Ferry High School, Birkenhead; Leicester University; Manchester University; Newcastle upon Tyne University. Lecturer, Flintshire College of Technology, 1970-71; Senior Lecturer, Department of Town and Country Planning, Liverpool John Moores University, 1971-77; Principal Lecturer/Deputy Head of Department, Department of Urban and Regional Planning, Coventry University, 1978-86; Senior Research Manager, ECOTEC Research and Consulting, Birmingham, 1987; Professor of Urban Planning, Leeds Metropolitan University, and Joint Director, Regional Research Observatory, 1988-94. Trustee and Council Member, Town and Country Planning Association; Board Member, The Planning Exchange; Director, Urban Mines Ltd. Publications include: Environmentally Sustainable Business (Co-author); Europe: A Handbook for Local Authorities (Co-author); Energy Efficiency in Housing (Co-author); Mineral Resources in Regional and Strategic Planning (Co-author). Recreations: hill-walking; collecting and reading books; restoring classic cars; listening to opera and classical music; watching cricket. Address: (b.) Centre for Planning Research, School of Town and Regional Planning, 13 Perth Road, Dundee DD1 4HT; T.-01382 345236.

Roberts, Professor Ronald John, BVMS, FRCVS, PhD, FRCPath, FIBiol, FRSE. Professor of Aquatic Pathobiology and Director, Institute of Aquaculture, Stirling University, 1971-96, Emeritus Professor since 1996; Scientific Adviser, Lithgow Group; Non-Executive Director, Landcatch Ltd., since 1996; b. 28.3.41; m., Helen Macgregor; 2 s. Educ. Campbeltown Grammar School; Glasgow University. Lecturer, Glasgow University, 1964-71; Consultant: Department of Agriculture and Fisheries for Scotland, 1967-70, Overseas Development Administration, since 1974, United Nations, since 1976; World Bank, since 1989; Council Member, Royal Society of Edinburgh, 1980-83; Member, Cabinet Office, Scientific Advisory Panel, 1994; Buckland Professor of Fisheries, Buckland Foundation, 1985; BVA Dalrymple-Champneys Medallist, 1990; Scientific Director, Machrihanish Marine Environmental

Research Laboratory, 1991-96; Chairman, Kintyre Enterprise Trust; Chairman, Argyll and Bute Countryside Trust; Editor, Journal of Fish Diseases, Aquaculture Research. Commander of Most Noble Order of the Crown (Thailand). Publications: Fish Pathology; Handbook of Salmon and Trout Diseases; Bacterial Diseases of Fishes; Recent Advances in Aquaculture; Diseases of Asian Catfishes (Co-author). Recreations: golf at Machrihanish Golf Club; squash; forestry; rhododendron culture. Address: (h.) Carrick Point Farm, Ardnacross, Peninver, by Campbeltown, Argyll; T.-01586 554417.

Robertson, Alistair John, BMedBiol (Hons), MB, ChB, FRCPath, MIAC. Clinical Director in Pathology, Dundee Teaching Hospitals NHS Trust, since 1993; Consultant Histopathologist, Tayside Health Board, since 1982; Honorary Senior Lecturer in Pathology, Dundee University, since 1982; b. 29.6.50, Aberdeen; m., Frances Elizabeth Smith. Educ. Aberdeen Grammar School; Aberdeen University. House Physician, Ninewells Hospital, Dundee, 1975; House Surgeon, Aberdeen Royal Infirmary, 1976; Senior House Officer in Pathology, Ninewells Hospital, 1976; Lecturer in Pathology, Ninewells Hospital, 1977; Consultant in Administrative Charge, Perth and Kinross Unit Laboratories, 1982. Recreations: golf; curling; caravanning; philately; photography; theatre. Address: (b.) Pathology Department, Ninewells Hospital and Medical School, Dundee; T.-Dundee 660111.

Robertson, Andrew Ogilvie, OBE, LLB. Partner, T.C. Young & Son, Solicitors and Notaries, since 1968; Secretary, Erskine Hospital, since 1976; Chairman, Post Office Users Council for Scotland, since 1988; Secretary, Princess Royal Trust for Carers, since 1990; Chairman, Greater Glasgow Community and Mental Health Services NHS Trust, since 1993; Chairman, Scottish Housing Association Charitable Trust, since 1991; Director, Scottish Building Society, since 1994; b. 30.6.43, Glasgow; m., Sheila Sturton; 2 s. Educ Glasgow Academy; Sedbergh School; Edinburgh University. Director, Merchants House of Glasgow, since 1978; Secretary, Clydeside Federation of Community Based Housing Associations, 1978-93; Secretary, The Briggait Company Ltd., 1982-88; Director, Glasgow Chamber of Commerce, 1982-93. Recreations: climbing; swimming; sailing; running; fishing. Address: (b.) 30 George Square, Glasgow, G2 1LH; T.-0141-221 5562.

Robertson, Brenda Margaret, JP. Member, Orkney Islands Council, 1974-94; b. 8.9.24, Scarborough; m., John MacDonald Robertson, BL, NP; 1 s.; 1 d. Educ. Scarborough Girls' High School; University College, St. Andrews. Wartime service, WRNS; decoding, at Bletchley Park; formerly: District Commissioner for Guides, Stromness and West Mainland; Member, Stromness Town Council, 1961-74; Orkney County Councillor; Member, Executive Council, NHS; Governor, Aberdeen College of Education. Recreations: reading; arts generally. Address: (h.) Berridale, Stromness, Orkney.

Robertson, Rev. Charles, JP, MA. Minister, Canongate Kirk, since 1978; Chaplain to The Queen, since 1991; b. 22.10.40, Glasgow; m., Alison Margaret Malloch; 1 s.; 2 d. Educ. Camphill School, Paisley; Edinburgh University. Assistant Minister, North Morningside Church, Edinburgh, 1964-65; Minister, Kiltearn, Ross and Cromarty, 1965-78. Secretary, Panel on Worship, General Assembly, 1982-95, Convener, since 1995; Church of Scotland Representative on Joint Liturgical Group, since 1984, and Chairman, since 1994; Chaplain to Lord High Commissioner, 1990, 1991 and to Her Grace The Princess Royal, 1996; Chaplain to: High Constables and Guard of Honour, since 1993, Elsie Inglis Memorial Maternity Hospital, 1982-89, New Club, since 1986, Moray House, since 1986, No. 2 (City of Edinburgh) Maritime HQ Unit RAAF, since 1987; President, Church Service Society, 1988-91 (Hon. President, since 1991); Chairman, Board, Queensberry

House Hospital, 1989-96; Chairman, Queensberry House Trust, since 1996; Governor, St. Columba's Hospice, Edinburgh, since 1986; Member, Executive Committee, Scottish Veteran's Residences, since 1978; Lecturer in Church Praise, St. Colm's College, 1980-93; Member, Broadcasting Standards Council, 1988-91 and 1992-93; Member, Historic Buildings Council for Scotland, since 1990; Trustee, Church Hymnary Trust, since 1987; Trustee, Edinburgh Old Town Trust, 1987-91; Trustee, Edinburgh Old Town Charitable Trust, since 1991; edited Singing the Faith, 1990, Common Order, 1994; St. Margaret Queen of Scotland and Her Chapel, 1994. Recreations: Recreations: books; music; history; Canongate. Address: Manse of Canongate, Edinburgh EH8 8BR; T.-0131-556 3515.

Robertson, Sheriff Daphne Jean Black, MA, LLB, WS. Sheriff of Lothian and Borders at Edinburgh (formerly Sheriff of Glasgow and Strathkelvin); b. 31.3.37. Address: Sheriff Court House, 27 Chambers Street, Edinburgh, EH1 1LB.

Robertson, David Alexander, CA, IRRV. Director of Finance, Orkney Islands Council, since 1994; Finance Director, Orkney Ferries Ltd., since 1992; b. 31.12.59, Glasgow; m., Ruth Elizabeth; 1 s.; 1 d. Educ. Inverness Royal Academy; Dundee College of Technology. Address: (b.) Council Offices, Kirkwall, Orkney; T.-01856 873535.

Robertson, David Greig, CBE, MA, MEd, HonLLD (Dundee). Chairman of Court, Dundee University, since 1993; Chairman, LEAD — Scotland, 1991-95; b. 29.12.24, Dundee; m., Margaret J.D. Keay; 3 s. Educ. Morgan Academy, Dundee; St. Andrews University. Education Officer, Royal Navy, 1945-47; Teacher, Dundee High School, 1952-54, Dollar Academy, 1954-58; Assistant Director of Education, Berwickshire, 1958-61, Dundee, 1961-64; Director of Education, Selkirkshire, 1964-72, Dundee, 1972-75, Tayside, 1975-89. President, Association of Directors of Education in Scotland, 1977-78; Trustee, Central Bureau for Educational Visits and Exchanges, 1975-84; Member, Scottish Consultative Council on the Curriculum, 1980-90; President, Scottish Amateur Music Association, since 1984; Vice-President, British Association for Early Childhood Education, since 1988; President, Scottish Institute of Adult Education, 1987-90; Vice Chairman, National Youth Orchestra of Scotland, 1988-94; Member, Scottish Commission on Education, since 1994. Recreations: reading; music. Address: (h.) 4 Glamis Terrace, Dundee DD2 1NA; T.-01382 665586.

Robertson, Professor Edmund Frederick, BSc, MSc, PhD, FRSE. Professor of Mathematics, St. Andrews University, since 1995; b. 1.6.43, St. Andrews; m., Helena Francesca; 2 s. Educ. Madras College, St. Andrews; St. Andrews University; Warwick University. Lecturer in Pure Mathematics, then Senior Lecturer, St. Andrews University, 1968-95. Partnership Award, 1992; European Academic Software Award, 1994; American Computational Engineering and Science Award, 1995. Publications: 26 books; 100 papers. Recreations: history of mathematics; computers. Address: (b.) Mathematical Institute, North Haugh, St. Andrews KY16 9SS; T.-01334 463738.

Robertson, George F., CBE, FRICS. Chartered Surveyor, Arbiter; Sole Principal, G.F. Robertson, Chartered Surveyors, Edinburgh; President, Rent Assessment Panel for Scotland, since 1987; b. 14.7.32, Edinburgh; m., Anne McGonigle; 3 d. Educ. George Heriot's School, Edinburgh; Heriot-Watt College, Edinburgh. Partner, Robertson and Dawson, Chartered Surveyors, Edinburgh, 1970-93; Lecturer (part-time), School of Architecture, Edinburgh College of Art/Heriot-Watt University, 1964-84; Chairman, Joint Standing Committee of Architects, Surveyors and Building Contractors in Scotland, 1976-78; Chairman, Board of Governors, Leith Nautical College, 1976-78; Chairman, Scottish Branch, Royal Institution of Chartered

Surveyors, 1984-85; Director, Queensberry House Hospital, Edinburgh, 1983-86; Chairman, Scottish Building Contract Committee, 1983-88; Board Member, Scottish Development Agency, 1987-91; Hon. Secretary, Royal Institution of Chartered Surveyors in Scotland, 1988-90; Lay Member, Scottish Solicitors Discipline Tribunal, 1976-94. Recreations: working; gardening; travel; researching Scottish market crosses. Address: (h.) Gladsheil, Campbell Court, Longniddry, East Lothian EH32 0NR.

Robertson, Rt. Hon. George Islay MacNeill, MA. MP (Labour), Hamilton South; Secretary of State for Defence, since 1997; Member, Shadow Cabinet, 1993-97; Shadow Scottish Secretary, 1993-97; b. 12.4.46, Port Ellen, Islay; m., Sandra Wallace; 2 s.; 1 d. Educ. Dunoon Grammar School; Dundee University; St. Andrews University. Tayside Study Economics Group, 1968-69; Scottish Organiser, General, Municipal, Boilermakers Union, 1969-78; Chairman, Scottish Labour Party, 1977-78; Member, Scottish Executive, Labour Party, 1973-79; MP, Hamilton, since 1978; PPS to Secretary of State for Social Services, 1979; Opposition Spokesman on Scottish Affairs, 1979-80, on Defence, 1980-81, on Foreign and Commonwealth Affairs, 1981-93, on Scottish Affairs, 1993-97; Principal Spokesman on Europe, 1984-93; Member of Board, Scottish Development Agency, 1976-78, Scottish Tourist Board, 1974-76; Board of Governors, Scottish Police College, 1975-78; Vice Chairman, British Council, 1985-93; Vice-Chairman, Westminster Foundation for Democracy, 1992-93. Recreations: family; photography. Address: (b.) House of Commons, London SW1A 0AA.

Robertson, George Slessor, MD, FFARCS, SBStJ. Consultant Anaesthetist, since 1969; Honorary Senior Lecturer in Anaesthesia, Aberdeen University; b. 30.12.33, Peterhead; m., Audrey E. McDonald; 1 s.; 2 d. Educ. Peterhead Academy; Aberdeen University. Early medical training, Aberdeen, London and Winnipeg. Publications: papers on the ethical dilemmas of non-treatment decisions in the demented elderly and advance directives. Recreations: golf; hill-walking; picture-framing. Address: (h.) 12 Queen's Den, Woodend, Aberdeen AB15 8BW; T.-01224 311903.

Robertson, Harry, CPFA. Chief Executive, Perth and Kinross Council, since 1995; b. 7.9.49, Dunfermline; m., Rosemary Elizabeth; 2 s. Educ. Dunfermline High School; Glasgow College of Commerce. Trainee Accountant, Burgh of Burntisland; Accountancy Assistant, Assistant Town Chamberlain, Depute Town Chamberlain, Burgh of Barrhead; Depute Director of Finance, Director of Finance, Depute Chief Executive, Chief Executive, Perth and Kinross District Council. Secretary/Treasurer, Perth Repertory Theatre Ltd.; Chairman, Scottish Branch, CIPFA, 1987-88; Council Member, CIPFA; Clerk to Lord Lieutenancy, Perth and Kinross; Chief Executive and Secretary, Perth and Kinross Recreational Facilities Ltd.; Hon. Secretary, Bowerswell Memorial Homes (Perth) Ltd.; Member, Society of High Constables of the City of Perth. Recreations: golf; theatre; badminton; tropical fish. Address: (b.) 2 High Street, Perth PH1 5PH; T.-01738 475001.

Robertson, Iain Alasdair, CBE, LLB. Chief Executive, Highlands and Islands Enterprise, since 1990; Board Member, Scottish Tourist Board, 1993-95; b. 30.10.49, Perth; m., Judith Helen Stevenson; 2 s.; 1 d. Educ. Perth Academy; Aberdeen University. Qualified as a Solicitor, 1973; service at home and abroad with British Petroleum, 1975-90, latterly as BP America's Director of Acquisitions. Recreations: skiing; sailing; music. Address: (b.) Bridge House, Bridge Street, Inverness; T.-01463 244204.

Robertson, Iain Samuel, LLB, CA. Managing Director, Corporate and Institutional Banking Division, Royal Bank of Scotland plc, since 1992; b. 27.12.45, Glasgow; m.,

Morag; 2 s.; 2 d. Educ. Jordanhill College School; Glasgow University. Civil Servant, Department of Trade and Industry and Department of Energy, 1973-78; Assistant Secretary, Scottish Office, 1978-83; Director, Locate in Scotland, Scottish Office, 1984-87; Chief Executive, Scottish Development Agency, 1987-90; Group Finance Director, County Natwest Ltd., 1990-92. Recreations: golf; football; music and arts.

Robertson, Maj.-Gen. Ian Argyll, CB (1968), MBE (1947), MA. Deputy Lieutenant, Highland Region (Nairn), 1973-88; b. 17.7.13, Richmond, Surrey; m., Marjorie Violet Isobel Duncan; 2 d. Educ. Winchester College; Trinity College, Oxford. Commissioned Seaforth Highlanders, 1934; commanded 1st Bn., 1954-57; commanded School of Infantry, 1963-64; commanded 51 Highland Division, 1964-66; retired, 1968. Vice-Chairman and Chairman, Royal British Legion Scotland, 1971-74. Recreations: golf; gardening. Address: (h.) Gardeners Cottage, Brackla, Cawdor, Nairn.

Robertson, Ian Barr, MA, LLB. Solicitor (retired); Advocate in Aberdeen; Honorary Sheriff, Grampian, Highland and Islands, at Stonehaven; b. Aberdeen; m., Vi L. Johnston; 2 s.; 1 d. Educ. Mackie Academy; Fettes College; Aberdeen University. King's Regiment and KAR, 1939-46 (Captain); Partner, Cunningham & Robertson, Solicitors, Stonehaven, 1951-89; Joint Town Clerk, then Town Clerk, Stonehaven, 1957-75; President, Society of Town Clerks in Scotland, 1973-75; Member, Grampian Regional Council, 1974-86 (Chairman, Transportation and Roads, 1978-86); Member, Aberdeen Harbour Board, 1975-86; Member, Peterhead Bay Authority, 1978-88; Elder, Stonehaven South. Address: (h.) 15 Bath Street, Stonehaven; T.-Stonehaven 762879.

Robertson, Hon. Lord (Ian Macdonald Robertson), TD (1946), BA, LLB, QC. Senator of the College of Justice in Scotland, 1966-87; Chairman of Governors, Merchiston Castle School, 1971-96; b. 30.10.12, Edinburgh; m., Anna Love Glen; 1 s.; 2 d. Educ. Merchiston Castle School, Edinburgh; Balliol College, Oxford; Edinburgh University. Admitted Faculty of Advocates, 1939; served War of 1939-45, 8th Bn., The Royal Scots (The Royal Regiment) - commissioned 1939; Captain/Staff Officer, 44th Lowland Infantry Brigade (15th Scottish Division); Normandy and North West Europe, 1944-45; mentioned in Despatches; Advocate Depute, 1949-51; QC, 1954; Sheriff Principal of Ayr and Bute, 1961-66; Sheriff Principal of Perth and Angus, 1966; Chairman, Medical Appeals Tribunal, 1957-63; Chairman, Scottish Joint Council for Teachers Salaries, 1965-81; Chairman, Scottish Valuation Advisory Council, 1977-86; UK Representative on Central Council, International Association of Judges, 1974-87; General Council Assessor, Edinburgh University Court, 1967-81; Chairman, Edinburgh Centre of Rural Economy and Edinburgh Centre for Tropical Veterinary Medicine, 1967-86; Governor, Merchiston Castle School, 1954-96; Captain, Honourable Company of Edinburgh Golfers at Muirfield, 1970-72. Recreation: golf. Address: (h.) 13 Moray Place, Edinburgh EH3 6DT; T.-0131-225 6637.

Robertson, John Davie Manson, CBE, BL, FRSA. Chairman, Robertson Group of Companies, since 1980; Director, Stanley Services Ltd., Falkland Islands, since 1987; Chairman, North of Scotland Water Authority, since 1995; Chairman, Lloyds TSB Foundation for Scotland, since 1997; b. 6.11.29, Golspie; m., Elizabeth Amelia Macpherson; 2 s.; 2 d. Educ. Kirkwall Grammar School; Edinburgh University. Honorary Sheriff, Grampian, Highland and Islands, since 1977; Honorary Vice Consul for Denmark, since 1972; Honorary Consul, Federal Republic of Germany, since 1976; Trustee, Lloyds TSB Foundation for Scotland, 1989-97; Member, National Health Service Tribunal, 1990-97; Chairman, Highland Health Board, 1991-97; Chairman, Scottish Health

Management Efficiency Group (SCOTMEG), 1985-95; Chairman, Orkney Health Board, 1983-91 (Vice Chairman, 1979-83, Member, 1974-79); Member, Board of Management, Orkney Hospitals, 1970-74; Board Member, Highlands and Islands Enterprise, 1990-95; Member, Highlands and Islands Development Consultative Council, 1989-91; Chairman, Highlands and Islands Savings Committee, 1975-78; Chairman, Children's Panel for Orkney, 1971-76; Chairman, Children's Panel, Orkney Advisory Committee, 1977-82. OBE, 1978; Royal Order of Knight of Dannebrog, 1982; Cavalier's Cross of the Order of Merit, 1986. Publications: Uppies and Doonies, 1967; An Orkney Anthology, 1991. Recreations: fly fishing; shooting. Address: (h.) Spinningdale House, Spinningdale, Sutherland IV24 3AD.

Robertson, John Shaw, MA. Rector, Dollar Academy, since 1994; b. 7.4.50, Glasgow; m., Mary; 1 s.; 1 d. Educ. Jordanhill College School; Glasgow University. English Master, Housemaster, Assistant Headmaster, Stewart's Melville, Edinburgh, 1973-87; Deputy Rector, Dollar Academy, 1987-94. Publication: Stewart's Melville: the first Ten Years (Co-author). Recreations: cricket (Scottish); music (English); literature (international). Address: 2 Academy Place, Dollar FK14 7DZ; T.-01259 742511.

Robertson, John William, WS, MA. Secretary, British Linen Bank Ltd., since 1986; Solicitor, since 1971; b. 12.11.43, Dunfermline; m., Alice Rudland; 1 s.; 3 d. Educ. Dunfermline High School; Edinburgh University. Assistant Law Secretary, Bank of Scotland, 1975; Manager, Law Department, Bank of Scotland, London, 1978; Assistant Secretary, British Linen Bank Ltd., 1983. Address: (b.) 4 Melville Street, Edinburgh EH3 7NZ.

Robertson, Sir Lewis, CBE, FRSE, FRSA. Chairman, Carnegie Trust for the Universities of Scotland, since 1990; b. 28.11.22, Dundee; m., Elspeth Badenoch; 2 s.; 1 s. (dec.); 1 d. Educ. Trinity College, Glenalmond. Apprentice Chartered Accountant, 1939-42; RAF Intelligence, 1942-46; entered family textile business, 1946; appointed Managing Director, Robertson Industrial Textiles, 1954; first Managing Director, Scott & Robertson, 1965 (Chairman, 1968); resigned, 1970; Chief Executive, Grampian Holdings, Glasgow, 1971-76 (also Deputy Chairman, 1972-76); Non-Executive Director, Scottish & Newcastle Breweries, 1975-87; Chairman: Triplex Lloyd plc, 1982-90, Girobank Scotland, 1984-90, Borthwicks plc, 1985-89, Lilley plc, 1986-93, Havelock Europe plc, 1989-92, Stakis plc, 1991-95, Postern Executive Group, 1991-96; Director, Whitman International, Geneva, 1987-90; Chairman, Scottish Board (and UK Council Member), British Institute of Management, 1981-83; Chairman, Eastern Regional Hospitals Board, 1960-70; Member, Committee of Enquiry into the Relationship of the Pharmaceutical Industry with the NHS, 1965-67; Member, Monopolies (later Monopolies and Mergers) Commission, 1969-76; Deputy Chairman and first Chief Executive, Scottish Development Agency, 1976-81; Member, Scottish Economic Council, 1977-83; Member, Restrictive Practices Court, 1983-97; Member, Scottish Post Office Board, 1984-90; Member, Court, Dundee University, 1967-70 (first Finance Chairman); Council Member, Scottish Business School, 1978-83; Chairman, Scottish Arts Council, and Member, Arts Council of GB, 1970-71; Chairman, Scottish Advisory Committee, British Council, 1978-87; Council Member, Scottish History Society, 1984-89; first Chairman, Policy Committee, Scottish Episcopal Church, 1974-76; Trustee, Foundation for the Study of Christianity and Society, 1983-89; Member, Advisory Board, Edinburgh Edition of the Waverley Novels, since 1986; Director, Friends of Royal Scottish Academy, 1986-95; Royal Society of Edinburgh: Fellow, since 1978, Member, Council, since 1992, Treasurer, since 1994; Chairman, Scottish Division, Imperial Society of Knights Bachelor, since 1995; Director and Trustee, Advanced Management

Programme Scotland, since 1996; Trustee and Vice-Patron, Scottish Council for Research in Education, since 1997; Hon. Doctorate of Laws, Dundee University, 1971; Hon. Doctorate of Business Administration, Napier University, 1992; Hon. DUniv, Stirling, 1993. Recreations: work; foreign travel; computer use; music; list-making. Address: 32 Saxe Coburg Place, Edinburgh EH3 5BP; T.-0131-332 5221.

Robertson, Professor Noel Farnie, CBE, MA, BSc, PhD, FRSE, FIBiol; b. 24.12.23, Dundalk; m., Doreen Colina Gardner; 2 s.; 2 d. Educ. Trinity Academy; Edinburgh University; Trinity College, Cambridge. Plant Pathologist, West African Cacao Research Institute, Ghana, 1946-48; Lecturer, Plant Pathology, Cambridge University, 1948-59; Professor of Botany, Hull University, 1959-69; Professor of Agriculture, Edinburgh University, and Principal, East of Scotland College of Agriculture, 1969-83. Publications: Britain's First Chair in Agriculture (Co-author), 1990; From Dearth to Plenty (Co-author), 1995. Recreations: gardening; natural history. Address: (h.) Woodend, Juniper Bank, Walkerburn, Peebles-shire EH43 6DE; T.-01896 810523.

Robertson, Raymond. Chairman, Scottish Conservative Party; former MP (Conservative), Aberdeen South; former Minister for Education, Housing and Fisheries, Scottish Office. Address: (b.) Suite 1/1, 14 Links Place, Leith, Edinburgh EH6 7EZ.

Robertson, Richard Ross, RSA, FRBS, DA. Sculptor; b. 10.9.14, Aberdeen; m., Kathleen May Matts; 2 d. Educ. Paisley Grammar School; Glasgow School of Art; Aberdeen Art School. Work exhibited in Aberdeen public parks and several public buildings in city and county of Aberdeen; also exhibited in several private collections in Britain, America and Holland; retired Lecturer in Sculpture, Gray's School of Art, Aberdeen. Recreations: carving; gardening; walking. Address: (h.) Creaguir, Woodlands Road, Rosemount, Blairgowrie, Perthshire; T.-01250 4970.

Robertson, Roderick. Managing Director, Robertsons of Tain Ltd.; Honorary Sheriff, Tain and Dingwall, 1976; b. 24.8.35, Tain; m., Elizabeth Martin Steele; 1 s. Educ. Tain Royal Academy. Agricultural engineering, 1951-56; Army, 1956-59; commenced business (agricultural engineering), 1959; elected, Tain Town Council, 1965 (Chairman of Development, Dean of Guild and Senior Bailie); JP, 1975; appointed Member, Valuation Appeal Committee, Ross and Cromarty, Skye and Lochalsh, 1980; Director, Royal Highland and Agricultural Society of Scotland; Director, Ross and Cromarty Enterprise, 1991; Chairman, Justice of the Peace Committee, Ross and Cromarty, 1980; Chairman, Local Royal British Legion Housing Association, 1984; Chairman, Tain Community Council. Recreations: flying; shooting; fishing; judo. Address: (h.) Viewfield Farm, Tain, Ross-shire IV19 1PX; T.-01862 892151.

Robertson, Brigadier Sidney Park, MBE, TD, JP, DL, BCom. Director, S. & J.D. Robertson Group Ltd. (Chairman, 1965-79); Honorary Sheriff, Grampian, Highlands and Islands, since 1969; Vice Lord Lieutenant of Orkney, 1987-90; b. 12.3.14, Kirkwall; m., Elsa Miller Croy; 1 s.; 1 d. Educ. Kirkwall Grammar School; MIBS; Edinburgh University. Commissioned, Royal Artillery, 1940 (Despatches, NW Europe, 1945); managerial posts, Anglo-Iranian Oil Co., Middle East, 1946-51; Manager Operations/Sales, Southern Division, Shell-Mex and BP, 1951-54; founder, Robertson firm, 1954; Major Commanding 861 (Independent) Light Anti-Aircraft Battery RA (Orkney and Zetland), TA, 1956-61; Lt. Col. Commanding Lovat Scouts, 1962-65; Brigadier, CRA 51st Highland Division, 1966-67; Chairman, Orkney Hospitals Board of Management/Orkney Health Board, 1965-79; DL, 1968; Honorary Vice-President, Royal British Legion Scotland, Highlands and Islands Area, since 1975; President, Royal British Legion Scotland, Kirkwall Branch,

1957-97; Chairman, RNLI, Kirkwall Station Committee, 1972-97 (President, since 1997); Honorary Colonel, 102 (Ulster and Scottish) Light Air Defence Regiment, Royal Artillery, 1975-80; Hon. Colonel Commandant, Royal Regiment of Artillery, 1977-80; Vice President, National Artillery Association, since 1977; Chairman, Royal Artillery Council of Scotland, 1980-84; Honorary President, Orkney Bn., Boys' Brigade; Vice-President, RNLI, since 1985; President, Villars Curling Club, 1978-80, 1986-88; Honorary President: Friends of St. Magnus Cathedral, since 1994, Orkney Family History Society, since 1996; Freedom of Orkney, 1990; Honorary Fellowship, Edinburgh University, since 1996. Recreations: travel, hill-walking; angling. Address: (h.) Daisybank, Kirkwall, Orkney; T.-01856 87 2085.

Robertson, Stephen Andrew Cormack, MBE, MUniv, MA, LLB, NP. Humorist and Actor; founder Member and co-author, Scotland The What?; b. 21.4.33, Aberdeen; m., Eva Mary Stephen; 1 s.; 1 d. Educ. Aberdeen Grammar School; Aberdeen University. National service (2nd Lt. in Royal Signals), 1957-59; supply teaching and legal and administrative assistant in various offices, 1960-63; Solicitor in Aberdeen, 1963-83, mostly as Partner, latterly Consultant, Wilsone & Duffus, Advocates; full-time participation in Scotland The What?, 1983-95; semi-retired, 1996. Recreations: watching sport; country pottering and hill-walking; golf; theatre; reading; drystane dyking. Address: (h.) Flat 1, Sillerton House, 15 Albyn Terrace, Aberdeen AB10 1YP; T.-01224 626728.

Robertson, Sue, BA, MSocSci. Director, One Parent Families Scotland, since 1988; b. 12.7.50, Carlisle; m., Paul Hare; 1 s.; 2 d. Educ. Penrith Queen Elizabeth Grammar School; Oxford University; Birmingham University. Senior Economic Assistant, Scottish Economic Planning Department, 1973-78; Co-ordinator, Scottish Women's Aid, 1978-83; Training Officer, Scottish Council for Single Parents, 1983-88. Committee Member, Cairn Housing Association. Recreations: hill-walking; cycling; reading. Address: (b.) 13 Gayfield Square, Edinburgh EH1 3NX; T.-0131-556 3899.

Robertson, William Archibald, QPM, LLB, MPhil, FIMgt. Chief Constable, Northern Constabulary, since 1996; b. 16.10.43, Motherwell; m., Isabel Cook; 3 s. Educ. Hamilton Academy; Glasgow University; University of Strathclyde. Joined Lanarkshire Constabulary, 1962; Head, Fraud Squad, Strathclyde Police, 1980-81; Head of Personnel, 1981-82; appointed Assistant Chief Constable, Strathclyde Police, 1982; Director of Training, Scottish Police College, 1986-88; Deputy Chief Constable, Cleveland Constabulary, 1992. Publication: Scottish Crime Prevention "Strategy for the 90s" (Co-author). Recreations: golf; Rotary. Address: (b.) Police Headquarters, Inverness, IV2 3SY; T.-01463 715555.

Robertson, William Nelson, CBE, MA, FCII. Director: Morrison Construction, since 1995; Director, since 1996: Alliance Investment Trust, Second Alliance Investment Trust, Edinburgh New Tiger Investment Trust, Caledonian Foundation; Member, Court, University of Abertay, Dundee, since 1996; Group Chief Executive, General Accident, 1990-95, Director, 1984-95; Board Member, Association of British Insurers, 1991-95; b. 14.12.33, Berwick upon Tweed; m., Sheila Catherine; 2 d. Educ. Berwick Grammar School; Edinburgh University. Joined General Accident, 1958; Deputy Chief General Manager, 1989-90. Recreations: hill-walking; gardening.

Robertson-Rae, Avril Margaret, FHCIMA. Director, Strathclyde Region Catering Services, 1988-96; b. 17.7.35, Edinburgh; 2 s. Educ. Eastwood Secondary School; Queen's College, Glasgow. Began career as assistant housekeeper, 1956; former domestic science teacher and catering manager; Principal Officer (Catering), Strathclyde

Regional Council, 1982-88. Vice-Chairman, Board of Management, Glasgow College of Food Technology; Member, Court, Glasgow Caledonian University; Director, Glasgow Chamber of Commerce, 1994-96. Industrial Caterer of the Year, 1992. Recreations: walking; reading; studying Portuguese; gardening; travel. Address: (h.) 4 Trigoni Court, Largs, Ayrshire; T.-01475 675360.

Robins, Professor David John, BSc, PhD, DSc, CChem, FRSC, FRSE. Professor of Bio-organic Chemistry, Glasgow University, since 1990; b. 12.8.45, Purley; m., Helen Dorothy Skinner; 1 s.; 1 d. Educ. Purley Grammar School; Exeter University. NIH Postdoctoral Fellowship, University of Pittsburgh, 1969-71; SRC Fellowship, Surrey University, 1971-72; Tutorial Fellow in Organic Chemistry, Reading University, 1973-74; Lecturer in Organic Chemistry, Glasgow University, 1974-87, Senior Lecturer, 1987-88, Reader, 1988-90. Recreations: badminton; gardening; music; hill-walking; cycling. Address: (b.) Department of Chemistry, Glasgow University, Glasgow, G12 8QQ; T.-0141-330 4378.

Robins, John F. Company Secretary, Animal Concern, since 1988 (Company Secretary, Scottish Anti-Vivisection Society, 1981-88); Co-ordinator, Scottish Animal Rights Network, since 1983; Managing Director, Ethical Promotions Ltd., since 1988; Co-ordinator, Save Scotland's Seals Funds, 1988-96; Secretary, Save Our Seals Fund, since 1996; b. 2.1.57, Glasgow; m., Mary E.; 1 s.; 1 d. Educ. St. Ninian's High School. Co-ordinator, Glasgow Energy Group, 1978-80; Green Party activist and candidate, 1978-81; Delegate, Anti-Nuclear Campaign, 1978-81; Vice-Chair, Friends of the Earth (Scotland) Ltd., 1981-82. Recreations: campaigning against hunting, shooting and fishing; catching up on lost sleep. Address: (b.) 62 Old Dumbarton Road, Glasgow G3 8RE; T.-0141-334 6014.

Robinson, Christopher Peter, FHCIMA. Chief Executive, Heart of Midlothian Football Club, since 1994; Chairman, Wheatsheaf Catering Ltd., since 1978; b. 23.3.51, Edinburgh; m., Elizabeth; 3 d. Educ. Bo'ness Academy; Napier University. Trainee Manager, Open Arms Hotel Group, 1972-78. Guest Lecturer, International Hotel Schools, Paris and Cornell; President, Hotel and Catering Institutional Management Association, 1992-93. Recreations: football; golf. Address: (b.) Tynecastle Park, Gorgie Road, Edinburgh EH11 2NL; T.-0131-200 7200.

Robinson, Ernest Thomson, OBE, TD, KLJ, MB, ChB, FRCGP, DRCOG. Chairman, Council, St. Andrew's Ambulance Association, since 1994; retired General Medical Practitioner; b. 18.3.34, Gartcosh; m., Margaret; 4 s.; 3 d. Educ. Coatbridge Secondary School; Glasgow University. Principal General Medical Practitioner, Woodside Health Centre, Glasgow (retired); former Regimental Medical Officer (rank Major), 154 Lowland Regiment RCT (TA). Publication: First Aid Book for Young People. Recreations: salmon and trout fishing. Address: (h.) 132 Prestonfield, Milngavie, Glasgow G62 7QA; T.-0141-563 7409.

Robinson, Helen Mairi Johnstone, MA. Freelance Book Editor, Researcher and Lecturer; Managing Editor, Larousse plc, formerly W. & R. Chambers, 1990-96; Research Associate, Edinburgh Edition of the Waverley Novels, 1987-91; Kerr-Fry Award holder, Edinburgh University, 1985-90; b. 21.1.45, Glasgow; 1 s.; 1 d. Educ. George Watson's Ladies' College, Edinburgh; Edinburgh University. Scottish National Dictionary: Junior Assistant Editor, 1966, Assistant Editor, 1967, Senior Assistant Editor, 1972; Editor-in-Chief, Concise Scots Dictionary, 1973-85; Member, Advisory Committee, Private Papers of James Boswell, Yale University, since 1987. Publications: Concise Scots Dictionary, 1985; Chambers 21st Century

Dictionary, 1996. Recreations: music; theatre; reading; travel. Address: (b.) 23 Dundas Street, Edinburgh, EH3 6QQ.

Robinson, Ian, BSc, FEng. Chief Executive, Scottish Power plc, since 1995; b. 3.5.42, Boldon, Co. Durham; m., Kay Robinson; 1 s.; 1 d. Educ. Middlesbrough High School; Leeds University. Managing Director, Parsons Corporation, 1985-86; Managing Director, John Brown Engineering and Construction, 1986-92; Chief Executive, John Brown plc, 1992-95; Director, Trafalgar House plc, 1992-95. Non-Executive Director: ASDA plc, Scottish Enterprise. Recreations: golf; gardening. Address: (b.) 1 Atlantic Quay, Glasgow G2 8SP; T.-0141-636 4503.

Robinson, Stanley Scott, MBE (Mil), TD, BL, SSC. Sheriff of Grampian, Highland and Islands (retired); Honorary Sheriff of Inverness; Honorary Sheriff of Angus; b. 27.3.13, Edinburgh; m., Helen Annan Hardie; 3 s. Educ. Boroughmuir School, Edinburgh; Edinburgh University. Admitted Solicitor, 1935; TA commission, 1936; War service, Royal Artillery, 1939-45; Major; mentioned in Despatches (2); France and Belgium, 1939-40, France and Germany, 1944-45; admitted SSC, 1962; Vice President, Law Society of Scotland, 1970-72; appointed Sheriff, Fort William/Skye/Inverness/Western Isles, 1972; retired, 1985. Publications: Law of Inderdict, 1987; Law of Game and Salmon Fishing, 1990; Encyclopedia of Laws of Scotland (Contributor). bowling; caravanning. Address: (h.) Drumalin House, 16 Drummond Road, Inverness IV2 4NB; T.-01463 233488.

Robson, Agnes, MA. Director, Directorate of Primary Care, NHS Management Executive, Scottish Office Home and Health Department, since 1992; b. 6.10.46, Edinburgh; 1 s. Educ. Holy Cross Academy; Edinburgh University. Civil Servant, since 1968; Head, Energy Division, 1988-89; Head, Nuclear Energy Division, 1989-90; Head, Urban Policy Division, 1990-92. Recreations: music; theatre. Address: (b.) St. Andrews House, Edinburgh.

Robson, Euan Macfarlane, BA, MSc, MICA. Scottish Manager, Gas Consumers' Council, since 1986; b. 17.2.54, Northumberland; m., Valerie; 2 d. Educ. Trinity College, Glenalmond; Newcastle-upon-Tyne University; Strathclyde University. Teacher, 1976-79; Deputy Secretary, Gas Consumers' Northern Council, 1981-86. Member, Northumberland County Council, 1981-89; Honorary Alderman, Northumberland CC, since 1989; Liberal/SDP Alliance candidate, Hexham, 1983, 1987. Address: (b.) 86 George Street, Edinburgh, EH2 3BU.

Robson, Professor Peter William Greenwell, LLB, PhD. Solicitor; Professor of Social Welfare Law, Strathclyde University, since 1992; Chair, Child Support Appeal Tribunal, since 1993; Chair, Social Security Appeal Tribunal, since 1995; b. 28.3.47, Birmingham; m., Andrina Ann Marie Smith. Educ. Slough Grammar School; St. Andrews University. Solicitor, 1967-70; Lecturer, 1970-82; Senior Lecturer, 1982-89, Reader, 1989-92, Strathclyde University; Visiting Lecturer, Universities of Stirling, Heriot-Watt and Glasgow, since 1982. Deputy Chair, Shelter; Chair, East End Advice Centre, Glasgow; Director, Weslo Housing Management, Bathgate; Board Member, Adviser (rights journal). Publications: Homeless People and the Law; Residential Tenancies; Family Law Encyclopaedia (Joint Editor). Recreations: football; golf; rollerblading; country music; swimming. Address: (b.) Law School, Strathclyde University, Glasgow G4 0RQ; T.-0141-552 4400/548 3340.

Rochester, Professor Colin Herbert, BSc, PhD, DSc, CChem, FRSC, FRSE. Baxter Professor of Chemistry, Dundee University, since 1980; b. 20.3.37, Coventry; m., Jennifer Mary Orrell; 2 s.; 2 d. Educ. Hymers College, Hull; Royal Liberty School, Romford; King's College, London University. Nottingham University: Assistant Lecturer in Physical Chemistry, 1962-64, Lecturer, 1964-72, Reader, 1972-80. Publication: Acidity Functions, 1970. Recreations: fossil collecting; swimming. Address: (b.) Chemistry Department, The University, Dundee DD1 4HN; T.-01382 344327.

Rochford, Professor Gerard, BA, BSc. Psychotherapist; b. 17.12.32, Dorking; m., Anne Prime (dec.); 3 s.; 7 d. Educ. Worcester Royal Grammar School; Hull University; Oxford University. Medical Research Council, 1960-63; Lecturer in Psychology: Aberdeen University, 1963-67, Hong Kong University, 1967-70; Lecturer/Senior Lecturer, 1970-78, Professor of Social Work Studies, 1978-88, Aberdeen University. Member, Scottish Association of Psychoanalytical Psychotherapists. Recreations: family; friends; poetry; pottery. Address: (h.) 47 Waverley Place, Aberdeen; T.-Aberdeen 644873.

Rodger of Earlsferry, Rt. Hon. Lord (Alan Ferguson Rodger), QC, MA, LLB, DCL. Lord Justice General; b. 18.9.44. Educ. Kelvinside Academy, Glasgow; Glasgow University; New College, Oxford. Fellow, New College, Oxford, 1970-72; Member, Faculty of Advocates, 1974; Clerk of Faculty, 1976-79; Advocate Depute, 1985-88; Home Advocate Depute, 1986-88; Member, Mental Welfare Commission for Scotland, 1981-84; UK Delegation to CCBE, 1984-89; Maccabaean Lecturer, British Academy, 1991; Solicitor General for Scotland, 1989-92; Lord Advocate, 1992-96. Address: (b.) Supreme Court, 2 Parliament House, Parliament Square, Edinburgh, EH1 1RQ.

Rodger, Willie, ARSA, RGI, DA (Glas). Artist in lino and woodcuts; b. 3.3.30, Kirkintilloch; m., Anne Charmian Henry; 2 s.; 2 d. Educ. Lenzie Academy; Glasgow School of Art. Visualiser, London advertising agency, 1953-54; Art Teacher, Lenzie Acacady, 1955-68; Head, Art Department, Clydebank High School, 1968-87. Artist in Residence, Sussex University, 1971; Scottish Historical Playing Cards, 1975; Saltire Awards for Art in Architecture, 1984-89; work in permanent collections in Scotland and England. Recreations: gardening; jazz. Address: Stenton, Bellevue Road, Kirkintilloch, Glasgow G66 1AP; T.-0141-776 2116.

Roe, Professor Nicholas Hugh, MA (Oxon), DPhil (Oxon). Professor of English Literature, St. Andrews University, since 1996; b. 14.12.55, Fareham; m., Dr. Susan Jane Stabler. Educ. Royal Grammar School, High Wycombe; Trinity College, Oxford. Lecturer in English, Queen's University of Belfast, 1982-85; St. Andrews University: Lecturer in English, 1985-94, Reader in English, 1994-96; Visiting Professor, University of Sao Paulo, 1989; Leverhulme Research Fellow, 1994-95; Director, Coleridge Conference, since 1994. Publications: Coleridge's Imagination, 1985; Wordsworth and Coleridge, 1988; The Politics of Nature, 1992; Selected Poetry of William Wordsworth, 1992; Keats and History, 1995; Selected Poems of John Keats, 1995; John Keats and the Culture of Dissent, 1997. Recreations: walking; gardening; cookery; France. Address: (b.) School of English, St. Andrews University, St. Andrews KY16 9AL; T.-01334 476161.

Roebuck, Michael Stuart, BSc, MEd, CertEd. Principal, Kilmarnock College, since 1996; b. 5.12.49, Huddersfield; m., Margaret Jane; 1 s.; 1 d. Educ. Marlborough Grammar School; University of Ulster; Edinburgh University. Trainee Town Planner; Lecturer/Senior Lecturer/Depute Head of Department, Stevenson College of F.E.; Assistant to the Director of Education, Lothian Region; TVEI Coordinator, Senior Adviser, Lothian Region; Principal, Lews Castle College. Recreation: cricket (retired). Address: (b.) Kilmarnock College, Holehouse Road, Kilmarnock KA3 7AT; T.-01563 523501.

Roger, Peter Charles Marshall, CA. Director, Speirs & Jeffrey Ltd., since 1974; b. 11.4.42, Glasgow; m., Fiona Ann Murray; 2 s.; 1 d. Educ. Glasgow High School. Qualified CA, 1964; Thomson McLintock & Co., 1964-71; joined Speirs & Jeffrey Ltd., 1971. Recreation: golf. Address: (b.) 36 Renfield Street, Glasgow G2 1NA; T.-0141-248 4311.

Rogerson, Robert William Kelly Cupples, OBE, BArch, FRIBA, FRIAS, FSA Scot, MRSH. Vice Chairman, Scottish Council on Disability, 1987-89; Chairman, Committee on Access for Scotland, 1980-89; Council Member, National Trust for Scotland, 1980-86; b. 14.5.17, Glasgow; m., Mary Clark MacNeill; 1 s.; 1 d. Educ. High School of Glasgow; Strathclyde University. Architect in private practice, 1955-56 and 1958-82 (Partner, Watson Salmond & Gray, 1956-58); Lecturer, School of Architecture, Glasgow School of Art; Past Chairman, Glasgow Building Guardian Committee; Past Chairman, RIAS Trustees of The Hill House, Helensburgh; Founder and Chairman, Glasgow Summer School; former Member, Committee on Artistic Matters, Church of Scotland. Publications: A Place at Work (Co-author); Jack Coia, His Life & Work. Recreations: gardening; travelling abroad. Address: (h.) Beinn Bhuidhe House, Glen Shira, Inverary, Argyll PA32 8XH; T.-01499 302472.

Rolfe, Lord Provost Mervyn James, OStJ, MEd, FRSA, FSAScot, JP. Lord Provost of Dundee; b. 31.7.47, Wisbech; m., Christine; 1 s. Educ. Buckhaven High School; Dundee University. Civil servant, until 1983; Co-ordinator, Dundee Resources Centre for the Unemployed, 1983-87; Vice-Chair, Dundee Trades Council, 1981-82; Leader, Labour Group, Tayside Regional Council, 1994-96; Convener, Tayside Education Committee, 1986-94; Member, Executive Committee, COSLA, 1990-96; Governor, Dundee (now Northern) College of Education, 1986-94; Member, Dundee University Court, since 1986; Member, Scottish Community Education Council, 1986-88; Member, General Teaching Council, 1986-95; Member, Scottish Committee for Staff Development in Education, 1987-91; Board Member, Scottish Enterprise, Tayside, 1991-96; Member, Scottish Cooperative Development Committee, since 1984; Member, Dundee Heritage Trust, since 1986; Executive Member, Campaign for a Scottish Assembly, 1989-91. Recreations: reading; politics. Address: (h.) 17 Mains Terrace, Dundee; T.-01382 450073.

Rolfe, William David Ian, PhD, FRSE, FGS, FMA. Keeper of Geology, National Museums of Scotland, 1986-96; b. 24.1.36; m., Julia Mary Margaret Rayer; 2 d. Educ. Royal Liberty Grammar School, Romford; Birmingham University. Geology Curator, University Lecturer, then Senior Lecturer in Geology, Hunterian Museum, Glasgow University, 1962-81; Deputy Director, 1981-86. President, Geological Society of Glasgow, 1973-76; Editor, Scottish Journal of Geology, 1967-72; President, Edinburgh Geological Society, 1989-91; President, Palaeontological Association, 1992-94; President, Society for the History of Natural History, since 1996. Recreations: visual arts; walking; swimming; music. Address: 4A Randolph Crescent, Edinburgh, EH3 7TH; T.-0131-226 2094.

Rolland, Lawrence Anderson Lyon, DA, PPRIBA, PPRIAS, FRSE, FRSA. Senior Partner, Hurd Rolland Partnership, 1980-97, Chairman and Consultant, since 1997; General Trustee, Church of Scotland, since 1979; Member of Court, Dundee University, and Chairman of Audit Committee, since 1994; b. 6.11.37, Leven; m., Mairi May Melville; 2 s.; 2 d. Educ. George Watson's Boys College; Duncan of Jordanstone College of Art. Entered father's practice, 1959; joined partnership with Ian Begg bringing L.A. Rolland and Partners and Robert Hurd and Partners together as one partnership; developed the firm into a national practice; President, Royal Incorporation of Architects in Scotland, 1979-81; President, Royal Institute of British Architects, 1985-87. Recreations: music; fishing. Address: (b.) Rossend Castle, Burntisland, Fife KY3 0DF; T.-01592 873535.

Rollo, 13th Lord (Eric John Stapylton Rollo); b. 3.12.15; m.; 2 s.; 1 d. Address: Pitcairns, Dunning, Perthshire, PH2 9BX.

Romanis, William Wright. Director, Administration and Services, National Farmers' Union of Scotland, since 1994; Organiser, ScotGrow, since 1987; Organiser, DairyScot, since 1994; b. 15.10.42, Musselburgh; m., Fiona MacGregor; 1 s.; 1 d. Educ. Musselburgh Grammar School. Administrative staff, Royal Highland & Agricultural Society of Scotland, 1957-65; Assistant Secretary, Scottish Association of Young Farmers' Clubs, 1965-67; Sales Officer/Promotion Officer, Scottish Milk Marketing Board, 1967-77; Organiser, then Director of Services, National Farmers' Union of Scotland, since 1977. Recreations: golf; hill-walking. Address: (b.) Rural Centre, West Mains, Ingliston, Newbridge, Midlothian EH28 8LT; T.-0131-335 3111.

Rooke, Matthew Andre Paul, MA (Hons), FRSA. Music Director, Scottish Arts Council, since 1991; b. 14.2.63, Oxford; m., Georgina Verity Dawson. Educ. St. Andrews University; Berklee College of Music. Music Officer, Arts Council of G.B., 1989-91. Recreation: cookery. Address: (b.) 12 Manor Place, Edinburgh EH3 7PD; T.-0131-225 6051.

Rorke, Professor John, CBE, PhD, BSc, DEng, CEng, FIMechE, FRSE. Professor Emeritus, formerly Professor of Mechanical Engineering, Heriot-Watt University, 1980-88, and Vice-Principal, 1984-88; b. 2.9.23, Dumbarton; m., Jane Craig Buchanan; 2 d. Educ. Dumbarton Academy; Royal Technical College, Glasgow. Lecturer, Strathclyde University, 1946-51; Assistant to Engineering Director, Alexander Stephen & Sons Ltd., 1951-56; Technical Manager, then General Manager and Engineering Director, William Denny & Bros. Ltd., 1956-63; Technical Director, then Sales Director, Managing Director and Chairman, Brown Bros. & Co. Ltd. and Chairman, John Hastie of Greenock Ltd., 1963-78; Managing Director, Vickers Offshore Group, 1978 (Director of Planning, Vickers PLC, 1979-80). President, Institution of Engineers and Shipbuilders in Scotland, 1985-87; Chairman, Institute of Offshore Engineering Group, 1990-94. Recreations: bridge; golf. Address: (h.) 3 Barnton Park Grove, Edinburgh; T.-0131-336 3044.

Rose, Barry Michael, BSc, FIA. Chief Executive, Scottish Provident UK, since 1993; b. 10.3.45, Southend; m., Sandra Jane; 2 d. Educ. Manchester University. Assistant Investment Manager, Cooperative Insurance Society, 1971-76; Investment Secretary, then Investment Manager, Scottish Life Assurance, 1976-88; General Manager (Investment), Scottish Provident Institution, 1988-93. Address: (b.) 6 St. Andrew Square, Edinburgh EH2 2YA, T.-0131-556 9181.

Rose, David, BA, NDA, CertEd, ARAgS. Principal, The Barony College, Dumfries, since 1980; b. 6.7.40, Denton, Manchester; m., Pauline Anne Rose; 1 s.; 1 d. Educ. Seale-Hayne College of Agriculture; Open University. Assistant Farm Manager, Wiltshire, 1962-66; Lecturer in Agriculture, Cumbria College of Agriculture and Forestry, 1967-70; Senior Lecturer in Agriculture, Bishop Burton College of Agriculture, 1970-74; Vice-Principal, Oatridge College of Agriculture, 1974-80. Recreation: hill-walking. Address: (b.) Parkgate, Dumfries; T.-01387 860251.

Rose, Dilys Lindsay, BA. Writer of fiction, poetry, drama, since 1980; b. 7.2.54, Glasgow; 2 d. Educ. Edinburgh University. Publications include: fiction: Our Lady of the

Pickpockets, Red Tides, War Dolls; poetry: Beauty is a Dangerous Thing, Madame Doubtfire's Dilemma. Winner, first Macallan/Scotland on Sunday short story competition, 1991; Hawthornden Fellow; RLS Memorial Award recipient, 1997. Address: (h.) 12 Panmure Place, Edinburgh; T.-0131-229 0800.

Rose, Professor Richard, BA, DPhil, FBA. Director and Professor of Public Policy, Centre for the Study of Public Policy, Strathclyde University, since 1976; b. 9.4.33; m., Rosemary J.; 2 s.; 1 d. Educ. Clayton High School, Missouri, USA; Johns Hopkins University; London School of Economics; Lincoln and Nuffield Colleges, Oxford University. Political public relations, Mississippi Valley, 1954-55; Reporter, St. Louis Post-Dispatch, 1955-57; Lecturer in Government, Manchester University, 1961-66; Professor of Politics, Strathclyde University, 1966-82; Consultant Psephologist, The Times, Independent Television, Daily Telegraph, STV, UTV, etc., since 1964; Scientific Adviser, Paul Lazarsfeld Society, Vienna, since 1991; American SSRC Fellow, Stanford University, 1967; Visiting Lecturer in Political Sociology, Cambridge University, 1967; Director, ISSC European Summer School, 1973; Secretary, Committee on Political Sociology, International Sociological Association, 1970-85; Founding Member, European Consortium for Political Research, 1970; Member: US/UK Fulbright Commission, 1971-75, Eisenhower Fellowship Programme, 1971; Guggenheim Foundation Fellow, 1974; Visiting Scholar: Woodrow Wilson International Centre, Washington DC, 1974, Brookings Institute, Washington DC, 1976, American Enterprise Institute, Washington, 1980, Fiscal Affairs Department, IMF, Washington, 1984; Visiting Professor, European University Institute, Florence, 1977, 1978; Visitor, Japan Foundation, 1984; Hinkley Professor, Johns Hopkins University, 1987; Guest Professor, Wissenschaftzentrum, Berlin, 1988, 1990, Central European University, Prague, 1992-95, Max Planck Institute, Berlin, 1996; Ransone Lecturer, University of Alabama, 1990; Consultant Chairman, NI Constitutional Convention, 1976; Home Office Working Party on Electoral Register, 1975-77; Co-Founder, British Politics Group, 1974; Convenor, Work Group on UK Politics, Political Studies Association, 1976-88; Member, Council, International Political Science Association, 1976-82; Keynote Speaker, Australian Institute of Political Science, Canberra, 1978; Technical Consultant, OECD, World Bank; Director, ESRC (formerly SSRC) Research Programme, Growth of Government, 1982-86; Honorary Vice President, Political Studies Association, UK, 1986; Editor, Journal of Public Policy, since 1985 (Chairman, 1981-85); Foreign Member, Finnish Academy of Science and Letters, 1985; Member, American Academy of Arts and Sciences, 1994; Robert Marjolin AMEX Prize in International Economics, 1992. Publications: The British General Election of 1959 (Co-author), 1960; Must Labour Lose? (Co-author), 1960; Politics in England, 1964; Studies in British Politics (Editor), 1966; Influencing Voters, 1967; Policy Making in Britain (Editor), 1969; People in Politics, 1970; European Politics (Joint Editor), 1971; Governing Without Consensus — An Irish Perspective, 1971; International Almanack of Electoral History (Co-author), 1974; Electoral Behaviour — A Comparative Handbook (Editor), 1974; Lessons From America (Editor), 1974; The Problem of Party Government, 1974; The Management of Urban Change in Britain and Germany (Editor), 1974; Northern Ireland — A Time of Choice, 1976; Managing Presidential Objectives, 1976; The Dynamics of Public Policy (Editor), 1976; New Trends in British Politics (Joint Editor), 1977; Comparing Public Policies (Joint Editor), 1977; What is Governing? — Purpose and Policy in Washington, 1978; Elections Without Choice (Joint Editor), 1978; Can Government Go Bankrupt? (Co-author), 1978; Britain — Progress and Decline (Joint Editor), 1980; Do Parties Make a Difference?, 1980; Challenge to Governance (Editor), 1980; Electoral Participation (Editor), 1980;

Presidents and Prime Ministers (Joint Editor), 1980; Understanding the United Kingdom, 1982; United Kingdom Facts (Co-author), 1982; The Territorial Dimension in United Kingdom Politics (Joint Editor), 1982; Fiscal Stress in Cities (Joint Editor), 1982; Understanding Big Government, 1984; The Nationwide Competition for Votes (Co-author), 1984; Public Employment in Western Nations, 1985; Voters Begin to Choose (Co-author), 1986; Patterns of Parliamentary Legislation (Co-author), 1986; The Welfare State East and West (Joint Editor), 1986; Ministers and Ministries, 1987; Taxation By Political Inertia (Co-author), 1987; The Post-Modern President — The White House Meets the World, 1988; Ordinary People in Public Policy, 1989; Training Without Trainers? (Co-author), 1990; The Loyalty of Voters (Co-author), 1990; Lesson-Drawing in Public Policy, 1993; Inheritance before Choice, 1994; What Is Europe?, 1996; How Russia Votes (Co-author), 1997. Recreations: architecture (historical, Britain; modern, America); music; writing. Address: (b.) CSPP, Strathclyde University, Livingstone Tower, Glasgow G1 1XH; T.-0141-548 3217.

Rosebery, 7th Earl of (Neil Archibald Primrose), DL; b. 11.2.29; m., Alison Mary Deirdre Reid; 1 s.; 4 d. Educ. Stowe; New College, Oxford. Address: (h.) Dalmeny House, South Queensferry, West Lothian.

Rosie, George. Freelance Writer and Broadcaster; b. 27.2.41, Edinburgh; m., Elizabeth Ann Burness; 2 s.; 1 d. Educ. Trinity Academy, Edinburgh; Edinburgh School of Architecture. Editor, Interior Design magazine, 1966-68; freelance magazine writer, 1968-76; Scottish Affairs Correspondent, Sunday Times, 1976-86; Reporter, Channel 4 TV series Down the Line, 1986-87, Scottish Eye, 1988; Reporter/Writer, The Englishing of Scotland, 1988, Selling Scotland, 1989; Scotching the Myth, 1990; Losing the Heid, 1991; Independence Day, 1996; Secret Scotland, 1997; Editor, Observer Scotland, 1988-89; award winner, RSPB birds and countryside awards, 1988. Publications: British in Vietnam, 1970; Cromarty, 1975; The Ludwig Initiative, 1978; Hugh Miller, 1982; The Directory of International Terrorism, 1986; as contributor: Headlines, the Media in Scotland, 1978; Scottish Government Yearbook, 1982; Scotland, Multinationals and the Third World, 1982; World Offshore Oil and Gas Industry Report, 1987; stage plays: The Blasphemer, 1990; Carlucco and the Queen of Hearts, 1991 (winner, Fringe First, The Independent Theatre Award); It Had To Be You, 1994. Recreation: hill-walking. Address: (h.) 70 Comiston Drive, Edinburgh EH10 5QS; T.-0131-447 9660.

Ross, Alastair Robertson, OStJ, DA, ARSA, FRBS, FSA Scot, FRSA, MBIM, Hon. FRIAS. Artist; Lecturer in Fine Art, Duncan of Jordanstone College University of Dundee, since 1994; Lecturer in Fine Art, Duncan of Jordanstone College of Art, Dundee, 1966-94; Honorary Lecturer, Dundee University, 1969-94; Vice President, Royal Society of British Sculptors, 1988-90; Council Member, British School at Rome, 1990-96; b. 8.8.41, Perth; m., Kathryn Margaret Greig Wilson; 1 d. Educ. St. Mary's Episcopal School, Dunblane; McLaren High School, Callander; Duncan of Jordanstone College of Art, Dundee. SED Postgraduate Scholarship, 1965-66; Dickson Prize for Sculpture, 1962; Holokrome (Dundee) Sculpture Prize and Commission, 1962; SED Travelling Scholarship, 1963; Royal Scottish Academy Chalmers Bursary, 1964; Royal Scottish Academy Carnegie Travelling Scholarship, 1965; Duncan of Drumfork Scholarship, 1965; award winner, Paris Salon, 1967; Medaille de Bronze, Societe des Artistes Francais, 1968; Professional Member, Society of Scottish Artists, 1969; Medaille D'Argent, 1970; Membre Associe, Societe des Artistes Francais, 1970; Scottish Representative and Member, Council, Royal Society of British Sculptors, 1972-92; Sir Otto Beit Medal, Royal Society of British Sculptors, 1988; Freeman, City of London, 1989; Sir William Gillies Bequest Award, Royal Scottish Academy,

1989; Council Member, Society of Scottish Artists, 1972-75; Hon. Fellow, Royal Incorporation of Architects in Scotland, 1992; Visiting Lecturer, University of Texas, Arlington, USA, 1996; Member, Board of Directors, Studio and Artists' Workshop Provision Scotland Ltd., since 1997; exhibited work widely in UK and abroad; work in: Scottish Arts Council Collection, Perth Art Gallery and Museum, Dundee Education Authority Collection, private collections in Austria, Switzerland, Egypt, USA, Norway, Bahamas, Canada, Portugal, India, UK. Recreations: genealogy; heraldry; travel. Address: (h.) Ravenscourt, 28 Albany Terrace, Dundee, DD3 6HS; T.-01382 224235.

Ross, Alexander (Sandy), LLB, CYCW. Deputy Chief Executive, Scottish Television Enterprises, since 1995; b. 17.4.48, Grangemouth; m., Alison Fraser; 2 s.; 1 d. Educ. Grangemouth High School; Edinburgh University; Moray House College. Apprentice lawyer, 1971-73; Lecturer, Paisley College, 1974-75; Producer, Granada TV, 1978-86; Controller, Arts and Entertainment, Scottish Television, 1986-95. Member, Edinburgh Town Council, 1971-74; Member, Edinburgh District Council, 1974-78; President, Moray House Students Union, 1976. Recreations: golf; music; reading; watching football. Address: (h.) 7 Murrayfield Avenue, Edinburgh EH12 6AU; T.-0131-539 1192.

Ross, Rev. Andrew Christian, MA, BD, STM, PhD, FRHistS. Senior Lecturer in Ecclesiastical History, Edinburgh University, since 1966 (Principal of New College and Dean, Faculty of Divinity, 1978-84); b. 10.5.31, Millerhill, Lothian; m., I. Joyce Elder; 4 s.; 1 d. (deceased). Educ. Dalkeith High School; Edinburgh University; Union Theological Seminary, New York. RAF, 1952-54; Minister, Church of Central Africa Presbyterian (Malawi), 1958-65; Chairman, Lands Tribunal of Nyasaland, then Malawi Government, 1963-65; Vice Chairman, National Tenders Board, Nyasaland, then Malawi Government, 1963-65. Member, University Court, 1971-73; Convener, Student Affairs Committee, 1977-83; Kerr Lecturer, Glasgow University, 1984; Lecturer, Assembly's College, Belfast, 1985; Visiting Professor, Yale University and Dartmouth College, 1992. Publications: John Philip: Missions, Race and Politics in South Africa; Vision Betrayed: the Jesuits in China and Japan; Blantyre Mission and the Development of Malawi. Recreation: coaching and watching football. Address: (h.) 27 Colinton Road, Edinburgh; T.-0131-447 5987.

Ross, Professor David Alexander, BSc (Hons), PhD, DipEdTech, CChem, FRSC. Head, School of Molecular and Life Sciences, since 1991, and Director, Centre for the Enhancement of Learning and Teaching, University of Abertay, since 1995; b. 6.7.52, Stirling; m., Lyn; 3 d. Educ. Kilsyth Academy; Strathclyde University. Procter and Gamble Ltd., Newcastle, 1977-85; Senior Lecturer, University of Abertay, Dundee, 1985-91. Recreations: golf; fishing; gardening. T.-01382 308651.

Ross, Rev. David Sinclair, BSc (Hons), MSc, PhD, BD (Hons). Minister, Old Parish Church, Peterhead, since 1978; b. 24.7.45, Aberdeen; m., Pamela Ann Anderson Nimmo; 2 s. by pr. m.; 1 d. Educ. Aberdeen Academy; Aberdeen University; Glasgow University. Research Chemist, Philips, Aachen, W. Germany, 1971-73; Assistant Minister, Northfield, Aberdeen, 1977-78. Past Chaplain, Peterhead Prison; Chaplain, RAF Buchan, Peterhead Community Hospital; Port Chaplain; Chairman, Local Action Group, Grampian Heart Campaign. Recreations: President, Peterhead R.F.C.; tenor, Peterhead Choral; swimming and sub aqua. Address: (h.) 1 Hawthorn Road, Peterhead AB42 2DW; T.-01779 472618.

Ross, Donald Forrester, MA, CA. General Treasurer, Church of Scotland, since 1995; b. 14.6.42, Aberdeen; m., Dorothy Reid Nelson; 2 s. Educ. Aberdeen Grammar School; Aberdeen University. CA Apprentice, G. & J. McBain, CA, Aberdeen, 1963-67; Audit Assistant, Thomson McLintock, CA, Glasgow, 1967-69; Assistant Treasurer, Church of Scotland, 1969-75; Deputy General Treasurer, Church of Scotland, 1975-95. Address: (b.) 121 George Street, Edinburgh EH2 4YN; T.-0131-225 5722.

Ross, Rt. Hon. Lord (Donald MacArthur Ross), PC, MA, LLB. Lord Justice Clerk and President of the Second Division of the Court of Session, 1985-97; a Senator of the College of Justice, 1977-97; Chairman, Judicial Studies Committee, Scotland, since 1997; Lord High Commissioner to the General Assembly of the Church of Scotland, 1990 and 1991; b. 29.3.27, Dundee; m., Dorothy Margaret Annand; 2 d. Educ. High School of Dundee; Edinburgh University. Advocate, 1952; QC, 1964; Vice-Dean, Faculty of Advocates, 1967-73; Dean of Faculty, 1973-76; Sheriff Principal of Ayr and Bute, 1972-73; Member, Scottish Committee, Council of Tribunals, 1970-76; Member, Committee on Privacy, 1970; Deputy Chairman, Boundary Commission for Scotland, 1977-85; Member, Court, Heriot-Watt University, 1978-90, Chairman, 1984-90; Member, Parole Board for Scotland, since 1997. Hon. LLD, Edinburgh, Dundee, Abertay Dundee; Hon. DUniv, Heriot Watt; FRSE. Recreation: gardening; walking; travel. Address: (h.) 33 Lauder Road, Edinburgh EH9 2JG; T.-0131-667 5731.

Ross, Ernest. MP (Labour), Dundee West, since 1979; Chair, PLP Foreign Affairs Committee; Member, Foreign Affairs Select Committee; Chair, Board of Governors, Westminster Foundation for Democracy; Chair, All Party Group on Poverty; b. 27.7.42, Dundee; m., June; 2 s.; 1 d. Educ. St. John's Junior Secondary School. Apprentice Marine Fitter, Caledon Shipyard; Quality Control Inspector/Engineer, Timex. Recreations: football; cricket. Address: (b.) Constituency Office, 13 Cowgate, Dundee; T.-01382 200329.

Ross, Helen Elizabeth, BA, MA (Oxon), PhD (Cantab), FBPsS, CPsychol, FRSE. Honorary Reader, Stirling University, since 1994; b. 2.12.35, London. Educ. South Hampstead High School; Somerville College, Oxford; Newnham College, Cambridge. Assistant Mistress, schools in London and Oxfordshire, 1959-61; Research Assistant and student, Psychological Laboratory, Cambridge University, 1961-65; Lecturer in Psychology: Hull University, 1965-68, Stirling University, 1969-72; Senior Lecturer in Psychology, Stirling University, 1972-83; Research Fellow, DFVLR Institute for Aerospace Medicine, Bonn, 1980-81; Leverhulme Fellowship, 1983-84; Reader in Psychology, Stirling University, 1983-94. Member, S.E. Regional Board, Nature Conservancy Council for Scotland, 1991-92; Fellowship Secretary, Royal Society of Edinburgh, 1994-97. Publications: Behaviour and Perception in Strange Environments, 1974; E.H. Weber: The Sense of Touch (Co-translator), 1978; E.H. Weber on the Tactile Senses (Co-translator), 1996. Recreations: skiing; curling; hill-walking; traditional music. Address: (b.) Department of Psychology, Stirling University, Stirling FK9 4LA; T.-01786 467647.

Ross, John Alexander, CBE, FRAgS. President, National Farmers' Union of Scotland, 1990-96; Chairman, Dumfries and Galloway Health Board, since 1997; b. 19.2.45, Stranraer; m., Alison Jean Darling; 2 s.; 1 d. Educ. George Watson's College, Edinburgh. NFU of Scotland: Convener, Hill Farming Sub-Committee, 1984-90, Convener, Livestock Committee, 1987-90, Vice-President, 1986-90, Wigtown Area President, 1985-86. Chairman, Stranraer School Council, 1980-89; Session Clerk, Portpatrick Parish Church, 1975-80; Elder, Church of Scotland; Director, Animal Diseases Research Association; Commissioner, Meat and Livestock Commission, since 1996; Director, NFU Mutual Insurance Society, since 1996. Recreations:

golf; curling. Address: Low Auchenree Farm, Portpatrick, Stranraer, Wigtownshire DG9 8TN.

Ross, Sheriff Kenneth A., LLB (Hons). Sheriff of Lothian and Borders at Linlithgow; b. 21.4.49. Educ. Hutchesons Grammar School, Glasgow; Edinburgh University. Former Partner, Gillespie Gifford and Brown, Solicitors, Dumfries. Address: (b.) Sheriff Court House, High Street, Linlithgow EH49 7EQ.

Ross, Michael David, FFA, CIMgt. Group Chief Executive, Scottish Widows, since 1991; b. 9.7.46, Edinburgh; m., Pamela Marquis Speakman. Joined Scottish Widows, 1964, as Trainee Actuary; Assistant General Manager, 1986-88; appointed Actuary, 1988; General Manager (Finance), 1988-90; Deputy Managing Director, 1990-91. Hon. Secretary, Faculty of Actuaries. Fellow, Royal Society of Arts Manufacture & Commerce. Publication: Transactions of Faculty of Actuaries. Recreations: golf; curling; skiing; gardening. Address: (b.) 15 Dalkeith Road, Edinburgh EH16 5BU; T.-0131-655 6000.

Ross, Neil Kilgour, MA, LLB. Partner, Grigor & Young, Solicitors, since 1989; b. 17.5.54, Sutton Coldfield; m., Kathleen Rae; 1 d. Educ. Inverurie Academy; Aberdeen University. Legal apprentice, Western Isles Islands Council, 1977-79; Legal Assistant, Angus District Council, 1979-82; Depute Director of Legal Services, Clerk of the Peace and Clerk to the Licensing Board, Western Isles Islands Council, 1982-85. Director, Moray Council on Addictions; contributor, Stair Memorial Encyclopedia; Member, Council, Law Society of Scotland, since 1994. Recreations: wine; gardening. Address: (b.) 1 North Street, Elgin IV30 1UA; T.-01343 544077.

Ross, Philip Wesley, TD, MD, FRCPE, FRCPath, CBiol, FIBiol, FLS. Consultant, Edinburgh Royal Infirmary, and Reader in Medical Microbiology, Edinburgh University; b. 6.6.36, Aberdeen; m., Stella Joyce Shand; 2 s.; 1 d. Educ. Turriff Academy; Robert Gordon's College, Aberdeen; Aberdeen University (President, SRC, 1958-59). Senior Warden, Edinburgh University, 1972-83. Lt.-Col., RAMC (TA); Officer Commanding Medical Division and Edinburgh Detachment 205 Scottish General Hospital, 1975-80; Chairman: Lothian Area Division of Laboratory Medicine, 1986-89, Scottish Branch Institute of Biology, 1991-93; Examiner: Royal College of Surgeons of Edinburgh, Royal College of Pathologists; President, Scottish Microbiology Association; Inspector, Clinical Pathology Accreditation (UK) Ltd.; Liberal Democrat Parliamentary Candidate, Monklands East, 1992; Chairman, Edinburgh East Liberal Democrats; Elder, Duddingston Kirk, Edinburgh. Publications on streptococci, diseases of the mouth, throat and genital tract, infection of the newborn, antibiotics and hospital infection. Recreations: music; playing church organs (organist and choirmaster, Woodside Congregational Church, Bucksburn Parish Church, Holburn Central Church, Aberdeen, 1954-64); travel; walking; old churches; art galleries; politics. Address: (h.) 18 Old Church Lane, Duddingston Village, Edinburgh EH15 3PX; T.-0131-661 5415.

Ross, Raymond, MA, PhD, DipEd. Writer, Editor, Lecturer; b. 17.10.53, Bangour; m., Jennifer; 1 d. Educ. Scotus Academy, Edinburgh; Edinburgh University; Stirling University. Editor, Cencrastus, which he co-founded in 1979; co-editor of books on the poets Sorley MacLean and Norman MacCaig; has organised many literary and music events on the Edinburgh Festival Fringe and Edinburgh International Folk Festival; contributor to most Scottish literary publications and newspapers; teaches creative writing, Department of Continuing Education, Edinburgh University; tutor, summer schools in Scottish literature. Address: 42 Spottiswoode Street, Edinburgh; T.-0131-229 4730.

Ross, Robert Fowler. Farming Editor, The Herald, since 1994; b. 9.3.40, Crossgates; m., Jeanette Miller; 1 s.; 1 d. Educ. Dunfermline High School. Trainee Reporter, Dunfermline Press; Reporter, Glasgow Herald, Scottish Daily Mail, Scotsman; Scottish Office Correspondent, The Herald, 1972-87; Edinburgh News Editor, The Herald, 1987-94. Recreations: gardening; walking. Address: (h.) 57 Oatlands Park, Linlithgow EH49 6AS; T.-01506 842892.

Ross, Susan, MA (Hons), MSc, CQSW, PhD. Director of Social Work, East Renfrewshire Council, since 1995; b. 4.7.52, Nottingham; partner, Andy Bilson; 2 d. Educ. Nottingham Bluecoat School; St. Andrews University; Oxford University; Keele University. Social Worker, Newcastle upon Tyne, 1974; Groupworker, Nottinghamshire Social Services Department, 1978; Lecturer, Social Work, Trent Polytechnic, 1983; Principal Officer, Leicestershire Social Services Department, 1985; Children's Society in Wales Director of Wales Centre for Juvenile Justice, 1986; Area Manager, Social Work Department, Fife, 1989; Assistant Director of Social Work, Borders Regional Council, 1995. Recreations: "mummy" things with children, Emma and Anna; ice-skating; listening to 70s music and pretending it's not 20 years old. Address: (h.) 22 Millbrae Crescent, Langside, Glasgow; T.-0141-649 8734.

Ross Stewart, David Andrew, OBE, BA (Cantab). Chairman, Edinburgh Income Trust; b. 30.11.30, Edinburgh; m., Susan Olive Routh; 2 s. Educ. Rugby School; Cambridge University. Assistant General Manager, Alex. Cowan & Sons (NZ) Ltd., 1959-62; General Manager, Alex. Cowan & Sons (Stationery) Ltd., 1962-66; General Manager, Spicers (Stationery) Ltd., 1966-68; Managing Director, John Bartholomew & Son Ltd., 1968-89. Chairman, St. Andrew Trust plc; Chairman, Quayle Munro plc; Director, Lothian Investment Fund for Enterprise Ltd.; Hon. Fellow, University of Edinburgh; Fellow, Scottish Council (Development and Industry); Convener, Finance Committee, National Trust for Scotland. Recreations: fishing; gardening; golf. Address: (b.) 13 Blacket Place, Edinburgh EH9 1RN; T.-0131-667 3221.

Rotter, Professor John Michael, BA, MA, PhD, FIEAust. Professor of Civil Engineering, Edinburgh University, since 1989; Head, Planning Unit for Chemical, Civil and Environmental and Mechanical Engineering, since 1992; b. 31.10.48, Chesterfield; 1 s.; 1 d. Educ. Monkton Combe School, Bath; Cambridge University. Temporary Lecturer in Civil Engineering, then Lecturer, then Senior Lecturer, University of Sydney, 1975-89. Visiting Professor, University of Washington, St. Louis, 1983-84; Visiting Research Fellow, Liverpool University, 1984; Visiting Professor: Insa, Lyon, France, 1996, T.U. Graz, Austria, 1997, University of Metz, Nancy, France, 1997. Publications: 180 technical papers. Recreations: classical music; eating; foreign places; hill-walking. Address: (b.) Edinburgh University, King's Buildings, Edinburgh EH9 3JN; T.-0131-650 5719.

Rousseau, Professor George Sebastian, PhD. Regius Professor of English Literature, Aberdeen University, since 1994, and Director, Thomas Reid Institute; b. 23.2.41. Educ. Amherst College; Princeton University. Instructor, then Assistant Professor, Harvard University, 1966-68; University of California, Los Angeles: Assistant Professor of English, 1968-69, Associate Professor, 1969-76, Professor, 1976-94; Fulbright Research Professor, West Germany, 1970; Cambridge University: Hon. Fellow, Wolfson College, 1974-75, Overseas Fellow, 1979; Visiting Fellow Commoner, Trinity College, 1982; Senior Fulbright Research Scholar, Sir Thomas Browne Institute, Netherlands, 1983; Visiting Exchange Professor, King's College, Cambridge, 1984; Clarke Libby Professor, University of California, 1985-86; Senior Fellow, NEH, 1986-87; Visiting Fellow and Waynflete Lecturer,

Magdalen College, Oxford, 1993-94; book reviewer, New York Times (Sunday), since 1967; FRSocMed, 1967; FRSA, 1973. Recent publications include: The Languages of Psyche: mind and body in enlightenment thought, 1990; Perilous Enlightenment: pre- and post-modern discourses – sexual, historical, 1991; Enlightenment Crossings: pre- and post-modern discourses – anthropological, 1991; Enlightenment Borders: pre- and post-modern discourses – medical, scientific, 1991; Hysteria Before Freud (jointly), 1993; Gout: the patrician malady (jointly), 1997. Recreations: chamber music; opera; skiing; walking; hiking. Address: (b.) Department of English, Taylor Building, King's College, Aberdeen University, Aberdeen AB24 3UB; T.-01224 273683.

Rowallan, Lord (John Polson Cameron), ARICS. Director, Rowallan Holdings Ltd., since 1989; Chairman: Rowallan Ltd., since 1997, Southgate Retail Park, since 1997; Secretary, Rowallan Activity Centre, since 1989; b. 8.3.47, Glasgow; m., Claire Rowallan; 2 s.; 2 d; 1 steps.; 1 stepd. Educ. Eton College; Royal Agricultural College. Estate Agent, 1969-74; Farmer, since 1974; Company Director, since 1989; Commentator, since 1986. Recreations: skiing; commentating. Address: (h.) Meiklemosside, Fenwick, Ayrshire KA3 6AY.

Rowan, Professor Alistair John, DipArch, PhD, FRSE. Principal, Edinburgh College of Art, since 1990; Professor, Heriot-Watt University, since 1991; b. 3.6.38, Belfast; m., Ann Martha Wrinch; 1 d. Educ. Campbell College, Belfast; Edinburgh College of Art; Magdalene College, Cambridge; University of Padua. Country Life magazine: Architectural Editor, 1966-67, Scottish Correspondent, 1967-77; Lecturer in Fine Art, Edinburgh University, 1967-77; Professor of History of Art, University College, Dublin, 1977-90; Slade Professor of Fine Art, Oxford University, 1988. Member, Historic Buildings Council for Scotland, 1986-94; President: Society of Architectural Historians of Great Britain, 1992-96, Architectural Heritage Society of Scotland; Chairman, The Paxton Trust; Cavaliere Del Ordine Al Merito, 1983. Publications: The Buildings of Ireland: North West Ulster, 1979, North Leinster, 1994; Designs for Castles and Country Villas by Robert and James Adam, 1985; Catalogue of Robert Adam Drawings (Victoria and Albert Museum), 1988. Recreation: gardening. Address: (b.) Edinburgh College of Art, Lauriston Place, Edinburgh EH3 9DF; T.-0131-221 6060.

Rowan, John O'Donnell, PhD, CPhys, FInstP, CEng, FIEE, FIEM. Deputy Director, West of Scotland Health Boards Department of Clinical Physics and Bio-Engineering, since 1983; Head, Department of Clinical Physics and Bio-engineering, Glasgow Royal Infirmary NHS Trust, since 1994; Honorary Clinical Senior Lecturer in Clinical Physics, Glasgow University, since 1991; Member, National Panel of Assessors for NHS Scientists in Scotland, 1982-97; b. 5.4.36, Glasgow; m., Anne Kerr Wotherspoon; 2 d by pr m. Educ. Victoria Drive Senior Secondary School, Glasgow; Glasgow University. Research Physicist, Barr and Stroud, Glasgow, 1961-63; Electronics Engineer, Scottish Research Reactor Centre, East Kilbride, 1963-66; West of Scotland Health Boards Department of Clinical Physics and Bio-Engineering: Senior Physicist, 1966-71, Principal Physicist, 1971-81, Top Grade Physicist, 1981-83; Chief Physicist, Institute of Neurological Sciences, Glasgow, 1966-83. Honorary Treasurer, Scottish Branch, Institute of Physics, 1972-77; Honorary Secretary, Hospital Physicists Association, 1976-78, and President, 1982-84; Deputy Editor, Physics in Medicine and Biology, 1980-82; President, Institute of Physical Sciences in Medicine, 1982-84; Member, Scottish Health Service National Scientific Services Advisory Committee, since 1989. Address: (b.) Glasgow Royal Infirmary, Glasgow G4; T.-0141-211 4934.

Professor Richard Jeremy, MA, LLM, FRSA. Solicitor (England and Wales); Legal Associate, Royal Town Planning Institute; Professor of Planning and Environmental Law, Aberdeen University, since 1989; Director, Aberdeen University Centre for Environmental Law and Policy; Consultant in Planning and Environmental Law, Paull and Williamsons, Solicitors, Aberdeen, since 1992; b. 29.3.44, Edinburgh; m., Yvonne Joan Elizabeth; 2 s. Educ. University of Kent; Aberdeen University; Law Society College of Law. Assistant Solicitor, LB of Redbridge, 1966; Senior Assistant Solicitor, LB of Hillingdon, 1969; Deputy Clerk, Westmorland County Council, 1972; Solicitor, Lake District Special Planning Board, 1975; Lecturer, then Senior Lecturer, Department of Land Economy, Aberdeen University, 1978-89. Address: (b.) Department of Law, Aberdeen University, Taylor Building, King's College, Old Aberdeen; T.-01228 272358.

Rowley, Alexander A.P., MA (Hons), MSc. Leader of Administration, Fife Council, since 1995; b. 30.11.63, Dunfermline; m., Susan Carden; 2 d. Educ. St. Columba's High School, Dunfermline; Newbattle Abbey College, Dalkeith; Edinburgh University. Address: (b.) Fife House, North Street, Glenrothes, Fife; T.-01592 414141.

Rowley, Professor David Ian, MB, ChB, BMedBiol, MD, FRCS. Professor of Orthopaedic and Trauma Surgery, Dundee University, since 1988; b. 4.7.51, Dewsbury; m., Ingrid Ginette; 1 s.; 1 d. Educ. Wheelwright Grammar School, Dewsbury; Aberdeen University; Sheffield University. Lecturer in Orthopaedic Surgery, Sheffield University, 1981; Senior Lecturer in Orthopaedic Surgery, Manchester University, and Senior Lecturer in Orthopaedic Mechanics, Salford University, 1985-88. Orthopaedic Editor, Journal of Royal College of Surgeons of Edinburgh; Regional Advisor in Surgery, NE Region, Royal College of Surgeons of Edinburgh; Examiner, Royal College of Surgeons, Edinburgh. Recreations: gardening; reading history. Address: (h.) Marclann Cottage, Kellie Castle, Arbroath; T.-01241 876466.

Rowlings, Professor Cherry, BA. Professor of Social Work, Stirling University, since 1991; Member, CCETSW Council and Scottish Committee, since 1992; b. 10.11.44, Bristol. Educ. Duncan House School, Bristol; York University; Oxford University. Social Worker, London Borough of Croydon; Team Leader, London Borough of Lewisham; Research Officer, Oxford University; Senior Research Fellow, Keele University; Lecturer/Senior Lecturer, Bristol University. Publications: on social work and services for older people and on social work education in Europe. Address: (b.) Department of Applied Social Science, Stirling University, Stirling FK9 4LA; T.-01786 467710.

Roxburghe, 10th Duke of (Guy David Innes-Ker), b. 18.11.54; m., 1, Lady Jane Meriel Grosvenor (m. diss.); 2 s.; 1 d.; 2, Virginia Mary Wynn-Williams; 1 s.; 1 d. Educ. Eton; Sandhurst; Magdalene College, Cambridge. Address: (h.) Floors Castle, Kelso.

Roy, Frank. MP (Labour), Motherwell and Wishaw, since 1997; b. 1958.

Roy, Kenneth. Founder Publisher: Who's Who in Scotland, since 1985, The Scottish Review, since 1994; b. 26.3.45, Falkirk; m., Margaret H. Campbell; 2 s. Educ. Denny High School. Local journalism, 1962-1965; Glasgow Herald, 1965-67; public relations, 1967-69; Founder Editor, Scottish Theatre magazine, 1969-72; news and current affairs anchorman, BBC Scotland, 1972-80; Founder Managing Director, West Sound, 1980-82; Founder Editor, The Journalist's Handbook, 1985-93; Deputy Chairman, European Editions plc, since 1996; former weekly Columnist: Scotland on Sunday, The Herald, The Observer; former daily Columnist, The Scotsman. Critic of the Year,

Scottish Press Awards, 1990, 1993; Columnist of the Year, UK Press Gazette Awards, 1994. Publications: Travels in a Small Country, 1987; Conversations in a Small Country, 1989; The Closing Headlines, 1993; Scenes from a Small Country, 1994. Address: (b.) Carrick Media, 2/1 Galt House, 31 Bank Street, Irvine KA12 0LL; T.-01294 311322.

Roy, Lindsay Allan, BSc. Rector, Inverkeithing High School, since 1989; Chairman, Higher Still Group Awards Steering Committee, since 1996; Member, Board of Management, Lauder College; b. 19.1.49, Perth; m., Irene Elizabeth Patterson; 2 s.; 1 d. Educ. Perth Academy; Edinburgh University. Assistant Rector, Kirkcaldy High School, 1983-86; Depute Rector, Glenwood High School, Glenrothes, 1986-89; Chairman, Modern Studies Association, 1976-79; Chairman, Modern Studies Panel, Scottish Examination Board, 1980-83; Member, Consultative Committee on the Curriculum Central Committee for Social Subjects, 1978-85. Recreation: angling. Address: (b.) Inverkeithing High School, Hillend Road, Inverkeithing, Fife; T.-01383 313400.

Roy, William Gordon Begg, CA. Company Secretary, Grampian Holdings plc, since 1976; b. 31.1.43, Irvine; m., Doris Doughty; 1 s.; 1 d. Educ. Irvine Royal Academy; Glasgow University. Trainee Accountant, Hourston Macfarlane & Co., CA, 1961-67; qualified as CA, 1967, and joined McClelland Moores & Co., 1967-69; joined Grampian Holdings as Assistant Group Accountant, 1969; Group Accountant, 1973-76. Recreations: golf; most other sports; reading; music; Indian food. Address: (b.) Grampian Holdings plc, Stag House, Castlebank Street, Glasgow G11 6DY; T.-0141-357 2000.

Royan, Professor Bruce, BA (Hons), FLA, MBA, MIInfSc, FIMgt. Chief Executive, Scottish Cultural Resources Access Network, since 1996; Principal Consultant, Infologistix Ltd., since 1988; Visiting Professor of Publishing and Communications, Napier University, since 1997; b. 22.1.47, Luton; m., Ann Elizabeth Wilkins; 1 s.; 1 d. Educ. Dunstable Grammar School; North West Polytechnic; Glasgow University. Systems Development Manager, British Library, 1975-77; Head of Systems, National Library of Scotland, 1977-85; Director, Singapore Integrated Library Automation Service, 1985-88; Director of Information Services and University Librarian, Stirling University, 1989-96. Secretary, Working Party on Access to the National Database, 1980-83; Member, Council, Library Association of Singapore, 1987-88; Convenor, Higher Education IT Directors in Scotland, 1991-93; Executive Chairman, Bath Information and Data Services, 1991-96; Councillor, The Library Association, since 1994; Chair, National Datasets Steering Group, 1994-96; Board Member, Croydon Libraries Internet Project, 1995-96; Chair, Scottish Collaborative On Demand Publishing Enterprise, since 1996. Recreations: choral singing; antique maps; travel. Address: (b.) SCRAN, Abden House, 1 Marchhall Crescent, Edinburgh EH16 5HW.

Royle, Trevor Bridge, MA, FRSE. Author and Journalist; Associate Editor, Scotland on Sunday; b. 26.1.45, Mysore, India; m., Dr. Hannah Mary Rathbone; 3 s. Educ. Madras College, St. Andrews; Aberdeen University. Editor, William Blackwood & Sons Ltd.; Literature Director, Scottish Arts Council, 1971-79; Council Member, Scottish National Dictionary Association; Scottish Arts Council Book Award, 1983. Publications: We'll Support You Evermore: the Impertinent Saga of Scottish Fitba' (Co-Editor), 1976; Jock Tamson's Bairns (Editor), 1977; Precipitous City: The Story of Literary Edinburgh, 1980; A Diary of Edinburgh, 1981; Edinburgh, 1982; Death Before Dishonour: The True Story of Fighting Mac, 1982; The Macmillan Companion to Scottish Literature, 1983; James and Jim: The Biography of James Kennaway, 1983; The Kitchener Enigma, 1985; The Best Years of their Lives:

The Post-War National Service Experience, 1986; War Report: The War Correspondents' View of Battle from the Crimea to the Falklands, 1987; The Last Days of the Raj, 1989; A Dictionary of Military Quotations, 1989; Anatomy of a Regiment, 1990; In Flanders Fields: poetry and prose of the First World War, 1990; Glubb Pasha, 1992; Mainstream Companion to Scottish Literature, 1993; Orde Wingate: Irregular Soldier, 1995; Winds of Change, 1996; radio plays: Magnificat, 1984; Old Alliances, 1985; Foreigners, 1987; Huntingtower, 1988; A Man Flourishing, 1988; The Pavilion on the Links, 1991; The Suicide Club, 1992; Tunes of Glory, 1995; stage play: Buchan of Tweedsmuir, 1991. Recreations: rugby football; hill-walking; restoring Craigiemeg. Address: (h.) 6 James Street, Edinburgh EH15 2DS; T.-0131-669 2116.

Ruckley, Professor Charles Vaughan, MB, ChM, FRCSEdin, FRCPEdin. Consultant Surgeon, Royal Infirmary, Edinburgh, since 1971; Professor of Vascular Surgery, Edinburgh University, since 1992; President, Vascular Surgical Society, Great Britain and Ireland, 1993-94; b. 14.5.34, Wallasey; m., Valerie Anne Brooks; 1 s.; 1 d. Educ. Wallasey Grammar School; Edinburgh University. Research Fellow, University of Colorado, 1967-68. Secretary/Treasurer, Vascular Surgical Society of Great Britain and Ireland; Member, Council, Association of Surgeons of Great Britain and Ireland. Recreations: angling; music; skiing. Address: (b.) Vascular Surgery Unit, Royal Infirmary, Edinburgh; T.-0131-229 2477.

Rugg, Professor Michael Derek, BSc, PhD. Professor of Psychology and Wellcome Research Fellow, School of Psychology, St. Andrews University, since 1994; b. 23.9.54, Ely; m., Elizabeth Louise. Educ. Leicester University. Lecturer, Department of Psychology, St. Andrews University, 1979-88, Reader, 1988-92, Professor and Head of School, 1992-94. Committee Member, Experimental Psychology Society; Member, Medical Research Council Advisory Board; Henri Hecaen Award for contributions to neuropsychology, 1989. Publications: approx. 100 scientific articles; three edited books. Fellow, Royal Society of Edinburgh, 1996. Recreations: rock climbing; mountaineering; skiing. Address: (b.) School of Psychology, St. Andrews University, St. Andrews KY16 9JU; T.-01334 462069.

Runciman, William Chisholm, LLB. Secretary, Carnegie Dunfermline and Hero Fund Trusts; b. 15.11.41, Greenock; m., Eileen; 2 s. Educ. Greenock Academy; Edinburgh University. Police Officer in Edinburgh and Lothian & Borders, retiring in 1987 as Chief Superintendent; former Director, National Playing Fields Association — Scotland. Recreations: mountaineering; fishing; photography. Address: (h.) 11 East Harbour Road, Charlestown, Fife KY11 3EA.

Rundell, David Richard, BSc, MSc, CStat. Director of Computing Services, Heriot-Watt University, since 1990; b. 5.9.48, Plymouth; 3 d. Educ. Harwich County High, Harwich, Essex; St. Andrews University; Heriot-Watt University. Statistician, Medical School, Edinburgh University, 1970-76; Applications Team, Regional Computing Centre, University of Bath, 1976-79; User Services Manager, Computer Centre, Heriot-Watt University, 1979-90. Hon. Secretary, Universities and Colleges Information Systems Association (UCISA). Address: (b.) Computer Centre, Heriot-Watt University, Riccarton, Edinburgh EH14 4AS; T.-0131-449 5111.

Runnalls, Professor Graham Arthur, BA, MA, DipGenLing, DLitt. Professor of French, Edinburgh University; b. 21.11.37, Exmouth; m., Anne K.; 2 d. Educ. Exmouth Grammar School; Exeter University. Assistant Lecturer in French, Exeter University, 1962-63; Lecturer in French, North London Polytechnic, 1963-66; joined Edinburgh University as Lecturer, 1966. Honorary

President, International Society for the Study of Medieval Theatre. Recreations: opera; sport, especially tennis and running. Address: (h.) 85A Colinton Road, Edinburgh EH10 5DF; T.-0131-337 1737.

Rush, Christopher, MA (Hons). Writer; Teacher, George Watson's College, Edinburgh, since 1972; b. 23.11.44, St. Monans; m., Patricia Irene Boyd (deceased); 1 s.; 1 d. Educ. Waid Academy; Aberdeen University. Has won two Scottish Arts Council bursaries, two SAC book awards, twice been short-listed for Scottish Book of the Year Award; shortlisted for McVitie Scottish Writer of the Year, 1988; Screenwriter, Venus Peter (based on own book). Publications include: Peace Comes Dropping Slow; A Resurrection of a Kind; A Twelvemonth and A Day; Two Christmas Stories; Into the Ebb; With Sharp Compassion; Venus Peter Saves the Whale; Last Lesson of the Afternoon. Recreations: music; reading; cross-country running; sea-watching. Address: (h.) 2 Peel Terrace, Edinburgh EH9 2AY; T.-0131-667 1248.

Russell, (Alastair) Muir, BSc. Secretary and Head of Department, Scottish Office Agriculture, Environment and Fisheries Department, since 1995; b. 9.1.49; m., Eileen Alison Mackay. Educ. High School of Glasgow; Glasgow University. Joined Scottish Office, 1970; seconded as Secretary to Scottish Development Agency, 1975-76; Assistant Secretary, 1981; Principal Private Secretary to Secretary of State for Scotland, 1981-83; Under Secretary, 1990; seconded to Cabinet Office, 1990-92; Under Secretary (Housing), Scottish Office Environment Department, 1992-95; Deputy Secretary, Secretary, Scottish Office Agriculture and Fisheries Department, February-October, 1995. Non-Executive Director, Stagecoach Holdings, 1992-95. Recreations: music; food; wine. Address: (b.) Pentland House, 47 Robb's Loan, Edinburgh EH14 1TY; T.-0131-244 6021.

Russell, Sheriff Albert Muir Galloway, CBE, QC, BA (Oxon), LLB. Sheriff, Grampian, Highland and Islands, at Aberdeen, 1971-91; b. 26.10.25, Edinburgh; m., Margaret Winifred Millar; 2 s.; 2 d. Educ. Edinburgh Academy; Wellington College; Brasenose College, Oxford; Edinburgh University. Lt., Scots Guards, 1944-47; Member, Faculty of Advocates, 1951; Standing Junior Counsel to Board of Trade, Department of Agriculture and Forestry Commission; QC (Scot), 1965; Vice Chairman, Board of Management, Southern Group of Hospitals, Edinburgh, 1966-70; Governor, Moray House College of Education, 1965-70. Recreations: golf; music. Address: (h.) Tulloch House, 1 Aultbea, Ross-shire IV22 2JB.

Russell, Sheriff Dan Chapman, MA, LLB. Sheriff of South Strathclyde, Dumfries and Galloway at Hamilton, since 1992; b. 25.12.39. Qualified as Solicitor, 1963; in private practice, 1963-92.

Russell, Professor Elizabeth Mary, MD, DipSocMed, DObstRCOG, FFCM, FRCPGlas, FRCPEdin, FRSE. Professor of Social Medicine, Aberdeen University; Hon. Consultant in Public Health Medicine, since 1972; b. 27.1.36, Preston. Educ. Marr College, Troon; Glasgow University. General practice until 1964; medical management and social medicine, 1964-72; academic public health and health services research, since 1972. Recreations: skiing; gardening; music. Address: (b.) Department of Public Health, Medical School, Foresterhill, Aberdeen AB25 2ZD; T.-01224 681818, Ext. 53861.

Russell, Frank. Councillor, City of Edinburgh Council, since 1996; Convener of Personnel, since 1996; b. 23.2.48, Edinburgh; m., Janice Russell; 1 s.; 1 d. Educ. Forrester High School, Edinburgh. Elected, Edinburgh District Council, 1988; Chair of Personnel, 1992-96; Chair, Labour Group, 1992; Depute Leader of Council, 1993-96. Member, Board, Edinburgh International Jazz Festival. Recreations:

reading; watching Hearts F.C. Address: (b.) City Chambers, High Street, Edinburgh; T.-0131-529 3289.

Russell, George Stuart, OBE, BL, CA, WS. Former Senior Partner, Strathern and Blair WS, now Anderson Strathern, WS; b. 21.1.14, Edinburgh; m., Nicholas Mary Gillespie; 1 s.; 3 d. Educ. Edinburgh Academy; Belhaven Hill; Harrow; Edinburgh University. CA, 1937; served Second World War, 1939-45 (Lt. Col.); OBE (Mil); Belgian Ordre de la Couronne; Polish Golden Cross of Merit with Swords; pursued a legal career; Fiscal, WS Society, 1973-79; Solicitor to the National Trust for Scotland, 1951-82, now Councillor Emeritus, Treasurer, Iona Community, 1947-65; President, Edinburgh Abbeyfield Society, 1978-92, now Vice-President; Vice President, UK, Abbeyfield Society, 1975-83; Trustee, New Club; Trustee, Scottish Churches Architectural Heritage Trust, 1982-95; Member, Queen's Bodyguard for Scotland (Royal Company of Archers). Recreations: fishing; walking; erecting plaques and view indicators. Address: 59 Braid Road, Edinburgh EH10 6AR; T.-0131-447 6009.

Russell, Ian Simon Macgregor, BComHons. Finance Director, Scottish Power PLC, since 1994; b. 16.1.53, Edinburgh; m., Fiona; 1 s.; 1 d. Educ. George Heriot's School; Edinburgh University. Recreations: golf; rugby. Address: (b.) 1 Atlantic Quay, Glasgow G2 8SP; T.-0141-636 4511.

Russell, Rev. John, MA. Minister, Tillicoultry Parish Church, since 1978; b. 29.5.33, Glasgow; m., Sheila Spence; 2 s. Educ. Cathedral School, Bombay; High School of Glasgow; Glasgow University. Licensed by Glasgow Presbytery, 1957; ordained by United Church of Canada, 1959; Assistant Minister: Trinity United Church, Kitchener, Ontario, 1958-60, South Dalziel Church, Motherwell, 1960-62; Minister: Scots Church, Rotterdam, 1963-72, Southend Parish Church, Kintyre, 1972-78; Member of various General Assembly Committees, since 1972; Convener, General Assembly's Committee on Unions and Readjustments, 1987-90; Convener, Parish Reappraisal Committee, 1990-94; Vice Convener, Board of National Mission, 1994-95; Convener, Board of National Mission, 1995-96; Moderator, Presbytery of Stirling, 1993-94. Recreations: travel; reading. Address: The Manse, Dollar Road, Tillicoultry, Clackmannanshire FK13 6PD; T.-01259 750340.

Russell, John Graham, FCIT. Chairman and Managing Director, John G. Russell (Transport) Ltd., since 1969; Chairman, Fife Warehousing Ltd., since 1988; Director: Combined Transport Ltd., since 1991, Freight Transport Association, since 1994, Alloa Warehousing, since 1988; Chairman: SCOTIA ATT Limited, since 1995, The Scottish Business Crime Centre, since 1996; b. Edinburgh; m., Isobel Margaret Hogg; 2 s.; 2 d. Educ. Merchiston Castle School, Edinburgh. Address: (b.) Gartcosh, Glasgow G69 8ES; T.-01236 873511.

Russell, Professor Michael John, EurIng, PGD, FIMM. Dixon Professor of Applied Geology, Glasgow University, since 1989; b. 12.3.39, Sutton, Surrey. Educ. London University; Durham University. Professor and Head, Department of Applied Geology, Strathclyde University, 1984-89. Recreation: science. Address: (b.) Department of Geology and Applied Geology, Glasgow University, Glasgow; T.-0141-330 6863.

Russell, Michael William, MA. Chief Executive, Scottish National Party; b. 9.8.53; m., Cathleen Macaskill; 1 s. Educ. Marr College, Troon; Edinburgh University. Creative Producer, Church of Scotland, 1974-77; Director, Cinema Sgire, Western Isles, 1977-81; Founder and first Director, Celtic Film and Television Festival, 1980; Secretary General, Association for Film and Television in the Celtic Countries, 1981-83; Chief Executive, Network Scotland

Ltd., 1983-91; Director, Eala Bhan Ltd., since 1991. Parliamentary candidate (SNP), Clydesdale, 1987; Executive Vice Convenor in charge of Publicity, SNP, 1987-91; Chairman, Save a Life in Scotland Campaign, 1986-88; Trustee, Celtic Film and TV Association, 1990-95; Board Director, Glasgow Film Theatre, 1992-96. Publication: A Poem of Remote Lives, 1997. Recreations: gardening; cookery. Address: (h.) Feorlean, Glendaruel, Argyll PA22 3AH; T.-01369 820139.

Russell, Peter MacLeod, MA. Director, North and East, Scottish Prison Service; b. 22.1.51, Edinburgh; m., Patricia Anne Kelly; 4 s.; 1 d. Educ. Royal High School, Edinburgh; Edinburgh University. Entered Scottish Office, 1973; Private Secretary to Parliamentary Under Secretary of State, 1976-78; Principal, 1978-86: Royal Commission on Legal Services in Scotland, 1978-80, SDD, 1980-84, Industry Department for Scotland, 1985-86; appointed Assistant Secretary, Scottish Office Home and Health Department, 1986. Address: (b.) Calton House, 5 Redheughs Rigg, Edinburgh EH12 9HW; T.-0131-244 8741.

Russell, Sir Robert Mark, MA (Oxon), KCMG. Chairman, Centre for Commonwealth, United Nations and International Affairs, 1990-95; Chairman, Margaret Blackwood Housing Association, since 1990; Chairman, C-Mist Ltd. (Centre for Maritime and Industrial Safety Technology), since 1993; b. 3.9.29, India; m., Virginia Mary Rogers; 2 s.; 2 d. Educ. Trinity College, Glenalmond; Exeter College, Oxford University. Royal Artillery, 1952-54; H.M. Diplomatic Service, 1954-89; Assistant Under Secretary of State, F.C.O., 1978-82; H.M. Ambassador to Turkey, 1983-86; Deputy Under Secretary of State, F.C.O., 1986-89. Recreations: music; travel. Address: (h.) 20 Meadow Place, Edinburgh EH9 1JR.

Russell, Robin Irvine, MD, PhD, FRCPEdin, FRCPGlas, FACN, FACP. Consultant in Charge, Department of Gastroenterology, Royal Infirmary, Glasgow, since 1970; Consultant Physician and Gastroenterologist, Royal Infirmary, Glasgow, and Glasgow University, since 1970; b. 21.12.36, Wishaw; m., Ann Tindal Wallace; 1 s.; 1 d. Educ. Glasgow University. Member, medical and scientific staff: Medical Research Council Gastroenterology Unit, London, National Institutes of Health, USA. Chairman, British Digestive Diseases Foundation (Scotland); Member: Association of Physicians, British Society of Gastroenterology, American Gastroenterological Association. Publications: Elemental Diets; Investigative Tests and Techniques in Gastroenterology; Nutrition in Gastro-Intestinal Disease; papers on mechanisms of cellular damage and protection in the gastro-intestinal tract, physiology of intestinal absorption, NSAID and Helicobacter damage in gastrointestinal tract, coeliac disease, Crohn's disease, clinical and experimental nutrition. Recreations: golf; travel; literature; music. Address: (h.) 28 Ralston Road, Bearsden, Glasgow G61 3BA; T.-0141-942 6613.

Russell, Shendl, DCE. Chairman, Scottish Official Board of Highland Dancing, since 1986; Ilead Teacher; b. 29.3.56, Ayr; m., Robert D. Harvey. Educ. Ayr Academy; Craigie College. Scottish Official Board of Highland Dancing: Delegate, South Africa, Australia; former Scottish champion. Recreations: dancing; football; rugby. Address: (h.) 3 Greenside Avenue, Prestwick KA9 2HB; T.-01292 478577.

Russell, Sheriff Terence Francis, BL. Sheriff, North Strathclyde, at Kilmarnock, since 1983; b. 12.4.31, Glasgow; m., Mary Ann Kennedy; 2 d. Educ. St. Mungo's Academy, Glasgow; Glasgow University. Solicitor: Glasgow, 1955-58, Bombay High Court, 1958-63, Glasgow, 1963-81; Sheriff, North Strathclyde, at Oban and Campbeltown and Grampian, Highland and Islands, at Fort William, 1981-83. Recreations: gardening; painting.

Russell, Thomas, BSc (Hons), MB, ChB, FRCS Edin, FRCS Glas. Consultant Neurosurgeon, since 1987; Senior Lecturer in Neurosurgery, Edinburgh University, since 1989; b. 8.3.50, Lanark; m., Donna; 1 d. Educ. Wishaw High School; Glasgow University. MRC Fellow in Neurosurgery, Institute of Neurological Sciences, Glasgow; Senior Registrar, Neurosurgery, Bristol; Exchange Neurosurgical Resident, Memphis; Consultant Neurosurgeon, Western General Hospital, Edinburgh. Recreation: medical ethics/philosophy. Address: (h.) 15 White Dales, Edinburgh EH10 7JQ; T.-0131-445 5920.

Russell-Johnston, Lord (David Russell Russell-Johnston), MA (Hons). MP (Liberal Democrat), Inverness, Nairn and Lochaber (formerly Inverness), 1964-97; b. 28.7.32, Edinburgh; m., Joan Graham Menzies; 3 s. Educ. Carbost Public School; Portree High School; Edinburgh University; Moray House College of Education. National Service: commissioned into Intelligence Corps and 2nd i/c British Intelligence Unit, Berlin, 1958-59; History Teacher, Liberton Secondary School, Edinburgh, 1961-63; Research Assistant, Scottish Liberal Party, 1963-64; Joint Parliamentary Adviser, Educational Institute of Scotland, 1964-70; Member, Royal Commission on Local Government in Scotland, 1966-69; Parliamentary Spokesman for Scottish National Federation for the Welfare of the Blind, since 1967; Parliamentary Representative, Royal National Institute for the Blind, 1977-97; Member, Select Committee on Scottish Affairs, 1969; Parliamentary Adviser, Scottish Police Federation, 1971-75; Scottish Liberal Party: elected to Executive, 1961, and Organisation Committee, 1962, Vice Chairman, 1965, Chairman, 1970-74, Leader, 1974-88, President, 1988-94; Liberal Party Spokesman on Education, 1964-66, on Foreign Affairs, 1970-75 and 1979-85, on Scotland, 1970-73, 1975-83, 1985-88, on Devolution, 1975, on Defence, 1983-88; Member, House of Commons Committee on Privileges, 1988-92; Liberal Democrat Parliamentary Spokesman, Foreign and Commonwealth Affairs, 1988-89, European Affairs, 1988-94, East/West Relations, 1989-94, Central and Eastern Europe, 1994-97; Leader, Council of Europe Liberal Democrat and Reform Group, since 1994; President, Council of Europe Sub Committee on Youth and Sport, 1992-94; Chairman, Council of Europe Committee on Culture and Education; Vice President, Liberal International, since 1994; Member, European Parliament, 1973-75 and 1976-79; Vice President, European Liberal Group and Group Spokesman on Regional Policy, 1973-75; Vice President of the Parliament's Political Committee, 1976-79; Member, Assemblies of Western European Union and Council of Europe, 1984-85, and since 1987; President, Scottish Liberal Democrats, 1988-94; Deputy Leader, Parliamentary Party, 1988-92; Vice President, ELDR, 1990-92. Created Knight Bachelor, 1985. Recreations: reading; photography; shinty (Vice Chief, Camanachd Association, 1987-90). Address: House of Lords, London, SW1A OPW; T.-0171-219 5353.

Rutherford, Alan Gray, OBE, BSc, PhD, CChem, CEng, FRSC, CEng, FInstE, FRSA. Scotch Whisky Production Director, United Distillers plc, since 1988; b. 9.10.42, Cramlington; m., Roslyn Anne Moore; 1 s.; 1 d. Educ. Gosforth Grammar School, Newcastle upon Tyne; Sheffield University; Newcastle upon Tyne University. Cookson Group of companies, three years; Scottish & Newcastle Breweries, 14 years, latterly as Group Personnel Director; joined Distillers Company Ltd. as Head of Research and Development, 1984. Executive Member, Scottish Council Development & Industry; Council Member, Scotch Whisky Association; President, Malt Distillers' Association of Scotland, 1991-94; Hon. Col., 4 Para (V); Member, Parachute Regimental Council; President, Ayrshire Branch, Parachute Regimental Association; Co-founder and Vice Chairman, The Airborne Initiative (Scotland) Ltd.; Member, Board of Management, International Centre for Brewing and Distilling. Recreations: TA; hill-walking;

rugby football. Address: (b.) United Distillers plc, 33 Ellersly Road, Edinburgh EH12 6JW; T.-0131-337 7373.

Rutherford, Rev. Brian Craig, BSc, BD. Minister, Mastrick Parish, Aberdeen, since 1990; b. 8.6.47, Glasgow; m., Jean Walker; 2 s. Educ. King's Park Secondary School, Glasgow; Glasgow University; Edinburgh University. Assistant Minister, Carrick Knowe Parish, Edinburgh, 1976-77; Minister, Strathbrock Parish, West Lothian, 1977-83; Minister, Greyfriars/St. Ann's Church, Trinidad, 1983-87; General Treasurer, Blantyre Synod, Church of Central Africa Presbyterian, Blantyre, Malawi, 1988-89. Former Member: Edinburgh Corporation, Edinburgh District Council (JP, 1977-80), West Lothian District Council, Aberdeen District Council, 1992-96. Address: (h.) 13 Beechgrove Avenue, Aberdeen AB15 5EZ; T.-01224 638011.

Rutherford, Colin, BA, CA. Chief Executive, RMD Group plc, since 1997; Managing Partner, RMD CAs, since 1986; b. 17.2.59, Edinburgh; m., Karen Elizabeth; 1 s.; 1 d. Educ. Royal High School; Heriot-Watt University. Touche Ross & Co., CAs, Edinburgh and London (Audit and Corporate Finance), 1981-85; Waverley Asset Management, Edinburgh (Unit and Investment Trust), 1985-86; founded Rutherford Manson Dowds (RMD), 1986. Recreations: fishing; shooting; travel; wines; food. Address: (b.) 25 Melville Street, Edinburgh EH3 7PE; T.-0131-225 4727.

Rutherford, William Hay, MA, LLB. Advocate in Aberdeen, since 1949; Consultant, Raeburn Christie & Co. (Partner, 1978-87); Honorary Sheriff, Grampian, Highland and Islands, since 1974; b. 9.11.16, Forres; m., Dr. Jean Aitken Steel Wilson; 1 s.; 2 d. Educ. Forres Academy; Aberdeen University. Law Apprentice, James & George Collie, Advocates, Aberdeen, 1936-39; 51st Highland Division, Royal Signals, 1939-46 (taken prisoner, St. Valery, France, 1940; held prisoner, Stalag VIIIB, Upper Silesia, 1940-45); Legal Assistant, John Angus, Advocate, Aberdeen, 1946-61; Partner, Christie, Buthlay & Rutherford, Advocates, Aberdeen, 1962-78; President, Society of Advocates, Aberdeen, 1985-86; Session Clerk, Kirk of St. Nicholas (City Kirk of Aberdeen), 1954-88; President, Royal Northern Agricultural Society, 1980; holder of British Horse Society 1994 Horse Trials Award for outstanding service to the sport. Recreations: country walking and wildlife study. Address: 38 Gladstone Place, Queen's Cross, Aberdeen AB10 6XA.

Ruthven, Ian Scott, MB, ChB, FRCPEdin, FRCPGlas, DObstRCOG. Consultant Paediatrician, Ayrshire and Arran Health Board, since 1969; b. 9.3.37, Glasgow; m., Louisa Mary Jolly; 1 s.; 2 d. Educ. High School of Glasgow; Glasgow University. Junior hospital appointments, various Glasgow hospitals and in New Jersey, USA; Clinical Director, Hospital Paediatric Services in Ayrshire; Chairman, Ayrshire and Arran Division, BMA, 1987-88; currently Ayrshire Representative, Scottish Council, BMA; National Panellist for paediatric appointments in Scotland. Recreations: golf; angling; hill-walking. Address: (h.) Westholme, 10 Victoria Drive, Troon KA10 6EN; T.-01292 313006.

Ryall, Michael Leslie (Mike), BSc, CEng, FIMechE, MInstPet, FRSA. Engineering Consultant (independent and retained by Weir Group), since 1991; Chairman, Scottish Design, since 1994; b. 25.3.31, Carshalton; m., Patricia; 2 s. Educ. George Watson's College; Watford Grammar School; Glasgow University. Research Director, Weir Pumps, 1971-75; Technical Director, Weir Pumps, 1975-91. National runner-up, Prince of Wales Award for Innovation and Production, 1984. Recreations: skiing; windsurfing; hill-walking; music; singing; gardening. Address: 18 Drumbeg Loan, Killearn, Glasgow G63 9LG; T.-01360 550713.

Ryan, Jack, DipComEd. Chief Executive, Crossroads (Scotland), since 1997; b. 9.6.61, Hamilton; m., Janine Barbour; 1 s. Educ. Hamilton Grammar School; Moray House, Edinburgh. Draughtsman, 1978-81; professional musician, 1981-83; Community Musician, Strathclyde Regional Council, 1983-88; Senior Development Officer, Govan Initiative Ltd., 1990-91; Project Manager, CAVOC Motherwell, 1991-92; Director, Govan Community Organisations Council, 1992-96; Lottery Officer, South Lanarkshire Council, 1997. Member, Glasgow YMCA Youth and Community Committee. Recreations: musician; computer programming; running/swimming. Address: (b.) 24 George Square, Glasgow; T.-0141-226 3793.

Rycroft, Philip John, BA, DPhil. Assistant Secretary, Scottish Office, since 1997 (Head of Agricultural Policy, Marketing and IT Support Divisions, Agriculture, Environment and Fisheries Department); b. 22.5.61, Skipton; m., Kate Richards; 2 s. Educ. Leys School, Cambridge; Wadham College, Oxford. Scottish Office Agriculture Department, Research Division, 1989-90; Private Secretary to Scottish Office Agriculture and Fisheries Minister, 1990-91; Principal, Scottish Office Industry Department, European Central Support Unit, 1992-94; Principal, Scottish Office Fisheries Group, Fisheries Policy Branch, 1994; Cabinet of Sir Leon Brittan, European Commission, 1995-97. Recreations: hill-walking; woodwork. Address: (b.) Pentland House, 47 Robb's Loan, Edinburgh EH14 1TY; T.-0131-244 6363.

S

Sadler, Professor Peter John, MA, DPhil, CChem, FRSC. Crum Brown Professor of Chemistry, Edinburgh University, since 1996; UK Representative, EC Technical Committee for Cost Chemistry, since 1995; Chairman, EC Cost Action on Chemistry of Metals in Medicine, since 1996; Member, Editorial Boards, several international research journals; b. 6.4.46, Norwich; m., Tessa Elizabeth Halstead; 2 s.; 1 d. Educ. City of Norwich School; Magdalen College, Oxford. Medical Research Council Research Fellow, Cambridge University, 1971-72, National Institute for Medical Research, Mill Hill, 1972-73; Lecturer, Reader in Biological Chemistry and Professor of Chemistry, Birkbeck College, London University, 1973-96. Royal Society of Chemistry Award, 1993. Publications: 230 research publications. Recreations: gardening; music; sport. Address: (b.) Department of Chemistry, Edinburgh University, West Mains Road, Edinburgh EH9 3JJ; T.-0131-650 4729.

Salmon, Professor Trevor C., MA (Hons), MLH, PhD, FRSA. Chair of International Relations and Jean Monnet Chair of European Integration, Aberdeen University, since 1996; Professor, College of Europe, since 1995; b. 7.9.48, Cambridge; m., June Veronica Miller; 1 d. Educ. Soham Grammar School; Aberdeen University; St. Andrews University. Lecturer, National Institute for Higher Education, Limerick, 1973-78; Lecturer in International Relations, then Senior Lecturer, St. Andrews University, 1978-90; Jean Monnet Professor of European Integration, St. Andrews University, 1990-95. Elder, Church of Scotland. Publications: Building European Union (Co-author); Understanding the New European Community (Co-author). Address: (b.) Department of Politics and International Relations, Edward Wright Building, Aberdeen University, Aberdeen AB24 3QY; T.-01224 272707.

Salmond, Alexander Elliot Anderson, MA (Hons). Economist; MP (SNP), Banff and Buchan, since 1987; National Convener, Scottish National Party, since 1990; b. 31.12.54, Linlithgow; m., Moira McGlashan. Educ. Linlithgow Academy; St. Andrews University. Vice-President; Federation of Student Nationalists, 1974-77, St. Andrews University SRC, 1977-78; Founder Member, SNP 79 Group, 1979; Assistant Agricultural and Fisheries Economist, DAFS, 1978-80; Economist, Royal Bank of Scotland, 1980-87. Hon. Vice-President, Scottish Centre for Economic and Social Research; former Member, Select Committee on Energy; Parliamentary Spokesman on constitution, fishing. Recreations: golf; reading; football. Address: (b.) 17 Maiden Street, Peterhead, AB42 1EE; T.-01779 470444.

Salmond, Rev. James Sommerville, BA, BD, MTh, ThD. Minister, Holytown Parish Church, since 1979; b. 13.1.51, Broxburn; m., Catherine F. Wildy; 1 s.; 4 d. Educ. West Calder High School; Whitburn Academy; Leeds University; Edinburgh University; Central School of Religion. Serves on the Committees of Scottish Reformation Society, National Church Association, etc. Publications: Evangelicals within the Kirk 1690-1843; Moody Blues; Any Dream Will Do. Recreations: field sports; riding. Address: The Manse, Holytown, Motherwell; T.-Holytown 832622.

Salter, Professor Stephen Hugh, MA (Cantab), FRSE. Professor of Engineering Design, Edinburgh University, since 1986; b. 7.12.38, Johannesburg; m., Professor Margaret Donaldson. Educ. Framlingham College; Sidney Sussex College, Cambridge. Apprentice aircraft fitter and tool-maker; Research Assistant, Department of Psychology, Cambridge University; Research Fellow, then Lecturer,

Department of Artificial Intelligence, then Reader in Mechanical Engineering, Edinburgh University. Recreations: photography; inventing and designing instruments and tools. Address: (b.) Department of Mechanical Engineering, Mayfield Road, Edinburgh University, Edinburgh EH9 3JL; T.-0131-650 5703.

Saltoun, Lady (Flora Marjory). Peer of the Realm, since 1979; Chief of the Name of Fraser, since 1979; b. 18.10.30, Edinburgh; 3 d. Educ. St. Mary's School, Wantage. Address: House of Lords, London, SW1A 0PW.

Salvesen, Robin Somervell, DL, FBIM, Chevalier de Dannebrog 1st Class. Director, Christian Salvesen plc; Chairman, Association for the Protection of Rural Scotland; Chairman, Scottish Council, King George's Fund for Sailors; b. 4.5.35, Edinburgh; m., Sari; 3 s.; 4 d. Educ. Fettes College; Oxford University. National Service commission, The Royal Scots, Queen's Own Nigeria Regiment; TA, 7/9 Bn., The Royal Scots, 8/9 Bn., The Royal Scots 52 Lowland Volunteers; retired Major; Director, shipping companies, A.F. Henry & Macgregor, Christian Salvesen plc; Lloyds Register of Shipping, 1974-87; Chamber of Shipping, 1974-88; British Shipowners Association, 1969-87; Chairman, Lights Advisory Committee, since 1987; Royal Danish Consul, 1972-87. Recreations: archery; shooting. Address: Eaglescairnie House, Haddington, EH41.

Samson, Brian George, DPE, DMS. Director of Sports Development, formerly Director of Operations, Scottish Sports Council, since 1994; b. 9.9.47, Cupar; m., Penny; 2 s.; 1 d. Educ. Bell Baxter High School, Cupar; Jordanhill College of Education; Napier University. Teacher of Physical Education, 1970-74; Principal Teacher of P.E., 1974-84; Development Officer, then Senior Development Officer, Scottish Sports Council, 1984-94. Recreations: rugby; jogging/keep fit; skiing; walking; cycling; music; theatre; ornithology. Address: (b.) South Gyle, Edinburgh EH12 9DQ; T.-0131-317 7200.

Samson, George Carmichael. Director of Administration, Law Society of Scotland, since 1986; b. 17.12.46, Dundee; m., Irene Josephine Ball; 1 d. Sidlaw Industries (Organisation and Methods), 1967-77; Divisional Systems Co-ordinator, Watson & Philip PLC, 1977-86. Law Society of Scotland: Secretary, Practice Management/Client Care Committee, Secretary, Working Party on Electronic Services, Secretary, Services Supra Committee; Member, Scottish Group Committee, Society for Computers and Law; Member, Centre for Law, Computers and Technology Advisory Council, University of Strathclyde Law School. Recreations: guitar; photography; golf; Mah Jong. Address: (b.) 26 Drumsheugh Gardens, Edinburgh EH3 7YR; T.-0131-226 7411.

Sandeman, Robert John, LLB, NP, WS, DL. Solicitor, since 1979; Deputy Lieutenant, Stirling and Falkirk, since 1986; Member, Southern Area Committee, Highland TA&VRA, since 1978; b. 8.1.29, India; m., Enid; 1 s.; 1 d. Educ. Trinity College, Glenalmond; RMA, Sandhurst; Glasgow University. Infantry Officer, 1948-76; Second-in-Command, 1st Bn., The Royal Scots (The Royal Regiment), 1965-67; staff appointments, 1967-76; retired from Regular Army as Major, 1976; law student, 1976-79; commanded Number One Company, Home Service Force (Black Watch), Territorial Army, 1982-85. Member, Queen's Bodyguard for Scotland (Royal Company of Archers), since 1967; former Director, Glasgow, Stirlingshire and Sons of the Rock Society; former Chairman, Stirling Members' Centre, National Trust for Scotland. Recreations: archery; walking; shooting. Address: (b.) Khyber House, Upper Glen Road, Bridge of Allan, FK9 4PX; T.-01786 832180.

Sanderson, Professor Jeffrey John, BSc, PhD. Professor of Theoretical Plasma Physics, St. Andrews University, since 1985 (Reader in Applied Mathematics, 1975-85); Proctor, since 1997; b. 25.4.37, Birmingham; m., Mirjana Adamovic; 1 s.; 1 d. Educ. George Dixon Grammar School, Birmingham; Birmingham University; Manchester University. Research Associate, Maryland University, 1961-64; Theoretical Physicist, English Electric Co., Whetstone, 1964-66; Lecturer, then Senior Lecturer in Applied Mathematics, St. Andrews University, 1966-75; Visiting Professor, Department of Physics, College of William and Mary, USA, 1976-77. Publications: Plasma Dynamics (Co-author), 1969; Laser Plasma Interactions (Joint Editor), 1979. Recreations: chess; Scottish country dancing; five-a-side football; cricket; hill-walking; choral singing. Address: (b.) College Gate, North Street, St. Andrews KY16 9AJ; T.: 01334 472547.

Sanderson, William. Farmer; Director, Royal Highland and Agricultural Society of Scotland; b. 9.3.38, Lanark; m., Netta; 4 d. Educ. Dalkeith High School. Past Chairman, South Midlothian and Lothians and Peeblesshire Young Farmers Clubs; Past Chairman, Dalkeith Agricultural Society; President, Royal Caledonian Curling Club, 1984-85; Past President, Oxenfoord and Edinburgh Curling Clubs; Scottish Curling Champion, 1971 and 1978 (2nd, World Championship, 1971). Recreations: curling; exhibiting livestock. Address: (h.) Blackshiels Farm, Blackshiels, Pathhead, Midlothian; T.-Humbie 833288.

Sanderson, Very Rev. William Roy, MA, DD. Minister, Church of Scotland; Extra Chaplain to The Queen in Scotland, since 1977 (Chaplain-in-Ordinary, 1965-77); b. 23.9.07, Leith; m., Muriel Easton; 3 s.; 2 d. Educ. Fettes College; Oriel College, Oxford; New College, Edinburgh. Ordained, 1933; Assistant Minister, St. Giles' Cathedral, 1932-34; Minister: St. Andrew's, Lochgelly, 1935-39, The Barony of Glasgow, 1939-63, Stenton with Whittingehame, 1963-73; Moderator, Glasgow Presbytery, 1958 and Haddington and Dunbar Presbytery, 1972-74; Moderator, General Assembly, 1967; Hon. DD (Glasgow), 1959; Chairman, Scottish Religious Advisory Committee, BBC, 1961-71; Member, Central Religious Advisory Committee, BBC and ITA, 1961-71; Governor, Fettes College, 1967-77; Honorary President, Church Service Society; President, New College Union, 1975. Recreations: reading; walking. Address: (h.) 1A York Road, North Berwick, EH39 4LS; T.-01620 892780.

Sanderson of Bowden, Lord (Charles Russell Sanderson), KB. Life Peer; Chairman, Scottish Mortgage and Trust, since 1993; Chairman, Hawick Cashmere Co., since 1990; Deputy Chairman, Clydesdale Bank, since 1996; Director: Union Auctions Ltd., Watson and Philip PLC, Morrison Construction PLC; Vice Chairman, Scottish Peers Association, since 1996; Chairman, Scottish Conservative Party, 1990-93; b. 30.4.33, Melrose; m., Frances Elizabeth Macaulay; 1 s.; 1 s. deceased; 2 d. Educ. St. Mary's School, Melrose; Glenalmond College; Bradford University; Scottish College of Textiles. Commissioned, Royal Signals; Partner, Charles P. Sanderson, 1958-87; former Director, Johnston of Elgin, Illingworth Morris, Edinburgh Woollen Mills; former Chairman, Shires Investment PLC, Edinburgh Financial Trust, Scottish Pride Holdings; President, Scottish Conservative and Unionist Association, 1977-79; Chairman, National Union of Conservative and Unionist Associations Executive Committee, 1981-86; Minister of State, Scottish Office, 1987-90; Chairman, Eildon Housing Association, 1976-83; Member, Court, Napier University; Chairman, Glenalmond Council, since 1994; DL. Recreations: golf; amateur dramatics; photography; fishing. Address: (h.) Becketts Field, Bowden, Melrose, Roxburgh, TD6 0ST.

Sandison, Bruce Macgregor. Writer and Journalist; b. 26.9.38, Edinburgh; m., Dorothy Ann Rhodes; 2 s.; 2 d. Educ. Royal High School, Edinburgh. Commissioned into Royal Army Service Corps, 1956-60; sometime poultry farmer and agricultural contractor; full-time writing, since 1981; Angling Correspondent, The Scotsman; Columnist, The Herald; writer on hill-walking and environmental matters; regular contributor to UK game fishing magazines and other journals; Tales of the Loch (series), Radio Scotland and Radio 4. Publications: The Trout Lochs of Scotland; The Sporting Gentleman's Gentleman; Game Fishing in Scotland; The Hillwalker's Guide to Scotland; The Heather Isles; Tales of the Loch; Long Walks with Little People; Trout and Salmon Rivers and Lochs of Scotland. Recreations: hill-walking; game fishing; photography; swimming; music; reading; chess; bridge. Address: Hysbackie, Tongue, by Lairg, IV27 4XJ; T.-01847 55 274.

Sanford, Professor Anthony John, BSc, PhD, FBPsS, CPsychol. Professor of Psychology, Glasgow University, since 1982 (Head, Department of Psychology, 1983-86); b. 5.7.44, Birmingham; m., Linda Mae Moxey; 1 s.; 2 d. Educ. Waverley Grammar School; Leeds University; Cambridge University. MRC Research Scholar, Applied Psychology Unit, Cambridge; Postdoctoral Research Fellow, then Lecturer in Psychology, Dundee University; Senior Lecturer, then Reader in Psychology, Glasgow University. Gifford Lecturer in Natural Theology, Glasgow, 1983. Publications: Understanding Written Language (Co-author); Models, Mind and Man; Cognition and Cognitive Psychology; The Mind of Man; Communicating Quantities (Co-author). Recreations: hill-walking; industrial archaeology; music; cooking. Address: (b.) Department of Psychology, Glasgow University, Glasgow; T.-0141-330 4085.

Sang, Christopher T.M., MB, ChB, FRCSEdin, FRCPEdin. Consultant Cardiothoracic Surgeon, Lothian Health Board, since 1982; b. 14.6.43, Georgetown, Guyana; m., Jean Cowan (divorced); 1 s.; 2 d. Educ. George Watson's College, Edinburgh; Edinburgh University. General surgery training, Edinburgh, and general medicine and cardiology training, Edinburgh and Canada, 1966-73; cardiovascular and thoracic surgery training, Toronto, Edinburgh, London (Guy's) and Baltimore (Johns Hopkins), 1973-82. Address: (h.) 29 Blackford Hill Grove, Edinburgh, EH2 3HA; T.-0131-667 6046.

Sangster, Professor Alan John, BSc (Eng), MSc, PhD, CEng, FIEE. Professor, Electromagnetic Engineering, Heriot Watt University, since 1990; b. 21.11.40, Aberdeen; m., Barbara Macleod Wilkie; 1 s.; 1 d. Educ. Aberdeen Grammar School; Aberdeen University. Research Engineer, Ferranti Ltd., Edinburgh, 1964-69; Plessey Radar Ltd., 1969-72; Lecturer, Heriot Watt University, 1972-79, Senior Lecturer, 1979-86, Reader, 1986-90. Publications: 105 papers. Recreation: golf. Address: (b.) Computing and Electrical Engineering Department, Heriot Watt University, Edinburgh; T.-0131-451 3358.

Sarkar, Professor Susanta, BTech (Hons), DCT, PhD, CEng, MIStructE. Professor of Civil Engineering and Director of Overseas Affairs, University of Abertay Dundee, since 1978; b. 22.9.34, West Bengal; m., Delphine; 2 s. Educ. Indian Institute of Technology; Leeds University. Postdoctoral Fellow, Leeds University; Senior Scientific Officer and Head of Concrete Structures, Structural Engineering Research Centre, 1965-68; Senior Lecturer/Acting Head, Department of Civil Engineering, National University of Singapore, 1968-71; Director of Studies, Civil Engineering, Hatfield Polytechnic, 1971-78; Head, School of Construction and Environment, University of Abertay, Dundee, 1978-97. Past Chairman, Tayside Community Relations Council; Past Chairman, Dundee Voluntary Association. Recreations: travelling; photography; squash; badminton. Address: (h.) Carphin, 81 Camphill Road, Broughty Ferry, Dundee, DD5 2NA; T.-01382 730777.

Sarwar, Mohammed. MP, Glasgow Govan, since 1997. Address: House of Commons, London SW1A 1AA.

Saunders, Professor Alison Marilyn, BA, PhD. Professor of French, Aberdeen University, since 1990; b. 23.12.44, Darlington. Educ. Wimbledon High School GPDST; Durham University. Lectrice, the Sorbonne, 1968-69; Lecturer in French, Aberdeen University, 1970-85; Senior Lecturer in French, 1985-90. Recreations: swimming; gardening; DIY; cooking; antiquarian book-collecting. Address: (h.) 75 Dunbar Street, Old Aberdeen, Aberdeen; T.-01224 494806.

Saunders, Ann Walker, BA, ALA, MIMgt. Director of Community and Leisure, East Renfrewshire Council, since 1995; b. 12.8.52, Glasgow; m., Christopher Saunders; 1 s.; 2 d. Educ. Hutchesons' Grammar School, Glasgow; Strathclyde University, Glasgow. Director of Arts and Libraries, then Director of Leisure Services, Renfrew District Council, 1991-95. Recreations: reading; travelling. Address: (b.) Council Offices, Eastwood Park, Giffnock, G46 6UG; T.-0141-577 3096.

Saunders, Professor David Stanley, BSc, PhD, FIBiol, FRES, FRSE. Professor of Insect Physiology, Edinburgh University, since 1990; b. 12.3.35, Pinner; m., Jean Margaret Comrie Doughty; 3 s. Educ. Pinner County Grammar School; King's College, London; London School of Hygiene and Tropical Medicine. Joined academic staff, Zoology Department, Edinburgh, 1958; Visiting Professor: Stanford University, California, 1971-72, North Carolina University, 1983. Publications: Insect Clocks; Introduction to Biological Rhythms. Recreations: cycling; gardening; photography. Address: (b.) Institute of Cell, Animal and Population Biology, West Mains Road, Edinburgh, EH9 3JT.

Saunders, Professor William Philip, BDS, PhD, FDSRCS(Edin), FDSRCPS(Glas), MRD. Professor in Clinical Dental Practice, Glasgow University, 1993-95, Professor of Endodontology, since 1995; b. 12.10.48, Carlisle; m., Elizabeth; 1 s.; 2 step s.; 1 d.; 1 step d. Educ. Maidstone Grammar School; Royal Dental Hospital of London. Dental Officer, RAF, 1970-75; general dental practice, 1975-81; Lecturer, Department of Conservative Dentistry, Dundee University, 1981-88; Senior Lecturer in Clinical Practice, Glasgow Dental Hospital and School, 1988-93. Postgraduate Dental Hospital Tutor, Glasgow Dental Hospital, 1992-95; Editor, International Endodontic Journal; President, British Endodontic Society, 1997-98. Publications: numerous papers. Recreations: ornithology; natural history; Scottish art; golf; endodontics. Address: (h.) The Old Smiddy, Knapp, Inchture, PH14 9SW; T.-01828 86478.

Savage, Rev. Gordon Matthew Alexander, MA, BD. Minister, Maxwelltown West Church, Dumfries, since 1984; Clerk, Presbytery of Dumfries and Kirkcudbright, since 1987; b. 25.8.51, Old Kilpatrick; m., Mairi Janet MacKenzie; 2 s. Educ. Glasgow Academy; Edinburgh University. Assistant Minister: Dyce Parish Church, 1975-76, Dunblane Cathedral, 1976-77; Minister, Almondbank-Tibbermore with Logiealmond, 1977-84; Junior Clerk, Presbytery of Perth, 1981-84. Recreations: railways; model railways; Clyde steamers; music. Address: Maxwelltown West Manse, 11 Laurieknowe, Dumfries DG2 7AH; T.-01387 252929.

Savidge, Malcolm Kemp, MP, MA (Hons), FRGU. MP (Labour), Aberdeen North, since 1997; b. 9.5.46, Redhill. Educ. Wallington County Grammar School, Surrey; University of Aberdeen; Aberdeen College of Education. Production/ Stock Control and Computer Assistant, Bryans' Electronics Ltd., 1970-71; Mathematics Teacher, Greenwood Dale Secondary School, Nottingham, 1971; Mathematics and Religious and Social Education Teacher,

Peterhead Academy, 1972-73; Mathematics Teacher, Kincorth Academy, Aberdeen, 1973-97. Member, Aberdeen City Council, 1980-96: Vice-Chair, Labour Group, 1980-88, Finance Convener, Policy Vice-Convener, Deputy Leader, 1994-96; Governor, Robert Gordon's Institute of Technology, 1980-88; Governor, Aberdeen College of Education, 1980-87; JP, 1984-96; Fellow, Robert Gordon University, 1997. Recreations: exploring life; puzzles; reading; real ale; spectator sport. Address: (b.) House of Commons, London SW1A 0AA; T.-0171-219 3570.

Saville, Alan, BA, FSA, MIFA, FSA Scot. Archaeologist; Head, Artefact Research Unit, National Museums of Scotland, since 1989; b. 31.12.46, London; m., Annette Carruthers. Educ. Colfe's Grammar School, London; Birmingham University. Archaeological Research Assistant, Department of the Environment, London, 1972-74; Archaeologist, Cheltenham Art Gallery and Museum, 1974-76; Field Officer, Western Archaeological Trust, Bristol, 1976-85; Archaeological Consultant, Cheltenham, 1985-89. Treasurer, Society of Antiquaries of Scoland, since 1992; Chairman, The Lithic Studies Society, 1983-90; Conservation Co-ordinator, The Prehistoric Society, 1989-93; Joint Editor, Transactions of the Bristol and Gloucestershire Archaeological Society, 1983-89. Recreations: book collecting; cinema. Address: (b.) Archaeology Department, National Museums of Scotland, Chambers Street, Edinburgh EH1 1JF; T.-0131-247 4054.

Savin, John Andrew, MA, MD (Cantab), FRCP, FRCPEdin, DIH. Consultant Dermatologist, Edinburgh Royal Infirmary, since 1971; Senior Lecturer, Dermatology Department, Edinburgh University, since 1971; b. 10.1.35, London; m., Patricia Margaret Steel; 2 s.; 2 d. Educ. Epsom College; Trinity Hall, Cambridge; St. Thomas's Hospital, London. Royal Naval Medical Service, 1960-64; Registrar to Skin Department, St. George's Hospital, London; Senior Registrar, St. John's Hospital for Diseases of the Skin, and St. Thomas's Hospital, London; Co-Editor, Recent Advances in Dermatology; Associate Editor, British Journal of Dermatology; former Secretary, Scottish Dermatological Society; President, British Association of Dermatologists, 1993-94; President, Section of Dermatology, Royal Society of Medicine, 1987-88. Recreations: golf; literature. Address: (h.) 86 Murrayfield Gardens, Edinburgh; T.-0131-337 7768.

Saxon, Professor David Harold, MA, DPhil, DSc, CPhys, FInstP, FRSE. Kelvin Professor of Physics, Glasgow University, since 1990; Head, Department of Physics and Astronomy, since 1996; b. 27.10.45, Stockport; m., Margaret Flitcroft; 1 s.; 1 d. Educ. Manchester Grammar School; Balliol College, Oxford; Jesus College, Oxford. Research Officer, Nuclear Physics Department, Oxford University, 1969-70; Research Associate, Columbia University, New York, 1970-73; Rutherford Appleton Laboratory, Oxon: Research Associate, 1974-75, Senior Scientific Officer, 1975-76, Principal Scientific Officer, 1976-89; Chairman, PPARC Particle Physics Committee, 1992-95; Member: Scientific Policy Committee, CERN, Geneva, since 1993, Physics Research Committee, DESY, Hamburg, since 1993, Research Assessment Panel (Physics), 1996; PPARC Council Member, since 1997. Address: (b.) Department of Physics and Astronomy, Glasgow University, Glasgow, G12 8QQ; T.-0141-330 4673.

Scaife, Geoffrey Richard. Chief Executive, NHS in Scotland, since 1993; b. 12.1.49, Workington; m. Janet Elizabeth Woodward; 2 s.; 2 d. Educ. Workington Grammar School. Department of Health, London, 1968-71 and 1975-83; secondment to Prime Minister's Private Office, 1971-74; NHS Manager, Mersey Region, 1983-93 (including 1989-93 as Chief Executive, Mersey Regional Health Authority). Recreations: sport; countryside. Address: (b.)

St. Andrew's House, Regent Road, Edinburgh, EH1 3DS; T.-0131-244 2410.

Scanlan, Patrick D., MA. Headteacher, St. Margaret Mary's Secondary School, Glasgow, since 1996; b. 1.3.50, Johnstone; m., Patricia; 2 s. Educ. St. Mirin's Academy, Paisley; Glasgow University; Notre Dame College of Education. Assistant Teacher, St. Cuthbert's High, Johnstone, 1971-73; Principal Teacher of English, then Assistant Head Teacher, St. Brendan's High, Linwood, 1973-90; Depute Head Teacher, St. Mirin's High, Paisley, 1990-96. Recreations: sport; reading; music; travel; theatre and cinema. Address: (b.) 65 Dougrie Road, Glasgow G45 9NJ; T.-0141-634 1169.

Schaw-Miller, Jean-Clare. Deputy Lieutenant, West Lothian, since 1980; Council Member (representing Scotland), Guide Dogs for the Blind Association, since 1992; Executive Committee Member, The Trefoil Holiday Centre for the Disabled, since 1993; b. 22.2.37, Gloucestershire; m., Robert Grant Schaw-Miller; 1 s.; 1 d. Educ. Clifton High School for Girls; Edinburgh College of Domestic Science. Scottish Chief Commissioner, Girl Guides Association, 1987-92. Address: (h.) Newgardens House, Dalmeny, South Queensferry, West Lothian, EH30 9TF; T.-0131-331 4612.

Schlesinger, Professor Philip Ronald, BA, PhD, FRSA. Professor of Film and Media Studies, Stirling University, since 1989; b. 31.8.48, Manchester; m., Sharon Joy Rose; 2 d. Educ. North Manchester Grammar School; Queen's College, Oxford; London School of Economics. University of Greenwich: Lecturer, 1974, Senior Lecturer, 1977, Principal Lecturer, 1981; Head, Division of Sociology, 1981-88, Professor of Sociology, 1987-89; Social Science Research Fellow, Nuffield Foundation, 1982-83; Jean Monnet Fellow, European University Institute, Florence, 1985-86; Chair, Research Assessment Panel for Comunication, Cultural and Media Studies, 1995-96; Visiting Professor of Media and Communication, University of Oslo, since 1993; Co-Editor, Media, Culture and Society, since 1982; Media Adviser, Know How Fund, since 1994; Board Member, Scottish Screen, since 1997. Publications: Putting "Reality" Together, 1978, 1987; Televising "Terrorism", 1983; Communicating Politics, 1986; Media, Culture and Society, 1986; Los Intelectuales en la Sociedad de la Informacion, 1987; Media, State and Nation, 1991; Women Viewing Violence, 1992; Culture and Power, 1992; Reporting Crime, 1994; European Transformations, 1994; International Media Research, 1996; European Communication Council Report, 1997. Recreations: the arts; walking; travel. Address: Department of Film and Media Studies, Stirling University, Stirling FK9 4LA; T.-01786 467520.

Schofield, Rev. Melville Frederick, MA. Chaplain to Western General and Associated Hospitals, Edinburgh, since 1988; b. 3.10.35, Glasgow; m., Christina Skirving Crookston. Educ. Irvine Royal Academy; Dalkeith High School; Edinburgh University and New College. Ordained Assistant, Bathgate High, 1960-61; Minister, Canal Street, Paisley, 1961-67; Minister, Laigh Kirk, Kilmarnock, 1967-88. Former Moderator, Presbytery of Irvine and Kilmarnock; former Moderator, Synod of Ayr; radio and TV broadcaster; Past President, No. 0 Kilmarnock Burns Club. Recreations: international Burns engagements; golf; after-dinner speaking. Address: (h.) 25 Rowantree Grove, Currie, Midlothian, EH14 5AT; T.-0131-449 4745.

Scholes, Thomas Alexander, MSc, IPFA, IRRV, MIMgt. Chief Executive, Renfrewshire Council, since 1995; b. 30.4.49, Glasgow; m., Irene Elizabeth; 2 d. Educ. Hamilton Academy; Central College of Commerce; Strathclyde University. Strathclyde Regional Council: Principal Officer, 1975-80, Assistant Director of Finance, 1981-85, Senior Depute Director of Finance, 1986-95. Recreations: football

supporting; watercolour painting; DIY. Address: (H.) 18 Glenfield Crescent, Paisley, PA2; T.-0141-884 5596.

Sclater, Robert Chalmers. Director of Harbours, Orkney Islands Council, since 1989; Oil Pollution Officer, Orkney, since 1989; Executive Director, Orkney Towage Company, since 1989; Executive Director, Orkney Islands Shipping Co.; Master Mariner; b. 7.8.41, Kirkwall; m., Anna Margaret; 1 s.; 2 d. Educ. Kirkwall Grammar School; Leith Nautical College; Robert Gordon's Institute of Technology. Merchant Navy, 1956-76; Marine Officer/1st Class Pilot, Orkney Islands Council, 1976-85; Depute Director of Harbours and Pilotage Superintendent, 1985-89. Member, Kirkwall Sea Cadets Management Committee; DLA, RNLI, for Kirkwall Lifeboat; Elder, St. Magnus Cathedral. Recreations: swimming; gardening; walking. Address: (b.) Council Offices, Kirkwall, Orkney, KW15 1NY.

Scobie, Rev. Andrew John, MA, BD. Minister, Cardross Parish Church, since 1965; b. 9.7.35, Windygates; m., Elizabeth Jeannette; 1 s.; 1 d. Educ. Whitehill Senior Secondary School, Glasgow; Glasgow University (Medal in Systematic Theology); Gottingen University; Tubingen University; Marburg University. Assistantship, New Kilpatrick Church, Bearsden; Moderator, Dumbarton Presbytery, 1973-74; Convener, General Assembly's Parish Education Commitee, 1978-80; Convener, General Assembly's Panel on Worship, 1986-90; Member, Joint Liturgical Group, 1987-91; Chairman or Vice-Chairman, Cardross Community Council, since inception; former Co-Chairman, Presbytery of Dumbarton/Archdiocese of Glasgow Liaison Group; Vice-Convener, General Assembly's Artistic Matters Committee, since 1995. Publications: Studies in the Historical Jesus (Translator); contributions to New Ways to Worship, 1980, Prayers for Sunday Services, 1980, Three Orders for Holy Communion, 1986, Songs of God's People, 1988; Worshipping Together, 1991; Common Order, 1994. Recreations: golf; photography; wine making; visual arts. Address: The Manse, Cardross, Dumbarton G82 5LB; T.-01389 841289.

Scobie, William Galbraith, MB, ChB, FRCSEdin, FRCSGlas. Consultant Paediatric Surgeon, Lothian Health Board, since 1971; part-time Senior Lecturer, Department of Clinical Surgery, Edinburgh University, 1971-92; Assistant Director, Edinburgh Postgraduate Board for Medicine, 1986-92; b. 13.10.36, Maybole; m., Elizabeth Caldwell Steel; 1 s.; 1 d. Educ. Carrick Academy, Maybole; Glasgow University. Registrar, General Surgery, Kilmarnock Infirmary; Senior Registrar, Royal Hospital for Sick Children, Glasgow; Senior Registrar, Hospital for Sick Children, London; Senior Paediatric Surgeon, Abu Dhabi, 1980-81. Recreations: fishing; golf; gardening; music. Address: (h.) 133 Caiyside, Fairmilehead, Edinburgh EH10 7HR; T.-0131-445 7404.

Scothorne, Professor Raymond John, BSc, MD, FRSE, FRCSG. Regius Professor of Anatomy, Glasgow University, 1973-90; b. 13.6.20, Nottingham; m., Audrey Gillott; 1 s.; 2 d. Educ. Royal Grammar School, Newcastle-upon-Tyne; Leeds University; Chicago University. Lecturer in Anatomy, Leeds University, 1944-50; Senior Lecturer, Glasgow University, 1950-60; Professor of Anatomy, Newcastle-upon-Tyne University, 1960-73. Anatomical Society of Gt. Britain and Ireland: Honorary Secretary, 1967-71, President, 1971-73; President, British Association of Clinical Anatomists, 1986-89; Hon. Member, American Association of Clinical Anatomists, 1995; Foundation Editor, Clinical Anatomy, since 1988. Recreations: the countryside; labrador dogs. Address: (b.) Southern Knowe, Friars Brae, Linlithgow, West Lothian, EH49 6BQ.

Scothorne, Richard Mark, MA, MPhil. Managing Director, Partners in Economic Development Ltd., since 1992; b. 17.7.53, Glasgow; m., Dr. Sarah Gledhill; 1 s. Educ. Royal Grammar School, Newcastle upon Tyne; St.

Catharine's College, Cambridge; Edinburgh University. Various posts in local government, 1977-86; Scottish Director, British Shipbuilders Enterprise Ltd., 1986-87; Economic Development Manager (Depute Director of Planning), Lothian Regional Council, 1987-92; Specialist Adviser to Select Committee on Education and Employment, since 1997. Publication: The Vital Economy: integrating training and enterprise, 1990. Recreations: hill-walking; Scottish art; windsurfing. Address: (h.) 71 Murrayfield Gardens, Edinburgh, EH12 6DL; T.-0131-337 5476.

Scott, Alan William Alexander, FCIBS. Secretary, Committee of Scottish Clearing Bankers, since 1991; b. 11.3.39, Glasgow; m., Doreen; 1 s.; 1 d. Educ. Eastwood High School. Savings Bank of Glasgow: branch network, 1958-64, Organisation and Methods, 1964-68; Data Processing Manager, TSB Scotland Computer Consortium, 1968-79; Management Services, West of Scotland TSB, 1980-83; Assistant General Manager, TSB Bank Scotland, 1983-84, Assistant General Manager, Technology, 1984-89, and of Strategic Planning, 1989-91. Recreations: computing; music; reading. Address: (b.) 19 Rutland Square, Edinburgh, EH1 2DD; T.-0131-229 1326.

Scott, Alastair, BA. Travel writer, freelance photographer, and broadcaster; b. 19.3.54, Edinburgh; m., Sheena. Educ. Blairmore; Sedbergh; Stirling University. Travelled around the world, 1978-83; wrote three travel books, 1984-87 – Scot Free, A Scot Goes South, A Scot Returns; cycled 5,000 miles in E. Europe, 1987-88; wrote Tracks Across Alaska (800-mile sled dog journey), 1988-90; travelled Scotland, 1993-94, wrote Native Stranger; presented BBC film version of Native Stranger, 1995. Recreations: reading; running; camping; carpentry; playing concertina. Address: Arroch, Kylerhea, Isle of Skye, IV40 8NH; T.-01599 522329.

Scott, Alexander, MA, MSc, PhD. Professorial Fellow, Heriot-Watt University, since 1989; b. 7.3.45, Lerwick; m., Anne Elliot; 3 d. Educ. Anderson Educational Institute; Boroughmuir Secondary; Edinburgh University. Research Assistant, Edinburgh University, 1967-70; Research Fellow, Heriot-Watt University, 1970-89; Director, The Polecon Co., 1972-89; External Examiner, CNAA, 1981-85; Member, Joint Working Party on Economics, Scottish Examination Board, 1989-90; Chairman, Southfield Housing Society, 1977-80; Executive Director, Edinburgh Business School, since 1997. Publications: Economics in Action (Co-author); Running the British Economy (Co-author); numerous papers. Recreations: hill-walking; swimming; music. Address: (b.) Edinburgh Business School, Heriot-Watt University, Edinburgh; T.-0131-451 3090.

Scott, Professor Bill, RSA. Sculptor; Professor of Sculpture, Edinburgh College of Art (Lecturer, since 1972); b. 16.8.35, Moniaive; m., Phyllis Owen Scott; 1 s.; 2 d. Educ. Dumfries Academy; Edinburgh College of Art; Ecole des Beaux Arts, Paris. One-man exhibitions: Compass Gallery, 1972, Stirling Gallery, 1974, New 57 Gallery, 1979, Lamp of Lothian, 1980, Artspace Gallery, 1980, Kirkcaldy Museum and Gallery, 1985, Talbot Rice Gallery, Edinburgh, 1995; numerous group exhibitions. Address: (h.) 45 St. Clair Crescent, Roslin, Midlothian, EH25 9NG.

Scott, Esme (Lady Scott), CBE, WS, MA, LLB, NP. Chair, The Volunteer Centre UK, 1993-95; b. 7.1.32, Edinburgh; m., 1, Ian Macfarlane Walker (deceased); 1 s.; 2, Kenneth Bertram Adam Scott, KCVO, CMG; 1 step-s.; 1 step-d. Educ. St. George's School for Girls, Edinburgh; Edinburgh University. Lawyer; Vice Chairman, National Consumer Council, 1984-87; Chairman, Scottish Consumer Council, 1980-85; Member, Equal Opportunities Commission, 1985-90; Past Chair, Scottish Association of Citizens Advice Bureaux; Chair, Volunteer Development

Scotland, 1989-92; Member, Securities and Investments Board, 1991-93; Member, Court, Edinburgh University, 1989-92; Member, Scottish Committee, Council on Tribunals, 1986-92; Member, Social Security Advisory Committee, 1990-96; Member, National Council for Voluntary Organisations Board, 1993-95. Address: (h.) 13 Clinton Road, Edinburgh.

Scott, Gavin William Thomson, BCom, CA. Company Secretary and Treasurer, Scottish Agricultural College, since 1991; b. 19.7.55, Edinburgh; m., Elizabeth Moira Davidson; 2 s. Educ. George Watson's College; Edinburgh University. Deloitte Haskins & Sells, CAs, 1979-82; Keir International Ltd., 1982-87; United Nations Adviser, West Africa, 1987-91. Captain, Gambian Rugby Team, 1987; Scottish International Swimming and Water Polo, 1970s. Recreation: almost any sport. Address: (b.) S.A.C., West Mains Road, Edinburgh, EH9 3JG; T.-0131-535 4000.

Scott, Hugh Johnstone, DA, CertEd. Writer; b. Paisley; m., Mary (Margo) Smith Craig Hamilton; 1 s.; 1 d. Educ. Paisley Grammar School; Glasgow School of Art. Various jobs, then art school; art teacher, until 1984; full-time writing since 1984, including Writing Fellow, City of Aberdeen, 1991; Lecturer in Creative Writing, Glasgow University Adult and Continuing Education Department, since 1988; Tutor in Creative Writing; winner, Woman's Realm children's short story competition, 1982; winner, children's category, Whitbread Book of the Year, 1989, for Why Weeps the Brogan?; short-listed, Mcvitie's Prize, 1990; Tutor, Arvon Foundation Ltd., 1994. Recreations: weight training; exploring England; day-dreaming; reading, of course.

Scott, Iain William St. Clair, CA, FCIBS. General Manager, UK Banking – East, Bank of Scotland, since 1996; Chairman, Stevenson College, Edinburgh, since 1991; b. 14.5.46, Edinburgh; m., Noelle Margaret Gilmour; 1 s.; 1 d. Educ. George Watson's College. J.W. & R.N. Oswalds, CAs, 1963-70; joined Bank of Scotland, 1970. Recreations: golf; squash; curling. Address: (b.) Uberior House, 61 Grassmarket, Edinburgh, EH1 2JF; T.-0131-243 5919.

Scott, Ian Edward. Deputy Chief Executive, Scottish Court Service, since 1995; Regional Sheriff Clerk, Glasgow and Strathkelvin, since 1996; Regional Sheriff Clerk, North Strathclyde, since 1997; m., Maureen Ferrie; 1 s.; 1 d. Educ. Bellahouston Academy. Regional Sheriff Clerk, Lothian and Borders, 1992-95; Sheriff Clerk, Edinburgh, 1992-95; Sheriff Clerk of Chancery,1992-95; Hon. Member, Royal Faculty of Procurators, Glasgow. Recreations: amateur astronomy; rugby; making changes. Address: (h.) Meadowbank, Annandale Avenue, Lockerbie; T.-01576 203132.

Scott, Rev. Ian Gray, BSc, BD, STM. Minister, Greenbank Parish Church, Edinburgh, since 1983; b. 31.5.41, Kirkcaldy; m., Alexandrina Angus; 1 d. Educ. Kirkcaldy High School; St. Andrews University; Union Theological Seminary, New York. Assistant Minister, St. Mungo's, Alloa, 1965-66; Minister: Holy Trinity Church, Bridge of Allan, 1966-76, Holburn Central, Aberdeen, 1976-83; Convener, Panel on Doctrine, General Assembly, 1978-82; part-time Lecturer, Faculty of Divinity, Aberdeen University, 1977-79; founder Member, Ministry and Psychotherapy Group; Convener, Board of Parish Education, Church of Scotland, 1993-97; Member, Joint Commission on Doctrine, Church of Scotland/Roman Catholic Church. Recreations: reading; photography; caravanning; golf (so called). Address: 112 Greenbank Crescent, Edinburgh, EH10 5SZ; T.-0131-447 4032.

Scott, James Archibald, CB, LVO, FRSE, FScotVec, MA. Director, Damyat Investment Trust PLC, since 1995; Member of Court, Heriot-Watt University, since 1995; b.

5.3.32, Palestine; m., Dr. Elizabeth Agnes Joyce Scott; 3 s.; 1 d. Educ. Dollar Academy; St. Andrews University; Queen's University of Ontario. RAF Pilot, 1954-56; Commonwealth Relations Office, 1956-65, serving in New Delhi and New York; Scottish Office, 1965; Private Secretary to Secretary of State for Scotland, 1969-71; Secretary, Scottish Education Department, 1984-88; Secretary, Industry Department for Scotland, 1988-91; Chief Executive, Scottish Development Agency, 1991-92; Executive Director, Scottish Financial Enterprise, 1992-95; Director, Scottish Power plc, 1993-96. Recreations: flying; golf. Address: (h.) 38 Queen's Crescent, Edinburgh EH9 2BA; T.-0131-667 8417.

Scott, James Niall, LLB. Partner, McGrigor Donald, since 1979; b. 5.4.52, Glasgow; m., Judith; 2 s.; 2 d. Educ. Jordanhill College School; Aberdeen University. External Examiner, Glasgow University Law School, 1990-92; Managing Partner, McGrigor Donald, 1994-97; currently heads McGrigor Donald's Media Law Group and Public Sector Unit. Governor, Glasgow School of Art; Chairman, Mark Scott Foundation; Trustee, Real Young Scots Trust; Member, various working parties, Law Society of Scotland. Recreations: swimming; golf; hill-walking. Address: (b.) Pacific House, 70 Wellington Street, Glasgow G2 2SB; T.- 0141-248 6677.

Scott, James Orrock, FCCA. Partner, Henderson and Loggie, Accountants, since 1967; Board Member, Angus, East of Scotland Housing Association, since 1988; Treasurer, SHARP (Scottish Heart and Arterial Disease Risk Prevention), since 1992; b. 13.12.40, Dundee; m., Alva; 1 s. Educ. Grove Academy. President, Scottish Branch Executive, Society of Certified Accountants; first President, Scottish Athletics Federation; Council Member, British Athletic Federation. Recreations: athletics; bowling. Address: (h.) 3 Menzieshill Road, Dundee, DD2 1PS; T.- 01382 665813.

Scott, Jayne Patricia, BA, CA. Director of Finance and Contracts, Fife Health Board, since 1994; b. 25.9.63, Edinburgh. Educ. Glenwood High School, Glenrothes; Napier College. Audit Manager, Coopers and Lybrand, 1988; Contracts and Finance Manager, Lothian Health Board, 1992; Assistant Director of Finance, Fife Health Board, 1993. Address: (b.) Springfield House, Cupar, Fife, KY15 5UP; T.-01334 656200.

Scott, John, DL, JP. Member, Orkney Islands Council, 1962-94; Director, Orkney Islands Shipping Company, 1962-93, latterly as Chairman; b. 3.9.21, Papa Stronsay; m., Margaret Ann Pottinger; 4 d. Educ. Stromness Academy. Home Guard; Auxiliary in Charge, HM Coastguard, Westray (retired); Army Cadet Force (Honorary Captain, retired); Past President, Local Committee, National Farmers Union; Secretary, Westray Baptist Church, 1943-86. Recreations: flying (PPL); sailing; golf; badminton. Address: (h.) Leckmelm, Annfield Crescent, Kirkwall, Orkney, KW15 1NS; T.-01856 873917.

Scott, John. Editor, Evening Times, since 1994. Address: (b.) 195 Albion Street, Glasgow G1 1QP.

Scott, John Andrew Ross, JP. Member, Scottish Borders Council, since 1995 (Chairman, Technical Services Committee); Chief Reporter, Southern Reporter, since 1986; b. 6.5.51, Hawick; 2 s. Educ. Hawick High School. Worked on father's farm, 1966-74; Journalist, Hawick News, 1977-78, Tweeddale Press Group, since 1978; first SDP Member, Roxburgh District Council (1980-85) and Borders Regional Council; Chairman, Roxburgh District Licensing Board, 1984-85; first Chairman, Borders Area Party, SDP, 1981-84; Secretary, Roxburgh and Berwickshire Liberal Democrats, 1988-89, Vice Chairman, 1993-94; Chairman, Scottish Association of Direct Labour Organisations Highways Division, 1994-96. Recreations:

writing; music; travel; tennis. Address: (h.) 8 Union Street, Hawick, Roxburghshire; T.-01450 76324.

Scott, John Dominic, LLB, DipLP. Solicitor, Gilfedder and McInnes, since 1991; Chair, Scottish Council for Civil Liberties, since 1997; Member, Council, Edinburgh Bar Association; b. 20.7.64, Glasgow. Educ. Holyrood Secondary School, Glasgow; Glasgow University. Trainee and Assistant, Hughes, Dowdall & Company, Glasgow, 1985-88; joined Gilfedder & McInnes, Edinburgh, 1988. Recreations: football; tennis. Address: (b.) 34 Leith Walk, Edinburgh EH6 5AA; T.-0131-552 7346.

Scott, John Hamilton. Farmer; Lord-Lieutenant, Shetland; Chairman: Woolgrowers of Shetland Ltd., Shetland Arts Trust, Sail Shetland Ltd., Belmont Trust; b. 30.11.36; m., Wendy Ronald; 1 s.; 1 d. Nature Conservancy Council Committee for Scotland, 1984-91; N.E. Scotland Board, Scottish Natural Heritage, 1992-97; Chairman, Shetland Crofting, Farming and Wildlife Advisory Group, 1984-94. Recreations: hills; music; pruning. Address: (h.) Gardie House, Bressay, Shetland, ZE2 9EL; T.-01595 820281.

Scott, Rev. John Miller, MA, BD, DD, FSA (Scot). Minister, St. Andrew's Scots Memorial Church, Jerusalem, 1985-88; b. 14.8.22, Glasgow; m., Dorothy Helen Loraine Bushnell; 2 s.; 1 d. Educ. Hillhead High School; Glasgow University and Trinity College. War Service, Egypt, Italy, India, 1942-46; Assistant Minister, Barony of Glasgow, 1948-49; Minister: Baxter Park Parish, Dundee, 1949-54; High Kirk of Stevenston, 1954-63; Kirk of the Crown of Scotland (Crown Court Church, Westminster), 1963-85; Moderator, Presbytery of England, 1971, 1979; Moderator, Presbytery of Jerusalem, 1986-88; Chairman, Israel Council, 1986-88; various periods of service on General Assembly Committees; Representative, World Alliance of Reformed Churches, Ecumenical Patriarchate, Istanbul, 1988. President, Caledonian Society of London, 1983-84; instituted Kirking Service for Scottish MPs and peers, 1966; Member, UNA Religious Advisory Committee, 1983-85. Recreations: travel; historical research; reading; gardening. Address: (h.) St. Martins, 6 Trinity Place, St. Andrews KY16 8SG; T.-01334 479518.

Scott, Sir Kenneth Bertram Adam, KCVO, CMG. Extra Equerry to The Queen, since 1996; b. 23.1.31, Belfast; m., Esme Scott (qv); 1 s.; 1 d; 1 step. s. Educ. George Watson's College; Edinburgh University. HM Diplomatic Service, 1954-85; HM Ambassador to Yugoslavia, 1982-85; Assistant Private Secretary/Deputy Private Secretary to The Queen, 1985-96; Acting Chairman, Provisional Election Commission for Bosnia, 1996. Deputy Chairman, Hopetoun House Preservation Trust; Governor, George Watson's College; President, British Southern Slav Society; Member, Central Council, Royal Overseas League. Recreations: travel; music; golf; gardening. Address: (h.) 13 Clinton Road, Edinburgh EH9 2AW; T.-0131-447 5191.

Scott, Malcolm Charles Norman, QC, BA, LLB; b. 8.9.51. Advocate, 1978. Address: (b.) Advocates' Library, Parliament House, Edinburgh, EH1 1RF.

Scott, Paul Henderson, CMG, MA, MLitt. Vice-President, Scottish National Party, since 1992; President, Scottish Centre, International PEN, since 1992; President, Saltire Society, since 1996; Convener, Advisory Council for the Arts in Scotland, since 1981; Honorary Fellow, Glasgow University, since 1996; b. 7.11.20, Edinburgh; m., B.C. Sharpe; 1 s.; 1 d. Educ. Royal High School, Edinburgh; Edinburgh University. HM Forces, 1941-47 (Major, RA); HM Diplomatic Service in Foreign Office, Warsaw, La Paz, Havana, Montreal, Vienna, Milan, 1947-80. Rector, Dundee University, 1989-92; Convener, Scottish Centre for Economic and Social Research, 1990-95; President, Edinburgh Sir Walter Scott Club, 1996. Publications: 1707, The Union of Scotland and England, 1979; Walter Scott and

Scotland, 1981; John Galt, 1985; The Age of MacDiarmid (Co-Editor), 1980; In Bed with an Elephant: The Scottish Experience, 1985; A Scottish Postbag (Co-Editor), 1986; The Thinking Nation, 1989; Towards Independence — essays on Scotland, 1991; Andrew Fletcher and the Treaty of Union, 1992; Scotland in Europe: a dialogue with a sceptical friend, 1992; Scotland: a Concise Cultural History (Editor), 1993; Defoe in Edinburgh and Other Papers, 1995; Scxotland's Ruine (Co-Editor), 1995; Scotland: An Unwon Cause, 1997. Recreation: skiing. Address: (h.) 3 Drumsheugh Gardens, Edinburgh, EH3 7RN; T.-0131-225 1038.

Scott, Sheriff Richard John Dinwoodie, MA, LLB. Sheriff of Lothian and Borders at Edinburgh, since 1986 (of Grampian, Highland and Islands, at Aberdeen and Stonehaven, 1977-86); Honorary Reader, Aberdeen University, 1980-86; b. 28.5.39, Manchester; m., Josephine Moretta Blake; 2 d. Educ. Edinburgh Academy; Edinburgh University. Lektor, Folkuniversitet of Sweden, 1960-61; admitted to Faculty of Advocates, 1965; Standing Junior Counsel, Ministry of Defence (Air), 1969; Parliamentary candidate, 1974. Address: (b.) Sheriffs' Chambers, Sheriff Court House, Edinburgh, EH1 1LB; T.-031-226 7181.

Scott, Robert Avisson. Group Chief Executive, General Accident plc, since 1996; b. 6.1.42; m., Joanne Rose Adams; 2 d. Educ. Scots College, Wellington, NZ. Associate: Australian Insurance Institute, Insurance Institute NZ; South British Insurance Co. Ltd., later NZI Corp Ltd., then General Accident plc, since 1959; Assistant General Manager, NZ, 1981-83; Australia: Assistant General Manager, 1983-85, General Manager, 1985-87, Chief General Manager, 1987-90; Deputy General Manager, UK, 1990-91, General Manager, 1991-94, Deputy Chief Executive, 1994-96. Recreations: sporting interests; walking; do-it-yourself. Address: (b.) General Accident plc, Pitheavlis, Perth, PH2 0NH; T.-01738 621202.

Scott, Professor Roger Davidson, BSc, PhD, CPhys, FInstP, FRSE. Director, Scottish Universities Research and Reactor Centre, since 1991; Personal Professorship, University of Glasgow, 1994; b. 17.12.41, Lerwick; m., Marion McCluckie; 2 s.; 1 d. Educ. Anderson Institute, Lerwick; Edinburgh University. Demonstrator, Edinburgh University, 1965-68; Lecturer, then Depute Director, SURRC, 1968-91. Recreations: watching football; walking dogs; home maintenance. Address: (b.) Scottish Universities Research and Reactor Centre, East Kilbride, Glasgow, G75 0QU; T.-013552 23332, Ext. 102.

Scott, Sheriff Thomas. Sheriff of North Strathclyde. Address: (b.) Dumbarton Sheriff Court, Sheriff Court House, Church Street, Dumbarton, G82 1QR.

Scott, William, BSc, MSc, MRPharmS. Chief Pharmaceutical Officer, Scottish Office, since 1992; b. 26.10.49, Bellshill; m., Catherine Muir Gilmour; 1 s.; 1 d. Educ. Wishaw High School; Heriot Watt University; Strathclyde University. Resident Pharmacist, Nottingham City Hospital, 1975-76; Staff Pharmacist, Eastern General Hospital, Edinburgh, 1976-79; Principal Pharmacist, Western General Hospital, Edinburgh, 1979-86; Chief Administrative Pharmaceutical Officer, Tayside Health Board, 1986-90; Deputy Chief Pharmacist, Scottish Office, 1990-92. Recreations: walking; reading; golf. Address: (b.) St. Andrews House, Edinburgh; T.-0131-244 2518.

Scott, Professor William Talbot, MA, PhD, DipEd, CertEd. Professor and Head, Department of Language and Media, Glasgow Caledonian University, since 1984; b. 28.2.42, Glasgow; m., Wendy Elizabeth Murray; 1 s.; 1 d. Educ. Woodside Secondary, Glasgow; Glasgow University; Sheffield University. Features Writer, D.C. Thomson & Co.; Lecturer/Senior Lecturer/Principal Lecturer in Communication Studies, Sheffield City Polytechnic.

Publication: The Possibility of Communication, 1990. Recreations: running; gardening. Address: (b.) Department of Language and Media, Glasgow Caledonian University, Cowcaddens Road, Glasgow, G4 0BA; T.-0141-331 3260.

Scott Brown, Ronald, MA, LLB, LLD. Director, Aberdeen Asset Management PLC, since 1983, Chairman, 1989-91; b. 14.2.37, Madras; m., Jean Leslie Booth; 3 s. Educ. Aberdeen Grammar School; Aberdeen University. Qualified Solicitor, 1961; Assistant, then Partner, Brander & Cruickshank, Advocates, 1961-83. Member, Board of Governors, Northern College of Education, 1983-95; Member, Court, Aberdeen University, since 1990. Address: (b.) 10 Queen's Terrace, Aberdeen, AB10 1QJ; T.-01224 631999.

Scrimgeour, John Beecher, MB, ChB, DObst, RCOG, FRCOG, FRCS(Edin), FRCP (Edin). Consultant Obstetrician and Gynaecologist, since 1972; Honorary Senior Lecturer in Obstetrics and Gynaecology, Edinburgh University, since 1972; Medical Director, Western General Hospitals Unit, Edinburgh, since 1993; President, Edinburgh Obstetrical Society, since 1996; Vice Chairman, Scottish Association of Trust Medical Directors, since 1996; b. 22.1.39, Elgin; m., Joyce Morrin; 1 s.; 1 d. Educ. Hawick High School; Edinburgh University. General Practitioner, Edinburgh, 1963-65; Senior House Officer; Stirling Royal Infirmary, 1965, and Registrar, Eastern General Hospital, Edinburgh, 1966-69; Senior Registrar, Edinburgh Royal Infirmary, 1970-72; Senior Secretary, Edinburgh Obstetrical Society, 1980-85; Chairman, Area Division of Obstetrics and Gynaecology, 1984-88; Member, Council, Royal College of Obstetricians and Gynaecologists, 1976-81. Publication: Towards the Prevention of Fetal Malformation, 1978. Recreations: gardening; golf. Address: (h.) 16 Belgrave Crescent, Edinburgh EH4 3AJ; T.-0131-332 6480.

Seafield, 13th Earl of (Ian Derek Francis Ogilvie-Grant), b. 20.3.39; m., 1, Mary Dawn Mackenzie Illingworth (m. diss.); 2 s.; 2, Leila Refaat. Educ. Eton. Address: (h.) Old Cullen, Cullen, Banffshire.

Seagrave, David Robert, LLB (Hons), SSC, NP. Solicitor and Notary Public; Council Member, Law Society of Scotland, 1981-87; Partner, Seagrave & Co., Solicitors, Dumfries; b. 29.4.43, Berwick-on-Tweed; m., Fiona Lesley Thomson; 1 s.; 1 d. Educ. Newcastle-upon-Tyne; Glasgow University. Banking, insurance, police; Secretary, Enterprise Trust for Nithsdale, Annandale/Eskdale and the Stewartry, 1984-92. Recreations: choral singing; shooting; fishing; golf. Address: (h.) Amulree, Islesteps, Dumfries; T.-Dumfries 264523.

Sealey, Barry Edward, CBE, BA (Hons) (Cantab), CBIM. Director: Wilson Byard PLC (Chairman), Interface Graphics Ltd. (Chairman), Stagecoach Holdings PLC, The Caledonian Brewing Company Ltd., Scottish Equitable plc, Scottish American Investment Trust plc, Morago Ltd., and other companies; Chairman, Edinburgh Healthcare NHS Trust; b. 3.2.36, Bristol; m., Helen Martyn; 1 s.; 1 d. Educ. Dursley Grammar School; St. John's College, Cambridge. RAF, 1953-55. Joined Christian Salvesen as trainee, 1958; joined Board, Christian Salvesen PLC (responsible for Food Services Division), 1969; appointed Managing Director, 1981, Deputy Chairman and Managing Director, 1987; retired from Christian Salvesen, 1990. Council Member, The Industrial Society. Address: (h.) 4 Castlelaw Road, Edinburgh, EH13 0DN.

Searle, Rev. David Charles, MA, DipTh. Minister of the Church of Scotland, since 1965; Warden, Rutherford House, Edinburgh, since 1993; b. 14.11.37, Swansea; m., Lorna Christine Wilson; 2 s.; 1 d. Educ. Arbroath High School; St. Andrews University; London University; Aberdeen University. Teacher, 1961-64; Assistant Minister,

St. Nicholas Church, Aberdeen, 1964-65; Minister: Newhills Parish Church, 1965-75, Larbert Old, 1975-85, Hamilton Road Presbyterian Church, Bangor, Co. Down, 1985-93; Contributor, Presbyterian Herald; Editor, Rutherford Journal of Church and Ministry. Publications: Be Strong in the Lord; Truth and Love in a Sexually Disordered World. Recreations: sail-boarding; gardening; hill-walking. Address: (b.) Rutherford House, 17 Claremont Park, Edinburgh, EH6 7PJ; T.-0131-554 1206.

Seaton, Professor Anthony, CBE, BA, MD (Cantab), FRCPLond, FRCPEdin, FFOM. Professor of Environmental and Occupational Medicine, Aberdeen University, since 1988; b. 20.8.38, London; m., Jillian Margaret Duke; 2 s. Educ. Rossall School, Fleetwood; King's College, Cambridge; Liverpool University. Assistant Professor of Medicine, West Virginia University, 1969-71; Consultant Chest Physician, Cardiff, 1971-77; Director, Institute of Occupational Medicine, Edinburgh, 1978-90. Editor, Thorax, 1977-82; Chairman, Department of Environment Expert Panel on Air Quality Standards, since 1992; Member, Department of Health Committee on Medical Aspects of Air Pollution, MRC Committee on Toxic Hazards in the Environment. Publications: books and papers on occupational and respiratory medicine. Recreations: keeping fit; opera; painting. Address: (h.) 8 Avon Grove, Cramond, Edinburgh, EH4 6RF; T.-031-336 5113; 71 Urquhart Terrace, Aberdeen AB24 1NJ.

Seaton, Robert, MA, LLB. Secretary of the University, Dundee University, since 1973; b. 2.8.37, Clarkston, Renfrewshire; m., Jennifer Graham Jack; 2 s.; 2 d. Educ. Eastwood Secondary School; Glasgow University; Balliol College, Oxford; Edinburgh University. Administrative Assistant, then Senior Administrative Officer, then Assistant Secretary, Edinburgh University, 1962-73. Director, Dundee University Utility Supply Company Ltd., Dundee University Project Management Ltd. Address: (b.) Dundee University, Dundee DD1 4HN.

Seckl, Professor Jonathan Robert, BSc, MB, BS, MRCP(UK), PhD, FRCPE. Moncrieff-Arnott Professor of Molecular Medicine, Edinburgh University, since 1997; Professor of Endocrinology, since 1996; Chairman, Molecular Medicine Centre, since 1996; b. 15.8.56, London; m., Molly; 1 s.; 1 d. Educ. William Ellis School, London; University College Hospital Medical School, London. Sir Jules Thorn Research Fellow in Neuroendocrinology, Charing Cross and Westminster Medical School, 1984-87; Honorary Clinical Assistant, National Hospital for Nervous Diseases, London, 1984-87; Lecturer in Medicine, Edinburgh University, 1987-89; Wellcome Trust/Royal Society of Edinburgh Senior Clinical Research Fellow, 1989-96. Address: (b.) Molecular Medicine Centre, Edinburgh University, Western General Hospital, Crewe Road, Edinburgh EH4 2XU; T.-0131-651 1035.

Sefton, Rev. Henry Reay, MA, BD, STM, PhD. Co-ordinator in Christian Studies, Aberdeen University, 1995-97; Clerk, Aberdeen Presbytery, 1993-95; b. 15.1.31, Rosehearty. Educ. Brechin High School; St. Andrews University; Glasgow University; Union Theological Seminary, New York. Assistant Minister, Glasgow Cathedral, 1957-58, St. Margaret's, Knightswood, Glasgow, 1958-61; Acting Chaplain, Hope Waddell Training Institution, Nigeria, 1959; Associate Minister, St. Mark's, Wishaw, 1962; Minister, Newbattle, 1962-66; Assistant Secretary, Church of Scotland Department of Education, 1966-72; Lecturer in Church History, Aberdeen University, 1972-90, Senior Lecturer, 1991-92; Master of Christ's College, Aberdeen, 1982-92; Alexander Robertson Lecturer, Glasgow University, 1995; Moderator, Aberdeen Presbytery, 1982-83, Synod of Grampian, 1991-92; Convener, Church of Scotland Board of Education, 1987-91; Chairman, Association of University Teachers

(Scotland), 1982-84. Recreations: hill-walking; church architecture; stamp and coin collecting. Address: (h.) 25 Albury Place, Aberdeen, AB11 6TQ; T.-01224 572305.

Selkirk of Douglas, Rt. Hon. Lord (James Alexander Douglas-Hamilton), MA, LLB. MP (Conservative), Edinburgh West, 1974-97; b. 31.7.42, Strathaven; m., (Priscilla) Susan (Susie) Buchan; 4 s. Educ. Eton; Balliol College, Oxford; Edinburgh University. Officer, TAS 6/7 Bn. Cameronians Scottish Rifles, 1961-66, TAVR, 1971-73, Captain 2 Bn. Lowland Volunteers; Advocate, 1968-74; Scottish Conservative Whip, 1977; a Lord Cmnr., HM Treasury, 1979-81, PPS to Malcolm Rifkind MP, at Foreign Office, later as Secretary of State for Scotland, 1983-87; Parliamentary Under Secretary of State: at the Scottish Office for Home Affairs and Environment, 1987-89; for Home Affairs and Environment, 1989-92 (with additional responsibility for local government finance 1989-90, and with additional responsibility for the arts in Scotland, 1990-92); for Education and Housing, Scottish Office, 1992-95; Minister of State for Home Affairs and Health, Scottish Office, 1995-97. Member, Scottish Select Committee Scottish Affairs 1981-83; Honorary Secretary: Conservative Parliamentary Constitutional Committee, Conservative Parliamentary Aviation Committee, since 1983; Chairman, Scottish Parliamentary All-Party Penal Affairs Committee, 1983; Honorary President, Scottish Amateur Boxing Association, 1975; President: Royal Commonwealth Society (Scotland), 1979-87, Scottish National Council of UN Association, 1981-87; Member, Council, National Trust for Scotland, 1977-82; Honorary Air Commodore No. 2 (City of Edinburgh) Maritime Headquarters Unit and President International Service Rescue, 1995. Oxford Boxing Blue, 1961; President, Oxford Union, 1964. Publications: Motive For A Mission: The Story Behind Hess's Flight to Britain, 1971; The Air Battle for Malta: The Diaries of a Fighter Pilot, 1981; Roof of the World: Man's First Flight over Everest, 1983; The Truth about Rudolf Hess, 1993. Recreations: golf; forestry; debating; history; boxing. Address: House of Lords, London.

Semple, David, WS, LLB, NP. Partner, Semple Fraser WS, since 1990; b. 29.12.43, Glasgow; m., Jet; 2 s.; 1 d. Educ. Loretto School; Glasgow University. Partner, Bird Son & Semple, 1968-73; Bird Semple and Crawford Herron, 1973-88; Bird Semple Fyfe Ireland, 1988-90. President, Glasgow Chamber of Commerce, 1996-97; Member, Board, Interactive Media Alliance Scotland; Chairman, Centre for Dispute Resolution, Scotland. Recreations: golf; hill-walking; bagpipes. Address: (b.) 130 St. Vincent Street, Glasgow G2 5HF; T.-0141-221 3771.

Semple, Peter d'Almaine, MD, FRCPGlas, FRCPEdin, FRCPLond. Consultant Physician and Chest Specialist, Inverclyde District, since 1979; b. 30.10.45, Glasgow; m., Judith Mairi Abercromby; 2 d. Educ. Belmont House; Loretto School; Glasgow University. Consultant Physician, Inverclyde Royal Hospital, 1979; former Postgraduate Medical Tutor, Inverclyde District; Honorary Clinical Senior Lecturer, Glasgow University. Past Chairman, Medical Audit Sub-Committee, Scottish Office; Past President, Greenock and District Faculty of Medicine; Past Chairman, West of Scotland Branch, British Deer Society; Director, Medical Audit, Royal College of Physicians and Surgeons of Glasgow. Recreations: field sports; gardening; golf. Address: (h.) High Lunderston, Inverkip, PA16 0DU; T.-01475 522342.

Semple, Walter George, BL, NP, ACI Arb. Solicitor; Partner, Bird Semple, Solicitors; b. 7.5.42, Glasgow; m., Dr. Lena Ohrstrom; 3 d. Educ. Belmont House, Glasgow; Loretto School; Glasgow University. President, Glasgow Juridical Society, 1968; Tutor and Lecturer (part-time), Glasgow University, 1970-79; Council Member, Law Society of Scotland, 1976-80; Chairman, Scottish Lawyers European Group, 1978-81; Member, Commission

Consultative des Barreaux Europeens, 1978-80, 1984-87; President, Association Internationale des Jeunes Avocats, 1983-84; Chairman, Scottish Branch, Institute of Arbitrators, 1989-91; Member, Business Committee, Glasgow University General Council. Recreations: golf; fishing; skiing; music. Address: (h.) 79 Lancefield Quay, Glasgow G3 8HA.

Sewel, Lord (John Buttifant Sewel), CBE. Parliamentary Under-Secretary of State, Scottish Office, with responsibility for Agriculture, Environment and Fisheries, since 1997; House of Lords Spokesman on all Scottish Affairs; created Peer, 1996; b. 1946. Educ. Hanson Boys' Grammar School, Bradford; Durham University; University College Swansea; Aberdeen University. Councillor, Aberdeen City Council, 1974-84 (Leader of the Council, 1977-80); President, COSLA, 1982-84; Member, Accounts Commission for Scotland, 1987-96; Member, Scottish Constitutional Convention, 1994-95; successively Research Fellow, Lecturer, Senior Lecturer, Professor, Aberdeen University, from 1969; Dean, Faculty of Economic and Social Sciences, 1989-94; Vice Principal and Dean, Faculty of Social Sciences and Law, 1995-96. Recreations: hill-walking; skiing; watching cricket. Address: (b.) Scottish Office, Pentland House, 47 Robb's Loan, Edinburgh EH14 1TY.

Sewell, Professor John Isaac, PhD, DSc, CEng, FIEEE. Professor of Electronic Systems, Glasgow University, since 1985 (Dean, Faculty of Engineering, 1990-93); b. 13.5.42, Kirkby Stephen; m., Ruth Alexandra Baxter; 1 d. Educ. Kirkby Stephen Grammar School; Durham University; Newcastle-upon-Tyne University. Lecturer, Senior Lecturer, Reader, Department of Electronic Engineering, Hull University, 1968-85. Publications: 123 papers. Recreations: swimming; climbing. Address: (h.) 16 Paterson Place, Bearsden, Glasgow, G61 4RU; T.-0141-943 0729.

Seymour, Professor Philip Herschel Kean, BA, MEd, PhD. Professor of Cognitive Psychology, Dundee University, since 1988; b. 9.3.38, London; m., Margaret Jean Dyson Morris; 2 s.; 2 d. Educ. Kelly College, Tavistock; Exeter College, Oxford; St. Andrews University. Dundee University: Lecturer, 1966-75, Senior Lecturer, 1975-82, Reader, 1982-88. Chairman, Scottish Dyslexia Association, 1982-85. Publications: Human Visual Cognition, 1979; Cognitive Analysis of Dyslexia, 1986. Address: (b.) Department of Psychology, Dundee University, Dundee; T.-Dundee 223181.

Shand, Jimmy, MBE. Musician and Scottish Country Dance Band Leader; b. 28.1.08, East Wemyss; m., Anne Anderson; 2 s. Educ. East Wemyss School. Has played the accordion and led Scottish danceband at thousands of concert and theatre performances at home and overseas; numerous recordings; several thousand broadcasts. Recreations: motor bikes; sailing.

Shanks, Duncan Faichney, RSA, RGI, RSW. Artist; b. 30.8.37, Airdrie; m., Una Brown Gordon. Educ. Uddingston Grammar School; Glasgow School of Art. Part-time Lecturer, Glasgow School of Art, until 1979; now full-time painter; one-man shows: Stirling University, Scottish Gallery, Fine Art Society, Talbot Rice Art Gallery, Edinburgh University, Crawford Centre, Maclaurin Art Gallery, Glasgow Art Gallery, Fine Art Society, touring exhibition (Wales); taken part in shows of Scottish painting, London, 1986, Toulouse, Rio de Janeiro, 1985, Wales, 1988; Scottish Arts Council Award; Latimer and MacAulay Prizes, RSA; Torrance Award, Cargill Award, MacFarlane Charitable Trust Award, RGI; May Marshall Brown Award, RSW; The Lord Provost's Prize for painting (GOMA), 1996; tapestry commissioned by Coats Viyella, woven by Edinburgh Tapestry Company, presented to Glasgow Royal Concert Hall, 1991. Recreations: music; gardening.

Shanks, Rev. Norman James, MA, BD. Leader, Iona Community, since 1995; b. 15.7.42, Edinburgh; m., Ruth Osborne Douglas; 2 s.; 1 d. Educ. Stirling High School; St. Andrews University; Edinburgh University. Scottish Office, 1964-79; Chaplain, Edinburgh University, 1985-88; Lecturer in Practical Theology, Glasgow University, 1988-95; Convener, Acts Commission on Justice, Peace, Social and Moral Issues, 1991-95; Chairman, Edinburgh Council of Social Service, 1985-88; Chairman, Secretary of State's Advisory Committee on Travelling People, 1985-88; Convener, Church and Nation Committee, Church of Scotland, 1988-92; Member, Broadcasting Council for Scotland, 1988-93; Member, Scottish Constitutional Convention and Executive Committee, since 1989. Recreations: armchair cricket; occasional golf. Address: (h.) 1 Marchmont Terrace, Glasgow, G12 9LT; T.-0141-339 4421.

Shanks, Thomas Henry, MA, LLB. Solicitor and Notary Public, since 1956; Honorary Sheriff, Lanark, since 1982; b. 22.10.30, Lanark; m., Marjorie A. Rendall; 1 s.; 1 d. (by pr. m.); 3 step s.; 1 step d. Educ. Lanark Grammar School; Glasgow University. Intelligence Corps (National Service), 1954-56. Depute Clerk of Peace, County of Lanark, 1961-74; Chairman, Royal Burgh of Lanark Community Council, 1977-80 and 1983-86; Captain, Lanark Golf Club, 1962; Lanark Lord Cornet, 1968. Recreation: golf. Address: (h.) Clydesholm Braes, Lanark.

Sharp, Sir George, Kt (1976), OBE, JP, DL. Chairman, Glenrothes Development Corporation, 1978-86; Member, Economic and Social Committee, EEC, 1982-86; b. 8.4.19; m., Elsie May Rodger; 1 s. Educ. Buckhaven High School. Fife County Council: Member, 1945-75, Chairman, Water and Drainage Committee, 1955-61, Chairman, Finance Committee, 1961-72, Convener, 1972-75; Convener, Fife Regional Council, 1974-78; President: Association of County Councils, 1972-74, COSLA, 1975-78; Chairman: Kirkcaldy District Council, 1958-75, Fife and Kinross Water Board, 1967-75, Forth River Purification Board, 1955-67 and 1975-78, Scottish River Purification Advisory Committee, 1967-75, Scottish Tourist Consultative Council, 1979-82; Member, Tay Road Bridge Committee, 1961-72, Vice-Chairman, 1972-78; Vice-Chairman, Forth Road Bridge Committee, 1972-78; Member, Scottish Water Advisory Committee, 1962-69, Potato Marketing Board, 1965-71, Committee of Enquiry into Salmon and Trout Fishing, 1963, Scottish Valuation Advisory Committee, 1972, Committee of Enquiry into Local Government Finance, 1974-76, Scottish Development Agency, 1975-80, Royal Commission on Legal Services in Scotland, 1978-80; Director, Grampian Television, 1975-89; Member, Scottish Board, National Girobank, 1982-90; Managing Trustee, Municipal Mutual Insurance Ltd., 1979-91. Recreations: golf; reading; gardening; football spectating. Address: (h.) Strathlea, 56 Station Road, Thornton, Fife; T.-Glenrothes 774347.

Sharratt, John, DPA, DCA, MITSA. Chief Trading Standards Officer, Scottish Borders Council (formerly Borders Regional Council), since 1988; b. 16.8.47, Manchester; m., Yvonne; 4 s. Educ. Horwich Secondary School; Bell College of Technology. Trainee, Lancashire CC, 1964-69; Senior Trading Standards Officer, Glasgow Corporation/Strathclyde RC, 1969-79; Assistant Divisional Trading Standards Officer, 1979-84, Principal TSO (Research, Development and Training), 1984-88, Strathclyde RC. Education Secretary, Institute of Trading Standards Administration (Scottish Branch), 1985-91, Chairman, 1991-92. Recreations: squash; golf; fishing; watching rugby. Address: (b.) St. Dunstan's, High Street, Melrose, TD6 9RU; T.-0189 682 3922.

Shaw, Rev. Alistair Neil, MA (Hons), BD (Hons). Minister, Laigh Kirk, Kilmarnock, since 1988; b. 6.7.53, Kilbarchan; m., Brenda Bruce; 2 d. Educ. Paisley Grammar

School; Glasgow University. Minister, Relief Parish Church, Bourtreehill, Irvine, 1982-88; Moderator, Presbytery of Irvine and Kilmarnock, 1995-96. Recreations: wine-making; visiting archaeological sites; foreign travel; swimming. Address: (h.) 1 Holmes Farm Road, Kilmarnock KA1 1TP; T.-01563 525416.

Shaw, Charles M., BA (Economics), DipMktg, MInstM. Director/General Manager, Invergordon Distillers, since 1994; b. 27.3.51, Greenock; m., Elizabeth Shaw; 2 s. Educ. St. Columba's School; Strathclyde University. Product Manager, Golden Wonder Ltd.; Marketing Manager, Canada Dry Corp; Marketing Manager/Marketing Director/Group Marketing and Corporate Development Director, Whyte and Mackay Group. Committee Member, Scotch Whisky Association. Address: (b.) Invergordon Distillers, Salamander Place, Leith, Edinburgh; T.-0131-554 4404.

Shaw, Rev. Professor Douglas William David, MA, LLB, BD, DD, WS. Professor of Divinity, St. Andrews University, 1979-91 (Dean, Faculty of Divinity, 1983-86, Principal, St. Mary's College, 1986-92; Minister, Church of Scotland, since 1960; b. 25.6.28, Edinburgh; m., Edinburgh Academy; Loretto; Ashbury College, Ottawa; St. John's College, Cambridge; Edinburgh University. Practised law as WS (Partner, Davidson and Syme, WS, Edinburgh), 1952-57; Assistant Minister, St. George's West Church, Edinburgh, 1960-63; Official Observer, Second Vatican Council, Rome, 1962; Lecturer in Divinity, Edinburgh University, 1963-79; Principal, New College, and Dean, Faculty of Divinity, Edinburgh, 1973-78; Visiting Fellow, Fitzwilliam College, Cambridge, 1978; Visiting Lecturer, Virginia University, 1979. Publications: Who is God?, 1968; The Dissuaders, 1978, In Divers Manners (Editor), 1990; Dimensions, 1992; Theology in Scotland. Recreations: squash; golf; hill-walking. Address: (h.) 4 Alexandra Court, St. Andrews, Fife, KY16 9XH; T.-01334 477254.

Shaw, Rev. Duncan, BD (Hons), MTh. Minister, St. John's, Bathgate, since 1978; b. 10.4.47, Blantyre; m., Margaret S. Moore; 2 s.; 1 d. Educ. St. John's Grammar School, Hamilton; Hamilton Academy; Trinity College, Glasgow University. Assistant Minister, Netherlee Parish Church, Glasgow, 1974-77. Clerk, West Lothian Presbytery, since 1982 (Moderator, 1989-90). Recreations: gardening; travel (in Scotland). Address: St. John's Parish Church Manse, Mid Street, Bathgate, EH48 1QD; T.-Bathgate 653146.

Shaw, Professor Sir John Calman, CBE, KStJ, BL, FRSE, CA, FCMA.. Deputy Governor, Bank of Scotland, since 1991; Chairman, Scottish Higher Education Funding Council, since 1992; b. 10.7.32, Perth; m., Shirley Botterill; 3 d. Educ. Strathallan; Edinburgh University. Qualified as Chartered Accountant, 1954; Partner, Graham, Smart & Annan, CA, Edinburgh, latterly Deloitte Haskins & Sells, 1960-1987; President, Institute of Chartered Accountants of Scotland, 1983-84; Johnstone Smith Professor of Accountancy, Glasgow University, 1977-83. Director: Scottish Mortgage and Trust PLC, Scottish American Investment Company PLC (Chairman), Scottish Financial Enterprise (Chairman), Scottish Metropolitan Property PLC, Templeton Emerging Markets Investment Trust PLC, Templeton Latin America Investment Trust PLC, TR European Growth Trust PLC, US Smaller Companies Trust PLC (Chairman); Director, Scottish Enterprise; Member, Scottish Economic Council; Lay Director, Scottish Chamber Orchestra; Deputy Chairman, Edinburgh Festival Society; Chairman, David Hume Institute; Vice-President, Scottish Council for International Arbitration; author of various texts and publications on accountancy. Recreations: music; walking; travel. Address: (b.) The Mound, Edinburgh, EH1 1YZ.

Shaw, Mark Robert, BA, MA, DPhil. Keeper of Geology and Zoology, National Museums of Scotland, since 1996; b. 11.5.45, Sutton Coldfield; m., Francesca Dennis Wilkinson; 2 d. Educ. Dartington Hall School; Oriel College, Oxford. Research Assistant (Entomology), Zoology Department, Manchester University, 1973-76; University Research Fellow, Reading University, 1977-80; Assistant Keeper, Department of Natural History, Royal Scottish Museum, 1980-83; Keeper of Natural History, National Museums of Scotland, 1983-96. Recreations: field entomology; family life. Address: (h.) 48 St. Albans Road, Edinburgh, EH9 2LU; T.-0131-667 0577.

Shaw, Richard Wright, CBE, MA. Principal, University of Paisley; b. 22.9.41, Preston; m., Susan Angela; 2 s. Educ. Lancaster Royal Grammar School; Sidney Sussex College, Cambridge. Assistant Lecturer in Management, then Lecturer in Economics, Leeds University, 1964-69; Lecturer in Economics, then Senior Lecturer, Stirling University, 1969-84; part-time Lecturer, Glasgow University, 1978-79; Visiting Lecturer, Newcastle University, NSW, 1982; Head, Department of Economics, Stirling University, 1982-84; Professor and Head, Department of Economics and Management, Paisley College, 1984-86; Vice Principal, 1986. Director, Renfrewshire Enterprise; Member: Board of Management, Reid Kerr College; Scottish Economic Council; Convener, Committee of Scottish Higher Education Principals, since 1996; Fellow, Scottish Vocational Education Council, since 1995. Recreations:walking; listening to music. Address: (b.) University of Paisley, High Street, Paisley, PA1 2BE; T.-0141-848 3670.

Shaw, Professor Susan Angela, MA (Cantab), FCIM. Deputy Principal, Strathclyde University, since 1995; Professor of Marketing, since 1991; b. 1.6.43, Bristol; m., Richard Shaw; 2 s. Educ. Kingswood Grammar School, Bristol; Girton College, Cambridge. Marketing Executive, ICI Fibres; Lecturer, Senior Lecturer, Professor, Stirling University. Council Member, Food from Britain; Member, Food Policy Directorate, BBSRC; Director, Strathclyde University Food Project. Recreations: hill-walking; tennis; opera. Address: (b.) Department of Marketing, Strathclyde University, Stenhouse Building, 173 Cathedral Street, Glasgow, G4 0RQ; T.-0141-552 4400.

Shaw-Stewart, Sir Houston (Mark), 11th Bt, MC (1950), TD. Deputy Lieutenant (formerly Vice Lord Lieutenant), Strathclyde Region (Eastwood, Renfrew and Inverclyde Districts); b. 24.4.31; m., Lucinda Victoria Fletcher; 1 s. Educ. Eton. Coldstream Guards, 1949; 2nd Lt., Royal Ulster Rifles, Korea, 1950; Ayrshire Yeomanry, 1952; Member, Queen's Bodyguard for Scotland (Royal Company of Archers). Address: (h.) Ardgowan, Inverkip, Renfrewshire, PA16 0DW.

Shaw-Stewart, Lady (Lucinda Victoria), FRSA. National Trust for Scotland: Vice President, since 1994, Member, Executive Committee, since 1985, Convener, Curatorial Committee, since 1993; Trustee, Wallace Collection, since 1987; Trustee, Burrell Collection, since 1992; b. 29.9.49, Harrogate; m., Sir Houston Shaw-Stewart Bt; 1 s. Educ. Cranborne Chase School; diploma from Study Centre for the History of the Fine and Decorative Arts. Freelance Lecturer in Fine and Decorative Arts, 1969-82; National Trust for Scotland: London Representative, 1978-82, Member, Council, 1983-88. Honorary Vice President, Ardgowan Hospice, Greenock. Address: (h.) Ardgowan, Inverkip, Renfrewshire PA16 0DW; T.-01475 521226.

Shea, Michael Sinclair MacAuslan, CVO, MA, PhD. Chairman, Connoisseurs Scotland, since 1992; Political Consultant, Hanson PLC, since 1993; b. 10.5.38, Carluke; m., Mona Grec Stensen; 2 d. Educ. Lenzie Academy; Gordonstoun; Edinburgh University. Entered Foreign Office, 1963; seconded to Cabinet Office; Deputy Director

General, British Information Services, New York; Press Secretary to the Queen; Head of Political and Government Affairs, Hanson PLC; remains Vice-Chairman of Melody Radio Ltd. (wholly-owned Hanson subsidiary). Visiting Professor, Graduate School, Strathclyde University; Trustee, National Galleries of Scotland; Governor, Gordonstoun; Board Member, Murray Johnstone companies; Non-Excecutive Director, P&A Group; Vice-Chairman, Foundation for Skin Research; Member, Board of Directors, Edinburgh Military Tattoo; has published 21 books of fiction and non-fiction. Address: (b.) 11 Moray Place, Edinburgh EH3 6DT; T.-0131-220 1456.

Shearer, Magnus MacDonald, JP. Lord Lieutenant of Shetland, 1982-94; Honorary Consul for Sweden in Shetland and Orkney, 1958-94; Honorary Consul for Federal Republic of Germany in Shetland, 1972-87; b. 27.2.24; m., Martha Nicolson Henderson; 1 s. Educ. Anderson Educational Institute, Shetland; George Watson's College, Edinburgh. Royal Navy, Atlantic, Mediterranean and Far East, 1942-46; Royal Artillery TA, commissioned 2nd Lt., 1949; TARO, rank Captain, 1959; Honorary Secretary, Lerwick Station, RNLI, 1968-92; Chairman, Lerwick Harbour Trust, 1966-72; Member, Lerwick Town Council, 1963-69; Deputy Lieutenant of Shetland, 1973-82. Recreations: reading; bird watching; ships. Address: (h.) 4 Queens Place, Lerwick, Shetland ZE1 0BZ; T.-01595 696612.

Shedden, Alfred Charles, MA, LLB. Senior Partner, McGrigor Donald, since 1993; b. 30.6.44, Edinburgh; m., Irene; 1 s.; 1 d. Educ. Arbroath High School; Aberdeen University. McGrigor Donald: Apprentice, 1967-69, Assistant, 1969-70, Partner, 1971, Managing Partner, 1985-92. Director, Scottish Financial Enterprise, since 1989; Director, Martin Currie Japan Investment Trust plc, since 1995; Director, Standard Life Assurance Society, since 1992. Address: (b.) Pacific House, 70 Wellington Street, Glasgow; T.-0141-248 6677.

Sheed, Ronald McLean, BSc, CEng, MICE. Director of Commercial Operations, South Ayrshire Council, since 1995; b. 8.5.47, Glasgow; m., Beth; 1 s.; 2 d. Educ. Duncanrig Senior Secondary School, East Kilbride; Strathclyde University. Lanark County Council, 1969-75; Strathclyde Regional Council, 1975-95, latterly as Contracts Manager, Roads Direct. Recreation: sport. Address: (b.) County Buildings, Wellington Square, Ayr, KA7 1DS; T.-01292 012421.

Sheehan, Sheriff Albert Vincent, MA, LLB. Sheriff of Tayside, Central and Fife, at Falkirk, since 1983; b. 23.8.36, Edinburgh; m., Edna Georgina Scott Hastings; 2 d. Educ. Bo'ness Academy; Edinburgh University. 2nd Lt., 1st Bn., Royal Scots (The Royal Regiment), 1960; Captain, Directorate of Army Legal Services, 1961; Depute Procurator Fiscal, Hamilton, 1961-71; Senior Depute Procurator Fiscal, Glasgow, 1971-74; Deputy Crown Agent for Scotland, 1974-79; Scottish Law Commission, 1979-81; Sheriff of Lothian and Borders, at Edinburgh, 1981-83. Leverhulme Fellow, 1971. Publications: Criminal Procedure in Scotland and France, 1975; Criminal Procedure, 1990. Recreations: naval history; travel. Address: (b.) Sheriff Court House, Falkirk; T.-Falkirk 20822.

Shelton, Richard Graham John, BSc, PhD. Officer-in-Charge, Scottish Office Freshwater Fisheries Laboratory, Pitlochry, since 1982; b. 3.7.42, Aylesbury; m., Freda Carstairs; 2 s. Educ. Royal Grammar School, High Wycombe; St. Andrews University. Research work, Burnham-on-Crouch Laboratory, MAFF, 1968-72; Assistant to Controller of Fisheries Research and Development, MAFF Fisheries Laboratory, Lowestoft, 1972-76 and (from 1974) Marine Laboratory, Aberdeen; worked on the population ecology of Crustacea, 1976-82.

Address: (b.) Scottish Office Freshwater Fisheries Laboratory, Faskally, Pitlochry, PH16 5LB; T.-01796 2060.

Shepherd, Lt.-Col. Ian. Regional Organiser (Scotland), Army Benevolent Fund; b. 6.4.39; m., Belinda Buchanan-Dunlop; 2 s.; 1 d. Educ. Queen's College of British Guiana; Dollar Academy; RMA Sandhurst. Commissioned into Royal Highland Fusiliers, 1960; Assistant Military Attache (Tech), Moscow, 1981-82; CO Scot Infantry Depot (Bridge of Don), 1984-86; CO, University of Aberdeen OTC, 1986-88, retired 1992. Chairman, Management Committee, Lady Haig's Poppy Factory; Member, North, South, East Committee, The Officers' Association Scotland. Recreation: being an old soldier. Address: c/o Bank of Scotland, The Mound, Edinburgh, EH1 1YZ.

Shepherd, Professor James, BSc, MB, ChB, PhD, FRCPath, FRCP (Glas). Professor in Pathological Biochemistry, Glasgow University, since 1987 (Reader, 1984-87); b. 8.4.44, Motherwell; m., Janet Bulloch Kelly; 1 s.; 1 d. Educ. Hamilton Academy; Glasgow University. Lecturer, Glasgow University: Biochemistry, 1968-72, Pathological Biochemistry, 1972-77; Assistant Professor of Medicine, Baylor College of Medicine, Houston, Texas, 1976-77; Senior Lecturer in Pathological Biochemistry, Glasgow University, 1977-84; Visiting Professor of Medicine, Geneva University, 1984; Director, West of Scotland Coronary Prevention Study; Chairman, European Atherosclerosis Society, 1993-96; author of textbooks and papers on lipoprotein metabolism and heart disease prevention. Address: (b.) Department of Biochemistry, Royal Infirmary, Glasgow, G4 OSF; T.-0141-304 4628.

Shepherd, Janet, CertEd. Secretary for Scotland, Duke of Edinburgh's Award, since 1994; b. 6.8.52, Chipping Sodbury. Educ. Rodway School; Bognor Regis College of Education. Royal Forest of Dean Grammar School; Plas Pencelli Outdoor Education Centre; Faskally Outdoor Centre; Dolcorsllwyn Hall Outdoor Education Centre, Knowsley; Howtown Outdoor Education Centre, Co. Durham; Bewerley Park Outdoor Education Centre, North Yorkshire. Recreations: travelling; ornithology; mountaineering; skiing; canoeing; embroidery; Scottish folk music. Address: (b.) 69 Dublin Street, Edinburgh EH3 6NS; T.-0131-556 9097.

Shepherd, Peter Charles, LLB, NP. Solicitor; b. 7.2.58, Aberdeen; m., Sheila Catherine; 2 s.; 1 d. Educ. Robert Gordon's College; Aberdeen University. Apprentice, 1978-80; Assistant, 1980-83; Partner, Aberdein Considine & Co., since 1984. President, Aberdeen Bar Association, 1994-95. Recreations: golf; fishing; gardening. Address: (b.) 8 Bon Accord Crescent, Aberdeen; T.-01224 589700.

Shepherd, Robert Horne (Robbie), AScA. Freelance Broadcaster, since 1976; b. 30.4.36, Dunecht, Aberdeen; m., Agnes Margaret (Esma); 1 s. Educ. Robert Gordon's College, Aberdeen. Left school at 15 to work in accountant's office; National Service, two years; joined fish firm as Assistant Accountant, then with fish group for 13 years as Management Accountant; left to become self-employed in that capacity; now full-time on radio and television. Recreations: golf; gardening; traditional music.

Sheridan, Rt. Rev. Mgr. John. Prelate of Honour; Parish Priest, St. Paul's, Whiteinch, Glasgow, since 1986; b. 22.8.29, Clydebank. Educ. Holyrood Senior Secondary School, Glasgow; Campion House, Osterley; Royal Scots College, Valladolid, Spain. Ordained Priest, 1956; Curate in Glasgow, 1956-63; Spiritual Director, Royal Scots College, Valladolid, Spain, 1963-69; Curate in Glasgow, 1969-84; Parish Priest, Our Lady and St. Margaret's, Kinning Park, 1984-86; Chancellor, Archdiocese of Glasgow, 1983-92. Scout Area Chaplain, Glasgow, 1960-63; Scout District Commissioner, N.E. and N.W.II Districts, Glasgow, 1970-78; National Scout Chaplain, 1978-94; Hon. Vice

Chairman, Scottish Catholic Scout Advisory Council, 1995; awarded Scout Silver Acorn, 1987. Recreations: golf; painting; caravanning. Address: St. Paul's, 1213 Dumbarton Road, Glasgow G14 9UP; T.-0141-950 2488.

Sherrard, Mary Stephen, MBE, BA. National President, Woman's Guild, Church of Scotland, 1993-96; Representative on Women's National Commission, since 1993; b. 22.4.23, Renfrew; m., Rev. John A. Sherrard; 2 s.; 1 d. Educ. Girls' High School, Glasgow; Open University. Journalist; service in W.R.N.S.; playgroup work; Citizens Advice Bureau Manager; Chairman, Angus Citizens Advice Bureau; Vice-Chair, Scottish CAB. Elder, Buckhaven Parish Church. Recreations: crosswords; writing; walking on holiday. Address: (h.) Fair Havens, West Wynd, Buckhaven, KY8 1AS; T.-01592 716457.

Sherriff, Robert Mark, CBE, MSI, BA, DL. Stockbroker, since 1960; Vice Chairman, Executive Committee, Erskine Hospital, since 1988; Chairman, The MacRoberts Trusts Tarland, since 1994; b. 29.3.36, Kilmacolm; m., Margaret Fraser; 2 s.; 2 d. Educ. Cargilfield; Sedbergh; Trinity College, Cambridge. Joined R.C. Greig & Co., Stockbroker, Glasgow, 1959; became a Partner (now Director); Vice Chairman, Greig Middleton & Co. Ltd., Glasgow; Director, King & Shaxson, London; Vice Chairman, Scottish Building Society; retired as Chairman, Highland TAVR, 1996. Member, Erskine Hospital Committee. Recreations: tennis; golf; shooting; skiing. Address: (b.) 155 St. Vincent Street, Glasgow, G2 5NN; T.-0141-240 4000.

Sherwood, Professor John Neil, DSc, PhD, CChem, FRSC, FRSE. Burmah Professor of Physical Chemistry, Strathclyde University, since 1983; Vice Principal, since 1995; b. 8.11.33, Redruth, Cornwall; m., Margaret Enid Shaw; 2 d. Educ. Aireborough Grammar School; Bede College, Durham University. Research Fellow, Hull University, 1958-60; Lecturer, Reader and Personal Professor, Strathclyde University, 1960-83. Recreations: hill-walking; photography; gardening. Address: (b.) Department of Pure and Applied Chemistry, Strathclyde University, Glasgow, G1 1XL; T.-041-552 4400.

Shewan, Rev. Michael Richard Rennie, BD, CPS. Minister, Ratho Parish Church, since 1985; b. 23.3.56; m., Judith Ann Alexander; 1 s.; 2 d. Educ. Insch School; Aberdeen University. Assistant Minister, Northfield Church, Aberdeen, 1985-85. Recreations: gardening; swimming; cycling; walking; frequent visitor to Israel. Address: (h.) 2 Freelands Road, Ratho, Midlothian; T.-0131-333 1346.

Shiach, Allan G., BA. Chairman, Macallan-Glenlivet PLC, 1979-96; Chairman, Scottish Film Council, 1991-97; Chairman, Scottish Film Production Fund, 1991-96; b. Elgin; m., Kathleen Breck; 2 s.; 1 d. Educ. Gordonstoun School; McGill University, Montreal. Writer/Producer, since 1970; Writer/Co-Writer: Don't Look Now, The Girl from Petrovia, Daryl, Joseph Andrews, Castaway, The Witches, Cold Heaven, Regeneration, In Love and War, and other films; Member: Broadcasting Council for Scotland, 1988-91; Member, Council, Scotch Whisky Association, 1984-96; Chairman, Writers' Guild of G.B., 1989-91; Director, Rafford Films, since 1982; Director, Scottish Media Group plc, since 1993; Director, Caledonian Publishing Ltd., since 1994; Freeman, City of London, 1988.

Shiach, Sheriff Gordon Iain Wilson, MA, LLB, BA (Hons). Sheriff of Lothian and Borders, at Edinburgh, 1984-97, and at Peebles, 1996-97; b. 15.10.35, Elgin; m., Margaret Grant Smith; 2 d. (1 deceased). Educ. Lathallan; Gordonstoun; Edinburgh University; Open University. Admitted Advocate, 1961; practised as Advocate, 1960-72; Sheriff of Fife and Kinross, later Tayside, Central and Fife, at Dunfermline, 1972-79; Sheriff of Lothian and Borders, at

Linlithgow, 1979-84; Hon. Sheriff, Elgin, since 1986; Member: Council of Sheriffs' Association, 1989-95 (President, 1993-95); Standing Committee on Criminal Procedure, 1989-93; Board, Lothian Family Conciliation Service, 1989-93; Parole Board for Scotland, since 1990 (Vice Chairman, since 1995); Council, Faculty of Advocates, 1993-95; Shrieval Training Group, 1994-95; Review Group on Social Work National Standards for Throughcare, 1994-95; Chairman, The Scottish Society, 1992-93, The Edinburgh Sir Walter Scott Club, since 1995. Recreations: walking; swimming; music; art; film; theatre.

Shields, Sir Robert, MD, DL, PRCSEd, FRCSEng, FRCPS, DSc, HonFACS, HonFRCSI, HonFRCSHK, HonFRCPEdin, FAcadMedSingap. President, Royal College of Surgeons of Edinburgh, since 1994; Professor of Surgery, Liverpool University; Consultant Surgeon, Royal Liverpool Hospital, 1969-96; b. 8.11.30, Paisley; m., Marianne; 1 s.; 2 d. Educ. John Neilson Institution, Paisley; Glasgow University. House Officer, Western Infirmary, Glasgow; Research Associate, Mayo Clinic, Rochester, USA; Lecturer in Surgery, Western Infirmary, Glasgow; Senior Lecturer and Reader, Welsh National School of Medicine; Honorary Consultant Surgeon, Royal Infirmary, Cardiff. President, James IV Association; Past President, Association of Surgeons of Great Britain and Ireland; Past President, British Society of Gastroenterology; Past President, Surgical Research Society. Recreations: walking; reading. Address: (b.) Royal College of Surgeons of Edinburgh, Nicolson Street, Edinburgh, EH8 9DW; T.-0131-527 1635.

Shinwell, Sir (Maurice) Adrian, Kt, LLB, NP, ACIArb. Solicitor; Senior Partner, Kerr, Barrie & Duncan, Glasgow, since 1991; b. 27.2.51; m., Lesley McLean; 2 s.; 1 d. Educ. Hutchesons' Boys' Grammar School; Glasgow University. Admitted Solicitor, 1975; joined Kerr, Barrie & Duncan, 1976; Notary Public, since 1976; Tutor (part-time), Law Faculty, Glasgow University, 1980-84; ACI Arbitrators, since 1990; Solicitor-Mediator, since 1994; Director, Kerr Barrie Nominees Ltd. Scottish Conservative and Unionist Association: Member, Scottish Council, since 1982; Chairman, Eastwood Association, 1982-85; Chairman, Cumbernauld and Kilsyth Association, 1989-91; Vice-President, 1989-92; President, 1992-94; Member, Central Advisory Committee on Justices of the Peace, since 1996. Recreations: family; politics. Address: (h.) Sarona, South Road, Busby, Glasgow, G76 8JB; T.-0141-221 6844.

Shirreffs, Murdoch John, MB, ChB, DObstRCOG, FRCGP, MFHom. General Medical Practitioner, Aberdeen, since 1974; Medical Hypnotherapist and Homoeopathic Physician; b. 25.5.47, Aberdeen; m., Jennifer McLeod. Educ. Aberdeen Grammar School; Aberdeen University. General Practice Trainer, since 1977; Secretary, Grampian Division, British Medical Association, since 1978; Member, BMA Scottish Council. Past President, North of Scotland Veterans' Hockey Club. Recreations: hockey; opera and classical music; big band jazz; DIY; gardening; food and wine; travel. Address: (h.) 72 Gray Street, Aberdeen, AB10 6JE; T.-01224 321998.

Short, Agnes Jean, BA (Hons), MLitt. Writer; b. Bradford, Yorkshire; m., Anthony Short (qv); 3 s.; 2 d. Educ. Bradford Girls' Grammar School; Exeter University; Aberdeen University. Various secretarial, research and teaching jobs, both in UK and abroad; took up writing, 1966; 19 novels, most of which have a Scottish setting; also short stories and radio; Constable Award, 1976. Recreations: dog-walking; whisky-tasting; good food; small hills. Address: (h.) Khantore, Crathie, by Ballater, Aberdeenshire, AB35 5TJ.

Shorter, Bob, BA, MHSM, MMS. Director of Primary Care, Lanarkshire Health Board, since 1995; b. 20.8.50, Epsom; m., Hilary; 2 s. Educ. Glyn Grammar School;

Heriot-Watt University. Address: (b.) 14 Beckford Street, Hamilton ML3 0TA; T.-01698 281313.

Siann, Professor Gerda, BSc, MSc, PhD, FBPsS. NCR Professor of Gender Relations, Dundee University, since 1996; b. 2.12.37, Cape Town; m., Julian Siann; 1 s.; 2 d. Educ. Wynberg Girls High School, Cape Town; University of Cape Town; University of Zambia; Edinburgh University. Lecturer in Psychology, Moray House Institute of Education, 1972-84; Senior Lecturer, Reader, Professor of Psychology, Glasgow Caledonian University, 1984-95. Member, British Council Gender and Development Task Force. Publications: Educational Psychology in a Changing World, 1980, 1988; Accounting for Aggression, 1985; Gender, Sex and Sexuality, 1994. Recreations: films; theatre; travel; reading contemporary fiction. Address: (h.) 9 Bay Road, Wormit, Fife DD6 8LU; T.-01382 543041.

Sibbald, Michael Robert, BA, MBA, MInstM. Group Personnel Director, Argos PLC, since 1996; b. 30.8.48, Edinburgh; m., Margaret; 2 s.; 1 d. Educ. George Heriot's School; Heriot-Watt University; Glasgow University. Scottish and Newcastle Breweries, 1972-75; Butler Manufacturing Co., 1975-79; Scottish Brick Corporation Ltd., 1979-81; ICL Plastics Ltd., 1981-82; Grand Metropolitan PLC, 1982-90; Director Human Resources: Stakis PLC, 1990-91, United Eng Steels Ltd., 1991-94, NHS in Scotland, 1994-96. Member, Advisory Board, Glasgow Business School, since 1996. Recreations: reading; sports cars; athletics; football. Address: (h.) 18 Craigmount Bank West, Edinburgh, EH4 8HG; T.-0131-538 4513.

Sibbett, Professor Wilson, BSc, PhD. Professor of Physics, St. Andrews University (Director of Research, since 1994, Chairman, Department of Physics and Astronomy, 1985-94); b. 15.3.48, Portglenone, N. Ireland; m., Barbara Anne Brown; 3 d. Educ. Ballymena Technical College; Queen's University, Belfast. Postdoctoral Research Fellow, Blackett Laboratory, Imperial College, London, 1973-76; Lecturer in Physics, then Reader, Imperial College, 1976-85. Fellow: Institute of Physics, Royal Society of Edinburgh, Royal Society (of London). Recreation: golf (to low standard). Address: (b.) Department of Physics and Astronomy, St. Andrews University, North Haugh, St. Andrews, KY16 9SS; T.-01334 463100.

Sidgwick, Richard Twining, JP, DL, MSc, FRICS. Partner, West Highland Estates Office, since 1974; b. 17.7.44; m., Alison Janet Baggallay; 1 s.; 2 d. Educ. Fort Augustus Abbey School; Reading University. JP, Highland area, 1990; Deputy Lieutenant, Lochaber, Inverness, Badenoch and Strathspey, 1991; Director, Lochaber Limited, 1991, Vice-Chairman, 1992; Member, Red Deer Commission, 1993; Honorary Sheriff Fort William, 1994. Recreations: country sports; gardening; amenity woodlands. Address: (h.) Inverlair Lodge, Roy Bridge, Inverness-shire, PH31 4AR; T.-01397 732 246.

Sillars, James. Management Consultant; Assistant to Secretary General, Arab-British Chamber of Commerce, since 1993; b. 4.10.37, Ayr; m., Margo MacDonald (qv); 1 s.; 3 d. Educ. Ayr Academy. Member, Ayr Town Council and Ayr County Council Education Committee, 1960s; Member, Western Regional Hospital Board, 1965-70; Head, Organisation Department, Scottish TUC, 1968-70; MP, South Ayrshire, 1970-79; Co-Founder, Scottish Labour Party, 1976; MP, Glasgow Govan, 1988-92.

Silver, Alan William, CEng, DipTE, FICE, FIHT, MRTPI. Assistant Director of Property and Technical Services – Roads, Aberdeen City Council, since 1996; b. 22.6.41, Aberdeen; m., Margaret Eileen; 2 s. Educ. Aberdeen Grammar School; Aberdeen University; Robert Gordon's Institute of Technology. Worked for Sir Robert McAlpine

& Sons on M1 Motorway; former Design Engineer, Sir William Halcrow, and Site Agent, C. Bryant & Sons; joined City Engineer's Department, Aberdeen, 1971; Chief Assistant, Traffic/Transportation/Road Safety, Roads Department, Grampian Regional Council, 1975, Director of Roads, 1993. Recreations: amateur opera; bowls; curling; steam vehicles. Address: (b.) Property and Technical Services Department, Roads Section, St. Nicholas House, Broad Street, Aberdeen AB10 1WL.

Silver, Frederick Philip, MA. Editor, Stornoway Gazette, since 1991; b. 15.7.54, Manchester; m., Stephanie Blyth Sargent; 2 d. Educ. Bolton School; Jesus College, Oxford; Victoria University, Wellington. Journalist: Reading Evening Post, Western Mail (Cardiff), Western Daily Press (Bristol), China Daily (Beijing), Dominion/Dominion Sunday Times, Wellington, New Zealand. Address: (b.) Address: (b.) 10 Francis Street, Stornoway HS1 2XE.

Silver, Gillian M., LLB, NP. Partner, MacNeill and Critchley, Solicitors, Inverness, since 1983; Member, Local Government Boundary Commission for Scotland, since 1995; b. 13.5.56, Aberdeen; m., Chris. Educ. Inverness Royal Academy; Edinburgh University. Past Chairman, Highland Solicitors Property Centre Ltd.; Past Chairman, Solicitors Property Centres Scotland; Senator, Junior Chamber International. Recreations: golf; curling; choral singing; running; theatre. Address: (h.) Chanonry Green, Kincurdie, Rosemarkie IV10 8SJ; T.-01381 621211.

Sim, Ian Allan, BSc, CA. Secretary General, Scottish Kennel Club, since 1997; Partner, Johnston Smillie, Chartered Accountants, since 1977; b. 2.8.48, Edinburgh; 2 s. Educ. Lochaber High School; Edinburgh University. Manager, Deloittes, Chartered Accountants, 1973-76. Treasurer, St. George's West Church; Chairman, Association of Independent Accountants in Scotland; Chairman/Vice Chairman, Kennel Club committees. Recreations: swimming; music. Address: (h.) 22 Craigmount Avenue, Edinburgh EH12 8HQ; T.-0131-317 7377.

Sime, Martin, MA. Director, Scottish Council for Voluntary Organisations, since 1991; b. 23.9.53, Edinburgh. Educ. George Heriot's; St. Andrews University; Edinburgh University. Social and Economic History Researcher, 1976-78; Sheep Farmer, 1978-81; Freelance Researcher, 1982; Project Manager, Sprout Market Garden, 1983-85; Development/Principal Officer (Day Services), Scottish Association for Mental Health, then Director, 1985-91; Secretary, Scottish Civic Assembly. Recreations: cinema; food; bridge. Address: (b.) 18/19 Claremont Crescent, Edinburgh, EH7 4QD; T.-0131-556 3882.

Simmers, Graeme Maxwell, OBE, CA. Chairman, Scottish Sports Council, since 1992; Non-Executive Director, Stirling Royal Infirmary NHS Trust, since 1993; b. 2.5.35, Glasgow; m., Jennifer M.H. Roxburgh; 2 s.; 2 d. Educ. Glasgow Academy; Loretto School. Qualified CA, 1959; commissioned Royal Marines, 1959-61. Former Partner, Kidsons Simmers CA; Chairman, Scottish Highland Hotels Group Ltd., 1972-92; Member, Scottish Tourist Board, 1979-86; Chairman, HCBA (Scotland), 1984-86; Past Chairman, Board of Management, Member of National Executive, BHA; Elder and Treasurer, Killearn Kirk; Governor, Queen's College, Glasgow, 1989-93; Chairman of Governors, Loretto School; Past Chairman, Championship Committee, Royal and Ancient Golf Club of St. Andrews. Recreations: rugby; golf; skiing. Address: (h.) Kincaple, Boquhan, Balfron, near Glasgow, G63 0RW; T.-01360 440375.

Simmons, Professor John Edmund Leonard, BSc, PhD, CEng, FIMechE, FIEE. Professor of Mechanical Engineering, Heriot Watt University, since 1992, and Head, Department of Mechanical and Chemical Engineering, since 1994; Vice-Chairman, Engineering Manufacturing Industries Division, IMechE, since 1995; b. 24.9.47, Faversham; m., Anne; 2 s.; 2 d. Educ. Birmingham University; Cambridge University. Production Manager, Baker Perkins Chemical Machinery, Stoke on Trent, 1977-80; Design Manager, Vickers plc–Michell Bearings, Newcastle upon Tyne, 1981-84; Lecturer in Engineering, Durham University, 1984-91. Recreations: gardening; walking; travelling; cinema. Address: (b.) Heriot Watt University, Edinburgh, EH14 4AS; T.-0131-451 3132.

Simpson, Andrew Rutherford, MB, ChB, D(Obst)RCOG. Principal, general practice, 1965-94; Non Executive Director, Borders Community Health Services NHS Trust; Chairman, Borders Research Ethics Committee; b. 13.7.32, Hawick; m., Helen Margaret Douglas; 3 d. Educ. Merchiston Castle School, Edinburgh; Edinburgh University. BMA: former Member, Scottish Council; Past Chairman, Scottish Borders Division, 1980, former Representative for Borders on Scottish Council; Past President and Life Member, Hawick Rugby Club (club doctor, over 30 years); Past President, Hawick Callants Club; Chairman, Douglas Haig Court. Recreations: rugby involvement; golf; philately; Rotary. Address: (h.) Netherfield, Buccleuch Road, Hawick, TD9 0EL; T.-01450 372459.

Simpson, Brian Middleton, MIBiol, FRAgS. Chief Executive, Scotch Quality Beef and Lamb Association, since 1991; b. 24.9.52, Perth; m., Helena; 1 s.; 2 d. Educ. Perth High School; West of Scotland Agricultural College. Agricultural Adviser, Scottish Agricultural College; Marketing Adviser, Kemira Fertilisers; Senior Project Executive, Scottish Enterprise. Recreation: hill-walking. Address: (b.) Rural Centre, West Mains, Ingliston, Newbridge, EH28 8NZ; T.-0131-472 4040.

Simpson, David, CBE, DSc, CEng, FIEE. Chairman: Simpson Research Ltd., Isocom Components Ltd., Albacom Ltd., Bookham Technology Ltd., Syntaq Ltd., Icon Research Ltd.; Vice-Chairman: Scotish Opto Electronic Association, Genesis Consultancy Ltd.; Director, Healthscribe Inc.; b. 23.11.26, Ceres; m., Janice Ann; 1 s.; 2 d. Educ. Bell Baxter School, Cupar; Dundee Technical College; Stanford University. R. & D. Engineer, Marconi, 1952-56; Managing Director, Microcell Electronics, 1956-60; General Manager, Hughes Microelectronics, 1960-62; Managing Director, Hewlett Packard Ltd., 1962-70; President, Gould Corp., Chicago, 1976-88; Chairman, various UK companies, 1988-92. Recreations: hill-walking; wood-carving. Address: (h.) Elvingston House, Tranent, EH33 1EH; T.-01875 852878.

Simpson, George Alexander. Chairman, Thainstone House Hotel Ltd., Carden Place Investments Ltd.; b. 13.1.43; m., Lorraine; 1 s.; 1 d. Educ. Peterhead Academy. Founded Kildonnan Investments Ltd., late '60s; sold, 1989; founded Craigendarroch Group, 1983; Director, North of Scotland Radio Ltd. (Northsound). Recreations: golf; swimming; football. Address: (h.) 22 Rubislaw Den North, Aberdeen, AB15 4AN; T.-01224 208584.

Simpson, Professor Hugh Walter, MB, ChB, MD, PhD, FRCPath, FRCP(Glas). Head of Pathology, Glasgow Royal Infirmary, 1984-93, now Senior Research Fellow, University Department of Surgery, Glasgow University and Royal Infirmary; b. 4.4.31, Ceres Fife; m., Myrtle Emslie (see Myrtle Simpson); 3 s.; 1 d. Educ. Bryanston; Edinburgh University. Leader of numerous expeditions to polar and tropical regions; awarded Polar Medal, Mungo Park and Pery Medals. Publications: 160 scientific publications, especially on breast cancer. Recreation: skiing. Address: (h.) 7 Cleveden Crescent, Glasgow, G12 0PD; T.-0141-357 1091.

Simpson, Ian Christopher, LLB. Sheriff of South Strathclyde, Dumfries and Galloway, since 1988, at Airdrie, since 1991; b. 5.7.49, Edinburgh; m., Christine Margaret Anne Strang; 2 s. Educ. Glenalmond; Edinburgh University. Admitted to Faculty of Advocates, 1974. Captain, Scottish Universities Golfing Society, 1989-90; President, All Sphere Club, 1989-90. Recreation: golf. Address: (b.) Airdrie Sheriff Court, Graham Street, Airdrie, ML6 6EE; T.-01236 751121.

Simpson, Rev. James Alexander, BSc (Hons), BD, STM, DD. Minister, Dornoch Cathedral, 1976-97; Chaplain to the Queen in Scotland; Moderator, General Assembly of the Church of Scotland, 1994; b. 9.3.34, Glasgow; m., Helen Gray McCorquodale; 3 s.; 2 d. Educ. Eastwood Secondary School; Glasgow University; Union Seminary, New York. Minister: Grahamston Church, Falkirk, 1960-66, St. John's Renfield, Glasgow, 1966-76. Publications: There is a time to ....; Marriage Questions Today; Doubts are not Enough; Holy Wit; Laughter Lines; The Master Mind; Dornoch Cathedral; More Holy Wit; Keywords of Faith; All About Christmas. Recreations: golf; photography; writing. Address: The Manse, Dalcrue Road, Pitcairngreen, Perth PH1 3LU; T.- 01738 583217.

Simpson, James Walter Thorburn, BArch, RIBA, FRIAS. Partner, Simpson & Brown, Architects, since 1977; b. 27.7.44, Edinburgh; m., Ann Mary Bunney; 2 d. Educ. Trinity College, Glenalmond; Edinburgh College of Art. Lecturer, Heriot Watt University, 1975-80; co-founded Simpson & Brown, 1977, and Acanthus Associated Architectural Practices, 1985; Architect to St. Giles' Cathedral, 1983-90; Member, Ancient Monuments Board for Scotland, 1983-95; Architectural Advisor, Scottish Historic Buildings Trust, since 1985; Surveyor of the Fabric of York Minster, 1994-95; Chairman, RIAS Conservation Committee, 1992-94; UK Committee Member, International Council for Monuments and Sites, since 1992. Recreations: architectural history and geography; walking; piping; Scotland. Address: (b.) 179 Canongate, Edinburgh, EH8 8BN; T.-0131-557 3880.

Simpson, J.W., BSc, MCIT, MRIN, MNI. Chief Harbour Master, Firth of Forth, and Manager, Marine Services, since 1996; Divisional Manager, Marine Services, Forth Ports PLC, 1986-96; Director, Forth Estuary Towage Ltd., since 1986; b. 30.8.44, St. Andrews; m., Barbara Hutton; 1 s.; 1 d. Educ. Grangemouth High School; Buckhaven High School; Leith Nautical College; Plymouth Polytechnic. Cadet, Furness Prince Lines, 1961-64; Navigating Officer: Shaw Savill Line, 1965-68, Overseas Containers Ltd., 1969-70; Assistant Harbour Master, then Assistant to Port Superintendent, Grangemouth, 1973-77; Port Superintendent, Leith and Granton, 1978-82; Port Manager, Grangemouth, 1982-86. Recreation: sailing. Address: (b.) Forth Ports PLC, Tower Place, Leith, EH6 7DB; T.-0131-554 6473.

Simpson, John Douglas, BSc(Hons). Headteacher, Fortrose Academy, since 1989; b. 2.3.51, Kilbirnie; m., Linda; 2 s.; 2 d. Educ. Spier's School, Beith; Glasgow University. Teacher of Biology, 1975; Principal Teacher, 1979; Assistant Headteacher, Merksworth High School, Paisley, 1983; Depute Headteacher, Cowdenknowes High School, Greenock, 1985. Recreations: golf; snooker. Address: (b.) Fortrose Academy, Fortrose, Ross-shire; T.-01381 620310.

Simpson, John William, IPFA. Secretary General, General Synod, Scottish Episcopal Church, since 1993; b. 19.11.44, Bournemouth; m., Joyce Carol Pollock; 2 s. Bournemouth CBC, 1961-68; Basingstoke BC, 1968-70; Poole BC, 1970-74, Bournemouth BC, 1974-81; Open University, 1981-87; Scottish Hydro-Electric PLC, 1988-90; KPMG Peat Marwick, 1990-93. Address: 21 Grosvenor Crescent, Edinburgh, EH12 5EE.

Simpson, Myrtle Lillias, DL. Author and Lecturer; Member, Scottish Sports Council; Past Chairman, Scottish National Ski Council; b. 5.7.31, Aldershot; m., Professor Hugh Simpson (qv); 3 s.; 1 d. Educ. 19 schools (father in Army). Writer/Explorer; author of 12 books, including travel, biography, historical and children's; first woman to ski across Greenland; attempted to ski to North Pole (most northerly point reached by a woman unsupported); numerous journeys in polar regions on ski or canoe; exploration in China and Peru; Mungo Park Medal; Editor, Avenue (University of Glasgow magazine). Recreations: climbing; skiing; canoeing. Address: (h.) 7 Cleveden Crescent, Glasgow, G12 0PD; T.-0141-357 1091.

Simpson, Robert Keith, FCCA, IPFA. Governor, Royal Scottish Academy of Music and Drama; b. 26.7.43, Barrow-in-Furness; m., Brenda Mary Baines; 2 s. Educ. Barrow-in-Furness Grammar School. Accountant, Barrow-in-Furness County Borough Council, 1959-72; Principal Auditor, Bristol City Council, 1972-74; Chief Auditor, Avon County Council, 1974-77; Assistant Director of Finance, South Yorkshire County Council, 1977-82; Depute Controller of Audit, Commission for Local Authority Accounts in Scotland, 1982-85; Controller of Audit, Commission for Local Authority Accounts in Scotland, 1985-89. Former Editor, Audit Bulletin, CIPFA. Publications: Internal Audit in the Public Sector; Audit in the Public Sector (Co-author). Recreations: golf; hill-walking; drama. Address: (h.) Torr Beag, Killiecrankie; T.-01796 473602.

Sims, Graeme Lindsay, BA (Hons). Deputy Director General (Scotland), Office of Electricity Regulation, since 1994; b. 31.10.63, Glasgow; m., June Kennedy Russell; 1 d. Educ. Calday Grange Grammar School, Wirral; Magdalen College, Oxford. Associate Consultant, Boston Consulting Group, 1985-87; Development Officer, Scottish Cooperatives Development Committee, 1988-91; Economic Adviser, OFFER, 1991-93. Recreations: cooking; eating out; film; music. Address: (b.) OFFER, Regent Court, 70 West Regent Street, Glasgow G2 2QZ.

Sinclair, Alexander, OBE, DL, FCII. President, The Golf Foundation, 1991-96; b. 6.7.20, West Kilbride; m., Elizabeth Tennant; 2 s.; 1 d. Educ. Ardrossan Academy. Clerk, Norwich Union, 1938-40; Royal Artillery, 1940-46; joined Alexander Stenhouse Insurance Brokers, 1957 (Director, 1962); Chairman, British Insurance Brokers Association in Scotland, 1985; retired, 1985. Deputy Lieutenant, Lanarkshire, 1988; Captain, Royal & Ancient Golf Club, 1988-89; Chairman, R. & A. Selection Committee, 1969-75; President, European Golf Association, 1981-83; President, Scottish Golf Union, 1976-77; former Scottish golf internationalist and Scottish golf captain; awarded Frank Moran Award, 1979, for contribution to golf; West of Scotland Champion, 1950; semi-finalist, Scottish Amateur Championship, 1947-56; Lanarkshire Champion, three times; Scottish Senior Champion, 1979-84. Recreations: golf; curling; painting. Address: (h.) 17 Blairston Avenue, Bothwell, G71 8RZ; T.-01698 853359.

Sinclair, 17th Lord (Charles Murray Kennedy St. Clair), CVO. Lord Lieutenant, Dumfries and Galloway Region (District of Stewartry), 1982- 89; Extra Equerry to the Queen Mother, since 1953; Member, Queen's Bodyguard for Scotland (Royal Company of Archers); b. 21.6.14; m., Anne Lettice Cotterell; 1 s.; 2 d. Educ. Eton; Magdalene College, Cambridge. Served Second World War (mentioned in Despatches); retired Major, Coldstream Guards. Address: (h.) Knocknalling, St. John's Town of Dalry, Castle Douglas, Kirkcudbrightshire.

Sinclair, Rev. Colin Andrew Macalister, BA (Hons), BD (Hons). Minister, Palmerston Place Church of Scotland, since 1996; b. 16.9.53, Glasgow; m., Ruth Mary Murray; 1 s.; 3 d. Educ. Glasgow Academy; Stirling University; Edinburgh University. Training Officer, Scripture Union, Zambia, 1974-77; Assistant Minister, Palmerston Place Church of Scotland, Edinburgh, 1980-82; Church of Scotland Minister, Newton on Ayr, 1982-88; General Director, Scripture Union Scotland, 1988-96. Chairman, Evangelical Alliance Scotland; Board Member, Mission Scotland; Chairman, Scottish Lausanne Committee; Member, Council of Management, Spring Harvest. Recreations: family; reading; sport. Address: (b.) Annan House, 10 Palmerston Place, Edinburgh EH12 5AA.

Sinclair, Derek Urquhart, MA (Hons), MB, ChB, MRCGP, DPM. Consultant in Learning Disability, Central Scotland Healthcare NHS Trust, since 1992; b. 10.10.40, Falkirk; m., Dorothy Aalbregt; 1 s.; 2 d. Educ. Grangemouth High School; Falkirk High School; Glasgow University. Norwegian State Stipendiary, 1965-66; Principal in general practice, Falkirk, 1972-86; Regional Medical Officer, 1986-87, Medical Officer, 1987-88, Senior Medical Officer, 1988-92, Scottish Office Home and Health Department; Royal Scottish National Hospital and Community NHS Trust, Larbert: Unit Medical Manager, 1992-93, Medical Director, 1993-94; Medical Director, Central Scotland Healthcare NHS Trust, 1994-97. Recreations: gardening; walking; fishing. Address: (b.) Central Scotland Healthcare NHS Trust, Larbert FK5 4SD; T.-01324 570700.

Sinclair, Douglas, MA (Hons). Chief Executive, Convention of Scottish Local Authorities (COSLA), since 1995; b. 28.1.46, Ellon; m., Mairi; 2 d. Educ. Inverness Royal Academy; Edinburgh University. Administrative Assistant, Midlothian CC, 1969-72; Administrative Officer, Barnardo's Scotland, 1972-75; Depute Director of Administration, then Director of Administration, Western Isles Islands Council, 1975-85; Chief Executive, Ross and Cromarty DC, 1985-90; Chief Executive, Central Regional Council, 1990-95. Recreations: gardening; Scottish literature; walking. Address: (h.) 1 Queens Road, Stirling, FK8 2QY.

Sinclair, Eric T.A., MA, DipEd. Rector, Kirkwall Grammar School, since 1991; b. 20.9.48, Edinburgh; m., Johanna Beckley; 3 c. Educ. Bell Baxter High School, Cupar; St. Andrews University; Edinburgh University; Moray House College. Taught, Teacher Training Colleges, Cameroon, Nigeria; Head of English, English High School, Istanbul; Assistant Rector, Forres Academy; Depute Rector, Bridge of Don Academy. Recreations: orienteering; squash; chess; gardening; reading. Address: (h.) Inganess Cottage, St. Ola, Kirkwall, Orkney; T.-01856 874289.

Sinclair, Isabel Lillias, MA, BL, QC. Honorary Sheriff of Lothian and Borders, since 1979; b. Glasgow; m., J. Gordon MacDonald, BL. Educ. Shawlands Academy; Glasgow University. Newspaperwoman, 1933-46; Scottish Editor, BBC Woman's Hour, 1948; called to Scottish Bar, 1949; appointed Queen's Counsel, 1964; Sheriff Substitute, Lanarkshire at Airdrie, 1966-68; Sheriff of Lothian and Borders at Selkirk and Peebles, then Peebles and Edinburgh, 1968-79. Address: 30 Ravelston Garden, Edinburgh, EH4 3LE; T.-0131-337 9797.

Sinclair, Professor John Henderson, BA, LLB. Professor of Conveyancing, Strathclyde University, since 1991; b. 5.11.35, Glasgow; m., Sandra Gunn Fraser; 1 s.; 1 d. Educ. Strathallan; Queen's University of Belfast; Glasgow University. Admitted Solicitor in Scotland, 1962; Lecturer in Conveyancing, Strathclyde University, 1970; Clerk, Royal Faculty of Procurators in Glasgow, 1983-93. Publications: Handbook of Conveyancing in Scotland; Contributor to Stair Memorial Encyclopaedia. Recreation: walking. Address: (b.) 173 Cathedral Street, Glasgow G4; T.-0141-552 4400.

Sinclair, Martin Fraser, MA, CA. Partner, Chiene & Tait, CA, since 1973; Director, Albyn Trust Ltd., since 1973;

Director, NESSCO Ltd., since 1982; b. 18.7.45, Greenock; m., Patricia Anne Ogilvy Smith; 1 s.; 2 d. Educ. Edinburgh Academy; Edinburgh University. Apprentice, Chiene & Tait, CA; qualified, 1970; Peat Marwick Mitchell & Co., Vancouver, 1970-73. President, Institute of Chartered Accountants Benevolent Association, 1983-84. Athletics Blue, Edinburgh University; Captain, Scottish Universities Athletics Team, 1969. Recreations: skiing; squash; orienteering. Address: (b.) 3 Albyn Place, Edinburgh, EH2 4NQ; T.-0131-225 7515.

Sinclair, Professor Roy Stuart, BSc, MSc, PhD, FSDC, FRSC, CCol, CChem. Personal Professor, Chemistry and Chemical Engineering, Paisley University, since 1991; Assistant Chief Commissioner (Scotland West), Scout Association, 1990-97; b. 21.4.33, Glasgow; m., Ellen Catherine Murray; 2 s. Educ. Allan Glen's School, Glasgow; London University (External); Paisley University; Strathclyde University. Research Assistant, J. & P. Coats, Paisley, 1950-56; Lecturer in Chemistry, Paisley College, 1956-80, Senior Lecturer, 1980-91. Vice President, Paisley Philosophical Institution. Recreations: Scouting; hill-walking; occasional golf. Address: (b.) Paisley University, Paisley PA1 2BE; T.-0141-848 3201.

Singleton, Major John Francis Maxwell, MA, DL; b. 26.8.16, Colwall; m., Jean Osborne (deceased); 1 s.; 2 d. Educ. Uppingham; Pembroke College, Cambridge. Commissioned Royal Artillery, 1938; served Second World War, BEF, MEF, CMF, BLA; Instructor, Mons Officer Cadet School, 1949-52; Malayan emergency, 1953-54. Deputy Lieutenant, Kincardineshire; Vice Chairman, NE TAVRA; County Commissioner for Scouts, Kincardineshire. Recreations: physical training; outdoor games. Address: Hillhead, St. Cyrus, Montrose.

Sischy, Judith, BA, MA. Director, Scottish Council of Independent Schools, since 1990; b. 20.12.47, Halifax; m., Mark Sischy. Educ. Newcastle upon Tyne Church High School; Bristol University; University of Toronto. Previously: Teacher of Modern Languages, Assistant and Deputy Secretary, Edinburgh Merchant Company. Director, Edinburgh Chamber of Commerce and Edinburgh Common Purpose; non-executive Director, Edinburgh Sick Children's Trust. Recreations: walking; swimming; cinema; music. Address: (b.) 21 Melville Street, Edinburgh EH3 7PE; T.-0131-220 2106.

Sizer, Professor John, CBE, DLitt, BA, FCMA, FIM, FRSA. Chief Executive, Scottish Higher Education Funding Council, since 1992; b. 14.9.38, Grimsby; m., Valerie; 3 s. Educ. Grimsby Technical Secondary School; Nottingham and Loughborough Universities. Financial Advisor, GKN PLC; Lecturer, Edinburgh University; Senior Lecturer, London Business School; Professor and Director, Business School, Loughborough University; Member, University Grants Committee. Leverhulme Prize, Chartered Institute of Management Accountants. Publications: An Insight Into Management Accounting; other books and papers. Recreations: walking; enjoying Scotland. Address: (b.) Donaldson House, 97 Haymarket Terrace, Edinburgh, EH12 5HD; T.-0131-313 6502.

Skene, Charles Pirie, OBE, FBIPP, ARPS, FRSA. Chairman, Skene Group of companies, developers and owners of first continuing care retirement community in Scotland; Visiting Professor of Entrepreneurship, Robert Gordon University; Member, Task Force to investigate under-achievement in schools, 1996-97; Chairman, CBI (Scotland) Enterprise Group, since 1994; b. 30.4.35, Aberdeen; m., Alison; 1 s.; 2 d. Educ. Loretto. Past President of numerous organisations, including Aberdeen Chamber of Commerce and Association of Scottish Chambers of Commerce; Past Chairman, CBI Education and Training Committee; initiated Skene Young Entrepreneur's Award, Grampian, 1986; Member, Board,

Young Enterprise Grampian; Trustee: Photographic Arts and Science Foundation, Oklahoma City, Haddo Arts Trust, Gordon Cook Foundation. Address: (b.) 23 Rubislaw Den North, Aberdeen, AB15 4AL; T.-01224 326221.

Skilbeck, Bruce. Chief Executive, Western Isles Health Board; Acting General Manager, Orkney Health Board. Address: (b.) 37 South Beach Street, Stornoway, Isle of Lewis.

Skinner, Professor Andrew, MA, BLitt, FRSE, FBA. Adam Smith Professor of Political Economy, since 1994, Vice-Principal, 1991-96, Glasgow University; b. 11.1.35, Glasgow; m., Margaret Mary Robertson. Educ. Keil School, Dumbarton; Glasgow University; Cornell University, New York. Address: (h.) Glen House, Cardross, G82 5ES; T.-0138 9841 603.

Skinner, Angus, MBA, BSc, CQSW. Chief Inspector of Social Work Services, Scotland, since 1991; b. 9.1.50, Pakistan; 1 s.; 2 d. Educ. Daniel Stewart's, Edinburgh; Edinburgh University; London University; Strathclyde University. Cheshire County Council, 1971-72; Kent County Council, 1973-75; Lothian Region Social Work Department, 1976-88; Borders Region Social Work Department, 1988-91. Address: (b.) Scottish Office Home Department, Social Work Services Group, James Craig Walk, Edinburgh EH1 3BA.

Skinner, Robert Gordon, LLB (Hons). Advocate, since 1987; part-time Chairman, Social Security Appeals Tribunal, since 1988; part-time Chairman, Disability Appeals Tribunal, since 1991; b. 14.6.57, Glasgow; m., Eileen Mary Judith Paterson; 2 s. Educ. Bishopbriggs High School; Glasgow University. Law Apprentice, Hughes, Dowdall & Co., Solicitors, Glasgow; Solicitor, Dorman Jeffrey & Co., Solicitors, Glasgow, 1980-86; called to the Bar, 1987. Recreations: football; swimming; golf; opera. Address: (h.) Whitehall, Springkell Avenue, Pollokshields, Glasgow.

Skorupski, Professor John Maria, MA, PhD. Professor of Moral Philosophy, St. Andrews University, since 1990; b. 19.9.46, Italy; m., Barbara Mary; 2 d. Educ. St. Benedict's, Ealing; Christ's College, Cambridge. Visiting Lectureships, Nigeria and Belgium, 1971-74; University of Wales Research Fellow, University College of Swansea, 1974-76; Lecturer in Philosophy, Glasgow University, 1976-84; Professor of Philosophy, Sheffield University, 1984-90. Fellow, Royal Society of Edinburgh. Publications: Symbol and Theory, 1976; John Stuart Mill, 1989; English Language Philosophy 1750-1945, 1993. Recreations: music; walking; skiing. Address: (h.) Cedar Lodge, Hepburn Gardens, St. Andrews, KY16 9LP; T.-01334 477590.

Slack, Rev. William G., DipTh. General Secretary, Baptist Union of Scotland, since 1995; b. 29.4.49, Edinburgh; m., Vivienne; 1 d. Educ. Trinity Academy, Edinburgh; Hamilton Academy; Baptist Theological College of Scotland. Minister, Ladywell, Livingston, 1974-82; Minister, International Baptist Church, Aberdeen, 1982-95. Recreations: philately; swimming; music. Address: (b.) 14 Aytoun Road, Glasgow, G41 5RT.

Slane, John Kerr, BSc. Factory Manager, Tarka Controls Ltd., Inverness, since 1984; former Chairman, Highland Area Group, CBI; b. 16.2.53, Dundee; m., Linda Jean. Educ. Morgan Academy; Dundee College of Technology. Recreation: hill-walking. Address: (b.) Tarka Controls Ltd., Lochiel Road, Inverness, IV2 3XR; T.-01463 237311.

Slater, Professor Peter James Bramwell, BSc, PhD, DSc, FIBiol, FRSE. Kennedy Professor of Natural History, St. Andrews University, since 1984, Head, School of Biological and Medical Sciences, 1992-97; b. 26.12.42,

Edinburgh; m., Elisabeth Vernon Smith; 2 s. Educ. Edinburgh Academy; Glenalmond; Edinburgh University. Demonstrator in Zoology, Edinburgh University, 1966-68; Lecturer in Biology, Sussex University, 1968-84. Secretary, Association for the Study of Animal Behaviour, 1973-78, President, 1986-89; European Editor, Animal Behaviour, 1979-82; Editor, Advances in the Study of Behavior. Recreations: walking; ornithology; music. Address: (b.) School of Environmental and Evolutionary Biology, St. Andrews, Fife; T.-01334 463500.

Slater, Stephen Oakley, BA (Hons). Senior Producer, Tramway, Glasgow City Council, since 1995; b. 13.2.62, Wirksworth, Derbyshire; m., Charlotte Mary Oakley. Educ. Anthony Gell Secondary School, Wirksworth; Howard Gardens College of Art, Cardiff. Performance Artist, Stanslat Performance Company, 1985-89; Co-Founder, Situation Cinema, multi media group, Brighton, 1985-88; Art Reach Co-ordinator, Third Eye Centre, Glasgow, 1988-91; Administrator, Paisley Arts Centre, 1992-95. Recreations: painting; hill-walking; cycling; astronomy; science fiction. Address: (h.) 12 Kensington Gate, Dowanhill, Glasgow G12 9LG; T.-0141-357 4363.

Slavin, Rev. William J., MA, STL, CPsychol.Chaplain, Royal Hospital for Sick Children, Glasgow; b. 17.1.40, Bristol. Educ. Blairs College, Aberdeen; Scots College, Rome; Glasgow University. Assistant Priest, Broomhill, Glasgow, 1965-70; Educational Psychologist, Glasgow Child Guidance Service, 1970-75; Deputy Director, Jessore Training Centre, Bangladesh, 1975-80; Secretary, RC Justice and Peace Commission, 1980-85; Co-ordinator, Scottish Drugs Forum, 1986-92; Parish Priest, St. Alphonsus, The Barras, Glasgow, 1992-97. Recreation: An rud Gaidhealach. Address: (h.) 1 Kelvinside Gardens, Glasgow G20 6BG; T.-0141-946 7622.

Sleeman, Professor Derek Henry, BSc, PhD, FBCS, FRSE. Professor of Computing Science, Aberdeen University, since 1986; b. 11.1.41, Penzance; m., Margaret G. Rankine; 1 d. Educ. Penzance Grammar School; King's College, London. Leeds University: Computing Assistant, 1965-67, Lecturer in Computational Science, 1967-82, Associate Director, Computer Based Learning Project, 1969-82; Visiting Scientist: Rutgers University, 1979, Carnegie-Mellon University, 1980-81; Senior Consultant, Teknowledge, Palo Alto, CA, 1983-86; Senior Research Associate/Associate Professor, Stanford University, 1982-86. Secretary, SS AISB, 1979-82; Academic Co-ordinator, European Network of Excellence in Machine Learning, 1992-95. Publications: 100 technical papers. Recreations: hill and coastal path walking; medieval architecture; photography. Address: (b.) Computing Science Department, King's College, Aberdeen University, Aberdeen, AB9 2FX; T.-01224 272288/96.

Sloan, Professor David McPheator, BSc, MSc, PhD, DSc, FRSE. Professor of Mathematics, Strathclyde University; b. 24.12.38, Cronberry; m., Margaret Templeton Kirk; 3 s.; 1 d. Educ. Cumnock Academy; Glasgow University; Keele University; Strathclyde University. Mathematician, English Electric Co., Stafford, 1962-64; Lecturer, Stafford Polytechnic, 1964-65; Lecturer, Senior Lecturer, Reader, Professor, Strathclyde University, from 1965. Recreations: hill-walking; folk music; reading. Address: (b.) Department of Mathematics, Strathclyde University, Glasgow; T.-0141-548 3819.

Sloan, Rev. Robert P., MA, BD. Minister, Braemar linked with Crathie, since 1996; Domestic Chaplain, Balmoral. Ordained, 1968. Address: Crathie, Ballater AB35 5UL.

Sloane, Professor Peter James, BA (Econ), PhD, FRSA, FRSE. Professor of Political Economy, Aberdeen University, since 1984; Vice Principal and Dean, Faculty of Social Sciences and Law, since 1996; b. 6.8.42, Cheadle

Hulme; m., Avril Mary Urquhart; 1 s. Educ. Cheadle Hulme School; Sheffield University; Strathclyde University. Assistant Lecturer and Lecturer, Department of Political Economy, Aberdeen University, 1966-69; Lecturer in Industrial Economics, Nottingham University, 1969-75; Economic Adviser, Department of Employment Unit for Manpower Studies (on secondment), 1973-74; Professor of Economics and Management, Paisley College, 1975-84. Member, Economic and Social Research Council, 1979-85; Council Member, Scottish Economic Society, since 1983; Member, Mergers Committee, Scottish Higher Education Funding Council, since 1994. Publications: Sex Discrimination in the Labour Market, 1976; Women and Low Pay, 1980; Sport in the Market?, 1980; Equal Employment Issues, 1981; Tackling Discrimination in the Workplace, 1982; Labour Economics, 1985. Recreation: sport. Address: (b.) Department of Economics, Aberdeen University, Edward Wright Building, Dunbar Street, Old Aberdeen, Aberdeen, AB24 3QY.

Slowey, Professor Maria, BComm, DipSocSci, M.Litt. Professor and Director, Department of Adult and Continuing Education, University of Glasgow, since 1992; b. 14.10.52, Dublin. Educ. Dominican Convent, Cabra; University College, Dublin; Trinity College, Dublin. Research Fellow, National Association of Adult Education of Ireland, 1976-79; Research Officer, DES National Survey of Adult Learners, 1980-82; Head, Adult Education Centre, LB of Waltham Forest, 1982-83; Lecturer in Adult Education, St Patrick's College, Maynooth, 1983-84; Senior Lecturer in Recurrent Education, subsequently Head, Centre for Continuing Education and External Relations, University of Northumbria, 1985-92. Consultant to international bodies, including OECD, Council of Europe, EC; Visiting Fellow, Centre for Policy Studies in H.E., University of California, Berkeley. Honorary Specialist Adviser on Continuing Education to the Committee of Scottish Higher Education Principals. Member: Executive, Universities Association of Continuing Education; Women Returner's Network; Board of Management, Scottish Centre for Community Development; Committee on Community Education Validation and Endorsement, Scottish Community Education Council; Higher Education Policy Group, National Institute of Adult and Continuing Education; Quality Assurance Consultative Group, Higher Education Quality Council; Advisory Group on the Funding of Continuing Education, Scottish Higher Education Funding Council; Chair, Society for Research into Higher Education Continuing Education Research Group. Publications: three co-authored books and numerous official reports, papers and articles on continuing and higher education. Address: (b.) Department of Adult and Continuing Education, University of Glasgow, 59 Oakfield Avenue, Glasgow, G12 8LW; T.– 0141-330 4392.

Smail, Peter James, MA, BM, BCh, FRCP, DCH. Consultant Paediatrician and Clinical Director of Child Health, Aberdeen Royal Hospitals Trust, since 1992; Honorary Senior Lecturer in Child Health, Aberdeen University, since 1980; b. 10.10.43, Harrow; m., Janice Lockhart; 3 s.; 1 d. Educ. Merchant Taylors', Northwood; St. John's College, Oxford; Oxford Clinical Medical School. Paediatric House Officer, Inverness Hospitals, 1970; Medical Registrar, Royal Cornwall Hospital (Treliske), 1972; Lecturer in Child Health, Dundee University, 1975; Fellow in Paediatric Endocrinology, University of Manitoba, Winnipeg, 1979. Member, Health Services Human Growth Hormone Committee, 1982-87; Secretary, Scottish Study Group for the Care of Young Diabetics, 1984-89. Recreations: Member, Aberdeen Bach Choir; Lay Clerk, St. Andrew's Cathedral, Aberdeen. Address: (b.) Royal Aberdeen Children's Hospital, Aberdeen, AB9 2ZG; T.-0224 681818, Ext. 53037.

Small, Christopher. Writer; b. 15.11.19, London; 3 d. Educ. Dartington Hall; Pembroke College, Oxford.

Journalist and miscellaneous writer; Literary Editor and Dramatic Critic, Glasgow Herald, 1955-80. Publications:Ariel Like A Harpy: Shelley, Mary & Frankenstein; The Road to Miniluv: George Orwell, the State & God; The Printed Word. Recreation: gardening. Address: (h.) 26 Bell Place, Edinburgh, EH3 5HT; T.-0131-332 6591.

Small, Professor John Rankin, CBE, DLitt, BSc (Econ), FCCA, FCMA. Professor, Department of Accountancy and Finance, Heriot-Watt University, since 1967; Chairman, Commission for Local Authority Accounts in Scotland, 1983-92; b. 28.2.33, Dundee; m., Catherine Wood; 1 s.; 2 d. Educ. Harris Academy; Dundee School of Economics. Industry and commerce; Lecturer, Edinburgh University; Senior Lecturer, Glasgow University. Consultant to various organisations; Council Member, Chartered Association of Certified Accountants (President, 1982-83); Vice-Principal, Heriot-Watt University, 1974-78, 1987-90, Deputy Principal, 1990-94; Chairman, National Appeal Panel for Entry to Pharmaceutical Lists (Scotland), 1987-95; Board Member, Scottish Homes, since 1993. Recreation: golf. Address: (b.) Heriot-Watt University, Riccarton, Edinburgh; T.-0131-451 3001.

Smart, John Dalziel Beveridge, DL. Chairman, British Polyolefin Textiles Association, 1986-97; b. 12.8.32, Edinburgh; m., Valerie Blaber; 2 s. Educ. Harrow; Administrative Staff College. 2nd Lt., Black Watch (RHR), Korea, 1952; J. & J. Smart (Brechin) Ltd., 1953 (Director, 1954); Director, Don Brothers, Buist & Co. Ltd., 1964 (Managing Director, 1985; retired, 1987). DL, Kincardineshire; Member, Queen's Bodyguard for Scotland, Royal Company of Archers; Dean, Guildry of Brechin, 1991-93; Chairman, Scottish American Community Relations Council, 1990-93. Recreations: shooting; skiing. Address: (h.) Woodmyre, Edzell, Angus, DD9 7UX; T.-01356 648416.

Smethurst, Professor Colin, BA, BLitt, MA, Officier Palmes Academiques. Marshall Professor of French, Glasgow University, since 1980; b. 3.8.37, Bedford; m., Claudine Rozenberg; 2 d. Educ. Slough Grammar School; Keble College, Oxford. Assistant Lecturer, Lecturer, Senior Lecturer in French, Liverpool University, 1962-80. President, Institut Francais D'Ecosse, 1989-96; Secretary, Association of University Professors of French, 1983-87. Publications: Zola: Germinal; Chateaubriand: Atala, Rene. Address: (b.) Department of French, Glasgow University, Glasgow G12 8QL; T.-0141-339 8855.

Smillie, Anne. Chief Executive, Scottish Badminton Union, since 1989; b. 17.8.56, Glasgow. Educ. Victoria Drive Secondary School; Anniesland College. Joined Scottish Badminton Union, 1980; Director of major badminton events, including 1992 European Championships, 1994 World Team Championships, 1997 World Team and Individual Championships. Recreations: music; reading. Address: (h.) 55 Westerton Avenue, Westerton, Glasgow; T.-0141-942 9804.

Smillie, Carol. Television Presenter. Credits include: Wheel of Fortune; The Travel Show; Good Morning with Anne and Nick; Holiday; The National Lottery Live; The Big Breakfast; Hearts of Gold; Get It On; Smillie's People; Changing Rooms; Midweek National Lottery Live; Holiday Memories.

Smith of Gilmorehill, Baroness, MA. Peeress, House of Lords, since 1995; Deputy Lieutenant, City of Edinburgh; Non-Executive Director, Morgan Grenfell (Scotland) Ltd.; Chairman, Edinburgh Festival Fringe Society, since 1995; Council Member, Edinburgh International Festival; Member, Press Complaints Commission; Member, BP Scottish Advisory Board; Council Member, British Heart Foundation; Council Member, Russo-British Chamber of Commerce; Trustee, Centre for European Reform; Trustee, Scottish Television Pension Fund; Governor, English Speaking Union; b. 4.6.40, Ayr; m., Rt. Hon. John Smith, MP (deceased); 3 d. Educ. Hutchesons Girls Grammar School; Glasgow University. Recreations: family; garden; the arts. Address: (b.) House of Lords, London, SW1A 0PN.

Smith, Professor Adam Neil, MD, DSc, FRCSE, FRCPE, FIBiol, FRSE. Formerly Wade Professor of Surgical Studies, RCSEd; formerly Consultant Surgeon, Gastro-Intestinal Unit, Edinburgh (retired); b. 27.6.26, Hamilton; m., Sibyl Mary Veitch Johnstone; 1 s., 3 d. Educ. Lanark Grammar School; Glasgow University. Academic and Health Service appointments, since 1948; Lecturer in Surgery, Glasgow University; Medical Research Council Fellow; Reader, Edinburgh University and Western General Hospital. Vice-President and Council Member, Royal College of Surgeons of Edinburgh; awarded Medal of RCSEd, 1997; Council Member, Association of Coloproctology; Past President, British Group for Research into Pelvic Function and Disease; President, Scottish Society of Coloproctology; former Surgical Traveller, James IV Surgical Association; Commonwealth Fund Travelling Fellow in Medical Education; Trustee, Melville Trust for Care and Cure of Cancer; Trustee, Soutra Project. Recreation: golf. Address: (h.) 2 Ravelston House Park, Edinburgh, EH4 3LU; T.-0131-332 4077.

Smith, Sir Alan, Kt (1982), CBE (1976), DFC (1941) and Bar (1942), DL, JP. President, Dawson International plc, Kinross, since 1982; Chairman, Quayle Munro PLC, Edinburgh, 1982-93; b. 14.3.17, South Shields; m., 1, Margaret Stewart Todd (deceased); 2, Alice Elizabeth Moncur; 3 s.; 2 d. Educ. Bede College, Sunderland. Self-employed, 1931-36; Unilever, 1936-39; RAF, 1939-45; Managing Director, Todd & Duncan Ltd., Kinross, 1946-60; Chairman and Chief Executive, Dawson International, Kinross, 1960-82. Board Member, Scottish Development Agency, 1982-87; Kinross Burgh Councillor, 1952-65; Provost of Kinross, 1959-65; Tayside Regional Councillor, 1979-90; Financial Convenor, Tayside Region, 1980-86. Recreations: work; sailing. Address: (h.) Ardgairney House, Cleish, by Kinross; T.-01577 850265.

Smith, Professor Alan Gordon Rae, MA, PhD, FRAS, FRHistS, FRSE. Professor of Early Modern History, Glasgow University, since 1995; b. 22.12.36, Glasgow; m., Isabel Robertson; 1 s.; 1 d. Educ. Glasgow High School; Glasgow University; University College, London. Research Fellow, Institute of Historical Research, London University, 1961-62; Assistant in History, 1962-64, then Lecturer, Glasgow University, 1964-75; Senior Lecturer in Modern History, 1975-85; Reader, 1985-92, Professor in Modern History, 1992-95; Review Editor, History (Journal of the Historical Association), 1984-87; Member, Council, Royal Historical Society, 1990-94; Member, Governing Board, Institute of Historical Research, London University, since 1994. Publications: The Government of Elizabethan England, 1967; The New Europe, 1969; Science and Society in the Sixteenth and Seventeenth Centuries, 1972; Servant of the Cecils: The Life of Sir Michael Hickes, 1977; The Emergence of a Nation State: The Commonwealth of England 1529-1660, 1984; The Anonymous Life of William Cecil, Lord Burghley, 1990; The Last Years of Mary Queen of Scots, 1990; Tudor Government, 1990; William Cecil, Lord Burghley, Minister of Queen Elizabeth I, 1991. Recreation: watching sport. Address: (h.) 5 Cargil Avenue, Kilmacolm, Renfrewshire; T.-Kilmacolm 2055.

Smith, Alex. Member, European Parliament for South of Scotland, since 1989; b. 2.12.43, Kilwinning; 1 s.; 1 d. Educ. (b.) Damside, Ayr, KA8 8ER; T.-01292 280096.

Smith, Allan Keppie. CBE, DUniv, BSc, FEng, FIMechE, FWeldI. Cahirman, Railcare Ltd., since 1995; Managing Director, Facilities Management Division, Babcock International Group PLC, Rosyth Royal Dockyard, until 1997; b. 18.5.32. Joined Army for National Service, 1953; commissioned, REME, 1954; Babcock & Wilcox: joined as Graduate Trainee, 1955; appointed: Industrial Engineering Manager, Renfrew Works, 1965, Production Director, Renfrew Works, 1974, Managing Director, Renfrew and Dumbarton Works, 1976; Managing Director, Babcock Thorn Limited and Chairman, Rosyth Royal Dockyard plc, 1986; Director, Babcock International Group PLC, 1989. Past President, Scottish Engineering; Past Chairman, Council of the Welding Institute; Honorary Doctor, University of Paisley; awarded Institute of Marketing Scottish Marketer of the Year, 1992. Address: (h.) The Forts, Hawes Brae, South Queensferry EH30 9TE; T.-0131-319 1668.

Smith, Anne, QC, LLB (Hons). Admitted, Faculty of Advocates, 1980. Address: (b.) Advocates' Library, Parliament House, Edinburgh, EH1 1RF.

Smith, Professor Brian Clive, BA, MA, PhD. Professor of Political Science and Social Policy, Dundee University, since 1989; b. 23.1.38, London; m., Jean Baselow; 1 s.; 1 d. Educ. Colfe's Grammar School; Exeter University; McMaster University, Canada. Lecturer in Politics, Exeter University; Lecturer in Public Administration, Civil Service College, 1970-72; Senior Lecturer/Reader in Politics, Bath University, 1972-89. Publications include: Decentralisation; Bureaucracy and Political Power; Understanding Third World Politics. Recreations: walking; opera. Address: (b.) Dundee University, Dundee, DD1 4HN; T.-01382 223181.

Smith, Bruce Livingstone, BSc, CEng, FIMarE, MRINA, FCMS, ACIArb. Hon. Secretary, Scottish Branch, Chartered Institute of Arbiters, since 1997; Chairman, Yacht Brokers, Designers, Surveyors Association, since 1977; b. 29.8.45, Glasgow; m., Jacqueline McLean; 1 s.; 1 d. Educ. Bearsden Academy; Glasgow University. After honours degree, served apprenticeship as fitter in various Clyde yards and abroad; joined John Brown Engineering as Test Engineer on gas turbines; employed in, and bought, E.K. Wallace and Son Ltd., Marine Consultants (Chairman/Managing Director); Principal Partner, Bruce L. Smith & Associates, since 1992; Past Chairman, Scottish Branch, Chartered Institute of Arbiters. Recreations: sailing; shooting; fishing. Address: (b.) Whittinghame House, 1099 Great Western Road, Glasgow G12 0AA; T.-0141-334 7222.

Smith, Sheriff Charles, MA, LLB, NP. Sheriff of Tayside, Central and Fife, at Cupar and Dundee, since 1991, at Perth, 1986-91; b. 15.8.30, Methil; m., Janet Elizabeth Hurst; 1 s.; 1 d. Educ. Perth Academy; St. Andrews University. Solicitor, 1956; private practice as Principal, 1962-82; Member, Perth Town Council, 1966-68; Interim Depute Procurator Fiscal, 1974-82; Tutor, Dundee University, 1980-82; Member, Council, Law Society of Scotland (Convener, various Committees), 1977-82; Temporary Sheriff, 1977-82; Honorary Tutor, Dundee University, since 1982; Sheriff of Glasgow and Strathkelvin, 1982-86; Member, Council, Sheriffs' Association, 1987-90. Recreations: tennis; golf; bridge. Address: (b.) c/o Sheriff Clerk, Sheriff Court, Cupar, KY15 4LX; T.-01334 652121.

Smith, C. Christopher, MB, FRCP, FRCPE. Consultant Physician, Aberdeen Royal Infirmary NHS Trust, since 1973; Honorary Senior Lecturer in Medicine, University of Aberdeen (Elected Member, Senatus Academicus, 1988-92); b. 16.5.39, West Indies; m., Sheila Anne Calder, MRCPsych; 2 s., 1 d. by pr. m. Educ. Lodge School, Barbados; Edinburgh University. Registrar, Department of Medicine, Edinburgh Royal Infirmary; Registrar, Thoracic Medicine, then Senior Registrar, Infectious Diseases, City Hospital, Edinburgh; Senior Registrar, Department of Therapeutics and Clinical Pharmacology, Edinburgh Royal Infirmary. Elected Member, Council, Royal College of Physicians of Edinburgh, 1991-94; Member, Fellowship Committee, 1991-94 and Committees on Examinations and Education, 1992-97; External Examiner, Final MB, University of Dundee, 1992-95; former Member, Part I MRCP Examination Board; Examiner, MRCP, since 1977; External, MRCP, in Hong Kong, Malaysia and Ireland; External Examiner, M.Med., Malaysia, 1996; Member, United Examination Board (UEB) and Member, Examination Committee; Chairman, Written Paper Panel, UEB, 1992-97; Chairman, Specialty Advisory Committee (JCHMT) on Infection and Tropical Medicine, 1991-95 and Member, JCHMT; Chairman, Scottish National Advisory Committee on Hospital Infection, 1996-97; Visitor for JCHMT Accreditation in Internal Medicine, Infection/Tropical Medicine; Regional Adviser, RCPs and Member, Aberdeen and NE Scotland Postgraduate Medical Education Committee; author of papers, chapters and leading articles on topics in medicine, infection, post-infective phenomena, and antimicrobial chemotherapy; Invited Lecturer, Hong Kong, Singapore, Malaysia, Kenya, Zimbabwe, Saudi Arabia, Iceland, South Africa, and Ireland, since 1982. Recreations: watching cricket; golf; live theatre; jazz music. Address: (b.) Wards 25/26 and Infection Unit, Aberdeen Royal Infirmary, Foresterhill, Aberdeen, AB25 2ZN; T.-Aberdeen 681818.

Smith, David Bruce Boyter, OBE, MA, LLB, FRSA, FInstD, NP. Director and Chief Executive, Dunfermline Building Society, since 1987; b. 11.3.42, St. Andrews; m., Christine Anne; 1 s.; 1 d. Educ. High School, Dunfermline; Edinburgh University. Legal training, Balfour & Manson, Edinburgh; admitted Solicitor, 1968; Solicitor, Standard Life Assurance Co., 1969-73; Dunfermline Building Society: Secretary, 1974-81, General Manager (Admin.), 1981-86, Deputy Chief Executive, 1986. Chairman, Scottish Committee, Building Societies Association; Member of Council, Building Societies Association; Chairman, Northern Association of Building Societies; Member, Council, NHBC (Scotland); Member, Scottish Conveyancing and Executry Services Board; Chairman, Institute of Directors, Scottish Division, 1994-97; Director, Fife Enterprise Ltd.; Director, Scottish Fisheries Museum; Member, Building Societies Investor Protection Board; Vice Chairman of Court and Finance Convener, Edinburgh University; Vice Chairman, Lauder College; Life Trustee, Carnegie Trust. Recreations: golf; sailing; the arts. Address: (b.) Caledonia House, Carnegie Avenue, Dunfermline, Fife; T.-01383 627727.

Smith, Sheriff David Buchanan, MA, LLB, FSAScot. Sheriff of North Strathclyde at Kilmarnock, since 1975; b. 31.10.36, Paisley; m., Hazel Mary Sinclair; 1 s.; 1 d. Educ. Paisley Grammar School; Glasgow University; Edinburgh University. Advocate, 1961; Standing Junior Counsel to Scottish Education Department, 1968-75; Tutor, Faculty of Law, Edinburgh University, 1964-72; Trustee, Scottish Curling Museum Trust, since 1980. President, Kilmarnock and District History Group; Trustee Scottish National Dictionary Association, since 1994; President, Ayr Curling Club, 1995-96. Publications: Curling: An Illustrated History, 1981; The Roaring Game: Memories of Scottish Curling, 1985; contributions to The Laws of Scotland: Stair Memorial Encyclopedia, Vol. 6; George Washington Wilson in Ayrshire, 1991. Recreations: Scotland — history and culture; curling; collecting curliana; music; architecture. Address: (b.) Sheriff Court House, Kilmarnock, KA1 1ED; T.-01563 520211.

Smith, Sir David Cecil, Kt, MA, DPhil, FRS, FRSE. Principal and Vice-Chancellor, Edinburgh University, 1987-94; President, Wolfson College, Oxford, since 1994; m., Lesley Margaret Mollison Mutch; 2 s.; 1 d. Educ. St. Paul's School, London; Queen's College, Oxford. Browne

Research Fellow, Queen's College, Oxford, 1956-59; Harkness Fellow, University of California, Berkeley, 1959-60; University Lecturer, Department of Agriculture, Oxford University, 1960-74; Fellow and Tutor, Wadham College, Oxford, 1964-74; Melville Wills Professor of Botany, Bristol University, 1974-80; Sibthorpian Professor of Rural Economy, Oxford University, 1980-87. President, British Lichen Society, 1972-74; President, British Mycological Society, 1980; President, Society for Experimental Biology, 1983-85. Publication: The Biology of Symbiosis (Co-author), 1987. Address: Wolfson College, Oxford OX2 6UD; T.-01865 274101; The Steading, Balquhidder, Perthshire FK19 8NY; T.-01877 384316.

Smith, Professor David John, MA. Professor of Criminology, Edinburgh University, since 1994; b. 10.7.41, Egypt; m., Colette Marie Obadia; 1 s. Educ. Bootham School, York; Christ Church, Oxford. Trainee Research Executive, 1963-64; Research Officer, 1964-66; Senior Research Officer, then Board Director, Interscan Ltd., 1966-71; Senior Research Associate, Political and Economic Planning, 1972-78; Senior Fellow, Policy Studies Institute, and Head, Social Justice and Social Order Group, 1979-94. Additional Commissioner, Commission for Racial Equality, 1978-84; Specialist Adviser to Home Affairs and Employment Committees, House of Commons, 1981-82, 1986; Visiting Fellow, Lincoln College, Oxford, 1988-89. Recreations: large format photography; piano; squash. Address: (b.) Faculty of Law, Edinburgh University, Old College, South Bridge, Edinburgh, EH8 9YL; T.-0131-650 2027.

Smith, Very Rev. David Macintyre Bell Armour, MA, BD, DUniv, JP. Minister, Logie, 1965-89; Moderator, General Assembly of the Church of Scotland, 1985; b. 5.4.23, Fort Augustus; m., Mary Kulvear Cumming; 3 s. Educ. Monckton Combe; Peebles High School; St. Andrews University. Minister, Warrender Church, Edinburgh, 1951-61; Exchange Preacher, USA, 1958 and 1961; Minister, Old Partick, Glasgow, 1961-65; Moderator, Stirling and Dunblane Presbytery, 1972-73; Moderator, Perth and Stirling Synod, 1975-76; Vice Convener, Joint Working Party, Church of Scotland, 1980-82; Convener, Church of Scotland Board of Education, 1979-83; Church of Scotland Representative, Stirlingshire Education Committee, 1969-79; Governor, Moray House College of Education, 1983; Member, Central Regional Education Committee, 1986-94; Member, Church of Scotland Assembly Council, 1989-93, Board of Practice and Procedure, 1982-90; Honorary Brother, Guildry of Stirling, 1986. Recreations: philately; gardening. Address: (h.) 34 Annfield Gardens, Stirling, FK8 3BJ.

Smith, Donald Alexander, MA, PhD. Director, Netherbow Arts Centre, since 1983; Curator, John Knox House, since 1989; Director, Scottish International Storytelling Festival, since 1987; b. 15.2.56, Glasgow; m., Alison; 3 s.; 2 d. Educ. Stirling High School; Edinburgh University. Researcher, School of Scottish Studies, 1979-82; Administrator, Netherbow, 1982-83. Programme Organiser, St. Margaret 900; Chairperson, Scotland 97 (anniversaries of St. Ninian and St. Columba). Publications: The Scottish Stage, 1994; Edinburgh Old Town Pilgrims' Way, 1995; John Knox House: Gateway to Edinburgh's Old Town,1996; Celtic Travellers: Scotland in the Age of the Saints, 1997. Address: (b.) The Netherbow, 43-45 High Street, Edinburgh EH1 1SR; T.-0131-556 2647.

Smith, (Edward) Alistair, CBE, MA, PhD. Director, Aberdeen University International Office, since 1990 (Director, Aberdeen University University Development Trust, 1982-90); Deputy Chairman, Scottish Conservative Party, 1981-86; b. 16.1.39, Aberdeen. Educ. Aberdeen Grammar School; Aberdeen University. Lecturer in Geography, Aberdeen University, 1963-88; President, Scottish Conservative and Unionist Association, 1979-81;

Member, Grampian Health Board, 1983-91; Board Member, SCOTVEC, 1989-93; Member, Committee for Scotland, Nature Conservancy Council, 1989-91; Member, N.E. Regional Committee, Nature Conservancy Council, 1991-92. Publications: Europe: A Geographical Survey of the Continent (Co-author), 1979; Scotland's Future Development (Contributor), 1983. Recreations: travel; photography; music. Address: (h.) 68A Beaconsfield Place, Aberdeen, AB2 4AJ; T.-01224 642932.

Smith, Elaine Constance. Actress; b. 2.8.58, Baillieston; m., Robert Morton; 2 d. Educ. Braidhurst High School, Motherwell; Royal Scottish Academy of Music and Drama; Moray House College of Education. Teacher of Speech and Drama, Firrhill High School, Edinburgh, 1979-82; joined 7:84 Theatre Company, 1982; moved to Wildcat Stage Productions, 1982; since 1986, worked with Borderline Theatre Co., Royal Lyceum, Dundee Rep., Tron Theatre; TV work includes City Lights and Naked Video; plays Mary Nesbitt in Rab C. Nesbitt (BBC2); original cast member, The Steamie. Board Member, Scottish Youth Theatre; Patron, Family Mediation Scotland. Recreations: swimming; aerobics; reading. Address: (b.) c/o Crossan Communications, 10 Bernard Street, Edinburgh, EH6 6PP.

Smith, Rev. Graham Walton, BA, BD, FSA Scot. Minister, Livingston Old Parish Church, since 1995; b. 17.9.46, Edinburgh; m., Rosemary Sheila James. Educ. Lenzie Academy; London University; Glasgow University. Bookseller; sales manager; publisher; company director. Recreations: reading; music; railways. Address: The Manse of Livingston, Livingston EH54 7AJ; T.-01506 420227.

Smith, Professor Grahame Francis, MA, PhD. Professor, Department of English Studies, Stirling University, since 1993; b. 30.5.33, London; m., Angela Mary; 2 s.; 1 d. Educ. Woodside Senior Secondary School, Glasgow; Aberdeen University; Cambridge University. Taught at California University, Los Angeles, 1963-65, University College, Swansea, 1965-70; secondment to Malawi University, 1982-83. Publications: Dickens, Money and Society, 1968; The Novel and Society: From Defoe to George Elliot, 1984; The Achievement of Graham Greene, 1985; A Literary Life of Charles Dickens, 1996. Recreations: cinema; opera; jazz; walking. Address: (b.) Department of English Studies, Stirling University, Stirling, FK9 4LA; T.-01786 467499.

Smith, Professor Hamilton, BSc, PhD, CChem, FRSC, FRCPath, FRSE. Professor of Forensic Medicine (Toxicology), Glasgow University, since 1987; b. 27.4.34, Stirling; m., Jacqueline Ann Spittal. Educ. Kilsyth Academy; Glasgow University. Glasgow University: MRC Fellow, 1960, Special Research Fellow, 1963, Lecturer in Forensic Medicine Department, 1964, Senior Lecturer, 1973, Reader, 1984. Publication: Glaister's Medical Jurisprudence and Toxicology, 13th edition. Recreations: golf (New Club, St. Andrews); gardening. Address: (b.) Department of Forensic Medicine and Science, Glasgow University, Glasgow, G12 8QQ; T.-0141-339 8855.

Smith, Ian, BSc, PhD, CBiol, MIBiol. Rector, Kinlochbervie High School, since 1995; b. 2.7.52, Edinburgh; m., Dianne; 2 d. Educ. Galashiels Academy; Heriot Watt University; Glasgow University. Research Biochemist, Knightswood Hospital, Glasgow; Teacher of Biology, Kelso High School, 1981-84; Assistant Principal Teacher of Biology, Nicolson Institute, 1984; Principal Teacher of Biology, Selkirk High School, 1984-88, Hawick High School, 1988-95. Publications: research papers on muscular dystrophy. Recreations: football; rugby; cycling; walking. Address: (b.) Kinlochbervie High School, Kinlochbervie, Sutherland IV27 4RG; T.-01971 521767.

Smith, Iain Crichton, OBE, LLD (Dundee), DLitt (Glasgow), DLitt (Aberdeen), MA (Hons). Writer; b. 1.1.28, Glasgow; m., Donalda Gillies Logan; 2 step s. Educ.

Nicolson Institute, Stornoway; Aberdeen University. Teacher, Oban High School, 1955-77; full-time Writer, since 1977; former Member, STV Gaelic Advisory Committee; former Member, Scottish Arts Council; Hon. President, Scottish Poetry Library and Scottish Association for the Speaking of Verse; Fellow, Royal Literary Society; books in English: 10 novels, six volumes of short stories, 13 volumes of poetry; books in Gaelic: two novels, five volumes of short stories, four volumes of poetry; translations from Gaelic into English; numerous radio plays in both languages; Poetry Book Society Choice and five recommendations; eight Arts Council awards; awards for Gaelic plays and short stories; award for Gaelic television play; PEN Award, 1970; Scotsman Short Story Award, 1983; Commonwealth Poetry Prize (European Section), 1986; Cholmondoley Award; Travelling Scholarship, Society of Authors, 1987; Saltire Prize, 1992. Recreation: reading detective stories. Address:Tigh Na Fuaran, Taynuilt, Argyll; T.-Taynuilt 463.

Smith, Ian Fraser, LLB. Chief Executive, Dumfries and Galloway Council, since 1995; Chief Executive, Dumfries and Galloway Regional Council, 1992-95; Chair, Scottish Branch, SOLACE, since 1996; b. 27.6.50, Dunfermline; m., Pat; 1 s.; 1 d. Educ. Kirkcaldy High School; Dundee University. Solicitor; held posts, Fife Region; Depute Chief Executive, Clackmannan District Council, 1977, Chief Executive, 1985. Recreations: gardening; modern painting; sculpture; watching rugby. Address: (b.) Dumfries and Galloway Council, Council Offices, English Street, Dumfries, DG1 2DD; T.-01387 260000.

Smith, James Aikman, TD, BA, LLB. Advocate; Honorary Sheriff, since 1976; b. 13.6.14, Kilmarnock; m., Katharine Ann Millar; 3 d. Educ. Glasgow Academy; Oxford University; Edinburgh University. Admitted Faculty of Advocates, 1939; served Royal Artillery, 1939-46 (Lt. Col., 1944), North Africa, Italy and Austria; Despatches, Bronze Star US; Sheriff Substitute, Renfrew and Argyll, 1948-52, Roxburgh, Berwick and Selkirk, 1952-57, Aberdeen, Kincardine and Banff, 1957-68; Sheriff of Lothians and Borders, 1968-76; President, Sheriffs' Association, 1969-72; Member, UK Departmental Committee on Probation Service, 1959-62; Member, After Care Council (Scotland), 1962-65; UK Delegate to UN Congress on Crime, Japan, 1970; Chairman, Edinburgh and East of Scotland Branch, English Speaking Union, 1970-74; Vice-President, Cairngorm Club, 1962-65; Chairman, Allelon Society, 1970-76; Elder, Church of Scotland, 1948-90. Recreations: hill-walking; gardening; travel. Address: (h.) 16 Murrayfield Avenue, Edinburgh, EH12 6AX; T.-0131-337 8205.

Smith, James David, OBE, MA, LLB. Retired Solicitor; Honorary Sheriff of North Strathclyde at Greenock, since 1976; b. 27.10.19, Dumbarton; m., Margaret McGregor Grant; 2 s. Educ. Dumbarton Academy; Glasgow University. Commissioned Highland Light Infantry, 1940; Town Clerk, Dumbarton, 1951-67; Chief Executive, Corporation of Greenock, 1967-75; Visiting Lecturer in Law, Paisley College of Technology, 1976-87. Address: (h.) 42 Octavia Terrace, Greenock, PA16 7SR; T.-01475 723788.

Smith, Sheriff James R., LLB. Sheriff of South Strathclyde, Dumfries and Galloway at Stranraer. Address: (b.) Sheriff Court House, Lewis Street, Stranraer, DG9 7AA.

Smith, Professor Keith, BA, PhD, FRSE. Professor of Environmental Science, Stirling University, since 1986; Dean, Faculty of Natural Sciences, Stirling University, since 1994; b. 9.1.38, Marple; m., Muriel Doris Hyde; 1 s.; 1 d. Educ. Hyde County Grammar School; Hull University. Tutor in Geography, Liverpool University, 1963-65; Lecturer in Geography, Durham University, 1965-70;

Strathclyde University: Senior Lecturer, 1971-75, Reader, 1975-82, Personal Professor, 1982-84, Professor and Head of Department, 1984-86. Drapers' Company Visiting Lecturer, Adelaide University, 1978; Visiting Principal Scientist, Illinois State Water Survey, 1988; Visiting Professor of Geography, University of Illinois, 1988. Publications: Water in Britain; Principles of Applied Climatology; Human Adjustment to Flood Hazard; Environmental Hazards. Recreations: hill-walking; badminton. Address: (b.) Department of Environmental Science, Stirling University, Stirling, FK9 4LA; T.-01786 467750.

Smith, Professor Lawrence D., BSc. Professor of Agricultural Economics, Glasgow University, since 1989; b. 1939, Bedfordshire; m., Evelyn Mavis Stead; 1 s.; 2 d. Educ. Bedford Modern School; Wye College, London University; Linacre College, Oxford. Departmental Lecturer, Agricultural Economics Research Institute, Oxford University, 1963-66; Lecturer, Senior Lecturer, Reader in Agricultural Economics, Department of Economics, Glasgow University. Director, Scottish Agricultural College, since 1990. Recreation: gardening. Address: (b.) Department of Economics, Glasgow University, Glasgow; T.-0141-330 5063.

Smith, Lewis Shand, MA, BD. Rector, St. Magnus Episcopal Church, St. Colman's Church, since 1980; Canon, St. Andrews Cathedral, Aberdeen, since 1993; Convener, Shetland Islands Council, since 1994; Member, Convention of the Highlands and Islands; Member, Executive, Scottish Constitutional Convention; b. 16.3.52, Lerwick; m., Annette; 1 s. Educ. Anderson Educational Institute, Lerwick; Aberdeen University; Edinburgh University; Edinburgh Theological College. Curate, St. Andrews, Wishaw and Holy Trinity, Motherwell, 1977-80. Convener, Orkney and Shetland Joint Valuation Board, since 1996; Hon. President, Shetland-Vagsoy Twinning Association; Chairman, Hunter-Morrison Trust. Recreations: amateur theatre; music; swimming; gardening. Address: (b.) Papilgarth, 1 Greenrig, Lerwick, Shetland, ZE1 0AW; T.-01595 693862.

Smith, Professor Lorraine Nancy, BScN, MEd, PhD. Professor of Nursing Studies, Glasgow University, since 1990 (Head of Department, since 1990); b. 29.6.49, Ottawa; m., Christopher Murray Smith; 1 s.; 1 d. Educ. Hillcrest High School, Ottawa; University of Ottawa; Manchester University. Co-opted to English National Board, 1988-90; Member, Scottish Alcohol Advisory Group, 1991-95; Member, Clinical and Biomedical Research Committee (Scotland), 1992-94; Member, Clinical Standards Advisory Group (UK), since 1994. Recreations: reading; bridge; sailing. Address: (b.) 68 Oakfield Avenue, Glasgow University, Glasgow, G12 8LS; T.-0141-330 4051.

Smith, Matt, JP. Scottish Secretary, UNISON, since 1993; Treasurer, Scottish TUC, since 1996; b. 4.2.52, Irvine; m., Eileen; 1 s.; 1 d. Educ. Stevenson High School; Ardrossan Academy. NALGO: employee from 1973; Senior Scottish Officer, Scottish Organiser, 1981-93; Member: STUC General Council, Executive of Scottish Council Development and Industry, Scottish Constitutional Convention, Church and Nation Committee of Church of Scotland, Scottish Local Government Information Unit, John Wheatley Centre, Scotland FORward, Ayrshire Industrial Forum, North Ayrshire Justices Committee; former Stevenston Burgh councillor; Parliamentary candidate, Labour, 1979. Recreations: family; travel; gardening; music; politics. Address: (b.) UNISON House, 14 West Campbell Street, Glasgow, G2 6RX; T.-0141-332 0006.

Smith, Nigel R. Managing Director, David Auld Valves Ltd., since 1976; b. 9.6.41, Girvan; m., Jody; 2 s.; 2 d. Educ. Dollar Academy. Lt., 4/5 Bn., Royal Scots Fusiliers

(TA), 1960-67; staff and management appointments, Bowater Paper, Richard Costain, Rank Hovis McDougall. Member, Executive, Scottish Engineering Employers Association, 1985-90; Member, Broadcasting Council for Scotland, 1986-90; Member, BBC General Advisory Council, 1991-93; Member, Glasgow Development Agency, Strategy Review Panel, 1993-94; Member, Scottish Constitutional Commission, 1993-94; Chairman, Broadcasting for Scotland Campaign, 1993-97; Chairman, Scotland Forward Campaign, 1997. Recreations: hill-walking; offshore sailing; opera and choral; reading, particularly biography. Address: (b.) David Auld Valves, Cowlairs Industrial Estate, Finlas Street, Glasgow, G22 5DQ; T.-0141-557 0515.

Smith, Sir Robert, Bt. MP (Liberal Democrat), Aberdeenshire West and Kincardine; b. 15.4.58; m.; 1 d. Educ. Merchant Taylors' School; Aberdeen University. Runs family estate at Crowmallie. Address: (b.) House of Commons, London SW1A 0AA.

Smith, Robert Lupton, OBE, FRICS. Vice-President, Association for the Protection of Rural Scotland, since 1993 (Director, 1981-93); Chartered Surveyor in private practice, 1954-96; b. 26.4.24, Cheadle Hulme; m.; 3 d. Educ. George Watson's College; College of Estate Management; Heriot-Watt College. Chairman, Scottish Junior Branch, RICS, 1952; Member, Scottish Executive Committee, RICS, 1952-60; elected, Edinburgh Town Council, 1962-74 and Edinburgh District Council, 1974-77; Governor, Edinburgh College of Art, 1963-89; fought European Election, 1979, as Liberal; Deputy Traffic Commissioner, 1974-78; Chairman, Good Neighbours Housing Association, 1984-87; Scottish Liberal Party: Chairman, Executive Committee, 1971-74, Chairman, 1974, President, 1976-82; Council Member, Royal Scottish Geographical Society, 1957-92; Chairman, A9 Highland Hosts Group, since 1995; Director, Cockburn Conservation Trust Ltd., 1976-90; Chairman, Logierait Bridge Co. Ltd. Recreations: visiting Orkney; reading; looking at fine art. Address: (h.) Charleston, Dalguise, near Dunkeld, PH8 0JX; T.-01350 728968.

Smith, Roger W. Writer and Editor; b. 28.11.38, London; 2 d. Educ. Latymer Upper School, London. Editor, The Great Outdoors, 1977-86; Editor, Environment Now, 1987-89; Editor, Scottish World, 1989-90; Past Chairman, Scottish Wild Land Group; Member, Executive Committee, National Trust for Scotland. Publications include: The Winding Trail, 1981; Weekend Walking, 1982; Visitor's Guide to Scottish Borders, 1983; The Great Outdoors Book of the Walking Year, 1988; Classic Walks in Scotland (Co-author), 1988; Chambers Guide to the Highlands and Islands, 1992; Catastrophes and Disasters, 1992; The Great Flood of Perth, 1993; 25 Walks: Highland Perthshire 1994; 25 Walks: Edinburgh and Lothian, 1995; Mapreading for Beginners, 1996; Insight Guide to the Scottish Highlands, 1997. Recreations: hill-walking; Scottish history. Address: (h.) 43 Kilnknowe Place, Galashiels TD1 1RH; T.-01896 751003.

Smith, Roger Galbraith, MB, ChB, FRCPEdin, FRCPLond, FRCPGlas. Consultant Physician in Geriatric Medicine, Royal Victoria Hospital, Edinburgh, and Honorary Senior Lecturer in Geriatric Medicine, Edinburgh University, since 1989; b. 7.7.42, Edinburgh; m., Margaret Lawson; 1 s.; 1 d. Educ. George Watson's College, Edinburgh; Edinburgh University. Surgeon Lieutenant, Royal Navy, 1967-72; Senior Registrar in Geriatric Medicine, 1973-76; Senior Lecturer, Department of Geriatric Medicine, Edinburgh University, 1976-89. Member, Board of Directors, Queensberry House Hospital, Edinburgh. Recreations: golf; curling. Address: (h.) 56 Alnwickhill Road, Edinburgh; T.-0131-664 1745.

Smith, Ronald A., MA. General Secretary, Educational Institute of Scotland, since 1995; Member, General Council,

STUC, since 1995, Chair, STUC Education Committee; Member, Executive Board, European Trade Union Committee for Education, since 1995; Member, European Regional Committee, Education International; b. 9.6.51, Lerwick; m., Mae; 1 s.; 1 d. Educ. Anderson Educational Institute; Aberdeen University; Aberdeen College of Education. Teacher of Latin, then A.P.T. of Latin, then Principal Teacher of Modern Studies, Broxburn Academy, 1973-88; Assistant Secretary, EIS, 1988-95. Address: (b.) 46 Moray Place, Edinburgh, EH3 6BH.

Smith, Sheriff Ronald Good, BL. Sheriff of North Strathclyde, since 1984; b. 24.7.33. Address: (b.) Sheriff Court House, 106 Renfrew Road, Paisley, PA3 4DD.

Smith, Emeritus Professor Stanley Desmond, BSc, PhD, DSc, FRS, FRSE. Professor of Physics, Heriot-Watt University, 1970-96; Chairman, Edinburgh Instruments Ltd., since 1971; Chairman, Edinburgh Sensors Ltd., since 1988; b. 3.3.31, Bristol; m., Gillian Anne Parish; 1 s.; 1 d. Educ. Cotham Grammar School; Bristol University; Reading University. SSO, RAE, Farnborough, 1956-58; Research Assistant, Department of Meteorology, Imperial College, London, 1958-59; Lecturer, then Reader, Reading University, 1960-70; Head, Department of Physics, Heriot-Watt University, 1970-96. Member: Advisory Council for Applied Research and Development, 1985-87, Advisory Council on Science and Technology, 1987-88, Defence Scientific Advisory Council, 1985-91, SERC Astronomy and Planetary Science and Engineering Boards, 1985-88, Council, Institute of Physics, 1984-87; Chairman, Scottish Optoelectronics Association, since 1996. Recreations: tennis; skiing; mountaineering; golf; raising the temperature. Address: (b.) Edinburgh Sensors Ltd., 2 Bein Square, Livingston, EH54 7DQ; T.-01506 425300.

Smith, Professor Stanley William, MA, PhD (Cantab). Chair of English, Dundee University, since 1989 (Reader in English, 1988-89, Head of Department, 1989-94); b. 12.1.43, Warrington; 2 s.; 1 d. Educ. Boteler Grammar School, Warrington; Jesus College, Cambridge. Assistant Lecturer in English, Aberdeen University, 1967-68; Lecturer in English, Dundee University, 1968-85; Senior Lecturer, 1985-88; Visiting Professor, University of Florence, 1987; Visiting Professor, University of Zaragoza, 1996; Chair, Council for University English, 1991-93; British Representative, Board, European Society for the Study of English, 1992-93; Member, Board, Standing Committee for Arts and Social Sciences, since 1989; Member, Board, Scotscass, since 1992; Vice-Chair, Scottish Committee of Professors of English, 1992-94. Publications: A Sadly Contracted Hero: The Comic Self in Post-War American Fiction, 1981; Inviolable Voice: History and Twentieth Century Poetry, 1982; 20th Century Poetry, 1983; W.H. Auden, 1985; Edward Thomas, 1986; W.B. Yeats, 1990; The Origins of Modernism, 1994; W.H. Auden, 1997; General Editor, Longman Critical Reader series and Longman Studies in 20th-century Literature series. Recreations: the arts; classical music; history and archaeology; travel. Address: (b.) English Department, Dundee University, Dundee, DD1 4HN; T.-01382 344412.

Smith, Vincent, PhB, LLB. Secretary, Glasgow Bar Association, since 1996; b. 21.4.54, Glasgow. Address: (b.) 49 Main Street, Thornliebank, Glasgow G46 7SF; T.-0141-638 2141.

Smith, William Angus, BEM, FEIS, JP. Chairman, Education Committee, Shetland Islands Council, since 1975 (Vice Chairman, Housing Committee, 1982-85); Vice-Chairman, Lerwick Harbour Trust; b. 20.8.19, Burra Isle, Shetland; m., Daisy Manson; 3 s. Educ. Anderson Educational Institute. Engineer, British Telecomms, 1937-83; Royal Signals, UK, Middle East, Burma, India, Germany, 1940-46; Member, Lerwick Town Council and Zetland County Council, 1967-75; Member, Lerwick

Harbour Trust, since 1967 (except for short break); Provost of Lerwick, 1971-74; Member, Shetland Islands Council, since 1975; Member, Shetland Area Health Board, 1974-89; Member, Electricity Consultative Council for North of Scotland District, 1974-90; Member, Shetland Recreational Trust. Recreations: crosswords; reading. Address: (h.) 14 Bruce Crescent, Lerwick, Shetland, ZE1 OPB; T.-01595 696428.

Smith, Professor William Ewen, BSc, DIC, PhD, DSc, FRSC, FRSE. Professor of Inorganic Chemistry, since 1987, and Head of Department, Strathclyde University, since 1995; b. 21.2.41, Glasgow; m., Frances Helen Williamson; 1 s.; 1 d. Educ. Hutchesons' Boys Grammar School; Strathclyde University. Visiting Scientist, Oak Ridge National Laboratory, 1965-67; SERC and ICI Fellow, University College, London, 1967-69; Lecturer, Reader, Professor, Strathclyde University, since 1969. Publications: 170 papers and reviews. Recreations: golf; sailing. Address: (b.) Department of Pure and Applied Chemistry, Strathclyde University, Glasgow, G1 1XL; T.-0141-552 4400.

Smith, William Leggat, CBE, MC, TD, JP, DL, BA (Oxon), LLB, LLD; b. 30.1.18, Kilmarnock; m., Yvonne Menna Williams; 1 s.; 2 d. Educ. Glasgow Academy; Queen's College, Oxford; Glasgow University. Commissioned (TA), Cameronians (Scottish Rifles), 1939; served Second World War in UK, Europe, USA; Solicitor, 1947-86; Chairman, Governors, Glasgow Academy, 1972-80; Deacon Convener, Trades of Glasgow, 1964-65; Dean, Royal Faculty of Procurators in Glasgow, 1976-79; Member, Reviewing Committee on Export of Works of Art, 1980-82; Convener, Retirement Scheme of Church of Scotland, 1976-80; Chairman, Charles Rennie Mackintosh Society, 1985-88; Chairman, Indigent Gentlewomen of Scotland Fund, 1985-93; Chairman, Glasgow School of Art, 1975-88. Recreations: gardening; salmon fishing. Address: (h.) The Cottage, Clachan of Campsie, Glasgow; T.-01360 311434.

Smith, William Wilson Campbell, MA (Cantab), LLB (Glas). Managing Partner, Biggart Baillie, Solicitors, Glasgow and Edinburgh; b. 17.5.46, Glasgow; m., Elizabeth Margaret Richards; 2 d. Educ. Glasgow Academy; St. Catharine's College, Cambridge; Glasgow University. Qualified as a Solicitor, 1972; Assistant Solicitor, Herbert Smith & Co., London, 1972-73; Partner, Biggart Baillie, since 1974. Member, various committees, Law Society of Scotland; Trustee, Glassford Sheltered Housing Trust; Member of Convocation, Strathclyde University; Member, Joint Insolvency Examination Board, 1986-95; Deacon, Incorporation of Barbers, Glasgow, 1989-90. Recreations: croquet; golf; barbershop singing. Address: (b.) Dalmore House, 310 St. Vincent Street, Glasgow, G2 5QR; T.-0141-228 8000.

Smout, Professor Thomas Christopher, CBE, MA, PhD, FRSE, FSA (Scot), FBA. HM Historiographer in Scotland; b. 19.12.33. Member, Royal Commission on the Ancient and Historic Monuments of Scotland. Address: (b.) School of History, St. Andrews University, St. Andrews, Fife.

Smuga, George Muirhead Russell, MA (Hons), DipEd. Headteacher, North Berwick High School, since 1990; seconded as Manager, Quality Assurance for East Lothian Department of Education and Community Services, since 1997; b. 6.11.47, Broughty Ferry; m., Isabel Ann; 1 s.; 1 d. Educ. Kirkcaldy High School; Edinburgh University. Principal Teacher, Modern Studies, then Assistant Headteacher, Portobello High School; Depute Headteacher, Beeslack High School. Member, Understanding British Industry Scotland and Northern Ireland Advisory Committee; co-author of four modern studies textbooks. Recreations: golf; supporting Hibernian F.C. Address: (h.)

47 Morton Street, Edinburgh, EH15 2DA; T.-0131-669 9690.

Smyth, Professor John Crocket, OBE, BSc, PhD, HonDUniv (Paisley), DipEd, CBiol, FIBiol, FLS, FRSA. Emeritus Professor of Biology, Paisley University, since 1988; Honorary Professor (Department of Educational Policy and Development), Stirling University; Chairman, Scottish Environmental Education Council, 1983-91, President, since 1991; Chairman, Secretary of State for Scotland's Working Group on Environmental Education, 1990-93; b. 21.3.24, Edinburgh; m., Elizabeth Wallace Learmond; 1 s.; 1 d. Educ. George Watson's College; Edinburgh University. Assistant Lecturer in Zoology, Edinburgh University; Lecturer to Head, Department of Biology, Paisley College; Commissioner, Countryside Commission for Scotland, 1990-92; Vice-President, Royal Zoological Society of Scotland; Institute of Biology Charter Award for 1989; former Secretary and Chairman, Scottish Branch, Institute of Biology; Member, IUCN Commission on Education and Communication; IUCN Tree of Learning Award, 1990; Chairman, N.W. Europe Committee, 1980-85; Consultant for UNESCO-UNEP and UNCED on environmental education; Founder-Leader, Scottish Boys' Club. Address: (h.) Glenpark, Johnstone, Renfrewshire, PA5 0SP; T.-01505 320219.

Smyth, Professor John Fletcher, MA, MB, BChir, MD (Cantab), MSc (Lond), FRCPE, FRCP, FRCSE, FRSE. Professor of Medical Oncology, Edinburgh University, since 1979 (Head, Department of Clinical Oncology, since 1980); Honorary Director, Imperial Cancer Research Fund Medical Oncology Unit, Edinburgh University, since 1980; b. 26.10.45, Dursley; m., Catherine Ellis; 2 d. Educ. Bryanston School; Trinity College, Cambridge. Trained, St. Bartholomews Hospital, Royal Postgraduate Medical School and Institute of Cancer Research, London; National Cancer Institute, Bethesda; University of Chicago; Honorary Consultant Physician, Royal Marsden Hospital and Senior Lecturer, Institute of Cancer Research, London, 1976-79. Address: (b.) Department of Clinical Oncology, Western General Hospital, Crew Road, Edinburgh, EH4 2XU.

Snaith, Professor David William, MSc, PhD, CEng, MIM, CChem, FRSC, FInstM, FRSA. Principal, Stow College, Glasgow, since 1983; b. 30.6.40; m., Susan Willoughby Tucker; 1 s.; 2 d. Educ. Kings Norton Grammar School, Birmingham; Aston University. Research Chemist, Birmingham Small Arms Co. Ltd., 1961; Lecturer in Chemistry: Matthew Boulton College, Birmingham, 1965; Suffolk College, 1969; Deputy Head, Department of Science and Metallurgy, North Lindsey College, Scunthorpe, 1974; Head, Department of Science, North East Liverpool Technical College, 1980. Royal Society of Chemistry: Assistant Secretary, East Anglia, and Chairman (Southumbria) Sections, 1972-78; Chair, West of Scotland Access Consortium, 1996. Recreations: hill-walking; music-making; photography. Address: (b.) Stow College, 43 Shamrock Street, Glasgow, G4 9LD; T.-0141-332 1786.

Sneddon, Brian M., BSc(Econ) (Hons), ACIB. Area Manager, Scotland, Midland Bank plc, since 1996; Member, Supervisory Committee, Scottish Equity Partnership, since 1996; b. 15.5.57, Kitale, Kenya; m., Nicola; 2 s. Educ. King's College, Taunton; Southampton University. Hongkong and Shanghai Banking Corporation, 1979-90; Credit Lyonnais Scotland, 1990-95. Address: (b.) 76 Hanover Street, Edinburgh EH2 1HQ; T.-0131-456 3256.

Sneddon, Hutchison Burt, CBE, JP. Lord Lieutenant of Lanarkshire; b. 17.4.29, Wishaw; m., Elizabeth Jardine; 1 s.; 2 d. Educ. Wishaw High School. Former Scottish Divisional Director, Nationwide Anglia Building Society; Chairman, Cumbernauld Development Corporation, 1979-

83; Vice-Chairman, Scottish National Housing and Town Planning Council, 1965-71; Chairman, Burns Heritage Trail, 1971-83; President, World Federation of Burns Clubs, 1989-90; Deputy President, COSLA, 1974-76; Chairman, Motherwell District Council, 1974-77; Provost, Burgh of Motherwell and Wishaw, 1971-75. Recreations: football (watching); philately. Addrerss: (h.) 36 Shand Street, Wishaw, ML2 8HN; T.-01698 373685.

Sneddon, Ian Naismith, OBE (1969), BSc, DSc, BA, MA, FRS, FRSE, FIMA. Honorary Senior Research Fellow and Emeritus Professor of Mathematics, Glasgow University; Board of Directors, Capella Nova; b. 8.12.19, Glasgow; m., Mary Campbell Macgregor; 2 s.; 1 d. Educ. Hyndland School, Glasgow; Glasgow University; Trinity College, Cambridge. Junior Scientific Officer, Ministry of Supply, 1942-45; William Bryce Fellow, Glasgow University, 1945-46; Lecturer in Natural Philosophy, Glasgow University, 1946-50; Professor of Mathematics, University College of North Staffordshire, 1950-56; Simson Professor of Mathematics, Glasgow University, 1956-85. Hon DSc: Warsaw University, Heriot-Watt University, Hull University, Strathclyde University; Kelvin Medal, Glasgow University; Makdougall-Brisbane Prize, Royal Society of Edinburgh, 1959; Eringen Medal, Society of Engineering Science, 1979; Copernicus Medal, Polish Academy of Sciences, 1973; Gold Medal for Culture (Poland), 1983; Member, Order of the Long Leaf Pine (North Carolina), 1964; Commander, Order of Polonia Restituta, 1969; Commander, Order of Merit of Poland, 1979. Recreations: music; painting in oils; photography. Address: (h.) 19 Crown Terrace, Glasgow, G12 9ES; T.-0141-339 4114.

Sneller, David Bruce, BSc (Hons). Leader, East Ayrshire Council, since 1995; Councillor, Cumnock South, since 1984; b. 16.1.58, Sheffield; m., Jean. Educ. Firth Park School, Sheffield; Nottingham University. Geologist, British Coal (Opencast), 1981-92; Area Geologist, Scottish Coal, since 1995. Board Member, Enterprise Ayrshire, since 1991; Chair, Carrick, Cumnock and Doon Valley C.L.P. Recreations: golf; reading; swimming. Address: (h.) 3 Kings Drive, Cumnock, KA18 1AG; T.-01290 421568.

Sole, David Michael Barclay, OBE, BA (Hons). Rugby Player; b. 8.5.62, Aylesbury; m., Jane; 3 s.; 1 d. Educ. Trinity College, Glenalmond; Exeter University. Played rugby for Scotland, 1986-92 (44 caps); also British Lions and Barbarians; Captain of Scotland, 1989-92; tour to New Zealand; 1991 World Cup; tour to Australia, 1992. Address: (b.) 33 Ellersly Road, Edinburgh; T.-0131-337 7373.

Somerville, David Wilkie, DipPE. Head of Community Services, Fife Council, since 1995; b. Edinburgh; m., Fiona; 1 s.; 1 d. Educ. Lasswade High School. Football: Hearts, Berwick Rangers; P.E. Teacher, Penicuik High School; Depute Director, National Sports Training Centre; Sport Development, Scottish Sports Council; Senior Assistant Director of Education, Fife Regional Council. Recreations: golf; swimming. Address: (b.) Fife Council, Fife House, North Street, Glenrothes; T.-01592 414141.

Somerville, Les, LLB, DipLP, NP. Solicitor, Pollock Stewart & Co., Stirling, since 1987; b. 6.5.61, Stirling; m., Fay. Educ. Lenzie Academy; Strathclyde University. Training in Glasgow, 1982-84; partnership, C. & D. Mactaggart, 1984-87; Assistant Solicitor, Pollock Stewart & Co., 1987-88, Partner, since 1988; Secretary, Stirling Faculty of Solicitors, since 1990. Recreations: Triathlon; golf; swimming. Address: (b.) 75 Murray Place, Stirling FK8 1AU; T.-01786 450346.

Sommerville, John Kenneth, CA. Partner, French Duncan, CA, Glasgow, since 1970; Council Member, Institute of Chartered Accountants of Scotland, 1984-90; Council Member, Association of Accounting Technicians, since 1989 (President, 1995-96); b. 1.3.42, Glasgow; m., Iris

Alexa Hutchison; 3 d. Educ. Kelvinside Academy. Member, Board of Governors, Kelvinside Academy, 1976-94 (Chairman of Board, 1985-94). Recreations: golf; running. Address: (b.) 375 West George Street, Glasgow, G2 4LH; T.-0141-221 2984.

Somerville, Lynda Margaret, RGN, SCM. Director, Mental Health Foundation Scotland, since 1991; b. Paisley. Educ. Paisley Grammar School. Registered general nurse; midwife; medical sales; Marketing Director, Ross Hall Hospital; Director, Mackay Somerville Marketing; Marketing Manager, Britannia Life Ltd. Recreations: studying; music; dance. Address: (b.) 24 George Square, Glasgow, G2 1EG; T.-0141-221 2092.

Spalding, Julian, BA, FMA. Director, Glasgow Museums and Art Galleries, since 1989; b. 15.6.47, London; 1 s. Educ. Chislehurst and Sidcup Grammar School for Boys; Nottingham University. Art Assistant: Leicester Museum & Art Gallery, 1970-71, Durham Light Infantry Museum & Arts Centre, 1971-72; Keeper, Mappin Art Gallery, 1972-76, Depute Director, 1976-82; Director of Arts, Sheffield City Council, 1982-85; Director, Manchester City Art Galleries, 1985-89; Director, National Museum of Labour History, 1987-89. Member, Arts Council of GB, 1978-82; Founder, Art Galleries Association, 1976; Director, Guild of St. George, since 1983, Master of Guild, since 1996; Director, Mayfest, since 1989; Member, Crafts Council, since 1986; Member, British Council, since 1987; Advisory Member, new British Library; Director, Scottish Football Museum, since 1994; Director, Niki de St. Phalle Foundation, since 1994. Publications: L.S. Lowry, 1979; Three Little Books on Painting, 1984; Art for People; various exhibition catalogues. Recreations: cycling; gardening; painting. Address: (b.) Art Gallery and Museum, Kelvingrove, Glasgow, G3 8AG; T.-0141-287 2600.

Sparks, Professor Leigh, MA, PhD, FRSA. Professor of Retail Studies, Stirling University, since 1992; Dean, Faculty of Management, since 1995; b. 15.2.57, Bridgend, Wales; m., Janice Lewis. Educ. Brynteg C.S.; Christ's College, Cambridge; Lampeter College, Wales. Researcher, Lecturer, Senior Lecturer, Professor, Institute for Retail Studies, Department of Marketing, Stirling University. Recreation: watching sport, especially rugby. Address: (b.) Faculty of Management, Stirling University, Stirling FK9 4LA; T.-01786 467278.

Spawforth, David Meredith, MA (Oxon), FRSA. Headmaster, Merchiston Castle School, since 1981; b. 2.1.38, Wakefield; m., Yvonne Mary Gude; 1 s.; 1 d. Educ. Silcoates School; Hertford College, Oxford. Assistant Master, Winchester College, 1961-64; Housemaster, Wellington College, 1964-80; BP Education Fellow, Keble College, Oxford, 1977. Recreations: travel - especially France and Italy; theatre; walking. Address: (b.) Merchiston Castle School, Colinton, Edinburgh.

Speirs, Robert, ACIS, FRSA. Finance Director, Royal Bank of Scotland plc, since 1993, b. 23.10.36, Liverpool; m., Patricia; 2 s. Educ. Alleynes Grammar School. Inland Revenue, 1953-64; Coopers & Lybrand, 1964-68; Texaco Ltd., 1968-77; Treasurer, British National Oil Corporation, 1977-83; Treasurer/Finance Director, Britoil plc, 1983-88; Finance Director, Olympia and York Canary Wharf Ltd., 1988-93. Recreations: DIY; walking; music. Address: (b.) 42 St. Andrew's Square, Edinburgh; T.-0131-523 2033.

Speirs, William MacLeod, BA (Hons), FRSA. Deputy General Secretary, Scottish TUC; Chairperson, 7:84 Theatre Company (Scotland), since 1988; b. 8.3.52, Dumbarton; 1 s.; 1 d. Educ. John Neilson High School, Paisley; Strathclyde University. Assistant Secretary, Scottish TUC, 1979-88. Chairperson, Labour Party in Scotland, 1987-88; Chairperson, Scottish Friends of Palestine, since 1982; Director, Scottish Trade Union Review. Recreations:

reading; losing money on horses; watching St. Mirren F.C. Address: (b.) STUC, 16 Woodlands Terrace, Glasgow, G3 6DF; T.-(b.) 0141-332 4946; (h.) 0141-333 1807.

Spence, Alan, MA. Writer (poet, playwright, novelist, short-story writer); b. 5.12.47, Glasgow; m., Janani (Margaret). Educ. Allan Glen's School, Glasgow; Glasgow University. Writer in Residence, Glasgow University, 1975-77, Deans Community School, 1978, Traverse Theatre, Edinburgh, 1983, City of Edinburgh, 1986-87, Edinburgh University, 1989-92, Aberdeen University, since 1996; winner, People's Prize, 1991; Macallan/Scotland on Sunday Short Story competition, 1993; McVitie's Prize, 1996; TMA Drama Award, 1996. Publications: poetry: ah!; Glasgow Zen; short stories: Its Colours They Are Fine, Stone Garden; novels: The Magic Flute, Way to Go; plays: Sailmaker; Space Invaders; Changed Days. Recreations: meditation; running; playing flute. Address: 21 Waverley Park, Edinburgh, EH8 8ER; T.-0131-661 8403.

Spence, Professor Alastair Andrew, CBE, MD, FRCA, FRCP (Glas & Edin), FRCS (Ed & Eng), Hon FDS, RCS Eng. Professor of Anaesthetics, Edinburgh University, since 1984; Honorary Consultant Anaesthetist, Royal Infirmary, Edinburgh; President, Royal College of Anaesthetists, 1991-94; b. 18.9.36, Glasgow; m., Maureen Isobel Aitchison; 2 s. Educ. Ayr Academy; Glasgow University. Professor and Head, University Department of Anaesthesia, Western Infirmary, Glasgow, 1969-84; Editor, British Journal of Anaesthesia, 1973-83; Hunterian Professor, Royal College of Surgeons of England, 1974; Joseph Clover Lecturer, 1990; Member, Advisory Committee on Distinction Awards, since 1992; Medical Director, since 1996. Recreations: golf; gardening. Address: (h.) Harewood, Kilmacolm, PA13 4HX; T.-Kilmacolm 872962.

Spence, James William, KFO (Norway), RON (Netherlands), BSc, MNI, MICS, DL. Master Mariner, since 1971; Shipbroker, since 1975; Company Director, since 1977; b. 19.1.45, St. Ola, Orkney; m., Margaret Paplay Stevenson; 3 s. Educ. Leith Nautical College, Edinburgh; Robert Gordon's Institute of Technology, Aberdeen; University of Wales, Cardiff. Merchant Navy, 1961-74 (Member, Nautical Institute, 1972, Member, Royal Institute of Navigation, 1971); Micoperi SpA, 1974-75 (Temporary Assistant Site Co-ordinator on Scapa Flow Project); John Jolly (Shipbrokers, Stevedores, Shipping and Forwarding Agents) since 1975 (Manager, 1975, Junior Partner, 1976-77, Proprietor and Managing Director, since 1977). Vice-Consul for Norway, 1976, Consul, 1978; Vice-Consul for the Netherlands, 1978-94; Member, Kirkwall Community Council, 1978-82; Member, Orkney Pilotage Committee, 1979-88; Chairman, Kirkwall Port Employers' Association, 1979-87 (Member, since 1975); Chairman, RNLI, Kirkwall Lifeboat, 1997 (Station Hon. Secretary, 1987-96, Deputy Launching Authority, 1976-87); Chairman, Pier Arts Centre Trust, 1989-91 (Trustee, 1980-91); Chairman, Association of Honorary Norwegian Consuls in the UK and Ireland, 1993-95. Recreations: oenology; equestrian matters; Orcadian history. Address: (h.) Alton House, Kirkwall, Orkney KW15 1NA; T.-01856 872268.

Spence, Professor John, ARCST, BSc, MEng, PhD, DSc, FEng, FRSE, FIMechE. Pro Vice-Principal, Strathclyde University (Trades House of Glasgow Professor of Mechanics of Materials, since 1982); b. 5.11.37, Chapelhall; m., Margaret Gray Hudson; 2 s. Educ. Airdrie Academy; Royal College of Science and Technology; Sheffield University. Engineering apprenticeship, Stewarts & Lloyds (now British Steel Corporation); Senior Engineer, then Head of Stress Analysis, Babcock & Wilcox Research Division; Strathclyde University: Lecturer, 1966, Senior Lecturer, Reader, Professor since 1979. Serves on several national committees: Deputy President, Institution of Mechanical Engineers; EPSRC College; British Standards

Institution; Engineering Professors Council (Vice Chairman). Address: (b.) Department of Mechanical Engineering, Strathclyde University, 75 Montrose Street, Glasgow, G1 1XJ; T.-0141-552 4400, Ext. 2324.

Spence, William Arthur, QPM, LLB, BA. Chief Constable of Tayside; b. 20.11.43, Ellon. Educ. Ellon Academy; Strathclyde University. Served in Renfrew and Bute Constabulary and Strathclyde Police prior to appointment to Tayside Police, 1988; Member, Scottish Victim Support Funding Panel, 1988-96; Chairman, ACPOS Traffic Standing Committee, 1995; President, Association of Chief Police Officers in Scotland, 1996-97; Chairman, Tayside Drugs Action Team; Fellow, RSA; Member of Court, University of Abertay, Dundee. Recreations: reading; genealogy; theatre; gardening. Address: (b.) Tayside Police, PO Box 59, West Bell Street, Dundee, DD1 9JU.

Spencely, John Despenser, MA, BArch, DipTP, RIBA, PPRIAS, MRTPI, FCIArb. Chairman, Reiach and Hall; Chairman, Buildings Investigation Centre; b. 5.10.39, Westerham, England; m., Marilyn Anne Read; 1 d. (by pr. m.). Educ. Bryanston School; Cambridge University; Edinburgh University. Architect, Town Planner; former Member, Scottish Building Contract Committee; President: Edinburgh Architectural Association, 1984-86; Royal Incorporation of Architects in Scotland, 1989-91; Lay Member, Scottish Solicitors Discipline Tribunal; Member, Advisory Committee on Arbitration to Scottish Law Commission; Board Member, Scottish Homes; Visiting Professor, Napier University; Freeman of the City of London; Liveryman, Worshipful Company of Arbitrators. Recreations: sailing; reading; collecting some unfashionable 20th century authors; making jam. Address: (b.) 6 Darnaway Street, Edinburgh EH3 6BG; T.-0131-225 8444.

Spencer, Alec P., BA (Hons), MA. Governor, Edinburgh Prison, since 1996; b. 12.3.46, London; m., Joan; 2 s.; 1 d. Educ. Dame Alice Owen School; Keele University. Joined Scottish Prison Service, 1972, as Assistant Governor: Polmont Borstal, Perth Prison, Glenochil; Deputy Governor, Aberdeen Prison, 1978; Prison Department HQ, 1981; Warden, Glenochil D.C., 1983; Deputy Governor, Glenochil Complex, 1987; Governor, Dungavel Prison, 1989; Governor, Peterhead Prison, 1992; Operational Adviser, PFI prison project 8PS HQ, 1996. Chairman, Scottish Forum on Prisons and Families; Butler Trust Award, 1987; Editor, ASPG Journal, 1982-90; Chairman, Governors' Committee, NUCPS, 1991-92; Hon. Senior Research Fellow, Dundee University. Recreations: music; walking; writing; collecting Penguin books. Address: (b.) Edinburgh Prison, 33 Stenhouse Road, Edinburgh EH11 3LN; T.-0131-444 3003.

Spencer, Very Rev. Paul Francis, CP. Rector, Saint Mungo's, Glasgow, since 1996; Provincial Consultor, Congregation of the Passion, since 1992; b. 2.3.54. Educ. Saint Mungo's Academy, Glasgow; University College, Dublin; Milltown Institute, Dublin; Pontifical Gregorian University, Rome. Professed as Member of Passionist Congregation, 1977; Ordained Priest, 1980; Vicar, Saint Mungo's, Glasgow, 1981-86; Master of Novices, Cochin, India, 1986-87; post-graduate studies, Rome, 1987-89; Rector, Anglophone de France, Paris, 1989-96. Advisor to the Passionist Nuns, since 1988; Postulator of the Cause of Canonisation of Elizabeth Prout CP, since 1994; Member, Historical Commission for the Cause of Ignatius Spencer CP, since 1993; awarded Cross Pro piis meritis, Sovereign Military Order of Malta, 1995. Publications: To Heal the Broken-Hearted: The Life of Blessed Charles of Mount Argus, 1988; As a Seal upon your Heart: The Life of Saint Paul of the Cross, Founder of the Passionists, 1994. Recreation: music. Address: (h.) Saint Mungo's Retreat, 52 Parson Street, Glasgow G4 0RX; T.-0141-552 1823.

Spiers, Rev. John McLaren, LTh, MTh. Minister, Orchardhill Church, Giffnock, since 1977; b. 12.12.43, Edinburgh; m., Janet Diane Watson; 2 d. Educ. George Watson's College, Edinburgh; Glasgow University. Probationer Assistant, Drumchapel Old Parish Church, Glasgow, 1971-72; Minister, South Church, Barrhead, 1972-77; Convener, Board of World Mission, since 1996. Recreations: music; art; family life. Address: 23 Huntly Avenue, Giffnock, Glasgow, G46 6LW.

Spilg, Walter Gerson Spence, MB, ChB (Hons), FRCPath, FRCPG. Consultant Pathologist, Victoria Infirmary, Glasgow, since 1972, in Administrative Charge, since 1986; Honorary Clinical Senior Lecturer, Glasgow University, since 1973; b. 27.10.37, Glasgow; m., Vivien Anne Burns; 1 s.; 2 d. Educ. Hutchesons' Boys' Grammar School, Glasgow; Glasgow University. Registrar in Pathology, Glasgow Royal Infirmary, 1965-68; Senior Registrar in Pathology, Victoria Infirmary, Glasgow, 1968-69; Lecturer in Pathology, Glasgow University (Western Infirmary), 1969-72. Member, Greater Glasgow Health Board Area Medical Sub-Committee in Laboratory Medicine; Examiner, Royal College of Physicians and Surgeons of Glasgow; Member, Forensic Pathology Liaison Committee. Recreations: bridge; golf. Address: (h.) 4B Newton Court, Newton Mearns, Glasgow, G77 5QL.

Spiller, Professor Eric, MA, FRSA. Assistant Principal/Dean, Faculty of Design, Robert Gordon University, since 1992; b. 19.8.46, Staffordshire; m., Carolyn; 2 s.; 1 d. Educ. Central School of Art and Design, London; Royal College of Art. Jewellery designer and lecturer; Head, School of Design, Portsmouth College of Art Design and Further Education, 1985-87, Grays School of Art, Robert Gordon's Institute of Technology, Aberdeen, 1987-92; public collections include: Goldsmiths Hall, Crafts Council, W. Midlands Arts, NW Arts, Aberdeen Art Gallery, Scottish Crafts Collection; private collections worldwide; numerous exhibitions; Council Member and Chair, Craft Committee, Scottish Arts Council. Recreation: hill-walking. Address: (b.) Faculty of Design, Garthdee Road, Aberdeen; T.-01224 263750.

Spratt, Col. Douglas Norman, CBE, TD. Director, Cameo of Edinburgh, since 1984; b. 18.9.20, Ramsgate; m., Margaret; 1 d. Educ. Sir Roger Manwood's Grammar School, Sandwich, Kent. President, Edinburgh Branch, Institute of Marketing; Chairman, Friends of the Reserve Forces Association, Scotland; Regional Chairman, Action Research in Scotland; Member, High Constables of Edinburgh; Deputy Lieutenant, City of Edinburgh; Member of the Military Attaches London. Recreations: fishing; sailing. Address: (h.) 6 Fernielaw Avenue, Edinburgh, EH13 OEE; T.-0131-441 1962.

Sprent, Professor Janet I., OBE, BSc, ARCS, PhD, DSc, FRSE. Professor of Plant Biology, Dundee University, since 1989; Deputy Principal of the University; b. 10.1.34, Siough; m., Emeritus Professor Peter Sprent. Educ. Slough High School; Imperial College, London; Tasmania University. Has spent 28 years at Dundee University; research focussed on nitrogen fixing legumes, both tree and crop species; currently involved in international collaboration, mainly in Africa and Brazil; Dean of Science and Engineering, 1987-89. Council Member, NERC, 1991-95; Member, Scottish Higher Education Funding Council, 1992-96; Member, Joint Nature Conservation Committee, since 1994. Publications:three books and over 100 chapters/papers. Recreations: flying; hill walking. Address: Department of Biological Sciences, Dundee University, Dundee DD1 4HN; T.-01382 344279.

Sprot of Haystoun, Lt.-Col. Aidan Mark, MC, JP. Landowner (Haystoun Estate) and Farmer, since 1965; b. 17.6.19, Lilliesleaf. Educ. Belhaven Hill; Stowe. Commissioned, Royal Scots Greys, 1940; served Palestine, 1941-42, Western Desert, 1942-43, Italy, 1943-44, NW Europe, 1944-45; continued serving with Regiment in Germany until 1952, Libya, Egypt and Jordan, 1952-55, UK, 1955-58, Germany, 1958-62; Adjutant, 1944-45; Commanding Officer, 1959-62; retired, 1962. County Councillor, Peeblesshire, 1963-75; DL (Peeblesshire), 1966-80; Lord Lieutenant, Tweeddale, 1980-94; Member, Queen's Bodyguard for Scotland (Royal Company of Archers), since 1950; County Director, Peeblesshire Branch, Red Cross, 1966-74, Patron, since 1983; County Commissioner, Peeblesshire Scout Association, 1968-73, Chairman, 1975-80, President, 1980-94; President, Borders Area Scout Association, since 1994; Scout Medal of Merit, 1994; Honorary Secretary, Royal Caledonian Hunt, 1964-74; President, Lowlands of Scotland TA&VRA, 1986-89; President, Lothian Federation of Boys' Clubs, 1989-96, now Hon. President; Honorary Freeman, Tweeddale District, 1994. Recreations: country sports; motor cycle touring. Address: (h.) Crookston, by Peebles, EH45 9JQ; T.-Kirkton Manor 740209.

Sprott, Gavin, MA, FSAScot. Keeper, Department of Social and Technological History, National Museums of Scotland; b. 23.7.43, Dundee; m., Maureen Turnbull; 2 s.; 1 d. Educ. Edinburgh University. Research Assistant, Scottish Country Life Section, National Museum of Antiquities of Scotland, 1972-79; Curator, Scottish Agricultural Museum, 1979-86. Recreations: cycling; walking. Address: (b.) National Museums of Scotland, Chambers Street, Edinburgh, EH1 1JF; T.-0131-247 4256.

Sproul-Cran, Robert Scott, MA (Cantab), PhD. Director, Northlight Productions Ltd., since 1991; b. 14.8.50; m., Elizabeth Ann; 3 s.; 1 d. Educ. Daniel Stewart's College; Pembroke College, Cambridge; Edinburgh University. Trainee, Phillips & Drew, Stockbrokers, London, 1971-72; Announcer, then Head of Presentation, BBC Radio Scotland, 1979-85; Radio Manager, BBC Aberdeen, 1986-90; Scottish Correspondent, BBC Daytime Television, 1990-91; freelance Graphic Designer and Underwater Photographer, since 1976; Winner, Scottish Corporate Communications Award, RTS Award for video graphics; illustrated Maurice Lindsay's Glasgow. Recreations: oil painting; printmaking; windsurfing; sub aqua; playing bad rock guitar. Address: (b.) The Media Village, Grampian TV, Queens Cross, Aberdeen AB15 4XJ; T.-01224 646460.

Spry, Christopher. Chief Executive, Greater Glasgow Health Board. Address: (b.) Dalian House, P.O. Box 15329, 350 St. Vincent Street, Glasgow G3 8YZ.

Spy, Sheriff James, LLB (Hons). Sheriff of North Strathclyde at Paisley, since 1988; b. 1.12.52. Admitted Solicitor, 1976; Advocate, 1979. Address: (b.) Sheriff Court House, 106 Renfrew Road, Paisley, PA3 4DD.

Squire, Rachel Anne, BA, CQSW. MP (Labour), Dunfermline West, since 1992; b. 13.7.54, Carshalton, Surrey; m., Allan Mason. Educ. Godolphin and Latymer Girls' School; Durham University. Social Worker, Birmingham Social Services, 1975-81; National Union of Public Employees, 1981-92. Address: (b.) House of Commons, London, SW1A 0AA.

Stafford, William, MIWM, MREHIS. Director of Community Services, East Ayrshire Council, since 1995; b. 25.3.54, Galston; m., Margaret Ann; 1 s. Educ. Galston High School; Loudoun Academy; College of Food Technology, Glasgow. Ayr County Council, 1971-75; various posts in Environmental Health, Cumnock and Doon Valley District Council, 1975-95. Chairman, Strathclyde Food and Drugs Liaison Group. Recreations: motor sport; gardening. Address: (b.) Council Headquarters, London Road, Kilmarnock; T.-01563 576023.

Stanforth, Professor Anthony William, BA, MA, Drphil. Professor of Languages, Heriot-Watt University, since 1981 (Head, Department of Languages, 1981-89; Dean, Faculty of Economic and Social Studies, 1989-92; Head, School of Languages, 1995-98); b. 27.7.38, Ipswich; m., Susan Margaret Vale; 2 s. Educ. Ipswich School; King's College, Newcastle (Durham University); Marburg University. Earl Grey Memorial Fellow, Newcastle-upon-Tyne University, 1962-64; Assistant Lecturer, Manchester University, 1964-65; Lecturer, Senior Lecturer, Newcastle-upon-Tyne University, 1965-81; Visiting Assistant Professor, Wisconsin University, 1970-71. Fellow, Royal Society of Arts; Honorary Fellow, Institute of Linguists. Recreation: opera. Address: (b.) School of Languages, Heriot-Watt University, Riccarton, Edinburgh, EH14 4AS; T.-0131-449 5111.

Stanners, Ian Cram, FRICS. Chartered Quantity Surveyor; b. 30.11.38, Glasgow; m., Louise Robertson; 2 d. Educ. Hutchesons' Boys' Grammar School. Chairman, Quantity Surveyors Divisional Committee, Scottish Branch, RICS, 1980-81; Chairman, RICS in Scotland, 1986-87; Chairman, Scottish Building Contract Committee. Honorary Vice-President, Clyde Amateur Rowing Club. Recreations: rowing; curling. Address: (b.) 21 Woodlands Terrace, Glasgow, G3 6DF; T.-0141-332 6032.

Stansfeld, John Raoul Wilmot, JP, DL, MA (Oxon), FIFM. Director, Joseph Johnston & Sons Ltd., since 1962; b. 15.1.35, London; m., Rosalinde Rachel Buxton; 3 s. Educ. Eton; Christ Church, Oxford. Lt., Gordon Highlanders, 1954-58; Chairman, North Esk District Salmon Fishery Board, 1967-80; Esk Fishery Board Committee, 1980-85; Vice Chairman, Association of Scottish District Salmon Fishery Boards, 1970-85; Director and Chairman, Montrose Chamber of Commerce, since 1984; Editor, Salmon Net Magazine, 1978-85; Chairman, Scottish Fish Farmers Association, 1970-73; Secretary, Diocese of Brechin, 1968-76. Member, Royal Company of Archers (Queen's Bodyguard for Scotland). Recreations: reading; jigsaw puzzles; trees. Address: (h.) Dunninald, Montrose, Angus, DD10 9TD; T.-01674 672666.

Stark, Edi, MA (Hons), ALA. Presenter, Fair Deal, Stark Talk, BBC Radio Scotland; b. Edinburgh; m., Gavin Stark; 1 s.; 1 d. Educ. Aberdeen University; RGIT. Community Librarian, Glasgow and Livingston; Northsound Radio: Community Co-ordinator, 1981, Senior Producer, 1982, Head of Speech Programming, 1983-89; freelance journalist, since 1990. Recreations: conversation, food and drink, travel, reading, contemporary art. Address: (b.) c/o BBC Scotland, Beechgrove Terrace, Aberdeen, AB9 2ZT; T.- 01224 625233.

Starszakowna, Professor Norma, DA, FCSD, FRSA. Textile Designer/Artist; Chair in Design, Duncan of Jordanstone College of Art; b. 9.5.45, Crosshill; m., Andrew Taylor; 2 s. Educ. Kirkcaldy High School; Duncan of Jordanstone College of Art. Design and production of printed and dyed textiles for fashion and interior; commissioned work includes Crest Hotel, Antwerp, General Accident HQ, Perth, Issey Miyake, Winchester, and Scottish Arts Council; exhibited widely, UK and abroad. SAC Award, 1977; Saltire Art in Architecture Award, 1983; Member: Crafts Council Index, Board of Texprint, Board of ETN (Brussels), Point, Axis, AHDFT, CNAA, Textile Institute H.E. Committee, SHEFC Teaching Quality Assessment, HEFCE Research Assessment Panel for Art and Design and various other national bodies. Recreation: travel. Address: (h.) 9 Fort Street, Magdalen Green, Dundee, DD2 1BS; T.-01382 644654.

Steedman, Robert Russell, OBE, RSA, RIBA, FRSA, FRIAS, ALI, DA, MLA. Partner, Morris and Steedman, Architects and Landscape Architects; b. 3.1.29, Batu Gajah, Malaysia; m., 1, Susan Scott (m. diss.); 1 s.; 2 d.; 2, Martha

Hamilton. Educ. Loretto School; School of Architecture, Edinburgh College of Art; Pennsylvania University. Governor, Edinburgh College of Art, since 1974; Commissioner, Countryside Commission for Scotland, 1980-88; Chairman, Central Scotland Woodlands Project, 1984-88; Association for the Protection of Rural Scotland Award Panel, since 1995; ARSA, 1973, Academician, 1979; Council Member, RSA, 1981 (Deputy President, 1982-83, Secretary, 1983-91); Commissioner, Royal Fine Art Commission for Scotland, 1983-96; former Member, Council, RIAS; nine Civic Trust Awards, 1963-78; British Steel Award, 1971; RIBA Award for Scotland, 1974; European Heritage Medal, 1975; Association for the Protection of Rural Scotland, 1977; Borders Region Award, 1984. Address: (h.) 11B Belford Mews, Edinburgh; T.-0131-225 1697.

Steel, Professor Christopher Michael, BSc, MB, ChB, PhD, DSc, FRCPEdin, FRCPath, FRCSEdin, FRSE. Professor in Medical Science, St. Andrews University, since 1994; b. 25.1.40, Buckhaven; m., Dr. Judith Margaret Spratt; 2 s.; 1 d. Educ. Prince of Wales School, Nairobi; George Watson's College, Edinburgh; Edinburgh University. House Physician/House Surgeon/Resident/Senior House Officer, Edinburgh Teaching Hospitals; Graduate Research Fellow in Medicine, 1968; joined MRC staff, 1971; MRC Travelling Research Fellow, University of Nairobi, 1972-73; Assistant Director, MRC Human Genetics Unit, Edinburgh, 1979. Editor, Disease Markers; published over 200 scientific papers and book chapters; Member, Government Gene Therapy Advisory Committee. Recreations: golf; skiing; music; theatre. Address: (b.) Bute Medical Building, St. Andrews, KY16 9TS; T.-01334 476161.

Steel, Very Rev. David, MA, BD, DD, LLD. Minister Emeritus, St. Michael's, Linlithgow, since 1977; b. 5.10.10, Hamilton; m., Sheila E.N. Martin (deceased); 3 s. (eldest son: Rt. Hon. Lord Steel of Aikwood, KBE, PC, DL (qv)); 2 d. Educ. St. John's Grammar School, Hamilton; Peterhead Academy; Robert Gordon's College, Aberdeen; Aberdeen University. Minister: Denbeath, Fife, 1936-41, Bridgend, Dumbarton, 1941-46; Associate Secretary, Foreign Mission Committee, Edinburgh, 1946-49; Minister, St. Andrew's, Nairobi and East Africa, 1949-57; Locum, St. Cuthbert's, Edinburgh, 1957-58; Minister, St. Michael's, Linlithgow, 1959-76; Moderator, General Assembly of the Church of Scotland, 1974-75; Visiting Preacher and Lecturer: in America, 1953-87, St. Columba's, Pont Street, 1977, Lausanne, 1978, Tanzania, 1980; Chairman, Callendar Park College of Education, 1972-78; Vice-President: Boys' Brigade, National Bible Society of Scotland, West Lothian Historical and Amenity Society. Publications: History of St. Michael's; The Belief; Preaching through the Year. Recreations: trout fishing; travel. Address: (h.) 39 Newbattle Terrace, Edinburgh, EH10 4SF; T.-0131-447 2180.

Steel of Aikwood, Rt. Hon. Lord (David Steel), KBE, PC, DL. MP, Tweeddale, Ettrick and Lauderdale, 1983-97 (Roxburgh, Selkirk and Peebles, 1965-83); Leader, Liberal Party, 1976-88; b. 31.3.38, Kirkcaldy; m., Judith MacGregor; 2 s.; 1 d. Educ. Prince of Wales School, Nairobi; George Watson's College, Edinburgh; Edinburgh University (MA, LLB). Assistant Secretary, Scottish Liberal Party, 1962-64; Interviewer, BBC TV Scotland, 1964-65; Presenter, weekly religious programme, STV, 1966-67, for Granada, 1969, for BBC, 1971-76; Liberal Chief Whip, 1970-75; Sponsor, Private Member's Bill to reform law on abortion, 1966-67; President, Anti-Apartheid Movement of Great Britain, 1966-69; Chairman, Shelter, Scotland, 1969-73; Member, British Council of Churches, 1971-75; Past President, Liberal International (President, 1994-96); Rector, Edinburgh University, 1982-85; Chubb Fellow, Yale, 1987; Hon. DUniv (Stirling), 1991; DLitt, University of Buckingham, 1994; Hon. Doctorate, Heriot

Watt University, Edinburgh, 1996; HonLLD, Edinburgh, 1997; awarded Freedom of Tweeddale, 1988, and Ettrick and Lauderdale, 1990; The Commander's Cross of the Order of Merit (Germany), 1992; DL, 1989; contested Central Italy seat, European elections, 1989; President, Liberal International, since 1994; Executive Chairman, Countryside Movement, 1995-97. Publications: Boost for the Borders, 1964; Out of Control, 1968; No Entry, 1969; The Liberal Way Forward, 1975; Militant for the Reasonable Man, 1977; High Ground of Politics, 1979; A House Divided, 1980; Border Country (with Judy Steel), 1985; The Time Has Come (with David Owen), 1987; Mary Stuart's Scotland (with Judy Steel), 1987; Against Goliath, 1989. Recreations: angling; vintage motoring. Address: (b.) House of Lords, London, SW1A 0PW; T.-0171-219 4433.

Steel, David Robert, MA, DPhil. Head of Health Gain, NHS in Scotland, since 1995; b. 29.5.48, Oxford; m., Susan Elizabeth Easton; 1 s.; 1 d. Educ. Birkenhead School; Jesus and Nuffield Colleges, Oxford. Lecturer in Public Administration, Exeter University, 1972-84; Assistant Director, National Association of Health Authorities, 1984-86; Secretary, Health Board Chairmen's and General Managers' Groups and SCOTMEG, 1986-90; Director of Corporate Affairs, NHS in Scotland, 1990-95. Address: (b.) St. Andrew's House, Edinburgh, EH1 3DE; T.-0131-244 2455.

Steele, Alexander Allison, OBE (1986). Honorary Sheriff, Perth, since 1985; b. 5.10.25, Oakley, Fife; m., Patricia Joyce Hipkins; 1 s.; 2 d. Educ. Boroughmuir Secondary School. Entered Scottish Home Department, 1942; Royal Navy, 1943-46; Scottish Court Service (Sheriff Clerk's Branch), 1950; Sheriff Clerk: Dingwall, 1969-71, Perth, 1971-81, Dundee, 1981-85; Member, Lord Stewart's Committee on Alternatives to Prosecution, 1977-83; Honorary Life Member, Society of Sheriff Court Auditors. Recreations: gardening; swimming; wine-making. Address: (h.) Lyndhurst, Hillend Road, Perth; T.-01738 626611.

Steele, Professor Robert James Campbell, BSc, MB,ChB, MD, FRCSEd, FRCSEng, FCSHK. Professor of Surgical Oncology, Dundee University, since 1996; b. 5.3.52, Edinburgh; m., Susan Margaret Cachia; 1 s.; 2 d. Educ. Daniel Stewart's College, Edinburgh; Edinburgh University. Surgical training, Edinburgh, 1977-85; Lecturer in Surgery, Chinese University of Hong Kong, 1985-86; Lecturer in Surgery, Aberdeen University, 1986-90; Senior Lecturer and Reader in Surgery, Nottingham University, 1990-96. Publications in: breast cancer, gastrointestinal surgery and colorectal cancer. Recreations: music; Scottish country dancing; country sports. Address:(b.) Department of Surgery, Ninewells Hospital, Dundee DD1 9SY; T.-01382 660111.

Steele, Thomas Graham. Managing Director: Radio Forth, Scottish Radio Network Sales, Cliar Sheanachain; b. 11.5.45, Lanark; m., Fiona MacAuslane; 1 s.; 1 d. Educ. Larkhall Academy, Larkhall; Skerry's College, Glasgow. Lobby Correspondent, Scottish Daily Mail; TV and Radio Presenter, BBC Glasgow; Producer, BBC Local Radio; Broadcaster, Radio Clyde; Head of News and Current Affairs, Radio Forth; Director of Programmes (Group); Creator, Festival City Radio; Member, Radio Academy Council. Recreations: sailing; walking; reading; conversation. Address: (b.) Forth House, Forth Street, Edinburgh; T.-0131-556 9255.

Steenbergen, Rev. Pauline, MA (Hons), BD. Minister, St. Luke's and Queen Street Church, Broughty Ferry, Dundee, since 1996; b. 2.3.69, Glasgow. Educ. Hazlehead Academy, Aberdeen; Aberdeen University; New College, Edinburgh University. Assistant Minister, Queensferry, 1994-96. Publication: Christian Values (Contributor). Recreations: cinema; reading; dog walking; travel; classical guitar. Address: (h.) 22 Albert Road, Broughty Ferry DD5 1AZ.

Steer, Christopher Richard, BSc (Hons), MB, ChB, DCH, FRCPE, FRCPCH. Consultant Paediatrician; Clinical Tutor, Department of Child Life and Health, Edinburgh University; Hon. Senior Lecturer, Department of Biomedical Science, St. Andrews University; Clinical Director of Obstetrics, Gynaecology and Paediatrics; b. 30.5.47, Clearbrook, near Plymouth; m., Patricia Mary Lennox. Educ. St. Olaves and St. Saviours Grammar School, London; Edinburgh University. Publications: Textbook of Paediatrics (Contributor); Treatment of Neurological Disorders (Contributor). Recreation: our garden. Address: (b.) Paediatric Unit, Kirkcaldy Acute Hospitals NHS Trust, Victoria Hospital, Kirkcaldy, Fife; T.-01592 643355.

Stein, Sheriff Colin Norman Ralph, BA (Hons), LLB. Floating Sheriff of Tayside, Central and Fife at Arbroath, since 1991; b. 14.6.48. Advocate, 1975. Address: (b.) Sheriff Court House, 88 High Street, Arbroath, DD11 1HL.

Stein, Rev. Jock, MA, BD. Joint Warden, Carberry, since 1986 (Minister, Steeple Church, Dundee, 1976-86); b. 8.11.41, Edinburgh; m., Margaret E. Munro; 3 d. Educ. Sedbergh School; Cambridge University; Edinburgh University. Work Study Officer, United Steel Companies, Sheffield; Assistant Warden, St. Ninian's Lay Training Centre, Crieff; publishing and lay training, Presbyterian Church of East Africa. Publications: Ministers for the '80s (Editor); Our One Baptism; In Christ All Things Hold Together (Co-author); Ministry and Mission in the City; Mission and the Crisis of Western Culture (Editor); Scottish Self-Government: Some Christian Viewpoints (Editor). Recreations: music; skiing. Address: Carberry Tower, Musselburgh, EH21 8PY.

Steiner, Eleanor Margaret, MB, ChB, DPH, MFCM, MRCGP, MICGP, FRSH. Formerly General Practitioner at Appin and Easdale, formerly Principal in general practice in Perthshire; Executive Member, Scottish Child Law Centre; Medical Member, Disability Appeals Tribunal; Medical Assessor, Social Security Appeal Tribunals; Aeromedical Doctor, St. John International Air Ambulance; Member, SACOT (Scottish Advisory Committee on Telecommunications); Member, DIEL (OFTEL Committee for Advice on Disabled and Elderly); Founder, National Society of Associate GPs; b. 21.5.37, Glasgow; m., Mark Rudie Steiner (qv); 1 s. Educ. Albyn School, Aberdeen; Aberdeen University. Surgical Assistant, Freiburg; worked in hospitals, Switzerland, Canada, USA; Departmental Medical Officer/Senior Medical Officer, Aberdeen City; Organiser, Family Planning Services, Aberdeen; Member, Rubella Working Party; Adviser, Aberdeen Telephone Samaritans; Assistant, Psychiatry, Murray Royal Hospital, Perth; Contributor, Scientific Congress, Institute of Advanced Medical Sciences, Moscow. Recreations: sailing; hill-walking; international contacts. Address: (h.) Atlantic House, Ellenabeich, Isle of Seil, by Oban, Argyll, PA34 4RF; T.-Balvicar 300 593.

Steiner, Mark Rudie, LLB, NP. Legal Consultant and Defence Lawyer; Chairman, Scotland Patients Association; former part-time Chairman, Social Security Appeal Tribunal and Disability Appeal Tribunal; former Scottish Representative, Consumers in the European Community Group; Member, Potato Marketing Board Consumer Liaison Committee; Member, National Pharmaceutical Consultative Committee Working Group on Quality Assurance; m., Dr. Eleanor Steiner, DPH, MFCM, MRCGP, MICGP; 1 s. Educ. Aberdeen University. Editor, Canadian Broadcasting Corporation, Toronto and Montreal; Editor, Swiss Broadcasting Corporation, Berne; Procurator Fiscal in Scotland; Partner and Director of various firms and companies; Past Chairman, Perth Community Relations Council; Delegate, Scottish Council for Racial Equality; neutral observer at various overseas political trials; contributor to various international journals; retired

Principal, Goodman Steiner & Co., Defence Lawyers and Notaries in Central Scotland; former Member, Scottish Consumer Council. Recreations: sailing; developing international exchanges. Address: (h.) Atlantic House, Ellenabeich, Isle of Seil, by Oban, Argyll, PA34 4RF; T.- Balvicar 300 593.

Stell, Geoffrey Percival, BA, FSA, FSA Scot. Head of Architecture, Royal Commission on the Ancient and Historical Monuments of Scotland, since 1991; b. 21.11.44, Keighley; m., Evelyn Florence Burns; 1 s.; 1 d. Educ. Keighley Boys' Grammar School; Leeds University; Glasgow University. Historic Buildings Investigator, RCAHMS, since 1969; sometime Chairman, Scottish Vernacular Buildings Working Group; sometime Chairman, Scottish Urban Archaeological Trust; sometime Vice-President, Council for Scottish Archaeology. Publications include: Dumfries and Galloway, 1986; Monuments of Industry (Co-author); Buildings of St. Kilda (Co-author); Loads and Roads in Scotland (Co-editor); The Scottish Medieval Town (Co-editor); Galloway, Land and Lordship (Co-Editor); Materials and Traditions in Scottish Building (Co-Editor). Recreations: gardening; music; travel, particularly in Scotland and France. Address: (h.) Beechmount, Borrowstoun, Bo'ness, West Lothian, EH51 9RS; T.-01506 510366.

Stenning, Professor Keith, MA, PhD. Director, Human Communication Research Centre, Edinburgh and Glasgow Universities, since 1989; Personal Chair, Edinburgh University, since 1989; b. 15.6.48, London; m., Dr. Lynn Michell; 2 s. Educ. High Wycombe Grammar School; Oxford University; Rockefeller University, NY. Lecturer in Psychology, Liverpool University; Lecturer in Psychology and Cognitive Science, Edinburgh University, 1983-88. Publications: papers on human information processing. Recreation: being blown hither and thither. Address: (b.) H.C.R.C., 2 Buccleuch Place, Edinburgh, EH8 9LW; T.- 0131-650 4444.

Stephen, Alex, FCCA. Chief Executive, Dundee City Council, since 1995; (Chief Executive, City of Dundee District Council, 1991-95); b. 17.9.48, Dundee; m., Joyce; 1 s.; 1 d. Local government since 1970. Recreation: voluntary work. Address: (b.) 21 City Square, Dundee; T.-01382 434201.

Stephen, Rev. Donald Murray, TD, MA, BD, ThM. Minister, Marchmont St. Giles' Parish Church, Edinburgh, since 1974; b. 1.6.36, Dundee; m., Hilda Swan Henriksen; 2 s.; 1 d. Educ. Brechin High School; Richmond Grammar School, Yorkshire; Edinburgh University; Princeton Theological Seminary. Assistant Minister, Westover Hills Presbyterian Church, Arkansas, 1962-64; Minister, Kirkoswald, 1964-74; Chaplain, TA, 1965-85 (attached to 4/5 Bn., RSF, 205 Scottish General Hospital, 2nd Bn., 52nd Lowland Volunteers); Convener, Committee on Chaplains to Her Majesty's Forces, General Assembly, 1985-89. Recreations: golf; curling. Address: 19 Hope Terrace, Edinburgh, EH9 2AP; T.-0131-447 2834.

Stephen, Eric John. Farmer; Director, McIntosh Donald Ltd., since 1995; b. 2.1.38, Turriff; 1 s.; 3 d. Educ. Inverurie Academy. Former Member, Scottish Agricultural Wages Board; former Convener, Employment and Technology Committee, National Farmers Union of Scotland; Elder, Auchterless Parish Church, 35 years; Past President, Aberdeen and Kincardine Executive, NFU of Scotland; Past President, Royal Northern Agricultural Society; Past President, Aberdeen Fatstock Club; former Director: Aberdeen and Northern Marts, Aberdeen and Northern Estates; President, Turriff Show, 1992; elected Grampian Regional Councillor, 1993; Regional Member, British Wool Marketing Board, since 1993. Recreation: bowling. Address: Lower Thorneybank, Rothienorman, Inverurie, AB51 8XT; T.-018885 11233.

Stephen, Professor Kenneth William, BDS, DDSc, HDDRCPS, FDSRCS. Professor of Dental Public Health, Glasgow University; b. 1.10.37, Glasgow; m., Anne Seymour Gardiner; 1 s.; 1 d. Educ. Hillhead High School, Glasgow; Glasgow University. General Dental Practitioner, 1960-64; House Officer, Department of Oral Surgery, Glasgow Dental Hospital, 1964-65; Lecturer, Department of Conservative Dentistry, 1965-68, Lecturer, Department of Oral Medicine and Pathology, Glasgow University, 1968-71; Visiting Lecturer, Department of Oral Physiology, Newcastle-upon-Tyne University, 1969-70; Senior Lecturer, Department of Oral Medicine and Pathology, Glasgow University, 1971-80; Reader, 1980-84. Co-President, European Organisation for Caries Research, 1978-79. Recreations: swimming; hill-walking; skiing; gardening. Address: (b.) Dental School, 378 Sauchiehall Street, Glasgow, G2 3JZ; T.-0141-211 9854.

Stephen, Mark, DSD. Presenter, The Scottish Connection, Radio Scotland, since 1997; b. 11.9.60, Aberdeen; m., Jean; 3 d. Educ. Inverurie Academy; Royal Scottish Academy of Music and Drama. Commercial Producer, Northsound ILR; Assistant Floor Manager, Researcher, Trails Producer, Senior Announcer (TV), Radio Producer, BBC Scotland. Recreations: reading; water colour painting; DIY. Address: (h.) Kingsford, Whiterashes, Aberdeenshire; T.-01651 882740.

Stephen, Sheriff Mhairi. Floating Sheriff, Lothian and Borders, based at Edinburgh. Address: (b.) Sheriff Court House, 27 Chambers Street, Edinburgh EH1 1LB.

Stephens, Professor William Peter, MA, BD, DesSR. Professor of Church History, Aberdeen University, since 1986 (Dean, Faculty of Divinity, 1987-89, Provost, Faculty of Divinity, 1989-90); Methodist Minister, since 1958; President Designate, Conference of the British Methodist Church; b. 16.5.34, Penzance. Educ. Truro School; Clare College, Cambridge, and Wesley House, Cambridge; Universities of Lund, Strasbourg, Muenster. Assistant Tutor, Hartley Victoria College, Manchester, 1958-61; Minister and University Chaplain, Nottingham University, 1961-65; Minister, Shirley Methodist Church, Croydon, 1967-71; Chair of Church History, Hartley Victoria College, Manchester, 1971-73; Chair of Historical and Systematic Theology, Wesley College, Bristol, 1973-80; Research Fellow, then Lecturer in Church History, The Queen's College, Birmingham, 1980-86. Secretary, Society for the Study of Theology, 1963-77; President, Society for Reformation Studies, since 1995; Max Geilinger Prize, 1997. Publications: The Holy Spirit in the Theology of Martin Bucer; Faith and Love; Methodism in Europe; The Theology of Huldrych Zwingli; Zwingli: an Introduction to His Thought; The Bible, the Reformation and the Church (Editor). Recreations: squash; tennis; hill-walking; skiing; swimming; theatre. Address: (b.) Faculty of Divinity, King's College, Aberdeen University, Aberdeen; T.-01224 272383.

Stevely, Professor William Stewart, BSc, DPhil, DipEd, FIBiol. Principal and Vice Chancellor, The Robert Gordon University, since 1997; b. 6.4.43, West Kilbride; m., Sheila Anne Stalker; 3 s.; 2 d. Educ. Ardrossan Academy; Glasgow University; Oxford University. Lecturer and Senior Lecturer in Biochemistry, Glasgow University, 1968-88; Professor and Head, Department of Biology, Paisley College, 1988-92; Vice Principal, Paisley University, 1992-97. Member, Scottish Higher Education Funding Council, since 1994; Member, National Board for Nursing, Midwifery and Health Visiting for Scotland, since 1993. Address: (b.) The Robert Gordon University, Schoolhill, Aberdeen, AB10 1FR; T.-01224 262001.

Steven, George, MBE. Convener, North Ayrshire Council, since 1995; b. 19.11.29, Glengarnock; m., Janet Ferguson Wilson; 2 s.; 1 d. Educ. Kilbirnie Central School; Glasgow

University. Probation Officer, 1963-68; Residential Social Work (Officer in Charge), 1968-88; Assistant Director of Social Work, Salvation Army, 1988-94; Cunninghame District Council: Vice-Chairman, Leisure Committee, 1980-84, Chairman, Planning Committee, 1984-88, Vice-Convener of Council, 1992-96. Recreations: hill-walking; bowling; swimming; football (spectator); music. Address: (h.) 13 Western Crescent, Kilbirnie, KA25 6JE; T.-01505 682698.

Steven, Ian Rollo, BL. Dean, Faculty of Solicitors and Procurators, Dundee, since 1997; b. 5.2.35, Dundee; m., Hilary Joy; 2 d. Educ. Glenalmond; St. Andrews University. Qualified, 1957; Senior Partner, Rollo, Steven & Bond, since 1975. Recreations: skiing; sailing; hill-walking. Address: (b.) 21 Dock Street, Dundee.

Steven, John Douglas, MB, ChB, FRCOG. Consultant Obstetrician and Gynaecologist, Stirling Royal Infirmary, since 1981; Member, Scottish Council, British Medical Association; b. 20.4.46, Perth. Educ. Douglas Ewart High School, Newton Stewart; Edinburgh University. Registrar in Obstetrics and Gynaecology, Western General Hospital, Edinburgh; Senior Registrar, Obstetrics and Gynaecology, Ninewells Hospital, Dundee. Address: (b.) Stirling Royal Infirmary, Stirling, FK8 2AU; T.-01786 434000.

Stevens, Professor Paul John, BA (Cantab), MA, PhD. Professor of Petroleum Policy and Economics, Dundee University, since 1993; b. 30.4.47, Liverpool; m., Cassie Stevens; 1 s.; 1 d. Educ. Alsop High School, Liverpool; Clare College, Cambridge; London University. Assistant Professor, American University of Beirut, 1973-75; oil consultant, Beirut, 1975-77; Assistant Professor, American University of Beirut, 1977-79; Lecturer in Economics, then Senior Lecturer, University of Surrey, 1979-93. Publications: numerous books and papers on oil and gas. Recreations: travel; food and drink; golf; carpentry. Address: (b.) CPMLP, Dundee University, Dundee, DD1 4HN; T.-01382 344300.

Stevenson, Celia Margaret Stirton. Director of Locations, Scottish Screen, since 1997; Director, Scottish Screen Locations Ltd., 1995-97; b. Ballantrae; m., Charles William Forbes Judge; 2 s.; 1 d. Educ. Wellington School, Ayr; Edinburgh College of Art. Interior design business, 1970-80; Reporter/Presenter, West Sound, Ayr, 1981-84; Scottish Television: Reporter/Presenter, 1984-86, Promotions trailer-maker, 1987-89, Head of Programme Planning and Film Acquisition, 1990-95. Director, South West Scotland Screen Commission; Trustee, Studio Drama Gaidhlig, Stornoway. Recreations: cooking; reading; study of 20th-century art; interior design. Address: (b.) 74 Victoria Crescent Road, Glasgow, G12 9JN.

Stevenson, Professor David, BA, PhD, DLitt. Emeritus Professor, Scottish History, St. Andrews University, since 1994; b. 30.4.42, Largs; m., Wendy B. McLeod; 2 s. Educ. Gordonstoun; Dublin University; Glasgow University. Aberdeen University: Lecturer in History, 1970-80, Senior Lecturer in History, 1980-84; Reader in Scottish History, 1984-90; St. Andrews University: Reader in Scottish History, 1990-91; Professor of Scottish History, 1991-94. Honorary Secretary, Scottish History Society, 1976-84; Fellow, Royal Historical Society. Publications: The Scottish Revolution 1637-44, 1973; Revolution and Counter-Revolution in Scotland 1644-51, 1977; Alasdair MacColla and the Highland Problem in the 17th Century, 1980; Scottish Covenanters and Irish Confederates, 1981; The Government of Scotland under the Covenanters 1637-51, 1982; Scottish Texts and Calendars (with Wendy B. Stevenson), 1987; The Origins of Freemasonry, 1988; The First Freemasons: The Early Scottish Lodges and their members, 1988; The Covenanters: the National Covenant and Scotland, 1988; King's College, Aberdeen, 1560-1641, 1990; Scotland's Lost Royal Wedding, 1997; King or

Covenant, 1998; Union, Revolution and Religion in 17th Century Scotland, 1998. Address: (h.) 5 Forgan Way, Newport on Tay, Fife DD6 8JQ.

Stevenson, David Deas, CBE, DSc, BCom, CA. Chairman Edinburgh Woollen Mill; b. 28.11.41, Hawick; m., Alix Jamieson; 2 d. Educ. Langholm Academy; Dumfries Academy; Edinburgh University. British Steel Corporation, 1966-67; Langholm Dyeing Co., 1967-70. Recreations: golf; horses; running. Address: (b.) Waverley Mills, Langholm, Dumfriesshire, DG13 OEB; T.-013873 80611.

Stevenson, Gerda. Actress, Singer, Writer, Book Illustrator, Director; b. 10.4.56, West Linton; m., Aonghas MacNeacail; 1 s. Educ. Peebles High School; Royal Academy of Dramatic Art, London (DDA, Vanbrugh Award). Has performed with 7:84 Theatre Co., Scottish Theatre Company, Royal Lyceum Theatre (Edinburgh), Traverse Theatre, Communicado, Monstrous Regiment, Victoria Theatre (Stoke on Trent), Contact Theatre (Manchester) and with Freefall at Lilian Baylis Theatre, London, and Birmingham Rep; directed Uncle Jesus for Edinburgh Festival Fringe; Assistant Director, Royal Lyceum, on Merchant of Venice and A Doll's House; Founder Member and Director, Stellar Quines Theatre Co.; TV work includes Clay, Smeddum and Greenden, Square Mile of Murder, Grey Granite, Horizon: Battered Baby, The Old Master, Taggart, Dr. Finlay, The Bill; films: The Stamp of Greatness, Tickets to the Zoo, Blue Black Permanent (BAFTA Scotland Best Film Actress Award, 1993), Braveheart; directed short film, An Iobairt, in Gaelic for BBC; extensive radio work includes title roles in Bride of Lammermoor and Catriona; freelance producer for Radio Scotland; wrote and illustrated children's book, The Candlemaker. Recreation: walking in the country.

Stevenson, John Meikle, DL, BSc (Agric), FInstD. Farmer; b. 20.1.31, Aberlady; m., Eileen A.; 2 s.; 1 d. Educ. Trinity College, Glenalmond; Aberdeen University. Councillor, East Lothian County Council, 1961-66; President, East Lothian, National Farmers' Union, 1968-69; Council Member, NFU, 1966-70; Member, Governing Body, British Society for Research in Agricultural Engineering, 1968-96; Chairman, Committee, Scottish Centre of Agricultural Engineering, 1987-95; Governor, East of Scotland College of Agriculture; Chairman, Royal Scottish Agricultural Benevolent Institution; Deputy Lieutenant, East Lothian. Recreations: shooting; fishing; gardening; golf. Address: (h.) Luffness Mains, Aberlady, East Lothian EH32 0PZ; T.-01875 870212.

Stevenson, Miranda Faye, BA (Hons), MBA, PhD. Curator of Animals, Royal Zoological Society of Scotland, since 1979, Deputy Director, since 1996; b. 26.3.47, Glasgow. Educ. Wesley College, Dublin; Trinity College, Dublin; University of Wales, Aberystwyth. Keeper, Chester Zoo; Biologist, Welsh Plant Breeding Centre; Research Assistant, University of Wales, Aberystwyth. International studbook keeper for the Diana monkey; EEP (European Endangered Species Programme) Co-ordinator; Chair, EEP Primate and Penguin TAGs; Winston Churchill Travelling Fellowship, 1976; Chair, Federation of Zoos Joint Management of Species Committee; Member, two IUCN specialist groups. Recreations: country walking; theatre; film. Address: (b.) Royal Zoological Society of Scotland, Murrayfield, Edinburgh EH12 6TS; T-0131-334 9171.

Stevenson, Peter David, MA (Cantab); b. 6.3.47, Edinburgh; m., The Hon. Susan Blades; 1 s.; 1 d. Educ. Edinburgh Academy; Trinity College, Cambridge. Chairman: Mackays Stores (Holdings) PLC; Director, British Energy plc; Director, Scottish Nuclear Ltd. Address: (b.) 22 Rutland Street, Edinburgh EH1 2AN; T.-0131-229 0550.

Stevenson, Ronald, DUniv (Stirling), FRMCM, HonFRIAS. Composer and Pianist; Broadcaster; Author; b. 6.3.28, Blackburn; m., Marjorie Spedding; 1 s.; 2 d. Educ. Royal Manchester College of Music; Conservatorio Di Santa Cecilia, Rome. Senior Lecturer, Cape Town University, 1963-65; BBC Prom debut in own 2nd Piano Concerto, 1972; Aldeburgh Festival recital with Sir Peter Pears, 1973; Busoni documentary, BBC TV, 1974; BBC Radio Scotland extended series on the bagpipe, clarsach and fiddle music of Scotland, 1980-84; Artist in Residence: Melbourne University, 1980, University of W. Australia, 1982, Conservatory of Shanghai, 1985; York University, 1987; published and recorded compositions: Passacaglia for Piano, two Piano Concertos, Violin Concerto (commissioned by Menuhin), Prelude, Fugue and Fantasy for Piano, Prelude and Fugue for Organ, In Memoriam Robert Carver, St. Mary's May Songs, A Child's Garden of Verse (BBC commission), Voces Vagabundae, Salute to Nelson Mandela (march for brass band), Cello Concerto (RSNO commission), A Carlyle Suite (piano). Publications: Western Music; Alan Bush - a symposium; The Paderewski Paradox. Recreations: hill-walking; reading poetry, biographies and politics. Address: (h.) Townfoot House, West Linton, Peeblesshire; T.-01968 60511.

Stevenson, Sir Simpson, LLD. Provost, Inverclyde District Council, 1984-88; Chairman, Scottish Health Services Common Services Agency, 1983-87; b. 18.8.21, Greenock; m., Jean Holmes Henry. Educ. Greenock High School. Provost of Greenock, 1962-65; Chairman, Western Regional Hospital Board, 1967-73; Chairman, Greater Glasgow Health Board, 1973-83; knighted, 1976; Hon. LLD, Glasgow University, 1982; Member, Royal Commission on NHS, 1976-79. Address: (h.) The Gables, Reservoir Road, Gourock; T.-01475 631774.

Stevenson, William Trevor, CBE, DL, FCIT; b. 21.3.21, Peebles; m., Alison Wilson Roy. Educ. Edinburgh Academy. Apprentice Engineer, 1937-41; Engineer, 1941-45; entered family food manufacturing business, Cottage Rusks, 1945; Managing Director, 1948-54; Chairman, 1954-59; Chief Executive, Cottage Rusks Associates, 1965-69; Regional Director, Ranks Hovis McDougall, 1969-74; Director, various companies in food, engineering, hotel and aviation industries, since 1974; Chairman, Alex. Wilkie Ltd., 1977-90; founder Chairman, Gleneagles Hotels, 1981-83; Chairman, Scottish Transport Group, 1981-86; Master, Company of Merchants of City of Edinburgh, 1978-80; Vice President, Edinburgh Chamber of Commerce, 1983-87; Chairman, Scottish Export Association, since 1993. Recreations: flying; sailing; curling.

Stewart, A.J. (Ada F. Kay). Playwright and Author; b. 5.3.29, Tottington, Lancashire. Educ. Grammar School, Fleetwood. ATS Scottish Command; first produced play, 1951; repertory actress, 1952-54; BBC TV Staff Writer/Editor/Adaptor, Central Script Section, 1956-59; returned to Scotland, 1959, as stage and TV writer; winner, BBC New Radio Play competition, 1956; The Man from Thermopylae, presented in Festival of Contemporary Drama, Rheydt, West Germany, 1959, as part of Edinburgh International Festival, 1965, and at Masquers' Theatre, Hollywood, 1972; first recipient, Wendy Wood Memorial Grant, 1982; Polish Gold Cross for achievements in literary field. Publications: Falcon - The Autobiography of His Grace, James the 4, King of Scots, 1970; Died 1513-Born 1929 - The Autobiography of A.J. Stewart, 1978; The Man from Thermopylae, 1981. Recreation: work. Address: 15 Oxford Street, Edinburgh EH8.

Stewart, Sheriff Alastair Lindsay, QC, BA (Oxon), LLB(Edin). Sheriff of Tayside, Central and Fife at Dundee, since 1990; Temporary Judge, Court of Session and High Court of Justiciary, since 1996; b. 28.11.38, Aberdeen; m., 1, Annabel Claire Stewart (m. diss.); 2 s.; 2, Sheila Anne Mackinnon. Educ. Edinburgh Academy; St. Edmund Hall,

Oxford; Edinburgh University. Admitted to Faculty of Advocates, 1963; Tutor, Faculty of Law, Edinburgh University, 1963-73; Standing Junior Counsel to the Registrar of Restrictive Trading Agreements, 1968-70; Advocate Depute, 1970-73; Sheriff of Lanarkshire (later South Strathclyde, Dumfries and Galloway) at Airdrie, 1973-79; Sheriff of Grampian, Highland and Islands at Aberdeen and Stonehaven, 1979-90. Chairman, Scottish Association of Family Conciliation Services, 1986-89; Editor, Scottish Civil Law Reports, 1992-95. Publications: Sheriff Court Practice (Contributor), 1988; The Scottish Criminal Courts in Action, 1990, 1997. Recreations: music; reading; walking. Address: (b.) Sheriffs' Chambers, Sheriff Court House, 6 West Bell Street, Dundee DD1 9AD; T.-01382 229961.

Stewart, Alexander Donald, BA, LLB, WS, DL. Director, Murray Split Capital Trust PLC; Chairman, Scottish Amicable Life Assurance Society; b. 18.6.33, Edinburgh; m., Virginia Mary Washington; 1 s.; 5 d. Educ. Wellington College, Berkshire; Oxford University; Edinburgh University. Hon. Consul for Thailand in Scotland; DL, Perthshire. Recreations: music; field sports; winter sports. Address: (h.) Ardvorlich, Lochearnhead, Perthshire.

Stewart, Alexander Reavell Macdonald, FRICS. Chartered Surveyor; Chairman, Scottish Branch, Royal Institution of Chartered Surveyors, 1985-86; b. 14.2.29, Bearsden; m., Keris Duguid Keir; 2 s.; 2 d. Educ. Merchiston Castle School. President: Property Owners and Factors Association Glasgow, 1968-69, National Federation of Property Owners Scotland, 1978-80. Recreations: trout fishing; piping. Address: (b.) 21 Winton Lane, Glasgow; T.-0141-332 2752.

Stewart, Angus, QC, BA, LLB; b. 14.12.46. Called to Scottish Bar, 1975; Keeper of the Library, Faculty of Advocates. Address: (b.) Advocates' Library, Parliament House, Edinburgh, EH1 1RF.

Stewart, Archibald Ian Balfour, CBE, BL (Dist), FSA (Scot). Retired Solicitor; Honorary Sheriff; b. 19.5.15, Campbeltown; m., Ailsa Rosamund Mary Massey; 3 s. Educ. Cheltenham College; Glasgow University. Solicitor, 1938; Town Clerk, Lochgilphead, 1939-46, Campbeltown, 1947-54; Procurator Fiscal of Argyll at Campbeltown, 1941-74; Temporary Sheriff, 1975-88; Secretary, Clyde Fishermen's Association, 1941-70; Churchill Fellow, 1966; President, Scottish Fishermen's Federation, 1970-75; Hon. President, Clyde Fishermen's Association and Scottish Fishermen's Federation; former Director, Scottish Fishermen's Organisation and Scottish Board, Phoenix Insurance Co. Ltd.; Past President, Kintyre Antiquarian Society; Past Chairman, Argyll and Bute National Insurance Committee, Kintyre Employment Committee; Adviser, North East Atlantic Fisheries Conference, UN Law of Sea Conference; Editor, Kintyre Antiquarian and Natural History Society Magazine; Editor, List of Inhabitants upon the Duke of Argyle's Kintyre Estates 1792. Recreations: local history; genealogy; wine; gardening; idling. Address: (h.) Askomel End, Campbeltown, Argyll PA28 6EP; T.-01586 52353.

Stewart (nee Muir), Professor Averil M., BA, FCOT, TDip, SROT. Head, Department of Occupational Therapy, Queen Margaret College, Edinburgh, since 1986; b. 7.4.43, Edinburgh; m., J. Gavin Stewart. Educ. Dunfermline High School; Occupational Therapy Training Centre, Edinburgh. Lecturer, Glasgow School of Occupational Therapy, 1972-74; Senior Occupational Therapist, Head and District Occupational Therapist, Worthing District, 1975-83; Educational Development Officer, Council for Professions Supplementary to Medicine (secondment), 1978-80; Senior Lecturer, Department of Occupational Therapy, Queen Margaret College, 1983-86. Member, Vice-Chairman and Chairman, Occupational Therapists Board, CPSM, 1980-92;

Trustee, Dementia Services Development Centre, since 1996; Chairman, CAB Leith, since 1997. Publications: Occupational Therapy Teaching Resources in UK; Contributor: Occupational Therapy in Short-Term Psychiatry; Occupational Therapy in Mental Health. Recreations: wilderness travel; gardening. Address: (b.) Queen Margaret College, Edinburgh EH6 8HF.

Stewart, Brian John, CBE, MSc, CA. Group Chief Executive and Deputy Chairman, Scottish & Newcastle plc, since 1991; Director (Non-Executive), Standard Life and Booker PLC, since 1993; b. 9.4.45, Stirling; m., Shona (Seonaid); 2 s.; 1 d. Educ. Perth Academy; Edinburgh University. J. & R. Morrison, CA, Perth, 1962-67; Chief Management Accountant, Ethicon Ltd., 1969-76; joined Scottish & Newcastle plc, 1976; Corporate Development Director, 1985; Group Finance Director, 1988. Recreations: skiing; golf. Address: (b.) 111 Holyrood Road, Edinburgh EH8 8YS; T.-0131-556 2591.

Stewart, Brian West, BSc, MRTPI. Chief Executive, Western Isles Islands Council, now Western Isles Council, since 1993; b. 27.6.58, Edinburgh; m., Alicia Dolores Giles-Stewart; 1 s.; 1 d. Educ. George Heriot's, Edinburgh; Heriot-Watt University, Edinburgh. Graduate Trainee, UK Atomic Energy Authority, Risley; entered local government with posts in Newbury, Farnborough, Dingwall and Stornoway. Recreations: reading; current affairs; planning foreign holidays. Address: (b.) Council Offices, Sandwick Road, Stornoway, Isle of Lewis; T.-01851 703773.

Stewart, David John, MP, BA (Hons). MP (Labour), Inverness East, Nairn and Lochaber, since 1997; b. 5.5.56; m., Linda; 1 s.; 1 d. Educ. Inverness High School; Paisley College; Stirling University. Lecturer in Community Care, Esk Valley College, 1981; Social Worker, Dumfries and Dingwall, 1981-87; Social Work Team Manager, Highland Council, 1987-97. Patron, Shopmobility Highland. Recreations: sport; spending time with family; reading. Address: (b.) Queensgate Business Centre, Fraser Street, Inverness; T.-01463 237441.

Stewart, David Roger, TD, MA, BA (Hons), FEIS. Honorary Sheriff, Selkirk, since 1983; b. 3.2.20, Glasgow; m., Gwyneth Ruth Morris; 2 s.; 1 d. Educ. Hyndland Secondary School; Glasgow High School; Glasgow University; London University. Army, 1939-46; Schoolmaster, 1947-65 (Kelvinside Academy, Galashiels Academy); Rector, Selkirk High School, 1965-81; Member: Selkirk Town Council, 1967-75, Borders Education Committee, 1975-81, Borders Regional Council, 1982-86; TA, 1939-64; Chairman, Selkirk Committee, Cancer Research Campaign. Recreations: golf; gardening; reading. Address: (h.) Cairncoed, Hillside Terrace, Selkirk TD7 4ND; T.-01750 21755.

Stewart, Ena Lamont. Playwright; b. 10.2.12, Glasgow; m., Jack Stewart (deceased); 1 s. Educ. Woodside School, Glasgow; Esdaile School, Edinburgh. Assistant, Public Library, Aberdeen, 1930-34; Medical Secretary, Radcliffe, Lancashire, 1934-37; Secretary/Receptionist, Royal Hospital for Sick Children, Glasgow, 1937-41; Baillie's Reference Library, Glasgow: Assistant Librarian, 1953-57, Librarian-in-charge, 1957-66; author of plays: Starched Aprons, Men Should Weep, The Heir to Ardmally, Business in Edinburgh, After Tomorrow (unperformed), Walkies Time, Knocking on the Wall, Towards Evening, High Places. Recreations: reading; listening to music. Address: (h.) 5a Monkton Road, Prestwick KA9 1AP.

Stewart, Francis John, MA (Oxon), LLB, TD. Writer to the Signet (retired); Member, Queen's Bodyguard for Scotland (Royal Company of Archers); b. 11.5.17, Edinburgh; m., Olga Margaret Mounsey; 3 s.; 1 d. Educ. Cargilfield School, Edinburgh; Loretto School; Trinity College, Oxford; Edinburgh University. 1st Bn., Lothians

and Borders Yeomanry; Senior Partner, Murray Beith & Murray, WS, Edinburgh (retired); Past Chairman of Governors, Loretto School; Honorary Consul for Principality of Monaco, 1964-85; Chevalier of the Order of St. Charles. Recreation: gardening. Address: (b.) 39 Castle Street, Edinburgh; T.-0131-225 1200.

Stewart, Sir Frederick Henry, KB, BSc, PhD, FRSA, DSc Hon. (Aberdeen, Leicester, Heriot-Watt, Durham, Glasgow), FRS, FRSE, FGS. Professor Emeritus, Edinburgh University, since 1982; Trustee, British Museum (Natural History), 1983-88; Council Member, Scottish Marine Biological Association, 1983-89; b. 16.1.16, Aberdeen; m., Mary Florence Elinor Rainbow. Educ. Fettes College, Edinburgh; Robert Gordon's College, Aberdeen; Aberdeen University; Emmanuel College, Cambridge. Mineralogist, Research Department, Imperial Chemical Industries, 1941-43; Lecturer in Geology, Durham University, 1943-56; Regius Professor of Geology and Mineralogy, Edinburgh University, 1956-82; Member, Council for Scientific Policy, 1967-71 (Assessor, 1971-73); Chairman, Natural Environment Research Council, 1971-73; Chairman, Advisory Board for the Research Councils, 1973-79; Member, Advisory Council for Research and Development, 1976-79; University Grants Committee Earth Sciences Review, 1986-87. Lyell Fund Award, 1951 and Lyell Medal, 1970, Geological Society of London; Mineralogical Society of America Award, 1952; Clough Medal, Edinburgh Geological Society; Sorby Medal, Yorkshire Geological Society. Publications: The British Caledonides, 1963; Marine Evaporites, 1963. Recreations: fishing; collecting fossil fish. Address: (h.) 79 Morningside Park, Edinburgh, EH10 5EZ; T.-0131-447 2620; House of Letterawe, Lochawe, Argyll, PA33 1AH; T.-01838 200 329.

Stewart, George Girdwood, CB, MC, TD, BSc, FICFor, Hon. FLI. Cairngorm Estate Adviser to Highlands and Islands Enterprise, since 1988; b. 12.12.19, Glasgow; m., Shelagh Jean Morven Murray; 1 s.; 1 d. Educ. Kelvinside Academy, Glasgow; Glasgow University; Edinburgh University. Royal Artillery, 1940-46 (mentioned in Despatches); Forestry Commission: District Officer, 1949-60, Assistant Conservator, 1960-67, Conservator (Glasgow), 1967-69, Commissioner, Forest and Estate Management, 1969-79. Commanding Officer, 278 (Lowland) Field Regiment RA (TA), 1956-59; President, Scottish Ski Club, 1971-75; Vice President, National Ski Federation of Great Britain, 1975-78; National Trust for Scotland: Member of Council, 1975-79, Representative, Branklyn Garden, 1980-84, Regional Representative, Central and Tayside, 1984-88; Forestry Consultant, 1989-93; Chairman, Scottish Wildlife Trust, 1981-87; Member, Countryside Commission for Scotland, 1981-88; Member, Environment Panel, British Railways Board, 1980-90; Associate Director, Oakwood Environmental, since 1990; Member, Cairngorm Recreation Trust, since 1986; President, Scottish National Ski Council, 1988-94; Specialist Adviser to House of Lords Select Committee on EEC Forestry Policy, 1986; National Service to Sport Award, 1995. Fellow, Royal Society of Arts. Recreations: skiing; tennis; studying Scottish painting. Address: (h.) Stormont House, 11 Mansfield Road, Scone, Perth PH2 6SA; T.-01738 551815.

Stewart, Gillian Mary, BA (Hons). Head of Group, Scottish Office Home Department, since 1992; b. 2.6.45, Gosforth; 2 s. Educ. Blyth Grammar School; Durham University. Joined Scottish Office, 1970, as Assistant Principal; posts held in Education, Social Work Services Group, Environment. Recreations: swimming; walking; theatre; music. Address: (b.) James Craig Walk, Edinburgh EH1 3BA; T.-0131-244 3670.

Stewart, Professor Graham George, BSc, PhD, DSc, FIBrew. Director, International Centre for Brewing and

Distilling, since 1994; b. 22.3.42, Cardiff; m., Olga Leonara. Educ. Cathays High School, Cardiff; University College Cardiff; Bath University. Lecturer in Biochemistry, Portsmouth College of Technology, 1967-69; various technical positions, J. Labatt Ltd., Canada, 1969-94. Recreations: rugby; music; travel. Address: (b.) Heriot-Watt University, Riccarton, Edinburgh, EH14 4AS; T.-0131-451 3184.

Stewart, Rev. James Charles, MA, BD, STM. Minister, Kirk of St. Nicholas, Aberdeen (The City Kirk), since 1980; b. 29.3.33, Glasgow. Educ. Glasgow Academy; St. Andrews University; Union Theological Seminary, New York. Assistant Minister, St. John's Kirk of Perth, 1959-64; Minister: St. Andrew's Church, Drumchapel, 1964-74, East Parish Church of St. Nicholas, Aberdeen, 1974-80. Trustee, Aberdeen Endowments Trust and other trusts; President, Church Service Society; Past Chairman, Aberdeen Civic Society; Past Chairman, Third World Centre, Aberdeen. Address: (b.) The New Vestry, Kirk of St. Nicholas, Back Wynd, Aberdeen AB10 1JZ; T.-01224 314056.

Stewart, John Barry Bingham, OBE, BA, CA. Past Chairman, Martin Currie Ltd.; b. 21.2.31, Edinburgh; m., Ailsa Margaret Crawford. Educ. The Leys School, Cambridge; Magdalene College, Cambridge. Accountancy training, Edinburgh; worked in London, United States and Canada; joined Martin Currie, 1960. Recreations: fishing; shooting; golf; skiing. Address: 18 Hope Terrace, Edinburgh EH9 2AR; T.-0131-447 1626.

Stewart, Sheriff John Hall, LLB. Sheriff of Strathclyde, Dumfries and Galloway, at Hamilton, since 1985; b. 15.3.44, Bellshill; m., Marion MacCalman; 1 s.; 2 d. Educ. Airdrie Academy; St. Andrews University. Admitted Solicitor, 1971; Advocate, 1978. President, Uddingston RFC. Address: (b.) Sheriff Court House, Beckford Street, Hamilton, ML3 6AA.

Stewart, Kathleen Margaret, MA, LLB, WS, NP. Partner, McGrigor Donald, Solicitors, Edinburgh, Glasgow and London, since 1988 (Partner, Balfour & Manson, Solicitors, Edinburgh, 1983-87); b. St. Andrews. Educ. Bell Baxter High School, Cupar; St. Andrews University; Sweet Briar College, USA; Edinburgh University. Assistant Lawyer (Corporate Department) in London firm of commercial lawyers, 1975-79, and Scottish firms of commercial lawyers, 1980-83. Member, Company Law Panel, CBI; Member, EEC Sub-Committee, Company Law Committee, Law Society of Scotland. Recreations: horse riding; tennis; squash; bad bridge. Address: (b.) Erskine House, Queen Street, Edinburgh; T.-0131-226 7777.

Stewart, Rev. Norma Drummond, MA, MEd, DipTh, BD. Minister, Strathbungo Queen's Park Church, Glasgow, since 1979; b. 20.5.36, Glasgow. Educ. Hyndland Secondary School, Glasgow; Glasgow University; Bible Training Institute, Glasgow; Trinity College, Glasgow. Teacher, Garrioch Secondary School, Glasgow, 1958-62; Missionary, Overseas Missionary Fellowship, West Malaysia, 1965-74; ordained to ministry, Church of Scotland, 1977. Selection School Assessor; Convener, Education for the Ministry Committee, Glasgow Presbytery; Member, Church of Scotland Panel on Doctrine; occasional Lecturer in Old Testament, Glasgow University; Participant in Congress on World Evangelisation, Manila, 1989; Member, Council, Evangelical Alliance Scotland; Pastoral Adviser, Glasgow Presbytery; Member, Council of Christians and Jews; Member, Judicial Commission, Church of Scotland. Recreation: research in Old Testament studies. Address: 5 Newark Drive, Glasgow G41 4QJ; T.-0141-423 4818.

Stewart, Norman MacLeod, BL, SSC. Senior Partner, Allan, Black & McCaskie, Solicitors, Elgin, since 1984; Chairman, Elgin and Lossiemouth Harbour Board, since 1993; President, Law Society of Scotland, 1985-86; b. 2.12.34, Lossiemouth; m., Mary Slater Campbell; 4 d. Educ. Elgin Academy; Edinburgh University. Training and Legal Assistant, Alex. Morison & Co., WS, Edinburgh, 1954-58; Legal Assistant: McLeod, Solicitor, Portsoy, 1958-59, Allan, Black & McCaskie, Solicitors, Elgin, 1959-61 (Partner, 1961); Council Member, Law Society of Scotland, 1976-87 (Convener, Public Relations Committee, 1979-81, and Professional Practice Committee, 1981-84). Past President, Elgin Rotary Club; Past Chairman, Moray Crime Prevention Panel; President, Edinburgh University Club of Moray, 1987-89. Recreations: walking; golf; music; Spanish culture. Address: (h.) Argyll Lodge, Lossiemouth, Moray; T.-0134381 3150.

Stewart, Patrick Loudon McIain, LLB, WS, DL. Senior Partner, Stewart Balfour & Sutherland, Solicitors, since 1982; Secretary, Clyde Fishermen's Association, since 1970; Honorary Sheriff at Campbeltown; b. 25.7.45, Campbeltown; m., Mary Anne McLellan; 1 s.; 1 d. Educ. Edinburgh Academy; Edinburgh University. Partner, Stewart Balfour & Sutherland, Campbeltown, 1970; former Executive Member, Scottish Fishermen's Federation; former Director, Scottish Fishermen's Organisation Ltd.; member of many Scottish fishing industry committees; Chairman, Argyll & Bute Trust; Secretary, Campbeltown and Kintyre Enterprise Trust Ltd.; Clerk, General Commissioners of Income Tax — Islay; HQ Staff Officer Legal Affairs, Sea Cadet Corps; Honorary Legal Adviser, Sea Cadet Association; Cadet Forces Medal. Recreations: sailing; shooting; youth work. Address: Craigadam, Campbeltown, Argyll PA28 6EP; T.-01586 552161.

Stewart, Robert Armstrong, BA, DipTP, FRTPI, MIMgt. Director of Economic Development and Planning, The Moray Council; formerly Director of Planning and Development, Moray District Council; b. Stirling. Planning Assistant, Lanark County Council, 1968-69; Planner, Glasgow, 1969-70; Senior Assistant, then Group Leader: Development Control, West Lothian County, 1970-75; Depute Director: Planning, East Lothian District, 1975-79; joined Moray District Council, 1979. Address: (b.) Council Office, High Street, Elgin, IV30 1BX.

Stewart, Lt. Col. Robert Christie, CBE, TD; Lord Lieutenant, Clackmannanshire, since 1994; b. 3.8.26, Dollar; m., Ann Grizel Cochrane; 3 s.; 2 d. Educ. Eton; University College, Oxford. Lt., Scots Guards, 1944-49; 7th Bn., Argyll and Sutherland Highlanders TA, 1951-66; Lt.-Col., 1963-66; Hon. Col., 1/51 Highland Volunteers, 1972-75; Landowner; Lord Lieutenant, Kinross-shire, 1966-74; Member, Perth and Kinross County Council, 1953-75; Chairman, Kinross County Council, 1963-73; Chairman and President, Board of Governors, East of Scotland College of Agriculture, 1970-83. Recreations: shooting; golf; the countryside. Address: (h.) Arndean, by Dollar, FK14 7NH; T.-01259 742527.

Stewart-Clark, Sir Jack, Bt, MEP. Member of European Parliament for East Sussex and Kent South, since 1979; Vice President, European Parliament, 1992-97; b. 17.9.29, West Lothian; m., Lydia Loudon; 1 s.; 4 d. Educ. Eton; Balliol College, Oxford; Harvard Business School. Coldstream Guards, 1948-49; J. & P. Coats, 1952-70; Philips Industries, 1970-79 (Managing Director, Philips Electrical Ltd., 1970-74, Pye of Cambridge Ltd., 1974-79). Member, Queen's Bodyguard for Scotland, Royal Company of Archers. Publications: European Competition Law; Drugs Education, It's My Problem as Well. Recreations: golf; tennis; photography; classic cars. Address: (h.) Dundas Castle, South Queensferry, near Edinburgh, EH30 9SP; T.-0131-331 1114.

Steyn, John H., CStJ, PhD, MB, ChB, FRCSEd, FRCSEng. Hon. Treasurer, Royal College of Surgeons, Edinburgh, 1993-97; Chairman, Albyn Hospital, Aberdeen, since 1985; b. 3.10.29, Johannesburg; m., Daphne Mary Nelson; 5 s.; 2 d. Educ. St. John's College, Johannesburg; Cape Town University. Consultant in Administrative Charge, Department of Urology, Aberdeen Royal Infirmary, 1969-93. Address: (b.) Albyn Hospital, 21 Albyn Place, Aberdeen AB10 1RW; T.-01224 595993.

Stillwell, Peter. Chief Executive, Edinburgh Chamber of Commerce; b. 16.6.37, London; m., Lindsay; 3 d. Educ. Holloway (London) Boys Grammar School. Overseas banking, Africa; Marks and Spencer. Chairman, Board of Governors, Moray House Institute of Education; Director, Lothian Region Transport. Recreation: agriculture. Address: (h.) Firth House, Roslin, Midlothian; T.-01968 674184.

Stimson, Professor William Howard, BSc, PhD, CBiol, FIBiol, FRSE. Professor of Immunology and Head, Department of Immunology, Strathclyde University, since 1981; Director, Immunogene Biomedical Ltd.; b. 2.11.43, Liverpool; m., Jean Scott Baird; 1 s.; 1 d. Educ. Prince of Wales School, Nairobi; St. Andrews University. Research Fellow, Department of Obstetrics and Gynaecology, Dundee University, 1970-72; Lecturer, then Senior Lecturer, Biochemistry Department, Strathclyde University, 1973-80. Patron, Scottish Motor Neurone Disease Association; holder, Glasgow Loving Cup, 1982-83; Member, Editorial Boards,five scientific journals. Recreations: mechanical engineering; walking; golf. Address: (b.) Department of Immunology, Strathclyde University, 31 Taylor Street, Glasgow G4 ONR; T.-0141-552 4400, Ext. 3729.

Stirling, Professor Colin, MA, DPhil. Professor of Computation Theory, Edinburgh University, since 1995; b. 13.3.54, Walsall; partner, Sarah Erskine; 1 d. Educ. St. Andrews University; York University. Research Fellow in Computer Science, 1979-84; Lecturer, 1985-92; Reader, 1992-95. Recreations: reading; walking; cooking. Address: (b.) Edinburgh University, Department of Computer Science, Kings Buildings, Edinburgh; T.-0131-650 5186.

Stirling, Sheriff Hamish, MA, LLB. Sheriff of South Strathclyde Dumfries and Galloway, at Hamilton, since 1992; b. 9.7.38, Liverpool; m., Margaret Davidson Bottomley; 2 s.; 1 d. Educ. Liverpool College; Robert Gordon's College, Aberdeen; Aberdeen University. Solicitor, 1961-62; Procurator Fiscal Depute: Dundee, 1963-70, Borders, 1970-74, Glasgow, 1974-75; Advocate, 1975-92; Temporary Sheriff, 1987-92. Recreations: foreign travel; golf. Address: (b.) Sheriff Court House, Beckford Street, Hamilton ML3 6AA; T.-01698 282957.

Stirling of Garden, Col. James, CBE, TD, KStJ, BA, FRICS. Lord Lieutenant of Stirling and Falkirk, since 1983; Chartered Surveyor; b. 8.9.30; m., Fiona; 2 s.; 2 d. Educ. Rugby; Trinity College, Cambridge. Partner, Ryden and Partners, 1962-89; Director, Scottish Widows Life Assurance Society, 1974-96. President, Highland TAVRA, since 1990. Address: (h.) Garden, Buchlyvie, Stirlingshire.

Stirling, Robin Colin Baillie, OBE, JP; b. 6.4.25, Bo'ness; m., Jean R. Hendrie, MA. Educ. Dalziel High School, Motherwell. Editor: Motherwell Times, 1957-85, Motherwell Times Series, 1959-85. Former Secretary, Lanarkshire Branch, NUJ; elected Life Member, NUJ, 1985; Guild of British Newspaper Editors: former Scottish Secretary, Chairman, 1967-70; NCTJ: Member, Scottish Training Committee, 1961-85, Chairman, Scottish Committee, 1978-81. Convener, Motherwell Guild of Help, since 1953; Chairman, Strathclyde Police P Division Crime Prevention Panel, 1976-84; Member: Management Committee, Motherwell and Wishaw CAB, 1971-95 (Chairman, 1978-80), Motherwell and District Christian Aid Committee 1970-82; Honorary Vice President: Motherwell ASC, since 1986, Motherwell CC, since 1985, Lanarkshire Little Theatre; President, Motherwell Probus

Club, 1987-88; Founder Chairman, Motherwell and District Music Society (Chairman, 1984-93). Recreations: gardening; music (including jazz); steam locomotives; Motherwell FC; Scottish Opera; cinema organs. Address: (h.) 37 The Loaning, Motherwell ML1 3HE; T.-63762.

Stirling of Fairburn, Roderick William Kenneth, TD, JP. Lord Lieutenant, Ross and Cromarty and Skye and Lochalsh, since 1988; Landowner and Estate Manager; Member, Red Deer Commission, 1964-89; Chairman, Highland Region Valuation Appeal Committee, 1983-91; Chairman, Scottish Salmon and White Fish Co. Ltd., 1980-91; b. 17.6.32; m., Penelope Jane Wright; 4 d. Educ. Wellesley House; Harrow; Aberdeen University. National Service, Scots Guards, 1950-52 (commissioned, 1951); TA service, Seaforth and Queen's Own Highlanders, 1953-69 (retired with rank of Captain); Member, Regional Advisory Committee to Forestry Commission, 1964-85; Local Director, Eagle Star Insurance Co., 1966-85; Director, Moray Firth Salmon Fishing Co. Ltd., 1973-91; Member, Highland River Purification Board, 1975-90; Ross and Cromarty County Councillor, 1970-74 (Chairman of Highways, 1973-74); Member, Ross and Cromarty District Council, and its Representative on Scottish Accident Prevention Council, 1984-96. Recreations: wild life management; gardening; curling. Address: (h.) Arcan, Muir of Ord, Ross-shire IV6 7UL; T.-01997 433207.

Stirrups, Professor David Robert, MSc, BA, BDS, FDS, DOrth(RCSEng), FDS, MOrth(RCPS) Glasgow. Professor of Orthodontics, Dundee University, since 1993; b. 23.6.48, Gillingham; m., Anne; 1 s.; 1 d. Educ. Gillingham Grammar School; Sheffield University. Senior Registrar, Northern Health Authority, 1977-80; Consultant Orthodontist, Greater Glasgow Health Board, 1980-93. Recreations: orienteering; mountain marathons; philately. Address: (b.) Dundee University, Dundee DD1 4HN; T.-01382 635961.

Stobie, David Henry, BSc, MSc, DMS, FIMgt. Head, Postgraduate Programmes, Napier University, since 1997; Chairman, Edinburgh Branch, British Institute of Management, 1988-91, President, 1991-94; b. 21.10.41, Edinburgh; m., June Moffat; 1 s.; 1 d. Educ. Tynecastle Senior Secondary School, Edinburgh; Heriot-Watt University, Edinburgh. Production Planning Engineer, Ferranti Ltd., 1965; various line management positions, Hewlett-Packard Ltd., 1966-73; Works Manager, Hall and Hall Ltd., 1973-74; Senior Systems Analyst, Hewlett-Packard Ltd., 1974-75; joined Napier as Lecturer, 1975; Head, Department of Management Studies, 1984-97. Recreations: hill-walking; classical music; wine-tasting. Address: (b.) Napier University Business School, Bevan Villa, Craighouse Road, Edinburgh, EH10 5LG.

Stobie, David Johnston, FRSA, MCIBS. Non-Executive Director, Shaw Marketing & Design Ltd., since 1994; Non-Executive Chairman, Macnaughton Holdings Ltd., since 1997; Chairman, Queen Margaret NHS Trust, since 1997; Chairman, Children 1st (RSSPCC), since 1996; Trustee: Carnegie Dunfermline and Hero Fund Trust, since 1990, Carnegie United Kingdom Trust, since 1995; b. 29.6.37, Galashiels; m., Nancy R. McIntosh; 1 s.; 1 d. Educ. George Heriot's School, Edinburgh. British Linen Bank, 1954-71; Noble Grossart Ltd., 1971-81 (Treasurer, 1976-81); British Linen Bank Ltd., 1981-96 (Business Development Director, 1986-96). Recreations: family; walking; gardening. Address: (h.) Strathmore, 17 Venturefair Avenue, Dunfermline KY12 OPF; T.-01383 721396.

Stobo, James, CBE, DL, FRAgS. Farmer; Chairman, Moredun Foundation for Animal Health and Welfare, since 1994; Chairman of Governors, Longridge Towers School, since 1982; Chairman, Scottish Seed Potato Development Council, 1988-95; Chairman, Pentland Science Park Ltd., since 1995; b. 9.12.34, Lanark; m., Pamela Elizabeth Mary Herriot; 1 s.; 2 d. Educ. Edinburgh Academy. Farming, since 1951; Past Chairman and President, Scottish Association of Young Farmers Clubs; Member, Home-Grown Cereals Authority, 1971-76; President, National Farmers' Union of Scotland, 1973-74; President, Animal Diseases Research Foundation, 1980-95; Director, John Hogarth Ltd., Kelso Mills; Member, Secretary of State for Scotland's Panel of Agricultural Arbiters. Vice-President: Scottish National Fat Stock Club, Royal Smithfield Club; Deputy Lieutenant, County of Berwick, 1987. Recreations: game shooting; photography. Address: Nabdean, Berwick-upon-Tweed TD15 1SZ; T.-01289 386224.

Stockdale, Elizabeth Joan Noel, MB, ChB, DMRD, FRCR, FRCPCH, MBA. Consultant Radiologist, Royal Aberdeen Children's Hospital and Aberdeen Royal Infirmary, since 1980; Clinical Senior Lecturer, Aberdeen University, since 1980; b. Chippenham; m., Christopher Leo Stockdale; 2 s.; 1 d. Educ. Aberdeen University. House Surgeon, Aberdeen Royal Infirmary; Senior House Surgeon, Professorial Surgical Unit, Hospital for Sick Children, Great Ormond Street; Registrar, St. George's Hospital; Senior Registrar, Royal National Orthopaedic Hospital, Royal Marsden Hospital, Atkinson Morley's Hospital; Chairman, Grampian Division, BMA, 1995-97. Recreations: theatre; classical music; travel. Address: (h.) 1 Grant Road, Banchory, Kincardineshire AB31 5UW; T.-013302 823096.

Stodart of Leaston, Rt. Hon. Lord (James Anthony Stodart), PC (1974); b. 6.6.16, Exeter; m., Hazel Usher (deceased). Educ. Wellington. MP (Conservative), Edinburgh West, 1959-74; Joint Under Secretary of State, Scottish Office, 1963-64; Parliamentary Secretary, later Minister of State, Ministry of Agriculture, Fisheries and Food, 1970-74; Chairman: Agricultural Credit Corporation Ltd., 1975-87, Committee of Enquiry into Local Government in Scotland, 1980, Manpower Review of Veterinary Profession in UK, 1984-85. Publication: Land of Abundance: a study of Scottish agriculture in the 20th century. Recreations: music; preserving a sense of humour. Addresses: Lorimers, North Berwick; Leaston, Humbie, East Lothian.

Stoddart, Sheriff Charles Norman, LLB, LLM, PhD. Sheriff of Lothian and Borders at Edinburgh, since 1995; b. 4.4.48, Dunfermline; m., Anne Lees; 1 d. Educ. Dunfermline High School; Edinburgh University; McGill University, Montreal. Private practice as Solicitor, 1972-73; Lecturer in Scots Law, Edinburgh University, 1973-80; private practice, 1980-88; Sheriff of North Strathclyde at Paisley, 1988-95. Publications: (as Co-author) The Law and Practice of Legal Aid in Scotland; Cases and Materials on Criminal Law; Cases and Materials on Criminal Procedure; (as author) Criminal Warrants; Bible John. Recreations: music; sport. Address: (b.) Sheriff's Chambers, Sheriff Court, 27 Chambers Street, Edinburgh, EH1 1LB; T.-0131-225 2525.

Stoddart, Sheila Grahame, LLB, WS, NP. Solicitor, since 1980; b. 20.11.43, Duns. Educ. Esdaile School for Girls, Edinburgh; Edinburgh University. Travel representative; beautician; BBC make-up artist; solicitor. Member, Council, Law Society of Scotland. Recreations: breeder/exhibitor/judge of Australian terriers; travel; reading. Address: (b.) Ayton, Berwickshire TD14 5QH; T.-018907 81209.

Stone, Professor Frederick Hope, OBE, MB, ChB, FRCP, FRCPsych. Professor of Child and Adolescent Psychiatry, Glasgow University, 1977-86; Consultant Psychiatrist, Royal Hospital for Sick Children, Glasgow, since 1954; b. 11.9.21, Glasgow; m., Zelda Elston, MA; 2 s.; 1 d. Educ. Hillhead High School, Glasgow; Glasgow University. Acting Director, Lasker Mental Hygiene Clinic, Hadassah, Jerusalem, 1952-54; World Health Organisation Visiting Consultant, 1960, 1964; Member, Kilbrandon Committee,

1963-65; Secretary-General, International Association of Child Psychiatry, 1962-66; Member, Houghton Committee on Adoption, 1968-72; Chairman, Scottish Division, Royal College of Psychiatrists, 1981-84; President, Young Minds; Chairman, Strathclyde Children's Panel Advisory Committee, 1988-94. Publication: Child Psychiatry for Students (Co-author). Address: (h.) 14A Hamilton Avenue, Pollokshields, Glasgow, G41 4JF; T.-0141-427 0115.

Stone, Gordon Victor, MBChB, FFCM, MFCMI, DCM. General Manager, Highland Health Board, since 1994; b. 4.10.45, London; m., Aileen S. Wilson; 1 s.; 1 d. Educ. Aberdeen Grammar School; Aberdeen University; Edinburgh University. Medical Officer, RAF, 1970-75; Scottish Health Service Fellow in Community Medicine, 1975-78; Specialist in Community Medicine, Grampian Health Board, 1978-89; Chief Administrative Medical Officer/Director of Public Health Medicine, Highland Health Board, 1989-94. Recreations: golf; skiing. Address: (b.) Beechwood Park, Inverness, IV2 3NG; T.-01463 717123.

Stone, Sheriff Marcus, MA, LLB. Accredited Mediator, since 1994; Director, The Mediation Bureau; Hon. President, Association of Mediators; b. 22.3.21, Glasgow; m., Jacqueline Barnoin; 3 s.; 2 d. Educ. High School of Glasgow; Glasgow University. Served Second World War; admitted Solicitor, 1949; admitted Faculty of Advocates, 1965; Sheriff of North Strathclyde, at Dumbarton, 1971-76; Sheriff of Glasgow and Strathkelvin, at Glasgow, 1976-84; Sheriff of Lothian and Borders, at Linlithgow, 1984-93. Publications: Proof of Fact in Criminal Trials, 1984; Cross-examination in Criminal Trials, 1988; Fact-Finding for Magistrates, 1990. Publication: Mediation Advocacy. Recreations: swimming; music. Address: (b.) Advocates Library, Parliament House, Edinburgh.

Stone, Professor Trevor W., BPharm, PhD, DSc. Professor and Head of Pharmacology, Glasgow University, since 1989; b. 7.10.47, Mexborough; m., Anne Corina. Educ. Mexborough Grammar School; London University; Aberdeen University. Lecturer in Physiology, Aberdeen University, 1970-77; Senior Lecturer/Reader in Neuroscience, then Professor of Neuroscience, London University, 1977-88. Editor, British Journal of Pharmacology, 1980-86. Publications: Microiontophoresis and Pressure Ejection, 1985; Purines: Basic and Clinical Aspects, 1991. Recreations: photography; snooker; working. Address: (b.) Department of Pharmacology, Glasgow University, Glasgow G12; T.-0141-330 4481.

Storie, Roy G., MA (Hons), DipEd. Headteacher, Prestwick Academy, since 1987; b. 16.9.34, Edinburgh; m.; 1 s.; 1 d. Educ. Royal High School; Edinburgh University; Moray House College of Education. Address: (b.) Prestwick Academy, Newdykes Road, Prestwick KA9 2LB.

Stormonth Darling, Sir Jamie Carlisle, Kt, CBE, MC, TD, WS, LLB, MA, Hon. FRIAS, DUniv (Stirling), Hon. LLD (Aberdeen); b. 18.7.18, Battle, Sussex; m., Mary Finella Gammell, BEM, DL; 1 s.; 2 d. Educ. Winchester College; Christ Church, Oxford; Edinburgh University. 2nd Lt., KOSB (Territorial); 1937: Adjutant, 1941, to Lt.-Col. Commanding 52nd (L) Division; Reconnaissance Regiment, RAC, 1945-46; studied law, Edinburgh University, 1946-49; appointed Chief Executive as Secretary, then Director, National Trust for Scotland, 1949-83, then Vice-President (Emeritus); Scottish Conservation Projects Trust: first President, 1984-89, Vice-President, 1989-97; concerned with various Scottish charities such as Scotland's Churches Scheme (Vice Chairman, 1994), Scottish Churches Architectural Heritage Trust, Scotland's Gardens Scheme, Pollok Trust (Glasgow), Edinburgh Old Town Charitable Trust; Patron, The Woodland Trust, Edinburgh Green Belt Trust. Recreations: gardening;

countryside; golf. Address: (h.) Chapelhill House, Dirleton, North Berwick EH39 5HG; T.-01620 850 296.

Stormonth Darling, Lady (Mary Finella), BEM, DL (East Lothian); b. 15.4.24, Farnborough; m., Sir Jamie Carlisle Stormonth Darling, qv; 1 s.; 2 d. Educ. Southover Manor School, Lewes; Architectural Association, London. Special Operations Executive (SOE), 1942-45. Designed own house, 1974; Elder, Dirleton Kirk and Convener, Fabric Committee, since 1976; Member, Church and Nation Committee, Church of Scotland, 1978-86; Convener, Sub-Committee on International Interests, 1982-84; Member, British Council of Churches, 1980-83; voluntary and charitable work. Recreations: painting, sculpting and gardening. Address: Chapelhill House, Dirleton, North Berwick EH39 5HG; T.-01620 850 296.

Stott, Professor David James, MB, ChB, MD(Glas), FRCP(Glas), FRCP(Edin). Professor of Geriatric Medicine, Glasgow University, since 1994; b. 4.6.59, Rugby; m., Shiona; 1 s.; 1 d. Educ. Eastwood High School; Glasgow University. Trained in research methodology, MRC Blood Pressure Unit, 1982-84; Senior Lecturer (Honorary Consultant) in Geriatric Medicine, 1991-94. Recreations: golf; hill-walking; acoustic guitar. Address: (b.) Academic Section of Geriatric Medicine, Glasgow Royal Infirmary G4 0SF; T.-0141-211 4976.

Stott, Rt. Hon. Lord (George Gordon Stott), PC (1964), QC (Scot), MA, LLB, DipEd; b. 22.12.09; m., Nancy Braggins; 1 s.; 1 d. Educ. Edinburgh Academy; Edinburgh University. Advocate, 1936; QC (Scot), 1950; Advocate Depute, 1947-51; Sheriff of Roxburgh, Berwick and Selkirk, 1961-64; Lord Advocate, 1964-67; Senator of the College of Justice, 1967-85. Publications: Lord Advocate's Diary, 1992; Judge's Diary, 1995; Editor, Edinburgh Clarion. Address: (h.) 12 Midmar Gardens, Edinburgh; T.-0131-447 4251.

Stott, Rev. Kenneth David, MA (Hons), BD (Hons). Parish Minister, Chalmers Ardler, Dundee, since 1997; b. 14.12.62, Montrose; m., Anne Herron; 3 d. Educ. Tynecastle High School, Edinburgh; Edinburgh University. Probationery period, Brightons, Falkirk, 1985-89; ordained and inducted into Partick South, Glasgow, 1989. Recreations: modern history; politics; football; reading. Address: The Manse, Turnberry Avenue, Dundee DD2 3TP; T.-01382 827439.

Strachan, Professor Hew Francis Anthony, MA, PhD, FRHistS. Professor of Modern History, Glasgow University, since 1992; Director, Scottish Centre for War Studies, since 1996; Life Fellow, Corpus Christi College, Cambridge, since 1992; b. 1.9.49, Edinburgh; m., Pamela Dorothy Tennant (née Symes); 1 s.; 1 step s.; 2 d.; 1 step d. Educ. Rugby School; Corpus Christi College, Cambridge. Senior Lecturer, Department of War Studies and International Affairs, Royal Military Academy, Sandhurst, 1978-79; Research Fellow, Corpus Christi College, Cambridge, 1975-78; Fellow, Corpus Christi College, since 1979; Tutor for Admissions, 1981-88, Director of Studies in History, 1986-92, Senior Tutor, 1987 and 1989-92. Governor, Rugby School, since 1985, and Stowe School, since 1990; Member, Council, Society for Army Historical Research, 1980-95, Army Records Society, 1990-94, Council, National Army Museum, since 1994; Joint Editor, War in History; Member, Queen's Bodyguard for Scotland (Royal Company of Archers). Publications: British Military Uniforms; History of the Cambridge University Officers Training Corps; European Armies and the Conduct of War; Wellington's Legacy: the Reform of the British Army 1830-54; From Waterloo to Balaclava: Tactics, Technology, and the British Army 1815-1854 (Templer Medal, 1986); The Politics of the British Army; numerous articles and reviews. Recreations: shooting; rugby fives; rugby football. Address:

(b.) Department of Modern History, Glasgow University, Glasgow G12 8QQ; T.-0141-339 8855.

Strachan, Michael Francis, CBE (Civil), MBE (Military), MA, FRSE. Writer; b. 23.10.19, Watford; m., Iris Winifred Hemingway; 2 s.; 2 d. Educ. Rugby School; Corpus Christi College, Cambridge. Served in Army, 1939-46; demobilised (Lt.-Col.), 1946; joined Wm. Thomson & Co., Edinburgh, managers of Ben Line, 1946; Partner, 1950-64; Joint Managing Director, Ben Line Steamers Ltd., 1964. Chairman, Associated Container Transportation Ltd., 1971-75; Trustee: National Galleries of Scotland, 1972 74, National Library of Scotland, since 1974 (Chairman, 1974-90), Carnegie Trust for Universities of Scotland, since 1976; Member, Queen's Bodyguard for Scotland (Royal Company of Archers). Publications: The Life and Adventures of Thomas Coryate, 1962; The East India Company Journals of Captain William Keeling and Master Thomas Bonner 1615-17, (Joint Editor), 1971; Sir Thomas Roe (1581-1644), A Life, 1989; contributor to Oxford Book of Military Anecdotes, 1987; The Ben Line, 1825-1982, 1992; Esmond S. de Beer (1895-1990), Scholar and Benefactor, 1995; contributor to various journals. Recreations: country pursuits; silviculture. Address: (h.) Glenhighton, Broughton, by Biggar ML12 6JF; T.-01899 830 273.

Strang, Gavin Steel, BSc (Hons), DipAgriSci, PhD. MP (Labour), East Edinburgh, since 1970; Minister for Transport, since 1997; b. 10.7.43, Dundee; m., Bettina Smith; 1 s. Educ. Morrison's Academy, Crieff; Edinburgh University. Parliamentary Under Secretary of State, Department of Energy, February to October, 1974; Parliamentary Secretary, Ministry of Agriculture, 1974-79; Principal Labour Agriculture Spokesman, since 1992. Recreations: golf; swimming; the countryside. Address: (b.) House of Commons, Westminster, London; T.-0171-219 3000.

Strang, William Frank Gourlay, BA (Oxon). Secretary to Forestry Commission, since 1997; b. 30.6.61, Glasgow; m., Eleanor Ann Munro-Faure. Educ. Loretto; St. Edmund Hall, Oxford. Administration Trainee, Ministry of Agriculture Fisheries and Food, 1984; Private Secretary to Permanent Secretary, 1987-88; Private Secretary to Parliamentary Secretary, 1988-89; Agricultural Attache, British Embassy, Paris, 1990-94; Principal Private Secretary to Minister of Agriculture, 1994-97. Recreations: hill-walking; bagpipes. Address: (b.) Forestry Commission, 231 Corstorphine Road, Edinburgh; T.-0131-314 6432.

Strange, Lady (Jean Cherry), MA, FIMarE, FSAScot. Peer of the Realm, since 1986; President, War Widows Association of Great Britain, since 1990; b. 17.12.28, London; m., Humphrey Drummond of Megginch; 3 s.; 3 d. Educ. Oxenfoord Castle School; St. Andrews University; Cambridge University. Member, All Party Parliamentary Defence Group; Member, Executive Committee, Association of Conservative Peers, 1990-93; Member, All Party Committee for Children. Publications: Love from Belinda; Lalage in Love; Creatures Great and Small; Love is Forever (poems); The Remarkable Life of Victoria Drummond, Marine Engineer. Address: (b.) Megginch Castle, Errol, Perthshire; T.-01821 642222.

Strang Steel, Sir (Fiennes) Michael, 3rd Bt; b. 22.2.43; m., Sally Russell; 2 s.; 1 d. Educ. Eton. Retired Major, 17th/21st Lancers, 1962-80. Forestry Commissioner, since 1988; DL. Address: (h.) Philiphaugh, Selkirk, TD7 5LX.

Strang Steel, Malcolm Graham, BA (Cantab), LLB, WS. Partner, W. & J. Burness, WS, since 1973; b. 24.11.46, Selkirk; m., Margaret Philippa Scott; 1 s.; 1 d. Educ. Eton; Trinity College, Cambridge; Edinburgh University. Sometime Chairman, Albyn Housing Society Ltd., Scottish Dyslexia Trust; Member, Council, Law Society of Scotland,

1984-90. Recreations: shooting; fishing; skiing; tennis; reading. Address: (b.) 16 Hope Street, Edinburgh EH2 4DD; T.-0131-226 2561.

Strathmore and Kinghorne, 18th Earl of (Michael Fergus Bowes Lyon); b. 7.6.57; m.; 3 s. President, Boys' Brigade, since 1994; DL, Angus, since 1993. Address: Glamis Castle, Forfar, DD8 1QJ.

Straton, Timothy Duncan, TD, CA, ATII. Partner, Scott-Moncrieff Downie Wilson, CA; Treasurer, Scottish Society for the Prevention of Cruelty to Animals; b. 1.10.42, Edinburgh; m., Gladys Margaret George; 1 s.; 1 d. Educ. Edinburgh Academy. Honorary Treasurer: Bruntsfield Links Golfing Society, Royal British Legion Scotland, SSAFA Forces Help (Edinburgh and Midlothian Branch); Major, AGC (SPS), TA. Recreations: TA; driving; photography; golf. Address: (b.) 17 Melville Street, Edinburgh EH3 7PH; T.-0131-473 3500.

Street, Margaret Dobson; b. 18.10.20, Hawick; m., Richard Andrew Rutherford Street (deceased); 2 s. Educ. Hawick High School; Alva Academy. Civil Servant, 1938-48; Ministry of Labour and National Service, 1938-47; Ministry of National Insurance (Inspectorate), 1947-48; voluntary work since 1948, apart from freelance writing on household and conservation topics; Honorary Secretary (Past Chairman), Leith Civic Trust; Convener, Friends of North Carr Lightship; Member, North East Fife District Council, North Carr Management Committee; Saltire Society Representative, Council, National Trust for Scotland, 1986-95; Secretary, Mungo Park Commemoration Committee; Trustee, Robert Hurd Memorial Fund; Appeal Convener, Wallace Statue, Lanark; Member, Steering Committee, Brownsbank; Appeal Convener, Wallace Statue, Dryburgh; Vice-Chairman, Saltire Society, 1983-94, Chairman, 1995-97; Saltire Society's Andrew Fletcher of Saltoun Award for services to Scotland, 1992. Recreations: promotion of Scottish cultural activity; conservation; good cooking. Address: (h.) 115 Trinity Road, Edinburgh; T.-0131-552 2409.

Stretton, James, BA, FFA. Chief Executive (UK Operations), Standard Life Assurance Company, since 1994; b. 16.12.43, Peterborough; m., Isobel Robertson; 2 d. Educ. Laxton Grammar School, Oundle; Worcester College, Oxford. Joined Standard Life, 1965. Recreations: music; gardening; reading; golf. Address: (b.) Standard Life House, 30 Lothian Road, Edinburgh, EH1 2DH; T.-0131-245 6012.

Stringer, Joan Kathleen, BA, CertEd, PhD, MIMgt, FRSA. Principal, Queen Margaret College, Edinburgh, since 1996; Commissioner (with responsibility for Scotland), Equal Opportunities Commission, since 1995; Member, Human Fertilisation and Embryology Authority, since 1996; Member, CVCP Commission on University Career Opportunities; b. 12.5.48, Stoke on Trent; m., Roel Mali. Educ. Portland House High School, Stoke on Trent; Stoke on Trent College of Art; Keele University. Assistant Principal, Robert Gordon University, 1991-96, having joined as Lecturer, 1980; Visiting Lecturer, Aberdeen University, 1984-86; Member, Management Board, North of Scotland Consortium on Wider Access, 1988-92; Auditor, Higher Education Quality Council, 1992-95; Member, Royal Institute of Public Administration, 1984-91; Member, Joint University Council for Social and Public Administration, 1982-91; Member, Scottish Committee, National Committee of Inquiry into Higher Education (The Dearing Committee), 1996-97; Member, Grampian Health Board, 1995-96; Member, Board of Management, Aberdeen College, 1993-96. Address: (b.) Queen Margaret College, Clerwood Terrace, Edinburgh, EH12 8TS; T.-01651 842430.

Strong, Hilary. Director, Edinburgh Festival Fringe, since 1994; b. 3.6.57, Chichester. Educ. Chichester High School for Girls; Lombard School of Dancing, London; Avery Hill College of Education, London. Stage manager and actress, 1979-83; administration and PR, 1984-85; Administrator: Merlin Theatre, Frome, 1986-88, Natural Theatre Company, Bath, 1989-94; freelance lecturer and director, 1987-94. Member, Board of Directors, National Campaign for the Arts, 1991-93; Drama Adviser, Arts Council of England, 1991-94. Recreations: travel; cooking; dancing. Address: (b.) Festival Fringe Society Ltd., 180 High Street, Edinburgh, EH1 1QS; T.-0131-226 5257.

Stuart, Charles Murray. Chairman, Scottish Power PLC, since 1992; Chairman, Intermediate Capital Group, since 1993; Chairman, Hammersmith Hospitals NHS Trust, since 1996; non-executive Director: Willis Corroon Group PLC, since 1996,The Royal Bank of Scotland plc, since 1996; Member, Meteorological Committee, since 1994; b. 28.7.33, Gourock; m., Netta Caroline; 1 s.; 1 d. Educ. Glasgow Academy; Glasgow University. MB Group PLC (formerly Metal Box), 1981-90, latterly as Executive Chairman; Chief Executive, Berisford International plc, 1990-91. Recreations: sailing; ballet; theatre. Address: (b.) 1 Atlantic Quay, Glasgow G2 8SP; T.-0141-248 8200.

Stuart of Findhorn, 2nd Viscount (David Randolph Moray Stuart); b. 20.6.24; m.; 2 s.; 3 d. Address: Findhorn, Forres, IV36 0YE.

Stuart, Jamie. Author of A Glasgow Bible; b. 10.9.20, Glasgow; widower; 2 d. Educ. Whitehill School, Glasgow. Flying Officer/Wireless Operator/Air Gunner, RAF, 1941-46; Actor/Social Worker/Evangelist; athlete: Scottish two-miles steeplechase champion, 1948. Address: (h.) 436 Edinburgh Road, Glasgow G33 2PW; T.-0141-778 2437.

Stuart, John Forester, MA (Cantab). Secretary General, General Synod, Scottish Episcopal Church, since 1996; b. 26.5.59, Broughty Ferry; m., Sally Ann Bell; 1 s. Educ. Dundee High School; Daniel Stewart's and Melville College; Queens' College Cambridge, College of Law, Guildford.Articled Clerk and subsequently Solicitor, MacFarlanes, London, 1982-86; Solicitor and subsequently Partner, J. & F. Anderson, Solicitors, Edinburgh (merged, 1992, to become Anderson Strathern), 1986-96. Recreations: music; walking; astronomy. Address: (b.) 21 Grosvenor Crescent, Edinbrugh EH12 5EE; T.-0131-225 6357.

Stuart, Michael John, BSc (Hons). Headteacher, Kincorth Academy, since 1990; b. 24.11.46, Fraserburgh; m., Daniele Madeleine; 2 s.; 1 d. Educ. Fraserburgh Academy; Aberdeen University. Assistant Teacher, Fraserburgh Academy, 1970-71, Kelvinside Academy, Glasgow, 1971-72; Principal Teacher, Greenwood Academy, Irvine, 1972-81; Assistant Head Teacher, Loudoun Academy, Galston, 1981-89; Depute Head Teacher, Carrick Academy, Maybole, 1989-90. Recreations: golf; angling; hill-walking. Address: (b.) Kincorth Academy, Kincorth Circle, Aberdeen, AB1 5NL; T.-01224 872881.

Stubbs, Ian Michael, LLB, CA, FTII. Partner, Maclay Murray & Spens, Solicitors, since 1973; b. 14.11.43, Birmingham; m., Joan Baird Crowther; 2 s.; 1 d. Educ. Marr College, Troon; Glasgow University. Thomson McLintock, Glasgow, 1965-68; Apprentice/Assistant, Maclay Murray & Spens, 1968-73; Council Member, Law Society of Scotland, since 1995; Council Member, Institute of Chartered Accountants of Scotland, 1986-92; Past Chairman, Board of Examiners, Law Society of Scotland; Senior Tutor, Wills Trusts and Executries, Glasgow University, 1980-86. Address: (h.) Suffolk Lodge, Methven Road, Whitecraigs, Glasgow, G46; T.-0141-639 6580.

Sturgeon, David, BL, MLitt. Registrar and Deputy Secretary, Heriot-Watt University, 1967-95; b. 10.12.35, Kilwinning; m., Nancy McDougall; 1 d.; 2 s. Educ. Dalry High School, Ayrshire (Blair Medallist, 1950); Glasgow University. National Service (RASC - War Office), 1957-59; Trainee Actuary, Scottish Widows Fund, 1959-61; Administrative Assistant, Royal College of Science and Technology (later, Strathclyde University), 1961-67. Secretary and Treasurer, Edinburgh Society of Glasgow University Graduates, since 1971; Hon. degree, Heriot-Watt University, 1996. Recreations: golf; music (particularly Scottish country dance music). Address: (h.) 10 Dalhousie Road, Eskbank, Midlothian EH22 3AS; T.-0131-663 1059.

Sturrock, Professor Robert Ralph, MB, ChB, DSc. Professor of Anatomy, Dundee University, since 1992; b. 1.7.43, Dundee; m., Norma Duncan; 1 d. Educ. Dundee High School; St. Andrews University. House Surgeon, Perth Royal Infirmary, 1967-68; House Physician, Stirling Royal Infirmary, 1968; Demonstrator, then Lecturer, Anatomy Department, Dundee University, 1968-77; Visiting Associate Professor of Neuroanatomy, Iowa University, 1976; Senior Lecturer, Dundee, 1977-81, Reader in Anatomy, 1981-92. Symington Memorial Prize in Anatomy, 1978; Convener, Tayforth Universities Military Education Committee, since 1997. Address: (b.) Dundee University, Dundee, DD1 4HN.

Sturrock, Professor Roger Davidson, MB, BS, MRCS, MD, FRCPLond, FRCPGlas. McLeod/ARC Professor of Rheumatology, Glasgow University, since 1990; b. 20.10.46, Dundee; m., Helen; 3 d. Educ. Llanelli Boys' Grammar School; Queen Mary's School, Basingstoke; London University. Senior Lecturer and Hon. Consultant, Westminster Medical School, 1977-79; Senior Lecturer in Medicine and Hon. Consultant, Centre for Rheumatic Diseases, Glasgow Royal Infirmary, 1979-90. Recreations: hill-walking; music; choral singing. Address: (b.) University Department of Medicine, Royal Infirmary, Glasgow G31 2ER; T.-0141-211 4687.

Subak-Sharpe, Professor John Herbert, CBE, FInstBiol, BSc, PhD, FRSE. Professor Emeritus, Glasgow University and Honorary Senior Research Fellow in Virology, since 1994; Professor of Virology, Glasgow University, 1968-94; Honorary Director, MRC Virology Unit, Institute of Virology, Glasgow, 1968-94; b. 14.2.24, Vienna; m., Barbara Naomi Morris; 2 s.; 1 d. Educ. Humanistisches Gymnasium, Vienna; Birmingham University. Assistant Lecturer, Glasgow University, 1954-56; Member, ARC scientific staff, AVRI Pirbright, 1956-61; Visiting Fellow, California Institute of Technology, 1961; Member, MRC Experimental Virus Unit scientific staff, Glasgow, 1961-68; Visiting Professor, NIH, Bethesda, 1967-68. Visiting Fellow, Clare Hall, Cambridge, 1986; elected Member (Past Chairman, Course and Workshops Committee), EMBO, since 1969; Trustee (former Secretary and Vice-President), Genetical Society, since 1971; Member, Genetic Manipulation Advisory Group, 1976-80; Chairman, MRC Training Awards Panel, 1986-89; Member, Governing Body, West of Scotland Oncological Organisation, since 1974, and Governing Body, Animal Virus Research Institute, 1986-88; Member, Scientific Advisory Group, Equine Virology Research Foundation, since 1987; Member, Medical Research Council Cell Biology and Disorders Board, 1988-92; Biochemical Society CIBA Medal and Prize, 1994. Recreations: travel; bridge. Address: (h.) 63 Kelvin Court, Glasgow G12 0AG; T.-0141-339 1863.

Suckling, Professor Colin James, BSc, PhD, DSc, CChem, FRSC, FRSA, FRSE. Professor of Chemistry, Strathclyde University, since 1984 (Deputy Principal, 1996); b. 24.3.47, Birkenhead; m., Catherine Mary Faulkner; 2 s.; 1 d. Educ. Quarry Bank High School, Liverpool; Liverpool University. Lecturer, Department of Pure and Applied Chemistry, Strathclyde University, 1972; Royal Society Smith and Nephew Senior Research Fellow, 1980; Dean, Faculty of Science, 1992-96. Convener, RSE Chemistry Committee, 1989-91; Member of Council, RSE, 1989-92; Member, General Teaching Council, 1993-95; Chairman, West of Scotland Schools Symphony Orchestra Board.Publications: Chemistry Through Models (Co-author), 1978; Biological Chemistry (Co-author), 1980; Enzyme Chemistry, Impact and Applications (Co-author), 1984, 1989, 1998. Recreations: music; horn playing. Address: (b.) Department of Pure and Applied Chemistry, Strathclyde Universtiy, 295 Cathedral Street Glasgow, G1 1XL; T.-0141-548 2271.

Suckling, David E., CBiol, MIBiol. Member, Scottish Borders Council, since 1995 (Chairman of Education, since 1996); Convener, Tweeddale District Council, 1992-96; b. 6.4.43, New Quay, Dyfed; m., Anne E. Robertson; 1 s.; 1 d. Educ. Dulwich College. District Council 1988; Board Member: Garvald Home Farm, since 1989 (Chairman, since 1997), Scottish Museums Council, 1991-97 (Vice Chair, 1992-97), Borders 1996 Ltd., since 1996, Borders Careers Ltd., since 1996; COSLA appointment to Board of Governors, Moray House College, since 1997; Chairman, West Linton Community Council, 1986-91; West Linton Whipman, 1987; President, Whipman Play, since 1992. Recreations: gardening; walking; MGBs; reading. Address: (h.) The Dean, West Linton, Peeblesshire EH46 7AU.

Sugden, Chris, BA. Rector, Buckie High School; b. 25.5.46, Paignton; m., Lynne; 1 s.; 1 d. Educ. Newcastle upon Tyne University. Gordonstoun School, Moray; Castlebrae High School, Edinburgh; Knox Academy, Haddington; Harlaw Academy, Aberdeen. Recreations: exploration and outdoor activities. Address: (b.) Buckie High School, West Cathcart Street, Buckie, AB56 1QB; T.-Buckie 832605.

Suggett, Gavin Robert, MA, MSc, FCA. Director (Managing), The Alliance Trust PLC, since 1995, The Second Alliance Trust PLC, since 1995; Director, Alliance Trust Savings Ltd., since 1986; b. 11.5.44, Sunderland; m., Louise Thomson; 1 s.; 2 d. Educ. Felsted; Christ's College Cambridge; London Business School. Deloitte Haskins & Sells; Weir Group PLC; Alliance Trust PLC: Assistant Company Secretary, Company Secretary, Director, Deputy Managing Director. Recreations: skiing; golf; gardening; keep-fit. Address: (b.) Meadow House, 64 Reform Street, Dundee DD1 1TJ; T.-01382 201700.

Sunter, Thomas Lacey Murray, FIMgt, FRSA, MNI. Director, Institute of Directors (Scotland), since 1997; Chief Executive, Business Enterprise Scotland, 1996-97; Deputy Lieutenant, Fife; b. 14.8.41, Liverpool; m., Margaret; 3 d. Educ. Merchant Taylors School, Crosby; Royal Naval College, Dartmouth. Royal Navy, 1960-96, including command of HMS Scylla, 1984-86 and HMS Endurance, 1987-89; UN Treaty Inspector, Antarctica, 1987-89; Ministry of Defence, 1989-91; Commander, RN Forces Hong Kong, 1991-94; Naval Base Commander, Rosyth, 1994-96. Trustee, Hong Kong Military Trust; Trustee, China Fleet Trust. Recreations: golf; tennis; reading. Address: (h.) 5 Briar Place, Dunfermline, Fife; T.-01383 734547.

Surber, Elizabeth, MA (Hons). Headmistress, Laurel Park School, Glasgow, since 1995; b. 10.5.54, Kingston upon Thames. Educ. Tiffin Girls' School, Kingston upon Thames; Exeter University; Oxford University. Teacher of French, Hadleigh High School, 1976-77; Lectrice, Universite de Haute, Bretagne, 1977-78; Teacher of French, Tiffin Girls' School, Kingston upon Thames, 1979-82; Cheltenham Ladies' College, 1982-88; Second Deputy Headmistress, Bedford High School, 1988-94. Recreations: ballet; walking; travel. Address: (b.) Laurel Park School, 4 Lilybank Terrace, Glasgow, G12 8RX.

Sutherland, Colin John MacLean, QC, LLB (Hons); b. 20.5.54. Advocate, 1977; Treasurer, Faculty of Advocates, since 1994. Address: (b.) Advocates' Library, Parliament House, Edinburgh, EH1 1RF.

Sutherland, David George Carr, CBE, MC and bar, TD. Landowner and Farmer, since 1962; Consultant, Control Risks Group Ltd., since 1985; b. 2.10.20, London; m., 1, Jean Henderson; 2, Christine Hotchkiss; 1 s.; 2 d. Educ. Eton; Sandhurst. War Service, Black Watch and Special Air Service Regiment, Dunkirk, Western Desert, Aegean, Adriatic; wounded; mentioned in Despatches; Greek War Cross; command and staff appointments, 1945-55, including British Military Mission to Greece, instructor at Sandhurst, Gold Staff Officer at The Queen's Coronation; retired from the Army, 1955; Ministry of Defence, 1955-80; commanded 21 SAS Regiment, Artists Rifles, TA, 1956-60; Deputy Lieutenant for Tweeddale, since 1974; Non-Executive Director, Asset Protection International Ltd., 1981-85. Member, Queen's Bodyguard for Scotland, Royal Company of Archers, since 1949; Fellow, Royal Geographical Society. Recreations: fishing; shooting; walking. Address: Ferniehaugh, Dolphinton, West Linton; T.-Dolphinton 82257.

Sutherland, David I.M., MA, MEd, DLitt, FCCEA, FIMgt, FRSA. Registrar, The General Teaching Council for Scotland, since 1985; b. 22.1.38, Wick; m., Janet H. Webster; 2 s. Educ. Aberdeen Grammar School; Aberdeen University; University of Zurich. Teacher of Modern Languages, Aberdeen Grammar School, 1962-66; Lecturer in Education, Stranmillis College of Education, Belfast, 1966-69; Lecturer in Educational Psychology, Craigie College of Education, Ayr, 1969-72; Assistant Director of Education, Sutherland County Council, 1972-75; Divisional Education Officer (Inverness), then Depute Director of Education, Highland Regional Council, 1975-85. Assessor, Committee of Scottish Higher Education Principals (Teacher Education Committee); Member: Scottish Education Department Planning Group on Teacher Supply, Scottish Association for Educational Management and Administration, Council, British Educational Management and Administration Society, Board, Commonwealth Council for Educational Administration and Management, Standing Conference on Studies in Education, Scottish Educational Research Association, Professional Advisory Committee to Department of Education, Stirling University; Associate Member: Association of Directors of Education in Scotland; Consultant, National Board for Nursing, Midwifery and Health Visiting for Scotland. Recreations: golf; walking; theatre; reading. Address: (b.) 5 Royal Terrace, Edinburgh EH7 5AF; T.-0131-556 0072.

Sutherland, Donald Gilmour, CA. Regional Managing Partner — South, Ernst & Young, 1990-95; b. 15.4.40, Edinburgh; m., Linda Malone; 2 s.; 1 d. Educ. George Watson's College. Joined Brown Fleming & Murray, London, 1963; Partner, Whinney Murray & Co., Glasgow, 1968, Edinburgh, 1974; Managing Partner, Ernst & Whinney, Edinburgh, 1985; Regional Managing Partner, 1987; Director, Murray Johnstone Ltd., Murray International Trust plc, Murray Income plc, Murray Smaller Markets Trust plc, 1987-89; Regional Managing Partner — North, Ernst & Young, 1989-90; Director: Standard Life Assurance Company, since 1990, CALA plc, since 1995, Murray Smaller Markets Trust plc, since 1995, Alexander Russell plc, since 1995, Quayle Munro Holdings plc, since 1995 (Chairman, since 1996). Recreations: conservation; golf; antiques. Address: (h.) Woodside House, Gladsmuir, East Lothian, EH33 2AL; T.-01875 852327.

Sutherland, Elizabeth (Elizabeth Margaret Marshall), FSA Scot. Writer; b. 24.8.26, Kemback, Cupar; m., Rev. John D. Marshall; 2 s.; 1 d. Educ. St. Leonard's Girls' School, St. Andrews; Edinburgh University. Social Worker for Scottish Episcopal Church, 1974-80; Curator, Groam House Museum, Rosemarkie, 1982-93; author of: Lent Term (Constable Trophy), 1973, The Seer of Kintail, 1974, Hannah Hereafter (Scottish Arts Council Book Award), 1976, The Eye of God, 1977, The Weeping Tree, 1980, Ravens and Black Rain: The Story of Highland Second Sight, 1985, The Gold Key and The Green Life, 1986; In Search of the Picts, 1994; Guide to the Pictish Stones, 1997. Recreations: Highland history; Gaelic language; the Picts; walking. Address: (h.) 17 Mackenzie Terrace, Rosemarkie, Ross-shire IV10 8UH; T.-Fortrose 620924.

Sutherland, Countess of (Elizabeth Millicent Sutherland). Chief of Clan Sutherland; b. 30.3.21; m., Charles Noel Janson; 2 s.; 1 d. (deceased); 1 d. Educ. Queen's College, London; abroad. Land Army, 1939-41; Laboratory Technician, Raigmore Hospital, Inverness, and St. Thomas's Hospital, London, 1941-45. Address: (h.) Dunrobin Castle, Sutherland; House of Tongue, Lairg, Sutherland.

Sutherland, George O., CA, MCT, FIMgt, FRSA. Director of Finance, Edinburgh University, since 1994; b. 5.11.44, Dundee; m., Jane; 1 s.; 3 d. Educ. Morgan Academy; St.Andrews University. TA, 1962-72. Shell International Petroleum Co. Ltd., 1969-92, serving in Libya, Hong Kong, United Arab Emirates, Norway, Brunei and Syria; set up a major World Bank power project in Pakistan, 1992-93; Member of Joint Universities of Edinburgh Military Education Committee; Member, Advisory Board, Centre for Second World War Studies. Recreations: military and aviation history; organised and led expeditions in Sahara desert and Borneo jungle, the latter identifying historically significant aircraft wrecks; battlefields; flying; hill-walking; water sports; a young family; an old Morgan sports car. Address: (b.) Old College, South Bridge, Edinburgh, EH8 9YL; T.-0131-650 2182.

Sutherland, George William Douglas, FCMA. Managing Director – Finance – North of Scotland Water, since 1995; b. 7.3.53, Dunoon; m., Mary; 1 s.; 2 d. Educ. Inverness High School. Dunlops; Rediffusion; Black and Decker (senior finance posts, latterly Group Financial Controller); Director of Financial Control, Grand Met; Finance Director, Express Foods Group; Finance Director, latterly Managing Director, Dairy Crest Dairies. Recreations: music; family; art. Address: (b.) North of Scotland Water, Cairngorm House, Beechwood Park, Inverness IV2 3ED; T.-01463 245400.

Sutherland, Ian, DL, DipYCS; b. 22.11.38, Edinburgh. Educ. Boroughmuir Secondary School; Moray House College of Education. Clerical, book-keeping, administrative posts, 1956-65; youth and community course, 1965-67; Youth Leader, Greenock and Kirkcaldy, 1967-71; Area Youth and Community Officer, Clackmannan County Council, 1971-73; Area Community Education Council, Central Regional Council, 1973-93. Trustee and Hon. Secretary, Scottish Silver Jubilee and Children's Bursary Fund; Elder, St. Serf's Church of Scotland, Tullibody; Deputy Lieutenant, Clackmannanshire. Recreations: singing; gardening; hand-crafts. Address: (h.) 1 Woodside Road, Tullibody, Alloa, FK10 2QQ; T.-01259 723935.

Sutherland, Ian Douglas, FRICS. Managing Partner, D.M. Hall & Son, Chartered Surveyors, Partner since 1975 (joined as Trainee Surveyor, 1965); b. 23.10.45, Colombo, Ceylon; m., Kathryn Wallace; 1 s.; 1 d. Educ. St. Bees School, Cumberland. Member, Company of Merchants of the City of Edinburgh. Address: (b.) 36 Melville Street, Edinburgh EH3 7HA; T.-0131-477 6000.

Sutherland, Professor Ian Wishart, BSc, PhD, DSc. Professor of Microbial Physiology, Edinburgh University, since 1991; b. 6.12.35, Perth; m., Ann Mary Barker; 1 d. Educ. Pitlochry High School; Dollar Academy; Edinburgh

University. Lecturer in Bacteriology, Edinburgh University Medical School, 1961-75, Senior Lecturer, then Reader, in Microbiology, 1975-91. Member, Council, Society of General Microbiology, 1984-93; Chair, British Co-ordinating Committee for Biotechnology, 1993-96. Recreations: mountain walking; photography. Address: (b.) Institute of Cell and Molecular Biology, Edinburgh University, Edinburgh EH9 3JH; T.-0131-650 5331.

Sutherland, James, CBE (1974), MA, LLB, LLD. McClure Naismith, Solicitors, Glasgow, Edinburgh and London (Partner, 1951-87, Consultant, 1987-90); b. 15.2.20; m . 1, Elizabeth Kelly Barr, 2 s.; 2, Grace Williamson Dawson. Educ. Queens Park Secondary School, Glasgow; Glasgow University. Royal Signals, 1940-46; Examiner in Scots Law, 1951-55, and Mercantile Law and Industrial Law, 1968-69, Glasgow University; Chairman, Glasgow South National Insurance Tribunal, 1964-66; Member, Board of Management, Glasgow Maternity and Women's Hospitals, 1964-74 (Chairman, 1966-74); Council Member, Law Society of Scotland, 1959-77 (Vice-President, 1969-70, President, 1972-74); Council Member, International Bar Association, since 1972 (Chairman, General Practice Section, 1978-80, Secretary General, 1980-84, President, 1984-86); Vice-Chairman, Glasgow Eastern Health Council, 1975-77; Council Member, General Dental Council, 1975-89; Deacon, Incorporation of Barbers, Glasgow, 1962-63; Dean, Royal Faculty of Procurators in Glasgow, 1977-80; Member, Court, Strathclyde University, 1977-92. Recreation: golf. Address: (h.) Greenacres, 20/1 Easter Belmont Road, Edinburgh EH12 6EX; T.-0131-337 1888.

Sutherland, Paul John, LLB (Hons), DipLP. Solicitor, since 1991; Partner, Drever and Heddle, Solicitors, Kirkwall, since 1995; President, Society of Procurators of Orkney, since 1996; b. 27.10.67, Aberdeen. Educ. Kirkwall Grammar School; Edinburgh University. Recreation: local history. Address: (b.) 56A Albert Street, Kirkwall, Orkney; T.-01856 872216.

Sutherland, Hon. Lord (Ranald Iain Sutherland), QC (Scot). Senator of the College of Justice, since 1985; b. 23.1.32. Advocate Depute, 1962-64, 1971-77; QC (Scot), 1969.

Sutherland, Professor Sir Stewart Ross, FBA, FRSE, MA. Principal and Vice-Chancellor, Edinburgh University, since 1994; b. 25.2.41, Aberdeen; m., Sheena Robertson; 1 s.; 2 d. Educ. Robert Gordon's College; Aberdeen University; Cambridge University. Assistant Lecturer, Philosophy, UCNW, 1965-68; Lecturer, Senior Lecturer, Reader, Stirling University, 1968-77; Professor, Philosophy of Religion, King's College, London, 1977-90 (Vice-Principal, 1981-85, Principal, 1985-90); Vice-Chancellor, London University, 1990-94, and HM Chief Inspector of Schools (England), 1992-94; Visiting Fellow, Australian National University, 1974; Chairman, Brit. Acad. Postgraduate Studentships, 1987-94; Member, Council for Science and Technology, since 1993, Hong Kong University Grants Com., since 1995, Higher Education Funding Council, England, since 1996; Editor, Religious Studies, 1984-90; Chairman, Secretary of State's Committee on Appeal Procedures, since 1994-96; Chairman, Royal Institute of Philosophy, since 1988; President, Society for Study of Theology, 1985, 1986. Publications: several books and papers. Recreations: jazz; theatre; rough gardening. Address: (b.) Edinburgh University, Old College, South Bridge, EH8 9YL; T.-0131-650 2150.

Sutherland, Sir William George MacKenzie, Kt. (1988), QPM. HM Chief Inspector of Constabulary for Scotland, since 1996; Chief Constable, Lothian and Borders Police, 1983-96; b. 12.11.33, Inverness; m., Jennie Abbott; 2 d. Educ. Inverness Technical High School. Cheshire Police, 1954-73; Surrey Police, 1973-75; Hertfordshire Police,

1975-79; Chief Constable, Bedfordshire Police, 1979-83. Recreations: squash; hill-walking. Address: (b.)2 Greenside Lane, Edinburgh, EH1 3AH; T.-0131-244 5614.

Sutter, Art. Broadcaster; b. 27.8.41, Airdrie; m., Janette; 2 d. Educ. Airdrie Academy. Studied piano/organ/voice; most of career spent in Scotch whisky industry (sales); Presenter, BBC Radio Scotland, 1985-93; chatshow, Grampian TV, since 1989. Recreations: golf; badminton; gardening.

Suttie, James Michael Peter, MRTPI. Director of Planning and Economic Development, Aberdeenshire Council, since 1995; b. 24.3.48, Arbroath; m., Sylvia; 1 s.; 2 d. Educ. Dundee High School; Duncan of Jordanstone College of Art, Dundee. Principal Planning Officer, Dundee Corporation, 1973-75; Principal Planning Assistant, Tayside Regional Council, 1975; Chief Assistant Planning Officer, Fife Regional Council, 1975-80; Director of Planning and Development, Banff and Buchan District Council, 1980-95. Recreations: golf; hill-walking; orienteering; driving. Address: (b.) Woodhill House, Westburn Road, Aberdeen; T.-01224 665540.

Swaffield, Professor John Arthur, BSc, MPhil, PhD, CEng, MRAeS, FIWEM, MCIBSE. Professor of Building Services Engineering, Heriot-Watt University, Edinburgh, since 1985; b. 4.3.43, Aberystwyth; m., Jean Winnan; 2 d. Educ. Ardwyn Grammar School, Aberystwyth; Bristol University. Research Fellow, Mechanical Engineering Department, City University, London, 1966-70; Deputy Head, Systems Laboratory, British Aircraft Corporation, Filton, Bristol, 1970-72; Senior Lecturer, South Bank Polytechnic, 1972-74; Lecturer and Senior Lecturer, Department of Building Technology, Brunel University, 1974-83; Reader in Mechanical Engineering, Brunel University, 1983-85; Dean of Engineering, Heriot-Watt University, 1990-93; Head, Department of Building Engineering and Surveying, Heriot-Watt University, 1995. Recreations: skiing; hill-walking; cinema; political/military history. Address: (b.) Department of Building Engineering and Surveying, Heriot-Watt University, Riccarton, Edinburgh EH14 4AS; T.-0131-449 5111.

Swan, John B.S., BSc (Hons), DipEd. Rector, The Gordon Schools, Huntly, since 1991; b. 18.10.46, Glasgow; m., Maureen; 1 s.; 2 d. Educ. High School of Glasgow; Aberdeen College of Education; Glasgow University. Teacher of Mathematics, Colston Secondary School, Glasgow, 1969-71; Teacher of Mathematics, then Principal Teacher of Remedial Education, Riverside Secondary School, Glasgow, 1972-79; Regional Staff Tutor, Strathclyde Region, 1979-80; Principal Teacher of Remedial Education, Whitehill Secondary School, Glasgow, 1980-84; Assistant Head Teacher, Acting Depute Head Teacher, Eastbank Academy, Glasgow, 1984-90; Depute Head Teacher, Victoria Drive Secondary School, Glasgow, 1990-91. Founder and Editor, Hard Words, 1980-84. Publication: Aye Nowyir Talkin'. Recreations: fine art; water colour painting; reading; music; hill walking, all sport; season ticket-holder, Huntly F.C. Address: (b.) Castle Street, Huntly AB54 4SE; T.-01466 79 2181.

Swanson, Alexander James Grenville, MB, ChB, FRCS Edin. Consultant Orthopaedic Surgeon, since 1980; b. 18.10.41, Ecclefechan; 2 s. Educ. Dingwall Academy; St. Andrews University. Postgraduate training: St. Andrews, 1967-68, Edinburgh, 1968-69, Glasgow, 1969-70, Edinburgh, 1970-74, Dunfermline, 1974-75; Lecturer, then Senior Lecturer and Honorary Consultant, Dundee University, 1975-83. Recreations: downhill skiing; cross-country skiing; travel. Address: (b.) Department of Orthopaedic and Trauma Surgery, Royal Infirmary, Dundee DD1 9ND; T.-01382 660111.

Swanson, Kenneth M., BSc, PhD, JP, DL. Farmer; Assistant Director, Technology, Dounreay Nuclear Power

Development Establishment, 1986-91; Vice Lord Lieutenant, Caithness, since 1996; b. 14.2.30, Canisbay, Caithness; m., Elspeth J.W. Paton; 2 s.; 1 d. Educ. Wick High School; St. Andrews University. Flying Officer, Pilot, RAF, 1952; Lecturer in Physics, University of Wales, 1955; joined UKAEA, Dounreay, on Fast Reactors, 1958; appointed JP, 1970; DL, Caithness, 1977; Chairman, Caithness Jobs Commission, 1988; Director, Caithness and Sutherland Local Enterprise Company, 1990 (Vice-Chairman, 1994); Member, N.W. Board, Scottish Natural Heritage, 1992; author of papers and patents on the development of plutonium fuels for electricity production. Address: Knockglass, Westfield, Thurso; T.-0184 787 1201.

Swanston, Professor Michael Timothy, MA (Cantab), PhD. Professor, University of Abertay Dundee, since 1995; Head, School of Social and Health Sciences, since 1995; b. 6.6.47, Bristol; m., Georgina Mary; 1 s.; 2 d. Educ. Rugby School; Cambridge University (Pembroke College). Psychologist, Army Personnel Research Establishment, 1969-72; Lecturer in Psychology, Dundee Institute of Technology, 1972-84; Reader in Psychology, 1984-95; Honorary Research Fellow, Dundee university, since 1989. Publications: one book; 40 papers. Recreations: golf; gardening: Address: (b.) School of Social and Health Sciences, University of Abertay Dundee, Marketgait House, 158 Marketgait, Dundee DD1 1NJ.

Swapp, George David, OBE, DL, MA (Hons), DipEd. Deputy Lieutenant, Kincardineshire, since 1990; Member Aberdeenshire Council, since 1995; b. 25.5.31, Labuan; m., Eva Jane MacNab; 2 s.; 2 d. Educ. Mackie Academy, Stonehaven; Aberdeen University. RAF Staff College, graduate and directing staff, 1965-68; Ministry of Defence (Training Policy), 1971-74 and 1978-80; promoted Wing Commander, 1971; Board Chairman, RAF Officer and Aircrew Selection Centre, 1974-78; Head, RAF Officer Training Establishment, Bracknell, 1980-83; retired from RAF, 1983. Former Member, Grampian Regional Council; President, Stonehaven Branch, Royal British Legion; founder Member, Stonehaven Heritage Society and Dunnottar Woodland Park Association; Church Elder. Recreations: hill-walking; local history; travel; geography; protection and enhancement of amenities and woodlands. Address: (h.) 9 Urie Crescent, Stonehaven AB39 2DY; T.-Stonehaven 764124.

Sweeney, Sister Dorothea, MA (Hons), BA(Soc) (Hons), PhD. Consultant and former Vice Principal, St. Andrew's College, 1985-97; b. Glasgow. Educ. Notre Dame High School, Glasgow; Glasgow University; Notre Dame College of Education; Bedford College and LSE, London University; Strathclyde University. Assistant Teacher of English, Our Lady & St. Francis Secondary School, Glasgow, 1960-63; entered Congregation of Sisters of Notre Dame, Sussex, 1963; Assistant Teacher of English, Notre Dame High School, London, 1966-67; Notre Dame College of Education: Lecturer, Department of Psychology, 1970-76, Senior Lecturer, Department of Educational Science, 1976-80, Assistant Principal, 1980-85. Member, Board of Governors, St. Andrew's College, 1980-97; Member, CNAA Inservice Education Board, 1982-87, Committee for Teacher Education, 1987-89, and Committee for Scotland, 1990-92; Member, National Inter-College Committee for Educational Research, 1982-89; Convener, School Boards, Headteacher Training, Steering Committee, 1988-89; School Boards Members Training, 1989-90; Training Consultant, National Staff Development & Appraisal Training, 1991-92; Myers-Briggs Qualified Trainer, since 1990; part-time Counsellor, since 1968. Recreations: creative writing; dance; music; art; sport; drama; technology.

Sweeney, Patrick, MA (Hons). Head Teacher, Holy Rood High School, Edinburgh, since 1994; b. 13.4.49, Wanlockhead; m., May Grant. Educ. Blairs College, Aberdeen; Glasgow University. Taught French and Latin in various schools, 1973-85; Assistant Head Teacher, St. Augustine's High School, Edinburgh, 1985-88; on staff of Quality Assurance Division, Lothian Regional Council, 1988-94, as Co-ordinator of Lothian TVEI Project and then Regional Adviser. Recreations: travel; squash; poor golf; The Herald newspaper; books of all descriptions. Address: (b.) Holy Rood High School, Duddingston Road, Edinburgh, EH15 1ST.

Swinfen, Professor David Berridge, MA, DPhil, FRHistS. Professor of Commonwealth History, Dundee University, since 1990 (Head, Department of Modern History, 1988-92, Deputy Principal, 1992-94, Vice Principal, since 1994); Chairman, Scottish Advisory Committee on Credit and Access, since 1997; b. 8.11.36, Kirkcaldy; m., Ann Pettit; 2 s.; 3 d. Educ. Fettes College, Edinburgh; Hertford College, Oxford. Assistant Lecturer in Modern History, then Lecturer, Queen's College, Dundee, 1963-75; Director, School of American Studies, Dundee University, 1970-85; Senior Lecturer, Modern History, Dundee University, 1975-90. Publications: five books. Recreation: music. Address: (h.) 14 Cedar Road, Broughty Ferry, Dundee, DD5 3BB; T.-01382 776496.

Swinney, John Ramsay, MP, MA (Hons). MP (SNP), North Tayside, since 1997; SNP Treasury Spokesman, since 1995; b. 13.4.64, Edinburgh; m., Lorna Ann King; 1 s.; 1 d. Educ. Forrester High School, Edinburgh; Edinburgh University. Research Officer, Scottish Coal Project, 1987-88; Senior Managing Consultant, Development Options Ltd., 1998-92; Strategic Planning Principal, Scottish Amicable, 1992-97. Recreation: hill-walking. Address: (b.) 35 Perth Street, Blairgowrie PH10 6DL; T.-01250 876576.

Swinton, Major General Sir John, KCVO, OBE, JP. Lord Lieutenant, Berwickshire, since 1989; President, Royal Highland and Agricultural Society of Scotland, 1993-94; Member, Queen's Bodyguard for Scotland (Royal Company of Archers), since 1977 (Ensign, since 1996); President, Borders Branch, SSAFA, since 1993; Council Member, Commonwealth Ex-Services League, since 1984; Trustee, Scottish National War Memorial, since 1988 (Chairman, since 1995); President, Berwickshire Civic Society (Chairman, 1982-96); President, Lowland TA & VRA, 1992-96; Chairman, Berwickshire Recreation Sports Trust, since 1997; Chairman, St. Abbs Head National Nature Reserve Joint Management Committee, since 1991; Trustee, The Scots at War Trust, since 1996; Trustee, Berwick Military Tattoo, since 1996; President, Berwickshire Naturalists Club, 1996-97; Patron, POWER, since 1995; b. 21.4.25, London; m., Judith Balfour Killen; 3 s.; 1 d. Educ. Harrow School. Enlisted Scots Guards, 1943; commissioned, 1944; served NW Europe (twice wounded); Malaya, 1948-51 (Despatches); ADC to Field Marshal Sir William Slim, Governor General of Australia, 1953-54; Regimental Adjutant, Scots Guards, 1960-62; Adjutant, RMA, Sandhurst, 1962-64; comd. 2nd Bn., Scots Guards, 1966-68; Lt.-Col. commanding Scots Guards, 1970-71; Commander, 4th Guards Armoured Brigade, BAOR, 1972-73; Brigadier, Lowlands and Commander, Edinburgh and Glasgow Garrisons, 1975-76; GOC London District and Major General comd. Household Division, 1976-79. Honorary Colonel, 2nd Bn., 52nd Lowland Volunteers, 1983-90; National Chairman, Royal British Legion Scotland, 1986-89; Coordinator for Scotland, Duke of Edinburgh's Award 25th Anniversary Appeal, 1980 (Honorary Liaison Officer for the Borders, 1983-85); Chairman, Roxburgh and Berwickshire Conservative Association, 1983-85; Chairman, Thirlestane Castle Trust, 1984-90; Trustee, Army Museums Ogilby Trust, 1978-91; Member, Central Advisory Committee on War Pensions, 1986-89. Address: (h.) Kimmerghame, Duns, Berwickshire; T.-01361 883277.

Sword, Ian Pollock, BSc, PhD, CChem, FRSC, FRSE. Chairman, Inveresk Research International, since 1979; Director, Inveresk Clinical Research, since 1988; Director, SGS UK Holding Ltd., since 1989; Senior Executive Vice President, SGS Geneva, since 1994; Member, Medical Research Council, since 1994; b. 6.3.42, Kilmarnock; m., Flora Collins; 2 s.; 1 d. Educ. Coatbridge High School; Glasgow University. Princeton University, New Jersey, 1967-69; Oxford University, 1969-70; Huntingdon Research Centre, 1970-73; Inveresk Research International, since 1973. Publications: editor of two books; scientific papers. Recreations: music; golf. Address: (b.) Inveresk Research International Ltd., Tranent EH33 2NE; T.-01875 614545.

Syme, Peter William, MA, DipAfrSts. Scottish Director, The Open University, and Vice-Chancellor's Delegate in Scotland, since 1997; b. 27.1.50, Brechin. Educ. Brechin High School; Trinity College, Glenalmond; Trinity College, Cambridge; Edinburgh University. VSO, Nigeria, 1972-74; Department of Education and Science, London, 1975-89, including Private Secretary to Sir James Hamilton, Permanent Secretary, 1979-80; seconded to Edinburgh University, 1983-85; Secretary to Review of University Grants Committee, 1985-87; Regional Director, Open University, London, 1990-97. Recreations: travel; photography; Africa. Address: (b.) The Open University in Scotland, 10 Drumsheugh Gardens, Edinburgh EH3 7QJ; T.-0131-226 3851.

Symington, Rev. Alastair Henderson, MA, BD. Minister, New Kilpatrick Parish Church, Bearsden, since 1985; Chaplain to The Queen in Scotland, since 1996; b. 15.4.47, Edinburgh; m., Eileen Margaret Jenkins; 2 d. Educ. Daniel Stewart's College, Edinburgh; Edinburgh University; Tubingen University, West Germany. Assistant Minister, Wellington Church, Glasgow, 1971-72; Chaplain, RAF, 1972-76; Minister, Craiglockhart Parish Church, Edinburgh, 1976-85. Contributor, Scottish Liturgical Review. Publications: Westminster Church Sermons, 1984; Reader's Digest Family Guide to the Bible (Co-author), 1985; For God's Sake, Ask!, 1993. Recreations: golf; rugby; music; computing. Address: 51 Manse Road, Bearsden, Glasgow G61 3PN; T.-0141-942 0035.

T

Tait, A. Margaret, BSc. Convenor, General Council, University of Edinburgh Business Committee; Member, St. Margaret's Chapel Guild; Vice Chairman, Lothian Healthy Volunteers Medical Ethics Committee; Member, Lothian Health Council; Public Affairs Consultant, Scotland, British Federation of Women Graduates; b. 8.10.44, Edinburgh; m., J. Haldane Tait; 1 s.; 1 d. Educ. George Watson's Ladies' College, Edinburgh; Edinburgh University; Jordanhill College of Education. Teacher of Mathematics, Bellahouston Academy, Glasgow; former Member, Lothian Children's Panel; former Honorary Secretary, Scottish Association of Children's Panels; former Chairman, Dean House Children's Home, Edinburgh; Volunteer, Edinburgh Citizens' Advice Bureau; former Member, Edinburgh Youth Orchestra Committee; formerly Secretary of State's Nominee to General Teaching Council; former Member, Scottish Legal Aid Board. Recreations: golf; speaking in Spanish and Japanese; entertaining. Address: (h.) 6 Ravelston House Park, Edinburgh EH4 3LU; T.-0131-332 6795.

Tait, Rev. Thomas William, BD, RAFVR (Rtd). Parish Minister, Rattray, Blairgowrie, 1972-97; Chairman, Tayside Health Council, since 1992; Convener, Scottish Association of Health Councils; Principal Chaplain, Scotland and Northern Ireland, Air Training Corps, since 1996; b. 11.11.31, Dunfermline; m., Irene Pope; 1 s.; 2 d. Educ. Dunfermline High School; St. Colm's College, Edinburgh; Edinburgh University; Christ's College, Aberdeen; Aberdeen University. HQ Staff, Boys' Brigade, 1954-61; Missionary, Church of Scotland, South Arabia, 1962-67; ordained and inducted, 1972; Member, Assembly Council, 1984-88; Chaplain, 2519 (Strathmore) Squadron, Air Training Corps, since 1974; Chairman, Blairgowrie Schools Council, 1975-89; Member, Perth and Kinross Health Council, 1980-91 (Chairman, 1984-91); Chairman, Blairgowrie and District Branch, Royal British Legion Scotland, and Chaplain, Angus and Perthshire Area; commissioned RAFVR, 1977 (retired Flt. Lt., 1988); Member, Secretary of State's Consultative Panel on Registration of Nursing Homes and Private Hospitals, since 1993; Member, Tayside Health Board Quality Monitoring Team, since 1993; Member, CRAG Clinical Audit Sub-Committee. Recreations: encouraging others to work in voluntary organisations; swimming; reading; overseas travel. Address: 20 Cedar Avenue, Blairgowrie, Perthshire; T.-01250 4833.

Tankel, Henry I., OBE, MD, FRCSEdin, FRCSGlas. Chairman, Glasgow Jewish Housing Association, since 1996; Surgeon, Southern General Hospital, Glasgow, 1962-91; b. 14.1.26, Glasgow; m., Judith Woolfson; 2 s.; 2 d. Educ. High School of Glasgow; Glasgow University. Fulbright Scholar, 1954-55; President, Glasgow Jewish Representative Council, 1974-77; Chairman, Glasgow Hospital Medical Services Committee, 1974-79; Board of Science and Education, 1978-81; President, United Synagogues of Scotland, 1978-85; Treasurer, Scottish Committee for Hospital Medical Services, 1978-91; Member, National Panel of Specialists, 1978-82 and 1987-91; invited to address General Assembly of Church of Scotland, 1984; Chairman, Scottish Joint Consultants Committee, 1989-92; Member, Scottish Health Service Advisory Council, 1989-93; Non-Executive Director, Southern General Hospital NHS Trust, 1993-97; Chairman, Glasgow Board of Jewish Education, 1985-90. Recreations: walking; making model boats. Address: (h.) 26 Dalziel Drive, Glasgow G41 4PU; T.-0141-423 5830.

Tannahill, Professor Andrew James, MB, ChB, MSc, FFPHM, FRCPE, MHSM. Chief Executive, Health Education Board for Scotland, since 1991; Visiting Professor, Glasgow University, since 1997; Honorary Senior Lecturer, Department of Epidemiology and Public Health, University of Dundee, since 1993; Honorary Fellow, Department of Public Health Sciences, University of Edinburgh, since 1994; Honorary Clinical Senior Lecturer, Department of Public Health, Glasgow University, since 1996; b. 28.4.54, Inchinnan; m., Carol Elizabeth Fyfe. Educ. John Neilson Institution, Paisley; Glasgow University; Edinburgh University. Lecturer in Pathology, Glasgow University; Senior Registrar in Community Medicine, Lothian Health Board/Honorary Clinical Tutor, Edinburgh University; Regional Specialist in Community Medicine, East Anglian Regional Health Authority/Associate Lecturer, Cambridge University; Senior Lecturer in Public Health Medicine, Glasgow University/Honorary Consultant in Public Health Medicine, Greater Glasgow Health Board. Publications: Health Promotion: Models and Values (Co-author); contributor to Health Promotion: Disciplines and Diversity; papers on health education, prevention and health promotion. Recreations: countryside and bird-watching; music; theatre; photography; drawing and painting; reading (especially humour). Address: (b.) Health Education Board for Scotland, Woodburn House, Canaan Lane, Edinburgh EH10 4SG; T.-0131-447 8044.

Tate, Professor Austin, BA (Hons), PhD, CEng, MBCS, FBIS. Technical Director, AIAI (Artificial Intelligence Applications Institute), since 1985; Chair in Knowledge-Based Systems, Edinburgh University, since 1995; b. 12.5.51, Knottingley; m., Margaret. Educ. King's School, Pontefract; Lancaster University; Edinburgh University. Elected Fellow, American Association of Artificial Intelligence, since 1993. Address: (b.) AIAI, University of Edinburgh, 80 South Bridge, Edinburgh EH1 1HN; T.-0131-650 2732.

Tavener, Alan, MA, ARCO, ARCM. Director of Music, Strathclyde University, since 1980; Artistic Director, Cappella Nova, since 1982; b. 22.4.57, Weston-Super-Mare; m., Rebecca Jane Gibson. Educ. City of Bath Boys' School; Brasenose College, Oxford. Conducted several world premieres of choral works and several CDs of early and contemporary music. Recreations: architecture; exhibitions; Scottish country dancing; food and drink. Address: (b.) Strathclyde University, Livingstone Tower, Richmond Street, Glasgow G1 1XH; T.-0141-548 3444.

Taylor, Brian, MA (Hons). Political Editor, BBC Scotland; b. 9.1.55, Dundee; m., Pamela Moira Niven; 2 s. Educ. High School of Dundee; St. Andrews University. Reporter, Press and Journal, Aberdeen, 1977-80; Lobby Correspondent, Thomson Regional Newspapers, Westminster, 1980-85; Reporter, BBC Scotland, Glasgow, 1985-86; Co-Presenter, Left, Right and Centre, BBC Scotland, 1986-88; Political Correspondent, BBC Scotland, 1988-90. Recreations: golf; theatre. Address: (b.) BBC Scotland, Queen Margaret Drive, Glasgow G12 8DG.

Taylor, Cameron Sutherland, MA (Hons). Chief Executive, Orkney Tourist Board, since 1994; b. 20.10.58, Kirkwall; m., Angela; 1 s.; 1 d. Educ. Kirkwall Grammar School; Aberdeen University. Civil Service, 1980-91, including two years as Duty Clerk at 10 Downing Street and four years, IT Services Agency; IT Project Manager, North Western Regional Health Authority, 1991-92; rejoined IT Services Agency, 1992-94. Recreations: archaeology; walking. Address: (b.) Orkney Tourist Board, 6 Broad Street, Kirkwall, Orkney, KW15 1JH; T.-01856 872856.

Taylor, Charles Edwin, CBE, BSc, PhD, FRSE, CBiol, FIBiol. Director, Scottish Crop Research Institute, 1972-86; President, Association of Applied Biologists, 1989; NATO Senior Research Fellow, Istituto di Nematologia Agraria CNR, Bari, Italy; b. 11.9.23, Oystermouth; 1 d. Educ.

Cardiff High School; University College, Cardiff. Pilot, RAF, 1943-46; Lecturer in Applied Zoology, Nottingham University School of Agriculture, 1949-56; Senior Entomologist, Federation of Rhodesia and Nyasaland, 1956-59; Head, Zoology Section, Scottish Horticultural Research Institute, 1959-72. President, European Society of Nematologists, 1980-84; Editor, Nematologica, 1990-96. Address: (b.) Westcroft, Longforgan, Dundee DD2 5EX; T.-01382 360 243.

Taylor, David Alexander, LLB (Hons), MSc, MBA. Director, Scottish Trade International, since 1994; Chairman, Scottish Development Overseas Ltd.; Director, Trade Development Centre Ltd.; b. 14.3.54, Forfar; m., Catherine Taylor; 2 s. Educ. Dundee High School; Edinburgh University; Strathclyde University. Senior Solicitor, City of Glasgow Council, 1979-84; SDA, 1985-91; Head of Consumer Products, Scottish Enterprise, 1991-94 (also part-time Tutor, Open University). Recreations: Partick Thistle; golf; the pursuit of knowledge. Address: (b.) 123 Bothwell Street, Glasgow, G2 7JP; T.-0141-228 2747.

Taylor, Elizabeth (Liz) Dewar, MA (Hons). Journalist and Author; b. 25.4.31, Newport, Fife; m., Adam McNeill Taylor (deceased); 1 s.; 3 d. Educ. Morgan Academy, Dundee; Galashiels Academy; King's College, Aberdeen. Reporter, Edinburgh Evening Dispatch, 1954-56; freelance stringer, Bombay, 1960-65; freelance journalist and broadcaster, since 1971. Publications include: Living with Loss; Bringing Up Children On Your Own; Living Alone; The Writing Business; 20th Century Antiques; also several books as Elisabeth McNeill. Recreations: gardening; crossword puzzles; bridge; Scrabble; cinema; horse-racing. Address: (h.) Cairnhill, Newstead, Melrose TD6 9DX; T.-0189682 2972.

Taylor, George Lamberton, MA, LLB. Managing Partner, Brodies WS, since 1990; b. 1.11.42, Paisley; m., Helen Jean; 2 d. Educ. Paisley Grammar School; Glasgow University. Partner, Torrance Baird, Solicitors, Glasgow, 1967-89; Commercial Property Partner, Brodies, since 1989. Trustee, Stanley Morrison Charitable Trust. Recreations: music; golf. Address: (b.) 15 Atholl Crescent, Edinburgh EH3 8HA; T.-0131-228 3777.

Taylor, Rev. Howard, BSc (Hons), BD (Hons). Minister, St. David's Church, Knightswood, Glasgow, since 1986; Part-time Lecturer in Apologetics, Glasgow Bible College, since 1989; b. 6.6.44, Stockport; m., Eleanor Clark; 3 s. Educ. Gravesend Technical School, Kent; Nottingham University; Edinburgh University. Maths and Physics Teacher, Malawi University; Missionary in Malawi (minister of town and rural African churches, theological teacher, teacher of African languages to missionaries); Minister, Toward and Innellan Churches, Argyll. Publications: Faith Seeks Understanding, 1980; Pray Today 1982/83, 1982; In Christ All Things Hold Together; World Hope in the Middle East; The Delusion of Unbelief in a Scientific Age; Faith and Understanding; Israel — People of God; The Uniqueness of Christ in a Pluralist World, 1994; Is the New Testament the Source of Anti-Semitism?,1994. Recreations: hill walking; reading; classical music. Address: 60 Southbrae Drive, Glasgow G13 1QD; T.-0141-959 2904.

Taylor, Rev. Ian, BSc, MA, LTh, DipEd. Lecturer on music and the arts, broadcaster, opera producer; b. 12.10.32, Dundee; m., Joy Coupar, LRAM; 2 s.; 1 d. Educ. Dundee High School; St. Andrews University; Durham University; Sheffield University; Edinburgh University. Teacher, Mathematics Department, Dundee High School; Lecturer in Mathematics, Bretton Hall College of Education; Senior Lecturer in Education, College of Ripon and York St. John; Assistant Minister, St. Giles' Cathedral,

Edinburgh; Minister, Abdie & Dunbog and Newburgh, 1983-97; Moderator, Presbytery of St. Andrews, 1995-96; Secretary, History of Education Society, 1968-73; extensive work in adult education (appreciation of music and the arts); Director, Summer Schools in Music, St. Andrews University; numerous courses for St. Andrews, Edinburgh and Hull Universities and WEA; has played principal roles in opera and operetta; Producer, Gilbert and Sullivan Society of Edinburgh, 1979-87; compiled Theatre Music Quiz series, Radio Tay; presented own operetta, My Dear Gilbert...My Dear Sullivan, BBC; Writer of revues and documentary plays with music, including Tragic Queen (Mary Queen of Scots), St. Giles' Cathedral, Edinburgh Festival Fringe, 1982, and John Knox (Church of Scotland Video). Publications: How to Produce Concert Versions of Gilbert Sullivan; The Gilbert and Sullivan Quiz Book; The Opera Lover's Quiz Book. Address: Lundie Cottage, Arncroach, Fife KY10 2RN; T.-01333 720 222.

Taylor, James Alastair, BSc, LLB. Partner, McGrigor Donald, Solicitors, since 1988, Head of Litigation Department, since 1992; Convener, Rights of Audience Civil Training Course, since 1995; b. 21.2.51, Inverness; m., Lesley Macleod; 2 s. Educ. Nairn Academy; Aberdeen University. Apprenticed to Brander & Cruickshank, Advocates in Aberdeen, 1975-77; apprenticed to, Assistant with, Lefevre & Co., Advocates in Aberdeen, 1977-78; Assistant, later Partner, A.C. Morrison & Richards, Advocates in Aberdeen, 1978-87; attained rights of audience in Supreme Courts in Scotland, 1993. Recreations: golf; music; good food and wine. Address: (b.) Erskine House, 63-73 Queen Street, Edinburgh EH2 4NF; T.-0131-226 7777.

Taylor, James Bradley. Chief Executive, Northern Lighthouse Board, since 1993; Nautical Assessor to the Court of Session, since 1996; Trustee, Scotland's Lighthouse Museum, since 1995; Trustee, Bell's Nautical Trust, since 1996; b. 12.8.45, Paisley; m., Elizabeth Sherwood. Educ. George Watson's College, Edinburgh; Britannia Royal Naval College; Defence School of Languages; Royal College of Defence Studies. Royal Navy, 1963-93; commanded HM submarines: Grampus, 1974-75, Orpheus, 1975-77, Spartan, 1980-82, HM ship London, 1989-90; Chief of Staff, Submarine Flotilla, 1990-91; Royal College of Defence Studies, 1992. Recreations: shooting; stalking; history; classic cars. Address: (b.) 84 George Street, Edinburgh, EH2 3DA; T.-0131-226 7051.

Taylor, Rev. John Henry Bindon, MA, BD, DipEd, FEIS. Vice-President, Christian Education Movewment (Scotland), since 1990; b. 4.11.26, Swansea; m., Jean Taylor, MBE; 3 s.; 1 d. Educ. Swansea Grammar School; Worcester College, Oxford; Glasgow University. Minister, Lincluden, Cumfries, 1952-56; St. Mary's, Woolston, Southampton, 1956-60; St. Andrew's, Irvine, 1960-69; Teacher, Ravenspark Academy, Irvine, 1969 (Assistant Rector, 1974); Depute Rector, Garnock Academy, 1978; Rector, Auchenharvie Academy, Stevenston, 1980, till retirement, 1989; Associate Minister, Galston Parish Church, since 1991; Convener, Scottish Examination Board Panel on Religious Studies, 1982-88; Convener, Church of Scotland Education Committee, 1989-95; Chairman, Forum on Scottish Education, 1989-96. Recreations: walking; railway history. Address: (h.) 62 Woodlands Grove, Kilmarnock; T.-01563 526698.

Taylor, Rt. Rev. John Mitchell, MA. Bishop of Glasgow and Galloway; b. 23.5.32, Aberdeen; m., Edna Elizabeth Maitland; 1 s.; 1 d. Educ. Banff Academy; Aberdeen University; Theological College, Edinburgh. Curate, St. Margaret's, Aberdeen; Rector: Holy Cross, Knightswood, Glasgow, St. Ninian's, Pollokshields, Glasgow, St. John the Evangelist, Dumfries; Canon, St. Mary's Cathedral, Glasgow. Recreations: angling; hill-walking; sketching;

music. Address: Bishop's House, 25 Quadrant Road, Glasgow G43 2QP.

Taylor, John Murray, MA, DipEd, MIM, FRSA. Principal, Clackmannan College, since 1987; b. 18.7.42; m., Katie Forsyth; 2 d. Educ. Banchory Academy; Aberdeen University. Teacher, Dunfermline High School, 1965-70; Principal Teacher of Classics, Kirkcudbright, Liberton, Callander, 1970-78; Assistant Director of Education, Central Region, 1978-87. Recreations: music; cycling; travel; railways; DX radio. Address: (b.) Clackmannan College of Further Education, Branshill Road, Alloa FK10 3BT; T.-01259 215121.

Taylor, Margie, MSc, MBA, BDS. Consultant in Dental Public Health, Lanarkshire Health Board, since 1994; Honorary Senior Lecturer, Glasgow University; b. Edinburgh. Educ. James Gillespie's High School for Girls; Edinburgh University; Heriot-Watt University. Formerly Chief Administrative Dental Officer, Fife Health Board, and Honorary Senior Lecturer, St. Andrews University. Vice-President, Royal Odonto-Chirurgical Society of Scotland. Recreations: calligraphy; golfing (badly); cooking. Address: (b.) Lanarkshire Health Board, 14 Beckford Street, Hamilton ML3 0TA; T.-01698 281313.

Taylor, Rt. Rev. Maurice, STD. Bishop of Galloway, since 1981; b. 5.5.26, Hamilton. Educ. St. Aloysius College, Glasgow; Our Lady's High School, Motherwell; Pontifical Gregorian University, Rome. Royal Army Medical Corps, UK, India, Egypt, 1944-47; Assistant Priest: St. Bartholomew's, Coatbridge, 1951-52, St. Bernadette's, Motherwell, 1954-55; Lecturer, St. Peter's College, Cardross, 1955-65; Rector, Royal Scots College, Spain, 1965-74; Parish Priest, Our Lady of Lourdes, East Kilbride, 1974-81. Episcopal Secretary, Bishops' Conference of Scotland; Vice President, Catholic Institute for International Relations; Chairman, Episcopal Board, International Commission on English in the Liturgy. Publications: The Scots College in Spain, 1971; Guatemala, A Bishop's Journey, 1991; El Salvador: Portrait of a Parish, 1992; Opening Our Lives to the Saviour (Co-author), 1995; Listening at the Foot of the Cross (Co-author), 1996. Address: 8 Corsehill Road, Ayr KA7 2ST; T.-01292 266750.

Taylor, Michael Thomas, MA, MEd. Rector, Dyce Academy, Aberdeen, since 1980; b. 17.2.47, Newcastle upon Tyne; m., Sheena Robertson; 1 s.; 2 d. Educ. Rutherford Grammar School, Newcastle upon Tyne; Trinity College, Cambridge; Aberdeen University. Teacher of Chemistry, Cannock Grammar School, 1969-75; Ellon Academy: Principal Teacher of Guidance, 1975-76, Assistant Head Teacher, 1977-78, Depute Rector, 1978-80. Secretary, Newmachar Community Council. Recreations: hill-walking; music. Address: (h.) Loch-An-Eilan, Newmachar, Aberdeen; T.-01651 862234. 46 6UG.

Taylor, Ronald Shaw McDonald, BA. Managing Director, Parklands Nursing Homes, since 1997; b. 15.2.59, Dumfries; m., Moira Margaret; 2 s.; 1 d. Educ. Buckie High School; Robert Gordon's University. Graduate Trainee, Unigate PLC, 1981-84; Partner, C.B. Milne, newsagents, 1984-91; Chief Executive, Moray Enterprise Trust, 1991-94; Chief Executive, Aberdeen Enterprise Trust, 1994-97. Recreations: fly fishing; skiing. Address: (h.) Whiteash, Letterfourie, Drybridge, Buckie AB56 5JB; T.-01542 832650.

Taylor, Professor Samuel Sorby Brittain, BA, PhD, Officier dans l'Ordre des Palmes Academiques. Professor of French, St. Andrews University, 1977-95; b. 20.9.30, Dore and Totley, Derbyshire; m., Agnes McCreadie Ewan; 2 d. Educ. High Storrs Grammar School, Sheffield; Birmingham University; Paris University. Royal Navy, 1956-58 (Sub Lt.,

RNVR); Personnel Research Officer, Dunlop Rubber Co., 1958-60; Institut et Musee Voltaire, Geneva, 1960-63; St. Andrews University: Lecturer, 1963, Reader, 1972, Professor, 1977; Chairman, National Council for Modern Languages, 1981-85; Member, Executive Committee, Complete Works of Voltaire, 1970-85; Project Leader, Inter-University French Language Teaching Research and Development Project, 1980-88; Director, Nuffield Foundation project (French for science students), 1991-97; Chairman, Scottish Joint Working Party for Standard Grade in Modern Languages, 1982-84; Secretary, Scottish Applied French Language Association, since 1965. Recreations: athletics timekeeping; photography. Address: (h.) 11 Irvine Crescent, St. Andrews KY16 8LG; T.-01334 472588.

Taylor of Gryfe, Lord (Thomas Johnston Taylor), Hon. LLD (Strathclyde); b. 27.4.12, Glasgow; m., Isobel. Educ. Bellahouston Academy. Member, Board, Scottish Television, 1968-83; Director: Whiteaway Laidlaw (Bankers), since 1971, Friends Provident, 1972-83, Scottish Metropolitan Property, 1972-88; Member, International Advisory Board, Morgan Grenfell, 1972-88; Chairman, Forestry Commission, 1967-72; Chairman, Economic Forestry, 1972-82; Chairman, Scottish Railways Board, 1969-80; Chairman, Wolfson Trust (Scotland), since 1975; Trustee, Dulverton Trust, since 1979; Chairman, Scottish Peers Association, 1988; Chairman, All-Party Parliamentary Group on Forestry; Commander Order of merit — Federal Republic of Germany.

Taylor, Tom, BSc, PhD. Rector, Kingussie High School, since 1990; m., Anne; 2 d. Educ. Glasgow University. Address: (b.) Kingussie High School, Ruthven Road, Kingussie PH21 1ES; T.-01540 661475.

Taylor, William James, QC, MA (Hons), LLB. Advocate, since 1971; Barrister, since 1990; b. 13.9.44, Nairn. Educ. Robert Gordon's College; Aberdeen University. Called to Scots Bar, 1971; called to Bar of England and Wales, 1990. Councillor, Edinburgh Corporation, 1973-75, Lothian Regional Council, 1974-82. Recreations: music; theatre; hill-walking. Address: (b.) Parliament House, Parliament Square, Edinburgh, EH1 1RF.

Teasdale, Professor Graham Michael, MB, BS, MRCP, FRCSEdin, FRCSGlas. Professor and Head, Department of Neurosurgery, Glasgow University, since 1981; Consultant Neurosurgeon, Institute of Neurological Sciences, Glasgow, since 1975; b. 23.9.40, Spennymoor; m.; 3 s. Educ. Johnston Grammar School, Durham; Durham University. Postgraduate clinical training, Newcastle-upon-Tyne, London and Birmingham, 1963-69; Assistant Lecturer in Anatomy, Glasgow University, 1969-71; specialist training in surgery and neurosurgery, Southern General Hospital, Glasgow, 1971-75; Senior Lecturer, then Reader in Neurosurgery, Glasgow University, 1975-81. President, International Neurotrauma Society, 1993; Chairman, European Brain Injury Consortium, 1995. Publication: The Management of Head Injuries. Recreations: hill-walking; inshore fishing. Address: (b.) University Department of Neurosurgery, Institute of Neurological Sciences, Southern General Hospital, Glasgow; T.-0141-445 2466.

Tedford, Professor David John, OBE, BSc, PhD, ScD, ARCST, CEng, FIEE, SMIEEE, CPhys, FInstP, FRSE, FRSA, Order of Merit of Poland, DTech (Hon. Abertay, Dundee), DSc (Hon. Robert Gordon University); DUniv (Strathclyde University). Emeritus Professor; formerly Professor of Electrical Engineering (Foundation Chair), Strathclyde University; Chief Scientific Adviser to Secretary of State for Scotland, 1994-96; Secretary of State Scientific Adviser to Scottish Office Industry Department, 1992-94; b. 12.7.31, Coatbridge; m., Mary White Gardner; 3 s.; 1 d. Educ. Coatbridge High School; Royal Technical College; Glasgow University. Research Engineer, Ferranti Ltd., Edinburgh, 1955-57; joined Strathclyde University as

Lecturer, 1957; Deputy Principal, 1982-84, Vice-Principal, 1986-88, Deputy Principal (International Affairs), 1988-91; Special Adviser to Principal, 1991-92; Member: Council, IEE, 1992-95; British National Committee and Executive Committee, CIGRE; Council and Vice President, Royal Society of Edinburgh, 1992-95; International Relations Committee, Royal Society, 1992-95; Management Board, Bell College of Technology, Hamilton; Management Board, SCOTVEC. Recreations: hill-walking; music; amateur astronomy. Address: (h.) 76 Woodlands Drive, Coatbridge, ML5 1LB; T.-01236 422016.

Templeton, Ian Godfrey, MA, BA. Warden, Glenalmond College, Perth, since 1992; b. 1.2.44, Edinburgh; m., Elisabeth Aline Robin; 1 s.; 1 d. Educ. Gordonstoun; Edinburgh University; Bedford College, London University. Assistant Master, then Housemaster, Melville College, Edinburgh, 1969-73; Housemaster, Daniel Stewart's and Melville College, Edinburgh, 1973-78; Assistant Headmaster, Robert Gordon's College, Aberdeen, 1978-85; Headmaster, Oswestry School, 1985-92. Governor, Belhaven Preparatory School; Director, Lathallan Preparatory School. Recreations: golf; skiing; choral singing. Address: Glenalmond College, Glenalmond, Perth PH1 3RY; T.-01738 880227.

Tennant, Sir Iain Mark, KT (1986). Chairman, Grampian Television PLC, 1968-89 (Vice-Chairman, 1960-68); Director, Caledonian Associated Cinemas PLC, 1950-90; Director, Clydesdale Bank PLC, 1969-89; Director, Abbey National Building Society (Chairman, Scottish Advisory Board, 1969-89); Director, Moray and Nairn Newspaper Company Ltd.; Member, Royal Company of Archers (Queen's Bodyguard in Scotland), since 1950; Crown Estate Commissioner, 1969-89; Honorary Director, Seagram Company Ltd., Montreal; Lord Lieutenant of Morayshire, 1963-94; Lord High Commissioner to the General Assembly of the Church of Scotland, 1988, 1989; b. 11.3.19, North Berwick; m., Lady Margaret Ogilvy; 2 s.; 1 d. Educ. Eton College; Magdalene College, Cambridge. Learned about film production, Welwyn Garden City Film Studios; served in Egypt with 2nd Bn., Scots Guards, 1940-42; became Intelligence Officer, 201 Guard's Brigade; captured at the surrender of Tobruk; prisoner of war, Italy and Germany, until 1945; Founder Member, Moray Sea School, 1949; Council Member, Outward Bound Trust, 15 years; joined Board, Gordonstoun School, 1951 (Chairman, 1957-72); Member, Moray and Nairn County Council, 1956-64 (latterly Vice-Chairman, Education Committee); Member, The Times Publishing Co. Ltd., 1962-66; Member, Board, Cairngorm Sports Development Ltd., 1964-76; appointed Chairman, local Disablement Advisory Committee, 1964; Chairman, Glenlivet and Glen Grant Distilleries Ltd., 1964-70; Chairman, Glenlivet Distillers Ltd., 1970-77; Trustee, King George's Jubilee Trust, London, 1967-71; FRSA, 1971; Trustee, Churchill Trust, 1973-76; Member, Board, Courage Ltd., 1974-77; Chairman, Seagram Distillers Ltd. (in London), 1977-82; CBIM, 1983. Recreations: shooting; fishing. Address: (b.) Lochnabo, Lhanbryde, Moray; T.-01343 842228.

Terrell, Harry, MA, JP. Chief Executive, Dundee and Tayside Chamber of Commerce and Industry, since 1978; Member, Industrial Tribunals, since 1986; b. 2.8.38, Dundee; m., Patricia Mary Milgate; 1 s. Educ. Royal High School, Edinburgh; Dundee University. H.M. Diplomatic Service, 1955-66; Confederation of British Industry, 1970-76; Export Group for the Constructional Industries, 1976-77. Member, Advisory Board, Salvation Army, Dundee; Member, Management Committee, Dundee Citizens' Advice Bureau. Recreations: curling; reading. Address: (b.) Panmure Street, Dundee, DD1 1ED; T.-01382 201122.

Terry, Peter Brian, MB, ChB, MD, FRCS Edin, FRCOG. Consultant Obstetrician and Gynaecologist, since 1986; b. 3.6.52, Hillingdon; m., Gillian Margaret; 3 s. Educ. Merchant Taylors'; Edinburgh University Medical School. SHO, Simpson Memorial Maternity Pavilion, Edinburgh, 1977, Cumberland Infirmary, Carlisle, 1978; Registrar, Obstetrics and Gynaecology, Dudley Road Hospital, Birmingham, 1979; Research Registrar, 1982; Senior Registrar, Obstetrics and Gynaecology, Aberdeen, 1983; Consultant, 1986. Recreations: gardening; golf; walking. Address: (h.) 60 Forest Road, Aberdeen, AB15 4BP; T.-01224 317560.

Tervet, David John, BSc, MSc, PhD, CChem, MRSC, FCIWEM, MIMgt. Divisional Manager, Scottish Environment Protection Agency, since 1996 (Director, Solway River Purification Board, 1994-96); b. 29.6.47, Woodford Green; m., Janie; 3 s. Educ. Chigwell; Edinburgh University; Strathclyde University; Dundee University. Assistant Chemist, Fife and Kinross Water Board, 1973-74; Chemist, Chief Chemist, Chief Scientist/Depute Director, Solway River Purification Board, 1974-94. Publications: papers on water quality. Recreations: cricket; music; gardening; railways (Life Member, Festiniog Railway Society). Address: (b.) Rivers House, Irongray Road, Dumfries, DG2 0JE; T.-01387 720502.

Thin, David Ainslie, BSc. Chairman and Managing Director, James Thin Ltd., since 1962; Chairman, Book Tokens Ltd., 1987-95; Director, Edinburgh Book Festival; Member, Finance Committee, National Trust for Scotland; b. 9.7.33, Edinburgh; m., Elspeth J.M. Scott; 1 s.; 2 d. Educ. Edinburgh Academy; Loretto School; Edinburgh University. President, Booksellers Association of GB and Ireland, 1976-78. Recreations: golf; travelling; reading. Address: (h.) 60 Fountainhall Road, Edinburgh EH9 2LP; T.-0131-667 2725.

Thomaneck, Professor Jurgen Karl Albert, JP, MEd, Drphil, FRSA. Professor in German, Aberdeen University, since 1992; Aberdeen City Councillor, since 1996; President, Aberdeen Trades Council, since 1982; Convenor, Grampian Joint Police Board, since 1995; b. 12.6.41, Germany; m., Guinevere Ronald; 2 d. Educ. Universities of Kiel, Tubingen, Aberdeen. Lecturer in German, Aberdeen University, since 1968. Grampian Regional Councillor, 1984-96; Board Member, Grampian Enterprise Ltd., until 1995; President, KIMO UK, since 1996; author/editor of ten books, eight contributions to books, 28 articles in learned journals, all in German studies. Recreation: football. Address: (b.) Aberdeen University, Aberdeen AB25 3UB.

Thomas, Jeremy St. John, MA (Oxon), FRCPE, FRCPath. Consultant Pathologist, Western General Hospital, Edinburgh, since 1988; Secretary, Royal College of Physicians of Edinburgh, since 1993; b. 29.8.53, Cardiff; m., Dr. Valerie Doherty; 1 s.; 1 d. Educ. Lincoln College, Oxford; St. Thomas's Hospital, London. Trained in general medicine and pathology, Western Infirmary, Glasgow, 1979-88. Recreations: rugby football; antique rugs; photography. Address: (b.) Department of Pathology, Western General Hospital, Edinburgh; T.-0131-537 1961.

Thomas, Joseph Healy. Provost, West Lothian Council, since 1995; b. 13.10.36, Fauldhouse; m., Mary Anna Welsh; 2 s.; 3 d. Educ. St. Mary's Senior Secondary School, Bathgate; Falkirk Technical College. JP, 1977-97; mine deputy, 1984-85; Depute Leader, West Lothian District Council, 1992-95. Recreations: walking; hill-climbing; reading; football as a spectator. Address: (b.) West Lothian House, Almondvale Boulevard, Livingston EH54 6QG; T.-01506 777022.

Thomas, Professor Lyn Carey, MA, DPhil (Oxon), FIMA, FRSE. Professor of Management Science, Edinburgh University, since 1985 (Head, Department of Business Studies, 1987-90); b. 10.8.46, Dowlais; m., Margery Wynn Bright; 2 s.; 1 d. Educ. Lewis School, Pengam; Jesus College, Oxford. Research Fellow, University College,

Swansea, 1971-74; Lecturer in Decision Theory, then Senior Lecturer, Manchester University, 1974-85; Senior NRC Fellow, Naval Postgraduate School, Monterey, California, 1982-83; President, Operational Research Society, 1994-95; Associate Editor, Naval Research Logistics; Editor, IMA Journal of Mathematics applied in Business and Industry. Publications: Games, Theory and Applications, 1984; Operational Research Techniques, 1986; Credit Scoring and Credit Control, 1992. Recreations: reading; rugby; walking. Address: (b.) Department of Business Studies, William Robertson Building, 50 George Square, Edinburgh; T.-0131-650 3798.

Thomas, Professor Michael Frederic, MA, PhD, FGS, FRSE. Professor of Environmental Science, Stirling University, since 1980; b. 15.9.33, London; m., Elizabeth Anne Dadley (deceased); 1 s.; 1 d. Educ. Royal Grammar School, Guildford; Reading University. Assistant Lecturer in Geography, Magee University College, Londonderry, 1957-60; Lecturer, Ibadan University, Nigeria, 1960-64; Lecturer, then Senior Lecturer, St. Andrews University, 1964-79; visiting appointments, Universities of Canterbury (New Zealand), New South Wales, Natal, and Sierra Leone. Council Member, Royal Scottish Geographical Society; Past Chairman, British Geomorphological Research Group; Vice Chairman, Scottish Environmental Education Council. Publications: Tropical Geomorphology, 1974; Geomorphology in the Tropics, 1994. Recreations: listening to music; hill-walking; travel. Address: (b.) Department of Environmental Science, Stirling University, Stirling FK9 4LA; T.-01786 67840.

Thomas, Professor Michael James, OM (Poland), BSc, MBA, FRSA, FCIM. Professor of Marketing, Strathclyde University, since 1987; b. 15.7.33; m.; 1 s.; 1 d. Educ. University College London; Indiana University. Metal Box Co. Ltd., London, 1957-60; Syracuse University Management School, 1960-71; Lancaster University, 1972-86; former National Chairman, Chartered Institute of Marketing. Recreation: ornithology. Address: (b.) Strathclyde University, Glasgow G4 ORQ.

Thomas, Professor Phillip Charles, BSc, PhD, FIBiol, CBiol, FRAgS, FRSE. Principal and Chief Executive, The Scottish Agricultural College, since 1990; Professor of Agriculture, Glasgow University, since 1987; Honorary Professor, Edinburgh University, since 1991; b. 17.6.42, Pontypool; m., Pamela Mary Hirst; 1 s.; 1 d. Educ. Abersychan Grammar School; University College of North Wales, Bangor. Lecturer, Department of Animal Nutrition and Physiology, Leeds University, 1966-71; Research Scientist, Hannah Research Institute, Ayr, 1971-87; Principal, West of Scotland College, Ayr, 1987-90. Publications: Nutritional Physiology of Farm Animals, 1983; Silage for Milk Production, 1983. Address: (b.) The Scottish Agricultural College, Central Office, West Mains Road, Edinburgh EH9 3JG.

Thompson, Professor Alan Eric, MA (Hons), PhD, FRSA, FSA(Scot). Emeritus Professor of the Economics of Government, Heriot-Watt University; b. 16.9.24; m., Mary Heather Long; 3 s.; 1 d. Educ. Edinburgh University. Edinburgh University: Assistant in Political Economy, 1952-53, Lecturer in Economics, 1953-59 and 1964-71; Professor of the Economics of Government, Heriot-Watt University, 1972-87; Parliamentary Labour candidate, Galloway, 1950, 1951; MP (Labour), Dunfermline, 1959-64; Member, Royal Fine Art Commission for Scotland, 1975-80; Chairman, Northern Offshore Maritime Resources Study, 1974-83; Governor, Newbattle Abbey College, 1975-85 (Chairman, 1980-83); Member, Local Government Boundaries Commission for Scotland, 1975-80; Member, Scottish Council for Adult Education in HM Forces, since 1973; BBC National Governor for Scotland, 1975-79; Governor, Leith Nautical College, 1981-85; Trustee, Bell's Nautical Trust, 1981-85; Parliamentary Adviser, Scottish

Pharmaceutical General Council, since 1984. Publications: Development of Economic Doctrine (Co-author), 1980; articles in academic journals. Recreation: writing children's stories and plays. Address: (h.) 11 Upper Gray Street, Edinburgh EH9 1SN; T.-0131-667 2140.

Thompson, Colin, CBE, DUniv, FRSE, MA, FMA. Writer, Lecturer and Broadcaster on art and museums; b. 2.11.19, Berkhamstead; m., Jean A.J. O'Connell; 1 s.; 1 d. Educ. Sedbergh; King's College, Cambridge; Chelsea Polytechnic. Lecturer, Bath Academy of Art, Corsham, 1948-54; joined National Gallery of Scotland as Assistant Keeper, 1954; Director, National Galleries of Scotland, 1977-84. Member: Scottish Arts Council, 1976-83, Edinburgh Festival Society, since 1979, Expert Advisory Panel on Museums to Heritage Lottery Fund, since 1995; Chairman, Scottish Museums Council, 1984-87; Chairman, Board of Governors, Edinburgh College of Art, 1989-91; Trustee, Buccleuch Heritage Trust, since 1988; Member, Scottish Mining Museum Trust, since 1987 (Chairman, 1992-96). Publications: Pictures for Scotland, 1972; Hugo Van Der Goes and the Trinity Panels in Edinburgh (Co-author), 1974; Exploring Museums: Scotland, 1990. Address: (h.) Edenkerry, Lasswade, Midlothian EH18 1LW; T.-0131-663 7927.

Thompson, David George, MITSA, MAPEA, DCA, FIMgt. Director of Protective Services, Highland Council, since 1996 (Director of Trading Standards, Highland Regional Council, 1986-96); b. 20.9.49, Lossiemouth; m., Veronica; 1 s.; 3 d. Educ. Lossiemouth High School. Trainee, then Trading Standards Officer, Banff, Moray and Nairn Joint CC, 1967-73; Assistant Chief Trading Standards Officer, Ross & Cromarty County Council, 1973-75; Chief Trading Standards Officer, Western Isles Islands Council, 1975-83; Depute Director of Trading Standards, Highland Regional Council, 1983-86. Secretary/Treasurer, Scottish Branch, Institute of Trading Standards Administration, 1985-87, Chairman, 1988-89; Secretary/Treasurer, Society of Directors of Trading Standards in Scotland, 1987-89, Chairman, 1991-93. Recreations: golf; DIY; reading; Speakers' Club. Address: (h.) Balnafettack Farmhouse, Leachkin Road, Inverness; T.-01463 221555.

Thompson, Francis George, IEng, FIElecIE, MIExE, FSA (Scot). Author of books on Highland subjects; retired Senior Lecturer, Lews Castle College, Stornoway; Director, Western Isles Development Fund; b. 29.3.31, Stornoway; m., Margaret Elaine Pullar; 1 s.; 3 d. Educ. Nicolson Institute, Stornoway. From 1946: supply maintenance electrician, technical writer, assistant publicity manager, lecturer; has held various offices within An Comann Gaidhealach, including editorship of Sruth, bilingual newspaper, 1967-71; books include: Harris and Lewis, 1968; Harris Tweed, 1969; Highlands and Islands, 1974; Crofting Years, 1985; Shell Guide to Northern Scotland, 1987; The Western Isles, 1988; The First Hundred, 1992. Recreation: writing! Address: Am Fasgadh, 5 Rathad na Muilne, Stornoway, Lewis; T.-01851 703812.

Thompson, Professor Paul Ian, BA (Hons), PhD. Professor of Management, Edinburgh University, since 1994; b. 1.1.51, Wallasey; 1 d. Educ. Maghull Grammar School; Liverpool University. Lecturer in Sociology, St. Helen's College of Technology, 1974-84; appointed Senior Lecturer in Organisation Studies, Lancashire Polytechnic, 1984, going on to become Principal Lecturer and Professor in new University of Central Lancashire; Visiting Professor, Institute for Advanced Studies, Vienna, 1987, Institute of Business, Beijing, 1989; Visiting Principal Fellow, University of Wollongong, Australia, 1997; Editor, Renewal (a journal of New Labour politics), since 1993. Recreations: music; cinema; playing and watching football, especially Everton F.C. Address: (b.) Department of Business Studies, Edinburgh University, 50 George Square, Edinburgh EH8 5JY; T.-0131-650 3811.

Thomson, Brian M. Managing Director, D. C. Thomson & Co. Ltd. Address: (b.) Courier Buildings, 2 Albert Square, Dundee, DD1 9QJ.

Thomson, Professor Derick S., MA (Aberdeen), BA (Cantab), DLitt (Univ. of Wales), DLitt (Univ. of Aberdeen), FRSE, FBA. Professor of Celtic, Glasgow University, 1963-91; b. 5.8.21, Stornoway; m., Carol Galbraith; 5 s.; 1 d. Educ. Nicolson Institute, Stornoway; Aberdeen University; Cambridge University; University College of North Wales, Bangor. Taught at Edinburgh, Glasgow and Aberdeen Universities before returning to Glasgow as Professor, 1963; Chairman, Gaelic Books Council, 1968-91; Hon. President, Scottish Gaelic Texts Society; former Member, Scottish Arts Council; first recipient, Ossian Prize, 1974; author of numerous books and articles, including An Introduction to Gaelic Poetry, The Companion to Gaelic Scotland, European Poetry in Gaelic and collections of Gaelic poetry, including collected poems Creachadh na Clarsaich and Meall Garbh/Rugged Mountain; Editor, Gairm, since 1952. Address: (h.) 15 Struan Road, Cathcart, Glasgow G44 3AT; T.-0141-637 3704.

Thomson, Sir (Frederick Douglas) David, Bt, BA. Chairman, Britannia Steam Ship Insurance Association Limited, since 1986 (Director, since 1965); Director, Cairn Energy PLC, since 1971; Chairman, Through Transport Marine Mutual Assurance Association (Bermuda) Ltd., since 1983 (Director, since 1973); Director, Danae Investment Trust Ltd., since 1979; Chairman, Jove Investment Trust PLC, since 1983; Director, Martin Currie Pacific Trust PLC, since 1985; Chairman, Abtrust European Index Investment Trust PLC, since 1990; Chairman, Ptarmigan International Capital Trust PLC, since 1990; Director, Kynoch Group PLC, since 1991; Director, James Fisher and Sons PLC, since 1993; Chairman, Wright & Jobson (Galashiels) Ltd., since 1996; Chairman, S.A. Meacock & Co. Ltd., since 1996; Director, Ionian Group Ltd., since 1994. Chairman, Laurence J. Smith Ltd., since 1993; Director, Asset Management Investment Company PLC, since 1994; Member, Royal Company of Archers (Queen's Bodyguard for Scotland); b. 14.2.40, Edinburgh; 2 s.; 1 d. Educ. Eton; University College, Oxford. Recreations: shooting; skiing; tennis; bonfires. Address: (h.) Holylee, Walkerburn, Peeblesshire; T.-01896 870673.

Thomson, Geddes, MA (Hons). Writer, former teacher; b. 20.9.39, Dalry; m., Lucy Faulkner; 2 s. Educ. Dalry High School; Glasgow University. Principal Teacher of English, Allan Glen's School, Glasgow, 1972-89; Shawlands Academy, Glasgow, 1989-93; Extra-Mural Lecturer, Department of Adult and Continuing Education, Glasgow University, 1985-93. Publications include: A Spurious Grace, 1981; Identities (Editor), 1981; The Poetry of Edwin Morgan, 1986. Recreations: supporting Partick Thistle; fishing; browsing in bookshops. Address: (h.) 48 Windyedge Crescent, Glasgow G13 1YF; T.-0141-959 5277.

Thomson, George Buchanan, FCIBS; b. 10.1.24, Glasgow, m., Margaret Irene Williams. Educ. Eastwood Secondary School. Joined Union Bank of Scotland, 1940; War Service, 1942-46 with RAF (Navigator, Bomber Command); held various banking appointments, 1947-86; retired as Assistant General Manager (Branch Administration, West), Bank of Scotland; Past President, Institute of Bankers in Scotland; Director and Chairman, Association for the Relief of Incurables; Hon. Treasurer, Scottish Civic Trust; former Convener, Board of Stewardship and Finance, Church of Scotland; Director, Ian Skelly Holdings Ltd., 1986-89; Director, Clydesdale Development Company, 1988-95. Recreations: curling; bowling. Address: (h.) Kingswood, 26 Waverley Avenue, Helensburgh G84 7JU; T.-01436 672915.

Thomson, George Preston. Board Director, United Distillers, responsible for Specialist Off-Licence Division, since 1996; b. 31.5.54, Lenzie; m., Gillian Kidd; 1 s.; 1 d. Educ. Lenzie Academy; Central College of Commerce, Glasgow; Glasgow College of Technology. Export Correspondent, White Horse Distillers, 1973-78; Sales Administration Manager, Export Sales Manager, Bass Export Ltd., 1978-84; External Accounts Manager, Charles Wells Ltd., 1984-87; joined United Distillers, 1987. Recreations: reading; music (eclectic); running; rugby; football. Address: (b.) United Distillers, Cherrybank, Perth PH2 0NG; T.-01738 621111.

Thomson, Rev. Iain Urquhart. Minister, Parish of Skene, since 1972; Clerk, Presbytery of Gordon, since 1988; b. 13.12.45, Dundee; m., Christine Freeland; 1 s.; 2 d. Educ. Harris Academy, Dundee; Inverness Royal Academy; Aberdeen University; Christ's College, Aberdeen. Assistant Minister, Castlehill Church, Ayr, 1970-72. Clerk and Treasurer, Synod of Grampian Trusts Committee, since 1993; Member, Skene School Board. Recreations: golf; theatre. Address: The Manse, Kirkton of Skene, Westhill, Aberdeenshire AB32 6LX; T.-01224 743277.

Thomson, Sir John Adam, GCMG. Chairman, Minority Rights Group, since 1991; International Adviser, ANZ Grindlays Bank, since 1996; Chairman, Flemings Emerging Markets Investment Trust, since 1990; b. 27.4.27, Bieldside, Aberdeen; m., 1, Elizabeth Anne McClure (deceased); 3 s.; 1 d.; 2, Judith Ogden Bullitt. Educ. Aberdeen University; Trinity College, Cambridge. Joined Foreign Office, 1950; seconded to Cabinet Office as Chief of Assessment Staff, 1968-71; Minister and Deputy Permanent Representative, NATO, 1972; Head of UK Delegation, MBFR Exploratory Talks, Vienna, 1973; Assistant Under Secretary for Defence and Disarmament, 1973-76; British High Commissioner in India, 1977-82; British Permanent Representative and Ambassador to UN, 1982-87; Principal Director, 21st Century Trust, 1987-90; Director, ANZ Grindlays, 1987-96; Director's Visitor, Institute for Advanced Studies, Princeton, 1995-96. Trustee, National Museums of Scotland; Member, Council, International Institute of Strategic Studies; Trustee, Aberdeen University Development Trust; Trustee, Indian National Trust for Art and Cultural Heritage; Member, Governing Body, IDS and ODI. Recreations: hill-walking; tennis. Address: (h.) Kirkpatrick Durham, Castle Douglas, Dumfries and Galloway.

Thomson, Professor John Aidan Francis, MA, DPhil, FRHistS. Professor of Mediaeval History, Glasgow University, since 1995; b. 26.7.34, Edinburgh; m., Katherine J.V. Bell; 1 s.; 1 d. Educ. George Watson's Boys' College, Edinburgh; Edinburgh University; Balliol College, Oxford. Glasgow University: Assistant in Mediaeval History, 1960, Lecturer, 1961, Senior Lecturer, 1974, Reader, 1983, Titular Professor, 1994. President, Glasgow Archaeological Society, 1978-81. Publications: The Later Lollards 1414-1520, 1965; Popes and Princes 1417-1517, 1980; The Transformation of Mediaeval England 1370-1529, 1983; Towns and Townspeople in the Fifteenth Century (Editor), 1988; The Early Tudor Church and Society, 1485-1529, 1993. Recreations: travel and sightseeing; walking; gardening. Address: (b.) Department of Medieval History, Glasgow University, Glasgow G12 8QQ; T.-0141-339 8855.

Thomson, John Alexander, MD, PhD, FRCPGlas, FRCPLond. Reader in Medicine, University Department of Medicine, Glasgow University, since 1981; Honorary Consultant Physician, Glasgow Royal Infirmary, since 1968; b. 19.4.33, Airdrie; m., Fiona Jane Reid; 2 s.; 2 d. Educ. Hamilton Academy; Glasgow University. House Physician, then House Surgeon, Glasgow Royal Infirmary, 1956-57; Royal Army Medical Corps, 1957-59 (Regimental Medical Officer, 13/18 Royal Hussars); House Surgeon,

Glasgow Royal Maternity and Women's Hospital, 1959-60; McIntyre Clinical Research Scholar in Medicine, University Department of Medicine, 1960-61; Registrar in Medicine, then Senior Registrar, University Medical Unit, Glasgow Royal Infirmary, 1961-68; Senior Lecturer in Medicine and Consultant Endocrinologist, Glasgow Royal Infirmary, 1968-81. Address: (b.) University Department of Medicine, Royal Infirmary, 10 Alexandra Parade, Glasgow G31 2ER; T.-0141-211 5410.

Thomson, Rev. John Morria Arnott, TD, BD, ThM. Minister, Lanark St. Nicholas, since 1988; b. 27.2.49, Buckhaven; m., Marlene Jeffrey Logan; 1 s.; 1 d. Educ. Irvine Royal Academy; Glasgow University; Columbia Theological Seminary, Atlanta, Georgia. Journalist, Irvine Herald; Executive Officer, Environment Research Council; Finance/Administration Officer, Irvine New Town Corporation; Assistant Project Co-ordinator, Wiltshire County Council; Minister, Houston and Killellan Kirk, 1978-88. Chaplain, Clyde Division RNR, 1986-92; Chaplain, 105 Regt. RA (V), since 1992; Chaplain, Lanark Lord Cornets Club; Depute Clerk, Lanark Presbytery. Recreations: sailing; writing; music; Romanian and Eastern Europe aid. Address: St. Nicholas Manse, 32 Braxfield Road, Lanark ML11 9BS; T.-01555 662600.

Thomson, Professor Joseph McGeachy, LLB, FRSE, FRSA. Regius Professor of Law, Glasgow University, since 1991; Deputy General Editor, Stair Memorial Encyclopaedia of the Laws of Scotland, since 1985; b. 6.5.48, Campbeltown. Educ. Keil School, Dumbarton; Edinburgh University. Lecturer in Law, Birmingham University, 1970-74; Lecturer in Laws, King's College, London, 1974-84; Professor of Law, Strathclyde University, 1984-90. Recreations: opera; ballet; food and wine. Address: (h.) 2 Kew Terrace, Glasgow; T.-0141-334 6682.

Thomson, Professor Kenneth James, MA, MSc, MS. Professor of Agricultural Economics, Aberdeen University, since 1986; b. 30.9.45, Aberdeen; m., Lydia. Educ. Aberdeen Grammar School; Aberdeen University; London University; Iowa State University. Lecturer and Senior Lecturer, Department of Agricultural Economics, Newcastle upon Tyne University, 1972-86. Editor, Journal of Agricultural Economics, 1987-93. Publication: The Cost of the Common Agricultural Policy, 1982. Recreations: viola-playing; mountaineering. Address: (b.) School of Agriculture, 581 King Street, Aberdeen, AB24 5UA; T.-01224 274139.

Thomson, Kirsteen Isabel Scott, MSc, AADip, ARIAS, MRTPI. Executive Director, Edinburgh Old Town Renewal Trust, since 1996; b. 31.8.49, Cardiff; 1 s.; 1 d. Educ. Malvern Girls College; Architectural Association, London; Edinburgh University. Principal, Scott Thomson, 1980-85; Programme Manager, The Planning Exchange, Glasgow, 1985-87; Principal, Scott Thomson, 1987-90; Economic Development Officer, Stirling District Council, 1990-92; Project Executive, Edinburgh Old Town Renewal Trust, 1992-96. Recreations: family; gardening; old buildings; walking; rock climbing. Address: (b.) 343 High Street, Edinburgh, EH1 1PW; T.-0131-225 8818.

Thomson, Malcolm George, QC, LLB. Practice at Scottish Bar, since 1974; b. 6.4.50, Edinburgh; m., Susan Gordon; 2 d. Educ. Edinburgh Academy; Edinburgh University. Standing Junior Counsel, Department of Agriculture and Fisheries and Forestry Commission, 1982-87; QC (Scotland), 1987; called to the Bar, Lincoln's Inn, 1991; Chairman, National Health Service Tribunal, Scotland, since 1995. Editor, Scots Law Times Reports, since 1989; Scottish Case Editor, Current Law, since 1977. Recreations: sailing; skiing. Address: (h.)12 Succoth Avenue, Edinburgh EH12 6BT; T.-0131-337 4911.

Thomson, Michael Stuart MacGregor, MA, CA. Director of Finance and Administration, Royal Scottish Society for Prevention of Cruelty to Children, since 1991; b. 4.5.38, Perth; m., Rosemary; 2 s.; 1 d. Educ. Gordonstoun; St. Andrews University. CA apprenticeship, 1960-63; Director, then Managing Director, Peter Thomson (Perth) Ltd., 1963-85; Michael Thomson & Co., 1985-91; Balbirnie House Hotel Ltd., 1987-91. Lord Dean of the Guildry Incorporation of Perth, 1973-76, Publication: Background to Collecting Doulton Art Pottery. Recreations: grandparenting; footering; adventures; travel; sport. Address: (b.) 41 Polwarth Terrace, Edinburgh EH11 1NU; T.-0131-337 8539.

Thomson, Sheriff Nigel Ernest Drummond, CBE, MA, LLB. Sheriff of Lothian and Borders, at Edinburgh, 1976-96; b. 19.6.26, Aberdeen; m., Snjolaug Magnusson; 1 s.; 1 d. Educ. George Watson's Boys' College; St. Andrews University; Edinburgh University. Called to Scottish Bar, 1953; appointed Sheriff at Hamilton, 1966; Member, Scottish Arts Council, 1978 (Chairman, Music Committee, 1979-84). Hon. President, Strathaven Arts Guild; Hon. Vice-President, Tenovus-Scotland; Hon. President, Scottish Association for Counselling, 1986-89; Vice President, British Association for Counselling, since 1992; Chairman, Edinburgh Youth Orchestra Society, 1986-92; Convenor, Council for Music in Hospitals in Scotland, since 1992; Honorary Texas Ranger, 1994. Recreations: music; woodwork; golf. Address: (h.) 50 Grange Road, Edinburgh; T.-0131-667 2166.

Thomson, Rev. Peter David, MA, BD. Minister, Comrie and Strowan with Dundurn, since 1978; b. 4.11.41, St. Andrews; m., Margaret Celia Murray; 1 s.; 1 d. Educ. Dundee High School; Edinburgh University; Glasgow University; Tubingen University. Minister, Balmaclellan with Kells, 1968-78; Moderator, Kirkcudbright Presbytery, 1974-75; Convener, Nomination Committee, General Assembly, 1982-85. Chairman, New Galloway and Kells Community Council, 1976-78; Moderator, Perth Presbytery, 1988-89. Recreations: haphazardly pursued interests in photography, wildlife, music, theology, current affairs. Address: The Manse, Comrie, Perthshire, PH6 2HE; T.-01764 670269.

Thomson, Professor Richard Ian, MA, DipHistArt (Oxon), MA, PhD. Watson Gordon Professor of Fine Art, Edinburgh University, since 1996; b. 1.3.53, Tenterden; m., Belina Jane Greaves; 2 s. Educ. Dragon School, Oxford; Shrewsbury School; St. Catherine's College, Oxford; Courtauld Institute of Art, London University. Lecturer/Senior Lecturer/Reader, Manchester University, 1977-96; Curator or Co-Curator of several exhibitions. Publications: Toulouse-Lautrec, 1977; Seurat, 1985; Degas: The Nudes, 1988; Edgar Degas: Waiting, 1995. Recreations: jazz; gardening. Address: (b.) Department of Fine Art, Edinburgh University, 19 George Square, Edinburgh EH8 9LD; T.-0131-650 4124.

Thomson, Roy Hendry, CStJ, MA (Hons). President, Scottish Liberal Democrats; President, Mental Health Aberdeen; Chairman, Friends of Aberdeen University Library; Director, Kaleidoscope, Aberdeen International Children's Festival; Marketing Director, Aberdeen International's Youth Festival; b. 27.8.32, Aberdeen; m., Nancy; 3 d. Educ. Aberdeen Grammar School; Aberdeen University. National Service, Gordon Highlanders, 1955-57; personnel and market research, Rowntree & Co. Ltd., 1957-60; Chairman/Director, family motor business, until 1986; former Director, The Scottish Ballet (Chairman, 1983-87); former Member, City of Aberdeen District Council; Past President: Rotary Club of Aberdeen, Mountain Rescue Association, Aberdeen; former Chairman, Scottish Liberal Democrats. Recreations: skiing; hill-walking. Address: (h.) 5 Baillieswells Grove, Bieldside, Aberdeen AB5 9BH; T.-Aberdeen 861628.

Thomson, Professor Samuel J., BSc, PhD, DSc, CChem, FRSC, FRSE. Professor Emeritus, Glasgow University, since 1987; Honorary Senior Research Fellow, since 1987; Adviser to BR Transrail, then to EWS Railway, since 1996; b. 27.9.22, Hamilton; m., Christina M. Mactaggart, BSc, PhD; 1 s.; 1 d. Educ. Hamilton Academy; Glasgow University. Lt., Royal Signals, 1944; Lecturer in Radiochemistry, Durham University, 1951; Lecturer, Senior Lecturer, Reader, Titular Professor, Glasgow University, 1957-87. Member, British Railways Board, Scottish Committee, 1989-94; Adviser to BR Railfreight Distribution, 1994-96. Publications: books and papers on surface chemistry and catalysis, etc. Recreations: visual perception; reading. Address: (h.) 10 Balfleurs Street, Milngavie, Glasgow G62 8HW; T.-0141-956 2622.

Thomson, S. Kenneth, MHSM, DipHSM. Chief Executive, Yorkhill NHS Trust, since 1997; Conductor, Glasgow Gaelic Musical Association, since 1983; b. 20.8.49, Campbeltown; m., Valerie Ferguson; 1 s.; 1 d. Educ. Keil School, Dumbarton. Administrative trainee, Scottish Health Service; hospital administrator; Unit Administrator, Argyll and Clyde Health Board, Renfrew Unit; Unit General Manager, Argyll and Dumbarton Unit; Unit General Manager, Lanarkshire Health Board, Law Hospital Unit; Chief Executive, Law Hospital NHS Trust. National Mod Gold Medallist, 1979; Governor, Keil School, since 1995. Recreations: opera; Gaelic language and culture; theatre; The Archers; EastEnders; swimming. Address: (b.) Yorkshire NHS Trust, Royal Hospital for Sick Children, Yorkhill, Glasgow G3 8SJ; T.-0141-201 0473.

Thomson, Stuart James, HND (Agric). Chief Executive, Ayrshire Cattle Society of GB and Ireland, since 1984; Managing Director, Cattle Services (Ayr) Ltd.; Managing Director, Ayrshire's Milk Marketing Ltd.; Executive Director, World Federation Ayrshire Breed Societies; b. 29.8.54, Kirkwall; m., Carolynne Henderson; 1 s. Educ. Kirkwall Grammar School; School of Agriculture, Aberdeen. Regional Officer, North of Scotland Milk Marketing Board, 1976-84. served, Executive Committee, National Cattle Association. Recreations: gardening; golf; fishing. Address: (b.) 1 Racecourse Road, Ayr KA7 2DE; T.-01292 267123.

Thomson, Sir Thomas James, Kt (1991), CBE (1983), OBE (1978), MB, ChB, FRCPGlas, FRCPLond, FRCPEdin, FRCPIre. Chairman, Greater Glasgow Health Board, 1987-93; Member, Court, University of Strathclyde, 1992-97; b. 8.4.23, Airdrie; m., Jessie Smith Shotbolt; 2 s.; 1 d. Educ. Airdrie Academy; Glasgow University. Lecturer, Department of Materia Medica, Glasgow University, 1953-61; Postgraduate Adviser to Glasgow Northern Hospitals, 1961-80; Honorary Secretary, RCPSGlas, 1965-73; Secretary, Specialist Advisory Committee for General Internal Medicine for UK, 1970-74; Chairman: Medico-Pharmaceutical Forum, 1978-80 (Chairman, Education Advisory Board, 1979-83); Conference of Royal Colleges and Faculties in Scotland, 1982-85; National Medical Consultative Committee for Scotland, 1982-87; President, RCPSGlas, 1982-84; Hon.FACP, 1983; Hon. LLD, Glasgow University, 1988, DUniv, Strathclyde University, 1997. Publications: Dilling's Pharmacology (Co-Editor); Gastroenterology - an integrated course. Recreations: swimming; golfing. Address: (h.) 1 Varna Road, Glasgow G14 9NE; T.-0141-959 5930.

Thorley, George William Faulds, BA (Hons), DipTP, MSc, FRSA, MRTPI. Chief Executive, South Ayrshire Council, since 1995; Assistant Chief Executive, Strathclyde Regional Council, 1990-95; b. 19.1.48, Dundee; m., Anne; 2 d. Educ. St. Michael's Secondary School, Dundee; Lawside Academy, Dundee; Strathclyde University. Joined Strathclyde Regional Council, 1975, as Senior Planner/Economist; joined Chief Executive's Department, 1980, as Senior Executive (Economic Strategy).

Recreations: gardening; badminton; music; visual arts. Address: (b.) County Buildings, Wellington Square, Ayr, KA7 1DR; T.-01292 612170.

Thornton-Kemsley, Nigel Scott, CBE (1987), DL. Managing Director, Thornton Enterprises Ltd.; Managing Director, Thornton Farms Ltd., 1956-88; Chairman, North of Scotland College of Agriculture, 1982-88; Director, Royal Highland and Agricultural Society of Scotland, 1971-88; Director, Scottish Agricultural Colleges, 1987-88; Governor, Rowett Research Institute, 1981-88; b. 14.8.33, Chigwell, Essex; m., Judith Gay Sanders; 1 s.; 2 d. Educ. Fettes College; East of Scotland College of Agriculture. National Service: Royal Signals, 1954-56, TA 51st Highland Signal Regiment, 1957-63, 3rd Bn., Gordon Highlanders, 1963-71, OC TAVR Company; Major on retiral; Deputy Lieutenant, Kincardineshire, 1978; Member, Grampian Health Board, 1989-93; President, Aberdeen-Angus Cattle Society, 1981-82; Member, Scottish American Community Relations Council, 1971-80; Chairman, Council, Scottish Agricultural Colleges, 1982-84; Life Governor, Imperial Cancer Research Council, since 1978; Past President, Royal Northern Agricultural Society; Past President, Fettercairn Farmers' Club. Recreation: fishing. Address: Thornton Castle, Laurencekirk, Kincardineshire; T.-01561 377301.

Thorpe, John Elton, BA, PhD. Leverhulme Emeritus Fellow, 1995-97, and Visiting Professor, Glasgow University Institute of Biomedical and Life Sciences; Professor, University of Bergen Institute of Biology; Emeritus Fellow, American Institute of Fishery Biologists; formerly Senior Principal Scientific Officer, Freshwater Fisheries Laboratory, Pitlochry; b. 24.1.35, Wolverhampton; m., Judith Anne Johnson; 2 s. Educ. Kingswood School, Bath; Jesus College, Cambridge. Cambridge Expedition to British Honduras, 1959-60 (Leader); Shell International Chemical Co. Ltd., London, 1960-62; joined DAFS Freshwater Fisheries Laboratory, Pitlochry, 1963. Vice-President, Fisheries Society of British Isles, 1988-93; Editor, Journal of Fish Biology, since 1991; Member, Editorial Board: Journal of Animal Ecology, since 1988, Reviews in Fish and Fisheries, since 1989, Fisheries Management, 1978-84, and Aquaculture and Fisheries Management, since 1985; Chairman, Killiecrankie and Fincastle Community Council, 1976-78. Special Medal, University of Lodz, Poland, 1992. Publications: nine books; 220 scientific papers. Recreations: travelling; Baroque music. Address: (h.) Piper's Croft, Killiecrankie, Perthshire PH16 5LW; T.-01796 47 3886.

Thrower, Rev. Charles George, BSc. Minister, Carnbee linked with Pittenweem, since 1970; Moderator, St. Andrews Presbytery, 1991-92; b. 22.11.37, Barton Turf, Norfolk; m., Dr. Stephanie A.M. Thrower; 1 s.; 3 d. Educ. King Edward VI School, Norwich; Britannia Royal Naval College, Dartmouth. Electrical branch training H.M.S. Girdle-Ness (Malta), 1960-61; divinity student, St. Mary's, 1961-64; probationer, St. Andrews Church, Dundee, 1964-65; missionary appointment, Hampden with Falmouth, Trelawny, Jamaica, 1966-70. Synod of Fife Youth Adviser, 1971-74; Chairman, East Neuk of Fife Committee, Children 1st, since 1974, and Member, Children 1st Policy and Resources Committee. Recreations: art; photography; sailing; gardening; local church history. Address: The Manse, 2 Milton Place, Pittenweem, Fife, KY10 2LR; T.-01333 311255.

Thrower, Professor James Arthur, BLitt, MA, PhD, FRAS. Professor of the History of Religions and Director, Centre for the Study of Religions, Aberdeen University, since 1994; b. 5.10.36, Guisborough; m., Judith Elizabeth Gauss; 3 d. Educ. Guisborough Grammar School; St. Chad's College, Durham; St. Edmund Hall, Oxford. Staff-Tutor, Eastern District, WEA, 1962-64; Lecturer in Philosophy of Religion, Ghana University, 1964-68;

Lecturer in Religious Studies, Bede College, Durham, 1968-70; Lecturer in Religious Studies, Aberdeen University, 1970 (Senior Lecturer, 1981, Reader, 1993, Head of Department, 1984-87); Riddoch Lecturer, since 1984; Visiting Professor: Helsinki University, 1974, Polish Academy of Sciences, 1976, Aligarh Muslim University, India, 1988; British Council Exchange Scholar, Leningrad University, 1976 and 1978; Visiting Scholar, Gdansk University, 1981 and 1982; British Academy exchange scholar Chinese Academy of Social Sciences, 1989; GLCA-Scotland, Visiting Fellow, De Pauw University, Indiana, 1998; Warden, Balgownie Lodge, Aberdeen University, 1971-82. Author of a number of books and articles about the history of religions. Recreations: travel and exploration; classical music; opera; ballet. (h.) 2 Riverside Mill Cottages, Bridge of Don AB23 8LZ; T.- Aberdeen 822127.

Thyne, Malcolm Tod, MA, FRSE. Headmaster, Fettes College, since 1988; b. 6.11.42, Edinburgh; m., Eleanor Christine Scott; 2 s. Educ. The Leys School, Cambridge; Clare College, Cambridge. Assistant Master, Edinburgh Academy, 1965-69; Assistant Master, Oundle School, 1969-80 (Housemaster, 1972-80); Headmaster, St. Bees School, Cumbria, 1980-88. Publications: Periodicity, Atomic Structure and Bonding (Revised Nuffield Chemistry), 1976; contributions to Revised Nuffield Chemistry Handbook for Pupils and Teachers Guides, 1978. Recreations: mountaineering; ski-ing. Address: (b.) Fettes College, Edinburgh EH4 1QX; T.-0131-332 2281.

Tiefenbrun, Ivor Sigmund, MBE. Managing Director, Linn Products Ltd., Glasgow; Member, Design Council; b. 18.3.46, Glasgow; m., Evelyn Stella Balarksy; 2 s.; 1 d. Educ. Strathbungo Senior Secondary School; Strathclyde University (Sixties dropout). Worked overseas, 1971-73; founded Linn Products, 1973. Chairman, Federation of British Audio, 1983-87; Council Member, Design Council, since 1995. Recreations: thinking; music; reading; sailing. Address: (b.) Linn Products Ltd., Floors Road, Waterfoot, Eaglesham, Glasgow G76 0EP; T.-0141-307 7777.

Tierney, David A., BA (Hons). Rector, Speyside High School, Aberlour, since 1987; b. 15.1.50, Glasgow; m., Valerie Lauder; 2 s. Educ. Queen's Park School, Glasgow; Strathclyde University; Jordanhill College of Education; Glasgow University. Teacher, Govan High School, Glasgow, 1973-76; Principal Teacher of Modern Studies, Mackie Academy, 1976-83; Depute Rector, Speyside High School, 1983-87. Recreations: hill-walking; cycling; reading; gardening. Address: (b.) Speyside High School, Mary Avenue, Aberlour, Banff; T.-01340 871522.

Tildesley, James Michael. Director, Scottish Maritime Museum, since 1989; Chairman, Ayrshire and Arran Tourist Board; b. 10.3.47, Southminster; m., Janet Birks; 2 s.; 1 d. Educ. Chelmsford Technical High School; Goldsmiths' College, London University. Assistant Master, Mayfield School, Redbridge; Assistant Curator, then Deputy Curator, Passmore Edwards Museum; Assistant Director of Leisure, L.B. of Newham. Address: (b.) Scottish Maritime Museum, Laird Forge, Gottries Road, Irvine, KA12 8QE; T.-01294 278283.

Timms, Professor Peter Kenneth, MBE. Chairman, Board of Management, Glasgow University Business School, since 1991; Chairman and Managing Director, Flexible Technology Ltd., Bute, since 1981; Member, Highlands and Islands Enterprise, since 1990; Member, Scottish Industrial Development Advisory Board, since 1989; b. 2.12.43, Witney, Oxon; m., Patricia; 3 s. Educ. St. Edmund's School, Canterbury, Kent. Production Engineer, Texas Instruments Ltd., 1964; Manufacturing Engineer, then Process Engineering Manager, IBM UK Ltd., 1967; Director and General Manager, AFA Minerva, 1978. Non-Executive Director: Ferranti Technologies Ltd (Chairman, since 1995), Murray Enterprise plc, Scottish Electronics Technology Group Ltd. Recreations: boating; travel. Address: Millbrae, Ascog, Rothesay, Bute PA20 9ET; T.- 01700 504515.

Titterington, Professor (Donald) Michael, BSc, PhD, DipMathStat, FRSE. Professor of Statistics, Glasgow University, since 1988; b. 20.11.45, Marple, Cheshire; m., Mary Hourie Philp; 1 s. Educ. High School of Stirling; Edinburgh University; Cambridge University. Lecturer, then Senior Lecturer, then Titular Professor, Department of Statistics, Glasgow University, 1972-88; visiting appointments: Princeton University, 1978, State University of New York, 1980, Wisconsin University, 1982, Australian National University, 1982, 1994, 1995; Associate Editor, Biometrika, 1979-85, Annals of Statistics, 1983-85 and 1995-96, Journal, American Statistical Association, 1986-88 and 1991-96, and IEEE Transactions on Pattern Analysis and Machine Intelligence, 1994-96; Joint Editor, Journal of the Royal Statistical Society, Series B, 1986-89, and Statistical Science, 1992-94; Editor, Biometrika, since 1996; Council Member, Royal Statistical Society, 1987-92; elected Fellow, Institute of Mathematical Statistics, 1986; elected Member, International Statistical Institute, 1991. Publications: Statistical Analysis of Finite Mixture Distributions (Co-author); many journal articles. Recreation: being a father. Address: (b.) Department of Statistics, Glasgow University, Glasgow, G12 8QQ; T.- 0141-330 5022.

Tobin, Patrick Francis John, MA, PGCE, FRSA. Principal, Mary Erskine School and Daniel Stewart's & Melville College, since 1989; b. 4.10.41, London; m., Margery Ann Sluce; 1 s.; 3 d. Educ. St. Benedict's, Ealing; Christ Church, Oxford; London University. Head of Economics, St. Benedict's, Ealing, 1963-71; Head of History, Christ College, Brecon, 1971-75; Head of History, Tonbridge School, 1975-81; The King's School, Parramatta, NSW, 1980; Headmaster, Prior Park College, Bath, 1981-89. Chairman Elect, HMC. Recreations: reading; writing; canal boating; hill-walking; travel. Address: (h.) 11 Queensferry Terrace, Edinburgh EH4 3EQ.

Tod, Stewart, DA (Edin), RIBA, FRIAS, FSA Scot. Consultant to Stewart Tod & Partners, Architects, Edinburgh, formerly David Carr Architects; b. 30.4.27, West Wemyss; m., A. Vivienne J. Nixon; 2 s.; 2 d. Educ. Buckhaven High School; Edinburgh College of Art. RAF, 1945-48; Stratton Davis & Yates, 1952-55; Falkirk District Council, 1955-57; Carr and Matthew, 1957-60; David Carr Architects, 1960-77. Executive Committee Member, Association for the Protection of Rural Scotland, Chairman, Historic Roads and Bridges Committee; General Trustee, Church of Scotland. Recreations: bee-keeping; gardening; sketching. Address: (b.) 43 Manor Place, Edinburgh; T.- 0131-225 7988.

Todd, Professor Adrian Christopher, BTech, PhD, CEng, FIChemE, FInstPet. Professor of Petroleum Engineering, Heriot Watt University, since 1990 (Head of Department, 1991-96); b. 1944, Leicester; m., Valerie H. Todd; 1 d. Educ. Lutterworth Grammar School; Loughborough University of Technology. Research Scientist, Shell, 1969-72; joined Heriot Watt University as Lecturer in Chemical Engineering, 1972. Recreation: Christian activities. Address: (b.) Department of Petroleum Engineering, Heriot Watt University, Riccarton, Edinburgh; T.-0131-451 3124.

Todd, Rev. Andrew Stewart, MA, BD, DD. Minister, St. Machar's Cathedral, Old Aberdeen, 1967-93; Extra Chaplain to The Queen in Scotland, since 1996 (Chaplain-in-Ordinary, 1991-96); b. 26.5.26, Alloa; m., Janet Agnes Brown Smith; 2 s.; 2 d. Educ. High School of Stirling; Edinburgh University; Basel University. Assistant Minister, St. Cuthbert's, Edinburgh, 1951-52; Minister: Symington, Lanarkshire, 1952; North Leith, 1960; Member, Church

Hymnary Revision Comittee, 1963-73; Convener, General Assembly's Committee on Public Worship and Aids to Devotion, 1974-78; Moderator, Aberdeen Presbytery, 1980-81; Convener, Panel on Doctrine, 1990-95; Member, Church Hymnary Trust; awarded Honorary Doctorate, Aberdeen University, 1982; translator of three theological books from German into English; Honorary President, Church Service Society; Honorary President, Scottish Church Society. Recreations: music; gardening. Address: (h.) Culearn, Balquhidder, Lochearnhead, Perthshire FK19 8PB; T.-01877 384662.

Toft, Anthony Douglas, CBE, BSc, MD, FRCPE, FRCPGlas, FRCPLond, FRCPI, FACP(Hon), FRACP(Hon), FRCSE, FRCPC(Hon), FRCGP(Hon), FFPM (Hon), FFAEM (Hon), FCPS Pakistan (Hon), FCPS Bangladesh (Hon), FAM Singapore (Hon), MAM Malaysia (Hon). Consultant Physician, Royal Infirmary, Edinburgh, since 1978; Physician to the Queen in Scotland, since 1996; Chief Medical Officer, Scottish Equitable Life Assurance, since 1987; President, Royal College of Physicians of Edinburgh, 1991-94; b. 29.10.44, Perth; m., Maureen Darling; 1 s.; 1 d. Educ. Perth Academy; Edinburgh University. Chairman, Collegiate Members' Committee, Royal College of Physicians of Edinburgh, 1978; Vice-President, Royal College of Physicians, 1989-91; Chairman, Scottish Royal Colleges, 1992-94; Chairman, Joint Committee of Higher Medical Training, 1993-96; Member, Health Advisory Committee, since 1994. Recreations: golf; gardening. Address: (h.) 41 Hermitage Gardens, Edinburgh EH10 6AZ; T.-0131-447 2221.

Togneri, Martin, MA (Hons), MBA. Director, Locate in Scotland, since 1995; b. 27.4.56, Stirling; m., Kathleen; 2 s. Educ. St. Modan's High School, Stirling; Glasgow University; Strathclyde University. Burroughs Machines Ltd., 1978-80; postgraduate study, 1980-83; Accounts Commission, 1983-84; joined Locate in Scotland, 1984. Recreations: reading; relaxing. Address: (b.) 120 Bothwell Street, Glasgow, G2 7JP; T.-0141-228 2247.

Tolley, David Anthony, MB, BS (Lond), FRCS, FRCSEdin. Consultant Urological Surgeon, Western General Hospital, Edinburgh, since 1980; Honorary Senior Lecturer, Department of Surgery/Urology, Edinburgh University, since 1980; Director, Scottish Lithotriptor Centre; b. 29.11.47, Warrington; m., Judith Anne Finn; 3 s.; 1 d. Educ. Manchester Grammar School; Kings College Hospital Medical School, London University. House Surgeon and Physician, Kings College Hospital; Lecturer in Human Morphology, Southampton University; Lecturer in Anatomy and Fulbright Fellow, University of Texas at Houston; Surgical Registrar, Hammersmith and Ealing Hospitals, London; Senior Surgical Registrar (Urology), Kings College Hospital, London; Senior Urological Registrar, Yorkshire Regional Training Scheme. Member: MRC Working Party on Urological Cancer; MRC Working Party on Superficial Bladder Cancer; Editorial Board, British Journal of Urology; Member, Council, British Association of Urological Surgeons; Standing Commitee on Postgraduate Education, British Association of Urological Surgeons; President, British Society for Endourology; Board, Minimal Access Therapy Training Unit Scotland; Education Committee, Royal College of Surgeons of Edinburgh; Past Chairman, Scottish Urological Oncology Group. Recreations: golf; motor racing; sailing. Address: (b.) Murrayfield Hospital, Corstorphine Road, Edinburgh; T.-0131-334 0363.

Tombs, Sebastian Martineau, BArch, DipArch (Cantab), FRIAS, ACIArb. Secretary, Royal Incorporation of Architects in Scotland, since 1995; b. 11.10.49, Sussex; m., Eva Hierman; 4 s.; 2 d. Educ. Bryanston; Cambridge University. RMJM, Edinburgh, 1975-76; Roland Wedgwood, Edinburgh, 1976-77; Fountainbridge Housing Association, Edinburgh, 1977-78; Housing Corporation,

1978-81; Edinburgh District Council Housing Department, 1982-86; Depute Secretary, RIAS, 1986-94; Founder and first Secretary, Scottish Ecological Design Association, 1991-94, Chairman, 1994-97. Founder and first Chairman, Association of Planning Supervisors, 1995-97. Recreation: choral music. Address: (b.) 15 Rutland Square, Edinburgh, EH1 2BE; T.-0131-229 7545.

Topping, Professor Barry H.V., BSc, PhD, CEng, CMath, MBCS, MICE, MIStructE, MIMechE, FIMA. Professor of Computational Mechanics, Department of Mechanical and Chemical Engineering, Heriot-Watt University, Edinburgh, since 1995; b. 14.2.52, Manchester. Educ. Bedford Modern School; City University, London. Lecturer in Civil Engineering, Edinburgh University, 1978-88; Von-Humboldt Research Fellow, Stuttgart University, 1986-87; Senior Lecturer, Heriot-Watt University, 1988-89, Reader, 1989-90, Professor of Structural Engineering, 1990-95. Co-Editor, Computers and Structures; Co-Editor, Advances in Engineering Software. Address: (b.) Department of Mechanical and Chemical Engineering, Heriot-Watt University, Riccarton, Edinburgh EH14 4AS; T.-0131-449 5111.

Torrance, Rev. Dr. Iain Richard, TD, MA, BD, DPhil. Senior Lecturer in Divinity, Aberdeen University, since 1997 (Lecturer, 1993-97); Co-Editor, Scottish Journal of Theology, since 1982; b. 13.1.49, Aberdeen; m., Morag Ann MacHugh; 1 s.; 1 d. Educ. Edinburgh Academy; Monkton Combe School, Bath; Edinburgh University; St. Andrews University; Oriel College, Oxford University. Minister, Northmavine, Shetland, 1982-85; Lecturer in New Testament and Ethics, Queen's College, Birmingham, 1985-89; Lecturer in New Testament and Patristics, Birmingham University, 1989-93; Chaplain to the Moderator of the General Assembly, 1976; Member, International Dialogue between the Orthodox and the Reformed Churches, since 1992; Member, General Assembly's Panel on Doctrine, since 1993; Member, Ethics Committee, Grampian Health Board, since 1996; Hon. Secretary, Aberdeen A.U.T., since 1995; Secretary, Society for the Study of Christian Ethics, since 1995; Judge, Templeton (UK) Awards, since 1994; TA Chaplain, 1982-97; ACF Chaplain, since 1996. Publications: Christology after Chalcedon, 1988; Human Genetics: a Christian perspective (Co-author), 1995. Recreations: historical Scottish culture (tartan, castles, battles, literature, art). Address: (h.) Concraig Smiddy, Clinterty, Kingswells, AB15 8RN; T.-01224 790902.

Torrance, Rev. Professor James Bruce, MA (Hons), BD. Professor of Systematic Theology, Aberdeen University, 1977-89 (Dean, Faculty of Divinity, 1978-81); Minister, Church of Scotland, since 1950; b. 3.2.23, Chengtu, Szechwan, West China; m., Mary Heather Aitken; 1 s.; 2 d. Educ. Royal High School, Edinburgh; Edinburgh University and New College; Marburg University; Basle University; Oxford University. RAF, 1943-45; ordained, Invergowrie, Dundee, 1954; Lecturer in Divinity and Dogmatics in History of Christian Thought, 1961, and Senior Lecturer in Christian Dogmatics, 1972, New College, Edinburgh; Visiting Professor of New Testament, Union Theological Seminary, Richmond, Virginia, 1960, of Theology, Columbia Theological Seminary, 1965, and Vancouver School of Theology, 1974-75; Visiting Professor in South Africa, USA, New Zealand, Australia, Fiji, W. Samoa, Canada. Convenor, Panel on Doctrine, General Assembly, 1982-86; Joint Convener, British Council of Churches Commission on Doctrine of the Trinity, 1983-89; Joint Convenor, World Alliance of Reformed Churches, Lutheran World Federation Conversations, 1985-88. Publications: John Duns Scotus in a Nutshell (Co-author), 1992; Worship, Community and the Triune God of Grace, 1994; Nature of Atonement (Editor), 1995; Scottish Theology, 1996. Recreations: bee-keeping; fishing; swimming; gardening. Address: (h.) 3 Greenbank Crescent, Edinburgh EH10 5TE; T.-0131-447 3230.

Torrance, Very Rev. Professor Thomas Forsyth, MBE, MA, BD, DrTheol, DLitt, DD, DrTeol, DTheol, DSc, FBA, FRSE. Emeritus Professor, Edinburgh University, since 1979; b. 30.8.13, Chengdu, Sichuan, China; m., Margaret Edith Spear; 2 s.; 1 d. Educ. Canadian School, Chengdu, China; Bellshill Academy, Lanarkshire; Edinburgh University; Basel University; Oriel College, Oxford. Minister: Alyth Barony Parish Church, 1940-47; served as Church of Scotland Chaplain, 1943-45; Minister, Beechgrove Parish Church, Aberdeen, 1947-50; Edinburgh University: Professor of Church History, 1950-52, Professor of Christian Dogmatics, 1952-79; Templeton Prize, 1978; Moderator, General Assembly of the Church of Scotland, 1976-77. Cross of St. Mark, First Class, 1970; Protoprebyter of Greek Orthodox Church (Hon.), 1973; President, Academie Internationale des Sciences Religieuses, 1972-81. Publications: The Doctrine of Grace in the Apostolic Fathers, 1949; Calvin's Doctrine of Man, 1949; Royal Priesthood, 1955; Kingdom and Church, 1956; The School of Faith, 1959; Conflict and Agreement in the Church, 1959; Karl Barth: An Introduction to his Early Theology, 1962; Theology in Reconstruction, 1965; Theological Science, 1969 (Collins Prize); Space, Time and Incarnation, 1969; God and Rationality, 1971; Theology in Reconciliation, 1975; Space, Time and Resurrection, 1976; The Ground and Grammar of Theology, 1980; Christian Theology and Scientific Culture, 1980; Divine and Contingent Order, 1981; Reality and Evangelical Theology, 1982; Juridical and Physical Law, 1982; The Mediation of Christ, 1983; Transformation and Convergence in the Frame of Knowledge, 1984; Reality and Scientific Theology, 1985; The Trinitarian Faith, 1988; The Hermeneutics of John Calvin, 1988; Karl Barth: Biblical and Evangelical Theologian, 1990; Trinitarian Perspectives, 1993; Preaching Christ Today, 1993; Divine Meaning, 1995; The Christian Doctrine of God, 1995. Founding Editor of Scottish Journal of Theology. Recreations: formerly golf, squash, fishing; now walking. Address: (h.) 37 Braid Farm Road, Edinburgh EH10 6LE; T.-0131-447 3224.

Toth, Professor Akos George, Dr. Jur., PhD. Professor of Law, Strathclyde University, since 1984; Jean Monnet Chair of European Law, since 1991; b. 9.2.36, Mezotur, Hungary; m., Sarah Kurucz. Educ. Budapest University; Szeged University; Exeter University. Strathclyde University: Lecturer in Law, 1971-76, Senior Lecturer, 1976-82, Reader, 1982-84; British Academy Research Readership, 1993-95. Publications: Legal Protection of Individuals in the European Communities, 1978; The Oxford Encyclopaedia of European Community Law, 1990. Recreations: travel; music; opera; theatre; swimming; walking. Address: (b.) Strathclyde University, Law School, 173 Cathedral Street, Glasgow, G4 0RQ; T.-0141-552 4400, Ext. 3338.

Toulmin, David. Hon. MLitt (Aberdeen). Writer; b. 1.7.13, Rathen, Aberdeenshire; m., Margaret Jane Willox; 3 s. Educ. five public/parish schools. From the age of 14 to 65, earned living by manual labour (farm worker); his first article was published by Farmer and Stock Breeder, 1947; wrote short stories in dialect for local newspapers and the Scots Magazine; five stories broadcast on radio by the BBC; a collection was published as Hard Shining Corn, 1972; has published a further eight books; awarded grant by the Scottish Arts Council, 1983; Spring Book Award, 1993, for Collected Short Stories; real name, John Reid. Recreations: writing; reading; popular music; cinema; video; television; antiquarian research. Address: (h.) 49 Westdyke Avenue, Elrick, Skene, Aberdeenshire, AB32 6QX.

Townell, Nicholas Howard, MB, BS (Lond), FRCS (Eng), FRCS (Edin). Consultant General Surgeon and Urologist, Dundee and Angus Hospitals, since 1985; Honorary Senior Lecturer in Surgery, Dundee University Medical School, since 1985; b. 19.4.49, Redhill; m., Hoang Anh Vuong; 1 s.; 2 d. Educ. Davenant Foundation Grammar School; London University; Royal Free Hospital School of Medicine. Various House Surgeon, House Physician and Registrar posts; Senior Registrar in General Surgery and Urology, Royal Free Hospital. Fellow, Royal Society of Medicine. Specialist interest: minimally invasive urology. Recreations: classical music; golf; squash; hill-walking. Address: (h.) Rosebank, Hillside, Angus, DD10 9HZ; T.-0167 4830296.

Trainer, Professor James, MA, PhD. Professor of German, Stirling University, since 1969 (Deputy Principal, 1973-78, 1981-87, 1989-92); b. 2.3.32; m., Barbara Herta Reinhard (deceased); 2 s.; 1 d. Educ. St. Andrews University; Free University of Berlin. Lecturer in German, St. Andrews University, 1958-67; Visiting Professor, Yale University, 1964-65; Visiting Scholar, University of California at Santa Barbara, 1989; Vice-Convener, SUCE, 1987-94; Convener, SUCE Modern Languages Panel, 1979-86; Member, Inter University and Polytechnic Council, since 1983; Member, Scottish Examination Board, 1975-82; Chairman, SED Postgraduate Awards Committee, since 1989; Member, UK Fulbright Committee, 1985-93; Trustee, National Library of Scotland, 1986-91; Chairman, Scottish Conference of University Teachers of German, 1978-80; Member, National Academic Audit Unit; Member, SHEFCO Quality Assessment Committee; Member Overseas Research Students Awards Committee, CVCP; Governor, Morrison's Academy, Crieff. Recreations: music; cricket; translating. Address: (b.) Stirling University, Stirling; T.-01786 473171.

Trainor, Professor Richard Hughes, BA, MA, DPhil, FRHistS, FRSA. Vice-Principal, Glasgow University, since 1996; Professor of Social History, Glasgow University, since 1995; b. 31.12.48, New Jersey; m., Dr. Marguerite Wright Dupree; 1 s.; 1 d. Educ. Calvert Hall High School, Maryland; Brown University; Princeton University; Merton and Nuffield Colleges, Oxford University. Junior Research Fellow, Wolfson College, Oxford, 1977-79; Lecturer, Balliol College, Oxford, 1978-79; Glasgow University: Lecturer in Economic History, 1979-89, Senior Lecturer in Economic and Social History, 1989-95, Director, Design and Implementation of Software in History Project, 1985-89, Co-Director, Computers in Teaching Initiative Centre for History, since 1989, Dean of Social Sciences, 1992-96. Rhodes Scholar; Council Member, Economic History Society, since 1993; Member, Scottish University Principals Working Party on Educational Technology and Innovative Teaching, 1991-92; Joint Editor, Economic and Social History, 1989-94. Publication: Black Country Elites: the exercise of authority in an industrialised area 1830-1900, 1993. Recreations: parenting; observing politics; tennis. Address: (h.) 45 Mitre Road, Glasgow G14 9LE; T.-0141-959 0006.

Tranter, Nigel, OBE, KCLJ, DLitt, MA (Hon.). Author and Novelist, since 1935; b. 23.11.09, Glasgow; m., May Jean Campbell Grieve (deceased); 1 s. (deceased); 1 d. Educ. St. James' Episcopal School; George Heriot's, Edinburgh. Professional Writer, since 1946; published more than 120 books, including over 80 novels; Vice-Convener, Scottish Covenant Association, 1951-55; President, East Lothian Liberal Association, 1960-70; Chairman, National Forth Road Bridge Committee, 1953-57; Chairman, St. Andrew Society of East Lothian, since 1966; President, Scottish PEN, 1962-66 (now Honorary President); Chairman, Society of Authors, Scotland, 1966-70; Chairman, National Book League, Scotland, 1971-73. Vice-Chancellor, Order of St. Lazarus of Jerusalem, 1982-88; Hon. Vice-President, Scottish Association of Teachers of History; Honorary Freeman of Blackstone, Virginia, USA, 1980; BBC Radio Scot of the Year, 1989; Hon. President, Saltire Society; Trustee, Scottish Flag Fund; Hon. Member, Scottish Library Association. Recreations: walking;

climbing; genealogy; castle architecture. Address: (h.) Quarry House, Aberlady, East Lothian; T.-Aberlady 258.

Travers, Andrew Keith Buchanan, BSc. Chief Executive, Scottish Design Ltd., since 1996; b. 3.1.62, Lanark. Educ. Earnock High School, Hamilton; Strathclyde University. Consultant Engineer, IBM Greenock, 1989-94; Director, Centre for Integrated Product Development, 1994-96. Recreations: rugby; tennis; sailing; skiing. Address: (b.) Scottish Design, Stock Exchange House, 7 Nelson Mandela Place, Glasgow, G2 7JN; T.-0141-221 6121.

Travers, John, BA, MA. Director of Education, North Ayrshire Council, since 1995; b. 22.1.48, Catterick; m., Joy; 1 s.; 2 d. Educ. St. Patrick's High School, Dumbarton; Glasgow University. Teaching, Glasgow and Barrhead, 1977-82; Assistant Head Teacher, St. Patrick's High School, Coatbridge, 1982-84; TVEI Coordinator, James Watt College, Greenock, 1984-86; Strathclyde Regional Council: Education Officer, Renfrew Division, 1986-89, Assistant Director of Education, 1989-90, Senior Education Officer, 1990-92; Senior Depute Director of Education, Fife Regional Council, 1992-95. Address: (b.) Cunninghame House, Irvine, KA12 8EE; T.-01294 324412.

Travis, Christopher Douglas, BSc (Soc Sci). Chief Executive, Kincardine and Deeside Enterprise Trust Ltd.; b. 12.5.59, Kaduna, Nigeria. Educ. Dollar Academy; Edinburgh University. Previously: Lecturer in Economics/research student, Dundee College of Technology, Business Counsellor, SDA, Economic Development Manager, Gordon District Council, Executive Director, Clydesdale Development Co. Ltd., Chairman, Lanarkshire Enterprise Training Ltd. Recreations: cooking; reading; hill-walking; golf. Address: (b.) Unit 1, Aboyne Business Centre, Huntly Road, Aboyne AB34 5HE; T.-013398 87222.

Trayhurn, Professor Paul, BSc, DPhil, DSc, FRSE. Assistant Director (Academic Affairs) and Head, Division of Biomedical Science, Rowett Research Institute, since 1988; Department of Biomedical Sciences and Department of Molecular and Cell Biology, Aberdeen University, since 1992 (Honorary); b. 6.5.48, Exeter; m., Deborah Hartland Gigg; 3 s.; 1 d. Educ. Colyton Grammar School, Devon; Reading University; Oxford University. Graduate student, Linacre College, Oxford, 1969-72; NATO European Research Fellow, Strasbourg, 1972-73; Postdoctoral Fellow, Oxford, 1973-75; MRC Scientific/Senior Scientific Staff, Dunn Nutrition Laboratory, Cambridge, 1975-86; Professor and Heritage Scholar, University of Alberta, 1986-88; Evelyn Williams Visiting Professor, University of Sydney, 1992. Member, Council, Nutrition Society, 1982-84, 1991-93; Chairman, Scottish Section, Nutrition Society, 1993-95; Chairman, BBSRC Human Nutrition Advisory Panel; Chairman, Scientific Committee, 8th European Congress on Obesity; Executive Council, Korean Collaboration Centre; Member, BBSRC Agri-Food Directorate. Publications: over 275 scientific publications. Address: (b.) Division of Biomedical Science, Rowett Research Institute, Bucksburn, Aberdeen, AB21 9SB; T.-01224 716610.

Trewavas, Professor Anthony James, BSc, PhD, FRSE., FRSA. Professor, Institute of Cell and Molecular Biology, Edinburgh University, since 1990; b. 17.6.39, London; m., Valerie; 1 s.; 2 d. Educ. Roan Grammar School; University College, London. Lecturer/Reader, Edinburgh University; Visiting Professor, Universities of Michigan State, Calgary, California (Davis), Bonn, Illinois, North Carolina, National University of Mexico; University of Milan. Publications: 170 scientific papers; two books. Recreations: music (particularly choral); reading. Address: (h.) 1 Rullion Road, Penicuik, Midlothian; T.-01968 673372.

Trotter, Alexander Richard, DL, FRSA; President, Scottish Landowners' Federation, since 1996; b. 20.2.39, London; m., Julia Henrietta Greenwell; 3 s. Educ. Eton

College; City of London Technical College. Royal Scots Greys, 1958-68; Member, Berwickshire County Council, 1969-75 (Chairman, Roads Committee, 1974-75); Manager, Charterhall Estate and Farm, since 1969; Chairman, Meadowhead Ltd. (formerly Mortonhall Park Ltd.), since 1974; Director, Timber Growers' GB Ltd., 1977-82; Vice Chairman, Border Grain Ltd., since 1984; Council Member, Scottish Landowners' Federation, since 1975 (Chairman, Land Use Committee, 1975-78, Convener, 1982-85); Member, Department of Agriculture Working Party on the Agricultural Holding (Scotland) Legislation, 1981-82; Chairman, Scottish Committee, Nature Conservancy Council, 1985-90; Member, UK Committee for Euro Year of the Environment, 1986-88; Member, Scottish Tourist Board Graded Holiday Parks Overseeing Committee, since 1993; Member, Queen's Bodyguard for Scotland (Royal Company of Archers). Recreations: skiing; tennis; hunting; shooting. Address: Charterhall, Duns, Berwickshire, TD11 3RE; T.-01890 840210.

Trudgill, David L., BSc, PhD, CBiol, FBIBiol. Head, Zoology Department, Scottish Crop Research Institute, since 1972; b. 2.5.42, Leeds; m., Margaret Jean Luckraft; 3 s. Educ. Leeds Grammar School; Ulverston Grammar School; Leeds University; London University. Nematologist, Rothamsted Experimental Station, 1966-72. Chairman, European Plant Protection Organisation ad hoc committee on potato cyst nematodes; President, European Society of Nematologists. Recreations:hill-walking; fishing. Address: (b.) Nematology Department, Scottish Crop Research Institute, Invergowrie, Dundee DD2 5DA; T.-01382 562731.

Truman, Donald Ernest Samuel, BA, PhD, FIBiol, CBiol, FRSA. Vice-Dean and Vice-Provost, Faculty of Science and Engineering, University of Edinburgh, since 1989; b. 23.10.36, Leicester; m., Kathleen Ramsay; 1 s.; 1 d. Educ. Wyggeston School, Leicester; Clare College, Cambridge. NATO Research Fellow, Wenner-Grenn Institute, Stockholm, 1962-63; MRC Epigenetics Research Group, Edinburgh, 1963-72; Lecturer, Department of Genetics, Edinburgh University, 1972-78; Senior Lecturer, 1978-89, Head of Department, 1984-89, Director of Biology Teaching Unit, 1985-89; Aneurin Bevan Memorial Fellow, Government of India, 1978; Chairman, Edinburgh Centre for Rural Research, since 1993; Member, Council, Scottish Agricultural College, since 1995; Chairman, Purchasing Consortium of Universities of Scotland and Northern Ireland, since 1996. Publications: The Biochemistry of Cytodifferentiation, 1974; Differentiation in Vitro (Joint Editor), 1982; Stability and Switching in Cellular Differentiation, 1982; Coordinated Regulation of Gene Expression, 1986. Recreation: gardening; books. Address: (b.) Faculty of Science and Engineering Office, West Mains Road, Edinburgh, EH9 3JY; T.-0131-650 5758.

Tuck, Ronald Moore Sinclair, MA, DMS. H.M. Chief Executive, Scottish Qualifications Authority, since 1997, b. 20.3.49, Edinburgh; m., Anne; 1 s.; 1 d. Educ. George Heriot's; Edinburgh University; Dundee Institute of Technology. Lecturer/Senior Lecturer, Angus College, 1974-85; H.M. Inspector of Schools, 1985-92; HM Chief Inspector of Schools, 1992-96. Recreations: watching football; travelling; reading; cooking. Address: (b.) Hanover House, 24 Douglas Street, Glasgow G2 7NQ.

Tucker, Derek Alan. Editor, Press and Journal, Aberdeen, since 1992; b. 31.10.53, Liverpool; 1 s.; 1 d. Educ. Quarry Bank High School, Liverpool; Municipal Grammar School, Wolverhampton. Reporter/Chief Reporter/News Editor/Deputy Editor, Express and Star, Wolverhampton, 1972-92. Member, Press Complaints Commission, since 1995; Officer, RAFVR. Recreations: golf; travel; watching any sport not involving horses. Address: (b.) Lang Stracht, Mastrick, Aberdeen; T.-01224 690222.

Tucker, Professor John Barry, BA, MA, PhD, FRSE. Professor of Cell Biology, St. Andrews University, since 1990; b. 17.3.41, Arundel; m., Janet Stephen Murray; 1 s. Educ. Queen Elizabeth Grammar School, Atherstone; Peterhouse, Cambridge. Fulbright Travel Scholar and Research Associate, Department of Zoology, Indiana University, 1966-68; SERC Research Fellow, Department of Zoology, Cambridge, 1968-69; Lecturer in Zoology, St. Andrews University, 1969-79 (Chairman, Zoology Department, 1982-84); Reader in Zoology, 1979-90. Member: SERC Advisory Group II, 1977-80, SERC Molecular Biology and Genetics Sub-committee, 1986-89, Editorial Board of Development, 1979-88. Recreations: cycling; hill-walking; tennis; reluctant gardener. Address: (b.) School of BioMedical Sciences, Bute Building, St. Andrews University, St. Andrews, Fife KY16 9TS; T.-01334 463560.

Tumelty, Michael, MA (Hons). Music Critic, The Herald, since 1983; b. 31.5.46, Hexham; m., Frances McGinniss; 2 s.; 1 d. Educ. St. Aloysius College, Glasgow; Aberdeen University. Postgraduate research into the music of Debussy, 1974-75; entered teaching, St. Columba's High School, Clydebank (Principal Teacher, 1980-83); served on a variety of working groups on curriculum development; freelance Music Critic, Jewish Echo, 1979-82, and Daily Telegraph, 1982-83; Member, Scottish Central Committee on Music, 1982-83. Recreations: family; avid collector of records. Address: (b.) The Herald, Albion Street, Glasgow.

Tunstall-Pedoe, Professor Hugh David, MA, MD, FRCP, FRCPE, FFCM, FESC. Professor and Director, Cardiovascular Epidemiology Unit, and Senior Lecturer in Medicine, Ninewells Hospital and Medical School, Dundee, since 1981; Honorary Consultant Cardiologist, since 1981; Honorary Specialist in Public Health Medicine, since 1981; b. 30.12.39, Southampton; m., Jacqueline Helen; 2 s.; 1 d. Educ. Haberdashers' Aske's School; Dulwich College; King's College, Cambridge; Guy's Hospital Medical School. Junior hospital posts, Guy's, Brompton, National Queen Square and London Hospitals; MRC Social Medicine Unit, 1969-71; Lecturer in Medicine, The London Hospital, 1971-74; Senior Lecturer in Epidemiology and Honorary Physician, and Honorary Community Physician, St. Mary's Hospital and Medical School, London, 1974-81. Chairman, European Society of Cardiology Working Group on Epidemiology and Prevention, 1983-85; Toshiba Year of Invention Award, 1991; BUPA National Epidemiology Award, 1996. Recreations: hill-walking; bee-keeping; golf. Address: (b.) Cardiovascular Epidemiology Unit, Ninewells Hospital and Medical School, Dundee, DD1 9SY; T.-01382 644255.

Turley, Mark John, BSc (Hons), MBA, MCIOH. Director of Housing, City of Edinburgh Council, since 1996; Executive Director of Housing, City of Edinburgh District Council, since 1993; b. 25.6.60, Dudley. Educ. High Arcal Grammar School, Sedgley; Leicester University. Sheffield City Council, 1981-91; Head of Tenant Services, York City Council, 1991-93. Recreations: playing violin; reading. Address: (b.) Housing Department, 23 Waterloo Place, Edinburgh, EH1 3BH; T.-0131-529 7325.

Turmeau, Professor William Arthur, CBE, FRSE, Dr. h.c., Doctor of Education (Napier University), BSc, PhD, CEng, FIMechE. Chairman, Scottish Environment Protection Agency, since 1995; Principal and Vice-Chancellor, Napier University, 1982-94; b. 19.9.29, London; m., Margaret Moar Burnett; 1 d. Educ. Stromness Academy, Orkney; Edinburgh University; Moray House College of Education; Heriot-Watt University. Royal Signals, 1947-49; Research Engineer, Northern Electric Co. Ltd., Montreal, 1952-54; Mechanical Engineer, USAF, Goose Bay, Labrador, 1954-56; Contracts Manager, Godfrey Engineering Co. Ltd., Montreal, 1956-61; Lecturer, Bristo Technical Institute, Edinburgh, 1962-64;

Napier College: Lecturer and Senior Lecturer, 1964-68, Head, Department of Mechanical Engineering, 1968-75, Assistant Principal and Dean, Faculty of Technology, 1975-82. Member, Steering Committee, University of the Highlands and Islands Project; Member, IMechE Academic Standards Committee; Trustee, Dynamic Earth Charitable Trust. Recreations: modern jazz; Leonardo da Vinci. Address: (h.) 71 Morningside Park, Edinburgh, EH10 5EZ; T.-0131-447 4639.

Turnbull, Wilson Mark, DipArch, MLA (Penn), MBCS, RIBA, FRIAS, FLI. Turnbull Jeffrey Partnership, Landscape Architects, since 1982; b. 1.4.43, Edinburgh. Educ. George Watson's; Edinburgh College of Art; University of Pennsylvania. Assistant Professor of Architecture, University of Southern California, 1970-74; Partner, W.J. Cairns and Partners, Environmental Consultants, 1974-82; Partner, Design Innovations Research, 1976-81; Council Member, Cockburn Association (Edinburgh Civic Trust), 1986-95; Commissioner, Countryside Commission for Scotland, 1988-92; Commissioner, Royal Fine Art Commission for Scotland, 1996; Chairman, Edinburgh Greenbelt Initiative, 1988-91; Director, Edinburgh Greenbelt Trust, since 1991, Vice-Chairman, since 1993. Recreation: sailing. Address: (b.) Sandeman House, 55 High Street, Edinburgh EH1 1SR; T.-0131-557 5050.

Turner, Donald Ian, CA. Regional Managing Partner Scotland and Northern Ireland, Ernst and Young, since 1986; b. 20.9.44, Kilmarnock; m., Trish; 1 s.; 1 d. Educ. Strathallan School. McClelland Moores & Co., 1962-67; Peat Marwick Mitchell & Co., Paris, 1967-69; Turner Hutton & Lawson, 1969-81; Arthur Young, 1981-89. Non-Executive Director, Scottish Knowledge plc; Board Member, Scottish Council Development and Industry; Member, Scottish Economic Council; Chairman, Scottish Fundraising Committee, Princess Royal Trust for Carers. Recreations: golf; fishing; shooting. Address: (b.) Ernst and Young, George House, 50 George Square, Glasgow G2 1RR; T.-0141-553 4363.

Turner, John R., MA, HonMA, MusB, FRCO. Organist and Director of Music, Glasgow Cathedral, since 1965; Lecturer, Royal Scottish Academy of Music, since 1965; Organist, Strathclyde University, since 1965; b. Halifax. Educ. Rugby; Jesus College, Cambridge. Recreations: gardening; travel. Address: (h.) Binchester, 1 Cathkin Road, Rutherglen, Glasgow G73 4SE; T.-0141-634 7775.

Turner, Professor Kenneth John, BSc, PhD. Professor of Computing Science, Stirling University, since 1987; b. 21.2.49, Glasgow; m., Elizabeth Mary Christina; 2 s. Educ. Hutchesons' Boys Grammar School; Glasgow University; Edinburgh University. Data Communications Designer, International Computers Ltd., 1974-76; Senior Systems Analyst, Central Regional Council, 1976-77; Data Communications Consultant, International Computers Ltd., 1977-87. Recreations: choral singing; craft work; sailing. Address: (b.) Department of Computing Science, Stirling University, Stirling, FK9 4LA; T.-01786 467420.

Turner, Malcolm, OBE, JP, DL. Deputy Lieutenant, Dunbartonshire, since 1989; Vice Chairman, Scottish National Housing and Town Planning Council; Vice-President, Clydebank Rugby Club; b. 13.12.21, Clydebank; m., Margaret Balfour; 1 s. Educ. Clydebank High School. Member: Clydebank Town Council, 1957-75 (Provost, 1966-69), Dunbarton County Council, 1957-75; Strathclyde Regional Council, 1974-95; Member, Cumbernauld Development Corporation, 1975-83; former Chairman, Central Water Development Board; Vice-Chairman, Convention of Royal Burghs, 1967-73; Hon. Freeman, Clydebank District; former Chairman, Forth and Clyde Advisory Committee. Recreations: angling; caravanning;

bowling; golf. Address: (h.) 14 Mossgiel Drive, Clydebank, Dunbartonshire G81 2BY; T.-0141-952 3992.

Turner, Norman William, LLB, MILAM, ALA, FIMgt, FSA(Scot). Director of Leisure Services, North Lanarkshire Council, since 1995; Past Chairman, Association of Directors of Leisure, Recreation and Tourism; b. 12.4.48, Portsmouth; m. Ann Malloy. Educ. Portsmouth Technical High School; Brighton Polytechnic; Strathclyde University. District Librarian, Motherwell District Council; Depute Director of Libraries and Museums, Falkirk District Council; Deputy District Librarian, City of Southampton District; Deputy Borough Librarian, Andover Borough Council; Director of Leisure, Motherwell District Council, 1985-95. Former Vice-Chairman, Public Libraries Group; former Hon. Treasurer, Scottish Library Association. Recreations: season ticket holder, Motherwell FC; sport; theatre; cinema; music; natural history. Address: (b.) Buchanan Tower, Buchanan Business Park, Stepps, G33 6HR.

Turner, Susan Morag, MA, DipEd, DIDCE, CTD, FISW, FCollP, FRSA. Consultant in deafness issues, since 1997; Director, Scottish Association for the Deaf, 1991-97; b. 5.4.35, Glasgow. Educ. Rutherglen Academy; Glasgow University; Manchester University. Teacher of hearing-impaired children, Glasgow School for the Deaf; Head Teacher: Paisley School for the Deaf, Dundee School for the Deaf; Lecturer, Professional Curriculum Support Services Department, Moray House College; Director, Scottish Centre for the Education of the Deaf, 1971-91. Vice President, Scottish Association for the Deaf, 1971-91; Scottish President, National Association of Special Educational Needs; Council Member, International Centre for Special Education; Member, Board of Trustees, Royal National Institute for Deaf People; Member, Church Advisorate on Special Educational Needs; Chairman, J.S. Lochrie Memorial Trust. Address: (h.) 15 Bonaly Brae, Colinton, Edinburgh EH13 0QF; T.-0131-441 7520.

Turner Thomson, Ann Denise. Interior Designer; b. 23.5.29, Molesey; m., Gordon Turner Thomson; 1 s.; 3 d. Educ. Sherborne School for Girls, Dorset; St. James's Secretarial College, London. Council Member, Scottish Arts Council, 1983-88; Council Member, National Trust for Scotland, 1990-95; Council Member, Edinburgh International Festival, 1991-97; Member, Board of Directors, Art in Partnership; Member, Saltire Society Housing Awards Panel, Art in Architecture Award Panel; Convenor, Saltire Society/Royal Scottish Academy Permanent Collection Award; Convenor, Scottish Committee, Iwate Art Festival UK, 1998. Recreations: theatre; opera; visual arts. Address: 8 Middleby Street, Edinburgh EH9 1TD; T.-0131-667 3997.

Turok, Professor Ivan Nicholas, BSc, MSc, PhD, MRTPI. Professor of Urban Economic Development, Glasgow University, since 1996; b. 7.8.56, Cape Town; m., Elizabeth; 1 s.; 1 d. Educ. William Ellis School, London; Bristol University. Lecturer, Glasgow University, 1984-87; Senior Lecturer and Professor, Strathclyde University, 1987-96. Publications; over 30 articles and books. Recreations: hill-walking; cycling; current affairs. Address: (b.) 25 Bute Gardens, Glasgow G12 8RS; T.-0141-330 6274.

Tweedie, Douglas Kay, DL. Land Owner; farming, since 1963; estate management, since 1991; b. 30.3.42, Gordon; m., Senga Anne; 1 s.; 1 d. Educ. Tabley House, Cheshire. M.F.H., Berwickshire Hunt, 1982-92; Church Elder and Treasurer. Recreation: hunting. Address: Middlethird, Gordon, Berwickshire, TD3 6JX; T.-01573 410297.

Tyre, Alistair McKenzie, FHCIMA, DipSHS, MIMgt. Principal and Chief Executive, Langside College, Glasgow, since 1991; b. 6.12.40, Glasgow; m., Jenice Elizabeth Cleat; 1 d. Educ. Dunoon Grammar School; Strathclyde University. Hotel management, 1960-67; Lecturer and Head of Department, Ayr College, 1967-87; Depute Principal, James Watt College, Greenock, 1987-91. Director, Association of Scottish Colleges; Director and Company Secretary, West of Scotland Colleges Partnership; Hampden Training Enterprises Ltd.; Member, General Convocation, Strathclyde University. Recreations: golf; squash; hill-walking; gardening; theatre. Address: (b.) 50 Prospecthill Road, Glasgow, G42 9LB; T.-0141-649 4991.

Tyre, Colin Jack, LLB, DESU. Advocate, since 1987; b. 17.4.56, Dunoon; m., Elaine Patricia Carlin; 1 s.; 2 d. Educ. Dunoon Grammar School; Edinburgh University; Universite d'Aix Marseille. Lecturer in Scots Law, Edinburgh University, 1980-83; Tax Editor, CCH Editions Ltd., Bicester, 1983-86. Publications: CCH Inheritance Tax Reporter; contributor to Stair Memorial Encyclopaedia; Standing Junior Counsel to Scottish Office Environment Department in planning matters. Recreations: orienteering; golf; mountain walking; contemporary music. Address: (b.) Advocates' Library, 1 Parliament Square, Edinburgh; T.-0131-226 5071.

U

U'ren, William Graham, BSc (Hons), DipTP, FRTPI. Director and Scottish Policy Officer, Royal Town Planning Institute in Scotland; b. 28.12.46, Glasgow; m., Wenuy; 2 d. Educ. Aberdeen Grammar School; Aberdeen University; Strathclyde University. Planning Assistant: Clackmannan County Council, 1970-72, Lanark County Council, 1972-75; Principal and Chief Planning Officer, Clydesdale District Council, 1975-82; Director of Planning and Technical Services, Clydesdale District Council, 1982-96; Environment Services Manager, Planning and Economic Development, South Lanarkshire Council, 1996-97. Past Chairman, Scottish Society of Directors of Planning; Vice Convener, Historic Burghs Association of Scotland. Recreations: town-twinning; cricket; bird watching; philately. Address: (b.) 125 Hyndford Road, Lanark ML11 9AU.

Urquhart, Celia Margaret Lloyd. Chief Executive, C U Group of Companies; Member, Board, Scottish Enterprise; a Director, Glasgow Chamber of Commerce; Chairman, Arran Haulage; Member, Advisory Committee, Imperial Cancer Research. b. 7.4.47, Glasgow; 1 s.; 2 d. Founded C U Data, 1986; Winner, Scottish Free Enterprise Award, 1990; Fellow, Institute of Management; Patron, Arran Cancer Support. Recreations: hill-walking; sailing; working late. Address: (b.) 6 Woodside Place, Glasgow G3 7QF.

Urquhart, John, LLB. Scottish Solicitor to Nationwide Building Society, since 1986; b. 10.1.48, Larkhall; m., Janice; 1 s.; 2 d. Educ. Glasgow High School; Glasgow University. Various legal posts in local government, 1968-76; Director, Cool Foods Ltd., 1976-82; Jeffrey Aitken & Co., Solicitors, 1982-86. Chairman, Ramblers Association, Edinburgh Group; Convener, Education and Training Committee, Law Society of Scotland; Scottish Representative, European Company Lawyers Association. Recreation: hill-walking. Address: (b.) 71 George Street, Edinburgh; T.-0131-456 0200.

Urquhart, John Munro, CBE, MA, MEd, FEIS; b. 16.9.10, Gairloch; m., Adela Margaret Sutherland; 1 s.; 1 d. Educ. Lochgilphead Secondary School; Oban High School; Glasgow University. Schoolmaster, Hutchesons' Boys' Grammar School; Assistant Director of Education, Banffshire; Depute Director of Education, Glasgow; Director of Education, Selkirkshire; Director, Scottish Certificate of Education Examination Board, 1965-75; Consultant Registrar, Caribbean Examinations Council, 1977-78; President, Association of Directors of Education, 1963-64. Boy Scouts County Commissioner, Selkirkshire; edited Statistical Account of Selkirkshire, 1964; District Governor, Rotary District 102, 1980. Recreations: angling; walking; reading; gardening. Address: (h.) 29 Craiglockhart Drive South, Edinburgh EH14 1JA; T.-0131-443 3085.

Urwin, Professor Derek William, BA, MA (Econ), PhD. Professor of Politics and International Relations, Aberdeen University, since 1990; b. 27.10.39, Consett; m., Patricia Anne Ross; 2 s. Educ. Consett Grammar School; Wolsingham Grammar School; Keele University; Manchester University. Lecturer, Strathclyde University, 1963-72; Associate Professor, University of Bergen, 1972-80; Professor, Warwick University, 1981-90. Publications: Western Europe since 1945; The Community of Europe; From Ploughshare to Ballot Box; Politics in Western Europe Today; Centre-Periphery Structures in Europe; Dictionary of European History and Politics, since 1945; Scottish Political Behaviour. Recreations: walking; reading; marquetry. Address: (b.) Department of Politics and International Relations, Aberdeen University, Old Aberdeen, AB9 2TY; T.-01224 272716/272713.

Usher, Professor Michael Barham, BSc, PhD, DUniv, CBiol, FIBiol, MIEEM, FRES. Chief Scientist, Scottish Natural Heritage, since 1991; b. 19.11.41, Old Colwyn; m., Kathleen Fionna Munro; 1 s.; 1 d. Educ. Portsmouth Grammar School; Edinburgh University. Lecturer, Senior Lecturer, Reader, Department of Biology, University of York, 1967-91; Adviser on termite research, British Technical Assistance to the Government of Ghana, 1971-73; research in Antarctica and Sub-Antarctica, 1980-81; joined Nature Conservancy Council for Scotland as Chief Scientific Adviser, 1991. Member/Chairman, several Natural Environment Research Council and Economic and Social Research Council Committees. Publications: c. 190 scientific papers; 10 books. Recreations: walking; gardening; natural history photography; philately. Address: (b.) Scottish Natural Heritage, 2 Anderson Place, Edinburgh, EH6 5NP; T.-0131-446 2401.

V

Valentine, Ian Balfour, CA, FRSA. Scottish Senior Partner, BDO Stoy Hayward, Chartered Accountants; Non-Executive Board Member, Ayrshire and Arran Health Board, 1981-93; b. 17.10.40, Glasgow; m., Elaine; 1 s.; 1 d. Educ. Hutchesons' Boys' Grammar School. Partner, J. Wyllie Guild & Ballantine, 1965 (subsequently BDO Stoy Hayward). Member, Council, Institute of Chartered Accountants of Scotland, 1989-97; Chairman, Ayrshire Association of Chartered Accountants of Scotland, 1976-78; President, Junior Chamber Ayr, 1972-73; Member, Ayr Schools Council, 1976-78; Director, Federation of Scottish Junior Chambers of Commerce, 1973-74; Honorary Secretary and Treasurer, Ayr Rugby Football Club, 1979-84; Captain, Royal Troon Golf Club, 1994-97. Recreations: golf; rugby (as spectator); bridge. Address: (b.) 64 Dalblair Road, Ayr; T.-01292 263277.

Vanderheijden, Professor Cornelius A.J.M. Professor of Strategic Management, Strathclyde University, since 1991; b. 31.10.32, Rotterdam; m., Haverkamp Henderika. Educ. Technological University, Delft. General and business planning, Shell Group; Head, Internal Consultancy, then Head, Scenario Planning, Shell International; Member, Shell's Planning Management Team. Address: (h.) Flat 7, 166 Ingram Street, Glasgow; T.-0141-552 7899.

Vanezis Professor Peter, MD, PhD, FRCPath, MRCP (Glas), DMJ. Regius Professor of Forensic Medicine and Science, Glasgow University, since 1993; Director, Human Identification Centre, since 1996; Senior Civilian Consultant in Forensic Medicine to the British Army, since 1992; b. 11.12.47, Nicosia; m., Maria; 1 s.; 1 d. Educ. Wanstead High School, London; Bristol University. Lecturer/Senior Lecturer in Forensic Medicine, London Hospital Medical College, 1974-90; Reader in Forensic Medicine, Charing Cross and Westminster Medical School, 1990-93; Hon. Consultant to Cyprus Government, since 1985, Kenyons International Emergency Services, since 1993. Publications: Pathology of Neck Injury, 1989; Suspicious Death – Scene Investigation, 1996. Recreations: golf; painting. Address: (b.) Department of Forensic Medicine and Science, Glasgow University, Glasgow G12 8QQ; T.-0141-330 4573.

van Heyningen, Veronica, MA, MS, DPhil, FRSE. Staff Scientist, MRC Human Genetics Unit, Edinburgh, since 1977; Hon. Treasurer, The Genetical Society, since 1994; Trustee, National Museums of Scotland, since 1994; b. 12.11.46, Hungary; m., Dr. Simon van Heyningen; 1 s.; 1 d. Educ. Humphrey Perkins School, Leicestershire; Girton College, Cambridge; Northwestern University, Illinois; Lady Margaret Hall, Oxford. Beit Memorial Fellow, 1973-76; Howard Hughes International Research Scholar, since 1993; Honorary Professor, Edinburgh University, 1995. Recreations: visiting museums; travel; talking to people. Address: (b.) MRC Human Genetics Unit, Edinburgh, EH4 2XU; T.-0131-467 8405.

Vannet, Alfred Douglas, LLB, FRSA. Regional Procurator Fiscal, Glasgow and Strathkelvin, since 1997; b. 31.7.49, Dundee; m., Pauline Margaret Renfrew; 1 s.; 1 d. Educ. High School of Dundee; Dundee University. Procurator Fiscal Depute, Dundee, 1976-77; Procurator Fiscal Depute, then Senior Procurator Fiscal Depute, Glasgow, 1977-84; Assistant Solicitor, Crown Office, 1984-90; Deputy Crown Agent, 1990-94; Regional Procurator Fiscal, Grampian, Highland and Islands at Aberdeen, 1994-97. Recreations: music; walking. Address: (b.) 10 Ballater Street, Glasgow G5 9PS.

Vardy, Professor Alan Edward, BSc, PhD, EurIng, CEng, FICE, FASCE, MIAHR, FRSA. Research Professor in Civil Engineering, Dundee University, since 1995; Professor of Civil Engineering, 1979-95 (Deputy Principal, 1985-89, Vice-Principal, 1988-89); Director, Wolfson Bridge Research Unit, 1980-90; b. 6.11.45, Sheffield; m., Susan Janet; 2 s.; 1 d. Educ. High Storrs Grammar School, Sheffield; Leeds University. Lecturer in Civil Engineering, Leeds University, 1972-75; Royal Society Warren Research Fellow, Cambridge University, 1975-79; Royal Society/SERC Industrial Fellow, 1990-94. Dunholm, 512 Perth Road, Dundee, DD2 1LW; T.-Dundee 566123.

Varwell, Rev. Dr. Adrian P.J., BA, BD. Director, St. Ninian's Centre, Crieff, since 1994. Educ. Aberdeen University; Durham University; Edinburgh University. Research Fellow, Aberdeen University, 1969-73; Social Development Officer, Ross and Cromarty County Council/Highland Regional Council, 1973-78; Research Fellow, Edinburgh University, 1978-79; Assistant Minister, Dunblane Cathedral, 1982-83; Minister, Benbecula, 1983-97; Clerk, Presbytery of Uist, 1985-97. Address: (b.) St. Ninian's Centre, Comrie Road, Crieff; T.-01764 653766.

Vas, Professor Peter, MSc, PhD, CSc, DSc, MIEEE, FIEE. Professor in Engineering, Department of Engineering, Aberdeen University, since 1990; b. 1.6.48, Budapest; m., S. Vasne; 2 s. Educ. Technical University of Budapest. United Electrical Machine Works, 1973-77; Newcastle University, 1977-87; Chalmers University of Technology, Lund University of Technology, 1987-90. Laureate of George Montefiore International Award, Belgium, 1990. Publications: over 100 papers; four books; several patents. Address: (b.) Department of Engineering, University of Aberdeen, Aberdeen; T.-01224 272818.

Vaughan, Barbara, BSc, MA. Chairman, Scottish Community Education Council, since 1988; b. 12.2.40, Thornton Heath; m., Dr. Robin A. Vaughan; 2 s.; 2 d. Educ. St. Anne's College, Sanderstead; Nottingham University; Dundee University. Teacher, Derbyshire, 1962-64; Lecturer in Economics, Dundee Institute of Technology, 1979-83; Councillor, Tayside Region, 1980; Chairman, Further Education Sub-Committee, 1981-82; Chairman, Education Committee, 1982-86; Member, MSC Committee for Scotland, 1983-86; Commissioner, MSC, 1986. Address: (b.) Rosebery House, 9 Haymarket Terrace, Edinburgh, EH12 5EZ.

Veal, Sheriff Kevin Anthony, KSG, KHS, LLB. Sheriff of Tayside Central and Fife at Forfar, since 1993; b. 16.9.46, Chesterfield; m., Monica Flynn; 2 s.; 2 d. Educ. Lawside Academy, Dundee; St. Andrews University. Partner, Burns Veal and Gillan, Dundee, 1971-93; Legal Aid Reporter, 1978-93; Temporary Sheriff, 1984-93; Tutor, Department of Law, Dundee University, 1978-85; Dean, Faculty of Procurators and Solicitors in Dundee, 1991-93. Musical Director, Cecilian Choir, Dundee, since 1975. Recreations: organ and classical music; hill-walking. Address: (h.) Viewfield, 70 Blackness Avenue, Dundee, DD2 1JL; T.-01382 668633.

Vernon, Kenneth Robert, CBE, BSc, FEng, FIEE, FIMechE. Deputy Chairman and Chief Executive, North of Scotland Hydro-Electric Board, 1973-88; b. 15.3.23, Dumfries; m., Pamela Hands; 1 s.; 3 d.; 1 d. deceased. Educ. Dumfries Academy; Glasgow University. BTH Co., Edinburgh Corporation, British Electricity Authority, 1948-55; South of Scotland Electricity Board, 1955-56; North of Scotland Hydro Electric Board: Chief Electrical and Mechanical Engineer, 1964, General Manager, 1966, Board Member, 1970; Director, British Electricity International Ltd., 1976-88; Board Member, Northern Ireland Electricity Service, 1979-85. Recreation: fishing. Address: (h.) 10 Keith Crescent, Edinburgh EH4 3NH; T.-0131-332 4610.

Vernon, Richard Geoffrey, BSc, PhD, FIBiol. Head, Science Planning and Development and Head, Molecular Homeorhesis Group, Hannah Research Intitute; Honorary Lecturer, Glasgow University; b. 19.2.43, Maidstone; m., Mary Christine Cunliffe; 1 s.; 1 d. Educ. Newcastle High School; Birmingham University. Research Fellow, University of Toronto, 1969-72; Senior Scientist then Head of Department, Hannah Research Institute, 1972-95; Consultant Editor, Journal of Dairy Research; Member, Editorial Board, British Journal of Nutrition, 1981-87, Domestic Animal Endocrinology (USA), 1992-95; Chairman, Scottish Section, Nutrition Society, 1989-91; Member, AFRC Animals Research Grants Board, 1991-94; Past President, Birmingham University Mountaineering Club; Chairman, Belmont Academy School Board, 1989-93. Publications: Physiological Strategies in Lactation (Co-editor); 200 scientific papers. Recreations: hill-walking; ornithology; bridge; photography. Address: (h.) 29 Knoll Park, Ayr, KA7 4RH; T.-01292 42195.

Vettese, Raymond John, DipEd, BA (Hons). Teacher and Writer; b. 1.11.50, Arbroath; m., Maureen Elizabeth. Educ. Montrose Academy; Dundee College of Education; Open Univesity. Journalist, Montrose Review, 1968-72; student, 1972-75; barman, 1975-77; factory worker/farmer, 1977-78; clerical officer, 1978-85; teacher, since 1985; Preses, Scots Language Society, 1991-94; William Soutar Fellowship, 1989-90. Publications: Four Scottish Poets, 1985; The Richt Noise, 1988 (Saltire Society Best First Book); A Keen New Air, 1995. Recreations: reading; music; cooking; chess. Address: (h.) 9 Tayock Avenue, Montrose, DD10 9AP; T.-01674 678943.

Vickerman, Professor Keith, BSc, PhD, DSc, FLS, FRSE, FRS. Regius Professor of Zoology, Glasgow University, since 1984; Consultant Expert on Parasitic Diseases, World Health Organisation, since 1973; b. 21.3.33, Huddersfield; m., Moira Dutton; 1 d. Educ. King James Grammar School, Almondbury; University College, London (Fellow, 1985). Wellcome Lecturer in Protozoology, University College, London, 1958-63; Tropical Research Fellow, Royal Society, 1963-68; Glasgow University: Reader in Zoology, 1968-74; Professor of Zoology, 1974-84; Head, Department of Zoology, 1979-85. Leeuwenhoek Lecturer, Royal Society, 1994; Linnean Society Gold Medal for contributions to science, 1996. Publications: The Protozoa (Co-author), 1967; many papers in scientific and medical journals. Recreations: drawing and painting; gardening. Address: (h.) 16 Mirrlees Drive, Glasgow G12 OSH; T.-0141-334 2794.

Vincent, Catherine Lindsey, BA (Hons). Director of Corporate Strategy, Scottish Sports Council, since 1989; b. 30.7.56, Oxford; m., Jonathan Nicholas Crook; 2 d. Educ. Rosebery Grammar School, Epsom; Newnham College, Cambridge. Research Assistant, Sheffield University, 1978; Assistant Editor, Athlone Press, 1979; Freelance Writer, 1980; Development Officer, Scottish Community Education Council, 1981; Senior Policy Analyst, Fife Regional Council, 1986. Former Chairman, Spiritual Assembly of the Baha'is of Edinburgh; former Director, Baha'i Information Scotland. Publication: Discovering Edinburgh, 1981. Recreations: reading; walking; tennis; badminton; enjoying family. Address: (b.) Scottish Sports Council, Caledonia House, South Gyle, Edinburgh EH12 9DQ; T.-0131-317 7200.

Vowles, Kenneth Leslie, FIME, FIEE, MBIM, CEng. Executive Director, Scottish Power, since 1996; b. 22.3.42, Newport, Gwent; m., Christine; 2 d. Educ. University of Wales. Generation Manager, National Power (Northern Group); Station Manager, Rugeley and Ironbridge Power Station. Director, Quality Scotland; Vice-President, Scottish Engineering. Recreation: golf. Address: (b.) 1 Atlantic Quay, Glasgow; T.-0141-636 4509.

W

Waddell, John MacLaren Ogilvie, LLB, WS. Director of Legal Services, Christian Salvesen PLC, since 1989, and Member, Management Board, since 1997; b. 12.4.56, Inverness; m., Alice Emily Bain; 1 s.; 1 d. Educ. Inverness Royal Academy; George Watson's College; Edinburgh University. Qualified as a Solicitor, 1980; Assistant, 1980, Partner, 1983, Steedman Ramage WS. Chairman, Fotofeis Ltd. Recreations: skiing; the arts. Address: (h.) 50 East Fettes Avenue, Edinburgh; T.-0131-559 3616.

Waddell, William A.H., BA (Hons). Head Teacher, Bishopbriggs High School, since 1994; b. 22.6.51, Paisley; m., Alison; 2 d. Educ. John Neilson, Paisley; Strathclyde University. Teacher of Mathematics, then Assistant Principal Teacher of Mathematics, Park Mains High School, 1974-80; Principal Teacher of Mathematics, Dumbarton Academy, 1980-85; Assistant Head Teacher, Boclair Academy, 1985-90; Depute Head Teacher, Hermitage Academy, 1990-94. Recreations: sport; gardening; family pursuits. Address: (h.) 66 Stuart Road, Bishopton, Renfrewshire.

Wade, Professor Nicholas James, BSc, PhD, FRSE. Professor of Visual Psychology, Dundee University, since 1991; b. 27.3.42, Retford, Nottinghamshire; m., Christine Whetton; 2 d. Educ. Queen Elizabeth's Grammar School, Mansfield; Edinburgh University; Monash University. Postdoctoral Research Fellow, Max-Planck Institute for Behavioural Physiology, Germany, 1969-70; Lecturer in Psychology, Dundee University, 1970-78, Reader, 1978-91. Publications: The Art and Science of Visual Illusions, 1982; Brewster and Wheatstone on Vision, 1983; Visual Allusions: Pictures of Perception, 1990; Visual Perception: an introduction, 1991; Psychologists in Word and Image, 1995; A Natural History of Vision, 1998. Recreations: cycling. Address: (h.) 36 Norwood, Newport-on-Tay, Fife DD6 8DW; T.-01382 543136.

Wade, Paul Francis Joseph, LLB. Solicitor, since 1976; Solicitor Advocate, since 1993; b. 19.3.53, Derby; m., Gilllian Ann; 1 s.; 1 d. Educ. Queen Margaret Academy, Ayr; Glasgow University. Biggart, Baillie and Gifford, 1974-79; Partner, Cochran Sayers & Cook, Glasgow, 1981-93; Partner, Simpson & Marwick WS, Glasgow, since 1993. Recreations: sailing; rural pursuits; travel. Address: (b.) 93 West George Street, Glasgow G2 1PB; T.-0141-248 2666.

Wade, Professor Terence Leslie Brian, BA, PhD, FIL. Emeritus Professor in Russian Studies, Strathclyde University; b. 19.5.30, Southend-on-Sea; m., Mary Isobel McEwan; 2 d. Educ. Southend-on-Sea High School for Boys; Durham University; Cologne University. National Service, Intelligence Corps, 1953-55; War Office Language Instructor, 1955-63; Lecturer, Scottish College of Commerce, Glasgow, 1963-64; Lecturer, Senior Lecturer, Reader, Professor, Strathclyde University, from 1964; Chairman, Department of Modern Languages, 1986-94; Professor, Research Fellow, since 1995. Convener, West of Scotland Association of Teachers of Russian; Editor, Journal of Russian Studies, 1980-86; Chairman, Association of Teachers of Russian, 1986-89; President, Association of Teachers of Russian, 1989-90; Member, Presidium, International Association of Teachers of Russian Language and Literature, since 1991. Publications: Russian Exercises for Language Laboratories (Co-author); The Russian Preposition "do" and the Concept of Extent; Prepositions in Modern Russian; Russia Today (Co-Editor); The Gender of Soft-Sign Nouns in Russian; A Comprehensive Russian Grammar; A Russian Grammar Workbook; Russian Etymological Dictionary. Address: 1 Cleveden Crescent, Glasgow, G12 OPD; T.-0141-339 3947.

Waigh, Professor Roger David, BPharm, PhD, FRPharmS, CChem, FRSC. Professor of Medicinal Chemistry, Strathclyde University, since 1991; b. 8.8.44, Loughborough; m., Sally Joy Bembridge; 1 s.; 1 d. Educ. Sir George Monoux Grammar School, Walthamstow; Bath University. Lecturer, Strathclyde University, 1970-76; Lecturer, then Senior Lecturer, Manchester University, 1976-91. Recreations: bird-watching; golf; photography. Address: (b.) Department of Pharmaceutical Sciences, Strathclyde University, Glasgow G1 1XW; T.-0141-548 4355.

Waite, James A., MA. Rector, Perth Academy, since 1986; b. 9.10.42, Edinburgh; m., Sandra R. MacKenzie; 2 d. Educ. Royal High School, Edinburgh; Edinburgh University. Teacher of English, George Heriot's School, 1965-70; Principal Teacher of English, Campbeltown Grammar School, 1970-71; Principal Teacher of English, then Assistant Head Teacher, Boroughmuir High School, 1971-83; Depute Head Teacher, James Gillespie's High School, 1983-86. Recreations: theatre; literature; music; hill-walking. Address: (b.) Perth Academy, Murray Place, Perth, PH1 1NJ; T.-01738 623491.

Wake, Joseph Robert, MA, CPA. Secretary, Scotland, Central Bureau for Educational Visits and Exchanges, since 1972; b. 16.5.42, Corbridge; 1 s.; 2 d. Educ. Royal Grammar School, Newcastle upon Tyne; Edinburgh University; Moray House College of Education. Teacher, Kirkcaldy High School, 1966-69, St. Modan's High School, Stirling, 1969-71; Principal Teacher of Modern Languages, Grangemouth High School, 1971-72. Recreations: cricket; philately; Scottish dancing. Address: (b.) 3 Bruntsfield Crescent, Edinburgh EH10 4HD; T.-0131-447 8024.

Wakeford, Air Marshal Sir Richard (Gordon), KCB (1976), LVO (1961), OBE (1958), AFC (1952). Chairman, MacRobert Trustees, 1982-94; b. 20.4.22, Torquay; m., Anne Butler; 2 s.; 1 d.; 1 d. (deceased). Educ. Montpelier School, Paignton; Kelly College, Tavistock. Entered RAF, 1941; Coastal Command, 1941-45; Transport Command, 1945-47; Training Command, 1947-52; staff duties, including Director of Ops Staff, Malaya, 1952-58; CO, The Queens' Flight, 1958-61; IDC, 1969; Director, Service Intelligence, 1970-73; Commander, Anzuk Force Singapore, 1974-75; Deputy Chief of Defence Staff (Intelligence), 1975-78; retired Air Marshal, 1978. Director, RAF Benevolent Fund, Scotland, 1978-89; Commissioner, Queen Victoria School, Dunblane, 1980-90; Director, Thistle Foundation; Director, Cromar Nominess; Commander, Order of St. John, 1986. Recreation: fishing. Address: (h.) Sweethome Cottage, Inchberry Road, Fochabers, IV32 7QA; T.-01343 820 436.

Walde, Professor Thomas W., LLM, Driur. Professor of International Economic, Natural Resources and Energy Law, University of Dundee, since 1991; Executive Director, Centre for Energy, Petroleum and Mineral Law and Policy; b. 1949, Germany; 1 s. Educ. Universities of Heildelberg, Frankfurt and Harvard. Institute for International Economic Law, Frankfurt, 1975-80; U.N. Natural Resources and Energy Division, 1980-85; Adviser to Governments on mineral development policies, legislation, and contract negotiations; Interregional Advisor on Petroleum and Mineral Legislation, U.N. (D.T.C.D.), 1985-90; EC Jean Monnet Professor of European Economic and Energy Law; Editor, Journal of Energy and Natural Resources Law; Visiting Professor, Universite de Paris II - Pantheon - Assosc.; Corresp. Editor, International Legal Materials; Chief Adviser EC-Tacis/Synergy legislative reform projects. Address: (b.) Park Place, Dundee DD1 4HN; T.-01382 344300.

Walkden, Gordon Mark, BSc, PhD. Head, Department of Geology and Petroleum Geology, Aberdeen University; Geological Consultant to industry; b. 8.6.44, Edinburgh; m.,

K. Mary M. Begg; 3 c. Educ. Quintin School, London; Manchester University. Former Member and Vice Convener, Kincardine and Deeside District Council; Past Chairman, Banchory Community Council; scientific author and local historian. Recreations: building restoration; palaeontology; landscape gardening. Address: (h.) Banchory, Kincardineshire.

Walker, Alexander William, MBE, JP. Honorary Sheriff, since 1970; Chairman, Finance and General Purposes Committee, Tweeddale District Council, 1977-92 (Member of Council, 1974-92; Chairman, Tweeddale Licensing Board, since 1975; Chairman, Tweeddale Local Sports Council; b. 10.5.24, Peebles; m., Dorothy Margaret. Educ. Kingsland School; Scottish Woollen and Worsted Technical College. D.B. Ballantyne Bros., 1939-70; Air Training Corps, 1941-43, RAF, 1943-46 (Sergeant); former Director, Sonido International Ltd. (formerly Fidelitone International Ltd.); elected, Peebles Town Council, 1960-75; Provost, 1967-70; Burgh Treasurer, 1971-75; held every office, Peebles Town Council; Member, Peeblesshire County Council, 1960-70 (Vice Chairman, Finance Committee); Vice Chairman, Tweeddale District Council, 1974-77; Warden, Neidpath Castle, 1971; former Dean, Guildry Corporation of Peebles; Honorary President, Peebles Callants Club; Dean, Guildry Corporation of Peebles, since 1990-93. Recreations: football in younger days; now enjoys reading political biographies; and, of course, local government, which unfortunately is no longer local or indeed democratic. Address: (h.) Gadeni, 59 High Street, Peebles; T.-Peebles 21011.

Walker, Professor Andrew Charles, BA, MSc, PhD, FInstP, FRSE, CPhys. Professor of Modern Optics, Heriot-Watt University, since 1988; b. 24.6.48, Wembley; m., Margaret Elizabeth; 1 s.; 1 d. Educ. Kingsbury County Grammar School; Essex University. Postdoctoral Fellowship, National Research Council of Canada, 1972-74; SRC Research Fellowship, Essex University, 1974-75; Higher/Senior Scientific Officer, UKAEA Culham Laboratory, 1975-83; Lecturer/Reader, Heriot-Watt University, 1983-88. Honorary Secretary, Quantum Electronics Group, Institute of Physics, 1982-85; Chairman, Scottish Branch, Institute of Physics, 1993-95. Recreations: music; skiing; sailing. Address: (b.) Department of Physics, Heriot-Watt University, Riccarton, Edinburgh EH14 4AS; T.-0131-451 3036.

Walker, Audrey R., BA, ALA. Librarian, Signet Library, since 1994; b. 18.10.57, Glasgow. Educ. Clydebank High School; Robert Gordon University, Aberdeen. Library Assistant, 1975-80; Senior Library Assistant, Telford College, Edinburgh, 1980-84; Assistant Librarian: Scottish Office Library, 1987, Post-Graduate Medical Library, 1988-90, Advocates Library, 1990-94. Scottish Library Association: Chair, East Branch, and Chair, Membership Services Committee; Committee Member, Meadowbank National Track League. Recreations: cycling; reading; cross-stitch; cinema. Address: (b.) Signet Library, Parliament Square, Edinburgh EH1 1RF; T.-0131-225 4923.

Walker, Professor David Maxwell, CBE, QC, MA, PhD, LLD, Hon. LLD, FBA, FRSE, FRSA. Regius Professor of Law, Glasgow University, 1958-90; Honorary Senior Research Fellow, since 1990; b. 9.4.20, Glasgow; m., Margaret Knox, OBE. Educ. High School of Glasgow; Glasgow University; Edinburgh University; London University. HLI and Indian Army, 1939-46; Advocate, 1948; in practice, Scottish Bar, 1948-54; Professor of Jurisprudence, Glasgow University, 1954-58; Barrister (Middle Temple), 1957; QC (Scot), 1958; Dean, Faculty of Law, Glasgow University, 1956-59; Convener, School of Law, 1984-88. Chairman, High School of Glasgow Trust. Publications: Law of Damages in Scotland; The Scottish Legal System; Law of Delict in Scotland; Law of Civil Remedies in Scotland; Law of Prescription in Scotland; Law of Contracts in Scotland; Oxford Companion to Law; Principles of Scottish Private Law (four volumes); The Scottish Jurists; Stair's Institutions (Editor); Stair Tercentenary Studies (Editor); A Legal History of Scotland, (5 Vols). Recreations: book collecting; Scottish history; motoring. Address: (b.) School of Law, Glasgow University, Glasgow G12 8QQ; T.-0141-339 8855, Ext. 4556.

Walker, Professor David Morrison, OBE, DA, FSA, FSA Scot, FRSE, HFRIAS, Hon. LLD (Dundee). Honorary Professor of Art History, University of St. Andrews, since 1994; Chief Inspector of Historic Buildings, Scottish Office Environment Department, 1988-93; b. 31.1.33, Dundee; m., Averil Mary Stewart McIlwraith (deceased); 1 s. Educ. Morgan Academy, Dundee; Dundee College of Art. Voluntary work for National Buildings Record, Edinburgh, 1952-56; National Service, Royal Engineers, 1956-58; Glasgow Education Authority, 1958-59; Dundee Education Authority, 1959-61; Historic Buildings Branch, Scottish Office: Senior Investigator of Historic Buildings, 1961-76, Principal Investigator of Historic Buildings, 1976-78; Principal Inspector of Historic Buildings, 1978-88. Alice Davis Hitchcock Medallion, 1970. Publications: Dundee Nineteenth Century Mansions, 1958; Architecture of Glasgow (Co-author), 1968 (revised and enlarged edition, 1987); Buildings of Scotland: Edinburgh (Co-author), 1984; Dundee: An Illustrated Introduction (Co-author), 1984; St. Andrew's House: an Edinburgh Controversy 1912-1939, 1989; Central Glasgow: an illustrated architectural guide (Co-author), 1989. Address: (h.) 22 Inverleith Row, Edinburgh EH3 5QH.

Walker, Douglas William, TD, BSc, CEng, MICE, MIBC. Director of Technical Services, East Dunbartonshire Council, since 1995; b. 18.6.50, Edinburgh; 2 d. Educ. George Heriot's School, Edinburgh; Edinburgh University. Perth and Kinross County Surveyor's Department, 1972-75; T. Harley Haddow and Partners, Consulting Engineers, 1975-80; Strathclyde Regional Council Roads Department, 1980-83; Glasgow City Council Building Control Department, 1984-95 (Depute Director, 1991-95). Service with TA Royal Engineers, 1968-86, retired 1986 with rank of Major. Recreations: golf; cycling; travel; reading. Address: (b.) East Dunbartonshire Council, Technical Services, Cleddens House, Wester Cleddens Road, Bishopbriggs, Glasgow G64 2LW.

Walker, Drew, BSc, MB, ChB, MSc, MFCM. Director of Health Planning and Public Health, Chief Administrative Medical Officer, Executive Board Member, Ayrshire and Arran Health Board, since 1991; b. 30.8.54, Bridge of Allan. Educ. Perth Academy; Edinburgh University. House Officer/SHO, 1978-80; District Medical Officer, Zimbabwe, 1980-82; Registrar/Senior Registrar in public health, 1983-87; Consultant in public health, 1987-91. National Vice President, Medical Practitioners Union, 1988-90. Recreations: football; climbing; skiing; reading Viz. Address: (h.) Schaw House, by Stair, Ayrshire.

Walker, (Edward) Michael, FRICS. Chairman, Walker Group (Scotland) Ltd., Westerwood Ltd., and associated companies, since 1986 (Founder, 1969); Chairman, Lothian and Edinburgh Ltd. (LEEL), since 1996 (Director, since 1991); b. 12.4.41, Aberdeen; m., Flora Margaret; 2 s.; 1 d. Educ. Aberdeen Grammar School. President, Edinburgh and District Master Builders Association, 1987 and 1996; Past President, Scottish House Builders Association; former Committee Member, NHBC (Scotland) Ltd., 1990-96; former Lord Dean of Guild, City of Edinburgh, 1992-96; Captain of Industry Award, Livingston Industrial and Commercial Association, 1987; Chairman, Livingston Youth Trust, since 1993. Recreations: skiing; scuba diving; walking; reading. Address: (b.) Walker Group (Scotland)

Ltd., Westerwood House, Royston Road, Deans Industrial Estate, Livingston, W. Lothian; T.-01506 413101.

Walker, Ernest John Munro, CBE. Chairman, UEFA Stadia Committee; b. 20.7.28, Glasgow; m., Anne; 1 s.; 2 d. Educ. Queen's Park Secondary School. Army (Royal Horse Artillery), 1946-48; Assistant Secretary, industrial textile company, 1948-58; Assistant Secretary, Scottish Football Association, 1958-77, Secretary, 1977-90. Director, Euro-Sporting; Director, Scotball Travel and Leisure Ltd.; Director, Eastern European Assistance Bureau; Member: FIFA Board of Appeal; Chairman, Scottish Stadia Committee; Chairman, Scottish Football's Independent Rview Commission; Vice-President, Newspaper Press Fund; Independent Adviser to Secretary of State for Scotland on Appointments to Public Bodies. Recreations: golf (past Captain, Haggs Castle GC); fishing; music; travel.

Walker, Hugh A.D. Principal, Clydebank College, since 1997; b. 26.10.43. Educ. Bournemouth School; St. David's College, Lampeter; Institute of Education, London. Taught in comprehensive school and adult education, London, 1968-71; taught in school and continuing education centre, Mid West State, Nigeria; Diploma, Applied Linguistics, Edinburgh University, 1974; Appleton Scholar, Edinburgh, 1975; Teacher, Stevenson College, 1975-85; Assistant to Director of Education, Lothian Region, 1985-88; Head of Department, West Lothian College, 1988-89; Depute Principal, Anniesland College, 1989, Principal, 1992-97; Chair, Higher Still Further Education Implementation Studies Group; Director, West of Scotland Colleges' Partnership; Director, Leven Valley Initiative. Recreations: hill-running; tennis; squash. Address: (b.) Kilbowie Road, Clydebank G81 2AA; T.-0141-952 7771.

Walker, Irene, MBA, BSc (Hons). Chief Executive, Dumfries and Galloway Enterprise Ltd., since 1994; b. 28.1.52, Larbert; m., Neil Walker. Educ. Larbert High School; Edinburgh University; St. Andrews University. Local government, 1975-86; Glasgow Garden Festival, 1986-88; Scottish Development Agency, 1989-91; Grampian Enterprise Ltd., 1991-93. Recreations: windsurfing; skiing. Address: (b.) Solway House, Dumfries Enterprise Park, Tinwald Downs Road, Heathhall, Dumfries DG1 3SJ. Tel.: 01387 245000.

Walker, Rev. James Bernard, MA, BD, DPhil. Chaplain, St. Andrews University, since 1993; b. 7.5.46, Malawi; m., Sheila Mary Easton; 3 s. Educ. Hamilton Academy; Edinburgh University; Merton College, Oxford. Church of Scotland Minister: Mid Craigie linked with Wallacetown, Dundee, 1975-78, Old and St. Paul's, Galashiels, 1978-87; Principal, The Queen's College, Birmingham, 1987-93. Publication: Israel — Covenant and Land, 1988. Recreations: hill-walking; tennis; squash; golf. Address: 3A St. Mary's Place, St. Andrews KY16 9UY; T.-01334 462865.

Walker, Leslie Gresson, MA, PhD, DipClinPsychol, CPsychol, CBiol, MIBiol, AFBPsS. Senior Lecturer, Department of Mental Health, Aberdeen University, since 1989; Director, Behavioural Oncology Unit, Departments of Mental Health and Surgery, Aberdeen University; Honorary Consultant Clinical Psychologist, Aberdeen Royal Hospitals NHS Trust; b. 17.5.49, Glasgow; m., Mary Birnie; 2 s. Educ. Banff Academy; Aberdeen University. Clinical Psychologist, Grampian Health Board, 1974-76; Lecturer, Aberdeen University, 1976-89; elected Member, National Committee of Scientists in Professions Allied to Medicine (Clinical Psychology Sub-Committee), Scottish Home and Health Department, 1979-85; External Assessor, Children's Panel Advisory Committee, Grampian Regional Council, 1982-90; Council Member, British Society of Experimental and Clinical Hypnosis, since 1991; Consultant Editor, Contemporary Hypnosis, since 1991; Editorial Advisory

Board Member, Psycho-Oncology, since 1996; Chairman, British Psychosocial Oncology Society, since 1996; Elder, Church of Scotland. Publications: numerous scientific papers and three books, including Police Stress at Work (Co-author), 1993. Address: (b.)Behavioural Oncology Unit, Departments of Mental Health and Surgery, Medical School, Foresterhill, Aberdeen AB9 2ZD; T.-01224 681818, Ext. 53881.

Walker, Michael Giles Neish, CBE, MA (Cantab). Chairman, Sidlaw Group, since 1988 (Chief Executive, 1976-88); b. 28.8.33, Fife; m., Margaret R. Hills; 2 s.; 1 d. Educ. Shrewsbury School, St. John's College, Cambridge. National Service, Royal Dragoons, 1952-54 (2nd Lt.); TA, Fife and Forfar Yeomanry, 1954-72 (Major); joined Jute Industries Ltd., 1958 (subsequently name changed to Sidlaw Group). Address: (b.) Sidlaw Group plc, Keith House, South Gyle, Edinburgh EH12 9DQ; T.-0131-317 2600.

Walker, Stewart. Director, Edinburgh Convention Bureau, since 1994; b. 13.10.53, Glasgow; m., Linda McPherson; 2 d. Educ. Queen's Park Secondary School, Glasgow; Glasgow College of Food Technology. Resident Manager, Caledonian Hotel, 1985-88; General Manager, North British Hotel, 1988-89; General Manager, St. James Club, Los Angeles, 1989-90; Managing Director, HCI Ltd., 1991-94. Recreations: golf; skiing. Address: (b.) 4 Rothesay Terrace, Edinburgh EH3 7RY; T.-0131-226 6888.

Walker, Professor William Barclay, BSc, MSc. Professor of International Relations, St. Andrews University, since 1996; b. 7.12.46, Longforgan; m., Carolyn Scott; 1 s. Educ. Shrewsbury School; Edinburgh University. Design Engineer, Ferranti Ltd., 1970-72; Research Fellow, Science Policy Research Unit, Sussex University, 1974-78; Research Fellow, Royal Institute of International Affairs, and Secretary, International Consultative Group on Nuclear Energy, 1978-80; Science Policy Research Unit, Sussex University: Senior Fellow, 1981-92, Professorial Fellow and Director of Research, 1993-96. Publications: Plutonium and Highly Enriched Uranium: World Inventories, Capabilities and Policies (Co-author), 1997. Recreations: piano-playing; tennis; ornithology. Address: (b.) Department of International Relations, University of St. Andrews, St. Andrews KY16 9AL; T.-01334 462934.

Walker, Professor William Farquhar, DSc, ChM, FRCS (Edin and Eng), FRSE. Consultant General Surgeon, since 1965; Emeritus Professor of Vascular Surgery, Surgery, Dundee University; b. 26.5.25, Aberdeen; m., Bettie Stanley; 2 s.; 1 d. Educ. Fraser Academy; St. Andrews University. RAF, 1949-51; Senior Lecturer in Surgery (Consultant), Dundee Royal Infirmary, 1956-75. President, Association of Surgeons of Great Britain and Ireland, 1984; President, Vascular Society of Great Britain and Ireland, 1989. Recreations: golf; fishing; gardening. Address: (h.) 438 Blackness Road, Dundee; T.-01382 68179.

Walkingshaw, Francis, NP. Solicitor; Procurator Fiscal, District of Wigtown, since 1983, and Kirkcudbright, since 1993; b. 9.12.42, Edinburgh; m., Penelope Marion Theodosia Brooks McKissock; 2 s. Educ. George Watson's College, Edinburgh. Private practice; joined Procurator Fiscal service, 1975; Depute Fiscal, Kirkcaldy, 1976-78; Depute Fiscal, Glasgow, 1978-81; Depute Fiscal, Perth, 1982. Dean, Faculty of Wigtown District Solicitors, 1985-87. Recreations: shooting; fishing; food and wine. Address: (b.) Sheriff Court House, Lewis Street, Stranraer; T.-01776 704321.

Wallace, Archibald Duncan, MB, ChB. Medical Practitioner, Campbeltown, since 1950; Hon. Sheriff of North Strathclyde at Campbeltown, since 1980; b. 4.1.26, Glasgow; m., Rona B. MacLennan; 1 s.; 2 d. Educ. High School of Glasgow; Glasgow University. Sector Medical

Officer, Argyll and Clyde Health Board, until 1988; Civilian MO to RAF Machrihanish, until 1988. Chairman, Campbeltown Branch, RNLI; Past President, Campbeltown Rotary Club; Past Captain, Machrihanish Golf Club. Recreations: golf; gardening. Address: (h.) Lilybank House, Low Askomil, Campbeltown; T.-01586 52658.

Wallace of Campsie, Baron (George Wallace), JP, DL. Life President, Wallace, Cameron (Holdings) Ltd., since 1981; b. 13.2.15; m. Educ. Queen's Park School, Glasgow; Glasgow University. Solicitor, since 1950; Honorary Sheriff, Hamilton, since 1971; Chairman, East Kilbride and Stonehouse Development Corporation, 1969-75; Member, South of Scotland Electricity Board, 1966-68; Member, Board, Scottish Development Agency, 1975-78; President, Glasgow Chamber of Commerce, 1974-76; Chairman, Scottish Executive Committee, British Heart Foundation, 1973-76; Patron, Scottish Retirement Council, since 1975. Address: (h.) 14 Fernleigh Road, Newlands, Glasgow G43 2UE.

Wallace, James Fleming, QC, MA, LLB. Counsel (Draftsman), Scottish Law Commission, 1979-93; Part-time Chairman, Industrial Tribunals, since 1993; b. 19.3.31, Edinburgh; m., Valerie Mary Lawrence (deceased); 2 d.; 2, Linda Ann Lilleker. Educ. Edinburgh Academy; Edinburgh University. National Service, 1954-56 (2nd Lt., Royal Artillery); TA (Lt., Royal Artillery), 1956-60; practised at Scottish Bar, 1957-60; Parliamentary Draftsman and Legal Secretary to Lord Advocate, 1960-79. Publications: The Businessman's Lawyer (Scottish Supplement); Stair Memorial Encyclopaedia (Contributor). Recreations: hill-walking; choral singing; golf; badminton. Address: (h.) 24 Corrennie Gardens, Edinburgh EH10 6DB; T.-0131-447 1224.

Wallace, James Robert, QC, MA (Cantab), LLB (Edinburgh). MP (Liberal Democrat, formerly Liberal), Orkney and Shetland, since 1983; Leader, Scottish Liberal Democrats, since 1992; Advocate, 1979; QC (Scot.), 1997; b. 25.8.54, Annan; m., Rosemary Janet Fraser; 2 d. Educ. Annan Academy; Downing College, Cambridge; Edinburgh University. Called to Scottish Bar, 1979; contested Dumfries, 1979, and South of Scotland Euro Constituency, 1979; Member, Scottish Liberal Party Executive, 1976-85 (Vice-Chairman, Policy, 1982-85); Honorary President, Scottish Young Liberals, 1984-85; Liberal Democrat Spokesman on Fisheries, 1988-97, and on Scotland, since 1992. Publication: New Deal for Rural Scotland (Co-Editor), 1983. Recreations: golf; reading; travelling (especially between London and the Northern Isles). Address: (h.) Northwood House, Tankerness, Orkney KW17 2QS; T.-01856 861383.

Wallace, John David, MA, DipEd, FSA Scot. International Arbiter and Chairman, Arbiters Council, Federation Internationale des Echecs; President, Scottish Junior Chess Association, 1986-89; Council Member, Scottish Chess Association; b. 21.11.21, Bulford; m., Jenefer M.H. Bell (deceased); 1 s.; 1 d. Educ. Tonbridge School; St. Andrews University. Army Service, 1940-46 (Captain, Royal Artillery); teaching appointments in Orkney and Fife, 1954-73; Assistant Rector, Madras College, St. Andrews, 1971-73; founding Headmaster, Abbotsgrange Middle School, Grangemouth, 1974-84. Recreations: bridge; chess; curling; hill-walking. Address: (h.) Kirkheugh Cottage, The Shorehead, St. Andrews, Fife KY16 9RG.

Wallace, Rev. William Fitch, BDS, BD. Minister, Pultneytown and Thrumster Church, since 1990; Convener, Church of Scotland Board of Social Responsibility, 1993-97; b. 6.10.39, Falkirk; m., Jean Wyness Hill; 1 s.; 3 d. Educ. Allan Glen's School; Glasgow University; Edinburgh University. Minister, Wick St. Andrew's and Thrumster Church, 1974-90; former missionary dentist. Vice-Convener, Board of Social Responsibility, 1989-92.

Recreations: family; golf; gardening. Address: The Manse, Coronation Street, Wick KW1 5LS; T.-01955 603166.

Wallace, Professor William Villiers, MA, FRHistS. Director, Institute of Russian and East European Studies, Glasgow University, 1979-92, now Senior Research Fellow; Visiting Professor, Sunderland University, since 1995; Vice-President, Council for Education in World Citizenship, since 1996; Features Editor, eurobüro, since 1997; b. 15.12.26, Glasgow; m., Gulli Fyfe; 2 s.; 1 d. Educ. Hutchesons' Boys' Grammar School; Glasgow University; London University. RNVR, 1944-47; appointments in History, Pittsburgh University, London University, Aberdeen University, Durham University, 1953-67; Professor of History, New University of Ulster, 1967-79. Foreign Member, Russian Academy of Technological Sciences. Address: (b.) Institute of Russian and East European Studies, Glasgow University, 29 Bute Gardens, Glasgow G12 8RS; T.-0141-330 5585.

Walls, Professor Andrew Finlay, OBE, MA, BLitt, DD, FSA Scot. Curator of Collections, Centre for the Study of Christianity in the Non-Western World, since 1996; b. 21.4.28; m., Doreen Mary Harden; 1 s.; 1 d. Librarian, Tyndale House, Cambridge, 1952-57; Lecturer in Theology, Fourah Bay College, Sierra Leone, 1957-62; Head, Department of Religion, Nigeria University, 1962-65; Aberdeen University: Lecturer in Church History, 1966-69, Senior Lecturer, 1969, first Head, Department of Religious Studies, and Riddoch Lecturer in Comparative Religion, 1970, Reader, 1975, Professor of Religious Studies, 1979-85, Emeritus Professor, 1985; Director, Centre for the Study of Christianity in the Non-Western World, 1982-96; Honorary Professor, Edinburgh University, 1987-96; Visiting Professor of World Christianity, Yale University, 1988; Visiting Professor of Ecumenics and Mission, Princeton Theological Seminary, since 1997; Co-opted Member, Aberdeen Education Committee, 1971-74; Aberdeen City Councillor, 1974-80; Convener, Arts and Recreation, COSLA, 1978-80; Chairman, Council for Museums and Galleries in Scotland, 1978-81; Vice-Chairman, Committee of Area Museums Councils, 1980-81; Member, Williams Committee on the future of the national museums, 1979-82; Trustee, National Museum of Antiquities of Scotland, 1982-85; Member, Museums Advisory Board for Scotland, 1984-85; Trustee, National Museums of Scotland, 1985-87; Methodist Preacher; Past Chairman, Disablement Income Group, Scotland; President, British Association for the History of Religions, 1977-80; Secretary, Scottish Institute of Missionary Studies; Editor, Journal of Religion in Africa, 1967-86; Henry Martyn Lectures, Cambridge University, 1988; Margaret Harris Lectures, Dundee University, 1989; Annual Missiology Lecturer, Fuller Theological Seminary, 1996; Co-chair, Yale-Edinburgh Group on the History of the Missionary Movement. Address: (b.) Centre for the Study of Christianity in the Non-Western World, Edinburgh University, New College, Mound Place, Edinburgh EH1 2LX; T.-0131-650 8952.

Walsh, James Richard Thomas. Leader, Argyll and Bute Council, since 1995 (Chairman, Finance and Personnel, Chairman, Policy); Chairman, Finance and Manpower, Argyll and Bute District Council, since 1992; b. 19.12.46, Dunoon; m., Allison; 2 s. Educ. Dunoon Grammar School. Member, Strathclyde Regional Council, since 1982. Recreations: painting; golf; walking dogs. Address: (h.) Castleton Villa, Innellan, Dunoon, Argyll; T.-01369 830383.

Walters, Professor David Gareth, BA, PhD. Stevenson Professor of Hispanic Studies, Glasgow University, since 1995; b. 1.1.48, Neath; m., Christine Ellen Knott; 1 s.; 1 d. Educ. Rhondda County Grammar School for Boys; University College, Cardiff. Temporary Lecturer in Spanish, Leeds University, 1972-73; Glasgow University,

1973-95: Lecturer in Hispanic Studies, Senior Lecturer, Titular Professor. Publications: books on Francisco de Quevedo and Francisco de Aldana; editor, Poems to Lisi and collection of essays on Antonio Machado; numerous articles on Spanish, Portuguese and Catalan literature. Recreations:music; playing the piano; poetry; travel; tennis and most sports. Address: (h.) 32 Golf View, Bearsden, Glasgow G61 4HJ; T.-0141-942 4948.

Walton, Professor Henry John, MD, PhD, FRCPE, FRCPsych, DPM, Hon.MD. Physician; Professor of International Medical Education, Edinburgh, since 1986; b. 15.2.24, South Africa; m., Sula Wolff. Educ. University of Cape Town; London University; Columbia University, NY; Edinburgh University. Registrar in Neurology and Psychiatry, University of Cape Town, 1946-54; Head, Department of Psychiatry, 1957-60; Senior Registrar, Maudsley Hospital, London, 1955-57; Senior Lecturer in Psychiatry, then Professor of Psychiatry, Edinburgh University, 1962-85; Editor, Medical Education, since 1976; President, Association for Medical Education in Europe, 1972-86, Hon. Life President, since 1986; Immediate Past-President, World Federation for Medical Education (Member, Executive Council); frequent Consultant to WHO; Member, Academies of Medicine of Argentina, Belgium and Poland. Publications: as Editor: Small Group Psychotherapy, 1974; Dictionary of Psychiatry, 1985; as Co-Editor: Newer Developments in Assessing Clinical Competence, 1986; as Co-Author: Alcoholism, 1988; Report of the World Conference on Medical Education, 1988; Report on World Summit of Medical Education, 1993. Recreations: literature; visual arts, particularly Western painting and Chinese and Japanese art. Address: 38 Blacket Place, Edinburgh, EH9 1RL; T.-0131-667 7811.

Walton, Professor John Christopher, BSc, PhD, DSc, FRSE. Professor of Reactive Chemistry, St. Andrews University, since 1997; b. 4.12.41, St. Albans; m., Jane Lehman; 1 s.; 1 d. Educ. Watford Grammar School for Boys; Sheffield University. Assistant Lecturer: Queen's College, St. Andrews, 1966-67, Dundee University, 1967-69; Lecturer in Chemistry, United College, St. Andrews, 1969-80; Senior Lecturer, 1980-86, Reader, 1986-96. Elder, Seventh-day Adventist Church. Recreations: music; philosophy. Address: (b.) School of Chemistry, St. Andrews University, St. Andrews, Fife, KY16 9ST; T.-01334 463864.

Wannop, Professor Urlan Alistair, MA, MCD, MRTPI. Emeritus Professor of Urban and Regional Planning, Strathclyde University; b. 16.4.31, Newtown St. Boswells; 1 s.; 1 d. Educ. Aberdeen Grammar School; Edinburgh University; Liverpool University. Appointments in public and private practice, 1956-68; Team Leader, Coventry-Solihull-Warwickshire Sub-Regional Planning Study, 1968-71; Director, West Central Scotland Plan, 1972-74; Senior Deputy Director of Planning, Strathclyde Regional Council, 1975-81, appointed Professor of Urban and Regional Planning, Strathclyde University, 1981. Member, Parliamentary Boundary Commission for Scotland, since 1983. Address: (h.) 43 Lomond Street, Helensburgh G84 7ES; T.-01436 74622.

Ward, Colin, BA, CA. Chief Executive, Student Loans Company, Glasgow, since 1996; b. 23.6.47, Edinburgh; m., Marjory. Educ. Daniel Stewart's College, Edinburgh; Heriot-Watt University. Ernst and Young, 1970-74; Price Waterhouse, Glasgow, 1974-75; British Steel Corporation, 1975-77; Scottish Development Agency, 1977-90, latterly as Chief Accountant; Student Loans Company, since 1990. Recreations: sailing; gardening; classical music. Address: (b.) 100 Bothwell Street, Glasgow, G2 7JD; T.-0141-306 2010.

Ward, David Romen, MA, CertEd. Rector, Hutchesons' Grammar School, since 1987; b. 21.12.35, Newcastle upon Tyne; m., Stella Barbara Anderson; 1 s.; 2 d. Educ. St. Mary's, Melrose; Sedbergh School; Emmanuel College, Cambridge. Assistant Master: Winchester College, Wellington College; Senior History Master, City of London School; Deputy Headmaster, Portsmouth Grammar School; Head Master, Hulme Grammar School. Member, Admiralty Interview Board; Deputy Chairman (Staff), Court, Strathclyde University; Member, Quality Assessment Committee, Scottish Higher Education Funding Council; Freeman, City of London. Publications: Fall of Metternich and the Revolution of 1848; British Foreign Policy 1815-1865; Explorations. Address: (h.) 192 Nithsdale Road, Glasgow, G41 5EU; (b.) Hutchesons' Grammar School, Beaton Road, Glasgow G41 4NW; T.-0141-423 2933.

Ward, Professor Geoffrey Christopher, BA, MA. Professor of English and Head of Department, Dundee University, since 1995; b. 18.2.54, Oldham; m., Marion Lynne-David; 1 s. Educ. Manchester Grammar School; Clare College, Cambridge. Lecturer, then Senior Lecturer, English Department, Liverpool University, 1978-95. Member, Editorial Board, The Cambridge Quarterly; has lectured widely. Publications: Statutes of Liberty: the New York School of Poets, 1992; Language Poetry and the American Avant-Garde, 1993; Bloomsbury Guide to Romantic Literature (Editor). Recreations: poetry; music; food; beach-combing. Address: (b.) English Department, Dundee University, Dundee DD1 4HN; T.-01382 344412.

Ward, Professor John Macqueen, CBE, CA, Companion, IEE. Chairman, Scottish Post Office Board; Chairman, Scottish Homes; Chairman, European Assets Trust NV; Director: Macfarlane Group (Clansman) PLC, Dunfermline Building Society; former Resident Director, Scotland and North of England, IBM United Kingdom Ltd, now Member, Advisory Board; Professor, Heriot Watt University; b. 1.8.40, Edinburgh; m., Barbara Macintosh; 1 s.; 3 d. Educ. Edinburgh Academy; Fettes College. Joined IBM UK Ltd. at Greenock plant, 1966; worked in France and UK; appointed European Director of Information Systems, 1975, and Havant Site Director, 1981. Past Chairman, Scottish CBI; Chairman, Quality Scotland Foundation; Chairman, Advisory Scottish Council for Education and Training Targets; Chairman, Scottish Electronics Forum; Chairman, Institute of Technology Management; Director, Scottish Business in the Community; Member, Council, Institute of Chartered Accountants; Director, IIP Scotland; Director, Greater Easterhouse Development Company, 1991-93; Honorary Doctorate, Napier University, Strathclyde University. Address: (b.) 102 West Port, Edinburgh EH3 9HS; T.-0131-228 7300.

Ward, Leslie Graeme. Director, Advocates for Animals, since 1989; Secretary, St.Andrew Animal Fund, since 1994; b. 12.1.51, Dunbar; m., Erika Gillian; 1 d. Educ. Dunbar Grammar School. RAF, 1969-79. Member, Home Secretary's Animal Procedures Committee; Fellow, Winston Churchill Travelling Fellowship Trust. Recreations: sports; walking the dogs. Address: (b.) 10 Queensferry Street, Edinburgh. EH2 4PG; T.-0131-225 6039.

Ward, Professor Mark Gordon, BA. Dean, Faculty of Arts, since 1995, Professor of German Language and Literature, since 1997, Glasgow University; Principal Examiner, CSYS German, since 1987; b. 4.2.51, Hemel Hempstead; m., Janet Helen; 2 s. Educ. Leeds Grammar School; King's College, London University. Tutorial Research Scholar, Bedford College, London University, 1974-75; Lecturer, then Senior Lecturer, Department of German, Glasgow University, 1975-97. Publications include: Theodor Storm: Der Schimmelreiter, 1988; Laughter, Comedy and Aesthetics: Kleist's Der Zerbrochne Krug, 1995; Perspectives on German Realism. Recreations:

music; gardening; sport. Address: (b.) Faculty of Arts, Glasgow University, Glasgow G12 8QQ; T.-0141-330 5253.

Ward, Maxwell Colin Bernard, MA. Partner, Baillie Gifford & Co., since 1975; Director, Scottish Equitable Policyholders' Trust, since 1994; Director, Scottish Equitable plc, since 1995; Director, Scottish Equitable Life Assurance Society, 1988-94; b. 22.8.49, Sherborne; m., Sarah Marsham; 2 s.; 2 d. Educ. Harrow; St. Catharine's, Cambridge. Trainee, Baillie Gifford & Co., 1971-75. Board Member, Capability Scotland. Recreations: tennis; squash; bridge; country pursuits. Address: (h.) Stobshiel House, Humbie, East Lothian EH36 5PD; T.-01875 833646.

Wardrop, James Arneil, DL, FCIBS, FSA (Scot). Retired Banker; Deputy Lieutenant, Renfrewshire; Vice Chairman, Accord, The Renfrewshire Hospice, since 1993; Vice Chairman, Japan Society of Scotland, since 1990; Secretary, Society of Friends of Paisley Abbey, since 1969; b. 19.4.40, Paisley. Educ. John Neilson Institution, Paisley. Joined National Bank of Scotland, by a process of mergers absorbed into Royal Bank of Scotland; Deputy Agent, San Francisco, 1978-81; Manager, Business Development International Division, 1981-94. Elder, Paisley Abbey; Trustee, Miss Kibble's Trust; Director, Past Chairman, Incorporated Glasgow Renfrewshire Society; Director, Kibble Education and Care Centre; Council Member, Society of Friends of Glasgow Cathedral; Member, Committee, Scotland's Gardens Scheme, Renfrewshire and Inverclyde; Member, Master Court, Paisley Hammermen Society (Deacon, 1996-97); Lay Member of Council, Paisley Art Institute. Recreations: country pursuits; gardening; music. Address: (h.) Saint Kevins, Meikleriggs, Paisley, PA2 9PT; T.-0141-887 3627.

Ward Thompson, Catharine J., BSc, DipLA, ALI. Head, School of Landscape Architecture, Edinburgh College of Art/Heriot Watt University, since 1989; b. 5.12.52; m., Henry Swift Thompson; 3 c. Educ. Holy Cross Convent, Chalfont St. Peter; Southampton University; Edinburgh University. Landscape Assistant/Landscape Architect/ Senior Landscape Architect, 1973-81; Lecturer and Studio Instructor, School of Landscape Architecture, Edinburgh College of Art, 1981-88. Consultant, Landscape Design and Research Unit, Heriot-Watt University, since 1989. Recreations: dance; choreography. Address: (h.) 11 Douglas Crescent, Edinburgh EH12 5BB; T.-0131-337 6818.

Wark, Kirsty, MA. Partner, Wark, Clements and Company, since 1990; b. 1955, Dumfries; m., Alan Clements; 1 s.; 1 d. Former Researcher and Producer, BBC; presented Seven Days, Reporting Scotland, Left Right and Centre, Up Front, Breakfast Time, etc.; formed production company with husband, presenting Words with Wark, One Foot in the Past; General Election night and Referendum coverage; Presenter, The Late Show, 1990-93, Newsnight, since 1993. BAFTA Scotland Journalist of the Year, 1993; BAFTA Scotland Best Television Presenter, 1997. Publication: Restless Nation (Co-author). Recreations: family; tennis; swimming; cooking; beach-combing; reading. Address: (b.) Wark, Clements and Co. Ltd., The Production Centre, The Tollgate, 19 Marine Crescent, Glasgow G51 1HD.

Warlow, Professor Charles Picton, BA, MB, BChir, MD, FRCP (Lond), FRCP (Edin), FRCP (Glas). Professor of Medical Neurology, Edinburgh, since 1987; Honorary Consultant Neurologist, Western General Hospital; b. 29.9.43; m.; 2 s.; 1 d. Educ. Cambridge University. Lecturer in Medicine, Aberdeen University, 1971-74; Registrar and Senior Registrar in Neurology, National Hospitals for Nervous Diseases, London, and University College Hospital, London, 1974-76; Clinical Lecturer in Neurology, then Clinical Reader, Oxford University, 1976-86.

Recreations: sailing; photography; mountains. Address: 3 Mortonhall Hall Road, Edinburgh EH9 2HS.

Warner, Gerald, OStJ, MA, FSAScot. Author; Columnist, Scotland on Sunday, since 1997; b. 22.3.45, Falkirk. Educ. St. Aloysius' College, Glasgow; Glasgow University. Administrative Assistant, Glasgow University, 1971-74; author and broadcaster, 1974-89; Diarist (under pseudonym Henry Cockburn), Sunday Times Scotland, 1989-95; columnist, 1992-95; Special Adviser to Secretary of State for Scotland, 1995-97. Council Member, 1745 Association, 1967-70; Member, Scottish Council of Monarchist League, 1969-71; Chairman, The Monday Club – Scotland, 1973-74; Secretary, Conservative Party's Scottish Policy Committee on Education, 1976-77; Parliamentary candidate, Hamilton, October 1974. Knight of Grace and Devotion, Sovereign Military Order of Malta, 1979; Knight, Jure Sanguinis, Sacred Military Constantinian Order of St. George, 1994. Publications: Homelands of the Clans, 1980; Being of Sound Mind, 1980; Tales of the Scottish Highlands, 1982; Conquering by Degrees, 1985; The Scottish Tory Party: A History, 1988. Recreations: literature; genealogy; Brummelliana. Address: 17 Huntly Gardens, Glasgow G12 9AT.

Warner, Sheriff Graeme Christopher, LLB, WS, NP. Sheriff of Grampian, Highland and Islands, at Aberdeen and Stonehaven, since 1992; in private practice as a Solicitor, 1969-91; b. 20.10.48, Glasgow; divorced; 1 s.; 1 d. Educ. Strathallan; Edinburgh University. Recreations: staying alive. Address: (b.) Sheriff Court House, Aberdeen; T.-01224 648316.

Waterman, Professor Peter George, BPharm (Hons), PhD, FLS, DSc, FRSE. Professor in Phytochemistry, Department of Pharmaceutical Sciences, Strathclyde University, since 1987; b. 28.4.46, Langley, Kent; m., Margaret Humble. Educ. Judd School, Tonbridge; London University. Postgraduate Research Assistant, London University, 1968-69; Lecturer, Senior Lecturer, Reader, Department of Pharmacy, Strathclyde University, 1969-87. Pharmaceutical Society Young Scientist of the Year Award, 1979; Phytochemical Society of Europe Tate & Lyle Award for contribution to Phytochemistry, 1984; Executive Editor, Journal of Biochemical Systematics and Ecology; Dhc, Universite de Franche-Compte, 1995. Recreations: travel; ornithology; walking. Address: (b.) Phytochemistry Research Laboratories, Department of Pharmaceutical Sciences, Strathclyde University, Glasgow G1 1XW; T.-0141-548 2028.

Waters, Donald Henry, OBE. Deputy Chairman and Chief Executive, Grampian Television PLC, since 1993 (Chief Executive and Director, 1987-93); b. 17.12.37, Edinburgh; m., June Leslie Hutchison; 1 s.; 2 d. Educ. George Watson's, Edinburgh; Inverness Royal Academy. Director, John M. Henderson and Co. Ltd., 1972-75; Grampian Television PLC: Company Secretary, 1975, Director of Finance, 1979; Director: Scottish Television and Grampian Sales Ltd., since 1980, Moray Firth Radio Ltd., since 1982, Independent Television Publications Ltd., 1987-90, Cablevision Scotland PLC, 1987-91; Chairman, Celtic Film and Television Association, 1994-96; Vice-Chairman, BAFTA Scotland; Visiting Professor of Film and Media Studies, Stirling University; Chairman, Police Dependant Trust for Grampian, 1992-96; Past Chairman, Royal Northern and University Club, Aberdeen; Chairman, Glenburnie Properties Ltd., since 1993; Director: Central Scotland Radio Ltd., 1994-96 (Chairman, 1995-96), GRT Bus Group PLC, 1994-96, British Linen Bank Group Ltd., since 1995, British Linen Bank Ltd., since 1995, Scottish Post Office Board, since 1996; Member, ITV Council and ITV Broadcast Board; Fellow, Royal Society of Arts; Council Member, CBI Scotland, since 1994; Director, Aberdeen Royal Hospital NHS Trust, since 1996; Member of Council, Aberdeen Chamber of Commerce, since 1996;

Member of Council, SATRO; Burgess of Guild Assessor, since 1997. Address: (h.) Balquhidder, 141 North Deeside Road, Milltimber, Aberdeen AB13 0JS; T.-Aberdeen 867131.

Waters, Fergus Cameron. Director, Scottish Mining Museum, since 1996; b. 15.2.57, Tanzania; m., Alison Crawford. Educ. Rannoch School; Moray College of Further Education. Marketing Manager, Castlewynd Studios, 1984-88; Commercial and Marketing Manager, Ford and Etal Estates, 1988-94; General Manager, Hartlepool Historic Quay, 1994-96. Recreations: motorbiking; skiing; sailing. Address: (b.) Scottish Mining Museum, Lady Victoria Colliery, Newtongrange EH22 4QN; T.-0131-663 7519.

Watling, Roy, MBE, BSc, PhD, DSc, FRSE, FIBiol, FLS, CBiol. Senior Principal Scientific Officer and Head of Pycology and Plant Pathology, Royal Botanic Garden Edinburgh, since 1987; b. 22.7.38, London; m., Ann Elizabeth; 1 s.; 1 d. Educ. Heath Grammar School, Halifax; Sheffield University; Edinburgh University. Senior Scientific Officer, then Principal Scientific Officer, Royal Botanic Garden; Hon. Reader in Plant and Soil Science, Aberdeen University, 1993; Centenary Vice-President, British Mycological Society, and Hon. Fellow; Hon. Fellow, Botanical Society of Edinburgh; Past President: British Mycological Society, Botanical Society of Scotland. Publications: 11 books; 150 scientific articles, book chapters. Recreations: hill-walking; gardening; natural history. Address: (h.) 26 Blinkbonny Avenue, Edinburgh EH4 3HU.

Watson, Adam, BSc, PhD, DSc, FRSE. Senior Principal Scientific Officer and Leader of grouse research team, Institute of Terrestrial Ecology, 1971-90; Environmental Consultant; Member, Cairngorms Partnership Board, since 1995; b. 14.4.30, Turriff; m., Jenny; 1 s.; 1 d. Educ. Aberdeen University. Demonstrator in Zoology, McGill University, Montreal, 1952-53; Zoologist on Baird expedition to Baffin Island, 1953; Assistant Lecturer in Zoology, Aberdeen University, 1953-55; Teacher of Science, Aberdeen Academy, 1957; Senior Research Fellow, Aberdeen University, 1957-60; Senior Scientific Officer, then Principal Scientific Officer, Nature Conservancy, 1961-66; Officer in charge, Nature Conservancy Council Mountain and Moorland Ecology Station, Banchory, 1968-71; Neill Prize, Royal Society of Edinburgh, for "outstanding contribution to natural history". Recreations: mountaineering; skiing. Address: (h.) Clachnaben, Crathes, Banchory AB31 5JE.

Watson, Professor Alan Albert, JP, MA, BD, MB, BS, FRCP, FRCPath, DMJ, DTM&H. Emeritus Regius Professor of Forensic Medicine, Glasgow University; Honorary Consultant in Forensic Medicine, Greater Glasgow Health Board, since 1978; Committee Member, Forensic Medicine (Scotland) Committee, since 1982; b. 20.2.29, Reading; m., Jeannette Anne Pitts; 3 s. Educ. Reading School; St. Mary's Hospital, London; Queens' College, Cambridge. Lecturer in Pathology, Glasgow University, 1964-69; University Senior Assistant Pathologist, Cambridge University, 1969-71; elected Fellow of Queen's College and Assistant Director of Studies, 1970; Consultant in Forensic Medicine, SE Asia Region, Delhi, WHO, 1977. Hon. President, Scottish Band of Hope Union. Recreations: Church activities (Baptist lay preacher). Address: (h.) 76 Arrol Drive, Ayr KA7 4AW; T.-01292 266365.

Watson, Alexander Bell, MA, MEd, FIMgt, FSA Scot, FRSA. Chief Executive, Angus Council, since 1995 (Chief Executive, Tayside Regional Council, 1995); b. 20.5.45, Airdrie; m., Jean; 3 s. Educ. Airdrie Academy; Glasgow University; Jordanhill College of Education. Teacher of Classics, Morrison's Academy, Crieff, 1968; Principal

Teacher of Classics: Portree High School, 1971, McLaren High School, Callander, 1973; Assistant Director of Education: Central, 1975, Strathclyde, 1983; Senior Depute Director of Education, Central Regional Council, 1986; Director of Education, Tayside Regional Council, 1990-94. General Secretary, Association of Directors of Education in Scotland, 1993-95; Chair, National Co-ordinating Committee on Staff Development of Teachers, 1994-95; Member, Board of Management and Chair, Personnel Committee, Angus College, since 1997. Recreations: music; reading; fishing; Scottish heritage; DIY. Address: (b.) Angus Council, The Cross, Forfar DD8 1BX; T.-01307 473020.

Watson, Garry Sanderson, CA. Scottish Legal Services Ombudsman, since 1994; b. 31.7.40, Glasgow; m., Elizabeth Ann; 4 d. Educ. Glasgow Academy. Hill Samuel Bank, 1969-91: Managing Director, Hill Samuel Pacific, Hong Kong, 1974-76, Director, Hill Samuel Bank, 1976, President, Hill Samuel, New York, 1979-82, a Managing Director, Hill Samuel Bank, 1990; Chairman, All Seasons Wholefoods, 1993-94. Director, Macaulay Land Use Research Institute, since 1997; Director, Business in the Community, 1985-88; Hon. Treasurer, National Association of Citizens' Advice Bureaux, 1986-91; Hon. Treasurer, Scottish Association of CAB, 1992-95; Director, Edinvar Housing Association, 1992 (Chair, 1997). Recreations: tennis; hill-walking; shooting. Address: (h.) Newlandburn House, Newlandrig, by Gorebridge, Midlothian, EH23 4NS; T.-01875 820939.

Watson, Professor George Alistair, BSc, MSc, PhD, FIMA, FRSE. Professor, Department of Mathematics and Computer Science, Dundee University, since 1988; b. 30.9.42, Aberfeldy; m., Hilary Mackay; 1 d. Educ. Breadalbane Academy; Edinburgh University; Australian National University. Demonstrator, Computer Unit, Edinburgh University, 1964-66; Dundee University: Research Fellow, then Lecturer, Mathematics Department, 1969-82; Senior Lecturer, Mathematical Sciences Department, 1982-84; Reader, Department of Mathematics and Computer Science, 1984-88. Recreation: gardening. Address: (h.) 7 Albany Road, West Ferry, Dundee DD5 1NS; T.-Dundee 779473.

Watson, Harry Duff, MA, BA, DipEd, FSAScot. Senior Editor, Dictionary of the Older Scottish Tongue, Edinburgh University, since 1985; b. 17.6.46, Crail; m., Susan Margaret Saul; 2 s. Educ. Waid Academy, Anstruther; Edinburgh University; University College, London. Teacher of English/English as a Foreign Language, Scotland, England, Sweden, West Germany, 1970-79; appointed Editor, Dictionary of the Older Scottish Tongue, 1979. Past Senior Vice-President, Scottish Swedish Society; Member, Council, Scottish Text Society; Member, Board, Scottish Studies, Edinburgh University. Publication: Kilrenny and Cellardyke. Recreations: reading; writing; music; genealogy; literary translation. Address: (h.) 14 Braehead Grove, Edinburgh EH4 6BG; T.-0131-339 6911.

Watson, Hugh, OBE, QPM. Commandant, Scottish Police College, Tulliallan Castle, since 1991; b. 24.2.38, Edinburgh; m., Evelyn Scrimger; 1 s.; 2 d. Educ. Dunfermline High School. RAF, 1955-58; Lothian and Peebles Constabulary, 1958-75; Lothian and Borders Police, 1975-91; Assistant Chief Constable, 1984-91. Recreations: gardening; reading; DIY. Address: (b.) Tulliallan Castle, Kincardine-on-Forth FK10 4BE; T.-01259 732000.

Watson, Professor John, BSc, ARCST, PhD, DSc. Professor in Biochemistry, Strathclyde University, since 1988 (Reader, 1985-88); Head, Department of Bioscience and Biotechnology; b. 17.6.42, Glasgow; m., Anne Brown; 2 d. Educ. Whitehill Secondary, Glasgow; Glasgow University; Strathclyde University. MRC Research Fellow,

Glasgow University; Lecturer, Senior Lecturer, Reader, Professor, Strathclyde University. Recreations: golf; swimming; skiing; reading. Address: (b.) Bioscience and Biotechnology, Strathclyde University, Todd Centre, Glasgow G4 0NR; T.-0141-548 3822.

Watson of Invergowrie, Lord (Michael Goodall Watson), BA (Hons). MP (Labour), Glasgow Central, 1989-97; b. 1.5.49, Cambuslang; m., Lorraine Therese McManus. Educ. Dundee High School; Heriot-Watt University. Development Officer, WEA East Midlands District, 1974-77; Industrial Officer, ASTMS, 1977-79; Regional Officer, ASTMS (latterly MSF), 1979-89. Member, Scottish Executive Committee, Labour Party, 1987-90. Publication: Rags to Riches: the official history of Dundee United FC. Recreations: watching Dundee United FC; jogging; reading, especially political biographies. Address: (b.) House of Lords, London SW1A 0PW.

Watson, Peter, BA, LLB, SSC. Solicitor (Levy & McRae); b. 22.1.54, Greenock; m., Claire Watson; 2 d. Educ. Eastwood High School, Glasgow; Strathclyde University; Edinburgh University; Scandinavian Maritime Law Institute, Norway; Dundee Petroleum Law Institute. Qualified, 1981; Solicitor to the Supreme Courts; Notary Public; Temporary Sheriff; President, Society of Solicitor Advocates, 1997; Chairman, Association of Mediators; Visiting Professor, Nova University, Fort Lauderdale, Florida; Member, Steering Committee, and Negotiator, Piper Alpha Disaster Group; Secretary, Braer Disaster Group; Secretary, Lockerbie Air Disaster Group; former Official Collaborator, International Labour Organisation, Geneva; Member, Criminal Rules Council; Member, Board, Sports Law Centre, Anglia University; Honorary Citizen of Nashville, Tennessee; large media practice based in Glasgow. Publications: Civil Justice System in Britain; Crimes of War – The Antony Gecas Story; The Truth Written in Blood; Dunblane – A Predictable Tragedy; DNA and the Criminal Trial; In Pursuit of Pan Am. Recreations: working out; drinking fine wine. Address: (b.) Levy & McRae, 266 St. Vincent Street, Glasgow G2 5RL; T.-0141-307 2311.

Watson, Professor Roderick, MA, PhD, FRSE. Poet; Literary Critic and Writer; Professor in English, Stirling University; Director, Stirling Institute for International Scottish Studies; b. 12.5.43, Aberdeen; m., Celia Hall Mackie; 1 s.; 1 d. Educ. Aberdeen Grammar School; Aberdeen University; Peterhouse, Cambridge. Lecturer in English, Victoria University, British Columbia, 1965-66; collections of poetry include Trio and True History on the Walls; other books include The Penguin Book of the Bicycle, The Literature of Scotland, MacDiarmid, The Poetry of Norman MacCaig and The Poetry of Scotland (Editor). Recreation: cycling; motor cycling. Address: (h.) 19 Millar Place, Stirling; T.-Stirling 475971.

Watson, Tom. Actor, Playwright, Poet; b. 21.3.32, Auchinleck; m., Joyce; 2 d. Educ. Hamilton Academy. Byre Theatre/Perth Theatre, 1955-57; BBC Radio Repertory Company; broadcasting work includes: The Physicist, Dr Finlay's Casebook, Treasure Island, Churchill's People, Village Hall, Benny Lynch, The Mourning Brooch, The Standard, Govan Ghost Story, Prime Suspect, Cardiac Arrest, Hamish MacBeth, Your Cheating Heart; stage work includes: Fool for Love, National Theatre and West End; The Treatment, Some Voices, A Wholly Healthy Glasgow, Royal Court; Translations, Lyceum; The Government Inspector, Almeida. Gold Medal, New York International Radio Awards. Publication: The Dark Whistle (poetry). Recreations: natural history; observing; old-time music hall. Address: (b.) Kerry Gardner Management, 15 Kensington High Street, London.

Watt, Archibald, MBE, JP, MA, MEd, FEIS, FSA Scot. Honorary Sheriff, Grampian, Highlands and Islands, since 1979; b. 20.5.14, Aberdeen; m., 1, Anne D.M. Ashton (deceased); 2, Elizabeth P. White. Educ. Robert Gordon's College, Aberdeen; Aberdeen University; Aberdeen College of Education. Teacher of English, Elgin Academy, 1938; Flt.-Lt., RAF Administrative and Special Duties Branch and RAF Regiment, 1941-46; Mackie Academy: Principal Teacher of English, 1949, Deputy Rector, 1962, retired, 1977; Organist, HM Prison, Aberdeen, 1930-38; WEA Organiser for Adult Education, Elgin, 1946-49; WEA Tutor in Psychology, 1946-51; Founder and Organising Secretary, Stonehaven Music Club, since 1949; Member, National Council, and Chairman, Regional and District Committees, Scottish Community Drama Association, 1949-67; Member, National Executive and District Chairman, School Library Association in Scotland, 1952-73; Elder, Church of Scotland, since 1954; Chairman and/or Member, Kincardine District Committee, EIS, 1956-77; Member, Joint Consultative Committee, Kincardine County Council, 1965-77; Queen's Jubilee Medal, 1977; Organist, South Church, Stonehaven, 1976-94; Director, Kinneff Old Church Preservation Trust Ltd., since 1979; Founder Member and President, Stonehaven Probus Club, 1981-82; Committee Member, National Trust for Scotland (Kincardine and Deeside Centre), 1984-88; Member, Aberdeen Choral Society, 1978-91; Aberdeen Proms Chorus, since 1985, BB Centenary Band, since 1991; Chairman, Stonehaven Heritage Society, since 1988; author of Reading Lists for the Secondary School, 1966; Highways and Byways Round Stonehaven, 1976; Highways and Byways Round Kincardine, 1985; A Goodly Heritage, 1991; The Roman Camp of Raedykes, 1992; Early Stonehaven Settlers, 1994. Recreations: concert and theatre-going; travel; antiquities and archaeology; brass bands; research; golf; choral singing. Address: (h.) Rutlands, Arduthie Road, Stonehaven; T.-Stonehaven 762712.

Watt, Brian, MD, FRCPath, FRCP Edin, CBiol, FIBiol. Consultant Bacteriologist, City Hospital, Edinburgh, since 1982; Honorary Senior Lecturer, Department of Bacteriology, Edinburgh University, since 1974; Director, Scottish Mycobacteria Reference Laboratory; Clinical Director, Medical Microbiology Services, RIE Unit; b. 6.12.41, Edinburgh; m., Hilary Watt; 2 d. Educ. Rudolf Steiner School; Edinburgh University. Lecturer, Department of Bacteriology, Edinburgh University, 1968-73; Consultant Microbiologist, Western General Hospital, 1973-82. Recreations: fishing; gardening; golf; tennis; singing. Address: (h.) Silverburn House, by Penicuik, Midlothian; T.-01968 672085.

Watt, Iain Alasdair, BSc (Econ). Chief Executive, Edinburgh Fund Managers; b. 30.3.45, Edinburgh; m., Lynne Neilson; 3 s.; 1 d. Educ. Edinburgh Academy; Hull University. Recreations: golf; tennis. Address: (b.) Donaldson House, 97 Haymarket Terrace, Edinburgh; T.-0131-313 1000.

Watt, Jim, MBE (1980). Boxer; b. 18.7.48, Glasgow. Turned professional, 1968; British Lightweight Champion, 1972-73, 1975-77; European Lightweight Champion, 1977-79; World Lightweight Champion, 1979-81; four successful defences of World title; Freedom of Glasgow, 1981.

Watt, Professor Roger, BA, PhD, FRSE. Professor of Psychology and Dean, Faculty of Human Sciences, Stirling University, since 1990; b. 26.11.54, London; m., Helen; 2 s.; 1 d. Educ. St. Olaves Grammar School; Downing College, Cambridge. Research Fellow: Durham University, University College London, Cambridge University; Scientist, MRC Applied Psychology Unit, Cambridge; Royal Society of Edinburgh BP Research Fellow, Stirling University. Editor, Ben Ledi View (Callander local paper). Recreations: music; hill-walking; family life. Address: (b.)

Department of Psychology, Stirling University, Stirling, FK9 4LA; T.-01786 467640.

Watters, Michael. Chief Executive, West Dunbartonshire Council. Address: (b.) Council Offices, Garshake Road, Dumbarton, G82 3PU.

Waugh, Alan, BSc (Hons), DipEd, FRSA. Head Teacher, Penicuik High School, since 1992; b. 9.2.49, Loanhead; m., Margo Watt; 1 s.; 1 d. Educ. Lasswade Senior Secondary School; Edinburgh University. Head of Chemistry, then Assistant Head Teacher, Lasswade High School Centre, 1976-86; Depute Head Teacher, James Gillespie's High School, 1986-92. Address: (b.) Penicuik High School, Carlops Road, Penicuik EH26 9EP; T.-Penicuik 674165.

Weatherhead, Alexander Stewart, OBE, TD, MA, LLB. Solicitor; Consultant, Brechin Tindal Oatts (formerly Tindal Oatts), Solicitors, Glasgow, since 1997 (Partner, 1960-97); b. 3.8.31, Edinburgh; m., Harriett Foye; 2 d. Educ. Glasgow Academy; Glasgow University. Royal Artillery, 1950-52; TA, 1952; Lt. Col. Commanding 277 (A&SH) Field Regiment, RA (TA), 1965-67, The Lowland Regiment, RA (T), 1967 and Glasgow and Strathclyde Universities OTC, 1970-73; Colonel, 1974; TAVR Colonel, Lowlands (West), 1974-76; ADC (TAVR) to The Queen, 1977-81; Honorary Colonel, Glasgow and Strathclyde Universities OTC, 1982-98; Chairman, Lowlands TAVRA, 1990-93; Council Member, Law Society of Scotland, 1971-84 (Honorary Vice-President, 1983-84); Member, Royal Commission on Legal Services in Scotland, 1976-80; Council Member, Society for Computers and Law, 1973-86 (Chairman, 1981-84); Temporary Sheriff, 1985-92; Dean, Royal Faculty of Procurators in Glasgow, 1991-95; Commodore, Royal Western Yacht Club, 1995-98. Recreations: tennis; sailing; reading; music. Address: (h.) 52 Partickhill Road, Glasgow, G11 5AB; T.-0141-334 6277.

Weatherhead, Very Rev. Dr. James Leslie, CBE, MA, LLB. Former Principal Clerk, General Assembly of the Church of Scotland; Moderator, General Assembly, 1993; b. 29.3.31, Dundee; m., Dr. Anne Elizabeth Shepherd (see Anne E. Weatherhead); 2 s. Educ. High School of Dundee; Edinburgh University and New College, Edinburgh. Temporary Sub-Lt., RNVR (National Service), 1955-56. Licensed by Presbytery of Dundee, 1960, Presbytery of Ayr, 1960; Assistant Minister, Auld Kirk of Ayr, 1960-62; Minister: Trinity Church, Rothesay, 1962-69, Old Church, Montrose, 1969-85. Member, Broadcasting Council for Scotland, 1978-82.

Weaver, C. Giles H., FCA, MBA. Managing Director, Murray Johnstone Ltd., since 1993; Proprietor, Greywalls Hotel, Gullane, since 1976; b. 4.4.46; m., Rosamund B. Mayhew; 2 s.; 2 d. Educ. Eton College; London Business School. Ernst & Young, 1966-70; London Business School, 1971-73; Jessel Securities/Berry Wiggins, 1973-76; Director, Ivory & Sime plc, 1976-86; Managing Director Pensions, Prudential Portfolio Managers, 1986-90. Trustee, Lutyens Trust. Recreations: golf; bridge; skiing; stalking. Address: (b.) Murray Johnstone Ltd., 7 West Nile Street, Glasgow G1 2PX; T.-0141-226 3131.

Webb, Professor David John, MD, FRCP, FRCPE, FFPM. Christison Professor of Therapeutics and Clinical Pharmacology, Clinical Pharmacology Unit and Research Centre, Edinburgh University, since 1995; Head, University Department of Medicine, Western General Hospital, Edinburgh, since 1997; Head, Centre for Research in Cardiovascular Biology, Edinburgh University, since 1997; Director, Clinical Research Centre and Honorary Consultant Physician, Western General Hospital, Edinburgh, since 1990; b. 1.9.53, Greenwich; m., Dr. Margaret Jane Cullen. Educ. Dulwich College, London; London University: Royal London Hospital. Junior hospital appointments, 1977-79; Medical Registrar, Royal London

rotation, 1979-82; MRC Research Fellow, MRC Blood Pressure Unit, Glasgow, and Honorary Lecturer, Glasgow University, 1982-85; Lecturer in Pharmacology and Clinical Pharmacology, St. George's Hospital Medical School, London, and Honorary Medical Senior Registrar, St. George's Hospital, London, 1985-89; Senior Lecturer in Medicine, Edinburgh University. Executive Member, British Hypertension Society, since 1991; Member, MRC Scientific Advisory Board, since 1996; Member, Wellcome Trust Physiology and Pharmacology Panel, since 1997; Member, Multi-Centre Research Ethics Committee for Scotland, since 1997; Honorary Trustee and Joint Research Director, High Blood Pressure Foundation and Endocrine Research Trust, since 1991; Member, Association of Clinical Professors of Medicine and of Association of Physicians of Great Britain and Ireland. Recreations: opera; bridge; summer and winter mountaineering. Address: (h.) 26 Inverleith Gardens, Edinburgh EH3 5PS; T.-0131-332 1205.

Webb, Professor Jeffrey R.L., BSc, DPhil, FRSE. Professor of Mathematics, Glasgow University, since 1987 (Reader, 1982-87); b. 19.12.45, Stourport-on-Severn; m., Angela Millard; 1 s.; 1 d. Educ. King Charles I School, Kidderminster; Sussex University. Royal Society European Programme Fellowship, 1970-71; Science Research Council Fellowship, Sussex University, 1971-73; Lecturer in Mathematics, Glasgow University, 1973-78 and 1979-82; Visiting Associate Professor, Indiana University, 1978-79; Visiting Professor, Tulane University, New Orleans, 1982. Member, Editorial Board, Glasgow Mathematical Journal. Recreations:chess; books; listening to music. Address: (b.) Mathematics Department, Glasgow University, Glasgow G12 8QW; T.-0141-339 8855, Ext. 5181.

Webster, Ann, BSc (Hons). National Secretary, Girls' Brigade in Scotland, since 1996; b. 16.11.43, Oxford; m., Robert Webster; 1 s.; 2 d. Educ. Stobswell Girls' Junior Secondary School, Dundee; Scottish College of Textiles, Galashiels. Analyst, WRAC, 1963-68; Assistant Domestic Services Manager, Ninewells Hospital, 1973-78. Girls' Brigade Officer, 19 years. Recreations: reading; cross-stitch; knitting; bird-watching. Address: (b.) Girls' Brigade Scotland, Boys' Brigade House, 168 Bath Street, Glasgow G2 4TQ; T.-0141-332 1765.

Webster, David Pirie, OBE, DPE. Author; Chairman, Commonwealth Games Council for Scotland, 1990-95; b. 18.9.28, Aberdeen; 4 s.; 2 d. Educ. Crowlees Boys School; Aberdeen Training College; Woolmanhill College. Senior Technical Representative, Scottish Council of Physical Recreation, 1954-72; Head of Facilities Planning Division, Scottish Sports Council, 1972-74; Director/Administrator, Magnum Leisure Centre, 1974-75; Director of Leisure, Recreation and Tourism, Cunninghame District Council, 1975-87. Director of Weightlifting, Commonwealth Games; Secretary General, International Federation of Strength Athletes. Recreations: writing (more than 30 books); Highland Games; fitness and weight training. Address: (h.) 43 West Road, Irvine KA12 8RE; T.-01294 272257.

Webster, G.E. (Ted), FRICS. Managing Partner Scotland, Richard Ellis, Chartered Surveyors, appointed to Board, 1997; b. 28.2.48, Glasgow; m.; 4 children. Joined Richard Ellis Glasgow, 1975, admitted to partnership, 1985. Executive Member, Scottish Council Development and Industry; Governor, Glasgow School of Art; Member, Court, Glasgow University. Recreations: Glasgow Art Club; Western Gailes Golf Club. Address: (b.) Pacific House, 70 Wellington Street, Glasgow; T.-0141-204 1931.

Webster, Jack (John Barron). Author and Journalist; Columnist, The Herald; b. 8.7.31, Maud, Aberdeenshire; m., Eden Keith; 3 s. Educ. Maud School; Peterhead Academy; Robert Gordon's College, Aberdeen. Reporter, Turriff Advertiser; Reporter/Sub Editor, Aberdeen Press &

Journal/Evening Express; Chief Sub-Editor, Scottish Sunday Express; Feature Writer, Scottish Daily Express; Feature Writer, Sunday Standard. Columnist of the Year, 1996; Speaker of the Year, 1996. Publications: The Dons, 1978; A Grain of Truth, 1981; Gordon Strachan, 1984; Another Grain of Truth, 1988; 'Tis Better to Travel, 1989; Alistair MacLean (biography), 1991; Famous Ships of the Clyde, 1993; The Flying Scots, 1994; The Express Years, 1994; In the Driving Seat, 1996; The Herald Years, 1996; television films: The Roup, 1985; As Time Goes By, 1987; Northern Lights, 1989; Webster Goes West, 1991; John Brown: The Man Who Drew a Legend, 1994; Walking Back to Happiness, 1996; video film: The Glory of Gothenburg, 1993. Address: (b.) The Herald, 195 Albion Street, Glasgow G1; T.-0141-552 6255.

Webster, Michael Alan, BA, DMS, MIMgt, FRSA. Principal, Perth College, since 1991; b. 7.12.45, Manchester. Educ. Chetham's School, Manchester; Moseley Hall Grammar School; Exeter University. FE Lecturer and Head of Department, 1972-84; Education Adviser, Shropshire County Council, 1984-88, Principal Adviser, 1988-91. Recreations: hill-walking; skiing; theatre; fishing. Address: (b.) Perth College, Crieff Road, Perth, PH1 2NX; T.-01738 621171.

Webster, Professor Nigel Robert, BSc, MB, ChB, PhD, FRCA, FRCPEdin. Professor of Anaesthesia and Intensive Care, Aberdeen University, since 1994; b. 14.6.53, Walsall; m., Diana C.S. Webster; 1 s.; 2 d. Educ. Edward Shelley High School, Walsall; Leeds University. Member, scientific staff/Consultant, Clinical Research Centre, Northwick Park Hospital, Harrow; Consultant in Anaesthesia and Intensive Care, St. James's University Hospital, Leeds. Address: (b.) Institute of Medical Sciences, Foresterhill, Aberdeen AB25 2ZD; T.-01224 681818.

Webster, Professor Robin Gordon Maclennan, MA (Cantab), MA (Arch), RIBA, FRIAS, ARSA. Professor of Architecture and Head of School, Scott Sutherland School of Architecture, The Robert Gordon University, Aberdeen, since 1984; Senior Partner, Robin Webster & Associates, Aberdeen, since 1984; Commissioner, Royal Fine Art Commission for Scotland, since 1990; b. 24.12.39, Glasgow; m., Katherine S. Crichton; 1 s.; 2 d. Educ. Glasgow Academy; Rugby School; St. John's College, Cambridge. Assistant, Gillespie Kidd & Coia, Architects, Glasgow, 1963-64; National Building Agency, London, 1965-67; Senior Partner, Spence and Webster, Architects, 1972-84; Lecturer, Bartlett School of Architecture, 1969-74; Visiting Lecturer, Washington University, St. Louis, 1975, Cambridge University, 1976-77, and Mackintosh School, Glasgow School of Art, 1978-84. Winner, New Parliamentary Building Competition, Westminster, 1972; 1st prize, New York Waterfront Competition, 1988; Winner, 1997 Sellic library competition for University of Edinburgh; Chairman, Association of Scottish Schools of Architecture, 1986-90; President, Aberdeen Society of Architects, 1989-91. Recreations: drawing and painting; sailing. Address: (b.) Scott Sutherland School of Architecture, The Robert Gordon University, Garthdee Road, Aberdeen; T.-01224 263500.

Webster, Robin Maclean, MBE, RD, BA (Cantab), FCIArb. Industrial Tribunal Chairman, Glasgow, since 1994; b. 22.4.40; m., Janice Helen Reid; 2 d. Educ. Fettes College, Edinburgh; Christ's College, Cambridge University. Solicitor (Scotland), 1966; NP, 1970; Partner, Haddow & McLay, Solicitors, Glasgow, 1968-70; Deputy Secretary, Law Society of Scotland, 1970-76; Secretary, Scottish Lawyers' European Group, 1971-77; Office of Solicitor to Secretary of State for Scotland, 1976-86; seconded as Legal Draftsman, Seychelles Government, 1980-82; Assistant Parliamentary Draftsman, Lord Advocate's Department, 1982-83; Senior Parliamentary Counsel, Kenya Government, 1985-86; Attorney-General,

Tuvalu, S. Pacific, 1986-88; Judge of the Supreme Court of Tonga, S. Pacific, 1988-91; Temporary Sheriff, 1991-96; part-time Industrial Tribunal Chairman, 1991-94; Legal Consultant, Overseas Development Administration, 1992-95. Royal Naval Reserve, 1962-90; Lt. Commander (Rtd); Chairman, Queensferry and District Unit, Sea Cadet Corps, since 1994; Hon. Secretary, Royal Scottish Pipers' Society, 1973-76; Elder, Palmerston Place Church of Scotland. Recreations: piping; Scottish dancing; reading; dog walking. Address: (b.) COIT (Scotland), Eagle Building, 215 Bothwell Street, Glasgow G2 7TS; T.-0141-204 0730.

Webster, Roderick Brenton. Managing Director, Northsound Radio, since 1997; b. 22.12.44, Inverness; m., Elizabeth Anne; 2 s.; 1 d. Educ. Portobello Secondary School. Moray Firth Radio, Inverness, 1980-89 (Head of Sales); on award of licence, established Radio Borders, 1989-97 (Managing Director); Sony "Station of the Year", 1991. Address: (b.) 45 Kingsgate, Aberdeen AB15 4EL; T.-01224 337000.

Weeple, Edward John, MA. Under Secretary, Lifelong Learning Group, Scottish Office Education and Industry Department, since 1990; b. 15.5.45, Glasgow; 3 s.; 1 d. Educ. St. Aloysius' College, Glasgow; Glasgow University. Entered DHSS, London, 1968; Assistant Principal, 1968-73 (Private Secretary to Minister of Health, 1971-73); Principal, 1973-78; transferred to Scottish Office, 1978; Principal (Industrial Development Division, SEPD), 1978-80; Assistant Secretary, Scottish Home and Health Department, 1980-85; Assistant Secretary, Department of Agriculture and Fisheries for Scotland, 1985-90. Address: (b.) Victoria Quay, Edinburgh, EH6 6QQ; T.-0131-244 0623.

Weir, Professor Alexander Douglas, MA, MEd. Professor of Education, Strathclyde University, since 1993; Vice Dean, Faculty of Education, since 1997; b. 2.9.42, Falkirk; m., Alison Marion Cook; 1 s.; 1 d. Educ. Falkirk High School; Edinburgh University. Lecturer, Falkirk College of Technology, 1965-67; Senior Research Officer, Scottish Council for Research in Education, 1967-74; Lecturer, Glasgow University, 1974-79; Director, Scottish Vocational Preparation Unit, 1979-85; Director, Vocational Initiatives Unit, Glasgow University, 1985-88; Director of Research, Jordanhill College of Education, 1988-91, Assistant Principal, 1991-93; Vice Dean (Research), Faculty of Education, Strathclyde University, 1993-97. Member, National Executive, Boys' Brigade, 1976-84; Chair, Strathclyde Regional Conference of Voluntary Youth Organisations, 1991-94; author of five books and 75 articles. Recreation: youth work. Address: (b.) Faculty of Education, Strathclyde University, Southbrae Drive, Glasgow G13 1PP; T.-0141-950 3200.

Weir, Hon. Lord (David Bruce Weir), QC (Scot), MA, LLB. Senator of the College of Justice in Scotland, 1985-97; b. 19.12.31. Advocate Depute, 1979-82; Chairman, Medical Appeal Tribunal, 1972-77; Chairman, Pensions Appeals Tribunal for Scotland, 1978-84; Chairman, NHS Tribunal Scotland, 1983-85; Member, Parole Board, Scotland, 1989-92.

Weir, Sharman Elizabeth, BMus (Hons), FRSA. General Manager, Citizens' Theatre, Glasgow, since 1994; b. 31.3.59, Barrhead. Educ. John Neilson High School, Paisley; Glasgow University. Professional musician, 1981-85; Project Manager and Consultant, BP Exploration, 1985-92; Business Manager, Citizens' Theatre, Glasgow, 1992-94. Director, Scottish Early Music Consort. Recreations: music (flute, singing, piano); travel. Address: (b.) Citizens' Theatre, 119 Gorbals Street, Glasgow, G5; T.-0141-429 5561.

Weir, Tom, MBE, FRSGS. Journalist and Photographer. Former Ordnance Surveyor; climbed in the Himalayas and began professional photography; author of several books on climbing and Scotland; Presenter, Weir's Way, Scottish Television.

Weir, Walter, CPFA. Chief Executive, Falkirk Council, since 1995; b. 21.12.39, Falkirk; m., Helen; 1 s.; 1 d. Educ. Falkirk High School. Trainee/Assistant Accountant, Stirling County Council, 1958; Senior Accountant, Falkirk Town Council, 1969; Depute Director of Finance, Director of Finance, Chief Executive, Falkirk District Council, 1974-95. Recreations: working; music; reading; walking. Address: (b.) Municipal Buildings, Falkirk, FK1 5RS; T.-01324 506002.

Weir, Viscount (William Kenneth James Weir), BA, Hon. DEng (Glasgow), Hon. FEng. Chairman, The Weir Group PLC, since 1966; Director and former Vice-Chairman, St. James' Place Capital plc; Chairman, BICC plc, since 1996 (Deputy Chairman, 1992-96, Director, since 1977); Director, Canadian Pacific Limited; b. 9.11.33, Glasgow; m., 1, Diana MacDougall (m. diss.); 2, Jacqueline Mary Marr (m. diss.); 3, Marina Sevastopoulo; 2 s.; 1 d. Educ. Eton; Trinity College, Cambridge. Member, London Advisory Committee, Hongkong and Shanghai Banking Corporation, 1980-92; Deputy Chairman, Charterhouse J. Rothschild PLC, 1983-85; Member, Court, Bank of England, 1972-84; Co-Chairman, RIT and Northern PLC, 1982-83; Director, 1970, Chairman, 1975-82, Great Northern Investment Trust Ltd.; Member, Scottish Economic Council, 1972-85; Director, British Steel Corporation, 1972-76; Chairman, Patrons of National Galleries of Scotland, 1984-95; Member, Queen's Bodyguard for Scotland (Royal Company of Archers). Recreations: shooting; golf; fishing. Address: (h.) Rodinghead, Mauchline, Ayrshire.

Wells, Margaret J., MA, CQSW. Director of Social Work, Aberdeenshire, since 1995; b. 22.7.55, Berwick upon Tweed; m., Tony Wells. Educ. Berwickshire High School, Duns; Edinburgh University; Glasgow University. Social worker, Perth, 1977-87; Area Fieldwork Manager (Hospitals), Tayside, 1987-89; District Manager, Dundee, 1989-92; Assistant Director of Social Work, then Depute Director, Grampian, 1992-95. Director, Opportunities Unlimited. Recreation: singing. Address: (h.) 257 Union Grove, Aberdeen; T.-01224 665490.

Welsh, Andrew Paton, MA (Hons), DipEd. MP (SNP), Angus East, since 1987; National Vice-President, SNP, since 1987; b. 19.4.44, Glasgow; m., Sheena Margaret Cannon (see Sheena Margaret Welsh); 1 d. Educ. Govan High School; Glasgow University. Member, Stirling District Council, 1974; MP (SNP), South Angus, 1974-79; SNP Parliamentary Spokesman on Housing, 1974-78 and since 1987, Self-Employed and Small Businesses, 1975-79 and 1987-97, Agriculture, 1975-79 and 1987-97, Education, since 1997; Parliamentary Chief Whip, 1977-79 and since 1987; Member, Select Committee on Members' Interests, 1989-92; Member, Scottish Affairs Committee, since 1992; SNP Executive Vice Chairman for Administration, 1979-83; Member, National Executive Committee, SNP, since 1983; Parliamentary candidate, East Angus, 1983; Member, Church and Nation Committee, Church of Scotland, 1984-85; Member, Dundee University Court, 1984-87; Provost, Angus District Council, 1984-87; Member, Angus District Health Council; Member, SCOTVEC Public Administration and Moderating Committees. Recreations: music; horse riding. Address: (h.) Montquhir, Carmyllie, Arbroath; T.-01241 860317.

Welsh, Frederick Wright, JP. Member, Dundee City Council, since 1995; Spokesperson, Joint Boards (Police, Fire, Valuation); Director/Chairman, Taywide Services, Dundee, since 1991; Member, Central Advisory Committee on Justices of the Peace, since 1991; Member, Justices Committee, Dundee District; Member, Scottish Housing

Forum; Vice-Chair, Post Office and Telecommunications Advisory Committee for Tayside; b. Dundee; m., Margaret; 3 s. Educ. Rockwell Secondary School, Dundee. Member, Dundee Corporation, 1973-75 (Convener, Public Libraries, Museums and Art Galleries, 1973-75); Member, Tayside Regional Council, 1974-77 (Labour Group Chief Whip and Further Education Opposition Spokesman, 1974-77); Member, Dundee District Council, 1977-95 (Chairman, Community Services Committee, 1992-95, Convener of Housing, 1992-95); Director, Local Government Information Unit, 1991-92; National Chair, Association of Direct Labour Organisations, 1991-92; Chair, Dundee East Constituency Labour Party, Member, Central Committee, Gas Consumers Council for Scotland; Member, Perth Prison Visiting Committee; Member, Management Committee, Dundee Resources Centre for Unemployed; Chairman, ADLO Scottish Region and Member, National Council, ADLO; Vice Convener, COSLA Miscellaneous Services Committee; Depute Chair, Heat Development (Dundee) Ltd., since 1986; Member, Fire Services Scotland Examination Board, 1973-75; Member, British Standards Institute OC/4 Committee. Recreations: gardening; DIY; watching all sports; walking. Address: (h.) 2 McKinnon Street, Dundee DD3 6JN; T.-01382 27669.

Welsh, Ian, MA (Hons), MA, DPSE, FRSA. Leader, South Ayrshire Council; Director of Human Resources and Public Affairs, Glasgow Prestwick International Airport; Director, Enterprise Ayrshire; Director, Ayr College; b. 23.11.53, Ayr; m., Elizabeth; 2 s. Educ. Prestwick Academy; Ayr Academy; Glasgow University; Jordanhill College; Open University. Councillor, Kyle and Carrick, 1989-95, Leader, 1990-92. Former Governor, Craigie College of Education; former professional footballer; Director, Prestwick International Airport, since 1992; Director, Borderline Theatre Company, since 1990; Member, Council, National Trust for Scotland; Member, COSLA Strategy Forum; Chair, Ayrshire Economic Forum; Chair, North Ayr Partnership. Recreations: reading non-fiction, crime fiction. Address: (h.) 35 Ayr Road, Prestwick, Ayrshire; T.-01292 476502.

Wemyss and March, Earl of (Francis David Charteris), KT (1966), Hon. LLD (St. Andrews), Hon. DUniv (Edinburgh), JP, BA. Lord Lieutenant, East Lothian, 1967-87; b. 19.1.12, London; m., Mavis Lynette Gordon Murray (deceased); 1 s.; 1 d.; 1 s. (deceased); 1 d. (deceased); 2, Shelagh Kennedy. Educ. Eton; Balliol College, Oxford. Commissioned, Lovat Scouts (TA), 1932-44; Basutoland Administrative Service, 1937-44; War Service, African Auxiliary Pioneer Corps, Middle East, 1941-44; Chairman, Council, National Trust for Scotland, 1947-67 (President, 1967-91); Chairman, Scottish Churches Council, 1964-71; Chairman, Royal Commission on Ancient and Historical Monuments of Scotland, 1949-84; Vice-President, Marie Curie Memorial Foundation; President, Royal Scottish Geographical Society, 1958-62; President, National Bible Society of Scotland, 1960-83; Lieutenant, Queen's Bodyguard for Scotland (Royal Company of Archers). Recreations: countryside and conservation. Address: (h.) Gosford House, Longniddry, East Lothian; T.-01875 870200.

West, Professor Anthony Roy, BSc, PhD, DSc, CChem, FRSC, FIM, FRSE. Professor of Chemistry, Aberdeen University, since 1989; b. 21.1.47, Sandwich; m., Sheena Cruickshank; 1 s.; 1 d. Educ. Harvey Grammar School, Folkestone; University College Swansea; Aberdeen University. Lecturer, 1971, Senior Lecturer, 1984, Reader, 1986, Professor, 1989, Aberdeen University; Visiting Professor: National University of Mexico, 1976-77, University of Stockholm, 1986, Moscow State University, 1991, Tokyo Institute of Technology, 1993, University of Barcelona, 1996, University of Bahia Blanca, 1997; Founding Editor, Journal of Materials Chemistry, 1991-94; Founding Chairman, Materials Chemistry Forum, since

1993; Member, various Engineering and Physical Sciences Research Council committees, since 1989; Member, SEB Chemistry Panel, 1990-96. Recreations: athletics; gardening. Address: (b.) Department of Chemistry, Meston Walk, Aberdeen AB24 3UE; T.-01224 272918.

West, Peter William Alan, MA, DUniv. Secretary to the University, Strathclyde University, since 1990; b. 16.3.49, Edinburgh; m., Margaret Clark; 1 s.; 1 d. Educ. Edinburgh Academy; St. Andrews University. Administrator, Edinburgh University, 1972-77; Assistant Secretary, Leeds University, 1977-83; Deputy Registrar, Strathclyde University, 1983-89. Doctor of the University of Rostov. Recreations: supporting Scotland's leading football team (Hibernian) through thick and thin. Address: (b.) Strathclyde University, McCance Building, 16 Richmond Street, Glasgow G1 1XQ; T.-0141-552 4400, Ext. 2001.

West, Professor Thomas Summers, CBE, BSc, PhD, DSc, FRSC, FRSE, FRS. Former Director, Macaulay Institute for Soil Research, Aberdeen; b. 18.11.27, Peterhead; m., Margaret O. Lawson; 1 s.; 2 d. Educ. Tarbat School, Portmahomack; Tain Royal Academy; Aberdeen University; Birmingham University. Lecturer in Chemistry, Birmingham University, 1955-63; Imperial College of Science and Technology, London: Reader in Chemistry, 1963-65, Professor of Chemistry, 1965-75. Meldola Medal, Royal Institute of Chemistry; Gold Medal, Society for Analytical Chemistry; President, Society for Analytical Chemistry, 1969-71; Honorary Secretary, Royal Society of Chemistry, 1972-75; President, Analytical Division, International Union of Pure and Applied Chemistry, 1979-81; Secretary General, IUPAC, 1983-91; Honorary Research Professor, Aberdeen University, 1983-87; Emeritus Professor, since 1987. Recreations: gardening; motoring; reading; music; fishing. Address:(h.) 31 Baillieswells Drive, Bieldside, Aberdeen AB15 9AT; T.-01224 868294.

Westcott, Michael John Herbert, BSc (Hons) (Glasgow), Hon. MA (Edinburgh). Retired Assistant Secretary, Edinburgh University; b. 16.4.19, Plymouth. Educ. Hillhead High School; Glasgow University. Ministry of Home Grown Timber Production, 1940-43; Army (Royal Signals), 1943-48 (retired as Major); Colonial Service, Sierra Leone (Administrative Officer), 1948-61; Administrative Officer, Edinburgh University, 1962-86. Honorary Vice-President, National Youth Music Theatre; Honorary President, Edinburgh and SE Scotland VSO Group; Trustee, UK Foundation for the Peoples of the South Pacific. Recreations: walking; theatre; music. Address: (h.) 2 Kilgraston Court, Kilgraston Road, Edinburgh EH9 2ES; T.-0131-447 8282.

Westwood, Alan, BSc, MSc, PhD, CChem, MRSC, FRCPath. Director of Clinical and Information Services, Royal Hospital for Sick Children, Edinburgh, since 1994; Honorary Senior Lecturer, Edinburgh University, since 1981; b. 2.3.48, Luton; m., Jennifer Anne; 1 s.; 1 d. Educ. Luton Technical School; Liverpool University; Birmingham University. Clinical Biochemist: Broadgreen Hospital, Liverpool, 1969, Birmingham Children's Hospital, 1970, Liverpool Royal Infirmary, 1976, Edinburgh Royal Hospital for Sick Children, 1979. Chairman, Scottish Region, Association of Clinical Biochemists, 1984-87 (Member of Association Council, 1982-85). Recreations: cycling; curling; microcomputing. Address: (h.) Fawnspark, Loanstone, by Penicuik, Midlothian EH26 8PH; T.-Penicuik 678407.

Whatley, Professor Christopher Allan, BA, PhD, FRHistS. Professor in Scottish History and Head, Department of Modern History, Dundee University, since 1995; b. 29.5.48, Birmingham; 1 s.; 1 d. Educ. Bearsden Academy; Strathclyde University. Lecturer, Ayr College, 1975-79, Dundee University, 1979-88, St. Andrews University, 1988-92, Dundee University, 1992-94; Senior Lecturer, 1994. Editor, Scottish Economic and Social History; Chairman, SCCC Review Group, Scottish History in the Curriculum. Publications: The Industrial Revolution in Scotland; The Scottish Salt Industry, 1570-1850; Onwards from Osnaburgs: the rise and progress of a Scottish textile company; Bought and Sold for English Gold?: explaining the union of 1707; The Manufacture of Scottish History (Co-editor); The Life and Times of Dundee (Co-author); The Remaking of Juteopolis: Dundee 1891-1991 (Editor); John Galt. Recreations: walking; watching Dundee United FC; theatre. Address: (h.) Viewlands, 2 Moor Road, Ceres, KY15 5LR; T.-01382 223181.

Wheater, Professor Roger John, OBE, CBiol, FIBiol, FRSA, FRSGS (Hon), FRSE. Director, Royal Zoological Society of Scotland, since 1972; Honorary Professor, Edinburgh University, since 1993; b. 24.11.33, Brighton; m., Jean Ord Troup; 1 s.; 1 d. Educ. Brighton, Hove and Sussex Grammar School; Brighton Technical College. Commissioned, Royal Sussex Regiment, 1953; served Gold Coast Regiment, 1953-54; 4/5th Bn., Royal Sussex Regiment (TA), 1954-56; Colonial Police, Uganda, 1956-61; Chief Warden, Murchison Falls National Park, 1961-70; Director, Uganda National Parks, 1970-72; Member, Co-ordinating Committee, Nuffield Unit of Tropical Animal Ecology; Member, Board of Governors, Mweka College of Wildlife Management, Tanzania; Director, National Park Lodges Ltd.; Member, Uganda National Research Council; Vice Chairman, Uganda Tourist Association; Council Member, 1980, and President, 1988-91, International Union of Directors of Zoological Gardens; Chairman, Federation of Zoological Gardens of Great Britain and Ireland, 1993-96; Chairman, Anthropoid Ape Advisory Panel, 1977-91; Member, International Zoo Year Book Editorial Board, since 1987; President, Association of British Wild Animal Keepers, since 1984; Chairman, Membership and Licensing Committee, 1984-91; Chairman, Working Party on Zoo Licensing Act, 1981-84; Council Member, Zoological Society of London, 1991-92, since 1995; Member, Board, Whipsnade Wild Animal Park; Vice-President, World Pheasant Association, since 1994; Trustee Dian Fossey Gorilla Fund, since 1995; Chairman, European Association of Zoos and Aquaria, 1994-97; Member of Council, National Trust for Scotland, 1973-78, Executive Committee, 1982-87; Chairman, Cammo Estate Advisory Committee, 1980-95; Member, Meetings Committee, Royal Society of Edinburgh, since 1996; ESU William Thyne Scholar, 1975 (Trustee, Thyne Scholarship, since 1997); Assessor, Council, Scottish Wildlife Trust, 1973-92; Consultant, World Tourist Organisation (United Nations), since 1980; Member, Secretary of State for Scotland's Working Group on Environmental Education, 1990-94; Board Member, Scottish Natural Heritage, since 1995 (Vice-Chairman, since 1997); Chairman, Access Forum, since 1996; Founder Patron, Dynamic Earth, since 1994; Vice-Chairman, Edinburgh Branch, English Speaking Union, 1977-81; President, Edinburgh Special Mobile Angling Club, 1982-86; President, Cockburn Trout Angling Club, since 1997. Recreations: country pursuits; painting; gardening. Address: (b.) Scottish National Zoological Park, Edinburgh EH12 6TS; T.-0131-334 9171.

Wheatley, Sheriff John Francis, QC, BL. Sheriff, Perthshire and Kinross-shire, at Perth, since 1980; b. 9.5.41, Edinburgh; m., Bronwen Catherine Fraser; 2 s. Educ. Mount St. Mary's College, Derbyshire; Edinburgh University. Called to Scottish Bar, 1966; Standing Counsel to Scottish Development Department, 1968-74; Advocate Depute, 1974-78. Recreations: music; gardening. Address: Braefoot Farmhouse, Fossoway, Kinross-shire; T.-Fossoway 212.

Wheeler, Sir (Harry) Anthony, Kt (1988), OBE, PPRSA, Hon. RA, Hon. RHA, Hon. RGI, Hon. DDes, Hon. RBS, PPRIAS, FRIBA, FRSA, BArch, MRTPI, DipTP.

Consultant, Wheeler & Sproson, Architects and Town Planners, Edinburgh and Kirkcaldy, since 1986; Hon. President, Saltire Society, since 1995; b. 7.11.19, Stranraer; m., Dorothy Jean Campbell; 1 d. Educ. Stranraer High School; Glasgow School of Architecture; Strathclyde University. War Service, Royal Artillery, 1939-46; John Keppie Scholar and Sir Rowand Anderson Studentship, RIBA Grissell Medallist, Neale Bursar; Assistant to City Architect, Oxford, to Sir Herbert Baker & Scott, London; Senior Architect, Glenrothes Development Corporation; began private practice in Fife; Senior Lecturer, Dundee School of Architecture, 1952-58; Saltire Awards and Commendations (22), Civic Trust Awards and Commendations (12); Trustee, Scottish Civic Trust, 1970-83; Member, Royal Fine Art Commission for Scotland, 1967-85; President, Royal Scottish Academy, 1983-90. Recreations: sketching and water colours; fishing; music; drama; gardens. Address: (h.) Hawthornbank House, Dean Village, Edinburgh EH4 3BH.

Wheeler, Professor Simon Jonathan, MA, DPhil, CEng, MICE. Cormack Professor of Civil Engineering, Glasgow University, since 1996; b. 30.4.58, Warlingham, Surrey; m., Noelle Patricia O'Rourke; 2 d. Educ. Whitehaven Grammar School; St. John's College, Cambridge; Balliol College, Oxford. University Lecturer in Soil Mechanics, Queen's University of Belfast, 1984-88; Lecturer in Soil Mechanics, Sheffield University, 1988-92; Lecturer in Civil Engineering, Oxford University, and Fellow of Keble College, Oxford, 1992-95. Committee Member, British Geotechnical Society, Scottish Geotechnical Group. Recreation: mountaineering. Address: (b.) Department of Civil Engineering, Rankine Building, Glasgow G12 8LT; T.-0141-330 5202.

Wherrett, Professor Brian Spencer, BSc, PhD, FInstP, FRSE. Chair of Theoretical Physics, Heriot-Watt University, since 1986; b. 8.5.46, Bromley; m., Shirley Ruth; 1 s.; 1 d. Educ. Westcliff High School; Reading University. Lecturer, Department of Physics, Heriot-Watt University, 1971; promoted to Senior Lecturer and Reader; Visiting Professor, North Texas State University, 1981-82; Past Chairman, SERC Committee on Atomic, Molecular and Plasma Physics and Optical Sciences. Recreation: golf. Address: (b.) Department of Physics, Heriot-Watt University, Riccarton, Edinburgh EH14 4AS; T.-0131-451 3039.

White, Iain, BSc (Hons), MEd, MIBiol, CBiol. Head Teacher, Govan High School, Glasgow, since 1994; b. 2.2.54, Greenock; m., Gail. Educ. Greenock High School; Glasgow University. Biology Teacher, then Principal Biology Teacher, Cowdenknowes High School, Greenock, 1977-87; Assistant Rector, Rothesay Academy, 1987-92; Depute Head Teacher, Port Glasgow High School, 1992-94. Vice Captain, Greenock Golf Club. Recreations: golf; skiing; travel; watching football; Robert Burns; after-dinner speaking. Address: (b.) Govan High School, 12 Ardnish Street, Glasgow G51 4NB; T.-0141-445 4464.

White, Michael, MA (Hons), CertEd, MIPD. Director of Education, Aberdeenshire Council, since 1995; b. 3.7.47, Llwynpia; 3 s. Educ. Grangemouth High School; Falkirk High School; Edinburgh University. Teacher, 1969-77; Headteacher, 1977-84; Divisional Education Officer, Grampian, 1984-90; Assistant Director, Dumfries and Galloway Regional Council, 1990-95. Recreations: sport; pop music; hospital radio; football history. Address: (b.) Woodhill House, Westburn Road, Aberdeen, AB16 5GB; T.-01224 665420.

White, Paul Charles, BA, IPFA, MBA. Director of Finance/Deputy General Manager, Lothian Health Board, since 1993; b. 9.8.49, Londonderry; m., Alison Perry; 4 d. Educ. St. Columb's College, Londonderry; Queen's University, Belfast; Henley Business School. Director of

Finance and Information, Western Health Board, N.I., 1985-90; General Manager, Altnagelvin Group of Hospitals, Londonderry, 1990-93. Recreations: family; North Berwick; golf; theatre. Address: (h.) 13 Macnair Avenue, North Berwick, East Lothian.

White, Professor Stephen Leonard, MA, PhD, DPhil. Professor of Politics, Glasgow University, since 1991; b. 1.7.45, Dublin; m., Ishbel MacPhie; 1 s. Educ. St. Andrew's College, Dublin; Trinity College, Dublin; Glasgow University; Wolfson College, Oxford. Lecturer in Politics, Glasgow University, 1971-85, Reader, 1985-91; Head of Department, since 1992. President, British Association for Slavonic and East European Studies, 1994-97; European Editor, International Politics; General Editor, Cambridge Russian, Soviet and Post-Soviet Series; Chief Editor, Journal of Communist Studies and Transition Politics. Publications include: Political Culture and Soviet Politics, 1979; Britain and the Bolshevik Revolution, 1980; Origins of Detente, 1986; The Bolshevik Poster, 1988; After Gorbachev, 1993; Russia Goes Dry, 1996; How Russia Votes (with others), 1996; Values and PoliticalChange in Postcommunist Europe (with others), 1997. Address: (h.) 11 Hamilton Drive, Glasgow G12 8DN; T.-0141-334 9541.

Whitelaw, Brian Murray, LLB, DipLP, MIMgt, NP. Caithness Area Manager, The Highland Council, since 1995; Clerk to Lord Lieutenant of Caithness; Depute Chief Executive, Caithness District Council, 1990-95; Solicitor and Notary Public; b. 25.12.53, Glasgow; m., Joan Harte; 1 s.; 2 d. Educ. St. Columba's, Clydebank; Strathclyde University. Trainee Solicitor, Joseph Mellick, Solicitors, Glasgow, 1981-83; Assistant Solicitor, Borders Regional Council, 1983-85; Senior Solicitor, Dumbarton District Council, 1985-86; Principal Solicitor, Dumbarton District Council, 1986-90. Recreations: sky diving; photography; cycling. Address: (b.) The Highland Council – Caithness, Market Square, Wick, KW1 4AB; T.-01955 607701.

Whitelaw, Robert George, MA, MD, FRCOG, DL. Deputy Lieutenant, Fife, since 1969; Honorary Sheriff, since 1978; b. 29.4.13, Motherwell; m., Cicely Mary Ballard; 1 s. Educ. Wishaw High School; Glasgow University. Consultant Obstetrician and Gynaecologist, West Fife Group of Hospitals, 1956-78; External Examiner, Edinburgh University, 1967-71; Examiner: Central Midwives Board for Scotland, General Nursing Council for Scotland, Royal College of Surgeons of Edinburgh, PLAB. Past President, Fife Branch, BMA; Past President, Dunfermline Rotary Club. Publications: various papers, mainly on obstetrical and gynaecological subjects. Recreations: golf; photography; travel. Address: (h.) 64 Garvock Hill, Dunfermline, Fife KY12 7UU; T.-01383 721209.

Whiteman, Professor Arthur John, BSc, PhD. Professor Emeritus, Aberdeen University, since 1993; Professor of Petroleum Geology, 1974-93; b. 1.1.28, Ormskirk; m., Sally Janet Pettet; 2 s.; 2 d. Educ. University College, London; Stanford University; Columbia University. Geologist, Humble Oil and Refining Co. Research Fellowship, Columbia University, 1949-51; Geologist, HM Geologist Survey, Great Britain, 1951-56; Exploration Geologist, Compagnie Des Petroles D'Algerie, Royal Dutch Shell, 1956-60; Consultant Petroleum Geologist, since 1960; Professor of Geology, Khartoum, 1960-68; Professor of Petroleum Geology, Ibadan University, 1968-72; Professor of Petroleum Geology, Bergen University, 1972-74. Publications: Geology of Sudan Republic, 1971; Nigeria: Its Petroleum Geology, Resources and Potential, 1982; Rift Systems — Hydrocarbon Habitat and Potential, 1989. Recreation: gardening; water colour. Address: (h.) Garden Cottage, Inchmarlo, Banchory AB31 4BT; T.-01330 825214.

Whiten, Professor David Andrew, BSc, PhD, FBPS. Professor of Evolutionary and Developmental Psychology, St. Andrews University, since 1997; b. 20.4.48, Grimsby; m., Dr. Susie Challoner; 2 d. Educ. Wintringham School, Grimsby; Sheffield University; Bristol University; Oxford University. Research Fellow, Oxford University, 1972-75; Lecturer, then Reader, St. Andrews University, 1975-97; Visiting Professor, Zurich University, 1992, Emory University, 1996. Publications: Machiavellian Intelligence (Co-author), 1988; Natural Theories of Mind, 1991; Foraging Strategies of Monkeys, Apes and Humans (Co-author), 1992; Machiavellian Intelligence II, 1997. Recreations: painting; walking; wildlife; good-lifing. Address: (b.) School of Psychology, St. Andrews University, St. Andrews KY16 9JU.

Whitley, Rev. Laurence Arthur Brown, MA, BD, PhD. Minister, Montrose Old Parish, since 1985 (Busby East and West, 1975-85); b. 19.9.49, Port Glasgow; m., Catherine MacLean MacFadyen; 1 s.; 1 d. Educ. Edinburgh Academy; Edinburgh University; St. Andrews University. Assistant Minister, St. Andrews, Dundee, 1974-75. Parliamentary candidate (SNP), Dumfriesshire, February and October, 1974. Recreation: Sesquipedalianism. Address: (h.) 2 Rosehill Road, Montrose, Angus DD10 8ST; T.-Montrose 672447.

Whittemore, Professor Colin Trengove, BSc, PhD, DSc, NDA, CBiol, FIBiol, FRSE. Head, Institute of Ecology and Resource Management, Edinburgh University, since 1990, and Professor of Agriculture and Rural Economy, since 1990; b. 16.7.42, Chester; m., Chris; 1 s.; 3 d. Educ. Rydal School; Newcastle-upon-Tyne University. Lecturer in Agriculture, Edinburgh University and Head, Animal Production, Advisory and Development, Edinburgh School of Agriculture; Professor of Animal Production, Head, Animal Division, Edinburgh School of Agriculture; Head, Department of Agriculture, Edinburgh University. Sir John Hammond Memorial Prize for scientific contribution to an understanding of nutrition and growth; Oxford University Blackman Lecture; Royal Agricultural Society of England Gold Medal for research; Mignini Oscar; David Black Award. Publications: author of five text books of animal sciences. Recreations: skiing; riding. Address: (b.) Edinburgh University, School of Agriculture, West Mains Road, Edinburgh EH9 3JG; T.-0131-667 1041.

Whyte, Christopher, MA (Hons), PhD. Writer and Critic; Lecturer in Scottish Literature, Glasgow University, since 1990; b. 29.10.52, Glasgow. Educ. St. Aloysius College, Glasgow; Pembroke College, Cambridge. Lector, Rome University, 1977-85; Lecturer in English Literature, Edinburgh University, 1986-89. Publications: In The Face of Eternity: Eight Gaelic Poets, 1991; Uirsgeul/Myth, 1991; Euphemia MacFarrigle and the Laughing Virgin, 1995; Gendering the Nation, 1995; The Warlock of Strathearn, 1997. Recreations: classical music; walking; cooking. Address: (h.) 15 Hart Street, Edinburgh EH1 3RN; T.-0131-558 3907.

Whyte, David James, MA. Rector, Golspie High School, since 1983; b. 21.2.40, Cupar; m., Judith; 4 s. Educ. Bell Baxter High School; St. Andrews University. Assistant Teacher of English, Strathallan School, 1964-67; Special Assistant, Kirkcaldy High School, 1967-69; Principal Teacher of English, Brechin High School, 1969-73; Assistant Headteacher, Arbroath Academy, 1973-79; Depute Rector, Peterhead Academy, 1979-83. British Athletics International, 1958-61; Scottish Rugby International, 1964-67; President, Rotary Club of East Sutherland, 1996. Recreations: bridge; tennis. Address: (b.) Golspie High School, Main Street, Golspie KW10 6RF; T.-01408 633451.

Whyte, David Malcolm, BAcc, CA. Director Scotland, British Red Cross Society, since 1997; b. 25.5.55, Magherafelt, N. Ireland; m., Frances; 1 s.; 1 d. Educ. Greenock Academy; Glasgow University. Various posts to Audit Manager, Deloitte Haskins & Sells, 1975-84; Group Financial Accountant/Company Secretary, Clydesdale Group Ltd., 1984-87; Financial Director, Glen Rentals Ltd., 1987-91; joined Red Cross (Scottish Central Council Branch) as Director of Finance, 1991. Recreations: golf; skiing; walking. Address: (b.) 204 Bath Street, Glasgow G2 4HL; T.-0141-332 9591.

Whyte, Donald, JP, FHG, FSG. Consultant Genealogist, Author and Lecturer; b. 13.3.26, Newtongrange; m., Mary Burton; 3 d. Educ. Crookston School, Musselburgh; Institute of Heraldic and Genealogical Studies, Canterbury. Agricultural and horticultural work, 1940-68; professional genealogist, 1968-76; Member, Kirkliston and Winchburgh District Council, 1964-75 (Chairman, 1970-73); Member, West Lothian County Council, 1970-75; founder Member and Vice-President, Scottish Genealogy Society; President, Association of Scottish Genealogists and Record Agents, since 1981. Publications: Kirkliston: A Short Parish History; Dictionary of Scottish Emigrants to USA; Introducing Scottish Genealogical Research; Dictionary of Scottish Emigrants to Canada before Confederation, 2 vols; Walter MacFarlane: Clan Chief and Antiquary; Scottish Clock and Watchmakers, 1453-1900; Scottish Surnames and Families. Address: (h.) 4 Carmel Road, Kirkliston EH29 9DD; T.-0131-333 3245.

Whyte, Rev. Iain Alexander, BA, BD, STM. Chaplain, University of Edinburgh, since 1994; b. 3.9.40, Stirling; m., Isabel Helen Martin; 2 s.; 1 d. Educ. Sherborne School, Dorset; St. Peter's College, Oxford; Glasgow University; Union Theological Seminary, NY. Assistant Minister, Kildrum, Cumbernauld, 1967-69; Minister and Youth Worker in Ghana, 1969-71; Chaplain to Overseas Students in Glasgow, 1971-74; Lecturer, Falkirk Technical College, 1974-75; Minister, Merksworth Parish Church, Paisley, 1976-81; Chaplain, St. Andrews University, 1981-87; Minister, Blairhill Dundyvan Parish Church, Coatbridge, 1987-90; National Secretary for Scotland, Christian Aid, 1990-94. Scottish Churches Representative, Board, Christian Aid, 1980-86 (Chairman, Christian Aid Middle East Committee, 1982-86); Chairman, Scottish Churches Council Race and Community Relations Group, 1981-83; Scottish Representative, Britain/Zimbabwe Society; former Chair, Glasgow Anti-Apartheid Group. Recreations: travel; squash; watching St. Mirren; numismatics; candle-making. Address: (h.) 34 Shandon Crescent, Edinburgh EH11 1QF; T.-0131-337 0886.

Whyte, Iain Wilson, BA, DCE, DMS. Director and General Secretary, Church of Scotland Board of Parish Education, since 1993; b. 2.12.56, Johnstone; m., Elaine; 2 d. Educ. Paisley Grammar School; Jordanhill College; Open University. Adult Education Tutor, Glasgow, 1978-82; Development Officer, Priesthill, Glasgow, 1982-84; Adult Education Officer, European Social Fund Project, Strathclyde, 1984-86; Lecturer, Cardonald College, Glasgow, 1986-90, Senior Lecturer, 1990-93. Elder, Colinton Parish Church, Edinburgh. Recreations: playing guitar, piano, organ; singing; songwriting; golf. Address: (b.) St. Colm's, 18 Inverleith Terrace, Edinburgh, EH3 5NS; T.-0131-332 0343.

Whyte, Rev. James, BD, DipCE. Parish Minister, Broom, Newton Mearns, since 1987; b. 26.4.46, Glasgow; m., Norma Isabella West; 1 s.; 2 d. Educ. Glasgow; Jordanhill College; Glasgow University. Trained as planning engineer; studied community education (Glasgow and Boston, Mass., USA); Community Organiser with Lamp of Lothian Collegiate Trust, Haddington; Organiser of Community Education, Dumbarton, 1971-73; Assistant Principal Community Education Officer, Renfrew Division,

Strathclyde Region, 1973-77; entered ministry, Church of Scotland, 1977; Assistant Minister: Barrhead Arthurlie, 1977-78, St. Marks, Oldhall, Paisley, 1978-80; Minister, Coupar Angus Abbey, 1981-87. Recreations: gardening; reading. Address: Manse of Broom, 3 Laigh Road, Newton Mearns, Glasgow G77; T.-0141-639 2916.

Whyte, Very Rev. Professor James Aitken, MA, LLD, DD, DUniv. Moderator, General Assembly of the Church of Scotland, 1988-89; Professor of Practical Theology and Christian Ethics, St. Andrews University, 1958-87; b. 28.1.20, Leith; m., 1, Elisabeth Wilson Mill (deceased); 2 s.; 1 d.; 2, Ishbel Christina Macaulay or Rathie. Educ. Daniel Stewart's College, Edinburgh; Edinburgh University. Ordained and commissioned as Chaplain to the Forces, 1945; Minister: Dunollie Road Church, Oban, 1948-54, Mayfield North Church, Edinburgh, 1954-58; Dean of Divinity, St. Andrews University, 1968-72; Principal, St. Mary's College, 1978-82; Kerr Lecturer, Glasgow University, 1969-72; Croall Lecturer, Edinburgh University, 1972-73; Hon. LLD, Dundee University, 1981; Hon.DD, St. Andrews University, 1989; Hon. DUniv., Stirling University, 1994; President, Society for the Study of Theology, 1983-84; Margaret Harris Lecturer, Dundee University, 1990. Publication: Laughter and Tears, 1993. Address: (h.) 13 Hope Street, St. Andrews, Fife; T.-St. Andrews 472323.

Whyte, Richard Brodie, LLB, DFM, SSC, NP. Solicitor Advocate, since 1995; Solicitor, since 1981; b. 1.8.47, Edinburgh; m., Gail; 2 s.; 1 d. Educ. Broxburn High School; Edinburgh University; Glasgow University. Principal in private practice, since 1983. Recreations: reading; golf; football; cinema; art galleries. Address: (b.) Lammermuir House, Livingston EH54 6NB; T.-01506 415281.

Whyte, Robert, MB, ChB, FRCPsych, DPM. Consultant Psychotherapist, Carswell House, Glasgow, since 1979; b. 1.6.41, Edinburgh; m., Susan Frances Milburn; 1 s.; 1 d. Educ. George Heriot's, Edinburgh; St. Andrews University. House Officer in Surgery, Arbroath Infirmary, 1966; House Officer in Medicine, Falkirk and District Royal Infirmary, 1967; Trainee in Psychiatry, Dundee Psychiatric Services, 1967-73; Consultant Psychiatrist, Duke Street Hospital, Glasgow, 1973. Past Chairman, Scottish Association of Psychoanalytical Psychotherapists; Member, Scottish Institute of Human Relations. Address: (h.) Waverley, 70 East Kilbride Road, Busby, Glasgow G76 8HU; T.-0141-644 1659.

Wickham-Jones, Caroline R., MA, MIFA, FSA, FSA Scot. Archaeologist; b. 25.4.55, Middlesborough; m.; 1 s. Educ. Teesside High School; Edinburgh University. Freelance archaeologist and author with research interests in early (postglacial) settlement of Scotland, stone tools, and the preservation of the cultural heritage; former Council Member, National Trust for Scotland; Council Member, Institute of Field Archaeologists, 1986-90; former Secretary, Society of Antiquaries of Scotland; former Trustee, John Muir Trust; Livery Woman of the City of London (Skinners Company). Publications: Scotland's First Settlers; Arthurs Seat and Holyrood Park, a Visitor's Guide. Recreations: travel; wilderness walking; socialising. Address: (h.) 21 Dudley Gardens, Edinburgh EH6 4PU.

Wigglesworth, Rev. Chris, MBE, BSc, PhD, BD. General Secretary, Church of Scotland Board of World Mission; b. 8.4.37, Leeds; m., Ann Livesey; 1 s.; 3 d. Educ. Grangefield Grammar School, Stockton-on-Tees; University College, Durham; New College, Edinburgh. Church of North India, 1967-72; St. Andrew's and St. Columba's Church, Bombay, 1972-79; University Lecturer in Practical Theology, Aberdeen, 1979-86. Recreations: painting; hill-walking. Address: (h.) 12 Leven Terrace, Edinburgh; T.-0131-228 335.

Wight, Robin A.F., MA, FCA. Chairman, Arville Holdings, since 1995; b. 5.6.38, Edinburgh; m., Sheila; 3 s.; 1 d. Educ. Dollar Academy; Magdalene College, Cambridge. Partner, Coopers & Lybrand, 1971-96; Regional Partner, Scotland, 1977-95; Member, Executive Committee, 1978-87; Member, Governing Board, 1987-89; Member, Council, 1989-93. Recreations: skiing; golf; reading; theatre. Address: (h.) 22 Regent Terrace, Edinburgh; T.-0131-556 2100.

Wightman, Very Rev. William David, BA (Hons). Provost, St. Andrews Cathedral, Aberdeen, since 1991, also Priest-in-Charge, St. Ninian's, Aberdeen; Hon. Canon, Christchurch Cathedral, Hartford, Conn., since 1991. b. 29.1.39, Leicester; m., Karen Elizabeth Harker; 2 s.; 2 d. Educ. Alderman Newton's Grammar School, Leicester; George Dixon Grammar School, Birmingham; Birmingham University; Wells Theological College. Ordained Deacon, 1963; ordained Priest, 1964. Director, Training for Ministry (Diocese of Aberdeen and Orkney), 1989-91. Recreations: fishing; swimming; choral music. Address: (h.) 15 Morningfield Road, Aberdeen AB15 4AP; T.-01224 314765.

Wilcox, Christine Alison, BA (Hons), ALA. Librarian, S.S.C. Library, Edinburgh, since 1991; b. 18.7.63, New Zealand; m., Michael Wilcox; 2 s. Educ. South Wilts Grammar School, Salisbury; Manchester Polytechnic Library School. Assistant Librarian, Barow Lyde and Gilbert, Solicitors, London, 1984-86; Librarian, Beaumont and Son, Solicitors, London, 1986-89; posting to Bahrain accompanying husband, 1989-91. Secretary, Scottish Law Librarians Group, 1993-95. Publications: Directory of Legal Libraries in Scotland; Union List of Periodical and Law Report Holdings in Scotland. Recreations: needlework; hill-walking. Address: (b.) S.S.C. Library, 11 Parliament Square, Edinburgh EH1 1RF; T.-0131-225 6268.

Wild, John Robin, JP, BDS, DPD, FDSRCS(Edin), DGDP. Chief Dental Officer, Scottish Office Department of Health, and Director of Dental Services for the NHS in Scotland, 1993-97 (Deputy Chief Dental Officer, 1987-93); b. 12.9.41, Scarborough; m., Eleanor Daphne Kerr; 1 s.; 2 d. Educ. Sedbergh School; Edinburgh University; Dundee University. General Dental Practitioner, Scarborough, 1965-71; Dental Officer, East Lothian, 1971-74; Chief Administrative Dental Officer, Borders Health Board, 1974-87; Regional Dental Postgraduate Adviser, S.E. Regional Committee for Postgraduate Medical Education, 1982-87; Hon. Senior Lecturer, Dundee Dental School, since 1993; JP for District of Ettrick and Lauderdale, since 1982; Past Chairman, Scottish Council, British Dental Association. Recreations: vintage cars (restoration and driving); music; gardening. Address: (h.) Braehead House, St. Boswells, Roxburghshire; T.-01835 823203.

Wildgoose, James Richmond, BSc, DPhil. Head of Animal Health and Welfare and Food Safety Division, Scottish Office Agriculture, Environment and Fisheries Department; formerly Chief Agricultural Economist; b. 17.4.49, Edinburgh; m., Charlotte Dorothy; 1 s.; 1 d. Educ. Melville College; Edinburgh University; Oxford University. Economic Assistant/Economic Adviser, Ministry of Agriculture, Fisheries and Food, 1976-86; Administrative Principal, MAFF Tropical Foods Division, 1986-90; Admnistrative Principal, Scottish Office (SDD), 1990. Address: (b.) Room 352, Pentland House, Robb's Loan, Edinburgh; T.-0131-244 6128.

Wildsmith, Professor John Anthony Winston, MD, FRCA, FRCPEd. Foundation Professor of Anaesthesia, Dundee University, since 1995; Honorary Consultant Anaesthetist, Dundee Teaching Hospitals, since 1995; b. 22.2.46, Newent, Glos; m., Angela Fay Smith; 3 d. Educ. King's School, Gloucester; Edinburgh University Medical School. Spent greater part of early professional career in

Edinburgh, either at University or Royal Infirmary, apart from a year at Brigham and Women's Hospital, Boston, USA; final post in Edinburgh, Consultant/Senior Lecturer; Clinical Director for Anaesthetics, Intensive Care and Operating Theatres, Royal Infirmary, Edinburgh, 1992-95. Member, Council, Royal College of Anaesthetists; Member, Editorial Board, British Journal of Anaesthesia. Recreations: golf; wine; travel. Address: (b.) University Department of Anaesthesia, Ninewells Hospital and Medical School, Dundee DD1 9SY; T.-01382 632427.

Wilkie, Rev. James Lindsay, MA, BD. Secretary for relations with churches in Africa, Board of World Mission, Church of Scotland, since 1984; b. 13.4.34, Dunfermline; m., Dr. Irene A. Wilkie; 1 s.; 3 d. Educ. Aberdeen Grammar School; Aberdeen University and Christ's College. Assistant Minister, St. Machar's Cathedral, Aberdeen, 1959-60; District Missionary and Minister, United Church of Zambia, 1961-70; Chaplain, University of Zambia, 1970-76; Africa Secretary, then Divisional Secretary and Deputy General Secretary, British Council of Churches, 1976-84; member of team which translated Bible into Chinamwanga language of Zambia. Recreation: DIY. Address: (h.) 7 Comely Bank Avenue, Edinburgh EH4 1EW; T.-0131-343 1552.

Wilkie, Neil Keith, OBE, MA (Hons), FRSA. Headmaster, Gairloch High School, since 1978; b. 5.4.39, Perth; m., Margaret Rawlinson; 1 s. Educ. Perth Academy; Dundee University; Dundee College of Education; East of Scotland College of Agriculture. Sugar planter, Trinidad, six years; resumed academic studies, 1966; Teacher of History and Modern Studies, then Principal Teacher of History, Golspie High School, 1972-78. Elder, Gairloch and Dundonnell Parish Church; Member, Gairloch Community Council. Recreations: sport; travel; gardening. Address: (h.) Rohallion, Achtercairn, Gairloch, Ross-shire; T.-01445 712221.

Wilkie, Professor (William) Roy, MA. Emeritus Professor, Department of Human Resource Management, Strathclyde University, since 1974; b. 10.6.30, Rutherglen; m., Jill Henzell; 1 s.; 3 d. Educ. Rutherglen Academy; Aberdeen University. Lecturer and Senior Lecturer, Department of Administration, Strathclyde University, 1963-66; Director, J. & J. Denholm (Management) Ltd., 1966-70; Reader and Head, Department of Administration, Strathclyde University, 1966-73. Publications: The Concept of Organization, 1974; Managing the Police, 1986. Recreations: swimming; movies; jazz; reading. Address: (b.) Graham Hill Building, 50 Richmond Street, Glasgow; T.-0141-552 4400.

Wilkins, Professor Malcolm Barrett, BSc, PhD, DSc, AKC, FRSE. Regius Professor of Botany, Glasgow University, since 1970 (Dean, Faculty of Science, 1985-87; Member, University Court, since 1993); b.27.2.33, Cardiff; m., Mary Patricia Maltby; 1 s.; 1 d. (deceased). Educ. Monkton House School, Cardiff; King's College, London University. Lecturer in Botany, King's College, London, 1958-64; Lecturer in Biology, then Professor of Biology, East Anglia University, 1964-67; Professor of Plant Physiology, Nottingham University, 1967-70. Rockefeller Foundation Fellow, Yale University, 1961-62; Corporation Research Fellow, Harvard University, 1962-63; Darwin Lecturer, British Association for the Advancement of Science, 1967; elected Corresponding (Honorary) Member, American Society of Plant Physiologists, 1984; Chairman, Life Science Working Group, European Space Agency, 1987-89; Trustee, Royal Botanic Garden, Edinburgh, since 1990, Chairman, since 1994; Vice President, Royal Society of Edinburgh, since 1994; Member, Advisory Council, Scottish Agricultural College, since 1992. Recreations: sailing; fishing; model engineering. Address: (b.) Botany Department, Glasgow University, Glasgow G12 8QQ; T.-0141-330 4450.

Wilkinson, Sheriff Alexander Birrell, QC, MA, LLB. Sheriff of Lothian and Borders at Edinburgh (formerly of Glasgow and Strathkelvin at Glasgow); Temporary Judge, Court of Session, since 1993; b. 2.2.32, Perth; m., Wendy Imogen Barrett; 1 s.; 1 d. Educ. Perth Academy; St. Andrews University; Edinburgh University. Advocate, 1959; practised at Scottish Bar, 1959-69; Lecturer in Scots Law, Edinburgh University, 1965-69; Sheriff of Stirling, Dunbarton and Clackmannan, at Stirling and Alloa, 1969-72; Professor of Private Law, Dundee University, 1972-86 (Dean, Faculty of Law, 1974-76 and 1986); Sheriff of Tayside, Central and Fife at Falkirk, 1986-91; a Chairman, Industrial Tribunals (Scotland), 1972-86; Chancellor, Dioceses of Brechin and of Argyll and the Isles, Scottish Episcopal Church; Chairman, Scottish Marriage Guidance Council, 1974-77; Chairman, Legal Services Group, Scottish Association of CAB, 1979-83. Publications: Gloag and Henderson's Introduction to the Law of Scotland, 8th and 9th editions (Co-editor); The Scottish Law of Evidence; The Law of Parent and Child in Scotland (Co-author). Recreations: collecting books and pictures; reading; travel.

Wilkinson, Professor Paul, MA. Professor of International Relations, St. Andrews University; Writer on conflict and terrorism; b. 9.5.37, Harrow, Middlesex; m., Susan; 2 s.; 1 d. Educ. John Lyon School; University College, Swansea; University of Wales. RAF, 1959-65; Assistant Lecturer in Politics, University College, Cardiff, 1966-68; University of Wales: Lecturer, 1968-75, Senior Lecturer, 1975-77, Reader in Politics, 1978-79; Professor of International Relations, Aberdeen University, 1979-89; Editor, Terrorism and Political Violence; Member, Editorial Board, Security Handbook, Social Intelligence, and Violence and Aggression; Editor, Key Concepts in International Relations; Scottish Free Enterprise Award, 1982; Honorary Fellow, University College, Swansea, 1986; Special Consultant, CBS America, 1989-90, BBC, since 1989; Aviation Security Adviser to IFAPA, 1988; Safety Adviser, World Tourism and Travel Council; FRSA, 1995; Visiting Fellow, Trinity Hall, Cambridge, 1997-98. Publications: Social Movement, 1971; Political Terrorism, 1974; Terrorism and the Liberal State, 1986 (revised edition); The New Fascists, 1983; Terrorism: Theory and Practice (Co-author), 1979; British Perspectives on Terrorism (Editor), 1981; Contemporary Research on Terrorism (Joint Editor), 1987; Technology and Terrorism (Editor), 1994; Terrorism: British Perspectives (Editor), 1993; Research Report for Inquiry into Legislation Against Terrorism, Vol. II, 1996. Recreations: modern art; poetry; walking. Address: (b.) Department of International Relations, St. Andrews University, St. Andrews KY16 9AL; T.-01334 462900.

Wilkinson, (William) Roderick, DAA, FIPM. Novelist and Scriptwriter; b. 31.3.17, Glasgow; 1 s.; 2 d. Educ. North Kelvinside Secondary, Glasgow. Director of advertising agency, 1946-59; Director of Personnel, 1959-80. Publications: 10 books, fiction and non-fiction; plays, articles and stories. Recreation: fishing. Address: (h.) 61 Norwood Park, Bearsden, Glasgow G61 2RZ; T.-0141-570 1689.

Wilks, Antony Hugh Francis, MBE, FNI. Chairman, Forth Estuary Forum; Member, Board, Scottish Environment Protection Agency (East); Member, Board, Scottish Natural Heritage (East); Direct, CoastNet; Member, Scottish Coastal Forum; b. 29.12.36, Watford; m., Susan Chaloner Reed; 1 s.; 1 d. Educ. Oundle. Royal Navy, 1958-90, latterly Naval Base Commander, Rosyth, 1985-90. Contributor, The Naval Review; knighthood, State of Brunei. Recreations: lawn tennis and rackets. Address: (b.) Easter Fossoway, Kinross-shire; T.-01577 840255.

Will, David Houston, BL, NP. Vice-President, FIFA, since 1990; Chairman, FIFA Referees Committee, and Legal Matters Committee; Member, FIFA Executive Committee, World Cup Organising Committee and Security Committee

b. 20.11.36, Glasgow; m., Margaret; 2 d. Educ. Brechin High School; Edinburgh University. Chairman, Brechin City FC, 1966-91; appointed to SFA Council, 1970; President, SFA, 1984-89; Vice-President, UEFA, 1986-90. Recreations: golf; curling. Address: (h.) Norandale, 32 Airlie Street, Brechin, Angus; T.-01356 622273.

Willett, Emeritus Professor Frank, CBE, MA, FRSE. Hon. Senior Research Fellow, since 1990, Director, Hunterian Museum & Art Gallery, Glasgow, 1976-90; b. 18.8.25, Bolton; m., Mary Constance Hewitt; 1 s.; 3 d. Educ. Bolton Municipal Secondary School; University College, Oxford. Keeper of Ethnology and General Archaeology, Manchester Museum, 1950-58; Government Archaeologist, Nigeria, 1958-63; Leverhulme Research Fellow, 1964; Research Fellow, Nuffield College, Oxford, 1964-66; Professor of Art History, African Studies and Interdisciplinary Studies, Northwestern University, Evanston, Illinois, 1966-76; Visiting Fellow, Clare Hall, Cambridge, 1970-71; Hon. Corresponding Member, Manchester Literary and Philosophical Society, since 1958; Vice Chairman, Scottish Museums Council, 1986-89; Fellow, Royal Anthropological Institute; Fellow, Royal Society of Edinburgh, 1979, Curator, RSE, 1992-97; Leadership Award, Arts Council of the African Studies Association, 1995. Publications: Ife in the History of West African Sculpture, 1967; African Art: An Introduction, 1971; Treasures of Ancient Nigeria, Co-author, 1980. Recreation: walking. Address: (b.) Hunterian Museum, University of Glasgow, Glasgow G12 8QQ; T.-0141-330 4221.

Willetts, Professor Brian Benjamin, MA, PhD, CEng, FICE, FRSE. Professor of Civil Engineering, Aberdeen University, since 1985 (Head, Engineering Department, 1991-94); b. 12.6.36, Old Hill; m., Patricia Margaret Jones; 1 s.; 1 d. Educ. King Edward VI School, Stourbridge; Emmanuel College, Cambridge. Assistant Engineer, City of Birmingham, 1959-61; Executive Engineer, Government of Northern Nigeria, 1961-63; Lecturer/Senior Lecturer, Lanchester Polytechnic, 1963-66; Lecturer/Senior Lecturer, Aberdeen University, 1967-85. Address: (h.) Mosscroft, Upper Lochton, Banchory, Kincardineshire; T.-0133 082 2674.

Willey, Professor Roger James, BSc, PhD, CPhys, MIOSH, MBIM. Chief Executive, Centre for Environmental and Waste Management, Paisley University, since 1992; b. 11.6.46, Rhondda; m., Jennifer; 2 d. Educ. Porth County Grammar School; University College, Swansea. Specialist in the treatment of hazardous materials, especially asbestos; consultancy work in Europe, USA, Canada, India, Middle East and Japan; presented at conferences in Europe, America and Japan; Past Chairman, Institute of Occupational Safety and Health (West of Scotland); Member, IOSH Professional Standards Committee; Member, Secretary of State for Scotland Advisory Group on Sustainable Development; former Board Member, South West Region, Scottish Natural Heritage; Member, Appeals Board, Entrust, since 1997; Consultant to World Bank, since 1997. Publications: 75 papers/technical articles. Recreations: sport; travel. Address: (b.) Westerfield House, 25 High Calside, Paisley PA2 6BY; T.-0141-848 3146.

Williams, Sir Alwyn, Kt, PhD, FRS, FRSE, MRIA, FGS, Hon. FRCPS, Hon. DSc, Hon. LLD. Honorary Research Fellow, Department of Geology, Glasgow University (Principal and Vice-Chancellor, Glasgow University, 1976-88); Non-Executive Director, Scottish Daily Record and Sunday Mail Ltd., 1984-90; b. 8.6.21, Aberdare, Wales; m., Edythe Joan Bevan; 1 s.; 1 d. Educ. Aberdare Boys' Grammar School; University College of Wales, berystwyth. Commonwealth Fund Fellow, US National useum, 1948-50; Lecturer in Geology, Glasgow versity, 1950-54; Professor of Geology, Queen's University, Belfast, 1954-74; Lapworth Professor Geology, Birmingham University, 1974-76; Chairman Scottish Hospital Endowments Research Trust, 1989-96; Member, Scottish Tertiary Education Advisory Council, 1984-86; President, Palaeontological Association, 1968-70; President, Royal Society of Edinburgh, 1985-88; Trustee and Chairman, Board of British Museum (Natural History), 1971-79; Chairman, Committee on National Museums and Galleries of Scotland, 1979-81; Honorary Fellow, Geological Society of America, since 1970; Foreign Member, Polish Academies of Science, since 1981; Hon. DSc, Universities of Wales, Queen's (Belfast) and Edinburgh; Hon. DCL, Oxford; Hon. LLD, Glasgow, Strathclyde; Hon. DUniv, Paisley; Hon. FRSAMD; Fellow, University College of Wales. Address: (h.) 25 Sutherland Avenue, Pollokshields, Glasgow G41 4HG; T.-0141-427 0589.

Williams, Professor Howard Peter, MSc. Professor, Management Science Department, Strathclyde University, since 1990; Director, Network and Resource Management Centre; b. 27.2.54, St. Albans. Educ. Exeter University; Newcastle upon Tyne University. Economist, ICI Plant Protection Division, International Wool Secretariat, British Ship Research Association; Senior Research Fellow, Newcastle-upon-Tyne University. Member, Scottish Advisory Committee on Telecommunications, Glasgow Advisory Committee on Posts and Telecommunications. Recreations: windsurfing; opera; breadmaking. Address: (b.) Department of Management Science, Sir Graham Hills Building, Strathclyde University, Glasgow G1 1XH; T.-0141-548 3143.

Williams, Professor Morgan Howard, BSc Hons, PhD, DSc, CEng, FBCS, FRSA. Professor of Computer Science, Heriot-Watt University, since 1980 (Head of Department, 1980-88); b. 15.12.44, Durban; 2 s. Educ. Grey High School, Port Elizabeth; Rhodes University, Grahamstown. Physicist in Antarctic Expedition, 1968-69; Rhodes University: Lecturer in Computer Science, 1970-72, Senior Lecturer, 1972-77, Professor and Head of Department, 1977-80. Address: Department of Computing and Electrical Engineering, Heriot-Watt University, Riccarton, Edinburgh EH14 4AS; T.-0131-451 3430.

Williamson, David, CBE, BL. Honorary President, SSC (a club for the youth of Scotland), Chairman, 1964-89; Chairman, North Merchiston Club, Edinburgh, since 1982; Trustee, Stanley Nairne Memorial Trust, since 1969; b. 13.1.20, Edinburgh; m., Agnes Margaret. Educ. George Heriot's School, Edinburgh; Edinburgh University. Army Service, 1940-46 (Gunner, Lance Bombadier, Bombadier, Sergeant, Officer Cadet, Second Lieutenant, Lieutenant, Captain); Keeper of the Registers of Scotland, 1973-82 (supervised introduction of Registration of Title to Scotland, 1981); Honorary Member, Law Society of Scotland, since 1982; received Keystone Gold Award for services to Boys' Clubs, 1985. Publications: Registration of Title Practice Book (Co-author); The Story of the Scottish Schoolboys' Club (Editor and Co-author); Stanley Nairne, The Boys' Club Pioneer. Recreations: walking; enjoying countryside; reading; appreciating music (including opera); watching rugby. Address: (h.) 10 Homeross House, Mount Grange, Edinburgh EH9 2QX; T.-0131-447 3050.

Williamson, Professor Edwin Henry, MA, PhD. Professor of Hispanic Studies, Edinburgh University, since 1990; b. 2.10.49; m., Susan Jane Fitchie; 2 d. Educ. Edinburgh University. Lecturer in Spanish, Trinity College, Dublin, 1974-77; Lecturer in Spanish, Birkbeck College, London, 1977-90. Publications: The Half-Way House of Fiction: Don Quixote and Arthurian Romance, 1984; El Quijote Y Los Libros de Caballerias, 1991; The Penguin History of Latin America, 1992; Cervantes and the Modernists, 1994. Recreations: theatre; art; film; hill-walking. Address: (b.) Department of Hispanic Studies, Edinburgh University,

avid Hume Tower, George Square, Edinburgh EH8 9JX;
T.-0131-650 3673.

Williamson, Professor James, CBE, MB, ChB, FRCPEdin, DSc (Hon.). Past Chairman, Chest, Heart and Stroke, Scotland; Past President, British Geriatrics Society; Past Chairman, Age Concern Scotland; Professor Emeritus, Geriatric Medicine, Edinburgh University; b. 22.11.20, Wishaw; m., Sheila Mary Blair; 3 s.; 2 d. Educ. Wishaw High School; Glasgow University. General medical training in Glasgow hospitals; general practice; training in respiratory medicine, becoming Consultant in Edinburgh, 1954; converted to geriatric medicine, 1959; Consultant, Edinburgh, until 1973; first occupant, Chair of Geriatric Medicine, Liverpool University; first occupant, Chair of Geriatric Medicine, Edinburgh University, 1976-86; Visiting Professor to several North American medical schools. Recreations: reading; walking. Address: (h.) 8 Chester Street, Edinburgh EH3 7RA; T.-0131-477 0282.

Williamson, Raymond MacLeod, MA, LLB, FRSA. Solicitor, since 1968 (Partner, MacRoberts, Solicitors, Glasgow and Edinburgh, since 1972); Secretary, High School of Glasgow Educational Trust; Governor, Royal Scottish Academy of Music and Drama; Chairman, John Currie Singers Ltd.; b. 24.12.42, Glasgow; m., Brenda; 1 s.; 1 d. Educ. High School of Glasgow; Glasgow University. Chairman, Royal Scottish National Orchestra, 1985-91; Chairman, Children's Music Foundation in Scotland; Chairman, National Youth Choir of Scotland; Deputy Chairman, Scottish International Piano Competition. Recreation: music. Address: (h.) 11 Islay Drive, Newton Mearns, Glasgow G77 6UD; T.-0141-639 4133.

Williamson, Professor Timothy, MA, DPhil, FBA, FRSE. Professor of Logic and Metaphysics, Edinburgh University, since 1995; b. 6.8.55, Uppsala, Sweden; m., Elisabetta Perosino; 1 s.; 1 d. Educ. Henley Grammar School; Balliol College and Christ Church, Oxford. Lecturer in Philosophy, Trinity College Dublin, 1980-88; Fellow in Philosophy, University College Oxford, 1988-94; Visiting Professor, MIT, 1994; Visiting Fellow, Australian National University, 1990 and 1995; Erskine Visiting Fellow, University of Canterbury (NZ), 1995. Publications: Identity and Discrimination, 1990; Vagueness, 1994; articles in learned journals. Recreation: conventional behaviour. Address: (b.) Department of Philosophy, Edinburgh University, David Hume Tower, George Square, Edinburgh EH8 9JX; T.-0131-650 3665.

Willock, Professor Ian Douglas, MA, LLB, PhD. Professor of Jurisprudence, Dundee University. Educ. Aberdeen University. Address: (b.) Department of Law, Dundee University, Dundee; T.-01382 223181.

Wills, Jonathan W.G., MA (Hons), PhD. Partner, Shetland News Agency; Writer, Illustrator and Painter; b. 17.6.47, Oxford; m., Lesley M. Roberts; 3 s.; 1 d. Educ. Warwick School; Anderson Educational Institute, Lerwick; Edinburgh University. Reporter, Shetland Times, 1969; Warden and boatman, Noss National Nature Reserve, 1970; Rector, Edinburgh University (first student Rector), 1971; Scottish and NI Organiser, Third World First (Oxfam), 1972; Boatman, Muckle Flugga Lighthouse, Unst, 1974; Reporter, Shetland Times, 1976; Senior Producer/Presenter, BBC Radio Shetland, 1977; News Editor, Shetland Times, 1981; Scottish Correspondent, The Times, 1982; Producer, BBC Radio Scotland, 1983; Freelance and Research Assistant to Alex. Falconer, MEP, 1984; Tutor, Media Studies, STUC and individual trade unions, 1984; Senior Reporter, Shetland Times, 1985, Editor, 1987-90; Fraser Press Award, 1981-82 and 1990, for work on Shetland Times; Labour candidate, Orkney and Shetland, 1974 (twice). Publications: Magnus Pole, 1975; Linda and the Lighthouse, 1976; A Place in the Sun — Shetland and oil,

1991; Innocent Passage — the wreck of the tanker Braer (Co-author), 1993.

Wilson, Alan Oliver Arneil, MB, ChB, DPM, FRCPsych. Consultant in private practice, Murrayfield Hospital, Edinburgh; Consultant Psychiatrist, Bangour Hospitals, 1977-89; former Member, Clinical Teaching Staff, Faculty of Medicine, Edinburgh University; Member, Executive Group of Board of Directors, and Past President, World Association for Psychosocial Rehabilitation; Consultant (in Scotland), Ex-Services Mental Welfare Society; b. 4.1.30, Douglas; m., Dr. Fiona Margaret Davidson; 3 s. Educ. Biggar High School; Edinburgh University. RAMC, 1953-55; psychiatric post, Stobhill General Hospital, Glasgow, and Garlands Hospital, Carlisle, 1955-63; Consultant Psychiatrist and Deputy Physician Superintendent, St. George's Hospital, Morpeth, 1963-77. Joint Honorary Secretary, Northern Counties Psychiatric Association; Chairman, Group for Study of Rehabilitation and Community Care, Scottish Division, RCPsych; Member, Ethics Committee, World Association for Social Psychiatry; Chairman, Psychosocial Rehabilitation Scotland. V.M. Bekhterev Medal awarded by Bekhterev Psychoneurological Research Institute, St. Petersburg. Recreations: golf; folk singing; guitar; "blethering"; former Hibernian FC footballer. Address: (h.) 14 Cammo Hill, Edinburgh EH4 8EY; T.-0131-339 2244.

Wilson, Brian, MA (Hons), FSA (Scot). MP (Labour), Cunninghame North, since 1987; Minister of State, Scottish Office (Minister for Education and Industry), since 1997; b. 13.12.48, Dunoon; m., Joni Buchanan; 2 s.; 1 d. Educ. Dunoon Grammar School; Dundee University; University College, Cardiff. Journalist; Publisher and Founding Editor, West Highland Free Press; Contributor to The Guardian, Glasgow Herald, etc.; first winner, Nicholas Tomalin Memorial Award for Journalism; contested Ross and Cromarty, Oct., 1974, Inverness, 1979, Western Isles, 1983; front-bench spokesman on Scottish Home Affairs etc., 1988-92, Transport, 1992-94 and 1995-96, Trade and Industry, 1994-95. Address: House of Commons, London SW1A 0AA.

Wilson, Brian, OBE, LLB. Depute Chief Executive, The Highland Council, since 1995; b. 20.2.46, Perth; m., Isobel Esson; 3 d. Educ. Buckie High School; Aberdeen University. Management trainee, Marks and Spencer, 1966-68; Apprentice, then Legal Assistant, Banff County Council, 1969-72; Senior Legal Assistant, Inverness County Council, 1972-73; Depute County Clerk, Banff County Council, 1973-75; Director of Administration and Legal Services, Banff and Buchan District Council, 1975-78; Chief Executive, Inverness District Council, 1978-95; Clerk, Highland River Purification Board, 1989-95; Hon. Secretary SOLACE (Scottish Branch) 1986-95; Recreations: garden; fishing. Address: (b.) Glenurquhart Road, Inverness, IV3 5NX; T.-01463 702844.

Wilson, Christina Kerr. Joint Managing Director and Co-Editor, Books in Scotland, since 1987; b. 7.1.24, Edinburgh; m., Norman Wilson (deceased); 2 d. Educ. Leith Academy. Compiled monthly magazine, New Books, for John Menzies & Co. Ltd., 1943; continued working for Menzies until 1960 (left to raise family); contributor, Books in Scotland, 1976. Recreations: cinema; swimming; reading. Address: (h.) 15 Gloucester Place, Edinburgh; T.-0131-225 5646.

Wilson of Tillyorn, Baron (David Clive Wilson), GCMG, MA (Oxon), PhD. Life Peer (1992); Chairman, Scottish Hydro Electric PLC, since 1993; Chairman, Scottish Committee, British Council, since 1993; Chancellor, Aberdeen University, since 1997; Member, Council, Glenalmond College, since 1994; President, Bhutan Societ of the UK, since 1993; Member, Board, Martin Cur Pacific Trust; Member, Governing Body, School of Orie and African Studies, since 1992; b. 14.2.34, Alloa; m., Natasha Helen Mary Alexander; 2 s. Educ. Trinity College, Glenalmond; Keble College, Oxford. Entered Foreign Service, 1958; Third Secretary, Vientiane, 1959-60; language student, Hong Kong, 1960-62; Second, later First Secretary, Peking, 1963-65; FCO, 1965-68; resigned, 1968; Editor, China Quarterly, 1968-74; Visiting Scholar, Columbia University, New York, 1972; rejoined Diplomatic Service, 1974; Cabinet Office, 1974-77; Political Adviser, Hong Kong, 1977-81; Head, S. European Department, FCO, 1981-84; Assistant Under Secretary of State, FCO, 1984-87. Hon.LLD (Aberdeen); Hon.DLitt (Sydney); Hon.DLitt (Abertay, Dundee); Hon. LLD, Chinese University, Hong Kong. KStJ. Recreations: mountaineering; skiing; reading. Address: (b.) Scottish Hydro Electric plc, Dunkeld Road, Perth PH1 5WA; T.-01738 455200.

Wilson, David Steel, DipM. Chef/Proprietor, The Peat Inn, since 1972; Director, Taste of Scotland Ltd., since 1996; b. 21.1.36, Bishopbriggs; m., Patricia Ann; 1 s.; 1 d. Educ. Bishopbriggs High School; Glasgow College of Commerce. Sales/Marketing Manager in industry, 1967-71; trainee chef, 1971-72. Master Chef of G.B.; Chef Laureate; Fellow, RSA, 1992; Hon. Doctor of Laws, Dundee University, 1997. Recreations: travel; art; sport; music; theatre. Address: (b.) The Peat Inn, by Cupar, Fife KY15 5LH; T.-0133840 206.

Wilson, Gerald R., CB, MA. Secretary, The Scottish Office Education and Industry Department, since 1988; b. 7.9.39, Edinburgh; m., Margaret; 1 s.; 1 d. Educ. Holy Cross Academy; Edinburgh University. Assistant Principal, Scottish Home and Health Department, 1961-65; Private Secretary, Minister of State for Scotland, 1965-66; Principal, Scottish Home and Health Department, 1966-72; Private Secretary to Lord Privy Seal, 1972-74, to Minister of State, Civil Service Department, 1974; Assistant Secretary, Scottish Economic Planning Department, 1974-77; Counsellor, Office of the UK Permanent Representative to the Economic Communities, Brussels, 1977-82; Assistant Secretary, Scottish Office, 1982-84; Under Secretary, Industry Department for Scotland, 1984-88. Recreation: music. Address: (b.) Victoria Quay, Edinburgh EH6 6QQ; T.-0131-244 7114.

Wilson, Professor Gordon McAndrew, MA, PhD, FRSA. Assistant Principal and Director of Craigie Campus in Ayr, Paisley University, since 1993; b. 4.12.39, Glasgow; m., Alison Rosemary Cook; 2 s.; 1 d. Educ. Eastwood Secondary School; Glasgow University; Jordanhill College of Education. Teacher of History and Modern Studies: Eastwood Secondary School, 1963-65, Eastwood High School, 1965-67; Lecturer in Social Studies, Hamilton College of Education, 1967-73 (Head of Department, 1973-81); Principal Lecturer in Inservice Education, then Assistant Principal, Jordanhill College of Education, 1981-88; Principal, Craigie College of Education, 1988-93; Member, General Teaching Council for Scotland, 1991-94; Chairman, Review and Development Group on English Language 5-14; Member, Committee on Curriculum and Examinations S5-S6 (Howie Committee), 1990-92; Specialist Adviser on Student Affairs, COSHEP, since 1993; Member: Board of Directors, Ayrshire Chamber of Commerce and Industry, 1992-96, Board of Directors, Enterprise Ayrshire, since 1994. Publications: Teaching Local History in Lanarkshire, 1972; Alexander McDonald, Leader of the Miners, 1982; Dictionary of Scottish Business Biography (Contributor), 1986. Recreations: reading; gardening; walking; music. Address: (b.) Paisley University, Craigie Campus in Ayr, Beech Grove, Ayr KA8 0SR; T.-01292 886200.

Wilson, Hamish Robert McHattie, MA (Aberdeen), MA, D (Cantab), FHSM. Director of Primary Care, Grampian Health Board, since 1991 (Unit General Manager, 1987- b. 19.1.46, Aberdeen. Educ. Robert Gordon's College,

Aberdeen; Aberdeen University; Emmanuel College, Cambridge. Entered Health Service administration, 1972; held posts with Grampian Health Board in planning, primary care and as Secretary. Recreations: music; reading; theatre; cinema; good food and wine. Address: (b.) Summerfield House, 2 Eday Road, Aberdeen AB15 6RE; T.-01224 663456.

Wilson, Ian Matthew, CB, MA. Secretary of Commissions for Scotland, 1987-92 (Under Secretary, Scottish Education Department, 1977-86); Member, RSAMD Governing Body, since 1992; President, University of Edinburgh Graduates' Association, 1995-97; b. 12.12.26, Edinburgh; m., 1, Anne Chalmers (deceased); 3 s.; 2, Joyce Town. Educ. George Watson's College; Edinburgh University. Assistant Principal, Scottish Home Department, 1950; Private Secretary to Permanent Under Secretary of State, Scottish Office, 1953-55; Principal, Scottish Home Department, 1955; Assistant Secretary: Scottish Education Department, 1963, Scottish Home and Health Department, 1971; Assistant Under Secretary of State, Scottish Office, 1974-77. Address: (h.) 1 Bonaly Drive, Edinburgh EH13 OEJ; T.-0131-441 2541.

Wilson, James Wiseman, OBE, SBStJ. Director, Barcapel Foundation, since 1970; Director, Wilson Management Ltd., since 1970; b. 31.5.33, Glasgow; m., Valerie Grant; 1 s.; 3 d. Educ. Trinity College, Glenalmond; Harvard Business School. Marketing Director, Scottish Animal Products, 1959-63; Sales Director, then Managing Director, then Chairman, Robert Wilson & Sons (1849) Ltd., 1964-85. National Trust for Scotland: Member of Council, 1977-82 and 1984-89, President, Ayrshire Members' Centre; Chairman, Management Committee, Scottish Civic Trust; Honorary President, Skelmorlie Golf Club and Irvine Pipe Band; won Aims of Industry Free Enterprise Award (Scotland), 1980. Recreations: golf; backgammon; skiing; bridge; travelling. Address: (h.) Skelmorlie Castle, Skelmorlie, Ayrshire PA17 5EY; T.-01475 521127.

Wilson, Janette Sylvia, LLB, NP. Solicitor of the Church of Scotland and Law Agent to the General Assembly, since 1995; b. 11.5.51, Inverness; m., Stuart Ronald Wilson. Educ. Inverness Royal Academy; Edinburgh University. Law Apprentice, then Assistant, Dundas & Wilson, CS, Edinburgh, 1973-77; Assistant, then Partner, Ross Harper & Murphy, Edinburgh, 1977-81; Depute Solicitor, Church of Scotland, 1981-95. Member, Law Society Conveyancing Committee and Public Service and Commerce Group. Recreations: keeping fit; reading; gardening. Address: (b.) 121 George Street, Edinburgh; T.-0131-225 5722.

Wilson, Les. Documentary Producer/Director, since 1980; Director, Caledonia, Sterne and Wyld Ltd., since 1992; b. 17.7.49, Glasgow; m., Adrienne Cochrane; 2 d. Educ. Grove Academy, Broughty Ferry. Trainee Journalist, 1969-70; hippy trail, 1970-71; Reporter, Greenock Telegraph, 1972-73; Reporter, STV, 1973-78; Editor, STV political programme, Ways and Means, 1979-80; Producer/Director, STV, 1981-92. Winner, Celtic Film Festival Award, 1991; BAFTA Scotland and British Telecom Factual/Current Affairs awards, 1997. Publication: Scotland's War (Co-author), 1995. Recreation: Islay – the island, its people, its malts. Address: (b.) 5 Queens Crescent, Glasgow G4 9BW; T.-0141-353 3153.

Wilson, Leslie, BSc, FCCA, MIMIS, DipStat, DipMS. Director of Finance, Historic Scotland, since 1997; b. 10.5.47, Glasgow; m., Maureen S. Borrowman; 1 s.; 2 d. Educ. Allan Glen's School; Glasgow University. British Gas (Edinburgh and London), 1969-91; Head of Finance, Scottish Homes, 1991-92; Head of Finance and Information Systems, Historic Scotland, 1992-97. Recreations: golf; music; languages. Address: (b.) Longmore House, Salisbury Place, Edinburgh EH9 1SH; T.-0131-668 8874.

Wilson, Paul, MBA, DMS, DN, RGN, RMN. Director of NHS Trusts, NHS in Scotland, since 1994; b. 2.8.47, Newcastle upon Tyne; 1 s. Educ. Brunel University; Henley Management College. Registered mental nurse training and registered general nurse training; nursing appointments; Divisional Nursing Officer, Roehampton Health District, 1977-82; Chief Nursing Officer, then Director Policy and Planning, Maidstone Health Authority, 1982-87; General Manager, Mental Health Services, Greater Glasgow Health Board, 1987-91; Director of Operations, then Director, Health Care Contracting, Lothian Health Board, 1991-95. Recreations: cats; children; food; travel; music. Address: (b.) Scottish Office, St. Andrews House, Edinburgh, EH1 3QG; T.-0131-244 2179.

Wilson, Peter Liddell, BSc, MA, FIMgt, FIPD. Secretary, Heriot-Watt University, since 1991; b. 8.12.42, Douglas; m., Joy Janet Gibson; 2 d. Educ. Lanark Grammar School; Glasgow University; Birkbeck College, London University. Mathematics Teacher, Lanark Grammar School, 1964-67; Royal Navy (Instructor Lieutenant), 1967-70; Army (Royal Army Educational Corps), 1970-90: Commander Education, 1st Armoured Division (Lt. Col.), 1983-85, SOI Education HQ BAOR (Lt. Col.), 1986-88, MOD (Resettlement) (Colonel), 1988-90. Chairman, Edinburgh Confrence Centre, since 1991. Recreations: golf; jogging; hill-walking; theatre. Address: (b.) Heriot-Watt University, Riccarton, Edinburgh EH14 4AS; T.-0131-449 5111.

Wilson, Professor Peter Northcote, CBE, BSc, MSc, Dip. Animal Genetics, PhD, CBiol, FBiol, FRSE, FRSA. Emeritus Professor of Agriculture and Rural Economy, Edinburgh University; General Secretary, Royal Society of Edinburgh, since 1996; b. 4.4.28, Beckenham, Kent; m., Maud Ethel Bunn; 2 s.; 1 d. Educ. Whitgift School, Croydon; Wye College, London University; Edinburgh University. Lecturer in Agriculture, Makerere College, East Africa; Senior Lecturer in Agriculture, Imperial College of Tropical Agriculture, Trinidad; Professor of Tropical Agriculture, University of West Indies, Trinidad; Head of Biometrics, Unilever Research Laboratory, Bedford; Agricultural Development Director, SLF Ltd., Liverpool; Chief Agricultural Adviser, BOCM Silcock Ltd., Basingstoke. Life Fellow, Wye College, University of London; Past President, British Society of Animal Production; Past Vice President, Institute of Biology; Chairman, Frank Parkinson Agricultural Trust, since 1978; Hon. Secretary, Institute of Biology, 1992-96; Scientific Director, Edinburgh Centre for Rural Research, 1990-95; Past President, Edinburgh Agricultural Society; Member, Council, SAC, since 1995; Vice-Convener, Business Committee, University of Edinburgh Council, since 1996. Publications: Agriculture in the Tropics (Co-author); Improved Feeding of Cattle and Sheep (Co-author). Recreations: walking; photography; natural history. Address: 8 St. Thomas Road, Edinburgh EH9 2LQ.

Wilson, Robert Gordon, BL, LLD. Vice-President, Scottish National Party, 1992-97; Solicitor; b. 16.4.38, Glasgow; m., Edith M. Hassall; 2 d. Educ. Douglas High School for Boys; Edinburgh University. National Secretary, SNP, 1963-71; MP, Dundee East, 1974-87; Chairman and National Convener, SNP, 1979-90; Rector, Dundee University, 1983-86; Member, Court, University of Abertay Dundee 1992-96. Recreation: reading; sailing; walking. Address: (h.) 48 Monifieth Road, Dundee DD5 2RX.

Wilson, Roy. General Manager, Pitlochry Festival Theatre, 1961-95, Art Exhibitions Director, since 1995; b. St. Andrews. Educ. Burgh School and Madras College, St. Andrews. Proprietor, grocer's business, St. Andrews, 1953-58; Assistant Manager, Pitlochry Festival Theatre, 1958-61. Winner David K. Thomson Award, 1995, in recognition of his contribution to Pitlochry Festival Theatre. Recreations: plays and theatre in general; most forms of classical music, with particular interest in choral singing; listening to records; reading; art and antiques. Address: (h.) Kilrymont, Bruach Lane, Pitlochry, Perthshire PH16 5DG; T.-Pitlochry 472897.

Wilson, R. Ross, BSc, PhD, MInstP, CPhys. Managing Director, James Howden & Co. Ltd., since 1992; Director, Renfrewshire Enterprise, since 1996; b. 13.3.47, Glasgow; m., Margaret; 2 s. Educ. Hamilton Academy; Glasgow University. Research Officer, then Vibration Group Leader, Central Electricity Research Laboratories, CEGB; Section Head, Design Analysis, Corporate Engineering Laboratory, British Steel; Design Manager, then Technical Director, James Howden Ltd. Recreations: golf; reading; gardening. Address: (b.) Old Govan Road, Renfrew PA4 8XJ; T.-0141-886 6711.

Wilson, Thomas Black, BSc (Hons), CEng, MBCS. Principal, Glasgow College of Building and Printing, since 1989; b. 23.12.43, Airdrie; m., Barbara Smith; 1 s.; 1 d. Educ. Cumnock Academy; Glasgow University; Jordanhill College. Principal Teacher, Prestwick Academy, 1969-74; Head, Computing Department, Ayr College, 1974-84; Depute Principal: Barmulloch College, Glasgow, 1984-86, Cardonald College, Glasgow, 1986-89. Member, Scottish Central Committee (Mathematics), 1975-82; Governor, Scottish Council for Educational Technology, since 1995; Hon. Professor, Glasgow Caledonian University, since 1995. Recreations: reading; writing; music. Address: (b.) 60 North Hanover Street, Glasgow G1 2BP; T.-0141-332 9969.

Wilson, Emeritus Professor Thomas Brendan, CBE, MA, BMus, ARCM, FRSE. Composer; b. 10.10.27, Trinidad, Colorado; m., Margaret Rayner; 3 s. Educ. St. Mary's College, Aberdeen; Glasgow University; Royal College of Music. RAF, 1945-48; Glasgow University: Lecturer in Music, Extra-Mural Studies, 1957, Reader in Music, Extra-Mural Studies, 1972, Professor, 1977; Member, Scottish Arts Council, 1966-72; Past Chairman, Composers Guild; President, Scottish Society of Composers; Member, Advisory Commitee, Scottish Music Information Centre; elected Member, Royal Society of Musicians; compositions include orchestral, choral-orchestral, chamber-orchestral, opera (including The Confessions of a Justified Sinner), ballet, brass band, vocal music of different kinds, and works for a wide variety of chamber ensembles and solo instruments; numerous commissions; Hon. Doctorate of Music, Glasgow University, 1991; Fellow, Royal Scottish Academy of Music and Drama, since 1991. Recreations: golf; talking shop. Address: (h.) 120 Dowanhill Street, Glasgow G12 9DN; T.-0141-339 1699.

Wilson, Professor Thomas Michael Aubrey, BSc (Hons), PhD, CBiol, MIBiol. Deputy Director, Scottish Crop Research Institute, since 1995; b. 10.10.51, Hawick; m., Judith Lindsey Dring; 2 s.; 1 d. Educ. Hawick High School; Edinburgh University; Cambridge University. Lecturer in Biochemistry, Liverpool University; Senior Scientific Officer, then Principal Scientific Officer, John Innes Institute, Norwich; Professor, AgBiotech Center, Rutgers University, NJ; Head, Virology Department, SCRI, Dundee, 1992-95; Senior Editor, Journal of General Virology; published 85 papers, reviews, and book chapters; edited or co-authored two books; first recipient, SGM Herpes Vaccine Research Trust Prize, 1985. Recreations: hill-walking. Address: (b.) Invergowrie, Dundee, DD2 5DA; T.-01382 562731.

Wilson, William John McKinley, QPM. Chief Constable, Central Scotland Police, since 1990; b. 27.6.43, Kinghorn; m., Catherine; 3 s. Educ. Kirkcaldy High School. Joined Fife Constabulary, 1962: Chief Superintendent, 198*; Deputy Chief Constable, 1984. Recreations: football; go*; Address: (b.) Central Scotland Police, Randolphfie*, Stirling; T.-01786 456000.

Wilson, William Murray, MB, ChB, MRCGP. General Medical Practitioner, Dalry, Ayrshire, 1949-89; Medical Advisor, Roche Products, Dalry, Ayrshire, since 1965; Medical Referee, Cunninghame District Council, since 1972; Member, Ayrshire and Arran Health Board; b. 19.1.25, Glasgow; m., Elizabeth Carbine; 3 s. Educ. Eastwood Secondary School; Glasgow University. Past Chairman, Local Medical Committee/GP Committee, Area Medical Committee, BMA Ayrshire Division; former Member, General Medical Services Committee, London and Edinburgh; Elder, St. Margaret's Church, Dalry; former Member, Education for the Ministry Committee, Church of Scotland; Honorary Lecturer, British Red Cross Society, St. Andrew's Ambulance Association. Recreations: travel; photography. Address: (h.) 22 Courthill Street, Dalry, Ayrshire KA24 5AN; T.-Dalry 832165.

Wilson, W. Stewart, BSc. Educational Consultant, since 1995; Rector, Banchory Academy, 1978-95; b. 15.5.37, Aberdeen; m., Elizabeth Gorrod; 1 s.; 1 d. Educ. Aberdeen Grammar School; Aberdeen University. Teacher, Aberdeen Grammar School, 1961-66; Principal Teacher of Mathematics, Deputy Rector, Banchory Academy, 1966-78. Elder, Banchory Ternan West Parish Church; Past President; Banchory and District Round Table, Rotary Club of Banchory Ternan; Chairman, Kincardine and Deeside National Trust Members' Centre; Assistant Chief Commissioner for Scouts in Scotland. Recreations: philately; Robert Burns - his life and works; antique maps of Kincardineshire. Address: (h.) Ibiscus, Rosehill Crescent, Banchory; T.-01330 823194.

Windsor, Malcolm L., PhD, FRSC. Secretary, North Atlantic Salmon Conservation Organization, since 1984; b. 12.4.38, Bristol; m., Sally; 2 d. Educ. Cotham Grammar School, Bristol; Bristol University. Researcher, University of California, 1965-67; fisheries research, Humber Laboratory, Hull, 1967-75; Fisheries Adviser to Chief Scientist, Ministry of Agriculture and Fisheries, London, 1975-84. Secretary, Duddingston Village Conservation Society. Publication: book on fishery products. Recreations: local conservation work; jazz; walking. Address: (b.) 11 Rutland Square, Edinburgh EH1 2AS; T.-0131-228 2551.

Windsor, Col. Rodney Francis Maurice, CBE, DL. Farmer; b. 22.2.25, Redhill; m., Deirdre Chichester (deceased); m. Angela Stainton; 2 s.; 1 d. Educ. Tonbridge School. Enlisted Royal Armoured Corps, 1943; commissioned The Queen's Bays, 1944-52; Captain, 1949; ADC to CINC and High Commissioner Austria, 1949-50; served in North Irish Horse (TA), 1959-67; Lt. Col. Commanding, 1964-67; Colonel TA N. Ireland, 1967-71; ADC (TA) to HM The Queen, 1970-75; Member, Highland TA Association, 1971-77; Member, Banff and Buchan District Valuation Appeal Committee, 1982-96 (Chairman, 1989-96); Deputy Lieutenant:, Co. Antrim, 1967-97, Aberdeenshire, since 1989. Recreations: field sports; golf. Address: (h.) Byth House, New Byth, Turriff, Aberdeenshire AB53 7XN; T.-01888 544230.

Winney, Robin John, MB, ChB, FRCPEdin. Consultant Renal Physician, Edinburgh Royal Infirmary, since 1978; b. 8.5.44, Dunfermline. Educ. Dunfermline High School; Edinburgh University. Recreations: badminton; curling. Address: (h.) 74 Lanark Road West, Currie, Midlothian EH14 5JZ.

Winning, His Eminence Thomas Joseph Cardinal, STL, DCL, DD, DUniv, GCHS, FEIS. Archbishop of Glasgow and Metropolitan, since 1974; President, Bishops' Conference of Scotland, since 1985; b. 3.6.25, Wishaw. Educ. Our Lady's High School, Motherwell; St. Mary's College, Blairs; St. Peter's College; Scots College; Gregorian University, Rome. Ordained Priest, Rome, 1948; Assistant Priest, Chapelhall, 1949-50; Rome (DCL, "Cum   "), 1953; Assistant Priest, St. Mary's Hamilton, 1953-

57; Cathedral, Motherwell, 1957-58; Chaplain, Franciscan of the Immaculate Conception, Bothwell, 1958-61; Diocesan Secretary, Motherwell, 1956-61; Spiritual Director, Scots College, Rome, 1961-66; Advocate of the Sacred Roman Rota, 1965; Parish Priest, St. Luke's Motherwell, 1966-70; Officialis and Vicar Episcopal, Motherwell Diocese, 1966-70; first President, Scottish Catholic Marriage Tribunal, 1970; nominated Titular Bishop of Louth and Bishop Auxiliary, 1971, and ordained by James Donald Scanlan, Archbishop of Glasgow, November, 1971; Parish Priest, Our Holy Redeemer's Clydebank, 1972-74; translated to Glasgow as Archbishop, 1974; created Cardinal Priest of the title of S. Andrea delle Frate, 1994; (Honorary DD (Glasgow), 1983; awarded Glasgow Loving Cup, 1983; Grand Prior of Scotland, Equestrian Order of the Holy Sepulchre of Jerusalem, 1989; Hon. D.Univ. (Strathclyde), 1992; Hon. LLD, Aberdeen University, 1996; Hon. Professor, Glasgow University, 1996. Recreations: watching football; listening to music. Address: (h.) 40 Newlands Road, Glasgow G43 2JD; T.-0141-226 5898.

Winton, Alexander, CBE, QFSM, MIFireE. HM Chief Inspector of Fire Services for Scotland, 1990-93; b. 13.7.32, Perth; m., Jean; 2 s. Perth and Kinross Fire Brigade, 1958; Instructor, Scottish Fire Service Training School, 1962; Lancashire County Fire Brigade, 1967; East Riding of Yorkshire Fire Brigade, 1970; Angus Area Fire Brigade, 1973; Tayside Fire Brigade, 1975; Deputy Firemaster, Tayside Fire Brigade, 1981; Firemaster, 1985-89. Recreations:golf; curling. Address: (h.) 5 Ferndale Drive, Broughty Ferry, Dundee DD5 3DB; T.-Dundee 778156.

Wiseman, Alan William. Director and Chairman, Robert Wiseman Dairies, since 1979; President, Scottish Dairy Trade Federation, 1988-95; b. 20.8.50, Giffnock; m., Margaret. Educ. Duncanrig Senior Secondary School, East Kilbride. Left school to be one of his father's milkmen, 1967; has been a milkman ever since. Scottish Businessman of the Year, 1992; former Chairman, Scottish Dairy Council; Scottish Business Achievement Award, 1994. Recreations: golf; shooting. Address: (b.) Cadzow House, High Parks Farm, Hamilton; T.-01698 425481.

Wishart, David, BSc, PhD, CEng, CStat. Director, Clustan Ltd.; b. 5.7.43, London; m., Doreen Pamela Craig Wishart; 3 s. Educ. Kilburn Grammar School; Truro School; St. Andrews University. Statistician, Civil Service Department, London, 1970-75; Principal, Scottish Office, 1975-77; Chief Statistician, Scottish Office, 1977-81; Director of Statistics, Scottish Office, 1981-84; Assistant Secretary, Scottish Office, 1984-95. Fellow: British Computer Society, Royal Statistical Society (Vice President, 1986-88), Royal Society of Arts; Member, Institute of Directors; Director, Wishart Society. Recreations: golf; skiing; opera. Address: (h.) 16 Kingsburgh Road, Edinburgh EH12; T.-0131-337 1448.

Wishart, Ruth. Columnist, The Herald; Broadcaster, BBC Radio, since 1989; b. Glasgow; m., Rod McLeod. Educ. Eastwood Senior Secondary School. TV Editor, Daily Record, 1970-73; Woman's Editor, Daily Record, 1973-78; Assistant Editor, Sunday Mail, 1978-82; Assistant Editor, Sunday Standard, 1982-83; Freelance Writer, 1983-86; Senior Assistant Editor, The Scotsman, 1986-88.

Withers, Professor Charles William John, BSc, PhD, FRGS. Professor of Geography, Edinburgh University, since 1992; b. 6.12.54, Edinburgh; m., Anne; 2 s.; 1 d. Educ. Daniel Stewart's College, Edinburgh; St. Andrews University; Cambridge University. Lecturer, Senior Lecturer, Principal Lecturer, Professor of Geography, College of St. Paul and St. Mary/Cheltenham and Gloucester College of Higher Education. Hon. Editor, Historical Geography Research series; Editor, History and Philosophy of Geography; author of five books, 80 cademic articles. Recreations: reading; hill-walking. Address: (b.) Department of Geography, Edinburgh University, Drummond Street, Edinburgh; T.-0131-650 2559.

Withers, John Alexander (Jack), FCIL. Writer; b. Glasgow; m., Beate (Bea) Haertel. Educ. North Kelvinside School; Jordanhill College of Education (Youth and Community Diploma). Left school at 14; worked in garage, electrical industry, labouring, National Service, unemployment, razor-blade salesman; long periods abroad, wandering, wondering, working: France, FRG, Italy, Scandinavia, Spain, North Africa; youth worker; freelance writer; ski instructor; librarian; performance poet; Scottish republican and radical; plays for radio, TV, theatre; James Kennoway Screenplay Award (shared); Scottish Arts Council Awards; short stories published in numerous journals in UK, Denmark and West Germany; Editor, Two Tongues — Two Cities; books: Glasgow Limbo, A Real Glasgow Archipelago, Balancing on a Barbed Wire Fence. Address: (h.) 16 Belmont Crescent, Glasgow; T.-0141-339 9492.

Witney, Eur. Ing. Professor Brian David, BSc, MSc, PhD, CEng, FIMechE, Hon.FIAgrE, MemASAE. Director, Land Technology Ltd., since 1995; Hon. Professor of Agricultural Engineering, Edinburgh University, since 1989; Professor of Terramechanics, Scottish Agricultural College, Edinburgh, since 1994; b. 8.6.38, Edinburgh; m., Maureen M.I. Donnelly; 1 s.; 2 d. Educ. Daniel Stewart's College, Edinburgh; Edinburgh University; Durham University; Newcastle University. Senior Research Associate, Newcastle upon Tyne University, 1962-66; Research Fellow, US Army Research Office, Duke Univ., 1966-67; Senior Scientific Officer, Military Engineering Experimental Establishment, Christchurch, 1967-70; Head, Agricultural Engineering Department, East of Scotland College of Agriculture, Edinburgh, 1970-86; Director, Scottish Centre of Agricultural Engineering, 1987-95, and Vice-Dean, Scottish Agricultural College, 1990-95. President, Institution of Agricultural Engineers, 1988-90; President, European Society of Agricultural Engineers, 1993-94; Managing Editor, Landwards, since 1996; Managing Editor, Land Technology, 1994-96; Member, Editorial Board, Journal of Agricultural Engineering Research, since 1988; Trustee, Douglas Bomford Trust, since 1997. Publication: Choosing and Using Farm Machines. Address: (b.) Land Technology Ltd., 33 South Barnton Avenue, Edinburgh EH4 6AN; T.-0131-336 3129.

Wolfe, William Cuthbertson, CA, JP. Member, National Council, Scottish National Party, since 1991; b. 22.2.24; 2 s.; 2 d. Educ. Bathgate Academy; George Watson's College, Edinburgh. Army Service, 1942-47, NW Europe and Far East; Air OP Pilot. Hon. Publications Treasurer, Saltire Society, 1953-60; Scout County Commissioner, West Lothian, 1960-64; Hon. President (Rector), Students' Association, Heriot-Watt University, 1966-69; contested (SNP) West Lothian, 1962, 1964, 1966, 1970, Feb. and Oct. 1974, 1979, North Edinburgh, Nov. 1973; Chairman, SNP, 1969-79, President, 1980-82; Treasurer, Scottish CND, 1982-85; Secretary, Scottish Poetry Library, 1985-91. Publication: Scotland Lives.

Wolfe Murray, Angus Malcolm. Film Critic, The Scotsman, since 1988; b. 20.5.37, Edinburgh; m., Stephanie; 4 s. Educ. Eton. Greensman, bank clerk, oil worker, insurance broker, journalist, novelist, publisher's editor, roadie for rock band, publisher, building worker, long-distance lorry driver, fine art transporter, film critic. Recreations: skiing; cricket. Address: (h.) Stobo Hopehead, Peebles, EH45 8NY.

Wolfram, Professor Julian, BSc, CEng, PhD, FRINA, MSaRS. Total Oil Marine Chair of Offshore Research and Development, Heriot-Watt University, since 1990; b.

2.8.46, London; m., Margaret Mary Lockhart; 1 s., 1 d., by pr. m. Educ. Gordonstoun; Reading University; Newcastle University. Research and Development Officer, Vickers Shipbuilders Ltd.; Lecturer (latterly Senior Lecturer) in Naval Architecture, Sunderland Polytechnic; Lecturer (latterly Senior Lecturer) in Marine Technology, Strathclyde University; Tutor, Open University; Chief Examiner, Ship Structures and Dynamics, Engineering Council; Consultant to several companies in the marine field. Publications: over 50 technical papers and reports. Recreations: sailing; squash; hill walking. Address: (b.) Heriot-Watt University, Edinburgh EH14 4AS; T.-0131-449 5111.

Wong, Professor Henry H.Y., BSc, PhD, DIC, CEng, FRAeS. Emeritus Professor, Department of Aeronautics and Fluid Mechanics, Glasgow University; Senior Research Fellow, since 1987; Adviser to the Guangdong Higher Education Bureau, China, since 1985; Adviser to Glasgow University on Chinese Affairs, since 1986; Chair Professor, Nanjing University of Aeronautics and Astronautics, since 1987; "Concurrent" Professor, National University of Defense Technology, Changsha, since 1989; b. 23.5.22, Hong Kong; m., Joan Anstey; 2 s.; 1 d. Educ. St. Stephen College, Hong Kong; Jiao-Tong University, Shanghai; Imperial College, London; Glasgow University. Assistant Lecturer, Jiao-Tong University, 1947-48; Engineer, Armstrong Siddeley, 1949; Structural Engineer, Hunting Percival Aircraft, 1949-51; Senior Structural Engineer, de Havilland Aircraft, 1952-57; Senior Lecturer, Hatfield Polytechnic, 1957-59; Lecturer, Senior Lecturer, then Reader in Aeronautics and Fluid Mechanics, Glasgow University, from 1960; Economic and Technological Consultant to Shantou Special Economic Zone, China, since 1988. Former Treasurer and Vice-Chairman, Kilmardinny Music Circle; Chairman, Glasgow Summer School, 1979-95; City of Glasgow Lord Provost's Award, 1988. Recreations: reading; music; painting; swimming. Address: (h.) 77 Antonine Road, Bearsden, Glasgow; T.-0141-942 8346.

Wood, Arthur Murdoch Mactaggart, OBE, MA, LLB. Chief Executive, Children 1st, since 1968; b. 15.12.37, Kilbarchan; 2 s.; 2 d. Educ. George Watson's College, Edinburgh; Edinburgh University. Standard Life Assurance Company, 1960-61; Assistant Secretary, RSSPCC, 1961-68. Address: (b.) Children 1st, Melville House, 41 Polwarth Terrace, Edinburgh EH11 1NU; T.-0131-337 8539.

Wood, Brian Charles Thallon, BL (Dist.), NP. Solicitor, since 1955; Consultant, Charles Wood & Son, Solicitors, Kirkcaldy; Honorary Sheriff; b. 8.8.34, Kirkcaldy; m., Tessa; 1 s.; 1 d. Educ. Fettes; Edinburgh University. Part-time Chairman, Industrial Tribunals, 1972-77; part-time Chairman, Rent Assessment Committee, 1987-96; Member, Council, Law Society of Scotland, since 1992-94; Accredited ADR Mediator. Recreations: gardens; skiing; curling; mending anything. Address: (h.) 4 Kilcruik Road, Kinghorn, Fife; T.-01592 891218.

Wood, Brian James, JP, BSc (Hons), FRSA. Rector, Hazlehead Academy, Aberdeen, since 1993 (Rector, Mearns Academy, 1989-93); Chairman, Justices of the Peace, Aberdeenshire; Hon. Sheriff, Stonehaven; b. 6.12.49, Banff; m., Doreen A. Petrie; 1 s.; 1 d. Educ. Banff Academy; Aberdeen Academy; Aberdeen University; Aberdeen College of Education. Teacher of Physics, George Heriot's School, Edinburgh, 1972-75; Mackie Academy, 1975-89, latterly as Depute Rector. Chairman, Justices of the Peace for Kincardine and Deeside; Member, Chairmen of Justices Committee for Scotland; Eld Church of Scotland. Recreations: sport; reading; m travel; theatre; DIY. Address: (h.) 13 Edinview Ga Stonehaven; T.-01569 763888.

Wood, David Crawford, BCom. Development and Communications Director, Royal Botanic Garden Edinburgh, since 1996; Managing Director, Botanics Trading Company Ltd., since 1996; b. 14.8.61, Odense, Denmark; m., Patricia; 2 s.; 1 d. Educ. Kirkcudbright Academy; Edinburgh University. General Manager, Local Investment Networking Company, 1986; Business Development Manager, Peter Dominic Ltd., 1989; Regional Manager, Thorntons PLC, 1992. Recreations: current affairs; sport; playing with my children. Address: (b.) Royal Botanic Garden Edinburgh, 20a Inverleith Row, Edinburgh EH3 5LR; T.-0131-552 7171.

Wood, Emeritus Professor Hamish Christopher Swan, CBE, BSc, PhD, CChem, FRSC, FRSE, DUniv, LLD, FScotvec, FSQA; b. 8.5.26, Hawick; m., Jean Dumbreck Mitchell; 1 s.; 1 d. Educ. Hawick High School; St. Andrews University. Lecturer in Chemistry, St. Andrews University, 1950-51; Research Fellow, Australian National University, 1951-53; Lecturer, Senior Lecturer and Reader, Strathclyde University, 1953-69, Professor of Organic Chemistry, 1969-91, Deputy Principal, 1982-84, Vice-Principal, 1984-86; Member, Universities Funding Council, 1989-92; Chairman, Court, Glasgow Caledonian University, 1993-94; Member, Council, Royal Society of Edinburgh, 1992-95. Address: (b.) Thomas Graham Building, Strathclyde University, 295 Cathedral Street, Glasgow G1 1XL; T.-0141-552 4400.

Wood, Sir Ian Clark, CBE (1982), LLD, BSc, CBIM. Chairman and Managing Director, John Wood Group PLC, since 1967; Chairman, J.W. Holdings, since 1982; Chairman, Scottish Enterprise Board, since 1997; b. 21.7.42, Aberdeen; m., Helen Macrae; 3 s. Educ. Robert Gordon's College, Aberdeen; Aberdeen University. Joined family business, John Wood & Sons, 1964; Member, Scottish Economic Council; Chairman, Oil, Gas and Petrochemicals Supplies Office Board; Fellow, Royal Society of Arts; Board Director, Royal Bank of Scotland; Grampian Industrialist of the Year, 1978; Young Scottish Businessman of the Year, 1979; Scottish Free Enterprise Award, 1985; Scottish Business Achievement Award Trust — joint winner, 1992, corporate elite leadership award services category; Hon. LLD, 1984; Corporate Elite "World Player" Award, 1996; Fellow: Scottish Vocational Educational Council, Scottish Qualifications Authority. Recreations: tennis; family; art. Address: (b.) John Wood Group PLC, John Wood House, Greenwell Road, East Tullos, Aberdeen; T.-01224 851000.

Wood, Professor Robert Anderson, BSc, MB, ChB, FRCPEdin and Glas, FRCSEdin. Professor of Postgraduate Medicine, Aberdeen University, since 1992; b. 26.5.39, Edinburgh; m., Dr. Sheila Pirie; 1 s.; 3 d. Educ. Edinburgh Academy; Edinburgh University. Consultant Physician, Perth Royal Infirmary, 1972-92; Deputy Director of Postgraduate Medical Education, Dundee University, 1985-91; Dean, RCPE, 1992-95, and Councillor, 1990-92. Address: (h.) Ballomill House, Abernethy, Perthshire; T.-Abernethy 0201.

Wood, Stephen Charles, BA, MA, FSA, FRSA, FSA Scot, Chevalier de l'Ordre des Palmes Académiques, France. Keeper, Scottish United Services Museum, Edinburgh Castle, since 1983; b. 29.1.52, Wells, Somerset; 1 s. Educ. The Blue School, Wells; Bishop Wordsworth's School, Salisbury; Birkbeck College, London University. Curator, Department of Uniform, National Army Museum, London, 1971-83. Publications: The Scottish Soldier, 1987; In the Finest Tradition, 1988; The Auld Alliance, 1989; The Legendary 51st, 1990. Recreations: travel; gastronomy; historical research. Address: (b.) Edinburgh Castle, Edinburgh.

Woodcock, Brian, BEd (Hons). Director of Arts and Recreation, Aberdeen City Council, since 1996; Hon. Chairman, Scottish Association of Directors of Leisure Services, since 1995; b. 22.4.59, St. Andrews; m., Susan; 1 s.; 1 d. Educ. Waid Academy, Anstruther; Jordanhill College. Sports Development Assistant, Central Regional Council, 1983-87; Sports Officer, Stirling District Council, 1987-89; Sport and Leisure Manager, Strathkelvin District Council, 1989-90; Chief Leisure Officer, Derwentside District Council, 1990-92; Director of Leisure Services, Kilmarnock and Loudoun District Council, 1992-96. Recreations: sport; music; theatre. Address: (b.) Aberdeen City Council, St. Nicholas House, Broad Street, Aberdeen AB10 1XJ; T.-01224 522472.

Woodruff, Professor Sir Michael (Francis Addison), Kt (1969), DSc, MD, MS, FRCS, FRCSE, FRACS, Hon. FACS, FRSE, FRS. Professor Emeritus, Surgery, Edinburgh University; b. 3.4.11, London; m., Hazel Gwenyth Ashby; 2 s.; 1 d. Educ. Wesley College, Melbourne; Queens College, Melbourne University. House Physician and House Surgeon, Royal Melbourne Hospital; Captain, Australian Army Medical Corps (PoW Singapore); Tutor in Surgery, Sheffield University, 1946; Lecturer in Surgery, Aberdeen University, 1948; Professor of Surgery, Otago University, 1953, Edinburgh University, 1957-76; research worker, MRC Clinical and Population Cytogenetics Unit, Edinburgh, 1976-86. President, The Transplantation Society, 1972-74. Publications: Deficiency Diseases in Japanese Prison Camps; Surgery for Dental Students; The Transplantation of Tissues and Organs; On Science and Surgery; The Interaction of Cancer and Host; Cellular Variation and Adaptation in Cancer, 1990. Recreations: sailing; music; tennis. Address: (h.) The Bield, 506 Lanark Road, Juniper Green, Edinburgh EH14 5DH; T.-0131-453 3653.

Woods, Kevin James, BSc, PhD, MHSM. Director of Strategy and Performance Management, NHS Management Executive, Scottish Office, since 1995; Hon. Fellow, Health Services Management Unit, Manchester University, since 1990; b. 9.2.53, Sale; m., Helen Denise; 3 d. Educ. Sale County Grammar School; Queen Mary College, London University. Lecturer in Health Care, Queen Mary College and London Hospital Medical College, 1979-85; Consumer and Operational Research Officer/Deputy District General Manager, North Derbyshire Health Authority, 1985-89; District General Manager, Chester Health Authority, 1990; Regional Director of Corporate Planning/Regional General Manager, Trent Regional Health Authority, 1991-94. Recreations: gardening; golf; soccer. Address: (b.) NHS Management Executive, Scottish Office, St. Andrews House, Edinburgh, EH1 3DG; T.-0131-244 1727.

Woodward, Michael Trevor, PhD, MA (Hons), MBA. Director, Ivory and Sime Investment Management plc; Investment Director, Ivory and Sime plc, 1990-94; b. 25.11.57, Birmingham; m., Anne McWalter Russell; 2 d. Educ. Dartmouth Comprehensive School; Aberdeen University; Edinburgh University. Ivory and Sime plc, since 1983. Recreations: family; golf; squash; racketball. Address: (b.) 1 Charlotte Square, Edinburgh EH2 4DZ; T.-0131-225 1357.

Wooton, Professor Ian, MA, MA, MPhil, PhD. Bonar-Macfie Professor of Economics, Glasgow University, since 1995; Research Fellow, Centre for Economic Policy Research, London, since 1994; b. 4.4.57, Kirkcaldy; m., Norma Begg; 1 s.; 1 d. Educ. Kirkcaldy High School; St. Andrews University; Columbia University, New York. Associate Professor of Economics, University of Western Ontario, London, Canada, 1982-95. Recreations: reading; architecture; calligraphy. Address: (b.) Department of Economics, Adam Smith Building, Glasgow University, Glasgow G12 8RT; T.-0141-330 4672.

Worrall, Ernest Paterson, MB, ChB, FRCPsych, DPM. Consultant Psychiatrist, Southern General Hospital, Glasgow, since 1980; Medical Director, Langside Priory Hospital; b. 28.10.42, Hamilton; m., Jean Price; 1 s.; 1 d. Educ. Hamilton Academy; Glasgow University. Lecturer in Psychiatry, Dundee University, 1973-75; Senior Lecturer in Psychological Medicine, Glasgow University, 1975-80. Recreations: cycling; bowling. Address: (b.) Department of Psychiatry, Southern General Hospital, Glasgow G51 1TF; T.-0141-201 1900.

Worthington, Tony, BA, MEd. MP (Labour), Clydebank and Milngavie, since 1987; Parliamentary Under Secretary of State, Northern Ireland Office, since 1997; b. 11.10.41, Hertfordshire; m., Angela; 1 s.; 1 d. Educ. City School, Lincoln; London School of Economics; York University; Glasgow University. Recreations: running; fishing; gardening. Address: (h.) 24 Cleddans Crescent, Hardgate, Clydebank; T.-01389 73195.

Wotherspoon (John Munro) Iain, TD, DL. Senior Partner, MacAndrew & Jenkins, WS, since 1954; Deputy Lieutenant, Districts of Lochaber, Inverness, Badenoch and Strathspey, since 1982, and Clerk, since 1985; b. 19.7.24, Inverness; m., Victoria Avril Jean Edwards; 2 s.; 2 d. Educ. Inverness Royal Academy; Loretto School; Trinity College, Oxford; Edinburgh University. Lt., Royal Signals, Europe and Burma, 1944-46; TA, 1948-78; Lt.-Col. commanding 51 (Highland) Division Signals, 1963-70; Col. Dep. Cdr. 13 Signals Gp., 1970-72; Hon. Col. 32 (Scottish) Signal Regiment, 1972-78; ADC to The Queen, 1972-76; WS, 1950; Solicitor and Land Owner. Recreations: shooting; fishing; stalking. Address: (h.) Maryfield, 62 Midmills Road, Inverness IV2 3QL; T.-01463 233642.

Wray, Professor David, MD (Hons), BDS, MB, ChB, FDSRCPS, FDSRCS (Edin). Professor of Oral Medicine, Glasgow University, since 1993; Hon. Consultant, Greater Glasgow Health Board, since 1993; b. 3.1.51, Carshalton; m., Alyson P.M. Wray; 2 s. Educ. Uddingston Grammar School; Glasgow University. Fogarty Fellow, N.I.H. Bethesda, USA, 1979-81; Wellcome Research Fellow, Royal Dental, London, 1982; Senior Lecturer, Edinburgh University, 1983-92. Recreations: golf; curling; skiing. Address: (h.) 3 Kirklee Gardens, Glasgow G12 0SG.

Wray, James. MP (Labour), Glasgow Baillieston (formerly Glasgow Provan); b. 28.4.38. Address: (b.) House of Commons, London SW1A 0AA.

Wright, Andrew Paul Kilding, BArch, RIBA, PPRIAS, FRSA. Partner, Law & Dunbar-Nasmith, since 1981; President, Royal Incorporation of Architects in Scotland, 1995-97; b. 11.2.47, Walsall; m., Jean Patricia; 1 s.; 2 d. Educ. Queen Mary's Grammar School, Walsall; Liverpool University School of Architecture. Practising architect, since 1972; President, Inverness Architectural Association, 1986-88; Council, RIAS, 1985-94 and since 1995; External Examiner, Robert Gordon University, since 1990; Council, Royal Institute of British Architects, 1988-94 and 1995-97; Diocesan Architect, Diocese of Moray, Ross and Caithness, since 1989; UK Delegate, Architects Council of Europe, since 1995; Consultant Architect to National Trust for Scotland for Mar Lodge Estate, since 1995; Board Director, Executive Board, City of Architecture and Design Glasgow 1999, since 1995; Member, Ancient Monuments Board for Scotland, since 1996; Commissioner, Royal Fine Art Commission for Scotland, since 1997; Hon. Adviser, Scottish Redundant Churches Trust, since 1996. Recreations: music; railway history; fishing. Address: (b.) 29 St. Leonards Road, Forres, IV36 0DN; T.-01309 673221.

Wright, Professor Crispin James Garth, MA, PhD, FBA, BPhil, DLitt, FRSE. Professor of Logic and Metaphysics, St. Andrews University, since 1978; Leverhulme Personal Research Professor, since 1998; Bishop Wardlaw Professor, since 1997; b. 21.12.42, Bagshot, Surrey; m., Catherine; 2 s. Educ. Birkenhead School; Trinity College, Cambridge. Junior Research Fellow, Trinity College, Oxford, 1967-69; Fellow/Research Fellow, All Souls College, Oxford, 1969-78. Publications: Wittgenstein on the Foundations of Mathematics, 1980; Frege's Conception of Numbers as Objects, 1983; Realism, Meaning and Truth, 1986; Truth and Objectivity, 1992. Recreations: mountaineering; gardening; travel. Address: (b.) Department of Logic and Metaphysics, St. Andrews University, St. Andrews KY16 9AL.

Wright, David, BEd, MEd. Headteacher, Dunbar Grammar School, since 1997; b. 21.7.55, Kirkcaldy; m., Katrina; 1 s.; 1 d. Educ. Kirkcaldy High School; Edinburgh University; Moray House. Biology Teacher, Ainslie Park High School, 1979; Principal Teacher of Biology, Balerno Community High School, 1983; Assistant Head, Musselburgh Grammar School, 1988; Depute Head, Firrhill High School, 1993. Publication: The Biosphere, 1989. Recreations: golf; football. Address: (b.) Dunbar Grammar School, Summerfield Road, Dunbar EH42 1NJ; T.-01368 863339.

Wright, David Frederick, MA (Cantab). Senior Lecturer in Ecclesiastical History, Edinburgh University, since 1973; b. 2.10.37, Hayes, Kent; m., Anne-Marie; 1 s.; 1 d. Educ. Christ's College, Cambridge; Lincoln College, Oxford. Edinburgh University: Lecturer, 1964-73, Associate Dean, Faculty of Divinity, 1972-76, Dean, 1988-92, Member, University Court, 1984-87; External Examiner, Universities of Sussex, Liverpool, Durham, Cambridge, etc.; Member, Council of Management, Keston College; Chairman, Tyndale Fellowship for Biblical and Theological Research; Associate Editor, Tyndale Bulletin; Editor, Scottish Bulletin of Evangelical Theology; Member of Praesidium, International Congress on Calvin Research; recipient of Festschrift, 1997. Publications: Common Places of Martin Bucer, 1972; Essays in Evangelical Social Ethics (Editor), 1979; Lion Handbook History of Christianity (Consultant Editor), 1977; New Dictionary of Theology (Joint Editor), 1988; The Bible in Scottish Life and Literature (Contributor and Editor), 1988; Chosen by God: Mary in Evangelical Perspective (Contributor and Editor), 1989; Dictionary of Scottish Church History and Theology (Chief General Editor), 1993; Calvin's Old Testament Commentaries (General Editor), 1993; Martin Bucer: Reforming Church and Community (Contributor and Editor), 1994; Disruption to Diversity: Edinburgh Divinity 1846-1996 (Co-Editor and Contributor), 1996. Recreations: walking; gardening; DIY. Address: (h.) 3 Camus Road East, Edinburgh EH10 6RE; T.-0131-445 1960.

Wright, David John, MB, BS, FRCA. Consultant Anaesthetist, Western General Hospital, Edinburgh, since 1979; b. 13.4.44, Oswestry; m., Bronwen; 2 s.; 1 d. Educ. Bristol Grammar School; St. Bartholomew's Hospital Medical College, London. Honorary Editor, Scottish Society of the History of Medicine. Address: (h.) 20 Lennox Row, Edinburgh EH5 3JW; T.-0131-552 3439.

Wright, Rev. David Livingston, MA, BD. Minister of Religion, Church of Scotland, since 1957; b. 18.5.30, Aberdeen; m., Margaret Brown; 2 s.; 1 d. Educ. Robert Gordon's College, Aberdeen; King's College, Aberdeen University. Assistant, Garthdee, Aberdeen, 1955-56, West St. Andrew's, 1956-57; licensed by Aberdeen Presbytery, 1957; Assistant, St. Andrew's, Dundee, till December 1957; Minister: Cockenzie Chalmers Memorial, 1957-64, Forfar Lowson Memorial, 1964-71, Hawick Old, 1971-72, linked with Teviothead, 1972-86, Stornoway St. Columba's Old Parish, since 1986. Former Moderator, Jedburgh Presbytery and Synod of Borders; twice Moderator, Lewis Presbytery; Chairman, Scottish Reformation Society; former Chairman, National Church Association. Recreations: golf; walking dog; reading; occasional TV; playing piano and organ.

Address: (b.) St. Columba's Old Parish Manse, Lewis Street, Stornoway, Isle of Lewis H51 2JF; T.-01851 703350.

Wright, Professor George, BSc, MPhil, PhD. Deputy Director and Professor of Business Administration, Strathclyde Graduate Business School, since 1991; b. 24.11.52, Louth; m., Josephine Elizabeth; 2 s. Educ. Queen Elizabeth I Grammar School; NE London Polytechnic; Brunel University. Research Assistant, Brunel University, 1974-79; Research Fellow, Huddersfield Polytechnic, 1979-81; Senior Lecturer, City of London Polytechnic, 1981-86; Reader, then Professor, Bristol Business School, 1986-91. Publications: seven books; 100 journal articles. Recreation: visiting public houses. Address: (b.) Strathclyde Graduate Business School, 130 Rottenrow, Glasgow G4 0GE; T.-0141-553 6000.

Wright, George Gordon. Publisher; b. 25.6.42, Edinburgh; m., Carmen Ilie; 1 s. Educ. Darroch Secondary School; Heriot Watt College. Started publishing as a hobby, 1969; left printing trade, 1973, to develop own publishing company; founder Member, Scottish General Publishers Association; Past Chairman, Scottish Young Publishers Society; Oliver Brown Award, 1994; Secretary/Treasurer, 200 Burns Club, since 1991. Publications: MacDiarmid: An Illustrated Biography, 1977; A Guide to the Royal Mile, 1979; Orkney From Old Photographs, 1981; A Guide to Holyrood Park and Arthur's Seat, 1987. Recreations: history of Edinburgh; photography; jazz. Address: (h.) 25 Mayfield Road, Edinburgh EH9 2NQ; T.-0131-667 1300.

Wright, Grahame Alan, BA (Econ), MPhil (Cantab). Assistant Principal External Relations, University of Abertay Dundee, since 1993; Chairman, Product Development Tayside Ltd., since 1994; Director, Dundee Incubator Ltd., since 1997; Trustee, Dundee Heritage Trust, since 1997; b. 5.8.47, Sunderland; m., Joan Margaret; 2 s.; 1 d. Educ. Mortimer County Secondary, South Shields; Open University; Newcastle Polytechnic; Clare College, Cambridge. Musical instrument retailer, 1963-77; Research Assistant, Lecturer, Senior Lecturer, Principal Lecturer, Newcastle Polytechnic, 1980-91; Head, Department of Accountancy, Economics and Law, Dundee Institute of Technology, 1991-93. Recreations: music; preacher, Methodist Church. Address: (h.) 12 Woodlands Park, Blairgowrie, PH10 6UW; T.-01250 875243.

Wright, Professor Howard David, BEng, PhD, CEng, FIStructE, FICE, FRSA. Professor of Structures (in association with Thorburn Colquhoun), Strathclyde University, since 1991; b. 5.10.52, Holmes Chapel; m., Elizabeth Mary Warren Baynham; 2 s.; 1 d. Educ. Sandbach School; Sheffield University. Assistant Engineer, CEGB, 1974-78; Structural Engineer, Boots the Chemists, 1978-82; Lecturer in Structural Design, University of Wales, Cardiff, 1982-91. Council Member, Institution of Structural Engineers, 1988-91; Committee Member, Building Standards Advisory Board, 1991-97. Publications: papers on composite construction and engineering education. Recreations: hill-walking; music; mechanics. Address: (b.) Department of Civil Engineering, 107 Rottenrow, Glasgow G4 0NG; T.-0141-552 4400, Ext. 3251.

Wright, Rev. Kenyon Edward, MA, BA, BSc, MTh. Director, Kairos (Centre for a Sustainable Society), since 1990; Convener, Scottish Ecumenical Environment Network; Consultant on Justice and Peace to ACTS (Action of Churches Together in Scotland); Chair, Executive, Scottish Constitutional Convention; Vice-Chair, Scottish Environmental Forum; Co-ordinating Secretary, The Christian Peace Conference (International); Patron, Scottish Refugee Council; Canon Emeritus and Companion of the Order of the Cross of Nails, Coventry Cathedral; b. 31.8.32, Paisley; m., Betty Robinson; 3 d. Educ. Paisley Grammar School; Glasgow University; Cambridge University.

Missionary in India, 1955-70; Director, Ecumenical Social and Industrial Institute, Durgapur, India, 1963-70; Director, Urban Ministry, Coventry Cathedral, 1970-74; Canon Residentiary and Director of International Ministry, Coventry Cathedral, 1974-81; General Secretary, Scottish Churches Council and Director, Scottish Churches House, 1981-90. Recreations: reading; walking; travel; living life to the full. Address: (b.) Kairos Centre, c/o The Rectory, Glencarse, Perth, PH2 7LX; T.-01738 860386.

Wright, Malcolm Robert, MHSM, DipHSM. Chief Executive, Edinburgh and Sick Children's NHS Trust, since 1994; b. 1.9.57, Blyth; m., Hilary; 1 s.; 1 d. Educ. Kings School, Tynemouth; Penicuik High School. Hospital Manager, Great Ormond Street, London, 1989-92; Unit General Manager, Lothian Health Board, 1992-94. Chairman, National Association for Child Health Services, since 1995. Recreations: cycling; reading; architecture. Address: (h.) Royal Hospital for Sick Children, Sciennes Road, Edinburgh; T.-0131-536 0002.

Wright, Philip, BSc, CEng, MICE. Head, European Environment and Engineering Unit, and Chief Water Engineer, Scottish Office Agriculture Environment and Fisheries Department, since 1997; b. 15.4.49, Edinburgh; m., Anne Margaret; 3 d. Educ. St. Anthony's Secondary School; Tynecastle Secondary School; Heriot Watt University. Civil Engineer, Edinburgh Corporation, 1971-75, Lothian Regional Council, 1975-82; joined Scottish Office as Senior Civil Engineer, 1982; Assistant Chief Engineer, 1991. Director, Scotland and Northern Ireland Forum for Environmental Research; Director, Foundation for Water Research. Recreations: football; squash; golf; walking. Address: (b.) Victoria Quay, Edinburgh EH6 6QQ; T.-0131-244 0193.

Wright, Tom, BA (Hons). Writer; b. 8.3.23, Glasgow. Educ. Coatbridge High School; Strathclyde University. Served apprenticeship in embossing and stained glass; Army, 1943-47; served in Europe and Far East, including Japan; began to publish poems and short stories after demobilisation; had first play performed, Edinburgh Festival, 1960; author of There Was A Man; began to write radio and television drama, 1963; former Creative Writing Fellow; former Script Editor, BBC Scotland Drama Department; has also been Script Editor and Story Line Editor, Take The High Road, STV; won Festival Fringe Award, 1984, for Talk of the Devil; recent work includes The Hunter and the Hill, 1994, and Forgotten Army, 1995; Past Chairman, Scottish Committee, Writers' Guild, and Scottish Society of Playwrights. Recreation: listening to music. Address: 318 Churchill Drive, Glasgow G11.

Wyke, John Anthony, MA, PhD, VetMB, MRCVS, FRSE. Director, Beatson Institute for Cancer Research, since 1987; Visiting Professor, Glasgow University; b. 5.4.42, Cleethorpes. Educ. Dulwich College; Cambridge University; Glasgow University; London University. Leukemia Society of America Fellow, Universities of Washington and Southern California, 1970-72; Staff Scientist, Imperial Cancer Research Fund, 1972-85; Assistant Director of Research, 1985-87. Address: (b.) Beatson Institute for Cancer Research, CRC Beatson Laboratories, Garscube Estate, Switchback Road, Bearsden, Glasgow G61 1BD; T.-0141-942 9361.

Wylie, Alexander Featherstonhaugh, QC, LLB, FCIArb. Lawyer; Member of the Scottish Bar, since 1978; b. 2.6.51, Perth; m., Gail Elizabeth Watson Duncan; 2 d. Educ. Edinburgh University. Qualified Solicitor in Scotland, 1976; called to Scottish Bar, 1978; Standing Junior Counsel to Accountant of Court, 1986-89; Advocate Depute, 1989-92; called to English Bar, 1990; QC (Scot), 1991. Part-time Joint Chairman, Discipline Committee, Institute of Chartered Accountants of Scotland, since 1994; Member, Scottish Legal Aid Board, since 1994. Address: (b.)

Advocates Library, Parliament House, Edinburgh, EH1 1RF; T.-0131-226 2881.

Wylie, Rt. Hon. Lord (Norman Russell Wylie), PC (1970), VRD (1961), BA (Oxon), LLB (Glas). Senator of the College of Justice in Scotland, 1974- 90; b. 26.10.23, Elderslie; m., Gillian Mary Verney; 3 s. Educ. Paisley Grammar School; St. Edmund Hall, Oxford (Hon. Fellow, since 1975); Glasgow University; Edinburgh University. Fleet Air Arm, 1942-46 (subsequently RNR, Lt.-Cdr, 1954). Admitted Faculty of Advocates, 1952; Standing Junior Counsel to Air Ministry, 1956; Advocate Depute, 1958; QC, 1964; Solicitor General for Scotland, April to October, 1964; MP (Conservative), Edinburgh Pentlands, 1964-74; Lord Advocate, 1970-74. Chairman, Scottish National Committee, English Speaking Union of Commonwealth, 1978-84; Trustee, Carnegie Trust for Universities of Scotland, 1975-95; Justice of Appeal, Republic of Botswana, 1994-96. Recreations: shooting; sailing. Address: (h.) 30 Lauder Road, Edinburgh; T.-0131-667 8377.

Wylie, Rev. William Andrew, MA. Crisis Management Consultant; b. 17.5.27, London; m., Jennifer Barclay Mack; 4 d. by pr. m. Educ. Glasgow Academy; Glasgow University and Trinity College. Royal Navy, 1944-47; Chaplain, Clyde Division, RNVR, 1954-59; Minister: Stepps, 1953-59, Scots Kirk, Lausanne, 1959-67; General Secretary, Scottish Churches Council, 1967-71; Minister, St. Andrew's and St. George's, Edinburgh, 1972-85; Chaplain, Inverclyde Industrial Mission, 1985-86; Chaplain to the offshore oil industry, 1986-91; elected Hon. Fellow, Institute of Petroleum, 1990; elected Burgess of Aberdeen, 1990; Chairman of Governors, Aiglon College, Switzerland, 1984-91; Governor, Fettes College, 1978-85. Recreations: gardening; writing music; labradors; not playing golf. Address: (h.) Wellrose Cottage, Peat Inn, Fife KY15 5LH; T.-01334 840600.

Wylie, William Iain, LLB, DMS, DipM. Director of Corporate Affairs, Strathclyde Passenger Transport Authority, since 1997; b. 7.3.55, Perth; m., Catherine Anne; 2 d. Educ. Perth Academy; Aberdeen University; Robert Gordon's Institute of Technology. Strathclyde Regional Council, 1977-96. Recreations: reading; music; theatre. Address: Consort House, 12 West George Street, Glasgow; T.-0141-333 3179.

Wyllie, George. Artist; b. 1921, Glasgow. Installations; performances; events; best known for "paper boat" installation and exhibition, Glasgow, Liverpool, London and New York, 1989-90; Visiting Lecturer, Glasgow School of Art; Associate, Royal Scottish Academy; Hon. DLitt, Strathclyde University, Glasgow.

Wyllie, Gordon Malcolm, LLB, FSA Scot, NP, TEP, WS. Partner, Biggart Baillie, Solicitors; Clerk to the Trades House of Glasgow and to Grand Antiquity Society of Glasgow; Clerk to General Commissioners of Inland Revenue, Glasgow North and South Divisions; b. Newton Mearns. Educ. Dunoon Grammar School; Glasgow University. Honorary Treasurer, Edinburgh Summer School in Ancient Greek; Director, Bailford Trustees Ltd.; Chairman, Edinburgh Subscription Ball Committee; Freeman of Glasgow; Deacon, Incorporation of Hammermen of Edinburgh; Member, Edinburgh West End Community Council; wrote Scottish contribution to International Bar Association's International Dictionary of Succession Terms. Recreations: music; history and the arts generally; country walks; foreign travel. Address: (b.) 310 St. Vincent Street, Glasgow; T.-0141-228 8000.

Wyllie, Very Rev. Hugh Rutherford, MA, Hon.DD (Aberdeen), FCIBS. Minister, Old Parish Church of Hamilton, since 1981; Moderator, General Assembly of the Church of Scotland, 1992-93; admitted as Hon. Freeman,

District of Hamilton, 1992; b. 11.10.34, Glasgow; m., Eileen E. Cameron, MA; 2 d. Educ. Shawlands Academy; Hutchesons' Grammar School, Glasgow. Union Bank of Scotland, 1951-53; RAF, 1953-55; Glasgow University, 1956-62; Assistant Minister, Glasgow Cathedral, 1962-65; Minister, Dunbeth Church, Coatbridge, 1965-72; Minister, Cathcart South Church, Glasgow, 1972-81; Moderator, Presbytery of Hamilton, 1989-90, Convener, Business Committee, 1991-95; President, Hamilton Burns Club, 1990; founder Member, Hamilton Centre for Information for the Unemployed, 1983; introduced Dial-a-Fact on drugs and alcohol, 1986; established Hamilton Church History Project, 1984-87; Convener, General Assembly's Stewardship and Budget Committee, 1978-83; Convener, Stewardship and Finance Board, 1983-86; Convener, Assembly Council, 1987-91; Member, Board of Nomination to Church Chairs, 1985-91 and since 1993; Member, General Assembly's Board of Practice and Procedure, 1991-95; Non-Executive Director, Lanarkshire Health Care NHS Trust, since 1995, a Vice-Chairman, since 1996; Dr William Barclay Memorial Lecturer, 1994; elected Member, Council, Scout Association, 1993; Master, Hamilton Hospital, since 1982; Chaplain, Royal British Legion, Hamilton, since 1981, Lanarkshire Burma Star Association, since 1983. Recreations: gardening; DIY; yellow labrador. Address: Mansewood, Union Street, Hamilton ML3 6NA; T.-01698 420002.

Wyllie, James Hogarth, BA, MA. Senior Lecturer in International Relations and Director, Postgraduate Strategic Studies Programme, Aberdeen University, since 1979; International Affairs Analyst, Grampian Television, 1989-94; Specialist Correspondent, Jane's Intelligence Review, since 1992; Member, JDM Marketing Associates, Aberdeen, since 1992; b. 7.3.51, Dumfries; m., Claire Helen Beaton; 2 s. Educ. Sanquhar Academy; Dumfries Academy; Stirling University; Lancaster University. Research Officer, Ministry of Defence, 1974-75; Tutor in Politics, Durham University, 1975-77; Lecturer in Politics, University of East Anglia, 1977-79; freelance journalism; frequent current affairs comment and analysis, BBC Radio; Commonwealth Fellow, University of Calgary, 1988. Publications: Influence of British Arms; European Security in the Nuclear Age; Economist Pocket Guide to Defence (Co-author); International Politics since 1945 (Contributor); European Security in the New Political Environment. Recreations: travelling; cinema; badminton; walking. Address: (b.) Department of Politics and International Relations, Aberdeen University, Aberdeen AB24 3QY; T.-01224 272725.

Wyllie, Willilam, JP, DL. Dean of Guild, City of Aberdeen, since 1981; Governor, Robert Gordon University, Aberdeen, since 1991; b. 5.2.32, Aberdeen; m., Mary Anne; 3 d. Educ. Robert Gordon's College, Aberdeen; Gordonstoun School, Elgin; North of Scotland College of Agriculture. W. Smith & Son, seedsmen; Hazlehead Nurseries, Aberdeen, 1952-85, retiring as Managing Director. Secretary, NE Scotland Horticultural Training Board; former Chairman, Aberdeen Airport Consultative Committee; Chairman, British Chambers of Commerce Aviation Committee. Recreations: gardening; swimming; reading. Address: (h.) 156 Kings Gate, Aberdeen, AB15 6BR; T.-01224 317811.

Wynd, Andrew H.D., DipSW (CQSW). General Secretary, Scottish Spina Bifida Association, since 1989; b. 7.10.53, Hamilton. Educ. Bellshill Academy; Stirling University. Local government officer; Senior Officer, National Voluntary Childcare Organisation. Past Chair, Scottish Association of Voluntary Service Co-ordinators; former Chair, Strathclyde Regional Council Pre-five Voluntary Sector Forum. Address: (b.) Scottish Spina Bifida Association, 190 Queensferry Road, Edinburgh EH4 2BW; T.-0131-332 0743.

Y

Yadav, Professor Pradeep Kumar, BSc (Hons), MSc (Physics), MSc (Financial Studies), PhD. Professor of Finance, since 1993, Head, Department of Accounting and Finance, since 1995, Strathclyde University; b. 31.8.53, India; m., Mamta; 1 s.; 1 d. Educ. St. Xaviers School, Delhi; St. Stephen's College, University of Delhi; Strathclyde University. Member, Indian Administrative Service (formerly Indian Civil Service), 1976-86; Lecturer in Finance/Senior Lecturer in Finance, Department of Accounting and Finance, Strathclyde University, 1987-93. Publications: 25 articles in journals and books. Address: (b.) Department of Accounting and Finance, Strathclyde University, 100 Cathedral Street, Glasgow G4 0LN; T.-0141-548 3939.

Yarrow, Sir Eric Grant, MBE, DL, CEng, MRINA, FRSE. Chairman, Clydesdale Bank PLC, 1985-91 (Director, since 1962); Director, National Australia Bank Ltd., 1987-91; b. 23.4.20, Glasgow; m., 1, Rosemary Ann Young (deceased); 1 s. (deceased); 2, Annette Elizabeth Francoise Steven (m. diss.); 3 s.; 3, Joan Botting; 3 step d. Educ. Marlborough College; Glasgow University. Served engineering apprenticeship, G. & J. Weir, 1938-39; Royal Engineers, 1939-45; served Burma, 1942-45 (Major, RE, 1945); Yarrow & Co. Ltd. (later Yarrow PLC): Assistant Manager, 1946, Director, 1948, Managing Director, 1958-67, Chairman, 1962-85, President, 1985-87; Director, Standard Life Assurance Company, 1958-91; Chairman, Princess Louise Scottish Hospital, Erskine, 1980-86, Hon. President, since 1986; President, Scottish Convalescent Home for Children, 1957-70; Council Member, Royal Institution of Naval Architects, since 1957 (Vice President, 1965, Honorary Vice President, 1972); Member, General Committee, Lloyd's Register of Shipping, 1960-89; Deacon, Incorporation of Hammermen in Glasgow, 1961-62; Chairman, Yarrow (Shipbuilders) Ltd., 1962-79; Officer (Brother), Order of St. John, since 1965; Deputy Lieutenant, County of Renfrewshire, 1970-96; Prime Warden, Worshipful Company of Shipwrights, 1970-71; Council Member, Institute of Directors, 1983-90; President, Smeatonican Society of Civil Engineers, 1983-84; President, The Marlburian Club, 1984; President, Scottish Area, Burma Star Association, since 1990; Vice President, Royal Highland and Agricultural Society for Scotland, 1990. Recreation: golf. Address: (h.) Cloak, Kilmacolm, Renfrewshire PA13 4SD; T.-Kilmacolm 2067.

Yates, Keith. Chief Executive, Stirling Council, since 1995. Address: (b.) c/o Viewforth, Stirling, FK8 2ET.

Yemm, Professor Robert, BDS, BSc, PhD, FDS RCS(Edin). Professor and Head, Department of Dental Prosthetics and Gerontology, Dundee University, since 1984; b. 31.1.39, Bristol; m., Glenys Margaret; 1 s.; 1 d. Educ. Bristol Grammar School; Bristol University. Lecturer in Dental Prosthetics, Bristol University; Associate Professor, Department of Oral Biology, Alberta University; Lecturer in Dental Medicine (Oral Biology), then Dental Prosthetics, Bristol University; Senior Lecturer (Honorary Consultant), Dental Prosthetics, Dundee University. Recreation: sailing. Address: (h.) 10 Birkhill Avenue, Wormit, Newport-on-Tay, Fife DD6 8PX; T.-01382 541819.

Yewe-Dyer, Mervyn Richard, BDS, BSc, FDS, MSc, MGDS. Deputy Chief Dental Officer, Scottish Office, since 1994; Chief Dental Adviser, since 1996; b. 4.8.43, London; m., Melanie Dorcas Gould; 1 s.; 2 d. Educ. Christ's Hospital; London University. Nuffield Research Fellow, 1966-68; Lecturer, Manchester University, 1969-73; general dental practice, 1974-93; Lecturer (part-time), Guy's

Hospital Dental School, 1979-87; Board Member, Dental Practice Board England, 1985-91. Publication: Notes on Prosthetic Dentistry. Recreations: photography; golf; bee-keeping. Address: (b.) Room 54 H, St. Andrew's House, Edinburgh, EH1 3DG; T.-0131-244 2305.

Young, Alastair Duncan, BSc (Hons), CEng, MICE. Director of Roads and Transportation, Glasgow City Council, since 1995; Director, RTI Focus, since 1996; Director, Susiephone Ltd., since 1997; b. 7.6.48, Glasgow; m., Janet U.H. Young; 1 s. Educ. Uddingston Grammar School; Strathclyde University. Technician, Leitch and Sharp; Strathclyde Regional Council, joining as Technician/Engineer, latterly as Regional Network Manager. Recreations: golf; cooking. Address: (b.) Richmond Exchange, 20 Cadogan Street, Glasgow, G2 7AD; T.-0141-287 9100.

Young, Alexander Grant, MA (Hons). Head Teacher, Kyle Academy, Ayr, since 1996; b. 9.6.51, Stornoway; m., Patricia; 1 s.; 1 d. Educ. Ayr Academy; Edinburgh University; Moray House College of Education. Began teaching, Penicuik High School; moved to Cumnock Academy, 1975; exchange teacher, Orange County, S. California, 1979-80; Principal Teacher of Geography, James Hamilton Academy, Kilmarnock, 1982-86; Assistant Head Teacher, Kilwinning Academy, 1986-91; Area Development Officer, TVEI Extension Team, Ayrshire, 1991-94; Depute Head Teacher, Grange Academy, Kilmarnock, 1994-96. Member, Higher Still Specialist Group on Guidance; former Vice President, Ayr Seaforth Athletic Club; Vice President, Mauchline Burns Club. Recreations: sport; family; reading; music; travel; gardening. Address: (b.) Kyle Academy, Overmills Road, Ayr KA7 3LR; T.-01292 262234.

Young, Charles Whiteford, LLB, CA. Director, British Linen Bank Ltd., since 1991; Director, United Auctions (Scotland) plc, since 1993; b. 18.5.53, Glasgow; m., Sharon M.M. Stevenson; 3 d. Educ. Glasgow Academy; Trinity College, Glenalmond; Aberdeen University; Glasgow University. Arthur Young McClelland Moores & Co., Glasgow, 1975-78; Corporate Finance Department, British Linen Bank, since 1979. Recreations: golf; tennis; swimming. Address: (b.) 4 Melville Street, Edinburgh EH3 7NZ; T.-0131-243 8326.

Young, Chick. Football Correspondent, BBC Television and Radio, since 1988; b. 4.5.51, Glasgow. Educ. Glasgow High School; Bellahouston Academy, Glasgow. Daily Record, 1969-72; Carrick Herald, Girvan, 1972; Irvine Herald, 1972-73; Charles Buchan's Football Monthly, London, 1973-74; Editor, Scottish Football magazine, 1974-75; Scottish Daily News, 1975; Scottish Daily Express, 1976; Evening Times, Glasgow, 1977-88; Radio Clyde, 1977-95; BBC, since 1988; Sunday People, 1988-89; Scotland on Sunday, 1989-91; Columnist, Daily Star, since 1996. Fraser Award, Young Journalist of the Year, 1973; British Provincial Sports Journalist of the Year, 1987; Sony Award, British Sports Broadcaster of the Year (Bronze), 1997; Scottish Sports Journalist of the Year (Runner-up), 1997. Publications: Rebirth of the Blues; Mo. Address: (b.) BBC TV Sport, Queen Margaret Drive, Glasgow G12 8DG; T.-0141-338 2622.

Young, Professor Daniel Greer, MB, ChB, FRCSEdin, FRCSGlas, DTM&H. Professor of Paediatric Surgery, Glasgow University; Honorary Consultant Paediatric Surgeon; former President, British Association of Paediatric Surgeons; b. Skipness, Argyll; m., Agnes Gilchrist Donald; 1 s.; 1 d. Educ. Wishaw High School; Glasgow University. Resident Assistant Surgeon, Hospital for Sick Children, London; Senior Lecturer, Institute of Child Health, London University; Honorary Consultant Surgeon, Hospital for Sick Children, London, and Queen Elizabeth Hospital, Hackney, London; Senior Lecturer and Head, Department of

Paediatric Surgery, Glasgow University, Honorary Consultant Surgeon, Royal Hospital for Sick Children and Stobhill General Hospital, Glasgow. Honorary Secretary, Lanarkshire Division, British Medical Association; Past President, Royal Medico-Chirurgical Society of Glasgow; Honorary President, Scottish Spina Bifida Association; Member of Council, Royal College of Physicians and Surgeons; Past Chairman, Intercollegiate Board in Paediatric Surgery; Honorary Member: Hungarian Paediatric Surgical Association, South African Paediatric Surgical Association, American Surgical Paediatric Association. Recreations: curling; fishing; gardening. Address: (b.) Department of Paediatric Surgery, Royal Hospital for Sick Children, Yorkhill, Glasgow G3 8SJ; T.-0141-201 0170.

Young, Lt.-Gen. Sir David (Tod), KBE (1980), CB (1977), DFC (1952). Chairman, Cairntech Ltd., Edinburgh, 1983-93, Director, 1993-96; b. 17.5.26, Edinburgh; m., 1, Joyce Marian Melville (deceased); 2 s.; 2, Joanna Myrtle Oyler (nee Torin). Educ. George Watson's College, Edinburgh. Commissioned The Royal Scots, 1945; Brevet Lt.-Col., 1964; Mil. Assistant, MoD, 1964-67; commanded 1st Bn., The Royal Scots, 1967-69; Col. GS, Staff College, 1969-70; Commander, 12 Mechanized Brigade, 1970-72; Deputy Military Secretary, MoD, 1972-74; Commander Land Forces, Northern Ireland, 1975-77; Director of Infantry, MoD, 1977-80; GOC Scotland and Governor, Edinburgh Castle, 1980-82; Colonel, The Royal Scots, 1975-80; Colonel Commandant: Scottish Division, 1980-82, Ulster Defence Regiment, 1986-91; Honorary Colonel, Northern Ireland Regiment Army Air Corps, 1988-93; Vice President, Scottish Partnership Agency for Palliative and Cancer Care, since 1993; Member, Scottish Committee, Marie Curie Foundation, since 1983 (Chairman, 1986); Trustee, Marie Curie, since 1986; President, Army Cadet Force Association Scotland, since 1984; HM Commissioner, Queen Victoria School, 1984-93; Chairman, St. Mary's Cathedral Workshop, 1986-92; Member, Board of Governors, St. Columba's Hospice, since 1986; Honorary President, St. Mary's Cathedral Workshop, since 1993. Recreations: golf; sports; music. Address: c/o Adam & Company plc, 22 Charlotte Square, Edinburgh EH2 4DF.

Young, Dennis James, MA, LLB, TEP. Senior Partner, Blackadder Reid Johnston, Solicitors, Dundee; b. 23.1.42, Forfar; m., Enid; 2 s. Educ. Brechin High School; St. Andrews University. Lectured part-time, Dundee University, for several years; trained, Gray Robertson & Wilkie, Dundee; joined present firm, 1967, becoming Partner, 1969; Founder Secretary, Committee, Dundee Solicitors' Property Centre, Chairman, 1978-86; Member, Society of Trust and Estates Practitioners (Leader, Tayside and Aberdeen Regional Discussion Group); Dean, Faculty of Procurators and Solicitors in Dundee, 1993-95; Member, Council, Law Society of Scotland, 1996-97. Member, Executive Committee, Scottish Heart and Arterial Disease Risk Prevention (charity). Recreations: golf; football/rugby spectating; listening to music. Address: (b.) 30-34 Reform Street, Dundee DD1 1RJ; T.-01382 229222.

Young, Hugh Kenneth, TD, CA, FCIBS. Vice-Chairman, Lowland Employers Liaison Committee; Chairman, Trustees, Royal Scots Benevolent Society; Trustee, Royal Scots (War Memorial) Club; General Manager and Secretary and Member, Management Board, Bank of Scotland, 1984-96; b. 6.5.36, Galashiels; m., Marjory Bruce Wilson; 2 s.; 1 d. Educ. Edinburgh Academy. National Service, 1959-61; commissioned as 2nd Lt., Royal Scots; TA service, 1957-59, 1961-69 and 1986-92, latterly as Major; with ICFC Ltd., 1962-67; with Schroders Ltd. group, 1967-73, latterly as Manager, J. Henry Schroder Wagg & Co. Ltd.; Local Director in Edinburgh, Edward Bates & Sons Ltd., 1973-75; joined Bank of Scotland, 1975; Head of Corporate Finance, Bank of Scotland Finance Company Ltd., 1976; Director, The British Linen Bank

Ltd., 1978-84 (Deputy Chief Executive, 1982-84). Recreations: squash; tennis; hill-walking. Address: (h.) 30 Braid Hills Road, Edinburgh EH10 6HY; T.-0131-447 3101.

Young, James Drummond, LLB, NP. Solicitor (Partner, McGrigor Donald, since 1985); b. 26.2.50, Broughty Ferry; m., Gillian Anne Boyd; 1 s.; 1 d. Educ. Hutchesons' Grammar School; Glasgow University. Apprentice, then Legal Assistant, McGrigor Donald & Co., 1971-75; Legal Officer, West Lothian District Council, 1975-77; Legal Assistant, then Partner, Moncrieff Warren Paterson & Co., 1977-85. Elder, Greenbank Church; Scottish Editor, Employment Precedents and Company Policy Documents. Recreations: golf; contemporary art; cricket. Address: (b.) Erskine House, 68/73 Queen Street, Edinburgh; T.-0131-226 7777.

Young, Sheriff J. N. Sheriff of Tayside, Central and Fife at Dundee. Address: (b.) Dundee Sheriff Court, 6 West Bell Street, Dundee, DD1 9AD.

Young, John Graeme Bennett, MA, PhD, DipEd. Director of Education, Falkirk Council, since 1995; b. 31.10.50, Bridge of Allan; m., Shena; 2 s. Educ. High School of Stirling. Teacher of History/Modern Studies, Dalziel High School, Motherwell, 1976-81; Principal Teacher, Tain Royal Academy, 1981-85; Assistant Divisional Education Officer, Highland Region, 1985-88; Assistant Director of Education, Head of Resources, Acting Director of Education, Central Regional Council, 1988-95. Recreations: reading; music; sport; local history; gardening; walking. Address: (b.) McLaren House, Marchmont Avenue, Polmont, FK2 0NZ; T.-01324 506680.

Young, John Henderson, OBE, JP, DL, KSJ, MIMgt. Deputy Lieutenant of Glasgow, since 1981; Chairman, Association of Scottish Conservative Councillors, 1991-94, Hon. President, since 1994; Member, SPTA, since 1996; b. 21.12.30, Glasgow; m., Doris Paterson; 1 s. Educ. Hillhead High School, Glasgow; Scottish College of Commerce. RAF, 1949-51. Councillor, Glasgow Corporation, 1964-73, Glasgow District Council, 1974-96, City of Glasgow Council, from 1996; Police Judge, 1971-72; Bailie/Magistrate of Glasgow on four occasions; Leader, Glasgow City Council, 1977-79, Leader of the Opposition, 1979-80, 1988-92, from 1996 (new City of Glasgow Council); former Chairman/Vice-Chairman, Council committees; Parliamentary candidate (Conservative), Rutherglen, 1966, Cathcart, 1992; Chairman, Cathcart Conservatives, 1964-65, 1968-71, 1987-88; Chairman, Glasgow Euro Constituency, 1987-91; Vice-Chairman, Scottish Tory Reform Group, since 1993; Vice Chairman, Glasgow Conservatives, 1969-72; Export Manager, Teacher's Whisky; Public Relations Consultant; former Vice-Chairman, Scottish Pakistani Association; Secretary, Scottish/South African Society, 1986-88; Governor, Hutcheson's Educational Trust, 1991-97; Member, Glasgow Sports Promotion Council; Life Member, Merchants House of Glasgow; Kentucky Colonel, 1984; Hon. Don Cossack (Russia), 1989; Lord Provost's Award, 1989. Publication: A History of Cathcart Conservative Association, 1918-93. Recreations: meeting people; history; reading; animal welfare. Address: (h.) 4 Deanwood Avenue, Muirend, Glasgow G44 3RJ; T.-0141-637 9535.

Young, Provost John Maclennan, OBE, JP. Farmer, since 1949; Caithness Area Provost, The Highland Council (Member of Housing Committee, Environmental Health Committee, Special Programmes Committee, Leisure and General Purposes Committee, Caithness District Licensing Board); Honorary Sheriff, Grampian, Highland and Islands; b. 6.6.33, Thurso. Educ. Thurso Miller Academy. Member, Caithness County Council, 1961-75 (Chairman, Housing Committee, 1968-73, Chairman, Planning Committee,

1973-75); Member, Caithness Western District Council, 1961-75 (Chairman, 1968-75); Elected to Caithness District Council, 1974; Member, Highland Regional Council, 1974-90 (Chairman, Manpower Committee, 1974-78, Chairman, Roads and Transport Committee, 1978-90, Member of Roads and Transport Committee, 1974-90, Policy and Resources Committee, 1974-90, Finance Committee, 1974-90, Water and Sewerage Committee, 1986-90, Planning Committee, 1974-90, Development Committee, 1974-90, Northern Joint Police Committee, 1975-90); Member, Council, National Farmers Union of Scotland, 1961-69 (President, Thurso Branch, 1961 and 1962, President, Caithness Area Executive Committee, 1963 and 1964); Conservative Candidate, Caithness and Sutherland, 1970. Address: (h.) Sordale, Halkirk, Caithness KW12 6XB; T.-01847 831228.

Young, Rev. John Nicol, MA, PhD, BD. Minister, Liberton Kirk, Edinburgh, since 1996; b. 5.12.55, W. Pakistan; m., C.S. Lindsay Wormald; 1 s.; 1 d. Educ. George Heriot's School, Edinburgh; Edinburgh University. Co-ordinator, Multi-Cultural Education Centre, Leith, 1982-88; Research Worker, Diocese of Hyderabad, Church of Pakistan, 1988-92. Address: (b.) The Manse, 7 Kirk Park, Edinburgh EH16 6HZ; T.-0131-664 3067.

Young, Margaret Rose, JP, MPAH (Scot), CMH, CHyp, DipCouns. Hypnotherapist and Counsellor, Honorary Sheriff; b. 5.1.51, Canada; m., Simon George Young; 3 d. Educ. St. Mary's School, Calne; St. Andrews University. Member, Justices of the Peace Committee, Ross and Cromarty, since 1985. Recreations: reading; music; theatre; walking. Address: (h.) Tarrel, by Tain, Ross-shire, IV20 1SL; T.-01862 871248.

Young, Mark Richard, BSc, PhD, FRES, FIBiol, CBiol. Senior Lecturer, Aberdeen University, since 1989; Director, Culterty Field Station, since 1996; Member, North Board, Scottish Environment Protection Agency, since 1996; b. 27.10.48, Worcester; m., Jennifer Elizabeth Tully; 1 s.; 1 d. Educ. Kings School, Worcester; Birmingham University. Lecturer, Aberdeen University, 1973-89. Recreations: natural history; walking; ball sports; visiting Hebridean islands. Address: (b.) Culterty Field Station, Department of Zoology, University of Aberdeen, Newburgh, Ellon, Aberdeenshire AB41 6AA; T.-01358 789631.

Young, Roger, BSc, MBA. Chief Executive, Scottish Hydro-Electric plc, since 1988; Non-Executive Director: Ivory and Sime PLC, since 1993, Bank of Scotland, since 1994; b. 14.1.44, Edinburgh; m., Susan; 1 s.; 2 d. Educ. Gordonstoun School; Edinburgh University; Cranfield Business School. Rolls-Royce Ltd.; Alidair Ltd.; Wavin Plastics Ltd.; Aurora Holdings Ltd.; Low and Bonar plc. Recreations: hill-walking; aviation; family. Address: (b.) 10 Dunkeld Road, Perth PH1 5WA; Tel.: 01738 455040.

Young, Professor Stephen, BCom, MSc. Professor of International Business, Strathclyde University, since 1987, Head, Department of Marketing, 1992-96; b. 20.8.44, Berwick upon Tweed; 1 s.; 1 d. Educ. Berwick Grammar School; Liverpool University; Newcastle University. Economist, Government of Tanzania; Head, International Economics Department, Milk Marketing Board, 1969-73; Lecturer/Senior Lecturer, Paisley College of Technology, 1973-79; Senior Lecturer, Department of Marketing, Strathclyde Business School, 1980-87 (Director, Strathclyde International Business Unit, from 1983); Director, Licensing Centre Ltd. Recreations: mountaineering; cycling; running. Address: (h.) 42 Brierie Gardens, Crosslee, Johnstone PA6 7BZ; T.-01505 615554.

Young, Sheriff Sir Stephen Stewart Templeton, 3rd Bt. Sheriff of North Strathclyde at Greenock, since 1984; b. 24.5.47; m.; 2 s. Educ. Rugby; Trinity College, Oxford; Edinburgh University. Sheriff, Glasgow and Strathkelvin,

1984. Address: (b.) Sheriff Court House, Nelson Street, Greenock, PA15 1TR.

Young, William Smith Geates, LLB (Hons), NP. Managing Partner, Brechin Tindal Oatts, since 1997; b. 21.12.55, Girvan; m., Margot Glanville. Educ. Girvan Academy; Glasgow University. Joined Tindall Oatts & Rodger, 1978; admitted as Solicitor, 1980; Managing Partner, Tindal Oatts, 1993. SFA Class 1 Referee List, 1990; FIFA List of International Linesmen, 1992; FIFA List of International Referees, 1994. Recreations: football; golf; after-dinner speaking. Address: (b.) 48 St. Vincent Street, Glasgow G2 5HS; T.-0141-221 8012.

Younger of Leckie, Rt. Hon. Viscount (George Kenneth Hotson Younger), KT, KCVO, TD, DL. Chairman, The Royal Bank of Scotland Group plc, since 1991; b. 22.9.31; m., Diana Rhona Tuck; 3 s.; 1 d. Educ. Cargilfield School, Edinburgh; Winchester College; New College, Oxford. Argyll and Sutherland Highlanders, 1950-51; 7th Bn., Argyll and Sutherland Highlanders (TA), 1951-65; Honorary Colonel, 154 (Lowland) Transport Regiment, RCT T&AVR, 1977-85; Director: George Younger & Son Ltd., 1958-68; J.G. Thomson & Co. Ltd., Leith, 1962-66; Maclachlans Ltd., 1968-70; Tennant Caledonian Breweries, 1977-79, Non Executive Director: The Royal Bank of Scotland Group plc, 1989; Murray International Trust PLC, 1989 (Chairman); Murray Smaller Markets Trust PLC, 1989 (Chairman); Murray Income Trust PLC, 1989 (Chairman); Murray Ventures PLC, 1989 (Chairman); Siemens Plessey Electronic Systems Ltd., 1990 (Chairman); Banco Santander S.A., 1991; SPEED, 1992 (Chairman); PIK Holdings Ltd., 1991 (Chairman); Scottish Equitable plc, 1993; Royal Armouries Board of Trustees, 1994 (Chairman); The Fleming Mercantile Investment Trust PLC, 1994; contested North Lanarkshire, 1959; Unionist Candidate, Kinross and West Perthshire, 1963 (stood down in favour of Sir Alec Douglas-Home); MP (Conservative), Ayr, 1964-92; Scottish Conservative Whip, 1965-67; Parliamentary Under-Secretary of State for Development, Scottish Office, 1970-74; Minister of State for Defence, 1974; Secretary of State for Scotland, 1979-86; Chairman, Conservative Party in Scotland, 1974-75 (Deputy Chairman, 1967-70); Secretary of State for Defence, 1986-89; President, National Union of Conservative and Unionist Associations, 1987-88. Brigadier, Queen's Bodyguard for Scotland (Royal Company of Archers); DL, Stirlingshire, 1968. Recreations: music; tennis; sailing; golf. Address: (b.) 42 St. Andrew Square, Edinburgh EH2 2YE; T.-0131-556 8555.

Younger, John David Bingham. Lord Lieutenant of Tweeddale, since 1994; Managing Director, Broughton Brewery Ltd., 1979-95; Director, Broughton Ales, 1995-96; b. 20.5.39, Doune; m., Anne Rosaleen Logan; 1 s.; 2 d. Educ. Eton College; Royal Military Academy, Sandhurst. Argyll and Sutherland Highlanders, 1957-69; Scottish and Newcastle Breweries, 1969-79; Broughton Brewery Ltd., 1979-95; Deputy Lieutenant, Tweeddale, 1987. Chairman, Board of Governors, Belhaven Hill School Trust, 1988; Chairman, Scottish Borders Tourist Board, 1989; Member, A&SH Regimental Trust and Committee, 1985; Director, Queen's Hall (Edinburgh) Ltd; Member, Queen's Bodyguard for Scotland (Royal Company of Archers) since 1969, Secretary, since 1993; Vice President, RHASS, 1994. Recreation: the countryside. Address: (h.) Kirkurd House, Blyth Bridge, Peeblesshire EH46 7AH; T.-01721 752223.

Younger, Sheriff Robert Edward Gilmour, MA, LLB. Sheriff of Tayside, Central and Fife, since 1992 (Stirling and Alloa, 1987-92); b. 25.9.40, Stirling; m., Helen Jane Hayes; 1 s.; 1 d. Educ. Winchester; New College, Oxford; Edinburgh University; Glasgow University. Advocate, 1968-79; Sheriff of Glasgow and Strathkelvin, at Glasgow, 1979-82, and of Tayside, Central and Fife, at

Stirling and Falkirk, 1982-87. Recreations: out of doors. Address: (h.) Old Leckie, Gargunnock, Stirling; T.-01786 860213.

Youngson, George Gray, MB, ChB, PhD, FRCSEdin. Consultant Surgeon, Royal Aberdeen Children's Hospital and Aberdeen Royal Infirmary, since 1985; Honorary Senior Lecturer in Clinical Surgery, Aberdeen University, since 1985; b. 13.5.49, Glasgow; m., Sandra Jean Lister; 1 s.; 2 d. Educ. Buckhaven High School; Aberdeen University. House Officer to Professor George Smith, 1973; Research Fellow, 1975; Registrar in General Surgery, 1975-77; Senior Resident in Cardiac and Thoracic Surgery, University Hospital, London, Ontario, 1979; Lecturer in Clinical Surgery, Aberdeen University, 1981; Clinical Fellow, Paediatric Surgery, Hospital for Sick Children, Toronto, 1983; Lecturer in Surgical Paediatrics and Transplantation, Aberdeen University, 1984; Regional Advisor and Examiner, Royal College of Surgeons of Edinburgh. Recreations: sport (tennis and squash); music (piobaireachd, guitar). Address: (h.) 10 Kennerty Park, Peterculter, Aberdeen.

Z

Zealley, Andrew King, MB, ChB, FRCP, FRCPsych, DPM. Consultant Psychiatrist, Lothian Health Board, since 1971, and Honorary Senior Lecturer, Edinburgh University; b. 28.10.35, Stockton-on-Tees; m., Dr. Helen Elizabeth Zealley (qv); 1 s.; 1 d. Educ. Sherborne School; Edinburgh University. Chairman, Lothian Area Medical Committee, 1978-88; Chairman, Lothian Research Ethics Committee, since 1988; Physician Superintendent, Royal Edinburgh Hospital, 1984-94; Medical Director, Edinburgh Healthcare NHS Trust, 1994-96. Publications include: Companion to Psychiatric Studies, 6th edition (Co-editor). Recreations: running; sailing; skiing. Address: (h.) Viewfield House, Tipperlinn Road, Edinburgh EH10 5ET; T.-0131-447 5545.

Zealley, Helen Elizabeth, QHP, MD, FRCPE, FFPHM. Chief Administrative Medical Officer and Director of Public Health, Lothian Health Board, since 1988; Honorary Senior Lecturer, Edinburgh University, since 1988; b. 10.6.40; m., Dr. Andrew Zealley (qv); 1 s.; 1 d. Educ. St. Albans High School; Edinburgh University. Former Member, Council, Royal College of Physicians, Edinburgh; former Member, Board, Faculty of Public Health Medicine; Hon. President, Lothian Branch, British Association of Early Childhood; Member, Court, Edinburgh University. Recreations: family and home; sailing; skiing; travel. Address: (b.) Lothian Health Board, 148 Pleasance, Edinburgh EH8 9RS; T.-0131-536 9163.

von Zugbach de Sugg, Professor Reginald (Reggie) Gordon Leslie, CLJ, MA, PhD, MBIM, FMS, ACP. Professor in Management, Paisley University, since 1990; b. 20.2.44, Derbyshire; m., 1, Moira Doreen Murphy (m. dissolved); 2, Claudia Bettina Hein (m. dissolved). Educ. City of London School; Brighton Polytechnic; London University Institute of Education; UMIST. Regular Army Officer (Major), 1968-86; Director of Undergraduate Studies, Glasgow Business School, Glasgow University, 1986-90; author of numerous papers; books: Power and Prestige in the British Army, 1988; The Winning Manager, 1995. Commander, Military and Hospitaler Order of St. Lazarus of Jerusalem. Recreations: horses; dogs; real tennis; literature. Address: (h.) 7 Dowanside Road, Dowanhill, Glasgow; T.-0141-337 2228.